بسم الله الرحمن الرحيم
الحمد لله رب العالمين
والصلاة والسلام على خاتم الأنبياء والمرسلين

In the Name of Allah,
the Compassionate, the Merciful,
Praise be to Allah, Lord of the Universe,
and Peace and Prayers be upon
His Final Prophet and Messenger.

AN APPEAL TO OUR READERS

Amana Corporation had devoted its best efforts to produce an error-free copy of this edition of the Meaning of the Holy Qur'ān.

We will greatly appreciate it if our readers inform us of any typographical errors that may have escaped our proofreaders in the translation and commentary of this edition.

The Editorial Board
Amana Corporation
4411 41st Street
Brentwood, Maryland 20722
U.S.A.

The Meaning of The Holy Qur'ān

The Meaning of

THE HOLY QUR'ÁN

'ABDULLAH YŪSUF 'ALĪ

New Edition with Revised
Translation and Commentary

Amana Corporation
Brentwood, Maryland, U.S.A.

Published by Amana Corporation

4411 41st Street
Brentwood, Maryland 20722
Phone (301) 779-7777 TWX 901153 WASH USA
Fax (301) 779-0570

Library of Congress Cataloging-in-Publication Data

'Alī, Abdullah Yūsuf, 1872-1948 A.C. (1288-1367 A.H.).
The meaning of the Holy Qur'ān/'Abdullah Yūsuf 'Alī.—
New ed. with rev. translation and commentary.

p. cm.

Arabic and English.
New rev. (4th) ed. published as: The Holy
Qur'ān. 1989.
Includes index.
ISBN 0-915957-08-6.
I. Koran. English & Arabic. 1991. II. Title.
BP109, 1991 90-25084
297'.122521—dc20 CIP

طبع النص القرآني بالرسم العثماني
على مصحف المدينة المنورة

5 4 3 2 1
95 94 93 92 91

PUBLISHER'S NOTE

Al Ḥamd li Allah (Praise be to Allah), this Revised Edition is a culmination of experiences in the last two decades in publishing translations of the meaning of the Qur'ān in several languages. With the Grace of Allah, Amana Corporation has succeeded in publishing this great work of the late 'Abdullah Yūsuf 'Alī, revised for the first time after his death with the highest standard of scholarship and authenticity that it deserves.

About eight years ago, the work for this edition began when we started the selection of the most recognised and authentic available English translation of the meaning of the Qur'ān. The selection committee, comprised of highly reputable Muslim scholars, decided on the work of 'Abdullah Yūsuf 'Alī and solicited opinions and criticisms from Islamic institutions and scholars around the world. A number of committees reviewed all the responses carefully, examined the text meticulously, updated the material and refined the commentaries. The last complete review was undertaken by the late Isma'īl Rājī al Fārūqī, who was then President of the International Institute of Islamic Thought (IIIT) in the United States of America.

Guided by its own commitment to serve the Qur'ān, Amana Corporation undertook this tremendous task, and in cooperation with the IIIT completed this honorable work. Amana Corporation and IIIT established an editorial board whose effort was to implement the final recommendations of the committees and to concentrate on the manuscript preparation, overall editorial changes, and revisions in style and format (discussed in the Preface to the Revised Edition). All praise be to Allah for enabling us to serve the Qur'ān by making available this Revised Edition.

We acknowledge with deep appreciation the efforts of IIIT and all those who helped produce this monumental work of 'Abdullah Yūsuf 'Alī. May Allah bless his soul and reward him generously; *wa al Ḥamd li Allah Rabb al 'Ālamīn* (All Praise and Gratitude is due to Allah, the Lord and Sustainer of the Worlds).

Jumādā al Ākhirah 1409 A.H.
January, 1989 A.C.
Washington, D.C.

Fakhri al Barzinji, President
Amana Corporation

N.B.:

We thank those readers of our 1409 AH/1989 AC edition who expressed their concern over the use of the expression "New Revised Edition."

In this edition we have removed the words "New Revised Edition" to avoid any misconception by our non-Muslim readers. This is therefore a new edition of the English meaning of the Holy Qur'ān, with revised translation and commentary.

Sha'bān 1411 A.H.
February, 1991 A.C.
Washington, D.C.

'ABDULLAH YŪSUF 'ALĪ

In 1872 A.C. 1289 A.H., 'Abdullah Yūsuf 'Alī was born in a family of the Bohra community in Bombay, India. His father, a merchant, was a very religious man who made sure that his son learned Qur'ān before anything else. Upon the completion of young Yūsuf's committing the entire Qur'ān to memory, his father celebrated the occasion with a grand banquet, thus showing to his son the importance of his achievement and the importance of the Qur'ān. In addition to studying contemporary knowledge at school, 'Abdullah continued to receive lessons in Arabic language and never ceased in his studies of the Qur'ān. He was a superior student who excelled in academic achievement and won the much coveted Indian Civil Service Award, a prestigious honour resulting from the extremely competetive entrance examinations for high positions in the Indian Civil Service which wealthy families would aspire for their sons to receive. 'Abdullah was easily able to absorb English literature and was considered to be among the best of his fellow countrymen in writing English. Many of the most well-known scholarly magazines in India published his works and expressed their appreciation for his beautiful literary style. Later, 'Abdullah Yūsuf left India for Europe and visited many European capitals and eventually resided in London for a considerable period of time. While in London, he was exposed to many translations of the Qur'ān and continued to have a tremendous interest in it and its studies. He then began to closely study the Qur'ān giving special attention to its various interpretations, both old and new. After studying what was written about the Qur'ān in both European and Eastern languages, he returned to India and took up new residence in Lahore where he became the Dean of the Islamic College. He then began his monumental work of translating and commentating on the Qur'ān and later died in Lahore in 1948 A.C. 1367 A.H.

PREFACE TO THE NEW REVISED EDITION

It has been more than half a century since the first appearance of 'Abdullah Yūsuf 'Alī's superlative work, *The Holy Qur'ān—Text, Translation and Commentary.* Since that time, there have been innumerous reprintings and millions of copies distributed throughout the world. It is, by far, the best known, most studied, and most respected English translation of the Qur'ān. It was the first monumental and authoritative work of its kind and it subsequently inspired many such similar endeavours. The eloquent poetic style of the translation and the authenticity of the extensive commentaries and explanatory notes, have, no doubt, contributed greatly to its much deserved reputation as *the* English translation of the Qur'ān.

The tremendous impact that this work has made upon the English-reading Muslims (as well as, many non-Muslims) of the world, has never been greater than it is today and shall continue—*in sha̱ā'a Allah*—for generations to come. It has enabled interested readers of English, who do not have a proficiency in reading and comprehending Quranic Arabic, to greatly enrich their understanding of the meaning and the incomparable beauty and perfection of the Glorious Qur'ān. It has given them a more authentic and reliable translation and commentary from which they could make a serious study.

'A. Yūsuf 'Alī was quick to point out that there can be *no* absolute or perfect translation of the Qur'ān and, at best, only an interpretation of its understood meaning can be offered. Probably, he never envisaged how universal his work would someday become, for he was primarily attempting to explain his understanding of the Qur'ān to his fellow-countrymen—both Muslim and non-Muslim alike. Therefore, he was apt to occasionally use references which could not be easily appreciated outside the milieu of the Indian Subcontinent.

Although it may not have been the intention of the author to reach such a wide range of readers as exists today, there nevertheless has long been a need for a revised new edition reflecting the needs and demands of today's enthusiastic readership. In response to this need, the present edition represents the first major revision since the initial printing over fifty years ago.

Revisions have been made in both the content and form of the original work. Where necessary, the content has been brought up-to-date and within the current understanding and interpretation of the Qur'ān. In the translation, the Sūrah introductions, and the commentaries, such changes were relatively few and infrequent and have been duly noted as having been revised. The reader will, however, find such notable changes as the use of the name 'Allah' for the word 'God' (as used in previous editions) since it was felt that the use of this Most Glorious Name is more widely understood and accepted by the general reader today. Also, the word 'Messenger' has been given preference over the word 'Apostle' for the meaning of the original Quranic word in Arabic, *'Rasūl'.* The reason being, it was felt, that the former term more clearly expresses the Islamic usage of the term without any negative connotations which may be associated with the latter term resulting from inaccuracies in its use by other religious or historical works.

The explanatory footnotes and the appendices, however, were subject to more frequent, and occasionally more substantial, changes than those in the translation and the commentaries. The reason being there was a greater need of general updating of information and clarification of certain explanations which were subject to misinterpretation. There were also a few instances in which certain portions of the material were deleted, either due to its outdatedness or due to its proneness to misinterpretation.

The form of this newly revised edition has undergone a more dramatic change in style and has been vastly improved in order to facilitate its readability and studyability. The Arabic script has been completely changed using the script of the highly acclaimed and recently published *Muṣḥaf al Madīnah al Munawwarah*. The type for the English text has been completely reset for the first time thereby making the character definition more legible after many years of reprintings.

In addition, the spelling has been modernised and the system of transliteration of Arabic into English has also been modernised and standardised. For reasons of practicality, the title of each Sūrah appears in its transliterated form at the head of each page within the Sūrah. This should enable the non-Arabic reader to not only become more familiar with the names of the Sūrahs in Arabic, but also to begin to associate the content of what he is reading with the name of the Sūrah in which he is reading. Also, the 'Abbreviated' Letters (or *al Muqaṭṭa'āt)* have been transliterated as they are spelled out in Arabic so as to make it possible to learn their pronunciation.

Furthermore, a new system of Quranic notation of the Sūrah and *Āyah* numbers used in the English text has been adopted. The Roman numerals used in the original system have been converted to Arabic numerals, thus, making it easier for most readers to readily understand the notations and to encourage them to investigate the frequent references and cross-references found in the Table of Contents, Index, and Footnotes. Finally, the method of indicating each *Juz'* (or 1/30th part of the Qur'ān) has been modified in order to incorporate the more conventional method of notation commonly used today and thereby reduce the potential for confusion to the reader.

In sum, the editors have acted out of a sincere desire to improve upon this great work. It is hoped that this will—*in shā'a Allah*—help in furthering the aim of 'Abdullah Yūsuf 'Alī by enhancing the usefulness and relevance of his work to the ever-changing needs and demands of the countless readers of today. May Allah bless him for his truly extraordinary efforts in producing this invaluable work of translation and commentary.

International Institute of Islamic Thought

Jumādā al Ākhirah, 1409 A.H.
January, 1989 A.C.
Herndon, Virginia
U.S.A.

PREFACE TO FIRST EDITION

I DO not wish to write a long Preface. I wish merely to explain the history of my Project, the scope and plan of this work, and the objects I have held in view.

In separate introductory Notes I have mentioned the useful books to which I have referred, under the headings: Commentaries on the Qur'ān; Translations of the Qur'ān; and Useful Works of Reference. I have similarly explained the system which I have followed in the Transliteration of Arabic Words and Names; the Abbreviations I have used; and the Principal Divisions of the Qur'ān.

It may be asked: Is there any need for a fresh English Translation? To those who ask this question I commend a careful consideration of the facts which I have set out in my note on Translations of the Qur'ān. After they have read it, I would invite them to take any particular passage say 2:74, or 2:102, or 2:164 and compare it with any previous version they choose. If they find that I have helped them even the least bit further in understanding its meaning, or appreciating its beauty, or catching something of the grandeur of the original, I would claim that my humble attempt is justified.

It is the duty of every Muslim—man, woman, or child—to read the Qur'ān and understand it according to his own capacity. If any one of us attains to some knowledge or understanding of it by study, contemplation, and the test of life, both outward and inward, it is his duty, according to his capacity, to instruct others, and share with them the joy and peace which result from contact with the spiritual world. The Qur'ān—indeed every religious book—has to be read, not only with the tongue and voice and eyes, but with the best light that our intellect can supply, and even more, with the truest and purest light which our heart and conscience can give us. It is in this spirit that I would have my readers approach the Qur'ān.

It was between the ages of four and five that I first learned to read its Arabic words, to revel in its rhythm and music, and wonder at its meaning. I have a dim recollection of the Khatm ceremony which closed that stage. It was called "completion": it really just *began* a spiritual awakening that has gone on ever since. My revered father taught me Arabic, but I must have imbibed from him into my innermost being something more, something which told me that all the world's thoughts, all the world's most beautiful languages and literatures, are but vehicles for that ineffable message which comes to the heart in rare moments of ecstasy. The soul of mysticism and ecstasy is in the Qur'ān, as well as the plain guidance for the plain man which a world in a hurry affects to consider as sufficient. It is good to make this personal confession, to an age in which it is in the highest degree unfashionable to speak of religion or spiritual peace or consolation, an age in which words like these draw forth only derision, pity, or contempt.

I have explored Western lands, Western manners, and the depths of Western thought and Western learning, to an extent which has rarely fallen to the lot of an Eastern mortal. But I have never lost touch with my Eastern heritage. Through all my successes and failures I have learned to rely more and more upon the one true thing in all life—the voice that speaks in a tongue above that of mortal man. For me the embodiment of that voice has been in the noble words of the Arabic Qur'ān, which I have tried to translate for myself and apply to my experience again and again. The service of the Qur'ān has been the pride and the privilege of many Muslims. I felt that with such life-experience as has fallen to my lot, my service to the Qur'ān should be to present it in a fitting garb in English. That ambition I have cherished in my mind for more than forty years. I have collected books and materials for it. I have visited places, undertaken journeys, taken notes, sought the society of men, and tried to explore their thoughts and hearts, in order to equip myself for the task. Sometimes I have considered it too stupendous for me—the double task of understanding the original, and reproducing its nobility, its beauty, its poetry, its grandeur, and its sweet practical reasonable application to everyday experience. Then I have blamed myself for lack of courage—the spiritual courage of men who dared all in the Cause which was so dear to them.

Two sets of apparently accidental circumstances at last decided me. A man's life is subject to inner storms far more devastating than those in the physical world around him. In such a storm, in the bitter anguish of a personal sorrow which nearly unseated my reason and made life seem meaningless, a new hope was born out of a systematic pursuit of my long-cherished project. Watered by tears, my manuscript began to grow in depth and earnestness if not in bulk.

I guarded it like a secret treasure. Wanderer that I am, I carried it about, thousands of miles, to all sorts of countries and among all sorts of people. At length, in the city of Lahore, I happened to mention the matter to some young people who held me in respect and affection. They showed an enthusiasm and an eagerness which surprised me. They almost took the matter out of my hands. They asked for immediate publication. I had various bits ready, but not even one complete *Sīpārah**. They made me promise to complete at least one *Sīpārah** before I left Lahore. As if by magic, a publisher, a *kātib* (calligraphist to write the Arabic Text), an engraver of blocks for such text, a printer were found, all equally anxious to push forward the scheme. Blessed be youth, for its energy and determination. "Where others flinch, rash youth will dare!"

Gentle and discerning reader! what I wish to present to you is an English Interpretation, side by side with the Arabic Text. The English shall be, not a mere substitution of one word for another, but the best expression I can give to the fullest meaning which I can understand from the Arabic Text. The rhythm, music, and exalted tone of the original should be reflected in the English Interpretation. It may be but a faint reflection, but such beauty and power as my pen can command shall be brought to its service. I want to make English itself an Islamic language, if such a person as I can do it. And I must give you all the accessory aid which I can. In rhythmic prose, or free verse (whichever you like to call it), I prepare the atmosphere for you in a running Commentary. Introducing the subject generally, I come to the actual *Sūrahs.* Where they are short, I give you one or two paragraphs of my rhythmic Commentary to prepare you for the Text. Where the *Sūrah* is long, I introduce the subject matter in short appropriate paragraphs of the Commentary from time to time, each indicating the particular verses to which it refers. The paragraphs of the running Commentary are numbered consecutively, with some regard to the connection with the preceding and the following paragraphs. It is possible to read this running rhythmic Commentary by itself to get a general bird's-eye view of the contents of the Holy Book before you proceed to the study of the Book itself.

The text in English is printed in larger type than the running Commentary, in order to distinguish, at a glance, the substance from the shadow. It is also displayed differently, in parallel columns with the Arabic Text. Each *Sūrah* and the verse of each *Sūrah* is separately numbered, and the numbers are shown page by page. The system of numbering the verses has not been uniform in previous translations. European editors and translators have allowed their numbering to diverge considerably from that accepted in the East. This causes confusion in giving and verifying references. The different *Qirā'ahs* sometimes differ as to the punctuation stops and the numbering of the verses. This is not a vital matter, but it causes confusion in references. It is important that at least in Islamic countries one system of numbering should be adopted. I have adopted mainly that of the Egyptian edition published under the authority of the King of Egypt. This will probably be accepted in Egypt and in Arabic-speaking countries, as those countries generally look up to Egypt in matters of literature. I am glad to see that the text shortly to be published by the *Anjumani Ḥimāyati Islam* of Lahore is following the same system of numbering. I recommend to other publishers in India the same good example. If once this is done we shall have a uniform system of numbering. I have retained the numbering of Sections, as it is universally used in the Arabic copies, and marks a logical division of the *Sūrahs.* I have supplied a further aid to the reader in indicating subdivision of the Sections into paragraphs. They are not numbered, but are distinguished by the use of a flowery initial letter.

In translating the Text I have aired no views of my own, but followed the received Commentators. Where they differ among themselves, I have had to choose what appeared to me to be the most reasonable opinion from all points of view. Where it is a question merely of words, I have not considered the question important enough to discuss in the Notes, but where it is a question of substance, I hope adequate explanations will be found in the Notes. Where I have departed from the literal translation in order to express the spirit of the original better in English, I have explained the literal meaning in the Notes. For example, see 2:104 n. and 2:26 n. In choosing an English word for an Arabic word, a translator necessarily exercises his own judgement and may be unconsciously expressing a point of view, but that is inevitable.

**Sīpārah* (Urdu) = *Juz'* (Arabic) = one-thirtieth part of the Qur'ān (see Divisions of the Qur'ān) [Eds.].

Let me explain the scope of the Notes. I have made them as short as possible consistently with the object I have in view, *viz.*, to give to the English reader, scholar as well as general reader, a fairly complete but concise view of what I understand to be the meaning of the Text. To discuss theological controversies or enter into polemical arguments I have considered outside my scope. Such discussions and arguments may be necessary and valuable, but they should find a place in separate treatises, if only out of respect to the Holy Book. Besides, such discussions leave no room from more important matters on which present-day readers desire information. In this respect our Commentators have not always been discreet. On questions of law, the Qur'ān lays down general principles, and these I have explained. I have avoided technical details: these will be found discussed in their proper place in my book on "Anglo-Muḥammadan Law". Nor have I devoted much space to grammatical or philological Notes. On these points I consider that the labours of the vast body of our learned men in the past have left little new to say now. There is usually not much controversy, and I have accepted their conclusions without setting out the reasons for them. Where it has been necessary for the understanding of the Text to refer to the particular occasion for the revelation of a particular verse, I have done so briefly, but have not allowed it to absorb a disproportionate amount of space. It will be found that every verse revealed for a particular occasion has also a general meaning. The particular occasion and the particular people concerned have passed away, but the general meaning and its application remain true for all time. What we are concerned about now, in the fourteenth century of the Hijrah, is: what guidance can we draw for ourselves from the message of Allah?

I spoke of the general meaning of the verses. Every earnest and reverent student of the Qur'ān, as he proceeds with his study, will find, with an inward joy difficult to describe, how this general meaning also enlarges as his own capacity for understanding increases. It is like a traveller climbing a mountain: the higher he goes, the farther he sees. From a literary point of view the poet Keats has described his feeling when he discovered Chapman's Homer:

> Then felt I like some watcher of the skies
> When a new planet swims into his ken,
> Or like stout Cortez when with eagle eyes
> He stared at the Pacific—and all his men
> Looked at each other with a wild surmise—
> Silent, upon a peak in Darien.

How much greater is the joy and sense of wonder and miracle when the Qur'ān opens our spiritual eyes! The meaning which we thought we had grasped expands. New worlds are opened out. As we progress, still newer, and again newer worlds "swim into our ken". The miracle deepens and deepens, and almost completely absorbs us. And yet we know that the "face of God"—our final goal—has not yet been reached. We are in the *mulk* of Sulayman (Q. 2:102), which the evil ones denied, belied, and even turned into blasphemy. But we can ignore blasphemy, ridicule and contempt, for we are on the threshold of Realities, and a little perfume from the garden of the Holy One has already gladdened our nostrils.

Such meaning it is most difficult to express. But where I can, I have indicated it in the Notes, in the Commentary, and with the help of the rhythm and the elevated language of the Text.

The Arabic Text* I have had printed from photographic blocks made for me by Master Muḥammad S͟harīf. The calligraphy is from the pen of Pir Abd al Ḥamīd, with whom I have been in touch and who has complied with my desire for a bold round hand, with the words clearly separated, the vowel points accurately placed over or under the letters to which they relate, and the verses duly numbered and placed in juxtaposition with their English equivalents. Calligraphy occupies an important place in Muslim Art, and it is my desire that my version should not in any way be deficient in this respect.

I have been fortunate in securing the cooperation of Professor Ẓafar Iqbal in looking over the proofs of the Arabic Text. In connection with the *Anjuman's* edition of the Arabic Qur'ān he has devoted much time and thought to the correct punctuation of the Text, and he has also investigated its history and problems. I hope he will some day publish these valuable notes. I have been privileged to see the *Anjuman's* Text before its formal publication. I consider it the

---

*This refers to the original copy of 1934. In this edition the Qur'anic text is taken from "Muṣhaf al Madīnah al Munawwarah". (eds)

most carefully prepared Text of any produced in India, and I have generally followed it in punctuation and the numbering of verses—the only points on which any difficulties are likely to arise on the Quranic Text.

It has been my desire to have the printing done in the best style possible, with new type, on good glazed paper, and with the best ink procurable. I hope the result will please those who are good enough to approve of the more essential features of the work. The proprietors of the Ripon Press and all their staff, but especially Mr. Badruddin Badr, their Proof Examiner, have taken a keen interest in their work. The somewhat unusual demands made on their time and attention they have met cheerfully, and I am obliged to them. The publisher, S̲hayk̲h̲ Muḥammad As̲h̲raf, has thrown himself heart and soul into his work, and I hope the public will appreciate his efforts.

My plan is to issue each *Sīpārah* or *Juz'* as it is ready, at intervals of not more than three months. As the work proceeds, I hope it will be possible to accelerate the pace. The paging will be continuous in the subsequent volumes. The final binding will be in either three or two volumes. It is my intention to provide a complete analytical Index to the whole. I hope all interested will sign the publisher's subscription order in advance.

One final word to my readers. Read, study, and digest the Holy Book. Read slowly, and let it sink into your heart and soul. Such study will, like virtue, be its own reward. If you find anything in this volume to criticise, please let it not spoil your enjoyment of the rest. If you write to me, quoting chapter and verse, I shall be glad to consider your criticism, but let it not vex you if I exercise my own judgement in deciding for myself. Any corrections accepted will be gratefully acknowledged. On the other hand, if there is something that specially pleases you or helps you, please do not hesitate to write to me. I have given up other interests to help you. It will be a pleasure to know that my labour has not been in vain. If you address me in care of my Publisher at his Lahore address, he will always forward the letters to me.

D̲h̲ū al Ḥijjah 18, 1352 A.H., A. Yūsuf 'Alī
April 4, 1934 A.C.
Lahore

COMMENTARIES ON THE QUR'ĀN

QURANIC literature is so voluminous that no single man can compass a perusal of the whole. Besides the extant works there were innumerable works written for special groups of people or from special points of view or for special purposes, which have perished. And more works are being added everyday. The activity in this line has never been greater than it is now.

There is no Book in the world in whose service so much talent, so much labour, so much time and money have been expended as has been the case with the Qur'ān. A mere glance at Suyūṭī's (d. 911 A.H.) *Itqān* or Ḥajī Khalīfah's (d. 1059 A.H.) *Kashf al Ẓunūn* will show the encyclopaedic volume of the Quranic sciences in their day.

Since then the volume has continued to go on increasing, although it must be admitted that the quality of the later literature on the subject leaves much to be desired. With the retrogression of the Islamic nations in original work in science, art, and philosophy, and the concomitant limitation in their outlook and experience in various phases of intellectual and spiritual life, has come a certain limitation in the free spirit of research and enquiry. The new Renaissance of Islam which is just beginning will, it is hoped, sweep away cobwebs and let in the full light of reason and understanding.

The need for an explanation of the verses of the Qur'ān arose quite early. Even before the whole of the Qur'ān was revealed, people used to ask the Prophet all sorts of questions as to the meaning of certain words in the verses revealed, or of their bearing on problems as they arose, or details of certain historical or spiritual matters on which they sought more light. The Prophet's answers were carefully stored in the memory of the Companions (*aṣḥāb*) and were afterwards written down. In the next generation, the *Tābi'ūn*, were those who had not personally conversed with the Prophet, like the Companions, but had conversed with the Companions and learned from them. Subsequent generations always went back to establish a chain of evidence through the *Tābi'ūn* and the Companions. Through them grew up the science of *Ḥadīth* or Traditions. As this literature grew, it became necessary to establish strict rules by which the evidence could be examined and tested, so as to separate that which was considered to be established from that which was doubtful or weak, and that which was to be rejected as unproved. In the evolution of the science of *Ḥadīth*, it became clear that even among the Companions certain persons had better memories than others, or better opportunities of becoming really acquainted with the Prophet's true meaning. Similarly the claims of the *Tābi'ūn* came to be examined and graded, and so on. Thus arose a new science, in which the names and positions of persons in *Ḥadīth* literature were examined biographically and in other ways. (R).

The *Ḥadīth* literature dealt with all sorts of matters, including Theology, Ethics, and Exegesis (explanation of the Qur'ān). Exegesis soon became an independent science by itself and was called *Tafsīr*, and the sphere of *Tafsīr* itself began to widen as the experience and knowledge of the Arabs and Arabic writers began to increase. Besides the examination of correct traditions from various kinds and grades of authorities, it began to examine the meaning of words philologically, collecting a vast amount of learning as to root meanings, the usage of the Quraysh tribe of Arabs, to which the Prophet belonged, the usage and meaning of words in the purest original Arabic before it became mixed up with foreign idioms and usages by the use of the Arabic language by non-Arabs in Islam, and by the influence of the enormous geographical expansion of the Arab race in the first few centuries of Islam. The increasing knowledge of history and of Jewish and Christian legends enabled the Commentators to illustrate the Text of the Holy Book with reference to these. Sometimes the amount of Jewish stuff (some of it absurd), which found its way into the Commentaries, was out of all proportion to its importance and relevance, and gave rise to the legend, which has been exploited by polemical Christian and Jewish writers, that Islam was built up on an imperfect knowledge of Christianity and Judaism, or that it accepts as true the illustrative legends from the Talmud or the Midrash or various fantastic schools of Christianity. Then came philosophy and the mystic doctrine of the Ṣūfī schools. The development of the science of *kalām* (built on formal logic), and its further offshoot the *'Ilm al 'Aqā'id* (the philosophical exposition of the grounds of our belief) introduced further elements on the intellectual side, while *Ta'wīl* (esoteric exposition of the hidden or inner meaning) introduced elements on the spiritual side, based on a sort of transcendental intuition of the expositor. The Ṣūfī mystics at least adhered to the rules of their own Orders, which were very strict. But many of the non-Ṣūfī writers on *Ta'wīl* indulged in an amount of licence in interpretation which has rightly called forth a protest on the part of the more sober 'Ulamā'.

For my part I agree with this protest. While freely reserving the right of individual judgement on the part of every earnest writer, I think the art of interpretation must stick as closely as possible to the text which it seeks to interpret. Every serious writer and thinker has a right to use all the knowledge and experience he possesses in the service of the Qur'ān. But he must not mix up his own theories and conclusions, however reasonable, with the interpretation of the Text itself, which is usually perfectly perspicuous, as it claims it to be. Our difficulties in interpretation often arise from various causes, of which I will mention just a few:

(1) Arabic words in the Text have acquired other meanings than those which were understood by the Prophet and his Companions. All living languages undergo such transformations. The early Commentators and Philologists went into these matters with a very comprehensive grasp, and we must accept their conclusions. Where they are not unanimous, we must use our judgement and historic sense in adopting the interpretation of that authority which appeals to us most. We must not devise new verbal meanings.

(2) Even since the early Commentators wrote, the Arabic language has further developed, and later Commentators often abandon the interpretations of earlier Commentators without sufficient reason. In exercising our selective judgement in such cases it would be a good rule to prefer the earlier to the later interpretation, though, where a later writer has reviewed the earlier interpretations and given good reasons for his own view, he has an advantage which we must freely concede to him.

(3) Classical Arabic has a vocabulary in which the meaning of each root word is so comprehensive that it is difficult to interpret it in a modern analytical language word for word, or by the use of the same word in all places where the original word occurs in the Text. A striking example is furnished by the word *Ṣabr,* about which see my notes on 2:45 and 2:153. Even though one particular shade of meaning may be predominant in any particular passage, the others are latent. So in a ray of light, when a prism analyses it, we may look at a portion of the field where a particular colour predominates, but other colours do not escape our glance. An Arabic word is often a full ray of light; when a translator looks at it through the prism of a modern analytical language, he misses a great deal of its meaning by confining his attention to one particular colour. European translators have often failed in this respect and sometimes even been landed in absurdities because these delicate rich tones are not studied in their languages or literatures, and they do not look for them or appreciate them in the best examples of Oriental style. If they despite them or think them fantastic, they had best leave the interpretation of Oriental literatures alone. This is all the more so in religious or spiritual literature. No human language can possibly be adequate for the expression of the highest spiritual thought. Such thought must be expressed symoblically in terse and comprehensive words, out of which people will perceive just as much light and colour as their spiritual eyes are capable of perceiving. It is possible that their prism will only show them a dark blue while a whole glorious symphony of colours is hidden from their eyes. And so it comes about that through the prism of a clever English translation, poor 'Umar (Omar) Khayyām emerges as a sensualist and cynic who sees no higher purpose in life than drinking wine, dallying with women, and holding up his hands in despair at "this sorry scheme of things entire". And so the parables of stern morality in the Qur'ān, its sublime earnestness, and its pictures of future beatitude are distorted into idle fables, incoherent effusions. and a sensual paradise! (R).

(4) An opposite error sometimes arises because in certain matters the rich vocabulary of the Qur'ān distinguishes between things and ideas of a certain kind by special words, for which there is only a general word in English. Instances are: *Raḥmān* and *Raḥīm* (Most Merciful), see 1:1, n. 19; *'afā, ṣafaḥa, ghafara* (to forgive), see 2:109 n. 110; and the various words for Creation, see 2:117, n 120. The fact is that it gives us a very limited idea of Allah's Mercy, when we only use the English word "mercy": the Quranic idea implies not only pity and forgiveness but the Grace which protects us and keeps us from sin, and indeed guides us to the light of His "Countenance." So the "forgiveness" of Allah is a thing totally different in quality from the forgiveness which a man can give to his brother man. The equation implied in "Forgive us our trespasses as we forgive those that trespass against us" is a misleading fallacy. So, again, "Creation" is not just a simple process done by Allah at some remote time and finished with: the Quranic idea implies various processes and the continuous presence and activity of Allah in His Creation. (R).

(5) Allah's purpose is eternal, and His plan is perfect, but man's intelligence is limited at its very best. In the same individual it grows and declines according to the strength of his

powers and the width of his experience. If we take mankind collectively the variations are even greater from age to age and from people to people. There is thus no finality in human interpretation. And in the thing interpreted—Allah's Creation—there is constant flux and change. So that the impact of the one on the other must yield diverse results. The view of Kunchinjunga must vary infinitely according to the position of the observer, even if Kunchinjunga remained the same. But if Kunchinjunga itself varies, there is a double cause of variation in the view. So I believe in progressive interpretation, in the need for understanding and explaining spiritual matters from different angles. The difficulties that confront me may not be the same as those that confront you. The problems which our age has to meet may not be the same as the problems which puzzled earnest minds of the fourth or sixth or later centuries of the Hijrah. Therefore it is no merit to hug the solutions offered in the fourth or sixth centuries when our souls cry out in hunger for solace in the fourteenth century of the Hijrah.

The distinction drawn by Commentators between matters of report (*manqūlāt*) and matters of judgement (*ma'qūlāt*) is a sound one, and I heartily accept it. But I would extend the scope of the *ma'qūlāt* far beyond questions of idiom and meaning. In the former the issues are: what actually happened, or what was actually said; or how were certain things done? Here the closer we go back to contemporary authority, the better. In the latter, the issues are: what is the bearing of this truth on our lives, or what illustration helps us best to grasp this, or what is the wisdom we can extract from this? In such matters, the closer we come to our own circumstances and experiences, the better. It is not only right but our duty to seek honestly our own solutions, and while we respect authority, we must not neglect or despise the gifts which Allah has accumulated for us through the ages.

The principles on which I have worked may be briefly stated. In matters of philology and language I accept the best authority among those who were competent to deal with these questions: the older the better. In matters of narration, contemporary authorities are best, subject to such corrections as have to be applied for their points of view. As to the particular occasions on which particular verses were revealed, the information is interesting and valuable from a historical point of view, and our older writers have collected ample material for it. But to lay too much stress on it today puts the picture out of all perspective. The Qur'ān was not revealed for a particular occasion only, but for all time. The particular occasion is now past. Our chief interest now is to see how it can guide us in our present lives. Its meaning is so manifold, and when tested, it is so true, that we should be wise to concentrate on the matters that immediately help us. So in nature plants seek out of the soil just that food which gives them nourishment. There is plenty of other food left in the soil, which other plants take, which can digest it. In matters of remote history or folklore, we must take the results of the latest researches. In interpreting Jewish or Christian legends or beliefs we must go to Jewish or Christian sources, but by way of illustration only, not in the direction of incorporating such beliefs or systems. Though they were true in their original purity, we are not sure of the form which they subsequently took, and in any case the fuller light of the sun obscures the lesser light of the stars.

In the application of spiritual truths to our own times and our own lives, we must use every kind of knowledge, science, and experience which we possess, but we must not obtrude irrelevant matter into our discussions. Let us take simple examples. When we speak of the rising of sun in the east, we do not go on to reconcile the expression with the Copernican system of astronomy. What we *mean* is as true under the Copernican system as it was under the Ptolemaeic system. When we speak of the endless plains of India, we are not put on our defence because the earth is round. Nor will such expressions as the seven firmaments raise questions as to the nature of space in modern astronomy. Man's intellect is given to him to investigate the nature of the physical world around him. He forms different conceptions of it at different times. Spiritual truths are quite independent of the question which of these conceptions are true. They deal with matters which are beyond the ken of physical science. In explaining or illustrating them we shall use such language as is current among the people to whom we speak. (R).

Let me set out the names of the most important *Tafsīrs*, especially those to which I have from time to time referred. They are not, however, in any sense my authorities. They belong to widely different schools of thought, and some of them express extreme views with which I do not agree. I only adopt the general sense of accepted Commentaries.

(1) The monumental work of Abū Ja'far Muḥammad ibn Jarīr *al Ṭabarī*, d. 310 A.H. A pefect mine of historical information, as the author was both a historian and a Traditionist. Copies are not easily accessible.

(2) *Al Mufradāt*, a dictionary of difficult words and phrases in the Qur'ān, by Abū al Qāsim Ḥusayn Rāghib, of Ispahān, d. 503 A.H. Also explains allusions.

(3) *Al Kashshāf*, by Abū al Qāsim Maḥmūd ibn 'Umar al *Zamakhshari*, of Khwārizm, d. 538 A.H. Very full in the explanation of words and idioms; takes a decidedly rational and ethical view of doctrine. Numerous Commentaries have been written on this Commentary.

(4) *Al Tafsīr al Kabīr*, by Abū al Faḍl Muḥammad Fakhr al Dīn al Rāzī; d. 606 A.H. Very comprehensive. Strong in interpretations from a Ṣūfī, or spiritual point of view.

(5) *Anwār al Tanzīl*, by al Qaḍī Nāṣir al Dīn Abū Sa'īd 'Abd Allah ibn 'Umar al *Bayḍāwī*, d. 685 A.H. Has drawn largely from *Al Mufradāt*, *Al Kashshāf* and *Al Tafsīr al Kabīr*, but incorporates a good deal of original matter. A very popular Commentary, on which again numerous Commentaries have been written.

(6) The Tafsīr of Abū al Fidā' Ismā'īl ibn Kathīr, d. 774 A.H. Voluminous, but has great authority among the 'Ulamā'.

(7) *Al Itqān fī 'Ulūm al Qur'ān*, by Jalāl al Dīn al Suyūṭī, d. 911 A.H. A comprehensive review of the sciences of the Qur'ān, being an introduction to his *Majma' al Baḥrayn*.

(8) *Tafsīr al Jalālayn*—Written by Jalāl al Dīn al Suyūṭī, d. 911 A.H., and Jalāl al Dīn al Maḥallī, d. 894 A.H. A concise and meritorious Commentary, on which again a number of Commentaries have been written.

(9) Our country has produced some notable scholars in the realm of *Tafsīr*. They wrote in Arabic and Persian, and the latter ones have written in Urdu.

The earliest I can trace is Shaykh 'Alī ibn Aḥmad Mahaymi (of Mahim, near Bombay), d. 835 A.H. or 1432 A.C., author of the *Tafsīr Raḥmānī*. Almost contemporary with him was 'Allāmah Shams al Dīn, of Dawlatābād and Delhi, who lived during the brilliant reign of Ibrahīm Sharqī of Jawnpur (1400—1440 A.C.). He wrote in Persian. During the nineteenth century, the famous Muḥaddith of Delhi, Shāh Walī Allah, and his two sons Shāh 'Abd al 'Azīz (d. 1824 A.C.) and Shāh 'Abd al Qādir (d. 1826 A.C.) wrote both translations and Commentaries. Shāh 'Abd al 'Azīz wrote in Persian and Shāh 'Abd al Qādir in Urdu. The Urdu Commentary of Sir Sayyid Aḥmad Khan of 'Alīgarh (d. 1898 A.C.) has not met the approval of the 'Ulamā'. On the other hand the more recent Urdu Commentary of Mawlvi 'Abd al Ḥaqq, the *Tafsīr Ḥaqqānī*, which has passed through several editions, is quite modern in tone and manageable in bulk, and is widely circulated in India. I have derived much instruction from it and have used it constantly. The Commentary of Mawlvi Abū al Kalām Azād has been planned on a spacious scale and has not yet been finished.

(10) The Modernist school in Egypt got a wise lead from the late Shaykh Muḥammad 'Abduh (d. 1323 A.H. or 1905 A.C.), whose unfinished Commentary is being completed by Muḥammad Rashīd Riḍā, the talented editor of the *Manār* newspaper. The work of Shaykh Ṭanṭawī Jawharī, a pupil of 'Abduh, finds the "jewels" of the Qur'ān and of the sciences mutually illuminative, and suggests many new lines of thought. 'Allāmah Farīd Wajdī is also spoken of as a good modern Commentator: I have not yet been able to get a copy of his work.

(11) It has been said that the Qur'ān is its own best Commentary. As we proceed with the study of the Book, we find how true this is. A careful comparison and collation of passages from the Qur'ān removes many difficulties. Use a good Concordance, such as the one I have named among the Works of Reference, and you will find that one passage throws light on another.

TRANSLATIONS OF THE QUR'ĀN

ALMOST all languages spoken by Muslims have translations of the Qur'ān in them. Usually the Text is printed with the Translation. If the language is undeveloped, many of the Arabic words of the Qur'ān are taken over bodily into it for want of corresponding words in the language. Even in cultivated languages like Persian or Turkish, the introduction of religious terms from Arabic gave a body of words which were common to the whole Islamic world, and thus cemented that unity of the Muslim Brotherhood which is typified by the Qiblah. Where the notion itself is new to the speakers of polished languages, they are glad to borrow the Arabic word expressing that notion and all the associations connected with it. Such a word is *Qiblah.* Where the language is undeveloped, the translation is nothing more than a rough explanation of the Arabic Text. The translation has neither grammatical finish nor a form which can stand independently by itself. That is what happened with the earlier Urdu translations. They were really rough explanations. The ambition of every learned Muslim is to read the Qur'ān in Arabic. The ambition of every Muslim is to read the *sounds* of the Arabic Text. I wish that his or her ambition were also to *understand* the Qur'ān, either in Arabic or in the mother tongue or some well-developed tongue which he or she understands. Hence the need for good and accurate translations.

The translations into non-European languages known to me are: Persian, Turkish, Urdu, Tamil (used by Moplas), Pashto (for Afghans), Bengali, Malay, some of the languages of the Eastern Archipelago, and some of the African languages. I believe there is also a Chinese (dialectical) translation.

The earliest Urdu translation was by S͟hāh 'Abd al Qādīr of Delhi (d. 1826 A.C.). He has aready been mentioned among the Indian Commentators. Since then numerous Urdu translations have followed, some of which have been left incomplete. Among the complete ones, much used at the time of this writing, may be mentioned those of S͟hāh Rafī' al Dīn of Delhi, S͟hāh As͟hraf 'Alī T͟hānawī, and Mawlvi Nad͟hīr Aḥmad (d. 1912 A.C.). Personally I prefer the last. The projected Urdu translation by Ḥakīm Aḥmad S͟hujā' has not yet been published.

Before the development of the modern European vernaculars, the cultivated language of Europe was Latin. A Latin translation was made for the Monastery of Clugny about 1143 A.C. (in the sixth century of the Hijrah) but not published till 1543 A.C. The place of publication was Basle and the publisher Bibliander. This was translated into Italian, German, and Dutch. Schweigger's German translation was published at Nurenburg (Bavaria) in 1616 A.C. A French translation by Du Ryer was published at Paris in 1647 A.C., and a Russian one at St. Petersburg in 1776 A.C. Savary's French translation appeared in 1783 A.C., and Kasimirski's French translation (which has passed through several editions) first appeared in 1840 A.C., the French interest in Islam having been stimulated by French conquests in Algeria and North Africa. The Germans have followed up Schweigger with Boysen's translation in 1773 A.C., Wahl's in 1828 A.C., and Ullmann's (first edition in 1840 A.C.). I believe the Aḥmadīyah Association of Lahore have in hand a fresh translation into German and Dutch.

Meanwhile Maracci had produced in 1689 A.C. a Latin version of the Qur'ān with the Arabic Text and quotations from various Arabic Commentaries, carefully selected and garbled, so as to give the worst possible impression of Islam to Europe. Maracci was a learned man, and there is no pretence about the object he had in view, *viz.*, to discredit Islam by an elaborate show of quotations from Muslim authorities themselves. Maracci was himself a Confessor to Pope Innocent XI; his work is dedicated to the holy Roman Emperor Leopold I; and he introduces it by an introductory volume containing what he calls a "Refutation of the Qur'ān."

The first English translation by A. Ross was but a translation of the first French translation of Du Ryer of 1647 A.C., and was published a few years after Du Ryer's. George Sale's translation (1737 A.C.) was based on Maracci's Latin version, and even his notes and his Preliminary Discourse are based mainly on Maracci. Considering that Maracci's object was to discredit Islam in the eyes of Europe, it is remarkable that Sale's translation should be looked upon as a standard translation in the English-speaking world, and should pass through edition after edition, being even included in the series called the Chandos Classics and receiving the benediction of Sir E. Denison Ross, The Rev. J.M. Rodwell arranged the Sūrahs in a rough chronological order. His translation was first published in 1861 A.C. Though he tries to render the idiom fairly, his notes show the mind of a Christian clergyman, who was more concerned to "show up," the Book than to appreciate or expound its beauties. Prof. E. H. Palmer's translation (first published in 1876 A.C.) suffers from the idea that the Qur'ān ought to be translated into colloquial language. He failed to realise the beauty and grandeur of style in the original Arabic. To him that style was "rude and rugged": we may more justifiably call his translation careless and slipshod.

The amount of mischief done by these versions of non-Muslim and anti-Muslim writers has led Muslim writers to venture into the field of English translation. The first Muslim to undertake an English translation was Dr. Muḥammad 'Abd al Ḥakīm Khan, of Patiala, 1905 A.C. Mīrza Hayrat of Delhi also published a translation, (Delhi 1919 A.C.): the Commentary which he intended to publish in a separate volume of Introduction was, as far as I know, never published. My dear friend, the late Nawwāb 'Imād al Mulk Sayyid Ḥusayn Bilgrāmī of Hyderabad, Deccan, translated a portion, but he did not live to complete his work. The Aḥmadīyah Sect* has also been active in the field. Its Qādiyān Anjuman published a version of the first *Sipārah* in 1915 A.C. Apparently no more was published. Its Lahore Anjuman has published Mawlvi Muḥammad 'Alī's translation (first edition in 1917 A.C.), which has passed through more than one edition. It's a scholarly work, and is equipped with adequate explanatory matter in the notes and the Preface, and a fairly full Index. But the English of the Text is decidedly weak, and is not likely to appeal to those who know no Arabic. There are two other Muslim translations of great merit. But they have been published without the Arabic Text. Ḥafiẓ Ghulām Sarwar's translation (published in 1930 A.C. or 1929 A.C.) deserves to be better known than it is. He has provided fairly full summaries of the Sūrahs, section by section, but he has practically no notes to his Text. I think such notes are necessary for a full understanding of the Text. In many cases the Arabic words and phrases are so pregnant of meaning that a Translator would be in despair unless he were allowed to explain all that he understands by them. Mr. Marmaduke Pickthall's translation was published in 1930 A.C. He is an English Muslim, a literary man of standing, and an Arabic scholar. But he has added very few notes to elucidate the Text. His rendering is "almost literal": it can hardly be expected that it can give an adequate idea of a Book which (in his own words) can be described as "that inimitable symphony the very sounds of which move men to tears and ecstasy." Perhaps the attempt to catch something of that symphony in another language is impossible. Greatly daring, I have made that attempt. We do not blame an artist who tries to catch in his picture something of the glorious light of a spring landscape.

The English language being widely spread over the world, many people interested in Islam will get their ideas of the Qur'ān from English translations. It is good that qualified Muslims should make the attempt to present the picture which their own mental and spiritual vision presents to themselves. The Indian educational system has enthroned English as the common language of culture for a population of 350 millions. The most educated of its 80 millions of Muslims—unless they know Arabic—look to English as the most cultivated medium of expression. Their non-Muslim fellow countrymen judge—usually misjudge— their religion by the material which is available to them in English. We should improve and increase this material as much as we can and from as many points of view as we can. Some Muslim nations—like the Turks—have now determined to provide their religious literature (including the Holy Book) in their own national language. In order to keep them in touch with the thought and points of view of their brethren in faith, the English language would under present conditions be the most convenient medium. These are the considerations which have moved me to undertake the stupendous task of providing an English Interpretation of the Qur'ān. I pray for strength and light, so that I may be enabled to succeed in this service to Islam.

---

*The Muslim *Ummah* is agreed that since Mirza Ghulam Ahmad of Qadiyan claimed to be a prophet and messenger of Allah, all those who consider him their religious leader are outside the fold of Islam. [Eds.]

USEFUL WORKS OF REFERENCE

THE wide compass of the Qur'ān makes it necessary to consult works of reference on almost every conceivable subject, to enable us to elucidate the various points that arise. To deal adequately with such a Book, the widest reading is necessary as well as the most varied experience in life. But the interests of readers require that a handy Commentary should not roam too far afield. Bearing this in view the three essential kinds of books would be: (a) Previous Commentaries; (b) Previous Translations; (c) Dictionaries and General Works of Reference, easily accessible. I have set out (a) and (b) in the previous two Notes. I note a few under (c):

1. Abū al Qāsim Ḥusayn ibn Muḥammad al Rāghib al Aṣfahāni's, *Al Mufraddāt:* a concise Arabic dictionary of words and phrases in the Qur'ān. Already mentioned under Commentaries.
2. The well-known Arabic Dictionary, *Al Qāmūs,* by Muḥammad ibn Ya'qūb al Fayrūzabādī.
3. The well-known Arabic Dictionary, *Lisān al 'Arab,* by Abū al Faḍl Jamāl al Dīn Muḥammad ibn Mukram ibn Manẓūr.
4. The concise Arabic-Perisan Dictionary, Ṣurāḥ.
5. J. Penrice's *Dictionary & Glossary of the Koran.*
6. E. W. Lane: *Arabic-English Lexicon.*
7. Jalāl al Dīn al Suyūṭī's *Al Itqān fī 'Ulūm al Qur'ān:* a veritable encyclopaedia of Quranic sciences.
8. Noldeke and Schwally: *Geschichte des Qorans.* A German Essay on the Chronology of the Qur'ān. Its criticisms and conclusions are from a non-Muslim point of view and to us not always acceptable, though it is practically the last word of European scholarship on the subject.
9. *Encyclopaedia of Islam.* Nearly completed. Very unequal in its various parts.
10. *Encyclopaedia Britannica,* 14th edition. A great advance on previous editions, as regards the attention it devotes to Arabic learning.
11. Hughes's *Dictionary of Islam.* Out of date, but still useful.
12. Muḥammad ibn Hishām: *Sīrah al Rasūl.* A fairly detailed Life of the Prophet.
13. Mawlvi Shiblī Nu'māni (d. 1914 or 1334 A.H.): *Sīrah al Nabī* (an Urdu Life of the Prophet).
14. *Fatḥ al Raḥmān,* an Arabic Concordance to the Qur'ān, by Fayḍ Allāh Bayk Ḥasani, printed in Cairo in 1346 A.H. Full and well arranged, and easy to use.

Since then the meaning of the Qur'ān has been rendered into many languages, Asian, European and African. Some such major works include:

1. Marmaduke William Muhammad Picktall, *Meaning of the Glorious Qur'ān,* (London, 1356/1937).
2. Syed Abul Ala Maudoodi's six-volume Urdu work, *Tafhīm ul Qur'ān* (1369-1392/1949-1972) translated and published in English under the title *The Meaning of the Qur'ān* by Islamic Publications, Lahore, Pakistan. A new translation is currently being released by the Islamic Foundation, Leicester, U.K.
3. Syed Qutb's *Fī Ẓilāl al Qur'ān* (Beirut: Dar al Shuruq, 1393/1973) in 6 vols. [Trans. into Turkish, Farsi, and Urdu. Vol. 30 of English trans. *In the Shade of the Qur'ān* published by (MWH, London, U.K. 1399/1979.)
4. The noteworthy modern English translations are Muhammad Asad's *The Message of the Qur'ān* (Gibralter: Dār al Andalus 1400/1980); Dr. T. B. Irving's *The Qur'ān—The First American Version* (Brattleboro, Vermont: Amana Books 1405/1986), and Prof. Ahmad Ali's *Al Qur'ān a contemporary translation,* (Akrash Publishing 1404/1984, Karachi).
5. Dr. Hamidullah's French rendering *Le Saint Coran* (1382/1963). [Eds.]

TRANSLITERATION OF ARABIC WORDS AND NAMES

THE following table shows the system which I have followed in transliterating the letters of the Arabic alphabet:

ا	= Alif	= a	ط	= Ṭā'	= ṭ	
		= ā (long vowel)	ظ	= Ẓā'	= ẓ	
ب	= Bā'	= b	ع	= 'Ayn	= '	(inverted apostrophe)
ت	= Tā'	= t	غ	= Ghayn	= gh	
ث	= Thā'	= th	ف	= Fā'	= f	
ج	= Jīm	= j	ق	= Qāf	= q	
ح	= Ḥā'	= ḥ	ك	= Kāf	= k	
خ	= Khā'	= kh	ل	= Lām	= l	
د	= Dāl	= d	م	= Mīm	= m	
ذ	= Dhāl	= dh	ن	= Nūn	= n	
ر	= Rā'	= r	ه	= Hā'	= h	
ز	= Zāy	= z	و	= Wāw	= w	(consonantal)
س	= Sīn	= s			= ū	(long vowel)
ش	= Shīn	= sh	ي	= Yā'	= y	(consonantal)
ص	= Ṣād	= ṣ			= ī	(long vowel)
ض	= Ḍād	= ḍ	ء	= Hamzah	= '	(apostrophe)

Short vowels: ——— (fatḥah) = a
——— (kasrah) = i
——— (ḍammah) = u

1. In internationalised words and names I have used the spelling ordinarily current in English; *e.g.*, Mawlvi, Urdu, Islam, Israel, Abraham, Jacob. Here the boundary is thin and rather ill-defined, and possibly my practice and that of my proofreaders, have not been absolutely uniform.

2. Some names, *e.g.*, Ishmael, Hagar, etc., have acquired a contemptuous association in their European forms, while the persons they represent are sacred personages held in great honour in Islam. I have, therefore, avoided the European forms and used the Arabic forms, Ismā'īl, Hājar, etc.

ABBREVIATIONS USED

I have not used many abbreviations. Those I have used are shown below:

A.C.	=	After Christ = year of the Christian Calendar.
B.C.	=	Before Christ = year of Christian Calendar.
A.H.	=	After Hijrah = Year of the Islamic Calendar.
Bk.	=	Book.
C.	=	The running Commentary, in rhythmic prose.
Cf.	=	compare.
d.	=	date of death of an author (to show the age in which he lived),
Deut.	=	The Book of Deuteronomy in the Old Testament.
E. B.	=	*Encyclopaedia Britannica*, 14th edition.
e.g.	=	*exempli gratia* = for example.
Exod.	=	The Book of Exodus, Old Testament.
Gen.	=	The Book of Genesis, Old Testament.
H.G.S.	=	Ḥāfiẓ G͟hulām Sarwar's Translation of the Qur'ān.
i.e.	=	*id est* = that is.
Josh.	=	Book of Joshua, Old Testament.
Matt.	=	Gospel of St. Matthew, New Testament.
M.M.A.	=	Mawlvi Muḥammad 'Ali's translation of the Qur'ān.
M.P.	=	Mr. M. Pickthall's *The Meaning of the Glorious Koran*.
n.	=	note.
nn.	=	notes.
Num.	=	The Book of Numbers, Old Testament.
p.	=	page.
pp.	=	pages.
Q.	=	Qur'ān.
20:25	=	Qur'ān, Sūrah 20, *Āyah* 25.
Rev.	=	Revelation of St. John, New Testament.
re	=	reference.
S.	=	Sūrah.
v.	=	verse.
vv.	=	verses.
viz.	=	*videlicet* = namely.
[Eds.]	=	Editors.
(R)	=	Revised by Editors.

PUNCTUATION MARKS IN THE ARABIC TEXT

The system of Quranic punctuations used in the Arabic script selected for this new revised edition, incorporates several kinds of signs or symbols indicating variations in methods of *Qirā'ah* (or recitation of the Qur'ān). The following table of symbols, known as the *'Alāmāt al Waqf* (or Signs for Stops), gives a brief description of their meaning and a reference giving an example of their use:

م *Waqf Lāzim*—must stop at place indicated; for example, see 6:36;

لا *Waqf Mamnū'*—must not stop at place indicated; for example,, see 16:32;

ج *Waqf Jā'iz*—may or may not stop at place indicated (there is no preference); for example, see 18:31;

صلى *Waqf Jā'iz, al Waṣl Awlā*—may or may not stop at place indicated, but first preference is not to stop; for example, see 6:17;

قلى *Waqf Jā'iz, al Waqf Awlā*—may or may not stop at place indicated, but first preference is to stop; for example, see 18:22;

∴ ∴ *Ta'ānuq al Waqf*—may stop at either place indicated, but not both places; for example, see 2:2. (R).

DIVISIONS OF THE QUR'ĀN

THE reading of the Qur'ān is considered a pious duty by every Muslim and is actually performed in practice by every literate person—man, woman, and child. For the convenience of those who wish to complete the whole reading in a given time, the whole Text is divided into thirty equal parts. The thirtieth Part is called *Juz'* in Arabic. and *Sīpārah* or simply *Pārah* in Persian and Urdu. If you read a *Juz'* every day, you complete the whole reading in a month of thirty days. Usually the arithmetical quarters of a *Juz'* (one-fourth, one-half, three-quarters) are also marked in the Arabic copies as *al rub', al nisf,* and *al thalāthah arbā'.*

According to subject matter, the division is different. The whole of the Qur'ān is arranged in 114 Sūrahs of very unequal size. The Sūrahs are numbered and the consecutive number is shown just before the title of the Sūrah in English. In Arabic, the number of the *Juz'* and the title of the Sūrah are given at the head of every page in the Sūrah. Each Sūrah consists of a number of *Āyāt*. Sūrah 1 contains 7 *Āyāt* and Sūrah 2 contains 286. For the meaning of Sūrah and *Āyah* see C. 42 nn. 15-17. The most convenient form of quotation is to name the Sūrah and the *Āyāt:* thus 2:120 means the 120th *Āyah* of the second Sūrah. A Sūrah is usually spoken of as a Chapter in English, but that translation is hardly satisfactory. If you examine the order you will find that Sūrah is a step in a gradation. I have left the word untranslated, as a technical term in our religious literature. The *Āyah* or verse division is usually determined by the rhythm and cadence in the Arabic Text. Sometimes an *Āyah* contains many sentences. Sometimes a sentence is divided by a break in an *Āyah*. But usually there is a pause in meaning at the end of an *Āyah*. (R).

DIVISIONS OF THE QUR'AN

[illegible]

[illegible]

Sūrah 2: ***Baqarah***—(Cont.).

Sūrah 3: ***Āli 'Imrān.*** سورة ٣: آل عمران

Sūrah 24: ***Al Nūr.*** سورة ٢٤: النور

Sūrah 25: ***Al Furqān.*** سورة ٢٥: الفرقان

Sūrah 26: ***Al Shu'arā'.*** سورة ٢٦: الشعراء

Juz' 28/30

بِسْمِ ٱللَّهِ ٱلرَّحْمَٰنِ ٱلرَّحِيمِ

INTRODUCTION

C. 1.—Glory to Allah Most High, full of Grace and Mercy;
He created All, including Man.
To Man He gave a special place in His Creation.
He honoured man to be His Agent,
And to that end, endued him with understanding.
Purified his affections, and gave him spiritual insight;
So that man should understand Nature,
Understand himself,
And know Allah through His wondrous Signs,
And glorify Him in Truth, reverence, and unity.

C. 2.—For the fulfilment of this great trust
Man was further given a Will,
So that his acts should reflect Allah's universal Will and Law,
And his mind, freely choosing,
Should experience the sublime joy
Of being in harmony with the Infinite,
And with the great drama of the world around him,
And with his own spiritual growth.

C. 3.—But, created though he was in the best of moulds,
Man fell from Unity when his Will was warped,
And he chose the crooked path of Discord.
And sorrow and pain, selfishness and degradation.
Ignorance and hatred, despair and unbelief
Poisoned his life, and he saw shapes of evil
In the physical, moral, and spiritual world,
And in himself.

C. 4.—Then did his soul rise against himself,
And his self-discord made discord between kith and kin:
Men began to fear the strong and oppress the weak,
To boast in prosperity, and curse in adversity.
And to flee each other, pursuing phantoms,
For the truth and reality of Unity
Was gone from their minds.

C. 5.—When men spread themselves over the earth,
And became many nations,
Speaking diverse languages,
And observing diverse customs and laws;

The evils became multiplied,
As one race or nation
Became alienated from another.
The Brotherhood of Man was now doubly forgotten—
First, between individuals, and secondly, between nations.
Arrogance, selfishness, and untruth

Were sown and reaped in larger fields;
And Peace, Faith, Love and Justice
Were obscured over masses of men,
As large tracts of land are starved
Of sunshine by clouds floating far on high.

C. 6.—But Allah, in His infinite mercy and love,
Who forgives and guides individuals and nations,
And turns to good even what seems to us evil,
Never forsakes the struggling soul that turns to Him,
Nor the groups of men and women
Who join together to obey His Will and Law
And strengthen each other in unity and truth,
Nor the Nations that dwell
In mountain or valley, heat or cold,
In regions fertile or arid,
In societies that roam over land or seas,
Or hunt, or tend flocks, or till the soil,
Or seek the seas for food or oil or fat or gems,
Or dig out from the bowels of the earth
Precious stones or metals or stored-up heat and energy,
Or practise arts and crafts, or produce abundant wealth
By machines of ingenious workmanship,
Or live a frugal life of contemplation:
For all are creatures of One God,
And share His loving care
And must be brought within the pale
Of His eternal unity and harmony.

C. 7.—And so this light of eternal Unity
Has shone in all ages and among all nations,
Through chosen Messengers of Allah, who came
As men to dwell among men,
To share their joys and sorrows,
To suffer for them and with them—
Aye, and to suffer more than falls
To ordinary mortal lot—
That so their message and their life
Might fulfil the eternal

And unchanging purpose of the Most High—
To lead man to his noblest destiny.

C. 8.—Ever this eternal light of Unity,
This mystic light of Allah's own Will,
Has shone and shines with undiminished splendour.
The names of many Messengers are inscribed
In the records of many nations and many tongues,
And many were the forms in which their message was delivered,
According to the needs of the times and the understanding of the people;
And manifold were the lives of the Messengers,
And manifold also was the response of their people;
But they all witnessed to the One Truth:
Of Allah's unity, might, grace and love.

C. 9.—As the records of man are imperfect,
And the memory of man unstable:
The names of many of these messengers
Are known in one place and not in another,
Or among one people and not among others;
And some of their names may have perished utterly;
But their message stands one and indivisible,
Even though it may have been forgotten,
Or twisted by ignorance, error, superstition or perversity;
Or misunderstood in the blinding light
Of time or tortuous Circumstances.

C. 10.—Many were the faiths in the composite world
Of Western Asia, Northern Africa, and Europe,
And many were the fragments of ancient wisdom,
Saved, transfomed, renewed, or mingled;
And many new streams of wisdom were poured through the crucibles
Of noble minds—prophets, poets, preachers,
Philosophers, and thinking men of action;
And many were the conflicts, and many
The noble attempts reaching out towards Unity,
And many were the subtle influences
Interchanged with the other worlds
Of further and Eastern Asia—
Aye, and perchance with the scattered Isles
Of the Pacific and the world between
The Atlantic and the Pacific.

C. 11.—At length came the time when the Voice of Unity
Should speak and declare to the People,

Without the need of Priests or Priest-craft,
Without miracles save those that happen
Now and always in the spiritual world,
Without mystery, save those mysteries
Which unfold themselves in the growing
Inner experience of man and his vision of Allah—
To declare with unfaltering voice
The Unity of Allah, the Brotherhood of Man,
And Grace and Mercy, Bounty and Love,
Poured out in unstinted measure forever and ever.

C. 12.—And this great healing light shone
Among a people steeped in ignorance,
Brave and free, but without cohesion or union,
Simple and rude, but with an easy familiarity with Nature,
Accustomed to Nature's hardships and her rugged resistance
to man,
But dreaming of the delights of gardens and fruitful fields,
Cruel, yet with a rough sense of equality,
And wielding a tongue, flexible, beautiful,
And able to respond, with brevity and eloquence,
To the sublimest thoughts which man could conceive.

C. 13.—Who were fit to be vehicles of this light?—
Not men intoxicated with words and mysteries,
Men whom politics had debauched or tyranny had subdued,
Men whose refinement had ended in vices,
Who saw Nature only through books or artificial conceits,
Or in moods which bred softness, indolence, or luxury,
Who spoke of love and justice, but practised
Gross selfishness between class and class,
Sex and sex, condition and condition;
And had perverted their language, once beautiful,
Into jargons of empty elegance and unmeaning futility.

C. 14.—For the glory of Hellas, and her freedom and wisdom had
departed;
Rome's great systems of law, organisation, and universal citizenship
Had sunk into the mire of ecclesiastical formalism,
And dogmatism, and exclusive arrogance;
The living fire of Persia's prophet scarce smouldered
In her votaries of luxury;
In India, countless castes and kingdoms
Cancelled the unity of Buddha's teaching;
The wounds of China had not yet been healed by T'ang culture;
And Japan was still a disciple of China.

C. 15.—Then, in the sacred city of pagan Arabia,
Shone a light that spread in all directions.
It was centrally placed for the bounds of the world
Of men's habitations in Asia, Europe, and Africa.
It made the Arabs the leading nation of culture and
science,
Of organised enterprise, law, and arts,
With a zeal for the conquest of Nature and her mysteries.

C. 16.—Behold! There was born into the world of sense
The unlettered Prophet, the comely child,
Noble of birth, but nobler still
In the grace and wisdom of human love
And human understanding; dowered with the key
Which opened to him the enchanted palace
Of nature; marked out to receive—
To receive and preach in burning words
The spiritual truth and message of the Most High.

C. 17.—Others before him had been born
In darkness, beyond the reach
Of history; others again it pleased Allah
To send as Messengers, preaching, working
In the dim twilight of history,
Wherein men fashion legends
After their own hearts and dimly seek
A light afar, remote from the lives
Mean and sordid, such as they knew.

C. 18.—But Muhammad came in the fullest blaze
Of history; with no learning he put to shame
The wisdom of the learned; with pasture folk
He lived and worked, and won their love; in hills
And valleys, caves and deserts, he wandered,
But never lost his way to truth and righteousness;
From his pure and spotless heart the Angels washed
Off the dust that flew around him; through the ways
Of crooked city folk, he walked upright and straight,
And won from them the ungrudging name
Of the Man of Faith[1] who never broke his word.

C. 19.—To the Praiseworthy[2] indeed be praise:
Born in the Sacred City[3] he destroyed
Its superstition; loyal to his people to the core,

1. Al Amīn.
2. Muḥammad.
3. Makkah.

He stood for all humanity; orphan-born
And poor, he envied not the rich,
And made his special care all those
Whom the world neglected or oppressed—
Orphans, women, slaves, and those in need
Of food or comforts, mental solace, spiritual strength,
Or virtues downtrodden in the haunts of men.

C. 20.—His mother[4] and his foster-mother[5]
Loved and wondered at the child;
His grandfather, 'Abd al Muṭṭalib,
Of all his twice-eight children and their offspring,
Loved him best and all his sweet and gentle ways;
His uncle Abū Ṭālib, loth though he was
To give up the cult of his fathers,
Knew well the purity of Muḥammad's
Mind and soul, and was his stoutest champion
When the other chiefs of Makkah sought to kill
The man who challenged in his person
Their narrow Pagan selfish lives.

C. 21.— To his cousin 'Alī, the well-beloved,[6]
Born when he was thirty, he appeared
As the very pattern of a perfect man,
As gentle as he was wise and true and strong,
The one in whose defence and aid
He spent his utmost strength and skill,
Holding life cheap in support of a cause so high,
And placing without reserve his chivalry,
His prowess, his wit and learning, and his sword
At the service of this mighty Messenger of Allah.

C. 22.—Not till the age of forty[7] did he receive
The Commission to stand forth and proclaim
The Bounty of Allah, and His gift, to lowly Man,
Of knowledge by Word and Pen; but all through
His years of preparation he did search
The Truth: he sought it in Nature's forms and laws,
Her beauty and her stern unflinching ways;
He sought it in the inner world
Of human lives, men's joys and sorrows;
Their kindly virtues and their sins

---

4. 'Āmīnah.
5. Ḥalīmah.
6. Murtaḍā.
7. The Arabian year preceding 10 A.H. was roughly luni-solar: See Appendix. IX.

Of pride, injustice, cruel wrong,
And greed of gain; scarce checked by the inner voice
That spoke of duty, moral law, and higher still,
The Will Supreme of Allah, to which the will
Of man must tune itself to find its highest bliss.

C. 23.—But he grew steadfastly in virtue and purity;
Untaught by men, he learnt from them, and learned
To teach them; even as a boy of nine,
When he went in a trade caravan with Abū Ṭālib
To Syria,[8] his tender soul marked inwardly
How Allah did speak in the wide expanse
Of deserts, in the stern grandeur of rocks,
In the refreshing flow of streams, in the smiling
Bloom of gardens, in the art and skill with which
Men and birds and all life sought for light
From the Life of Lives, even as every plant
Seeks through devious ways the light of the Sun.

C. 24.—Nor less was he grieved at Man's ingratitude
When he rebelled and held as naught the Signs
Of Allah, and turned His gifts to baser uses,
Driving rarer souls to hermit life,
Clouding the heavenly mirror of pure affections
With selfish passions, mad unseemly wrangles,
And hard unhallowed loathsome tortures of themselves.

C. 25.—He worked, and joyed in honest labour;
He traded with integrity to himself and to others;
He joined the throngs of cities and their busy life,
But saw its good and evil as types
Of an inner and more lasting life hereafter;
People gladly sought his help as umpire
And peacemaker because they knew his soul
Was just and righteous: he loved the society
Of old and young, but oft withdrew to solitude
For Prayer and inward spiritual strength;
He despised not wealth but used it for others;
He was happy in poverty and used it as his badge

---

8. It was on such visits that he met and conversed with Nestorian Christian monks like Baḥīrah who were quick to recognise his spiritual worth. Perhaps the meeting was in Busra (بُصرى) in the Jabal Druze district of Syria, some 70 miles south of Damascus. There was another Busra in Edom, north of Petra in Transjordania. Busra was famous for trade in costly red dyes, and is referred to as Bozrah in Isaiah, xliii:i. Neither of these towns is to be confounded with the modern Basra. [The Prophet, peace be on him, went to Syria twice, and the incident of meeting Baḥīrah took place in one of these visits. (Eds.)].

And his pride[9] when wealth was within his reach
But not within his grasp, as a man among men.

C. 26.—At twenty-five he was united in the holy bonds
Of wedlock with Khadījah the Great, the noble lady
Who befriended him when he had no worldly resources,
Trusted him when his worth was little known,
Encouraged and understood him in his spiritual struggles,
Believed in him when with trembling steps
He took up the Call and withstood obloquy,
Persecution, insults, threats, and tortures,
And was a life-long helpmate till she was gathered
To the saints in his fifty-first year—
A perfect woman, the mother of those that believe.

C. 27.—There is a cave in the side of Mount Ḥirā'
Some three miles north of the city of Makkah,
In a valley which turns left from the road to 'Arafāt.
To which Muḥammad used to retire for peaceful contemplation:
Often alone, but sometimes with Khadījah.[9-A]
Days and nights he spent there with his Lord.
Hard were the problems he revolved in his mind—
Harder and more cross-grained than the red granite
Of the rock around him—problems not his own,
But his people's, yea, and of human destiny,
Of the Mercy of Allah, and the age-long conflict
Of evil and righteousness, sin and abounding Grace.

C. 28.—Not till forty years of earthly life had passed
That the veil was lifted from the Preserved Tablet
And its contents began to be transferred to the tablet of his mind,
To be proclaimed to the world, and read and studied
For all time—a fountain of mercy and wisdom,
A warning to the heedless, a guide to the erring,
An assurance to those in doubt, a solace to the suffering,
A hope to those in despair—to complete the chain
Of Revelation through the mouths
Of divinely inspired Prophets.

C. 29.—The Chosen One[10] was in the Cave of Ḥirā'.
For two years and more he had prayed there and adored
His Creator and wondered at the mystery
Of man with his corruptible flesh, just growing

9. *Al faqru fakhrī:* "Poverty is my pride."
9-A. This statement is not supported by any authentic evidence on record. [Eds.].
10. Al Muṣṭafā.

Out of a clot,[10-A] and the soul in him
Reaching out to knowledge sublime, new
And ever new, taught by the bounty
Of Allah, and leading to that which man himself
Knoweth not. And now, behold! a dazzling
Vision of beauty and light overpowered his senses,
And he heard the word "*Iqra'!*"

C. 30.—"*Iqra'!*" which being interpreted may mean
"Read!" or "Proclaim!" or "Recite!"
The unlettered Prophet was puzzled;
He could not read. The Angel seemed
To press him to his breast in a close embrace,
And the cry rang clear "*Iqra'!*"
And so it happened three times; until
The first overpowering sensation yielded
To a collected grasp of the words which made clear
His Mission; its Author, Allah, the Creator,
Its subject, Man, Allah's wondrous handiwork,
Capable, by Grace, of rising to heights sublime;
And the instrument of that mission, the sanctified Pen,
And the sanctified Book, the Gift of Allah,
Which men might read, or write, or study, or treasure in their souls.

C. 31.—The veil was lifted from the Chosen One's eyes,
And his soul for a moment was filled with divine
Ecstasy. . .When this passed,
And he returned to the world of Time
And Circumstance and this world of Sense,
He felt like one whose eyes had seen
A light of dazzling beauty, and felt dazed
On his return to common sights.
The darkness now seemed tenfold dark;
The solitude seemed tenfold empty;
The mount of Ḥira', henceforth known
As the Mountain of Light,[11] the mere shell
Of an intense memory. Was it a dream?
Terror seized his limbs and he straightway sought
Her who shared his inmost life,
And told her of his sense of exaltation,
And the awful void when the curtain closed.

C. 32.—She understood, rejoiced, and comforted him;
Gave strength to his shaken senses;

10-A. See 96:2 and n. 6205.

11. Jabal al Nūr (The place where Prophet Muḥammad received the first revelation) (R).

Wrapped up in warmth his shivering body,
Unused as yet to bear the strain and stress
Of an experience rare to mortal men.
She knew it was no dream or delusion.
She went and consulted her cousin Waraqah,
A devout worshipper of Allah in the Faith of Christ,
Learned in spiritual lore. He listened
And with her rejoiced that he, Muḥammad,
Was Allah's Chosen One to renew the Faith.

C. 33.—She said: 'Blessed be thou, Chosen One!
Do we not see thy inner life—true and pure?
Do not all see thy outer life—kind and gentle?—
Loyal to kin, hospitable to strangers?
No thought of harm or mischief ever stained thy mind
Nor word ever passed thy lips that was not true
Or stilled not the passions of narrower men.
Ever ready in the service of Allah, thou art he
Of whom I bear witness: there's no god but He,
And thou art His Chosen Prophet.'

C. 34.—Khadījah believed, exalted in faith
Above all women; 'Alī, the well-beloved,
Then a child of ten, but lion-hearted,
Plighted his faith, and became from that moment
The right hand of Islam; Abū Bakr, the Sincere,[12]
The True-hearted, the man of wealth and influence,
Who used both without stint for the Cause,
The sober counsellor, the inseparable friend,
Never hesitated to declare his faith;
And Zayd, the freedman of Muḥammad,
Counted his freedom as naught compared
With the service of Muḥammad and Islam.
These were the first fruits of the mission:
A woman, a child, a man of affairs, and a freedman,
All banded together in the equality of Islam.

C. 35.—The revelation had come, the mission
And the inspiration. But what was it leading to?
It was a miracle, but not in the sense
Of a reversing of Nature: Al Muṣṭafā's vision
Was linked with Eternity, but he was no soothsayer
Foretelling passing events; the mysteries

12. Ṣadīq or Ṣiddīq, the title of Abū Bakr.

Of knowledge were being opened out, but his message
Was no mere esoteric doctrine, to be grasped
By a few in contemplation, fleeing from action;
Nor was it the practice of single or social monasticism,
Undisturbed by the whims or passions of life.
He was asked to stand forth, to preach, to declare
The One Universal God, the Gracious, the Merciful,
And to lead men to the Right and forbid the Wrong.

C. 36.—The wrong?—The selfish pride of birth,
The massing of power and wealth in the hands
Of a few, the slaughter of female infants,
The orgies of gambling and drunkenness,
The frauds of temples and idols and priests,
The feuds and arrogance of tribes and races,
The separation of Sacred and Profane,
As if the unity of All Life and All Truth
Did not flow from the unity of Allah, Most High.

C. 37.—He was loyal to his family, but could he support
Their monopoly of power?—To his tribe,
But were the Quraysh the only creatures
Of Allah? To the temple of Makkah, but
Could he wink at Lāt and 'Uzzā, and the other monsters,
Whose worship killed the spiritual growth of Man?—
To the earlier Revelations, but could he hold
With the superstitions and falsehoods, the dogmas and creeds
Which went against reason and nature, and the inner light
Which was now fanned into flame by the Will of Allah?

C. 38.—And so his very virtues and loyalties pointed
To offence and conflict, mockery and misrepresentation,
Hatred and persecution, threats, tortures, and exile
For him and his, and martyrdoms, wars, revolutions,
And the shaking of the foundations of history
And the social order. But Islam meant
The willing submission of his will to Allah,
The active attainment of Peace through Conflict.

C. 39.—And he gave that submission, not without effort,
Even as Moses[13] did before him,
And Jesus[14] in the agony of the garden of Gethsemane.

---

13. Qur'ān 20:25-32.
14. Matt. xxvi.

C. 40.—For three and twenty years, in patience,
Conflict, hope, and final triumph,
Did this Prophet of Allah receive
And teach the Message of the Most High.
It came, like the fruit of the soul's own yearning,
To teach profound spiritual truths,
Answer questions, appeal to men
In their doubts and fears, help and put heart
In them in moments of trial, and ordain
For them laws by which they could live
In society lives of purity, goodness and peace.

C. 41.— These messages came as inspiration
To Muḥammad as the need arose,
On different occasions and in different places:
He recited them, and they were recorded
By the Pen: they were imprinted on his heart
And mind, and on the memory
Of his loving disciples: as the body
Of sacred Scripture grew, it was arranged
For purposes of public prayer and reading:
This is the Book, or the Reading, or the Qur'ān.

INTRODUCTION TO SŪRAH 1—*AL FĀTIHAH*

C. 42.—First comes that beautiful Sūrah,[15]
The Opening Chapter[16] of Seven Verses,[17]
Rightly called the Essence of the Book.
It teaches us the perfect Prayer.
For if we can pray aright, it means
That we have some knowledge of Allah
And His attributes, of His relations
To us and His creation, which includes
Ourselves; that we glimpse the source
From which we come, and that final goal
Which is our spiritual destiny
Under Allah's true judgement: then
We offer ourselves to Allah and seek His light.

C. 43.—Prayer is the heart of Religion and Faith
But how shall we pray? What words shall convey
The yearnings of our miserable ignorant hearts
To the Knower of all? Is it worthy of Him
Or of our spiritual nature to ask
For vanities, or even for such physical needs
As our daily bread? The Inspired One
Taught us a Prayer that sums up our faith,
Our hope, and our aspiration in things that matter.
We think in devotion of Allah's name and His Nature;
We praise Him for His creation and His Cherishing care;
We call to mind the Realities, seen and unseen;
We offer Him worship and ask His guidance;
And we know the straight from the crooked path
By the light of His grace that illumines the righteous.

---

15. Each chapter or portion of the Qur'ān is called a Sūrah, which means a Degree or Step, by which we mount up. Sometimes whole Sūrahs were revealed, and sometimes portions, which were arranged under the Prophet's directions. Some Sūrahs are long, and some are short, but a logical thread runs through them all. Each verse of the Sūrah is called an *Āyah* (plural, *Āyāt*), which means also a sign. A verse of revelation is a Sign of Allah's wisdom and goodness just as much as Allah's beautiful handiwork in the material creation or His dealings in history are signs to us, if we would understand. Some *Āyāt* are long, and some are short. The *Āyah* is the true unit of the Qur'ān.

16. *Fātihah* = Opening Chapter.

17. These seven verses form a complete unit by themselves, and are recited in every prayer and on many other occasions. *Cf.* 15:87.

Sūrah 1.

الجزء الأول — سورة الفاتحة

1/30

Al Fātiḥah (The Opening)[18]

1. *In the name of Allah, Most Gracious, Most Merciful.*[19]
2. Praise be to Allah The Cherisher and Sustainer[20] of the Worlds;
3. Most Gracious, Most Merciful;
4. Master of the Day of Judgement.
5. Thee do we worship,[21] And Thine aid we seek.

(١) بِسْمِ اللَّهِ الرَّحْمَٰنِ الرَّحِيمِ
(٢) الْحَمْدُ لِلَّهِ رَبِّ الْعَالَمِينَ
(٣) الرَّحْمَٰنِ الرَّحِيمِ
(٤) مَالِكِ يَوْمِ الدِّينِ
(٥) إِيَّاكَ نَعْبُدُ وَإِيَّاكَ نَسْتَعِينُ

---

18. By universal consent it is rightly placed at the beginning of the Qur'ān, as summing up, in marvellously terse and comprehensive words, man's relation to Allah in contemplation and prayer. In our spiritual contemplation the first words should be those of praise. If the praise is from our inmost being, it brings us into union with Allah's Will. Then our eyes see all good, peace, and harmony. Evil, rebellion, and conflict are purged out. They do not exist for us, for our eyes are lifted up above them in praise. Then we see Allah's attributes better (verses 2-4). This leads us to the attitude of worship and acknowledgment (verse 5). And finally comes prayer for guidance, and a contemplation of what guidance means (verses 6-7).

Allah needs no praise, for He is above all praise; He needs no petition, for He knows our needs better than we do ourselves; and His bounties are open without asking, to the righteous and the sinner alike. The prayer is for our own spiritual education, consolation, and confirmation.

That is why the words in this Sūrah are given to us in the form in which we should utter them. When we reach enlightenment, they flow spontaneously from us.

19. The Arabic words "*Raḥmān* and *Raḥīm*," translated "Most Gracious" and "Most Merciful" are both intensive forms referring to different aspects of Allah's attribute of Mercy. The Arabic intensive is more suited to express Allah's attributes than the superlative degree in English. The latter implies a comparison with other beings, or with other times or places, while there is no being like unto Allah, and He is independent of Time and Place. Mercy may imply pity, long-suffering, patience, and forgiveness, all of which the sinner needs and Allah Most Merciful bestows in abundant measure. But there is a Mercy that goes before even the need arises, the Grace which is ever watchful, and flows from Allah Most Gracious to all His creatures, protecting them, preserving them, guiding them, and leading them to clearer light and higher life. For this reason the attribute *Raḥmān* (Most Gracious) is not applied to any but Allah, but the attribute *Raḥīm* (Merciful), is a general term, and may also be applied to Men. To make us contemplate these boundless gifts of Allah, the formula: "In the name of Allah Most Gracious, Most Merciful": is placed before every Sūrah of the Qur'ān (except the ninth), and repeated at the beginning of every act by the Muslim who dedicates his life to Allah, and whose hope is in His Mercy.

Opinion is divided whether the *Bismillāh* should be numbered as a separate verse or not. It is unanimously agreed that it is a part of the Qur'ān. Therefore it is better to give it an independent number in the first Sūrah. For subsequent Sūrahs it is treated as an introduction or headline, and therefore not numbered.

20. The Arabic word *Rabb*, usually translated Lord, has also the meaning of cherishing, sustaining, bringing to maturity. Allah cares for all the worlds He has created.

There are many worlds—astronomical and physical worlds, worlds of thought, spiritual world, and so on. In every one of them, Allah is all-in-all. We express only one aspect of it when we say: "In Him we live, and move, and have our being." The mystical division between (1) *Nāsūt*, the human world knowable by the senses, (2) *Malakūt*, the invisible world of angels, and (3) *Lāhūt*, the divine world of Reality, requires a whole volume to explain it.

21. On realizing in our souls Allah's love and care, His grace and mercy, and His power and justice (as Ruler of the Day of Judgement), the immediate result is that we bend in the act of worship, and see both our shortcomings and His all-sufficient power. The emphatic form means that not only do we reach the position of worshipping Allah and asking for His help, but we worship Him alone and ask for His aid only. For there is none other than He worthy of our devotion and able to help us. Then plural "we" indicates that we associate ourselves with all who seek Allah, thus strengthening ourselves and strengthening them in a fellowship of faith.

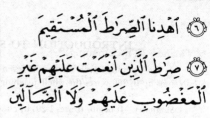

6. Show[22] us the straight way,

اهْدِنَا الصِّرَاطَ الْمُسْتَقِيمَ ۝٦

7. The way of those on whom
Thou hast bestowed Thy Grace,
Those whose (portion)
Is not wrath,[23]
And who go not astray.[24]

صِرَاطَ الَّذِينَ أَنْعَمْتَ عَلَيْهِمْ غَيْرِ الْمَغْضُوبِ عَلَيْهِمْ وَلَا الضَّالِّينَ ۝٧

22. If we translate by the English word "guide," we shall have to say: "Guide us to and in the straight Way." For we may be wandering aimlessly, and the first step is to find the Way; and the second need is to keep in the Way: Our own wisdom may fail in either case. The straight Way is often the narrow Way, or the steep Way, which many people shun (90:11). By the world's perversity the straight Way is sometimes stigmatized and the crooked Way praised. How are we to judge? We must ask for Allah's guidance. With a little spiritual insight we shall see which are the people who walk in the light of Allah's grace, and which are those that walk in the darkness of Wrath. This also would help our judgement.

23. Note that the words relating to Grace are connected actively with Allah; those relating to Wrath are impersonal. In the one case Allah's Mercy encompasses us beyond our deserts. In the other case our own actions are responsible for the Wrath—the negative of Grace, Peace, or Harmony.

24. Are there two categories?—those who are in the darkness of Wrath and those who stray? The first are those who deliberately break God's law; the second those who stray out of carelessness or negligence. Both are responsible for their own acts or omissions. In opposition to both are the people who are in the light of Allah's Grace: for His Grace not only protects them from active wrong (if they will only submit their will to Him) but also from straying into paths of temptation or carelessness. The negative _ghayr_ should be construed as applying not to the way, but as describing men protected from two dangers by Allah's Grace.

INTRODUCTION TO SŪRAH 2—*AL BAQARAH*

As the Opening Sūrah sums up in seven beautiful verses the essence of the Qur'ān, so this Sūrah sums up in 286 verses the whole teaching of the Qur'ān. It is a closely reasoned argument.

Summary—It begins (verses 1-29) by classifying men into three broad categories, depending on how they receive Allah's message.

This leads to the story of the creation of man, the high destiny intended for him, his fall, and the hope held out to him (2:30-39).

Israel's story is then told according to their own records and traditions—what privileges they received and how they abused them (2:40-86), thus illustrating again as by a parable the general story of man.

In particular, reference is made to Moses and Jesus and their struggles with an unruly people: how people of the Book played false their own lights and in their pride rejected Muḥammad, who came in the true line of Prophets (2:87-121). (R).

They falsely laid claim to the virtues of Father Abraham: he was indeed a righteous Imām, but he was the progenitor of Ismā'īl's line (Arabs) as well as of Israel's line, and he with Ismā'īl built the Ka'bah (the House of Allah in Makkah) and purified it, thus establishing a common religion, of which Islam is the universal exponent (2:122-141). (R).

The Ka'bah was now to be the center of universal worship and the symbol of Islamic unity (2:142-167).

The Islamic *Ummah* (brotherhood) having thus been established with its definite centre and symbol, ordinances are laid down for the social life of the community, with the proviso (2:177) that righteousness does not consist in formalities, but in faith, kindness, prayer, charity, probity, and patience under suffering. The ordinances relate to food and drink, bequests, fasts, jihād, wine and gambling, treatment of orphans and women, etc. (2:168-242).

Lest the subject of jihād should be misunderstood, it is taken up again in the story of Saul, Goliath and David, in contrast to the story of Jesus (2:243-253).

And so the lesson is enforced that true virtue lies in practical deeds of manliness, kindness, and good faith (2:254-283), and Allah's nature[24-A] is called to mind in the sublime *Ayah al Kursī*, the Verse of the Throne (2:255).

The Sūrah ends with an exhortation to Faith, Obedience, a sense of Personal Responsibility, and Prayer (2:284-286).

This is the longest Sūrah of the Qur'ān, and in it occurs the longest verse (2:282). The name of the Sūrah is from the Parable of the Heifer in 2:67-71, which illustrates the insufficiency of carping obedience. When faith is lost, people put off obedience with various excuses: even when at last they obey in the letter, they fail in the spirit, which means that they get fossilised, and their self-sufficiency prevents them from seeing that spiritually they are not alive but dead. For life is movement, activity, striving, fighting against baser things. And this is the burden of the Sūrah.

This is in the main an early Madīnah.

C. 44.—The Message of Allah, is a guide that is sure
(2:1-29.) To those who seek His light. But those
Who reject faith are blind: their hearts
Are sealed. Woe to the hypocrites,
Self-deceived and deceiving others,
With mockery on their lips, and mischief
In their hearts, and fear; the clouds
That bring fertilizing rain to others,
To them bring but deafening thunder-peals
And lightning flashes blinding to their eyes.

24-A. By the expression "Allah's nature" the author means Allah's attributes. [Eds.].

Sūrah 2.

***Al Baqarah* (The Heifer)**

In the name of Allah, Most Gracious,
Most Merciful.

1. Alif Lām Mīm.[25]

2. This is the Book;
In it is guidance sure, without doubt,
To those who fear[26] Allah;

3. Who believe in the Unseen,
Are steadfast in prayer,
And spend out of what We
Have provided for them;[27]

4. And who believe in the Revelation
Sent to thee,
And sent before thy time,
And (in their hearts)
Have the assurance of the Hereafter.[28]

الجزء الأول سُورَةُ البَقَرَة

بِسْمِ ٱللَّهِ ٱلرَّحْمَٰنِ ٱلرَّحِيمِ

(١) الٓمٓ

(٢) ذَٰلِكَ ٱلْكِتَٰبُ لَا رَيْبَ فِيهِ
هُدًى لِّلْمُتَّقِينَ

(٣) ٱلَّذِينَ يُؤْمِنُونَ بِٱلْغَيْبِ وَيُقِيمُونَ ٱلصَّلَوٰةَ
وَمِمَّا رَزَقْنَٰهُمْ يُنفِقُونَ

(٤) وَٱلَّذِينَ يُؤْمِنُونَ بِمَآ أُنزِلَ إِلَيْكَ
وَمَآ أُنزِلَ مِن قَبْلِكَ
وَبِٱلْءَاخِرَةِ هُمْ يُوقِنُونَ

---

25. These are abbreviated letters, the *Muqaṭṭaʻāt,* on which a general discussion will be found in Appendix I (at the end of this Sūrah).

The particular letters, *Alif, Lām, Mīm,* are found prefixed to this Sūrah, and Sūrahs 3, 29, 30, 31 and 32 (six in all). In 2 and 3 the argument is about the rise and fall of nations, their past, and their future in history, with ordinances for the new universal people of Islam. In 29 a similar argument about nations leads off to the mystery of Life and Death, Failure and Triumph, Past and Future, in the history of individual souls. The burden of 30 is that Allah is the source of all things and all things return to Him. In 31 and 32 the same lesson is enforced: Allah is the Creator and He will be the Judge on the Last Day. There is therefore a common thread, the mystery of Life and Death, Beginning and End.

Much has been written about the meaning of these letters, but most of it is pure conjecture. Some commentators are content to recognize them as some mystic symbols of which it is unprofitable to discuss the meaning by more verbal logic. (R).

26. *Taqwā,* and the verbs and nouns connected with the root, signify: (1) the fear of Allah, which, according to the writer of Proverbs (i. 7) in the Old Testament, is the beginning of Wisdom; (2) restraint, or guarding one's tongue, hand, and heart from evil; (3) hence righteousness, piety, good conduct. All these ideas are implied: in the translation, only one or other of these ideas can be indicated, according to the context. See also 47:17; and 74:56, n. 5808.

27. All bounties proceed from Allah. They may be physical gifts, *e.g.* food, clothing, houses, gardens, wealth, etc. or intangible gifts, *e.g.*, influence, power, birth and the opportunities flowing from it, health, talents, etc. or spiritual gifts, *e.g.*, insight into good and evil, understanding of men, the capacity for love, etc. We are to use all in humility and moderation. But we are also to give out of every one of them something that contributes to the well-being of others. We are to be neither ascetics nor luxurious sybarites, neither selfish misers nor thoughtless prodigals.

28. Righteousness comes from a secure faith, from sincere devotion to Allah, and from unselfish service to Man.

5. They are on (true guidance),
From their Lord, and it is
These who will prosper.[29]

(٥) أُولَٰٓئِكَ عَلَىٰ هُدًى مِّن رَّبِّهِمْ
وَأُولَٰٓئِكَ هُمُ ٱلْمُفْلِحُونَ

6. As to those who reject Faith,[30]
It is the same to them
Whether thou warn them
Or do not warn them;
They will not believe.

(٦) إِنَّ ٱلَّذِينَ كَفَرُوا۟ سَوَآءٌ عَلَيْهِمْ
ءَأَنذَرْتَهُمْ أَمْ لَمْ تُنذِرْهُمْ لَا يُؤْمِنُونَ

7. Allah hath set a seal[31]
On their hearts and on their hearing,
And on their eyes is a veil;
Great is the penalty they (incur).[32]

(٧) خَتَمَ ٱللَّهُ عَلَىٰ قُلُوبِهِمْ وَعَلَىٰ سَمْعِهِمْ
وَعَلَىٰٓ أَبْصَٰرِهِمْ غِشَٰوَةٌ
وَلَهُمْ عَذَابٌ عَظِيمٌ

SECTION 2.

8. Of the people there are some who say:[33]
"We believe in Allah and the Last day;"
But they do not (really) believe.

(٨) وَمِنَ ٱلنَّاسِ مَن يَقُولُ ءَامَنَّا بِٱللَّهِ
وَبِٱلْيَوْمِ ٱلْءَاخِرِ وَمَا هُم بِمُؤْمِنِينَ

9. Fain would they deceive
Allah and those who believe,
But they only deceive themselves,
And realize (it) not!

(٩) يُخَٰدِعُونَ ٱللَّهَ وَٱلَّذِينَ ءَامَنُوا۟
وَمَا يَخْدَعُونَ إِلَّآ أَنفُسَهُمْ وَمَا يَشْعُرُونَ

10. In their hearts is a disease;

(١٠) فِى قُلُوبِهِم مَّرَضٌ

---

29. Prosperity must be taken as referring to all the kinds of bounty which we discussed in the note to 2:3 above. The right use of one kind leads to an increase in that and other kinds, and that is prosperity.

30. *Kafara, kufr, kāfir,* and derivative forms of the word, imply a deliberate rejection of Faith as opposed to a mistaken idea of Allah or faith, which is not inconsistent with an earnest desire to see the truth. Where there is such desire, the Grace and Mercy of Allah gives guidance. But that guidance is not efficacious when it is deliberately rejected, and the possibility of rejection follows from the grant of free will. The consequence of the rejection is that the spiritual faculties become dead or impervious to better influences, See also n. 93 to 2:88.

31. All actions are referred to Allah. Therefore when we get the penalty of our deliberate sin, and our senses become impervious to good, the penalty is referred to the justice of Allah.

32. The penalty here is the opposite of the prosperity referred to in 2:5. As we go down the path of sin, our penalty gathers momentum, just as goodness brings its own capacity for greater goodness.

33. We now come to a third class of people, the hypocrites. They are untrue to themselves, and therefore their hearts are diseased (2:10). The disease tends to spread, like all evil. They are curable but if they harden their hearts, they soon pass into the category of those who deliberately reject light.

And Allah has increased their
disease:[34]
And grievous is the penalty they
(incur),
Because they are false
(to themselves).

فَزَادَهُمُ ٱللَّهُ مَرَضًا
وَلَهُمْ عَذَابٌ أَلِيمٌۢ بِمَا كَانُوا۟ يَكْذِبُونَ

11. When it is said to them:
"Make not mischief on the earth,"
They say: "Why, we only
Want to make peace!"

١١ وَإِذَا قِيلَ لَهُمْ لَا تُفْسِدُوا۟ فِى ٱلْأَرْضِ
قَالُوٓا۟ إِنَّمَا نَحْنُ مُصْلِحُونَ

12. Of a surety, they are the ones
Who make mischief,
But they realize (it) not.[35]

١٢ أَلَآ إِنَّهُمْ هُمُ ٱلْمُفْسِدُونَ
وَلَٰكِن لَّا يَشْعُرُونَ

13. When it is said to them:
"Believe as the others believe:"
They say: "Shall we believe
As the fools believe?"—
Nay, of a surety they are the
fools,
But they do not know.[36]

١٣ وَإِذَا قِيلَ لَهُمْ ءَامِنُوا۟ كَمَآ ءَامَنَ ٱلنَّاسُ
قَالُوٓا۟ أَنُؤْمِنُ كَمَآ ءَامَنَ ٱلسُّفَهَآءُ ۗ
أَلَآ إِنَّهُمْ هُمُ ٱلسُّفَهَآءُ وَلَٰكِن لَّا يَعْلَمُونَ

14. When they meet those who
believe,[37]
They say: "We believe;"
But when they are alone
With their evil ones,
They say: "We are really with you
We (were) only jesting."

١٤ وَإِذَا لَقُوا۟ ٱلَّذِينَ ءَامَنُوا۟ قَالُوٓا۟ ءَامَنَّا
وَإِذَا خَلَوْا۟ إِلَىٰ شَيَٰطِينِهِمْ قَالُوٓا۟ إِنَّا مَعَكُمْ
إِنَّمَا نَحْنُ مُسْتَهْزِءُونَ

15. Allah will throw back
Their mockery on them,
And give them rope in
their trespasses;
So they will wander like blind
ones (to and fro).

١٥ ٱللَّهُ يَسْتَهْزِئُ بِهِمْ
وَيَمُدُّهُمْ فِى طُغْيَٰنِهِمْ يَعْمَهُونَ

16. These are they who have
bartered
Guidance for error:

١٦ أُو۟لَٰٓئِكَ ٱلَّذِينَ ٱشْتَرَوُا۟
ٱلضَّلَٰلَةَ بِٱلْهُدَىٰ

---

34. The insincere man who thinks he can get the best of both worlds by compromising with good and evil only increases the disease of his heart, because he is not true to himself. Even the good which comes to him he can pervert to evil. So the rain which fills out the ear of corn or lends fragrance to the rose also lends strength to the thorn or adds strength to the poison of the deadly nightshade.

35. Much mischief is caused (sometimes unwittingly) by people who think that they have a mission of peace, when they have not even a true perception of right and wrong. By their blind arrogance they depress the good and encourage the evil.

36. This is another phase of the hypocrite and the cynic. "Faith," he says, "is good enough to fools." But his cynicism may be the greatest folly in the eyes of Allah.

37. A deeper phase of insincerity is actual duplicity. But it never pays in the end. If we compare such a man to a trader, he loses in the bargain.

But their traffic is profitless,
And they have lost true direction.

فَمَا رَبِحَت تِّجَـٰرَتُهُمْ وَمَا كَانُوا۟ مُهْتَدِينَ

17. Their similitude is that of a man[38]
Who kindled a fire;
When it lighted all around him,
Allah took away their light
And left them in utter darkness.
So they could not see.

١٧ مَثَلُهُمْ كَمَثَلِ ٱلَّذِى ٱسْتَوْقَدَ نَارًا
فَلَمَّآ أَضَآءَتْ مَا حَوْلَهُۥ ذَهَبَ ٱللَّهُ بِنُورِهِمْ
وَتَرَكَهُمْ فِى ظُلُمَـٰتٍ لَّا يُبْصِرُونَ

18. Deaf, dumb, and blind,
They will not return (to the path).

١٨ صُمٌّۢ بُكْمٌ عُمْىٌ فَهُمْ لَا يَرْجِعُونَ

19. Or (another similitude)[39]
Is that of a rain-laden cloud
From the sky: in it are zones
Of darkness, and thunder and lightning:
They press their fingers in their ears
To keep out the stunning thunderclap,
The while they are in terror of death.
But Allah is ever round
The rejecters of Faith!

١٩ أَوْ كَصَيِّبٍ مِّنَ ٱلسَّمَآءِ
فِيهِ ظُلُمَـٰتٌ وَرَعْدٌ وَبَرْقٌ
يَجْعَلُونَ أَصَـٰبِعَهُمْ فِىٓ ءَاذَانِهِم
مِّنَ ٱلصَّوَٰعِقِ حَذَرَ ٱلْمَوْتِ
وَٱللَّهُ مُحِيطٌۢ بِٱلْكَـٰفِرِينَ

20. The lightning all but snatches away
Their sight; every time the light
(Helps) them, they walk therein,
And when the darkness grows on them,
They stand still,
And if Allah willed, He could take away
Their faculty of hearing and seeing;
For Allah hath power over all things.

٢٠ يَكَادُ ٱلْبَرْقُ يَخْطَفُ أَبْصَـٰرَهُمْ
كُلَّمَآ أَضَآءَ لَهُم مَّشَوْا۟ فِيهِ
وَإِذَآ أَظْلَمَ عَلَيْهِمْ قَامُوا۟
وَلَوْ شَآءَ ٱللَّهُ
لَذَهَبَ بِسَمْعِهِمْ وَأَبْصَـٰرِهِمْ
إِنَّ ٱللَّهَ عَلَىٰ كُلِّ شَىْءٍ قَدِيرٌ

38. The man wanted light; he only kindled a fire. It produced a blaze, and won the applause of all around. But it did not last long. When the flame went out as was inevitable, the darkness was worse than before. And they all lost their way. So hypocrisy, deception, arrogant compromise with evil, cynicism, or duplicity may win temporary applause. But the true light of faith and sincerity is wanting, and therefore it must mislead and ruin all concerned. In the consternation they cannot speak or hear each other, and of course they cannot see; so they end like the deliberate rejecters of Faith (2:7), wildly groping about, dumb, deaf and blind.

39. A wonderfully graphic and powerful simile applying to those who reject Faith. In their self-sufficiency they are undisturbed normally. But what happens when a great storm breaks over them? They cover their ears against thunder-claps, and the lightning nearly blinds them. They are in mortal fear, but Allah encompasses them around—even them, for He at all times encompasses all. He gives them rope. In the intervals of deafening noise and blinding flashes, there are moments of steady light, and these creatures take advantage of them, but again they are plunged into darkness. Perhaps they curse; perhaps they think that the few moments of effective light are due to their own intelligence! How much wiser would they be if they humbled themselves and sought the light of Allah!

SECTION 3.

21. O ye people!
Adore your Guardian Lord,
Who created you
And those who came before you,
That ye may become righteous,[40]

يَٰٓأَيُّهَا ٱلنَّاسُ ٱعْبُدُوا۟ رَبَّكُمُ ﴿٢١﴾
ٱلَّذِى خَلَقَكُمْ وَٱلَّذِينَ مِن قَبْلِكُمْ
لَعَلَّكُمْ تَتَّقُونَ

22. Who has made the earth your couch
And the heavens your canopy;
And sent down rain from the heavens;
And brought forth therewith
Fruits for your sustenance;
Then set not up rivals[41] unto Allah
When ye know (the truth).

ٱلَّذِى جَعَلَ لَكُمُ ٱلْأَرْضَ فِرَٰشًا ﴿٢٢﴾
وَٱلسَّمَآءَ بِنَآءً وَأَنزَلَ مِنَ ٱلسَّمَآءِ مَآءً
فَأَخْرَجَ بِهِۦ مِنَ ٱلثَّمَرَٰتِ رِزْقًا لَّكُمْ
فَلَا تَجْعَلُوا۟ لِلَّهِ أَندَادًا
وَأَنتُمْ تَعْلَمُونَ

23. And if ye are in doubt
As to what We have revealed
From time to time to Our servant,
Then produce a Sūrah
Like thereunto;
And call your witnesses or helpers
(If there are any) besides Allah,
If your (doubts) are true.[42]

وَإِن كُنتُمْ فِى رَيْبٍ مِّمَّا نَزَّلْنَا عَلَىٰ عَبْدِنَا ﴿٢٣﴾
فَأْتُوا۟ بِسُورَةٍ مِّن مِّثْلِهِۦ
وَٱدْعُوا۟ شُهَدَآءَكُم مِّن دُونِ ٱللَّهِ
إِن كُنتُمْ صَٰدِقِينَ

24. But if ye cannot—
And of a surety ye cannot—
Then fear the Fire
Whose fuel is Men and Stones—

فَإِن لَّمْ تَفْعَلُوا۟ وَلَن تَفْعَلُوا۟ ﴿٢٤﴾
فَٱتَّقُوا۟ ٱلنَّارَ ٱلَّتِى وَقُودُهَا ٱلنَّاسُ وَٱلْحِجَارَةُ

40. For *Taqwā* see 2:2, n. 26. I connect this dependent clause with "adore, etc." above, though it could be connected with "created." According to my construction the argument will be as follows. Adoration is the act of the highest and humblest reverence and worship. When you get into that relationship with Allah, Who is your Creator and Guardian, your faith produces works of righteousness. It is a chance given you: will you exercise your free will and take it? If you do, your whole nature will be transformed.

41. Further proofs of Allah's goodness to you are given in this verse. Your whole life, physical and spiritual, depends upon Him. The spiritual is figured by the Canopy of Heaven. The truth has been brought plainly before you. Will you still resist it and go after false gods, the creation of your own fancy? The false gods may be idols, superstitions, self, or even great or glorious things like Poetry, Art, or Science, when set up as rivals to Allah. They may be pride of race, pride of birth, pride of wealth or position, pride of power, pride of learning, or even spiritual pride.

42. How do we know that there is revelation, and that it is from Allah? Here is a concrete test. The Teacher of Allah's Truth has placed before you many Sūrahs. Can you produce one like it? If there is any one besides Allah, who can inspire spiritual truth in such noble language, produce your evidence. Or is it that your doubts are merely argumentative, refractory, against your own inner light, or conscience? All true revelation is itself a miracle, and stands on its own merits.

Which is prepared for those
Who reject Faith.[43]

أُعِدَّتْ لِلْكَٰفِرِينَ

25. But give glad tidings
To those who believe
And work righteousness,
That their portion is Gardens,
Beneath which rivers flow.
Every time they are fed
With fruits therefrom,
They say: "Why, this is
What we were fed with before,"
For they are given things in similitude;
And they have therein
Companions pure (and holy);[44]
And they abide therein (forever).

٢٥ وَبَشِّرِ ٱلَّذِينَ ءَامَنُوا۟
وَعَمِلُوا۟ ٱلصَّٰلِحَٰتِ
أَنَّ لَهُمْ جَنَّٰتٍ تَجْرِى مِن تَحْتِهَا ٱلْأَنْهَٰرُ ۖ
كُلَّمَا رُزِقُوا۟ مِنْهَا مِن ثَمَرَةٍ رِّزْقًا ۙ قَالُوا۟
هَٰذَا ٱلَّذِى رُزِقْنَا مِن قَبْلُ ۖ
وَأُتُوا۟ بِهِۦ مُتَشَٰبِهًا ۖ
وَلَهُمْ فِيهَآ أَزْوَٰجٌ مُّطَهَّرَةٌ ۖ
وَهُمْ فِيهَا خَٰلِدُونَ

26. Allah disdains not to use
The similitude of things,
Lowest[45] as well as highest.

٢٦ إِنَّ ٱللَّهَ لَا يَسْتَحْىِۦٓ أَن يَضْرِبَ مَثَلًا
مَّا بَعُوضَةً فَمَا فَوْقَهَا ۚ

43. According to commentators the "Stones" mentioned in this verse refer to the idols which the polytheists worshipped. Thus, far from coming to the aid of their worshippers, the false gods would be a means of aggravating their torment. [Eds.].

44. What can be more delightful than a Garden where you observe from a picturesque height a beautiful landscape round you—rivers flowing with crystal water, and fruit trees of which the choicest fruit is before you. The fruit of goodness is goodness, similar, but choicer in every degree of ascent. You think it is the same, but it is because of your past experiences and associations of memory. (R).

45. The word for "the lowest" in the original Arabic means a gnat, a byword in the Arabic language for the weakest of creatures. In 29:41, which was revealed before this Sūrah, the similitude of the Spider was used, and similarly in 22:73, there is the similitude of the fly. For similitudes taken from magnificent forces of nature, expressed in exalted language, see 2:19 above. To Allah all His creation has some special meaning appropriate to itself, and some of what we consider the lowest creatures have wonderful aptitudes, *e.g.*, the spider or the fly. Parables like these may be an occasion of stumbling to those "who forsake the path": in other words those who deliberately shut their eyes to Allah's Signs, and their Penalty is attributed to Allah, the Cause of all causes. But lest there should be misunderstanding, it is immediately added that the stumbling and offence only occur as the result of the sinner's own choice of the wrong course. Verses 26 and 27 form one sentence and should be read together. "Forsaking the path" is defined in 2:27; *viz.*, breaking solemn covenants which the sinner's own soul had ratified, causing division among mankind, who were meant to be one brotherhood, and doing as much mischief as possible in the life on this earth, for the life beyond will be on another plane, where no rope will be given to evil.

The mention of the Covenant (2:27) has a particular and a general signification. The particular one has reference to the Jewish tradition that a Covenant was entered into with "Father Abraham" that in return for Allah's favours the seed of Abraham would serve Allah faithfully. But as a matter of fact a great part of Abraham's progeny were in constant spiritual rebellion against Allah, as is testified by their own Prophets and Preachers and by Muḥammad Muṣṭafā. The general signification is that a similar Covenant is entered into by every creature of Allah: for Allah's loving care, we at least owe Him the fullest gratitude and willing obedience. The Sinner, before he darkens his own conscience, knows this, and yet he not only "forsakes the path" but resists the Grace of Allah which comes to save him. That is why his case becomes hopeless. But the loss is his own. He cannot spoil Allah's design. The good man is glad to retrace his steps from any lapses of which he may have been guilty, and in his case Allah's Message reclaims him with complete understanding. (R).

Those who believe know
That it is truth from their Lord;
But those who reject faith say:
"What means Allah by this
similitude?"
By it He causes many to stray,
And many He leads into the right
path;
But He causes not to stray,
Except those who forsake
(the path)—

فَأَمَّا ٱلَّذِينَ ءَامَنُوا۟
فَيَعْلَمُونَ أَنَّهُ ٱلْحَقُّ مِن رَّبِّهِمْ
وَأَمَّا ٱلَّذِينَ كَفَرُوا۟ فَيَقُولُونَ
مَاذَآ أَرَادَ ٱللَّهُ بِهَٰذَا مَثَلًا
يُضِلُّ بِهِۦ كَثِيرًا وَيَهْدِى بِهِۦ كَثِيرًا
وَمَا يُضِلُّ بِهِۦٓ إِلَّا ٱلْفَٰسِقِينَ

27. Those who break Allah's
Covenant
After it is ratified,
And who sunder what Allah
Has ordered to be joined,
And do mischief on earth:
These cause loss (only) to
themselves.

٢٧ ٱلَّذِينَ يَنقُضُونَ عَهْدَ ٱللَّهِ
مِنۢ بَعْدِ مِيثَٰقِهِۦ
وَيَقْطَعُونَ مَآ أَمَرَ ٱللَّهُ بِهِۦٓ أَن يُوصَلَ
وَيُفْسِدُونَ فِى ٱلْأَرْضِ
أُو۟لَٰٓئِكَ هُمُ ٱلْخَٰسِرُونَ

28. How can ye reject[46]
The faith in Allah?—Seeing that
ye were without life,
And He gave you life;
Then will He cause you to die,
And will again bring you to life;
And again to Him will ye return.

٢٨ كَيْفَ تَكْفُرُونَ بِٱللَّهِ
وَكُنتُمْ أَمْوَٰتًا فَأَحْيَٰكُمْ
ثُمَّ يُمِيتُكُمْ ثُمَّ يُحْيِيكُمْ
ثُمَّ إِلَيْهِ تُرْجَعُونَ

29. It is He Who hath created for
you
All things that are on earth;
Then He turned to the heaven
And made them into seven
firmaments.
And of all things
He hath perfect knowledge.

٢٩ هُوَ ٱلَّذِى خَلَقَ لَكُم
مَّا فِى ٱلْأَرْضِ جَمِيعًا
ثُمَّ ٱسْتَوَىٰٓ إِلَى ٱلسَّمَآءِ
فَسَوَّىٰهُنَّ سَبْعَ سَمَٰوَٰتٍ
وَهُوَ بِكُلِّ شَىْءٍ عَلِيمٌ

C. 45.—Yet man! What wonderful destiny
(2:30-39.) Is thine! Created to be
Allah's viceregent on earth!

---

46. In the preceding verses Allah has used various arguments. He has recalled His goodness (2:21-22); resolved doubts (2:23); plainly set forth the penalty of wrongdoing (2:24); given glad tidings (2:25); shown how misunderstandings arise from a deliberate rejection of the light and breach of the Covenant (2:26-27). Now (2:28-29) He pleads with His creatures and appeals to their own subjective feelings. He brought you into being. The mysteries of life and death are in His hands. When you die on this earth, that is not the end. You were of Him and you must return to Him. Look around you and realize your own dignity: it is from Him. The immeasurable depths of space above and around you may stagger you. They are part of His plan. What you have imagined as the seven firmaments (and any other scheme you may construct) bears witness to His design of order and perfection, for His knowledge (unlike yours) is all-comprehending. And yet will you deliberately reject or obscure or deaden the faculty of Faith which has been put into you?

Yet beguiled by evil! Set for a season
On this earth on probation
To purge thy stain, with the promise
Of guidance and hope from on high,
From the Oft-Returning, Merciful!
Wilt thou choose right and regain
Thy spiritual home with Allah?

SECTION 4.

30. Behold, thy Lord said to the angels: "I will create
A vicegerent on earth." They said:
"Wilt Thou place therein one who will make
Mischief therein and shed blood?—
Whilst we do celebrate Thy praises
And glorify Thy holy (name)?"
He said: "I know what ye know not."[47]

٣٠ وَإِذْ قَالَ رَبُّكَ لِلْمَلَٰٓئِكَةِ
إِنِّي جَاعِلٌ فِي ٱلْأَرْضِ خَلِيفَةً
قَالُوٓا۟ أَتَجْعَلُ فِيهَا مَن يُفْسِدُ فِيهَا
وَيَسْفِكُ ٱلدِّمَآءَ
وَنَحْنُ نُسَبِّحُ بِحَمْدِكَ
وَنُقَدِّسُ لَكَ
قَالَ إِنِّيٓ أَعْلَمُ مَا لَا تَعْلَمُونَ

31. And He taught Adam the names[48]
Of all things; then He placed them
Before the angels, and said: "Tell Me
The names of these if ye are right."

٣١ وَعَلَّمَ ءَادَمَ ٱلْأَسْمَآءَ كُلَّهَا
ثُمَّ عَرَضَهُمْ عَلَى ٱلْمَلَٰٓئِكَةِ
فَقَالَ أَنۢبِـُٔونِي بِأَسْمَآءِ هَٰٓؤُلَآءِ
إِن كُنتُمْ صَٰدِقِينَ

32. They said: "Glory to Thee: of knowledge

٣٢ قَالُوا۟ سُبْحَٰنَكَ

47. It would seem that the angels, though holy and pure, and endued with power from Allah, yet represented only one side of Creation. We may imagine them without passion or emotion, of which the highest flower is love. If man was to be endued with emotions, those emotions could lead him to the highest and drag him to the lowest. The power of will or choosing would have to go with them, in order that man might steer his own bark. This power of will (when used aright) gave him to some extent a mastery over his own fortunes and over nature, thus bringing him nearer to the God-like nature, which has supreme mastery and will. We may suppose the angels had no independent wills of their own: their perfection in other ways reflected Allah's perfection but could not raise them to the dignity of vicegerency. The perfect vicegerent is he who has the power of initiative himself, but whose independent action always reflects perfectly the will of his Principal. The distinction is expressed by Shakespeare (Sonnet 94) in those fine lines: "They are the lords and owners of their faces. Others but stewards of their excellence." The angels in their one-sidedness saw only the mischief consequent on the misuse of the emotional nature by man: perhaps they also. being without emotions, did not understand the whole of Allah's nature, which gives and asks for love. In humility and true devotion to Allah, they remonstrate: we must not imagine the least tinge of jealousy, as they are without emotion. This mystery of love being above them, they are told that they do not know, and they acknowledge (in 2:32 below) not their fault (for there is no question of fault but their imperfection of knowledge. At the same time, the matter is brought home to them when the actual capacities of man are shown to them (2:31.33).

48. "The names of things:" according to commentators means the inner nature and qualities of things, and things here would include feelings. The particular qualities or feelings which were outside the nature of angels were put by Allah into the nature of man. Man was thus able to love and understand love, and thus plan and initiate, as becomes the office of vicegerent. The angels acknowledged this. These things they could only know from the outside, but they had faith, or belief in the Unseen. And they knew that Allah saw all—what others see, what others do not see, what others may even wish to conceal. Man has many qualities which are latent or which he may wish to suppress or conceal, to his own detriment. (R).

We have none, save what Thou
Hast taught us: in truth it is Thou
Who art perfect in knowledge and wisdom."

لَا عِلْمَ لَنَآ إِلَّا مَا عَلَّمْتَنَآ
إِنَّكَ أَنتَ ٱلْعَلِيمُ ٱلْحَكِيمُ

33. He said: "O Adam! tell them
Their names." When he had told them,
Allah said: "Did I not tell you
That I know the secrets of heaven
And earth, and I know what ye reveal
And what ye conceal?"

٣٣ قَالَ يَـٰٓـَٔادَمُ أَنۢبِئْهُم بِأَسْمَآئِهِمْ
فَلَمَّآ أَنۢبَأَهُم بِأَسْمَآئِهِمْ قَالَ أَلَمْ أَقُل لَّكُمْ
إِنِّىٓ أَعْلَمُ غَيْبَ ٱلسَّمَـٰوَٰتِ وَٱلْأَرْضِ
وَأَعْلَمُ مَا تُبْدُونَ وَمَا كُنتُمْ تَكْتُمُونَ

34. And behold, We said to the angels:
"Bow down to Adam:" and they bowed down:
Not so Iblīs:[49] he refused and was haughty:
He was of those who reject Faith.

٣٤ وَإِذْ قُلْنَا لِلْمَلَـٰٓئِكَةِ ٱسْجُدُوا۟ لِءَادَمَ
فَسَجَدُوٓا۟ إِلَّآ إِبْلِيسَ أَبَىٰ
وَٱسْتَكْبَرَ وَكَانَ مِنَ ٱلْكَـٰفِرِينَ

35. We said: "O Adam! dwell thou
And thy wife in the Garden;[50]
And eat of the bountiful things therein
As (where and when) ye will; but
approach not this tree,
Or ye run into harm and transgression."[51]

٣٥ وَقُلْنَا يَـٰٓـَٔادَمُ ٱسْكُنْ أَنتَ وَزَوْجُكَ ٱلْجَنَّةَ
وَكُلَا مِنْهَا رَغَدًا حَيْثُ شِئْتُمَا
وَلَا تَقْرَبَا هَـٰذِهِ ٱلشَّجَرَةَ
فَتَكُونَا مِنَ ٱلظَّـٰلِمِينَ

36. Then did Satan[52] make them slip
From the (Garden), and get them out

٣٦ فَأَزَلَّهُمَا ٱلشَّيْطَـٰنُ عَنْهَا
فَأَخْرَجَهُمَا

49. The Arabic may also be translated: "They bowed down, except Iblīs." In that case Iblīs (Satan) would be one of the angels. But the theory of fallen angels is not accepted in Muslim theology. In 18:50, Iblīs is spoken of as a Jinn. We shall discuss later the meaning of this word. (R).

50. Was the Garden of Eden a place on this earth? Obviously not. For, in verse 36 below, it was after the Fall that the sentence was pronounced: "On earth will be your dwelling-place." Before the Fall, we must suppose Man to be on another plane altogether—of felicity, innocence, trust, a spiritual existence,. with the negation of enmity, want of faith, and all evil. (R).

51. *Ẓulm* in Arabic implies harm, wrong, injustice. or transgression, and may have reference to oneself; when the wrong is done to others it implies tyranny and oppression; the idea of wrong naturally connects itself with darkness, which is another shade of meaning carried with the root word.

52. The word Iblīs in the verse 34 above is derived from the root idea of desperateness or rebellion whereas "Satan" conveys the idea of perversity or enmity. Note the appropriateness of the term on each occasion. Also, "slipping" from the Garden denotes the idea of Evil gradually tempting man from a higher to a lower state. (R).

Of the state (of felicity) in which
They had been. We said:
"Get ye down, all (ye people[53]),
With enmity between yourselves.
On earth will be your dwelling place
And your means of livelihood[54] —
For a time."

مِمَّا كَانَا فِيهِ
وَقُلْنَا ٱهْبِطُوا۟ بَعْضُكُمْ لِبَعْضٍ عَدُوٌّ
وَلَكُمْ فِى ٱلْأَرْضِ مُسْتَقَرٌّ
وَمَتَٰعٌ إِلَىٰ حِينٍ

37. Then learnt Adam from his Lord
Words of inspiration,[55] and his Lord
Turned towards him; for He
Is Oft-Returning, Most Merciful.

٣٧ فَتَلَقَّىٰٓ ءَادَمُ مِن رَّبِّهِۦ كَلِمَٰتٍ
فَتَابَ عَلَيْهِ
إِنَّهُۥ هُوَ ٱلتَّوَّابُ ٱلرَّحِيمُ

38. We said: "Get ye down all from here:
And if, as is sure, there comes to you
Guidance from Me,[56] whosoever
Follows My guidance, on them
Shall be no fear, nor shall they grieve.

٣٨ قُلْنَا ٱهْبِطُوا۟ مِنْهَا جَمِيعًا
فَإِمَّا يَأْتِيَنَّكُم مِّنِّى هُدًى
فَمَن تَبِعَ هُدَاىَ
فَلَا خَوْفٌ عَلَيْهِمْ وَلَا هُمْ يَحْزَنُونَ

39. "But those who reject Faith
And belie Our Signs,
They shall be Companions of the Fire;
They shall abide therein."[57]

٣٩ وَٱلَّذِينَ كَفَرُوا۟ وَكَذَّبُوا۟ بِـَٔايَٰتِنَآ
أُو۟لَٰٓئِكَ أَصْحَٰبُ ٱلنَّارِ
هُمْ فِيهَا خَٰلِدُونَ

C. 46. — Amongst men what nation had higher chances
(2:40-86.) In the realm of the Spirit than the Children of Israel?
But again and again did they fail in the Spirit.

---

53. Allah's decree is the result of man's action. Note the transition in Arabic from the singular number in 2:33, to the dual in 2:35, and the plural here, which I have indicated in English by "All ye people." Evidently Adam is the type of all mankind, and the sexes go together in all spiritual matters. Moreover, the expulsion applied to Adam, Eve, and Satan, and the Arabic plural is appropriate for any number greater than two.

54. Man's sojourn in this lower state, where he is partly an animal of this earth, is for a time. But he must fulfill his lower duties also, for they too are a part of his spiritual training.

55. As "names" in verse 31 above is used for the "nature of things", so "words" here mean "inspiration," "spiritual knowledge." The Arabic word used for "learn" here implies some effort on his part, to which Allah's Grace responded.

The Arabic word for "Repentance" (*tawbah*) means "turning," and the intensive word (*tawwāb*) for Allah's forgiveness ("Oft-Returning" or "Ever-Returning") is from the same root. For repentance, three things are necessary: the sinner must acknowledge his wrong; he must give it up; and he must resolve to eschew it for the future. Man's nature is weak, and he may have to return again and again for mercy. So long as he does it sincerely, Allah is Oft-Returning, Most Merciful. For His grace helps out the sinner's shortcomings.

56. Note the transition from the plural "We" at the beginning of the verse to the singular "Me" later in the same verse, Allah speaks of Himself usually in the first person plural "We"; it is the plural of respect and honour and is used in human language in Royal proclamations and decrees. But where a special personal relationship is expressed the singular, "I" or "Me" is used *Cf.* 26:52, etc.

In spite of Man's fall, and in consequence of it, assurance of guidance is given. In case man follows the guidance he is free from any fear for the present or the future, and any grief or sorrow for the past. The soul thus freed grows nearer to Allah.

57. As their rejection of faith was deliberate and definite, so the consequences must be of an abiding character. (R).

They rebelled against Moses and murmured
In the wilderness; the Prophets they slew
And the Signs they rejected; they falsified
Scripture and turned their back on righteousness.

SECTION 5.

40. O Children of Israel! call to mind
The (special) favour which I bestowed
Upon you, and fulfil your Covenant[58]
With Me as I fulfil My Covenant
With you, and fear none but Me.

٤٠ يَٰبَنِىٓ إِسْرَٰٓءِيلَ ٱذْكُرُوا۟ نِعْمَتِىَ
ٱلَّتِىٓ أَنْعَمْتُ عَلَيْكُمْ وَأَوْفُوا۟ بِعَهْدِىٓ
أُوفِ بِعَهْدِكُمْ وَإِيَّٰىَ فَٱرْهَبُونِ

41. And believe in what I reveal,[59]
Confirming the revelation
Which is with you,
And be not the first to reject
Faith therein, nor sell My Signs
For a small price; and fear Me,
And Me alone.

٤١ وَءَامِنُوا۟ بِمَآ أَنزَلْتُ
مُصَدِّقًا لِّمَا مَعَكُمْ وَلَا تَكُونُوٓا۟ أَوَّلَ كَافِرٍۭ بِهِۦ
وَلَا تَشْتَرُوا۟ بِـَٔايَٰتِى
ثَمَنًا قَلِيلًا وَإِيَّٰىَ فَٱتَّقُونِ

42. And cover not Truth
With falsehood, nor conceal
The Truth when ye know
(what it is).

٤٢ وَلَا تَلْبِسُوا۟ ٱلْحَقَّ بِٱلْبَٰطِلِ
وَتَكْتُمُوا۟ ٱلْحَقَّ وَأَنتُمْ تَعْلَمُونَ

43. And be steadfast in prayer;
Practise regular charity;
And bow down your heads[60]
With those who bow down
(in worship).

٤٣ وَأَقِيمُوا۟ ٱلصَّلَوٰةَ
وَءَاتُوا۟ ٱلزَّكَوٰةَ
وَٱرْكَعُوا۟ مَعَ ٱلرَّٰكِعِينَ

44. Do ye enjoin right conduct
On the people, and forget
(To practise it) yourselves.
And yet ye study the Scripture?
Will ye not understand?

٤٤ أَتَأْمُرُونَ ٱلنَّاسَ بِٱلْبِرِّ وَتَنسَوْنَ
أَنفُسَكُمْ وَأَنتُمْ تَتْلُونَ ٱلْكِتَٰبَ ۚ أَفَلَا تَعْقِلُونَ

---

58. The appeal is made to Israel subjectively in terms of their own tradition. You claim to be a favoured nation: have you forgotten My favours? You claim a special Covenant with Me: I have fulfilled My part of the Covenant by bringing you out of the land of bondage and giving you Canaan, the land "flowing with milk and honey": how have you fulfilled your part of the Covenant? Do you fear for your national existence? If you fear Me, nothing else will matter.

59. You received revelations before: now comes one confirming it: its first appeal should be to you—are you to be the first to reject it? And reject it for what? Allah's Signs are worth more than all your paltry considerations. And the standard of duty and righteousness is to be taken from Allah, and not from priests and customs.

60. The argument is still primarily addressed to the Jews, but is of universal application, as in all the teachings of the Qur'ān. The chief feature of Jewish worship was and is the bowing of the head.

45. Nay, seek (Allah's) help
With patient perseverance[61]
And prayer:
It is indeed hard, except
To those who bring a lowly spirit—

٤٥ وَٱسۡتَعِينُواْ بِٱلصَّبۡرِ وَٱلصَّلَوٰةِۚ
وَإِنَّهَا لَكَبِيرَةٌ إِلَّا عَلَى ٱلۡخَٰشِعِينَ

46. Who bear in mind the certainty
That they are to meet their Lord,
And that they are to return to Him.

٤٦ ٱلَّذِينَ يَظُنُّونَ أَنَّهُم مُّلَٰقُواْ رَبِّهِمۡ
وَأَنَّهُمۡ إِلَيۡهِ رَٰجِعُونَ

SECTION 6.

47. O Children of Israel! call to mind
The (special) favour which I bestowed
Upon you,[62] and that I preferred you
To all others (for My Message).

٤٧ يَٰبَنِيٓ إِسۡرَٰٓءِيلَ ٱذۡكُرُواْ
نِعۡمَتِيَ ٱلَّتِيٓ أَنۡعَمۡتُ عَلَيۡكُمۡ
وَأَنِّي فَضَّلۡتُكُمۡ عَلَى ٱلۡعَٰلَمِينَ

48. Then guard yourselves against a day
When one soul shall not avail another
Nor shall intercession be accepted for her,
Nor shall compensation be taken from her,
Nor shall anyone be helped (from outside).[63]

٤٨ وَٱتَّقُواْ يَوۡمٗا
لَّا تَجۡزِي نَفۡسٌ عَن نَّفۡسٖ شَيۡـٔٗا
وَلَا يُقۡبَلُ مِنۡهَا شَفَٰعَةٞ
وَلَا يُؤۡخَذُ مِنۡهَا عَدۡلٞ
وَلَا هُمۡ يُنصَرُونَ

49. And remember, We delivered you
From the people of Pharaoh: they set you
Hard tasks and punishments, slaughtered

٤٩ وَإِذۡ نَجَّيۡنَٰكُم مِّنۡ ءَالِ فِرۡعَوۡنَ
يَسُومُونَكُمۡ سُوٓءَ ٱلۡعَذَابِ يُذَبِّحُونَ

61. The Arabic word *Ṣabr* implies many shades of meaning, which it is impossible to comprehend in one English word. It implies (1) patience in the sense of being thorough, not hasty; (2) patient perseverance, constancy, steadfastness, firmness of purpose; (3) systematic as opposed to spasmodic or chance action; (4) a cheerful attitude of resignation and understanding in sorrow, defeat, or suffering, as opposed to murmuring or rebellion, but saved from mere passivity or listlessness, by the element of constancy or steadfastness.

62. These words are recapitulated from 2:40, which introduced a general account of Allah's favours to Israel; now we are introduced to a particular account of incidents in Israel's history. Each incident is introduced by the Arabic words *Idh*, which is indicated in the translation by "Remember."

63. Before passing to particular incidents, the conclusion is stated. Be on your guard: do not think that special favours exempt you from the personal responsibility of each soul.

Your sons and let your
womenfolk live;[64]
Therein was a tremendous trial
from your Lord.

أَبْنَآءَكُمْ وَيَسْتَحْيُونَ نِسَآءَكُمْ
وَفِي ذَٰلِكُم بَلَآءٌ مِّن رَّبِّكُمْ عَظِيمٌ

50. And remember We divided
The Sea for you and saved you
And drowned Pharaoh's people
Within your very sight.[65]

(٥٠) وَإِذْ فَرَقْنَا بِكُمُ ٱلْبَحْرَ فَأَنجَيْنَٰكُمْ
وَأَغْرَقْنَآ ءَالَ فِرْعَوْنَ وَأَنتُمْ تَنظُرُونَ

51. And remember We appointed
Forty nights for Moses,[66]
And in his absence ye took
The calf (for worship),
And ye did grievous wrong.

(٥١) وَإِذْ وَٰعَدْنَا مُوسَىٰٓ أَرْبَعِينَ لَيْلَةً
ثُمَّ ٱتَّخَذْتُمُ ٱلْعِجْلَ مِنۢ بَعْدِهِۦ
وَأَنتُمْ ظَٰلِمُونَ

52. Even then We did forgive you,[67]
There was a chance for you
To be grateful.

(٥٢) ثُمَّ عَفَوْنَا عَنكُم مِّنۢ بَعْدِ ذَٰلِكَ
لَعَلَّكُمْ تَشْكُرُونَ

53. And remember We gave
Moses the Scripture and the
Criterion[68]

(٥٣) وَإِذْ ءَاتَيْنَا مُوسَى ٱلْكِتَٰبَ وَٱلْفُرْقَانَ

---

64. The bondage of Egypt was indeed a tremendous trial. Even the Egyptians' wish to spare the lives of Israel's females when the males were slaughtered, added to the bitterness of Israel. Their hatred was cruel, but their "love" was still more cruel. About the hard tasks, see Exod. i. 14: "They made their lives bitter with hard bondage, in mortar and in brick, and in all manner of service in the field: all their service, wherein they made them serve, was with rigour." Pharaoh's taskmasters gave no straw, yet ordered the Israelites to make bricks without straw: Exod. v. 5-19. Pharaoh's decree was: "Every son that is born ye shall cast into the river, and every daughter ye shall save alive": Exod. i. 22. It was in consequence of this decree that Moses was hidden three months after he was born, and when he could be hidden no longer, he was put into an ark of bulrushes and cast into the Nile, where he was found by Pharaoh's daughter and wife (28:9), and adopted into the family: Exod. ii.2-10. *Cf.* 20:37-40. Thus Moses was brought up by the enemies of his people. He was chosen by Allah to deliver his people, and Allah's wisdom made the learning and experience and even cruelties of the Egyptian enemies themselves to contribute to the salvation of his people.

65. When the Israelites at last escaped from Egypt, they were pursued by Pharaoh and his host. By a miracle the Israelites crossed the Red Sea, but the host of Pharaoh was drowned: Exod. xiv. 5-31.

66. This was after the Ten Commandments and the Laws and Ordinances had been given on Mount Sinai. Moses was asked up into the Mount, and he was there forty days and forty nights: Exod. xxiv. 18. But the people got impatient of the delay, made a calf of melted gold, and offered worship and sacrifice to it: Exod. xxxii. 1-8.

67. Moses prayed for his people, and Allah forgave them. This is the language of the Qur'ān. The Old Testament version is rougher: "The Lord repented of the evil which He thought to do unto His people"; Exod. xxxii. 14. The Muslim position has always been that the Jewish (and Christian) scriptures as they stand cannot be traced direct to Moses or Jesus, but are later compilations. Modern scholarship and Higher Criticism has left no doubt on the subject. But the stories in these traditional books may be used in an appeal to those who use them: only they should be spiritualized, as they are here, and especially in 2:54 below.

68. Allah's revelation, the expression of Allah's Will, is the true standard of right and wrong. It may be in a Book or in Allah's dealings in history. All these may be called His Signs or Miracles. In this passage some commentators take the Scripture and the Criterion *(Furqān)* to be identical. Others take them to be two distinct things: Scripture being the written Book and the Criterion being other Signs. I agree with the latter view. The word *Furqān* also occurs in 21:48 in connection with Moses and Aaron and in the first verse of Sūra 25, as well as in its title, in connection with Muḥammad. As Aaron received no Book, Furqān must mean the other Signs. Al Muṣṭafā had both the Book and the other Signs: perhaps here too we take the other Signs as supplementing the Book. *Cf.* Wordsworth's "Arbiter undisturbed of right and wrong." (Prelude. Book 4).

(Between right and wrong), there was
A chance for you to be guided aright.

لَعَلَّكُمْ تَهْتَدُونَ

54. And remember Moses said
To his people: "O my people!
Ye have indeed wronged
Yourselves by your worship of the calf:
So turn (in repentance) to your Maker,
And slay yourselves
(the wrongdoers);[69]
That will be better for you
In the sight of your Maker."
Then He turned towards you
(in forgiveness):
For He is Oft-Returning, Most Merciful.

٥٤ وَإِذْ قَالَ مُوسَىٰ لِقَوْمِهِۦ يَٰقَوْمِ
إِنَّكُمْ ظَلَمْتُمْ أَنفُسَكُم
بِٱتِّخَاذِكُمُ ٱلْعِجْلَ
فَتُوبُوٓا۟ إِلَىٰ بَارِئِكُمْ
فَٱقْتُلُوٓا۟ أَنفُسَكُمْ ذَٰلِكُمْ
خَيْرٌ لَّكُمْ عِندَ بَارِئِكُمْ
فَتَابَ عَلَيْكُمْ
إِنَّهُۥ هُوَ ٱلتَّوَّابُ ٱلرَّحِيمُ

55. And remember ye said:[70]
"O Moses!
We shall never believe in thee
Until we see Allah manifestly,"
But ye were dazed
By thunder and lightning
Even as ye looked on.

٥٥ وَإِذْ قُلْتُمْ يَٰمُوسَىٰ
لَن نُّؤْمِنَ لَكَ
حَتَّىٰ نَرَى ٱللَّهَ جَهْرَةً
فَأَخَذَتْكُمُ ٱلصَّٰعِقَةُ وَأَنتُمْ تَنظُرُونَ

56. Then We raised you up
After your death;
Ye had the chance
To be grateful.

٥٦ ثُمَّ بَعَثْنَٰكُم
مِّنۢ بَعْدِ مَوْتِكُمْ
لَعَلَّكُمْ تَشْكُرُونَ

57. And We gave you the shade of clouds
And sent down to you

٥٧ وَظَلَّلْنَا عَلَيْكُمُ ٱلْغَمَامَ
وَأَنزَلْنَا عَلَيْكُمُ

---

69. Moses's speech may be construed literally, as translated, in which case it reproduces Exod. xxxii. 27-28 but in a much softened form, for the Old Testament says: "Go in and out from gate to gate throughout the camp, and slay every man his brother, and every man his companion, and every man his neighbour. . .and there fell of the people that day 3,000 men." (R).

The word here translated Maker *(Bārī')* has also in it a touch of the root-meaning of "liberator"—an apt word as referring to the Israelites, who had just been liberated from bondage in Egypt.

70. We have hitherto had instances from the Jewish traditional *Tawrāh* (or Pentateuch). Now we have some instances from Jewish tradition in the Talmud, or body of exposition in the Jewish theological schools. They are based on the Jewish scriptures, but add many marvellous details and homilies. As to seeing Allah, we have in Exod. xxxiii. 20: "And He said, 'Thou canst not see My face: for there shall no man see Me and live'." The punishment for insisting on seeing Allah was therefore death: but those who rejected faith were forgiven, and yet they were ungrateful.

Manna[71] and quails, saying:
"Eat of the good things
We have provided for you:"
(But they rebelled);
To Us they did no harm,
But they harmed their own souls.

ٱلۡمَنَّ وَٱلسَّلۡوَىٰۖ
كُلُواْ مِن طَيِّبَٰتِ مَا رَزَقۡنَٰكُمۡۖ
وَمَا ظَلَمُونَا وَلَٰكِن كَانُوٓاْ أَنفُسَهُمۡ يَظۡلِمُونَ

58. And remember We said:
"Enter this town,[72] and eat
Of the plenty therein
As ye wish; but enter
The gate with humility,
In posture and in words,
And We shall forgive you your faults
And increase (the portion of)
Those who do good."

٥٨ وَإِذۡ قُلۡنَا
ٱدۡخُلُواْ هَٰذِهِ ٱلۡقَرۡيَةَ فَكُلُواْ مِنۡهَا
حَيۡثُ شِئۡتُمۡ رَغَدٗا
وَٱدۡخُلُواْ ٱلۡبَابَ سُجَّدٗا
وَقُولُواْ حِطَّةٞ نَّغۡفِرۡ لَكُمۡ خَطَٰيَٰكُمۡۚ
وَسَنَزِيدُ ٱلۡمُحۡسِنِينَ

59. But the transgressors
Changed the word from that
Which had been given them;
So We sent on the transgressors
A plague from heaven,
For that they infringed
(Our command) repeatedly.

٥٩ فَبَدَّلَ ٱلَّذِينَ ظَلَمُواْ قَوۡلًا
غَيۡرَ ٱلَّذِي قِيلَ لَهُمۡ
فَأَنزَلۡنَا عَلَى ٱلَّذِينَ ظَلَمُواْ
رِجۡزٗا مِّنَ ٱلسَّمَآءِ بِمَا كَانُواْ يَفۡسُقُونَ

SECTION 7.

60. And remember Moses prayed
For water for his people;
We said: "Strike the rock
With thy staff." Then gushed forth

٦٠ وَإِذِ ٱسۡتَسۡقَىٰ مُوسَىٰ لِقَوۡمِهِۦ
فَقُلۡنَا ٱضۡرِب بِّعَصَاكَ ٱلۡحَجَرَۖ فَٱنفَجَرَتۡ

---

71. *Manna*=Hebrew, *Man hu*: Arabic *Mā huwa*?=What is it? In Exod. xvi. 14 it is described as "a small round thing, as small as the hoar frost on the ground." It usually rotted if left over till next day; it melted in the hot sun; the amount necessary for each man was about an Omer, a Hebrew measure of capacity equal to about 2½ quarts. This is the Hebrew account, probably distorted by traditional exaggeration. The actual Manna found to this day in the Sinai region is a gummy saccharine secretion found on a species of Tamarisk. It is produced by the puncture of a species of insect like the cochineal, just as lac is produced by the puncture of the lac insect on certain trees in India. As to quails, large flights of them are driven by winds in the Eastern Mediterranean in certain seasons of the year, as was witnessed during the Great War of 1914-1918. (R).

72. This probably refers to Shittim. It was the "town of acacias," just east of the Jordan, where the Israelites were guilty of debauchery and the worship of and sacrifices to false gods (Num. xxv. 1-2, also 8-9): a terrible punishment ensued, including the plague, of which 24,000 died. The word which the transgressors changed may have been a password. In the Arabic text it is *Hittatun* which implies humility and a prayer of forgiveness, a fitting emblem to distinguish them from their enemies. From this particular incident a more general lesson may be drawn: in the hour of triumph we are to behave humbly as in Allah's sight, and our conduct should be exemplary according to Allah's word: otherwise our arrogance will draw its own punishment.

These verses 58-59, may be compared with 7:161-162. There are two verbal differences. Here (2:58) we have "*enter* the town" and in 7:161 we have "dwell in this town." Again in 2:59 here we have "infringed (Our command)." and in 7:162, we have "transgressed." The verbal differences make no difference to the sense.

Therefrom twelve springs.
Each group[73] knew its own place
For water. So eat and drink
Of the sustenance provided by
Allah.
And do no evil nor mischief
On the (face of the) earth.

مِنْهُ ٱثْنَتَا عَشْرَةَ عَيْنًا
قَدْ عَلِمَ كُلُّ أُنَاسٍ مَّشْرَبَهُمْ
كُلُوا۟ وَٱشْرَبُوا۟ مِن رِّزْقِ ٱللَّهِ
وَلَا تَعْثَوْا۟ فِى ٱلْأَرْضِ مُفْسِدِينَ

61. And remember ye said:
"O Moses! we cannot endure
One kind of food (always);
So beseech thy Lord for us
To produce for us of what the
earth
Groweth—its pot-herbs, and
cucumbers,
Its garlic, lentils, and onions."
He said: "Will ye exchange
The better for the worse?
Go ye down to any town,[74]
And ye shall find what ye want!"

٦١ وَإِذْ قُلْتُمْ
يَـٰمُوسَىٰ لَن نَّصْبِرَ عَلَىٰ طَعَامٍ وَٰحِدٍ
فَٱدْعُ لَنَا رَبَّكَ يُخْرِجْ لَنَا مِمَّا تُنۢبِتُ ٱلْأَرْضُ مِنۢ
بَقْلِهَا وَقِثَّآئِهَا وَفُومِهَا وَعَدَسِهَا وَبَصَلِهَا
قَالَ أَتَسْتَبْدِلُونَ
ٱلَّذِى هُوَ أَدْنَىٰ بِٱلَّذِى هُوَ خَيْرٌ
ٱهْبِطُوا۟ مِصْرًا فَإِنَّ لَكُم مَّا سَأَلْتُمْ

73. Here we have a reference to the tribal organization of the Jews, which played a great part in their forty-years' march through the Arabian deserts (Num. i and ii) and their subsequent settlement in the land of Canaan (Josh. xiii. and xiv.). The twelve tribes were derived from the sons of Jacob, whose name was changed to Israel (soldier of Allah) after he had wrestled, says Jewish tradition, with Allah (Genesis xxxii. 28). Israel had twelve sons (Gen. xxxv. 22-26), including Levi and Joseph. The descendants of these twelve sons were the "Children of Israel." Levi's family got the priesthood and the care of the Tabernacle; they were exempted from military duties, for which the census was taken (Num. i. 47-53), and therefore from the distribution of Land in Canaan (Josh. xiv. 3); they were distributed among all the Tribes, and were really a privileged caste and not numbered among the Tribes; Moses and Aaron belonged to the house of Levi. On the other hand Joseph, on account of the high position to which he rose in Egypt as the Pharaoh's minister, was the progenitor of two tribes, one in the name of each of his two sons Ephraim and Manasseh. Thus there were twelve Tribes in all, as Levi was cut out and Joseph represented two tribes. Their having fixed stations and watering places in camp and fixed territorial areas later in the Promised Land prevented confusion and mutual jealousies and is pointed to as an evidence of the Providence of Allah acting through His Prophet Moses. *Cf.* also 7:160.

The gushing of twelve springs from a rock evidently refers to a local tradition well known to Jews and Arabs in Al Muṣṭafā's time. Near Horeb close to Mount Sinai, where the Law was given to Moses, is a huge mass of red granite, twelve-feet high and about fifty feet in circumference, where European travellers (*e.g.*, Breydenbach in the 15th Century after Christ saw abundant springs of water twelve in number (see Sale's notes on this passage). It existed in Al Muṣṭafā's time and may still exist to the present day, for anything we know to the contrary. The Jewish tradition would be based on Exod. xvii. 6: "Thou shalt smite the rock, and there shall come water out of it that the people may drink."

The story is used as a parable, as is clear from the latter part of the verse. In the desolation and among the rocks of this life people grumble. But they will not be left starving or thirsty of spiritual life. Allah's Messenger can provide abundant spiritual sustenance even from such unpromising things as the hard rocks of life. And all the nations can be grouped round it, each different, yet each in perfect order and discipline. We are to use with gratitude all spiritual food and drink provided by Allah, and He sometimes provides from unexpected places. We must restrain ourselves from mischief, pride, and every kind of evil, for our higher life is based on our probation on this very earth.

74. The declension of the word *Misr* in the Arabic text here shows that it is treated as a common noun meaning any town, but this is not conclusive, and the reference may be to the Egypt of Pharaoh. The *Tanwīn* expressing indefiniteness may mean "any Egypt", *i.e.*, any country as fertile as Egypt. There is here a subtle reminiscence as well as a severe reproach. The rebellious children of Israel murmured at the sameness of the food they got in the desert. They were evidently hankering after the delicacies of the Egypt which they had left, although they should have known that the only thing certain for them in Egypt was their bondage and harsh treatment. Moses's reproach to them was twofold: (1) Such variety of foods you can get in any town: would you, for their sake, sell your freedom? Is not freedom better than delicate food? (2) In front of the rich Promised Land, which you are reluctant to march to; behind is Egypt, the land of bondage. Which is better? Would you exchange the better for the worse?

They were covered with
humiliation[75]
And misery; they drew
On themselves the wrath of Allah.
This because they went on
Rejecting the Signs of Allah
And slaying His Messengers
Without just cause.
This because they rebelled
And went on transgressing.

وَضُرِبَتْ عَلَيْهِمُ ٱلذِّلَّةُ
وَٱلْمَسْكَنَةُ وَبَآءُو بِغَضَبٍ مِّنَ ٱللَّهِ
ذَٰلِكَ بِأَنَّهُمْ كَانُوا۟ يَكْفُرُونَ بِـَٔايَٰتِ ٱللَّهِ
وَيَقْتُلُونَ ٱلنَّبِيِّـۧنَ بِغَيْرِ ٱلْحَقِّ
ذَٰلِكَ بِمَا عَصَوا۟ وَّكَانُوا۟ يَعْتَدُونَ

SECTION 8.

62. Those who believe (in the
Qur'ān),
And those who follow the Jewish
(scriptures),
And the Christians and the
Sabians[76] —
Any who believe in Allah
And the Last Day,
And work righteousness,
Shall have their reward

(٦٢) إِنَّ ٱلَّذِينَ ءَامَنُوا۟
وَٱلَّذِينَ هَادُوا۟
وَٱلنَّصَٰرَىٰ وَٱلصَّٰبِـِٔينَ
مَنْ ءَامَنَ بِٱللَّهِ
وَٱلْيَوْمِ ٱلْءَاخِرِ
وَعَمِلَ صَٰلِحًا فَلَهُمْ أَجْرُهُمْ

---

75. From here the argument becomes more general. They got the Promised Land. But they continued to rebel against Allah. And their humiliation and misery became a national disaster. They were carried in captivity to Assyria. They were restored under the Persians, but still remained under the Persian yoke, and they were under the yoke of the Greeks, the Romans, and Arabs. They were scattered all over the earth, and have been a wandering people ever since, because they rejected faith, slew Allah's messengers, and went on transgressing.

The slaying of the Prophets begins with the murder of Abel, who was in the ancestry of Israel. The elder sons of Jacob attempted the murder of Joseph when they dropped him into the well, and if he was afterwards rescued by strangers, their blood-guilt was none the less. In later history they attempted to slay Jesus, in as much as they got the Roman Governor to crucify one in his likeness, and they attempted to take the life of Muṣṭafā.

But the moral goes wider than the Children of Israel. It applies to all nations and all individuals. If they are stiff-necked, if they set a greater value on perishable goods than on freedom and eternal salvation, if they break the law of Allah and resist His grace, their portion must be humiliation and misery in the spiritual world and probably even on this earth if a long view is taken.

76. Latest researches have revealed a small remnant of a religious community numbering about 2,000 souls in Lower Irāq, near Basra. In Arabic they are called *Ṣubbī* (plural *Ṣubbā*). They are also called Sabians and Nasoraeans, or Mandaeans, or Christians of St. John. They claim to be Gnostics, or Knowers of the Great Life. They dress in white, and believe in frequent immersions in water. Their Book Ginza is in a dialect of Aramaic. They have theories of Darkness and Light as in Zoroastrianism. They use the name *Yardan* (Jordan) for any river. They live in peace and harmony among their Muslim neighbours. They resemble the Ṣābi'ūn mentioned in the Qur'ān, but are not probably identical with them.

The pseudo-Sabians of Ḥarrān, who attracted the attention of Khalifah Ma'mūn al Rashīd in 830 A.C. by their long hair and peculiar dress probably adopted the name as it was mentioned in the Qur'ān, in order to claim the privileges of the People of the Book. They were Syrian Star-worshippers with Hellenistic tendencies, like the Jews contemporary with Jesus.

There was another people called the Sabaens, who played an important part in the history of early Arabia, and are known through their inscriptions in an alphabet allied to the Phoenician and Babylonian. They had a flourishing kingdom in the Yemen tract in South Arabia about 800-700 B.C., though their origin may have been in North Arabia. They worshipped the planets and stars (Moon, Sun, Venus). Probably the Queen of Sheba is connected with them. They succumbed to Abyssinia about 350 A.C. and to Persia about 579 A.C. Their capital was near San'ā. They had beautiful stone buildings, in which the pointed arch is noticeable. *Cf.* 5:72 and n. 779. (See E.B. on Sabaeans.) (R).

With their Lord; on them
Shall be no fear, nor shall they
grieve.[77]

عِندَ رَبِّهِمْ
وَلَا خَوْفٌ عَلَيْهِمْ وَلَا هُمْ يَحْزَنُونَ

63. And remember We took
Your Covenant
And We raised above you
(The towering height
Of Mount (Sinai)[78]
(Saying): "Hold firmly
To what We have given you
And bring (ever) to remembrance
What is therein:
Perchance ye may fear Allah."

(٦٣) وَإِذْ أَخَذْنَا مِيثَاقَكُمْ
وَرَفَعْنَا فَوْقَكُمُ الطُّورَ
خُذُوا مَا آتَيْنَاكُم بِقُوَّةٍ
وَاذْكُرُوا مَا فِيهِ لَعَلَّكُمْ تَتَّقُونَ

64. But ye turned back thereafter;
Had it not been for the Grace
And Mercy of Allah to you,
Ye had surely been
Among the lost.

(٦٤) ثُمَّ تَوَلَّيْتُم مِّن بَعْدِ ذَٰلِكَ
فَلَوْلَا فَضْلُ اللَّهِ عَلَيْكُمْ وَرَحْمَتُهُ
لَكُنتُم مِّنَ الْخَاسِرِينَ

65. And well ye knew
Those amongst you
Who transgressed
In the matter of the Sabbath;
We said to them:
"Be ye apes,
Despised and rejected."[79]

(٦٥) وَلَقَدْ عَلِمْتُمُ
الَّذِينَ اعْتَدَوْا مِنكُمْ
فِي السَّبْتِ
فَقُلْنَا لَهُمْ كُونُوا قِرَدَةً خَاسِئِينَ

66. So We made it an example
To their own time

(٦٦) فَجَعَلْنَاهَا نَكَالًا لِّمَا بَيْنَ يَدَيْهَا

77. *Cf.* 2:38, where the same phrase occurs. And it recurs again and again afterwards. The point of the verse is that Islam does not teach an exclusive doctrine, and is not meant exclusively for one people. The Jews claimed this for themselves, and the Christians in their origin were a sect of the Jews. Even the modern organized Christian churches, though they have been, consciously or unconsciously, influenced by the Time Spirit, including the historical fact of Islam, yet cling to the idea of Vicarious Atonement, which means that all who do not believe in it or who lived previously to the death of Christ are at a disadvantage spiritually before the Throne of Allah. The attitude of Islam is entirely different. Islam existed before the preaching of Muḥammad on this earth: the Qur'ān expressly calls Abraham a Muslim (3:67). Its teaching (submission to Allah's will) has been and will be the teaching of Religion for all time and for all peoples.

78. The Mountain of Sinai (*Ṭūr al Sīnīn*), a prominent mountain in the Arabian desert, in the peninsula between the two arms of the Red Sea. Here the Ten Commandments and the Law were given to Moses. Hence it is now called the Mountain of Moses (*Jabal Mūsa*). The Israelites encamped at the foot of it for nearly a year. The Covenant was taken from them under many portents (Exods. xix. 5, 8, 16, 18), which are described in Jewish tradition in great detail. Under thunder and lightning the mountain must indeed have appeared an awe-inspiring sight above to the Camp at its foot. And the people solemnly entered into the Covenant: all the people answered together and said, "All that the Lord hath spoken we will do."

79. The punishment for breach of the Sabbath under the Mosaic law was death. "Every one that defileth it (the Sabbath) shall surely be put to death: for whosoever doeth any work therein, that soul shall be cut off from among his people": (Exod. xxxi. 14). There must have been a Jewish tradition about a whole fishing community in a seaside town, which persisted in breaking the Sabbath and were turned into apes: *cf.* 7:163-166.

And to their posterity,
And a lesson
To those who fear Allah.

وَمَا خَلْفَهَا وَمَوْعِظَةً لِّلْمُتَّقِينَ

67. And remember Moses said
To his people: "Allah commands
That ye sacrifice a heifer."[80]
They said: "Makest thou
A laughing-stock of us?"
He said: "Allah save me
From being an ignorant (fool)!"

(٦٧) وَإِذْ قَالَ مُوسَىٰ
لِقَوْمِهِۦٓ إِنَّ ٱللَّهَ يَأْمُرُكُمْ أَن تَذْبَحُوا۟ بَقَرَةً
قَالُوٓا۟ أَتَتَّخِذُنَا هُزُوًا
قَالَ أَعُوذُ بِٱللَّهِ أَنْ أَكُونَ مِنَ ٱلْجَٰهِلِينَ

68. They said: "Beseech on our behalf
Thy Lord to make plain to us
What (heifer) it is!"
He said: "He says: the heifer
Should be neither too old
Nor too young, but of middling
Age: now do what ye are commanded!"

(٦٨) قَالُوا۟
ٱدْعُ لَنَا رَبَّكَ يُبَيِّن لَّنَا مَا هِىَ
قَالَ إِنَّهُۥ يَقُولُ إِنَّهَا بَقَرَةٌ لَّا فَارِضٌ
وَلَا بِكْرٌ عَوَانٌۢ بَيْنَ ذَٰلِكَ
فَٱفْعَلُوا۟ مَا تُؤْمَرُونَ

69. They said: "Beseech on our behalf
Thy Lord to make plain to us
Her colour." He said: "He says:
A fawn-coloured heifer,
Pure and rich in tone,
The admiration of beholders!"

(٦٩) قَالُوا۟
ٱدْعُ لَنَا رَبَّكَ يُبَيِّن لَّنَا مَا لَوْنُهَا
قَالَ إِنَّهُۥ يَقُولُ إِنَّهَا بَقَرَةٌ صَفْرَآءُ
فَاقِعٌ لَّوْنُهَا تَسُرُّ ٱلنَّٰظِرِينَ

70. They said: "Beseech on our behalf
Thy Lord to make plain to us
What she is: to us are all heifers
Alike: we wish indeed for guidance
If Allah wills."

(٧٠) قَالُوا۟
ٱدْعُ لَنَا رَبَّكَ يُبَيِّن لَّنَا مَا هِىَ
إِنَّ ٱلْبَقَرَ تَشَٰبَهَ عَلَيْنَا وَإِنَّآ
إِن شَآءَ ٱللَّهُ لَمُهْتَدُونَ

---

80. This story or parable of the heifer in 2:67-71 should be read with the parable of the dead man brought to life in 2:72-73. The stories were accepted in Jewish traditions, which are themselves based on certain sacrificial directions in the Old Testament. The heifer story of Jewish tradition is based on Num. xix. 1-10, in which Moses and Aaron ordered the Israelites to sacrifice a red heifer without spot or blemish; her body was to be burnt and the ashes were to be kept for the purification of the congregation from sin. The parable of the dead man we shall refer to later.

The lesson of the heifer parable is plain, Moses announced the sacrifice to the Israelites, and they treated it as a jest. When Moses continued solemnly to ask for the sacrifice, they put him off on one pretext and another, asking a number of questions which they could have answered themselves if they had listened to Moses's directions. Their questions were carping criticisms rather than the result of a desire for information. It was a mere thin pretence that they were genuinely seeking for guidance. When at last they were driven into a corner, they made the sacrifice, but the will was wanting, which would have made the sacrifice efficacious for purification from sin. The real reason for their prevarications was their guilty conscience, as we see in the parable of the dead man (2:72-73).

71. He said: "He says: a heifer
Not trained to till the soil
Or water the fields; sound
And without blemish." They said:
"Now hast thou brought
The truth." Then they offered
Her in sacrifice,
But not with goodwill.

٧١ قَالَ إِنَّهُۥ يَقُولُ إِنَّهَا بَقَرَةٌ
لَّا ذَلُولٌ تُثِيرُ ٱلْأَرْضَ وَلَا تَسْقِى ٱلْحَرْثَ
مُسَلَّمَةٌ لَّا شِيَةَ فِيهَا ۚ قَالُوا۟
ٱلْـَٔـٰنَ جِئْتَ بِٱلْحَقِّ ۚ فَذَبَحُوهَا
وَمَا كَادُوا۟ يَفْعَلُونَ

SECTION 9.

72. Remember ye slew a man[81]
And fell into a dispute
Among yourselves as to the crime:
But Allah was to bring forth
What ye did hide.

٧٢ وَإِذْ قَتَلْتُمْ نَفْسًا
فَٱدَّٰرَْٰٔتُمْ فِيهَا ۖ
وَٱللَّهُ مُخْرِجٌ مَّا كُنتُمْ تَكْتُمُونَ

73. So We said: "Strike the (body)
With a piece of the (heifer)."
Thus Allah bringeth the dead
To life and showeth you His Signs:
Perchance ye may understand.

٧٣ فَقُلْنَا ٱضْرِبُوهُ بِبَعْضِهَا ۚ
كَذَٰلِكَ يُحْىِ ٱللَّهُ ٱلْمَوْتَىٰ وَيُرِيكُمْ ءَايَـٰتِهِۦ
لَعَلَّكُمْ تَعْقِلُونَ

74. Thenceforth were your hearts
Hardened: they became
Like a rock and even worse
In hardness. For among rocks
There are some from which
Rivers gush forth; others
There are which when split
Asunder send forth water;
And others which sink

٧٤ ثُمَّ قَسَتْ قُلُوبُكُم مِّنۢ بَعْدِ ذَٰلِكَ
فَهِىَ كَٱلْحِجَارَةِ أَوْ أَشَدُّ قَسْوَةً ۚ وَإِنَّ مِنَ ٱلْحِجَارَةِ
لَمَا يَتَفَجَّرُ مِنْهُ ٱلْأَنْهَـٰرُ ۚ
وَإِنَّ مِنْهَا لَمَا يَشَّقَّقُ فَيَخْرُجُ مِنْهُ ٱلْمَآءُ ۚ
وَإِنَّ مِنْهَا لَمَا يَهْبِطُ

81. In Deut. xxi.1-9 it is ordained that if the body of a slain man be found in a field and the slayer is not known, a heifer shall be beheaded, and the elders of the city next to the slain man's domicile shall wash their hands over the heifer and say that they neither did the deed nor saw it done, thus clearing themselves from the blood-guilt.

The Jewish story based on this was that in a certain case of this kind, every one tried to clear himself of guilt and lay the blame at the door of others. In the first place they tried to prevaricate and prevent a heifer being slain as in the last parable. When she was slain, Allah by a miracle disclosed the real person. A portion of the sacrificed heifer was ordered to be placed on the corpse, which came to life and disclosed the whole story of the crime.

The lesson of this parable is that men may try to hide their crimes individually or collectively, but Allah will bring them to light in unexpected ways. Applying this further to Jewish national history, the argument is developed in the following verses that the Children of Israel played fast and loose with their own rites and traditions, but they could not thus evade the consequences of their own sin.

For fear of Allah. And Allah is
Not unmindful of what ye do.[82]

مِنْ خَشْيَةِ ٱللَّهِ ۗ وَمَا ٱللَّهُ بِغَٰفِلٍ عَمَّا تَعْمَلُونَ

75. Can ye (O ye men of Faith)
Entertain the hope that they
Will believe in you?—
Seeing that a party of them
Heard the Word of Allah,
And perverted it knowingly
After they understood it.

٧٥ أَفَتَطْمَعُونَ أَن يُؤْمِنُوا۟ لَكُمْ
وَقَدْ كَانَ فَرِيقٌ مِّنْهُمْ يَسْمَعُونَ كَلَٰمَ ٱللَّهِ
ثُمَّ يُحَرِّفُونَهُۥ مِنۢ بَعْدِ مَا عَقَلُوهُ
وَهُمْ يَعْلَمُونَ

76. Behold! when they meet[83]
The men of Faith, they say:
"We believe": but when
They meet each other in private,
They say: "Shall you tell them
What Allah hath revealed to you,
That they may engage you
In argument about it
Before your Lord?"—
Do ye not understand (their aim)?

٧٦ وَإِذَا لَقُوا۟
ٱلَّذِينَ ءَامَنُوا۟ قَالُوٓا۟ ءَامَنَّا وَإِذَا
خَلَا بَعْضُهُمْ إِلَىٰ بَعْضٍ قَالُوٓا۟ أَتُحَدِّثُونَهُم
بِمَا فَتَحَ ٱللَّهُ عَلَيْكُمْ لِيُحَآجُّوكُم بِهِۦ
عِندَ رَبِّكُمْ ۚ أَفَلَا تَعْقِلُونَ

77. Know they not that Allah
Knoweth what they conceal
And what they reveal?

٧٧ أَوَلَا يَعْلَمُونَ أَنَّ ٱللَّهَ
يَعْلَمُ مَا يُسِرُّونَ وَمَا يُعْلِنُونَ

---

82. The sinner's heart gets harder and harder. It is even harder than rocks, of which a beautiful poetical allegory is placed before us. In nature we think there is nothing harder than rocks. But there are rocks that weep voluntarily, like repentant hearts that come to Allah of their own accord. Such are the rocks from which rivers and springs flow spontaneously, sometimes in small trickles, sometimes in big volumes. Then there are rocks which have to be split or dug into or blown up with dynamite, and underneath we find abundant waters, as in wells beneath rocky soil. Such are the hearts of a less degree of fineness, which yet melt into tears when some great blow or calamity calls the mind to higher things. (R).

83. The immediate argument applies to the Jews of Madīnah, but the more general argument applies to the people of Faith and the people without Faith, as we shall see below. If the Muslims of Madīnah ever entertained the hope that the Jews in their city would, as a body, welcome Muḥammad Muṣṭafā as the Prophet prophesied in their own books, they were mistaken. In Deut. xviii. 18, they read: "I will raise them up a Prophet from among their brethren, like unto thee," (*i.e.,* like unto Moses): which was interpreted by some of their doctors as referring to Muḥammad, and they came into Islam. The Arabs are a kindred branch of the Semitic family, and are correctly described in relation to the Jews as, "their brethren"; and there is no question that there was not another Prophet "like unto Moses" until Muḥammad came; in fact the postscript of Deuteronomy, which was written many centuries after Moses, says: "There arose not a prophet since in Israel like unto Moses, whom the Lord Knew face to face." But the Jews as a body were jealous of Muḥammad, and played a double part. When the Muslim community began to grow stronger they pretended to be of them, but really tried to keep back any knowledge of their own Scriptures from them, lest they should be beaten by their own arguments.

The more general interpretation holds good in all ages. Faith and Unfaith are pitted against each other. Faith has to struggle against power, position, organization, and privilege. When it gains ground, Unfaith comes forward insincerely and claims fellowship. But in its own mind it is jealous of the armoury of science and knowledge which Faith brings into the service of Allah. But Allah knows all, and if the people of Faith will only seek knowledge sincerely wherever they can find it—even as far afield as China, as Muḥammad said, they can defeat Unfaith on its own ground. [Even though the directive that Muslims should derive knowledge regardless of its location is an acceptable proposition from the Islamic viewpoint, the tradition to which the author refers here is not authentic. (Eds.)]

78. And there are among them[84]
Illiterates, who know not the Book,
But (see therein their own) desires,
And they do nothing but
conjecture.

٧٨ وَمِنۡهُمۡ
أُمِّيُّونَ لَا يَعۡلَمُونَ ٱلۡكِتَٰبَ إِلَّآ أَمَانِيَّ
وَإِنۡ هُمۡ إِلَّا يَظُنُّونَ

79. Then woe to those who write
The Book with their own hands,
And then say: "This is from
Allah,"
To traffic with it
For a miserable price!—
Woe to them for what their hands
Do write, and for the gain
They make thereby.

٧٩ فَوَيۡلٌ لِّلَّذِينَ يَكۡتُبُونَ ٱلۡكِتَٰبَ بِأَيۡدِيهِمۡ
ثُمَّ يَقُولُونَ هَٰذَا مِنۡ عِندِ ٱللَّهِ لِيَشۡتَرُواْ بِهِۦ
ثَمَنًا قَلِيلًاۖ فَوَيۡلٌ لَّهُم مِّمَّا كَتَبَتۡ أَيۡدِيهِمۡ
وَوَيۡلٌ لَّهُم مِّمَّا يَكۡسِبُونَ

80. And they say: "The Fire[85]
Shall not touch us
But for a few numbered days;"
Say: "Have ye taken a promise
From Allah, for He never
Breaks His promise?
Or is it that ye say of Allah
What ye do not know?"

٨٠ وَقَالُواْ لَن تَمَسَّنَا ٱلنَّارُ
إِلَّآ أَيَّامًا مَّعۡدُودَةًۚ قُلۡ أَتَّخَذۡتُمۡ عِندَ ٱللَّهِ
عَهۡدًا فَلَن يُخۡلِفَ ٱللَّهُ عَهۡدَهُۥٓۖ
أَمۡ تَقُولُونَ عَلَى ٱللَّهِ مَا لَا تَعۡلَمُونَ

81. Nay, those who seek gain[86]
In Evil, and are girt round
By their sins—
They are Companions of the Fire:
Therein shall they abide
(Forever).

٨١ بَلَىٰ مَن كَسَبَ سَيِّئَةً وَأَحَٰطَتۡ بِهِۦ
خَطِيٓـَٔتُهُۥ فَأُوْلَٰٓئِكَ أَصۡحَٰبُ ٱلنَّارِۖ
هُمۡ فِيهَا خَٰلِدُونَ

82. But those who have faith
And work righteousness.
They are Companions of the
Garden:

٨٢ وَٱلَّذِينَ ءَامَنُواْ وَعَمِلُواْ ٱلصَّٰلِحَٰتِ
أُوْلَٰٓئِكَ أَصۡحَٰبُ ٱلۡجَنَّةِۖ

84. The argument of 1:76 is continued. The Jews wanted to keep back knowledge, but what knowledge had they? Many of them, even if they could read, were no better than illiterates, for they knew not their own true Scriptures, but read into them what they wanted, or at best their own conjectures. They palmed off their own writings for the Message of Allah. Perhaps it brought them profit for the time being: but it was a miserable profit if they "gained the whole world and lost their own souls" (Matt. xvi. 26). "Writing with their own hands" means inventing books themselves, which had no divine authority.

The general argument is similar. Unfaith erects its own false gods. It atttributes things to causes which only exist in its own imagination. Sometimes it even indulges in actual dishonest traffic in the ignorance of the multitude. It may pay for a time, but the bubble always bursts.

85. The Jews, in their arrogance might say: Whatever the terror of Hell may be for other people, our sins will be forgiven, because we are the children of Abraham; at worst, we shall suffer a short definite punishment and then be restored to the "bosom of Abraham." This bubble is pricked here. Read this verse with 2:81-82.

The general application is also clear. If Unfaith claims some special prerogative, such as race, "civilization," political power, historical experience, and so on, these will not avail in Allah's sight. His promise is sure, but His promise is for those who seek Allah in Faith, and show it in their conduct.

86. This is many degrees worse than merely falling into evil; it is going out to "earn evil," as the Arabic text has it, *i.e.*, to seek gain in evil. Such a perverse attitude means that the moral and spiritual fortress erected around us by the Grace of Allah is voluntarily surrendered by us and demolished by Evil, which erects its own fortress, so that access to Good may be more and more difficult.

Therein shall they abide
(Forever).

هُمْ فِيهَا خَٰلِدُونَ

SECTION 10.

83. And remember We took[87]
A Covenant from the Children
Of Israel (to this effect):
Worship none but Allah;
Treat with kindness
Your parents and kindred,
And orphans and those in need;
Speak fair to the people;
Be steadfast in prayer;
And practise regular charity.
Then did ye turn back,
Except a few among you,
And ye backslide (even now).

٨٣ وَإِذْ أَخَذْنَا مِيثَٰقَ بَنِىٓ إِسْرَٰٓءِيلَ
لَا تَعْبُدُونَ إِلَّا ٱللَّهَ وَبِٱلْوَٰلِدَيْنِ إِحْسَانًا
وَذِى ٱلْقُرْبَىٰ وَٱلْيَتَٰمَىٰ وَٱلْمَسَٰكِينِ
وَقُولُوا۟ لِلنَّاسِ حُسْنًا وَأَقِيمُوا۟ ٱلصَّلَوٰةَ
وَءَاتُوا۟ ٱلزَّكَوٰةَ ثُمَّ تَوَلَّيْتُمْ
إِلَّا قَلِيلًا مِّنكُمْ
وَأَنتُم مُّعْرِضُونَ

84. And remember We took[88]
Your Covenant (to this effect):
Shed no blood amongst you,
Nor turn out your own people
From your homes: and this
Ye solemnly ratified,
And to this ye can bear witness.

٨٤ وَإِذْ أَخَذْنَا مِيثَٰقَكُمْ لَا تَسْفِكُونَ
دِمَآءَكُمْ وَلَا تُخْرِجُونَ أَنفُسَكُم مِّن دِيَٰرِكُمْ
ثُمَّ أَقْرَرْتُمْ وَأَنتُمْ تَشْهَدُونَ

85. After this it is ye, the same people,
Who slay among yourselves,
And banish a party of you
From their homes; assist
(Their enemies) against them,
In guilt and transgression;
And if they come to you
As captives, ye ransom[89] them,
Though it was not lawful

٨٥ ثُمَّ أَنتُمْ هَٰٓؤُلَآءِ تَقْتُلُونَ أَنفُسَكُمْ
وَتُخْرِجُونَ فَرِيقًا مِّنكُم مِّن دِيَٰرِهِمْ
تَظَٰهَرُونَ عَلَيْهِم بِٱلْإِثْمِ وَٱلْعُدْوَٰنِ
وَإِن يَأْتُوكُمْ أُسَٰرَىٰ تُفَٰدُوهُمْ وَهُوَ مُحَرَّمٌ

87. So far from the Covenant being of the kind you suggest in 2:80, the real Covenant is about the moral law, which is set out in 2:83. This moral law is universal, and if you break it, no privileges will lighten your punishment or help you in any way (2:86). "Speak fair to the people" not only means outward courtesy from the leaders to the meanest among the people, but the protection of the people from being exploited, deceived, defrauded, or doped with things to lull their intelligence.

88. Verse 83 referred to the universal moral law. This verse 84 refers to its application under a special Covenant entered into with the Jews of Madīnah by the newborn Muslim Commonwealth under its Guide and teacher Muḥammad. This Covenant is given in Ibn Hishām's *Sīrat-ur-Rasūl*, and comments on it will be found in Ameer 'Ali's *Spirit of Islam* (London, 1922), pp. 57-61. It was entered into in the second year of the Hijrah, and was treacherously broken by the Jews almost immediately afterwards.

89. I understand "ransom them" here to mean "take ransom for them," though most of the Commentators take it to mean "give ransom for them," Al Muṣṭafā had made a Pact which, if it had been faithfully observed by all parties, would have brought a reign of law and order for Madīnah. But some of the treacherous Jews never intended to observe its terms. They fought and slew each other and not only banished those who were obnoxious to them but intrigued with their enemies. If by any chance they came back into their hands as captives, they demanded ransom for them to return to their homes although they had no right to banish them at all. If we understand by "ransom them" pay "ransom for them to release them from the hands of their enemies," it would mean that they did this pious act for show, although they were themselves the authors of their unlawful banishment. I think the former makes better sense.

For you to banish them.
Then is it only a part of the Book
That ye believe in,
And do ye reject the rest?
But what is the reward for those
Among you who behave like this
But disgrace in this life?—
And on the Day of Judgement
They shall be consigned
To the most grievous penalty.
For Allah is not unmindful
Of what ye do.

عَلَيْكُمْ إِخْرَاجُهُمْ ۚ أَفَتُؤْمِنُونَ بِبَعْضِ
الْكِتَابِ وَتَكْفُرُونَ بِبَعْضٍ ۚ
فَمَا جَزَاءُ مَنْ يَفْعَلُ ذَٰلِكَ مِنْكُمْ
إِلَّا خِزْيٌ فِي الْحَيَاةِ الدُّنْيَا ۖ وَيَوْمَ الْقِيَامَةِ
يُرَدُّونَ إِلَىٰ أَشَدِّ الْعَذَابِ ۗ
وَمَا اللَّهُ بِغَافِلٍ عَمَّا تَعْمَلُونَ

86. These are the people who buy
The life of this world at the price
Of the Hereafter: their penalty
Shall not be lightened
Nor shall they be helped.

٨٦ أُولَٰئِكَ الَّذِينَ اشْتَرَوُا
الْحَيَاةَ الدُّنْيَا بِالْآخِرَةِ ۖ فَلَا يُخَفَّفُ عَنْهُمُ
الْعَذَابُ وَلَا هُمْ يُنْصَرُونَ

C. 47. —The people of Moses and the people of Jesus
(2:87-121.) Were given revelations, but alas!
They played false with their own lights
And, in their selfishness, made narrow
Allah's universal message. To them
It seemed incredible that His light
Should illumine Arabia and reform
The world. But His ways are wondrous,
And they are clear to those who have Faith.

SECTION 11.

87. We gave Moses the Book
And followed him up
With a succession of Messengers;
We gave Jesus, the son of Mary,[90]
Clear (Signs) and strengthened him
With the Holy Spirit. Is it
That whenever there comes to you
A Messenger with what ye
Yourselves desire not, ye are
Puffed up with pride?—
Some ye called imposters,
And others ye slay![91]

٨٧ وَلَقَدْ آتَيْنَا مُوسَى الْكِتَابَ
وَقَفَّيْنَا مِنْ بَعْدِهِ بِالرُّسُلِ ۖ
وَآتَيْنَا عِيسَى ابْنَ مَرْيَمَ الْبَيِّنَاتِ
وَأَيَّدْنَاهُ بِرُوحِ الْقُدُسِ ۗ
أَفَكُلَّمَا جَاءَكُمْ رَسُولٌ بِمَا لَا تَهْوَىٰ
أَنْفُسُكُمُ اسْتَكْبَرْتُمْ فَفَرِيقًا كَذَّبْتُمْ
وَفَرِيقًا تَقْتُلُونَ

90. As to the birth of Jesus, *cf.* 19:16-34. Why is he called the "Son of Mary"? What are his clear signs"? What is the "holy spirit" by which he was strengthened? We reserve to a later stage a discussion of the Quranic teaching on these questions. See 3:62 n. 401.

91. Notice the sudden transition from the past tense in "some ye *called* imposters" to the present tense in "others ye slay." There is a double significance. First, reviewing the long course of Jewish history, we have come to the time of Jesus: they have often given the lie to Allah's Prophets, and even now they are trying to slay Jesus. Secondly, extending the review of that history to the time of Muḥammad, they are even now trying to take the life of that Holy Prophet. This would be literally true at the time the words were promulgated to the people. And this transition leads on naturally to the next verse, which refer to the actual conditions before Muḥammad in Madīnah in the second year of the Hijrah.

Sections 11-13 (2:87-121) refer to the People of the Book generally, Jews and Christians. Even where Moses and the Law of Sinai are referred to, those traditions are common to both Jews and Christians. The argument is about the people who ought to have learnt from previous Revelations and welcomed Muḥammad's teaching, and yet they both took up an attitude of arrogant rejection.

88. They say, "Our hearts
Are the wrappings[92] (which preserve
Allah's Word: we need no more)."
Nay, Allah's curse is on them
For their blasphemy:[93]
Little is it they believe.

٨٨ وَقَالُوا قُلُوبُنَا غُلْفٌ
بَل لَّعَنَهُمُ اللَّهُ بِكُفْرِهِمْ
فَقَلِيلًا مَّا يُؤْمِنُونَ

89. And when there comes to them
A Book[94] from Allah, confirming
What is with them—although
From of old they had prayed
For victory against those
Without Faith—when there comes
To them that which they
(Should) have recognized.
They refuse to believe in it
But the curse of Allah
Is on those without Faith.

٨٩ وَلَمَّا جَاءَهُمْ كِتَابٌ
مِّنْ عِندِ اللَّهِ مُصَدِّقٌ لِّمَا مَعَهُمْ
وَكَانُوا مِن قَبْلُ يَسْتَفْتِحُونَ
عَلَى الَّذِينَ كَفَرُوا فَلَمَّا جَاءَهُم
مَّا عَرَفُوا كَفَرُوا بِهِ
فَلَعْنَةُ اللَّهِ عَلَى الْكَافِرِينَ

90. Miserable is the price
For which they have sold
Their souls, in that they
Deny (the revelation)
Which Allah has sent down,
In insolent envy that Allah
Of His Grace should send it
To any of His servants He pleases:[95]

٩٠ بِئْسَمَا اشْتَرَوْا بِهِ أَنفُسَهُمْ
أَن يَكْفُرُوا بِمَا أَنزَلَ
اللَّهُ بَغْيًا أَن يُنَزِّلَ اللَّهُ مِن فَضْلِهِ
عَلَىٰ مَن يَشَاءُ مِنْ عِبَادِهِ

92. The Jews in their arrogance claimed that all wisdom and all knowledge of Allah were enclosed in their hearts. But there were more things in heaven and earth than were dreamt of in their philosophy. Their claim was not only arrogance but blasphemy. In reality they were men without Faith. (I take *Ghulfun* here to be the plural of *Ghilāfun* the wrapping or cover of a book, in which the book is preserved.)

As usual, there is a much wider meaning. How many people at all times and among all nations close their hearts to any extension of knowledge or spiritual influence because of some little fragment which they have got and which they think is the whole of Allah's Truth? Such an attitude shows really want of faith and is a blasphemous limitation of Allah's unlimited spiritual gifts to His creatures. [According to another view, the verse refers to the Jewish claim that a covering had been placed over their hearts which prevented them from grasping the message of the Prophet (peace be on him). See Ibn Kathīr's commentary on the verse. See also verse 4:155, [Eds.].

93. The root *kafara* has many shades of meaning: (1) to deny Allah's goodness, to be ungrateful, (2) to reject Faith, deny His revelation, (3) to blaspheme, to ascribe some limitation or attribute to Allah which is derogatory to His nature. In a translation, one shade or another must be put forward according to the context, but all are implied.

94. The Jews, who pretended to be so superior to the people without Faith—the Gentiles—should have been the first to recognize the new Truth—or the Truth renewed—which it was Muḥammad's mission to bring because it was so similar in form and language to what they had already received. But they had more arrogance than faith. It is this want of faith that brings on the curse, *i.e.*, deprives us (if we adopt such an attitude) of the blessings of Allah.

Again the lesson applies to a much wider circle than the Jews. We are all apt, in our perverseness, to reject an appeal from our brother even more summarily than one from an outsider. If we have a glimmering of the truth, we are apt to make ourselves impervious to further truth, and thus lose the benefit of Allah's Grace.

95. Racial arrogance made the Jews adverse to the reception of Truth when it came through a servant of Allah, not of their own race. Again the lesson is wider. Is that adverseness unknown in our own times, and among other races? Yet how can a race or a people set bounds to Allah's choice? Allah is the Creator and Cherisher of all races and all worlds.

Thus have they drawn
On themselves Wrath upon
Wrath,
And humiliating is the
punishment
Of those who reject Faith.

فَبَآءُو بِغَضَبٍ عَلَىٰ غَضَبٍ
وَلِلْكَٰفِرِينَ عَذَابٌ مُّهِينٌ

91. When it is said to them,
"Believe in what Allah
Hath sent down," they say,
"We believe in what was sent
down
To us;" yet they reject
All besides, even if it be Truth
Confirming what is with them.
Say: "Why then have ye slain
The prophets of Allah in times
Gone by, if ye did indeed
Believe?"[96]

٩١ وَإِذَا قِيلَ لَهُمْ
ءَامِنُوا۟ بِمَآ أَنزَلَ ٱللَّهُ
قَالُوا۟ نُؤْمِنُ بِمَآ أُنزِلَ عَلَيْنَا
وَيَكْفُرُونَ بِمَا وَرَآءَهُۥ وَهُوَ ٱلْحَقُّ مُصَدِّقًا
لِّمَا مَعَهُمْ ۗ قُلْ فَلِمَ تَقْتُلُونَ أَنۢبِيَآءَ ٱللَّهِ مِن قَبْلُ
إِن كُنتُم مُّؤْمِنِينَ

92. There came to you Moses
With clear (Signs); yet
Ye worshipped the Calf
(Even) after that, and ye
Did behave wrongfully.

٩٢ وَلَقَدْ جَآءَكُم مُّوسَىٰ بِٱلْبَيِّنَٰتِ
ثُمَّ ٱتَّخَذْتُمُ ٱلْعِجْلَ مِنۢ بَعْدِهِۦ
وَأَنتُمْ ظَٰلِمُونَ

93. And remember We took
Your Covenant and We raised
Above you (the towering height)
Of Mount (Sinai):
(Saying): "Hold firmly
To what We have given you,
And hearken (to the Law)":[97]
They said: "We hear,
And we disobey":[98]
And they had to drink[99]
Into their hearts

٩٣ وَإِذْ أَخَذْنَا مِيثَٰقَكُمْ
وَرَفَعْنَا فَوْقَكُمُ ٱلطُّورَ
خُذُوا۟ مَآ ءَاتَيْنَٰكُم بِقُوَّةٍ وَٱسْمَعُوا۟
قَالُوا۟ سَمِعْنَا وَعَصَيْنَا
وَأُشْرِبُوا۟ فِى قُلُوبِهِمُ

---

96. Even the race argument is often a flimsy and hollow pretext. Did not the Jews reject Prophets of their own race who told them unpleasant truths? And do not other nations do likewise? The real trouble is selfishness, narrowness, a mean dislike of anything which runs counter to habits, customs or inclinations.

97. *Cf.* the introductory words of 2:63, which are the same as the introductory words here, but the argument is developed in a different direction in the two places. In 2:63, after they are reminded of the solemn Covenant under the towering height of Mount Sinai they are told how they broke the Covenant in after ages. Here, after they are reminded of the same solemn Covenant, they are told that even then they never meant to observe it. Their thought is expressed in biting words of sarcasm. They said in words: "All that the Lord hath spoken, we will do." But they said in their hearts: "We shall disobey."

98. What they should have said was: "We hear and we obey": this is the attitude of the true men of Faith (2:285).

99. After the Commandments and the Law had been given at Mount Sinai, and the people had solemnly given their Covenant, Moses went up to the Mount, and in his absence, the people made the golden calf. [The word *ūshribū* which occurs in the verse seems to suggest, as noted Tābi'i Qatādah is reported to have said, that their hearts were saturated with the love for the calf. See Ibn Kathīr, Commentary on the verse 2:93, (Eds.)]

(Of the taint) of the Calf
Because of their Faithlessness.
Say: "Vile indeed
Are the behests of your Faith
If ye have any faith!"

ٱلْعِجْلَ بِكُفْرِهِمْ ۚ قُلْ بِئْسَمَا
يَأْمُرُكُم بِهِۦٓ إِيمَـٰنُكُمْ إِن كُنتُم مُّؤْمِنِينَ

94. Say: "If the last Home,
with Allah, be for you specially,
And not for anyone else,
Then seek ye for death,
If ye are sincere."

قُلْ إِن كَانَتْ لَكُمُ ٱلدَّارُ ٱلْـَٔاخِرَةُ ﴿٩٤﴾
عِندَ ٱللَّهِ خَالِصَةً مِّن دُونِ ٱلنَّاسِ
فَتَمَنَّوُا۟ ٱلْمَوْتَ إِن كُنتُمْ صَـٰدِقِينَ

95. But they will never seek
For death, on account of the (sins)
Which their hands have sent
On before them.[100]
And Allah is well-acquainted
With the wrongdoers.

وَلَن يَتَمَنَّوْهُ أَبَدًۢا ﴿٩٥﴾
بِمَا قَدَّمَتْ أَيْدِيهِمْ ۗ
وَٱللَّهُ عَلِيمٌۢ بِٱلظَّـٰلِمِينَ

96. Thou wilt indeed find them,
Of all people, most greedy
Of life—even more
Than the idolaters:
Each one of them wishes
He could be given a life
Of a thousand years:
But the grant of such life
Will not save him
From (due) punishment.
For Allah sees well
All that they do.

وَلَتَجِدَنَّهُمْ أَحْرَصَ ٱلنَّاسِ ﴿٩٦﴾
عَلَىٰ حَيَوٰةٍ وَمِنَ ٱلَّذِينَ أَشْرَكُوا۟ ۚ
يَوَدُّ أَحَدُهُمْ لَوْ يُعَمَّرُ أَلْفَ سَنَةٍ
وَمَا هُوَ بِمُزَحْزِحِهِۦ
مِنَ ٱلْعَذَابِ أَن يُعَمَّرَ ۗ
وَٱللَّهُ بَصِيرٌۢ بِمَا يَعْمَلُونَ

SECTION 12.

97. Say: Whoever is an enemy[101]
To Gabriel—for he brings down

قُلْ مَن كَانَ عَدُوًّا لِّجِبْرِيلَ فَإِنَّهُۥ نَزَّلَهُۥ ﴿٩٧﴾

100. The phrase "What their hands have sent on before them" frequently occurs in the Qur'ān. Here and in many places, it refers to sins. In such passages as 78:40 or 81:14, it is implied that both good and bad deeds go before us to the Judgement Seat of Allah before we do ourselves. In 2:110, it is the good that goes before us. Our deeds are personified. They are witnesses for or against us, and they always go before us. Their good or bad influence begins to operate before we even know it. This is more general than the New Testament idea in the First Epistle of St. Paul to Timothy, v. 24: "Some men's sins are open beforehand, going before to judgement; and some men they follow after."

101. A party of the Jews in the time of Muḥammad ridiculed the Muslim belief that Gabriel brought down revelations to Muḥammad Al Muṣṭafā. Michael was called in their books "the great prince which standeth for the children of thy people": (Daniel, xii. 1). The vision of Gabriel inspired fear (Daniel, viii. 16-17). But this pretence—that Michael was their friend and Gabriel their enemy—was merely a manifestation of their unbelief in angels, Prophets and Allah Himself; and such unbelief could not win the love of Allah. In any case it was disingenuous to say that they believed in one angel and not in another. Muḥammad's inspiration was through visions of Gabriel. Muḥammad had been helped to the highest spiritual light, and the message which he delivered and his spotless integrity and exemplary life were manifest Signs which every one could understand except those who were obstinate and perverse. Besides, the verses of the Qur'ān were in themselves reasonable and clear.

The (revelation) to thy heart
By Allah's will, a confirmation
Of what went before.
And guidance and glad tidings
For those who believe—

عَلَىٰ قَلْبِكَ بِإِذْنِ ٱللَّهِ مُصَدِّقًا لِّمَا بَيْنَ
يَدَيْهِ وَهُدًى وَبُشْرَىٰ لِلْمُؤْمِنِينَ

98. Whoever is an enemy to Allah
And His angels and prophets,
To Gabriel and Michael—
Lo! Allah is an enemy to those
Who reject Faith.

٩٨ مَن كَانَ عَدُوًّا لِّلَّهِ وَمَلَٰٓئِكَتِهِۦ
وَرُسُلِهِۦ وَجِبْرِيلَ وَمِيكَىٰلَ
فَإِنَّ ٱللَّهَ عَدُوٌّ لِّلْكَٰفِرِينَ

99. We have sent down to thee
Manifest Signs *(āyāt);*
And none reject them
But those who are perverse.

٩٩ وَلَقَدْ أَنزَلْنَآ إِلَيْكَ ءَايَٰتٍۭ بَيِّنَٰتٍ ۖ
وَمَا يَكْفُرُ بِهَآ إِلَّا ٱلْفَٰسِقُونَ

100. Is it not (the case) that
Every time they make a
Covenant,
Some party among them
Throw it aside?—Nay,
Most of them are faithless.

١٠٠ أَوَكُلَّمَا عَٰهَدُوا۟ عَهْدًا
نَّبَذَهُۥ فَرِيقٌ مِّنْهُم ۚ
بَلْ أَكْثَرُهُمْ لَا يُؤْمِنُونَ

101. And when there came to them
A Messenger from Allah,
Confirming what was with them,
A Party of the People of the
Book
Threw away the Book of Allah[102]
Behind their backs.
As if (it had been something)
They did not know!

١٠١ وَلَمَّا جَآءَهُمْ رَسُولٌ مِّنْ عِندِ ٱللَّهِ
مُصَدِّقٌ لِّمَا مَعَهُمْ نَبَذَ فَرِيقٌ مِّنَ
ٱلَّذِينَ أُوتُوا۟ ٱلْكِتَٰبَ كِتَٰبَ ٱللَّهِ
وَرَآءَ ظُهُورِهِمْ كَأَنَّهُمْ لَا يَعْلَمُونَ

102. They followed what the evil
ones[103]
Gave out (falsely)
Against the power
Of Solomon: the blasphemers
Were, not Solomon, but
The evil ones, teaching men

١٠٢ وَٱتَّبَعُوا۟ مَا تَتْلُوا۟ ٱلشَّيَٰطِينُ عَلَىٰ مُلْكِ
سُلَيْمَٰنَ ۖ وَمَا كَفَرَ سُلَيْمَٰنُ وَلَٰكِنَّ
ٱلشَّيَٰطِينَ كَفَرُوا۟ يُعَلِّمُونَ ٱلنَّاسَ

---

102. I think that by "the Book of Allah" here is meant, not the Qur'ān, but the Book which the People of the Book had been given, *viz.*, the previous Revelations. The argument is that Muḥammad's Message was similar to Revelations which they had already received, and if they had looked into their own Books honestly and sincerely, they would have found proofs in them to show that the new Message was true and from Allah. But they ignored their own Books or twisted or distorted them according to their own fancies. Worse, they followed something which was actually false and mischievous and inspired by the evil one. Such was the belief in magic and sorcery. These are described in the next verse in terms referring to the beliefs and practices of the "People of the Book."

103. This is a continuation of the argument in 2:101. The People of the Book, instead of sticking to the plain Books of Revelations, and seeking to do the will of Allah, ran after all sorts of occult knowledge, most of which was false and evil. Many wonderful tales of occult power attributed the power of Solomon to magic. But Solomon dealt in no arts of evil. It was the powers of evil that pretended to force the laws of nature and the will of Allah; such a pretence is plainly blasphemy.

Magic, and such things
As came down at Babylon
To the angels Hārūt and Mārūt.[104]
But neither of these taught anyone
(Such things) without saying:
"We are only for trial;
So do not blaspheme."
They learned from them[105]
The means to sow discord
Between man and wife.
But they could not thus
Harm anyone except
By Allah's permission.
And they learned what harmed them,
Not what profited them.
And they knew that the buyers
Of (magic) would have
No share in the happiness
Of the Hereafter. And vile
Was the price for which
They did sell their souls,
If they but knew!

103. If they had kept their Faith
And guarded themselves from evil,

ٱلسِّحْرَ وَمَآ أُنزِلَ عَلَى ٱلْمَلَكَيْنِ بِبَابِلَ
هَٰرُوتَ وَمَٰرُوتَ ۚ وَمَا يُعَلِّمَانِ مِنْ أَحَدٍ
حَتَّىٰ يَقُولَآ إِنَّمَا نَحْنُ فِتْنَةٌ
فَلَا تَكْفُرْ ۖ
فَيَتَعَلَّمُونَ مِنْهُمَا مَا يُفَرِّقُونَ بِهِۦ
بَيْنَ ٱلْمَرْءِ وَزَوْجِهِۦ ۚ وَمَا هُم بِضَآرِّينَ بِهِۦ
مِنْ أَحَدٍ إِلَّا بِإِذْنِ ٱللَّهِ ۚ وَيَتَعَلَّمُونَ
مَا يَضُرُّهُمْ وَلَا يَنفَعُهُمْ ۚ
وَلَقَدْ عَلِمُوا۟ لَمَنِ ٱشْتَرَىٰهُ
مَا لَهُۥ فِى ٱلْءَاخِرَةِ مِنْ خَلَٰقٍ ۚ
وَلَبِئْسَ مَا شَرَوْا۟ بِهِۦٓ أَنفُسَهُمْ ۚ
لَوْ كَانُوا۟ يَعْلَمُونَ

١٠٣ وَلَوْ أَنَّهُمْ ءَامَنُوا۟ وَٱتَّقَوْا۟

104. Hārūt and Mārūt lived in Babylon, a very ancient seat of science, especially the science of astronomy. The period may be supposed to be anywhere about the time when the ancient Eastern Monarchies were strong and enlightened: probably even earlier, as Mā-rū-tu or Madruk was a deified hero afterwards worshipped as a god of magic in Babylon. Being good men, Hārūt and Mārūt of course dabbled in nothing evil, and their hands were certainly clean of fraud. But knowledge and the arts, if learned by evil men, can be applied to evil uses. The evil ones, besides their fraudulent magic, also learnt a little of this true science and applied it to evil uses. Hārūt and Mārūt did not withhold knowledge, yet never taught anyone without plainly warning them of the trial and temptation of knowledge in the hands of evil men. Being men of insight, they also saw the blasphemy that might rise to the lips of the evil ones puffed up with science and warned them against it. Knowledge is indeed a trial or temptation: if we are warned, we know its dangers: if Allah has endowed us with free will, we must be free to choose between the benefit and the danger.

Among the Jewish traditions in the Midrash (Jewish *Tafsīrs*) was a story of two angels who asked Allah's permission to come down to earth but succumbed to temptation, and were hung up by their feet at Babylon for punishment. Such stories about sinning angels who were cast down to punishment were believed in by the early Christians also. (See the Second Epistle of Peter. ii. 4, and the Epistle of Jude, verse 6). (R).

105. What the evil ones learnt from Hārūt and Mārūt (see last note) they turned to evil. When mixed with fraud and deception, it appeared as charms and spells and love potions. They did nothing but cause discord between the sexes. But of course their power was limited to the extent to which Allah permitted the evil to work, for His grace protected all who sought His guidance and repented and returned to Him. But apart from the harm that these false pretenders might do to others, the chief harm which they did was to their own souls. They sold themselves into slavery to the Evil One, as is shown in the allegory of Goethe's *Faust*. That allegory dealt with the individual soul. Here the tragedy is shown to occur not only to individuals but to whole groups of people, for example, the People of the Book. Indeed the story might be extended indefinitely.

Far better had been
The reward from their Lord,
If they but knew!

لَمَثُوبَةٌ مِّنْ عِندِ ٱللَّهِ خَيْرٌ
لَّوْ كَانُوا۟ يَعْلَمُونَ

SECTION 13.

104. O ye of Faith!
Say not (to the Prophet)
Words of ambiguous import,[106]
But words of respect;
And hearken (to him):
To those without Faith
Is a grievous punishment.

١٠٤ يَـٰٓأَيُّهَا ٱلَّذِينَ ءَامَنُوا۟
لَا تَقُولُوا۟ رَٰعِنَا وَقُولُوا۟ ٱنظُرْنَا
وَٱسْمَعُوا۟ وَلِلْكَـٰفِرِينَ عَذَابٌ أَلِيمٌ

105. It is never the wish
Of those without Faith
Among the People of the Book,
Nor of the Pagans,
That anything good
Should come down to you
From your Lord.
But Allah will choose
For His special Mercy
Whom He will—for Allah is
Lord of grace abounding.

١٠٥ مَّا يَوَدُّ ٱلَّذِينَ كَفَرُوا۟
مِنْ أَهْلِ ٱلْكِتَـٰبِ وَلَا ٱلْمُشْرِكِينَ
أَن يُنَزَّلَ عَلَيْكُم مِّنْ خَيْرٍ مِّن رَّبِّكُمْ
وَٱللَّهُ يَخْتَصُّ بِرَحْمَتِهِۦ مَن يَشَآءُ
وَٱللَّهُ ذُو ٱلْفَضْلِ ٱلْعَظِيمِ

106. None of Our revelations[107]
Do We abrogate
Or cause to be forgotten,
But We substitute

١٠٦ مَا نَنسَخْ مِنْ ءَايَةٍ أَوْ نُنسِهَا نَأْتِ

106. The word disapproved is *Rā'inā*, which as used by the Muslims meant "Please look at us, attend to us." But it was ridiculed by enemies by a little twist to suggest some insulting meaning. So an unambiguous word "Unzurnā," with the same meaning is suggested. The general lesson is that we must guard ourselves against the cynical trick of using words which sound complimentary to the ear but have a hidden barb in them. Not only must we be plain and honest in our words. We must respectfully hearken to the words of a Teacher whom we have addressed. Thoughtless people use vain words or put foolish questions, and straightaway turn their minds to something else.

107. The word which I have translated by the word "revelations" is Āyāt. See C. 41 and n. 15. It is not only used for verses of the Qur'ān, but in a general sense for Allah's revelations, as in 2:39 and for other Signs of Allah in history or nature, or miracles, as in 2:61. It has even been used for human signs and tokens of wonder, as, for example, monuments or landmarks built by the ancient people of 'Ād (26:128). What is the meaning here? If we take it in a general sense, it means that Allah's Message from age to age is always the same, but that its form may differ according to the needs and exigencies of the time. That form was different as given to Moses and then to Jesus and then to Muḥammad. Some commentators apply it also to The Āyāt of the Qur'ān. There is nothing derogatory in this if we believe in progressive revelation. In 3:7 we are told distinctly about the Qur'ān, that some of its verses are clear (and of established meaning), and others are not entirely clear, and it is mischievous to treat the verses that are not entirely clear and to follow them (literally). On the other hand, it is absurd to treat such a verse as 2:115 as if it were abrogated by 2:144 about Qiblah.

There may be express abrogation, or there may be "causing or permitting to forget." How many good and wise institutions gradually become obsolete by afflux of time? Then there is the gradual process of disuse or forgetting in evolution. This does not mean that eternal principles change. It is only a sign of Allah's infinite Power that His creation should take so many forms and shapes not only in the material world but in the world of man's thought and expression.

Something better or similar:
Knowest thou not that Allah
Hath power over all things?

بِخَيْرٍ مِّنْهَآ أَوْ مِثْلِهَآ ۗ
أَلَمْ تَعْلَمْ أَنَّ ٱللَّهَ عَلَىٰ كُلِّ شَىْءٍ قَدِيرٌ

107. Knowest thou not
That to Allah belongeth
The dominion of the heavens
And the earth?
And besides Him ye have
Neither patron nor helper.

١٠٧ أَلَمْ تَعْلَمْ
أَنَّ ٱللَّهَ لَهُۥ مُلْكُ ٱلسَّمَٰوَٰتِ وَٱلْأَرْضِ ۗ
وَمَا لَكُم مِّن دُونِ ٱللَّهِ مِن وَلِىٍّ وَلَا نَصِيرٍ

108. Would ye question
Your Messenger as Moses[108]
Was questioned of old?
But whoever changeth
From Faith to Unbelief,
Hath strayed without doubt
From the even way.[109]

١٠٨ أَمْ تُرِيدُونَ أَن تَسْـَٔلُوا۟
رَسُولَكُمْ كَمَا سُئِلَ مُوسَىٰ مِن قَبْلُ ۗ
وَمَن يَتَبَدَّلِ ٱلْكُفْرَ بِٱلْإِيمَٰنِ
فَقَدْ ضَلَّ سَوَآءَ ٱلسَّبِيلِ

109. Quite a number of the People
Of the Book wish they could
Turn you (people) back
To infidelity after ye have
believed.
From selfish envy,
After the Truth hath become
Manifest unto them:
But forgive and overlook,[110]
Till Allah accomplishes
His purpose:[111] for Allah
Hath power over all things.[112]

١٠٩ وَدَّ كَثِيرٌ مِّنْ أَهْلِ ٱلْكِتَٰبِ
لَوْ يَرُدُّونَكُم مِّنۢ بَعْدِ إِيمَٰنِكُمْ كُفَّارًا
حَسَدًا مِّنْ عِندِ أَنفُسِهِم
مِّنۢ بَعْدِ مَا تَبَيَّنَ لَهُمُ ٱلْحَقُّ ۖ
فَٱعْفُوا۟ وَٱصْفَحُوا۟ حَتَّىٰ يَأْتِىَ ٱللَّهُ بِأَمْرِهِۦٓ ۗ
إِنَّ ٱللَّهَ عَلَىٰ كُلِّ شَىْءٍ قَدِيرٌ

---

108. Moses was constantly harassed with foolish, impertinent, or disingenuous questions by his own people. We must not follow that bad example. In spiritual matters, posers do no good: questions should be asked only for real instruction.

109. "Even way": the Arabic word *sawā'a* signifies smoothness as opposed to roughness; symmetry as opposed to want of plan; equality or proportion as opposed to want of design; rectitude as opposed to crookedness; a mean as opposed to extremes; and fitness for the object held in view as opposed to faultiness.

110. Three words are used in the Qur'ān, with a meaning akin to "forgive", but each with a different shade of meaning. *'Afā* (here translated "forgive") means to forget, to obliterate from one's mind. *Ṣafaḥa* (here translated "overlook") means to turn away from, to ignore, to treat a matter as if it did not affect one. *Ghafara* (which does not occur in this verse) means to cover up something as Allah does to our sins with His grace: this word is particularly appropriate in Allah's attribute to *Ghaffār*, the One who forgives again and again.

111. The word, *Amr*, is comprehensive, and includes (1) an order or command as in 94:12; or (2) a purpose, design, will, as in 18:82; or (3) affairs, working, doing, carrying out or execution of a design, as in 89. 5. In many cases some of these meanings run together.

112. Note how this phrase, seemingly repeated from 2:106, and occurring in many other places, has an appropriate signification in each place. In 2:106 we were told about progressive revelation, how the same thing may take different forms, and seeming human infirmity contribute to the fulfilment of Allah's design, for Allah's power is unlimited. Here we are told to be patient and forgiving against envy and injustice; this too may be fulfilling Allah's purpose, for His power is infinite.

110. And be steadfast in prayer
And regular in charity:
And whatever good
Ye send forth for your souls[113]
Before you, ye shall find it
With Allah: for Allah sees
Well all that ye do.

(١١٠) وَأَقِيمُوا۟ ٱلصَّلَوٰةَ وَءَاتُوا۟ ٱلزَّكَوٰةَ ۚ
وَمَا تُقَدِّمُوا۟ لِأَنفُسِكُم مِّنْ خَيْرٍ تَجِدُوهُ
عِندَ ٱللَّهِ ۗ إِنَّ ٱللَّهَ بِمَا تَعْمَلُونَ بَصِيرٌ

111. And they say: "None
Shall enter Paradise unless
He be a Jew or a Christian."
Those are their (vain) desires.
Say: "Produce your proof
If ye are truthful."

(١١١) وَقَالُوا۟ لَن يَدْخُلَ ٱلْجَنَّةَ إِلَّا مَن كَانَ
هُودًا أَوْ نَصَٰرَىٰ ۗ تِلْكَ أَمَانِيُّهُمْ ۗ قُلْ هَاتُوا۟
بُرْهَٰنَكُمْ إِن كُنتُمْ صَٰدِقِينَ

112. Nay—whoever submits
His whole self[114] to Allah
And is a doer of good—
He will get his reward
With his Lord;
On such shall be no fear,
Nor shall they grieve.[115]

(١١٢) بَلَىٰ مَنْ أَسْلَمَ وَجْهَهُۥ لِلَّهِ
وَهُوَ مُحْسِنٌ فَلَهُۥٓ أَجْرُهُۥ عِندَ رَبِّهِۦ
وَلَا خَوْفٌ عَلَيْهِمْ وَلَا هُمْ يَحْزَنُونَ

Section 14.

113. The Jews say: "The Christians
Have naught (to stand) upon";
And the Christians say:
"The Jews have naught
(To stand) upon." Yet they
(Profess to) study the (same) Book.
Like unto their word
Is what those say who know not;[116]
But Allah will judge
Between them in their quarrel
On the Day of Judgement.

(١١٣) وَقَالَتِ ٱلْيَهُودُ لَيْسَتِ ٱلنَّصَٰرَىٰ
عَلَىٰ شَىْءٍ وَقَالَتِ ٱلنَّصَٰرَىٰ لَيْسَتِ ٱلْيَهُودُ
عَلَىٰ شَىْءٍ وَهُمْ يَتْلُونَ ٱلْكِتَٰبَ ۗ كَذَٰلِكَ قَالَ
ٱلَّذِينَ لَا يَعْلَمُونَ مِثْلَ قَوْلِهِمْ ۚ
فَٱللَّهُ يَحْكُمُ بَيْنَهُمْ يَوْمَ ٱلْقِيَٰمَةِ
فِيمَا كَانُوا۟ فِيهِ يَخْتَلِفُونَ

---

113. *Cf.* 2:95 n. 100.

114. The word translated "self" is *Wajh*, a comprehensive Arabic word. It means (1) literally face, but it may imply (2) countenance or favour, as in 92:20; (3) honour, glory. Presence as applied to Allah, as in 4:72; (4) cause, sake ("for the sake of") as in 76:8; (5) the first part, the beginning, as in 3:71; (6) nature, inner being, essence, self, as in 5:111, 27:88, and perhaps also 55:27. Here I understand meaning 6; the face expresses the personality or the whole inner self of man. (R).

115. This phrase comes in aptly in its own context many times. In this Surah it occurs in 2:38, 62, 112, 262, 274, and 277. (R).

116. It is a sure sign of ignorance and prejudice when you study the same book as another or a similar one and yet are absolutely intolerant of the meaning which the other draws from it. You should know better, but you speak like the ignorant. In this case the primary reference in the word "ignorant" may be to the Pagan Arabs.

114. And who is more unjust
Than he who forbids[117]
That in places for the worship
Of Allah, His name should be
Celebrated?—whose zeal
Is (in fact) to ruin them?
It was not fitting that such
Should themselves enter them
Except in fear. For them
There is nothing but disgrace
In this world, and in the world
To come, an exceeding torment.

﴿١١٤﴾ وَمَنْ أَظْلَمُ مِمَّن مَّنَعَ
مَسَٰجِدَ ٱللَّهِ أَن يُذْكَرَ فِيهَا ٱسْمُهُۥ
وَسَعَىٰ فِى خَرَابِهَآ ۚ أُو۟لَٰٓئِكَ مَا كَانَ لَهُمْ
أَن يَدْخُلُوهَآ إِلَّا خَآئِفِينَ ۚ
لَهُمْ فِى ٱلدُّنْيَا خِزْىٌ
وَلَهُمْ فِى ٱلْءَاخِرَةِ عَذَابٌ عَظِيمٌ

115. To Allah belong the East
And the West: whithersoever
Ye turn, there is Allah's
countenance.[118]
For Allah is All-Embracing,
All-Knowing.

﴿١١٥﴾ وَلِلَّهِ ٱلْمَشْرِقُ وَٱلْمَغْرِبُ ۚ
فَأَيْنَمَا تُوَلُّوا۟ فَثَمَّ وَجْهُ ٱللَّهِ ۚ
إِنَّ ٱللَّهَ وَٰسِعٌ عَلِيمٌ

116. They say: "Allah hath begotten
A son": Glory be to Him—Nay,
To Him belongs all
That is in the heavens
And on earth: everything
Renders worship to Him.[119]

﴿١١٦﴾ وَقَالُوا۟ ٱتَّخَذَ ٱللَّهُ وَلَدًا ۗ
سُبْحَٰنَهُۥ ۖ بَل لَّهُۥ مَا فِى ٱلسَّمَٰوَٰتِ
وَٱلْأَرْضِ ۖ كُلٌّ لَّهُۥ قَٰنِتُونَ

117. To Him is due
The primal origin

﴿١١٧﴾ بَدِيعُ

117. There were actually Pagans in Makkah who tried to shut out Muslim Arabs from the Ka'bah, the universal place of Arab worship. The Pagans themselves called it the House of Allah. With what face could they exclude the Muslims, who wanted to worship the true Allah instead of worshipping idols? If these Pagans had succeeded, they would only have caused violent divisions among the Arabs and destroyed the sanctity and the very existence of the Ka'bah.

This verse, taken in a general sense, establishes the principle of freedom of worship in a public mosque or place dedicated to the worship of Allah. This is recognised in Muslim law. (R).

118. That is, you will face Allah whichsoever direction you turn your face. See note 2:112 above. (R).

119. It is a derogation from the glory of Allah—in fact it is blasphemy—to say that Allah begets sons, like a man or an animal. The Christian doctrine is here emphatically repudiated. If words have any meaning, it would mean an attribution to Allah of a material nature, and of the lower animal functions of sex. (R).

Of the heavens and the earth:[120]
When He decreeth a matter,
He saith to it: "Be,"
And it is.

ٱلسَّمَٰوَٰتِ وَٱلْأَرْضِ ۖ
وَإِذَا قَضَىٰٓ أَمْرًا فَإِنَّمَا يَقُولُ لَهُۥ كُن فَيَكُونُ

118. Say those without knowledge:
"Why speaketh not Allah
Unto us? Or why cometh not
Unto us a Sign?"
So said the people before them
Words of similar import.
Their hearts are alike.
We have indeed made clear
The Signs unto any people
Who hold firmly
To Faith (in their hearts).

١١٨ وَقَالَ ٱلَّذِينَ لَا يَعْلَمُونَ
لَوْلَا يُكَلِّمُنَا ٱللَّهُ أَوْ تَأْتِينَآ ءَايَةٌ ۗ
كَذَٰلِكَ قَالَ ٱلَّذِينَ مِن قَبْلِهِم
مِّثْلَ قَوْلِهِمْ ۘ تَشَٰبَهَتْ قُلُوبُهُمْ ۗ
قَدْ بَيَّنَّا ٱلْءَايَٰتِ لِقَوْمٍ يُوقِنُونَ

119. Verily, We have sent thee
In truth as a bearer
Of glad tidings and a warner:
But of thee no question
Shall be asked of the companions
Of the Blazing Fire.

١١٩ إِنَّآ أَرْسَلْنَٰكَ
بِٱلْحَقِّ بَشِيرًا وَنَذِيرًا ۖ
وَلَا تُسْـَٔلُ عَنْ أَصْحَٰبِ ٱلْجَحِيمِ

120. Never will the Jews
Or the Christians be satisfied
With thee unless thou follow
Their form of religion. Say:

١٢٠ وَلَن تَرْضَىٰ عَنكَ ٱلْيَهُودُ
وَلَا ٱلنَّصَٰرَىٰ حَتَّىٰ تَتَّبِعَ مِلَّتَهُمْ ۗ قُلْ

---

120. The previous verse told us that everything in heaven and earth celebrates the glory of Allah. Lest anyone should think that the heavens and the earth were themselves primeval and eternal, we are now told that they themselves are creatures of Allah's will and design. *Cf.* 6:102, where the word *bada'a* is used as here for the creation of the heavens and the earth, and *khalaqa* is used for the creation of all things. *Bada'a* goes back to the very primal beginning, as far as we can conceive it. The materialists might say that primeval matter was eternal: other things, *i.e.*, the forms and shapes as we see them now, were called into being at some time or other, and will perish. When they perish, they dissolve into primeval matter again, which stands at the base of all existence. We go further back. We say that if we postulate such primeval matter, it owes its origin itself to Allah. Who is the final basis of existence, the Cause of all Causes. If this is conceded, we proceed to argue that the process of Creation is not then completed. " All things in the heavens and on the earth" are created by gradual processes. In "things" we include abstract as well as material things. We see the abstract things and ideas actually growing before us. But that also is Allah's creation, to which we can apply the word *khalaqa*, for in it is involved the idea of measuring, fitting it into a scheme of other things. *Cf.* 54:49; also 25:59. Here comes in what we know as the process of evolution. On the other hand, the "*amr*" (=Command, Direction, Design) is a single thing, unrelated to Time. "like the twinkling of an eye" (54:50). Another word to note in this connection is *ja'ala* "making" which seems to imply new shapes and forms, new dispositions, as the making of the Signs of the Zodiac in the heavens, or the setting out of the sun and moon for light, or the establishment of the succession of day and night (25:61-62). A Further process with regard to the soul is described in the word *sawwā*, bringing it to perfection (91:7) but this we shall discuss in its place. *Faṭara* (42:11) implies, like *bada'a*, the creating of a thing out of nothing and after no pre-existing similitude, but perhaps *faṭara* implies the creation of primeval matter to which further processes have to be applied later, as when one prepares dough but leaves the leavening to be done after. *Badaa* (without the 'ain), 30:27, implies beginning the process of creation: this is made further clear in 32:7 where the beginning of the creation of pristine man from clay refers to his physical body, leaving the further processes of reproduction and the breathing in of the soul to be described in subsequent verses. Lastly, *bara'a* is creation implying liberation from pre-existing matter or circumstance, *e.g.*, man's body from clay (59:24) or a calamity from previously existing circumstances (57:22). See also 6:94 n. 916; 6:98 n. 923; 59:24 nn. 5405-6.

"The Guidance of Allah—that
Is the (only) Guidance,"
Wert thou to follow their desires
After the knowledge
Which hath reached thee,
Then wouldst thou find
Neither Protector nor Helper
Against Allah.

إِنَّ هُدَى ٱللَّهِ هُوَ ٱلْهُدَىٰ
وَلَئِنِ ٱتَّبَعْتَ أَهْوَآءَهُم
بَعْدَ ٱلَّذِى جَآءَكَ مِنَ ٱلْعِلْمِ
مَا لَكَ مِنَ ٱللَّهِ مِن وَلِىٍّ وَلَا نَصِيرٍ

121. Those to whom We have sent
The Book study it as it
Should be studied: they are
The ones that believe therein:
Those who reject faith therein—
The loss is their own.

١٢١ ٱلَّذِينَ ءَاتَيْنَٰهُمُ ٱلْكِتَٰبَ
يَتْلُونَهُۥ حَقَّ تِلَاوَتِهِۦٓ أُو۟لَٰٓئِكَ يُؤْمِنُونَ بِهِۦ
وَمَن يَكْفُرْ بِهِۦ فَأُو۟لَٰٓئِكَ هُمُ ٱلْخَٰسِرُونَ

C. 48.—If the People of the Book rely
(2:122-141.) Upon Abraham, let them study
His history. His posterity included
Both Israel and Ismā'īl. Abraham
Was a righteous man of Allah,
A Muslim, and so were his children.
Abraham and Ismā'īl built
The Ka'ba as the house of Allah,
And purified it, to be a centre
Of worship for all the world:
For Allah is the God of all Peoples.[121]

SECTION 15.

122. O Children of Israel! call to mind
The special favour which I
bestowed
Upon you, and that I preferred
you
To all others (for My Message).

١٢٢ يَٰبَنِىٓ إِسْرَٰٓءِيلَ ٱذْكُرُوا۟
نِعْمَتِىَ ٱلَّتِىٓ أَنْعَمْتُ عَلَيْكُمْ
وَأَنِّى فَضَّلْتُكُمْ عَلَى ٱلْعَٰلَمِينَ

123. Then guard yourselves against
a Day

١٢٣ وَٱتَّقُوا۟ يَوْمًا

121. The argument now proceeds on another line. Ye People of the Book who go back to Abraham! not only is your claim to exclusive knowledge of Allah false and derogatory to the Lord of All the Worlds. If you must appeal to Abraham, he was also the progenitor of the Arab race through Ismā'īl. Indeed Abraham and Ismā'īl together built the House of Allah in Makkah (long before the Temple of Jerusalem was built). They purified it and laid the foundations of the universal religion, which is summed up in word Islam, or complete submission to the Will of Allah. Abraham and Ismā'īl were thus true Muslims. Whence then your rancour against Islam?

Historically the House of Allah at Makkah must have been far more ancient place of worship than the Temple of Jerusalem. Arab tradition connects various places in and around Makkah with the name of Abraham and identifies the well of Zam-zam with the well in the story of the child Ismā'īl. Arab tradition also refers the story of the Sacrifice to Ismā'īl and not to Isaac, therein differing from the Jewish tradition in Gen. xxii. 1-19. (R).

When one soul shall not avail
another.
Nor shall compensation be
accepted from her
Nor shall intercession profit her
Nor shall anyone be helped
(from outside).[122]

لَا تَجْزِى نَفْسٌ عَن نَّفْسٍ شَيْـًٔا
وَلَا يُقْبَلُ مِنْهَا عَدْلٌ
وَلَا تَنفَعُهَا شَفَٰعَةٌ وَلَا هُمْ يُنصَرُونَ

124. And remember that Abraham
Was tried by his Lord
With certain Commands,[123]
Which he fulfilled:
He said: "I will make thee
An Imām[124] to the Nations."
He pleaded: "And also
(Imāms) from my offspring!"
He answered: "But My Promise
Is not within the reach
Of evildoers."

١٢٤ وَإِذِ ٱبْتَلَىٰٓ إِبْرَٰهِـۧمَ
رَبُّهُۥ بِكَلِمَٰتٍ فَأَتَمَّهُنَّ
قَالَ إِنِّى جَاعِلُكَ لِلنَّاسِ إِمَامًا
قَالَ وَمِن ذُرِّيَّتِى قَالَ لَا يَنَالُ
عَهْدِى ٱلظَّٰلِمِينَ

125. Remember We made the House[125]
A place of assembly for men
And a place of safety;
And take ye the Station
Of Abraham as a place
Of prayer; and We covenanted
With Abraham and Ismā'īl,

١٢٥ وَإِذْ جَعَلْنَا ٱلْبَيْتَ مَثَابَةً لِّلنَّاسِ
وَأَمْنًا وَٱتَّخِذُوا۟ مِن مَّقَامِ إِبْرَٰهِـۧمَ مُصَلًّى
وَعَهِدْنَآ إِلَىٰٓ إِبْرَٰهِـۧمَ وَإِسْمَٰعِيلَ

122. Verses 122-123 repeat verses 47-48 (except for a slight verbal variation in 2:123, which does not affect the sense). The argument about the favours to Israel is thus beautifully rounded off, and we now proceed to the argument in favour of the Arabs as succeeding to the spiritual inheritance of Abraham.

123. *Kalimāt*: literally "words": here used in the sense of Allah's Will or Decree or Purpose. This verse may be taken to be the sum of the verses following. In everything Abraham fulfilled Allah's wish: he purified Allah's house; he built the sacred refuge of the Ka'bah; he submitted his will to Allah's, and thus became the type of Islam. He was promised the leadership of the world; he pleaded for his progeny, and his prayer was granted, with the limitation that if his progeny was false to Allah, Allah's promise did not reach the people who proved themselves false.

124. *Imām*: the primary sense is that of being foremost: hence it may mean: (1) leader in religion; (2) leader in congregational prayer; (3) model, pattern, example; (4) a book of guidance and instruction (11:17); (5) a book of evidence or record (36:12). Here, meanings 1 and 3 are implied. In 9:12 the word is applied to leaders of Unbelief or Blasphemy.

125. The Ka'bah, the House of Allah. Its foundation goes back by Arab tradition to Abraham. Its fourfold character is here referred to (1) It was the centre to which all the Arab tribes resorted for trade, for poetic contests, and for worship. (2) It was sacred territory, and was respected by friend and foe alike. At certain seasons, all fighting was and is forbidden within its limits, and even arms are not allowed to be carried, and no game or other thing is allowed to be killed. Like the Cities of Refuge under the Mosaic Dispensation, to which manslayers could flee (Num. xxxv. 6), or the Sanctuaries in Mediaeval Europe, to which criminals could not be pursued. Makkah was recognised by Arab custom as inviolable for the pursuit of revenge or violence. (3) It was a place of prayer: even to-day there is a Station of Abraham. (4) It must be held pure and sacred for all purposes.

Though the verse as a whole is expressed in the First Person Plural, the House is called "My House," to emphasise the personal relation of Allah, the One True God, to it, and repudiate the Polytheism which defiled it before it was purified again by Muḥammad. (R).

That they should sanctify
My House for those who
Compass it round, or use it
As a retreat, or bow, or
Prostrate themselves (therein[126]
In Prayer).

أَن طَهِّرَا بَيْتِيَ لِلطَّآئِفِينَ
وَٱلْعَٰكِفِينَ وَٱلرُّكَّعِ ٱلسُّجُودِ

126. And remember Abraham said:
"My Lord, make this a City
Of Peace,[127] and feed its People
With fruits[128]—such of them
As believe in Allah and the
Last Day."
He said: "(Yea), and such as
Reject Faith—for a while
Will I grant them their pleasure,
But will soon drive them
To the torment of Fire—
An evil destination (indeed)!"

١٢٦ وَإِذْ قَالَ إِبْرَٰهِـۧمُ
رَبِّ ٱجْعَلْ هَٰذَا بَلَدًا ءَامِنًا وَٱرْزُقْ أَهْلَهُۥ
مِنَ ٱلثَّمَرَٰتِ مَنْ ءَامَنَ مِنْهُم بِٱللَّهِ وَٱلْيَوْمِ ٱلْءَاخِرِ
قَالَ وَمَن كَفَرَ فَأُمَتِّعُهُۥ قَلِيلًا ثُمَّ أَضْطَرُّهُۥٓ
إِلَىٰ عَذَابِ ٱلنَّارِ وَبِئْسَ ٱلْمَصِيرُ

127. And remember Abraham
And Ismā'īl raised
The foundations of the House
(With this prayer): "Our Lord!
Accept (this service) from us:
For Thou art the All-Hearing,
The All-Knowing.

١٢٧ وَإِذْ يَرْفَعُ إِبْرَٰهِـۧمُ ٱلْقَوَاعِدَ
مِنَ ٱلْبَيْتِ وَإِسْمَٰعِيلُ
رَبَّنَا تَقَبَّلْ مِنَّآ إِنَّكَ أَنتَ ٱلسَّمِيعُ ٱلْعَلِيمُ

128. "Our Lord! make of us
Muslims, bowing to Thy (Will),
And of our progeny a people
Muslim, bowing to thy (Will);
And show us our places for
The celebration of (due) rites;
And turn unto us (in Mercy);
For Thou art the Oft-Returning,
Most Merciful.

١٢٨ رَبَّنَا وَٱجْعَلْنَا مُسْلِمَيْنِ لَكَ
وَمِن ذُرِّيَّتِنَآ أُمَّةً مُّسْلِمَةً لَّكَ
وَأَرِنَا مَنَاسِكَنَا وَتُبْ عَلَيْنَآ
إِنَّكَ أَنتَ ٱلتَّوَّابُ ٱلرَّحِيمُ

---

126. Four rites are here enumerated, which have now acquired a technical meaning. (1) Compassing the sacred territory, or going round the Ka'bah: *Ṭawāf*. (2) Retiring to the place as a spiritual retreat, for contemplation and prayer: *I'tikāf*. (3) The posture of bending the back in prayer: *Rukū'*. (4) The posture of prostrating oneself on the ground in prayer: *Sujūd*. The protection of the holy territory is for all, but special cleanliness and purity is required for the sake of the devotees who undertake these rites. (R).

127. The root *salama* in the word Islam implies (among other ideas) the idea of Peace and therefore when Makkah is the city of Islam, it is also the City of Peace. The same root occurs in the latter part of the name Jerusalem, the Jewish City of Peace. When the day of Jerusalem passed (see verse 134 or 141 below). Makkah became the "New Jerusalem"—or rather the old and original "City of Peace" restored and made universal.

128. The territory of Makkah is barren and rocky, compared with, say, Ṭā'if, a city to the east of Makkah. A prayer for the prosperity of Makkah therefore includes a prayer for the good things of material life. (R).

129. "Our Lord! send amongst them
A Messenger of their own,
Who shall rehearse Thy Signs
To them and instruct them
In Scripture and Wisdom,
And sanctify them:
For Thou art the Exalted in Might
The Wise."[129]

﴿١٢٩﴾ رَبَّنَا وَابْعَثْ فِيهِمْ
رَسُولًا مِّنْهُمْ يَتْلُوا عَلَيْهِمْ ءَايَٰتِكَ
وَيُعَلِّمُهُمُ ٱلْكِتَٰبَ وَٱلْحِكْمَةَ وَيُزَكِّيهِمْ
إِنَّكَ أَنتَ ٱلْعَزِيزُ ٱلْحَكِيمُ

SECTION 16.

130. And who turns away
From the religion of Abraham
But such as debase their souls
With folly? Him We chose[130]
And rendered pure in this world:
And he will be in the Hereafter
In the ranks of the Righteous.

﴿١٣٠﴾ وَمَن يَرْغَبُ عَن مِّلَّةِ إِبْرَٰهِـۧمَ
إِلَّا مَن سَفِهَ نَفْسَهُۥ وَلَقَدِ ٱصْطَفَيْنَٰهُ فِى ٱلدُّنْيَا
وَإِنَّهُۥ فِى ٱلْءَاخِرَةِ لَمِنَ ٱلصَّٰلِحِينَ

131. Behold! his Lord said
To him: "Bow (thy will to Me):"
He said: "I bow (my will)
To the Lord and Cherisher
Of the Universe."

﴿١٣١﴾ إِذْ قَالَ لَهُۥ رَبُّهُۥٓ أَسْلِمْ
قَالَ أَسْلَمْتُ لِرَبِّ ٱلْعَٰلَمِينَ

132. And this was the legacy
That Abraham left to his sons,
And so did Jacob;
"Oh my sons! Allah hath chosen
The Faith for you; then die not
Except in the state of submission (to Allah).

﴿١٣٢﴾ وَوَصَّىٰ بِهَآ إِبْرَٰهِـۧمُ بَنِيهِ
وَيَعْقُوبُ يَٰبَنِىَّ إِنَّ ٱللَّهَ ٱصْطَفَىٰ لَكُمُ ٱلدِّينَ
فَلَا تَمُوتُنَّ إِلَّا وَأَنتُم مُّسْلِمُونَ

129. How beautiful this prayer is, and how aptly it comes in here in the argument! Such Paganism or star-worship or planet-worship as there was in Abraham's time was first cleared out of Makkah by Abraham. This is the chief meaning of "sanctification" or "purification" in 2:125, although of course physical cleanliness is (in physical conditions) a necessary element of purification in the higher sense. Abraham and his elder son Ismā'īl then built the Ka'bah and established the rites and usages of the sacred city. He was thus the founder of the original Islam (which is as old as mankind) in Arabia. As becomes a devout man, he offers and dedicates the work to Allah in humble supplication, addressing Him as the All-Hearing and the All-Knowing. He then asks for a blessing on himself and progeny generally, both the children of his eldest-born Ismā'īl and his younger son Isaac. With prophetic vision he foresees that there will be corruption and backsliding in both branches of his family: Makkah will house 360 idols, Jerusalem will became a harlot city (Ezekiel xvi. 15), a city of abomination. But the light of Islam will shine, and reclaim the lost people in both branches and indeed in all the world. So he prays for Allah's mercy, addressing Him as the Oft-Returning, Most Merciful. And finally he foresees in Makkah a Prophet teaching the people as one "of their own." and in their own beautiful Arabic language: he asks for a blessing on Muḥammad's ministry, appealing to the Power and Wisdom of Allah.

130. *Iṣṭafā* chose: chose because of purity; chose and purified. It is the same root from which *Muṣṭafā* is derived, one of the titles of Muḥammad.

133. Were ye witnesses[131]
When Death appeared before
Jacob?
Behold, he said to his sons:
"What will ye worship after me?"
They said: "We shall worship
Thy God and the God of thy
fathers,[132]—
Of Abraham, Ismā'īl and Isaac—
The One (True) God:
To him we bow (in Islam)."

(١٣٣) أَمْ كُنتُمْ شُهَدَآءَ
إِذْ حَضَرَ يَعْقُوبَ ٱلْمَوْتُ إِذْ قَالَ لِبَنِيهِ
مَا تَعْبُدُونَ مِنۢ بَعْدِى قَالُوا۟ نَعْبُدُ
إِلَٰهَكَ وَإِلَٰهَ ءَابَآئِكَ إِبْرَٰهِـۧمَ وَإِسْمَٰعِيلَ
وَإِسْحَٰقَ إِلَٰهًا وَٰحِدًا وَنَحْنُ لَهُۥ مُسْلِمُونَ

134. That was a People that hath
Passed away. They shall reap
The fruit of what they did,
And ye of what ye do!
Of their merits
There is no question in your
case![133]

(١٣٤) تِلْكَ أُمَّةٌ قَدْ خَلَتْ
لَهَا مَا كَسَبَتْ وَلَكُم مَّا كَسَبْتُمْ
وَلَا تُسْـَٔلُونَ عَمَّا كَانُوا۟ يَعْمَلُونَ

135. They say: "Become Jews
Or Christians if ye would be guided
(To salvation)." Say thou:
"Nay! (I would rather) the
Religion
Of Abraham, the True,[134]
And he joined not gods with
Allah."

(١٣٥) وَقَالُوا۟ كُونُوا۟ هُودًا
أَوْ نَصَٰرَىٰ تَهْتَدُوا۟ قُلْ بَلْ مِلَّةَ إِبْرَٰهِـۧمَ
حَنِيفًا وَمَا كَانَ مِنَ ٱلْمُشْرِكِينَ

136. Say ye: "We believe
In Allah, and the revelation
Given to us, and to Abraham,
Ismā'īl, Isaac, Jacob,
And the Tribes, and that given
To Moses and Jesus, and that given
To (all) Prophets from their Lord:

(١٣٦) قُولُوٓا۟ ءَامَنَّا بِٱللَّهِ وَمَآ أُنزِلَ إِلَيْنَا
وَمَآ أُنزِلَ إِلَىٰٓ إِبْرَٰهِـۧمَ وَإِسْمَٰعِيلَ وَإِسْحَٰقَ وَيَعْقُوبَ
وَٱلْأَسْبَاطِ وَمَآ أُوتِىَ مُوسَىٰ وَعِيسَىٰ وَمَآ أُوتِىَ
ٱلنَّبِيُّونَ مِن رَّبِّهِمْ

131. The whole of the Children of Israel are called to witness one of their slogans, that they worshipped "the God of their fathers." The idea in their minds got narrowed down to that of a tribal God. But they are reminded that their ancestors had the principle of Islam in them—the worship of Allah, the One True and Universal God. The death-bed scene is described in Jewish tradition.

132. "Fathers" means ancestors, and includes uncles, grand-uncles, as well as direct ascendants.

133. I have made a free paraphrase of what would read literally: "Ye shall not be asked about what they used to do." On the Day of Judgement each soul would have to answer for its own deeds: it cannot claim merit from others, nor be answerable for the crimes or sins of others. Here the argument is: if the Jews or Christians claim the merits of Father Abraham and the Patriarchs or of Jesus, we cannot follow them. Because there were righteous men in the past, it cannot help us unless we are ourselves righteous. The doctrine of personal responsibility is a cardinal feature of Islam.

134. *Ḥanīf*: inclined to right opinion, orthodox (in the literal meaning of the Greek words.), firm in faith, sound and well-balanced, true. Perhaps the last word, True, sums up most of the other shades.

The Jews, though taught Unity, went after false gods, and the Christians invented the Trinity or borrowed it from Paganism. We go back to pure, *ḥanīf* doctrine of Abraham, to live and die in faith in the One True God.

We make no difference
Between one and another of them:
And we bow to Allah (in Islam).[135]

137. So if they believe
As ye believe, they are indeed
On the right path; but if
They turn back, it is they
Who are in schism; but Allah will
Suffice thee as against them,[136]
And He is the All-Hearing,
The All-Knowing.

138. (Our religion is)
The Baptism of Allah:[137]
And who can baptize better
Than Allah? And it is He
Whom we worship.

139. Say: Will ye dispute
With us about Allah, seeing
That He is our Lord
And your Lord; that we
Are responsible for our doings
And ye for yours; and that
We are sincere (in our faith)
In Him?

140. Or[138] do ye say that
Abraham, Ismā'īl, Isaac,
Jacob and the Tribes were

لَا نُفَرِّقُ بَيْنَ أَحَدٍ مِّنْهُمْ وَنَحْنُ لَهُۥ مُسْلِمُونَ

(١٣٧) فَإِنْ ءَامَنُوا۟ بِمِثْلِ مَآ ءَامَنتُم بِهِۦ
فَقَدِ ٱهْتَدَوا۟ ۖ وَّإِن تَوَلَّوْا۟ فَإِنَّمَا هُمْ فِى شِقَاقٍ ۖ
فَسَيَكْفِيكَهُمُ ٱللَّهُ ۚ
وَهُوَ ٱلسَّمِيعُ ٱلْعَلِيمُ

(١٣٨) صِبْغَةَ ٱللَّهِ ۖ
وَمَنْ أَحْسَنُ مِنَ ٱللَّهِ صِبْغَةً ۖ
وَنَحْنُ لَهُۥ عَٰبِدُونَ

(١٣٩) قُلْ أَتُحَآجُّونَنَا فِى ٱللَّهِ
وَهُوَ رَبُّنَا وَرَبُّكُمْ وَلَنَآ
أَعْمَٰلُنَا وَلَكُمْ أَعْمَٰلُكُمْ
وَنَحْنُ لَهُۥ مُخْلِصُونَ

(١٤٠) أَمْ تَقُولُونَ إِنَّ إِبْرَٰهِۦمَ وَإِسْمَٰعِيلَ
وَإِسْحَٰقَ وَيَعْقُوبَ وَٱلْأَسْبَاطَ كَانُوا۟

135. Here we have the Creed of Islam: to believe in (1) the One Universal God, (2) the Message to us through Muḥammad and the Signs (*āyāt*) as interpreted on the basis of personal responsibility, (3) the Message delivered by other Teachers in the past. These are mentioned in three groups: (1) Abraham, Ismā'īl, Isaac, Jacob and the Tribes: of these Abraham had apparently a Book (lxxxvii. 19) and the others followed his tradition: (2) Moses and Jesus, who each left a scripture; these scriptures are still extant though not in their pristine form; and (3) other scriptures, Prophets, or Messengers of Allah, not specifically mentioned in the Qur'ān (11:78). We make no difference between any of these. Their Message (in essentials) was one, and that is the basis of Islam.

136. We are thus in the true line of those who follow the one and indivisible Message of the One Allah, wherever delivered. If others narrow it or corrupt it, it is they who have left the faith and created a division or schism. But Allah sees and knows all. And He will protect His own, and His support will be infinitely more precious than the support which men can give.

137. *Ṣibghah:* the root-meaning implies a dye or colour; apparently the Arab Christians mixed a dye or colour in the baptismal water, signifying that the baptized person got a new colour in life. [We do not believe that it is necessary to be baptized to be saved. Eds.].

138. The alternative is with the question in the last verse. Do you dispute with us although we worship the same God as you and claim that ours is the same religion as that of your ancestors? Or do you really assert that Abraham and his son and his sons' sons, who founded the Tribes long before Moses, followed your Jewish religion as you know it? History of course proves that claim absurd. If the Christians claim that these Patriarchs knew of and followed the teaching of Jesus, the claim is still more absurd—except in the sense of Islam that Allah's teaching is one in all ages.

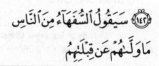

Jews or Christians?
Say: Do ye know better
Than Allah? Ah! who
Is more unjust than those
Who conceal the testimony
They have from Allah?
But Allah is not unmindful
Of what ye do!

هُودًا أَوْ نَصَٰرَىٰ ۗ قُلْ ءَأَنتُمْ أَعْلَمُ أَمِ ٱللَّهُ ۗ
وَمَنْ أَظْلَمُ مِمَّن كَتَمَ شَهَٰدَةً عِندَهُۥ
مِنَ ٱللَّهِ ۗ وَمَا ٱللَّهُ بِغَٰفِلٍ عَمَّا تَعْمَلُونَ

141. That was a people that hath
Passed away. They shall reap
The fruit of what they did
And ye of what ye do!
Of their merits
There is no question in your
case:[139]

(١٤١) تِلْكَ أُمَّةٌ قَدْ خَلَتْ ۖ
لَهَا مَا كَسَبَتْ وَلَكُم مَّا كَسَبْتُمْ ۖ
وَلَا تُسْـَٔلُونَ عَمَّا كَانُوا۟ يَعْمَلُونَ

C. 49.—But those people have passed away,
(2:142-167.) Who promised to uphold the Law of Allah.
Their progeny having been found
Unworthy, their place was taken
By a new people looking towards Makkah—
A new people, with a new Messenger,
To bear witness to Allah's Law,
To proclaim the truth, maintain
His Symbols, and strive and fight
For Unity in Allah's Way.

SECTION 17

2
30

142. The Fools among the people[140]
Will say: "What hath turned
Them from the Qiblah[141] to which

(١٤٢) سَيَقُولُ ٱلسُّفَهَآءُ مِنَ ٱلنَّاسِ
مَا وَلَّىٰهُمْ عَن قِبْلَتِهِمُ

139. Verse 134 began a certain argument, which is now rounded off in the same words in this verse. To use a musical term, the *motif* is now completed. The argument is that it is wrong to claim a monopoly for Allah's Message: it is the same peoples and in all ages: if it undergoes local variations or variations according to times and seasons those variations pass away. This leads to the argument in the remainder of the Sūrah that with the renewal of the Message and the birth of a new people, a new symbolism and new ordinances become appropriate, and they are now expounded.

140. *Nās*=People, the unthinking multitude that sway to and fro, instead of being firm in Allah's Way. The reference here is to the idolaters, the Hypocrites, and the party of Jews who were constantly seeking to "entangle in their talk." Al Muṣṭafā and his disciples in Madīnah even as the Pharisees and the Sadducees of Jesus's day tried to entangle Jesus (Matt. xxii. 15, 23).

141. *Qiblah*=the direction to which Muslims turn in prayer. Islam lays great stress on social prayer in order to emphasise our universal Brotherhood and mutual cooperation. For such prayer, order, punctuality, precision, symbolical postures, and a common direction are essential, so that the Imām (leader) and all his congregation may face one way and offer their supplications to Allah. In the early days, before they were organised as a people, they followed as a symbol for their *Qiblah* the sacred city of Jerusalem, scared both to the Jews and the Christians, the people of the Book. This symbolised their allegiance to the continuity of Allah's revelation. When, despised and persecuted, they were turned out of Makkah and arrived in Madīnah, Al Muṣṭafā under divine direction began to organise its people as an *Ummah*, an independent people, with laws and rituals of their own. At that stage the Ka'bah was established as *Qiblah,* thus going back to the earliest centre, with which the name of Abraham was connected, and traditionally also the name of Adam. Jerusalem still remained (and remains) sacred in the eyes of Islam on account of its past, but Islam is a progressive religion, and its new symbolism enabled it to shake off the tradition of a dead past and usher in the era of untrammelled freedom dear to the spirit of Arabia. The change took place about 16½ months after Hijrah.

They were used?" Say:
To Allah belong East and West:
He guideth whom He will
To a Way that is straight

ٱلَّتِى كَانُوا۟ عَلَيْهَا ۚ قُل لِّلَّهِ ٱلْمَشْرِقُ وَٱلْمَغْرِبُ ۚ
يَهْدِى مَن يَشَآءُ إِلَىٰ صِرَٰطٍ مُّسْتَقِيمٍ

143. Thus[142] have We made of you
An *Ummah* justly balanced,[143]
That ye might be witnesses[144]
Over the nations,
And the Messenger a witness
Over yourselves;
And We appointed the Qiblah
To which thou wast used,
Only to test those who followed
The Messenger from those
Who would turn on their
heels[145]
(From the Faith). Indeed it was
(A change) momentous, except
To those guided by Allah.
And never would Allah
Make your faith of no effect.[146]
For Allah is to all people
Most surely full of kindness,
Most Merciful.

١٤٣ وَكَذَٰلِكَ جَعَلْنَٰكُمْ أُمَّةً وَسَطًا
لِّتَكُونُوا۟ شُهَدَآءَ عَلَى ٱلنَّاسِ
وَيَكُونَ ٱلرَّسُولُ عَلَيْكُمْ شَهِيدًا ۗ
وَمَا جَعَلْنَا ٱلْقِبْلَةَ ٱلَّتِى كُنتَ عَلَيْهَآ
إِلَّا لِنَعْلَمَ مَن يَتَّبِعُ ٱلرَّسُولَ
مِمَّن يَنقَلِبُ عَلَىٰ عَقِبَيْهِ ۚ
وَإِن كَانَتْ لَكَبِيرَةً
إِلَّا عَلَى ٱلَّذِينَ هَدَى ٱللَّهُ ۗ
وَمَا كَانَ ٱللَّهُ لِيُضِيعَ إِيمَٰنَكُمْ ۚ
إِنَّ ٱللَّهَ بِٱلنَّاسِ لَرَءُوفٌ رَّحِيمٌ

142. *Thus*: By giving you a Qiblah of your own, most ancient in history, and most modern as a symbol of your organisation as a new nation (*Ummah*).

143. *Justly balanced:* The essence of Islam is to avoid all extravagances on either side. It is a sober, practical religion. But the Arabic word (*wasat*) also implies a touch of the literal meaning of Intermediacy. Geographically, Arabia is in an intermediate position in the Old World, as was proved in history by the rapid expansion of Islam, north, south, west and east.

144. *Witnesses*: When two persons dispute, they advance extravagant claims. A just witness comes between them, and brings the light of reason to bear on them, pruning all their selfish extravagances. So the mission of Islam is to curb, for instance, the extreme formalism of the Mosaic law and the extreme "other-worldliness" professed by Christianity. The witness must be unselfish, equipped with first-hand knowledge, and ready to intervene in the cause of justice. Such is the position claimed by Islam among rival systems. Similarly, within Islam itself, the position of witness to whom disputants can appeal is held by Muḥammad Al Muṣṭafā.

145. The Qiblah of Jerusalem might itself have seemed strange to the Arabs, and the change from it to the Ka'bah might have seemed strange after they had become used to the other. In reality one direction or another, or east or west, in itself did not matter. What mattered was the sense of discipline, on which Islam lays so much stress: which of us is willing to follow the directions of the chosen Prophet of Allah? Mere quibblers about non-essential matters are tested by this. (R).

146. What became of prayer with the Jerusalem Qiblah? It was equally efficacious before the new Qiblah was ordained. Allah regards our faith: every act of true and genuine faith is efficacious with Him, even if formalists pick holes in such acts.

144. We see the turning
Of thy face (for guidance)
To the heavens:[147] now
Shall We turn thee
To a Qiblah that shall
Please thee. Turn then
Thy face in the direction
Of the Sacred Mosque:[148]
Wherever ye are, turn
Your faces in that direction.
The people of the Book[149]
Know well that that is
The truth from their Lord,
Nor is Allah unmindful
Of what they do.

١٤٤ قَدْ نَرَىٰ تَقَلُّبَ
وَجْهِكَ فِي السَّمَآءِ
فَلَنُوَلِّيَنَّكَ قِبْلَةً تَرْضَىٰهَا
فَوَلِّ وَجْهَكَ شَطْرَ الْمَسْجِدِ الْحَرَامِ
وَحَيْثُ مَا كُنتُمْ فَوَلُّوا وُجُوهَكُمْ شَطْرَهُ
وَإِنَّ الَّذِينَ أُوتُوا الْكِتَٰبَ لَيَعْلَمُونَ أَنَّهُ الْحَقُّ
مِن رَّبِّهِمْ وَمَا اللَّهُ بِغَٰفِلٍ عَمَّا يَعْمَلُونَ

145. Even if thou wert to bring
To the people of the Book
All the Signs (together),
They would not follow
Thy Qiblah; nor art thou
Going to follow their Qiblah;

١٤٥ وَلَئِنْ أَتَيْتَ الَّذِينَ أُوتُوا الْكِتَٰبَ
بِكُلِّ ءَايَةٍ مَّا تَبِعُوا قِبْلَتَكَ
وَمَا أَنتَ بِتَابِعٍ قِبْلَتَهُمْ

147. This shows the sincere desire of Al Muṣṭafā to seek light from above in the matter of the Qiblah. Until the organisation of his own People into a well-knit community, with its distinctive laws and ordinances, he followed a practice based on the fact that the Jews and Christians looked upon Jerusalem as a sacred city. But there was no universal Qiblah among them. Some Jews turned towards Jerusalem, especially during the Captivity, as we shall see later. At the time of our Prophet, Jerusalem was in the hands of the Byzantine Empire, which was Christian. But the Christians oriented their churches to the East (hence the word "orientation"), which is a point of the compass, and not the direction of any sacred place. The fact of the altar being in the East does not mean that every worshipper has his face to the east: for, according at least to modern practice, the seats in a church are so placed that different worshippers may face in different directions. The Preacher of Unity naturally wanted, in this as in other matters, a symbol of complete unity, and his heart was naturally delighted when the Qiblah towards the Ka'bah was settled. Its connection with Abraham gave it great antiquity: its character of being an Arab centre made it appropriate when the Message came in Arabic, and was preached through the union of the Arabs; at the time it was adopted, the little Muslim community was shut out of it, being exiles in Madīnah, but it became a symbol of hope and eventual triumph, of which Muḥammad lived to see the fulfilment; and it also became the centre and gathering ground of all peoples in the universal pilgrimage, which was instituted with it.

148. *The Sacred Mosque*: *i.e.* the mosque wherein the Ka'bah is located, in the sacred city of Makkah. It is not correct to suggest that the command making the Ka'bah the Qiblah abrogates 2:115, where it is stated that East and West belong to Allah. This is perfectly true at all times, before and after the institution of the Qiblah. As if to emphasise this, the same words about East and West are repeated in this very passage, see 2:142 above. Where the *Itqān* mentions *mansūkh* in this connection. I am sorry I cannot follow that opinion, unless *mansūkh* is defined in a special way, as some of the commentators do. (R).

149. Glimmerings of such a Qiblah were already foreshadowed in Jewish and Christian practice but its universality was only perfected in Islam.

Nor indeed will they follow[150]
Each other's Qiblah. If thou
After the knowledge hath reached thee,
Wert to follow their (vain)
Desires—then wert thou
Indeed (clearly) in the wrong.

وَمَا بَعْضُهُم بِتَابِعٍ قِبْلَةَ بَعْضٍ وَلَئِنِ
اتَّبَعْتَ أَهْوَاءَهُم مِّن بَعْدِ مَا جَاءَكَ
مِنَ الْعِلْمِ إِنَّكَ إِذًا لَّمِنَ الظَّالِمِينَ

146. The people of the Book
Know this as they know
Their own sons;[151] but some
Of them conceal the truth
Which they themselves know.

١٤٦ الَّذِينَ آتَيْنَاهُمُ الْكِتَابَ يَعْرِفُونَهُ
كَمَا يَعْرِفُونَ أَبْنَاءَهُمْ وَإِنَّ فَرِيقًا مِّنْهُمْ
لَيَكْتُمُونَ الْحَقَّ وَهُمْ يَعْلَمُونَ

147. The Truth is from thy Lord[152]
So be not at all in doubt.

١٤٧ الْحَقُّ مِن رَّبِّكَ فَلَا تَكُونَنَّ مِنَ الْمُمْتَرِينَ

Section 18

148. To each is a goal
To which Allah[153] turns him;
Then strive together (as in a race)
Towards all that is good.
Wheresoever ye are,

١٤٨ وَلِكُلٍّ وِجْهَةٌ هُوَ مُوَلِّيهَا
فَاسْتَبِقُوا الْخَيْرَاتِ أَيْنَ مَا تَكُونُوا

150. See n. 147 to 2:144 above.

The Jews and Christians had a glimmering of the Qiblah idea, but in their attitude of self-sufficiency they were not likely to welcome the Qiblah idea as perfected in Islam. Nor is Islam, after the fuller knowledge which it has received, likely to revert to the uncertain, imperfect, and varying ideas of orientation held previously.

A very clear glimpse of the old Jewish practice in the matter of the Qiblah and the importance attached to it is found in the book of Daniel. 6:10. Dainel was a righteous man of princely lineage and lived about 506-538 B.C. He was carried off to Babylon by Nebuchadnezzar, the Assyrian, but was still living when Assyria was overthrown by the Medes and Persians. In spite of the "captivity" of the Jews, Daniel enjoyed the highest offices of state at Babylon, but he was ever true to Jerusalem. His enemies (under the Persian monarch) got a penal law passed against any one who "asked a petition of any god or man for 30 days" except the Persian King. But Daniel continued true to Jerusalem. "His windows being open in his chamber towards Jerusalem, he kneeled upon his knees three times a day, and prayed, and gave thanks before his God, as he did aforetime."

151. The People of the Book should have known all this as well as "they knew their own sons," as their past traditions and teaching should have made them receptive of the new Message. Some commentators construe the demonstrative pronoun "this" to refer to the Prophet. In that case the interpretation would be: The People of the Book know Muḥammad as well as they know their own sons; they know him to be true and upright, they know him to be in the line of Abraham: they know him to correspond to the description of the prophet foretold among themselves; but selfishness induces some of them to act against their own knowledge and conceal the truth.

152. Truth only comes from Allah, and it remains truth, however men might try to conceal it or throw doubts on it.

153. The question is how we are to construe the pronoun, *huwa,* in the original. The alternative translation would be: "To each is a goal to which he turns."

The simile of life being a race in which we all zealously run forward to the one goal, *viz.*, the goal of good, may be applied individually and nationally. This supplies another argument of the Ka'bah Qiblah, *viz.*, the unity of goal, with diversity of races, traditions and temperaments.

Allah will bring you
Together. For Allah
Hath power over all things.

يَأْتِ بِكُمُ ٱللَّهُ جَمِيعًا ۚ
إِنَّ ٱللَّهَ عَلَىٰ كُلِّ شَيْءٍ قَدِيرٌ

149. From whencesoever
Thou startest forth[154] turn
Thy face in the direction
Of the Sacred Mosque;
That is indeed the truth
From thy Lord. And Allah
Is not unmindful
Of what ye do.

﴿١٤٩﴾ وَمِنْ حَيْثُ خَرَجْتَ فَوَلِّ وَجْهَكَ
شَطْرَ ٱلْمَسْجِدِ ٱلْحَرَامِ ۖ وَإِنَّهُۥ لَلْحَقُّ مِن رَّبِّكَ ۗ
وَمَا ٱللَّهُ بِغَٰفِلٍ عَمَّا تَعْمَلُونَ

150. So from whencesoever
Thou startest forth, turn
Thy face in the direction
Of the Sacred Mosque;
And wheresoever ye are,
Turn your face thither:
That there be no ground
Of dispute against you
Among the people,
Except those of them that are
Bent on wickedness; so fear
Them not, but fear Me;
And that I may complete
My favours on you, and ye
May (consent to) be guided;

﴿١٥٠﴾ وَمِنْ حَيْثُ خَرَجْتَ
فَوَلِّ وَجْهَكَ شَطْرَ ٱلْمَسْجِدِ ٱلْحَرَامِ ۚ
وَحَيْثُ مَا كُنتُمْ فَوَلُّوا۟ وُجُوهَكُمْ شَطْرَهُۥ
لِئَلَّا يَكُونَ لِلنَّاسِ عَلَيْكُمْ حُجَّةٌ إِلَّا ٱلَّذِينَ
ظَلَمُوا۟ مِنْهُمْ فَلَا تَخْشَوْهُمْ وَٱخْشَوْنِى
وَلِأُتِمَّ نِعْمَتِى عَلَيْكُمْ وَلَعَلَّكُمْ تَهْتَدُونَ

151. A similar (favour
Have ye already received)[155]
In that We have sent

﴿١٥١﴾ كَمَآ أَرْسَلْنَا

154. The simile of a race is continued, and so the Qiblah command is repeated from that point of view In 2:144 it was mentioned as the new symbol of the new nation (Muslim); now it is shown as the symbol of Good, at which we should all aim, from whichever point we started. *e.g.* as Jews or Christians, or our individual point of view; the Qiblah will unite us as a symbol of the Goal of the Future. In 2:150 below, it is repeated; first for the individual, on the ground of uniformity and the removal of all occasions of dispute and argument; and secondly for the Muslim people, on the same ground, as a matter of discipline. There is another little harmony in the matter of the repetitions. Note that the race and starting point argument begins at 2:149 and is rounded off in the first part of 2:150; while the national and general argument beginning at 2:144 is rounded off in the latter part of 2:150. The latter argument includes the former, and is more widely worded: "wheresoever ye are"; which in the Arabic expression would imply three things: in whatever circumstances ye are, or at whatever time ye are, or in whatever place ye are. I have spoken before of a sort musical harmony in verbal repetitions: here there is a sort of pictorial harmony, as of a larger circle symmetrically a including smaller concentric circle.

155. This verse should be read with 2:150, of which the sentence is here completed. The argument is that in the grant of the Ka'bah Qiblah, Allah was perfecting religion and fulfilling the prayer for the future made by Abraham. That prayer was threefold: (1) That Makkah should be a sacred Sanctuary (2:126): (2) that a truly believing (Muslim) nation should be raised, with places of devotion there (2:128); and (3) that a Messenger should be sent among the Arabs with certain qualities (2:129), which are set out there and again repeated here to complete the argument.

Among you a Messenger
Of your own, rehearsing to you
Our Signs, and purifying
You, and instructing you
In Scripture and Wisdom,
And in new Knowledge.

فِيكُمْ رَسُولًا مِّنكُمْ يَتْلُوا۟ عَلَيْكُمْ
ءَايَٰتِنَا وَيُزَكِّيكُمْ وَيُعَلِّمُكُمُ ٱلْكِتَٰبَ
وَٱلْحِكْمَةَ وَيُعَلِّمُكُم مَّا لَمْ تَكُونُوا۟ تَعْلَمُونَ

152. Then do ye remember[156]
Me; I will remember
You. Be grateful to Me,
And reject not Faith.

١٥٢ فَٱذْكُرُونِىٓ أَذْكُرْكُمْ
وَٱشْكُرُوا۟ لِى وَلَا تَكْفُرُونِ

SECTION 19.

153. O ye who believe! seek help
With patient Perseverance[157]
And Prayer: for Allah is with those
Who patiently persevere.

١٥٣ يَٰٓأَيُّهَا ٱلَّذِينَ ءَامَنُوا۟ ٱسْتَعِينُوا۟ بِٱلصَّبْرِ
وَٱلصَّلَوٰةِ ۚ إِنَّ ٱللَّهَ مَعَ ٱلصَّٰبِرِينَ

154. And say not of those
Who are slain in the way[158]
Of Allah: "They are dead."
Nay, they are living,
Though ye perceive (it) not.

١٥٤ وَلَا تَقُولُوا۟ لِمَن يُقْتَلُ
فِى سَبِيلِ ٱللَّهِ أَمْوَٰتٌۢ ۚ
بَلْ أَحْيَآءٌ وَلَٰكِن لَّا تَشْعُرُونَ

155. Be sure we shall test you
With something of fear
And hunger, some loss
In goods or lives or the fruits
(Of your toil), but give
Glad tidings[159] to those
Who patiently persevere—

١٥٥ وَلَنَبْلُوَنَّكُم بِشَىْءٍ مِّنَ ٱلْخَوْفِ
وَٱلْجُوعِ وَنَقْصٍ مِّنَ ٱلْأَمْوَٰلِ
وَٱلْأَنفُسِ وَٱلثَّمَرَٰتِ ۗ وَبَشِّرِ ٱلصَّٰبِرِينَ

---

156. The word "remember" is too pale a word for *dhikr*, which has now acquired a large number of associations in our religious literature. In its verbal signification it implies; to remember; to praise by frequently mentioning; to rehearse; to celebrate or commemorate; to make much of; to cherish the memory of as a precious possession.(R).

157. See 2:45 and n. 61. An additional meaning implied in *ṣabr* is self-restraint. Ḥaqqāni defines it in his *Tafsīr* as following Reason and restraining Fear, Anger, and Desire. What can be a higher reward for patience, perseverance, self-restraint and constancy than that Allah should be with us? For this promise opens the door to every kind of spiritual well-being.

158. The "patient perseverance and prayer" mentioned in the last verse is not mere passivity. It is active striving in the way of Truth, which is the way of Allah. Such striving is the spending of one's self in Allah's way, either through our property or through our own lives, or the lives of those nearest and dearest to us, or it may be the loss of all the fruits of a lifetime's labour not only in material goods but in some intellectual or moral gain, some position which seemed in our eyes to be eminently desirable in itself, but which we must cheerfully sacrifice if necessary for the Cause. With such sacrifice, our apparent loss may be our real gain; he that loses his life may really gain it; and the rewards or "fruits" that seem lost were mere impediments on our path to real inward progress. (R).

159. The glad tidings are the blessings of Allah in 2:157 or (which is the same thing) the promise in 2:153 that Allah will be with them.

156. Who say, when afflicted
With calamity: "To Allah
We belong, and to Him
Is our return"—

١٥٦ الَّذِينَ إِذَا أَصَابَتْهُم مُّصِيبَةٌ قَالُوا
إِنَّا لِلَّهِ وَإِنَّا إِلَيْهِ رَاجِعُونَ

157. They are those on whom
(Descend) blessings from their
Lord,
And Mercy,
And they are the ones
That receive guidance.

١٥٧ أُولَٰئِكَ عَلَيْهِمْ صَلَوَاتٌ مِّن رَّبِّهِمْ
وَرَحْمَةٌ وَأُولَٰئِكَ هُمُ الْمُهْتَدُونَ

158. Behold! Ṣafā and Marwah
Are among the Symbols[160]
Of Allah. So if those who visit
The House[161] in the Season
Or at other times,
Should compass them round,
It is no sin in them.
And if any one obeyeth his own
Impulse to Good—[162]
Be sure that Allah
Is He Who recogniseth
And knoweth.

١٥٨ إِنَّ الصَّفَا وَالْمَرْوَةَ
مِن شَعَائِرِ اللَّهِ
فَمَنْ حَجَّ الْبَيْتَ أَوِ اعْتَمَرَ
فَلَا جُنَاحَ عَلَيْهِ أَن يَطَّوَّفَ بِهِمَا
وَمَن تَطَوَّعَ خَيْرًا فَإِنَّ اللَّهَ شَاكِرٌ عَلِيمٌ

159. Those who conceal
The clear (Signs) We have
Sent down, and the Guidance,
After We have made it
Clear for the People
In the Book—on them
Shall be Allah's curse,

١٥٩ إِنَّ الَّذِينَ يَكْتُمُونَ مَا أَنزَلْنَا
مِنَ الْبَيِّنَاتِ وَالْهُدَىٰ مِن بَعْدِ مَا بَيَّنَّاهُ
لِلنَّاسِ فِي الْكِتَابِ أُولَٰئِكَ يَلْعَنُهُمُ اللَّهُ

160. The virtue of patient perseverance in faith leads to the mention of two symbolic monuments of that virtue. These are the two little hills of Ṣafā and Marwah now absorbed in the city of Makkah, and close to the well of Zamzam. Here, according to tradition, the lady Hājar, mother of the infant Ismā'īl, prayed for water in the parched desert, and in her eager quest round these hills, she found her prayer answered and saw the Zamzam spring. Unfortunately the Pagan Arabs had placed a male and a female idol here, and their gross and superstitious rites caused offense to the early Muslims. They felt some hesitation in going round these places during the Pilgrimage. As a matter of fact they should have known that the Ka'bah (the House of Allah) had been itself defiled with idols, and was sanctified again by the purity of Muḥammad's life and teaching. The lesson is that the most sacred things may be turned to the basest uses; that we are not therefore necessarily to ban a thing misused; that if our intentions and life are pure, Allah will recognise them even if the world cast stones at us because of some evil associations which they join with what we do, or with the people we associate with, or with the places which claim our reverence.

161. *The House*=the Sacred Mosque, the Ka'bah. The Season of regular Hajj culminates in the visit to Arafāt on the ninth day of the month of *Dhu al Ḥijjah,* followed by the circumambulation of Ka'bah. A visit to the Sacred Mosque and the performance of the rites of pilgrimage at any other time is called an *Umrah*. The symbolic rites are the same in either case, except that the *'Arafāt* rites are omitted in the *Umrah*. The Ṣafā and Marwah are included among the Monuments, as pointing to one of the highest of Muslim virtues.

162. The impulse should be to Good; if once we are sure of this, we must obey it without hesitation, whatever people may say.

And the curse of those
Entitled to curse—[163]

وَيَلۡعَنُهُمُ ٱللَّٰعِنُونَ

160. Except those who repent
And make amends
And openly declare (the Truth):
To them I turn;
For I am Oft-Returning,
Most Merciful.

١٦٠ إِلَّا ٱلَّذِينَ تَابُواْ وَأَصۡلَحُواْ وَبَيَّنُواْ
فَأُوْلَٰٓئِكَ أَتُوبُ عَلَيۡهِمۡۚ
وَأَنَا ٱلتَّوَّابُ ٱلرَّحِيمُ

161. Those who reject Faith,
And die rejecting—
On them is Allah's curse,
And the curse of angels,
And of all mankind;

١٦١ إِنَّ ٱلَّذِينَ كَفَرُواْ وَمَاتُواْ وَهُمۡ
كُفَّارٌ أُوْلَٰٓئِكَ عَلَيۡهِمۡ لَعۡنَةُ ٱللَّهِ
وَٱلۡمَلَٰٓئِكَةِ وَٱلنَّاسِ أَجۡمَعِينَ

162. They will abide therein:[164]
Their penalty will not
Be lightened, nor will
Respite be their (lot).

١٦٢ خَٰلِدِينَ فِيهَاۖ لَا يُخَفَّفُ
عَنۡهُمُ ٱلۡعَذَابُ وَلَا هُمۡ يُنظَرُونَ

163. And your God
Is One God:
There is no god
But He,
Most Gracious,
Most Merciful.[165]

١٦٣ وَإِلَٰهُكُمۡ إِلَٰهٞ وَٰحِدٞۖ
لَّآ إِلَٰهَ إِلَّا هُوَ
ٱلرَّحۡمَٰنُ ٱلرَّحِيمُ

SECTION 20.

164. Behold! In the creation
Of the heavens and the earth;
In the alternation
Of the Night and the Day;

١٦٤ إِنَّ فِي خَلۡقِ ٱلسَّمَٰوَٰتِ وَٱلۡأَرۡضِ
وَٱخۡتِلَٰفِ ٱلَّيۡلِ وَٱلنَّهَارِ

---

163. *Those entitled to curse: i.e.*, angels and mankind (see 2:161 below): the cursed ones will deprive themselves of the protection of Allah and of the angels, and of the good wishes of mankind, because by contumaciously rejecting Faith, they not only sin against Allah but are false to their own manhood, which Allah created in the "best of moulds" (Q. 95:4). The terrible curses denounced in the Old Testament are set out in Deut. xxviii. 15-68. There is one difference. Here it is for the deliberate rejection of Faith, a theological term for the denying of our higher nature. There it is for a breach of the least part of the ceremonial Law. (R).

164. *Therein*=in the curse. A curse is not a matter of words: it is a terrible spiritual state, opposite to the state of Grace. Can man curse? Not of course in the same sense in which we speak of the curse of Allah. A mere verbal curse is of no effect. Hence the English saying: "A causeless curse will not come." But if men are oppressed or unjustly treated, their cries can ascend to Allah in prayer, and then it becomes Allah's "wrath" or curse, the deprivation of Allah's Grace as regards the wrongdoer.

165. Where the terrible consequences of Evil, *i.e.*, the rejection of Allah, are mentioned, there is always stress laid on Allah's attributes of Grace and Mercy. In this case Unity is also stressed, because we have just been told about the Qiblah symbol of unity and are about to pass the theme of unity in diversity, in Nature and in the social laws of human society.

In the sailing of the ships
Through the Ocean
For the profit of mankind;
In the rain which Allah
Sends down from the skies,
And the life which He gives
therewith
To an earth that is dead;
In the beasts of all kinds
That He scatters
Through the earth;
In the change of the winds,
And the clouds which they
Trail like their slaves
Between the sky and the earth—
(Here) indeed are Signs
For a people that are wise.[166]

165. Yet there are men
Who take (for worship)
Others besides Allah,
As equal (with Allah):
They love them
As they should love Allah,
But those of Faith are
Overflowing in their love
For Allah. If only
The unrighteous could see,
Behold, they would see
The Punishment: that to Allah
Belongs all power, and Allah

وَٱلْفُلْكِ ٱلَّتِى تَجْرِى فِى ٱلْبَحْرِ
بِمَا يَنفَعُ ٱلنَّاسَ وَمَآ أَنزَلَ ٱللَّهُ
مِنَ ٱلسَّمَآءِ مِن مَّآءٍ فَأَحْيَا بِهِ
ٱلْأَرْضَ بَعْدَ مَوْتِهَا
وَبَثَّ فِيهَا مِن كُلِّ دَآبَّةٍ
وَتَصْرِيفِ ٱلرِّيَٰحِ وَٱلسَّحَابِ
ٱلْمُسَخَّرِ بَيْنَ ٱلسَّمَآءِ وَٱلْأَرْضِ
لَءَايَٰتٍ لِّقَوْمٍ يَعْقِلُونَ
(١٦٥) وَمِنَ ٱلنَّاسِ
مَن يَتَّخِذُ مِن دُونِ ٱللَّهِ أَندَادًا
يُحِبُّونَهُمْ كَحُبِّ ٱللَّهِ
وَٱلَّذِينَ ءَامَنُوٓا۟ أَشَدُّ حُبًّا لِّلَّهِ
وَلَوْ يَرَى ٱلَّذِينَ ظَلَمُوٓا۟ إِذْ يَرَوْنَ
ٱلْعَذَابَ أَنَّ ٱلْقُوَّةَ لِلَّهِ جَمِيعًا وَأَنَّ ٱللَّهَ

166. This magnificent Nature passage stands out like a hill in a landscape, enhancing the beauty of our view, and preparing us for the everyday laws and ordinances which follow.

Note its literary architecture. Allah is One: and among His wondrous Signs is the unity of design in the widest diversity of Nature. The Signs are taken from the features of beauty, power, and utility to man himself, and lead up to an appeal to Man's own intelligence and wisdom. We begin with the glory of the heavens and the earth, the wide spaces covered by man's imagination, remote and yet so near to his own life. The most striking everyday phenomenon resulting from the interrelations of the heavens and the earth is the alternation of day and night, regular and yet changing in duration with the seasons and the latitudes of our globe. The night for rest, and the day for work; and we can think of the work in terms of nature's beauty; the stately ships "flowing" (as the original text has it) across the seas, for communications and merchandise as between men and men. The seas thus serve us no less than land, and the give-and-take as between sea, sky, and land, is further exemplified by the rain. The rain leads to the fertility of the land, and here we are reminded of the contrast between the Winter's death of Nature and her revivification in the Spring. Here we are reminded of agriculture and the use we make of cattle and all kinds of living creatures. The word translated "beasts" has a wide meaning, including crawling creatures, insects, etc.—all contributing to the round of Nature's operations. This leads us on to the wonderful winds, the region of the air, which man is just beginning to explore and navigate. The personified winds drive the clouds in the sky like "slaves." Here is another aspect of clouds besides that of giving rain. The fleecy clouds are things of sunset beauty; at midday they temper the glare of the sun; at all times they affect radiation and other processes going on in the sky. So we come back to the sky, rounding off the argument, and correlating our human life with the Will and Power of Allah, if we had the wisdom to see!

Will strongly enforce
The Punishment.[167]

شَدِيدُ ٱلْعَذَابِ

166. Then would those
Who are followed
Clear themselves of those
Who follow (them):
They would see the Penalty,
And all relations
Between them would be cut off.

١٦٦ إِذْ تَبَرَّأَ ٱلَّذِينَ ٱتُّبِعُوا۟
مِنَ ٱلَّذِينَ ٱتَّبَعُوا۟ وَرَأَوُا۟ ٱلْعَذَابَ
وَتَقَطَّعَتْ بِهِمُ ٱلْأَسْبَابُ

167. And those who followed
Would say: "If only
We had one more chance,
We would clear ourselves
Of them, as they have
Cleared themselves of us."
Thus will Allah show them
(The fruits of) their deeds
As (nothing but) regrets.
Nor will there be a way
For them out of the Fire.[168]

١٦٧ وَقَالَ ٱلَّذِينَ ٱتَّبَعُوا۟
لَوْ أَنَّ لَنَا كَرَّةً فَنَتَبَرَّأَ مِنْهُمْ
كَمَا تَبَرَّءُوا۟ مِنَّا ۗ كَذَٰلِكَ يُرِيهِمُ ٱللَّهُ
أَعْمَٰلَهُمْ حَسَرَٰتٍ عَلَيْهِمْ ۖ
وَمَا هُم بِخَٰرِجِينَ مِنَ ٱلنَّارِ

C. 50.—The Society thus organised
(2:168-242.) Must live under laws
That would guide their everyday life—
Based on eternal principles
Of righteousness and fair dealing.
Cleanliness and sobriety,
Honesty and helpfulness,
One to another—yet shaped
Into concrete forms, to suit
Times and circumstances,
And the varying needs

---

167. Everything around and within us points to unity of purpose and design—points to Allah. Yet there are foolish persons (unrighteous=those who deliberately use the choice given them to go wrong). They think something else is equal to Allah. Perhaps they even do lip service to Allah, but their heart is in their fetish—unlike the heart of the righteous, who are wholly devoted and absorbed in the love of Allah. If only the unrighteous could see the consequences, they would see the terrible Penalty, and that all Power is in Allah's hands, not in that of any one else. Who are these others who are used as fetishes by the misguided? It may be: (1) creatures of their own imagination, or of their faculties misused; the idea lying behind idols is akin to this, for no intelligent idol-worshipper owns to worshipping stocks and stones; or (2) good leaders whose names have been misused out of perversity to erect them to a position of equality with Allah; or (3) Powers of evil that deliberately mislead. When it comes to the inevitable consequences of blasphemy and the rejection of Allah, the eyes of all are opened and these false and artificial relations dissolve. The idea which was created into a fetish disowns its follower, *i.e.* is seen to have no reasonable basis in the life of the follower, and the follower is forced to renounce it as false. The good leaders whose names were misused would of course disown the misuse of their names, and the evil ones would take an unholy delight in exposing the facts. The Reality is now irresistible, but alas! at what cost?

168. Cf. 3:156, 7:36, 19:39, 69:50, 25:23. [Eds.].

Of average men and women:
The food to be clean and wholesome;
Blood-feuds to be abolished;
The rights and duties of heirs
To be recognised after death,
Not in a spirit of Formalism,
But to help the weak and the needy
And check all selfish wrongdoing;
Self-denial to be learnt by fasting;
The courage to fight in defence
Of right, to be defined;
The Pilgrimage to be sanctified
As a symbol of unity;
Charity and help to the poor
To be organised; unseemly riot
And drink and gambling
To be banished; orphans to be protected;
Marriage, divorce, and widowhood
To be regulated; and the rights of women,
Apt to be trampled under foot,
Now clearly affirmed.

SECTION 21.

168. O ye people!
Eat of what is on earth,
Lawful and good;[169]
And do not follow
The footsteps of the Evil One,
For he is to you
An avowed enemy.

١٦٨ يَـٰٓأَيُّهَا ٱلنَّاسُ كُلُوا۟ مِمَّا فِى ٱلْأَرْضِ
حَلَـٰلًا طَيِّبًا وَلَا تَتَّبِعُوا۟ خُطُوَٰتِ ٱلشَّيْطَـٰنِ ۚ
إِنَّهُۥ لَكُمْ عَدُوٌّ مُّبِينٌ

169. For he commands you
What is evil
And shameful,
And that ye should say
Of Allah that of which
Ye have no knowledge.

١٦٩ إِنَّمَا يَأْمُرُكُم بِٱلسُّوٓءِ
وَٱلْفَحْشَآءِ وَأَن تَقُولُوا۟ عَلَى ٱللَّهِ
مَا لَا تَعْلَمُونَ

169. We now come to the regulations about food. First (2:168-71) we have an appeal to all people, Muslims, Pagans, as well as the People of the Book; then (2:172-73) to the Muslims specially; then (2:174-76) to the sort of men who then (as some do now) either believe in too much formalism or believe in no restrictions at all. Islam follows the Golden Mean. All well-regulated societies lay down reasonable limitations. These become incumbent on all loyal members of any given society, and show what is "lawful" in that society. But if the limitations are reasonable, as they should be, the "lawful" will also coincide more and more with what is "good."

Good: Tayyib = Pure, clean, wholesome, nourishing, pleasing to the taste.

The general principle then would be: what is lawful and what is good, should be followed, not what is evil, or shameful, or foisted on by false ascription to divine injunctions, or what rests merely on the usage of ancestors, even though the ancestors were ignorant or foolish. An example of a shameful custom would be that among the Pagan Arabs of taking congealed blood and eating it fried.

170. When it is said to them:
"Follow what Allah hath
revealed:"
They say: "Nay! we shall follow
The ways of our fathers:"
What! even though their fathers
Were void of wisdom and
guidance?

١٧٠ وَإِذَا قِيلَ لَهُمُ ٱتَّبِعُوا مَآ أَنزَلَ ٱللَّهُ
قَالُوا بَلْ نَتَّبِعُ مَآ أَلْفَيْنَا عَلَيْهِ ءَابَآءَنَآ
أَوَلَوْ كَانَ ءَابَآؤُهُمْ
لَا يَعْقِلُونَ شَيْـًٔا وَلَا يَهْتَدُونَ

171. The parable of those
Who reject Faith is
As if one were to shout
Like a goat-herd, to things
That listen to nothing
But calls and cries:[170]
Deaf, dumb, and blind,[171]
They are void of wisdom.

١٧١ وَمَثَلُ ٱلَّذِينَ كَفَرُوا
كَمَثَلِ ٱلَّذِى يَنْعِقُ بِمَا لَا يَسْمَعُ
إِلَّا دُعَآءً وَنِدَآءً ۚ صُمٌّ بُكْمٌ عُمْىٌ
فَهُمْ لَا يَعْقِلُونَ

172. O ye who believe!
Eat of the good things
That We have provided for you
And be grateful to Allah,
If it is Him ye worship.[172]

١٧٢ يَـٰٓأَيُّهَا ٱلَّذِينَ ءَامَنُوا
كُلُوا مِن طَيِّبَـٰتِ مَا رَزَقْنَـٰكُمْ
وَٱشْكُرُوا لِلَّهِ إِن كُنتُمْ إِيَّاهُ تَعْبُدُونَ

173. He hath only forbidden you
Dead meat,[173] and blood,
And the flesh of swine,
And that on which
Any other name hath been invoked
Besides that of Allah.[174]

١٧٣ إِنَّمَا حَرَّمَ عَلَيْكُمُ
ٱلْمَيْتَةَ وَٱلدَّمَ وَلَحْمَ ٱلْخِنزِيرِ
وَمَآ أُهِلَّ بِهِۦ لِغَيْرِ ٱللَّهِ

170. If you reject all faith, the highest wisdom and the most salutary regulations are lost on you. You are like "dumb driven cattle" who can merely hear calls, but cannot distinguish intelligently between shades of meaning or subtle differences of values.

171. *Cf.* 2:18, where we are told that the rejectors of faith are "deaf, dumb and blind: they will not return to the path." Here the consequence of their not using their senses is that they have no wisdom. In each context there is just the appropriate deduction.

172. Gratitude for Allah's gifts is one form of worship.

173. Dead meat: *maytah*: carrion: animal that dies of itself: the original Arabic has a slightly wider meaning given to it in *Fiqh* (Religious Law): anything that dies of itself and is not expressly killed for food with the *Takbīr* duly pronounced on it. But there are exceptions, *e.g.*, fish and locust are lawful, though they have not been made specially *ḥalāl* with the *Takbīr*. But even fish or locusts as carrion would be obviously ruled out.

174. For prohibited foods, *cf.* also 5:4-5; 6:121, 138-146; etc. The teachers of *Fiqh* (Religious Law) work out the details with great elaboration. My purpose is to present general principles, not technical details. Carrion or dead meat and blood as articles of food would obviously cause disgust to any refined person. So would swine's flesh were the swine lives on offal. Where swine are fed artifically on clean food, the objections remain: (1) that they are filthy animals in other respects, and the flesh of filthy animals taken as food affects the eater; (2) that swine's flesh has more fat than muscle-building material; and (3) that it is more liable to desease than other kinds of meat; *e.g.*, trichinosis, characterized by hair-like worms in the muscular tissue. As to food dedicated to idols or false gods, it is obviously unseemly for the Children of Unity to partake of it.

But if one is forced by
necessity,
Without willful disobedience,
Nor transgressing due limits—
Then is he guiltless.
For Allah is Oft-Forgiving
Most Merciful.

فَمَنِ اضْطُرَّ غَيْرَ بَاغٍ
وَلَا عَادٍ فَلَآ إِثْمَ عَلَيْهِ
إِنَّ اللَّهَ غَفُورٌ رَّحِيمٌ

174. Those who conceal
Allah's revelations in the Book,
And purchase for them
A miserable profit—
They swallow into themselves[175]
Naught but Fire;
Allah will not address them
On the Day of Resurrection,
Nor purify them:
Grievous will be
Their Penalty.

١٧٤ إِنَّ الَّذِينَ يَكْتُمُونَ
مَآ أَنزَلَ اللَّهُ مِنَ الْكِتَٰبِ
وَيَشْتَرُونَ بِهِۦ ثَمَنًا قَلِيلًا
أُولَٰٓئِكَ مَا يَأْكُلُونَ فِي بُطُونِهِمْ إِلَّا النَّارَ
وَلَا يُكَلِّمُهُمُ اللَّهُ يَوْمَ الْقِيَٰمَةِ
وَلَا يُزَكِّيهِمْ وَلَهُمْ عَذَابٌ أَلِيمٌ

175. They are the ones
Who buy Error
In place of Guidance
And Torment in place
Of Forgiveness.
Ah! what boldness
(They show) for the Fire!

١٧٥ أُولَٰٓئِكَ الَّذِينَ اشْتَرَوُا الضَّلَٰلَةَ
بِالْهُدَىٰ وَالْعَذَابَ بِالْمَغْفِرَةِ
فَمَآ أَصْبَرَهُمْ عَلَى النَّارِ

176. (Their doom is) because
Allah sent down the Book
In truth but those who seek
Causes of dispute in the Book
Are in a schism[176]
Far (from the purpose).

١٧٦ ذَٰلِكَ بِأَنَّ اللَّهَ نَزَّلَ الْكِتَٰبَ
بِالْحَقِّ وَإِنَّ الَّذِينَ اخْتَلَفُوا
فِي الْكِتَٰبِ لَفِي شِقَاقٍ بَعِيدٍ

175. "They eat nothing but fire into their bellies" is a literal translation that produces an effect of rude inelegance which is not in the Arabic words. Even in the matter of food and drinks, the mission of Islam is to avoid the extremes of lawlessness on the one hand and extreme formalism on the other. It has laid down a few simple and very reasonable rules. Their infraction causes loss of health or physical powers in any case. But if there is further a spirit of subjective rebellion or fraud—passing off in the name of religion something which is far from the purpose—the consequences become also moral and spiritual. Then it becomes a sin against Faith and Spirit. Continuing the physical simile, we actually swallow fire into ourselves. Imagine the torments which we should have if we swallowed fire into our physical body! They would be infinitely worse in our spiritual state, and they would go on to the Day of Resurrection, when we shall be deprived even of the words which the Judge speaks to a reasonable culprit, and we shall certainly not win His Grace and Mercy.

176. From the mere physical regulation we are at once lifted up into the sphere of morals and faith. For the one acts and reacts on the other. If we are constantly carping at wholesome regulations, we shall do nothing but cause division and schisms among the people, and ordered society would tend to break up.

Section 22

177. It is not righteousness
That ye turn your faces
Towards East or West;
But it is righteousness—[177]
To believe in Allah[178]
And the Last Day,
And the Angels,
And the Book,
And the Messengers;
To spend of your substance,[179]
Out of love for Him,
For your kin,
For orphans,
For the needy,
For the wayfarer,
For those who ask,
And for the ransom of slaves;
To be steadfast in prayer,[180]
And practise regular charity,
To fulfil the contracts
Which ye have made;
And to be firm and patient,[181]
In pain (or suffering)
And adversity,

﴿١٧٧﴾ لَّيْسَ ٱلْبِرَّ أَن تُوَلُّوا۟ وُجُوهَكُمْ
قِبَلَ ٱلْمَشْرِقِ وَٱلْمَغْرِبِ
وَلَـٰكِنَّ ٱلْبِرَّ مَنْ ءَامَنَ بِٱللَّهِ وَٱلْيَوْمِ ٱلْـَٔاخِرِ
وَٱلْمَلَـٰٓئِكَةِ وَٱلْكِتَـٰبِ وَٱلنَّبِيِّـۧنَ
وَءَاتَى ٱلْمَالَ عَلَىٰ حُبِّهِۦ ذَوِى ٱلْقُرْبَىٰ
وَٱلْيَتَـٰمَىٰ وَٱلْمَسَـٰكِينَ
وَٱبْنَ ٱلسَّبِيلِ وَٱلسَّآئِلِينَ وَفِى ٱلرِّقَابِ
وَأَقَامَ ٱلصَّلَوٰةَ وَءَاتَى ٱلزَّكَوٰةَ
وَٱلْمُوفُونَ بِعَهْدِهِمْ إِذَا عَـٰهَدُوا۟ۖ
وَٱلصَّـٰبِرِينَ فِى ٱلْبَأْسَآءِ وَٱلضَّرَّآءِ

---

177. As if to emphasise again a warning against deadening formalism, we are given a beautiful description of the righteous and God-fearing man. He should obey salutary regulations, but he should fix his gaze on the love of Allah and the love of his fellow-men. We are given four heads: (1) our faith should be true and sincere; (2) we must be prepared to show it in deeds of charity to our fellow-men; (3) we must be good citizens, supporting social organisation; and (4) our own individual soul must be firm and unshaken in all circumstances. They are interconnected, and yet can be viewed separately.

178. Faith is not merely a matter of words. We must realise the presence and goodness of Allah. When we do so, the scales fall from our eyes: all the falsities and fleeting nature of the Present cease to enslave us, for we see the Last Day as if it were today. We also see Allah's working in His world and in us: His Angels. His Messengers and His Message are no longer remote from us, but come within our experience. (R).

179. Practical deeds of charity are of value when they proceed from love and from no other motive. In this respect, also, our duties take various forms, which are shown in reasonable gradation: our kith and kin: orphans (including any persons who are without support or help); people who are in real need but who never ask (it is our duty to find them out, and they come before those who ask); the stranger, who is entitled to laws of hospitality; the people who ask and are entitled to ask, *i.e.*, not merely lazy beggars, but those who seek our assistance in some form or another (it is our duty to respond to them); and the slaves (we must do all we can to give or buy their freedom). Slavery has many insidious forms, and all are included.

180. Charity and piety in individual cases do not complete our duties. In prayer and charity we must also look to our organised effort. Where there is a Muslim State, these are made through the State in facilities for public prayer, and public assistance, and for the maintenance of contracts and fair dealing in all matters.

181. Then come the Muslim virtues of firmness and patience. They are to "preserve the dignity of man, with soul erect" (Burns). Three sets of circumstances are specially mentioned for the exercise of this virtue: (1) bodily pain or suffering, (2) adversities or injuries of all kinds, deserved and undeserved, and (3) periods of public panic, such as war, violence, pestilence, etc.

And throughout
All periods of panic.
Such are the people
Of truth, the God-fearing.

178. O ye who believe!
The law of equality[182]
Is prescribed to you
In cases of murder:[183]
The free for the free,
The slave for the slave,
The woman for the woman.
But if any remission
Is made by the brother[184]
Of the slain, then grant
Any reasonable demand,[185]
And compensate him
With handsome gratitude.
This is a concession
And a Mercy
From your Lord.

وَحِينَ ٱلْبَأْسِ ۗ أُولَٰٓئِكَ ٱلَّذِينَ صَدَقُوا۟ ۖ
وَأُولَٰٓئِكَ هُمُ ٱلْمُتَّقُونَ

﴿١٧٨﴾ يَٰٓأَيُّهَا ٱلَّذِينَ ءَامَنُوا۟
كُتِبَ عَلَيْكُمُ ٱلْقِصَاصُ فِى ٱلْقَتْلَى ۖ
ٱلْحُرُّ بِٱلْحُرِّ وَٱلْعَبْدُ بِٱلْعَبْدِ وَٱلْأُنثَىٰ بِٱلْأُنثَىٰ ۚ
فَمَنْ عُفِىَ لَهُۥ مِنْ أَخِيهِ شَىْءٌ
فَٱتِّبَاعٌۢ بِٱلْمَعْرُوفِ
وَأَدَآءٌ إِلَيْهِ بِإِحْسَٰنٍ ۗ
ذَٰلِكَ تَخْفِيفٌ مِّن رَّبِّكُمْ وَرَحْمَةٌ ۗ

182. Note first that this verse and the next make it clear that Islam has much mitigated the horrors of the pre-Islamic custom of retaliation. In order to meet the strict claims of justice, equality is prescribed, with a strong recommendation for mercy and forgiveness. To translate *qiṣās*, therefore, by retaliation, is I think incorrect. The Latin legal term *Lex Talionis* may come near it, but even that is modified here. In any case it is best to avoid technical terms for things that are very different. "Retaliation" in English has a wider meaning, equivalent almost to returning evil for evil, and would more fitly apply to the blood-feuds of the Days of Ignorance. Islam says: if you *must* take a life for a life, at least there should be some measure of equality in it; the killing of the slave of a tribe should not involve a blood feud where many free men would be killed; but the law of mercy, where it can be obtained by consent, with reasonable compensation, would be better.

Our law of equality only takes account of three conditions in civil society; free for free, slave for slave, woman for woman. Among free men or women, all are equal: you cannot ask that because a wealthy, or high-born, or influential man is killed, his life is equal to two or three lives among the poor or the lowly. Nor, in cases of murder, can you go into the value or abilities of a slave. A woman is mentioned separately because her position as a mother or an economic worker is different. She does not form a third class, but a division in the other two classes. One life having been lost, do not waste many lives in retaliation: at most, let the Law take one life under strictly perscribed conditions, and shut the door to private vengeance or tribal retaliation. But if the aggrieved party consents (and this condition of consent is laid down to prevent worse evils), forgiveness and brotherly love is better, and the door of Mercy is kept open. In Western law, no felony can be compounded.

183. The jurists have carefully laid down that the law of *qiṣāṣ* refers to murder only. *Qiṣāṣ* is not applicable to manslaughter, due to a mistake or an accident. There, there would be no capital punishment.

184. *The brother*: the term is perfectly general; all men are brothers in Islam. In this, and in all questions of inheritance, females have similar rights to males, and therefore the masculine gender imports both sexes. Here we are considering the rights of the heirs in the light of the larger brotherhood. In 2:178-179 we have the rights of the heirs to life (as it were): in 2:180-182 we proceed to the heirs to property.

185. The demand should be such as can be met by the party concerned, *i.e.*, within his means, and reasonable according to justice and good conscience. For example, a demand could not be made affecting the honour of a woman or a man. The whole penalty can be remitted if the aggrieved party agrees, out of brotherly love. In meeting that demand the culprit or his friends should equally be generous and recognise the good will of the other side. There should be no subterfuges, no bribes. no unseemly byplay: otherwise the whole intention of mercy and peace is lost.

After this, whoever
Exceeds the limits
Shall be in grave penalty.

فَمَنِ اعْتَدَىٰ بَعْدَ ذَٰلِكَ فَلَهُۥ عَذَابٌ أَلِيمٌ

179. In the Law of Equality
There is (saving of) Life
To you, O ye men of understanding;
That ye may
Restrain yourselves.

١٧٩ وَلَكُمْ فِى الْقِصَاصِ حَيَوٰةٌ
يَٰٓأُو۟لِى الْأَلْبَٰبِ
لَعَلَّكُمْ تَتَّقُونَ

180. It is perscribed,
When death approaches
Any of you, if he leave
Any goods, that he make a bequest
To parents and next of kin,[186]
According to reasonable usage;
This is due
From the God-fearing.

١٨٠ كُتِبَ عَلَيْكُمْ
إِذَا حَضَرَ أَحَدَكُمُ الْمَوْتُ
إِن تَرَكَ خَيْرًا الْوَصِيَّةُ لِلْوَٰلِدَيْنِ
وَالْأَقْرَبِينَ بِالْمَعْرُوفِ ۖ حَقًّا عَلَى الْمُتَّقِينَ

181. If anyone changes the bequest
After hearing it,
The guilt shall be on those
Who make the change.
For Allah hears and knows
(All things).

١٨١ فَمَنۢ بَدَّلَهُۥ بَعْدَ مَا سَمِعَهُۥ
فَإِنَّمَآ إِثْمُهُۥ عَلَى الَّذِينَ يُبَدِّلُونَهُۥٓ ۚ
إِنَّ اللَّهَ سَمِيعٌ عَلِيمٌ

182. But if anyone fears
Partiality or wrongdoing[187]
On the part of the testator,
And makes peace between
(The parties concerned),
There is no wrong in him:

١٨٢ فَمَنْ خَافَ مِن مُّوصٍ جَنَفًا
أَوْ إِثْمًا فَأَصْلَحَ بَيْنَهُمْ
فَلَآ إِثْمَ عَلَيْهِ ۚ

186. There are rules of course for the disposal of intestate property. But it is a good thing that a dying man or woman should, of his own free will, think of his parents and his next of kin, not in a spirit of injustice to others, but in a spirit of love and reverence for those who have cherished him. He must, however, do it "according to reasonable usage": the limitations will be seen further on.

187. A verbal will is allowed but it is expected that the testator will be just to his heirs and not depart from what is considered equitable. For this reason definite shares were laid down for heirs later (see Q. 5:11, etc.). These define or limit the testamentary power, but do not abrogate it. For example, amongst kin there are persons (*e.g.*, an orphan grandson in the presence of surviving sons) who would not inherit under the intestate scheme, and the testator might like to provide for them. Again, there may be outsiders for whom he may wish to provide, and jurists have held that he has powers of disposition up to one-third of his property. But he must not be partial to one heir at the expense of another, or attempt to defeat lawful creditors. If he tries to do this, those who are witnesses to his oral disposition may interfere in two ways. One way would be to persuade testator to change his bequest before he dies. The other way would be, after death, to get the interested parties together and ask them to agree to a more equitable arrangement. In such a case they are acting in good faith, and there is no fraud. They are doing nothing wrong. Islam approves of every lawful device for keeping brethren at peace, without litigation and quarrels. Except for this, the changing of the provisions of a Will is a crime, as it is under all Law.

For Allah is Oft-Forgiving,
Most Merciful.

إِنَّ ٱللَّهَ غَفُورٌ رَّحِيمٌ

SECTION 23.

183. O ye who believe!
Fasting is prescribed to you
As it was prescribed[188]
To those before you,
That ye may (learn)
Self-restraint—

١٨٣ يَـٰٓأَيُّهَا ٱلَّذِينَ ءَامَنُوا۟ كُتِبَ عَلَيْكُمُ
ٱلصِّيَامُ كَمَا كُتِبَ عَلَى ٱلَّذِينَ
مِن قَبْلِكُمْ لَعَلَّكُمْ تَتَّقُونَ

184. (Fasting) for a fixed[189]
Number of days;
But if any of you is ill,
Or on a journey,[190]
The prescribed number
(Should be made up)
From days later.
For those who can do it[191]
(With hardship), is a ransom,
The feeding of one
That is indigent
But he that will give
More, of his own free will—
It is better for him.
And it is better for you
That ye fast,
If ye only knew.

١٨٤ أَيَّامًا مَّعْدُودَٰتٍ
فَمَن كَانَ مِنكُم مَّرِيضًا
أَوْ عَلَىٰ سَفَرٍ فَعِدَّةٌ مِّنْ أَيَّامٍ أُخَرَ
وَعَلَى ٱلَّذِينَ يُطِيقُونَهُۥ
فِدْيَةٌ طَعَامُ مِسْكِينٍ
فَمَن تَطَوَّعَ خَيْرًا فَهُوَ خَيْرٌ لَّهُۥ
وَأَن تَصُومُوا۟ خَيْرٌ لَّكُمْ
إِن كُنتُمْ تَعْلَمُونَ

188. *As it was prescribed*: this does not mean that the Muslim fast is like the other fasts previously observed, in the number of days, in the time or manner of the fast, or in other incidents; it only means that the principle of self-denial by fasting is not a new one.

189. This verse should be read with the following verses, 185-188, in order that the incidents of the physical fast may be fully understood with reference to its spiritual meaning.

The Muslim fast is not meant for self-torture. Although it is stricter than other fasts, it also provides alleviations for special circumstances. If it were merely a temporary abstention from food and drink, it would be salutary to many people, who habitually eat and drink to excess. The instincts for food, drink, and sex are strong in the animal nature, and temporary restraint from all these enables the attention to be directed to higher things. This is necessary through prayer, contemplation and acts of charity, not of the showy kind, but by seeking out those really in need. Certain standards are prescribed, but much higher standards are recommended.

190. For journeys, a minimum standard of three marches is prescribed by some Commentators; others make it more precise by naming a distance of 16 *farsakhs,* equivalent to 48 miles. A journey of 8 or 9 miles on foot is more tiring than a similar one by bullock cart. There are various degrees of fatigue in riding a given distance on horseback or by camel or in a comfortable train or by motor car or by steamer, aeroplane, or airship. In my opinion the standard must depend on the means of locomotion and on the relative resources of the traveller. It is better to determine it in each case according to circumstances. (R).

191. *Those who can do it with hardship:* such as aged people, or persons specially circumstanced. The Shāfi'is would include a woman expecting a child, or one who is nursing a baby, but on this point opinion is not unanimous, some holding that they ought to put in the fasts later, when they can.

185. Ramaḍān is the (month)
In which was sent down
The Qur'ān, as a guide
To mankind, also clear (Signs)
For guidance and judgement[192]
(Between right and wrong).
So every one of you
Who is present (at his home)
During that month
Should spend it in fasting,
But if any one is ill,
Or on a journey,
The prescribed period
(Should be made up)
By days later.
Allah intends every facility
For you; He does not want
To put you to difficulties.
(He wants you) to complete
The prescribed period,
And to glorify Him[193]
In that He has guided you;
And perchance ye shall be
grateful.

186. When My servants
Ask thee concerning Me,
I am indeed
Close (to them): I listen
To the prayer of every
Suppliant when he calleth on
Me:
Let them also, with a will,
Listen to My call,
And believe in Me:
That they may walk
In the right way.[194]

187. Permitted to you,
On the night of the fasts,

١٨٥ شَهْرُ رَمَضَانَ ٱلَّذِىٓ أُنزِلَ فِيهِ
ٱلْقُرْءَانُ هُدًى لِّلنَّاسِ
وَبَيِّنَٰتٍ مِّنَ ٱلْهُدَىٰ وَٱلْفُرْقَانِ ۚ
فَمَن شَهِدَ مِنكُمُ ٱلشَّهْرَ فَلْيَصُمْهُ ۖ
وَمَن كَانَ مَرِيضًا أَوْ عَلَىٰ سَفَرٍ
فَعِدَّةٌ مِّنْ أَيَّامٍ أُخَرَ ۗ يُرِيدُ ٱللَّهُ بِكُمُ
ٱلْيُسْرَ وَلَا يُرِيدُ بِكُمُ ٱلْعُسْرَ
وَلِتُكْمِلُوا۟ ٱلْعِدَّةَ
وَلِتُكَبِّرُوا۟ ٱللَّهَ عَلَىٰ مَا هَدَىٰكُمْ
وَلَعَلَّكُمْ تَشْكُرُونَ

١٨٦ وَإِذَا سَأَلَكَ
عِبَادِى عَنِّى فَإِنِّى قَرِيبٌ ۖ
أُجِيبُ دَعْوَةَ ٱلدَّاعِ إِذَا دَعَانِ ۖ
فَلْيَسْتَجِيبُوا۟ لِى وَلْيُؤْمِنُوا۟ بِى
لَعَلَّهُمْ يَرْشُدُونَ

١٨٧ أُحِلَّ لَكُمْ لَيْلَةَ ٱلصِّيَامِ

---

192. Judgement (between right and wrong): *Furqān* = the criterion or standard by which we judge between right and wrong. See 2:5 n. 68.

193. The regulations are again and again coupled with an insistence on two things: (a) the facilities and concessions given, and (b) the spiritual significance of the fast, without which it is like an empty shell without a kernel. If we realise this, we shall look upon Ramadan, not as a burden, but as a blessing, and shall be duly grateful for the lead given to us in this matter.

194. These verses 186 and 188 are not foreign to the subject of Ramaḍān, but emphasise its spiritual aspect. Here we are told of prayer and the nearness of Allah, and in 188 we are asked not to "eat up" other people's substance.

Is the approach to your wives.
They are your garments
And ye are their garments.[195]
Allah knoweth what ye
Used to do secretly among
yourselves;
But He turned to you
And forgave you;
So now associate with them,
And seek what Allah
Hath ordained for you,[196]
And eat and drink,
Until the white thread
Of dawn appear to you
Distinct from its black thread;[197]
Then complete your fast
Till the night appears;[198]
But do not associate
With your wives
While ye are in retreat[199]
In the mosques. Those are[200]
Limits (set by) Allah:
Approach not nigh thereto.
Thus doth Allah make clear
His Signs to men: that
They may learn self-restraint.

ٱلرَّفَثُ إِلَىٰ نِسَآئِكُمْۚ
هُنَّ لِبَاسٌ لَّكُمْ وَأَنتُمْ لِبَاسٌ لَّهُنَّۗ عَلِمَ ٱللَّهُ
أَنَّكُمْ كُنتُمْ تَخْتَانُونَ أَنفُسَكُمْ
فَتَابَ عَلَيْكُمْ وَعَفَا عَنكُمْۖ
فَٱلْـَٔـٰنَ بَـٰشِرُوهُنَّ وَٱبْتَغُوا۟ مَا كَتَبَ ٱللَّهُ لَكُمْۚ
وَكُلُوا۟ وَٱشْرَبُوا۟ حَتَّىٰ يَتَبَيَّنَ لَكُمُ ٱلْخَيْطُ ٱلْأَبْيَضُ
مِنَ ٱلْخَيْطِ ٱلْأَسْوَدِ مِنَ ٱلْفَجْرِۖ ثُمَّ أَتِمُّوا۟ ٱلصِّيَامَ
إِلَى ٱلَّيْلِۚ وَلَا تُبَـٰشِرُوهُنَّ وَأَنتُمْ عَـٰكِفُونَ
فِى ٱلْمَسَـٰجِدِۗ تِلْكَ حُدُودُ ٱللَّهِ فَلَا تَقْرَبُوهَاۗ
كَذَٰلِكَ يُبَيِّنُ ٱللَّهُ ءَايَـٰتِهِۦ لِلنَّاسِ
لَعَلَّهُمْ يَتَّقُونَ

188. And do not eat up
Your property among yourselves
For vanities, nor use it
As bait for the judges,

١٨٨ وَلَا تَأْكُلُوٓا۟ أَمْوَٰلَكُم بَيْنَكُم بِٱلْبَـٰطِلِ
وَتُدْلُوا۟ بِهَآ إِلَى ٱلْحُكَّامِ

195. Men and women are each other's garments: *i.e.*, they are for mutual support, mutual comfort, and mutual protection, fitting into each other as a garment fits the body. A garment also is both for show and concealment. The question of sex is always delicate to handle: here we are told that even in such matters a clear, open, and honest course is better than fraud or self-deception. The sex instinct is classed with eating and drinking, an animal thing to be restrained, but not to be ashamed of. The three things are prohibited during the fast by day, but permitted after the fast is broken at night till the next fast commences.

196. There is difference of opinion as to the exact meaning of this. I would connect this as a parallel clause with the clause "eat and drink", which follows, all three being governed by "until the white thread", etc. That is, all three things must stop when the fast begins again in the early morning. Or it may mean: What is permitted is well enough, but seek the higher things ordained for you.

197. Those in touch with Nature know the beautiful effects of early dawn. First appear thin white indefinable streaks of light in the east; then a dark zone supervenes; followed by a beautiful pinkish white zone clearly defined from the dark; after that the fast begins.

198. *Till the night appears*: From the actual practice of the Holy Prophet, this is rightly interpreted to mean: "Till sunset".

199. This verse refers to the known Islamic practice called *i'tikāf* which means retreating to mosques for devotion and worship. The Prophet (peace be on him) used to retreat to the mosque during the last ten days of Ramaḍān. [Eds.].

200. I construe these limits as applying to the whole of the regulations about fasts.

With intent that ye may
Eat up wrongfully and knowingly
A little of (other) people's
property.[201]

لِتَأْكُلُوا فَرِيقًا مِّنْ أَمْوَالِ النَّاسِ
بِالْإِثْمِ وَأَنتُمْ تَعْلَمُونَ

Section 24

189. They ask thee
Concerning the New Moons.[202]
Say: They are but signs
To mark fixed periods of time
In (the affairs of) men,
And for Pilgrimage.
It is no virtue if ye enter
Your houses from the back:
It is virtue if ye fear Allah.
Enter houses
Through the proper doors:[203]
And fear Allah:
That ye may prosper.

١٨٩ يَسْـَٔلُونَكَ عَنِ الْأَهِلَّةِ ۖ
قُلْ هِيَ مَوَاقِيتُ لِلنَّاسِ وَالْحَجِّ ۗ وَلَيْسَ الْبِرُّ
بِأَن تَأْتُوا الْبُيُوتَ مِن ظُهُورِهَا وَلَٰكِنَّ الْبِرَّ
مَنِ اتَّقَىٰ ۗ وَأْتُوا الْبُيُوتَ مِنْ أَبْوَابِهَا ۚ
وَاتَّقُوا اللَّهَ لَعَلَّكُمْ تُفْلِحُونَ

190. Fight in the cause of Allah
Those who fight you,[204]
But do not transgress limits;
For Allah loveth not transgressors.

١٩٠ وَقَاتِلُوا فِي سَبِيلِ اللَّهِ الَّذِينَ يُقَاتِلُونَكُمْ وَلَا
تَعْتَدُوا ۚ إِنَّ اللَّهَ لَا يُحِبُّ الْمُعْتَدِينَ

201. Besides the three primal physical needs of man, which are apt to make him greedy, there is a fourth greed in society, the greed of wealth and property. The purpose of fasts is not completed until this fourth greed is also restrained. Ordinarily honest men are content if they refrain from robbery, theft, or embezzlement. Two more subtle forms of the greed are mentioned here. One is where one uses one's own property for corrupting others—judges or those in authority—so as to obtain some material gain even under the cover and protection of the law. The words translated "other people's property" may also mean "public property". A still more subtle form is where we use our own property or property under our own control— "among yourselves" in the Text—for vain or frivolous uses. Under the Islamic standard this is also greed. Property carries with it its own reponsibilities. If we fail to understand or fulfil them, we have not learnt the full lesson of self-denial by fasts.

202. There were many superstitions connected with the New Moon, as there are to the present day. We are told to disregard such superstitions. As a measure of time, where the lunar calendar is used, the New Moon is one great sign, for which people watch with eagerness. Muslim festivals, including the Pilgrimage are fixed by the appearance of the New Moon. The Arabs, among other superstitions, had one which made them enter their houses by the back door during or after the Pilgrimage. This is disapproved, for there is no virtue in any such artificial restrictions. All virtue proceeds from the love and fear of Allah.

203. This is a Muslim proverb now, and much might be written about its manifold meanings. A few may be noted here. (1) If you enter a society, respect its manners and customs. (2) If you want to achieve an object honourably, go about it openly and not "by a backdoor." (3) Do not beat about the bush. (4) If you wish success in an undertaking, provide all the necessary instruments for it.

The subject of the New Moon provides a good transition between the Ramaḍān fast, which begins and ends with the New Moon, the Pilgrimage, whose ten days commence with the New Moon, and the War which Islam had to wage in self-defence against the Pagans, who wanted to exclude them from the Pilgrimage after they had driven them out of house and home.

204. War is permissible in self-defence, and under well-defined limits. When undertaken, it must be pushed with vigour (but not relentlessly), but only to restore peace and freedom for the worship of Allah. In any case strict limits must not be transgressed: women, children, old and infirm men should not be molested, nor trees and crops cut down, nor peace withheld when the enemy comes to terms. (R).

191. And slay them
Wherever ye catch them,
And turn them out
From where they have
Turned you out;
For tumult and oppression
Are worse than slaughter;
But fight them not[205]
At the Sacred Mosque,
Unless they (first)
Fight you there;
But if they fight you,
Slay them.
Such is the reward
Of those who suppress faith.[206]

(١٩١) وَٱقۡتُلُوهُمۡ حَيۡثُ ثَقِفۡتُمُوهُمۡ
وَأَخۡرِجُوهُم مِّنۡ حَيۡثُ أَخۡرَجُوكُمۡۚ
وَٱلۡفِتۡنَةُ أَشَدُّ مِنَ ٱلۡقَتۡلِۚ
وَلَا تُقَٰتِلُوهُمۡ عِندَ ٱلۡمَسۡجِدِ ٱلۡحَرَامِ
حَتَّىٰ يُقَٰتِلُوكُمۡ فِيهِۖ فَإِن قَٰتَلُوكُمۡ فَٱقۡتُلُوهُمۡۗ
كَذَٰلِكَ جَزَآءُ ٱلۡكَٰفِرِينَ

192. But if they cease,
Allah is Oft-Forgiving,
Most Merciful.

(١٩٢) فَإِنِ ٱنتَهَوۡاْ فَإِنَّ ٱللَّهَ غَفُورٞ رَّحِيمٞ

193. And fight them on
Until there is no more
Tumult or oppression,
And there prevail
Justice and faith in Allah;[207]

(١٩٣) وَقَٰتِلُوهُمۡ حَتَّىٰ لَا تَكُونَ فِتۡنَةٞ
وَيَكُونَ ٱلدِّينُ لِلَّهِۖ

205. This passage is illustrated by the events that happened at Ḥudaybiyyah in the sixth year of the Hijrah, though it is not clear that it was revealed on that occasion, The Muslims were by this time a strong and influential community. Many of them were exiles from Makkah, where the Pagans had established an intolerant autocracy, persecuting Muslims, preventing them from visiting their homes, and even keeping them out by force from performing the Pilgrimage during the universally recognised period of truce. This was intolerance, oppression, and autocracy to the last degree, and the mere readiness of the Muslims to enforce their rights as Arab citizens resulted without bloodshed in an agreement which the Muslims faithfully observed. The Pagans, however, had no scruples in breaking faith, and it is unnecessary here to go into subsequent events.

In general, it may be said that Islam is the religion of peace, good will, mutual understanding, and good faith. But it will not acquiesce in wrongdoing, and its men will hold their lives cheap in defence of honour, justice, and the religion which they hold sacred. Their ideal is that of heroic virtue combined with unselfish gentleness and tenderness, such as is exemplified in the life of the Prophet. They believe in courage, obedience, discipline, duty, and a constant striving by all the means in their power, physical, moral, intellectual, and spiritual, for the establishment of truth and righteousness. They know that war is an evil, but they will not flinch from it if their honour demands it and a righteous *Imām* (such as Muḥammad was *par excellence*) commands it, for then they know they are not serving carnal ends. In other cases, war has nothing to do with their faith, except that it will always be regulated by its humane precepts. (R).

206. *Suppress faith*: in the narrower as well as the larger sense. If they want forcibly to prevent you from exercising your sacred rites, they have declared war on your religion, and it would be cowardice to ignore the challenge or to fail in rooting out the tyranny.

207. *Justice and faith*. The Arabic word is *Dīn*, which is comprehensive. It implies the ideas of indebtedness, duty, obedience, judgment, justice, faith, religion, customary rites, etc. The clause means: "until there is *Dīn* for Allah."

But if they cease,[208]
Let there be no hostility
Except to those
Who practise oppression.

فَإِنِ انتَهَوْا
فَلَا عُدْوَانَ إِلَّا عَلَى الظَّالِمِينَ

194. The prohibited month—[209]
For the prohibited month,
And so for all things
prohibited—
There is the law of equality.
If then any one transgresses
The prohibition against you,
Transgress ye likewise
Against him.
But fear Allah, and know[210]
That Allah is with those
Who restrain themselves.

(١٩٤) الشَّهْرُ الْحَرَامُ
بِالشَّهْرِ الْحَرَامِ وَالْحُرُمَاتُ قِصَاصٌ ۚ
فَمَنِ اعْتَدَىٰ عَلَيْكُمْ فَاعْتَدُوا
عَلَيْهِ بِمِثْلِ مَا اعْتَدَىٰ عَلَيْكُمْ ۚ
وَاتَّقُوا اللَّهَ وَاعْلَمُوا أَنَّ اللَّهَ مَعَ الْمُتَّقِينَ

195. And spend of your substance
In the cause of Allah,
And make not your own hands
Contribute to (your) destruction;[211]
But do good;
For Allah loveth those
Who do good.

(١٩٥) وَأَنفِقُوا فِي سَبِيلِ اللَّهِ
وَلَا تُلْقُوا بِأَيْدِيكُمْ إِلَى التَّهْلُكَةِ ۛ
وَأَحْسِنُوا ۛ إِنَّ اللَّهَ يُحِبُّ الْمُحْسِنِينَ

---

208. If the opposite party ceases, to persecute you, your hostility ends with them as a party, but it does not mean that you become friends to oppression. Your fight is against wrong; there should be no rancour against men.

209. *Ḥarām*=prohibited, sacred. The month of Pilgrimage (*Dhu al Ḥajja*) was a sacred month, in which warfare was prohibited by Arab custom. The month preceding (*Dhu al Qa'da*) and the month following (*Muḥarram*) were included in the prohibition, and *Muḥarram* was specially called *al Ḥarām*. Possibly *Muḥarram* is meant in the first line, and the other months and other prohibited things in "all things prohibited." In *Rajab*, also, war was prohibited, If the pagan enemies of Islam broke that custom and made war in the prohibited months, the Muslims were free also to break that custom but only to the same extent as the others broke it. Similarly the territory of Makkah was sacred, in which war was prohibited. If the enemies of Islam broke that custom, the Muslims were free to do so to that extent. Any convention is useless if one party does not respect it. There must be a law of equality. Or perhaps the word reciprocity may express it better.

210. At the same time the Muslims are commanded to exercise self-restraint as much as possible. Force is a dangerous weapon. It may have to be used for self-defence or self-preservation, but we must always remember that self-restraint is pleasing in the eyes of Allah. Even when we are fighting, it should be for a principle, not out of passion.

211. Every fight requires the wherewithals for the fight, the "sinews of war." If the war is just and in the cause of Allah, all who have wealth must spend it freely. That may be their contribution to the Cause, in addition to their personal effort, or if for any reason they are unable to fight. If they hug their wealth, perhaps their own hands are helping in their own self-destruction. Or if their wealth is being spent, not in the Cause of Allah, but in something which pleases their fancy, it may be that the advantage goes to the enemy, and they are by their action helping their own destruction. In all things, their standard should be, not selfishness, but the good of their brethren, for such good is pleasing to Allah.

196. And complete
The *Ḥajj* or *Umrah*[212]
In the service of Allah,
But if ye are prevented
(From completing it),
Send an offering
For sacrifice,
Such as ye may find,
And do not shave your heads
Until the offering reaches
The place of sacrifice.
And if any of you is ill,[213]
Or has an ailment in his scalp,
(Necessitating shaving),
(He should) in compensation
Either fast, or feed the poor,
Or offer sacrifice;
And when ye are
In peaceful conditions (again),[214]
If any one wishes
To continue the *Umrah*
On to the *Ḥajj*,
He must make an offering
Such as he can afford,
But if he cannot afford it,
He should fast
Three days during the *Ḥajj*

١٩٦ وَأَتِمُّوا۟ ٱلْحَجَّ وَٱلْعُمْرَةَ لِلَّهِ ۚ
فَإِنْ أُحْصِرْتُمْ
فَمَا ٱسْتَيْسَرَ مِنَ ٱلْهَدْىِ ۖ
وَلَا تَحْلِقُوا۟ رُءُوسَكُمْ حَتَّىٰ يَبْلُغَ ٱلْهَدْىُ مَحِلَّهُۥ ۚ
فَمَن كَانَ مِنكُم مَّرِيضًا
أَوْ بِهِۦٓ أَذًى مِّن رَّأْسِهِۦ
فَفِدْيَةٌ مِّن صِيَامٍ أَوْ صَدَقَةٍ أَوْ نُسُكٍ ۚ
فَإِذَآ أَمِنتُمْ فَمَن تَمَتَّعَ بِٱلْعُمْرَةِ إِلَى ٱلْحَجِّ
فَمَا ٱسْتَيْسَرَ مِنَ ٱلْهَدْىِ ۚ
فَمَن لَّمْ يَجِدْ فَصِيَامُ
ثَلَٰثَةِ أَيَّامٍ فِى ٱلْحَجِّ

212. See 2:158, n. 161. The Ḥajj is the complete pilgrimage, of which the chief rites are performed during the first twelve or thirteen days of the month of *Dhu al Hijjah*. The *Umrah* is a less formal pilgrimage at any time of the year. In either case, the intending pilgrim commences by putting on a simple garment of unsewn cloth in two pieces when he is some distance yet from Makkah. The putting on of the pilgrim garb (*iḥrām*) is symbolical of his renouncing the vanities of the world. After this and until the end of the pilgrimage he must not wear other clothes, or ornaments, anoint his hair, use perfumes, hunt, or do other prohibited acts. The completion of the pilgrimage is symbolised by the shaving of the head for men and the cutting off of a few locks of the hair of the head for women, the putting off of the *iḥrām* and the resumption of the ordinary dress.

Here we are told: (1) that having once undertaken the pilgrimage, we must complete it; (2) that we must do it not for worldly ends, but as a symbol of our service and worship to Allah; (3) that if we are prevented, for any reason, from completing the rites, a symbolical completion can be made by sending an offering for sacrifice; sacrifice would have been offered if we had been present personally; here we would send the sacrifice vicariously, and when it is likely to reach the place of sacrifice, we could then shave our heads and resume our ordinary dress and avocations. (R).

213. If any one is taken ill after putting on the *iḥrām*, so that he has to put on other clothes, or if he has trouble or skin disease in his head or insects in his hair, and he has to shave his head before completion, he should fast (three days, say the Commentators), or feed the poor, or offer sacrifice.

214. When this was revealed, the city of Makkah was in the hands of the enemies of Islam, and the regulations about the fighting and the pilgrimage came together and were interconnected. But the revelation provides, as always, for the particular occasion, and also for normal conditions. Makkah soon passed out of the hands of the enemies of Islam. People sometimes came long distances to Makkah before the Pilgrimage season began. Having performed the *Umrah*, they stayed on for the formal *Ḥajj*. In case the pilgrim had spent his money, he is shown what he can do, rich or poor, and yet hold his head high among his fellows, as having performed all rites as prescribed.

And seven days on his return,
Making ten days in all.
This is for those
Whose household
Is not in (the precincts[215]
Of) the Sacred Mosque,
And fear Allah,
And know that Allah,
Is strict in punishment.[216]

وَسَبْعَةٍ إِذَا رَجَعْتُمْ تِلْكَ عَشَرَةٌ كَامِلَةٌ
ذَٰلِكَ لِمَن لَّمْ يَكُنْ أَهْلُهُۥ حَاضِرِى
ٱلْمَسْجِدِ ٱلْحَرَامِ وَٱتَّقُوا۟ ٱللَّهَ
وَٱعْلَمُوٓا۟ أَنَّ ٱللَّهَ شَدِيدُ ٱلْعِقَابِ

SECTION 25

197. For *Ḥajj*
Are the months well-known.[217]
If any one undertakes
That duty therein,
Let there be no obscenity,
Nor wickedness,
Nor wrangling
In the *Ḥajj*
And whatever good
Ye do, (be sure)
Allah knoweth it.

(١٩٧) ٱلْحَجُّ أَشْهُرٌ مَّعْلُومَٰتٌ
فَمَن فَرَضَ فِيهِنَّ ٱلْحَجَّ فَلَا رَفَثَ
وَلَا فُسُوقَ وَلَا جِدَالَ فِى ٱلْحَجِّ
وَمَا تَفْعَلُوا۟ مِنْ خَيْرٍ
يَعْلَمْهُ ٱللَّهُ

215. There is disagreement among jurists whether residents of Makkah are allowed to make *tamattu'* or not. However, the four schools of law are agreed that sacrificial offering is not obligatory for the residents of Makkah. [Eds.].

216. This closes the section about the duties of fighting and introduces the connected question of pilgrimage in a sort of transition. Fighting is connected with fear, and while it is meritorious to obey Allah, we are warned that we must not allow our selfish passions to carry us away, because it is in such times of stress that our spirit is tested. Verse 195 ended with a benediction for those who do good. This verse ends with a warning to those who take advantage of Allah's cause to transgress the limits, for the punishment is equally sure. The next verse shows us the pitfalls we must avoid in a large concourse of people.

217. *The months well known*: the months of *Shawwāl*, *Dhu al Qa'dah*, and *Dhu al Ḥijjah* (up to the 10th or the 13th) are set apart for the rites of *Ḥajj*. That is to say, the first rites may begin as early as the beginning of Shawwāl, with a definite approach to Makkah, but the chief rites are concentrated on the first ten days of *Dhu al Ḥijjah*, and specially on the 8th, 9th and 10th of that month, when the concourse of pilgrims reaches its height. The chief rites may be briefly enumerated: (1) The wearing of the pilgrim garment (*iḥrām*) from certain points definitely fixed on all the roads to Makkah; after this the pilgrimage prohibitions come into operation and the pilgrim is dedicated to worship and prayer and the denial of vanities; (2) the going round the Ka'bah seven times *(ṭawāf)*, typifying activity, with the kissing of the little Black Stone built into the wall, the symbol of concentration in the love of Allah; (3) after a short prayer at the Station of Abraham (Q. 2:125), the pilgrim goes to the hills Ṣafā and Marwah (Q. 2:158), the symbols of patience and perseverance; (4) the great Sermon (*Khuṭbah*) on the 7th of *Dhu al Ḥijjah*, when the whole assembly listens to an exposition of the meaning of *Ḥajj*; (5) the visit on the eighth, of the whole body of pilgrims to the Valley of Minā (about six miles north of Makkah), where the pilgrims halt and stay the night, proceeding on the ninth to the plain and hill of 'Arafāt, about five miles further north, which is also called the Mount of Mercy; (5) the tenth day, the 'Id Day, the day of Sacrifice, when the sacrifice is offered in the Valley of Minā, the head is shaved or the hair trimmed, the *ṭawāf al ifāḍah* and the symbolic ceremony of casting seven stones at the Evil One is performed on the first occasion; it is continued on subsequent days; both rites are connected with the story of Abraham: this is the *'Īd al Aḍḥā*; note that the ceremony is symbolically connected with the rejection of evil in thought, word, and deed. A stay of two or three days after this is prescribed; these days are called *Tashrīq* days. (R).

And take a provision[218]
(With you) for the journey,
But the best of provisions
Is right conduct.
So fear Me,
O ye that are wise.

وَتَزَوَّدُوا
فَإِنَّ خَيْرَ الزَّادِ التَّقْوَىٰ
وَاتَّقُونِ يَا أُولِي الْأَلْبَابِ

198. It is no crime in you
If ye seek of the bounty
Of your Lord (during
pilgrimage).[219]
Then when ye pour down
From (Mount) 'Arafāt,
Celebrate the praises of Allah
At the Sacred Monument,[220]
And celebrate His praises
As He has directed you,
Even though, before this,
Ye went astray.[221]

١٩٨ لَيْسَ عَلَيْكُمْ جُنَاحٌ
أَنْ تَبْتَغُوا فَضْلًا مِنْ رَبِّكُمْ
فَإِذَا أَفَضْتُمْ مِنْ عَرَفَاتٍ
فَاذْكُرُوا اللَّهَ عِنْدَ الْمَشْعَرِ الْحَرَامِ
وَاذْكُرُوهُ كَمَا هَدَاكُمْ
وَإِنْ كُنْتُمْ مِنْ قَبْلِهِ لَمِنَ الضَّالِّينَ

199. Then pass on
At a quick pace from the place
Whence it is usual
For the multitude[222]
So to do, and ask
For Allah's forgiveness.
For Allah is Oft-Forgiving,
Most Merciful.

١٩٩ ثُمَّ أَفِيضُوا
مِنْ حَيْثُ أَفَاضَ النَّاسُ
وَاسْتَغْفِرُوا اللَّهَ
إِنَّ اللَّهَ غَفُورٌ رَحِيمٌ

---

218. It is recommended that pilgrims should come with provisions, so that they should not be compelled to resort to begging. But, as usual, our thought is directed at once from the physical to the spiritual. If provisions are required for a journey on earth, how much more important to provide for the final journey into the future world? The best of such provisions is right conduct, which is the same as the fear of Allah.

219. Legitimate trade is allowed, in the interests both of the honest trader, who can thus meet his own expenses, and of the generality of pilgrims, who would otherwise be greatly inconvenienced for the necessaries of life. But the profit must be sought as from the "bounty of Allah." There should be no profiteering, or trade "tricks." Good honest trade is a form of service to the community, and therefore to Allah.

220. About midway between 'Arafāt and Minā (see n. 217 to 2:197) is a place called Muzdalifah where the Holy Prophet offered up a long prayer. It has thus become a Sacred Monument and pilgrims are directed to follow that example on their return. A special reason for this is given in the note following.

221. Certain arrogant tribes living in Makkah used not to go to 'Arafāt with the crowd but to stop short at Muzdalifah. They are rebuked for their arrogance and told that they must perform all the rites like the rest of the pilgrims. There is equality in Islam.

222. See last note. Towards the end of the Pilgrimage the crowd is very great, and if any people loitered after 'Arafāt, it would cause great confusion and inconvenience. The pace has therefore to be quick for every one, a very salutary regulation. Every member of the crowd must think of the comfort and convenience of the whole mass.

200. So when ye have
Accomplished your holy rites,
Celebrate the praises of Allah,
As ye used to celebrate
The praises of your fathers—[223]
Yea, with far more
Heart and soul.
There are men who say:
"Our Lord! Give us
(Thy bounties) in this world!"
But they will have
No portion in the Hereafter.[224]

٢٠٠ فَإِذَا قَضَيْتُم مَّنَٰسِكَكُمْ
فَٱذْكُرُوا۟ ٱللَّهَ كَذِكْرِكُمْ ءَابَآءَكُمْ
أَوْ أَشَدَّ ذِكْرًا ۗ فَمِنَ ٱلنَّاسِ مَن
يَقُولُ رَبَّنَآ ءَاتِنَا فِى ٱلدُّنْيَا
وَمَا لَهُۥ فِى ٱلْءَاخِرَةِ مِنْ خَلَٰقٍ

201. And there are men who say:
"Our Lord! Give us
Good in this world
And good in the Hereafter,
And defend us
From the torment
Of the Fire!"

٢٠١ وَمِنْهُم مَّن يَقُولُ
رَبَّنَآ ءَاتِنَا فِى ٱلدُّنْيَا حَسَنَةً
وَفِى ٱلْءَاخِرَةِ حَسَنَةً وَقِنَا عَذَابَ ٱلنَّارِ

202. To these will be allotted[225]
What they have earned;
And Allah is quick in account.

٢٠٢ أُو۟لَٰٓئِكَ لَهُمْ نَصِيبٌ مِّمَّا كَسَبُوا۟ ۚ
وَٱللَّهُ سَرِيعُ ٱلْحِسَابِ

203. Celebrate the praises of Allah
During the Appointed Days.[226]
But if anyone hastens
To leave in two days,
There is no blame on him,
And if anyone stays on,
There is no blame on him,
If his aim is to do right.
Then fear Allah, and know
That ye will surely
Be gathered unto Him.

٢٠٣ وَٱذْكُرُوا۟ ٱللَّهَ فِىٓ أَيَّامٍ مَّعْدُودَٰتٍ ۚ
فَمَن تَعَجَّلَ فِى يَوْمَيْنِ فَلَآ إِثْمَ عَلَيْهِ
وَمَن تَأَخَّرَ فَلَآ إِثْمَ عَلَيْهِ ۚ لِمَنِ ٱتَّقَىٰ ۗ
وَٱتَّقُوا۟ ٱللَّهَ وَٱعْلَمُوٓا۟ أَنَّكُمْ إِلَيْهِ تُحْشَرُونَ

223. After the Pilgrimage, in Pagan times, the pilgrims used to gather in assemblies in which the praises of ancestors were sung. As the whole of the pilgrimage rites were spiritualised in Islam, so this aftermath of the Pilgrimage was also spiritualised. It was required from pilgrims to stay on two or three days after the Day of Sacrifice, but they must use them in prayer and praise to Allah. See 2:203 below. (R).

224. If you hasten to get all the good things of the world, and only think of them and pray for them, you would lose the higher things of the future. The proper Muslim attitude is neither to renounce this world nor to be so engrossed in it as to forget the spiritual future.

225. Our spiritual account is mounting up, both on the debit and credit side. In worldly accounts, both our profits and our losses may be delayed. But in Allah's books there is no delay. Our actions go before us. (See 2:95. n.100.)

226. *The Appointed Days*: the three days after the tenth, when the Pilgrims stay on in the Valley of Minā for prayer and praise. They are the days of *Tas̲h̲rīq* (see 2:200, n. 223). It is optional for pilgrims to leave on the second or third day.

204. There is the type of man[227]
Whose speech
About this world's life
May dazzle thee,
And he calls Allah to witness
About what is in his heart;
Yet is he the most contentious
Of enemies.

٢٠٤ وَمِنَ ٱلنَّاسِ مَن يُعْجِبُكَ
قَوْلُهُۥ فِى ٱلْحَيَوٰةِ ٱلدُّنْيَا
وَيُشْهِدُ ٱللَّهَ عَلَىٰ مَا فِى قَلْبِهِۦ
وَهُوَ أَلَدُّ ٱلْخِصَامِ

205. When he turns his back,
His aim everywhere
Is to spread mischief
Through the earth and destroy
Crops and cattle.
But Allah loveth not mischief.

٢٠٥ وَإِذَا تَوَلَّىٰ سَعَىٰ فِى ٱلْأَرْضِ
لِيُفْسِدَ فِيهَا وَيُهْلِكَ ٱلْحَرْثَ وَٱلنَّسْلَ ۗ
وَٱللَّهُ لَا يُحِبُّ ٱلْفَسَادَ

206. When it is said to him,
"Fear Allah,"
He is led by arrogance
To (more) crime.
Enough for him is Hell—
An evil bed indeed
(To lie on)![228]

٢٠٦ وَإِذَا قِيلَ لَهُ ٱتَّقِ ٱللَّهَ
أَخَذَتْهُ ٱلْعِزَّةُ بِٱلْإِثْمِ ۚ
فَحَسْبُهُۥ جَهَنَّمُ ۚ وَلَبِئْسَ ٱلْمِهَادُ

207. And there is the type of man
Who gives his life
To earn the pleasure of Allah;
And Allah is full of kindness
To (His) devotees.[229]

٢٠٧ وَمِنَ ٱلنَّاسِ مَن يَشْرِى نَفْسَهُ
ٱبْتِغَآءَ مَرْضَاتِ ٱللَّهِ ۗ
وَٱللَّهُ رَءُوفٌۢ بِٱلْعِبَادِ

208. O ye who believe!
Enter into Islam
Wholeheartedly;
And follow not
The footsteps
Of the Evil One;

٢٠٨ يَٰٓأَيُّهَا ٱلَّذِينَ ءَامَنُوا۟
ٱدْخُلُوا۟ فِى ٱلسِّلْمِ كَآفَّةً
وَلَا تَتَّبِعُوا۟ خُطُوَٰتِ ٱلشَّيْطَٰنِ ۚ

227. The two contrasted types of men mentioned in 2:200 and 201 are here further particularised: the glib hypocrite who appears worldly-wise but plans harm, contrasted with the sincere believer who is prepared to suffer martyrdom for his faith. The Commentators give names of people who exemplified these types. The mischief-maker has a smooth tongue and indulges in plausible talk with many oaths. He appears to be worldly-wise, and though you may despise him for his worldliness, you may not realise his frauds. Behind your back he is an implacable enemy. He stirs up quarrels, and causes all sorts of mischief to you or your friends. He can never win Allah's love, and we are warned against his tricks.

228. According to the English saying, "As you have made your bed, so you must lie in it."

229. This second type of man—firm, sincere, devoted, willing to give his life for the faith that is in him—was common in early Islam. Such men were its pillars. Through persecution, obloquy, torture, threat to their own lives or the lives of those dear to them, they stood by their leader and many of them gave their lives. That is what established Islam. We are asked in the next verse to follow this type and shun the other or evil type. If we do that, our Cause is safe.

For he is to you
An avowed enemy.

إِنَّهُۥ لَكُمۡ عَدُوّٞ مُّبِينٞ

209. If ye backslide
After the clear (Signs)
Have come to you,
Then know that Allah
Is Exalted in Power, Wise.[230]

٢٠٩ فَإِن زَلَلۡتُم مِّنۢ بَعۡدِ
مَا جَآءَتۡكُمُ ٱلۡبَيِّنَٰتُ
فَٱعۡلَمُوٓاْ أَنَّ ٱللَّهَ عَزِيزٌ حَكِيمٌ

210. Will they wait
Until Allah comes to them
In canopies of clouds,
With angels (in His train)
And the question
Is (thus) settled?
But to Allah
Do all questions
Go back (for decision).[231]

٢١٠ هَلۡ يَنظُرُونَ إِلَّآ أَن
يَأۡتِيَهُمُ ٱللَّهُ فِي ظُلَلٖ مِّنَ ٱلۡغَمَامِ
وَٱلۡمَلَٰٓئِكَةُ وَقُضِيَ ٱلۡأَمۡرُۚ
وَإِلَى ٱللَّهِ تُرۡجَعُ ٱلۡأُمُورُ

SECTION 26

211. Ask the Children of Israel[232]
How many Clear (Signs)
We have sent them.
But if anyone,
After Allah's favour
Has come to him,
Substitutes (something else),
Allah is strict in punishment.[233]

٢١١ سَلۡ بَنِيٓ إِسۡرَٰٓءِيلَ كَمۡ
ءَاتَيۡنَٰهُم مِّنۡ ءَايَةِۢ بَيِّنَةٖۗ
وَمَن يُبَدِّلۡ نِعۡمَةَ ٱللَّهِ مِنۢ بَعۡدِ مَا جَآءَتۡهُ
فَإِنَّ ٱللَّهَ شَدِيدُ ٱلۡعِقَابِ

212. The life of this world
Is alluring to those
Who reject faith,
And they scoff at those
Who believe.

٢١٢ زُيِّنَ لِلَّذِينَ كَفَرُواْ ٱلۡحَيَوٰةُ ٱلدُّنۡيَا
وَيَسۡخَرُونَ مِنَ ٱلَّذِينَ ءَامَنُواْۘ

230. If you backslide after the conviction has been brought home to you, you may cause some inconvenience to the Cause, or to those who counted upon you, but do not be so arrogant as to suppose that you will defeat Allah's Power and Wisdom. The loss will be your own.

231. If faith is wanting, all sorts of excuses are made to resist the appeal of Allah. They might and do say: "Oh yes! we shall believe if Allah appears to us with His angels in His glory!" In other words they want to settle the question their way, and not in Allah's way. That will not do. The decision in all questions belongs to Allah. If we are true to Him, we wait for His times and seasons, and do not expect Him to wait on ours.

232. The Israelites under Moses were shown Allah's glory and many clear Signs and yet they went after their own ways, and preferred their own whims and fancies. So do people in all ages. But let them not decieve themselves. Allah's justice is sure, and when it comes, it will be strict and unmistakable to those who reject His grace.

233 *Cf.* 2:196 (end) where the question was of those who do not fear Allah. Here the question is of those who reject Allah's Signs.

But the righteous
Will be above them
On the Day of Resurrection;
For Allah bestows His
abundance
Without measure
On whom He will.[234]

وَالَّذِينَ اتَّقَوْا فَوْقَهُمْ
يَوْمَ الْقِيَامَةِ ۗ
وَاللَّهُ يَرْزُقُ مَن يَشَاءُ بِغَيْرِ حِسَابٍ

213. Mankind was one single nation,
And Allah sent Messengers
With glad tidings and
warnings;
And with them He sent
The Book in truth,
To judge between people
In matters wherein
They differed;
But the People of the Book,
After the clear Signs
Came to them, did not differ
Among themselves,
Except through selfish
contumacy.
Allah by His Grace
Guided the Believers
To the Truth,
Concerning that
Wherein they differed.
For Allah guides
Whom He will
To a path
That is straight.

٢١٣ كَانَ النَّاسُ أُمَّةً وَاحِدَةً فَبَعَثَ اللَّهُ
النَّبِيِّينَ مُبَشِّرِينَ وَمُنذِرِينَ
وَأَنزَلَ مَعَهُمُ الْكِتَابَ بِالْحَقِّ
لِيَحْكُمَ بَيْنَ النَّاسِ فِيمَا اخْتَلَفُوا فِيهِ ۚ
وَمَا اخْتَلَفَ فِيهِ إِلَّا الَّذِينَ أُوتُوهُ مِن بَعْدِ
مَا جَاءَتْهُمُ الْبَيِّنَاتُ بَغْيًا بَيْنَهُمْ ۖ
فَهَدَى اللَّهُ الَّذِينَ آمَنُوا
لِمَا اخْتَلَفُوا فِيهِ مِنَ الْحَقِّ بِإِذْنِهِ ۗ
وَاللَّهُ يَهْدِي مَن يَشَاءُ إِلَىٰ صِرَاطٍ مُّسْتَقِيمٍ

214. Or do ye think
That ye shall enter
The Garden (of Bliss)
Without such (trials)
As came to those
Who passed away
Before you?
They encountered
Suffering and adversity,
And were so shaken in spirit
That even the Messenger
And those of faith
Who were with him

٢١٤ أَمْ حَسِبْتُمْ أَن تَدْخُلُوا
الْجَنَّةَ وَلَمَّا يَأْتِكُم
مَّثَلُ الَّذِينَ خَلَوْا مِن قَبْلِكُم ۖ
مَّسَّتْهُمُ الْبَأْسَاءُ وَالضَّرَّاءُ وَزُلْزِلُوا
حَتَّىٰ يَقُولَ الرَّسُولُ
وَالَّذِينَ آمَنُوا مَعَهُ

234. Allah's gifts in this world seem unequal, and sometimes those who get them seem to deserve them least. Allah's bounty is unlimited to the just as well as the unjust. In His wisdom He may give to whomsoever He pleases. The account is not taken now, but will be taken in the end, when the balance will be redressed.

Cried: "When (will come)
The help of Allah"
Ah! Verily, the help of Allah
Is (always) near!

مَتَىٰ نَصْرُ ٱللَّهِ
أَلَآ إِنَّ نَصْرَ ٱللَّهِ قَرِيبٌ

215. They ask thee
What they should spend
(In charity). Say: Whatever
Ye spend that is good,[235]
Is for parents and kindred
And orphans
And those in want
And for wayfarers.
And whatever ye do
That is good—Allah
Knoweth it well.

(٢١٥) يَسْـَٔلُونَكَ مَاذَا يُنفِقُونَ
قُلْ مَآ أَنفَقْتُم مِّنْ خَيْرٍ فَلِلْوَٰلِدَيْنِ
وَٱلْأَقْرَبِينَ وَٱلْيَتَـٰمَىٰ وَٱلْمَسَـٰكِينِ وَٱبْنِ ٱلسَّبِيلِ
وَمَا تَفْعَلُوا۟ مِنْ خَيْرٍ
فَإِنَّ ٱللَّهَ بِهِۦ عَلِيمٌ

216. Fighting is prescribed
Upon you, and ye dislike it.[236]
But it is possible
That ye dislike a thing
Which is good for you,
And that ye love a thing
Which is bad for you.
But Allah knoweth,
And ye know not.

(٢١٦) كُتِبَ عَلَيْكُمُ ٱلْقِتَالُ وَهُوَ كُرْهٌ لَّكُمْ
وَعَسَىٰٓ أَن تَكْرَهُوا۟ شَيْـًٔا وَهُوَ خَيْرٌ لَّكُمْ
وَعَسَىٰٓ أَن تُحِبُّوا۟ شَيْـًٔا وَهُوَ شَرٌّ لَّكُمْ
وَٱللَّهُ يَعْلَمُ وَأَنتُمْ لَا تَعْلَمُونَ

SECTION 27.

217. They ask thee
Concerning fighting
In the Prohibited Month.[237]
Say: "Fighting therein
Is a grave (offence);

(٢١٧) يَسْـَٔلُونَكَ
عَنِ ٱلشَّهْرِ ٱلْحَرَامِ قِتَالٍ فِيهِ
قُلْ قِتَالٌ فِيهِ كَبِيرٌ

235. Three questions arise in charity: (1) What shall we give? (2) to whom shall we give? and (3) how shall we give? The answer is here. Give anything that is good, useful, helpful, valuable. It may be property or money; it may be a helping hand; it may be advice; it may be a kind word; "whatever ye do that is good" is charity. On the other hand, if you throw away what is useless, there is no charity in it. Or if you give something with a harmful intent, *e.g.*, a sword to a madman, or a drug or sweets or even money to someone whom you want to entrap or corrupt, it is no charity but a gift of damnation. To whom should you give? It may be tempting to earn the world's praise by a gift that will be talked about, but are you meeting the needs of those who have the first claim on you? If you are not, you are like a person who defrauds creditors: it is no charity. Every gift is judged by its unselfish character: the degree of need or claim is a factor which you should consider; if you disregard it, there is something selfish behind it. How should it be given? As in the sight of Allah; this shuts out all pretence, show, and insincerity.

236. To fight in the cause of Truth is one of the highest forms of charity. What can you offer that is more precious than your own life? But here again the limitations come in. If you are a mere brawler, or a selfish aggressive person, or a vainglorious bully, you deserve the highest censure. Allah knows the value of things better than you do. (R).

237. *Prohibited Month*: See 2:194, n. 209.

But graver is it
In the sight of Allah
To prevent access
To the path of Allah,
To deny Him,
To prevent access
To the Sacred Mosque,
And drive out its members."[238]
Tumult and oppression[239]
Are worse than slaughter.
Nor will they cease
Fighting you until
They turn you back
From your faith
If they can.
And if any of you
Turn back from their faith
And die in unbelief,
Their works will bear no fruit
In this life
And in the Hereafter;
They will be
Companions of the Fire
And will abide therein.

وَصَدٌّ عَن سَبِيلِ ٱللَّهِ
وَكُفْرٌۢ بِهِۦ
وَٱلْمَسْجِدِ ٱلْحَرَامِ
وَإِخْرَاجُ أَهْلِهِۦ مِنْهُ أَكْبَرُ عِندَ ٱللَّهِ ۚ
وَٱلْفِتْنَةُ أَكْبَرُ مِنَ ٱلْقَتْلِ ۗ
وَلَا يَزَالُونَ يُقَٰتِلُونَكُمْ حَتَّىٰ يَرُدُّوكُمْ
عَن دِينِكُمْ إِنِ ٱسْتَطَٰعُوا۟ ۚ
وَمَن يَرْتَدِدْ مِنكُمْ عَن دِينِهِۦ
فَيَمُتْ وَهُوَ كَافِرٌ فَأُو۟لَٰٓئِكَ حَبِطَتْ
أَعْمَٰلُهُمْ فِى ٱلدُّنْيَا وَٱلْءَاخِرَةِ ۖ
وَأُو۟لَٰٓئِكَ أَصْحَٰبُ ٱلنَّارِ ۖ
هُمْ فِيهَا خَٰلِدُونَ

218. Those who believed
And those who suffered exile
And fought (and strove and
struggled)
In the path of Allah—
They have the hope
Of the Mercy of Allah:
And Allah is Oft-Forgiving,
Most Merciful.

٢١٨ إِنَّ ٱلَّذِينَ ءَامَنُوا۟
وَٱلَّذِينَ هَاجَرُوا۟ وَجَٰهَدُوا۟
فِى سَبِيلِ ٱللَّهِ أُو۟لَٰٓئِكَ
يَرْجُونَ رَحْمَتَ ٱللَّهِ ۚ
وَٱللَّهُ غَفُورٌ رَّحِيمٌ

219. They ask thee

٢١٩ يَسْـَٔلُونَكَ

238. The intolerance and persecution of the Pagan clique at Makkah caused untold hardships to the Holy Messenger of Islam and his early disciples. They bore all with meekness and long-suffering patience until the Holy One permitted them to take up arms in self-defence. Then they were twitted with breach of the custom about Prohibited Months, though they were driven to fight during that period against their own feeling in self defence. But their enemies not only forced them to engage in actual warfare, but interfered with their conscience, persecuted them and their families, openly insulted and denied Allah, kept out the Muslims from the Sacred Mosque, and exiled them. Such violence and intolerance are deservedly called worse than slaughter.

239. *Cf.* 2:191, 193, where a similar phrase occurs. *Fitnah* = trial, temptation, as in 2:102; or tumult, sedition, oppression, as here; M.M.A., H.G.S., and M.P. translate "persecution" in this passage, which is also legitimate, seeing that persecution is the suppression of some opinion by violence, force, or threats.

Concerning wine[240] and
gambling.[241]
Say: "In them is great sin,
And some profit, for men;
But the sin is greater
Than the profit."
They ask thee how much
They are to spend;
Say: "What is beyond[242]
Your needs."
Thus doth Allah
Make clear to you
His Signs: in order that
Ye may consider—

عَنِ ٱلْخَمْرِ وَٱلْمَيْسِرِ
قُلْ فِيهِمَآ إِثْمٌ كَبِيرٌ وَمَنَٰفِعُ لِلنَّاسِ
وَإِثْمُهُمَآ أَكْبَرُ مِن نَّفْعِهِمَا
وَيَسْـَٔلُونَكَ مَاذَا يُنفِقُونَ قُلِ ٱلْعَفْوَ
كَذَٰلِكَ يُبَيِّنُ ٱللَّهُ لَكُمُ ٱلْـَٔايَٰتِ
لَعَلَّكُمْ تَتَفَكَّرُونَ

220. (Their bearings) on
This life and the Hereafter.[243]
They ask thee
Concerning orphans.[244]
Say: "The best thing to do
Is what is for their good;
If ye mix
Their affairs with yours,
They are your brethren;

٢٢٠ فِى ٱلدُّنْيَا وَٱلْـَٔاخِرَةِ
وَيَسْـَٔلُونَكَ عَنِ ٱلْيَتَٰمَىٰ
قُلْ إِصْلَاحٌ لَّهُمْ خَيْرٌ
وَإِن تُخَالِطُوهُمْ فَإِخْوَٰنُكُمْ

240. *Wine: Khamr*: literally understood to mean the fermented juice of the grape; applied by analogy to all fermented liquor, and by further analogy to any intoxicating liquor or drug. There may possibly be some benefit in it, but the harm is greater than the benefit, especially if we look at it from a social as well as an individual point of view.

241. *Gambling: maysir*: literally, a means of getting something too easily, getting a profit without working for it; hence gambling. That is the principle on which gambling is prohibited. The form most familiar to the Arabs was gambling by casting losts by means of arrows, on the principle of a lottery: the arrows were marked and served the same purpose as a modern lottery ticket. Something, *e.g.*, the carcass of a slaughtered animal, was divided into unequal parts. The marked arrows were drawn from a bag. Some were blank and those who drew them got nothing. Others indicated prizes, which were big or small. Whether you got a big share or a small share, or nothing, depended on pure luck, unless there was fraud also on the part of some persons concerned. The principle on which the objection is based is: that, even if there is no fraud, you gain what you have not earned, or lose on a mere chance. Dice and wagering are rightly held to be within the definition of gambling. (R).

242. Hoarding is no use either to ourselves, or to any one else. We should use the wealth we need; any superfluities we must spend in good works or in charity.

243. Gambling and intemperance are social as well as individual sins. They may ruin us in our ordinary everyday worldly life, as well as our spiritual future. In case it is suggested that there is no harm in a little indulgence, we are asked to think over all its aspects, social and individual—worldly and spiritual.

244. For Orphans the best rule is to keep their property, household, and accounts separate, lest there should be any temptation to get a personal advantage to their guardian by mixing them with the guardian's property, household or accounts—also to keep clear of any ideas of marriage, where this fiduciary relation exists. Q. 6:152 may possibly suggest complete separation. But it may be an economy and an advantage to the orphan to have his property and accounts administered with the guardian's property and accounts and to have him live in the guardian's household, or to marry into the guardian's family, especially where the orphan's property is small and he or she has no other friend. The test is: what is best in the orphan's interests? If the guardian does fall into temptation, even if human law does not detect him, he is told he is sinning in Allah's sight and that should keep him straight.

But Allah knows
The man who means mischief
From the man who means good.
And if Allah had wished,
He could have put you
Into difficulties: he is indeed
Exalted in Power, Wise."[245]

وَاللَّهُ يَعْلَمُ الْمُفْسِدَ مِنَ الْمُصْلِحِ
وَلَوْ شَاءَ اللَّهُ لَأَعْنَتَكُمْ
إِنَّ اللَّهَ عَزِيزٌ حَكِيمٌ

221. Do not marry
Unbelieving[245-A] women
Until they believe:
A slave woman who believes
Is better than an unbelieving[245-A] woman.
Even though she allure you.
Nor marry (your girls)
To unbelievers until
They believe:
A man slave who believes
Is better than an unbeliever[245-A]
Even though he allure you.[246]
Unbelievers do (but)
Beckon you to the Fire.
But Allah beckons by His Grace
To the Garden (of Bliss)
And forgiveness,
And makes His Signs
Clear to mankind:
That they may
Receive admonition.

(٢٢١) وَلَا تَنكِحُوا الْمُشْرِكَاتِ
حَتَّىٰ يُؤْمِنَّ وَلَأَمَةٌ مُّؤْمِنَةٌ
خَيْرٌ مِّن مُّشْرِكَةٍ وَلَوْ أَعْجَبَتْكُمْ
وَلَا تُنكِحُوا الْمُشْرِكِينَ حَتَّىٰ يُؤْمِنُوا
وَلَعَبْدٌ مُّؤْمِنٌ خَيْرٌ مِّن
مُّشْرِكٍ وَلَوْ أَعْجَبَكُمْ
أُولَٰئِكَ يَدْعُونَ إِلَى النَّارِ وَاللَّهُ يَدْعُو
إِلَى الْجَنَّةِ وَالْمَغْفِرَةِ بِإِذْنِهِ
وَيُبَيِّنُ آيَاتِهِ لِلنَّاسِ
لَعَلَّهُمْ يَتَذَكَّرُونَ

SECTION 28

222. They ask thee
Concerning women's courses.

(٢٢٢) وَيَسْأَلُونَكَ عَنِ الْمَحِيضِ

---

245. The idea in Islam is not to make Allah's Law a burdensome fetter, but to ease a man's path in all kinds of difficult situations by putting him on his honour and trusting him. The strictest probity is demanded of him, but if he falls short of it, he is told that he cannot escape Allah's punishment even though he may evade human punishment.

245-A. Literally "pagan".

246. Marriage is a most intimate communion, and the mystery of sex finds its highest fulfilment when intimate spiritual harmony is combined with the physical link. If religion is at all a real influence in life to both parties or to either party, a difference in this vital matter must affect the lives of both more profoundly than differences of birth, race, language, or position in life. It is therefore only right that the parties to be married should have the same spiritual outlook. If two persons love each other, their outlook in the highest things of life must be the same. Note that religion is not here a mere label or a matter of custom or birth. The two persons may have been born in different religions, but if, by their mutual influence, they come to see the truth in the same way, they must openly accept the same rites and the same social brotherhood. Otherwise the position will become impossible individually and socially.

Say: They are A hurt and a pollution:[247] So keep away from women In their courses, and do not Approach them until They are clean. But when they have Purified themselves, Ye may approach them In any manner, time, or place[248] Ordained for you by Allah. For Allah loves those Who turn to Him constantly And He loves those Who keep themselves pure and clean.	قُلْ هُوَ أَذًى فَاعْتَزِلُوا النِّسَاءَ فِي الْمَحِيضِ وَلَا تَقْرَبُوهُنَّ حَتَّىٰ يَطْهُرْنَ فَإِذَا تَطَهَّرْنَ فَأْتُوهُنَّ مِنْ حَيْثُ أَمَرَكُمُ اللَّهُ إِنَّ اللَّهَ يُحِبُّ التَّوَّابِينَ وَيُحِبُّ الْمُتَطَهِّرِينَ
223. Your wives are As a tilth[249] unto you So approach your tilth When or how you will; But do some good act For your souls beforehand; And fear Allah, And know that ye are To meet Him (in the Hereafter), And give (these) good tidings[250] To those who believe.	﴿٢٢٣﴾ نِسَاؤُكُمْ حَرْثٌ لَكُمْ فَأْتُوا حَرْثَكُمْ أَنَّىٰ شِئْتُمْ وَقَدِّمُوا لِأَنْفُسِكُمْ وَاتَّقُوا اللَّهَ وَاعْلَمُوا أَنَّكُمْ مُلَاقُوهُ وَبَشِّرِ الْمُؤْمِنِينَ

247. *Adhān*: hurt, pollution. Both aspects must be remembered. Physical cleanliness and purity make for health, bodily and spiritual. But the matter should be looked at from the woman's point of view as well as the man's. To her there is danger of hurt, and she should have every consideration. In the animal world, instinct is a guide which is obeyed. Man should in this respect be better: he is often worse.

248. *Ḥaythu*: A comprehensive word referring to manner, time, or place. The most delicate matters are here referred to in the most discreet and yet helpful terms. In sex morality, manner, time, and place are all important: and the highest standards are set by social laws, by our own refined instinct of mutual consideration, and above all, by the light shed by the highest Teachers from the wisdom which they receive from our Maker, Who loves purity and cleanliness in all things.

249. Sex is not a thing to be ashamed of, or to be treated lightly, or to be indulged to excess. It is as solemn a fact as any in life. It is compared to a husbandman's tilth; it is a serious affair to him; he sows the seed in order to reap the harvest. But he chooses his own time and mode of cultivation. He does not sow out of season nor cultivate in a manner which will injure or exhaust the soil. He is wise and considerate and does not run riot. Coming from the simile to human beings, every kind of mutual consideration is required, but above all, we must remember that even in these matters there is a spiritual aspect. We must never forget our souls, and that we are responsible to Allah.

It was carnal-minded men who invented the doctrine of original sin: "Behold," says the Psalmist, "I was shapen in iniquity, and in sin did my mother conceive me" (Psalms li. 5). This is entirely repudiated by Islam, in which the office of father and mother is held in the highest veneration. Every child of pure love is born pure. Celibacy is not necessarily a virtue, and may be a vice.

250. Our highest spiritual ambition should be the hope of meeting Allah. To uphold such a hope is to give glad tidings to people of faith. It would only be unrepentant sinners who would fear the meeting. Note how the most sensuous matters are discussed frankly, and immediately taken up into the loftiest regions of spiritual upliftment.

224. And make not
Allah's (name) an excuse
In your oaths against
Doing good, or acting rightly,
Or making peace
Between persons;
For Allah is One
Who hearest and knoweth[251]
All things.

٢٢٤ وَلَا تَجْعَلُوا۟ ٱللَّهَ عُرْضَةً
لِّأَيْمَٰنِكُمْ أَن تَبَرُّوا۟ وَتَتَّقُوا۟
وَتُصْلِحُوا۟ بَيْنَ ٱلنَّاسِ ۗ
وَٱللَّهُ سَمِيعٌ عَلِيمٌ

225. Allah will not
Call you to account
For thoughtlessness
In your oaths,
But for the intention
In your hearts,[252]
And He is
Oft-Forgiving,
Most Forbearing.

٢٢٥ لَّا يُؤَاخِذُكُمُ ٱللَّهُ
بِٱللَّغْوِ فِىٓ أَيْمَٰنِكُمْ وَلَٰكِن
يُؤَاخِذُكُم بِمَا كَسَبَتْ قُلُوبُكُمْ ۗ
وَٱللَّهُ غَفُورٌ حَلِيمٌ

226. For those who take
An oath for abstention
From their wives,
A waiting for four months
Is ordained;
If then they return,
Allah is Oft-Forgiving,
Most Merciful.

٢٢٦ لِّلَّذِينَ يُؤْلُونَ مِن نِّسَآئِهِمْ
تَرَبُّصُ أَرْبَعَةِ أَشْهُرٍ ۖ فَإِن فَآءُو
فَإِنَّ ٱللَّهَ غَفُورٌ رَّحِيمٌ

227. But if their intention
Is firm for divorce,
Allah heareth
And knoweth all things.[253]

٢٢٧ وَإِنْ عَزَمُوا۟ ٱلطَّلَٰقَ
فَإِنَّ ٱللَّهَ سَمِيعٌ عَلِيمٌ

251. The Arabs had many special kinds of oaths, for each of which they had a special name in their language. Some of them related to sex matters, and caused misunderstanding, alienation, division, or separation between husband and wife. This and the following three verses refer to them all. In 2:224 we are first of all told in perfectly general terms that we are not to make an oath in the name of Allah as excuse for not doing the right thing when it is pointed out to us, or for refraining from doing something which will bring people together. If we were swayed by anger or passion or mere caprice, Allah knows our inmost hearts, and right conduct and not obstinacy or quibbling is what He demands from us.

252. It has been held that thoughtless oaths, if there is no intention behind them, can be expiated by an act of charity.

253. Verses 225-227 should be read together with verse 224. The latter, though it is perfectly general, leads up to the other three.

The Pagan Arabs had a custom very unfair to women in wedlock, and this was suppressed by Islam. Sometimes, in a fit of anger or caprice, a husband would take an oath by Allah not to approach his wife. This deprived her of conjugal rights, but at the same time kept her tied to him indefinitely, so that she could not marry again. If the husband was remonstrated with, he would say that his oath by Allah bound him. Islam in the first place disapproved of thoughtless oaths, but insisted on proper solemn intentional oaths being scrupulously observed. In a serious matter like that affecting a wife, if the oath was put forward as an excuse, the man is told that is not excuse at all. Allah looks to intention, not mere thoughtless words. The parties are allowed a period of four months to make up their minds and see if an adjustment is possible. Reconciliation is recommended, but if they are really determined against reconciliation, it is unfair to keep them tied indefinitely. (R).

228. Divorced women
Shall wait concerning themselves
For three monthly periods.
Nor is it lawful for them
To hide what Allah
Hath created in their wombs,
If they have faith
In Allah and the Last Day.
And their husbands
Have the better right
To take them back
In that period, if
They wish for reconciliation.[254]
And women shall have rights
Similar to the rights
Against them, according
To what is equitable;
But men have a degree
(Of advantage) over them.[255]
And Allah is Exalted in Power,
Wise.

٢٢٨ وَٱلْمُطَلَّقَٰتُ
يَتَرَبَّصْنَ بِأَنفُسِهِنَّ ثَلَٰثَةَ قُرُوٓءٍ
وَلَا يَحِلُّ لَهُنَّ أَن يَكْتُمْنَ مَا خَلَقَ ٱللَّهُ فِىٓ
أَرْحَامِهِنَّ إِن كُنَّ يُؤْمِنَّ بِٱللَّهِ وَٱلْيَوْمِ ٱلْءَاخِرِ
وَبُعُولَتُهُنَّ أَحَقُّ بِرَدِّهِنَّ فِى ذَٰلِكَ
إِنْ أَرَادُوٓا۟ إِصْلَٰحًا
وَلَهُنَّ مِثْلُ ٱلَّذِى عَلَيْهِنَّ بِٱلْمَعْرُوفِ
وَلِلرِّجَالِ عَلَيْهِنَّ دَرَجَةٌ
وَٱللَّهُ عَزِيزٌ حَكِيمٌ

SECTION 29

229. A divorce is only[256]
Permissible twice: after that,
The parties should either hold
Together on equitable terms,
Or separate with kindness.[257]

٢٢٩ ٱلطَّلَٰقُ مَرَّتَانِ
فَإِمْسَاكٌۢ بِمَعْرُوفٍ أَوْ تَسْرِيحٌۢ بِإِحْسَٰنٍ

254. Islam tries to maintain the married state as far as possible, especially where children are concerned, but it is against the restriction of the liberty of men and women in such vitally important matters as love and family life. It will check hasty action as far as possible, and leave the door to reconciliation open at many stages. Even after divorce a suggestion of reconciliation is made, subject to certain precautions (mentioned in the following verses) against thoughtless action. A period of waiting (*'iddah*) for three monthly courses is prescribed, in order to see if the marriage conditionally dissolved is likely to result in issue. But this is not necessary where the divorced woman is a virgin: Q. 33:49. Is it definitely declared that men and women shall have similar rights against each other.

255. The difference in economic position between the sexes makes the man's rights and liabilities a little greater than the woman's. Q. 4:34 refers to the duty of the man to maintain the woman, and to a certain difference in nature between the sexes. Subject to this, the sexes are on terms of equality in law, and in certain matters the weaker sex is entitled to special protection.

256. Where divorce for mutual incompatibility is allowed, there is danger that the parties might act hastily, then repent, and again wish to separate. To prevent such capricious action repeatedly, a limit is prescribed. Two divorces (with a reconciliation between) are allowed. After that the parties must definitely make up their minds, either to dissolve the union permanently, or to live honourable lives together in mutual love and forebearance—to "hold together on equitable terms," neither party worrying the other nor grumbling nor evading the duties and responsibilities of marriage.

257. If a separation is inevitable, the parties should not throw mud at each other, but recognise what is right and honourable on a consideration of all the circumstances. In any case a man is not allowed to ask back for any gifts or property he may have given to the wife. This is for the protection of the economically weaker sex. Lest that protective provision itself work against the woman's freedom, an exception is made in the next clause.

It is not lawful for you,
(Men), to take back
Any of your gifts (from your wives),
Except when both parties
Fear that they would be
Unable to keep the limits
Ordained by Allah.[258]
If ye (judges) do indeed
Fear that they would be
Unable to keep the limits
Ordained by Allah,
There is not blame on either
Of them if she give
Something for her freedom.
These are the limits
Ordained by Allah;
So do not transgress them
If any do transgress
The limits ordained by Allah,
Such persons wrong
(Themselves as well as others).[259]

وَلَا يَحِلُّ لَكُمْ أَن تَأْخُذُوا
مِمَّآ ءَاتَيْتُمُوهُنَّ شَيْـًٔا
إِلَّآ أَن يَخَافَآ
أَلَّا يُقِيمَا حُدُودَ ٱللَّهِ
فَإِنْ خِفْتُمْ أَلَّا يُقِيمَا حُدُودَ ٱللَّهِ
فَلَا جُنَاحَ عَلَيْهِمَا فِيمَا ٱفْتَدَتْ بِهِۦ
تِلْكَ حُدُودُ ٱللَّهِ فَلَا تَعْتَدُوهَا
وَمَن يَتَعَدَّ حُدُودَ ٱللَّهِ
فَأُولَٰٓئِكَ هُمُ ٱلظَّٰلِمُونَ

230. So if a husband
Divorces his wife
(irrevocably),[260]
He cannot, after that,
Remarry her until
After she has married
Another husband and
He has divorced her.
In that case there is
No blame on either of them
If they reunite, provided
They feel that they
Can keep the limits
Ordained by Allah.
Such are the limits

٢٣٠ فَإِن طَلَّقَهَا
فَلَا تَحِلُّ لَهُۥ مِنۢ بَعْدُ
حَتَّىٰ تَنكِحَ زَوْجًا غَيْرَهُۥ
فَإِن طَلَّقَهَا فَلَا جُنَاحَ عَلَيْهِمَآ
أَن يَتَرَاجَعَآ إِن ظَنَّآ أَن
يُقِيمَا حُدُودَ ٱللَّهِ
وَتِلْكَ حُدُودُ

258. All other prohibitions and limits prescribed here are in the interests of good and honourable lives for both sides, and in the interests of a clean and honourable social life, without public or private scandals. If there is any fear that in safeguarding her economic rights, her very freedom of person may suffer, the husband refusing the dissolution of marriage, and perhaps treating her with cruelty, then, in such exceptional cases, it is permissible to give some material consideration to the husband, but the need and equity of this should be submitted to the judgement of impartial judges, *i.e.*, properly constituted courts. A divorce of this kind is called *khula'*.

259. *Wrong (themselves as well as others): Zālimūn*: for the root meaning of *ẓulm* see n. 51. 2:35.

260. This is in continuation of the first sentence of 2:229. Two divorces followed by reunion are permissible; the third time the divorce becomes irrevocable, until the woman marries some other man and he divorces her. This is to set an almost impossible condition. The lesson is: if a man loves a woman he should not allow a sudden gust of temper or anger to induce him to take hasty action. What happens after two divorces, if the man takes her back? See n. 261 to 2:231.

Ordained by Allah,
Which He makes plain
To those who understand.

231. When ye divorce[261]
Women, and they fulfil
The term of their (*'Iddah*),
Either take them back
On equitable terms
Or set them free
On equitable terms;
But do not take them back
To injure them, (or) to take
Undue advantage;[262]
If any one does that,
He wrongs his own soul.
Do not treat Allah's Signs
As a jest,[263]
But solemnly rehearse[264]
Allah's favours on you,
And the fact that He
Sent down to you
The Book
And Wisdom,
For your instruction.
And fear Allah,
And know that Allah
Is well-acquainted
With all things.

SECTION 30.

232. When ye divorce
Women, and they fulfil
The term of their (*'Iddah*),

اللَّهِ يُبَيِّنُهَا لِقَوْمٍ يَعْلَمُونَ

٢٣١ وَإِذَا طَلَّقْتُمُ النِّسَاءَ
فَبَلَغْنَ أَجَلَهُنَّ فَأَمْسِكُوهُنَّ بِمَعْرُوفٍ
أَوْ سَرِّحُوهُنَّ بِمَعْرُوفٍ
وَلَا تُمْسِكُوهُنَّ ضِرَارًا لِتَعْتَدُوا
وَمَن يَفْعَلْ ذَٰلِكَ فَقَدْ ظَلَمَ نَفْسَهُ
وَلَا تَتَّخِذُوا آيَاتِ اللَّهِ هُزُوًا
وَاذْكُرُوا نِعْمَتَ اللَّهِ عَلَيْكُمْ
وَمَا أَنزَلَ عَلَيْكُم مِّنَ الْكِتَابِ
وَالْحِكْمَةِ يَعِظُكُم بِهِ وَاتَّقُوا اللَّهَ
وَاعْلَمُوا أَنَّ اللَّهَ بِكُلِّ شَيْءٍ عَلِيمٌ

٢٣٢ وَإِذَا طَلَّقْتُمُ النِّسَاءَ فَبَلَغْنَ أَجَلَهُنَّ

261. If the man takes back his wife after two divorces, he must do so only on equitable terms, *i.e.*, he must not put pressure on the woman to prejudice her rights in any way, and they must live clean and honourable lives, respecting each other's personalities. There are here two conditional clauses: (1) 'when ye divorce women,' and (2) 'when they fulfil their *'Iddah:'* followed by two consequential clauses, (3) 'take them back on equitable terms,' or (4) 'set them free with kindness.' The first is connected with the third and the second with the fourth. Therefore if the husband wishes to resume marital relations, he need not wait for *'Iddah*. But if he does not so wish, she is free to marry someone else after *'Iddah*. For the meaning of *'Iddah* see n. 254 above.

262. Let no one think that the liberty given to him can be used for his own selfish ends. If he uses the law for the injury of the weaker party, his own moral and spiritual nature suffers.

263. These difficult questions of sex relations are often treated as a joke. But they profoundly affect our individual lives, the lives of our children, and the purity and well-being of the society in which we live. This aspect of the question is reiterated again and again.

264. *Rehearse: dhikr. Cf.* 2:151 and n. 156. We are asked to remember in our own minds, and to proclaim and praise, and be proud of Allah's favours on us. His favours are immeasurable: not the least are His Revelations, and the wisdom which He has given to us to enable us to judge and act up to His guidance.

Do not prevent them[265]
From marrying
Their (former) husbands,
If they mutually agree
On equitable terms.
This instruction
Is for all amongst you,
Who believe in Allah
And the Last Day.
That is (the course
Making for) most virtue
And purity amongst you.
And Allah knows,
And ye know not.

233. The mothers shall give suck[266]
To their offspring
For two whole years,
If the father desires
To complete the term.
But he shall bear the cost
Of their food and clothing[266-A]
On equitable terms.
No soul shall have
A burden laid on it
Greater than it can bear.
No mother shall be
Treated unfairly
On account of her child.
Nor father
On account of his child,
An heir shall be chargeable
In the same way,

فَلَا تَعْضُلُوهُنَّ
أَن يَنكِحْنَ أَزْوَٰجَهُنَّ
إِذَا تَرَٰضَوْا بَيْنَهُم بِٱلْمَعْرُوفِ ۗ
ذَٰلِكَ يُوعَظُ بِهِۦ مَن كَانَ مِنكُمْ يُؤْمِنُ بِٱللَّهِ
وَٱلْيَوْمِ ٱلْءَاخِرِ ۗ ذَٰلِكُمْ أَزْكَىٰ لَكُمْ وَأَطْهَرُ ۗ
وَٱللَّهُ يَعْلَمُ وَأَنتُمْ لَا تَعْلَمُونَ

٢٣٣ وَٱلْوَٰلِدَٰتُ يُرْضِعْنَ
أَوْلَٰدَهُنَّ حَوْلَيْنِ كَامِلَيْنِ ۖ
لِمَنْ أَرَادَ أَن يُتِمَّ ٱلرَّضَاعَةَ ۚ
وَعَلَى ٱلْمَوْلُودِ لَهُۥ رِزْقُهُنَّ وَكِسْوَتُهُنَّ بِٱلْمَعْرُوفِ ۚ
لَا تُكَلَّفُ نَفْسٌ إِلَّا وُسْعَهَا ۚ
لَا تُضَآرَّ وَٰلِدَةٌۢ بِوَلَدِهَا
وَلَا مَوْلُودٌ لَّهُۥ بِوَلَدِهِۦ ۚ
وَعَلَى ٱلْوَارِثِ مِثْلُ ذَٰلِكَ ۗ

265. The termination of a marriage bond is a most serious matter for family and social life. And every lawful device is approved which can equitably bring back those who have lived together, provided only there is mutual love and they can live on honourable terms with each other. If these conditions are fulfilled, it is not right for outsiders to prevent or hinder reunion. They may be swayed by property or other considerations. This verse was occasioned by an actual case that was referred to the Holy Prophet in his lifetime.

266. As this comes in the midst of regulations on divorce, it applies primarily to cases of divorce, where some definite rule is necessary, as the father and mother would not, on account of the divorce, probably be on good terms, and the interests of the children must be safeguarded. As, however, the wording is perfectly general, it has been held that the principle applies equally to the father and mother in wedlock: each must fulfil his or her part in the fostering of the child. On the other hand, it is provided that the child shall not be used as an excuse for driving a hard bargain on either side. By mutual consent they can agree to some course that is reasonable and equitable, both as regards the period before weaning (the maximum being two years) and the engagement of a wet-nurse, or (by analogy) for artificial feeding. But the mother's privileges must not be curtailed simply because by mutual consent she does not nurse the baby. In a matter of this kind the ultimate appeal must be to godliness, for all legal remedies are imperfect and may be misused.

266-A. *I.e.*, in the case of divorce. [Eds.].

If they both decide
On weaning,
By mutual consent,
And after due consultation,
There is no blame on them.
If ye decide
On a foster-mother
For your offspring
There is no blame on you,
Provided ye pay (the mother)
What ye offered,
On equitable terms.
But fear Allah and know
That Allah sees well
What ye do.

فَإِنْ أَرَادَا فِصَالًا عَن تَرَاضٍ مِّنْهُمَا
وَتَشَاوُرٍ فَلَا جُنَاحَ عَلَيْهِمَا
وَإِنْ أَرَدتُّمْ أَن تَسْتَرْضِعُوٓا أَوْلَادَكُمْ
فَلَا جُنَاحَ عَلَيْكُمْ إِذَا سَلَّمْتُم مَّآ ءَاتَيْتُم بِالْمَعْرُوفِ
وَاتَّقُوا اللَّهَ وَاعْلَمُوٓا
أَنَّ اللَّهَ بِمَا تَعْمَلُونَ بَصِيرٌ

234. If any of you die
And leave widows behind,
They shall wait concerning themselves
Four months and ten days:[267]
When they have fulfilled
Their term, there is no blame
On you if they dispose
Of themselves in a just
And reasonable manner.
And Allah is well acquainted
With what ye do.

٢٣٤ وَالَّذِينَ يُتَوَفَّوْنَ مِنكُمْ
وَيَذَرُونَ أَزْوَاجًا يَتَرَبَّصْنَ بِأَنفُسِهِنَّ
أَرْبَعَةَ أَشْهُرٍ وَعَشْرًا فَإِذَا بَلَغْنَ أَجَلَهُنَّ
فَلَا جُنَاحَ عَلَيْكُمْ فِيمَا فَعَلْنَ فِىٓ أَنفُسِهِنَّ
بِالْمَعْرُوفِ وَاللَّهُ بِمَا تَعْمَلُونَ خَبِيرٌ

235. There is no blame
On you if you make
An offer of betrothal
Or hold it in your hearts.[268]
Allah knows that ye
Cherish them in your hearts:
But do not make a secret contract
With them except

٢٣٥ وَلَا جُنَاحَ عَلَيْكُمْ فِيمَا عَرَّضْتُم بِهِۦ
مِنْ خِطْبَةِ النِّسَآءِ أَوْ أَكْنَنتُمْ فِىٓ أَنفُسِكُمْ
عَلِمَ اللَّهُ أَنَّكُمْ سَتَذْكُرُونَهُنَّ
وَلَٰكِن لَّا تُوَاعِدُوهُنَّ سِرًّا

267. The *'Iddah* of widowhood (four months and ten days) is longer than the *'Iddah* of divorce (three monthly courses. 2:228). In the latter the only consideration is to ascertain if there is any unborn issue of the marriage dissolved. This is clear from 33:49, where it is laid down that there is no *'Iddah* for virgin divorcees. In the former there is in addition the consideration of mourning and respect for the deceased husband. In either case, if it is proved that there is unborn issue, there is of course no question of remarriage for the woman until it is born and for a reasonable time afterwards. Meanwhile her maintenance on a reasonable scale is chargeable to the late husband or his estate.

268. A definite contract of remarriage for the woman during her period of *'Iddah* of widowhood is forbidden as obviously unseemly, as also any secrecy in such matters. It would bind the woman at a time when she is not fitted to exercise her fullest judgement. But circumstances may arise when an *offer* (open for future consideration but not immediately decided) may be to her interests, and this is permissible. (R).

That you speak to them
In terms honourable, nor resolve
on the tie
Of marriage till the term
Prescribed is fulfilled.
And know that Allah
Knoweth what is in your hearts,
And take heed of Him;
And know that Allah is
Oft-Forgiving, Most Forbearing.

SECTION 31.

236. There is no blame on you
If ye divorce women
Before consummation
Or the fixation of their dower;
But bestow on them
(A suitable gift),
The wealthy
According to his means,
And the poor
According to his means—
A gift of reasonable amount
Is due from those
Who wish to do the right thing.

237. And if ye divorce them
Before consummation,
But after the fixation
Of a dower for them,
Then the half of the dower
(Is due to them), unless
They remit it
Or (the man's half) is remitted[269]
By him in whose hands
Is the marriage tie;[270]
And the remission
(Of the man's half)
Is the nearest to righteousness
And do not forget

إِلَّآ أَن تَقُولُواْ قَوْلًا مَّعْرُوفًاۚ وَلَا تَعْزِمُواْ
عُقْدَةَ ٱلنِّكَاحِ حَتَّىٰ يَبْلُغَ ٱلْكِتَٰبُ أَجَلَهُۥۚ
وَٱعْلَمُوٓاْ أَنَّ ٱللَّهَ يَعْلَمُ مَا فِىٓ أَنفُسِكُمْ
فَٱحْذَرُوهُۚ وَٱعْلَمُوٓاْ أَنَّ ٱللَّهَ غَفُورٌ حَلِيمٌ

٢٣٦ لَّا جُنَاحَ عَلَيْكُمْ
إِن طَلَّقْتُمُ ٱلنِّسَآءَ مَا لَمْ تَمَسُّوهُنَّ
أَوْ تَفْرِضُواْ لَهُنَّ فَرِيضَةًۚ
وَمَتِّعُوهُنَّ عَلَى ٱلْمُوسِعِ قَدَرُهُۥ
وَعَلَى ٱلْمُقْتِرِ قَدَرُهُۥ مَتَٰعًۢا بِٱلْمَعْرُوفِۖ
حَقًّا عَلَى ٱلْمُحْسِنِينَ

٢٣٧ وَإِن طَلَّقْتُمُوهُنَّ
مِن قَبْلِ أَن تَمَسُّوهُنَّ وَقَدْ فَرَضْتُمْ
لَهُنَّ فَرِيضَةً فَنِصْفُ مَا فَرَضْتُمْ
إِلَّآ أَن يَعْفُونَ أَوْ يَعْفُوَاْ ٱلَّذِى بِيَدِهِۦ
عُقْدَةُ ٱلنِّكَاحِۚ وَأَن تَعْفُوٓاْ أَقْرَبُ لِلتَّقْوَىٰۚ
وَلَا تَنسَوُاْ

269. The law declares that in such a case half the dower fixed shall be paid by the man to the woman. But it is open to the woman to remit the half due to her or to the man to remit the half which he is entitled to deduct, and thus pay the whole.

270. *Him is whose hands is the marriage tie*: According to Ḥanafī doctrine this is the husband himself, who can ordinarily by his act dissolve the marriage. It therefore behoves him to be all the more liberal to the woman and pay her the full dower even if the marriage was not consummated.

Liberality between yourselves.
For Allah sees well
All that ye do.

الْفَضْلَ بَيْنَكُمْ إِنَّ اللَّهَ بِمَا تَعْمَلُونَ بَصِيرٌ

238. Guard strictly
Your (habit) of prayers,
Especially the Middle Prayer;[271]
And stand before Allah
In a devout (frame of mind).

٢٣٨ حَٰفِظُواْ عَلَى ٱلصَّلَوَٰتِ
وَٱلصَّلَوٰةِ ٱلْوُسْطَىٰ
وَقُومُواْ لِلَّهِ قَٰنِتِينَ

239. If ye fear (an enemy),[272]
Pray on foot, or riding,
(As may be most convenient),
But when you are
In security, celebrate
Allah's praises in the manner
He has taught you,
Which ye knew not (before).

٢٣٩ فَإِنْ خِفْتُمْ
فَرِجَالًا أَوْ رُكْبَانًا فَإِذَآ أَمِنتُمْ
فَٱذْكُرُواْ ٱللَّهَ كَمَا عَلَّمَكُم
مَّا لَمْ تَكُونُواْ تَعْلَمُونَ

240. Those of you
Who die and leave widows
Should bequeath
For their widows
A year's maintenance
And residence;[273]
But if they leave
(The residence),
There is no blame on you
For what they do
With themselves,
Provided it is reasonable.
And Allah is Exalted in Power,
Wise.

٢٤٠ وَٱلَّذِينَ يُتَوَفَّوْنَ مِنكُمْ
وَيَذَرُونَ أَزْوَٰجًا وَصِيَّةً لِّأَزْوَٰجِهِم
مَّتَٰعًا إِلَى ٱلْحَوْلِ غَيْرَ إِخْرَاجٍ
فَإِنْ خَرَجْنَ فَلَا جُنَاحَ عَلَيْكُمْ
فِي مَا فَعَلْنَ فِيٓ أَنفُسِهِنَّ مِن مَّعْرُوفٍ
وَٱللَّهُ عَزِيزٌ حَكِيمٌ

241. For divorced women
Maintenance (should be provided)
On a reasonable (scale).
This is a duty
On the righteous.

٢٤١ وَلِلْمُطَلَّقَٰتِ مَتَٰعٌۢ بِٱلْمَعْرُوفِ
حَقًّا عَلَى ٱلْمُتَّقِينَ

271. *The Middle Prayer: Ṣalāt al wusṭā*: may be translated "the best or most excellent prayer." Authorities differ as to the exact meaning of this phrase. The weight of authorities seems to be in favour of interpreting this as the *'Aṣr* prayer (in the middle of the afternoon). This is apt to be most neglected, and yet this is the most necessary, to remind us of Allah in the midst of our worldly affairs. (R).

272. Verses 238-239 are parenthetical, introducing the subject of prayer in danger. This is more fully dealt with in 4:101-03.

273. Opinions differ whether the provision (of a year's maintenance, with residence), for a widow, is abrogated by the share which the widow gets (one-eighth or one-fourth) as an heir (Q. 4:12). I do not think it is. The bequest (where made) takes effect as a charge on the property, but the widow can leave the house before the year is out, and presumably maintenance then ceases.

242. Thus doth Allah
Make clear His Signs
To you: in order that
Ye may understand.

٢٤٢ كَذَٰلِكَ يُبَيِّنُ ٱللَّهُ
لَكُمْ ءَايَٰتِهِۦ لَعَلَّكُمْ تَعْقِلُونَ

C. 51.—Fighting in defence of Truth and Right
(2:234-235.) Is not to be undertaken lightheartedly,
Nor to be evaded as a duty.
Life and Death are in the hands of Allah.
Not all can be chosen to fight
For Allah. It requires constancy,
Firmness, and faith. Given these,
Large armies can be routed
By those who battle for Allah,
As shown by the courage of David,
Whose prowess single-handedly
Disposed of the Philistines.
The mission of some of the messengers,
Like Jesus, was different—
Less wide in scope than that
Of Muṣṭafā, and He carries it out
As He wills.

SECTION 32.

243. Didst thou not
Turn thy vision to those
Who abandoned their homes,
Though they were thousands
(In number), for fear of death?
Allah said to them: "Die":
Then He restored them to
life.[274]
For Allah is full of bounty
To mankind, but
Most of them are ungrateful.

٢٤٣ أَلَمْ تَرَ إِلَى ٱلَّذِينَ خَرَجُوا۟
مِن دِيَٰرِهِمْ وَهُمْ أُلُوفٌ حَذَرَ ٱلْمَوْتِ
فَقَالَ لَهُمُ ٱللَّهُ مُوتُوا۟ ثُمَّ أَحْيَٰهُمْ
إِنَّ ٱللَّهَ لَذُو فَضْلٍ عَلَى ٱلنَّاسِ
وَلَٰكِنَّ أَكْثَرَ ٱلنَّاسِ لَا يَشْكُرُونَ

244. Then fight in the cause
Of Allah, and know that Allah

٢٤٤ وَقَٰتِلُوا۟ فِى سَبِيلِ ٱللَّهِ وَٱعْلَمُوٓا۟ أَنَّ ٱللَّهَ

274. We now return to the subject of *Jihād*, which we left at 2:214-216. We are to be under no illusion about it. If we are not prepared to fight for our faith, with our lives and all our resources, both our lives and our resources will be wiped out by our enemies. As to life, Allah gave it, and a coward is not likely to save it. It has happened again and again in history that men who tamely submitted to be driven from their homes although they were more numerous than their enemies, had the sentence of death pronounced on them for their cowardice, and they deserved it. But Allah gives further and further chances in His mercy. This is a lesson to every generation. The Commentators differ as to the exact episode referred to, but the wording is perfectly general, and so is the lesson to be learnt from it.

Heareth and knoweth all things.[275]

سَمِيعٌ عَلِيمٌ

245. Who is he
That will loan to Allah
A beautiful loan,[276] which Allah
Will double unto his credit
And multiply many times?
It is Allah that giveth (you)
Want or Plenty,
And to Him shall be
Your return.

﴿٢٤٥﴾ مَن ذَا ٱلَّذِى يُقْرِضُ ٱللَّهَ قَرْضًا حَسَنًا
فَيُضَٰعِفَهُۥ لَهُۥٓ أَضْعَافًا كَثِيرَةً
وَٱللَّهُ يَقْبِضُ وَيَبْصُۜطُ
وَإِلَيْهِ تُرْجَعُونَ

246. Hast thou not
Turned thy vision to the Chiefs
Of the Children of Israel
After (the time of) Moses?[277]
They said to a Prophet[278]
(That was) among them:
"Appoint for us a King, that we
May fight in the cause of Allah."
He said: "Is it not possible,[279]

﴿٢٤٦﴾ أَلَمْ تَرَ إِلَى ٱلْمَلَإِ مِنۢ بَنِىٓ إِسْرَٰٓءِيلَ
مِنۢ بَعْدِ مُوسَىٰٓ إِذْ قَالُوا۟ لِنَبِىٍّ لَّهُمُ
ٱبْعَثْ لَنَا مَلِكًا نُّقَٰتِلْ فِى سَبِيلِ ٱللَّهِ
قَالَ هَلْ عَسَيْتُمْ

275. For Allah's cause we must fight, but never to satisfy our own selfish passions or greed, for the warning is repeated: "Allah heareth and knoweth all things"; all deeds, words, and motives are perfectly open before Him, however we might conceal them from men or even from ourselves. See 2:216. n. 236.

276. Spending in the cause of Allah is called metaphorically "a beautiful loan". It is excellent in many ways: (1) it shows a beautiful spirit of self-denial; (2) in other loans there may be a doubt as to the safety of your capital or any return thereon; here you give to the Lord of All, in Whose hands are the keys of want or plenty; giving, you may have manifold blessings, and withholding, you may even lose what you have. If we remember that our goal is Allah, can we turn away from His cause?

277. The next generation after Moses and Aaron was ruled by Joshua, who crossed the Jordan and settled the tribes in Palestine. His rule lasted for 25 years, after which there was a period of 320 years when the Israelites had a chequered history. They were not united among themselves, and suffered many reverses at the hands of the Midianites, Amalekites, and other tribes of Palestine. They frequently lapsed into idolatry and deserted the worship of the true God. From time to time a leader appeared among them who assumed dictatorial powers. Acting under a sort of theocratic commission from Allah, he pointed out their backslidings, reunited them under His banner, and restored, from time to time and place to place, the power of Israel. These dictators are called Judges in the English translation of the Old Testament. The last of their line was Samuel, who marks the transition towards the line of Kings on the one hand and of the later Prophets on the other. He may be dated approximately about the 11th century B.C.

278. This was Samuel. In his time Israel had suffered from much corruption within and many reverses without. The Philistines had made a great attack and defeated Israel with great slaughter. The Israelites, instead of relying on Faith and their own valour and cohesion, brought out their most sacred possession, the Ark of the Covenant, to help them in the fight. But the enemy captured it, carried it away, and retained it for seven months. The Israelites forgot that wickedness cannot screen itself behind a sacred relic. Nor can a sacred relic help the enemies of faith. The enemy found that the Ark brought nothing but misfortune for themselves, and were glad to abandon it. It apparently remained twenty years in the village (*qaryah*) of Ya'ārim (Kirjath jearim): I. Samuel, vii. 2. Meanwhile the people pressed Samuel to appoint them a king. They thought that a king would cure all their ills, whereas what was wanting was a spirit of union and discipline and a readiness on their part to fight in the cause of Allah.

279. Samuel knew as a Prophet that the people were fickle and only wanted to cover their own want of union and true spirit by asking for a king. They replied with spirit in words, but when it came to action, they failed. They hid themselves in caves and rocks, or ran away, and even those who remained "followed him trembling": I. Samuel, xiii. 6-7.

If ye were commanded To fight, that that ye Will not fight?" They said: "How could we refuse To fight in the cause of Allah, Seeing that we were turned out Of our homes and our families?" But when they were commanded To fight, they turned back, Except a small band Among them. But Allah Has full knowledge of those Who do wrong.	إِن كُتِبَ عَلَيْكُمُ ٱلْقِتَالُ أَلَّا تُقَٰتِلُوا۟ ۖ قَالُوا۟ وَمَا لَنَآ أَلَّا نُقَٰتِلَ فِى سَبِيلِ ٱللَّهِ وَقَدْ أُخْرِجْنَا مِن دِيَٰرِنَا وَأَبْنَآئِنَا ۖ فَلَمَّا كُتِبَ عَلَيْهِمُ ٱلْقِتَالُ تَوَلَّوْا۟ إِلَّا قَلِيلًا مِّنْهُمْ ۗ وَٱللَّهُ عَلِيمٌۢ بِٱلظَّٰلِمِينَ
247. Their Prophet said to them: "Allah hath appointed Ṭālūt[280] as king over you." They said: "How can he Exercise authority over us When we are better fitted Than he to exercise authority, And he is not even gifted, With wealth in abundance?" He said: Allah hath Chosen him above you, And hath gifted him Abundantly with knowledge And bodily prowess: Allah Granteth His authority to whom He pleaseth. Allah is All-Embracing, and He knoweth All things."	﴿٢٤٧﴾ وَقَالَ لَهُمْ نَبِيُّهُمْ إِنَّ ٱللَّهَ قَدْ بَعَثَ لَكُمْ طَالُوتَ مَلِكًا ۚ قَالُوٓا۟ أَنَّىٰ يَكُونُ لَهُ ٱلْمُلْكُ عَلَيْنَا وَنَحْنُ أَحَقُّ بِٱلْمُلْكِ مِنْهُ وَلَمْ يُؤْتَ سَعَةً مِّنَ ٱلْمَالِ ۚ قَالَ إِنَّ ٱللَّهَ ٱصْطَفَىٰهُ عَلَيْكُمْ وَزَادَهُۥ بَسْطَةً فِى ٱلْعِلْمِ وَٱلْجِسْمِ ۖ وَٱللَّهُ يُؤْتِى مُلْكَهُۥ مَن يَشَآءُ ۚ وَٱللَّهُ وَٰسِعٌ عَلِيمٌ
248. And (further) their Prophet Said to them: "A Sign Of his authority Is that there shall come To you the Ark of the Covenant,[281]	﴿٢٤٨﴾ وَقَالَ لَهُمْ نَبِيُّهُمْ إِنَّ ءَايَةَ مُلْكِهِۦٓ أَن يَأْتِيَكُمُ ٱلتَّابُوتُ

280. Ṭālūt is the Arabic name for Saul, who was tall and handsome, but belonged to the tribe of Benjamin, the smallest tribe in Israel. His worldly belongings were slender, and it was when he went out to search for some asses which had been lost from his father's house that he met Samuel and was anointed king by him. The people's fickleness appeared immediately after he was named. They raised all sorts of petty objections to him. The chief consideration in their minds was selfishness: each one wanted to be leader and king himself, instead of desiring sincerely the good of the people as a whole, as a leader should do.

281. *Ark of the Covenant: Tābūt*: a chest of acacia wood covered and lined with pure gold, about 5 ft. x 3 ft. x 3 ft. See Exod. xxv. 10-22. It was to contain the "testimony of Allah", or the Ten Commandments engraved on stone, with relics of Moses and Aaron. Its Gold lid was to be the "Mercy Seat." This was a sacred possession to Israel. It was lost to the enemy in the early part of Samuel's ministry: see n. 278 to 2:246. When it came back, it remained in a village for twenty years, and was apparently taken to the capital when kingship was instituted. It thus became a symbol of unity and authority. (R).

With (an assurance) therein
Of security[282] from your Lord,
And the relics left
By the family of Moses
And the family of Aaron,
Carried by angels.[283]
In this is a Symbol
For you if ye indeed
Have faith."

فِيهِ سَكِينَةٌ مِّن رَّبِّكُمْ وَبَقِيَّةٌ مِّمَّا
تَرَكَ ءَالُ مُوسَىٰ وَءَالُ هَٰرُونَ
تَحْمِلُهُ ٱلْمَلَٰٓئِكَةُ ۚ إِنَّ فِى ذَٰلِكَ لَءَايَةً
لَّكُمْ إِن كُنتُم مُّؤْمِنِينَ

SECTION 33.

249. When Ṭālūt set forth
With the armies, he said:[284]
"Allah will test you
At the stream; if any
Drinks of its water,
He goes not with my army;
Only those who taste not
Of it go with me;
A mere sip out of the hand
Is excused." But they all
Drank of it, except a few.
When they crossed the river—
He and the faithful ones with him,
They said: "This day[285]
We cannot cope
With Goliath and his forces."
But those who were convinced
That they must meet Allah,
Said: "How oft, by Allah's will,
Hath a small force
Vanquished a big one?
Allah is with those
Who steadfastly persevere."

٢٤٩ فَلَمَّا فَصَلَ طَالُوتُ بِٱلْجُنُودِ قَالَ
إِنَّ ٱللَّهَ مُبْتَلِيكُم بِنَهَرٍ
فَمَن شَرِبَ مِنْهُ فَلَيْسَ مِنِّى وَمَن لَّمْ يَطْعَمْهُ
فَإِنَّهُۥ مِنِّىٓ إِلَّا مَنِ ٱغْتَرَفَ غُرْفَةًۢ بِيَدِهِۦ ۚ
فَشَرِبُوا۟ مِنْهُ إِلَّا قَلِيلًا مِّنْهُمْ ۚ فَلَمَّا جَاوَزَهُۥ
هُوَ وَٱلَّذِينَ ءَامَنُوا۟ مَعَهُۥ قَالُوا۟
لَا طَاقَةَ لَنَا ٱلْيَوْمَ بِجَالُوتَ وَجُنُودِهِۦ ۚ
قَالَ ٱلَّذِينَ يَظُنُّونَ أَنَّهُم مُّلَٰقُوا۟ ٱللَّهِ
كَم مِّن فِئَةٍ قَلِيلَةٍ غَلَبَتْ فِئَةً
كَثِيرَةًۢ بِإِذْنِ ٱللَّهِ ۗ وَٱللَّهُ مَعَ ٱلصَّٰبِرِينَ

282. *Security: sakīnah*=safety, tranquillity, peace. Later Jewish writings use the same word for a symbol of Allah's Glory in the Tabernacle or tent in which the Ark was kept, or in the Temple when it was built by Solomon.

283. *Carried by angels*: these words refer to the Ṭābūt or Ark. (R).

284. A Commander is hampered by a large force if it is not in perfect discipline and does not wholeheartedly believe in its Commander. He must get rid of all the doubtful ones, as did Gideon before Saul, and Henry V, in Shakespeare's story long afterwards. Saul used the same test as Gideon: he gave a certain order when crossing a stream: the greater part disobeyed, and were sent back. Gideon's story will be found in Judges, vii. 2-7.

285. Even in the small band that remained faithful, there were some who were appalled by the number of the enemy when they met him face to face, and saw the size and strength of the enemy Commander, the giant Goliath (Jālūt). But there was a very small band who were determined to face all odds because they had perfect confidence in Allah and in the cause for which they were fighting. They were for making a firm stand and seeking Allah's help. Of that number was David: see next note.

250. When they advanced
To meet Goliath and his forces,
They prayed: "Our Lord!
Pour out constancy on us
And make our steps firm:
Help us against those
They reject faith."

٢٥٠ وَلَمَّا بَرَزُوا۟ لِجَالُوتَ وَجُنُودِهِۦ قَالُوا۟
رَبَّنَآ أَفْرِغْ عَلَيْنَا صَبْرًا وَثَبِّتْ أَقْدَامَنَا
وَٱنصُرْنَا عَلَى ٱلْقَوْمِ ٱلْكَـٰفِرِينَ

251. By Allah's will,
They routed them:
And David[286] slew Goliath:
And Allah gave him
Power and wisdom
And taught him
Whatever (else) He willed.[287]
And did not Allah
Check one set of people
By means of another,
The earth would indeed
Be full of mischief:
But Allah is full of bounty
To all the worlds.[288]

٢٥١ فَهَزَمُوهُم بِإِذْنِ ٱللَّهِ وَقَتَلَ
دَاوُۥدُ جَالُوتَ وَءَاتَىٰهُ ٱللَّهُ ٱلْمُلْكَ
وَٱلْحِكْمَةَ وَعَلَّمَهُۥ مِمَّا يَشَآءُ ۗ
وَلَوْلَا دَفْعُ ٱللَّهِ ٱلنَّاسَ بَعْضَهُم بِبَعْضٍ
لَّفَسَدَتِ ٱلْأَرْضُ وَلَـٰكِنَّ
ٱللَّهَ ذُو فَضْلٍ عَلَى ٱلْعَـٰلَمِينَ

252. These are the Signs
Of Allah: we rehearse them
To thee in truth: verily
Thou art one of the Messengers.

٢٥٢ تِلْكَ ءَايَـٰتُ ٱللَّهِ نَتْلُوهَا عَلَيْكَ
بِٱلْحَقِّ ۚ وَإِنَّكَ لَمِنَ ٱلْمُرْسَلِينَ

---

286. Note how the whole story is compressed into a few words as regards narration, but its spiritual lessons are dwelt upon from many points of view. The Old Testament is mainly interested in the narrative, which is full of detail, but says little about the universal truths of which every true story is a parable. The Qur'ān assumes the story, but tells the parable.

David was a raw youth, with no arms or armour. He was not known even in the Israelite camp, and the giant Goliath mocked him. Even David's own elder brother chid him for deserting his sheep, for he was a poor shepherd lad to outward appearance, but his faith had made him more than a match for the Philistine hosts. When Saul offered his own armour and arms to David, the young hero declined, as he had not tried them, while his shepherd's sling and staff were his well-tried implements. He picked up five smooth pebbles on the spot from the stream, and used his sling to such effect that he knocked down Goliath. He then used Goliath's own sword to slay him. There was consternation in the Philistine army: they broke and fled, and were pursued and cut to pieces.

Apart from the main lesson that if we would preserve our national existence and our faith it is our duty to fight with courage and firmness, there are other lessons in David's story: (1) numbers do not count, but faith, determination and the blessing of Allah; (2) size and strength are of no avail against truth, courage, and careful planning; (3) the hero tries his own weapons, and those that are available to him at the time and place, even though people may laugh at him; (4) if Allah is with us, the enemy's weapon may become an instrument of his own destruction; (5) personality conquers all dangers, and puts heart into our own wavering friends; (6) pure faith brings Allah's reward, which may take many forms: in David's case it was Power, Wisdom, and other gifts; see next note.

287. David was not only a shepherd, a warrior, a king, a wise man, and a prophet, but was also endowed with the gifts of poetry and music. (R).

288. Allah's plan is universal. He loves and protects *all* His creatures and His bounties are for all worlds (1:2 n. 98). To protect one He may have to check another, but we must never lose faith that His love is for all in boundless measure.

3/30

253. Those Messengers
We endowed with gifts,
Some above others:[289]
To one of them Allah spoke;[290]
Others He raised
To degrees (of honour);[291]
To Jesus, the son of Mary,
We gave Clear (Signs),[292]
And strengthened him
With the holy spirit.[292-A]
If Allah had so willed,
Succeeding generations
Would not have fought
Among each other, after
Clear (Signs) had come to them
But they (chose) to wrangle,
Some believing and others
Rejecting. If Allah had so willed,
They would not have fought
Each other; but Allah
Fulfilleth His plan.[293]

٢٥٣ تِلْكَ ٱلرُّسُلُ فَضَّلْنَا بَعْضَهُمْ عَلَىٰ بَعْضٍ
مِّنْهُم مَّن كَلَّمَ ٱللَّهُ ۖ وَرَفَعَ بَعْضَهُمْ دَرَجَٰتٍ ۚ
وَءَاتَيْنَا عِيسَى ٱبْنَ مَرْيَمَ ٱلْبَيِّنَٰتِ وَأَيَّدْنَٰهُ
بِرُوحِ ٱلْقُدُسِ ۗ وَلَوْ شَآءَ ٱللَّهُ مَا ٱقْتَتَلَ
ٱلَّذِينَ مِنۢ بَعْدِهِم
مِّنۢ بَعْدِ مَا جَآءَتْهُمُ ٱلْبَيِّنَٰتُ وَلَٰكِنِ ٱخْتَلَفُوا۟
فَمِنْهُم مَّنْ ءَامَنَ وَمِنْهُم مَّن كَفَرَ ۚ
وَلَوْ شَآءَ ٱللَّهُ مَا ٱقْتَتَلُوا۟
وَلَٰكِنَّ ٱللَّهَ يَفْعَلُ مَا يُرِيدُ

C. 52.—Who can describe the nature of Allah?
(2:254-283.) The Living, the Eternal: His Throne
Extends over worlds and worlds
That no imagination can compass.
His truth is clear as daylight: how
Can compulsion advance religion?
The keys of Life and Death, and the mysteries
Of everything around us, are in His hands.

---

289. Different gifts and different modes of procedure are prescribed to Allah's Messengers in different ages, and perhaps their degrees are different though it is not for mortals, with our imperfect knowledge, to make any difference between one and another of Allah's Messengers (2:136). As this winds up the argument about fighting, three illustrations are given from the past, how it affected Allah's Messengers. To Moses Allah spoke directly: he led his men for forty years through the wilderness, mainly fighting against the unbelief of his own people; he organised them to fight with the sword for Palestine, but was raised to Allah's mercy before his enterprise ripened, and it fell to Joshua to carry out his plan. David, though a mere shepherd boy, was chosen by Allah. He overthrew the greatest warrior of his time, became a king, and waged successful wars, being also a prophet, a poet, and musician. Jesus was "strengthened with the holy spirit": he was given no weapons to fight, and his mission was of a more limited character. In Muḥammad's mission these and other characters were combined. Gentler than Jesus, he organised on a vaster scale than Moses, and from Madīnah he ruled and gave laws, and the Qur'ān has a vaster scope than the Psalms of David.

290. Moses: see note above.

291. There is a two-fold sense: they were raised to high posts of honour, and they rose by degrees. I take the reference to be to David.

292. *Cf.* 2:87. See n. 401 to 3:62.

292-A. "Holy spirit," according to commentators signifies Gabriel. [Eds.].

293. If some power of choice was to be given to man, his selfishness inevitably caused divisions. It must not be supposed that it frustrates Allah's Plan. He carries it out as He will.

Our duty then is to seek the path
Of goodness, kindness, upright
Conduct and Charity—to grasp
At no advantage from a brother's need,
To stand by the word that is pledged,
To bear true witness, and remove all cause
Of misunderstandings in our dealings
As between man and man.

SECTION 34.

254. O ye who believe!
Spend out of (the bounties)[294]
We have provided for you,
Before the Day comes
When no bargaining
(Will avail), nor friendship
Nor intercession.[295]
Those who reject Faith—they
Are the wrongdoers.

٢٥٤ يَـٰٓأَيُّهَا ٱلَّذِينَ ءَامَنُوٓا۟ أَنفِقُوا۟
مِمَّا رَزَقْنَـٰكُم مِّن قَبْلِ أَن يَأْتِىَ
يَوْمٌ لَّا بَيْعٌ فِيهِ وَلَا خُلَّةٌ وَلَا شَفَـٰعَةٌ
وَٱلْكَـٰفِرُونَ هُمُ ٱلظَّـٰلِمُونَ

255. Allah! There is no god
But He—the Living,
The Self-subsisting, Eternal.[296]
No slumber can seize Him
Nor sleep. His are all things
In the heavens and on earth.
Who is there that can intercede
In His presence except
As He permitteth? He knoweth
What (appeareth to His
creatures

٢٥٥ ٱللَّهُ لَآ إِلَـٰهَ إِلَّا هُوَ
ٱلْحَىُّ ٱلْقَيُّومُ لَا تَأْخُذُهُۥ سِنَةٌ وَلَا نَوْمٌ
لَّهُۥ مَا فِى ٱلسَّمَـٰوَٰتِ وَمَا فِى ٱلْأَرْضِ
مَن ذَا ٱلَّذِى يَشْفَعُ عِندَهُۥٓ إِلَّا بِإِذْنِهِۦ
يَعْلَمُ مَا بَيْنَ

294. *Spend, i.e.*, give away in charity, or employ in good works, but do not hoard. Good works would in Islam include everything that advances the good of one that is in need whether a neighbour or a stranger, or that advances the good of the community, or even the good of the person himself to whom Allah has given the bounty. But it must be real good and there should be no admixture of baser motives, such as vainglory, or false indulgence, or encouragement of idleness, or playing off one person against another. The bounties include mental and spiritual gifts as well as wealth and material gifts.

295. *Cf.* 2:123 and 2:48.

296. This is the *Āyah al Kursī*, the "Verse of the Throne". Who can translate its glorious meaning, or reproduce the rhythm of its well-chosen and comprehensive words. Even in the original Arabic the meaning seems to be greater than can be expressed in words.

The attributes of Allah are different from anything we know in our present world: He lives, but His life is self-subsisting and eternal: it does not depend upon other beings and is not limited to time and space. Perhaps the attribute of *Qayyūm* includes not only the idea of "Self-subsisting" but also the idea of "Keeping up and maintaining all life." His life being the source and constant support of all derived forms of life. Perfect life is perfect activity, in contrast to the imperfect life which we see around us, which is not only subject to death but to the need for rest or slowed-down activity, (something which is between activity and sleep, for which I, in common with other translators, have used the word "slumber") and the need for full sleep itself. But Allah has no need for rest or sleep. His activity, like His life, is perfect and self-subsisting. Contrast with this the expression used in Psalms lxxviii. 65: "Then the Lord awaked as one out of sleep, and like a mighty man that shouteth by reason of wine." (R).

As) Before or After
Or Behind them.[297]
Nor shall they compass
Aught of His knowledge
Except as He willeth.
His Throne doth extend[298]
Over the heavens
And the earth, and He feeleth
No fatigue in guarding
And preserving them[299]
For He is the Most High,
The Supreme (in glory).

أَيْدِيهِمْ وَمَا خَلْفَهُمْ
وَلَا يُحِيطُونَ بِشَيْءٍ مِّنْ عِلْمِهِۦٓ إِلَّا بِمَا شَآءَ
وَسِعَ كُرْسِيُّهُ ٱلسَّمَٰوَٰتِ وَٱلْأَرْضَ
وَلَا يَـُٔودُهُۥ حِفْظُهُمَا
وَهُوَ ٱلْعَلِيُّ ٱلْعَظِيمُ

256. Let there be no compulsion[300]
In religion: Truth stands out
Clear from Error: whoever
Rejects Evil and believes
In Allah hath grasped
The most trustworthy
Handhold, that never breaks.[301]

٢٥٦ لَآ إِكْرَاهَ فِى ٱلدِّينِ قَد تَّبَيَّنَ ٱلرُّشْدُ مِنَ ٱلْغَىِّ
فَمَن يَكْفُرْ بِٱلطَّٰغُوتِ وَيُؤْمِنۢ بِٱللَّهِ
فَقَدِ ٱسْتَمْسَكَ بِٱلْعُرْوَةِ ٱلْوُثْقَىٰ لَا ٱنفِصَامَ لَهَا

297. After we realise that His Life is absolute Life, His Being is absolute Being, while others are contigent and evanescent, our ideas of heaven and earth vanish like shadows. What is behind that shadow is He. Such reality as our heavens and our earth possess is a reflection of His absolute Reality. The pantheist places the wrong accent when he says that everything is He. The truth is better expressed when we say that everything is His. How then can any creatures stand before Him as of right, and claim to intercede for a fellow-creature? In the first place both are His, and He cares as much for one as for the other. In the second place, they are both dependent on His will and command. But He in His Wisdom and Plan may grade His creatures and give one superiority over another. Then by His will and permission such a one may intercede or help according to the laws and duties laid on him. Allah's knowledge is absolute, and is not conditioned by Time or Space. To us, His creatures, these conditions always apply. His knowledge and our knowledge are therefore in different categories, and our knowledge only gets some reflection of Reality when it accords with His Will and Plan.

298. *Throne:* seat, power, knowledge, symbol of authority. In our thoughts we exhaust everything when we say "the heavens and the earth". Well, then, in everything is the working of Allah's power, and will, and authority. Everything of course includes spiritual things as well as things of sense. (R).

299. A life of activity that is imperfect or relative would not only need rest for carrying on its own activities, but would be in need of double rest when it has to look after and guard, or cherish, or help other activities. In contrast with this is the Absolute Life, which is free from any such need or contingency. For it is supreme above anything that we can conceive.

300. Compulsion is incompatible with religion: because (1) religion depends upon faith and will, and these would be meaningless if induced by force; (2) Truth and Error have been so clearly shown up by the mercy of Allah that there should be no doubt in the minds of any persons of good will as to the fundamentals of faith; (3) Allah's protection is continuous, and His Plan is always to lead us from the depths of darkness into the clearest light.

301. *Handhold*: something which the hands can grasp for safety in a moment of danger. It may be a loop or a handle, or anchor. If it is without flaw, so that there is no danger of breaking our safety is absolutely assured so long as we hold fast to it. Our safety then depends on our own will and faith: Allah's help and protection will always be unfailing if we hold firmly to Allah and trust in Him.

And Allah heareth
And knoweth all things.

وَٱللَّهُ سَمِيعٌ عَلِيمٌ

257. Allah is the Protector
Of those who have faith:
From the depths of darkness
He will lead them forth
Into light. Of those
Who reject faith the patrons
Are the Evil Ones: from light
They will lead them forth
Into the depths of darkness.
They will be Companions
Of the fire, to dwell therein
(Forever).

٢٥٧ ٱللَّهُ وَلِىُّ ٱلَّذِينَ ءَامَنُوا۟
يُخْرِجُهُم مِّنَ ٱلظُّلُمَٰتِ إِلَى ٱلنُّورِ ۖ
وَٱلَّذِينَ كَفَرُوٓا۟ أَوْلِيَآؤُهُمُ ٱلطَّٰغُوتُ
يُخْرِجُونَهُم مِّنَ ٱلنُّورِ إِلَى ٱلظُّلُمَٰتِ ۗ
أُو۟لَٰٓئِكَ أَصْحَٰبُ ٱلنَّارِ ۖ
هُمْ فِيهَا خَٰلِدُونَ

Section 35.

258. Hast thou not
Turned thy vision to one
Who disputed with Abraham[302]
About his Lord, because
Allah had granted him
Power? Abraham said:
"My Lord is He Who
Giveth life and death."
He said: "I give life and death."
Said Abraham: "But it is Allah
That causeth the sun
To rise from the East:
Do thou then cause him
To rise from the West?"
Thus was he confounded
Who (in arrogance) rejected
Faith. Nor doth Allah
Give guidance

٢٥٨ أَلَمْ تَرَ إِلَى ٱلَّذِى
حَآجَّ إِبْرَٰهِۦمَ فِى رَبِّهِۦٓ
أَنْ ءَاتَىٰهُ ٱللَّهُ ٱلْمُلْكَ إِذْ قَالَ إِبْرَٰهِۦمُ
رَبِّىَ ٱلَّذِى يُحْىِۦ وَيُمِيتُ
قَالَ أَنَا۠ أُحْىِۦ وَأُمِيتُ ۖ
قَالَ إِبْرَٰهِۦمُ فَإِنَّ ٱللَّهَ يَأْتِى بِٱلشَّمْسِ مِنَ
ٱلْمَشْرِقِ فَأْتِ بِهَا مِنَ ٱلْمَغْرِبِ
فَبُهِتَ ٱلَّذِى كَفَرَ ۗ
وَٱللَّهُ لَا يَهْدِى

302. The three verses 258-260 have been the subject of much controversy as to the exact meaning to be attached to the incidents and the precise persons alluded to, whose names are not mentioned. In such matters, where the Qur'ān has given no names and the Holy Prophet has himself given no indication, it seems to me useless to speculate, and still worse to put forward positive opinions. In questions of learning, speculations are often interesting. But it seems to me that the meaning of the Qur'ān is so wide and universal that we are in danger of missing the real and eternal meaning if we go on disputing about minor points. All three incidents are such as may happen again and again in any prophet's lifetime, and be seen in impersonal vision at any time. Here they are connected with Al Muṣṭafā's vision as shown by the opening words of verse 258. (R).

To a people unjust.[303]

259. Or (take) the similitude
Of one who passed
By a hamlet, all in ruins[304]
To its roofs. He said:
"Oh! how shall Allah
Bring it (ever) to life,
After (this) its death?"
But Allah caused him
To die for a hundred years,
Then raised him up (again).
He said: "How long
Didst thou tarry (thus)?"
He said: "(Perhaps) a day
Or part of a day." He said:
"Nay, thou hast tarried
Thus a hundred years;
But look at thy food
And thy drink; they show
No signs of age; and look
At thy donkey; and that
We may make of thee
A Sign unto the people,
Look further at the bones,
How We bring them together
And clothe them with flesh."[305]

ٱلْقَوْمَ ٱلظَّٰلِمِينَ

٢٥٩ أَوْ كَٱلَّذِى مَرَّ
عَلَىٰ قَرْيَةٍ وَهِىَ خَاوِيَةٌ عَلَىٰ عُرُوشِهَا
قَالَ أَنَّىٰ يُحْىِۦ هَٰذِهِ ٱللَّهُ بَعْدَ مَوْتِهَا
فَأَمَاتَهُ ٱللَّهُ مِاْئَةَ عَامٍ ثُمَّ بَعَثَهُۥ
قَالَ كَمْ لَبِثْتَ
قَالَ لَبِثْتُ يَوْمًا أَوْ بَعْضَ يَوْمٍ
قَالَ بَل لَّبِثْتَ مِاْئَةَ عَامٍ فَٱنظُرْ إِلَىٰ
طَعَامِكَ وَشَرَابِكَ لَمْ يَتَسَنَّهْ وَٱنظُرْ إِلَىٰ
حِمَارِكَ وَلِنَجْعَلَكَ ءَايَةً لِّلنَّاسِ
وَٱنظُرْ إِلَى ٱلْعِظَامِ كَيْفَ نُنشِزُهَا
ثُمَّ نَكْسُوهَا لَحْمًا

303. The first point illustrated is the pride of power, and the impotence of human power as against Allah's power. The person who disputed with Abraham may have been Nimrod or some ruler in Babylonia, or indeed elsewhere. I name Babylonia as it was the original home of Abraham (Ur of the Chaldees), and Babylon prided herself on her arts and sciences in the ancient world. Science can do many wonderful things; it could then; it can now. But the mystery of Life baffled science then, as it continues to baffle science now, after many centuries of progress. Abraham had faith, and referred back everything to the true Cause of Causes. A sceptical ruler might jestingly say: "I have the power of life and death." A man of science might say: "We have investigated the laws of life and death." Different kinds of powers lie in the hands of kings and men of knowledge. The claim in both cases is true in a very limited sense. But Abraham confounded the claimer by going back to fundamentals. "If you had the ultimate power, why could you not make the sun rise from the West?"

304. This incident is referred variously (1) to Ezekiel's vision of dry bones (Ezekiel, xxxvii. 1-10); (2) to Nehemiah's visit to Jerusalem in ruins after the Captivity, and to its rebuilding (Nehemiah, i. 12-20): and (3) to 'Uzayr, or Ezra, or Esdras, the scribe, priest, and reformer, who was sent by the Persian King after the Captivity to Jerusalem, and about whom there are many Jewish legends. As to (1), there are only four words in this verse about bones. As to (2) and (3), there is nothing specific to connect this verse with either. The wording is perfectly general, and we must understand it as general. I think it does refer not only to individual, but to national death and resurrection.

305. A man is in despair when he sees the destruction of a whole people, city, or civilisation. But Allah can cause resurrection as He has done many times in history, and as He will do at the final Resurrection. Time is nothing before Allah. The doubter thinks that he has been dead or "tarried thus" a day or less when the period has been a century. On the other hand, the food and drink which he left behind is intact, and as fresh as it was when he left it. But the donkey is not only dead, but nothing but bones is left of it. And before the man's eyes, the bones are reunited, clothed with flesh and blood, and restored to life. Moral: (1) Time is nothing to Allah; (2) It affects different things in different ways; (3) The keys of life and death are in Allah's hands; (4) Man's power is nothing; his faith should be in Allah.

When this was shown clearly
To him, he said: "I know
That Allah hath power
Over all things."

فَلَمَّا تَبَيَّنَ لَهُۥ قَالَ أَعۡلَمُ
أَنَّ ٱللَّهَ عَلَىٰ كُلِّ شَيۡءٖ قَدِيرٞ

260. Behold! Abraham said:
"My Lord! Show me how
Thou givest life to the dead."[306]
He said: "Dost thou not
Then believe?" He said:
"Yea! but to satisfy
My own understanding."[307]
He said: "Take four birds;
Tame them to turn to thee;
Put a portion[308] of them
On every hill, and call to them;
They will come to thee,
(Flying) with speed.
Then know that Allah
Is Exalted in Power, Wise."

(٢٦٠) وَإِذۡ قَالَ إِبۡرَٰهِـۧمُ رَبِّ أَرِنِي كَيۡفَ
تُحۡيِ ٱلۡمَوۡتَىٰۖ قَالَ أَوَلَمۡ تُؤۡمِنۖ قَالَ بَلَىٰ
وَلَٰكِن لِّيَطۡمَئِنَّ قَلۡبِيۖ قَالَ فَخُذۡ أَرۡبَعَةٗ مِّنَ
ٱلطَّيۡرِ فَصُرۡهُنَّ إِلَيۡكَ ثُمَّ ٱجۡعَلۡ عَلَىٰ كُلِّ جَبَلٖ
مِّنۡهُنَّ جُزۡءٗا ثُمَّ ٱدۡعُهُنَّ يَأۡتِينَكَ سَعۡيٗاۚ
وَٱعۡلَمۡ أَنَّ ٱللَّهَ عَزِيزٌ حَكِيمٞ

SECTION 36.

261. The parable of those
Who spend their substance
In the way of Allah is that
Of a grain of corn: it groweth
Seven ears, and each ear
Hath a hundred grains.
Allah giveth manifold increase
To whom He pleaseth:
And Allah careth for all
And He knoweth all things,

(٢٦١) مَّثَلُ ٱلَّذِينَ يُنفِقُونَ أَمۡوَٰلَهُمۡ
فِي سَبِيلِ ٱللَّهِ كَمَثَلِ حَبَّةٍ أَنۢبَتَتۡ
سَبۡعَ سَنَابِلَ فِي كُلِّ سُنۢبُلَةٖ مِّاْئَةُ حَبَّةٖۗ
وَٱللَّهُ يُضَٰعِفُ لِمَن يَشَآءُۚ
وَٱللَّهُ وَٰسِعٌ عَلِيمٌ

262. Those who spend
Their substance in the cause
Of Allah, and follow not up
Their gifts with reminders
Of their generosity

(٢٦٢) ٱلَّذِينَ يُنفِقُونَ أَمۡوَٰلَهُمۡ فِي سَبِيلِ ٱللَّهِ
ثُمَّ لَا يُتۡبِعُونَ مَآ أَنفَقُواْ مَنّٗا

306. Verse 258, we saw, illustrated Allah's power over Life and Death, contrasted with man's vain boasts or imaginings. Verse 259 illustrated how Time is immaterial to Allah's workings; things; individuals and nations are subject to laws of life and death, which are under Allah's complete control, however much we may be misled by appearances. (R).

307. Abraham had complete faith in Allah's power, but he wanted, with Allah's permission, to give an explanation of that faith to his own heart and mind. Where I have translated "satisfy my own understanding," the literal translation would be "satisfy my own heart."

308. A *portion* of them: *Juz'ān*. The Commentators understand this to mean that the birds were to be cut up and pieces of them were to be put on the hills. The cutting up or killing is not mentioned, but they say that it is implied by an ellipsis, as the question is how Allah gives life to the dead. (R).

Or with injury—for them
Their reward is with their Lord;
On them shall be no fear,
Nor shall they grieve.

وَلَآ أَذًى لَّهُمْ أَجْرُهُمْ عِندَ رَبِّهِمْ
وَلَا خَوْفٌ عَلَيْهِمْ وَلَا هُمْ يَحْزَنُونَ

263. Kind words[309]
And covering of faults
Are better than charity
Followed by injury.
Allah is Free of all wants,
And He is most Forbearing.

٢٦٣ قَوْلٌ مَّعْرُوفٌ وَمَغْفِرَةٌ
خَيْرٌ مِّن صَدَقَةٍ يَتْبَعُهَآ أَذًى
وَٱللَّهُ غَنِيٌّ حَلِيمٌ

264. O ye who believe!
Cancel not your charity
By reminders of your generosity
Or by injury—like those
Who spend their substance
To be seen of men,
But believe neither
In Allah nor in the Last Day.[310]
They are in Parable like a hard
Barren rock, on which
Is a little soil; on it
Falls heavy rain,
Which leaves it
(Just) a bare stone.
They will be able to do nothing
With aught they have earned.
And Allah guideth not
Those who reject faith.

٢٦٤ يَٰٓأَيُّهَا ٱلَّذِينَ ءَامَنُوا۟ لَا تُبْطِلُوا۟
صَدَقَٰتِكُم بِٱلْمَنِّ وَٱلْأَذَىٰ كَٱلَّذِى يُنفِقُ مَالَهُۥ
رِئَآءَ ٱلنَّاسِ وَلَا يُؤْمِنُ بِٱللَّهِ وَٱلْيَوْمِ ٱلْءَاخِرِ
فَمَثَلُهُۥ كَمَثَلِ صَفْوَانٍ عَلَيْهِ تُرَابٌ
فَأَصَابَهُۥ وَابِلٌ فَتَرَكَهُۥ صَلْدًا
لَّا يَقْدِرُونَ عَلَىٰ
شَىْءٍ مِّمَّا كَسَبُوا۟
وَٱللَّهُ لَا يَهْدِى ٱلْقَوْمَ ٱلْكَٰفِرِينَ

265. And the likeness of those
Who spend their substance,

٢٦٥ وَمَثَلُ ٱلَّذِينَ يُنفِقُونَ أَمْوَٰلَهُمُ

309. A very high standard is set for charity. (1) It must be in the way of Allah. (2) It must expect no reward in this world. (3) It must not be followed by references or reminders to the act of charity. (4) Still less should any annoyance or injury be caused to the recipient, *e.g.*, by boasting that the giver relieved the person in the hour of need. Indeed, the kindness and the spirit which turns a blind eye to other people's faults or shortcomings is the essence of charity: these things are better than charity if charity is spoilt by tricks that do harm. At the same time, while no reward is to be *expected*, there is abundant reward from Allah—material, moral, and spiritual—according to His own good pleasure and plan. If we spend in the way of Allah, it is not as if Allah was in need of our charity. On the contrary our shortcomings are so great that we require His utmost forbearance before any good that we can do can merit His praise or reward. Our motives are so mixed that our best may really be very poor if judged by a very strict standard.

310. False charity, "to be seen of men," is really no charity. It is worse, for it betokens a disbelief in Allah and the Hereafter. "Allah seeth well whatever ye do" (2:265). It is compared to hard barren rock on which by chance has fallen a little soil. Good rain, which renders fertile soil more fruitful, washes away the little soil which this rock had, and exposes its nakedness. What good can hypocrites derive even from the little wealth they may have amassed?

Seeking to please Allah
And to strengthen their souls,
Is as a garden, high
And fertile; heavy rain[311]
Falls on it but makes it yield
A double increase
Of harvest, and if it receives not
Heavy rain, light moisture
Sufficeth it. Allah seeth well
Whatever ye do.

ٱبْتِغَآءَ مَرْضَاتِ ٱللَّهِ وَتَثْبِيتًا مِّنْ أَنفُسِهِمْ
كَمَثَلِ جَنَّةٍۭ بِرَبْوَةٍ أَصَابَهَا وَابِلٌ فَـَٔاتَتْ
أُكُلَهَا ضِعْفَيْنِ فَإِن لَّمْ يُصِبْهَا
وَابِلٌ فَطَلٌّ ۗ وَٱللَّهُ بِمَا تَعْمَلُونَ بَصِيرٌ

266. Does any of you wish
That he should have a garden[312]
With date palms and vines
And streams flowing
Underneath, and all kinds
Of fruit, while he is stricken
With old age, and his children
Are not strong (enough[313]
To look after themselves)—
That it should be caught
In a whirlwind,
With fire therein,
And be burnt up?
Thus doth Allah make clear
To you (His) Signs:
That ye may consider.

٢٦٦ أَيَوَدُّ أَحَدُكُمْ أَن تَكُونَ لَهُۥ جَنَّةٌ
مِّن نَّخِيلٍ وَأَعْنَابٍ تَجْرِى مِن تَحْتِهَا
ٱلْأَنْهَٰرُ لَهُۥ فِيهَا مِن كُلِّ ٱلثَّمَرَٰتِ
وَأَصَابَهُ ٱلْكِبَرُ وَلَهُۥ ذُرِّيَّةٌ ضُعَفَآءُ
فَأَصَابَهَآ إِعْصَارٌ فِيهِ نَارٌ فَٱحْتَرَقَتْ ۗ
كَذَٰلِكَ يُبَيِّنُ ٱللَّهُ لَكُمُ ٱلْـَٔايَٰتِ
لَعَلَّكُمْ تَتَفَكَّرُونَ

311. True charity is like a field with good soil on a high situation. It catches good showers of rain, the moisture penetrates the soil, and yet its elevated situation keeps it well-drained, and healthy favourable conditions increase its output enormously. But supposing even that the rain is not abundant, it catches dew and makes the most of any little moisture it can get, and that is sufficient for it. So a man of true charity is spiritually healthy; he is best situated to attract the bounties of Allah, which he does not hoard selfishly but circulates freely. In lean times he still produces good works, and is content with what he has. He looks to Allah's pleasure and the strengthening of his own soul.

312. The truly spiritual nature of charity having been explained in three parables (2:261, 264, 265) a fourth parable is now added, explaining its bearing on the whole of our life. Suppose we had a beautiful garden well-watered and fertile, with delightful views of streams, and a haven of rest for mind and body; suppose old age were creeping in on us, and our children were either too young to look after themselves or too feeble in health; how should we feel if a sudden whirlwind came with lightning or fire in its train, and burnt it up, thus blasting the whole of our hopes for the present and for the future, and destroying the result of all our labour and savings in the past? Well, this life of ours is a probation. We may work hard, we may save, we may have good luck. We may make ourselves a goodly pleasance, and have ample means of support for ourselves and our children. A great whirlwind charged with lightning and fire comes and burns up the whole show. We are too old to begin again: our children are too young or feeble to help us to repair the mischief. Our chance is lost, because we did not provide against such a contingency. The whirlwind is the "wrath to come": the provision against it is a life of true charity and righteousness, which is the only source of true and lasting happiness in this world and the next. Without it we are subject to all the vicissitudes of this uncertain life. We may even spoil our so-called "charity" by insisting on the obligation which others owe to us or by doing some harm, because our motives are not pure.

313. *Not strong (enough): ḍu'afā'u:* literally weak, decrepit, infirm, possibly referring to both health and will or character.

SECTION 37.

267. O ye who believe!
Give of the good things
Which ye have (honourably)
earned,[314]
And of the fruits of the earth
Which We have produced
For you, and do not even aim[315]
At getting anything
Which is bad, in order that
Out of it ye may give away
Something, when ye yourselves
Would not receive it
Except with closed eyes.[316]
And know that Allah
Is free of all wants,
And worthy of all praise.[317]

٢٦٧ يَـٰٓأَيُّهَا ٱلَّذِينَ ءَامَنُوٓا۟
أَنفِقُوا۟ مِن طَيِّبَـٰتِ مَا كَسَبْتُمْ
وَمِمَّآ أَخْرَجْنَا لَكُم مِّنَ ٱلْأَرْضِ
وَلَا تَيَمَّمُوا۟ ٱلْخَبِيثَ
مِنْهُ تُنفِقُونَ
وَلَسْتُم بِـَٔاخِذِيهِ
إِلَّآ أَن تُغْمِضُوا۟ فِيهِ
وَٱعْلَمُوٓا۟ أَنَّ ٱللَّهَ غَنِىٌّ حَمِيدٌ

268. The Evil One threatens
You with poverty
And bids you to conduct
Unseemly. Allah promiseth
You His forgiveness

٢٦٨ ٱلشَّيْطَـٰنُ يَعِدُكُمُ ٱلْفَقْرَ
وَيَأْمُرُكُم بِٱلْفَحْشَآءِ
وَٱللَّهُ يَعِدُكُم مَّغْفِرَةً مِّنْهُ

314. According to the English proverb "Charity covers a multitude of sins". Such a sentiment is strongly disapproved in Islam. Charity has value only if (1) something good and valuable is given, (2) which has been honourably earned or acquired by the giver, or (3) which is produced in nature and can be referred to as a bounty of Allah. (1) may include such things as are of use and value to others though they may be of less use to us or superfluous to us on account of our having acquired something more suitable for our station in life: for example, discarded clothes, or an old horse or a used motor car; but if the horse is vicious, or the car engine so far gone that it is dangerous to use, then the gift is worse than useless; it is positively harmful, and the giver is a wrongdoer. (2) applies to fraudulent company-promoters, who earn great credit by giving away in charity some of their ill-gotten gains, or to robbers (even if they call themselves by high-sounding names) who "rob Peter to pay Paul". Islam will have nothing to do with tainted property. Its economic code requires that every gain should be honest and honourable. Even "charity" would not cover or destroy the taint. (3) lays down a test in cases of a doubtful gain. Can we refer to it as a gift of Allah? Obviously the produce of honest labour or agriculture can be so referred to. In modern commerce and speculation there is much of quite the contrary character, and charity will not cover the taint. Some kinds of art, skill or talent are God-given, it is the highest kind of charity to teach them or share their product. Others are the contrary: they are bad or tainted. In the same way some professions or services may be tainted, if these tend to moral harm.

315. The preceding note tries to indicate some of the things which are bad or tainted. We should not even think of acquiring them for ourselves, soothing our conscience by the salve that we shall practise charity out of them.

316. *Closed eyes* imply disgust or connivance because of some feature which we would not openly acknowledge.

317. To dedicate tainted things to Allah is a dishonour to Allah. Who is independent of all wants, and Who is worthy of all honour and praise.

And bounties.[318]
And Allah careth for all
And He knoweth all things.

وَفَضۡلٗاۗ وَٱللَّهُ وَٰسِعٌ عَلِيمٞ

269. He granteth wisdom
To whom He pleaseth;
And he to whom wisdom
Is granted receiveth
Indeed a benefit overflowing;
But none will grasp the Message
But men of understanding.

٢٦٩ يُؤۡتِي ٱلۡحِكۡمَةَ مَن يَشَآءُۚ
وَمَن يُؤۡتَ ٱلۡحِكۡمَةَ
فَقَدۡ أُوتِيَ خَيۡرٗا كَثِيرٗاۗ
وَمَا يَذَّكَّرُ إِلَّآ أُوْلُواْ ٱلۡأَلۡبَٰبِ

270. And whatever ye spend
In charity or devotion,
Be sure Allah knows it all.
But the wrongdoers
Have no helpers.

٢٧٠ وَمَآ أَنفَقۡتُم مِّن نَّفَقَةٍ أَوۡ نَذَرۡتُم
مِّن نَّذۡرٖ فَإِنَّ ٱللَّهَ يَعۡلَمُهُۥۗ
وَمَا لِلظَّٰلِمِينَ مِنۡ أَنصَارٍ

271. If ye disclose (acts[319]
Of) charity, even so
It is well,
But if ye conceal them,
And make them reach
Those (really) in need,
That is best for you:
It will remove from you
Some of your (stains
Of) evil. And Allah
Is well-acquainted
With what ye do.

٢٧١ إِن تُبۡدُواْ ٱلصَّدَقَٰتِ فَنِعِمَّا هِيَۖ
وَإِن تُخۡفُوهَا وَتُؤۡتُوهَا
ٱلۡفُقَرَآءَ فَهُوَ خَيۡرٞ لَّكُمۡۚ
وَيُكَفِّرُ عَنكُم
مِّن سَيِّـَٔاتِكُمۡۗ
وَٱللَّهُ بِمَا تَعۡمَلُونَ خَبِيرٞ

272. It is not required
Of thee (O Messenger),

٢٧٢ لَّيۡسَ عَلَيۡكَ

318. Good and evil draw us opposite ways and by opposite motives, and the contrast is well-marked out in charity. When we think of doing some real act of kindness or charity, we are assailed with doubts and fear of impoverishment; but Evil supports any tendency to selfishness, greed, or even to extravagant expenditure for show, or self-indulgence, or unseemly appetites. On the other hand, Allah draws us on to all that is kind and good, for that way lies the forgiveness of our sins, and greater real prosperity and satisfaction. No kind or generous act ever ruined any one. It is false generosity that is sometimes shown as leading to ruin. As Allah knows all our motives and cares for all, and has everything in His power, it is obvious which course a wise man will choose. But wisdom is rare, and it is only wisdom that can appreciate true well-being and distinguish it from the false appearance of well-being.

319. It is better to seek no publicity in charity. But if it is known there is no harm. If it is for public purposes, it must necessarily be known, and a pedantic show of concealment may itself be a fault. The harm of publicity lies in motives of ostentation. We can better reach the really deserving poor by quietly seeking for them. The spiritual benefit ensures to our own souls, provided our motives are pure, and we are really seeking the good pleasure of Allah.

To set them on the right path,[320]
But Allah sets on the right path
Whom He pleaseth.
Whatever of good ye give
Benefits your own souls,
And ye shall only do so
Seeking the "Face"[321]
Of Allah. Whatever good
Ye give, shall be
Rendered back to you,
And ye shall not
Be dealt with unjustly.

هُدَىٰهُمْ وَلَٰكِنَّ ٱللَّهَ يَهْدِى مَن يَشَآءُ
وَمَا تُنفِقُوا۟ مِنْ خَيْرٍ فَلِأَنفُسِكُمْ
وَمَا تُنفِقُونَ إِلَّا ٱبْتِغَآءَ وَجْهِ ٱللَّهِ
وَمَا تُنفِقُوا۟ مِنْ خَيْرٍ يُوَفَّ إِلَيْكُمْ
وَأَنتُمْ لَا تُظْلَمُونَ

273. (Charity is) for those
In need, who, in Allah's cause[322]
Are restricted (from travel),
And cannot move about
In the land, seeking
(For trade or work):
The ignorant man thinks,
Because of their modesty,
That they are free from want.
Thou shalt know them
By their (unfailing) mark:
They beg not importunately
From all and sundry,
And whatever of good
Ye give, be assured
Allah knoweth it well.

٢٧٣ لِلْفُقَرَآءِ ٱلَّذِينَ
أُحْصِرُوا۟ فِى سَبِيلِ ٱللَّهِ
لَا يَسْتَطِيعُونَ ضَرْبًا فِى ٱلْأَرْضِ
يَحْسَبُهُمُ ٱلْجَاهِلُ أَغْنِيَآءَ مِنَ
ٱلتَّعَفُّفِ تَعْرِفُهُم بِسِيمَٰهُمْ
لَا يَسْـَٔلُونَ ٱلنَّاسَ إِلْحَافًا
وَمَا تُنفِقُوا۟ مِنْ خَيْرٍ فَإِنَّ ٱللَّهَ بِهِۦ عَلِيمٌ

SECTION 38.

274. Those who (in charity)[323]

٢٧٤ ٱلَّذِينَ

320. In connection with charity this means that we must relieve those really in need, whether they are good or bad, on the right path or not, Muslims or otherwise. It is not for us to judge in these matters. Allah will give light according to His wisdom. Incidentally it adds a further meaning to the command, "Let there be no compulsion in religion" (2:256). For compulsion may not only be by force, but by economic necessity. In matters of religion we must not even compel by a bribe of charity. The chief motive in charity should be Allah's pleasure and our own spiritual good. This was addressed in the first instance to Al Muṣṭafā in Madīnah, but it is of universal application.

321. See note to 2:112, *Wajh* means literally: face, countenance; hence, favour, glory, Self, Presence.

322. Indiscriminate acts of so-called charity are condemned as they may do more harm than good (see 2:262). The real beneficiaries of charity are indicated. They must be in want. And the want must be due to some honourable cause. For example, they may be doing some unpaid service, such as teaching, or acquiring knowledge or skill, or be in exile for their faith, or in other ways be prevented from seeking employment or doing strenuous work. "Allah's cause" must not be narrowly interpreted. All sincere and real service to humanity comes within the definition. Such men do not beg from door to door. It is the duty of those who are well-to-do, or the Public Purse, to find them out. (R).

323. We recapitulate the beauty of charity (*i.e.*, unselfish giving of one's self or one's goods) before we come to its opposite, *i.e.*, the selfish grasping greed of usury against those in need or distress. Charity instead of impoverishing you will enrich you: you will have more happiness and less fear. Contrast it with what follows—the degradation of the grasping usurer.

Spend of their goods
By night and by day,
In secret and in public,
Have their reward
With their Lord:
On them shall be no fear,
Nor shall they grieve.

يُنفِقُونَ أَمْوَٰلَهُم بِٱلَّيْلِ وَٱلنَّهَارِ سِرًّا
وَعَلَانِيَةً فَلَهُمْ أَجْرُهُمْ عِندَ رَبِّهِمْ
وَلَا خَوْفٌ عَلَيْهِمْ وَلَا هُمْ يَحْزَنُونَ

275. Those who devour usury[324]
Will not stand except
As stands one whom
The Evil One by his touch
Hath driven to madness.[325]
That is because they say:
"Trade is like usury,"[326]
But Allah hath permitted trade
And forbidden usury.
Those who after receiving
Direction from their Lord,
Desist, shall be pardoned
For the past; their case
Is for Allah (to judge);
But those who repeat
(The offence) are Companions
Of the Fire; they will
Abide therein (forever).

٢٧٥ ٱلَّذِينَ يَأْكُلُونَ ٱلرِّبَوٰاْ لَا يَقُومُونَ
إِلَّا كَمَا يَقُومُ ٱلَّذِى يَتَخَبَّطُهُ ٱلشَّيْطَٰنُ
مِنَ ٱلْمَسِّ ذَٰلِكَ بِأَنَّهُمْ قَالُوٓاْ إِنَّمَا ٱلْبَيْعُ
مِثْلُ ٱلرِّبَوٰاْ وَأَحَلَّ ٱللَّهُ ٱلْبَيْعَ وَحَرَّمَ ٱلرِّبَوٰاْ
فَمَن جَآءَهُۥ مَوْعِظَةٌ مِّن رَّبِّهِۦ فَٱنتَهَىٰ فَلَهُۥ
مَا سَلَفَ وَأَمْرُهُۥٓ إِلَى ٱللَّهِ وَمَنْ عَادَ
فَأُوْلَٰٓئِكَ أَصْحَٰبُ ٱلنَّارِ
هُمْ فِيهَا خَٰلِدُونَ

276. Allah will deprive
Usury of all blessing,
But will give increase
For deeds of charity;
For He loveth not

٢٧٦ يَمْحَقُ ٱللَّهُ ٱلرِّبَوٰاْ
وَيُرْبِى ٱلصَّدَقَٰتِ وَٱللَّهُ لَا يُحِبُّ

324. Usury is condemned and prohibited in the strongest possible terms. There can be no question about the prohibition. When we come to the definition of usury there is room for difference of opinion. 'Umar, according to Ibn Kathīr, felt some difficulty in the matter, as the Prophet left this world before the details of the question were settled. This was one of the three questions on which he wished he had had more light from the Prophet, the other two being Khilāfah and Kalālah (see 4:12, n. 518). Our 'Ulamā', ancient and modern, have worked out a great body of literature on usury, based mainly on economic conditions as they existed at the rise of Islam. (R).

325. An apt simile: whereas legitimate trade or industry increases the prosperity and stability of men and nations, a dependence on usury would merely encourage a race of idlers, cruel blood-suckers, and worthless fellows who do not know their own good and therefore akin to madmen.

326. Owing to the fact that interest occupies a central position in modern economic life, and specially since interest is the very life blood of the existing financial institutions, a number of Muslims have been inclined to interpret it in a manner which is radically different from the understanding of Muslim scholars throughout the last fourteen centuries and is also sharply in confict with the categorical statements of the Prophet (peace be on him). According to Islamic teachings any excess on the capital is *ribā* (interest). Islam accepts no distinction, insofar as prohibition is concerned, between reasonable and exorbitant rates of interest, and thus what came to be regarded as the difference between usury and interest; nor between returns on bonus for consumption and those for production purposes and so on. [Eds.].

Creatures ungrateful
And wicked.

كُلَّ كَفَّارٍ أَثِيمٍ

277. Those who believe,
And do deeds of righteousness,
And establish regular prayers
And regular charity,
Will have their reward
With their Lord:
On them shall be no fear,
Nor shall they grieve.[327]

٢٧٧ إِنَّ ٱلَّذِينَ ءَامَنُوا۟ وَعَمِلُوا۟
ٱلصَّٰلِحَٰتِ وَأَقَامُوا۟ ٱلصَّلَوٰةَ وَءَاتَوُا۟ ٱلزَّكَوٰةَ
لَهُمْ أَجْرُهُمْ عِندَ رَبِّهِمْ وَلَا خَوْفٌ عَلَيْهِمْ
وَلَا هُمْ يَحْزَنُونَ

278. O ye who believe!
Fear Allah, and give up
What remains of your demand
For usury, if ye are
Indeed believers.

٢٧٨ يَٰٓأَيُّهَا ٱلَّذِينَ ءَامَنُوا۟ ٱتَّقُوا۟ ٱللَّهَ
وَذَرُوا۟ مَا بَقِىَ مِنَ ٱلرِّبَوٰٓا۟ إِن كُنتُم مُّؤْمِنِينَ

279. If ye do it not,
Take notice of war[328]
From Allah and His Messenger:
But if ye turn back,
Ye shall have
Your capital sums;
Deal not unjustly,
And ye shall not
Be dealt with unjustly.

٢٧٩ فَإِن لَّمْ تَفْعَلُوا۟
فَأْذَنُوا۟ بِحَرْبٍ مِّنَ ٱللَّهِ وَرَسُولِهِۦ
وَإِن تُبْتُمْ فَلَكُمْ رُءُوسُ أَمْوَٰلِكُمْ
لَا تَظْلِمُونَ وَلَا تُظْلَمُونَ

280. If the debtor is
In a difficulty,
Grant him time
Till it is easy
For him to repay.
But if ye remit it
By way of charity,
That is best for you
If ye only knew.

٢٨٠ وَإِن كَانَ ذُو عُسْرَةٍ
فَنَظِرَةٌ إِلَىٰ مَيْسَرَةٍ
وَأَن تَصَدَّقُوا۟ خَيْرٌ لَّكُمْ
إِن كُنتُمْ تَعْلَمُونَ

281. And fear the Day
When ye shall be
Brought back to Allah.

٢٨١ وَٱتَّقُوا۟ يَوْمًا تُرْجَعُونَ فِيهِ إِلَى ٱللَّهِ

327. The contrast between charity and unlawful grasping of wealth began at 2:274, where this phrase occurs as a theme. Here the theme finishes with the same phrase. The following four verses refer to further concessions on behalf of debtors, as creditors are asked to (a) give up even claims arising out of the past on account of usury, and (b) to give time for payment of capital if necessary, or (c) to write off the debt altogether as an act of charity.

328. This is not war for opinions, but an ultimatum of war for the liberation of debtors unjustly dealt with and oppressed.

Then shall every soul
Be paid what it earned,
And none shall be
Dealt with unjustly.

SECTION 39.

282. O ye who believe!
When ye deal with each other,
In transactions involving
Future obligations
In a fixed period of time,
Reduce them to writing[329]
Let a scribe write down
Faithfully as between
The parties; let not the scribe
Refuse to write: as Allah[330]
Has taught him,
So let him write.
Let him who incurs
The liability dictate,
But let him fear
His Lord Allah,
And not diminish
Aught of what he owes.
If the party liable
Is mentally deficient,
Or weak, or unable
Himself to dictate,[331]
Let his guardian
Dictate faithfully.
And get two witnesses,
Out of your own men,[332]

ثُمَّ تُوَفَّىٰ كُلُّ نَفْسٍ مَّا كَسَبَتْ
وَهُمْ لَا يُظْلَمُونَ

٢٨٢ يَـٰٓأَيُّهَا ٱلَّذِينَ ءَامَنُوٓا۟
إِذَا تَدَايَنتُم بِدَيْنٍ إِلَىٰٓ أَجَلٍ مُّسَمًّى فَٱكْتُبُوهُ ۚ
وَلْيَكْتُب بَّيْنَكُمْ كَاتِبٌۢ بِٱلْعَدْلِ ۚ وَلَا يَأْبَ
كَاتِبٌ أَن يَكْتُبَ كَمَا عَلَّمَهُ ٱللَّهُ ۚ
فَلْيَكْتُبْ وَلْيُمْلِلِ ٱلَّذِى عَلَيْهِ ٱلْحَقُّ
وَلْيَتَّقِ ٱللَّهَ رَبَّهُۥ وَلَا يَبْخَسْ مِنْهُ شَيْـًٔا ۚ
فَإِن كَانَ ٱلَّذِى عَلَيْهِ ٱلْحَقُّ سَفِيهًا أَوْ ضَعِيفًا
أَوْ لَا يَسْتَطِيعُ أَن يُمِلَّ هُوَ فَلْيُمْلِلْ وَلِيُّهُۥ
بِٱلْعَدْلِ ۚ وَٱسْتَشْهِدُوا۟ شَهِيدَيْنِ
مِن رِّجَالِكُمْ ۖ

329. The first part of the verse deals with transactions involving future payment or future consideration, and the second part with transactions in which payment and delivery are made on the spot. Examples of the former are if goods are brought now and payment is promised at a fixed time and place in the future, or if cash is paid now and delivery is contracted for at a fixed time and place in the future. In such cases a written document is recommended, but it is held that the words later on in this verse, that it is "juster. . .more suitable as evidence, and more convenient to prevent doubts," etc., imply that it is not obligatory in law. Examples of the latter kind—cash payment and delivery on the spot—require no evidence in writing, but apparently oral witnesses to such transactions are recommended.

330. The scribe in such matters assumes a fiduciary capacity; he should therefore remember to act as in the presence of Allah, with full justice to both parties. The art of writing he should look upon as a gift from Allah, and he should use it as in His service. In an illiterate population the scribe's position is still more responsible.

331. Possibly the person "mentally deficient, or weak, or unable to dictate," may also be incapable of making a valid contract, and the whole duty would be on his guardian, who again must act in perfect good faith, not only protecting but vigilantly promoting the interests of his ward.

332. It is desirable that the men (or women) who are chosen as witness should be from the circle to which the parties belong, as they would best be able to understand the transaction, and be most easily available if their evidence is required in future.

And if there are not two men,
Then a man and two women,
Such as ye choose,
For witnesses,
So that if one of them errs,
The other can remind her.
The witnesses
Should not refuse
When they are called on
(For evidence).
Disdain not to reduce
To writing (your contract)
For a future period,
Whether it be small
Or big: it is juster
In the sight of Allah,
More suitable as evidence,
And more convenient
To prevent doubts
Among yourselves
But if it be a transaction
Which ye carry out
On the spot among yourselves
There is no blame on you
If ye reduce it not
To writing.
But take witnesses
Whenever ye make
A commercial contract;
And let neither scribe
Nor witness suffer harm.
If ye do (such harm),
It would be wickedness
In you. So fear Allah;
For it is Allah
That teaches you.
And Allah is well acquainted
With all things.[333]

فَإِن لَّمْ يَكُونَا رَجُلَيْنِ
فَرَجُلٌ وَٱمْرَأَتَانِ مِمَّن تَرْضَوْنَ
مِنَ ٱلشُّهَدَآءِ أَن تَضِلَّ إِحْدَىٰهُمَا
فَتُذَكِّرَ إِحْدَىٰهُمَا ٱلْأُخْرَىٰ
وَلَا يَأْبَ ٱلشُّهَدَآءُ إِذَا مَا دُعُوا۟ وَلَا تَسْـَٔمُوٓا۟
أَن تَكْتُبُوهُ صَغِيرًا أَوْ كَبِيرًا إِلَىٰٓ أَجَلِهِۦ
ذَٰلِكُمْ أَقْسَطُ عِندَ ٱللَّهِ وَأَقْوَمُ لِلشَّهَـٰدَةِ
وَأَدْنَىٰٓ أَلَّا تَرْتَابُوٓا۟ إِلَّآ أَن تَكُونَ
تِجَـٰرَةً حَاضِرَةً تُدِيرُونَهَا بَيْنَكُمْ
فَلَيْسَ عَلَيْكُمْ جُنَاحٌ أَلَّا تَكْتُبُوهَا
وَأَشْهِدُوٓا۟ إِذَا تَبَايَعْتُمْ
وَلَا يُضَآرَّ كَاتِبٌ وَلَا شَهِيدٌ
وَإِن تَفْعَلُوا۟ فَإِنَّهُۥ فُسُوقٌۢ بِكُمْ
وَٱتَّقُوا۟ ٱللَّهَ وَيُعَلِّمُكُمُ ٱللَّهُ
وَٱللَّهُ بِكُلِّ شَىْءٍ عَلِيمٌ

283. If ye are on a journey,
And cannot find
A scribe, a pledge
With possession (may serve

٢٨٣ وَإِن كُنتُمْ عَلَىٰ سَفَرٍ
وَلَمْ تَجِدُوا۟ كَاتِبًا فَرِهَـٰنٌ مَّقْبُوضَةٌ

333. Commercial morality is here taught on the highest plane and yet in the most practical manner, both as regards the bargains to be made, the evidence to be provided, the doubts to be avoided, and the duties and rights of scribes and witnesses. Probity even in worldly matters is to be, not a mere matter of convenience or policy, but a matter of conscience and religious duty. Even our everyday transactions are to be carried out as in the presence of Allah.

The purpose).[334]
And if one of you
Deposits a thing
On trust with another,[335]
Let the trustee
(Faithfully) discharge
His trust, and let him
Fear his Lord.
Conceal not evidence;
For whoever conceals it—
His heart is tainted[336]
With sin. And Allah
Knoweth all that ye do.

فَإِنْ أَمِنَ بَعْضُكُم بَعْضًا
فَلْيُؤَدِّ ٱلَّذِى ٱؤْتُمِنَ أَمَٰنَتَهُۥ
وَلْيَتَّقِ ٱللَّهَ رَبَّهُۥ ۗ وَلَا تَكْتُمُوا۟ ٱلشَّهَٰدَةَ ۚ
وَمَن يَكْتُمْهَا فَإِنَّهُۥٓ ءَاثِمٌ قَلْبُهُۥ ۗ
وَٱللَّهُ بِمَا تَعْمَلُونَ عَلِيمٌ

C. 53.—(2:284-286.)

Our honesty and upright conduct
Are not mere matters of policy
Or convenience: all our life in this world
Must be lived as in the presence of Allah.
The finest example of Faith we have
In the Prophet's life; full of faith,
Let us render willing obedience
To Allah's Will. Our responsibility,
Though great, is not a burden
Greater than we can bear; let us
Pray for Allah's assistance, and He will help.

SECTION 40.

284. To Allah belongeth all
That is in the heavens
And on earth. Whether
Ye show what is in your minds
Or conceal it, Allah
Calleth you to account for it.
He forgiveth whom He pleaseth,
And punisheth whom He pleaseth.

(٢٨٤) لِّلَّهِ مَا فِى ٱلسَّمَٰوَٰتِ وَمَا فِى ٱلْأَرْضِ ۗ
وَإِن تُبْدُوا۟ مَا فِىٓ أَنفُسِكُمْ أَوْ تُخْفُوهُ
يُحَاسِبْكُم بِهِ ٱللَّهُ ۖ فَيَغْفِرُ لِمَن يَشَآءُ
وَيُعَذِّبُ مَن يَشَآءُ ۗ

334. A pledge or security stands on its own independent footing, though it is a very convenient form of closing the bargain where the parties cannot trust each other, and cannot get a written agreement with proper witnesses.

335. The Law of Deposit implies great trust in the Depositary on the part of the Depositor. The Depositary becomes a trustee, and the doctrine of Trust can be further developed on that basis. The trustee's duty is to guard the interests of the person on whose behalf he holds the trust and to render back the property and accounts when required according to the terms of the trust. This duty again is linked to the sanction of Religion, which requires a higher standard than Law.

336. It sometimes happens that if some inconvenient piece of evidence is destroyed or concealed, we gain a great advantage materially. We are warned not to yield to such a temptation. The concealment of evidence has a serious effect on our own moral and spiritual life, for it taints the very source of higher life, as typified by the heart. The heart is also the seat of our secrets. We are told that the sin will reach our most secret being, though the sin may not be visible or open to the world. Further, the heart is the seat of our affections, and false dealing taints all our affections.

For Allah hath power
Over all things.

285. The Messenger believeth
In what hath been revealed
To him from his Lord,
As do the men of faith.
Each one (of them) believeth
In Allah, His angels,
His books, and His Messengers.[337]
"We make no distinction (they say)
Between one and another[338]
Of His Messengers." And they say:
"We hear, and we obey:
(We seek) Thy forgiveness,[339]
Our Lord, and to Thee
Is the end of all journeys."

286. On no soul doth Allah
Place a burden greater
Than it can bear.[340]
It gets every good that it earns,
And it suffers every ill that it earns.
(Pray:) "Our Lord!
Condemn us not
If we forget or fall
Into error; our Lord!
Lay not on us a burden
Like that which Thou
Didst lay on those before us;[341]

وَاللَّهُ عَلَىٰ كُلِّ شَيْءٍ قَدِيرٌ

٢٨٥ ءَامَنَ الرَّسُولُ بِمَآ أُنزِلَ إِلَيْهِ مِن رَّبِّهِۦ
وَالْمُؤْمِنُونَ كُلٌّ ءَامَنَ بِاللَّهِ وَمَلَٰٓئِكَتِهِۦ وَكُتُبِهِۦ
وَرُسُلِهِۦ لَا نُفَرِّقُ بَيْنَ أَحَدٍ مِّن رُّسُلِهِۦ
وَقَالُوا سَمِعْنَا وَأَطَعْنَا
غُفْرَانَكَ رَبَّنَا
وَإِلَيْكَ الْمَصِيرُ

٢٨٦ لَا يُكَلِّفُ اللَّهُ نَفْسًا إِلَّا وُسْعَهَا
لَهَا مَا كَسَبَتْ وَعَلَيْهَا مَا اكْتَسَبَتْ
رَبَّنَا لَا تُؤَاخِذْنَآ إِن نَّسِينَآ أَوْ أَخْطَأْنَا
رَبَّنَا وَلَا تَحْمِلْ عَلَيْنَآ إِصْرًا
كَمَا حَمَلْتَهُۥ عَلَى الَّذِينَ مِن قَبْلِنَا

337. This Sūrah started with the question of faith (2:3-4), showed us various aspects of faith and the denial of faith, gave us ordinances for the new people of Islam as a community, and now rounds off the argument again with a confession of faith and of its practical manifestation in conduct ("we hear and we obey"), and closes on a note of humility, so that we may confess our sins, ask for forgiveness, and pray for Allah's help and guidance.

338. *Cf.* 2:253, n. 289. It is not for us to make any distinction between one and another of Allah's Messengers; we must honour them all equally, though we know that Allah in His wisdom sent them with different kinds of mission and gave them different degrees of rank.

339. When our faith and conduct are sincere, we realise how far from perfection we are, and we humbly pray to Allah for the forgiveness of our sins. We feel that Allah imposes no burden on us that we cannot bear, and with this realisation in our hearts and in the confession of our lips, we go to Him and ask for His help and guidance.

340. *Cf.* 2:233. In that verse the burden was in terms of material wealth; here it is in terms of spiritual duty. Assured by Allah that He will accept from each soul just such duty as it has the ability to offer, we pray further on for the fulfilment of that promise.

341. We must not be arrogant, and think that because Allah has granted us His favour and mercy we have no need to exert ourselves, or that we are ourselves superior to those before us. On the contrary, knowing how much they failed, we pray that our burdens should be lightened, and we confess our realisation that we have all the greater need for Allah's mercy and forgiveness.

And so we end the whole argument of the Sūrah with a prayer for Allah's help, not in our own selfish ends, but in our resolve to uphold Allah's truth against all Unbelief.

Our Lord! lay not on us A burden greater than we Have strength to bear.	رَبَّنَا وَلَا تُحَمِّلْنَا مَا لَا طَاقَةَ لَنَا بِهِۦ
Blot out our sins, And grant us forgiveness. Have mercy on us.	وَٱعْفُ عَنَّا وَٱغْفِرْ لَنَا وَٱرْحَمْنَآ
Thou art our Protector;	أَنتَ مَوْلَىٰنَا فَٱنصُرْنَا
Help us against those Who stand against Faith."	عَلَى ٱلْقَوْمِ ٱلْكَٰفِرِينَ

APPENDIX I.

The Abbreviated Letters (*Al Muqaṭṭaʿāt*)

Certain Sūrahs have certain initials prefixed to them, which are called the "Abbreviated Letters." A number of conjectures have been made as to their meaning. Opinions are divided as to the exact meaning of each particular letter or combination of letters, and it is agreed that only Allah knows their exact meaning. (R).

Their presence is not inconsistent with the character of the Qur'ān as a "plain book." The book of nature is also a plain book, but how few can fully understand it? Everyone can get out of the Qur'ān plain guidance for his life according to his capacity for spiritual understanding. As his capacity grows, so will his understanding grow. The whole Book is a record for all time. It must necessarily contain truths that only gradually unfold themselves to humanity.

This is not a mystery of the same class as "mysteries" by which we are asked to believe against the dictates of reason. If we are asked to believe that one is three and three is one, we can give no intelligible meaning to the words. If we are asked to believe that certain initials have a meaning which will be understood in the fullness of time or of spiritual development, we are asked to draw upon faith, but we are not asked to do any violence to our reason.

I shall try to discuss some of the probable meanings of any particular abbreviated letter or set of abbreviated letters on the first occasion on which it appears in the Qur'ān. But it may be desirable here to take a general view of the facts of their occurrence to help us in appreciating the various views which are held about them.

There are 29 letters in the Arabic alphabet (counting *hamzah* and *alif* as two letters), and there are 29 Sūrahs which have abbreviated letters prefixed to them. One of these Sūrahs (S. 42.) has two sets of abbreviated letters, but we need not count this Sūrah twice. If we take the half of the alphabet, omitting the fraction, we get 14, and this is the number of letters which actually occur in the *Muqaṭṭaʿāt*.

The 14 letters, which occur in various combinations, are:

Alif	أ	Qāf	ق
Ḥā'	ح	Kāf	ك
Rā'	ر	Lām	ل
Sīn	س	Mīm	م
Ṣād	ص	Nūn	ن
Ṭā'	ط	Hā'	هـ
'Ayn	ع	Yā'	ى

The science of phonetics tells us that our vocal sounds arise from the expulsion of the air from the lungs, and the sounds are determined by the way in which the breath passes through the various organs of speech, *e.g.*, the throat (guttural), or the various positions of the tongue to the middle or front of the palate or to the teeth, or the play of the lips. Everyone of these kinds of sounds is represented in these letters.

Let us now examine the combinations.

Three of these letters occur alone, prefixed each to only one Sūrah. The letters and Sūrahs are:

S. 38	Ṣād	ص
S. 50	Qāf	ق
S. 68	Nūn	نٓ

The combinations of two letters occur in ten Sūrahs as shown below. Three of them occur only once each, but the fourth Ḥā', Mīm (حٰمٓ) occurs in seven consecutive Sūrahs.

S. 20	Ṭā', Hā'	طٰه
S. 27	Ṭā', Sīn	طسٓ
S. 36	Yā', Sīn	يسٓ
S. 40, S. 41, S. 42, S. 43, S. 44, S. 45, S. 46	Ḥā', Mīm	حٰمٓ

Note that S. 42 has a double combination of abbreviated letters, one of two followed by one of three. See under combinations of five.

There are three combinations of three letters each, occurring as follows in 13 Sūrahs:

S. 2, S. 3, S. 29, S. 30, S. 31, S. 32	Alif, Lām, Mīm	الٓمٓ
S. 10, S. 11, S. 12, S. 14, S. 15	Alif, Lām, Rā	الٓر
S. 26, S. 28	Ṭā', Sīn, Mīm	طسٓمٓ

Combinations of four letters occur twice, each only once:

S. 7	Alif, Lām, Mīm, Ṣād	الٓمٓصٓ
S. 8*	Alif, Lām, Mīm, Rā'	الٓمٓر

Finally there remain the combinations of five letters, each of which occurs once only, as follows:

S. 19	Kāf, Hā', Yā', 'Ayn, Ṣād	كٓهيعٓصٓ
S. 42	Ḥā', Mīm — 'Ayn, Sīn, Qāf	حٰمٓ عٓسٓقٓ

*Note that the three preceding and the two following Sūrahs have the triple letters Alif, Lām, Mīm, Rā'.

In S. 42, the Ḥā', Mīm (حم) and 'Ayn Sīn, Qāf (عسق) are put in separate verses. From that point of view they may be considered two separate combinations. The first combination has already been listed under the group of two-letter combinations.

This arithmetical analysis brings certain facts into prominence. I do not know how far they have a bearing on the inner meaning of the *Muqaṭṭa'at*.

The combinations of abbreviated letters that run in a series in consecutive Sūrahs is noticeable. For example, Ḥā', Mīm (حم) occurs in seven consecutive Sūrahs from 40 to 46. The combination Alif, Lām, Rā' (الر) occurs in six consecutive Sūrahs, 10 to 15, but in one of them (S. 8) is modified to Alif, Lām, Mīm, Rā (المر) connecting it with the Alif, Lām, Mīm (الم) series. The Alif, Lām, Mīm (الم) series covers six Sūrahs. It begins with S. 2 and S. 3 which are practically the beginning of the Qur'ān, and ends with the four consecutive Sūrahs, 29 to 32. I call S. 2 and S. 3 practically the beginning of the Qur'ān, because S. 1 is considered a general introduction to the Qur'ān, and the first Sīpāra or *Juz'* is commonly known as Alif, Lām, Mīm, (الم) the first verse of S. 2. The combination Ṭā', Sīn, Mīm (طسم) is prefixed to S. 26 and S. 28, but the intervening S. 27 has the combination Ṭā', Sīn, (طس) which may be considered a syncopated form, or the three-letter combination Ṭā', Sīn, Mīm (طسم) may be considered an extended form of Ṭā', Sīn (طس). Again the question arises: does the Mīm (م) in Alif, Lām, Mīm (الم) and Ḥā', Mīm (حم), Ṭā', Sīn, Mīm (طسم) stand for the same signification, or does it mean a different thing in each case? We may generalise and say that there are three series of six, and one series of three, and the others occur all singly.

We should logically look for a common factor in the Sūrahs bearing the same initials, and this factor should be different for Sūrahs bearing other initials. In all cases where the abbreviated letters occur, there is some mention of the Qur'ān or the Book. The *Itqan* makes an exception in the case of three Sūrahs: *Al 'Ankabūt* (S. 29), *Al Rūm* (S. 30), and *Nūn* (S. 68). But a close perusal will show that these Sūrahs are no exceptions. In 29:27 we have a reference to the Book remaining in the family of Abraham, and later on we have a whole Section, devoted to the Book, with special reference to the continuity of revelation in the previous Books and the Qur'ān (29:45-51). In 30:58 there is express mention of the Qur'ān, and the whole argument of the Sūrah leads up to the intimate relation between Allah's "Signs" in nature (30:20-27) and His revelation in the Qur'ān. In S. 48:52, the very first verse begins the theme from the Pen as the instrument of writing, exhorts Muṣṭafā to stand forth boldly to proclaim the Message, and ends (48:52) with the declaration that it is a Message for all the worlds. (R).

These are general considerations, which I have thought it most convenient to present in the form of an Appendix.

INTRODUCTION TO SŪRAH 3—*ĀLI 'IMRĀN*

This Sūrah is cognate to Sūrah 2, but the matter is here treated from a different point of view. The references to Badr (*Ramaḍān.* A.H. 2) and Uḥud (*Shawwāl* A. Ḥ. 3) give a clue to the dates of those passages.

Like Sūrah 2, it takes a general view of the religious history of mankind, with special reference to the People of the Book, proceeds to explain the birth of the new people of Islam and their ordinances, insists on the need of struggle and fighting in the cause of Truth, and exhorts those who have been blessed with Islam to remain constant in Faith, pray for guidance, and maintain their spiritual hope for the future.

The new points of view developed are: (1) The emphasis is here laid on the duty of the Christians to accept the new light; the Christians are here specially appealed to, as the Jews were specially appealed to in the last Sūrah; (2) the lessons of the battles of Badr and Uḥud are set out for the Muslim community; and (3) the responsibilities of that community are insisted on both internally and in their relations to those outside.

Summary—Allah having revealed His Book, confirming previous revelations, we must accept it in all reverence, try to understand its meaning, and reject the base motives which make truth unacceptable to those who reject Faith. (3:1-20, and C. 54.)

The People of the Book had only a portion of the Book, and if they reject the complete Book, the People of Faith must part company with them, and their day is done. (3:21-30, and C. 55.)

The story of the family of 'Imrān (the father of Moses) leads us from the Mosaic Dispensation to the miracles connected with the birth of Jesus and his ministry. (3:31-63, and C. 56.)

Allah's revelation being continuous, all people are invited to accept its completion in Islam, and controversies are deprecated. The Muslims are asked to hold together in union and harmony, and are promised security from harm from their enemies, and enjoined to seek friendship among their own people. (3:64-120, and C. 57.)

The battle of Badr showed how Allah helps and upholds the virtuous, and how patience, perseverance, and discipline find their reward; on the other hand, the lessons of Uḥud must be learnt, not in despair, but in the exercise of the higher virtues and in contempt of pain and death. (3:121-148, and C. 58)

The misfortunes at Uḥud are shown to be due to the indiscipline of some, the indecision and selfishness of others, and cowardice on the part of the hypocrites, but no enemy can hurt Allah's Cause. (3:149-180, and C. 59.)

The taunts of the enemy should be disregarded, and sincere prayer offered to Allah Who would grant His servants success and prosperity. (3:181-200, and C. 60.)

C. 54.—The Qur'ān revelation has, step by step,
(3:1-20.) Confirmed the Law of Moses and the Gospel
Of Jesus. It is a guide from Allah,
And appeals to reason and understanding.
Let us understand it rightly, in reverence
And truth, unswayed by those who reject
Faith, and seeking ever the reward
Of the pleasure of Allah, through firmness,
Patience, discipline, and charity, and offering others
The light which we have ourselves received.

Sūrah 3.

Āli 'Imrān (The Family of 'Imrān)

In the name of Allah, Most Gracious,
Most Merciful.

1. Alif Lām Mīm.[342]

2. Allah! There is no god
But He—the Living,
The Self-Subsisting, Eternal.[343]

3. It is He Who sent down
To thee (step by step),
In truth, the Book,
Confirming what went before it;
And He sent down the Law
(Of Moses) and the Gospel[344]
(Of Jesus)

4. Before this, as a guide to
mankind,
And He sent down the Criterion[345]
(Of judgement between right and
wrong).
Then those who reject
Faith in the Signs of Allah
Will suffer the severest
Penalty, and Allah
Is Exalted in Might,
Lord of Retribution.

5. From Allah, verily
Nothing is hidden
On earth or in the heavens.

6. He it is Who shapes you
In the wombs as He pleases.[346]

الجزء الثالث سورة آل عمران

بسم الله الرحمن الرحيم

١ الٓمٓ

٢ ٱللَّهُ لَآ إِلَٰهَ إِلَّا هُوَ ٱلۡحَيُّ ٱلۡقَيُّومُ

٣ نَزَّلَ عَلَيۡكَ ٱلۡكِتَٰبَ
بِٱلۡحَقِّ مُصَدِّقٗا لِّمَا بَيۡنَ يَدَيۡهِ
وَأَنزَلَ ٱلتَّوۡرَىٰةَ وَٱلۡإِنجِيلَ

٤ مِن قَبۡلُ هُدٗى لِّلنَّاسِ
وَأَنزَلَ ٱلۡفُرۡقَانَۗ
إِنَّ ٱلَّذِينَ كَفَرُواْ بِـَٔايَٰتِ ٱللَّهِ
لَهُمۡ عَذَابٞ شَدِيدٞۗ
وَٱللَّهُ عَزِيزٞ ذُو ٱنتِقَامٍ

٥ إِنَّ ٱللَّهَ لَا يَخۡفَىٰ عَلَيۡهِ
شَيۡءٞ فِي ٱلۡأَرۡضِ وَلَا فِي ٱلسَّمَآءِ

٦ هُوَ ٱلَّذِي يُصَوِّرُكُمۡ فِي ٱلۡأَرۡحَامِ كَيۡفَ يَشَآءُۚ

342. See note to 2:1.

343. *Cf.* 2:255.

344. In some editions the break between verses 3 and 4 occurs here in the middle of the sentence, but in the edition of *Hāfiz 'Uthmān*, followed by the Egyptian Concordance *Fath-ur-Rahmān*, the break occurs at the word *Furqān*. In verse-divisions our classicists have mainly followed rhythm. As the word *Furqān* from this point of view is parallel to the word *Intiqām*, which ends the next verse, I have accepted the verse-division at *Furqān* as more in consonance with Qur'anic rhythm. It makes no real difference to the numbering of the verses, as there is only a question of whether one line should go into verse 3 or verse 4. (R).

345. *Criterion: Furqān*: for meaning see 2:53 n. 68.

346. Who can penetrate the mystery of life when a new life is just being born, except Allah? The reference to the mystery of birth prepares us for the mystery of the birth of Jesus mentioned in 3:41 and the following verses.

There is no god but He,
The Exalted in Might,
The Wise.

لَآ إِلَٰهَ إِلَّا هُوَ ٱلْعَزِيزُ ٱلْحَكِيمُ

7. He it is Who has sent down
To thee the Book;
In it are verses
Basic or fundamental
(Of established meaning);
They are the foundation[347]
Of the Book: others
Are not of well-established
meaning. But those
In whose hearts is perversity
follow
The part thereof that is not of
well-established meaning.
Seeking discord, and searching
For its hidden meanings,
But no one knows
Its true meanings except Allah.
And those who are firmly
grounded[348]
In knowledge say: "We believe
In the Book; the whole of it
Is from our Lord:" and none
Will grasp the Message
Except men of understanding.

(٧) هُوَ ٱلَّذِىٓ أَنزَلَ عَلَيْكَ ٱلْكِتَٰبَ
مِنْهُ ءَايَٰتٌ مُّحْكَمَٰتٌ هُنَّ أُمُّ
ٱلْكِتَٰبِ وَأُخَرُ مُتَشَٰبِهَٰتٌ
فَأَمَّا ٱلَّذِينَ فِى قُلُوبِهِمْ زَيْغٌ
فَيَتَّبِعُونَ مَا تَشَٰبَهَ مِنْهُ
ٱبْتِغَآءَ ٱلْفِتْنَةِ وَٱبْتِغَآءَ تَأْوِيلِهِۦ
وَمَا يَعْلَمُ تَأْوِيلَهُۥٓ إِلَّا ٱللَّهُ
وَٱلرَّٰسِخُونَ فِى ٱلْعِلْمِ يَقُولُونَ
ءَامَنَّا بِهِۦ كُلٌّ مِّنْ عِندِ رَبِّنَا
وَمَا يَذَّكَّرُ إِلَّآ أُو۟لُوا۟ ٱلْأَلْبَٰبِ

8. "Our Lord!" (they say),
"Let not our hearts deviate
Now after Thou hast guided us,
But grant us mercy
From Thine own Presence;
For Thou art the Grantor
Of bounties without measure.

(٨) رَبَّنَا لَا تُزِغْ قُلُوبَنَا بَعْدَ إِذْ هَدَيْتَنَا
وَهَبْ لَنَا مِن لَّدُنكَ رَحْمَةً
إِنَّكَ أَنتَ ٱلْوَهَّابُ

9. "Our Lord! Thou art He
That will gather mankind

(٩) رَبَّنَآ إِنَّكَ جَامِعُ ٱلنَّاسِ

347. This passage gives us an important clue to the interpretation of the Holy Qur'ān. Broadly speaking it may be divided into two portions, not given separately, but intermingled: *viz.* (1) the nucleus or foundation of the Book, literally "the mother of the Book", (2) the part which is not of well-established meaning. It is very fascinating to take up the latter, and exercise our ingenuity about its inner meaning, but it refers to such profound spiritual matters that human language is inadequate to it, and though people of wisdom may get some light from it, no one should be dogmatic, as the final meaning is known to Allah alone. The Commentators usually understand the verses "of established meaning" (*muhkam*) to refer to the categorical orders of the *Sharī'ah* (or the Law), which are plain to everyone's understanding. But perhaps the meaning is wider: the "mother of the Book" must include the very foundation on which all law rests, the essence of Allah's Message, as distinguished from the various illustrative parables, allegories, and ordinances. (R).

348. One reading, rejected by the majority of Commentators, but accepted by Mujāhid and others, would not make a break at the point here marked *Waqfa Lāzim*, but would run the two sentences together. In that case the construction would run: "No one knows its hidden meanings except Allah and those who are firm in knowledge. They say", etc.

Together against a Day about which
There is no doubt; for Allah
Never fails in His promise."[349]

لِيَوْمٍ لَّا رَيْبَ فِيهِ
إِنَّ ٱللَّهَ لَا يُخْلِفُ ٱلْمِيعَادَ

SECTION 2.

10. Those who reject Faith—
Neither their possessions
Nor their (numerous) progeny
Will avail them aught
Against Allah; they are themselves
But fuel for the Fire.

١٠ إِنَّ ٱلَّذِينَ كَفَرُوا۟ لَن تُغْنِىَ عَنْهُمْ
أَمْوَٰلُهُمْ وَلَآ أَوْلَٰدُهُم مِّنَ ٱللَّهِ شَيْـًٔا
وَأُو۟لَٰٓئِكَ هُمْ وَقُودُ ٱلنَّارِ

11. (Their plight will be)
No better than that
Of the people of Pharaoh,[350]
And their predecessors:
They denied our Signs,
And Allah called them to account
For their sins.
For Allah is strict
In punishment.

١١ كَدَأْبِ ءَالِ فِرْعَوْنَ
وَٱلَّذِينَ مِن قَبْلِهِمْ
كَذَّبُوا۟ بِـَٔايَٰتِنَا فَأَخَذَهُمُ ٱللَّهُ بِذُنُوبِهِمْ
وَٱللَّهُ شَدِيدُ ٱلْعِقَابِ

12. Say to those who reject Faith:
"Soon will ye be vanquished[351]
And gathered together
To Hell—an evil bed
Indeed (to lie on)!

١٢ قُل لِّلَّذِينَ كَفَرُوا۟ سَتُغْلَبُونَ
وَتُحْشَرُونَ إِلَىٰ جَهَنَّمَ وَبِئْسَ ٱلْمِهَادُ

13. "There has already been
For you a Sign
In the two armies

١٣ قَدْ كَانَ لَكُمْ ءَايَةٌ فِى فِئَتَيْنِ

349. This is the prayer of those who are firmly grounded in knowledge. The more they know, the more they realise how little they know of all the depths of Truth in the spiritual worlds. But they have Faith. The glimpses they get of Truth they wish to hold fast in their hearts, and they pray to Allah to preserve them from deviating even from what light they have got. They are sure of their eventual return to Allah, when all doubts will be solved.

350. From the beginning of the world, sin, oppression, arrogance, and want of Faith have gone together. The Pharaoh of the time of Moses relied upon his power, his territory, his armies, and his resources to mock at Moses the messenger of Allah and to oppress the people of Moses. Allah saved the Israelites and punished their oppressors through many plagues and calamities. (R).

351. As Moses warned the Egyptians, so the warning is here sounded to the Pagan Arabs, the Jews and the Christians, and all who resisted Faith, that their resistance would be in vain. Already the battle of Badr (referred to in the next verse) had been a warning how Faith must conquer with the help of Allah. The next few decades saw the Byzantine and the Persian Empires overthrown because of their arrogance and their resistance to the Law of Allah.

That met (in combat):[352]
One was fighting in the Cause
Of Allah, the other
Resisting Allah; these saw
With their own eyes
Twice their number.[353]
But Allah doth support
With His aid whom He pleaseth.
In this is a warning
For such as have eyes to see."

ٱلْتَقَتَا ۖ فِئَةٌ تُقَٰتِلُ فِى سَبِيلِ ٱللَّهِ
وَأُخْرَىٰ كَافِرَةٌ يَرَوْنَهُم مِّثْلَيْهِمْ
رَأْىَ ٱلْعَيْنِ ۚ وَٱللَّهُ يُؤَيِّدُ بِنَصْرِهِۦ مَن يَشَآءُ ۗ
إِنَّ فِى ذَٰلِكَ لَعِبْرَةً لِّأُو۟لِى ٱلْأَبْصَٰرِ

14. Fair in the eyes of men
Is the love of things they covet:[354]
Women and sons;
Heaped-up hoards
Of gold and silver; horses
Branded (for blood and excellence);
And (wealth of) cattle
And well-tilled land.
Such are the possessions
Of this world's life;
But in nearness to Allah
Is the best of the goals
(To return to).

(١٤) زُيِّنَ لِلنَّاسِ حُبُّ ٱلشَّهَوَٰتِ
مِنَ ٱلنِّسَآءِ وَٱلْبَنِينَ وَٱلْقَنَٰطِيرِ ٱلْمُقَنطَرَةِ
مِنَ ٱلذَّهَبِ وَٱلْفِضَّةِ
وَٱلْخَيْلِ ٱلْمُسَوَّمَةِ وَٱلْأَنْعَٰمِ وَٱلْحَرْثِ ۗ
ذَٰلِكَ مَتَٰعُ ٱلْحَيَوٰةِ ٱلدُّنْيَا ۖ
وَٱللَّهُ عِندَهُۥ حُسْنُ ٱلْمَـَٔابِ

15. Say: Shall I give you
Glad tidings of things
Far better than those?
For the righteous are Gardens

(١٥) قُلْ أَؤُنَبِّئُكُم بِخَيْرٍ مِّن ذَٰلِكُمْ ۚ
لِلَّذِينَ ٱتَّقَوْا۟ عِندَ رَبِّهِمْ جَنَّٰتٌ

---

352. This refers to the battle of Badr in *Ramaḍān* in the second year of the Hijrah. The little exiled community of Makkan Muslims, with their friends in Madīnah, had organised themselves into a God-fearing community, but were constantly in danger of being attacked by their Pagan enemies of Makkah, in alliance with some of the disaffected elements (Jews and Hypocrites) in or near Madīnah itself. The design of the Makkans was to gather all the resources they could, and with an overwhelming force, to crush and annihilate Muḥammad and his party. To this end Abū Sufyān was leading a richly-laden caravan from Syria to Makkah. He called for armed aid from Makkah. The battle was fought in the plain of Badr, about 50 miles southwest of Madīnah. The Muslim force consisted of only about 313 men, mostly ill-armed, but they were led by Muḥammad, and they were fighting for their Faith. The Makkan army, well-armed and well-equipped, numbered over a thousand and had among its leaders some of the most experienced warriors of Arabia, including Abū Jahl, the inveterate foe and persecutor of Islam. Against all odds the Muslims won a brilliant victory, and many of the enemy leaders, including Abū Jahl, were killed. (R).

353. It was impossible, without the miraculous aid of Allah, for such a small and ill-equipped force as was the Muslim band, to defeat the large and well-found force of the enemy. But their firmness, zeal, and discipline won them divine aid. Enemy prisoners stated that the enemy ranks saw the Muslim force to be many times larger than it was.

354. The pleasures of this world are first enumerated: women for love; sons for strength and pride; hoarded riches, which procure all luxuries; the best and finest pedigree horses; cattle, the measure of wealth in the ancient world, as well as the means and symbols of good farming in the modern world; and broad acres of well-tilled land. By analogy, we may include, for our mechanised age, machines of all kinds—tractors, motor-cars, aeroplanes, the best internal-combustion engines, etc.,etc. In "heaped-up hoards of gold and silver," the Arabic word translated *hoards* is *qanāṭīr* plural of *qinṭār*, which literally means a talent of 1,200 ounces of gold. (R).

In nearness to their Lord,
With rivers flowing beneath;
Therein is their eternal home;
With Companions pure (and holy)[355]
And the good pleasure of Allah.
For in Allah's sight
Are (all) His servants—

تَجْرِي مِن تَحْتِهَا ٱلْأَنْهَٰرُ خَٰلِدِينَ فِيهَا
وَأَزْوَٰجٌ مُّطَهَّرَةٌ
وَرِضْوَٰنٌ مِّنَ ٱللَّهِ
وَٱللَّهُ بَصِيرٌۢ بِٱلْعِبَادِ

16. (Namely), those who say;
"Our Lord! we have indeed
Believed: forgive us, then,
Our sins, and save us
From the agony of the Fire"—

١٦ ٱلَّذِينَ يَقُولُونَ رَبَّنَآ إِنَّنَآ ءَامَنَّا
فَٱغْفِرْ لَنَا ذُنُوبَنَا وَقِنَا عَذَابَ ٱلنَّارِ

17. Those who show patience,
Firmness and self-control;[356]
Who are true (in word and deed);
Who worship devoutly;
Who spend (in the way of Allah);
And who pray for forgiveness
In the early hours of the morning.[357]

١٧ ٱلصَّٰبِرِينَ وَٱلصَّٰدِقِينَ
وَٱلْقَٰنِتِينَ وَٱلْمُنفِقِينَ
وَٱلْمُسْتَغْفِرِينَ
بِٱلْأَسْحَارِ

18. There is no god but He:
That is the witness of Allah,
His angels, and those endued
With knowledge, standing firm[358]
On justice. There is no god but He
The Exalted in Power,
The Wise.

١٨ شَهِدَ ٱللَّهُ أَنَّهُۥ لَآ إِلَٰهَ إِلَّا هُوَ
وَٱلْمَلَٰٓئِكَةُ وَأُو۟لُوا۟ ٱلْعِلْمِ قَآئِمًۢا بِٱلْقِسْطِ
لَآ إِلَٰهَ إِلَّا هُوَ ٱلْعَزِيزُ ٱلْحَكِيمُ

19. The Religion before Allah
Is Islam (submission to His Will):
Nor did the People of the Book

١٩ إِنَّ ٱلدِّينَ عِندَ ٱللَّهِ ٱلْإِسْلَٰمُ
وَمَا ٱخْتَلَفَ ٱلَّذِينَ أُوتُوا۟ ٱلْكِتَٰبَ

355. *Cf.* 2:25 and n. 44.

356. *Ṣabr (Ṣābirīn)* includes many shades of meaning: I have specified three here, *viz.*, patience, firmness, and self-control. See 2:45 and 2:153 and notes thereon.

357. True servants of Allah are described in 3:16 and 17. They have faith, humility, and hope (3:16); and they have certain virtues (3:17) *viz.*, (1) patience, steadfastness, self-restraint, and all that goes under the full definition of *Ṣabr:* this shows a certain attitude of mind; (2) in all their dealings they are true and sincere as they are also in their promises and words; this marks them out in social conduct; (3) further, their spiritual worship is earnest and deep, an inner counterpart of their outward conduct; (4) their worship of Allah shows itself in their love of their fellow-men, for they are ready and liberal in charity; and (5) their self-discipline is so great that the first thing they do every morning is humbly to approach their God.

358. Allah Himself speaks to us through His revelations (through angels) and through His Creation, for all Nature glorifies Allah. No thinking mind, if it only judges the matter fairly, can fail to find the same witness in his own heart and conscience. All this points to the Unity of Allah. His exalted nature, and His wisdom.

Dissent therefrom except
Through envy of each other,[359]
After knowledge had come to them.
But if any deny the Signs of Allah,
Allah is swift in calling to account.

إِلَّا مِنۢ بَعۡدِ مَا جَآءَهُمُ ٱلۡعِلۡمُ بَغۡيَۢا بَيۡنَهُمۡۗ
وَمَن يَكۡفُرۡ بِـَٔايَٰتِ ٱللَّهِ
فَإِنَّ ٱللَّهَ سَرِيعُ ٱلۡحِسَابِ

20. So if they dispute with thee,
Say: "I have submitted
My whole self[360] to Allah
And so have those
Who follow me."
And say to the People of the Book
And to those who are unlearned:[361]
"Do ye (also) submit yourselves?"
If they do, they are in right guidance,
But if they turn back,
Thy duty is to convey the Message;
And in Allah's sight
Are (all) His servants.[362]

٢٠ فَإِنۡ حَآجُّوكَ فَقُلۡ أَسۡلَمۡتُ
وَجۡهِيَ لِلَّهِ وَمَنِ ٱتَّبَعَنِۗ
وَقُل لِّلَّذِينَ أُوتُواْ ٱلۡكِتَٰبَ
وَٱلۡأُمِّيِّـۧنَ ءَأَسۡلَمۡتُمۡۚ
فَإِنۡ أَسۡلَمُواْ فَقَدِ ٱهۡتَدَواْۖ
وَّإِن تَوَلَّوۡاْ فَإِنَّمَا عَلَيۡكَ ٱلۡبَلَٰغُۗ
وَٱللَّهُ بَصِيرُۢ بِٱلۡعِبَادِ

C. 55.—If the people who received
(3:21-30.) Earlier revelations confine themselves
To partial truths, and in their pride
Shut their eyes to the whole of the Book
Of Allah, their day is done;
Let the Muslims seek the society
And friendship of their own, and trust
In Allah, who knows all, and holds
Every soul responsible for its own deeds.

SECTION 3.

21. As to those who deny
The Signs of Allah, and in defiance
Of right,[363] slay the prophets,

٢١ إِنَّ ٱلَّذِينَ يَكۡفُرُونَ بِـَٔايَٰتِ ٱللَّهِ
وَيَقۡتُلُونَ ٱلنَّبِيِّـۧنَ بِغَيۡرِ حَقّٖ

359. *Baghyan:* through envy, through selfish contumacy or obstinacy, through sheer contrary- mindedness, or desire to resist or rebel. *Cf.* 2:90, and 2:213.

360. *Wajh*: whole self. See n. 114 to 2:112.

361. The People of the Book may be supposed to know something about the previous religious history of mankind. To them the appeal should be easy and intelligible, as all religion is one, and it is only being renewed in Islam. But the appeal is also made to the pagan Arabs, who are unlearned, and who can well be expected to follow the example of one of their own, who received divine enlightenment, and was able to bring new knowledge to them. A great many of both these classes did so. But the few who resisted Allah's grace, and actually threatened and persecuted those who believed, are told that Allah will look after His own.

362. Note the literary skill in the argument as it proceeds. The mystery of birth faintly suggests that we are coming to the story of Jesus. The exposition of the Book suggests that Islam is the same religion as that of the People of the Book. Next we are told that the People of the Book made their religion one-sided, and through the priesthood of the family of 'Imrān, we are brought to the story of Jesus, who was rejected by a body of the Jews as Muḥammad was rejected by a body of both Jews and Christians.

363. *Right: ḥaqq* has many shades of meaning: (1) right, in the sense of having a right to something; (2) right, in the sense of straight conduct, as opposed to wrong; (3) truth; (4) justice. All these shades are implied here.

And slay those who teach
Just dealing with mankind,[364]
Announce to them a grievous
penalty.

وَيَقْتُلُونَ ٱلَّذِينَ يَأْمُرُونَ بِٱلْقِسْطِ
مِنَ ٱلنَّاسِ فَبَشِّرْهُم بِعَذَابٍ أَلِيمٍ

22. They are those whose works
Will bear no fruit[365]
In this world
And in the Hereafter,
Nor will they have
Anyone to help.

٢٢ أُولَٰٓئِكَ ٱلَّذِينَ حَبِطَتْ أَعْمَٰلُهُمْ
فِى ٱلدُّنْيَا وَٱلْءَاخِرَةِ
وَمَا لَهُم مِّن نَّٰصِرِينَ

23. Hast thou not turned
Thy vision to those
Who have been given a portion[366]
Of the Book? They are
Invited to the Book of Allah,
To settle their dispute,
But a party of them
Turn back and decline
(The arbitration).[367]

٢٣ أَلَمْ تَرَ إِلَى ٱلَّذِينَ
أُوتُوا۟ نَصِيبًا مِّنَ ٱلْكِتَٰبِ
يُدْعَوْنَ إِلَىٰ كِتَٰبِ ٱللَّهِ لِيَحْكُمَ بَيْنَهُمْ
ثُمَّ يَتَوَلَّىٰ فَرِيقٌ مِّنْهُمْ وَهُم مُّعْرِضُونَ

24. This because they say:
"The Fire shall not touch us
But for a few numbered days";[368]
For their forgeries deceive them
As to their own religion.

٢٤ ذَٰلِكَ بِأَنَّهُمْ قَالُوا۟ لَن تَمَسَّنَا ٱلنَّارُ
إِلَّآ أَيَّامًا مَّعْدُودَٰتٍ وَغَرَّهُمْ فِى دِينِهِم
مَّا كَانُوا۟ يَفْتَرُونَ

25. But how (will they fare)
When We gather them together

٢٥ فَكَيْفَ إِذَا جَمَعْنَٰهُمْ

364. Examples of the Prophets slain were: "the righteous blood shed upon the earth, from the blood of righteous Abel unto the blood of Zacharias, son of Barachias, whom ye slew between the temple and the altar": Matt. xxiii. 35. *Cf.* Q. 2:61. n. 75. Again, John the Baptist (Yaḥyā, noble, chaste, a prophet, of the goodly company of the righteous, Q. 3:39), was bound, imprisoned, and beheaded, and his head presented to a dancing harlot: Matt. xiv. 1-11.

365. *Cf.* 2:217, end.

366. *A portion of the Book.* I conceive that Allah's revelation as a whole throughout the ages is "The Book". The Law of Moses, and the Gospel of Jesus were portions of the Book. The Qur'ān completes the revelation and is *par excellence* the Book of Allah.

367. The Commentators mention a particular incident when a dispute was submitted by the Jews for arbitration to the Holy Prophet. He appealed to the authority of their own books, but they tried to conceal and prevaricate. The general lesson is that the People of the Book should have been the first to welcome in Muḥammad the living exponent of the Message of Allah as a whole, and some of them did so; but others turned away from guilty arrogance, relying on corrupted texts and doctrines forged out of their own fancies, though they were not conformable to reason and good sense.

368. *Cf.* 2:80.

Against a Day about which
There is no doubt,
And each soul will be paid out
Just what it has earned,
Without (favour or) injustice?

لِيَوْمٍ لَّا رَيْبَ فِيهِ وَوُفِّيَتْ كُلُّ نَفْسٍ
مَّا كَسَبَتْ وَهُمْ لَا يُظْلَمُونَ

26. Say: "O Allah!
Lord of Power (and Rule),
Thou givest Power
To whom Thou pleasest,
And Thou strippest off Power
From whom Thou pleasest:
Thou enduest with honour
Whom Thou pleasest,
And Thou bringest low
Whom Thou pleasest:
In Thy hand is all Good.[369]
Verily, over all things
Thou hast power.

٢٦ قُلِ ٱللَّهُمَّ مَٰلِكَ ٱلْمُلْكِ
تُؤْتِي ٱلْمُلْكَ مَن تَشَآءُ
وَتَنزِعُ ٱلْمُلْكَ مِمَّن تَشَآءُ
وَتُعِزُّ مَن تَشَآءُ وَتُذِلُّ مَن تَشَآءُ
بِيَدِكَ ٱلْخَيْرُ
إِنَّكَ عَلَىٰ كُلِّ شَيْءٍ قَدِيرٌ

27. "Thou causest the Night
To gain on the Day,
And Thou causest the Day
To gain on the Night;[370]
Thou bringest the Living
Out of the Dead,
And Thou bringest the Dead
Out of the Living;[371]
And Thou givest sustenance
To whom Thou pleasest,
Without measure."[372]

٢٧ تُولِجُ ٱلَّيْلَ فِي ٱلنَّهَارِ
وَتُولِجُ ٱلنَّهَارَ فِي ٱلَّيْلِ
وَتُخْرِجُ ٱلْحَيَّ مِنَ ٱلْمَيِّتِ
وَتُخْرِجُ ٱلْمَيِّتَ مِنَ ٱلْحَيِّ
وَتَرْزُقُ مَن تَشَآءُ بِغَيْرِ حِسَابٍ

369. Another glorious passage, full of meaning. The governing phrase in it all is: "In Thy hand is all Good." What is the standard by which we may judge Good? It is Allah's Will. Therefore when we submit to Allah's Will, and real Islam illuminates us, we see the highest Good. There has been and is much controversy as to what is the Highest Good. To the Muslim there is no difficulty: it is the Will of Allah. He must ever strive to learn and understand that Will. But once in that fortress, he is secure. He is not troubled with the nature of Evil.

370. True in many senses. In every twenty-four hours, night merges into day, and day into night, and there is no clear boundary between them. In every solar year, the night gains on the day after the summer solstice, and the day gains on the night after the winter solstice. But further, if light and darkness are viewed as symbols of (a) knowledge and ignorance, (b) happiness and misery, (c) spiritual insight and spiritual blindness, Allah's Plan or Will works here too as in the physical world, and in His hand is all Good.

371. We can interpret Dead and Living in even more senses than Day and Night: death physical, intellectual, emotional, spiritual. Life and Death may also apply to collective, group, or national life. And who has ever solved the mystery of Life? But Faith refers it to Allah's Will and Plan.

372. Again true in all the senses suggested in the two previous notes. The only Eternal Reality is Allah. All else has its basis and sustenance in Him. Lest our little minds create fear out of "nicely calculated less or more", we are told at once that Allah's bounty is without measure or account.

28. Let not the Believers
Take for friends or helpers
Unbelievers rather than
Believers: if any do that,
In nothing will there be help
From Allah: except by way
Of precaution, that ye may
Guard yourselves from them.[373]
But Allah cautions you
(To remember) Himself;
For the final goal
Is to Allah.

٢٨ لَّا يَتَّخِذِ ٱلْمُؤْمِنُونَ ٱلْكَٰفِرِينَ أَوْلِيَآءَ
مِن دُونِ ٱلْمُؤْمِنِينَ ۖ وَمَن يَفْعَلْ ذَٰلِكَ فَلَيْسَ
مِنَ ٱللَّهِ فِى شَىْءٍ إِلَّآ أَن تَتَّقُوا۟ مِنْهُمْ
تُقَىٰةً ۗ وَيُحَذِّرُكُمُ ٱللَّهُ نَفْسَهُۥ ۗ
وَإِلَى ٱللَّهِ ٱلْمَصِيرُ

29. Say: "Whether ye hide
What is in your hearts
Or reveal it,
Allah knows it all:
He knows what is
In the heavens,
And what is on earth.
And Allah has power
Over all things.

٢٩ قُلْ إِن تُخْفُوا۟ مَا فِى صُدُورِكُمْ
أَوْ تُبْدُوهُ يَعْلَمْهُ ٱللَّهُ ۗ وَيَعْلَمُ مَا فِى
ٱلسَّمَٰوَٰتِ وَمَا فِى ٱلْأَرْضِ ۗ
وَٱللَّهُ عَلَىٰ كُلِّ شَىْءٍ قَدِيرٌ

30. "On the Day when every soul
Will be confronted
With all the good it has done,
And all the evil it has done,
It will wish there were
A great distance
Between it and its evil.
But Allah cautions you
(To remember) Himself.
And Allah is full of kindness
To those that serve Him."

٣٠ يَوْمَ تَجِدُ كُلُّ نَفْسٍ مَّا عَمِلَتْ
مِنْ خَيْرٍ مُّحْضَرًا وَمَا عَمِلَتْ مِن سُوٓءٍ تَوَدُّ
لَوْ أَنَّ بَيْنَهَا وَبَيْنَهُۥٓ أَمَدًۢا بَعِيدًا ۗ
وَيُحَذِّرُكُمُ ٱللَّهُ نَفْسَهُۥ ۗ
وَٱللَّهُ رَءُوفٌۢ بِٱلْعِبَادِ

C. 56.—Allah's truth is continuous, and His Prophets
(3:31-36.) From Adam, through Noah and Abraham,
Down to the last of the Prophets, Muḥammad,
Form one brotherhood. Of the progeny
Of 'Imrān, father of Moses and Aaron,
Sprang a woman, who devoted

373. If Faith is a fundamental matter in our lives our associations and friendships will naturally be with those who share our faith. "Evil communications corrupt good manners": and evil company may corrupt faith. In our ordinary everyday affairs of business, we are asked to seek the help of Believers rather than Unbelievers. Only in this way can our community be strong in organisation and unity. But where there is no question of preference, or where in self-defence we have to take the assistance of those not belonging to our faith, that is permissible. In any case we must not weaken our brotherhood: we must try to make it stronger if possible.

Her unborn offspring to Allah.
The child was Mary the mother of Jesus.
Her cousin was the wife of the priest
Zakariya, who took charge of Mary.
To Zakariya, in his old age, was born
A son Yaḥyā, amid prodigies:
Yaḥyā was the herald of Jesus
The son of Mary, and was known
As John the Baptist. Jesus
Was of virgin birth,
And performed many miracles.
But those to whom he came as Prophet
Rejected him, and plotted for his death.
Their plots failed, for Allah's Plan
Is above man's plots. So will it be
With Islam, the Truth from all eternity.

SECTION 4.

31. Say: "If ye do love Allah,
Follow me: Allah will love you
And forgive you your sins;
For Allah is Oft-Forgiving,
Most Merciful."

قُلْ إِن كُنتُمْ تُحِبُّونَ ٱللَّهَ فَٱتَّبِعُونِى يُحْبِبْكُمُ ٱللَّهُ وَيَغْفِرْ لَكُمْ ذُنُوبَكُمْ وَٱللَّهُ غَفُورٌ رَّحِيمٌ ﴿٣١﴾

32. Say: "Obey Allah
And His Messenger":
But if they turn back,
Allah loveth not those
Who reject Faith.

قُلْ أَطِيعُوا۟ ٱللَّهَ وَٱلرَّسُولَ فَإِن تَوَلَّوْا۟ فَإِنَّ ٱللَّهَ لَا يُحِبُّ ٱلْكَٰفِرِينَ ﴿٣٢﴾

33. Allah did choose
Adam and Noah, the family
Of Abraham, and the family
Of 'Imrān above all people—

إِنَّ ٱللَّهَ ٱصْطَفَىٰٓ ءَادَمَ وَنُوحًا وَءَالَ إِبْرَٰهِيمَ وَءَالَ عِمْرَٰنَ عَلَى ٱلْعَٰلَمِينَ ﴿٣٣﴾

34. Offspring, one of the other;[374]
And Allah heareth
And knoweth all things.

ذُرِّيَّةًۢ بَعْضُهَا مِنۢ بَعْضٍ وَٱللَّهُ سَمِيعٌ عَلِيمٌ ﴿٣٤﴾

374. The Prophets in the Jewish-Christian-Muslim dispensation form one family literally. But the argument is wider. All men of God form spiritually one family. If you love and obey Allah, love and obey His Messenger; your love, obedience, and discipline will be the test of your faith.

35. Behold! a woman of 'Imrān[375]
Said: "O my Lord! I do
Dedicate unto Thee
What is in my womb
For Thy special service:[376]
So accept this of me:
For Thou hearest
And knowest all things."

إِذْ قَالَتِ ٱمْرَأَتُ عِمْرَٰنَ رَبِّ إِنِّي نَذَرْتُ لَكَ مَا فِي بَطْنِي مُحَرَّرًا فَتَقَبَّلْ مِنِّيٓ إِنَّكَ أَنتَ ٱلسَّمِيعُ ٱلْعَلِيمُ ﴿٣٥﴾

36. When she was delivered,
She said: "O my Lord!
Behold! I am delivered
Of a female child!"—
And Allah knew best
What she brought forth—[377]
"And no wise is the male
Like the female.[378]
I have named her Mary,
And I commend her
And her offspring
To Thy protection
From the Evil One,
The Rejected."

فَلَمَّا وَضَعَتْهَا قَالَتْ رَبِّ إِنِّي وَضَعْتُهَآ أُنثَىٰ وَٱللَّهُ أَعْلَمُ بِمَا وَضَعَتْ وَلَيْسَ ٱلذَّكَرُ كَٱلْأُنثَىٰ وَإِنِّي سَمَّيْتُهَا مَرْيَمَ وَإِنِّيٓ أُعِيذُهَا بِكَ وَذُرِّيَّتَهَا مِنَ ٱلشَّيْطَٰنِ ٱلرَّجِيمِ ﴿٣٦﴾

37. Right graciously
Did her Lord accept her:
He made her grow
In purity and beauty;
To the care of Zakarīya
Was she assigned.

فَتَقَبَّلَهَا رَبُّهَا بِقَبُولٍ حَسَنٍ وَأَنۢبَتَهَا نَبَاتًا حَسَنًا وَكَفَّلَهَا زَكَرِيَّا ﴿٣٧﴾

375. Now we begin the story of Jesus. As a prelude we have the birth of Mary and the parallel story of John the Baptist, Yaḥyā the son of Zakariya. Yaḥyā's mother Elizabeth was a cousin of Mary the mother of Jesus (Luke i. 36), and therefore John and Jesus were cousins by blood, and there was a spiritual cousinhood in their birth and career. Elizabeth was of the daughters of Aaron (Luke i. 5), of a priestly family which went back to Aaron the brother of Moses and son of 'Imrān. Her husband Zakariya was actually a priest, and her cousin Mary was presumably also of a priestly family. By tradition Mary's mother was called Hannah (in Latin, Anna, and in English, Anne), and her father was called 'Imrān. Hannah is therefore both a descendant of the priestly house of 'Imrān and the wife of 'Imrān,—"a woman of 'Imrān" in a double sense.

376. *Muḥarrar*=freed from all worldly affairs and specially dedicated to Allah's service. She expected a son, who was to be a special devotee, a miraculous son of the old age of his parents, but Allah gave her instead a daughter. But that daughter was Mary the mother of Jesus, the chosen one among the women; 3:42.

377. The mother of Mary expected a male child. Was she disappointed that it was a female child? No, for she had faith, and she knew that Allah's Plan was better than any wishes of hers. Mary was no ordinary girl: only Allah knew what it was that her mother brought forth.

378. The female child could not be devoted to Temple service under the Mosaic law, as she intended. But she was marked out for a special destiny as a miracle-child, to be the mother of the miracle-child Jesus. She was content to seek Allah's protection for her against all evil. There is a certain sense of pride in the girl on the part of the mother.

Every time that he entered
(Her) chamber to see her,
He found her supplied
With sustenance. He said:
"O Mary! Whence (comes) this
To you?" She said:
"From Allah: for Allah
Provides sustenance
To whom He pleases,
Without measure."[379]

كُلَّمَا دَخَلَ عَلَيْهَا زَكَرِيَّا الْمِحْرَابَ
وَجَدَ عِندَهَا رِزْقًا قَالَ يَٰمَرْيَمُ
أَنَّىٰ لَكِ هَٰذَا قَالَتْ هُوَ مِنْ عِندِ اللَّهِ
إِنَّ اللَّهَ يَرْزُقُ مَن يَشَاءُ بِغَيْرِ حِسَابٍ

38. There did Zakarīya
Pray to his Lord, saying:
"O my Lord! Grant unto me
From Thee a progeny
That is pure: for Thou
Art He that heareth prayer!"[380]

٣٨ هُنَالِكَ دَعَا زَكَرِيَّا رَبَّهُ
قَالَ رَبِّ هَبْ لِي مِن لَّدُنكَ ذُرِّيَّةً
طَيِّبَةً إِنَّكَ سَمِيعُ الدُّعَاءِ

39. While he was standing
In prayer in the chamber,
The angels called unto him:
"Allah doth give thee
Glad tidings of Yaḥya,
Witnessing the truth
Of a Word from Allah,[381] and (be
Besides) noble, chaste,
And a Prophet—
Of the (goodly) company
Of the righteous."

٣٩ فَنَادَتْهُ الْمَلَٰئِكَةُ
وَهُوَ قَائِمٌ يُصَلِّي فِي الْمِحْرَابِ
أَنَّ اللَّهَ يُبَشِّرُكَ بِيَحْيَىٰ مُصَدِّقًا
بِكَلِمَةٍ مِّنَ اللَّهِ وَسَيِّدًا وَحَصُورًا
وَنَبِيًّا مِّنَ الصَّٰلِحِينَ

40. He said: "Oh my Lord!
How shall I have a son,
Seeing I am very old,
And my wife is barren?"
"Thus," was the answer,
"Doth Allah accomplish
What He willeth."

٤٠ قَالَ رَبِّ أَنَّىٰ يَكُونُ لِي غُلَٰمٌ
وَقَدْ بَلَغَنِيَ الْكِبَرُ وَامْرَأَتِي عَاقِرٌ
قَالَ كَذَٰلِكَ اللَّهُ يَفْعَلُ مَا يَشَاءُ

---

379. Mary grew under Allah's special protection. Her sustenance, under which we may include both her physical needs and her spiritual food, came from Allah, and her growth was indeed a "goodly growth" which I have tried to express in the text by the words "purity and beauty". Some aprocryphal Christian writings say that she was brought up in the Temple to the age of twelve like a dove, and that she was fed by angels.

380. The birth of Mary, the mother of Jesus, of John the Baptist, the precursor of Jesus, and of Jesus, the prophet of Israel, whom Israel rejected, occurred in that order chronologically, and are told in that order. They are all interconnected. Zakariya prayed for no ordinary son. He and his wife were past the age of parenthood. Seeing the growth of Mary, he prayed for some child from Allah,—"from Thee, a progeny that is pure". Perhaps he had adoption in his mind. Did he want to adopt Mary? To his surprise, he is given a son in the flesh, ushered in by a special Sign. (R).

381. Notice: "*a* Word from Allah", not "*the* Word of Allah", the epithet that mystical Christianity uses for Jesus. As stated in 3:59 below, Jesus was created by a miracle, by Allah's word "Be", and he was.

41. He said: "O my Lord!
Give me a Sign!"
"Thy Sign," was the answer,
"Shall be that thou
Shalt speak to no man
For three days
But with signals.
Then celebrate
The praises of thy Lord
Again and again,
And glorify Him
In the evening
And in the morning."

(٤١) قَالَ رَبِّ ٱجْعَل لِّىٓ ءَايَةً
قَالَ ءَايَتُكَ أَلَّا تُكَلِّمَ ٱلنَّاسَ
ثَلَٰثَةَ أَيَّامٍ إِلَّا رَمْزًا
وَٱذْكُر رَّبَّكَ كَثِيرًا
وَسَبِّحْ بِٱلْعَشِىِّ وَٱلْإِبْكَٰرِ

SECTION 5.

42. Behold! the angels said:
"O Mary! Allah hath chosen thee
And purified thee—chosen thee
Above the women of all nations.[382]

(٤٢) وَإِذْ قَالَتِ ٱلْمَلَٰٓئِكَةُ
يَٰمَرْيَمُ إِنَّ ٱللَّهَ ٱصْطَفَىٰكِ وَطَهَّرَكِ
وَٱصْطَفَىٰكِ عَلَىٰ نِسَآءِ ٱلْعَٰلَمِينَ

43. "O Mary! worship
Thy Lord devoutly:
Prostrate thyself,
And bow down (in prayer)
With those who bow down."

(٤٣) يَٰمَرْيَمُ ٱقْنُتِى لِرَبِّكِ وَٱسْجُدِى
وَٱرْكَعِى مَعَ ٱلرَّٰكِعِينَ

44. This is part of the tidings
Of the things unseen,[383]
Which We reveal unto thee
(O Prophet!) by inspiration:
Thou wast not with them
When they cast lots
With arrows,[384] as to which
Of them should be charged
With the care of Mary:
Nor wast thou with them

(٤٤) ذَٰلِكَ مِنْ أَنۢبَآءِ
ٱلْغَيْبِ نُوحِيهِ إِلَيْكَ
وَمَا كُنتَ لَدَيْهِمْ إِذْ يُلْقُونَ
أَقْلَٰمَهُمْ أَيُّهُمْ يَكْفُلُ مَرْيَمَ
وَمَا كُنتَ لَدَيْهِمْ

382. Mary, the mother of Jesus, was unique, in that she gave birth to a son by a special miracle, without the intervention of the customary physical means. This of course does not mean that she was more than human, any more than that her son was more than human. She had as much need to pray to Allah as anyone else. The Christian dogma, in all sects except the Unitarian, holds that Jesus was God and the son of God. The worship of Mary became the practice in the Roman Catholic Church, which calls Mary the "Mother of God". This seems to have been endorsed by the Council of Ephesus in 431 A.C., in the century before Muḥammad was born to sweep away the corruptions of the Church of Christ. For *'ālamīn* as meaning all nations, see 3:96, n. 423.

383. *Things unseen*: belong to a realm beyond the reach of human perception and therefore it would be unseemly to dispute or speculate about them. (R).

384. Literally, *reeds: aqlām*. For the Arab custom of casting lots with arrows, see 2:219, n. 241.

When they disputed (the point).[385]

إِذْ يَخْتَصِمُونَ

45. Behold! the angels said:
"O Mary! Allah giveth thee
Glad tidings of a Word
From Him: his name
Will be Christ Jesus.[386]
The son of Mary, held in honour
In this world and the Hereafter
And of (the company of) those
Nearest to Allah;[387]

٤٥ إِذْ قَالَتِ ٱلْمَلَٰٓئِكَةُ
يَٰمَرْيَمُ إِنَّ ٱللَّهَ يُبَشِّرُكِ بِكَلِمَةٍ مِّنْهُ
ٱسْمُهُ ٱلْمَسِيحُ عِيسَى ٱبْنُ مَرْيَمَ وَجِيهًا
فِى ٱلدُّنْيَا وَٱلْءَاخِرَةِ وَمِنَ ٱلْمُقَرَّبِينَ

46. "He shall speak to the people
In childhood and in maturity.[388]
And he shall be (of the company)
Of the righteous."

٤٦ وَيُكَلِّمُ ٱلنَّاسَ فِى ٱلْمَهْدِ
وَكَهْلًا وَمِنَ ٱلصَّٰلِحِينَ

47. She said: "O my Lord![389]
How shall I have a son
When no man hath touched me?"
He said: "Even so:
Allah createth
What He willeth:
When He hath decreed
A Plan, He but saith
To it, 'Be,' and it is!

٤٧ قَالَتْ رَبِّ أَنَّىٰ يَكُونُ لِى وَلَدٌ
وَلَمْ يَمْسَسْنِى بَشَرٌ قَالَ كَذَٰلِكِ
ٱللَّهُ يَخْلُقُ مَا يَشَآءُ إِذَا قَضَىٰٓ أَمْرًا
فَإِنَّمَا يَقُولُ لَهُۥ كُن فَيَكُونُ

48. "And Allah will teach him
The Book and Wisdom,
The Law and the Gospel,

٤٨ وَيُعَلِّمُهُ ٱلْكِتَٰبَ
وَٱلْحِكْمَةَ وَٱلتَّوْرَىٰةَ وَٱلْإِنجِيلَ

49. "And (appoint him)
A messenger to the Children
Of Israel, (with this message):
"'I have come to you,
With a Sign from your Lord,
In that I make for you

٤٩ وَرَسُولًا إِلَىٰ بَنِىٓ إِسْرَٰٓءِيلَ
أَنِّى قَدْ جِئْتُكُم بِـَٔايَةٍ مِّن رَّبِّكُمْ
أَنِّىٓ أَخْلُقُ لَكُم

385. Christian apocryphal writings mention the contention between the priests as to the honour of taking charge of Mary, and how it was decided by means of rods and reeds in favour of Zakarīya.

386. *Christ:* Greek, *Christos*=anointed: kings and priests were anointed to symbolise consecration to their office. The Hebrew and Arabic form is *Masīh*.

387. Nearest to Allah: *Muqarrabīn, Cf.* Q. 56:2.

388. The ministry of Jesus lasted only about three years, from 30 to 33 years of his age, when in the eyes of his enemies he was crucified. But the Gospel of Luke (ii. 46) describes him as disputing with the doctors in the Temple at the age of 12, and even earlier, as a child, he was "strong in spirit, filled with wisdom" (Luke ii. 40).Some apocryphal Gospels describe him as preaching from infancy.

389. She was addressed by angels, who gave her Allah's message. In reply she speaks as to Allah. In reply, apparently an angel again gives Allah's message.

Out of clay, as it were,
The figure of a bird,
And breathe into it,
And it becomes a bird
By Allah's leave:[390]
And I heal those
Born blind, and the lepers,
And I quicken the dead,
By Allah's leave;
And I declare to you
What ye eat, and what ye
store[391]
In your houses. Surely
Therein is a Sign for you
If ye did believe;

مِنَ الطِّينِ كَهَيْـَٔةِ الطَّيْرِ
فَأَنفُخُ فِيهِ فَيَكُونُ طَيْرًۢا بِإِذْنِ اللَّهِ
وَأُبْرِئُ الْأَكْمَهَ وَالْأَبْرَصَ
وَأُحْيِ الْمَوْتَىٰ بِإِذْنِ اللَّهِ
وَأُنَبِّئُكُم بِمَا تَأْكُلُونَ وَمَا تَدَّخِرُونَ
فِي بُيُوتِكُمْ إِنَّ فِي ذَٰلِكَ لَءَايَةً لَّكُمْ
إِن كُنتُم مُّؤْمِنِينَ

50. "(I have come to you),
To attest the Law
Which was before me.
And to make lawful
To you part of what was
(Before) forbidden to you;
I have come to you
With a Sign from your Lord.
So fear Allah
And obey me.

٥٠ وَمُصَدِّقًا لِّمَا بَيْنَ يَدَيَّ مِنَ التَّوْرَىٰةِ
وَلِأُحِلَّ لَكُم بَعْضَ الَّذِي حُرِّمَ عَلَيْكُمْ
وَجِئْتُكُم بِـَٔايَةٍ مِّن رَّبِّكُمْ
فَاتَّقُوا اللَّهَ وَأَطِيعُونِ

51. "It is Allah
Who is my Lord
And your Lord;
Then worship Him.
This is a Way
That is straight."

٥١ إِنَّ اللَّهَ رَبِّي
وَرَبُّكُمْ فَاعْبُدُوهُ
هَٰذَا صِرَٰطٌ مُّسْتَقِيمٌ

52. When Jesus found
Unbelief on their part
He said: "Who will be
My helpers to (the work
Of) Allah?" Said the Disciples:
"We are Allah's helpers:
We believe in Allah,

٥٢ فَلَمَّا أَحَسَّ عِيسَىٰ مِنْهُمُ الْكُفْرَ
قَالَ مَنْ أَنصَارِي إِلَى اللَّهِ قَالَ الْحَوَارِيُّونَ
نَحْنُ أَنصَارُ اللَّهِ ءَامَنَّا بِاللَّهِ

390. This miracle of the clay birds is found in some of the apocryphal Gospels; those of curing the blind and the lepers and raising the dead are in the canonical Gospels. The original Gospel (see 3:48) was not the various stories written afterwards by disciples, but the real Message taught direct by Jesus.

391. I do not know whether this clause refers to a particular incident, or generally to a prophetic knowledge of what is not known to ordinary people.

And do thou bear witness
That we are Muslims.[392]

وَاشْهَدْ بِأَنَّا مُسْلِمُونَ

53. "Our Lord! we believe
In what Thou hast revealed,
And we follow the Messenger;
Then write us down
Among those who bear witness."

(٥٣) رَبَّنَآ ءَامَنَّا بِمَآ أَنزَلْتَ وَاتَّبَعْنَا الرَّسُولَ
فَاكْتُبْنَا مَعَ الشَّٰهِدِينَ

54 And (the unbelievers)
Plotted and planned,
And Allah too planned,[393]
And the best of planners
Is Allah.

(٥٤) وَمَكَرُوا وَمَكَرَ اللَّهُ
وَاللَّهُ خَيْرُ الْمَٰكِرِينَ

SECTION 6.

55. Behold! Allah said:
"O Jesus! I will take thee[394]
And raise thee to Myself
And clear thee (of the
falsehoods)[395]
Of those who blaspheme;
I will make those
Who follow thee superior[396]
To those who reject faith,
To the Day of Resurrection:
Then shall ye all
Return unto me,
And I will judge
Between you of the matters
Wherein ye dispute.[397]

(٥٥) إِذْ قَالَ اللَّهُ يَٰعِيسَىٰٓ
إِنِّي مُتَوَفِّيكَ وَرَافِعُكَ إِلَيَّ وَمُطَهِّرُكَ
مِنَ الَّذِينَ كَفَرُوا وَجَاعِلُ الَّذِينَ اتَّبَعُوكَ
فَوْقَ الَّذِينَ كَفَرُوٓا إِلَىٰ يَوْمِ الْقِيَٰمَةِ
ثُمَّ إِلَيَّ مَرْجِعُكُمْ فَأَحْكُمُ بَيْنَكُمْ
فِيمَا كُنتُمْ فِيهِ تَخْتَلِفُونَ

392. The story of Jesus is told with special application to the time of the Prophet Muḥammad. Note the word helpers (*Anṣār*) in this connection, and the reference to plotters in 3:54. It was the one Religion—the Religion of Allah, which was in essence the religion of Abraham, Moses, and Jesus. The argument runs: who do ye then now make divisions and reject the living Teacher? Islam is: bowing to the Will of Allah. All who have faith should bow to the Will of Allah and be Muslims.

393. The Arabic *makara* has both a bad and a good meaning, that of making an intricate plan to carry out some secret purpose. The enemies of Allah are constantly doing that. But Allah—in whose hands is all good—has His plans also, against which the evil ones will have no chance whatever.

394. Read this with 4:157, where it is said that "whereas they slew him not nor they crucified him but it was made dubious unto". The guilt of the Jews remained, but Jesus was eventually taken up to Allah.

395. Jesus was charged by the Jews with blasphemy as claiming to be God or the son of God. The Christians (except a few early sects which were annihilated by persecution, and the modern sect of Unitarians), adopted the substance of the claim, and made it the cornerstone of their faith. Allah clears Jesus of such a charge or claim.

396. *Those who follow thee* refers to both Muslims (insofar as they truly follow the basic teachings of Jesus) and Christians (who claim to follow him). [Eds.].

397. All the controversies about dogma and faith will disappear when we appear before Allah. He will judge not by what we profess but by what we are.

56. "As to those who reject faith,
I will punish them
With terrible agony
In this world and in the
Hereafter,
Nor will they have
Anyone to help.

٥٦ فَأَمَّا الَّذِينَ كَفَرُوا
فَأُعَذِّبُهُمْ عَذَابًا شَدِيدًا
فِي الدُّنْيَا وَالْآخِرَةِ
وَمَا لَهُم مِّن نَّاصِرِينَ

57. "As to those who believe
And work righteousness,
Allah will pay them (in full)
Their reward:
But Allah loveth not
Those who do wrong.

٥٧ وَأَمَّا الَّذِينَ آمَنُوا وَعَمِلُوا
الصَّالِحَاتِ فَيُوَفِّيهِمْ أُجُورَهُمْ
وَاللَّهُ لَا يُحِبُّ الظَّالِمِينَ

58. "This is what we rehearse
Unto thee of the Signs
And the Message
Of Wisdom."

٥٨ ذَٰلِكَ نَتْلُوهُ عَلَيْكَ
مِنَ الْآيَاتِ وَالذِّكْرِ الْحَكِيمِ

59. The similitude of Jesus
Before Allah is as that of
Adam;[398]
He created him from dust,
Then said to him: "Be":
And he was.

٥٩ إِنَّ مَثَلَ عِيسَىٰ عِندَ اللَّهِ
كَمَثَلِ آدَمَ خَلَقَهُ مِن تُرَابٍ
ثُمَّ قَالَ لَهُ كُن فَيَكُونُ

60. The Truth (comes)
From thy Lord alone;
So be not of those
Who doubt.[399]

٦٠ الْحَقُّ مِن رَّبِّكَ
فَلَا تَكُن مِّنَ الْمُمْتَرِينَ

61. If anyone disputes
In this matter with thee,
Now after (full) knowledge
Hath come to thee,
Say: "Come! let us
Gather together—
Our sons and your sons,
Our women and your women,
Ourselves and yourselves:
Then let us earnestly pray,

٦١ فَمَنْ حَاجَّكَ فِيهِ
مِن بَعْدِ مَا جَاءَكَ مِنَ الْعِلْمِ
فَقُلْ تَعَالَوْا نَدْعُ أَبْنَاءَنَا وَأَبْنَاءَكُمْ
وَنِسَاءَنَا وَنِسَاءَكُمْ وَأَنفُسَنَا وَأَنفُسَكُمْ
ثُمَّ نَبْتَهِلْ

398. After a description of the high position which Jesus occupies as a prophet, we have a repudiation of the dogma that he was Allah, or the son of Allah, or anything more than a man. If it is said that he was born without a human father, Adam was also so born. Indeed Adam was born without either a human father or mother. As far as our physical bodies are concerned they are mere dust. In Allah's sight Jesus was as dust just as Adam was or humanity is. The greatness of Jesus arose from the Divine command "Be": for after that he was—more than dust—a great spiritual leader and teacher.

399. The truth does not necessarily come from priests, or from the superstitions of whole peoples. It comes from Allah, and where there is a direct revelation, there is no room for doubt.

And invoke the curse
Of Allah on those who lie!"[400]

فَنَجۡعَل لَّعۡنَتَ ٱللَّهِ عَلَى ٱلۡكَٰذِبِينَ

62. This is the true account;[401]
There is no god
Except Allah;
And Allah—He is indeed
The Exalted in Power,
The Wise.

إِنَّ هَٰذَا لَهُوَ ٱلۡقَصَصُ ٱلۡحَقُّۚ وَمَا مِنۡ إِلَٰهٍ إِلَّا ٱللَّهُۚ وَإِنَّ ٱللَّهَ لَهُوَ ٱلۡعَزِيزُ ٱلۡحَكِيمُ ٦٢

63. But if they turn back,
Allah hath full knowledge
Of those who do mischief.

فَإِن تَوَلَّوۡاْ فَإِنَّ ٱللَّهَ عَلِيمُۢ بِٱلۡمُفۡسِدِينَ ٦٣

C. 57.—Islam doth invite all people
(3:64-120.) To the Truth; there is no cause
For dissembling or disputing.
False are the people who corrupt
Allah's truth, or hinder men
From coming to Allah. Let the Muslims
Hold together in unity and discipline,
Knowing that they have a mission
Of righteousness for humanity.
No harm can come to them.
Though there are good men and true
In other Faiths, Muslims must
Be true to their own Brotherhood.
They should seek help and friendship
From their own, and stand firm
In constancy and patient perseverance.

---

400. In the year of Deputations, 10th of the Hijrah, came a Christian embassy from Najrān (towards Yaman, about 150 miles north of Ṣana'ā). They were much impressed on hearing this passage of the Qur'ān explaining the true position of Christ, and they entered into tributary relations with the new Muslim State. But ingrained habits and customs prevented them from accepting Islam as a body. The Holy Prophet, firm in his faith, proposed a *Mubāhalah, i.e.*, a solemn meeting, in which both sides should summon not only their men, but their women and children, earnestly pray to Allah, and invoke the curse of Allah on those who should lie. Those who had a pure and sincere faith would not hesitate. The Christians declined, and they were dismissed in a spirit of tolerance with a promise of protection from the State in return for tribute, "the wages of rule," as it is called in the *Ā'ini Akbari*.

401. We are now in a position to deal with the questions which we left over at 2:87, Jesus is no more than a man. It is against reason and revelation to call him Allah or the son of Allah. He is called the son of Mary to emphasise this. He had no human father, as his birth was miraculous. But it was not this which raised him to his high spiritual position as a prophet, but because Allah called him to his office. The praise is due to Allah. Who by His word gave him spiritual strength—"strengthened him with the holy spirit." The miracles which surround his story relate not only to his birth and his life and death, but also to his mother Mary and his precursor Yaḥyā. These were the "Clear Signs" which he brought. It was those who misunderstood him who obscured his clear Signs and surrounded him with mysteries of their own invention. (R).

SECTION 7.

64. Say: "O People
Of the Book! come
To common terms
As between us and you:
That we worship
None but Allah;
That we associate
No partners with Him;
That we erect not,
From among ourselves,
Lords and patrons
Other than Allah."[402]
If then they turn back,
Say ye: "Bear witness
That we (at least)
Are Muslims (bowing
To Allah's Will)."

(٦٤) قُلْ يَٰٓأَهْلَ ٱلْكِتَٰبِ تَعَالَوْا۟
إِلَىٰ كَلِمَةٍ سَوَآءٍۭ بَيْنَنَا وَبَيْنَكُمْ
أَلَّا نَعْبُدَ إِلَّا ٱللَّهَ وَلَا نُشْرِكَ بِهِۦ
شَيْـًٔا وَلَا يَتَّخِذَ بَعْضُنَا
بَعْضًا أَرْبَابًا مِّن دُونِ ٱللَّهِ ۚ
فَإِن تَوَلَّوْا۟ فَقُولُوا۟
ٱشْهَدُوا۟ بِأَنَّا
مُسْلِمُونَ

65. Ye People of the Book!
Why dispute ye
About Abraham,
When the Law and the Gospel
Were not revealed
Till after him?
Have ye no understanding?

(٦٥) يَٰٓأَهْلَ ٱلْكِتَٰبِ لِمَ تُحَآجُّونَ فِىٓ
إِبْرَٰهِيمَ وَمَآ أُنزِلَتِ ٱلتَّوْرَىٰةُ وَٱلْإِنجِيلُ
إِلَّا مِنۢ بَعْدِهِۦٓ ۚ أَفَلَا تَعْقِلُونَ

66. Ah! Ye are those
Who fell to disputing
(Even) in matters of which
Ye had some knowledge![403]
But why dispute ye
In matters of which
Ye have no knowledge?
It is Allah Who knows,
And ye who know not!

(٦٦) هَٰٓأَنتُمْ هَٰٓؤُلَآءِ حَٰجَجْتُمْ
فِيمَا لَكُم بِهِۦ عِلْمٌ فَلِمَ تُحَآجُّونَ
فِيمَا لَيْسَ لَكُم بِهِۦ عِلْمٌ ۚ
وَٱللَّهُ يَعْلَمُ وَأَنتُمْ لَا تَعْلَمُونَ

402. In the abstract the People of the Book would agree to all three propositions. In practice they fail. Apart from doctrinal lapses from the unity of the One True God, there is the question of a consecrated Priesthood (among the Jews it was hereditary also), as if a mere human being—Cohen, or Pope, or Priest, or Brahman—could claim superiority apart from his learning and the purity of his life, or could stand between man and Allah in some special sense. The same remarks apply to the worship of saints. They may be pure and holy, but no one can protect us or claim Lordship over us except Allah. For *Rabb*, see 1:2, n. 90. Abraham was a true man of God, but he could not be called a Jew or a Christian as he lived long before the Law of Moses or the Gospel of Jesus was revealed.

403. The number of sects among the Jews and Christians shows that they wrangled and disputed even about some of the matters of their own religion, of which they should have had some knowledge. But when they talk of Father Abraham, they are entirely out of court, as he lived before their peculiar systems were evolved.

67. Abraham was not a Jew
Nor yet a Christian;
But he was true in Faith,
And bowed his will to Allah's,
(Which is Islam),
And he joined not gods with
Allah.[404]

٦٧ مَا كَانَ إِبْرَٰهِيمُ يَهُودِيًّا وَلَا نَصْرَانِيًّا
وَلَٰكِن كَانَ حَنِيفًا مُّسْلِمًا
وَمَا كَانَ مِنَ ٱلْمُشْرِكِينَ

68. Without a doubt, among men,
The nearest of kin to Abraham,
Are those who follow him,
As are also this Prophet
And those who believe:
And Allah is the Protector
Of those who have faith.

٦٨ إِنَّ أَوْلَى ٱلنَّاسِ بِإِبْرَٰهِيمَ
لَلَّذِينَ ٱتَّبَعُوهُ وَهَٰذَا ٱلنَّبِيُّ وَٱلَّذِينَ ءَامَنُوا۟ ۗ
وَٱللَّهُ وَلِيُّ ٱلْمُؤْمِنِينَ

69. It is the wish of a section
Of the People of the Book
To lead you astray.
But they shall lead astray
(Not you), but themselves,
And they do not perceive!

٦٩ وَدَّت طَّآئِفَةٌ مِّنْ أَهْلِ ٱلْكِتَٰبِ
لَوْ يُضِلُّونَكُمْ وَمَا يُضِلُّونَ إِلَّآ أَنفُسَهُمْ
وَمَا يَشْعُرُونَ

70. Ye People of the Book!
Why reject ye
The Signs of Allah,
Of which ye are
(Yourselves) witnesses?

٧٠ يَٰٓأَهْلَ ٱلْكِتَٰبِ لِمَ تَكْفُرُونَ
بِـَٔايَٰتِ ٱللَّهِ وَأَنتُمْ تَشْهَدُونَ

71. Ye People of the Book!
Why do ye clothe
Truth with falsehood,
And conceal the Truth,
While ye have knowledge?[405]

٧١ يَٰٓأَهْلَ ٱلْكِتَٰبِ لِمَ تَلْبِسُونَ ٱلْحَقَّ
بِٱلْبَٰطِلِ وَتَكْتُمُونَ ٱلْحَقَّ وَأَنتُمْ تَعْلَمُونَ

SECTION 8.

72. A section of the People
Of the Book say:
"Believe in the morning[406]

٧٢ وَقَالَت طَّآئِفَةٌ مِّنْ أَهْلِ ٱلْكِتَٰبِ ءَامِنُوا۟

404. *Cf.* 2:135 and the whole argument in that passage.

405. There are many ways of preventing the access of people to the truth. One is to tamper with it, or trick it out in colours of falsehood: half-truths are often more dangerous than obvious falsehoods. Another is to conceal it altogether. Those who are jealous of a prophet of Allah, whom they actually see before them, do not allow his credentials or virtues to be known, or vilify him, or conceal facts which would attract people to him. When people do this of set purpose, against their own light ("of which ye are yourselves witnesses"), they are descending to the lowest depths of degradation, and they are doing more harm to themselves than to anyone else. (R).

406. *Wajh* here has the sense of "beginning", "early part". The cynics who plotted against Islam actually asked their accomplices to join the believers and then repudiate them.

What is revealed
To the Believers,
But reject it at the end
Of the day; perchance
They may (themselves)
Turn back;

بِالَّذِىٓ أُنزِلَ عَلَى الَّذِينَ ءَامَنُوا وَجْهَ النَّهَارِ
وَاكْفُرُوٓا ءَاخِرَهُۥ لَعَلَّهُمْ يَرْجِعُونَ

73. "And believe no one
Unless he follows
Your religion."
Say: "True guidance
Is the guidance of Allah;
(Fear ye) lest a revelation[407]
Be sent to someone (else)
Like unto that which was sent
Unto you? Or that those
(Receiving such revelation)
Should engage you in argument
Before your Lord?"[408]
Say: "All bounties
Are in the hand of Allah:
He granteth them
To whom He pleaseth:
And Allah careth for all,
And He knoweth all things."

٧٣ وَلَا تُؤْمِنُوٓا
إِلَّا لِمَن تَبِعَ دِينَكُمْ
قُلْ إِنَّ الْهُدَىٰ هُدَى اللَّهِ
أَن يُؤْتَىٰٓ أَحَدٌ مِّثْلَ مَآ أُوتِيتُمْ
أَوْ يُحَآجُّوكُمْ عِندَ رَبِّكُمْ
قُلْ إِنَّ الْفَضْلَ بِيَدِ اللَّهِ يُؤْتِيهِ مَن يَشَآءُ
وَاللَّهُ وَاسِعٌ عَلِيمٌ

74. For His Mercy He specially chooseth
Whom He pleaseth;
For Allah is the Lord
Of bounties unbounded.

٧٤ يَخْتَصُّ بِرَحْمَتِهِۦ مَن يَشَآءُ
وَاللَّهُ ذُو الْفَضْلِ الْعَظِيمِ

75. Among the People of the Book
Are some who, if entrusted
With a hoard of gold,[409]
Will (readily) pay it back;
Others, who, if entrusted
With a single silver coin,[410]

٧٥ وَمِنْ أَهْلِ الْكِتَٰبِ
مَنْ إِن تَأْمَنْهُ بِقِنطَارٍ يُؤَدِّهِۦٓ إِلَيْكَ
وَمِنْهُم مَّنْ إِن تَأْمَنْهُ بِدِينَارٍ

---

407. The two clauses following have been variously construed, and some translations leave the sense ambiguous. I have construed the conjunction "*an*" to mean "lest", as it undoubtedly does in 7:172, "*an taqūlū*", etc.

408. *Cf.* 2:26. The People of the Book were doubly annoyed at the Muslims: (1) that they should (being outside their ranks) receive Allah's revelations, and (2) that having received such revelations, they should be able to convict them out of their own scriptures before their Lord!

409. *Hoard of gold*: *qinṭār*: a talent of 1,200 ounces of gold. See 3:14, n. 354. (R).

410. *Silver coin: dīnār*. In the later Roman Empire, the denarius was a small silver coin. It must have been current in Syria and the markets of Arabia in the time of the Prophet. It was the coin whose name is translated in the English Bible by the word penny. Matt. xxii. 19; hence the abbreviation of a penny is *d*(=denarius). The later Arabian coin *dīnār*, coined by the Umayyads, was a gold coin after the pattern of the Byzantine (Roman) *denarius aureus* and weighed about 66349 grains troy.

Will not repay it unless
Thou constantly stoodest
Demanding, because,
They say, "there is no call
On us (to keep faith)
With these ignorant (Pagans)."[411]
But they tell a lie against Allah
And (well) they know it.

لَا يُؤَدِّهِۦٓ إِلَيْكَ إِلَّا مَا دُمْتَ عَلَيْهِ قَآئِمًا ۗ
ذَٰلِكَ بِأَنَّهُمْ قَالُوا۟ لَيْسَ عَلَيْنَا فِى
ٱلْأُمِّيِّـۧنَ سَبِيلٌ وَيَقُولُونَ عَلَى ٱللَّهِ
ٱلْكَذِبَ وَهُمْ يَعْلَمُونَ

76. Nay—those that keep
Their plighted faith
And act aright—verily
Allah loves those
Who act aright.

٧٦ بَلَىٰ مَنْ أَوْفَىٰ بِعَهْدِهِۦ وَٱتَّقَىٰ
فَإِنَّ ٱللَّهَ يُحِبُّ ٱلْمُتَّقِينَ

77. As for those who sell
The faith they owe to Allah
And their own plighted word
For a small price,[412]
They shall have no portion
In the Hereafter:
Nor will Allah
(Deign to) speak to them
Or look at them
On the Day of Judgement,
Nor will He cleanse them[413]
(Of sin): they shall have
A grievous Penalty.

٧٧ إِنَّ ٱلَّذِينَ يَشْتَرُونَ
بِعَهْدِ ٱللَّهِ وَأَيْمَٰنِهِمْ ثَمَنًا قَلِيلًا
أُو۟لَٰٓئِكَ لَا خَلَٰقَ لَهُمْ فِى ٱلْءَاخِرَةِ
وَلَا يُكَلِّمُهُمُ ٱللَّهُ وَلَا يَنظُرُ إِلَيْهِمْ
يَوْمَ ٱلْقِيَٰمَةِ وَلَا يُزَكِّيهِمْ
وَلَهُمْ عَذَابٌ أَلِيمٌ

78. There is among them
A section who distort
The Book with their tongues:
(As they read) you would think
It is a part of the Book,
But it is no part
Of the Book; and they say,
"That is from Allah,"
But it is not from Allah:

٧٨ وَإِنَّ مِنْهُمْ لَفَرِيقًا يَلْوُۥنَ أَلْسِنَتَهُم
بِٱلْكِتَٰبِ لِتَحْسَبُوهُ مِنَ ٱلْكِتَٰبِ
وَمَا هُوَ مِنَ ٱلْكِتَٰبِ وَيَقُولُونَ هُوَ
مِنْ عِندِ ٱللَّهِ وَمَا هُوَ مِنْ عِندِ ٱللَّهِ

---

411. Every race imbued with race arrogance resorts to this kind of moral or religious subterfuge. Even if its members are usually honest or just among themselves, they are contemptuous of those outside their circle, and cheat and deceive them without any qualms of conscience. This is a "lie against Allah".

412. All our duties to our fellow creatures are referred to the service and faith we owe to Allah. But in the matter of truth an appeal is made to our own self-respect as responsible beings: is it becoming that we should be false to our own word, to ourselves? And then we are reminded that the utmost we can gain by falsifying Allah's word or being untrue to ourselves is but a miserable price. We get at best something very paltry as the price for selling our very souls.

413. Even on sinners—ordinary sinners—Allah will look with compassion and mercy; He will speak words of kindness and cleanse them of their sins. But those who are in active rebellion against Allah and sin against their own light—what mercy can they expect?

It is they who tell
A lie against Allah,
And (well) they know it!

وَيَقُولُونَ عَلَى ٱللَّهِ ٱلْكَذِبَ وَهُمْ يَعْلَمُونَ

79. It is not (possible)
That a man, to whom
Is given the Book,
And Wisdom,
And the Prophetic Office,
Should say to people:
"Be ye my worshippers
Rather than Allah's":[414]
On the contrary
(He would say):
"Be ye worshippers
Of Him Who is truly
The Cherisher of all:
For ye have taught
The Book and ye
Have studied it earnestly."

٧٩ مَا كَانَ لِبَشَرٍ
أَن يُؤْتِيَهُ ٱللَّهُ ٱلْكِتَٰبَ وَٱلْحُكْمَ
وَٱلنُّبُوَّةَ ثُمَّ يَقُولَ لِلنَّاسِ كُونُوا۟ عِبَادًا لِّى
مِن دُونِ ٱللَّهِ وَلَٰكِن كُونُوا۟ رَبَّٰنِيِّـۧنَ
بِمَا كُنتُمْ تُعَلِّمُونَ ٱلْكِتَٰبَ
وَبِمَا كُنتُمْ تَدْرُسُونَ

80. Nor would he instruct you
To take angels and prophets[415]
For Lords and Patrons.
What! would he bid you
To unbelief after ye have
Bowed your will
(To Allah in Islam)?

٨٠ وَلَا يَأْمُرَكُمْ أَن تَتَّخِذُوا۟ ٱلْمَلَٰٓئِكَةَ
وَٱلنَّبِيِّـۧنَ أَرْبَابًا ۗ أَيَأْمُرُكُم بِٱلْكُفْرِ
بَعْدَ إِذْ أَنتُم مُّسْلِمُونَ

Section 9.

81. Behold! Allah took
The Covenant of the Prophets,[416]
Saying: "I give you
A Book and Wisdom;

٨١ وَإِذْ أَخَذَ ٱللَّهُ مِيثَٰقَ ٱلنَّبِيِّـۧنَ
لَمَآ ءَاتَيْتُكُم مِّن كِتَٰبٍ وَحِكْمَةٍ

414. It is not in reason or in the nature of things that Allah's messenger should preach against Allah. Jesus came to preach and convey the true message of Allah. (R).

415. Jesus was a prophet, and the Holy Spirit "with which he was strengthened" was the Angel who brought the revelations to him.

416. *Cf.* 2:63, n. 78. The argument is: You (People of the Book) are bound by your own oaths, sworn solemnly in the presence of your own Prophets. In the Old Testament as it now exists, Muḥammad is foretold in Deut. xviii; and the rise of the Arab nation in Isiah. xlii. 11, for Kedar was a son of Ismā'īl and the name is used for the Arab nation. Also, in the New Testament as it now exists, Muḥammad is foretold in the Gospel of St. John, xiv. 16, xv. 26, and xvi. 7; the *future* Comforter cannot be the "Holy Spirit" as understood by Christians, because the Holy Spirit already was present, helping and guiding Jesus. The Greek word translated "Comforter" is "Paracletos", which is an easy corruption from "Periclytos", which is almost a literal translation of "Muḥammad"or "Aḥmad"; see Q. 61:6. Further, there were other Gospels that have perished, but of which traces still remain, which were even more specific in their reference to Muḥammad; *e.g.*, the Gospel of St. Barnabas, of which an Italian translation is extant in the State Library at Vienna. It was edited in 1907 with an English translation by Mr. Lonsdale and Laura Ragg.

Then comes to you
A Messenger, confirming
What is with you;
Do you believe in him
And render him help."
Allah said: "Do ye agree,
And take this my Covenant
As binding on you?"
They said: "We agree."
He said: "Then bear witness,
And I am with you
Among the witnesses."

ثُمَّ جَآءَكُمْ رَسُولٌ
مُّصَدِّقٌ لِّمَا مَعَكُمْ لَتُؤْمِنُنَّ بِهِۦ وَلَتَنصُرُنَّهُۥ
قَالَ ءَأَقْرَرْتُمْ وَأَخَذْتُمْ عَلَىٰ ذَٰلِكُمْ إِصْرِى
قَالُوٓا أَقْرَرْنَا قَالَ فَاشْهَدُوا
وَأَنَا مَعَكُم مِّنَ الشَّٰهِدِينَ

82. If any turn back
After this, they are
Perverted transgressors.

٨٢ فَمَن تَوَلَّىٰ بَعْدَ ذَٰلِكَ
فَأُولَٰٓئِكَ هُمُ الْفَٰسِقُونَ

83. Do they seek
For other than the Religion
Of Allah?—while all creatures
In the heavens and on earth
Have, willing or unwilling,[417]
Bowed to His Will
(Accepted Islam),
And to Him shall they
All be brought back.

٨٣ أَفَغَيْرَ دِينِ اللَّهِ يَبْغُونَ
وَلَهُۥٓ أَسْلَمَ مَن فِى السَّمَٰوَٰتِ وَالْأَرْضِ
طَوْعًا وَكَرْهًا
وَإِلَيْهِ يُرْجَعُونَ

84. Say: "We believe
In Allah, and in what
Has been revealed to us
And what was revealed
To Abraham, Ismā'īl;
Isaac, Jacob, and the Tribes,
And in (the Books)
Given to Moses, Jesus,
And the Prophets,
From their Lord:
We make no distinction
Between one and another
Among them, and to Allah do we
Bow our will (in Islam)."

٨٤ قُلْ ءَامَنَّا بِاللَّهِ وَمَآ أُنزِلَ عَلَيْنَا
وَمَآ أُنزِلَ عَلَىٰٓ إِبْرَٰهِيمَ وَإِسْمَٰعِيلَ وَإِسْحَٰقَ
وَيَعْقُوبَ وَالْأَسْبَاطِ وَمَآ أُوتِىَ مُوسَىٰ
وَعِيسَىٰ وَالنَّبِيُّونَ مِن رَّبِّهِمْ
لَا نُفَرِّقُ بَيْنَ أَحَدٍ مِّنْهُمْ
وَنَحْنُ لَهُۥ مُسْلِمُونَ

417. Allah's Truth is manifest, and all that is good and true and sane and normal accepts it with joy. But even where there is "disease in the heart" (Q. 2:10), or judgement is obscured by perversity, every creature must eventually see and acknowledge Allah and His power (2:167), *Cf.* R. Bridges: "Testament of Beauty": iv. 1419-22—"For God's love is unescapable as nature's environment, which if a man ignore or think to thrust it off, he is the ill-natured fool that runneth blindly on death." All Nature adores Allah, and Islam asks for nothing peculiar or sectarian; it but asks that we follow our nature and make our will conformable to Allah's Will as seen in Nature, history, and revelation. Its message is universal.

85. If anyone desires
A religion other than
Islam (submission to Allah),[418]
Never will it be accepted
Of him; and in the Hereafter
He will be in the ranks
Of those who have lost
(All spiritual good).

٨٥ وَمَن يَبْتَغِ غَيْرَ
ٱلْإِسْلَٰمِ دِينًا فَلَن يُقْبَلَ مِنْهُ
وَهُوَ فِى ٱلْءَاخِرَةِ مِنَ ٱلْخَٰسِرِينَ

86. How shall Allah
Guide those who reject
Faith after they accepted it
And bore witness
That the Messenger was true
And that Clear Signs
Had come unto them?
But Allah guides not
A people unjust.

٨٦ كَيْفَ يَهْدِى ٱللَّهُ قَوْمًا كَفَرُوا۟
بَعْدَ إِيمَٰنِهِمْ وَشَهِدُوٓا۟ أَنَّ ٱلرَّسُولَ حَقٌّ
وَجَآءَهُمُ ٱلْبَيِّنَٰتُ ۚ وَٱللَّهُ لَا يَهْدِى
ٱلْقَوْمَ ٱلظَّٰلِمِينَ

87. Of such the reward
Is that on them (rests)
The curse of Allah,
Of His angels,
And of all mankind—

٨٧ أُو۟لَٰٓئِكَ جَزَآؤُهُمْ أَنَّ عَلَيْهِمْ لَعْنَةَ ٱللَّهِ
وَٱلْمَلَٰٓئِكَةِ وَٱلنَّاسِ أَجْمَعِينَ

88. In that will they dwell;
Nor will their penalty
Be lightened, nor respite
Be their (lot);[418-A]

٨٨ خَٰلِدِينَ فِيهَا لَا يُخَفَّفُ عَنْهُمُ ٱلْعَذَابُ
وَلَا هُمْ يُنظَرُونَ

89. Except for those that repent
(Even) after that,
And make amends;
For verily Allah
Is Oft-Forgiving,
Most Merciful.

٨٩ إِلَّا ٱلَّذِينَ تَابُوا۟ مِنۢ بَعْدِ ذَٰلِكَ
وَأَصْلَحُوا۟ فَإِنَّ ٱللَّهَ غَفُورٌ رَّحِيمٌ

90. But those who reject
Faith after they accepted it,
And then go on adding
To their defiance of Faith—

٩٠ إِنَّ ٱلَّذِينَ كَفَرُوا۟ بَعْدَ إِيمَٰنِهِمْ
ثُمَّ ٱزْدَادُوا۟ كُفْرًا

418. The Muslim position is clear. The Muslim does not claim to have a religion peculiar to himself. Islam is not a sect or an ethnic religion. In its view all Religion is one, for the Truth is one. It was the religion preached by all the earlier prophets. It was the truth taught by all the inspired Books. In essence it amounts to a consciousness of the Will and Plan of Allah and a joyful submission to that Will and Plan. If anyone wants a religion other than that, he is false to his own nature, as he is false to Allah's Will and Plan. Such a one cannot expect guidance, for he has deliberately renounced guidance.

418-A. *Cf.* 2:161-62.

Never will their repentance
Be accepted; for they
Are those who have
(Of set purpose) gone astray.

لَن تُقْبَلَ تَوْبَتُهُمْ
وَأُولَٰئِكَ هُمُ الضَّالُّونَ

91. As to those who reject
Faith, and die rejecting—
Never would be accepted
From any such as much
Gold as the earth contains,
Though they should offer it
For ransom. For such
Is (in store) a penalty grievous,
And they will find no helpers.

٩١ إِنَّ الَّذِينَ كَفَرُوا وَمَاتُوا وَهُمْ كُفَّارٌ فَلَن
يُقْبَلَ مِنْ أَحَدِهِم مِّلْءُ الْأَرْضِ ذَهَبًا
وَلَوِ افْتَدَىٰ بِهِ ۗ أُولَٰئِكَ لَهُمْ عَذَابٌ أَلِيمٌ
وَمَا لَهُم مِّن نَّاصِرِينَ

SECTION 10.

92. By no means shall ye
Attain righteousness unless
Ye give (freely) of that[419]
Which ye love; and whatever
Ye give, of a truth
Allah knoweth it well.

٩٢ لَن تَنَالُوا الْبِرَّ حَتَّىٰ تُنفِقُوا
مِمَّا تُحِبُّونَ ۚ وَمَا تُنفِقُوا مِن شَيْءٍ
فَإِنَّ اللَّهَ بِهِ عَلِيمٌ

93. All food was lawful
To the Children of Israel,
Except what Israel[420]
Made unlawful for itself,
Before the Law (of Moses)
Was revealed. Say:
"Bring ye the Law
And study it,
If ye be men of truth."

٩٣ كُلُّ الطَّعَامِ كَانَ حِلًّا لِّبَنِي إِسْرَائِيلَ
إِلَّا مَا حَرَّمَ إِسْرَائِيلُ عَلَىٰ نَفْسِهِ
مِن قَبْلِ أَن تُنَزَّلَ التَّوْرَاةُ ۗ قُلْ فَأْتُوا بِالتَّوْرَاةِ
فَاتْلُوهَا إِن كُنتُمْ صَادِقِينَ

94. If any, after this, invent
A lie and attribute it
To Allah, they are indeed
Unjust wrongdoers.

٩٤ فَمَنِ افْتَرَىٰ عَلَى اللَّهِ الْكَذِبَ
مِن بَعْدِ ذَٰلِكَ فَأُولَٰئِكَ هُمُ الظَّالِمُونَ

419. The test of charity is: do you give something that you value greatly, something that you love? If you give your life in a Cause, that is the greatest gift you can give. If you give yourself, that is, your personal efforts, your talents, your skill, your learning, that comes next in degree. If you give your earnings, your property, your possessions, that is also a great gift; for many people love them even more than other things. And there are less tangible things, such as position, reputation, the well-being of those we love, the regard of those who can help us, etc. It is unselfishness that Allah demands, and there is no act of unselfishness, however small or intangible, but is well within the knowledge of Allah.

420. The Arabs ate the flesh of the camel, which is lawful in Islam, but it was prohibited by the Jewish Law of Moses (Leviticus xi. 4). But that Law was very strict because of the "hardness of heart" of Israel, because of Israel's insolence and iniquity (Q 6:146). Before it was promulgated Israel was free to choose its own food. I take "Israel" here to stand for the people of Israel.

95. Say: "Allah speaketh
The Truth: follow
The religion of Abraham,
The sane in faith; he
Was not of the Pagans."[421]

٩٥ قُلْ صَدَقَ ٱللَّهُ فَٱتَّبِعُوا۟ مِلَّةَ إِبْرَٰهِيمَ
حَنِيفًا وَمَا كَانَ مِنَ ٱلْمُشْرِكِينَ

96. The first House (of worship)
Appointed for men
Was that at Bakka;[442]
Full of blessing
And of guidance
For all kinds of beings:[423]

٩٦ إِنَّ أَوَّلَ بَيْتٍ وُضِعَ لِلنَّاسِ لَلَّذِى
بِبَكَّةَ مُبَارَكًا وَهُدًى لِّلْعَٰلَمِينَ

97. In it are Signs
Manifest; (for example),
The Station of Abraham;[424]
Whoever enters it
Attains security;[425]
Pilgrimage thereto is a duty
Men owe to Allah—
Those who can afford
The journey; but if any
Deny faith, Allah stands not
In need of any of His creatures.

٩٧ فِيهِ ءَايَٰتٌۢ بَيِّنَٰتٌ مَّقَامُ إِبْرَٰهِيمَ ۖ
وَمَن دَخَلَهُۥ كَانَ ءَامِنًا ۗ وَلِلَّهِ عَلَى ٱلنَّاسِ
حِجُّ ٱلْبَيْتِ مَنِ ٱسْتَطَاعَ إِلَيْهِ سَبِيلًا ۚ
وَمَن كَفَرَ فَإِنَّ ٱللَّهَ غَنِىٌّ عَنِ ٱلْعَٰلَمِينَ

98. Say: "O People of the Book!
Why reject ye the Signs
Of Allah, when Allah
Is Himself witness
To all ye do?"

٩٨ قُلْ يَٰٓأَهْلَ ٱلْكِتَٰبِ لِمَ تَكْفُرُونَ
بِـَٔايَٰتِ ٱللَّهِ وَٱللَّهُ شَهِيدٌ عَلَىٰ مَا تَعْمَلُونَ

99. Say: "O ye People of the Book!
Why obstruct ye
Those who believe,
From the Path of Allah,
Seeking to make it crooked,
While ye were yourselves
Witnesses (to Allah's Covenant)?[426]

٩٩ قُلْ يَٰٓأَهْلَ ٱلْكِتَٰبِ
لِمَ تَصُدُّونَ عَن سَبِيلِ ٱللَّهِ مَنْ ءَامَنَ
تَبْغُونَهَا عِوَجًا وَأَنتُمْ شُهَدَآءُ

421. The greater freedom of Islam in the matter of the ceremonial law, compared with the Mosaic Law, is not a reproach but a recommendation. We go back to an older source than Judaism—the institutions of Abraham. By common consent his Faith was sound, and he was certainly not a pagan, a term contemptuously applied to the Arabs by the Jews.

422. *Bakka*: same as Makkah; perhaps an older name. The foundation of the Ka'ba goes back to Abraham, but there are place associations in the sacred territory with the names of Adam and Eve. (R).

423. *'Ālamīn:* all the worlds (1:2, 2); all kinds of beings; all nations (3:42); all creatures (3:97).

424. *Station of Abraham*: see 2:125 and n. 125.

425. See reference in last note.

426. *Cf.* 3:81.

But Allah is not unmindful
Of all that ye do."

وَمَا ٱللَّهُ بِغَٰفِلٍ عَمَّا تَعْمَلُونَ

100. O ye who believe!
If ye listen
To a faction
Among the People of the Book,
They would (indeed)
Render you apostates
After ye have believed!

١٠٠ يَٰٓأَيُّهَا ٱلَّذِينَ ءَامَنُوٓا۟ إِن تُطِيعُوا۟
فَرِيقًا مِّنَ ٱلَّذِينَ أُوتُوا۟ ٱلْكِتَٰبَ
يَرُدُّوكُم بَعْدَ إِيمَٰنِكُمْ كَٰفِرِينَ

101. And how would ye
Deny Faith while unto you
Are rehearsed the Signs
Of Allah, and among you
Lives the Messenger?
Whoever holds
Firmly to Allah
Will be shown
A Way that is straight.

١٠١ وَكَيْفَ تَكْفُرُونَ وَأَنتُمْ تُتْلَىٰ
عَلَيْكُمْ ءَايَٰتُ ٱللَّهِ وَفِيكُمْ رَسُولُهُۥ
وَمَن يَعْتَصِم بِٱللَّهِ فَقَدْ هُدِىَ
إِلَىٰ صِرَٰطٍ مُّسْتَقِيمٍ

Section 11.

102. O ye who believe!
Fear Allah as He should be[427]
Feared, and die not
Except in a state[428]
Of Islam.

١٠٢ يَٰٓأَيُّهَا ٱلَّذِينَ ءَامَنُوا۟ ٱتَّقُوا۟ ٱللَّهَ حَقَّ تُقَاتِهِۦ
وَلَا تَمُوتُنَّ إِلَّا وَأَنتُم مُّسْلِمُونَ

103. And hold fast,
All together, by the Rope[429]
Which Allah (stretches out
For you), and be not divided
Among yourselves;
And remember with gratitude
Allah's favour on you;
For ye were enemies[430]
And He joined your hearts
In love, so that by His Grace,
Ye became brethren;
And ye were on the brink

١٠٣ وَٱعْتَصِمُوا۟ بِحَبْلِ ٱللَّهِ جَمِيعًا
وَلَا تَفَرَّقُوا۟ وَٱذْكُرُوا۟ نِعْمَتَ ٱللَّهِ عَلَيْكُمْ
إِذْ كُنتُمْ أَعْدَآءً فَأَلَّفَ بَيْنَ قُلُوبِكُمْ
فَأَصْبَحْتُم بِنِعْمَتِهِۦٓ إِخْوَٰنًا
وَكُنتُمْ عَلَىٰ شَفَا

427. Fear is of many kinds: (1) the abject fear of the coward; (2) the fear of a child or an inexperienced person in the face of an unknown danger; (3) the fear of a reasonable man who wishes to avoid harm to himself or to people whom he wishes to protect; (4) the reverence which is akin to love, for it fears to do anything which is not pleasing to the object of love. The first is unworthy of man; the second is necessary for one spiritually immature; the third is a manly precaution against evil as long as it is unconquered; and the fourth is the seed-bed of righteousness. Those mature in faith cultivate the fourth; at earlier stages, the third or the second may be necessary; they are fears, but not the fear of Allah. The first is a feeling of which anyone should be ashamed.

Of the Pit of Fire,
And He saved you from it.
Thus doth Allah make
His Signs clear to you:
That ye may be guided.

حُفْرَةٍ مِّنَ ٱلنَّارِ فَأَنقَذَكُم مِّنْهَا
كَذَٰلِكَ يُبَيِّنُ ٱللَّهُ لَكُمْ ءَايَٰتِهِۦ لَعَلَّكُمْ تَهْتَدُونَ

104. Let there arise out of you
A band of people
Inviting to all that is good,
Enjoining what is right,
And forbidding what is wrong:
They are the ones
To attain felicity.[431]

١٠٤ وَلْتَكُن مِّنكُمْ أُمَّةٌ يَدْعُونَ إِلَى ٱلْخَيْرِ
وَيَأْمُرُونَ بِٱلْمَعْرُوفِ وَيَنْهَوْنَ عَنِ ٱلْمُنكَرِ
وَأُو۟لَٰٓئِكَ هُمُ ٱلْمُفْلِحُونَ

105. Be not like those
Who are divided
Amongst themselves
And fall into disputations
After receiving
Clear Signs:
For them
Is a dreadful Penalty—

١٠٥ وَلَا تَكُونُوا۟ كَٱلَّذِينَ تَفَرَّقُوا۟
وَٱخْتَلَفُوا۟ مِنۢ بَعْدِ مَا جَآءَهُمُ ٱلْبَيِّنَٰتُ
وَأُو۟لَٰٓئِكَ لَهُمْ عَذَابٌ عَظِيمٌ

106. On the Day when
Some faces will be (lit up
With) white, and some faces
Will be (in the gloom of) black:[432]
To those whose faces
Will be black, (will be said):
"Did ye reject Faith
After accepting it?

١٠٦ يَوْمَ تَبْيَضُّ وُجُوهٌ
وَتَسْوَدُّ وُجُوهٌ فَأَمَّا ٱلَّذِينَ ٱسْوَدَّتْ
وُجُوهُهُمْ أَكَفَرْتُم بَعْدَ إِيمَٰنِكُمْ

---

428. Our whole being should be permeated with Islam; it is not a mere veneer or outward show.

429. The simile is that of people struggling in deep water, to whom a benevolent Providence stretches out a strong and unbreakable rope of rescue. If all hold fast to it together, their mutual support adds to the chance of their safety.

430. Yathrib was torn with civil and tribal feuds and dissensions before the Messenger of Allah set his sacred feet on its soil. After that, it became the City of the Prophet, Madīnah, and unmatched Brotherhood and the pivot of Islam. This poor quarrelsome world is a larger Yathrib: can we establish the sacred feet on its soil, and make it a new and larger Madīnah?

431. *Mufliḥ, aflaḥa, falāḥ*: the root idea is attainment of desires; happiness, in this world and the next; success; prosperity; freedom from anxiety, care, or a disturbed state of mind—the opposite of *'adhāb* in the next verse, which includes: failure; misery; punishment or penalty; agony or anguish.

The ideal Muslim community is happy, untroubled by conflicts or doubts, sure of itself, strong, united, and prosperous; because it invites to all that is good, enjoins the right; and forbids the wrong—a master-stroke of description in three clauses.

432. The "face" (*wajh*) expresses our personality, our inmost being. White is the colour of Light; to become white is to be illumined with Light, which stands for felicity, the rays of the glorious Light of Allah. Black is the colour of darkness, sin, rebellion, misery; removal from the Grace and Light of Allah. These are the Signs of Heaven and Hell. The standard of decision in all questions is the justice of Allah.

Taste then the Penalty
For rejecting Faith."

فَذُوقُوا۟ ٱلْعَذَابَ بِمَا كُنتُمْ تَكْفُرُونَ

107. But those whose faces
Will be (lit with) white—
They will be in (the Light
Of) Allah's mercy; therein
To dwell (forever).

١٠٧ وَأَمَّا ٱلَّذِينَ ٱبْيَضَّتْ وُجُوهُهُمْ
فَفِى رَحْمَةِ ٱللَّهِ هُمْ فِيهَا خَٰلِدُونَ

108. These are the Signs
Of Allah: We rehearse them
To thee in Truth;
And Allah means
No injustice to any
Of His creatures.

١٠٨ تِلْكَ ءَايَٰتُ ٱللَّهِ نَتْلُوهَا عَلَيْكَ بِٱلْحَقِّ
وَمَا ٱللَّهُ يُرِيدُ ظُلْمًا لِّلْعَٰلَمِينَ

109. To Allah belongs all
That is in the heavens
And on earth; to Him
Do all questions
Go back (for decision).[433]

١٠٩ وَلِلَّهِ مَا فِى ٱلسَّمَٰوَٰتِ وَمَا فِى ٱلْأَرْضِ
وَإِلَى ٱللَّهِ تُرْجَعُ ٱلْأُمُورُ

SECTION 12.

110. Ye are the best
Of Peoples, evolved
For mankind,
Enjoining what is right,
Forbidding what is wrong,
And believing in Allah.[434]
If only the People of the Book
Had faith, it were best
For them: among them
Are some who have faith,
But most of them
Are perverted transgressors.

١١٠ كُنتُمْ خَيْرَ أُمَّةٍ أُخْرِجَتْ لِلنَّاسِ تَأْمُرُونَ
بِٱلْمَعْرُوفِ وَتَنْهَوْنَ عَنِ ٱلْمُنكَرِ
وَتُؤْمِنُونَ بِٱللَّهِ وَلَوْ ءَامَنَ أَهْلُ ٱلْكِتَٰبِ
لَكَانَ خَيْرًا لَّهُم مِّنْهُمُ ٱلْمُؤْمِنُونَ
وَأَكْثَرُهُمُ ٱلْفَٰسِقُونَ

111. They will do you no harm,
Barring a trifling annoyance;
If they come out to fight you,

١١١ لَن يَضُرُّوكُمْ إِلَّآ أَذًى وَإِن يُقَٰتِلُوكُمْ

433. *Cf.* 2:210.

434. The logical conclusion to the evolution of religious history is a non-sectarian, non-racial. non-doctrinal, universal religion, which Islam claims to be. For Islam is just submission to the Will of Allah. This implies (1) Faith, (2) doing right, being an example to others to do right, and having the power to see that the right prevails, (3) eschewing wrong, being an example to others to eschew wrong, and having the power to see that wrong and injustice are defeated. Islam therefore lives, not for itself, but for mankind. The People of the Book, if only they had faith, would be Muslims, for they have been prepared for Islam. Unfortunately there is Unfaith, but it can never harm those who carry the banner of Faith and Right, which must always be victorious.

They will show you their backs,
And no help shall they get.

يُوَلُّوكُمُ ٱلْأَدْبَارَ ثُمَّ لَا يُنصَرُونَ

112. Shame is pitched over them[435]
(Like a tent) wherever
They are found,
Except when under a covenant
(Of protection) from Allah
And from men; they draw
On themselves wrath from
Allah,
And pitched over them
Is (the tent of) destitution.
This because they rejected
The Signs of Allah, and slew
The Prophets in defiance of
right;[436]
This because they rebelled
And transgressed beyond
bounds.

(١١٢) ضُرِبَتْ عَلَيْهِمُ ٱلذِّلَّةُ أَيْنَ مَا ثُقِفُوٓا۟
إِلَّا بِحَبْلٍ مِّنَ ٱللَّهِ وَحَبْلٍ مِّنَ ٱلنَّاسِ
وَبَآءُو بِغَضَبٍ مِّنَ ٱللَّهِ
وَضُرِبَتْ عَلَيْهِمُ ٱلْمَسْكَنَةُ
ذَٰلِكَ بِأَنَّهُمْ كَانُوا۟ يَكْفُرُونَ بِـَٔايَٰتِ ٱللَّهِ
وَيَقْتُلُونَ ٱلْأَنۢبِيَآءَ بِغَيْرِ حَقٍّ
ذَٰلِكَ بِمَا عَصَوا۟ وَّكَانُوا۟ يَعْتَدُونَ

113. Not all of them are alike:
Of the People of the Book
Are a portion that stand
(For the right); they rehearse
The Signs of Allah all night
long,
And they prostrate themselves[437]
In adoration.

(١١٣) لَيْسُوا۟ سَوَآءً مِّنْ أَهْلِ ٱلْكِتَٰبِ
أُمَّةٌ قَآئِمَةٌ يَتْلُونَ ءَايَٰتِ ٱللَّهِ
ءَانَآءَ ٱلَّيْلِ وَهُمْ يَسْجُدُونَ

114. They believe in Allah
And the Last Day;
They enjoin what is right,
And forbid what is wrong;
And they hasten (in emulation)
In (all) good works:
They are in the ranks
Of the righteous.

(١١٤) يُؤْمِنُونَ بِٱللَّهِ وَٱلْيَوْمِ ٱلْءَاخِرِ
وَيَأْمُرُونَ بِٱلْمَعْرُوفِ وَيَنْهَوْنَ عَنِ ٱلْمُنكَرِ
وَيُسَٰرِعُونَ فِى ٱلْخَيْرَٰتِ
وَأُو۟لَٰٓئِكَ مِنَ ٱلصَّٰلِحِينَ

115. Of the good that they do,
Nothing will be rejected
Of them; for Allah knoweth well
Those that do right.

(١١٥) وَمَا يَفْعَلُوا۟ مِنْ خَيْرٍ فَلَن يُكْفَرُوهُ
وَٱللَّهُ عَلِيمٌۢ بِٱلْمُتَّقِينَ

435. *Ḍuribat*: I think there is a simile from the pitching of a tent. Ordinarily a man's tent is a place of tranquillity and honour for him. The tent of the wicked wherever they are found is ignominy, shame, and humiliation. It is pity from Allah or from men that gives them protection when their pride has a fall. Using the same simile of a tent in another way, their home will be destitution and misery.

436. *Cf.* 3:21. n. 363.

437. In Islam we respect sincere faith and true righteousness in whatever form they appear. This verse, according to Commentators, refers to those People of the Book who eventually embraced Islam. (R).

116. Those who reject Faith—
Neither their possessions
Nor their (numerous) progeny
Will avail them aught against
Allah:
They will be Companions
Of the Fire—dwelling
Therein (forever).[438]

١١٦ إِنَّ ٱلَّذِينَ كَفَرُوا۟ لَن تُغْنِىَ عَنْهُمْ
أَمْوَٰلُهُمْ وَلَآ أَوْلَـٰدُهُم مِّنَ ٱللَّهِ شَيْـًٔا ۖ
وَأُو۟لَـٰٓئِكَ أَصْحَـٰبُ ٱلنَّارِ ۚ هُمْ فِيهَا خَـٰلِدُونَ

117. What they spend
In the life
Of this (material) world
May be likened to a Wind
Which brings a nipping frost:
It strikes and destroys the harvest
Of men who have wronged
Their own souls; it is not Allah
That hath wronged them, but
They wrong themselves.[439]

١١٧ مَثَلُ مَا يُنفِقُونَ فِى هَـٰذِهِ ٱلْحَيَوٰةِ ٱلدُّنْيَا
كَمَثَلِ رِيحٍ فِيهَا صِرٌّ أَصَابَتْ حَرْثَ قَوْمٍ
ظَلَمُوٓا۟ أَنفُسَهُمْ فَأَهْلَكَتْهُ ۚ وَمَا ظَلَمَهُمُ
ٱللَّهُ وَلَـٰكِنْ أَنفُسَهُمْ يَظْلِمُونَ

118. O ye who believe!
Take not into your intimacy
Those outside your ranks:
They will not fail
To corrupt you. They
Only desire your ruin:
Rank hatred has already
Appeared from their mouths:
What their hearts conceal
Is far worse.
We have made plain
To you the Signs,
If ye have wisdom.

١١٨ يَـٰٓأَيُّهَا ٱلَّذِينَ ءَامَنُوا۟ لَا تَتَّخِذُوا۟ بِطَانَةً
مِّن دُونِكُمْ لَا يَأْلُونَكُمْ خَبَالًا وَدُّوا۟ مَا عَنِتُّمْ
قَدْ بَدَتِ ٱلْبَغْضَآءُ مِنْ أَفْوَٰهِهِمْ
وَمَا تُخْفِى صُدُورُهُمْ أَكْبَرُ ۚ
قَدْ بَيَّنَّا لَكُمُ ٱلْـَٔايَـٰتِ ۖ إِن كُنتُمْ تَعْقِلُونَ

119. Ah! ye are those
Who love them,
But they love you not—

١١٩ هَـٰٓأَنتُمْ أُو۟لَآءِ تُحِبُّونَهُمْ وَلَا يُحِبُّونَكُمْ

438. *Cf.* 3:10.

439. False "spending" may be either in false "charity" or in having a "good time". For the man who resists Allah's purpose, neither of them is any good. The essence of charity is faith and love. Where these are wanting, charity is not charity. Some baser motive is there: ostentation, or even worse, getting a person into the giver's power by a pretence of charity: something that is connected with the life of this grasping, material world. What happens? You expect a good harvest. But "while you think, good easy man, for surely your greatness is a-ripening," there comes a nipping frost, and destroys all your hopes. The frost is some calamity, or the fact that you are found out! Or perhaps it is "High blown pride," as in Shakespeare's *Henry VIII*, ii. 3. In your despair you may blame blind Fate or you may blame Allah! Blind Fate does not exist, for there is Allah's Providence, which is just and good. The harm or injustice has come, not from Allah, but from your own soul. You wronged your soul, and it suffered the frost. Your base motive brought you no good: it may have reduced you to poverty, shame, and disgrace. All the brave show of the wicked in this life is but a wind charged with evil to themselves.

Though ye believe
In the whole of the Book,[440]
When they meet you,
They say, "We believe":[441]
But when they are alone,
They bite off the very tips
Of their fingers at you
In their rage. Say:
"Perish in your rage;
Allah knoweth well
All the secrets of the heart."

وَتُؤۡمِنُونَ بِٱلۡكِتَٰبِ كُلِّهِۦ
وَإِذَا لَقُوكُمۡ قَالُوٓاْ ءَامَنَّا
وَإِذَا خَلَوۡاْ عَضُّواْ عَلَيۡكُمُ ٱلۡأَنَامِلَ مِنَ ٱلۡغَيۡظِۚ
قُلۡ مُوتُواْ بِغَيۡظِكُمۡۗ إِنَّ ٱللَّهَ عَلِيمُۢ بِذَاتِ ٱلصُّدُورِ

120. If aught that is good
Befalls you, it grieves them;
But if some misfortune
Overtakes you, they rejoice
At it. But if ye are constant
And do right,
Not the least harm
Will their cunning
Do to you; for Allah
Compasseth round about
All that they do.

(١٢٠) إِن تَمۡسَسۡكُمۡ حَسَنَةٞ تَسُؤۡهُمۡ
وَإِن تُصِبۡكُمۡ سَيِّئَةٞ يَفۡرَحُواْ بِهَاۖ
وَإِن تَصۡبِرُواْ وَتَتَّقُواْ لَا يَضُرُّكُمۡ
كَيۡدُهُمۡ شَيۡـًٔاۗ إِنَّ ٱللَّهَ بِمَا يَعۡمَلُونَ مُحِيطٞ

C. 58.—Allah's help comes to those who strive
(3:121-148.) With firmness, as it did at Badr.
Much can be learnt from the misfortunes
At Uḥud. It is not for us
To question Allah's Plan, which is full
Of wisdom and mercy for all. Our duty
Is to stand firm and unswerving,
To obey, and in steadfast courage
To persevere, to retrieve our mistakes,
Not in grief and despair, but in firm hope
In Allah and in contempt of pain and death.

SECTION 13.

121. Remember that morning
Thou didst leave
Thy household (early)
To post the Faithful

(١٢١) وَإِذۡ غَدَوۡتَ مِنۡ أَهۡلِكَ
تُبَوِّئُ ٱلۡمُؤۡمِنِينَ

440. Islam gives you the complete revelation, "the whole of the Book," though partial revelations have come in all ages. (*Cf.* 3:23, and n. 366.)

441. *Cf.* 2:14.

At their stations for battle;[442]
And Allah heareth
And knoweth all things:

مَقَـٰعِدَ لِلْقِتَالِ وَٱللَّهُ سَمِيعٌ عَلِيمٌ

122. Remember two of your parties[443]
Meditated cowardice;
But Allah was their protector,
And in Allah should the Faithful
(Ever) put their trust.

١٢٢ إِذْ هَمَّت طَّآئِفَتَانِ مِنكُمْ
أَن تَفْشَلَا وَٱللَّهُ وَلِيُّهُمَا
وَعَلَى ٱللَّهِ فَلْيَتَوَكَّلِ ٱلْمُؤْمِنُونَ

123. Allah had helped you
At Badr, when ye were
A contemptible little force;
Then fear Allah; thus
May ye show your gratitude.[444]

١٢٣ وَلَقَدْ نَصَرَكُمُ ٱللَّهُ بِبَدْرٍ وَأَنتُمْ أَذِلَّةٌ
فَٱتَّقُوا ٱللَّهَ لَعَلَّكُمْ تَشْكُرُونَ

124. Remember thou saidst
To the Faithful: "Is it not enough
For you that Allah should help you
With three thousand angels
(Specially) sent down?[445]

١٢٤ إِذْ تَقُولُ لِلْمُؤْمِنِينَ أَلَن يَكْفِيَكُمْ أَن
يُمِدَّكُمْ رَبُّكُم بِثَلَـٰثَةِ ءَالَـٰفٍ مِّنَ ٱلْمَلَـٰٓئِكَةِ مُنزَلِينَ

442. The Battle of Uḥud was a great testing time for the young Muslim community. Their mettle and the wisdom and strength of their Leader were shown in the battle of Badr (3:13 and note), in which the Makkan Pagans suffered a crushing defeat. The Makkans were determined to wipe off their disgrace and to annihilate the Muslims in Madīnah. To this end they collected a large force and marched to Madīnah. They numbered some 3,000 fighting men under Abū Sufyān, and they were so confident of victory that their women-folk came with them, and showed the most shameful savagery after the battle. To meet the threatened danger the Muslim Leader, Muḥammad Muṣṭafā, with his usual foresight, courage, and initiative, resolved to take his station at the foot of Mount Uḥud, which dominates the city of Madīnah some three miles to the north. Early in the morning, on the 7th of *Shawwāl*, A.H. 3 (January, 625), he made his dispositions for battle. Madīnah winters are notoriously rigorous, but the warriors of Islam (700 to 1000 in number) were up early. A torrent bed was to their south, and the passes in the hills at their back were filled with 50 archers to prevent the enemy attack from the rear. The enemy were set the task of attacking the walls of Madīnah, with the Muslims at their rear. In the beginning the battle went well for the Muslims. The enemy wavered, but the Muslim archers, in disobedience of their orders, left their posts to join in the pursuit and share in the booty. There was also treachery on the part of the 300 "Hypocrites" led by 'Abd Allah ibn Ubayy, who deserted. The enemy took advantage of the opening left by the archers, and there was severe hand-to-hand fighting, in which numbers told in favour of the enemy. Many of the Companions and Helpers were killed. But there was no rout. Among the Muslim martyrs was the gallant Ḥamzah, a brother of the Prophet's father. The graves of the martyrs are still shown at Uḥud. The Messenger himself was wounded in his head and face, and one of his front teeth was broken. Had it not been for his firmness, courage, and coolness, all would have been lost. As it was, the Prophet, in spite of his wound, and many of the wounded Muslims, inspired by his example, returned to the field the next day, and Abū Sufyān and his Makkah army thought it most prudent to withdraw. Madīnah was saved, but a lesson in faith, constancy, firmness, and steadfastness was learnt by the Muslims. (R).

443. The two parties wavering in their minds were probably the Banū Salmah Khazrajī and the Banū Ḥāritha, but they rallied under the Prophet's inspiration. That incident shows that man may be weak, but if he allows his weak will to be governed by the example of men of God, he may yet retrieve his weakness.

444. Gratitude to Allah is not to be measured by words. It should show itself in conduct and life. If all the Muslims had learnt the true lesson from the victory at Badr, their archers would not have left the posts appointed for them, nor the two tribes mentioned in the last note ever wavered in their faith.

445. Read verse 124 with the following five verses, to get its full signification.

125. "Yea—if ye remain firm,
And act aright, even if
The enemy should rush here
On you in hot haste,
Your Lord would help you
With five thousand angels
Making a terrific onslaught."[446]

١٢٥ بَلَىٰٓ إِن تَصۡبِرُواْ وَتَتَّقُواْ
وَيَأۡتُوكُم مِّن فَوۡرِهِمۡ هَٰذَا يُمۡدِدۡكُمۡ رَبُّكُم
بِخَمۡسَةِ ءَالَٰفٖ مِّنَ ٱلۡمَلَٰٓئِكَةِ مُسَوِّمِينَ

126. Allah made it but a message
Of hope for you, and an assurance
To your hearts: (in any case)
There is no help
Except from Allah,
The Exalted, the Wise:[447]

١٢٦ وَمَا جَعَلَهُ ٱللَّهُ إِلَّا بُشۡرَىٰ لَكُمۡ
وَلِتَطۡمَئِنَّ قُلُوبُكُم بِهِۦۗ وَمَا ٱلنَّصۡرُ
إِلَّا مِنۡ عِندِ ٱللَّهِ ٱلۡعَزِيزِ ٱلۡحَكِيمِ

127. That He might cut off
A fringe of the Unbelievers[448]
Or expose them to infamy,
And they should then
Be turned back,
Frustrated of their purpose.

١٢٧ لِيَقۡطَعَ طَرَفٗا
مِّنَ ٱلَّذِينَ كَفَرُوٓاْ أَوۡ يَكۡبِتَهُمۡ
فَيَنقَلِبُواْ خَآئِبِينَ

128. Not for thee, (but for Allah),
Is the decision:
Whether He turn in mercy
To them, or punish them;
For they are indeed wrong-
doers.[449]

١٢٨ لَيۡسَ لَكَ مِنَ ٱلۡأَمۡرِ شَيۡءٌ
أَوۡ يَتُوبَ عَلَيۡهِمۡ أَوۡ يُعَذِّبَهُمۡ
فَإِنَّهُمۡ ظَٰلِمُونَ

129. To Allah belongeth all
That is in the heavens

١٢٩ وَلِلَّهِ مَا فِي ٱلسَّمَٰوَٰتِ

446. *Musawwim*: this is the active voice of the verb, not to be confused with the passive voice in 3:14, which has a different signification.

447. Whatever happens, whether there is a miracle or not, all help proceeds from Allah. Man should not be so arrogant as to suppose that his own resources will change the current of the world plan. Allah helps those who show constancy, courage, and discipline, and use all the human means at their disposal, not those who fold their hands and have no faith. But Allah's help is determined on considerations exalted far above our petty human motive, and by perfect wisdoms, of which we can have only faint glimpses.

448. *A fringe of the Unbelievers*: an extremity, an end, either upper or lower. Here it may mean that the chiefs of the Makkan Pagans, who had come to exterminate the Muslims with such confidence, went back frustrated in their purpose. The shameless cruelty with which they and their women mutilated the Muslim corpses on the battlefield will stand recorded to their eternal infamy. Perhaps it also exposed their real nature to some of those who fought for them, *e.g.*, K͟hālid ibn Walid, who not only accepted Islam afterwards, but became one of the most notable champions of Islam. He was with the Muslims in the conquest of Makkah, and later on, won distinguished honours in Syria and 'Irāq.

449. Uḥud is as much a signpost for Islam as Badr. For us in these latter days it carries an ever greater lesson. Allah's help will come if we have faith, obedience, discipline, unity, and the spirit of acting in righteousness and justice. If we fail, His mercy is always open to us. But it is also open to our enemies, and those who seem to us His enemies. His Plan may be to bring sinners to repentance, and to teach us righteousness and wisdom through those who seem in our eyes to be rebellious or even defiant. There may be good in them that He sees and we do not—a humbling thought that must lead to our own self-examination and self-improvement.

And on earth.
He forgiveth whom He pleaseth
And punisheth whom He pleaseth;
But Allah is Oft-Forgiving,
Most Merciful.

وَمَا فِي الْأَرْضِ يَغْفِرُ لِمَن يَشَاءُ
وَيُعَذِّبُ مَن يَشَاءُ وَاللَّهُ غَفُورٌ رَّحِيمٌ

SECTION 14.

130. O ye who believe!
Devour not Usury,[450]
Doubled and multiplied;
But fear Allah; that
Ye may (really) prosper.[451]

١٣٠ يَا أَيُّهَا الَّذِينَ آمَنُوا لَا تَأْكُلُوا الرِّبَا
أَضْعَافًا مُّضَاعَفَةً وَاتَّقُوا اللَّهَ لَعَلَّكُمْ تُفْلِحُونَ

131. Fear the Fire, which is prepared
For those who reject Faith;

١٣١ وَاتَّقُوا النَّارَ الَّتِي أُعِدَّتْ لِلْكَافِرِينَ

132. And obey Allah
And the Messenger;
That ye may obtain mercy.

١٣٢ وَأَطِيعُوا اللَّهَ وَالرَّسُولَ
لَعَلَّكُمْ تُرْحَمُونَ

133. Be quick in the race
For forgiveness from your Lord,
And for a Garden whose width
Is that (of the whole)
Of the heavens
And of the earth,[452]
Prepared for the righteous—

١٣٣ وَسَارِعُوا إِلَىٰ مَغْفِرَةٍ مِّن رَّبِّكُمْ
وَجَنَّةٍ عَرْضُهَا السَّمَاوَاتُ وَالْأَرْضُ
أُعِدَّتْ لِلْمُتَّقِينَ

134. Those who spend (freely),[453]
Whether in prosperity,

١٣٤ الَّذِينَ يُنفِقُونَ فِي السَّرَّاءِ

450. *Cf.* 2:275 and note. The last verse spoke of forgiveness, even to enemies. If such mercy is granted by Allah to erring sinners, how much more is it incumbent on us, poor sinners to refrain from oppressing our fellow-beings in need, in matters of mere material and ephemeral wealth? Usury is the opposite extreme of charity, unselfishness, striving, and giving of ourselves in the service of Allah and of our fellow-men.

451. Real prosperity consists, not in greed, but in giving—the giving of ourselves and of our substance in the cause of Allah and Allah's truth and in the service of Allah's creatures.

452. The Fire (3:131) is, as always, contrasted with the Garden—in other words, Hell contrasted with Heaven. We are told that its width alone is that of the whole of the heavens and the earth—all the creation we can imagine. In other words our spiritual felicity covers not merely this or that part of our being, but all life and all existence. Who can measure its width, or length, or depth? (R).

453. Another definition of the righteous (*vv.* 134-35). So far from grasping material wealth, they give freely, of themselves and their substance, not only when they are well-off and it is easy for them to do so, but also when they are in difficulties, for other people may be in difficulties at the same time. They do not get ruffled in adversity, or get angry when the other people behave badly, or their own good plans fail. On the contrary they redouble their efforts. For the charity—or good deed—is all the more necessary in adversity. And they do not throw the blame on others. Even where such blame is due and correction is necessary, their own mind is free from a sense of grievance, for they forgive and cover other men's faults. This as far as other people are concerned. But we may be ourselves at fault, and perhaps we brought some calamity on ourselves. The righteous man is not necessarily perfect. In such circumstances his behaviour is described in the next verse.

Or in adversity; Who restrain anger, And pardon (all) men— For Allah loves those Who do good—	وَٱلضَّرَّآءِ وَٱلْكَٰظِمِينَ ٱلْغَيْظَ وَٱلْعَافِينَ عَنِ ٱلنَّاسِ ۗ وَٱللَّهُ يُحِبُّ ٱلْمُحْسِنِينَ
135. And those who,[454] Having done something To be ashamed of, Or wronged their own souls,[455] Earnestly bring Allah to mind, And ask for forgiveness For their sins— And who can forgive Sins except Allah?— And are never obstinate In persisting knowingly In (the wrong) they have done.	١٣٥ وَٱلَّذِينَ إِذَا فَعَلُوا۟ فَٰحِشَةً أَوْ ظَلَمُوٓا۟ أَنفُسَهُمْ ذَكَرُوا۟ ٱللَّهَ فَٱسْتَغْفَرُوا۟ لِذُنُوبِهِمْ وَمَن يَغْفِرُ ٱلذُّنُوبَ إِلَّا ٱللَّهُ وَلَمْ يُصِرُّوا۟ عَلَىٰ مَا فَعَلُوا۟ وَهُمْ يَعْلَمُونَ
136. For such the reward Is forgiveness from their Lord, And Gardens with rivers Flowing underneath— An eternal dwelling: How excellent a recompense For those who work (and strive)!	١٣٦ أُو۟لَٰٓئِكَ جَزَآؤُهُم مَّغْفِرَةٌ مِّن رَّبِّهِمْ وَجَنَّٰتٌ تَجْرِى مِن تَحْتِهَا ٱلْأَنْهَٰرُ خَٰلِدِينَ فِيهَا ۚ وَنِعْمَ أَجْرُ ٱلْعَٰمِلِينَ
137. Many were the Ways of Life[456] That have passed away Before you: travel through The earth, and see what was The end of those Who rejected Truth.	١٣٧ قَدْ خَلَتْ مِن قَبْلِكُمْ سُنَنٌ فَسِيرُوا۟ فِى ٱلْأَرْضِ فَٱنظُرُوا۟ كَيْفَ كَانَ عَٰقِبَةُ ٱلْمُكَذِّبِينَ
138. Here is a plain statement To men, a guidance And instruction to those Who fear Allah!	١٣٨ هَٰذَا بَيَانٌ لِّلنَّاسِ وَهُدًى وَمَوْعِظَةٌ لِّلْمُتَّقِينَ

454. The righteous man, when he finds he has fallen into sin or error, does not whine or despair, but asks for Allah's forgiveness, and his faith gives him hope. If he is sincere, that means that he abandons his wrong conduct and makes amends.

455. Sin is a sort of oppression of ourselves by ourselves. This follows from the doctrine of personal responsibility, as opposed to that of blind fate or of an angry God or gods lying in wait for revenge or injury on mankind.

456. *Cf.* Tennyson (In Memoriam): "Our little systems have their day. They have their day and cease to be: They are but broken lights of Thee, And Thou, O Lord! art more than they." Only Allah's Truth will last, and it will gain the mastery in the end. If there is defeat, we must not be dejected, lose heart, or give up the struggle. Faith means hope, activity, striving steadfastly on to the goal.

139. So lose not heart,
Nor fall into despair:
For ye must gain mastery
If ye are true in Faith.

١٣٩ وَلَا تَهِنُوا وَلَا تَحْزَنُوا
وَأَنتُمُ الْأَعْلَوْنَ إِن كُنتُم مُّؤْمِنِينَ

140. If a wound hath touched you,[457]
Be sure a similar wound
Hath touched the others.
Such days (of varying fortunes)
We give to men and men
By turns: that Allah may know
Those that believe,
And that He may take
To Himself from your ranks
Martyr-witnesses (to Truth).
And Allah loveth not
Those that do wrong.

١٤٠ إِن يَمْسَسْكُمْ قَرْحٌ
فَقَدْ مَسَّ الْقَوْمَ قَرْحٌ مِّثْلُهُ
وَتِلْكَ الْأَيَّامُ نُدَاوِلُهَا بَيْنَ النَّاسِ وَلِيَعْلَمَ
اللَّهُ الَّذِينَ آمَنُوا وَيَتَّخِذَ مِنكُمْ شُهَدَاءَ
وَاللَّهُ لَا يُحِبُّ الظَّالِمِينَ

141. Allah's object also is to purge[458]
Those that are true in Faith
And to deprive of blessing
Those that resist Faith.

١٤١ وَلِيُمَحِّصَ اللَّهُ الَّذِينَ آمَنُوا
وَيَمْحَقَ الْكَافِرِينَ

142. Did ye think that ye
Would enter Heaven[459]
Without Allah testing
Those of you who fought hard
(In His Cause) and
Remained steadfast?

١٤٢ أَمْ حَسِبْتُمْ أَن تَدْخُلُوا الْجَنَّةَ
وَلَمَّا يَعْلَمِ اللَّهُ الَّذِينَ جَاهَدُوا مِنكُمْ
وَيَعْلَمَ الصَّابِرِينَ

143. Ye did indeed
Wish for Death
Before ye met Him:
Now ye have seen Him
With your own eyes,
(And ye flinch!)

١٤٣ وَلَقَدْ كُنتُمْ تَمَنَّوْنَ الْمَوْتَ
مِن قَبْلِ أَن تَلْقَوْهُ فَقَدْ رَأَيْتُمُوهُ
وَأَنتُمْ تَنظُرُونَ

---

457. These general considerations apply in particular to the disaster in Uḥud. (1) In a fight for truth, if you are hurt, be sure the adversary has suffered hurt also, the more so as he has no faith to sustain him. (2) Success or failure in this world comes to all at varying times: we must not grumble, as we do not see the whole of Allah's Plan. (3) Men's true mettle is known in adversity as gold is assayed in fire: *Cf.* also 3:154, n. 467. (4) Martyrdom is in itself an honour and a privilege; how glorious is the fame of Ḥamzah the Martyr? (5) If there is any dross in us, it will be purified by resistance and struggle. (6) When evil is given rope a little, it works out its own destruction: the orgies of cruelty indulged in by the Pagans after what they supposed to be their victory at Uḥud filled up their cup of iniquity; it lost them the support and adherence of the best in their own ranks, and hastened the destruction of Paganism from Arabia, *Cf.* 3:127 and 2:448.

458. The purge or purification was in two senses. (1) It cleared out the Hypocrites from the ranks of the Muslim warriors. (2) The testing-time strengthened the faith of the weak and wavering: for suffering has its own mission in life. The Prophet's example—wounded but staunch, and firmer than ever—put new life into the Community.

459. *Cf.* 2:214.

SECTION 15.

144. Muḥammad is no more[460]
Than a Messenger: many
Were the Messengers that passed away
Before him. If he died
Or were slain, will ye then
Turn back on your heels?
If any did turn back
On his heels, not the least
Harm will he do to Allah;
But Allah (on the other hand)
Will swiftly reward those
Who (serve him) with gratitude.

١٤٤ وَمَا مُحَمَّدٌ إِلَّا رَسُولٌ
قَدْ خَلَتْ مِن قَبْلِهِ ٱلرُّسُلُ
أَفَإِيْن مَّاتَ أَوْ قُتِلَ ٱنقَلَبْتُمْ عَلَىٰٓ أَعْقَٰبِكُمْ
وَمَن يَنقَلِبْ عَلَىٰ عَقِبَيْهِ
فَلَن يَضُرَّ ٱللَّهَ شَيْـًٔا
وَسَيَجْزِى ٱللَّهُ ٱلشَّٰكِرِينَ

145. Nor can a soul die
Except by Allah's leave,
The term being fixed
As by writing. If any
Do desire a reward
In this life, We shall give it[461]
To him; and if any
Do desire a reward
In the Hereafter, We shall
Give it to him.
And swiftly shall We reward
Those that (serve us with) gratitude.

١٤٥ وَمَا كَانَ لِنَفْسٍ أَن تَمُوتَ
إِلَّا بِإِذْنِ ٱللَّهِ كِتَٰبًا مُّؤَجَّلًا
وَمَن يُرِدْ ثَوَابَ ٱلدُّنْيَا نُؤْتِهِۦ مِنْهَا
وَمَن يُرِدْ ثَوَابَ ٱلْءَاخِرَةِ نُؤْتِهِۦ مِنْهَا
وَسَنَجْزِى ٱلشَّٰكِرِينَ

146. How many of the Prophets
Fought (in Allah's way),
And with them (fought)
Large bands of godly men?
But they never lost heart
If they met with disaster

١٤٦ وَكَأَيِّن مِّن نَّبِىٍّ قَٰتَلَ
مَعَهُۥ رِبِّيُّونَ كَثِيرٌ
فَمَا وَهَنُوا۟ لِمَآ أَصَابَهُمْ

460. This verse primarily applies to the battle of Uḥud, in the course of which a cry was raised that the Messenger was slain. He had indeed been severely wounded, but Ṭalḥah, Abū Bakr, and 'Ali were at his side, and his own unexampled bravery saved the Muslim army from a rout. This verse was recalled again by Abū Bakr when the Messenger actually died a natural death eight years later, to remind people that Allah, Whose Message he brought, lives forever. And have need to remember this now and often for two reasons: (1) when we feel inclined to pay more than human honour to one who was the truest, the purest, and the greatest of men, and thus in a sense to compound for our forgetting the spirit of his teaching, and (2) when we feel depressed at the chances and changes of time, and forget that the eternal Allah lives and watches over us and over all His creatures now as in all history in the past and in the future.

461. There is a slight touch of irony in this. As applied to the archers at Uḥud, who deserted their post for the sake of plunder, they might have got some plunder, but they put themselves and the whole of their army into jeopardy. For a little worldly gain, they nearly lost their souls. On the other hand, those who took the long view and fought with staunchness and discipline—their reward was swift and sure. If they died, they got the crown of martyrdom. If they lived, they were heroes honoured in this life and the next.

In Allah's way, nor did
They weaken (in will)
Nor give in. And Allah
Loves those who are
Firm and steadfast.

فِي سَبِيلِ ٱللَّهِ وَمَا ضَعُفُوا
وَمَا ٱسْتَكَانُوا وَٱللَّهُ يُحِبُّ ٱلصَّٰبِرِينَ

147. All that they said was:
"Our Lord! forgive us
Our sins and anything
We may have done
That transgressed our duty:
Establish our feet firmly,
And help us against
Those that resist
Faith."

وَمَا كَانَ قَوْلَهُمْ إِلَّآ أَن قَالُوا ﴿١٤٧﴾
رَبَّنَا ٱغْفِرْ لَنَا ذُنُوبَنَا وَإِسْرَافَنَا فِيٓ أَمْرِنَا
وَثَبِّتْ أَقْدَامَنَا وَٱنصُرْنَا
عَلَى ٱلْقَوْمِ ٱلْكَٰفِرِينَ

148. And Allah gave them
A reward in this world,
And the excellent reward
Of the Hereafter. For Allah
Loveth those who do good.

فَـَٔاتَىٰهُمُ ٱللَّهُ ثَوَابَ ٱلدُّنْيَا ﴿١٤٨﴾
وَحُسْنَ ثَوَابِ ٱلْءَاخِرَةِ وَٱللَّهُ يُحِبُّ ٱلْمُحْسِنِينَ

C. 59. (3:149-180.) —Uḥud showed how dangerous it was
To lend ear to enemy suggestions,
To disobey orders, dispute, lose courage,
Or seek selfish ends; some even followed
The evil course of turning back.
But great is Allah's mercy; where He helps,
No harm can come. Trust your Leader.
The Hyprocrites, in withdrawing from battle,
Were really helping the Unbelievers,
But glorious were those who knew
No fear: those killed in the Cause of Allah
Yet live and thrive and do rejoice:
And never can those who fight against Faith
Hurt in the least the Cause of Allah.

SECTION 16.

149. O ye who believe!
If ye obey the Unbelievers,
They will drive you back
On your heels, and ye
Will turn back (from Faith)
To your own loss.

يَٰٓأَيُّهَا ٱلَّذِينَ ءَامَنُوٓا إِن تُطِيعُوا ﴿١٤٩﴾
ٱلَّذِينَ كَفَرُوا يَرُدُّوكُمْ عَلَىٰٓ
أَعْقَٰبِكُمْ فَتَنقَلِبُوا خَٰسِرِينَ

150. Nay, Allah is your Protector,
And He is the best of helpers.

بَلِ ٱللَّهُ مَوْلَىٰكُمْ وَهُوَ خَيْرُ ٱلنَّٰصِرِينَ ﴿١٥٠﴾

151. Soon shall We cast terror
Into the hearts of the
Unbelievers,
For that they joined companions
With Allah, for which He had sent
No authority; their abode
Will be the Fire; and evil
Is the home of the wrongdoers!

﴿١٥١﴾ سَنُلْقِي فِي قُلُوبِ ٱلَّذِينَ كَفَرُوا۟
ٱلرُّعْبَ بِمَآ أَشْرَكُوا۟ بِٱللَّهِ مَا لَمْ يُنَزِّلْ
بِهِۦ سُلْطَٰنًا ۖ وَمَأْوَىٰهُمُ ٱلنَّارُ ۚ
وَبِئْسَ مَثْوَى ٱلظَّٰلِمِينَ

152. Allah did indeed fulfil
His promise to you
When ye with His permission
Were about to annihilate
Your enemy—until ye flinched
And fell to disputing
About the order,[462]
And disobeyed it
After He brought you in sight
(Of the Booty) which ye covet.
Among you are some
That hanker after this world
And some that desire
The Hereafter. Then did He
Divert you from your foes
In order to test you.[463]
But He forgave you:
For Allah is full of grace
To those who believe.

﴿١٥٢﴾ وَلَقَدْ صَدَقَكُمُ ٱللَّهُ وَعْدَهُۥٓ إِذْ
تَحُسُّونَهُم بِإِذْنِهِۦ ۖ حَتَّىٰٓ إِذَا فَشِلْتُمْ
وَتَنَٰزَعْتُمْ فِي ٱلْأَمْرِ وَعَصَيْتُم مِّنۢ بَعْدِ
مَآ أَرَىٰكُم مَّا تُحِبُّونَ ۚ مِنكُم مَّن يُرِيدُ
ٱلدُّنْيَا وَمِنكُم مَّن يُرِيدُ ٱلْءَاخِرَةَ ۚ ثُمَّ
صَرَفَكُمْ عَنْهُمْ لِيَبْتَلِيَكُمْ ۖ وَلَقَدْ عَفَا
عَنكُمْ ۗ وَٱللَّهُ ذُو فَضْلٍ عَلَى ٱلْمُؤْمِنِينَ

153. Behold! ye were climbing up
The high ground, without even
Casting a side glance
At anyone, and the Messenger
In your rear was calling you
Back. There did Allah give you
One distress after another
By way of requital,[464]

﴿١٥٣﴾ إِذْ تُصْعِدُونَ وَلَا تَلْوُۥنَ
عَلَىٰٓ أَحَدٍ وَٱلرَّسُولُ يَدْعُوكُمْ
فِيٓ أُخْرَىٰكُمْ فَأَثَٰبَكُمْ غَمًّۢا بِغَمٍّ

462. The order was: not to run after booty, but strictly to maintain discipline. Uḥud was in the beginning a victory for the Muslims. Many of the enemy were slain, and they were retiring when a part of the Muslims, against orders, ran in pursuit, attracted by the prospects of booty. See note to 3:121.

463. The disobedience seemed at first pleasant: they were chasing the enemy, and there was the prospect of booty. But when the gap was noticed by the enemy, they turned the flank round the hill and, nearly overwhelmed the Muslims. Had it not been for Allah's grace, and the firmness of their Leader and his immediate Companions, they would have been finished.

464. It would seem that a party of horsemen led by the dashing Khālid ibn Walid came through the gap in the passes where the Muslim archers should have been, and in the confusion that arose, the retreating foe rallied and turned back on the Muslims. From the low ground on the bank of the Nullah, the Muslims retreated in their turn and tried to gain the hill. They had a double loss: (1) they were baulked of the booty they had run after, and (2) their own lives and the lives of their whole army were in danger, and many lives were actually lost from their ranks. Their own lives being in danger, they had hardly time to grieve for the loss of booty or the general calamity. But it steadied them, and some of them stood the test.

To teach you not to grieve
For (the booty) that had escaped
you
And for (the ill) that had befallen
you.
For Allah is well aware
Of all that ye do.

154. After (the excitement)
Of the distress, He sent down
Calm on a band of you
Overcome with slumber,[465]
While another band
Was stirred to anxiety
By their own feelings,
Moved by wrong suspicions
Of Allah—suspicions due
To Ignorance. They said:
"What affair is this of ours?"[466]
Say thou: "Indeed, this affair
Is wholly Allah's." They hide
In their minds what they
Dare not reveal to thee.
They say (to themselves):
"If we had had anything
To do with this affair,
We should not have been
In the slaughter here."
Say: "Even if you had remained
In your homes, those
For whom death was decreed
Would certainly have gone
forth
To the place of their death";
But (all this was)[467]
That Allah might test
What is in your breasts
And purge what is
In your hearts.

لِّكَيْلَا تَحْزَنُوا عَلَىٰ مَا فَاتَكُمْ
وَلَا مَآ أَصَٰبَكُمْ ۗ
وَٱللَّهُ خَبِيرٌۢ بِمَا تَعْمَلُونَ
١٥٤ ثُمَّ أَنزَلَ عَلَيْكُم مِّنۢ بَعْدِ ٱلْغَمِّ
أَمَنَةً نُّعَاسًا يَغْشَىٰ طَآئِفَةً مِّنكُمْ ۖ
وَطَآئِفَةٌ قَدْ أَهَمَّتْهُمْ أَنفُسُهُمْ يَظُنُّونَ
بِٱللَّهِ غَيْرَ ٱلْحَقِّ ظَنَّ ٱلْجَٰهِلِيَّةِ ۖ يَقُولُونَ
هَل لَّنَا مِنَ ٱلْأَمْرِ مِن شَىْءٍ ۗ قُلْ إِنَّ ٱلْأَمْرَ كُلَّهُۥ لِلَّهِ ۗ
يُخْفُونَ فِىٓ أَنفُسِهِم مَّا لَا يُبْدُونَ لَكَ ۖ
يَقُولُونَ لَوْ كَانَ لَنَا مِنَ ٱلْأَمْرِ
شَىْءٌ مَّا قُتِلْنَا هَٰهُنَا ۗ
قُل لَّوْ كُنتُمْ فِى بُيُوتِكُمْ لَبَرَزَ
ٱلَّذِينَ كُتِبَ عَلَيْهِمُ ٱلْقَتْلُ إِلَىٰ مَضَاجِعِهِمْ ۖ
وَلِيَبْتَلِىَ ٱللَّهُ مَا فِى صُدُورِكُمْ
وَلِيُمَحِّصَ مَا فِى قُلُوبِكُمْ ۗ

465. After the first surprise, when the enemy turned on them, a great part of the Muslims did their best, and seeing their mettle, the enemy withdrew to his camp. There was a lull; the wounded had rest; those who had fought the hard fight were visited by kindly Sleep, sweet Nature's nurse. In contrast to them was the band of hypocrites, whose behaviour is described in the next note.

466. The hypocrites withdrew from the fighting. Apparently they had been among those who had been counselling the defence of Madīnah within the walls instead of boldly coming out to meet the enemy. Their distress was caused by their own mental state: the sleep of the just was denied them; and they continued to murmur of what might have been. Only fools do so: wise men face actualities.

467. That testing by Allah is not in order that it may add to His knowledge, for He knows all. It is in order to help us subjectively, to mould our will, and purge us of any grosser motives, that will be searched out by calamity. If it is a hardened sinner, the test brings conviction out of his own self *Cf.* also 3:140.

For Allah knoweth well
The secrets of your hearts.

وَٱللَّهُ عَلِيمٌۢ بِذَاتِ ٱلصُّدُورِ

155. Those of you[468]
Who turned back
On the day the two hosts
Met—it was Satan
Who caused them to fail,
Because of some (evil)
They had done. But Allah
Has blotted out (their fault):
For Allah is Oft-Forgiving,
Most Forbearing.

إِنَّ ٱلَّذِينَ تَوَلَّوْا۟ مِنكُمْ ﴿١٥٥﴾
يَوْمَ ٱلْتَقَى ٱلْجَمْعَانِ إِنَّمَا ٱسْتَزَلَّهُمُ
ٱلشَّيْطَٰنُ بِبَعْضِ مَا كَسَبُوا۟
وَلَقَدْ عَفَا ٱللَّهُ عَنْهُمْ إِنَّ ٱللَّهَ غَفُورٌ حَلِيمٌ

Section 17.

156. O ye who believe!
Be not like the Unbelievers,
Who say of their brethren,
When they are travelling
Through the earth or engaged
In fighting: "If they had stayed
With us, they would not
Have died, or been slain."
This that Allah may make it
A cause of sighs and regrets
In their hearts. It is Allah
That gives Life and Death,[469]
And Allah sees well
All that ye do.

يَٰٓأَيُّهَا ٱلَّذِينَ ءَامَنُوا۟ لَا تَكُونُوا۟ كَٱلَّذِينَ ﴿١٥٦﴾
كَفَرُوا۟ وَقَالُوا۟ لِإِخْوَٰنِهِمْ إِذَا ضَرَبُوا۟ فِى ٱلْأَرْضِ
أَوْ كَانُوا۟ غُزًّى لَّوْ كَانُوا۟ عِندَنَا مَا مَاتُوا۟ وَمَا
قُتِلُوا۟ لِيَجْعَلَ ٱللَّهُ ذَٰلِكَ حَسْرَةً فِى قُلُوبِهِمْ
وَٱللَّهُ يُحْىِۦ وَيُمِيتُ
وَٱللَّهُ بِمَا تَعْمَلُونَ بَصِيرٌ

468. It was the duty of all who were able to fight, to fight in the sacred cause at Uḥud. But a small section were timid; they were not quite as bad as those who railed against Allah, or those who thoughtlessly disobeyed orders. But they still failed in their duty. It is our inner motives that Allah regards. These timorous people were forgiven by Allah. Perhaps they were given another chance: perhaps they rose to it and did their duty then.

469. It is want of faith that makes people afraid (1) of meeting death, (2) of doing their duty when it involves danger, as in travelling in order to earn an honest living, or fighting in a sacred cause. Such fear is part of the punishment for want of faith. If you have faith, there is no fear in meeting death, for it brings you nearer to your goal, nor in meeting danger for a sufficient cause, because you know that the keys of life and death are in Allah's hands. Nothing can happen without Allah's Will. If it is Allah's Will that you should die, your staying at home will not save you. If it is His Will that you should live, the danger you incur in a just cause brings you glory. Supposing it is His Will that you should lose your life in the danger, there are three considerations that would make you eager to meet it: (1) dying in doing your duty is the best means of reaching Allah's Mercy; (2) the man of faith knows that he is not going to an unknown country of which he has no news; he is going nearer to Allah; and (3) he is being "brought together" unto Allah: *i.e.*, he will meet all his dear ones in faith: instead of the separation which the souls without faith fear, he looks forward to a surer reunion than is possible in this life.

157. And if ye are slain, or die,
In the way of Allah,
Forgiveness and mercy
From Allah are far better
Than all they could amass.[470]

﴿١٥٧﴾ وَلَئِن قُتِلْتُمْ فِى سَبِيلِ ٱللَّهِ أَوْ مُتُّمْ
لَمَغْفِرَةٌ مِّنَ ٱللَّهِ وَرَحْمَةٌ خَيْرٌ مِّمَّا يَجْمَعُونَ

158. And if ye die, or are slain,
Lo! it is unto Allah
That ye are brought together.

﴿١٥٨﴾ وَلَئِن مُّتُّمْ أَوْ قُتِلْتُمْ لَإِلَى ٱللَّهِ تُحْشَرُونَ

159. It is part of the Mercy
Of Allah that thou dost deal
Gently with them.[471]
Wert thou severe
Or harsh-hearted,
They would have broken away
From about thee: so pass over
(Their faults), and ask
For (Allah's) forgiveness
For them; and consult
Them in affairs (of moment).
Then, when thou hast
Taken a decision,
Put thy trust in Allah.
For Allah loves those
Who put their trust (in Him).

﴿١٥٩﴾ فَبِمَا رَحْمَةٍ مِّنَ ٱللَّهِ لِنتَ لَهُمْ ۖ
وَلَوْ كُنتَ فَظًّا غَلِيظَ ٱلْقَلْبِ
لَٱنفَضُّوا۟ مِنْ حَوْلِكَ ۖ
فَٱعْفُ عَنْهُمْ وَٱسْتَغْفِرْ لَهُمْ
وَشَاوِرْهُمْ فِى ٱلْأَمْرِ ۖ
فَإِذَا عَزَمْتَ فَتَوَكَّلْ عَلَى ٱللَّهِ ۚ
إِنَّ ٱللَّهَ يُحِبُّ ٱلْمُتَوَكِّلِينَ

160. If Allah helps you,
None can overcome you:
If He forsakes you,
Who is there, after that,
That can help you?
In Allah, then,
Let Believers put their trust.

﴿١٦٠﴾ إِن يَنصُرْكُمُ ٱللَّهُ فَلَا غَالِبَ لَكُمْ ۖ
وَإِن يَخْذُلْكُمْ فَمَن ذَا ٱلَّذِى يَنصُرُكُم مِّنۢ
بَعْدِهِۦ ۗ وَعَلَى ٱللَّهِ فَلْيَتَوَكَّلِ ٱلْمُؤْمِنُونَ

470. Notice a beautiful little literary touch here. At first sight you would expect the second person here ("*you* could amass"), to match the second person in the earlier clause. But remember that the second person in the earlier clause refers to the man of faith, and the third person in the last line refers to the Unbelievers; as if it said: "Of course you as a man of faith would not be for hoarding riches: your wealth—duty and the mercy of Allah—is far more precious than anything the Unbelievers can amass in their selfish lives."

471. The extremely gentle nature of Muḥammad endeared him to all, and it is reckoned as one of the Mercies of Allah. One of the Prophet's titles is "A Mercy to all Creation." At no time was this gentleness, this mercy, this long-suffering with human weaknesses, more valuable than after a disaster like that at Uḥud. It is a God-like quality, which then, as always, bound and binds the souls of countless men to him.

161. No prophet could (ever)[472]
Be false to his trust.
If any person is so false,
He shall, on the Day
Of Judgement, restore
What he misappropriated;
Then shall every soul
Receive its due,
Whatever it earned—
And none shall be
Dealt with unjustly.

١٦١ وَمَا كَانَ لِنَبِيٍّ أَن يَغُلَّ ۚ
وَمَن يَغْلُلْ يَأْتِ بِمَا غَلَّ يَوْمَ الْقِيَامَةِ ۚ
ثُمَّ تُوَفَّىٰ كُلُّ نَفْسٍ مَّا كَسَبَتْ
وَهُمْ لَا يُظْلَمُونَ

162. Is the man who follows
The good pleasure of Allah
Like the man who draws
On himself the wrath
Of Allah, and whose abode
Is in Hell?—
A woeful refuge!

١٦٢ أَفَمَنِ اتَّبَعَ رِضْوَانَ اللَّهِ
كَمَنْ بَآءَ بِسَخَطٍ مِّنَ اللَّهِ
وَمَأْوَاهُ جَهَنَّمُ ۚ وَبِئْسَ الْمَصِيرُ

163. They are in varying grades
In the sight of Allah,
And Allah sees well,
All that they do.

١٦٣ هُمْ دَرَجَاتٌ عِندَ اللَّهِ ۗ
وَاللَّهُ بَصِيرٌ بِمَا يَعْمَلُونَ

164. Allah did confer
A great favour
On the Believers[473]
When He sent among them
A Messenger from among
Themselves, rehearsing
Unto them the Signs
Of Allah, sanctifying them,
And instructing them
In Scripture and Wisdom,
While, before that,

١٦٤ لَقَدْ مَنَّ اللَّهُ عَلَى الْمُؤْمِنِينَ
إِذْ بَعَثَ فِيهِمْ رَسُولًا مِّنْ أَنفُسِهِمْ يَتْلُوا عَلَيْهِمْ
ءَايَاتِهِۦ وَيُزَكِّيهِمْ وَيُعَلِّمُهُمُ الْكِتَابَ
وَالْحِكْمَةَ وَإِن كَانُوا مِن قَبْلُ

472. Besides the gentleness of his nature, Al Muṣṭafā was known from his earliest life for his trustworthiness. Hence his title of *Al Amīn*. Unscrupulous people often read their own low motives into other men, and their accusation, which is meant to injure, fastens on the various virtues for which the man they attack is well known. Some of the hypocrites after Uḥud raised some doubts about the division of the spoils, thinking to sow the seeds of poison in the hearts of the men who had deserted their posts in their craving for booty. Those low suspicions were never believed in by any sensible people, and they have no interest for us now. But the general principles were declared are of eternal value. (1) Prophets of Allah do not act from unworthy motives. (2) Those who act from such motives are spiritually the lowest of creatures, and they will make no profit. (3) A Prophet of Allah is not to be judged by the same standard as a greedy creature. (4) In Allah's eyes there are various grades of men, and we must try to understand and appreciate such grades. If we trust our Leader, we shall not question his honesty without cause. If he is dishonest, he is not fit to be a leader. (R).

473. *Cf.* 2:151.

They had been
In manifest error.

لَفِى ضَلَٰلٍ مُّبِينٍ

165. What! When a single
Disaster smites you,
Although ye smote (your enemies)
With one twice as great,
Do ye say?—
"Whence is this?"
Say (to them):
"It is from yourselves:
For Allah hath power
Over all things."[474]

١٦٥ أَوَلَمَّآ أَصَٰبَتْكُم مُّصِيبَةٌ
قَدْ أَصَبْتُم مِّثْلَيْهَا قُلْتُمْ أَنَّىٰ هَٰذَا ۖ
قُلْ هُوَ مِنْ عِندِ أَنفُسِكُمْ ۗ
إِنَّ ٱللَّهَ عَلَىٰ كُلِّ شَىْءٍ قَدِيرٌ

166. What ye suffered
On the day the two armies
Met, was with the leave
Of Allah, in order that
He might test[475] the Believers—

١٦٦ وَمَآ أَصَٰبَكُمْ يَوْمَ ٱلْتَقَى ٱلْجَمْعَانِ
فَبِإِذْنِ ٱللَّهِ وَلِيَعْلَمَ ٱلْمُؤْمِنِينَ

167. And the Hypocrites also.[476]
These were told: "Come,
Fight in the way of Allah,
Or (at least) drive
(The foe from your city)."
They said: "Had we known
There would be a fight, we should
Certainly have followed you."
They were that day
Nearer to Unbelief
Than to Faith,
Saying with their lips
What was not in their hearts.
But Allah hath full knowledge
Of all they conceal.

١٦٧ وَلِيَعْلَمَ ٱلَّذِينَ نَافَقُوا۟ ۚ وَقِيلَ لَهُمْ
تَعَالَوْا۟ قَٰتِلُوا۟ فِى سَبِيلِ ٱللَّهِ أَوِ ٱدْفَعُوا۟ ۖ
قَالُوا۟ لَوْ نَعْلَمُ قِتَالًا لَّٱتَّبَعْنَٰكُمْ ۗ
هُمْ لِلْكُفْرِ يَوْمَئِذٍ أَقْرَبُ مِنْهُمْ لِلْإِيمَٰنِ ۚ
يَقُولُونَ بِأَفْوَٰهِهِم مَّا لَيْسَ فِى قُلُوبِهِمْ ۗ
وَٱللَّهُ أَعْلَمُ بِمَا يَكْتُمُونَ

474. If Uḥud was a reverse to the Muslims, they had inflicted a reverse twice as great on the Makkans at Badr. This reverse was not without Allah's permission, for He wanted to test and purify the faith of those who followed Islam, and to show them that they must strive and do all in their power to deserve Allah's help. If they disobeyed orders and neglected discipline, they must attribute the disaster to themselves and not to Allah.

475. *Test*: literally *know*. See n. 467 to 3:154.

476. The testing of the hypocrites was the searching out of their motives and exposing them to the sight of their brethren, who might otherwise have been taken in. In the first place they gave counsels of caution: in their minds it was nothing but cowardice. In the second place, what they wished was not the good of the community but its being placed in a contemptible position. When the others were for self-sacrifice, they were for ease and fair words. Pretending to be Muslims, they were nearer to unbelief. Ironically they pretended to know nothing of fighting, and left their devout brethren to defend their faith and ideas. If that devout spirit did not appeal to them, they might at least have defended their city of Madinah when it was threatened—defended their hearths and homes as good citizens.

168. (They are) the ones that say, (Of their brethren slain), While they themselves Sit (at ease): "If only They had listened to us, They would not have been slain." Say: "Avert death From your own selves, If ye speak the truth."	١٦٨ ٱلَّذِينَ قَالُواْ لِإِخْوَٰنِهِمْ وَقَعَدُواْ لَوْ أَطَاعُونَا مَا قُتِلُواْۗ قُلْ فَٱدْرَءُواْ عَنْ أَنفُسِكُمُ ٱلْمَوْتَ إِن كُنتُمْ صَٰدِقِينَ
169. Think not of those Who are slain in Allah's way As dead. Nay, they live,[477] Finding their sustenance In the Presence of their Lord;	١٦٩ وَلَا تَحْسَبَنَّ ٱلَّذِينَ قُتِلُواْ فِي سَبِيلِ ٱللَّهِ أَمْوَٰتًاۚ بَلْ أَحْيَآءٌ عِندَ رَبِّهِمْ يُرْزَقُونَ
170. They rejoice in the Bounty Provided by Allah: And with regard to those Left behind, who have not Yet joined them (in their bliss), The (Martyrs) glory in the fact That on them is no fear, Nor have they (cause to) grieve.[478]	١٧٠ فَرِحِينَ بِمَآ ءَاتَىٰهُمُ ٱللَّهُ مِن فَضْلِهِۦ وَيَسْتَبْشِرُونَ بِٱلَّذِينَ لَمْ يَلْحَقُواْ بِهِم مِّنْ خَلْفِهِمْ أَلَّا خَوْفٌ عَلَيْهِمْ وَلَا هُمْ يَحْزَنُونَ
171. They glory in the Grace And the Bounty from Allah, And in the fact that Allah suffereth not The reward of the Faithful To be lost (in the least).	١٧١ يَسْتَبْشِرُونَ بِنِعْمَةٍ مِّنَ ٱللَّهِ وَفَضْلٍ وَأَنَّ ٱللَّهَ لَا يُضِيعُ أَجْرَ ٱلْمُؤْمِنِينَ
SECTION 18.	
172. Of those who answered The call of Allah	١٧٢ ٱلَّذِينَ ٱسْتَجَابُواْ لِلَّهِ

477. A beautiful passage about the Martyrs in the cause of Truth. They are not dead: they live—and in a far higher and deeper sense than in the life they have left. Even those who have no faith in the Hereafter honour those that die in their cause, with the crown of immortality in the minds and memories of generations unborn. But in Faith we see a higher, truer, and less relative immortality. Perhaps "immortality" is not the right word in this connection, as it implies a continuation of this life. In their case, through the gateway of death, they enter, the true real Life, as opposed to its shadow here. Our carnal life is sustained with carnal food, and its joys and pleasures at their best are those which are projected on the screen of this material world. Their real Life is sustained from the ineffable Presence and Nearness of Allah. *Cfr.* 2:154, and see how the idea is further developed here.

478. The Martyrs not only rejoice at the bliss they have themselves attained. The dear ones left behind are in their thoughts: it is part of their glory that they have saved their dear ones from fear, sorrow, humiliation, and grief, in this life, even before they come to share in the glories of the Hereafter.

Note how the refrain: "on them shall be no fear, nor shall they grieve": comes in here with a new and appropriate meaning. Besides other things, it means that the dear ones have no cause to grieve at the death of the Martyrs; rather have they cause to rejoice.

And the Messenger,
Even after being wounded,[479]
Those who do right
And refrain from wrong
Have a great reward—

وَالرَّسُولِ مِنۢ بَعْدِ مَآ أَصَابَهُمُ الْقَرْحُ ۚ
لِلَّذِينَ أَحْسَنُوا مِنْهُمْ وَاتَّقَوْا أَجْرٌ عَظِيمٌ

173. Men said to them:
"A great army is gathering
Against you, so fear them":
But it (only) increased
Their Faith; they said:
"For us Allah sufficeth,
And He is the best
Disposer of affairs."

﴿١٧٣﴾ الَّذِينَ قَالَ لَهُمُ النَّاسُ إِنَّ النَّاسَ قَدْ
جَمَعُوا لَكُمْ فَاخْشَوْهُمْ فَزَادَهُمْ إِيمَانًا
وَقَالُوا حَسْبُنَا اللَّهُ وَنِعْمَ الْوَكِيلُ

174. And they returned
With Grace and Bounty
From Allah; no harm
Ever touched them:
For they followed
The good pleasure of Allah:
And Allah is the Lord
Of bounties unbounded.

﴿١٧٤﴾ فَانقَلَبُوا بِنِعْمَةٍ مِّنَ اللَّهِ وَفَضْلٍ
لَّمْ يَمْسَسْهُمْ سُوٓءٌ وَاتَّبَعُوا رِضْوَانَ اللَّهِ ۗ
وَاللَّهُ ذُو فَضْلٍ عَظِيمٍ

175. It is only the Evil One
That suggests to you
The fear of his votaries:
Be ye not afraid
Of them, but fear Me,
If ye have Faith.

﴿١٧٥﴾ إِنَّمَا ذَٰلِكُمُ الشَّيْطَٰنُ يُخَوِّفُ أَوْلِيَآءَهُۥ
فَلَا تَخَافُوهُمْ وَخَافُونِ إِن كُنتُم مُّؤْمِنِينَ

176. Let not those grieve thee
Who rush headlong
Into Unbelief:
Not the least harm
Will they do to Allah:
Allah's Plan is that He
Will give them no portion
In the Hereafter,
But a severe punishment.

﴿١٧٦﴾ وَلَا يَحْزُنكَ الَّذِينَ يُسَٰرِعُونَ فِى الْكُفْرِ ۚ
إِنَّهُمْ لَن يَضُرُّوا اللَّهَ شَيْـًٔا ۗ يُرِيدُ اللَّهُ أَلَّا يَجْعَلَ
لَهُمْ حَظًّا فِى الْءَاخِرَةِ ۖ وَلَهُمْ عَذَابٌ عَظِيمٌ

479. After the confusion at Uḥud, men rallied round the Prophet. He was wounded, and they were wounded, but they were all ready to fight again. Abū Sufyān with his Makkans withdrew, but left a challenge with them to meet him and his army again at the fair of Badr Ṣughrā next year. The challenge was accepted, and a picked band of Muslims under their intrepid Leader kept the tryst, but the enemy did not come. They returned, not only unharmed, but enriched by the trade at the fair, and (it may be presumed) strengthened by the accession of new adherents to their cause.

177. Those who purchase
Unbelief at the price
Of faith—
Not the least harm
Will they do to Allah,
But they will have
A grievous punishment.

(١٧٧) إِنَّ ٱلَّذِينَ ٱشْتَرَوُا۟ ٱلْكُفْرَ بِٱلْإِيمَٰنِ
لَن يَضُرُّوا۟ ٱللَّهَ شَيْـًٔا
وَلَهُمْ عَذَابٌ أَلِيمٌ

178. Let not the Unbelievers
Think that Our respite
To them is good for themselves:
We grant them respite
That they may grow[480]
In their iniquity:
But they will have
A shameful punishment.

(١٧٨) وَلَا يَحْسَبَنَّ ٱلَّذِينَ كَفَرُوٓا۟
أَنَّمَا نُمْلِى لَهُمْ خَيْرٌ لِّأَنفُسِهِمْ ۚ
إِنَّمَا نُمْلِى لَهُمْ لِيَزْدَادُوٓا۟ إِثْمًا ۚ
وَلَهُمْ عَذَابٌ مُّهِينٌ

179. Allah will not leave
The Believers in the state
In which ye are now,
Until He separates
What is evil
From what is good.[481]
Nor will Allah disclose
To you the secrets
Of the Unseen,[482]
But He chooses
Of His Messengers
(For the purpose)
Whom He pleases.
So believe in Allah
And His Messengers;
And if ye believe
And do right,
Ye have a reward
Without measure.

(١٧٩) مَّا كَانَ ٱللَّهُ لِيَذَرَ ٱلْمُؤْمِنِينَ
عَلَىٰ مَآ أَنتُمْ عَلَيْهِ
حَتَّىٰ يَمِيزَ ٱلْخَبِيثَ مِنَ ٱلطَّيِّبِ ۗ
وَمَا كَانَ ٱللَّهُ لِيُطْلِعَكُمْ عَلَى ٱلْغَيْبِ
وَلَٰكِنَّ ٱللَّهَ يَجْتَبِى مِن رُّسُلِهِۦ مَن يَشَآءُ ۖ
فَـَٔامِنُوا۟ بِٱللَّهِ وَرُسُلِهِۦ ۚ
وَإِن تُؤْمِنُوا۟ وَتَتَّقُوا۟
فَلَكُمْ أَجْرٌ عَظِيمٌ

480. That the cup of their iniquity may be full. The appetite for sin grows with what it feeds on. The natural result is that the sinner sinks deeper into sin. If there is any freedom of will, this naturally follows, though Allah's Grace is always ready for the repentant. If the Grace is rejected, the increase of iniquity makes the nature of iniquity plainer to those who might otherwise be attracted by its glitter. The working of Allah's Law is therefore both just and merciful. See also the next verse.

481. The testing of good men by calamities and evil men by leaving them in the environment of good things is part of the Universal Plan, in which some freedom of choice is left to man. The psychological and subjective test is unfailing, and the separation is effected partly by the operation of the human wills, to which some freedom is allowed. But it must be effected, if only in the interests of the good.

482. Man in his weak state would be most miserable if he could see the secrets of the future or the secrets of the Unseen. But things are revealed to him from time to time as may be expedient for him, by Messengers chosen for the purpose. Our duty is to hold fast by faith and lead a good life.

180. And let not those
Who covetously withheld
Of the gifts which Allah
Hath given them of His Grace,[483]
Think that it is good for them:
Nay, it will be the worse
For them; soon shall the things
Which they covetously withheld
Be tied to their necks
Like a twisted collar,[484]
On the Day of Judgement.
To Allah belongs the heritage[485]
Of the heavens and the earth;
And Allah is well-acquainted
With all that ye do.

١٨٠ وَلَا يَحْسَبَنَّ ٱلَّذِينَ يَبْخَلُونَ
بِمَآ ءَاتَىٰهُمُ ٱللَّهُ مِن فَضْلِهِۦ
هُوَ خَيْرًا لَّهُم بَلْ هُوَ شَرٌّ لَّهُمْ
سَيُطَوَّقُونَ مَا بَخِلُوا۟ بِهِۦ يَوْمَ ٱلْقِيَـٰمَةِ
وَلِلَّهِ مِيرَٰثُ ٱلسَّمَـٰوَٰتِ وَٱلْأَرْضِ
وَٱللَّهُ بِمَا تَعْمَلُونَ خَبِيرٌ

C. 60.—Regard, unmoved, the taunts of those
(3:181-200.) Who laugh at faith; nor let their falsehood
Nor their seeming prosperity, raise
Questions in your minds. All
Who can read the Signs of Allah in Nature
Know His wisdom, goodness, power,
And justice. They know His promise
Is sure, and in humble prayer,
Wholly put their trust in Him.

SECTION 19.

181. Allah hath heard
The taunt of those
Who say: "Truly, Allah[486]

١٨١ لَّقَدْ سَمِعَ ٱللَّهُ قَوْلَ ٱلَّذِينَ قَالُوٓا۟ إِنَّ ٱللَّهَ

483. The gifts are of all kinds: material gifts, such as wealth, property, strength of limbs, etc., or intangible gifts, such as influence, birth in a given set, intellect, skill, insight, etc., or spiritual gifts of the highest kind. The spending of all these things (apart from what is necessary for ourselves) for those who need them, is charity, and purifies our own character. The withholding of them (apart from our needs) is similarly greed and selfishness, and is strongly condemned.

484. By an apt metaphor the miser is told that his wealth or the other gifts which he hoarded will cling round his neck and do him no good. He will wish he could get rid of them, but he will not be able to do so. According to the Biblical phrase in another connection they will hang like a millstone round his neck (Matt. xviii. 6). The metaphor here is fuller. He hugged his wealth or his gifts about him. They will become like a heavy collar, the badge of slavery, round his neck. They will be tied tight and twisted, and they will give him pain and anguish instead of pleasure, *Cf.* also 17:13.

485. Another metaphor is now introduced. Material wealth or property is only called ours during our short life here. So all gifts are ours in trust only; they ultimately revert to Allah, to Whom belongs all that is in the heavens or on earth. (R).

486. In 2:245 we read: "Who is he that will loan to Allah a beautiful loan?" In other places charity or spending in the way of Allah is metaphorically described as giving to Allah. The Holy Prophet often used that expression in appealing for funds to be spent in the way of Allah. The scoffers mocked and said: "So Allah is indigent and we are rich!" This blasphemy was of a piece with all their conduct in history, in slaying the Prophets and men of God.

Is indigent and we
Are rich!"—We shall
Certainly record their word
And (their act) of slaying
The Prophets in defiance[487]
Of right, and We shall say:
"Taste ye the Penalty
Of the Scorching Fire!

فَقِيرٌ وَنَحْنُ أَغْنِيَآءُ
سَنَكْتُبُ مَا قَالُوا۟
وَقَتْلَهُمُ ٱلْأَنۢبِيَآءَ بِغَيْرِ حَقٍّ
وَنَقُولُ ذُوقُوا۟ عَذَابَ ٱلْحَرِيقِ

182. "This is because
Of the (unrighteous deeds)
Which your hands
Sent on before ye;[488]
For Allah never harms
Those who serve Him."

﴿١٨٢﴾ ذَٰلِكَ بِمَا قَدَّمَتْ أَيْدِيكُمْ
وَأَنَّ ٱللَّهَ لَيْسَ بِظَلَّامٍ
لِّلْعَبِيدِ

183. They (also) said: "Allah took
Our promise not to believe
In a messenger unless
He showed us a sacrifice
Consumed by fire[489]
(From heaven)." Say:
"There came to you
Messengers before me,
With Clear Signs
And even with what
Ye ask for: why then
Did ye slay them,
If ye speak the truth?"

﴿١٨٣﴾ ٱلَّذِينَ قَالُوٓا۟ إِنَّ ٱللَّهَ عَهِدَ إِلَيْنَآ
أَلَّا نُؤْمِنَ لِرَسُولٍ حَتَّىٰ يَأْتِيَنَا بِقُرْبَانٍ
تَأْكُلُهُ ٱلنَّارُ قُلْ قَدْ جَآءَكُمْ رُسُلٌ
مِّن قَبْلِى بِٱلْبَيِّنَٰتِ وَبِٱلَّذِى قُلْتُمْ
فَلِمَ قَتَلْتُمُوهُمْ إِن كُنتُمْ صَٰدِقِينَ

184. Then if they reject thee,
So were rejected messengers
Before thee, who came
With Clear Signs,
And the Scriptures,

﴿١٨٤﴾ فَإِن كَذَّبُوكَ فَقَدْ كُذِّبَ رُسُلٌ
مِّن قَبْلِكَ جَآءُو بِٱلْبَيِّنَٰتِ وَٱلزُّبُرِ

487. For the expression "slaying in defiance of right," *Cf.* 3:21, and 3:112.

488. *Cf.* 2:95. and note.

489. Burnt sacrifices figured in the Mosaic Law, and in the religious ceremonies long before Moses, but it is not true that the Mosaic Law laid down a fire from heavens on a burnt sacrifice as a test of the credentials of Prophets. Even if it had been so, did the Jews obey the Prophets who showed this Sign? In Leviticus ix. 23-24, we are told a burnt offering prepared by Moses and Aaron: "and there came a fire out from before the Lord, and consumed upon the altar the burnt offering and the fat." Yet the people rebelled frequently against Moses, and rebellion against a Prophet is spiritually an attempt to kill him. Abel's offering (sacrifice) was probably a burnt offering: it was accepted by Allah, and he was killed by Cain out of jealousy: Gen. iv. 3-8. Mosaic sacrifices were no longer needed by the people of Jesus or the people of Muḥammad.

And the Book of
Enlightenment.[490]

185. Every soul shall have
A taste of death:[491]
And only on the Day
Of Judgement shall you
Be paid your full recompense.
Only he who is saved
Far from the Fire
And admitted to the Garden
Will have attained
The object (of Life):
For the life of this world
Is but goods and chattels
Of deception.[492]

186. Ye shall certainly
Be tried and tested
In your possessions
And in your personal selves;[493]
And ye shall certainly
Hear much that will grieve you,
From those who received
The Book before you
And from those who
Worship many gods.
But if ye persevere
Patiently, and guard
Against evil—then
That will be
A determining factor
In all affairs.

وَٱلْكِتَـٰبِ ٱلْمُنِيرِ

(١٨٥) كُلُّ نَفْسٍ ذَآئِقَةُ ٱلْمَوْتِ ۗ
وَإِنَّمَا تُوَفَّوْنَ أُجُورَكُمْ يَوْمَ ٱلْقِيَـٰمَةِ ۖ
فَمَن زُحْزِحَ عَنِ ٱلنَّارِ
وَأُدْخِلَ ٱلْجَنَّةَ فَقَدْ فَازَ ۗ
وَمَا ٱلْحَيَوٰةُ ٱلدُّنْيَآ إِلَّا مَتَـٰعُ ٱلْغُرُورِ

(١٨٦) لَتُبْلَوُنَّ فِىٓ أَمْوَٰلِكُمْ
وَأَنفُسِكُمْ وَلَتَسْمَعُنَّ
مِنَ ٱلَّذِينَ أُوتُوا۟ ٱلْكِتَـٰبَ مِن قَبْلِكُمْ
وَمِنَ ٱلَّذِينَ أَشْرَكُوٓا۟ أَذًى كَثِيرًا ۚ
وَإِن تَصْبِرُوا۟ وَتَتَّقُوا۟ فَإِنَّ ذَٰلِكَ
مِنْ عَزْمِ ٱلْأُمُورِ

490. The three things mentioned in the Text are: (1) Clear Signs (*bayyināt*); (2) *zubūr*, and (3) *kitāb al Munīr.* The signification of (1) I have explained in the note to 3:62, as far as they relate to Jesus. In a more general sense, it means the clear evidence which Allah's dealings furnish about a man of God having a true mission; *e.g.*, Moses in relation to Pharaoh, (2) The word *Zubūr* has been translated as scriptures. It comes from the root *Zabara* which implies something hard. The commentators are not agreed, but the prophetic writings which seemed to contemporaries difficult to understand may well be meant here. David's psalms (*Zabūr*, iv. 163) may also come under this description. As to (3), there is no doubt about the literal meaning of the words, "the Book of Enlightenment". But what does it precisely refer to? I take it to mean the fundamental guide to conduct—the clear rules laid down in all Dispensations to help men to lead good lives. (R).

491. The soul will not die; but the death of the body will give a taste of death to the soul when the soul separates from the body. The soul will then know that this life was but a probation. And seeming inequalities will be adjusted finally on the Day of Judgement.

492. *Cf.* Longfellow's Psalm of Life: "All this world's a fleeting show, For man's illusion given". The only Reality will be when we have attained our final goal.

493. Not wealth and possessions only (or want of them), are the means of our trial. All our personal talents, knowledge, opportunities, and their opposites—in fact everything that happens to us and makes up our personality is a means of our testing. So is our Faith; we shall have to put up for it many insults from those who do not share it.

187. And remember
Allah took a Covenant
From the People of the Book,[494]
To make it known
And clear to mankind,
And not to hide it;
But they threw it away
Behind their backs,[495]
And purchased with it
Some miserable gain!
And vile was the bargain
They made!

١٨٧ وَإِذْ أَخَذَ ٱللَّهُ مِيثَٰقَ
ٱلَّذِينَ أُوتُوا۟ ٱلْكِتَٰبَ لَتُبَيِّنُنَّهُۥ لِلنَّاسِ
وَلَا تَكْتُمُونَهُۥ فَنَبَذُوهُ وَرَآءَ ظُهُورِهِمْ
وَٱشْتَرَوْا۟ بِهِۦ ثَمَنًا قَلِيلًا ۖ
فَبِئْسَ مَا يَشْتَرُونَ

188. Think not that those
Who exult in what they
Have brought about, and love
To be praised for what
They have not done—[496]
Think not that they
Can escape the Penalty.
For them is a Penalty
Grievous indeed.

١٨٨ لَا تَحْسَبَنَّ ٱلَّذِينَ يَفْرَحُونَ بِمَآ أَتَوا۟
وَّيُحِبُّونَ أَن يُحْمَدُوا۟ بِمَا لَمْ يَفْعَلُوا۟
فَلَا تَحْسَبَنَّهُم بِمَفَازَةٍ مِّنَ ٱلْعَذَابِ ۖ
وَلَهُمْ عَذَابٌ أَلِيمٌ

189. To Allah belongeth
The dominion
Of the heavens
And the earth;
And Allah hath power
Over all things.

١٨٩ وَلِلَّهِ مُلْكُ
ٱلسَّمَٰوَٰتِ وَٱلْأَرْضِ ۗ
وَٱللَّهُ عَلَىٰ كُلِّ شَىْءٍ قَدِيرٌ

Section 20.

190. Behold! In the creation
Of the heavens and the earth,
And the alternation
Of Night and Day—[497]

١٩٠ إِنَّ فِى خَلْقِ ٱلسَّمَٰوَٰتِ وَٱلْأَرْضِ
وَٱخْتِلَٰفِ ٱلَّيْلِ وَٱلنَّهَارِ

494. Truth—Allah's Message—comes to any man or nation as a matter of sacred trust. It should be broadcast and published and taught and made clear to all within reach. Privileged priesthood at once erects a barrier. But worse—when such priesthood tampers with the truth, taking what suits it and ignoring the rest, it has sold Allah's gift for a miserable ephemeral profit; how miserable, it will learn when Nemesis comes.

495. *Cf.* 2:101.

496. A searching picture of the worldly wise! They may cause mischief and misery to others, but gloat over any glory it may bring them! They may trample down Allah's truths, and enthrone false standards of worship. They may take credit for virtues they do not possess and seeming successes that come in spite of their despicable deceptions.

497. See 2:164. The two items mentioned here are just brief symbols recalling the six or seven mentioned in the other passage. And those too are but brief symbols and reminders of the glorious majesty of Allah and His goodness to man.

There are indeed Signs
For men of understanding—

لَأٓيَٰتٍ لِّأُوْلِي ٱلْأَلْبَٰبِ

191. Men who celebrate
The praises of Allah,
Standing, sitting,
And lying down on their
sides,[498]
And contemplate
The (wonders of) creation
In the heavens and the earth,
(With the thought):
"Our Lord! not for naught
Hast Thou created (all) this!
Glory to Thee! Give us[499]
Salvation from the Penalty
Of the Fire.

(١٩١) ٱلَّذِينَ يَذْكُرُونَ ٱللَّهَ قِيَٰمًا
وَقُعُودًا وَعَلَىٰ جُنُوبِهِمْ
وَيَتَفَكَّرُونَ
فِي خَلْقِ ٱلسَّمَٰوَٰتِ وَٱلْأَرْضِ
رَبَّنَا مَا خَلَقْتَ هَٰذَا بَٰطِلًا
سُبْحَٰنَكَ فَقِنَا عَذَابَ ٱلنَّارِ

192. "Our Lord! any whom Thou
Dost admit to the Fire,
Truly Thou coverest with shame,
And never will wrongdoers
Find any helpers!

(١٩٢) رَبَّنَآ إِنَّكَ مَن تُدْخِلِ ٱلنَّارَ فَقَدْ أَخْزَيْتَهُۥ
وَمَا لِلظَّٰلِمِينَ مِنْ أَنصَارٍ

193. "Our Lord! we have heard
The call of one calling
(Us) to Faith, 'Believe ye
In the Lord,' and we
Have believed. Our Lord!
Forgive us our sins,
Blot out from us
Our iniquities, and take
To Thyself our souls
In the company of the righteous.

(١٩٣) رَّبَّنَآ إِنَّنَا سَمِعْنَا مُنَادِيًا يُنَادِي
لِلْإِيمَٰنِ أَنْ ءَامِنُوا۟ بِرَبِّكُمْ فَـَٔامَنَّا
رَبَّنَا فَٱغْفِرْ لَنَا ذُنُوبَنَا وَكَفِّرْ عَنَّا سَيِّـَٔاتِنَا
وَتَوَفَّنَا مَعَ ٱلْأَبْرَارِ

194. "Our Lord! Grant us
What Thou didst promise
Unto us through Thy Messengers,
And save us from shame
On the Day of Judgment;
For Thou never breakest
Thy promise."

(١٩٤) رَبَّنَا وَءَاتِنَا مَا وَعَدتَّنَا عَلَىٰ رُسُلِكَ
وَلَا تُخْزِنَا يَوْمَ ٱلْقِيَٰمَةِ
إِنَّكَ لَا تُخْلِفُ ٱلْمِيعَادَ

498. That is, in all postures, which again is symbolical of all circumstances—personal, social, economic, historical and other.

499. It is the thought of Salvation that connects all these glories with man. Otherwise man would be a miserable, contemptible creature in these beauties and wonders of Nature. With his high destiny of Salvation he can be lifted even higher than these glories! The Fire is a symbol of penalty. We pray for salvation from the penalty.

195. And their Lord hath accepted
Of them, and answered them:
"Never will I suffer to be lost
The work of any of you,
Be he male or female:
Ye are members, one of
another;[500]
Those who have left their homes,
And were driven out therefrom,
And suffered harm in My Cause,
And fought and were slain—
Verily, I will blot out
From them their iniquities,
And admit them into Gardens
With rivers flowing beneath—
A reward from the Presence[501]
Of Allah, and from His Presence
Is the best of rewards."

(١٩٥) فَٱسْتَجَابَ لَهُمْ رَبُّهُمْ
أَنِّى لَآ أُضِيعُ عَمَلَ عَٰمِلٍ مِّنكُم مِّن ذَكَرٍ أَوْ أُنثَىٰ ۖ
بَعْضُكُم مِّنۢ بَعْضٍ ۖ فَٱلَّذِينَ هَاجَرُوا۟ وَأُخْرِجُوا۟
مِن دِيَٰرِهِمْ وَأُوذُوا۟ فِى سَبِيلِى وَقَٰتَلُوا۟ وَقُتِلُوا۟
لَأُكَفِّرَنَّ عَنْهُمْ سَيِّـَٔاتِهِمْ وَلَأُدْخِلَنَّهُمْ
جَنَّٰتٍ تَجْرِى مِن تَحْتِهَا ٱلْأَنْهَٰرُ ثَوَابًا
مِّنْ عِندِ ٱللَّهِ ۗ وَٱللَّهُ عِندَهُۥ حُسْنُ ٱلثَّوَابِ

196. Let not the strutting about
Of the Unbelievers
Through the land
Deceive thee:

(١٩٦) لَا يَغُرَّنَّكَ تَقَلُّبُ
ٱلَّذِينَ كَفَرُوا۟ فِى ٱلْبِلَٰدِ

197. Little is it for enjoyment:
Their ultimate abode
Is Hell; what an evil bed
(To lie on)!

(١٩٧) مَتَٰعٌ قَلِيلٌ ثُمَّ مَأْوَىٰهُمْ
جَهَنَّمُ ۚ وَبِئْسَ ٱلْمِهَادُ

198. On the other hand, for those
Who fear their Lord,
Are Gardens, with rivers
Flowing beneath; therein
Are they to dwell (forever)—
A gift from the Presence
Of Allah; and that which is
In the Presence of Allah
Is the best (bliss)
For the righteous.

(١٩٨) لَٰكِنِ ٱلَّذِينَ ٱتَّقَوْا۟ رَبَّهُمْ
لَهُمْ جَنَّٰتٌ تَجْرِى مِن تَحْتِهَا ٱلْأَنْهَٰرُ
خَٰلِدِينَ فِيهَا نُزُلًا مِّنْ عِندِ ٱللَّهِ ۗ
وَمَا عِندَ ٱللَّهِ خَيْرٌ لِّلْأَبْرَارِ

199. And there are, certainly,
Among the People of the Book,

(١٩٩) وَإِنَّ مِنْ أَهْلِ ٱلْكِتَٰبِ

500. In Islam the equal status of the sexes is not only recognised but insisted on. If sex distinction, which is a distinction in nature, does not count in spiritual matters, still less of course would count artifical distinctions, such as rank, wealth, position, race, colour, birth, etc.

501. Here, and in 3:198 below, and in many places elsewhere, stress is laid on the fact that whatever gift, or reward, or bliss will come to the righteous, its chief merit will be that it proceeds from the Presence of Allah Himself. "Nearness to Allah" expresses it better than any other symbol.

Those who believe in Allah, In the revelation to you, And in the revelation to them, Bowing in humility to Allah: They will not sell The Signs of Allah For a miserable gain! For them is a reward With their Lord, And Allah is swift in account.	لَمَن يُؤْمِنُ بِٱللَّهِ وَمَآ أُنزِلَ إِلَيْكُمْ وَمَآ أُنزِلَ إِلَيْهِمْ خَـٰشِعِينَ لِلَّهِ لَا يَشْتَرُونَ بِـَٔايَـٰتِ ٱللَّهِ ثَمَنًا قَلِيلًا ۗ أُو۟لَـٰٓئِكَ لَهُمْ أَجْرُهُمْ عِندَ رَبِّهِمْ ۗ إِنَّ ٱللَّهَ سَرِيعُ ٱلْحِسَابِ
200. O ye who believe! Persevere in patience[502] And constancy; vie In such perseverance; Strengthen each other; And fear Allah; That ye may prosper.[503]	٢٠٠ يَـٰٓأَيُّهَا ٱلَّذِينَ ءَامَنُوا۟ ٱصْبِرُوا۟ وَصَابِرُوا۟ وَرَابِطُوا۟ وَٱتَّقُوا۟ ٱللَّهَ لَعَلَّكُمْ تُفْلِحُونَ

502. The full meaning of *Ṣabr* is to be understood here, viz.: patience, perseverance, constancy, self-restraint, refusing to be cowed down. These virtues we are to exercise for ourselves and in relation to others; we are to set an example, so that others may vie with us, and we are to vie with them, lest we fall short; in this way we strengthen each other and bind our mutual relations closer, in our common service to Allah.

503. Prosperity *(falāh)* here and in other passages is to be understood in a wide sense, including prosperity in our mundane affairs as well as in spiritual progress. In both cases it implies happiness and the attainment of our wishes, purified by the love of Allah.

INTRODUCTION TO SŪRAH 4—*AL NISĀ'*

This Sūrah is closely connected chronologically with Sūrah 3. Its subject matter deals with the social problems which the Muslim community had to face immediately after Uḥud. While the particular occasion made the necessity urgent, the principles laid down have permanently governed Muslim Law and social practice.

Broadly speaking, the Sūrah consists of two parts: (1) that dealing with women, orphans, inheritance, marriage, and family rights generally, and (2) that dealing with the recalcitrants in the larger family, the community at Madīnah, *viz.*, the Hypocrites and their accomplices.

Summary—It begins with an appeal to the solidarity of mankind, the rights of women and orphans, and the implications of family relationship, including an equitable distribution of property after death. (4:1-14 and C. 61.)

While the decencies of family life should be enforced, women should be held in honour and their rights recognised, in marriage, property, and inheritance; and this principle of goodness should be extended to all beings, great and small. (4:15-42, and C. 62.)

The sections in Madīnah, not yet in the Muslim community, should not go after false gods, but should accept the authority of the Prophet, and obey him. Then it will be their privilege to be admitted to a great and glorious Fellowship. (4:43-70, and C. 63.)

The Believers should organize in self-defence against their enemies, and beware of the secret plots and mischiefs of the Hypocrites; how deserters should be treated. (4:71-91, and C. 64.).

Caution about the taking of life; recommendations for leaving places inimical to Islam; religious duties in the midst of war. (4:92-104, and C. 65.)

Treachery and the lure of evil. (4:105-126, and C. 66.)

Women and orphans to be justly dealt with; Faith must go with justice, sincerity, and moderation in speech. (4:127-152, and C. 67.)

Where People of the Book went wrong, with honourable exceptions. (4:153-176, and C. 68.)

C. 61.—All mankind are one, and mutual rights
(4:1-14.) Must be respected; the sexes
Must honour, each the other;
Sacred are family relationships
That rise through marriage
And women bearing children;
Orphans need especial loving care;
In trust is held all property;
With duties well-defined;
And after death, due distribution
Should be made in equitable shares
To all whose affection, duty,
And trust shed light and joy
On this our life below.

Sūrah 4.

Al Nisā' (The Women)

In the name of Allah, Most Gracious,
Most Merciful.

1\. O mankind! reverence
Your Guardian-Lord,
Who created you
From a single Person,[504]
Created, of like nature,
His mate, and from them twain
Scattered (like seeds)
Countless men and women—
Fear Allah, through Whom[505]
Ye demand your mutual (rights),
And (reverence) the wombs[506]
(That bore you): for Allah
Ever watches over you.

2\. To orphans restore their property
(When they reach their age),
Nor substitute (your) worthless
things
For (their) good ones; and
devour not
Their substance (by mixing it
up)[507]

بِسْمِ ٱللَّهِ ٱلرَّحْمَٰنِ ٱلرَّحِيمِ

١ يَٰٓأَيُّهَا ٱلنَّاسُ ٱتَّقُوا۟ رَبَّكُمُ
ٱلَّذِى خَلَقَكُم مِّن نَّفْسٍ وَٰحِدَةٍ
وَخَلَقَ مِنْهَا زَوْجَهَا وَبَثَّ مِنْهُمَا رِجَالًا كَثِيرًا وَنِسَآءً
وَٱتَّقُوا۟ ٱللَّهَ ٱلَّذِى تَسَآءَلُونَ بِهِۦ وَٱلْأَرْحَامَ
إِنَّ ٱللَّهَ كَانَ عَلَيْكُمْ رَقِيبًا

٢ وَءَاتُوا۟ ٱلْيَتَٰمَىٰٓ أَمْوَٰلَهُمْ
وَلَا تَتَبَدَّلُوا۟ ٱلْخَبِيثَ بِٱلطَّيِّبِ
وَلَا تَأْكُلُوٓا۟ أَمْوَٰلَهُمْ

504\. *Nafs* may mean: (1) soul; (2) self; (3) person, living person; (4) will, good pleasure, as in 4:4 below. *Minhā*: I follow the construction suggested by Imām Rāzi. The particle *min* would then suggest here not a portion or a source of something else, but a species, a nature, a similarity. The pronoun *hā* refers of course to *Nafs*. (R).

505\. All our mutual rights and duties are referred to Allah. We are His creatures: His Will is the standard and measure of Good; and our duties are measured by our conformity with His Will. "Our wills are ours, to make them Thine," says Tennyson (*In Memoriam*). Among ourselves (human beings) our mutual rights and duties arise out of Allah's Law, the sense of Right that is implanted in us by Him.

506\. Among the most wonderful mysteries of our nature is that of sex. The unregenerate male is apt, in the pride of his physical strength, to forget the all-important part which the female plays in his very existence, and in all the social relationships that arise in our collective human lives. The mother that bore us must ever have our reverence. The wife, through whom we enter parentage, must have our reverence. Sex, which governs so much our physical life, and has so much influence on our emotional and higher nature, deserves—not our fear, or our contempt, or our amused indulgence, but—our reverence in the highest sense of the term. With this fitting introduction we enter on a discussion of women, orphans, and family relationships.

507\. Justice to orphans is enjoined, and three things are particularly mentioned as temptations in the way of a guardian: (1) He must not postpone restoring all his ward's property when the time comes; subject to 4:5 below. (2) If there is a list of property, it is not enough that that list should be technically followed: the property restored must be of equal value to the property received: the same principle applies where there is no list. (3) If property is managed together, or where perishable goods must necessarily be consumed, the strictest probity is necessary when the separation takes place, and this is insisted on. See also 2:220 and note.

إِلَىٰٓ أَمۡوَٰلِكُمۡۚ إِنَّهُۥ كَانَ حُوبٗا كَبِيرٗا

With your own. For this is
Indeed a great sin.

٣ وَإِنۡ خِفۡتُمۡ أَلَّا تُقۡسِطُواْ فِي ٱلۡيَتَٰمَىٰ
فَٱنكِحُواْ مَا طَابَ لَكُم مِّنَ ٱلنِّسَآءِ
مَثۡنَىٰ وَثُلَٰثَ وَرُبَٰعَۖ فَإِنۡ خِفۡتُمۡ أَلَّا تَعۡدِلُواْ
فَوَٰحِدَةً أَوۡ مَا مَلَكَتۡ أَيۡمَٰنُكُمۡۚ
ذَٰلِكَ أَدۡنَىٰٓ أَلَّا تَعُولُواْ

3. If ye fear that ye shall not
Be able to deal justly
With the orphans,[508]
Marry women of your choice,
Two, or three, or four;
But if ye fear that ye shall not
Be able to deal justly (with them),
Then only one, or (a captive)
That your right hands possess.
That will be more suitable,
To prevent you
From doing injustice.[509]

٤ وَءَاتُواْ ٱلنِّسَآءَ صَدُقَٰتِهِنَّ نِحۡلَةٗۚ
فَإِن طِبۡنَ لَكُمۡ عَن شَيۡءٖ مِّنۡهُ نَفۡسٗا
فَكُلُوهُ هَنِيٓـٔٗا مَّرِيٓـٔٗا

4. And give the women
(On marriage) their dower
As a free gift; but if they,
Of their own good pleasure,
Remit any part of it to you,
Take it and enjoy it
With right good cheer.

٥ وَلَا تُؤۡتُواْ ٱلسُّفَهَآءَ أَمۡوَٰلَكُمُ ٱلَّتِي جَعَلَ ٱللَّهُ لَكُمۡ
قِيَٰمٗا وَٱرۡزُقُوهُمۡ فِيهَا وَٱكۡسُوهُمۡ

5. To those weak of understanding[510]
Make not over your property,[511]
Which Allah hath made
A means of support for you,
But feed and clothe them

508. Notice the conditional clause about orphans, introducing the rules about marriage. This reminds us of the immediate occasion of the promulgation of this verse. It was after Uḥud, when the Muslim community was left with many orphans and widows and some captives of war. Their treatment was to be governed by principles of the greatest humanity and equity. The occasion is past, but the principles remain. Marry the orphans if you are quite sure that you will in that way protect their interests and their property, with perfect justice to them and to your own dependants if you have any. If not, make other arrangements for the orphans.

509. The unrestricted number of wives of the "Times of Ignorance" was now strictly limited to a maximum of four, provided you could treat them with equality. (R).

510. This applies to orphans, but the wording is perfectly general, and defines principles like those of Chancery in English Law and the Court of Wards in Indian Law. Property has not only its rights but also its responsibilities. The owner may not do just what he likes absolutely: his right is limited by the good of the community of which he is a member, and if he is incapable of understanding it, his control should be removed. This does not mean that he is harshly dealt with. On the contrary his interest must be protected, and he must be treated with special kindness because of his incapacity.

511. *Your property:* Ultimately all property belongs to Allah, and is intended for the support of the community. It is held in trust by a particular individual. If he is incapable, he is put aside but gently and with kindness. While his incapacity remains, the duties and responsibilities devolve on his guardian even more strictly than in the case of the original owner: for he may not take any of the profits for himself unless he is poor, and in that case his remuneration for his trouble must be on a scale that is no more than just and reasonable.

Therewith, and speak to them
Words of kindness and justice.

وَقُولُوا لَهُمْ قَوْلًا مَّعْرُوفًا

6. Make trial of orphans
Until they reach the age[512]
Of marriage; if then ye find
Sound judgement in them,
Release their property to them;
But consume it not wastefully,
Nor in haste against their growing up.
If the guardian is well-off,
Let him claim no remuneration,
But if he is poor, let him
Have for himself what is
Just and reasonable.
When ye release their property
To them, take witnesses
In their presence:
But all-sufficient
Is Allah in taking account.[513]

٦ وَابْتَلُوا الْيَتَامَىٰ حَتَّىٰ إِذَا بَلَغُوا النِّكَاحَ
فَإِنْ آنَسْتُم مِّنْهُمْ رُشْدًا فَادْفَعُوا إِلَيْهِمْ أَمْوَالَهُمْ
وَلَا تَأْكُلُوهَا إِسْرَافًا وَبِدَارًا أَن يَكْبَرُوا
وَمَن كَانَ غَنِيًّا فَلْيَسْتَعْفِفْ
وَمَن كَانَ فَقِيرًا فَلْيَأْكُلْ بِالْمَعْرُوفِ
فَإِذَا دَفَعْتُمْ إِلَيْهِمْ أَمْوَالَهُمْ فَأَشْهِدُوا عَلَيْهِمْ
وَكَفَىٰ بِاللَّهِ حَسِيبًا

7. From what is left by parents
And those nearest related[514]
There is a share for men
And a share for women,
Whether the property be small
Or large—a determinate share.

٧ لِّلرِّجَالِ نَصِيبٌ مِّمَّا تَرَكَ الْوَالِدَانِ
وَالْأَقْرَبُونَ وَلِلنِّسَاءِ نَصِيبٌ مِّمَّا تَرَكَ الْوَالِدَانِ
وَالْأَقْرَبُونَ مِمَّا قَلَّ مِنْهُ أَوْ كَثُرَ نَصِيبًا مَّفْرُوضًا

8. But if at the time of division
Other relatives, or orphans,
Or poor, are present,
Feed them out of the (property),
And speak to them
Words of kindness and justice.

٨ وَإِذَا حَضَرَ الْقِسْمَةَ أُولُو الْقُرْبَىٰ وَالْيَتَامَىٰ
وَالْمَسَاكِينُ فَارْزُقُوهُم مِّنْهُ
وَقُولُوا لَهُمْ قَوْلًا مَّعْرُوفًا

9. Let those (disposing of an estate)
Have the same fear in their minds
As they would have for their own

٩ وَلْيَخْشَ الَّذِينَ لَوْ تَرَكُوا مِنْ خَلْفِهِمْ

---

512. The age of marriage is the age when they reach their majority.

513. It is good to take human witnesses when you faithfully discharge your trust; but remember that, however fully you satisfy your fellow-men when you give your account to them, there is a stricter account due from you to Allah. If you are righteous in Allah's eyes, you must follow these stricter standards.

514. I have resisted the temptation to translate "next of kin," as this phrase has a technical meaning in Indian Law, referring to certain kinds of heirs, whereas here the people meant are those whose inheritance is to be divided. The shares are specified. Here the general principles are laid down that females inherit as well as males, and that relatives who have no legal shares, orphans, and indigent people are not to be treated harshly, if present at the division. (R).

If they had left a helpless
family behind:
Let them fear Allah, and speak
Words of appropriate
(comfort).[515]

ذُرِّيَّةً ضِعَٰفًا خَافُوا۟ عَلَيْهِمْ
فَلْيَتَّقُوا۟ ٱللَّهَ وَلْيَقُولُوا۟ قَوْلًا سَدِيدًا

10. Those who unjustly
Eat up the property
Of orphans, eat up
A Fire into their own
Bodies: they will soon
Be enduring a blazing Fire!

١٠ إِنَّ ٱلَّذِينَ يَأْكُلُونَ أَمْوَٰلَ ٱلْيَتَٰمَىٰ
ظُلْمًا إِنَّمَا يَأْكُلُونَ فِى بُطُونِهِمْ نَارًا ۖ
وَسَيَصْلَوْنَ سَعِيرًا

Section 2.

11. Allah (thus) directs you
As regards your children's[516]
(Inheritance): to the male,
A portion equal to that
Of two females: if only
Daughters, two or more,[517]
Their share is two-thirds
Of the inheritance;
If only one, her share
Is a half.

For parents, a sixth share
Of the inheritance to each,
If the deceased left children;
If no children, and the parents
Are the (only) heirs, the mother
Has a third; if the deceased
Left brothers (or sisters)

١١ يُوصِيكُمُ ٱللَّهُ فِىٓ أَوْلَٰدِكُمْ ۖ
لِلذَّكَرِ مِثْلُ حَظِّ ٱلْأُنثَيَيْنِ ۚ
فَإِن كُنَّ نِسَآءً فَوْقَ ٱثْنَتَيْنِ فَلَهُنَّ ثُلُثَا مَا تَرَكَ ۖ
وَإِن كَانَتْ وَٰحِدَةً فَلَهَا ٱلنِّصْفُ ۚ
وَلِأَبَوَيْهِ لِكُلِّ وَٰحِدٍ مِّنْهُمَا ٱلسُّدُسُ مِمَّا
تَرَكَ إِن كَانَ لَهُۥ وَلَدٌ ۚ فَإِن لَّمْ يَكُن لَّهُۥ وَلَدٌ وَوَرِثَهُۥٓ
أَبَوَاهُ فَلِأُمِّهِ ٱلثُّلُثُ ۚ فَإِن كَانَ لَهُۥٓ إِخْوَةٌ

515. It is a touching argument addressed to those who have to divide an estate. 'How anxious would you be if you had left a helpless family behind?' If others do so, help and be kind.

516. The principles of inheritance law are laid down in broad outline in the Qur'ān; the precise details have been worked out on the basis of the Prophet's practice and that of his Companions, and by interpretation and analogy. Muslim jurists have collected a vast amount of learning on this subject, and this body of law is enough by itself to form the subject of life-long study. Here we shall deal only with the broad principles to be gathered from the Text, as interpreted by the Jurists.

(1) The power of testamentary disposition extends over only one-third of the Property; the remaining two-thirds are distributed among heirs as laid down. (2) All distribution takes place after the legacies and debts (including funeral expenses) have first been paid. (3) Legacies cannot be left to any of the heirs included in the scheme of distribution; or it will amount to upsetting the shares and undue preference of one heir to another. (4) Generally, but not always, the male takes a share double that of a female in his own category.

517. At first sight, the Arabic words seem to mean: "If more than two daughters." But the alternative in the next clause is: "if only one daughter." Logically, therefore, the first clause must mean: "if daughters, two or more." This is the general interpretation, and is confirmed by the supplementary provision in 4:176 at the end of the Sūrah, which should be read along with this.

The mother has a sixth.
(The distribution in all cases
Is) after the payment
Of legacies and debts.
Ye know not whether
Your parents or your children
Are nearest to you
In benefit. These are
Settled portions ordained[518]
By Allah; and Allah is
All-Knowing, All-Wise.

فَلِأُمِّهِ ٱلسُّدُسُ مِنۢ بَعۡدِ وَصِيَّةٖ يُوصِي
بِهَآ أَوۡ دَيۡنٍۗ ءَابَآؤُكُمۡ وَأَبۡنَآؤُكُمۡ لَا تَدۡرُونَ
أَيُّهُمۡ أَقۡرَبُ لَكُمۡ نَفۡعٗاۚ فَرِيضَةٗ مِّنَ ٱللَّهِۗ
إِنَّ ٱللَّهَ كَانَ عَلِيمًا حَكِيمٗا

12. In what your wives leave,
Your share is a half,
If they leave no child;
But if they leave a child,
Ye get a fourth; after payment
Of legacies and debts.
In what ye leave,
Their share is a fourth,[519]
If ye leave no child;
But if ye leave a child,
They get an eighth; after payment
Of legacies and debts.

If the man or woman
Whose inheritance is in question,
Has left neither ascendants nor descendants,[520]

١٢ وَلَكُمۡ نِصۡفُ مَا تَرَكَ أَزۡوَٰجُكُمۡ
إِن لَّمۡ يَكُن لَّهُنَّ وَلَدٞۚ فَإِن كَانَ لَهُنَّ وَلَدٞ
فَلَكُمُ ٱلرُّبُعُ مِمَّا تَرَكۡنَۚ مِنۢ بَعۡدِ وَصِيَّةٖ
يُوصِينَ بِهَآ أَوۡ دَيۡنٖۚ وَلَهُنَّ ٱلرُّبُعُ مِمَّا
تَرَكۡتُمۡ إِن لَّمۡ يَكُن لَّكُمۡ وَلَدٞۚ فَإِن كَانَ
لَكُمۡ وَلَدٞ فَلَهُنَّ ٱلثُّمُنُ مِمَّا تَرَكۡتُمۚ
مِّنۢ بَعۡدِ وَصِيَّةٖ تُوصُونَ بِهَآ أَوۡ دَيۡنٖۗ
وَإِن كَانَ رَجُلٞ يُورَثُ كَلَٰلَةً أَوِ ٱمۡرَأَةٞ

518. The verse deals with the portions allotted to (a) children, and (b) parents. The next verse deals with the portions allotted to (c) husband or wife of the deceased, and (d) collaterals. The children's shares are fixed, but their amount will depend upon what goes to the parents. If both parents are living, and there are also children, both father and mother take a sixth each; if only one parent is living, he or she takes his or her sixth; and the rest goes to the children. If the parents are living, and there is no child or other heir, the mother gets a third (and the father the remaining two-thirds); if there are no children, but there are brothers or sisters (this is interpreted strictly in the plural), the mother has a sixth, and the father apparently the residue, as the father excludes collaterals. This is far from being an exhaustive statement, but it establishes the proposition that children and parents have always some share if they survive, but their shares are affected by the existence and number of the heirs in these categories.

519. The husband takes a half of his deceased wife's properety if she leaves no child, the rest going to residuaries; if she leaves a child, the husband gets only a fourth. Following the rule that the female share is generally half the male share, the widow gets a fourth of her deceased husband's property, if he leaves no children, and an eighth if he leaves children. If there are more widows than one, their collective share is a fourth or an eighth as the case may be: *inter se* they divide equally.

520. The word in Arabic is *kalālah*, which is so construed usually. But it was nowhere defined authoritatively in the lifetime of the Messenger. This was one of the three terms about which Umar wished that the Messenger had defined them in his lifetime, the other two being *Khilāfah*, and *ribā* (usury). On the accepted definition, we are concerned with the inheritance of a person who has left no descendant or ascendant (however distant), but only collaterals, with or without a widow or widower. If there is a widow or widower surviving, she or he takes the share as already defined, before the collaterals come in.

But has left a brother[521]
Or a sister, each one of the two
Gets a sixth; but if more
Than two, they share in a third;
After payment of legacies
And debts; so that no loss[522]
Is caused (to anyone).
Thus is it ordained by Allah;
And Allah is All-Knowing,
Most Forbearing.

وَلَهُۥٓ أَخٌ أَوْ أُخْتٌ فَلِكُلِّ وَٰحِدٍ مِّنْهُمَا ٱلسُّدُسُ ۚ
فَإِن كَانُوٓا۟ أَكْثَرَ مِن ذَٰلِكَ فَهُمْ شُرَكَآءُ
فِى ٱلثُّلُثِ ۚ مِنۢ بَعْدِ وَصِيَّةٍ يُوصَىٰ بِهَآ أَوْ دَيْنٍ
غَيْرَ مُضَآرٍّ ۚ وَصِيَّةً مِّنَ ٱللَّهِ ۗ وَٱللَّهُ عَلِيمٌ حَلِيمٌ

13. Those are limits
Set by Allah; those who
Obey Allah and His Messenger
Will be admitted to Gardens
With rivers flowing beneath,
To abide therein (forever)
And that will be
The Supreme achievement.[522-A]

١٣ تِلْكَ حُدُودُ ٱللَّهِ ۚ وَمَن يُطِعِ ٱللَّهَ
وَرَسُولَهُۥ يُدْخِلْهُ جَنَّٰتٍ تَجْرِى مِن
تَحْتِهَا ٱلْأَنْهَٰرُ خَٰلِدِينَ فِيهَا ۚ
وَذَٰلِكَ ٱلْفَوْزُ ٱلْعَظِيمُ

14. But those who disobey
Allah and His Messenger
And transgress His limits
Will be admitted
To a Fire, to abide therein:
And they shall have
A humiliating punishment.

١٤ وَمَن يَعْصِ ٱللَّهَ وَرَسُولَهُۥ وَيَتَعَدَّ
حُدُودَهُۥ يُدْخِلْهُ نَارًا خَٰلِدًا فِيهَا
وَلَهُۥ عَذَابٌ مُّهِينٌ

C. 62.—What can be a holier cement to Society
(4:15-42) Than that women should be chaste and pure,
And crimes against sex rooted out?
Let decency, kindness, and justice
Prevail in all sex relationships;
Let marriage be cherished and carefully guarded;
Women's rights secured; family jars

---

521. A "brother or sister" is here interpreted to mean a uterine brother or sister, *i.e.*, a brother or sister by the same mother but not by the same father, as the case of full brothers and sisters or brothers and sisters by the same father but different mothers is understood to be dealt with later, in the last verse of this Sūrah. The uterine brother or sister, if only one survives, takes a sixth, if more than one survives, they take a third collectively, and divide among themselves; this on the supposition that there are no descendants or ascendants, however remote. There may, however, be a widow or widower surviving: she or he takes her or his share, as already specified.

The shares of collaterals generally are calculated on a complicated system which cannot be described in a brief note. For these, and the rules about Residuaries (*'Asaba*) reference should be made to special legal treatises.

522. Debts (in which funeral expenses take first rank) and legacies are the first charge on the estate of a deceased person, before distribution takes place. But equity and fair dealing should be observed in all matters, so that no one's interests are prejudiced. Thus funeral expenses should be reasonable; debts must be genuine and not reckless debts; and the shares must be calculated with fairness.

522-A. *Cf.* 44:57, n. 4733. (R).

Adjusted; and all life lived
In faith, charity, and kindness sincere
To all our fellow-creatures.

SECTION 3.

15. If any of your women
Are guilty of lewdness,[523]
Take the evidence of four[524]
(Reliable) witnesses from amongst you
Against them; and if they testify,
Confine them to houses until
Death do claim them,
Or Allah ordain for them
Some (other) way.[525]

١٥ وَٱلَّٰتِى يَأْتِينَ ٱلْفَٰحِشَةَ مِن
نِّسَآئِكُمْ فَٱسْتَشْهِدُوا۟ عَلَيْهِنَّ أَرْبَعَةً
مِّنكُمْ ۖ فَإِن شَهِدُوا۟ فَأَمْسِكُوهُنَّ فِى
ٱلْبُيُوتِ حَتَّىٰ يَتَوَفَّىٰهُنَّ ٱلْمَوْتُ
أَوْ يَجْعَلَ ٱللَّهُ لَهُنَّ سَبِيلًا

16. If two men among you
Are guilty of lewdness,
Punish them both.
If they repent and amend,
Leave them alone; for Allah
Is Oft-Returning, Most Merciful.

١٦ وَٱلَّذَانِ يَأْتِيَٰنِهَا مِنكُمْ فَـَٔاذُوهُمَا ۖ
فَإِن تَابَا وَأَصْلَحَا فَأَعْرِضُوا۟ عَنْهُمَآ ۗ
إِنَّ ٱللَّهَ كَانَ تَوَّابًا رَّحِيمًا

17. Allah accepts the repentance
Of those who do evil
In ignorance and repent
Soon afterwards; to them
Will Allah turn in mercy:
For Allah is full of knowledge
And wisdom.

١٧ إِنَّمَا ٱلتَّوْبَةُ عَلَى ٱللَّهِ لِلَّذِينَ يَعْمَلُونَ
ٱلسُّوٓءَ بِجَهَٰلَةٍ ثُمَّ يَتُوبُونَ مِن قَرِيبٍ فَأُو۟لَٰٓئِكَ
يَتُوبُ ٱللَّهُ عَلَيْهِمْ ۗ وَكَانَ ٱللَّهُ عَلِيمًا حَكِيمًا

18. Of no effect is the repentance

١٨ وَلَيْسَتِ ٱلتَّوْبَةُ

523. Most commentators understand this to refer to adultery or fornication: in that case they consider that the punishment was altered to 100 stripes by the later verse, 24:2. But I think it refers to unnatural crime between women, analogous to unnatural crime between men in 4:16 below; because (1) no punishment is specified here for the man, as would be the case where a man was involved in the crime; (2) the word, *al lātī*, the purely feminine plural of *al latī*, is used for the parties to the crime; (3) the punishment is indefinite; see the next note but one.

524. To protect the honour of women, stricter evidence is required, *i.e.*, the evidence of four instead of the usual two witnesses. It is the same for adultery (see 24:4.)

525. Keep them in prison until some definite order is received. Those who take the crime to be adultery or fornication construe this definite order ("some other way") to mean some definite pronouncement by the Prophet under inspiration; this was the punishment of flogging under 24:2. for fornication, and stoning to death under the Prophet's directives for adultery. If we understand the crime to be unnatural crime, we might presume, in the absence of any definite order ("some other way") that the punishment would be similar to that for men in the next verse. The Prophet's Sunnah has prescribed capital punishment although the exact method is left indefinite. (R).

Of those who continue[526]
To do evil, until Death
Faces one of them, and he says,
"Now have I repented indeed;"
Nor of those who die
Rejecting Faith; for them
Have we prepared
A punishment most grievous.

لِلَّذِينَ يَعْمَلُونَ ٱلسَّيِّـَٔاتِ حَتَّىٰٓ إِذَا
حَضَرَ أَحَدَهُمُ ٱلْمَوْتُ قَالَ إِنِّى تُبْتُ ٱلْـَٔـٰنَ
وَلَا ٱلَّذِينَ يَمُوتُونَ وَهُمْ كُفَّارٌ ۚ
أُو۟لَـٰٓئِكَ أَعْتَدْنَا لَهُمْ عَذَابًا أَلِيمًا

19. O ye who believe!
Ye are forbidden to inherit
Women against their will.[527]
Nor should ye treat them
With harshness, that ye may
Take away part of the dower[528]
Ye have given them—except
Where they have been guilty
Of open lewdness;
On the contrary live with them
On a footing of kindness and equity.
If ye take a dislike to them
It may be that ye dislike
A thing, and Allah brings about
Through it a great deal of good.

١٩ يَـٰٓأَيُّهَا ٱلَّذِينَ ءَامَنُوا۟ لَا يَحِلُّ لَكُمْ
أَن تَرِثُوا۟ ٱلنِّسَآءَ كَرْهًا ۖ وَلَا تَعْضُلُوهُنَّ لِتَذْهَبُوا۟
بِبَعْضِ مَآ ءَاتَيْتُمُوهُنَّ إِلَّآ أَن يَأْتِينَ بِفَـٰحِشَةٍ
مُّبَيِّنَةٍ ۚ وَعَاشِرُوهُنَّ بِٱلْمَعْرُوفِ ۚ
فَإِن كَرِهْتُمُوهُنَّ فَعَسَىٰٓ أَن تَكْرَهُوا۟ شَيْـًٔا
وَيَجْعَلَ ٱللَّهُ فِيهِ خَيْرًا كَثِيرًا

20. But if ye decide to take
One wife in place of another,
Even if ye had given the latter
A whole treasure[529] for dower,
Take not the least bit of it back;
Would ye take it by slander
And a manifest wrong?

٢٠ وَإِنْ أَرَدتُّمُ ٱسْتِبْدَالَ زَوْجٍ مَّكَانَ
زَوْجٍ وَءَاتَيْتُمْ إِحْدَىٰهُنَّ قِنطَارًا فَلَا تَأْخُذُوا۟
مِنْهُ شَيْـًٔا ۚ أَتَأْخُذُونَهُۥ بُهْتَـٰنًا وَإِثْمًا مُّبِينًا

21. And how could ye take it
When ye have gone in
Unto each other, and they have
Taken from you a solemn covenant?

٢١ وَكَيْفَ تَأْخُذُونَهُۥ وَقَدْ أَفْضَىٰ بَعْضُكُمْ
إِلَىٰ بَعْضٍ وَأَخَذْنَ مِنكُم مِّيثَـٰقًا غَلِيظًا

---

526. Note the fine touch. A sin may be fashionable, and people may sin together without compunction. When one of them is faced with Death, he repents, but that sort of repentance is no good.

527. Among many nations, including Arabs in the Days of Ignorance, a step-son or brother took possession of a dead man's widow or widows along with his goods and chattels. This shameful custom is forbidden. See also 4:22 below.

528. Another trick, to detract from the freedom of married women was to treat them badly and force them to sue for a *Khul'* a divorce (see 2:229, n. 258) or its equivalent in pre-Islamic custom, when the dower could be claimed back. This is also forbidden. Or the harshness may be exercised in another way; a divorced woman may be prevented by those who have control of her, from re-marrying unless she remits her dower. All kinds of harshness are forbidden.

529. Treasure: *Qinṭār*=a talent of gold: see 3:14, first note.

22. And marry not women
Whom your fathers married—
Except what is past:
It was shameful and odious—
An abominable custom indeed.[530]

٢٢ وَلَا تَنكِحُوا۟ مَا نَكَحَ ءَابَآؤُكُم مِّنَ
ٱلنِّسَآءِ إِلَّا مَا قَدْ سَلَفَ ۚ إِنَّهُۥ كَانَ
فَٰحِشَةً وَمَقْتًا وَسَآءَ سَبِيلًا

SECTION 4.

23. Prohibited to you
(For marriage) are—[531]
Your mothers, daughters,[532]
Sisters; father's sisters,
Mother's sisters; brother's daughters,
Sister's daughters; foster-mothers[533]
(Who gave you suck), foster-sisters;
Your wives' mothers;
Your step-daughters under your[534]
Guardianship, born of your wives
To whom ye have gone in—
No prohibition if ye have not gone in—
(Those who have been)
Wives of your sons[535] proceeding
From your loins;
And two sisters in wedlock
At one and the same time,[536]
Except for what is past;
For Allah is Oft-Forgiving,
Most Merciful—

٢٣ حُرِّمَتْ عَلَيْكُمْ أُمَّهَٰتُكُمْ
وَبَنَاتُكُمْ وَأَخَوَٰتُكُمْ وَعَمَّٰتُكُمْ
وَخَٰلَٰتُكُمْ وَبَنَاتُ ٱلْأَخِ وَبَنَاتُ ٱلْأُخْتِ
وَأُمَّهَٰتُكُمُ ٱلَّٰتِىٓ أَرْضَعْنَكُمْ
وَأَخَوَٰتُكُم مِّنَ ٱلرَّضَٰعَةِ وَأُمَّهَٰتُ
نِسَآئِكُمْ وَرَبَٰٓئِبُكُمُ ٱلَّٰتِى فِى
حُجُورِكُم مِّن نِّسَآئِكُمُ ٱلَّٰتِى دَخَلْتُم
بِهِنَّ فَإِن لَّمْ تَكُونُوا۟ دَخَلْتُم بِهِنَّ
فَلَا جُنَاحَ عَلَيْكُمْ وَحَلَٰٓئِلُ
أَبْنَآئِكُمُ ٱلَّذِينَ مِنْ أَصْلَٰبِكُمْ
وَأَن تَجْمَعُوا۟ بَيْنَ ٱلْأُخْتَيْنِ إِلَّا مَا
قَدْ سَلَفَ ۗ إِنَّ ٱللَّهَ كَانَ غَفُورًا رَّحِيمًا

530. See above; 4:19, n. 527.

531. This Table of Prohibited Degrees agrees in the main with what is usually accepted among all nations, except in minor details. It begins in the last verse (with father's widows or divorcees). The scheme is drawn upon the assumption that the person who proposes to marry is a man; if it is a woman, the same scheme will apply, *mutatis mutandis;* it will read: "your fathers, sons, brothers," etc.; or you can always read it from the husband's view of relationship, as there must always be a husband in a marriage.

532. "Mother" includes grandmother (through the father or mother), great-grandmother, etc.; "daughter" includes granddaughter through son or daughter), great-granddaughter, etc.; "sister," includes full-sister and half-sister. "Father's sister" includes grandfather's sister, etc. and "mother's sister" includes grandmother's sister, etc.

533. "Fosterage" or milk-relationships play an important part in Muslim Law, and count like blood-relationships; it would therefore seem that not only foster-mothers and foster-sisters, but foster-mother's sister, etc., all come within the prohibited degrees.

534. It is generally held that "under your guardianship" is a description, not a condition. (R).

535. "Sons" includes grandsons, but excludes adopted sons, or persons treated as such, on account of the words "proceeding from your loins."

536. The bar against two sisters in marriage together applies to aunt and niece together, but not to deceased wife's sister after the wife dies.

5/30

24. Also (prohibited are)
Women already married,
Except those
Whom your right hands possess:[537]
Thus hath Allah ordained
(Prohibitions) against you:
Except for these, all others
Are lawful, provided
Ye seek (them in marriage)
With gifts from your property—
Desiring chastity, not lust.[538]
Seeing that ye derive
Benefit from them, give them
Their dowers (at least)[539]
As prescribed; but if,
After a dower is prescribed, ye agree
Mutually (to vary it),
There is no blame on you,
And Allah is All-Knowing,
All-Wise.

٢٤ وَٱلْمُحْصَنَٰتُ مِنَ ٱلنِّسَآءِ
إِلَّا مَا مَلَكَتْ أَيْمَٰنُكُمْ
كِتَٰبَ ٱللَّهِ عَلَيْكُمْ وَأُحِلَّ لَكُم
مَّا وَرَآءَ ذَٰلِكُمْ أَن تَبْتَغُوا۟ بِأَمْوَٰلِكُم
مُّحْصِنِينَ غَيْرَ مُسَٰفِحِينَ فَمَا ٱسْتَمْتَعْتُم بِهِۦ
مِنْهُنَّ فَـَٔاتُوهُنَّ أُجُورَهُنَّ فَرِيضَةً
وَلَا جُنَاحَ عَلَيْكُمْ فِيمَا تَرَٰضَيْتُم بِهِۦ
مِنۢ بَعْدِ ٱلْفَرِيضَةِ
إِنَّ ٱللَّهَ كَانَ عَلِيمًا حَكِيمًا

25. If any of you have not
The means wherewith
To wed free believing women,
They may wed believing
Girls from among those
Whom your right hands possess:[540]
And Allah hath full knowledge
About your Faith.
Ye are one from another:
Wed them with the leave
Of their owners, and give them
Their dowers, according to what

٢٥ وَمَن لَّمْ يَسْتَطِعْ مِنكُمْ طَوْلًا أَن
يَنكِحَ ٱلْمُحْصَنَٰتِ ٱلْمُؤْمِنَٰتِ فَمِن مَّا
مَلَكَتْ أَيْمَٰنُكُم مِّن فَتَيَٰتِكُمُ ٱلْمُؤْمِنَٰتِ
وَٱللَّهُ أَعْلَمُ بِإِيمَٰنِكُم بَعْضُكُم مِّنۢ بَعْضٍ
فَٱنكِحُوهُنَّ بِإِذْنِ أَهْلِهِنَّ
وَءَاتُوهُنَّ أُجُورَهُنَّ

537. *Whom your right hands possess: i.e.*, captives in a Jihād. (R).

538. After defining the prohibited degrees, the verse proceeds to say that women other than those specified may be sought in marriage, but even so, not from motives of lust, but in order to promote chastity between the sexes. Marriage in the original Arabic is here described by a word which suggests a fortress (*ḥiṣn)*; marriage is, therefore, the fortress of chastity.

539. As the woman in marriage surrenders her person, so the man also must surrender (besides some part of his independence) at least some of his property according to his means. And this gives rise to the law of dower. A minimum dower is prescribed, but it is not necessary to stick to the minimum, and in the new relationship created, the parties are recommended to act towards each other with the greatest confidence and liberality.

540. That is, captives taken in *Jihād: Your right hands* does not mean necessarily that she has been assigned to you, or is your property. All captures in war belong to the community, they are "yours" in that sense. If you seek such a person in marriage, do it from no base motives. Safeguard your faith, and see that she too does believe. In that case, after all, she is of the human brotherhood, and her condition is accidental and redeemable. If the slave bore a child to her master, she would become free. (R).

Is reasonable: they should be
Chaste, not lustful, nor taking
Paramours: when they
Are taken in wedlock,
If they fall into shame,
Their punishment is half
That for free women.
This (permission) is for those
Among you who fear sin;
But is better for you
That ye practise self-restraint.
And Allah is Oft-Forgiving,
Most Merciful.

بِٱلۡمَعۡرُوفِ مُحۡصَنَٰتٍ غَيۡرَ مُسَٰفِحَٰتٖ وَلَا
مُتَّخِذَٰتِ أَخۡدَانٖۚ فَإِذَآ أُحۡصِنَّ فَإِنۡ أَتَيۡنَ
بِفَٰحِشَةٖ فَعَلَيۡهِنَّ نِصۡفُ مَا عَلَى ٱلۡمُحۡصَنَٰتِ
مِنَ ٱلۡعَذَابِۚ ذَٰلِكَ لِمَنۡ خَشِيَ ٱلۡعَنَتَ
مِنكُمۡۚ وَأَن تَصۡبِرُواْ خَيۡرٞ لَّكُمۡۗ
وَٱللَّهُ غَفُورٞ رَّحِيمٞ

Section 5.

26. Allah doth wish
To make clear to you
And to show you
The ordinances of those
Before you; and (He
Doth wish to) turn to you
(In Mercy); and Allah
Is All-Knowing, All-Wise.

٢٦ يُرِيدُ ٱللَّهُ لِيُبَيِّنَ لَكُمۡ
وَيَهۡدِيَكُمۡ سُنَنَ ٱلَّذِينَ
مِن قَبۡلِكُمۡ وَيَتُوبَ عَلَيۡكُمۡۗ
وَٱللَّهُ عَلِيمٌ حَكِيمٞ

27. Allah doth wish
To turn to you,
But the wish of those
Who follow their lusts
Is that ye should turn
Away (from Him)—
Far, far away.

٢٧ وَٱللَّهُ يُرِيدُ أَن يَتُوبَ عَلَيۡكُمۡ
وَيُرِيدُ ٱلَّذِينَ يَتَّبِعُونَ ٱلشَّهَوَٰتِ
أَن تَمِيلُواْ مَيۡلًا عَظِيمٗا

28. Allah doth wish
To lighten your (difficulties):
For man was created
Weak (in flesh).

٢٨ يُرِيدُ ٱللَّهُ أَن يُخَفِّفَ عَنكُمۡۚ
وَخُلِقَ ٱلۡإِنسَٰنُ ضَعِيفٗا

29. O ye who believe![541]
Eat not up your property

٢٩ يَٰٓأَيُّهَا ٱلَّذِينَ ءَامَنُواْ
لَا تَأۡكُلُوٓاْ أَمۡوَٰلَكُم

541. Let me paraphrase this verse, for there is profound meaning in it. (1) All your property you hold in trust, whether it is in your name, or belongs to the community, or to people over whom you have control. To waste is wrong. (2) In 2:188 the same phrase occurred, to caution us against greed. Here it occurs, to encourage us to increase property by economic use (traffic and trade), recalling Christ's parable of the Talents (Matt. 25:14-30), where the servants who had increased their master's wealth were promoted and the servant who had hoarded was cast into darkness. (3) We are warned that our waste may mean our own destruction ("nor kill or destroy yourselves.") But there is a more general meaning also: we must be careful of our own and other people's lives. We must commit no violence. This is the opposite of "trade and traffic by mutual good will." (4) Our violence to our own brethren is particularly preposterous, seeing that Allah has loved and showered His mercies on us and all His creatures.

Among yourselves in vanities;
But let there be amongst you
Traffic and trade
By mutual good will:
Nor kill (or destroy)
Yourselves: for verily
Allah hath been to you
Most Merciful!

بَيْنَكُم بِالْبَٰطِلِ إِلَّآ أَن تَكُونَ تِجَٰرَةً
عَن تَرَاضٍ مِّنكُمْ ۚ وَلَا تَقْتُلُوٓا۟ أَنفُسَكُمْ ۚ
إِنَّ ٱللَّهَ كَانَ بِكُمْ رَحِيمًا

30. If any do that
In rancour and injustice—
Soon shall We cast them
Into the Fire: and easy
It is for Allah.

(٣٠) وَمَن يَفْعَلْ ذَٰلِكَ عُدْوَٰنًا وَظُلْمًا فَسَوْفَ
نُصْلِيهِ نَارًا ۚ وَكَانَ ذَٰلِكَ عَلَى ٱللَّهِ يَسِيرًا

31. If ye (but) eschew
The most heinous
Of the things
Which ye are forbidden to do,
We shall expel
Out of you
All the evil in you,
And admit you to a Gate
Of great honour.

(٣١) إِن تَجْتَنِبُوا۟ كَبَآئِرَ
مَا تُنْهَوْنَ عَنْهُ نُكَفِّرْ عَنكُمْ سَيِّـَٔاتِكُمْ
وَنُدْخِلْكُم مُّدْخَلًا كَرِيمًا

32. And in nowise covet[542]
Those things in which Allah
Hath bestowed His gifts
More freely on some of you
Than on others: to men
Is allotted what they earn,
And to women what they earn:
But ask Allah of His bounty.
For Allah hath full knowledge
Of all things.

(٣٢) وَلَا تَتَمَنَّوْا۟ مَا فَضَّلَ ٱللَّهُ بِهِۦ بَعْضَكُمْ
عَلَىٰ بَعْضٍ ۚ لِّلرِّجَالِ نَصِيبٌ مِّمَّا ٱكْتَسَبُوا۟ ۖ
وَلِلنِّسَآءِ نَصِيبٌ مِّمَّا ٱكْتَسَبْنَ ۚ وَسْـَٔلُوا۟ ٱللَّهَ مِن
فَضْلِهِۦٓ ۗ إِنَّ ٱللَّهَ كَانَ بِكُلِّ شَىْءٍ عَلِيمًا

33. To (benefit) every one,
We have appointed
Sharers and heirs[543]

(٣٣) وَلِكُلٍّ جَعَلْنَا مَوَٰلِىَ

542. Men and women have gifts from Allah—some greater than others. They seem unequal, but we are assured that Providence has allotted them by a scheme by which people receive what they earn. If this does not appear clear in our sight, let us remember that we have no full knowledge but Allah has. We must not be jealous if other people have more than we have—in wealth or position or strength or honour or talent or happiness. Probably things are equalized in the aggregate or in the long run, or equated to needs and merits on a scale which we cannot appraise. If we want more, instead of being jealous or covetous, we should pray to Allah and place before Him our needs. Though He knows all, and has no need of our prayer, our prayer may reveal to ourselves our shortcomings and enable us to deserve more of Allah's bounty or make ourselves fit for it.

543. *Mawālī*, plural of *Mawlā*; from the root *walā*, to be near in place or relationship, to follow. *Mawlā* may therefore mean: (1) nearly related, (2) heir, (3) sharer or partner; these three meanings are implied here; (4) neighbour, or friend, or protector, or client (44:44); (5) lord or master (16:76).

To property left
By parents and relatives.
To those, also, to whom
Your right hand was pledged,[544]
Give their due portion.
For truly Allah is witness
To all things.

SECTION 6.

34\. Men are the protectors[545]
And maintainers of women,
Because Allah has given
The one more (strength)
Than the other, and because
They support them
From their means.
Therefore the righteous women
Are devoutly obedient, and guard
In (the husband's) absence
What Allah would have them guard.[546]
As to those women
On whose part ye fear
Disloyalty and ill-conduct,
Admonish them (first),[547]
(Next), refuse to share their beds,
(And last) beat them (lightly);
But if they return to obedience,

مِمَّا تَرَكَ ٱلْوَٰلِدَانِ وَٱلْأَقْرَبُونَ وَٱلَّذِينَ
عَقَدَتْ أَيْمَٰنُكُمْ فَـَٔاتُوهُمْ نَصِيبَهُمْ
إِنَّ ٱللَّهَ كَانَ عَلَىٰ كُلِّ شَىْءٍ شَهِيدًا

٣٤ ٱلرِّجَالُ قَوَّٰمُونَ عَلَى ٱلنِّسَآءِ
بِمَا فَضَّلَ ٱللَّهُ بَعْضَهُمْ عَلَىٰ بَعْضٍ
وَبِمَآ أَنفَقُوا۟ مِنْ أَمْوَٰلِهِمْ
فَٱلصَّٰلِحَٰتُ قَٰنِتَٰتٌ
حَٰفِظَٰتٌ لِّلْغَيْبِ
بِمَا حَفِظَ ٱللَّهُ
وَٱلَّٰتِى تَخَافُونَ نُشُوزَهُنَّ
فَعِظُوهُنَّ وَٱهْجُرُوهُنَّ فِى ٱلْمَضَاجِعِ
وَٱضْرِبُوهُنَّ فَإِنْ أَطَعْنَكُمْ

544. When the emigration took place from Makkah to Madīnah, bonds and links of brotherhood were established between the "Emigrants" and the "Helpers," and they shared in each other's inheritance. Later, when the Community was solidly established, and relations with those left behind in Makkah were resumed, the rights of blood-relations in Makkah, and the Helper-brethren in Madīnah were both safeguarded. This is the particular meaning. The more general meaning is similar; respect your ties of blood, of neighbourhood, and of friendly compacts and understandings. Be just to all.

545. *Qawwām*: one who stands firm in another's business, protects his interests, and looks after his affairs; or it may be, standing firm in his own business, managing affairs, with a steady purpose. *Cf.* 4:135.

546. Or the sentence may be rendered: "and protect (the husband's interests) in his absence, as Allah has protected them." If we take the rendering as in the text, the meaning is: the good wife is obedient and harmonious in her husband's presence, and in his absence guards his reputation and property and her own virtue, as ordained by Allah. If we take the rendering as in the note, we reach the same result in a different way: the good wife, in her husband's absence, remembering how Allah has given her a sheltered position, does everything to justify that position by guarding her own virtue and his reputation and property.

547. In case of family jars four steps are mentioned, to be taken in that order: (1) perhaps verbal advice or admonition may be sufficient; (2) if not, sex relations may be suspended; (3) if this is not sufficient, some slight physical correction may be administered; but Imām Shāfi'i considers this inadvisable, though permissible, and all authorities are unanimous in deprecating any sort of cruelty, even of the nagging kind, as mentioned in the next clause; (4) if all this fails, a family council is recommended in 4:35 below.

Seek not against them[548]
Means (of annoyance):
For Allah is Most High,
Great (above you all).

35. If ye fear a breach
Between them twain,
Appoint (two) arbiters,
One from his family,
And the other from hers;[549]
If they wish for peace,
Allah will cause
Their reconciliation:
For Allah hath full knowledge,
And is acquainted
With all things.

36. Serve Allah, and join not[550]
Any partners with Him;
And do good—
To parents, kinsfolk,
Orphans, those in need,
Neighbours who are near[551]
Neighbours who are strangers,
The Companion by your side,[552]
The wayfarer (ye meet),
And what your right hands
possess:[553]
For Allah loveth not

فَلَا تَبْغُوا۟ عَلَيْهِنَّ سَبِيلًا
إِنَّ ٱللَّهَ كَانَ عَلِيًّا كَبِيرًا

٣٥ وَإِنْ خِفْتُمْ شِقَاقَ بَيْنِهِمَا
فَٱبْعَثُوا۟ حَكَمًا مِّنْ أَهْلِهِۦ
وَحَكَمًا مِّنْ أَهْلِهَآ
إِن يُرِيدَآ إِصْلَـٰحًا يُوَفِّقِ ٱللَّهُ بَيْنَهُمَآ
إِنَّ ٱللَّهَ كَانَ عَلِيمًا خَبِيرًا

٣٦ وَٱعْبُدُوا۟ ٱللَّهَ وَلَا تُشْرِكُوا۟ بِهِۦ شَيْـًٔا
وَبِٱلْوَٰلِدَيْنِ إِحْسَـٰنًا وَبِذِى ٱلْقُرْبَىٰ
وَٱلْيَتَـٰمَىٰ وَٱلْمَسَـٰكِينِ وَٱلْجَارِ ذِى ٱلْقُرْبَىٰ
وَٱلْجَارِ ٱلْجُنُبِ وَٱلصَّاحِبِ بِٱلْجَنۢبِ
وَٱبْنِ ٱلسَّبِيلِ وَمَا مَلَكَتْ أَيْمَـٰنُكُمْ
إِنَّ ٱللَّهَ لَا يُحِبُّ

548. Temper, nagging, sarcasm, speaking at each other in other people's presence, reverting to past faults which should be forgiven and forgotten—all this is forbidden. And the reason given is characteristic of Islam. You must live all your life as in the presence of Allah, Who is high above us, but Who watches over us. How petty and contemptible will our little squabbles appear in His presence!

549. An excellent plan for settling family disputes, without too much publicity or mud-throwing, or resort to the chicaneries of the law. The Latin countries recognise this plan in their legal systems. It is a pity that Muslims do not resort to it universally, as they should. The arbiters from each family would know the idiosyncrasies of both parties, and would be able, with Allah's help to effect a real reconciliatiion.

550. The essence of Islam is to serve Allah and do good to your fellow-creatures. This is wider and more comprehensive than "Love God and love your neighbour". For it includes duties to animals as our fellow-creatures, and emphasises practical service rather than sentiment.

551. *Neighbours who are near*: that is, in local situation as well as intimate relationships, just as *neighbours who are strangers* includes those whom we do not know or who live away from us or in a different sphere altogether.

552. The *Companion by your side* may be your intimate friends and associates, just as the *wayfarer you meet* may be a casual acquaintance on your travels. This last is much wider than the "stranger within your gate."

553. *What your right hands possess*: For the meaning of the phrase see n. 537 above. (R).

The arrogant, the
vainglorious—[554]

مَن كَانَ مُخۡتَالٗا فَخُورًا

37. (Nor) those who are niggardly,
Or enjoin niggardliness on others,
Or hide the bounties
Which Allah hath bestowed[555]
On them; for We have prepared,
For those who resist Faith,
A Punishment that steeps[556]
Them in contempt—

٣٧ ٱلَّذِينَ يَبۡخَلُونَ وَيَأۡمُرُونَ ٱلنَّاسَ
بِٱلۡبُخۡلِ وَيَكۡتُمُونَ مَآ ءَاتَىٰهُمُ ٱللَّهُ
مِن فَضۡلِهِۦۗ وَأَعۡتَدۡنَا لِلۡكَٰفِرِينَ
عَذَابٗا مُّهِينٗا

38. Nor those who spend
Of their substance, to be seen[557]
Of men, but have no faith
In Allah and the Last Day:
If any take the Evil One
For their intimate,
What a dreadful intimate he is!

٣٨ وَٱلَّذِينَ يُنفِقُونَ أَمۡوَٰلَهُمۡ رِئَآءَ
ٱلنَّاسِ وَلَا يُؤۡمِنُونَ بِٱللَّهِ وَلَا بِٱلۡيَوۡمِ ٱلۡأٓخِرِۗ
وَمَن يَكُنِ ٱلشَّيۡطَٰنُ لَهُۥ قَرِينٗا فَسَآءَ قَرِينٗا

39. And what burden
Were it on them if they
Had faith in Allah
And in the Last Day,
And they spent
Out of what Allah hath
Given them for sustenance?[558]
For Allah hath full
Knowledge of them.

٣٩ وَمَاذَا عَلَيۡهِمۡ لَوۡ ءَامَنُواْ بِٱللَّهِ
وَٱلۡيَوۡمِ ٱلۡأٓخِرِ وَأَنفَقُواْ
مِمَّا رَزَقَهُمُ ٱللَّهُۚ
وَكَانَ ٱللَّهُ بِهِمۡ عَلِيمًا

40. Allah is never unjust
In the least degree:
If there is any good (done),

٤٠ إِنَّ ٱللَّهَ لَا يَظۡلِمُ مِثۡقَالَ ذَرَّةٖۖ
وَإِن تَكُ حَسَنَةٗ

554. Real deeds of service and kindness proceed, not from showing off or from a superior sort of condescension (*cf.* "White Man's Burden"), but from a frank recognition of our own humility and the real claims, before Allah, of all our fellow-creatures. For in our mutual needs we are equal before Allah, or perhaps the best of us (as the world sees us) may be worse than the worst of us (from the same point of view).

555. Arrogance is one reason why our deeds of love and kindness do not thrive. Another is niggardliness or selfishness. Allah does not love either the one or the other, for they both proceed from want of love of Allah, or faith in Allah. Niggardly is the worldly-wise man who not only refuses to spend himself in service, but by example and precept prevents others from doing so, as otherwise he would be made odious by comparison, before his fellow-creatures. So he either makes a virtue of his caution, or hides the gifts which have been given him—wealth, position, talent, etc.

556. Note how the punishment fits the crime. The niggard holds other people in contempt, and in doing so, becomes himself contemptible.

557. A fault opposed to niggardliness, and equally opposed to true charity, is to spend lavishly to be seen of men. It is mere hypocrisy; there is no love in it, either for Allah or for man.

558. *Sustenance*: physical, intellectual, spiritual—everything pertaining to life and growth. Our being is from Allah, and we must therefore spend ourselves freely for Allah. How can it be a burden? It is merely a response to the demand of our own healthy nature.

He doubleth it,
And giveth from His own
Presence a great reward.[559]

يُضَـٰعِفْهَا وَيُؤْتِ مِن لَّدُنْهُ أَجْرًا عَظِيمًا

41. How then if We brought
From each People a witness,
And We brought thee
As a witness against
These People![560]

فَكَيْفَ إِذَا جِئْنَا مِن كُلِّ أُمَّةٍۭ بِشَهِيدٍ وَجِئْنَا بِكَ عَلَىٰ هَـٰٓؤُلَآءِ شَهِيدًا ﴿٤١﴾

42. On that day
Those who reject Faith
And disobey the Messenger
Will wish that the earth
Were made one with them:[561]
But never will they hide
A single fact from Allah!

يَوْمَئِذٍ يَوَدُّ ٱلَّذِينَ كَفَرُوا۟ وَعَصَوُا۟ ٱلرَّسُولَ لَوْ تُسَوَّىٰ بِهِمُ ٱلْأَرْضُ وَلَا يَكْتُمُونَ ٱللَّهَ حَدِيثًا ﴿٤٢﴾

C. 63.—Be clean and pure, and seek not occasions
(4:43-70.) For quibbles, nor go after sorcery
Or false gods. Be faithful
In your trusts, learn obedience,
And settle your quarrels under the guidance
Of Allah's Messenger. Ever keep away
From hypocrisy and every kind of falsehood.
Then will you be admitted to a glorious Fellowship
With the highest and noblest in the spiritual world.

SECTION 7.

43. O ye who believe!
Approach not prayers
With a mind befogged,[562]
Until ye can understand
All that ye say—

يَـٰٓأَيُّهَا ٱلَّذِينَ ءَامَنُوا۟ لَا تَقْرَبُوا۟ ٱلصَّلَوٰةَ وَأَنتُمْ سُكَـٰرَىٰ حَتَّىٰ تَعْلَمُوا۟ مَا تَقُولُونَ ﴿٤٣﴾

559. Any little good of our own comes from the purity of our heart. Its results in the world are doubled and multiplied by Allah's grace and mercy; but an even greater reward comes from His own Presence, His good pleasure, which brings us nearer to Him.

560. Each Prophet and Leader is a witness for his People and his contemporaries—for those who accept Allah, and against those who reject Him.

561. Those who reject Allah's message will wish, when their eyes are opened, that they were reduced to dust, for existence itself will be agony to them. They might like to hide in the dust, but nothing is hidden from Allah. All their past will stand out clear before Him.

562. The reference is either to a state of intoxication or to a dazed state of mind on account of drowsiness or some other cause; or perhaps both are implied. Before the prohibition of intoxicants altogether was promulgated, it was at least unbecoming that people should come to prayers in such a state. For prayers it is only right that we should collect our whole minds and approach Allah in a spirit of reverence. "Prayers" (*Ṣalāh*) here may mean "a place of prayers," a Mosque: the resulting meaning would be the same.

Nor in a state
Of ceremonial impurity
(Except when travelling on the road),
Until after washing
Your whole body.
If ye are ill,
Or on a journey,
Or one of you cometh
From offices of nature,
Or ye have been
In contact with women,
And ye find no water,[563]
Then take for yourselves
Clean sand or earth,
And rub therewith
Your faces and hands.
For Allah doth blot out sins
And forgive again and again.

44. Hast thou not turned
Thy vision to those
Who were given a portion[564]
Of the Book? They traffic
In error, and wish that ye
Should lose the right path.

45. But Allah hath full knowledge
Of your enemies:
Allah is enough for a Protector,
And Allah is enough for a Helper.

46. Of the Jews there are those
Who displace words
From their (right) places,
And say: "We hear
And we disobey";[565]

وَلَا جُنُبًا إِلَّا عَابِرِي سَبِيلٍ
حَتَّىٰ تَغْتَسِلُوا۟
وَإِن كُنتُم مَّرْضَىٰٓ أَوْ عَلَىٰ سَفَرٍ
أَوْ جَآءَ أَحَدٌ مِّنكُم مِّنَ ٱلْغَآئِطِ
أَوْ لَٰمَسْتُمُ ٱلنِّسَآءَ فَلَمْ تَجِدُوا۟ مَآءً
فَتَيَمَّمُوا۟ صَعِيدًا طَيِّبًا فَٱمْسَحُوا۟
بِوُجُوهِكُمْ وَأَيْدِيكُمْ
إِنَّ ٱللَّهَ كَانَ عَفُوًّا غَفُورًا

٤٤ أَلَمْ تَرَ إِلَى ٱلَّذِينَ أُوتُوا۟ نَصِيبًا
مِّنَ ٱلْكِتَٰبِ يَشْتَرُونَ ٱلضَّلَٰلَةَ
وَيُرِيدُونَ أَن تَضِلُّوا۟ ٱلسَّبِيلَ

٤٥ وَٱللَّهُ أَعْلَمُ بِأَعْدَآئِكُمْ
وَكَفَىٰ بِٱللَّهِ وَلِيًّا وَكَفَىٰ بِٱللَّهِ نَصِيرًا

٤٦ مِّنَ ٱلَّذِينَ هَادُوا۟
يُحَرِّفُونَ ٱلْكَلِمَ عَن مَّوَاضِعِهِۦ
وَيَقُولُونَ سَمِعْنَا وَعَصَيْنَا

563. The strictest cleanliness and purity of mind and body are required, especially at the time of prayer. But there are circumstances when water for ablutions is not easily obtainable, especially in the dry conditions of Arabia, and then washing with dry sand or clean earth is recommended. Four such circumstances are mentioned: the two last when washing is specially required; the two first when washing may be necessary, but it may not be easy to get water. For a man, when he is ill, cannot walk out far to get water, and a man on a journey has no full control over his supplies. In all four cases, where water cannot be got, cleaning with dry sand or dry earth is recommended. This is called *Tayammum.*

564. *Cf.* 3:23 and n. 366.

565. See 2:93, n. 98. A trick of the Jews was to twist words and expressions, so as to ridicule the most solemn teachings of Faith. Where they should have said, "We hear and we obey," they said aloud, "We hear," and whispered, "We disobey." Where they should have said respectfully, "We hear," they added in a whisper, "May you not hear," by way of ridicule. Where they claimed the attention of the Teacher, they used an ambiguous word apparently harmless, but in their intention disrespectful. (R).

And "Hear, may you not
Hear;" and "*Rā'inā*";[566]
With a twist of their tongues
And a slander to Faith.
If only they had said:
"We hear and we obey";
And "Do hear";
And "Do look at us":
It would have been better
For them, and more proper;
But Allah hath cursed them
For their Unbelief; and but few
Of them will believe.

وَٱسْمَعْ غَيْرَ مُسْمَعٍ
وَرَٰعِنَا لَيًّۢا بِأَلْسِنَتِهِمْ وَطَعْنًا فِى ٱلدِّينِ ۚ
وَلَوْ أَنَّهُمْ قَالُوا۟ سَمِعْنَا وَأَطَعْنَا وَٱسْمَعْ وَٱنظُرْنَا
لَكَانَ خَيْرًا لَّهُمْ وَأَقْوَمَ وَلَٰكِن لَّعَنَهُمُ ٱللَّهُ
بِكُفْرِهِمْ فَلَا يُؤْمِنُونَ إِلَّا قَلِيلًا

47. O ye People of the Book!
Believe in what We
Have (now) revealed, confirming
What was (already) with you,
Before We change the face and fame[567]
Of some (of you) beyond all recognition,
And turn them hindwards,
Or curse them as We cursed
The Sabbath-breakers,[568]
For the decision of Allah
Must be carried out.

(٤٧) يَٰٓأَيُّهَا ٱلَّذِينَ أُوتُوا۟ ٱلْكِتَٰبَ
ءَامِنُوا۟ بِمَا نَزَّلْنَا مُصَدِّقًا لِّمَا مَعَكُم
مِّن قَبْلِ أَن نَّطْمِسَ وُجُوهًا
فَنَرُدَّهَا عَلَىٰٓ أَدْبَارِهَآ
أَوْ نَلْعَنَهُمْ كَمَا لَعَنَّآ أَصْحَٰبَ ٱلسَّبْتِ ۚ
وَكَانَ أَمْرُ ٱللَّهِ مَفْعُولًا

48. Allah forgiveth not
That partners should be set up
With Him; but He forgiveth
Anything else, to whom
He pleaseth; to set up
Partners with Allah
Is to devise a sin[569]
Most heinous indeed.

(٤٨) إِنَّ ٱللَّهَ لَا يَغْفِرُ أَن يُشْرَكَ بِهِۦ
وَيَغْفِرُ مَا دُونَ ذَٰلِكَ لِمَن يَشَآءُ ۚ
وَمَن يُشْرِكْ بِٱللَّهِ
فَقَدِ ٱفْتَرَىٰٓ إِثْمًا عَظِيمًا

566. See 2:104, n. 106, *Rā'inā* if used respectfully in the Arabic way, would have meant "Please attend to us." With a twist of their tongue, they suggested an insulting meaning, such as "O thou that takes us to pasture!" or in Hebrew, "Our bad one!"

567. Literally, "before We obliterate some features (or faces) and turn them front to back (or back to front)": an Arabic idiom, which must be translated freely to yield its proper meaning in English. The face is the chief expression of a man's own real essence; it is also the index of his fame and estimation. The People of the Book had been specially favoured by Allah with spiritual revelations. If they proved themselves unworthy, they lost their "face". Their eminence, would, owing to their own conduct, be turned into degradation. Others would take their place. The first shall be last and the last shall be first: Matt. 19:30.

568. *Cf.* 2:65 and n. 79.

569. Just as in an earthly kingdom the worst crime is that of treason, as it cuts at the very existence of the State, so in the spiritual kingdom, the unforgivable sin is that of contumacious treason against Allah by putting up Allah's creatures in rivalry against Him. This is rebellion against the essence and source of spiritual Life. It is what Plato would call the "lie in the soul." But even here, if the rebellion is through ignorance, and is followed by sincere repentance and amendment, Allah's Mercy is always open (4:17).

49. Hast thou not turned
Thy vision to those
Who claim sanctity
For themselves?[570]
Nay—but Allah
Doth sanctify
Whom He pleaseth.
But never will they
Fail to receive justice
In the least little thing.[571]

٤٩ أَلَمْ تَرَ إِلَى
ٱلَّذِينَ يُزَكُّونَ أَنفُسَهُم
بَلِ ٱللَّهُ يُزَكِّي مَن يَشَآءُ
وَلَا يُظْلَمُونَ فَتِيلًا

50. Behold! how they invent
A lie against Allah!
But that by itself
Is a manifest sin!

٥٠ ٱنظُرْ كَيْفَ يَفْتَرُونَ عَلَى ٱللَّهِ ٱلْكَذِبَ
وَكَفَىٰ بِهِۦٓ إِثْمًا مُّبِينًا

SECTION 8.

51. Hast thou not turned
Thy vision to those
Who were given a portion[572]
Of the Book? They believe
In Sorcery and Evil,[573]
And say to the Unbelievers
That they are better guided
In the (right) way
Than the Believers!

٥١ أَلَمْ تَرَ إِلَى ٱلَّذِينَ أُوتُوا۟ نَصِيبًا مِّنَ
ٱلْكِتَٰبِ يُؤْمِنُونَ بِٱلْجِبْتِ وَٱلطَّٰغُوتِ
وَيَقُولُونَ لِلَّذِينَ كَفَرُوا۟ هَٰٓؤُلَآءِ أَهْدَىٰ
مِنَ ٱلَّذِينَ ءَامَنُوا۟ سَبِيلًا

52. They are (men) whom
Allah hath cursed:
And those whom Allah
Hath cursed, thou wilt find,
Have no one to help.[574]

٥٢ أُو۟لَٰٓئِكَ ٱلَّذِينَ لَعَنَهُمُ ٱللَّهُ
وَمَن يَلْعَنِ ٱللَّهُ فَلَن تَجِدَ لَهُۥ نَصِيرًا

53. Have they a share
In dominion or power?

٥٣ أَمْ لَهُمْ نَصِيبٌ مِّنَ ٱلْمُلْكِ

570. The sanctimonious or self-sanctified people are the farthest from sanctity or purity, which can only proceed from Allah. They cannot play with Allah's Truth and yet go on claiming to be guided and purified or justified by Allah. Their falsehood in itself condemns them; no further proof is needed of their selfishness and evil.

571. Literally, the small skin in the groove of a date stone, a thing of no value: *fatīla*.

572. *Cf.* 3:23 and n. 366. The phrase also occurs in 4:44.

573. The word I have translated *Sorcery* is *jibt*, which may mean divination, sorcery, magic, or any false object of belief or worship, such as an idol. The word I have translated *Evil* (here and in 2:256) is *Ṭāghūt*, which means the evil one, the one who exceeds all bounds, Satan; or it may refer to some idol worshipped by the Pagan Arabs, with whom the Jews of Madīnah were intriguing against the Holy Prophet. The Jews had taken much to sorcery, magic, divination, and such superstitions.

574. The Jews were then seeking the aid of the Makkan Pagans against Muḥammad, but far from getting any help from them, they and the Pagans were both overthrown. That was the immediate occasion, but the words have a perfectly general—a universal—meaning.

Behold, they give not a farthing[575]
To their fellow-men?

فَإِذًا لَّا يُؤْتُونَ النَّاسَ نَقِيرًا

54. Or do they envy mankind
For what Allah hath given them
Of His bounty? But We
Had already given the people
Of Abraham the Book
And Wisdom, and conferred
Upon them a great kingdom.[576]

٥٤ أَمْ يَحْسُدُونَ النَّاسَ عَلَىٰ مَا آتَاهُمُ اللَّهُ
مِن فَضْلِهِ ۖ فَقَدْ آتَيْنَا آلَ إِبْرَاهِيمَ الْكِتَابَ
وَالْحِكْمَةَ وَآتَيْنَاهُم مُّلْكًا عَظِيمًا

55. Some of them believed,
And some of them averted
Their faces from him; and enough
Is Hell for a burning fire.[577]

٥٥ فَمِنْهُم مَّنْ آمَنَ بِهِ وَمِنْهُم مَّن
صَدَّ عَنْهُ ۚ وَكَفَىٰ بِجَهَنَّمَ سَعِيرًا

56. Those who reject
Our Signs, We shall soon
Cast into the Fire;
As often as their skins
Are roasted through,
We shall change them
For fresh skins,
That they may taste
The Penalty: for Allah
Is Exalted in Power, Wise.

٥٦ إِنَّ الَّذِينَ كَفَرُوا بِآيَاتِنَا سَوْفَ
نُصْلِيهِمْ نَارًا كُلَّمَا نَضِجَتْ جُلُودُهُم
بَدَّلْنَاهُمْ جُلُودًا غَيْرَهَا لِيَذُوقُوا الْعَذَابَ ۗ
إِنَّ اللَّهَ كَانَ عَزِيزًا حَكِيمًا

57. But those who believe
And do deeds of righteousness,
We shall soon admit to Gardens,
With rivers flowing beneath—
Their eternal home;
Therein shall they have
Companions pure and holy:[578]
We shall admit them
To shades, cool and ever
deepening.[579]

٥٧ وَالَّذِينَ آمَنُوا وَعَمِلُوا الصَّالِحَاتِ
سَنُدْخِلُهُمْ جَنَّاتٍ تَجْرِي مِن تَحْتِهَا الْأَنْهَارُ
خَالِدِينَ فِيهَا أَبَدًا ۖ لَّهُمْ فِيهَا أَزْوَاجٌ مُّطَهَّرَةٌ ۖ
وَنُدْخِلُهُمْ ظِلًّا ظَلِيلًا

575. The word I have translated *farthing* is *naqīr*, the groove in a date stone, a thing of no value whatever. Close-fistedness and envy are among the worst forms of selfishness, and appear specially incongruous in people of power, authority, or influence, from whom is expected generosity in giving and generosity in seeing other people's prosperity or happiness.

576. Such as the kingdoms of David and Solomon, for they had international fame.

577. Envy is like the eternal fire, which is in itself a hell.

578. *Cf.* 2:25 and n. 44.

579. The Garden is contrasted with the Fire: the shade is contrasted with the roasting. Evil grows with what it feeds on. So goodness and felicity grow with their practice. The good may be alone to start with, but (unlike evil ones) they get Holy Companions. Just as agony increases with what it suffers (typified by fresh skins growing as the old ones burn out), so felicity finds deeper and deeper meaning (typified by the shades in a garden, which grow deeper and cooler as you proceed into the interior).

58. Allah doth command you
To render back your Trusts
To those to whom they are due;
And when ye judge
Between man and man,
That ye judge with justice:
Verily how excellent
Is the teaching which He giveth
you!
For Allah is He Who heareth
And seeth all things.

٥٨ إِنَّ ٱللَّهَ يَأۡمُرُكُمۡ أَن تُؤَدُّواْ ٱلۡأَمَٰنَٰتِ
إِلَىٰٓ أَهۡلِهَا وَإِذَا حَكَمۡتُم بَيۡنَ ٱلنَّاسِ
أَن تَحۡكُمُواْ بِٱلۡعَدۡلِۚ
إِنَّ ٱللَّهَ نِعِمَّا يَعِظُكُم بِهِۦٓۗ
إِنَّ ٱللَّهَ كَانَ سَمِيعَۢا بَصِيرٗا

59. O ye who believe!
Obey Allah, and obey the
Messenger,
And those charged
With authority among you.[580]
If ye differ in anything
Among yourselves, refer it
To Allah and His Messenger,
If ye do believe in Allah
And the Last Day:
That is best, and most suitable
For final determination.

٥٩ يَٰٓأَيُّهَا ٱلَّذِينَ ءَامَنُوٓاْ أَطِيعُواْ ٱللَّهَ
وَأَطِيعُواْ ٱلرَّسُولَ وَأُوْلِي ٱلۡأَمۡرِ مِنكُمۡۖ
فَإِن تَنَٰزَعۡتُمۡ فِي شَيۡءٖ فَرُدُّوهُ إِلَى ٱللَّهِ وَٱلرَّسُولِ
إِن كُنتُمۡ تُؤۡمِنُونَ بِٱللَّهِ وَٱلۡيَوۡمِ ٱلۡأٓخِرِۚ
ذَٰلِكَ خَيۡرٞ وَأَحۡسَنُ تَأۡوِيلًا

SECTION 9.

60. Hast thou not turned
Thy vision to those[581]
Who declare that they believe
In the revelations
That have come to thee
And to those before thee?
Their (real) wish is
To resort together for judgement
(In their disputes)
To the Evil One,
Though they were ordered
To reject him.
But Satan's wish

٦٠ أَلَمۡ تَرَ إِلَى ٱلَّذِينَ
يَزۡعُمُونَ أَنَّهُمۡ ءَامَنُواْ بِمَآ
أُنزِلَ إِلَيۡكَ وَمَآ أُنزِلَ مِن قَبۡلِكَ
يُرِيدُونَ أَن يَتَحَاكَمُوٓاْ إِلَى ٱلطَّٰغُوتِ
وَقَدۡ أُمِرُوٓاْ أَن يَكۡفُرُواْ بِهِۦ
وَيُرِيدُ ٱلشَّيۡطَٰنُ

580. *Ūlī al amr* = those charged with authority or responsibility or decision, or the settlement of affairs. All ultimate authority rests in Allah. Prophets of Allah derive their authority from Him. As Islam makes no sharp division between sacred and secular affairs, it expects governments to be imbued with righteousness. Likewise Islam expects Muslims to respect the authority of such government for otherwise there can be no order or discipline. (R).

581. The immediate reference was to the hypocrites (*Munāfiqīn*) of Madīnah, but the words are general, and the evil of hypocrisy has to be dealt with in all ages. This type of man is what is called Mr. Facing-both-ways in Bunyan's "Pilgrim's Progress." Such men declare that they are always with the Right, but calmly intrigue with evil and injustice, and even make injustice their judge if their personal interests are served in that way.

Is to lead them astray
Far away (from the Right).

أَن يُضِلَّهُمْ ضَلَٰلًۢا بَعِيدًا

61. When it is said to them:
"Come to what Allah hath revealed,
And to the Messenger":
Thou seest the Hypocrites avert
Their faces from thee in disgust.

٦١ وَإِذَا قِيلَ لَهُمْ تَعَالَوْا۟ إِلَىٰ مَآ أَنزَلَ
ٱللَّهُ وَإِلَى ٱلرَّسُولِ رَأَيْتَ ٱلْمُنَٰفِقِينَ
يَصُدُّونَ عَنكَ صُدُودًا

62. How then, when they are
Seized by misfortune,
Because of the deeds
Which their hands have sent forth?
Then they come to thee,
Swearing by Allah:
"We meant no more
Than goodwill and conciliation!"

٦٢ فَكَيْفَ إِذَآ أَصَٰبَتْهُم مُّصِيبَةٌۢ بِمَا
قَدَّمَتْ أَيْدِيهِمْ ثُمَّ جَآءُوكَ يَحْلِفُونَ بِٱللَّهِ
إِنْ أَرَدْنَآ إِلَّآ إِحْسَٰنًا وَتَوْفِيقًا

63. Those men—Allah knows
What is in their hearts;
So keep clear of them,[582]
But admonish them,
And speak to them a word
To reach their very souls.

٦٣ أُو۟لَٰٓئِكَ ٱلَّذِينَ يَعْلَمُ ٱللَّهُ مَا
فِى قُلُوبِهِمْ فَأَعْرِضْ عَنْهُمْ وَعِظْهُمْ
وَقُل لَّهُمْ فِىٓ أَنفُسِهِمْ قَوْلًۢا بَلِيغًا

64. We sent not a Messenger,
But to be obeyed, in accordance
With the Will of Allah.
If they had only,
When they were unjust
To themselves,
Come unto thee
And asked Allah's forgiveness,
And the Messenger had asked
Forgiveness for them,
They would have found
Allah indeed Oft-Returning,
Most Merciful.

٦٤ وَمَآ أَرْسَلْنَا مِن رَّسُولٍ
إِلَّا لِيُطَاعَ بِإِذْنِ ٱللَّهِ
وَلَوْ أَنَّهُمْ إِذ ظَّلَمُوٓا۟ أَنفُسَهُمْ جَآءُوكَ
فَٱسْتَغْفَرُوا۟ ٱللَّهَ وَٱسْتَغْفَرَ لَهُمُ ٱلرَّسُولُ
لَوَجَدُوا۟ ٱللَّهَ تَوَّابًا رَّحِيمًا

65. But no, by the Lord,
They can have
No (real) Faith,

٦٥ فَلَا وَرَبِّكَ لَا يُؤْمِنُونَ

582. How should hypocrites be treated? To take them into your confidence would of course be foolish. To wage unrelenting war against them may destroy the hope of reforming them and purging them of their hypocrisy. The Prophet of Allah keeps clear of their wiles, but at the same time, does not hesitate to show them the error of their ways, nor to put in a word in season, to penetrate their hearts and win them back to Allah.

Until they make thee judge
In all disputes between them,
And find in their souls
No resistance against
Thy decisions, but accept
Them with the fullest
conviction.[583]

حَتَّىٰ يُحَكِّمُوكَ فِيمَا شَجَرَ بَيْنَهُمْ
ثُمَّ لَا يَجِدُوا فِي أَنفُسِهِمْ حَرَجًا
مِّمَّا قَضَيْتَ وَيُسَلِّمُوا تَسْلِيمًا

66. If We had ordered them
To sacrifice their lives
Or to leave their homes,
Very few of them
Would have done it:[584]
But if they had done
What they were (actually) told,
It would have been best
For them, and would have gone
Farthest to strengthen their (faith);

٦٦ وَلَوْ أَنَّا كَتَبْنَا عَلَيْهِمْ أَنِ اقْتُلُوا
أَنفُسَكُمْ أَوِ اخْرُجُوا مِن دِيَارِكُم مَّا فَعَلُوهُ
إِلَّا قَلِيلٌ مِّنْهُمْ ۖ وَلَوْ أَنَّهُمْ فَعَلُوا مَا يُوعَظُونَ بِهِ
لَكَانَ خَيْرًا لَّهُمْ وَأَشَدَّ تَثْبِيتًا

67. And We should then have
Given them from Our Presence
A great reward;

٦٧ وَإِذًا لَّآتَيْنَاهُم مِّن لَّدُنَّا أَجْرًا عَظِيمًا

68. And We should have
Shown them the Straight Way.[585]

٦٨ وَلَهَدَيْنَاهُمْ صِرَاطًا مُّسْتَقِيمًا

69. All who obey Allah
And the Messenger
Are in the Company
Of those on whom
Is the Grace of Allah—
Of the Prophets (who teach),
The Sincere (lovers of Truth),
The Witnesses (who testify),

٦٩ وَمَن يُطِعِ اللَّهَ وَالرَّسُولَ
فَأُولَٰئِكَ مَعَ الَّذِينَ أَنْعَمَ اللَّهُ عَلَيْهِم
مِّنَ النَّبِيِّينَ وَالصِّدِّيقِينَ
وَالشُّهَدَاءِ

583. The test of true Faith is not mere lip profession, but bringing all our doubts and disputes to the one in whom we profess faith. Further, when a decision is given we are not only to accept it, but find in our inmost souls no difficulty and no resistance, but on the contrary a joyful acceptance springing from the conviction of our own faith.

584. The highest in faith willingly sacrifice their lives, their homes, and all that they hold dearest, in the cause of Allah. Those whose faith is not so strong are expected at least to do what a loyal member of any society does, submit his doubts and disputes to the head of the society and cheerfully accept his decision and submit to it. The contrast is between the hypocrites who will not even do this, and the really devoted men and women who would voluntarily sacrifice their lives.

585. Four advantages of obedience to Allah are mentioned, in the order in which they will appeal to the beginner in faith: (1) his own benefit ("best for them"); (2) strengthening of his faith, as he becomes more and more at home in the spiritual world; (3) reward from Allah's own Presence, such intense conviction that no further arguments are needed; (4) the Straight Way, in which there is no doubt or difficulty whatever in our practical conduct.

And the Righteous (who do good):
Ah! what a beautiful Fellowship![586]

وَٱلصَّٰلِحِينَ وَحَسُنَ أُو۟لَٰٓئِكَ رَفِيقًا

70. Such is the Bounty
From Allah; and sufficient
Is it that Allah knoweth all.[587]

٧٠ ذَٰلِكَ ٱلْفَضْلُ مِنَ ٱللَّهِ ۚ وَكَفَىٰ بِٱللَّهِ عَلِيمًا

C. 64. — Keep together in your noble Brotherhood:
(4:71-91.) Share its joys and sorrows: strive
And fight the good fight and never fear:
For this life is short, and the Hereafter
Eternal. Allow not yourselves to be drawn
Into unbelief and cowardice:
Maintain the Right. Protect yourselves
Against Hypocrites and Deserters,
But pursue them not unrelentingly.

SECTION 10.

71. O ye who believe!
Take your precautions,
And either go forth in parties
Or go forth all together.[588]

٧١ يَٰٓأَيُّهَا ٱلَّذِينَ ءَامَنُوا۟ خُذُوا۟ حِذْرَكُمْ فَٱنفِرُوا۟ ثُبَاتٍ أَوِ ٱنفِرُوا۟ جَمِيعًا

72. There are certainly among you
Men who would tarry behind;[589]

٧٢ وَإِنَّ مِنكُمْ لَمَن لَّيُبَطِّئَنَّ

586. A passage of the deepest spiritual meaning. Even the humblest man who accepts Faith and does good becomes at once an accepted member of a great and beautiful spiritual Fellowship. It is a company which lives perpetually in the sunshine of Allah's Grace. (This passage partly illustrates Q. 1:5). It is a glorious hierarchy, of which four grades are specified: (1) The highest is that of the Prophets or Apostles, who get plenary inspiration from Allah, and who teach mankind by example and precept. That rank in Islam is held by Muḥammad Muṣṭafā. (2) The next are those whose badge is sincerity and truth; they love and support the truth with their person, their means, their influence, and all that is theirs. That rank was held by the special companions of Muḥammad, among whom the type was that of Abū Bakr Ṣiddiq. (3) The next are the noble army of Witnesses, who testify to the truth. The testimony may be by martyrdom. Or it may be by the tongue of the true preacher or the pen of the devoted scholar, or the life of the man devoted to service. (4) Lastly, there is the large company of righteous people, the ordinary folk who do their ordinary business, but always in a righteous way. They are the rank and file of the beautiful Fellowship, in which each has his place and yet all feel that they derive glory from the common association. (R).

587. If a generous General gives the private soldier the privilege of sitting with his comrades and officers, high and low, in one common Brotherhood, people may perhaps wonder: how may this be? If we are admitted to that Fellowship, we want to know no more. It is enough to us that Allah knows our humility and our unworthiness, and with His full knowledge admits us to that glorious Fellowship!

588. No fight should be undertaken without due preparations and precautions. When these are taken, we must go boldly forward. "Go forth" is therefore repeated for emphasis. But we must go forth in a collective spirit—either in small parties or all together, as our Leader determines. We must not tarry like the doubter in the next two verses.

589. The doubter detaches himself in thought and action from the community. If the general body has a reverse, he blesses Allah that he was not among them, instead of being ashamed of himself for desertion. If the general body wins a success, he does not rejoice from the common cause, but only regrets for himself that he was not here to share in the glory and the gains!

If a misfortune befalls you,
They say: "Allah did favour us
In that we were not
Present among them."

فَإِنْ أَصَٰبَتْكُم مُّصِيبَةٌ قَالَ قَدْ أَنْعَمَ ٱللَّهُ عَلَىَّ
إِذْ لَمْ أَكُن مَّعَهُمْ شَهِيدًا

73. But if good fortune comes to you
From Allah, they would be sure
To say—as if there had never been
Ties of affection between you and them—
"Oh! I wish I had been with them;
A fine thing should I then
Have made of it!"[590]

٧٣ وَلَئِنْ أَصَٰبَكُمْ فَضْلٌ
مِّنَ ٱللَّهِ لَيَقُولَنَّ كَأَن لَّمْ تَكُنۢ
بَيْنَكُمْ وَبَيْنَهُۥ مَوَدَّةٌ
يَٰلَيْتَنِى كُنتُ مَعَهُمْ
فَأَفُوزَ فَوْزًا عَظِيمًا

74. Let those fight
In the cause of Allah
Who sell the life of this world
For the Hereafter.[591]
To him who fighteth
In the cause of Allah—
Whether he is slain
Or gets victory—
Soon shall We give him
A reward of great (value).

٧٤ فَلْيُقَٰتِلْ فِى سَبِيلِ ٱللَّهِ ٱلَّذِينَ
يَشْرُونَ ٱلْحَيَوٰةَ ٱلدُّنْيَا بِٱلْءَاخِرَةِ
وَمَن يُقَٰتِلْ فِى سَبِيلِ ٱللَّهِ فَيُقْتَلْ
أَوْ يَغْلِبْ فَسَوْفَ نُؤْتِيهِ أَجْرًا عَظِيمًا

75. And why should ye not
Fight in the cause of Allah
And of those who, being weak,[592]
Are ill-treated (and oppressed)?—
Men, women, and children,
Whose cry is: "Our Lord!
Rescue us from this town,
Whose people are oppressors;
And raise for us from Thee
One who will protect;

٧٥ وَمَا لَكُمْ لَا تُقَٰتِلُونَ فِى سَبِيلِ ٱللَّهِ
وَٱلْمُسْتَضْعَفِينَ مِنَ ٱلرِّجَالِ
وَٱلنِّسَآءِ وَٱلْوِلْدَٰنِ ٱلَّذِينَ يَقُولُونَ
رَبَّنَآ أَخْرِجْنَا مِنْ هَٰذِهِ ٱلْقَرْيَةِ ٱلظَّالِمِ أَهْلُهَا
وَٱجْعَل لَّنَا مِن لَّدُنكَ وَلِيًّا

---

590. Just a selfish man's thought. Such men are far from being a source of strength to their community. They are no use in a fight, and the next verse by implication discards them.

591. It is not everyone—least of all, poltroons and fainthearted persons—who is fit to fight in the cause of Allah. To do so is a privilege, and those who understand the privilege are prepared to sacrifice all their interests in this life, and this life itself; for they know that it is the sacrifice of something fleeting and of little value, for the sake of something everlasting, and of immense value. Whether (in appearance) they win or lose, in reality they win the prize for which they are fighting—*viz.*, honour and glory in the sight of Allah. Note that the only alternatives here are death or victory! The true fighter knows no defeat.

592. *Mustadh'af*=one reckoned weak, and therefore ill-treated and oppressed. *Cf.* 4:98, and 7:150.

And raise for us from Thee
One who will help!"[593]

وَاجْعَل لَّنَا مِن لَّدُنكَ نَصِيرًا

76. Those who believe
Fight in the cause of Allah,
And those who reject Faith
Fight in the cause of Evil:
So fight ye against the
Friends[594] of Satan: feeble indeed
Is the cunning of Satan.

٧٦ الَّذِينَ آمَنُوا يُقَاتِلُونَ فِي سَبِيلِ اللَّهِ وَالَّذِينَ
كَفَرُوا يُقَاتِلُونَ فِي سَبِيلِ الطَّاغُوتِ فَقَاتِلُوا
أَوْلِيَاءَ الشَّيْطَانِ إِنَّ كَيْدَ الشَّيْطَانِ كَانَ ضَعِيفًا

SECTION 11.

77. Hast thou not turned
Thy vision to those
Who were told to hold back[595]
Their hands (from fight)
But establish regular prayers
And spend in regular Charity?
When (at length) the order
For fighting was issued to them,
Behold! a section of them
Feared men as—
Or even more than—
They should have feared Allah:
They said: "Our Lord!
Why hast Thou ordered us
To fight? Wouldst Thou not
Grant us respite
To our (natural) term,[596]

٧٧ أَلَمْ تَرَ إِلَى الَّذِينَ
قِيلَ لَهُمْ كُفُّوا أَيْدِيَكُمْ
وَأَقِيمُوا الصَّلَاةَ وَآتُوا الزَّكَاةَ
فَلَمَّا كُتِبَ عَلَيْهِمُ الْقِتَالُ إِذَا فَرِيقٌ مِّنْهُمْ
يَخْشَوْنَ النَّاسَ كَخَشْيَةِ اللَّهِ أَوْ أَشَدَّ خَشْيَةً
وَقَالُوا رَبَّنَا لِمَ كَتَبْتَ عَلَيْنَا الْقِتَالَ
لَوْلَا أَخَّرْتَنَا إِلَىٰ أَجَلٍ

593. Even from the human point of view the cause of Allah is the cause of justice, the cause of the oppressed. In the great persecution, before Makkah was won again, what sorrows, threats, tortures, and oppressions, were suffered by those whose faith was unshaken? Muḥammad's life and that of his adherents was threatened: they were mocked, assaulted, insulted and beaten; those within the power of the enemy were put into chains and cast into prison; others were boycotted, and shut out of trade, business, and social intercourse; they could not even buy the food they wanted, or perform their religious duties. The persecution was redoubled for the believing slaves, women, and children after the Hijrah. Their cry for a protector and helper from Allah was answered when Muḥammad, the Chosen One, brought freedom and peace to Makkah again.

594. *Awliyā* plural of *walī*, friend, supporter, protector, patron: from the same root as *mawlā*, for which see 4:33,n. 543.

595. Before the command for fighting was issued there were some who were impatient, and could scarcely be held back. They wanted fighting from human motives—pugnacity, the love of plunder, hatred against their enemies, the gaining of personal ends. Fighting from such motives is wrong at all times. When the testing time came, and they had to fight, not for their own land, but for a Sacred Cause, in which there was much suffering and little personal gain, the hypocrites held back and were afraid.

596. "Our natural term of life," they would say, "is short enough: why should we jeopardize it by fighting in which there is no personal gain?" The answer is begun in this verse and continued in the next.

Briefly, the answer is: (1) in any case the pleasures of this world are short: this life is fleeting; the first thing for a righteous man to do is to emancipate himself from its obsessions; (2) to do your duty is to do right; therefore turn your attention mainly to duty; (3) when duty calls for self-sacrifice, be sure that Allah's call is never unjust, and never such as to exceed your capacity; and (4) if you fear death, you will not by fear escape death; it will find you out wherever you are; why not face it boldly when duty calls?

Near (enough)?" Say: "Short
Is the enjoyment of this world:
The Hereafter is the best
For those who do right;
Never will ye be
Dealt with unjustly
In the very least!

قَرِيبٍ قُلْ مَتَٰعُ ٱلدُّنْيَا قَلِيلٌ
وَٱلْءَاخِرَةُ خَيْرٌ لِّمَنِ ٱتَّقَىٰ
وَلَا تُظْلَمُونَ فَتِيلًا

78. "Wherever ye are,
Death will find you out,
Even if ye are in towers
Built up strong and high!"

If some good befalls them,
They say, "This is from Allah";
But if evil, they say,
"This is from thee" (O Prophet).[597]
Say: "All things are from Allah."
But what hath come
To these people,
That they fail
To understand
A single fact?

٧٨ أَيْنَمَا تَكُونُوا۟ يُدْرِككُّمُ
ٱلْمَوْتُ وَلَوْ كُنتُمْ فِى بُرُوجٍ مُّشَيَّدَةٍ
وَإِن تُصِبْهُمْ حَسَنَةٌ يَقُولُوا۟ هَٰذِهِۦ مِنْ عِندِ ٱللَّهِ
وَإِن تُصِبْهُمْ سَيِّئَةٌ يَقُولُوا۟ هَٰذِهِۦ مِنْ عِندِكَ
قُلْ كُلٌّ مِّنْ عِندِ ٱللَّهِ فَمَالِ هَٰٓؤُلَآءِ ٱلْقَوْمِ
لَا يَكَادُونَ يَفْقَهُونَ حَدِيثًا

79. Whatever good, (O man!)
Happens to thee, is from Allah;
But whatever evil happens
To thee, is from thy (own) soul.
And We have sent thee
As a Messenger[598]
To (instruct) mankind.
And enough is Allah
For a witness.

٧٩ مَّآ أَصَابَكَ مِنْ حَسَنَةٍ فَمِنَ ٱللَّهِ
وَمَآ أَصَابَكَ مِن سَيِّئَةٍ فَمِن نَّفْسِكَ
وَأَرْسَلْنَٰكَ لِلنَّاسِ رَسُولًا
وَكَفَىٰ بِٱللَّهِ شَهِيدًا

80. He who obeys
The Messenger, obeys Allah;

٨٠ مَّن يُطِعِ ٱلرَّسُولَ فَقَدْ أَطَاعَ ٱللَّهَ

597. The Hypocrites were inconsistent, and in this reflect unregenerate mankind. If a disaster happens, due to their own folly, they blame somebody else; but if they are fortunate, they claim reflected credit by pretending that Heaven has favoured them because of their own superior merits. The modern critic discards even this pretence, eliminates Heaven altogether, and claims all credit direct to himself, unless he brings in blind chance, but that he does mostly to "explain" misfortune. If we look to the Ultimate Cause of all things, all things come from Allah. But if we look to the proximate cause of things, our own merit is so small, that we can hardly claim credit for good ourselves with any fairness. In Allah's hand is all good: 3:26. On the other hand, the proximate cause of our evil is due to some wrong in our own inner selves; for never are we dealt with unjustly in the very least: 4:77.

598. To blame a man of God for our misfortunes is doubly unjust. For he comes to save us from misfortune, and it is because we flout him or pay no heed to him, that our own rebellion, brings its own punishment. If we realise this truth we shall be saved from two sins: (1) the sin of injustice to Allah's Messengers, who come for our good, and not for our harm; (2) the sin of not realising our own shortcomings or rebellion, and thus living in spiritual darkness. If the message is from Allah, that carries its own authority: "enough is Allah for a witness."

But if any turn away,
We have not sent thee
To watch over
Their (evil deeds).[599]

وَمَن تَوَلَّىٰ فَمَآ أَرْسَلْنَٰكَ عَلَيْهِمْ حَفِيظًا

81. They have "Obedience"
On their lips; but
When they leave thee,
A section of them
Meditate all night
On things very different
From what thou tellest them.
But Allah records
Their nightly (plots):
So keep clear of them,
And put thy trust in Allah,
And enough is Allah
As a disposer of affairs.[600]

(٨١) وَيَقُولُونَ طَاعَةٌ فَإِذَا بَرَزُوا۟ مِنْ عِندِكَ بَيَّتَ طَآئِفَةٌ مِّنْهُمْ غَيْرَ ٱلَّذِى تَقُولُ ۖ وَٱللَّهُ يَكْتُبُ مَا يُبَيِّتُونَ ۖ فَأَعْرِضْ عَنْهُمْ وَتَوَكَّلْ عَلَى ٱللَّهِ ۚ وَكَفَىٰ بِٱللَّهِ وَكِيلًا

82. Do they not consider
The Qur'ān (with care)?
Had it been from other
Than Allah, they would surely
Have found therein
Much discrepancy.[601]

(٨٢) أَفَلَا يَتَدَبَّرُونَ ٱلْقُرْءَانَ ۚ وَلَوْ كَانَ مِنْ عِندِ غَيْرِ ٱللَّهِ لَوَجَدُوا۟ فِيهِ ٱخْتِلَٰفًا كَثِيرًا

83. When there comes to them
Some matter touching
(Public) safety or fear,
They divulge it.
If they had only referred it
To the Messenger or to those

(٨٣) وَإِذَا جَآءَهُمْ أَمْرٌ مِّنَ ٱلْأَمْنِ أَوِ ٱلْخَوْفِ أَذَاعُوا۟ بِهِۦ ۖ وَلَوْ رَدُّوهُ إِلَى ٱلرَّسُولِ وَإِلَىٰٓ

599. The Messenger was sent to preach, guide, instruct, and show the Way—not to drive people to good. That is not Allah's Plan, which trains the human will. The Messenger's duty is therefore to convey the Message of Allah, in all the ways of persuasion that are open to him. If men perversely disobey that Message, they are not disobeying him but they are disobeying Allah. In the same way those who obey the Message are obeying Allah. They are not obliging the Messenger; they are merely doing their duty.

600. If we trust people who are not true, they are more likely to hinder than to help. But Allah is All-Good as well as All-Powerful, and all our affairs are best entrusted to His care. He is the best Guardian of all interests.

Therefore we should not trust the lip professions of hypocrites, but trust in Allah. Nor should our confidence in Allah be shaken by any secret plots that enemies hatch against us. We should take all human precautions against them, but having done so, we should put our trust in Allah, Who knows the inner working of events better than any human mind can conceive.

601. The unity of the Qur'ān is admittedly greater than that of any other sacred book. And yet how can we account for it except through the unity of Allah's purpose and design? From a mere human point of view, we should have expected much discrepancy, because (1) the Messenger who promulgated it was not a learned man or philosopher, (2) it was promulgated at various times and in various circumstances, and (3) it is addressed to all grades of mankind. Yet, when properly understood, its various pieces fit together better than a jig-saw puzzle even when arranged without any regard to chronological order. There was just the One Inspirer and the One Inspired.

Charged with authority
Among them, the proper
Investigators would have
Tested it from them (direct).
Were it not for the Grace
And Mercy of Allah unto you,
All but a few of you
Would have followed Satan.[602]

أُوْلِي ٱلْأَمْرِ مِنْهُمْ لَعَلِمَهُ ٱلَّذِينَ يَسْتَنۢبِطُونَهُۥ
مِنْهُمْ ۗ وَلَوْلَا فَضْلُ ٱللَّهِ عَلَيْكُمْ وَرَحْمَتُهُۥ
لَٱتَّبَعْتُمُ ٱلشَّيْطَٰنَ إِلَّا قَلِيلًا

84. Then fight in Allah's cause—
Thou art held responsible
Only for thyself—
And rouse the Believers.
It may be that Allah
Will restrain the fury
Of the Unbelievers;
For Allah is the strongest
In might and in punishment.[603]

٨٤ فَقَٰتِلْ فِي سَبِيلِ ٱللَّهِ
لَا تُكَلَّفُ إِلَّا نَفْسَكَ ۚ وَحَرِّضِ ٱلْمُؤْمِنِينَ ۖ
عَسَى ٱللَّهُ أَن يَكُفَّ بَأْسَ ٱلَّذِينَ كَفَرُوا۟ ۚ
وَٱللَّهُ أَشَدُّ بَأْسًا وَأَشَدُّ تَنكِيلًا

85. Whoever recommends
And helps a good cause
Becomes a partner therein:
And whoever recommends
And helps an evil cause,
Shares in its burden:
And Allah hath power[604]
Over all things.

٨٥ مَّن يَشْفَعْ شَفَٰعَةً حَسَنَةً يَكُن لَّهُۥ
نَصِيبٌ مِّنْهَا ۖ وَمَن يَشْفَعْ شَفَٰعَةً سَيِّئَةً يَكُن
لَّهُۥ كِفْلٌ مِّنْهَا ۗ وَكَانَ ٱللَّهُ عَلَىٰ كُلِّ شَيْءٍ مُّقِيتًا

86. When a (courteous) greeting
Is offered you, meet it
With a greeting still more
Courteous, or (at least)

٨٦ وَإِذَا حُيِّيتُم بِتَحِيَّةٍ فَحَيُّوا۟
بِأَحْسَنَ مِنْهَآ أَوْ

602. In times of war or public panic, thoughtless repetition of gossip is rightly restrained by all effective States. If false, such news may cause needless alarm: if true, it may frighten the timid and cause some misgiving even to the bravest, because the counterpart of it—the preparations made to meet the danger—is not known. Thoughtless news, true or false, may also encourage the enemy. The proper course is quietly to hand all news direct to those who are in a position to investigate it. They can then sift it and take suitable measures to checkmate the enemy. Not to do so, but to deal with news either thoughtlessly or maliciously, is to fall directly into the snares of Evil.

603. The courage of Muḥammad was as notable as his wisdom, his gentleness, and his trust in Allah. Facing fearful odds, he often stood alone, and took the whole responsibility on himself. But his example and visible trust in Allah inspired and roused the Muslims, and also—speaking purely from a human point of view—restrained the fury of his enemies. When we consider that he was Allah's inspired Messenger to carry out His Plan, we can see that nothing can resist that Plan. If the enemy happens to have strength, power, or resources, Allah's strength, power, and resources are infinitely greater. If the enemy is meditating punishment on the righteous for their righteousness, Allah's punishment for such wickedness will be infinitely greater and more effective.

604. In this fleeting world's chances, Allah's providence and justice may not always appear plain to our eyes. But we are asked to believe that if we help and support a good cause, we share in all its credit and in its eventual victory. And conversely, we cannot support a bad cause without sharing in all its evil consequences. If appearances seem against this faith, let us not be deceived by appearances. For Allah has power over all things.

Of equal courtesy.
Allah takes careful account[605]
Of all things.

رُدُّوهَآ إِنَّ ٱللَّهَ كَانَ عَلَىٰ كُلِّ شَىْءٍ حَسِيبًا

87. Allah! There is no god
But He: of a surety
He will gather you together
Against the Day of Judgement,
About which there is no doubt.
And whose word can be
Truer than Allah's?

(٨٧) ٱللَّهُ لَآ إِلَٰهَ إِلَّا هُوَ ۚ
لَيَجْمَعَنَّكُمْ إِلَىٰ يَوْمِ ٱلْقِيَٰمَةِ لَا رَيْبَ فِيهِ ۗ
وَمَنْ أَصْدَقُ مِنَ ٱللَّهِ حَدِيثًا

SECTION 12.

88. Why should ye be
Divided into two parties
About the Hypocrites?[606]
Allah hath upset them
For their (evil) deeds.
Would ye guide those
Whom Allah hath thrown
Out of the Way? For those
Whom Allah hath thrown
Out of the Way, never
Shalt thou find the Way.

(٨٨) فَمَا لَكُمْ فِى ٱلْمُنَٰفِقِينَ فِئَتَيْنِ
وَٱللَّهُ أَرْكَسَهُم بِمَا كَسَبُوٓا۟ ۚ
أَتُرِيدُونَ أَن تَهْدُوا۟ مَنْ
أَضَلَّ ٱللَّهُ ۖ وَمَن يُضْلِلِ ٱللَّهُ
فَلَن تَجِدَ لَهُۥ سَبِيلًا

89. They but wish that ye
Should reject Faith,
As they do, and thus be
On the same footing (as they):
So take not friends
From their ranks

(٨٩) وَدُّوا۟ لَوْ تَكْفُرُونَ
كَمَا كَفَرُوا۟ فَتَكُونُونَ سَوَآءً ۖ
فَلَا تَتَّخِذُوا۟ مِنْهُمْ أَوْلِيَآءَ

605. The necessary correlative to the command to fight in a good cause is the command to cultivate sweetness and cordiality in our manners at all times. For fighting is an exceptional necessity while the sweetness of daily human intercourse is a normal need. Further, we give kindness and courtesy without asking, and return it if possible in even better terms than we recieved, or at least in equally courteous terms. For we are all creatures of One God, and shall be brought together before Him.

606. When the desertion of the hypocrites at Uḥud nearly caused a disaster to the Muslim cause there was great feeling among the Muslims of Madīnah against them. One party wanted to put them to the sword: another to leave them alone. The actual policy pursued avoided both extremes, and was determined by these verses. It was clear that they were a danger to the Muslim community if they were admitted into its counsels, and in any case they were a source of demoralisation. But while every caution was used, no extreme measures were taken against them. On the contrary, they were given a chance of making good. If they made a sacrifice for the cause ("flee from what is forbidden," see next verse), their conduct purged their previous cowardice, and their sincerity entitled them to be taken back. But if they deserted the Muslim community again, they were treated as enemies, with the additional penalty of desertion which is enforced by all nations actually at war. Even so, a humane exception was made in the two cases specified in 4:90.

Until they flee[607]
In the way of Allah
(From what is forbidden).
But if they turn renegades,
Seize them and slay them
Wherever ye find them;
And (in any case) take
No friends or helpers
From their ranks—

90. Except those who join
A group between whom
And you there is a treaty[608]
(Of peace), or those who
approach[609]
You with hearts restraining
Them from fighting you
As well as fighting their own
People. If Allah had pleased,
He could have given them
Power over you, and they
Would have fought you:
Therefore if they withdraw
From you but fight you not,
And (instead) send you
(Guarantees of) peace, then Allah

حَتَّىٰ يُهَاجِرُوا فِي سَبِيلِ اللَّهِ
فَإِن تَوَلَّوْا فَخُذُوهُمْ وَاقْتُلُوهُمْ
حَيْثُ وَجَدتُّمُوهُمْ وَلَا تَتَّخِذُوا
مِنْهُمْ وَلِيًّا وَلَا نَصِيرًا
٩٠ إِلَّا الَّذِينَ يَصِلُونَ إِلَىٰ قَوْمٍ
بَيْنَكُمْ وَبَيْنَهُم مِّيثَاقٌ أَوْ جَاءُوكُمْ
حَصِرَتْ صُدُورُهُمْ أَن يُقَاتِلُوكُمْ
أَوْ يُقَاتِلُوا قَوْمَهُمْ وَلَوْ شَاءَ اللَّهُ
لَسَلَّطَهُمْ عَلَيْكُمْ فَلَقَاتَلُوكُمْ
فَإِنِ اعْتَزَلُوكُمْ فَلَمْ يُقَاتِلُوكُمْ
وَأَلْقَوْا إِلَيْكُمُ السَّلَمَ فَمَا جَعَلَ اللَّهُ

607. *Flee*: the verbal form from which the noun *hijrah* is derived. Bukhārī interprets this rightly as fleeing from all that is forbidden. This would include *hijrah* in the technical sense of leaving a place in which the practice of religion is not allowed. But it is more general. In time of war, if a man is willing to submit to discipline and refrains from infringing orders issued, he has proved his fidelity and may be treated as a member of the community at war.

On the other hand, if he by false pretences comes into the inner counsels merely to betray them, he may rightly be treated as a traitor or deserter and be punished for his treason or desertion; or if he escapes, he can be treated as an enemy and is entitled to no mercy. He is worse than an enemy; he has claimed to be one of you in order to spy on you, and been all the time helping the enemy.

608. *Except*: the exception refers to "seize them and slay them", the death penalty for repeated desertion. Even after such desertion, exemption is granted in two cases. One is where the deserter took asylum with a tribe with whom there was a treaty of peace and amity. Presumably such a tribe (even though outside the pale of Islam) might be trusted to keep the man from fighting against the forces of Islam—in the modern phrase, to disarm him and render him harmless. The second case for exemption is where the man from his own heart desires never to take up arms against Islam, though he does not wish to join the forces of Islam, to fight against a hostile tribe (perhaps his own) fighting against Islam. But he must make a real approach, giving guarantees of his sincerity. In the modern phrase he would be "on parole". But this provision is much milder than that in modern military codes, which grant the privilege only to enemy prisoners, not to those who have deserted from the army granting them parole. The hypocrites were in that position, but humanity as well as policy treated them with great leniency.

609. *Approach* or come: refers not to the physical act of coming, but to the mental attitude; the heart is mentioned for sincerity. When they sincerely promise not to fight against you, do not pursue them. Remember that if they had fought against you, your difficulties would have been increased. Their neutrality itself may be a great advantage to you. So long as you are satisfied that they are sincere and their acts support their declarations of peace with you, you should not consider yourself justified in pursuing them and warring against them.

Hath opened no way
For you (to war against them).

لَكُمْ عَلَيْهِمْ سَبِيلًا

91. Others you will find
That wish to gain
Your confidence as well
As that of their people:
Every time they are sent back[610]
To temptation, they succumb
Thereto; if they withdraw not
From you nor give you
(guarantees)
Of peace besides
Restraining their hands,
Seize them and slay them
Wherever ye get them;
In their case
We have provided you
With a clear argument
Against them.

سَتَجِدُونَ ءَاخَرِينَ ﴿٩١﴾
يُرِيدُونَ أَن يَأْمَنُوكُمْ وَيَأْمَنُواْ قَوْمَهُمْ
كُلَّ مَا رُدُّوٓاْ إِلَى ٱلْفِتْنَةِ أُرْكِسُواْ فِيهَا
فَإِن لَّمْ يَعْتَزِلُوكُمْ وَيُلْقُوٓاْ إِلَيْكُمُ ٱلسَّلَمَ
وَيَكُفُّوٓاْ أَيْدِيَهُمْ فَخُذُوهُمْ
وَٱقْتُلُوهُمْ حَيْثُ ثَقِفْتُمُوهُمْ
وَأُوْلَٰٓئِكُمْ جَعَلْنَا لَكُمْ عَلَيْهِمْ
سُلْطَٰنًا مُّبِينًا

C. 65.—The lives of those who believe
(4:92-104.) Are sacred; if one is slain
By mistake, full compensation
Should be made. Nor should
A stranger, even in time of war,
Be treated as an enemy, without
The fullest investigation. Live not
In places hostile to Islam,
If ye are able to migrate—
And spacious is Allah's earth.
Devotion and prayer may be
Shortened in times of danger.
Take every precaution for safety,
But be bold and undaunted in fight.

SECTION 13.

92. Never should a Believer
Kill a Believer; but

وَمَا كَانَ لِمُؤْمِنٍ أَن يَقْتُلَ مُؤْمِنًا إِلَّا ﴿٩٢﴾

610. As opposed to the two classes of deserters to whom clemency may be shown, there is a class which is treacherous and dangerous and cannot be left alone. They try to win your confidence, and are all the time in the confidence of the enemy. Every time they get a chance, they succumb to the temptation of double-dealing. The best way of dealing with them is to treat them as open enemies. Keep them not in your midst. If they give you guarantees of peace and do not actually fight against you, well and good. If not, they are deserters actively fighting in the ranks of the enemy. They have openly given you proof, and you can fairly seize and slay them in war as deserters and enemies.

(If it so happens) by mistake,[611]
(Compensation is due);
If one (so) kills a Believer,
It is ordained that he
Should free a believing slave,
And pay compensation
To the deceased's family,
Unless they remit it freely.
If the deceased belonged
To a people at war with you,
And he was a Believer,
The freeing of a believing slave
(Is enough). If he belonged
To a people with whom
Ye have a treaty of mutual
Alliance, compensation should
Be paid to his family,
And a believing slave be freed.
For those who find this
Beyond their means, (is prescribed)
A fast for two months
Running: by way of repentance
To Allah; for Allah hath
All knowledge and all wisdom.

93. If a man kills a Believer
Intentionally, his recompense[612]
Is Hell, to abide therein
(Forever): and the wrath
And the curse of Allah

خَطَـًٔا
وَمَن قَتَلَ مُؤْمِنًا خَطَـًٔا فَتَحْرِيرُ رَقَبَةٍ
مُّؤْمِنَةٍ وَدِيَةٌ مُّسَلَّمَةٌ إِلَىٰٓ أَهْلِهِۦٓ إِلَّآ أَن
يَصَّدَّقُوا۟ ۚ فَإِن كَانَ مِن قَوْمٍ عَدُوٍّ لَّكُمْ
وَهُوَ مُؤْمِنٌ فَتَحْرِيرُ رَقَبَةٍ مُّؤْمِنَةٍ ۖ
وَإِن كَانَ مِن قَوْمٍۭ بَيْنَكُمْ
وَبَيْنَهُم مِّيثَـٰقٌ فَدِيَةٌ مُّسَلَّمَةٌ
إِلَىٰٓ أَهْلِهِۦ وَتَحْرِيرُ رَقَبَةٍ مُّؤْمِنَةٍ ۖ
فَمَن لَّمْ يَجِدْ فَصِيَامُ شَهْرَيْنِ
مُتَتَابِعَيْنِ تَوْبَةً مِّنَ ٱللَّهِ ۗ
وَكَانَ ٱللَّهُ عَلِيمًا حَكِيمًا
﴿٩٣﴾ وَمَن يَقْتُلْ مُؤْمِنًا مُّتَعَمِّدًا
فَجَزَآؤُهُۥ جَهَنَّمُ خَـٰلِدًا فِيهَا
وَغَضِبَ ٱللَّهُ عَلَيْهِ وَلَعَنَهُۥ

611. Life is absolutely sacred in the Islamic Brotherhood. But mistakes will sometimes happen, as did happen in the melee at Uḥud, when some Muslims were killed (being mistaken for the enemy) by Muslims. There was no guilty intention: therefore there was no murder. But all the same, the family of the deceased was entitled to compensation unless they freely remitted it, and in addition it was provided that the unfortunate man who made the mistake should free a believing slave. Thus a deplorable mistake was made the occasion for winning the liberty of a slave who was a Believer, for Islam discountenances slavery. The compensation could only be paid if the deceased belonged to a Muslim society or to some people at peace with the Muslim society. Obviously it could not be paid if, though the deceased was a Believer, his people were at war with the Muslim society; even if his people could be reached, it is not fair to increase the resources of the enemy. If the deceased was himself an enemy at war, obviously the laws of war justify his being killed in warfare unless he surrendered. If the man who took life unintentionally has no means from which to free a believing slave or to give compensation, he must still by an act of strict self-denial (fasting for two whole months running) show that he is cognizant of the grave nature of the deed he has done and sincerely repentant. I take this to apply to all three cases mentioned: that is, where a Believer killed a Believer unintentionally and the deceased (1) belonged to the same community as you, or (2) belonged to a community at war with you, or (3) belonged to a community in alliance with you.

612. What is mentioned here is the punishment in the Hereafter, the spiritual consequences. The legal consequences, enforceable by human society, are mentioned in 2:178, under the rules of *Qiṣāṣ*. That is, a life should be taken for a life destroyed, but this should be on a scale of equality: a single murder should not commit a whole tribe to a perpetual blood-feud, as in the days of ignorance. But if the heirs of the man slain accept reasonable compensation, this should be accepted, and the taking of a life for a life should be put a stop to. This course leads to the saving of life, and is commanded to men of understanding.

Are upon him, and
A dreadful penalty
Is prepared for him.

وَأَعَدَّ لَهُۥ عَذَابًا عَظِيمًا

94. O ye who believe!
When ye go abroad[613]
In the cause of Allah,
Investigate carefully,
And say not to anyone
Who offers you a salutation:
"Thou art none of a Believer!"
Coveting the perishable goods
Of this life: with Allah
Are profits and spoils abundant.
Even thus were ye yourselves
Before, till Allah conferred
On you His favours: therefore
Carefully investigate.
For Allah is well aware
Of all that ye do.

٩٤ يَٰٓأَيُّهَا ٱلَّذِينَ ءَامَنُوٓا۟
إِذَا ضَرَبْتُمْ فِى سَبِيلِ ٱللَّهِ فَتَبَيَّنُوا۟
وَلَا تَقُولُوا۟ لِمَنْ أَلْقَىٰٓ إِلَيْكُمُ ٱلسَّلَٰمَ
لَسْتَ مُؤْمِنًا تَبْتَغُونَ عَرَضَ ٱلْحَيَوٰةِ
ٱلدُّنْيَا فَعِندَ ٱللَّهِ مَغَانِمُ كَثِيرَةٌ
كَذَٰلِكَ كُنتُم مِّن قَبْلُ
فَمَنَّ ٱللَّهُ عَلَيْكُمْ فَتَبَيَّنُوٓا۟
إِنَّ ٱللَّهَ كَانَ بِمَا تَعْمَلُونَ خَبِيرًا

95. Not equal are those
Believers who sit (at home)
And receive no hurt,
And those who strive
And fight in the cause
Of Allah with their goods
And their persons.
Allah hath granted
A grade higher to those
Who strive and fight
With their goods and persons
Than to those who sit (at home).
Unto all (in Faith)[614]

٩٥ لَّا يَسْتَوِى ٱلْقَٰعِدُونَ مِنَ ٱلْمُؤْمِنِينَ
غَيْرُ أُو۟لِى ٱلضَّرَرِ وَٱلْمُجَٰهِدُونَ
فِى سَبِيلِ ٱللَّهِ بِأَمْوَٰلِهِمْ وَأَنفُسِهِمْ
فَضَّلَ ٱللَّهُ ٱلْمُجَٰهِدِينَ بِأَمْوَٰلِهِمْ
وَأَنفُسِهِمْ عَلَى ٱلْقَٰعِدِينَ دَرَجَةً
وَكُلًّا

613. *Go abroad: daraba*—to travel, to go abroad, either for *jihād*, or for honest trade or other service, which if done with pure motives, counts as service in the cause of Allah. The immediate occasion was in connection with *jihād*, but the words are general, and can be applied to all circumstances in which a man falls through spiritual pride: he thinks he is not as other men are, but forgets that, but for the grace of Allah, he is himself a sinner! In war (or in peace) we are apt to catch some worldly advantage by pluming ourselves on our superiority in Faith. In war perhaps we want to gain glory or booty by killing a supposed enemy! In peace we make light of other people in order to steal some advantage or material gain! This is wrong. The righteous man, if he is really out in Allah's service, has more abundant and richer gifts to think of in the spiritual world.

614. Allah's goodness is promised to all people of Faith. But there are degrees among men and women of Faith. There are people with natural inertia: they do the minimum that is required of them, but no more. There are people who are weak in will: they are easily frightened. There are people who are so strong in will and so firm in faith that they are determined to conquer every obstacle, whether in their own physical or other infirmities or in the external world around them. In a time of *jihād*, when people give their all, and even their lives, for the common cause, they must be accounted more glorious than those who sit at home, even though they have goodwill to the cause and carry out minor duties in aid. The special reward of such self-sacrifice is high spiritual rank, and special forgiveness and mercy, as proceeding from the direct approbation and love of Allah.

Hath Allah promised good:
But those who strive and fight
Hath He distinguished
Above those who sit (at home)
By a special reward—

وَعَدَ ٱللَّهُ ٱلْحُسْنَىٰ ۚ وَفَضَّلَ ٱللَّهُ
ٱلْمُجَٰهِدِينَ عَلَى ٱلْقَٰعِدِينَ أَجْرًا عَظِيمًا

96. Ranks specially bestowed
By Him and Forgiveness
And Mercy, For Allah is
Oft-Forgiving, Most Merciful.

٩٦ دَرَجَٰتٍ مِّنْهُ وَمَغْفِرَةً وَرَحْمَةً ۚ
وَكَانَ ٱللَّهُ غَفُورًا رَّحِيمًا

SECTION 14.

97. When angels take
The souls of those
Who die in sin
Against their souls,[615]
They say: "In what (plight)
Were ye?" They reply:
"Weak and oppressed
Were we in the earth."
They say: "Was not
The earth of Allah
Spacious enough for you
To move yourselves away
(From evil)?" Such men
Will find their abode
In Hell—What an evil
Refuge!—

٩٧ إِنَّ ٱلَّذِينَ تَوَفَّىٰهُمُ
ٱلْمَلَٰٓئِكَةُ ظَالِمِىٓ أَنفُسِهِمْ
قَالُوا۟ فِيمَ كُنتُمْ ۖ
قَالُوا۟ كُنَّا مُسْتَضْعَفِينَ فِى ٱلْأَرْضِ ۚ
قَالُوٓا۟ أَلَمْ تَكُنْ أَرْضُ ٱللَّهِ وَٰسِعَةً فَتُهَاجِرُوا۟ فِيهَا ۚ
فَأُو۟لَٰٓئِكَ مَأْوَىٰهُمْ جَهَنَّمُ ۖ
وَسَآءَتْ مَصِيرًا

98. Except those who are
(Really) weak and oppressed—
Men, women, and children
Who have no means
In their power, nor (a guide post)[616]
To direct their way.

٩٨ إِلَّا ٱلْمُسْتَضْعَفِينَ
مِنَ ٱلرِّجَالِ وَٱلنِّسَآءِ وَٱلْوِلْدَٰنِ
لَا يَسْتَطِيعُونَ حِيلَةً وَلَا يَهْتَدُونَ سَبِيلًا

615. The immediate occasion for this passage was the question of migration (*hijrah*) from places where Islam was being persecuted and suppressed. Obviously the duty of Muslims was to leave such places, even if it involved forsaking their homes, and join and strengthen the Muslim community among whom they could live in peace and with whom they could help in fighting the evils around them. But the meaning is wider. Islam does not say: "Resist not evil." On the contrary it requires a constant, unceasing struggle against evil. For such struggle it may be necessary to forsake home and unite and organise and join our brethren in assaulting and overthrowing the fortress of evil. For the Muslim's duty is not only to enjoin good but to prohibit evil. To make our assault we must be prepared to put ourselves in a position from which such assault would be possible, and Allah's earth is spacious enough for the purpose. "Position" includes not only local position, but moral and material position. For example, we must shun evil company where we cannot put it down, but organise a position from which we can put it down.

616. If through physical, mental, or moral incapacity, we are unable to fight the good fight, we must nevertheless guard ourselves from it. Allah's gracious Mercy will recognise and forgive our weakness if it is real weakness, and not merely an excuse. (R).

99. For these, there is hope
That Allah will forgive:
For Allah doth blot out (sins)
And forgive again and again.

٩٩ فَأُولَٰٓئِكَ عَسَى ٱللَّهُ أَن يَعۡفُوَ عَنۡهُمۡۚ
وَكَانَ ٱللَّهُ عَفُوًّا غَفُورًا

100. He who forsakes his home
In the cause of Allah,
Finds in the earth
Many a refuge,
Wide and spacious:
Should he die
As a refugee from home
For Allah and His Messenger,
His reward becomes due
And sure with Allah:
And Allah is Oft-Forgiving,
Most Merciful.

١٠٠ وَمَن يُهَاجِرۡ فِي سَبِيلِ ٱللَّهِ
يَجِدۡ فِي ٱلۡأَرۡضِ مُرَٰغَمٗا كَثِيرٗا وَسَعَةٗۚ
وَمَن يَخۡرُجۡ مِنۢ بَيۡتِهِۦ مُهَاجِرًا إِلَى ٱللَّهِ وَرَسُولِهِۦ
ثُمَّ يُدۡرِكۡهُ ٱلۡمَوۡتُ فَقَدۡ وَقَعَ أَجۡرُهُۥ عَلَى ٱللَّهِۗ
وَكَانَ ٱللَّهُ غَفُورٗا رَّحِيمٗا

SECTION 15.

101. When ye travel
Through the earth,
There is no blame on you
If ye shorten your prayers,[617]
For fear the Unbelievers
May attack you:
For the Unbelievers are
Unto you open enemies.

١٠١ وَإِذَا ضَرَبۡتُمۡ فِي ٱلۡأَرۡضِ
فَلَيۡسَ عَلَيۡكُمۡ جُنَاحٌ أَن تَقۡصُرُواْ مِنَ ٱلصَّلَوٰةِ
إِنۡ خِفۡتُمۡ أَن يَفۡتِنَكُمُ ٱلَّذِينَ كَفَرُوٓاْۚ
إِنَّ ٱلۡكَٰفِرِينَ كَانُواْ لَكُمۡ عَدُوّٗا مُّبِينٗا

102. When thou (O Messenger)
Art with them, and standest
To lead them in prayer,
Let one party of them
Stand up (in prayer) with thee,
Taking their arms with them;
When they finish
Their prostrations, let them
Take their position in the rear.

١٠٢ وَإِذَا كُنتَ فِيهِمۡ فَأَقَمۡتَ لَهُمُ
ٱلصَّلَوٰةَ فَلۡتَقُمۡ طَآئِفَةٞ مِّنۡهُم مَّعَكَ
وَلۡيَأۡخُذُوٓاْ أَسۡلِحَتَهُمۡ فَإِذَا سَجَدُواْ
فَلۡيَكُونُواْ مِن وَرَآئِكُمۡ

617. Verse 101 gives permission to shorten congregational prayers when people are on a journey: verses 102-104 deal with cases when they are in danger at war, in face of the enemy. The shortening of congregational prayers in both cases is further governed as to details by the practice of the Messenger and his companions. As to journeys, two questions arise: (1) what constitutes a journey for this purpose? (2) is the fear of an attack an essential condition for the shortening of the congregational prayers? As to (1), it is best to leave the matter to discretion, having regard to all the circumstances of the journey, as in the case of the journeys which excuse a fast: see 2:84, n. 190. The text leaves it to discretion. As to (2), the practice of the Prophet shows that danger is not an essential condition; it is merely mentioned as a possible incident. The Messenger usually shortened the prayers from four Rak'ahs to two Rak'ahs in *Ẓuhr* (midday prayer). *'Aṣr* (afternoon prayer) and *'Ishā'* (night prayer): the other two are in any case short, *Fajr* (morning prayer) having two Rak'ahs and *Maghrib* (evening prayer) having three. (R).

And let the other party come up
Which hath not yet prayed—
And let them pray with thee,
Taking all precautions,
And bearing arms:
The Unbelievers wish,
If ye were negligent
Of your arms and your baggage,
To assault you in a single rush.[618]
But there is no blame on you
If ye put away your arms
Because of the inconvenience
Of rain or because ye are ill;
But take (every) precaution
For yourselves. For the Unbelievers
Allah hath prepared
A humiliating punishment.

وَلْتَأْتِ طَآئِفَةٌ أُخْرَىٰ
لَمْ يُصَلُّوا فَلْيُصَلُّوا مَعَكَ
وَلْيَأْخُذُوا حِذْرَهُمْ وَأَسْلِحَتَهُمْ
وَدَّ ٱلَّذِينَ كَفَرُوا لَوْ تَغْفُلُونَ
عَنْ أَسْلِحَتِكُمْ وَأَمْتِعَتِكُمْ فَيَمِيلُونَ
عَلَيْكُم مَّيْلَةً وَٰحِدَةً وَلَا جُنَاحَ عَلَيْكُمْ
إِن كَانَ بِكُمْ أَذًى مِّن مَّطَرٍ أَوْ كُنتُم مَّرْضَىٰٓ
أَن تَضَعُوٓا أَسْلِحَتَكُمْ وَخُذُوا حِذْرَكُمْ
إِنَّ ٱللَّهَ أَعَدَّ لِلْكَٰفِرِينَ عَذَابًا مُّهِينًا

103. When ye pass[619]
(Congregational) prayers,
Celebrate Allah's praises,
Standing, sitting down,
Or lying down on your sides;
But when ye are free
From danger, set up
Regular Prayers:
For such prayers
Are enjoined on Believers
At stated times.

١٠٣ فَإِذَا قَضَيْتُمُ ٱلصَّلَوٰةَ
فَٱذْكُرُوا ٱللَّهَ قِيَٰمًا وَقُعُودًا
وَعَلَىٰ جُنُوبِكُمْ فَإِذَا ٱطْمَأْنَنتُمْ
فَأَقِيمُوا ٱلصَّلَوٰةَ إِنَّ ٱلصَّلَوٰةَ كَانَتْ
عَلَى ٱلْمُؤْمِنِينَ كِتَٰبًا مَّوْقُوتًا

104. And slacken not
In following up the enemy:
If ye are suffering hardships,
They are suffering similar
Hardships; but ye have

١٠٤ وَلَا تَهِنُوا فِى ٱبْتِغَآءِ ٱلْقَوْمِ إِن تَكُونُوا
تَأْلَمُونَ فَإِنَّهُمْ يَأْلَمُونَ كَمَا تَأْلَمُونَ

618. The congregational prayer in danger in face of the enemy rests on the principle that the congregation should be divided into two parties; one party prays while the other watches the enemy, and then the second party comes up to prayers while the first falls back to face the enemy; either party does only one or two Rak'ahs, or about half the congregational prayer; every precaution is taken to prevent a rush by the enemy; even while at prayers armour and arms need not be put off except when rain is likely to cause inconvenience to the wearer and damage to the arms, or when illness or fatigue causes the wearer's strength to fail. Details can be varied according to circumstances, as was actually done by the Prophet at different times.

619. Two interpretations are possible: (1) "when ye have finished congregational prayers", or (2) "when (on account of extreme danger) ye have to pass over congregational prayers altogether—even the shorter form indicated for times of danger." I prefer the latter, as it accords better with the following sentence, which allows you to remember Allah individually in any posture possible during the danger. But when the danger is past, the full prayers should be offered at the stated times.

Hope from Allah, while they[620]
Have none. And Allah
Is full of knowledge and wisdom.

وَتَرْجُونَ مِنَ ٱللَّهِ مَا لَا يَرْجُونَ
وَكَانَ ٱللَّهُ عَلِيمًا حَكِيمًا

C. 66.—(4:105-126.) Beware of treachery, that would use
The good and pious for its wicked
Ends: its plots will but recoil
On its own head. The righteous
Have no cause for secrecy, except
In doing good. 'Tis evil that
Misleads, deceives, and even dares
Deface fair Nature, as by Allah
Created. Shun all evil, and be firm
In righteousness and faith in Allah.

SECTION 16.

105. We have sent down
To thee the Book in truth,
That thou mightest judge
Between men, as guided
By Allah: so be not (used)
As an advocate by those
Who betray their trust;[621]

١٠٥ إِنَّآ أَنزَلْنَآ إِلَيْكَ ٱلْكِتَٰبَ بِٱلْحَقِّ
لِتَحْكُمَ بَيْنَ ٱلنَّاسِ بِمَآ أَرَىٰكَ ٱللَّهُ
وَلَا تَكُن لِّلْخَآئِنِينَ خَصِيمًا

106. But seek the forgiveness
Of Allah; for Allah is
Oft-Forgiving, Most Merciful.

١٠٦ وَٱسْتَغْفِرِ ٱللَّهَ
إِنَّ ٱللَّهَ كَانَ غَفُورًا رَّحِيمًا

107. Contend not on behalf
Of such as betray

١٠٧ وَلَا تُجَٰدِلْ عَنِ ٱلَّذِينَ يَخْتَانُونَ

620. Religion should be a source of strength and not of weakness in all our affairs. If we have to struggle hard and suffer hardships, those without faith have to do the same, with this difference, that the man of Faith is full of hope in Allah, whereas the man without faith has nothing to sustain him.

621. The Commentators explain this passage with reference to the case of Ṭa'imah ibn Ubayraq, who was nominally a Muslim but really a hypocrite, and given to all sorts of wicked deeds. He was suspected of having stolen a set of armour, and when the trail was hot, he planted the stolen property in the house of a Jew, where it was found. The Jew denied the charge and accused Ṭa'ima, but the sympathies of the Muslim community were with Ṭa'ima on account of his nominal profession of Islam. The case was brought to the Prophet, who acquitted the Jew according to the strict principle of justice, as "guided by Allah". Attempts were made to prejudice him and deceive him into using his authority to favour Ṭa'ima. When Ṭa'ima realized that his punishment was imminent he fled and turned apostate. (R).

The general lesson is that the righteous man is faced with all sorts of subtle wiles: the wicked will try to appeal to his highest sympathies and most honourable motives to deceive him and use him as an instrument for defeating justice. He should be careful and cautious, and seek the help of Allah for protection against deception and for firmness in dealing the strictest justice without fear or favour. To do otherwise is to betray a sacred trust; the trustee must defeat all attempts made to mislead him.

Their own souls;[622]
For Allah loveth not
One given to perfidy
And crime;

أَنفُسَهُمْ إِنَّ ٱللَّهَ لَا يُحِبُّ
مَن كَانَ خَوَّانًا أَثِيمًا

108. They may hide
(Their crimes) from men,
But they cannot hide
(Them) from Allah, seeing that
He is with them
When they plot by night,
In words that He cannot
Approve; and Allah
Doth compass round[623]
All that they do.

﴿١٠٨﴾ يَسْتَخْفُونَ مِنَ ٱلنَّاسِ
وَلَا يَسْتَخْفُونَ مِنَ ٱللَّهِ وَهُوَ مَعَهُمْ
إِذْ يُبَيِّتُونَ مَا لَا يَرْضَىٰ مِنَ ٱلْقَوْلِ
وَكَانَ ٱللَّهُ بِمَا يَعْمَلُونَ مُحِيطًا

109. Ah! these are the sort
Of men on whose behalf
Ye may contend in this world;
But who will contend with Allah
On their behalf on the Day
Of Judgement, or who
Will carry their affairs through?

﴿١٠٩﴾ هَٰٓأَنتُمْ هَٰٓؤُلَآءِ جَٰدَلْتُمْ عَنْهُمْ فِى
ٱلْحَيَوٰةِ ٱلدُّنْيَا فَمَن يُجَٰدِلُ ٱللَّهَ عَنْهُمْ يَوْمَ
ٱلْقِيَٰمَةِ أَم مَّن يَكُونُ عَلَيْهِمْ وَكِيلًا

110. If anyone does evil
Or wrongs his own soul
But afterwards seeks
Allah's forgiveness, he will find
Allah Oft-Forgiving,
Most Merciful.

﴿١١٠﴾ وَمَن يَعْمَلْ سُوٓءًا
أَوْ يَظْلِمْ نَفْسَهُۥ ثُمَّ يَسْتَغْفِرِ ٱللَّهَ
يَجِدِ ٱللَّهَ غَفُورًا رَّحِيمًا

111. And if any one earns[624]

﴿١١١﴾ وَمَن يَكْسِبْ

622. Our souls are a sort of trust with us. We have to guard them against all temptation. Those who surrender to crime or evil, betray that trust. We are warned against being deceived into taking their part, induced either by plausible appearances, or by such incentives to partiality as that they belong to our own people or that some link connects them with us, whereas when we are out to do justice, we must not allow any irrelevant considerations to sway us.

623. The plots of sinners are known fully to Allah, and He can fully circumvent them if necessary, according to the fulness of His wisdom. The words used are: *Compass them round: muhīṭ*: not only does Allah know all about it, but He is all round it: if in His wisdom He allows it, it is not because He has not complete control over it, but because, having it as it were enclosed in a complete circle, He can use it to further His own Plan. Even out of evil He can bring good.

624. *Kasaba*=to earn, to gain, to work for something valuable, to lay up a provision for the future life. We do a day's labour to earn our livelihood; so in a spiritual sense, whatever good or evil we do in this life, earns us good or evil in the life to come. In verses 110-112 three cases are considered: (1) if we do ill, and repent, Allah will forgive: (2) if we do ill and do not repent, thinking that we can hide it, we are wrong; nothing is hidden from Allah, and we shall suffer the full consequences in the life to come, for we can never evade our personal responsibility: (3) if we do ill, great or small, and impute it to another, our original responsibility for the ill remains, but we add to it something else; for we tie round our necks the guilt of falsehood, which converts even our minor fault into a great sin, and in any case brands us even in this life with shame and ignominy.

Sin, he earns it against
His own soul: for Allah
Is full of knowledge and wisdom.

إِثْمًا فَإِنَّمَا يَكْسِبُهُۥ عَلَىٰ نَفْسِهِۦ ۚ
وَكَانَ ٱللَّهُ عَلِيمًا حَكِيمًا

112. But if anyone earns
A fault or a sin
And throws it on to one
That is innocent,
He carries (on himself)
(Both) a falsehood
And a flagrant sin.

﴿١١٢﴾ وَمَن يَكْسِبْ
خَطِيٓـَٔةً أَوْ إِثْمًا ثُمَّ يَرْمِ بِهِۦ بَرِيٓـًٔا
فَقَدِ ٱحْتَمَلَ بُهْتَٰنًا وَإِثْمًا مُّبِينًا

SECTION 17.

113. But for the Grace of Allah
To thee and His Mercy,
A party of them would
Certainly have plotted
To lead thee astray.
But (in fact) they will only
Lead their own souls astray,
And to thee they can do
No harm in the least.
For Allah hath sent down
To thee the Book and Wisdom
And taught thee what thou
Knewest not (before):
And great is the Grace
Of Allah unto thee.

﴿١١٣﴾ وَلَوْلَا فَضْلُ ٱللَّهِ عَلَيْكَ وَرَحْمَتُهُۥ
لَهَمَّت طَّآئِفَةٌ مِّنْهُمْ أَن
يُضِلُّوكَ وَمَا يُضِلُّونَ إِلَّآ أَنفُسَهُمْ ۖ
وَمَا يَضُرُّونَكَ مِن شَىْءٍ ۚ وَأَنزَلَ ٱللَّهُ عَلَيْكَ
ٱلْكِتَٰبَ وَٱلْحِكْمَةَ وَعَلَّمَكَ مَا لَمْ تَكُن
تَعْلَمُ ۚ وَكَانَ فَضْلُ ٱللَّهِ عَلَيْكَ عَظِيمًا

114. In most of their secret talks
There is no good; but if
One exhorts to a deed
Of charity or justice
Or conciliation between men,[625]
(Secrecy is permissible):
To him who does this,
Seeking the good pleasure

﴿١١٤﴾ لَّا خَيْرَ فِى كَثِيرٍ مِّن نَّجْوَىٰهُمْ
إِلَّا مَنْ أَمَرَ بِصَدَقَةٍ أَوْ مَعْرُوفٍ
أَوْ إِصْلَٰحٍۭ بَيْنَ ٱلنَّاسِ ۚ
وَمَن يَفْعَلْ ذَٰلِكَ ٱبْتِغَآءَ مَرْضَاتِ

625. Usually secrecy is for evil ends, or from questionable motives, or because the person seeking secrecy is ashamed of himself and knows that if his acts or motives became known, he would make himself odious. Islam therefore disapproves of secrecy and loves and enjoins openness in all consultations and doings. But there are three things in which secrecy is permissible, and indeed laudable, provided the motive be purely unselfish, to earn "the good pleasure of Allah": (1) if you are doing a deed of charity or beneficence, whether in giving material things or in helping in moral, intellectual, or spiritual matters; here publicity may not be agreeable to the recipient of your beneficence, and you have to think of his feelings; (2) where an unpleasant act of justice or correction has to be done; this should be done, but there is no virtue in publishing it abroad and causing humiliation to some parties or adding to their humiliation by publicity; (3) where there is a delicate question of conciliating parties to a quarrel; they may be very touchy about publicity but quite amenable to the influence of a man acting in private.

Of Allah, We shall soon give
A reward of the highest (value).

115. If anyone contends with
The Messenger even after
Guidance has been plainly
Conveyed to him, and follows
A path other than that
Becoming to men of Faith,
We shall leave him
In the path he has chosen,
And land him in Hell—
What an evil refuge!

SECTION 18.

116. Allah forgiveth not
(The sin of) joining other gods[626]
With Him; but He forgiveth
Whom He pleaseth other sins
Than this: one who joins
Other gods with Allah,
Hath strayed far, far away
(From the Right).

117. (The Pagans), leaving Him,
Call but upon female deities:[627]
They call but upon Satan
The persistent rebel!

118. Allah did curse him,
But he said: "I will take
Of Thy servants a portion[628]
Marked off;

اللَّهِ فَسَوْفَ نُؤْتِيهِ أَجْرًا عَظِيمًا

(١١٥) وَمَن يُشَاقِقِ الرَّسُولَ
مِنۢ بَعْدِ مَا تَبَيَّنَ لَهُ الْهُدَىٰ وَيَتَّبِعْ
غَيْرَ سَبِيلِ الْمُؤْمِنِينَ نُوَلِّهِۦ مَا تَوَلَّىٰ
وَنُصْلِهِۦ جَهَنَّمَ وَسَآءَتْ مَصِيرًا

(١١٦) إِنَّ اللَّهَ لَا يَغْفِرُ أَن يُشْرَكَ بِهِۦ
وَيَغْفِرُ مَا دُونَ ذَٰلِكَ لِمَن يَشَآءُ
وَمَن يُشْرِكْ بِاللَّهِ فَقَدْ ضَلَّ ضَلَٰلًا بَعِيدًا

(١١٧) إِن يَدْعُونَ مِن دُونِهِۦٓ إِلَّآ إِنَٰثًا
وَإِن يَدْعُونَ إِلَّا شَيْطَٰنًا مَّرِيدًا

(١١٨) لَّعَنَهُ اللَّهُ وَقَالَ لَأَتَّخِذَنَّ
مِنْ عِبَادِكَ نَصِيبًا مَّفْرُوضًا

626. *Cf.* 4:48 and n. 569. Blasphemy in the spiritual kingdom is like treason in the political kingdom.

627. The unity, power, and goodness of Allah are so manifest in nature and in the human mind when it is in accord with the universal spirit, that only the most abject perversion can account for the sin of spiritual treason. That sin arises from perverted ideas of sex or perverted ideas of self. The perversion of sex is to suppose that sex rules in spiritual matters. From it arise such horrible creations of the imagination as Kāli, the blood-thirsty goddess of Hindus, or Hecate, the goddess of revenge and hate in Greek mythology. Even in beautiful forms like Saraswati (the goddess of learning) or Minerva (the virgin goddess of sport and arts), to say nothing of Venus (the goddess of carnal pleasures), the emphasis laid on sex destroys a right view of spiritual nature. Perverted ideas of self are typified in the story of Satan, who was so puffed up with arrogance that he disobeyed Allah, and Allah cursed him. Both these perversions, if allowed lodgment, completely ruin our spiritual nature and deface Allah's handiwork. Hence it is not merely an outer sin but one that corrupts us through and through.

628. Satan obtained Allah's permission to tempt man, and this was implied in such free will as was granted to man by Allah. Satan's boast is that the portion of mankind seduced by him will be so corrupted in their nature that they will bear a sort of brand that will mark them off as his own; or that they will be like a portion assigned to himself.

119. "I will mislead them,[629]
And I will create
In them false desires; I will
Order them to slit the ears[630]
Of cattle, and to deface
The (fair) nature created[631]
By Allah." Whoever,
Forsaking Allah, takes Satan
For a friend, hath
Of a surety suffered
A loss that is manifest.

(١١٩) وَلَأُضِلَّنَّهُمْ وَلَأُمَنِّيَنَّهُمْ
وَلَآمُرَنَّهُمْ فَلَيُبَتِّكُنَّ ءَاذَانَ
ٱلْأَنْعَٰمِ وَلَآمُرَنَّهُمْ فَلَيُغَيِّرُنَّ خَلْقَ ٱللَّهِ
وَمَن يَتَّخِذِ ٱلشَّيْطَٰنَ وَلِيًّا مِّن دُونِ
ٱللَّهِ فَقَدْ خَسِرَ خُسْرَانًا مُّبِينًا

120. Satan makes them promises,
And creates in them false desires;
But Satan's promises
Are nothing but deception.

(١٢٠) يَعِدُهُمْ وَيُمَنِّيهِمْ
وَمَا يَعِدُهُمُ ٱلشَّيْطَٰنُ إِلَّا غُرُورًا

121. They (his dupes)
Will have their dwelling
In Hell, and from it
They will find no way
Of escape.

(١٢١) أُو۟لَٰٓئِكَ مَأْوَىٰهُمْ جَهَنَّمُ
وَلَا يَجِدُونَ عَنْهَا مَحِيصًا

122. But those who believe
And do deeds of righteousness—
We shall soon admit them
To Gardens, with rivers
Flowing beneath—to dwell
Therein forever.
Allah's promise is the truth,
And whose word can be
Truer than Allah's?

(١٢٢) وَٱلَّذِينَ ءَامَنُوا۟ وَعَمِلُوا۟ ٱلصَّٰلِحَٰتِ
سَنُدْخِلُهُمْ جَنَّٰتٍ تَجْرِى مِن تَحْتِهَا
ٱلْأَنْهَٰرُ خَٰلِدِينَ فِيهَآ أَبَدًا وَعْدَ ٱللَّهِ حَقًّا
وَمَنْ أَصْدَقُ مِنَ ٱللَّهِ قِيلًا

123. Not your desires, nor those[632]

(١٢٣) لَّيْسَ بِأَمَانِيِّكُمْ وَلَآ أَمَانِىِّ

629. Satan's deceptions are with false desires, false superstitions, and false fears.

630. Slitting the ears of cattle is just one instance of the superstitions to which men become slaves when they run after false gods. Astrology, magic, and vain beliefs in things that do not exist lead men away from Allah, the one true God. (R).

631. To deface the (fair) nature created by Allah: there is both a physical and a spiritual meaning. We see many kinds of defacements practised on men and animals, against their true nature as created by Allah, partly on account of superstition, partly on account of selfishness. Spiritually the case is even worse. How many natures are dwarfed or starved and turned from their original instincts by cruel superstitions or customs? Allah created man pure: the Evil One defaces the image.

632. Personal responsibility is again and again insisted on as the keynote of Islam. In this are implied faith and right conduct. Faith is not an external thing; it begins with an act of will, but if true and sincere, it affects the whole being, and leads to right conduct. In this it is distinguished from the kind of faith which promises salvation because someone else in whom you are asked to believe has borne away the sins of men, or the kind of faith which says that because you are born of a certain race ("Children of Abraham") or a certain caste, you are privileged, and your conduct will be judged by a different standard from that of other men. Whatever you are, if you do evil, you must suffer the consequences, unless Allah's Mercy comes to your help.

Of the People of the Book
(Can prevail): whoever
Works evil, will be
Requited accordingly.
Nor will he find, besides Allah,
Any protector or helper.

أَهْلِ ٱلْكِتَٰبِ ۗ
مَن يَعْمَلْ سُوٓءًا يُجْزَ بِهِۦ
وَلَا يَجِدْ لَهُۥ مِن دُونِ ٱللَّهِ وَلِيًّا وَلَا نَصِيرًا

124. If any do deeds
Of righteousness—
Be they male or female—
And have faith,
They will enter Heaven,
And not the least injustice[633]
Will be done to them.

١٢٤ وَمَن يَعْمَلْ مِنَ ٱلصَّٰلِحَٰتِ
مِن ذَكَرٍ أَوْ أُنثَىٰ وَهُوَ مُؤْمِنٌ فَأُو۟لَٰٓئِكَ
يَدْخُلُونَ ٱلْجَنَّةَ وَلَا يُظْلَمُونَ نَقِيرًا

125. Who can be better
In religion than one
Who submits his whole self
To Allah, does good,
And follows the way
Of Abraham the true in faith?
For Allah did take
Abraham for a friend.[634]

١٢٥ وَمَنْ أَحْسَنُ دِينًا مِّمَّنْ
أَسْلَمَ وَجْهَهُۥ لِلَّهِ وَهُوَ مُحْسِنٌ
وَٱتَّبَعَ مِلَّةَ إِبْرَٰهِيمَ حَنِيفًا ۗ
وَٱتَّخَذَ ٱللَّهُ إِبْرَٰهِيمَ خَلِيلًا

126. But to Allah belong all things
In the heavens and on earth;
And He it is that
Encompasseth all things.[635]

١٢٦ وَلِلَّهِ مَا فِى ٱلسَّمَٰوَٰتِ وَمَا فِى ٱلْأَرْضِ ۚ
وَكَانَ ٱللَّهُ بِكُلِّ شَىْءٍ مُّحِيطًا

C. 67.—Justice to women and orphans
(4:127-152.) Is part of religion and the fear
Of Allah. Stand out firmly
For justice to all, even against
Yourselves or your nearest of kin.
Remain firm in faith, and consort not
With evil or hypocrisy. Be true
In speech, and wound not others;
Nor distinguish between Teachers of Truth,
For Allah's Truth is one and should be believed.

---

633. *Naqīr*=the groove in a date stone, a thing of no value whatever. *Cf.* n. 575 to 4:53.

634. Abraham is distinguished in Muslim theology with the title of "Friend of Allah". This does not of course mean that he was anything more than a mortal. But his faith was pure and true, and his conduct was firm and righteous in all circumstances. He was the fountainhead of the present monotheistic tradition, the Patriarch of the prophetic line, and is revered alike by Jews, Christians and Muslims. (R).

635. *Muḥīṭ*. *Cf.* 4:108, and n. 623.

SECTION 19.

127. They ask thy instruction
Concerning the Women.
Say: Allah doth
Instruct you about them:
And (remember) what hath
Been rehearsed unto you[636]
In the Book, concerning
The orphans of women to whom
Ye give not the portions
Prescribed, and yet whom ye
Desire to marry, as also
Concerning the children
Who are weak and oppressed;[637]
That ye stand firm
For justice to orphans.
There is not a good deed
Which ye do, but Allah
Is well-acquainted therewith.

١٢٧ وَيَسْتَفْتُونَكَ فِي ٱلنِّسَآءِ
قُلِ ٱللَّهُ يُفْتِيكُمْ فِيهِنَّ
وَمَا يُتْلَىٰ عَلَيْكُمْ
فِي ٱلْكِتَٰبِ فِي يَتَٰمَى ٱلنِّسَآءِ
ٱلَّٰتِي لَا تُؤْتُونَهُنَّ مَا كُتِبَ لَهُنَّ
وَتَرْغَبُونَ أَن تَنكِحُوهُنَّ
وَٱلْمُسْتَضْعَفِينَ مِنَ ٱلْوِلْدَٰنِ
وَأَن تَقُومُوا۟ لِلْيَتَٰمَىٰ بِٱلْقِسْطِ ۚ
وَمَا تَفْعَلُوا۟ مِنْ خَيْرٍ فَإِنَّ ٱللَّهَ كَانَ بِهِۦ عَلِيمًا

128. If a wife fears
Cruelty or desertion
On her husband's part,
There is no blame on them
If they arrange
An amicable settlement
Between themselves;
And such settlement is best;
Even though men's souls

١٢٨ وَإِنِ ٱمْرَأَةٌ خَافَتْ مِنۢ بَعْلِهَا نُشُوزًا
أَوْ إِعْرَاضًا فَلَا جُنَاحَ عَلَيْهِمَآ
أَن يُصْلِحَا بَيْنَهُمَا صُلْحًا ۚ
وَٱلصُّلْحُ خَيْرٌ ۗ
وَأُحْضِرَتِ ٱلْأَنفُسُ

636. Again and again is it impressed on the community of Islam to be just in their dealings with women, orphans, children, and all whose weakness requires special consideration. The law about widows and orphans, inheritance, dower, and marriage had already been declared in 4:2-35, and further instructions are now given on a further reference. The words translated *orphans of women* mean, I think, the orphaned children of widows, of whom there were several after the battle of Uḥud, and whom it was the duty of the community to provide for. But some Commentators take them to mean "female orphans." In any case, because women were orphans or widows, it was not right that anyone should take advantage of their helpless position to deprive them of dower or of their portion in inheritance.

637. *Cf.* 4:75, n. 592.

Both widows and orphans are to be helped because they are ordinarily weak, ill-treated, and oppressed. In communities which base their civil rights on brute strength, the weaker go to the wall, and public opinion expects nothing else. In Nietzsche's philosophy of the Superman that doctrine is stressed strongly, and some of the militarist nations in our own time seem inclined to support this reversion to our primitive instincts. Even in modern democracies of the saner sort, we are often told that it is the fate of minorities to suffer: strength of numbers here becomes the passport to power and privilege. Islam, while upholding sane manly views in general, enjoins the most solicitous care for the weak and oppressed in every way—in rights of property, in social rights, and in the right to opportunities of development. Spiritual strength or weakness does not necessarily go with physical or numerical strength.

Are swayed by greed.[638]
But if ye do good
And practise self-restraint,
Allah is well-acquainted
With all that ye do.

ٱلشُّحَّۚ وَإِن تُحۡسِنُواْ وَتَتَّقُواْ
فَإِنَّ ٱللَّهَ كَانَ بِمَا تَعۡمَلُونَ خَبِيرٗا

129. Ye are never able
To be fair and just
As between women,
Even if it is
Your ardent desire:
But turn not away
(From a woman) altogether,
So as to leave her (as it were)
Hanging (in the air).[639]
If ye come to a friendly
Understanding, and practise
Self-restraint, Allah is
Oft-Forgiving, Most Merciful.

١٢٩ وَلَن تَسۡتَطِيعُوٓاْ أَن تَعۡدِلُواْ
بَيۡنَ ٱلنِّسَآءِ وَلَوۡ حَرَصۡتُمۡۖ
فَلَا تَمِيلُواْ كُلَّ ٱلۡمَيۡلِ
فَتَذَرُوهَا كَٱلۡمُعَلَّقَةِۚ
وَإِن تُصۡلِحُواْ وَتَتَّقُواْ
فَإِنَّ ٱللَّهَ كَانَ غَفُورٗا رَّحِيمٗا

130. But if they disagree
(And must part), Allah
Will provide abundance
For all from His
All-Reaching bounty:
For Allah is He
That careth for all
And is Wise.

١٣٠ وَإِن يَتَفَرَّقَا
يُغۡنِ ٱللَّهُ كُلّٗا مِّن سَعَتِهِۦۚ
وَكَانَ ٱللَّهُ وَٰسِعًا حَكِيمٗا

131. To Allah belong all things
In the heavens and on earth.[640]

١٣١ وَلِلَّهِ مَا فِي ٱلسَّمَٰوَٰتِ وَمَا فِي ٱلۡأَرۡضِۗ

638. To protect the woman's economic interests, various rules are prescribed for dower in marriage. But the sanctity of marriage itself is greater than any economic interests. Divorce is, of all things permitted, most hateful to Allah. Therefore if a breach between husband and wife can be prevented by some economic consideration, it is better to make that concession than to imperil the future of the wife, the children, and probably the husband also. Such concessions are permissible, in view of the love of wealth ingrained in unregenerate man, but a recommendation is made that we should practise self-restraint, and do what we can to come to an amicable settlement without any economic sacrifice on the part of the woman.

639. In this material world there are two principal causes of division between man and wife, money and "the other woman" or "the other man". Money was dealt with in the last verse. Here is the case of "the other woman". Legally more than one wife (up to four) are permissible on the condition that the man can be perfectly fair and just to all. But this is a condition almost impossible to fulfil. If, in the hope that he might be able to fulfil it, a man puts himself in that impossible position, it is only right to insist that he should not discard one but at least fulfil all the outward duties that are incumbent on him in respect of her.

640. Notice the refrain: "To Allah belong all things in the heavens and on earth": repeated three times, each time with a new application. In the first instance it follows the statement of Allah's universal providence and love. If two persons, in spite of every sincere desire to love and comfort each other, fail to achieve that end, and have to separate, Allah's all-reaching bounty never fails, for He is the Lord of all things. In the second instance it is connected with Allah's Self-Existence, Self-Excellence, and independence of all creatures; all His commands are for our good, and they are given to all His creatures, according to their capacities. In the third instance, it is connected with His universal power; for He could destroy any individual or nation and create a new one without any loss to himself; but He gives a chance to all again and again, and even rewards them beyond their own ambitions.

Verily We have directed
The People of the Book
Before you, and you (O Muslims)
To fear Allah. But if ye
Deny Him, lo! unto Allah
Belong all things
In the heavens and on earth,
And Allah is free
Of all wants, worthy[641]
Of all praise.

وَلَقَدْ وَصَّيْنَا ٱلَّذِينَ أُوتُوا۟ ٱلْكِتَـٰبَ
مِن قَبْلِكُمْ وَإِيَّاكُمْ أَنِ ٱتَّقُوا۟ ٱللَّهَ ۚ
وَإِن تَكْفُرُوا۟ فَإِنَّ لِلَّهِ مَا فِى ٱلسَّمَـٰوَٰتِ
وَمَا فِى ٱلْأَرْضِ ۚ وَكَانَ ٱللَّهُ غَنِيًّا حَمِيدًا

132. Yea, unto Allah belong
All things in the heavens
And on earth, and enough
Is Allah to carry through[642]
All affairs.

(١٣٢) وَلِلَّهِ مَا فِى ٱلسَّمَـٰوَٰتِ
وَمَا فِى ٱلْأَرْضِ ۚ وَكَفَىٰ بِٱللَّهِ وَكِيلًا

133. If it were His Will,
He could destroy you,
O mankind, and create
Another race; for He
Hath power this to do.

(١٣٣) إِن يَشَأْ يُذْهِبْكُمْ أَيُّهَا ٱلنَّاسُ
وَيَأْتِ بِـَٔاخَرِينَ ۚ وَكَانَ ٱللَّهُ عَلَىٰ ذَٰلِكَ قَدِيرًا

134. If anyone desires
A reward in this life,
In Allah's (gift) is the reward
(Both) of this life
And of the Hereafter;[643]
For Allah is He that heareth
And seeth (all things).

(١٣٤) مَّن كَانَ يُرِيدُ ثَوَابَ ٱلدُّنْيَا
فَعِندَ ٱللَّهِ ثَوَابُ ٱلدُّنْيَا وَٱلْءَاخِرَةِ ۚ
وَكَانَ ٱللَّهُ سَمِيعًۢا بَصِيرًا

SECTION 20.

135. O ye who believe!
Stand out firmly

(١٣٥) يَـٰٓأَيُّهَا ٱلَّذِينَ ءَامَنُوا۟ كُونُوا۟ قَوَّٰمِينَ

641. Allah's existence is absolute existence. It does not depend on any other person or any other thing. And it is worthy of all praise, for it is all-good and comprises every possible excellence. It is necessary to stress this point in order to show that the moral law for man is not a mere matter of transcendental commands, but really rests on the essential needs of mankind itself. If therefore such schools of thought as Behaviourism proved their theories up to the hilt, they do not affect the position of Islam in the least. The highest ethical standards are enjoined by Islam, not as dogmatic imperatives, but because they can be shown to follow from the needs of man's nature and the results of man's experience.

642. This refers to the next verse. He does not need us, but we need Him. Our hopes, our happiness, our success centre in Him; but He is Self-sufficient. He has the power to supersede us, but His goodness is ever seeking to give us every chance in this world as well as in the Hereafter.

643. Man in this life can only see up to the horizon of this life. The highest rewards which his wishes or ambitions can conceive of are conceived in the terms of this life. But Allah can give him not only these but something infinitely higher—the rewards of the Hereafter—which it did not even enter his heart to ask for or his imagination to conceive.

For justice, as witnesses[644]
To Allah, even as against
Yourselves, or your parents,
Or your kin, and whether
It be (against) rich or poor:[645]
For Allah can best protect both.
Follow not the lusts
(Of your hearts), lest ye
Swerve, and if ye
Distort (justice) or decline
To do justice, verily
Allah is well-acquainted
With all that ye do.

بِالْقِسْطِ شُهَدَآءَ لِلَّهِ وَلَوْ عَلَىٰٓ
أَنفُسِكُمْ أَوِ الْوَٰلِدَيْنِ وَالْأَقْرَبِينَ ۚ
إِن يَكُنْ غَنِيًّا أَوْ فَقِيرًا فَاللَّهُ أَوْلَىٰ بِهِمَا ۖ
فَلَا تَتَّبِعُوا الْهَوَىٰٓ أَن تَعْدِلُوا ۚ
وَإِن تَلْوُۥٓا أَوْ تُعْرِضُوا
فَإِنَّ اللَّهَ كَانَ بِمَا تَعْمَلُونَ خَبِيرًا

136. O ye who believe!
Believe in Allah
And His Messenger,
And the scripture which He
Hath sent to His Messenger
And the scripture which He sent
To those before (him).[646]
Any who denieth Allah,
His angels, His Books,
His Messengers, and the Day
Of Judgement, hath gone
Far, far astray.

١٣٦ يَٰٓأَيُّهَا الَّذِينَ ءَامَنُوٓا ءَامِنُوا بِاللَّهِ
وَرَسُولِهِۦ وَالْكِتَٰبِ الَّذِى نَزَّلَ عَلَىٰ رَسُولِهِۦ
وَالْكِتَٰبِ الَّذِىٓ أَنزَلَ مِن قَبْلُ ۚ
وَمَن يَكْفُرْ بِاللَّهِ وَمَلَٰٓئِكَتِهِۦ وَكُتُبِهِۦ
وَرُسُلِهِۦ وَالْيَوْمِ الْءَاخِرِ فَقَدْ ضَلَّ
ضَلَٰلًۢا بَعِيدًا

137. Those who believe,
Then reject Faith,
Then believe (again)
And (again) reject Faith,
And go on increasing

١٣٧ إِنَّ الَّذِينَ ءَامَنُوا ثُمَّ كَفَرُوا
ثُمَّ ءَامَنُوا ثُمَّ كَفَرُوا
ثُمَّ ازْدَادُوا

644. Justice is Allah's attribute, and to stand firm for justice is to be a witness to Allah, even if it is detrimental to our own interests (as we conceive them) or the interests of those who are near and dear to us. According to the Latin saying, "Let justice be done though heaven should fall."

But Islamic justice is something higher than the formal justice of Roman Law or any other human law. It is even more penetrative than the subtler justice in the speculations of the Greek philosophers. It searches out the innermost motives, because we are to act as in the presence of Allah, to whom all things, acts, and motives are known.

645. Some people may be inclined to favour the rich, because they expect something from them. Some people may be inclined to favour the poor because they are generally helpless. Partiality in either case is wrong. Be just, without fear or favour. Both the rich and the poor are under Allah's protection as far as their legitimate interests are concerned, but they cannot expect to be favoured at the expense of others. And He can protect their interests far better than any man.

646. If your belief is by habit or birth or the example of those you love or respect or admire, make that belief more specific and personal to yourself. We must not only have faith, but realise that faith in our inmost being. The chief objects of our Faith are Allah, His Messenger, and His Revelations. To all these we must give a home in our hearts. The angels we do not see and realise as we realise Allah, who is nearer to us than the vehicle of our life-blood, and the Day of Judgement is for our future experience, but we must not deny them, or we cut off a part of our spiritual view.

In Unbelief—Allah
Will not forgive them
Nor guide them on the Way.[647]

كُفْرًا لَّمْ يَكُنِ ٱللَّهُ لِيَغْفِرَ لَهُمْ
وَلَا لِيَهْدِيَهُمْ سَبِيلًا

138. To the Hypocrites give
The glad tidings that
There is for them
(But) a grievous Penalty—

١٣٨ بَشِّرِ ٱلْمُنَٰفِقِينَ
بِأَنَّ لَهُمْ عَذَابًا أَلِيمًا

139. Yea, to those who take
For friends Unbelievers
Rather than Believers:
Is it honour they seek
Among them? Nay—
All honour is with Allah.[648]

١٣٩ ٱلَّذِينَ يَتَّخِذُونَ ٱلْكَٰفِرِينَ أَوْلِيَآءَ
مِن دُونِ ٱلْمُؤْمِنِينَ أَيَبْتَغُونَ
عِندَهُمُ ٱلْعِزَّةَ فَإِنَّ ٱلْعِزَّةَ لِلَّهِ جَمِيعًا

140. Already has He sent you[649]
Word in the Book, that when
Ye hear the Signs of Allah
Held in defiance and ridicule,
Ye are not to sit with them
Unless they turn to a different
Theme: if ye did, ye would be
Like them. For Allah will
Collect the Hypocrites and those
Who defy Faith—all in Hell—

١٤٠ وَقَدْ نَزَّلَ عَلَيْكُمْ فِى ٱلْكِتَٰبِ
أَنْ إِذَا سَمِعْتُمْ ءَايَٰتِ ٱللَّهِ يُكْفَرُ بِهَا وَيُسْتَهْزَأُ بِهَا
فَلَا تَقْعُدُوا۟ مَعَهُمْ حَتَّىٰ يَخُوضُوا۟ فِى حَدِيثٍ
غَيْرِهِۦٓ إِنَّكُمْ إِذًا مِّثْلُهُمْ إِنَّ ٱللَّهَ جَامِعُ ٱلْمُنَٰفِقِينَ
وَٱلْكَٰفِرِينَ فِى جَهَنَّمَ جَمِيعًا

141. (These are) the ones who
Wait and watch about you:
If ye do gain
A victory from Allah,
They say: "Were we not
With you?"—but if
The Unbelievers gain
A success, they say

١٤١ ٱلَّذِينَ يَتَرَبَّصُونَ بِكُمْ
فَإِن كَانَ لَكُمْ فَتْحٌ مِّنَ ٱللَّهِ
قَالُوٓا۟ أَلَمْ نَكُن مَّعَكُمْ
وَإِن كَانَ لِلْكَٰفِرِينَ نَصِيبٌ قَالُوٓا۟

---

647. Those who go on changing sides again and again can have no real Faith at any time. Their motives are mere worldly double-dealing. How can they expect Allah's grace or forgiveness?

Here is a clear warning against those who make their religion a mere matter of worldly convenience. True religion goes far deeper. It transforms the very nature of man. After that transformation it is as impossible for him to change as it is for light to become darkness.

648. If the motive is some advantage, some honour—the fountain of all good is Allah. How can it really be expected from those who deny Faith? And if there is some show of worldly honour, what is it worth against the contempt they earn in the spiritual world?

649. *Cf.* 6:68, an earlier and Makkan verse.

Where we see or hear Truth held in light esteem, we ought to make our protest and withdraw from such company, not out of arrogance, as if we thought ourselves superior to other people, but out of real humility, lest our own nature be corrupted in such society. But it is possible that our protest or our sincere remonstrance may change the theme of discourse. In that case we have done good to those who were inclined to hold Truth in light esteem, if we have saved them for ridiculing Truth.

(To them): "Did we not
Gain an advantage over you,
And did we not guard
You from the Believers?"
But Allah will judge
Betwixt you on the Day
Of Judgement. And never
Will Allah grant
To the Unbelievers
A way (to triumph)
Over the Believers.[650]

أَلَمْ نَسْتَحْوِذْ عَلَيْكُمْ
وَنَمْنَعْكُم مِّنَ ٱلْمُؤْمِنِينَ ۚ
فَٱللَّهُ يَحْكُمُ بَيْنَكُمْ يَوْمَ ٱلْقِيَٰمَةِ ۗ
وَلَن يَجْعَلَ ٱللَّهُ لِلْكَٰفِرِينَ
عَلَى ٱلْمُؤْمِنِينَ سَبِيلًا

SECTION 21.

142. The Hypocrites—they think
They are over-reaching Allah
But He will over-reach them:
When they stand up to prayer,
They stand without earnestness,
To be seen of men,
But little do they hold
Allah in remembrance;

١٤٢ إِنَّ ٱلْمُنَٰفِقِينَ يُخَٰدِعُونَ ٱللَّهَ
وَهُوَ خَٰدِعُهُمْ وَإِذَا قَامُوٓا۟ إِلَى ٱلصَّلَوٰةِ
قَامُوا۟ كُسَالَىٰ يُرَآءُونَ ٱلنَّاسَ
وَلَا يَذْكُرُونَ ٱللَّهَ إِلَّا قَلِيلًا

143. (They are) distracted in mind
Even in the midst of it—
Being (sincerely) for neither
One group nor for another.
Whom Allah leaves straying—
Never wilt thou find
For him the Way.[651]

١٤٣ مُّذَبْذَبِينَ بَيْنَ ذَٰلِكَ
لَآ إِلَىٰ هَٰٓؤُلَآءِ وَلَآ إِلَىٰ هَٰٓؤُلَآءِ ۚ
وَمَن يُضْلِلِ ٱللَّهُ فَلَن تَجِدَ لَهُۥ سَبِيلًا

144. O ye who believe!
Take not for friends
Unbelievers rather than
Believers: do ye wish
To offer Allah an open
Proof against yourselves?

١٤٤ يَٰٓأَيُّهَا ٱلَّذِينَ ءَامَنُوا۟ لَا تَتَّخِذُوا۟ ٱلْكَٰفِرِينَ
أَوْلِيَآءَ مِن دُونِ ٱلْمُؤْمِنِينَ ۚ أَتُرِيدُونَ
أَن تَجْعَلُوا۟ لِلَّهِ عَلَيْكُمْ سُلْطَٰنًا مُّبِينًا

650. The methods and motives of Hypocrisy are thoroughly unmasked here. It has no principles, but watches for an opportunity to turn any event to its own advantage. If battle is joined between two inconsistent principles, it has no belief in either, but watches the result. There is unceasing fight between Good and Evil in this world. If the Good seems to win, the hypocrites range themselves on its side with unctuous words, taking a great part of the credit to themselves. Perhaps the balance tips the other way later, and they have to make their peace with Evil. "Oh!" they say, we were in the ranks of your enemy before, on purpose to protect you when they were too strong for you!" This may suit the ways of the world. But the day of their account will come eventually. For the Good must ultimately triumph.

651. If we choose evil deliberately and double our guilt by fraud and deception, we do not deceive Allah, but we deceive ourselves. We deprive ourselves of the Grace of Allah, and are left straying away from the Path. In that condition who can guide us or show us the Way? Our true and right instincts become blunted; our fraud makes us unstable in character; when our fellow-men find out our fraud, any advantages we may have gained by the fraud are lost; and we become truly distracted in mind.

145. The Hypocrites will be
In the lowest depths
Of the Fire; no helper
Wilt thou find for them—

إِنَّ ٱلْمُنَٰفِقِينَ فِى ٱلدَّرْكِ ٱلْأَسْفَلِ مِنَ ٱلنَّارِ وَلَن تَجِدَ لَهُمْ نَصِيرًا ﴿١٤٥﴾

146. Except for those who repent,
Mend (their life), hold fast
To Allah, and purify their religion
As in Allah's sight; if so
They will be (numbered)[652]
With the Believers.
And soon will Allah
Grant to the Believers
A reward of immense value.

إِلَّا ٱلَّذِينَ تَابُوا۟ وَأَصْلَحُوا۟ وَٱعْتَصَمُوا۟ بِٱللَّهِ وَأَخْلَصُوا۟ دِينَهُمْ لِلَّهِ فَأُو۟لَٰٓئِكَ مَعَ ٱلْمُؤْمِنِينَ ۖ وَسَوْفَ يُؤْتِ ٱللَّهُ ٱلْمُؤْمِنِينَ أَجْرًا عَظِيمًا ﴿١٤٦﴾

147. What can Allah gain
By your punishment,
If ye are grateful
And ye believe?
Nay, it is Allah
That recogniseth[653]
(All good), and knoweth
All things.

مَّا يَفْعَلُ ٱللَّهُ بِعَذَابِكُمْ إِن شَكَرْتُمْ وَءَامَنتُمْ ۚ وَكَانَ ٱللَّهُ شَاكِرًا عَلِيمًا ﴿١٤٧﴾

6/30

148. Allah loveth not that evil
Should be noised abroad[654]
In public speech, except
Where injustice hath been
Done; for Allah
Is He who heareth
And knoweth all things.

لَّا يُحِبُّ ٱللَّهُ ٱلْجَهْرَ بِٱلسُّوٓءِ مِنَ ٱلْقَوْلِ إِلَّا مَن ظُلِمَ ۚ وَكَانَ ٱللَّهُ سَمِيعًا عَلِيمًا ﴿١٤٨﴾

---

652. Even Hypocrites can obtain forgiveness, on four conditions: (1) sincere repentance, which purifies their mind; (2) amendment of their conduct, which purifies their outer life; (3) steadfastness and devotion to Allah, which strengthens their faith and protects them from the assaults of evil; and (4) sincerity in their religion, or their whole inner being, which brings them as full members into the goodly Fellowship of Faith.

653. There is no pleasure nor advantage to Allah in punishing His own creatures, over whom He watches with loving care. On the contrary He recognises any good—however little—which He finds in us, and delights to give us a reward beyond all measure. His recognition of us is compared by a bold metaphor to our gratitude to Him for His favours. The epithet *Shākir* is applied to Allah, as here, in 2:158, and other passages. In 16:121 it is applied to Abraham: "he showed his gratitude for the favours of Allah, who chose him and guided him to a Straight Way."

654. We can make a public scandal of evil in many ways. (1) It may be idle sensation-mongering: it often leads to more evil by imitation, as where criminal deeds are glorified in a cinema, or talked about shamelessly in a novel or drama. (2) It may be malicious gossip of a foolish, personal kind: it does no good, but it hurts people's feelings. (3) It may be malevolent slander or libel: it is intended deliberately to cause harm to people's reputation or injure them in other ways, and is rightly punishable under all laws. (4) It may be a public rebuke or correction or remonstrance, without malice. (1), (2) and (3) are absolutely forbidden. (4) may be by a person in authority; in which case the exception applies, for all wrong or injustice must be corrected openly, to prevent its recurrence. Or (4) may be by a person not vested with authority, but acting either from motives of public spirit, or in order to help some one who has been wronged; here again the exception will apply. But if the motive is different, the exception does not apply. (4) would also include a public complaint by a person who has suffered a wrong; he has every right to seek public redress.

149. Whether ye publish
A good deed or conceal it
Or cover evil with pardon,
Verily Allah doth blot out
(Sins) and hath power
(In the judgement of values).[655]

١٤٩ إِن تُبْدُوا۟ خَيْرًا أَوْ تُخْفُوهُ
أَوْ تَعْفُوا۟ عَن سُوٓءٍ فَإِنَّ ٱللَّهَ كَانَ عَفُوًّا قَدِيرًا

150. Those who deny Allah
And His Messengers, and (those
Who) wish to separate
Allah from His Messengers,
Saying: "We believe in some
But reject others":
And (those who) wish
To take a course midway—[656]

١٥٠ إِنَّ ٱلَّذِينَ يَكْفُرُونَ بِٱللَّهِ وَرُسُلِهِۦ
وَيُرِيدُونَ أَن يُفَرِّقُوا۟ بَيْنَ ٱللَّهِ وَرُسُلِهِۦ
وَيَقُولُونَ نُؤْمِنُ بِبَعْضٍ وَنَكْفُرُ بِبَعْضٍ
وَيُرِيدُونَ أَن يَتَّخِذُوا۟ بَيْنَ ذَٰلِكَ سَبِيلًا

151. They are in truth
(Equally) Unbelievers;
And We have prepared
For Unbelievers a humiliating
Punishment.

١٥١ أُو۟لَٰٓئِكَ هُمُ ٱلْكَٰفِرُونَ حَقًّا
وَأَعْتَدْنَا لِلْكَٰفِرِينَ عَذَابًا مُّهِينًا

152. To those who believe
In Allah and His Messengers
And make no distinction
Between any of the messengers,
We shall soon give
Their (due) rewards:
For Allah is Oft-Forgiving,
Most Merciful.

١٥٢ وَٱلَّذِينَ ءَامَنُوا۟ بِٱللَّهِ وَرُسُلِهِۦ
وَلَمْ يُفَرِّقُوا۟ بَيْنَ أَحَدٍ مِّنْهُمْ
أُو۟لَٰٓئِكَ سَوْفَ يُؤْتِيهِمْ أُجُورَهُمْ
وَكَانَ ٱللَّهُ غَفُورًا رَّحِيمًا

C. 68.—The People of the Book went wrong:
(4:153-176.) The Jews in breaking their Covenant,
And slandering Mary and Jesus,
And in their usury and injustice;
And the Christians in raising
Jesus the Messenger to equality

---

655. *Qadīr*: I have translated it more fully than most translators. The root *qadara* not only implies power, ability, strength, but two other ideas which it is difficult to convey in a single word, *viz.*, the act and power of estimating the true value of a thing or persons, as in 6:91; and the act and power of regulating something so as to bring it into correspondence with something. "Judgement of values" I think sums up these finer shades of meaning. Allah forgives what is wrong and is able to fully appreciate and judge the value of our good deeds whether we publish them or conceal them.

656. Unbelief takes various forms. Three are mentioned here:(1) denial of Allah and His revelation to mankind through inspired men; (2) a sort of nominal belief in Allah and His Prophets, but one which is partial, and mixed up with racial pride, which does not allow for the recognition of any Messengers beyond those of a particular race; and (3) a nominal belief in universal revelation, but so hedged around with peculiar doctrines of exclusive salvation, that it practically approaches to a denial of Allah's universal love for all mankind and all Creation. All three amount to Unbelief, for they really deny Allah's universal love and care.

With Allah. Allah's revelation
Is continued in the Qur'ān,
Which comes with manifest proof
And a clear light to those who understand.

SECTION 22.

153. The People of the Book
Ask thee to cause
A book to descend to them
From heaven: indeed
They asked Moses
For an even greater
(Miracle), for they said:
"Show us Allah in public,"[657]
But they were dazed
For their presumption,
By thunder and lightning.
Yet they worshipped the calf
Even after Clear Signs
Had come to them;
Even so We forgave them;
And gave Moses manifest
Proofs of authority.

(١٥٣) يَسْـَٔلُكَ أَهْلُ ٱلْكِتَٰبِ
أَن تُنَزِّلَ عَلَيْهِمْ كِتَٰبًا مِّنَ ٱلسَّمَآءِ
فَقَدْ سَأَلُوا۟ مُوسَىٰٓ أَكْبَرَ مِن ذَٰلِكَ
فَقَالُوٓا۟ أَرِنَا ٱللَّهَ جَهْرَةً
فَأَخَذَتْهُمُ ٱلصَّٰعِقَةُ بِظُلْمِهِمْ
ثُمَّ ٱتَّخَذُوا۟ ٱلْعِجْلَ مِنۢ بَعْدِ مَا جَآءَتْهُمُ
ٱلْبَيِّنَٰتُ فَعَفَوْنَا عَن ذَٰلِكَ
وَءَاتَيْنَا مُوسَىٰ سُلْطَٰنًا مُّبِينًا

154. And for their Covenant
We raised over them
(The towering height)
Of Mount (Sinai);[658]
And (on another occasion)
We said: "Enter the gate
With humility"; and (once again)
We commanded them:
"Transgress not in the matter
Of the Sabbath."
And We took from them
A solemn Covenant.

(١٥٤) وَرَفَعْنَا فَوْقَهُمُ ٱلطُّورَ
بِمِيثَٰقِهِمْ وَقُلْنَا لَهُمُ
ٱدْخُلُوا۟ ٱلْبَابَ سُجَّدًا
وَقُلْنَا لَهُمْ
لَا تَعْدُوا۟ فِى ٱلسَّبْتِ
وَأَخَذْنَا مِنْهُم مِّيثَٰقًا غَلِيظًا

657. *Cf.* 2:55, for the thunder and lightning which dazed those who were presumptuous enough to ask that they should see Allah face to face, and 2:51 and n. 66, for the worship of the golden calf.

The lesson is that it is presumptuous on the part of man to judge of spiritual things in terms of material things, or to ask to see Allah with their material eyes when Allah is above material forms and is independent of time and space.

658. In this verse there is a recapitulation of three salient incidents of Jewish refractoriness already referred to in the second Sūrah: *viz.*, (1) the Covenant under the towering height of Sinai, 2:63; (2) their arrogance where they were commanded humility in entering a town, 2:58; and (3) their transgression of the Sabbath, 2:65.

155. (They have incurred divine[659]
Displeasure): in that they
Broke their Covenant;
That they rejected the Signs
Of Allah; that they slew
The Messengers in defiance[660]
Of right; that they said,
"Our hearts are the wrappings[661]
(Which preserve Allah's Word;
We need no more)"—nay,
Allah hath set the seal on
their hearts
For their blasphemy,
And little is it they believe—

﴿١٥٥﴾ فَبِمَا نَقْضِهِم مِّيثَٰقَهُمْ
وَكُفْرِهِم بِـَٔايَٰتِ ٱللَّهِ
وَقَتْلِهِمُ ٱلْأَنۢبِيَآءَ بِغَيْرِ حَقٍّ
وَقَوْلِهِمْ قُلُوبُنَا غُلْفٌۢ
بَلْ طَبَعَ ٱللَّهُ عَلَيْهَا بِكُفْرِهِمْ
فَلَا يُؤْمِنُونَ إِلَّا قَلِيلًا

156. That they rejected Faith;
That they uttered against Mary
A grave false charge;[662]

﴿١٥٦﴾ وَبِكُفْرِهِمْ وَقَوْلِهِمْ
عَلَىٰ مَرْيَمَ بُهْتَٰنًا عَظِيمًا

157. That they said (in boast),
"We killed Christ Jesus
The son of Mary,
The Messenger of Allah"—
But they killed him not,

﴿١٥٧﴾ وَقَوْلِهِمْ إِنَّا قَتَلْنَا ٱلْمَسِيحَ عِيسَى
ٱبْنَ مَرْيَمَ رَسُولَ ٱللَّهِ
وَمَا قَتَلُوهُ

659. In verses 155, 156, 157, 160 (latter half), and 161 with parenthetical clauses including those in verses 158-159, and 160 (first half), there is a catalogue of the iniquities of which the Jews were guilty, and for these iniquities we must understand some such words as: "They are under divine displeasure." Each clause of the indictment I have indicated by prefixing the word "that."

660. *Cf.* 3:21, and nn. 363 and 364.

661. *Cf.* 2:88, and n. 92, where the full meaning is explained.

Note the crescendo (heightening effect) in the argument. Their iniquities were: (1) that they broke their Covenant; (2) that they rejected Allah's guidance as conveyed in His signs; (3) that they killed Allah's Messengers and incurred a double guilt, *viz.*, that of murder and that of a deliberate defiance of Allah's law; and (4) that they imagined themselves arrogantly self-sufficient, which means a blasphemous closing of their hearts forever against the admission of Allah's grace. Then begins another series of iniquities from a different point of view: (1) that they rejected Faith; (2) that they made false charges against a saintly woman like Mary, who was chosen by Allah to be the mother of Jesus; (3) that they boasted of having killed Jesus when they were victims of their own self-hallucination; (4) that they hindered people from Allah's way; and (5) that by means of usury and fraud they oppressed their fellow-men.

662. The false charge against Mary was that she was unchaste, *Cf.* 19:27-28. Such a charge is bad enough to make against any woman, but to make it against Mary, the mother of Jesus, was to bring into ridicule Allah's power itself. Islam is specially strong in guarding the reputation of women. Slanderers of women are bound to bring four witnesses in support of their accusations, and if they fail to produce four witnesses, they are to be flogged with eighty stripes and debarred forever from being competent witnesses: 24:4.

Nor crucified him,[663] But so it was made To appear to them, And those who differ Therein are full of doubts, With no (certain) knowledge, But only conjecture to follow, For of a surety They killed him not—	وَمَا صَلَبُوهُ وَلَٰكِن شُبِّهَ لَهُمْ وَإِنَّ الَّذِينَ اخْتَلَفُوا فِيهِ لَفِي شَكٍّ مِّنْهُ مَا لَهُم بِهِ مِنْ عِلْمٍ إِلَّا اتِّبَاعَ الظَّنِّ وَمَا قَتَلُوهُ يَقِينًا
158. Nay, Allah raised him up[664] Unto Himself; and Allah Is Exalted in Power, Wise—	١٥٨ بَل رَّفَعَهُ اللَّهُ إِلَيْهِ وَكَانَ اللَّهُ عَزِيزًا حَكِيمًا
159. And there is none Of the People of the Book But must believe in him Before his death;[665] And on the Day of Judgement He will be a witness[666] Against them—	١٥٩ وَإِن مِّنْ أَهْلِ الْكِتَابِ إِلَّا لَيُؤْمِنَنَّ بِهِ قَبْلَ مَوْتِهِ وَيَوْمَ الْقِيَامَةِ يَكُونُ عَلَيْهِمْ شَهِيدًا

663. The end of the life of Jesus on earth is as much involved in mystery as his birth, and indeed the greater part of his private life, except the three main years of his ministry. It is not profitable to discuss the many doubts and conjectures among the early Christian sects and among Muslim theologians. The Orthodox Christian Churches make it a cardinal point of their doctrine that his life was taken on the Cross, that he died and was buried, that on the third day he rose in the body with his wounds intact, and walked about and conversed, and ate with his disciples, and was afterwards taken up bodily to heaven. This is necessary for the theological doctrine of blood sacrifice and vicarious atonement for sins, which is rejected by Islam. But some of the early Christian sects did not believe that Christ was killed on the Cross. The Basilidans believed that someone else was substituted for him. The Docetae held that Christ never had a real physical or natural body, but only an apparent or phantom body, and that his Crucifixion was only apparent, not real. The Marcionite Gospel (about A.C. 138) denied that Jesus was born, and merely said that he appeared in human form. The Gospel of St. Barnabas supported the theory of substitution on the Cross. The Qur'anic teaching is that Christ was not crucified nor killed by the Jews, notwithstanding certain apparent circumstances which produced that illusion in the minds of some of his enemies; that disputations, doubts, and conjectures on such matters are vain; and that he was taken up to Allah (see next verse and note).

664. There is difference of opinion as to the exact interpretation of this verse. The words are: The Jews did not kill Jesus, but Allah raised him up (*rafa'a*) to Himself. One school holds that Jesus did not die the usual human death, but still lives in the body in heaven, which is the generally accepted Muslim view. Another holds that he did die (v. 120) but not when he was supposed to be crucified, and that his being "raised up" unto Allah means that instead of being disgraced as a malefactor, as the Jews intended, he was on the contrary honoured by Allah as His Messenger: see also next verse. The same word *rafa'a* is used in association with honour in connection with Muṣṭafā in 94:4. (R).

665. *Before his death.* Interpreters are not agreed as to the exact meaning. Those who hold that Jesus did not die (see last note) refer the pronoun "his" to Jesus. They say that Jesus is still living in the body and that he will appear just before the Final Day, after the coming of the Mahdi, when the world will be purified of sin and unbelief. There will be a final death before the final Resurrection, but all will have believed before that final death. Others think that "his" is better referred to "none of the People of the Book", and that the emphatic form "must believe" (*layu'minanna*) denotes more a question of duty than of fact. (R).

666. *Cf.* 4:41.

160. For the iniquity of the Jews
We made unlawful for them[667]
Certain (foods) good and wholesome
Which had been lawful for them—
In that they hindered many
From Allah's Way—

١٦٠ فَبِظُلْمٍ مِّنَ الَّذِينَ هَادُوا
حَرَّمْنَا عَلَيْهِمْ طَيِّبَاتٍ
أُحِلَّتْ لَهُمْ وَبِصَدِّهِمْ
عَن سَبِيلِ اللَّهِ كَثِيرًا

161. That they took usury,
Though they were forbidden;
And that they devoured
Men's substance wrongfully—
We have prepared for those
Among them who reject Faith
A grievous punishment.

١٦١ وَأَخْذِهِمُ الرِّبَوٰا وَقَدْ نُهُوا عَنْهُ
وَأَكْلِهِمْ أَمْوَٰلَ النَّاسِ بِالْبَٰطِلِ
وَأَعْتَدْنَا لِلْكَٰفِرِينَ مِنْهُمْ عَذَابًا أَلِيمًا

162. But those among them
Who are well-grounded in knowledge,
And the Believers,
Believe in what hath been
Revealed to thee and what was
Revealed before thee:
And (especially) those
Who establish regular prayer
And practise regular charity
And believe in Allah
And in the Last Day:
To them shall We soon
Give a great reward.

١٦٢ لَّٰكِنِ الرَّٰسِخُونَ فِي الْعِلْمِ مِنْهُمْ
وَالْمُؤْمِنُونَ يُؤْمِنُونَ بِمَا أُنزِلَ إِلَيْكَ
وَمَا أُنزِلَ مِن قَبْلِكَ
وَالْمُقِيمِينَ الصَّلَوٰةَ
وَالْمُؤْتُونَ الزَّكَوٰةَ
وَالْمُؤْمِنُونَ بِاللَّهِ وَالْيَوْمِ الْآخِرِ
أُولَٰٓئِكَ سَنُؤْتِيهِمْ أَجْرًا عَظِيمًا

SECTION 23.

163. We have sent thee
Inspiration, as We sent it
To Noah and the Messengers[668]
After him: We sent

١٦٣ إِنَّآ أَوْحَيْنَآ إِلَيْكَ كَمَآ أَوْحَيْنَآ
إِلَىٰ نُوحٍ وَالنَّبِيِّـۧنَ مِنۢ بَعْدِهِۦ

667. *Cf.* 6:146. The ceremonial law of the Jews forbade the eating of the flesh of the camel, rabbit and hare (Leviticus xi. 4-6), and the fat of oxen, sheep, and goats (Leviticus vii. 23), and was in other respects very strict.

668. First we have a general statement: that inspiration was sent to many Messengers, and the inspiration was of the same kind as that sent to the Prophet Muḥammad, for Allah's Message is one. Note that what is spoken of here is Inspiration, not necessarily a Book. Every nation or group of people had a messenger: 10:47. Some of these messengers have been mentioned by name in the Qur'ān, and some not; 4:164.

Inspiration to Abraham,[669]
Ismā'īl, Isaac, Jacob
And the Tribes, to Jesus,
Job, Jonah, Aaron, and Solomon,
And to David We gave
The Psalms.

وَأَوْحَيْنَآ إِلَىٰٓ إِبْرَٰهِيمَ وَإِسْمَٰعِيلَ وَإِسْحَٰقَ
وَيَعْقُوبَ وَٱلْأَسْبَاطِ وَعِيسَىٰ وَأَيُّوبَ
وَيُونُسَ وَهَٰرُونَ وَسُلَيْمَٰنَ ۚ وَءَاتَيْنَا دَاوُۥدَ زَبُورًا

164. Of some messengers We have
Already told thee the story;
Of others we have not—
And to Moses Allah spoke
direct—[670]

١٦٤ وَرُسُلًا قَدْ قَصَصْنَٰهُمْ عَلَيْكَ مِن قَبْلُ
وَرُسُلًا لَّمْ نَقْصُصْهُمْ عَلَيْكَ ۚ
وَكَلَّمَ ٱللَّهُ مُوسَىٰ تَكْلِيمًا

165. Messengers who gave good news[671]
As well as warning,
That mankind, after (the coming)
Of the messengers, should have
No plea against Allah:
For Allah is Exalted in Power,
Wise.

١٦٥ رُّسُلًا مُّبَشِّرِينَ وَمُنذِرِينَ
لِئَلَّا يَكُونَ لِلنَّاسِ عَلَى ٱللَّهِ حُجَّةٌۢ بَعْدَ ٱلرُّسُلِ ۚ
وَكَانَ ٱللَّهُ عَزِيزًا حَكِيمًا

166. But Allah beareth witness
That what He hath sent
Unto thee He hath sent
From His (own) knowledge,[672]
And the angels bear witness:
But enough is Allah for a witness.

١٦٦ لَّٰكِنِ ٱللَّهُ يَشْهَدُ بِمَآ أَنزَلَ إِلَيْكَ ۖ
أَنزَلَهُۥ بِعِلْمِهِۦ ۖ وَٱلْمَلَٰٓئِكَةُ يَشْهَدُونَ ۚ
وَكَفَىٰ بِٱللَّهِ شَهِيدًا

167. Those who reject Faith
And keep off (men)
From the Way of Allah,
Have verily strayed far,
Far away from the Path.

١٦٧ إِنَّ ٱلَّذِينَ كَفَرُوا۟ وَصَدُّوا۟ عَن
سَبِيلِ ٱللَّهِ قَدْ ضَلُّوا۟ ضَلَٰلًۢا بَعِيدًا

168. Those who reject Faith
And do wrong—Allah

١٦٨ إِنَّ ٱلَّذِينَ كَفَرُوا۟ وَظَلَمُوا۟ لَمْ يَكُنِ ٱللَّهُ

---

669. *Cf.* 2:136 and 3:84. The list here given is in three groups. (1) The first group, Abraham's family, is the same as in 2:136 (where see the note) and in 3:84. (2) Then we have the Prophets Jesus, Job and Jonah, who symbolise patience and perseverance. (3) Then we have Aaron the priest and Solomon the King, both great figures, but each subordinate to another primary figure, *viz.*, Moses (mentioned in the next verse) and David (mentioned at the end of this verse). David's distinction was the Psalms, which are still extant. Though their present form may possibly be different from the original and they do undoubtedly include Psalms not written by David, the collection contains much devotional poetry of a high order. (R).

670. Allah spoke to Moses on Mount Sinai. Hence the title of Moses in Muslim theology: *Kalīm Allāh*: the one to whom Allah spoke. (R).

671. Every prophet proclaims Allah's goodness to the righteous and forgiveness to those who repent, (good news), and the Wrath to come for those who reject Faith and live in iniquity (warning). Their mission of warning is a prelude and complement to their mission of good news. No one can then say that he or she did not know.

672. Inspiration, though it is clothed in human language, and shaped to the personality of the inspired one, proceeds from the knowledge of Allah. (R).

Will not forgive them Nor guide them To any way—	لِيَغْفِرَ لَهُمْ وَلَا لِيَهْدِيَهُمْ طَرِيقًا
169. Except the way of Hell, To dwell therein forever. And this to Allah is easy.[673]	١٦٩ إِلَّا طَرِيقَ جَهَنَّمَ خَٰلِدِينَ فِيهَآ أَبَدًا وَكَانَ ذَٰلِكَ عَلَى ٱللَّهِ يَسِيرًا
170. O mankind! the Messenger Hath come to you in truth From Allah: believe in him; It is best for you.[674] But if Ye reject Faith, to Allah Belong all things in the heavens And on earth: and Allah Is All-Knowing, All-Wise.	١٧٠ يَٰٓأَيُّهَا ٱلنَّاسُ قَدْ جَآءَكُمُ ٱلرَّسُولُ بِٱلْحَقِّ مِن رَّبِّكُمْ فَـَٔامِنُوا۟ خَيْرًا لَّكُمْ وَإِن تَكْفُرُوا۟ فَإِنَّ لِلَّهِ مَا فِى ٱلسَّمَٰوَٰتِ وَٱلْأَرْضِ وَكَانَ ٱللَّهُ عَلِيمًا حَكِيمًا
171. O People of the Book! Commit no excesses[675] In your religion: nor say Of Allah aught but the truth. Christ Jesus the son of Mary Was (no more than) A Messenger of Allah, And His Word, Which He bestowed on Mary, And a Spirit proceeding From Him: so believe In Allah and His Messengers. Say not "Trinity": desist:[676]	١٧١ يَٰٓأَهْلَ ٱلْكِتَٰبِ لَا تَغْلُوا۟ فِى دِينِكُمْ وَلَا تَقُولُوا۟ عَلَى ٱللَّهِ إِلَّا ٱلْحَقَّ إِنَّمَا ٱلْمَسِيحُ عِيسَى ٱبْنُ مَرْيَمَ رَسُولُ ٱللَّهِ وَكَلِمَتُهُۥٓ أَلْقَىٰهَآ إِلَىٰ مَرْيَمَ وَرُوحٌ مِّنْهُ فَـَٔامِنُوا۟ بِٱللَّهِ وَرُسُلِهِۦ وَلَا تَقُولُوا۟ ثَلَٰثَةٌ ٱنتَهُوا۟

673. *Easy*—not in the sense that Allah takes any pleasure in any of His creatures going astray. The contrary is the case: for Allah's Grace recognises all good in us to such an extent that it is compared to gratitude in 4:147; see n. 653. We must understand *easy* in the sense that Allah is Supreme in knowledge and power; if any forces of rebellion foolishly think that they can evade punishment, they are mistaken. Punishment comes as a matter of course. It is not a matter of difficulty or exertion on the part of Allah.

674. Allah's solicitude for us is for our own good, not because He gets any advantage from it. For He is independent of all things, and everything declares His glory and praise.

675. Just as a foolish servant may go wrong by excess of zeal for his master, so in religion people's excesses may lead them to blasphemy or a spirit the very opposite of religion. The Jewish excesses in the direction of formalism, racialism, exclusiveness, and rejection of Christ Jesus have been denounced in many places. Here the Christian attitude is condemned, which raises Jesus to an equality with Allah; in some cases venerates Mary almost to idolatry; attributes a physical son to Allah; and invents the doctrine of the Trinity, opposed to all reason, which according to the Athanasian Creed, unless a man believes, he is doomed to hell forever. Let our Muslims also beware lest they fall into excesses either in doctrine or in formalism.

676. Christ's attributes are mentioned: (1) that he was the son of a woman, Mary, and therefore a man; (2) but a messenger, a man with a mission from Allah, and therefore entitled to honour; (3) a Word bestowed on Mary, for he was created by Allah's word "Be" (*kun*), and he was; 3:59; (4) a spirit proceeding from Allah, but not Allah: his life and his mission were more limited than in the case of some other Messengers, though we must pay equal honour to him as a Prophet of Allah. The doctrines of Trinity, equality with Allah, and sonship, are repudiated as blasphemies. Allah is independent of all needs and has no need of a son to manage His affairs. The Gospel of John (whoever wrote it) has put in a great deal of Alexandrian and Gnostic mysticism round the doctrine of the Word (Greek, Logos), but it is simply explained here. (R).

It will be better for you: For Allah is One God: Glory be to Him: (Far Exalted is He) above Having a son. To Him Belong all things in the heavens And on earth. And enough Is Allah as a Disposer of affairs.	خَيْرًا لَّكُمْ إِنَّمَا ٱللَّهُ إِلَٰهٌ وَٰحِدٌ سُبْحَٰنَهُۥٓ أَن يَكُونَ لَهُۥ وَلَدٌ لَّهُۥ مَا فِى ٱلسَّمَٰوَٰتِ وَمَا فِى ٱلْأَرْضِ وَكَفَىٰ بِٱللَّهِ وَكِيلًا

SECTION 24.

172. Christ disdaineth not To serve and worship Allah,[677] Nor do the angels, those Nearest (to Allah): Those who disdain His worship and are arrogant— He will gather them all Together unto Himself[678] To (answer).	١٧٢ لَّن يَسْتَنكِفَ ٱلْمَسِيحُ أَن يَكُونَ عَبْدًا لِّلَّهِ وَلَا ٱلْمَلَٰٓئِكَةُ ٱلْمُقَرَّبُونَ وَمَن يَسْتَنكِفْ عَنْ عِبَادَتِهِۦ وَيَسْتَكْبِرْ فَسَيَحْشُرُهُمْ إِلَيْهِ جَمِيعًا
173. But to those who believe And do deeds of righteousness, He will give their (due) Rewards—and more, Out of His bounty: But those who are Disdainful and arrogant, He will punish With a grievous penalty; Nor will they find, Besides Allah, any To protect or help them.	١٧٣ فَأَمَّا ٱلَّذِينَ ءَامَنُوا۟ وَعَمِلُوا۟ ٱلصَّٰلِحَٰتِ فَيُوَفِّيهِمْ أُجُورَهُمْ وَيَزِيدُهُم مِّن فَضْلِهِۦ وَأَمَّا ٱلَّذِينَ ٱسْتَنكَفُوا۟ وَٱسْتَكْبَرُوا۟ فَيُعَذِّبُهُمْ عَذَابًا أَلِيمًا وَلَا يَجِدُونَ لَهُم مِّن دُونِ ٱللَّهِ وَلِيًّا وَلَا نَصِيرًا
174. O mankind! Verily There hath come to you A convincing proof From your Lord: For We have sent unto you A light (that is) manifest.[679]	١٧٤ يَٰٓأَيُّهَا ٱلنَّاسُ قَدْ جَآءَكُم بُرْهَٰنٌ مِّن رَّبِّكُمْ وَأَنزَلْنَآ إِلَيْكُمْ نُورًا مُّبِينًا

677. Christ often watched and prayed, as a humble worshipper of Allah; and his agony in the Garden of Gethsemane was full of human dignity, suffering, and self-humiliation (see Matt. xxvi. 36-45).

678. The disdainful and the arrogant are the crew of Satan, who will be gathered together before the Supreme Throne for punishment.

679. The Proof and the Light are the Qur'ān and the Personality, Life and Teaching of Muḥammad Muṣṭafā.

175. Then those who believe
In Allah, and hold fast
To Him—soon will He
Admit them to Mercy
And Grace from Himself,[680]
And guide them to Himself
By a straight Way.

١٧٥ فَأَمَّا ٱلَّذِينَ ءَامَنُوا۟ بِٱللَّهِ
وَٱعْتَصَمُوا۟ بِهِۦ فَسَيُدْخِلُهُمْ فِى رَحْمَةٍ مِّنْهُ
وَفَضْلٍ وَيَهْدِيهِمْ إِلَيْهِ صِرَٰطًا مُّسْتَقِيمًا

176. They ask thee
For a legal decision.
Say: Allah directs (thus)
About those who leave
No descendants or ascendants
As heirs. If it is a man[681]
That dies, leaving a sister
But no child, she shall
Have half the inheritance:
If (such a deceased was)
A woman, who left no child,
Her brother takes her inheritance:
If there are two sisters,
They shall have two-thirds
Of the inheritance
(Between them): if there are
Brothers and sisters, (they share),
The male having twice
The share of the female.
Thus doth Allah make clear
To you (His law), lest
Ye err. And Allah
Hath knowledge of all things.

١٧٦ يَسْتَفْتُونَكَ
قُلِ ٱللَّهُ يُفْتِيكُمْ فِى ٱلْكَلَٰلَةِ
إِنِ ٱمْرُؤٌا۟ هَلَكَ لَيْسَ لَهُۥ وَلَدٌ
وَلَهُۥٓ أُخْتٌ فَلَهَا نِصْفُ مَا تَرَكَ
وَهُوَ يَرِثُهَآ إِن لَّمْ يَكُن لَّهَا وَلَدٌ
فَإِن كَانَتَا ٱثْنَتَيْنِ
فَلَهُمَا ٱلثُّلُثَانِ مِمَّا تَرَكَ
وَإِن كَانُوٓا۟ إِخْوَةً رِّجَالًا وَنِسَآءً
فَلِلذَّكَرِ مِثْلُ حَظِّ ٱلْأُنثَيَيْنِ
يُبَيِّنُ ٱللَّهُ لَكُمْ أَن تَضِلُّوا۟
وَٱللَّهُ بِكُلِّ شَىْءٍ عَلِيمٌ

680. From Himself = From His Presence: see 3:195 and n. 501. The Mercy and Grace are expressed here as specially flowing from Him.

681. This verse supplements the rule of inheritance of the estate of a deceased person who has left as heir neither a descendant nor an ascendant. We shall call such a person *A*, who may be either a male or a female. In 4:12 (second half), *A's* case was considered where he had left uterine brothers or sisters. Here *A's* case is considered where he has left brothers and/or sisters by the father's side, whether the mother was the same or not. "Brothers" and "sisters" in this verse must be construed to be such brothers and sisters.

For the sake of clearness I have expanded the terse language of the original in the translation. Let me explain it more concretely in this note. *A*, and "brother" and "sister" being strictly defined as above, we proceed to consider how *A's* inheritance would be divided. If *A* left a widow or widower, the widow's or widower's share would first be calculated as in the first half of 4:12; if *A* left no spouse, this calculation would not be necessary. Then if *A* left a single "sister," she would have a half share, the remaining half (insofar as it, or a part of it, does not fall to a spouse, if any) going to remoter heirs; if a single "brother," he would have the whole (subject to the spouse's right if there is a spouse); if more than one "brother," they divide the whole (subject to, etc.). If *A* left two or more "sisters," they get between them two-thirds, subject to the spouse's right, if any. If *A* left a "brother" and "sister," or "brothers" and "sisters," they divide on the basis that each "brother's" share is twice that of the "sister" (subject to, etc.). In all cases debts, funeral expenses, and legacies (to the amount allowed) have priority as in n. 522.

INTRODUCTION TO SŪRAH 5—*AL MĀ'IDAH*

This Sūrah deals, by way of recapitulation, with the backsliding of the Jews and Christians from their pure religions, to which the coping stone was placed by Islam. It refers particularly to the Christians, and to their solemn Sacrament of the Last Supper, to whose true meaning they are declared to have been false. (R).

As a logical corollary to the corruption of the earlier religions of Allah, the practical precepts of Islam, about food, cleanliness, justice, and fidelity are recapitulated.

The third verse contains the memorable declaration: "This day have I perfected your religion for you": which was promulgated in 10 H., during the Prophet's last Pilgrimage to Makkah. Chronologically it was the last verse to be revealed.

Summary—Beginning with an appeal to fulfil, as sacred, all obligations, human and divine, it points to certain regulations about food, as conducive to a sober and social life, without superstition and without bias or hatred (5:1-5, and C. 69).

Cleanliness of body, and justice and uprightness of dealing are nearest to Piety (5:12-26, and C. 70).

If the Jews and the Christians turned back from the Truth and violated their Covenants, they have had their warning (5:12-26, and C. 71).

The murder of Abel by Cain is the type of the treatment which the just man suffers from the envious. There is punishment from Allah. The just man must not grieve (5:27-43, and C. 72).

Muslims must do impartial justice, but must protect their own Brotherhood and their Faith from insult and scorn; they must appreciate piety, humility, and other good points among the Christians (5:46-86, and C. 73).

They must enjoy with gratitude all that is good and lawful, but guard themselves against excess. Swearing, intoxication, gambling, violation of the Sanctuary, superstitions of all kinds, and false evidence are condemned (5:87-108, and C. 74).

The miracles of Jesus, and how they were misused by those who bore his name (5:109-120, and C. 75).

C. 69.—All obligations are sacred, human
(5:1-6.) Or divine. In the spiritual world
We owe duties to Allah, which must
Be fulfilled. But whilst we are
In this world of sense, those duties
Are by no means isolated
From what we owe to ourselves
And our fellows in the world
Of men. We must respect the laws
And customs of the Sacred Mosque
And the Sacred Sanctuary.
In food our laws are simple:
All things good and pure are lawful.
We refuse not social intercourse
With men and women—
People of the Book.

Sūrah 5.

Al Mā'idah (The Repast)

In the name of Allah, Most Gracious, Most Merciful.

الجزء السادس سورة المائدة

بِسْمِ ٱللَّهِ ٱلرَّحْمَٰنِ ٱلرَّحِيمِ

1. O ye who believe!
Fulfil (all) obligations.[682]

يَٰٓأَيُّهَا ٱلَّذِينَ ءَامَنُوٓا۟ أَوْفُوا۟ بِٱلْعُقُودِ ۚ

Lawful unto you (for food)
Are all four-footed animals
With the exceptions named:[683]
But animals of the chase
Are forbidden while ye
Are in the Sacred Precincts
Or in pilgrim garb:[684]
For Allah doth command
According to His Will and Plan.[685]

أُحِلَّتْ لَكُم بَهِيمَةُ
ٱلْأَنْعَٰمِ إِلَّا مَا يُتْلَىٰ عَلَيْكُمْ
غَيْرَ مُحِلِّى ٱلصَّيْدِ وَأَنتُمْ حُرُمٌ ۗ
إِنَّ ٱللَّهَ يَحْكُمُ مَا يُرِيدُ

2. O ye who believe!
Violate not the sanctity
Of the Symbols of Allah,[686]

يَٰٓأَيُّهَا ٱلَّذِينَ ءَامَنُوا۟ لَا تُحِلُّوا۟ شَعَٰٓئِرَ ٱللَّهِ

682. This line has been justly admired for its terseness and comprehensiveness. Obligations: *'uqūd*: the Arabic word implies so many things that a whole chapter of Commentary can be written on it. First, there are the divine obligations that arise from our spiritual nature and our relation to Allah. He created us and implanted in us the faculty of knowledge and foresight; besides the intuition and reason which He gave us, He made Nature responsive to our needs, and His Signs in Nature are so many lessons to us in our own inner life; He further sent Messengers and Teachers, for the guidance of our conduct in individual, social, and public life. All these gifts create corresponding obligations which we must fulfil. But in our own human and material life we undertake mutual obligations express and implied. We make a promise; we enter into a commercial or social contract; we enter into a contract of marriage: we must faithfully fulfil all obligations in all these relationships. Our group of our State enters into a treaty: every individual in that group or State is bound to see that as far as lies in his power, such obligations are faithfully discharged. There are tacit obligations: living in civil society, we must respect its tacit conventions unless they are morally wrong, and in that case we must get out of such society. There are tacit obligations in the characters of host and guest, wayfarer or companion, employer or employed, etc., etc., which every man of Faith must discharge conscientiously. The man who deserts those who need him and goes to pray in a desert is a coward who disregards his obligations. All these obligations are inter-connected. Truth and fidelity are parts of religion in all relations of life.

This verse is numbered separately from the succeeding verses. (R).

683. That is, the exceptions named not only in the Qur'ān but in the Sunnah as well. See 5:4 below. (R).

684. *Cf.* 5:94-96. Hunting and the use of game are forbidden "while ye are *hurumun*," *i.e.*, while ye are (1) in the Sacred Precincts, or (2) in the special pilgrim garb (iḥrām), as to which see n. 212, 2:196. In most cases the two amount to the same thing. The Sacred Precincts are sanctuary both for man and beast.

685. Allah's commands are not arbitrary. His Will is the perfect Archetype or Plan of the world. Everything He wills has regard to His Plan, in which are reflected His perfect wisdom and goodness.

686. *Cf.* 2:158, where Ṣafā and Marwa are called "Symbols (*sha'ā'ir*) of Allah". Here the Symbols are everything connected with the Pilgrimage, *viz.*, (1) the places (like Ṣafā and Marwa, or the Ka'bah or 'Arafāt, etc.); (2) the rites and ceremonies prescribed; (3) prohibitions (such as that of hunting, etc.); (4) the times and seasons prescribed. There is spiritual and moral symbolism in all these. See notes on 2:158, 2:194-200.

Nor of the Sacred Month,[687]
Nor of the animals brought
For sacrifice, nor the garlands
That mark out such animals,
Nor the people resorting
To the Sacred House,[688]
Seeking of the bounty
And good pleasure
Of their Lord.
But when ye are clear
Of the Sacred Precincts[689]
And of pilgrim garb,
Ye may hunt
And let not the hatred
Of some people
In (once) shutting you out
Of the Sacred Mosque
Lead you to transgression
(And hostility on your part).[690]
Help ye one another
In righteousness and piety,
But help ye not one another
In sin and rancour:
Fear Allah: for Allah
Is strict in punishment.

وَلَا ٱلشَّهْرَ ٱلْحَرَامَ
وَلَا ٱلْهَدْىَ وَلَا ٱلْقَلَٰٓئِدَ
وَلَآ ءَآمِّينَ ٱلْبَيْتَ ٱلْحَرَامَ
يَبْتَغُونَ فَضْلًا مِّن رَّبِّهِمْ وَرِضْوَٰنًا
وَإِذَا حَلَلْتُمْ فَٱصْطَادُوا۟
وَلَا يَجْرِمَنَّكُمْ
شَنَـَٔانُ قَوْمٍ أَن صَدُّوكُمْ
عَنِ ٱلْمَسْجِدِ ٱلْحَرَامِ أَن تَعْتَدُوا۟
وَتَعَاوَنُوا۟ عَلَى ٱلْبِرِّ وَٱلتَّقْوَىٰ
وَلَا تَعَاوَنُوا۟ عَلَى ٱلْإِثْمِ وَٱلْعُدْوَٰنِ
وَٱتَّقُوا۟ ٱللَّهَ إِنَّ ٱللَّهَ شَدِيدُ ٱلْعِقَابِ

3. Forbidden to you (for food)
Are: dead meat, blood,
The flesh of swine, and that
On which hath been invoked
The name of other than Allah;[691]

٣ حُرِّمَتْ عَلَيْكُمُ ٱلْمَيْتَةُ وَٱلدَّمُ
وَلَحْمُ ٱلْخِنزِيرِ وَمَآ أُهِلَّ لِغَيْرِ ٱللَّهِ بِهِۦ

---

687. The month of pilgrimage, or else, collectively, the four sacred months (9:36), *viz, Rajab* (7th), *Dhu al Qa'dah* (11th), *Dhu al Hijjah* (12th, the month of Pilgrimage), and *Muharram* (the first of the year). In all these months War was prohibited. Excepting *Rajab* the other three months are consecutive.

688. The immunity from attack or interference extended to the animals brought as offerings for sacrifice and the garlands or fillets or distinguishing marks which gave them immunity. They were treated as sacred symbols. And of course every protection or immunity was enjoyed by the Pilgrims.

689. This is the state opposite to that described in n. 684, *i.e.*, when ye have left the Sacred Precincts, and have doffed the special pilgrim garb, showing your return to ordinary life.

690. See n. 205 to 2:191. In the sixth year of the Hijrah the Pagans, by way of hatred and persecution of the Muslims, had prevented them from access to the Sacred Mosque. When the Muslims were re-established in Makkah, some of them wanted to retaliate and exclude the Pagans or in some way to interfere with them in the Pilgrimage. This is condemned. Passing from the immediate event to the general principle, we must not retaliate or return evil for evil. The hatred of the wicked does not justify hostility on our part. We have to help each other in righteousness and piety, not in perpetuating feuds of hatred and enmity. We may have to fight and put down evil, but never in a spirit of malice or hatred, but always in a spirit of justice and righteousness.

691. *Cf.* 2:173 and nn. 173 and 174. The prohibition of dead meat, blood, the flesh of swine, and that on which other names than that of Allah have been invoked, has been there explained.

That which hath been
Killed by strangling,
Or by a violent blow,
Or by a headlong fall,
Or by being gored to death;
That which hath been (partly)
Eaten by a wild animal;
Unless ye are able
To slaughter it (in due form);[692]
That which is sacrificed[693]
On stone (altars);
(Forbidden) also is the division[694]
(Of meat) by raffling
With arrows: that is impiety.

وَٱلْمُنْخَنِقَةُ وَٱلْمَوْقُوذَةُ
وَٱلْمُتَرَدِّيَةُ وَٱلنَّطِيحَةُ
وَمَآ أَكَلَ ٱلسَّبُعُ إِلَّا مَا ذَكَّيْتُمْ
وَمَا ذُبِحَ عَلَى ٱلنُّصُبِ
وَأَن تَسْتَقْسِمُوا۟ بِٱلْأَزْلَٰمِ
ذَٰلِكُمْ فِسْقٌ

This day have those who
Reject Faith given up
All hope of your religion:[695]
Yet fear them not
But fear Me.
This day have I
Perfected your religion[696]
For you, completed
My favour upon you,
And have chosen for you
Islām as your religion.

ٱلْيَوْمَ يَئِسَ ٱلَّذِينَ كَفَرُوا۟ مِن دِينِكُمْ
فَلَا تَخْشَوْهُمْ وَٱخْشَوْنِ
ٱلْيَوْمَ أَكْمَلْتُ لَكُمْ دِينَكُمْ
وَأَتْمَمْتُ عَلَيْكُمْ نِعْمَتِى
وَرَضِيتُ لَكُمُ ٱلْإِسْلَٰمَ دِينًا

But if any is forced
By hunger, with no inclination
To transgression, Allah is
Indeed Oft-Forgiving,
Most Merciful.

فَمَنِ ٱضْطُرَّ فِى مَخْمَصَةٍ غَيْرَ مُتَجَانِفٍ
لِّإِثْمٍ فَإِنَّ ٱللَّهَ غَفُورٌ رَّحِيمٌ

4. They ask thee what is
Lawful to them (as food).[697]

٤ يَسْـَٔلُونَكَ مَاذَآ أُحِلَّ لَهُمْ

692. If an animal dies by strangling, or by a violent blow, or a headlong fall, or by being gored to death, or by being attacked by a wild animal, the presumption is that it becomes carrion, as the life-blood is congealed before being taken out of the body. But the presumption can be rebutted. If the life-blood still flows and the solemn mode of slaughter (*zabḥ*) in the name of Allah as a sacrifice is carried out, it becomes lawful as food.

693. This was also an idolatrous rite, different from that in which a sacrifice was devoted to a particular idol or a false god.

694. Gambling of all kinds is forbidden: 2:291. A sort of lottery or raffle practised by Pagan Arabs has been described in n. 241. Division of meat in this way is here forbidden, as it is a form of gambling.

695. So long as Islam was not organised, with its own community and its own laws, the Unbelievers had hoped to wean the Believers from the new Teaching. (Now that hope was gone, with the complete organisation of Islam).

696. The last verse revealed chronologically, marking the approaching end of Muṣṭafā's ministry in his earthly life.

697. The previous verse was negative: it defined what was not lawful for food, *viz.*, things gross, or disgusting, or dedicated to superstition. This verse is positive: it defines what is lawful, *viz.*, all things that are good and pure.

Say: Lawful unto you
Are (all) things good and pure:
And what ye have taught
Your trained hunting animals
(To catch) in the manner
Directed to you by Allah:
Eat what they catch for you,[698]
But pronounce the name
Of Allah over it: and fear
Allah; for Allah is swift
In taking account.

قُلْ أُحِلَّ لَكُمُ ٱلطَّيِّبَٰتُ
وَمَا عَلَّمْتُم مِّنَ ٱلْجَوَارِحِ مُكَلِّبِينَ
تُعَلِّمُونَهُنَّ مِمَّا عَلَّمَكُمُ ٱللَّهُ فَكُلُوا۟ مِمَّآ أَمْسَكْنَ عَلَيْكُمْ
وَٱذْكُرُوا۟ ٱسْمَ ٱللَّهِ عَلَيْهِ وَٱتَّقُوا۟ ٱللَّهَ
إِنَّ ٱللَّهَ سَرِيعُ ٱلْحِسَابِ

5. This day are (all) things
Good and pure made lawful
Unto you. The food
Of the People of the Book[699]
Is lawful unto you
And yours is lawful
Unto them.
(Lawful unto you in marriage)
Are (not only) chaste women
Who are believers, but
Chaste women among
The People of the Book,[700]
Revealed before your time—
When ye give them
Their due dowers, and desire
Chastity, not lewdness,

٥ ٱلْيَوْمَ أُحِلَّ لَكُمُ ٱلطَّيِّبَٰتُ
وَطَعَامُ ٱلَّذِينَ أُوتُوا۟ ٱلْكِتَٰبَ حِلٌّ لَّكُمْ
وَطَعَامُكُمْ حِلٌّ لَّهُمْ
وَٱلْمُحْصَنَٰتُ مِنَ ٱلْمُؤْمِنَٰتِ
وَٱلْمُحْصَنَٰتُ مِنَ ٱلَّذِينَ أُوتُوا۟ ٱلْكِتَٰبَ
مِن قَبْلِكُمْ إِذَآ ءَاتَيْتُمُوهُنَّ أُجُورَهُنَّ
مُحْصِنِينَ غَيْرَ مُسَٰفِحِينَ

698. In the matter of the killing for meat, the general rule is that the name of Allah, the true God should be pronounced as a rite in order to call our attention to the fact that we do not take life thoughtlessly but solemnly for food, with the permission of Allah, to whom we render the life back. The question of hunting is then raised. How can this solemn rite be performed when we send forth trained hawks, trained hounds, or trained cheetahs or other animals trained for the chase? They must necessarily kill at some distance from their masters. Their game is legalised on these conditions: (1) that they are trained to kill, not merely for their own appetite, or out of mere wantonness, but for their master's food; the training implies that something of the solemnity which Allah has taught us in this matter goes into their action; and (2) we are to pronounce the name of Allah over the quarry; this is interpreted to mean that the *Takbīr* should be pronounced when the hawk or dog, etc., is released to the quarry. (R).

699. The question is for food generally, such as is ordinarily "good and pure": in the matter of meat it should be killed with some sort of solemnity analogous to that of the *Takbīr*. The rules of Islam in this respect being analogous to those of the People of the Book, there is no objection to mutual recognition, as opposed to meat killed by Pagans with superstitious rites. In this respect the Christian rule is the same: "That ye abstain from meats offered to idols, and from blood, and from things strangled, and from fornication." (Acts. xv. 29). Notice the bracketing of fornication with things unlawful to eat.

700. Islam is not exclusive. Social intercourse, including inter-marriage, is permitted with the People of the Book. A Muslim man may marry a woman from their ranks on the same terms as he would marry a Muslim woman, *i.e.*, he must give her an economic and moral status, and must not be actuated merely by motives of lust or physical desire. A Muslim woman may not marry a non-Muslim man, because her Muslim status would be affected: the wife ordinarily takes the nationality and status given by her husband's law. A non-Muslim woman marrying a Muslim husband would be expected eventually to accept Islam. Any man or woman, of any race or faith, may, on accepting Islam, freely marry any Muslim woman or man, provided it be from motives of purity and chastity and not of lewdness.

Nor secret intrigues.
If anyone rejects faith,[701]
Fruitless is his work,
And in the Hereafter
He will be in the ranks
Of those who have lost
(All spiritual good).

وَلَا مُتَّخِذِىٓ أَخْدَانٍ ۗ
وَمَن يَكْفُرْ بِٱلْإِيمَٰنِ فَقَدْ حَبِطَ عَمَلُهُۥ
وَهُوَ فِى ٱلْءَاخِرَةِ مِنَ ٱلْخَٰسِرِينَ

C. 70.—(5:6-11) Allah wishes us to be clean and pure,
At prayer and at other times.
But justice and right conduct,
Even in the face of spite and hatred,
Are nearest to Piety and the love
Of Allah: in Him we put our trust.

SECTION 2.

6. O ye who believe!
When ye prepare
For prayer, wash[702]
Your faces, and your hands
(And arms) to the elbows;
Rub your heads (with water);
And (wash) your feet
To the ankles.
If ye are in a state
Of ceremonial impurity,[703]
Bathe your whole body.
But if ye are ill,
Or on a journey,
Or one of you cometh
From offices of nature,
Or ye have been
In contact with women,
And ye find no water,
Then take for yourselves
Clean sand or earth,[704]
And rub therewith

يَٰٓأَيُّهَا ٱلَّذِينَ ءَامَنُوٓا۟ إِذَا ٦
قُمْتُمْ إِلَى ٱلصَّلَوٰةِ فَٱغْسِلُوا۟ وُجُوهَكُمْ
وَأَيْدِيَكُمْ إِلَى ٱلْمَرَافِقِ وَٱمْسَحُوا۟
بِرُءُوسِكُمْ وَأَرْجُلَكُمْ إِلَى ٱلْكَعْبَيْنِ ۚ
وَإِن كُنتُمْ جُنُبًا فَٱطَّهَّرُوا۟ ۚ
وَإِن كُنتُم مَّرْضَىٰٓ أَوْ عَلَىٰ سَفَرٍ
أَوْ جَآءَ أَحَدٌ مِّنكُم مِّنَ ٱلْغَآئِطِ
أَوْ لَٰمَسْتُمُ ٱلنِّسَآءَ فَلَمْ تَجِدُوا۟ مَآءً
فَتَيَمَّمُوا۟ صَعِيدًا طَيِّبًا فَٱمْسَحُوا۟

701. As always, food, cleanliness, social intercourse, marriage and other interests in life, are linked with our duty to Allah and faith in Him. Duty and faith are for our own benefit, here and in the Hereafter.

702. These are the essentials of Wuḍū, or ablutions preparatory to prayers, *viz.* (1) to bathe the whole face in water, and (2) both hands and arms to the elbows, with (3) a little rubbing of the head with water (as the head is usually protected and comparatively clean), and (4) the bathing of the feet to the ankles. In addition, following the practice of the Prophet, it is usual first to wash the mouth, the throat, and the nose, before proceeding with the face, etc.

703. *Cf.* 4:43 and n. 563. Ritual impurity arises from sex pollution.

704. This is *Tayammum*, or washing with clean sand or earth where water is not available. I take it that this substitute is permissible both for Wuḍū and for a full bath, in the circumstances mentioned.

Your faces and hands.
Allah doth not wish
To place you in a difficulty,
But to make you clean,
And to complete
His favour to you,
That ye may be grateful.

بِوُجُوهِكُمْ وَأَيْدِيكُم مِّنْهُ مَا يُرِيدُ ٱللَّهُ
لِيَجْعَلَ عَلَيْكُم مِّنْ حَرَجٍ وَلَٰكِن يُرِيدُ
لِيُطَهِّرَكُمْ وَلِيُتِمَّ نِعْمَتَهُۥ عَلَيْكُمْ
لَعَلَّكُمْ تَشْكُرُونَ

7. And call in remembrance
The favour of Allah
Unto you, and His Covenant,[705]
Which He ratified
With you, when ye said:
"We hear and we obey":
And fear Allah, for Allah
Knoweth well
The secrets of your hearts.

٧ وَٱذْكُرُوا۟ نِعْمَةَ ٱللَّهِ عَلَيْكُمْ
وَمِيثَٰقَهُ ٱلَّذِى وَاثَقَكُم بِهِۦٓ إِذْ قُلْتُمْ
سَمِعْنَا وَأَطَعْنَا ۖ وَٱتَّقُوا۟ ٱللَّهَ ۚ
إِنَّ ٱللَّهَ عَلِيمٌۢ بِذَاتِ ٱلصُّدُورِ

8. O ye who believe!
Stand out firmly
For Allah, as witnesses[706]
To fair dealing, and let not
The hatred of others
To you make you swerve[707]
To wrong and depart from
Justice. Be just: that is
Next to Piety: and fear Allah.
For Allah is well-acquainted
With all that ye do.

٨ يَٰٓأَيُّهَا ٱلَّذِينَ ءَامَنُوا۟
كُونُوا۟ قَوَّٰمِينَ لِلَّهِ شُهَدَآءَ بِٱلْقِسْطِ ۖ
وَلَا يَجْرِمَنَّكُمْ شَنَـَٔانُ قَوْمٍ عَلَىٰٓ
أَلَّا تَعْدِلُوا۟ ۚ ٱعْدِلُوا۟ هُوَ أَقْرَبُ لِلتَّقْوَىٰ ۖ
وَٱتَّقُوا۟ ٱللَّهَ ۚ إِنَّ ٱللَّهَ خَبِيرٌۢ بِمَا تَعْمَلُونَ

9. To those who believe
And do deeds of righteousness
Hath Allah promised forgiveness
And a great reward.

٩ وَعَدَ ٱللَّهُ ٱلَّذِينَ ءَامَنُوا۟ وَعَمِلُوا۟
ٱلصَّٰلِحَٰتِ ۙ لَهُم مَّغْفِرَةٌ وَأَجْرٌ عَظِيمٌ

10. Those who reject faith
And deny Our Signs

١٠ وَٱلَّذِينَ كَفَرُوا۟ وَكَذَّبُوا۟ بِـَٔايَٰتِنَآ

705. There is a particular and a general meaning. The particular meaning refers to the solemn Pledge and Covenant taken by two groups of people at 'Aqaba, a valley near Minā, the first about fourteen months before the Hijrah, and the second a little later. These were Pledges of fealty to the Messenger of Allah, comparable to the Covenant under Mount Sinai taken in the time of Moses (See 2:63 and n. 78). The general meaning has been explained in n. 682 to 5:1: man is under a spiritual obligation under an implied Covenant with Allah; Allah has given man reason, judgement, the higher faculties of the soul, and even the position of Allah's vicegerent on earth (2:30), and man is bound to serve Allah faithfully and obey His Will. That obedience begins with cleanliness in bodily functions, food, etc. It goes on to cleanliness of mind and thought, and culminates in purity of motives in the inmost recesses of his heart and soul.

706. *Cf.* 4:135.

707. To do justice and act righteously in a favourable or neutral atmosphere is meritorious enough, but the real test comes when you have to do justice to people who hate you or to whom you have an aversion. But no less is required of you by the higher moral law.

Will be Companions
Of Hell-fire.

أُولَٰٓئِكَ أَصْحَٰبُ ٱلْجَحِيمِ

11. O ye who believe!
Call in remembrance
The favour of Allah
Unto you when
Certain men formed the design
To stretch out
Their hands against you,
But (Allah) held back
Their hands from you:[708]
So fear Allah. And on Allah
Let Believers put
(All) their trust.

(١١) يَٰٓأَيُّهَا ٱلَّذِينَ ءَامَنُوا۟
ٱذْكُرُوا۟ نِعْمَتَ ٱللَّهِ عَلَيْكُمْ
إِذْ هَمَّ قَوْمٌ أَن يَبْسُطُوٓا۟ إِلَيْكُمْ أَيْدِيَهُمْ
فَكَفَّ أَيْدِيَهُمْ عَنكُمْ ۖ وَٱتَّقُوا۟ ٱللَّهَ ۚ
وَعَلَى ٱللَّهِ فَلْيَتَوَكَّلِ ٱلْمُؤْمِنُونَ

C. 71.—If the men who received revelations
(5:12-26.) Before were false to their trust,
If they broke their agreements
And twisted Allah's Message from its aim,
If they rebelled against Truth and followed
Their fancies, Allah's grace was withdrawn
From them and they wandered in the wilderness.

SECTION 3.

12. Allah did aforetime
Take a Covenant from
The Children of Israel,[709]
And We appointed twelve
Captains among them.
And Allah said: "I am
With you: if ye (but)
Establish regular Prayers,
Practise regular Charity,
Believe in My messengers,
Honour and assist them,

(١٢) وَلَقَدْ أَخَذَ ٱللَّهُ مِيثَٰقَ بَنِىٓ إِسْرَٰٓءِيلَ
وَبَعَثْنَا مِنْهُمُ ٱثْنَىْ عَشَرَ نَقِيبًا ۖ
وَقَالَ ٱللَّهُ إِنِّى مَعَكُمْ ۖ لَئِنْ
أَقَمْتُمُ ٱلصَّلَوٰةَ وَءَاتَيْتُمُ ٱلزَّكَوٰةَ
وَءَامَنتُم بِرُسُلِى وَعَزَّرْتُمُوهُمْ

708. In the lifetime of the Prophet it happened again and again that the enemies of Islam stretched out their hands against him, his people, and his teaching. The odds were, from a worldly point of view, in their favour, but their hands were rendered inert and powerless because they were fighting against the truth of Allah. So does it happen always, now as it did then. True faith must take heart, and at the same time humbly recognise Allah's favour and mercy, and be grateful.

709. *Cf.* 2:63 and n. 78, "Moses. . .called for the elders of the people. . .and all the people answered together and said, 'All that the Lord hath spoken we will do'." (Exod. xix. 7-8.) This was under the towering height of Mount Sinai.

The captains or elders or leaders of the people were selected, one from each of the twelve tribes (see 2:60 and n. 73). For census purposes the names of the elders of the tribes are given in Num. i. 4-16: they are called "every one the head of the house of his fathers". Later, twelve other "heads of the Children of Israel" were selected to spy out of the land of Canaan: their names are mentioned in Num. xiii. 1-16. See also, below, 5:22-29 and notes.

And loan to Allah
A beautiful loan,[710]
Verily I will wipe out
From you your evils,
And admit you to Gardens
With rivers flowing beneath;
But if any of you, after this,
Resisteth faith, he hath truly
Wandered from the path
Of rectitude."[711]

وَأَقْرَضْتُمُ ٱللَّهَ قَرْضًا حَسَنًا لَّأُكَفِّرَنَّ
عَنكُمْ سَيِّـَٔاتِكُمْ وَلَأُدْخِلَنَّكُمْ جَنَّـٰتٍ
تَجْرِى مِن تَحْتِهَا ٱلْأَنْهَـٰرُ ۚ فَمَن كَفَرَ بَعْدَ
ذَٰلِكَ مِنكُمْ فَقَدْ ضَلَّ سَوَآءَ ٱلسَّبِيلِ

13. But because of their breach
Of their Covenant, We
Cursed them,[712] and made
Their hearts grow hard:
They change the words
From their (right) places
And forget a good part
Of the Message that was
Sent them, nor wilt thou
Cease to find them—
Barring a few—ever
Bent on (new) deceits:[713]
But forgive them, and overlook[714]
(Their misdeeds): for Allah
Loveth those who are kind.

١٣ فَبِمَا نَقْضِهِم مِّيثَـٰقَهُمْ
لَعَنَّـٰهُمْ وَجَعَلْنَا قُلُوبَهُمْ قَـٰسِيَةً ۖ
يُحَرِّفُونَ ٱلْكَلِمَ عَن مَّوَاضِعِهِۦ ۙ
وَنَسُوا۟ حَظًّا مِّمَّا ذُكِّرُوا۟ بِهِۦ ۚ وَلَا تَزَالُ تَطَّلِعُ
عَلَىٰ خَآئِنَةٍ مِّنْهُمْ إِلَّا قَلِيلًا مِّنْهُمْ ۖ فَٱعْفُ عَنْهُمْ
وَٱصْفَحْ ۚ إِنَّ ٱللَّهَ يُحِبُّ ٱلْمُحْسِنِينَ

14. From those, too, who call
Themselves Christians,
We did take a Covenant,[715]
But they forgot a good part
Of the Message that was
Sent them: so We estranged

١٤ وَمِنَ ٱلَّذِينَ قَالُوٓا۟ إِنَّا نَصَـٰرَىٰٓ
أَخَذْنَا مِيثَـٰقَهُمْ فَنَسُوا۟ حَظًّا
مِّمَّا ذُكِّرُوا۟ بِهِۦ فَأَغْرَيْنَا

710. *Cf.* 2:245, n. 276. The phrase means "spending in the cause of Allah." Allah in His infinite grace looks upon this as a loan, for which He gives a recompense manifold.

711. *The path of rectitude*: or the even way: see 2:108, n. 109.

712. *Cursed them*: that means that because of the breach of their Covenant, Allah withdrew His overflowing Grace from them. The withdrawal of Grace made their hearts grow hard in two ways: (1) they were no longer protected from the assaults of evil, and (2) they became impervious even to the message of forgiveness and mercy which is open to all Allah's creatures.

713. Israel, when it lost Allah's grace as above, began to sin against truth and religion in three ways: (1) they began to misuse Scripture itself, by either taking words out of their right meaning, or applying them to things for which they were never meant; (2) in doing so, they conveniently forgot a part of the Message and purpose of Allah; and (3) they invented new deceits to support the old ones.

714. *Cf.* 2:109 and n. 110, where I have explained the different shades of meaning in the words for "forgiveness."

715. The Christian Covenant may be taken to be the charge which Jesus gave to his disciples, and which the disciples accepted, to welcome Ahmad (Q. 61:6). Glimpses of this are to be found in the Gospel of St. John even as it exists now (John xv. 26, xvi. 7). It is those who call themselves "Christians" who reject this. True Christians have accepted it. The enmity between those who call themselves Christians and the Jews will continue till the Last Day.

Them, with enmity and hatred
Between the one and the other,
To the Day of Judgement.
And soon will Allah[715-A] show
Them what it is
They have done.

بَيْنَهُمُ ٱلْعَدَاوَةَ وَٱلْبَغْضَآءَ إِلَىٰ
يَوْمِ ٱلْقِيَٰمَةِ ۚ وَسَوْفَ يُنَبِّئُهُمُ ٱللَّهُ
بِمَا كَانُوا۟ يَصْنَعُونَ

15. O People of the Book!
There hath come to you
Our Messenger, revealing
To you much that ye
Used to hide in the Book,
And passing over much
(That is now unnecessary):

There hath come to you
From Allah a (new) light
And a perspicuous Book—[716]

١٥ يَٰٓأَهْلَ ٱلْكِتَٰبِ قَدْ جَآءَكُمْ
رَسُولُنَا يُبَيِّنُ لَكُمْ كَثِيرًا مِّمَّا
كُنتُمْ تُخْفُونَ مِنَ ٱلْكِتَٰبِ
وَيَعْفُوا۟ عَن كَثِيرٍ ۚ قَدْ جَآءَكُم
مِّنَ ٱللَّهِ نُورٌ وَكِتَٰبٌ مُّبِينٌ

16. Wherewith Allah guideth all
Who seek His good pleasure
To ways of peace and safety,
And leadeth them out
Of darkness, by His Will,
Unto the light—guideth them
To a Path that is Straight.

١٦ يَهْدِى بِهِ ٱللَّهُ مَنِ ٱتَّبَعَ
رِضْوَٰنَهُۥ سُبُلَ ٱلسَّلَٰمِ وَيُخْرِجُهُم
مِّنَ ٱلظُّلُمَٰتِ إِلَى ٱلنُّورِ بِإِذْنِهِۦ
وَيَهْدِيهِمْ إِلَىٰ صِرَٰطٍ مُّسْتَقِيمٍ

17. In blasphemy indeed
Are those that say
That Allah is Christ
The son of Mary.
Say: "Who then
Hath the least power
Against Allah, if His Will
Were to destroy Christ
The son of Mary, his mother,
And all—everyone
That is on the earth?
For to Allah belongeth

١٧ لَّقَدْ كَفَرَ ٱلَّذِينَ قَالُوٓا۟
إِنَّ ٱللَّهَ هُوَ ٱلْمَسِيحُ ٱبْنُ مَرْيَمَ ۚ
قُلْ فَمَن يَمْلِكُ مِنَ ٱللَّهِ شَيْـًٔا إِنْ
أَرَادَ أَن يُهْلِكَ ٱلْمَسِيحَ ٱبْنَ مَرْيَمَ
وَأُمَّهُۥ وَمَن فِى ٱلْأَرْضِ جَمِيعًا ۗ وَلِلَّهِ

715-A. The change from the First Person in the beginning of the verse to the Third Person here illustrates the change from the personal relationship of the Covenant, to the impersonal operation of Justice at Judgement. *Cf.* 35:9.

716. *Mubīn*: I wish I could translate by a simpler word than "perspicuous". But "plain" may mean unadorned, the opposite of beautiful, and this Book is among the most beautiful that it is the privilege of mankind to read. "Clear" would be right as far as it means "unambiguous, self-evident, not involved in mysteries of origin, history, or meaning, one which everyone can understand as to the essentials necessary for him, without the intervention of priests or privileged persons". *Mubīn* has all these meanings, but it suggests, besides, some quality of a shining light, by which we are able to *make* things clear, to distinguish the true from the false. This I think is suggested better by "perspicuous" than by the word "clear". Besides it is hardly good idiom to speak of "a clear Book."

The dominion of the heavens
And the earth, and all
That is between. He createth[717]
What He pleaseth. For Allah
Hath power over all things."

مُلْكُ ٱلسَّمَٰوَٰتِ وَٱلْأَرْضِ وَمَا بَيْنَهُمَا ۚ
يَخْلُقُ مَا يَشَآءُ ۚ وَٱللَّهُ عَلَىٰ كُلِّ شَىْءٍ قَدِيرٌ

18. (Both) the Jews and the Christians
Say: "We are sons
Of Allah, and His beloved."[718]
Say: "Why then doth He
Punish you for your sins?
Nay, ye are but men—
Of the men He hath created:
He forgiveth whom He pleaseth,
And He punisheth whom He pleaseth:
And to Allah belongeth[719]
The dominion of the heavens
And the earth, and all
That is between:
And unto Him
Is the final goal (of all)."

١٨ وَقَالَتِ ٱلْيَهُودُ وَٱلنَّصَٰرَىٰ
نَحْنُ أَبْنَٰٓؤُا۟ ٱللَّهِ وَأَحِبَّٰٓؤُهُۥ ۚ
قُلْ فَلِمَ يُعَذِّبُكُم بِذُنُوبِكُم ۖ
بَلْ أَنتُم بَشَرٌ مِّمَّنْ خَلَقَ ۚ
يَغْفِرُ لِمَن يَشَآءُ وَيُعَذِّبُ مَن يَشَآءُ ۚ
وَلِلَّهِ مُلْكُ ٱلسَّمَٰوَٰتِ وَٱلْأَرْضِ
وَمَا بَيْنَهُمَا ۖ وَإِلَيْهِ ٱلْمَصِيرُ

19. O People of the Book!
Now hath come unto you,
Making (things) clear unto you,
Our Messenger, after the break[720]
In (the series of) our messengers,
Lest ye should say:
"There came unto us
No bringer of glad tidings

١٩ يَٰٓأَهْلَ ٱلْكِتَٰبِ
قَدْ جَآءَكُمْ رَسُولُنَا
يُبَيِّنُ لَكُمْ عَلَىٰ فَتْرَةٍ مِّنَ ٱلرُّسُلِ
أَن تَقُولُوا۟ مَا جَآءَنَا مِنۢ بَشِيرٍ

717. The most honoured of the prophets of Allah are but men. All power belongs to Allah, and not to any man. Allah's creation may take many forms, but because in any particular form it is different from what we see daily around us, it does not cease to be Creation, or to be subject to the power of Allah. No creature can be God.

718. *Sons of God: Cf.* Job, xxxviii. 7: "When the morning stars sang together, and all the sons of God shouted for joy." In the 29th Psalm, 1st verse, the authorised Translation "O ye mighty" should apparently be "O ye sons of Elim". El being a name of God. *Cf.* also Genesis, vi. 2: "The sons of God saw the daughters of men."

Beloved: Cf. Psalms, cxxvii. 2: "He giveth his beloved sleep."

If used figuratively, these and like words refer to the love of Allah. Unfortunately, "son" used in a physical sense, or "beloved" in an exclusive sense as if Allah loved only the Jews, make a mockery of religion.

719. This refrain in the last verse negatives the idea of sonship, and in this verse negatives the idea of an exclusive "Beloved". In both cases it means that Allah is independent of physical relationships or exclusive partiality.

720. The six hundred years (in round figures) between Christ and Muḥammad were truly the dark ages of the world. Religion was corrupted; the standard of morals fell low; many false systems and heresies, arose; and there was a break in the succession of prophets until the advent of Muḥammad.

And no warner (from evil)";
But now hath come
Unto you a bringer
Of glad tidings
And a warner (from evil).
And Allah hath power
Over all things.

وَلَا نَذِيرٍ ۖ
فَقَدْ جَآءَكُم بَشِيرٌ وَنَذِيرٌ ۗ
وَٱللَّهُ عَلَىٰ كُلِّ شَىْءٍ قَدِيرٌ

SECTION 4.

20. Remember Moses said
To his people: "O my People!
Call in remembrance the favour
Of Allah unto you, when He
Produced prophets among you,[721]
Made you kings,[722] and gave
You what He had not given
To any other among the peoples.[723]

(٢٠) وَإِذْ قَالَ مُوسَىٰ لِقَوْمِهِۦ
يَٰقَوْمِ ٱذْكُرُوا۟ نِعْمَةَ ٱللَّهِ عَلَيْكُمْ
إِذْ جَعَلَ فِيكُمْ أَنۢبِيَآءَ وَجَعَلَكُم مُّلُوكًا
وَءَاتَىٰكُم مَّا لَمْ يُؤْتِ أَحَدًا مِّنَ ٱلْعَٰلَمِينَ

21. "O my people! enter[724]
The holy land which
Allah hath assigned unto you,
And turn not back
Ignominiously, for then
Will ye be overthrown,
To your own ruin."

(٢١) يَٰقَوْمِ ٱدْخُلُوا۟ ٱلْأَرْضَ ٱلْمُقَدَّسَةَ
ٱلَّتِى كَتَبَ ٱللَّهُ لَكُمْ وَلَا تَرْتَدُّوا۟ عَلَىٰٓ أَدْبَارِكُمْ
فَتَنقَلِبُوا۟ خَٰسِرِينَ

22. They said: "O Moses!
In this land are a people
Of exceeding strength:[725]

(٢٢) قَالُوا۟ يَٰمُوسَىٰٓ إِنَّ فِيهَا قَوْمًا جَبَّارِينَ

---

721. There was a long line of patriarchs and prophets before Moses, *e.g.*, Abraham, Isaac, Ismā'īl, Jacob, etc.

722. From the slavery of Egypt the Children of Israel were made free and independent, and thus each man became as it were a king, if only he had obeyed Allah and followed the lead of Moses.

723. *Cf.* Exod. xix. 5: "Now, therefore, if ye will obey my voice indeed, and keep my covenant, then ye shall be a peculiar treasure unto me above all people." Israel was chosen to be the vehicle of Allah's message, the highest honour which any nation can receive.

724. We now come to the events detailed in the 13th and 14th chapters of the Book of Numbers in the Old Testament. Read these as a Commentary, and examine a good map of the Sinai Peninsula, showing its connections with Egypt on the west, Northwest Arabia on the east, and Palestine on the northeast. We may suppose that Israel crossed from Egypt into the Peninsula somewhere near the northern extremity of the Gulf of Suez. Moses organised and numbered the people, and instituted the Priesthood. They went south about 200 miles to Mount Sinai where the Law was received. Then, perhaps a hundred and fifty miles north, was the desert of Paran, close to the southern borders of Canaan. From the camp there, twelve men were sent to spy out the land, and they penetrated as far as Hebron, say about 150 miles north of their camp, about 20 miles south of the future Jerusalem. They saw a rich country, and brought from it pomegranates and figs and a bunch of grapes so heavy that it had to be carried by two men on a staff. They came back and reported that the land was rich, but the men there were too strong for them. The people of Israel had no courage and no faith, and Moses remonstrated with them.

725. The people were not willing to follow the lead of Moses, and were not willing to fight for their "inheritance." In effect they said: "Turn out the enemy first, and then we shall enter into possession." In Allah's Law we must work and strive for what we wish to enjoy.

Never shall we enter it
Until they leave it:
If (once) they leave,
Then shall we enter."

وَإِنَّا لَن نَّدْخُلَهَا حَتَّىٰ يَخْرُجُوا مِنْهَا
فَإِن يَخْرُجُوا مِنْهَا فَإِنَّا دَاخِلُونَ

23. (But) among (their) God-fearing men
Were two on whom
Allah had bestowed His grace:[726]
They said: "Assault them
At the (proper) Gate:
When once ye are in,
Victory will be yours;

But on Allah put your trust
If ye have faith."

٢٣ قَالَ رَجُلَانِ
مِنَ الَّذِينَ يَخَافُونَ أَنْعَمَ اللَّهُ عَلَيْهِمَا
ادْخُلُوا عَلَيْهِمُ الْبَابَ فَإِذَا دَخَلْتُمُوهُ
فَإِنَّكُمْ غَالِبُونَ ۚ وَعَلَى اللَّهِ فَتَوَكَّلُوا
إِن كُنتُم مُّؤْمِنِينَ

24. They said: "O Moses!
While they remain there,
Never shall we be able
To enter, to the end of time.
Go thou, and thy Lord,
And fight ye two,
While we sit here[727]
(And watch)."

٢٤ قَالُوا يَا مُوسَىٰ
إِنَّا لَن نَّدْخُلَهَا أَبَدًا مَّا دَامُوا فِيهَا ۖ
فَاذْهَبْ أَنتَ وَرَبُّكَ فَقَاتِلَا
إِنَّا هَاهُنَا قَاعِدُونَ

25. He said: "O my Lord!
I have power only
Over myself and my brother:[728]
So separate us from this
Rebellious people!"

٢٥ قَالَ رَبِّ إِنِّي لَا أَمْلِكُ إِلَّا نَفْسِي وَأَخِي ۖ
فَافْرُقْ بَيْنَنَا وَبَيْنَ الْقَوْمِ الْفَاسِقِينَ

26. Allah said: "Therefore
Will the land be out

٢٦ قَالَ فَإِنَّهَا

---

726. Among those who returned after spying out the land were two men who had faith and courage. They were Joshua and Caleb. Joshua afterwards succeeded Moses in the leadership after 40 years. These two men pleaded for an immediate entry through the proper Gate, which I understand to mean, "after taking all due precautions and making all due preparations". *Cf.* 2:189 and n. 203. But of course, they said, they must put their trust in Allah for victory.

727. The advice of Joshua and Caleb, and the proposals of Moses under divine instructions were unpalatable to the crowd, whose prejudices were further inflamed by the other ten men who had gone with Joshua and Caleb. They made an "evil report," and were frightened by the great stature of the Canaanites. The crowd was in open rebellion, was prepared to stone Moses, Aaron, Joshua, and Caleb, and return to Egypt. Their reply to Moses was full of irony, insolence, blasphemy, and cowardice. In effect they said: "You talk of your God and all that: go with your God and fight there if you like: we shall sit here and watch."

728. "Moses and Aaron fell on their faces before all the assembly of the congregation." (Num. xiv. 5). According to the words in the Old Testament story, God said: "I will smite them with the pestilence, and disinherit them." (Num. xiv. 12). Moses prayed and interceded. But as we are told here, (a spiritual touch not found in the Jewish story), Moses was careful to separate himself and his brother from the rebellion.

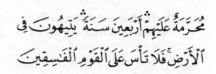

Of their reach for forty years:[729]
In distraction will they
Wander through the land:
But sorrow thou not
Over these rebellious people.

مُحَرَّمَةٌ عَلَيْهِمْ أَرْبَعِينَ سَنَةً يَتِيهُونَ فِي الْأَرْضِ فَلَا تَأْسَ عَلَى الْقَوْمِ الْفَاسِقِينَ

C. 72.—The jealousy of Cain against Abel,
(5:27-43.) Which led to the murder
Of innocent Abel, is the type
Of the jealousy between the People
Of the Book and their younger brethren
In Islam. Jealousy leads to envy
And murder. Such crimes against
Individuals are often crimes
Against whole peoples. There are
Men who are ready to catch up
Every lie told against a just man.
The just man should not grieve,
For that is their way.

SECTION 5.

27. Recite to them the truth[730]
Of the story of the two sons[731]
Of Adam. Behold! they each
Presented a sacrifice (to Allah):
It was accepted from one,
But not from the other.
Said the latter: "Be sure
I will slay thee." "Surely,"
Said the former, "Allah

وَاتْلُ عَلَيْهِمْ نَبَأَ ابْنَيْ آدَمَ بِالْحَقِّ ﴿٢٧﴾
إِذْ قَرَّبَا قُرْبَانًا فَتُقُبِّلَ مِنْ أَحَدِهِمَا
وَلَمْ يُتَقَبَّلْ مِنَ الْآخَرِ
قَالَ لَأَقْتُلَنَّكَ قَالَ

729. The punishment of the rebellion of these stiff-necked people, rebellion that was repeated "these ten times" (Num. xiv. 22) and more, was that they were left to wander distractedly hither and thither, through the wilderness for forty years. That generation was not to see the Holy Land. All those that were twenty years old and upwards were to die in the wilderness: "your carcasses shall fall in this wilderness." (Num. xiv. 29). Only those who were then children would reach the promised land. And so it happened. From the desert of Paran they wandered south, north, and east for forty years. From the head of what is now the Gulf of 'Aqaba, they travelled north, keeping to the east side of the depression of which the Dead Sea and the river Jordan are portions. Forty years afterwards they crossed the Jordan opposite what is now Jericho, but by that time Moses, Aaron, and the whole of the elder generation had died.

730. Literally, "recite to them in truth the story", etc. The point is that the story in Gen. iv. 1-15 is a bare narrative, not including the lessons now to be enforced. The Prophet is told now to supply the truth of the matter, the details that will enforce the lessons.

731. The two sons of Adam were Hābīl (in the English Bible, Abel) and Qābīl (in English, Cain). Cain was the elder, and Abel the younger—the righteous and innocent one. Presuming on the right of the elder, Cain was puffed up with arrogance and jealously, which led him to commit the crime of murder. Among the Christians, Cain was the type of the Jew as against Abel the Christian. The Jew tried to kill Jesus and exterminate the Christian. In the same way, as against Muḥammad, the younger brother of the Semitic family, Cain was the type of the Old Testament and New Testament people, who tried to resist and kill Muḥammad and put down his people.

Doth accept of the sacrifice
Of those who are righteous.

إِنَّمَا يَتَقَبَّلُ ٱللَّهُ مِنَ ٱلْمُتَّقِينَ

28. "If thou dost stretch thy hand
Against me, to slay me,
It is not for me to stretch
My hand against thee
To slay thee: for I do fear
Allah, the Cherisher of the Worlds.

٢٨ لَئِنۢ بَسَطتَ إِلَىَّ يَدَكَ لِتَقْتُلَنِى
مَآ أَنَا۠ بِبَاسِطٍ يَدِىَ إِلَيْكَ لِأَقْتُلَكَ ۖ
إِنِّىٓ أَخَافُ ٱللَّهَ رَبَّ ٱلْعَٰلَمِينَ

29. "For me, I intend to let
Thee draw on thyself
My sin as well as thine,[732]
For thou wilt be among
The Companions of the Fire,
And that is the reward
Of those who do wrong."[733]

٢٩ إِنِّىٓ أُرِيدُ أَن تَبُوٓأَ بِإِثْمِى وَإِثْمِكَ
فَتَكُونَ مِنْ أَصْحَٰبِ ٱلنَّارِ ۚ
وَذَٰلِكَ جَزَٰٓؤُا۟ ٱلظَّٰلِمِينَ

30. The (selfish) soul of the other
Led him to the murder
Of his brother: he murdered
Him, and became (himself)
One of the lost ones.[734]

٣٠ فَطَوَّعَتْ لَهُۥ نَفْسُهُۥ قَتْلَ أَخِيهِ
فَقَتَلَهُۥ فَأَصْبَحَ مِنَ ٱلْخَٰسِرِينَ

31. Then Allah sent a raven,
Who scratched the ground,
To show him how to hide
The shame of his brother.[735]
"Woe is me!" said he;
"Was I not even able
To be as this raven,
And to hide the shame

٣١ فَبَعَثَ ٱللَّهُ غُرَابًا يَبْحَثُ فِى ٱلْأَرْضِ
لِيُرِيَهُۥ كَيْفَ يُوَٰرِى سَوْءَةَ أَخِيهِ ۚ
قَالَ يَٰوَيْلَتَىٰٓ أَعَجَزْتُ أَنْ أَكُونَ مِثْلَ هَٰذَا
ٱلْغُرَابِ فَأُوَٰرِىَ سَوْءَةَ

---

732. *My sin as well as thine.* There are two possible interpretations: (1) The obvious one is that the unjust murderer not only carried on himself the burden of his own sin, but also the burden of his victim's sins. The victim, in suffering a wrong or injustice, is forgiven his own sins, and the wrongdoer, having been warned, aggravates his own sin. (2) "My sin" has also been interpreted as "the sin against me, in that thou slayest me": in that case "thy sin" may mean either "thy crime in committing a murder," or "thy sin against thyself, for the crime causes real loss to thyself in the Hereafter." See the last clause of the next verse.

733. Abel's speech is full of meaning. He is innocent and God-fearing. To the threat of death held out by the other, he returns a calm reply, aimed at reforming the other. "Surely," he pleads, "if your sacrifice was not accepted, there was something wrong in you, for Allah is just and accepts the sacrifice of the righteous. If this does not deter you, I am not going to retaliate, though there is as much power in me against you as you have against me. I fear my Maker, for I know He cherishes all His Creation. Let me warn you that you are doing wrong. I do not intend even to resist, but do you know what the consequences will be to you? You will be in spiritual torment."

734. The innocent unselfish pleading of the younger brother had no effect, for the soul of the other was full of pride, selfishness and jealousy. He committed the murder, but in doing so, ruined his own self.

735. *Saw'ah* may mean "corpse", with a suggestion of nakedness and shame in two senses: (1) the sense of being exposed without burial, and (2) the sense of being insulted by being violently deprived by the unwarranted murder, of the soul which inhabited it—the soul, too, of a brother.

Of my brother?" Then he became
Full of regrets—[736]

أَخِي فَأَصْبَحَ مِنَ ٱلنَّٰدِمِينَ

32. On that account: We ordained
For the Children of Israel
That if anyone slew
A person—unless it be
For murder or for spreading
Mischief in the land—
It would be as if
He slew the whole people:[737]
And if anyone saved a life,
It would be as if he saved
The life of the whole people.
Then although there came
To them Our Messengers
With Clear Signs, yet,
Even after that, many
Of them continued to commit
Excesses in the land.

﴿٣٢﴾ مِنْ أَجْلِ ذَٰلِكَ كَتَبْنَا
عَلَىٰ بَنِيٓ إِسْرَٰٓءِيلَ أَنَّهُۥ مَن قَتَلَ نَفْسًۢا
بِغَيْرِ نَفْسٍ أَوْ فَسَادٍ فِي ٱلْأَرْضِ فَكَأَنَّمَا
قَتَلَ ٱلنَّاسَ جَمِيعًا وَمَنْ أَحْيَاهَا
فَكَأَنَّمَآ أَحْيَا ٱلنَّاسَ جَمِيعًا ۚ
وَلَقَدْ جَآءَتْهُمْ رُسُلُنَا بِٱلْبَيِّنَٰتِ
ثُمَّ إِنَّ كَثِيرًا مِّنْهُم بَعْدَ ذَٰلِكَ
فِي ٱلْأَرْضِ لَمُسْرِفُونَ

33. **T**he punishment of those
Who wage war against Allah
And His Messenger, and strive
With might and main
For mischief through the land[738]
Is: execution, or crucifixion,
Or the cutting off of hands
And feet from opposite sides,[739]
Or exile from the land:

﴿٣٣﴾ إِنَّمَا جَزَٰٓؤُاْ ٱلَّذِينَ يُحَارِبُونَ ٱللَّهَ وَرَسُولَهُۥ
وَيَسْعَوْنَ فِي ٱلْأَرْضِ فَسَادًا أَن يُقَتَّلُوٓاْ
أَوْ يُصَلَّبُوٓاْ أَوْ تُقَطَّعَ أَيْدِيهِمْ
وَأَرْجُلُهُم مِّنْ خِلَٰفٍ أَوْ يُنفَوْاْ مِنَ ٱلْأَرْضِ ۚ

736. The thought at last came home to the murderer. It was dreadful indeed to slay anyone—the more so as he was a brother, and an innocent righteous brother! But worse still, the murderer had not even the decency to bury the corpse, and of this simple duty he was reminded by a raven—a blackbird usually held in contempt! His regret was on that account. That was no true repentance.

737. The story of Cain is referred to in a few graphic details in order to tell the story of Israel. Israel rebelled against Allah, slew and insulted righteous men who did them no harm but on the contrary came in all humility. When Allah withdrew His favour from Israel because of its sins and bestowed it on a brother nation, the jealousy of Israel plunged it deeper into sin. To kill or seek to kill an individual because he represents an ideal is to kill all who uphold the ideal. On the other hand, to save an individual life in the same circumstances is to save a whole community. What could be stronger condemnation of individual assassination and revenge?

738. For the double crime of treason against the State, combined with treason against Allah, as shown by overt crimes, four alternative punishments are mentioned, any one of which is to be applied according to circumstances, *viz.*, execution (cutting off of the head), crucifixion, maiming, or exile. These were features of the Criminal Law then and for centuries afterwards, except that tortures such as "hanging, drawing, and quartering" in English Law, and piercing of eyes and leaving the unfortunate victim exposed to a tropical sun, which was practised in Arabia, and all such tortures were abolished. In any case sincere repentance before it was too late was recognised as a ground for mercy.

739. Understood to mean the right hand and the left foot.

That is their disgrace
In this world, and
A heavy punishment is theirs
In the Hereafter;

ذَٰلِكَ لَهُمْ خِزْيٌ فِي الدُّنْيَا
وَلَهُمْ فِي الْآخِرَةِ عَذَابٌ عَظِيمٌ

34. Except for those who repent
Before they fall
Into your power:
In that case, know
That Allah is Oft-Forgiving,
Most Merciful.

٣٤ إِلَّا الَّذِينَ تَابُوا مِن قَبْلِ
أَن تَقْدِرُوا عَلَيْهِمْ فَاعْلَمُوا
أَنَّ اللَّهَ غَفُورٌ رَّحِيمٌ

SECTION 6.

35. O ye who believe!
Do your duty to Allah,[740]
Seek the means
Of approach unto Him,
And strive with might
And main in His cause:
That ye may prosper.[741]

٣٥ يَا أَيُّهَا الَّذِينَ آمَنُوا
اتَّقُوا اللَّهَ وَابْتَغُوا إِلَيْهِ الْوَسِيلَةَ
وَجَاهِدُوا فِي سَبِيلِهِ لَعَلَّكُمْ تُفْلِحُونَ

36. As to those who reject
Faith—if they had
Everything on earth,
And twice repeated,
To give as ransom
For the penalty of the Day
Of Judgement, it would
Never be accepted of them.
Theirs would be
A grievous Penalty.

٣٦ إِنَّ الَّذِينَ كَفَرُوا لَوْ أَنَّ لَهُم
مَّا فِي الْأَرْضِ جَمِيعًا وَمِثْلَهُ مَعَهُ
لِيَفْتَدُوا بِهِ مِنْ عَذَابِ يَوْمِ الْقِيَامَةِ
مَا تُقُبِّلَ مِنْهُمْ وَلَهُمْ عَذَابٌ أَلِيمٌ

37. Their wish will be
To get out of the Fire,
But never will they
Get out therefrom:
Their Penalty will be
One that endures.

٣٧ يُرِيدُونَ أَن يَخْرُجُوا مِنَ النَّارِ
وَمَا هُم بِخَارِجِينَ مِنْهَا
وَلَهُمْ عَذَابٌ مُّقِيمٌ

740. *Taqwā* here too might be translated "fear of Allah", but the very next clause shows that "fear of Allah" does not mean "fear" in the ordinary sense, which would make you avoid the object of fear. On the contrary the "fear of Allah" is the intense desire to avoid everything that is against His Will and Law. It is in fact duty to Allah, for we are told to seek ardently the means by which we may approach Him, and that can only be done by striving with might and main for His cause.

741. "Prosper" in the spiritual sense, for that is all that matters, as the life of this world is brief and fleeting, and of small account as against Eternity.

38. As to the thief,[742]
Male or female,
Cut off his or her hands:
A punishment by way
Of example, from Allah,
For their crime:
And Allah is Exalted in Power,
Full of Wisdom.

٣٨ وَٱلسَّارِقُ وَٱلسَّارِقَةُ
فَٱقْطَعُوٓا۟ أَيْدِيَهُمَا جَزَآءًۢ
بِمَا كَسَبَا نَكَٰلًا مِّنَ ٱللَّهِ ۗ
وَٱللَّهُ عَزِيزٌ حَكِيمٌ

39. But if the thief repents
After his crime,
And amends his conduct,
Allah turneth to him
In forgiveness; for Allah
Is Oft-Forgiving, Most Merciful.

٣٩ فَمَن تَابَ مِنۢ بَعْدِ ظُلْمِهِۦ
وَأَصْلَحَ فَإِنَّ ٱللَّهَ يَتُوبُ عَلَيْهِ ۗ
إِنَّ ٱللَّهَ غَفُورٌ رَّحِيمٌ

40. Knowest thou not[743]
That to Allah (alone)
Belongeth the dominion
Of the heavens and the earth?
He punisheth whom He pleaseth,
And He forgiveth whom He pleaseth:
And Allah hath power
Over all things.

٤٠ أَلَمْ تَعْلَمْ أَنَّ ٱللَّهَ لَهُۥ
مُلْكُ ٱلسَّمَٰوَٰتِ وَٱلْأَرْضِ
يُعَذِّبُ مَن يَشَآءُ وَيَغْفِرُ لِمَن يَشَآءُ ۗ
وَٱللَّهُ عَلَىٰ كُلِّ شَىْءٍ قَدِيرٌ

41. O Messenger! let not
Those grieve thee, who race
Each other into Unbelief:[744]
(Whether it be) among those
Who say "We believe"
With their lips but
Whose hearts have no faith;
Or it be among the Jews—

٤١ يَٰٓأَيُّهَا ٱلرَّسُولُ لَا يَحْزُنكَ
ٱلَّذِينَ يُسَٰرِعُونَ فِى ٱلْكُفْرِ
مِنَ ٱلَّذِينَ قَالُوٓا۟ ءَامَنَّا بِأَفْوَٰهِهِمْ
وَلَمْ تُؤْمِن قُلُوبُهُمْ ۛ وَمِنَ ٱلَّذِينَ هَادُوا۟

742. Here we touch upon jurisprudence. The Canon Law jurists are not unanimous as to the value of the property stolen, which would involve the penalty of the cutting off of the hand. The majority hold that petty thefts are exempt from this punishment. The general opinion is that only one hand should be cut off for the first theft, on the principle that "if thy hand or thy foot offend thee, cut them off, and cast them from thee" (Matt. xviii. 8). Apparently in the age of Jesus thieves were crucified (Matt. xxvii. 38).

743. Punishment really does not belong to mortals, but to Allah alone. Only, in order to keep civil society together, and protect innocent people from crime, certain principles are laid down on which people can build up their criminal law. But we must always remember that Allah not only punishes but forgives, and forgiveness is the attribute which is more prominently placed before us. It is not our wisdom that can really define the bounds of forgiveness or punishment, but His Will or Plan, which is the true standard of righteousness and justice.

744. Two classes of men are meant, *viz.*, the Hypocrites and the Jews. For both of them Muṣṭafā laboured earnestly and assiduously, and it must have been a cause of great grief and disappointment to him that some among them showed so much insincerity, cunning, and hardness of heart. These are types not yet extinct.

Men who will listen
To any lie—will listen
Even to others who have
Never so much as come[745]
To thee. They change the words
From their (right) times[746]
And places: they say,
"If ye are given this,
Take it, but if not,
Beware!" If anyone's trial
Is intended by Allah, thou hast
No authority in the least
For him against Allah.
For such—it is not
Allah's will to purify
Their hearts. For them
There is disgrace
In this world, and
In the Hereafter
A heavy punishment.

سَمَّٰعُونَ لِلۡكَذِبِ
سَمَّٰعُونَ لِقَوۡمٍ ءَاخَرِينَ لَمۡ يَأۡتُوكَۖ
يُحَرِّفُونَ ٱلۡكَلِمَ مِنۢ بَعۡدِ مَوَاضِعِهِۦۖ
يَقُولُونَ إِنۡ أُوتِيتُمۡ هَٰذَا فَخُذُوهُ
وَإِن لَّمۡ تُؤۡتَوۡهُ فَٱحۡذَرُواْۚ وَمَن يُرِدِ ٱللَّهُ
فِتۡنَتَهُۥ فَلَن تَمۡلِكَ لَهُۥ مِنَ ٱللَّهِ شَيۡـًٔاۚ
أُوْلَٰٓئِكَ ٱلَّذِينَ لَمۡ يُرِدِ ٱللَّهُ أَن يُطَهِّرَ
قُلُوبَهُمۡۚ لَهُمۡ فِي ٱلدُّنۡيَا خِزۡيٞۖ
وَلَهُمۡ فِي ٱلۡأٓخِرَةِ عَذَابٌ عَظِيمٞ

42. (They are fond of) listening
To falsehood, of devouring[747]
Anything forbidden.
If they do come to thee,
Either judge between them,
Or decline to interfere.[748]
If thou decline, they cannot
Hurt thee in the least.
If thou judge, judge
In equity between them.
For Allah loveth those
Who judge in equity.

٤٢ سَمَّٰعُونَ لِلۡكَذِبِ
أَكَّٰلُونَ لِلسُّحۡتِۚ فَإِن جَآءُوكَ
فَٱحۡكُم بَيۡنَهُمۡ أَوۡ أَعۡرِضۡ عَنۡهُمۡۖ
وَإِن تُعۡرِضۡ عَنۡهُمۡ فَلَن يَضُرُّوكَ شَيۡـٔٗاۖ
وَإِنۡ حَكَمۡتَ فَٱحۡكُم بَيۡنَهُم بِٱلۡقِسۡطِۚ
إِنَّ ٱللَّهَ يُحِبُّ ٱلۡمُقۡسِطِينَ

---

745. There were men among the Jews who were eager to catch up any lie against the Prophet. They had their ears open even to tales from people who had never so much as come near to the Prophet. If we understand "for" instead of "to" before "others" (for the Arabic word would bear both meanings), the sense will be: They are keen listeners or spies for any lies they can catch: and they will act as spies for others (their Rabbis, etc.) who are in the background but to whom they carry false tales.

746. *Cf.* 5:14. The addition of the words *min ba'di* here suggests the change of words from their right *times* as well as places. They did not deal honestly with their Law, and misapplied it, by distorting the meaning. Or it may be that as tale-bearers they distorted the meaning by misrepresenting the context.

747. *Devouring anything forbidden*: both in a literal and in a figurative sense. In the figurative sense, it would be: the taking of usury or bribes, or taking undue advantage of people's weak position or their own fiduciary powers to add to their own wealth.

748. Where it is merely a trick to catch out the unwary, a just man may honourably decline to interfere in a cause submitted to him, as also in a case where the parties are not honestly desirous of justice, but each hopes that some partiality will be shown to it.

43. But why do they come[749]
To thee for decision,
When they have (their own)
Law before them?—
Therein is the (plain)
Command of Allah; yet
Even after that, they would
Turn away. For they
Are not (really)
People of Faith.

وَكَيْفَ يُحَكِّمُونَكَ ﴿٤٣﴾
وَعِندَهُمُ ٱلتَّوْرَىٰةُ
فِيهَا حُكْمُ ٱللَّهِ
ثُمَّ يَتَوَلَّوْنَ مِنۢ بَعْدِ ذَٰلِكَ
وَمَآ أُو۟لَـٰٓئِكَ بِٱلْمُؤْمِنِينَ

C. 73.—True justice accords with Allah's Law.
(5:46-86.) Follow not men's selfish desires,
But Allah's Will, which was revealed
To Moses and Jesus, and now to Muḥammad.
Take not for friends and protectors
Those in whose hearts is a disease—
To whom religion is a mockery
Or a plaything—who worship evil.
Proclaim the Truth of Allah, and be
Not afraid. Eschew their iniquities,
Which were denounced by David
And Jesus. But recognise with justice
Those who are sincere and humble,
Though they may be themselves
Not of your flock, if they witness to Truth.

SECTION 7.

44. It was We who revealed
The Law (to Moses): therein
Was guidance and light.[750]
By its standard have been judged
The Jews, by the Prophets
Who bowed (as in Islam)
To Allah's Will, by the Rabbis[751]

إِنَّآ أَنزَلْنَا ٱلتَّوْرَىٰةَ ﴿٤٤﴾
فِيهَا هُدًى وَنُورٌ يَحْكُمُ بِهَا
ٱلنَّبِيُّونَ ٱلَّذِينَ أَسْلَمُوا۟
لِلَّذِينَ هَادُوا۟ وَٱلرَّبَّـٰنِيُّونَ

749. This is a searching question as to the motive of the Jews in bringing their cases for decisions to the Prophet. They came either (1) to ridicule whatever he said, or (2) to deceive him as to facts and snatch a favourable decision which was against equity. If their own Law did not suit their selfish interests, they sometimes twisted it. But Muḥammad was always inflexible in his justice.

750. *Guidance*, with reference to conduct; *light*, with reference to insight into the higher realms of the spirit.

751. *Rabbāniyyūn* may, I think, be rightly translated by the Jewish title of *Rabbi* for their learned men. Jewish learning is identified with Rabbinical literature. *Aḥbār* is the plural of *ḥibr* or *ḥabr*, by which we may understand Jewish Doctors of Law. Later the term was applied to those of other religions. Query: Is the word connected with the same root as "Hebrew", or "Eber" (Gen. x. 21), the ancestor of the Hebrew race? This seems negatived by the the fact that the Arabic root connected with the word "Hebrew" is *'Abar*, not *Ḥabar*.

And the Doctors of Law:
For to them was entrusted
The protection of Allah's Book,
And they were witnesses thereto:[752]
Therefore fear not men,
But fear Me, and sell not
My Signs for a miserable price.[753]
If any do fail to judge
By (the light of) what Allah
Hath revealed, they are
(No better than) Unbelievers.

وَٱلْأَحْبَارُ بِمَا ٱسْتُحْفِظُوا۟
مِن كِتَٰبِ ٱللَّهِ وَكَانُوا۟ عَلَيْهِ شُهَدَآءَ ۚ
فَلَا تَخْشَوُا۟ ٱلنَّاسَ وَٱخْشَوْنِ
وَلَا تَشْتَرُوا۟ بِـَٔايَٰتِى ثَمَنًا قَلِيلًا ۚ وَمَن لَّمْ يَحْكُم
بِمَآ أَنزَلَ ٱللَّهُ فَأُو۟لَٰٓئِكَ هُمُ ٱلْكَٰفِرُونَ

45. We ordained therein for them:[754]
"Life for life, eye for eye,
Nose for nose, ear for ear,
Tooth for tooth, and wounds
Equal for equal." But if
Anyone remits the retaliation
By way of charity, it is
An act of atonement for himself.[755]
And if any fail to judge
By (the light of) what Allah
Hath revealed, they are
(No better than) wrongdoers.[756]

٤٥ وَكَتَبْنَا عَلَيْهِمْ فِيهَآ أَنَّ ٱلنَّفْسَ بِٱلنَّفْسِ
وَٱلْعَيْنَ بِٱلْعَيْنِ وَٱلْأَنفَ بِٱلْأَنفِ
وَٱلْأُذُنَ بِٱلْأُذُنِ وَٱلسِّنَّ بِٱلسِّنِّ
وَٱلْجُرُوحَ قِصَاصٌ ۚ فَمَن تَصَدَّقَ بِهِۦ
فَهُوَ كَفَّارَةٌ لَّهُۥ ۚ وَمَن لَّمْ يَحْكُم
بِمَآ أَنزَلَ ٱللَّهُ فَأُو۟لَٰٓئِكَ هُمُ ٱلظَّٰلِمُونَ

46. And in their footsteps
We sent Jesus the son
Of Mary, confirming

٤٦ وَقَفَّيْنَا عَلَىٰٓ ءَاثَٰرِهِم
بِعِيسَى ٱبْنِ مَرْيَمَ مُصَدِّقًا

752. They were living witnesses to the truth of Scripture, and could testify that they had made it known to the people; *Cf.* 2:143, and 4:135.

753. Two charges are made, against the Jews: (1) that even the books which they had, they twisted in meaning, to suit their own purposes, because they feared men rather than Allah: (2) that what they had was but fragments of the original Law given to Moses, mixed up with a lot of semi-historical and legendary matter, and some fine poetry. The *Tawrāh* mentioned in the Qur'ān is not the Old Testament as we have it: nor is it even the Pentateuch (the first five books of the Old Testament, containing the Law embedded in a great deal of semi-historical and legendary narrative). See Appendix II, on the *Tawrāh* (printed at the end of this Sūrah).

754. The retaliation is prescribed in three places in the Pentateuch, *viz.*, Exod. xxi. 23-25; Leviticus xxiv. 18-21, and Deut. xix. 21. The wording in the three quotations is different, but in none of them is found the additional rider for mercy, as here. Note that in Matt. v. 38, Jesus quotes the Old Law "eye for eye." etc., and modifies it in the direction of forgiveness, but the Qur'anic injunction is more practical. This appeal for mercy is as between man and man in the spiritual world. Even where the injured one forgives, the State or Ruler is competent to take such action as is necessary for the preservation of law and order in Society. For crime has a bearing that goes beyond the interests of the person injured: the Community is affected: see 5:32.

755. This is not part of the Mosaic Law, but the teaching of Jesus and of Muḥammad. Notice how the teaching of Jesus is gradually introduced as leading up to the Qur'ān.

756. The seeming repetitions at the end of verses 44, 45 and 46 are not real repetitions. The significant words in the three cases are: Unbelievers, wrongdoers, and rebellious: and each fits the context. If the Jews tamper with their books they are Unbelievers; if they give false judgments, they are wrongdoers. If the Christians follow not their light, they are rebellious.

The Law that had come
Before him: We sent him
The Gospel: therein
Was guidance and light,[757]
And confirmation of the Law
That had come before him:
A guidance and an admonition
To those who fear Allah.

لِّمَا بَيْنَ يَدَيْهِ مِنَ ٱلتَّوْرَىٰةِ
وَءَاتَيْنَٰهُ ٱلْإِنجِيلَ فِيهِ هُدًى وَنُورٌ
وَمُصَدِّقًا لِّمَا بَيْنَ يَدَيْهِ مِنَ ٱلتَّوْرَىٰةِ
وَهُدًى وَمَوْعِظَةً لِّلْمُتَّقِينَ

47. Let the People of the Gospel
Judge by what Allah hath revealed
Therein. If any do fail
To judge by (the light of)
What Allah hath revealed,
They are (no better than)
Those who rebel.[758]

٤٧ وَلْيَحْكُمْ أَهْلُ ٱلْإِنجِيلِ بِمَآ أَنزَلَ ٱللَّهُ
فِيهِ ۚ وَمَن لَّمْ يَحْكُم بِمَآ أَنزَلَ ٱللَّهُ
فَأُو۟لَٰٓئِكَ هُمُ ٱلْفَٰسِقُونَ

48. To thee We sent the Scripture
In truth, confirming
The scripture that came
Before it, and guarding it[759]
In safety: so judge
Between them by what
Allah hath revealed,
And follow not their vain
Desires, diverging
From the Truth that hath come
To thee. To each among you
Have We prescribed a Law
And an Open Way.[760]
If Allah had so willed,

٤٨ وَأَنزَلْنَآ إِلَيْكَ ٱلْكِتَٰبَ بِٱلْحَقِّ
مُصَدِّقًا لِّمَا بَيْنَ يَدَيْهِ مِنَ ٱلْكِتَٰبِ
وَمُهَيْمِنًا عَلَيْهِ ۖ فَٱحْكُم بَيْنَهُم
بِمَآ أَنزَلَ ٱللَّهُ ۖ وَلَا تَتَّبِعْ أَهْوَآءَهُمْ
عَمَّا جَآءَكَ مِنَ ٱلْحَقِّ ۚ
لِكُلٍّ جَعَلْنَا مِنكُمْ شِرْعَةً
وَمِنْهَاجًا ۚ وَلَوْ شَآءَ ٱللَّهُ

757. *Guidance and light*: see n. 750 above. For the meaning of the Gospel (Injīl), see Appendix III, "On the *Injīl*", (printed at the end of this Sūrah).

758. See n. 756 above.

759. After the corruption of the older revelations, the Qur'ān comes with a twofold purpose: (1) to confirm the true and original Message, and (2) to guard it, or act as a check to its interpretation. The Arabic word *Muhaymin* is very comprehensive in meaning. It means one who safeguards, watches over, stands witness, preserves, and upholds. The Qur'ān safeguards "the Book", for it has preserved within it the teachings of all the former Books. It watches over these Books in the sense that it will not let their true teachings to be lost. It supports and upholds these Books in the sense that it corroborates the Word of Allah which has remained intact in them. It stands as a witness because it bears testimony to the Word of Allah contained in these Books and helps to sort it out from the interpretations and commentaries of the people which were mixed with it; what is confirmed by the Qur'ān is the Word of Allah and what is against it is that of the people. (R).

760. *Law: shir'ah* = rules of practical conduct. *Open Way: Minhāj* = the finer things which are above the law, but which are yet available to everyone, like a sort of open highway. The *light* in verses 44 and 46 above, I understand to be something in the still higher regions of the spirit, which is common to mankind, though laws and rules may take different forms among different Peoples.

He would have made you[761]
A single People, but (His
Plan is) to test you in what
He hath given you; so strive
As in a race in all virtues.
The goal of you all is to Allah;
It is He that will show you
The truth of the matters
In which ye dispute;[762]

لَجَعَلَكُمْ أُمَّةً وَٰحِدَةً وَلَٰكِن
لِّيَبْلُوَكُمْ فِي مَآ ءَاتَىٰكُمْ فَاسْتَبِقُوا۟
الْخَيْرَٰتِ إِلَى اللَّهِ مَرْجِعُكُمْ جَمِيعًا
فَيُنَبِّئُكُم بِمَا كُنتُمْ فِيهِ تَخْتَلِفُونَ

49. And this (He commands):
Judge thou between them
By what Allah hath revealed,
And follow not their vain
Desires, but beware of them
Lest they beguile thee
From any of that (teaching)
Which Allah hath sent down
To thee. And if they turn
Away, be assured that
For some of their crimes
It is Allah's purpose to punish
Them. And truly most men
Are rebellious.

(٤٩) وَأَنِ احْكُم بَيْنَهُم
بِمَآ أَنزَلَ اللَّهُ وَلَا تَتَّبِعْ أَهْوَآءَهُمْ
وَاحْذَرْهُمْ أَن يَفْتِنُوكَ
عَنۢ بَعْضِ مَآ أَنزَلَ اللَّهُ إِلَيْكَ فَإِن تَوَلَّوْا۟ فَاعْلَمْ
أَنَّمَا يُرِيدُ اللَّهُ أَن يُصِيبَهُم بِبَعْضِ ذُنُوبِهِمْ
وَإِنَّ كَثِيرًا مِّنَ النَّاسِ لَفَٰسِقُونَ

50. Do they then seek after
A judgement of (the Days[763]
Of) Ignorance? But who,
For a people whose faith
Is assured, can give
Better judgement than Allah?

(٥٠) أَفَحُكْمَ الْجَٰهِلِيَّةِ يَبْغُونَ
وَمَنْ أَحْسَنُ مِنَ اللَّهِ حُكْمًا
لِّقَوْمٍ يُوقِنُونَ

SECTION 8.

51. O ye who believe!
Take not the Jews

(٥١) يَٰٓأَيُّهَا الَّذِينَ ءَامَنُوا۟ لَا تَتَّخِذُوا۟ الْيَهُودَ

761. By origin mankind were a single people or nation: 4:1, and 2:213. That being so, Allah could have kept us all alike, with one language, one kind of disposition, and one set of physical conditions (including climate) to live in. But in His wisdom, He gives us diversity in these things, not only at any given time, but in different periods and ages. This tests our capacity for Unity *(Waḥdāniyah)* still more, and accentuates the need of Unity and Islam.

762. Men are wont to make conflicting claims regarding Allah, the ultimate destiny of man, and other questions of vital importance. No matter how vehement and eloquent the proponents of false doctrines might be, their efforts will prove fruitless and it will be indisputably clear on the Day of Judgement as to who entertained false notions and who cherished the truth. (Eds.).

763. The Days of Ignorance were the days of tribalism, feuds and selfish accentuation of differences in man. Those days are really not yet over. It is the mission of Islam to take us away from that false mental attitude, towards the true attitude of Unity. If our Faith is certain (and not merely a matter of words), Allah will guide us to that Unity.

And the Christians
For your friends and protectors;[764]
They are but friends and
protectors
To each other. And he
Amongst you that turns to them
(For friendship) is of them.
Verily Allah guideth not
A people unjust.

وَٱلنَّصَٰرَىٰٓ أَوۡلِيَآءَۘ
بَعۡضُهُمۡ أَوۡلِيَآءُ بَعۡضٖۚ
وَمَن يَتَوَلَّهُم مِّنكُمۡ فَإِنَّهُۥ مِنۡهُمۡۗ
إِنَّ ٱللَّهَ لَا يَهۡدِي ٱلۡقَوۡمَ ٱلظَّٰلِمِينَ

52. Those in whose hearts[765]
Is a disease—thou seest
How eagerly they run about
Amongst them, saying:
"We do fear lest a change
Of fortune bring us disaster."
Ah! perhaps Allah will give
(Thee) victory, or a decision
According to His Will.
Then will they repent
Of the thoughts which they secretly
Harboured in their hearts.

٥٢ فَتَرَى ٱلَّذِينَ فِي قُلُوبِهِم
مَّرَضٞ يُسَٰرِعُونَ فِيهِمۡ
يَقُولُونَ نَخۡشَىٰٓ أَن تُصِيبَنَا دَآئِرَةٞۚ
فَعَسَى ٱللَّهُ أَن يَأۡتِيَ بِٱلۡفَتۡحِ أَوۡ أَمۡرٖ مِّنۡ عِندِهِۦ
فَيُصۡبِحُواْ عَلَىٰ مَآ أَسَرُّواْ فِيٓ أَنفُسِهِمۡ نَٰدِمِينَ

53. And those who believe
Will say: "Are these
The men who swore
Their strongest oaths by Allah,
That they were with you?"[766]
All that they do
Will be in vain,
And they will fall
Into (nothing but) ruin.

٥٣ وَيَقُولُ ٱلَّذِينَ ءَامَنُوٓاْ
أَهَٰٓؤُلَآءِ ٱلَّذِينَ أَقۡسَمُواْ بِٱللَّهِ جَهۡدَ أَيۡمَٰنِهِمۡ
إِنَّهُمۡ لَمَعَكُمۡۚ حَبِطَتۡ أَعۡمَٰلُهُمۡ
فَأَصۡبَحُواْ خَٰسِرِينَ

54. O ye who believe!
If any from among you
Turn back from his Faith,
Soon will Allah produce
A people whom He will love
As they will love Him—
Lowly with the Believers,

٥٤ يَٰٓأَيُّهَا ٱلَّذِينَ ءَامَنُواْ مَن يَرۡتَدَّ مِنكُمۡ
عَن دِينِهِۦ فَسَوۡفَ يَأۡتِي ٱللَّهُ بِقَوۡمٖ يُحِبُّهُمۡ
وَيُحِبُّونَهُۥٓ أَذِلَّةٍ عَلَى ٱلۡمُؤۡمِنِينَ

764. That is, look not to them for help and comfort. They are more likely to combine against you than to help you. And this happened more than once in the lifetime of the Prophet, and in after-ages again and again. He who associates with them and shares their counsels must be counted as of them. The trimmer loses whichever way the wheel of fortune turns.

765. *Cf.* 2:10.

766. The Hypocrites, while matters were doubtful, pretended to be with Muslims, but were in league with their enemies. When matters came to a decision and Allah granted victory to Islam, their position was awkward. They were not only disowned by the Muslims, but the Muslims could well say in reproach to their enemies: "Are these the men who swore friendship for you? What was their friendship worth to you? Where are they now?"

Mighty against the Rejecters,
Fighting in the Way of Allah,
And never afraid
Of the reproaches
Of such as find fault.[767]
That is the Grace of Allah,
Which He will bestow
On whom He pleaseth.
And Allah encompasseth all,
And He knoweth all things.

أَعِزَّةٍ عَلَى ٱلْكَٰفِرِينَ يُجَٰهِدُونَ فِى
سَبِيلِ ٱللَّهِ وَلَا يَخَافُونَ لَوْمَةَ لَآئِمٍ
ذَٰلِكَ فَضْلُ ٱللَّهِ يُؤْتِيهِ مَن يَشَآءُ
وَٱللَّهُ وَٰسِعٌ عَلِيمٌ

55. Your (real) friends are
(No less than) Allah,
His Messenger, and the (Fellowship
Of) Believers—those who
Establish regular prayers
And regular charity,
And they bow
Down humbly (in worship).

(٥٥) إِنَّمَا وَلِيُّكُمُ ٱللَّهُ وَرَسُولُهُۥ
وَٱلَّذِينَ ءَامَنُوا۟ ٱلَّذِينَ يُقِيمُونَ ٱلصَّلَوٰةَ
وَيُؤْتُونَ ٱلزَّكَوٰةَ وَهُمْ رَٰكِعُونَ

56. As to those who turn
(For friendship) to Allah,
His Messenger, and the (Fellowship
Of) Believers—it is
The Fellowship of Allah
That must certainly triumph.

(٥٦) وَمَن يَتَوَلَّ ٱللَّهَ
وَرَسُولَهُۥ وَٱلَّذِينَ ءَامَنُوا۟
فَإِنَّ حِزْبَ ٱللَّهِ هُمُ ٱلْغَٰلِبُونَ

Section 9.

57. O ye who believe!
Take not for friends
And protectors those
Who take your religion
For a mockery or sport—[768]
Whether among those

(٥٧) يَٰٓأَيُّهَا ٱلَّذِينَ ءَامَنُوا۟ لَا تَتَّخِذُوا۟
ٱلَّذِينَ ٱتَّخَذُوا۟ دِينَكُمْ
هُزُوًا وَلَعِبًا مِّنَ

767. As "most men are rebellious" (5:49), it is inevitable that there should be apostates even from such a religion of reason and common-sense as Islam. But here is a warning to the Muslim body that they should not repeat the history of the Jews, and become so self-satisfied or arrogant as to depart from the spirit of Allah's teaching. If they do, the loss will be their own. Allah's bounty is not confined to one group or section of humanity. He can always raise up people who will follow the true spirit of Islam. That spirit is defined in two ways: first in general terms; they will love Allah and Allah will love them; and secondly, by specific signs; amongst the Brethren, their attitude will be that of humility, but to wrongdoers they will offer no mealy-mouthed compromises; they will always strive and fight for truth and right; they will know no fear, either physical, or that more insidious form, which says: "What will people say if we act thus?" They are too great in mind to be haunted by any such thought. For, as the next verse says, their friends are Allah, His Prophet, and His people, the people who judge rightly, without fear or favour.

768. It is not right that we should be in intimate association with those to whom religion is either a subject of mockery or at best is nothing but a plaything. They may be amused, or they may have other motives for encouraging you. But your association with them will sap the earnestness of your faith, and make you cynical and insincere.

Who received the Scripture
Before you, or among those
Who reject Faith;
But fear ye Allah,
If ye have Faith (indeed).

ٱلَّذِينَ أُوتُوا۟ ٱلْكِتَٰبَ مِن قَبْلِكُمْ
وَٱلْكُفَّارَ أَوْلِيَآءَ ۚ وَٱتَّقُوا۟ ٱللَّهَ إِن كُنتُم مُّؤْمِنِينَ

58. When ye proclaim
Your call to prayer,
They take it (but)
As mockery and sport;
That is because they are
A people without understanding.

٥٨ وَإِذَا نَادَيْتُمْ إِلَى ٱلصَّلَوٰةِ
ٱتَّخَذُوهَا هُزُوًا وَلَعِبًا ۚ
ذَٰلِكَ بِأَنَّهُمْ قَوْمٌ لَّا يَعْقِلُونَ

59. Say: "O People of the Book!
Do ye disapprove of us
For no other reason than
That we believe in Allah,
And the revelation
That hath come to us
And that which came
Before (us), and (perhaps)
That most of you
Are rebellious and disobedient?"[769]

٥٩ قُلْ يَٰٓأَهْلَ ٱلْكِتَٰبِ
هَلْ تَنقِمُونَ مِنَّآ إِلَّآ أَنْ ءَامَنَّا بِٱللَّهِ
وَمَآ أُنزِلَ إِلَيْنَا وَمَآ أُنزِلَ مِن قَبْلُ
وَأَنَّ أَكْثَرَكُمْ فَٰسِقُونَ

60. Say: "Shall I point out
To you something much worse
Than this, (as judged)
By the treatment it received
From Allah? Those who
Incurred the curse of Allah
And His wrath, those of whom some
He transformed into apes and swine,[770]
Those who worshipped Evil—
These are (many times) worse
In rank, and far more astray
From the even Path!"

٦٠ قُلْ هَلْ أُنَبِّئُكُم بِشَرٍّ مِّن
ذَٰلِكَ مَثُوبَةً عِندَ ٱللَّهِ ۚ مَن
لَّعَنَهُ ٱللَّهُ وَغَضِبَ عَلَيْهِ
وَجَعَلَ مِنْهُمُ ٱلْقِرَدَةَ وَٱلْخَنَازِيرَ
وَعَبَدَ ٱلطَّٰغُوتَ ۚ أُو۟لَٰٓئِكَ شَرٌّ مَّكَانًا
وَأَضَلُّ عَن سَوَآءِ ٱلسَّبِيلِ

769. There is the most biting irony in this and the next verse. 'You People of the Book! Do you hate us because we believe in Allah and not only our scripture, but yours also? Perhaps you hate us because we obey and you are in rebellion against Allah! Why hate us? There are worse things than our obedience and our faith. Shall I tell you some of them? Our test will be: what treatment Allah meted out to the things I mention. Who were the people who incurred the curse of Allah? (See Deut. xi. 28, and xxviii. 15-68; and numerous passages like Hosea viii. 14, and ix. 1.). Who provoked Allah's wrath? (See numerous passages like Deut. i. 34; Matt. iii. 7.) Who forsook Allah, and worshipped evil? (See Jeremiah, xvi. 11-13). That is your record. Is that why you hate us?'

770. For apes see Q. 2:65. For men possessed by devils, and the devils being sent into swine, see Matt. viii. 28-32. Or perhaps both apes and swine are allegorical: those who falsified Allah's scriptures became lawless like apes, and those who succumbed to filth, gluttony, or gross living became like swine.

61\. When they come to thee,
They say: "We believe":
But in fact they enter
With a mind against Faith,
And they go out
With the same.
But Allah knoweth fully
All that they hide.

٦١ وَإِذَا جَآءُوكُمْ قَالُوٓا۟ ءَامَنَّا
وَقَد دَّخَلُوا۟ بِٱلْكُفْرِ
وَهُمْ قَدْ خَرَجُوا۟ بِهِۦ
وَٱللَّهُ أَعْلَمُ بِمَا كَانُوا۟ يَكْتُمُونَ

62\. Many of them dost thou
See, racing each other
In sin and transgression
And their eating of things [771]
Forbidden. Evil indeed
Are the things that they do.

٦٢ وَتَرَىٰ كَثِيرًا مِّنْهُمْ يُسَٰرِعُونَ
فِى ٱلْإِثْمِ وَٱلْعُدْوَٰنِ وَأَكْلِهِمُ
ٱلسُّحْتَ لَبِئْسَ مَا كَانُوا۟ يَعْمَلُونَ

63\. Why do not the Rabbis
And the doctors of law forbid
Them from their (habit
Of) uttering sinful words
And eating things forbidden?
Evil indeed are their works.

٦٣ لَوْلَا يَنْهَىٰهُمُ ٱلرَّبَّٰنِيُّونَ وَٱلْأَحْبَارُ
عَن قَوْلِهِمُ ٱلْإِثْمَ وَأَكْلِهِمُ ٱلسُّحْتَ
لَبِئْسَ مَا كَانُوا۟ يَصْنَعُونَ

64\. The Jews say: "Allah's hand[772]
Is tied up." Be *their* hands
Tied up and be they accursed
For the (blasphemy) they utter.
Nay, both His hands
Are widely outstretched:
He giveth and spendeth
(Of His bounty) as He pleaseth.
But the revelation that
Cometh to thee from Allah
Increaseth in most of them
Their obstinate rebellion[773]

٦٤ وَقَالَتِ ٱلْيَهُودُ يَدُ ٱللَّهِ مَغْلُولَةٌ
غُلَّتْ أَيْدِيهِمْ وَلُعِنُوا۟ بِمَا قَالُوا۟
بَلْ يَدَاهُ مَبْسُوطَتَانِ
يُنفِقُ كَيْفَ يَشَآءُ
وَلَيَزِيدَنَّ كَثِيرًا مِّنْهُم
مَّآ أُنزِلَ إِلَيْكَ مِن رَّبِّكَ طُغْيَٰنًا

771\. *Eating of things forbidden*: maybe construed in a literal or a figurative sense. From its juxtaposition with sin and hatred, it is better to construe it in a figurative sense, as referring to their fraudulent misappropriations of other people's property or trust property. "Eating" is used in 5:66 below in the general sense of enjoyment and happiness.

772\. *Cf.* 5:12 and 2:245, for a "beautiful loan to Allah", and 3:81, for the blasphemous taunt, "Then Allah is poor!" It is another form of the taunt to say, "Then Allah's hands are tied up. He is close-fisted. He does not give!" This blasphemy is repudiated. On the contrary, boundless is Allah's bounty, and He gives, as it were, with both hands outstretched—a figure of speech for unbounded liberality.

773\. Their jealousy—because Muṣṭafā is chosen for Allah's Message—is so great that it only confirms and strengthens their rebellion and blasphemy.

And blasphemy. Amongst them
We have placed enmity[774]
And hatred till the Day
Of Judgement. Every time
They kindle the fire of war,
Allah doth extinguish it;
But they (ever) strive
To do mischief on earth.
And Allah loveth not
Those who do mischief.[775]

وَكُفْرًا وَأَلْقَيْنَا بَيْنَهُمُ ٱلْعَدَٰوَةَ
وَٱلْبَغْضَآءَ إِلَىٰ يَوْمِ ٱلْقِيَٰمَةِ
كُلَّمَآ أَوْقَدُوا۟ نَارًا لِّلْحَرْبِ أَطْفَأَهَا ٱللَّهُ
وَيَسْعَوْنَ فِى ٱلْأَرْضِ فَسَادًا
وَٱللَّهُ لَا يُحِبُّ ٱلْمُفْسِدِينَ

65. If only the People of the Book
Had believed and been righteous,
We should indeed have
Blotted out their iniquities
And admitted them
To Gardens of Bliss.

٦٥ وَلَوْ أَنَّ أَهْلَ ٱلْكِتَٰبِ ءَامَنُوا۟
وَٱتَّقَوْا۟ لَكَفَّرْنَا عَنْهُمْ سَيِّـَٔاتِهِمْ
وَلَأَدْخَلْنَٰهُمْ جَنَّٰتِ ٱلنَّعِيمِ

66. If only they had stood fast
By the Law, the Gospel,
And all the revelation that was sent
To them from their Lord,
They would have enjoyed
Happiness from every side.[776]
There is from among them
A party on the right course:
But many of them
Follow a course that is evil.

٦٦ وَلَوْ أَنَّهُمْ أَقَامُوا۟ ٱلتَّوْرَىٰةَ
وَٱلْإِنجِيلَ وَمَآ أُنزِلَ إِلَيْهِم مِّن رَّبِّهِمْ
لَأَكَلُوا۟ مِن فَوْقِهِمْ وَمِن
تَحْتِ أَرْجُلِهِم مِّنْهُمْ أُمَّةٌ مُّقْتَصِدَةٌ
وَكَثِيرٌ مِّنْهُمْ سَآءَ مَا يَعْمَلُونَ

774. *Cf.* 5:14, where the eternal warring of the Christian sects, among themselves and against the Jews, is referred to. The reference is to the whole of the People of the Book, Jews and Christians—their internal squabbles and their external disputes, quarrels, and wars.

775. The argument of the whole verse may be thus stated. The Jews blaspheme and mock, and because of their jealousy, the more they are taught, the more obstinate they become in their rebellion. But what good will it do to them? Their selfishness and spite sow quarrels among themselves, which will not be healed till the Day of Judgement. When they stir up wars, especially against the innocent, Allah's Mercy is poured down like a flood of water to extinguish them. But their wickedness continues to devise ever new mischief. And Allah loves not mischief or those who do mischief.

776. The literal translation of the two lines would be: "They would have eaten from above them and from below their feet." To eat (*akala*) is a very comprehensive word, and denotes enjoyment generally, physical, social, mental and moral, and spiritual. "To eat what is forbidden" in verses 65 and 66 referred to taking unlawful profit, from usury or trust funds or in other ways. Here "eating" would seem to mean receiving satisfaction or happiness in this life as well as in the life to come. "From above them" may refer to heavenly or spiritual satisfaction, and "from below their feet" to earthly satisfaction. But it is better to take the words as a general idiom, and understand "satisfaction or happiness from every side." (R).

SECTION 10.

67. O Messenger! proclaim
The (Message) which hath been
Sent to thee from thy Lord.[777]
If thou didst not, thou
Wouldst not have fulfilled
And proclaimed His Mission.
And Allah will defend thee
From men (who mean mischief).
For Allah guideth not
Those who reject Faith.

٦٧ يَٰٓأَيُّهَا ٱلرَّسُولُ
بَلِّغْ مَآ أُنزِلَ إِلَيْكَ مِن رَّبِّكَ
وَإِن لَّمْ تَفْعَلْ فَمَا بَلَّغْتَ رِسَالَتَهُۥ
وَٱللَّهُ يَعْصِمُكَ مِنَ ٱلنَّاسِ
إِنَّ ٱللَّهَ لَا يَهْدِى ٱلْقَوْمَ ٱلْكَٰفِرِينَ

68. Say: "O People of the Book!
Ye have no ground
To stand upon unless
Ye stand fast by the Law,
The Gospel, and all the revelation
That has come to you from
Your Lord." It is the revelation
That cometh to thee from
Thy Lord, that increaseth in most
Of them their obstinate
Rebellion and blasphemy.
But sorrow thou not
Over (these) people without Faith.[778]

٦٨ قُلْ يَٰٓأَهْلَ ٱلْكِتَٰبِ
لَسْتُمْ عَلَىٰ شَىْءٍ حَتَّىٰ تُقِيمُوا۟ ٱلتَّوْرَىٰةَ
وَٱلْإِنجِيلَ وَمَآ أُنزِلَ إِلَيْكُم مِّن رَّبِّكُمْ
وَلَيَزِيدَنَّ كَثِيرًا مِّنْهُم مَّآ أُنزِلَ
إِلَيْكَ مِن رَّبِّكَ طُغْيَٰنًا وَكُفْرًا
فَلَا تَأْسَ عَلَى ٱلْقَوْمِ ٱلْكَٰفِرِينَ

69. Those who believe (in the Qur'ān),
Those who follow the Jewish (scriptures),
And the Sabians and the Christians—
Any who believe in Allah
And the Last Day,

٦٩ إِنَّ ٱلَّذِينَ ءَامَنُوا۟
وَٱلَّذِينَ هَادُوا۟
وَٱلصَّٰبِـُٔونَ وَٱلنَّصَٰرَىٰ
مَنْ ءَامَنَ بِٱللَّهِ وَٱلْيَوْمِ ٱلْءَاخِرِ

777. Muḥammad had many difficulties to contend with, many enemies and dangers to avoid. This is to assure him that his Message was true and from Allah. His mission must be fulfilled. And he must—as he did—go forward and proclaim that Message and fulfil his mission, trusting Allah for protection, and unconcerned if people who had lost all sense of right rejected it or threatened him.

778. In 5:26 Moses was told not to sorrow over a rebellious people. Here Muḥammad is told not to sorrow over people without faith. The second situation is even more trying than the first. Rebellion may be a passing phase. Want of faith is an attitude of mind that is well-nigh hopeless. Yet the Prophet patiently reasoned with them and bore their taunts and insults. If, the argument runs, you do not believe in anything, even in the things that you may be expected to believe in, how can you receive, in faith, Allah's Message that has come in another form? In fact your jealousy adds to your obstinacy and unbelief.

And work righteousness—[779]
On them shall be no fear,
Nor shall they grieve.

وَعَمِلَ صَٰلِحًا فَلَا خَوْفٌ عَلَيْهِمْ وَلَا هُمْ يَحْزَنُونَ

70. We took the Covenant
Of the Children of Israel
And sent them Messengers.
Every time there came
To them a Messenger
With what they themselves
Desired not—some
(Of these) they called
Imposters, and some they
(Go so far as to) slay.[780]

٧٠ لَقَدْ أَخَذْنَا مِيثَٰقَ بَنِىٓ إِسْرَٰٓءِيلَ
وَأَرْسَلْنَآ إِلَيْهِمْ رُسُلًا ۖ كُلَّمَا جَآءَهُمْ
رَسُولٌۢ بِمَا لَا تَهْوَىٰٓ أَنفُسُهُمْ
فَرِيقًا كَذَّبُوا۟ وَفَرِيقًا يَقْتُلُونَ

71. They thought there would be
No trial (or punishment);
So they became blind and deaf;[781]
Yet Allah (in mercy) turned
To them; yet again many
Of them became blind and deaf.
But Allah sees well
All that they do.

٧١ وَحَسِبُوٓا۟ أَلَّا تَكُونَ فِتْنَةٌ
فَعَمُوا۟ وَصَمُّوا۟ ثُمَّ تَابَ ٱللَّهُ عَلَيْهِمْ
ثُمَّ عَمُوا۟ وَصَمُّوا۟ كَثِيرٌ مِّنْهُمْ ۚ
وَٱللَّهُ بَصِيرٌۢ بِمَا يَعْمَلُونَ

72. They do blaspheme who say:
"Allah is Christ the son
Of Mary." But said Christ:[782]

٧٢ لَقَدْ كَفَرَ ٱلَّذِينَ قَالُوٓا۟ إِنَّ ٱللَّهَ هُوَ
ٱلْمَسِيحُ ٱبْنُ مَرْيَمَ ۖ وَقَالَ ٱلْمَسِيحُ

779. Here, as in Sūrah Al Baqarah (2:62), the Qur'ān underscores the importance of true and genuine faith, which is to be judged by a sincere belief in Allah and man's accountability to Him backed by righteous conduct rather than by mere forms or labels. In both places it repudiates the false claims of the People of the Book that they had a special relationship with Allah for they were the children of Abraham; that they were a chosen people with special privileges, and no matter what they did, their high status would remain unaffected. Here this false notion is refuted and the People of the Book are being reminded that it is through sincere belief and righteous conduct rather than pretentious claims that man can win his Lord's pleasure and achieve ultimate success. The verse does not purport to lay down an exhaustive list of the articles of faith. Nor does it seek to spell out the essentials of a genuine belief in Allah, which has no meaning unless it is accompanied by belief in His Prophets for it is through their agency alone that we know Allah's Will and can abide by it in our practical lives. This is especially true of His final Prophet, Muḥammad (peace be on him) whose message is universal, and not confined to any particular group or section of humanity. Belief in the Prophethood of Muḥammad (peace be on him) is thus an integral part and a logical corollary of belief in Allah. Moreover, it is also an essential test of genuineness of such belief. This becomes clear when the verse is read in conjunction with other relevant verses of the Qur'ān. See, for instance, 4:170, 5:16, 21, 7:157, 158, 21:107, 25:1, 33:40, 61:6. See also 2:40, 3:31-32. 4:150-151. (Eds.).

780. *Cf.* 2:87, and n. 91.

781. That is, they turned away their eyes from Allah's Signs and they turned a deaf ear to Allah's Message.

782. *Cf.* Matt. iv. 10, where Christ rebukes Satan for desiring the worship of other than Allah; John xx. 17, where Christ says to Mary Magdalene, "Go unto my brethren, and say unto them, I ascend unto my Father and your Father; and to my God and your God." *Cf.* also Luke xviii, 19, where Christ rebukes a certain ruler for calling him Good Master: "Why callest thou me good? None is good, save One, that is, God." In Mark xii. 25 Jesus says: "The first of all the commandments is, Hear O Israel: the Lord our God is One Lord."

"O Children of Israel!
Worship Allah, my Lord
And your Lord." Whoever
Joins other gods with Allah—
Allah will forbid him
The Garden, and the Fire
Will be his abode. There will
For the wrongdoers
Be no one to help.

يَٰبَنِيٓ إِسۡرَٰٓءِيلَ ٱعۡبُدُواْ ٱللَّهَ رَبِّي
وَرَبَّكُمۡۖ إِنَّهُۥ مَن يُشۡرِكۡ بِٱللَّهِ فَقَدۡ
حَرَّمَ ٱللَّهُ عَلَيۡهِ ٱلۡجَنَّةَ وَمَأۡوَىٰهُ ٱلنَّارُۖ
وَمَا لِلظَّٰلِمِينَ مِنۡ أَنصَارٖ

73. They do blaspheme who say:
Allah is one of three
In a Trinity: for there is
No god except One God.
If they desist not
From their word (of blasphemy),
Verily a grievous penalty
Will befall the blasphemers
Among them.

٧٣ لَّقَدۡ كَفَرَ ٱلَّذِينَ قَالُوٓاْ إِنَّ ٱللَّهَ
ثَالِثُ ثَلَٰثَةٖۘ وَمَا مِنۡ إِلَٰهٍ إِلَّآ إِلَٰهٞ وَٰحِدٞۚ
وَإِن لَّمۡ يَنتَهُواْ عَمَّا يَقُولُونَ لَيَمَسَّنَّ
ٱلَّذِينَ كَفَرُواْ مِنۡهُمۡ عَذَابٌ أَلِيمٌ

74. Why turn they not to Allah
And seek His forgiveness?
For Allah is Oft-Forgiving,
Most Merciful.

٧٤ أَفَلَا يَتُوبُونَ إِلَى ٱللَّهِ
وَيَسۡتَغۡفِرُونَهُۥۚ وَٱللَّهُ غَفُورٞ رَّحِيمٞ

75. Christ, the son of Mary,
Was no more than
A Messenger; many were
The Messengers that passed away
Before him. His mother
Was a woman of truth.[783]
They had both to eat
Their (daily) food.
See how Allah doth make
His Signs clear to them;[784]
Yet see in what ways
They are deluded
Away from the truth!

٧٥ مَّا ٱلۡمَسِيحُ ٱبۡنُ مَرۡيَمَ
إِلَّا رَسُولٞ قَدۡ خَلَتۡ مِن قَبۡلِهِ
ٱلرُّسُلُ وَأُمُّهُۥ صِدِّيقَةٞۖ
كَانَا يَأۡكُلَانِ ٱلطَّعَامَۗ
ٱنظُرۡ كَيۡفَ نُبَيِّنُ لَهُمُ ٱلۡأٓيَٰتِ
ثُمَّ ٱنظُرۡ أَنَّىٰ يُؤۡفَكُونَ

76. Say: "Will ye worship,
Besides Allah, something
Which hath no power either

٧٦ قُلۡ أَتَعۡبُدُونَ
مِن دُونِ ٱللَّهِ مَا لَا يَمۡلِكُ

---

783. She never claimed that she was a mother of God, or that her son was God. She was a pious and virtuous woman.

784. Note how logically the argument has led up from Jewish backslidings and want of faith, to blasphemies associated with the names of Jesus and Mary, and in the following verses to the worship of senseless sticks and stones. Allah is One; His Message is one; yet how people's perversity transforms truth into falsehood, religion into superstition!

To harm or benefit you?
But Allah—He it is
That heareth and knoweth
All things."

لَكُمْ ضَرًّا وَلَا نَفْعًا
وَاللَّهُ هُوَ السَّمِيعُ الْعَلِيمُ

77. Say: "O People of the Book!
Exceed not in your religion[785]
The bounds (of what is proper),
Trespassing beyond the truth,
Nor follow the vain desires
Of people who went wrong
In times gone by—who misled
Many, and strayed (themselves)
From the even Way.

٧٧ قُلْ يَٰٓأَهْلَ الْكِتَٰبِ لَا تَغْلُوا فِي
دِينِكُمْ غَيْرَ الْحَقِّ وَلَا تَتَّبِعُوٓا أَهْوَآءَ قَوْمٍ
قَدْ ضَلُّوا مِن قَبْلُ وَأَضَلُّوا كَثِيرًا
وَضَلُّوا عَن سَوَآءِ السَّبِيلِ

SECTION 11.

78. Curses were pronounced
On those among the Children
Of Israel who rejected Faith,
By the tongue of David[786]
And of Jesus, the son of Mary,[787]
Because they disobeyed
And persisted in Excesses.

٧٨ لُعِنَ الَّذِينَ كَفَرُوا مِنۢ بَنِىٓ
إِسْرَٰٓءِيلَ عَلَىٰ لِسَانِ دَاوُۥدَ وَعِيسَى ابْنِ
مَرْيَمَ ذَٰلِكَ بِمَا عَصَوا وَّكَانُوا يَعْتَدُونَ

79. Nor did they (usually)
Forbid one another[788]
The iniquities which they
Committed: evil indeed
Were the deeds which they did.

٧٩ كَانُوا لَا يَتَنَاهَوْنَ عَن مُّنكَرٍ
فَعَلُوهُ لَبِئْسَ مَا كَانُوا يَفْعَلُونَ

80. Thou seest many of them
Turning in friendship
To the Unbelievers.

٨٠ تَرَىٰ كَثِيرًا مِّنْهُمْ
يَتَوَلَّوْنَ الَّذِينَ كَفَرُوا

785. Excess, as opposed to moderation and reason, is the simplest test by which a hypocrite or a selfish man who "trades" on religion, is known from a sincere, pious, and truly religious man. Excess means that truth is sometimes concealed or trampled upon, that the fashions of ancestors or contemporaries are copied or overdone, and Allah's name is dishonoured by blasphemies or the setting up of false gods or fetishes, or that good (or even bad) men are deified and worshipped. The true path is the even path, the path of rectitude. (*Cf.* 2:108, and 5:13).

786. The Psalms of David have several passages of imprecations against the wicked. *Cf.* Psalms cix 17-18; lxxviii. 21-22 ("Therefore the Lord heard this and was wroth: so a fire was kindled against Jacob, and anger also came up against Israel; because they believed not in God, and trusted not in His salvation"); Psalms lxix. 22-28, and Psalms v. 10.

787. *Cf.* Matt. xxiii. 33 ("Ye serpents, ye generation of vipers, how can ye escape the damnation of Hell?); also Matt. xii. 34.

788. There are bad men in every community, but if leaders connive at the misdeeds of the commonalty—and even worse, if leaders themselves share in the misdeeds, as happened with the Pharisees and Scribes against whom Jesus spoke out, then that community is doomed.

Evil indeed are (the works) which
Their souls have sent forward
Before them (with the result),
That Allah's wrath
Is on them,
And in torment
Will they abide.

لَبِئْسَ مَا قَدَّمَتْ لَهُمْ أَنفُسُهُمْ
أَن سَخِطَ ٱللَّهُ عَلَيْهِمْ
وَفِى ٱلْعَذَابِ هُمْ خَٰلِدُونَ

81. If only they had believed
In Allah, in the Prophet,
And in what hath been
Revealed to him, never
Would they have taken
Them for friends and protectors,
But most of them are
Rebellious wrongdoers.

﴿٨١﴾ وَلَوْ كَانُوا۟ يُؤْمِنُونَ بِٱللَّهِ وَٱلنَّبِىِّ
وَمَآ أُنزِلَ إِلَيْهِ مَا ٱتَّخَذُوهُمْ أَوْلِيَآءَ
وَلَٰكِنَّ كَثِيرًا مِّنْهُمْ فَٰسِقُونَ

7/30

82. Strongest among men in enmity
To the Believers wilt thou
Find the Jews and Pagans;
And nearest among them in love
To the Believers wilt thou
Find those who say,[789]
"We are Christians":
Because amongst these are
Men devoted to learning[790]
And men who have renounced
The world, and they
Are not arrogant.

﴿٨٢﴾ لَتَجِدَنَّ أَشَدَّ ٱلنَّاسِ عَدَٰوَةً لِّلَّذِينَ ءَامَنُوا۟
ٱلْيَهُودَ وَٱلَّذِينَ أَشْرَكُوا۟ وَلَتَجِدَنَّ
أَقْرَبَهُم مَّوَدَّةً لِّلَّذِينَ ءَامَنُوا۟ ٱلَّذِينَ قَالُوٓا۟
إِنَّا نَصَٰرَىٰ ذَٰلِكَ بِأَنَّ مِنْهُمْ قِسِّيسِينَ
وَرُهْبَانًا وَأَنَّهُمْ لَا يَسْتَكْبِرُونَ

83. And when they listen
To the revelation received
By the Messenger, thou wilt
See their eyes overflowing
With tears, for they
Recognise the truth:
They pray: "Our Lord!
We believe; write us
Down among the witnesses.

﴿٨٣﴾ وَإِذَا سَمِعُوا۟ مَآ أُنزِلَ إِلَى ٱلرَّسُولِ
تَرَىٰٓ أَعْيُنَهُمْ تَفِيضُ مِنَ ٱلدَّمْعِ
مِمَّا عَرَفُوا۟ مِنَ ٱلْحَقِّ يَقُولُونَ رَبَّنَآ
ءَامَنَّا فَٱكْتُبْنَا مَعَ ٱلشَّٰهِدِينَ

84. "What cause can we have
Not to believe in Allah

﴿٨٤﴾ وَمَا لَنَا لَا نُؤْمِنُ بِٱللَّهِ

789. The meaning is not that they merely call themselves Christians, but that they are such sincere Christians that they appreciate Muslim virtues, as did the Abyssinians to whom Muslim refugees went during the persecution in Makkah. (R).

790. *Qissīs*: I have translated as "devoted to learning," following the Commentators. It seems to be a foreign word, possibly Abyssinian rather than Syriac, as the reference seems to be to the Abyssinian Christians. Their real devotion to learning and the renunciation of the world by the Monastic Orders are contrasted with the hypocrisy and arrogance of the Pharisees and Scribes.

And the truth which has
Come to us, seeing that
We long for our Lord
To admit us to the company
Of the righteous?"

وَمَا جَآءَنَا مِنَ ٱلْحَقِّ وَنَطْمَعُ
أَن يُدْخِلَنَا رَبُّنَا مَعَ ٱلْقَوْمِ ٱلصَّٰلِحِينَ

85. And for this their prayer
Hath Allah rewarded them
With Gardens, with rivers
Flowing underneath—their eternal
Home. Such is the recompense
Of those who do good.

٨٥ فَأَثَٰبَهُمُ ٱللَّهُ بِمَا قَالُوا۟ جَنَّٰتٍ
تَجْرِى مِن تَحْتِهَا ٱلْأَنْهَٰرُ خَٰلِدِينَ فِيهَا
وَذَٰلِكَ جَزَآءُ ٱلْمُحْسِنِينَ

86. But those who reject Faith
And belie Our Signs—
They shall be Companions
Of Hell-fire.

٨٦ وَٱلَّذِينَ كَفَرُوا۟ وَكَذَّبُوا۟ بِـَٔايَٰتِنَآ
أُو۟لَٰٓئِكَ أَصْحَٰبُ ٱلْجَحِيمِ

C. 74.—In the physical pleasures of life
(5:87-108.) The crime is excess: there is no merit
In abstention from things that are good
And lawful. Take no rash vows,
But to solemn oaths be faithful. Shun
As abominations drinking and gambling,
And superstitions of all kinds.
But be reverent to what is sacred
In rites and associations. Not the same
Are things good and things evil.
Learn to distinguish, but pry not
Into questions beyond your ken.
Guard your own souls in truth
And justice, and no harm can befall you.

SECTION 12.

87. O ye who believe!
Make not unlawful
The good things which Allah
Hath made lawful for you,
But commit no excess;[791]
For Allah loveth not
Those given to excess.

٨٧ يَٰٓأَيُّهَا ٱلَّذِينَ ءَامَنُوا۟
لَا تُحَرِّمُوا۟ طَيِّبَٰتِ مَآ أَحَلَّ ٱللَّهُ لَكُمْ
وَلَا تَعْتَدُوٓا۟ ۚ إِنَّ ٱللَّهَ لَا يُحِبُّ ٱلْمُعْتَدِينَ

791. In pleasures that are good and lawful the crime is excess. There is no merit merely in abstention or asceticism, though the humility or unselfishness that may go with asceticism may have its value. In 5:82 Christian monks are praised for particular virtues, though here and elsewhere monasticism is disapproved of. Use Allah's gifts of all kinds with gratitude, but excess is not approved of by Allah.

88. Eat of the things which
Allah hath provided for you,
Lawful and good; but fear
Allah, in Whom ye believe.

٨٨ وَكُلُوا مِمَّا رَزَقَكُمُ اللَّهُ حَلَٰلًا طَيِّبًا ۚ
وَاتَّقُوا اللَّهَ الَّذِي أَنتُم بِهِۦ مُؤْمِنُونَ

89. Allah will not call you
To account for what is
Futile in your oaths,[792]
But He will call you
To account for your deliberate
Oaths: for expiation, feed
Ten indigent persons,
On a scale of the average
For the food of your families;
Or clothe them; or give
A slave his freedom.
If that is beyond your means,
Fast for three days.
That is the expiation
For the oaths ye have sworn.
But keep to your oaths.
Thus doth Allah make clear
To you His Signs, that ye
May be grateful.

٨٩ لَا يُؤَاخِذُكُمُ اللَّهُ بِاللَّغْوِ فِي أَيْمَٰنِكُمْ
وَلَٰكِن يُؤَاخِذُكُم بِمَا عَقَّدتُّمُ الْأَيْمَٰنَ ۖ
فَكَفَّٰرَتُهُۥ إِطْعَامُ عَشَرَةِ مَسَٰكِينَ
مِنْ أَوْسَطِ مَا تُطْعِمُونَ أَهْلِيكُمْ
أَوْ كِسْوَتُهُمْ أَوْ تَحْرِيرُ رَقَبَةٍ ۖ
فَمَن لَّمْ يَجِدْ فَصِيَامُ ثَلَٰثَةِ أَيَّامٍ ۚ
ذَٰلِكَ كَفَّٰرَةُ أَيْمَٰنِكُمْ إِذَا حَلَفْتُمْ ۚ
وَاحْفَظُوا أَيْمَٰنَكُمْ ۚ كَذَٰلِكَ يُبَيِّنُ اللَّهُ
لَكُمْ ءَايَٰتِهِۦ لَعَلَّكُمْ تَشْكُرُونَ

90. O ye who believe!
Intoxicants and gambling,[793]
(Dedication of) stones,[794]
And (divination by) arrows,[795]
Are an abomination—
Of Satan's handiwork;
Eschew such (abomination),
That ye may prosper.

٩٠ يَٰأَيُّهَا الَّذِينَ ءَامَنُوا إِنَّمَا الْخَمْرُ وَالْمَيْسِرُ
وَالْأَنصَابُ وَالْأَزْلَٰمُ رِجْسٌ مِّنْ عَمَلِ
الشَّيْطَٰنِ فَاجْتَنِبُوهُ لَعَلَّكُمْ تُفْلِحُونَ

792. Vows of penance or abstention may sometimes be futile, or even stand in the way of really good or virtuous act. See 2:224-226, and notes. The general principles established are: (1) take no futile oaths; (2) use not Allah's name, literally or in intention, to fetter yourself against doing a lawful or good act; (3) keep to your solemn oaths to the utmost of your ability; (4) where you are unable to do so, expiate your failure by feeding or clothing the poor, or obtaining some one's freedom, or if you have not the means, by fasting. This is from a spiritual aspect. If any party suffers damage from your failure, compensation will be due to him, but that would be a question of law or equity.

793. *Cf.* 2:219, and notes 240 and 241.

794. *Cf.* 5:3. The stones there referred to were stone altars or stone columns on which oil was poured for consecration, or slabs on which meat was sacrificed to idols. Any idolatrous or superstitious practices are here condemned. The *anṣāb* were objects of worship, and were common in Arabia before Islam. See Renan, "History of Israel", Chapter iv. and *Corpus Inscriptionum Semiticarum*, Part I. p. 154: Illustrations Nos. 123 and 123 *bis* are Phoenician columns of that kind, found in Malta.

795. *Cf.* 5:3. The arrows there referred to were used for the division of meat by a sort of lottery or raffle. But arrows were also used for divination, *i.e.*, for ascertaining lucky or unlucky moments, or learning the wishes of the heathen gods, as to whether men should undertake certain actions or not. All superstitions are condemned.

91. Satan's plan is (but)
To excite enmity and hatred
Between you, with intoxicants
And gambling, and hinder you
From the remembrance
Of Allah, and from prayer:
Will ye not then abstain?

٩١ إِنَّمَا يُرِيدُ ٱلشَّيْطَٰنُ أَن يُوقِعَ بَيْنَكُمُ
ٱلْعَدَٰوَةَ وَٱلْبَغْضَآءَ فِى ٱلْخَمْرِ وَٱلْمَيْسِرِ وَيَصُدَّكُمْ
عَن ذِكْرِ ٱللَّهِ وَعَنِ ٱلصَّلَوٰةِ ۖ فَهَلْ أَنتُم مُّنتَهُونَ

92. Obey Allah, and obey the
Messenger,[796]
And beware (of evil):
If ye do turn back,
Know ye that it is
Our Messenger's duty
To proclaim (the Message)[797]
In the clearest manner.

٩٢ وَأَطِيعُوا۟ ٱللَّهَ وَأَطِيعُوا۟
ٱلرَّسُولَ وَٱحْذَرُوا۟ ۚ فَإِن تَوَلَّيْتُمْ
فَٱعْلَمُوٓا۟ أَنَّمَا عَلَىٰ
رَسُولِنَا ٱلْبَلَٰغُ ٱلْمُبِينُ

93. On those who believe
And do deeds of righteousness
There is no blame
For what they ate (in the past),
When they guard themselves
From evil, and believe,
And do deeds of righteousness—
(Or) again, guard themselves
From evil and believe—
(Or) again, guard themselves
From evil and do good.
For Allah loveth those
Who do good.[798]

٩٣ لَيْسَ عَلَى ٱلَّذِينَ ءَامَنُوا۟ وَعَمِلُوا۟
ٱلصَّٰلِحَٰتِ جُنَاحٌ فِيمَا طَعِمُوٓا۟
إِذَا مَا ٱتَّقَوا۟ وَّءَامَنُوا۟
وَعَمِلُوا۟ ٱلصَّٰلِحَٰتِ ثُمَّ ٱتَّقَوا۟
وَّءَامَنُوا۟ ثُمَّ ٱتَّقَوا۟ وَّأَحْسَنُوا۟ ۗ
وَٱللَّهُ يُحِبُّ ٱلْمُحْسِنِينَ

796. We are asked to obey the commands of Allah (which are always reasonable), instead of following superstitions (which are irrational), or seeking undue stimulation in intoxicants or undue advantage in gambling. To some there may be temporary excitement or pleasure in these, but that is not the way either of prosperity or piety.

797. *Cf.* 5:67. Both the worldly and the spiritual aspects of loss are pointed out. Can Allah's Message do more?

798. There is a subtle symphony in what appears at first sight to be a triple repetition. The relation of such simple regulations as those of food, or game, or the reverence due to a sacred place or sacred institution, has to be explained *vis-a-vis* man's higher duties. Baiḍāwi is right in classifying such duties under three heads: those due to Allah, those due from a man to himself (his self-respect), and those due to other creatures of Allah. Or perhaps all duties have this threefold aspect. The first may be called *believing* or *faith*; the second, *guarding* ourselves from evil, or *conscience*; and the third, doing good or *righteousness.* But the simplest physical rules, *e.g.*, those about eating, cleanliness, etc., if they are good, refer also to the higher aspects. If we eat bad food, we hurt ourselves, we cause offence to our neighbours, and we disobey Allah. If we have faith and righteousness, we are likely to be wanting in conscience? If we have conscience and faith, are we likely to fail in righteousness? If we have conscience and righteousness, what can be their foundation but faith? All three manifest themselves in a willing obedience to Allah, and love for Him. We realise His love in loving and doing good to His creatures, and our love to Him is meaningless without such good.

SECTION 13.

94. O ye who believe!
Allah doth but make a trial of you
In a little matter
Of game well within reach
Of your hands and your lances,
That He may test[799]
Who feareth Him unseen;
Any who transgress
Thereafter, will have
A grievous penalty.

٩٤ يَٰٓأَيُّهَا ٱلَّذِينَ ءَامَنُوا۟ لَيَبْلُوَنَّكُمُ ٱللَّهُ
بِشَىْءٍ مِّنَ ٱلصَّيْدِ تَنَالُهُۥٓ أَيْدِيكُمْ وَرِمَاحُكُمْ
لِيَعْلَمَ ٱللَّهُ مَن يَخَافُهُۥ بِٱلْغَيْبِ ۚ
فَمَنِ ٱعْتَدَىٰ بَعْدَ ذَٰلِكَ
فَلَهُۥ عَذَابٌ أَلِيمٌ

95. O ye who believe!
Kill not game
While in the Sacred
Precincts or in pilgrim garb.[800]
If any of you doth so
Intentionally, the compensation
Is an offering, brought
To the Ka'bah, of a domestic animal
Equivalent to the one he killed,[801]
As adjudged by two just men
Among you; or by way
Of atonement, the feeding
Of the indigent; or its
Equivalent in fasts; that he
May taste of the penalty
Of his deed. Allah
Forgives what is past:
For repetition Allah will
Exact from him the penalty.
For Allah is Exalted,
And Lord of Retribution.

٩٥ يَٰٓأَيُّهَا ٱلَّذِينَ ءَامَنُوا۟
لَا تَقْتُلُوا۟ ٱلصَّيْدَ وَأَنتُمْ حُرُمٌ ۚ
وَمَن قَتَلَهُۥ مِنكُم مُّتَعَمِّدًا
فَجَزَآءٌ مِّثْلُ مَا قَتَلَ مِنَ ٱلنَّعَمِ يَحْكُمُ بِهِۦ
ذَوَا عَدْلٍ مِّنكُمْ هَدْيًۢا بَٰلِغَ ٱلْكَعْبَةِ
أَوْ كَفَّٰرَةٌ طَعَامُ مَسَٰكِينَ
أَوْ عَدْلُ ذَٰلِكَ صِيَامًا لِّيَذُوقَ
وَبَالَ أَمْرِهِۦ ۗ عَفَا ٱللَّهُ عَمَّا سَلَفَ ۚ
وَمَنْ عَادَ فَيَنتَقِمُ ٱللَّهُ مِنْهُ ۗ
وَٱللَّهُ عَزِيزٌ ذُو ٱنتِقَامٍ

799. Literally, "know", *Cf.* 3:166 and 3:154, n. 467. Game is forbidden in the Sacred Precincts. If we deliberately break that injunction, we have no faith and reverence.

800. See 2:1 and n. 684. The pilgrim garb, *Iḥrām*, has been explained in n. 212, 2:196.

801. For an inadvertent breach of the game rule there is apparently no penalty. Intentional breach will be prevented, if possible, by previous action. If in some case the preventive action is not effective, the penalty is prescribed. The penalty is in three alternatives: an equivalent animal should be brought to the Ka'ba for sacrifice; If so, the meat would be distributed to the poor; *or* the poor must be fed, with grain or money, according to the value of the animal if one had been sacrificed; *or* the offender must fast as many days as the number of the poor who would have been fed under the second alternative. Probably the last alternative would only be open if the offender is too poor to afford the first or second, but on this point Commentators are not agreed. The "equivalent animal" in the first alternative would be a domestic animal of similar value or weight in meat or of similar shape (*e.g.*, goat to antelope), as adjudged by two just men on the spot.

The alternatives about the penalty and its remission ("Allah forgives what is past") or exaction explain the last two lines of the verse: being "Exalted and Lord of Retribution", Allah can remit or regulate according to His just laws.

96. Lawful to you is the pursuit[802]
Of water-game and its use
For food—for the benefit
Of yourselves and those who
Travel; but forbidden
Is the pursuit of land-game—
As long as ye are
In the Sacred Precincts
Or in pilgrim garb.
And fear Allah, to Whom
Ye shall be gathered back.

٩٦ أُحِلَّ لَكُمْ صَيْدُ الْبَحْرِ
وَطَعَامُهُ مَتَاعًا لَّكُمْ وَلِلسَّيَّارَةِ
وَحُرِّمَ عَلَيْكُمْ صَيْدُ الْبَرِّ
مَا دُمْتُمْ حُرُمًا وَاتَّقُوا اللَّهَ
الَّذِي إِلَيْهِ تُحْشَرُونَ

97. Allah made the Ka'bah,
The Sacred House, an asylum
Of security for men, as
Also the Sacred Months,[803]
The animals for offerings,
And the garlands that mark
them:[804]
That ye may know
That Allah hath knowledge
Of what is in the heavens
And on earth and that Allah
Is well-acquainted
With all things.[805]

٩٧ جَعَلَ اللَّهُ الْكَعْبَةَ الْبَيْتَ الْحَرَامَ
قِيَامًا لِّلنَّاسِ وَالشَّهْرَ الْحَرَامَ
وَالْهَدْيَ وَالْقَلَائِدَ
ذَٰلِكَ لِتَعْلَمُوا أَنَّ اللَّهَ يَعْلَمُ
مَا فِي السَّمَاوَاتِ وَمَا فِي الْأَرْضِ
وَأَنَّ اللَّهَ بِكُلِّ شَيْءٍ عَلِيمٌ

98. Know ye that Allah
Is strict in punishment
And that Allah is
Oft-Forgiving, Most Merciful.

٩٨ اعْلَمُوا أَنَّ اللَّهَ شَدِيدُ الْعِقَابِ
وَأَنَّ اللَّهَ غَفُورٌ رَّحِيمٌ

99. The Messenger's duty is
But to proclaim (the Message).
But Allah knoweth all
That ye reveal and ye conceal.

٩٩ مَّا عَلَى الرَّسُولِ إِلَّا الْبَلَاغُ
وَاللَّهُ يَعْلَمُ مَا تُبْدُونَ وَمَا تَكْتُمُونَ

100. Say: "Not equal are things
That are bad and things
That are good, even though

١٠٠ قُل لَّا يَسْتَوِي الْخَبِيثُ وَالطَّيِّبُ وَلَوْ

802. *Water game: i.e.*, game found in water, *e.g.*, water fowl, fish, etc. "Water" includes sea, river, lake, pond, etc.

803. The Sacred or Prohibited Months are explained in n. 209, 2:194, and n. 687, 5:3.

804. See 5:2 and n. 688.

805. All sorts of people from all parts of the earth gather during the Pilgrimage. They must not think that they are strangers, that nobody knows them, and that they may behave as they like. It is the House of Allah, and He has supreme knowledge of all things, of all thoughts, and all motives. As the next verse says, while He is Oft-Forgiving, Most Merciful. He is also strict in enforcing respect for His ordinances.

The abundance of the bad
May dazzle thee;[806]
So fear Allah, O ye
That understand;
That (so) ye may prosper."

أَعۡجَبَكَ كَثۡرَةُ ٱلۡخَبِيثِۚ فَٱتَّقُواْ ٱللَّهَ
يَٰٓأُوْلِي ٱلۡأَلۡبَٰبِ لَعَلَّكُمۡ تُفۡلِحُونَ

Section 14.

101. O ye who believe!
Ask not questions
About things which,
If made plain to you,
May cause you trouble.
But if ye ask about things
When the Qur'ān is being
Revealed, they will be
Made plain to you,[807]
Allah will forgive those:
For Allah is Oft-Forgiving,
Most Forbearing.

١٠١ يَٰٓأَيُّهَا ٱلَّذِينَ ءَامَنُواْ لَا تَسۡـَٔلُواْ
عَنۡ أَشۡيَآءَ إِن تُبۡدَ لَكُمۡ تَسُؤۡكُمۡ
وَإِن تَسۡـَٔلُواْ عَنۡهَا حِينَ يُنَزَّلُ
ٱلۡقُرۡءَانُ تُبۡدَ لَكُمۡ عَفَا ٱللَّهُ عَنۡهَاۗ
وَٱللَّهُ غَفُورٌ حَلِيمٞ

102. Some people before you
Did ask such questions,[808]
And on that account
Lost their faith.

١٠٢ قَدۡ سَأَلَهَا قَوۡمٞ مِّن قَبۡلِكُمۡ
ثُمَّ أَصۡبَحُواْ بِهَا كَٰفِرِينَ

103. It was not Allah
Who instituted (superstitions[809]

١٠٣ مَا جَعَلَ ٱللَّهُ

806. *Cf.* 2:204. People often judge by quantity rather than quality. They are dazzled by numbers: their hearts are captured by what they see everywhere around them. But the man of understanding and discrimination judges by a different standard. He knows that good and bad things are not to be lumped together, and carefully chooses the best, which may be the scarcest, and avoids the bad, though evil may meet him at every step.

807. Many secrets are wisely hidden from us. If the future were known to us, we need not necessarily be happy. In many cases we should be miserable. If the inner meaning of some of the things we see before our eyes were disclosed to us, it might cause a lot of mischief. Allah's Message, insofar as it is necessary for shaping our conduct, is plain and open to us. But there are many things too deep for us to understand, either individually or collectively. It would be foolish to pry into them, as some people tried to do in the time of the Prophet. Where a matter is mentioned in the Qur'ān, we can reverently ask for its meaning. That is not forbidden. But we should never pass the bounds of (1) our own capacity to understand, (2) the time and occasion when we ask questions, and (3) the part of the Universal Plan which it is Allah's purpose to reveal to us.

808. For example, the merely fractious questions asked of Moses by the Jews; 2:68-71. They showed that they had no faith. When foolish questions are asked, and there is no answer, it also shakes the faith of the foolish ones.

809. A number of Arab Pagan superstitions are referred to. The Pagan mind, not understanding the hidden secrets of nature, attributed certain phenomena to divine anger and were assailed by superstitious fears which haunted their lives. If a she-camel or other female domestic animal had a large number of young, she (or one of her offspring) had her ear slit and she was dedicated to a god; such an animal was a *bahīra*. On return in safety from a journey, or on recovery from an illness a she-camel was similarly dedicated and let loose for free pasture; she was called a *sāiba*. Where an animal bore twins, certain sacrifices or dedications were made to idols; an animal so dedicated was a *waṣīla*. A stallion-camel dedicated to the gods by certain rites was a *ḥām*. The particular examples lead to the general truth; that superstition is due to ignorance, and is degrading to men and dishonouring to Allah.

Like those of) a slit-ear
She-camel, or a she-camel
Let loose for free pasture,
Or idol sacrifices for
Twin-births in animals,
Or stallion-camels
Freed from work:
It is blasphemers
Who invent a lie
Against Allah; but most
Of them lack wisdom.

مِنۢ بَحِيرَةٖ وَلَا سَآئِبَةٖ
وَلَا وَصِيلَةٖ وَلَا حَامٖ
وَلَٰكِنَّ ٱلَّذِينَ كَفَرُواْ
يَفۡتَرُونَ عَلَى ٱللَّهِ ٱلۡكَذِبَۖ
وَأَكۡثَرُهُمۡ لَا يَعۡقِلُونَ

104. When it is said to them:
"Come to what Allah
Hath revealed; come
To the Messenger":
They say: "Enough for us[810]
Are the ways we found
Our fathers following."
What! even though their fathers
Were void of knowledge
And guidance?

١٠٤ وَإِذَا قِيلَ لَهُمۡ تَعَالَوۡاْ
إِلَىٰ مَآ أَنزَلَ ٱللَّهُ وَإِلَى ٱلرَّسُولِ
قَالُواْ حَسۡبُنَا مَا وَجَدۡنَا عَلَيۡهِ ءَابَآءَنَآۚ
أَوَلَوۡ كَانَ ءَابَآؤُهُمۡ لَا يَعۡلَمُونَ
شَيۡـٔٗا وَلَا يَهۡتَدُونَ

105. O ye who believe!
Guard your own souls:
If ye follow (right) guidance,
No hurt can come to you
From those who stray.
The goal of you all
Is to Allah: it is He
That will show you
The truth of all
That ye do.[811]

١٠٥ يَٰٓأَيُّهَا ٱلَّذِينَ ءَامَنُواْ عَلَيۡكُمۡ أَنفُسَكُمۡۖ
لَا يَضُرُّكُم مَّن ضَلَّ إِذَا ٱهۡتَدَيۡتُمۡۚ
إِلَى ٱللَّهِ مَرۡجِعُكُمۡ جَمِيعٗا
فَيُنَبِّئُكُم بِمَا كُنتُمۡ تَعۡمَلُونَ

106. O ye who believe!
When death approaches
Any of you, (take) witnesses
Among yourselves when making
Bequests—two just men
Of your own (brotherhood)
Or others from outside
If ye are journeying
Through the earth,

١٠٦ يَٰٓأَيُّهَا ٱلَّذِينَ ءَامَنُواْ شَهَٰدَةُ بَيۡنِكُمۡ
إِذَا حَضَرَ أَحَدَكُمُ ٱلۡمَوۡتُ حِينَ ٱلۡوَصِيَّةِ
ٱثۡنَانِ ذَوَا عَدۡلٖ مِّنكُمۡ أَوۡ ءَاخَرَانِ
مِنۡ غَيۡرِكُمۡ إِنۡ أَنتُمۡ ضَرَبۡتُمۡ فِي ٱلۡأَرۡضِ

810. *Cf.* 2:170. Where a Messenger of Truth comes to teach us the better way, it is foolish to say: "What our ancestors did is good enough for us."

811. *Cf.* 5:48. There the unity of Allah will reconcile different views. The unity of the one Judge will do perfect justice to each one's conduct, however different in form it may have appeared in this world.

And the chance of death
Befalls you (thus).
If ye doubt (their truth),
Detain them both
After prayer, and let them both
Swear by Allah:
"We wish not in this
For any worldly gain,
Even though the (beneficiary)
Be our near relation:
We shall hide not
The evidence before Allah:
If we do, then behold!
The sin be upon us!"[812]

فَأَصَـٰبَتْكُم مُّصِيبَةُ ٱلْمَوْتِ ۚ
تَحْبِسُونَهُمَا مِنۢ بَعْدِ ٱلصَّلَوٰةِ
فَيُقْسِمَانِ بِٱللَّهِ إِنِ ٱرْتَبْتُمْ
لَا نَشْتَرِى بِهِۦ ثَمَنًا
وَلَوْ كَانَ ذَا قُرْبَىٰ ۙ
وَلَا نَكْتُمُ شَهَـٰدَةَ ٱللَّهِ
إِنَّآ إِذًا لَّمِنَ ٱلْـَٔاثِمِينَ

107. But if it gets known
That these two were guilty
Of the sin (of perjury),
Let two others stand forth
In their places—nearest
In kin from among those
Who claim a lawful right:[813]
Let them swear by Allah;
"We affirm that our witness
Is truer than that
Of those two, and that we
Have not trespassed (beyond
The truth): if we did,
Behold! the wrong be
Upon us!"

(١٠٧) فَإِنْ عُثِرَ عَلَىٰٓ أَنَّهُمَا ٱسْتَحَقَّآ
إِثْمًا فَـَٔاخَرَانِ يَقُومَانِ مَقَامَهُمَا
مِنَ ٱلَّذِينَ ٱسْتَحَقَّ عَلَيْهِمُ ٱلْأَوْلَيَـٰنِ
فَيُقْسِمَانِ بِٱللَّهِ لَشَهَـٰدَتُنَآ
أَحَقُّ مِن شَهَـٰدَتِهِمَا
وَمَا ٱعْتَدَيْنَآ
إِنَّآ إِذًا لَّمِنَ ٱلظَّـٰلِمِينَ

108. That is most suitable:
That they may give the evidence
In its true nature and shape,
Or else they would fear
That other oaths would be
Taken after their oaths.
But fear Allah, and listen
(To His counsel): for Allah
Guideth not a rebellious people.

(١٠٨) ذَٰلِكَ أَدْنَىٰٓ أَن يَأْتُوا۟
بِٱلشَّهَـٰدَةِ عَلَىٰ وَجْهِهَآ أَوْ يَخَافُوٓا۟
أَن تُرَدَّ أَيْمَـٰنٌۢ بَعْدَ أَيْمَـٰنِهِمْ ۗ وَٱتَّقُوا۟ ٱللَّهَ
وَٱسْمَعُوا۟ ۗ وَٱللَّهُ لَا يَهْدِى ٱلْقَوْمَ ٱلْفَـٰسِقِينَ

812. Ordinarily this oath should be decisive, and the matter must rest here. But if it gets known that the oath was false, other evidence may be taken as in the next verse.

813. *Istaḥaqqa* = Deserved having something (good or evil) attributed to one; hence the alternative meanings: (1) committed or was guilty (of a sin); (2) had or claimed a lawful right (to property). The procedure was followed in an actual case in the Prophet's lifetime. A man from Madīnah died abroad, having made over his goods, to two friends, to be delivered to his designated heirs in Madīnah. They however, kept back a valuable silver cup. When this was found out, oaths were taken from those who knew, and justice was done.

C. 75.—Jesus did feed his disciples by miracles,
(5:109-120.) But he claimed not divinity: he was
A true servant of Allah, to Whom doth belong
The dominion of the heavens and the earth:
Glory and Power are His, and His alone.

SECTION 15.

109. One day will Allah
Gather the Messengers together,
And ask: "What was
The response ye received
(From men to your teaching)?"
They will say: "We
Have no knowledge: it is Thou
Who knowest in full
All that is hidden."[814]

١٠٩ يَوْمَ يَجْمَعُ ٱللَّهُ ٱلرُّسُلَ
فَيَقُولُ مَاذَآ أُجِبْتُمْ
قَالُوا۟ لَا عِلْمَ لَنَآ
إِنَّكَ أَنتَ عَلَّٰمُ ٱلْغُيُوبِ

110. Then will Allah say:
"O Jesus the son of Mary!
Recount My favour[815]
To thee and to thy mother.
Behold! I strengthened thee[816]
With the holy spirit,
So that thou didst speak
To the people in childhood
And in maturity.[817]
Behold! I taught thee
The Book and Wisdom,[818]
The Law and the Gospel.
And behold! thou makest[819]
Out of clay, as it were,
The figure of a bird,
By My leave,

١١٠ إِذْ قَالَ ٱللَّهُ يَٰعِيسَى ٱبْنَ مَرْيَمَ
ٱذْكُرْ نِعْمَتِى عَلَيْكَ وَعَلَىٰ وَٰلِدَتِكَ
إِذْ أَيَّدتُّكَ بِرُوحِ ٱلْقُدُسِ
تُكَلِّمُ ٱلنَّاسَ فِى ٱلْمَهْدِ وَكَهْلًا
وَإِذْ عَلَّمْتُكَ ٱلْكِتَٰبَ وَٱلْحِكْمَةَ
وَٱلتَّوْرَىٰةَ وَٱلْإِنجِيلَ وَإِذْ تَخْلُقُ
مِنَ ٱلطِّينِ كَهَيْـَٔةِ ٱلطَّيْرِ بِإِذْنِى

---

814. A scene of the Day of Reckoning is put before us in graphic words, showing the responsibility and the limitations of the Prophets of Allah, sent to preach His Message to men, with special reference to the Message of Jesus. The Messengers are sent to preach the Truth. What fantastic forms the Message takes in men's reactions to it was beyond their knowledge at the time, and beyond their responsibility. (R).

815. In a solemn scene before the Court of Judgement, Jesus is asked to recount all the mercies and favours shown to him, so that his followers should become ashamed of their ingratitude in corrupting that Message, when they could have done so much in profiting by its purity and spiritual truth. This argument continues to the end of the Sūrah.

816. *Cf.* 2:87 and 3:62, n. 401.

817. *Cf.* 3:46, and n. 388.

818. *Cf.* 3:48.

819. *Cf.* 3:49, and n. 390.

And thou breathest into it,
And it becometh a bird
By My leave,
And thou healest those
Born blind, and the lepers,
By My leave.
And behold! thou
Bringest forth the dead
By My leave.[820]
And behold! I did
Restrain the Children of Israel
From (violence to) thee[821]
When thou didst show them
The Clear Signs,
And the unbelievers among them
Said: 'This is nothing
But evident magic.'[822]

فَتَنفُخُ فِيهَا فَتَكُونُ طَيۡرَۢا
بِإِذۡنِيۖ وَتُبۡرِئُ ٱلۡأَكۡمَهَ
وَٱلۡأَبۡرَصَ بِإِذۡنِيۖ
وَإِذۡ تُخۡرِجُ ٱلۡمَوۡتَىٰ بِإِذۡنِيۖ
وَإِذۡ كَفَفۡتُ بَنِيٓ إِسۡرَٰٓءِيلَ
عَنكَ إِذۡ جِئۡتَهُم بِٱلۡبَيِّنَٰتِ
فَقَالَ ٱلَّذِينَ كَفَرُواْ مِنۡهُمۡ
إِنۡ هَٰذَآ إِلَّا سِحۡرٞ مُّبِينٞ

111. "And behold! I inspired
The Disciples to have faith
In Me and Mine Messenger;
They said, 'We have faith,
And do thou[823] bear witness
That we bow to Allah
As Muslims'."[824]

(١١١) وَإِذۡ أَوۡحَيۡتُ إِلَى ٱلۡحَوَارِيِّـۧنَ
أَنۡ ءَامِنُواْ بِي وَبِرَسُولِي قَالُوٓاْ
ءَامَنَّا وَٱشۡهَدۡ بِأَنَّنَا مُسۡلِمُونَ

112. Behold! the Disciples said:
"O Jesus the son of Mary!
Can thy Lord send down to us
A Table set (with viands)
From heaven?" Said Jesus:

(١١٢) إِذۡ قَالَ ٱلۡحَوَارِيُّونَ يَٰعِيسَى ٱبۡنَ مَرۡيَمَ
هَلۡ يَسۡتَطِيعُ رَبُّكَ أَن يُنَزِّلَ عَلَيۡنَا
مَآئِدَةٗ مِّنَ ٱلسَّمَآءِۖ قَالَ

---

820. Note how the words "by My leave" are repeated with each miracle to emphasise the fact that they arose, not out of the power or will of Jesus, but by the leave and will and power of Allah, who is supreme over Jesus as He is over all other mortals.

821. The Jews were seeking to take the life of Jesus long before their final attempt to crucify him; see Luke iv. 28-29. Their attempt to crucify him was also foiled, according to the teaching we have received: Q. 4:157.

822. According to Luke (xi. 15), when Christ performed the miracle of casting out devils, the Jews said he did it through the chief of the devils, *i.e.*, they accused him of black magic. No such miracle of casting out devils is mentioned in the Qur'ān. But Moses, Jesus, and Muḥammad were all accused of magic and sorcery, by those who could find no other explanation of Allah's power. (R).

823. "Thou" refers to Jesus, who is being addressed by his Disciples. *Cf.* 3:52.

824. Before or after Muḥammad's life on this earth, all who bowed to Allah's Will were Muslims, and their religion is Islam, *Cf.* 3:52 and n. 392.

"Fear Allah, if ye have faith."[825]

اتَّقُواْ اللَّهَ إِن كُنتُم مُّؤْمِنِينَ

113. They said: "We only wish
To eat thereof and satisfy
Our hearts, and to know
That thou hast indeed
Told us the truth; and
That we ourselves may be
Witnesses to the miracle."

قَالُواْ نُرِيدُ أَن نَّأْكُلَ مِنْهَا وَتَطْمَئِنَّ قُلُوبُنَا وَنَعْلَمَ أَن قَدْ صَدَقْتَنَا وَنَكُونَ عَلَيْهَا مِنَ الشَّاهِدِينَ ﴿١١٣﴾

114. Said Jesus the son of Mary:
"O Allah our Lord!
Send us from heaven
A Table set (with viands),[826]
That there may be for us—
For the first and the last of us—
A solemn festival
And a Sign from Thee;
And provide for our sustenance,[827]
For Thou art the best
Sustainer (of our needs)."

قَالَ عِيسَى ابْنُ مَرْيَمَ اللَّهُمَّ رَبَّنَا أَنزِلْ عَلَيْنَا مَائِدَةً مِّنَ السَّمَاءِ تَكُونُ لَنَا عِيدًا لِّأَوَّلِنَا وَآخِرِنَا وَآيَةً مِّنكَ وَارْزُقْنَا وَأَنتَ خَيْرُ الرَّازِقِينَ ﴿١١٤﴾

115. Allah said: "I will
Send it down unto you;
But if any of you
After that resisteth faith,
I will punish him
With a penalty such
As I have not inflicted
On anyone among
All the peoples."[828]

قَالَ اللَّهُ إِنِّي مُنَزِّلُهَا عَلَيْكُمْ فَمَن يَكْفُرْ بَعْدُ مِنكُمْ فَإِنِّي أُعَذِّبُهُ عَذَابًا لَّا أُعَذِّبُهُ أَحَدًا مِّنَ الْعَالَمِينَ ﴿١١٥﴾

---

825. The request of the Disciples savours a little of (1) want of faith, (2) too much attention to physical food, and (3) a childish desire for miracles or Signs. All these three can be proved from the Canonical Gospels, (1) Simon Peter, quite early in the story, asked Jesus to depart from him, as he (Simon) was a sinful man (Luke v. 8). The same Peter afterwards denied his "Master" three times shamelessly when the Master was in the power of his enemies. And one of the Disciples (Judas) actually betrayed Jesus. (2) Even in the Canonical Gospels, so many of the miracles are concerned with food and drink, *e.g.*, the turning of the water into wine (John, ii. 1-11); the conversion of five loaves and two small fishes into food for 5,000 men (John vi. 5-13), this being the *only* miracle recorded in all the four Gospels; the miraculous number of fishes caught for food (Luke v. 4-11); the cursing of the fig tree because it had no fruit (Matt. xxi. 18-19); the allegory of eating Christ's flesh and drinking his blood (John vi. 53-57). (3) Because the Samaritans would not receive Jesus into their village, the Disciples James and John wanted a fire to come down from heaven and consume them (Luke ix. 54).

826. The words of the Prayer seem to suggest the Last Supper, *Cf.* also the vision of Peter in "The Acts of the Apostles," x. 9-16.

827. As in Islam, so in Christ's Prayer, sustenance should be taken for both physical and spiritual strength, especially the latter. "Give us this day our daily bread" seems the rendering of a literalist whose attention was fixed too much on bread.

828. It is a wicked generation that asks for Signs and Miracles. Usually they are not vouchsafed. But where they are, the responsibility of those who ask for them is increased. If, after that, they reject faith, invent lies, and go after false gods or false ideals, their penalty will be worse than that of other people. How this works out practically among those who call themselves Christians is exemplified in such books as the late Mr. W.T. Stead's "If Christ Came to Chicago?" (R).

SECTION 16.

116. And behold! Allah will say:
"O Jesus the son of Mary!
Didst thou say unto men,
'Worship me and my mother
As gods in derogation of Allah'?"
He will say: "Glory to Thee!
Never could I say
What I had no right
(To say). Had I said
Such a thing, Thou wouldst
Indeed have known it.
Thou knowest what is
In my heart, though I
Know not what is
In Thine. For Thou
Knowest in full
All that is hidden.[829]

(١١٦) وَإِذْ قَالَ ٱللَّهُ يَٰعِيسَى ٱبْنَ مَرْيَمَ
ءَأَنتَ قُلْتَ لِلنَّاسِ ٱتَّخِذُونِى
وَأُمِّىَ إِلَٰهَيْنِ مِن دُونِ ٱللَّهِ
قَالَ سُبْحَٰنَكَ مَا يَكُونُ لِىٓ أَنْ
أَقُولَ مَا لَيْسَ لِى بِحَقٍّ إِن كُنتُ قُلْتُهُۥ
فَقَدْ عَلِمْتَهُۥ تَعْلَمُ مَا فِى
نَفْسِى وَلَآ أَعْلَمُ مَا فِى نَفْسِكَ
إِنَّكَ أَنتَ عَلَّٰمُ ٱلْغُيُوبِ

117. "Never said I to them
Aught except what Thou
Didst command me
To say, to wit, 'Worship
Allah, my Lord and your Lord';[830]
And I was a witness
Over them whilst I dwelt
Amongst them; when thou
Didst take me up
Thou wast the Watcher
Over them, and Thou
Art a witness to all things.[831]

(١١٧) مَا قُلْتُ لَهُمْ
إِلَّا مَآ أَمَرْتَنِى بِهِۦٓ أَنِ ٱعْبُدُوا۟
ٱللَّهَ رَبِّى وَرَبَّكُمْ وَكُنتُ عَلَيْهِمْ شَهِيدًا
مَّا دُمْتُ فِيهِمْ فَلَمَّا تَوَفَّيْتَنِى كُنتَ أَنتَ
ٱلرَّقِيبَ عَلَيْهِمْ وَأَنتَ عَلَىٰ كُلِّ شَىْءٍ شَهِيدٌ

118. "If Thou dost punish them,
They are Thy servants:
If Thou dost forgive them,
Thou art the Exalted in power,
The Wise."[832]

(١١٨) إِن تُعَذِّبْهُمْ فَإِنَّهُمْ عِبَادُكَ
وَإِن تَغْفِرْ لَهُمْ فَإِنَّكَ أَنتَ ٱلْعَزِيزُ ٱلْحَكِيمُ

829. Jesus disclaims here any knowledge of the sort of things that are attributed to him by those who take his name. The worship of Mary, though repudiated by the Protestants, was widely spread in the earlier Churches, both in the East and the West.

830. *Cf.* 5:72 and n. 782.

831. Jesus here acknowledges that he was mortal, and that his knowledge was limited like that of a mortal.

832. The Master can justly punish His servants for disobedience: no one can say to Him nay, for He is high above all. But if He chooses to forgive. He in His wisdom sees things that we mortals cannot see. This is the limit of intercession that men of God can make on behalf of sinners.

119. Allah will say: "This is
A day on which
The truthful will profit
From their truth: theirs
Are Gardens, with rivers
Flowing beneath—their eternal
Home: Allah well-pleased
With them, and they with Allah:
That is the great Salvation.[833]
(The fulfilment of all desires).

١١٩ قَالَ ٱللَّهُ هَٰذَا يَوْمُ
يَنفَعُ ٱلصَّٰدِقِينَ صِدْقُهُمْ لَهُمْ جَنَّٰتٌ
تَجْرِى مِن تَحْتِهَا ٱلْأَنْهَٰرُ خَٰلِدِينَ فِيهَآ أَبَدًا
رَّضِىَ ٱللَّهُ عَنْهُمْ وَرَضُوا۟ عَنْهُ ذَٰلِكَ ٱلْفَوْزُ ٱلْعَظِيمُ

120. To Allah doth belong the dominion
Of the heavens and the earth,
And all that is therein,
And it is He who hath power
Over all things.

١٢٠ لِلَّهِ مُلْكُ
ٱلسَّمَٰوَٰتِ وَٱلْأَرْضِ وَمَا فِيهِنَّ
وَهُوَ عَلَىٰ كُلِّ شَىْءٍ قَدِيرٌۢ

833. *Fauz* = Felicity, happiness, achievement, salvation, the attainment or fulfilment of desires. What a beautiful definition of salvation or the end of life!—that we should win Allah's good pleasure and that we should reach the stage at which His good pleasure is all-in-all to us.

APPENDIX II.

On the *Tawrāh* (see 5:47, n. 753)

The *Tawrāh* is frequently referred to in the Qur'ān. It is well to have clear ideas as to what it exactly means. Vaguely we may say that it was the Jewish Scripture. It is mentioned with honour as having been, in its purity, a true revelation from Allah.

To translate it by the words "The Old Testament" is obviously wrong. The "Old Testament" is a Christian term, applied to a body of old Jewish records. The Protestants and the Roman Catholics are not agreed precisely as to the number of records to be included in the canon of the "Old Testament." They use the term in contradistinction to the "New Testament," whose composition we shall discuss in Appendix III.

Nor is it correct to translate *Tawrāh* as the "Pentateuch," a Greek term meaning the "Five Books." These are the first five books of the Old Testament, known as Genesis, Exodus, Leviticus, Numbers, and Deuteronomy. They contain a semi-historical and legendary narrative of the history of the world from the Creation to the time of the arrival of the Jews in the Promised Land. There are in them some beautiful idylls but there are also stories of incest, fraud, cruelty, and treachery, not always disapproved. A great part of the Mosaic Law is embodied in this narrative. The books are traditionally ascribed to Moses, but it is certain that they were not written by Moses or in an age either contemporary with Moses or within an appreciable distance of time from Moses. They were in their present form probably compiled some time after the return of the Jews from the Babylonian Captivity. The decree of Cyrus permitting such return was in 536 B.C. Some books now included in the Old Testament, such as Haggai, Zechariah, and Malachi were admittedly written after the return from the captivity. Malachi being as late as 420-397 B.C. The compilers of the Pentateuch of course used some ancient material: some of the material is actually named. Egyptian and Chaldaean terms are relics of local colour and contemporary documents.

But there are some ludicrous slips, which show that the compilers did not always understand their material. Modern criticism distinguishes two distinct sources among the documents of different dates used by the editors. For the sake of brevity and convenience they may be called (a) Jehovistic, and (b) Elohistic. Then there are later miscellaneous interpolations. They sometimes overlap and sometimes contradict each other.

Logically speaking, the Book of Joshua, which describes the entry into the Promised Land, should be bracketed with the Pentateuch, and many writers speak of the six books together as the Hexateuch (Greek term for Six Books).

The Apocrypha contain certain Books which are not admitted as Canonical in the English Bible. But the early Christians received them as part of the Jewish Scriptures, and the Council of Trent (A.C. 1545-1563) seems to have recognised the greater part of them as Canonical. The statement in 2 Esdras (about the first century A.C.) that the law was burnt and Ezra (say, about 458-457 B.C.) was inspired to rewrite it, is probably true as to the historical fact that the law was lost, and that what we have now is no earlier than the time of Ezra, and some of it a good deal later.

So far we have spoken of the Christian view of the Old Testament. What is the Jewish view? The Jews divide their Scripture into three parts: (1) the Law (*Torah*), (2) the Prophets (*Nebiim*), and (3) the Writings (*Kethubim*). The corresponding Arabic words would be: (1) *Tawrāh*, (2) *Nabˉiyīn*, and (3) *Kutub*. This division was probably current in the time of Jesus. In Luke xxiv. 44 Jesus refers to the Law, the Prophets and the Psalms. In other places (*e.g.*, Matt. vii. 12) Jesus refers to the Law and the Prophets as summing up the whole Scripture. In the Old Testament Book, II. Chronicles xxxiv. 30, the reference to the Book of the Covenant must be to the *Torah* or the original Law. This is interesting, as the Qur'ān frequently refers to the Covenant with reference to the Jews. The modern Christian terms "Old Testament" and "New Testament" are substitutes for the older terms "Old Covenant" and "New Covenant." The Samaritans, who claim to be the real Children of Israel and disavow the Jews as schismatics from their Law of Moses, only recognise the Pentateuch, of which they have their own version slightly different from that in the Old Testament.

The view of the school of Higher Criticism is radically destructive. According to Renan it is doubtful whether Moses was not a myth. Two versions of Sacred History existed, different in language, style, and spirit, and they were combined together into a narrative in the reign of Hezekiah (B.C. 727-697). This forms the greater part of the Pentateuch as it exists today, excluding the greater part of Deuteronomy and Leviticus. In the reign of Josiah about 622 B.C., certain priests and scribes (with Jeremiah the prophet) promulgated a new code, pretending that they had found it in the Temple (II. Kings, xxii. 8). This Law (*Torah* = Tawrāh) was the basis of Judaism, the new religion then founded in Palestine. This was further completed by the sacerdotal and Levitical *Torah*, compiled under the inspiration of Ezekiel, say, about 575 B.C., and contained mainly in the Book of Leviticus, with scattered fragments in Exodus, Numbers, and Joshua. We are entitled to accept the general results of a scientific examination of documents, probabilities, and dates, even though we reject the premise which we believe to be false, *viz.*, that Allah does not send inspired Books through inspired Prophets. We believe that Moses existed; that he was an inspired man of God; that he gave a message which was afterwards distorted or lost; that attempts were made by Israel at various times to reconstruct that message; and that the *Tawrāh* as we have it is (in view of the statement in 2 Esdras) no earlier than the middle of the fifth century B.C.

The primitive *Torah* must have been in old Hebrew, but there is no Hebrew manuscript of the Old Testament which can be dated with certainty earlier than 916 A.C. Hebrew ceased to be a spoken language with the Jews during or after the Captivity, and by the time we come to the period of Jesus, most cultivated Hebrews used the Greek language, and others used Aramaic (including Syriac and Chaldee), Latin, or local dialects. There were also Arabic versions. For historical purposes the most important versions were the Greek version, known as the Septuagint, and the Latin version, known as the Vulgate. The Septuagint was supposed to have been prepared by 70 or 72 Jews (Latin, septuaginta = seventy) working independently and at different times, the earliest portion dating from about 284 B.C. This version was used by the Jews of Alexandria and the Hellenized Jews who were spread over all parts of the Roman Empire. The Vulgate was a Latin translation made by the celebrated Father of the Christian Church, St. Jerome, from Hebrew, early in the fifth century A.C., superseding the older Latin versions. Neither the Septuagint nor the Vulgate have an absolutely fixed or certain text. The present standard text of the Vulgate as accepted by the Roman Catholic Church was issued by Pope Clement VIII (A.C. 1592-1605).

It will be seen therefore that there is no standard text of the Old Testament in its Hebrew form. The versions differ from each other frequently in minor particulars and sometimes in important particulars. The Pentateuch itself is only a small portion of the Old Testament. It is in narrative form, and includes the laws and regulations associated with the name of Moses, but probably compiled and edited from older sources by Ezra (or Esdras Arabic, 'Uzair) in the 5th century B.C. As Renan remarks in the preface to his *History of the People of Israel*, the "definite constitution of Judaism" may be dated only from the time of Ezra. The very early Christians were divided into two parties. One was a Judaizing party, which wished to remain in adherence to the Jewish laws and customs while recognising the mission of Jesus. The other, led by Paul, broke away from Jewish customs and traditions. Ultimately Pauline Christianity won. But both parties recognised the Old Testament in its present form (in one or another of its varying versions) as Scripture. It was the merit of Islam that it pointed out that as scripture it was of no value, although it recognised Moses as an inspired messenger and his original Law as having validity in his period until it was superseded. In its criticism of the Jewish position it said in effect: "You have lost your original Law; even what you have now as its substitute, you do not honestly follow; is it not better, now that an inspired Teacher is living among you, that you should follow him rather than quibble over uncertain texts?"

But the Jews in the Prophet's time (and since) went a great deal by the Talmud, or a body of oral exposition, reduced to writing in different Schools of doctors and learned men. "Talmud" in Hebrew is connected with the Arabic root in *Tilmīdh*, "disciple" or "student." The Talmudists took the divergent texts of the Old Testament and in interpreting them by a mass of traditional commentary and legendary lore, evolved a standard body of teaching. The Talmudists are of special interest to us, as, in the sixth century A.C., just before the preaching of Islam, they evolved the Massorah, which may be regarded as the body of authoritative Jewish Ḥadīth, to which references are to be found in passages addressed to the Jews in the Qur'ān.

The first part of the Talmud is called the *Mishna*—a collection of traditions and decisions prepared by the Rabbi Judah about 150 A.C. He summed up the results of a great mass of previous rabbinical writings. The *Mishna* is the "Second Law". *Cf.* the Arabic *Thānī* = second. "It bound heavy burdens, grievous to be borne, and laid them on men's shoulders"; Matt. xxiii. 4.

There were also many Targums or paraphrases of the Law among the Jews. "Targum" is connected in root with the Arabic *Tarjama*, "he translated." There were many Targums, mostly in Aramaic, and they constituted the teaching of the Law to the masses of the Jewish people.

The correct translation of the *Tawrāh* is therefore "The Law." In its original form it was promulgated by Moses, and is recognised in Islam as having been an inspired Book. But it was lost before Islam was preached. What passed as "The Law" with the Jews in the Prophet's time was the mass of traditional writing which I have tried to review in this Appendix.

Authorities: *Encyclopaedia Britannica*, "Bible"; *Helps to the Study of the Bible*, Oxford University Press; A.F. Kirkpatrick, *Divine Library of the Old Testament*; C.E. Hammond, *Outline of Textual Criticism*; E. Renan, *History of Israel*; G.F. Moore, *Literature of the Old Testament*, and the bibliography therein (Home University Library); Sir Frederic Kenyon, *The Story of the Bible*, 1936.

APPENDIX III

On the *Injīl* (see 5:49, n. 757)

Just as the *Tawrāh* is not the Old Testament, or the Pentateuch, as now received by the Jews and Christians, so the *Injīl* mentioned in the Qur'ān is certainly not the New Testament, and it is not the four Gospels, as now received by the Christian Church, but an original Gospel which was promulgated by Jesus as the *Tawrāh* was promulgated by Moses and the Qur'ān by Muḥammad Muṣṭafā.

The New Testament as now received consists of (a) four Gospels with varying contents (Matthew, Mark, Luke, and John); and other miscellaneous matter; *viz.*, (b) the Acts of the Apostles (probably written by Luke and purporting to describe the progress of the Christian Church under St. Peter and St. Paul from the supposed Crucifixion of Jesus to about 61 A.C.); (c) twenty-one Letters or Epistles (the majority written by St. Paul to various churches or individuals, but a few written by other Disciples, and of a general nature); and (d) the Book of Revelation or Apocalypse (ascribed to St. John, and containing mystic visions and prophecies, of which it is difficult to understand the meaning).

As Prof. F.C. Burkitt remarks (*Canon of the New Testament*), it is an odd miscellany. "The four biographies of Jesus Christ. . .are not all independent of each other, and neither of them was intended by its writer to form one of a quartette. But they are all put side by side, unharmonised, one of them being actually imperfect at the end, and one being only the first volume of a larger work." All this body of unmethodical literature was casual in its nature. No wonder, because the early Christians expected the end of the world very soon. The four canonical Gospels were only four out of many, and some others besides the four have survived. Each writer just wrote down some odd sayings of the Master that he recollected. Among the miracles described there is only one which is described in all the four Gospels, and others were described and believed in other Gospels, which are not mentioned in any of the four canonical Gospels. Some of the Epistles contain expositions of doctrine, but this has been interpreted differently by different Churches. There must have been hundreds of such Epistles, and not all the Epistles now received as canonical were always so received or intended to be so received. The Apocalypse also was not the only one in the field. There were others. They were prophecies of "things which must shortly come to pass"; they could not have been meant for long preservation, "for the time is at hand."

When were these four Gospels written? By the end of the second century A.C. they were in existence, but it does not follow that they had been selected by that date to form a canon. They were merely pious productions comparable to Dean Farrar's *Life of Christ*. There were other Gospels besides. And further, the writers of two of them, Mark and Luke, were not among the Twelve Disciples "called" by Jesus. About the Gospel of St. John there is much controversy as to authorship, date, and even as to whether it was all written by one person. Clement of Rome (about 97 A.C.) and Polycarp (about 112 A.C.) quote sayings of Jesus in a form different from those found in the present canonical Gospels. Polycarp (Epistle, vii) inveighs much against men "who pervert the sayings of the Lord to their own lusts," and he wants to turn "to the Word handed down to us from the beginning," thus referring to a Book (or a Tradition) much earlier than the four orthodox Gospels. An Epistle of St. Barnabas and an Apocalypse of St. Peter were recognized by Presbyter Clement of Alexandria (flourished about 180 A.C.). The Apocalypse of St. John, which is a part of the present canon in the West, forms no part of the Peshitta (Syriac) version of the Eastern Christians, which was produced about 411-433 A.C. and which was used by the Nestorian Christians. It is probable that the Peshitta was the version (or an Arabic form of it) used by the Christians in Arabia in the time of the Prophet. The final form of the New Testament canon for the West was fixed in the fourth century A.C. (say, about 367 A.C.) by Athanasius and the Nicene creed. The beautiful Codex Sinaiticus which was acquired for the British Museum in 1934, and is one of the earliest complete manuscripts of the Bible, may be dated about the fourth century. It is written in the Greek language. Fragments of unknown Gospels have also been discovered, which do not agree with the received canonical Gospels.

The *Injīl* (Greek, Evangel = Gospel) spoken of by the Qur'ān is not the New Testament. It is not the four Gospels now received as canonical. It is the single Gospel which, Islam teaches, was revealed to Jesus, and which he taught. Fragments of it survive in the received canonical Gospels and in some others, of which traces survive (*e.g.*, the Gospel of Childhood or the Nativity, the Gospel of St. Barnabas, etc.). Muslims are therefore right in respecting the present Bible (New Testament and Old Testament), though they reject the peculiar doctrines taught by orthodox Christianity or Judaism. They claim to be in the true tradition of Abraham, and therefore all that is of value in the older revelations, it is claimed, is incorporated in the teaching of the Last of the Prophets.

In 5:85 we are told that nearest in love to the Believers among the People of the Book are the Christians. I do not agree that this does not apply to modern Christians "because they are practically atheists or freethinkers." I think that Christian thought (like the world's thought) has learnt a great deal from the protest of Islam against priest domination, class domination, and sectarianism, and its insistence on making this life pure and beautiful while we are in it. We must stretch a friendly hand to all who are sincere and in sympathy with our ideals.

Authorities: The first two mentioned for Appendix II, and in addition: Prof. F.C. Burkitt, on the Canon of the New Testament, in *Religion*, June 1934, the Journal of Transactions of the Society for Promoting the Study of Religions; R.W. Mackay, *Rise and Progress of Christianity*; G.R.S. Mead. *The Gospel and the Gospels*; B.W. Bacon, *Making of the New Testament*, with its Bibliography; Sir Frederic Kenyon, *The Story of the Bible*; R. Hone, *The Apocryphal New Testament*, London 1820; H.I. Bell and T.C. Skeat, *Fragments of an Unknown Gospel and other Christian Papyri*, published by the British Museum, 1935. See also chapter 15 of Gibbon's *Decline and Fall of the Roman Empire*, where the genesis of the early churches and sects in the Roman Empires is briefly reviewed.

INTRODUCTION TO SŪRAH 6—*AL AN'ĀM*

This is a Sūrah of the late Makkan period. The greater part of it was revealed entire. Its place in the traditional order of arrangement is justified by logical considerations. We have already had the spiritual history of mankind, a discussion of the earlier revelations and how they were lost or corrupted, the regulations for the outer life of the new Community, and the points in which the Jews and Christians failed to maintain the central doctrine of Islām—the unity of Allah. The next step now taken is to expound this doctrine in relation to Pagan Arabia.

Summary—The nature of Allah and the method by which He reveals Himself are first expounded, and the weakness of Paganism is exposed (6:1-30, and C. 76).

The emptiness of this world's life is contrasted with the evidence of Allah's wonderful handiwork in all Creation. It is He who holds the keys of the Unseen and the secrets of all that we see (6:31-60, and C. 77).

Allah's working in His world and His constant care and guidance should give a clue to His unity as it did to Abraham when he argued with those who worshipped false gods (6:61-82, and C. 78).

The succession of prophets after Abraham kept Allah's truth alive, and led up to the Qur'ān. How can man fail to understand the majesty and goodness of Allah, when he contemplates Allah's creation and His Messages to mankind? (6:83-110, and C. 79). (R).

The obstinate and the rebellious are deceived; they should be avoided. Though they turn for assistance to each other, they will receive due punishment (6:111-129, and C. 80).

Allah's decrees will come to pass, in spite of all the crimes and superstitions of the ungodly (6:130-150, and C. 81).

The better course is to follow the straight Way, the Way of Allah, as directed in the Qur'ān, with unity and the full dedication of our lives (6:151-165, and C. 82). (R).

C. 76.—Allah did separate Light from Darkness;
(6:1-30.) He reigns not only in heaven but also
On earth; Mercy is His Law;
To Him shall we all return
At the end of all things. How can we
Then depart from truth and forge lies
Against Him? It is folly to say that there is
Nothing beyond this our present life.

Al An'ām (The Cattle)

In the name of Allah, Most Gracious, Most Merciful.

بِسْمِ ٱللَّهِ ٱلرَّحْمَٰنِ ٱلرَّحِيمِ

1. Praise be to Allah,
Who created the heavens
And the earth,
And made the Darkness
And the Light.
Yet those who reject Faith
Hold (others) as equal[834]
With their Guardian-Lord.[835]

١ ٱلْحَمْدُ لِلَّهِ ٱلَّذِى
خَلَقَ ٱلسَّمَٰوَٰتِ وَٱلْأَرْضَ
وَجَعَلَ ٱلظُّلُمَٰتِ وَٱلنُّورَ
ثُمَّ ٱلَّذِينَ كَفَرُوا۟ بِرَبِّهِمْ يَعْدِلُونَ

2. He it is Who created[836]
You from clay, and then
Decreed a stated term[837]
(For you). And there is
In His Presence another
Determined term; yet
Ye doubt within yourselves!

٢ هُوَ ٱلَّذِى خَلَقَكُم مِّن طِينٍ
ثُمَّ قَضَىٰٓ أَجَلًا وَأَجَلٌ مُّسَمًّى عِندَهُۥ
ثُمَّ أَنتُمْ تَمْتَرُونَ

3. And He is Allah
In the heavens
And on earth.
He knoweth what ye
Hide, and what ye reveal,
And He knoweth
The (recompense) which
Ye earn (by your deeds).[838]

٣ وَهُوَ ٱللَّهُ فِى
ٱلسَّمَٰوَٰتِ وَفِى ٱلْأَرْضِ
يَعْلَمُ سِرَّكُمْ وَجَهْرَكُمْ
وَيَعْلَمُ مَا تَكْسِبُونَ

834. *'Adala* has various meanings: (1) to hold something as equal to something else, as here; to balance nicely; (2) to deal justly, as between one party and another, 42:15; (3) to give compensation or reparation, or something as equivalent to something else, 11:70; (4) to turn the balance the right way, to give a right disposition, to give a just bias or proportion, 82:7; (5) to turn the balance the wrong way, to swerve, to show bias, 4:135.

835. The argument is threefold: (1) Allah created everything you see and know: how can you then set up any of His own creatures as equal to Him? (2) He is your own Guardian-Lord; He cherishes and loves you, how can you be so ungrateful as to run after something else? (3) Darkness and Light are to help you to distinguish between the true from the false: how then can you confound the true God with your false ideas and superstitions? There may also be a repudiation of the Duality of old Persian theology; Light and Darkness are not conflicting Powers; they are both creatures of Allah.

836. After the general argument, the argument comes to man personally. Can such a miserable creature, created from clay, put himself in opposition to his Creator? And can man forget or doubt that he is here only for a short term of probation? And then, after a period, comes the Day of Account before Allah.

837. This life is a period of probation. The other term leads up to Judgement.

838. It is folly to suppose that Allah only reigns in the heavens. He also reigns on earth. He knows all our secret thoughts and motives, and the real worth of all that is behind what we care to show. It is by our deeds that He judges us; for our deeds, whether good or evil, we shall get due recompense in due time.

4. But never did a single
One of the Signs
Of their Lord reach them,
But they turned
Away therefrom.

٤ وَمَا تَأْتِيهِم مِّنْ ءَايَةٍ مِّنْ
ءَايَٰتِ رَبِّهِمْ إِلَّا كَانُوا۟ عَنْهَا مُعْرِضِينَ

5. And now they reject
The truth when it reaches
Them; but soon shall they
Learn the reality of what
They used to mock at.

٥ فَقَدْ كَذَّبُوا۟ بِٱلْحَقِّ لَمَّا جَآءَهُمْ
فَسَوْفَ يَأْتِيهِمْ أَنۢبَٰٓؤُا۟ مَا كَانُوا۟ بِهِۦ يَسْتَهْزِءُونَ

6. See they not how many
Of those before them
We did destroy?—[839]
Generations We had established
On the earth, in strength
Such as We have not given
To you—for whom
We poured out rain
From the skies in abundance,
And gave (fertile) streams
Flowing beneath their (feet):
Yet for their sins
We destroyed them,
And raised in their wake
Fresh generations
(To succeed them).

٦ أَلَمْ يَرَوْا۟ كَمْ أَهْلَكْنَا مِن قَبْلِهِم
مِّن قَرْنٍ مَّكَّنَّٰهُمْ فِى ٱلْأَرْضِ
مَا لَمْ نُمَكِّن لَّكُمْ
وَأَرْسَلْنَا ٱلسَّمَآءَ عَلَيْهِم مِّدْرَارًا
وَجَعَلْنَا ٱلْأَنْهَٰرَ تَجْرِى مِن تَحْتِهِمْ
فَأَهْلَكْنَٰهُم بِذُنُوبِهِمْ
وَأَنشَأْنَا مِنۢ بَعْدِهِمْ قَرْنًا ءَاخَرِينَ

7. If We had sent
Unto thee a written
(Message) on parchment,[839-A]
So that they could
Touch it with their hands,
The Unbelievers would
Have been sure to say:

٧ وَلَوْ نَزَّلْنَا عَلَيْكَ كِتَٰبًا
فِى قِرْطَاسٍ فَلَمَسُوهُ بِأَيْدِيهِمْ
لَقَالَ ٱلَّذِينَ كَفَرُوٓا۟

839. Now comes the argument from history, looking backwards and forwards. If we are so short-sighted or arrogant as to suppose that we are firmly established on the earth, secure in our privileges, we are reminded of much greater nations in the past, who failed in their duty and were wiped out. In their fate we must read our own fate, if we fail likewise! But those without faith, instead of facing facts squarely "turn away therefrom."

839-A. *Qirṭās*, in the Prophet's life, could only mean "parchment," which was commonly used as writing material in Western Asia from the 2nd century B.C. The word was derived from the Greek, *Charles* (*Cf.* Latin, *"Charta"*). Paper, as we know it, made from rags, was first used by the Arabs after the conquest of Smarqand in 751 A.C. The Chinese had used it by the 2nd century B.C. The Arabs introduced it into Europe; it was used in Greece in the 11th or 12th century, and in Spain through Sicily in the 12th century. The Papyrus, made from an Egyptian reed, was used in Egypt as early as 2500 B.C. It gave place to paper in Egypt in the 10th century.

"This is nothing but
Obvious magic!"[840]

إِنْ هَٰذَآ إِلَّا سِحْرٌ مُّبِينٌ

8. They say: "Why is not
An angel sent down to him?"
If We did send down
An angel, the matter
Would be settled at once,
And no respite
Would be granted them.[841]

٨ وَقَالُوا۟ لَوْلَآ أُنزِلَ عَلَيْهِ مَلَكٌ
وَلَوْ أَنزَلْنَا مَلَكًا لَّقُضِىَ ٱلْأَمْرُ
ثُمَّ لَا يُنظَرُونَ

9. If We had made it
An angel, We should
Have sent him as a man,
And We should certainly
Have caused them confusion
In a matter which they have
Already covered with confusion.[842]

٩ وَلَوْ جَعَلْنَٰهُ مَلَكًا
لَّجَعَلْنَٰهُ رَجُلًا وَلَلَبَسْنَا
عَلَيْهِم مَّا يَلْبِسُونَ

10. Mocked were (many)
Messengers before thee;
But their scoffers
Were hemmed in
By the thing that they mocked.[843]

١٠ وَلَقَدِ ٱسْتُهْزِئَ بِرُسُلٍ مِّن قَبْلِكَ
فَحَاقَ بِٱلَّذِينَ سَخِرُوا۟ مِنْهُم
مَّا كَانُوا۟ بِهِۦ يَسْتَهْزِءُونَ

SECTION 2.

11. Say: "Travel through the earth
And see what was the end
Of those who rejected Truth."

١١ قُلْ سِيرُوا۟ فِى ٱلْأَرْضِ ثُمَّ ٱنظُرُوا۟
كَيْفَ كَانَ عَٰقِبَةُ ٱلْمُكَذِّبِينَ

12. Say: "To whom belongeth
All that is in the heavens

١٢ قُل لِّمَن مَّا فِى ٱلسَّمَٰوَٰتِ

---

840. The materialists want to see actual physical material things before them, but if such a thing came from an unusual source or expressed things they cannot understand, they give it some name like magic, or superstition, or whatever name is in fashion, and they are not helped at all in attaining faith, because their "hearts are diseased" (2:10).

841. *Cf.* 2:210. An angel is a heavenly being, a manifestation of Allah's glory, invisible to men who live gross material lives. Such men are given plenty of respite in which to turn in repentance to Allah and make themselves worthy of His light. But if their prayer to see an angel were granted, it would do them no good, for they would be destroyed as darkness is destroyed by light.

842. Supposing an angel should appear to their grosser senses, he could only do it in human form. In that case their present confused notions about spiritual life would be still more confounded. They would say: "We wanted to see an angel, and we have only seen a man!"

843. "The scoffers were mocked by the thing that they mocked" would express epigrammatically part of the sense, but not the whole. "Hemmed in" implies that the logic of events turned the tables, and as a man might be besieged and surrounded by an enemy in war, and would be forced to surrender, so these mockers will find that events would justify Truth, not them. The mockers of Jesus—where were they when Titus destroyed Jerusalem? The mockers who drove out Muḥammad from Makkah—what was their plight when Muḥammad came back in triumph and they sued for mercy—*and he gave it to them*! According to the Latin proverb, Great is Truth, and must prevail.

And on earth?" Say:
"To Allah. He hath inscribed
For Himself (the rule of) Mercy.[844]
That He will gather you
Together for the Day of Judgment,
There is no doubt whatever.
It is they who have lost
Their own souls, that will
Not believe.

وَالْأَرْضِ ۖ قُل لِّلَّهِ ۚ
كَتَبَ عَلَىٰ نَفْسِهِ الرَّحْمَةَ ۚ
لَيَجْمَعَنَّكُمْ إِلَىٰ يَوْمِ الْقِيَامَةِ لَا رَيْبَ فِيهِ ۚ
الَّذِينَ خَسِرُوا أَنفُسَهُمْ فَهُمْ لَا يُؤْمِنُونَ

13. To him belongeth all
That dwelleth (or lurketh)[845]
In the Night and the Day.
For He is the One
Who heareth and knoweth
All things."[846]

١٣ وَلَهُ مَا سَكَنَ
فِي اللَّيْلِ وَالنَّهَارِ ۚ
وَهُوَ السَّمِيعُ الْعَلِيمُ

14. Say: "Shall I take
For my protector
Any other than Allah,
The Maker of the heavens
And the earth?
And He it is that
Feedeth but is not fed."[847]
Say: "Nay! but I am
Commanded to be the first
Of those who bow
To Allah (in Islam),
And be not thou
Of the company of those
Who join gods with Allah."

١٤ قُلْ أَغَيْرَ اللَّهِ أَتَّخِذُ وَلِيًّا
فَاطِرِ السَّمَاوَاتِ وَالْأَرْضِ
وَهُوَ يُطْعِمُ وَلَا يُطْعَمُ ۗ
قُلْ إِنِّي أُمِرْتُ أَنْ أَكُونَ
أَوَّلَ مَنْ أَسْلَمَ ۖ وَلَا تَكُونَنَّ
مِنَ الْمُشْرِكِينَ

---

844. History, travel, human experience, all prove the Mercy of Allah and the law that without it those who reject Truth tend to lose their own souls and destroy themselves.

845. *Sakan* = (1) to dwell; (2) to rest, to be still, to stop (moving), to lurk; (3) to be quiescent, as a letter which is not moved with a vowel.

If we imagine Night and Day to be places, and each to have (dwelling in them) things that are open and things that are concealed, things that move and things that are still, things that are sounded and things that are quiescent, we get some idea of the imagery implied. The mystery of Time (which seems more absract than Space) is thus explained and illustrated by the idea of Place or Space, which also is a notion and not a concrete thing. But He Who has control of all these things is the one true Allah.

846. Throughout this section we have a sort of implied dialogue, of which one part is understood from the other part, which is expressed. In verse 11, we might have an imaginary objector saying: "Why go back to the past?" The answer is: "Well travel through the world, and see whether it is not true that virtue and godliness exalt a nation, and the opposite are causes of ruin. Both the past and the present prove this." In verse 12 the objector may say: "But you speak of Allah's power?" The man of God replies: "Yes, but Mercy is Allah's own attribute, and knowledge and wisdom beyond what man can conceive."

847. *Feedeth but is not fed:* true both literally and figuratively. To Allah we owe the satisfaction of all needs, but He is independent of all needs.

15. Say: "I would, if I
Disobeyed my Lord,
Indeed have fear
Of the Penalty
Of a Mighty Day.

١٥ قُلْ إِنِّيٓ أَخَافُ إِنْ عَصَيْتُ
رَبِّي عَذَابَ يَوْمٍ عَظِيمٍ

16. "On that day, if the Penalty
Is averted from any,
It is due to Allah's Mercy;
And that would be (Salvation),
The obvious fulfilment
Of all desire.[848]

١٦ مَّن يُصْرَفْ عَنْهُ يَوْمَئِذٍ فَقَدْ
رَحِمَهُۥ ۚ وَذَٰلِكَ ٱلْفَوْزُ ٱلْمُبِينُ

17. "If Allah touch thee
With affliction, none
Can remove it but He;
If He touch thee with happiness,
He hath power over all things.[849]

١٧ وَإِن يَمْسَسْكَ ٱللَّهُ بِضُرٍّ
فَلَا كَاشِفَ لَهُۥٓ إِلَّا هُوَ ۖ
وَإِن يَمْسَسْكَ بِخَيْرٍ فَهُوَ عَلَىٰ كُلِّ شَيْءٍ قَدِيرٌ

18. "He is the Irresistible, (watching)
From above over His worshippers;
And He is the Wise,
Acquainted with all things."

١٨ وَهُوَ ٱلْقَاهِرُ فَوْقَ عِبَادِهِۦ ۚ
وَهُوَ ٱلْحَكِيمُ ٱلْخَبِيرُ

19. Say: "What thing is most
Weighty in evidence?"
Say: "Allah is witness
Between me and you;
This Qur'ān hath been
Revealed to me by inspiration.
That I may warn you
And all whom it reaches.
Can ye possibly bear witness
That besides Allah there is
Another God?" Say:
"Nay! I cannot bear witness!"
Say: "But in truth
He is the One God,

١٩ قُلْ أَيُّ شَيْءٍ أَكْبَرُ شَهَٰدَةً ۖ
قُلِ ٱللَّهُ ۖ شَهِيدٌۢ بَيْنِي وَبَيْنَكُمْ ۚ
وَأُوحِيَ إِلَيَّ هَٰذَا ٱلْقُرْءَانُ
لِأُنذِرَكُم بِهِۦ وَمَنۢ بَلَغَ ۚ
أَئِنَّكُمْ لَتَشْهَدُونَ أَنَّ مَعَ ٱللَّهِ
ءَالِهَةً أُخْرَىٰ ۚ قُل لَّآ أَشْهَدُ ۚ
قُلْ إِنَّمَا هُوَ إِلَٰهٌ وَٰحِدٌ

848. We continue the implied dialogue suggested in n. 846. In verse 14, the objector might say: "But we have other interests in life than religion and Allah." "No," says the man of God. "My Creator is the one and only Power whose protection I seek; and I strive to be first in the race." In verse 15, the objector suggests: "Enjoy the good things of this life; it is short." The answer is: "The Hereafter is more real to me, and promises the true fulfilment of all desire; happiness or affliction comes not from the fleeting pettinesses or illusions of this life, but from the power and wisdom of Allah." In verse 19, the objector makes his final splash: "What evidence is there for all this?" The reply is: "I know it is true for Allah's voice is within me, and my living Teacher awakens that voice; and there is the Book of Inspiration. Allah is one, and there is none other besides."

849. The vulgar worship false gods out of fear that they would harm them or hope that they would confer some benefit on them. These false gods can do neither. All power, all goodness in the hands of Allah. All else is pretence or illusion.

And I truly am innocent
Of (your blasphemy of) joining
Others with Him."

وَإِنَّنِي بَرِيٓءٞ مِّمَّا تُشۡرِكُونَ

20. Those to whom
We have given the Book
Know this as they know[850]
Their own sons.
Those who have lost
Their own souls
Refuse therefore to believe.

٢٠ ٱلَّذِينَ ءَاتَيۡنَٰهُمُ ٱلۡكِتَٰبَ
يَعۡرِفُونَهُۥ كَمَا يَعۡرِفُونَ أَبۡنَآءَهُمُۘ
ٱلَّذِينَ خَسِرُوٓاْ أَنفُسَهُمۡ فَهُمۡ لَا يُؤۡمِنُونَ

SECTION 3.

21. Who doth more wrong
Than he who inventeth
A lie against Allah
Or rejecteth His Signs?
But verily the wrongdoers
Never shall prosper.

٢١ وَمَنۡ أَظۡلَمُ مِمَّنِ ٱفۡتَرَىٰ
عَلَى ٱللَّهِ كَذِبًا أَوۡ كَذَّبَ بِـَٔايَٰتِهِۦٓۚ
إِنَّهُۥ لَا يُفۡلِحُ ٱلظَّٰلِمُونَ

22. One day shall We gather
Them all together: We
Shall say to those
Who ascribed partners (to Us):
"Where are the partners
Whom ye (invented
And) talked about!"

٢٢ وَيَوۡمَ نَحۡشُرُهُمۡ جَمِيعٗا ثُمَّ نَقُولُ
لِلَّذِينَ أَشۡرَكُوٓاْ أَيۡنَ شُرَكَآؤُكُمُ
ٱلَّذِينَ كُنتُمۡ تَزۡعُمُونَ

23. There will then be (left)
No subterfuge for them[851]
But to say: "By Allah
Our Lord, we were not
Those who joined gods
With Allah."

٢٣ ثُمَّ لَمۡ تَكُن فِتۡنَتُهُمۡ
إِلَّآ أَن قَالُواْ وَٱللَّهِ
رَبِّنَا مَا كُنَّا مُشۡرِكِينَ

24. Behold! how they lie
Against their own souls!
But the (lie) which they

٢٤ ٱنظُرۡ كَيۡفَ كَذَبُواْ عَلَىٰٓ أَنفُسِهِمۡۚ

850. *Cf.* 2:146 and n. 151. In both passages the pronoun translated "this" may mean "him" and refer to Muḥammad the Messenger of Allah, as some Commentators think.

851. *Fitnah* has various meanings, from the root idea of "to try, to test, to tempt;" *e.g.*, (1) a trial or temptation, as in 2:102; (2) trouble, tumult, oppression, persecution, as in 2:191, 193, 217; (3) discord, as in 3:7. (4) subterfuge, an answer that amounts to a sedition, and excuse founded on a falsehood, as here. Other shades of meaning will be noticed as they occur.

Those who blasphemed Allah in imagining false gods will now see the vanity of their imaginations for themselves. What answer can they give now? In their perversity they will deny that they *ever* entertained the notion of false gods.

Invented will leave them[852]
In the lurch.

وَضَلَّ عَنْهُم مَّا كَانُوا يَفْتَرُونَ

25. Of them there are some
Who (pretend to) listen to thee;
But We have thrown
Veils on their hearts,
So they understand it not,[852-A]
And deafness in their ears;
If they saw every one
Of the Signs, they will
Not believe in them;
In so much that
When they come to thee,
They (but) dispute with thee;
The Unbelievers say:
"These are nothing
But tales of the ancients."

٢٥ وَمِنْهُم مَّن يَسْتَمِعُ إِلَيْكَ
وَجَعَلْنَا عَلَىٰ قُلُوبِهِمْ أَكِنَّةً
أَن يَفْقَهُوهُ وَفِي آذَانِهِمْ وَقْرًا
وَإِن يَرَوْا كُلَّ آيَةٍ لَّا يُؤْمِنُوا بِهَا
حَتَّىٰ إِذَا جَاءُوكَ يُجَادِلُونَكَ
يَقُولُ الَّذِينَ كَفَرُوا
إِنْ هَٰذَا إِلَّا أَسَاطِيرُ الْأَوَّلِينَ

26. Others they keep away from it,
And themselves they keep away;
But they only destroy
Their own souls,
And they perceive it not.

٢٦ وَهُمْ يَنْهَوْنَ عَنْهُ وَيَنْأَوْنَ عَنْهُ
وَإِن يُهْلِكُونَ إِلَّا أَنفُسَهُمْ وَمَا يَشْعُرُونَ

27. If thou couldst but see
When they are confronted
With the Fire!
They will say:
"Would that we were
But sent back!
Then would we not reject
The Signs of our Lord,
But would be amongst those
Who believe!"

٢٧ وَلَوْ تَرَىٰ إِذْ وُقِفُوا عَلَى النَّارِ
فَقَالُوا يَا لَيْتَنَا نُرَدُّ
وَلَا نُكَذِّبَ بِآيَاتِ رَبِّنَا
وَنَكُونَ مِنَ الْمُؤْمِنِينَ

28. Yea, in their own (eyes)
Will become manifest
What before they concealed.
But if they were returned,
They would certainly relapse

٢٨ بَلْ بَدَا لَهُم مَّا كَانُوا يُخْفُونَ مِن قَبْلُ
وَلَوْ رُدُّوا لَعَادُوا

852. The lies which they used to tell have now "wandered" from the channels which they used to occupy, and left the liars in the lurch. In denying the indubitable fact that they took false gods, they admit the falsity of their notions and thus are practically convicted out of their own mouths.

852-A. *It* = The Qur'ān.

To the things they were forbidden,
For they are indeed liars.[853]

لِمَا نُهُوا۟ عَنْهُ وَإِنَّهُمْ لَكَٰذِبُونَ

29. And they (sometimes) say:
"There is nothing except
Our life on this earth,
And never shall we be
Raised up again."

٢٩ وَقَالُوٓا۟ إِنْ هِىَ إِلَّا حَيَاتُنَا ٱلدُّنْيَا
وَمَا نَحْنُ بِمَبْعُوثِينَ

30. If thou couldst but see
When they are confronted
With their Lord!
He will say:
"Is not this the truth?"
They will say:
"Yea, by our Lord!"
He will say:
"Taste ye then the Penalty,
Because ye rejected Faith."

٣٠ وَلَوْ تَرَىٰٓ إِذْ وُقِفُوا۟ عَلَىٰ رَبِّهِمْ
قَالَ أَلَيْسَ هَٰذَا بِٱلْحَقِّ
قَالُوا۟ بَلَىٰ وَرَبِّنَا
قَالَ فَذُوقُوا۟ ٱلْعَذَابَ
بِمَا كُنتُمْ تَكْفُرُونَ

C. 77.—The life of this world is but empty:
(6:31-60.) What is serious is the life hereafter.
The teacher of Allah's truth is not baulked
By frivolous objections or insults
Or persecution. The wicked will be
Cut off to the last remnant. Allah's wisdom
Pervades the whole of His Creation,
And in His hands are the keys of the Unseen,
And the secrets of all that we see.

SECTION 4.

31. Lost indeed are they
Who treat it as a falsehood
That they must meet Allah—
Until on a sudden
The hour is on them,
And they say: "Ah! woe
Unto us that we took
No thought of it";

٣١ قَدْ خَسِرَ ٱلَّذِينَ كَذَّبُوا۟ بِلِقَآءِ ٱللَّهِ
حَتَّىٰٓ إِذَا جَآءَتْهُمُ ٱلسَّاعَةُ بَغْتَةً
قَالُوا۟ يَٰحَسْرَتَنَا
عَلَىٰ مَا فَرَّطْنَا فِيهَا

853. Their falsity was not due to want of knowledge, but to perversity and selfishness. In their hearts was a disease (2:10): therefore neither their understanding, nor their ears, nor their eyes do their proper work. They twist what they see, hear, or are taught, and go deeper and deeper into the mire. The deceptions which they used to practise on other people will, before the Seat of Judgement, become clear in their own eyes.

For they bear their burdens[854]
On their backs,
And evil indeed are
The burdens that they bear.

وَهُمْ يَحْمِلُونَ أَوْزَارَهُمْ عَلَىٰ ظُهُورِهِمْ
أَلَا سَآءَ مَا يَزِرُونَ

32. What is the life of this world
But play and amusement?[855]
But best is the Home
In the Hereafter, for those
Who are righteous.
Will ye not then understand?

٣٢ وَمَا ٱلْحَيَوٰةُ ٱلدُّنْيَآ إِلَّا لَعِبٌ وَلَهْوٌ
وَلَلدَّارُ ٱلْءَاخِرَةُ خَيْرٌ لِّلَّذِينَ يَتَّقُونَ
أَفَلَا تَعْقِلُونَ

33. We know indeed the grief
Which their words do cause thee:
It is not thee they reject:
It is the Signs of Allah,
Which the wicked condemn.

٣٣ قَدْ نَعْلَمُ إِنَّهُۥ لَيَحْزُنُكَ
ٱلَّذِى يَقُولُونَ فَإِنَّهُمْ لَا يُكَذِّبُونَكَ
وَلَٰكِنَّ ٱلظَّٰلِمِينَ بِـَٔايَٰتِ ٱللَّهِ يَجْحَدُونَ

34. Rejected were the Messengers
Before thee: with patience
And constancy they bore
Their rejection and their wrongs,
Until Our aid did reach
Them: there is none
That can alter the Words
(And Decrees) of Allah.
Already hast thou received
Some account of those Messengers.

٣٤ وَلَقَدْ كُذِّبَتْ رُسُلٌ مِّن قَبْلِكَ
فَصَبَرُوا۟ عَلَىٰ مَا كُذِّبُوا۟ وَأُوذُوا۟ حَتَّىٰٓ أَتَىٰهُمْ نَصْرُنَا
وَلَا مُبَدِّلَ لِكَلِمَٰتِ ٱللَّهِ
وَلَقَدْ جَآءَكَ مِن نَّبَإِى۟ ٱلْمُرْسَلِينَ

35. If their spurning is hard
On thy mind, yet if
Thou wert able to seek
A tunnel in the ground
Or a ladder to the skies
And bring them a Sign—[856]

٣٥ وَإِن كَانَ كَبُرَ عَلَيْكَ إِعْرَاضُهُمْ
فَإِنِ ٱسْتَطَعْتَ أَن تَبْتَغِىَ نَفَقًا فِى ٱلْأَرْضِ
أَوْ سُلَّمًا فِى ٱلسَّمَآءِ فَتَأْتِيَهُم بِـَٔايَةٍ

854. Grievous is the burden of sins which the wicked will bear on their backs when they become conscious of them. Some Commentators personify sins as ugly demons riding on the backs of men, while the men's good deeds become the strong and patient mounts which will carry the men on their backs. If the good deeds are few and the sins many, the man and his good deeds will be crushed under the load of the Evil which they carry.

855. Play and amusement are for preparing our minds for the serious things of life: in themselves they are not serious. So this life is a preparation for the Eternal Home to which we are going, which is far more important than the ephemeral pleasures which may possibly seduce us in this life.

856. There were many Signs of a divine mission in the Prophet's life and in the Message which he delivered. If these did not convince the Unbelievers, was it not vain to seek a miraculous Sign from the bowels of the earth or by a visible ascent to the skies? If in the Prophet's eagerness to get all to accept his Message he was hurt at their callousness, active opposition, and persecution of him, he is told that a full knowledge of the working of Allah's Plan would convince him that impatience was misplaced. This was in the days of persecution before the Hijrah. The history in Madīnah and after shows how Allah's truth was ultimately and triumphantly vindicated. Who among the sincere devotees of Muḥammad can fail to read 6:33-35 without tears in his eyes?

(What good?). If it were
Allah's Will, He could
Gather them together
Unto true guidance:
So be not thou
Amongst those who are swayed
By ignorance (and impatience)!

وَلَوْ شَآءَ ٱللَّهُ
لَجَمَعَهُمْ عَلَى ٱلْهُدَىٰ
فَلَا تَكُونَنَّ مِنَ ٱلْجَٰهِلِينَ

36. Those who listen (in truth),[857]
Be sure, will accept:
As to the dead, Allah will
Raise them up; then will they
Be returned unto Him.

٣٦ إِنَّمَا يَسْتَجِيبُ ٱلَّذِينَ يَسْمَعُونَ
وَٱلْمَوْتَىٰ يَبْعَثُهُمُ ٱللَّهُ ثُمَّ إِلَيْهِ يُرْجَعُونَ

37. They say: "Why is not
A Sign sent down
To him from his Lord?"
Say: "Allah hath certainly
Power to send down a Sign:
But most of them
Understand not."[858]

٣٧ وَقَالُوا۟ لَوْلَا نُزِّلَ عَلَيْهِ ءَايَةٌ مِّن رَّبِّهِۦ
قُلْ إِنَّ ٱللَّهَ قَادِرٌ عَلَىٰٓ أَن يُنَزِّلَ ءَايَةً
وَلَٰكِنَّ أَكْثَرَهُمْ لَا يَعْلَمُونَ

38. There is not an animal
(That lives) on the earth,
Nor a being that flies
On its wings, but (forms
Part of) communities like you.[859]
Nothing have We omitted
From the Book, and they (all)
Shall be gathered to their Lord
In the end.

٣٨ وَمَا مِن دَآبَّةٍ فِى ٱلْأَرْضِ وَلَا طَٰٓئِرٍ
يَطِيرُ بِجَنَاحَيْهِ إِلَّآ أُمَمٌ أَمْثَالُكُم
مَّا فَرَّطْنَا فِى ٱلْكِتَٰبِ مِن شَىْءٍ
ثُمَّ إِلَىٰ رَبِّهِمْ يُحْشَرُونَ

857. There is a double meaning here. (1) If people listen to truth sincerely and earnestly, they must believe; even if the spiritual faculty is dead. Allah will by His grace revive it and they will come to Him, if they really try earnestly to understand. (2) The sincere will believe; but those whose hearts are dead will not listen, yet they cannot escape being brought to the Judgement Seat before Him.

858. Signs are all around them, but they do not understand. If they want a particular Sign to suit their gross ignorance, they will not be humoured, for they can always pick holes in anything that descends to their level.

859. "Animals living on the earth" include those living in the water—fishes, reptiles, crustaceans, insects, as well as four-footed beasts. Life on the wing is separately mentioned. "Ṭā'ir," which is ordinarily translated as "bird," is anything that flies, including mammals like bats. In our pride we may exclude animals from our purview, but they all live a life, social and individual, like ourselves, and all life is subject to the Plan and Will of Allah. In 6:59 we are told that not a leaf falls but by His Will, and things dry and green are recorded in His Book. In other words they all obey His archetypal Plan, the Book which is also mentioned here. They are all answerable in their several degrees to His Plan ("shall be gathered to their Lord in the end"). This is not Pantheism: it is ascribing all life, activity, and existence to the Will and Plan of Allah.

39. Those who reject our Signs
Are deaf and dumb—[860]
In the midst of darkness
Profound: whom Allah willeth,
He leaveth to wander;
Whom He willeth, He placeth
On the Way that is Straight.

٣٩ وَالَّذِينَ كَذَّبُوا بِآيَاتِنَا صُمٌّ وَبُكْمٌ
فِي الظُّلُمَاتِ مَن يَشَإِ اللَّهُ يُضْلِلْهُ
وَمَن يَشَأْ يَجْعَلْهُ عَلَىٰ صِرَاطٍ مُّسْتَقِيمٍ

40. Say: "Think ye to yourselves,
If there come upon you
The Wrath of Allah,
Or the Hour (that ye dread),
Would ye then call upon
Other than Allah?—
(Reply) if ye are truthful!

٤٠ قُلْ أَرَأَيْتَكُمْ إِنْ أَتَاكُمْ
عَذَابُ اللَّهِ أَوْ أَتَتْكُمُ السَّاعَةُ
أَغَيْرَ اللَّهِ تَدْعُونَ إِن كُنتُمْ صَادِقِينَ

41. "Nay—On Him would ye
Call, and if it be
His Will, He would remove
(The distress) which occasioned
Your call upon Him,
And ye would forget
(The false gods) which ye
Join with Him!"

٤١ بَلْ إِيَّاهُ تَدْعُونَ
فَيَكْشِفُ مَا تَدْعُونَ إِلَيْهِ إِن شَاءَ
وَتَنسَوْنَ مَا تُشْرِكُونَ

SECTION 5.

42. Before thee We sent
(Messengers) to many nations,
And We afflicted the nations
With suffering and adversity,
That they might learn humility.

٤٢ وَلَقَدْ أَرْسَلْنَا إِلَىٰ أُمَمٍ مِّن قَبْلِكَ
فَأَخَذْنَاهُم بِالْبَأْسَاءِ وَالضَّرَّاءِ لَعَلَّهُمْ يَتَضَرَّعُونَ

43. When the suffering reached
Them from Us, why then
Did they not learn humility?[861]
On the contrary their hearts
Became hardened, and Satan
Made their (sinful) acts
Seem alluring to them.

٤٣ فَلَوْلَا إِذْ جَاءَهُم بَأْسُنَا تَضَرَّعُوا
وَلَٰكِن قَسَتْ قُلُوبُهُمْ وَزَيَّنَ لَهُمُ الشَّيْطَانُ
مَا كَانُوا يَعْمَلُونَ

---

860. The limited free will of man makes a little difference. If he sees the Signs but shuts his ears to the true Message, and refuses (like a dumb thing) to speak out the Message which all Nature proclaims, then according to the Plan (of his limited free will) he must suffer and wander, just as, in the opposite case, he will receive grace and salvation.

861. Sorrow and suffering may (if we take them rightly) turn out to be the best gifts of Allah to us. According to the Psalms (xciv. 12). "Blessed is the man whom Thou chastenest, O Lord!" Through suffering we learn humility, the antidote to many vices and the fountain of many virtues. But if we take them the wrong way, we grumble and complain, we become fainthearted; and Satan gets his opportunity to exploit us by putting forward the alluring pleasures of his Vanity Fair.

44. But when they forgot
The warning they had received,
We opened to them the gates
Of all (good) things,[862]
Until, in the midst
Of their enjoyment
Of Our gifts,
On a sudden, We called
Them to account, when lo!
They were plunged in despair!

٤٤ فَلَمَّا نَسُوا۟ مَا ذُكِّرُوا۟ بِهِۦ
فَتَحْنَا عَلَيْهِمْ أَبْوَٰبَ كُلِّ شَىْءٍ
حَتَّىٰٓ إِذَا فَرِحُوا۟ بِمَآ أُوتُوٓا۟
أَخَذْنَٰهُم بَغْتَةً
فَإِذَا هُم مُّبْلِسُونَ

45. Of the wrongdoers the last
Remnant was cut off.
Praise be to Allah,
The Cherisher of the Worlds.[863]

٤٥ فَقُطِعَ دَابِرُ ٱلْقَوْمِ ٱلَّذِينَ ظَلَمُوا۟ ۚ
وَٱلْحَمْدُ لِلَّهِ رَبِّ ٱلْعَٰلَمِينَ

46. Say: "Think ye, if Allah
Took away your hearing
And your sight, and sealed up[864]
Your hearts, who—a god
Other than Allah—could
Restore them to you?"
See how We explain
The Signs by various (symbols);
Yet they turn aside.

٤٦ قُلْ أَرَءَيْتُمْ إِنْ أَخَذَ ٱللَّهُ سَمْعَكُمْ
وَأَبْصَٰرَكُمْ وَخَتَمَ عَلَىٰ قُلُوبِكُم مَّنْ إِلَٰهٌ
غَيْرُ ٱللَّهِ يَأْتِيكُم بِهِ ۗ ٱنظُرْ كَيْفَ
نُصَرِّفُ ٱلْءَايَٰتِ ثُمَّ هُمْ يَصْدِفُونَ

47. Say: "Think ye, if
The Punishment of Allah
Comes to you,
Whether suddenly or openly,[865]
Will any be destroyed
Except those who do wrong?

٤٧ قُلْ أَرَءَيْتَكُمْ إِنْ أَتَىٰكُمْ
عَذَابُ ٱللَّهِ بَغْتَةً أَوْ جَهْرَةً
هَلْ يُهْلَكُ إِلَّا ٱلْقَوْمُ ٱلظَّٰلِمُونَ

862. Learning the inner truth of ourselves and the world presupposes a certain advanced stage of sensitiveness and spiritual development. There is a shallower stage, at which prosperity and the good things of life may teach us sympathy and goodness and cheerfulness like that of Mr. Cheeribyles in Dickens. In such cases the Message takes root. But there is another type of character which is puffed up in prosperity. For them prosperity is a trial or even a punishment from the higher point of view. They go deeper and deeper into sin, until they are pulled up of a sudden and then instead of being contrite they merely become desperate.

863. Allah's punishment of wrongdoers is a measure of justice, to protect the true and righteous from their depredations and maintain His righteous decrees. It is an aspect of His character which is emphasised by the epithet "Cherisher of the Worlds."

864. *Cf.* 2:7 and n. 31.

865. *Suddenly* = without warning. *Openly* = with many warnings, even to the sinners, though they heed them not. As to those who understand and read the signs of Allah, they could always tell that all wrongdoing must eventually have its punishment. But it will affect the wrongdoers, not the righteous. It is justice, not revenge.

48. We send the Messengers
Only to give good news[866]
And to warn: so those
Who believe and mend
(Their lives)—upon them
Shall be no fear,
Nor shall they grieve.

٤٨ وَمَا نُرْسِلُ ٱلْمُرْسَلِينَ إِلَّا مُبَشِّرِينَ
وَمُنذِرِينَ فَمَنْ ءَامَنَ وَأَصْلَحَ
فَلَا خَوْفٌ عَلَيْهِمْ وَلَا هُمْ يَحْزَنُونَ

49. But those who reject
Our Signs—them
Shall punishment touch,
For that they ceased not
From transgressing.

٤٩ وَٱلَّذِينَ كَذَّبُوا۟ بِـَٔايَٰتِنَا
يَمَسُّهُمُ ٱلْعَذَابُ بِمَا كَانُوا۟ يَفْسُقُونَ

50. Say: "I tell you not
That with me
Are the Treasures of Allah,[867]
Nor do I know
What is hidden,
Nor do I tell you I am
An angel. I but follow
What is revealed to me."
Say: "Can the blind
Be held equal to the seeing?"[868]
Will ye then consider not?

٥٠ قُل لَّآ أَقُولُ لَكُمْ عِندِى
خَزَآئِنُ ٱللَّهِ وَلَآ أَعْلَمُ ٱلْغَيْبَ
وَلَآ أَقُولُ لَكُمْ إِنِّى مَلَكٌ إِنْ أَتَّبِعُ إِلَّا
مَا يُوحَىٰٓ إِلَىَّ قُلْ هَلْ يَسْتَوِى ٱلْأَعْمَىٰ
وَٱلْبَصِيرُ أَفَلَا تَتَفَكَّرُونَ

SECTION 6.

51. Give this warning to those[869]
In whose (hearts) is the fear
That they will be brought
(To Judgement) before their Lord:
Except for Him
They will have no protector
Nor intercessor;

٥١ وَأَنذِرْ بِهِ ٱلَّذِينَ يَخَافُونَ
أَن يُحْشَرُوٓا۟ إِلَىٰ رَبِّهِمْ
لَيْسَ لَهُم مِّن دُونِهِۦ وَلِىٌّ وَلَا شَفِيعٌ

866. The Prophets are not sent to cancel man's limited free will. They are sent to preach and teach—to preach hope to the repentant ("good news"), and to warn the rebellious of the Wrath to come.

867. Literally, it might mean that the men of God are not like vulgar soothsayers, who pretend to reveal hidden treasures, or peer into the future, or claim to be something of a different nature from men. But the meaning is wider: they deal out Allah's great treasures of truth, but the treasures are not theirs, but Allah's; they have greater insight into the higher things, but that insight is not due to their own wisdom, but to Allah's inspiration; they are of the same flesh and blood with us, and the sublimity of their words and teachings arises through Allah's grace—to them and to those who hear them.

868. Therefore compare not the men of God ("the seeing") with ordinary men ("the blind"). The men of God, although they be but men, have the higher light with them; therefore do not exact of them petty ephemeral services. Though they are men, they are not as other men, and are entitled to reverence.

869. There are some men, sinners, who yet believe in Judgement; let them be warned of their personal responsibility to guard against evil; let them not rely upon protectors or intercessors before Allah; their sins can only be forgiven by Allah's own Mercy.

That they may guard
(Against evil).

لَعَلَّهُمْ يَتَّقُونَ

52. Send not away those
Who call on their Lord
Morning and evening,
Seeking His Face.[870]
In naught art thou accountable
For them, and in naught are they
Accountable for thee,[871]
That thou shouldst turn
Them away, and thus be
(One) of the unjust.

٥٢ وَلَا تَطْرُدِ ٱلَّذِينَ يَدْعُونَ رَبَّهُم
بِٱلْغَدَوٰةِ وَٱلْعَشِيِّ يُرِيدُونَ وَجْهَهُۥ
مَا عَلَيْكَ مِنْ حِسَابِهِم مِّن شَىْءٍ
وَمَا مِنْ حِسَابِكَ عَلَيْهِم مِّن شَىْءٍ
فَتَطْرُدَهُمْ فَتَكُونَ مِنَ ٱلظَّٰلِمِينَ

53. Thus did We try
Some of them by comparison[872]
With others, that they
Should say: "Is it these
Then that Allah hath
Favoured from amongst us?"
Doth not Allah know best
Those who are grateful?

٥٣ وَكَذَٰلِكَ فَتَنَّا
بَعْضَهُم بِبَعْضٍ لِّيَقُولُوٓا۟ أَهَٰٓؤُلَآءِ
مَنَّ ٱللَّهُ عَلَيْهِم مِّنۢ بَيْنِنَآ
أَلَيْسَ ٱللَّهُ بِأَعْلَمَ بِٱلشَّٰكِرِينَ

54. When those come to thee
Who believe in Our Signs,
Say: "Peace be on you;"[873]
Your Lord hath inscribed
For Himself (the rule[874]
Of) Mercy: verily,
If any of you did evil
In ignorance, and thereafter

٥٤ وَإِذَا جَآءَكَ ٱلَّذِينَ
يُؤْمِنُونَ بِـَٔايَٰتِنَا فَقُلْ سَلَٰمٌ عَلَيْكُمْ
كَتَبَ رَبُّكُمْ عَلَىٰ نَفْسِهِ ٱلرَّحْمَةَ
أَنَّهُۥ مَنْ عَمِلَ مِنكُمْ سُوٓءًۢا بِجَهَٰلَةٍ ثُمَّ

---

870. *Face: wajh*: see 2:112 and n. 114. (R).

871. Some of the rich and influential Quraysh thought it beneath their dignity to listen to Muḥammad's teaching in company with the lowly disciples, who were gathered round him. But he refused to send away these lowly disciples, who were sincere seekers after Allah. From a worldly point of view they had nothing to gain from Muḥammad as he was himself poor, and he had nothing to gain from them as they had no influence. But that was no reason for turning them away; indeed their true sincerity entitled them to precedence over worldly men in the kingdom of Allah, Whose justice was vindicated in Muḥammad's daily life in this as in other things. If their sincerity was in any way doubtful, it involved no responsibility for the Preacher.

872. Pursue the argument of the last note. The influential people who were not given precedence over the poor and humble but sincere disciples, were on their trial as to their spiritual insight. Their temptation was to say (and they said it in scorn): "We are much greater than they: has Allah then selected these lowly people for His teaching?" But that was so. And Allah knew best those who were grateful to Him for His guidance.

873. The humble who had sincere faith, were not only not sent away to humour the wealthy: they were honoured and were given a special salutation, which has become the characteristic salutation in Islam: "Peace be on you"—the word peace, "*salām*" having special affinity with the word "*Islām*." In words they are given the salutation; in life they are promised Mercy by the special grace of Allah.

874. *Cf.* 6:12.

Repented, and amended
(His conduct), lo! He is
Oft-Forgiving, Most Merciful.

تَابَ مِنۢ بَعۡدِهِۦ وَأَصۡلَحَ فَأَنَّهُۥ غَفُورٞ رَّحِيمٞ

55. Thus do We explain
The Signs in detail:
That the way of the sinners
May be shown up.[875]

٥٥ وَكَذَٰلِكَ نُفَصِّلُ ٱلۡأٓيَٰتِ
وَلِتَسۡتَبِينَ سَبِيلُ ٱلۡمُجۡرِمِينَ

SECTION 7.

56. Say:[876] "I am forbidden
To worship those—others
Than Allah—whom ye
Call upon." Say: "I will
Not follow your vain desires:
If I did, I would stray
From the path, and be not
Of the company of those
Who receive guidance."

٥٦ قُلۡ إِنِّي نُهِيتُ أَنۡ أَعۡبُدَ
ٱلَّذِينَ تَدۡعُونَ مِن دُونِ ٱللَّهِۚ قُل
لَّآ أَتَّبِعُ أَهۡوَآءَكُمۡ قَدۡ ضَلَلۡتُ إِذٗا
وَمَآ أَنَا۠ مِنَ ٱلۡمُهۡتَدِينَ

57. Say: "For me, I (work)
On a clear Sign from my Lord,
But ye reject Him. What ye[877]
Would see hastened, is not
In my power. The Command
Rests with none but Allah:
He declares the Truth,
And He is the best of judges."

٥٧ قُلۡ إِنِّي عَلَىٰ بَيِّنَةٖ مِّن رَّبِّي وَكَذَّبۡتُم بِهِۦۚ
مَا عِندِي مَا تَسۡتَعۡجِلُونَ بِهِۦٓۚ إِنِ ٱلۡحُكۡمُ
إِلَّا لِلَّهِۖ يَقُصُّ ٱلۡحَقَّۖ وَهُوَ خَيۡرُ ٱلۡفَٰصِلِينَ

58. Say: "If what ye would see
Hastened were in my power,
The matter would be settled
At once between you and me.[878]

٥٨ قُل لَّوۡ أَنَّ عِندِي مَا تَسۡتَعۡجِلُونَ بِهِۦ
لَقُضِيَ ٱلۡأَمۡرُ بَيۡنِي وَبَيۡنَكُمۡۗ

---

875. If the way of the sinners (in jealousy and worldly pride) is shown up, and details are given how to honour the truly sincere, it forms the best illustration of the teaching of Allah.

876. There are a number of arguments now put forward against the Makkans who refused to believe in Allah's Message. Each argument is introduced with the word "Say." Here are the first four: (1) I have received Light and will follow it; (2) I prefer my Light to your vain desires; (3) your challenge—"if there is a God, why does He not finish the blasphemers at once?"—it is not for me to take up; punishment rests with Allah; (4) if it rested with me, it would be for me to take up your challenge; all I know is that Allah is not unacquainted with the existence of folly and wickedness, and many other things besides, that no mortal can know; you can see little glimpses of His Plan, and you can be sure that He will not be tardy in calling you to account.

877. *What ye would see hastened*: what ye, deniers of Allah, are so impatient about, the punishment which ye mockingly say does not come to you. *Cf.* 8:6.

878. The Messenger of Allah is not here to settle scores with the wicked. It is not a matter between them and him. It is a matter between them and Allah; he is only a warner against sin, and a declarer of the gospel of salvation.

But Allah knoweth best
Those who do wrong."

وَٱللَّهُ أَعْلَمُ بِٱلظَّٰلِمِينَ

59. With Him are the keys[879]
Of the Unseen, the treasures
That none knoweth but He.
He knoweth whatever there is
On the earth and in the sea.
Not a leaf doth fall
But with His knowledge:
There is not a grain
In the darkness (or depths)
Of the earth, nor anything
Fresh or dry (green or withered),
But is (inscribed) in a Record[880]
Clear (to those who can read).

٥٩ وَعِندَهُۥ مَفَاتِحُ ٱلْغَيْبِ
لَا يَعْلَمُهَآ إِلَّا هُوَ ۚ وَيَعْلَمُ مَا فِى
ٱلْبَرِّ وَٱلْبَحْرِ ۚ وَمَا تَسْقُطُ مِن وَرَقَةٍ
إِلَّا يَعْلَمُهَا وَلَا حَبَّةٍ فِى ظُلُمَٰتِ
ٱلْأَرْضِ وَلَا رَطْبٍ وَلَا يَابِسٍ
إِلَّا فِى كِتَٰبٍ مُّبِينٍ

60. It is He Who doth take
Your souls by night,
And hath knowledge of all
That ye have done by day;
By day doth He raise
You up again; that a term
Appointed be fulfilled;
In the end unto Him
Will be your return;[881]
Then will He show you
The truth of all
That ye did.

٦٠ وَهُوَ ٱلَّذِى يَتَوَفَّىٰكُم بِٱلَّيْلِ
وَيَعْلَمُ مَا جَرَحْتُم بِٱلنَّهَارِ
ثُمَّ يَبْعَثُكُمْ فِيهِ
لِيُقْضَىٰٓ أَجَلٌ مُّسَمًّى
ثُمَّ إِلَيْهِ مَرْجِعُكُمْ ثُمَّ يُنَبِّئُكُم
بِمَا كُنتُمْ تَعْمَلُونَ

C. 78.—Allah's loving care doth encompass
(6:61-82.) Us round throughout life,
And delivers us from dangers
By land and sea. He is the only
Protector: how can we then
Forget Him or run after things
That are mere creatures of His,

---

879. *Mafātiḥ*: Plural of either *miftāḥ* = a key, or *miftaḥ* = a treasure. Both meanings are implied, and I have accordingly put them both in my translation.

880. This is the mystic Record, the archetypal Plan, the Eternal Law, according to which everything seen and unseen is ordered and regulated. The simplest things in Nature are subject to His Law. The fresh and the withered, the living and the lifeless—nothing is outside the Plan of His Creation. (R).

881. As the rest of His Creation is subject to His Law and Plan, so is man's life in every particular and at every moment, awake or asleep. The mystery of Sleep—"the twin brother of death"—is called the taking of our soul by Him, with the record of all we have done in our waking moments, and this record sometimes appears to us in confused glimpses in dreams. By day we awaken again to our activities, and so it goes on until we fulfil the term of our life appointed for this earth. Then comes the other Sleep (death), with the longer record of our Day (life); and then, in the end comes the Resurrection and Judgement, at which we see everything clearly and not as in dreams, for that is the final Reality.

And shall perish—while He
Is the Eternal God, adored
By Abraham and all the prophets?

SECTION 8.

61. He is Irresistible, (watching)
From above over His worshippers,
And He sets guardians[882]
Over you. At length,
When death approaches
One of you, Our angels[883]
Take his soul, and they
Never fail in their duty.

٦١ وَهُوَ ٱلْقَاهِرُ فَوْقَ عِبَادِهِۦ وَيُرْسِلُ عَلَيْكُمْ حَفَظَةً حَتَّىٰٓ إِذَا جَآءَ أَحَدَكُمُ ٱلْمَوْتُ تَوَفَّتْهُ رُسُلُنَا وَهُمْ لَا يُفَرِّطُونَ

62. Then are men returned
Unto Allah, their True Protector,
Surely His is the Command,[884]
And He is the Swiftest
In taking account.

٦٢ ثُمَّ رُدُّوٓا۟ إِلَى ٱللَّهِ مَوْلَىٰهُمُ ٱلْحَقِّ ۚ أَلَا لَهُ ٱلْحُكْمُ وَهُوَ أَسْرَعُ ٱلْحَٰسِبِينَ

63. Say:[885] "Who is it
That delivereth you
From the dark recesses[886]
Of land and sea,
When ye call upon Him
In humility
And silent terror:[887]

٦٣ قُلْ مَن يُنَجِّيكُم مِّن ظُلُمَٰتِ ٱلْبَرِّ وَٱلْبَحْرِ تَدْعُونَهُۥ تَضَرُّعًا وَخُفْيَةً

882. *Guardians*: most Commentators understand this to mean guardian angels. The idea of guardianship is expressed in a general term. Allah watches over us and guards us, and provides all kinds of agencies, material, moral, and spiritual, to help our growth and development, keep us from harm, and bring us nearer to our Destiny.

883. *Angels*: the word used is *rusul*, the Sent Ones—the same word as for human Messengers sent by Allah to teach mankind. The agents who come to take our souls at death are accurate in the performance of their duty. They come neither before nor after their appointed time, nor do they do it in any manner other than that fixed by the Command of Allah.

884. *The Reality: Al Ḥaqq*, the Truth, the only True One. The point is that our illusions of the life of this lower world now vanish, when we are rendered back to Allah, from Whom we came. And now we find that far from the results of our actions being delayed, they follow more swiftly than we can express in terms of Time. Here is the answer to the taunt of those who were impatient of the working of Allah's Plans (6:57-58). (R).

885. In continuation of the four heads of argument referred to in n. 876, we have three more heads here in 6:63-65: (5) your calling upon Him in times of danger shows that in the depths of your hearts you feel His need; (6) Allah's Providence saves you, and yet you ungratefully run after false gods; (7) it is not only physical calamities that you have to fear; your mutual discords and vengeances are even more destructive, and only faith in Allah can save you from them.

886. *Ẕulumāt*: dark recesses, terrible lurking dangers, as in deserts or mountains, or forests, or seas.

887. There are two readings, but they both ultimately yield the same meaning. (1) *Khufyatan*, silently, secretly, from the depth of your inner heart, suggesting unspeakable terror. (2) *Khīfatan*, out of terror or fear or reverence, as in 7:205.

'If He only delivers us
From these (dangers),
(We vow) we shall truly
Show our gratitude.'?"

لَئِنْ أَنجَىٰنَا مِنْ هَٰذِهِۦ لَنَكُونَنَّ مِنَ ٱلشَّٰكِرِينَ

64. Say: "It is Allah
That delivereth you
From these and all (other)
Distresses: and yet
Ye worship false gods!"

٦٤ قُلِ ٱللَّهُ يُنَجِّيكُم مِّنْهَا وَمِن كُلِّ كَرْبٍ ثُمَّ أَنتُمْ تُشْرِكُونَ

65. Say: "He hath power
To send calamities[888]
On you, from above
And below, or to cover
You with confusion
In party strife,
Giving you a taste
Of mutual vengeance—
Each from the other."
See how We explain
The Signs by various (symbols);[889]
That they may understand.

٦٥ قُلْ هُوَ ٱلْقَادِرُ عَلَىٰٓ أَن يَبْعَثَ عَلَيْكُمْ عَذَابًا مِّن فَوْقِكُمْ أَوْ مِن تَحْتِ أَرْجُلِكُمْ أَوْ يَلْبِسَكُمْ شِيَعًا وَيُذِيقَ بَعْضَكُم بَأْسَ بَعْضٍ ٱنظُرْ كَيْفَ نُصَرِّفُ ٱلْءَايَٰتِ لَعَلَّهُمْ يَفْقَهُونَ

66. But thy people reject
This, though it is
The Truth. Say: "Not mine
Is the responsibility
For arranging your affairs;[890]

٦٦ وَكَذَّبَ بِهِۦ قَوْمُكَ وَهُوَ ٱلْحَقُّ قُل لَّسْتُ عَلَيْكُم بِوَكِيلٍ

67. For every Message
Is a limit of time,
And soon shall ye
Know it."

٦٧ لِّكُلِّ نَبَإٍ مُّسْتَقَرٌّ وَسَوْفَ تَعْلَمُونَ

68. When thou seest men
Engaged in vain discourse
About Our Signs, turn
Away from them unless

٦٨ وَإِذَا رَأَيْتَ ٱلَّذِينَ يَخُوضُونَ فِيٓ ءَايَٰتِنَا فَأَعْرِضْ عَنْهُمْ حَتَّىٰ

888. *Calamities from above and below*: such as storms and blizzards, torrential rain, etc., or earthquakes, floods, landslides, etc.

889. *Cf.* 6:46, where this refrain commences the argument now drawing to a close.

890. At the date of this revelation, the Messenger's people had as a body not only rejected Allah's truth, but were persecuting it. The Messenger's duty was to deliver his Message, which he did. He was not responsible for their conduct. But he told them plainly that all warnings from Allah had their time limit, as they would soon find out. And they did find out within a very few years. For the leaders of the resistance came to an evil end, and their whole system of fraud and selfishness was destroyed, to make room for the purer Faith of Islam. Apart from that particular application, there is the more general application for the present time and for all time.

They turn to a different[891]
Theme. If Satan ever
Makes thee forget, then
After recollection, sit not
Thou in the company
Of those who do wrong.

69. On their account
No responsibility
Falls on the righteous,[892]
But (their duty)
Is to remind them,
That they may (learn
To) fear Allah.

70. Leave alone those
Who take their religion
To be mere play
And amusement,[893]
And are deceived
By the life of this world.
But proclaim (to them)
This (truth): that every soul
Delivers itself to ruin
By its own acts;[894]
It will find for itself
No protector or intercessor
Except Allah; if it offered
Every ransom, (or
Reparation), none
Will be accepted; such is
(The end of) those who
Deliver themselves to ruin
By their own acts:
They will have for drink
(Only) boiling water,
And for punishment,
One most grievous;

يَخُوضُواْ فِي حَدِيثٍ غَيْرِهِۦۚ
وَإِمَّا يُنسِيَنَّكَ ٱلشَّيْطَٰنُ فَلَا تَقْعُدْ بَعْدَ
ٱلذِّكْرَىٰ مَعَ ٱلْقَوْمِ ٱلظَّٰلِمِينَ
٦٩ وَمَا عَلَى ٱلَّذِينَ يَتَّقُونَ
مِنْ حِسَابِهِم مِّن شَيْءٍ وَلَٰكِن
ذِكْرَىٰ لَعَلَّهُمْ يَتَّقُونَ
٧٠ وَذَرِ ٱلَّذِينَ
ٱتَّخَذُواْ دِينَهُمْ لَعِبًا وَلَهْوًا
وَغَرَّتْهُمُ ٱلْحَيَوٰةُ ٱلدُّنْيَاۚ
وَذَكِّرْ بِهِۦٓ أَن تُبْسَلَ نَفْسٌۢ
بِمَا كَسَبَتْ لَيْسَ لَهَا
مِن دُونِ ٱللَّهِ وَلِيٌّ وَلَا شَفِيعٌ
وَإِن تَعْدِلْ كُلَّ عَدْلٍ لَّا يُؤْخَذْ مِنْهَآۗ
أُوْلَٰٓئِكَ ٱلَّذِينَ أُبْسِلُواْ بِمَا كَسَبُواْۖ
لَهُمْ شَرَابٌ مِّنْ حَمِيمٍ
وَعَذَابٌ أَلِيمٌۢ

891. *Cf.* 4:140. If in any gathering truth is ridiculed, we must not sit in such company. If we find ourselves in it, as soon as we realise it, we must show our disapproval by leaving.

892. Every man is responsible for his own conduct. But the righteous have two duties: (1) to protect themselves from infection, and (2) to proclaim Allah's truth, for even in the most unlikely circumstances, it is possible that it may have some effect. (R).

893. *Cf.* 6:22, where we are told that the life of this world is mere play and amusement, and Religion and the Hereafter are the serious things that require our attention. Worldly people reverse this, because they are deceived by the allurements of this life. But their own acts will find them out.

894. We must never forget our own personal responsibility for all we do, or deceive ourselves by the illusion of vicarious atonement.

For they persisted
In rejecting Allah.

بِمَا كَانُوا۟ يَكْفُرُونَ

SECTION 9.

71. Say:[895] "Shall we indeed
Call on others besides Allah—
Things that can do us
Neither good nor harm—
And turn on our heels
After receiving guidance
From Allah—like one
Whom the evil ones
Have made into a fool,
Wandering bewildered
Through the earth, his friends
Calling 'Come to us',
(Vainly) guiding him to the Path?"

Say: "Allah's guidance
Is the (only) guidance,
And we have been directed
To submit ourselves
To the Lord of the worlds—

(٧١) قُلْ أَنَدْعُوا۟ مِن دُونِ ٱللَّهِ
مَا لَا يَنفَعُنَا وَلَا يَضُرُّنَا
وَنُرَدُّ عَلَىٰٓ أَعْقَابِنَا بَعْدَ إِذْ هَدَىٰنَا ٱللَّهُ
كَٱلَّذِى ٱسْتَهْوَتْهُ ٱلشَّيَٰطِينُ
فِى ٱلْأَرْضِ حَيْرَانَ لَهُۥٓ أَصْحَٰبٌ
يَدْعُونَهُۥٓ إِلَى ٱلْهُدَى ٱئْتِنَا ۗ
قُلْ إِنَّ هُدَى ٱللَّهِ هُوَ ٱلْهُدَىٰ ۖ
وَأُمِرْنَا لِنُسْلِمَ لِرَبِّ ٱلْعَٰلَمِينَ

72. "To establish regular prayers
And to fear Allah:
For it is to Him
That we shall be
Gathered together."

(٧٢) وَأَنْ أَقِيمُوا۟ ٱلصَّلَوٰةَ وَٱتَّقُوهُ ۚ
وَهُوَ ٱلَّذِىٓ إِلَيْهِ تُحْشَرُونَ

73. It is He Who created
The heavens and the earth
In true (proportions):[896]
The day He saith, "Be,"
Behold! it is. His Word
Is the Truth. His will be

(٧٣) وَهُوَ ٱلَّذِى خَلَقَ ٱلسَّمَٰوَٰتِ
وَٱلْأَرْضَ بِٱلْحَقِّ ۖ وَيَوْمَ يَقُولُ كُن
فَيَكُونُ ۚ قَوْلُهُ ٱلْحَقُّ ۚ وَلَهُ

895. In continuation of the seven heads of argument referred to in nn. 876 and 885, we have here the final two heads: (8) who would, after receiving guidance from the living, eternal God, turn to lifeless idols? To do so would indeed show that we were made into fools, wandering to a precipice; (9) therefore accept the only true guidance, the guidance of Allah, and obey His Law, for we shall have to answer before His Judgement Seat.

896. The argument mounts up here, leading to the great insight of Abraham the true in faith, who did not stop short at the wonders of nature, but penetrated "from nature up to nature's God." Allah not only created the heavens and the earth: with every increase of knowledge we see in what true and perfect proportions all Creation is held together. Creatures are subject to Time, but the Creator is not: His word is the key that opens the door of existence. It is not only the starting point of existence, but the whole measure and standard of Truth and Right. There may possibly be, to our sight in this great world, aberrations of human or other wills, but the moment the trumpet sounds for the last day, His Judgement Seat will, with perfect justice, restore the dominion of Right and Reality. For His Knowledge and Wisdom cover all reality.

The dominion the day
The trumpet will be blown.
He knoweth the Unseen
As well as that which is
Open. For He
Is the Wise, well-acquainted
(With all things).

ٱلْمُلْكُ يَوْمَ يُنفَخُ فِى ٱلصُّورِ ۚ
عَـٰلِمُ ٱلْغَيْبِ وَٱلشَّهَـٰدَةِ ۚ
وَهُوَ ٱلْحَكِيمُ ٱلْخَبِيرُ

74. Lo! Abraham said
To his father Āzar:
"Takest thou idols for gods?
For I see thee
And thy people
In manifest error."

٧٤ وَإِذْ قَالَ إِبْرَٰهِيمُ لِأَبِيهِ ءَازَرَ
أَتَتَّخِذُ أَصْنَامًا ءَالِهَةً ۖ إِنِّىٓ أَرَىٰكَ
وَقَوْمَكَ فِى ضَلَـٰلٍ مُّبِينٍ

75. So also did We show[897]
Abraham the power
And the laws of the heavens
And the earth, that he
Might (with understanding)
Have certitude.

٧٥ وَكَذَٰلِكَ نُرِىٓ إِبْرَٰهِيمَ
مَلَكُوتَ ٱلسَّمَـٰوَٰتِ وَٱلْأَرْضِ
وَلِيَكُونَ مِنَ ٱلْمُوقِنِينَ

76. When the night
Covered him over,
He saw a star:
He said: "This is my Lord."
But when it set,
He said: "I love not
Those that set."[898]

٧٦ فَلَمَّا جَنَّ عَلَيْهِ ٱلَّيْلُ
رَءَا كَوْكَبًا ۖ قَالَ هَـٰذَا رَبِّى ۖ
فَلَمَّآ أَفَلَ قَالَ لَآ أُحِبُّ ٱلْـَٔافِلِينَ

77. When he saw the moon
Rising in splendour,
He said: "This is my Lord."
But when the moon set,

٧٧ فَلَمَّا رَءَا ٱلْقَمَرَ بَازِغًا
قَالَ هَـٰذَا رَبِّى ۖ فَلَمَّآ أَفَلَ

---

897. Now comes the story of Abraham. He lived among the Chaldeans, who had great knowledge of the stars and heavenly bodies. But he got beyond that physical world and saw the spiritual world behind. His ancestral idols meant nothing to him. That was the first step. But Allah took him many degrees higher. Allah showed him with certitude the spiritual glories behind the magnificent powers and laws of the physical universe.

898. This shows the stages of Abraham's spiritual enlightenment. It should not be supposed that he literally worshipped stars or heavenly bodies. Having seen through the folly of ancestral idol worship, he began to see the futility of worshipping distant beautiful things that shine, which the vulgar endue with a power which does not reside in them. A type of such is a star shining in the darkness of the night. Superstition might read fortunes in it, but truer knowledge shows that it rises and sets according to laws whose author is Allah. And its light is extinguished in the broader light of day. Its worship is therefore futile. It is not a Power, much less the Supreme Power.

According to some commentators the whole thrust of Abraham's reasoning in verses 76-78 is directed against the superstitious beliefs of his people and demonstrates the folly of worshipping stars and other heavenly bodies. As such his statements may be seen as premises of his arguments against Polytheism rather than as stages in his spiritual enlightenment. (R).

He said: "Unless my Lord
Guide me, I shall surely
Be among those
Who go astray."[899]

قَالَ لَئِن لَّمْ يَهْدِنِى رَبِّى
لَأَكُونَنَّ مِنَ الْقَوْمِ الضَّالِّينَ

78. When he saw the sun
Rising in splendour,
He said: "This is my Lord;
This is the greatest (of all)."
But when the sun set,
He said: "O my people!
I am indeed free
From your (guilt)
Of giving partners to Allah.[900]

٧٨ فَلَمَّا رَءَا الشَّمْسَ بَازِغَةً
قَالَ هَٰذَا رَبِّى هَٰذَا أَكْبَرُ
فَلَمَّا أَفَلَتْ قَالَ يَٰقَوْمِ
إِنِّى بَرِىٓءٌ مِّمَّا تُشْرِكُونَ

79. "For me, I have set
My face, firmly and truly,
Towards Him Who created
The heavens and the earth,
And never shall I give
Partners to Allah."

٧٩ إِنِّى وَجَّهْتُ وَجْهِىَ لِلَّذِى
فَطَرَ السَّمَٰوَٰتِ وَالْأَرْضَ حَنِيفًا
وَمَآ أَنَا۠ مِنَ الْمُشْرِكِينَ

80. His people disputed[901]
With him. He said:
"(Come) ye to dispute
With me, about Allah,
When He (Himself)
Hath guided me?
I fear not (the beings)
Ye associate with Allah:
Unless my Lord willeth,
(Nothing can happen).
My Lord comprehendeth

٨٠ وَحَآجَّهُۥ قَوْمُهُۥ قَالَ
أَتُحَٰٓجُّوٓنِّى فِى اللَّهِ وَقَدْ هَدَىٰنِ
وَلَآ أَخَافُ مَا تُشْرِكُونَ بِهِۦٓ
إِلَّآ أَن يَشَآءَ رَبِّى شَيْـًٔا
وَسِعَ رَبِّى

899. The moon, though it looks bigger and brighter than the star, turns out on closer knowledge, not only to set like the star, but to change its shape from hour to hour, and even to depend for its light on some other body! How deceptive are appearances! This is not Allah! At that stage you begin to search for something more reliable than appearances to the eye in the darkness of the night. You ask for guidance from Allah. (R).

900. The next stage in the allegory is the sun. You are in the open light of Day. Now you have the right clue. You see the biggest object in the heavens. But is it the biggest? There are thousands of stars in the universe bigger than the sun. And every day the sun appears and disappears from your sight. Such is not God who created you and all these wonderful works of His. What folly to worship creatures, when we might turn to the true God? Let us abjure all these follies and proclaim the one true God.

901. The story of Abraham is highly instructive for all men in quest of truth. If spiritual enlightenment goes so far as to take a man beyond his ancestral worship, people will come to dispute with him. They will frighten him with the dire consequences of his dissent. What does he care? He has found the truth. He is free from superstitious fears, for has he not found the true God, without Whose Will nothing can happen? On the contrary, he knows that it is the godless who have just grounds for fear. And he offers admonition to them, and arguments that should bring them the clearness of truth instead of the vagueness and mystery of superstition—the security of Faith instead of the haunting fear of those who have no clear guidance. (R).

In His knowledge all things.
Will ye not (yourselves)
Be admonished?

كُلَّ شَىْءٍ عِلْمًا
أَفَلَا تَتَذَكَّرُونَ

81. "How should I fear
(The beings) ye associate
With Allah, when ye
Fear not to give partners
To Allah without any warrant
Having been given to you?
Which of (us) two parties
Hath more right to security?
(Tell me) if ye know.

(٨١) وَكَيْفَ أَخَافُ مَآ أَشْرَكْتُمْ وَلَا
تَخَافُونَ أَنَّكُمْ أَشْرَكْتُم بِاللَّهِ
مَا لَمْ يُنَزِّلْ بِهِۦ عَلَيْكُمْ سُلْطَٰنًا
فَأَىُّ الْفَرِيقَيْنِ أَحَقُّ بِالْأَمْنِ إِن كُنتُمْ تَعْلَمُونَ

82. "It is those who believe
And confuse not their beliefs
With wrong[901-A]—that are
(Truly) in security, for they
Are on (right) guidance."

(٨٢) الَّذِينَ ءَامَنُوا وَلَمْ يَلْبِسُوٓا إِيمَٰنَهُم بِظُلْمٍ
أُولَٰٓئِكَ لَهُمُ الْأَمْنُ وَهُم مُّهْتَدُونَ

C. 79.—The good men and true, who succeeded
(6:83-110.) Abraham, received the gifts
Of revelation and guidance, and kept
Alive Allah's Message, which now
Is proclaimed in the Qur'ān,
In which is blessing and confirmation
Of all that went before. In the daily
Pageants of Nature—the dawn
And the restful night, the sun,
The moon, the stars that guide
The mariner in distant seas,
The rain-clouds pouring abundance,
And the fruits that delight the heart
Of man—can ye not read
Signs of Allah? No vision can
Comprehend Him, yet He
Knoweth and comprehendeth all.

SECTION 10.

83. That was the reasoning
About Us, which
We gave to Abraham
(To use) against his people:[902]

(٨٣) وَتِلْكَ حُجَّتُنَآ
ءَاتَيْنَٰهَآ إِبْرَٰهِيمَ عَلَىٰ قَوْمِهِۦ

901-A. The word "wrong" here refers to ascribing partners to Allah as has been stated by the Prophet (peace be on him) in his explanation of the verse. [Eds.].

902. The spiritual education of Abraham raised him many degrees above his contemporaries, and he was expected to use that knowledge and dignity for preaching the truth among his own people.

We raise whom We will,
Degree after degree:
For thy Lord is full
Of wisdom and knowledge.

نَرْفَعُ دَرَجَـٰتٍ مَّن نَّشَآءُ ۗ
إِنَّ رَبَّكَ حَكِيمٌ عَلِيمٌ

84. We gave him Isaac
And Jacob: all (three)
We guided:[903]
And before him,
We guided Noah,[904]
And among his progeny,
David, Solomon, Job,
Joseph, Moses, and Aaron:
Thus do We reward
Those who do good:

(٨٤) وَوَهَبْنَا لَهُۥٓ إِسْحَـٰقَ وَيَعْقُوبَ ۚ
كُلًّا هَدَيْنَا ۚ وَنُوحًا هَدَيْنَا مِن قَبْلُ ۖ
وَمِن ذُرِّيَّتِهِۦ دَاوُۥدَ وَسُلَيْمَـٰنَ وَأَيُّوبَ
وَيُوسُفَ وَمُوسَىٰ وَهَـٰرُونَ ۚ
وَكَذَٰلِكَ نَجْزِى ٱلْمُحْسِنِينَ

85. And Zakariyyā and John,[905]
And Jesus and Elias:
All in the ranks
Of the Righteous:

(٨٥) وَزَكَرِيَّا وَيَحْيَىٰ وَعِيسَىٰ وَإِلْيَاسَ ۖ
كُلٌّ مِّنَ ٱلصَّـٰلِحِينَ

86. And Ismā'īl and Elisha,[906]
And Jonah, and Lot:
And to all We gave
Favour above the nations:

(٨٦) وَإِسْمَـٰعِيلَ وَٱلْيَسَعَ وَيُونُسَ وَلُوطًا ۚ
وَكُلًّا فَضَّلْنَا عَلَى ٱلْعَـٰلَمِينَ

---

903. We have now a list of eighteen Prophets in four groups, covering the great Teachers accepted among the three great religions based on Moses, Jesus, and Muḥammad. The first group to be mentioned is that of Abraham, his son Isaac, and Isaac's son, Jacob. Abraham was the first to have a Book. His Book is mentioned in Q. 87:19, though it is now lost. They were therefore the first to receive Guidance in the sense of a Book.

904. In the second group, we have the great founders of families, apart from Abraham, *viz.*, Noah, of the time of the Flood; David and Solomon, the real establishers of the Jewish monarchy; Job, who lived 140 years, saw four generations of descendants, and was blessed at the end of his life with large pastoral wealth (Job xlii. 16, 12); Joseph, who as Minister of State did great things in Egypt and was the progenitor of two Tribes; and Moses and Aaron, the leaders of the Exodus from Egypt. They led active lives and are called "doers of good."

905. The third group consists not of men of action, but Preachers of Truth, who led solitary lives. Their epithet is: "the Righteous." They form a connected group round Jesus. Zakariyyā was the father of John the Baptist, the precursor of Jesus (3:37-41); and Jesus referred to John the Baptist as Elias: "this is Elias, which was to come" (Matt. xi. 14); and Elias is said to have been present and talked to Jesus at the Transfiguration on the Mount (Matt. xvii. 3). Elias is the same as Elijah. (R).

906. This is the last group, described as those "favoured above the nations." It consists of four men who had all great misfortunes to contend with, and were concerned in the clash of nations, but they kept in the path of Allah, and came through above the clash of nations. Ismā'īl was the eldest son of Abraham; when he was a baby, he and his mother had nearly died of thirst in the desert round Makkah; but they were saved by the well of Zamzam, and he became the founder of the new Arab nation. Elisha (Al Yasa') succeeded to the mantle of the Prophet Elijah (same as Elias, see last note); he lived in troublous times for both the Jewish kingdoms (of Judah and Israel); there were wicked kings, and other nations were pressing in on them; but he performed many miracles, and some check was given to the enemies under his advice. The story of Jonah (Yūnus) is well-known: he was swallowed by a fish or whale, but was saved by Allah's mercy: through his preaching, his city (Nineveh) was saved (10:98). Lot was a contemporary and nephew of Abraham: when the city of Sodom was destroyed for its wickedness, he was saved as a just man (7:80-84).

87. (To them) and to their fathers,[907]
And progeny and brethren:
We chose them,
And We guided them
To a straight Way.

٨٧ وَمِنْ ءَابَآئِهِمْ وَذُرِّيَّٰتِهِمْ وَإِخْوَٰنِهِمْ ۖ
وَٱجْتَبَيْنَٰهُمْ وَهَدَيْنَٰهُمْ إِلَىٰ صِرَٰطٍ مُّسْتَقِيمٍ

88. This is the Guidance
Of Allah: He giveth
That guidance to whom
He pleaseth of His worshippers.
If they were to join
Other gods with Him,
All that they did
Would be vain for them.

٨٨ ذَٰلِكَ هُدَى ٱللَّهِ
يَهْدِى بِهِۦ مَن يَشَآءُ مِنْ عِبَادِهِۦ ۚ
وَلَوْ أَشْرَكُوا۟ لَحَبِطَ عَنْهُم
مَّا كَانُوا۟ يَعْمَلُونَ

89. These were the men
To whom We gave
The Book, and Authority,
And Prophethood: if these
(Their descendants) reject them,[908]
Behold! We shall entrust
Their charge to a new People
Who reject them not.

٨٩ أُو۟لَٰٓئِكَ ٱلَّذِينَ ءَاتَيْنَٰهُمُ
ٱلْكِتَٰبَ وَٱلْحُكْمَ وَٱلنُّبُوَّةَ ۚ
فَإِن يَكْفُرْ بِهَا هَٰٓؤُلَآءِ فَقَدْ وَكَّلْنَا
بِهَا قَوْمًا لَّيْسُوا۟ بِهَا بِكَٰفِرِينَ

90. Those were the (prophets)
Who received Allah's guidance:
Copy the guidance they received;
Say: "No reward for this
Do I ask of you:
This is no less than
A Message for the nations."

٩٠ أُو۟لَٰٓئِكَ ٱلَّذِينَ هَدَى ٱللَّهُ ۖ
فَبِهُدَىٰهُمُ ٱقْتَدِهْ ۗ
قُل لَّآ أَسْـَٔلُكُمْ عَلَيْهِ أَجْرًا ۖ
إِنْ هُوَ إِلَّا ذِكْرَىٰ لِلْعَٰلَمِينَ

SECTION 11.

91. No just estimate of Allah[909]
Do they make when they say:
"Nothing doth Allah send down
To man (by way of revelation)":

٩١ وَمَا قَدَرُوا۟ ٱللَّهَ حَقَّ قَدْرِهِۦٓ إِذْ قَالُوا۟
مَآ أَنزَلَ ٱللَّهُ عَلَىٰ بَشَرٍ مِّن شَىْءٍ ۗ

907. I take verse 87 to refer back to all the four groups just mentioned.

908. *Them, i.e.*, the Book, and Authority and Prophethood. They were taken away from the other People of the Book and entrusted to the Holy Prophet Muḥammad and his People.

909. *Qadara*: to weigh, judge, or estimate the value of capacity of anything; to have power so to do. *Cf. Qadīr* in 4:149 and n. 655. The Jews who denied the inspiration of Muḥammad had a good answer in their own books about the inspiration of Moses. To those who do not believe in Moses, the answer is more general: is it a just estimate of Allah to think either that He has not the power or the will to guide mankind, seeing that He is Omnipotent and the Source of all good? If you say that guidance comes, not through an inspired book or man, but through our general intelligence, we point to the spiritual ignorance of "you and your ancestors" the sad spiritual darkness of men and nations high in the intellectual scale.

Say: "Who then sent down
The Book which Moses brought?—
A light and guidance to man:[910]
But ye make it into
(Separate) sheets for show,[911]
While ye conceal much
(Of its contents): therein
Were ye taught that
Which ye knew not—
Neither ye nor your fathers."
Say: "Allah (sent it down)":
Then leave them to plunge
In vain discourse and trifling.

قُلْ مَنْ أَنزَلَ ٱلْكِتَـٰبَ ٱلَّذِى
جَآءَ بِهِۦ مُوسَىٰ نُورًا وَهُدًى لِّلنَّاسِ ۖ
تَجْعَلُونَهُۥ قَرَاطِيسَ تُبْدُونَهَا وَتُخْفُونَ كَثِيرًا ۖ
وَعُلِّمْتُم مَّا لَمْ تَعْلَمُوٓا۟ أَنتُمْ وَلَآ ءَابَآؤُكُمْ ۖ
قُلِ ٱللَّهُ ۖ ثُمَّ ذَرْهُمْ فِى خَوْضِهِمْ يَلْعَبُونَ

92. And this is a Book
Which We have sent down,
Bringing blessings,[912] and confirming
(The revelations) which came
Before it: that thou
Mayest warn the Mother[913]
Of Cities and all around her.
Those who believe
In the Hereafter,
Believe in this (Book),
And they are constant
In guarding their Prayers.[914]

(٩٢) وَهَـٰذَا كِتَـٰبٌ أَنزَلْنَـٰهُ
مُبَارَكٌ مُّصَدِّقُ ٱلَّذِى بَيْنَ يَدَيْهِ
وَلِتُنذِرَ أُمَّ ٱلْقُرَىٰ وَمَنْ حَوْلَهَا ۚ
وَٱلَّذِينَ يُؤْمِنُونَ بِٱلْـَٔاخِرَةِ يُؤْمِنُونَ بِهِۦ ۖ
وَهُمْ عَلَىٰ صَلَاتِهِمْ يُحَافِظُونَ

93. Who can be more wicked
Than one who inventeth
A lie against Allah,
Or said, "I have
Received inspiration,"

(٩٣) وَمَنْ أَظْلَمُ مِمَّنِ ٱفْتَرَىٰ عَلَى
ٱللَّهِ كَذِبًا أَوْ قَالَ أُوحِىَ إِلَىَّ

---

910. *Cf.* 5:47 and n. 750, and 5:49. In those passages Guidance (in practical conduct) is put before Light (or spiritual insight), as they refer to ordinary or average men. Here Light (or spiritual insight) is put first as the question is: does Allah send inspiration?

911. The Message to Moses had unity: it was one Book. The present Old Testament is a collection of odd books ("sheets") of various kinds: see Appendix II, end of S. 5. In this way you can make a show, but there is no unity, and much of the spirit of the original is lost or concealed or overlaid. The same applies to the New Testament: see Appendix III, after Appendix II.

912. *Mubārak*: blessed, as having received Allah's blessing; bringer of blessings to others, as having been blessed by Allah. Allah's highest blessing is the Guidance and Light which the Book brings to us, and which brings us nearer to Him.

913. *Mother of Cities*: Makkah, now the Qiblah and Centre of Islam. If this verse was (like the greater part of the Chapter) revealed in Makkah before the Hijrah, and before Makkah was made the Qiblah of Islam, Makkah was nonetheless the Mother of Cities, being traditionally associated with Abraham and with Adam and Eve (see 2:125, and n. 217 to 2:197).

All round Makkah: would mean, the whole world if we look upon Makkah as the Centre.

914. An earnest study of the Qur'ān is true worship; so is Prayer, and so are all deeds of goodness and charity.

When he hath received
None, or (again) who saith,
"I can reveal the like
Of what Allah hath revealed"?
If thou couldst but see
How the wicked (do fare)
In the flood of confusion
At death!—the angels
Stretch forth their hands,
(Saying), "Yield up your souls:[915]
This day shall ye receive
Your reward—a penalty
Of shame, for that ye used
To tell lies against Allah,
And scornfully to reject
Of His Signs!"

94. "And behold! ye come
To Us bare and alone
As We created you
For the first time:[916]
Ye have left behind you
All (the favours) which
We bestowed on you:
We see not with you
Your intercessors
Whom ye thought to be
Partners in your affairs:
So now all relations
Between you have been
Cut off, and your (pet) fancies
Have left you in the lurch!"[917]

وَلَمْ يُوحَ إِلَيْهِ شَىْءٌ وَمَن قَالَ
سَأُنزِلُ مِثْلَ مَآ أَنزَلَ ٱللَّهُ
وَلَوْ تَرَىٰٓ إِذِ ٱلظَّـٰلِمُونَ فِى غَمَرَٰتِ
ٱلْمَوْتِ وَٱلْمَلَـٰٓئِكَةُ بَاسِطُوٓا۟ أَيْدِيهِمْ
أَخْرِجُوٓا۟ أَنفُسَكُمُ
ٱلْيَوْمَ تُجْزَوْنَ عَذَابَ ٱلْهُونِ
بِمَا كُنتُمْ تَقُولُونَ عَلَى ٱللَّهِ غَيْرَ ٱلْحَقِّ
وَكُنتُمْ عَنْ ءَايَـٰتِهِۦ تَسْتَكْبِرُونَ

٩٤ وَلَقَدْ جِئْتُمُونَا فُرَٰدَىٰ
كَمَا خَلَقْنَـٰكُمْ أَوَّلَ مَرَّةٍ
وَتَرَكْتُم مَّا خَوَّلْنَـٰكُمْ وَرَآءَ ظُهُورِكُمْ
وَمَا نَرَىٰ مَعَكُمْ شُفَعَآءَكُمُ
ٱلَّذِينَ زَعَمْتُمْ أَنَّهُمْ فِيكُمْ شُرَكَـٰٓؤُا۟
لَقَد تَّقَطَّعَ بَيْنَكُمْ وَضَلَّ
عَنكُم مَّا كُنتُمْ تَزْعُمُونَ

915. *Yield up your souls*: or "get your souls to come out of your bodies." The wicked, we may suppose, are not anxious to part with the material existence in their bodies for the "reward" which in irony is stated to be there to welcome them.

916. Some of the various ideas connected with "Creation" are noted in n. 120 to 2:117. In the creation of man there are various processes. If his body was created out of clay, *i.e.*, earthy matter, there was an earlier process of the creation of such earthy matter. Here the body is left behind, and the soul is being addressed. The soul underwent various processes of fashioning and adapting to its various functions in its various surroundings (32:7-9). But each individual soul, after release from the body, comes back as it was created, with nothing more than its history, "the deeds which it has earned," which are really a part of it. Any exterior things given to help in its development, "the favours which We bestowed on you," it must necessarily leave behind, however it may have been proud of them. These exterior things may be material things, *e.g.*, wealth, property, signs of power, influence and pride such as sons, relatives, and friends, etc., or they may be intangible things, like talents, intellect, social gifts. etc.

917. The false ideas of intercessors, demi-gods, gods, saviours, etc., now vanish like unsubstantial visions, "leaving not a wrack behind." Now the soul is face to face with reality. Its personal responsibility is brought home to it.

SECTION 12.

95. It is Allah Who causeth[918]
The seed grain
And the date stone
To split and sprout.[919]
He causeth the living
To issue from the dead,
And He is the One
To cause the dead
To issue from the living.[920]
That is Allah: then how
Are ye deluded
Away from the truth?

96. He it is that cleaveth
The daybreak (from the dark):
He makes the night
For rest and tranquillity,

٩٥ إِنَّ ٱللَّهَ فَالِقُ
ٱلْحَبِّ وَٱلنَّوَىٰ
يُخْرِجُ ٱلْحَيَّ مِنَ ٱلْمَيِّتِ
وَمُخْرِجُ ٱلْمَيِّتِ مِنَ ٱلْحَيِّ
ذَٰلِكُمُ ٱللَّهُ فَأَنَّىٰ تُؤْفَكُونَ

٩٦ فَالِقُ ٱلْإِصْبَاحِ
وَجَعَلَ ٱلَّيْلَ سَكَنًا

918. Another beautiful nature passage, referring to Allah's wonderful artistry in His Creation. In how few and how simple words, the whole pageant of Creation is placed before us. Beginning from our humble animal needs and dependence on the vegetable world, we are asked to contemplate the interaction of the living and the dead. Here is mystic teaching, referring not only to physical life but to the higher life above the physical plane—not only to individual life but to the collective life of nations. Then we take a peep into the daily miracle of morning, noon, and night, and pass on to the stars that guide the distant mariner. We rise still higher to the mystery of the countless individuals from the one human soul—their sojourn and their destiny. So we get back to the heavens: the description of the luscious fruits which the "gentle rain from heaven" produces, leaves us to contemplate the spiritual fruits which faith will provide for us, with the aid of the showers of Allah's mercy.

919. The seed grain and the date stone are selected as types in the vegetable kingdom, showing how our physical life depends on it. The fruits mentioned later (in 6:99) start another allegory which we shall notice later. Botanists will notice that the seed grain includes the cereals (such as wheat, barley, rice, millet, etc.) which are monocotyledons, as well as the pulses (such as beans, peas, gram, etc.) and other seeds which are dicotyledons. These two represent the most important classes of food grains, while the date palm, a monocotyledon, represents for Arabia both food, fruit, confectionery, thatch and pillars for houses, shady groves in oases, and a standard measure of wealth and well-being. *"Split and sprout"*: both ideas are included in the root *falaqa,* and a third is expressed by the word "cleave" in the next verse, for the action of evolving daybreak from the dark. I might almost have used the word "churn," familiar to students of Hindu lore in the Hindu allegory of the "churning of the ocean." For vegetables, "split and sprout" represents a double process: (1) the seed divides, and (2) one part shoots up, seeking the light, and forming leaves and the visible parts of the future tree, and the other part digs down into the dark, forming the roots and seeking just that sustenance from the soil, which is adapted for the particular plant. This is just one small instance of the "judgement and ordering" of Allah, referred to in the next verse.

920. This does not mean that in physical nature there are no limits between life and non-life, between the organic and the inorganic. In fact physicists are baffled at the barrier between them and frankly confess that they cannot solve the mystery of Life. If there is such a barrier in physical nature, is it not all the more wonderful that Allah can create Life out of nothing? He has but to say, "Be," and it is. He can bring Life from non-Life and annihilate Life. But there are two other senses in which we can contemplate the contrast between the living and the dead. (1) We have just been speaking of the botanical world. Take it as a whole, and see the contrast between the winter of death, the spring of revivification, the summer of growth, and the autumn of decay, leading back to the death of winter. Here is a cycle of living from dead, and dead from living. (2) Take our spiritual life, individual or collective; we rise from the darkness of spiritual nothingness to the light of spiritual life; and if we do not follow the spiritual laws, Allah will take away that life and we shall be again as dead. We may die many deaths. The keys of life and death are in Allah's hands. Neither Life nor Death are fortuitous things. Behind them both is the Cause of Causes—and only He.

And the sun and moon
For the reckoning (of time):
Such is the judgement[921]
And ordering of (Him),
The Exalted in Power,
The Omniscient.

وَٱلشَّمْسَ وَٱلْقَمَرَ حُسْبَانًا
ذَٰلِكَ تَقْدِيرُ ٱلْعَزِيزِ ٱلْعَلِيمِ

97. It is He Who maketh
The stars (as beacons) for you,
That ye may guide yourselves,
With their help,
Through the dark spaces
Of land and sea:[922]
We detail Our Signs
For people who know.

٩٧ وَهُوَ ٱلَّذِى جَعَلَ لَكُمُ ٱلنُّجُومَ
لِتَهْتَدُوا۟ بِهَا فِى ظُلُمَٰتِ ٱلْبَرِّ وَٱلْبَحْرِ
قَدْ فَصَّلْنَا ٱلْءَايَٰتِ لِقَوْمٍ يَعْلَمُونَ

98. It is He Who hath
Produced you[923]
From a single Person;
Here is a place of sojourn
And a place of departure:[924]
We detail Our signs
For people who understand.

٩٨ وَهُوَ ٱلَّذِىٓ أَنشَأَكُم
مِّن نَّفْسٍ وَٰحِدَةٍ فَمُسْتَقَرٌّ وَمُسْتَوْدَعٌ
قَدْ فَصَّلْنَا ٱلْءَايَٰتِ لِقَوْمٍ يَفْقَهُونَ

99. It is He Who sendeth down
Rain from the skies;[925]
With it We produce
Vegetation of all kinds:
From some We produce
Green (crops), out of which

٩٩ وَهُوَ ٱلَّذِىٓ أَنزَلَ مِنَ ٱلسَّمَآءِ مَآءً
فَأَخْرَجْنَا بِهِۦ نَبَاتَ كُلِّ شَىْءٍ
فَأَخْرَجْنَا مِنْهُ خَضِرًا نُّخْرِجُ

921. The night, the day, the sun, the moon—the great astronomical universe of Allah. How far, and yet how near to us! Allah's universe is boundless, and we can barely comprehend even its relations to us. But this last we must try to do if we want to be numbered with "the people who know." *Taqdīr: Cf.* 6:91 and n. 909, and 4:149 and n. 655.

922. See the last note. At sea, or in deserts or forests, or "in fairy scenes forlorn"—whenever we sweep over wide spaces, it is the stars that act as our guides, just as the sun and moon have already been mentioned as our measures of time.

923. *Produced: ansha'a* = made you grow, increase, develop, reach maturity: another of the processes of creation. This supplements n. 120 to 2:117 and n. 916 to 6:94. It is one of the wonders of Allah's Creation, that from one person we have grown to be so many, and each individual has so many faculties and capacities, and yet we are all one. In the next verse we have the allegory of grapes and other fruits: all grapes may be similar to look at, yet each variety has a distinctive flavour and other distinctive qualities, and each individual grape may have its own special qualities. So for man.

924. In the sojourn of this life we must respond to Allah's hand in fashioning us, by making full use of all our faculties, and we must get ready for our departure into the Life that will be eternal.

925. Our allegory now brings us to maturity, the fruit, the harvest, the vintage. Through the seed we came up from nothingness of life; we lived our daily life of rest and work and passed the milestones of time; we had the spiritual experience of traversing through vast spaces in the spiritual world, guiding our course through the star of Faith; we grew; and now for the harvest or the vintage! So will man if he has produced the fruits of Faith!

We produce grain,
Heaped up (at harvest);
Out of the date palm
And its sheaths (or spathes)
(Come) clusters of dates
Hanging low and near:
And (then there are) gardens
Of grapes, and olives,
And pomegranates,
Each similar (in kind)
Yet different (in variety):[926]
When they begin to bear fruit,
Feast your eyes with the fruit
And the ripeness thereof.[927]
Behold! in these things
There are Signs for people
Who believe.[928]

مِنْهُ حَبًّا مُّتَرَاكِبًا
وَمِنَ ٱلنَّخْلِ مِن طَلْعِهَا
قِنْوَانٌ دَانِيَةٌ وَجَنَّٰتٍ مِّنْ
أَعْنَابٍ وَٱلزَّيْتُونَ وَٱلرُّمَّانَ
مُشْتَبِهًا وَغَيْرَ مُتَشَٰبِهٍ ۗ
ٱنظُرُوٓا۟ إِلَىٰ ثَمَرِهِۦٓ إِذَآ أَثْمَرَ وَيَنْعِهِۦٓ ۚ
إِنَّ فِى ذَٰلِكُمْ لَءَايَٰتٍ
لِّقَوْمٍ يُؤْمِنُونَ

100. Yet they make
The Jinns equals[929]
With Allah, though Allah
Did create the Jinns;

وَجَعَلُوا۟ لِلَّهِ ١٠٠
شُرَكَآءَ ٱلْجِنَّ وَخَلَقَهُمْ ۖ

926. Each fruit—whether it is grapes, or olives, or pomegranates—looks alike in its species, and yet each variety may be different in flavour, consistency, shape, size, colour, juice or oil contents, proportion of seed to fruit, etc. In each variety individuals may be different. Apply the allegory to man, whose varied spiritual fruit may be equally different and yet equally valuable!

927. And so we finish this wonderful allegory. Search through the world's literature, and see if you can find another such song or hymn—so fruity in its literary flavour, so profound in its spiritual meaning!

928. There is a refrain in this song, which is subtly varied. In verse 97 it is: "We detail our Signs for people who *know*." So far we were speaking of the things we see around us everyday. Knowledge is the appropriate instrument for these things. In verse 98 we read: "We detail Our Signs for people who *understand*." Understanding is a higher faculty than knowledge, and is necessary for seeing the mystery and meaning of this life. At the end of verse 99 we have: "In these things there are Signs for people who *believe*." Here we are speaking of the real fruits of spiritual life. For them Faith is necessary, as bringing us nearer to Allah.

929. *Jinns*: who are they? In 18:50 we are told that Iblis was one of the Jinns, and it is suggested that that was why he disobeyed the Command of Allah. But in that passage and other similar passages, we are told that Allah commanded the angels to bow down to Adam, and they obeyed except Iblīs. That implies that Iblīs had been of the company of angels. In many passages Jinns and men are spoken of together. In 55:14-15, man is stated to have been created from clay, while Jinns from a flame of fire. The root meaning of *junna, yujannu*, is "to be covered or hidden," and *janna yajunnu*, in the active voice, "to cover or hide," as in 6:76. Some people say that *jinn* therefore means the hidden qualities or capacities in man; others that it means wild or jungle folk hidden in the hills or forests. I do not wish to be dogmatic, but I think, from a collation and study of the Quranic passages, that the meaning is simply "a spirit," or an invisible or hidden force. In folklore stories and romances like the Arabian Nights they become personified into fantastic forms, but with them we are not concerned here. Both the Qur'ān and the Hadith describe the Jinn as a definite species of living beings. They are created out of fire and are like man, may believe or disbelieve, accept or reject guidance. The authoritative Islamic texts show that they are not merely a hidden force, or a spirit. They are personalized beings who enjoy a certain amount of free will and thus will be called to account. (Eds.).

And they falsely,
Having no knowledge,
Attribute to Him
Sons and daughters.
Praise and glory be
To Him! (for He is) above
What they attribute to Him!

وَخَرَقُوا لَهُ بَنِينَ وَبَنَاتٍ بِغَيْرِ عِلْمٍ
سُبْحَانَهُ وَتَعَالَىٰ
عَمَّا يَصِفُونَ

SECTION 13.

101. To Him is due
The primal origin
Of the heavens and the earth:[930]
How can He have a son
When He hath no consort?
He created all things,
And He hath full knowledge
Of all things.

١٠١ بَدِيعُ السَّمَاوَاتِ وَالْأَرْضِ
أَنَّىٰ يَكُونُ لَهُ وَلَدٌ وَلَمْ تَكُن لَّهُ صَاحِبَةٌ
وَخَلَقَ كُلَّ شَيْءٍ وَهُوَ بِكُلِّ شَيْءٍ عَلِيمٌ

102. That is Allah, your Lord!
There is no god but He,
The Creator of all things;
Then worship ye Him;
And He hath power
To dispose of all affairs.

١٠٢ ذَٰلِكُمُ اللَّهُ رَبُّكُمْ لَا إِلَٰهَ إِلَّا هُوَ
خَالِقُ كُلِّ شَيْءٍ فَاعْبُدُوهُ
وَهُوَ عَلَىٰ كُلِّ شَيْءٍ وَكِيلٌ

103. No vision can grasp Him.
But His grasp is over
All vision: He is
Above all comprehension,[931]
Yet is acquainted with all things.

١٠٣ لَّا تُدْرِكُهُ الْأَبْصَارُ
وَهُوَ يُدْرِكُ الْأَبْصَارَ
وَهُوَ اللَّطِيفُ الْخَبِيرُ

104. "Now have come to you,
From your Lord, proofs
(To open your eyes):
If any will see,
It will be for (the good
Of) his own soul;
If any will be blind,
It will be to his own
(Harm): I am not (here)
To watch over your doings."[932]

١٠٤ قَدْ جَاءَكُم بَصَائِرُ مِن رَّبِّكُمْ
فَمَنْ أَبْصَرَ فَلِنَفْسِهِ
وَمَنْ عَمِيَ فَعَلَيْهَا
وَمَا أَنَا عَلَيْكُم بِحَفِيظٍ

930. *Cf.* 2:117 and n. 120.

931. *Latif*: fine, subtle, so fine and subtle as to be invisible to the physical eye; so fine as to be imperceptible to the senses; so pure as to be above the mental or spiritual vision of men. The active meaning should also be understood: 'one who understands the finest mysteries.' *Cf.* 22:63, and n. 2844.

932. I understand "Say" to be understood in the beginning of this verse. The words would then be the words of the Prophet, as in fact is suggested in verse 107 below. That is why I have enclosed them in inverted commas.

105. Thus do We explain
The Signs by various
(symbols)[933]
That they may say,
"Thou hast learnt this
(From somebody),"
And that We may make
The matter clear
To those who know.[934]

١٠٥ وَكَذَٰلِكَ
نُصَرِّفُ ٱلْأَيَٰتِ
وَلِيَقُولُواْ دَرَسْتَ
وَلِنُبَيِّنَهُۥ لِقَوْمٍ يَعْلَمُونَ

106. Follow what thou art taught
By inspiration from thy Lord:
There is no god but He:
And turn aside from those
Who join gods with Allah.

١٠٦ ٱتَّبِعْ مَآ أُوحِىَ إِلَيْكَ مِن رَّبِّكَ
لَآ إِلَٰهَ إِلَّا هُوَ وَأَعْرِضْ عَنِ
ٱلْمُشْرِكِينَ

107. If it had been Allah's Plan,[935]
They would not have taken
False gods: but We
Made thee not one
To watch over their doings,
Nor art thou set
Over them to dispose
Of their affairs.

١٠٧ وَلَوْ شَآءَ ٱللَّهُ
مَآ أَشْرَكُواْ
وَمَا جَعَلْنَٰكَ عَلَيْهِمْ حَفِيظًا
وَمَآ أَنتَ عَلَيْهِم بِوَكِيلٍ

108. Revile not ye
Those whom they call upon
Besides Allah, lest
They out of spite
Revile Allah
In their ignorance.
Thus have We made

١٠٨ وَلَا تَسُبُّواْ ٱلَّذِينَ
يَدْعُونَ مِن دُونِ ٱللَّهِ
فَيَسُبُّواْ ٱللَّهَ عَدْوًۢا بِغَيْرِ عِلْمٍ
كَذَٰلِكَ

933. *Cf.* 6:65 and n. 889.

934. The teaching in the Qur'ān explains things by various symbols, parables, narratives, and appeals to nature. Each time, a new phase of the question is presented to our minds. This is what a diligent and earnest teacher would do, such as was Muḥammad Muṣṭafā. Those who were in search of knowledge and had thus acquired some knowledge of spiritual things were greatly helped to understand more clearly the things of which, before the varied explanations, they had only one-sided knowledge.

935. Allah's Plan is to use the human will to cooperate in understanding Him and His relations to us. This is the answer to an objector who might say: "If He is All-Powerful, why does sin or evil exist in the world? Can He not destroy it?" He can, but His Plan is different, and in any case it is not for a Teacher to force anyone to accept the truths which he is inspired to preach and proclaim.

Alluring to each people[936]
Its own doings.
In the end will they
Return to their Lord,
And We shall then
Tell them the truth
Of all that they did.

زَيَّنَّا لِكُلِّ أُمَّةٍ عَمَلَهُمْ
ثُمَّ إِلَىٰ رَبِّهِم مَّرْجِعُهُمْ
فَيُنَبِّئُهُم بِمَا كَانُوا۟ يَعْمَلُونَ

109. They swear their strongest
Oaths by Allah, that if
A (special) Sign came
To them, by it they would
Believe. Say: "Certainly
(All) Signs are in the power
Of Allah: but what will
Make you (Muslims) realise
That (even) if (special) Signs
Came, they will not believe?"[937]

١٠٩ وَأَقْسَمُوا۟ بِٱللَّهِ جَهْدَ أَيْمَٰنِهِمْ
لَئِن جَآءَتْهُمْ ءَايَةٌ لَّيُؤْمِنُنَّ بِهَا
قُلْ إِنَّمَا ٱلْـَٔايَٰتُ عِندَ ٱللَّهِ
وَمَا يُشْعِرُكُمْ أَنَّهَآ إِذَا
جَآءَتْ لَا يُؤْمِنُونَ

110. We (too) shall turn
To (confusion) their hearts[938]
And their eyes, even as they
Refused to believe in this
In the first instance:
We shall leave them

١١٠ وَنُقَلِّبُ أَفْـِٔدَتَهُمْ
وَأَبْصَٰرَهُمْ كَمَا لَمْ يُؤْمِنُوا۟ بِهِۦٓ
أَوَّلَ مَرَّةٍ وَنَذَرُهُمْ

936. A man's actual personal religion depends upon many things: his personal psychology, the background of his life, his hidden or repressed feelings, tendencies, or history (which psychoanalysis tries to unravel), his hereditary dispositions or antipathies, and all the subtle influences of his education and his environment. The task before the man of God is: (1) to use any of these which can subserve the higher ends; (2) to purify such as have been misused; (3) to introduce new ideas and modes of looking at things; and (4) to combat what is wrong and cannot be mended—all for the purpose of leading to the truth and gradually letting in spiritual light where there was darkness before. If that is not done with discretion and the skill of a spiritual Teacher, there may be not only a reaction of obstinacy, but an unseemly show of dishonour to the true God and His Truth, and doubts would spread among the weaker brethren whose faith is shallow and infirm. What happens to individuals is true collectively of nations or groups of people. They think in their self-obsession that their own ideas are right. Allah in His infinite compassion bears with them, and asks those who have purer ideas of faith not to vilify the weaknesses of their neighbours, lest the neighbours in their turn vilify the real truth and make matters even worse than before. Insofar as there are mistakes, Allah will forgive and send His grace for helping ignorance and folly. Insofar as there is active evil, He will deal with it in His own way. Of course the righteous man must not hide his light under a bushel, or compromise with evil, or refuse to establish right living where he has the power to do so.

937. If the unbelievers are merely obstinate, nothing will convince them. There is no story more full of miracles than the story of Jesus. Yet in that same story we are told that Jesus said: "A wicked adulterous generation seeketh after a sign; and there shall no sign be given unto it, but the sign of the Prophet Jonah": Matt. xvi. 4. There are Signs given by Allah everyday—understood by those who believe. A mere insistence upon some particular or special Sign means mere contumacy and misunderstanding of the spiritual world.

938. Where there is sheer obstinacy and ridicule of faith, the result will be that such a sinner's heart will be hardened and his eyes will be sealed, so that he cannot even see the things visible to ordinary mortals. The sinner gathers impetus in his descent towards wrong.

In their trespasses,
To wander in distraction.[939]

فِي طُغْيَٰنِهِمْ يَعْمَهُونَ

C. 80.—(6:111-129.) Those in obstinate rebellion
Against Allah are merely deceived
And deceive each other. Leave them
Alone, but trust and obey Allah
Openly and in the inmost recesses
Of your heart. The plots of the wicked
Are but plots against their own souls.

SECTION 14.

111. Even if We did send
Unto them angels,
And the dead did speak
Unto them, and We gathered
Together all things before[940]
Their very eyes, they are not
The ones to believe,
Unless it is in Allah's Plan.
But most of them
Ignore (the truth).

١١١ وَلَوْ أَنَّنَا نَزَّلْنَآ إِلَيْهِمُ ٱلْمَلَٰٓئِكَةَ
وَكَلَّمَهُمُ ٱلْمَوْتَىٰ وَحَشَرْنَا عَلَيْهِمْ كُلَّ شَىْءٍ قُبُلًا
مَّا كَانُوا۟ لِيُؤْمِنُوٓا۟ إِلَّآ أَن يَشَآءَ ٱللَّهُ
وَلَٰكِنَّ أَكْثَرَهُمْ يَجْهَلُونَ

112. Likewise did We make
For every Messenger
An enemy—evil ones[941]
Among men and Jinns,
Inspiring each other
With flowery discourses
By way of deception.
If thy Lord had so planned,
They would not have
Done it: so leave them
And their inventions alone.

١١٢ وَكَذَٰلِكَ جَعَلْنَا لِكُلِّ نَبِىٍّ
عَدُوًّا شَيَٰطِينَ ٱلْإِنسِ وَٱلْجِنِّ
يُوحِى بَعْضُهُمْ إِلَىٰ بَعْضٍ زُخْرُفَ
ٱلْقَوْلِ غُرُورًا وَلَوْ شَآءَ رَبُّكَ مَا فَعَلُوهُ
فَذَرْهُمْ وَمَا يَفْتَرُونَ

113. To such (deceit)
Let the hearts of those
Incline, who have no faith

١١٣ وَلِتَصْغَىٰٓ إِلَيْهِ أَفْـِٔدَةُ
ٱلَّذِينَ لَا يُؤْمِنُونَ

939. *Cf.* 2:15. Allah's grace is always ready to help human weakness or ignorance, and to accept repentance and give forgiveness. But where the sinner is in actual rebellion, he will be given rope, and it will be his own fault if he wanders about distractedly, without any certain hope or refuge.

940. The most stupendous miracles even according to their ideas would not have convinced them. If the whole pageant of the spiritual world were brought before them, they would not have believed, because they—of their own choice and will—refuse knowledge and faith.

941. What happened in the history of the Holy Prophet happens in the history of all righteous men who have a Message from Allah. The spirit of evil is ever active and uses men to practise deception by means of highly embellished words and plausible excuses and objections. Allah permits these things in His Plan. It is not for us to complain. Our faith is tested, and we must stand the test steadfastly.

In the Hereafter: let them
Delight in it, and let them
Earn from it what they may.[942]

بِٱلۡأٓخِرَةِ وَلِيَرۡضَوۡهُ
وَلِيَقۡتَرِفُواْ مَا هُم مُّقۡتَرِفُونَ

114. Say: "Shall I seek
For judge other than Allah?—
When He it is
Who hath sent unto you
The Book, explained in detail."[943]
They know full well,
To whom We have given
The Book, that it hath been
Sent down from thy Lord
In truth. Never be then
Of those who doubt.

﴿١١٤﴾ أَفَغَيۡرَ ٱللَّهِ أَبۡتَغِي حَكَمٗا
وَهُوَ ٱلَّذِيٓ أَنزَلَ إِلَيۡكُمُ ٱلۡكِتَٰبَ مُفَصَّلٗاۚ
وَٱلَّذِينَ ءَاتَيۡنَٰهُمُ ٱلۡكِتَٰبَ يَعۡلَمُونَ
أَنَّهُۥ مُنَزَّلٞ مِّن رَّبِّكَ بِٱلۡحَقِّۖ
فَلَا تَكُونَنَّ مِنَ ٱلۡمُمۡتَرِينَ

115. The Word of thy Lord
Doth find its fulfilment
In truth and in justice:
None can change His Words:
For He is the one Who
Heareth and knoweth all.

﴿١١٥﴾ وَتَمَّتۡ كَلِمَتُ رَبِّكَ صِدۡقٗا
وَعَدۡلٗاۚ لَّا مُبَدِّلَ لِكَلِمَٰتِهِۦۚ
وَهُوَ ٱلسَّمِيعُ ٱلۡعَلِيمُ

116. Wert thou to follow
The common run of those
On earth, they will lead
Thee away from the Way
Of Allah. They follow
Nothing but conjecture: they
Do nothing but lie.

﴿١١٦﴾ وَإِن تُطِعۡ أَكۡثَرَ مَن فِي ٱلۡأَرۡضِ
يُضِلُّوكَ عَن سَبِيلِ ٱللَّهِۚ إِن يَتَّبِعُونَ
إِلَّا ٱلظَّنَّ وَإِنۡ هُمۡ إِلَّا يَخۡرُصُونَ

117. Thy Lord knoweth best
Who strayeth from His Way:
He knoweth best
Who they are that receive
His guidance.

﴿١١٧﴾ إِنَّ رَبَّكَ هُوَ أَعۡلَمُ مَن يَضِلُّ عَن سَبِيلِهِۦۖ
وَهُوَ أَعۡلَمُ بِٱلۡمُهۡتَدِينَ

118. So eat of (meats)
On which Allah's name
Hath been pronounced,

﴿١١٨﴾ فَكُلُواْ مِمَّا ذُكِرَ ٱسۡمُ ٱللَّهِ عَلَيۡهِ

---

942. People who have no faith in the future destiny of man listen to and are taken in by the deceit of evil. If they take a delight in it, let them. See what they gain by it. Their gains will be as deceitful as their delight. For the end of evil must be evil.

943. The righteous man seeks no other standard of judgement but Allah's Will. How can he, when Allah in His grace has explained His Will in the Qur'ān, with details which men of every capacity can understand? The humblest can learn lessons of right conduct in daily life, and the most advanced can find the highest wisdom in its spiritual teaching, enriched as it is with all kinds of beautiful illustrations from nature and the story of man.

If ye have faith
In His Signs.

إِن كُنتُم بِـَٔايَـٰتِهِۦ مُؤْمِنِينَ

119. Why should ye not
Eat of (meats) on which
Allah's name hath been
Pronounced, when He hath
Explained to you in detail
What is forbidden to you—
Except under compulsion[944]
Of necessity?
But many do mislead (men)
By their appetites unchecked
By knowledge. Thy Lord
Knoweth best those who transgress.

(١١٩) وَمَا لَكُمْ أَلَّا تَأْكُلُوا۟ مِمَّا
ذُكِرَ ٱسْمُ ٱللَّهِ عَلَيْهِ وَقَدْ فَصَّلَ لَكُم
مَّا حَرَّمَ عَلَيْكُمْ إِلَّا مَا ٱضْطُرِرْتُمْ إِلَيْهِ
وَإِنَّ كَثِيرًا لَّيُضِلُّونَ بِأَهْوَآئِهِم بِغَيْرِ عِلْمٍ
إِنَّ رَبَّكَ هُوَ أَعْلَمُ بِٱلْمُعْتَدِينَ

120. Eschew all sin,
Open or secret:
Those who earn sin
Will get due recompense
For their "earnings."

(١٢٠) وَذَرُوا۟ ظَـٰهِرَ ٱلْإِثْمِ وَبَاطِنَهُۥٓ إِنَّ ٱلَّذِينَ
يَكْسِبُونَ ٱلْإِثْمَ سَيُجْزَوْنَ بِمَا كَانُوا۟ يَقْتَرِفُونَ

121. Eat not of (meats)
On which Allah's name
Hath not been pronounced:
That would be impiety.
But the evil ones
Ever inspire their friends
To contend with you
If ye were to obey them,
Ye would indeed be Pagans.

(١٢١) وَلَا تَأْكُلُوا۟ مِمَّا لَمْ يُذْكَرِ
ٱسْمُ ٱللَّهِ عَلَيْهِ وَإِنَّهُۥ لَفِسْقٌ
وَإِنَّ ٱلشَّيَـٰطِينَ لَيُوحُونَ إِلَىٰٓ أَوْلِيَآئِهِمْ
لِيُجَـٰدِلُوكُمْ وَإِنْ أَطَعْتُمُوهُمْ إِنَّكُمْ لَمُشْرِكُونَ

SECTION 15.

122. Can he who was dead,[945]
To whom We gave life,
And a Light whereby
He can walk amongst men,
Be like him who is

(١٢٢) أَوَمَن كَانَ مَيْتًا فَأَحْيَيْنَـٰهُ وَجَعَلْنَا لَهُۥ
نُورًا يَمْشِى بِهِۦ فِى ٱلنَّاسِ كَمَن مَّثَلُهُۥ

---

944. *Cf.* 5:4. When a clear law has explained what is lawful and unlawful in food, it is wrong to raise fresh scruples and mislead the ignorant.

945. Here is an allegory of the good man with his divine mission and the evil man with his mission of evil. The former, before he got his spiritual life, was like one dead. It was Allah's grace that gave him spiritual life, with a Light by which he could walk and guide his own footsteps as well as the footsteps of those who are willing to follow Allah's light. The opposite type is that which hates Allah's light, which lives in the depths of darkness, and which plots and burrows against all that is good. But the plots of evil recoil on itself, although it thinks that they will hurt the good. Can these two types be for a moment compared with each other? Perhaps the lead in every centre of populations is taken by the men of evil. But the good men should not be discouraged. They should work in righteousness and fulfil their mission.

In the depths of darkness,
From which he can
Never come out?
Thus to those without Faith
Their own deeds seem pleasing.

فِي الظُّلُمَٰتِ لَيْسَ بِخَارِجٍ مِّنْهَا كَذَٰلِكَ
زُيِّنَ لِلْكَٰفِرِينَ مَا كَانُوا يَعْمَلُونَ

123. Thus have We placed
Leaders in every town,
Its wicked men, to plot
(And burrow) therein:
But they only plot
Against their own souls,
And they perceive it not.

(١٢٣) وَكَذَٰلِكَ جَعَلْنَا فِي كُلِّ قَرْيَةٍ
أَكَٰبِرَ مُجْرِمِيهَا لِيَمْكُرُوا فِيهَا
وَمَا يَمْكُرُونَ إِلَّا بِأَنفُسِهِمْ وَمَا يَشْعُرُونَ

124. When there comes to them
A Sign (from Allah),
They say: "We shall not
Believe until we receive
One (exactly) like those
Received by Allah's messengers."[946]
Allah knoweth best where
(And how) to carry out
His mission. Soon
Will the wicked
Be overtaken by
Humiliation before Allah,
And a severe punishment,
For all their plots.

(١٢٤) وَإِذَا جَآءَتْهُمْ ءَايَةٌ
قَالُوا لَن نُّؤْمِنَ حَتَّىٰ نُؤْتَىٰ
مِثْلَ مَآ أُوتِيَ رُسُلُ اللَّهِ
اللَّهُ أَعْلَمُ حَيْثُ يَجْعَلُ رِسَالَتَهُۥ
سَيُصِيبُ الَّذِينَ أَجْرَمُوا
صَغَارٌ عِندَ اللَّهِ وَعَذَابٌ
شَدِيدٌ بِمَا كَانُوا يَمْكُرُونَ

125. Those whom Allah (in His Plan)
Willeth to guide—He openeth[947]
Their breast to Islam;
Those whom He willeth
To leave straying—He maketh

(١٢٥) فَمَن يُرِدِ اللَّهُ أَن يَهْدِيَهُۥ يَشْرَحْ
صَدْرَهُۥ لِلْإِسْلَٰمِ وَمَن يُرِدْ أَن يُضِلَّهُۥ يَجْعَلْ

946. Besides the teaching in Allah's Word, and the teaching in Allah's world, of nature and history and human contacts, many Signs come to the men of God, which they humbly receive and try to understand; and many Signs also come to the ungodly, in the shape of warnings or otherwise, which the ungodly either do not heed, or deliberately reject. The Signs in the two cases are not the same, and that becomes one of their perverse arguments against faith. But Allah's working will be according to His own Will and Plan, and not according to the wishes or whims of the ungodly.

947. Allah's Universal Plan is the *Qaḍā wa Qadr,* which is so much misunderstood. That Plan is unalterable, and that is His Will. It means that in the spiritual world, as in the physical world, there are laws of justice, mercy, grace, penalty, etc., which work as surely as anything we know. If, then, a man refuses Faith, becomes a rebel, with each step he goes further and further down, and his pace will be accelerated; he will scarcely be able to take spiritual breath, and his recovery—in spite of Allah's mercy which he has rejected—will be as difficult as if he had to climb up to the skies. On the other hand, the godly will find, with each step, the next step easier. Jesus expressed this truth paradoxically: "He that hath, to him shall be given; but he that hath not, from him shall be taken away even that which he hath": Mark. iv. 25. John (vi. 65) makes Jesus say: "No man can come unto me, except it were given unto him of my Father."

Their breast close and constricted,
As if they had to climb
Up to the skies: thus
Doth Allah (heap) the penalty
On those who refuse to believe.

صَدْرَهُۥ ضَيِّقًا حَرَجًا كَأَنَّمَا يَصَّعَّدُ
فِى ٱلسَّمَآءِ ۚ كَذَٰلِكَ يَجْعَلُ ٱللَّهُ ٱلرِّجْسَ
عَلَى ٱلَّذِينَ لَا يُؤْمِنُونَ

126. This is the Way
Of thy Lord, leading straight:
We have detailed the Signs
For those who
Receive admonition.

(١٢٦) وَهَٰذَا صِرَٰطُ رَبِّكَ مُسْتَقِيمًا ۗ
قَدْ فَصَّلْنَا ٱلْءَايَٰتِ لِقَوْمٍ يَذَّكَّرُونَ

127. For them will be a Home[948]
Of Peace in the presence
Of their Lord: He will be
Their Friend, because
They practised (righteousness).

(١٢٧) لَهُمْ دَارُ ٱلسَّلَٰمِ عِندَ رَبِّهِمْ ۖ
وَهُوَ وَلِيُّهُم بِمَا كَانُوا۟ يَعْمَلُونَ

128. One day will He gather
Them all together, (and say):
"O ye assembly of Jinns![949]
Much (toll) did ye take
Of men." Their friends
Amongst men will say:
"Our Lord! we made profit[950]
From each other: but (alas!)
We reached our term—
Which Thou didst appoint
For us." He will say:
"The Fire be your dwelling place:
You will dwell therein forever,
Except as Allah willeth."[951]
For thy Lord is full
Of wisdom and knowledge.

(١٢٨) وَيَوْمَ يَحْشُرُهُمْ جَمِيعًا
يَٰمَعْشَرَ ٱلْجِنِّ قَدِ ٱسْتَكْثَرْتُم مِّنَ ٱلْإِنسِ ۖ
وَقَالَ أَوْلِيَآؤُهُم مِّنَ ٱلْإِنسِ رَبَّنَا ٱسْتَمْتَعَ
بَعْضُنَا بِبَعْضٍ وَبَلَغْنَآ أَجَلَنَا ٱلَّذِىٓ
أَجَّلْتَ لَنَا ۚ قَالَ ٱلنَّارُ مَثْوَىٰكُمْ
خَٰلِدِينَ فِيهَآ إِلَّا مَا شَآءَ ٱللَّهُ ۗ إِنَّ
رَبَّكَ حَكِيمٌ عَلِيمٌ

129. Thus do We make
The wrongdoers turn
To each other, because
Of what they earn.[952]

(١٢٩) وَكَذَٰلِكَ نُوَلِّى بَعْضَ ٱلظَّٰلِمِينَ بَعْضًۢا
بِمَا كَانُوا۟ يَكْسِبُونَ

948. *Cf.* 10:25.

949. Jinns are spirits—here evil spirits. See 6:100, n. 929.

950. It is common experience that the forces of evil make an alliance with each other, and seem thus to make a profit by their mutual log-rolling. But this is only in this material world. When the limited term expires, their unholy bargains will be exposed, and there will be nothing but regrets.

951. Eternity and infinity are abstract terms. They have no precise meaning in our human experience. The qualification, "except as Allah willeth," makes it more intelligble, as we can form some idea—however inadequate—of a Will and Plan, and we know Allah by His attribute of Mercy as well as of Justice.

952. See n. 950 above. Evil consorts with evil because of their mutual bargains. But in doing so they save the righteous from further temptation.

C. 81.—Allah punishes not mere shortcoming:
(6:130-150.) There are degrees in good and evil
Deeds. Allah is Merciful, but
His Plan is sure, and none
Can stand in its way. We must
Avoid all superstition, and all excess,
And humbly ask for His guidance.

SECTION 16.

130. "O ye assembly of Jinns
And men! came there not
Unto you messengers from
amongst you,[953]
Setting forth unto you
My Signs, and warning you
Of the meeting of this Day
Of yours?" They will say:
"We bear witness against
Ourselves." It was
The life of this world
That deceived them. So
Against themselves will they
Bear witness that they
Rejected Faith.

١٣٠ يَٰمَعۡشَرَ ٱلۡجِنِّ وَٱلۡإِنسِ
أَلَمۡ يَأۡتِكُمۡ رُسُلٞ مِّنكُمۡ
يَقُصُّونَ عَلَيۡكُمۡ ءَايَٰتِي
وَيُنذِرُونَكُمۡ لِقَآءَ يَوۡمِكُمۡ هَٰذَاۚ
قَالُواْ شَهِدۡنَا عَلَىٰٓ أَنفُسِنَاۖ
وَغَرَّتۡهُمُ ٱلۡحَيَوٰةُ ٱلدُّنۡيَا وَشَهِدُواْ
عَلَىٰٓ أَنفُسِهِمۡ أَنَّهُمۡ كَانُواْ كَٰفِرِينَ

131. (The messengers were sent) thus,
For thy Lord would not
Destroy, for their wrongdoing
Men's habitations whilst
Their occupants were unwarned.

١٣١ ذَٰلِكَ أَن لَّمۡ يَكُن رَّبُّكَ مُهۡلِكَ
ٱلۡقُرَىٰ بِظُلۡمٖ وَأَهۡلُهَا غَٰفِلُونَ

132. To all are degrees (or ranks)[954]
According to their deeds:
For thy Lord
Is not unmindful
Of anything that they do.

١٣٢ وَلِكُلّٖ دَرَجَٰتٞ مِّمَّا عَمِلُواْۚ
وَمَا رَبُّكَ بِغَٰفِلٍ عَمَّا يَعۡمَلُونَ

133. Thy Lord is Self-sufficient,[955]
Full of Mercy: if it were

١٣٣ وَرَبُّكَ ٱلۡغَنِيُّ ذُو ٱلرَّحۡمَةِۚ إِن

953. *Messengers from amongst you.* This is addressed to the whole gathering of men and Jinns. (R).

954. On good and evil there are infinite degrees, in our deeds and motives: so will there be degrees in our spiritual position. For everything is known to Allah, better than it is to ourselves.

955. Allah is not dependent on our prayer or service. It is out of His Mercy that He desires our own good. Any race or people to whom He gives chances should understand that its failure does not affect Allah. He could create others in their place, as He did in times past, and is doing in our own day, if only we had the wit to see it.

His Will, He could destroy
You, and in your place
Appoint whom He will
As your successors, even as
He raised you up
From the posterity
Of other people.

يَشَأْ يُذْهِبْكُمْ وَيَسْتَخْلِفْ
مِنۢ بَعْدِكُم مَّا يَشَآءُ كَمَآ أَنشَأَكُم
مِّن ذُرِّيَّةِ قَوْمٍ ءَاخَرِينَ

134. All that hath been[956]
Promised unto you
Will come to pass:
Nor can ye frustrate it
(In the least bit).

١٣٤ إِنَّ مَا تُوعَدُونَ لَءَاتٍ
وَمَآ أَنتُم بِمُعْجِزِينَ

135. Say: "O my people!
Do whatever ye can:[957]
I will do (my part):
Soon will ye know
Who it is whose end
Will be (best) in the Hereafter:
Certain it is that
The wrongdoers will not prosper."

١٣٥ قُلْ يَٰقَوْمِ ٱعْمَلُوا۟ عَلَىٰ مَكَانَتِكُمْ
إِنِّى عَامِلٌ فَسَوْفَ تَعْلَمُونَ
مَن تَكُونُ لَهُۥ عَٰقِبَةُ ٱلدَّارِ
إِنَّهُۥ لَا يُفْلِحُ ٱلظَّٰلِمُونَ

136. Out of what Allah
Hath produced in abundance
In tilth and in cattle,
They assigned Him a share:
They say, according to their
fancies:[958]
"This is for Allah, and this—
For Our 'partners'"!
But the share of their "partners"

١٣٦ وَجَعَلُوا۟ لِلَّهِ مِمَّا ذَرَأَ مِنَ
ٱلْحَرْثِ وَٱلْأَنْعَٰمِ نَصِيبًا
فَقَالُوا۟ هَٰذَا لِلَّهِ بِزَعْمِهِمْ وَهَٰذَا لِشُرَكَآئِنَا
فَمَا كَانَ لِشُرَكَآئِهِمْ

956. Both the good news and the warning which Allah's messengers came to give will be fulfilled. Nothing can stop Allah's Universal Plan. See n. 947 to 6:125.

957. Insofar as this is addressed to the Unbelievers it is a challenge: "Do your utmost; nothing will deter me from my duty: we shall see who wins in the end." Passing from the particular occasion, we can understand it in a more general sense, which is true for all time. Let the evil ones do their worst. Let those who believe do all they can, according to their opportunities and abilities. The individual must do the straight duty that lies before him. In the end Allah will judge, and His judgement is always true and just.

958. There is scathing sarcasm here, which some of the commentators have missed. The Pagans have generally a big Pantheon, though above it they have a vague idea of a Supreme God. But the material benefits go to the godlings, the fancied "partners" of Allah; for they have temples, priests, dedications, etc., while the True and Supreme God has only lip-worship, or at best a share with numerous "partners." This was so in Arabia also. The shares assigned to the "partners" went to the priests and hangers-on of the "partners", who were many and clamorous for their rights. The share assigned to Allah possibly went to the poor, but more probably went to the priests who had the cult of the "partners", for the Supreme God had no separate priests of His own. It is also said that when heaps were thus laid out, if any portion of Allah's heap fell into the heaps of the "partners" the priests greedily and promptly appropriated it, while in the contrary case the "partners" priests were careful to reclaim any portion from what they called "Allah's heap." The absurdity of the whole thing is ridiculed. Allah created everything: how can He have a *share*?

Reacheth not Allah, whilst
The share of Allah reacheth
Their "partners"! Evil
(And unjust) is their assignment!

فَلَا يَصِلُ إِلَى ٱللَّهِ وَمَا كَانَ لِلَّهِ
فَهُوَ يَصِلُ إِلَىٰ شُرَكَآئِهِمْ
سَآءَ مَا يَحْكُمُونَ

137. Even so, in the eyes
Of most of the Pagans,[959]
Their "partners" made alluring
The slaughter of their children,
In order to lead them
To their own destruction,
And cause confusion
In their religion.
If Allah had willed,
They would not have done so:
But leave alone
Them and their inventions.

﴿١٣٧﴾ وَكَذَٰلِكَ زَيَّنَ لِكَثِيرٍ مِّنَ
ٱلْمُشْرِكِينَ قَتْلَ أَوْلَٰدِهِمْ
شُرَكَآؤُهُمْ لِيُرْدُوهُمْ وَلِيَلْبِسُوا۟
عَلَيْهِمْ دِينَهُمْ وَلَوْ شَآءَ ٱللَّهُ مَا فَعَلُوهُ
فَذَرْهُمْ وَمَا يَفْتَرُونَ

138. And they say that
Such and such cattle and crops[960]
Are taboo, and none should
Eat of them except those
Whom—so they say—We
Wish; further, there are
Cattle forbidden to yoke[961]
Or burden, and cattle
On which, (at slaughter),
The name of Allah is not[962]
Pronounced—inventions
Against Allah's name: soon
Will He requite them
For their inventions.

﴿١٣٨﴾ وَقَالُوا۟ هَٰذِهِۦٓ أَنْعَٰمٌ وَحَرْثٌ
حِجْرٌ لَّا يَطْعَمُهَآ إِلَّا مَن
نَّشَآءُ بِزَعْمِهِمْ وَأَنْعَٰمٌ حُرِّمَتْ
ظُهُورُهَا وَأَنْعَٰمٌ لَّا يَذْكُرُونَ
ٱسْمَ ٱللَّهِ عَلَيْهَا ٱفْتِرَآءً عَلَيْهِ
سَيَجْزِيهِم بِمَا كَانُوا۟ يَفْتَرُونَ

139. They say: "What is
In the wombs of
Such and such cattle

﴿١٣٩﴾ وَقَالُوا۟ مَا فِى بُطُونِ هَٰذِهِ ٱلْأَنْعَٰمِ

959. The false gods and idols—among many nations, including the Arabs—were supposed to require human sacrifices. Ordinarily such sacrifices are revolting to man, but they are made "alluring"—a sacred rite—by Pagan custom, which falsely arrogates to itself the name of religion. Such customs, if allowed, would do nothing but destroy the people who practise them, and make their religion but a confused bundle of revolting superstitions.

960. A taboo of certain foods is sometimes a device of the priesthood to get special things for itself. It has to be enforced by pretending that the prohibition for others is by the Will of Allah. It is a lie or invention against Allah—most superstitions are.

961. Cattle dedicated to heathen gods may be reserved from all useful work; in that case they are a dead loss to the community, and they may, besides, do a great deal of damage to fields and crops.

962. If meat is killed in the name of heathen gods, it would naturally not be killed by the solemn rite in Allah's name, by which alone the killing can be justified for food. See n. 698 to 5:5.

Is specially reserved
(For food) for our men,
And forbidden to our women;
But if it is stillborn,
Then all have shares therein.[963]
For their (false) attribution
(Of superstitions to Allah),
He will soon punish them:
For He is full
Of wisdom and knowledge.

خَالِصَةٌ لِّذُكُورِنَا
وَمُحَرَّمٌ عَلَىٰٓ أَزْوَٰجِنَا
وَإِن يَكُن مَّيْتَةً فَهُمْ فِيهِ شُرَكَآءُ
سَيَجْزِيهِمْ وَصْفَهُمْ إِنَّهُۥ حَكِيمٌ عَلِيمٌ

140. Lost are those who slay
Their children, from folly,
Without knowledge, and forbid
Food which Allah hath provided
For them, inventing (lies)
Against Allah. They have
Indeed gone astray
And heeded no guidance.

(١٤٠) قَدْ خَسِرَ ٱلَّذِينَ قَتَلُوٓا۟
أَوْلَٰدَهُمْ سَفَهًۢا بِغَيْرِ عِلْمٍ وَحَرَّمُوا۟
مَا رَزَقَهُمُ ٱللَّهُ ٱفْتِرَآءً عَلَى ٱللَّهِ
قَدْ ضَلُّوا۟ وَمَا كَانُوا۟ مُهْتَدِينَ

Section 17.

141. It is He who produceth[964]
Gardens, with trellises
And without, and dates,
And tilth with produce
Of all kinds, and olives
And pomegranates,
Similar (in kind)
And different (in variety):[965]
Eat of their fruit
In their season, but render
The dues that are proper
On the day that the harvest
Is gathered. But waste not[966]
By excess: for Allah
Loveth not the wasters.

(١٤١) وَهُوَ ٱلَّذِىٓ أَنشَأَ جَنَّٰتٍ مَّعْرُوشَٰتٍ
وَغَيْرَ مَعْرُوشَٰتٍ وَٱلنَّخْلَ وَٱلزَّرْعَ
مُخْتَلِفًا أُكُلُهُۥ وَٱلزَّيْتُونَ
وَٱلرُّمَّانَ مُتَشَٰبِهًا وَغَيْرَ مُتَشَٰبِهٍ
كُلُوا۟ مِن ثَمَرِهِۦٓ إِذَآ أَثْمَرَ وَءَاتُوا۟ حَقَّهُۥ
يَوْمَ حَصَادِهِۦ وَلَا تُسْرِفُوٓا۟
إِنَّهُۥ لَا يُحِبُّ ٱلْمُسْرِفِينَ

963. These are further Pagan superstitions about cattle. Some have already been noted in 5:106, which may be consulted with the notes.

964. *Ansha'a*: see 6:98, n. 923.

965. A beautiful passage, with music to match the meaning. *Cf.* 6:99 and notes.

966. "Waste not, want not," says the English proverb. Here the same wisdom is preached from a higher motive. See what magnificent means Allah provides in nature for the sustenance of all His creatures, because He loves them all. Enjoy them in moderation and be grateful. But commit no excess, and commit no waste: the two things are the same from different angles of vision. If you do, you take away something from other creatures and Allah would not like your selfishness.

142. Of the cattle are some
For burden and some for meat:[967]
Eat what Allah hath provided
For you, and follow not
The footsteps of Satan:
For he is to you
An avowed enemy.

١٤٢ وَمِنَ ٱلۡأَنۡعَـٰمِ حَمُولَةً وَفَرۡشًاۚ
كُلُواْ مِمَّا رَزَقَكُمُ ٱللَّهُ وَلَا تَتَّبِعُواْ
خُطُوَٰتِ ٱلشَّيۡطَـٰنِۚ إِنَّهُۥ لَكُمۡ عَدُوٌّ مُّبِينٌ

143. (Take) eight (head of cattle)[968]
In (four) pairs:
Of sheep a pair,
And of goats a pair;
Say, hath He forbidden
The two males,
Or the two females,
Or (the young) which the wombs
Or the two females enclose?
Tell me with knowledge
If ye are truthful:

١٤٣ ثَمَـٰنِيَةَ أَزۡوَٰجٍۖ مِّنَ
ٱلضَّأۡنِ ٱثۡنَيۡنِ وَمِنَ ٱلۡمَعۡزِ ٱثۡنَيۡنِۗ
قُلۡ ءَآلذَّكَرَيۡنِ حَرَّمَ أَمِ ٱلۡأُنثَيَيۡنِ
أَمَّا ٱشۡتَمَلَتۡ عَلَيۡهِ أَرۡحَامُ ٱلۡأُنثَيَيۡنِۖ
نَبِّـُٔونِي بِعِلۡمٍ إِن كُنتُمۡ صَـٰدِقِينَ

144. Of camels a pair,
And of oxen a pair;
Say, hath He forbidden
The two males,
Or the two females,
Or (the young) which the wombs
Of the two females enclose?—
Were ye present when Allah
Ordered you such a thing?
But who doth more wrong
Than one who invents
A lie against Allah,
To lead astray men
Without knowledge?
For Allah guideth not
People who do wrong.

١٤٤ وَمِنَ ٱلۡإِبِلِ ٱثۡنَيۡنِ وَمِنَ ٱلۡبَقَرِ ٱثۡنَيۡنِۗ
قُلۡ ءَآلذَّكَرَيۡنِ حَرَّمَ أَمِ ٱلۡأُنثَيَيۡنِ
أَمَّا ٱشۡتَمَلَتۡ عَلَيۡهِ أَرۡحَامُ ٱلۡأُنثَيَيۡنِۖ
أَمۡ كُنتُمۡ شُهَدَآءَ إِذۡ وَصَّىٰكُمُ
ٱللَّهُ بِهَـٰذَاۚ فَمَنۡ أَظۡلَمُ مِمَّنِ ٱفۡتَرَىٰ عَلَى ٱللَّهِ
كَذِبًا لِّيُضِلَّ ٱلنَّاسَ بِغَيۡرِ عِلۡمٍۗ
إِنَّ ٱللَّهَ لَا يَهۡدِي ٱلۡقَوۡمَ ٱلظَّـٰلِمِينَ

SECTION 18.

145. Say: "I find not
In the Message received

١٤٥ قُل لَّآ أَجِدُ فِي مَآ أُوحِيَ

967. Superstition kills true religion. We come back to the Arab Pagan superstitions about cattle for food. The horse is not mentioned, because horse flesh was not an article of diet and there were no superstitions about it. Sheep and goats, camels and oxen were the usual sources of meat. Sheep and goats were not used as beasts of burden, but camels (of both sexes) were used for carrying burdens, and oxen for the plough, though cows were mainly used for milk and meat. The words "some for burden and some for meat" do not differentiate whole species, except that they give you the first two and the last two as categories.

968. The superstitions referred to in 6:139 and 5:106 are further ridiculed in this verse and the next.

By me by inspiration
Any (meat) forbidden
To be eaten by one
Who wishes to eat it,
Unless it be dead meat,
Or blood poured forth,[969]
Or the flesh of swine—
For it is an abomination—
Or what is impious, (meat)
On which a name has been
Invoked other than Allah's."
But (even so), if a person
Is forced by necessity,
Without willful disobedience,
Nor transgressing due limits—
Thy Lord is Oft-Forgiving,
Most Merciful.

إِلَىَّ مُحَرَّمًا عَلَىٰ طَاعِمٍ
يَطْعَمُهُۥٓ إِلَّآ أَن يَكُونَ مَيْتَةً
أَوْ دَمًا مَّسْفُوحًا أَوْ لَحْمَ خِنزِيرٍ
فَإِنَّهُۥ رِجْسٌ أَوْ فِسْقًا
أُهِلَّ لِغَيْرِ ٱللَّهِ بِهِۦ ۚ
فَمَنِ ٱضْطُرَّ غَيْرَ بَاغٍ وَلَا عَادٍ
فَإِنَّ رَبَّكَ غَفُورٌ رَّحِيمٌ

146. For those who followed
The Jewish Law, We forbade
Every (animal) with
Undivided hoof,[970]
And We forbade them
The fat of the ox[971]
And the sheep, except
What adheres to their backs
Or their entrails,
Or is mixed up
With a bone:
This in recompense
For their willful disobedience:
For We are True
(In Our ordinances).

١٤٦ وَعَلَى ٱلَّذِينَ هَادُوا۟ حَرَّمْنَا
كُلَّ ذِى ظُفُرٍ ۖ وَمِنَ ٱلْبَقَرِ
وَٱلْغَنَمِ حَرَّمْنَا عَلَيْهِمْ شُحُومَهُمَآ
إِلَّا مَا حَمَلَتْ ظُهُورُهُمَآ
أَوِ ٱلْحَوَايَآ أَوْ مَا ٱخْتَلَطَ بِعَظْمٍ ۚ
ذَٰلِكَ جَزَيْنَٰهُم بِبَغْيِهِمْ ۖ
وَإِنَّا لَصَٰدِقُونَ

147. If they accuse thee
Of falsehood, say:
"Your Lord is Full

١٤٧ فَإِن كَذَّبُوكَ فَقُل رَّبُّكُمْ ذُو

969. *Blood poured forth*: as distinguished from blood adhering to flesh, or the liver, or such other internal organs purifying the blood.

970. *Zufur* may mean claw or hoof; it is in the singular number; but as no animal has a single claw, and there is no point in a division of claws, we must look to a hoof for the correct interpretation. In the Jewish Law (Leviticus. xi. 3-6), "whatsoever parteth the hoof, and is cloven footed, and cheweth the cud, among the beasts" was lawful as food, but the camel, the coney (rabbit), and the hare were not lawful, because they do not "divide the hoof". Undivided hoof therefore is the correct interpretation. These three animals, unlawful to the Jews, are lawful in Islam. *Cf.* 4:160.

971. In Leviticus (vii. 23) it is laid down that "ye shall eat no manner of fat, of ox, or of sheep, or of goat." As regards the exceptions, it is to be noticed that priests were enjoined (Leviticus. vii. 6) to eat of the fat in the trespass offering, which was considered holy, *viz.*, "the rump" (back and bone) "and the fat that covereth the inwards" (entails), (Leviticus, vii. 3).

Of Mercy, All-Embracing;"
But from people in guilt
Never will His wrath
Be turned back.

رَحْمَةٍ وَٰسِعَةٍ وَلَا يُرَدُّ
بَأْسُهُۥ عَنِ ٱلْقَوْمِ ٱلْمُجْرِمِينَ

148. Those who give partners
(To Allah) will say:
"If Allah had wished,
We should not have
Given partners to Him,
Nor would our fathers:
Nor should we have had[972]
Any taboos." So did
Their ancestors argue
Falsely, until they tasted
Of Our wrath. Say:
"Have ye any (certain)
Knowledge? If so, produce
It before us. Ye follow
Nothing but conjecture:
Ye do nothing but lie."

١٤٨ سَيَقُولُ ٱلَّذِينَ أَشْرَكُوا۟
لَوْ شَآءَ ٱللَّهُ مَآ أَشْرَكْنَا
وَلَآ ءَابَآؤُنَا وَلَا حَرَّمْنَا مِن شَىْءٍ
كَذَٰلِكَ كَذَّبَ ٱلَّذِينَ
مِن قَبْلِهِمْ حَتَّىٰ ذَاقُوا۟ بَأْسَنَا
قُلْ هَلْ عِندَكُم مِّنْ عِلْمٍ فَتُخْرِجُوهُ لَنَآ
إِن تَتَّبِعُونَ إِلَّا ٱلظَّنَّ وَإِنْ أَنتُمْ إِلَّا تَخْرُصُونَ

149. Say: "With Allah is the argument[973]
That reaches home: if it had
Been His Will, He could
Indeed have guided you all."

١٤٩ قُلْ فَلِلَّهِ ٱلْحُجَّةُ ٱلْبَٰلِغَةُ
فَلَوْ شَآءَ لَهَدَىٰكُمْ أَجْمَعِينَ

150. Say: "Bring forward your witnesses
To prove that Allah did
Forbid so and so." If they
Bring such witnesses,
Be not thou amongst them:[974]
Nor follow thou the vain
Desires of such as treat
Our Signs as falsehoods,
And such as believe not

١٥٠ قُلْ هَلُمَّ شُهَدَآءَكُمُ ٱلَّذِينَ
يَشْهَدُونَ أَنَّ ٱللَّهَ حَرَّمَ هَٰذَا
فَإِن شَهِدُوا۟ فَلَا تَشْهَدْ مَعَهُمْ
وَلَا تَتَّبِعْ أَهْوَآءَ ٱلَّذِينَ كَذَّبُوا۟
بِـَٔايَٰتِنَا وَٱلَّذِينَ لَا يُؤْمِنُونَ

972. As used by the Pagans, the argument is false, for it implies (a) that men have no personal responsibility, (b) that they are the victims of a Determinism against which they are helpless, and (c) that they might therefore go on doing just what they liked. It is also inconsistent, for if (b) is true, (c) cannot be true. Nor is it meant to be taken seriously.

973. On the other hand, the argument cuts true and deep, as from Allah to His creatures. Allah is Omnipotent, and can do all that we can conceive. But He, in His Plan, has given man some responsibility, and some choice in order to train man's will. If man fails, he is helped in various ways by Allah's mercy and grace. But man cannot go on sinning, and in a state of sin, expect Allah to be pleased with him (6:147).

974. The Pagan superstitions were of course baseless, and in many cases harmful and debasing. If Allah's name was taken as supporting them, no true man of God could be taken in, or join in support simply because Allah's name was taken in vain.

In the Hereafter: for they
Hold others as equal
With their Guardian-Lord.[975]

بِٱلۡأٓخِرَةِ وَهُم بِرَبِّهِمۡ يَعۡدِلُونَ

C. 82.—Allah's commands are not irrational
(6:151-165.) Taboos, but based on the moral law,
And conformable to reason. His Way
Is the straight Way, of justice and truth.
In unity and faith must we dedicate
All our life to His service, and His
Alone, to Whom we shall return.

SECTION 19.

151. Say: "Come, I will rehearse
What Allah hath (really)[976]
Prohibited you from": join not
Anything as equal with Him;
Be good to your parents;
Kill not your children
On a plea of want—We
Provide sustenance for you
And for them—come not
Nigh to shameful deeds,
Whether open or secret;
Take not life, which Allah
Hath made sacred, except
By way of justice and law:[977]
Thus doth He command you,
That ye may learn wisdom.

١٥١ قُلۡ تَعَالَوۡاْ أَتۡلُ مَا حَرَّمَ رَبُّكُمۡ
عَلَيۡكُمۡۖ أَلَّا تُشۡرِكُواْ بِهِۦ شَيۡـٔٗاۖ
وَبِٱلۡوَٰلِدَيۡنِ إِحۡسَٰنٗاۖ وَلَا تَقۡتُلُوٓاْ أَوۡلَٰدَكُم
مِّنۡ إِمۡلَٰقٖ نَّحۡنُ نَرۡزُقُكُمۡ وَإِيَّاهُمۡۖ
وَلَا تَقۡرَبُواْ ٱلۡفَوَٰحِشَ مَا ظَهَرَ مِنۡهَا وَمَا
بَطَنَۖ وَلَا تَقۡتُلُواْ ٱلنَّفۡسَ ٱلَّتِي حَرَّمَ
ٱللَّهُ إِلَّا بِٱلۡحَقِّۚ ذَٰلِكُمۡ وَصَّىٰكُم بِهِۦ لَعَلَّكُمۡ تَعۡقِلُونَ

152. And come not nigh
To the orphan's property,

١٥٢ وَلَا تَقۡرَبُواْ مَالَ ٱلۡيَتِيمِ

975. *Cf.* 6:1. Allah, who created and who cherishes and cares for all, should have the first claim on our attention. Those who set up false gods fail to understand Allah's true governance or their own true destiny.

976. Instead of following Pagan superstitions, and being in constant terror of imaginary taboos and prohibitions, we should study the true moral law, whose sanction is Allah's Law. The first step is that we should recognise that He is the One and Only Lord and Cherisher. The mention of goodness to parents immediately afterwards suggests: (1) that Allah's love of us and care for us may—on an infinitely higher plane—be understood by our ideal of parental love, which is purely unselfish; (2) that our first duty among our fellow creatures is to our father and mother, whose love leads us to the conception of divine love. Arising from that is the conception of our converse duties to our children. Allah provides sustenance (material and spiritual) not only for us, but for them; hence any custom like the Pagan custom of sacrificing children to Moloch stands condemned. Then come the moral prohibitions against lewdness and all unseemly acts, relating to sex or otherwise, open or secret. This is followed by the prohibition of killing or fighting. All these things are conformable to our own interests, and therefore true wisdom from our own point of view.

977. For the comprehensive word, *ḥaqq*, I have used the two words, "justice and law": other significations implied are: right, truth, what is becoming, etc. It is not only that human life is sacred, but all life is sacred. Even in killing animals for food, a dedicatory formula "in the name of Allah" has to be employed, to make it lawful: see n. 698 to 5:5 and n. 962 to 6:138.

Except to improve it,
Until he attains the age
Of full strength; give measure
And weight with (full) justice—
No burden do We place
On any soul, but that
Which it can bear—
Whenever ye speak, speak justly,
Even if a near relative
Is concerned; and fulfil
The Covenant of Allah:[978]
Thus doth He command you,
That ye may remember.

إِلَّا بِٱلَّتِي هِيَ أَحۡسَنُ حَتَّىٰ يَبۡلُغَ أَشُدَّهُۥۖ
وَأَوۡفُواْ ٱلۡكَيۡلَ وَٱلۡمِيزَانَ بِٱلۡقِسۡطِۖ
لَا نُكَلِّفُ نَفۡسًا إِلَّا وُسۡعَهَاۖ
وَإِذَا قُلۡتُمۡ فَٱعۡدِلُواْ وَلَوۡ كَانَ ذَا قُرۡبَىٰۖ
وَبِعَهۡدِ ٱللَّهِ أَوۡفُواْۚ ذَٰلِكُمۡ
وَصَّىٰكُم بِهِۦ لَعَلَّكُمۡ تَذَكَّرُونَ

153. Verily, this is My Way
Leading straight: follow it;
Follow not (other) paths:
They will scatter you about
From His (great) Path;
Thus doth He command you,
That ye may be righteous.[979]

١٥٣ وَأَنَّ هَٰذَا صِرَٰطِي مُسۡتَقِيمٗا فَٱتَّبِعُوهُۖ
وَلَا تَتَّبِعُواْ ٱلسُّبُلَ فَتَفَرَّقَ بِكُمۡ عَن سَبِيلِهِۦۚ
ذَٰلِكُمۡ وَصَّىٰكُم بِهِۦ لَعَلَّكُمۡ تَتَّقُونَ

154. Moreover, We gave Moses
The Book, completing
(Our favour) to those
Who would do right,
And explaining all things[980]
In detail—and a guide
And a mercy, that they
Might believe in the meeting
With their Lord.

١٥٤ ثُمَّ ءَاتَيۡنَا مُوسَى
ٱلۡكِتَٰبَ تَمَامًا عَلَى ٱلَّذِيٓ أَحۡسَنَ
وَتَفۡصِيلٗا لِّكُلِّ شَيۡءٖ وَهُدٗى وَرَحۡمَةٗ
لَّعَلَّهُم بِلِقَآءِ رَبِّهِمۡ يُؤۡمِنُونَ

SECTION 20.

155. And this is a Book
Which We have revealed
As a blessing: so follow it

١٥٥ وَهَٰذَا كِتَٰبٌ أَنزَلۡنَٰهُ مُبَارَكٞ فَٱتَّبِعُوهُ

978. *Cf.* 5:1 and n. 682.

979. Note again the refrain with variations, in 6:151, 152 and 153. In verse 151, we have the moral law, which it is for our own good to follow: "Thus doth He command you, that ye may learn wisdom." In verse 152, we have to deal justly and rightly with others; we are apt to think too much of ourselves and forget others: "Thus doth He command you, that ye may remember." In verse 153 our attention is called to the Straight Way, the Way of Allah, the only Way that leads to righteousness: "Thus doth He command you, that ye may be righteous."

980. The revelation to Moses went into the details of people's lives, and thus served as a practical guide to the Jews and after them to the Christians. Admittedly the Message delivered by Christ dealt with general principles only and in no way with details. The message of Islam as in the Qur'ān is the next complete guide in point of time after that of Moses.

And be righteous, that ye
May receive mercy;

وَاتَّقُوا لَعَلَّكُمْ تُرْحَمُونَ

156. Lest ye should say:
"The Book was sent down
To two Peoples before us,
And for our part, we
Remained unacquainted[981]
With all that they learned
By assiduous study;"

(١٥٦) أَن تَقُولُوٓا إِنَّمَآ أُنزِلَ ٱلْكِتَٰبُ
عَلَىٰ طَآئِفَتَيْنِ مِن قَبْلِنَا وَإِن كُنَّا
عَن دِرَاسَتِهِمْ لَغَٰفِلِينَ

157. Or lest ye should say:
"If the Book had only
Been sent down to us,
We should have followed
Its guidance better than they."
Now then hath come
Unto you a Clear (Sign)[982]
From your Lord—and a guide
And a mercy: then who
Could do more wrong
Than one who rejecteth
Allah's Signs, and turneth
Away therefrom? In good time
Shall We requite those
Who turn away from Our Signs,
With a dreadful penalty,
For their turning away.

(١٥٧) أَوْ تَقُولُوا لَوْ أَنَّآ أُنزِلَ
عَلَيْنَا ٱلْكِتَٰبُ لَكُنَّآ أَهْدَىٰ مِنْهُمْ
فَقَدْ جَآءَكُم بَيِّنَةٌ
مِّن رَّبِّكُمْ وَهُدًى
وَرَحْمَةٌ فَمَنْ أَظْلَمُ مِمَّن كَذَّبَ
بِـَٔايَٰتِ ٱللَّهِ وَصَدَفَ عَنْهَا
سَنَجْزِى ٱلَّذِينَ يَصْدِفُونَ عَنْ ءَايَٰتِنَا
سُوٓءَ ٱلْعَذَابِ بِمَا كَانُوا يَصْدِفُونَ

158. Are they waiting to see
If the angels come to them,
Or thy Lord (Himself),
Or certain of the Signs
Of thy Lord!
The day that certain
Of the Signs of thy Lord
Do come, no good
Will it do to a soul[983]
To believe in them then,
If it believed not before

(١٥٨) هَلْ يَنظُرُونَ إِلَّآ أَن تَأْتِيَهُمُ ٱلْمَلَٰٓئِكَةُ
أَوْ يَأْتِىَ رَبُّكَ أَوْ يَأْتِىَ بَعْضُ ءَايَٰتِ رَبِّكَ
يَوْمَ يَأْتِى بَعْضُ ءَايَٰتِ رَبِّكَ
لَا يَنفَعُ نَفْسًا إِيمَٰنُهَا
لَمْ تَكُنْ ءَامَنَتْ مِن قَبْلُ

981. Because the diligent studies of the earlier People of the Book were in languages foreign to the new People of Islam, or because they were meant for circumstances different from those of the new world after Islam.

982. The Qur'ān and the life and the teaching of Muḥammad, the Messenger of Allah.

983. There is no merit in faith in things that you are compelled to acknowledge when they actually happen. Faith is belief in things which you do not see with your eyes but you understand with your spiritual sense: if your whole will consents to it, it results in deeds of righteousness, which are the evidence of your faith.

Nor earned righteousness
Through its Faith. Say:
"Wait ye: we too
Are waiting."[984]

أَوْ كَسَبَتْ فِىٓ إِيمَٰنِهَا خَيْرًا ۗ
قُلِ ٱنتَظِرُوٓا۟ إِنَّا مُنتَظِرُونَ

159. As for those who divide[985]
Their religion and break up
Into sects, thou hast
No part in them in the least:
Their affair is with Allah:
He will in the end
Tell them the truth
Of all that they did.

(١٥٩) إِنَّ ٱلَّذِينَ فَرَّقُوا۟ دِينَهُمْ
وَكَانُوا۟ شِيَعًا لَّسْتَ مِنْهُمْ فِى شَىْءٍ ۚ
إِنَّمَآ أَمْرُهُمْ إِلَى ٱللَّهِ ثُمَّ
يُنَبِّئُهُم بِمَا كَانُوا۟ يَفْعَلُونَ

160. He that doeth good
Shall have ten times
As much to his credit:
He that doeth evil
Shall only be recompensed
According to his evil:[986]
No wrong shall be done
Unto (any of) them.

(١٦٠) مَن جَآءَ بِٱلْحَسَنَةِ فَلَهُۥ عَشْرُ أَمْثَالِهَا ۖ
وَمَن جَآءَ بِٱلسَّيِّئَةِ فَلَا يُجْزَىٰٓ إِلَّا مِثْلَهَا
وَهُمْ لَا يُظْلَمُونَ

161. Say: "Verily, my Lord
Hath guided me to
A Way that is straight—
A religion of right—
The Path (trod) by Abraham
The true in faith,
And he (certainly)
Joined not gods with Allah."

(١٦١) قُلْ إِنَّنِى هَدَىٰنِى رَبِّىٓ إِلَىٰ صِرَٰطٍ
مُّسْتَقِيمٍ دِينًا قِيَمًا مِّلَّةَ إِبْرَٰهِيمَ حَنِيفًا ۚ
وَمَا كَانَ مِنَ ٱلْمُشْرِكِينَ

162. Say: "Truly, my prayer
And my service of sacrifice,
My life and my death,
Are (all) for Allah,
The Cherisher of the Worlds;

(١٦٢) قُلْ إِنَّ صَلَاتِى وَنُسُكِى وَمَحْيَاىَ
وَمَمَاتِى لِلَّهِ رَبِّ ٱلْعَٰلَمِينَ

---

984. The waiting in the two cases is in quite different senses: the foolish man without faith is waiting for things which will not happen, and is surprised by the real things which do happen; the righteous man of faith is waiting for the fruits of righteousness, of which he has an assured hope; in a higher state of spiritual elevation, even the fruits have no personal meaning to him, for Allah is to him All-in-All: 6:162.

985. *Divide their religion: (farraqū) i.e.*, (1) make a distinction between one part of it and another, take the part which suits them and reject the rest; or (2) have religion one day of the week and the world the rest of the six days; or (3) keep "religion in its right place," as if it did not claim to govern the whole life; make a sharp distinction between the secular and the religious, or (4) show a sectarian bias, seek differences in views, so as to break up the unity of Islam.

986. Allah is just as well as genereous. To the good, the reward is multiplied ten times (*i.e.*, far above merits) on account of His generosity. To the evil, the punishment is no more than commensurate with their sin, and even so the door of mercy is always open to those who sincerely repent and show it by their conduct.

163. No partner hath He:
This am I commanded,
And I am the first
Of those who bow
To His Will.

﴿١٦٣﴾ لَا شَرِيكَ لَهُۥ ۖ وَبِذَٰلِكَ أُمِرْتُ
وَأَنَا۠ أَوَّلُ ٱلْمُسْلِمِينَ

164. Say: "Shall I seek
For (my) Cherisher
Other than Allah,
When He is the Cherisher
Of all things (that exist)?
Every soul draws the meed
Of its acts on none[987]
But itself: no bearer
Of burdens can bear
The burden of another.
Your goal in the end
Is towards Allah: He will tell
You the truth of the things
Wherein ye disputed."

﴿١٦٤﴾ قُلْ أَغَيْرَ ٱللَّهِ أَبْغِى رَبًّا
وَهُوَ رَبُّ كُلِّ شَىْءٍ ۚ
وَلَا تَكْسِبُ
كُلُّ نَفْسٍ إِلَّا عَلَيْهَا ۚ
وَلَا تَزِرُ وَازِرَةٌ وِزْرَ أُخْرَىٰ ۚ
ثُمَّ إِلَىٰ رَبِّكُم مَّرْجِعُكُمْ فَيُنَبِّئُكُم
بِمَا كُنتُمْ فِيهِ تَخْتَلِفُونَ

165. It is He Who hath made
You (His) agents, inheritors[988]
Of the earth: He hath raised
You in ranks, some above
Others: that He may try you
In the gifts He hath given you:
For thy Lord is quick
In punishment: yet He
Is indeed Oft-Forgiving,
Most Merciful.

﴿١٦٥﴾ وَهُوَ ٱلَّذِى جَعَلَكُمْ
خَلَٰٓئِفَ ٱلْأَرْضِ وَرَفَعَ بَعْضَكُمْ فَوْقَ
بَعْضٍ دَرَجَٰتٍ لِّيَبْلُوَكُمْ فِى مَآ ءَاتَىٰكُمْ ۗ
إِنَّ رَبَّكَ سَرِيعُ ٱلْعِقَابِ
وَإِنَّهُۥ لَغَفُورٌ رَّحِيمٌۢ

987. The doctrine of personal responsibility again. We are fully responsible for our acts ourselves, we cannot transfer the consequences to someone else. Nor can anyone vicariously atone for our sins. If people have honest doubts or differences about important questions of religion, they should not start futile disputes. All will be clear in the end. Our duty here is to maintain unity and discipline, and do the duty that comes to us.

988. *Cf.* 2:30 and n., where I have translated "Khalīfah" as "Vicegerent", it being Allah's Plan to make Adam (as representing mankind) His vicegerent on earth. In C. 1, I have construed the same word by the word "Agent." Another idea implied in "Khalīfah" is that of "successor, heir, or inheritor," *i.e.*, one who has the ultimate ownership after the present possessors, to whom a life tenancy has been given by the owner, have passed away. In 15:23 occurs the striking word, "heirs" (*wārithūn*), applied to Allah: "We give life and death, and We are the Heirs (or Inheritors)." The same idea occurs in 3:180, where see n. 485. The translation here attempts to express both the ideas which I understand from the original.

INTRODUCTION TO SŪRAH 7—*AL A'RĀF*

This Sūrah is closely connected, both chronologically and in respect of the argument, with the previous Sūrah. But it expounds the doctrine of revelation and man's spiritual history by illustrations from Adam onwards, through various Prophets, and the details of Moses's struggles, to the time of the Prophet Muḥammad, in whom Allah's revelation is completed.

***Summary.*—The note, "learn from the past," is struck from the very beginning. The opposition of Evil to Good is illustrated by the story of Adam and Iblīs. Arrogance leads to rebellion; the rebel is jealous and tempts the natural man, who is warned against deceit and all excess (7:1-31, and C. 83).**

If the warning is not heeded, the future penalties are indicated, while the privileges and the bliss and peace of the righteous are shown in a picture of the Hereafter, as well as in the power and goodness of Allah in the world that we see around us (7:32-58, and C. 84).

The story of Noah and the Flood, and the stories of Hūd, Ṣāliḥ, Lot, and Shu'ayb, all point to the lesson that the Prophets were resisted and rejected, but truth triumphed in the end, and evil was humbled, for Allah's Plan never fails (7:59-99, and C. 85).

The story of Moses is told in greater detail, not only in his struggles with Pharaoh, but in his preparation for his mission, and his struggles with his own rebellious people. Even from the time of Moses, the coming of the unlettered Prophet was foreshadowed (7:100-157, and C. 86).

But the people of Moses frequently lapsed from Allah's Law as promulgated to them, and transgressed Allah's Covenant, and they were scattered through the earth in sections (7:158-171, and C. 87).

The children of Adam have multiplied, but many of them have rejected truth and go by degrees to destruction in ways that they do not realise. The righteous listen to the Message of Allah, and serve Him in humility (7:172-206, and C. 88).

C. 83.—Revelation should ease the difficulties
(7:1-31.) Of heart and mind, for it tells
The story of man's spiritual past,
And teaches the end of good and evil.
Iblis fell from jealousy and arrogance,
And Adam fell because he listened
To his deceit. But Allah did grant
In His Mercy gifts and guidance
To men, warned them against excess,
And taught them moderation and justice.

Sūrah 7.

Al A'rāf (The Heights)

الجزء الثامن سورة الأعراف

In the name of Allah, Most Gracious, Most Merciful.

بِسْمِ اللَّهِ الرَّحْمَٰنِ الرَّحِيمِ

1. Alif Lām Mīm Ṣād.[989]

المص ﴿١﴾

2. A Book revealed unto thee—
So let thy heart be oppressed[990]
No more by any difficulty
On that account—
That with it thou mightest
Warn (the erring) and teach
The Believers.

كِتَٰبٌ أُنزِلَ إِلَيْكَ ﴿٢﴾
فَلَا يَكُن فِى صَدْرِكَ حَرَجٌ مِّنْهُ
لِتُنذِرَ بِهِۦ وَذِكْرَىٰ لِلْمُؤْمِنِينَ

3. Follow (O men!) the revelation
Given unto you from your Lord,
And follow not, as friends
Or protectors, other than Him.
Little it is ye remember
Of admonition.[991]

اتَّبِعُوا۟ مَآ أُنزِلَ إِلَيْكُم مِّن رَّبِّكُمْ ﴿٣﴾
وَلَا تَتَّبِعُوا۟ مِن دُونِهِۦٓ أَوْلِيَآءَ
قَلِيلًا مَّا تَذَكَّرُونَ

4. How many towns have We
Destroyed (for their sins)?
Our punishment took them
On a sudden by night
Or while they slept
For their afternoon rest.

وَكَم مِّن قَرْيَةٍ أَهْلَكْنَٰهَا ﴿٤﴾
فَجَآءَهَا بَأْسُنَا بَيَٰتًا
أَوْ هُمْ قَآئِلُونَ

989. This is a combination of four Abbreviated Letters. For Abbreviated Letters generally, see Appendix I (at the end of Sūrah 2). The combination here includes the three letters *Alif, Lām, Mīm,* which occurred at the beginning of Sūrah 2, and are discussed in n. 25 to 2:1.

The additional letter *Ṣād* occurs in combination here and in Sūrah 19, and by itself at the beginning of S. 38, and nowhere else. The factor common to S. 7, S. 19, and S. 38 is that in each case the core of the Sūrah consists in the stories *(qaṣaṣ)* of the Prophets. In this Sūrah we have the stories of Noah, Hūd, Ṣāliḥ, Lot, Shu'ayb, and Moses, leading up to Muḥammad, and in S. 38, the stories of David, Solomon, and Job similarly lead up to Muḥammad, occupying three out of the five sections. Sūrah 19 consists almost entirely of such stories. Can we understand *Ṣād* to stand for *qaṣaṣ,* of which it is the most characteristic letter? In this Sūrah 7, we have also the spiritual history of mankind traced—the Beginning, the Middle, and the End, which, as explained in n. 25, might be represented symbolically by *Alif, Lām, Mīm.* If so, this Sūrah, dealing with the Beginning, Middle, and End of man's spiritual story, and illustrating it by the stories of the Prophets, might well be represented symbolically by the letters, *Alif, Lām, Mīm, Ṣād.* But no one can be dogmatic about these symbols. (R).

990. *Heart*: in the original, *breast.* I have used the word most appropriate to the English idiom. The meaning is that Al Muṣṭafā is consoled for all the difficulties which he encountered in his mission, with the fact that he had clear guidance in the Book for his preaching.

991. This is added in order that men might not be puffed up with such little knowledge as they possessed, for there are great heights to be scaled in the spiritual kingdom.

5. When (thus) Our punishment
Took them, no cry
Did they utter but this:
"Indeed we did wrong."[992]

فَمَا كَانَ دَعْوَىٰهُمْ إِذْ جَآءَهُم بَأْسُنَآ ﴿٥﴾
إِلَّآ أَن قَالُوٓا۟ إِنَّا كُنَّا ظَـٰلِمِينَ

6. Then shall We question
Those to whom Our Message
Was sent and those by whom[993]
We sent it.

فَلَنَسْـَٔلَنَّ ٱلَّذِينَ أُرْسِلَ إِلَيْهِمْ ﴿٦﴾
وَلَنَسْـَٔلَنَّ ٱلْمُرْسَلِينَ

7. And verily We shall recount
Their whole story
With knowledge, for We
Were never absent
(At any time or place).[994]

فَلَنَقُصَّنَّ عَلَيْهِم بِعِلْمٍ ۖ ﴿٧﴾
وَمَا كُنَّا غَآئِبِينَ

8. The balance that day
Will be true (to a nicety):
Those whose scale (of good)
Will be heavy, will prosper:

وَٱلْوَزْنُ يَوْمَئِذٍ ٱلْحَقُّ ۚ فَمَن ثَقُلَتْ ﴿٨﴾
مَوَٰزِينُهُۥ فَأُو۟لَـٰٓئِكَ هُمُ ٱلْمُفْلِحُونَ

9. Those whose scale will be light,
Will find their souls
In perdition, for that they
Wrongfully treated Our Signs.

وَمَنْ خَفَّتْ مَوَٰزِينُهُۥ فَأُو۟لَـٰٓئِكَ ٱلَّذِينَ خَسِرُوٓا۟ ﴿٩﴾
أَنفُسَهُم بِمَا كَانُوا۟ بِـَٔايَـٰتِنَا يَظْلِمُونَ

10. It is We Who have
Placed you with authority
On earth, and provided
You therein with means
For the fulfilment of your life:[995]
Small are the thanks
That ye give!

وَلَقَدْ مَكَّنَّـٰكُمْ ﴿١٠﴾
فِى ٱلْأَرْضِ وَجَعَلْنَا لَكُمْ فِيهَا
مَعَـٰيِشَ ۗ قَلِيلًا مَّا تَشْكُرُونَ

992. The spiritual story of man begins with a prelude. Think of the towns and nations ruined by their iniquity. Allah gave them many opportunities, and sent them warners and teachers. But they arrogantly went on in their evil ways, till some dreadful calamity came like a thief in the night and wiped out their traces. In a warm climate the disturbance in the heat of the midday rest is even more than the disturbance at night. It was when the catastrophe came that the people realised their sins, but it was too late.

993. In the final reckoning, the warners and teachers will give evidence of their preaching the truth, and the wicked will themselves have to acknowledge the truth. We picture it like a court scene, when the story is related, but the Judge knows all, even more than the parties can tell.

994. Allah (being All-Knowing) is never absent from any place or at any time, for time and place are relative conceptions for our limited natures, while He is the Absolute, independent of such relative conceptions. (R).

995. That is, all the material things which are necessary to sustain, beautify, and refine life, as well as all those powers, faculties, and opportunities which are instrumental in bringing up life to a higher plane and preparing man for his high spiritual destiny.

SECTION 2.

11. It is We Who created you
And gave you shape;[996]
Then We bade the angels
Bow down to Adam, and they
Bowed down; not so Iblīs;
He refused to be of those[997]
Who bow down.

(١١) وَلَقَدْ خَلَقْنَٰكُمْ ثُمَّ صَوَّرْنَٰكُمْ
ثُمَّ قُلْنَا لِلْمَلَٰٓئِكَةِ ٱسْجُدُوا۟ لِءَادَمَ فَسَجَدُوٓا۟
إِلَّآ إِبْلِيسَ لَمْ يَكُن مِّنَ ٱلسَّٰجِدِينَ

12. (Allah) said: "What prevented
Thee from bowing down
When I commanded thee?"
He said: "I am better
Than he: Thou didst create
Me from fire, and him from
clay."[998]

(١٢) قَالَ مَا مَنَعَكَ أَلَّا تَسْجُدَ
إِذْ أَمَرْتُكَ قَالَ أَنَا۠ خَيْرٌ مِّنْهُ خَلَقْتَنِى
مِن نَّارٍ وَخَلَقْتَهُۥ مِن طِينٍ

13. (Allah) said: "Get thee down
From this:[999] it is not
For thee to be arrogant
Here: get out, for thou
Art of the meanest (of
creatures)."

(١٣) قَالَ فَٱهْبِطْ مِنْهَا فَمَا
يَكُونُ لَكَ أَن تَتَكَبَّرَ فِيهَا
فَٱخْرُجْ إِنَّكَ مِنَ ٱلصَّٰغِرِينَ

14. He said: "Give me respite
Till the day they are
Raised up."

(١٤) قَالَ أَنظِرْنِىٓ إِلَىٰ يَوْمِ يُبْعَثُونَ

15. (Allah) said: "Be thou
Amongst those who have
respite."[1000]

(١٥) قَالَ إِنَّكَ مِنَ ٱلْمُنظَرِينَ

---

996. *Shape* or form must be interpreted not only to refer to the physical form, which changes day by day, but also the various forms or shapes which our ideal and spiritual existence may take from time to time according to our inner experiences: *Cf.* 82:8. It was after Adam (as standing for all mankind) had been so taught that the angels were asked to bow down to him, for, by Allah's grace, his status had actually been raised higher. Note the transition from "you" (plural) in the first clause to "Adam" in the second clause: Adam and mankind are synonymous: the plural is reverted to in 7:14, 16-18. (R).

997. Iblīs not only refused to bow down: he refused to be of those who bowed down. In other words he arrogantly despised the angels who bowed down as well as man to whom they bowed down and he was in rebellion against Allah for not obeying His order. Arrogance, jealousy, and rebellion were his triple crime.

998. Notice the subtle wiles of Iblīs: his egotism in putting himself above men, and his falsehood in ignoring the fact that Allah had not merely made man's body from clay, but had given him spiritual form—in other words, had taught him the nature of things and raised him above the angels.

999. *"This"*: the situation as it was then—a rebellious creature impertinent to His Creator. At every step Iblīs falls lower: arrogance, jealousy, disobedience, egotism and untruth.

1000. Are there others under respite? Yes, Iblīs has a large army of wicked seducers, and those men who are their dupes. For though degradation takes effect at once, its appearance may be long-delayed.

16. He said: "Because Thou
Hast thrown me out[1001]
Of the Way, lo! I will
Lie in wait for them
On Thy Straight Way:

١٦ قَالَ فَبِمَآ أَغْوَيْتَنِى
لَأَقْعُدَنَّ لَهُمْ صِرَٰطَكَ ٱلْمُسْتَقِيمَ

17. "Then will I assault them
From before them and behind
them,
From their right and their left:
Nor wilt Thou find,
In most of them,
Gratitude (for Thy mercies)."[1002]

١٧ ثُمَّ لَءَاتِيَنَّهُم مِّنۢ بَيْنِ أَيْدِيهِمْ
وَمِنْ خَلْفِهِمْ وَعَنْ أَيْمَٰنِهِمْ وَعَن شَمَآئِلِهِمْ
وَلَا تَجِدُ أَكْثَرَهُمْ شَٰكِرِينَ

18. (Allah) said: "Get out
From this, disgraced
And expelled. If any
Of them follow thee—
Hell will I fill
With you all.

١٨ قَالَ ٱخْرُجْ مِنْهَا مَذْءُومًا مَّدْحُورًا
لَّمَن تَبِعَكَ مِنْهُمْ لَأَمْلَأَنَّ
جَهَنَّمَ مِنكُمْ أَجْمَعِينَ

19. "O Adam! dwell thou[1003]
And thy wife in the Garden,
And enjoy[1004] (its good things)
As ye wish: but approach not
This tree, or ye run
Into harm and transgression."

١٩ وَيَٰٓـَٔادَمُ ٱسْكُنْ أَنتَ وَزَوْجُكَ ٱلْجَنَّةَ
فَكُلَا مِنْ حَيْثُ شِئْتُمَا وَلَا تَقْرَبَا
هَٰذِهِ ٱلشَّجَرَةَ فَتَكُونَا مِنَ ٱلظَّٰلِمِينَ

20. Then began Satan[1005] to whisper
Suggestions to them,
In order to reveal to them

٢٠ فَوَسْوَسَ لَهُمَا ٱلشَّيْطَٰنُ لِيُبْدِىَ لَهُمَا

1001. Another instance of Iblīs's subtlety and falsehood. He waits till he gets the respite. Then he breaks out into a lie and impertinent defiance. The lie is in suggesting that Allah had thrown him out of the Way, in other words misled him; whereas his own conduct was responsible for his degradation. The defiance is in his setting snares on the Straight Way to which Allah directs men. Iblīs now falls a step lower than the five steps mentioned in n. 999. His sixth step is defiance.

1002. The assault of evil is from all sides. It takes advantage of every weak point, and sometimes even our good and generous sympathies are used to decoy us into the snares of evil. Man has every reason to be grateful to Allah for all His loving care and yet man in his folly forgets his gratitude and does the very opposite of what he should do.

1003. Now the story turns to man. He was placed in a spiritual Garden of innocence and bliss, but it was Allah's Plan to give him a limited faculty of choice. All that he was forbidden to do was to approach the Tree, but he succumbed to Satan's suggestions. (R).

1004. *Enjoy*: literally, "eat." *Cf.* the meaning of *ṭa'ama* in 6:14, n. 847 and *akala* in 5:66, n. 776.

1005. The transition from the name "Iblīs" to the name "Satan" is similar to that in 2:36, where it is explained in n. 52.

Their shame[1006]
That was hidden from them
(Before): he said: "Your Lord
Only forbade you this tree,
Lest ye should become angels
Or such beings as live forever."

مَا وُۥرِيَ عَنْهُمَا مِن سَوْءَٰتِهِمَا وَقَالَ
مَا نَهَىٰكُمَا رَبُّكُمَا عَنْ هَٰذِهِ ٱلشَّجَرَةِ
إِلَّآ أَن تَكُونَا مَلَكَيْنِ أَوْ تَكُونَا مِنَ ٱلْخَٰلِدِينَ

21. And he swore to them
Both, that he was
Their sincere adviser.

٢١ وَقَاسَمَهُمَآ إِنِّى لَكُمَا لَمِنَ ٱلنَّٰصِحِينَ

22. So by deceit he brought about
Their fall: when they
Tasted of the tree,
Their shame became manifest
To them, and they began
To sew together the leaves
Of the Garden over their
bodies.
And their Lord called
Unto them: "Did I not
Forbid you that tree,
And tell you that Satan
Was an avowed
Enemy unto you?"

٢٢ فَدَلَّىٰهُمَا بِغُرُورٍ فَلَمَّا ذَاقَا ٱلشَّجَرَةَ
بَدَتْ لَهُمَا سَوْءَٰتُهُمَا وَطَفِقَا
يَخْصِفَانِ عَلَيْهِمَا مِن وَرَقِ ٱلْجَنَّةِ
وَنَادَىٰهُمَا رَبُّهُمَآ أَلَمْ أَنْهَكُمَا
عَن تِلْكُمَا ٱلشَّجَرَةِ وَأَقُل
لَّكُمَآ إِنَّ ٱلشَّيْطَٰنَ لَكُمَا عَدُوٌّ مُّبِينٌ

23. They said: "Our Lord!
We have wronged our own
souls:
If Thou forgive us not
And bestow not upon us
Thy Mercy, we shall
Certainly be lost."

٢٣ قَالَا رَبَّنَا ظَلَمْنَآ أَنفُسَنَا
وَإِن لَّمْ تَغْفِرْ لَنَا وَتَرْحَمْنَا
لَنَكُونَنَّ مِنَ ٱلْخَٰسِرِينَ

24. (Allah) said: "Get ye down,
With enmity between yourselves.
On earth will be your
dwelling-place
And your means of livelihood—
For a time."

٢٤ قَالَ ٱهْبِطُوا۟ بَعْضُكُمْ لِبَعْضٍ
عَدُوٌّ وَلَكُمْ فِى ٱلْأَرْضِ مُسْتَقَرٌّ
وَمَتَٰعٌ إِلَىٰ حِينٍ

25. He said: "Therein shall ye
Live, and therein shall ye

٢٥ قَالَ فِيهَا تَحْيَوْنَ وَفِيهَا

1006. Our first parents as created by Allah (and this applies to all of us) were innocent in matters material as well as spiritual. They knew no evil. But the faculty of choice, which was given to them and which raised them above the angels, also implied that they had the capacity of evil, which by the training of their own will, they were to reject. They were warned of the danger. When they fell, they realised the evil. They were (and we are) still given the chance, in this life on a lower plane, to make good and recover the lost status of innocence and bliss.

Die; but from it shall ye
Be taken out (at last)."[1007]

تَمُوتُونَ وَمِنْهَا تُخْرَجُونَ

Section 3.

26. O ye Children of Adam!
We have bestowed raiment[1008]
Upon you to cover
Your shame, as well as
To be an adornment to you.
But the raiment of
righteousness—
That is the best.
Such are among the Signs
Of Allah, that they
May receive admonition!

(٢٦) يَٰبَنِىٓ ءَادَمَ قَدْ أَنزَلْنَا
عَلَيْكُمْ لِبَاسًا يُوَٰرِى سَوْءَٰتِكُمْ
وَرِيشًا ۖ وَلِبَاسُ ٱلتَّقْوَىٰ
ذَٰلِكَ خَيْرٌ ۚ ذَٰلِكَ مِنْ ءَايَٰتِ
ٱللَّهِ لَعَلَّهُمْ يَذَّكَّرُونَ

27. O ye Children of Adam!
Let not Satan seduce you,
In the same manner as[1009]
He got your parents out
Of the Garden, stripping them
Of their raiment, to expose
Their shame: for he
And his tribe watch you
From a position where ye
Cannot see them: We made
The Evil Ones friends
(Only) to those without Faith.

(٢٧) يَٰبَنِىٓ ءَادَمَ لَا يَفْتِنَنَّكُمُ ٱلشَّيْطَٰنُ
كَمَآ أَخْرَجَ أَبَوَيْكُم مِّنَ ٱلْجَنَّةِ يَنزِعُ عَنْهُمَا
لِبَاسَهُمَا لِيُرِيَهُمَا سَوْءَٰتِهِمَآ ۗ إِنَّهُۥ
يَرَىٰكُمْ هُوَ وَقَبِيلُهُۥ مِنْ حَيْثُ لَا تَرَوْنَهُمْ ۗ
إِنَّا جَعَلْنَا ٱلشَّيَٰطِينَ أَوْلِيَآءَ لِلَّذِينَ لَا يُؤْمِنُونَ

1007. *Cf.* this whole passage about Adam with the passage in 2:30-39, and with other passages in subsequent Sūrahs. In places the words are precisely the same, and yet the whole argument is different. In each case it exactly fits the context. In S. 2, the argument was about the origin of man. Here the argument is a prelude to his history on earth, and so it continues logically in the next section to address the Children of Adam, and goes on afterwards with the story of the various prophets that came to guide mankind. Truth is one, but its apt presentment in human words shows a different facet in different contexts.

1008. There is a double philosophy of clothes here, to correspond with the double signification of verse 20 above, as explained in n. 1006. Spiritually, Allah created man "bare and alone" (6:94): the soul in its naked purity and beauty knew no shame because it knew no guilt: after it was touched by guilt and soiled by evil, its thoughts and deeds became its clothing and adornments, good or bad, honest or meretricious, according to the inner motives which gave them colour. So in the case of the body: it is pure and beautiful, as long as it is not defiled by misuse; its clothing and ornaments may be good or meretricious, according to the motives in the mind and character; if good, they are the symbols of purity and beauty; but the best clothing and ornament we could have comes from righteousness, which covers the nakedness of sin, and adorns us with virtues. (R).

1009. That is, by fraud and deceit—by putting you off your guard and telling lies. Adam's story here becomes an introduction to the later spiritual history of mankind: 7:20-22. In the Garden, Satan's deceit stripped off their raiment of honour and innocence. In this life, on a lower plane, he seeks to strip us of the raiment of righteousness. And he can take up positions on a vantage ground of worldly power or influence or riches, in which he and his confederates are not seen in their true colours. They may assume a fair-seeming disguise of disinterested friendship or high motives of patriotism or public spirit, or loyalty to ancestors, when beneath it there is nothing but spite and selfishness.

28. When they do aught
That is shameful, they say:
"We found our fathers
Doing so"; and "Allah
Commanded us thus;"
Say: "Nay, Allah never
Commands what is shameful:
Do ye say of Allah
What ye know not?"

﴿٢٨﴾ وَإِذَا فَعَلُوا۟ فَٰحِشَةً قَالُوا۟
وَجَدْنَا عَلَيْهَآ ءَابَآءَنَا وَٱللَّهُ أَمَرَنَا بِهَا ۗ
قُلْ إِنَّ ٱللَّهَ لَا يَأْمُرُ بِٱلْفَحْشَآءِ ۖ
أَتَقُولُونَ عَلَى ٱللَّهِ مَا لَا تَعْلَمُونَ

29. Say: "My Lord hath commanded
Justice; and that ye set
Your whole selves (to Him)[1010]
At every time and place
Of prayer, and call upon Him,
Making your devotion sincere
As in His sight:
Such as He created you[1011]
In the beginning, so
Shall ye return."

﴿٢٩﴾ قُلْ أَمَرَ رَبِّى بِٱلْقِسْطِ ۖ
وَأَقِيمُوا۟ وُجُوهَكُمْ عِندَ كُلِّ
مَسْجِدٍ وَٱدْعُوهُ مُخْلِصِينَ لَهُ ٱلدِّينَ ۚ
كَمَا بَدَأَكُمْ تَعُودُونَ

30. Some He hath guided:
Others have (by their choice)
Deserved the loss of their way;[1012]
In that they took
The Evil Ones, in preference
To Allah, for their friends
And protectors, and think
That they receive guidance.

﴿٣٠﴾ فَرِيقًا هَدَىٰ وَفَرِيقًا حَقَّ عَلَيْهِمُ
ٱلضَّلَٰلَةُ ۗ إِنَّهُمُ ٱتَّخَذُوا۟ ٱلشَّيَٰطِينَ
أَوْلِيَآءَ مِن دُونِ ٱللَّهِ وَيَحْسَبُونَ
أَنَّهُم مُّهْتَدُونَ

31. O Children of Adam!
Wear your beautiful apparel[1013]

﴿٣١﴾ يَٰبَنِىٓ ءَادَمَ خُذُوا۟ زِينَتَكُمْ

1010. For *wajh,* see 2:112 and n. 114. Our devotion should be sincere, not as in other men's sight, but by presenting our whole selves, heart and soul, to Allah. Even so, it may not be enough; for the sight of our heart and soul may be faulty. We should call upon Allah to give us the light, by which our sincerity may commend itself to Him as true sincerity "as in His sight".

1011. *Cf.* 6:94. Our sincerity should be real sincerity, as in His sight, for when we return to Him, we shall be stripped of all pretence, even such self-deception as may satisfy us in this life.

1012. Guidance is for all. But in some it takes effect; in others the doors are closed against it, because they have taken Evil for their friend. If they have lost their way, they have richly deserved it; for they deliberately took their choice, even though, in their self-righteousness, they may think that their sin is their virtue, and that their Evil is their Good.

1013. *Beautiful apparel: zīnah:* adornments or apparel for beautiful living: construed to mean not only clothes that add grace to the wearer, but toilet and cleanliness, attention to hair, and other small personal details which no self-respecting man or woman ought to neglect when going solemnly even before a great human dignitary, if only out of respect for the dignity of the occasion. How much more important it is to attend to these details when we solemnly apply our minds to the Presence of Allah. But the caution against excess applies: men must not go to prayer in silks or ornaments appropriate to women. Similarly sober food, good and wholesome, is not to be divorced from offices of religion; only the caution against excess applies strictly. A dirty, unkept, slovenly *Faqīr* could not claim sanctity in Islam. (R).

At every time and place
Of prayer: eat and drink:
But waste not by excess,
For Allah loveth not the wasters.

عِندَ كُلِّ مَسْجِدٍ وَكُلُوا وَاشْرَبُوا
وَلَا تُسْرِفُوٓا۟ إِنَّهُۥ لَا يُحِبُّ ٱلْمُسْرِفِينَ

C. 84.—Allah has forbidden the things
(7:32-58.) That are evil, not those that are good,
For these were created for man's
Enjoyment. The transgressors
Are those who reject Allah's Signs.
They will have no share in the Bliss
Of the Hereafter. But the righteous
Will dwell in Peace, and the Hope
That was promised will be theirs.

SECTION 4.

32. Say: Who hath forbidden
The beautiful (gifts) of Allah,[1014]
Which He hath produced
For His servants,
And the things, clean and pure,
(Which He hath provided)
For sustenance?
Say: They are, in the life
Of this world, for those
Who believe, (and) purely[1015]
For them on the Day
Of Judgement. Thus do We
Explain the Signs in detail
For those who understand.

قُلْ مَنْ حَرَّمَ زِينَةَ ٱللَّهِ ﴿٣٢﴾
ٱلَّتِىٓ أَخْرَجَ لِعِبَادِهِۦ
وَٱلطَّيِّبَٰتِ مِنَ ٱلرِّزْقِ
قُلْ هِىَ لِلَّذِينَ ءَامَنُوا۟ فِى ٱلْحَيَوٰةِ
ٱلدُّنْيَا خَالِصَةً يَوْمَ ٱلْقِيَٰمَةِ
كَذَٰلِكَ نُفَصِّلُ ٱلْءَايَٰتِ لِقَوْمٍ يَعْلَمُونَ

33. Say: The things that my Lord
Hath indeed forbidden are:[1016]
Shameful deeds, whether open

قُلْ إِنَّمَا حَرَّمَ رَبِّىَ ٱلْفَوَٰحِشَ مَا ظَهَرَ ﴿٣٣﴾

1014. Asceticism often means the negation of art and beauty, it has no necessary sanctity attached to it.

1015. The beautiful and good things of life are really meant for, and should be the privilege of those with faith in Allah. If they do not always have them in this life, and if there is sometimes the semblance of others having them who do not deserve them, let us at least consider the matter in another light. Our Faith in Allah's wisdom is unshaken and we know that these are but fleeting and mixed types of the things in the spiritual world. Their pure counterparts in the spiritual world will be only for those who proved, in all the trials of this world, that they had faith.

1016. The forbidden things are described in four categories: (1) what is shameful or unbecoming; the sort of things which have also legal and social sanctions, not of a local but of a universal kind; they may be called offences against society; (2) sins against self and trespasses or excesses of every sort; these are against truth and reason; here would come in indiscipline, failure in doing intangible duties not clearly defined by law; selfishness or self-aggrandisement, which may be condoned by custom and not punished by law, etc.; (3) erecting fetishes or false gods; this is treason against the true God; and (4) corrupting religion by debasing superstitions, etc.

Or secret; sins and trespasses
Against truth or reason; assigning
Of partners to Allah, for which
He hath given no authority;
And saying things about Allah
Of which ye have no knowledge.

مِنْهَا وَمَا بَطَنَ وَالْإِثْمَ وَالْبَغْيَ بِغَيْرِ الْحَقِّ
وَأَن تُشْرِكُوا بِاللَّهِ مَا لَمْ يُنَزِّلْ بِهِ سُلْطَانًا
وَأَن تَقُولُوا عَلَى اللَّهِ مَا لَا تَعْلَمُونَ

34. To every People is a term[1017]
Appointed: when their term
Is reached, not an hour
Can they cause delay,
Nor (an hour) can they
Advance (it in anticipation).

٣٤ وَلِكُلِّ أُمَّةٍ أَجَلٌ
فَإِذَا جَاءَ أَجَلُهُمْ لَا يَسْتَأْخِرُونَ
سَاعَةً وَلَا يَسْتَقْدِمُونَ

35. O ye Children of Adam!
Whenever there come to you
Messengers from amongst you,
Rehearsing My Signs unto you—
Those who are righteous
And mend (their lives)—
On them shall be no fear
Nor shall they grieve.

٣٥ يَا بَنِي آدَمَ إِمَّا يَأْتِيَنَّكُمْ رُسُلٌ مِّنكُمْ
يَقُصُّونَ عَلَيْكُمْ آيَاتِي فَمَنِ اتَّقَىٰ وَأَصْلَحَ
فَلَا خَوْفٌ عَلَيْهِمْ وَلَا هُمْ يَحْزَنُونَ

36. But those who reject
Our Signs and treat them
With arrogance—they
Are Companions of the Fire,
To dwell therein (forever).

٣٦ وَالَّذِينَ كَذَّبُوا بِآيَاتِنَا وَاسْتَكْبَرُوا عَنْهَا
أُولَٰئِكَ أَصْحَابُ النَّارِ هُمْ فِيهَا خَالِدُونَ

37. Who is more unjust
Than one who invents
A lie against Allah
Or rejects His Signs?
For such, their portion[1018]
Appointed must reach them
From the Book (of Decrees):

٣٧ فَمَنْ أَظْلَمُ مِمَّنِ افْتَرَىٰ
عَلَى اللَّهِ كَذِبًا أَوْ كَذَّبَ بِآيَاتِهِ
أُولَٰئِكَ يَنَالُهُمْ نَصِيبُهُم مِّنَ الْكِتَابِ

1017. People: *ummah*. I do not know whether "generation" would not be more appropriate here. If so, it would refer to the Time-Spirit, for it affects a whole number of people living contemporaneously, and while we deal grammatically with a group, we really have in mind the individuals composing the group. Anyway, the lesson is what is suggested in the following verses. There is only a limited time for an individual or for a group of people. If they do not make good during that time of probation, the chance is lost, and it cannot come again. We cannot retard or advance the march of time by a single hour or minute. ("Hour" in the text expresses an indefinite but short period of time.)

1018. It must not be supposed that the rebels against Allah would at once be cut off in this life for their sins. They will get the portion allotted to them, including the good things of life and the chance of repentance and reformation, during their probationary period on this earth. During that period they will have a full run. After that period expires, they will be called to account. They will themselves see that the false things in which they put their trust, were false, and they will confess their sin, but it will be too late.

Until, when Our messengers
(Of death) arrive and take
Their souls, they say:
"Where are the things
That ye used to invoke
Besides Allah?"
They will reply, "They
Have left us in the lurch,"
And they will bear witness
Against themselves, that they
Had rejected Allah.

حَتَّىٰٓ إِذَا جَآءَتْهُمْ رُسُلُنَا يَتَوَفَّوْنَهُمْ
قَالُوٓاْ أَيْنَ مَا كُنتُمْ تَدْعُونَ
مِن دُونِ ٱللَّهِ
قَالُواْ ضَلُّواْ عَنَّا وَشَهِدُواْ
عَلَىٰٓ أَنفُسِهِمْ أَنَّهُمْ كَانُواْ كَٰفِرِينَ

38. He will say: "Enter ye
In the company of
The Peoples who passed away
Before you—men and Jinns—
Into the Fire. Every time
A new People enters,
It curses its sister-People
(That went before), until
They follow each other, all
Into the Fire. Saith the last
About the first: "Our Lord!
It is these that misled us:
So give them a double
Penalty in the Fire."
He will say: "Doubled[1019]
For all": but this
Ye do not understand.

٣٨ قَالَ ٱدْخُلُواْ فِىٓ أُمَمٍ قَدْ خَلَتْ
مِن قَبْلِكُم مِّنَ ٱلْجِنِّ وَٱلْإِنسِ
فِى ٱلنَّارِ كُلَّمَا دَخَلَتْ أُمَّةٌ لَّعَنَتْ أُخْتَهَا
حَتَّىٰٓ إِذَا ٱدَّارَكُواْ فِيهَا جَمِيعًا
قَالَتْ أُخْرَىٰهُمْ لِأُولَىٰهُمْ رَبَّنَا
هَٰٓؤُلَآءِ أَضَلُّونَا فَـَٔاتِهِمْ
عَذَابًا ضِعْفًا مِّنَ ٱلنَّارِ قَالَ
لِكُلٍّ ضِعْفٌ وَلَٰكِن لَّا تَعْلَمُونَ

39. Then the first will say
To the last: "See then!
No advantage have ye
Over us; so taste ye
Of the Penalty for all
That ye did!"[1020]

٣٩ وَقَالَتْ أُولَىٰهُمْ لِأُخْرَىٰهُمْ
فَمَا كَانَ لَكُمْ عَلَيْنَا مِن فَضْلٍ
فَذُوقُواْ ٱلْعَذَابَ بِمَا كُنتُمْ تَكْسِبُونَ

1019. The earlier generations committed a double crime: (1) their own sins, (2) the bad example they set for those that followed. We are responsible not only for our own misdeeds, but for those which our example and our teaching to our juniors may induce them to commit. But it does not lie in the mouth of the juniors to ask for a double punishment for seniors: the motive is not justice, but pure spite, which is itself a sin. Further, the later generations have to answer for two things: (1) their own sins, and (2) their failure to learn from the past, from the experiences of those who preceded them. They should have an advantage in this respect, being "in the foremost files of Time," but they did not learn. Thus there was nothing to choose between the earlier and later generations in the matter of guilt. But how few people understand this!

In 6:160, we were told that good was rewarded tenfold, but evil was punished according to its guilt, in perfect justice. This verse is in no way inconsistent with it. Two crimes must have a double penalty. (R).

1020. Wrongdoers have really no sense of honour towards each other. "Honour among thieves" is an exceptional, not an ordinary, experience. In real life, guilt and crime are apt to indulge in mean spite and bitter recriminations against accomplices.

SECTION 5.

40. To those who reject
Our Signs and treat them
With arrogance, no opening
Will there be of the gates
Of heaven, nor will they
Enter the Garden, until
The camel can pass
Through the eye of the needle:
Such is Our reward
For those in sin.

٤٠ إِنَّ ٱلَّذِينَ كَذَّبُوا۟ بِـَٔايَـٰتِنَا
وَٱسْتَكْبَرُوا۟ عَنْهَا لَا تُفَتَّحُ لَهُمْ أَبْوَٰبُ
ٱلسَّمَآءِ وَلَا يَدْخُلُونَ ٱلْجَنَّةَ حَتَّىٰ يَلِجَ ٱلْجَمَلُ
فِى سَمِّ ٱلْخِيَاطِ ۚ وَكَذَٰلِكَ
نَجْزِى ٱلْمُجْرِمِينَ

41. For them there is
Hell, as a couch
(Below) and folds and folds
Of covering above: such
Is Our requital of those
Who do wrong.

٤١ لَهُم مِّن جَهَنَّمَ مِهَادٌ
وَمِن فَوْقِهِمْ غَوَاشٍ ۚ
وَكَذَٰلِكَ نَجْزِى ٱلظَّـٰلِمِينَ

42. But those who believe
And work righteousness—
No burden do We place
On any soul, but that
Which it can bear—
They will be Companions
Of the Garden, therein
To dwell (forever).

٤٢ وَٱلَّذِينَ ءَامَنُوا۟ وَعَمِلُوا۟
ٱلصَّـٰلِحَـٰتِ لَا نُكَلِّفُ نَفْسًا
إِلَّا وُسْعَهَآ أُو۟لَـٰٓئِكَ أَصْحَـٰبُ
ٱلْجَنَّةِ ۖ هُمْ فِيهَا خَـٰلِدُونَ

43. And We shall remove
From their hearts any
Lurking sense of injury—[1021]
Beneath them will be
Rivers flowing—and they
Shall say: "Praise be to Allah,
Who hath guided us
To this (felicity): never
Could we have found
Guidance, had it not been
For the guidance of Allah:

٤٣ وَنَزَعْنَا مَا فِى صُدُورِهِم
مِّنْ غِلٍّ تَجْرِى مِن تَحْتِهِمُ ٱلْأَنْهَـٰرُ ۖ
وَقَالُوا۟ ٱلْحَمْدُ لِلَّهِ ٱلَّذِى هَدَىٰنَا
لِهَـٰذَا وَمَا كُنَّا لِنَهْتَدِىَ
لَوْلَآ أَنْ هَدَىٰنَا ٱللَّهُ ۖ

1021. A man who may have suffered or been disappointed may have a lurking sense of injury at the back of his mind, which may spoil his enjoyment on account of past memory intruding in the midst of felicity. In such cases memory itself is pain. Even sorrow is intensified by memory: as Tennyson says, "A sorrow's crown of sorrows is remembering happier things." But that is in this our imperfect life. In the perfect felicity of the righteous, all such feelings will be blotted out. No "heartaches" then and no memories of them! The clouds of the past will have dissolved in glorious light, and no past happiness will be comparable with the perfect happiness which will have then been attained. Nor will any sense of envy or shortcoming be possible in that perfect bliss.

Indeed it was the truth
That the Messengers of our Lord
Brought unto us." And they
Shall hear the cry:
"Behold! the Garden before you!
Ye have been made[1022]
Its inheritors, for your
Deeds (of righteousness)."

لَقَدْ جَآءَتْ رُسُلُ رَبِّنَا بِالْحَقِّ
وَنُودُوٓا أَن تِلْكُمُ الْجَنَّةُ
أُورِثْتُمُوهَا بِمَا كُنتُمْ تَعْمَلُونَ

44. The Companions of the Garden
Will call out to the Companions
Of the Fire: "We have
Indeed found the promises
Of our Lord to us true:
Have you also found
Your Lord's promises true?"
They shall say, "Yes"; but[1023]
A Crier shall proclaim
Between them: "The curse
Of Allah is on the wrongdoers—

٤٤ وَنَادَىٰٓ أَصْحَٰبُ الْجَنَّةِ أَصْحَٰبَ النَّارِ
أَن قَدْ وَجَدْنَا مَا وَعَدَنَا رَبُّنَا حَقًّا
فَهَلْ وَجَدتُّم مَّا وَعَدَ رَبُّكُمْ حَقًّا
قَالُوا نَعَمْ فَأَذَّنَ مُؤَذِّنٌۢ بَيْنَهُمْ أَن
لَّعْنَةُ اللَّهِ عَلَى الظَّٰلِمِينَ

45. "Those who would hinder (men)
From the path of Allah
And would seek in it
Something crooked:[1024]
They were those who
Denied the Hereafter."

٤٥ الَّذِينَ يَصُدُّونَ
عَن سَبِيلِ اللَّهِ وَيَبْغُونَهَا عِوَجًا
وَهُم بِالْءَاخِرَةِ كَٰفِرُونَ

46. Between them shall be
A veil, and on the Heights[1025]

٤٦ وَبَيْنَهُمَا حِجَابٌ وَعَلَى الْأَعْرَافِ

1022. Jesus said: "Blessed are the meek, for they shall inherit the earth": Matt. v. 5. Here we are told: blessed are the righteous, for they shall inherit the kingdom of heaven. The stress here is on actual practical deeds of righteousness: whether they find their rewards on earth or not is immaterial: their attention is directed to an infinitely greater reward, the kingdom of Heaven. In the Sermon on the Mount this is promised to the "poor in spirit": Matt. v. 3.

1023. The Companions of the Fire can only answer a single word, "Yes," such is their state of misery. Even so, their voice is drowned in the voice of the Crier, who explains their state: they are in a state of curse, that is, deprivation of the Grace and Mercy of Allah. Such deprivation is the highest misery that souls can suffer.

1024. The unrighteous reflect their own crooked minds when the path of Allah is before them. Instead of going straight, they try to find something in it that suits their own crooked ideas. Frankly they have no faith in the final Goal, the Hereafter.

1025. This is a difficult passage, and Commentators have interpreted it in different ways. Three distinct schools of thought may be discerned in the interpretation. (1) One school thinks that the men on the Heights are Angels, or such men of exalted spiritual dignity (*e.g.*, the great Prophets), as will be able to know the souls at sight as regards their spiritual worth: the Heights will be their exalted stations, from which they will welcome the righteous with a salutation of peace, even before the righteous have entered heaven; the salutation of peace being itself an assurance of salvation to those whom they salute. (2) Another school of thought thinks that the men on the Heights are such souls as are not decidedly on the side of merit or decidedly on the side of sin, but evenly balanced on a partition between heaven and hell. Their case is yet to be decided, but their salutation to the righteous is a wistful salutation, because they hope for Allah's Mercy. (3) The third line of interpretation, with which I agree, is close to the first, with this exception, that the partition and the Heights are figurative. The higher souls will rejoice at the approaching salvation of the righteous.

Will be men
Who would know everyone
By his marks: they will call
Out to the Companions
Of the Garden, "Peace on you":
They will not have entered,
But they will have
An assurance (thereof).

رِجَالٌ يَعْرِفُونَ كُلًّا بِسِيمَـٰهُمْ
وَنَادَوْا۟ أَصْحَـٰبَ ٱلْجَنَّةِ أَن سَلَـٰمٌ عَلَيْكُمْ
لَمْ يَدْخُلُوهَا وَهُمْ يَطْمَعُونَ

47. When their eyes[1026] shall be turned
Towards the Companions
Of the Fire, they will say:
"Our Lord! send us not
To the company
Of the wrongdoers."

٤٧ وَإِذَا صُرِفَتْ أَبْصَـٰرُهُمْ
تِلْقَآءَ أَصْحَـٰبِ ٱلنَّارِ قَالُوا۟ رَبَّنَا
لَا تَجْعَلْنَا مَعَ ٱلْقَوْمِ ٱلظَّـٰلِمِينَ

SECTION 6.

48. The men on the Heights
Will call to certain men
Whom they will know
From their marks, saying:[1027]
"Of what profit to you
Were your hoards and your
Arrogant ways?

٤٨ وَنَادَىٰٓ أَصْحَـٰبُ ٱلْأَعْرَافِ رِجَالًا
يَعْرِفُونَهُم بِسِيمَـٰهُمْ قَالُوا۟ مَآ أَغْنَىٰ عَنكُمْ
جَمْعُكُمْ وَمَا كُنتُمْ تَسْتَكْبِرُونَ

49. "Behold! are these not
The men whom you swore
That Allah with His Mercy
Would never bless?
Enter ye the Garden:
No fear shall be on you,
Nor shall ye grieve."

٤٩ أَهَـٰٓؤُلَآءِ ٱلَّذِينَ أَقْسَمْتُمْ
لَا يَنَالُهُمُ ٱللَّهُ بِرَحْمَةٍ ٱدْخُلُوا۟ ٱلْجَنَّةَ
لَا خَوْفٌ عَلَيْكُمْ وَلَآ أَنتُمْ تَحْزَنُونَ

50. The Companions of the Fire
Will call to the Companions
Of the Garden: "Pour down
To us water or anything

٥٠ وَنَادَىٰٓ أَصْحَـٰبُ ٱلنَّارِ أَصْحَـٰبَ
ٱلْجَنَّةِ أَنْ أَفِيضُوا۟ عَلَيْنَا مِنَ ٱلْمَآءِ أَوْ

1026. *Their eyes*: according to interpretation (2) of the last note, *"their"* would refer to the people whose fate has not yet been decided, and the speech would be theirs; according to interpretations (1) and (3) in that note, "their" would refer to the Companions of the Garden, who would realise the terrible nature of hell, and express their horror of it. I prefer the latter. Then the mention of the "men on the Heights" and their speech in verse 48 comes in naturally as a different kind of speech from a different kind of men.

1027. This speech is in three parts: (1) the last lines of this verse are addressed to the Companions of the Fire, reminding them (as a bench of judges might speak to a prisoner) of the futility of their wealth and riches and arrogance in their earthly life; (2) the second part, in the first half of verse 49, recalls to their minds how false was their contempt of the good but lowly men who are now to be the inheritors of Heaven; and (3) the latter part of verse 49, "enter ye the Garden" is addressed to the Blessed, to give them a welcome to their state of felicity.

That Allah doth provide
For your sustenance."
They will say: "Both
These things hath Allah forbidden
To those who rejected Him—[1028]

مِمَّا رَزَقَكُمُ ٱللَّهُ ۚ قَالُوٓا۟
إِنَّ ٱللَّهَ حَرَّمَهُمَا عَلَى ٱلْكَـٰفِرِينَ

51. "Such as took their religion
To be mere amusement
And play, and were deceived
By the life of the world."
That day shall We forget them[1029]
As they forgot the meeting
Of this day of theirs,
And as they were wont
To reject Our Signs.

(٥١) ٱلَّذِينَ ٱتَّخَذُوا۟ دِينَهُمْ لَهْوًا
وَلَعِبًا وَغَرَّتْهُمُ ٱلْحَيَوٰةُ ٱلدُّنْيَا ۚ
فَٱلْيَوْمَ نَنسَىٰهُمْ كَمَا نَسُوا۟ لِقَآءَ
يَوْمِهِمْ هَـٰذَا وَمَا كَانُوا۟ بِـَٔايَـٰتِنَا يَجْحَدُونَ

52. For We had certainly
Sent unto them a Book,
Based on knowledge,
Which We explained
In detail—a guide
And a mercy
To all who believe.

(٥٢) وَلَقَدْ جِئْنَـٰهُم بِكِتَـٰبٍ
فَصَّلْنَـٰهُ عَلَىٰ عِلْمٍ هُدًى
وَرَحْمَةً لِّقَوْمٍ يُؤْمِنُونَ

53. Do they just wait
For the final fulfilment
Of the event? On the day
The event is finally fulfilled,[1030]
Those who disregarded it
Before will say: "The Messengers
Of our Lord did indeed
Bring true (tidings). Have we
No intercessors now to intercede
On our behalf? Or could we
Be sent back? Then should we

(٥٣) هَلْ يَنظُرُونَ إِلَّا تَأْوِيلَهُۥ ۚ
يَوْمَ يَأْتِى تَأْوِيلُهُۥ يَقُولُ ٱلَّذِينَ نَسُوهُ
مِن قَبْلُ قَدْ جَآءَتْ رُسُلُ رَبِّنَا بِٱلْحَقِّ
فَهَل لَّنَا مِن شُفَعَآءَ فَيَشْفَعُوا۟
لَنَآ أَوْ نُرَدُّ

1028. The Companions of the Fire will thirst for water and not get it, and for sustenance which will not be theirs, while the Companions of the Garden will have the crystal waters of the springs and rivers and they will enjoy the bliss of Allah's Countenance, which will be their supreme nourishment and the fruit of their life of probation and seeking. These things will not be transferable. *Cf.* also 37:41-47, 62-67. (R).

1029. "Forgetfulness" may be involuntary, from a defect of memory, or figuratively, a deliberate turning away from, or ignoring of, something we do not want, as when we say in an argument, "you conveniently forget that so-and-so is so-and-so." Here the latter kind is meant. If men deliberately ignored the Hereafter in spite of warnings, can they expect to be received by Allah, Whom they themselves rejected?

1030. If those without faith want to wait and see what happens in the Hereafter, they will indeed learn the truth, but it will be too late for them to profit by it then. All the false ideals and false gods which they put their trust upon will leave them in the lurch. If they thought that the goodness or greatness of others would help them, they will be undeceived on the day when their personal responsibility will be enforced. There will be no salvation except on their own record. How they will then wish that they had another chance! But their chance will be gone.

Behave differently from our
Behaviour in the past."
In fact they will have lost
Their souls, and the things
They invented will leave
Them in the lurch.

فَنَعْمَلَ غَيْرَ ٱلَّذِى كُنَّا نَعْمَلُ
قَدْ خَسِرُوٓا۟ أَنفُسَهُمْ وَضَلَّ
عَنْهُم مَّا كَانُوا۟ يَفْتَرُونَ

SECTION 7.

54. Your Guardian-Lord
Is Allah, Who created
The heavens and the earth[1031]
In six Days, then He
Established Himself on the Throne[1032]
(Of authority): He draweth
The night as a veil
O'er the day, each seeking
The other in rapid succession:
He created the sun,
The moon, and the stars,
(All) governed by laws
Under His Command.
Is it not His to create
And to govern? Blessed
Be Allah, the Cherisher
And Sustainer of the Worlds!

٥٤ إِنَّ رَبَّكُمُ ٱللَّهُ ٱلَّذِى خَلَقَ
ٱلسَّمَٰوَٰتِ وَٱلْأَرْضَ فِى سِتَّةِ أَيَّامٍ
ثُمَّ ٱسْتَوَىٰ عَلَى ٱلْعَرْشِ
يُغْشِى ٱلَّيْلَ ٱلنَّهَارَ يَطْلُبُهُۥ
حَثِيثًا وَٱلشَّمْسَ وَٱلْقَمَرَ
وَٱلنُّجُومَ مُسَخَّرَٰتٍۭ بِأَمْرِهِۦٓ
أَلَا لَهُ ٱلْخَلْقُ وَٱلْأَمْرُ
تَبَارَكَ ٱللَّهُ رَبُّ ٱلْعَٰلَمِينَ

55. Call on your Lord
With humility and in private:[1033]
For Allah loveth not
Those who trespass beyond bounds.

٥٥ ٱدْعُوا۟ رَبَّكُمْ تَضَرُّعًا وَخُفْيَةً
إِنَّهُۥ لَا يُحِبُّ ٱلْمُعْتَدِينَ

1031. A sublime verse, comparable to the Throne Verse, 2:255. The Creation in *six Days* is of course metaphorical. In 45:14, the "Days of Allah" refer not so much to time as to the growth in us of a spiritual sense, a sense of sin and a sense of Allah's Mercy. In 22:47, we are told that a Day in the sight of Allah is *like* a thousand years of our reckoning, and in 70:4, the comparison is with 50,000 of our years. In the history of our material earth, we may reckon six great epochs of evolution. The significance of the figure *six* will be discussed in connection with 41:9-12, where the matter is referred to in more detail.

1032. Here, we are told of the creation of the Heavens and the Earth in six days. But lest we should be obsessed with the Jewish idea that Allah *rested* on the seventh day, we are told that the Creation was but a prelude to Allah's work: for His authority is exercised constantly by the laws which He establishes and enforces in all parts of His Creation. The beautiful imagery of night and day seeking out each other in rapid succession is still further enforced in the Arabic by the double accusative of the very *yughshī*, showing the *mutual* interactions of the day and the night, each covering the other in turn. The Heavenly bodies show an order which is evidence of His *constant* care and government. Not only that, but it is only He Who creates, maintains, and governs, and no one else. (R).

1033. In prayer, we must avoid any arrogance or show or loudness, or vanity of requests or words. If excess is condemned in all things, it is specially worthy of condemnation when we go humbly before our Lord—we poor creatures before the Omnipotent, Who knoweth all.

56. Do no mischief on the earth,
After it hath been[1034]
Set in order, but call
On Him with fear[1035]
And longing (in your hearts):
For the Mercy of Allah
Is (always) near
To those who do good.

(٥٦) وَلَا تُفْسِدُوا فِي الْأَرْضِ
بَعْدَ إِصْلَاحِهَا وَادْعُوهُ خَوْفًا وَطَمَعًا
إِنَّ رَحْمَتَ اللَّهِ قَرِيبٌ
مِنَ الْمُحْسِنِينَ

57. It is He Who sendeth
The Winds like heralds
Of glad tidings, going before[1036]
His Mercy: when they have
Carried the heavy-laden
Clouds, We drive them
To a land that is dead,
Make rain to descend thereon,
And produce every kind
Of harvest therewith: thus
Shall We raise up the dead:
Perchance ye may remember.

(٥٧) وَهُوَ الَّذِي يُرْسِلُ
الرِّيَاحَ بُشْرًا بَيْنَ يَدَيْ رَحْمَتِهِ حَتَّىٰ إِذَا
أَقَلَّتْ سَحَابًا ثِقَالًا سُقْنَاهُ لِبَلَدٍ مَيِّتٍ
فَأَنْزَلْنَا بِهِ الْمَاءَ فَأَخْرَجْنَا بِهِ مِنْ كُلِّ الثَّمَرَاتِ
كَذَٰلِكَ نُخْرِجُ الْمَوْتَىٰ لَعَلَّكُمْ تَذَكَّرُونَ

58. From the land that is clean
And good, by the Will
Of its Cherisher, springs up
Produce, (rich) after its kind:[1037]
But from the land that is
Bad, springs up nothing
But that which is niggardly:
Thus do we explain the Signs

(٥٨) وَالْبَلَدُ الطَّيِّبُ
يَخْرُجُ نَبَاتُهُ بِإِذْنِ رَبِّهِ
وَالَّذِي خَبُثَ لَا يَخْرُجُ إِلَّا نَكِدًا
كَذَٰلِكَ نُصَرِّفُ الْآيَاتِ

1034. The man who prays with humility and earnestness finds the ground prepared by Allah for his spiritual advancement. It is all set in order, and cleared of weeds. He does not, like the wicked, upset that order, to introduce evil or mischief into it.

1035. *Fear and longing*: the fear of Allah is really a fear lest we should diverge from His Will, or do anything which would not be pleasing to Him: unlike ordinary fear, it therefore brings us nearer to Allah, and in fact nourishes our longing and desire for Him.

1036. The Parable is complete in its triple significance. (1) In the physical world the winds go like heralds of glad tidings; they are the advance guard, behind which is coming a great army of winds driving heavily laden clouds before it; the wise Providence of Allah is their General, who directs them towards a parched land, on which the clouds deliver their gladdening showers of mercy, which convert the dead land into a living, fertile, and beautiful land bearing a rich harvest. (2) In the spiritual world, the winds are the great motive forces in the mind of man, or in the world around him, that bring the clouds or instruments of Allah's Mercy, which descend and fertilise souls hitherto spiritually dead. (3) If we can see or experience such things in our life here below, can we doubt the resurrection?

1037. The triple parable explained in the last note is here continued. (1) In the physical world, the fertilising showers of rain yield a rich harvest on good soil, but bad soil yields little or nothing, (2) In the, spiritual world, also, Allah's Mercy evokes no response in some souls which have chosen evil. (3) In the final reckoning, though all will be raised, not all will achieve the fulfilment of their lives.

By various (symbols) to those
Who are grateful.[1038]

لِقَوْمٍ يَشْكُرُونَ

C. 85.—Noah's warning was rejected by his
(7:59-99.) Generation, and they were destroyed
In the Flood. Hūd was defied
By his own people 'Ād, but they were
Swept away by a terrible blast.
Their successors, the Thamūd, were puffed up
With pride and injustice, but behold!
An earthquake buried them for their sins
After Ṣāliḥ had warned them from Allah.
With a rain of brimstone and fire
Were overwhelmed the Cities of the Plain
For their unexampled lusts, against which
Lot did warn them. The people of Midian
Were given to mischief and fraud: Shu'ayb
Did warn them, but they heeded not,
And perished in an earthquake.
Allah's punishment is sure for wickedness and sin.

SECTION 8.

59. We sent Noah to his people.[1039]
He said: "O my people!
Worship Allah! ye have
No other god but Him.
I fear for you the Punishment
Of a dreadful Day!

(٥٩) لَقَدْ أَرْسَلْنَا نُوحًا إِلَىٰ قَوْمِهِۦ فَقَالَ يَٰقَوْمِ
ٱعْبُدُوا۟ ٱللَّهَ مَا لَكُم مِّنْ إِلَٰهٍ غَيْرُهُۥٓ
إِنِّىٓ أَخَافُ عَلَيْكُمْ عَذَابَ يَوْمٍ عَظِيمٍ

60. The leaders of his people
Said: "Ah! we see thee
Evidently wandering (in mind)."

(٦٠) قَالَ ٱلْمَلَأُ مِن قَوْمِهِۦٓ إِنَّا لَنَرَىٰكَ
فِى ضَلَٰلٍ مُّبِينٍ

61. He said: "O my people!
No wandering is there
In my (mind): on the contrary
I am a messenger from
The Lord and Cherisher
Of the Worlds!

(٦١) قَالَ يَٰقَوْمِ لَيْسَ بِى
ضَلَٰلَةٌ وَلَٰكِنِّى رَسُولٌ
مِّن رَّبِّ ٱلْعَٰلَمِينَ

1038. *Those who are grateful* are those who joyfully receive Allah's Message, and respond to it by deeds of holiness and righteousness.

1039. The story of Noah in greater detail will be found in 6:25-49. Here the scheme is to tell briefly the stories of some of the Prophets between Noah and Moses, and lead up thus to a lesson for the contemporaries of the Prophet Muḥammad himself. When Noah attacked the wickedness of his generation, he was laughed at for a madman, for he mentioned the Great Day to come in the Hereafter. Allah's retribution came soon afterwards—the great Flood, in which his unbelieving people were drowned, but he and those who believed in him and came into the Ark were saved.

62. "I but fulfil towards you
The duties of my Lord's mission:
Sincere is my advice to you,
And I know from Allah
Something that ye know not.

﴿٦٢﴾ أُبَلِّغُكُمْ رِسَٰلَٰتِ رَبِّي وَأَنصَحُ لَكُمْ
وَأَعْلَمُ مِنَ ٱللَّهِ مَا لَا تَعْلَمُونَ

63. "Do ye wonder that
There hath come to you
A message from your Lord,
Through a man of your own
People, to warn you—
So that ye may fear Allah
And haply receive His Mercy?"

﴿٦٣﴾ أَوَعَجِبْتُمْ أَن جَآءَكُمْ ذِكْرٌ مِّن
رَّبِّكُمْ عَلَىٰ رَجُلٍ مِّنكُمْ لِيُنذِرَكُمْ
وَلِتَتَّقُوا۟ وَلَعَلَّكُمْ تُرْحَمُونَ

64. But they rejected him,
And We delivered him,
And those with him
In the Ark:
But We overwhelmed
In the Flood those
Who rejected Our Signs.
They were indeed
A blind people!

﴿٦٤﴾ فَكَذَّبُوهُ فَأَنجَيْنَٰهُ
وَٱلَّذِينَ مَعَهُۥ فِى ٱلْفُلْكِ
وَأَغْرَقْنَا ٱلَّذِينَ كَذَّبُوا۟ بِـَٔايَٰتِنَآ
إِنَّهُمْ كَانُوا۟ قَوْمًا عَمِينَ

SECTION 9.

65. To the 'Ād people,[1040]
(We sent) Hūd, one
Of their (own) brethren:
He said: "O my people!
Worship Allah! ye have
No other god but Him.
Will ye not fear (Allah)?"

﴿٦٥﴾ وَإِلَىٰ عَادٍ أَخَاهُمْ هُودًا
قَالَ يَٰقَوْمِ ٱعْبُدُوا۟ ٱللَّهَ مَا لَكُم
مِّنْ إِلَٰهٍ غَيْرُهُۥٓ أَفَلَا تَتَّقُونَ

66. The leaders of the unbelievers
Among his people said:

﴿٦٦﴾ قَالَ ٱلْمَلَأُ ٱلَّذِينَ كَفَرُوا۟ مِن قَوْمِهِۦٓ

1040. The 'Ād people, with their prophet Hūd, are mentioned in many places. See especially 26:123-140, and 46:21-26. Their story belongs to Arabian tradition. Their eponymous ancestor 'Ād was fourth in generation from Noah, having been a son of 'Aus, the son of Aram, the son of Sām, the son of Noah. They occupied a large tract of country in Southern Arabia, extending from 'Ummān at the mouth of the Persian Gulf to Ḥaḍramūt and Yemen at the southern end of the Red Sea. The people were tall in stature and were great builders. Probably the long, winding tracts of sands *(aḥqāf)* in their dominions (46:21) were irrigated with canals. They forsook the true God, and oppressed their people. A three-year famine visited them, but yet they took no warning. At length a terrible blast of wind destroyed them and their land, but a remnant, known as the second 'Ād or the Thamūd (see below) were saved, and afterwards suffered a similar fate for their sins.

The tomb of the Prophet Hūd (*qabr Nabī Hūd*) is still traditionally shown in Ḥaḍramūt, latitude 15°N and longitude 49½°E, about 90 miles north of Mukalla. There are ruins and inscriptions in the neighbourhood. See "Ḥaḍramūt. Some of its Mysteries Unveiled," by D. van der Meulen and H. von Wissmann, Leyden, 1932. (R).

"Ah! we see thou art
An imbecile!" and "We think
Thou art a liar!"

إِنَّا لَنَرَىٰكَ فِي سَفَاهَةٍ وَإِنَّا لَنَظُنُّكَ
مِنَ ٱلْكَٰذِبِينَ

67. He said "O my people!
I am no imbecile, but
(I am) a messenger from
The Lord and Cherisher
Of the Worlds!

٦٧ قَالَ يَٰقَوْمِ لَيْسَ بِي سَفَاهَةٌ وَلَٰكِنِّي
رَسُولٌ مِّن رَّبِّ ٱلْعَٰلَمِينَ

68. "I but fulfil towards you
The duties of my Lord's mission:
I am to you a sincere
And trustworthy adviser.

٦٨ أُبَلِّغُكُمْ رِسَٰلَٰتِ رَبِّي
وَأَنَا۠ لَكُمْ نَاصِحٌ أَمِينٌ

69. "Do ye wonder that
There hath come to you
A message from your Lord
Through a man of your own
People, to warn you?
Call in remembrance
That He made you
Inheritors after the people
Of Noah, and gave you
A stature tall among the nations.
Call in remembrance
The benefits (ye have received)
From Allah: that so
Ye may prosper."

٦٩ أَوَعَجِبْتُمْ أَن جَآءَكُمْ ذِكْرٌ
مِّن رَّبِّكُمْ عَلَىٰ رَجُلٍ مِّنكُمْ لِيُنذِرَكُمْ
وَٱذْكُرُوٓا۟ إِذْ جَعَلَكُمْ خُلَفَآءَ مِنۢ بَعْدِ قَوْمِ
نُوحٍ وَزَادَكُمْ فِي ٱلْخَلْقِ بَصْۜطَةً
فَٱذْكُرُوٓا۟ ءَالَآءَ ٱللَّهِ
لَعَلَّكُمْ تُفْلِحُونَ

70. They said: "Comest thou
To us, that we may worship
Allah alone, and give up
The cult of our fathers?
Bring us what thou
Threatenest us with,
If so be that thou
Tellest the truth!"

٧٠ قَالُوٓا۟ أَجِئْتَنَا لِنَعْبُدَ
ٱللَّهَ وَحْدَهُۥ وَنَذَرَ مَا كَانَ
يَعْبُدُ ءَابَآؤُنَا فَأْتِنَا بِمَا تَعِدُنَآ
إِن كُنتَ مِنَ ٱلصَّٰدِقِينَ

71. He said: "Punishment
And wrath have already[1041]
Come upon you from your Lord:
Dispute ye with me

٧١ قَالَ قَدْ وَقَعَ عَلَيْكُم
مِّن رَّبِّكُمْ رِجْسٌ وَغَضَبٌ أَتُجَٰدِلُونَنِي

1041. The past tense may be understood in three ways. (1) A terrible famine had already afflicted the 'Ād as a warning before they were overwhelmed in the final blast of hot wind (see the last note). (2) The terrible insolence and sin into which they had fallen was itself a punishment. (3) The prophetic past is used, as much as to say: "Behold! I see a dreadful calamity: it is already on you!"

Over names which ye[1042]
Have devised—ye
And your fathers—
Without authority from Allah?
Then wait: I am
Amongst you, also waiting."

فِي أَسْمَاءٍ سَمَّيْتُمُوهَا أَنتُمْ
وَءَابَاؤُكُم مَّا نَزَّلَ ٱللَّهُ بِهَا مِن سُلْطَٰنٍ
فَٱنتَظِرُوٓا۟ إِنِّي مَعَكُم مِّنَ ٱلْمُنتَظِرِينَ

72. We saved him and those
Who adhered to him,
By Our Mercy and We
Cut off the roots of those
Who rejected Our Signs
And did not believe.

٧٢ فَأَنجَيْنَٰهُ وَٱلَّذِينَ مَعَهُۥ بِرَحْمَةٍ مِّنَّا
وَقَطَعْنَا دَابِرَ ٱلَّذِينَ كَذَّبُوا۟ بِـَٔايَٰتِنَا
وَمَا كَانُوا۟ مُؤْمِنِينَ

SECTION 10.

73. To the Thamūd people[1043]
(We sent) Ṣāliḥ, one
Of their own brethren:
He said: "O my people!
Worship Allah; ye have
No other god but Him.
Now hath come unto you
A clear (Sign) from your Lord!
This she-camel of Allah
Is a Sign unto you:
So leave her to graze

٧٣ وَإِلَىٰ ثَمُودَ أَخَاهُمْ صَٰلِحًا
قَالَ يَٰقَوْمِ ٱعْبُدُوا۟ ٱللَّهَ مَا لَكُم
مِّنْ إِلَٰهٍ غَيْرُهُۥ قَدْ جَآءَتْكُم
بَيِّنَةٌ مِّن رَّبِّكُمْ هَٰذِهِۦ نَاقَةُ ٱللَّهِ
لَكُمْ ءَايَةً فَذَرُوهَا تَأْكُلْ

1042. Why dispute over names and imaginary gods, the inventions of your minds? Come to realities. If you ask for the punishment and are waiting in insolent defiance, what can I do but also wait?—in fear and trembling for you, for I know that Allah's punishment is sure!

1043. The Thamūd people were the successors to the culture and civilisation of the 'Ād people, for whom see n. 1040 and 7:65 above. They were cousins to the 'Ād, apparently a younger branch of the same race. Their story also belongs to Arabian tradition, according to which their eponymous ancestor Thamūd was a son of 'Ābir (a brother of Aram), the son of Sām, the son of Noah. Their seat was in the northwest corner of Arabia (Arabia Petraea), between Madīnah and Syria. It included both rocky country (*hijr,* 15:80), and the spacious fertile valley (Wādi) and plains country of Qurā, which begins just north of the City of Madīnah and was traversed by the Ḥijāz Railway. When the Holy Prophet in the 9th year of the Hijrah led his expedition to Tabūk (about 400 miles north of Madīnah) against the Roman forces, on a reported Roman invasion from Syria, he and his men came across the archaeological remains of the Thamūd. The recently excavated rock city of Petra, near Ma'ān, may go back to the Thamūd, though its architecture has many features connecting it with Egyptian and Graeco-Roman culture overlaying what is called by European writers Nabataean culture. Who were the Nabataeans? They were an old Arab tribe which played a considerable part in history after they came into conflict with Antigonus 1 in 312 B.C. Their capital was Petra, but they extended their territory right up to the Euphrates. In 85 B.C. they were lords of Damascus under their king Ḥāritha (Aretas of Roman history). For some time they were allies of of the Roman Empire and held the Red Sea littoral. The Emperor Trajan reduced them and annexed their territory in A.C. 105. The Nabataeans succeeded the Thamūd of Arabian tradition. The Thamūd are mentioned by name in an inscription of the Assyrian King Sargon, dated 715 B.C., as a people of Eastern and Central Arabia (*Encyclopaedia of Islam*). See also Appendix VII to S. 26.

With the advance of material civilisation, the Thamūd people became godless and arrogant, and were destroyed by an earthquake. Their prophet and warner was Ṣāliḥ, and the crisis in their history is connected with the story of a wonderful she-camel: see next note.

In Allah's earth, and let her
Come to no harm,
Or ye shall be seized
With a grievous punishment.[1044]

فِىٓ أَرْضِ ٱللَّهِ وَلَا تَمَسُّوهَا بِسُوٓءٍ
فَيَأْخُذَكُمْ عَذَابٌ أَلِيمٌ

74. "And remember how He
Made you inheritors
After the 'Ād people
And gave you habitations
In the land: ye build
For yourselves palaces and castles
In (open) plains, and carve out
Homes in the mountains;
So bring to remembrance
The benefits (ye have received)
From Allah, and refrain
From evil and mischief
On the earth."

٧٤ وَٱذْكُرُوٓا۟ إِذْ جَعَلَكُمْ خُلَفَآءَ
مِنۢ بَعْدِ عَادٍ وَبَوَّأَكُمْ فِى ٱلْأَرْضِ
تَتَّخِذُونَ مِن سُهُولِهَا قُصُورًا
وَتَنْحِتُونَ ٱلْجِبَالَ بُيُوتًا
فَٱذْكُرُوٓا۟ ءَالَآءَ ٱللَّهِ وَلَا تَعْثَوْا۟
فِى ٱلْأَرْضِ مُفْسِدِينَ

75. The leaders of the arrogant
Party among his people said
To those who were reckoned
Powerless—those among them[1045]
Who believed: "Know ye
Indeed that Ṣāliḥ is
A messenger from his Lord?"
They said: "We do indeed
Believe in the revelation[1046]
Which hath been sent
Through him."

٧٥ قَالَ ٱلْمَلَأُ ٱلَّذِينَ ٱسْتَكْبَرُوا۟
مِن قَوْمِهِۦ لِلَّذِينَ ٱسْتُضْعِفُوا۟
لِمَنْ ءَامَنَ مِنْهُمْ أَتَعْلَمُونَ
أَنَّ صَـٰلِحًا مُّرْسَلٌ مِّن رَّبِّهِۦ ۚ
قَالُوٓا۟ إِنَّا بِمَآ أُرْسِلَ بِهِۦ مُؤْمِنُونَ

1044. The story of this wonderful she-camel, that was a sign to the Thamūd, is variously told in tradition. We need not follow the various versions in the traditional story. What we are told in the Qur'ān is: that (1) she was a Sign or Symbol, which the Prophet Ṣāliḥ, used for a warning to the haughty oppressors of the poor; (2) there was scarcity of water, and the arrogant or privileged classes tried to prevent the access of the poor or their cattle to the springs, while Ṣāliḥ intervened on their behalf (26:155, 54:28); (3) like water, pasture was considered a free gift of nature, in this spacious earth of Allah (7:73), but the arrogant ones tried to monopolise the pasture also; (4) this particular she-camel was made a test case (54:27) to see if the arrogant ones would come to reason; (5) the arrogant ones, instead of yielding to the reasonable rights of the people, hamstrung the poor she-camel and slew her, probably secretly (91:14, 54:29); the cup of their iniquities was full, and the Thamūd people were destroyed by a dreadful earthquake, which threw them prone on the ground and buried them with their houses and their fine buildings.

1045. As usually happens in such cases, the Believers were the lowly and the humble, and the oppressors were the arrogant, who in selfishly keeping back nature's gifts (which are Allah's gifts) from the people, were deaf to the dictates of justice and kindness. Ṣāliḥ took the side of the unprivileged, and was therefore himself attacked.

1046. Notice the relation between the question and the answer. The godless chiefs wanted to discredit Ṣāliḥ, and put a personal question, as much as to say, "Is he not a liar?" The Believers took back the issue to the higher plane, as much as to say, "We know he is a man of Allah, but look at the justice for which he is making a stand: to resist it is to resist Allah". The answer of the godless was to reject Allah in words, and in action to commit a further act of cruelty and injustice in hamstringing and killing the she-camel, at the same time hurling defiance at Ṣāliḥ and his God.

76. The arrogant party said:
"For our part, we reject
What ye believe in."

٧٦ قَالَ ٱلَّذِينَ ٱسْتَكْبَرُوٓا۟ إِنَّا بِٱلَّذِىٓ ءَامَنتُم بِهِۦ كَـٰفِرُونَ

77. Then they hamstrung
The she-camel, and insolently
Defied the order of their Lord,
Saying: "O Ṣāliḥ! bring about
Thy threats, if thou art
A messenger (of Allah)!"

٧٧ فَعَقَرُوا۟ ٱلنَّاقَةَ وَعَتَوْا۟ عَنْ أَمْرِ رَبِّهِمْ وَقَالُوا۟ يَـٰصَـٰلِحُ ٱئْتِنَا بِمَا تَعِدُنَآ إِن كُنتَ مِنَ ٱلْمُرْسَلِينَ

78. So the earthquake took them[1047]
Unawares, and they lay
Prostrate in their homes
In the morning!

٧٨ فَأَخَذَتْهُمُ ٱلرَّجْفَةُ فَأَصْبَحُوا۟ فِى دَارِهِمْ جَـٰثِمِينَ

79. So Ṣāliḥ left them,[1048]
Saying: "O my people!
I did indeed convey to you
The message for which
I was sent by my Lord:
I gave you good counsel,
But ye love not good counsellors!"

٧٩ فَتَوَلَّىٰ عَنْهُمْ وَقَالَ يَـٰقَوْمِ لَقَدْ أَبْلَغْتُكُمْ رِسَالَةَ رَبِّى وَنَصَحْتُ لَكُمْ وَلَـٰكِن لَّا تُحِبُّونَ ٱلنَّـٰصِحِينَ

80. We also (sent) Lūṭ:[1049]
He said to his people:
"Do ye commit lewdness
Such as no people
In creation (ever) committed
Before you?

٨٠ وَلُوطًا إِذْ قَالَ لِقَوْمِهِۦٓ أَتَأْتُونَ ٱلْفَـٰحِشَةَ مَا سَبَقَكُم بِهَا مِنْ أَحَدٍ مِّنَ ٱلْعَـٰلَمِينَ

81. "For ye practise your lusts
On men in preference

٨١ إِنَّكُمْ لَتَأْتُونَ ٱلرِّجَالَ شَهْوَةً مِّن دُونِ

1047. The retribution was not long delayed. A terrible earthquake came and buried the people and destroyed their boasted civilisation. The calamity must have been fairly extensive in area and intense in the terror it inspired, for it is described (54:31) as a "single mighty blast" (*ṣayḥatan wāḥidatan*), the sort of terror-inspiring noise which accompanies all big earthquakes.

1048. Ṣāliḥ was saved by Allah's mercy as a just and righteous man. His speech here may be either a parting warning, or it may be a soliloquy lamenting the destruction of his people for their sin and folly.

1049. Lūṭ is the Lot of the English Bible. His story is biblical, but freed from some shameful features which are a blot on the biblical narrative, (*e.g.*, see Gen. xix, 30-36). He was a nephew of Abraham, and was sent as a Prophet and warner to the people of Sodom and Gomorrah, cities utterly destroyed for their unspeakable sins. They cannot be exactly located, but it may be supposed that they were somewhere in the plain east of the Dead Sea. The story of their destruction is told in the 19th chapter of Genesis. Two angels in the shape of handsome young men came to Lot in the evening and became his guests by night. The inhabitants of Sodom in their lust for unnatural crime invaded Lot's house but were repulsed. In the morning, the angels warned Lot to escape with his family. "Then the Lord rained upon Sodom and upon Gomorrah brimstone and fire from the Lord out of heaven; and He overthrew those cities, and all the plain, and all the inhabitants of the cities, and that which grew upon the ground. But his wife looked back from behind him, and she became a pillar of salt." (Gen. xix. 24-26).

Note that Lūṭ's people are the people to whom he is sent on a mission. He was not one of their own brethren, as was Ṣāliḥ or Shu'ayb. But he looked upon his people as his brethren (50:13), as a man of God always does.

To women: ye are indeed
A people transgressing
Beyond bounds."

ٱلنِّسَآءِ بَلْ أَنتُمْ قَوْمٌ مُّسْرِفُونَ

82. And his people gave
No answer but this:
They said, "Drive them out
Of your city: these are
Indeed men who want
To be clean and pure!"[1050]

﴿٨٢﴾ وَمَا كَانَ جَوَابَ قَوْمِهِۦٓ إِلَّآ
أَن قَالُوٓا۟ أَخْرِجُوهُم مِّن قَرْيَتِكُمْ ۖ
إِنَّهُمْ أُنَاسٌ يَتَطَهَّرُونَ

83. But We saved him
And his family, except
His wife: she was
Of those who lagged behind[1051]

﴿٨٣﴾ فَأَنجَيْنَٰهُ وَأَهْلَهُۥٓ إِلَّا
ٱمْرَأَتَهُۥ كَانَتْ مِنَ ٱلْغَٰبِرِينَ

84. And we rained down on them
A shower (of brimstone):[1052]
Then see what was the end
Of those who indulged
In sin and crime!

﴿٨٤﴾ وَأَمْطَرْنَا عَلَيْهِم مَّطَرًا ۖ فَٱنظُرْ
كَيْفَ كَانَ عَٰقِبَةُ ٱلْمُجْرِمِينَ

Section 11.

85. To the Madyan people[1053]

﴿٨٥﴾ وَإِلَىٰ مَدْيَنَ

1050. An instance of the withering sarcasm that hardened sinners use against the righteous. They wound with words, and follow up the insult with deeds of injustice, thinking that they would bring the righteous into disgrace. But Allah looks after His own, and in the end, the wicked themselves are overthrown when the cup of their iniquity is full.

1051. In the biblical narrative she looks back, a physical act (see n. 1049): here she is a type of those who lag behind, *i.e.* whose mental and moral attitude, in spite of their association with the righteous, is to hark back to the glitter of wickedness and sin. The righteous should have one sole objective, the Way of Allah. They should not look behind, nor yet to the right or the left.

1052. The shower is expressly stated in Q. 11:82 to have been of stones. In 15:73-74, we are told that there was a terrible blast or noise (*sayḥah*) in addition to the shower of stones. Taking these passages into consideration along with Gen. xix. 24. (see n. 1049 above), I think it is legitimate to translate: "a shower of brimstone."

1053. "Madyan" may be identified with "Midian." Midian and the Midianites are frequently mentioned in the Old Testament, though the particular incident here mentioned belongs to Arab rather than to Jewish tradition. The Midianites were of Arab race, though, as neighbours of the Canaanites, they probably intermixed with them. They were a wandering tribe; it was Midianite merchants to whom Joseph was sold into slavery, and who took him to Egypt. Their principal territory in the time of Moses was in the northeast of the Sinai Peninsula, and east of the Amalekites. Under Moses the Israelites waged a war of extermination against them: they slew the kings of Midian, slaughtered all the males, burnt their cities and castles, and captured their cattle (Num. xxxi. 7-11). This sounds like total extermination. Yet a few generations afterwards, they were so powerful that the Israelites for their sins were delivered into the captivity of the Midianites for seven years: both the Midianites and their camels were without number: and the Israelites hid from them in "dens. . .caves, and strongholds" (Judges vii. 1-6). Gideon destroyed them again, (Judges vii. 1-25), say about two centuries after Moses. As the decisive battle was near the hill of Moreh, not far south of Mount Tabor, we may localise the Midianites on this occasion in the northern parts of the Jordan valley, at least 200 miles north of the Sinai Peninsula.

This and the previous destruction under Moses were local, and mention no *town* of Midian. In later times there was a town of Madyan on the east side of the Gulf of 'Aqaba. It is mentioned in Josephus, Eusebius, and Ptolemy: (*Encyclopaedia of Islam*). Then it disappears from geography. In Muslim times it was a revived town with quite a different kind of population, but it never flourished. The Midianites disappeared from history.

We sent Shu'ayb,[1054] one
Of their own brethren: he said:
"O my people! worship Allah;
Ye have no other god
But Him. Now hath come
Unto you a clear (Sign)
From your Lord! Give just
Measure and weight, nor withhold
From the people the things
That are their due; and do
No mischief on the earth
After it has been set
In order: that will be best
For you, if ye have Faith.

أَخَاهُمْ شُعَيْبًا قَالَ يَٰقَوْمِ ٱعْبُدُوا۟ ٱللَّهَ
مَا لَكُم مِّنْ إِلَٰهٍ غَيْرُهُۥ قَدْ جَآءَتْكُم
بَيِّنَةٌ مِّن رَّبِّكُمْ فَأَوْفُوا۟
ٱلْكَيْلَ وَٱلْمِيزَانَ وَلَا تَبْخَسُوا۟
ٱلنَّاسَ أَشْيَآءَهُمْ وَلَا تُفْسِدُوا۟
فِى ٱلْأَرْضِ بَعْدَ إِصْلَٰحِهَا
ذَٰلِكُمْ خَيْرٌ لَّكُمْ إِن كُنتُم مُّؤْمِنِينَ

86. "And squat not on every road,
Breathing threats, hindering
From the path of Allah
Those who believe in Him,
And seeking in it
Something crooked;
But remember how ye were
Little, and He gave you increase.
And hold in your mind's eye
What was the end

٨٦ وَلَا تَقْعُدُوا۟ بِكُلِّ صِرَٰطٍ
تُوعِدُونَ وَتَصُدُّونَ عَن سَبِيلِ ٱللَّهِ
مَنْ ءَامَنَ بِهِۦ وَتَبْغُونَهَا عِوَجًا
وَٱذْكُرُوٓا۟ إِذْ كُنتُمْ قَلِيلًا فَكَثَّرَكُمْ
وَٱنظُرُوا۟ كَيْفَ كَانَ عَٰقِبَةُ

1054. Shu'ayb belongs to Arab rather than to Jewish tradition, to which he is unknown. His identification with Jethro, the father-in-law of Moses, has no warrant, and I reject it. There is no similarity either in names or incidents, and there are chronological difficulties (see 1064 below). If, as the Commentators tell us, Shu'ayb was in the fourth generation from Abraham, being a great-grandson of Madyan (a son of Abraham), he would be only about a century from the time of Abraham, whereas the Hebrew Bible would give us a period of four to six centuries between Abraham and Moses. The mere fact that Jethro was a Midianite and that another name, Hobab, is mentioned for a father-in-law of Moses in Num. x. 29, is slender ground for identification. As the Midianites were mainly a nomad tribe, we need not be surprised that their destruction in one or two settlements did not affect their life in wandering sections of the tribe in other geographical regions. Shu'ayb's mission was apparently in one of the settled towns of the Midianites, which was completely destroyed by an earthquake (7:91). If this happened in the century after Abraham, there is no difficulty in supposing that they were again a numerous tribe three or five centuries later, in the time of Moses (see last note). As they were a mixed wandering tribe, both their resilience and their eventual absorption can be easily understood. But the destruction of the settlement or settlements (if the Wood or Ayka was a separate settlement, see n. 2000 to 15:78) to which Shu'ayb was sent to preach was complete, and no traces of it now remain.

The name of the highest mountain of Yemen, Nabi Shu'ayb (11,000 ft.) has probably no connection with the geographical territory of the nomad Midianites, unless we suppose that their wanderings extended so far south from the territories mentioned in the last note.

Of those who did mischief.[1055]

ٱلْمُفْسِدِينَ

87. "And if there is a party
Among you who believes
In the Message with which
I have been sent, and a party
Which does not believe,[1056]
Hold yourselves in patience
Until Allah doth decide
Between us: for He
Is the best to decide."[1057]

﴿٨٧﴾ وَإِن كَانَ طَآئِفَةٌ مِّنكُمْ ءَامَنُوا۟ بِٱلَّذِىٓ أُرْسِلْتُ بِهِۦ وَطَآئِفَةٌ لَّمْ يُؤْمِنُوا۟ فَٱصْبِرُوا۟ حَتَّىٰ يَحْكُمَ ٱللَّهُ بَيْنَنَا ۚ وَهُوَ خَيْرُ ٱلْحَٰكِمِينَ

9/30

88. The leaders, the arrogant
Party among his people, said:[1058]

﴿٨٨﴾ قَالَ ٱلْمَلَأُ ٱلَّذِينَ ٱسْتَكْبَرُوا۟ مِن قَوْمِهِۦ

1055. The Midianites were in the path of a commercial highway of Asia, *viz.*, that between two such opulent and highly organised nations as Egypt and the Mesopotamian group comprising Assyria and Babylonia. Their besetting sins are thus characterised here: (1) giving short measure or weight, whereas the strictest commercial probity is necessary for success, (2) a more general form of such fraud, depriving people of rightful dues, (3) producing mischief and disorder, whereas peace and order had been established (again in a literal as well as a metaphorical sense); (4) not content with upsetting settled life, taking to highway robbery, literally as well as (5) metaphorically, in two says, *viz.*, cutting off people from access to the worship of Allah, and abusing religion and piety for crooked purposes, *i.e.*, exploiting religion itself for their crooked ends, as when a man builds houses of prayer out of unlawful gains or ostentatiously gives charity out of money which he has obtained by force or fraud, etc. After setting out this catalogue of besetting sins Shu'ayb makes two appeals to the past: (1) You began as an insignificant tribe, and by Allah's favour you increased and multiplied in numbers and resources; do you not then owe a duty to Allah to fulfil His Law? (2) What was the result in the case of those who fell into sin? Will you not take warning by their example?

So Shu'ayb began his argument with faith in Allah as the source of all virtue, and ended it with destruction as the result of all sin. In the next verse he pleads with them to end their controversies and come to Allah.

1056. Madyan is torn by internal conflict. Shu'ayb comes as a peacemaker, not in virtue of his own wisdom, but by an appeal to the truth, righteousness and justice of Allah. As we see later, the real motives of his opponents were selfishness, arrogance, violence, lawlessness, and injustice. But he appeals to their better nature, and is prepared to argue on the basis that the party which wants to suppress those who believe in Allah's Message and in righteousness, has some sincere mental difficulty in accepting Shu'ayb's mission. "If," he says to them, "that is the case, do you think it justifies your intolerance, your violence, or your persecution? On the contrary, events will prove by themselves who is right and who is wrong." To the small band who believe in his mission and follow his teaching, he would preach patience and perseverance. His argument to them would be: "You have faith; surely your faith is strong enough to sustain you in the hope that Allah's truth will triumph in the end; there is no cause for despair or dejection."

How exactly these past experiences fit the times of our Holy Guide Muḥammad! And it is for that analogy and that lesson that the stories of Noah, Hūd, Ṣāliḥ, Lūṭ, and Shu'ayb are related to us—all different, and yet all pointing to the great lessons in Muḥammad's life.

1057. See the argument in the last note. Allah's decision may come partly in this very life, either for the same generation or for succeeding generations, by the logic of external events. But in any case it is bound to come spiritually on a higher plane eventually, when the righteous will be comforted and the sinners will be convinced of sin from their own inner conviction.

1058. The gentle, all-persuasive arguments of Shu'ayb fell on hard hearts. Their only reply was: "Turn him out!—him and his people." When courtesy and a plea for toleration are pitted against bigotry, what room is there for logic? But bigotry and unrighteousness have their own crooked ways of pretending to be tolerant. "O yes!" they said, "we are very tolerant and long-suffering! But we are for our country and religion. Come back to the ways of our fathers, and we shall graciously forgive you!" "Ways of their fathers!"—they meant injustice and oppression, highhandedness to the poor and the weak, fraud under cover of religion, and so on! Perhaps the righteous were the poor and the weak. Were they likely to love such ways? Perhaps there was implied a bribe as well as a threat. "If you come back and wink at our iniquities, you shall have scraps of prosperity thrown at you. If not, out you go in disgrace!"

O Shu'ayb! we shall
Certainly drive thee out
Of our city—(thee) and those
Who believe with thee;
Or else ye (thou and they)
Shall have to return
To our ways and religion."
He said: "What! even
Though we do detest (them)?

لَنُخْرِجَنَّكَ يَٰشُعَيْبُ
وَٱلَّذِينَ ءَامَنُوا۟ مَعَكَ مِن قَرْيَتِنَآ
أَوْ لَتَعُودُنَّ فِى مِلَّتِنَا ۚ
قَالَ أَوَلَوْ كُنَّا كَٰرِهِينَ

89. "We should indeed invent[1059]
A lie against Allah,
If we returned to your ways
After Allah hath rescued
Us therefrom; nor could we
By any manner of means
Return thereto unless it be
As in the will and plan of Allah,[1060]
Our Lord. Our Lord
Can reach out to the utmost
Recesses of things by His
knowledge.
In Allah is our trust.
Our Lord! Decide thou[1061]
Between us and our people
In truth, for thou
Art the best to decide."

٨٩ قَدِ ٱفْتَرَيْنَا عَلَى ٱللَّهِ كَذِبًا
إِنْ عُدْنَا فِى مِلَّتِكُم بَعْدَ إِذْ نَجَّىٰنَا
ٱللَّهُ مِنْهَا ۚ وَمَا يَكُونُ لَنَآ أَن
نَّعُودَ فِيهَآ إِلَّآ أَن يَشَآءَ ٱللَّهُ رَبُّنَا ۚ
وَسِعَ رَبُّنَا كُلَّ شَىْءٍ عِلْمًا ۚ
عَلَى ٱللَّهِ تَوَكَّلْنَا ۚ رَبَّنَا ٱفْتَحْ بَيْنَنَا وَبَيْنَ
قَوْمِنَا بِٱلْحَقِّ وَأَنتَ خَيْرُ ٱلْفَٰتِحِينَ

90. The leaders, the Unbelievers
Among his people, said:
"If ye follow Shu'ayb,
Be sure then ye are ruined!"[1062]

٩٠ وَقَالَ ٱلْمَلَأُ ٱلَّذِينَ كَفَرُوا۟ مِن قَوْمِهِۦ
لَئِنِ ٱتَّبَعْتُمْ شُعَيْبًا إِنَّكُمْ إِذًا لَّخَٰسِرُونَ

1059. The answer of the righteous is threefold. (1) "Coming back is all very well. But do you mean that we should practise the vices we detest?" (2) "You want us to lie against our consciences and our Lord, after we have seen the evil of your ways." (3) "Neither bribes nor threats, nor specious appeals to patriotism or ancestral religion can move us: the matter rests with Allah, Whose will and pleasure we obey, and on Whom alone we rely. His knowledge will search out all your specious pretences."

1060. This of course, does not mean that anyone can ever return to evil ways with Allah's consent. Shu'ayb has already emphatically repudiated the idea of returning "to your ways after Allah hath rescued us therefrom." But even if their ways had been good, the human will, he goes on to say, has no data to rely upon, and he and his followers would only be guided by Allah's Will and Plan.

1061. Having answered the insincere quibblers among the godless, the righteous turn to Allah in earnest prayer. The endless controversies in this world about abstract or speculative things never end even where both sides are sincere in their beliefs. The decision must be taken to Allah, Who sits on the throne of Truth, and Whose decisions will, therefore, be free from the errors and imperfections of all human judgement. The sincere have nothing to fear in the appeal to Him, as their motives are pure.

1062. The answer of the Unbelievers is characteristic. As all their bribes and subtleties have failed, they resort to threats, which are worse than the argument of the stick. "All right," they say, "there is nothing but ruin before you!" That means that the Believers will be persecuted, held up to obloquy, ostracised, and prevented from access to all means of honourable livelihood; their families and dependants will be insulted, reviled, and tortured, if they could but be got into the enemy's power; their homes destroyed, and their names held up to ridicule and contempt even when they are gone. But, as verse 92 says, their wicked designs recoiled on themselves: it was the wicked who were ruined and blotted out.

91. But the earthquake took them
Unawares, and they lay
Prostrate in their homes
Before the morning![1063]

٩١ فَأَخَذَتْهُمُ ٱلرَّجْفَةُ
فَأَصْبَحُوا۟ فِى دَارِهِمْ جَٰثِمِينَ

92. The men who rejected
Sh̲u'ayb became as if
They had never been
In the homes where they
Had flourished: the men
Who rejected Sh̲u'ayb—
It was they who were ruined!

٩٢ ٱلَّذِينَ كَذَّبُوا۟ شُعَيْبًا كَأَن
لَّمْ يَغْنَوْا۟ فِيهَا ۚ ٱلَّذِينَ كَذَّبُوا۟ شُعَيْبًا
كَانُوا۟ هُمُ ٱلْخَٰسِرِينَ

93. So Sh̲u'ayb left them,
Saying: "O my people!
I did indeed convey to you
The Messages for which
I was sent by my Lord:
I gave you good counsel,
But how shall I lament
Over a people who refuse
To believe!"[1064]

٩٣ فَتَوَلَّىٰ عَنْهُمْ
وَقَالَ يَٰقَوْمِ لَقَدْ أَبْلَغْتُكُمْ
رِسَٰلَٰتِ رَبِّى وَنَصَحْتُ لَكُمْ ۖ
فَكَيْفَ ءَاسَىٰ عَلَىٰ قَوْمٍ كَٰفِرِينَ

Section 12.

94. Whenever We sent a prophet
To a town, We took up
Its people in suffering

٩٤ وَمَآ أَرْسَلْنَا فِى قَرْيَةٍ مِّن نَّبِىٍّ إِلَّآ
أَخَذْنَآ أَهْلَهَا بِٱلْبَأْسَآءِ

1063. The fate of the Madyan people is described in the same terms as that of the *Th̲amūd* in verse 78 above. An earthquake seized them by night, and they were buried in their own homes, no longer to vex Allah's earth. But a supplementary detail is mentioned in Q. 26:189, "the punishment of a day of overshadowing gloom," which may be understood to mean a shower of ashes and cinders accompanying a volcanic eruption. Thus a day of terror drove them into their homes, and the earthquake finished them. The lament of Sh̲u'ayb in verse 93 is almost the same as that of Ṣāliḥ in verse 79, with two differences: (1) Sh̲u'ayb's messages attacked the many sins of his people (see n. 1055) and are, therefore, expressed in the plural, while Ṣāliḥ's fight was chiefly against selfish arrogance, and his message is expressed in the singular; (2) the Th̲amūd were the more cultured people of the two, and perished in their own pride; as Ṣāliḥ said, "ye love not good counsellors"; the Midianites were a rougher people, and their minds were less receptive of argument or faith; as Sh̲u'ayb said, they were a people who "refused to believe."

1064. Can we get any idea of the chronological place of the destruction of the Midianites? In n. 1053 (7:85) we have discussed the geographical aspects. The following considerations will help us in getting some idea of their period: (1) The stories of Noah, Hūd, Ṣāliḥ, Lūṭ, and Sh̲u'ayb seem to be in chronological order. Therefore Sh̲u'ayb came after Abraham, whose nephew Lūṭ was; (2) If Sh̲u'ayb was in the fourth generation from Abraham, (see 11:89, n. 1590), it would be impossible for him to have been a contemporary of Moses, who came many centuries later—this difficulty is recognised by Ibn Kath̲īr and other classical commentators; (3) The identification of Sh̲u'ayb with Jethro the father-in-law of Moses is without warrant; see n. 1054 (7:85); (4) Sh̲u'ayb must have been before Moses; see 7:103; (5) The Midianites who were destroyed by Moses and by Gideon after him (n. 1053) were local remnants, as we may speak of the Jews at the present day; but their existence as a nation in their original homelands seems to have ended before Moses: "they became as if they had never been in the homes where they had flourished" (7:92); (6) Josephus, Eusebius, and Ptolemy mention a town of Madyan, but it was not of any importance (n. 1053); (7) After the first centuries of the Christian era, Madyan as a town appears as an unimportant place resting on its past.

And adversity, in order
That they might learn humility.[1065]

وَٱلضَّرَّآءِ لَعَلَّهُمْ يَضَّرَّعُونَ

95. Then We changed their suffering
Into prosperity, until they grew[1066]
And multiplied, and began
To say: "Our fathers (too)
Were touched by suffering
And affluence". . Behold!
We called them to account
Of a sudden, while they
Realised not (their peril).

٩٥ ثُمَّ بَدَّلْنَا مَكَانَ ٱلسَّيِّئَةِ ٱلْحَسَنَةَ
حَتَّىٰ عَفَوا وَّقَالُوا قَدْ مَسَّ
ءَابَآءَنَا ٱلضَّرَّآءُ وَٱلسَّرَّآءُ فَأَخَذْنَٰهُم
بَغْتَةً وَهُمْ لَا يَشْعُرُونَ

96. If the people of the towns
Had but believed and feared
Allah, We should indeed
Have opened out to them
(All kinds of) blessings
From heaven and earth;
But they rejected (the truth),
And We brought them
To book for their misdeeds.

٩٦ وَلَوْ أَنَّ أَهْلَ ٱلْقُرَىٰٓ
ءَامَنُوا وَٱتَّقَوْا لَفَتَحْنَا عَلَيْهِم بَرَكَٰتٍ
مِّنَ ٱلسَّمَآءِ وَٱلْأَرْضِ وَلَٰكِن كَذَّبُوا
فَأَخَذْنَٰهُم بِمَا كَانُوا يَكْسِبُونَ

97. Did the people of the towns
Feel secure against the coming[1067]
Of Our wrath by night
While they were asleep?

٩٧ أَفَأَمِنَ أَهْلُ ٱلْقُرَىٰٓ أَن يَأْتِيَهُم
بَأْسُنَا بَيَٰتًا وَهُمْ نَآئِمُونَ

98. Or else did they feel
Secure against its coming
In broad daylight while they
Played about (carefree)?

٩٨ أَوَأَمِنَ أَهْلُ ٱلْقُرَىٰٓ أَن يَأْتِيَهُم
بَأْسُنَا ضُحًى وَهُمْ يَلْعَبُونَ

99. Did they then feel secure
Against the Plan of Allah?—
But no one can feel

٩٩ أَفَأَمِنُوا مَكْرَ ٱللَّهِ فَلَا يَأْمَنُ

1065. Man was originally created pure. The need of a Prophet arises when there is some corruption and iniquity, which he is sent to combat. His coming means much trial and suffering, especially to those who join him in his protest against wrong. Even so peaceful a Prophet as Jesus said: "I came not to send peace but a sword" (Matt. x. 34). But it is all in Allah's Plan, for we must learn humility if we would be worthy of Him.

1066. Allah gives enough rope to the sinful. They grow and multiply, and become scornful. Neither suffering nor affluence teaches them the lessons which they are meant to learn, *viz.*, patience and humility, gratitude and kindness to others. They take adversity and prosperity alike as a matter of chance. "O yes!" they say, "such things have happened in all ages! Our fathers had such experience before us, and our sons will have them after us. Thus goes on the world for all time!" But does it? What about the Plan of the Architect? They are found napping when Nemesis overtakes them in the midst of their impious tomfoolery!

1067. This and the two following verses should be read together. They furnish a commentary on the story of the five Prophets that has already been related. Allah's wrath may come by night or by day, whether people are arrogantly defying Allah's laws or are sunk in lethargy or vain dreams of unreality. Who can escape Allah's Plan, and who can feel themselves outside it except those who are seeking their own ruin?

Secure from the Plan
Of Allah, except those
(Doomed) to ruin![1068]

مَكْرَ ٱللَّهِ إِلَّا ٱلْقَوْمُ ٱلْخَٰسِرُونَ

C. 86.—While the story of the prophets who preached
(7:100-157.) In vain to their people prefigures
The struggles in the early careers
Of all Prophets, the story of Moses—
His struggles, with an alien and arrogant
People, his final deliverance
Of his people from foreign domination,
And his leading them within sight
Of the Promised Land, in spite
Of the forces that resisted—prefigures
The early struggles and eventual triumph
Of Muḥammad, the Holy Prophet of Allah.

SECTION 13.

100. To those who inherit
The earth in succession
To its (previous) possessors,
Is it not a guiding (lesson)
That, if We so willed,
We could punish them (too)
For their sins, and seal up
Their hearts so that they
Could not hear?[1069]

أَوَلَمْ يَهْدِ لِلَّذِينَ ﴿١٠٠﴾
يَرِثُونَ ٱلْأَرْضَ مِنۢ بَعْدِ أَهْلِهَآ
أَن لَّوْ نَشَآءُ أَصَبْنَٰهُم بِذُنُوبِهِمْ ۚ
وَنَطْبَعُ عَلَىٰ قُلُوبِهِمْ فَهُمْ لَا يَسْمَعُونَ

101. Such were the towns
Whose story We (thus)
Relate unto thee:
There came indeed to them
Their Messengers with clear
(Signs):

تِلْكَ ٱلْقُرَىٰ ﴿١٠١﴾
نَقُصُّ عَلَيْكَ مِنْ أَنۢبَآئِهَا ۚ
وَلَقَدْ جَآءَتْهُمْ رُسُلُهُم بِٱلْبَيِّنَٰتِ

1068. This closes that chapter of the narrative which deals with Prophets who were rejected by their own people, but who stood firm on Allah's message and were able to rescue a remnant who believed. In each case there were special circumstances and special besetting sins, which have been explained in the notes. The nations which as a body could not be won over to Allah's Law perished. So far we have been dealing with the corruptions and iniquities within each nation. In the story of Moses we have first a struggle against the bondage of Egypt, one of the foremost powers then in the world, the rescue of the Israelites and their wanderings, and their proving themselves unworthy and being left to wander in a new sense when they rejected the new Prophet (Muḥammad) who came to renew Allah's Message.

1069. The stories which have been related should give a warning to present and future generations which have inherited the land, the power, or the experience of the past. They should know that if they fall into the same sins they will meet with the same fate: when through their contumacy their hearts are hardened, they do not listen to the advice that falls on their ears.

But they would not believe
What they had rejected before.[1070]
Thus doth Allah seal up
The hearts of those
Who reject Faith.

فَمَا كَانُوا لِيُؤْمِنُوا بِمَا كَذَّبُوا مِن قَبْلُ ۚ
كَذَٰلِكَ يَطْبَعُ اللَّهُ عَلَىٰ قُلُوبِ الْكَافِرِينَ

102. Most of them We found not
Men (true) to their covenant:
But most of them We found
Rebellious and disobedient.

(١٠٢) وَمَا وَجَدْنَا لِأَكْثَرِهِم مِّنْ عَهْدٍ ۖ
وَإِن وَجَدْنَا أَكْثَرَهُمْ لَفَاسِقِينَ

103. Then after them We sent
Moses with Our Signs
To Pharaoh and his chiefs,
But they wrongfully rejected them:
So see what was the end
Of those who made mischief.

(١٠٣) ثُمَّ بَعَثْنَا مِن بَعْدِهِم مُّوسَىٰ بِآيَاتِنَا
إِلَىٰ فِرْعَوْنَ وَمَلَئِهِ فَظَلَمُوا بِهَا ۖ
فَانظُرْ كَيْفَ كَانَ عَاقِبَةُ الْمُفْسِدِينَ

104. Moses[1071] said: "O Pharaoh![1072]
I am a messenger from
The Lord of the Worlds—

(١٠٤) وَقَالَ مُوسَىٰ يَا فِرْعَوْنُ
إِنِّي رَسُولٌ مِّن رَّبِّ الْعَالَمِينَ

105. "One for whom it is right
To say nothing but truth
About Allah. Now have I

(١٠٥) حَقِيقٌ عَلَىٰ أَن لَّا أَقُولَ عَلَى اللَّهِ إِلَّا الْحَقَّ ۚ

1070. Those who have heard the Message and rejected it find it more difficult afterwards to retrace their steps. Evil has blocked the channels of Allah's grace to them. It begins with their breaking their Covenant with Allah; with each step afterwards they fall deeper and deeper into the mire.

1071. The story of Moses is told in many places in the Holy Qur'ān, with a special lesson in each context. In 2:49-71, the story is an appeal to the Jews from their own scripture and traditions, to show their true place in the religious history of mankind, and how they forfeited it. Here we have an instructive parallelism in that story to the story of Muḥammad's mission—how both these men of Allah had to fight against (1) a foreign foe, arrogant, unjust, faithless, and superstitious, and (2) against the same class of internal foe among their own people. Both of them won through. In the case of Moses, the foreign foe was Pharaoh and his Egyptians, who boasted of their earlier and superior civilisation; in the case of the Prophet Muḥammad the foreign foes were the Jews themselves and the Christians of his day. Moses led his people nearly to the Land of promise in spite of rebellions among his own people; Muḥammad succeeded completely in overcoming the resistance of his own people by his own virtues and firmness of character, and by the guidance of Allah. What was a hope when these Makkan verses were revealed became an accomplishment before the end of his life and mission on earth.

1072. "Pharaoh" (Arabic, *Fir'awn*) is a dynastic title, not the name of any particular king in Egypt. It has been traced to the ancient Hieroglyphic words, *Per-āa*, which mean "Great House." The *nūn* is an "infirm" letter added in the process of Arabisation. Who was the Pharaoh in the story of Moses? If the Inscriptions had helped us, we could have answered with some confidence, but unfortunately the Inscriptions fail us. It is probable that it was an early Pharaoh of the XVIIIth Dynasty, say Thothmes I, about 1540 B.C. See Appendix IV, on Egyptian Chronology and Israel, printed at the end of this Sūrah.

Come unto you (people), from[1073]
Your Lord, with a clear (Sign):
So let the Children of Israel
Depart along with me."

قَدْ جِئْتُكُم بِبَيِّنَةٍ مِّن رَّبِّكُمْ
فَأَرْسِلْ مَعِيَ بَنِيٓ إِسْرَٰٓءِيلَ

106. (Pharaoh) said: "If indeed
Thou hast come with a Sign,
Show it forth—
If thou tellest the truth."[1074]

١٠٦ قَالَ إِن كُنتَ جِئْتَ بِـَٔايَةٍ
فَأْتِ بِهَآ إِن كُنتَ مِنَ ٱلصَّٰدِقِينَ

107. Then (Moses) threw his rod,
And behold! it was
A serpent, plain (for all to see)![1075]

١٠٧ فَأَلْقَىٰ عَصَاهُ فَإِذَا هِيَ ثُعْبَانٌ مُّبِينٌ

108. And he drew out his hand,
And behold! it was white
To all beholders![1076]

١٠٨ وَنَزَعَ يَدَهُۥ فَإِذَا هِيَ بَيْضَآءُ لِلنَّٰظِرِينَ

1073. Notice that Moses,in addressing Pharaoh and the Egyptians, claims his mission to be not from *his* God, or *his people's* God but from "*your* Lord," from "the Lord of the Worlds," And his mission is not to *his* people only: "I come unto *you* (Egyptian people) from *your* Lord." The spirit of our version is entirely different from the spirit of the same story as told in the Old Testament (Exod. chapters i. to xv.). In Exod. iii. 18, the mission of Moses is expressed to be as from "the Lord God of the Hebrews."

The essence of the whole Islamic story is this: Joseph's sufferings and good fortune were not merely a story in a romance. Joseph was a prophet; his sufferings and his subsequent rise to power and position in Egypt were to be a lesson (a) to his wicked brothers who sold him into slavery, (b) to his people who were stricken with famine and found a welcome in Egypt, and (c) to the Egyptians, who were arrogant over their high material civilisation, but had yet to be taught the pure faith of Abraham. Israel prospered in Egypt, and stayed there perhaps two to four centuries. (Renan allows only one century). Times changed, and the racial bigotry of the Egyptians showed its head again, and Israel was oppressed. Moses was raised up with a threefold mission again (a) to learn all the learning of the Egyptians and preach Allah's Truth to them as one who had been brought up among themselves, (b) to unite and reclaim his own people, and (c) to rescue them and lead them to a new world, which was to open out their spiritual horizon and lead them to the Psalms of David and the glories of Solomon.

1074. The ensuing dialogue shows the psychology on the two sides. Pharaoh is sitting in his court, with his ministers and chiefs around him. In their arrogance they are only amused at the effrontery and apparent revolt of the Israelite leaders, and they rely upon their own superior worldly power, aided by the magic which was a part of the Egyptian religion. Confronting them stand two men, Moses with his mission from Allah, and his brother Aaron who was his lieutenant. They are confident, not in their own powers, but in the mission they had received. The first thing they have to do is to act on the subjective mind of the Egyptians, and by methods which by Allah's miracle show that Egyptian magic was nothing before the true power of Allah.

1075. The serpent played a large part in Egyptian mythology. The great sun-god Ra won a great victory over the serpent Apophis, typifying the victory of light over darkness. Many of their gods and goddesses took the forms of snakes to impress their foes with terror. Moses's rod as a type of a serpent at once appealed to the Egyptian mentality. The contempt which the Egyptians had entertained in their minds before was converted into terror. Here was some one who could control the reptile which their great god Ra himself had such difficulty in overcoming!

1076. But the second Sign displayed by Moses was even more puzzling to the Egyptians. Moses drew out his hand from the folds of the garments on his breast, and it was white and shining as with divine light! This was to counter any suggestions of evil, which the serpent might have created. This was no work of evil—of black magic, or a trick or illusion. His hand was transfigured—with a light which no Egyptian sorcerers could produce. In Islam the "white hand" of Moses has passed into a proverb, for a symbol of divine glory dazzling to the beholders.

SECTION 14.

109. Said the Chiefs of the people
Of Pharaoh: "This is indeed
A sorcerer well-versed.

110. "His plan is to get you out
Of your land: then
What is it ye counsel?"[1077]

111. They said: "Keep him
And his brother in suspense
(For awhile); and send
To the cities men to collect—

112. And bring up to thee
All (our) sorcerers well-versed."[1078]

113. So there came
The sorcerers to Pharaoh:
They said, "Of course
We shall have a (suitable)
Reward if we win!"[1079]

114. He said: "Yea, (and more)—
For ye shall in that case
Be (raised to posts)
Nearest (to my person)."

115. They said: "O Moses!
Wilt thou throw (first),
Or shall we have
The (first) throw?"

١٠٩ قَالَ ٱلْمَلَأُ مِن قَوْمِ فِرْعَوْنَ
إِنَّ هَٰذَا لَسَٰحِرٌ عَلِيمٌ

١١٠ يُرِيدُ أَن يُخْرِجَكُم مِّنْ أَرْضِكُمْ ۖ فَمَاذَا تَأْمُرُونَ

١١١ قَالُوٓا۟ أَرْجِهْ وَأَخَاهُ
وَأَرْسِلْ فِى ٱلْمَدَآئِنِ حَٰشِرِينَ

١١٢ يَأْتُوكَ بِكُلِّ سَٰحِرٍ عَلِيمٍ

١١٣ وَجَآءَ ٱلسَّحَرَةُ فِرْعَوْنَ قَالُوٓا۟ إِنَّ
لَنَا لَأَجْرًا إِن كُنَّا نَحْنُ ٱلْغَٰلِبِينَ

١١٤ قَالَ نَعَمْ وَإِنَّكُمْ
لَمِنَ ٱلْمُقَرَّبِينَ

١١٥ قَالُوا۟ يَٰمُوسَىٰٓ إِمَّآ أَن تُلْقِىَ
وَإِمَّآ أَن نَّكُونَ نَحْنُ ٱلْمُلْقِينَ

1077. The two Signs had the desired effect on the Egyptians. They were impressed, but they judged them by their own standards. They thought to themselves, "These are ordinary sorcerers: let us search out our best sorcerers and show them that they have superior powers." But like all worldly people, they began to fear for their own power and possessions. It was far from Moses's intention to drive out the Egyptians from their own land. He merely wanted to end the Egyptian oppression. But the Egyptians had a guilty conscience, and they judged other people's motives by their own. They discussed the matter in council on quite wrong premises.

1078. The advice of the Council to Pharaoh shows a misreading of the situation. They were in a panic about what the magic of this evidently powerful sorcerer could do against them. So they advised the Pharaoh to summon their most powerful sorcerers from all over the country, and in the meantime to hold Moses and Aaron in suspense—neither to yield to them nor definitely to oppose them. The Prophets of Allah could well afford to wait. Time is always in favour of Truth. (R).

1079. The most noted sorcerers of Pharaoh came. Their art was built up on trickery and imposture, and the first thing they could think of was to make a selfish bargain for themselves. The Pharaoh and his Council would, in their present state of panic, agree to anything. And so they did. Pharaoh not only promised them any rewards they desired if they foiled the strange power of these men, but he also promised them the highest dignities round his own person. And so the contest begins, with due observance of the amenities observed by combatants before they come to close grips.

116. Said Moses: "Throw ye (first)."
So when they threw,
They bewitched the eyes
Of the people, and struck
Terror into them: for they
Showed a great (feat of) magic.[1080]

قَالَ أَلْقُوا۟ فَلَمَّآ أَلْقَوْا۟ ﴿١١٦﴾
سَحَرُوٓا۟ أَعْيُنَ ٱلنَّاسِ
وَٱسْتَرْهَبُوهُمْ وَجَآءُو بِسِحْرٍ عَظِيمٍ

117. We put it into Moses's mind
By inspiration: "Throw (now)
Thy rod": and behold!
It swallows up straightway
All the falsehoods
Which they fake!

وَأَوْحَيْنَآ إِلَىٰ مُوسَىٰٓ ﴿١١٧﴾
أَنْ أَلْقِ عَصَاكَ فَإِذَا هِىَ
تَلْقَفُ مَا يَأْفِكُونَ

118. Thus truth was confirmed.
And all that they did
Was made of no effect.

فَوَقَعَ ٱلْحَقُّ وَبَطَلَ مَا كَانُوا۟ يَعْمَلُونَ ﴿١١٨﴾

119. So the (great ones) were vanquished
There and then, and were
Made to look small.[1081]

فَغُلِبُوا۟ هُنَالِكَ وَٱنقَلَبُوا۟ صَـٰغِرِينَ ﴿١١٩﴾

120. But the sorcerers fell down
Prostrate in adoration.

وَأُلْقِىَ ٱلسَّحَرَةُ سَـٰجِدِينَ ﴿١٢٠﴾

121. Saying: "We believe
In the Lord of the Worlds.

قَالُوٓا۟ ءَامَنَّا بِرَبِّ ٱلْعَـٰلَمِينَ ﴿١٢١﴾

122. "The Lord of Moses and Aaron."

رَبِّ مُوسَىٰ وَهَـٰرُونَ ﴿١٢٢﴾

123. Said Pharaoh: "Believe ye
In Him before I give
You permission? Surely
This is a trick which ye

قَالَ فِرْعَوْنُ ءَامَنتُم بِهِۦ قَبْلَ أَنْ ﴿١٢٣﴾
ءَاذَنَ لَكُمْ إِنَّ هَـٰذَا لَمَكْرٌ

1080. Moses and his brother Aaron were pitted against the most skillful magic-men of Egypt, but they were calm and confident and let the magic-men have their innings first. As is usual in this world, the magicians trickery made a great impression on the people, but when Moses threw his rod, the illusion was broken, and the falsehood was all shown up. In the Old Testament story (Exod. vii. 10-12) it was Aaron that threw the rod, and he threw it before the magicians. Aaron's rod became a serpent. Then the magicians threw their rods, and they became serpents, but Aaron's rod swallowed up their rods. The story given to us is more dramatic and less literal. We are told in general terms that Moses first allowed the magic-men to play their tricks. The rod of Moses was the symbol of his authority. It must have been a simple shepherd's crook with which he used to feed his flocks. With Allah's grace behind him, he was able to expose all false trickery and establish the Truth.

1081. The proud ones of the Court—Pharaoh and his chiefs—were hard-hearted, and the exposure of the imposture only made them wreak their rage on those whom they could reach. On the other hand the effect on the humbler ones—those who had been made the dupes and instruments of the imposture—was quite different. Their conscience was awakened. They fell down to the ground in adoration of the Lord of the Worlds, and confessed their faith.

Have planned in the City
To drive out its people:
But soon shall ye know
(The consequences).[1082]

مَكَرْتُمُوهُ فِي ٱلْمَدِينَةِ لِتُخْرِجُوا۟ مِنْهَآ أَهْلَهَا
فَسَوْفَ تَعْلَمُونَ

124 "Be sure I will cut off
Your hands and your feet
On opposite sides, and I
Will cause you all
To die on the cross."

(١٢٤) لَأُقَطِّعَنَّ أَيْدِيَكُمْ وَأَرْجُلَكُم
مِّنْ خِلَٰفٍ ثُمَّ لَأُصَلِّبَنَّكُمْ أَجْمَعِينَ

125. They said: "For us,
We are but sent back
Unto our Lord:

(١٢٥) قَالُوٓا۟ إِنَّآ إِلَىٰ رَبِّنَا مُنقَلِبُونَ

126. "But thou dost wreak
Thy vengeance on us
Simply because we believed
In the Signs of our Lord
When they reached us!
Our Lord! pour out on us
Patience and constancy, and take
Our souls unto Thee
As Muslims (who bow
To Thy Will)!"[1083]

(١٢٦) وَمَا تَنقِمُ مِنَّآ
إِلَّآ أَنْ ءَامَنَّا بِـَٔايَٰتِ رَبِّنَا
لَمَّا جَآءَتْنَا
رَبَّنَآ أَفْرِغْ عَلَيْنَا صَبْرًا
وَتَوَفَّنَا مُسْلِمِينَ

1082. Pharaoh and his Court were doubly angry: first because they were made to look small when confronted by the power of Allah, and secondly, because their dupes and instruments were snatched away from them. These men, the sorcerers, at once recognised the Signs of Allah, and in their case the mission of Moses and Aaron was fulfilled. They turned back on their past life of imposture, make-believe, false worship, and oppression of the weak, and confessed the One true God. As usually happens, hardened sinners resent all the more the saving of any of their companions from sin and error. Judging other people's motives by their own, they accuse them of duplicity, and if they have the power, they take cruel revenge. Here the Pharaoh threatens the repentant sinners with the extreme punishment for treason and apostasy (cutting off of hands and feet, combined with an ignominious death on the cross, as in the case of the worst malefactors). But they remained firm, and prayed to Allah for patience and constancy. Probably their influence spread quietly in the commonality. Ultimately it appeared on the Throne itself, in the person of Amenophis IV about five or six generations afterwards. See Appendix V, on Egyptian Religion, printed at the end of this Sūrah.

1083. These Egyptians, by their patience and constancy, show that their repentance was true. Thus in their case the mission of Moses was fulfilled directly, and their number must have amounted to a considerable figure. They were martyrs to their faith, and their martyrdom affected their nation in two ways. In the first place, as they were the pick of those who practised the false superstition in Egypt, their conversion and disappearance dealt a staggering blow to the whole system. Secondly, the indirect effect of their martyrdom on the commonalty of Egypt must have been far greater than can be measured by numbers. The banner of Allah was planted, and the silent spiritual fight must have gone on ever since, though history, in recording outward events, is silent on the slow and gradual processes of transformation undergone by Egyptian religion. From a chaotic pantheon of animals and animal gods, the worship of the sun and the heavenly bodies, and the worship of the Pharaoh as the embodiment of power, they gradually came to realise the oneness and mercy of the true God. After many glimpses of Monotheism on Egyptian soil itself, the Gospel of Jesus reached them, and eventually Islam.

SECTION 15.

127. Said the chiefs of Pharaoh's
People: "Wilt thou leave
Moses and his people,
To spread mischief in the land,
And to abandon thee
And thy gods?" He said
"Their male children will we
Slay; (only) their females
Will we save alive;
And we have over them
(Power) irresistible."[1084]

﴿١٢٧﴾ وَقَالَ ٱلْمَلَأُ مِن قَوْمِ فِرْعَوْنَ أَتَذَرُ
مُوسَىٰ وَقَوْمَهُۥ لِيُفْسِدُوا۟ فِى ٱلْأَرْضِ
وَيَذَرَكَ وَءَالِهَتَكَ ۚ قَالَ
سَنُقَتِّلُ أَبْنَآءَهُمْ وَنَسْتَحْىِۦ نِسَآءَهُمْ
وَإِنَّا فَوْقَهُمْ قَٰهِرُونَ

128. Said Moses to his people:
"Pray for help from Allah,"
And (wait) in patience and constancy:
For the earth is Allah's,
To give as a heritage
To such of His servants
As He pleaseth; and the end
Is (best) for the righteous.[1085]

﴿١٢٨﴾ قَالَ مُوسَىٰ لِقَوْمِهِ
ٱسْتَعِينُوا۟ بِٱللَّهِ وَٱصْبِرُوٓا۟ ۖ
إِنَّ ٱلْأَرْضَ لِلَّهِ يُورِثُهَا مَن
يَشَآءُ مِنْ عِبَادِهِۦ ۖ وَٱلْعَٰقِبَةُ لِلْمُتَّقِينَ

129. They said: "We have had
(Nothing but) trouble, both before
And after thou camest[1086]
To us." He said:
"It may be that your Lord
Will destroy your enemy
And make you inheritors[1087]

﴿١٢٩﴾ قَالُوٓا۟ أُوذِينَا مِن قَبْلِ أَن تَأْتِيَنَا
وَمِنۢ بَعْدِ مَا جِئْتَنَا ۚ قَالَ عَسَىٰ رَبُّكُمْ
أَن يُهْلِكَ عَدُوَّكُمْ وَيَسْتَخْلِفَكُمْ

1084. Pharaoh's order against the sorcerers was drastic enough. But his Council is not satisfied. What about Moses and the Israelites? They had a seeming victory, and will now be more mischievous than ever. They appeal to Pharaoh's vanity and his superstition and sense of power. "If you leave them alone," they say, "where will be your authority? You and your gods will be defied!" Pharaoh has a ready answer. He was really inwardly cowed by the apparent power of Moses. He dared not openly act against him. But he had already, before the birth of Moses, passed a cunning order to destroy the whole people of Israel. Through the instrumentality of midwives (Exod. i. 15) all the male children were to be destroyed, and the females would then be for the Egyptians: the race of Israel would thus be at an end. This order was still in force, and would remain in force until the despised race was absorbed. But Egyptian cunning and wickedness had no power against Allah's Plan for those who had faith. See verse 129 below.

1085. Notice the contrast between the arrogant tone of Pharaoh and the humility and faith taught by Moses. In the end the arrogance was humbled, and humility and faith were protected and advanced.

1086. There is a slight note of querulousness in the people's answer. But Moses allays it by his own example and courage, and his vision of the future: which was amply fulfilled in time. See verse 137 below.

1087. The Israelites, despised and enslaved, were to be rescued and made rulers in Palestine. David and Solomon were great kings and played a notable part in history. But the greatness of Israel was conditional; they were to be judged by their deeds. When they fell from grace, other people were given honour and power. And so it came to be the turn of the Arab race, and so on. Allah gives His gifts to those who are righteous and obey His Law.

In the earth; that so He may try you By your deeds."	فِي ٱلْأَرْضِ فَيَنظُرَ كَيْفَ تَعْمَلُونَ

Section 16.

130. We punished the people Of Pharaoh with years (Of drought) and shortness Of crops; that they might Receive admonition.	وَلَقَدْ أَخَذْنَآ ءَالَ فِرْعَوْنَ بِٱلسِّنِينَ وَنَقْصٍ مِّنَ ٱلثَّمَرَٰتِ لَعَلَّهُمْ يَذَّكَّرُونَ ﴿١٣٠﴾
131. But when good (times) came, They said, "This is due To us;" when gripped By calamity, they ascribed it To evil omens connected With Moses and those with him! Behold! in truth the omens Of evil are theirs [1088] In Allah's sight, but most Of them do not understand!	فَإِذَا جَآءَتْهُمُ ٱلْحَسَنَةُ قَالُوا۟ لَنَا هَٰذِهِۦ ۖ وَإِن تُصِبْهُمْ سَيِّئَةٌ يَطَّيَّرُوا۟ بِمُوسَىٰ وَمَن مَّعَهُۥٓ ۗ أَلَآ إِنَّمَا طَٰٓئِرُهُمْ عِندَ ٱللَّهِ وَلَٰكِنَّ أَكْثَرَهُمْ لَا يَعْلَمُونَ ﴿١٣١﴾
132. They said (to Moses): "Whatever be the Signs Thou bringest, to work Therewith thy sorcery on us,[1089] We shall never believe In thee."	وَقَالُوا۟ مَهْمَا تَأْتِنَا بِهِۦ مِنْ ءَايَةٍ لِّتَسْحَرَنَا بِهَا فَمَا نَحْنُ لَكَ بِمُؤْمِنِينَ ﴿١٣٢﴾
133. So We sent (plagues) on them: Wholesale Death,[1090] Locusts, Lice, Frogs, And Blood: Signs openly[1091] Self-explained: but they	فَأَرْسَلْنَا عَلَيْهِمُ ٱلطُّوفَانَ وَٱلْجَرَادَ وَٱلْقُمَّلَ وَٱلضَّفَادِعَ وَٱلدَّمَ ءَايَٰتٍ مُّفَصَّلَٰتٍ

1088. Their superstition ascribed the punishment of their own wickedness to some evil omen. They thought Moses and his people brought them ill-luck. They did not look within themselves to see the root of evil, and the cause of their punishment! So it happens in all ages. People blame the righteous for something which they do, different from other men, instead of searching out their own lapses from rectitude, which are punished by Allah.

1089. A type of obstinacy and resistance to Allah's message. As they believed in sorcery and magic, they thought anything unusual was but sorcery and magic, and hardened their hearts against Truth.

1090. *Ṭūfān* = a widespread calamity, causing wholesale death and destruction. It may be a flood, or a typhoon, or an epidemic, among men or cattle. Perhaps the last is meant, if we may interpret by the Old Testament story. See also Exod. ix. 3, 9, 15; xii. 29.

1091. In 17:101, the reference is to nine Clear Signs. These are: (1) the Rod (7:107), (2) the Radiant Hand (7:108), (3) the years of drought or shortage of water (7:130), (4) short crops (7:130), and the five mentioned in this verse, *viz.*, (5) epidemics among men and beasts, (6) locusts, (7) lice, (8) frogs, and (9) the water turning to blood.

Were steeped in arrogance,
A people given to sin.

فَاسْتَكْبَرُوا وَكَانُوا قَوْمًا مُّجْرِمِينَ

134. Every time the Penalty
Fell on them, they said:
"O Moses! on our behalf
Call on thy Lord in virtue
Of His promise to thee:
If thou wilt remove
The Penalty from us,
We shall truly believe in thee,
And we shall send away
The Children of Israel
With thee."[1092]

١٣٤ وَلَمَّا وَقَعَ عَلَيْهِمُ ٱلرِّجْزُ قَالُوا
يَـٰمُوسَى ٱدْعُ لَنَا رَبَّكَ بِمَا عَهِدَ عِندَكَ
لَئِن كَشَفْتَ عَنَّا ٱلرِّجْزَ لَنُؤْمِنَنَّ لَكَ
وَلَنُرْسِلَنَّ مَعَكَ
بَنِىٓ إِسْرَٰٓءِيلَ

135. But every time We removed
The Penalty from them
According to a fixed term
Which they had to fulfil—[1093]
Behold! they broke their word!

١٣٥ فَلَمَّا كَشَفْنَا عَنْهُمُ ٱلرِّجْزَ
إِلَىٰٓ أَجَلٍ هُم بَـٰلِغُوهُ إِذَا هُمْ يَنكُثُونَ

136. So We exacted retribution
From them: We drowned them[1094]
In the sea, because they
Rejected Our Signs, and failed
To take warning from them.[1095]

١٣٦ فَٱنتَقَمْنَا مِنْهُمْ فَأَغْرَقْنَـٰهُمْ فِى ٱلْيَمِّ
بِأَنَّهُمْ كَذَّبُوا بِـَٔايَـٰتِنَا وَكَانُوا عَنْهَا غَـٰفِلِينَ

137. And We made a people,
Considered weak (and of no
account),
Inheritors of lands

١٣٧ وَأَوْرَثْنَا ٱلْقَوْمَ ٱلَّذِينَ
كَانُوا يُسْتَضْعَفُونَ

1092. The demand of Moses was two-fold: (1) come to Allah and cease from oppression, and (2) let me take Israel out of Egypt. At first it was laughed at and rejected with scorn. When the Plagues came for punishment, each time the Egyptians suffered, they promised amendment and begged Moses to intercede and cause the plague to cease. But every time it ceased, they went back to their evil attitude, until the final retribution came. This is a type of the sinner's attitude for all times.

1093. The intercession of Moses was limited to prayer. Each plague or penalty had its appointed term in Allah's decree. That term was duly fulfilled before the plague ceased. Allah's law is firm: it does not vacillate like the human will. The intercession only meant two things: (1) that Allah's name was invoked and His presence duly brought home to the mind and heart of the sinner who promised repentance, and (2) that the sinner was given a further chance if the prayer was accepted. This again is a universal truth.

1094. When at last Pharaoh let Israel go, they selected, not the highway to Canaan, along the Mediterranean and by Gaza, because they were unarmed and would have encountered immediate opposition there, but by way of the wilderness of Sinai. They crossed the Red Sea, while Pharaoh's host which came in pursuit was drowned. *Cf.* 2:50. (R).

1095. Where was the Council of Pharaoh held in which Moses addressed Pharaoh? Egypt's primary capital in the XVIIIth Dynasty was Thebes (= No-Ammon), but that was more than 400 miles to the south of the Delta, in whose corner Israel dwelt. Memphis, on the apex of the Delta, a little south of where Cairo is now, was also over 100 miles from Israel's habitations. The interview must have been either in a Palace near Goshen, where the Israelites dwelt, or in Zoan (= Tanis), the Deltaic capital built by a former dynasty, which was of course still available for the reigning dynasty, and which was not far from the Israelite settlement.

In both East and West—
Lands whereon We sent
Down Our blessings.
The fair promise of thy Lord
Was fulfilled for the Children
Of Israel, because they had
Patience and constancy,
And We levelled to the ground
The Great Works and fine
Buildings
Which Pharaoh and His people
Erected (with such pride).[1096]

مَشَـٰرِقَ ٱلْأَرْضِ وَمَغَـٰرِبَهَا
ٱلَّتِى بَـٰرَكْنَا فِيهَا
وَتَمَّتْ كَلِمَتُ رَبِّكَ ٱلْحُسْنَىٰ
عَلَىٰ بَنِىٓ إِسْرَٰٓءِيلَ بِمَا صَبَرُوا۟
وَدَمَّرْنَا مَا كَانَ يَصْنَعُ
فِرْعَوْنُ وَقَوْمُهُۥ وَمَا كَانُوا۟ يَعْرِشُونَ

138. We took the Children of Israel
(With safety) across the sea.
They came upon a people
Devoted entirely to some idols[1097]
They had. They said:
"O Moses! fashion for us
A god like unto the gods
They have." He said:
"Surely ye are a people
Without knowledge.

١٣٨ وَجَـٰوَزْنَا بِبَنِىٓ إِسْرَٰٓءِيلَ ٱلْبَحْرَ
فَأَتَوْا۟ عَلَىٰ قَوْمٍ يَعْكُفُونَ
عَلَىٰٓ أَصْنَامٍ لَّهُمْ قَالُوا۟
يَـٰمُوسَى ٱجْعَل لَّنَآ إِلَـٰهًا كَمَا لَهُمْ
ءَالِهَةٌ قَالَ إِنَّكُمْ قَوْمٌ تَجْهَلُونَ

139. "As to these folk—

١٣٩ إِنَّ هَـٰٓؤُلَآءِ

1096. Israel, which was despised, became a great and glorious nation under Solomon. He had goodly territory, and was doubly-blest. His land and people were prosperous, and he was blessed with wisdom from Allah. His sway and his fame spread east and west. And thus Allah's promise to Israel was fulfilled. Note that Syria and Palestine had once been under the sway of Egypt. At the same time the proud and rebellious Pharaoh and his people were brought low. The splendid monuments which they had erected with so much skill and pride were mingled with the dust. Their great cities—Thebes (or No-Ammon), Memphis (or Noph, sacred to the Bull of Osiris), and the other splendid cities, became as if they had not existed, and archaeologists have had to dig up their ruins from the sands. The splendid monuments—temples, palaces, tombs, statues, columns, and stately structures of all kinds—were buried in the sands. Even monuments like the Great Sphinx, which seem to defy the ages, were partly buried in the sands, and owe their rescue to the comparatively recent researches of archaeologists. As late as 1743 Richard Pococke in his *Travels in Egypt* (p. 41), remarked: "Most of those pyramids are very much ruined." (R).

1097. Who were these people? We are now in the Sinai Peninsula. Two conjectures are possible: (1) The Amalekites of the Sinai Peninsula were at perpetual war with the Israelites. They were probably an idolatrous nation, but we have very little knowledge of their cult; (2) From Egyptian history we know that Egypt had worked from very ancient times some copper mines in Sinai. An Egyptian settlement may have been here. Like all mining camps it contained from the beginning the dregs of the population. When the mines ceased to be worked, the settlement, or what remained of it, must have degenerated further. Cut off from civilisation, its cult must have become still narrower, without the refining influences which a progressive nation applies even to its idolatry. Perhaps Apis, the sacred bull of Memphis, lost all its allegorical meaning for them, and only gross and superstitious rites remained among them. The text speaks of "*some idols they had,*" implying that they had merely a detached fragment of a completer religion. This was a snare in the path of the Israelites, whom many generations of slavery in Egypt had debased into ignorance and superstition.

The cult they are in
Is (but) a fragment of a ruin,[1098]
And vain is the (worship)
Which they practise."

مُتَبَّرٌ مَّا هُمْ فِيهِ
وَبَٰطِلٌ مَّا كَانُوا۟ يَعْمَلُونَ

140. He said: "Shall I seek for you
A god other than the (true)
God, when it is Allah
Who hath endowed you
With gifts above the nations?"

١٤٠ قَالَ أَغَيْرَ ٱللَّهِ أَبْغِيكُمْ إِلَٰهًا
وَهُوَ فَضَّلَكُمْ عَلَى ٱلْعَٰلَمِينَ

141. And remember We rescued you
From Pharaoh's people,
Who afflicted you with
The worst of penalties,
Who slew your male children
And saved alive your females:
In that was a momentous
Trial from your Lord.[1099]

١٤١ وَإِذْ أَنجَيْنَٰكُم مِّنْ ءَالِ فِرْعَوْنَ
يَسُومُونَكُمْ سُوٓءَ ٱلْعَذَابِ يُقَتِّلُونَ
أَبْنَآءَكُمْ وَيَسْتَحْيُونَ نِسَآءَكُمْ
وَفِى ذَٰلِكُم بَلَآءٌ مِّن رَّبِّكُمْ عَظِيمٌ

SECTION 17.

142. We appointed for Moses
Thirty nights, and completed
(The period) with ten (more):
Thus was completed the term
(Of communion) with his Lord,[1100]
Forty nights. And Moses
Had charged his brother Aaron
(Before he went up):
"Act for me amongst my people:
Do right, and follow not
The way of those
Who do mischief."[1101]

١٤٢ وَوَٰعَدْنَا مُوسَىٰ ثَلَٰثِينَ لَيْلَةً
وَأَتْمَمْنَٰهَا بِعَشْرٍ فَتَمَّ مِيقَٰتُ رَبِّهِۦٓ
أَرْبَعِينَ لَيْلَةً وَقَالَ مُوسَىٰ لِأَخِيهِ
هَٰرُونَ ٱخْلُفْنِى فِى قَوْمِى وَأَصْلِحْ
وَلَا تَتَّبِعْ سَبِيلَ ٱلْمُفْسِدِينَ

1098. If conjecture 2 in the last note is correct, this idolatrous worship was but the fragment of a ruin from Egypt, and Moses's reproach is biting: "You, who have been rescued from the bondage of living Egypt—do you hanker after the bondage of a dead cult debased even from that from which you have been rescued?" *Mutabbar* = broken in pieces, smashed into fragments, destroyed.

1099. This is Allah's reminder to Israel through the mouth of Moses. There was a double trial: (1) while the bondage lasted, the people were to learn patience and constancy in the midst of affliction; (2) when they were rescued, they were to learn humility, justice, and righteous deeds of prosperity.

1100. The forty nights' communion of Moses with Allah on the Mount may be compared with the forty-day fast of Jesus in the wilderness before he took up his ministry (Matt. iv. 2), and with the forty years of Al Muṣṭafā's preparation in life before he took up his Ministry. In each case the Prophets lived alone apart from their people, before they came into the full blaze of the events of their Ministry.

1101. When for any reason the man of God is absent from his people, his duty of leadership (*khilāfah*) should be taken up by his brother—not necessarily a blood-brother, but one of his society or brotherhood. The deputy should discharge it in all humility, remembering three things: (1) that he is only a deputy, and bound to follow the directions of his Principal, (2) that right and justice are the essence of power, and (3) that mischief gets its best chance to raise its head in the absence of the Principal, and that the deputy should always guard against the traps laid for him in the Principal's absence.

143. When Moses came
To the place appointed by Us,
And his Lord addressed him,
He said: "O my Lord!
Show (Thyself) to me,
That I may look upon Thee."[1102]
Allah said: "By no means
Canst thou see Me (direct);
But look upon the mount;
If it abide
In its place, then
Shalt thou see Me."[1103]
When his Lord manifested
His glory on the Mount,
He made it as dust,
And Moses fell down
In a swoon. When he
Recovered his senses he said:
"Glory be to Thee! To Thee
I turn in repentance, and I
Am the first to believe."[1104]

١٤٣ وَلَمَّا جَآءَ مُوسَىٰ لِمِيقَٰتِنَا
وَكَلَّمَهُۥ رَبُّهُۥ قَالَ رَبِّ
أَرِنِىٓ أَنظُرْ إِلَيْكَ ۚ قَالَ لَن تَرَىٰنِى
وَلَٰكِنِ ٱنظُرْ إِلَى ٱلْجَبَلِ فَإِنِ
ٱسْتَقَرَّ مَكَانَهُۥ فَسَوْفَ تَرَىٰنِى ۚ
فَلَمَّا تَجَلَّىٰ رَبُّهُۥ لِلْجَبَلِ
جَعَلَهُۥ دَكًّا وَخَرَّ مُوسَىٰ صَعِقًا ۚ
فَلَمَّآ أَفَاقَ قَالَ سُبْحَٰنَكَ
تُبْتُ إِلَيْكَ وَأَنَا۠ أَوَّلُ ٱلْمُؤْمِنِينَ

144. (Allah) said: "O Moses!
I have chosen thee
Above (other) men,[1105]
By the mission I (have
Given thee) and the words
I (have spoken to thee):
Take then the (revelation)
Which I give thee,
And be of those
Who give thanks."[1106]

١٤٤ قَالَ يَٰمُوسَىٰٓ
إِنِّى ٱصْطَفَيْتُكَ عَلَى ٱلنَّاسِ
بِرِسَٰلَٰتِى وَبِكَلَٰمِى
فَخُذْ مَآ ءَاتَيْتُكَ
وَكُن مِّنَ ٱلشَّٰكِرِينَ

1102. Even the best of us may be betrayed into overweening confidence or spiritual ambition not yet justified by the stage we have reached. Moses had already seen part of the glory of Allah in his Radiant White Hand, that shone with the glory of Divine light (7:108, n. 1076). But he was still in the flesh, and the mission to his people was to begin after the Covenant of Sinai. It was premature of him to ask to see Allah.

1103. But Allah—the Cherisher of all His creatures—treats even our improper requests with mercy, compassion, and understanding. Even the reflected glory of Allah is too great for the grosser substance of matter. The peak on which it shone became as powder before the ineffable glory, and Moses could only live by being taken out of his bodily senses. When he recovered from his swoon, he saw the true position, and the distance between our grosser bodily senses and the true splendour of Allah's glory. He at once turned in penitence to Allah, and confessed his faith. Having been blinded by the excessive Glory, he could not see with the physical eye. But he could get a glimpse of the reality through faith, and he hastened to proclaim his faith. (R).

1104. *"First to believe." Cf.* the expression "first of those who bow to Allah in Islam" in 6:14 and 6:163. "First" means here not the first in time, but most zealous in faith. It has the intensive and not the comparative meaning.

1105. *"Above (other) men": i.e.* among his contemporaries. He had a high mission, and he had the honour of speaking to Allah.

1106. Allah's revelation is for the benefit of His creatures, who should receive it with reverence and gratitude. While Moses was having these great spiritual experiences on the Mount, his people below were ungrateful enough to forget Allah and make a golden calf for worship (7:147).

145. And We ordained laws For him in the Tablets In all matters, both Commanding and explaining All things, (and said): "Take and hold these With firmness, and enjoin Thy people to hold fast By the best in the precepts:[1107] Soon shall I show you[1108] The homes of the wicked—[1109] (How they lie desolate)."	وَكَتَبْنَا لَهُۥ فِى ٱلْأَلْوَاحِ ﴿١٤٥﴾ مِن كُلِّ شَىْءٍ مَّوْعِظَةً وَتَفْصِيلًا لِّكُلِّ شَىْءٍ فَخُذْهَا بِقُوَّةٍ وَأْمُرْ قَوْمَكَ يَأْخُذُوا۟ بِأَحْسَنِهَا سَأُو۟رِيكُمْ دَارَ ٱلْفَٰسِقِينَ
146. Those who behave arrogantly On the earth in defiance Of right—them will I Turn away from My Signs:[1110] Even if they see all the Signs, They will not believe in them; And if they see the way Of right conduct, they will Not adopt it as the Way; But if they see the way Of error, that is The Way they will adopt. For they have rejected[1111]	سَأَصْرِفُ عَنْ ءَايَٰتِىَ ﴿١٤٦﴾ ٱلَّذِينَ يَتَكَبَّرُونَ فِى ٱلْأَرْضِ بِغَيْرِ ٱلْحَقِّ وَإِن يَرَوْا۟ كُلَّ ءَايَةٍ لَّا يُؤْمِنُوا۟ بِهَا وَإِن يَرَوْا۟ سَبِيلَ ٱلرُّشْدِ لَا يَتَّخِذُوهُ سَبِيلًا وَإِن يَرَوْا۟ سَبِيلَ ٱلْغَىِّ يَتَّخِذُوهُ سَبِيلًا ذَٰلِكَ بِأَنَّهُمْ كَذَّبُوا۟

1107. The Tablets of the Law contained the essential spiritual Truth, from which were derived the positive injunctions and prohibitions, explanations and interpretations, which it was the function of the prophetic office to hold up for the people to follow. The precepts would contain, as the *Sharī'ah* does, matters absolutely prohibited, matters not prohibited but disapproved, matters about which there was no prohibition or injunction, but in which conduct was to be regulated by circumstances; matters of positive and universal duty, matters recommended for those whose zeal was sufficient to enable them to work on higher than minimum standards, and matters which were sought by persons of the highest spiritual eminence. No soul is burdened beyond its capacity; but we are asked to seek the best and highest possible for us in conduct.

1108. Notice the transition from the "We" of authority and honour and impersonal dignity, to the "I" of personal concern in specially guiding the righteous.

1109. There are two meanings, one literal and the other figurative. Literally, the homes of the wicked, both individuals and nations, lie desolate, as in the case of the ancient Egyptians, the 'Ād, and the Thamūd. Figuratively, the "home" shows the inner and more intimate condition of people. If you are dazzled by the outward prosperity of the ungodly, examine their inner anguish and fear and insecurity, and you will thank Allah for His gracious guidance.

1110. The argument may be simplified thus in paraphrase. The right is established on the earth as Allah created it: Nature recognises and obeys Allah's law as fixed for each portion of Creation. But man, because of the gift of Will, sometimes upsets this balance. The root-cause is his arrogance, as it was in the case of Iblis. Allah's Signs are everywhere, but if they are rejected with scorn and blasphemy, Allah will withdraw His grace, for sin hardens the heart and makes it impervious to the truth. Want of faith produces a kind of blindness to spiritual facts, a kind of deafness to the warnings of a Day of Account. If we had contumaciously rejected faith, can we hope for anything but justice—the just punishment of our sins? (R).

1111. *Rejected Our Signs*: again a return to the Plural of impersonal Dignity and Authority, from the singular of personal concern in granting grace and guidance to the righteous.

Our Signs, and failed
To take warning from them.

بِـَٔايَـٰتِنَا وَكَانُوا۟ عَنْهَا غَـٰفِلِينَ

147. Those who reject Our Signs
And the Meeting in the Hereafter—
Vain are their deeds:
Can they expect to be rewarded
Except as they have wrought?

١٤٧ وَٱلَّذِينَ كَذَّبُوا۟ بِـَٔايَـٰتِنَا
وَلِقَآءِ ٱلْـَٔاخِرَةِ حَبِطَتْ أَعْمَـٰلُهُمْ
هَلْ يُجْزَوْنَ إِلَّا مَا كَانُوا۟ يَعْمَلُونَ

SECTION 18.

148. The people of Moses made,
In his absence, out of their ornaments,[1112]
The image of a calf, (for worship):[1113]
It seemed to low: did they[1114]
Not see that it could
Neither speak to them, nor
Show them the Way?
They took it for worship
And they did wrong.

١٤٨ وَٱتَّخَذَ قَوْمُ مُوسَىٰ مِنۢ بَعْدِهِۦ
مِنْ حُلِيِّهِمْ عِجْلًا جَسَدًا
لَّهُۥ خُوَارٌ ۚ أَلَمْ يَرَوْا۟ أَنَّهُۥ لَا
يُكَلِّمُهُمْ وَلَا يَهْدِيهِمْ سَبِيلًا ۘ
ٱتَّخَذُوهُ وَكَانُوا۟ ظَـٰلِمِينَ

149. When they repented, and saw
That they had erred,
They said: "If our Lord
Have not mercy upon us
And forgive us, we shall
Indeed be of those who perish."

١٤٩ وَلَمَّا سُقِطَ فِىٓ أَيْدِيهِمْ وَرَأَوْا۟ أَنَّهُمْ
قَدْ ضَلُّوا۟ قَالُوا۟ لَئِن لَّمْ يَرْحَمْنَا رَبُّنَا
وَيَغْفِرْ لَنَا لَنَكُونَنَّ مِنَ ٱلْخَـٰسِرِينَ

1112. The making of the golden calf and its worship by the Israelites during the absence of Moses on the Mount were referred to in 2:51 and some further details are given in 20:85-97. Notice how in each case only those points are referred to which are necessary to the argument in hand. A narrator whose object is mere narration, tells the story in all its details, and is done with it. A consummate artist, whose object is to enforce lessons, brings out each point in its proper place. Master of all details, he does not ramble, but with supreme literary skills, just adds the touch that is necessary in each place to complete the spiritual picture. His object is not a story but a lesson. Here notice the contrast between the intense spiritual communion of Moses on the Mount and the simultaneous corruption of his people in his absence. We can understand his righteous indignation and bitter grief (7:150). The people had melted all their gold ornaments, and made the image of a calf like the bull of Osiris in the city of Memphis in the wicked Egypt that they had turned their backs upon.

1113. *Image of a Calf: Jasad* is literally a body, especially the body of a man according to Khalil quoted by Rāghib. In 21:8 it is used obviously for the human body, as also in 38:34; but in the latter case, the idea of an image, without any real life or soul, is also suggested. In the present passage I understand many suggestions: (1) that it was a mere image, without life; (2) as such, it could not low, therefore the appearance of lowing, mentioned immediately afterwards, was a fraud; (3) unlike its prototype, the bull of Osiris, it had not even the symbolism of Osiris behind it; the Osiris myth, in the living religion of Egypt, had at least some ethical principles behind it.

1114. The lowing of the golden calf was obviously a deception practised by the Egyptian promoters of the cult. Lytton in his "Last Days of Pompeii" exposes the deception practised by the priests of Isis. Men hidden behind images imposed on the credulity of the commonalty.

150. When Moses came back
To his people, angry and grieved,
He said: "Evil it is that ye
Have done in my place
In my absence: did ye[1115]
Make haste to bring on
The judgement of your Lord?"
He put down the Tablets,[1116]
Seized his brother by (the hair
Of) his head, and dragged him[1117]
To him. Aaron said:
"Son of my mother! The people
Did indeed reckon me
As naught, and went near
To slaying me! Make not
The enemies rejoice over
My misfortune, nor count thou
Me amongst the people
Of sin."[1118]

(١٥٠) وَلَمَّا رَجَعَ مُوسَىٰٓ
إِلَىٰ قَوْمِهِۦ غَضْبَٰنَ أَسِفًا
قَالَ بِئْسَمَا خَلَفْتُمُونِى مِنۢ بَعْدِىٓ
أَعَجِلْتُمْ أَمْرَ رَبِّكُمْ وَأَلْقَى ٱلْأَلْوَاحَ
وَأَخَذَ بِرَأْسِ أَخِيهِ يَجُرُّهُۥٓ إِلَيْهِ
قَالَ ٱبْنَ أُمَّ إِنَّ ٱلْقَوْمَ ٱسْتَضْعَفُونِى
وَكَادُوا۟ يَقْتُلُونَنِى فَلَا تُشْمِتْ
بِىَ ٱلْأَعْدَآءَ وَلَا تَجْعَلْنِى
مَعَ ٱلْقَوْمِ ٱلظَّٰلِمِينَ

151. Moses prayed: "O my Lord!
Forgive me and my brother![1119]
Admit us to Thy mercy!
For Thou art the Most Merciful
Of those who show mercy!"

(١٥١) قَالَ رَبِّ ٱغْفِرْ لِى وَلِأَخِى وَأَدْخِلْنَا فِى
رَحْمَتِكَ وَأَنتَ أَرْحَمُ ٱلرَّٰحِمِينَ

1115. *Did ye make haste*...? 'In your impatience, could you not wait for me? Your lapse into idolatry has only hastened Allah's wrath. If you had only waited. I was bringing to you in the Tablets the most excellent teaching in the commands of Allah.' There is subtle irony in the speech of Moses. There is also a play upon words: *'ijl* = calf; and *'ajila* = to make haste: no translation can bring out these niceties.

1116. *Put down the Tablets*: we are not told that the Tablets were broken; in fact 7:154 (below) shows that they were whole. They contained Allah's Message. There is a touch of disrespect (if not blasphemy) in supposing that Allah's Messenger broke the Tablets in his incontinent rage, as is stated in the Old Testament: "Moses's anger waxed hot, and he cast the tablets out of his hands, and brake them beneath the Mount." (Exod. xxxii. 10). On this point and also on the point that Aaron (in the Old Testament story) ordered the gold to be brought, made a molten calf, fashioned it with a graving tool, and built an altar before the calf (Exod. xxxii. 2-5), our version differs from that of the Old Testament. We cannot believe that Aaron, who was appointed by Allah to assist Moses as Allah's Messenger, could descend so low as to seduce the people into idolatry, whatever his human weaknesses might be.

1117. Moses was but human. Remembering the charge he had given to Aaron (7:142) he had a just grievance at the turn events had taken. But he did not wreak his vengeance on the Tablets of Allah's Law by breaking them. He laid hands on his brother, and his brother at once explained.

1118. Aaron's speech is full of tenderness and regret. He addresses Moses as "son of my mother"—an affectionate term. He explains how the turbulent people nearly killed him for resisting them. And he states in the clearest terms that the idolatry neither originated with him nor had his consent. In 20:85 we are told that a fellow described as the Sāmiri had led them astray. We shall discuss this when we come to that passage.

1119. As Moses was convinced that his brother was guiltless, his wrath was turned to gentleness. He prayed for forgiveness—for himself and his brother: for himself because of his wrath and for his brother because he had been unable to suppress idolatry among his people. And like a true leader that he is, he identifies himself with his lieutenant for all that has happened. Even more, he identifies himself with his whole people in his prayer in verse 155 below. Herein, again, is a type of what the Holy Prophet Muḥammad did for his people.

SECTION 19.

152. Those who took the calf
(For worship) will indeed
Be overwhelmed with wrath
From their Lord, and with
Shame in this life:[1120]
Thus do We recompense
Those who invent (falsehoods).

١٥٢ إن الذين اتخذوا العجل سينالهم
غضب من ربهم وذلة في الحيوة الدنيا ۚ
وكذلك نجزي المفترين

153. But those who do wrong
But repent thereafter and
(Truly) believe—verily
Thy Lord is thereafter
Oft-Forgiving, Most Merciful.

١٥٣ والذين عملوا السيئات ثم تابوا من بعدها
وءامنوا إن ربك من بعدها لغفور رحيم

154. When the anger of Moses
Was appeased, he took up
The Tablets: in the writing
Thereon was Guidance and
Mercy
For such as fear their Lord.

١٥٤ ولما سكت عن موسى الغضب
أخذ الألواح ۖ وفي نسختها هدى ورحمة
للذين هم لربهم يرهبون

155. And Moses chose seventy[1121]
Of his people for Our place
Of meeting: when they
Were seized with violent
quaking,[1122]
He prayed: "O my Lord!
If it had been Thy Will
Thou couldst have destroyed,
Long before, both them
And me: wouldst Thou
Destroy us for the deeds
Of the foolish ones among us?
This is no more than[1123]

١٥٥ واختار موسى قومه سبعين
رجلا لميقتنا ۖ فلما أخذتهم
الرجفة قال رب لو شئت
أهلكتهم من قبل وإيي ۖ
أتهلكنا بما فعل السفهاء منا ۖ
إن هي إلا

1120. The consequences were twofold: (1) spiritual, in that Allah's grace is withdrawn, and (2) even in the present life of this world, in that godly men also shun the sinner's company, and he is isolated.

1121. Seventy of the elders were taken up to the Mount, but left at some distance from the place where Allah spoke to Moses. They were to be silent witnesses, but their faith was not yet complete, and they dared to say to Moses: "We shall never believe in thee until we see Allah in public" (2:55). They were dazed with thunder and lightning, and might have been destroyed but for Allah's mercy on the intercession of Moses.

1122. *Rajfah*: violent quaking, earthquake. I take it to refer to the same event as is described by the word *Ṣā'iqah* in 2:55, the thunder and lightning that shook the mountainside.

1123. Moses was guiltless, but he identifies himself with his whole people, and intercedes with Allah on their behalf. He recognises that it was a trial, in which some of his people failed to stand the test. Such failure was worthy of punishment. But he pleads for mercy for such as erred from weakness and not from contumacy, and were truly repentant, although all who erred were in their several degrees worthy of punishment.

Thy trial: by it Thou causest
Whom Thou wilt to stray,[1124]
And Thou leadest whom
Thou wilt into the right path.
Thou art our Protector:
So forgive us and give us
Thy mercy; for Thou art
The Best of those who forgive.

فِتْنَتُكَ تُضِلُّ بِهَا مَن تَشَآءُ
وَتَهْدِى مَن تَشَآءُ أَنتَ وَلِيُّنَا
فَٱغْفِرْ لَنَا وَٱرْحَمْنَا
وَأَنتَ خَيْرُ ٱلْغَٰفِرِينَ

156. "And ordain for us
That which is good,
In this life
And in the Hereafter:
For we have turned unto Thee."
He said: "With My Punishment
I visit whom I will;
But My Mercy extendeth[1125]
To all things. That (Mercy)
I shall ordain for those
Who do right, and practise
Regular charity, and those
Who believe in Our Signs—[1126]

١٥٦ وَٱكْتُبْ لَنَا فِى هَٰذِهِ ٱلدُّنْيَا
حَسَنَةً وَفِى ٱلْءَاخِرَةِ إِنَّا هُدْنَآ إِلَيْكَ
قَالَ عَذَابِىٓ أُصِيبُ بِهِۦ مَنْ أَشَآءُ
وَرَحْمَتِى وَسِعَتْ كُلَّ شَىْءٍ
فَسَأَكْتُبُهَا لِلَّذِينَ يَتَّقُونَ وَيُؤْتُونَ
ٱلزَّكَوٰةَ وَٱلَّذِينَ هُم بِـَٔايَٰتِنَا يُؤْمِنُونَ

157. "Those who follow the Messenger,
The unlettered Prophet,
Whom they find mentioned
In their own (Scriptures)—[1127]
In the Law and the Gospel—
For he commands them
What is just and forbids them
What is evil; he allows
Them as lawful what is good
(And pure) and prohibits them

١٥٧ ٱلَّذِينَ يَتَّبِعُونَ ٱلرَّسُولَ ٱلنَّبِىَّ ٱلْأُمِّىَّ
ٱلَّذِى يَجِدُونَهُۥ مَكْتُوبًا عِندَهُمْ فِى ٱلتَّوْرَىٰةِ
وَٱلْإِنجِيلِ يَأْمُرُهُم بِٱلْمَعْرُوفِ وَيَنْهَىٰهُمْ
عَنِ ٱلْمُنكَرِ وَيُحِلُّ لَهُمُ ٱلطَّيِّبَٰتِ
وَيُحَرِّمُ عَلَيْهِمُ

1124. *Cf.* 2:26.

1125. Allah's mercy is in and for all things. All nature subserves a common purpose, which is for the good of all His creatures. Our faculties and our understandings are all instances of His grace and mercy. Each unit or factor among His creatures benefits from the others and receives them as Allah's mercy to itself; and in its turn, each contributes to the benefit of the others and is thus an instance of Allah's mercy to them. His mercy is universal and all-pervasive; while His justice and punishment are reserved for those who swerve from His plan and (to use a medieval juridicial formula) go out of His Peace.

1126. The personal grace and mercy—and their opposite—are referred to the singular pronoun "I", while the impersonal Law, by which Allah's Signs operate in His universe, is referred to the plural pronoun of authority and dignity, "We".

1127. In this verse is a prefiguring, to Moses, of the Arabian Messenger, the last and greatest of the Messengers of Allah. Prophecies about him will be found in the *Tawrāh* and the *Injīl*. In the reflex of the *Tawrāh* as now accepted by the Jews, Moses says: "The Lord thy God will raise up unto thee a Prophet from the midst of thee, of thy brethren, like unto me" (Deut. xviii. 15): the only Prophet who brought a Sharī'ah like that of Moses was Muḥammad Muṣṭafā, and he came of the house of Ismā'īl, the brother of Isaac, the father of Israel. In the reflex of the Gospel as now accepted by the Christians, Christ promised another Comforter (John xiv. 16): the Greek word *Paraclete* which the Christians interpret as referring to the Holy Spirit is by our Doctors taken to be *Periclyte*, which would be the Greek form of Aḥmad. See Q. 61:6.

From what is bad (and impure);
He releases them
From their heavy burdens
And from the yokes[1128]
That are upon them.
So it is those who believe
In him, honour him,
Help him, and follow the Light
Which is sent down with him—[1129]
It is they who will prosper."[1130]

ٱلْخَبَٰٓئِثَ وَيَضَعُ عَنْهُمْ إِصْرَهُمْ
وَٱلْأَغْلَٰلَ ٱلَّتِى كَانَتْ عَلَيْهِمْ ۚ
فَٱلَّذِينَ ءَامَنُوا۟ بِهِۦ وَعَزَّرُوهُ وَنَصَرُوهُ
وَٱتَّبَعُوا۟ ٱلنُّورَ ٱلَّذِىٓ أُنزِلَ مَعَهُۥٓ ۙ
أُو۟لَٰٓئِكَ هُمُ ٱلْمُفْلِحُونَ

C. 87.—With the advent of the Holy Prophet,
(7:158-171.) The light and guidance which he brought
For all mankind from Allah
Superseded the earlier Law for the Jews.
The good and the upright among them
Followed the new Light, but
The rest were scattered through the earth.

SECTION 20.

158. Say: "O men! I am sent[1131]
Unto you all, as the Messenger
Of Allah, to Whom belongeth
The dominion of the heavens
And the earth: there is no god
But He: it is He that giveth
Both life and death. So believe
In Allah and His Messenger,

١٥٨ قُلْ يَٰٓأَيُّهَا ٱلنَّاسُ إِنِّى رَسُولُ ٱللَّهِ
إِلَيْكُمْ جَمِيعًا ٱلَّذِى لَهُۥ مُلْكُ ٱلسَّمَٰوَٰتِ
وَٱلْأَرْضِ ۖ لَآ إِلَٰهَ إِلَّا هُوَ يُحْىِۦ وَيُمِيتُ ۖ
فَـَٔامِنُوا۟ بِٱللَّهِ وَرَسُولِهِ

1128. *Aghlāl:* plural of *ghullun*, a yoke, an iron collar. In the formalism and exclusiveness of the Jews there were many restrictions which were removed by Islam, a religion for freedom in the faith of Allah, of universality in the variety of races, languages, manners and customs.

1129. *Light which is sent down with him*: the words are "with him", not "to him", emphasising the fact that the Light which he brought illumines everyone who has the privilege of joining his great and universal Fellowship.

1130. *Falāh* = prosperity in its general sense as well as in its spiritual sense. In the general sense it means that right conduct is the only door to happiness and well-being. In the spiritual sense it means that Faith and its fruits (right conduct) are the only gates to salvation.

1131. Our attention having been directed to various prophets, who were sent with missions to their several peoples, and in each of whose careers there is some prefigurement of the life of the last and greatest of them, we are now asked to listen to the proclamation of Muḥammad's universal mission. We contemplate no longer, after this, partial truths. It is not now a question of saving Israel from the bondage of Egypt, nor teaching Midian the ethics of business, nor reclaiming the people of Lūṭ from sexual sin or Thamūd from the sin of oppression in power, or 'Ād from arrogance and ancestor-worship. Now are set forth plainly the issues of Life and Death, the Message of Allah, the One Universal God to all mankind.

The unlettered Prophet,[1132]
Who believeth in Allah
And His Words: follow him
That (so) ye may be guided."

ٱلنَّبِيِّ ٱلْأُمِّيِّ ٱلَّذِى يُؤْمِنُ بِٱللَّهِ
وَكَلِمَٰتِهِۦ وَٱتَّبِعُوهُ
لَعَلَّكُمْ تَهْتَدُونَ

159. Of the people of Moses
There is a section
Who guide and do justice
In the light of truth.

١٥٩ وَمِن قَوْمِ مُوسَىٰٓ أُمَّةٌ
يَهْدُونَ بِٱلْحَقِّ وَبِهِۦ يَعْدِلُونَ

160. We divided them into twelve Tribes[1133]
Or nations. We directed
Moses by inspiration,
When his (thirsty) people asked
Him for water: "Strike the rock
With thy staff": out of it
There gushed forth twelve springs:
Each group knew its own place
For water. We gave them
The shade of clouds, and sent
Down to them manna and quails,
(Saying): "Eat of the good things
We have provided for you":
(But they rebelled); to Us
They did no harm, but
They harmed their own souls.[1134]

١٦٠ وَقَطَّعْنَٰهُمُ ٱثْنَتَىْ عَشْرَةَ أَسْبَاطًا أُمَمًا
وَأَوْحَيْنَآ إِلَىٰ مُوسَىٰٓ إِذِ ٱسْتَسْقَىٰهُ قَوْمُهُۥٓ
أَنِ ٱضْرِب بِّعَصَاكَ ٱلْحَجَرَ فَٱنۢبَجَسَتْ
مِنْهُ ٱثْنَتَا عَشْرَةَ عَيْنًا قَدْ عَلِمَ كُلُّ أُنَاسٍ
مَّشْرَبَهُمْ وَظَلَّلْنَا عَلَيْهِمُ ٱلْغَمَٰمَ وَأَنزَلْنَا
عَلَيْهِمُ ٱلْمَنَّ وَٱلسَّلْوَىٰ كُلُوا۟ مِن
طَيِّبَٰتِ مَا رَزَقْنَٰكُمْ وَمَا ظَلَمُونَا
وَلَٰكِن كَانُوٓا۟ أَنفُسَهُمْ يَظْلِمُونَ

161. And remember it was
Said to them:
"Dwell in this town
And eat[1135] therein as ye wish,
But say the word of humility
And enter the gate

١٦١ وَإِذْ قِيلَ لَهُمُ ٱسْكُنُوا۟ هَٰذِهِ
ٱلْقَرْيَةَ وَكُلُوا۟ مِنْهَا حَيْثُ شِئْتُمْ
وَقُولُوا۟ حِطَّةٌ وَٱدْخُلُوا۟ ٱلْبَابَ

1132. "Unlettered," as applied to the Prophet here and in verse 157 above, has three special significations. (1) He was not versed in human learning; yet he was full of the highest wisdom, and had a most wonderful knowledge of the previous Scriptures. This was a proof of his inspiration. It was a miracle of the highest kind, a "Sign", which everyone could test then, and everyone can test now. (2) All organised human knowledge tends to be crystallised, to acquire a partial bias or flavour of some "school" of thought. The highest Teacher had to be free from any such taint, just as a clean slate is necessary if a perfectly clear and bold message has to be written on it. (3) In 3:20 and 62:2, the epithet is applied to the Pagan Arabs, because, before the advent of Islam, they were unlearned. That the last and greatest of the Prophets should arise among them, and they and their language be made the vehicle of the new, full and universal light, has also a meaning, which is explained in C. 12-15.

1133. We now come to some incidents in Jewish history, which have been referred to in 2:57-60. Here they have special reference to their bearing on the times when early Islam was preached. The Twelve Tribes and the parable drawn from them have been explained in n. 73 to 2:60.

1134. *Cf.* 2:57 and n. 71.

1135. As in 7:19, we may construe "eat" here to mean not only eating literally, but enjoying the good things of life.

In a posture of humility:
We shall forgive you
Your faults; We shall increase
(The portion of) those who do
good."

سُجَّدًا نَّغْفِرْ لَكُمْ
خَطِيٓـَٔـٰتِكُمْ ۚ سَنَزِيدُ ٱلْمُحْسِنِينَ

162. But the transgressors among them
Changed the word from that
Which had been given them
So we sent on them
A plague from heaven.
For that they repeatedly
transgressed.[1136]

١٦٢ فَبَدَّلَ ٱلَّذِينَ ظَلَمُوا۟ مِنْهُمْ قَوْلًا غَيْرَ
ٱلَّذِى قِيلَ لَهُمْ فَأَرْسَلْنَا عَلَيْهِمْ رِجْزًا
مِّنَ ٱلسَّمَآءِ بِمَا كَانُوا۟ يَظْلِمُونَ

Section 21.

163. Ask them concerning the town
Standing close by the sea.
Behold! they transgressed
In the matter of the Sabbath.[1137]
For on the day of their Sabbath
Their fish did come to them,
Openly holding up their heads,
But on the day they had
No Sabbath, they came not:
Thus did We make a trial
Of them, for they were
Given to transgression.

١٦٣ وَسْـَٔلْهُمْ عَنِ ٱلْقَرْيَةِ
ٱلَّتِى كَانَتْ حَاضِرَةَ ٱلْبَحْرِ
إِذْ يَعْدُونَ فِى ٱلسَّبْتِ إِذْ تَأْتِيهِمْ
حِيتَانُهُمْ يَوْمَ سَبْتِهِمْ شُرَّعًا
وَيَوْمَ لَا يَسْبِتُونَ ۙ لَا تَأْتِيهِمْ ۚ
كَذَٰلِكَ نَبْلُوهُم بِمَا كَانُوا۟ يَفْسُقُونَ

164. When some of them said:
"Why do ye preach
To a people whom Allah
Will destroy or visit
With a terrible punishment?"—[1138]
Said the preachers: "To discharge

١٦٤ وَإِذْ قَالَتْ أُمَّةٌ مِّنْهُمْ لِمَ تَعِظُونَ
قَوْمًا ۙ ٱللَّهُ مُهْلِكُهُمْ أَوْ مُعَذِّبُهُمْ
عَذَابًا شَدِيدًا ۖ قَالُوا۟ مَعْذِرَةً

1136. *Cf.* 2:58-59, and n. 72. The story is here told by way of parable for the times of Islam. Hence we have a few verbal changes: *e.g.*, "dwell in this town" instead of "enter this town," etc.

1137. *Cf.* 2:65 and n. 79. Fishing, like every other activity, was prohibited to Israel on the Sabbath day. As this practice was usually observed, the fish used to come up with a sense of security to their water channels or pools openly on the Sabbath day, but not on other days when fishing was open. This was a great temptation to the law-breakers, which they could not resist. Some of their men of piety protested, but it had no effect. When their transgressions, which, we may suppose, extended to other commandments, passed beyond bounds, the punishment came. (R).

1138. There are always people who wonder, no doubt sincerely, what good it is to preach to the wicked. The answer is given to them here: (1) every man who sees evil must speak out against it; it is his duty and responsibility to Allah; (2) there is always a chance that the warning may have effect and save a precious soul. This passage has a special meaning for the times when our Holy Prophet was preaching in Makkah, apparently without results. But it applies to all times.

Our duty to your Lord,
And perchance they may fear
Him."

إِلَىٰ رَبِّكُمْ وَلَعَلَّهُمْ يَتَّقُونَ

165. When they disregarded the warnings
That had been given them,
We rescued those who forbade
Evil; but We visited
The wrongdoers with a
Grievous punishment, because
They were given to transgression.

١٦٥ فَلَمَّا نَسُوا۟ مَا ذُكِّرُوا۟ بِهِۦٓ
أَنجَيْنَا ٱلَّذِينَ يَنْهَوْنَ عَنِ ٱلسُّوٓءِ
وَأَخَذْنَا ٱلَّذِينَ ظَلَمُوا۟ بِعَذَابٍۭ بَـِٔيسٍۭ
بِمَا كَانُوا۟ يَفْسُقُونَ

166. When in their insolence
They transgressed (all) prohibitions,
We said to them:
"Be ye apes.
Despised and rejected."[1139]

١٦٦ فَلَمَّا عَتَوْا۟ عَن
مَّا نُهُوا۟ عَنْهُ قُلْنَا لَهُمْ
كُونُوا۟ قِرَدَةً خَـٰسِـِٔينَ

167. Behold! thy Lord did declare[1140]
That He would send
Against them, to the Day
Of Judgement, those who would
Afflict them with grievous
Penalty. Thy Lord is quick
In retribution, but He is also
Oft-Forgiving, Most Merciful.

١٦٧ وَإِذْ تَأَذَّنَ رَبُّكَ لَيَبْعَثَنَّ
عَلَيْهِمْ إِلَىٰ يَوْمِ ٱلْقِيَـٰمَةِ مَن يَسُومُهُمْ
سُوٓءَ ٱلْعَذَابِ ۗ إِنَّ رَبَّكَ لَسَرِيعُ
ٱلْعِقَابِ ۖ وَإِنَّهُۥ لَغَفُورٌ رَّحِيمٌ

168. We broke them up
Into sections on this earth.[1141]
There are among them some
That are the righteous, and some
That are the opposite.
We have tried them
With both prosperity and adversity:
In order that they
Might turn (to Us).

١٦٨ وَقَطَّعْنَـٰهُمْ فِى ٱلْأَرْضِ أُمَمًا ۖ
مِّنْهُمُ ٱلصَّـٰلِحُونَ وَمِنْهُمْ
دُونَ ذَٰلِكَ ۖ وَبَلَوْنَـٰهُم بِٱلْحَسَنَـٰتِ
وَٱلسَّيِّـَٔاتِ لَعَلَّهُمْ يَرْجِعُونَ

169. After them succeeded
An (evil) generation: they

١٦٩ فَخَلَفَ مِنۢ بَعْدِهِمْ خَلْفٌ

1139. *Cf.* 2:65, n. 79.

1140. See Deut. xi. 28: "A curse if ye will not obey the commandments of the Lord your God but turn aside out of the way which I command you this day"; also Deut. xxviii. 49; "The Lord shall bring a nation against thee from afar, from the end of the earth, as swift as the eagle flieth; a nation whose tongue thou shalt not understand"; and many other passages.

1141. The dispersal of the Jews is a great fact in the world's history. Neither has their persecution ended yet, nor is it likely to end as far as we can foresee.

Inherited the Book, but
They chose (for themselves)[1142]
The vanities of this world,
Saying (for excuse): "(Everything)
Will be forgiven us."
(Even so), if similar vanities
Came their way, they would
(Again) seize them.
Was not the Covenant[1143]
Of the Book taken from them,
That they would not
Ascribe to Allah anything
But the truth? And they
Study what is in the Book.
But best for the righteous
Is the Home in the Hereafter.
Will ye not understand?

وَرِثُوا۟ ٱلْكِتَـٰبَ يَأْخُذُونَ عَرَضَ
هَـٰذَا ٱلْأَدْنَىٰ وَيَقُولُونَ سَيُغْفَرُ لَنَا
وَإِن يَأْتِهِمْ عَرَضٌ مِّثْلُهُۥ يَأْخُذُوهُ
أَلَمْ يُؤْخَذْ عَلَيْهِم مِّيثَـٰقُ ٱلْكِتَـٰبِ
أَن لَّا يَقُولُوا۟ عَلَى ٱللَّهِ إِلَّا ٱلْحَقَّ
وَدَرَسُوا۟ مَا فِيهِ ۗ وَٱلدَّارُ ٱلْـَٔاخِرَةُ
خَيْرٌ لِّلَّذِينَ يَتَّقُونَ ۗ أَفَلَا تَعْقِلُونَ

170. As to those who hold fast
By the Book and establish
Regular Prayer—never
Shall We suffer the reward
Of the righteous to perish.

١٧٠ وَٱلَّذِينَ يُمَسِّكُونَ بِٱلْكِتَـٰبِ
وَأَقَامُوا۟ ٱلصَّلَوٰةَ إِنَّا لَا نُضِيعُ أَجْرَ ٱلْمُصْلِحِينَ

171. When We shook the Mount
Over them, as if it had been
A canopy, and they thought
It was going to fall on them
(We said): "Hold firmly[1144]
To what We have given you,
And bring (ever) to remembrance
What is therein;[1145]
Perchance ye may fear Allah."

١٧١ وَإِذْ نَتَقْنَا ٱلْجَبَلَ فَوْقَهُمْ
كَأَنَّهُۥ ظُلَّةٌ وَظَنُّوٓا۟ أَنَّهُۥ وَاقِعٌۢ بِهِمْ
خُذُوا۟ مَآ ءَاتَيْنَـٰكُم بِقُوَّةٍ وَٱذْكُرُوا۟
مَا فِيهِ لَعَلَّكُمْ تَتَّقُونَ

C. 88.—Mankind have the nature of good
(7:172-206.) Created within them: yet doth Allah
By His Signs keep up a constant
Reminder to men of His Holy Names.
Those who err scarce realise
How gradually they fall into sin.
Their respite has a term; the doom

1142. Merely inheriting a Book, or doing lip service to it, does not make a nation righteous. If they succumb to the temptations of the world, their hypocrisy becomes all the more glaring. "High finance" is one of these temptations. *Cf.* also 2:80: "the Fire shall not touch us except for a few numbered days": and 2:88, about their blasphemous self-sufficiency.

1143. *Cf.* Exod. xix. 5-8; xxiv. 3; xxxiv. 27; and many other passages.

1144. *Cf.* 2:63 and n. 78.

1145. *Therein* = in the Book or Revelation, in "what We have given you."

Must come, and it may be on a sudden.
So humbly draw nigh to the Lord,
Declare His glory, and rejoice in His service.

SECTION 22.

172. When thy Lord drew forth[1146]
From the Children of Adam
From their loins—
Their descendants, and made
them
Testify concerning themselves,
(saying):
"Am I not your Lord
(Who cherishes and sustains
you)?"—
They said: "Yea!
We do testify!"[1147] (This), lest
Ye should say on the Day
Of Judgement: "Of this we
Were never mindful."

﴿١٧٢﴾ وَإِذْ أَخَذَ رَبُّكَ مِنۢ بَنِىٓ ءَادَمَ
مِن ظُهُورِهِمْ ذُرِّيَّتَهُمْ
وَأَشْهَدَهُمْ عَلَىٰٓ أَنفُسِهِمْ
أَلَسْتُ بِرَبِّكُمْ
قَالُوا۟ بَلَىٰ شَهِدْنَآ
أَن تَقُولُوا۟ يَوْمَ ٱلْقِيَٰمَةِ
إِنَّا كُنَّا عَنْ هَٰذَا غَٰفِلِينَ

173. Or lest ye should say:
"Our fathers before us
May have taken false gods,
But we are (their) descendants
After them: wilt Thou then
Destroy us because of the deeds
Of men who were futile?"[1148]

﴿١٧٣﴾ أَوْ تَقُولُوٓا۟ إِنَّمَآ أَشْرَكَ ءَابَآؤُنَا مِن قَبْلُ
وَكُنَّا ذُرِّيَّةً مِّنۢ بَعْدِهِمْ
أَفَتُهْلِكُنَا بِمَا فَعَلَ ٱلْمُبْطِلُونَ

1146. This passage has led to differences of opinion in interpretation. According to the dominant opinion of commentators each individual in the posterity of Adam had a separate existence from the time of Adam, and a Covenant was taken from all of them, which is binding accordingly on each individual. The words in the text refer to the descendants of the Children of Adam, *i.e.*, to all humanity, born or unborn, without any limit of time. Adam's seed carries on the existence of Adam and succeeds to his spiritual heritage. Humanity has been given by Allah certain powers and faculties, whose possession creates on our side special spiritual obligations which we must faithfully discharge: see 5:l. and n. 682. These obligations may from a legal point of view be considered as arising from implied Covenants. In the preceding verse (7:171) a reference was made to the implied Covenant of the Jewish nation. Now we consider the implied Covenant of the whole of humanity, for the Holy Prophet's mission was worldwide. (R).

1147. The Covenant is completed in this way. We acknowledge that Allah is our Creator, Cherisher, and Sustainer: therefore we acknowledge our duty to Him: when we so testify concerning ourselves, the obligation is, as it were, assumed by us; for it follows from our very nature when it is pure and uncorrupted.

1148. The latent faculties in man are enough to teach him the distinction between good and evil, to warn him of the dangers that beset his life. But to awaken and stimulate them, a personal appeal is made to each individual through the "still small voice" within him. This, in its uncorrupted state, acknowledges the truth and, as it were, swears its Covenant with Allah. There is, therefore, no excuse for any individual to say, either (1) that he was unmindful, or (2) that he should not be punished for the sins of his fathers, because his punishment (if any) comes from his personal responsibility and is for his own rejection of faith and the higher spiritual influences. (R).

174. Thus do We explain
The Signs in detail;
And perchance they may turn
(Unto Us).

١٧٤ وَكَذَٰلِكَ نُفَصِّلُ ٱلْءَايَٰتِ
وَلَعَلَّهُمْ يَرْجِعُونَ

175. Relate to them the story[1149]
Of the man to whom
We sent Our Signs,
But he passed them by:
So Satan followed him up,
And he went astray.

١٧٥ وَٱتْلُ عَلَيْهِمْ نَبَأَ ٱلَّذِىٓ
ءَاتَيْنَٰهُ ءَايَٰتِنَا فَٱنسَلَخَ مِنْهَا
فَأَتْبَعَهُ ٱلشَّيْطَٰنُ فَكَانَ مِنَ ٱلْغَاوِينَ

176. If it had been Our Will,
We should have elevated him
With Our Signs; but he
Inclined to the earth,
And followed his own vain
desires.[1150]
His similitude is that
Of a dog: if you attack
Him, he lolls out his tongue,
Or if you leave him alone,
He (still) lolls out his tongue.[1151]
That is the similitude
Of those who reject Our Signs;
So relate the story;
Perchance they may reflect.

١٧٦ وَلَوْ شِئْنَا لَرَفَعْنَٰهُ بِهَا
وَلَٰكِنَّهُۥٓ أَخْلَدَ إِلَى ٱلْأَرْضِ
وَٱتَّبَعَ هَوَىٰهُ ۚ فَمَثَلُهُۥ كَمَثَلِ
ٱلْكَلْبِ إِن تَحْمِلْ عَلَيْهِ
يَلْهَثْ أَوْ تَتْرُكْهُ يَلْهَث ۚ
ذَّٰلِكَ مَثَلُ ٱلْقَوْمِ ٱلَّذِينَ كَذَّبُوا۟ بِـَٔايَٰتِنَا ۚ
فَٱقْصُصِ ٱلْقَصَصَ لَعَلَّهُمْ يَتَفَكَّرُونَ

177. Evil as an example are
People who reject Our Signs
And wrong their own souls.

١٧٧ سَآءَ مَثَلًا ٱلْقَوْمُ ٱلَّذِينَ
كَذَّبُوا۟ بِـَٔايَٰتِنَا وَأَنفُسَهُمْ كَانُوا۟ يَظْلِمُونَ

178. Whom Allah doth guide—
He is on the right path:

١٧٨ مَن يَهْدِ ٱللَّهُ فَهُوَ ٱلْمُهْتَدِى ۖ

1149. Commentators differ whether this story or parable refers to a particular individual, and if so, to whom. The story of Balaam, the seer, who was called out by Israel's enemies to curse Israel, but who blessed Israel instead. (Num. xxii., xxiii., xxiv) is quite different. It is better to take the parable in general sense. These are men, of talents and position, to whom great opportunities of spiritual insight come, but they perversely pass them by. Satan sees his opportunity and catches them up. Instead of rising higher in the spiritual world, their selfish and worldly desires and ambitions pull them down, and they are lost.

1150. Notice the contrast between the exalted spiritual honours which they would have received from Allah if they had followed His Will, and the earthly desires which eventually bring them low to the position of beasts and worse.

1151. The dog, especially in the hot weather, lolls out his tongue, whether he is attacked and pursued and is tired, or is left alone. It is part of his nature to slobber. So with the man who rejects Allah. Whether he is warned or left alone, he continues to throw out his dirty saliva. The injury he will do will be to his own soul. But there may be infection in his evil example. So we must protect others. And we must never give up hope of his own amendment. So we must continue to warn him and make him think.

Whom He rejects from His
guidance—
Such are the persons who perish.[1152]

وَمَن يُضْلِلْ فَأُولَٰٓئِكَ هُمُ ٱلْخَٰسِرُونَ

179. Many are the Jinns and men
We have made for Hell:
They have hearts wherewith they
Understand not, eyes wherewith[1153]
They see not, and ears wherewith
They hear not. They are
Like cattle—nay more
Misguided: for they
Are heedless (of warning).

١٧٩ وَلَقَدْ ذَرَأْنَا لِجَهَنَّمَ كَثِيرًا مِّنَ ٱلْجِنِّ
وَٱلْإِنسِ لَهُمْ قُلُوبٌ لَّا يَفْقَهُونَ بِهَا وَلَهُمْ أَعْيُنٌ
لَّا يُبْصِرُونَ بِهَا وَلَهُمْ ءَاذَانٌ لَّا يَسْمَعُونَ بِهَآ أُولَٰٓئِكَ
كَٱلْأَنْعَٰمِ بَلْ هُمْ أَضَلُّ أُولَٰٓئِكَ هُمُ ٱلْغَٰفِلُونَ

180. The most beautiful names[1154]
Belong to Allah:
So call on him by them;
But shun such men as
Use profanity in His names:
For what they do, they will
Soon be requited.

١٨٠ وَلِلَّهِ ٱلْأَسْمَآءُ ٱلْحُسْنَىٰ فَٱدْعُوهُ بِهَا
وَذَرُوا ٱلَّذِينَ يُلْحِدُونَ فِىٓ أَسْمَٰٓئِهِۦ
سَيُجْزَوْنَ مَا كَانُوا يَعْمَلُونَ

181. Of those We have created
Are people who direct
(Others) with truth,
And dispense justice therewith.

١٨١ وَمِمَّنْ خَلَقْنَآ أُمَّةٌ
يَهْدُونَ بِٱلْحَقِّ وَبِهِۦ يَعْدِلُونَ

SECTION 23.

182. Those who reject Our Signs,
We shall gradually visit
With punishment, in ways
They perceive not;[1154-A]

١٨٢ وَٱلَّذِينَ كَذَّبُوا بِـَٔايَٰتِنَا
سَنَسْتَدْرِجُهُم مِّنْ حَيْثُ لَا يَعْلَمُونَ

183. Respite will I grant
Unto them: for My scheme
Is strong (and unfailing).

١٨٣ وَأُمْلِى لَهُمْ إِنَّ كَيْدِى مَتِينٌ

1152. Those who reject Allah will be deprived of Allah's grace and guidance. His Mercy is always open for sincere repentance. But with each step downwards, they go lower and lower, until they perish.

1153. *Cf.* 2:18. Though they have apparently all the faculties of reason and perception, they have so deadened them that those faculties do not work, and they go headlong into Hell. They are, as it were, made for Hell.

1154. As we contemplate Allah's nature, we can use the most beautiful names we can think of, to express His attributes. There are hundreds of such attributes. In the opening Sūrah, we have these indicated in a few comprehensive words, such as *Raḥmān* (most Gracious), *Raḥīm* (most Merciful), *Rabb al 'ālamīn* (Cherisher and Sustainer of the worlds). Our bringing such names to remembrance is part of our Prayer and Praise. But we must not associate with people who use Allah's names profanely, or so as to suggest anything derogatory to His dignity or His unity. *Cf.* 17:110.

1154-A. See also 68:44 and n. 5626.

184. Do they not reflect?
Their Companion is not seized[1155]
With madness: he is but
A perspicuous warner.[1156]

١٨٤ أَوَلَمْ يَتَفَكَّرُوا مَا بِصَاحِبِهِم
مِّن جِنَّةٍ إِنْ هُوَ إِلَّا نَذِيرٌ مُّبِينٌ

185. Do they see nothing
In the government of the heavens
And the earth and all
That Allah hath created?[1157]
(Do they not see) that
It may well be that
Their term is nigh
Drawing to an end?
In what Message after this
Will they then believe?

١٨٥ أَوَلَمْ يَنظُرُوا فِي مَلَكُوتِ
السَّمَاوَاتِ وَالْأَرْضِ وَمَا خَلَقَ اللَّهُ مِن شَيْءٍ
وَأَنْ عَسَىٰ أَن يَكُونَ قَدِ اقْتَرَبَ أَجَلُهُمْ
فَبِأَيِّ حَدِيثٍ بَعْدَهُ يُؤْمِنُونَ

186. To such as Allah rejects
From His guidance, there can be
No guide: He will
Leave them in their trespasses,
Wandering in distraction.[1158]

١٨٦ مَن يُضْلِلِ اللَّهُ فَلَا هَادِيَ لَهُ
وَيَذَرُهُمْ فِي طُغْيَانِهِمْ يَعْمَهُونَ

187. They ask thee about
The (final) Hour—when
Will be its appointed time?
Say: "The knowledge thereof
Is with my Lord (alone):
None but He can reveal
As to when it will occur.[1159]
Heavy were its burden through

١٨٧ يَسْأَلُونَكَ عَنِ السَّاعَةِ
أَيَّانَ مُرْسَاهَا قُلْ إِنَّمَا عِلْمُهَا
عِندَ رَبِّي لَا يُجَلِّيهَا لِوَقْتِهَا
إِلَّا هُوَ ثَقُلَتْ فِي

1155. *Their companion, i.e.*, the Holy Prophet, who lived with and amongst them. He was accused of madness because he behaved differently from them. He had no selfish ambitions: he was always true, in thought, words, and deed: he was kind and considerate to the weak, and was not dazzled by worldly power or wealth or position: he was undeterred by fear of the strong, the mockery of the cynics, the bitterness of the evil, or the indifference of the heedless. That is why he stood out boldly against wrong: he did not mince his words, and his warnings were not mealy-mouthed.

1156. *Mubīn*: perspicuous. The reason why I have not used a simpler word, such as "plain" or "clear" is explained in n. 716 to 5:17. Al Muṣṭafā's sermons were not polite reminders, with an eye to the flattery of weaknesses in high places or national vanities or crowd passions. They brought out every foible into the glare of light, by a fiery eloquence fed by inspiration from Allah.

1157. An appeal to Allah's most wonderful universe should at once convince a thinking mind of man's nothingness, and Allah's power, glory, and goodness. Man's term here is fleeting. If he is not warned by the great Signs, and the Messages which call his attention to them, is he capable of any faith at all?

1158. *Cf.* 2:15. If Allah's light is removed, the best of them can only wander hither and thither, like blind men, in distraction.

1159. The fact of its coming is a certainty: the exact time appointed for it is not revealed by Allah. If it were it would be so momentous as to disturb our thoughts and life. It would be a heavy burden to us. Our duty is to be prepared for it at all times. It will come when we least expect it. In the present Gospels, Jesus says the same thing: he does not know the Hour, but it will come suddenly. "But of that day and that Hour knoweth no man, no, not the angels which are in heaven, neither the Son, but the Father. Take ye heed, watch and pray: for ye know not when the time is." (Mark. xiii. 32-33).

The heavens and the earth.
Only, all of a sudden
Will it come to you."
They ask thee as if thou
Wert eager in search thereof:[1160]
Say: "The knowledge thereof
Is with Allah (alone),
But most men know not."

ٱلسَّمَٰوَٰتِ وَٱلْأَرْضِ لَا تَأْتِيكُمْ إِلَّا بَغْتَةً
يَسْـَٔلُونَكَ كَأَنَّكَ حَفِيٌّ عَنْهَا
قُلْ إِنَّمَا عِلْمُهَا عِندَ ٱللَّهِ
وَلَٰكِنَّ أَكْثَرَ ٱلنَّاسِ لَا يَعْلَمُونَ

188. Say: "I have no power
Over any good or harm
To myself except as Allah
Willeth. If I had knowledge
Of the unseen, I should have
Multiplied all good, and no evil
Should have touched me:
I am but a warner,
And a bringer of glad tidings
To those who have faith."[1161]

١٨٨ قُل لَّآ أَمْلِكُ لِنَفْسِى نَفْعًا وَلَا ضَرًّا
إِلَّا مَا شَآءَ ٱللَّهُ وَلَوْ كُنتُ أَعْلَمُ ٱلْغَيْبَ
لَٱسْتَكْثَرْتُ مِنَ ٱلْخَيْرِ وَمَا مَسَّنِىَ ٱلسُّوٓءُ
إِنْ أَنَا۠ إِلَّا نَذِيرٌ وَبَشِيرٌ لِّقَوْمٍ يُؤْمِنُونَ

Section 24.

189. It is He Who created
You from a single person,
And made his mate
Of like nature,[1162] in order
That he might dwell with her
(In love). When they are
United, she bears a light
Burden and carries it about
(Unnoticed). When she grows
Heavy, they both pray[1163]
To Allah their Lord, (saying):
"If Thou givest us
A goodly child,[1164]

١٨٩ هُوَ ٱلَّذِى خَلَقَكُم مِّن نَّفْسٍ وَٰحِدَةٍ
وَجَعَلَ مِنْهَا زَوْجَهَا لِيَسْكُنَ إِلَيْهَا
فَلَمَّا تَغَشَّىٰهَا حَمَلَتْ
حَمْلًا خَفِيفًا فَمَرَّتْ بِهِۦ
فَلَمَّآ أَثْقَلَت دَّعَوَا ٱللَّهَ رَبَّهُمَا
لَئِنْ ءَاتَيْتَنَا صَٰلِحًا

1160. *Ḥafiyy* is usually construed to mean: "eagerly or anxiously in search of": the preposition following here is *'an* = concerning, about. Some commentators (including Rāghib) understand it in this passage to mean "well-acquainted." In 19:47, with the preposition *bi* following it, it signifies "well-disposed to", "favourable to, good to, kind to."

1161. A warner to all, and a bringer of glad tidings to those who have faith, because they will profit by the glad tidings. As everyone is invited to faith, the glad tidings are *offered* to all, but they are not necessarily accepted by all.

1162. *Cf.* 4:1. and n. 504, where the construction is explained.

1163. The mystery of the physical birth of man, as it affects the father and the mother, only touches the imagination of the parents in the later stages when the child is yet unborn and yet the life stirs within the body of the expectant mother. The coming of the new life is a solemn thing, and is fraught with much hope as well as much unknown risk to the mother herself. The parents in their anxiety turn to Allah. If this feeling of solemnity, hope, and looking towards Allah were maintained after birth, all would be well for the parents as well as for the rising generation. But the attitude changes, as the verses following show.

1164. *Goodly: ṣāliḥ*: includes the following ideas: sound in body and mind; healthy; righteous: of good moral disposition.

We vow we shall
(Ever) be grateful."

لَنَكُونَنَّ مِنَ الشَّٰكِرِينَ

190. But when He giveth them
A goodly child, they ascribe[1165]
To others a share in the gift
They have received:
But Allah is exalted
High above the partners
They ascribe to Him.

(١٩٠) فَلَمَّآ ءَاتَىٰهُمَا صَٰلِحًا
جَعَلَا لَهُۥ شُرَكَآءَ فِيمَآ ءَاتَىٰهُمَا
فَتَعَٰلَى ٱللَّهُ عَمَّا يُشْرِكُونَ

191. Do they indeed ascribe
To Him as partners things
That can create nothing,
But are themselves created?

(١٩١) أَيُشْرِكُونَ مَا لَا يَخْلُقُ
شَيْـًٔا وَهُمْ يُخْلَقُونَ

192. No aid can they give them,
Nor can they aid themselves!

(١٩٢) وَلَا يَسْتَطِيعُونَ لَهُمْ نَصْرًا
وَلَآ أَنفُسَهُمْ يَنصُرُونَ

193. If ye call them to guidance,
They will not obey:
For you it is the same
Whether ye call them
Or ye hold your peace![1166]

(١٩٣) وَإِن تَدْعُوهُمْ إِلَى ٱلْهُدَىٰ لَا يَتَّبِعُوكُمْ
سَوَآءٌ عَلَيْكُمْ أَدَعَوْتُمُوهُمْ أَمْ أَنتُمْ صَٰمِتُونَ

194. Verily those whom ye
Call upon besides Allah
Are servants like unto you:[1167]
Call upon them, and let them
Listen to your prayer,
If ye are (indeed) truthful!

(١٩٤) إِنَّ ٱلَّذِينَ تَدْعُونَ مِن دُونِ ٱللَّهِ عِبَادٌ
أَمْثَالُكُمْ فَٱدْعُوهُمْ فَلْيَسْتَجِيبُوا۟
لَكُمْ إِن كُنتُمْ صَٰدِقِينَ

195. Have they feet to walk with?
Or hands to lay hold with?
Or eyes to see with?
Or ears to hear with?

(١٩٥) أَلَهُمْ أَرْجُلٌ يَمْشُونَ بِهَآ أَمْ لَهُمْ أَيْدٍ
يَبْطِشُونَ بِهَآ أَمْ لَهُمْ أَعْيُنٌ يُبْصِرُونَ بِهَآ
أَمْ لَهُمْ ءَاذَانٌ يَسْمَعُونَ بِهَا

1165. When the child is born, the parents forget that it is a precious gift of Allah—a miracle of Creation, which should lift their minds up to the higher things of Allah. Instead, their gradual familiarity with the new life makes them connect it with many superstitious ideas or rites and ceremonies, or they take it as a matter of course, as a little plaything of the material world. This leads to idolatry or false worship, or the setting up of false standards, in derogation of the dignity of Allah.

1166. When false worship takes root, the teacher of Truth finds much to discourage him. As far as he is concerned, it seems as if he has produced no effect. Yet his duty is to continue his work, in the spirit of verse 199 below, forgiving all opposition, teaching what is right, and not joining the ignorant in their attitude of doubt and indecision.

1167. False gods, whether idols or deified men, or ideas and superstitions, have no existence of their own, independent of Allah's creation. They are Allah's creatures, and like servants are subject to His authority. Deified men are not real men, but false ideas of men. They cannot help themselves: how can they help others?

Say: "Call your 'god-partners',[1168]
Scheme (your worst) against me,
And give me no respite!

قُلِ ادْعُوا شُرَكَاءَكُمْ ثُمَّ كِيدُونِ فَلَا تُنظِرُونِ

196. "For my Protector is Allah,
Who revealed the Book
(From time to time),
And He will choose
And befriend the righteous.

١٩٦ إِنَّ وَلِيِّـۧ اللَّهُ الَّذِي نَزَّلَ الْكِتَابَ ۖ
وَهُوَ يَتَوَلَّى الصَّالِحِينَ

197. "But those ye call upon
Besides Him, are unable
To help you, and indeed
To help themselves."

١٩٧ وَالَّذِينَ تَدْعُونَ مِن دُونِهِ لَا يَسْتَطِيعُونَ
نَصْرَكُمْ وَلَا أَنفُسَهُمْ يَنصُرُونَ

198. If thou callest them
To guidance, they hear not.
Thou wilt see them
Looking at thee, but
They see not.[1169]

١٩٨ وَإِن تَدْعُوهُمْ إِلَى الْهُدَىٰ لَا يَسْمَعُوا ۖ
وَتَرَاهُمْ يَنظُرُونَ إِلَيْكَ وَهُمْ لَا يُبْصِرُونَ

199. Hold to forgiveness;
Command what is right;
But turn away from the
ignorant.[1170]

١٩٩ خُذِ الْعَفْوَ وَأْمُرْ بِالْعُرْفِ
وَأَعْرِضْ عَنِ الْجَاهِلِينَ

200. If a suggestion from Satan
Assail thy (mind),[1171]
Seek refuge with Allah;
For He heareth and knoweth
(All things).

٢٠٠ وَإِمَّا يَنزَغَنَّكَ مِنَ الشَّيْطَانِ نَزْغٌ
فَاسْتَعِذْ بِاللَّهِ ۚ إِنَّهُ سَمِيعٌ عَلِيمٌ

201. Those who fear Allah,
When a thought of evil
From Satan assaults them,

٢٠١ إِنَّ الَّذِينَ اتَّقَوْا إِذَا
مَسَّهُمْ طَائِفٌ مِّنَ الشَّيْطَانِ

1168. Here is a test and a challenge. If the false gods had any power or even existence, collect them all together, and, says the Prophet of Allah, "Let them do their worst against me." They cannot; because the whole thing is based on a superstition and a chimaera.

1169. The beauty and righteousness of Muṣṭafā's life were acknowledged on all hands, until he received the mission to preach and to fight against evil. What happened then? Evil erected barricades for itself. It had eyes, but it refused to see. It had ears, but it refused to hear. It had intelligence, but it blocked up its channels of understanding. Even now, after fourteen centuries, a life of unexampled purity, probity, justice, and righteousness is seen in false lights by blind detractors!

1170. Allah comforts the Prophet and directs his mind to three precepts: (1) to forgive injuries, insults, and persecution; (2) to continue to declare the faith that was in him, and not only to declare it, but to act up to it in all his dealings with friends and foes: (3) to pay no attention to ignorant fools, who raised doubts or difficulties, hurled taunts or reproaches, or devised plots to defeat the truth: they were to be ignored and passed by, not to be engaged in fights and fruitless controversies, or conciliated by compromises.

1171. Even a Prophet of Allah is but human. He might think that revenge or retaliation, or a little tactful silence when evil stalks abroad, or some compromise with ignorance, might be best for the cause. He is to reject such suggestions.

Bring Allah to remembrance,
When lo! they see (aright)![1172]

تَذَكَّرُواْ فَإِذَا هُم مُّبْصِرُونَ

202. But their brethren (the evil ones)[1173]
Plunge them deeper into error,
And never relax (their efforts).

٢٠٢ وَإِخْوَٰنُهُمْ يَمُدُّونَهُمْ
فِى ٱلْغَىِّ ثُمَّ لَا يُقْصِرُونَ

203. If thou bring them not
A revelation,[1174] they say:
"Why hast thou not
Got it together?"
Say: "I but follow
What is revealed to me
From my Lord:
This is (nothing but)
Lights from your Lord,[1175]
And Guidance, and Mercy,
For any who have Faith."

٢٠٣ وَإِذَا لَمْ تَأْتِهِم بِـَٔايَةٍ
قَالُواْ لَوْلَا ٱجْتَبَيْتَهَا ۚ
قُلْ إِنَّمَآ أَتَّبِعُ مَا يُوحَىٰٓ إِلَىَّ مِن رَّبِّى ۚ
هَٰذَا بَصَآئِرُ مِن رَّبِّكُمْ
وَهُدًى وَرَحْمَةٌ لِّقَوْمٍ يُؤْمِنُونَ

204. When the Qur'ān is read,
Listen to it with attention,
And hold your peace:
That ye may receive Mercy.

٢٠٤ وَإِذَا قُرِئَ ٱلْقُرْءَانُ فَٱسْتَمِعُواْ لَهُۥ
وَأَنصِتُواْ لَعَلَّكُمْ تُرْحَمُونَ

205. And do thou (O reader!)
Bring thy Lord to remembrance
In thy (very) soul,
With humility and in reverence,
Without loudness in words,
In the mornings and evenings;
And be not thou
Of those who are unheedful.

٢٠٥ وَٱذْكُر رَّبَّكَ فِى نَفْسِكَ
تَضَرُّعًا وَخِيفَةً وَدُونَ ٱلْجَهْرِ مِنَ ٱلْقَوْلِ
بِٱلْغُدُوِّ وَٱلْـَٔاصَالِ وَلَا تَكُن مِّنَ ٱلْغَٰفِلِينَ

1172. Allah protects His own, as no one else can. He is the sure refuge—and the only one—for men of faith. If we are confused or angry, being blinded by this world, He will open our eyes.

1173 We go back to consider the ungodly, whom we left at verse 198, in order to be taught our behaviour towards evil. The forces of evil never relax their efforts to draw their "brethren" (those who go into their family) deeper and deeper into the mire of sin and destruction.

1174. "Āyah" here, I think, means specially an Āyah of the Holy Qur'ān. The infidels did not believe in revelation, and used to taunt the Holy Prophet, as much as to say that he used to put together words and promulgate them as revelation. The answer is contained in the sentence that follows. No human composition could contain the beauty, power, and spiritual insight of the Qur'ān. Without inspiration it is impossible to suppose that a man, with or without literary and philosophic training could produce such a book as the Qur'ān.

1175. "*Lights*": eyes, faculty of spiritual insight. The revelation is for us (1) spiritual eyes, (2) guidance, and (3) mercy. (1) is the highest in degree: just as a blind man, if he is given eyes and the faculty of sight, is at once removed into an entirely new world, so those who can reach the stage of spiritual insight pass into and become citizens of a wholly new spiritual World. (2) is next in degree: the man of the world can act up to the teaching about right conduct and prepare for the Hereafter. (3) is the Mercy of Allah, free to every one, saint and sinner, who sincerely believes and puts his trust in Allah.

206. Those who are near[1176]
To thy Lord, disdain not
To do Him worship:
They celebrate His praises,
And bow down before Him.[1177]

إِنَّ ٱلَّذِينَ عِندَ رَبِّكَ لَا يَسْتَكْبِرُونَ عَنْ عِبَادَتِهِۦ وَيُسَبِّحُونَهُۥ وَلَهُۥ يَسْجُدُونَ ۩ ٢٠٦

1176. The higher you are in spiritual attainment, the more is your desire and your opportunity to serve and worship your Lord and Cherisher and the Lord and Cherisher of all the worlds; and the greater is your pride in that service and that worship.

1177. At this stage a *Sajdah* or prostration is indicated, as symbolical of our humble acceptance of the privilege of serving and worshipping Allah—a fitting close to a Sūrah in which we are led, through a contemplation of the stories of the Messengers of Allah, to the meaning of revelation and its relation to our moral and spiritual progress.

APPENDIX IV

Egyptian Chronology and Israel (see 7:104, n. 1072)

In order to get some idea of the comparative chronology of Egypt and Israel, we must first consider what data we have for Egyptian chronology. Israel's surviving records date from a time many centuries later than Israel's contact with Egypt. On the other hand, Egypt's records in monuments, inscriptions, tombs, etc., are rich and absolutely reliable as far as they go.

Of the surviving old civilisations, Egypt and China go back furthest in time with historical material. Egypt has more interest for us, because geographically it was centrally situated, and it influenced and was influenced by almost every important cultural movement in Asia, Europe, and Africa. Nothing happened in Mediterranean history that had not some points of contact with Egypt.

The first broad division in Egyptian chronology is between the pre-Dynastic and the Dynastic periods. The pre-Dynastic period is all prehistory. But recent researches have thrown a great deal of light on the culture of that period, and we know many more details about the arts and tools of that period in Egypt than we do for the corresponding periods of prehistory in other countries.

With the first Egyptian Dynasty of rulers begins the Dynastic period. What were the Egyptian Dynasties, and why is so much prominence given to them in Egyptian chronology? The reason is that though we can form a graphic idea of the sequence of events and in many cases of the details of events, arts, and crafts, manners and customs, cults and ceremonies, and social and economic conditions in the dynastic period, we are not yet able, except for occasional and isolated glimpses, to give any accurate figures of early dates to connect them with our chronology B.C. On the other hand, we have abundant materials to justify us in placing certain events or personages or ideas in some division of the Dynastic scheme. We can say that such and such ideas held sway under the 18th Dynasty or that such and such invasion, outwards or inwards, took place at the close of the 14th Dynasty.

The Dynastic scheme rests mainly on the lists and fragments preserved from the writings of one Manetho, an Egyptian priest and annalist, who lived under Ptolemy I and Ptolemy II (B.C. 313-246), the inheritors of the Egyptian portion of Alexander's Empire. For his Egyptian history in Greek he had access to Egyptian records. His scheme of Dynasties therefore supplies a rough chronological framework into which can be fitted our ever-increasing detailed knowledge derived from Egyptian monuments, tombs, and excavations. His first Dynasty begins with the unification of Upper and Lower Egypt, but its actual date B.C. has been placed at between such wide margins as 5500 B.C. and 3300 B.C.

The two Egypts may be considered distinct ethnical and perhaps geographical divisions, which tend to assimilate when they are united politically, but whose physical characteristics are different, as also their outlook when there is political division. Lower Egypt looks to the Mediterranean, and its population is mixed, containing almost all the Mediterranean and Arab elements, while Upper Egypt looks to interior Africa (Nubia, Sudan, Abyssinia, etc.). and its population tends to have more and more African characteristics. The whole of Egypt has had a ribbon development, the population and cultivation being confined to the banks of the Nile. Without the Nile Egypt would be just a desert forming a link in the long chain of tropical and subtropical deserts stretching from the Sahara, the Libyan desert, the Arabian deserts, through the Persian, Baluchistan, Sindh, and Rajputana deserts, to the Turki and Gobi deserts in Central Asia. But Upper Egypt is purely a long irregular line along the banks of the Nile, while Lower Egypt has the broad fan-link delta in which the many mouths of the Nile run into a very irregular coastline extending over about 200 miles. Lower Egypt had (and has) much marshland, and its low-lying configuration was subject to many physical changes, in the same way as invasions and foreign immigrations gave its population a less stable character. Its cities, such as Sais and Tanis (Zoan), were also less stable in character, and Memphis (near the site of modern Cairo) has to be just above the Delta. On the other hand the Capitals in Upper Egypt, such as Thebes (or No), with their magnificent temples and tombs were safe above Nile waters in the highest inundations until the modern dam of Aswān was built many miles above them. Even after the union of the two Egypts, the King wore a double crown. The boundary between Upper and Lower Egypt was never clearly defined, because in spite of frequent interruptions in the unity of the country, the identification of Egypt with the Nile made the unity of Egypt a political and economic necessity. The present boundary of Lower Egypt is just south of Cairo, making Lower Egypt include just the Delta. The tract between Cairo and Assyut is sometimes called Middle Egypt and is distinguished from the rest of Upper Egypt, which is higher up the river.

There being such wide variations in the estimate of ancient dates by competent authorities, the only practicable course is to refer ancient events to Dynasties according to Manetho's scheme. In the later dates it is sometimes possible to express a date in approximate figures B.C., but such figures are uncertain, whereas the sequence of Dynasties may be taken to be a stable fact in Egyptian history, although some of Manetho's material, when it can be tested, has proved to be inaccurate. But we have only Manetho secondhand. The inaccuracies may be due not to Manetho but to his transmitters. Thirty-one such Dynasties are reckoned, and they may be grouped into Periods as follows:

I. The Old Kingdom, Dynasties I to VIII, including (a) the first three Dynasties, with a new orientation in Egyptian Art, and (b) Dynasties IV to VI, the Pyramid Period, during which the Great Pyramid and the second and third Pyramids of Ghizeh were built. The capital now came to Lower Egypt, to the site of Memphis, near modern Cairo.

II. The Middle Kingdom, Dynasties IX to XVII. In Dynasties IX and X the centre of gravity moved from Memphis in Lower Egypt to Middle Egypt. In the XIIth Dynasty many of the great monuments of and near Thebes (Karnak, Luxor, etc.), were constructed. Perhaps the movement higher up the river was necessitated by foreign invasions in Lower Egypt. Dynasties XV to XVII are called the Hyksos Period, when a Syrian Dynasty was established in Lower Egypt, with a sort of lordship over the native Dynasties of Upper Egypt, and international connections in other Mediterranean countries. We shall presently speak of the Hyksos Pharaohs, who have been placed in the 17th, 18th, and even 26th century B.C.

III. The New Empire, Dynasties XVIII to XX, crowded with events. The dates now begin to be more definite: the period may be placed about 1580 B.C. and about 1200 B.C. The foreign Hyksos were driven out; the empire was extended to Syria and Nubia; perhaps even the Euphrates was reached. Some of the most wonderful works of Egyptian art date from this period.

IV. The Dynasties of the Delta. Dynasties XXI to XXXI, including a Dynasty at Sais (on one of the western branches of the Deltaic Nile). But Assyrian and Persian invasions were now weakening the power of Egypt. The dates now became more certain. The XXIst Dynasty was roughly about 1100 B.C. The XXVIIth Dynasty was ended by the invasion of the Persians under Cambyses in 525 B.C. The Persians held sway (with Egyptian local dynasties under them) until the XXXIst Dynasty, when the last Pharoah fled to Ethiopia about 340 B.C.

V. The Egyptian Dynasties have now ended, and we are in firm history: the Macedonian Period after Alexander's conquest, 332 B.C., and the Dynasty of the Ptolemies 323 B.C. to 30 B.C.; and the Roman Period 30 B.C. to 639 A.C., after which the Arab and Turkish conquests evolved modern Egypt and Muslim Egyptian civilisation.

Having cleared the chronological background, we are now in a position to examine the data about Israel's stay in Egypt in order to see if we can get some idea of the time in Egyptian history when the contact took place. We saw that Dynasties XV to XVII were concerned with the Hyksos (or Shepherd) kings. They were foreigners from Asia, but it is not quite clear exactly what race they belonged to. Josephus supposed that they were Israelites, but that theory is untenable. It has been conjectured that they were Phoenicians, or Amalekites, or Hittites. In any case they were Semites. They founded a city called Zoan (Tanis) on one of the eastern branches of the Deltaic Nile, and were in close communication with the Hittite city of Hebron in the south of Palestine. That would be their own city, but their capital would probably be the same as the old Egyptian capital at Memphis when they were well-established. They are credited with having invented the Semitic alphabet of 22 letters, which (through the Phoenicians) is the parent of all modern alphabets. Their invention probably helped in the process of converting old Egyptian Hieroglyphics from picture-writing to phonetic writing. As the Hyksos had close relations with Hebron in Palestine, and Abraham and Israel had settled in the Palestine country, a nexus would be established, by which the first Israelites would be attracted to Zoan in Egypt. It must also be remembered that southern Palestine was a poor country and subject to frequent famines, while Deltaic Egypt was well-watered by the Nile, and suffered from famines only on the rare occasions when the Nile failed to inundate. The attraction of Egypt for the famine-stricken lands of the neighborhood would therefore be strong. And this is proved in the story of Joseph and his brethren.

Can we form even a rough idea of the dates of the Hyksos occupation? At the latest the Hyksos period ended about 1600 B.C. Renan is therefore probably not far wrong when he places the Hyksos occupation about 2000 B.C. Possibly a date between 2000 B.C. and 1600 B.C. may be nearer the mark. If we suppose Joseph to have been the Wazīr of one of the Hyksos Pharaohs in the Delta, there is no great violence of probabilities in the suggestion, as Joseph and the Hyksos would be of kindred races. In that case Joseph's date would fall somewhere between the 19th and 17th century B.C.

No reference to Joseph or Moses has been found in Egyptian records. The solitary reference to Israel (*Ysraer*, r = l) in a stele of Mer-en-Ptah or Mineptah (about 1225 B.C.) seems to refer to Israel in Palestine rather than to Israel in Egypt. At this we need not wonder, as the Pharaoh who honoured Joseph was, strictly speaking, only a foreigner. When the reaction against the Hyksos took place and the Hyksos were overthrown, the Egyptians would not probably be anxious to remember the interrupted period or to preserve its memory. The Pharaoh who "knew not Joseph" looked upon the Israelites as contemptible slaves, not worthy of a thought except when they revolted, and then only as a despised race fit to be punished and kept in its place. It may be noticed, however, that the land of Goshen in which Israel dwelt and multiplied between the time of Joseph and the time of the Exodus, was a frontier tract of Egypt in the neighbourhood of the Hyksos city of Zoan in the Delta.

In seeking the approximate date of Moses, we must again look to the probabilities of Egyptian history. It was formerly the received opinion that Rameses II (say about 1250 B.C.) was the Pharaoh who oppressed Israel in Egypt, and that the exodus may have taken place under his immediate successor Mineptah (say about 1225 B.C.). The vigorous policy of Rameses II and the spirit of his time would be consistent with this view. But this date is almost certainly too late. There are indications pointing to the Israelites having already been settled in Canaan by this time. The Hyksos were turned out by the XVIIIth Dynasty, which established the New Empire in the 16th century B.C. Thothmes I (Tethmosis I, about 1540 B.C.) is more likely, in the first flush of his nationalist campaign, to have oppressed the Israelites and led to the exodus. His date fits in better. And his character also accords with the description in sacred history. He centralised the monarchy and made it a military autocracy. Militarism went with the lust of war and foreign conquest. He carried his arms as far as the Euphrates. Slaves, plunder, and foreign tribute made Egypt opulent and arrogant, and he added many monuments to Thebes. We can imagine him in his splendid Court, scarcely paying any attention to Moses, and viewing all his complaints with an amusement mingled with contempt and impatience. But retribution was to come in Allah's good time. The men who followed Allah's message—Israel in the time of Solomon (a little after 1000 B.C.), and more completely, the Muslims in the time of 'Umar and his successors—became lords of the East and the West (Q. 7:137), and ancient Egypt's glories were eventually buried in the sands.

It was this same Pharaoh, Thothmes I, who took for his partner on the Throne his daughter Hatshepshut. If Thothmes was the Pharaoh in Moses's story, we may suppose that it was this same celebrated strong-minded lady, Pharaoh's daughter, who found the child Moses (Exod. ii. 10), and brought him to her mother to be adopted into the family (Q. 28:9). Like her father, she was a great supporter of the national cults. Moses was nurtured in the palace, and learned all the wisdom of the Egyptians, then reputed to be the wisest of nations. With their own wisdom he foiled them. Thus in Allah's Plan the enemies of Allah and the enemies of Israel (Q. 20:39) were the very ones who were used as instruments for the purpose of Allah and the salvation of Israel.

References: E.B., *Egypt*; D.A. Mackenzie, *Egyptian Myth and Legend*; Renan, *History of the People of Israel*, 3 vols.; Joseph Cattanie Pasha, *Coup d'oeil sur la chronolgie de la nation Egyptienne*, Paris 1931; Sir W.M. Flinders Petrie, *History of Egypt*, 3 vols.; *Cambridge Ancient History*, vol. I, Chapter IV. (iii).

APPENDIX V

Egyptian Religion and its Steps Toward Islam (see 7:123 n. 1082)

This should be read along with Appendix IV in which a discussion of Egyptian chronology will be found.

Allah's Plan works silently but surely among all nations and at all times. In the most fantastic forms of religion appear gleams of His Light of Unity, calls to Islam, *i.e.*, man's submission of his will to the Will of Allah (see C. 7-10). From that point of view, the religious history of Egypt from the most ancient times to the present day is most interesting, as is indeed the religious history of any country for which we have records of thought and development. That of India touches us dearly, but it is not directly relevant in a translation and exposition of the Qur'ān. The religious history of Israel is just an earlier chapter of the history of Islam, and our doctors and commentators have written in great detail about it. Sometimes, I think, they have attached exaggerated importance to it. But none of them has paid much attention to Egypt from this point of view. Our people know very little of ancient Egypt and have shown little interest in it. It is a healthy sign that modern Egypt is showing much interest in it, and I hope that it will in time recognise in it a valuable unfoldment of religious ideas leading up to Islam.

The field of Egyptology is vast and is being extended everyday by the diligent researches of archaeologists and scholars. I do not propose to write an essay on Egyptian religion. But I wish to put forward a few considerations to show how Allah's Plan and Will worked steadily, in Egypt as elsewhere, towards a greater and greater appreciation, on the part of the people, of Allah's true nature and the real purpose of religion. The eternal light of Unity and Islam shines in many ways, and its rays give light to the spiritual aspirations of mankind in the darkest periods. With a gifted and artistic people like the Egyptians, their religious sense was led, in spite of many rebuffs, gradually to a purer and purer conception of man's eternal destiny, until Muḥammad's Message was preached to them in the very language in which it was originally preached in Arabia. And that language, Arabic, became and is now the language of the Egyptian people themselves.

In the pre-Dynastic Egypt, there must already have been a great deal of development in the religious conceptions which afterwards showed such vitality in Dynastic Egypt. The Old Kingdom, including the Pyramid Period, shows that the Egyptian mind was obsessed with the certainty of life after death. It was also impressed with ideas of grandeur, order, and precision in the universe—ideas which found eloquent expression in the grand conceptions and mathematical symmetry and simplicity of its architecture. Its massive dignity and repose are also reflected in the faces and poses of the figures in Egyptian statuary and painting. The unending expanse and the mystery of the desert seem to have acted on the Egyptian mind like a soporific and made it less active in mundane affairs and less practical in speculation than that of some other races of similar gifts. What mysteries are typified in the proportions of the Pyramids and their internal galleries and mysterious chambers, we shall probably never know with certainty. But a haunting sense of death and of the other world seems to oppress us in its atmosphere, as it does in the grim scenes of the "Book of the Dead". As Prof. T.E. Peet remarks (*Cambridge Ancient History,* vol. I, p. 354), "the Egyptian mind closely associated together men, gods, and the dead as merely three species of a single genus." Each of these it considered was subject to an irresistible force called *Hīke* or *Heka*: hence the force of Magic, Incantations to the Dead, and Rites and Formularies in daily life.

The Middle Kingdom brings us face to face with fresh ideas. We have no data with which to appraise the influence of foreign cults and foreign ideas during the period. But knowing, as we do, how Egypt acted as a magnet to the world at large and how many points of contact the Euphrates valley civilisations and the Nile valley civilisations had with each other, we may well suppose a broadening of Egyptian culture and civilisation in consequence. The Hyksos may have been Egyptianised in Egypt, but they could not have failed in their turn to contribute Syrian and Semitic ideas to Egypt. Among these were Monotheism, a patriarchal organisation of society, and an impatience of priestly or caste denomination. These must have contrasted strangely with the chaotic Pantheon of countless deities, the lash-driven slaves living huddled in the cities, and the dedicated priests and richly endowed temples, which catered for the privileged few, but lived by the sweat of the brow of the unprivileged many.

The New Empire was the flowering period of Egyptian genius and requires special consideration. The crudities of the old pre-Dynastic chaotic Pantheon had been in process of attrition through the centuries. Local gods tended to be absorbed into general gods. Some sort of rationalism and spiritualisation had been going on throughout the Dynastic period. A process of systemisation and unification was now consciously undertaken. The primitive worship of animals had gradually been transformed into a system of animal gods, with human bodies and animal heads. The human bodies represented the anthropomorphic tendencies, while the animal heads became types of qualities. For example, Anubis, with the dog emblem, was the doorkeeper, the messenger, the custodian of the dead. Apis, or Hapis, the sacred bull of Memphis, symbolised the renewal of life: he was identified with Osiris: there were great rejoicings when a new Apis (a black bull calf) was found, and great mourning and costly burial when one died. Thoth, the god of wisdom and magic, was symbolised by an ibis, that stately, mute, mysterious bird of passage in the Nile valley.

In addition to the symbolism of animals, there was the worship of the great phenomena of nature, the Nile, the giver of agricultural bounties to Egypt, and the sun, which, as the god Ra, became the supreme god in Egypt. Then there was the myth of Osiris the good, who came to the earth for the benefit of mankind, was killed by the magic of Set, the power of evil, and reigns as the judge of the dead in the lower world. His faithful wife Isis and his falcon-eyed son Horus figure in the mysteries. It is possible that the Osiris myth itself arose from a myth of the Nile or the sun.

There was a gradual perception of Monotheism, a realisation that Allah is One and above names. But the picturesque forms, festivals, and representations remained, and as the priests of all grades enjoyed special privileges and monopolised knowledge and learning, the people remained ignorant. They were exploited and practically enslaved. It was in the midst of such conditions that Moses came. He came to rescue his own people from the bondage of Egypt, a task which he performed. But it must not be forgotten that his mission was also addressed to the king of Egypt, and to the people of Egypt. Here also he sowed the seed, although he did not reap the fruit. The king, the Pharaoh, was almost looked upon as a god, and looked upon himself as a god. He had to be humbled, and he was humbled. But Allah's purpose is not merely to humble. It is also to lead from darkness to light. If the particular Pharaoh was too hard-hearted to respond, his descendant in the fifth or sixth generation made a public confession of the One True God, as we shall see presently. What of the people? The wise men of Egypt, who were confronted with Moses, repented of their deceit, and saw the light by the Grace of Allah, according to the Quranic narrative. Though they were threatened and perhaps martyred, their fate must have opened the eyes of the people and prepared them for the remarkable religious revolution which we shall now proceed to describe.

The Pharaoh of the Exodus was probably Thothmes I (about 1540 B.C.). The Pharaoh Amenophis IV (about 1350 B.C.) adopted the worship of the One Supreme God as the State religion. He had been a high priest of the Sungod at Heliopolis, but had begun to look upon the multiplicity of gods in the Egyptian Pantheon as a blot on Egyptian religion. His original name had been Ahmen-hotep ("Ammon is satisfied") as being devoted to Ammon the great god of the State religion at Thebes. He changed his name to Akhan-Aton ("Pious to Aton") and worshipped the Supreme God under the name of Aton. He abandoned the city of Thebes as being devoted to Ammon and founded a new city near the site of what is now Tel al Amarna, betwen Thebes and Memphis, and dedicated it to Aton the Supreme God. The clay tablets discovered at Tel al Amarna in 1887 throw much light on the relations of Egypt with her tributaries in Syria. The alphabet on the tablets is the Cuneiform of Assyria: the language is Semitic, and closely akin to Hebrew. Unfortunately the religious revolution of Amenophis IV did not last. The city was only inhabited twenty years. His second son-in-law and successor, Tutankh Aton, carried out a counter-revolution. He went back from Aton to the cult of Ammon. The recent finds from his tombs show what exquisite skill the artists and artisans of Egypt had then attained. The pure religion remained established on the throne only for two generations but we need not suppose it was rooted out of the minds of the people.

The later Dynasties, XXI to XXXI, saw the decay of Egypt as a Power. The Assyrian and Persian invasions ultimately extinguished the freedom of Egypt. With the coming of Alexander the Great (332 B.C.) and the foundation of the city of Alexandria, a new era dawned on the culture of Egypt. It mingled with Greek and other thought, and became cosmopolitan in nature. Already, in the time of Herodotus, the sensitive Greek mind had been impressed with the mystery and wisdom of Egypt. It now made the soil of Egypt cosmopolitan in religion, culture, and philosophy. The Ptolemaic dynasty held a broadly tolerant attitude, and even imported the rites of Serapis from the Black Sea and assimilated him to Apis the Bull of Memphis. The new cult of Serapis spread widely over the East, and later, when Egypt came under the Roman Empire (30 B.C.), into the very heart of that Empire. The Serapion in Alexandria, with its famous library, became for a few centuries the true intellectual centre of the world. The very unfavourable picture drawn of Egyptian religion in Lytton's *Last Days of Pompeii* must be referred to the somewhat hybrid cult of Isis as practised in foreign lands rather than to Egyptian religion generally. What course real Egyptian religion took in this period we have no means of judging accurately. In the light of earlier and later events we may suppose that the steady honest industrious Egyptian peasantry and people went on pursuing the even tenor of their career with the same mystic longing for a practical religion which was preparing them for purer forms of worship and a juster distribution of the fruits of labour.

Alexandria in the first centuries of the Christian era was resounding with the shouts of every kind of philosophy and the teaching of every kind of religious sect, from East and West, North and South, but mainly from the East, which has ever been a nursery of religious ideas. A special quarter was assigned to the Jews in the city. It became the true centre of Hellenised Judaism, and may claim Josephus among its disciples. Neo-Pythagoreanism, Neo-Platonism, Gnosticism, and Manichaeism found a home there. Mithraism, which was so widely spread in the Roman Empire, especially in the army, in the first three centuries A.C., was probably represented on its philosophic side in Alexandria. Its intermixture of races, creeds, philosophies, and religions, produced an atmosphere of chaos, which was not cleared until the advent of Islam.

But from a religious point of view our greatest interest in Egypt in the first seven centuries of the Christian era is in the development of Christianity itself. It is difficult to say when exactly Christianity began to displace the older Egyptian cults. But when Christianity was well-established, we find Egypt one of its most important centres. But the new Christianity which was evolved out of the ruins of Christ's simple teaching had four distinct attitudes towards organisation, speculative doctrine, asceticism and mysticism. (1) The native Egyptian or Coptic Church was contemplative, ascetic, and mystical. Monasticism became so rampant that it seriously affected the growth of population and degraded the position of women. (2) The Alexandrian school developed on Greek lines—political, ambitious, speculative, philosophical, and liable to break up into numerous sects and heresies, each party trying to dominate and put down the others as heretical by the strong arm of the law. (3) The Bishop of Rome, when the seat of the Empire was transferred to Constantinople in 330, gradually developed political power in Italy. He inherited the Roman genius for organisation, and the invasion of the Germanic tribes gave him an opportunity not only of extending the Roman Catholic Church over the whole of Central and Western Europe, but of establishing the Church as superior to the state when the Papacy became an established political power. (4) The Orthodox Eastern Church, and all the sects which it fought in the East, tended ultimately to vanish before the advance of Islam. Had it not been for the vast Slav territories over which it obtained sway, in and around Russia and afterwards in Siberia, the Orthodox Eastern Church would have been reduced to a negligible position like the Coptic Church in Egypt. With pretensions to rule the State, it had yet become, in Kingley's words in *Hypatia,* the "stipendiary slave-official" of the Empire, sharing in all its effete corruption.

But we are anticipating. Before the Roman Catholic Church parted from the Orthodox Eastern Church, the united Church fought with and suppressed many so-called "heresies", some of which represented the view of primitive Christianity, and the scene of many of these doctrinal fights was in Egypt. The one that interests us most is Arianism. Arius was an Alexandrian Presbyter early in the fourth century A.C. and fought hard for the doctrine of Unity, the simple conception of the Eternal God, as against all the hair splitting and irrational distinctions in the nature and persons of the Godhead, which finally crystallised in the doctrine of the Trinity, propounded and maintained with much personal acrimony by Athanasius. Athanasius himself was born in Alexandria and became Bishop of Alexandria. He may be counted as the father of Orthodoxy (as now understood by Christianity) and the real systematiser of the doctrine of the Trinity—"three in one and one in three." Up to the third century A.C. the Unitarians had been in the majority in the Christian Church, though subtle metaphysicians had started disputes as to the meaning of "God becoming man," the Logos or the Word, the Power of Allah, whether the Father and the Son were of the same substance or of similar substance, whether the Son could be said to have been created by the Father, and numerous questions of that kind. They do not interest us now, but they rent the Christian world into many jarring sects until the mission of our Holy Prophet dissipated the mists and reestablished the doctrine of Unity on a firm and rational basis.

As I have said, the Christian Churches in the East, as well as the Germanic nations which came later into the fold, adhered to Unity although not in the pure form which was made clear in the Holy Qur'ān. The issue was joined between Arius and Athanasius, and the first General Council on the Christian Church, that of Nicaea (in Bithynia) in 325, decided against Arius and Unitarianism. The controversy, however, still continued to rage until 381, when the Council of Constantinople, called by the Emperor Theodosius the Great, confirmed the Nicene doctrine of the Trinity and declared it to be the only Orthodox one. Though controversies, protests, and persecutions continued long afterwards, we may take that date as the date of the fall of Christianity. Even in Western Christianity, as late as 496, Clovis, the Frankish king, was the only Christian sovereign sophisticated enough to follow the subtle doctrine of the Trinity. The others were brought into line by political power later.

The Christian creed became narrower and narrower, less and less rational, more and more inclined to use earthly weapons to suppress the eternal truth of Allah. In 415 the Jews were expelled from Alexandria. In the same year and in the same city the beautiful, modest, eloquent philosopher and mathematician, Hypatia, was murdered—an outrage against both rationalism and the intellectual and religious position of woman in human society. The murder was a particularly brutal one. She was dragged from her chariot in the streets, stripped naked, and suffered a lingering death in a Christian Church. Her body was then cut to pieces and burned. The worst feature of the crime was the complicity of the Patriarch of Alexandria, who was not only the chief religious dignitary of the Orthodox Church in Egypt but the *de facto* repository of political power. Meanwhile the native Christian community—the Coptic Church—which had all along clung to the Monophysite doctrine, a corrupt form of Unitarianism, was out of the pale, and its members were held down as a depressed class by their Orthodox brethren. The latter also, basking in official sunshine, collected power and property into their own hands. As Kingsley remarks in *Hypatia*, the Egyptian Church "ended as a mere chaos of idolatrous sects, persecuting each other for metaphysical propositions, which, true or false, were equally heretical in their mouths because they used them as watchwords for division." The social conditions produced an amount of discontent, for which the redress came only with the advent of Islam.

It was for this reason that the Copts and the inhabitants of Egypt generally welcomed the forces of Islam under 'Amr as deliverers in 639 A.C. The power was taken over by the victorious army of Islam from Cyrus (called Muqawqas in Arabic through the Coptic), the Patriarch of Alexandria, but it was used by the army of deliverance to enlarge the liberties of the Egyptians, to admit them into the universal brotherhood of Islam, and to improve the resources of the country for the benefit of the people. Except a negligible remnant of conservatives, the Egyptians as a nation accepted the religion, the language, and the institutions of the Arabs and embarked on a new course of history, which it is necessary to follow further in this note.

It should be remarked, however, that what happened in Egypt happened generally in western Asia. The jarring sectarian irrational religions gave place before the triumphant religion of Unity and Brotherhood, and the Byzantine Empire receded and receded until it was swept out of existence. The feeble efforts made by the Emperor Leo the Isaurian in 726-731 to restrict the use of images were a reflection of the puritanical zeal of Islam. But they did not succeed in the area of his authority, and they completely alienated the Papacy from the Eastern Orthodox Church. The Bishop of Rome had been consolidating his power, and in the person of Gregory I (590-604) had already assumed the control of Italy and was seeking the aid and support of the Barbarian invaders who eventually became the pillars of the Papacy. The final and open rupture between the Orthodox Eastern Church and the Roman Catholic Church took place in 1054. But the earlier dates are remarkable. After the birth of the Holy Prophet of Islam the disruption of the Orthodox Christian Church (which had now become an anachronism) began. When Islam was making its triumphant march in the 8th century after Christ, the original (Greek) Church began to take some steps to put its own house in order. But it had lost its mission, and the new Islamic people took its place. The Western Church has since worked on definitely new lines, and its offshoots among the Protestant Church have, consciously or unconsciously, been influenced by the broad principles of Islam. What the course of future religion may be and how Allah will unfold His All-Wise Plan is not given to us mortals to know. In the Islamic Brotherhood many changes have taken place and are taking place. Egypt, in spite of her many vicissitudes in the Islamic period, is in the intellectual forefront among the Arabic-speaking nations of Islam. We pray that her people may be guided, through their educational, cultural, and religious channels, to work with a new spirit for the progress of Islam and the glory of Allah.

References: Those given for Appendix IV; and in addition: Sir E. A. Wallis Budge, Gods of the Egyptians: and his latest book From Fetish to God in Ancient Egypt (Oxford 1940: Budge. Book of the Dead; A.W. Shorter, Introduction to Egyptian Religion (1931); Adolf von Harnack, History of Dogma, 7 vols., is an elaborate detailed German account of how Christian Dogma grew up and may be read in an English translation; a handier book is R.W. Mackay, Rise and Progress of Christianity (1854); C. Kingsley's novel Hypatia gives a good picture of social and religious conditions in Christian Egypt in the fifth century. On the identity of al Muqawqas (Pkauchios) with Cyrus, see Dr. A.J. Butler's "Arab Conquest of Egypt,' (Oxford 1902), pp. 508-562.

INTRODUCTION TO SŪRAH 8—*AL ANFĀL*

In the previous Introductions to the Sūrahs we have shown how each Sūrah is a step or gradation in the teaching of the Qur'ān. The first seven Sūrahs, comprising a little less than one-third of the Qur'ān, form a gradation, sketching the early spiritual history of man and leading up to the formation of the new Ummah or Community of the Holy Messenger. Now we begin another gradation, consolidating that Ummah and directing us as to various phases in our new collective life.

In this chapter we have the lessons of the Battle of Badr enforced in their larger aspects: (1) the question of war booty; (2) the true virtues necessary for fighting the good fight; (3) victory against odds; (4) clemency and consideration for one's own and for others in the hour of victory.

As regards booty taken in battle, the first point to note is that that should never be our aim in war. It is only an adventitious circumstance, a sort of windfall. Secondly, no soldier or troop has any inherent right to it. A righteous war is a community affair, and any accessions resulting from it belong to Allah, or the community or Cause. Thirdly, certain equitable principles of division should be laid down to check human greed and selfishness. A fifth share goes to the Commander, and he can use it at his discretion; for his own expenses, and for the relief of the poor and suffering, and the orphans and widows (8:41). The remainder was divided, according to the Prophet's practice, not only among those who were actually in the fight physically, but all who were in the enterprise, young and old, provided they loyally did some duty assigned to them. Fourthly, there should be no disputes, as they interfere with internal discipline and harmony.

These principles are followed in the best modern practice of civilised nations. All acquisitions of war belong absolutely to the Sovereign as representing the commonwealth. In the distribution of booty not only the actual captors but also the "joint captors" and the "constructive captors" share. See Sir R. Phillimore's *International Law* (1885), vol. 3, pp. 209-10, 221-24.

As regards the military virtues, which are the types of virtues throughout life, we are shown by an analysis of the incidents of Badr how against the greatest odds, Allah's help will give victory if men are fighting not for themselves but for the sacred Cause of Allah. And directions are given for the treatment of prisoners and for maintaining the solidarity of the Muslim community.

The date of this Sūrah is shortly after the battle of Badr, which was fought on Friday, the 17th of Ramaḍān in the second year of the Hijrah. A short account of the battle is given in n. 352 to 3:13.

Summary—All booty is really at the disposal of Allah's Messenger under directions from Allah. Men of faith accept and obey these directions with cheerfulness. Victory and the prize of victory come from Allah, as was proved at Badr (8:1-19, and C. 89).

Obedience and intelligent discipline, zeal, faith, and gratitude to Allah, are the true passports to success and protection from the assaults of evil. Evil will be piled up with evil and destroyed (8:20-37, and C. 90).

The battle of Badr was a testing time, and showed how virtue and valour can conquer against odds. Steadfastness and obedience; faith, courage, and fearlessness; due preparation and free expenditure of resources and energy—these are expected from you by Allah, and His help is all-sufficient (8:38-64, and C. 91).

Even tenfold odds against you do not count if you are fighting for truth and faith against enemies of truth and faith; but remember clemency and consideration in the hour of victory (8:65-75, and C. 92).

C. 89.—Fight the good fight, but dispute not
(8:1-19.) About the prize: that is for Allah
To give. Men of faith act and obey.
'Tis nobler to fight for Truth
Than to seek worldly gain.
To the pure in faith Allah will give
The mind and the resources to conquer.
They but fight, with no thought
Of ever turning back: the victory
Should be ascribed to Allah, not men.

Sūrah 8.

الجزء التاسع سورة الأنفال

Al Anfāl (The Spoils of War)

In the name of Allah, Most Gracious,
Most Merciful.

بِسْمِ ٱللَّهِ ٱلرَّحْمَٰنِ ٱلرَّحِيمِ

1. They ask thee[1178] concerning
(Things taken as) spoils of war.
Say: "(Such) spoils are
At the disposal of Allah[1179]
And the Messenger: so fear
Allah, and keep straight
The relations between yourselves:
Obey Allah and His Messenger,
If ye do believe."

(١) يَسْـَٔلُونَكَ عَنِ ٱلْأَنفَالِ قُلِ ٱلْأَنفَالُ لِلَّهِ وَٱلرَّسُولِ فَٱتَّقُوا۟ ٱللَّهَ وَأَصْلِحُوا۟ ذَاتَ بَيْنِكُمْ وَأَطِيعُوا۟ ٱللَّهَ وَرَسُولَهُۥٓ إِن كُنتُم مُّؤْمِنِينَ

2. For, Believers are those
Who, when Allah is mentioned,
Feel a tremor in their hearts,
And when they hear
His Signs rehearsed, find
Their faith strengthened,
And put (all) their trust
In their Lord;

(٢) إِنَّمَا ٱلْمُؤْمِنُونَ ٱلَّذِينَ إِذَا ذُكِرَ ٱللَّهُ وَجِلَتْ قُلُوبُهُمْ وَإِذَا تُلِيَتْ عَلَيْهِمْ ءَايَٰتُهُۥ زَادَتْهُمْ إِيمَٰنًا وَعَلَىٰ رَبِّهِمْ يَتَوَكَّلُونَ

3. Who establish regular prayers
And spend (freely) out of
The gifts We have given
Them for sustenance:[1180]

(٣) ٱلَّذِينَ يُقِيمُونَ ٱلصَّلَوٰةَ وَمِمَّا رَزَقْنَٰهُمْ يُنفِقُونَ

4. Such in truth are the Believers:
They have grades of dignity
With their Lord, and forgiveness,
And generous sustenance:

(٤) أُو۟لَٰٓئِكَ هُمُ ٱلْمُؤْمِنُونَ حَقًّا لَّهُمْ دَرَجَٰتٌ عِندَ رَبِّهِمْ وَمَغْفِرَةٌ وَرِزْقٌ كَرِيمٌ

1178. The occasion was the question of the division of the booty after the battle of Badr. See Introduction to this Sūrah.

1179. Booty taken in a lawful and just war does not belong to any individual. If he fought for such accessory rewards, he fought from wrong motives. It belongs to the Cause, in this case the Cause of Allah, as administered by His Messenger. Any portion given out to individuals are accessory gifts, windfalls from the bounty of the Commander. The chief thing is to remain staunch to the Cause of Allah, and have no differences among those who stand for the Cause. Our internal relations must be kept straight: they must not be disturbed by cupidity or worldly considerations of gain, for any windfalls of this kind should be outside our calculations.

1180. *Sustenance*: again in both the literal and the metaphorical sense. The object is to warn off from the love of booty and worldly wealth. Why do we want these? To all true Believers Allah gives generous sustenance in any case, in both senses, but especially in the spiritual sense, for it is coupled with forgiveness and grades of dignity before Allah, in the next verse.

5. Just as[1181] thy Lord ordered thee
Out of thy house in truth,
Even though a party among
The Believers disliked it,

٥ كَمَآ أَخۡرَجَكَ رَبُّكَ مِنۢ بَيۡتِكَ بِٱلۡحَقِّ
وَإِنَّ فَرِيقٗا مِّنَ ٱلۡمُؤۡمِنِينَ لَكَٰرِهُونَ

6. Disputing with thee concerning
The truth after it was made
Manifest, as if they were
Being driven to death
And they (actually) saw it.[1182]

٦ يُجَٰدِلُونَكَ فِي ٱلۡحَقِّ بَعۡدَ مَا تَبَيَّنَ
كَأَنَّمَا يُسَاقُونَ إِلَى ٱلۡمَوۡتِ وَهُمۡ يَنظُرُونَ

7. Behold! Allah promised you
One of the two (enemy) parties,[1183]
That it should be yours:
Ye wished that the one
Unarmed should be yours,
But Allah willed
To justify the Truth
According to His words,
And to cut off the roots
Of the Unbelievers—

٧ وَإِذۡ يَعِدُكُمُ ٱللَّهُ إِحۡدَى ٱلطَّآئِفَتَيۡنِ
أَنَّهَا لَكُمۡ وَتَوَدُّونَ أَنَّ غَيۡرَ
ذَاتِ ٱلشَّوۡكَةِ تَكُونُ لَكُمۡ
وَيُرِيدُ ٱللَّهُ أَن يُحِقَّ ٱلۡحَقَّ بِكَلِمَٰتِهِۦ
وَيَقۡطَعَ دَابِرَ ٱلۡكَٰفِرِينَ

8. That He might justify Truth
And prove Falsehood false,
Distasteful though it be
To those in guilt.

٨ لِيُحِقَّ ٱلۡحَقَّ وَيُبۡطِلَ ٱلۡبَٰطِلَ
وَلَوۡ كَرِهَ ٱلۡمُجۡرِمُونَ

9. Remember ye implored
The assistance of your Lord,
And He answered you:

٩ إِذۡ تَسۡتَغِيثُونَ رَبَّكُمۡ فَٱسۡتَجَابَ لَكُمۡ

1181. *Just as*: the comparison takes us back to the first clause in verse 4: "such in truth are the Believers"—just as thy Lord also is just and true in ordering thee out to fight against heavy odds, when the alternative was to fight against the unarmed caravan which would have given thee abundant booty almost without a fight. To appreciate the full meaning, remember that the word *ḥaqq*, translated "truth" means also "right," "just", "what is becoming." The true Believers believe in truth and do right in obedience to Allah's command. So Allah also, in asking them to fight against odds, is not asking them to rush to destruction, but is providing them with an opportunity of vindicating the truth in scorn of worldly advantage. And He made good His promise by giving them victory.

1182. In verse 6 we have again the word "truth": some of the Believers disputed concerning "the truth": they did not feel sure that the course recommended was the true and right course. They thought it would be certain destruction: they saw death almost staring them in the face.

1183. Just before Badr there were two alternatives before the Muslims in Madīnah, to save themselves from being overwhelmed by the Makkan Quraysh with all their resources from the rich Syrian trade. One, which had least danger for the time being, and also promised much booty, was to fall upon the Quraysh caravan returning from Syria to Makkah richly laden, and led by Abū Sufyān with only 40 men unarmed. From a wordly point of view this was the safest and most lucrative course. The other alternative, which was actually adopted on the recommendation of the Prophet by the guidance of Allah, was to leave the booty alone and march out boldly against the well-armed and well-equipped Quraysh army of 1,000 men coming from Makkah. The Muslims had no more than 300 men, ill-armed, to oppose the force. But if they could defeat it, it would shake the selfish autocracy which was in possession of Makkah. By Allah's help they won a splendid victory, and the standard of Truth was established, never to be lowered again.

"I will assist you
With a thousand of the angels,
Ranks on ranks."[1184]

أَنِّي مُمِدُّكُم بِأَلْفٍ مِّنَ ٱلْمَلَٰٓئِكَةِ مُرْدِفِينَ

10. Allah made it but a message
Of hope, and an assurance
To your hearts: (in any case)[1185]
There is no help
Except from Allah:
And Allah is Exalted in Power,
Wise.

وَمَا جَعَلَهُ ٱللَّهُ إِلَّا بُشْرَىٰ وَلِتَطْمَئِنَّ بِهِۦ قُلُوبُكُمْ ۚ وَمَا ٱلنَّصْرُ إِلَّا مِنْ عِندِ ٱللَّهِ ۚ إِنَّ ٱللَّهَ عَزِيزٌ حَكِيمٌ ﴿١٠﴾

SECTION 2.

11. Remember He covered you
With a sort of drowsiness,[1186]
To give you calm as from
Himself, and he caused
Rain to descend on you[1187]
From heaven, to clean you
Therewith, to remove from you
The stain of Satan,[1188]
To strengthen your hearts,
And to plant your feet
Firmly therewith.

إِذْ يُغَشِّيكُمُ ٱلنُّعَاسَ أَمَنَةً مِّنْهُ وَيُنَزِّلُ عَلَيْكُم مِّنَ ٱلسَّمَآءِ مَآءً لِّيُطَهِّرَكُم بِهِۦ وَيُذْهِبَ عَنكُمْ رِجْزَ ٱلشَّيْطَٰنِ وَلِيَرْبِطَ عَلَىٰ قُلُوبِكُمْ وَيُثَبِّتَ بِهِ ٱلْأَقْدَامَ ﴿١١﴾

12. Remember thy Lord inspired
The angels (with the message):
"I am with you: give
Firmness to the Believers:
I will instil terror
Into the hearts of the Unbelievers:
Smite ye above their necks

إِذْ يُوحِى رَبُّكَ إِلَى ٱلْمَلَٰٓئِكَةِ أَنِّى مَعَكُمْ فَثَبِّتُوا۟ ٱلَّذِينَ ءَامَنُوا۟ ۚ سَأُلْقِى فِى قُلُوبِ ٱلَّذِينَ كَفَرُوا۟ ٱلرُّعْبَ فَٱضْرِبُوا۟ فَوْقَ ٱلْأَعْنَاقِ ﴿١٢﴾

1184. *Cf.* 3:123, 125, 126. The number of angels, a thousand at Badr and three thousand and five thousand at Uḥud, is probably not to be taken literally, but to express a strength at least equal to the strength of the enemy.

1185. All help comes ultimately from Allah. In special cases it may take special forms to put heart into us, and to fit in with our feelings and our psychology.

1186. *Cf.* 3:154 for Uḥud. Calm (presence of mind) is essential in battle and in all posts of danger. If the mind is too much in a state of excitement, it cannot carry out a well-considered or well-concerned plan. This spirit of calm confidence on the part of the Muslims won against the blustering violence of the Quraysh.

1187. The rain was welcome for many reasons. (1) Water was scarce both for drinking and ablutions; (2) the Muslim band, without baggage or equipment or comforts, found that their thirst aggravated their fatigue; (3) the sand was loose, and the rain consolidated it and enabled them "to plant their feet firmly."

1188. *"Stain of Satan"*: both literally and figuratively. Dirt is physically a symbol of evil, and the Muslims were particular about ablutions before prayer. But the rain also refreshed their spirits and removed any lurking doubts in their minds (suggestions of the Evil One) that victory might be impossible in such adverse circumstances.

And smite all their
Finger tips off them."[1189]

وَاضْرِبُوا مِنْهُمْ كُلَّ بَنَانٍ

13. This because they contended
Against Allah and His Messenger:
If any contend against Allah
And His Messenger, Allah
Is strict in punishment.

﴿١٣﴾ ذَٰلِكَ بِأَنَّهُمْ شَاقُّوا اللَّهَ وَرَسُولَهُ ۚ وَمَن
يُشَاقِقِ اللَّهَ وَرَسُولَهُ فَإِنَّ
اللَّهَ شَدِيدُ الْعِقَابِ

14. Thus (will it be said): "Taste ye
Then of the (punishment):
For those who resist Allah,
Is the penalty of the Fire."

﴿١٤﴾ ذَٰلِكُمْ فَذُوقُوهُ
وَأَنَّ لِلْكَافِرِينَ عَذَابَ النَّارِ

15. O ye who believe!
When ye meet
The Unbelievers
In hostile array,[1190]
Never turn your backs
To them.

﴿١٥﴾ يَا أَيُّهَا الَّذِينَ آمَنُوا
إِذَا لَقِيتُمُ الَّذِينَ كَفَرُوا زَحْفًا
فَلَا تُوَلُّوهُمُ الْأَدْبَارَ

16. If any do turn his back
To them on such a day—
Unless it be in a stratagem
Of war, or to retreat
To a troop (of his own)—
He draws on himself
The wrath of Allah,
And his abode is Hell—
An evil refuge (indeed)!

﴿١٦﴾ وَمَن يُوَلِّهِمْ يَوْمَئِذٍ دُبُرَهُ
إِلَّا مُتَحَرِّفًا لِّقِتَالٍ
أَوْ مُتَحَيِّزًا إِلَىٰ فِئَةٍ
فَقَدْ بَاءَ بِغَضَبٍ مِّنَ اللَّهِ
وَمَأْوَاهُ جَهَنَّمُ ۖ وَبِئْسَ الْمَصِيرُ

17. It is not ye who
Slew them; it was Allah:

﴿١٧﴾ فَلَمْ تَقْتُلُوهُمْ وَلَٰكِنَّ اللَّهَ قَتَلَهُمْ ۚ

1189. The vulnerable parts of an armed man are above the neck. A blow on the neck, face, or head, finishes him off. If he has armour it is difficult to get at his heart. But if his hands are put out of action, he is unable to wield his sword or lance or other weapon, and easily becomes a prisoner.

1190. The laws of spiritual fight are exactly similar to those enforced by military virtue and discipline. Meet your enemy fairly and squarely, not rashly, but after due preparation. *Zahfān* in the text (*meeting in hostile array*) implies a slow and well-planned proceeding towards a hostile army. When once in combat, carry it through: there is no room for second thoughts. Death or victory should be the motto of every soldier: it may be death for himself individually, but if he has faith, there is triumph in either case for his cause. Two exceptions are recognised: (1) *reculer pour mieux sauter,* to go back in order to jump forward; or to deceive the enemy by a feint; (2) if an individual or body is, by the chances of battle, isolated from his own force, he can fall back on his force in order to fight the battle. There is no virtue in mere single-handedness. Each individual must use his life and his resources to the best advantage for the common cause.

When thou threwest (a handful[1191]
Of dust), it was not
Thy act, but Allah's:
In order that He might
Test the Believers
By a gracious trial[1192]
From Himself: for Allah
Is He Who heareth
And knoweth (all things).

وَمَا رَمَيْتَ إِذْ رَمَيْتَ
وَلَٰكِنَّ ٱللَّهَ رَمَىٰ ۚ وَلِيُبْلِيَ
ٱلْمُؤْمِنِينَ مِنْهُ بَلَآءً حَسَنًا ۚ
إِنَّ ٱللَّهَ سَمِيعٌ عَلِيمٌ

18. That, and also because
Allah is He Who makes feeble
The Plans and stratagems
Of the Unbelievers.

١٨ ذَٰلِكُمْ وَأَنَّ ٱللَّهَ
مُوهِنُ كَيْدِ ٱلْكَٰفِرِينَ

19. (O Unbelievers!) if ye prayed
For victory and judgement,[1193]
Now hath the judgement
Come to you: if ye desist
(From wrong), it will be
Best for you: if ye return
(To the attack), so shall We.
Not the least good
Will your forces be to you
Even if they were multiplied:
For verily Allah
Is with those who believe!

١٩ إِن تَسْتَفْتِحُوا۟
فَقَدْ جَآءَكُمُ ٱلْفَتْحُ ۖ
وَإِن تَنتَهُوا۟ فَهُوَ خَيْرٌ لَّكُمْ ۖ وَإِن تَعُودُوا۟
نَعُدْ وَلَن تُغْنِيَ عَنكُمْ فِئَتُكُمْ شَيْـًٔا
وَلَوْ كَثُرَتْ وَأَنَّ ٱللَّهَ مَعَ ٱلْمُؤْمِنِينَ

C. 90.—Be ready to obey Allah's call, and to hold
(8:20-37.) All else as naught: He will give you
The light, turn away all evil from you,
And forgive you your sins and shortcomings.
Ever keep in remembrance His mercies and grace.
The godless may try to keep men
From Allah, but they will not thrive:
They will be hurled together to destruction.

SECTION 3.

20. O ye who believe!
Obey Allah and His Messenger,

٢٠ يَٰٓأَيُّهَا ٱلَّذِينَ ءَامَنُوٓا۟ أَطِيعُوا۟ ٱللَّهَ وَرَسُولَهُۥ

1191. When the battle began, the Holy Prophet prayed, and threw a handful of dust or sand at the enemy, which, as described in Traditions, struck the eyes of the enemy. This had a great psychological effect. Every act in the battle is ascribed to Allah, as it was in His cause and it was not undertaken except by His command. (R).

1192. Numerically the odds against the Muslims were three to one. In other ways they were at a disadvantage: of arms and equipment they had but little, while the enemy were well-found; they were inexperienced, while the Quraysh had brought their foremost warriors. In all this there was a test, but the test was accompanied by gracious favours of countless value: their Commander was one in whom they had perfect faith, and for whom they were ready to lay down their lives; the rain refreshed them; their spirit was unshaken; and they were fighting in Allah's cause. Thus the trial or test became itself a blessing.

1193. *Fatḥ* = victory, decision, judgement. The Quraysh in Makkah had prayed for victory; they were confident that their superior numbers, equipment, and experience would be decisive. With a play on the word, they are told that the decision had come, and the victory—but not in the sense they had hoped for!

And turn not away from him
When ye hear (him speak).

وَلَا تَوَلَّوْا عَنْهُ وَأَنتُمْ تَسْمَعُونَ

21. Nor be like those who say,
"We hear," but listen not:[1194]

(٢١) وَلَا تَكُونُوا كَالَّذِينَ قَالُوا
سَمِعْنَا وَهُمْ لَا يَسْمَعُونَ

22. For the worst of beasts
In the sight of Allah
Are the deaf and the dumb—[1195]
Those who understand not.

(٢٢) إِنَّ شَرَّ الدَّوَابِّ عِندَ اللَّهِ
الصُّمُّ الْبُكْمُ الَّذِينَ لَا يَعْقِلُونَ

23. If Allah had found in them
Any good, He would indeed
Have made them listen:
(As it is), if He had made them
Listen, they would but have
Turned back and declined (faith).

(٢٣) وَلَوْ عَلِمَ اللَّهُ فِيهِمْ خَيْرًا
لَّأَسْمَعَهُمْ وَلَوْ أَسْمَعَهُمْ
لَتَوَلَّوا وَّهُم مُّعْرِضُونَ

24. O ye who believe!
Give your response to Allah
And His Messenger, when He
Calleth you to that which
Will give you life;[1196]
And know that Allah
Cometh in between a man[1197]
And his heart, and that
It is He to Whom
Ye shall (all) be gathered.

(٢٤) يَا أَيُّهَا الَّذِينَ آمَنُوا اسْتَجِيبُوا
لِلَّهِ وَلِلرَّسُولِ إِذَا دَعَاكُمْ لِمَا يُحْيِيكُمْ
وَاعْلَمُوا أَنَّ اللَّهَ يَحُولُ بَيْنَ الْمَرْءِ
وَقَلْبِهِ وَأَنَّهُ إِلَيْهِ تُحْشَرُونَ

25. And fear tumult or oppression,[1198]
Which affecteth not in particular
(Only) those of you wo do wrong:

(٢٥) وَاتَّقُوا فِتْنَةً لَّا تُصِيبَنَّ الَّذِينَ
ظَلَمُوا مِنكُمْ خَاصَّةً

1194. *Cf.* 2:93.

1195. *Cf.* 2:18.

1196. There are two points to note. (1) Note that after Allah and His Messenger are mentioned, the pronoun and verb in the next clause are singular: everything that Allah's Messenger put forward as an injunction came by inspiration from Allah: the Messenger made his will coincide completely with Allah's will. (2) We are asked actively to give our response in deed and life to the call of duty and conscience, for that call leads to real life, the life eternal, even though it may apparently mean in this world the loss of things that make life dear or the loss of life itself. If we refer this to Jihād, *i.e.*, fighting in and for the Cause, both literally and metaphorically, the meaning becomes quite clear.

1197. If the human heart is refractory and refuses to obey the call of Allah, that is not the end of the matter. Allah has to be reckoned with. The refusal may be because there was some pet human scheme which the heart of man was not willing to give up for Allah's Cause. Will that scheme come to fruition by refusing to serve the higher Cause? By no means. Man proposes, but God disposes. If the scheme or motive was perfectly secret from men, it was not secret from Allah. The heart is the innermost seat of man's affections and desires; but Allah intervenes between man and his heart. (R).

1198. *Fitnah* has many meanings: (1) the root meaning is trial or temptation, as in 2:102 and 8:28; (2) an analogous meaning is trial or punishment, as in 6:74; (3) tumult or oppression, as in 2:193; and here; and in 8:39; (4) there is here (8:25) the further shade of meaning suggested, discord, sedition, civil war.

This warning against internal discord or tumult was very necessary in the Civil Wars of early Islam, and was never more necessary than it is now, for it affects innocent and guilty alike.

And know that Allah
Is strict in punishment.

وَٱعۡلَمُوٓاْ أَنَّ ٱللَّهَ شَدِيدُ ٱلۡعِقَابِ

26. Call to mind when ye
Were a small (band),
Despised through the land,
And afraid that men might
Despoil and kidnap you;[1199]
But He provided a safe asylum
For you, strengthened you
With His aid, and gave you
Good things for sustenance:
That ye might be grateful.

٢٦ وَٱذۡكُرُوٓاْ إِذۡ أَنتُمۡ قَلِيلٞ
مُّسۡتَضۡعَفُونَ فِي ٱلۡأَرۡضِ تَخَافُونَ
أَن يَتَخَطَّفَكُمُ ٱلنَّاسُ فَـَٔاوَىٰكُمۡ
وَأَيَّدَكُم بِنَصۡرِهِۦ وَرَزَقَكُم
مِّنَ ٱلطَّيِّبَٰتِ لَعَلَّكُمۡ تَشۡكُرُونَ

27. O ye that believe!
Betray not the trust
Of Allah and the Messenger,
Nor misappropriate knowingly
Things entrusted to you.[1200]

٢٧ يَٰٓأَيُّهَا ٱلَّذِينَ ءَامَنُواْ لَا تَخُونُواْ ٱللَّهَ
وَٱلرَّسُولَ وَتَخُونُوٓاْ أَمَٰنَٰتِكُمۡ وَأَنتُمۡ تَعۡلَمُونَ

28. And know ye
That your possessions
And your progeny
Are but a trial;[1201]
And that it is Allah

٢٨ وَٱعۡلَمُوٓاْ أَنَّمَآ أَمۡوَٰلُكُمۡ
وَأَوۡلَٰدُكُمۡ فِتۡنَةٞ
وَأَنَّ ٱللَّهَ

1199. On the immediate occasion the Muslims were reminded that they were a small band in Makkah; despised and rejected; living in a state of insecurity for their persons, their lives, their property, and those of their dependents; persecuted and exiled and how by the grace of Allah they found a safe asylum in Madīnah, how they found friends and helpers, how their many needs were cared for, and how at length they gathered strength and numbers enough to defeat the forces of godlessness, injustice, and oppression.

But for every individual, in some form or other, the lesson applies. His spiritual life begins humbly; he is despised and laughed at, perhaps persecuted and shut out from ordinary privileges open to all; but Allah gives him strength; friends spring up for him; and he is sustained until his highest spiritual desires are gradually fulfilled.

1200. Trusts may be of various kinds: (1) property, goods, credit, etc.; (2) plans, confidences, secrets, etc.; (3) knowledge, talents, opportunities, etc., which we are expected to use for our fellow men. Men may betray the trust of Allah and His Prophet by misusing property, or abusing the confidence reposed in them, or the knowledge or talents given to them. On that special occasion, when the plans for the protection of Allah's worshippers against annihilation were of special importance, the Prophet's trust and confidence had to be guarded with special care. Occasions for scrupulously respecting the trust and confidence of our fellow men occur every day in our life, and few of us can claim perfection in this respect. Hence the special distinction of the Prophet of Allah, who earned the title of *Al Amīn*, the one who was true to every trust reposed in him.

1201. A big family—many sons—was considered a source of power and strength: 3:10, 116. So in English, a man with many children is said to have his "quiver full;" *Cf.* Psalms, cxxvii. 4-5: "As arrows are in the hands of a mighty man, so are the children of thy youth. Happy is the man that hath his quiver full of them; they shall not be ashamed, but they shall speak with the enemies in the gate." So with property and possessions: they add to a man's dignity, power, and influence. But both possessions and a large family are a temptation and a trial. They may turn out to be a source of spiritual downfall, if they are mishandled, or if the love of them excludes the love of Allah.

With whom lies
Your highest reward.

عِندَهُۥٓ أَجۡرٌ عَظِيمٞ

SECTION 4.

29. O ye who believe!
If ye fear Allah,
He will grant you a Criterion[1202]
(To judge between right and wrong),
Remove from you (all) evil
(That may afflict) you,
And forgive you:
For Allah is the Lord
Of grace unbounded.

(٢٩) يَٰٓأَيُّهَا ٱلَّذِينَ ءَامَنُوٓاْ
إِن تَتَّقُواْ ٱللَّهَ يَجۡعَل لَّكُمۡ فُرۡقَانٗا
وَيُكَفِّرۡ عَنكُمۡ سَيِّـَٔاتِكُمۡ وَيَغۡفِرۡ لَكُمۡۗ
وَٱللَّهُ ذُو ٱلۡفَضۡلِ ٱلۡعَظِيمِ

30. Remember how the Unbelievers
Plotted against thee, to keep
Thee in bonds, or slay thee,
Or get thee out (of thy home).[1203]
They plot and plan,
And Allah too plans,
But the best of planners[1203-A]
Is Allah.

(٣٠) وَإِذۡ يَمۡكُرُ بِكَ ٱلَّذِينَ
كَفَرُواْ لِيُثۡبِتُوكَ أَوۡ يَقۡتُلُوكَ
أَوۡ يُخۡرِجُوكَۚ وَيَمۡكُرُونَ وَيَمۡكُرُ ٱللَّهُۖ
وَٱللَّهُ خَيۡرُ ٱلۡمَٰكِرِينَ

31. When Our Signs are rehearsed
To them, they say: "We
Have heard this (before):
If we wished, we could
Say (words) like these:
These are nothing
But tales of the ancients."[1204]

(٣١) وَإِذَا تُتۡلَىٰ عَلَيۡهِمۡ ءَايَٰتُنَا
قَالُواْ قَدۡ سَمِعۡنَا لَوۡ نَشَآءُ لَقُلۡنَا مِثۡلَ هَٰذَآ
إِنۡ هَٰذَآ إِلَّآ أَسَٰطِيرُ ٱلۡأَوَّلِينَ

32. Remember how they said:
"O Allah! if this is indeed
The Truth from Thee,
Rain down on us a shower

(٣٢) وَإِذۡ قَالُواْ ٱللَّهُمَّ إِن كَانَ هَٰذَا
هُوَ ٱلۡحَقَّ مِنۡ عِندِكَ فَأَمۡطِرۡ عَلَيۡنَا

1202. *Cf.* 2:53 and 2:185. The battle of Badr is called the *Furqān* in Muslim theology, because it was the first trial of strength by battle, in Islam, between the powers of good and evil. Evil was defeated, and those who had real faith were tested and sorted out from those who had not faith enough to follow the banner of Faith. See also 8:41 and n. 1210.

1203. The plots against Muṣṭafā in Makkah aimed at three things. They were not only foiled, but Allah's wonderful working turned the tables, and brought good out of evil in each case. (1) They tried to hold the Prophet in subjection in Makkah by putting pressure on his uncles, relatives, and friends. But the more they persecuted, the more the little Muslim community grew in faith and numbers. (2) They tried to injure or slay him. But the wonderful example of his humility, perseverance, and fearlessness furthered the cause of Islam. (3) They tried to get him and his followers out of their homes. But they found a new home in Madīnah, from which they eventually reconquered not only Makkah, but Arabia and the world.

1203-A. *Cf.* 3:54.

1204. *Cf.* 6:25.

Of stones from the sky,
Or send us a grievous Penalty."[1205]

حِجَارَةً مِّنَ السَّمَاءِ أَوِ ائْتِنَا بِعَذَابٍ أَلِيمٍ

33. But Allah was not going
To send them a Penalty
Whilst thou wast amongst them;
Nor was He going to send it
Whilst they could ask for pardon.

٣٣ وَمَا كَانَ اللَّهُ لِيُعَذِّبَهُمْ وَأَنتَ فِيهِمْ
وَمَا كَانَ اللَّهُ مُعَذِّبَهُمْ وَهُمْ يَسْتَغْفِرُونَ

34. But what plea have they
That Allah should not punish
Them, when they keep out
(Men) from the Sacred Mosque—
And they are not its guardians?
No men can be its guardians
Except the righteous; but most
Of them do not understand.

٣٤ وَمَا لَهُمْ أَلَّا يُعَذِّبَهُمُ اللَّهُ
وَهُمْ يَصُدُّونَ عَنِ الْمَسْجِدِ الْحَرَامِ
وَمَا كَانُوا أَوْلِيَاءَهُ إِنْ أَوْلِيَاؤُهُ إِلَّا الْمُتَّقُونَ
وَلَٰكِنَّ أَكْثَرَهُمْ لَا يَعْلَمُونَ

35. Their prayer at the House
(Of Allah) is nothing but
Whistling and clapping of hands:
(Its only answer can be),
"Taste ye the Penalty
Because ye blasphemed."

٣٥ وَمَا كَانَ صَلَاتُهُمْ
عِندَ الْبَيْتِ إِلَّا مُكَاءً وَتَصْدِيَةً
فَذُوقُوا الْعَذَابَ بِمَا كُنتُمْ تَكْفُرُونَ

36. The Unbelievers spend their wealth
To hinder (men) from the path
Of Allah, and so will they
Continue to spend; but
In the end they will have
(Only) regrets and sighs;
At length they will be overcome:
And the Unbelievers will be
Gathered together to Hell—

٣٦ إِنَّ الَّذِينَ كَفَرُوا يُنفِقُونَ
أَمْوَالَهُمْ لِيَصُدُّوا عَن سَبِيلِ اللَّهِ
فَسَيُنفِقُونَهَا ثُمَّ تَكُونُ
عَلَيْهِمْ حَسْرَةً ثُمَّ يُغْلَبُونَ
وَالَّذِينَ كَفَرُوا إِلَىٰ جَهَنَّمَ يُحْشَرُونَ

1205. This was actually a challenge thrown out by the Infidels in Makkah, not seriously but as a taunt. The answer is in the two following verses. Allah punishes in His own good time, not according to the foolish and frivolous taunts of the unbelievers. While the Holy Prophet was with them, he—the Mercy for the Worlds—conferred a certain amount of immunity to them. There were also other Muslims, just men who asked for forgiveness. And Allah keeps the door of repentance and forgiveness open to all as long as they make it possible. But let them not be puffed up with pride, or think that they have lasting immunity. What became of Abū Jahl? He and some of his greatest warriors were slain at Badr. The little autocratic clique that prevented Muslims from access to the Sacred Mosque had their Nemesis not long afterwards. They pretended to be its guardians. But were they? Could they be? Only the righteous could be true guardians to Allah's places of worship, and particularly to the Central House of the Ka'bah. It was to be a place of pure worship, while their idolatrous worship was mere mummery—whistling and clapping of hands. All false worship advertises itself by noise and unseemly riot: it is said that the Pagans used to go naked round the Ka'bah.

37. In order that Allah may separate[1206]
The impure from the pure,
Put the impure, one on another,
Heap them together, and cast them
Into Hell. They will be
The ones to have lost.

٣٧ لِيَمِيزَ ٱللَّهُ ٱلْخَبِيثَ مِنَ ٱلطَّيِّبِ وَيَجْعَلَ
ٱلْخَبِيثَ بَعْضَهُۥ عَلَىٰ بَعْضٍ فَيَرْكُمَهُۥ جَمِيعًا
فَيَجْعَلَهُۥ فِى جَهَنَّمَ ۚ أُو۟لَٰٓئِكَ هُمُ
ٱلْخَٰسِرُونَ

C. 91 — The battle of Badr brought to an issue
(8:38-64.) The fight between Truth and Unbelief.
It was the Day of Differentiation.
Not for spoils was it won, nor by numbers;
But by courage and planning, union of wills,
And pooling of strength and resources —
Above all by the help of Allah,
Whose help is ever all-sufficient.

SECTION 5.

38. Say to the Unbelievers,
If (now) they desist (from Unbelief),
Their past would be forgiven them;
But if they persist, the punishment
Of those before them is already
(A matter of warning for them).

٣٨ قُل لِّلَّذِينَ كَفَرُوٓا۟
إِن يَنتَهُوا۟ يُغْفَرْ لَهُم مَّا قَدْ سَلَفَ
وَإِن يَعُودُوا۟ فَقَدْ مَضَتْ سُنَّتُ ٱلْأَوَّلِينَ

39. And fight them on
Until there is no more
Tumult or oppression,
And there prevails
Justice and faith in Allah[1207]
Altogether and everywhere;
But if they cease, verily Allah
Doth see all that they do.[1208]

٣٩ وَقَٰتِلُوهُمْ حَتَّىٰ لَا تَكُونَ فِتْنَةٌ
وَيَكُونَ ٱلدِّينُ كُلُّهُۥ لِلَّهِ ۚ
فَإِنِ ٱنتَهَوْا۟ فَإِنَّ ٱللَّهَ
بِمَا يَعْمَلُونَ بَصِيرٌ

40. If they refuse, be sure
That Allah is your Protector —
The Best to protect
And the Best to help.

٤٠ وَإِن تَوَلَّوْا۟ فَٱعْلَمُوٓا۟ أَنَّ ٱللَّهَ مَوْلَىٰكُمْ ۚ
نِعْمَ ٱلْمَوْلَىٰ وَنِعْمَ ٱلنَّصِيرُ

1206. It is only when matters are brought to an issue that evil is separated distinctly from the good. Then evil consorts with evil, and good with good. The evil will be piled into a heap. When the cup is full, the punishment will come. There will be no mistake about it. The good should not be discouraged, because in fighting against them, all forces of evil join together and pool their resources together. The more they do so, the easier is the final arbitrament. It is all in Allah's Plan.

1207. *Cf.* 2:193 and n. 207.

1208. If they cease from fighting and from the persecution of truth, Allah judges them by their actions and their motives, and would not wish that they should be harassed with further hostility. But if they refuse all terms, the righteous have nothing to fear: Allah will help and protect them.

10
30

41. And know that out of
All the booty that ye
May acquire (in war),
A fifth share is assigned[1209]
To Allah—and to the Messenger,
And to near relatives,
Orphans, the needy,
And the wayfarer—
If ye do believe in Allah
And in the revelation
We sent down to our Servant
On the Day of Testing—[1210]
The Day of the meeting
Of the two forces.
For Allah hath power
Over all things.[1211]

٤١ وَٱعْلَمُوٓا أَنَّمَا غَنِمْتُم مِّن شَىْءٍ
فَأَنَّ لِلَّهِ خُمُسَهُۥ وَلِلرَّسُولِ وَلِذِى ٱلْقُرْبَىٰ
وَٱلْيَتَٰمَىٰ وَٱلْمَسَٰكِينِ وَٱبْنِ ٱلسَّبِيلِ
إِن كُنتُمْ ءَامَنتُم بِٱللَّهِ
وَمَآ أَنزَلْنَا عَلَىٰ عَبْدِنَا
يَوْمَ ٱلْفُرْقَانِ يَوْمَ ٱلْتَقَى ٱلْجَمْعَانِ ۗ
وَٱللَّهُ عَلَىٰ كُلِّ شَىْءٍ قَدِيرٌ

42. Remember ye were
On the hither side
Of the valley, and they
On the farther side,
And the caravan[1212]
On lower ground than ye.
Even if ye had made
A mutual appointment
To meet, ye would certainly
Have failed in the appointment:[1213]
But (thus ye met),

٤٢ إِذْ أَنتُم بِٱلْعُدْوَةِ ٱلدُّنْيَا وَهُم
بِٱلْعُدْوَةِ ٱلْقُصْوَىٰ وَٱلرَّكْبُ
أَسْفَلَ مِنكُمْ ۚ
وَلَوْ تَوَاعَدتُّمْ لَٱخْتَلَفْتُمْ
فِى ٱلْمِيعَٰدِ ۙ وَلَٰكِن

1209. The rule is that a fifth share is set apart for the Imām (the Commander) and the rest is divided among the forces. The fifth share reserved is expressed to be for Allah and the Prophet, and for charitable purposes for those to whom charity is due. Ultimately everything is at the disposal of Allah and His Prophet: 8:1: but four-fifths are divided, and only one-fifth is retained for the special purposes. The Imām has discretion as to the mode of division. In the Prophet's lifetime a certain portion was assigned to him and his near relatives.

1210. 'Testing': *Furqān*: Criterion between right and wrong, decision between the forces of faith and unbelief. The battle of Badr is called by this name. See 8:29 and n. 1202.

1211. Allah's power is shown in the events detailed in the three verses following (*vv.* 42-44), leading to the complete victory of the Muslims over the pagan Quraysh.

1212. The little Islamic force from Madīnah went out to meet the big Makkan army, and they met on the two sides of a valley at Badr, while the Quraysh caravan was on lower ground towards the sea, about 3 miles from Badr.

1213. They were all at cross purposes. The caravan was making for Makkah, but scarcely thought it could get there. The Quraysh force was trying to save the caravan and then annihilate the Muslims. The Muslims had decided to let the caravan alone but attack the Quraysh army from Makkah, which they thought was going to be small, but which turned out to be big, more than three times their number. Yet the two forces met, precisely at the spot and at the time when a decisive battle should take place and the Muslims dispose of the pretensions of the Makkans. If they had carefully planned a mutual appointment, they could not have carried it out more precisely.

On the Muslim side the few martyrs knew that the victory was theirs and those who survived the battle enjoyed the fruits of the victory. On the pagan side, both these who died and those who lived knew fully the issue joined. Even psychologically both sides went in with full determination to decide the issue.

That Allah might accomplish
A matter already enacted;
That those who died might
Die after a clear Sign
(Had been given), and those who lived
Might live after a Clear Sign
(Had been given). And verily
Allah is He who heareth
And knoweth (all things).

لِّيَقْضِيَ ٱللَّهُ أَمْرًا كَانَ مَفْعُولًا
لِّيَهْلِكَ مَنْ هَلَكَ عَنۢ بَيِّنَةٍ
وَيَحْيَىٰ مَنْ حَيَّ عَنۢ بَيِّنَةٍ
وَإِنَّ ٱللَّهَ لَسَمِيعٌ عَلِيمٌ

43. Remember in thy dream
Allah showed them to thee
As few: if He had shown
Them to thee as many,
Ye would surely have been
Discouraged, and ye would
Surely have disputed
In (your) decision: but Allah
Saved (you) for He knoweth
Well the (secrets) of (all) hearts.

٤٣ إِذْ يُرِيكَهُمُ ٱللَّهُ فِي مَنَامِكَ قَلِيلًا
وَلَوْ أَرَىٰكَهُمْ كَثِيرًا لَّفَشِلْتُمْ وَلَتَنَٰزَعْتُمْ
فِي ٱلْأَمْرِ وَلَٰكِنَّ ٱللَّهَ سَلَّمَ
إِنَّهُۥ عَلِيمٌۢ بِذَاتِ ٱلصُّدُورِ

44. And remember when ye met,
He showed them to you
As few in your eyes,
And He made you appear
As contemptible in their eyes:[1214]
That Allah might accomplish
A matter already enacted.
For to Allah do all questions
Go back (for decision).

٤٤ وَإِذْ يُرِيكُمُوهُمْ إِذِ ٱلْتَقَيْتُمْ
فِيٓ أَعْيُنِكُمْ قَلِيلًا وَيُقَلِّلُكُمْ فِيٓ أَعْيُنِهِمْ
لِيَقْضِيَ ٱللَّهُ أَمْرًا كَانَ مَفْعُولًا
وَإِلَى ٱللَّهِ تُرْجَعُ ٱلْأُمُورُ

SECTION 6.

45. O ye who believe!
When ye meet a force,
Be firm, and call Allah
In remembrance much (and often);
That ye may prosper:

٤٥ يَٰٓأَيُّهَا ٱلَّذِينَ ءَامَنُوٓا۟ إِذَا لَقِيتُمْ فِئَةً
فَٱثْبُتُوا۟ وَٱذْكُرُوا۟ ٱللَّهَ كَثِيرًا
لَّعَلَّكُمْ تُفْلِحُونَ

46. And obey Allah and His Messenger;
And fall into no disputes,

٤٦ وَأَطِيعُوا۟ ٱللَّهَ وَرَسُولَهُۥ وَلَا تَنَٰزَعُوا۟

1214. The Muslim army, though they knew their worldly disadvantage, did not realise the full odds against them. The Makkans came exulting in any case, and they despised the contemptible little force opposed to them. Even though they thought the Muslim force was twice as great as it was (3:13), still that number was contemptible, when taken with its poor equipment. Both these psychological mistakes subserved the Plan, which was to bring the matter to a decisive issue, whether the Pagans of Makkah were to continue their arrogant oppression, or the religion of Allah was to be established in freedom and honour.

Lest ye lose heart
And your power depart;
And be patient and persevering:
For Allah is with those
Who patiently persevere:[1215]

فَتَفْشَلُوا وَتَذْهَبَ رِيحُكُمْ
وَاصْبِرُوا إِنَّ اللَّهَ مَعَ الصَّابِرِينَ

47. And be not like those
Who started from their homes
Insolently and to be seen of men,
And to hinder (men)
From the path of Allah:[1216]
For Allah compasseth round about
All that they do.

(٤٧) وَلَا تَكُونُوا كَالَّذِينَ خَرَجُوا مِن
دِيَارِهِم بَطَرًا وَرِئَاءَ النَّاسِ وَيَصُدُّونَ
عَن سَبِيلِ اللَّهِ وَاللَّهُ بِمَا يَعْمَلُونَ مُحِيطٌ

48. Remember Satan made
Their (sinful) acts seem
Alluring to them, and said:
"No one among men
Can overcome you this day,
While I am near to you":
But when the two forces
Came in sight of each other,
He turned on his heels,
And said: "Lo! I am clear
Of you; lo! I see
What ye see not;
Lo! I fear Allah; for Allah
Is strict in punishment."[1217]

(٤٨) وَإِذْ زَيَّنَ لَهُمُ الشَّيْطَانُ أَعْمَالَهُمْ وَقَالَ
لَا غَالِبَ لَكُمُ الْيَوْمَ مِنَ النَّاسِ
وَإِنِّي جَارٌ لَّكُمْ فَلَمَّا تَرَاءَتِ الْفِئَتَانِ
نَكَصَ عَلَىٰ عَقِبَيْهِ وَقَالَ إِنِّي بَرِيءٌ مِّنكُمْ
إِنِّي أَرَىٰ مَا لَا تَرَوْنَ إِنِّي أَخَافُ اللَّهَ
وَاللَّهُ شَدِيدُ الْعِقَابِ

SECTION 7.

49. Lo! the Hypocrites say, and those
In whose hearts is a disease:[1218]
"These people—their religion
Has misled them." But

(٤٩) إِذْ يَقُولُ الْمُنَافِقُونَ وَالَّذِينَ
فِي قُلُوبِهِم مَّرَضٌ غَرَّ هَٰؤُلَاءِ دِينُهُمْ وَمَن

1215. A fine description of the Muslim virtues which make for success and whose loss brings about humiliation and failure. *"Power"*: literally, "wind"—the favourable wind for a sailing ship.

1216. A true description of the Makkan army which met its doom.

1217. It is the way with the leaders of evil, when they find their cause lost, that they wash their hands of their followers and leave them in the lurch. They see more clearly then their dupes. They are not simpletons: they know the consequences of the wrath of Allah. Satan's "fear" of Allah is terror combined with hatred—the very opposite of the feeling which is described in *Taqwā, viz.*, the desire to avoid doing anything against Allah's will, such desire being founded on trust in Allah and the love of Allah.

1218. *Cf.* 2:10, for "disease in the heart."

Trust in Allah brings its own reward: our eyes are opened, and we see how great, good, and wise is the Cherisher ofthe Worlds. Others may sneer and despise. But the blessing of Allah keeps our minds fresh and our hearts contented.

If any trust in Allah, behold!
Allah is Exalted in might, Wise.

يَتَوَكَّلْ عَلَى ٱللَّهِ فَإِنَّ ٱللَّهَ عَزِيزٌ حَكِيمٌ

50. If thou couldst see,
When the angels take the souls
Of the Unbelievers (at death),[1219]
(How) they smite their faces
And their backs, (saying):
"Taste the Penalty of the blazing
Fire—

٥٠ وَلَوْ تَرَىٰٓ إِذْ يَتَوَفَّى ٱلَّذِينَ كَفَرُوا۟
ٱلْمَلَٰٓئِكَةُ يَضْرِبُونَ وُجُوهَهُمْ وَأَدْبَٰرَهُمْ
وَذُوقُوا۟ عَذَابَ ٱلْحَرِيقِ

51. "Because of (the deeds) which[1220]
Your (own) hands sent forth:
For Allah is never unjust
To His servants:

٥١ ذَٰلِكَ بِمَا قَدَّمَتْ أَيْدِيكُمْ
وَأَنَّ ٱللَّهَ لَيْسَ بِظَلَّٰمٍ لِّلْعَبِيدِ

52. "(Deeds) after the manner
Of the People of Pharaoh
And of those before them:
They rejected the Signs of Allah,
And Allah punished them
For their crimes: for Allah
Is Strong, and Strict in
punishment:

٥٢ كَدَأْبِ ءَالِ فِرْعَوْنَ وَٱلَّذِينَ مِن قَبْلِهِمْ
كَفَرُوا۟ بِـَٔايَٰتِ ٱللَّهِ فَأَخَذَهُمُ ٱللَّهُ بِذُنُوبِهِمْ
إِنَّ ٱللَّهَ قَوِىٌّ شَدِيدُ ٱلْعِقَابِ

53. "Because Allah will never
change[1221]
The Grace which He hath
bestowed
On a people until they change
What is in their (own) souls:
And verily Allah is He
Who heareth and knoweth (all
things)."

٥٣ ذَٰلِكَ بِأَنَّ ٱللَّهَ لَمْ يَكُ
مُغَيِّرًا نِّعْمَةً أَنْعَمَهَا عَلَىٰ قَوْمٍ
حَتَّىٰ يُغَيِّرُوا۟ مَا بِأَنفُسِهِمْ
وَأَنَّ ٱللَّهَ سَمِيعٌ عَلِيمٌ

54. "(Deeds) after the manner
Of the People of the Pharaoh
And those before them":[1222]
They treated as false the Signs

٥٤ كَدَأْبِ ءَالِ فِرْعَوْنَ
وَٱلَّذِينَ مِن قَبْلِهِمْ كَذَّبُوا۟ بِـَٔايَٰتِ

1219. In contrast to the taunt against those who trust in Allah, "that their religion has misled them," is shown the terrible punishment, after death, of those who laughed at Faith.

1220. The punishment is shown to be due to their own deeds of wrong, because Allah is never unjust in the least to His servants.

1221. Allah bestows His grace freely, but He never withdraws it arbitrarily. Before He changes their state and circumstances, an actual state of rebellion and contumacy has arisen in their own souls, which brings about its inevitable punishment.

1222. These words from the address of the angels are quoted again, in order to add the comment that follows. Note that in verse 51, the words were that they *rejected* the Signs of Allah and were *punished*: here the words are that they treated the Signs as false and were *destroyed*—a higher degree of guilt deserved a severer punishment.

Of their Lord: so We
Destroyed them for their crimes,
And We drowned the People
Of Pharaoh: for they were all
Oppressors and wrongdoers.

رَبِّهِمْ فَأَهْلَكْنَٰهُم بِذُنُوبِهِمْ
وَأَغْرَقْنَآ ءَالَ فِرْعَوْنَ ۚ وَكُلٌّ كَانُوا۟ ظَٰلِمِينَ

55. For the worst of beasts
In the sight of Allah[1223]
Are those who reject Him:
They will not believe.

٥٥ إِنَّ شَرَّ ٱلدَّوَآبِّ عِندَ ٱللَّهِ
ٱلَّذِينَ كَفَرُوا۟ فَهُمْ لَا يُؤْمِنُونَ

56. They are those with whom
Thou didst make a covenant,[1224]
But they break their covenant
Every time, and they have not
The fear (of Allah).

٥٦ ٱلَّذِينَ عَٰهَدتَّ مِنْهُمْ ثُمَّ يَنقُضُونَ
عَهْدَهُمْ فِى كُلِّ مَرَّةٍ وَهُمْ لَا يَتَّقُونَ

57. If ye gain the mastery
Over them in war,
Disperse, with them, those
Who follow them,
That they may remember.[1224-A]

٥٧ فَإِمَّا تَثْقَفَنَّهُمْ فِى ٱلْحَرْبِ فَشَرِّدْ بِهِم
مَّنْ خَلْفَهُمْ لَعَلَّهُمْ يَذَّكَّرُونَ

58. If thou fearest treachery
From any group, throw back
(Their Covenant) to them, (so as
To be) on equal terms:
For Allah loveth not the
treacherous.

٥٨ وَإِمَّا تَخَافَنَّ مِن قَوْمٍ خِيَانَةً
فَٱنۢبِذْ إِلَيْهِمْ عَلَىٰ سَوَآءٍ ۚ
إِنَّ ٱللَّهَ لَا يُحِبُّ ٱلْخَآئِنِينَ

SECTION 8.

59. Let not the Unbelievers
Think that they can

٥٩ وَلَا يَحْسَبَنَّ ٱلَّذِينَ كَفَرُوا۟

1223. In 8:22 we were warned against "the worst of beasts in the sight of Allah", who do not make use of their faculties of hearing, speaking and understanding, in the service of Allah, and in fact misuse their faculties to blaspheme Allah. The same brute creatures are shown here in another light: they are faithless both to Allah and man.

1224. The immediate occasion was the repeated treachery of the Banū Qurayẓa after their treaties with the Muslims. But the general lesson remains, as noted in the two following verses. Treachery in war is doubly wrong, for it endangers so many lives. Such treachery should be punished in such a way that it gets no chance again. Not only the actual perpetrators but those who follow their standard should be rendered powerless. And the broken treaty should be denounced so that the innocent party can at least fight on equal terms. From actual physical warfare we can carry the same lesson to spiritual warfare. A truce or understanding is possible with those who respect definite principles, not with those who have no principles and are merely out for oppression and wickedness.

1224-A. The purpose of the verse is to urge Muslims to act against their enemies described above with a severity and resoluteness which would serve as a deterrent to other enemies of Islam who might be inclined to follow their example and act treacherously towards Muslims. (Eds.).

Get the better (of the godly):
They will never frustrate (them).

سَبَقُوٓا۟ إِنَّهُمْ لَا يُعْجِزُونَ

60. Against them make ready
Your strength to the utmost
Of your power, including[1225]
Steeds of war, to strike terror
Into (the hearts of) the enemies,
Of Allah and your enemies,
And others besides, whom
Ye may not know, but whom[1226]
Allah doth know. Whatever
Ye shall spend in the Cause
Of Allah, shall be repaid
Unto you, and ye shall not
Be treated unjustly.[1227]

٦٠ وَأَعِدُّوا۟ لَهُم مَّا ٱسْتَطَعْتُم
مِّن قُوَّةٍ وَمِن رِّبَاطِ ٱلْخَيْلِ
تُرْهِبُونَ بِهِۦ عَدُوَّ ٱللَّهِ وَعَدُوَّكُمْ
وَءَاخَرِينَ مِن دُونِهِمْ لَا تَعْلَمُونَهُمُ ٱللَّهُ يَعْلَمُهُمْ
وَمَا تُنفِقُوا۟ مِن شَىْءٍ فِى سَبِيلِ ٱللَّهِ
يُوَفَّ إِلَيْكُمْ وَأَنتُمْ لَا تُظْلَمُونَ

61. But if the enemy
Incline towards peace,
Do thou (also) incline
Towards peace, and trust
In Allah: for He is the One
That heareth and knoweth
(All things).[1228]

٦١ وَإِن جَنَحُوا۟ لِلسَّلْمِ
فَٱجْنَحْ لَهَا وَتَوَكَّلْ عَلَى ٱللَّهِ
إِنَّهُۥ هُوَ ٱلسَّمِيعُ ٱلْعَلِيمُ

62. Should they intend
To deceive thee—verily Allah
Sufficeth thee: He it is
That hath strengthened thee
With His aid and
With (the company of)
The Believers;[1229]

٦٢ وَإِن يُرِيدُوٓا۟ أَن يَخْدَعُوكَ
فَإِنَّ حَسْبَكَ ٱللَّهُ هُوَ ٱلَّذِىٓ أَيَّدَكَ
بِنَصْرِهِۦ وَبِٱلْمُؤْمِنِينَ

1225. The immediate occasion of this injunction was the weakness of cavalry and appointments of war in the early fights of Islam. But the general meaning follows. In every fight, physical, moral, or spiritual, arm yourself with the best weapons and the best arms against your enemy, so as to instil wholesome respect into him for you and the Cause you stand for.

1226. There are always lurking enemies whom you may not know, but whom Allah knows. It is your duty to be ready against all, for the sacred Cause under whose banner you are fighting.

1227. Be always ready and put all your resources into your Cause. You do not do so in vain. Allah's reward will come in various forms. He knows all, and His reward will always be more generous than you can possibly deserve.

1228. While we must always be ready for the good fight lest it be forced on us, even in the midst of the fight we must always be ready for peace if there is any inclination towards peace on the other side. There is no merit merely in a fight by itself. It should be a joyful duty not for itself, but to establish the reign of peace and righteousness and Allah's Law.

1229. In working for peace there may be certain risk of treachery on the other side. We must take that risk: because the men of Faith have Allah's aid to count upon and the strength of the united body of the righteous. (R).

63. And (moreover) He hath put
Affection between their hearts:
Not if thou hadst spent
All that is in the earth,
Couldst thou have produced
That affection, but Allah
Hath done it: for He
Is Exalted in might, Wise.[1230]

٦٣ وَأَلَّفَ بَيْنَ قُلُوبِهِمْ لَوْ أَنفَقْتَ مَا فِي الْأَرْضِ جَمِيعًا مَّا أَلَّفْتَ بَيْنَ قُلُوبِهِمْ وَلَٰكِنَّ اللَّهَ أَلَّفَ بَيْنَهُمْ إِنَّهُ عَزِيزٌ حَكِيمٌ

64. O Prophet! Sufficient
Unto thee is Allah—
(Unto thee) and unto those
Who follow thee
Among the Believers.[1231]

٦٤ يَا أَيُّهَا النَّبِيُّ حَسْبُكَ اللَّهُ وَمَنِ اتَّبَعَكَ مِنَ الْمُؤْمِنِينَ

C. 92.—No man of heart, spirit, or constancy
(8:65-75.) Can ever be cowed down by odds
Against him. We fight not for spoils
Or for captives, but for the glory
Of Allah, and for truth and faith.
We must be kind to all, but specially
Regard the needs of our comrades,
Linked to us by ties of duty and affection.
Our highest reward will be forgiveness
And grace from the Giver of all.

SECTION 9.

65. O Prophet! rouse the Believers
To the fight. If there are
Twenty amongst you, patient
And persevering, they will
Vanquish two hundred: if a
hundred,
They will vanquish a thousand

٦٥ يَا أَيُّهَا النَّبِيُّ حَرِّضِ الْمُؤْمِنِينَ عَلَى الْقِتَالِ إِن يَكُن مِّنكُمْ عِشْرُونَ صَابِرُونَ يَغْلِبُوا مِائَتَيْنِ وَإِن يَكُن مِّنكُم مِّائَةٌ يَغْلِبُوا أَلْفًا

1230. On the immediate occasion, the greatest miracle and most wonderful working of Allah's grace was the union of hearts produced among the jarring, war-like, excitable elements of Arabia under the gentle, firm, and wise guidance of Muḥammad, the Messenger of Allah. At all times we must pray to Allah for this gift above all—union, understanding, and pure and sincere affection among those who take Allah's name. With it there is strength and success. Without it there is humiliation, slavery, and moral degradation. There may be many causes of difference and dispute. The reconciliation can only come from the glory and wisdom of Allah.

1231. *The Believers*: mere lip-profession of belief, or even the kind of belief that does not result in action, is not enough. To those whose belief is so sincere that it results in complete trust in Allah and in fearless action in His service, the consequences on this earth do not matter. Allah's good pleasure is enough for them.

Of the Unbelievers: for these
Are a people without
understanding.[1232]

مِنَ ٱلَّذِينَ كَفَرُوا۟ بِأَنَّهُمْ قَوْمٌ لَّا يَفْقَهُونَ

66. For the present, Allah
Hath lightened your (task),
For He knoweth that there is
A weak spot in you:[1233]
But (even so), if there are
A hundred of you, patient
And persevering, they will
Vanquish two hundred, and if
A thousand, they will vanquish
Two thousand, with the leave
Of Allah: for Allah is with those
Who patiently persevere.

٦٦ ٱلْـَٔـٰنَ خَفَّفَ ٱللَّهُ عَنكُمْ
وَعَلِمَ أَنَّ فِيكُمْ ضَعْفًا
فَإِن يَكُن مِّنكُم مِّا۟ئَةٌ صَابِرَةٌ
يَغْلِبُوا۟ مِا۟ئَتَيْنِ وَإِن يَكُن مِّنكُمْ أَلْفٌ
يَغْلِبُوٓا۟ أَلْفَيْنِ بِإِذْنِ ٱللَّهِ
وَٱللَّهُ مَعَ ٱلصَّـٰبِرِينَ

67. It is not fitting
For a Prophet
That he should have
Prisoners of war until
He hath thoroughly subdued[1234]
The land. Ye look
For the temporal goods
Of this world; but Allah
Looketh to the Hereafter:
And Allah is Exalted in might,
Wise.

٦٧ مَا كَانَ لِنَبِىٍّ أَن يَكُونَ
لَهُۥٓ أَسْرَىٰ حَتَّىٰ يُثْخِنَ فِى ٱلْأَرْضِ
تُرِيدُونَ عَرَضَ ٱلدُّنْيَا
وَٱللَّهُ يُرِيدُ ٱلْـَٔاخِرَةَ
وَٱللَّهُ عَزِيزٌ حَكِيمٌ

1232. In a fight, odds of ten-to-one against anyone are appalling. But they do not daunt the men of faith. Whether they personally win or die, their Cause prevails. They are sure to win: because (1) they have divine aid, and (2) even humanly speaking, those who take up arms against truth and righteousness are fools, and their seeming power is but a broken reed.

1233. Given equal conditions, Muslims on account of their faith could win against odds of ten-to-one. But where their organisation and equipment are weak, as was the case about the time of Badr, they were set a lighter task, and asked to tackle no more than odds of two to one against them. As a matter of fact at Badr they won through against odds of more than three to one.

1234. An ordinary war may be for territory or trade, revenge or military glory—all "temporal goods of this world." Such a war is condemned. But a Jihād is fought under strict conditions laid down by Islam, and solely for the cause of Allah. All baser motives, therefore are strictly excluded. The greed of gain in the shape of ransom from captives has no place in such warfare. (R).

At the same time, if there has been heavy loss of life already, captives may be taken, and it would be for the Imām to exercise his discretion as to the time when it was safe to release them, and whether the release should be free or on parole or on a fine by way of punishment. Destruction and slaughter, however repugnant to a gentle soul like that of Muḥammad, were inevitable where evil tried to suppress the good. Even Jesus, whose mission was more limited, had to say: "Think not that I am come to send peace on earth: I came not to send peace but a sword." (Matt. x. 34).

Seventy captives were taken at Badr, and it was decided to take ransom for them. While the general principle of fighting for the purpose of taking captives in order to get their ransom is condemned, the particular action in this case was approved in *vv.* 68-71.

68. Had it not been for
A previous ordainment[1235]
From Allah, a severe penalty
Would have reached you
For the (ransom) that ye took.

٦٨ لَّوْلَا كِتَٰبٌ مِّنَ ٱللَّهِ سَبَقَ
لَمَسَّكُمْ فِيمَآ أَخَذْتُمْ عَذَابٌ عَظِيمٌ

69. But (now) enjoy[1236] what ye took
In war, lawful and good:
But fear Allah: for Allah
Is Oft-Forgiving, Most Merciful.

٦٩ فَكُلُوا۟ مِمَّا غَنِمْتُمْ حَلَٰلًا طَيِّبًا
وَٱتَّقُوا۟ ٱللَّهَ إِنَّ ٱللَّهَ غَفُورٌ رَّحِيمٌ

SECTION 10.

70. O Prophet! say to those
Who are captives in your hands:
"If Allah findeth any good[1237]
In your hearts, He will
Give you something better
Than what has been taken
From you, and He will
Forgive you: for Allah
Is Oft-Forgiving, Most Merciful."

٧٠ يَٰٓأَيُّهَا ٱلنَّبِىُّ قُل لِّمَن فِىٓ أَيْدِيكُم مِّنَ
ٱلْأَسْرَىٰٓ إِن يَعْلَمِ ٱللَّهُ فِى قُلُوبِكُمْ خَيْرًا
يُؤْتِكُمْ خَيْرًا مِّمَّآ أُخِذَ مِنكُمْ
وَيَغْفِرْ لَكُمْ وَٱللَّهُ غَفُورٌ رَّحِيمٌ

71. But if they have
Treacherous designs against thee,
(O Messenger!), they have already
Been in treason against Allah,[1238]

٧١ وَإِن يُرِيدُوا۟ خِيَانَتَكَ
فَقَدْ خَانُوا۟ ٱللَّهَ مِن قَبْلُ

1235. Though any motive of worldly gain, which may have been in the minds of some among the victorious Muslim army, is condemned as worthy of a severe penalty, what actually happened is ascribed to the Plan of Allah, which was pre-ordained. Among the prisoners taken were the Prophet's uncle 'Abbās and 'Alī's brother, 'Aqīl, who afterwards became Muslims. 'Abbās was an ancestor of the founder of the celebrated 'Abbāsi Dynasty which played such a notable part in Islamic history. In his case the promise made in verse 70 was amply fulfilled. In the case of all prisoners, if there was any good in their hearts, their very fight against Islam and their capture led to their being blessed with Islam. Thus does Allah's Plan work in a marvellous way, and evolve good out of seeming evil.

1236. *Enjoy*: literally, *eat*. See 7:19, n. 1004, and 5:69, n. 776.

1237. This is a consolation to the prisoners of war. In spite of their previous hostility, Allah will forgive them in His mercy if there was any good in their hearts, and confer upon them a far higher gift than anything they have ever lost. This gift in its highest sense would be the blessing of Islam, but even in a material sense, there was great good fortune awaiting them, *e.g.*, in the case of 'Abbās (see n. 1235).

Note how comprehensive is Allah's care. He encourages and strengthens the Muslims, at the same time condemning any baser motives that may have entered their minds. He consoles the prisoners of war and promises them better things if there is any good in them at all. And He offers comfort to those who have left their homes in His Cause, and knits them into closer fellowship with those who have helped them and sympathised with them.

1238. If the kindness shown to them is abused by the prisoners of war when they are released, it is not a matter of discouragement to those who showed the kindness. Such persons have in their treachery shown already their treason to Allah, in that they took up arms against Allah's Prophet, and sought to blot out the pure worship of Allah. The punishment of defeat, which opened the eyes of some of their comrades, evidently did not open their eyes. But Allah knows all, and in His wisdom will order all things for the best. The Believers have done their duty in showing such clemency as they could in the circumstances of war. For them "Allah sufficeth" (8:62).

And so hath He given
(Thee) power over them.
And Allah is He who hath
(Full) knowledge and wisdom.

فَأَمْكَنَ مِنْهُمْ
وَاللَّهُ عَلِيمٌ حَكِيمٌ

72. Those who believed,
And adopted exile,
And fought for the Faith,
With their property
And their persons,
In the cause of Allah,
As well as those
Who gave (them) asylum[1239]
And aid—these are (all)
Friends and protectors,
One of another.
As to those who believed
But came not into exile;
Ye owe no duty
Of protection to them
Until they come into exile;[1240]
But if they seek
Your aid in religion,
It is your duty
To help them,
Except against a people
With whom ye have
A treaty of mutual alliance.[1241]
And (remember) Allah
Seeth all that ye do.

(٧٢) إِنَّ الَّذِينَ ءَامَنُوا
وَهَاجَرُوا وَجَٰهَدُوا
بِأَمْوَٰلِهِمْ وَأَنفُسِهِمْ فِي سَبِيلِ
اللَّهِ وَالَّذِينَ ءَاوَوا وَّنَصَرُوٓا
أُولَٰٓئِكَ بَعْضُهُمْ أَوْلِيَآءُ بَعْضٍ
وَالَّذِينَ ءَامَنُوا وَلَمْ يُهَاجِرُوا
مَا لَكُم مِّن وَلَٰيَتِهِم مِّن شَيْءٍ حَتَّىٰ يُهَاجِرُوا
وَإِنِ اسْتَنصَرُوكُمْ فِي الدِّينِ
فَعَلَيْكُمُ النَّصْرُ إِلَّا عَلَىٰ قَوْمٍ
بَيْنَكُمْ وَبَيْنَهُم مِّيثَٰقٌ
وَاللَّهُ بِمَا تَعْمَلُونَ بَصِيرٌ

73. The Unbelievers are
Protectors, one of another:
Unless ye do this,

(٧٣) وَالَّذِينَ كَفَرُوا بَعْضُهُمْ أَوْلِيَآءُ
بَعْضٍ إِلَّا تَفْعَلُوهُ

1239. The reference is to the *Muhājirīn* and *Anṣār*, the Emigrants and the Helpers, the people who forsook their homes and adopted voluntary exile from Makkan company with their beloved Leader, and their good friends in Madīnah, who gave them asylum and every kind of assistance, moral and material. Under the magnetic personality of the Holy Prophet these two groups became like blood-brothers, and they were so treated in matters of inheritance during the period when they were cut off from their kith and kin.

1240. The Believers (Muslims) were entitled to all assistance in matters of religion. But if they were not strong enough to suffer voluntary exile on behalf of the Cause and make the personal sacrifices which their more ardent brethren in faith made, they could not reasonably ask for political or military assistance or protection.

1241. If a community suffers voluntary exile on account of persecution and oppression, and some of its weaker brethren stay behind, holding fast to faith but not prepared for the higher sacrifice, the exiles have still a duty to help their weaker brethren in matters of religion. The exiles, being at open war against the state which oppressed them, would be free to fight against such state. But if the weaker brethren are in a state in mutual alliance with the community, the community cannot in honour interfere with that state, whether it is Muslim or not. Presumably the alliance implies that the grievances of the weaker brethren will be redressed by the state itself. But it is not honourable to embarrass your own ally.

(Protect each other),
There would be
Tumult and oppression
On earth, and great mischief.[1242]

تَكُن فِتْنَةٌ فِى ٱلْأَرْضِ
وَفَسَادٌ كَبِيرٌ

74. Those who believe,
And adopt exile,
And fight for the Faith,
In the cause of Allah,
As well as those
Who give (them) asylum
And aid—these are (all)
In very truth the Believers:
For them is the forgiveness
Of sins and a provision
Most generous.[1243]

٧٤ وَٱلَّذِينَ ءَامَنُوا۟ وَهَاجَرُوا۟
وَجَٰهَدُوا۟ فِى سَبِيلِ ٱللَّهِ
وَٱلَّذِينَ ءَاوَوا۟ وَّنَصَرُوٓا۟ أُو۟لَٰٓئِكَ
هُمُ ٱلْمُؤْمِنُونَ حَقًّا
لَّهُم مَّغْفِرَةٌ وَرِزْقٌ كَرِيمٌ

75. And those who
Accept Faith subsequently,[1244]
And adopt exile,
And fight for the Faith
In your company—
They are of you.
But kindred by blood
Have prior rights
Against each other
In the Book of Allah.[1245]
Verily Allah is well-acquainted
With all things

٧٥ وَٱلَّذِينَ ءَامَنُوا۟
مِنۢ بَعْدُ وَهَاجَرُوا۟ وَجَٰهَدُوا۟
مَعَكُمْ فَأُو۟لَٰٓئِكَ مِنكُمْ
وَأُو۟لُوا۟ ٱلْأَرْحَامِ بَعْضُهُمْ
أَوْلَىٰ بِبَعْضٍ فِى كِتَٰبِ ٱللَّهِ
إِنَّ ٱللَّهَ بِكُلِّ شَىْءٍ عَلِيمٌ

1242. Evil consorts with evil. The good have all the more reason for drawing together and not only living in mutual harmony, but being ready at all times to protect each other. Otherwise the world will be given over to aggressions by unscrupulous people, and the good will fail in their duty to establish Allah's Peace and to strengthen all the forces of truth and righteousness.

1243. Believers who make all sacrifices in the cause of Allah have given the best possible proof of their Faith by their actions. They have loved Allah much,and much will be forgiven them. What they sacrificed was, perhaps, judged by universal standards, of small value, but its value will be estimated by the precious love behind it, and its reward will be of no ordinary kind. It will not be a reward in the ordinary sense at all, for a reward is given once and for all. It will be a provision which lasts forever, and is on the most generous scale.

1244. Those who come into the fold last are none the less brethren in the fullest acceptation of the term. But any special provisions made in the special circumstances of the first martyrs for the Cause will not of course apply to them as the special circumstances which made them necessary have ceased to exist. See next note.

1245. *The Book of Allah, i.e.,* the Universal Plan, the Eternal Decree, the Preserved Tablet (85:22). Blood-relationship and its rights and duties do not depend on special circumstances of a temporary nature. Any temporary rights of mutual inheritance established between the early Emigrants and Helpers (n. 1239) would not apply to later recruits, who would come under entirely different circumstances.

INTRODUCTION TO SŪRAH 9—*AL TAWBAH* or *BARĀ'AH*

Logically this Sūrah follows up the argument of the last Sūrah (8), and indeed may be considered a part of it, although chronologically the two are separated by an interval of seven years.

We saw that Sūrah 8 dealt with the large questions arising at the outset of the life of a new Ummah or organised nation: questions of defence under attack, distribution of war acquisitions after victory, the virtues needed for concerted action, and clemency and consideration for one's own and for enemies in the hour of victory. We pass on in this Sūrah to deal with the question: what is to be done if the enemy breaks faith and is guilty of treachery? No nation can go on with a treaty if the other party violates it at will; but it is laid down that a period of four months should be allowed by way of notice after denunciation of the treaty; that due protection should be accorded in the intervening period; that there should always be open the door to repentance and reunion with the people of Allah; and that if all these fail, and war must be undertaken, it must be pushed with the utmost vigour.

These are the general principles deducible from the Sūrah. The immediate occasion for their promulgation may be considered in connection with the chronological place of the Sūrah.

Chronologically, verses 1-29 were a notable declaration of state policy promulgated about the month of Shawwāl, A.H. 9, and read out by 'Alī at the Pilgrimage two months later in order to give the policy the widest publicity possible. The remainder of the Sūrah, verses 30-129, was revealed a little earlier, say about the month of Ramaḍān, A.H. 9, and sums up the lessons of the Prophet's Tabūk expedition in the late summer of A.H. 9 (say October 630).

Tabūk is a place near the frontier of Arabia, quite close to what was then Byzantine territory in the Province of Syria (which includes Palestine). It is on the Hijāz Railway, about 350 miles northwest of Madīnah, and 150 miles south of Ma'ān. It had a fort and a spring of sweet water. In consequence of strong and persistent rumours that the Byzantines (Romans) were preparing to invade Arabia and that the Byzantine Emperor himself had arrived near the frontier for the purpose, the Prophet collected as large a force as he could, and marched to Tabūk. The Byzantine invasion did not come off. But the Prophet took the opportunity of consolidating the Muslim position in that direction and making treaties of alliance with certain Christian and Jewish tribes near the Gulf of 'Aqabah. On his return to Madīnah he considered the situation. During his absence the Hypocrites had played, as always, a double game; and the policy hitherto followed, of free access to the sacred centre of Islam to Muslims and Pagans alike—was now altered, as it had been abused by the enemies of Islam.

This is the only Sūrah to which the usual formula of *Bismillāh* is not prefixed. It was among the last of the Sūrahs revealed, and though the Prophet had directed that it should follow Sūrah 8, it was not clear whether it was to form a separate Sūrah or only a part of Sūrah 8. It is now treated as a separate Sūrah, but the *Bismillāh* is not prefixed to it, as there is no warrant for supposing that the Prophet used the *Bismillāh* before it in his recitation of the Qur'ān. The Sūrah is known under many names: the most commonly used are (1) *Al Tawbah* (Repentance), with reference to 9:104 and (2) *Barā'ah* (The Disavowel), the opening word of the Sūrah.

Summary—Treaties with those Pagans who have treacherously broken their terms are denounced, but four months' time is given for adjustments or repentance. Pagans to be excluded from the sacred Mosques. Infidelity to be fought (9:1-29, and C. 93).

The People of the Book have obscured the light of Allah, but the Truth of Allah must prevail over all. We must be ready to fight for the Faith that is in us; otherwise we shall be unworthy to uphold Allah's banner, and He will raise other people in our place (9:30-42, and C. 94).

The Hypocrites and their double dealing: their evil ways pointed out. Their punishment will be as sure as the blessings of the righteous (9:43-72, and C. 95).

All evil should be resisted, unless there is repentance: falsehood is not content with breach of faith but mocks all good: it should not be envied but shunned (9:73-99, and C. 96).

The good pleasure of Allah is with those who are sincere and make sacrifices in His cause; He will forgive those who do wrong and repent, but not those who intend mischief and foment unbelief and disunion among believers. The Believers by their self-surrender obtain eternal Felicity. Allah will turn in mercy even to those who, though they waver or fail in duty, turn at last to Him (9:100-118, and C. 97).

Those who believe should associate with the righteous and the truthful, actively doing their duty. But if the Community marches out, a part of them should remain behind for the purpose of diligently studying religion and teaching their brethren when they return. Every Sūrah increases the faith of those who believe, though those diseased in heart may add doubt to doubt. Trust in Allah, Lord of the Throne of Glory (9:119-129, and C. 98).

C. 93.—If the Pagans repeatedly break
(9:1-29.) Their treaties, denounce the treaties,
But give them time either to repent
Or to prepare for the just punishment
Of their treachery. Punish the chiefs
Of the treacherous, and destroy them.
But if one of them seek asylum,
Give it: let him hear the Word
Of Allah and escort him to security.
Be true to the true, but fight those
Who are false to plighted word
And taunt you for your Faith.
No one has the right to approach
The mosques of Allah unless
He believes in Allah and follows
Allah's Law, the law of righteousness.

Al Tawbah (The Repentance) or *Barā'ah* (The Disavowel)

1. A (declaration) of immunity[1246]
From Allah and His Messenger,
To those of the Pagans
With whom ye have contracted
Mutual alliances—

(١) بَرَآءَةٌ مِّنَ ٱللَّهِ وَرَسُولِهِۦٓ
إِلَى ٱلَّذِينَ عَـٰهَدتُّم مِّنَ ٱلْمُشْرِكِينَ

2. Go ye, then, for four months,[1247]
Backwards and forwards,
(As ye will), throughout the land,
But know ye that ye cannot
Frustrate Allah (by your falsehood)
But that Allah will cover
With shame those who reject Him.

(٢) فَسِيحُوا۟ فِى ٱلْأَرْضِ أَرْبَعَةَ أَشْهُرٍ
وَٱعْلَمُوٓا۟ أَنَّكُمْ غَيْرُ مُعْجِزِى ٱللَّهِ ۙ
وَأَنَّ ٱللَّهَ مُخْزِى ٱلْكَـٰفِرِينَ

3. And an announcement from Allah
And His Messenger, to the people
(Assembled) on the day
Of the Great Pilgrimage—[1248]
That Allah and His Messenger
Dissolve (treaty) obligations
With the Pagans.
If, then, ye repent,
It were best for you;
But if ye turn away,
Know ye that ye cannot
Frustrate Allah. And proclaim
A grievous penalty to those
Who reject Faith.

(٣) وَأَذَٰنٌ مِّنَ ٱللَّهِ وَرَسُولِهِۦٓ
إِلَى ٱلنَّاسِ يَوْمَ ٱلْحَجِّ ٱلْأَكْبَرِ
أَنَّ ٱللَّهَ بَرِىٓءٌ مِّنَ ٱلْمُشْرِكِينَ ۙ وَرَسُولُهُۥ ۚ
فَإِن تُبْتُمْ فَهُوَ خَيْرٌ لَّكُمْ ۖ وَإِن تَوَلَّيْتُمْ
فَٱعْلَمُوٓا۟ أَنَّكُمْ غَيْرُ مُعْجِزِى ٱللَّهِ ۗ
وَبَشِّرِ ٱلَّذِينَ كَفَرُوا۟ بِعَذَابٍ أَلِيمٍ

1246. *Barā'ah*: usually translated "immunity". I do not think that word correctly represents the Arabic word in this context. The general sense is explained in the introduction to this Sūrah. In verse 3 below I use the periphrasis "dissolve treaty obligations," which goes some way to explain the meaning. The Pagans and enemies of Islam frequently made treaties of mutual alliances with the Muslims. The Muslims scrupulously observed their part, but the Pagans violated their part again and again when it suited them. After some years' experience it became imperative to denounce such treaties altogether. This was done in due form, with four months' notice, and a chance was given to those who faithfully observed their pledges, to continue their alliance. (R.).

1247. *Four Months.* Some Commentators understand by this the four forbidden months in which warfare by ancient Arabian custom was unlawful, *viz.*, Rajab, D͟hu al Qa'dah, D͟hu al Hijjah, and Muḥarram: See 2:194 n. But it is better to take the signification of the four months immediately following the Declaration. Assuming that the Sūrah was promulgated early in S͟hawwāl (see Introduction), the four months would be S͟hawwāl, D͟hu al Qa'dah, D͟hu al Hijjah, and Muḥarram, of which the last three would also be the customary Prohibited Months.

1248. The great day of Ḥajj is either the 9th of D͟hu al Hijjah,(*'Arafah*), or the 10th (the Day of Sacrifice).

4. (But the treaties are) not
dissolved[1249]
With those Pagans with whom
Ye have entered into alliance
And who have not subsequently
Failed you in aught,
Nor aided anyone against you.
So fulfil your engagements
With them to the end
Of their term: for Allah
Loveth the righteous.

٤ إِلَّا ٱلَّذِينَ عَٰهَدتُّم مِّنَ
ٱلْمُشْرِكِينَ ثُمَّ لَمْ يَنقُصُوكُمْ شَيْـًٔا
وَلَمْ يُظَٰهِرُوا۟ عَلَيْكُمْ أَحَدًا
فَأَتِمُّوٓا۟ إِلَيْهِمْ عَهْدَهُمْ إِلَىٰ مُدَّتِهِمْ ۚ
إِنَّ ٱللَّهَ يُحِبُّ ٱلْمُتَّقِينَ

5. But when the forbidden
months[1250]
Are past, then fight and slay[1251]
The Pagans wherever ye find
them,
And seize them, beleaguer them,
And lie in wait for them
In every stratagem (of war);
But if they repent,[1252]
And establish regular prayers
And practise regular charity,
Then open the way for them:
For Allah is Oft-Forgiving,
Most Merciful.

٥ فَإِذَا ٱنسَلَخَ ٱلْأَشْهُرُ ٱلْحُرُمُ فَٱقْتُلُوا۟
ٱلْمُشْرِكِينَ حَيْثُ وَجَدتُّمُوهُمْ وَخُذُوهُمْ
وَٱحْصُرُوهُمْ وَٱقْعُدُوا۟ لَهُمْ كُلَّ مَرْصَدٍ ۚ
فَإِن تَابُوا۟ وَأَقَامُوا۟ ٱلصَّلَوٰةَ
وَءَاتَوُا۟ ٱلزَّكَوٰةَ فَخَلُّوا۟ سَبِيلَهُمْ ۚ
إِنَّ ٱللَّهَ غَفُورٌ رَّحِيمٌ

6. If one amongst the Pagans[1253]
Ask thee for asylum,

٦ وَإِنْ أَحَدٌ مِّنَ ٱلْمُشْرِكِينَ ٱسْتَجَارَكَ

1249. The sacred duty of fulfilling all obligations of every kind, to Muslims and non Muslims, in public as well as private life, is a cardinal feature of Muslim ethics. The question of what is to be done with those who abuse this principle by failing in their duty but expect the Muslims to do their part is not to be solved (in the case of treaties) by a general denunciation of treaties but by a careful consideration of the cases where there has been fidelity and not treachery. There we are enjoined to give the strictest fidelity, as it is a part of righteousness and our duty to Allah.

1250. The emphasis is on the first clause: it is only when the four months of grace are past, and the other party show no signs of desisting from their treacherous designs by right conduct, that the state of war supervenes—between Faith and Unfaith.

1251. When war becomes inevitable, it must be prosecuted with vigour. According to the English phrase, you cannot fight with kid gloves. The fighting may take the form of slaughter, or capture, or siege, or ambush and other stratagems. But even then there is room for repentance and amendment on the part of the guilty party, and if that takes place, our duty is forgiveness and the establishment of peace.

1252. The repentance must be sincere, and that is shown by conduct—a religious spirit of true prayer and charity. In that case we are not to bar the gate against the repentant. On the contrary we must do all we can to make their way easy, remembering that Allah is Oft-Forgiving, Most Merciful.

1253. Even among the enemies of Islam, actively fighting against Islam, there may be individuals who may be in a position to require protection. Full asylum is to be given to them, and opportunities provided for hearing the Word of Allah. If they accept the Word, they become Muslims and brethren, and no further question arises. If they do not see their way to accept Islam, they will require double protection: (1) from the Islamic forces openly fighting against their people, and (2) from their own people, as they detached themselves from them. Both kinds of protection should be ensured for them, and they should be safely escorted to a place where they can be safe. Such persons only err through ignorance, and there may be much good in them.

Grant it to him,
So that he may hear the Word
Of Allah; and then escort him
To where he can be secure.[1254]
That is because they are
Men without knowledge.

فَأَجِرْهُ حَتَّىٰ يَسْمَعَ كَلَٰمَ ٱللَّهِ
ثُمَّ أَبْلِغْهُ مَأْمَنَهُۥ ذَٰلِكَ
بِأَنَّهُمْ قَوْمٌ لَّا يَعْلَمُونَ

SECTION 2.

7. How can there be a league,
Before Allah and His Messenger,
With the Pagans, except those[1255]
With whom ye made a treaty
Near the Sacred Mosque?
As long as these stand true
To you, stand ye true to them:
For Allah doth love the righteous.

٧ كَيْفَ يَكُونُ لِلْمُشْرِكِينَ
عَهْدٌ عِندَ ٱللَّهِ وَعِندَ رَسُولِهِۦٓ إِلَّا ٱلَّذِينَ
عَٰهَدتُّمْ عِندَ ٱلْمَسْجِدِ ٱلْحَرَامِ فَمَا ٱسْتَقَٰمُوا۟
لَكُمْ فَٱسْتَقِيمُوا۟ لَهُمْ إِنَّ ٱللَّهَ يُحِبُّ ٱلْمُتَّقِينَ

8. How (can there be such a league),[1256]
Seeing that if they get an advantage
Over you, they respect not
In you the ties either of kinship[1257]
Or of covenant? With (fair words
From) their mouths they entice you,
But their hearts are averse
From you; and most of them
Are rebellious and wicked.

٨ كَيْفَ وَإِن يَظْهَرُوا۟ عَلَيْكُمْ
لَا يَرْقُبُوا۟ فِيكُمْ إِلًّا وَلَا ذِمَّةً
يُرْضُونَكُم بِأَفْوَٰهِهِمْ
وَتَأْبَىٰ قُلُوبُهُمْ
وَأَكْثَرُهُمْ فَٰسِقُونَ

9. The Signs of Allah have they sold
For a miserable price,
And (many) have they hindered

٩ ٱشْتَرَوْا۟ بِـَٔايَٰتِ ٱللَّهِ ثَمَنًا قَلِيلًا فَصَدُّوا۟

1254. *Ma'manah:* place or opportunity of being secure from all harm.

1255. In this section we have the reasons why the treaties with treacherous Pagan foes were denounced. The clause introducing the exception is a parenthetical clause. The word "Pagans" must be connected with verse 8 which follows. In that verse the word *kayfa* resumes the clause introduced by the word *kayfa* at the beginning of verse 7. The exceptional Pagan tribes which remained true to their word were the Banū Ḥamzah and the Banū Kināna, who swore their treaty near the Sacred Mosque and faithfully observed it. They were to be given the full benefit of their fidelity even though their kindred tribes were treacherous.

1256. The exceptions having been stated parenthetically in verse 7, the indictment of the general mass of Pagan tribes is now set out briefly but fully and convincingly. After that kind of behaviour how can a treaty be possible with them? The counts are: (1) that whenever they got a slight advantage, they disregarded the ties both of kinship and of covenant as against the Muslims because of their Faith, thus proving doubly treacherous; (2) that they spoke fair words, but had venom in their hearts; (3) that their attitude was one of rebellion against their plighted word; (4) that they disregarded the solemn Signs of Allah for some miserable worldly gain; (5) that they tried to prevent other people from coming to the Way of Allah. The first clause is repeated again as the last clause, to emphasize their double treachery, and round off the argument.

1257. Among the Arabs, the ties of kinship were so strong as to be almost unbreakable. The Pagan Arabs went out of their way to break them in the case of the Muslims, who were kith and kin to them. Besides the bond of kinship there was the further bond of their plighted oath in the Treaty. They broke that oath because the other parties were Muslims.

From His Way: evil indeed
Are the deeds they have done.

عَن سَبِيلِهِۦٓۚ إِنَّهُمۡ سَآءَ مَا كَانُواْ يَعۡمَلُونَ

10. In a Believer they respect not
The ties either of kinship
Or of covenant! It is they
Who have transgressed all
bounds.[1258]

١٠ لَا يَرۡقُبُونَ فِي مُؤۡمِنٍ إِلّٗا وَلَا ذِمَّةٗۚ
وَأُوْلَٰٓئِكَ هُمُ ٱلۡمُعۡتَدُونَ

11. But (even so), if they repent,[1259]
Establish regular prayers,
And practise regular charity—
They are your brethren in Faith:
(Thus) do We explain the Signs
In detail, for those who
understand.

١١ فَإِن تَابُواْ وَأَقَامُواْ ٱلصَّلَوٰةَ
وَءَاتَوُاْ ٱلزَّكَوٰةَ فَإِخۡوَٰنُكُمۡ فِي ٱلدِّينِۗ
وَنُفَصِّلُ ٱلۡأٓيَٰتِ لِقَوۡمٖ يَعۡلَمُونَ

12. But if they violate their oaths
After their covenant,
And taunt you for your Faith—[1260]
Fight ye the chiefs of Unfaith:
For their oaths are nothing to
them:
That thus they may be restrained.

١٢ وَإِن نَّكَثُوٓاْ أَيۡمَٰنَهُم مِّنۢ بَعۡدِ عَهۡدِهِمۡ
وَطَعَنُواْ فِي دِينِكُمۡ فَقَٰتِلُوٓاْ أَئِمَّةَ ٱلۡكُفۡرِ
إِنَّهُمۡ لَآ أَيۡمَٰنَ لَهُمۡ لَعَلَّهُمۡ يَنتَهُونَ

13. Will ye not fight people
Who violated their oaths,
Plotted to expel the Messenger,[1261]
And took the aggressive
By being the first (to assault) you?
Do ye fear them? Nay,
It is Allah Whom ye should
More justly fear, if ye believe!

١٣ أَلَا تُقَٰتِلُونَ قَوۡمٗا نَّكَثُوٓاْ أَيۡمَٰنَهُمۡ
وَهَمُّواْ بِإِخۡرَاجِ ٱلرَّسُولِ وَهُم
بَدَءُوكُمۡ أَوَّلَ مَرَّةٍۚ أَتَخۡشَوۡنَهُمۡۚ
فَٱللَّهُ أَحَقُّ أَن تَخۡشَوۡهُ إِن كُنتُم مُّؤۡمِنِينَ

14. Fight them, and Allah will
Punish them by your hands,
Cover them with shame,
Help you (to victory) over them,

١٤ قَٰتِلُوهُمۡ يُعَذِّبۡهُمُ ٱللَّهُ
بِأَيۡدِيكُمۡ وَيُخۡزِهِمۡ وَيَنصُرۡكُمۡ عَلَيۡهِمۡ

1258. The catalogue of their sins being set out, it is clear that they were aggressors in the worst possible ways; and war became inevitable.

1259. The chance of repentance and mercy to the worst enemies is again emphasised, in order that people with any understanding may not be misled into thinking that war was an easy or light matter. This emphasis is balanced by the emphasis in the next verse on the causes which made war inevitable for those with any self-respect.

1260. Not only did the enemies break their oaths shamelessly, but they even taunted the Muslims on their Faith and the "simple-minded" way in which they continued to respect their part of the treaty, as if they were afraid to fight!

1261. The argument now takes a new turn. An appeal is made to the Muslims on various grounds: (1) the shameless disregard of treaties by the enemy, (2) the underhanded plots to discredit the Holy Prophet, and turn him out of Madīnah as he had been turned out of Makkah, (3) the aggression taken by the Quraysh and their confederates in Madīnah after the treaty to Hudaybīyah (A. H. 6, Dhu al Qa'dah, Feb. 628), (4) the manly attitude that fears Allah rather than men, and (5) the need to prove our sincere faith by test and trial and struggle and sacrifice (9:16).

Heal the breasts of Believers,[1262]

وَيَشْفِ صُدُورَ قَوْمٍ مُّؤْمِنِينَ

15. And still the indignation of their hearts.[1263]
For Allah will turn (in mercy)[1264]
To whom He will; and Allah
Is All-Knowing, All-Wise.

١٥ وَيُذْهِبْ غَيْظَ قُلُوبِهِمْ ۗ
وَيَتُوبُ ٱللَّهُ عَلَىٰ مَن يَشَآءُ ۗ وَٱللَّهُ عَلِيمٌ حَكِيمٌ

16. Or think ye that ye
Shall be abandoned,
As though Allah did not know[1265]
Those among you who strive
With might and main, and take
None for friends and protectors
Except Allah, His Messenger,
And the (community of) Believers?
But Allah is well-acquainted
With (all) that ye do.

١٦ أَمْ حَسِبْتُمْ أَن تُتْرَكُوا۟ وَلَمَّا يَعْلَمِ ٱللَّهُ
ٱلَّذِينَ جَٰهَدُوا۟ مِنكُمْ وَلَمْ يَتَّخِذُوا۟ مِن
دُونِ ٱللَّهِ وَلَا رَسُولِهِۦ وَلَا ٱلْمُؤْمِنِينَ وَلِيجَةً ۚ
وَٱللَّهُ خَبِيرٌۢ بِمَا تَعْمَلُونَ

SECTION 3.

17. It is not for such
As join gods with Allah,
To visit or maintain[1266]

١٧ مَا كَانَ لِلْمُشْرِكِينَ أَن يَعْمُرُوا۟

1262. *Heal the breasts of believers, i.e.*, of wounds that they may have sustained from the assaults, taunts, and cruelty of the enemy.

1263. When the victory comes and the wounds are healed, a great peace comes to the hearts of those who have suffered, striven, and struggled. The fighting was an abnormal necessity forced by injustice and oppression. When Allah's Law is established, the fire of indignation is quelled, and the true Peace of Islam is attained.

1264. Allah's mercy is unlimited. When evil is destroyed, many of those who were enticed by evil will come into the fold of truth and righteousness, and the cessation of war and conflict will bring peace, certainly to those who fought for the right, but also possibly to those whose eyes have been opened to the working of Allah's Law and who in healing reconciliation become members of the Brotherhood of Peace in Islam.

1265. Some translators have taken a different verbal construction of this passage, but the ultimate effect in meaning is the same: we must all be tested and tried, but Allah knows our inmost hearts, and He will support those who strive in His way, out of sincere love for Him, His Prophet, and the body of the true men of faith.

1266. *'Amara* as applied to mosques implies the following ideas: (1) to build or repair; (2) to maintain in fitting dignity; (3) to visit for purposes of devotion; and (4) fill with light and life and activity. For brevity I have only used the two words "visit and maintain" in the translation.

Before the preaching of Islam the Pagans built, repaired, and maintained the Mosque, and celebrated Pagan ceremonies in it, including naked circumambulation round the Ka'bah. They made an income out of it. Islam protested, and the Pagans ejected Muslims and their Leader from Makkah, and shut them out from the Ka'bah itself. When the Muslims were strong enough to retake Makkah (A. H. 8), they purified the Mosque and reestablished the worship of the true God. The families who previously held control could not after this be allowed *in a state of Paganism* to control the Mosque any longer. If they became Muslims, it was a different matter. The further question arose: should they be allowed to visit it and practise their unseemly Pagan rites? Obviously this would be derogatory to the dignity and honour of the Mosque, and was forbidden. This was the particular occasion to which the verse refers. The general deduction is clear. A house of Allah is a place of sincere devotion, not a theatre for vulgar rites nor a source of worldly income. Only sincere Believers have a right of entry. Who the sincere Believers are, is explained in the next verse.

The mosques of Allah
While they witness
Against their own souls
To infidelity. The works
Of such bear no fruit:
In Fire shall they dwell.

مَسَٰجِدَ ٱللَّهِ شَٰهِدِينَ
عَلَىٰٓ أَنفُسِهِم بِٱلْكُفْرِ ۚ أُو۟لَٰٓئِكَ
حَبِطَتْ أَعْمَٰلُهُمْ وَفِى ٱلنَّارِ هُمْ خَٰلِدُونَ

18. The mosques of Allah
Shall be visited and maintained
By such as believe in Allah
And the Last Day, establish
Regular prayers, and practise
Regular charity, and fear
None (at all) except Allah.[1267]
It is they who are expected
To be on true guidance.[1268]

(١٨) إِنَّمَا يَعْمُرُ مَسَٰجِدَ ٱللَّهِ مَنْ ءَامَنَ
بِٱللَّهِ وَٱلْيَوْمِ ٱلْءَاخِرِ وَأَقَامَ ٱلصَّلَوٰةَ
وَءَاتَى ٱلزَّكَوٰةَ وَلَمْ يَخْشَ إِلَّا ٱللَّهَ ۖ
فَعَسَىٰٓ أُو۟لَٰٓئِكَ أَن يَكُونُوا۟ مِنَ ٱلْمُهْتَدِينَ

19. Do ye make the giving[1269]
Of drink to pilgrims,
Or the maintenance of
The Sacred Mosque, equal
To (the pious service of) those
Who believe in Allah
And the Last Day, and strive
With might and main
In the cause of Allah?
They are not comparable
In the sight of Allah:
And Allah guides not
Those who do wrong.

(١٩) أَجَعَلْتُمْ سِقَايَةَ ٱلْحَآجِّ
وَعِمَارَةَ ٱلْمَسْجِدِ ٱلْحَرَامِ
كَمَنْ ءَامَنَ بِٱللَّهِ وَٱلْيَوْمِ ٱلْءَاخِرِ
وَجَٰهَدَ فِى سَبِيلِ ٱللَّهِ ۚ
لَا يَسْتَوُۥنَ عِندَ ٱللَّهِ ۗ
وَٱللَّهُ لَا يَهْدِى ٱلْقَوْمَ ٱلظَّٰلِمِينَ

20. Those who believe, and suffer
Exile and strive with might
And main, in Allah's cause,[1270]
With their goods and their
persons,

(٢٠) ٱلَّذِينَ ءَامَنُوا۟ وَهَاجَرُوا۟ وَجَٰهَدُوا۟
فِى سَبِيلِ ٱللَّهِ بِأَمْوَٰلِهِمْ وَأَنفُسِهِمْ

1267. See the previous note. Sincere Believers are those who have faith in Allah and the future, and have a spirit of devotion and charity—a true and abiding spirit, not merely isolated acts now and then. Moreover they must not bow to worldly greed or ambition, which produces fear of worldly power.

1268. Others may call themselves by what names they like. True guidance is shown by the tests here indicated.

1269. Giving drinks of cold water to thirsty pilgrims, and doing material services to a mosque are meritorious acts, but they are only external. If they do not touch the soul, their value is slight. Far greater, in the sight of Allah, are Faith, Endeavour, and self-surrender to Allah. Men who practise these will obtain honour in the sight of Allah. Allah's light and guidance comes to them, and not to those self-sufficient beings who think that a little show of what the world considers piety is enough.

1270. Here is a good description of *Jihād.* It may require fighting in Allah's cause, as a form of self-sacrifice. But its essence consists in (1) a true and sincere Faith, which so fixes its gaze on Allah, that all selfish or worldly motives seem paltry and fade away, and (2) in earnest and ceaseless activity, involving the sacrifice (if need be) of life, person, or property, in the service of Allah. Mere brutal fighting is opposed to the whole spirit of *Jihād,* while the sincere scholar's pen or preacher's voice or wealthy man's contributions may be the most valuable forms of *Jihād.*

Have the highest rank
In the sight of Allah:
They are the people
Who will achieve (salvation).

أَعْظَمُ دَرَجَةً عِندَ ٱللَّهِ
وَأُوْلَٰٓئِكَ هُمُ ٱلْفَآئِزُونَ

21. Their Lord doth give them
Glad tidings of a Mercy
From Himself, of His good pleasure,
And of Gardens for them,
Wherein are delights
That endure:

٢١ يُبَشِّرُهُمْ رَبُّهُم
بِرَحْمَةٍ مِّنْهُ وَرِضْوَٰنٍ
وَجَنَّٰتٍ لَّهُمْ فِيهَا نَعِيمٌ مُّقِيمٌ

22. They will dwell therein
Forever. Verily in Allah's presence
Is a reward, the greatest (of all).[1271]

٢٢ خَٰلِدِينَ فِيهَآ أَبَدًا ۚ إِنَّ ٱللَّهَ
عِندَهُۥٓ أَجْرٌ عَظِيمٌ

23. O ye who believe! Take not
For protectors your fathers
And your brothers if they love
Infidelity above Faith:
If any of you do so,
They do wrong.

٢٣ يَٰٓأَيُّهَا ٱلَّذِينَ ءَامَنُوا۟ لَا تَتَّخِذُوٓا۟ ءَابَآءَكُمْ
وَإِخْوَٰنَكُمْ أَوْلِيَآءَ إِنِ ٱسْتَحَبُّوا۟ ٱلْكُفْرَ عَلَى
ٱلْإِيمَٰنِ ۚ وَمَن يَتَوَلَّهُم مِّنكُمْ فَأُوْلَٰٓئِكَ هُمُ
ٱلظَّٰلِمُونَ

24. Say: If it be that your fathers,
Your sons, your brothers,
Your mates, or your kindred;
The wealth that ye have gained;
The commerce in which ye fear
A decline; or the dwellings
In which ye delight—[1272]
Are dearer to you than Allah,
Or His Messenger, or the striving
In His cause—then wait
Until Allah brings about[1273]

٢٤ قُلْ إِن كَانَ ءَابَآؤُكُمْ وَأَبْنَآؤُكُمْ وَإِخْوَٰنُكُمْ
وَأَزْوَٰجُكُمْ وَعَشِيرَتُكُمْ وَأَمْوَٰلٌ ٱقْتَرَفْتُمُوهَا
وَتِجَٰرَةٌ تَخْشَوْنَ كَسَادَهَا وَمَسَٰكِنُ تَرْضَوْنَهَآ
أَحَبَّ إِلَيْكُم مِّنَ ٱللَّهِ وَرَسُولِهِۦ وَجِهَادٍ
فِى سَبِيلِهِۦ فَتَرَبَّصُوا۟ حَتَّىٰ يَأْتِىَ ٱللَّهُ

1271. Those who strive and suffer in Allah's cause are promised (1) a mercy specially from Himself, (2) His own good pleasure, (3) gardens of perpetual delight, (4) the supreme reward, Allah's own Presence or nearness. These are in gradation: (1) is a special mercy, higher than flows out to all creatures; (2) is a consciousness of Allah's good pleasure, which raises the soul above itself; (3) is that state of permanent spiritual assurance, which is typified by gardens of perpetual delight, and (4) is the final bliss, which is the sight of Allah Himself. (R).

1272. Man's heart clings to (1) his own kith and kin—parents, children, brothers and sisters, husbands or wives, or other relatives, (2) wealth and prosperity, (3) commerce or means of profit and gain, or (4) noble buildings, for dignity or comfort. If these are a hindrance in Allah's cause, we have to choose which we love most. We must love Allah even if it involves the sacrifice of all else.

1273. If we love our earthly ties and comforts, profits and pleasures, more than we love Allah, and therefore fail to respond to Allah's cause, it is not Allah's cause which will suffer. Allah's purpose will be accomplished, with or without us. But our failure to respond to His will must leave us spiritually poorer, bereft of grace and guidance: "for Allah guides not the rebellious".

This is of universal application. But it was strikingly illustrated in the case of those faithful ones who obeyed the Prophet's call, left the comfort of their homes in Makkah and suffered exile in Madīnah, gave up their trade and their possessions, strove and fought for Allah's cause, sometimes against their own kith and kin or their own tribesmen who were enemies of Islam. They won through. Others were not prepared for such sacrifice, but their failure did not stop the accomplishment of Allah's plan and purpose.

His Decision: and Allah
Guides not the rebellious.

بِأَمْرِهِۦ ۗ وَٱللَّهُ لَا يَهْدِى ٱلْقَوْمَ ٱلْفَـٰسِقِينَ

SECTION 4.

25. Assuredly Allah did help you
In many battlefields
And on the day of Ḥunayn:[1274]
Behold! your great numbers
Elated you, but they availed
You naught: the land,
For all that it is wide,
Did constrain you, and ye
Turned back in retreat.[1275]

٢٥ لَقَدْ نَصَرَكُمُ ٱللَّهُ فِى مَوَاطِنَ كَثِيرَةٍ ۙ
وَيَوْمَ حُنَيْنٍ ۙ إِذْ أَعْجَبَتْكُمْ كَثْرَتُكُمْ فَلَمْ
تُغْنِ عَنكُمْ شَيْـًٔا وَضَاقَتْ عَلَيْكُمُ
ٱلْأَرْضُ بِمَا رَحُبَتْ ثُمَّ وَلَّيْتُم مُّدْبِرِينَ

26. But Allah did pour His calm[1276]
On the Messenger and on the Believers,
And sent down forces which ye
Saw not: He punished
The Unbelievers: thus doth He
Reward those without Faith.

٢٦ ثُمَّ أَنزَلَ ٱللَّهُ سَكِينَتَهُۥ عَلَىٰ رَسُولِهِۦ وَعَلَى
ٱلْمُؤْمِنِينَ وَأَنزَلَ جُنُودًا لَّمْ تَرَوْهَا وَعَذَّبَ
ٱلَّذِينَ كَفَرُوا۟ ۚ وَذَٰلِكَ جَزَآءُ ٱلْكَـٰفِرِينَ

27. Again will Allah, after this,[1277]
Turn (in mercy) to whom

٢٧ ثُمَّ يَتُوبُ ٱللَّهُ مِنۢ بَعْدِ ذَٰلِكَ عَلَىٰ مَن

1274. Ḥunayn is on the road to Ṭā'if from Makkah about fourteen miles to the east of Makkah. It is a valley in the mountainous country between Makkah and Ṭā'if. Immediately after the conquest of Makkah, (A.H. 8), the Pagan idolaters, who were surprised and chagrined at the wonderful reception which Islam was receiving, organised a great gathering near Ṭā'if to concert plans for attacking the Prophet. The Hawāzin and the Thaqif tribes took the lead and prepared a great expedition for Makkah, boasting of their strength and military skill. There was on the other hand a wave of confident enthusiasm among the Muslims at Makkah, in which the new Muslims joined. The enemy forces numbered about 4,000 but the Muslim force reached a total of ten or twelve thousand, as everyone wished to join. The battle was joined at Ḥunayn, as described in the next note.

1275. For the first time the Muslims had at Ḥunayn tremendous odds in their favour. But this itself constituted a danger. Many in their ranks had more enthusiasm than wisdom, more a spirit of elation than of faith and confidence in the righteousness of their cause. The enemy had the advantage of knowing the ground thoroughly. They laid an ambush in which the advance guard of the Muslim forces was caught. The country is hilly, in which the enemy concealed himself. As soon as the Muslim vanguard entered the Ḥunayn valley, the enemy fell upon them with fury and caused havoc with their arrows from their places of concealment. In such ground the numbers of the Muslims were themselves a disadvantage. Many were slain, and many turned back in confusion and retreat. But the Prophet, as ever, was calm in his wisdom and faith. He rallied his forces and inflicted the most crushing defeat on the enemy.

1276. *Sakīn*: calm, peace, security, tranquility. *Cf.* 2:248. The Prophet never approved of over-weening confidence, or reliance merely upon human strength, or human resources or numbers. In the hour of danger and seeming disaster, he was perfectly calm, and with cool courage relied upon the help of Allah, Whose standard he carried. His calmness inspired all around him, and stopped the rout of those who had turned their backs. It was with Allah's help that they won, and their victory was complete. They followed it up with an energetic pursuit of the enemies, capturing their camps, their flocks and herds, and their families, whom they had boastfully brought with them in expectation of an easy victory.

1277. Examples of Allah's mercy and grace in difficult circumstances in one case illustrate His grace and mercy at all times to those who have faith.

He will: for Allah
Is Oft-Forgiving, Most Merciful.

يَشَآءُ ۚ وَٱللَّهُ غَفُورٌ رَّحِيمٌ

28. O ye who believe! Truly
The Pagans are unclean;[1278]
So let them not,
After this year of theirs,[1279]
Approach the Sacred Mosque.
And if ye fear poverty,[1280]
Soon will Allah enrich you,
If He wills, out of His bounty,
For Allah is All-Knowing,
All-Wise.

٢٨ يَٰٓأَيُّهَا ٱلَّذِينَ ءَامَنُوٓا۟ إِنَّمَا ٱلْمُشْرِكُونَ
نَجَسٌ فَلَا يَقْرَبُوا۟ ٱلْمَسْجِدَ ٱلْحَرَامَ بَعْدَ
عَامِهِمْ هَٰذَا ۚ وَإِنْ خِفْتُمْ عَيْلَةً فَسَوْفَ
يُغْنِيكُمُ ٱللَّهُ مِن فَضْلِهِۦٓ إِن شَآءَ ۚ
إِنَّ ٱللَّهَ عَلِيمٌ حَكِيمٌ

29. Fight those who believe not
In Allah nor the Last Day,
Nor hold that forbidden
Which hath been forbidden
By Allah and His Messenger,
Nor acknowledge the Religion
Of Truth, from among
The People of the Book,
Until they pay the *Jizyah*[1281]
With willing submission,[1282]
And feel themselves subdued.

٢٩ قَٰتِلُوا۟ ٱلَّذِينَ لَا يُؤْمِنُونَ بِٱللَّهِ
وَلَا بِٱلْيَوْمِ ٱلْءَاخِرِ وَلَا يُحَرِّمُونَ مَا حَرَّمَ ٱللَّهُ
وَرَسُولُهُۥ وَلَا يَدِينُونَ دِينَ ٱلْحَقِّ
مِنَ ٱلَّذِينَ أُوتُوا۟ ٱلْكِتَٰبَ
حَتَّىٰ يُعْطُوا۟ ٱلْجِزْيَةَ عَن يَدٍ وَهُمْ صَٰغِرُونَ

1278. *Unclean*: both literally and metaphorically; because Muslims are enjoined to be strict in ablutions and physical cleanliness, as well as in purity of mind and heart, so that their word can be relied upon.

1279. *This year of theirs*: there is a two-fold meaning: (1) now that you have complete control of Makkah, and are charged with the purity of worship there, shut out all impurity from this year; (2) you have seen how the Pagans have behaved this year; their year of power and misuse of that power may be called *their* year; it is over, and now you Muslims are responsible.

1280. The concourse in Makkah added to the profits of trade and commerce. "But fear not," we are told; "the Pagans are a waning power, bound to disappear, and you should strengthen your own community, that they may more than counterbalance the apparent loss of custom; and Allah has other means of improving your economic position." This actually happened. The Pagans were extinguished from Arabia, and the concourse of Pilgrims from all parts of the world increased the numbers more than a hundredfold. Here is common-sense, wisdom, and statesmanship, even if we look at it from a purely human point of view.

1281. *Jizyah*: the root meaning is compensation. The derived meaning, which became the technical meaning, was a poll tax levied from those who did not accept Islam, but were willing to live under the protection of Islam, and were thus tacitly willing to submit to its ideals being enforced in the Muslim State. There was no amount permanently fixed for it, and in any case it was merely symbolical—an acknowledgment that those whose religion was tolerated would in their turn not interfere with the preaching and progress of Islam. Imām Shāfi'i suggests one dīnār per year, which would be the Arabian gold dīnār of the Muslim States, equivalent in value to about half a sovereign, or about 5 or 7 rupees. See n. 410 to 3:75. The tax varied in amount, and there were exemptions for the poor, for females and children (according to Abū Ḥanifa), for slaves, and for monks and hermits. Being a tax on able-bodied males of military age, it was in a sense a commutation for military service. But see the next note.

1282. *'An Yadin* (literally, from the hand) has been variously interpreted. The hand being the symbol of power and authority, I accept the interpretation "in token of willing submission." The Jizyah was thus partly symbolic and partly a commutation for military service, but as the amount was insignificant and the exemptions numerous, its symbolic character predominated. See the last note.

C. 94.—The enemies of Faith would fain put out
(9:30-42.) Allah's light, but Allah's light will shine
More glorious than ever. Wealth
Is for use and on trust for mankind:
Hoard not, nor misuse it. Fight
A straight fight in the cause of Right:
Go forth bravely to strive and struggle,
And prove yourselves worthy of Allah.

SECTION 5.

30. The Jews call 'Uzayr a son[1283]
Of God, and the Christians
Call Christ the Son of God.
That is a saying from their mouth;
(In this) they but imitate[1284]
What the Unbelievers of old
Used to say. Allah's curse
Be on them: how they are deluded
Away from the Truth![1285]

٣٠ وَقَالَتِ ٱلْيَهُودُ عُزَيْرٌ ٱبْنُ ٱللَّهِ وَقَالَتِ
ٱلنَّصَٰرَى ٱلْمَسِيحُ ٱبْنُ ٱللَّهِ ذَٰلِكَ
قَوْلُهُم بِأَفْوَٰهِهِمْ يُضَٰهِـُٔونَ قَوْلَ
ٱلَّذِينَ كَفَرُوا۟ مِن قَبْلُ قَٰتَلَهُمُ
ٱللَّهُ أَنَّىٰ يُؤْفَكُونَ

31. They take their priests[1286]
And their anchorites to be
Their lords in derogation of
Allah,[1287]
And (they take as their Lord)
Christ, the son of Mary;
Yet they were commanded
To worship but One God:
There is no god but He.

٣١ ٱتَّخَذُوٓا۟ أَحْبَارَهُمْ وَرُهْبَٰنَهُمْ
أَرْبَابًا مِّن دُونِ ٱللَّهِ وَٱلْمَسِيحَ ٱبْنَ
مَرْيَمَ وَمَآ أُمِرُوٓا۟ إِلَّا لِيَعْبُدُوٓا۟ إِلَٰهًا
وَٰحِدًا لَّآ إِلَٰهَ إِلَّا هُوَ

1283. In n. 718 to v. 20, I have quoted passages from the Old Testament, showing how freely the expression "sons of God" was used by the Jews. A sect of them called 'Uzayr a son of God, according to Baidhāwi. In Appendix II (Sūrah 5.) I have shown that the constitution of Judaism dates from 'Uzayr (Ezra). The Christians still call Christ the Son of God.

1284. Taking men for gods or sons of God was not a new thing. All ancient mythologies have fables of that kind. There was less excuse for such blasphemies after the Prophets of Allah had clearly explained our true relation to Allah than in the times of primitive ignorance and superstition.

1285. *Cf.* 5:78.

1286. *Aḥbār*: doctors of law; priests; learned men. *Cf.* 5:49, where they are associated with Rabbis. ***Ruhbān***: monks, ascetics, anchorites, men who have renounced the world; where there is a celibate clergy, the term can be applied to them as well as to members of monastic orders. It is also permissible to apply the term to "saints", where they are deified or credited with divine powers, or where people pray to them as they do in the Roman Catholic Church.

1287. Priest worship, and the worship of saints and ascetics is a form of superstition to which men have been prone in all ages. The growth of Jewish superstition is shown in the Talmud, and of Christian superstition in the doctrine of papal infallibility and the worship of saints. The mere idea of a separate order of priesthood to stand between Allah and man and be the exclusive repository of Allah's secrets is derogatory to the goodness and all-pervading grace of Allah. The worship of "lords many and gods many" was not confined only to the Pagans. The deification of the son of Mary is put here in a special clause by itself, as it held (and still holds) in its thrall a large portion of civilised humanity.

Praise and glory to Him:[1288]
(Far is He) from having
The partners they associate
(With Him).

سُبۡحَٰنَهُۥ
عَمَّا يُشۡرِكُونَ

32. Fain would they extinguish
Allah's Light with their mouths,[1289]
But Allah will not allow
But that His Light should be
Perfected, even though the
Unbelievers
May detest (it).

٣٢ يُرِيدُونَ أَن يُطۡفِـُٔواْ نُورَ ٱللَّهِ
بِأَفۡوَٰهِهِمۡ وَيَأۡبَى ٱللَّهُ إِلَّآ أَن يُتِمَّ نُورَهُۥ
وَلَوۡ كَرِهَ ٱلۡكَٰفِرُونَ

33. It is He Who hath sent
His Messenger with Guidance
And the Religion of Truth,
To proclaim it[1290]
Over all religion,
Even though the Pagans
May detest (it).

٣٣ هُوَ ٱلَّذِيٓ أَرۡسَلَ رَسُولَهُۥ بِٱلۡهُدَىٰ
وَدِينِ ٱلۡحَقِّ لِيُظۡهِرَهُۥ عَلَى ٱلدِّينِ كُلِّهِۦ
وَلَوۡ كَرِهَ ٱلۡمُشۡرِكُونَ

34. O ye who believe! There are
Indeed many among the priests
And anchorites, who in
falsehood[1291]
Devour the substance of men
And hinder (them) from the Way
Of Allah. And there are those
Who bury gold and silver[1292]
And spend it not in the Way

٣٤ يَٰٓأَيُّهَا ٱلَّذِينَ ءَامَنُوٓاْ إِنَّ كَثِيرٗا مِّنَ
ٱلۡأَحۡبَارِ وَٱلرُّهۡبَانِ لَيَأۡكُلُونَ أَمۡوَٰلَ ٱلنَّاسِ
بِٱلۡبَٰطِلِ وَيَصُدُّونَ عَن سَبِيلِ ٱللَّهِۗ
وَٱلَّذِينَ يَكۡنِزُونَ ٱلذَّهَبَ وَٱلۡفِضَّةَ
وَلَا يُنفِقُونَهَا فِي سَبِيلِ

1288. *Cf.* 6:100.

1289. *With their mouths*: there is a twofold meaning: (1) the old-fashioned open oil lamps were extinguished by blowing with the mouth: the Unbelievers would like to blow out Allah's Light as It is a cause of offence to them; (2) false teachers and preachers distort the Message of Allah by the false words of their mouth. Their wish is to put out the light of Truth for they are people of darkness; but Allah will perfect His Light, *i.e.*, make It shine all the brighter in the eyes of men. His Light in itself is ever perfect, but It will penetrate the hearts of men more and more, and so become more and more perfect for them.

1290. Every religion which commends itself widely to human beings and lasts through some space of time has a glimpse of Truth in it. But Islam being the perfect light of Truth is bound to prevail. As the greater Light, through its own strength, outshines all lesser lights, so will Islam outshine all else, in spite of the displeasure of those to whom light is an offence. See also 48:28, n. 4912, and 61:9, n. 5442.

1291. *Bil bāṭili* = in falsehood, *i.e.*, by false means, pretences, or in false or vain things. This was strikingly exemplified in the history of Mediaeval Europe, though the disease is apt to attack all peoples and organisations at all times. Priests got rich by issuing indulgences and dispensations; they made their office a stepping stone to worldly power and possessions. Even the Monastic Orders, which took vows of poverty for individuals grew rich with corporate property, until their wealth became a scandal, even among their own nations.

1292. Misuse of wealth, property, and resources is frequently condemned, and in three ways: (1) do not acquire anything wrongfully or on false pretences; (2) do not hoard or bury or amass wealth for its own sake but use it freely for good, whether for yourself or for your neighbours; and (3) be particularly careful not to waste it for idle purposes, but only so that it may fructify for the good of the people.

Of Allah: announce unto them
A most grievous penalty—

ٱللَّهِ فَبَشِّرْهُم بِعَذَابٍ أَلِيمٍ

35. On the Day when heat[1293]
Will be produced out of
That (wealth) in the fire
Of Hell, and with it will be
Branded their foreheads,
Their flanks, and their backs—
"This is the (treasure) which ye
Buried for yourselves:[1294] taste ye,
Then, the (treasures) ye buried!"

٣٥ يَوْمَ يُحْمَىٰ عَلَيْهَا فِى نَارِ جَهَنَّمَ
فَتُكْوَىٰ بِهَا جِبَاهُهُمْ وَجُنُوبُهُمْ
وَظُهُورُهُمْ هَٰذَا مَا كَنَزْتُمْ لِأَنفُسِكُمْ
فَذُوقُوا مَا كُنتُمْ تَكْنِزُونَ

36. The number of months[1295]
In the sight of Allah
Is twelve (in a year)—
So ordained by Him
The day He created
The heavens and the earth;
Of them four are sacred:
That is the straight usage.
So wrong not yourselves[1296]
Therein, and fight the Pagans
All together as they
Fight you all together.
But know that Allah

٣٦ إِنَّ عِدَّةَ ٱلشُّهُورِ عِندَ ٱللَّهِ ٱثْنَا عَشَرَ
شَهْرًا فِى كِتَٰبِ ٱللَّهِ يَوْمَ خَلَقَ ٱلسَّمَٰوَٰتِ
وَٱلْأَرْضَ مِنْهَآ أَرْبَعَةٌ حُرُمٌ ذَٰلِكَ ٱلدِّينُ
ٱلْقَيِّمُ فَلَا تَظْلِمُوا فِيهِنَّ أَنفُسَكُمْ
وَقَٰتِلُوا ٱلْمُشْرِكِينَ كَآفَّةً كَمَا
يُقَٰتِلُونَكُمْ كَآفَّةً وَٱعْلَمُوٓا أَنَّ ٱللَّهَ

1293. Gold and silver, symbolising wealth which these people cherished even more than the good pleasure of their Lord, will not only be the cause but the instrument whereby they would receive a grievous punishment. (Ed.).

1294. The voice enforces the moral: "did you expect satisfaction or salvation from the treasures that you misused? Behold! they add to your torment!"

1295. This and the following verse must be read together. They condemn the arbitrary and selfish conduct of the Pagan Arabs, who, because there was a long-established custom of observing four months as those in which fighting was forbidden, changed the months about or added or deducted months when it suited them, to get an unfair advantage over the enemy. The four Prohibited Months were: Dhu al Qa'dah, Dhu al Hijjah, Muḥarram, and Rajab. If it suited them they postponed one of these months, and so a prohibited month became an ordinary month: while their opponents might hesitate to fight, they got an undue advantage. It also upset the security of the Month of Pilgrimage. This very ancient usage made for fair dealing all round, and its infraction by the Pagans is condemned.

The question of a solar astronomical year as against the lunar Islamic year does not arise here. But it may be noted that the Arab year was roughly luni-solar like the Hindu year, the months being lunar and the intercalation of a month every three years brought the year nearly but not accurately up to the solar reckoning. From the year of the Farewell Pilgrimage (A.H. 10) the Islamic year was definitely fixed as a purely lunar year of roughly 354 days, the months being calculated by the actual appearance of the moon. After that, every month of the Islamic year came about 11 days earlier in the solar year, and thus the Islamic months travelled all round the seasons and the solar year. (R).

1296. The Muslims were at a disadvantage on account of their scruples about the Prohibited Months. They are told not to wrong themselves in this. If the Pagans fought in all months on one pretence or another, they were allowed to defend themselves in all months. But self-restraint was (as always) recommended as far as possible.

Is with those who restrain
Themselves.

مَعَ ٱلْمُتَّقِينَ

37. Verily the transposing[1297]
(Of a prohibited month)
Is an addition to Unbelief:
The Unbelievers are led
To wrong thereby: for they make
It lawful one year,
And forbidden another year,
In order to adjust the number
Of months forbidden by Allah
And make such forbidden ones
Lawful. The evil of their course
Seems pleasing to them.[1298]
But Allah guideth not
Those who reject Faith.

٣٧ إِنَّمَا ٱلنَّسِىٓءُ زِيَادَةٌ فِى
ٱلْكُفْرِ يُضَلُّ بِهِ ٱلَّذِينَ كَفَرُوا۟
يُحِلُّونَهُۥ عَامًا وَيُحَرِّمُونَهُۥ عَامًا
لِّيُوَاطِـُٔوا۟ عِدَّةَ مَا حَرَّمَ ٱللَّهُ
فَيُحِلُّوا۟ مَا حَرَّمَ ٱللَّهُ
زُيِّنَ لَهُمْ سُوٓءُ أَعْمَـٰلِهِمْ
وَٱللَّهُ لَا يَهْدِى ٱلْقَوْمَ ٱلْكَـٰفِرِينَ

SECTION 6.

38. O ye who believe! what
Is the matter with you,[1299]
That, when ye are asked
To go forth in the Cause of Allah,
Ye cling heavily to the earth?[1300]
Do ye prefer the life
Of this world to the Hereafter?
But little is the comfort
Of this life, as compared
With the Hereafter.

٣٨ يَـٰٓأَيُّهَا ٱلَّذِينَ ءَامَنُوا۟ مَا لَكُمْ إِذَا قِيلَ
لَكُمُ ٱنفِرُوا۟ فِى سَبِيلِ ٱللَّهِ ٱثَّاقَلْتُمْ إِلَى ٱلْأَرْضِ
أَرَضِيتُم بِٱلْحَيَوٰةِ ٱلدُّنْيَا مِنَ ٱلْـَٔاخِرَةِ
فَمَا مَتَـٰعُ ٱلْحَيَوٰةِ ٱلدُّنْيَا
فِى ٱلْـَٔاخِرَةِ إِلَّا قَلِيلٌ

1297. To meddle with an old-fashioned custom of close time for warfare during Prohibited or Sacred Months was not only a demonstration of the Unbelievers against the Muslims on account of their Faith, but was wrong and unjust in itself, as it abolished a wholesome check on unregulated warfare, and prejudiced the law-abiding side by arbitrary decisions.

1298. *Cf.* 6:122. The lawless man thinks he is doing a great thing in getting the better of those who are careful to observe a law they believe in. But the lawless man loses the guidance of Faith, which is a symbol of his being guided by Allah; he will therefore lose in the end.

1299. The immediate reference is to the expedition to Tabūk (A.H. 9), for which see the Introduction to this Sūrah. But the lesson is perfectly general. When a call is made on behalf of a great cause, the fortunate ones are those who have the privilege of responding to the call. The unfortunate ones are those who are so engrossed in their parochial affairs that they turn a deaf ear to the appeal. They are suffering from a spiritual disease.

1300. The choice is between two courses: will you choose a noble adventure and the glorious privilege of following your spiritual leader, or grovel in the earth for some small worldly gain or for fear of worldly loss? The people who hesitated to follow the call of Tabūk were deterred by (1) the heat of the summer, in which the expedition was undertaken on account of the threat to the existence of the little community, and (2) the fear of losing the fruit harvest, which was ripe for gathering.

39. Unless ye go forth,[1301]
He will punish you
With a grievous penalty,
And put others in your place;
But Him ye would not harm
In the least. For Allah
Hath power over all things.

﴿٣٩﴾ إِلَّا تَنفِرُوا يُعَذِّبْكُمْ عَذَابًا أَلِيمًا
وَيَسْتَبْدِلْ قَوْمًا غَيْرَكُمْ وَلَا تَضُرُّوهُ شَيْـًٔا ۗ
وَٱللَّهُ عَلَىٰ كُلِّ شَىْءٍ قَدِيرٌ

40. If ye help not (your Leader),
(It is no matter): for Allah
Did indeed help him,[1302]
When the Unbelievers
Drove him out: he had
No more than one companion:[1303]
The two were in the Cave,
And he said to his companion,
"Have no fear for Allah
Is with us": then Allah
Sent down His peace upon him,[1304]
And strengthened him with forces
Which ye saw not, and
humbled[1305]
To the depths the word
Of the Unbelievers.
But the word of Allah
Is exalted to the heights:
For Allah is Exalted in might,
Wise

﴿٤٠﴾ إِلَّا تَنصُرُوهُ فَقَدْ نَصَرَهُ ٱللَّهُ
إِذْ أَخْرَجَهُ ٱلَّذِينَ كَفَرُوا ثَانِىَ ٱثْنَيْنِ
إِذْ هُمَا فِى ٱلْغَارِ إِذْ يَقُولُ لِصَٰحِبِهِۦ
لَا تَحْزَنْ إِنَّ ٱللَّهَ مَعَنَا ۖ فَأَنزَلَ
ٱللَّهُ سَكِينَتَهُۥ عَلَيْهِ وَأَيَّدَهُۥ
بِجُنُودٍ لَّمْ تَرَوْهَا وَجَعَلَ
كَلِمَةَ ٱلَّذِينَ كَفَرُوا
ٱلسُّفْلَىٰ ۗ وَكَلِمَةُ ٱللَّهِ هِىَ
ٱلْعُلْيَا ۗ وَٱللَّهُ عَزِيزٌ حَكِيمٌ

1301. *Tanfirū* = go forth, march onward, be ready to strive and suffer. For this is the condition of all progress in the spiritual and moral, as well as in the physical, world. According to the homely English proverb, Allah helps those who help themselves. Inactivity and lethargy are fatal. No one can rest on his oars. Man is not necessary to Allah, but Allah is necessary to man. If a nation receives favours and fails to deserve them, it will be replaced by another: as has so often happened in history. We may take this as a special warning to Islamic nations.

1302. The Tabūk expedition was not a failure. Though some hesitated, many more joined in. But a more striking example was when the Prophet was forced to leave Makkah and performed his famous *Hijrah*. His enemies plotted for his life. He had already sent his followers on to Madīnah. Ali had volunteered to face his enemies in his house. His single companion was Abū Bakr. The two concealed themselves in the cave of Thaur, three miles from Makkah, for three nights, with the enemy prowling around in great numbers in fruitless search of them. "We are but two," said Abū Bakr. "Nay," said Muḥammad, "for Allah is with us." Faith gave their minds peace, and Allah gave them safety. They reached Madīnah, and a glorious chapter opened for Islam. The forces that helped them were not seen, but their power was irresistible. (R).

1303. Literally, "the second of two," which afterwards became Abū Bakr's proud title.

1304. *Cf.* 9:26.

1305. The superlatives in the Arabic I have rendered by the periphrases, "humbled to the depths" and "exalted to the heights," as they accord better with the genius of the English language. The enemies of Islam had boasted that they would root it out: the result showed them up as ridiculous and despicable.

41. Go ye forth, (whether equipped)[1306]
Lightly or heavily, and strive
And struggle, with your goods
And your persons, in the Cause
Of Allah. That is best
For you, if ye (but) knew.

﴿٤١﴾ انفروا خفافا وثقالا وجهدوا بأموالكم وأنفسكم في سبيل الله ذلكم خير لكم إن كنتم تعلمون

42. If there had been
Immediate gain (in sight),
And the journey easy,
They would (all) without doubt
Have followed thee, but
The distance was long,
(And weighed) on them.
They would indeed swear
By Allah, "If we only could,
We should certainly
Have come out with you:"
They would destroy their own souls;[1307]
For Allah doth know
That they are certainly lying.

﴿٤٢﴾ لو كان عرضا قريبا وسفرا قاصدا لاتبعوك ولكن بعدت عليهم الشقة وسيحلفون بالله لو استطعنا لخرجنا معكم يهلكون أنفسهم والله يعلم إنهم لكذبون

C. 95.—The Believers do their duty, and make
(9:43-72.) No excuses—unlike the Hypocrites,
Who are a burden whether they join you
Or hold back. No help should be accepted
From these last, as they are false and insincere,
And have a slanderous tongue. Alms
Are for the poor and the needy, not for those
Who come in hypocrisy and mock
At things solemn. But the Hypocrites
Will be found out and receive due punishment,
While the righteous will be rewarded
With bliss and the good pleasure of Allah.

1306. *Whether equipped lightly or heavily*: to be taken both literally and metaphorically. All were invited, and they were to bring such resources as they had—lightly armed or heavily armed, on foot or mounted, experienced men for posts of danger, raw men for duties for which they were fit—all would and should help. Even those who were too old or feeble to go could contribute such money or resources as they had.

1307. The arts and excuses of the Hypocrites are here exposed. If there had been booty in sight or an easy walk-over, they would have come. All their oaths are false, and in taking the false oaths they are destroying their spiritual life. Indeed the backsliders are jeopardising their own physical lives in hanging back. If the enemy succeeded, they would all suffer.

SECTION 7.

43. Allah give thee grace![1308] Why
Didst thou grant them exemption
Until those who told the truth
Were seen by thee in a clear light,
And thou hadst proved the liars?

عَفَا ٱللَّهُ عَنكَ لِمَ أَذِنتَ لَهُمْ حَتَّىٰ يَتَبَيَّنَ لَكَ ٱلَّذِينَ صَدَقُوا۟ وَتَعْلَمَ ٱلْكَٰذِبِينَ ﴿٤٣﴾

44. Those who believe in Allah
And the Last Day ask thee
For no exemption from fighting
With their goods and persons.
And Allah knoweth well
Those who do their duty.

لَا يَسْتَـْٔذِنُكَ ٱلَّذِينَ يُؤْمِنُونَ بِٱللَّهِ وَٱلْيَوْمِ ٱلْءَاخِرِ أَن يُجَٰهِدُوا۟ بِأَمْوَٰلِهِمْ وَأَنفُسِهِمْ ۗ وَٱللَّهُ عَلِيمٌۢ بِٱلْمُتَّقِينَ ﴿٤٤﴾

45. Only those ask thee for exemption
Who believe not in Allah
And the Last Day, and
Whose hearts are in doubt,
So that they are tossed[1309]
In their doubts to and fro.

إِنَّمَا يَسْتَـْٔذِنُكَ ٱلَّذِينَ لَا يُؤْمِنُونَ بِٱللَّهِ وَٱلْيَوْمِ ٱلْءَاخِرِ وَٱرْتَابَتْ قُلُوبُهُمْ فَهُمْ فِى رَيْبِهِمْ يَتَرَدَّدُونَ ﴿٤٥﴾

46. If they had intended
To come out, they would
Certainly have made
Some preparation therefor;
But Allah was averse
To their being sent forth;
So He made them lag behind,
And they were told,
"Sit ye among those
Who sit (inactive)."

وَلَوْ أَرَادُوا۟ ٱلْخُرُوجَ لَأَعَدُّوا۟ لَهُۥ عُدَّةً وَلَٰكِن كَرِهَ ٱللَّهُ ٱنۢبِعَاثَهُمْ فَثَبَّطَهُمْ وَقِيلَ ٱقْعُدُوا۟ مَعَ ٱلْقَٰعِدِينَ ﴿٤٦﴾

47. If they had come out
With you, they would not
Have added to your (strength)

لَوْ خَرَجُوا۟ فِيكُم مَّا زَادُوكُمْ ﴿٤٧﴾

1308. Literally, "Allah give thee forgiveness!" But there is no question of fault here, and Imām Rāzi understands the expression to mean an exclamation—as one might say in English, "God bless you!" In Shakespeare "God save you!" is a simple friendly greeting, without any question of danger: *e.g.*, in "Much Ado about Nothing," iii. 2. 82. Note that in Q. 3:152, last clause, "forgiveness" is put in juxtaposition to "grace" as having closely allied meanings. What the Holy Prophet had done in the Tabūk expedition was that he had been granting exemptions which may appear from a military point of view too liberal. He was actuated by motives of kindness as well as policy—kindness, because, in the urgency of the moment he did not wish anyone who had a real excuse to be refused exemption; and policy, because, if any one did not come with hearty good will, he would be a burden instead of a help to the army. The policy was justified, because in fact 30,000 men or more followed him. But that did not in any way jusify the slackers, and in a review of the position, the slackers and hypocrites are justly condemned.

1309. Doubt takes away all stability of conduct, while Faith makes a man firm in action and cool and collected in mind.

But only (made for) disorder,
Hurrying to and fro in your midst[1310]
And sowing sedition among you,
And there would have been
Some among you
Who would have listened to them.
But Allah knoweth well
Those who do wrong.

إِلَّا خَبَالًا وَلَأَوْضَعُوا خِلَٰلَكُمْ
يَبْغُونَكُمُ ٱلْفِتْنَةَ
وَفِيكُمْ سَمَّٰعُونَ لَهُمْ
وَٱللَّهُ عَلِيمٌۢ بِٱلظَّٰلِمِينَ

48. Indeed they had plotted
Sedition before, and upset
Matters for thee—until
The Truth arrived, and the Decree
Of Allah became manifest,
Much to their disgust.[1311]

٤٨ لَقَدِ ٱبْتَغَوُا ٱلْفِتْنَةَ مِن قَبْلُ
وَقَلَّبُوا لَكَ ٱلْأُمُورَ حَتَّىٰ جَآءَ ٱلْحَقُّ
وَظَهَرَ أَمْرُ ٱللَّهِ وَهُمْ كَٰرِهُونَ

49. Among them is (many) a man
Who says: "Grant me exemption
And draw me not[1312]
Into trial." Have they not
Fallen into trial already?
And indeed Hell surrounds
The Unbelievers (on all sides).

٤٩ وَمِنْهُم مَّن يَقُولُ ٱئْذَن لِّي
وَلَا تَفْتِنِّىٓ أَلَا فِي ٱلْفِتْنَةِ سَقَطُوا
وَإِنَّ جَهَنَّمَ لَمُحِيطَةٌۢ بِٱلْكَٰفِرِينَ

50. If good befalls thee,
It grieves them; but if
A misfortune befalls thee,
They say, "We took indeed
Our precautions beforehand,"
And they turn away rejoicing.

٥٠ إِن تُصِبْكَ حَسَنَةٌ تَسُؤْهُمْ وَإِن
تُصِبْكَ مُصِيبَةٌ يَقُولُوا قَدْ أَخَذْنَآ
أَمْرَنَا مِن قَبْلُ وَيَتَوَلَّوا وَّهُمْ فَرِحُونَ

1310. *Khilāl* has more than one meaning, but I follow the interpretation of Rāghib and the majority of accepted Commentators, who take it to mean "in your midst".

1311. Evil plotters against Truth are only too glad to get an opportunity of meddling from within with affairs which they want to spoil or upset. They plot from outside, but they like to get into the inner circle, that their chances of intrigue may be all the greater. They are, however, unwilling to incur any danger or any self-sacrifice. The whole of their activities are directed to mischief. Great wisdom is required in a leader to deal with such a situation, and the best of such leaders must need divine guidance, as was forthcoming in this case.

1312. *Fitnah*, as explained in n. 1198, 8:25, may mean either trial or temptation, or else tumult, turmoil, or sedition. The Commentators here take the former meaning, and explain that some Hypocrites claimed exemption from service in the Tabūk expedition in the direction of Syria on the plea that they could not withstand the charms of Syrian women and ought best to stay at home. The answer is: "But you have already fallen into temptation here by refusing service and disobeying the call." But perhaps the other meaning of "turmoil" may also be permissible as a secondary echo: in that case they object to be drawn into the turmoil of war, but they are told that they are already in a moral turmoil in advancing a disingenuous plea. In using the English word "trial" in the translation, I have also had in my mind the two shades of meaning associated with that word in English.

51. Say: "Nothing will happen to us
Except what Allah has decreed
For us: He is our Protector":
And on Allah let the Believers
Put their trust.

٥١ قل لن يصيبنا إلا ما كتب
الله لنا هو مولىنا وعلى الله فليتوكل
المؤمنون

52. Say: "Can you expect for us
(Any fate) other than one
Of two glorious things—
(Martyrdom or victory)?
But we can expect for you
Either that Allah will send
His punishment from Himself,
Or by your hands. So wait
(Expectant); we too
Will wait with you."[1313]

٥٢ قل هل تربصون بنا إلا إحدى
الحسنيين ونحن نتربص بكم أن يصيبكم
الله بعذاب من عنده أو بأيدينا
فتربصوا إنا معكم متربصون

53. Say: "Spend (for the Cause)
Willingly or unwillingly:[1314]
Not from you will it be
Accepted: for ye are indeed
A people rebellious and wicked."

٥٣ قل أنفقوا طوعا أو كرها لن يتقبل
منكم إنكم كنتم قوما فسقين

54. The only reasons why
Their contributions are not
Accepted are: that they reject
Allah and His Messenger;
That they come to prayer
Without earnestness; and that
They offer contributions
unwillingly.

٥٤ وما منعهم أن تقبل منهم نفقتهم
إلا أنهم كفروا بالله وبرسوله
ولا يأتون الصلوة إلا وهم كسالى
ولا ينفقون إلا وهم كرهون

55. Let not their wealth
Nor their (following in) sons[1315]
Dazzle thee: in reality

٥٥ فلا تعجبك أمولهم ولا أولدهم إنما

1313. The waiting of the Unbelievers and that of the Believers are in different senses. The Unbelievers wish for disaster to the Believers, but the Believers will either conquer or die as martyrs in the Cause, in either case happy in the issue. The Believers expect punishment for the Unbelievers for their infidelity, either through their own instrumentality, or in some other way in Allah's Plan, and the Unbelievers would not like it in either case. *Cf.* 6:158.

1314. The Hypocrites, who secretly plotted against Islam, might sometimes (and they did) make a show of making some contribution to the Cause in order to keep up their pretence. Their contributions were not acceptable, whether they seemed to give willingly or unwillingly, because rebellion and disobedience were in their hearts. Three reasons are specifically given for their rejection, in the next verse: (1) they did not believe; (2) their prayers were not earnest, but for mere show; and (3) in reality their hearts were not behind the contributions which they offered. Nothing is acceptable to Allah which does not proceed from a pure and sincere heart.

1315. If they appeared to be prosperous, with their purses and their quivers full (metaphorically), they were not to be envied. In reality their wealth and their sons might themselves be a snare: *Cf.* 8:28. On this particular occasion this was proved to the hilt. The wealth of the Pagans filled them with pride, darkened their understanding, and led to their destruction. Their sons and followers adopted the Faith which their fathers had fought against, much to the chagrin of the fathers, whose spiritual death was even worse than their discomfiture in this world.

Allah's Plan is to punish them
With these things in this life,[1316]
And that their souls may perish
In their (very) denial of Allah.

يُرِيدُ ٱللَّهُ لِيُعَذِّبَهُم بِهَا فِي ٱلْحَيَوٰةِ ٱلدُّنْيَا
وَتَزْهَقَ أَنفُسُهُمْ وَهُمْ كَٰفِرُونَ

56. They swear by Allah
That they are indeed
Of you; but they are not
Of you: yet they are afraid
(To appear in their true colours).

(٥٦) وَيَحْلِفُونَ بِٱللَّهِ إِنَّهُمْ لَمِنكُمْ
وَمَا هُم مِّنكُمْ وَلَٰكِنَّهُمْ قَوْمٌ يَفْرَقُونَ

57. If they could find
A place to flee to,
Or caves, or a place
Of concealment, they would
Turn straightway thereto,
With an obstinate rush.[1317]

(٥٧) لَوْ يَجِدُونَ مَلْجَـًٔا
أَوْ مَغَٰرَٰتٍ أَوْ مُدَّخَلًا
لَّوَلَّوْا۟ إِلَيْهِ وَهُمْ يَجْمَحُونَ

58. And among them are men
Who slander thee in the matter
Of (the distribution of) the alms.[1318]
If they are given part thereof,
They are pleased, but if not,
Behold! they are indignant!

(٥٨) وَمِنْهُم مَّن يَلْمِزُكَ فِي ٱلصَّدَقَٰتِ
فَإِنْ أُعْطُوا۟ مِنْهَا رَضُوا۟ وَإِن لَّمْ يُعْطَوْا۟
مِنْهَآ إِذَا هُمْ يَسْخَطُونَ

59. If only they had been content
With what Allah and His Messenger
Gave them, and had said,
"Sufficient unto us is Allah!
Allah and His Messenger will soon
Give us of His bounty:
To Allah do we turn our hopes!"
(That would have been the right course).[1319]

(٥٩) وَلَوْ أَنَّهُمْ رَضُوا۟
مَآ ءَاتَىٰهُمُ ٱللَّهُ وَرَسُولُهُۥ وَقَالُوا۟
حَسْبُنَا ٱللَّهُ سَيُؤْتِينَا ٱللَّهُ مِن فَضْلِهِۦ
وَرَسُولُهُۥٓ إِنَّآ إِلَى ٱللَّهِ رَٰغِبُونَ

1316. *Cf.* 3:176-178.

1317. ***Jamaḥa*** = to be ungovernable, to run like a runaway horse, to rush madly and obstinately.

1318. ***Ṣadaqāh*** = alms, that which is given in Allah's name, mainly to the poor and needy, and for the cognate purposes specified in the next verse but one. ***Zakāh*** is the regular and obligatory charity in an organised Muslim community, usually 2½ per cent of merchandise and 10 percent on the fruits of the earth. There is a vast body of literature on this subject. The main points may be studied in the ***Hidāya fil Furū***, of Shaikh Burhānud-din 'Ali. As against *zakah* the term *sadaqah* has a much wider connotation, and is inclusive of *zakat* as in the verse 60 of this sūrah. (R).

1319. Selfish men think that charitable funds are fair game for raids, but the Islamic standards on this subject are very high. The enforcement of such standards is always unpopular, and even the Holy Prophet was subjected to obloquy and slander for his strictness to principle. In doubtful cases, claimants who are disappointed should not blame the principles or those who enforce them, but put their trust in Allah, whose bounties are unbounded, and are given to all, whether rich or poor, according to their needs and their deserts. For everyone it is excellent advice to say: deserve before you desire.

SECTION 8.

60. Alms are for the poor
And the needy, and those
Employed to administer the
(funds);
For those whose hearts
Have been (recently) reconciled
(To the Truth); for those in
bondage
And in debt; in the cause
Of Allah; and for the
wayfarer:[1320]
(Thus is it) ordained by Allah,
And Allah is full of knowledge
And wisdom.

٦٠ إنما الصدقت
للفقراء والمسكين
والعملين عليها والمؤلفة قلوبهم
وفي الرقاب والغرمين وفي
سبيل الله وابن السبيل
فريضة من الله
والله عليم حكيم

61. Among them are men
Who molest the Prophet
And say, "He is (all) ear."[1321]
Say, "He listens to what is
Best for you: he believes
In Allah, has faith
In the Believers, and is a Mercy
To those of you who believe."
But those who molest the Prophet
Will have a grievous penalty.

٦١ ومنهم الذين يؤذون النبي
ويقولون هو أذن قل أذن خير
لكم يؤمن بالله ويؤمن للمؤمنين
ورحمة للذين ءامنوا منكم
والذين يؤذون رسول الله لهم عذاب أليم

62. To you they swear by Allah.
In order to please you:
But it is more fitting
That they should please
Allah and His Messenger,
If they are Believers.

٦٢ يحلفون بالله لكم ليرضوكم
والله ورسوله أحق أن يرضوه
إن كانوا مؤمنين

1320. Alms or charitable gifts are to be given to the poor and the needy and those who are employed in their service. That is, charitable funds are not to be diverted to other uses, but the genuine expenses of administering charity are properly chargeable to such funds. Who are the needy? Besides the ordinary indigent, there are certain classes of people whose need is great and should be relieved. Those mentioned here are: (1) men who have been weaned from hostility to Truth, who would probably be persecuted by their former associates, and require assistance until they establish new connections in their new environment; (2) those in bondage, literally and figuratively; captives of war must be redeemed; slaves should be helped to freedom; those in the bondage of ignorance or superstition or unfavourable environment should be helped to freedom to develop their own gifts; (3) those who are held in the grip of debt should be helped to economic freedom; (4) those who are struggling and striving in Allah's Cause by teaching or fighting or in duties assigned to them by the righteous Imam, who are thus unable to earn their ordinary living; and (5) strangers stranded on the way. All these have a claim to charity. They should be relieved by individual or organised effort, but in a responsible way. In this verse, the word *ṣadaqah* refers to obligatory charity (*zakāh*). See n. 1318 above. (R).

1321. The assonance of the Arabic words "*yu'dhūna*" and "*udhnun*" is of course lost in the Translation. But the sense remains. Detractors of the Prophet said: "O! he listens to everybody!" "Yes," is the answer, "he listens for their good; he is a mercy and a blessing to all men of Faith, but specially to you (who are addressed)." The general statement is emphasised for the particular people addressed.

63. Know they not that for those
Who oppose Allah and His
Messenger,
Is the Fire of Hell?—
Wherein they shall dwell.
That is the supreme disgrace.

٦٣ أَلَمْ يَعْلَمُوٓا۟ أَنَّهُۥ مَن يُحَادِدِ
ٱللَّهَ وَرَسُولَهُۥ فَأَنَّ لَهُۥ نَارَ جَهَنَّمَ خَٰلِدًا فِيهَا ۚ
ذَٰلِكَ ٱلْخِزْىُ ٱلْعَظِيمُ

64. The Hypocrites are afraid[1322]
Lest a Sūrah should be sent down
About them, showing them what
Is (really passing) in their hearts.
Say: "Mock ye! But verily
Allah will bring to light all
That ye fear (should be revealed)."

٦٤ يَحْذَرُ ٱلْمُنَٰفِقُونَ أَن تُنَزَّلَ عَلَيْهِمْ
سُورَةٌ تُنَبِّئُهُم بِمَا فِى قُلُوبِهِمْ ۚ قُلِ ٱسْتَهْزِءُوٓا۟
إِنَّ ٱللَّهَ مُخْرِجٌ مَّا تَحْذَرُونَ

65. If thou dost question them,
They declare (with emphasis):
"We were only talking idly
And in play." Say: "Was it
At Allah, and His Signs,
And His Messenger, that ye
Were mocking?"

٦٥ وَلَئِن سَأَلْتَهُمْ لَيَقُولُنَّ إِنَّمَا
كُنَّا نَخُوضُ وَنَلْعَبُ ۚ قُلْ أَبِٱللَّهِ وَءَايَٰتِهِۦ
وَرَسُولِهِۦ كُنتُمْ تَسْتَهْزِءُونَ

66. Make ye no excuses:
Ye have rejected Faith
After ye had accepted it.
If We pardon some of you,
We will punish others amongst
you,
For that they are in sin.[1323]

٦٦ لَا تَعْتَذِرُوا۟ قَدْ كَفَرْتُم
بَعْدَ إِيمَٰنِكُمْ ۚ إِن نَّعْفُ عَن طَآئِفَةٍ مِّنكُمْ
نُعَذِّبْ طَآئِفَةًۢ بِأَنَّهُمْ كَانُوا۟ مُجْرِمِينَ

Section 9.

67. The Hypocrites, men and women,
(Have an understanding) with
each other:[1324]
They enjoin evil, and forbid
What is just, and are close[1325]

٦٧ ٱلْمُنَٰفِقُونَ وَٱلْمُنَٰفِقَٰتُ بَعْضُهُم مِّنۢ
بَعْضٍ ۚ يَأْمُرُونَ بِٱلْمُنكَرِ وَيَنْهَوْنَ
عَنِ ٱلْمَعْرُوفِ وَيَقْبِضُونَ

1322. The dissection of the motives of the Hypocrites alarmed them. For it meant that they would fail in their policy of having the best of both worlds and undermining the loyalty of the weaker members of the Muslim community. So they turn it off as a jest. But they are sharply rebuked: "Can you make such solemn matters subjects of playful jokes? Fie upon you! You are found out, and your guile is of no effect." (R).

1323. See last note. Hypocrisy is a halfway house, a state of indecision in the choice between good and evil. Those who definitely range themselves with good obtain forgiveness; those who pass definitely to evil suffer the penalties of evil.

1324. Literally, "the Hypocrites. . .are of each other". The forms of hypocrisy may vary, but they are all alike, and they understand each other's hypocrisy. They hold together.

1325. The English phrase "close-fisted" would cover only a part of the meaning. The hand is the symbol of power, help, and assistance. They may be financial, or it may be in other ways. The Hypocrites pretend a great deal, but are of no use or real help to anyone.

With their hands. They have
Forgotten Allah; so He[1326]
Hath forgotten them. Verily
The Hypocrites are rebellious
And perverse.

أَيْدِيَهُمْ نَسُوا۟ ٱللَّهَ فَنَسِيَهُمْ
إِنَّ ٱلْمُنَـٰفِقِينَ هُمُ ٱلْفَـٰسِقُونَ

68. Allah hath promised the Hypocrites
Men and women, and the rejecters,
Of Faith, the fire of Hell:
Therein shall they dwell:
Sufficient is it for them:
For them is the curse of Allah,[1327]
And an enduring punishment—

وَعَدَ ٱللَّهُ ٱلْمُنَـٰفِقِينَ ﴿٦٨﴾
وَٱلْمُنَـٰفِقَـٰتِ وَٱلْكُفَّارَ
نَارَ جَهَنَّمَ خَـٰلِدِينَ فِيهَا ۚ هِىَ حَسْبُهُمْ ۚ
وَلَعَنَهُمُ ٱللَّهُ ۖ وَلَهُمْ عَذَابٌ مُّقِيمٌ

69. As in the case of those
Before you: they were
Mightier than you in power,
And more flourishing in wealth
And children. They had
Their enjoyment of their portion:
And ye have of yours, as did
Those before you; and ye
Indulge in idle talk
As they did. They!—
Their works are fruitless
In this world and in the Hereafter,
And they will lose
(All spiritual good).

كَٱلَّذِينَ مِن قَبْلِكُمْ كَانُوٓا۟ أَشَدَّ ﴿٦٩﴾
مِنكُمْ قُوَّةً وَأَكْثَرَ أَمْوَٰلًا وَأَوْلَـٰدًا فَٱسْتَمْتَعُوا۟
بِخَلَـٰقِهِمْ فَٱسْتَمْتَعْتُم بِخَلَـٰقِكُمْ كَمَا ٱسْتَمْتَعَ
ٱلَّذِينَ مِن قَبْلِكُم بِخَلَـٰقِهِمْ وَخُضْتُمْ كَٱلَّذِى
خَاضُوٓا۟ ۚ أُو۟لَـٰٓئِكَ حَبِطَتْ أَعْمَـٰلُهُمْ فِى
ٱلدُّنْيَا وَٱلْـَٔاخِرَةِ ۖ وَأُو۟لَـٰٓئِكَ هُمُ ٱلْخَـٰسِرُونَ

70. Hath not the story reached them
Of those before them?—
The people of Noah, and 'Ād,[1328]
And Thamūd; the people
Of Abraham, the men[1329]
Of Midian, and the Cities overthrown.[1330]

أَلَمْ يَأْتِهِمْ نَبَأُ ٱلَّذِينَ مِن قَبْلِهِمْ ﴿٧٠﴾
قَوْمِ نُوحٍ وَعَادٍ وَثَمُودَ وَقَوْمِ إِبْرَٰهِيمَ
وَأَصْحَـٰبِ مَدْيَنَ وَٱلْمُؤْتَفِكَـٰتِ ۚ

1326. *Cf.* 7:51 and n. 1029. They ignore Allah: and Allah will ignore them.

1327. "Curse," here as elsewhere, is deprivation of grace and mercy, brought about by the rejection of Allah by the Unbelievers.

1328. The story of Noah is told in 7:59-64; of 'Ād in 7:65-72; and of Thamūd in 7:73-79; of Abraham in numerous places, but see specially 6:74-82; of Midianites in 7:85-93; and of Lot and the Cities of the Plain overthrown for their wickedness, in 7:80-84.

1329. In the case of Noah and Abraham, the word I have translated as "people of..." is *qawm*; these prophets were messengers each to his own people or nation, as was also Hūd to the 'Ād people and Ṣāliḥ to the Thamūd people. The word used for the Midianites is *Aṣḥābi Madyan,* which I have translated "men of Midian" for want of a better word. The Midianites were for the greater part of their history nomads, with pasture grounds but no settled territory or town. The town of Madyan on the Gulf of 'Aqabah refers to much later times when the Midianites as a people had ceased to count. See n. 1053 to 7:85.

1330. The Cities of Plain, Sodom and Gomorrah, to whom Lot preached in vain to desist from their abominations: 7:80-84.

To them came their messengers
With Clear Signs. It is
Not Allah Who wrongs them,
But they wrong their own souls.

أَتَتْهُمْ رُسُلُهُم بِالْبَيِّنَٰتِ فَمَا كَانَ اللَّهُ
لِيَظْلِمَهُمْ وَلَٰكِن كَانُوٓا أَنفُسَهُمْ يَظْلِمُونَ

71. The Believers, men
And women, are protectors,
One of another: they enjoin
What is just, and forbid
What is evil: they observe
Regular prayers, practice
Regular charity, and obey
Allah and His Messenger.
On them will Allah pour
His Mercy: for Allah
Is Exalted in power, Wise.

﴿٧١﴾ وَالْمُؤْمِنُونَ وَالْمُؤْمِنَٰتُ بَعْضُهُمْ
أَوْلِيَآءُ بَعْضٍ يَأْمُرُونَ بِالْمَعْرُوفِ وَيَنْهَوْنَ
عَنِ الْمُنكَرِ وَيُقِيمُونَ الصَّلَوٰةَ وَيُؤْتُونَ
الزَّكَوٰةَ وَيُطِيعُونَ اللَّهَ وَرَسُولَهُۥٓ
أُولَٰٓئِكَ سَيَرْحَمُهُمُ اللَّهُ إِنَّ اللَّهَ عَزِيزٌ حَكِيمٌ

72. Allah hath promised to Believers—
Men and women—Gardens
Under which rivers flow,
To dwell therein,
And beautiful mansions
In Gardens of everlasting bliss.
But the greatest bliss
Is the Good Pleasure of Allah:
That is the supreme felicity.

﴿٧٢﴾ وَعَدَ اللَّهُ الْمُؤْمِنِينَ وَالْمُؤْمِنَٰتِ جَنَّٰتٍ
تَجْرِى مِن تَحْتِهَا الْأَنْهَٰرُ خَٰلِدِينَ فِيهَا
وَمَسَٰكِنَ طَيِّبَةً فِى جَنَّٰتِ عَدْنٍ وَرِضْوَٰنٌ
مِّنَ اللَّهِ أَكْبَرُ ذَٰلِكَ هُوَ الْفَوْزُ الْعَظِيمُ

C. 96.—The hardest striving and fighting are needed
(9:73-99.) To combat evil and hypocrisy; for sin
Can reach a stage when the doors of forgiveness
Are closed. The good must shun all evil
As unclean, and gladly welcome all chance
Of service and sacrifice, as bringing them closer
To the Presence and Mercy of Allah.

SECTION 10.

73. O Prophet! strive hard against
The Unbelievers and the
Hypocrites,
And be firm against them.
Their abode is Hell—
An evil refuge indeed.

﴿٧٣﴾ يَٰٓأَيُّهَا النَّبِىُّ جَٰهِدِ الْكُفَّارَ
وَالْمُنَٰفِقِينَ وَاغْلُظْ عَلَيْهِمْ
وَمَأْوَىٰهُمْ جَهَنَّمُ وَبِئْسَ الْمَصِيرُ

74. They swear by Allah that they
Said nothing (evil), but indeed
They uttered blasphemy,
And they did it after accepting

﴿٧٤﴾ يَحْلِفُونَ بِاللَّهِ مَا قَالُوا وَلَقَدْ
قَالُوا كَلِمَةَ الْكُفْرِ وَكَفَرُوا بَعْدَ

Islam; and they meditated[1331]
A plot which they were unable
To carry out: this revenge
Of theirs was (their) only return
For the bounty with which
Allah and His Messenger had enriched
Them! If they repent,
It will be best for them;
But if they turn back
(To their evil ways),
Allah will punish them
With a grievous penalty
In this life and in the Hereafter:
They shall have none on earth
To protect or help them.

إِسْلَٰمِهِمْ وَهَمُّوا۟ بِمَا لَمْ يَنَالُوا۟ۚ
وَمَا نَقَمُوٓا۟ إِلَّآ أَنْ أَغْنَىٰهُمُ
ٱللَّهُ وَرَسُولُهُۥ مِن فَضْلِهِۦۚ
فَإِن يَتُوبُوا۟ يَكُ خَيْرًا لَّهُمْۖ
وَإِن يَتَوَلَّوْا۟ يُعَذِّبْهُمُ ٱللَّهُ
عَذَابًا أَلِيمًا فِى ٱلدُّنْيَا وَٱلْءَاخِرَةِۚ
وَمَا لَهُمْ فِى ٱلْأَرْضِ مِن وَلِىٍّ وَلَا نَصِيرٍ

75. Amongst them are men
Who made a Covenant with Allah,
That if He bestowed on them
Of His bounty, they would give
(Largely) in charity, and be truly
Amongst those who are righteous.

٧٥ وَمِنْهُم مَّنْ عَٰهَدَ ٱللَّهَ لَئِنْ
ءَاتَىٰنَا مِن فَضْلِهِۦ لَنَصَّدَّقَنَّ
وَلَنَكُونَنَّ مِنَ ٱلصَّٰلِحِينَ

76. But when He did bestow
Of His bounty, they became
Covetous, and turned back
(From their Covenant), averse
(From its fulfilment).

٧٦ فَلَمَّآ ءَاتَىٰهُم مِّن فَضْلِهِۦ
بَخِلُوا۟ بِهِۦ وَتَوَلَّوا۟ وَّهُم مُّعْرِضُونَ

77. So He hath put as a consequence[1332]
Hypocrisy into their hearts,
(To last) till the Day whereon
They shall meet Him: because
They broke their Covenant
With Allah, and because they
Lied (again and again).

٧٧ فَأَعْقَبَهُمْ نِفَاقًا فِى قُلُوبِهِمْ
إِلَىٰ يَوْمِ يَلْقَوْنَهُۥ بِمَآ أَخْلَفُوا۟
ٱللَّهَ مَا وَعَدُوهُ وَبِمَا كَانُوا۟
يَكْذِبُونَ

1331. The reference is to a plot made by the Prophet's enemies to kill him when he was returning from Tabūk. The plot failed. It was all the more dastardly in that some of the conspirators were among the men of Madīnah, who were enriched by the general prosperity that followed the peace and good government established through Islam in Madīnah. Trade flourished; justice was firmly administered with an even hand. And the only return that these men could make was a return of evil for good. That was their revenge, because Islam aimed at suppressing selfishness, stood for the rights of the poorest and humblest, and judged worth by righteousness rather than by birth or position.

1332. If men are false to their covenants and words, the natural consequence will be hypocrisy to cover their falsehood. All consequences of our own acts are in Quranic language ascribed to Allah. Such consequences will last till the Day of Judgement, when they will have to account for their deeds. They may think that they are deceiving men by their hypocrisy, but they cannot deceive Allah, to Whom all their most secret thoughts and plots and doings are known.

78. Know they not that Allah
Doth know their secret (thoughts)
And their secret counsels,
And that Allah knoweth well
All things unseen?

(٧٨) أَلَمْ يَعْلَمُوٓا۟ أَنَّ ٱللَّهَ يَعْلَمُ سِرَّهُمْ
وَنَجْوَىٰهُمْ وَأَنَّ ٱللَّهَ عَلَّٰمُ ٱلْغُيُوبِ

79. Those who slander such
Of the Believers as give themselves
Freely to (deeds of) charity,
As well as such as can find
Nothing to give except
The fruits of their labour—
And throw ridicule on them—[1333]
Allah will throw back
Their ridicule on them:
And they shall have
A grievous penalty.

(٧٩) ٱلَّذِينَ يَلْمِزُونَ ٱلْمُطَّوِّعِينَ
مِنَ ٱلْمُؤْمِنِينَ فِى ٱلصَّدَقَٰتِ
وَٱلَّذِينَ لَا يَجِدُونَ إِلَّا جُهْدَهُمْ
فَيَسْخَرُونَ مِنْهُمْ سَخِرَ ٱللَّهُ مِنْهُمْ
وَلَهُمْ عَذَابٌ أَلِيمٌ

80. Whether thou ask
For their forgiveness,
Or not, (their sin is unforgivable):
If thou ask seventy times[1334]
For their forgiveness, Allah
Will not forgive them:
Because they have rejected
Allah and His Messenger; and Allah
Guideth not those
Who are perversely rebellious.

(٨٠) ٱسْتَغْفِرْ لَهُمْ أَوْ لَا تَسْتَغْفِرْ لَهُمْ
إِن تَسْتَغْفِرْ لَهُمْ سَبْعِينَ مَرَّةً
فَلَن يَغْفِرَ ٱللَّهُ لَهُمْ ذَٰلِكَ بِأَنَّهُمْ
كَفَرُوا۟ بِٱللَّهِ وَرَسُولِهِۦ
وَٱللَّهُ لَا يَهْدِى ٱلْقَوْمَ ٱلْفَٰسِقِينَ

SECTION 11.

81. Those who were left behind
(In the Tabūk expedition)
Rejoiced in their inaction
Behind the back of the Messenger
Of Allah: they hated to strive
And fight, with their goods
And their persons, in the Cause
Of Allah: they said,

(٨١) فَرِحَ ٱلْمُخَلَّفُونَ بِمَقْعَدِهِمْ
خِلَٰفَ رَسُولِ ٱللَّهِ وَكَرِهُوٓا۟
أَن يُجَٰهِدُوا۟ بِأَمْوَٰلِهِمْ وَأَنفُسِهِمْ
فِى سَبِيلِ ٱللَّهِ وَقَالُوا۟

1333. When financial help is necessary for the Cause, every Muslim contributes what he can. Those who can afford large sums are proud to bring them in of their own free will, and those who are very poor contribute their mite or their labour. Both kinds of gifts are equally precious because of the faith and good will behind them, and only cynics will laugh at the scantiness of the one or the lavishness of the other. Sometimes they not only laugh, but attribute wrong motives to the givers. Such conduct is here reprimanded.

1334. An awful warning for those who actively oppose the Cause of Allah. The Holy Prophet was by nature full of mercy and forgiveness. He prayed for his enemies. But in such a case even his prayers are nullified by their attitude of rejecting Allah.

"Go not forth in the heat."[1335]
Say, "The fire of Hell
Is fiercer in heat." If
Only they could understand!

لَا تَنفِرُوا فِي الْحَرِّ قُلْ نَارُ جَهَنَّمَ
أَشَدُّ حَرًّا لَّوْ كَانُوا يَفْقَهُونَ

82. Let them laugh a little:
Much will they weep:[1336]
A recompense for the (evil)
That they do.

﴿٨٢﴾ فَلْيَضْحَكُوا قَلِيلًا وَلْيَبْكُوا كَثِيرًا
جَزَاءً بِمَا كَانُوا يَكْسِبُونَ

83. If, then, Allah bring thee back
To any of them, and they ask
Thy permission to come out
(With thee), say: "Never shall ye
Come out with me, nor fight
An enemy with me:
For ye preferred to sit
Inactive on the first occasion:
Then sit ye (now)
With those who lag behind."

﴿٨٣﴾ فَإِن رَّجَعَكَ اللَّهُ إِلَىٰ طَائِفَةٍ مِّنْهُمْ
فَاسْتَأْذَنُوكَ لِلْخُرُوجِ فَقُل لَّن تَخْرُجُوا
مَعِيَ أَبَدًا وَلَن تُقَاتِلُوا مَعِيَ عَدُوًّا إِنَّكُمْ رَضِيتُم
بِالْقُعُودِ أَوَّلَ مَرَّةٍ فَاقْعُدُوا مَعَ الْخَالِفِينَ

84. Nor do thou ever pray
For any of them that dies,
Nor stand at his grave;[1337]
For they rejected Allah
And His Messenger, and died
In a state of perverse rebellion.

﴿٨٤﴾ وَلَا تُصَلِّ عَلَىٰ أَحَدٍ مِّنْهُم مَّاتَ أَبَدًا
وَلَا تَقُمْ عَلَىٰ قَبْرِهِ إِنَّهُمْ كَفَرُوا بِاللَّهِ
وَرَسُولِهِ وَمَاتُوا وَهُمْ فَاسِقُونَ

85. Nor let their wealth
Nor their (following in) sons
Dazzle thee: Allah's Plan
Is to punish them
With these things in this world,
And that their souls may perish
In their (very) denial of Allah.[1338]

﴿٨٥﴾ وَلَا تُعْجِبْكَ أَمْوَالُهُمْ وَأَوْلَادُهُمْ
إِنَّمَا يُرِيدُ اللَّهُ أَن يُعَذِّبَهُم بِهَا فِي الدُّنْيَا
وَتَزْهَقَ أَنفُسُهُمْ وَهُمْ كَافِرُونَ

1335. The Tabūk expedition had to be undertaken hurriedly in the heat of summer, because of a threat or fear of Byzantine invasion. They marched from Madīnah about the month of September or October in the solar calendar.

1336. They may sneer or ridicule or rejoice now: that will be only for a little; much will they have to weep for afterwards.

1337. On the death of a Muslim, it is the pious duty of every neighbouring Muslim who can, to assist in the simple funeral ceremonies—the prayer for mercy before the body is consigned to the grave, and the consignment of the body to the grave, by a simple, solemn, and dignified ritual. For those who have shown hostility to Islam, this would not be seemly and is forbidden. (R).

1338. Except for the omission of a single word ("life"), this verse repeats verse 55 above. But the repetition indicates the harmonious closing of the same argument in two aspects. In 9:55 it occurred in connection with the reasons for refusing to receive the contributions of such persons to the expenses of an enterprise which though vital to Islam's defence was secretly opposed by such persons. Here (in 9:85) it is a question of refusing to participate in the obsequies of such persons after their death: it is natural to omit the word "life" in this case.

86. When a Sūrah comes down,
Enjoining them to believe
In Allah and to strive and fight
Along with His Messenger,
Those with wealth and influence
Among them ask thee
For exemption, and say:
"Leave us (behind): we
Would be with those
Who sit (at home)."

٨٦ وَإِذَآ أُنزِلَتْ سُورَةٌ أَنْ ءَامِنُوا۟
بِٱللَّهِ وَجَٰهِدُوا۟ مَعَ رَسُولِهِ
ٱسْتَـْٔذَنَكَ أُو۟لُوا۟ ٱلطَّوْلِ مِنْهُمْ
وَقَالُوا۟ ذَرْنَا نَكُن مَّعَ ٱلْقَٰعِدِينَ

87. They prefer to be with
(the women),
Who remain behind (at home):[1339]
Their hearts are sealed
And so they understand not.

٨٧ رَضُوا۟ بِأَن يَكُونُوا۟ مَعَ ٱلْخَوَالِفِ
وَطُبِعَ عَلَىٰ قُلُوبِهِمْ فَهُمْ لَا يَفْقَهُونَ

88. But the Messenger, and those
Who believe with him,
Strive and fight with their wealth
And their persons: for them
Are (all) good things:[1340]
And it is they
Who will prosper.

٨٨ لَٰكِنِ ٱلرَّسُولُ وَٱلَّذِينَ ءَامَنُوا۟ مَعَهُۥ
جَٰهَدُوا۟ بِأَمْوَٰلِهِمْ وَأَنفُسِهِمْ ۚ وَأُو۟لَٰٓئِكَ
لَهُمُ ٱلْخَيْرَٰتُ ۖ وَأُو۟لَٰٓئِكَ هُمُ ٱلْمُفْلِحُونَ

89. Allah hath prepared for them
Gardens under which rivers flow,
To dwell therein:
That is the supreme felicity.[1341]

٨٩ أَعَدَّ ٱللَّهُ لَهُمْ جَنَّٰتٍ تَجْرِى مِن تَحْتِهَا
ٱلْأَنْهَٰرُ خَٰلِدِينَ فِيهَا ۚ ذَٰلِكَ ٱلْفَوْزُ ٱلْعَظِيمُ

SECTION 12.

90. And there were, among
The desert Arabs (also),
Men who made excuses
And came to claim exemption;

٩٠ وَجَآءَ ٱلْمُعَذِّرُونَ مِنَ
ٱلْأَعْرَابِ لِيُؤْذَنَ لَهُمْ

1339. *Khawālif*, plural of *Khālifah*, those (feminine) who remain behind at home when the men go to war; women. There is a stinging taunt in this, a suggestion that such men were cowards, preferring to remain behind like women when stiff work was to be done by men in defending their homes. They were not only cowards, but fools; as they did not understand their own best interests. If the enemy got the better of their brethren, they would themselves be crushed. "Their hearts are sealed": the habits of cowardice and hypocrisy which they have adopted have become their second nature.

1340. "Good things," and "prosperity," are to be understood both in the physical and in the highest spiritual sense as the next verse makes clear.

1341. In this verse there is a reminiscence, but not an exact repetition, of verse 72 above. This balances the parallel repetition or reminiscence in verse 85 above. See n. 1338. The symmetry of the argument is thus completed, as regards the Hypocrites of Madīnah, before we pass on to consider the case of the Hypocrites among the desert Bedouins in section 12.

And those who were false
To Allah and His Messenger
(Merely) sat inactive.[1342]
Soon will a grievous penalty
Seize the Unbelievers
Among them.

وَقَعَدَ ٱلَّذِينَ كَذَبُوا۟ ٱللَّهَ وَرَسُولَهُۥ ۚ سَيُصِيبُ ٱلَّذِينَ كَفَرُوا۟ مِنْهُمْ عَذَابٌ أَلِيمٌ

91. There is no blame[1343]
On those who are infirm,
Or ill, or who find
No resources to spend
(On the Cause), if they
Are sincere (in duty) to Allah
And his Messenger:
No ground (of complaint)
Can there be against such
As do right: and Allah
Is Oft-Forgiving, Most Merciful.

٩١ لَّيْسَ عَلَى ٱلضُّعَفَآءِ وَلَا عَلَى ٱلْمَرْضَىٰ وَلَا عَلَى ٱلَّذِينَ لَا يَجِدُونَ مَا يُنفِقُونَ حَرَجٌ إِذَا نَصَحُوا۟ لِلَّهِ وَرَسُولِهِۦ ۚ مَا عَلَى ٱلْمُحْسِنِينَ مِن سَبِيلٍ ۚ وَٱللَّهُ غَفُورٌ رَّحِيمٌ

92. Nor (is there blame)
On those who came to thee
To be provided with mounts,[1344]
And when thou saidst,
"I can find no mounts
For you," they turned back,
Their eyes streaming with tears
Of grief that they had
No resources wherewith
To provide the expenses.

٩٢ وَلَا عَلَى ٱلَّذِينَ إِذَا مَآ أَتَوْكَ لِتَحْمِلَهُمْ قُلْتَ لَآ أَجِدُ مَآ أَحْمِلُكُمْ عَلَيْهِ تَوَلَّوا۟ وَّأَعْيُنُهُمْ تَفِيضُ مِنَ ٱلدَّمْعِ حَزَنًا أَلَّا يَجِدُوا۟ مَا يُنفِقُونَ

1342. Not only had the Hypocrites a nest in Madīnah, but their tactics affected some of the village or desert Bedouins, who loved war and would have followed a standard of war even if no question of Faith or a sacred Cause was involved. But some of them, though professing Islam, were frightened by the hardships of the Tabūk expedition and the prospect of meeting the trained armies of the great Roman (Byzantine) Empire. They made all sorts of lying excuses, but really their want of faith made them ineligible for being enlisted in a sacred Cause, in the terms of 9:46-47 and 9:53-54. Some came to make excuses; others did not even come, but sat at home, ignoring the summons.

1343. Though active service in person or by contributing resources is expected in emergencies of every person who believes in the Cause, there are some who must necessarily be exempted without the least blame attached to them. Such would be those who are weak in body on account of age, sex, infirmity, or illness. Personal service in their case is out of the question, but they could contribute towards expenses if they are able. But if they are too poor to afford even such assistance, they are excused. But in all cases the motive must be sincere, and there should be a desire to serve and do such duty as they can. With such motives people are doing good or right in whatever form they express their service: sometimes, in Milton's words, "they also serve who only stand and wait." In any case their purity of motive would get Allah's grace and forgiveness, and we must not criticise even if we thought they might have done more.

1344. *Ḥamala, yaḥmilu*, here seems to mean: to provide means of transport, *viz.* mounts (horses, camels, etc.) for riding, and perhaps beasts of burden for carrying equipment and baggage, suitable to the rank of those concerned. It may possibly mean other facilities for getting about, such as boots and shoes, or provisions: for any army's march depends upon all these things. Where people fight as volunteers for a cause, without an extensive war fund, those who can afford it provide such things for themselves, but those without means, yet anxious to serve, have to be left behind. Their disappointment is in proportion to their eagerness to serve.

93. The ground (of complaint)
Is against such as claim
Exemption while they are rich.
They prefer to stay
With the (women) who remain
Behind: Allah hath sealed
Their hearts; so they know not
(What they miss).[1345]

٩٣ إِنَّمَا ٱلسَّبِيلُ عَلَى ٱلَّذِينَ
يَسْتَـْٔذِنُونَكَ وَهُمْ أَغْنِيَآءُ
رَضُوا۟ بِأَن يَكُونُوا۟ مَعَ ٱلْخَوَالِفِ
وَطَبَعَ ٱللَّهُ عَلَىٰ قُلُوبِهِمْ فَهُمْ لَا يَعْلَمُونَ

94. They will present their excuses
To you when ye return
To them. Say thou: "Present
No excuses: we shall not
Believe you: Allah hath already
Informed us of the true state
Of matters concerning you:
It is your actions that Allah
And His Messenger will observe:
In the end will ye
Be brought back to Him
Who knoweth what is hidden
And what is open:
Then will He show you
The truth of all
That ye did."

٩٤ يَعْتَذِرُونَ إِلَيْكُمْ
إِذَا رَجَعْتُمْ إِلَيْهِمْ قُل لَّا تَعْتَذِرُوا۟
لَن نُّؤْمِنَ لَكُمْ
قَدْ نَبَّأَنَا ٱللَّهُ مِنْ أَخْبَارِكُمْ
وَسَيَرَى ٱللَّهُ عَمَلَكُمْ وَرَسُولُهُۥ
ثُمَّ تُرَدُّونَ إِلَىٰ عَٰلِمِ ٱلْغَيْبِ
وَٱلشَّهَٰدَةِ فَيُنَبِّئُكُم بِمَا كُنتُمْ تَعْمَلُونَ

95. They will swear to you by Allah,
When ye return to them,
That ye may leave them alone.
So leave them alone:
For they are an abomination,
And Hell is their dwelling place—
A fitting recompense
For the (evil) that they did.

٩٥ سَيَحْلِفُونَ بِٱللَّهِ لَكُمْ إِذَا ٱنقَلَبْتُمْ
إِلَيْهِمْ لِتُعْرِضُوا۟ عَنْهُمْ فَأَعْرِضُوا۟ عَنْهُمْ
إِنَّهُمْ رِجْسٌ وَمَأْوَىٰهُمْ جَهَنَّمُ
جَزَآءًۢ بِمَا كَانُوا۟ يَكْسِبُونَ

96. They will swear unto you,
That ye may be pleased with them.
But if ye are pleased with them,
Allah is not pleased
With those who disobey.

٩٦ يَحْلِفُونَ لَكُمْ لِتَرْضَوْا۟ عَنْهُمْ
فَإِن تَرْضَوْا۟ عَنْهُمْ فَإِنَّ ٱللَّهَ لَا يَرْضَىٰ
عَنِ ٱلْقَوْمِ ٱلْفَٰسِقِينَ

97. The Arabs of the desert
Are the worst in unbelief
And hypocrisy, and most fitted
To be in ignorance

٩٧ ٱلْأَعْرَابُ أَشَدُّ كُفْرًا
وَنِفَاقًا وَأَجْدَرُ أَلَّا يَعْلَمُوا۟

1345. *Cf.* 9:87, where similar phrases are used for a similar shirking of duty by townsfolk, while here we are considering the desert folk. It is not only a duty, but a precious privilege, to serve a great Cause by personal self-sacrifice. Those who shirk such an opportunity know not what they miss.

Of the command which Allah
Hath sent down to His Messenger
But Allah is All-Knowing,
All-Wise.

حُدُودَ مَآ أَنزَلَ ٱللَّهُ عَلَىٰ رَسُولِهِۦۗ
وَٱللَّهُ عَلِيمٌ حَكِيمٌ

98. Some of the desert Arabs
Look upon their payments[1346]
As a fine, and watch
For disasters for you: on them
Be the disaster of Evil:
For Allah is He that heareth
And knoweth (all things).

(٩٨) وَمِنَ ٱلْأَعْرَابِ مَن يَتَّخِذُ مَا يُنفِقُ
مَغْرَمًا وَيَتَرَبَّصُ بِكُمُ ٱلدَّوَآئِرَۚ عَلَيْهِمْ
دَآئِرَةُ ٱلسَّوْءِۗ وَٱللَّهُ سَمِيعٌ عَلِيمٌ

99. But some of the desert Arabs
Believe in Allah and the Last Day,
And look on their payments
As pious gifts bringing them
Nearer to Allah and obtaining
The prayers of the Messenger.
Aye, indeed they bring them
Nearer (to Him): soon will Allah
Admit them to His Mercy:[1347]
For Allah is Oft-Forgiving,
Most Merciful.

(٩٩) وَمِنَ ٱلْأَعْرَابِ
مَن يُؤْمِنُ بِٱللَّهِ وَٱلْيَوْمِ ٱلْءَاخِرِ
وَيَتَّخِذُ مَا يُنفِقُ قُرُبَٰتٍ عِندَ ٱللَّهِ
وَصَلَوَٰتِ ٱلرَّسُولِۚ أَلَآ إِنَّهَا قُرْبَةٌ لَّهُمْۚ
سَيُدْخِلُهُمُ ٱللَّهُ فِى رَحْمَتِهِۦٓۗ
إِنَّ ٱللَّهَ غَفُورٌ رَّحِيمٌ

C. 97.—The vanguard of Faith think nothing
(9:100-118.) Of self-sacrifice. Their reward is God's
Good Pleasure. Even those who do wrong
But repent will obtain His Mercy: not so
Those who peresist in Unfaith, Hypocrisy,
And Mischief. Allah's grace is free and abounding
For the righteous. Even if they waver
Or fail, He will turn to them in Mercy,
If only they repent and come back unto Him.

1346. The payments refer to the regular Charity established by Islam—the obligatory alms. If you look upon them as a fine or a burden, their virtue is lost. If you rejoice that you have there an opportunity of helping the Community to maintain its standards of public assistance and to suppress the unseemly beggary and loathsome importunity whose relief is only governed by motives of getting rid of awkward obstacles on the way, then your outlook is entirely different. You wish for organised and effective efforts to solve the problems of human poverty and misery. In doing so, you get nearer to Allah, and you earn the good wishes and prayers of godly men, led by our Holy Leader, Muṣṭafā.

1347. The Mercy of Allah is always present, as the sun is always shining. But when we have prepared ourselves to receive it, we come to the full enjoyment of it, as a man who was in a shade comes out by his effort into the open, and basks in sunshine.

SECTION 13.

100. The vanguard (of Islam)—[1348]
The first of those who forsook
(Their homes) and of those
Who gave them aid, and (also)
Those who follow them
In (all) good deeds—
Well-pleased is Allah with them,
As are they with Him:
For them hath He prepared
Gardens under which rivers
flow,[1349]
To dwell therein forever:
That is the supreme Felicity.

(١٠٠) وَٱلسَّٰبِقُونَ ٱلْأَوَّلُونَ
مِنَ ٱلْمُهَٰجِرِينَ وَٱلْأَنصَارِ
وَٱلَّذِينَ ٱتَّبَعُوهُم بِإِحْسَٰنٍ
رَّضِىَ ٱللَّهُ عَنْهُمْ وَرَضُوا۟ عَنْهُ
وَأَعَدَّ لَهُمْ جَنَّٰتٍ تَجْرِى تَحْتَهَا
ٱلْأَنْهَٰرُ خَٰلِدِينَ فِيهَآ أَبَدًا ۚ ذَٰلِكَ ٱلْفَوْزُ ٱلْعَظِيمُ

101. Certain of the desert Arabs
Round about you are Hypocrites,
As well as (desert Arabs) among
The Madīnah folk:[1350] they are
Obstinate in hypocrisy: thou
Knowest them not: We know them:
Twice shall We punish them:[1351]
And in addition shall they be
Sent to a grievous Penalty.

(١٠١) وَمِمَّنْ حَوْلَكُم مِّنَ ٱلْأَعْرَابِ
مُنَٰفِقُونَ ۖ وَمِنْ أَهْلِ ٱلْمَدِينَةِ ۖ مَرَدُوا۟ عَلَى
ٱلنِّفَاقِ لَا تَعْلَمُهُمْ ۖ نَحْنُ نَعْلَمُهُمْ ۚ سَنُعَذِّبُهُم
مَّرَّتَيْنِ ثُمَّ يُرَدُّونَ إِلَىٰ عَذَابٍ عَظِيمٍ

102. Others (there are who) have
Acknowledged their wrongdoings:
They have mixed an act
That was good with another[1352]

(١٠٢) وَءَاخَرُونَ ٱعْتَرَفُوا۟ بِذُنُوبِهِمْ
خَلَطُوا۟ عَمَلًا صَٰلِحًا وَءَاخَرَ

1348. The vanguard of Islam—those in the first rank—are those who dare and suffer for the Cause and never flinch. The first historical examples are the Muhājirs and the Anṣār. The Muhājirs—those who forsook their homes in Makkah and migrated to Madīnah, the Holy Prophet being among the last to leave the post of danger, are mentioned first. Then come the Anṣār, the Helpers, the citizens of Madīnah who invited them, welcomed them, and gave them aid, and who formed the pivot of the new Community. Then are mentioned all who follow them in good deeds: not only the early heroes and ordinary men and women who had been Companions of the Prophet or had seen him, but men and women in all ages who have lived noble lives. In spite of all their sacrifices and suffering they rejoice in the precious gift of the Good Pleasure of Allah, and their Salvation is the Supreme Felicity which such Good Pleasure gives, symbolised by the Gardens of Heaven.

1349. Note the description of the final accomplishment of the destiny of man. In mathematical science it would be like a letter or formula which would sum up a long course of reasoning. In this very Sūrah it occurs before in 9:72 and 9:89, where see n. 1341. (R).

1350. The desert Arabs were not all simple folk. There were cunning hypocrites among them: both among certain tribes encamped round about Madīnah and certain others in Madīnah itself. I understand that both groups are of the *A'rāb,* to whom the context refers, and not of the settled citizens of Madīnah, whose Hypocrites were already referred to in previous sections. They might look simple, but they were, in their ignorance, all the more obstinate and hypocritical.

1351. Their punishment in this world was double, *viz.*, not only in their discomfiture, but because in their obstinate ignorance, they failed to understand the accomplished facts, while cleverer men realised that their hostility to Islam was hopeless. In addition to their discomfiture in this life, they would have to meet the penalties to come.

1352. There were some whose will was weak and succumbed to evil, although there was much good in them. To them is held out the promise of forgiveness if they would repent and undertake all acts of Muslim charity, which would purify their souls, aided by the prayers of Allah's Messenger. Then would they get the Peace that comes from purity and right conduct.

That was evil. Perhaps Allah
Will turn unto them (in mercy):
For Allah is Oft-Forgiving,
Most Merciful.

سَيِّئًا عَسَى ٱللَّهُ أَن يَتُوبَ عَلَيْهِمْ ۚ
إِنَّ ٱللَّهَ غَفُورٌ رَّحِيمٌ

103. Of their goods take alms,
That so thou mightest
Purify and sanctify them;
And pray on their behalf,
Verily thy prayers are a source
Of security for them:
And Allah is One
Who heareth and knoweth.

(١٠٣) خُذْ مِنْ أَمْوَٰلِهِمْ صَدَقَةً تُطَهِّرُهُمْ
وَتُزَكِّيهِم بِهَا وَصَلِّ عَلَيْهِمْ ۖ
إِنَّ صَلَوٰتَكَ سَكَنٌ لَّهُمْ ۗ
وَٱللَّهُ سَمِيعٌ عَلِيمٌ

104. Know they not that Allah
Doth accept repentance from
His votaries and receives
Their gifts of charity, and that
Allah is verily He,
The Oft-Returning, Most
Merciful?

(١٠٤) أَلَمْ يَعْلَمُوٓا۟ أَنَّ ٱللَّهَ هُوَ يَقْبَلُ
ٱلتَّوْبَةَ عَنْ عِبَادِهِۦ وَيَأْخُذُ ٱلصَّدَقَٰتِ
وَأَنَّ ٱللَّهَ هُوَ ٱلتَّوَّابُ ٱلرَّحِيمُ

105. And say: "Work
(righteousness):[1353]
Soon will Allah observe your work,
And His Messenger, and the
Believers:
Soon will ye be brought back
To the Knower of what is
Hidden and what is open:
Then will He show you
The truth of all that ye did."

(١٠٥) وَقُلِ ٱعْمَلُوا۟ فَسَيَرَى
ٱللَّهُ عَمَلَكُمْ وَرَسُولُهُۥ وَٱلْمُؤْمِنُونَ ۖ
وَسَتُرَدُّونَ إِلَىٰ عَٰلِمِ ٱلْغَيْبِ وَٱلشَّهَٰدَةِ
فَيُنَبِّئُكُم بِمَا كُنتُمْ تَعْمَلُونَ

106. There are (yet) others,
Held in suspense for the command
Of Allah, whether He will
Punish them, or turn in mercy[1354]
To them: and Allah
Is All-Knowing, Wise.

(١٠٦) وَءَاخَرُونَ مُرْجَوْنَ لِأَمْرِ
ٱللَّهِ إِمَّا يُعَذِّبُهُمْ وَإِمَّا يَتُوبُ عَلَيْهِمْ ۗ
وَٱللَّهُ عَلِيمٌ حَكِيمٌ

1353. The repentant should be encouraged, after their repentance, to amend their conduct. The kindly interest of their brethren in them will strengthen them in virtue and blot out their past. When they go back into Eternity, they will understand the healing grace which saved them, just as the evil ones will then have their eyes opened to the real truth of their spiritual degradation (9:94). The similar words, in verse 84 and here, clench the contrast.

1354. Three categories of men are mentioned, whose faith was tested and found wanting in the Tabūk affair, but their characteristics are perfectly general, and we may here consider them in their general aspects: (1) the deep-dyed hypocrites, who when found out make excuses because otherwise they will suffer ignominy; they are unregenerate and obstinate, and there is no hope for them (9:101); (2) there are those who have lapsed into evil, but are not altogether evil; they repent and amend, and are accepted (9:102-105); and (3) there are doubtful cases, but Allah will judge them (9:106). A fourth category is mentioned in 9:107, which will be discussed later.

107. And there are those[1355]
Who put up a mosque
By way of mischief and infidelity—
To disunite the Believers—
And in preparation for one[1356]
Who warred against Allah
And His Messenger aforetime.
They will indeed swear
That their intention is nothing
But good; but Allah doth declare
That they are certainly liars.

﴿١٠٧﴾ وَٱلَّذِينَ ٱتَّخَذُواْ مَسۡجِدٗا ضِرَارٗا
وَكُفۡرٗا وَتَفۡرِيقَۢا بَيۡنَ ٱلۡمُؤۡمِنِينَ
وَإِرۡصَادٗا لِّمَنۡ حَارَبَ ٱللَّهَ وَرَسُولَهُۥ مِن قَبۡلُۚ
وَلَيَحۡلِفُنَّ إِنۡ أَرَدۡنَآ إِلَّا ٱلۡحُسۡنَىٰۖ
وَٱللَّهُ يَشۡهَدُ إِنَّهُمۡ لَكَٰذِبُونَ

108. Never stand thou forth therein.
There is a mosque whose foundation[1357]
Was laid from the first day
On piety; it is more worthy
Of thy standing forth (for prayer)
Therein. In it are men who
Love to be purified; and Allah
Loveth those who make themselves pure.[1358]

﴿١٠٨﴾ لَا تَقُمۡ فِيهِ أَبَدٗاۚ لَّمَسۡجِدٌ أُسِّسَ
عَلَى ٱلتَّقۡوَىٰ مِنۡ أَوَّلِ يَوۡمٍ أَحَقُّ أَن
تَقُومَ فِيهِۚ فِيهِ رِجَالٞ يُحِبُّونَ
أَن يَتَطَهَّرُواْۚ وَٱللَّهُ يُحِبُّ ٱلۡمُطَّهِّرِينَ

109. Which then is best?—he that
Layeth his foundation
On piety to Allah
And His Good Pleasure?—or he
That layeth his foundation
On an undermined sand cliff[1359]

﴿١٠٩﴾ أَفَمَنۡ أَسَّسَ بُنۡيَٰنَهُۥ عَلَىٰ تَقۡوَىٰ
مِنَ ٱللَّهِ وَرِضۡوَٰنٍ خَيۡرٌ أَم مَّنۡ أَسَّسَ
بُنۡيَٰنَهُۥ عَلَىٰ شَفَا جُرُفٍ هَارٍ

1355. Three categories of Hypocrites having already been mentioned (n. 1354), a fourth class of insidious evildoers is now mentioned, whose type is illustrated in the story of the Qubā "Mosque of mischief (*ḍirār*)". Qubā is a suburb of Madīnah, about three miles to the southeast. When the Holy Prophet arrived at Madīnah for Hijrah, he rested four days in Qubā before entering the town of Madīnah. Here was built the first mosque, the "Mosque of Piety" (*Taqwā*, or the mosque of the power of Islam (*Qūwah al Islam*), to which he frequently came during his subsequent stay in Madīnah. Taking advantage of these sacred associations, some Hypocrites of the Tribe of Banī Ghanam built an opposition mosque in Qubā, pretending to advance Islam. In reality they were in league with a notorious enemy of Islam, one Abū 'Āmir, who had fought against Islam at Uhud and who was now, after the battle of Ḥunayn (A.H. 9), in Syria; his confederates wanted a mosque for him to come to, but it would only be a source of mischief and division, and the scheme was disapproved.

1356. Abū 'Āmir, surnamed the *Rāhib* (Monk), as he had been in touch with Christian monks. See last note.

1357. The original "Mosque of Piety" built by the Holy Prophet himself.

1358. The true Muslim must be pure in body, mind, and heart. His motives should always be sincere, and his religion without any alloy of worldly gain.

1359. A man who builds his life on Piety (which includes sincerity and the purity of all motives) and his hopes on the Good Pleasure of Allah, builds on a firm foundation of rock that will never be shaken. In contrast to him is the man who builds on a shifting sand cliff on the brink of an abyss, already undermined by forces which he does not see. The cliff and the foundations all crumble to pieces along with him, and he is plunged into the Fire of misery from which there is no escape.

Ready to crumble to pieces?
And it doth crumble to pieces
With him, into the fire
Of Hell. And Allah guideth not
People that do wrong.

فَانْهَارَ بِهِ فِي نَارِ جَهَنَّمَ
وَاللَّهُ لَا يَهْدِي الْقَوْمَ الظَّالِمِينَ

110. The foundation of those
Who so build is never free
From suspicion and shakiness[1360]
In their hearts, until
Their hearts are cut to pieces.
And Allah is All-Knowing, Wise.

١١٠ لَا يَزَالُ بُنْيَانُهُمُ الَّذِي بَنَوْا رِيبَةً
فِي قُلُوبِهِمْ إِلَّا أَنْ تَقَطَّعَ قُلُوبُهُمْ
وَاللَّهُ عَلِيمٌ حَكِيمٌ

SECTION 14.

111. Allah hath purchased of the Believers
Their persons and their goods;
For theirs (in return)
Is the Garden (of Paradise):[1361]
They fight in His Cause,
And slay and are slain:
A promise binding on Him
In Truth, through the Law,
The Gospel, and the Qur'ān:[1362]
And who is more faithful
To his Covenant than Allah?

١١١ إِنَّ اللَّهَ اشْتَرَى مِنَ الْمُؤْمِنِينَ
أَنْفُسَهُمْ وَأَمْوَالَهُمْ بِأَنَّ لَهُمُ الْجَنَّةَ
يُقَاتِلُونَ فِي سَبِيلِ اللَّهِ فَيَقْتُلُونَ
وَيُقْتَلُونَ وَعْدًا عَلَيْهِ حَقًّا فِي
التَّوْرَاةِ وَالْإِنْجِيلِ وَالْقُرْآنِ
وَمَنْ أَوْفَى بِعَهْدِهِ مِنَ اللَّهِ

1360. The parable is continued further. The heart of man is the seat of his hopes and fears, the foundation of his moral and spiritual life. If that foundation is on an undermined sand cliff already crumbling to pieces, what security or stability can he have? He is being shaken by alarms and suspicions and superstitions, until like the edge of a sand cliff they are cut clean away and fall into a heap of ruin and his spiritual life and all its landmarks are destroyed.

1361. In a human bargain both sides give something and receive some advantage. In the divine bargain of Allah with man, Allah takes man's will and soul and his wealth and goods, and gives him in return everlasting Felicity. Man fights in Allah's Cause and carries out His will. All that he has to give up is the ephemeral things of this world, while he gains eternal salvation, the fulfilment of his highest spiritual hopes—a supreme achievement indeed.

1362. We offer our whole selves and our possessions to Allah, and Allah gives us Salvation. This is the true doctrine of redemption; and we are taught that this is the doctrine not only of the Qur'ān but of the earlier Revelations—the original Law of Moses and the original Gospel of Jesus. Any other view of redemption is rejected by Islam, especially that of corrupted Christianity, which thinks that some other person suffered for our sins and we are redeemed by his blood. It is our self-surrender that counts, not other people's merits. Our complete self-surrender may include fighting for the cause, both spiritually and physically. As regards actual fighting with the sword there has been some difference in theological theories at different times, but very little in the practice of those who framed those theories. The Jewish wars were ruthless wars of extermination. The Old Testament does not mince matters on the subject. In the New Testament St. Paul, in commending the worthy fruits of Faith, mentions Gideon, Barak, and other warriors of the Old Testament as his ideals, "Who through faith subdued kingdoms. . .waxed valiant in fight, turned to flight the armies of the aliens. . ." (Hebrews, xi. 32-34). The monkish morality of the Gospels in their present form has never been followed by any self-respecting Christian or other nation in history. Nor is it common sense to ignore lust of blood in unregenerate man as a form of evil which has to be combatted "within the limits set by Allah" (Q. 9:112). (R).

Then rejoice in the bargain
Which ye have concluded:
That is the achievement supreme.

فَٱسْتَبْشِرُوا۟ بِبَيْعِكُمُ ٱلَّذِى بَايَعْتُم بِهِۦ ۚ
وَذَٰلِكَ هُوَ ٱلْفَوْزُ ٱلْعَظِيمُ

112. Those that turn (to Allah)[1363]
In repentance; that serve Him,
And praise Him; that wander
In devotion to the Cause of Allah;
That bow down and prostrate themselves
In prayer; that enjoin good
And forbid evil; and observe
The limits set by Allah—
(These do rejoice). So proclaim
The glad tidings to the Believers.

١١٢ ٱلتَّٰٓئِبُونَ ٱلْعَٰبِدُونَ
ٱلْحَٰمِدُونَ ٱلسَّٰٓئِحُونَ
ٱلرَّٰكِعُونَ ٱلسَّٰجِدُونَ ٱلْءَامِرُونَ
بِٱلْمَعْرُوفِ وَٱلنَّاهُونَ عَنِ ٱلْمُنكَرِ
وَٱلْحَٰفِظُونَ لِحُدُودِ ٱللَّهِ ۗ وَبَشِّرِ ٱلْمُؤْمِنِينَ

113. It is not fitting,
For the Prophet and those
Who believe, that they should
Pray for forgiveness
For Pagans, even though
They be of kin, after it is
Clear to them that they
Are companions of the Fire.[1364]

١١٣ مَا كَانَ لِلنَّبِىِّ وَٱلَّذِينَ ءَامَنُوٓا۟ أَن
يَسْتَغْفِرُوا۟ لِلْمُشْرِكِينَ وَلَوْ كَانُوٓا۟
أُو۟لِى قُرْبَىٰ مِنۢ بَعْدِ مَا تَبَيَّنَ لَهُمْ
أَنَّهُمْ أَصْحَٰبُ ٱلْجَحِيمِ

114. And Abraham prayed
For his father's forgiveness
Only because of a promise
He had made to him.[1365]
But when it became clear
To him that he was
An enemy to Allah, he
Dissociated himself from him:

١١٤ وَمَا كَانَ ٱسْتِغْفَارُ إِبْرَٰهِيمَ لِأَبِيهِ
إِلَّا عَن مَّوْعِدَةٍ وَعَدَهَآ إِيَّاهُ
فَلَمَّا تَبَيَّنَ لَهُۥٓ أَنَّهُۥ
عَدُوٌّ لِّلَّهِ تَبَرَّأَ مِنْهُ

1363. We are to rejoice that by giving up such small things as ourselves and our possessions we are to be rewarded with such a great thing as the eternal life of felicity. The truly righteous, whose lives in various aspects are described in this verse, do so rejoice. The good news is to be proclaimed to all Believers, including the weakest among us, so that they may profit by that example.

1364. This is usually understood to refer to the prayer for the dead, (1) if they died unrepentant after Islam was preached to them, (2) if they actively resisted or opposed the Faith *to the last*, and (3) if the person praying knows that on account of deliberate contumacy the deceased may be said to have had the doors of mercy closed to him. How is he to know? The knowledge must come from special commands as declared by the Holy Prophet in his lifetime regarding individuals. Where no light is available from this source we must follow the best judgement we can.

1365. Abraham and his unbelieving father are referred to in 6:74. Apparently when Abraham was convinced that the conditions mentioned in the last note applied to his father, he gave up praying for him, as the physical bond was cut off by the spiritual hostility. For the promise to pray for his father, see 19:47.

For Abraham was most
Tender-hearted, forbearing.[1366]

إِنَّ إِبْرَٰهِيمَ لَأَوَّٰهٌ حَلِيمٌ

115. And Allah will not mislead[1367]
A people after He hath
Guided them, in order that
He may make clear to them
What to fear (and avoid)—
For Allah hath knowledge
Of all things.

(١١٥) وَمَا كَانَ ٱللَّهُ لِيُضِلَّ قَوْمًۢا
بَعْدَ إِذْ هَدَىٰهُمْ حَتَّىٰ يُبَيِّنَ لَهُم
مَّا يَتَّقُونَ ۚ إِنَّ ٱللَّهَ بِكُلِّ شَىْءٍ عَلِيمٌ

116. Unto Allah belongeth
The dominion of the heavens
And the earth. He giveth life
And He taketh it. Except for Him
Ye have no protector
Nor helper.

(١١٦) إِنَّ ٱللَّهَ لَهُۥ مُلْكُ ٱلسَّمَٰوَٰتِ
وَٱلْأَرْضِ ۖ يُحْىِۦ وَيُمِيتُ ۚ وَمَا لَكُم مِّن
دُونِ ٱللَّهِ مِن وَلِىٍّ وَلَا نَصِيرٍ

117. Allah turned with favour
To the Prophet, the Muhājirs,[1368]
And the Anṣār— who followed
Him in a time of distress,
After that the hearts of a part[1369]
Of them had nearly swerved
(From duty); but He turned
To them (also): for He is
Unto them Most Kind,
Most Merciful.

(١١٧) لَّقَد تَّابَ ٱللَّهُ عَلَى ٱلنَّبِىِّ
وَٱلْمُهَٰجِرِينَ وَٱلْأَنصَارِ ٱلَّذِينَ
ٱتَّبَعُوهُ فِى سَاعَةِ ٱلْعُسْرَةِ مِنۢ بَعْدِ مَا
كَادَ يَزِيغُ قُلُوبُ فَرِيقٍ مِّنْهُمْ
ثُمَّ تَابَ عَلَيْهِمْ ۚ إِنَّهُۥ بِهِمْ رَءُوفٌ رَّحِيمٌ

118. (He turned in mercy also)
To the three who were left

(١١٨) وَعَلَى ٱلثَّلَٰثَةِ ٱلَّذِينَ خُلِّفُوا۟

1366. Abraham was loyal and tender-hearted, and bore with much that he disapproved, being in this a prototype of Muṣṭafā, and it must have gone against his grain to cut off relations in that way. But it would obviously be wrong for a human being to entreat Allah for mercy on people who had finally rejected Allah.

1367. Allah's clear commands are given, so that Believers may not be misled by their human frailty into unbecoming conduct.

1368. *Cf.* 9:100. The Muhājirs were the people who originally forsook their homes in Makkah and followed Muṣṭafā in exile to Madīnah. The Anṣār were the Madīnah people who received them with honour and hospitality into their city. Both these groups were staunch supports of Islam, and proved their Faith by great sacrifices. But in the difficult days of the Tabūk expedition some of them, not perversely, but out of lethargy and human weakness, had failed to follow the standard. They were forgiven, and they afterwards acquitted themselves with zeal.

1369. Note that the "swerving from duty" was merely an inclination due to the weakness of human nature in the face of new difficulties; that it only affected a part of the men for a time; and that it was overcome even in their case by the grace of Allah, so that they all did their duty, and were freely forgiven their incipient weakness, which they conquered. There were three exceptions, which are referred to in the next verse.

Behind; (they felt guilty)[1370]
To such a degree that the earth
Seemed constrained to them,
For all its spaciousness,
And their (very) Souls seemed
Straitened to them—
And they perceived that
There is no fleeing from Allah
(And no refuge) but to Himself.
Then He turned to them,
That they might repent:
For Allah is Oft-Returning,
Most Merciful.

حَتَّىٰٓ إِذَا ضَاقَتۡ
عَلَيۡهِمُ ٱلۡأَرۡضُ بِمَا رَحُبَتۡ
وَضَاقَتۡ عَلَيۡهِمۡ أَنفُسُهُمۡ
وَظَنُّوٓاْ أَن لَّا مَلۡجَأَ مِنَ ٱللَّهِ إِلَّآ إِلَيۡهِ
ثُمَّ تَابَ عَلَيۡهِمۡ لِيَتُوبُوٓاْۚ
إِنَّ ٱللَّهَ هُوَ ٱلتَّوَّابُ ٱلرَّحِيمُ

C. 98.—To be true in word and deed is to hold
(9:119-129.) Our selfish desires at bay, and follow
Allah's Call: in this is our fullest satisfaction
And reward. But our striving should include
Study and teaching, for the Brethren's benefit.
For Allah's Message increases our Faith
And leads us to love Him and trust Him,
The Lord of the Throne of Glory Supreme.

SECTION 15.

119. O ye who believe! Fear Allah
And be with those
Who are true (in word and deed).

١١٩ يَٰٓأَيُّهَا ٱلَّذِينَ ءَامَنُواْ ٱتَّقُواْ ٱللَّهَ
وَكُونُواْ مَعَ ٱلصَّٰدِقِينَ

120. It was not fitting
For the people of Madīnah
And the Bedouin Arabs
Of the neighbourhood, to refuse
To follow Allah's Messenger,
Nor to prefer their own lives
To his: because nothing
Could they suffer or do,

١٢٠ مَا كَانَ لِأَهۡلِ ٱلۡمَدِينَةِ وَمَنۡ حَوۡلَهُم
مِّنَ ٱلۡأَعۡرَابِ أَن يَتَخَلَّفُواْ عَن رَّسُولِ ٱللَّهِ
وَلَا يَرۡغَبُواْ بِأَنفُسِهِمۡ عَن نَّفۡسِهِۦۚ
ذَٰلِكَ بِأَنَّهُمۡ لَا يُصِيبُهُمۡ

1370. Among the Faithful, the largest number consisted of those who were perfectly staunch and ever ready to do their duty. They obtained the love and good pleasure of Allah. Next came a few who wavered because their will was weak and they were daunted by the dangers and difficulties that faced them; Allah's saving grace protected them and they conquered their weakness, and did not fail in their duty; Allah forgave them and accepted their repentance. Lastly, in the illustration taken from the Tabūk affair, there were some who actually failed in their duty, not from contumacy or ill will, but from thoughtlessness, slackness, and human weakness: they actually failed to obey the Holy Prophet's summons, and were naturally called on to explain, and were excluded from the life of the Community. Their mental state is here described graphically. Though the earth is spacious, to them it was constrained. In their own souls they had a feeling of constraint. In worldly affluence they felt poor in spirit. They realised that they could not flee from Allah, but could only find solace and refuge in coming back to Him. They freely repented and showed it in their deeds, and Allah freely forgave them and took them to His grace. Though illustrated by the particular examples of the Anṣār, *viz.*, Ka'b, Marār, and Hilāl, the lesson is perfectly general and is good for all times.

But was reckoned to their credit
As a deed of righteousness—
Whether they suffered thirst,
Or fatigue, or hunger, in the Cause
Of Allah, or trod paths
To raise the ire of the Unbelievers,
Or received any injury[1371]
Whatever from an enemy:
For Allah suffereth not
The reward to be lost
Of those who do good—

ظَمَأٌ وَلَا نَصَبٌ وَلَا مَخْمَصَةٌ
فِي سَبِيلِ ٱللَّهِ وَلَا يَطَـُٔونَ مَوْطِئًا يَغِيظُ
ٱلْكُفَّارَ وَلَا يَنَالُونَ مِنْ عَدُوٍّ نَّيْلًا
إِلَّا كُتِبَ لَهُم بِهِۦ عَمَلٌ صَٰلِحٌ
إِنَّ ٱللَّهَ لَا يُضِيعُ أَجْرَ ٱلْمُحْسِنِينَ

121. Nor could they spend anything
(For the Cause)—small or great—
Nor cut across a valley,[1372]
But the deed is inscribed
To their credit; that Allah
May requite their deed
With the best (possible reward).

١٢١ وَلَا يُنفِقُونَ نَفَقَةً صَغِيرَةً وَلَا كَبِيرَةً
وَلَا يَقْطَعُونَ وَادِيًا إِلَّا كُتِبَ لَهُمْ
لِيَجْزِيَهُمُ ٱللَّهُ أَحْسَنَ مَا كَانُوا۟ يَعْمَلُونَ

122. Nor should the Believers
All go forth together:
If a contingent
From every expedition
Remained behind,
They could devote themselves
To studies in religion,
And admonish the people
When they return to them—
That thus they (may learn)[1373]
To guard themselves (against evil).

١٢٢ وَمَا كَانَ ٱلْمُؤْمِنُونَ لِيَنفِرُوا۟ كَآفَّةً
فَلَوْلَا نَفَرَ مِن كُلِّ فِرْقَةٍ مِّنْهُمْ طَآئِفَةٌ
لِّيَتَفَقَّهُوا۟ فِى ٱلدِّينِ
وَلِيُنذِرُوا۟ قَوْمَهُمْ إِذَا رَجَعُوٓا۟
إِلَيْهِمْ لَعَلَّهُمْ يَحْذَرُونَ

1371. Again, the illustration is that of Tabūk, but the lesson is general. We must not hold our own comfort or lives dearer than that of our Leader, nor desert him in the hour of danger. If we have true devotion, we shall hold our own lives or comfort cheap in comparison to his. But whatever service we render to the Cause of Allah, and whatever sufferings, hardships, or injuries we endure, or whatever resources we spend for the Cause—all goes to raise our degree in the spiritual world. Nothing is lost. Our reward is far greater in worth than any little service we can render, or any little hardship we can suffer, or any little contributions we can make to the Cause. We "painfully attain to joy".

1372. *Cut across a valley*: this is specially mentioned in a symbolical way, as denoting an individual act of heroism, dash, or bravery. To march with the troops along valleys, or, spiritually, tread paths of danger along with our Comrades, is good and praiseworthy; but one that dashes across a stream, all alone, for some special deed of bravery where the *elan* of comradeship does not sustain him, needs special mention. Notice that both the things mentioned in this verse—the spending of resources and the dashing across a valley—are individual acts, while those mentioned in the last verse are collective acts, which are in some ways easier. The individual acts having been mentioned, the next verse follows naturally.

1373. Fighting may be inevitable, and where a call is made by the *Amīr al Mu'minīn,* ruler of an Islamic State, it should be obeyed. But fighting is not to be glorified to the exclusion of all else. Even among those who are able to go forth, a party should remain behind—one in each township or circle—for purposes of study; so that when the fighters return home, their minds may be attuned again to the more normal interests of religious life, under properly instructed teachers. The students and teachers are soldiers of the *Jihād* in their spirit of obedience and discipline. (R).

SECTION 16.

123. O ye who believe! Fight
The Unbelievers who gird you
about,[1374]
And let them find firmness
In you: and know that Allah
Is with those who fear Him.

يَٰٓأَيُّهَا ٱلَّذِينَ ءَامَنُوا۟ قَٰتِلُوا۟ ٱلَّذِينَ يَلُونَكُم مِّنَ ٱلْكُفَّارِ وَلْيَجِدُوا۟ فِيكُمْ غِلْظَةً ۚ وَٱعْلَمُوٓا۟ أَنَّ ٱللَّهَ مَعَ ٱلْمُتَّقِينَ ﴿١٢٣﴾

124. Whenever there cometh down[1375]
A Sūrah, some of them say:
"Which of you has had
His faith increased by it?"
Yea, those who believe—
Their faith is increased,
And they do rejoice.

وَإِذَا مَآ أُنزِلَتْ سُورَةٌ فَمِنْهُم مَّن يَقُولُ أَيُّكُمْ زَادَتْهُ هَٰذِهِۦٓ إِيمَٰنًا ۚ فَأَمَّا ٱلَّذِينَ ءَامَنُوا۟ فَزَادَتْهُمْ إِيمَٰنًا وَهُمْ يَسْتَبْشِرُونَ ﴿١٢٤﴾

125. But those in whose hearts[1376]
Is a disease—it will add doubt
To their doubt, and they will die
In a state of Unbelief.

وَأَمَّا ٱلَّذِينَ فِى قُلُوبِهِم مَّرَضٌ فَزَادَتْهُمْ رِجْسًا إِلَىٰ رِجْسِهِمْ وَمَاتُوا۟ وَهُمْ كَٰفِرُونَ ﴿١٢٥﴾

126. See they not that they
Are tried every year[1377]
Once or twice? Yet they
Turn not in repentance,
And they take no heed.

أَوَلَا يَرَوْنَ أَنَّهُمْ يُفْتَنُونَ فِى كُلِّ عَامٍ مَّرَّةً أَوْ مَرَّتَيْنِ ثُمَّ لَا يَتُوبُونَ وَلَا هُمْ يَذَّكَّرُونَ ﴿١٢٦﴾

127. Whenever there cometh down
A Sūrah, they look at each other,
(Saying), "Doth anyone see you?"
Then they turn aside:

وَإِذَا مَآ أُنزِلَتْ سُورَةٌ نَّظَرَ بَعْضُهُمْ إِلَىٰ بَعْضٍ هَلْ يَرَىٰكُم مِّنْ أَحَدٍ ثُمَّ ٱنصَرَفُوا۟ ۚ

1374. When conflict becomes inevitable, the first thing is to clear our surroundings of all evil, for it is only evil that we can rightly fight. To evil we must put up a stout and stiff resistance. Mealy-mouthed compromises are not right for soldiers of truth and righteousness. They are often a compound of cowardice, weariness, greed, and corruptibility.

1375. The incompatibility of Unfaith and Faith are contrasted in this section in respect of revelation and the divine teacher. The Unbelievers laugh at revelation, and say to each other mockingly: "Does this increase your faith?" To the Believer every new aspect of Allah's truth as revealed increases his faith, and wonder, and gratitude. He rejoices, because he gets added strength for life and achievement.

1376. *Cf.* 2:10 and several similar passages. Just as the light, which to healthy eyes gives enlightenment, causes pain to the diseased eye, which emits unclean matter, so to those spiritually diseased, Allah's grace is unwelcome, and they put forth more doubts to cover their disease. And they die in their disease, and of their disease. Note the aptness of the metaphor.

1377. Yet, in spite of their infidelity, one or two chances are given them every year. The door is not closed to them. Yet they deliberately turn away, and take no heed of all the warnings which their own nature and the teaching and example of good men should give them.

Allah hath turned their hearts[1378]
(From the light); for they
Are a people that understand not.

صَرَفَ ٱللَّهُ قُلُوبَهُم بِأَنَّهُمْ قَوْمٌ لَّا يَفْقَهُونَ

128. Now hath come unto you
A Messenger from amongst
Yourselves: it grieves him
That ye should perish:
Ardently anxious is he
Over you: to the Believers
Is he most kind and merciful.[1379]

١٢٨ لَقَدْ جَآءَكُمْ رَسُولٌ مِّنْ أَنفُسِكُمْ عَزِيزٌ عَلَيْهِ مَا عَنِتُّمْ حَرِيصٌ عَلَيْكُم بِٱلْمُؤْمِنِينَ رَءُوفٌ رَّحِيمٌ

129. But if they turn away,
Say: "Allah sufficeth me:
There is no god but He:
On Him is my trust—
He the Lord of the Throne
(Of Glory) Supreme!"[1380]

١٢٩ فَإِن تَوَلَّوْا فَقُلْ حَسْبِيَ ٱللَّهُ لَآ إِلَٰهَ إِلَّا هُوَ عَلَيْهِ تَوَكَّلْتُ وَهُوَ رَبُّ ٱلْعَرْشِ ٱلْعَظِيمِ

1378. Even the Unbelievers, in their hearts and conscience, feel uncomfortable when they turn aside from Faith and Truth, and therefore their turning aside is figured by furtive glances, such as we may suppose literally to have been cast by the Hypocrites in the assemblies of the Holy Prophet. Then they slink away feeling superior in their minds. And yet, if they only knew it, their contumacy deprives them of Allah's grace and light. They are turning Grace away, and when Allah withdraws it altogether, they perish utterly.

1379. The tender heart of the Teacher is grieved that any among his flock should rush headlong to ruin. He watches ardently over them, and whenever any of them show signs of Faith, his kindness and mercy surround him and rejoice over him.

1380. But if the Message is rejected, he still proclaims the burning Faith of his heart, which is unquenchable, Allah is All in All. To trust Him is to find the accomplishment of all spiritual desire. His grandeur is figured by a lofty Throne, supreme in glory!

Thus have we been led, through a notable incident in Muṣṭafā's earthly career, to truths of the highest spiritual import.

INTRODUCTION TO SŪRAH 10—*YŪNUS*

Chronologically this Sūrah and the five that follow (Sūrahs 11, 12, 13, 14, and 15) are closely connected, and were revealed in the late Makkan period, as the great event of the Hijrah was gradually approaching down the stream of Time. But their chronology has no particular significance.

On the other hand their arrangement in the gradation of Quranic teaching fits in with the subject matter. S. 8 and S. 9 were mainly concerned with the first questions that arose on the formation of the new and organised Community of Islam in its conflict with those who wished to suppress or destroy it or use force to prevent its growth and the consolidation of its ideals. See Introductions to those Sūrahs. The present group leads us to the questions that face us when external hostility has been met, and our relations to Allah have to be considered from a higher standpoint than that of self-preservation. How does revelation work? What is the meaning of divine grace and its withdrawal? How do the Messengers of Allah deliver their Message? How should we receive it?

All these questions revolve around the revelation of the Qur'ān and each Sūrah of this group except the 13th has the Abbreviated Letters Alif, Lām, Rā', attached to it. S. 13 has the letters, Alif, Lām, Mīm, Rā', and we shall discuss this variation when we come to S. 13.

As shown in Appendix I, the Abbreviated Letters are mystic symbols, about whose meaning there is no authoritative explanation. If the theory advanced in n. 25 to 2:1 has any validity, and the present group, Alif, Lām, Rā', is cognate to the group Alif, Lām, Mīm, we have to consider and form some idea in our minds as to the probable meaning of the variation. We took Alif, Lām, Mīm to be a symbol of those Sūrahs that deal with the beginning, the middle, and the end of man's spiritual history—the origin, the present position, and the things to come in the Last Days (eschatology, to use a theological term). We took Alif, Lām, to stand as symbols of the first two, and Mīm, of the last. In the present group of Sūrahs we find hardly any eschatological matter, and therefore we can understand the absence of Mīm, the symbol standing for such matter. In its place comes Rā', which is phonetically allied to Lām. Lām is produced by the impact of the tongue to the front of the palate, and Rā' to the middle of the palate. In many languages the letters Lām, and Rā' are interchangeable; *e.g.*, in Arabic, *Al Raḥmān* becomes ar-Raḥmān, and Rā' in imperfect enunciation Lām, in Chinese lallations. If Lām is a symbol of present-day things looking to the future, we may take Rā' as a symbol of present-day things looking within, *i.e.*, into the interior of the organization of the Ummah. And this symbolism fits in with the subject matter of the Sūrahs in question. But no one should be dogmatic in spectulation about mystic Symbols.

Let us now consider Sūrah 10 alone. The central theme is that Allah's wonderful Creation must not be viewed by us as a creation of material things only, once made and finished with. Most wonderful of all is how He reveals Himself to men through Prophets and Scriptures; how prophets are rejected by men, and the Message disbelieved until it is too late for repentance; and how, as in the case of Yūnus (Jonah) and his people, even the rejection (when repentance supervenes) does not prevent Allah's grace and mercy from working, and how far that working is beyond man's comprehension.

Summary—The wonderful working of the Spirit through man by revelation seems like magic to men; yet they could find Signs and Messages from Him in the sun and the moon and the constantly varying yet regular phenomena of nature, from which men should take a lesson of constancy and Faith (10:1-20, and C. 99).

All the goodness or beauty that man meets in the life around him proceeds from Allah. Yet man is blind and will not understand (10:21-40, and C. 100).

As all things and beings proceed from Allah, so will they return to Him, and He is ever true. Why then does ungrateful man make untrue phantoms for himself instead of rejoicing in the good news which He sends? (10:41-70, and C. 101).

Allah revealed Himself through Noah, but Noah's people rejected him and perished. He spoke through Moses to Pharaoh, but Pharaoh was stiff-necked and arrogant, and when he repented at all, it was too late (10:71-92, and C. 102).

Everywhere want of faith causes people to perish. But the people of Yūnus repented, and Allah saved them by His wonderful grace. So Allah will deliver the Believers. When the Truth comes from Allah, follow it and be patient, for Allah is the most righteous of Judges (10:93-109, and C. 103).

C. 99.—Men may wonder that a man
(10:1-20.) Like unto them should bring a Message
From Allah, but Allah's Message shines
Forth through all nature and Creation.
He guides the human spirit, if only
Man will have Faith and put his hope
In Allah. Wonderful are Allah's relations
With man, yet man is ungrateful
And runs to fancies and fanciful gods.
Glory to the One True Allah, Who made
Mankind as One, and holds alone
The secrets of the Unseen in His
Great and good Universal Plan.

Sūrah 10.

Yūnus, (Jonah)

الجزء الحادي عشر سورة يونس

*In the name of Allah, Most Gracious,
Most Merciful*

بِسْمِ اللَّهِ الرَّحْمَٰنِ الرَّحِيمِ

1. Alif Lām Rā'[1381]
These are the Ayāt[1382]
Of the Book of Wisdom.

١ الٓر تِلْكَ ءَايَٰتُ ٱلْكِتَٰبِ ٱلْحَكِيمِ

2. Is it a matter
Of wonderment to men
That We have sent
Our inspiration to a man
From among themselves?—[1383]
That he should warn mankind
(Of their danger), and give
The good news to the Believers
That they have before their Lord
The lofty rank of Truth.[1384]
(But) say the Unbelievers:
"This is indeed
An evident sorcerer!"

٢ أَكَانَ لِلنَّاسِ عَجَبًا أَنْ أَوْحَيْنَآ إِلَىٰ رَجُلٍ مِّنْهُمْ أَنْ أَنذِرِ ٱلنَّاسَ وَبَشِّرِ ٱلَّذِينَ ءَامَنُوٓا۟ أَنَّ لَهُمْ قَدَمَ صِدْقٍ عِندَ رَبِّهِمْ قَالَ ٱلْكَٰفِرُونَ إِنَّ هَٰذَا لَسَٰحِرٌ مُّبِينٌ

3. Verily your Lord is Allah,
Who created the heavens
And the earth in six Days,[1385]

٣ إِنَّ رَبَّكُمُ ٱللَّهُ ٱلَّذِى خَلَقَ ٱلسَّمَٰوَٰتِ وَٱلْأَرْضَ فِى سِتَّةِ أَيَّامٍ

1381. For the Abbreviated Letters generally as mystic Symbols, see Appendix I. For this particular combination see the Introduction to this Sūrah.

1382. *Āyāt* = Signs, or Verses of the Qur'ān. Here both meanings are to be understood. Each verse is a nugget of wisdom. And in the verses immediately following, *e.g.*, 10:3-6, examples are given of the wonders of Allah's material Creation. If the starry heavens impress us with their sublimity as signs of Allah's wisdom and power, how much more wonderful is it that He should speak to lowly man through His Messengers, in man's language, so that he can understand?

1383. Is it not still more wonderful that the inspired man should be one of ourselves? The Arabs had known Muḥammad in other relations and conditions, and when the mighty Message came through his mouth—the message of Wisdom and Power, such as no man could speak as from himself, least of all a man not instructed in human learning—they could only in their wonder attribute it to magic and sorcery. They failed to understand that magic and sorcery were projections of their own mind, while here was solid, enduring Truth from Allah!

1384. Allah's Message was and is not all smooth and agreeable. The first thing is to convince us of our sin and wrongdoing, and warn us of our danger. If we have Faith, we then learn what a high rank we obtain in the sight of Allah, through His glorious Truth, which makes us pure and free. According to another view the word "*qadama*" here refers to the fact that the acts of a person precede him to his Lord. The word *ṣidq* qualifies these acts with sincerity and genuineness. (R).

1385. See note 1031 to 7:54.

Then He established Himself[1386]
On the Throne (of authority),
Regulating and governing all
things.
No intercessor (can plead with
Him)
Except after His leave
(Hath been obtained). This
Is Allah your Lord; Him therefore
Serve ye: will ye not
Receive admonition?[1387]

ثُمَّ ٱسْتَوَىٰ
عَلَى ٱلْعَرْشِ ۖ يُدَبِّرُ ٱلْأَمْرَ ۖ
مَا مِن شَفِيعٍ إِلَّا مِنۢ بَعْدِ إِذْنِهِۦ ۚ
ذَٰلِكُمُ ٱللَّهُ رَبُّكُمْ
فَٱعْبُدُوهُ ۚ أَفَلَا تَذَكَّرُونَ

4. To Him will be your return—
Of all of you. The promise
Of Allah is true and sure.[1388]
It is He who beginneth
The process of Creation,[1389]
And repeateth it, that He
May reward with justice
Those who believe
And work righteousness;
But those who reject Him
Will have draughts[1390]
Of boiling fluids,
And a Penalty grievous,
Because they did reject Him.

٤ إِلَيْهِ مَرْجِعُكُمْ جَمِيعًا ۖ وَعْدَ ٱللَّهِ حَقًّا ۚ
إِنَّهُۥ يَبْدَؤُا۟ ٱلْخَلْقَ ثُمَّ يُعِيدُهُۥ لِيَجْزِىَ ٱلَّذِينَ
ءَامَنُوا۟ وَعَمِلُوا۟ ٱلصَّٰلِحَٰتِ بِٱلْقِسْطِ ۚ
وَٱلَّذِينَ كَفَرُوا۟ لَهُمْ
شَرَابٌ مِّنْ حَمِيمٍ وَعَذَابٌ أَلِيمٌۢ
بِمَا كَانُوا۟ يَكْفُرُونَ

5. It is He who made the sun
To be a shining glory[1391]
And the moon to be a light
(Of beauty), and measured out

٥ هُوَ ٱلَّذِى جَعَلَ ٱلشَّمْسَ
ضِيَآءً وَٱلْقَمَرَ نُورًا وَقَدَّرَهُۥ

1386. *Istawā*, with the preposition *ilā* after it, means He turned to or He directed Himself by His will; hence, in 2:29, I have translated, "His design comprehended the heavens," to emphasise the fact that the heavens were not eternal or co-eternal with Him, but were a part of His design, and in a sense, as they appear to man subjectively, a complement to the creation of man's Earth. With the preposition *'alā* after it, as and in 7:54 and elsewhere, the meaning seems to be "to mount or ascend," and to be firmly established, to sit firm and unshaken, beyond question." The Throne of authority represents many ideas: *e.g.*, (1) that Allah is high above all His Creation; (2) that He regulates and governs it, as a king does, whose authority is unquestionably recognised; (3) that He is not, therefore, like the gods of Greece and paganism, who were imagined to be in a world apart, careless of mankind, or jealous of mankind, but on the contrary, He (4) disposes of their affairs and all affairs continuously and with justice; (5) that the authority of His prophets, ministers, and messengers is derived from Him, and such intercession as they can make is by His will and permission. (R).

1387. *Cf.* 6:80.

1388. *Haqq*: true, right, for just ends, in right proportions, sure and certain: all these ideas are implied.

1389. *Cf.* n. 120 to 2:117. Allah's creation is not a simple act, once done and finished with. It is continuous, and there are many stages, not the least important of which is the Hereafter, when the fruits of our life will be achieved.

1390. *Hamīm*: boiling fluid; it is associated as in 38:57, with *ghassāq*, a dark, murky, or intensely cold fluid: both symbols of the grievous penalty that results from rebellion against Allah.

1391. The fitting epithet for the sun is *ḍiya'*, "splendour and glory of brightness", and for the moon is "a light" (of beauty), the cool light that illuminates and helps in the darkness of the night. But the sun and moon also measure time. The simplest observation can keep pace with the true lunar months and lunar years, which are all that is required by a pastoral people. For agriculture solar years are required, as they indicate the changes of the seasons, but ordinary solar years are never exact; even the solar year of 365¼ days requires correction by advanced astronomical calculation.

Stages for it; that ye might
Know the number of years
And the count (of time).
Nowise did Allah create this
But in truth and righteousness.[1392]
(Thus) doth He explain His Signs
In detail, for those who
understand.[1393]

مَنَازِلَ لِتَعْلَمُوا عَدَدَ السِّنِينَ وَالْحِسَابَ
مَا خَلَقَ اللَّهُ ذَٰلِكَ إِلَّا بِالْحَقِّ
يُفَصِّلُ الْآيَاتِ لِقَوْمٍ يَعْلَمُونَ

6. Verily, in the alternation
Of the Night and the Day,
And in all that Allah
Hath created, in the heavens
And the earth, are Signs
For those who fear Him.[1394]

٦ إِنَّ فِي اخْتِلَافِ اللَّيْلِ وَالنَّهَارِ
وَمَا خَلَقَ اللَّهُ فِي السَّمَاوَاتِ وَالْأَرْضِ
لَآيَاتٍ لِقَوْمٍ يَتَّقُونَ

7. Those who rest not their hope
On their meeting with Us,
But are pleased and satisfied
With the life of the Present,
And those who heed not
Our Signs—[1395]

٧ إِنَّ الَّذِينَ لَا يَرْجُونَ لِقَاءَنَا
وَرَضُوا بِالْحَيَاةِ الدُّنْيَا وَاطْمَأَنُّوا بِهَا
وَالَّذِينَ هُمْ عَنْ آيَاتِنَا غَافِلُونَ

8. Their abode is the Fire,
Because of the (evil)
They earned.

٨ أُولَٰئِكَ مَأْوَاهُمُ النَّارُ
بِمَا كَانُوا يَكْسِبُونَ

9. Those who believe,
And work righteousness—
Their Lord will guide them
Because of their Faith:[1396]
Beneath them will flow
Rivers in Gardens of Bliss.

٩ إِنَّ الَّذِينَ آمَنُوا وَعَمِلُوا الصَّالِحَاتِ
يَهْدِيهِمْ رَبُّهُمْ بِإِيمَانِهِمْ تَجْرِي مِنْ
تَحْتِهِمُ الْأَنْهَارُ فِي جَنَّاتِ النَّعِيمِ

1392. Everything in Allah's creation has use and purpose, and fits into a Design. It is true in every sense of the word and it is good and just. It is not merely a matter of sport or freak (21:16). Though so varied, it proclaims Allah's Unity; though a limited free will is granted to creatures, the results of evil (which is rebellion) are neutralised and harmony is restored. *Cf.* 3:191.

1393. *Cf.* 9:11.

1394. *Cf.* 2:164.

1395. Those who fall from Grace are described by three epithets: (1) the meeting with Allah is not the object of their hope and earnest desire, but something else, *viz.* (2) the material good of this world, which not only attracts them but apparently gives them complete satisfaction, so that there is no glow of the Future in their horizon, and (3) they are deaf and dead to the resounding and living Message of Allah. (1) and (2) refer to the extinction of Faith in them, and (3) to their falling prey to the evils of this world in their conduct. They are contrasted in 10:9 with the Faith and the Righteousness of those who accept Grace.

1396. Their Faith is the cause as well as the instrument of their Guidance—the Kindly Light which leads them as well as the Joy which fills their Soul. The usual symbols of Garfdens and Fire are again contrasted—in each case the result of Good or Evil in Life.

10. (This will be) their cry therein:
"Glory to Thee, O Allah!"
And "Peace" will be their
greeting therein!
And the close of their cry[1397]
Will be: "Praise be to Allah,
The Cherisher and Sustainer
Of the Worlds!"

(١٠) دَعْوَىٰهُمْ فِيهَا سُبْحَٰنَكَ
ٱللَّهُمَّ وَتَحِيَّتُهُمْ فِيهَا سَلَٰمٌ ۚ
وَءَاخِرُ دَعْوَىٰهُمْ أَنِ ٱلْحَمْدُ لِلَّهِ
رَبِّ ٱلْعَٰلَمِينَ

SECTION 2.

11. If Allah were to hasten for men
The ill (they have earned)
As they would fain hasten on
The good—then would
Their respite be settled at once.[1398]
But We leave those
Who rest not their hope
On their meeting with Us,
In their trespasses, wandering
In distraction to and fro.

(١١) وَلَوْ يُعَجِّلُ ٱللَّهُ لِلنَّاسِ
ٱلشَّرَّ ٱسْتِعْجَالَهُم بِٱلْخَيْرِ
لَقُضِىَ إِلَيْهِمْ أَجَلُهُمْ ۖ فَنَذَرُ
ٱلَّذِينَ لَا يَرْجُونَ لِقَآءَنَا
فِى طُغْيَٰنِهِمْ يَعْمَهُونَ

12. When trouble toucheth a man,
He crieth unto Us
(In all postures)—lying down[1399]
On his side, or sitting,
Or standing. But when We
Have solved his trouble,
He passeth on his way as if
He had never cried to Us
For a trouble that touched him!
Thus do the deeds of transgressors
Seem fair in their eyes![1400]

(١٢) وَإِذَا مَسَّ ٱلْإِنسَٰنَ ٱلضُّرُّ
دَعَانَا لِجَنۢبِهِۦٓ أَوْ قَاعِدًا أَوْ قَآئِمًا
فَلَمَّا كَشَفْنَا عَنْهُ ضُرَّهُۥ مَرَّ كَأَن
لَّمْ يَدْعُنَآ إِلَىٰ ضُرٍّ مَّسَّهُۥ ۚ كَذَٰلِكَ زُيِّنَ
لِلْمُسْرِفِينَ مَا كَانُوا۟ يَعْمَلُونَ

1397. A beautiful piece of spiritual melody! They sing and shout with joy, but their joy is in the Glory of Allah! The greetings they receive and the greetings they give are of Peace and Harmony! From first to last they realise that it is Allah Who cherished them and made them grow, and His rays are their Light.

1398. Those who have no spiritual hope for the Future grasp at any temporary advantage, and in their blindness even mockingly ask for immediate punishment for their sins (8:32), thus vainly challenging Allah, in Whom they do not believe. If the beneficent Allah were to take them at their word, they would have no chance at all. Their doom would be sealed. But even the respite they get they use badly. They merely wander about distractedly like men, to and fro. *Cf.* 2:15.

1399. Not only do men fail to use their respite: even those who have a superficial belief in Allah call on Him in their trouble but forget Him when He has relieved their trouble. Their Faith is not strong enough to make them realise that all good proceeds from Allah. But in moments of trouble they use every position, literally and figuratively, to appeal to Him.

1400. Those without Faith are selfish, and are so wrapped up in themselves that they think every good that comes to them is due to their own merits or cleverness. That is itself a cause of their undoing. They do not see their own faults.

13. Generations before you
We destroyed when they
Did wrong: their Messengers
Came to them with Clear Signs,
But they would not believe!
Thus do We requite
Those who sin!

﴿١٣﴾ وَلَقَدْ أَهْلَكْنَا الْقُرُونَ مِن قَبْلِكُمْ لَمَّا
ظَلَمُوا ۙ وَجَاءَتْهُمْ رُسُلُهُم بِالْبَيِّنَاتِ وَمَا كَانُوا
لِيُؤْمِنُوا ۚ كَذَٰلِكَ نَجْزِي الْقَوْمَ الْمُجْرِمِينَ

14. Then We made you heirs
In the land after them,
To see how ye would behave![1401]

﴿١٤﴾ ثُمَّ جَعَلْنَاكُمْ خَلَائِفَ فِي الْأَرْضِ
مِن بَعْدِهِمْ لِنَنظُرَ كَيْفَ تَعْمَلُونَ

15. But when Our Clear Signs
Are rehearsed unto them,
Those who rest not their hope
On their meeting with Us,
Say: "Bring us a Reading[1402]
Other than this, or change this,"
Say: "It is not for me,
Of my own accord,
To change it: I follow
Naught but what is revealed
Unto me: if I were
To disobey my Lord,
I should myself fear the Penalty
Of a Great Day (to come)."

﴿١٥﴾ وَإِذَا تُتْلَىٰ عَلَيْهِمْ آيَاتُنَا بَيِّنَاتٍ ۙ
قَالَ الَّذِينَ لَا يَرْجُونَ لِقَاءَنَا
ائْتِ بِقُرْآنٍ غَيْرِ هَٰذَا أَوْ بَدِّلْهُ ۚ
قُلْ مَا يَكُونُ لِي أَنْ أُبَدِّلَهُ مِن تِلْقَاءِ
نَفْسِي ۖ إِنْ أَتَّبِعُ إِلَّا مَا يُوحَىٰ إِلَيَّ ۖ إِنِّي أَخَافُ
إِنْ عَصَيْتُ رَبِّي عَذَابَ يَوْمٍ عَظِيمٍ

16. Say: "If Allah had so willed,
I should not have rehearsed it
To you, or would He
Have made it known to you.[1403]
A whole lifetime before this
Have I tarried amongst you:
Will ye not then understand?"[1404]

﴿١٦﴾ قُل لَّوْ شَاءَ اللَّهُ مَا تَلَوْتُهُ عَلَيْكُمْ
وَلَا أَدْرَاكُم بِهِ ۖ فَقَدْ لَبِثْتُ فِيكُمْ
عُمُرًا مِّن قَبْلِهِ ۚ أَفَلَا تَعْقِلُونَ

1401. This is addressed to the Quraysh in the first instance, for they have succeeded to the 'Ād and the Thamūd heritage. But the application is universal, and was true to the 'Abbāsi Empire in the time of Hārūn al Rashid, or the Muslim Empire in Spain or the Turkish Empire in its palmiest days, and indeed, aparta from political power, to the Muslims and non-Muslims of our own days.

1402. *Reading:* in the Arabic, the word is "*Qur'ān*", which may mean Reading or in the special sense, the Qur'ān. The duty of Allah's Messenger is to deliver Allah's Message as it is revealed to him, whether it please or displease those who hear it. Selfish men want to read their own desires or fancies into religious precepts, and thus they are often willing to use Religion for their own ends. Most of the corruptions of Religion are due to this cause. But Religion is not to be so prostituted.

1403. It is in Allah's Plan that He should reveal Himself in certain ways to His creatures, and His Messengers are the instruments that carry out His Will. It is in itself gracious Mercy that He should thus make His Will known. We should be grateful for His guidance instead of carping at it.

1404. Muḥammad Musṭafā had lived his whole life of purity and virtue amongst his people, and they knew and acknowledged it before he received his mission. They knew he loved his nation and was loyal to it. Why should they turn against him when he had to point out under inspiration all their sins and wrong-doing? It was for their own good. And he had to plead again and again with them: "Will you not understand, and see what a glorious privilege it is for you to receive true guidance from Allah?"

17. Who doth more wrong
Than such as forge a lie
Against Allah, or deny
His Signs? But never
Will prosper those who sin.

١٧ فَمَنْ أَظْلَمُ مِمَّنِ افْتَرَىٰ عَلَى
اللَّهِ كَذِبًا أَوْ كَذَّبَ بِآيَاتِهِ ۚ إِنَّهُ
لَا يُفْلِحُ الْمُجْرِمُونَ

18. They serve, besides Allah,
Things that hurt them not
Nor profit them, and they say:
"These are our intercessors
With Allah." Say: "Do ye
Indeed inform Allah of something
He knows not, in the heavens[1405]
Or on earth?—Glory to Him!
And far is He above the partners
They ascribe (to Him)!"

١٨ وَيَعْبُدُونَ مِن دُونِ اللَّهِ مَا لَا يَضُرُّهُمْ
وَلَا يَنفَعُهُمْ وَيَقُولُونَ هَٰؤُلَاءِ شُفَعَاؤُنَا
عِندَ اللَّهِ ۚ قُلْ أَتُنَبِّئُونَ اللَّهَ بِمَا
لَا يَعْلَمُ فِي السَّمَاوَاتِ وَلَا فِي الْأَرْضِ ۚ
سُبْحَانَهُ وَتَعَالَىٰ عَمَّا يُشْرِكُونَ

19. Mankind was but one nation,[1406]
But differed (later). Had it not
Been for a Word[1407]
That went forth before
From thy Lord, their differences
Would have been settled
Between them.

١٩ وَمَا كَانَ النَّاسُ إِلَّا أُمَّةً وَاحِدَةً
فَاخْتَلَفُوا ۚ وَلَوْلَا كَلِمَةٌ سَبَقَتْ مِن
رَّبِّكَ لَقُضِيَ بَيْنَهُمْ فِيمَا فِيهِ يَخْتَلِفُونَ

20. They say: "Why is not
A Sign sent down to him
From his Lord?" Say:
"The Unseen is only
For Allah (to know).
Then wait ye: I too
Will wait with you."[1408]

٢٠ وَيَقُولُونَ لَوْلَا أُنزِلَ عَلَيْهِ
آيَةٌ مِّن رَّبِّهِ ۖ فَقُلْ إِنَّمَا الْغَيْبُ لِلَّهِ
فَانتَظِرُوا إِنِّي مَعَكُم مِّنَ الْمُنتَظِرِينَ

1405. When we shut our eyes to Allah's glory and goodness, and go after false gods, we give some plausible excuse to ourselves, such as that they will intercede for us. But how can sticks and stones intercede for us? And how can men intercede for us, when they themselves have need of Allah's Mercy? Even the best and noblest cannot intercede as of right, but only with His permission (10:3). To pretend that there are other powers than Allah is to invent lies and to teach Allah. There is nothing in heaven or earth that He does not know, and there is no other like unto Him.

1406. *Cf.* 2:213. All mankind was created one, and Allah's Message to mankind is in essence one, the Message of Unity and Truth. But as selfishness and egotism got hold of man, certain differences sprang up between individuals, races, and nations, and in His infinite Mercy He sent them messengers and messages to suit their varying mentality, to test them by His gifts, and stir them up to emulation in virtue and piety (5:51).

1407. *Cf.* 6:115, 9:40, and 4:171. "Word" is the Decree of Allah, the expression of His Universal Will or Wisdom in a particular case. When men began to diverge from one another (see last note). Allah made their very differences subserve the higher ends by increasing their emulation in virtue and piety, and thus pointing back to the ultimate Unity and Reality. (R).

1408. Their demand for a Sign is disingenuous. All nature and revelation furnishes them with incontestable Signs. What they want is the Book of the Unseen opened out to them like the physical leaves of a book. But they forget that a physical Book is on a wholly different plane from Allah's Mysteries, and that their physical natures cannot apprehend the mysteries. They must wait. Truth will also wait. But the waiting in two cases is in quite different senses. *Cf.* 6:158 and 9:52.

C. 100.—(10:21-40.)
The good, the beautiful, and the useful
In man's life are derived from Allah;
Yet man is ungrateful. He runs
After the ephemeral things of this life;
Yet they are no better than the green
Of the fields, that lasts for a season
Ere it perish! Allah's call is to an eternal
Home of Peace. Will ye not answer it?
Know ye not that it is He Who sustains
And cherishes? No partner has He.
And He speaks to His creatures and guides them
Through His wonderful Book unmatched.

Section 3.

21. When We make mankind
Taste of some mercy after
Adversity hath touched them,
Behold! they take to plotting
Against Our Signs! Say:
"Swifter to plan is Allah!"
Verily, Our messengers record
All the plots that ye make![1409]

٢١ وَإِذَآ أَذَقْنَا ٱلنَّاسَ رَحْمَةً مِّنۢ بَعْدِ ضَرَّآءَ
مَسَّتْهُمْ إِذَا لَهُم مَّكْرٌ فِىٓ ءَايَاتِنَا ۚ قُلِ ٱللَّهُ أَسْرَعُ
مَكْرًا ۚ إِنَّ رُسُلَنَا يَكْتُبُونَ مَا تَمْكُرُونَ

22. He it is who enableth you
To traverse through land
And sea; so that ye even board
Ships—they sail with them
With a favourable wind,
And they rejoice thereat;
Then comes a stormy wind
And the waves come to them
From all sides, and they think
They are being overwhelmed:
They cry unto Allah, sincerely
Offering (their) duty unto Him,
Saying, "If Thou dost deliver us
From this, we shall truly
Show our gratitude!"[1410]

٢٢ هُوَ ٱلَّذِى يُسَيِّرُكُمْ فِى ٱلْبَرِّ
وَٱلْبَحْرِ ۖ حَتَّىٰٓ إِذَا كُنتُمْ فِى ٱلْفُلْكِ
وَجَرَيْنَ بِهِم بِرِيحٍ طَيِّبَةٍ وَفَرِحُوا۟ بِهَا
جَآءَتْهَا رِيحٌ عَاصِفٌ وَجَآءَهُمُ ٱلْمَوْجُ
مِن كُلِّ مَكَانٍ وَظَنُّوٓا۟ أَنَّهُمْ أُحِيطَ بِهِمْ ۙ دَعَوُا۟
ٱللَّهَ مُخْلِصِينَ لَهُ ٱلدِّينَ لَئِنْ أَنجَيْتَنَا مِنْ هَٰذِهِۦ
لَنَكُونَنَّ مِنَ ٱلشَّٰكِرِينَ

1409. Man turns his thoughts in adversity to Allah. But as soon as the trouble is past, he not only forgets Him but actually strives against His cause. But such people are poor ignorant creatures, not realising that the Universal Plan of Allah is swifter to stop their petty plans, and that though they fail, the record of them remains eternally against them. (R).

1410. All the great inventions and discoveries on which man prides himself are the fruit of that genius and talent which Allah has freely given of His grace. But the spirit of man remains petty, as is illustrated by the parable from the sea. How the heart of man rejoices when the ship goes smoothly with favourable winds! How in adversity it turns, in terror and helplessness, to Allah, and makes vows for deliverance! and how those vows are disregarded as soon as the danger is past! *Cf.* 6:63.

23. But when he delivereth them,
Behold! they transgress
Insolently through the earth
In defiance of right!
O mankind! your insolence[1411]
Is against your own souls—
An enjoyment of the life
Of the Present: in the end,
To Us is your return,
And We shall show you
The truth of all that ye did.

(٢٣) فَلَمَّآ أَنجَىٰهُمْ إِذَا هُمْ
يَبْغُونَ فِى ٱلْأَرْضِ بِغَيْرِ ٱلْحَقِّ
يَـٰٓأَيُّهَا ٱلنَّاسُ إِنَّمَا بَغْيُكُمْ عَلَىٰٓ أَنفُسِكُم
مَّتَـٰعَ ٱلْحَيَوٰةِ ٱلدُّنْيَا ثُمَّ إِلَيْنَا مَرْجِعُكُمْ
فَنُنَبِّئُكُم بِمَا كُنتُمْ تَعْمَلُونَ

24. The likeness of the life
Of the Present is
As the rain which We
Send down from the skies:[1412]
By its mingling arises
The produce of the earth—
Which provides food
For men and animals:
(It grows) till the earth
Is clad with its golden
Ornaments and is decked out
(In beauty): the people to whom
It belongs think they have
All powers of disposal over it:
There reaches it Our command
By night or by day,
And We make it
Like a harvest clean-mown,
As if it had not flourished
Only the day before!
Thus do We explain
The Signs in detail
For those who reflect.

(٢٤) إِنَّمَا مَثَلُ ٱلْحَيَوٰةِ
ٱلدُّنْيَا كَمَآءٍ أَنزَلْنَـٰهُ مِنَ ٱلسَّمَآءِ
فَٱخْتَلَطَ بِهِۦ نَبَاتُ ٱلْأَرْضِ
مِمَّا يَأْكُلُ ٱلنَّاسُ وَٱلْأَنْعَـٰمُ
حَتَّىٰٓ إِذَآ أَخَذَتِ ٱلْأَرْضُ زُخْرُفَهَا
وَٱزَّيَّنَتْ وَظَنَّ أَهْلُهَآ
أَنَّهُمْ قَـٰدِرُونَ عَلَيْهَآ
أَتَىٰهَآ أَمْرُنَا لَيْلًا أَوْ نَهَارًا
فَجَعَلْنَـٰهَا حَصِيدًا
كَأَن لَّمْ تَغْنَ بِٱلْأَمْسِ
كَذَٰلِكَ نُفَصِّلُ ٱلْـَٔايَـٰتِ
لِقَوْمٍ يَتَفَكَّرُونَ

1411. In our insolence and pride we do not see how small and ephemeral is that part of us which is mortal. We shall see it at last when we appear before our Judge. In the meantime our ridiculous pretensions only hurt ourselves.

1412. Another beautiful Parable, explaining the nature of our present life. The rain comes down in drops and mingles with the earth. Through it, by Allah's matchless artistry, the womb of the earth is made fruitful. All kinds of good, useful, and beautiful grains, vegetables, and fruits are produced for men and animals. The earth is covered in its bravery of green and gold and all kinds of colours. Perhaps the "owner" takes all the credit to himself, and thinks that this will last eternally. A hailstorm or blast, a frost or a volcanic eruption, comes and destroys it, or it may be even normally, that the time of harvest comes, and the fields and orchards are stripped bare by some blight or disease. Where is the beauty and bravery of yesterday? All that is left is dust and ashes! What more can we get from this physical material life?

25. But Allah doth call
To the Home of Peace:[1413]
He doth guide whom He pleaseth
To a Way that is straight.

٢٥ وَٱللَّهُ يَدْعُوٓا۟ إِلَىٰ دَارِ ٱلسَّلَٰمِ
وَيَهْدِى مَن يَشَآءُ إِلَىٰ صِرَٰطٍ مُّسْتَقِيمٍ

26. To those who do right
Is a goodly (reward)—
Yea, more (than in measure)![1414]
No darkness nor shame
Shall cover their faces![1415]
They are Companions of the Garden;
They will abide therein
(For aye)!

٢٦ لِّلَّذِينَ أَحْسَنُوا۟ ٱلْحُسْنَىٰ وَزِيَادَةٌ
وَلَا يَرْهَقُ وُجُوهَهُمْ قَتَرٌ وَلَا ذِلَّةٌ
أُو۟لَٰٓئِكَ أَصْحَٰبُ ٱلْجَنَّةِ
هُمْ فِيهَا خَٰلِدُونَ

27. But those who have earned
Evil will have a reward
Of like evil:[1416] ignominy
Will cover their (faces):
No defender will they have
From (the wrath of) Allah:
Their faces will be covered,
As it were, with pieces
From the depth of the darkness[1417]
Of Night: they are Companions
Of the Fire: they will
Abide therein (for aye)!

٢٧ وَٱلَّذِينَ كَسَبُوا۟ ٱلسَّيِّـَٔاتِ
جَزَآءُ سَيِّئَةٍۭ بِمِثْلِهَا وَتَرْهَقُهُمْ ذِلَّةٌ
مَّا لَهُم مِّنَ ٱللَّهِ مِنْ عَاصِمٍ كَأَنَّمَآ
أُغْشِيَتْ وُجُوهُهُمْ قِطَعًا مِّنَ ٱلَّيْلِ مُظْلِمًا
أُو۟لَٰٓئِكَ أَصْحَٰبُ ٱلنَّارِ هُمْ فِيهَا خَٰلِدُونَ

28. One Day shall We gather them
All together. Then shall We say
To those who joined gods (with Us):
"To your place! ye and those
Ye joined as 'partners'."

٢٨ وَيَوْمَ نَحْشُرُهُمْ
جَمِيعًا ثُمَّ نَقُولُ لِلَّذِينَ أَشْرَكُوا۟
مَكَانَكُمْ أَنتُمْ وَشُرَكَآؤُكُمْ

1413. In contrast with the ephemeral and uncertain pleasures of this material life, there is a higher life to which Allah is always calling. It is called the Home of Peace. For there is no fear, nor disappointment nor sorrow there. And all are called, and those will be chosen who have sought, not material advantages, but the Good Pleasure of Allah. *Salām*, Peace, is from the same root as *Islām*, the Religion of Unity and Harmony.

1414. The reward of the righteous will be far more than in proportion to their merits. For they will have the supreme bliss of being near to Allah, and "seeing His face". (R).

1415. The face is the symbol of the Personality, the inner and real Self, which is the antithesis of the outer and ephemeral Self. It will be illuminated with Allah's Light, behind which is no shadow or darkness. All its old shortcomings will be blotted out, with their sense of shame, for there will be Perfection, as in Allah's sight.

1416. Note that the evil reward is for those who have "earned" evil, *i.e.*, brought it on themselves by the deliberate choice of evil. Further, in the justice of Allah, they will be requited with evil similar to, and not greater in quantity or intensity, than the evil they had done—unlike the good, who, in Allah's generosity, get a reward far greater than anything they have earned or could possibly earn.

1417. Night is the negation of Light and metaphorically of joy and felicity. The intensive is indicated by "the depth of the darkness of Night."

We shall separate them,
And their "partners" shall say:
"It was not us
That ye worshipped![1418]

فَزَيَّلْنَا بَيْنَهُمْ ۖ وَقَالَ شُرَكَآؤُهُم
مَّا كُنتُمْ إِيَّانَا تَعْبُدُونَ

29. "Enough is Allah for a witness
Between us and you: we
Certainly knew nothing
Of your worship of us!"[1419]

٢٩ فَكَفَىٰ بِٱللَّهِ شَهِيدًۢا بَيْنَنَا وَبَيْنَكُمْ
إِن كُنَّا عَنْ عِبَادَتِكُمْ لَغَٰفِلِينَ

30. There will every soul prove
(The fruits of) the deeds
It sent before[1420]: they will
Be brought back to Allah
Their rightful Lord,
And their invented falsehoods
Will leave them in the lurch.[1421]

٣٠ هُنَالِكَ تَبْلُوا۟ كُلُّ نَفْسٍ مَّآ أَسْلَفَتْ ۚ
وَرُدُّوٓا۟ إِلَى ٱللَّهِ مَوْلَىٰهُمُ ٱلْحَقِّ ۖ
وَضَلَّ عَنْهُم مَّا كَانُوا۟ يَفْتَرُونَ

SECTION 4.

31. Say: "Who is it that
Sustains you (in life)
From the sky and from the
earth?[1422]
Or who is it that
Has power over hearing[1423]
And sight? And who
Is it that brings out
The living from the dead
And the dead from the living?[1424]
And who is it that

٣١ قُلْ مَن يَرْزُقُكُم
مِّنَ ٱلسَّمَآءِ وَٱلْأَرْضِ
أَمَّن يَمْلِكُ ٱلسَّمْعَ وَٱلْأَبْصَٰرَ
وَمَن يُخْرِجُ ٱلْحَىَّ مِنَ ٱلْمَيِّتِ
وَيُخْرِجُ ٱلْمَيِّتَ مِنَ ٱلْحَىِّ وَمَن

1418. The false gods are not real: they are only the figments of the imaginations of those who indulged in the false worship. But the prophets or great or good men whose names were vainly taken in competition with the name of Allah, and the personified Ideas or Idols treated in the same way would themselves protest against their names being used in that way, and show that the worship was paid not to them, but to the ignorance or superstition or selfish lusts of the false worshippers.

1419. See last note. They did not even know that they were being falsely worshipped in that way.

1420. *Cf.* 2:95, where the verb used is *qaddama*. The verb *aslafa*, used here, is nearly synonymous.

1421. Instead of their false ideas helping them, they will desert them and leave them in the lurch. *Cf.* 6:24.

1422. Sustenance may be understood in the sense of all the provision necessary for maintaining physical life as well as mental and spiritual development and well-being. Examples of the former are light and rain from heaven and the produce of the earth and facilities of movement on land and sea and in air. Examples of the latter are the moral and spiritual influences that come from our fellow-men, and from the great Teachers and Prophets.

1423. Just two of our ordinary faculties, hearing and sight, are mentioned, as examples of the rest. All the gifts of Allah, physical and spiritual, are enjoyed and incorporated by us by means of the faculties and capacities with which He has endowed us.

1424. *Cf.* 3:27 and n. 371; 6:95 and n. 920: and 30:19.

Rules and regulates all affairs?"[1425]
They will soon say, "Allah".
Say, "Will ye not then
Show piety (to Him)?"

يُدَبِّرُ ٱلْأَمْرَ ۚ فَسَيَقُولُونَ ٱللَّهُ ۚ
فَقُلْ أَفَلَا تَتَّقُونَ

32. Such is Allah, your real
Cherisher and Sustainer:
Apart from Truth,
What (remains) but error?[1426]
How then are ye turned away?

٣٢ فَذَٰلِكُمُ ٱللَّهُ رَبُّكُمُ ٱلْحَقُّ ۖ
فَمَاذَا بَعْدَ ٱلْحَقِّ إِلَّا ٱلضَّلَٰلُ ۖ فَأَنَّىٰ تُصْرَفُونَ

33. Thus is the Word
Of thy Lord proved true[1427]
Against those who rebel:
Verily they will not believe.

٣٣ كَذَٰلِكَ حَقَّتْ كَلِمَتُ رَبِّكَ
عَلَى ٱلَّذِينَ فَسَقُوٓا۟ أَنَّهُمْ لَا يُؤْمِنُونَ

34. Say: "Of your 'partners',[1428]
Can any originate creation
And repeat it?" Say:
"It is Allah Who originates
Creation and repeats it:
Then how are ye deluded
Away (from the truth)?"

٣٤ قُلْ هَلْ مِن شُرَكَآئِكُم مَّن يَبْدَؤُا۟ ٱلْخَلْقَ
ثُمَّ يُعِيدُهُۥ ۚ قُلِ ٱللَّهُ يَبْدَؤُا۟ ٱلْخَلْقَ
ثُمَّ يُعِيدُهُۥ ۖ فَأَنَّىٰ تُؤْفَكُونَ

35. Say: "Of your 'partners'
Is there any that
Can give any guidance
Towards Truth?" Say: "It is Allah
Who gives guidance
Towards Truth. Is then He
Who gives guidance to Truth
More worthy to be followed,
Or he who finds not guidance
(Himself) unless he is guided?

٣٥ قُلْ هَلْ مِن شُرَكَآئِكُم مَّن يَهْدِىٓ
إِلَى ٱلْحَقِّ ۚ قُلِ ٱللَّهُ يَهْدِى لِلْحَقِّ ۗ
أَفَمَن يَهْدِىٓ إِلَى ٱلْحَقِّ أَحَقُّ أَن يُتَّبَعَ
أَمَّن لَّا يَهِدِّىٓ إِلَّآ أَن يُهْدَىٰ ۖ

1425. This is the general summing-up of the argument. The government of the whole Creation and its maintenance and sustenance is in the hands of Allah. How futile then would it be to neglect His true worship and go after false gods?

1426. The wonderful handiwork and wisdom of Allah having been referred to, as the real Truth, as against the false worship and false gods that men set up, it follows that to disregard the Truth must lead us into woeful wrong, not only in our beliefs but in our conduct. We shall err and stray and be lost. How then can we turn away from the Truth?

1427. Disobedience to Allah brings its own terrible consequences on ourselves. The Law, the Word, the Decree, of Allah must be fulfilled. If we go to false gods, our Faith will be dimmed, and then extinguished. Our spiritual faculties will be dead.

1428. The argument is now turned in another direction. The false gods can neither create out of nothing nor sustain the creative energy which maintains the world. Nor can they give any guidance which can be of use for the future destiny of mankind: on the contrary they themselves (assuming they were men who were deified) stand in need of such guidance. Why then follow vain fancies, instead of going to the source of all knowledge, truth, and guidance, and worship, serve, and obey Allah, the One True God?

What then is the matter
With you? How judge ye?"

فَمَا لَكُمْ كَيْفَ تَحْكُمُونَ

36. But most of them follow
Nothing but fancy: truly
Fancy can be of no avail
Against Truth. Verily Allah
Is well aware of all
That they do.

٣٦ وَمَا يَتَّبِعُ أَكْثَرُهُمْ إِلَّا ظَنًّا
إِنَّ الظَّنَّ لَا يُغْنِي مِنَ الْحَقِّ شَيْئًا
إِنَّ اللَّهَ عَلِيمٌ بِمَا يَفْعَلُونَ

37. This Qur'ān is not such
As can be produced
By other than Allah;
On the contrary it is
A confirmation of (revelations)
That went before it,
And a fuller explanation[1429]
Of the Book—wherein
There is no doubt—
From the Lord of the Worlds.

٣٧ وَمَا كَانَ هَٰذَا الْقُرْءَانُ أَن يُفْتَرَىٰ
مِن دُونِ اللَّهِ وَلَٰكِن تَصْدِيقَ
الَّذِي بَيْنَ يَدَيْهِ وَتَفْصِيلَ
الْكِتَٰبِ لَا رَيْبَ فِيهِ
مِن رَّبِّ الْعَٰلَمِينَ

38. Or do they say,
"He forged it"?
Say: "Bring then
A Sūrah like unto it,
And call (to your aid)
Anyone you can,
Besides Allah, if it be
Ye speak the truth!"[1430]

٣٨ أَمْ يَقُولُونَ افْتَرَىٰهُ
قُلْ فَأْتُوا بِسُورَةٍ مِّثْلِهِ
وَادْعُوا مَنِ اسْتَطَعْتُم مِّن دُونِ اللَّهِ
إِن كُنتُمْ صَٰدِقِينَ

39. Nay, they charge with falsehood
That whose knowledge they
Cannot compass, even before
The elucidation thereof[1431]
Hath reached them: thus
Did those before them
Make charges of falsehood:

٣٩ بَلْ كَذَّبُوا بِمَا لَمْ يُحِيطُوا بِعِلْمِهِ
وَلَمَّا يَأْتِهِمْ تَأْوِيلُهُ كَذَٰلِكَ كَذَّبَ
الَّذِينَ مِن قَبْلِهِمْ

1429. *The Book: Cf.* 3:23 and n. 366. Allah's revelation throughout the ages is one. The Qur'ān confirms, fulfils, completes, and further explains the one true revelation, which has been sent by the One True God in all ages.

1430. *Cf.* 2:23 and n. 42.

1431. *Ta'wīl*: elucidation, explanation, final fulfilment, *Cf.*, 7:53. The Message of Allah not only gives us rules of our everyday conduct, but speaks of high matters of religious significance, which require elucidation in three ways: (1) by instruction from Teachers of great spiritual experince, (2) by experience from the actual facts of life, and (3) by the final fulfilment of the hopes and warnings which we now take on trust through our Faith. The Unbelievers reject Allah's Message simply because they cannot understand it and without giving it even a chance of elucidation in any of these ways. (R).

But see what was the end
Of those who did wrong![1432]

فَانظُرْ كَيْفَ كَانَ عَٰقِبَةُ ٱلظَّٰلِمِينَ

40. Of them there are some
Who believe therein,
And some who do not:
And thy Lord knoweth best
Those who are out for mischief.

﴿٤٠﴾ وَمِنْهُم مَّن يُؤْمِنُ بِهِۦ وَمِنْهُم مَّن لَّا يُؤْمِنُ بِهِۦ ۚ وَرَبُّكَ أَعْلَمُ بِٱلْمُفْسِدِينَ

C. 101.—Men but wrong their own souls in shutting out
(10:41-70.) The truth of Allah. To Him will be
Their return. They have been warned
At all times and among all peoples
By chosen Prophets of Allah, whom they
Have flouted. The Day will come
When they will see the majesty, the glory,
The goodness, and the justice of Allah.
But they invent fancies and falsehoods.
Let not their blasphemies and falsehoods
Grieve the men of Allah: for falsehoods
And false ones will never prosper.

SECTION 5.

41. If they charge thee
With falsehood, say:
"My work to me,
And yours to you![1433]
Ye are free from responsibility
For what I do and I
For what ye do!"

﴿٤١﴾ وَإِن كَذَّبُوكَ فَقُل لِّى عَمَلِى وَلَكُمْ عَمَلُكُمْ ۖ أَنتُم بَرِيٓـُٔونَ مِمَّآ أَعْمَلُ وَأَنَا۠ بَرِىٓءٌ مِّمَّا تَعْمَلُونَ

42. Among them are some who
(Pretend to) listen to thee:
But canst thou make the deaf
To hear—even though
They are without
understanding?[1434]

﴿٤٢﴾ وَمِنْهُم مَّن يَسْتَمِعُونَ إِلَيْكَ ۚ أَفَأَنتَ تُسْمِعُ ٱلصُّمَّ وَلَوْ كَانُوا۟ لَا يَعْقِلُونَ

1432. Wrongdoers always came to grief ultimately. The true course of history shows it from a broad standpoint. But they are so headstrong that they prejudge issues in their ignorance before they are decided.

1433. When the Prophet of Allah is rejected and charged with falsehood, he does not give up his work, but continues to teach and preach his Message. He can well say to those who interfere with him: "Mind your own business: supposing your charge against me is true, you incur no responsibility: I have to answer for it before Allah: and if I do my duty and deliver my Message, your rejection does not make me liable for your wrongdoing: you will have to answer before Allah."

1434. *Cf.* 6:25, 36, 39 and notes. Hypocrites go to hear and see some great Teacher, but they get no profit out of it because they are not sincerely seeking the truth. They are like the blind, or the deaf, or the imbeciles. It is impossible to guide them, because they have not the will to be guided.

43. And among them are some
Who look at thee:
But canst thou guide
The blind—even though
They will not see?

٤٣ ومنهم من ينظر إليك أفأنت
تهدي العمى ولو كانوا لا يبصرون

44. Verily Allah will not deal
Unjustly with man in aught:
It is man that wrongs
His own soul.[1435]

٤٤ إن الله لا يظلم الناس شيئا
ولكن الناس أنفسهم يظلمون

45. One day He will
Gather them together:
(It will be) as if
They had tarried[1436]
But an hour of a day:
They will recognise each other:[1437]
Assuredly those will be lost
Who denied the meeting
With Allah and refused
To receive true guidance.

٤٥ ويوم يحشرهم
كأن لم يلبثوا إلا ساعة
من النهار يتعارفون بينهم
قد خسر الذين كذبوا
بلقاء الله وما كانوا مهتدين

46. Whether We show thee
(Realised in thy lifetime)
Some part of what We
Promise them—or We
Take thy soul (to Our Mercy)
(Before that)—in any case,
To Us is their return:
Ultimately Allah is witness[1438]
To all that they do.

٤٦ وإما نرينك
بعض الذي نعدهم
أو نتوفينك
فإلينا مرجعهم
ثم الله شهيد على ما يفعلون

1435. Allah cannot be blamed for man's evil, nor will He deal unjustly with man. He has given him faculties and means of guidance. If man goes wrong, it is because he wrongs himself.

1436. In eternity our life on this earth will look as if it had been just a little part of our little day, and so also will appear any interval between our death and the call to Judgement.

1437. We shall retain some perception of our mutual relations on earth, so that the righteous judgement which will be pronounced will be intelligible to us, and we shall be convinced of its righteousness.

1438. The Prophet is assured that the end of evil is evil, just as the end of good is good. Whether this result is made plain before his very eyes in his own lifetime or afterwards, makes no difference. The wicked should not rejoice if they are given rope and seem to have the upper hand for a time, nor should the righteous lose heart: for Allah's promise is sure and must come to pass. And in any case, the scales can only be partially, if at all, adjusted in this life. There is the final and complete adjustment on the Day of Judgement. Allah is All-Knowing, and all truth will be before Him.

47. To every people (was sent)
A Messenger: when their
Messenger[1439]
Comes (before them), the matter
Will be judged between them
With justice, and they
Will not be wronged.

٤٧ وَلِكُلِّ أُمَّةٍ رَّسُولٌ
فَإِذَا جَآءَ رَسُولُهُمْ قُضِىَ
بَيْنَهُم بِٱلْقِسْطِ وَهُمْ لَا يُظْلَمُونَ

48. They say: "When
Will this promise
Come to pass—
If ye speak the truth?"

٤٨ وَيَقُولُونَ مَتَىٰ هَٰذَا ٱلْوَعْدُ
إِن كُنتُمْ صَٰدِقِينَ

49. Say: "I have no power[1440]
Over any harm or profit
To myself except as Allah
Willeth. To every People[1441]
Is a term appointed:
When their term is reached,
Not an hour can they cause
Delay, nor (an hour) can they
Advance (it in anticipation)."

٤٩ قُل لَّآ أَمْلِكُ لِنَفْسِى
ضَرًّا وَلَا نَفْعًا إِلَّا مَا شَآءَ ٱللَّهُ
لِكُلِّ أُمَّةٍ أَجَلٌ إِذَا جَآءَ أَجَلُهُمْ
فَلَا يَسْتَـْٔخِرُونَ سَاعَةً وَلَا يَسْتَقْدِمُونَ

50. Say: "Do ye see—
If His punishment should come
To you by night or by day,[1442]
What portion of it
Would the Sinners
Wish to hasten?

٥٠ قُلْ أَرَءَيْتُمْ إِنْ
أَتَىٰكُمْ عَذَابُهُۥ بَيَٰتًا أَوْ نَهَارًا
مَّاذَا يَسْتَعْجِلُ مِنْهُ ٱلْمُجْرِمُونَ

51. "Would ye then believe in it
At last, when it actually cometh
To pass? (It will then be said:)

٥١ أَثُمَّ إِذَا مَا وَقَعَ ءَامَنتُم بِهِۦٓ

1439. Every people or generation or nation had its Message or Messenger: Allah revealed Himself to it in some way or another. If that Messenger was ignored or rejected, or his Message was twisted or misused, the Day of Reckoning will come, when perfect justice will be done and the whole Truth revealed. The Unbelievers mockingly say: "If that is true, pray tell us when that Day will come!" The answer of the Messenger is: "It will come in good time: no one can either hasten or retard it. If you want me then to save you or if you fear that I shall harm you for your treatment of me, know that this matter is in the hands of Allah alone, Who will do perfect justice. Even in regard to myself, any harm or good that befalls me is by the command and in the power of Allah."

1440. *Cf.* 7:188.

1441. This repeats 7:34, but the significance is different in the two contexts. Here the reply is to the Unbelievers' mocking incredulity (seen n. 1439) as to whether there is such a thing as a Hereafter: they suggest to the Prophet of Allah that if his claim to inspiration from Allah is true, he should get them punished at once for rejecting him. In 7:34 the reference is to the punishment of iniquity as described in 7:33: sin is not necessarily punished at once: every People or generation gets a chance; when their term is fulfilled, the final adjustment is made.

1442. The mockery of Unbelievers will be turned into panic when the wrath of Allah descends on them. It may do so suddenly, by night or by day, when they least expect it. Will they then say of any bit of it: "Let it be hastened"?

ءَآلْـَٰٔنَ وَقَدْ كُنتُم بِهِۦ تَسْتَعْجِلُونَ

'Ah! now? and ye wanted
(Aforetime) to hasten it on!'

ثُمَّ قِيلَ لِلَّذِينَ ظَلَمُوا۟ ذُوقُوا۟ عَذَابَ ٱلْخُلْدِ هَلْ تُجْزَوْنَ إِلَّا بِمَا كُنتُمْ تَكْسِبُونَ ﴿٥٢﴾

52. "At length will be said
To the wrongdoers: 'Taste ye
The enduring punishment![1443]
Ye get but the recompense
Of what ye earned!'"

وَيَسْتَنۢبِـُٔونَكَ أَحَقٌّ هُوَ قُلْ إِى وَرَبِّىٓ إِنَّهُۥ لَحَقٌّ وَمَآ أَنتُم بِمُعْجِزِينَ ﴿٥٣﴾

53. They seek to be informed
By thee: "Is that true?"
Say: "Aye! by my Lord!
It is the very truth!
And ye cannot frustrate it!"

SECTION 6.

وَلَوْ أَنَّ لِكُلِّ نَفْسٍ ظَلَمَتْ مَا فِى ٱلْأَرْضِ لَٱفْتَدَتْ بِهِۦ وَأَسَرُّوا۟ ٱلنَّدَامَةَ لَمَّا رَأَوُا۟ ٱلْعَذَابَ وَقُضِىَ بَيْنَهُم بِٱلْقِسْطِ وَهُمْ لَا يُظْلَمُونَ ﴿٥٤﴾

54. Every soul that hath sinned,
If it possessed all
That is on earth,
Would fain give it in ransom:[1444]
They would declare (their)
repentance[1445]
When they see the Penalty:
But the judgement between them
Will be with justice,
And no wrong will be done
Unto them.

أَلَآ إِنَّ لِلَّهِ مَا فِى ٱلسَّمَـٰوَٰتِ وَٱلْأَرْضِ ﴿٥٥﴾

55. Is it not (the case) that to Allah
Belongeth whatever is
In the heavens and on earth?

1443. This will be the final doom, and they will themselves have brought it on themselves!

The psychology of the Unbelievers is here analysed and exposed. This particular argument begins at 10:47 and ends at 10:53. It begins with the general statement that every People has had due warning and explanation by means of a Prophet specially sent to them; that Prophet will be a relevant witness at the final Judgement, when the matter will be judged in perfect equity. Then follows a dialogue. The Unbelievers mock and say, "Why not bring on the Punishment now?" The reply to the Unbelievers is, "It will come in Allah's good time". The Believers are told to watch and see how the sinners would take it if the Punishment were to come at once. Would they not think it too sudden? When it actually comes, their panic will be indescribable. "Is that true?" say the Unbelievers. "It is the very truth," is the answer, "and nothing can ward it off."

1444. *Cf.* 3:91.

1445. *Declare their repentance*: the verb in the original is *asarrū*, which may mean either "declare" or "reveal" or else "conceal" or "hide". The classical Commentators are divided as to the meaning to be adopted here. If the first, which I prefer, the sense would be: "When the Penalty stares the sinners in the face, they would give anything to escape it, and they would even openly declare their repentance, which would be a source of shame and ignominy to them." If the latter meaning be taken, the sense would be: "They would give anything to escape the Penalty; but the hardest thing of all for them is frankly to confess and repent, and so they conceal their sense of shame and ignominy."

Is it not (the case) that
Allah's promise is assuredly true?
Yet most of them understand not.

أَلَآ إِنَّ وَعْدَ ٱللَّهِ حَقٌّ وَلَٰكِنَّ أَكْثَرَهُمْ لَا يَعْلَمُونَ

56. It is He who giveth life
And who taketh it,
And to Him shall ye
All be brought back.

هُوَ يُحْىِۦ وَيُمِيتُ ٥٦
وَإِلَيْهِ تُرْجَعُونَ

57. O mankind! there hath come
To you a direction from your Lord
And a healing for the (diseases)[1446]
In your hearts—and for those
Who believe, a Guidance
And a Mercy.

يَٰٓأَيُّهَا ٱلنَّاسُ قَدْ جَآءَتْكُم ٥٧
مَّوْعِظَةٌ مِّن رَّبِّكُمْ وَشِفَآءٌ لِّمَا فِى
ٱلصُّدُورِ وَهُدًى وَرَحْمَةٌ لِّلْمُؤْمِنِينَ

58. Say: "In the Bounty of Allah.
And in His Mercy—in that
Let them rejoice": that is better
Than the (wealth) they hoard.

قُلْ بِفَضْلِ ٱللَّهِ وَبِرَحْمَتِهِۦ فَبِذَٰلِكَ ٥٨
فَلْيَفْرَحُوا۟ هُوَ خَيْرٌ مِّمَّا يَجْمَعُونَ

59. Say: "See ye what things[1447]
Allah hath sent down to you
For sustenance? Yet ye
Hold forbidden some things
Thereof and (some things) lawful."
Say: "Hath Allah indeed
Permitted you, or do ye invent
(Things) to attribute to Allah?"

قُلْ أَرَءَيْتُم مَّآ أَنزَلَ ٱللَّهُ لَكُم ٥٩
مِّن رِّزْقٍ فَجَعَلْتُم مِّنْهُ حَرَامًا وَحَلَٰلًا
قُلْ ءَآللَّهُ أَذِنَ لَكُمْ
أَمْ عَلَى ٱللَّهِ تَفْتَرُونَ

60. And what think those
Who invent lies against Allah,
Of the Day of Judgement?[1448]
Verily Allah is full of Bounty

وَمَا ظَنُّ ٱلَّذِينَ يَفْتَرُونَ عَلَى ٱللَّهِ ٱلْكَذِبَ ٦٠
يَوْمَ ٱلْقِيَٰمَةِ إِنَّ ٱللَّهَ لَذُو فَضْلٍ

1446. Those who do wrong have a disease in their hearts, which will cause their spiritual death. Allah in His Mercy declares His Will to them, which should direct their lives and provide a healing for their spiritual disease. If they accept Faith, the remedy acts; they find themselves in right guidance and receive Allah's forgiveness and mercy. Surely those are far better gifts than material advantages, wealth, or possessions.

1447. "Sustenance" is to be taken in both the literal and the metaphorical sense. In the literal sense, what fine and varied things Allah has provided for us on land and in sea and air, in the vegetable, animal, and mineral kingdoms? Yet narrow minds put artificial barriers against their use. In the metaphorical sense, what enchanting fields of knowledge and spiritual endeavour are provided in our individual and social lives? And who is to say that some are lawful and others forbidden? Supposing they were so in special circumstances, it is not right to attribute artificial restrictions of that kind to Allah and falsely erect religious sanctions against them.

1448. People who lie in Religion or invent false gods, or false worship—have they any idea of the Day of Judgement, when they will be called to account, and will have to answer for their deeds?

To mankind, but most
Of them are ungrateful.[1449]

عَلَى ٱلنَّاسِ وَلَٰكِنَّ أَكْثَرَهُمْ لَا يَشْكُرُونَ

SECTION 7.

61. In whatever business thou
Mayest be, and whatever portion
Thou mayest be reciting
From the Qur'ān—and whatever
Deed ye (mankind) may be
doing—
We are Witnesses thereof
When ye are deeply engrossed
Therein. Nor is hidden
From the Lord (so much as)
The weight of an atom
On the earth or in heaven.
And not the least
And not the greatest
Of these things but are recorded
In a clear Record.[1450]

٦١ وَمَا تَكُونُ فِي شَأْنٍ
وَمَا تَتْلُوا۟ مِنْهُ مِن قُرْءَانٍ
وَلَا تَعْمَلُونَ مِنْ عَمَلٍ
إِلَّا كُنَّا عَلَيْكُمْ شُهُودًا إِذْ تُفِيضُونَ فِيهِ
وَمَا يَعْزُبُ عَن رَّبِّكَ مِن مِّثْقَالِ ذَرَّةٍ
فِي ٱلْأَرْضِ وَلَا فِي ٱلسَّمَآءِ وَلَآ أَصْغَرَ مِن
ذَٰلِكَ وَلَآ أَكْبَرَ إِلَّا فِي كِتَٰبٍ مُّبِينٍ

62. Behold! verily on the friends
Of Allah there is no fear,[1451]
Nor shall they grieve;

٦٢ أَلَآ إِنَّ أَوْلِيَآءَ ٱللَّهِ
لَا خَوْفٌ عَلَيْهِمْ وَلَا هُمْ يَحْزَنُونَ

63. Those who believe
And (constantly) guard
Against evil—

٦٣ ٱلَّذِينَ ءَامَنُوا۟ وَكَانُوا۟ يَتَّقُونَ

64. For them are Glad Tidings,
In the life of the Present
And in the Hereafter:
No change can there be
In the Words of Allah.

٦٤ لَهُمُ ٱلْبُشْرَىٰ فِي ٱلْحَيَوٰةِ ٱلدُّنْيَا
وَفِي ٱلْأَخِرَةِ لَا تَبْدِيلَ لِكَلِمَٰتِ ٱللَّهِ

1449. Allah is most kind, and gracious, and generous with His gifts of all kinds, material and spiritual. But men do not understand, and are ungrateful in forgetting the Giver of all and setting up false objects of worship and false standards of pride.

1450. There is nothing that men can do but Allah is a witness to it. We may be deeply engrossed in some particular thing and for the time being be quite unconscious of other things. But Allah's knowledge not only comprehends all things, but has all things actively before it. Nothing is hidden from Him. And His knowledge has another quality which human knowledge has not. Human knowledge is subject to time, and is obliterated by time. Allah's knowledge is like a Record and endures forever. And His Record has a further quality which human records have not. The most permanent human record may be quite intelligible to those who make it but may be ambiguous to others and may become unintelligible with the progress of time, as happens almost invariably to the most enduring inscriptions from very ancient times: but in Allah's "Record" or knowledge there is no ambiguity, for it is independent of time, or place, or circumstance. This is the force of *Mubīn* ("clear") here.

1451. Allah's all-embracing knowledge and constant watchful care over all His creatures, may be a source of fear to sinners, but there is no fear for those whom He honours with His love and friendship—neither in this world nor in the world to come.

This is indeed
The supreme Felicity.

ذَٰلِكَ هُوَ ٱلْفَوْزُ ٱلْعَظِيمُ

65. Let not their speech[1452]
Grieve thee: for all power
And honour belong to Allah:
It is He Who heareth
And knoweth (all things).

٦٥ وَلَا يَحْزُنكَ قَوْلُهُمْ إِنَّ
ٱلْعِزَّةَ لِلَّهِ جَمِيعًا هُوَ ٱلسَّمِيعُ ٱلْعَلِيمُ

66. Behold! verily to Allah
Belong all creatures,
In the heavens and on earth.
What do they follow
Who worship as His "partners"
Other than Allah? They follow
Nothing but fancy, and
They do nothing but lie.[1453]

٦٦ أَلَآ إِنَّ لِلَّهِ مَن فِى ٱلسَّمَٰوَٰتِ وَمَن
فِى ٱلْأَرْضِ وَمَا يَتَّبِعُ ٱلَّذِينَ يَدْعُونَ
مِن دُونِ ٱللَّهِ شُرَكَآءَ إِن يَتَّبِعُونَ إِلَّا
ٱلظَّنَّ وَإِنْ هُمْ إِلَّا يَخْرُصُونَ

67. He it is that hath
Made you the Night
That ye may rest therein,
And the Day to make
Things visible (to you).[1454]
Verily in this are Signs
For those who listen
(To His Message).

٦٧ هُوَ ٱلَّذِى جَعَلَ لَكُمُ
ٱلَّيْلَ لِتَسْكُنُوا۟ فِيهِ
وَٱلنَّهَارَ مُبْصِرًا إِنَّ فِى ذَٰلِكَ
لَءَايَٰتٍ لِّقَوْمٍ يَسْمَعُونَ

68. They say, "Allah hath begotten
A son!"—Glory be to Him!
He is Self-Sufficient! His
Are all things in the heavens
And on earth! No warrant
Have ye for this! Say ye
About Allah what ye know not?

٦٨ قَالُوا۟ ٱتَّخَذَ ٱللَّهُ وَلَدًا سُبْحَٰنَهُۥ
هُوَ ٱلْغَنِىُّ لَهُۥ مَا فِى ٱلسَّمَٰوَٰتِ وَمَا فِى ٱلْأَرْضِ
إِنْ عِندَكُم مِّن سُلْطَٰنٍ بِهَٰذَآ
أَتَقُولُونَ عَلَى ٱللَّهِ مَا لَا تَعْلَمُونَ

1452. Sometimes the words of the unrighteous or their revilings hurt or grieve the righteous man, but there is no occasion for either anger or sorrow: they have no power and they can do no real dishonour, for all power and honour are from Allah.

1453. All creatures are subject to Allah. If, therefore, any false worship is set up, the false gods—so called "partners"—are merely creatures of imagination or false inventions.

1454. Our physical life—and our higher life in so far as it is linked with the physical—is sustained by the alternation of rest and activity, and the fit environment for this alternation is the succession of Nights and Days in our physical world. The Day makes the things "visible to us"—a beautiful symbol, not only of the physical work for which we go about by day, but of the higher activities which are fitly associated with seeing, perception and inquiry. Intuition (insight) is a little out of that circle because that may come by night, when our other faculties are resting.

69. Say: "Those who invent
A lie against Allah
Will never prosper."[1455]

٦٩ قُلْ إِنَّ ٱلَّذِينَ يَفْتَرُونَ
عَلَى ٱللَّهِ ٱلْكَذِبَ لَا يُفْلِحُونَ

70. A little enjoyment
In this world!—
And then, to Us
Will be their return.
Then shall We make them
Taste the severest Penalty
For their blasphemies.

٧٠ مَتَٰعٌ فِى ٱلدُّنْيَا
ثُمَّ إِلَيْنَا مَرْجِعُهُمْ
ثُمَّ نُذِيقُهُمُ ٱلْعَذَابَ ٱلشَّدِيدَ
بِمَا كَانُوا۟ يَكْفُرُونَ

C. 102. (10:71-92.) — Allah works in His world—in mercy
For His servants, and in just punishment
For those who do wrong. Thus was it
In Noah's story, for he worked unselfishly
For his people, though rejected by them.
So was it with Moses: he preached
To Pharaoh and the Egyptians; but most
Of them preferred falsehood and pride
To the Truth of Allah, and perished. Even
Pharaoh's confession of Allah at the last
Was too late, as his life had been spent
In luxury, pride, and oppression.

SECTION 8.

71. Relate to them the story[1456]
Of Noah. Behold! he said
To his People: "O my People,
If it be hard on your (mind)
That I should stay (with you)
And commemorate the Signs
Of Allah—yet I put
My trust in Allah.
Get ye then an agreement
About your plan and among

٧١ وَٱتْلُ عَلَيْهِمْ نَبَأَ نُوحٍ إِذْ قَالَ
لِقَوْمِهِۦ يَٰقَوْمِ إِن كَانَ كَبُرَ عَلَيْكُم
مَّقَامِى وَتَذْكِيرِى بِـَٔايَٰتِ ٱللَّهِ
فَعَلَى ٱللَّهِ تَوَكَّلْتُ
فَأَجْمِعُوٓا۟ أَمْرَكُمْ

1455. In Quranic language "prosperity" refers both to our everyday life and to the higher life within us—to the Present and the Future—health and strength, opportunities and resources, a spirit of contentment and the power of influencing others. Here there seems to be an extra touch of meaning. A liar not only deprives himself of prosperity in all senses, but his "lie" itself against Allah will not succeed: it will and must be found out.

1456. The reference to Noah's story here is only incidental, to illustrate a special point. The fuller story will be found in 11:25-49, and in many other passages, *e.g.*, 7:59-64, 26:105-122, and 37:75-82. At each place there is a special point in the context. The special point here is that Noah's very life and preaching among his wicked people was a cause of offence to them. But he feared nothing, trusted in Allah, delivered his message, and was saved from the Flood.

Your Partners, so your plan[1457]
Be not to you dark and dubious.
Then pass your sentence on me,
And give me no respite.

وَشُرَكَآءَكُمْ ثُمَّ لَا يَكُنْ أَمْرُكُمْ عَلَيْكُمْ غُمَّةً
ثُمَّ ٱقْضُوٓا۟ إِلَىَّ وَلَا تُنظِرُونِ

72. "But if ye turn back, (consider):
No reward have I asked[1458]
Of you: my reward is only
Due from Allah, and I
Have been commanded to be
Of those who submit
To Allah's Will (in Islām)."

﴿٧٢﴾ فَإِن تَوَلَّيْتُمْ فَمَا سَأَلْتُكُم مِّنْ أَجْرٍ
إِنْ أَجْرِىَ إِلَّا عَلَى ٱللَّهِ وَأُمِرْتُ
أَنْ أَكُونَ مِنَ ٱلْمُسْلِمِينَ

73. They rejected him,
But We delivered him,
And those with him,
In the Ark, and We made
Them inherit (the earth),
While We overwhelmed
In the Flood those
Who rejected Our Signs.[1459]
Then see what was the end
Of those who were warned
(But heeded not)!

﴿٧٣﴾ فَكَذَّبُوهُ فَنَجَّيْنَٰهُ
وَمَن مَّعَهُۥ فِى ٱلْفُلْكِ
وَجَعَلْنَٰهُمْ خَلَٰٓئِفَ
وَأَغْرَقْنَا ٱلَّذِينَ كَذَّبُوا۟ بِـَٔايَٰتِنَا
فَٱنظُرْ كَيْفَ كَانَ عَٰقِبَةُ ٱلْمُنذَرِينَ

74. Then after him We sent
(Many) messengers to their
Peoples:
They brought them Clear Signs,
But they would not believe
What they had already rejected[1460]
Beforehand. Thus do We seal
The hearts of the transgressors.

﴿٧٤﴾ ثُمَّ بَعَثْنَا مِنۢ بَعْدِهِۦ رُسُلًا
إِلَىٰ قَوْمِهِمْ فَجَآءُوهُم بِٱلْبَيِّنَٰتِ
فَمَا كَانُوا۟ لِيُؤْمِنُوا۟ بِمَا كَذَّبُوا۟ بِهِۦ مِن قَبْلُ
كَذَٰلِكَ نَطْبَعُ عَلَىٰ قُلُوبِ ٱلْمُعْتَدِينَ

1457. Firm in his sense of Truth from Allah, Noah plainly told his people to condemn him to death if they liked, openly and in concert, so that he should at least know who would listen to his Message and who would not. He wanted them to be frank and direct, for he feared nothing.

1458. The Prophet of Allah preaches for the good of his people. He claims no reward from them; but, on the contrary, is reviled, persecuted, banished, and often slain.

1459. *Cf.* 7:64.

1460. I understand the meaning to be that there is a sort of spiritual influence descending from generation to generation, among the Unbelievers as among the men of Faith. In history we find the same spiritual problems in many ages—denial of Allah's grace, defiance of Allah's law, rejection of Allah's Message. These influences cause the hearts of the contumacious to be sealed and impervious to the Truth. *Cf.* 2:7 and notes. What they do is prejudges the issues even before the Prophet explains them.

75. Then after them sent We
Moses and Aaron to Pharaoh[1461]
And his chiefs with Our Signs.
But they were arrogant:
They were a people in sin.

٧٥ ثُمَّ بَعَثْنَا مِنۢ بَعْدِهِم مُّوسَىٰ
وَهَٰرُونَ إِلَىٰ فِرْعَوْنَ وَمَلَإِيْهِۦ بِـَٔايَٰتِنَا
فَٱسْتَكْبَرُوا۟ وَكَانُوا۟ قَوْمًا مُّجْرِمِينَ

76. When the Truth did come
To them from Us, they said:
"This is indeed evident sorcery!"

٧٦ فَلَمَّا جَآءَهُمُ ٱلْحَقُّ مِنْ عِندِنَا
قَالُوٓا۟ إِنَّ هَٰذَا لَسِحْرٌ مُّبِينٌ

77. Said Moses: "Say ye (this)
About the Truth when
It hath (actually) reached you?
Is sorcery (like) this?
But sorcerers will not prosper."[1462]

٧٧ قَالَ مُوسَىٰٓ أَتَقُولُونَ لِلْحَقِّ لَمَّا جَآءَكُمْ
أَسِحْرٌ هَٰذَا وَلَا يُفْلِحُ ٱلسَّٰحِرُونَ

78. They said: "Hast thou
Come to us to turn us
Away from the ways
We found our fathers following—
In order that thou and thy brother
May have greatness in the land?[1463]
But not we shall believe in you!"

٧٨ قَالُوٓا۟ أَجِئْتَنَا لِتَلْفِتَنَا عَمَّا
وَجَدْنَا عَلَيْهِ ءَابَآءَنَا وَتَكُونَ لَكُمَا
ٱلْكِبْرِيَآءُ فِى ٱلْأَرْضِ وَمَا نَحْنُ لَكُمَا بِمُؤْمِنِينَ

79. Said Pharaoh: "Bring me
Every sorcerer well-versed."

٧٩ وَقَالَ فِرْعَوْنُ ٱئْتُونِى بِكُلِّ سَٰحِرٍ عَلِيمٍ

80. When the sorcerers came,
Moses said to them:
"Throw ye what ye (wish)
To throw!"

٨٠ فَلَمَّا جَآءَ ٱلسَّحَرَةُ قَالَ لَهُم مُّوسَىٰٓ
أَلْقُوا۟ مَآ أَنتُم مُّلْقُونَ

81. When they had had their throw,[1464]
Moses said: "What ye
Have brought is sorcery:
Allah will surely make it
Of no effect: for Allah

٨١ فَلَمَّآ أَلْقَوْا۟ قَالَ مُوسَىٰ مَا جِئْتُم بِهِ
ٱلسِّحْرُ إِنَّ ٱللَّهَ سَيُبْطِلُهُۥٓ إِنَّ ٱللَّهَ

1461. The story of Moses, Aaron, and Pharaoh is fully told in 7:103-137, and there are references to it in many places in the Qur'ān. The incidental reference here is to illustrate a special point, *viz.*, that the wicked are arrogant and bound up in their sin, and prefer deception to Truth: they do not hesitate to charge the men of God, who work unselfishly for them, with mean motives, such as would actuate them in similar circumstances!

1462. Sorcery is the very opposite of Truth—being deception of plausible shows by the powers of evil. But these cannot succeed or last permanently, and Truth must ultimately prevail.

1463. Notice how they attribute evil motives to the men of God, motives of ambition and lust for power, which the men of God had been sent expressly to put down. The same device was used against Al Muṣṭafā.

1464. When they threw their rods, the rods became snakes by a trick of sorcery, but Moses's miracles were greater than any tricks of sorcery, and had real Truth behind them.

Prospereth not the work
Of those who make mischief.

لَا يُصْلِحُ عَمَلَ ٱلْمُفْسِدِينَ

82. "And Allah by His Words[1465]
Doth prove and establish
His Truth, however much
The Sinners may hate it!"

٨٢ وَيُحِقُّ ٱللَّهُ ٱلْحَقَّ بِكَلِمَٰتِهِۦ
وَلَوْ كَرِهَ ٱلْمُجْرِمُونَ

SECTION 9.

83. But none believed in Moses
Except some children of his
People,[1466]
Because of the fear of Pharaoh
And his chiefs, lest they
Should persecute them; and
certainly
Pharaoh was mighty on the earth
And one who transgressed all
bounds.

٨٣ فَمَآ ءَامَنَ لِمُوسَىٰٓ إِلَّا ذُرِّيَّةٌ مِّن قَوْمِهِۦ
عَلَىٰ خَوْفٍ مِّن فِرْعَوْنَ وَمَلَإِيْهِمْ أَن يَفْتِنَهُمْ ۚ
وَإِنَّ فِرْعَوْنَ لَعَالٍ فِى ٱلْأَرْضِ
وَإِنَّهُۥ لَمِنَ ٱلْمُسْرِفِينَ

84. Moses said: "O my People!
If ye do (really) believe
In Allah, then in Him
Put your trust if ye
Submit (your will to His)."

٨٤ وَقَالَ مُوسَىٰ يَٰقَوْمِ إِن كُنتُمْ ءَامَنتُم بِٱللَّهِ
فَعَلَيْهِ تَوَكَّلُوٓا۟ إِن كُنتُم مُّسْلِمِينَ

85. They said: "In Allah
Do we put our trust.
Our Lord! make us not
A trial for those[1467]
Who practise oppression;

٨٥ فَقَالُوا۟ عَلَى ٱللَّهِ تَوَكَّلْنَا
رَبَّنَا لَا تَجْعَلْنَا فِتْنَةً لِّلْقَوْمِ ٱلظَّٰلِمِينَ

86. "And deliver us by Thy Mercy
From those who reject (Thee)."

٨٦ وَنَجِّنَا بِرَحْمَتِكَ مِنَ ٱلْقَوْمِ ٱلْكَٰفِرِينَ

1465. Allah's Words or Commands have real power, while sorcerer's tricks only seem wonderful by deceiving the eye.

1466. The pronoun "his" in "his People" is taken by some Commentators to refer to Pharaoh. The majority of Pharaoh's people refused to believe at the time, but the sorcerers believed (7:120-122), and so did Pharaoh's wife (66:11), and ultimately Pharaoh himself, though too late (10:90). If we took "his" to refer to Moses, it would mean that the Israelites were hardhearted and grumbled (7:129) even when they were being delivered from Egypt, and only a few of them had any real faith in Allah's providence and the working of His Law, and they feared Pharaoh even more than they feared Allah.

1467. *A trial for those who practise oppression*: the various meanings of *Fitnah* have been explained in n. 1198 to 8:25. The prayer is that the righteous people, being weak, should be saved from being used as objects of oppression or punishment at the hands of powerful enemies. Weakness tempts power to practise oppression, and is thus an occasion of trial for the oppressors.

87. We inspired Moses and his brother
With this Message: "Provide[1468]
Dwellings for your People
In Egypt, make your dwellings
Into places of worship,
And establish regular prayers:
And give Glad Tidings
To those who believe!"

(٨٧) وَأَوْحَيْنَآ إِلَىٰ مُوسَىٰ وَأَخِيهِ أَن تَبَوَّءَا لِقَوْمِكُمَا
بِمِصْرَ بُيُوتًا وَٱجْعَلُوا۟ بُيُوتَكُمْ قِبْلَةً
وَأَقِيمُوا۟ ٱلصَّلَوٰةَ ۗ وَبَشِّرِ ٱلْمُؤْمِنِينَ

88. Moses prayed: "Our Lord!
Thou hast indeed bestowed
On Pharaoh and his Chiefs
Splendour and wealth in the life[1469]
Of the Present, and so,
Our Lord, they mislead (men)
From Thy Path. Deface,
Our Lord, the features of their wealth,[1470]
And send hardness to their hearts,
So they will not believe
Until they see
The grievous Penalty."

(٨٨) وَقَالَ مُوسَىٰ رَبَّنَآ إِنَّكَ ءَاتَيْتَ
فِرْعَوْنَ وَمَلَأَهُۥ زِينَةً وَأَمْوَٰلًا فِى ٱلْحَيَوٰةِ
ٱلدُّنْيَا رَبَّنَا لِيُضِلُّوا۟ عَن سَبِيلِكَ ۖ
رَبَّنَا ٱطْمِسْ عَلَىٰٓ أَمْوَٰلِهِمْ
وَٱشْدُدْ عَلَىٰ قُلُوبِهِمْ فَلَا يُؤْمِنُوا۟
حَتَّىٰ يَرَوُا۟ ٱلْعَذَابَ ٱلْأَلِيمَ

89. Allah said: "Accepted is
Your prayer (O Moses and Aaron)!
So stand ye straight,
And follow not the path
Of those who know not."[1471]

(٨٩) قَالَ قَدْ أُجِيبَت دَّعْوَتُكُمَا
فَٱسْتَقِيمَا وَلَا تَتَّبِعَآنِّ سَبِيلَ ٱلَّذِينَ لَا يَعْلَمُونَ

90. We took the Children
Of Israel across the sea:

(٩٠) وَجَٰوَزْنَا بِبَنِىٓ إِسْرَٰٓءِيلَ ٱلْبَحْرَ

1468. This instruction, we may suppose, was given when the sorcerers were brought to confusion, and some of the Egyptians believed. Moses was for a little while to remain in Egypt, so that his Message should have time to work, before the Israelites were led out of Egypt. They were to make their houses into places of prayer (*Qiblah*), as Pharaoh would not probably allow them to set up public places of prayer, and they were now to be only sojourners in Egypt. The *Qiblah* was to be symbolical of their later wanderings in Arabia, and the still later restoration of Allah's pure worship at the Ka'bah under Al Muṣṭafā. These were the glad tidings (the Gospel) of Islam, which was preached under Noah, Abraham, Moses, and Jesus, and completed under Muḥammad.

1469. Moses's prayer, in which Aaron joined, for he was always with him, may be paraphrased thus: "O Allah! we understand that the glitter and the wealth of the Egyptians are not to be envied. They are but the ephemeral goods of this life. They are a disadvantage, in that in their pride of possessions the Egyptians mislead themselves and others. Let their pride be their undoing! Turn their wealth into bitterness and their hearts into hardness, for they reject Thee, and they will not believe until they actually see the Punishment of their sins!"

1470. A terrible curse! Let their wealth and splendour become so defaced in their features, that instead of being objects of desire, they become objects of loathing! The heart is the seat of affections and joy: let it be so hardened by their unbelief that it becomes the seat of hatred and grief! It is when they see the Penalty that they will believe!

1471. Be not dazzled by their splendour, but stand out straight for Truth, for that is your salvation! Addressed in form to Moses and Aaron, in substance it is addressed to the Israelites.

Pharaoh and his hosts followed them
In insolence and spite.[1472]
At length, when overwhelmed
With the flood, he said:
"I believe that there is no god
Except Him Whom the Children
Of Israel believe in:[1473]
I am of those who submit
(To Allah in Islām)."

فَأَتْبَعَهُمْ فِرْعَوْنُ وَجُنُودُهُۥ بَغْيًا وَعَدْوًا
حَتَّىٰٓ إِذَآ أَدْرَكَهُ ٱلْغَرَقُ قَالَ
ءَامَنتُ أَنَّهُۥ لَآ إِلَٰهَ إِلَّا ٱلَّذِىٓ ءَامَنَتْ بِهِۦ بَنُوٓاْ
إِسْرَٰٓءِيلَ وَأَنَا۠ مِنَ ٱلْمُسْلِمِينَ

91. (It was said to him:)
"Ah now!—But a little while
Before, wast thou in rebellion!—
And thou didst mischief (and violence)!

٩١ ءَآلْـَٔنَ وَقَدْ عَصَيْتَ قَبْلُ
وَكُنتَ مِنَ ٱلْمُفْسِدِينَ

92. "This day shall We save thee
In thy body, that thou
Mayest be a Sign to those
Who come after thee!
But verily, many among mankind
Are heedless of Our Signs!"

٩٢ فَٱلْيَوْمَ نُنَجِّيكَ بِبَدَنِكَ
لِتَكُونَ لِمَنْ خَلْفَكَ ءَايَةً
وَإِنَّ كَثِيرًا مِّنَ ٱلنَّاسِ عَنْ ءَايَٰتِنَا لَغَٰفِلُونَ

C. 103.—Allah's purpose of Mercy and Forgiveness
(10:93-109.) Was shown in the mission of Jonah, when
Nineveh was pardoned on repentance, and given
A new lease of life. We must
Be patient and strive with constancy and perseverance,
For all suffering and sorrow as well as
All bounties proceed from Allah, Whose plan
Is righteous and for the good of His creatures.

SECTION 10.

93. We settled the Children
Of Israel in a beautiful[1474]

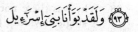

٩٣ وَلَقَدْ بَوَّأْنَا بَنِىٓ إِسْرَٰٓءِيلَ

1472. Notice the swiftness of the action in the narrative. The execution of poetic justice could not have been described in fewer words.

1473. That is, in the One True God. This was deathbed repentance, and even so it was forced by the terror of the catastrophe. So it was not accepted (*cf.* 4:18) in its entirety. Only this concession was made, that the body was saved from the sea, and presumably, according to Egyptian custom, it was embalmed and the mummy was given due rites of the dead. But the story commemorated forever Allah's working, in mercy for His people, and in just punishment of oppressors.

1474. After many wanderings the Israelites were settled in the land of Canaan, described as "a land flowing with milk and honey" (Exod. iii. 8). They had a prosperous land; and they were supplied with spiritual sustenance by men sent to deliver Allah's Message. They should have known better than to fall into disputes and schisms, but they did so. This was all the more inexcusable considering what bounties they had received from Allah. The schisms arose from selfish arrogance, and Allah will judge between them on the Day of Judgement.

Dwelling place, and provided
For them sustenance of the best;
It was after knowledge had been
Granted to them, that they
Fell into schisms. Verily
Allah will judge between them
As to the schisms amongst them
On the Day of Judgement.

مُبَوَّأَ صِدْقٍ وَرَزَقْنَٰهُم مِّنَ ٱلطَّيِّبَٰتِ
فَمَا ٱخْتَلَفُوا۟ حَتَّىٰ جَآءَهُمُ ٱلْعِلْمُ
إِنَّ رَبَّكَ يَقْضِى بَيْنَهُمْ يَوْمَ ٱلْقِيَٰمَةِ
فِيمَا كَانُوا۟ فِيهِ يَخْتَلِفُونَ

94. If thou wert in doubt
As to what We have revealed
Unto thee, then ask those
Who have been reading
The Book from before thee:[1475]
The Truth hath indeed come
To thee from thy Lord:
So be in nowise
Of those in doubt.[1476]

٩٤ فَإِن كُنتَ فِى شَكٍّ مِّمَّآ أَنزَلْنَآ إِلَيْكَ
فَسْـَٔلِ ٱلَّذِينَ يَقْرَءُونَ ٱلْكِتَٰبَ مِن قَبْلِكَ
لَقَدْ جَآءَكَ ٱلْحَقُّ مِن رَّبِّكَ
فَلَا تَكُونَنَّ مِنَ ٱلْمُمْتَرِينَ

95. Nor be of those who reject
The Signs of Allah,
Or thou shalt be of those
Who perish.

٩٥ وَلَا تَكُونَنَّ مِنَ ٱلَّذِينَ كَذَّبُوا۟
بِـَٔايَٰتِ ٱللَّهِ فَتَكُونَ مِنَ ٱلْخَٰسِرِينَ

96. Those against whom the Word
Of thy Lord hath been verified[1477]
Would not believe—

٩٦ إِنَّ ٱلَّذِينَ حَقَّتْ عَلَيْهِمْ
كَلِمَتُ رَبِّكَ لَا يُؤْمِنُونَ

97. Even if every Sign was brought
Unto them—until they see
(For themselves) the Grievous
Penalty.

٩٧ وَلَوْ جَآءَتْهُمْ كُلُّ ءَايَةٍ
حَتَّىٰ يَرَوُا۟ ٱلْعَذَابَ ٱلْأَلِيمَ

98. Why was there not
A single township (among those
We warned), which believed—

٩٨ فَلَوْلَا كَانَتْ قَرْيَةٌ ءَامَنَتْ

1475. Allah's Truth is all one, and even in different forms men sincere in Religion recognise the oneness. So sincere Jews like 'Abd Allah ibn Salām, and sincere Christians like Waraqa or the Nestorian monk Baḥīrah, were ready to recognise the mission of Muḥammad Muṣṭafā. "The Book" in this connection is Revelation generally, including pre-Islamic revelations.

1476. *Cf.* 3:60 and n. 399.

1477. Allah has given frequent warnings against Evil and want of Faith in all ages, through Signs and through inspiration—the latter ("the Word") being even more direct and personal than the former. Those who did not heed the warning found to their cost that it was true, and they perished. Such contumacy in the rejection of Truth only yields when the actual penalty is in sight. Belief then is induced by irresistible facts: it is not efficacious as Faith, as was proved against Pharaoh. See 10:90 and n. 1473.

So its Faith should have Profited it—except the People[1478] Of Jonah? When they believed, We removed from them The Penalty of Ignominy In the life of the Present, And permitted them to enjoy (Their life) for awhile.[1479]	فَنَفَعَهَآ إِيمَٰنُهَآ إِلَّا قَوْمَ يُونُسَ لَمَّآ ءَامَنُواْ كَشَفْنَا عَنْهُمْ عَذَابَ ٱلْخِزْيِ فِى ٱلْحَيَوٰةِ ٱلدُّنْيَا وَمَتَّعْنَٰهُمْ إِلَىٰ حِينٍ
99. If it had been the Lord's Will, They would all have believed— All who are on earth! Wilt thou then compel mankind, Against their will, to believe![1480]	﴿٩٩﴾ وَلَوْ شَآءَ رَبُّكَ لَءَامَنَ مَن فِى ٱلْأَرْضِ كُلُّهُمْ جَمِيعًا ۚ أَفَأَنتَ تُكْرِهُ ٱلنَّاسَ حَتَّىٰ يَكُونُواْ مُؤْمِنِينَ
100. No soul can believe, except By the Will of Allah,[1481]	﴿١٠٠﴾ وَمَا كَانَ لِنَفْسٍ أَن تُؤْمِنَ إِلَّا بِإِذْنِ ٱللَّهِ ۚ

1478. Allah in His infinite Mercy points out the contumacy of Sin as a warning, and the exceptional case of Nineveh and its Prophet Jonah is alluded to. The story of Jonah is told in 37:139-148, which would be an appropriate place for further comments. Here it is sufficient to note that Nineveh was a very ancient town which is now no longer on the map. Its site is believed to be marked by the two mounds on the left bank of the Tigris, opposite the flourishing city of Mosul on the right bank, about 230 miles north-northwest of Baghdād. One of the mounds bears the name of the "the Tomb of Nabi Yūnus." Archaeologists have not yet fully explored its antiquities, but it is clear that it was a very old Sumerian town, perhaps older than 3500 B.C. It became the capital of Assyria. The first Assyrian Empire under Shalmanester I, about 1300 B.C., became the supreme power in Western Asia. Babylon, whose tributary Assyria had formerly been, now became tributary to Assyria. The second Assyrian Empire arose about 745 B.C., and Sennacherib (705-681 B.C.) beautified the town with many public works. It was destroyed by the Scythians (so-called Medes) in 612 B.C. If the date of Jonah were assumed to be about 800 B.C., it would be between the First and Second Assyrian Empire; when the City was nearly destroyed for its sins, but on account of its repentance was given a new lease of glorious life in the Second Empire.

1479. The point of the allusion here may be thus explained: Nineveh was a great and glorious City; but it became, like Babylon, a city of sin. Allah sent the prophet Yūnus (Jonah) to warn it. Full of iniquities though it was, it listened to the warning, perhaps in the person of a few just men. For their sakes, the All-Merciful Allah spared it, and gave it a new lease of glorious life. According to the chronology in the last note the new lease would be for about two centuries, after which it perished completely for its sins and abominations. Note that its new lease of life was for its collective life as a City, the life of the Present, *i.e.*, of this World. It does not mean that individual sinners escaped the spiritual consequences of their sin, unless they individually repented and obtained Allah's mercy and forgiveness.

1480. If it had been Allah's Plan or Will not to grant the limited Free Will that He has granted to man, His omnipotence could have made all mankind alike: all would then have had Faith, but that Faith would have reflected no merit on them. In the actual world as it is, man has been endowed with various faculties and capacities, so that he should strive and explore, and bring himself into harmony with Allah's Will. Hence Faith becomes a moral achievement, and to resist Faith becomes a sin. As a complementary proposition, men of Faith must not be impatient or angry if they have to contend against Unfaith, and most important of all, they must guard against the temptation of forcing Faith, *i.e.*, imposing it on others by physical compulsion, or any other forms of compulsion such as social pressure, or inducements held out by wealth or position, or other adventitious advantages. Forced faith is no faith. They should strive spiritually and let Allah's Plan work as He wills.

1481. To creatures endued with Will, Faith comes out of an active use of that Will. But we must not be so arrogant as to suppose that that is enough. At best, man is weak and in need of Allah's grace and help. If we sincerely wish to understand, He will help our Faith; but if not, our doubts and difficulties will only be increased. This follows as a necessary consequence, and in Quranic language all consequences are ascribed to Allah, the Cause of Causes.

And He will place Doubt[1482]
(Or obscurity) on those
Who will not understand.

وَيَجْعَلُ ٱلرِّجْسَ عَلَى ٱلَّذِينَ لَا يَعْقِلُونَ

101. Say: "Behold all that is
In the heavens and on earth";
But neither Signs nor Warners
Profit those who believe not.[1483]

١٠١ قُلِ ٱنظُرُواْ مَاذَا فِي ٱلسَّمَٰوَٰتِ وَٱلْأَرْضِۚ
وَمَا تُغْنِي ٱلْأٓيَٰتُ وَٱلنُّذُرُ عَن قَوْمٍ لَّا يُؤْمِنُونَ

102. Do they then expect
(Anything) but (what happened
In) the days of the men
Who passed away before them?
Say: "Wait ye then:
For I, too, will wait with you."[1484]

١٠٢ فَهَلْ يَنتَظِرُونَ إِلَّا مِثْلَ أَيَّامِ
ٱلَّذِينَ خَلَوْاْ مِن قَبْلِهِمْۚ قُلْ فَٱنتَظِرُوٓاْ
إِنِّي مَعَكُم مِّنَ ٱلْمُنتَظِرِينَ

103. In the end We deliver
Our messengers and those who
believe:
Thus is it fitting on Our part
That We should deliver
Those who believe!

١٠٣ ثُمَّ نُنَجِّي رُسُلَنَا وَٱلَّذِينَ ءَامَنُواْۚ
كَذَٰلِكَ حَقًّا عَلَيْنَا
نُنجِ ٱلْمُؤْمِنِينَ

SECTION 11.

104. Say: "O ye men!
If ye are in doubt
As to my religion, (behold!)[1485]
I worship not what ye
Worship other than Allah!
But I worship Allah—
Who will take your souls[1486]
(At death): I am commanded[1487]

١٠٤ قُلْ يَٰٓأَيُّهَا ٱلنَّاسُ إِن كُنتُمْ فِي شَكٍّ
مِّن دِينِي فَلَآ أَعْبُدُ ٱلَّذِينَ تَعْبُدُونَ مِن دُونِ
ٱللَّهِ وَلَٰكِنْ أَعْبُدُ ٱللَّهَ ٱلَّذِي يَتَوَفَّىٰكُمْۖ وَأُمِرْتُ

1482. *Rijs* (from *rajisa, yarjisu,* or *rajasa, yarjasu*) has various meanings: *e.g.*, (1) filth, impurity, uncleanness, abomination, as in 9:95; (2) hence, filthy deeds, foul conduct, crime, abomination, thus shading off into (1), as in 5:93; (3) hence punishment for crime, penalty, as in 6:125; (4) a form of such punishment, *viz.*, doubt, obscurity, or unsettlement of mind, anger, indignation, as in 9:125, and here, but perhaps the idea of punishment is also implied here.

1483. If Faith results from an active exertion of our spiritual faculties or understanding, it follows that if we let those die, Allah's Signs in His Creation or in the spoken Word which comes by inspiration through the mouths of His Messengers will not reach us any more than music reaches a deaf man.

1484. *Cf.* 10:20 and n. 1408. The argument about Allah's revelation of Himself to man was begun in those early sections of this Sūrah and is being now rounded off towards the end of this Sūrah with the same formula.

1485. Other people may hesitate, or doubt, or wonder. But the righteous man has no doubt in his own mind, and he declares his Faith clearly and unambiguously to all, as did Al Mustafā.

1486. The worship of the One and True God is not a fancy worship, to be arrived at merely by reasoning and philosophy. It touches the vital issues of life and death, which are in His hands and His alone.

1487. Nor is the worship of One God an invention of the Prophet. It comes as a direct command through him and to all.

To be (in the ranks)
Of the Believers,[1488]

أَنْ أَكُونَ مِنَ ٱلْمُؤْمِنِينَ

105. "And further (thus): 'set thy face
Towards Religion with true piety,
And never in anywise
Be of the Unbelievers;

١٠٥ وَأَنْ أَقِمْ وَجْهَكَ لِلدِّينِ حَنِيفًا
وَلَا تَكُونَنَّ مِنَ ٱلْمُشْرِكِينَ

106. "'Nor call on any,
Other than Allah—
Such will neither profit thee
Nor hurt thee: if thou dost,
Behold! thou shalt certainly
Be of those who do wrong.'"

١٠٦ وَلَا تَدْعُ مِن دُونِ ٱللَّهِ
مَا لَا يَنفَعُكَ وَلَا يَضُرُّكَ
فَإِن فَعَلْتَ فَإِنَّكَ إِذًا مِّنَ ٱلظَّٰلِمِينَ

107. If Allah do touch thee
With hurt, there is none
Can remove it but He:
If He do design some benefit
For thee, there is none
Can keep back His favour:
He causeth it to reach
Whomsoever of His servants
He pleaseth. And He is
The Oft-Forgiving, Most
Merciful.[1489]

١٠٧ وَإِن يَمْسَسْكَ ٱللَّهُ بِضُرٍّ
فَلَا كَاشِفَ لَهُۥٓ إِلَّا هُوَ
وَإِن يُرِدْكَ بِخَيْرٍ فَلَا رَآدَّ لِفَضْلِهِۦ
يُصِيبُ بِهِۦ مَن يَشَآءُ مِنْ عِبَادِهِۦ
وَهُوَ ٱلْغَفُورُ ٱلرَّحِيمُ

108. Say: "O ye men! Now
Truth hath reached you
From your Lord! Those who
receive
Guidance, do so for the good
Of their own souls; those
Who stray, do so to their own loss:
And I am not (set) over you
To arrange your affairs."[1490]

١٠٨ قُلْ يَٰٓأَيُّهَا ٱلنَّاسُ قَدْ جَآءَكُمُ
ٱلْحَقُّ مِن رَّبِّكُمْ فَمَنِ ٱهْتَدَىٰ
فَإِنَّمَا يَهْتَدِى لِنَفْسِهِۦ وَمَن ضَلَّ فَإِنَّمَا
يَضِلُّ عَلَيْهَا وَمَآ أَنَا۠ عَلَيْكُم بِوَكِيلٍ

1488. Individual Faith is good, but it is completed and strengthened by joining or forming a Righteous Society, in which the individual can develop and expand. Islam was never a religion of monks and anchorites. It laid great stress on social duties, which in many ways test and train the individual's character.

1489. Allah is Oft-Forgiving, Most Merciful. Even when we suffer under trials and tribulations, it is for our good, and no one can remove them except He, when, in His Plan, He sees it to be best for all concerned. On the other hand, there is no power that can intercept His blessings and favours, and His bounty flows freely when we are worthy, and often when we are not worthy of it.

1490. The *Furqān,* the Criterion between right and wrong, has been sent to us from Allah. If we accept guidance, it is not as if we confer favours on those who bring us guidance. They suffer unselfishly for us, in order that we may be guided for our own good. On the other hand, if we reject it, it is our own loss. We have a certain amount of free will, and the responsibility is ours and cannot be shifted to the Teachers sent by Allah.

109. Follow thou the inspiration
Sent unto thee, and be
Patient and constant, till Allah
Doth decide: for He
Is the Best to decide.[1491]

١٠٩ وَٱتَّبِعْ مَا يُوحَىٰٓ إِلَيْكَ
وَٱصْبِرْ حَتَّىٰ يَحْكُمَ ٱللَّهُ ۚ وَهُوَ خَيْرُ ٱلْحَٰكِمِينَ

1491. When, in spite of all the efforts of the Prophets of Allah, people do not accept Truth, and evil seems to flourish for a time, we must wait and be patient, but at the same time we must not give up hope or persevering effort. For thus only can we carry out our part in the Plan of Allah.

INTRODUCTION TO SŪRAH 11—*HŪD*

For the chronological place of this Sūrah and the general argument of Sūrahs 10 to 15, see Introduction to S. 10.

In subject matter this Sūrah supplements the preceding one. In the last Sūrah stress was laid on that side of Allah's dealings with man which leans to Mercy: here stress is laid on the side which deals with justice and the punishment of Sin when all Grace is resisted.

Summary—Allah's revelation of mercy, His dealing with man, and His long-suffering patience are contrasted with man's ingratitude, his love of falsehood and vanity, and his crookedness (11:1-24, and C. 104).

Noah's unselfishness and humility in teaching his people the Truth of Allah were traduced by the ungodly, and his Message ridiculed and rejected. But he built his Ark under directions from Allah, and was saved, with peace and blessings, while his rejecters perished (11:25-49, and C. 105).

The prophet Hūd preached to his people, the 'Ād, against false gods, and the prophet Ṣāliḥ to his people, the Thamūd, against dishonouring the symbol of Allah's bounty. In both cases Allah's Signs were rejected, and the rejecters were blotted out (11:50-68, and C. 106).

Lot's people were given to abominations: Abraham pleaded for them, and Lot was sent out to them, but they went deeper and deeper into sin and suffered the Penalty. Shu'ayb's people, the Midianites, were warned against fraud and mischief, but they reproached him with helplessness and were themselves destroyed (11:69-95, and C. 107).

It is arrogant leaders like Pharaoh who mislead men, and men bring ruin on themselves. But Allah is Just. The penalty for sin is real and abiding; therefore shun all wrongdoing, and serve Allah wholeheartedly (11:96-123, and C. 108).

C. 104.—Allah's Revelation teaches the Truth: it warns
(11:1-24.) Against wrong and gives glad tidings to the righteous:
Ungrateful man folds up his heart
And fails to see how all Nature points
To Allah and to the Hereafter: he but seeks
Petty issues, forgetting the Cause of Causes.
Not all the wisdom of man can produce
Aught like the Message which comes from Allah,
As the Light that leads and the Mercy
That forgives. Who then but will humble
Himself before Allah, seeking His light and His voice?

Sūrah 11.

Hūd (The Prophet Hūd)

In the name of Allah, Most Gracious,
Most Merciful.

بِسْمِ ٱللَّهِ ٱلرَّحْمَٰنِ ٱلرَّحِيمِ

1. Alif Lām Rā.[1492]
(This is) a Book,
With verses basic or
fundamental[1493]
(Of established meaning)—
Further explained in detail—
From One Who is Wise
And Well-Acquainted (with all
things):

١ الٓر
كِتَٰبٌ أُحْكِمَتْ ءَايَٰتُهُۥ
ثُمَّ فُصِّلَتْ مِن لَّدُنْ حَكِيمٍ خَبِيرٍ

2. (It teacheth) that ye should
Worship none but Allah.
(Say:) "Verily I am[1494]
(Sent) unto you from Him
To warn and to bring
Glad tidings:

٢ أَلَّا تَعْبُدُوٓا۟ إِلَّا ٱللَّهَ
إِنَّنِى لَكُم مِّنْهُ
نَذِيرٌ وَبَشِيرٌ

3. "(And to preach thus), 'Seek ye
The forgiveness of your Lord,
And turn to Him in repentance;
That He may grant you
Enjoyment, good (and true),
For a term appointed,
And bestow His abounding grace
On all who abound in merit![1495]
But if ye turn away,
Then I fear for you
The Penalty of a Great Day:

٣ وَأَنِ ٱسْتَغْفِرُوا۟ رَبَّكُمْ
ثُمَّ تُوبُوٓا۟ إِلَيْهِ يُمَتِّعْكُم مَّتَٰعًا حَسَنًا
إِلَىٰٓ أَجَلٍ مُّسَمًّى وَيُؤْتِ كُلَّ ذِى فَضْلٍ فَضْلَهُۥ
وَإِن تَوَلَّوْا۟ فَإِنِّىٓ أَخَافُ عَلَيْكُمْ
عَذَابَ يَوْمٍ كَبِيرٍ

4. "'To Allah is your return
And He hath power
Over all things.'"

٤ إِلَى ٱللَّهِ مَرْجِعُكُمْ وَهُوَ عَلَىٰ كُلِّ شَىْءٍ قَدِيرٌ

1492. For the meaning of these Letters, see Introduction to S. 10.

1493. Seen n. 347 to 3:7. Every basic principle is included in Allah's Revelation, and it is further illustrated and explained in detail.

1494. Al Muṣṭafā's Message—as was the Message of all prophets—was to warn against evil, and to bring the glad tidings of Allah's Mercy and Grace to all who would receive it in Faith and trust in Allah. This double Message is preached illustratively in this Sūrah.

1495. The enjoyment of all good and true things in life refers, I think, to the present life with its limited term, and the abounding Grace refers to the higher spiritual reward, which begins here but is completed in the life to come.

5. Behold! they fold up[1496]
Their hearts, that they may lie
Hid from Him! Ah! even
When they cover themselves
With their garments, He knoweth
What they conceal, and what
They reveal: for He knoweth
Well the (inmost secrets)
Of the hearts.[1497]

٥ أَلَآ إِنَّهُمْ يَثْنُونَ صُدُورَهُمْ لِيَسْتَخْفُوا۟ مِنْهُ ۚ
أَلَا حِينَ يَسْتَغْشُونَ ثِيَابَهُمْ
يَعْلَمُ مَا يُسِرُّونَ وَمَا يُعْلِنُونَ ۚ
إِنَّهُۥ عَلِيمٌۢ بِذَاتِ ٱلصُّدُورِ

6. There is no moving creature
On earth but its sustenance[1498]
Dependeth on Allah: He knoweth
The time and place of its
Definite abode and its
Temporary deposit:[1499]
All is in a clear Record.[1500]

٦ وَمَا مِن دَآبَّةٍ فِى ٱلْأَرْضِ إِلَّا عَلَى
ٱللَّهِ رِزْقُهَا وَيَعْلَمُ مُسْتَقَرَّهَا وَمُسْتَوْدَعَهَا ۚ
كُلٌّ فِى كِتَـٰبٍ مُّبِينٍ

7. He it is Who created
The heavens and the earth
In six Days[1501]—and His Throne
Was over the Waters—[1502]
That He might try you,[1503]
Which of you is best
In conduct. But if
Thou wert to say to them,
"Ye shall indeed be raised up
After death," the Unbelievers
Would be sure to say,[1504]

٧ وَهُوَ ٱلَّذِى خَلَقَ ٱلسَّمَـٰوَٰتِ وَٱلْأَرْضَ
فِى سِتَّةِ أَيَّامٍ وَكَانَ عَرْشُهُۥ
عَلَى ٱلْمَآءِ لِيَبْلُوَكُمْ أَيُّكُمْ أَحْسَنُ عَمَلًا ۗ
وَلَئِن قُلْتَ إِنَّكُم مَّبْعُوثُونَ
مِنۢ بَعْدِ ٱلْمَوْتِ لَيَقُولَنَّ ٱلَّذِينَ كَفَرُوٓا۟

1496. The heart (literally *breast* in Arabic) is already well-guarded in the body; and secrets are supposed to be hidden in the heart or breast. Foolish persons might further cover up their hearts with cloaks, but even so, nothing can be hidden from Allah.

1497. *Cf.* 3:119.

1498. *Cf.* 6:59. Nothing happens in Creation except by the Word of Allah and with the knowledge of Allah. Not a leaf stirs but by His Will. Its maintenance in every sense is dependent on His Will.

1499. *Mustaqarr* = definite abode; where a thing stops or stays for some time, where it is established. *Mustawda'* = where a thing is laid up or deposited for a little while. Referring to animals, the former denotes its life on this earth; the latter its temporary prenatal existence in the egg or the womb and its after-death existence in the tomb or whatever state it is in until its resurrection.

1500. *Cf.* 6:59 and n. 880, and 10:61 and n. 1450.

1501. See n. 1031 to 7:54.

1502. It is scientifically correct to say that all life was evolved out of the waters, and this statement also occurs in the Qur'ān, 21:30. Some such meaning, I think, also attaches to the Gen. i. 2. The past tense "was" refers to the time before life developed in solid forms, on land and in air. (R).

1503. The Creation we see around us is not idle sport or play (in Hindi, *Lila*) or whim on the part of Allah. It is the medium through which our spiritual life is to develop, with such free will as we have. This life is our testing time.

1504. The Unbelievers, who do not believe in a Future life, think all talk of it is like a sorcerer's talk, empty of reality. But in this they show their ignorance, and they are begging the question.

"This is nothing but
Obvious sorcery!"

إِنْ هَٰذَآ إِلَّا سِحْرٌ مُّبِينٌ

8. If We delay the penalty
For them for a definite term,
They are sure to say,
"What keeps it back?"[1505]
Ah! On the day it (actually)
Reaches them, nothing will
Turn it away from them,
And they will be completely
Encircled by that which
They used to mock at!

(٨) وَلَئِنْ أَخَّرْنَا عَنْهُمُ ٱلْعَذَابَ إِلَىٰٓ
أُمَّةٍ مَّعْدُودَةٍ لَّيَقُولُنَّ مَا يَحْبِسُهُۥٓ
أَلَا يَوْمَ يَأْتِيهِمْ لَيْسَ مَصْرُوفًا عَنْهُمْ
وَحَاقَ بِهِم مَّا كَانُوا۟ بِهِۦ يَسْتَهْزِءُونَ

SECTION 2.

9. If We give man a taste
Of mercy from Ourselves,
And then withdraw it from him,
Behold! he is in despair
And (falls into) blasphemy.[1506]

(٩) وَلَئِنْ أَذَقْنَا ٱلْإِنسَٰنَ مِنَّا رَحْمَةً
ثُمَّ نَزَعْنَٰهَا مِنْهُ إِنَّهُۥ لَيَـُٔوسٌ كَفُورٌ

10. But if We give him a taste
Of (Our) favours after
Adversity hath touched him,
He is sure to say,
"All evil has departed from
me;"[1507]
Behold! he falls into exultation
And pride.

(١٠) وَلَئِنْ أَذَقْنَٰهُ نَعْمَآءَ
بَعْدَ ضَرَّآءَ مَسَّتْهُ لَيَقُولَنَّ
ذَهَبَ ٱلسَّيِّـَٔاتُ عَنِّىٓ إِنَّهُۥ لَفَرِحٌ فَخُورٌ

11. Not so do those who show
Patience and constancy, and
work[1508]
Righteousness; for them
Is forgiveness (of sins)
And a great reward.

(١١) إِلَّا ٱلَّذِينَ صَبَرُوا۟ وَعَمِلُوا۟
ٱلصَّٰلِحَٰتِ أُو۟لَٰٓئِكَ لَهُم
مَّغْفِرَةٌ وَأَجْرٌ كَبِيرٌ

12. Perchance thou mayest (feel
The inclination) to give up

(١٢) فَلَعَلَّكَ تَارِكٌۢ

1505. As much as to say: "Oh! all this talk of punishment is nonsense. There is no such thing!"

1506. He does not realise that some kinds of chastening are good for discipline and the training of our spiritual faculties.

1507. He takes it as a matter of course, or as due to his own merit or cleverness! He does not realise that both in good and ill fortune there is a beneficent purpose in the Plan of Allah.

1508. Their attitude is the right one: to take ill fortune with fortitude and good fortune with humility, and in either case go on persevering in good deeds to their fellow creatures.

A part of what is revealed[1509]
Unto thee, and thy heart
Feeleth straitened lest they say,
"Why is not a treasure sent down
Unto him, or why does not
An angel come down with him?"
But thou art there only to warn!
It is Allah that arrangeth
All affairs!

بَعْضَ مَا يُوحَىٰٓ إِلَيْكَ وَضَآئِقٌۢ بِهِۦ صَدْرُكَ
أَن يَقُولُوا۟ لَوْلَآ أُنزِلَ عَلَيْهِ كَنزٌ أَوْ جَآءَ
مَعَهُۥ مَلَكٌ ۚ إِنَّمَآ أَنتَ نَذِيرٌ ۚ
وَٱللَّهُ عَلَىٰ كُلِّ شَىْءٍ وَكِيلٌ

13. Or they may say, "He forged it."
Say, "Bring ye then ten Sūrahs
Forged, like unto it, and call
(To your aid) whomsoever
Ye can, other than Allah!—
If ye speak the truth![1510]

١٣ أَمْ يَقُولُونَ ٱفْتَرَىٰهُ ۖ قُلْ فَأْتُوا۟ بِعَشْرِ سُوَرٍ
مِّثْلِهِۦ مُفْتَرَيَٰتٍ وَٱدْعُوا۟ مَنِ ٱسْتَطَعْتُم
مِّن دُونِ ٱللَّهِ إِن كُنتُمْ صَٰدِقِينَ

14. "If then they (your false gods)
Answer not your (call),
Know ye that this Revelation
Is sent down (replete) with the knowledge
Of Allah, and that there is
No god but He! Will ye
Even then submit (to Islam)?"

١٤ فَإِلَّمْ يَسْتَجِيبُوا۟ لَكُمْ
فَٱعْلَمُوٓا۟ أَنَّمَآ أُنزِلَ بِعِلْمِ ٱللَّهِ
وَأَن لَّآ إِلَٰهَ إِلَّا هُوَ ۖ فَهَلْ أَنتُم مُّسْلِمُونَ

15. Those who desire
The life of the Present
And its glitter—to them
We shall pay (the price
Of) their deeds therein—
Without diminution.[1511]

١٥ مَن كَانَ يُرِيدُ ٱلْحَيَوٰةَ ٱلدُّنْيَا
وَزِينَتَهَا نُوَفِّ إِلَيْهِمْ أَعْمَٰلَهُمْ فِيهَا
وَهُمْ فِيهَا لَا يُبْخَسُونَ

16. They are those for whom
There is nothing in the Hereafter
But the Fire: vain
Are the designs they frame therein,

١٦ أُو۟لَٰٓئِكَ ٱلَّذِينَ لَيْسَ لَهُمْ فِى ٱلْءَاخِرَةِ
إِلَّا ٱلنَّارُ ۖ وَحَبِطَ مَا صَنَعُوا۟ فِيهَا

1509. Every Prophet of Allah, when he not only encounters opposition, but is actually accused of falsehood and those very evils which he is protesting against, may feel inclined, in his human weakness, to ask himself the question, "Supposing I omit this little point, will Allah's Truth then be accepted more readily? Or he may think to himself, "If I had only more money to organise my campaign, or something which will draw people's attention, like the company of an angel, how much better can I push my Message?" He is told that truth must be delivered as it is revealed, even though portions of it may be unpalatable, and that resources and other means to draw people to him are beside the point. He must use just such resources and opportunities as he has, and leave the rest to Allah.

1510. *Cf.* 2:23 and 10:38.

1511. If worldly men desire the glitter of this world, they shall have it in full measure, but it is false glitter, and it involves the negation of that spiritual life which comes from the guidance of the inner light and from the revelation of Allah, as described in verse 17 below.

And of no effect
Are the deeds that they do!

وَبَٰطِلٌ مَّا كَانُوا۟ يَعْمَلُونَ

17. Can they be (like) those
Who accept a Clear (Sign)
From their Lord, and whom
A witness from Himself[1512]
Doth teach, as did the Book
Of Moses before it—a guide[1513]
And a mercy? They believe
Therein; but those of the Sects
That reject it—the Fire
Will be their promised
Meeting place. Be not then
In doubt thereon: for it is
The Truth from thy Lord:
Yet many among men
Do not believe!

١١٧ أَفَمَن كَانَ عَلَىٰ بَيِّنَةٍ
مِّن رَّبِّهِۦ وَيَتْلُوهُ شَاهِدٌ مِّنْهُ
وَمِن قَبْلِهِۦ كِتَٰبُ مُوسَىٰٓ إِمَامًا وَرَحْمَةً ۚ
أُو۟لَٰٓئِكَ يُؤْمِنُونَ بِهِۦ ۚ وَمَن يَكْفُرْ بِهِۦ
مِنَ ٱلْأَحْزَابِ فَٱلنَّارُ مَوْعِدُهُۥ ۚ فَلَا تَكُ
فِى مِرْيَةٍ مِّنْهُ ۚ إِنَّهُ ٱلْحَقُّ مِن رَّبِّكَ
وَلَٰكِنَّ أَكْثَرَ ٱلنَّاسِ لَا يُؤْمِنُونَ

18. Who doth more wrong
Than those who invent a lie
Against Allah? They will be
Turned back to the presence
Of their Lord, and the witnesses
Will say, "There are the ones
Who lied against their Lord!
Behold! the Curse of Allah
Is on those who do wrong!—

١١٨ وَمَنْ أَظْلَمُ مِمَّنِ ٱفْتَرَىٰ عَلَى ٱللَّهِ كَذِبًا ۚ
أُو۟لَٰٓئِكَ يُعْرَضُونَ عَلَىٰ رَبِّهِمْ
وَيَقُولُ ٱلْأَشْهَٰدُ هَٰٓؤُلَآءِ ٱلَّذِينَ كَذَبُوا۟
عَلَىٰ رَبِّهِمْ ۚ أَلَا لَعْنَةُ ٱللَّهِ عَلَى ٱلظَّٰلِمِينَ

19. "Those who would hinder (men)
From the path of Allah
And would seek in it
Something crooked: these were
They who denied the
Hereafter!"[1514]

١١٩ ٱلَّذِينَ يَصُدُّونَ عَن سَبِيلِ ٱللَّهِ
وَيَبْغُونَهَا عِوَجًا وَهُم
بِٱلْءَاخِرَةِ هُمْ كَٰفِرُونَ

20. They will in nowise
Frustrate (His design) on earth,

١٢٠ أُو۟لَٰٓئِكَ لَمْ يَكُونُوا۟ مُعْجِزِينَ فِى ٱلْأَرْضِ

1512. *"A witness from Himself"*: *i.e.*, the Book which was given to Al Muṣṭafā, the Holy Qur'ān, which is compared to the original Revelation given to Moses. We make no difference between one true and genuine Message and another, nor between one prophet and another—for they all come from the One True God.

1513. "Guide": the Arabic word here is *Imām*, a leader, a guide, one that directs to the true Path. Such a direction is an instance of the Mercy and Goodness of Allah to man. The Qur'ān and the Prophet Muḥammad are also called, each, a Guide and a Mercy, and so are these epithets applicable to previous Books and Prophets.

1514. *Cf.* 7:45.

Nor have they protectors
Besides Allah! Their penalty[1515]
Will be doubled! They lost
The power to hear,
And they did not see!

وَمَا كَانَ لَهُم مِّن دُونِ ٱللَّهِ مِنْ أَوْلِيَآءَ يُضَٰعَفُ
لَهُمُ ٱلْعَذَابُ مَا كَانُوا۟ يَسْتَطِيعُونَ ٱلسَّمْعَ
وَمَا كَانُوا۟ يُبْصِرُونَ

21. They are the ones who
Have lost their own souls:
And the (fancies) they invented
Have left them in the lurch!

٢١ أُو۟لَٰٓئِكَ ٱلَّذِينَ خَسِرُوٓا۟ أَنفُسَهُمْ
وَضَلَّ عَنْهُم مَّا كَانُوا۟ يَفْتَرُونَ

22. Without a doubt, these
Are the very ones who
Will lose most in the Hereafter!

٢٢ لَا جَرَمَ أَنَّهُمْ فِى ٱلْءَاخِرَةِ هُمُ ٱلْأَخْسَرُونَ

23. But those who believe
And work righteousness,
And humble themselves
Before their Lord—[1516]
They will be Companions
Of the Garden, to dwell
Therein for aye!

٢٣ إِنَّ ٱلَّذِينَ ءَامَنُوا۟ وَعَمِلُوا۟ ٱلصَّٰلِحَٰتِ
وَأَخْبَتُوٓا۟ إِلَىٰ رَبِّهِمْ أُو۟لَٰٓئِكَ أَصْحَٰبُ
ٱلْجَنَّةِ هُمْ فِيهَا خَٰلِدُونَ

24. These two kinds (of men)
May be compared to
The blind and deaf,
And those who can see
And hear well. Are they
Equal when compared?
Will ye not then take heed?

٢٤ مَثَلُ ٱلْفَرِيقَيْنِ كَٱلْأَعْمَىٰ
وَٱلْأَصَمِّ وَٱلْبَصِيرِ وَٱلسَّمِيعِ
هَلْ يَسْتَوِيَانِ مَثَلًا أَفَلَا تَذَكَّرُونَ

C. 105.—Noah walked righteously and humbly
(11:25-49.) As in the sight of Allah. With unselfish
Love for his people he warned them
And taught them. But they did flout
And reject his Message with scorn
And insults. Allah gave him directions
To build an ark against the impending
Flood which was to purify the world
From Sin and Unrighteousness. In it
Were saved Noah and those who believed.

1515. *Cf.* 7:38. In this context, it is implied that they committed a twofold wrong: (1) in inventing falsehoods against Allah, which deadened their own soul, and (2) in leading others astray or hindering them from Allah's path. Thus they lost the faculty of hearing, which they might have used to hear the Word of Allah, and they blinded the faculty of sight by shutting out Allah's light.

1516. Note that the humility is to be "before their Lord," *i.e.*, in Allah's sight. There is no virtue, quite the contrary, in rubbing our noses to the ground before men. We are not to be arrogant even before men because we are humble as in Allah's sight. Nor does true humility lose self-confidence: for that self-confidence arises from confidence in the support and help of Allah.

So were promised salvation and Allah's Peace,
And Blessings to the Righteous evermore.

SECTION 3.

25. We sent Noah to his People
(With a mission): "I have come
To you with a Clear Warning:

٢٥ وَلَقَدْ أَرْسَلْنَا نُوحًا إِلَىٰ قَوْمِهِۦٓ
إِنِّى لَكُمْ نَذِيرٌ مُّبِينٌ

26. "That ye serve none but Allah:
Verily I do fear for you
The Penalty of a Grievous
Day."[1517]

٢٦ أَن لَّا تَعْبُدُوٓا۟ إِلَّا ٱللَّهَ ۖ إِنِّىٓ أَخَافُ
عَلَيْكُمْ عَذَابَ يَوْمٍ أَلِيمٍ

27. But the Chiefs of the
Unbelievers
Among his People said:
"We see (in) thee nothing
But a man like ourselves:
Nor do we see that any
Follow thee but the meanest
Among us, in judgement
immature:
Nor do we see in you (all)
Any merit above us:
In fact we think ye are
liars!"[1518]

٢٧ فَقَالَ ٱلْمَلَأُ ٱلَّذِينَ كَفَرُوا۟ مِن قَوْمِهِۦ
مَا نَرَىٰكَ إِلَّا بَشَرًا مِّثْلَنَا وَمَا نَرَىٰكَ
ٱتَّبَعَكَ إِلَّا ٱلَّذِينَ هُمْ أَرَاذِلُنَا بَادِىَ
ٱلرَّأْىِ وَمَا نَرَىٰ لَكُمْ عَلَيْنَا مِن فَضْلٍۭ
بَلْ نَظُنُّكُمْ كَٰذِبِينَ

28. He said: "O my People!
See ye if (it be that)
I have a Clear Sign
From my Lord, and that He
Hath sent Mercy unto me
From His own Presence, but
That the Mercy hath been
Obscured from your sight?[1519]

٢٨ قَالَ يَٰقَوْمِ أَرَءَيْتُمْ إِن كُنتُ
عَلَىٰ بَيِّنَةٍ مِّن رَّبِّى وَءَاتَىٰنِى رَحْمَةً
مِّنْ عِندِهِۦ فَعُمِّيَتْ عَلَيْكُمْ

1517. Noah's mission was to a wicked world, plunged in sin. The mission had a double character, as in the mission of all Prophets of Allah: it had to warn men against evil and call them to repentance, and it had to give them the glad tidings of Allah's Grace in case they turned back to Allah: it was a Guidance and Mercy.

1518. The Unbelievers were impelled by three powerful human motives of evil to resist Grace: (1) jealousy of other men; they said, "Why, you are no better than ourselves," half perceiving the Prophet's superiority, and half ignoring it; (2) contempt of the weak and lowly, who are often better intellectually, morally, and spiritually; they said, "We cannot believe or do what these fellows, our inferiors in social rank, believe or do!"; (3) arrogance and self-sufficiency, which is a vice cognate to (2), looked at from a different angle; they said, "We are really better than the lot of you!" Now the claim made on behalf of Allah's Message attacked all these three attitudes. And all they could say against it was to abuse it impatiently, and call it a lie.

1519. Noah's answer (like that of the Prophet of Allah who spoke in later ages in Makkah and Madīnah) is a pattern of humility, gentleness, firmness, persuasiveness, truth, and love for his own people. First, he meekly (not exultingly) informs them that he has got a Message from Allah. Secondly, he tells them that it is a Message of Mercy even in its warning, though in their arrogance the Mercy may be hidden from them. Thirdly, he tells them plainly that there can be no compulsion in Religion: but will they not accept with goodwill what is for their own benefit? He pleads with them as one of their own.

Shall we compel you
To accept it when ye
Are averse to it?

أَنُلْزِمُكُمُوهَا وَأَنتُمْ لَهَا كَارِهُونَ

29. "And O my People!
I ask you for no wealth
In return: my reward
Is from none but Allah:[1520]
But I will not drive away
(In contempt) those who believe:
For verily they are
To meet their Lord, and ye,
I see, are the ignorant ones!

(٢٩) وَيَٰقَوْمِ لَآ أَسْـَٔلُكُمْ عَلَيْهِ مَالًا إِنْ أَجْرِىَ إِلَّا عَلَى ٱللَّهِ وَمَآ أَنَا۠ بِطَارِدِ ٱلَّذِينَ ءَامَنُوٓا۟ إِنَّهُم مُّلَٰقُوا۟ رَبِّهِمْ وَلَٰكِنِّىٓ أَرَىٰكُمْ قَوْمًا تَجْهَلُونَ

30. "And O my People!
Who would help me against Allah
If I drove them away?
Will ye not then take heed?[1521]

(٣٠) وَيَٰقَوْمِ مَن يَنصُرُنِى مِنَ ٱللَّهِ إِن طَرَدتُّهُمْ أَفَلَا تَذَكَّرُونَ

31. "I tell you not that[1522]
With me are the Treasures[1523]
Of Allah, nor do I know
What is hidden,
Nor claim I to be
An angel. Nor yet
Do I say, of those whom
Your eyes do despise[1524]
That Allah will not grant them
(All) that is good:
Allah knoweth best
What is in their souls:

(٣١) وَلَآ أَقُولُ لَكُمْ عِندِى خَزَآئِنُ ٱللَّهِ وَلَآ أَعْلَمُ ٱلْغَيْبَ وَلَآ أَقُولُ إِنِّى مَلَكٌ وَلَآ أَقُولُ لِلَّذِينَ تَزْدَرِىٓ أَعْيُنُكُمْ لَن يُؤْتِيَهُمُ ٱللَّهُ خَيْرًا ٱللَّهُ أَعْلَمُ بِمَا فِىٓ أَنفُسِهِمْ

1520. The fourth point in Noah's address meets their accusation that he was a liar, implying that he was serving some selfish end of his own: on the contrary, he says, he seeks no reward from them but will bear any insults they heap on him, for he looks to Allah rather than men. But, fifthly if they insult the poor and needy who come to him in Faith, and think that he would send them away in order to attract the great ones of the land, he tells them plainly that they are mistaken. In fact, (sixthly), he has no hesitation in telling the blunt truth that *they* are the ignorant ones, and not the poor who came to seek Allah's Truth!

1521. But (seventhly) again he pleads, with as much earnestness as ever, that he is one of themselves, and just doing his truest duty. Would they have him do less? Indeed, would they not themselves see the Truth and come into the goodly company of Believers?

1522. The eighth point that Noah urges is that he is not a mere vulgar soothsayer pretending to reveal secrets not worth knowing, nor an angel living in another world, with no ties to them. He is their real well-wisher, delivering a true Message from Allah.

1523. *Cf.* 6:50 and n. 867.

1524. But Noah will not close his argument without defending the men of Faith, whom the Chiefs despise because they are lacking in worldly goods. He tells them plainly that Allah perhaps sees in them something in which they, the arrogant Chiefs, are lacking. Their spiritual faculties can only be appreciated truly by Him to Whom all the secrets of the spirit are open. But he, Noah, must declare boldly his own Faith, and this is the ninth point in his argument.

I should, if I did,
Indeed be a wrongdoer."

إِنِّيٓ إِذًا لَّمِنَ ٱلظَّٰلِمِينَ

32. They said: "O Noah!
Thou hath disputed with us,
And (much) hast thou prolonged
The dispute with us: now
Bring upon us what thou
Threatenest us with, if thou
Speakest the truth!?"[1525]

قَالُوا۟ يَٰنُوحُ قَدْ جَٰدَلْتَنَا
فَأَكْثَرْتَ جِدَٰلَنَا فَأْتِنَا بِمَا تَعِدُنَآ
إِن كُنتَ مِنَ ٱلصَّٰدِقِينَ ﴿٣٢﴾

33. He said: "Truly, Allah
Will bring it on you
If He wills—and then,
Ye will not be able
To frustrate it![1526]

قَالَ إِنَّمَا يَأْتِيكُم بِهِ ٱللَّهُ إِن شَآءَ
وَمَآ أَنتُم بِمُعْجِزِينَ ﴿٣٣﴾

34. "Of no profit will be
My counsel to you,
Much as I desire
To give you (good) counsel,
If it be that Allah
Willeth to leave you astray:[1527]
He is your Lord!
And to Him will ye return!"

وَلَا يَنفَعُكُمْ نُصْحِيٓ إِنْ أَرَدتُّ أَنْ
أَنصَحَ لَكُمْ إِن كَانَ ٱللَّهُ يُرِيدُ أَن يُغْوِيَكُمْ
هُوَ رَبُّكُمْ وَإِلَيْهِ تُرْجَعُونَ ﴿٣٤﴾

35. Or do they say,
"He has forged it?" Say:
"If I had forged it,
On me were my sin!
And I am free

أَمْ يَقُولُونَ ٱفْتَرَىٰهُ ﴿٣٥﴾
قُلْ إِنِ ٱفْتَرَيْتُهُۥ فَعَلَيَّ إِجْرَامِي وَأَنَا۠ بَرِيٓءٌ

1525. To Noah's address the worldly Chiefs give a characteristic reply. In its aggressive spirit it is the very antithesis of the gentle remonstrances of Noah. Because he had gently and patiently argued with them, they impatiently accuse him of "disputing with them" and "prolonging the dispute". They are unable to deal with his points. So they arrogantly throw out their challenge, which is a compound of hectoring insolence, unreasoning skepticism, and biting irony. "You foretell disaster to us if we don't mend our ways! Let us see you bring it on! Now, if you please! Or shall we have to call you a liar?"

1526. To the blasphemous challenge addressed to Noah his only answer could be: "I never claimed that I could punish you. All punishment is in the hands of Allah, and He knows best when His punishment will descend. But this I can tell you! His punishment is sure if you do not repent, and when it comes, you will not be able to ward it off!"

1527. But Noah's heart bleeds for his people. They are preparing their own undoing! All his efforts are to be vain! Obstinate as they are, Allah's grace must be withdrawn, and then who can help them, and what use is any counsel? But again he will try to remind them of their Lord, and turn their face to Him. For their ultimate return to His Judgement Seat is certain, to answer for their conduct.

Of the sins of which
Ye are guilty!"[1528]

مِّمَّا تُجْرِمُونَ

SECTION 4.

36. It was revealed to Noah:
"None of thy People will believe[1529]
Except those who have believed
Already! So grieve no longer
Over their (evil) deeds.

وَأُوحِيَ إِلَىٰ نُوحٍ أَنَّهُۥ لَن ﴿٣٦﴾
يُؤْمِنَ مِن قَوْمِكَ إِلَّا مَن قَدْ ءَامَنَ
فَلَا تَبْتَئِسْ بِمَا كَانُوا۟ يَفْعَلُونَ

37. "But construct an Ark
Under Our eyes and Our[1530]
Inspiration, and address Me
No (further) on behalf
Of those who are in sin:
For they are about to be
Overwhelmed (in the Flood)."

وَٱصْنَعِ ٱلْفُلْكَ بِأَعْيُنِنَا ﴿٣٧﴾
وَوَحْيِنَا وَلَا تُخَٰطِبْنِى فِى ٱلَّذِينَ
ظَلَمُوٓا۟ إِنَّهُم مُّغْرَقُونَ

38. Forthwith he (starts)
Constructing the Ark:
Every time that the Chiefs
Of his People passed by him,
They threw ridicule on him.[1531]
He said: "If ye ridicule
Us now, we (in our turn)

وَيَصْنَعُ ٱلْفُلْكَ وَكُلَّمَا ﴿٣٨﴾
مَرَّ عَلَيْهِ مَلَأٌ مِّن قَوْمِهِۦ سَخِرُوا۟ مِنْهُ
قَالَ إِن تَسْخَرُوا۟ مِنَّا فَإِنَّا

1528. The fine narrative of dramatic power is here interrupted by a verse which shows that the story of Noah is also a parable for the time and the ministry of Muḥammad, the Prophet. The wonderful force and aptness of the story cannot be denied. The enemy therefore turns and says, "Oh! but you invented it!" The answer is, "No! but it is Allah's own truth! You may be accustomed to dealing in falsehoods, but I protest that I am free from such sins." The place of this verse here corresponds to the place of verse 49 at the end of the next Section.

While understanding this verse to refer to Al Muṣṭafā, as most of the accepted Commentators understand it, it is possible also, I think, to read it into the story of Noah, for all Prophets have similar spiritual experiences.

1529. The story of Noah is resumed. A point was reached, when it was clear that there was no hope of saving the sinners, who were courting their own destruction. It was to be a great Flood. So Noah was ordered to construct a great Ark or Ship, not a sailing ship, but a heavy vessel to remain afloat in the Flood, so that the righteous could be saved in it.

1530. It was to be built under the special instructions of Allah, to serve the special purpose it was intended to serve.

1531. The ridicule of the sinners, from their own point of view, was natural. Here was a preacher turned carpenter! Here was a plain in the higher reaches of the Mesopotamian basin, drained by the majestic Tigris, over 800 to 900 miles from the sea (the Persian Gulf) in a straight line! Yet he talks of a flood like the Sea! All material civilisations pride themselves on their Public Works and their drainage schemes. And here was a fellow relying on Allah! But did not their narrow pride seem ridiculous also to the Prophet of Allah! Here were men steeped in sin and insolence! And they pit themselves against the power and the promise of Allah! Truly a contemptible race is man!

Can look down on you
With ridicule likewise![1532]

نَسْخَرُ مِنكُمْ كَمَا تَسْخَرُونَ

39. "But soon will ye know
Who it is on whom
Will descend a Penalty
That will cover them
With shame—on whom will be
Unloosed a Penalty lasting:"

٣٩ فَسَوْفَ تَعْلَمُونَ
مَن يَأْتِيهِ عَذَابٌ يُخْزِيهِ
وَيَحِلُّ عَلَيْهِ عَذَابٌ مُّقِيمٌ

40. At length, behold!
There came Our Command,
And the fountains of the
earth[1533]
Gushed forth! We said:
"Embark therein, of each kind
Two, male and female,[1534]
And your family—except
Those against whom the Word
Has already gone forth—[1535]
And the Believers."
But only a few
Believed with him.

٤٠ حَتَّىٰٓ إِذَا جَآءَ
أَمْرُنَا وَفَارَ ٱلتَّنُّورُ
قُلْنَا ٱحْمِلْ فِيهَا مِن كُلٍّ
زَوْجَيْنِ ٱثْنَيْنِ وَأَهْلَكَ
إِلَّا مَن سَبَقَ عَلَيْهِ ٱلْقَوْلُ وَمَنْ ءَامَنَ
وَمَآ ءَامَنَ مَعَهُۥٓ إِلَّا قَلِيلٌ

41. So he said: "Embark ye
On the Ark
In the name of Allah,
Whether it move
Or be at rest!

٤١ وَقَالَ ٱرْكَبُوا۟ فِيهَا
بِسْمِ ٱللَّهِ مَجْر۪ىٰهَا وَمُرْسَىٰهَآ

1532. The Arabic Aorist may be construed either by the present tense or the future tense, and both make good sense here. Following Zamakhsharī, I construe in the present tense, because the future is so tragic for the sinners. For the time being the worldly ones looked down on the Believers as they always do; but the Believers relied on Allah, and pitied their critics for knowing no better!—for their arrogance was really ridiculous.

1533. *Fār al tannūru.* Two interpretations have been given: (1) the fountains or the springs on the surface of the earth bubbled over or gushed forth; or (2) the oven (of Allah's Wrath) boiled over. The former has the weight of the best authority behind it and I prefer it. Moreover, the same phrase occurs in 23:27, where it is a clause coordinated (as here) with the coming of Allah's Command. These two passages may be compared with 54:11-12, where it is said that water poured forth from the skies and gushed forth from the springs. This double action is familiar to anyone who has seen floods on a large scale. The rain from above would saturate the great Ararat Plateau, and give great force to the springs and fountains in the valley of the Tigris below.

1534. *Zawjayni*: the dual number refers to the two individuals in each pair of opposite sexes. Some of the most authoritative Commentators (*e.g.*, Imām Rāzī) construe it in this sense, though others construe it to mean two pairs of each species.

1535. A disobedient and recalcitrant son (or step-son or grandson) of Noah is mentioned below (11:42-43, 45-46). A member of the family, who breaks away from the traditions of the family in things that matter, ceases to share in the privileges of the family.

For my Lord is, be sure,
Oft-Forgiving, Most Merciful!"

إِنَّ رَبِّى لَغَفُورٌ رَّحِيمٌ

42. So the Ark floated
With them on the waves
(Towering) like mountains,[1536]
And Noah called out
To his son, who had
Separated himself (from the rest):
"O my son! embark
With us, and be not
With the Unbelievers!"

وَهِىَ تَجْرِى بِهِمْ فِى مَوْجٍ ﴿٤٢﴾
كَالْجِبَالِ وَنَادَىٰ نُوحٌ ٱبْنَهُۥ
وَكَانَ فِى مَعْزِلٍ
يَٰبُنَىَّ ٱرْكَب مَّعَنَا
وَلَا تَكُن مَّعَ ٱلْكَٰفِرِينَ

43. The son replied: "I will
Betake myself to some mountain:[1537]
It will save me from
The water." Noah said:
"This day nothing can save,
From the Command of Allah,
Any but those on whom
He hath mercy!"—
And the waves came
Between them, and the son
Was among those
Overwhelmed in the Flood.

قَالَ سَـَٔاوِىٓ إِلَىٰ جَبَلٍ ﴿٤٣﴾
يَعْصِمُنِى مِنَ ٱلْمَآءِ
قَالَ لَا عَاصِمَ ٱلْيَوْمَ مِنْ أَمْرِ ٱللَّهِ
إِلَّا مَن رَّحِمَ وَحَالَ بَيْنَهُمَا ٱلْمَوْجُ
فَكَانَ مِنَ ٱلْمُغْرَقِينَ

44. Then the word went forth:[1538]
"O earth! swallow up
Thy water, and O sky!
Withhold (thy rain)!"
And the water abated,
And the matter was ended.

وَقِيلَ يَٰٓأَرْضُ ٱبْلَعِى ﴿٤٤﴾
مَآءَكِ وَيَٰسَمَآءُ أَقْلِعِى
وَغِيضَ ٱلْمَآءُ وَقُضِىَ ٱلْأَمْرُ

1536. The simile of mountains applies to the waves, which were mountain high—literally, for the peaks were being submerged.

1537. The Unbelievers refuse to believe in Allah, but have great faith in material things! This young man was going to save himself on mountain peaks, not knowing that the peaks were themselves being submerged.

1538. A wonderful passage. The whole picture is painted in just a few words. The chain of material facts are linked together, not only in their relations to each other, but also in their relation to the spiritual forces that control them, and the spiritual consequences of Sin and wrongdoing. The drowning in the material sense was the last part of the Penalty. A whole new world came into existence after the Deluge. (R).

The Ark rested on Mount[1539]
Jūdī, and the word
Went forth: "Away
With those who do wrong!"

وَٱسْتَوَتْ عَلَى ٱلْجُودِيِّ وَقِيلَ
بُعْدًا لِّلْقَوْمِ ٱلظَّٰلِمِينَ

45. And Noah called upon
His Lord, and said:
"O my Lord! surely
My son is of my family!
And Thy promise is true,
And Thou art
The Justest of Judges!"

٤٥ وَنَادَىٰ نُوحٌ رَّبَّهُۥ فَقَالَ رَبِّ إِنَّ
ٱبْنِى مِنْ أَهْلِى وَإِنَّ وَعْدَكَ ٱلْحَقُّ
وَأَنتَ أَحْكَمُ ٱلْحَٰكِمِينَ

46. He said: "O Noah!
He is not of thy family:[1540]
For his conduct is unrighteous.
So ask not of Me
That of which thou
Hast no knowledge!
I give thee counsel, lest
Thou act like the ignorant!"

٤٦ قَالَ يَٰنُوحُ إِنَّهُۥ لَيْسَ مِنْ أَهْلِكَ
إِنَّهُۥ عَمَلٌ غَيْرُ صَٰلِحٍ فَلَا تَسْـَٔلْنِ
مَا لَيْسَ لَكَ بِهِۦ عِلْمٌ إِنِّىٓ أَعِظُكَ
أَن تَكُونَ مِنَ ٱلْجَٰهِلِينَ

47. Noah said: "O my Lord!
I do seek refuge with Thee,
Lest I ask Thee for that
Of which I have no knowledge.
And unless Thou forgive me

٤٧ قَالَ رَبِّ إِنِّىٓ أَعُوذُ بِكَ أَنْ أَسْـَٔلَكَ
مَا لَيْسَ لِى بِهِۦ عِلْمٌ وَإِلَّا تَغْفِرْ لِى

1539. Let us get a little idea of the geography of the place. The letters Jīm, Bā', and Kāf are philologically interchangeable, and Jūdī, Gūdī, Kūdī are sounds that can pass into each other. There is no doubt that the name is connected with the name "Kurd", in which the letter *r* is a later interpolation, for the oldest Sumerian records name a people called Kūti or Gūtū as holding the middle Tigris region not later than 2000 B.C. (see E.B., Kurdistan). That region comprises the modern Turkish district of Bohtan, in which Jabal Jūdī is situated (near the frontiers of modern Turkey, modern Iraq, and modern Syria), and the town of Jazīrah ibn 'Umar, (on the present Turco-Syrian frontier), and it extends into Iraq and Iran. The great mountain mass of the Ararat plateau dominates this district. This mountain system "is unique in the Old World in containing great sheets of water that are bitter lakes without outlets, Lake Van and Lake Urumiya being the chief" (E.B., Asia). Such would be the very region for a stupendous Deluge if the usual scanty rainfall were to be changed into a very heavy downpour. A glacier damming of Lake Van in the Ice Age would have produced the same result. The region has many local traditions connected with Noah and the Flood. The Biblical legend of Mount Ararat being the resting place of Noah's Ark is hardly plausible, seeing that the highest peak of Ararat is over 16,000 feet high. If it means one of the lower peaks of the Ararat system, it agrees with the Muslim tradition about Mount Jūdī (or Gūdī), and this is in accordance with the oldest and best local traditions. These traditions are accepted by Josephus, by the Nestorian Christians, and indeed by all the Eastern Christians and Jews, and they are the best in touch with local traditions. See (Viscount) J. Bryce. "*Transcaucasia and Ararat*," 4th ed., 1896, p. 216.

1540. See n. 5135 above. Like all Prophets of Allah, Noah was kind-hearted, but he is told that there can be no compromise with evil. And Noah acknowledges the reproof. There was a wife of Noah, who was also an unbelieving woman (66:10), and she suffered the fate of Unbelievers.

And have Mercy on me,
I should indeed be lost!"[1541]

وَتَرْحَمْنِيٓ أَكُن مِّنَ ٱلْخَٰسِرِينَ

48. The word came: "O Noah!
Come down (from the Ark)
With Peace from Us,
And Blessing on thee
And on some of the Peoples
(Who will spring) from those
With thee: but (there will be
Other) Peoples to whom We
Shall grant their pleasures[1542]
(For a time), but in the end
Will a grievous Penalty
Reach them from Us."[1543]

(٤٨) قِيلَ يَٰنُوحُ ٱهْبِطْ
بِسَلَٰمٍ مِّنَّا وَبَرَكَٰتٍ عَلَيْكَ
وَعَلَىٰٓ أُمَمٍ مِّمَّن مَّعَكَ
وَأُمَمٌ سَنُمَتِّعُهُمْ ثُمَّ يَمَسُّهُم
مِّنَّا عَذَابٌ أَلِيمٌ

49. Such are some of the stories
Of the Unseen, which We
Have revealed unto thee:
Before this, neither thou
Nor thy People knew them.
So persevere patiently:
For the End is for those
Who are righteous.[1544]

(٤٩) تِلْكَ مِنْ أَنۢبَآءِ ٱلْغَيْبِ
نُوحِيهَآ إِلَيْكَ مَا كُنتَ تَعْلَمُهَآ أَنتَ
وَلَا قَوْمُكَ مِن قَبْلِ هَٰذَا فَٱصْبِرْ
إِنَّ ٱلْعَٰقِبَةَ لِلْمُتَّقِينَ

C. 106. — Awful were the fates of the 'Ād
(11:50-68.) And the Thamūd, two mighty peoples
Of ancient Arabia. They rejected
Allah and His Message and went on
In their evil ways — the 'Ād
In their superstitions and arrogance,
And the Thamūd in their entrenched
Selfishness, denying to others the gifts
Of Allah's spacious earth! How swiftly
Were they wiped out, as if they
Had never been? But wrong can never stand!

1541. Noah, in his natural affection and respect for ties of relationship, was overcome with human weakness in wishing to reverse the law of spiritual Justice. It was not sin but ignorance. His ignorance was corrected by divine inspiration, and he immediately saw the full Truth, acknowledged his error, and asked for Allah's forgiveness and mercy. This is the standard set for us all.

1542. *Cf.* 2:126.

1543. Those who truly seek Allah's light and guidance and sincerely bend their will to His Will are freely admitted to Allah's grace. Notwithstanding any human weaknesses in them, they are advanced higher in the spiritual stage on account of their Faith, Trust, and Striving after Right. They are given Allah's Peace, which gives the soul true calmness and strength, and all the blessings that flow from spiritual life. This was given not only to Noah and his family but to all the righteous people who were saved with him. And their descendants were also promised those blessings on condition of righteousness. But some of them fell from grace, as we know in history. Allah's grace is not a social or family privilege. Each people and each individual must earnestly strive for it and earn it.

1544. *Cf.* n. 1528 to 9:35. The sum of the whole matter is that the righteous, who work for Allah and their fellow-men, may be traduced, insulted, and persecuted. But they will be sustained by Allah's Mercy. They must go on working patiently, for the End will all be for them and their Cause.

SECTION 5.

50. To the 'Ād People
(We sent) Hūd, one
Of their own brethren.
He said: "O my people!
Worship Allah! ye have
No other god but Him.[1545]
(Your other gods) ye do nothing
But invent!

٥٠ وَإِلَىٰ عَادٍ أَخَاهُمْ هُودًا ۚ
قَالَ يَٰقَوْمِ ٱعْبُدُوا۟ ٱللَّهَ
مَا لَكُم مِّنْ إِلَٰهٍ غَيْرُهُۥٓ ۖ
إِنْ أَنتُمْ إِلَّا مُفْتَرُونَ

51. "O my people! I ask of you
No reward for this (Message).
My reward is from none
But Him who created me:
Will ye not then understand?

٥١ يَٰقَوْمِ لَآ أَسْـَٔلُكُمْ عَلَيْهِ أَجْرًا ۖ
إِنْ أَجْرِىَ إِلَّا عَلَى ٱلَّذِى فَطَرَنِىٓ ۚ أَفَلَا تَعْقِلُونَ

52. "And O my people! Ask
Forgiveness of your Lord,
And turn to Him (in
repentance):
He will send you the skies[1546]
Pouring abundant rain,
And add strength
To your strength:[1547]
So turn ye not back
In sin!"

٥٢ وَيَٰقَوْمِ ٱسْتَغْفِرُوا۟ رَبَّكُمْ
ثُمَّ تُوبُوٓا۟ إِلَيْهِ يُرْسِلِ ٱلسَّمَآءَ
عَلَيْكُم مِّدْرَارًا وَيَزِدْكُمْ قُوَّةً
إِلَىٰ قُوَّتِكُمْ وَلَا تَتَوَلَّوْا۟ مُجْرِمِينَ

53. They said: "O Hūd!
No Clear (Sign) hast thou
Brought us, and we are not
The ones to desert our gods

٥٣ قَالُوا۟ يَٰهُودُ مَا جِئْتَنَا بِبَيِّنَةٍ
وَمَا نَحْنُ بِتَارِكِىٓ ءَالِهَتِنَا

1545. *Cf.* the story of Hūd the Messenger to the 'Ād People, in 7:65-72. There the argument was how other Peoples treated their prophets as the Makkans were treating Al Muṣṭafā. Here we see another point emphasised: the insolence of the 'Ād in obstinately adhering to false gods after the true God had been preached to them, Allah's long-suffering grace to them, and finally Allah's justice in bringing them to book while the righteous were saved.

The locality in which the 'Ād flourished is indicated in n. 1040 to 7:65.

1546. The beautiful metaphor about the skies coming down with rain has been obscured unnecessarily in most translations. The country of the 'Ād was an arid country, and rain was the greatest blessing they could receive. We can imagine this being said in a time of famine, when the people performed all sorts of superstitious rites and invocations instead of turning to the true God in faith and repentance. Further, when we remember that there were, in this tract in ancient times, dams like that at Ma'ārib, for the storage of rain water, the effect is still further heightened in pointing to Allah's care and mercy in His dealing with men.

1547. Adding strength to strength may refer to an increase of population, as some Commentators think. While other parts of Arabia were sparsely populated, the irrigated lands of the 'Ād supported a comparatively dense population and added to their natural strength in the arts of peace and war. But the term used is perfectly general. They were a powerful people in their time. If they obeyed Allah and followed the law of righteousness, they would be still more powerful, for "righteousness exalteth a nation."

On thy word! Nor shall we
Believe in thee![1548]

عَن قَوْلِكَ وَمَا نَحْنُ لَكَ بِمُؤْمِنِينَ

54. "We say nothing but that
(Perhaps) some of our gods
May have seized thee[1549]
With imbecility." He said:
"I call Allah to witness,
And do ye bear witness,
That I am free from the sin
Of ascribing, to Him,

٥٤ إِن نَّقُولُ إِلَّا ٱعْتَرَىٰكَ
بَعْضُ ءَالِهَتِنَا بِسُوٓءٍ قَالَ
إِنِّىٓ أُشْهِدُ ٱللَّهَ وَٱشْهَدُوٓا۟
أَنِّى بَرِىٓءٌ مِّمَّا تُشْرِكُونَ

55. "Other gods as partners!
So scheme (your worst) against me,
All of you, and give me
No respite.[1550]

٥٥ مِن دُونِهِۦ فَكِيدُونِى
جَمِيعًا ثُمَّ لَا تُنظِرُونِ

56. "I put my trust in Allah,
My Lord and your Lord!
There is not a moving
Creature, but He hath
Grasp of its forelock.[1551]
Verily, it is my Lord
That is on a straight Path.[1552]

٥٦ إِنِّى تَوَكَّلْتُ عَلَى ٱللَّهِ رَبِّى وَرَبِّكُم
مَّا مِن دَآبَّةٍ إِلَّا هُوَ ءَاخِذٌۢ بِنَاصِيَتِهَآ
إِنَّ رَبِّى عَلَىٰ صِرَٰطٍ مُّسْتَقِيمٍ

57. "If ye turn away—
I (at least) have conveyed
The Message with which I
Was sent to you. My Lord
Will make another People

٥٧ فَإِن تَوَلَّوْا۟ فَقَدْ أَبْلَغْتُكُم مَّآ أُرْسِلْتُ
بِهِۦٓ إِلَيْكُمْ وَيَسْتَخْلِفُ رَبِّى قَوْمًا

1548. The argument of the Unbelievers is practically this: "We are not convinced by you; we don't want to be convinced: we think you are a liar—or perhaps a fool!" (See next verse).

1549. See n. 1548 above. Continuing their argument, the Unbelievers make a show of making all charitable allowances for Hūd, but in reality cut him to the quick by bringing in their false gods. "To be quite polite," said they, "we will not say that you are exactly a liar! Perhaps you have been touched with imbecility! Ah yes! You rail against what you call our false gods! Some of them have paid you out, and made you a fool! Ha! ha!" This mockery is even worse than their other false accusations. For it sets up false gods against the One True God, even in dealing with Hūd. So Hūd replies, with spirit and indignation: "At least keep Allah's name out of your futile talk! You know as well as I do, that I worship the One True God! You pretend that your false gods can smite a true Prophet of Allah! I accept the challenge. Scheme and plot against me as you may, all of you—you and your gods! See if you have any power! I ask for no quarter from you! My trust is in Allah."

1550. *Cf.* 7:195 and n. 1168.

1551. *Grasp of the forelock*: an Arabic idiom, referring to a horse's forelock. The man who grasps it has complete power over the horse, and for the horse the forelock is as it were the crown of his beauty, the sum of his power of self-assertion. So Allah's power over all creatures is unlimited and no one can withstand His decree. *Cf.* 96:15-16.

1552. That is, the standard of all virtue and righteousness is in the Will of Allah, the Universal Will that controls all things in goodness and justice. You are on a crooked Path. Allah's Path is a straight Path.

To succeed you, and you
Will not harm Him[1553]
In the least. For my Lord
Hath care and watch
Over all things."

غَيْرَكُمْ وَلَا تَضُرُّونَهُۥ شَيْـًٔا
إِنَّ رَبِّى عَلَىٰ كُلِّ شَىْءٍ حَفِيظٌ

58. So when Our decree
Issued, We saved Hūd
And those who believed
With him, by (special) Grace[1554]
From Ourselves: We saved them
From a severe Penalty.

٥٨ وَلَمَّا جَآءَ أَمْرُنَا نَجَّيْنَا هُودًا
وَٱلَّذِينَ ءَامَنُوا۟ مَعَهُۥ بِرَحْمَةٍ مِّنَّا
وَنَجَّيْنَٰهُم مِّنْ عَذَابٍ غَلِيظٍ

59. Such were the 'Ād People:
They rejected the Signs
Of their Lord and Cherisher;
Disobeyed His Messengers;
And followed the command
Of every powerful, obstinate
Transgressor.[1555]

٥٩ وَتِلْكَ عَادٌ جَحَدُوا۟ بِـَٔايَٰتِ
رَبِّهِمْ وَعَصَوْا۟ رُسُلَهُۥ
وَٱتَّبَعُوٓا۟ أَمْرَ كُلِّ جَبَّارٍ عَنِيدٍ

60. And they were pursued
By a Curse in this Life—
And on the Day of Judgement.
Ah! Behold! For the 'Ād
Rejected their Lord and Cherisher!
Ah! Behold! Removed (from sight)
Were 'Ād, the People of Hūd!

٦٠ وَأُتْبِعُوا۟ فِى هَٰذِهِ ٱلدُّنْيَا لَعْنَةً
وَيَوْمَ ٱلْقِيَٰمَةِ أَلَآ إِنَّ عَادًا كَفَرُوا۟ رَبَّهُمْ
أَلَا بُعْدًا لِّعَادٍ قَوْمِ هُودٍ

SECTION 6.

61. To the Thamūd People
(We sent) Ṣāliḥ, one
Of their own brethren.[1556]

٦١ وَإِلَىٰ ثَمُودَ أَخَاهُمْ صَٰلِحًا

1553. Hūd was dealing with a people of pride and obstinate rebellion. He tells them that their conduct will only recoil on themselves. It can do no harm to Allah or in any way frustrate the beneficent Plan of Allah. He will only put some other people in their place to carry out His Plan. That Plan is referred to in the next sentence as "care and watch" over all his Creation.

1554. A few just men might suffer for the iniquities of the many. But Allah's Plan is perfect and eventually saves His own people by special Grace, if they have Faith and Trust in Him.

1555. Instead of following the beneficent Lord who cherished them, they followed every rebel against Allah's Law, if he only obtained a little power to dazzle them.

1556. The story of Ṣāliḥ and the Thamūd people has been told from another point of view in 7:73-79. The difference in the point of view there and here is the same as in the story of Hūd: see n. 1545 to 11:50. Note how the story now is the same, and yet new points and details are brought out to illustrate each new argument. Note, also, how the besetting sin of the 'Ād—pride and obstinacy—is distinguished from the besetting sin of the Thamūd—the oppression of the poor, as illustrated by the test case and symbol of the she-camel: see n. 1044 to 7:73. All sin is in a sense pride and rebellion; yet sins take particular hues in different circumstances, and these colours are brought out as in a most artistically painted picture—with the greatest economy of words and the most piercing analysis of motives. For the locality and history of the Thamūd, see n. 1043 to 7:73.

He said: "O my People!
Worship Allah: ye have
No other god but Him.
It is He Who hath produced you[1557]
From the earth and settled you
Therein: then ask forgiveness
Of Him, and turn to Him
(In repentance): for my Lord
Is (always) near, ready
To answer."

قَالَ يَٰقَوۡمِ ٱعۡبُدُواْ ٱللَّهَ
مَا لَكُم مِّنۡ إِلَٰهٍ غَيۡرُهُۥۖ هُوَ أَنشَأَكُم
مِّنَ ٱلۡأَرۡضِ وَٱسۡتَعۡمَرَكُمۡ فِيهَا
فَٱسۡتَغۡفِرُوهُ ثُمَّ تُوبُوٓاْ إِلَيۡهِۚ
إِنَّ رَبِّي قَرِيبٞ مُّجِيبٞ

62. They said: "O Ṣaliḥ!
Thou hast been of us!—
A centre of our hopes[1558]
Hitherto! Dost thou (now)
Forbid us the worship
Of what our fathers worshipped?
But we are really
In suspicious (disquieting)
Doubt as to that to which
Thou invitest us."

٦٢ قَالُواْ يَٰصَٰلِحُ
قَدۡ كُنتَ فِينَا مَرۡجُوّٗا قَبۡلَ هَٰذَآۖ
أَتَنۡهَىٰنَآ أَن نَّعۡبُدَ مَا يَعۡبُدُ ءَابَآؤُنَا
وَإِنَّنَا لَفِي شَكّٖ مِّمَّا تَدۡعُونَآ إِلَيۡهِ مُرِيبٖ

63. He said: "O my people!
Do ye see?—If I have
A Clear (Sign) from my Lord
And He hath sent Mercy
Unto me from Himself—who[1559]
Then can help me
Against Allah if I were
To disobey Him? What
Then would ye add
To my (portion) but perdition?

٦٣ قَالَ يَٰقَوۡمِ أَرَءَيۡتُمۡ إِن كُنتُ
عَلَىٰ بَيِّنَةٖ مِّن رَّبِّي وَءَاتَىٰنِي مِنۡهُ رَحۡمَةٗ
فَمَن يَنصُرُنِي مِنَ ٱللَّهِ إِنۡ عَصَيۡتُهُۥۖ
فَمَا تَزِيدُونَنِي غَيۡرَ تَخۡسِيرٖ

64. "And O my people!
This she-camel of Allah is

٦٤ وَيَٰقَوۡمِ هَٰذِهِۦ نَاقَةُ ٱللَّهِ

1557. For *Ansha'a* as a process of creation see n. 923 to 6:98 and the further references given there. As to his body, man has been produced from earth or clay, and his settlement on earth is a fact of his material existence. Therefore we must conform to all the laws of our physical being, in order that through our life on this earth we may develop that higher Life which belongs to the other part of our being, our spiritual heritage. Through the use we make of our health, of our tilth, of our pastures, of material facts of all kinds, will develop our moral and spiritual nature.

1558. Ṣaliḥ's life with his people had been so righteous (like that of Al Amīn in later times) that he might have been chosen leader or king if he had only conformed to their superstitions and supported their sins. But he was born for a higher mission—that of a preacher of truth and righteousness and an ardent opponent of selfish privilege and a champion of the rights of humanity on Allah's free earth by the symbol of the she-camel: see n. 1044 to 7:73.

1559. "Allah has been good to me and bestowed on me His light and the inestimable privilege of carrying His mission to you. Don't you see that if I fail to carry out his mission, I shall have to answer before Him? Who can help me in that case? The only thing which you can add to my misfortunes would be total perdition in the spiritual world." *Cf.* 11:28.

A symbol to you:[1560]
Leave her to feed
On Allah's (free) earth,
And inflict no harm
On her, or a swift Penalty
Will seize you!"

لَكُمْ ءَايَةً فَذَرُوهَا تَأْكُلْ
فِىٓ أَرْضِ ٱللَّهِ وَلَا تَمَسُّوهَا بِسُوٓءٍ
فَيَأْخُذَكُمْ عَذَابٌ قَرِيبٌ

65. But they did hamstring her.
So he said: "Enjoy yourselves
In your homes for three days:[1561]
(Then will be your ruin):
(Behold) there a promise
Not to be belied!"

٦٥ فَعَقَرُوهَا فَقَالَ تَمَتَّعُوا۟
فِى دَارِكُمْ ثَلَٰثَةَ أَيَّامٍ
ذَٰلِكَ وَعْدٌ غَيْرُ مَكْذُوبٍ

66. When Our Decree issued,
We saved Ṣāliḥ and those
Who believed with him,
By (special) Grace from
Ourselves—[1562]
And from the Ignominy
Of that Day. For thy Lord—
He is the Strong One, and Able
To enforce His Will.

٦٦ فَلَمَّا جَآءَ أَمْرُنَا نَجَّيْنَا صَٰلِحًا
وَٱلَّذِينَ ءَامَنُوا۟ مَعَهُۥ بِرَحْمَةٍ مِّنَّا
وَمِنْ خِزْىِ يَوْمِئِذٍ إِنَّ رَبَّكَ
هُوَ ٱلْقَوِىُّ ٱلْعَزِيزُ

67. The (mighty) Blast[1563] overtook
The wrongdoers, and they
Lay prostrate in their homes
Before the morning—

٦٧ وَأَخَذَ ٱلَّذِينَ ظَلَمُوا۟ ٱلصَّيْحَةُ
فَأَصْبَحُوا۟ فِى دِيَٰرِهِمْ جَٰثِمِينَ

68. As if they had never
Dwelt and flourished there.
Ah! Behold! For the Thamūd
Rejected their Lord and Cherisher!
Ah! Behold! Removed
(From sight) were the Thamūd![1564]

٦٨ كَأَن لَّمْ يَغْنَوْا۟ فِيهَآ
أَلَآ إِنَّ ثَمُودَا۟ كَفَرُوا۟ رَبَّهُمْ
أَلَا بُعْدًا لِّثَمُودَ

1560. Ṣāliḥ does not merely take up a negative attitude, he puts forward the she-camel as a Symbol: see n. 1044 to 8:73. "Give up your selfish monopoly. Make Allah's gifts on this free earth available to all. Give the poor their rights, including grazing rights on common lands. Show your penitence and your new attitude by leaving this she-camel to graze freely. She is a Symbol, and therefore sacred to you." But their only reply was to defy the appeal and hamstring the camel. And so they went the way of all sinners—to total perdition.

1561. Just three days' time for further thought and repentance! But they paid no heed. A terrible earthquake came by night, preceded by a mighty rumbling blast (probably volcanic), such as is well-known in earthquake-prone areas. It came by night and buried them in their own fortress homes, which they thought such places of security! The morning found them lying on their faces hidden from the light. How the mighty were brought low!

1562. *Cf.* 11:58 above and n. 1554. For *'Azīz*, see n. 2818 to 21:40.

1563. *Cf.* 11:78 and n. 1047—also n. 1561 above.

1564. *Cf.* 11:60 above.

C. 107.— When the angels, on a mission to Sodom
(11:69-95.) And Gomorrah, Cities of the Plain,
Passed by Abraham, he entertained them
And received from them the Good News
Of the line of Prophets to spring from his loins.
He tried, in his goodness of heart, to intercede
For the wicked Cities, but they were steeped
In Sin and past all hope of repentance.
Lūṭ preached to them, but they flouted him
And went to their fate, as also did Midian.
The People of Shu'ayb destroyed their commerce
By fraudulent dealings and love of brute force.
Marvellous are Allah's Mercies, and strange
Are the ways of ungrateful man!

SECTION 7.

69. There came Our Messengers
To Abraham with glad tidings.
They said, "Peace!" He answered,
"Peace!" and hastened
To entertain them
With a roasted calf.[1565]

٦٩ وَلَقَدْ جَاءَتْ رُسُلُنَا إِبْرَٰهِيمَ
بِالْبُشْرَىٰ قَالُوا سَلَٰمًا قَالَ سَلَٰمٌ
فَمَا لَبِثَ أَن جَاءَ بِعِجْلٍ حَنِيذٍ

70. But when he saw
Their hands went not
Towards the (meal), he felt
Some mistrust of them,
And conceived a fear of
them.[1565-A]
They said: "Fear not:

٧٠ فَلَمَّا رَءَا أَيْدِيَهُمْ لَا تَصِلُ إِلَيْهِ
نَكِرَهُمْ وَأَوْجَسَ مِنْهُمْ خِيفَةً
قَالُوا لَا تَخَفْ

1565. According to the sequence of Sūrah 7, the next reference should be to the story of Lūṭ, and that story commences at 11:77 below, but it is introduced by a brief reference to an episode in the life of his uncle Abraham, from whose seed sprang the peoples to whom Moses, Jesus, and Muḥammad Muṣṭafā were sent with the major Revelations. Abraham had by this time passed through the fire of persecutions in the Mesopotamian valleys; he had left behind him the ancestral idolatry of Ur of the Chaldees; he had been tried and he had triumphed over the persecution of Nimrūd; he had now taken up his residence in Canaan, from which his nephew Lot (Lūṭ) was called to preach to the wicked Cities of the Plain east of the Dead sea which is itself called Baḥr Lūṭ. Thus prepared and sanctified, he was now ready to receive the Message that he was chosen to be the progenitor of a great line of Prophets, and the Message is now referred to.

Can we localise Nimrūd? If local tradition in place-names can be relied upon, this king must have ruled over the tract which includes the modern Nimrūd, on the Tigris, about twenty miles south of Mosul. This is the site of Assyrian ruins of great interest, but the rise of Assyria as an Empire was of course much later than the time of Abraham. The Assyrian city was called Kalakh (or Calah), and archaeological excavations carried out there have yielded valuable results, which are however irrelevant for our Commentary.

1565-A. Abraham received the strangers with a salutation of Peace, and immediately placed before them a sumptuous meal of roasted calf. The strangers were embarrassed. They were angels and did not eat. If hospitality is refused, it means that those who refuse it meditate no good to the would-be host. Abraham therefore had a feeling of mistrust and fear in his mind, which the strangers at once set at rest by saying that their mission was in the first place to help Lūṭ as a warner to the Cities of Plain. But in the second place they had good news for Abraham: he was to be the father of great peoples! (R).

We have been sent
Against the people of Lūṭ."[1566]

إِنَّآ أُرۡسِلۡنَآ إِلَىٰ قَوۡمِ لُوطٖ

71. And his wife was standing
(There), and she laughed:[1567]
But We gave her
Glad tidings of Isaac,
And after him, of Jacob.

٧١ وَٱمۡرَأَتُهُۥ قَآئِمَةٞ فَضَحِكَتۡ
فَبَشَّرۡنَٰهَا بِإِسۡحَٰقَ وَمِن وَرَآءِ إِسۡحَٰقَ يَعۡقُوبَ

72. She said: "Alas for me![1568]
Shall I bear a child,
Seeing I am an old woman,
And my husband here
Is an old man?
That would indeed
Be a wonderful thing!"

٧٢ قَالَتۡ يَٰوَيۡلَتَىٰٓ ءَأَلِدُ
وَأَنَا۠ عَجُوزٞ وَهَٰذَا بَعۡلِي شَيۡخًاۖ
إِنَّ هَٰذَا لَشَيۡءٌ عَجِيبٞ

73. They said: "Dost thou
Wonder at Allah's decree?
The grace of Allah
And His blessings on you,
O ye people of the house![1569]
For He is indeed
Worthy of all praise,
Full of all glory!"[1570]

٧٣ قَالُوٓاْ أَتَعۡجَبِينَ مِنۡ أَمۡرِ ٱللَّهِۖ
رَحۡمَتُ ٱللَّهِ وَبَرَكَٰتُهُۥ
عَلَيۡكُمۡ أَهۡلَ ٱلۡبَيۡتِۚ
إِنَّهُۥ حَمِيدٞ مَّجِيدٞ

74. When fear had passed
From (the mind of) Abraham
And the glad tidings[1571]
Had reached him, he

٧٤ فَلَمَّا ذَهَبَ عَنۡ إِبۡرَٰهِيمَ ٱلرَّوۡعُ
وَجَآءَتۡهُ ٱلۡبُشۡرَىٰ

1566. *The people of Lūṭ* means the people to whom Lūṭ was sent on his mission of warning, the people of the wicked Cities of the Plain, Sodom and Gomorrah.

1567. The narrative is very concise, and most of the details are taken for granted. We may suppose that the angels gave the news first to Abraham, who was already, according to Gen. xxi. 5, a hundred years of age, and his wife Sarah was not far short of ninety (Gen. xvii. 7). She was probably screened. She could hardly believe the news. In her scepticism (some say in her joy) she laughed. But the news was formally communicated to her that she was to be the mother of Isaac, and through Isaac, the grandmother of Jacob. Jacob was to be a fruitful tree, with his twelve sons. But, hitherto, Abraham had had no son by her, and Sarah was past the age of childbearing. "How could it be?" she thought. (R).

1568. This is as much a sigh of past regrets as of future wistfulness!

1569. *Ahl al bayt* = people of the house, a polite form of addressing the wife and members of the family. Blessings are invoked on the whole family.

1570. This little episode of Abraham's life comes in fitly as one of the illustrations of Allah's wonderful providence in His dealings with man. Abraham had had a tussle with his father on behalf of Truth and Unity (6:74); he had passed through the fire of temptation unscathed (21:68-69); he had travelled to far countries, and was now ready to receive his great mission as the fountainhead of prophets in his old age. Humanly speaking it seemed impossible that he should have a son at his age, and yet it came to pass and became a cornerstone of sacred history.

1571. *Glad-tidings*: not only that he was to have a son, but that he was to be a fountainhead of prophets. So he now begins to plead at once for the sinful people to whom Lūṭ was sent as a warner.

Began to plead with Us
For Lūṭ's people.

يُجَٰدِلُنَا فِي قَوْمِ لُوطٍ

75. For Abraham was,
Without doubt, forbearing
(Of faults), compassionate,
And given to look to Allah.[1572]

(٧٥) إِنَّ إِبْرَٰهِيمَ لَحَلِيمٌ
أَوَّٰهٌ مُّنِيبٌ

76. O Abraham! Seek not this.
The decree of thy Lord
Hath gone forth: for them
There cometh a Penalty
That cannot be turned back![1573]

(٧٦) يَٰٓإِبْرَٰهِيمُ أَعْرِضْ عَنْ هَٰذَآ إِنَّهُۥ قَدْ جَآءَ
أَمْرُ رَبِّكَ وَإِنَّهُمْ ءَاتِيهِمْ عَذَابٌ غَيْرُ مَرْدُودٍ

77. When Our Messengers
Came to Lūṭ, he was
Grieved on their account
And felt himself powerless
(To protect) them. He said:
"This is a distressful day."[1574]

(٧٧) وَلَمَّا جَآءَتْ رُسُلُنَا لُوطًا
سِيٓءَ بِهِمْ وَضَاقَ بِهِمْ ذَرْعًا
وَقَالَ هَٰذَا يَوْمٌ عَصِيبٌ

78. And his people came
Rushing towards him,
And they had been long
In the habit of practising
Abominations. He said:
"O my people! Here are
My daughters: they are purer
For you (if ye marry)![1575]
Now fear Allah, and cover me not
With shame about my guests!
Is there not among you
A single right-minded man?"

(٧٨) وَجَآءَهُۥ قَوْمُهُۥ يُهْرَعُونَ إِلَيْهِ
وَمِن قَبْلُ كَانُوا۟ يَعْمَلُونَ ٱلسَّيِّـَٔاتِ قَالَ
يَٰقَوْمِ هَٰٓؤُلَآءِ بَنَاتِى هُنَّ أَطْهَرُ لَكُمْ
فَٱتَّقُوا۟ ٱللَّهَ وَلَا تُخْزُونِ فِى ضَيْفِىٓ
أَلَيْسَ مِنكُمْ رَجُلٌ رَّشِيدٌ

1572. Like Al Muṣṭafā, Abraham had three qualities in a pre-eminent degree, which are here mentioned: (1) he was long-suffering with other people's faults; (2) his sympathies and compassion were very wide; and (3) for every difficulty or trouble he turned to Allah and sought Him in prayer.

1573. This is a sort of prophetic apostrophe. 'All your care and sympathy are useless, O Abraham! All your warning, O Lūṭ, will be unheeded! Alas! they are so deep in sin that nothing will reclaim them!' This is illustrated in verse 79 below. And now we proceed to Lūṭ and how he was dealt with by the wicked.

1574. The story of Lot, as referred to in 7:80-84, laid emphasis on the rejection of Lot's mission by men who practised unnatural abominations. See n. 1049 to 7:80. Here the emphasis is laid on Allah's dealings with men—in mercy for true spiritual service and in righteous wrath and punishment for those who defy the laws of nature established by Him; also, on men's dealings with each other and the contrast between the righteous and the wicked who respect no laws human or divine.

1575. The Biblical narrative suggests that the daughters were married and their husbands were close by (Gen. xix. 14) and that these same daughters afterwards committed incest with their father and had children by him (Gen. xix. 31). The Holy Qur'ān nowhere suggests such abominations. Some Commentators suggest that "my daughters" in the mouth of a venerable man like Lūṭ, the father of his people, may mean any young girls of those Towns. "My son" (*waladī*) is still a common mode of address in Arabic-speaking countries when an elderly man addresses a young man.

79. They said: "Well dost thou
Know we have no need
Of thy daughters: indeed
Thou knowest quite well
What we want!"

٧٩ قَالُوا۟ لَقَدْ عَلِمْتَ مَا لَنَا فِى بَنَاتِكَ
مِنْ حَقٍّ وَإِنَّكَ لَتَعْلَمُ مَا نُرِيدُ

80. He said: "Would that I
Had power to suppress you
Or that I could betake
Myself to some powerful
support."[1576]

٨٠ قَالَ لَوْ أَنَّ لِى بِكُمْ قُوَّةً
أَوْ ءَاوِىٓ إِلَىٰ رُكْنٍ شَدِيدٍ

81. (The Messengers) said: "O Lūṭ!
We are Messengers from thy Lord!
By no means shall they
Reach thee! Now travel
With thy family while yet
A part of the night remains,
And let not any of you
Look back: but thy wife[1577]
(Will remain behind):
To her will happen
What happens to the people.
Morning is their time appointed:
Is not the morning nigh?"

٨١ قَالُوا۟ يَٰلُوطُ إِنَّا رُسُلُ رَبِّكَ
لَن يَصِلُوٓا۟ إِلَيْكَ فَأَسْرِ بِأَهْلِكَ
بِقِطْعٍ مِّنَ ٱلَّيْلِ وَلَا يَلْتَفِتْ مِنكُمْ أَحَدٌ
إِلَّا ٱمْرَأَتَكَ إِنَّهُۥ مُصِيبُهَا مَآ أَصَابَهُمْ
إِنَّ مَوْعِدَهُمُ ٱلصُّبْحُ
أَلَيْسَ ٱلصُّبْحُ بِقَرِيبٍ

82. When Our decree issued,
We turned (the cities)
Upside down, and rained down
On them brimstones[1578]
Hard as baked clay,[1579]
Spread, layer on layer—

٨٢ فَلَمَّا جَآءَ أَمْرُنَا جَعَلْنَا
عَٰلِيَهَا سَافِلَهَا وَأَمْطَرْنَا عَلَيْهَا
حِجَارَةً مِّن سِجِّيلٍ مَّنضُودٍ

1576. Lūṭ seemed helpless in the situation in which he found himself—alone against a rabble of people inflamed with evil passions. He wished he had had the strength to suppress them himself or had had some powerful support to lean on! But the powerful support was there, though he had not realised it till then. It was the support of Allah. His guests were not ordinary men, but Angels who had come to test the people before they inflicted the punishment. They now declared themselves, and gave him directions to get away before the morning, when the punishment would descend on the doomed Cities of the Plain.

1577. Even in Lot's household was one who detracted from the harmony of the family. She was disobedient to her husband, and he was here obeying Allah's Command. She looked back and shared the fate of the wicked inhabitants of the Cities of the Plain: see also 66:10. The Biblical narrative suggests that she was turned into a pillar of salt (Gen. xix. 26).

1578. *Cf.* 7:84 and n. 1052.

1579. *Sijjīl*, a Persian word Arabicised, from *Sang-o-gil*, or *Sang-i-gil*, stone and clay, or hard as baked clay, according to the Qāmūs. Sodom and Gomorrah were in a tract of hard, caky, sulphurous soil, to which this description well applies. *Cf.* 51:33, where the words are "stones of clay" (*ḥijārah min ṭīn*) in connection with the same incident. On the other hand, in 105:4, the word *sijjīl* is used for pellets of hard-baked clay in connection with Abraha and the Companions of the Elephant.

83. Marked as from thy Lord:[1580]
Nor are they[1581] ever far
From those who do wrong!

٨٣ مُّسَوَّمَةً عِندَ رَبِّكَ
وَمَا هِيَ مِنَ الظَّٰلِمِينَ بِبَعِيدٍ

SECTION 8.

84. To the Madyan people[1582]
(We sent) Shu'ayb, one
Of their own brethren: he said:
"O my people! worship Allah:
Ye have no other god
But Him. And give not
Short measure or weight:
I see you in prosperity,[1583]
But I fear for you
The Penalty of a Day
That will compass (you) all round.

٨٤ وَإِلَىٰ مَدْيَنَ أَخَاهُمْ شُعَيْبًا قَالَ
يَٰقَوْمِ اعْبُدُوا اللَّهَ مَا لَكُم مِّنْ إِلَٰهٍ غَيْرُهُ
وَلَا تَنقُصُوا الْمِكْيَالَ وَالْمِيزَانَ
إِنِّي أَرَىٰكُم بِخَيْرٍ وَإِنِّي أَخَافُ عَلَيْكُمْ
عَذَابَ يَوْمٍ مُّحِيطٍ

85. "And O my people! give
Just measure and weight,
Nor withhold from the people
The things that are their due:[1584]
Commit not evil in the land
With intent to do mischief.

٨٥ وَيَٰقَوْمِ أَوْفُوا الْمِكْيَالَ
وَالْمِيزَانَ بِالْقِسْطِ وَلَا تَبْخَسُوا النَّاسَ
أَشْيَاءَهُمْ وَلَا تَعْثَوْا فِي الْأَرْضِ مُفْسِدِينَ

1580. If we take the words literally, they would mean that the showers of brimstones were marked with the destiny of the wicked as decreed by Allah. But would it not be better to take them figuratively, to mean that the shower of brimstones was especially appointed in Allah's Decree or Plan to mark the punishment for the crimes of Sodom and Gomorrah?

1581. *They*: Arabic, *hiya*: some Commentators take the pronoun to refer to the wicked cities so destroyed: the meaning then would be: those wicked cities were not so different from other cities that do wrong, for they would all suffer similar punishment! Perhaps it would be better to refer "they" to the stones of punishment by a metonymy for "punishment": 'punishment would not be far from any people that did wrong.'

1582. *Cf.* 7:85-93. The location of Madyan is explained in n. 1053 to 7:85 and the chronological place of Shu'ayb in n. 1064 to 7:93. The point of the reference here is different from that in S. 7. Here the emphasis is on Allah's dealings with men and men's crooked and obstinate ways: there the emphasis was rather on their treatment of their Prophet, thus throwing light on some of the sins of the Makkans in later times.

1583. The Midianites were a commercial people, and their besetting sin was commercial selfishness and fraudulent dealings in weights and measures. Their Prophet tells them that that is the surest way to cut short their "prosperity", both in the material and the spiritual sense. When the Day of Judgement comes, it will search out their dealings through and through: "it will compass them all round," and they will not be able to escape then, however much they may conceal their frauds in this world.

1584. Both Plato and Aristotle define justice as the virtue which gives everyone his due. From this point of view Justice becomes the master virtue, and includes most other virtues. It was the lack of this that ruined the Midianites. Their selfishness was "intent on mischief," *i.e.*, spoiling other people's business by not giving them their just dues.

86. "That which is left you
By Allah is best for you,[1585]
If ye (but) believed!
But I am not set
Over you to keep watch!"

٨٦ بَقِيَّتُ ٱللَّهِ خَيْرٌ لَّكُمْ إِن كُنتُم
مُّؤْمِنِينَ ۚ وَمَآ أَنَا۠ عَلَيْكُم بِحَفِيظٍ

87. They said: "O Shu'ayb!
Does thy (religion of) prayer
Command thee that we
Leave off the worship which
Our fathers practised, or
That we leave off doing
What we like with our property?[1586]
Truly, thou art the one
That forbeareth with faults
And is right-minded!"[1587]

٨٧ قَالُوا۟ يَٰشُعَيْبُ أَصَلَوٰتُكَ
تَأْمُرُكَ أَن نَّتْرُكَ مَا يَعْبُدُ ءَابَآؤُنَآ
أَوْ أَن نَّفْعَلَ فِىٓ أَمْوَٰلِنَا مَا نَشَٰٓؤُا۟ ۖ
إِنَّكَ لَأَنتَ ٱلْحَلِيمُ ٱلرَّشِيدُ

88. He said: "O my people!
See ye whether I have
A Clear (Sign) from my Lord,
And He hath given me
Sustenance (pure and) good[1588]
As from Himself? I wish not,
In opposition to you, to do
That which I forbid you to do.
I only desire (your) betterment
To the best of my power;
And my success (in my task)

٨٨ قَالَ يَٰقَوْمِ أَرَءَيْتُمْ إِن كُنتُ
عَلَىٰ بَيِّنَةٍ مِّن رَّبِّى وَرَزَقَنِى مِنْهُ رِزْقًا حَسَنًا ۚ
وَمَآ أُرِيدُ أَنْ أُخَالِفَكُمْ إِلَىٰ مَآ أَنْهَىٰكُمْ عَنْهُ ۚ
إِنْ أُرِيدُ إِلَّا ٱلْإِصْلَٰحَ مَا ٱسْتَطَعْتُ ۚ
وَمَا تَوْفِيقِىٓ

1585. Allah's Law does not require that a man should deprive himself of the things that are necessary for his own well-being and development. If he follows Allah's Law, what is left him after he renders to others their just dues will be not only enough, but will be the best possible provision for his own physical and spiritual growth. Even the kindness and consideration which Allah's Law inculcates are in the best interests of the man's own soul. But of course the kindness and consideration must be spontaneous. It must flow from the man's own will, and cannot be forced on him by the Teachers who come from Allah to show him the way.

1586. It is the say of selfish and material minded people (1) to scoff at spiritual things like prayer and worship and (2) to hug their own property rights as if there were not other rights even greater than those of property!

1587. They grow sarcastic against Shu'ayb. In effect they say: "You are a fine man! You teach us that we must be kind and forbearing with other people's faults, and now get at what you call our sins! You think you are the only right-minded man!"

1588. Shu'ayb's answer is gentle and persuasive. First, he would ask them not to fly into a passion but satisfy themselves that he had a mission from Allah, and was working in the discharge of his mission: he was not merely finding fault with them. Secondly, though he was a poor man, he asked them to note that he was happy and comfortable: Allah had given him good sustenance, material and spiritual, as from Himself, though he did not resort to the sort of tricks which they considered necessary for their prosperity. Thirdly, if he forbade them anything he wished to apply the same standards to himself. Fourthly, all the advice which he is giving them is for their own good, which he desires to advance to the utmost of his powers. Fifthly, he is humble for himself; he would not set himself up to be their teacher or guide, or expect to be obeyed; the success of any of his efforts on their behalf must come from Allah's grace; will they not therefore turn to Allah, so that Allah's grace can heal them?

Can only come from Allah.
In Him I trust,
And unto Him I look.

إِلَّا بِٱللَّهِ عَلَيْهِ تَوَكَّلْتُ وَإِلَيْهِ أُنِيبُ

89. "And O my people!
Let not my dissent (from you)[1589]
Cause you to sin,
Lest ye suffer
A fate similar to that
Of the people of Noah
Or of Hūd or of Ṣaliḥ,
Nor are the people of Lūṭ
Far off from you![1590]

٨٩ وَيَـٰقَوْمِ لَا يَجْرِمَنَّكُمْ
شِقَاقِىٓ أَن يُصِيبَكُم مِّثْلُ مَآ أَصَابَ
قَوْمَ نُوحٍ أَوْ قَوْمَ هُودٍ أَوْ قَوْمَ صَـٰلِحٍ
وَمَا قَوْمُ لُوطٍ مِّنكُم بِبَعِيدٍ

90. "But ask forgiveness
Of your Lord, and turn
Unto Him (in repentance):
For my Lord is indeed
Full of mercy and loving-kindness."

٩٠ وَٱسْتَغْفِرُوا۟ رَبَّكُمْ
ثُمَّ تُوبُوٓا۟ إِلَيْهِ ۚ إِنَّ رَبِّى رَحِيمٌ وَدُودٌ

91. They said: "O Shu'ayb!
Much of what thou sayest
We do not understand![1591]
In fact, among us we see
That thou hast no strength!
Were it not for thy family,
We should certainly
Have stoned thee!
For thou hast among us
No great position!"[1592]

٩١ قَالُوا۟ يَـٰشُعَيْبُ
مَا نَفْقَهُ كَثِيرًا مِّمَّا تَقُولُ
وَإِنَّا لَنَرَىٰكَ فِينَا ضَعِيفًا
وَلَوْلَا رَهْطُكَ لَرَجَمْنَـٰكَ
وَمَآ أَنتَ عَلَيْنَا بِعَزِيزٍ

92. He said: "O my people!
Is then my family
Of more consideration with you

٩٢ قَالَ يَـٰقَوْمِ أَرَهْطِىٓ أَعَزُّ عَلَيْكُم

1589. Finally, Shu'ayb appeals to them as man to man. "Because I differ from you, do not think I do not love you or feel for you. Let it not drive you into obstinacy and sin. I see things that you do not. My vision takes in the fate of previous generations who sinned, and perished on account of their sins. Turn therefore to Allah in repentance."

1590. The generation of Lūṭ was not far off from the generation of Shu'ayb chronologically, if Shu'ayb was only in the fourth generation from Abraham (see n. 1064 to 7:93). Nor was its habitat geographically far from that of Shu'ayb, as the Midianites wandered about from the Sinai Peninsula to the Jordan valley (see n. 1053 to 7:85).

1591. Spiritual things are easy to understand if we bring the right mind to them. But those who are contemptuous of them deliberately shut their eyes to Allah's Signs, and then pretend in their superior arrogance that they are 'quite beyond them'!

1592. What they do understand is brute strength. They practically say: "Don't you see that we have all the power and influence, and you, Shu'ayb, are only a poor Teacher? We could stone you or imprison you or do what we like with you! Thank us for our kindness that we spare you—for the sake of your family. It is more than you yourself deserve!"

Than Allah? For ye cast Him Away behind your backs (With contempt). But verily My Lord encompasseth On all sides All that ye do![1593]	مِنَ ٱللَّهِ وَٱتَّخَذْتُمُوهُ وَرَآءَكُمْ ظِهْرِيًّا ۖ إِنَّ رَبِّى بِمَا تَعْمَلُونَ مُحِيطٌ
93. "And O my people Do whatever ye can: I will do (my part):[1594] Soon will ye know Who it is on whom Descends the Penalty Of ignominy, and who Is a liar! And watch ye! For I too am watching With you!"[1595]	٩٣ وَيَٰقَوْمِ ٱعْمَلُوا۟ عَلَىٰ مَكَانَتِكُمْ إِنِّى عَٰمِلٌ ۖ سَوْفَ تَعْلَمُونَ مَن يَأْتِيهِ عَذَابٌ يُخْزِيهِ وَمَنْ هُوَ كَٰذِبٌ ۖ وَٱرْتَقِبُوٓا۟ إِنِّى مَعَكُمْ رَقِيبٌ
94. When Our decree issued, We saved Shu'ayb and those Who believed with him, By (special) Mercy from Ourselves:[1596] But the (mighty) Blast did seize The wrongdoers, and they Lay prostrate in their homes By the morning—	٩٤ وَلَمَّا جَآءَ أَمْرُنَا نَجَّيْنَا شُعَيْبًا وَٱلَّذِينَ ءَامَنُوا۟ مَعَهُۥ بِرَحْمَةٍ مِّنَّا وَأَخَذَتِ ٱلَّذِينَ ظَلَمُوا۟ ٱلصَّيْحَةُ فَأَصْبَحُوا۟ فِى دِيَٰرِهِمْ جَٰثِمِينَ
95. As if they had never Dwelt and flourished there![1597] Ah! Behold! How the Madyan Were removed (from sight) As were removed the <u>Th</u>amūd!	٩٥ كَأَن لَّمْ يَغْنَوْا۟ فِيهَآ ۗ أَلَا بُعْدًا لِّمَدْيَنَ كَمَا بَعِدَتْ ثَمُودُ

C. 108.—How the arrogant Pharaoh misled his people
(11:96-123.) In resisting Allah's Message through Moses!
Thus did they ruin themselves! It was they
Who wronged themselves: for Allah is ever kind

1593. *Cf.* 8:47.

1594. *Cf.* 6:135 and n. 957.

1595. If the wicked will continue to blaspheme and mock, what can the godly say but this?—"Watch and wait! Allah's Plan works without fail! I have faith, and I too will watch with you for its fulfilment." *Cf.* 10:102, and n. 1484.

1596. *Cf.* 11:66 and 11:58, n. 1554.

1597. *Cf.* 11:67-68. The blast was probably the tremendous noise which accompanies volcanic eruptions.

And His punishments are just. All men
Will be brought to His Judgement Seat, and the good
Will be rewarded with bliss, as the evil
Will be consigned to misery. Eschew evil;
Stand firm in righteousness; be not immersed
In the lusts of this world. Learn from the stories
Of the past, and seek the Lord's Mercy:
Trust Him and serve and praise Him forever!

SECTION 9.

96. And we sent Moses,[1598]
With our Clear (signs)
And an authority manifest,

وَلَقَدْ أَرْسَلْنَا مُوسَىٰ بِـَٔايَـٰتِنَا وَسُلْطَـٰنٍ مُّبِينٍ ﴿٩٦﴾

97. Unto Pharaoh and his Chiefs:
But they followed the command[1599]
Of Pharaoh, and the command
Of Pharaoh was no right (guide).

إِلَىٰ فِرْعَوْنَ وَمَلَإِيْهِۦ فَٱتَّبَعُوٓا۟ أَمْرَ فِرْعَوْنَ ۖ وَمَآ أَمْرُ فِرْعَوْنَ بِرَشِيدٍ ﴿٩٧﴾

98. He will go before his people
On the Day of Judgement,
And lead them into the Fire
(As cattle are led to water):[1600]
But woeful indeed will be
The place to which they are led!

يَقْدُمُ قَوْمَهُۥ يَوْمَ ٱلْقِيَـٰمَةِ فَأَوْرَدَهُمُ ٱلنَّارَ ۖ وَبِئْسَ ٱلْوِرْدُ ٱلْمَوْرُودُ ﴿٩٨﴾

99. And they are followed
By a curse in this (life)
And on the Day of Judgement:
And woeful is the gift
Which shall be given
(Unto them)!

وَأُتْبِعُوا۟ فِى هَـٰذِهِۦ لَعْنَةً وَيَوْمَ ٱلْقِيَـٰمَةِ ۚ بِئْسَ ٱلرِّفْدُ ٱلْمَرْفُودُ ﴿٩٩﴾

1598. The story of Moses and Pharaoh is referred to in many places in the Qur'ān, each in connection with some special point to be illustrated. Here the point is that Allah's dealings with man are in all things and at all times just. But man falls under false leadership by deliberate choice and perishes along with his false leaders accordingly. In exercise of the intelligence and choice given him, man should be particularly careful to understand his own responsibilities and to profit from Allah's Signs, so as to attain to Allah's Mercy and blessings.

1599. Pharaoh is the type of the arrogant, selfish, and false leader, who poses as a power in rivalry with that of Allah. Such an attitude seems to attract unregenerate humanity, which falls a willing victim, in spite of the teaching and warning given by the Prophets of Allah and the many moral and spiritual forces that beckon man towards Allah's Grace.

1600. *Awrada* = to lead, as cattle, down to their watering place. The metaphor is apt. The true herdsman is trusted by his normal flock, and he leads them in the heat of the day down to pleasant and cool watering places in order that they may slake their thirst and be happy. The false leader does the opposite: he takes them down to the fire of eternal misery! And yet men sin against their own intelligence, and follow the false leader like cattle without intelligence!

100. These are some of the stories
Of communities which We
Relate unto thee: of them
Some are standing,[1601] and some
Have been mown down
(By the sickle of time).[1602]

١٠٠ ذَٰلِكَ مِنْ أَنۢبَآءِ ٱلْقُرَىٰ
نَقُصُّهُۥ عَلَيْكَ ۖ مِنْهَا قَآئِمٌ
وَحَصِيدٌ

101. It was not We that wronged them:
They wronged their own souls:
The deities, other than Allah,
Whom they invoked, profited them
No whit when there issued
The decree of thy Lord:[1603]
Nor did they add aught
(To their lot) but perdition!

١٠١ وَمَا ظَلَمْنَٰهُمْ وَلَٰكِن ظَلَمُوٓا۟ أَنفُسَهُمْ ۖ
فَمَآ أَغْنَتْ عَنْهُمْ ءَالِهَتُهُمُ ٱلَّتِى يَدْعُونَ
مِن دُونِ ٱللَّهِ مِن شَىْءٍ لَّمَّا جَآءَ أَمْرُ رَبِّكَ ۖ
وَمَا زَادُوهُمْ غَيْرَ تَتْبِيبٍ

102. Such is the chastisement
Of thy Lord when He chastises
Communities in the midst of
Their wrong: grievous, indeed,
And severe is His chastisement.

١٠٢ وَكَذَٰلِكَ أَخْذُ رَبِّكَ إِذَآ أَخَذَ
ٱلْقُرَىٰ وَهِىَ ظَٰلِمَةٌ ۚ إِنَّ أَخْذَهُۥٓ أَلِيمٌ شَدِيدٌ

103. In that is a Sign
For those who fear
The Penalty of the Hereafter:
That is a Day for which mankind
Will be gathered together:
That will be a Day
Of Testimony.[1604]

١٠٣ إِنَّ فِى ذَٰلِكَ لَءَايَةً لِّمَنْ خَافَ عَذَابَ ٱلْءَاخِرَةِ ۚ
ذَٰلِكَ يَوْمٌ مَّجْمُوعٌ لَّهُ ٱلنَّاسُ
وَذَٰلِكَ يَوْمٌ مَّشْهُودٌ

104. Nor shall We delay it
But for a term appointed.

١٠٤ وَمَا نُؤَخِّرُهُۥٓ إِلَّا لِأَجَلٍ مَّعْدُودٍ

1601. *Some are standing*: like corn, which is ready to be reaped. Among the communities which remained was, and is, Egypt, although the Pharaoh and his wicked people have been swept away. The simile of standing corn also suggests that at no time can any town or community expect permanency, except in the Law of the Lord.

1602. Nations grow and ripen and are mown down. If they disobeyed Allah, their end is evil; if they were true and godly, their harvest was good.

1603. All false and fleeting shadows must vanish before the reality and permanence of the decree of Allah. If we worshipped the false, we earned nothing but perdition.

1604. *Yawmun mashhūdun:* To suggest the comprehensive meaning of the Arabic I have translated, "a Day of Testimony". I proceed to explain the various shades of meaning implied: (1) a Day to which all testimony points from every quarter; (2) a Day when testimony will be given before Allah's Judgement Seat, by all who are relevant witnesses, *e.g.*, the Prophets that preached, the men or women we benefited or injured, the angels who recorded our thoughts and deeds, or our thoughts and deeds personified; (3) a Day which will be witnessed, *i.e.*, seen by all, no matter how or where they died.

105. The day it arrives,
No soul shall speak[1605]
Except by His leave:
Of those (gathered) some
Will be wretched and some
Will be blessed.[1606]

١٠٥ يَوْمَ يَأْتِ لَا تَكَلَّمُ نَفْسٌ
إِلَّا بِإِذْنِهِۦ ۚ فَمِنْهُمْ
شَقِىٌّ وَسَعِيدٌ

106. Those who are wretched
Shall be in the Fire:
There will be for them
Therein (nothing but) the heaving
Of sighs and sobs:[1607]

١٠٦ فَأَمَّا ٱلَّذِينَ شَقُوا۟ فَفِى ٱلنَّارِ
لَهُمْ فِيهَا زَفِيرٌ وَشَهِيقٌ

107. They will dwell therein[1608]
For all the time that
The heavens and the earth
Endure, except as thy Lord
Willeth: for thy Lord
Is the (sure) Accomplisher
Of what He planneth.

١٠٧ خَٰلِدِينَ فِيهَا مَا دَامَتِ
ٱلسَّمَٰوَٰتُ وَٱلْأَرْضُ إِلَّا مَا شَآءَ رَبُّكَ ۚ
إِنَّ رَبَّكَ فَعَّالٌ لِّمَا يُرِيدُ

108. And those who are blessed
Shall be in the Garden:
They will dwell therein[1609]
For all the time that
The heavens and the earth

١٠٨ وَأَمَّا ٱلَّذِينَ سُعِدُوا۟ فَفِى ٱلْجَنَّةِ
خَٰلِدِينَ فِيهَا مَا دَامَتِ ٱلسَّمَٰوَٰتُ وَٱلْأَرْضُ

1605. *Speak: i.e.*, either in self-defence or in accusation of others or to intercede for others, or to enter into conversation or ask questions, one with another. It will be a solemn Day, before the Great Judge of all, to whom everything will be known and whose authority will be unquestioned. There will be no room for quibbling or equivocation or subterfuge of any kind, nor can anyone lay the blame on another or take the responsibility of another. Personal responsibility will be enforced strictly.

1606. *Shaqī* (wretched) and *Sa'īd* (blessed) have become almost technical theological terms. They are explained in the four following verses.

1607. The first word, *Zafīr*, translated "sighs", is applied to one part in the process of the braying of an ass, when he emits a deep breath. The second, *Shahīq*, translated "sobs", is the other process in the braying of an ass, when he draws in a long breath. This suggestion of an animal proverbial for his folly implies that the wicked, in spite of their arrogance and insolence in this world below, will at last realise that they have been fools after all, throwing away their own chances whenever they got them. In 67:7 the word *Shahīq* is applied to the tremendous roaring intake or devouring of Hell-fire.

1608. *Khālidīn*: This is the word which is usually translated "dwell forever" or "dwell for aye". Here it is definitely connected with two conditions, *viz*: (1) as long as the heavens and the earth endure, and (2) except as Allah wills. Some Muslim theologians deduce from this the conclusion that the penalties referred to are not eternal, because the heavens and the earth as we see them are not eternal, and the punishments for the deeds of a life that will end should not be such as will never end. The majority of Muslim theologians reject this view. They hold that the heavens and the earth here referred to are not those we see now, but others that will be eternal. They agree that Allah's Will is unlimited in scope and power, but that it has willed that the rewards and punishments of the Day of Judgement will be eternal. This is not the place to enter into this tremendous controversy.

1609. Exactly the same arguments apply as in the last note.

Endure, except as thy Lord
Willeth: a gift without break.[1610]

إِلَّا مَا شَآءَ رَبُّكَ عَطَآءً غَيْرَ مَجْذُوذٍ

109. Be not then in doubt
As to what these men
Worship. They worship nothing[1611]
But what their fathers worshipped
Before (them): but verily
We shall pay them back
(In full) their portion[1612]
Without (the least) abatement.

﴿١٠٩﴾ فَلَا تَكُ فِي مِرْيَةٍ مِّمَّا يَعْبُدُ هَٰٓؤُلَآءِ
مَا يَعْبُدُونَ إِلَّا كَمَا يَعْبُدُ ءَابَآؤُهُم مِّن قَبْلُ
وَإِنَّا لَمُوَفُّوهُمْ نَصِيبَهُمْ غَيْرَ مَنقُوصٍ

SECTION 10.

110. We certainly gave the Book
To Moses, but differences
Arose therein: had it not been
That a Word had gone forth
Before from thy Lord, the matter
Would have been decided[1613]
Between them: but they
Are in suspicious doubt
Concerning it.[1614]

﴿١١٠﴾ وَلَقَدْ ءَاتَيْنَا مُوسَى ٱلْكِتَٰبَ
فَٱخْتُلِفَ فِيهِ وَلَوْلَا كَلِمَةٌ
سَبَقَتْ مِن رَّبِّكَ لَقُضِيَ بَيْنَهُمْ
وَإِنَّهُمْ لَفِي شَكٍّ مِّنْهُ مُرِيبٍ

111. And, of a surety, to all
Will your Lord pay back
(In full the recompense)
Of their deeds: for He
Knoweth well all that they do.[1615]

﴿١١١﴾ وَإِنَّ كُلًّا لَّمَّا لَيُوَفِّيَنَّهُمْ رَبُّكَ
أَعْمَٰلَهُمْ إِنَّهُۥ بِمَا يَعْمَلُونَ خَبِيرٌ

1610. The felicity will be uninterrrupted, unlike any joy or happiness which we can imagine in this life and which is subject to chances and changes, as our daily experience shows.

1611. Their worship is not based on any spiritual attitude of mind. They merely follow the ways of their fathers.

1612. Allah will take fully into account all their motives in such mummery as they call worship, and they will have their full spiritual consequences in the future.

1613. *Cf.* 10:19. Previous revelations are not to be denied or dishonoured because those who nominally go by them have corrupted and deprived them of spiritual value by their vain controversies and disputes. It was possible to settle such disputes under the flag, as it were, of the old Revelations, but Allah's Plan was to revive and rejuvenate His Message through Islam, amongst a newer and younger people, unhampered by the burden of age-old prejudices.

1614. *Cf.* 11:62. There is always in human affairs the conflict between the old and the new—the worn out system of our ancestors, and the fresh living spring of Allah's inspiration fitting in with new times and new surroundings. The advocates of the former look upon this latter not only with intellectual doubt but with moral suspicion, as did the People of the Book upon Islam, with its fresh outlook and vigorous realistic way of looking at things.

1615. *Cf.* 11:109 above, with which the argument is now connected by recalling the characteristic word ("pay back") and leading to the exhortation (in the verses following) to stand firm in the right path freshly revealed.

112. Therefore stand firm (in the straight
Path) as thou art commanded—
Thou and those who with thee
Turn (unto Allah); and transgress not
(From the Path); for He seeth
Well all that ye do.

(١١٢) فَٱسْتَقِمْ كَمَآ أُمِرْتَ
وَمَن تَابَ مَعَكَ وَلَا تَطْغَوْا۟ ۚ
إِنَّهُۥ بِمَا تَعْمَلُونَ بَصِيرٌ

113. And incline not to those
Who do wrong, or the Fire
Will seize you; and ye have
No protectors other than Allah,
Nor shall ye be helped.

(١١٣) وَلَا تَرْكَنُوٓا۟ إِلَى ٱلَّذِينَ ظَلَمُوا۟
فَتَمَسَّكُمُ ٱلنَّارُ وَمَا لَكُم مِّن
دُونِ ٱللَّهِ مِنْ أَوْلِيَآءَ ثُمَّ لَا تُنصَرُونَ

114. And establish regular prayers
At the two ends of the day[1616]
And at the approaches of the night:[1617]
For those things that are good
Remove those that are evil:[1618]
Be that the word of remembrance
To those who remember (their Lord):

(١١٤) وَأَقِمِ ٱلصَّلَوٰةَ
طَرَفَىِ ٱلنَّهَارِ وَزُلَفًا مِّنَ ٱلَّيْلِ ۚ
إِنَّ ٱلْحَسَنَٰتِ يُذْهِبْنَ ٱلسَّيِّـَٔاتِ ۚ
ذَٰلِكَ ذِكْرَىٰ لِلذَّٰكِرِينَ

115. And be steadfast in patience;
For verily Allah will not suffer
The reward of the righteous
To perish.

(١١٥) وَٱصْبِرْ فَإِنَّ ٱللَّهَ
لَا يُضِيعُ أَجْرَ ٱلْمُحْسِنِينَ

116. Why were there not,
Among the generations before you,

(١١٦) فَلَوْلَا كَانَ مِنَ ٱلْقُرُونِ مِن قَبْلِكُمْ

1616. *The two ends of the day*: Morning and afternoon. The morning prayer is the *Fajr*, after the light is up but before sunrise: we thus get up betimes and begin the day with the remembrance of Allah and of our duty to Him. The early afternoon prayer, *Ẓuhr*, is immediately after noon: we are in the midst of our daily life, and again we remember Allah. (R).

1617. *Approaches of the night: Zulafun*, plural of *Zulfatun*, an approach, something near at hand. As Arabic has, like Greek, a dual number distinct from the plural, and the plural number is used here, and not the dual, it is reasonable to argue that at least three "approaches of the night" are meant. The late afternoon prayer, *'Aṣr*, can be one of these three, and the evening prayer, *Maghrib*, just after sunset, can be the second. The early night prayer, *'Ishā'*, at supper time when the glow of sunset is disappearing, would be the third of the "approaches of the night", when we commit ourselves to Allah before sleep. These are the five canonical prayers of Islām.

1618. *Those things that are good*: in this context the words refer primarily to prayers and sacred thoughts, but they include all good thoughts, good words, and good deeds. It is by them that we keep away everything that is evil, whether referring to the past, the present, or the future.

Persons possessed of balanced[1619]
Good sense, prohibiting (men)
From mischief in the earth—
Except a few among them
Whom We saved (from harm)?[1620]
But the wrongdoers pursued
The enjoyment of the good things
Of life which were given them,
And persisted in sin.

أُوْلُواْ بَقِيَّةٍ يَنْهَوْنَ عَنِ ٱلْفَسَادِ فِى ٱلْأَرْضِ
إِلَّا قَلِيلًا مِّمَّنْ أَنجَيْنَا مِنْهُمْ
وَٱتَّبَعَ ٱلَّذِينَ ظَلَمُواْ مَآ
أُتْرِفُواْ فِيهِ وَكَانُواْ مُجْرِمِينَ

117. Nor would thy Lord be
The One to destroy
Communities for a single
wrongdoing[1621]
If its members were likely
To mend.

(١١٧) وَمَا كَانَ رَبُّكَ
لِيُهْلِكَ ٱلْقُرَىٰ بِظُلْمٍ
وَأَهْلُهَا مُصْلِحُونَ

118. If thy Lord had so willed,
He could have made mankind[1622]
One People: but they
Will not cease to dispute,

(١١٨) وَلَوْ شَآءَ رَبُّكَ لَجَعَلَ ٱلنَّاسَ
أُمَّةً وَٰحِدَةً وَلَا يَزَالُونَ مُخْتَلِفِينَ

119. Except those on whom thy Lord
Hath bestowed His Mercy:
And for this did He create
Them: and the Word
Of thy Lord shall be fulfilled:

(١١٩) إِلَّا مَن رَّحِمَ رَبُّكَ
وَلِذَٰلِكَ خَلَقَهُمْ وَتَمَّتْ كَلِمَةُ رَبِّكَ

1619. *Baqiyyah*: some virtue or faculty that stands assault and is lasting; balanced good sense that stands firm to virtue and is not dazzled by the lusts and pleasures of this world, and is not deterred by fear from boldly condemning wrong if it was fashionable or customary. It is leaders possessed of such character that can save a nation from disaster or perdition. The scarcity of such leaders—and the rejection of the few who stood out—brought ruin among the nations whose example has already been set out to us as a warning.

In 11:86 the word has a more literal meaning.

1620. The exceptional men of firm virtue would have been destroyed by the wicked to whom they were an offence, had they not been saved by the Grace and Mercy of Allah. Or perhaps, but for such grace, they might themselves have succumbed to the evil around them, or been overwhelmed in the general calamity.

1621. There are different shades of interpretation for this verse. I follow Bayḍāwī in construing *ẓulmin* here as "a single wrong". He thinks that the wrong referred to is *shirk*, or polytheism; Allah will not destroy for mere wrong belief if the conduct is right. I am inclined to interpret it in more general terms. Allah is Long-Suffering and Oft-Forgiving: He is too Merciful to destroy for a single wrong, if there is any hope of reclaiming the wrongdoers to repentance and amendment or right life. An alternative interpretation is: "to destroy communities unjustly."...

1622. *Cf.* 10:19. All mankind might have been one. But in Allah's Plan man was to have a certain measure of free will, and this made differences inevitable. This would not have mattered if all had honestly sought Allah. But selfishness and moral wrong came in, and people's disputations became mixed up with hatred, jealousy, and sin, except in the case of those who accepted Allah's grace, which saved them. The object of their creation was to raise them up spiritually by Allah's grace. But if they will choose the path of evil and fall into sin, Allah's decree must be fulfilled, and His justice will take its course. In the course of that justice Hell will be filled with men and spirits, such is the number of those who go astray.

"I will fill Hell with jinns
And men all together."[1623]

لَأَمْلَأَنَّ جَهَنَّمَ مِنَ ٱلْجِنَّةِ وَٱلنَّاسِ أَجْمَعِينَ

120. All that we relate to thee
Of the stories of the
messengers—
With it We make firm
Thy heart: in them there
cometh
To thee the Truth, as well as
An exhortation and a message
Of remembrance to those who
believe.[1624]

١٢٠ وَكُلًّا نَّقُصُّ عَلَيْكَ مِنْ أَنۢبَآءِ
ٱلرُّسُلِ مَا نُثَبِّتُ بِهِۦ فُؤَادَكَ
وَجَآءَكَ فِى هَـٰذِهِ ٱلْحَقُّ
وَمَوْعِظَةٌ وَذِكْرَىٰ لِلْمُؤْمِنِينَ

121. Say to those who do not
Believe: "Do whatever ye can:
We shall do our part;[1624-A]

١٢١ وَقُل لِّلَّذِينَ لَا يُؤْمِنُونَ
ٱعْمَلُوا۟ عَلَىٰ مَكَانَتِكُمْ إِنَّا عَـٰمِلُونَ

122. "And wait ye!
We too shall wait."[1625]

١٢٢ وَٱنتَظِرُوٓا۟ إِنَّا مُنتَظِرُونَ

123. To Allah do belong
The unseen (secrets)
Of the heavens and the earth,
And to Him goeth back
Every affair (for decision):[1626]
Then worship Him,
And put thy trust in Him:
And thy Lord is not
Unmindful of aught
That ye do.

١٢٣ وَلِلَّهِ غَيْبُ ٱلسَّمَـٰوَٰتِ وَٱلْأَرْضِ
وَإِلَيْهِ يُرْجَعُ ٱلْأَمْرُ كُلُّهُۥ
فَٱعْبُدْهُ وَتَوَكَّلْ عَلَيْهِ
وَمَا رَبُّكَ بِغَـٰفِلٍ عَمَّا تَعْمَلُونَ

1623. *Cf.* 7:18 and 7:179. If Satan and his evil spirits tempt men from the path of rectitude, the responsibility of the tempted, who choose the path of evil, is no less than that of the tempters, and they will both be involved in punishment together.

1624. The stories of the Prophets in the Qur'ān are not mere narratives or histories: they involve three things: (1) they teach the highest spiritual Truth; (2) they give advice, direction, and warning, as to how we should govern our lives, and (3) they awaken our conscience and recall to us the working of Allah's Law in human affairs. The story of Joseph in the next Sūrah is an illustration in point.

1624-A. *Cf.* 11:93 and 6:135, n. 957. The worst that ye can do will not defeat Allah's Plan; and as for us who believe, our obvious duty is to do our part as taught to us by Allah's revelation.

1625. *Cf.* 11:93, n. 1595, and 10:102, n. 1484. If the wicked only wait, they will see how Allah's Plan unfolds itself. As for those who believe, they are glad to wait in perfect confidence, because they know that Allah is good and merciful, as well as just and true.

1626. *Cf.* 2:210. There is nothing, secret or open, in our world or in Creation, which does not depend ultimately on Allah's Will and Plan. Every affair goes back to Him for decision. Therefore we must worship Him and trust Him. Worship implies many things: e.g., (1) trying to understand His nature and His Will; (2) realising His goodness and glory, and His working in us; as a means to this end, (3) keeping Him in constant remembrance and celebrating His praise, to whom all praise is due; and (4) completely identifying our will with His, which means obedience to His Law, and service to Him and His creatures in all sincerity.

INTRODUCTION TO SŪRAH 12—*YŪSUF*

For the chronological place of this Sūrah and the general argument of Sūrahs 10 to 15, see Introduction to Sūrah 10.

In subject matter this Sūrah is entirely taken up with the story (recapitulated rather than told) of Joseph, the youngest (but one) of the twelve sons of the patriarch Jacob. The story is called the most beautiful of stories (12:3) for many reasons: (1) it is the most detailed of any in the Qur'ān; (2) it is full of human vicissitudes, and has therefore deservedly appealed to men and women of all classes; (3) it paints in vivid colours, with their spiritual implications, the most varied aspects of life—the patriarch's old age and the confidence between him and his little best-beloved son, the elder brothers' jealousy of this little son, their plot and their father's grief, the sale of the father's darling into slavery for a miserable little price, carnal love contrasted with purity and chastity, false charges, prison, the interpretation of dreams, low life and high life, Innocence raised to honour, the sweet "revenge" of Forgiveness and Benevolence, high matters of state and administration, humility in exaltation, filial love, and the beauty of Piety and Truth.

The story is similar to but not identical with the Biblical story; but the atmosphere is wholly different. The Biblical story is like a folktale in which morality has no place. Its tendency is to exalt the clever and financially-minded Jew against the Egyptian, and to explain certain ethnic and tribal peculiarities in later Jewish history. Joseph is shown as buying up all the cattle and the land of the poor Egyptians for the State under the stress of famine conditions, and making the Israelites "rulers" over Pharoah's cattle. The Quranic story, on the other hand, is less a narrative than a highly spiritual sermon or allegory explaining the seeming contradictions in life, the enduring nature of virtue in a world full of flux and change, and the marvellous working of Allah's eternal purpose in His Plan as unfolded to us on the wide canvas of history. This aspect of the matter has been a favourite with Muslim poets and Sūfi exegetists. (R).

Summary—Life is a dream and a vision, to be explained by stories and parables, as in the perspicuous Arabic Qur'ān. The truth, which Joseph the Prophet of Allah saw in his vision, was unpalatable to his ten half-brothers, who plotted against him and sold him into slavery to a merchant for a few pieces of silver. (12:1-20, and C. 109).

Joseph was taken by the merchant into Egypt, was bought by a great Egyptian court dignitary ('Aziz), who adopted him. The dignitary's wife sought, but in vain, to attract Joseph to the delights of earthly love. His resistance brought him disgrace and imprisonment, but he taught the truth even in prison and was known for his kindness. One of his fellow prisoners, to whom he had interpreted a dream, was released and received into favour as the King's cupbearer. (12:21-42, and C. 110).

The King had a vision, which Joseph (through the cupbearer) got an opportunity to explain. Joseph insisted that all the scandal that had been raised about him should be publicly cleared. He was received into favour, and was appointed wazīr by the King. His half-brothers (driven by famine) came to Egypt and were treated kindly by Joseph without their knowing his identity. He asks them to bring his full brother, the youngest son, Benjamin. (12:43-68, and C. 111).

Joseph detains Benjamin and by a stratagem convicts his half-brothers of their hatred and crime against himself, forgives them, and sends them to bring Jacob and the whole family from Canaan to Egypt. (12:69-93, and C. 112).

Israel (Jacob) comes, is comforted, and settles in Egypt. The name of Allah is glorified. The truth of Allah endures forever, and Allah's purpose is fully revealed in the Hereafter. (12:94-111, and C. 113).*

C. 109.—Life and Wisdom are explained by Signs,
(12:1-20.) Symbols, Parables, and moving Stories,
In the Holy Qur'ān. A beautiful story
Is that of Joseph, the best-beloved son
Of Jacob. His future greatness
Was prefigured in a vision, but his brothers
Were filled with envy and hate: they plotted
To get rid of him and threw him down
Into a well. Some merchants found him,
Bound for Egypt. The brothers sold him
Into slavery for a few silver coins—
Him, the noblest man of his age,
Marked out by Allah for a destiny
Of greatness, righteousness, and benevolence.

* It is to be noted that the author has in his notes on the Quranic version of the story of Joseph added many details which are drawn from unauthentic sources including popular fiction and poetry. [Eds.].

Sūrah 12.

Yūsuf (Joseph)

In the name of Allah, Most Gracious,
Most Merciful.

بِسْمِ ٱللَّهِ ٱلرَّحْمَٰنِ ٱلرَّحِيمِ

1. Alif Lām Rā.[1627] These are
The Symbols[1628] (or Verses)
Of the Perspicuous Book.[1629]

الٓر تِلْكَ ءَايَٰتُ ٱلْكِتَٰبِ ٱلْمُبِينِ ١

2. We have sent it down
As an Arabic Qur'ān,[1630]
In order that ye may
Learn wisdom.

إِنَّآ أَنزَلْنَٰهُ قُرْءَٰنًا عَرَبِيًّا
لَّعَلَّكُمْ تَعْقِلُونَ ٢

3. We do relate unto thee
The most beautiful of stories,[1631]
In that We reveal to thee
This (portion of the) Qur'ān:
Before this, thou too
Wast among those
Who knew it not.

نَحْنُ نَقُصُّ عَلَيْكَ أَحْسَنَ ٱلْقَصَصِ
بِمَآ أَوْحَيْنَآ إِلَيْكَ هَٰذَا ٱلْقُرْءَانَ
وَإِن كُنتَ مِن قَبْلِهِۦ لَمِنَ ٱلْغَٰفِلِينَ ٣

4. Behold, Joseph said
To his father: "O my father![1632]
I did see eleven stars
And the sun and the moon:

إِذْ قَالَ يُوسُفُ لِأَبِيهِ يَٰٓأَبَتِ إِنِّى رَأَيْتُ
أَحَدَ عَشَرَ كَوْكَبًا وَٱلشَّمْسَ وَٱلْقَمَرَ

1627. For the meaning of these mystic letters, see Introduction to S. 10.

1628. *Āyāt*: Signs, Symbols, verses of the Qur'ān. The Symbolic meaning is particularly appropriate here, as the whole of Joseph's story is a Sign or a Miracle—a working exposition of the Plan and Purpose of Allah.

1629. *Cf.* 5:15, n. 716. The predominant meaning of *Mubīn* here is: one that explains or makes things clear.

1630. *Qur'ān* means: something (1) to be read, or (2) recited, or (3) proclaimed. It may apply to a verse, or a Sūrah, or to the whole Book of Revelation.

1631. *Most beautiful of stories*: see Introduction to this Sūrah. Eloquence consists in conveying by a word or hint many meanings for those who can understand and wish to learn wisdom. Not only is Joseph's story "beautiful" in that sense; Joseph himself was renowned for manly beauty: the women of Egypt, called him a noble angel (12:31), and the beauty of his exterior form was a symbol of the beauty of his soul.

1632. For the Parable all that is necessary to know about Joseph is that he was one of the Chosen Ones of Allah. For the story it is necessary to set down a few more details. His father was Jacob, also called Israel the son of Isaac, the younger son of Abraham, (the elder son having been Ismā'īl, whose story is told in 2:124-129). Abraham may be called the Father of the line of Semitic prophecy. Jacob had four wives. From three of them he had ten sons. In his old age he had from Rachel (Arabic *Rāḥil*), a very beautiful woman, two sons Joseph and Benjamin (the youngest). At the time this story begins we may suppose that Joseph was about seventeen years of age. The place where Jacob and his family and his flocks were located was in Canaan, and is shown by tradition near modern Nāblūs (ancient Shechem), some thirty miles north of Jerusalem. The traditional site of the well into which Joseph was thrown by his brothers is still shown in the neighbourhood.

I saw them prostrate themselves
To me!"[1633]

رَأَيْتُهُمْ لِي سَاجِدِينَ

5. Said (the father):
"My (dear) little son!
Relate not thy vision
To thy brothers, lest they
Concoct a plot against thee:[1634]
For Satan is to man
An avowed enemy![1635]

قَالَ يَا بُنَيَّ لَا تَقْصُصْ رُؤْيَاكَ عَلَىٰ إِخْوَتِكَ فَيَكِيدُوا لَكَ كَيْدًا ۖ إِنَّ الشَّيْطَانَ لِلْإِنسَانِ عَدُوٌّ مُّبِينٌ ﴿٥﴾

6. "Thus will thy Lord
Choose thee and teach thee
The interpretation of stories[1636]
(and events)
And perfect His favour
To thee and to the posterity
Of Jacob—even as He
Perfected it to thy fathers
Abraham and Isaac aforetime!
For thy Lord is full of knowledge
And wisdom."[1637]

وَكَذَٰلِكَ يَجْتَبِيكَ رَبُّكَ وَيُعَلِّمُكَ مِن تَأْوِيلِ الْأَحَادِيثِ وَيُتِمُّ نِعْمَتَهُ عَلَيْكَ وَعَلَىٰ آلِ يَعْقُوبَ كَمَا أَتَمَّهَا عَلَىٰ أَبَوَيْكَ مِن قَبْلُ إِبْرَاهِيمَ وَإِسْحَاقَ ۚ إِنَّ رَبَّكَ عَلِيمٌ حَكِيمٌ ﴿٦﴾

SECTION 2.

7. Verily in Joseph and his brethren
Are Signs (or Symbols)
For Seekers (after Truth).[1638]

۞ لَّقَدْ كَانَ فِي يُوسُفَ وَإِخْوَتِهِ آيَاتٌ لِّلسَّائِلِينَ ﴿٧﴾

1633. Joseph was a mere lad of seventeen. But he was true and frank and righteous; he was a type of manly beauty and rectitude. His father loved him dearly. His half-brothers were jealous of him and hated him. His destiny was prefigured in the vision. He was to be exalted in rank above his eleven brothers (stars) and his father and mother (sun and moon), but as the subsequent story shows, he never lost his head, but always honoured his parents and repaid his brothers' craft and hatred with forgiveness and kindness.

1634. The young lad Yūsuf was innocent and did not even know of his brothers' guile and hatred, but the father knew and warned him.

1635. The story is brought up at once to its spiritual bearing. These wicked brothers were puppets in the hands of Evil. They allowed their manhood to be subjugated by Evil, not remembering that Evil was the declared opposite or enemy of the true nature and instincts of manhood.

1636. If Joseph was to be of the elect, he must understand and intepret Signs and events aright. The imagination of the pure sees truths, which those not so endowed cannot understand. The dreams of the righteous prefigure great events, while the dreams of the futile are mere idle futilities. Even things that happen to us are often like dreams. The righteous man receives disasters and reverses, not with blasphemies against Allah, but with humble devotion, seeking to ascertain His Will. Nor does he receive good fortune with arrogance, but as an opportunity for doing good, to friends and foes alike. His attitude to histories and stories is the same: he seeks the edifying material which leads to Allah.

1637. Whatever happens is the result of Allah's Will and Plan. And He is good and wise, and He knows all things. Therefore we must trust Him. In Joseph's case he could look back to his fathers, and to Abraham, the True, the Righteous, who through all adversities kept his Faith pure and undefiled, and won through.

1638. In Joseph's story we have good and evil contrasted in so many different ways. Those in search of true spiritual knowledge can see it embodied in concrete events in this story of many facets, matching the colours of Joseph's many-coloured coat.

8. They said: "Truly Joseph
And his brother are loved
More by our father than we:
But we are a goodly body![1639]
Really our father is obviously
Wandering (in his mind)!

إِذْ قَالُوا۟ لَيُوسُفُ وَأَخُوهُ أَحَبُّ إِلَىٰٓ أَبِينَا مِنَّا وَنَحْنُ عُصْبَةٌ إِنَّ أَبَانَا لَفِى ضَلَـٰلٍ مُّبِينٍ ﴿٨﴾

9. "Slay ye Joseph or cast him out
To some (unknown) land,
That so the favour
Of your father may be
Given to you alone:
(There will be time enough)
For you to be righteous after
that!"[1640]

ٱقْتُلُوا۟ يُوسُفَ أَوِ ٱطْرَحُوهُ أَرْضًا يَخْلُ لَكُمْ وَجْهُ أَبِيكُمْ وَتَكُونُوا۟ مِنۢ بَعْدِهِۦ قَوْمًا صَـٰلِحِينَ ﴿٩﴾

10. Said one of them: "Slay not
Joseph, but if ye must
Do something, throw him down
To the bottom of the well:
He will be picked up
By some caravan of travellers."[1641]

قَالَ قَآئِلٌ مِّنْهُمْ لَا تَقْتُلُوا۟ يُوسُفَ وَأَلْقُوهُ فِى غَيَـٰبَتِ ٱلْجُبِّ يَلْتَقِطْهُ بَعْضُ ٱلسَّيَّارَةِ إِن كُنتُمْ فَـٰعِلِينَ ﴿١٠﴾

11. They said: "O our father!
Why dost thou not
Trust us with Joseph—
Seeing we are indeed
His sincere well-wishers?[1642]

قَالُوا۟ يَـٰٓأَبَانَا مَا لَكَ لَا تَأْمَ۟نَّا عَلَىٰ يُوسُفَ وَإِنَّا لَهُۥ لَنَـٰصِحُونَ ﴿١١﴾

1639. The ten brothers envied and hated their innocent younger brothers, Joseph and Benjamin. Jacob had the wisdom to see that his young and innocent sons wanted protection and to perceive Joseph's spiritual greatness. But his wisdom, to them, was folly or madness or imbecility, because it touched their self-love, as truth often does. And they relied on the brute strength of numbers—the ten hefty brethren against old Jacob, the lad Joseph, and the boy Benjamin!

1640. There seems to be some irony here, consistent with the cynical nature of these callous, worldly-wise brethren. The goodness of Joseph was a reproach to their own wickedness. Perhaps the grieved father contrasted Joseph against them, and sometimes spoke of it: "Why don't you be good like Joseph?" This was gall and wormwood to them. Real goodness was to them nothing but a name. Perhaps it only suggested hypocrisy to them. So they plotted to get rid of Joseph. In their mean hearts they thought that would bring back their father's love whole to them. But they valued that love only for what material good they could get out of it. On the other hand their father was neither foolish nor unjustly partial. He only knew the difference beteween gold and dross. They say in irony, "Let us first get rid of Joseph. It will be time enough then to pretend to be 'good' like him, or to repent of our crime after we have had all its benefits in material things!"

1641. One of the brethren, perhaps less cruel by nature, or perhaps more worldly-wise, said: "Why undertake the risk of blood-guiltiness? Throw him into the well you see there! Some travellers passing by will pick him up and remove him to a far country. If not, at least *we* shall not have killed him." This was false casuistry, but such casuistry appeals to sinners of a certain kind of temperament. The well was apparently a dry well, deep enough to prevent his coming out, but with no water in which he could be drowned. It was Allah's Plan to save him alive, but not to make Joseph indebted to any of his brethren for his life!

1642. The plot having been formed, the brethren proceed to put it into execution. Jacob, knowing the situation, did not ordinarily trust his beloved Joseph with the brethren. The latter therefore remonstrate and feign brotherly affection.

12. "Send him with us tomorrow
To enjoy himself and play,
And we shall take
Every care of him."[1643]

١٢ أَرْسِلْهُ مَعَنَا غَدًا يَرْتَعْ
وَيَلْعَبْ وَإِنَّا لَهُۥ لَحَٰفِظُونَ

13. (Jacob) said: "Really
It saddens me that ye
Should take him away:
I fear lest the wolf
Should devour him
While ye attend not[1644]
To him."

١٣ قَالَ إِنِّى لَيَحْزُنُنِىٓ أَن
تَذْهَبُوا۟ بِهِۦ وَأَخَافُ أَن يَأْكُلَهُ
ٱلذِّئْبُ وَأَنتُمْ عَنْهُ غَٰفِلُونَ

14. They said: "If the wolf
Were to devour him
While we are (so large) a party,
Then should we indeed
(First) have perished ourselves!"[1645]

١٤ قَالُوا۟ لَئِنْ أَكَلَهُ ٱلذِّئْبُ
وَنَحْنُ عُصْبَةٌ إِنَّآ إِذًا لَّخَٰسِرُونَ

15. So they did take him away,
And they all agreed
To throw him down
To the bottom of the well:
And We put into his heart[1646]
(This Message): 'Of a surety
Thou shalt (one day)
Tell them the truth

١٥ فَلَمَّا ذَهَبُوا۟ بِهِۦ وَأَجْمَعُوٓا۟
أَن يَجْعَلُوهُ فِى غَيَٰبَتِ ٱلْجُبِّ
وَأَوْحَيْنَآ إِلَيْهِ لَتُنَبِّئَنَّهُم

1643. They did not expect their protestations to be believed. But they added an argument that might appeal both to Jacob and Joseph. 'They were going to give their young brother a good time. Why not let him come out with them and play and enjoy himself to his heart's content?'

1644. Jacob did not know the precise plot, but he had strong misgivings. But how could he put off these brethren? If they were driven to open hostility, they would be certain to cause him harm. He must deal with the brethren wisely and cautiously. He pleaded that he was an old man, and would miss Joseph and be sad without him. And after all, Joseph was not of an age to play with them. They would be attending to their own affairs, and a wolf might come and attack and kill Joseph. In saying this he was really unwittingly giving a cue to the wicked ones, for they use that very excuse in verse 17 below. Thus the wicked plot thickens, but there is a counter-plan also, which is drawing a noose of lies round the wicked ones, so that they are eventually driven into a corner, and have to confess their own guilt in verse 91 below, and through repentance obtain forgiveness.

1645. Jacob's objections as stated could be easily rebutted, and the brethren did so. They would be eleven in the party, and the ten strong and grown-up men would have to perish before the wolf could touch the young lad Joseph! So they prevailed, as verbal arguments are apt to prevail, when events are weaving their web on quite another Plan, which has nothing to do with verbal arguments. Presumably Benjamin was too young to go with them.

1646. Allah was with Joseph in all his difficulties, sorrows, and sufferings, as He is with all His servants who put their trust in Him. The poor lad was betrayed by his brothers, and left, perhaps to die or to be sold into slavery. But his heart was undaunted. His courage never failed him. On the contrary he had an inkling, a presentiment, of things that were to be—that his own rectitude and beauty of soul would land him on his feet, and perhaps some day, his brothers would stand in need of him, and he would be in a position to fulfil that need, and would do it gladly, putting them to shame for their present plotting and betrayal of him.

Of this their affair
While they know (thee) not."[1647]

بِأَمْرِهِمْ هَٰذَا وَهُمْ لَا يَشْعُرُونَ

16. Then they came
To their father
In the early part
Of the night,
Weeping.[1648]

١٦ وَجَاءُوٓ أَبَاهُمْ عِشَآءً يَبْكُونَ

17. They said: "O our father!
We went racing with one another,[1649]
And left Joseph with our things;
And the wolf devoured him...
But thou wilt never believe us
Even though we tell the truth."[1650]

١٧ قَالُوا۟ يَٰٓأَبَانَآ إِنَّا ذَهَبْنَا نَسْتَبِقُ وَتَرَكْنَا يُوسُفَ عِندَ مَتَٰعِنَا فَأَكَلَهُ ٱلذِّئْبُ وَمَآ أَنتَ بِمُؤْمِنٍ لَّنَا وَلَوْ كُنَّا صَٰدِقِينَ

18. They stained his shirt[1651]
With false blood. He said:
"Nay, but your minds
Have made up a tale
(That may pass) with you.[1652]
(For me) patience is most fitting:
Against that which ye assert,
It is Allah (alone)
Whose help can be sought."...

١٨ وَجَآءُو عَلَىٰ قَمِيصِهِۦ بِدَمٍ كَذِبٍ قَالَ بَلْ سَوَّلَتْ لَكُمْ أَنفُسُكُمْ أَمْرًا فَصَبْرٌ جَمِيلٌ وَٱللَّهُ ٱلْمُسْتَعَانُ عَلَىٰ مَا تَصِفُونَ

1647. This situation occurred when Joseph later on became the governor of Egypt and his brothers stood before him suing for his assistance although they did not know that he was their betrayed brother; see 12:89 below; also 12:58.

1648. The plotters were ready with their false tale for their father, but in order to make it appear plausible, they came sometime after sundown, to show that they had made an effort to search for their brother and save him.

1649. They wanted to make out that they were not negligent of Joseph. They were naturally having games and exercise, while the boy was left with their belongings. It was the racing that prevented them from seeing the wolf. And Jacob's fears about the wolf (12:13 above) made them imagine that he would swallow the wolf story readily.

1650. They were surprised that Jacob received the story about the wolf with cold incredulity. So they grew petulent, put on an air of injured innocence, and brought out the blood-stained garment described in the next verse.

1651. Joseph wore a garment of many colours, which was a special garment peculiar to him. If the brethren could produce it blood-stained before their father, they thought he would be convinced that Joseph had been killed by a wild beast. But the stain on the garment was a stain of "false blood"—not the blood of Joseph, but the blood of a goat which the brethren had killed expressly for this purpose. Their device, however, was not quite convincing because, as some Commentators have pointed out, the garment was intact which is inconceivable if a wolf had indeed devoured Joseph. (R).

1652. Jacob saw that there had been some foul play, and he did not hesitate to say so. In effect he said: "Ah me! the tale you tell may be good enough for you, who invented it! But what about me, your aged father? What is there left in life for me now, with my beloved son gone? And yet what can I do but hold my heart in patience and implore Allah's assistance? I have faith, and I know that all that He does is for the best!"

19. Then there came a caravan[1653]
Of travellers: they sent
Their water-carrier (for water),
And he let down his bucket
(Into the well)...He said:
"Ah there! Good news![1654]
Here is a (fine) young man!"
So they concealed him[1655]
As a treasure! But Allah
Knoweth well all that they do![1656]

١٩ وَجَآءَتْ سَيَّارَةٌ فَأَرْسَلُوا۟
وَارِدَهُمْ فَأَدْلَىٰ دَلْوَهُۥ ۖ قَالَ يَٰبُشْرَىٰ
هَٰذَا غُلَٰمٌ ۚ وَأَسَرُّوهُ بِضَٰعَةً ۚ
وَٱللَّهُ عَلِيمٌۢ بِمَا يَعْمَلُونَ

20. The (Brethren) sold him
For a miserable price—
For a few dirhams[1657] counted out:
In such low estimation
Did they hold him![1658]

٢٠ وَشَرَوْهُ بِثَمَنٍۭ بَخْسٍ دَرَٰهِمَ
مَعْدُودَةٍ وَكَانُوا۟ فِيهِ مِنَ ٱلزَّٰهِدِينَ

C. 110.—Joseph was bought by a man high at Court
(12:21-42.) In Egypt, who asked his wife Zulaykhā[1658-A]
To treat him with honour, with a view
To his adoption as a son. But she burnt
With a passion of earthly love for him.

1653. Then comes the caravan of unknown travellers—Midianite or Arab merchants travelling to Egypt with merchandise, such as the balm of Gilead in Transjordania. In accordance with custom the caravan was preceded by advance parties to search out water and pitch a camp near. They naturally went to the well and let down their bucket.

1654. The water carrier is surprised and taken aback, when he finds a youth of comely appearance, innocent like an angel, with a face as bright as the sun! What is he to make of it? Anyhow, to see him is a delight! And he shouts it out as a piece of good news. Some Commentators think that "*Bushrā*", the Arabic word for "Good news", is a proper noun, the name of the companion to whom he shouted. (R).

1655. It was a caravan of merchants, and they think of everything in terms of the money to be made out of it! Here was an unknown, unclaimed youth, of surpassing beauty, with apparently a mind as refined as was his external beauty. If he could be sold in the opulent slave markets of Memphis or whatever was the capital of the Hyksos Dynasty then ruling in Egypt (see Appendix IV following S. 7), what a price he would fetch! They had indeed lighted upon a treasure! And they wanted to conceal him lest he was another's slave and had run away from his master who might come and claim him! The circumstances were peculiar and the merchants were cautious. *Biḍā'ah* = stock in trade; capital; money; wealth; treasure.

1656. To different minds the situation appeared different. Joseph must have felt keenly the edge of his brethren's treason. His father Jacob was lost in the sorrow of the loss of his best-beloved son. The brethren were exulting in their plan of getting rid of one whom they hated. The merchants were gloating over their gains. But the horizon of all was limited. Allah knew their deeds and their feelings and motives, and He was working out His own Plan. Neither the best of us nor the worst of us know wither our Destiny is leading us—how evil plots are defeated and goodness comes to its own in marvellous ways!

1657. *Dirham;* from Greek, *drachma*, a small silver coin, which varied in weight and value at different times and in different States. (R).

1658. There was mutual deceit on both sides. The Brethren had evidently been watching to see what happened to Joseph: when they saw the merchants take him up and hide him, they came to claim his price as a run away slave, but dared not haggle over the price, lest their object, to get rid of him, should be defeated. The merchants were shrewd enough to doubt the claim in their own minds: but they dared not haggle lest they should lose a very valuable acquisition. And so the most precious of human lives in the age was sold into slavery for a few silver pieces! (R).

1658-A. In popular tradition the wife of the Egyptian courtier is identified as Zulaykha. [Eds.].

When Joseph refused to yield to her solicitations,
There was trouble and scandal, and Joseph
Had to go to prison. Here were shown
His greatness, and kindness, and wisdom.
The King's cupbearer came in disgrace
To prison. Joseph instructed him and others
In the eternal Gospel of Unity. When released
And restored to favour, the cupbearer
Forgot Joseph—for a time—until
It pleased Allah to put into Joseph's hands
The keys of the prosperity of Egypt and the world.

SECTION 3.

21. The man in Egypt[1659]
Who bought him, said
To his wife: "Make his stay
(Among us) honourable:[1660]
Maybe he will bring us
Much good, or we shall
Adopt him as a son."
Thus did We establish
Joseph in the land,[1661]
That We might teach him
The interpretation of stories[1662]

٢١ وَقَالَ ٱلَّذِى ٱشْتَرَىٰهُ
مِن مِّصْرَ لِٱمْرَأَتِهِۦٓ أَكْرِمِى مَثْوَىٰهُ
عَسَىٰٓ أَن يَنفَعَنَآ أَوْ نَتَّخِذَهُۥ وَلَدًا ۚ
وَكَذَٰلِكَ مَكَّنَّا لِيُوسُفَ فِى ٱلْأَرْضِ
وَلِنُعَلِّمَهُۥ مِن تَأْوِيلِ ٱلْأَحَادِيثِ ۚ

1659. Joseph is now clear of his jealous brethren in the land of Canaan. The merchants take him to Egypt. In the city of Memphis (or whatever was the Egyptian capital then) he was exposed for sale by the merchants. The merchants had not miscalculated. There was a ready market for him: his handsome presence, his winning ways, his purity and innocence, his intelligence and integrity, combined with his courtesy and noble manliness, attracted all eyes to him. There was the keenest competition to purchase him, and in the highest Court circles. Every competitor was outbid by a high court official, who is called in verse 30 below "the 'Aziz" (the Exalted in rank). (R).

1660. See last note. The 'Azīz's motive was perhaps worldly. Such a handsome, attractive, intelligent son would get him more honour, dignity, power and wealth. (R).

1661. How unerringly Allah's plan works! To teach Joseph wisdom and power, he had to be tested and proved in righteousness, and advanced in Egypt, and the way prepared for Israel and his posterity to proclaim Allah's truth to the world and to make possible the subsequent missions of Moses and Al Muṣṭafā. (R).

1662. *Aḥādīth* might be stories, things imagined or related, things that happened, in life or in true dreams. To suppose that phenomenal events are the only reality is a mark of one-sided materialism. As Hamlet said to Horatio, "there are more things in heaven and earth, Horatio, than are dreamt of in your philosophy." External events have their own limited reality, but there are bigger realities behind them, and sometimes appear darkly in the visions of ordinary men, but more clearly in the visions of poets, seers, sages, and prophets. Joseph had to be trained in seeing the realities behind events and visions. He was hated by his brothers and sold by them into slavery: they were sending him into the land of Egypt, where he was to rule men. He loved his father dearly and was separated from him, and his mother had died early; but his affection was not blunted, but drawn to a keener edge when his benevolent work benefited millions in Egypt, and in the world. His own vision of stars, sun, and moon prostrating themselves before him, was no idle dream of a selfish fool, but the prefigurement of a power, which, used rightly, was to make his own honour an instrument of service to millions he had not seen, through men and women whose own power and dignity were sanctified through him. He was to understand the hidden meaning of what seemed futilities, blunderings, snares, evil plottings, love gone wrong, and power used tyrannically. He was to interpret truth to those who would never have reached it otherwise.

(And events). And Allah
Hath full power and control
Over His affairs; but most
Among mankind know it not.[1663]

وَٱللَّهُ غَالِبٌ عَلَىٰٓ أَمْرِهِۦ
وَلَٰكِنَّ أَكْثَرَ ٱلنَّاسِ لَا يَعْلَمُونَ

22. When Joseph attained[1664]
His full manhood, We gave him
Power and knowledge: thus do We
Reward those who do right.[1665]

٢٢ وَلَمَّا بَلَغَ أَشُدَّهُۥٓ ءَاتَيْنَٰهُ
حُكْمًا وَعِلْمًا وَكَذَٰلِكَ نَجْزِى ٱلْمُحْسِنِينَ

23. But she in whose house
He was, sought to seduce him[1666]
From his (true) self: she fastened
The doors, and said:
"Now come, thou (dear one)!"
He said: "Allah forbid!
Truly (thy husband) is
My lord! he made
My sojourn agreeable!
Truly to no good
Come those who do wrong![1667]

٢٣ وَرَٰوَدَتْهُ ٱلَّتِى هُوَ فِى بَيْتِهَا
عَن نَّفْسِهِۦ وَغَلَّقَتِ ٱلْأَبْوَٰبَ
وَقَالَتْ هَيْتَ لَكَ قَالَ مَعَاذَ ٱللَّهِ
إِنَّهُۥ رَبِّىٓ أَحْسَنَ مَثْوَاىَ
إِنَّهُۥ لَا يُفْلِحُ ٱلظَّٰلِمُونَ

24. And (with passion) did she
Desire him, and he would
Have desired her, but that
He saw the evidence[1668]

٢٤ وَلَقَدْ هَمَّتْ بِهِۦ وَهَمَّ بِهَا
لَوْلَآ أَن رَّءَا بُرْهَٰنَ

1663. *Cf.*: "There is a divinity that shapes our ends, rough hew them as we will." Only, in Shakespeare, (Hamlet, V. 2), we have a vague and distant ideal, an irresolute striving, an unsuccessful attempt at getting beyond "this too, too solid flesh"! In Joseph we have the Prophet of Allah, sure in faith, above all carnal motives, and advancing the destiny of mankind with a conscious purpose, as the scroll of knowledge, wisdom, and power, unfolds itself before him by the grace of Allah, All-Good and All-Powerful.

1664. When Joseph left Canaan, he was a young and immature lad of seventeen or eighteen, but his nature was innocent and good. Through the vicissitudes of his fortune in Egypt, he grew in knowledge, judgement, and power.

1665. *Muhsinīn:* those who do right, those who do good. Both ideas are implied. In the following right conduct, you are necessarily doing good to yourself and to others.

1666. The 'Azīz had treated Joseph with honour: he was more his guest and son than his slave. In trying to seduce Joseph in these circumstances, his wife was guilty of a crime against Joseph's own honour and dignity. And there was a third fault in her earthly love. True love blots Self out: it thinks more of the loved one than of the Self. The 'Azīz's wife was seeking the satisfaction of her own selfish passion, and was in treason against Joseph's pure soul and his high destiny. It was inevitable that Joseph should repel the advances made by the wife of the courtier. (R).

1667. Joseph's plea in rejecting her advances is threefold: '(1) I owe a duty, and so do you, to your husband, the 'Azīz; (2) the kindness, courtesy, and honour, with which he has treated me entitled him to more than mere gratitude from me; (3) in any case, do you not see that you are harbouring a guilty passion, and that no good can come out of guilt? We must all obey laws, human and divine.' (R).

1668. She was blinded with passion, and his plea had no effect on her. He was human after all, and her passionate love and her beauty placed a great temptation in his path. But he had a sure refuge—his faith in Allah. His spiritual eyes saw something that her eyes, blinded by passion, did not see. She thought no one saw when the doors were closed. He knew that Allah was there and everywhere. That made him strong, and proof against temptation.

Of his Lord: thus
(Did We order) that We[1669]
Might turn away from him
(All) evil and shameful deeds:
For he was one of Our servants,
Sincere and purified.

رَبِّهِۦۚ كَذَٰلِكَ
لِنَصۡرِفَ عَنۡهُ ٱلسُّوٓءَ وَٱلۡفَحۡشَآءَۚ
إِنَّهُۥ مِنۡ عِبَادِنَا ٱلۡمُخۡلَصِينَ

25. So they both raced each other
To the door, and she
Tore his shirt from the back:[1670]
They both found her lord
Near the door. She said:
"What is the (fitting) punishment
For one who formed
An evil design against
Thy wife, but prison
Or a grievous chastisement?"[1671]

(٢٥) وَٱسۡتَبَقَا ٱلۡبَابَ وَقَدَّتۡ
قَمِيصَهُۥ مِن دُبُرٖ وَأَلۡفَيَا سَيِّدَهَا لَدَا ٱلۡبَابِۚ
قَالَتۡ مَا جَزَآءُ مَنۡ أَرَادَ بِأَهۡلِكَ سُوٓءًا
إِلَّآ أَن يُسۡجَنَ أَوۡ عَذَابٌ أَلِيمٞ

26. He said: "It was she
That sought to seduce me—[1672]
From my (true) self." And one
Of her household saw (this)
And bore witness, (thus)—[1673]
"If it be that his shirt
Is rent from the front, then
Is her tale true,
And he is a liar!

(٢٦) قَالَ هِيَ رَٰوَدَتۡنِي عَن نَّفۡسِيۚ
وَشَهِدَ شَاهِدٞ مِّنۡ أَهۡلِهَآ
إِن كَانَ قَمِيصُهُۥ قُدَّ مِن قُبُلٖ
فَصَدَقَتۡ وَهُوَ مِنَ ٱلۡكَٰذِبِينَ

1669. The credit of our being saved from sin is due, not to our weak earthly nature, but to Allah. We can only try, like Joseph, to be true and sincere; Allah will purify us and save us from all that is wrong. Tempted but true, we rise above ourselves.

1670. With his master's wife in her mad passion, the situation became intolerable, and Joseph made for the door. She ran after him to detain him. She tugged at his garment to detain him. As he was retreating, she could only catch hold of the back of his shirt, and in the struggle she tore it. He was determined to open the door and leave the place, as it was useless to argue with her in her mad passion. When the door was opened, it so happened, that the 'Aziz was not far off. We need not assume that he was spying, or had any suspicions either of his wife or Joseph. In his narrow limited way he was a just man. We can imagine his wife's consternation. One guilt leads to another. She had to resort to a lie, not only to justify herself but also to have her revenge on the man who had scorned her love. Slighted love (of the physical kind) made her ferocious, and she lost all sense of right and wrong. (R).

1671. Her lie and her accusation were plausible. Joseph was found with his dress disarranged. She wanted the inference to be drawn that he had assaulted her and she had resisted. For one in his position it was a dreadful crime. Should he not be consigned to a dungeon or at least scourged? Perhaps she hoped that in either case he would be more pliable to her designs in the future.

1672. Joseph bore himself with dignity. He was too great and noble to indulge in angry recrimination. But he had to tell the truth. And he did it with quiet simplicity, without argument or bitterness—and not caring whether he was believed or not. 'The love game was hers, not his, and it went too far in seeking to assault his person.'

1673. In the nature of things there was no eyewitness to what had happened between them. But as there was a scene and the whole household collected, wisdom came through one who was not immediately concerned. They say it was a child. If so, it illustrates the truth that the most obvious things are not noticed by people who are excited, but are plain to simple people who remain calm. Wisdom comes often through babes and sucklings.

27. "But if it be that his shirt
Is torn from the back,
Then is she the liar,
And he is telling the truth!"[1674]

٢٧ وَإِن كَانَ قَمِيصُهُۥ قُدَّ مِن دُبُرٍ
فَكَذَبَتْ وَهُوَ مِنَ ٱلصَّـٰدِقِينَ

28. So when he saw his shirt—
That it was torn at the back—
(Her husband) said: "Behold!
It is a snare of you women![1675]
Truly, mighty is your snare!

٢٨ فَلَمَّا رَءَا قَمِيصَهُۥ قُدَّ مِن دُبُرٍ قَالَ إِنَّهُۥ
مِن كَيْدِكُنَّ ۖ إِنَّ كَيْدَكُنَّ عَظِيمٌ

29. "O Joseph, pass this over!
(O wife), ask forgiveness
For thy sin, for truly
Thou hast been at fault!"[1676]

٢٩ يُوسُفُ أَعْرِضْ عَنْ هَـٰذَا ۚ وَٱسْتَغْفِرِى
لِذَنۢبِكِ ۖ إِنَّكِ كُنتِ مِنَ ٱلْخَاطِـِٔينَ

Section 4.

30. Ladies said in the City:
"The wife of the (great) 'Azīz[1677]
Is seeking to seduce her slave
From his (true) self:
Truly hath he inspired her
With violent love: we see
She is evidently going astray."[1678]

٣٠ وَقَالَ نِسْوَةٌ فِى ٱلْمَدِينَةِ ٱمْرَأَتُ ٱلْعَزِيزِ
تُرَٰوِدُ فَتَىٰهَا عَن نَّفْسِهِۦ ۖ قَدْ شَغَفَهَا
حُبًّا ۖ إِنَّا لَنَرَىٰهَا فِى ضَلَـٰلٍ مُّبِينٍ

1674. If Joseph's shirt was torn at the back, he must obviously have been retreating, and the wife of the 'Aziz must have been tugging from behind. No one could doubt who was the guilty party. Everybody saw it, and the 'Aziz was convinced. (R).

1675. When the real fact became clear to everyone, the 'Aziz as head of the household had to decide what to do. His own position was difficult, and it was made ridiculous. He was a high officer of state, say Grand Chamberlain. His dignity and rank were advanced by the so-called marriage with a high-born Princess. Was he going to proclaim to the world that his wife was running after a slave? He was probably fond of her, and he saw the innocence, loyalty, and sterling merit of Joseph. He must treat the whole affair as a woman's prank—the madness of sex-love, and the tricks and snares connected with sex-love. He must take no further action but to rate his life and do justice. (R).

1676. As was only fair, he apologised to Joseph and begged him to give no further throught to the injury that had been done to him, first by the love-snare of his wife, secondly, by the uttlerly false charge made against him, and thirdly, by the scene, which must have been painful to a man of such spotless character as Joseph. That was not enough. He must ask his wife humbly to beg Joseph's pardon for the wrong that she had done him. And he must further ask her to consider her unbecoming conduct in itself, apart from any wrong done to Joseph. (R).

1677. *'Azīz*: title of a nobleman or officer of Court, of high rank. Considering all the circumstances, the office of Grand Chamberlain or minister may be indicated. But "'Aziz" I think is a title, not an office. I have not translated the title but left it as it is. "Excellency" or "Highness" would have specialised modern associations which I want to avoid.

1678. The 'Aziz's just, wise, and discreet conduct would have closed the particular episode of his wife's guilty conduct if only Mrs. Grundy had left her alone and she had not foolishly thought of justifying her conduct to Mrs. Grundy. The 'Aziz had reproved her, and he had the right and authority so to do. He also probably understood her. Joseph by his behaviour had upheld the highest standard both for himself and for her. (R).

31. When she heard
Of their malicious talk,
She sent for them
And prepared a banquet[1679]
For them: she gave
Each of them a knife:
And she said (to Joseph),
"Come out before them."
When they saw him,
They did extol him,
And (in their amazement)
Cut their hands: they said,
"Allah preserve us! no mortal
Is this! This is none other
Than a noble angel!"

٣١ فَلَمَّا سَمِعَتْ بِمَكْرِهِنَّ
أَرْسَلَتْ إِلَيْهِنَّ وَأَعْتَدَتْ لَهُنَّ مُتَّكَـًٔا
وَءَاتَتْ كُلَّ وَٰحِدَةٍ مِّنْهُنَّ سِكِّينًا
وَقَالَتِ ٱخْرُجْ عَلَيْهِنَّ فَلَمَّا رَأَيْنَهُۥٓ
أَكْبَرْنَهُۥ وَقَطَّعْنَ أَيْدِيَهُنَّ وَقُلْنَ
حَٰشَ لِلَّهِ مَا هَٰذَا بَشَرًا
إِنْ هَٰذَآ إِلَّا مَلَكٌ كَرِيمٌ

32. She said: "There before you
Is the man about whom
Ye did blame me!
I did seek to seduce him from
His (true) self but he did
Firmly save himself guiltless![1680] . . .
And now, if he doth not
My bidding, he shall certainly
Be cast into prison,
And (what is more)
Be of the company of the vilest!"

٣٢ قَالَتْ فَذَٰلِكُنَّ ٱلَّذِى
لُمْتُنَّنِى فِيهِ وَلَقَدْ رَٰوَدتُّهُۥ
عَن نَّفْسِهِۦ فَٱسْتَعْصَمَ
وَلَئِن لَّمْ يَفْعَلْ مَآ ءَامُرُهُۥ
لَيُسْجَنَنَّ وَلَيَكُونًا مِّنَ ٱلصَّٰغِرِينَ

33. He said: "O my Lord!
The prison is more

٣٣ قَالَ رَبِّ ٱلسِّجْنُ

1679. When her reputation began to be pulled to pieces by Mrs. Grundy, with sundry exaggerations and distortions and malicious inuendos, the wife of 'Azīz invited all the ladies in society to a grand banquet. We can imagine them reclining at ease after the manner of fashionable banquets. When dessert was reached and the talk flowed freely about the gossip and scandal which made their hostess interesting, they were just about to cut the fruit with their knives, when, behold! Joseph was brought into their midst. Imagine the consternation which his beauty caused, and the havoc it played with their hearts! "Ah!", thought the wife of 'Azīz "now is your hypocrisy self-exposed! What about your reproaches to me? You have yourselves so lost your self-control that you have cut your fingers!" (R).

1680. Her speech is subtle, and shows that any repentance or compunction she may have felt is blotted out by the collective crowd mentality into which she has deliberately invited herself to fall. Her speech falls into two parts, with a hiatus between, which I have marked by the punctuation mark (. . .). In the first part there is a note of triumph, as much as to say, "Now you see! Mine was no vulgar passion! You are just as susceptible! You would have done the same thing!" Finding encouragement from their passion and their fellow-feelings, she openly avows as a woman amongst women (by a sort of freemasonry) what she would have been ashamed to acknowledge to others before. She falls a step lower and boasts of it. A step lower still, and she sneers at Joseph's innocence, his firmness in saving himself guiltless! There is a pause. The tide of passion rises still higher, and the dreadful second part of her speech begins. It is a sort of joint consultation, though she speaks in monologue. The women all agree that no man has a right to resist their solicitations. Beauty spurned is the highest crime. And so now she rises to the height of tragic guilt and threatens Joseph. She forgets all her finer feelings, and is overpowered by brute passion. After all, he is a slave and must obey his mistress! Or, there is prison, and the company of the vilest, instead of the caresses of beauty and fashion in high places!" Poor, deluded, fallen creature! She sank lower than herself, in seeking the support of the crowd around her! What pain and suffering and sorrow can expiate the depth of this crime? (R).

To my liking than that
To which they invite me:[1681]
Unless Thou turn away
Their snare from me,
I should (in my youthful folly)
Feel inclined towards them
And join the ranks of the
ignorant."[1682]

أَحَبُّ إِلَيَّ مِمَّا يَدْعُونَنِي إِلَيْهِ
وَإِلَّا تَصْرِفْ عَنِّي كَيْدَهُنَّ
أَصْبُ إِلَيْهِنَّ وَأَكُن مِّنَ الْجَاهِلِينَ

34. So his Lord hearkened to him
(In his prayer) and turned
Away from him their snare:[1683]
Verily He heareth and knoweth
(All things).

٣٤ فَاسْتَجَابَ لَهُ رَبُّهُ فَصَرَفَ
عَنْهُ كَيْدَهُنَّ إِنَّهُ هُوَ السَّمِيعُ الْعَلِيمُ

35. Then it occurred to the men[1684]
After they had seen the Signs,
(That it was best)
To imprison him
For a time.

٣٥ ثُمَّ بَدَا لَهُم مِّن بَعْدِ مَا رَأَوُا الْآيَاتِ
لَيَسْجُنُنَّهُ حَتَّىٰ حِينٍ

SECTION 5.

36. Now with him there came
Into the prison two young men.[1685]

٣٦ وَدَخَلَ مَعَهُ السِّجْنَ فَتَيَانِ

1681. *"To which they invite me."* Notice it is now "they" not "she". Where there was the snare of one woman before, it is now the collective snare of many women—of womankind!

1682. Joseph's speech is characteristic. Like a true Prophet of Allah, he takes refuge in Allah. He knows the weakness of human nature. He would not pit his own strength against the whole assault of evil. He will rely on Allah to turn evil away from him, and praise Him alone for any success he achieves in his fight. It is only the ignorant who do not know man's weakness and Allah's strength!

1683. Joseph was saved from the wiles of the women, which would have degraded him. But more, his truth and character were completely vindicated in the eyes of all concerned by the avowal of the wife of the 'Aziz. (R).

1684. When Joseph's character was completely vindicated, there was no disgrace on him in being sent to prison after that. On the contrary the blame now would attach to those who, for their own selfish motives, restricted his liberty for a time. As a matter of fact, various motives on the part of the many actors in this drama converged towards that end. For Joseph, prison was better than the importunities of the women, and now, not one woman, but all society women were after him. To the women themselves it looked as if that was a lever which they could use to force his compliance. Vain, deluded creatures, to think that a man of God could be forced from the path of rectitude by threats or bribes. To the 'Aziz it appears as if it might be in his wife's best interests that he should disappear from her view in prison. The decisive factor was the view of the men generally, who were alarmed at the consternation he had caused among the women. They knew that Joseph was righteous: they had seen the Signs of Allah in his wonderful personality and his calm and confident fortitude. But, it was argued, it was better that one man (even if righteous) should suffer in prison rather than that many should suffer from the extraordinary disturbance he was unwittingly causing in their social life. Not for the first nor for the last time did the righteous suffer plausibly for the guilt of the guilty. And so Joseph went to prison—for a time. (R).

1685 Now opens another chapter in Joseph's life. The Plan of Allah develops. The wicked might plot; the weak might be swayed by specious arguments: but everything is used by the Universal Plan for its own beneficent purposes. Joseph must get into touch with the Pharaoh, in order to work out the salvation of Egypt, and yet it must be through no obligation to smaller men. And he must diffuse his personality and teach the truth to men of all sorts in prison.

Said one of them: "I see
Myself (in a dream)
Pressing wine." Said the other:
"I see myself (in a dream)
Carrying bread on my head,
And birds are eating thereof."[1686]
"Tell us" (they said) "the truth
And meaning thereof: for we
See thou art one
That doth good (to all)."[1687]

قَالَ أَحَدُهُمَآ إِنِّيٓ
أَرَىٰنِيٓ أَعۡصِرُ خَمۡرٗاۖ وَقَالَ ٱلۡأٓخَرُ
إِنِّيٓ أَرَىٰنِيٓ أَحۡمِلُ فَوۡقَ رَأۡسِي خُبۡزٗا
تَأۡكُلُ ٱلطَّيۡرُ مِنۡهُۖ نَبِّئۡنَا بِتَأۡوِيلِهِۦٓۖ
إِنَّا نَرَىٰكَ مِنَ ٱلۡمُحۡسِنِينَ

37. He said: "Before any food
Comes (in due course)
To feed either of you
I will surely reveal
To you the truth
And meaning of this
Ere it befall you.[1688]
That is part of the (Duty)
Which my Lord hath taught
me.[1689]

I have (I assure you)
Abandoned the ways
Of a people that believe not
In Allah and that (even)
Deny the Hereafter.[1690]

٣٧ قَالَ لَا يَأۡتِيكُمَا طَعَامٞ
تُرۡزَقَانِهِۦٓ إِلَّا نَبَّأۡتُكُمَا
بِتَأۡوِيلِهِۦ قَبۡلَ أَن
يَأۡتِيَكُمَاۚ ذَٰلِكُمَا
مِمَّا عَلَّمَنِي رَبِّيٓۚ
إِنِّي تَرَكۡتُ مِلَّةَ قَوۡمٖ لَّا يُؤۡمِنُونَ
بِٱللَّهِ وَهُم بِٱلۡأٓخِرَةِ هُمۡ كَٰفِرُونَ

1686. Two men came to the prison about the same time as Joseph. They were both apparently officers of the king (the Pharaoh), who had incurred his wrath. One was a cupbearer (or butler or chief steward) whose duty was to prepare the king's wines and drinks. The other was the king's baker, whose duty was to prepare the king's bread. They were both in disgrace. The former dreamed that he was again carrying on his duties and pressing wine: the latter that he was carrying bread, but it did not reach his master, for the birds ate of it.

1687. Both these men saw the Signs of Allah about Joseph. They felt not only that he had wisdom, but that he was kind and benevolent, and would give of his wisdom even to strangers like themselves. They therefore told him their dreams and asked him to interpret them.

1688. The dream of one foreboded good to him, and of the other, evil to him. It was good that each should prepare for his fate. But Joseph's mission was far higher than that of merely foretelling events. He must teach the truth of Allah and the faith in the Hereafter to both men. He does that first before he talks of the events of their phenomenal life. And yet he does it so tenderely. He does not tantalise them. In effect he says, "You shall learn everything before our next meal, but let me first teach you Faith!"

1689. Joseph does not preach a pompous sermon, or claim any credit to himself for placing himself at their service. He is just doing his duty, and the highest good he can do to them is to teach them Faith.

1690. These men were Egyptians, perhaps steeped in materialism, idolatry, and polytheism. He must teach them the Gospel of Unity. And he does it simply, by appealing to his own experience: 'I have found the Lord good: in prosperity and adversity I have been supported by Faith: in life no man can live by error or evil: perhaps one of you has done some wrong for which you find yourself here: perhaps one of you is innocent: in either case, will you not accept Faith and live forever?

38. "And I follow the ways[1691]
Of my fathers—Abraham,
Isaac, and Jacob; and never
Could we attribute any partners
Whatever to Allah: that (comes)
Of the grace of Allah to us
And to mankind: yet
Most men are not grateful.

﴿٣٨﴾ وَٱتَّبَعْتُ مِلَّةَ ءَابَآءِىٓ إِبْرَٰهِيمَ
وَإِسْحَٰقَ وَيَعْقُوبَ مَا كَانَ لَنَآ أَن نُّشْرِكَ
بِٱللَّهِ مِن شَىْءٍ ذَٰلِكَ مِن فَضْلِ ٱللَّهِ عَلَيْنَا وَعَلَى
ٱلنَّاسِ وَلَٰكِنَّ أَكْثَرَ ٱلنَّاسِ لَا يَشْكُرُونَ

39. "O my two companions[1692]
Of the prison! (I ask you):
Are many lords differing
Among themselves better,
Or Allah, the One,
Supreme and Irresistible?

﴿٣٩﴾ يَٰصَٰحِبَىِ ٱلسِّجْنِ
ءَأَرْبَابٌ مُّتَفَرِّقُونَ خَيْرٌ
أَمِ ٱللَّهُ ٱلْوَٰحِدُ ٱلْقَهَّارُ

40. "If not Him, ye worship nothing
But names which ye have
named—[1693]
Ye and your fathers—
For which Allah hath sent down
No authority: the Command
Is for none but Allah: He
Hath commanded that ye worship
None but Him: that is
The right religion, but
Most men understand not . . .

﴿٤٠﴾ مَا تَعْبُدُونَ مِن دُونِهِۦٓ إِلَّآ أَسْمَآءً
سَمَّيْتُمُوهَآ أَنتُمْ وَءَابَآؤُكُم
مَّآ أَنزَلَ ٱللَّهُ بِهَا مِن سُلْطَٰنٍ إِنِ ٱلْحُكْمُ إِلَّا لِلَّهِ
أَمَرَ أَلَّا تَعْبُدُوٓا۟ إِلَّآ إِيَّاهُ ذَٰلِكَ ٱلدِّينُ ٱلْقَيِّمُ
وَلَٰكِنَّ أَكْثَرَ ٱلنَّاسِ لَا يَعْلَمُونَ

41. "O my two companions[1694]
Of the prison! As to one

﴿٤١﴾ يَٰصَٰحِبَىِ ٱلسِّجْنِ أَمَّآ أَحَدُكُمَا

1691. Again the same note of personal modesty. 'You may think I am as young as you, or younger. Yes, but I have the heritage of great men renowned for wisdom and truth, such as Abraham, Isaac, and Jacob. Surely what they knew is worthy of respect. Never did they swerve a hair's breadth from the Gospel of Unity. It is not that we boast. It was Allah's grace that taught us and Allah's grace is teaching all mankind. But men show their ingratitude by inventing other so-called gods.'

1692. Note the personal touch again. 'Are we not also companions in misfortune? And may I not speak to you on terms of perfect equality—as one prisoner to another? Well then, do you really think a conflict of heterogeneous gods is better than Allah, the One (and Only), Whose power is Supreme and Irresistible?" (R).

1693. 'If you name other gods, they are nothing but your inventions—names which you and your fathers put forward without any reality behind them. Who gave you authority to do any such thing? The only reality is Allah. Authority can come from Him alone. It is only for Him to command. And He has distinctly commanded you to worship none other than Him. That is the only religion that is right—that has stood and will stand and endure forever. He has revealed it at all times by His Messengers and by His Signs. If men fail to understand, it is their own fault.

1694. Having fulfilled his great duty, that touching the things of the spirit, Joseph now passes on, and comes to the things in which they were immediately interested—the questions which they had asked him about their dreams and what they prognosticated of their immediate future. Notice how Joseph again puts himself into sympathy with them by repeating the phrase of camaraderie, "my two companions of the prison!" For one he has good news, and for the other, bad news. He does not mince matters or waste words. He just barely tells the truth, hoping that the higher spiritual truths of which he has spoken will appear in their eyes, too, as of more importance than mere earthly triumphs or disasters—(in Kipling's words) "both impostors all the same."

Of you, he will pour out
The wine for his lord to drink:[1695]
As for the other, he will
Hang from the cross, and the birds
Will eat from off his head.[1696]
(So) hath been decreed
That matter whereof
Ye twain do enquire"...

فَيَسْقِي رَبَّهُۥ خَمْرًا
وَأَمَّا ٱلْآخَرُ فَيُصْلَبُ
فَتَأْكُلُ ٱلطَّيْرُ مِن رَّأْسِهِۦ
قُضِىَ ٱلْأَمْرُ ٱلَّذِى فِيهِ تَسْتَفْتِيَانِ

42. And of the two,
To that one whom he considered
About to be saved, he said:
"Mention me to thy lord."[1697]
But Satan made him forget[1698]
To mention him to his lord:
And (Joseph) lingered in prison
A few (more) years.[1699]

٤٢ وَقَالَ لِلَّذِى ظَنَّ أَنَّهُۥ نَاجٍ
مِّنْهُمَا ٱذْكُرْنِى عِندَ رَبِّكَ
فَأَنسَىٰهُ ٱلشَّيْطَـٰنُ ذِكْرَ رَبِّهِۦ
فَلَبِثَ فِى ٱلسِّجْنِ بِضْعَ سِنِينَ

C. 111. — The king of Egypt saw a vision
(12:43-68.) Which none of his grandees could explain.
The cupbearer referred to Joseph,
Who was sent for by the king. But Joseph
Insisted that the voice of scandal,
Which had pointed to him, should be declared
In public to be false. After Zulaykhā
Had paid a splendid ungrudging tribute

1695. The cupbearer had perhaps been proved innocent of the crime which had been charged against him, and was to be restored to the favour of the Pharaoh. He was to carry the cup and be the king's confidant again. How much more good he could do now, after the spiritual influence he had imbibed from Joseph, the Prophet of Allah! He was more fortunate in having had Joseph's company than in being restored to his intimate position with the king! Yet he was not a perfect man, as we shall see presently.

1696. For the baker, alas! he had bad news, and he tells it directly without tantalising him. Perhaps he had been found guilty—perhaps he had been really guilty—of some act of embezzlement or of joining in some palace intrigue, and he was to die a malefactor's death on the cross, followed by exposure to birds of the air—vultures pecking away at his eyes and cheeks, and all that had been his face and head! Poor man! If he was guilty, Joseph had taught him repentance, and we should like to think that he lost in this life but gained in the next. If he was innocent, the cruel death did not affect him. Joseph had shown him a higher and more lasting hope in the Hereafter.

1697. Joseph never mentioned himself in interpreting the dream, nor ever thought of himself in his kindness to his fellow-sufferers in prison. It was afterwards, when the cupbearer's dream came true, and he was being released on being restored to favour, that we can imagine him taking an affectionate leave of Joseph, and even asking him in his elation if he could do anything for Joseph. Joseph had no need of earthly favours—least of all, from kings or their favourites. The divine grace was enough for him. But he had great work to do, which he could not do in prison—work for Egypt and her king, and the world at large. If the cupbearer could mention him to the king, not by way of recommendation, but because the king's own justice was being violated in keeping an innocent man in prison, perhaps that might help to advance the cause of the king and the Egypt. And so he said, "Mention me to Pharaoh."

1698. The eternal Plan does not put Allah's Prophets under obligations to men commanding mere worldly favour or earthly power. If they are given a chance, the obligation is on the worldly men, however highly placed... In this case, the poor cupbearer was but human. When he was in the midst of the Court, he forgot the poor fellow-prisoner languishing in prison. In this he yielded to the lower part of his nature, which is guided by Satan. (R).

1699. *A few (more) years: biḍ'* in Arabic signifies a small indefinite number, say up to 3, 5, 7 or 9 years.

To his truth and righteousness, he came,
And was invested with supreme power
By the king. In times of plenty he organised
Great reserves to meet the needs
Of famine. When wide-spread famine at last
Prevailed, his brothers came from Canaan
In search of corn. He treated them kindly
And got them to bring his youngest brother
Benjamin; but they knew not that he was Joseph.

SECTION 6.

43. The king (of Egypt) said:[1700]
"I do see (in a vision)
Seven fat kine, whom seven
Lean ones devour—and seven
Green ears of corn, and seven
(others)
Withered. O ye chiefs!
Expound to me my vision,
If it be that ye can
Interpret visions."

٤٣ وَقَالَ الْمَلِكُ إِنِّي أَرَىٰ سَبْعَ بَقَرَاتٍ
سِمَانٍ يَأْكُلُهُنَّ سَبْعٌ عِجَافٌ وَسَبْعَ
سُنْبُلَاتٍ خُضْرٍ وَأُخَرَ يَابِسَاتٍ
يَا أَيُّهَا الْمَلَأُ أَفْتُونِي فِي رُؤْيَايَ
إِنْ كُنْتُمْ لِلرُّؤْيَا تَعْبُرُونَ

44. They said: "A confused medley
Of dreams: and we are not
Skilled in the interpretation
Of dreams."[1701]

٤٤ قَالُوا أَضْغَاثُ أَحْلَامٍ
وَمَا نَحْنُ بِتَأْوِيلِ الْأَحْلَامِ بِعَالِمِينَ

45. But the man who had been
Released, one of the two
(Who had been in prison)
And who now bethought him
After (so long) a space of time,
Said: "I will tell you
The truth of its interpretation:
Send ye me (therefor)."[1702]

٤٥ وَقَالَ الَّذِي نَجَا
مِنْهُمَا وَادَّكَرَ بَعْدَ أُمَّةٍ
أَنَا أُنَبِّئُكُمْ بِتَأْوِيلِهِ
فَأَرْسِلُونِ

1700. The Pharaoh is holding a Council. His confidential adviser the cupbearer is present. The Pharaoh relates his double dream—of seven fat kine being devoured by seven lean ones, and of seven fine full green ears of corn (presumably being devoured) by seven dry withered ears.

1701. No one in the Council apparently wanted to take the responsibility either of interpreting the dream, or of carrying out any measures consequent on the interpretation.

1702. At length the cupbearer's conscience was awakened. He thought of Joseph. He (Joseph) was a truthful man, and the cupbearer knew by personal experience how skillful he was in the interpretation of dreams. Perhaps he could get him released at this juncture by getting him to interpret the king's dream. If he had been frank, straight, and direct, he would have mentioned Joseph at once, and presented him to Pharaoh. But he had worldly subtlety. He wanted some credit for himself, at the same time that he fulfilled an old obligation. His petty conscience would be satisfied if he got Joseph's release, but meanwhile he wanted to see how much attention he could draw to himself in the court. So he just asked permission to withdraw in order to find the interpretation. He went straight to the prison, and addressed himself to Joseph, as in the following verse.

46. "O Joseph!" (he said).
"O man of truth! Expound
To us (the dream)
Of seven fat kine
Whom seven lean ones
Devour, and of seven
Green ears of corn
And (seven) others withered:
That I may return
To the people, and that
They may understand."[1703]

٤٦ يُوسُفُ أَيُّهَا ٱلصِّدِّيقُ
أَفْتِنَا فِي سَبْعِ بَقَرَٰتٍ سِمَانٍ
يَأْكُلُهُنَّ سَبْعٌ عِجَافٌ وَسَبْعِ
سُنۢبُلَٰتٍ خُضْرٍ وَأُخَرَ يَابِسَٰتٍ
لَّعَلِّيٓ أَرْجِعُ إِلَى ٱلنَّاسِ لَعَلَّهُمْ يَعْلَمُونَ

47. (Joseph) said: "For seven years
Shall ye diligently sow
As is your wont:
And the harvests that ye reap,
Ye shall leave them in the ear—[1704]
Except a little, of which
Ye shall eat.

٤٧ قَالَ تَزْرَعُونَ سَبْعَ سِنِينَ دَأَبًا
فَمَا حَصَدتُّمْ فَذَرُوهُ فِي سُنۢبُلِهِۦٓ
إِلَّا قَلِيلًا مِّمَّا تَأْكُلُونَ

48. "Then will come
After that (period)
Seven dreadful (years),
Which will devour
What ye shall have laid by
In advance for them—
(All) except a little[1705]
Which ye shall have
(Specially) guarded.

٤٨ ثُمَّ يَأْتِي مِنۢ بَعْدِ ذَٰلِكَ
سَبْعٌ شِدَادٌ يَأْكُلْنَ
مَا قَدَّمْتُمْ لَهُنَّ
إِلَّا قَلِيلًا مِّمَّا تُحْصِنُونَ

49. "Then will come
After that (period) a year

٤٩ ثُمَّ يَأْتِي مِنۢ بَعْدِ ذَٰلِكَ عَامٌ

1703. The speech must have been longer, to explain the circumstances. We are just given the points. From Joseph he conceals nothing. He knows that Joseph knows more than himself. He tells Joseph that if he got the meaning, he would go and tell the Council. It would be impertinent for the cupbearer to hold out to Joseph, the Prophet of Allah, the bribe of the hope of his release. Notice how blandly he avoids referring to his own lapse in having forgotten Joseph so long, and how the magnanimous Joseph has not a word of reproach, but gets straight on with the interpretation. (R).

1704. Joseph not only shows what will happen, but, unasked, suggests the measures to be taken for dealing with the calamity when it comes. There will be seven years of abundant harvest. With diligent cultivation they should get bumper crops. Of them they should take a little for their sustenance and store the rest in-the-ear, the better to preserve it from the pests that attack corn heaps when they have passed through the threshing floor.

1705. There will follow seven years of dreadful famine, which will devour all the stores which they will have laid by in the good years. They must be careful, even during the famine, not to consume all the grain; they must by special arrangement save a little for seed, lest they should be helpless even when the Nile brought down abundant waters from the rains at its sources.

In which the people will have
Abundant water, and in which
They will press (wine and oil)."[1706]

فِيهِ يُغَاثُ ٱلنَّاسُ وَفِيهِ يَعْصِرُونَ

SECTION 7.

50. So the king said:
"Bring ye him unto me."[1707]
But when the messenger
Came to him, (Joseph) said:
"Go thou back to thy lord,
And ask him, 'What is
The state of mind
Of the ladies
Who cut their hands'?[1708]
For my Lord is
Certainly well aware
Of their snare."[1709]

٥٠ وَقَالَ ٱلْمَلِكُ ٱئْتُونِي بِهِۦ
فَلَمَّا جَآءَهُ ٱلرَّسُولُ قَالَ
ٱرْجِعْ إِلَىٰ رَبِّكَ فَسْـَٔلْهُ مَا بَالُ
ٱلنِّسْوَةِ ٱلَّٰتِي قَطَّعْنَ أَيْدِيَهُنَّ
إِنَّ رَبِّي بِكَيْدِهِنَّ عَلِيمٌ

51. (The king) said (to the ladies):
"What was your affair
When ye did seek to seduce
Joseph from his (true) self?"[1710]
The ladies said: "Allah
Preserve us! no evil
Know we against him!"
Said the 'Azīz's wife:
"Now is the truth manifest
(To all): it was I
Who sought to seduce him
From his (true) self:

٥١ قَالَ مَا خَطْبُكُنَّ
إِذْ رَٰوَدتُّنَّ يُوسُفَ عَن نَّفْسِهِۦ
قُلْنَ حَٰشَ لِلَّهِ مَا عَلِمْنَا عَلَيْهِ مِن سُوٓءٍ
قَالَتِ ٱمْرَأَتُ ٱلْعَزِيزِ ٱلْـَٰٔنَ حَصْحَصَ
ٱلْحَقُّ أَنَا۠ رَٰوَدتُّهُۥ عَن نَّفْسِهِۦ

1706. This is a symbol of a very abundant year, following the seven years of drought. The Nile must have brought abundant fertilising waters and silt from its upper reaches, and there was probably some rain also in Lower Egypt. The vine and the olive trees, which must have suffered in the drought, now revived, and yielded their juice and their oil; among the annuals, also, the oil seeds, such as linseed, sesame, and the castor oil plant, must have been grown, as there was irrigated land to spare from the abundant grain crops. And the people's spirits revived, to enjoy the finer products of the earth, when their absolute necessities had been more than met in their grain crops.

1707. The cupbearer must have reported Joseph's interpretation to the king, and the king naturally wanted to see Joseph himself. He sent a messenger to fetch him.

1708. The king's messenger must have expected that a prisoner would be only too overjoyed at the summons of the king. But Joseph, sure of himself, wanted some assurance that he would be safe from the sort of nagging and persecution to which he had been subjected by the ladies. We saw in verse 33 above that he preferred prison to their solicitations. He must therefore know what was in the mind of the women now.

1709. If the king ("thy lord") did not know of all the snares which had been laid for Joseph by the ladies, Allah ("my Lord") knew all their secret motives and plots.

1710. Joseph's message was conveyed by the messenger to the king, who sent for the ladies concerned. Among them came the wife of 'Azīz. "What was this affair?" said the king: "tell me the whole truth." (R).

He is indeed of those
Who are (ever) true (and
virtuous).[1711]

وَإِنَّهُۥ لَمِنَ ٱلصَّٰدِقِينَ

52. "This (say I), in order that
He may know that I
Have never been false
To him in his absence,
And that Allah will never
Guide the snare of the false
ones.[1712]

٥٢ ذَٰلِكَ لِيَعْلَمَ أَنِّي
لَمْ أَخُنْهُ بِٱلْغَيْبِ وَأَنَّ ٱللَّهَ
لَا يَهْدِي كَيْدَ ٱلْخَآئِنِينَ

13
30

53. "Nor do I absolve my own self
(Of blame): the (human) soul
Is certainly prone to evil,[1712-A]
Unless my Lord do bestow
His Mercy: but surely
My Lord is Oft-Forgiving,
Most Merciful."[1713]

٥٣ وَمَآ أُبَرِّئُ نَفْسِيٓ إِنَّ ٱلنَّفْسَ
لَأَمَّارَةُۢ بِٱلسُّوٓءِ إِلَّا مَا رَحِمَ رَبِّيٓ
إِنَّ رَبِّي غَفُورٌ رَّحِيمٌ

54. So the king said:
"Bring him unto me;[1714]
I will take him specially
To serve about my own person."
Therefore when he had spoken

٥٤ وَقَالَ ٱلْمَلِكُ ٱئْتُونِي بِهِۦٓ أَسْتَخْلِصْهُ
لِنَفْسِي فَلَمَّا كَلَّمَهُۥ

1711. The wife of the 'Azīz stood by, while the other ladies answered. Their answer was the answer of Mrs. Grundy, grudgingly acknowledging the truth of Joseph's innocence and high principles, but holding a discreet silence about Mrs. Grundy's own part in egging on the 'Azīz's wife to sin, wrongdoing and revenge. When they had done, she began. She did not mince matters. She acknowledged her own guilt, freely and frankly. This was no time for her even to refer to other ladies—their jealousy, their gross mindedness, their encouragement of all that was frail or evil in herself. (R).

1712. I construe verses 52 and 53 to be a continuation of the speech of the 'Azīz's wife and have translated accordingly. There is both good reason and authority (*e.g.*, Ibn Kathīr) for this. But the majority of Commentators construe verses 52-53 to be spoken by Joseph, in which case they would mean that Joseph was referring to his fidelity to the 'Azīz, that he had never taken advantage of his absence to play false with his wife, although he (Joseph) was human and liable to err. In my view the 'Azīz's wife while fully reprobating her own guilty conduct, claims that she has at least been constant, and that she hopes for mercy, forgiveness, and the capacity to understand at last what true love is. Whatever false charge she made, she made it in a moment of passion and to his face, (never in cold blood, or behind his back).
Guide the snare of the false ones, i.e., allow such snare to attain its goal. (R).

1712-A. *Ammārah*: prone, impelling, headstrong, passionate. See n. 5810 to 75:2.

1713 See n. 1712. I construe this verse to be a continuation of the speech of the wife of the 'Azīz. It is more appropriate to her than to Joseph. (R).

1714. Joseph had not yet appeared before the king. The king's order in the same terms in verse 50 above had led to a message from Joseph and the subsequent public proceedings with the ladies. Now that Joseph's innocence, wisdom, truth, and trustworthiness had been proved, and confirmed by the splendid tribute of the courtier's wife, and Joseph's own manly bearing before the king, the king was much impressed, and took him specially to serve about his own person as his trusty and confidential Wazīr. If, as is probable, the 'Azīz had by this time died (for he is never mentioned again) Joseph succeeded to his office, and he is addressed as 'Azīz in verse 78 below. But Joseph got more than his rank and powers, as specially selected to carry out a great emergency policy to meet the very difficult times of depression that were foretold. He was given plenary powers and the fullest confidence that a king could give to his most trusted and best-proved Wazīr or Prime Minister, with special access to his Person, like a Grand Chamberlain. (R).

To him, he said: "Be assured this day, Thou art, before our own Presence, With rank firmly established. And fidelity fully proved!"[1715]	قَالَ إِنَّكَ ٱلۡيَوۡمَ لَدَيۡنَا مَكِينٌ أَمِينٞ
55. (Joseph) said: "Set me Over the storehouses[1716] Of the land: I will Indeed guard them, As one that knows (Their importance)."	٥٥ قَالَ ٱجۡعَلۡنِي عَلَىٰ خَزَآئِنِ ٱلۡأَرۡضِۖ إِنِّي حَفِيظٌ عَلِيمٞ
56. Thus did we give Established power to Joseph In the land, to take possession[1717] Therein as, when, or where He pleased. We bestow Of Our mercy on whom We please, and We suffer not, To be lost, the reward Of those who do good.	٥٦ وَكَذَٰلِكَ مَكَّنَّا لِيُوسُفَ فِي ٱلۡأَرۡضِ يَتَبَوَّأُ مِنۡهَا حَيۡثُ يَشَآءُۚ نُصِيبُ بِرَحۡمَتِنَا مَن نَّشَآءُۖ وَلَا نُضِيعُ أَجۡرَ ٱلۡمُحۡسِنِينَ
57. But verily the reward Of the Hereafter Is the best, for those Who believe, and are constant In righteousness.[1718]	٥٧ وَلَأَجۡرُ ٱلۡأٓخِرَةِ خَيۡرٞ لِّلَّذِينَ ءَامَنُواْ وَكَانُواْ يَتَّقُونَ

1715. Who was this Pharaoh, and what approximate date could we assign to him? He was probably a king of the Hyksos Dynasty, somewhere between the 19th and the 17th century B.C. See Appendix IV, on Egyptian Chronology and Israel (printed after S. 7).

1716. Joseph had been given plenary authority by the king. He could have enjoyed his dignity, drawn his emoluments, put the hard and perhaps unpopular work on the shoulders of others, and kept to himself the glitter and the kudos. But that was not his way, nor can it indeed be the way of anyone who wants to do real service. He undertook the hardest and most unpopular task himself. Such a task was that of organising reserves in times of plenty, against the lean years to come. He deliberately asked to be put in charge of the granaries and storehouses, and the drudgery of establishing them and guarding them, for the simple reason that he understood that need better than anyone else, and was prepared to take upon himself rather than throw on to another the obloquy of restricting supplies in times of plenty.

1717. What a wonderful example of the working of divine Providence! The boy whom his jealous brothers got rid of by selling him into slavery for a miserable price becomes the most trusted dignitary in a foreign land, chief minister in one of the greatest empires of the world of that day. And this not for himself only, but for his family, for the world at large, and for that noble example of righteousness and strenuous service, which he was to set for all time. According to tradition, Joseph's age was barely 30 at that time!

As, when, or where he pleased: ḥaythu refers to manner, time, or place. He had almost absolute powers, but as his fidelity was fully proved (12:53) these powers were for service rather than for self. (R).

1718. To the righteous, whatever rewards (if any) that come in this world are welcome for the opportunities of service which they open out. But the true and best reward is in the Hereafter.

SECTION 8.

58. Then came Joseph's brethren:[1719]
They entered his presence,
And he knew them,
But they knew him not.

٥٨ وَجَآءَ إِخْوَةُ يُوسُفَ فَدَخَلُوا۟ عَلَيْهِ
فَعَرَفَهُمْ وَهُمْ لَهُۥ مُنكِرُونَ

59. And when he had furnished
Them forth with provisions
(Suitable) for them, he said:
"Bring unto me a brother
Ye have, of the same father
As yourselves, (but a different mother):
See ye not that I pay out
Full measure, and that I
Do provide the best hospitality?[1720]

٥٩ وَلَمَّا جَهَّزَهُم
بِجَهَازِهِمْ قَالَ ٱئْتُونِى بِأَخٍ
لَّكُم مِّنْ أَبِيكُمْ
أَلَا تَرَوْنَ أَنِّىٓ أُوفِى ٱلْكَيْلَ
وَأَنَا۠ خَيْرُ ٱلْمُنزِلِينَ

60. "Now if ye bring him not
To me, ye shall have
No measure (of corn) from me,
Nor shall ye (even) come
Near me."

٦٠ فَإِن لَّمْ تَأْتُونِى بِهِۦ فَلَا
كَيْلَ لَكُمْ عِندِى وَلَا تَقْرَبُونِ

61. They said: "We shall
Certainly seek to get
Our wish about him

٦١ قَالُوا۟ سَنُرَٰوِدُ عَنْهُ

1719. Years pass; the times of prosperity go by; famine holds the land in its grip, and it extends to neighbouring countries. Joseph's preparations are complete. His reserves are ample to meet the calamity. Not only does Egypt bless him, but neighbouring countries send to Egypt to purchase corn. All are received with hospitality, and corn is sold to them according to judicious measure.

Now there has been one sorrow gnawing at Joseph's heart. His poor father Jacob! How he must have wept, as indeed he did, at the loss of his beloved Joseph! And Joseph's little brother Benjamin, born of the same mother as himself; would the other ten brothers, not by the same mother, have any affection for him, or would they treat him, as they treated Joseph? How would the whole family be in these hard times? A sort of answer came when the ten selfish brothers, driven by famine, came from Canaan to buy corn. Joseph, though so great a man, kept the details of the famine department in his own hands: otherwise there might have been waste. But to the public he was a mighty Egyptian administrator, probably in Egyptian dress, and with all the paraphernalia of his rank about him. When his brothers came, he knew them, but they did not know he was Joseph. In their thoughts Joseph was probably some menial slave in a remote houshold, perhaps already starved to death in these hard times!

1720. Joseph treated his brothers liberally. Perhaps he condescended to enter into conversation with these strangers, and enquired about their family. The ten brothers had come. Had they left a father behind them? What sort of a person was he? Very aged? Well, of course he could not come. Had they any other brothers? Doubtless the ten brothers said nothing about their lost Joseph, or told some lie about him. But perhaps their host's kindly insistence brought Benjamin into the conversation. How old was he? Why had they not brought him? Would they bring him next time? Indeed they must, or they would get no more corn, and he—the great Egyptian Wazīr—would not even see them.

From his father:[1721]
Indeed we shall do it."

أَبَاهُ وَإِنَّا لَفَٰعِلُونَ

62. And (Joseph) told his servants
To put their stock in trade[1722]
(With which they have bartered)
Into their saddlebags,
So they should know it only
When they returned to their people,
In order that they
Might come back.[1723]

٦٢ وَقَالَ لِفِتْيَٰنِهِ ٱجْعَلُوا۟
بِضَٰعَتَهُمْ فِى رِحَالِهِمْ لَعَلَّهُمْ
يَعْرِفُونَهَآ إِذَا ٱنقَلَبُوٓا۟ إِلَىٰٓ أَهْلِهِمْ
لَعَلَّهُمْ يَرْجِعُونَ

63. Now when they returned
To their father, they said:
"O our father! No more
Measure of grain shall we get
(Unless we take our brother):
So send our brother with us,
That we may get our measure;
And we will indeed
Take every care of him."[1724]

٦٣ فَلَمَّا رَجَعُوٓا۟ إِلَىٰٓ أَبِيهِمْ قَالُوا۟
يَٰٓأَبَانَا مُنِعَ مِنَّا ٱلْكَيْلُ
فَأَرْسِلْ مَعَنَآ أَخَانَا نَكْتَلْ
وَإِنَّا لَهُۥ لَحَٰفِظُونَ

64. He said: "Shall I trust you
With him with any result
Other than when I trusted you
With his brother aforetime?
But Allah is the best
To take care (of him),
And He is the Most Merciful
Of those who show mercy!"[1725]

٦٤ قَالَ هَلْ ءَامَنُكُمْ عَلَيْهِ إِلَّا كَمَآ
أَمِنتُكُمْ عَلَىٰٓ أَخِيهِ مِن قَبْلُ
فَٱللَّهُ خَيْرٌ حَٰفِظًا
وَهُوَ أَرْحَمُ ٱلرَّٰحِمِينَ

1721. The brothers said: "Certainly, we shall try to beg him of our father, and bring him away with us: we shall certainly comply with your desire." In reality they probably loved Benjamin no more than they loved Joseph. But they must get food when the present supply was exhausted, and they must humour the great Egyptian Wazīr. Note that they do not call Jacob "our father" but "his father": how little they loved their aged father, whom they identified with Joseph and Benjamin! Their trial and their instruction in their duties is now being undertaken by Joseph.

1722. *Biḍā'ah*: stock in trade; capital with which business is carried on; money when it is used as capital for trade. It is better here to suppose that they were bartering goods for grain. *Cf.* 12:19.

1723. It was most important for Joseph's plan that they should come back. If they came back at all, they could not come without Benjamin after what he had told them. As an additional incentive to their coming back, he returns the price of the grain in such a way that they should find it in their saddlebags when they reach home.

1724. On their return they no doubt told Jacob all that had transpired. But to beg Benjamin of him was no easy matter, as Jacob did not trust them and had no cause to trust them after their treatment of Joseph. So they use the argument of urgent necessity for all it is worth.

1725. I construe Jacob's answer to be a flat refusal to let Benjamin go with them. It would be like the former occasion when he trusted Joseph with them and they lost him. Did they talk of taking care of him? The only protection that he trusted was that of Allah. He at least showed mercy to old and young alike. Did man show such mercy? Witness his sad old age and his lost little Joseph! Would they bring down "his grey hairs with sorrow to the grave?"

65. Then when they opened
Their baggage, they found
Their stock in trade had been
Returned to them. They said:
"O our father! What (more)
Can we desire? This our
Stock in trade has been
returned[1726]
To us: so we shall get
(More) food for our family;
We shall take care of our brother;
And add (at the same time)
A full camel's load (of grain
To our provisions).
This is but a small quantity.[1727]

٦٥ وَلَمَّا فَتَحُوا مَتَاعَهُمْ
وَجَدُوا بِضَاعَتَهُمْ رُدَّتْ إِلَيْهِمْ
قَالُوا يَا أَبَانَا مَا نَبْغِي
هَٰذِهِ بِضَاعَتُنَا رُدَّتْ إِلَيْنَا
وَنَمِيرُ أَهْلَنَا وَنَحْفَظُ أَخَانَا
وَنَزْدَادُ كَيْلَ بَعِيرٍ
ذَٰلِكَ كَيْلٌ يَسِيرٌ

66. (Jacob) said: "Never will I
Send him with you until
Ye swear a solemn oath to me,
In Allah's name, that ye
Will be sure to bring him back
To me unless ye are yourselves
Hemmed in (and made
powerless).[1728]
And when they had sworn
Their solemn oath,
He said: "Over all
That we say, be Allah
The Witness and Guardian!"[1729]

٦٦ قَالَ لَنْ أُرْسِلَهُ مَعَكُمْ
حَتَّىٰ تُؤْتُونِ مَوْثِقًا مِنَ اللَّهِ
لَتَأْتُنَّنِي بِهِ إِلَّا
أَنْ يُحَاطَ بِكُمْ
فَلَمَّا آتَوْهُ مَوْثِقَهُمْ
قَالَ اللَّهُ عَلَىٰ مَا نَقُولُ وَكِيلٌ

1726. The ten brothers did not take their father's refusal as final. They opened their saddlebags, and found that the price they had paid for their provisions had been returned to them. They had got the grain free! What more could they desire? The spell which Joseph had woven now worked. If they only went back, this kind Wazīr would give more grain if they pleased him. And the only way to please him was to take back their younger brother with them. It would cost them nothing. Judging by past experience they would get a whole camel's load of grain now. And so they stated their case to the aged father.

1727. Two meanings are possible—either or perhaps both. 'What we have brought now is nothing compared to what we shall get if we humour the whim of the Egyptian Wazīr. And, moreover, Egypt seems to have plenty of grain stored up. What is a camel-load to her Wazīr to give away?'

1728. The appeal to the family's needs in the time of famine at length made Jacob relent, but he exacted a solemn promise from the brothers, under the most religious sanctions, that they would bring Benjamin back to him, unless they were themselves prevented, as the Insurance Policies say "by an act of God," so that they became really powerless. To that promise Jacob called Allah to witness.

1729. This is more than a formula. Allah is invoked as present and witnessing the bargain, and to Him both parties make over the affair to arrange and fulfil.

67. Further he said:
"O my sons! enter not[1730]
All by one gate: enter ye
By different gates. Not that
I can profit you aught
Against Allah (with my advice):
None can command except Allah:
On Him do I put my trust:
And let all that trust
Put their trust on Him."

٦٧ وَقَالَ يَٰبَنِيَّ لَا تَدْخُلُوا۟ مِنۢ بَابٍ وَٰحِدٍ
وَٱدْخُلُوا۟ مِنْ أَبْوَٰبٍ مُّتَفَرِّقَةٍ ۖ وَمَآ أُغْنِى عَنكُم
مِّنَ ٱللَّهِ مِن شَىْءٍ ۖ إِنِ ٱلْحُكْمُ إِلَّا لِلَّهِ ۖ
عَلَيْهِ تَوَكَّلْتُ ۖ وَعَلَيْهِ فَلْيَتَوَكَّلِ
ٱلْمُتَوَكِّلُونَ

68. And when they entered
In the manner their father
Had enjoined, it did not
Profit them in the least
Against (the Plan of) Allah:[1731]
It was but a necessity
Of Jacob's soul, which he[1732]
Discharged. For he was,
By Our instruction, full
Of knowledge (and experience):
But most men know not.[1733]

٦٨ وَلَمَّا دَخَلُوا۟ مِنْ حَيْثُ أَمَرَهُمْ أَبُوهُم
مَّا كَانَ يُغْنِى عَنْهُم مِّنَ ٱللَّهِ مِن شَىْءٍ
إِلَّا حَاجَةً فِى نَفْسِ يَعْقُوبَ قَضَىٰهَا ۚ وَإِنَّهُۥ
لَذُو عِلْمٍ لِّمَا عَلَّمْنَٰهُ وَلَٰكِنَّ أَكْثَرَ
ٱلنَّاسِ لَا يَعْلَمُونَ

C. 112.—When the brothers went back without Benjamin,
(12:69-93.) Jacob was overwhelmed with grief, but he bore

1730. The Commentators refer to a Jewish (or Eastern) custom (or superstition) which forbade members of a numerous family to go together in a mass for fear of "the evil eye". But apart from East or West, or custom or superstition, it would be ridiculous for any large family of ten or eleven to parade together in a procession among strangers. But there was even a better reason in this particular case, which made Jacob's advice sound, and Jacob was, as stated in the next verse, a man of knowledge and experience. Here were eleven strangers dressed alike, in a dress not of the country, talking a strange language, coming in a time of stress, on an errand for which they had no credentials. Would they not attract undue attention and suspicion if they went together? Would they not be taken for spies?—or for men bent on some mischief, theft, or organised crime? Such a suspicion is referred to in verse 73 below. By entering separately they would attract little attention. Jacob very wisely tells them to take all human precautions. But like a Prophet of Allah he warns them that human precautions would be no good if they neglect or run counter to far weightier matters—Allah's Will and Law. Above all, they must try to understand and obey this, and their trust should be on Allah rather than on human usages, institutions, or precautions, however, good and reasonable these might be. (R).

1731. See the last verse and n. 1730. Though they scrupulously observed their father's injunctions to the letter, their hearts were not yet pure, and they got into trouble, as the later story will show. They had the hardihood to cast aspersions on Joseph, not knowing that they were in Joseph's power. And Joseph took a noble revenge by planning a reunion of the whole family and shaming the ten brothers into repentance. He was the instrument for the fulfilment of Allah's Plan.

1732. It is a necessity of a Prophet's soul that he should speak out and teach all that he knows, to the worthy and unworthy alike. This, Jacob did to his unworthy sons, as well as to his worthy sons whom he loved best. It was not for him as a Prophet to guarantee any results. In this case he could not save his sons from getting into trouble merely because they followed the letter of his advice in a small matter. Apply this to the teaching of one who is greater than Jacob. Men who literally observe some small injunctions of the Holy Prophet Muḥammad and neglect the greater principles which he taught cannot blame him for their troubles and difficulties. If they examined the matter, they would find that they brought the troubles on themselves.

1733. The Prophets of Allah are full of knowledge—not as men, but as taught by the grace of Allah, for men, as such, are (as Carlyle said) mostly fools—devoid of knowledge and understanding. (R).

His affliction with patience and faith in Allah.
He refused to be comforted and sent his sons back,
To Egypt. At last Joseph revealed himself,
Forgave them, and sent his shirt by them
To Jacob, to tell him the good news
That Joseph lived and did great work
In Egypt, and had sent for his whole family
To come and rejoice and live in the land
Of Egypt, and be a blessing to all.

SECTION 9.

69. Now when they came
Into Joseph's presence,[1734]
He received his (full) brother[1735]
To stay with him. He said
(To him): "Behold! I am thy (own)
Brother; so grieve not
At aught of their doings."[1736]

٦٩ وَلَمَّا دَخَلُواْ عَلَىٰ يُوسُفَ
ءَاوَىٰٓ إِلَيْهِ أَخَاهُ قَالَ إِنِّيٓ أَنَا۠ أَخُوكَ
فَلَا تَبْتَئِسْ بِمَا كَانُواْ يَعْمَلُونَ

70. At length when he had furnished
Them forth with provisions
(Suitable) for them, he put
The drinking cup into
His brother's saddlebag.
Then shouted out a Crier:
"O ye (in) the Caravan!
Behold! ye are thieves,
Without doubt!"[1737]

٧٠ فَلَمَّا جَهَّزَهُم بِجَهَازِهِمْ
جَعَلَ ٱلسِّقَايَةَ فِى رَحْلِ أَخِيهِ
ثُمَّ أَذَّنَ مُؤَذِّنٌ أَيَّتُهَا ٱلْعِيرُ
إِنَّكُمْ لَسَٰرِقُونَ

1734. The ten brothers, with Benjamin, arrived in Egypt, and waited on the great Wazir. Joseph again received them hospitably, even more so than before, as they had complied with his request to bring Benjamin. No doubt many shrewd and probing questions were asked by Joseph, and no doubt it was clear that Benjamin was one apart from the other ten. Bayḍāwī fills up the picture of the great feast for us. The guests were seated two by two. Benjamin was the odd one, and Joseph courteously took him to his own table.

1735. After the feast the questions of lodgings arose. They were to be accommodated two by two. Again Benjamin was the odd one. What more natural than the Wazir should take him to himself? He thus got a chance of privacy with him. He disclosed his identity to him, charging him to keep it a secret, and to take no notice of any strange doings that might occur. He must have learnt from Benjamin about his father and about the inner doings of the family. He must get them all together into Egypt under his own eye. He had a plan, and he proceeded to put it into execution.

1736. The past tense of *kānū*, combined with the aorist of *ya'malūn*, signifies that the reference is to their brothers' doings, past, present, and future. Benjamin was not to mind what wrongs they had done in the past, or how they behaved in the present or the immediate future. Joseph had a plan that required Benjamin's silence in strange circumstances.

1737. Joseph's plan was to play a practical joke on them, which would achieve two objects. Immediately it would put them into some consternation, but nothing comparable to what he had suffered at their hands. When the plan was unravelled, it would make them thoroughly ashamed of themselves, and dramatically bring home their guilt to them. Secondly, it would give him an excuse to detain Benjamin and bring their aged father into Egypt. He contrived that a valuable drinking cup should be concealed in Benjamin's saddlebag. When it was found after an ostentatious search, he would detain the supposed culprit, and attain his object, as the story relates further on.

71. They said, turning towards them:
"What is it that ye miss?"

٧١ قَالُوا۟ وَأَقْبَلُوا۟ عَلَيْهِم مَّاذَا تَفْقِدُونَ

72. They said: "We miss
The great beaker of the king;
For him who produces it,
Is (the reward of)
A camel load; I
Will be bound by it."

٧٢ قَالُوا۟ نَفْقِدُ صُوَاعَ ٱلْمَلِكِ
وَلِمَن جَآءَ بِهِۦ حِمْلُ بَعِيرٍ
وَأَنَا۠ بِهِۦ زَعِيمٌ

73. (The brothers) said: "By Allah!
Well ye know that we
Came not to make mischief
In the land, and we are
No thieves!"[1738]

٧٣ قَالُوا۟ تَٱللَّهِ لَقَدْ عَلِمْتُم
مَّا جِئْنَا لِنُفْسِدَ فِى ٱلْأَرْضِ وَمَا كُنَّا سَٰرِقِينَ

74. (The Egyptians) said: "What then
Shall be the penalty of this,
If ye are (proved) to have lied?"[1739]

٧٤ قَالُوا۟ فَمَا جَزَٰٓؤُهُۥٓ إِن كُنتُمْ كَٰذِبِينَ

75. They said: "The penalty
Should be that he
In whose saddlebag
It is found, should be held
(As bondman) to atone[1740]
For the (crime). Thus it is
We punish the wrongdoers!"[1741]

٧٥ قَالُوا۟ جَزَٰٓؤُهُۥ مَن وُجِدَ فِى
رَحْلِهِۦ فَهُوَ جَزَٰٓؤُهُۥ ۚ كَذَٰلِكَ
نَجْزِى ٱلظَّٰلِمِينَ

1738. As strangers in a strange land, they were liable to be suspected as spies or men who meditated some unlawful design, or some crime, such as theft, which would be common in a season of scarcity. The brothers protested against the absurdity of such a suspicion after they had been entertained so royally by the Wazīr.

1739. "That might be all very well," said the Egyptians, "but what if it is found by a search that you have in fact abused the Wazīr's hospitality by stealing a valuable cup?"

1740. We must try to picture to ourselves the mentality of the ten. They understood each other perfectly, in their sins as well as in other things. For themselves, the search held out no fears. Besides they had had no opportunity of stealing. But what of that young fellow Benjamin? They were ready to believe anything against him, the more so as the Wazīr's partiality for him had lent a keen edge to their jealousy. Judging by their own standards, they would not be surprised if he had stolen, seeing that he had had such opportunities—sitting at the High Table and staying with the Wazīr. They felt very self-righteous at the same time that they indulged in the luxury of accusing in their thoughts the most innocent of men! Supposing he had stolen, here would be a fine opportunity of getting rid of him. What about their solemn oath to their father? Oh! that was covered by the exception. He had done for himself. They had done all they could to protect him, but they were powerless. The old man could come and see for himself.

1741. This was their family custom. It was of course long anterior to the Mosaic Law, which laid down full restitution for theft, and if the culprit had nothing, he was to be sold for his theft (Exod. xxii. 3). But here the crime was more than theft. It was theft, lying, and the grossest abuse of confidence and hospitality. While the ten felt a secret satisfaction in suggesting the penalty, they were unconsciously carrying out Joseph's plan. Thus the vilest motives often help in carrying out the most beneficient plans.

76\. So he[1742] began (the search)
With their baggage,
Before (he came to) the baggage[1743]
Of his brother: at length
He brought it[1744] out of his
Brother's baggage. Thus did We
Plan for Joseph. He could not
Take his brother by the law
Of the king except that Allah[1745]
Willed it (so). We raise
To degrees (of wisdom) whom[1746]
We please: but over all
Endued with knowledge is One,
The All-Knowing.

(٧٦) فَبَدَأَ بِأَوْعِيَتِهِمْ قَبْلَ وِعَاءِ أَخِيهِ
ثُمَّ ٱسْتَخْرَجَهَا مِن وِعَاءِ أَخِيهِ
كَذَٰلِكَ كِدْنَا لِيُوسُفَ مَا كَانَ
لِيَأْخُذَ أَخَاهُ فِي دِينِ ٱلْمَلِكِ
إِلَّآ أَن يَشَآءَ ٱللَّهُ نَرْفَعُ دَرَجَٰتٍ
مَّن نَّشَآءُ وَفَوْقَ كُلِّ ذِي عِلْمٍ عَلِيمٌ

77\. They said: "If he steals,
There was a brother of his
Who did steal before (him)."[1747]
But these things did Joseph
Keep locked in his heart,
Revealing not the secrets to
them.[1748]

(٧٧) قَالُوٓا۟ إِن يَسْرِقْ فَقَدْ
سَرَقَ أَخٌ لَّهُۥ مِن قَبْلُ فَأَسَرَّهَا يُوسُفُ
فِي نَفْسِهِۦ وَلَمْ يُبْدِهَا لَهُمْ

1742\. The pronoun "he" can only refer to Joseph. He may have been present all the time, or he may just have come up, as the supposed theft of the king's own cup (12:72 above) was a very serious and important affair, and the investigation required his personal supervision. All that his officers did by his orders was his own act. As the lawyers say: *Qui facit per alium, facit per se* (whoever does anything through another, does it himself).

1743\. The Arabic word here used is *wi'ā'i*, plural *aw'iya*, which includes bags, lockers, boxes, or any receptacles in which things are stored. Notice the appropriateness of the words used. The cut was concealed in a saddlebag (*raḥl*), verse 70 above. When it comes to searching, they must search *all* the baggage of every description if the search was to be convincing and effective.

1744\. *It* refers to the drinking cup, the *siqāyah*, which is a feminine noun: hence the feminine pronoun, *hā*, in Arabic.

1745\. Let no one suppose that it was a vulgar or wicked trick, such as we sometimes hear of in police courts, when property is planted on innocent men to get them into trouble. On the contrary, it was a device or stratagem whose purpose was to show up wickedness in its true colours, to give it a chance of repentance, to bring about forgiveness and reconciliation, to give solace to the aged father who had suffered so much, and above all, to further that larger plan for the instruction of the world, which is unfolded in Israel's religious history. Joseph was a Prophet of Allah, but he could not have carried out this plan or taken the first step, of detaining his brother, except with the will and permission of Allah, Whose Plan is universal and for all His creatures. (R).

1746\. If we examine this world's affairs, there are all sorts of plans, and all degrees of folly and wisdom. The wicked ones plan; the foolish ones plan; the simple ones plan; then there are men who think themselves wise and are perhaps thought to be wise, but who are foolish, and they have their plans: and there are degrees of real and beneficent wisdom among men. Allah, the Universal Planner, is above all. Anything good in our wisdom is but a reflection of His wisdom, and His wisdom can even turn folly and wickedness to good.

1747\. The hatred of the ten for Joseph and Benjamin comes out again. They are not only ready to believe evil of Benjamin, but they carry their thoughts back to Joseph and call him a thief as well. They had injured Joseph; and by a false charge of this kind they salve their conscience. Little did they suspect that Joseph was before them, under another guise, and their falsehood and treachery, would soon be exposed.

1748\. There were many secrets: (1) that he was Joseph himself; (2) that his brother, Benjamin, knew him; (3) that there was no guilt in Benjamin, but the whole practical joke was in furtherance of a great plan (see n. 1745 above); (4) that they were giving themselves away, and were unconsciously facilitating the plan, though their motives were not aboveboard.

He (simply) said (to himself):
"Ye are the worse situated;[1749]
And Allah knoweth best
The truth of what ye assert!"

قَالَ أَنتُمْ شَرٌّ مَّكَانًا
وَاللَّهُ أَعْلَمُ بِمَا تَصِفُونَ

78. They said: "O exalted one![1750]
Behold! he has a father,
Aged and venerable, (who will
Grieve for him); so take
One of us in his place;
For we see that thou art
(Gracious) in doing good."

٧٨ قَالُوا يَا أَيُّهَا الْعَزِيزُ إِنَّ لَهُ أَبًا
شَيْخًا كَبِيرًا فَخُذْ أَحَدَنَا مَكَانَهُ
إِنَّا نَرَاكَ مِنَ الْمُحْسِنِينَ

79. He said: "Allah forbid
That we take other than him
With whom we found
Our property: indeed
(If we did so), we should
Be acting wrongfully."[1751]

٧٩ قَالَ مَعَاذَ اللَّهِ أَن نَّأْخُذَ
إِلَّا مَن وَجَدْنَا مَتَاعَنَا عِندَهُ إِنَّا
إِذًا لَّظَالِمُونَ

SECTION 10.

80. Now when they saw
No hope of his (yielding),
They held a conference in private.
The leader among them said:[1752]
"Know ye not that your father
Did take an oath from you
In Allah's name, and how
Before this, ye did fail
In your duty with Joseph?
Therefore will I not leave

٨٠ فَلَمَّا اسْتَيْأَسُوا مِنْهُ خَلَصُوا نَجِيًّا
قَالَ كَبِيرُهُمْ أَلَمْ تَعْلَمُوا أَنَّ أَبَاكُمْ
قَدْ أَخَذَ عَلَيْكُم مَّوْثِقًا مِّنَ اللَّهِ وَمِن
قَبْلُ مَا فَرَّطتُمْ فِي يُوسُفَ فَلَنْ أَبْرَحَ

1749. "Ah!" thought Joseph, "you think that Benjamin is safely out of the way, and that Joseph was got rid of long since! Would you be surprised to know that you have given yourselves away, that you are now in the power of Joseph, and that Joseph is the very instrument of your exposure and (let us hope) of your repentance?"

1750. I have translated the title of *'Azīz* here as "the exalted one" when addressed to Joseph in order not to cause confusion with the other man, the 'Azīz, the Courtier, who had brought Joseph on arrival in Egypt. See 12:30 above, and notes 1677 and 1714. (R).

1751. There is a little sparring now between the Ten and Joseph. They are afraid of meeting their father's wrath, and he holds them strictly to the bargain which they had themselves suggested.

1752. *Kabīr* may mean the eldest. But in 12:78 above, *Kabīr* is distinguished from *Shaykh*, and I have translated the one as "venerable" and the other as "aged". In 20:71, *Kabīr* obviously means "leader" or "chief", and has no reference to age. I therefore translate here by the word "leader", that brother among them who took the most active part in these transactions. His name is not given in the Qur'ān. The eldest brother was Reuben. But according to the biblical story the brother who had taken the most active part in this transaction was Judah, one of the elder brothers, being the fourth son, after Reuben, Simeon, and Levi, and of the same mother as these. It was Judah who stood surety to Jacob for Benjamin (Gen. xliii. 9). It is therefore natural that Judah should, as here, offer to stay behind.

This land until my father
Permits me, or Allah[1753]
Commands me; and He
Is the best to command.

ٱلْأَرْضَ حَتَّىٰ يَأْذَنَ لِيٓ أَبِيٓ
أَوْ يَحْكُمَ ٱللَّهُ لِي ۖ وَهُوَ خَيْرُ ٱلْحَٰكِمِينَ

81. "Turn ye back to your father,
And say, 'O our father!
Behold! thy son committed theft!
We bear witness only to what
We know, and we could not
Well guard against the unseen![1754]

٨١ ٱرْجِعُوٓا۟ إِلَىٰٓ أَبِيكُمْ فَقُولُوا۟ يَٰٓأَبَانَآ
إِنَّ ٱبْنَكَ سَرَقَ وَمَا شَهِدْنَآ إِلَّا
بِمَا عَلِمْنَا وَمَا كُنَّا لِلْغَيْبِ حَٰفِظِينَ

82. "'Ask at the town where
We have been and the caravan
In which we returned,
And (you will find) we are
Indeed telling the truth.'"[1755]

٨٢ وَسْـَٔلِ ٱلْقَرْيَةَ ٱلَّتِي كُنَّا فِيهَا
وَٱلْعِيرَ ٱلَّتِيٓ أَقْبَلْنَا فِيهَا ۖ وَإِنَّا لَصَٰدِقُونَ

83. Jacob said: "Nay, but ye
Have yourselves contrived
A story (good enough) for you.[1756]
So patience is most fitting
(For me). Maybe Allah will
Bring them (back) all
To me (in the end).[1757]
For He is indeed full
Of knowledge and wisdom."

٨٣ قَالَ بَلْ سَوَّلَتْ لَكُمْ أَنفُسُكُمْ أَمْرًا ۖ
فَصَبْرٌ جَمِيلٌ ۖ عَسَى ٱللَّهُ أَن
يَأْتِيَنِي بِهِمْ جَمِيعًا ۚ إِنَّهُۥ هُوَ
ٱلْعَلِيمُ ٱلْحَكِيمُ

84. And he turned away from them,
And said: "How great
Is my grief for Joseph!"

٨٤ وَتَوَلَّىٰ عَنْهُمْ وَقَالَ يَٰٓأَسَفَىٰ عَلَىٰ يُوسُفَ

1753. The pledge he had given was to his father, and in Allah's name. Therefore he was bound both to his father, and to Allah. He must await his father's order and remain here as pledged, unless Allah opened out some other way. For example the Egyptian Wazir might relent: if so, he could go back with Benjamin to his father, and his pledge would be satisfied.

1754. 'He stole in secret and without our knowledge. How could we in the circumstances prevent it?' This may have been a good statement for the other nine brothers, but Judah was himself personally and specially pledged.

1755. To vouch for the truth of the story, the nine brothers are asked by Judah to appeal to their father to enquire at the place where they stayed and the caravan with which they came, and he would find that the facts were as they stated them. The nine brothers came back and told their father as they had been instructed by Judah.

1756. Jacob was absolutely stunned by the story. He knew his darling little Benjamin too well to believe that he had committed theft. He flatly refused to believe it, and called it a cock-and-bull story, which indeed it was, though not in the sense in which he reproached the nine brothers. With the eye of faith he saw clearly the innocence of Benjamin, though he did not see every detail of what had happened.

1757. With the eye of faith he clung to even a larger hope. Perhaps all three of his lost sons would come back—Joseph, Benjamin, and Judah. His faith in Allah was unswerving, although alas! the present facts altogether unnerved him. (R).

And his eyes became white[1758]
With sorrow, and he fell
Into silent melancholy.

وَٱبْيَضَّتْ عَيْنَاهُ مِنَ ٱلْحُزْنِ فَهُوَ كَظِيمٌ

85. They said: "By Allah!
(Never) wilt thou cease
To remember Joseph
Until thou reach the last
Extremity of illness,
Or until thou die!"?[1759]

٨٥ قَالُوا۟ تَٱللَّهِ تَفْتَؤُا۟
تَذْكُرُ يُوسُفَ حَتَّىٰ تَكُونَ حَرَضًا
أَوْ تَكُونَ مِنَ ٱلْهَٰلِكِينَ

86. He said: "I only complain[1760]
Of my distraction and anguish
To Allah, and I know from
Allah[1761]
That which ye know not...

٨٦ قَالَ إِنَّمَآ أَشْكُوا۟ بَثِّى وَحُزْنِىٓ
إِلَى ٱللَّهِ وَأَعْلَمُ مِنَ ٱللَّهِ مَا لَا تَعْلَمُونَ

87. "O my sons! go ye
And enquire about Joseph
And his brother, and never
Give up hope of Allah's
Soothing Mercy:[1762] truly
No one despairs of Allah's
Soothing Mercy, except
Those who have no faith."[1763]

٨٧ يَٰبَنِىَّ ٱذْهَبُوا۟ فَتَحَسَّسُوا۟ مِن يُوسُفَ
وَأَخِيهِ وَلَا تَا۟يْـَٔسُوا۟ مِن رَّوْحِ ٱللَّهِ ۖ إِنَّهُۥ
لَا يَا۟يْـَٔسُ مِن رَّوْحِ ٱللَّهِ إِلَّا ٱلْقَوْمُ ٱلْكَٰفِرُونَ

1758. The old father's grief is indescribable. Yet with what master-strokes it is described here! One sorrow brings up the memory of another and a greater one. 'Benjamin is now gone! Oh but Joseph! his pretty dream of boyhood! his greatness foretold! and now how dark was the world! If he could but weep! Tears might give relief, and his red and swollen eyes might yet regain their light!' But his grief was too deep for tears. His eyes lost their colour, and became a dull white. The light became a mere blur, a white glimmer. Darkness seemed to cover everything. So it was in the outside world. So was it in his mind. His grief was unshared, unexpressed, and uncomplaining. Who could share it? Who could understand it? He bore his sorrow in silence. Yet his faith was undimmed, and he trimmed the lamp of patience, that sovereign virtue for those who have faith.

1759. A speech full of jealousy, taunting malice, and lack of understanding—one that would have driven mad anyone less endowed with patience and wisdom than was Jacob, the Prophet of Allah. It shows that the sons were still unregenerate, though the time of their repentance and reclamation was drawing nigh. The cruel heartlessness of their words is particularly out of place, as Jacob bore his sorrow in silence and complained to no mortal, but poured out his distraction and grief only to Allah, as stated in the next verse.

1760. Jacob's plaint to Allah is about himself, not about Allah's doings. He bewails the distraction of his mind and his occasional breaking out of those bounds of patience which he had set for himself.

1761. He knew of Allah's merciful and beneficent dealings with man in a way his shallow sons did not. And his perfect faith in Allah also told him that all would be well. He never gave up hope for Joseph, as his directions in the next verse show. They may be supposed to have been spoken after a little silence of grief and thought. That silence I have indicated in punctuation by three dots.

1762. The word is *rawḥ*, not *rūḥ*, as some translators have mistakenly construed it. *Rawḥ* includes the idea of a Mercy that stills or calms our distracted state, and is particularly appropriate here in the mouth of Jacob.

1763. Jacob ignores and forgives the sting and malice in the speech of his sons, and like a true Prophet of Allah, still wishes them well, gives them sound advice, and sends them on an errand which is to open their eyes to the wonderful ways of Providence as much as it will bring consolation to his own distressed soul. He asks them to go again in search of Joseph and Benjamin. Perhaps by now he had an idea that they might be together in Egypt. In any case their stock of grain is again low, and they must seek its replenishment in Egypt. (R).

88. Then, when they came
(Back) into (Joseph's) presence[1764]
They said: "O exalted one!
Distress has seized us
And our family: we have
(Now) brought but scanty capital:
So pay us full measure,
(We pray thee), and treat it
As charity to us: for Allah
Doth reward the charitable."

٨٨ فَلَمَّا دَخَلُواْ عَلَيْهِ
قَالُواْ يَٰٓأَيُّهَا ٱلْعَزِيزُ مَسَّنَا
وَأَهْلَنَا ٱلضُّرُّ وَجِئْنَا بِبِضَٰعَةٍ مُّزْجَىٰةٍ
فَأَوْفِ لَنَا ٱلْكَيْلَ وَتَصَدَّقْ عَلَيْنَآ
إِنَّ ٱللَّهَ يَجْزِى ٱلْمُتَصَدِّقِينَ

89. He said: "Know ye
How ye dealt with Joseph[1765]
And his brother, not knowing
(What ye were doing)?"

٨٩ قَالَ هَلْ عَلِمْتُم مَّا فَعَلْتُم بِيُوسُفَ
وَأَخِيهِ إِذْ أَنتُمْ جَٰهِلُونَ

90. They said: "Art thou indeed[1766]
Joseph?" He said, "I am
Joseph, and this is my brother:
Allah has indeed been gracious
To us (all): behold, he that is
Righteous and patient—never
Will Allah suffer the reward
To be lost, of those
Who do right."

٩٠ قَالُوٓاْ أَءِنَّكَ لَأَنتَ يُوسُفُ
قَالَ أَنَا۠ يُوسُفُ وَهَٰذَآ أَخِى
قَدْ مَنَّ ٱللَّهُ عَلَيْنَآ إِنَّهُۥ مَن
يَتَّقِ وَيَصْبِرْ فَإِنَّ ٱللَّهَ
لَا يُضِيعُ أَجْرَ ٱلْمُحْسِنِينَ

91. They said: "By Allah! Indeed
Has Allah preferred thee

٩١ قَالُواْ تَٱللَّهِ لَقَدْ ءَاثَرَكَ ٱللَّهُ

1764. The nine brothers come back to Egypt according to their father's direction. Their first care is to see the Wazīr. They must tell him of all their father's distress and excite his pity, if perchance he might release Benjamin. They would describe the father's special mental distress as well as the distress which was the common lot of all in famine time. They had spent a great part of their capital and stock in trade. They would appeal to his charity. It might please so great a man, the absolute governor of a wealthy state. And they did so. Perhaps they mentioned their father's touching faith, and that brought Joseph out of his shell, as in the next verse.

1765. Joseph now wants to reveal himself and touch their conscience. He had but to remind them of the true facts as to their treatment of their brother Joseph, whom they pretended to have lost. He had by now also learnt from Benjamin what slights and injustice he too had suffered at their hands after Joseph's protection had been removed from him in their home. Had not Joseph himself seen them but too prone to believe the worst of Benjamin and to say the worst of Joseph? But Joseph would be charitable—not only in the sense which they meant when they asked for a charitable grant of grain, but in a far higher sense. He would forgive them and put the most charitable construction on what they did—that they knew not what they were doing!

1766. Their father's words, the way events were shaping themselves, Joseph's questionings, perhaps Benjamin's manner now—not a slave kept in subjection but one in perfect love and understanding with this great Wazīr—perhaps also a recollection of Joseph's boyish dream—all these things had prepared their minds and they ask the direct question. "Art thou Joseph?" They get the direct reply, "Yes, I am Joseph; and if you have still any doubt of my identity, here is Benjamin: ask him. We have suffered much, but patience and right conduct are at last rewarded by Allah!"

Above us, and we certainly
Have been guilty of sin!"[1767]

عَلَيْنَا وَإِن كُنَّا لَخَٰطِـِٔينَ

92. He said: "This day
Let no reproach be (cast)[1768]
On you: Allah will forgive you,
And He is the Most Merciful
Of those who show mercy!

٩٢ قَالَ لَا تَثْرِيبَ عَلَيْكُمُ ٱلْيَوْمَ
يَغْفِرُ ٱللَّهُ لَكُمْ وَهُوَ أَرْحَمُ ٱلرَّٰحِمِينَ

93. "Go with this my shirt,[1769]
And cast it over the face
Of my father: he will
Come to see (clearly). Then come
Ye (here) to me together
With all your family."

٩٣ ٱذْهَبُوا۟ بِقَمِيصِى هَٰذَا
فَأَلْقُوهُ عَلَىٰ وَجْهِ أَبِى يَأْتِ بَصِيرًا
وَأْتُونِى بِأَهْلِكُمْ أَجْمَعِينَ

C. 113.—Jacob was comforted with the news.
(12:94-111.) The whole family moved to Egypt,
Where Joseph received them with honour.
He forgave his brothers, thanked and praised
Allah, and lived and died a righteous man.
So the story shows how the Plan of Allah
Doth work without fail: it defeats
The wiles of the wicked, turns evil to good,
And ever leads those who are true
To beatitudes undreamt of. So
Did it happen in Al Muṣṭafā's life.
Will man not learn to rely on Allah
As the only Reality, turning away
From all that is fleeting or untrue?

1767. The scales fall from the eyes of the brothers. We may suppose that they had joined Judah at this interview, and perhaps what Judah had seen when he was alone helped in the process of their enlightenment. They are convicted of sin out of their own mouths, and now there is no *arrier pensee*, no reserve thought, in their minds. They freely confess their wrongdoing, and the justice of Joseph's preferment.

1768. Joseph is most generous. He is glad that they have at last seen the significance of what happened. But he will not allow them at this great moment of reconciliation to dwell on their conduct with reproaches against themselves. There is more urgent work to do. An aged and beloved father is eating out his heart in far Canaan in love and longing for his Joseph, and he must be told all immediately, and "comforted in body, mind, and estate," and so he tells the brothers to hurry back immediately with his shirt as a sign of recognition, as a proof of these wonderful happenings.

1769. It will be remembered that they had covered their crime by taking his shirt, putting on the stains of blood, and pretending that he had been killed by a wolf: see above, 12:17-18. Now that they have confessed their crime and been forgiven, and they have joyful news to tell Jacob about Joseph. Joseph gives them another shirt of his to prove the truth of their story. It is rich shirt, befitting a ruler of Egypt, to prove his good fortune, and yet perhaps its design and many colours (12:18. n. 1651) were reminiscent of the lost Joseph. The first shirt plunged Jacob into grief. This one will now restore him. See the verses following.

SECTION 11.

94. When the Caravan left (Egypt),
Their father said: "I do indeed
Scent the presence of Joseph:[1770]
Nay, think me not a dotard."

﴿٩٤﴾ وَلَمَّا فَصَلَتِ ٱلْعِيرُ قَالَ أَبُوهُمْ
إِنِّى لَأَجِدُ رِيحَ يُوسُفَ لَوْلَآ أَن تُفَنِّدُونِ

95. They[1771] said: "By Allah!
Truly thou art in
Thine old wandering mind."

﴿٩٥﴾ قَالُوا۟ تَٱللَّهِ إِنَّكَ لَفِى ضَلَٰلِكَ ٱلْقَدِيمِ

96. Then when the bearer[1772]
Of the good news came,
He cast (the shirt)
Over his face, and he
Forthwith[1773] regained clear
sight.[1774]

﴿٩٦﴾ فَلَمَّآ أَن جَآءَ ٱلْبَشِيرُ
أَلْقَىٰهُ عَلَىٰ وَجْهِهِۦ
فَٱرْتَدَّ بَصِيرًا

He said: "Did I not say
To you, 'I know from Allah
That which ye know not?' "[1775]

قَالَ أَلَمْ أَقُل لَّكُمْ
إِنِّىٓ أَعْلَمُ مِنَ ٱللَّهِ مَا لَا تَعْلَمُونَ

97. They said: "O our father!
Ask for us forgiveness
For our sins, for we
Were truly at fault."

﴿٩٧﴾ قَالُوا۟ يَٰٓأَبَانَا ٱسْتَغْفِرْ لَنَا
ذُنُوبَنَآ إِنَّا كُنَّا خَٰطِـِٔينَ

1770. Literally, 'I feel the scent, or the air, or the atmosphere or the breath of Joseph'; for *rīh* has all these significations. Or we might translate, 'I feel the presence of Joseph in the air'. When a long-lost friend is about to be found or heard of, many people have a sort of presentiment of it, which they call telepathy. In Jacob's case it was more definite. He had always had faith that Joseph was living and that his dream would be realised. Now that faith was proved true by his own sons; they had been undutiful, and hard, and ignorant; and circumstances had converged to prove it to them by ocular demonstration. Jacob's soul was more sensitive. No wonder he knew already before the news was actually brought to him.

1771. "They" must be the people around him, before the brothers actually arrived. These same brothers had sedulously cultivated the calumny that their father was an old dotard, and everybody around believed it, even after its authors had to give it up. Thus lies die hard, once they get a start.

1772. We may suppose this to have been Judah (see notes 1752 and 1753 above) who was pledged to his father for Benjamin, and who could now announce the good news not only of Benjamin but of Joseph. We can imagine him hurrying forward, to be the first to tell the news, though the plural pronoun for those whom Jacob addresses in this verse, and for those who reply in the next verse, shows that all the brothers practically arrived together.

1773. The particle *fa* ("then") has here the force of "forthwith".

1774. Jacob's sight had grown dim; his eyes had become white with much sorrow for Joseph (see 12:84 above). Both his physical and mental vision now became clear and bright as before.

1775. He had said this (12:86) when everything was against him, and his sons were scoffers. Now they themselves have come to say that his faith was justified and his vision was true.

98. He said: "Soon[1776] will I
Ask my Lord for forgiveness
For you: for He is indeed
Oft-Forgiving, Most Merciful."

قَالَ سَوْفَ أَسْتَغْفِرُ لَكُمْ رَبِّيٓ إِنَّهُۥ هُوَ ٱلْغَفُورُ ٱلرَّحِيمُ ﴿٩٨﴾

99. Then when they entered[1777]
The presence of Joseph,
He provided a home
For his parents with himself,
And said: "Enter ye[1778]
Egypt (all) in safety
If it please Allah."

فَلَمَّا دَخَلُوا۟ عَلَىٰ يُوسُفَ ءَاوَىٰٓ إِلَيْهِ أَبَوَيْهِ وَقَالَ ٱدْخُلُوا۟ مِصْرَ إِن شَآءَ ٱللَّهُ ءَامِنِينَ ﴿٩٩﴾

100. And he raised his parents
High on the throne (of dignity),[1779]
And they fell down in prostration,
(All) before him.[1779-A] He said:
"O my father! this is
The fulfilment of my vision
Of old! Allah hath made it
Come true! He was indeed
Good to me when He
Took me out of prison

وَرَفَعَ أَبَوَيْهِ عَلَى ٱلْعَرْشِ وَخَرُّوا۟ لَهُۥ سُجَّدًا ۖ وَقَالَ يَٰٓأَبَتِ هَٰذَا تَأْوِيلُ رُءْيَٰىَ مِن قَبْلُ قَدْ جَعَلَهَا رَبِّى حَقًّا ۖ وَقَدْ أَحْسَنَ بِىٓ إِذْ أَخْرَجَنِى مِنَ ٱلسِّجْنِ ﴿١٠٠﴾

1776. He fully intended to do this, but the most injured party was Joseph, and it was only fair that Joseph should be consulted. In fact Joseph had already forgiven his brothers all their past, and his father could confidently look forward to Joseph joining in the wish of the whole family to turn to Allah through their aged father Jacob in his prophetic office.

1777. At length the whole family arrived in Egypt and were reunited with Joseph. They were all entertained and provided with homes. But the parents were treated with special honour, as was becoming both to Joseph's character and ordinary, family ethics. His mother Rachel had long been dead, but he had been brought up by his mother's sister Leah, whom his father had also married. Leah was now his mother. They were lodged with Joseph himself.

1778. This is in Arabic in the plural, not in the dual number. The welcome is for all to Egypt, and under the auspices of the Wazir of Egypt. They came, therefore, under Allah's will, to a double sense of security: Egypt was secure from the famine unlike the neighbouring countries; and they were to be cared for by the highest in the land.

1779. Certainly metaphorically: probably also literally. By Eastern custom the place of honour at a ceremonial reception is on a seat on a dais, with a special cushion of honour, such as is assigned to a bridegroom at his reception. To show his high respect for his parents, Joseph made them sit on a throne of dignity. On the other hand, his parents and his brothers—all performed the ceremony of prostration before Joseph in recognition of his supreme rank in Egypt under the Pharaoh. And thus was fulfilled the dream or vision of his youth (12:4 above, and n. 1633).

1779-A. The ceremony of prostration for paying respect might have been allowed at the time of previous prophets, but with the advent of the complete and final revelation prostration before anyone other than Allah is a grave sin strictly prohibited. (Eds.).

And brought you (all here)[1780]
Out of the desert,
(Even) after Satan had sown
Enmity between me and my
brothers.
Verily my Lord understandeth
Best the mysteries of all
That he planneth to do.
For verily He is full
Of knowledge and wisdom.

وَجَآءَ بِكُم مِّنَ ٱلْبَدْوِ
مِنۢ بَعْدِ أَن نَّزَغَ ٱلشَّيْطَٰنُ
بَيْنِى وَبَيْنَ إِخْوَتِىٓ
إِنَّ رَبِّى لَطِيفٌ لِّمَا يَشَآءُ
إِنَّهُۥ هُوَ ٱلْعَلِيمُ ٱلْحَكِيمُ

101. "O my Lord! Thou hast
Indeed bestowed on me
Some power, and taught me
Something of the interpretation[1781]
Of dreams and events—O thou
Creator of the heavens[1782]
And the earth! Thou art
My Protector in this world
And in the Hereafter.
Take Thou my soul (at death)
As one submitting to Thy Will
(As a Muslim), and unite me
With the righteous."[1783]

١٠١ رَبِّ قَدْ ءَاتَيْتَنِى مِنَ ٱلْمُلْكِ
وَعَلَّمْتَنِى مِن تَأْوِيلِ ٱلْأَحَادِيثِ
فَاطِرَ ٱلسَّمَٰوَٰتِ وَٱلْأَرْضِ
أَنتَ وَلِىِّۦ فِى ٱلدُّنْيَا
وَٱلْءَاخِرَةِ
تَوَفَّنِى مُسْلِمًا
وَأَلْحِقْنِى بِٱلصَّٰلِحِينَ

1780. Note how modest Joseph is throughout. The first things he thinks of among Allah's gracious favours to him are: (1) that he was brought out of prison and publicly proclaimed to be honest and virtuous; and (2) that his dear father was restored to him, as well as the brothers who had persecuted him all his life. He will say nothing against them personally. In his *husn ẓann* (habit of interpreting everyone and everything in the most favourable and charitable light), he looks upon them as having been misled. It was Satan (the power of Evil) that set them against him. But now all is rectified by the grace of Allah, to Whom he renders due praise.

Latif: see n. 2844 to 22:63; the fourth meaning mentioned there applies here, with echoes of the other meanings.

1781. Then he turns to Allah in prayer, and again his modesty is predominant. He held supreme power under the king, but he calls it "some power" or authority. His reading of events and dreams had saved millions of lives in the great Egyptian famine; yet he refers to it as "something of the interpretation of dreams and events". And he takes no credit to himself. "All this," he says, "was Thy gift, O Allah! For such things can only come from the Creator of the heavens and the earth."

1782. Power in the doing of things as well as power in intelligent forecasts and plans—both must look to Allah: otherwise the deed and the plan would be futile.

1783. Joseph's prayer may be analysed thus: (1) I am nothing; all power and knowledge are Thine; (2) such things can only come from Thee, for Thou art the Creator of all; (3) none can protect me from danger and wrong, but only Thou; (4) Thy protection I need both in this world and the next; (5) may I till death remain constant to Thee; (6) may I yield up my soul to Thee in cheerful submission to Thy will; (7) in this moment of union with my family after many partings let me think of the final union with the great spiritual family of the righteous. How marvellously apt to the occasion!

102. Such is one of the stories
Of what happened unseen,[1784]
Which We reveal by inspiration
Unto thee: nor wast thou[1785]
(Present) with them when they
Concerted their plans together
In the process of weaving their
plots.

ذَٰلِكَ مِنْ أَنۢبَآءِ ٱلْغَيْبِ نُوحِيهِ إِلَيْكَ ۖ وَمَا كُنتَ لَدَيْهِمْ إِذْ أَجْمَعُوٓا۟ أَمْرَهُمْ وَهُمْ يَمْكُرُونَ ﴿١٠٢﴾

103. Yet no faith will
The greater part of mankind
Have, however ardently
Thou dost desire it.[1786]

وَمَآ أَكْثَرُ ٱلنَّاسِ وَلَوْ حَرَصْتَ بِمُؤْمِنِينَ ﴿١٠٣﴾

104. And no reward dost thou ask
Of them for this: it is
No less than a Message
For all creatures.[1787]

وَمَا تَسْـَٔلُهُمْ عَلَيْهِ مِنْ أَجْرٍ ۚ إِنْ هُوَ إِلَّا ذِكْرٌ لِّلْعَٰلَمِينَ ﴿١٠٤﴾

SECTION 12.

105. And how many Signs
In the heavens and the earth

وَكَأَيِّن مِّنْ ءَايَةٍ فِى ٱلسَّمَٰوَٰتِ وَٱلْأَرْضِ ﴿١٠٥﴾

1784. The story is finished. But is it a story? It is rather a recital of forces and motives, thoughts and feelings, complications and results, ordinarily not seen by men. However much they concert their plans and unite their forces, whatever dark plots they back with all their resources—the plan of Allah works irresistibly, and sweeps away all their machinations. The good win through in the end, but not always as they planned; the evil are foiled, and often their very plots help the good. What did the brothers desire in trying to get rid of Joseph, and what actually happened? How the Courtier's wife, encouraged by the corrupt women of her acquaintance, tried and failed to seduce Joseph and how Allah listened to his prayer and saved him from her vile designs? How wrong was it of the cupbearer to forget Joseph, and yet how his very forgetfulness kept Joseph safe and undisturbed in prison until the day came when he should tackle the great problems of Pharaoh's kingdom? With every character in the story there are problems, and the whole is a beautifully balanced picture of the working of Allah's Providence in man's chequered destiny. (R).

1785. The Holy Prophet was no actor in those scenes; yet by inspiration he was able to expound them in the Divine Light, as they had never been expounded before, whether in the Pentateuch or by any Seer before him. And allegorically they figured his own story—how his own brethren sought to betray and kill him, how by Allah's Providence he was not only saved but he won through. (R).

1786. In spite of such an exposition and such a convincing illustration, how few men really have true faith—such a faith as Jacob had in the old story, or Muḥammad the Chosen One had, in the story which was actually unfolding itself on the world's stage when this Sūrah was revealed, shortly before the Hijrah? Al Muṣṭafā's ardent wish and faith was to save his people and all mankind from the graceless condition of want of faith. But his efforts were flouted, and he had to leave his home and suffer all kinds of persecution; but, like Joseph, and more than Joseph, he was marked out for great work, which he finally achieved.

1787. The Divine Message was priceless; it was not for the Messenger's personal profit, nor did he ask of men any reward for bringing it for their benefit. It was for all creatures—literally, for all the worlds, as explained in 1:2. n. 20.

Do they pass by? Yet they
Turn (their faces) away
from them![1788]

يَمُرُّونَ عَلَيْهَا وَهُمْ عَنْهَا مُعْرِضُونَ

106. And most of them
Believe not in Allah
Without associating (others
As partners) with Him![1789]

١٠٦ وَمَا يُؤْمِنُ أَكْثَرُهُم بِاللَّهِ
إِلَّا وَهُم مُّشْرِكُونَ

107. Do they then feel secure
From the coming against them
Of the covering veil[1790]
Of the wrath of Allah—
Or of the coming against them
Of the (final) Hour
All of a sudden[1791]
While they perceive not?

١٠٧ أَفَأَمِنُوٓا۟ أَن تَأْتِيَهُمْ
غَٰشِيَةٌ مِّنْ عَذَابِ ٱللَّهِ
أَوْ تَأْتِيَهُمُ ٱلسَّاعَةُ بَغْتَةً
وَهُمْ لَا يَشْعُرُونَ

108. Say thou: "This is my Way:
I do invite unto Allah—
On evidence clear as
The seeing with one's eyes—[1792]
I and whoever follows me.
Glory to Allah! and never
Will I join gods with Allah!"

١٠٨ قُلْ هَٰذِهِۦ سَبِيلِىٓ أَدْعُوٓا۟ إِلَى ٱللَّهِ
عَلَىٰ بَصِيرَةٍ أَنَا۠ وَمَنِ ٱتَّبَعَنِى
وَسُبْحَٰنَ ٱللَّهِ وَمَآ أَنَا۠ مِنَ ٱلْمُشْرِكِينَ

1788. Not only can we learn through Scripture of the working of Allah's providence in human history and the history of individual souls, but also His Signs are scattered literally throughout nature—throughout Creation—for all who have eyes to see. And yet man is so arrogant that he turns away his very eyes from them!

1789. Even if people profess a nominal faith in Allah, they corrupt it by believing in other things as if they were Allah's partners, or had some share in the shaping of the world's destinies! In some circles, it is idolatry, the worship of stocks and stones. In others, it is Christolatry and Mariolatry, or the deification of heroes and men of renown. In others it is the powers of Nature or of Life, or of the human intellect personified in Science or Art or invention, and this is the more common form of modern idolatry. Others again worship mystery, or imaginary powers of good or even evil: greed and fear are mixed up with these forms of worship. Islam calls us to worship Allah, the One True God, and Him only. (R).

1790. *Ghāshīyah* = covering veil, pall; used for the Judgement to come, which will be so dark and appalling as to hide up all other and petty things, and be the one great reality for the souls that were slaves to evil.

1791. The metaphor is changed, from intensity of darkness to suddenness of time. It will come before they are aware of it. Let them not feel any sense of safety in sin.

1792. Islam holds fast to the one central fact in the spiritual world—the unity of Allah, and all Reality springing from Him and Him alone. There can be no one and nothing in competition with that one and only Reality. It is the essence of Truth. All other ideas or existences, including our perception of Self, are merely relative—mere projections from the wonderful faculties which He has given to us. This is not, to us, mere hypothesis. It is in our inmost experience. In the physical world, they say that seeing is believing. In our inner world this sense of Allah is as clear as sight in the physical world. Therefore, Al Muṣṭafā and those who really follow him in the truest sense of the world, call all the world to see this Truth, feel this experience, follow this Way. They will never be distracted by metaphysical speculations, whose validity will always be doubtful, nor be deluded with phantoms which lead men astray.

109. Nor did We send before thee
(As Messengers) any but men,[1793]
Whom We did inspire—
(Men) living in human habitations.
Do they not travel
Through the earth, and see
What was the end
Of those before them?
But the home of the Hereafter[1794]
Is best, for those who do right.
Will ye not then understand?

(١٠٩) وَمَآ أَرْسَلْنَا مِن قَبْلِكَ إِلَّا رِجَالًا
نُّوحِىٓ إِلَيْهِم مِّنْ أَهْلِ ٱلْقُرَىٰٓ ۗ
أَفَلَمْ يَسِيرُوا۟ فِى ٱلْأَرْضِ فَيَنظُرُوا۟
كَيْفَ كَانَ عَـٰقِبَةُ ٱلَّذِينَ مِن قَبْلِهِمْ ۗ
وَلَدَارُ ٱلْـَٔاخِرَةِ خَيْرٌ لِّلَّذِينَ ٱتَّقَوْا۟ ۗ
أَفَلَا تَعْقِلُونَ

110. (Respite will be granted)
Until, when the messengers
Give up hope (of their people)
And (come to) think that they
Were treated as liars,[1795]
There reaches them Our help,
And those whom We will
Are delivered into safety.
But never will be warded off
Our punishment from those
Who are in sin.

(١١٠) حَتَّىٰٓ إِذَا ٱسْتَيْـَٔسَ ٱلرُّسُلُ
وَظَنُّوٓا۟ أَنَّهُمْ قَدْ كُذِبُوا۟
جَآءَهُمْ نَصْرُنَا
فَنُجِّىَ مَن نَّشَآءُ ۖ
وَلَا يُرَدُّ بَأْسُنَا عَنِ
ٱلْقَوْمِ ٱلْمُجْرِمِينَ

111. There is, in their stories,[1796]
Instruction for men endued
With understanding. It is not
A tale invented, but a
confirmation

(١١١) لَقَدْ كَانَ فِى قَصَصِهِمْ عِبْرَةٌ لِّأُو۟لِى
ٱلْأَلْبَـٰبِ ۗ مَا كَانَ حَدِيثًا يُفْتَرَىٰ
وَلَـٰكِن تَصْدِيقَ

1793. It was men that Allah sent as His Messengers to explain Him to men. He did not send angels or gods. Into His chosen men He breathed His inspiration, so that they could see truer than other men. But they were men living with men—in men's habitations in town or country; not recluses or cenobites, who had no personal experience of men's affairs and could not be teachers of men in the fullest sense. Their deeds tell their own tale.

1794. The righteous, the men of Allah, had, as in Joseph's history, some evidence of Allah's Providence in this very world with all its imperfections as reflecting our imperfections. But this world is of no real consequence to them. Their home is in the Hereafter. Joseph's earthly home was in Canaan: but he attained his glory elsewhere; and his spiritual Home is in the great Society of the Righteous (3:39).

1795. *Ẓannū* (comes to think): I construe the nominative of this verb to be "the messengers" in agreement with the best authorities. *Kudhibū* is the usual reading, though *Kudhdhibū*, the alternative reading, also rests on good authority. I construe the meaning to be: that Allah gives plenty of rope to the wicked (as in Joseph's story) until His own Messengers feel almost that it will be hopeless to preach to them and come to consider themselves branded as liars by an unbelieving world; that the breaking-point is then reached; that Allah's help then comes swiftly to His men, and they are delivered from persecution and danger, while the wrath of Allah overtakes sinners, and nothing can then ward it off. This interpretation has good authority behind it, though there are differences of opinion.

1796. *Their stories, i.e.*, the stories of the Prophets or of the wicked; for the two threads intertwine, as in Joseph's story.

Of what went before it—[1797]
A detailed exposition
Of all things, and a Guide
And a Mercy to any such
As believe.

ٱلَّذِى بَيْنَ يَدَيْهِ وَتَفْصِيلَ كُلِّ شَىْءٍ
وَهُدًى وَرَحْمَةً لِّقَوْمٍ يُؤْمِنُونَ

1797. A story like that of Joseph is not a purely imaginary fable. The People of the Book have it in their sacred literature. It is confirmed here in its main outline, but here there is a detailed spiritual exposition that will be found nowhere in earlier literature. The exposition covers all sides of human life. If properly understood, it gives valuable lessons to guide our conduct—an instance of Allah's grace and mercy to people who will go to Him in faith and put their affairs in His hands.

INTRODUCTION TO SŪRAH 13—*AL RA'D*

The chronological place of this Sūrah and the general argument of Sūrahs 10 to 15 has been described in the Introduction to S. 10.

The special argument of this Sūrah deals with that aspect of Allah's revelation of Himself to man and His dealings with him, which is concerned with certain contrasts which are here pointed out. There is the revelation of the Prophets, which comes in spoken words adapted to the language of the various men and groups of men to whom it comes; and there is the parallel revelation or Signs in the constant laws of external nature, on this earth and in the visible heavens. There is the contrast between recurring life and death already in the external world: why should men disbelieve in the life after death? They mock at the idea of punishment because it is deferred: but can they not see Allah's power and glory in thunder and the forces of nature? All creation praises Him: it is the good that endures and the evil that is swept away like froth or scum. Not only in miracles but in the normal working of the world, are shown Allah's power and mercy. What is Punishment in this world, compared to that in the life to come? Even here there are Signs of the working of his law: plot or plan as men will, it is Allah's Will that must prevail. This is illustrated in Joseph's story in the preceding Sūrah.

Summary—The Book of Revelation is true, and is confirmed by the Signs to be seen in visible nature. Allah Who created such mighty forces in outer nature can raise up man again after death. Allah's knowledge is all-encompassing: so are His power and goodness (13:1-18, and C. 114).

The righteous seek the pleasure of Allah and find Peace; the evil ones break His Law, cavil and dispute, and reject faith; the wrath of Allah will take them unawares, but in His Own good time (13:19-31, and C. 115).

So was it with Prophets before: they were mocked, but the mockers were destroyed, while the righteous rejoiced and were established (13:32-43, and C. 116).

C. 114.—Allah's Truth comes to man in revelation
(13:1-18.) And in nature. How noble are His works!
How sublime His government of the world!
They all declare forth His glory!
Yet man must strangely resist Faith,
And ask to see the Signs of His power
Rather than the Signs of His Mercy!
Doth not His knowledge search through
The most hidden things? Are not
Lightning and Thunder the Signs of His Might
As well as of His Mercy? He alone
Is Worthy of praise, and His Truth
Will stand when all vanities pass
Away like scum on the torrent of Time.

Sūrah 13.

Al Ra'd (The Thunder)

In the name of Allah, Most Gracious,
Most Merciful.

بِسْمِ ٱللَّهِ ٱلرَّحْمَٰنِ ٱلرَّحِيمِ

1. Alif Lām Mīm Rā.[1798] These are
The Signs (or Verses)[1799]
Of the Book: that which
Hath been revealed unto thee
From thy Lord is the Truth;
But most men believe not.

١ الٓمٓر
تِلْكَ ءَايَٰتُ ٱلْكِتَٰبِ
وَٱلَّذِىٓ أُنزِلَ إِلَيْكَ مِن رَّبِّكَ ٱلْحَقُّ
وَلَٰكِنَّ أَكْثَرَ ٱلنَّاسِ لَا يُؤْمِنُونَ

2. Allah is He Who raised
The heavens without any pillars[1800]
That ye can see;
Then He established Himself
On the Throne (of Authority);[1801]
He has subjected the sun
And the moon (to his Law)!
Each one runs (its course)
For a term appointed.
He doth regulate all affairs,[1802]
Explaining the Signs in detail,

٢ ٱللَّهُ ٱلَّذِى رَفَعَ ٱلسَّمَٰوَٰتِ
بِغَيْرِ عَمَدٍ تَرَوْنَهَا
ثُمَّ ٱسْتَوَىٰ عَلَى ٱلْعَرْشِ
وَسَخَّرَ ٱلشَّمْسَ وَٱلْقَمَرَ
كُلٌّ يَجْرِى لِأَجَلٍ مُّسَمًّى
يُدَبِّرُ ٱلْأَمْرَ يُفَصِّلُ ٱلْءَايَٰتِ

1798. For Alif, Lām, Mīm, see 2:1, n. 25. For Alif, Lām, Rā', see Introduction to S. 10. For abbreviated Letters generally see Appendix I. Here there seems to be a combination of the groups Alif, Lām, Mīm and Alif, Lām, Rā'. We consider here not only the beginning (Alif), the middle (Lām), and the end (Mīm), of man's spiritual history, but also the immediate future of the interior of our organisation, such as it appeared to our Ummah towards the close of the Makkan period. But in trying to determine their meaning, we must not be dogmatic. The befitting attitude is to say: Allah knows best. (R).

1799. *Cf.* 10:1, n. 1382.

1800. Should we construe the clause "that ye can see" to refer to "pillars" or "to the heavens"? Either is admissible, but I prefer the former. The heavens are supported on no pillars that we can see. What we see is the blue vault of heaven, but there are invisible forces or conditions created by Allah, which should impress us with His power and glory.

1801. *Cf.* 10:3, and n. 1386. We must not think that anything came into being by itself or carries out its functions by itself. Allah is the active Force through which everything has its life and being and through which everything is maintained and supported, even though fixed laws are established for its regulation and government. The "term appointed" limits the duration of their functioning: its ultimate return is to Allah, as its beginning proceeded from Allah.

1802. *Cf.* 10:31, n. 1425. Where the laws of nature are fixed, and everything runs according to its appointed course, the government and regulation behind it is still that of Allah. Where there is limited free will as in man, yet the ultimate source of man's faculties is Allah. Allah cares for His creatures. He does not, as in the idea of polytheistic Greece, sit apart on Olympus, careless of His creatures.

That ye may believe with certainty In the meeting with your Lord.[1803]	لَعَلَّكُم بِلِقَاءِ رَبِّكُمْ تُوقِنُونَ
3. And it is He Who spread out The earth, and set thereon Mountains standing firm, And (flowing) rivers: and fruit Of every kind He made In pairs, two and two:[1804] He draweth the Night as a veil[1805] O'er the Day. Behold, verily In these things there are Signs For those who consider!	٣ وَهُوَ ٱلَّذِى مَدَّ ٱلْأَرْضَ وَجَعَلَ فِيهَا رَوَٰسِىَ وَأَنْهَٰرًا وَمِن كُلِّ ٱلثَّمَرَٰتِ جَعَلَ فِيهَا زَوْجَيْنِ ٱثْنَيْنِ يُغْشِى ٱلَّيْلَ ٱلنَّهَارَ إِنَّ فِى ذَٰلِكَ لَءَايَٰتٍ لِّقَوْمٍ يَتَفَكَّرُونَ
4. And in the earth are tracts (Diverse though) neighbouring, And gardens of vines And fields sown with corn, And palm trees—growing[1806] Out of single roots or otherwise: Watered with the same water, Yet some of them We make More excellent than others to eat.[1807] Behold, verily in these things There are Signs for those Who understand!	٤ وَفِى ٱلْأَرْضِ قِطَعٌ مُّتَجَٰوِرَٰتٌ وَجَنَّٰتٌ مِّنْ أَعْنَٰبٍ وَزَرْعٌ وَنَخِيلٌ صِنْوَانٌ وَغَيْرُ صِنْوَانٍ يُسْقَىٰ بِمَآءٍ وَٰحِدٍ وَنُفَضِّلُ بَعْضَهَا عَلَىٰ بَعْضٍ فِى ٱلْأُكُلِ إِنَّ فِى ذَٰلِكَ لَءَايَٰتٍ لِّقَوْمٍ يَعْقِلُونَ

1803. One manifestation of His caring for His creatures, even where a limited amount of free will is granted for their development, is that He is careful to explain His Signs both in nature and in express and detailed revelation through His Messengers, lest man should have any doubts whether he has to return ultimately to his Lord and account for all his actions during the "term appointed," when he was given some initiative by way of trial and preparation. If man attends carefully to the Signs, he should have no doubt whatever.

1804. I think that this refers to sex in plants, and I see M.P. has translated accordingly. Plants like animals have their reproductive apparatus—male stamens and female pistils. In most cases the same flower combines both stamens and pistils, but in some cases these organs are specialised in separate flowers, and in some cases, even in separate trees. The date palm of Arabia and the Papaya of India, are instances of fruit trees which are unisexual.

1805. *Cf.* 7:54 and n. 1032. The whole passage there may be compared with the whole passage here. Both their similarity and their variation show how closely reasoned each argument is, with expressions exactly appropriate to each occasion.

1806. Does "growing out of single roots or otherwise" qualify "palm trees" or "vines" and "corn" as well? The former construction is adopted by the classical Commentators: in which case the reference is to the fact either that two or more palm trees occasionally grow out of a single root, or that palm trees grow sometimes as odd trees and sometimes in great thick clusters. If the latter construction is adopted, the reference would be to the fact that date palm (and palms generally) and some other plants arise out of a single taproot, while the majority of trees arise out of a network of roots that spread out extensively. Here is adaptation to soil and water conditions—another Sign or wonder of Creation.

1807. The date palm, the crops of food-grains, and the grapevine are all fed by the same kind of water, yet how different the harvests which they yield! And that applies to all vegetation. The fruit or eatable produce may vary in shape, size, colour, flavour, etc., in endless variety.

5. If thou dost marvel
(At their want of faith),
Strange is their saying:
"When we are (actually) dust,[1808]
Shall we indeed then be
In a creation renewed?" They are
Those who deny their Lord! They
Are those round whose necks
Will be yokes (of servitude):[1809]
They will be Companions
Of the Fire, to dwell therein
(For aye)!

٥ وَإِن تَعْجَبْ فَعَجَبٌ قَوْلُهُمْ
أَءِذَا كُنَّا تُرَٰبًا أَءِنَّا لَفِى خَلْقٍ جَدِيدٍ ۗ
أُو۟لَـٰٓئِكَ ٱلَّذِينَ كَفَرُوا۟ بِرَبِّهِمْ ۖ
وَأُو۟لَـٰٓئِكَ ٱلْأَغْلَـٰلُ فِىٓ أَعْنَاقِهِمْ ۖ
وَأُو۟لَـٰٓئِكَ أَصْحَـٰبُ ٱلنَّارِ ۖ هُمْ فِيهَا خَـٰلِدُونَ

6. They ask thee to hasten on
The evil in preference to the
good:[1810]
Yet have come to pass,
Before them, (many) exemplary
Punishments! But verily
Thy Lord is full of forgiveness
For mankind for their
wrongdoing.
And verily thy Lord
Is (also) strict in punishment.

٦ وَيَسْتَعْجِلُونَكَ
بِٱلسَّيِّئَةِ قَبْلَ ٱلْحَسَنَةِ
وَقَدْ خَلَتْ مِن قَبْلِهِمُ ٱلْمَثُلَـٰتُ ۗ
وَإِنَّ رَبَّكَ لَذُو مَغْفِرَةٍ لِّلنَّاسِ عَلَىٰ ظُلْمِهِمْ ۖ
وَإِنَّ رَبَّكَ لَشَدِيدُ ٱلْعِقَابِ

7. And the Unbelievers say:
"Why is not a Sign sent down
To him from his Lord?"[1811]
But thou art truly
A warner, and to every people
A guide.[1812]

٧ وَيَقُولُ ٱلَّذِينَ كَفَرُوا۟
لَوْلَآ أُنزِلَ عَلَيْهِ ءَايَةٌ مِّن رَّبِّهِۦٓ ۗ
إِنَّمَآ أَنتَ مُنذِرٌ ۖ وَلِكُلِّ قَوْمٍ هَادٍ

1808. After seeing the Signs in nature and the Signs in revelation, it is indeed strange that people should deny their Creator. But if they admit the Signs of the Creator, Who works marvels before their very eyes everyday, why should they doubt that when they are reduced to dust, they can be raised up again? If one creation is possible, what difficulty can there be in accepting a renewed creation? It becomes then a question of obstinate and rebellious will, for which the punishment is described.

1809. *Aghlāl*: yokes (of servitude): *Cf.* 7:157 and n. 1128. The punishment may be conceived of in two stages: immediately, yokes of servitude to superstition, falsehood, etc., as against the freedom in Faith; and finally, the Fire which burns the very soul.

1810. The Unbelievers by way of a taunt say: "If there is a punishment, let us see it come down now." The answer to it is threefold. (1) Why do you want to see the punishment rather than the mercy of Allah? Which is better? (2) Have you not heard in history of terrible punishments for evil? And have you not before your very eyes seen examples of wickedness brought to book? (3) Allah works not only in justice and punishment, but also in mercy and forgiveness, and mercy and forgiveness come first.

1811. After all the Signs that have just been mentioned it is mere fractiousness to say, "Bring down a Sign." Al Muṣṭafā brought Signs and credentials as other Prophets did, and like them, refused to satisfy mere idle curiosity.

1812. The last sentence of this verse has usually been interpreted to mean that the Prophet's function was merely to warn, and that guidance was sent by Allah to every nation through its Prophets. I think the following interpretation is equally possible: 'it is itself a Sign that Al Muṣṭafā should warn and preach and produce the Qur'ān, and the guidance which he brings is universal guidance, as from Allah.'

SECTION 2.

8. Allah doth know what
Every female (womb) doth bear,[1813]
By how much the wombs
Fall short (of their time
Or number) or do exceed.
Every single thing is before
His sight, in (due) proportion.

٨ اللَّهُ يَعْلَمُ مَا تَحْمِلُ كُلُّ أُنثَىٰ
وَمَا تَغِيضُ الْأَرْحَامُ وَمَا تَزْدَادُ
وَكُلُّ شَيْءٍ عِندَهُ بِمِقْدَارٍ

9. He knoweth the Unseen
And that which is open:
He is the Great,
The most High.[1814]

٩ عَالِمُ الْغَيْبِ وَالشَّهَادَةِ
الْكَبِيرُ الْمُتَعَالِ

10. It is the same (to Him)
Whether any of you
Conceal his speech or
Declare it openly;
Whether he lie hid by night
Or walk forth freely by day.[1815]

١٠ سَوَاءٌ مِّنكُم مَّنْ أَسَرَّ الْقَوْلَ
وَمَن جَهَرَ بِهِ وَمَنْ هُوَ مُسْتَخْفٍ
بِاللَّيْلِ وَسَارِبٌ بِالنَّهَارِ

11. For each (such person)[1816]
There are (angels) in succession.
Before and behind him:
They guard him by command
Of Allah. Verily never
Will Allah change the condition
Of a people until they
Change it themselves
(With their own souls).[1817]

١١ لَهُ مُعَقِّبَاتٌ مِّن بَيْنِ يَدَيْهِ
وَمِنْ خَلْفِهِ يَحْفَظُونَهُ مِنْ أَمْرِ اللَّهِ
إِنَّ اللَّهَ لَا يُغَيِّرُ مَا بِقَوْمٍ
حَتَّىٰ يُغَيِّرُوا مَا بِأَنفُسِهِمْ

1813. The female womb is just an example, a type, of extreme secrecy. Not even the female herself knows what is in the womb—whether it is a male young or a female young, whether it is one or more, whether it is to be born short of the standard time or to exceed the standard time. But the most hidden and apparently unknowable things are clear to Allah's knowledge: there is no mere chance: all things are regulated by Allah in just measure and proportion. The general proposition comes in the last sentence: "every single thing is before His sight, in (due) proportion."

1814. A verse of matchless rhythm in Arabic.

1815. Our most hidden thoughts and motives are known to Him at all times.

1816. See last verse. Every person, whether he conceals or reveals his thoughts, whether he skulks in darkness or goes about by day—all are under Allah's watch and ward. His grace encompasses everyone, and again and again protects him, if he will only take the protection, from harm and evil. If in his folly he thinks he can secretly take some pleasure or profit, he is wrong, for recording angels record all his thoughts and deeds.

1817. Allah is not intent on punishment. He created man virtuous and pure: he gave him intelligence and knowledge; he surrounded him with all sorts of instruments of His grace and mercy. If, in spite of all this, man distorts his own will and goes against Allah's Will, yet is Allah's forgiveness open to him if he will take it. It is only when he has made his own sight blind and changed his own nature or soul away from the beautiful mould in which Allah formed it, that Allah's Wrath will descend on him and the favourable position in which Allah placed him will be changed. When once the punishment comes, there is no turning it back. None of the things which he relied upon—other than Allah—can possibly protect him.

But when (once) Allah willeth
A people's punishment,
There can be no
Turning it back, nor
Will they find, besides Him,
Any to protect.

وَإِذَآ أَرَادَ ٱللَّهُ بِقَوْمٍ
سُوٓءًا فَلَا مَرَدَّ لَهُۥ
وَمَا لَهُم مِّن دُونِهِۦ مِن وَالٍ

12. It is He Who doth show you
The lightning, by way
Both of fear and of hope:[1818]
It is He Who doth raise up
The clouds, heavy
With (fertilising) rain!

(١٢) هُوَ ٱلَّذِى يُرِيكُمُ
ٱلْبَرْقَ خَوْفًا وَطَمَعًا
وَيُنشِئُ ٱلسَّحَابَ ٱلثِّقَالَ

13. Nay, thunder repeateth His praises,[1819]
And so do the angels, with awe:[1820]
He flingeth the loud-voiced
Thunderbolts, and therewith
He striketh whomsoever He will...
Yet these (are the men)
Who (dare to) dispute
About Allah, with the strength
Of His power (supreme)![1821]

(١٣) وَيُسَبِّحُ ٱلرَّعْدُ بِحَمْدِهِۦ
وَٱلْمَلَٰٓئِكَةُ مِنْ خِيفَتِهِۦ وَيُرْسِلُ
ٱلصَّوَٰعِقَ فَيُصِيبُ بِهَا مَن يَشَآءُ
وَهُمْ يُجَٰدِلُونَ فِى ٱللَّهِ
وَهُوَ شَدِيدُ ٱلْمِحَالِ

14. For Him (alone) is prayer
In Truth:[1822] any others that they
Call upon besides Him hear them
No more than if they were
To stretch forth their hands
For water to reach their mouths
But it reaches them not:
For the prayer of those

(١٤) لَهُۥ دَعْوَةُ ٱلْحَقِّ وَٱلَّذِينَ يَدْعُونَ مِن دُونِهِۦ
لَا يَسْتَجِيبُونَ لَهُم بِشَىْءٍ إِلَّا كَبَٰسِطِ كَفَّيْهِ إِلَى
ٱلْمَآءِ لِيَبْلُغَ فَاهُ وَمَا هُوَ بِبَٰلِغِهِۦ
وَمَا دُعَآءُ

1818. Here then is the climax to the answer of the sarcastic challenge of the Unbelievers for punishment, in language of great sublimity. Why look to evil rather than to good?—to punishment rather than to mercy?—to the fear in the force and fire of the lightning rather than to the hope of good and abundant crops in the rain which will come behind the lightning clouds?

1819. Nay, thunder itself, which may frighten you, is but a tame and beneficent force before Him, declaring his praises, like the rest of creation. THUNDER thus aptly gives the name of this Sūrah of contrasts, where what we may think terrible is shown to be really a submissive instrument of good in Allah's hands.

1820. And the angels, whom we think to be beautiful creatures of power and glory nearest to Allah, yet feel reverence and awe even as they praise His Holy Name.

1821. Who is puny man, to call Allah in question? *Cf.* some variations on this theme in the Book of Job. *e.g.*, chapters 38 to 41.

1822. *Ḥāqq* = truth; right; what is due, befitting, proper. All these meanings are to be understood here. If we worship anything other than Allah (whether it is idols, stars, powers of nature, spirits, or deified men, or Self, or Power, or Wealth, Science of Art, Talent or Intellect), our worship is both foolish and futile.

Without Faith is nothing
But (futile) wandering (in the
mind).[1823]

ٱلْكَٰفِرِينَ إِلَّا فِى ضَلَٰلٍ

15. Whatever beings[1824] there are
In the heavens and the earth
Do prostrate themselves to
Allah[1825]
(Acknowledging subjection)—with
goodwill
Or in spite of themselves:[1826]
So do their shadows[1827]
In the mornings and evenings.

١٥ وَلِلَّهِ يَسْجُدُ
مَن فِى ٱلسَّمَٰوَٰتِ وَٱلْأَرْضِ
طَوْعًا وَكَرْهًا وَظِلَٰلُهُم
بِٱلْغُدُوِّ وَٱلْءَاصَالِ

16. Say: "Who is the Lord and
Sustainer[1828]
Of the heavens and the earth?"
Say: "(It is) Allah."
Say: "Do ye then take
(For worship) protectors other
Than Him, such as have
No power either for good
Or for harm to themselves?"[1829]
Say: "Are the blind equal
With those who see?
Or the depths of darkness
Equal with Light?"

١٦ قُلْ مَن رَّبُّ ٱلسَّمَٰوَٰتِ
وَٱلْأَرْضِ قُلِ ٱللَّهُ
قُلْ أَفَٱتَّخَذْتُم مِّن دُونِهِۦٓ
أَوْلِيَآءَ لَا يَمْلِكُونَ لِأَنفُسِهِمْ نَفْعًا وَلَا ضَرًّا
قُلْ هَلْ يَسْتَوِى ٱلْأَعْمَىٰ وَٱلْبَصِيرُ
أَمْ هَلْ تَسْتَوِى ٱلظُّلُمَٰتُ وَٱلنُّورُ

1823. Without Faith, it is obvious that prayer or worship has no meaning whatever. It is but an aberration of the mind. But there is a deeper meaning. You may have false faith, as in superstitions or in worshipping things other than Allah, as explained in the last note. In that case, too, you are pursuing mere phantoms of the mind. When you come to examine it, it is mere imbecility or futility. Worship and prayer are justified only to Allah, the One True God. (R).

1824. Notice that the original of what I have translated "whatever being" is the personal pronoun *man*, not *mā*. This then refers to beings with a personality, *e.g.*, angels, spirits, human beings, and possibly other things of objective (not necessarily material) existence, as contrasted with their Shadows or Simulacra or Appearances, or Phantasms, mentioned at the end of the verse. Both these Beings and their Shadows are subject to the Will of Allah. See notes 1825 and 1827.

1825. "Prostrate themselves": the posture means that they recognise their subjection to Allah's Will and Law, whether they wish it or not.

1826. "In spite of themselves": Satan and the Spirits of Evil. They would like to get away from the control of the All-Good Allah, but they cannot, and they have to acknowledge His supremacy and lordship over them.

1827. Even the Shadows—creations of the Imagination, or projections from other things and dependent on the other things for their existence, as shadows or to substance—even such shadows are subject to Allah's Laws and Will, and cannot arise or have any effect on our minds except by His permission. The Shadows are longest and therefore most prominent when the sun is level, and tend to disappear as the sun approaches the zenith. But even when they are longest and most prominent, they are still subject to Allah's Will and Law. (R).

1828. The meaning of *Rabb* is explained in n. 20, to 1:2.

1829. *Cf.* 5:79.

Or do they assign to Allah[1830]
Partners who have created
(Anything) as He has created,
So that the creation seemed
To them similar?
Say: "Allah is the Creator
Of all things: He is
The One, the Supreme and
Irresistible."

أَمْ جَعَلُوا۟ لِلَّهِ شُرَكَآءَ خَلَقُوا۟ كَخَلْقِهِۦ
فَتَشَٰبَهَ ٱلْخَلْقُ عَلَيْهِمْ ۚ
قُلِ ٱللَّهُ خَٰلِقُ كُلِّ شَىْءٍ
وَهُوَ ٱلْوَٰحِدُ ٱلْقَهَّٰرُ

17. He sends down water[1831]
From the skies, and the channels
Flow, each according to its
measure:
But the torrent bears away
The foam that mounts up
To the surface. Even so,
From that (ore) which they heat[1832]
In the fire, to make ornaments
Or utensils therewith,
There is a scum likewise.
Thus doth Allah (by parables)
Show forth Truth and Vanity.
For the scum disappears
Like froth cast out;
While that which is for the good
Of mankind remains
On the earth. Thus doth Allah
Set forth parables.

(١٧) أَنزَلَ مِنَ ٱلسَّمَآءِ مَآءً
فَسَالَتْ أَوْدِيَةٌۢ بِقَدَرِهَا
فَٱحْتَمَلَ ٱلسَّيْلُ زَبَدًا رَّابِيًا ۚ
وَمِمَّا يُوقِدُونَ عَلَيْهِ فِى ٱلنَّارِ
ٱبْتِغَآءَ حِلْيَةٍ أَوْ مَتَٰعٍ زَبَدٌ مِّثْلُهُۥ ۚ
كَذَٰلِكَ يَضْرِبُ ٱللَّهُ ٱلْحَقَّ وَٱلْبَٰطِلَ ۚ
فَأَمَّا ٱلزَّبَدُ فَيَذْهَبُ جُفَآءً ۖ
وَأَمَّا مَا يَنفَعُ ٱلنَّاسَ فَيَمْكُثُ فِى ٱلْأَرْضِ ۚ
كَذَٰلِكَ يَضْرِبُ ٱللَّهُ ٱلْأَمْثَالَ

1830 This verse may be analysed into six parts, each two parts going together like question and answer. Each except the fifth part is introduced by the word "Say", which is equivalent in old Arabic to inverted commas. The fifth part, "or do they assign... similar?" is not introduced by "Say", because it is in the indirect form.

(1) Who is the Lord and Sustainer of the Worlds? It is Allah. (2) And yet you worship other gods? No, no one can be equal to Him, any more than darkness is equal to light. (3) Your other gods have created nothing by which you can be misled? No indeed; He is the only Creator, the One and Supreme.

1831. This verse is full of parables. (1) It is Allah Who sends rain and sends it to all. See how it flows in different channels according to their capacities. Some are sluggish; some have a swift current. Some form great rivers and irrigate wide tracts of country; some are clear crystal streams, perhaps in hilly tracts, with beds of clean pebbles which you can see through the water. Some produce delicious edible fish: and some are infested by crocodiles or injurious monsters. And there are degrees, and degrees among brooks, streams, lakes, rivers, and seas. So with the rain of Allah's mercy and the knowledge and wisdom and guidance which He sends. All can receive it. Different ones will respond according to their capacities. (2) In the physical world, water is pure and beneficial. But froth and scum will gather according to local conditions. As the floods will carry off the scum and purify the water, so will the flood of Allah's spiritual mercy carry away our spiritual scum and purify the water. (3) The froth may make a greater show on the surface, but it will not last. So will there be frothy knowledge which will disappear, but Allah's Truth will endure.

1832. In continuation of the last note, the fourth parable is that of metal ones: (4) the ore is full of baser admixture, but the fire will separate the gold from the dross for ornaments, or (5) some metal of household utility, with which you make everyday utensils, which the fire will separate from admixtures which you do not want. So the fire of Allah's test, either by adversity or by affluence, will search out the true metal in us and reject the dross. It will show us what is valuable or what is useful, all sorts of scum and vanity which we collect and miscall knowledge.

18. For those who respond
To their Lord, are (all)
Good things. But those
Who respond not to Him—
Even if they had all
That is in the heavens
And on earth, and as much more,
(In vain) would they offer it[1833]
For ransom. For them
Will the reckoning be terrible:
Their abode will be Hell—
What a bed of misery!

﴿١٨﴾ لِلَّذِينَ ٱسْتَجَابُوا۟ لِرَبِّهِمُ ٱلْحُسْنَىٰ
وَٱلَّذِينَ لَمْ يَسْتَجِيبُوا۟ لَهُۥ لَوْ أَنَّ
لَهُم مَّا فِى ٱلْأَرْضِ جَمِيعًا وَمِثْلَهُۥ
مَعَهُۥ لَٱفْتَدَوْا۟ بِهِۦٓ أُو۟لَـٰٓئِكَ لَهُمْ
سُوٓءُ ٱلْحِسَابِ وَمَأْوَىٰهُمْ جَهَنَّمُ وَبِئْسَ ٱلْمِهَادُ

C. 115.—The seeing and the blind are not alike:
(13:19-31.) Nor are those blessed with Faith and those without.
The former seek Allah, and attain
Peace and blessedness in their hearts,
And a final Home of rest: the latter
Are in a state of Curse, and their End
Is terrible. If Allah in His wisdom
Postpones retribution, it is for a time.
His promise never fails: it will come
To pass in His own good time.
In all things it is for Him to command.

SECTION 3.

19. Is then one who doth know
That that which hath been
Revealed unto thee
From thy Lord is the Truth,
Like one who is blind?[1834]
It is those who are
Endued with understanding
That receive admonition—

﴿١٩﴾ أَفَمَن يَعْلَمُ أَنَّمَآ أُنزِلَ إِلَيْكَ
مِن رَّبِّكَ ٱلْحَقُّ كَمَنْ هُوَ أَعْمَىٰٓ
إِنَّمَا يَتَذَكَّرُ أُو۟لُوا۟ ٱلْأَلْبَـٰبِ

20. Those who fulfil the Covenant
Of Allah and fail not
In their plighted word;

﴿٢٠﴾ ٱلَّذِينَ يُوفُونَ بِعَهْدِ ٱللَّهِ
وَلَا يَنقُضُونَ ٱلْمِيثَـٰقَ

21. Those who join together
Those things which Allah

﴿٢١﴾ وَٱلَّذِينَ يَصِلُونَ مَآ أَمَرَ ٱللَّهُ

1833. *Cf.* 3:91 and 10:54.

1834. In this section the contrast between Faith and Righteousness on the one hand and Infidelity and Evil on the other is set out. The righteous man is known as one who (1) receives admoniton; (2) is true to his covenants; (3) follows the universal Religion of Faith and Practice joined together; (4) is patient and persevering in seeking Allah; and in practical matters he is known to be; (5) regular in prayer; (6) generous in true charity, whether open or secret; and (7) not revengeful, but anxious to turn off evil with good, thus breaking the chain of evil which tends to perpetuate itself.

Hath commanded to be joined,[1835]
Hold their Lord in awe,
And fear the terrible reckoning;

بِهِۦٓ أَن يُوصَلَ وَيَخْشَوْنَ رَبَّهُمْ
وَيَخَافُونَ سُوٓءَ ٱلْحِسَابِ

22. Those who patiently persevere,
Seeking the countenance of
their Lord;
Establish regular prayers; spend,
Out of (the gifts) We have
bestowed
For their sustenance, secretly
And openly; and turn off Evil
With good: for such there is
The final attainment
Of the (Eternal) Home—[1836]

٢٢ وَٱلَّذِينَ صَبَرُوا۟ ٱبْتِغَآءَ وَجْهِ رَبِّهِمْ
وَأَقَامُوا۟ ٱلصَّلَوٰةَ وَأَنفَقُوا۟
مِمَّا رَزَقْنَٰهُمْ سِرًّا وَعَلَانِيَةً
وَيَدْرَءُونَ بِٱلْحَسَنَةِ ٱلسَّيِّئَةَ
أُو۟لَٰٓئِكَ لَهُمْ عُقْبَى ٱلدَّارِ

23. Gardens of perpetual bliss:
They shall enter there,
As well as the righteous
Among their fathers, their spouses,
And their offspring:[1837]
And angels shall enter unto them
From every gate
(with the salutation):

٢٣ جَنَّٰتُ عَدْنٍ يَدْخُلُونَهَا
وَمَن صَلَحَ مِنْ ءَابَآئِهِمْ وَأَزْوَٰجِهِمْ وَذُرِّيَّٰتِهِمْ ۖ
وَٱلْمَلَٰٓئِكَةُ يَدْخُلُونَ عَلَيْهِم مِّن كُلِّ بَابٍ

24. "Peace unto you for that ye
Persevered in patience! Now
How excellent is the final Home!"

٢٤ سَلَٰمٌ عَلَيْكُم بِمَا صَبَرْتُمْ ۚ فَنِعْمَ عُقْبَى ٱلدَّارِ

25. But those who break
The Covenant of Allah, after
Having plighted their word
thereto,
And cut asunder those things[1838]
Which Allah has commanded
To be joined, and work mischief
In the land—on them

٢٥ وَٱلَّذِينَ يَنقُضُونَ
عَهْدَ ٱللَّهِ مِنۢ بَعْدِ مِيثَٰقِهِۦ
وَيَقْطَعُونَ مَآ أَمَرَ ٱللَّهُ بِهِۦٓ أَن يُوصَلَ
وَيُفْسِدُونَ فِى ٱلْأَرْضِ ۙ أُو۟لَٰٓئِكَ

1835. That is, join faith with practice, love of Allah with love of man, and respect for all Prophets alike, *i.e.*, follow the universal Religion, and not odd bits of it.

1836. Their journey in this life was at best a sojourn. The final Bliss is their eternal Home, which is further prefigured in the two following verses.

1837. The relationships of this life are temporal, but love in righteousness is eternal. In the eternal Gardens of Bliss the righteous will be reunited with all those near and dear ones whom they loved, provided only that they were righteous also; for in eternity nothing else counts. Blood-relationships and marriage relationships create certain physical bonds in this life, which may lead to much good, and possibly also to evil. All that is physical or evil will go. But the good will come forth with a new meaning in the final Reckoning. Thus ancestors and descendants, husbands and wives, brothers and sisters, (for *dhurriyyāt* includes them), whose love was pure and sanctified, will find new bliss in the perfecting of their love and will see a new and mystic meaning in the old and ephemeral bonds. Can we wonder at Jacob's reunion with Joseph, or that of Moses with Aaron, or of Muḥammad Al Muṣṭafā with the Lady Khadījah? In fact all the Righteous will be reunited in the Hereafter (12:101).

1838. This is the opposite of the things explained in 13:21 above, n. 1835.

Is the Curse; for them
Is the terrible Home![1839]

لَهُمُ ٱللَّعۡنَةُ وَلَهُمۡ سُوٓءُ ٱلدَّارِ

26. Allah doth enlarge, or grant
By (strict) measure, the
Sustenance[1840]
(Which He giveth) to whom so
He pleaseth. (The worldly) rejoice
In the life of this world:
But the life of this world
Is but little comfort
In the Hereafter.[1841]

٢٦ ٱللَّهُ يَبۡسُطُ ٱلرِّزۡقَ
لِمَن يَشَآءُ وَيَقۡدِرُۚ
وَفَرِحُواْ بِٱلۡحَيَوٰةِ ٱلدُّنۡيَا
وَمَا ٱلۡحَيَوٰةُ ٱلدُّنۡيَا فِي ٱلۡأٓخِرَةِ إِلَّا مَتَٰعٞ

SECTION 4.

27. The Unbelievers say: "Why
Is not a Sign sent down
To him from his Lord?"[1842]
Say: "Truly Allah leaveth,
To stray, whom He will;
But He guideth to Himself
Those who turn to Him
In penitence—

٢٧ وَيَقُولُ ٱلَّذِينَ كَفَرُواْ
لَوۡلَآ أُنزِلَ عَلَيۡهِ ءَايَةٞ مِّن رَّبِّهِۦۚ
قُلۡ إِنَّ ٱللَّهَ يُضِلُّ مَن يَشَآءُ
وَيَهۡدِيٓ إِلَيۡهِ مَنۡ أَنَابَ

28. "Those who believe, and whose
hearts
Find satisfaction in the
remembrance
Of Allah: for without doubt
In the remembrance of Allah
Do hearts find satisfaction.[1843]

٢٨ ٱلَّذِينَ ءَامَنُواْ
وَتَطۡمَئِنُّ قُلُوبُهُم بِذِكۡرِ ٱللَّهِۗ
أَلَا بِذِكۡرِ ٱللَّهِ تَطۡمَئِنُّ ٱلۡقُلُوبُ

29. "For those who believe
And work righteousness,

٢٩ ٱلَّذِينَ ءَامَنُواْ وَعَمِلُواْ ٱلصَّٰلِحَٰتِ

1839. This is in contrast to the state of the blessed, described in 13:22-24 above. The Curse is the opposite of the Bliss, and the Terrible Home is the opposite of the Eternal Home, the Gardens of perpetual bliss.

1840. Allah, the Sustainer and Cherisher of all His creatures, gives sustenance to all—the sustenance including all means for their physical, moral, intellectual, and spiritual growth and development according to their needs and capacities. To some He grants it in abundance; to others He gives it in strict measure. No one can question Him, for His Will is supreme, and it is the measure of all good.

1841. *Cf.* 9:38. The meaning here may also be: This present life is just a furniture, a convenience, a stepping stone, a probation, for the life to come. In itself it is less important than the Hereafter.

1842. The question is repeated from 8:7 above: for the line of reasoning there suggested in answer is now completed, and another line of reasoning is now taken up. Allah provides every guidance for those who turn to Him in penitence, but He will leave those to wander astray who deliberately close their eyes and their hearts to His grace and the comfort that comes from remembering Him and celebrating His praises.

1843. The Sign or Miracle is not something external: it is something internal, something in your mind, heart, and soul. It depends on your inner spiritual experience. If you turn to Allah, the light, that experience, will come. If you do not, Allah will not force you.

Is (every) blessedness,[1844]
And a beautiful place
Of (final) return."

طُوبَىٰ لَهُمْ وَحُسْنُ مَـَٔابٍ

30. Thus have We sent thee
Amongst a People before whom
(Long since) have (other) Peoples
(Gone and) passed away;[1845]
In order that thou mightest
Rehearse unto them what We
Send down unto thee by
inspiration;
Yet do they reject (Him),
The Most Gracious!
Say: "He is my Lord!
There is no god but He!
On Him is my trust,
And to Him do I turn!"[1846]

كَذَٰلِكَ أَرْسَلْنَـٰكَ فِىٓ ﴿٣٠﴾
أُمَّةٍ قَدْ خَلَتْ مِن قَبْلِهَآ أُمَمٌ
لِّتَتْلُوَا۟ عَلَيْهِمُ ٱلَّذِىٓ أَوْحَيْنَآ إِلَيْكَ
وَهُمْ يَكْفُرُونَ بِٱلرَّحْمَـٰنِ
قُلْ هُوَ رَبِّى لَآ إِلَـٰهَ إِلَّا هُوَ
عَلَيْهِ تَوَكَّلْتُ وَإِلَيْهِ مَتَابِ

31. If there were a Qur'ān
With which mountains were
moved,
Or the earth were cloven asunder,
Or the dead were made to speak,
(This would be the one!)
But, truly, the Command is
With Allah in all things![1847]
Do not the Believers know,
That, had Allah (so) willed,
He could have guided
All mankind (to the Right)?

But the Unbelievers—never
Will disaster cease to seize
Them for their (ill) deeds,
Or to settle close to their homes,
Until the Promise of Allah
Come to pass, for, verily,

وَلَوْ أَنَّ قُرْءَانًا سُيِّرَتْ بِهِ ٱلْجِبَالُ ﴿٣١﴾
أَوْ قُطِّعَتْ بِهِ ٱلْأَرْضُ أَوْ كُلِّمَ بِهِ ٱلْمَوْتَىٰ
بَل لِّلَّهِ ٱلْأَمْرُ جَمِيعًا
أَفَلَمْ يَا۟يْـَٔسِ ٱلَّذِينَ ءَامَنُوٓا۟
أَن لَّوْ يَشَآءُ ٱللَّهُ لَهَدَى
ٱلنَّاسَ جَمِيعًا
وَلَا يَزَالُ ٱلَّذِينَ كَفَرُوا۟
تُصِيبُهُم بِمَا صَنَعُوا۟ قَارِعَةٌ
أَوْ تَحُلُّ قَرِيبًا مِّن دَارِهِمْ حَتَّىٰ يَأْتِىَ وَعْدُ ٱللَّهِ

1844. "Blessedness": *Ṭūbā*: an internal state of satisfaction, an inward joy which is difficult to describe in words, but which reflects itself in the life of the good man, through good and ill fortune, through good report and evil. And then, there is always the final goal to which his eyes are turned, the beautiful Home of rest in the Hereafter, after this life's struggles are over. That goal is Allah Himself.

1845. Our Prophet came later in time than other Prophets, to complete their Message and universalise Religion. And certainly it is after his age that the process of the unification of the world began. That process is not complete yet, but is proceeding apace.

1846. Faith tells us that no amount of opposition from Unbelievers can ever stop Allah's Plan.

1847. Everything is possible and in Allah's power. His Plan is beneficent and all-embracing. But it is not for His creatures to dictate to Him, or demand what He should do, or how He should do it. The Command is with Allah in all things. The Believers know His Omnipotence, and they also know that He will order His world for the best.

Allah will not fail
In His promise.[1848]

إِنَّ ٱللَّهَ لَا يُخْلِفُ ٱلْمِيعَادَ

C. 116.—(13:32-43.)
The mockery of Allah's Messengers is an old game
Of the world. But Allah's Truth will come
To its own in good time. The End
Of the righteous is their Home of Bliss,
And they rejoice in the revelations
They receive. The Messengers of Allah
Take their due share in the life
Of the world; they win through by Allah's grace
Against all the plots of the world.
Their witness is from Allah, through His revelation.

SECTION 5.

32. Mocked were (many)
Messengers[1849]
Before thee: but I granted
Respite to the Unbelievers,
And finally I punished them:
Then how (terrible) was My
requital![1850]

٣٢ وَلَقَدِ ٱسْتُهْزِئَ بِرُسُلٍ مِّن قَبْلِكَ
فَأَمْلَيْتُ لِلَّذِينَ كَفَرُوا۟ ثُمَّ أَخَذْتُهُمْ
فَكَيْفَ كَانَ عِقَابِ

33. Is then He Who standeth
Over every soul (and knoweth)
All that it doth,
(Like any others)? And yet
They ascribe partners to Allah.
Say: "But name them![1851]
Is it that ye will
Inform Him of something
He knoweth not on earth,
Or is it (just) a show

٣٣ أَفَمَنْ هُوَ قَآئِمٌ
عَلَىٰ كُلِّ نَفْسٍۭ بِمَا كَسَبَتْ
وَجَعَلُوا۟ لِلَّهِ شُرَكَآءَ قُلْ سَمُّوهُمْ
أَمْ تُنَبِّـُٔونَهُۥ بِمَا لَا يَعْلَمُ فِى ٱلْأَرْضِ
أَم بِظَـٰهِرٍ

1848. Let not the Unbelievers think that if they seem to prosper for a time, that is the end of the matter. They are warned about three things. (1) Their ill deeds must carry evil consequences for them all the time, though they may not perceive them for a certain time. (2) Their homes, their places of resort, the circles in which they move, will also be haunted by their ill deeds and their consequences. For evil makes a complex of its environment. The walls of Jericho, when they fall, must bring down all Jericho in its ruins. (3) The ultimate Disaster, the final Reckoning, must come, for Allah never fails in His promise. True values must eventually be restored: the good to the good, and the evil to the evil.

The Commentators draw illustrations from the life of the Messenger, his exile from Makkah, and his restoration. A similar miracle works in all history. But the Command is with Allah.

1849. *Cf.* 6:10.

1850. The punishment was in many cases deferred. But when it did come, how terrible and exemplary it was!

1851. *Cf.* 12:40. 'You have but to name your false gods, and you will see that they are nothing but names. There is no reality behind them, whereas Allah is the One great Reality. He penetrates everything through and through and knows all things. Do you dare to tell Him of something on earth that He does not know? Or is it just a trick or a show of words?

Of words?" Nay! to those
Who believe not, their pretence[1852]
Seems pleasing, but they are
Kept back (thereby) from the Path.
And those whom Allah leaves
To stray, no one can guide.

مِنَ ٱلْقَوْلِ بَلْ زُيِّنَ لِلَّذِينَ كَفَرُوا۟ مَكْرُهُمْ
وَصُدُّوا۟ عَنِ ٱلسَّبِيلِ
وَمَن يُضْلِلِ ٱللَّهُ فَمَا لَهُۥ مِنْ هَادٍ

34. For them is a Penalty
In the life of this world,[1853]
But harder, truly, is the Penalty
Of the Hereafter: and defender
Have they none against Allah.

٣٤ لَّهُمْ عَذَابٌ فِى ٱلْحَيَوٰةِ ٱلدُّنْيَا
وَلَعَذَابُ ٱلْءَاخِرَةِ أَشَقُّ
وَمَا لَهُم مِّنَ ٱللَّهِ مِن وَاقٍ

35. The parable of the Garden
Which the righteous are
promised!—
Beneath it flow rivers:
Perpetual is the enjoyment
thereof[1854]
And the shade therein:[1855]
Such is the End
Of the Righteous; and the End
Of Unbelievers is the Fire.[1856]

٣٥ مَّثَلُ ٱلْجَنَّةِ ٱلَّتِى وُعِدَ ٱلْمُتَّقُونَ
تَجْرِى مِن تَحْتِهَا ٱلْأَنْهَـٰرُ
أُكُلُهَا دَآئِمٌ وَظِلُّهَا
تِلْكَ عُقْبَى ٱلَّذِينَ ٱتَّقَوا۟
وَّعُقْبَى ٱلْكَـٰفِرِينَ ٱلنَّارُ

36. Those to whom We have
Given the Book[1857] rejoice
At what hath been revealed
Unto thee: but there are

٣٦ وَٱلَّذِينَ ءَاتَيْنَـٰهُمُ ٱلْكِتَـٰبَ
يَفْرَحُونَ بِمَآ أُنزِلَ إِلَيْكَ

1852. All pretences and fancies seem attractive to their inventors, but alas! they are a great obstruction to the Path of Religion and Truth. However, if by their contumacy, they have cut themselves off from Allah's grace, who can guide them or reclaim them from their errors?

1853. The consequences of sin may be felt in this life itself, but they are nothing compared to the final penalties in the life to come.

1854. For the comprehensive meaning of the root *akala* (literally 'to eat'), see 5:69. n. 776. In its derived meaning, it means fruit and enjoyment of all kinds, spiritual as well as other. The joys of heaven are not like the joys of the earth, which fade away or cloy. The joys of heaven are pure, lasting, and without any of the drawbacks which we associate with the joys of the sense.

1855. *Ẓillun*: literally shade, hence, shelter, protection, security. All these meanings are implied. Shade is one of the delights of a garden. *Cf.* 4:57, and n. 579.

1856. In this, as no other place, the Fire is contrasted with the Garden, as misery is contrasted with bliss. We can also imagine other incidents in contrast with those of the Garden; *e.g.*, with the Fire will be drought, aridity, thirst, instead of beautiful rivers; pain and suffering, instead of perpetual delight; no protection against the fierceness of the heat, as contrasted with the cool shades ever deepening as you proceed in the Garden.

1857. *The Book*: in a general sense, Revelation. "Those to whom the Book hath been given" are both (1) the People of the Book of previous revelations, who study the new Revelation in Arabic without prejudice and find in it confirmation of what their ancestors had received; and (2) the Muslims who receive the Qur'an with such spiritual joy.

Among the clans[1858] those who reject
A part thereof. Say:
"I am commanded to worship
Allah, and not to join partners
With Him. Unto him
Do I call, and
Unto Him is my return."

وَمِنَ الأَحْزَابِ مَن يُنكِرُ بَعْضَهُ
قُلْ إِنَّمَا أُمِرْتُ أَنْ أَعْبُدَ اللَّهَ وَلَا أُشْرِكَ بِهِ
إِلَيْهِ أَدْعُوا
وَإِلَيْهِ مَآبِ

37. Thus have We revealed it
To be a judgement of authority[1859]
In Arabic. Wert thou to follow
Their (vain) desires after the knowledge
Which hath reached thee,
Then wouldst thou find
Neither protector nor defender[1860]
Against Allah.

(٣٧) وَكَذَٰلِكَ أَنزَلْنَاهُ حُكْمًا عَرَبِيًّا
وَلَئِنِ اتَّبَعْتَ أَهْوَاءَهُم
بَعْدَ مَا جَاءَكَ مِنَ الْعِلْمِ
مَا لَكَ مِنَ اللَّهِ مِن وَلِيٍّ وَلَا وَاقٍ

SECTION 6.

38. We did send messengers
Before thee, and appointed
For them wives and children:[1861]
And it was never the part
Of a messenger to bring a Sign
Except as Allah permitted[1862]

(٣٨) وَلَقَدْ أَرْسَلْنَا رُسُلًا مِّن
قَبْلِكَ وَجَعَلْنَا لَهُمْ أَزْوَاجًا وَذُرِّيَّةً
وَمَا كَانَ لِرَسُولٍ أَن يَأْتِيَ بِآيَةٍ إِلَّا بِإِذْنِ اللَّهِ

1858. *Aḥzāb* (plural of *ḥizb* = parties, sects, troops, clans. The reference may be to the clans mentioned in 30:20 and 22 (that whole Sūrah is called *Aḥzāb)*. But we can understand it in a perfectly general sense. Among all the sections of the people there are persons who would receive a portion of Allah's truth but reject whatever does not suit them or fall in with their selfish aims or vain desires. The proper answer to them is: surely, Allah's command is universal—to worship and serve Him and refuse to bend the knee to any other; the man of God finds his staff and support in it; but he must invite all to share in its blessings; it came from Allah, and to Allah shall we all return.

1859. The Qur'ān is in Arabic; therefore the Arabs, among whom it was promulgated, could have no difficulty in understanding its precepts and using it in the judging of right and wrong in all their affairs. But it is also universal; therefore no one should give preference to his own vain fancies against this authoritative declaration.

1860. *Cf.* 2:120. The variation is in the single word *"Wāq"* here in place of *"Naṣīr"* in 2:120. In each case the apt word is chosen not only for the rhythm in its own passage but for the general meaning in the argument.

1861. All the Prophets of whom we have any detailed knowledge, except one, had wives and children. The exception is Jesus, the son of Mary. But his life was incomplete: his ministry barely lasted three years; his mission was limited; and he was not called upon to deal with the many-sided problems that arise in a highly organised society or State. We pay equal respect to him, because he was Allah's Messenger; but that is not to say that his Message covers the same universal ground as that of Al Muṣṭafā. There is no reproach for a normal human being if he lives a normal human life; there is glory if he beautifies it and sets a nobler example of virtue than other men, as did Al Muṣṭafā.

1862. No Prophet performed any miracle or showed forth any "Signs," except as Allah willed. Allah's will (*Mashiyyah*) is an All-Wise, universal Plan, which is not formed for the benefit of one tribe or *millah* or of one age or country (see also next verse). The greatest Miracle in history was and is the Qur'ān. We can apprehend its beauty and grandeur today as much as did the people of Al Muṣṭafā's day—even more, as our collective knowledge of nature and of Allah's creation has increased.

(Or commanded). For each period
Is a Book (revealed).[1863]

لِكُلِّ أَجَلٍ كِتَابٌ

39. Allah doth blot out
Or confirm what He pleaseth:
With Him is
The Mother of the Book.[1864]

يَمْحُوا اللَّهُ مَا يَشَاءُ وَيُثْبِتُ ﴿٣٩﴾
وَعِندَهُ أُمُّ الْكِتَابِ

40. Whether We shall show thee
(Within thy lifetime)
Part of what We promised them
Or take to Ourselves thy soul
(Before it is all accomplished),
Thy duty is to make
(The Message) reach them:
It is Our part
To call them to account.

وَإِن مَّا نُرِيَنَّكَ ﴿٤٠﴾
بَعْضَ الَّذِي نَعِدُهُمْ أَوْ نَتَوَفَّيَنَّكَ
فَإِنَّمَا عَلَيْكَ الْبَلَاغُ
وَعَلَيْنَا الْحِسَابُ

41. See they not that We
Gradually reduce the land
(In their control) from its
Outlying border?[1865] (Where) Allah
Commands, there is none
To put back His command:
And He is Swift
In calling to account.

أَوَلَمْ يَرَوْا أَنَّا نَأْتِي الْأَرْضَ ﴿٤١﴾
نَنقُصُهَا مِنْ أَطْرَافِهَا
وَاللَّهُ يَحْكُمُ لَا مُعَقِّبَ لِحُكْمِهِ
وَهُوَ سَرِيعُ الْحِسَابِ

42. Those before them did (also)
Devise plots; but in all things
The master-planning is Allah's.[1866]
He knoweth the doings
Of every soul; and soon
Will the Unbelievers know
Who gets home in the End.

وَقَدْ مَكَرَ الَّذِينَ مِن قَبْلِهِمْ ﴿٤٢﴾
فَلِلَّهِ الْمَكْرُ جَمِيعًا يَعْلَمُ مَا تَكْسِبُ كُلُّ نَفْسٍ
وَسَيَعْلَمُ الْكُفَّارُ لِمَنْ عُقْبَى الدَّارِ

1863. *Kitāb*: I have translated "a Book (revealed)"; but it can also mean "a Law decreed" or "a Decree established." Ultimately the meaning is the same; for each age, according to Allah's wisdom, His Message is renewed.

1864. *Umm al Kitāb*: Mother of the Book: the original foundation of all revelation; the essence of Allah's Will and Law. *Cf.* 3:7. and n. 347.

1865. In the Prophet's ministry at Makkah, the most stiff-necked opposition came from the seat and centre of power in Makkah. The humbler people—the fringe of Makkan society—came in readily, as also did some tribes round about Makkah. After the Hijrah there was a hard struggle between Makkah and Madīnah, and at last the bloodless conquest of Makkah in 8 A. H. made the pagan structure finally collapse, though it had already been sapped to its foundations. So, generally, Truth finds easiest entrance through the humble and lowly, and not in the beginning at the headquarters of power, but in the fulness of time it makes its way everywhere with irresistible force.

1866. *Cf.* 3:54. and n. 393.

43. The Unbelievers say: "No
messenger[1867]
Art thou." Say: "Enough
For a witness between me
And you is Allah, and such
As have knowledge of the
Book."[1868]

وَيَقُولُ ٱلَّذِينَ كَفَرُوا۟ لَسْتَ مُرْسَلًا ۚ قُلْ كَفَىٰ بِٱللَّهِ شَهِيدًۢا بَيْنِى وَبَيْنَكُمْ وَمَنْ عِندَهُۥ عِلْمُ ٱلْكِتَٰبِ ﴿٤٣﴾

1867. The enemies of Islam have to acknowledge that Al Muṣṭafā was a great and noble character, but they deny his Prophethood. He could point to his credentials from Allah in the work which he achieved, and the Qur'ān which he brought.

1868. That is, those who have knowledge of revelation generally will recognise Allah's revelation in the Holy Qur'ān. An alternative reading is *"min 'indihi"*, which is written the same in Arabic, with only three vowel points different. If we adopt that, the last clause will be: "and from Him is (all) knowledge of the Book": *i.e.*, 'as all knowledge of the Book comes from Allah, the Qur'ān also bears witness to me.'

INTRODUCTION TO SŪRAH 14—*IBRĀHĪM*

For the chronology and the general argument of this Sūrah in the series Sūrahs 10 to 15, see Introduction to S. 10.

The special subject matter of this Sūrah is a continuation of the concluding portion of the last Sūrah, which explained how Allah's revelation gains ground in spite of selfish men's opposition. Here illustrations are given from the story of Moses and Abraham, and Abraham's Prayer for Makkah forms the core of the Sūrah.

Summary.—Revelation leads man from darkness to light. It comes to each nation in its own language and for its own special circumstances. So was it with Moses and other Prophets. There was a conflict of evil with good, but evil was destroyed. Parable of the Goodly Tree (14:1-27 and C. 117).

Why will men not receive Allah's grace? Why will they choose to go astray? Abraham prayed to be saved from infidelity, himself and his posterity, and he prayed for Makkah, the city of the new revelation through Arabia. Good and Evil will find their proper retribution, and Allah's Plan of Unity will prevail (14:28-52. and C. 118).

C. 117.—Revelation leads mankind from the depths
(14:1-27) Of darkness into light. It comes
To every age and nation in its own
Language. So was it before; so it is
Always. The Prophets were doubted,
Insulted, threatened, and persecuted,
But their trust was sure in Allah.
It is Evil that will be wiped out.
Allah's Truth is a goodly tree,
Firmly established on its roots,
Stretching its branches high and wide,
And bearing good fruit at all times.

Sūrah 14.

Ibrāhīm (Abraham)

In the name of Allah, Most Gracious,
Most Merciful.

بِسْمِ ٱللَّهِ ٱلرَّحْمَٰنِ ٱلرَّحِيمِ

1. Alif Lām Rā.[1869] A Book
Which We have revealed
Unto thee, in order that
Thou mightest lead mankind
Out of the depths of darkness
Into light—by the leave[1870]
Of their Lord—to the Way
Of (Him) the Exalted in Power,
Worthy of all Praise!—[1871]

الٓر ۚ كِتَٰبٌ أَنزَلْنَٰهُ إِلَيْكَ ١
لِتُخْرِجَ ٱلنَّاسَ مِنَ ٱلظُّلُمَٰتِ
إِلَى ٱلنُّورِ بِإِذْنِ رَبِّهِمْ
إِلَىٰ صِرَٰطِ ٱلْعَزِيزِ ٱلْحَمِيدِ

2. Of Allah, to Whom do belong
All things in the heavens
And on earth!
But alas for the Unbelievers[1872]
For a terrible Penalty
(Their Unfaith will bring
them)!—

ٱللَّهِ ٱلَّذِى لَهُۥ مَا فِى ٢
ٱلسَّمَٰوَٰتِ وَمَا فِى ٱلْأَرْضِ ۗ
وَوَيْلٌ لِّلْكَٰفِرِينَ مِنْ عَذَابٍ شَدِيدٍ

3. Those who love the life[1873]
Of this world more than
The Hereafter, who hinder
(men)
From the Path of Allah
And seek therein something
crooked:
They are astray
By a long distance.

ٱلَّذِينَ يَسْتَحِبُّونَ ٱلْحَيَوٰةَ ٣
ٱلدُّنْيَا عَلَى ٱلْءَاخِرَةِ وَيَصُدُّونَ
عَن سَبِيلِ ٱللَّهِ وَيَبْغُونَهَا عِوَجًا ۚ
أُو۟لَٰٓئِكَ فِى ضَلَٰلٍۭ بَعِيدٍ

1869. For those mystic Letters see Introduction to S. 10.

1870. It is insisted that every Prophet speaks not from himself but from Allah. His leading into the light is but by the Grace and Mercy of Allah, not by any power of his own, or by any merit of those who hear him.

1871. In this and the next verse where the sentence is completed, three qualities of Allah are mentioned, *viz.*, (1) His exalted position above all Creation; (2) His goodness, which entitles Him, and Him alone, to Praise; and (3) His Power in all heaven and earth. Thus He stands in no need of man's worship; His goodness is all for the good of man (and His creatures); and His control over His creatures is complete; so He can carry out His Will and Plan.

1872. See the last note. That being the case, in what a sad plight are those who reject the Faith and Grace offered to them, and draw down on themselves all the terrible consequence of that rejection—the Wrath to come!

1873. The Unbelievers are here characterised in three ways: (1) they love this ephemeral life and its vanities more than the true Life which goes into the Hereafter; (2) they not only harm themselves but mislead others; (3) their own crooked minds search for something crooked in Allah's straight Path (*Cf.* 7:45). But in doing so, they go farther and farther from the Truth.

4. We sent not a messenger
Except (to teach) in the language[1874]
Of his (own) people, in order
To make (things) clear to them.
Now Allah leaves straying
Those whom He pleases
And guides whom He pleases:[1875]
And He is Exalted in Power,
Full of Wisdom.

٤ وَمَآ أَرۡسَلۡنَا مِن رَّسُولٍ إِلَّا بِلِسَانِ قَوۡمِهِۦ لِيُبَيِّنَ لَهُمۡۖ فَيُضِلُّ ٱللَّهُ مَن يَشَآءُ وَيَهۡدِي مَن يَشَآءُۚ وَهُوَ ٱلۡعَزِيزُ ٱلۡحَكِيمُ

5. We sent Moses with Our Signs
(And the command). "Bring out
Thy people from the depths
Of darkness into light,
And teach them to remember
The Days of Allah."[1876] Verily
In this there are Signs
For such as are firmly patient
And constant—grateful and appreciative.[1877]

٥ وَلَقَدۡ أَرۡسَلۡنَا مُوسَىٰ بِـَٔايَٰتِنَآ أَنۡ أَخۡرِجۡ قَوۡمَكَ مِنَ ٱلظُّلُمَٰتِ إِلَى ٱلنُّورِ وَذَكِّرۡهُم بِأَيَّىٰمِ ٱللَّهِۚ إِنَّ فِي ذَٰلِكَ لَأٓيَٰتٖ لِّكُلِّ صَبَّارٖ شَكُورٖ

6. Remember! Moses said
To his people: "Call to mind
The favour of Allah to you
When He delivered you[1878]
From the people of Pharaoh:
They set you hard tasks
And punishments, slaughtered

٦ وَإِذۡ قَالَ مُوسَىٰ لِقَوۡمِهِ ٱذۡكُرُواْ نِعۡمَةَ ٱللَّهِ عَلَيۡكُمۡ إِذۡ أَنجَىٰكُم مِّنۡ ءَالِ فِرۡعَوۡنَ يَسُومُونَكُمۡ سُوٓءَ ٱلۡعَذَابِ وَيُذَبِّحُونَ

1874. If the object of a Message is to make things clear, it must be delivered in the language current among the people to whom the Messenger is sent. Through them it can reach all mankind. There is even a wider meaning for "language". It is not merely a question of alphabets, letters, or words. Each age or people—or world in a psychological sense—casts its thoughts in a certain mould or form. Allah's Message—being universal—can be expressed in all moulds and forms, and is equally valid and necessary for all grades of humanity, and must therefore be explained to each according to his or her capacity or receptivity. In this respect the Qur'ān is marvellous. It is for the simplest as well as the most advanced.

1875. *"Whom He pleases"*: the usual expression for *Mashiyyah*, the universal Will and Plan, which is All-Wise and on the highest plane of goodness and righteousness.

1876. *"The Days of Allah"*: the days when Allah's mercy was specially shown to them. Every day and every hour and minute, Allah's Grace flows to us abundantly, but there are special events in personal or national history which may be commemorated as Red-letter Days. Those to the Israelites were set out in great detail in 2:30-61 and on other places.

1877. *Ṣabbār* is the intensive form, and includes all the ideas implied in *Ṣabr* (2:45 and n. 61 and 2:153 n. 157) in an intensive degree. *Shakūr* and *Shākir* have in them the idea of appreciation, recognition, gratitude as shown in deeds of goodness and righteousness. Both terms are applied to Allah as well as to men. A slight distinction in shades of meaning may be noted. *Shakūr* implies that the appreciation is even for the smallest favours and response on the other side: it is mental attitude independent of specific facts. *Shākir* implies bigger and more specific things.

1878. *Cf.* 2:49. The reference back to Israel and Moses serves a double purpose—as an appeal to the People of the Book, and as a reminder to the Quraysh of the favour now conferred on them by the coming among them of a greater Prophet than Moses.

Your sons, and let your womenfolk
Live; therein was
A tremendous trial from your
Lord."

أَبْنَآءَكُمْ وَيَسْتَحْيُونَ نِسَآءَكُمْ
وَفِي ذَٰلِكُم بَلَآءٌ مِّن رَّبِّكُمْ عَظِيمٌ

SECTION 2.

7. And remember! your Lord
Caused to be declared (publicly):
"If ye are grateful, I will
Add more (favours) unto you;
But if ye show ingratitude,[1879]
Truly My punishment
Is terrible indeed."

وَإِذْ تَأَذَّنَ رَبُّكُمْ ۝٧
لَئِن شَكَرْتُمْ لَأَزِيدَنَّكُمْ
وَلَئِن كَفَرْتُمْ إِنَّ عَذَابِي لَشَدِيدٌ

8. And Moses said: "If ye
Show ingratitude,[1880] ye and all
On earth together—yet
Is Allah Free of all wants,[1881]
Worthy of all praise.

وَقَالَ مُوسَىٰٓ إِن تَكْفُرُوٓا۟ أَنتُمْ وَمَن ۝٨
فِي ٱلْأَرْضِ جَمِيعًا فَإِنَّ ٱللَّهَ لَغَنِيٌّ حَمِيدٌ

9. Has not the story
Reached you, (O people!), of those
Who (went) before you?—
Of the People of Noah,
And 'Ād, and Thamūd?—
And of those who (came)
After them? None knows them[1882]
But Allah. To them came
Messengers with Clear (Signs);
But they put their hands[1883]
Up to their mouths, and said:
"We do deny (the mission)

أَلَمْ يَأْتِكُمْ نَبَؤُا۟ ٱلَّذِينَ ۝٩
مِن قَبْلِكُمْ قَوْمِ نُوحٍ وَعَادٍ وَثَمُودَ
وَٱلَّذِينَ مِنۢ بَعْدِهِمْ لَا يَعْلَمُهُمْ إِلَّا ٱللَّهُ
جَآءَتْهُمْ رُسُلُهُم بِٱلْبَيِّنَٰتِ فَرَدُّوٓا۟
أَيْدِيَهُمْ فِيٓ أَفْوَٰهِهِمْ وَقَالُوٓا۟ إِنَّا كَفَرْنَا

1879. The various shades of meaning in *Shakara* are explained in n. 1877 above. *Kafara* implies: (1) to reject Faith, as in 2:6 and n. 30; (2) to be ungrateful for mercies and favours received, as here; (3) to resist Allah or Faith, as in 3:13; (4) to deny (the Signs of Allah), as in 3:21, or deny the mission of Messengers, as in 14:9. *Kāfir* in the most general sense may be translated "Unbeliever."

1880. Ingratitude not only in feeling or words, but in disobedience, and willful rejection and rebellion. If the whole of you band together against Allah, you do not detract from Allah's power one atom, because Allah does not depend upon you for anything, and His goodness and righteousness and praiseworthiness cannot be called into question by your contumacy.

1881. *Cf.* 22:64, 29:6, 25:15, 67:38. [Eds.].

1882. Even the names of all the Prophets are not known to men, much less the details of their story. If some "news" of them (for the word translated "story" may also be translated "news") reaches us, it is to give us spiritual instruction for our own lives.

1883. That is, either that the unbelievers metaphorically put their hands up to the mouths of the Prophets to try to prevent them from proclaiming their Message, or that the unbelievers put up their fingers to their own mouths, as much as to say "Don't listen to them," or bit their own fingers in token of incontinent rage. Whatever construction we adopt, the meaning is that they were intolerant of their prophets even as the Quraysh were intolerant of Al Muṣṭafā and did all they could to suppress Allah's Truth.

On which ye have been sent,
And we are really
In suspicious (disquieting)
doubt[1884]
As to that to which
Ye invite us."

بِمَآ أُرْسِلْتُم بِهِۦ
وَإِنَّا لَفِى شَكٍّ مِّمَّا
تَدْعُونَنَآ إِلَيْهِ مُرِيبٍ

10. Their messengers said: "Is there
A doubt about Allah,
The Creator of the heavens
And the earth." It is He[1885]
Who invites you, in order
That He may forgive you
Your sins and give you
Respite for a term appointed!"
They said: "Ah! ye are
No more than human,
Like ourselves! Ye wish
To turn us away from
The (gods) our fathers
Used to worship: then
Bring us some clear authority."[1886]

﴿١٠﴾ قَالَتْ رُسُلُهُمْ أَفِى ٱللَّهِ
شَكٌّ فَاطِرِ ٱلسَّمَٰوَٰتِ وَٱلْأَرْضِ
يَدْعُوكُمْ لِيَغْفِرَ لَكُم مِّن ذُنُوبِكُمْ
وَيُؤَخِّرَكُمْ إِلَىٰٓ أَجَلٍ مُّسَمًّى
قَالُوٓا۟ إِنْ أَنتُمْ إِلَّا بَشَرٌ مِّثْلُنَا تُرِيدُونَ
أَن تَصُدُّونَا عَمَّا كَانَ يَعْبُدُ ءَابَآؤُنَا
فَأْتُونَا بِسُلْطَٰنٍ مُّبِينٍ

11. Their messengers said to them:
"True, we are human
Like yourselves, but Allah
Doth grant His grace
To such of His servants
As He pleases. It is not
For us to bring you
An authority except as Allah
Permits. And on Allah
Let all men of faith
Put their trust.

﴿١١﴾ قَالَتْ لَهُمْ رُسُلُهُمْ
إِن نَّحْنُ إِلَّا بَشَرٌ مِّثْلُكُمْ وَلَٰكِنَّ ٱللَّهَ
يَمُنُّ عَلَىٰ مَن يَشَآءُ مِنْ عِبَادِهِۦ وَمَا كَانَ
لَنَآ أَن نَّأْتِيَكُم بِسُلْطَٰنٍ إِلَّا بِإِذْنِ ٱللَّهِ
وَعَلَى ٱللَّهِ فَلْيَتَوَكَّلِ ٱلْمُؤْمِنُونَ

1884. *Cf.* 11:62. The distinction between *Shakk* and *rayb* may be noted. *Shakk* is intellectual doubt, a doubt as to fact: is it so, or is it not? *Rayb* is something more than intellectual doubt; a suspicion that there is fraud or deception; something that upsets your moral belief, and causes a disquiet in your soul. In 52:30, it is used as equivalent to "calamity" or "disaster", some punishment or evil. Both kinds of doubts and suspicions are hinted at against Prophets of Allah.

1885. The Prophets (generally) clear both kinds of doubt. "You cannot doubt the existence of Allah! Behold His works! We are not speaking for ourselves or deceiving you. We speak according to the Message of inspiration from Allah." Notice that the doubters had said to the Prophets: "Ye invite us." The Prophets say: "It is Allah Who invites you, and He does it to save you by His grace, and give you plenty of time (but not indefinite time) for penitence and amendment."

1886. Infidelity is illogical and argues in a circle. If the Prophet speaks of Allah, the Unbeliever says, "You are only a man!" "But I speak from Allah!" "Oh well! Our ancestral ways of worship are good enough for us!" "What if they are wrong?" "What authority have you for saying so?" "The highest authority, that from Allah!" And so we come back full circle! Then the wicked rely on violence, but it recoils on them, and they perish.

12. "No reason have we why
We should not put our trust
On Allah. Indeed He
Has guided us to the Ways
We (follow). We shall certainly
Bear with patience all
The hurt you may cause us.
For those who put their trust
Should put their trust on Allah."

١٢ وَمَا لَنَآ أَلَّا نَتَوَكَّلَ
عَلَى ٱللَّهِ وَقَدْ هَدَىٰنَا سُبُلَنَا ۚ
وَلَنَصْبِرَنَّ عَلَىٰ مَآ ءَاذَيْتُمُونَا ۚ
وَعَلَى ٱللَّهِ فَلْيَتَوَكَّلِ ٱلْمُتَوَكِّلُونَ

SECTION 3.

13. And the Unbelievers said
To their messengers: "Be sure
We shall drive you out
Of our land, or ye shall
Return to our religion."[1887]
But their Lord inspired
(This Message) to them:
"Verily We shall cause
The wrongdoers to perish!

١٣ وَقَالَ ٱلَّذِينَ كَفَرُوا۟ لِرُسُلِهِمْ
لَنُخْرِجَنَّكُم مِّنْ أَرْضِنَآ
أَوْ لَتَعُودُنَّ فِى مِلَّتِنَا ۖ
فَأَوْحَىٰٓ إِلَيْهِمْ رَبُّهُمْ لَنُهْلِكَنَّ ٱلظَّـٰلِمِينَ

14. "And verily We shall
Cause you to abide
In the land, and succeed them.
This for such as fear[1888]
The Time when they shall stand
Before My tribunal—such
As fear the Punishment
denounced."

١٤ وَلَنُسْكِنَنَّكُمُ ٱلْأَرْضَ مِنۢ بَعْدِهِمْ ۚ
ذَٰلِكَ لِمَنْ خَافَ مَقَامِى
وَخَافَ وَعِيدِ

15. But they sought victory and
decision[1889]
(There and then), and frustration
Was the lot of every
Powerful obstinate transgressor.[1890]

١٥ وَٱسْتَفْتَحُوا۟
وَخَابَ كُلُّ جَبَّارٍ عَنِيدٍ

1887. The arguments in a circle were explained in the last note. But Infidelity looks upon argument merely as an amusement. Its chief weapon is physical force. As its only belief is in materialism, it thinks that threats of force will put down the righteous. It offers the choice between exile and violence against conformity to its own standards of evil, which it thinks to be good. But Faith is not to be cowed down by Force. Its source of strength is Allah, and it receives the assurance that violence will perish ultimately by violence, and that Faith and Goodness must stand and be established. In fact the good must inherit the earth and the evil ones be blotted out.

1888. "Fear" means here "have present before their minds something which should cause fear, so that they should shape their conduct in order to avoid the ill consequences of wickedness."

1889. *Cf.* 8:19. I have assumed that "they" in this verse is the same as "them" in the preceding verse, *i.e.*, the ungodly. Hoping for victory, they forced a decision, and they got it—against themselves. Or they challenged a punishment, and it came in good time. Some Commentators construe "they" here to mean "the Prophets"; in that case the verse would mean: "The Prophets prayed for a victory and decision, and the ungodly were frustrated in their efforts to suppress the Truth."

1890. *Cf.* 11:59.

16. In front of such a one
Is Hell, and he is given
For drink, boiling fetid water.

١٦ مِّن وَرَآئِهِۦ جَهَنَّمُ وَيُسۡقَىٰ مِن مَّآءٖ صَدِيدٖ

17. In gulps will he sip it,
But never will he be near
Swallowing it down his throat:
Death will come to him
From every quarter, yet
Will he not die: and
In front of him will be
A chastisement unrelenting.[1891]

١٧ يَتَجَرَّعُهُۥ وَلَا يَكَادُ يُسِيغُهُۥ
وَيَأۡتِيهِ ٱلۡمَوۡتُ مِن كُلِّ
مَكَانٖ وَمَا هُوَ بِمَيِّتٖۖ
وَمِن وَرَآئِهِۦ عَذَابٌ غَلِيظٞ

18. The parable of those who
Reject their Lord is that
Their works are as ashes,[1892]
On which the wind blows
Furiously on a tempestuous day:
No power have they over
Aught that they have earned:
That is the straying
Far, far (from the goal).

١٨ مَّثَلُ ٱلَّذِينَ كَفَرُواْ بِرَبِّهِمۡۖ
أَعۡمَٰلُهُمۡ كَرَمَادٍ ٱشۡتَدَّتۡ بِهِ ٱلرِّيحُ فِي يَوۡمٍ
عَاصِفٖۖ لَّا يَقۡدِرُونَ مِمَّا كَسَبُواْ عَلَىٰ شَيۡءٖۚ
ذَٰلِكَ هُوَ ٱلضَّلَٰلُ ٱلۡبَعِيدُ

19. Seest thou not that Allah
Created the heavens and the earth
In Truth?[1893] If He so will,
He can remove you
And put (in your place)
A new Creation?

١٩ أَلَمۡ تَرَ أَنَّ ٱللَّهَ خَلَقَ
ٱلسَّمَٰوَٰتِ وَٱلۡأَرۡضَ بِٱلۡحَقِّۚ
إِن يَشَأۡ يُذۡهِبۡكُمۡ وَيَأۡتِ بِخَلۡقٖ جَدِيدٖ

20. Nor is that for Allah
Any great matter.[1894]

٢٠ وَمَا ذَٰلِكَ عَلَى ٱللَّهِ بِعَزِيزٖ

21. They will all be marshalled
Before Allah together: then

٢١ وَبَرَزُواْ لِلَّهِ جَمِيعٗا

1891. A graphic and deterrent picture, from the preaching of the earlier Prophets, of unrelieved horror of the torments of Hell. The door of escape by annihilation is also closed to them.

1892. Note the fulness of the parable. The works of the ungoldy are in themselves light and unsubstantial like ashes: they are the useless rubbish that remains out of the faculties and opportunities which they have misused by burning them up. Further, the ashes are blown about hither and thither by the wind: the ungodly have no compass, direction, or purpose that can stand. The wind, too, which blows on them is no ordinary wind, nor the day on which they seek to enjoy the fruits of their labours an ordinary tranquil day: a furious gale is blowing, for such is the Wrath of Allah. They have neither internal peace nor external gain. In the scattering of the ashes they lose control even of such things as they might have earned but for their misdeeds. Their whole nature is contaminated. All their wishes go astray. They are carried so far, far away from what was on their minds. What did they aim at, and what did they achieve?

1893. *Ḥaqq*: Truth. Right. Righteousness. True proportions. Reality. Allah's creation is not to be trifled with. It is built on righteousness, and those who do not obey its laws must give place to others who do. This warning is repeated again and again in history and in revelation. *Cf.* 6:73.

1894. *'Azīz*: great, mighty, excellent, powerful, rare, precious.

Will the weak say to those[1895]
Who were arrogant: "For us,
We but followed you: can ye
Then avail us at all
Against the Wrath of Allah?"
They will reply, "If we
Had received the guidance[1896]
Of Allah, we should have
Given it to you: to us
It makes no difference (now)
Whether we rage, or bear
(These torments) with patience:
For ourselves there is no way
Of escape."

فَقَالَ ٱلضُّعَفَٰٓؤُاْ لِلَّذِينَ ٱسۡتَكۡبَرُوٓاْ
إِنَّا كُنَّا لَكُمۡ تَبَعٗا
فَهَلۡ أَنتُم مُّغۡنُونَ عَنَّا
مِنۡ عَذَابِ ٱللَّهِ مِن شَيۡءٖۚ
قَالُواْ لَوۡ هَدَىٰنَا ٱللَّهُ لَهَدَيۡنَٰكُمۡۖ
سَوَآءٌ عَلَيۡنَآ أَجَزِعۡنَآ أَمۡ صَبَرۡنَا
مَا لَنَا مِن مَّحِيصٖ

SECTION 4.

22. And Satan will say
When the matter is decided:[1897]
"It was Allah Who gave you
A promise of Truth: I too
Promised, but I failed
In my promise to you.
I had no authority over you
Except to call you, but ye
Listened to me: then
Reproach not me, but reproach
Your own souls. I cannot listen
To your cries, nor can ye
Listen to mine. I reject[1898]
Your former act in associating
Me with Allah.
For wrongdoers there must be
A Grievous Penalty."

(٢٢) وَقَالَ ٱلشَّيۡطَٰنُ لَمَّا قُضِيَ ٱلۡأَمۡرُ
إِنَّ ٱللَّهَ وَعَدَكُمۡ وَعۡدَ ٱلۡحَقِّ
وَوَعَدتُّكُمۡ فَأَخۡلَفۡتُكُمۡۖ وَمَا كَانَ لِيَ عَلَيۡكُم
مِّن سُلۡطَٰنٍ إِلَّآ أَن دَعَوۡتُكُمۡ فَٱسۡتَجَبۡتُمۡ لِيۖ
فَلَا تَلُومُونِي وَلُومُوٓاْ أَنفُسَكُمۖ
مَّآ أَنَا۠ بِمُصۡرِخِكُمۡ وَمَآ أَنتُم بِمُصۡرِخِيَّۖ
إِنِّي كَفَرۡتُ بِمَآ أَشۡرَكۡتُمُونِ مِن قَبۡلُۗ
إِنَّ ٱلظَّٰلِمِينَ لَهُمۡ عَذَابٌ أَلِيمٞ

1895. When the time for judgement comes, there are two kinds of disillusionment waiting for the ungodly. (1) Those who were misled and failed to see that each soul bears its own personal responsibility (2:134) and cannot shift it on to others, will turn to those who misled them, in the hope that they might intercede for them or do something to help them. They receive a plain answer as in the latter part of this verse. (2) Those who relied on Satan, the Power of Evil. His answer (in 14:22 below) is frank, cynical and brutal.

1896. Those whose power or specious intelligence or influence misled them—such as false priests or leaders—will find themselves in a perilous state. How can they help others? They themselves failed to profit from Allah's guidance, and they can with some justice retort that they put them in the wrong path as they followed it themselves!

1897. After the Judgement, Evil declares itself in its true colours. Frankly it says: 'I deceived you. The promise of Allah was true, but you believed me rather than Allah. I had no power to force you. I had but to call you, and you came running after me. You must blame yourselves. Did you think I was equal with Allah? I know too well that I was not and never could be. If you did wrong, you must suffer the Penalty.'

1898. See the last note. An alternative interpretation of this sentence may be: "I had already beforehand rebelled against Allah with Whom ye associated me."

23. But those who believe
And work righteousness
Will be admitted to Gardens
Beneath which rivers flow—
To dwell therein for aye
With the leave of their Lord.
Their greeting therein
Will be: "Peace!"[1899]

٢٣ وَأُدْخِلَ ٱلَّذِينَ ءَامَنُوا۟ وَعَمِلُوا۟
ٱلصَّٰلِحَٰتِ جَنَّٰتٍ تَجْرِى مِن تَحْتِهَا
ٱلْأَنْهَٰرُ خَٰلِدِينَ فِيهَا بِإِذْنِ رَبِّهِمْ ۖ
تَحِيَّتُهُمْ فِيهَا سَلَٰمٌ

24. Seest thou not how
Allah sets forth a parable?—
A goodly Word[1900]
Like a goodly tree,
Whose root is firmly fixed,
And its branches (reach)
To the heavens—

٢٤ أَلَمْ تَرَ كَيْفَ ضَرَبَ ٱللَّهُ مَثَلًا
كَلِمَةً طَيِّبَةً كَشَجَرَةٍ طَيِّبَةٍ
أَصْلُهَا ثَابِتٌ وَفَرْعُهَا فِى ٱلسَّمَآءِ

25. It brings forth its fruit[1901]
At all times, by the leave
Of its Lord.
So Allah sets forth parables
For men, in order that
They may receive admonition.

٢٥ تُؤْتِىٓ أُكُلَهَا كُلَّ حِينٍۭ بِإِذْنِ رَبِّهَا ۗ
وَيَضْرِبُ ٱللَّهُ ٱلْأَمْثَالَ لِلنَّاسِ
لَعَلَّهُمْ يَتَذَكَّرُونَ

26. And the parable
Of an evil Word
Is that of any evil tree:
It is torn up by the root
From the surface of the earth:
It has no stability.[1902]

٢٦ وَمَثَلُ كَلِمَةٍ خَبِيثَةٍ كَشَجَرَةٍ
خَبِيثَةٍ ٱجْتُثَّتْ مِن فَوْقِ ٱلْأَرْضِ
مَا لَهَا مِن قَرَارٍ

1899. How this contrasts with the misery and mutual self-recrimination of the ungodly!

1900. "Goodly word" is usually interpreted as the Divine Word, the Divine Message, the True Religion. It may also be interpreted in a more general sense as a word of truth, a word of goodness or kindness, which follows from a true appreciation of Religion. For Religion includes our duty to Allah and our duty to man. The "evil word" is opposite to this: false religion, blasphemy, false speech, or preaching or teaching unkindness and wrongdoing. (R).

1901. The goodly tree is known for: (1) its beauty: it gives pleasure to all who see it: (2) its stability; it remains firm and unshaken in storms, because its roots are firmly fixed in the earth; (3) its wide compass; its branches reach high, and it catches all the sunshine from heaven, and gives shade to countless birds in its branches and men and animals beneath it, and (4) its abundant fruit, which it yields at all times. So is the Good Word. It is as beautiful as it is true. It abides in all changes and chances of this life, and even beyond (see verse 27 below): it is never shaken by sorrow or what seems to us calamity; its roots are deep down in the bedrock facts of life. Its reach is universal, above, around, below: it is illuminated by the divine light from heaven, and its consolation reaches countless beings of all grades of life. Its fruit—the enjoyment of its blessings—is not confined to one season or one set of circumstances; furthermore the fortunate man who is the vehicle of that word has no self-pride: he attributes all its goodness, and his act in spreading it, to the Will and Leave of Allah. *Cf.* the New Testment Parable of the Sower (Matt. iv. 14-20) or of the Mustard-seed (Matt. iv. 30-32). In this Parable of the Qur'ān there are fewer words and more spiritual meaning, and the emphasis is on more essential things.

1902. The evil tree is the opposite of the goodly tree. The parallelism of contrast can be followed out in all the details of the last note.

27. Allah will establish in strength
Those who believe, with the Word
That stands firm, in this world
And in the Hereafter; but Allah
Will leave, to stray, those
Who do wrong: Allah doeth
What he willeth.[1903]

﴿٢٧﴾ يُثَبِّتُ ٱللَّهُ ٱلَّذِينَ ءَامَنُوا۟ بِٱلْقَوْلِ ٱلثَّابِتِ فِى ٱلْحَيَوٰةِ ٱلدُّنْيَا وَفِى ٱلْـَٔاخِرَةِ ۖ وَيُضِلُّ ٱللَّهُ ٱلظَّـٰلِمِينَ ۚ وَيَفْعَلُ ٱللَّهُ مَا يَشَآءُ

C. 118.—But the evil not only choose evil
(14:28-52.) For themselves but mislead others
To perdition. The godly should learn
From the Signs of Allah all around them,
And be on their guard against all
That is false. So Abraham prayed
Not only for his posterity, but for all:
For he foresaw the universality
Of Allah's Message in Islam.
That leads to the sublime doctrine
Of Oneness, which will be seen
In its fulness on the Great Day
When a new Earth and a new Heaven
Will proclaim the end of Evil
And the adjustment of all this life's accounts. (R).

SECTION 5.

28. Hast thou not turned
Thy vision to those who[1904]
Have changed the favour of Allah
Into blasphemy and caused
Their people to descend
To the House of Perdition?—

﴿٢٨﴾ أَلَمْ تَرَ إِلَى ٱلَّذِينَ بَدَّلُوا۟ نِعْمَتَ ٱللَّهِ كُفْرًا وَأَحَلُّوا۟ قَوْمَهُمْ دَارَ ٱلْبَوَارِ

29. Into Hell? They will burn
Therein—an evil place
To stay in!

﴿٢٩﴾ جَهَنَّمَ يَصْلَوْنَهَا ۖ وَبِئْسَ ٱلْقَرَارُ

1903. His Will and Plan may be above comprehension but will prevail over all things. It is not like the will of man, who may plan good things but is not necessarily able to carry them out.

1904. There is a particular and a general meaning. The particular meaning is understood to be a reference to the Makkan Pagans who turned the House of Allah into a place for the worship of horrible idols and the practice of unseemly rites and cults. There is no real difficulty in accepting this as part of a late Makkan Sūrah even without supposing it to be a prophecy. The Makkan Pagans had turned Religion into a blasphemous superstition, and were misguiding their people, persecuting the true Messenger of Allah and all who followed his teaching. Their cup of iniquity seemed about full, and they seemed to be heading to perdition, as later events indeed showed to be the case.

The general meaning is also clear. Selfish men, when they seize power, want worship for themselves or their Phantasies, in derogation of the true God. Power, which should have been an instrument of good, becomes in their hands an instrument of evil. They and their people rush headlong to perdition. "These be thy gods, O Israel!" has been a cry repeated again and again in history, in the face, or at the back, of men of God!

30. And they set up (idols)
As equal to Allah, to mislead
(Men) from the Path! Say:
"Enjoy (your brief power)!
But verily ye are making
Straightway for Hell!"

٣٠ وَجَعَلُوا لِلَّهِ أَندَادًا لِّيُضِلُّوا عَن سَبِيلِهِۦ قُلْ تَمَتَّعُوا فَإِنَّ مَصِيرَكُمْ إِلَى ٱلنَّارِ

31. Speak to my servants
Who have believed,[1905]
That they may establish
Regular prayers, and spend
(In charity) out of the
Sustenance[1906]
We have given them,
Secretly and openly, before
The coming of a Day
In which there will be
Neither mutual bargaining[1907]
Nor befriending.

٣١ قُل لِّعِبَادِىَ ٱلَّذِينَ ءَامَنُوا يُقِيمُوا ٱلصَّلَوٰةَ وَيُنفِقُوا مِمَّا رَزَقْنَٰهُمْ سِرًّا وَعَلَانِيَةً مِّن قَبْلِ أَن يَأْتِىَ يَوْمٌ لَّا بَيْعٌ فِيهِ وَلَا خِلَٰلٌ

32. It is Allah Who hath created
The heavens and the earth
And sendeth down rain
From the skies, and with it
Bringeth out fruits wherewith
To feed you: it is He
Who hath made the ships subject
To you, that they may sail
Through the sea by His
Command;

٣٢ ٱللَّهُ ٱلَّذِى خَلَقَ ٱلسَّمَٰوَٰتِ وَٱلْأَرْضَ وَأَنزَلَ مِنَ ٱلسَّمَآءِ مَآءً فَأَخْرَجَ بِهِۦ مِنَ ٱلثَّمَرَٰتِ رِزْقًا لَّكُمْ وَسَخَّرَ لَكُمُ ٱلْفُلْكَ لِتَجْرِىَ فِى ٱلْبَحْرِ بِأَمْرِهِۦ

1905. Putting ourselves back in the position which the Muslim community found themselves in Makkah just before the Hijrah, we can imagine how much encouragement and consolation they needed from the preaching, the Faith, and the steadfast character of Al Muṣṭafā. Intolerant persecution was the order of the day; neither the life nor the property or reputation of the Muslims was safe. They are asked to find strength and tranquillity in prayer and in helping each other according to their needs and resources.

1906. Here, as elsewhere, "Sustenance" is to be taken in the literal as well as the metaphorical sense. There were many among the Muslims who were poor, or slaves, or depressed, because they were deprived of the means of livelihood on account of their Faith. They were to be fed, clothed, and sheltered, by those who had means. There were those who were ignorant and needed spiritual sustenance: they were to be taught and strengthened by those to whom Allah had given knowledge and firmness of character. Charity was to be ordinarily secret, so as to cut out all show or parade, and perhaps also lest the enemy should dry up those sources by unprincipled violence; but there must be much that had to be open and organised, so that all the needy could know where to go to be relieved.

1907. The great Day of Reckoning would be one on which all values would be changed. Wealth, as understood in this world, would no longer count. Should we not therefore use any wealth we have in this life, to give here and receive there? *Bay'* includes all bargaining—barter, purchase and sale, etc. In this world, where wealth has some value, let us spend it and get for ourselves "treasures in heaven." In the next life each man will stand on his merits and personal responsibility. One man cannot help another. Let us here help each other to become true and righteous, so that our personal account may be favourable there.

And the rivers (also)
Hath He made subject to you.[1908]

وَسَخَّرَ لَكُمُ الْأَنْهَارَ

33. And He hath made subject
To you the sun and the moon,[1909]
Both diligently pursuing
Their courses: and the Night
And the Day hath He (also)
Made subject to you.

وَسَخَّرَ لَكُمُ ﴿٣٣﴾
الشَّمْسَ وَالْقَمَرَ دَائِبَيْنِ
وَسَخَّرَ لَكُمُ اللَّيْلَ وَالنَّهَارَ

34. And he giveth you
Of all that ye ask for.[1910]
But if ye count the favours
Of Allah, never will ye
Be able to number them.
Verily, man is given up
To injustice and ingratitude.[1911]

وَءَاتَىٰكُم مِّن كُلِّ مَا سَأَلْتُمُوهُ ﴿٣٤﴾
وَإِن تَعُدُّوا نِعْمَتَ اللَّهِ لَا تُحْصُوهَا
إِنَّ الْإِنسَٰنَ لَظَلُومٌ كَفَّارٌ

SECTION 6.

35. Remember Abraham said:[1912]
"O my Lord! make this city

وَإِذْ قَالَ إِبْرَٰهِيمُ رَبِّ اجْعَلْ هَٰذَا الْبَلَدَ ﴿٣٥﴾

1908. We must realise that behind all of our strength, skill, and intelligence there is the power and goodness of Allah, Who gave us all these things. Man can understand and control the forces of nature so as to bring them to his own service: he can only do so, because (1) he has got these gifts from Allah, and (2) Allah has fixed definite laws in nature, of which he can take advantage by Allah's command and permission. He has been made Vicegerent on earth (2:30): Allah commanded the highest creatures to bow down to Adam (2:34). Man, by Allah's command, can use rain to produce food for himself: make ships to sail the seas: use rivers as highways, and cut canals for traffic and irrigation. Not only this, but even the heavenly bodies can (by Allah's command) contribute to his needs (see next verse).

1909. The sun gives out heat, which is the source of all life and energy on this planet, and produces the seasons of the year, by utilising which, man can supply his needs, not only material, but immaterial in the shape of light, health, and other blessings. The sun and the moon together produce tides, and are responsible for atmospheric changes which are of the highest importance in the life of man. The succession of Day and Night is due to the apparent daily course of the sun through the skies; and the cool light of the moon performs other services different from those of warm daylight. Because there are laws here, which men can understand and calculate, he can use all such things for his own service, and in that sense the heavenly bodies are themselves made subject to him by Allah's command.

1910. Sincere and true prayer in faith is answered by Allah. Thus He gives us everything which a wise and benevolent Providence can give.

1911. I have tried to render the intensive forms of the Arabic by what I consider their near equivalent here: the phrase "given up to injustice and ingratitude" suggests habitual ignorance of just values and ingratitude for the innumerable gifts and favours which Allah has showered on mankind.

1912. The Prayer of Abraham, the True in Faith, the progenitor of the Semitic peoples and the Prototype of their Religion, is introduced in this place, to illustrate the points referred to in the preceding section 14:31-34, *viz.*, how the new Revelation through the Ka'bah bears out the universal Revelation of Prayer and Charity, Love of Allah and man, recognition of Allah's handiwork in nature, and insistence on man's turning away from false worship and ingratitude to Allah. Notice the four divisions into which it falls: (1) verses 35-36 are spoken by Abraham as on his own behalf ("O my Lord!"); (2) verse 37-38 are spoken on behalf of his progeny ("O our Lord!") but with special reference to the elder branch, the children of Ismā'īl; (3) verses 39-40 are again a personal appeal, but both branches of his family, *viz.*, the sons of Ismā'īl and Isaac, are expressly mentioned; (4) verse 41 is a Prayer for himself, his parents, and all Believers, typifying that in the universality of Islam all nations are to be blessed. Jerusalem, for the Mosaic Law and the Gospel of Jesus, was the centre and symbol for the Jews, though of course all Allah's Truth is universal; Makkah, the centre of the Arabs, was to throw off its tribal character and become universal in spite of the Makkans themselves.

One of peace and security:
And preserve me and my sons
From worshipping idols.[1913]

ءَامِنًا وَٱجْنُبْنِي وَبَنِيَّ أَن نَّعْبُدَ ٱلْأَصْنَامَ

36. "O my Lord! they have indeed
Led astray many among mankind;
He then who follows my (ways)
Is of me, and he that
Disobeys me—but Thou
Art indeed Oft-Forgiving,
Most Merciful.

٣٦ رَبِّ إِنَّهُنَّ أَضْلَلْنَ كَثِيرًا مِّنَ ٱلنَّاسِ
فَمَن تَبِعَنِي فَإِنَّهُۥ مِنِّي وَمَنْ عَصَانِي
فَإِنَّكَ غَفُورٌ رَّحِيمٌ

37. "O our Lord! I have made
Some of my offspring to dwell
In a valley without cultivation,[1914]
By Thy Sacred House;
In order, O our Lord, that they
May establish regular Prayer:
So fill the hearts of some
Among men with love towards
them,
And feed them with Fruits:[1915]
So that they may give thanks.

٣٧ رَّبَّنَآ إِنِّيٓ أَسْكَنتُ مِن ذُرِّيَّتِي
بِوَادٍ غَيْرِ ذِي زَرْعٍ عِندَ بَيْتِكَ ٱلْمُحَرَّمِ
رَبَّنَا لِيُقِيمُوا ٱلصَّلَوٰةَ فَٱجْعَلْ أَفْـِٔدَةً
مِّنَ ٱلنَّاسِ تَهْوِيٓ إِلَيْهِمْ وَٱرْزُقْهُم
مِّنَ ٱلثَّمَرَٰتِ لَعَلَّهُمْ يَشْكُرُونَ

38. "O our Lord! truly Thou
Dost know what we conceal
And what we reveal:
For nothing whatever is hiddden
From Allah, whether on earth
Or in heaven.[1916]

٣٨ رَبَّنَآ إِنَّكَ تَعْلَمُ مَا نُخْفِي وَمَا نُعْلِنُ
وَمَا يَخْفَىٰ عَلَى ٱللَّهِ مِن شَيْءٍ
فِي ٱلْأَرْضِ وَلَا فِي ٱلسَّمَآءِ

39. "Praise be to Allah. Who hath
Granted unto me in old age
Ismā'īl and Isaac: for truly
My Lord is He, the Hearer
Of Prayer![1917]

٣٩ ٱلْحَمْدُ لِلَّهِ ٱلَّذِي وَهَبَ لِي عَلَى ٱلْكِبَرِ
إِسْمَٰعِيلَ وَإِسْحَٰقَ إِنَّ رَبِّي لَسَمِيعُ ٱلدُّعَآءِ

1913. *Cf.* 2:125-129. Abraham (with Ismā'īl built the Ka'bah, and Abraham asks a blessing on his handiwork and forgivness for such lapses into idoltary as both branches of his family might fall into.

1914. The Makkan valley is enclosed by hills on all sides, unlike Madīnah, which has level cultivated plains. But just because of its natural isolation, it is fitted to be a centre for prayer and praise.

1915. *Cf.* 2:126, and n. 128.(The "Fruits" are there explained). The righteous, though they have to have sustenance, both in a literal and figurative sense, require also the love and sympathy of their fellow-men.

1916. In Abraham's prophetic mind was the secret and open enmity or contempt which the Children of Israel were to have for the Children of Ismā'īl (Arabs). He prays to Allah that they may be united in Islam, as indeed they were, except a small remnant.

1917. Abraham was 100 years old when Isaac was born (Gen. xxi. 5); and as Ismā'īl was 13 years old when Abraham was 99, (Gen. xvii. 24-25), Ismā'īl was also a son of his father's old age, having been born when Abraham was 86 years old. The younger son's progeny developed the Faith of Israel and that of Christ; the elder son's progeny perfected the more universal Faith of Islam, the Faith of Abraham the True.

40\. "O my Lord! make me
One who establishes regular
Prayer,
And also (raise such)
Among my offspring[1918]
O our Lord!
And accept Thou my Prayer.

﴿٤٠﴾ رَبِّ ٱجْعَلْنِى مُقِيمَ ٱلصَّلَوٰةِ
وَمِن ذُرِّيَّتِى ۚ
رَبَّنَا وَتَقَبَّلْ دُعَآءِ

41\. "O our Lord![1919] cover (us)[1920]
With Thy Forgiveness—me,
My parents,[1921] and (all) Believers,
On the Day that the Reckoning
Will be established!"[1922]

﴿٤١﴾ رَبَّنَا ٱغْفِرْ لِى وَلِوَٰلِدَىَّ
وَلِلْمُؤْمِنِينَ يَوْمَ يَقُومُ ٱلْحِسَابُ

SECTION 7.

42\. Think not that Allah
Doth not heed the deeds
Of those who do wrong.
He but giveth them respite
Against a Day when
The eyes will fixedly stare
In horror—

﴿٤٢﴾ وَلَا تَحْسَبَنَّ ٱللَّهَ غَٰفِلًا
عَمَّا يَعْمَلُ ٱلظَّٰلِمُونَ ۚ
إِنَّمَا يُؤَخِّرُهُمْ لِيَوْمٍ تَشْخَصُ فِيهِ ٱلْأَبْصَٰرُ

43\. They are running forward
With necks outstretched,
Their heads uplifted, their gaze
Returning not towards them,
And their hearts a (gaping)
void![1923]

﴿٤٣﴾ مُهْطِعِينَ مُقْنِعِى رُءُوسِهِمْ
لَا يَرْتَدُّ إِلَيْهِمْ طَرْفُهُمْ ۖ
وَأَفْـِٔدَتُهُمْ هَوَآءٌ

1918\. Abraham prays for both branches of his family, having a wider vision than some of the later Children of Israel.

1919\. Read again n. 1912 above. Having prayed for his progeny, Abraham now prays for Allah's Grace on himself, his parents, and the whole Brotherhood of Faith, irrespective of family or race or time, to be perfected in the ideal of Islam.

1920\. For the shades of meaning in the different words for forgiveness, see n. 110 to 2:109.

1921\. *My parents.* Abraham's father was an idolater (43:26; 6:74). Not only that, but he persecuted the Faith of Unity and threatened Abraham with stoning and exile (19:46); and he and his people cast him into the Fire to be burned (21:52, 68). Yet Abraham's heart was tender, and he prayed for forgiveness for his father because of a promise which he made (9:114), though he renounced the land of his fathers (Chaldea).

1922\. At the final Reckoning, all that may seem inequality or injustice in this world will be redressed. But the merits of the best of us will need Allah's Grace to establish us in that lasting felicity which is promised to the righteous. And Abraham, as the father of Prophecy, prayed for all—for the Universal Faith perfected in Islam.

1923\. A picture of horror. The evil ones, when they realise the situation, will be dazed: their eyes will stare without expression, and never move back; their necks will be outstretched; their heads uplifted in terror of the Judgement from on High; and their hearts become empty of all hope or intelligence as the physical heart might become empty of blood when circulation stops. In this state they will press forward to Judgement.

44. So warn mankind
Of the Day when the Wrath
Will reach them: then will
The wrongdoers say: "Our Lord!
Respite us (if only)
For a short Term: we will
Answer Thy Call, and follow
The messengers!"
"What! were ye not wont
To swear aforetime that ye
Should suffer no decline?[1924]

٤٤ وَأَنذِرِ ٱلنَّاسَ يَوْمَ يَأْتِيهِمُ ٱلْعَذَابُ
فَيَقُولُ ٱلَّذِينَ ظَلَمُوا۟ رَبَّنَآ أَخِّرْنَآ إِلَىٰٓ أَجَلٍ
قَرِيبٍ نُّجِبْ دَعْوَتَكَ وَنَتَّبِعِ ٱلرُّسُلَ ۗ
أَوَلَمْ تَكُونُوٓا۟ أَقْسَمْتُم مِّن قَبْلُ
مَا لَكُم مِّن زَوَالٍ

45. "And ye dwelt in the dwellings
Of men who wronged their own
Souls; ye were clearly shown
How We dealt with them;
And We put forth (many) Parables
In your behalf!"

٤٥ وَسَكَنتُمْ فِى مَسَٰكِنِ ٱلَّذِينَ
ظَلَمُوٓا۟ أَنفُسَهُمْ وَتَبَيَّنَ لَكُمْ كَيْفَ
فَعَلْنَا بِهِمْ وَضَرَبْنَا لَكُمُ ٱلْأَمْثَالَ

46. Mighty indeed were the plots
Which they made, but their plots
Were (well) within the sight
Of Allah, even though they were
Such as to shake the hills!

٤٦ وَقَدْ مَكَرُوا۟ مَكْرَهُمْ وَعِندَ ٱللَّهِ
مَكْرُهُمْ وَإِن كَانَ مَكْرُهُمْ
لِتَزُولَ مِنْهُ ٱلْجِبَالُ

47. Never think that Allah would fail
His messengers in His promise:
For Allah is Exalted in Power—
The Lord of Retribution.

٤٧ فَلَا تَحْسَبَنَّ ٱللَّهَ مُخْلِفَ وَعْدِهِۦ رُسُلَهُۥٓ ۗ
إِنَّ ٱللَّهَ عَزِيزٌ ذُو ٱنتِقَامٍ

48. One day the Earth will be
Changed to a different Earth,
And so will be the Heavens,[1925]
And (men) will be marshalled
Forth, before Allah, the One,
The Irresistible;

٤٨ يَوْمَ تُبَدَّلُ ٱلْأَرْضُ
غَيْرَ ٱلْأَرْضِ وَٱلسَّمَٰوَٰتُ ۖ
وَبَرَزُوا۟ لِلَّهِ ٱلْوَٰحِدِ ٱلْقَهَّارِ

49. And thou wilt see
The Sinners that day
Bound together in fetters—[1926]

٤٩ وَتَرَى ٱلْمُجْرِمِينَ يَوْمَئِذٍ
مُّقَرَّنِينَ فِى ٱلْأَصْفَادِ

1924. *Zawāl* = decline from the zenith, as that of the sun; decline from the highest point reached by a heavenly body in its course through the sky. The ungodly are apt to think that their power will remain in the ascendant, on account of some material advantages given them temporarily by Allah, but they are constantly receiving warnings in history and revelation and from the example of others before them. There is a warning to the contemporary Pagan Makkans here; but the warning is perfectly general, and for all time.

1925. "A new earth and a new heaven" refers to the entirely changed conditions at the end of things as we know them. *Cf.* 20:105-107. 39:67-69, 84:3. (R).

1926. *Cf.* 36:8, 60:71. 69:30. (Eds.).

50. Their garments[1927] of liquid
pitch,[1928]
And their faces covered with Fire;

٥٠ سَرَابِيلُهُم مِّن قَطِرَانٍ
وَتَغْشَىٰ وُجُوهَهُمُ ٱلنَّارُ

51. That Allah may requite
Each soul according
To its deserts;[1929]
And verily Allah is Swift
In calling to account.[1930]

٥١ لِيَجْزِيَ ٱللَّهُ كُلَّ نَفْسٍ مَّا كَسَبَتْ
إِنَّ ٱللَّهَ سَرِيعُ ٱلْحِسَابِ

52. Here is a Message for mankind:
Let them take warning therefrom,
And let them know that He
Is (no other than) One God:[1931]
Let men of understanding
Take heed.

٥٢ هَٰذَا بَلَٰغٌ لِّلنَّاسِ وَلِيُنذَرُوا۟ بِهِۦ
وَلِيَعْلَمُوٓا۟ أَنَّمَا هُوَ إِلَٰهٌ وَٰحِدٌ
وَلِيَذَّكَّرَ أُو۟لُوا۟ ٱلْأَلْبَٰبِ

1927. *Sirbāl*; plural, *Sarābīl:* a garment or coat of mail, breast plate; something covering the most vital parts of the body; like the shirt or the Indian *kurtā*.

1928. *Qaṭirān*: black pitch, a resinous substance exuding from certain kinds of trees like the terebinth or the pines, or distilled from wood or coal. It catches fire readily. Issuing from the upper garments (*Sarābīl*) the flames soon cover the face, the most expressive part of man's essence or being. The metaphor of fetters (n. 1926) is now changed to that of pitch, which darkens and sets on fire the soul of man.

1929. *Its deserts: i.e.*, according to what it earned by its own acts, good or evil, in its life of probation.

1930. *Swift in calling into account*: We understand this in two significations. (1) Let not the wicked think that because Allah, out of His infinite grace and mercy, grants respite, therefore the retribution will be slow in coming. When the time comes in accordance with Allah's Plan and Wisdom, the retribution will come so swiftly that the ungodly will be surprised and they will wish they could get more respite (14:44.). (2) On the great Day of Reckoning, let it not be supposed that, because there will be millions of souls to be judged, there will be any delay in judgement as in a human tribunal. It will be a new world and beyond the flight of Time. Or if a metaphor from time as we conceive it in this world can be taken, it will be as it were in a twinkling of an eye (16:77).

1931. Here is another aspect of Truth of Unity. Allah being One, all justice is of one standard, for Truth is one, and we see it as soon as the scales of phenomenal diversity fall from our eyes. The one true Reality then emerges. Blessed are those who treasured this Truth in their souls already in their life of probation.

INTRODUCTION TO SŪRAH 15—*AL ḤIJR*

This is the last of the six Sūrahs of the Alif, Lām, Mīm series (10 to 15). Its place in chronology is the late Makkan period, probably somewhere near the middle of that period. See Introduction to S. 10, where will be found also an indication of the general subject matter of the whole series in the gradation of Quranic teaching.

The special subject matter of this Sūrah is the protection of Allah's Revelation and Allah's Truth. Evil arose from Pride and the warping of man's will, but Allah's Mercy is the antidote, as was proved in the case of Abraham and Lot, and might have been proved by the people of the Aykah and the Ḥijr if they had only attended to Allah's "Signs". The Qur'ān, beginning with the Seven Oft-Repeated Verses, is the precious vehicle for the praises of Allah.

Summary—Allah will guard His Revelation, in spite of the cavils of the Unbelievers: Allah is the source of all things; He knows His own people, whom He will gather to Himself (15:1-25, and C. 119).

How Evil arose through the pride of Iblīs, to whom a respite was granted for a period; but neither fear nor evil affect those who receive Allah's Message (15:26-50, and C. 120).

The Mercy of Allah to Abraham was conveyed by the same messengers that were sent to destroy the people of Lot for their unspeakable crimes; Evil brought its retribution also on the Companions of the Wood (*Al Aykah*) and of the Rocky Tract (*Al Ḥijr*) (15:51-84, and C. 121).

The Qur'ān and its Sūrahs teach you to celebrate Allah's praises, learn humility in worship, and serve Allah all your life (15:85-99, and C. 122).

Sūrah 15.

Al Ḥijr[1931-A]

*In the name of Allah, Most Gracious,
Most Merciful.*

بِسْمِ ٱللَّهِ ٱلرَّحْمَٰنِ ٱلرَّحِيمِ

1. Alif Lām Rā.[1932] These are
The Āyāt[1933] of Revelation—
Of a Qur'ān
That makes things clear.[1934]

الٓر تِلْكَ ءَايَٰتُ ٱلْكِتَٰبِ ۝١
وَقُرْءَانٍ مُّبِينٍ

C. 119.—Allah's Truth makes all things clear, and He
(15:1-25.) Will guard it. But His Signs are not
For those who mock. Who fails to see
The majesty, beauty, order, and harmony
Blazoned in His Creation, and His goodness
To all His creatures, in the heavens
And on earth? With Him are the sources
Of all things, and He doth freely give
His gifts in due measure. He holds
The keys of Life and Death, and He will remain
When all else passes away.

2. Again and again will those
Who disbelieve, wish that they
Had bowed (to Allah's Will)
In Islam.[1935]

رُّبَمَا يَوَدُّ ٱلَّذِينَ كَفَرُوا۟ ۝٢
لَوْ كَانُوا۟ مُسْلِمِينَ

3. Leave them alone, to enjoy[1936]
(The good things of this life)

ذَرْهُمْ يَأْكُلُوا۟ ۝٣

1931-A. See nn. 2002 and 2003 for an explanation of *Al Hijr.*

1932. For these mystic letters, see Introduction to Sūrah 10.

1933. *Cf.* 10:1. and n. 1382.

1934. Note how appropriately the different phrases in which the Qur'ān is characterised bring out its different aspects as a Revelation. Let us just consider the phrases used at the beginning of the six Alif, Lām, Mīm Sūrahs of which this is the last in order of arrangement. In 10:1 we read, "Āyāt (or verses or Signs) of the Book of Wisdom", the theme being the wonders of Allah's creation, and its relation to His Revelation. In 11:1 we read, "a Book, with verses basic or fundamental, further explained in detail": the theme is Allah's Justice and Punishment, to preserve the fundamental scheme of His Laws. In 12:1 we read, "The Symbols (or verses) of the Perspicuous Book": the wonderful unfolding of Allah's Plan is explained in Joseph's story. In 13:1 we read, "The Signs (or verses) of the Book": the contrasts in the modes of Allah's Revelation and its reception by man are pointed out, but not illustrated by detailed examples as in Joseph's perspicuous story. In 14:1 we read "A Book...revealed...to lead...out of...darkness into light": the theme being Abraham's prayer for man to be rescued from the darkness of false worship into the light of Unity. Here in 15:1 we read, "Āyāt (or verses) of Revelation—of a Qur'ān that makes things clear (or perspicuous)": the theme being an explanation of evil, and how Allah's Truth is protected from it.

1935. The time must inevitably come when those who allow themselves to be deceived by falsehood or deliberately break Allah's Law will find themselves in a terrible plight. They will then wish ardently and again and again, that they had sought Allah's Will and walked in the light of Truth. That time may be early or late—in this life, or death, or at the Day of Judgement, but it must come. Man's own highest interest requires that he should awake to the Reality before it is too late for repentance.

1936. Literally, "to eat", *Cf.* 5:69 and n. 776.

And to please themselves:
Let (false) Hope amuse them: soon
Will knowledge (undeceive
them).[1937]

وَيَتَمَتَّعُوا۟ وَيُلْهِهِمُ ٱلْأَمَلُ ۖ
فَسَوْفَ يَعْلَمُونَ

4. Never did We destroy
A population that had not
A term decreed and assigned
Beforehand.[1938]

٤ وَمَآ أَهْلَكْنَا مِن قَرْيَةٍ إِلَّا
وَلَهَا كِتَابٌ مَّعْلُومٌ

5. Neither can a people anticipate
Its Term, nor delay it.[1939]

٥ مَّا تَسْبِقُ مِنْ أُمَّةٍ أَجَلَهَا وَمَا يَسْتَـْٔخِرُونَ

6. They say: "O thou to whom
The Message is being revealed!
Truly thou art mad
(or possessed)![1940]

٦ وَقَالُوا۟ يَـٰٓأَيُّهَا ٱلَّذِى
نُزِّلَ عَلَيْهِ ٱلذِّكْرُ إِنَّكَ لَمَجْنُونٌ

7. "Why bringest thou not
Angels to us if it be
That thou hast the Truth?"[1941]

٧ لَّوْ مَا تَأْتِينَا بِٱلْمَلَـٰٓئِكَةِ
إِن كُنتَ مِنَ ٱلصَّـٰدِقِينَ

8. We send not the angels
Down except for just cause:[1942]
If they came (to the ungodly),
Behold! no respite would they
have![1943]

٨ مَا نُنَزِّلُ ٱلْمَلَـٰٓئِكَةَ إِلَّا بِٱلْحَقِّ
وَمَا كَانُوٓا۟ إِذًا مُّنظَرِينَ

1937. The foolish and the wicked set great store by the pleasures of this world. In their pride they think they have all knowledge. In the fulness of knowledge they will see how wrong they were. Meanwhile those who have received the Light should not for a single moment wonder at the apparent prosperity of the ungodly in this world. They should leave them alone, confident in the goodness and justice of Allah.

1938. *Kitābun ma'lūmun*: literally, "a writing known". There are many shades of meaning implied. (1) For every people, as for every individual, there is a definite Term assigned: their faculty of choice gives them the opportunity of moulding their will according to Allah's Will, and thus identifying themselves with Allah's Universal Law. During that Term they will be given plenty of rope: after that Term is past, there will be no opportunity for repentance. (2) Neither the righteous nor the ungodly can hasten or delay the doom: Allah's Will must prevail, and He is All-Wise. (3) The destruction of a people is not an arbitrary punishment from Allah: the people bring it on themselves by their own choice: for the fixed Law or Decree of Allah is always made known to them beforehand, and in many ways.

1939. *Cf.* 7:34. Also see the last note.

1940. Al Muṣṭafā was accused by the ungodly of being mad or possessed, because he spoke of higher things than they knew, and acted from motives purer and nobler than they could understand. So, in a minor degree, is the lot of all the righteous in the presence of an ungodly world. Their motives, actions, words, hopes, and aspirations are unintelligible to their fellows, and they are accused of being mad or out of their senses. But they know that they are on the right path, and it is the ungodly who are really acting against their own best interests.

1941. *Cf.* 6:8-9 and notes 840, 841. On the part of the unbelievers, this is a mere taunt. They neither believe in Allah nor in angels nor in revelation nor in any but material things. It is ridiculous to suppose that they could be taken seriously.

1942. Angels are not sent down to satisfy the whim or curiosity of the unbelievers. They are sent to bring inspiration to Allah's messengers and to execute Allah's decrees.

1943. If the angels were to appear before the ungodly, it would mean that they came to execute just punishment, and then there would be no hope of respite possible for the ungodly.

9. We have, without doubt, Sent down the Message; And We will assuredly Guard it (from corruption).[1944]	إِنَّا نَحْنُ نَزَّلْنَا ٱلذِّكْرَ وَإِنَّا لَهُۥ لَحَٰفِظُونَ ﴿٩﴾
10. We did send messengers before thee Amongst the religious sects[1945] Of old:	وَلَقَدْ أَرْسَلْنَا مِن قَبْلِكَ فِى شِيَعِ ٱلْأَوَّلِينَ ﴿١٠﴾
11. But never came a messenger To them but they mocked him.	وَمَا يَأْتِيهِم مِّن رَّسُولٍ إِلَّا كَانُوا۟ بِهِۦ يَسْتَهْزِءُونَ ﴿١١﴾
12. Even so do We let it creep Into the hearts of the sinners—[1946]	كَذَٰلِكَ نَسْلُكُهُۥ فِى قُلُوبِ ٱلْمُجْرِمِينَ ﴿١٢﴾
13. That they should not believe In the (Message); but the ways Of the ancients have passed away.[1947]	لَا يُؤْمِنُونَ بِهِۦ ۖ وَقَدْ خَلَتْ سُنَّةُ ٱلْأَوَّلِينَ ﴿١٣﴾
14. Even if We opened out to them A gate from heaven,[1948] And they were to continue (All day) ascending therein,	وَلَوْ فَتَحْنَا عَلَيْهِم بَابًا مِّنَ ٱلسَّمَآءِ فَظَلُّوا۟ فِيهِ يَعْرُجُونَ ﴿١٤﴾
15. They would only say: "Our eyes have been intoxicated:	لَقَالُوٓا۟ إِنَّمَا سُكِّرَتْ أَبْصَٰرُنَا ﴿١٥﴾

1944. The purity of the text of the Qur'ān through fourteen centuries is a foretaste of the eternal care with which Allah's Truth is guarded through all ages. All corruptions, inventions, and accretions pass away, but Allah's Pure and Holy Truth will never suffer eclipse even though the whole world mocked at it and was bent on destroying it. (R).

1945. *Shiya'un*, plural of *Shī'atun* = a sect, a religious division. Mankind sees fragments of Truth at a time, and is apt to fall into fragments and divisions. All true Messengers of Allah come to reconcile these fragments or divisions, for they preach the true Gospel of Unity. So came Al Mustafā to bring back to Unity the many jarring sects among the Jews, Christians, and Pagans. His mission was held up to ridicule, but so was the mission of his predecessors. Mockery itself should not discourage the preachers of Truth.

1946. If evil and disbelief exist in the world, we must not be impatient or lose our faith. We must recognise that if such things are permitted, they are part of the Universal Plan and purpose of Allah, Who is All-Wise and All-Good, but Whose wisdom and goodness we cannot fully fathom. One consolation we have, and that is stated in the next verse and the next note.

1947. Sects, divisions, and systems invented by men tend to pass away, but Allah's pure Truth of Unity endures forever. This we see in history when we study it on a large scale. *Cf.* the parable in 14:24-26. *Khalat*: I have translated it here in the same sense as in 13:30, 10:102, and other places. Some Commentators give it a slightly different shade of meaning. The other meaning is seen in 48:23.

1948. *Cf.* 6:35. The spiritual kingdom is open to all to enter. But the entrance is not a mere matter of physical movement. It is a question of total change of heart. Evil must cease to be evil, before it can see or enjoy Good. If we could suppose Evil, like Bottom the weaver, to be "translated" or in some way carried up to Heaven, it would only think that the Truth was an illusion and the reality mere witchery. The taint is in its very nature, which must be purified and rendered fit for the reception of light, truth, and bliss.

Nay, we have been bewitched
By sorcery."

بَلْ نَحْنُ قَوْمٌ مَّسْحُورُونَ

SECTION 2.

16. It is We Who have set out[1949]
The Zodiacal Signs[1950] in the heavens,
And made them fair-seeming
To (all) beholders;

وَلَقَدْ جَعَلْنَا فِي ٱلسَّمَآءِ بُرُوجًا وَزَيَّنَّـٰهَا لِلنَّـٰظِرِينَ ﴿١٦﴾

17. And (moreover) We have guarded them[1951]
From every evil spirit accursed:[1952]

وَحَفِظْنَـٰهَا مِن كُلِّ شَيْطَـٰنٍ رَّجِيمٍ ﴿١٧﴾

18. But any that gains a hearing[1953]
By stealth, is pursued
By a flaming fire, bright (to see).[1954]

إِلَّا مَنِ ٱسْتَرَقَ ٱلسَّمْعَ فَأَتْبَعَهُۥ شِهَابٌ مُّبِينٌ ﴿١٨﴾

19. And the earth We have spread out[1955]
(Like a carpet); set thereon
Mountains firm and immovable;

وَٱلْأَرْضَ مَدَدْنَـٰهَا وَأَلْقَيْنَا فِيهَا رَوَٰسِىَ ﴿١٩﴾

1949. Evil having been described, not as an external thing, but as a taint of the soul, we have in this section a glorious account of the purity and beauty of Allah's Creation. Evil is a blot on it, not a normal feature of it. Indeed, the normal feature is the guard which Allah has put on it, to protect it from evil.

1950. In the countless millions of stars in the universe which we see, the first step in our astronomical knowledge is to find marvellous order, beauty, and harmony, on a scale of grandeur which we appreciate more and more as our knowledge increases. The first broad belt that we distinguish is the Zodiac, which marks the sun's path through the heavens year after year and the limit of the wanderings of the moon and the planets. We make twelve divisions of it and call them Signs of the Zodiac. Each marks the solar path through the heavens as we see it, month after month. We can thus mark off the seasons in our solar year, and express in definite laws the most important facts in meteorology, agriculture, seasonal winds, and tides. Then there are the mansions of the moon, the mapping out of the Constellations, and other marvellous facts of the heavens, some of which affect our physical life on this earth. But the highest lessons we can draw from them are spiritual. The author of this wonderful Order and Beauty is One, and He alone is entitled to our worship.

1951. Taking the physical heavens, we can imagine the supreme melody or harmony—the Music of the Spheres—guarded from every disturbing force. If by any chance any rebellious force of evil seeks to obtain, by stealth, a sound of that harmony to which all who make themselves consonant are freely invited, it is pursued by a shooting star, for there can be no consonance between evil and good.

1952. *Rajīm*: driven away with stones, rejected, accursed. *Cf.* 3:36.

1953. *Cf.* 72:8-9. (Eds.).

1954. A shooting star appears to be meant. *Cf.* 37:10.

1955. Majesty, order, beauty, and harmony are shown in all Allah's Creation, but especially in the heavens. Coming nearer to man, Allah's care for man and His goodness are shown (besides His other qualities) in His creation of the earth. In highly poetical language, the earth is described as spread out like a carpet, on which the eternal hills act as weights to keep it steady.

And produced therein all kinds
Of things in due balance.[1956]

وَأَنۢبَتۡنَا فِيهَا مِن كُلِّ شَيۡءٖ مَّوۡزُونٖ

20. And We have provided therein
Means of subsistence—for you
And for those for whose sustenance
Ye are not responsible.[1957]

٢٠ وَجَعَلۡنَا لَكُمۡ فِيهَا مَعَٰيِشَ
وَمَن لَّسۡتُمۡ لَهُۥ بِرَٰزِقِينَ

21. And there is not a thing
But its (sources and) treasures[1958]
(Inexhaustible) are with Us;
But We only send down
Thereof in due and ascertainable
measures.[1959]

٢١ وَإِن مِّن شَيۡءٍ إِلَّا عِندَنَا
خَزَآئِنُهُۥ وَمَا نُنَزِّلُهُۥٓ
إِلَّا بِقَدَرٖ مَّعۡلُومٖ

22. And We send the fecundating[1960]
winds,
Then cause the rain to descend
From the sky, therewith providing
You with water (in abundance),
Though ye are not the
guardians[1961]
Of its stores.[1962]

٢٢ وَأَرۡسَلۡنَا ٱلرِّيَٰحَ لَوَٰقِحَ
فَأَنزَلۡنَا مِنَ ٱلسَّمَآءِ مَآءٗ فَأَسۡقَيۡنَٰكُمُوهُ
وَمَآ أَنتُمۡ لَهُۥ بِخَٰزِنِينَ

1956. And every kind of thing is produced on the earth in due balance and measure. The mineral kingdom supports the vegetable and they, in their turn, support the animal, and there is a link of mutual dependence between them. Excess is eliminated. The waste of one is made the food of another, and *vice versa*. And this is an infinite chain of gradation and interdependence.

1957. See last note. 'We provide sustenance of every kind, physical, mental, spiritual, etc., for you (*i.e.*, for mankind). But We do more. We provide for every one of Our creatures. And there are those of which mankind is not even cognisant. We provide for them also. There are those who may at first sight appear hostile to man, or whom man may consider hostile, such as wild and noxious animals. They are Our creatures, and We provide for them also, as they are Our creatures. But there is due order and balance in the economy of Our Universal Plan.

1958. *Khazā'in*: treasures; store houses; places where valuable things are accumulated, from which supplies are distributed from time to time as need arises.

1959. All the wonderful gifts and forces and energies which we see in the world around us have their sources and fountainheads with Allah, the Creator and Sustainer of the Worlds. And what we see or perceive or imagine is just a small portion of what exists. That portion is sent out to us and to our world according to our needs or its needs from time to time as the occasion arises. It is strictly limited according to rule and plan. Its source is unlimited and inexhaustible. In the same way the forces which we see operating around us, in nature or in the spiritual world, according to laws which we can grasp and ascertain, are mere derived forces, in the 2nd, 3rd, or *n*th degree. Their source and ultimate fountainhead is with Allah.

1960. *Lawāqiḥ*, plural of *lāqiḥ*, from *laqaha*, to impregnate or fecundate the female date palm by putting the pollen of the male tree on to the ovaries of the female tree. The date palm is unisexual. The wind performs this office for many flowers. Here, by a bold metaphor, its fecundating quality is transferred to the clouds, which by means of rain produce all kinds of fruit, grain, and vegetation. The clouds as vapour are manipulated by the winds, which set up atmospheric currents resulting in condensation and the descent of rain. Note the appropriateness of the little particle "then", showing the connection of winds with rain.

1961. *Cf.* the previous verse, and n. 1958. Man may store water in cisterns, tanks, lakes, and headwaters of canals. But he has no control over its original sources, which are the clouds, which by the help of the winds, act as grand distributors of water over wide spaces of the world's surface.

1962. This verse must be understood as furnishing an example of illustration of what is said in the last verse.

23. And verily, it is We
Who give life, and Who give[1963]
Death: it is We Who remain
Inheritors[1964]
(After all else passes away).

وَإِنَّا لَنَحْنُ نُحْيِۦ وَنُمِيتُ وَنَحْنُ ٱلْوَٰرِثُونَ ﴿٢٣﴾

24. To Us are known those of you
Who hasten forward, and those
Who lag behind.[1965]

وَلَقَدْ عَلِمْنَا ٱلْمُسْتَقْدِمِينَ مِنكُمْ وَلَقَدْ عَلِمْنَا ٱلْمُسْتَـْٔخِرِينَ ﴿٢٤﴾

25. Assuredly it is thy Lord
Who will gather them together:
For He is Perfect in Wisdom
And Knowledge.

وَإِنَّ رَبَّكَ هُوَ يَحْشُرُهُمْ إِنَّهُۥ حَكِيمٌ عَلِيمٌ ﴿٢٥﴾

C. 120.—Man's origin was from dust, lowly;
(15:26-50) But his rank was raised above that
Of other creatures because Allah breathed
Into him His spirit. Jealousy and arrogance
Caused the fall of Iblīs, the power of Evil:
But no power has Evil o'er those sincere
Souls who worship Allah and seek His Way.
Many are the gates of Evil, but Peace
And dignified joy will be the goal
Of those whom the Grace of Allah has made His own.

SECTION 3.

26. We created man from sounding
clay,[1966]
From mud moulded into shape;

وَلَقَدْ خَلَقْنَا ٱلْإِنسَٰنَ مِن صَلْصَٰلٍ مِّنْ حَمَإٍ مَّسْنُونٍ ﴿٢٦﴾

1963. Note how the argument has mounted up from 15:16 onwards to 15:23—from things most remote from man to things touching his inmost being, and each of them in its own way is a wonderful instance of Allah's glory and goodness, and the beauty, order, and harmony of His creation. First, the heavens, the Zodiacal Signs, the stars, and the mysterious phenomena that we see above us; then the earth, and the perfect balance of life and forces therein, with man as an important factor, but not the only factor; then, the inexhaustible sources of energy, of which Allah alone is the fountainhead, but which come to us in measured proportions, as needed; and lastly, Life and Death itself, which will pass away but Allah will remain. A noble passage, and a fine vindication of Allah's wisdom and providence in dealing with His creatures.

1964. Literally, "We are the Heirs, or Inheritors." *Cf.* 3:180: "To Allah belongs the heritage of the heavens and the earth." See also the latter part of n. 988 to 6:165.

1965. *Cf.* 9:100, where the *Sābiqūn* may perhaps correspond to the *Mustaqdimīn* here. In that case the two classes are those who are the first to accept Faith and do deeds of righteousness and those who come later, but are still numbered with the righteous. A second alternative meaning may be: "those who preceded you in point of time and those who come after you in point of time: they are all known to Allah, and He will gather them all together on the Day of Judgement."

1966. *Ṣalṣāl*: dry clay which produces a sound, like pottery, *Cf.* 55:14. Taking verses 26 and 29 together, I understand the meaning to be: that man's body was formed from wet clay moulded into shape and then dried until it could emit sound (perhaps referring to speech); that it was then further fashioned and completed; that into the animal form thus fashioned was breathed the Spirit of Allah, which gave it a superiority over other Creation: and that the order for obeisance was then given.

27. And the Jinn race, We had
Created before, from the fire
Of a scorching wind.[1967]

وَٱلْجَآنَّ خَلَقْنَٰهُ مِن قَبْلُ مِن نَّارِ ٱلسَّمُومِ ٢٧

28. Behold! thy Lord said
To the angels: "I am about
To create man, from sounding clay
From mud moulded into shape;

وَإِذْ قَالَ رَبُّكَ لِلْمَلَٰٓئِكَةِ إِنِّى ٢٨
خَٰلِقٌۢ بَشَرًا مِّن صَلْصَٰلٍ مِّنْ حَمَإٍ مَّسْنُونٍ

29. "When I have fashioned him
(In due proportion) and breathed
Into him of My spirit,
Fall ye down in obeisance
Unto him."[1968]

فَإِذَا سَوَّيْتُهُۥ وَنَفَخْتُ فِيهِ مِن رُّوحِى ٢٩
فَقَعُوا۟ لَهُۥ سَٰجِدِينَ

30. So the angels prostrated
themselves,
All of them together:

فَسَجَدَ ٱلْمَلَٰٓئِكَةُ كُلُّهُمْ أَجْمَعُونَ ٣٠

31. Not so[1969] Iblīs:[1970] he refused to be
Among those who prostrated
themselves.[1971]

إِلَّآ إِبْلِيسَ أَبَىٰٓ أَن يَكُونَ مَعَ ٱلسَّٰجِدِينَ ٣١

32. (Allah) said: "O Iblīs!
What is your reason
For not being among those
Who prostrated themselves?"

قَالَ يَٰٓإِبْلِيسُ مَا لَكَ ٣٢
أَلَّا تَكُونَ مَعَ ٱلسَّٰجِدِينَ

33. (Iblīs) said: "I am not one
To prostrate myself to man,
Whom Thou didst create
From sounding clay, from mud
Moulded into shape."

قَالَ لَمْ أَكُن لِّأَسْجُدَ لِبَشَرٍ ٣٣
خَلَقْتَهُۥ مِن صَلْصَٰلٍ مِّنْ حَمَإٍ مَّسْنُونٍ

34. (Allah) said: "Then get thee out
From here: for thou art

قَالَ فَٱخْرُجْ مِنْهَا فَإِنَّكَ ٣٤

1967. *Cf.* 6:100 and n. 929. Hidden or invisible forces are aptly typified as arising "from the fire of scorching winds."

1968. Among other passages where the creation of Adam is referred to *cf.* the following: 2:30-39; 7:11-25. Note that here the emphasis is on three points: (1) the breathing of Allah's Spirit into man, *i.e.*, the faculty of God-like knowledge and will, which, if rightly used, would give man superiority over other creatures; (2) the origin of evil in arrogance and jealousy on the part of Satan, who saw only the lower side of man (his clay) and failed to see the higher side, the faculty brought in by the Spirit of Allah; (3) that this evil only touches those who yield to it, and has no power over Allah's sincere servants, purified by His grace (15:40, 42). Adam is not here mentioned by name, but only Man, whose symbol is Adam.

1969. *Cf.* n. 49 to 2:34.

1970. *Iblīs:* the name has in it the root idea of desperateness or rebellion. *Cf.* n. 52 to 2:36.

1971. Apparently Iblīs's arrogance has two grounds: (1) that man was made of clay while he was made of fire: (2) that he did not wish to do what others did. Both grounds were false: (1) because man had the spirit of Allah breathed into him; (2) because contempt of the angels who obeyed Allah's word showed not Iblīs's superiority but his inferiority. The word "*bashar*" for man (verse 33) suggests a gross physical body.

Rejected, accursed. رَجِيمٌ

35. "And the Curse shall be
On thee till the Day of
Judgement."[1972]
وَإِنَّ عَلَيْكَ ٱللَّعْنَةَ إِلَىٰ يَوْمِ ٱلدِّينِ ﴿٣٥﴾

36. (Iblīs) said: "O my Lord!
Give me then respite[1973]
Till the Day
The (dead) are raised."
قَالَ رَبِّ فَأَنظِرْنِىٓ إِلَىٰ يَوْمِ يُبْعَثُونَ ﴿٣٦﴾

37. (Allah) said: "Respite
Is granted thee—
قَالَ فَإِنَّكَ مِنَ ٱلْمُنظَرِينَ ﴿٣٧﴾

38. "Till the Day
Of the Time Appointed."
إِلَىٰ يَوْمِ ٱلْوَقْتِ ٱلْمَعْلُومِ ﴿٣٨﴾

39. (Iblīs) said: "O my Lord!
Because Thou hast put me[1974]
In the wrong, I will
Make (wrong) fair-seeming
To them on the earth,
And I will put them[1975]
All in the wrong—
قَالَ رَبِّ بِمَآ أَغْوَيْتَنِى لَأُزَيِّنَنَّ لَهُمْ فِى ٱلْأَرْضِ وَلَأُغْوِيَنَّهُمْ أَجْمَعِينَ ﴿٣٩﴾

40. "Except Thy servants among
them,
Sincere and purified
(By Thy grace)."
إِلَّا عِبَادَكَ مِنْهُمُ ٱلْمُخْلَصِينَ ﴿٤٠﴾

41. (Allah) said: "This (Way
Of My sincere servants) is
قَالَ هَـٰذَا صِرَٰطٌ ﴿٤١﴾

1972. After the Day of Judgement the whole constitution of the universe will be different. There will be a new world altogether, on a wholly different plane. (*Cf.* 21:104).

1973. What was this respite! The curse on Iblis remained, *i.e.*, he was deprived of Allah's Grace and became in the spiritual world what an outlaw is in a political kingdom. An earthly kingdom may not be able to catch and destroy an outlaw. But Allah is Omnipotent, and such power as Iblis may have had can only come through the respite granted by Allah. The respite then is what is expressed in 15:39 below. In Allah's grant of limited free will to man is implied the faculty of choosing between good and evil, and the faculty is exercised through the temptations and allurements put forward by Satan, "the open enemy" of man. This is for the period of man's probation on this earth. Even so, no temptations have power over the sincere worshippers of Allah, who are purified by His grace.

1974. *Aghwaytanī*: 'thrown me out of the way, put me in the wrong': *Cf.* 7:16. Satan as the Power of Evil cannot be straight or truthful even before Allah. By his arrogance and rebellion he fell; he attributes this to Allah. Between Allah's righteous judgement and Satan's snares and temptations there cannot be the remotest comparison. Yet he presumes to put them on an equal footing. He is taking advantage of the respite.

1975. Iblīs (the Rebellious) is powerless against Allah. He turns therefore against man and becomes Satan (the Enemy).

Indeed a Way that leads
Straight to Me.[1976]

عَلَيَّ مُسْتَقِيمٌ

42. "For over My servants
No authority shalt thou
Have, except such as
Put themselves in the wrong
And follow thee."

٤٢ إِنَّ عِبَادِي لَيْسَ لَكَ عَلَيْهِمْ سُلْطَٰنٌ
إِلَّا مَنِ ٱتَّبَعَكَ مِنَ ٱلْغَاوِينَ

43. And verily, Hell
Is the promised abode
For them all!

٤٣ وَإِنَّ جَهَنَّمَ لَمَوْعِدُهُمْ أَجْمَعِينَ

44. To it are seven Gates:[1977]
For each of those Gates
Is a (special) class
(Of sinners) assigned.

٤٤ لَهَا سَبْعَةُ أَبْوَٰبٍ لِّكُلِّ بَابٍ
مِّنْهُمْ جُزْءٌ مَّقْسُومٌ

SECTION 4.

45. The righteous (will be)
Amid Gardens
And fountains
(Of clear-flowing water).

٤٥ إِنَّ ٱلْمُتَّقِينَ فِي جَنَّٰتٍ
وَعُيُونٍ

46. (Their greeting will be):
"Enter ye here
In Peace and Security."

٤٦ ٱدْخُلُوهَا بِسَلَٰمٍ ءَامِنِينَ

47. And We shall remove
From their hearts any
Lurking sense of injury:[1978]
(They will be) brothers
(Joyfully) facing each other
On thrones (of dignity).

٤٧ وَنَزَعْنَا مَا فِي صُدُورِهِم
مِّنْ غِلٍّ إِخْوَٰنًا عَلَىٰ
سُرُرٍ مُّتَقَٰبِلِينَ

48. There no sense of fatigue
Shall touch them,

٤٨ لَا يَمَسُّهُمْ فِيهَا نَصَبٌ

1976. To be sincere in the worship of Allah is to obtain purification from all stain of evil and exemption from all influence of evil. It changes the whole nature of man. After that, evil cannot touch him. Evil will acknowledge him to be beyond its power and will not even tempt him. Apart from such purified souls, everyone who worships Allah invites Allah's grace to protect him. But if he puts himself in the way of wrong and deliberately chooses evil, he must take the consequences. The blame is not even on Satan, the power of evil: it is on the sinner himself, who puts himself into his power: 14:22; 15:42.

1977. The ways of sin are numerous, and if they are classified into seven, each of them points to a Gate that leads into Hell.

1978. *Cf.* 7:43, and n. 1021. The hearts and minds will be so purified that all past rancour, jealousy, or sense of injury will be obliterated. The true Brotherhood will be realised there, when each will have his own dignity; there will be no question of invidious comparisons; each will face the others with joy and confidence. There will be no sense of toil or fatigue, and joy will last forever.

Nor shall they (ever)
Be asked to leave.

وَمَا هُم مِّنْهَا بِمُخْرَجِينَ

49. Tell My servants[1979]
That I am indeed
The Oft-Forgiving,
Most Merciful;

﴿٤٩﴾ نَبِّئْ عِبَادِىٓ أَنِّىٓ أَنَا ٱلْغَفُورُ ٱلرَّحِيمُ

50. And that my Penalty
Will be indeed
The most grievous Penalty.

﴿٥٠﴾ وَأَنَّ عَذَابِى هُوَ ٱلْعَذَابُ ٱلْأَلِيمُ

C. 121.—(15:52-84.) Allah's Grace and Mercy are always
First, But His Justice and Wrath will seize
Those who defy His Law. Even when
The unspeakable crimes of the Cities
Of the Plain made their destruction
Inevitable, Allah's message of Mercy
To mankind was sent to Abraham
And of safety to Lot. The last remnants
Of sin will be cut off, and the Signs
And Tokens thereof are plain for all
To see. The proud Companions of the Wood
And the builders of Rocky Fortresses
Were all swept away because of their sins.

51. Tell them about
The guests of Abraham.[1980]

﴿٥١﴾ وَنَبِّئْهُمْ عَن ضَيْفِ إِبْرَٰهِيمَ

52. When they entered his presence
And said, "Peace!"
He said, "We feel
Afraid of you!"[1981]

﴿٥٢﴾ إِذْ دَخَلُوا۟ عَلَيْهِ فَقَالُوا۟ سَلَـٰمًا قَالَ إِنَّا مِنكُمْ وَجِلُونَ

53. They said: "Fear not!
We give thee glad tidings

﴿٥٣﴾ قَالُوا۟ لَا تَوْجَلْ إِنَّا نُبَشِّرُكَ

1979. We must realise both sides of Allah's attributes: His Mercy, Grace, and Forgiveness are unbounded; if we reject all this, His justice and punishment will also be beyond all that we can conceive.

1980. In illustration of the contrasts between Good and Evil, and the consequences that flow from them, we now have a reference to four incidents from the past, *viz.*,: (1) an incident from the story of Abraham; (2) from that of Lot, nephew of Abraham and the end of the Cities of the Plain, which he was sent to warn; (3) the People of the Wood; and (4) the People of the Rocky Tract *(Al Ḥijr),* after whom this Sūrah is called. As usual, the recital of Allah's abounding Grace comes first.

1981. For a full understanding of this reference to the angels who were Abraham's guests and came to announce the birth of a son to him in his old age, read 11:69-73 and notes. The appearance of two strangers of uncommon appearance, who refused to partake of the host's sumptuous hospitality, made Abraham at first suspicious and afraid.

Of a son endowed
With wisdom."1982

بِغُلَٰمٍ عَلِيمٍ

54. He said: "Do you give me
Glad tidings that old age
Has seized me? Of what
Then, is your good news?"

قَالَ أَبَشَّرْتُمُونِي عَلَىٰٓ أَن مَّسَّنِيَ ٱلْكِبَرُ فَبِمَ تُبَشِّرُونَ ٥٤

55. They said: "We give thee
Glad tidings in truth:
Be not then in despair!"

قَالُوا۟ بَشَّرْنَٰكَ بِٱلْحَقِّ فَلَا تَكُن مِّنَ ٱلْقَٰنِطِينَ ٥٥

56. He said: "And who
Despairs of the mercy
Of his Lord, but such
As go astray?"1983

قَالَ وَمَن يَقْنَطُ مِن رَّحْمَةِ رَبِّهِۦٓ إِلَّا ٱلضَّآلُّونَ ٥٦

57. Abraham said:1984 "What then
Is the business of which
Ye (have come), O ye
Messengers (of Allah)?"

قَالَ فَمَا خَطْبُكُمْ أَيُّهَا ٱلْمُرْسَلُونَ ٥٧

58. They said: "We have been
Sent to a people
(Deep) in sin.1985

قَالُوٓا۟ إِنَّآ أُرْسِلْنَآ إِلَىٰ قَوْمٍ مُّجْرِمِينَ ٥٨

59. "Excepting the adherents
Of Lūṭ: them we are certainly
(Charged) to save (from
harm)—1986
All—

إِلَّآ ءَالَ لُوطٍ إِنَّا لَمُنَجُّوهُمْ أَجْمَعِينَ ٥٩

60. "Except his wife, who,
We have ascertained,

إِلَّا ٱمْرَأَتَهُۥ قَدَّرْنَآ ٦٠

1982. The birth of a son in old age, to a sonless father was glad tidings to Abraham personally. The birth of a son endowed with wisdom promised something infinitely more. Considering that the angels were divine messengers, the wisdom referred to was divine wisdom, and the event became an event of prime importance in the world's religious history. For Abraham became, through his progeny, the root of the three great universal religions diffused throughout the world.

1983. *Cf.* 11:69. [Eds.].

1984. When cordial understanding was established between Abraham and his guests and probably when the guests were about to depart, Abraham put a question to them. "What is the mission on which you are going?" It was further implied: "Is there anything I can do to help?" But no. The mission was one of punishment for abominable sins. Note that the mention of Allah's Wrath is always linked with that of Allah's Mercy, and the Mercy comes first. The same angels that came to punish Sodom and Gomorrah were charged first to give the good news of Allah's Mercy to Abraham in the shape of a long line of teachers of righteousness.

1985. The Cities of the Plain round the Dead Sea, which to this day is called Bahr Lūṭ. They were given to unspeakable abominations. Read in this connection 11:77-83 and notes.

1986. Here, again, Allah's saving Grace is linked with His Wrath, and is mentioned first.

Will be among those
Who lag behind."[1987]

إِنَّهَا لَمِنَ ٱلْغَٰبِرِينَ

SECTION 5.

61. At length when the messengers
Arrived among the adherents[1988]
Of Lūṭ,

٦١ فَلَمَّا جَآءَ ءَالَ لُوطٍ ٱلْمُرْسَلُونَ

62. He said: "Ye appear
To be uncommon folk."

٦٢ قَالَ إِنَّكُمْ قَوْمٌ مُّنكَرُونَ

63. They said: "Yea
We have come to thee
To accomplish that
Of which they doubt.[1989]

٦٣ قَالُوا۟ بَلْ جِئْنَٰكَ
بِمَا كَانُوا۟ فِيهِ يَمْتَرُونَ

64. "We have brought to thee
That which is inevitably[1990]
Due, and assuredly
We tell the truth.

٦٤ وَأَتَيْنَٰكَ بِٱلْحَقِّ
وَإِنَّا لَصَٰدِقُونَ

65. "Then travel by night
With thy household,
When a portion of the night
(Yet remains), and do thou
Bring up the rear:
Let no one amongst you
Look back, but pass on
Whither ye are ordered."

٦٥ فَأَسْرِ بِأَهْلِكَ بِقِطْعٍ مِّنَ ٱلَّيْلِ
وَٱتَّبِعْ أَدْبَٰرَهُمْ وَلَا يَلْتَفِتْ مِنكُمْ أَحَدٌ
وَٱمْضُوا۟ حَيْثُ تُؤْمَرُونَ

66. And We made known
This decree to him,
That the last remnants

٦٦ وَقَضَيْنَآ إِلَيْهِ ذَٰلِكَ ٱلْأَمْرَ أَنَّ دَابِرَ

1987. See 11:81, and n. 1577.

1988. *Āl* means people who adhere to the ways and teaching of a great teacher; *e.g.*, *Āli Muḥammad*: it does not necessarily mean race or descendants. *Ahl* (15:65 below) usually implies "household" but may be taken in an extended sense to include people generally, see 15:67. *Qawm* (15:62) may be a collection of aggregate people. In 11:70 the hostile inhabitants of the Cities of the Plan are Called *qawmi Lūṭ* (the People of Lūṭ). *Ashāb* (companions) refers to a Group rather than to a People: *Cf.* 15:78. (R).

1989. The unusual appearance of the angels struck Lot as it had struck Abraham. Knowing the abominable vices to which the cities were addicted, he feared to entertain handsome young men. They at once disclosed their mission to him. In effect they said: "You, Lot, have been preaching in vain to these wicked cities. When you warn them of their inevitable end—Destruction—they laugh and doubt. Now their doubt will be resolved. Their destruction will be accomplished before the morning."

1990. Another meaning of *al Ḥaqq*: The Punishment which is justly and inevitably due, which must certainly come to pass *Cf.* 22:18.

Of those (sinners) should be
Cut off by the morning.[1991]

هَٰٓؤُلَآءِ مَقۡطُوعٞ مُّصۡبِحِينَ

67. The inhabitants of the City
Came in (mad) joy
(At news of the young men).[1992]

وَجَآءَ أَهۡلُ ٱلۡمَدِينَةِ يَسۡتَبۡشِرُونَ ٦٧

68. Lūṭ said: "These are
My guests: disgrace me not:

قَالَ إِنَّ هَٰٓؤُلَآءِ ضَيۡفِي فَلَا تَفۡضَحُونِ ٦٨

69. "But fear Allah
And shame me not."

وَٱتَّقُواْ ٱللَّهَ وَلَا تُخۡزُونِ ٦٩

70. They said: "Did we not
Forbid thee (to speak)
For all and sundry?"[1993]

قَالُوٓاْ أَوَلَمۡ نَنۡهَكَ عَنِ ٱلۡعَٰلَمِينَ ٧٠

71. He said: "There are
My daughters (to marry),
If ye must act (so)."[1994]

قَالَ هَٰٓؤُلَآءِ بَنَاتِيٓ إِن كُنتُمۡ فَٰعِلِينَ ٧١

72. Verily, by thy life (O Prophet),
In their wild intoxication,
They wander in distraction,
To and fro.[1995]

لَعَمۡرُكَ إِنَّهُمۡ لَفِي سَكۡرَتِهِمۡ يَعۡمَهُونَ ٧٢

73. But the (mighty) Blast[1996]
Overtook them before morning,

فَأَخَذَتۡهُمُ ٱلصَّيۡحَةُ مُشۡرِقِينَ ٧٣

74. And We turned (the Cities)
Upside down, and rained down

فَجَعَلۡنَا عَٰلِيَهَا سَافِلَهَا وَأَمۡطَرۡنَا ٧٤

1991. As the last remnants of the wicked were to be cut off, and as the Mercy of Allah wished to save every true soul who might be with Lot, Allah's decree was made known to Lot, so that he might save his adherents.

1992. They were addicted to unnatural crime, and the news of the advent of handsome young men inflamed them. How true it is that at the very verge of destruction, men rush blindly to their fate, and cut off any last hope of repentance and mercy for themselves. *Cf.* 15:72 below.

1993. I understand the meaning to be that Lot, the only righteous man in the city, had frequently remonstrated with the inhabitants against their unnatural crimes, and they had forbidden him to speak to them again on behalf of anyone, "as if" (they might tauntingly say) "he was the protector of all and sundry." Some Commentators understand the verse to mean: 'Did we not forbid thee to entertain any strangers?'

1994. *Cf.* 11:78, n. 1575. "My daughters" in the mouth of a venerable man may mean young girls of the city, which would be appropriate considering the large number of men who came to besiege Lot's house.

1995. The wild, mad fury of passion and sin attains its own destruction and cuts off the last hope of repentance or mercy.

1996 *Al Ṣayḥah*, the mighty Blast, is mentioned as accompanying earthquakes: *Cf.* 11:67-94. Here it was the violent wind and noise accompanying the shower of brimstones, possibly with some volcanic action.

On them brimstones
Hard as baked clay.[1997]

عَلَيْهِمْ حِجَارَةً مِّن سِجِّيلٍ

75. Behold! in this are Signs
For those who by tokens
Do understand.

إِنَّ فِي ذَٰلِكَ لَآيَاتٍ لِّلْمُتَوَسِّمِينَ ﴿٧٥﴾

76. And the (Cities were)
Right on the highroad.[1998]

وَإِنَّهَا لَبِسَبِيلٍ مُّقِيمٍ ﴿٧٦﴾

77. Behold! in this
Is a Sign
For those who believe![1999]

إِنَّ فِي ذَٰلِكَ لَآيَةً لِّلْمُؤْمِنِينَ ﴿٧٧﴾

78. And the Companions of the Wood[2000]
Were also wrongdoers;

وَإِن كَانَ أَصْحَابُ الْأَيْكَةِ لَظَالِمِينَ ﴿٧٨﴾

79. So We exacted retribution
From them. They were both[2001]
On an open highway,
Plain to see.

فَانتَقَمْنَا مِنْهُمْ ﴿٧٩﴾
وَإِنَّهُمَا لَبِإِمَامٍ مُّبِينٍ

SECTION 6.

80. The Companions of the Rocky Tract[2002]
Also rejected the messengers:

وَلَقَدْ كَذَّبَ أَصْحَابُ الْحِجْرِ الْمُرْسَلِينَ ﴿٨٠﴾

81. We sent them Our Signs,
But they persisted
In turning away from them.

وَآتَيْنَاهُمْ آيَاتِنَا فَكَانُوا عَنْهَا مُعْرِضِينَ ﴿٨١﴾

1997. *Cf.* 11:82 and notes, in which the word *Sijjīl* and its origin are explained.

1998. The cities of Sodom and Gomorrah were utterly destroyed, and even their precise position cannot be identified. But the brimstone plain of the tract still exits, right on the highway between Arabia and Syria. To the traveller in the neighbourhood of the Dead Sea, the whole locality presents a sense of dismal desolation which truly suggests the awful punishment for unspeakable crimes.

1999. Verse 75 refers to all who have the intelligence to grasp the Signs of Allah. Verses 76-77 especially refer to those who use the Arabia-Syrian highroad. The desolation is especially brought home to them.

2000. "Companions of the Wood": *Aṣhab al Aykah*. Perhaps *Aykah* is after all a proper noun, the name of a town or tract. Who were the Companions of the Aykah? They are mentioned four times in the Qur'ān, *viz.*, here, and in 26:176-191; 38:13; and 50:14. The only passage in which any details are given is 26:176-191. There we are told that their Prophet was Shu'ayb, and other details given correspond to those of the Madyan, to whom Shu'ayb was sent as Prophet: see 7:85-93. In my notes to that passage I have discussed the question of Shu'ayb and the Madyan people. It is reasonable to suppose that the Companions of the Wood were either the same as the Madyan, or a group among them or in their neighbourhood.

2001. Both: *i.e.*, The Cities of the Plain and the Companions of the Aykah.

2002. "The Rocky Tract" is undoubtedly a geographical name. On the maps of Arabia will be found a tract called the *Hijr,* north of Madīnah. Jabal *Hijr* is about 150 miles north of Madīnah. The tract would fall on the highway to Syria. This was the country of the Thamūd. For them and the country see 7:73, n. 1043.

82. Out of mountains[2003]
Did they hew (their) edifices,
(Feeling themselves) secure.

٨٢ وَكَانُوا۟ يَنْحِتُونَ مِنَ ٱلْجِبَالِ بُيُوتًا ءَامِنِينَ

83. But the (mighty) Blast[2004]
Seized them of a morning,

٨٣ فَأَخَذَتْهُمُ ٱلصَّيْحَةُ مُصْبِحِينَ

84. And of no avail to them
Was all that they did
(With such art and care)!

٨٤ فَمَآ أَغْنَىٰ عَنْهُم مَّا كَانُوا۟ يَكْسِبُونَ

C. 122.—But Allah's Creation doth bear witness
(15:85-99.) To Allah's Design and Mercy. His Plan
Is sure. His gift of the glorious Qur'ān
Is more than any worldly goods can be.
So, while we denounce Sin openly,
Let us be gentle and kind, and adore
And serve our Lord all our lives.

85. We created not the heavens,
The earth, and all between them,
But for just ends.[2005]
And the Hour is surely
Coming (when this will be
manifest).
So overlook (any human faults)
With gracious forgiveness.[2006]

٨٥ وَمَا خَلَقْنَا ٱلسَّمَٰوَٰتِ
وَٱلْأَرْضَ وَمَا بَيْنَهُمَآ إِلَّا بِٱلْحَقِّ
وَإِنَّ ٱلسَّاعَةَ لَءَاتِيَةٌ
فَٱصْفَحِ ٱلصَّفْحَ ٱلْجَمِيلَ

86. For verily it is thy Lord
Who is the Master-Creator,[2007]
Knowing all things.

٨٦ إِنَّ رَبَّكَ هُوَ
ٱلْخَلَّٰقُ ٱلْعَلِيمُ

87. And We have bestowed
Upon thee the Seven

٨٧ وَلَقَدْ ءَاتَيْنَٰكَ سَبْعًا

2003. Remains of these rock edifices in the *Ḥijr* are still found, and the City of Petra is not more than 380 miles fron Jabal *Hijr*. See n. 1043 to 7:73. "Petra" in Greek means "Rock". For the Inscriptions found there, and their significance, see Appendix VII to S. 26.

2004. The mighty rumbling noise and wind accompanying an earthquake. See 7:78, 1047.

2005. Allah's Creation is all for a true, just, and righteous purpose. *Cf.* 10:5. It is not for mere whim or sport: 21:16.

2006. The Hour will not be long delayed when the true Design and Pattern of Life will be manifest. We must not be impatient, if there appear to be, to our limited vision, apparent injustices. We must bear and forbear, and as far as our own personal feelings are concerned, we must overlook other people's faults with "a gracious forgiveness".

2007. *Khallāq*: the emphatic intensive form, as meaning the Creator, Who is perfected in His skill and knowledge, and Whose creation answers perfectly to His designs. Therefore no one should think that anything has gone wrong in Allah's creation. What may seem out of joint is merely the result of our shortsighted standards. It often happens that what appears to us to be evil or imperfect or unjust is a reflection of our own imperfect minds. See the next two verses and notes.

Oft-repeated (Verses)[2008]
And the Grand Qur'ān.

مِنَ ٱلْمَثَانِى وَٱلْقُرْءَانَ ٱلْعَظِيمَ

88. Strain not thine eyes,
(Wistfully) at what We
Have betowed on certain classes[2009]
Of them, nor grieve over them:[2010]
But lower thy wings (in
gentleness)[2011]
To the Believers.

٨٨ لَا تَمُدَّنَّ عَيْنَيْكَ إِلَىٰ مَا مَتَّعْنَا بِهِۦٓ
أَزْوَٰجًا مِّنْهُمْ وَلَا تَحْزَنْ عَلَيْهِمْ
وَٱخْفِضْ جَنَاحَكَ لِلْمُؤْمِنِينَ

89. And say: "I am indeed he
That warneth openly
And without ambiguity"—[2012]

٨٩ وَقُلْ إِنِّىٓ أَنَا ٱلنَّذِيرُ ٱلْمُبِينُ

90. (Of just such wrath)
As We sent down
On those who divided
(Scripture into arbitrary
parts)—[2013]

٩٠ كَمَآ أَنزَلْنَا عَلَى
ٱلْمُقْتَسِمِينَ

91. (So also on such)
As have made the Qur'ān
Into shreds (as they please).[2014]

٩١ ٱلَّذِينَ جَعَلُوا۟ ٱلْقُرْءَانَ عِضِينَ

92. Therefore, by thy Lord,
We will, of a surety,
Call them to account,

٩٢ فَوَرَبِّكَ لَنَسْـَٔلَنَّهُمْ أَجْمَعِينَ

2008. The Seven Oft-repeated Verses are ususally understood to be the Opening Sūrah, the *Fātiḥah*. They sum up the whole teaching of the Qur'ān. What can be a more precious gift to a Muslim than the glorious Qur'ān or any Sūrah of it? Worldly wealth, honour, possessions, or anything else, sinks into insignificance in comparison with it.

2009. It may be that other people have worldly goods which worldly men envy. Do they necessarily bring happiness? Even the temporary pleasure that they may give is not unmixed with spiritual poisons, and even so, will not last. The man of God looks with wistful eyes at other things—the favour and countenance of Allah.

2010. The Prophet of Allah, in his human love and sympathy, may grieve over certain classes of people who are puffed up with false notions and callous to the Message of Allah. But he should not make himself unhappy. There is no flaw in Allah's Plan, and it must prevail. This was addressed in the first instance to Al Muṣṭafā, but in a minor degree, it applies to all righteous men. (R).

2011. The metaphor is from a bird who lowers her wing in tender solicitude for her little ones. *Cf.* 17:24, where it is applied to "lowering the wing" to aged parents.

2012. In the ministry of Al Muṣṭafā there was no mincing of matters, no compromises with evil. Evil was denounced in unambiguous terms. *Mubīn* implies both openness and clearness. *i.e.*, freedom from ambiguity.

2013. The Commentators differ as to the precise significance of verses 90 and 91. Are the persons referred to in the two verses the same, or different? And who were they? I adopt the view, for which there is good authority, that the two classes of persons were different but similar. Verse 90, I think, refers to the Jews and Christians, who took out of Scripture what suited them, and ignored or rejected the rest: 2:85, 101. For verse 91 see next note.

2014. The Makkan Pagans, in the early days of Islam, in order to dishonour and ridicule the Qur'ān, divided what was so far revealed, into bits, and apportioned them to people coming on pilgrimage to Makkah by different routes, slandering and abusing the Prophet of Allah.

93. For all their deeds.[2015]

عَمَّا كَانُوا۟ يَعْمَلُونَ ﴿٩٣﴾

94. Therefore expound openly
What thou art commanded,
And turn away from those
Who join false gods with Allah.

فَٱصْدَعْ بِمَا تُؤْمَرُ ﴿٩٤﴾
وَأَعْرِضْ عَنِ ٱلْمُشْرِكِينَ

95. For sufficient are We
Unto thee against those
Who scoff—[2016]

إِنَّا كَفَيْنَٰكَ ٱلْمُسْتَهْزِءِينَ ﴿٩٥﴾

96. Those who adopt, with Allah,
Another god: but soon
Will they come to know.

ٱلَّذِينَ يَجْعَلُونَ مَعَ ٱللَّهِ إِلَٰهًا ءَاخَرَ ﴿٩٦﴾
فَسَوْفَ يَعْلَمُونَ

97. We do indeed know
How thy heart is distressed[2017]
At what they say.

وَلَقَدْ نَعْلَمُ أَنَّكَ يَضِيقُ صَدْرُكَ ﴿٩٧﴾
بِمَا يَقُولُونَ

98. But celebrate the praises
Of thy Lord, and be of those
Who prostrate themselves
In adoration.

فَسَبِّحْ بِحَمْدِ رَبِّكَ ﴿٩٨﴾
وَكُن مِّنَ ٱلسَّٰجِدِينَ

99. And serve thy Lord
Until there come unto thee
The Hour that is Certain.[2018]

وَٱعْبُدْ رَبَّكَ حَتَّىٰ يَأْتِيَكَ ٱلْيَقِينُ ﴿٩٩﴾

2015. Those who ridicule Scripture in any form will all be called to account for their insolence, for they are all alike.

2016. If the whole world is ranged against the Prophet of Allah, as was at one time the case with the Prophet, and scoffs at all that is sacred, the sense of Allah's presence and protection outweighs all. And after all, the scoffers are creatures of a day. Soon will they find their level, and be undeceived as to all their falsehoods. But the Truth of Allah endures forever. (R).

2017. Literally, 'that thy breast is constrained.'

2018. *Yaqīn*: Certainty; the Hour that is Certain; death.

INTRODUCTION TO SŪRAH 16—*AL NAḤL*

Chronologically this Sūrah, like the six which preceded it, belongs to the late Makkan period, except perhaps verse 110 and some of the verses that follow. But the chronology has no significance. In subject matter it sums up, from a new point of view, the arguments on the great questions of Allah's dealings with man, His Self-revelation to man, and how the Messengers and the Message are writ large in every phase of Allah's Creation and the life of Man. The new point of view is that Nature points to Nature's God.

Summary—Everything in Creation proclaims the glory of Allah. To man is given dominion over Nature, that man may recognise Allah's Unity and Allah's Truth (16:1-25. and C. 123).

Man should never lose sight of his goal, which is the good, or dispute with the great Teachers, who are sent to all Peoples, to bring about Unity: all creatures serve Allah (16:26-50, and C. 124).

Allah's favours and man's ingratitude recounted, His Signs in the rain-bearing clouds, the cattle that give milk, the bee that produces honey, the wonderful relations of family and social life, and the refinements and comforts of civilisation (16:51-83, and C. 125).

The Messengers of Truth will bear witness against those who reject the Truth. Allah will judge us according to our faith and deeds (16:84-100, and C. 126).

The Qur'ān is true: it guides and gives glad tidings. Believe, and make the most of life in all things good and lawful. Follow the example of Abraham: be true in Faith and righteousness, and do good (16:101-128, and C. 127).

C. 123.—Allah's Command must inevitably
(16:1-25) Come to pass. But all His Creation
Proclaims His glory, and leads to His Truth.
In all things has He furnished man
With favours innumerable,
To lead and guide him and bring him
To Himself. Why then does man
Refuse the Truth, except for arrogance?
Why does he run after false gods,
Thus acting against his own lights
And misleading others less blest in knowledge?

Sūrah 16.

Al Naḥl (Bees)

In the name of Allah, Most Gracious,
Most Merciful.

بِسْمِ ٱللَّهِ ٱلرَّحْمَـٰنِ ٱلرَّحِيمِ

1. (Inevitably) cometh (to pass)
The Command of Allah:[2019]
Seek ye not then
To hasten it: glory to Him,
And far is He above
Having the partners
They ascribe unto Him!

١ أَتَىٰٓ أَمْرُ ٱللَّهِ فَلَا تَسْتَعْجِلُوهُ ۚ
سُبْحَـٰنَهُۥ وَتَعَـٰلَىٰ
عَمَّا يُشْرِكُونَ

2. He doth send down His angels
With inspiration of His
Command,
To such of His servants
As He pleaseth, (saying):
"Warn (Man) that there is
No god but I: so do
Your duty unto Me."[2020]

٢ يُنَزِّلُ ٱلْمَلَـٰٓئِكَةَ بِٱلرُّوحِ مِنْ أَمْرِهِۦ
عَلَىٰ مَن يَشَآءُ مِنْ عِبَادِهِۦٓ أَنْ أَنذِرُوٓا۟
أَنَّهُۥ لَآ إِلَـٰهَ إِلَّآ أَنَا۠ فَٱتَّقُونِ

3. He has created the heavens
And the earth for just ends:[2021]
Far is He above having
The partners they ascribe to Him!

٣ خَلَقَ ٱلسَّمَـٰوَٰتِ وَٱلْأَرْضَ بِٱلْحَقِّ ۚ
تَعَـٰلَىٰ عَمَّا يُشْرِكُونَ

4. He has created man
From a sperm-drop
And behold this same (man)
Becomes an open disputer![2022]

٤ خَلَقَ ٱلْإِنسَـٰنَ مِن نُّطْفَةٍ
فَإِذَا هُوَ خَصِيمٌ مُّبِينٌ

5. And cattle He has created[2023]
For you (men): from them

٥ وَٱلْأَنْعَـٰمَ خَلَقَهَا ۗ لَكُمْ فِيهَا

2019. This is an answer to the taunt of the Pagans, who said: "If there is a god, the One True God, as you say, with unified control, why does He not punish the wrongdoers at once?" The answer is: "The decree of Allah will inevitably come to pass; it will come soon enough; when it comes, you will wish it were delayed; how foolish of you to wish even to cut off your last hope of forgiveness?"

2020. The Pagans, with their multiplicity of gods and goddesses, good and evil, could play one off against another. That is mere mockery of religion. With such conceptions, man cannot understand the Unity of Design in the Universe nor realise the Power and Glory of the One True God, to Whom alone worship and service are due.

2021. Not for sport, or fortuitously and without Design. *Cf.* 15:85. Surely the Unity of Design in Creation also proves the Unity of Allah their Creator.

2022. Man's physical origin is lowly. Yet do men go back to material things, and neglect or dispute about the highest things in Life.

2023. Why will you go back to material things, considering that material things are made subservient to your use and enjoyment in various ways as suggested in the clauses that follow.

Ye derive warmth,
And numerous benefits,[2024]
And of their (meat) ye eat.

دِفْءٌ وَمَنَٰفِعُ وَمِنْهَا تَأْكُلُونَ

6. And ye have a sense
Of pride and beauty in them
As ye drive them home
In the evening, and as ye
Lead them forth to pasture
In the morning.[2025]

وَلَكُمْ فِيهَا جَمَالٌ حِينَ تُرِيحُونَ وَحِينَ تَسْرَحُونَ ﴿٦﴾

7. And they carry your heavy loads
To lands that you could not
(Otherwise) reach except with[2026]
Souls distressed: for your Lord
Is indeed Most Kind, Most
Merciful.

وَتَحْمِلُ أَثْقَالَكُمْ إِلَىٰ بَلَدٍ لَّمْ تَكُونُوا۟ بَٰلِغِيهِ إِلَّا بِشِقِّ ٱلْأَنفُسِ ۚ إِنَّ رَبَّكُمْ لَرَءُوفٌ رَّحِيمٌ ﴿٧﴾

8. And (He has created) horses,
Mules, and donkeys, for you
To ride and use for show;[2027]
And He has created (other) things
Of which ye have no
knowledge.[2028]

وَٱلْخَيْلَ وَٱلْبِغَالَ وَٱلْحَمِيرَ لِتَرْكَبُوهَا وَزِينَةً ۚ وَيَخْلُقُ مَا لَا تَعْلَمُونَ ﴿٨﴾

9. And unto Allah leads straight[2029]
The Way, but there are ways
That turn aside: if Allah

وَعَلَى ٱللَّهِ قَصْدُ ٱلسَّبِيلِ وَمِنْهَا جَآئِرٌ ۚ ﴿٩﴾

2024. From wool, and hair, and skins, and milk. Camel's hair makes warm robes and blankets; and certain kinds of goats yield hair which makes similar fabrics. Sheep yield wool, and llamas alpaca for similar uses. The skins and furs of many animals yield warm raiment or make warm rugs or bedding. The females of many of these animals yield good warm milk, a nourishing and wholesome diet. Then the flesh of many of these animals is good to eat. There are other uses, which the animals serve, and which are referred to later.

2025. The good man is proud of his cattle and is good to them. As they go to, and return from, pasture, morning and evening, he has a sense of his power and wealth and their beauty and docility. Will not man turn from these material facts to the great spiritual truths and purpose behind them?

2026. The cattle and animals also carry loads, and thus make intercommunication between different lands easy. But for them there would have been many difficulties, not only physical, but psychological. Weary men carrying loads are in no mood for social and spiritual intercourse. This intercourse is made possible by the kindness and mercy of Allah.

2027. Horses, mules, and donkeys as well as other animals may be beasts of burden, but they may also be pedigree animals bred for beauty and for all those more refined uses, such as processions, in which grace and elegance is the predominant feature.

2028. If we examine the history of transport, there have been vast changes through the ages, from rude pack animals to fine equipages, and then through mechanical contrivances, such means of transport as elegant coaches, tramways, and railways, useful motor lorries and Rolls-Royce cars, and airships and aeroplanes of all descriptions. At any given point of time, many of those were yet unkown to man. Nor can we suppose the limits to have been reached now or that it will ever be reached at any future time. Through the mind and ingenuity of man it is Allah that creates new things hitherto unknown to man.

2029. Through material things "the Way" does always lead to Allah. But some minds are so obsessed with material things that they miss the pointers to the spiritual. Allah could have forced all to the true Way, but in His Will and Plan is the training of man's will, and that is done by the Signs in nature and Revelation.

Had willed, He could have
Guided all of you.

وَلَوْ شَآءَ لَهَدَىٰكُمْ أَجْمَعِينَ

SECTION 2.

10. It is He Who sends down
Rain from the sky.
From it ye drink,
And out of it (grows)
The vegetation on which
Ye feed your cattle.

(١٠) هُوَ ٱلَّذِىٓ أَنزَلَ مِنَ ٱلسَّمَآءِ مَآءً لَّكُم مِّنْهُ شَرَابٌ وَمِنْهُ شَجَرٌ فِيهِ تُسِيمُونَ

11. With it He produces
For you corn, olives,
Date palms, grapes,
And every kind of fruit:
Verily in this is a Sign
For those who give thought.[2030]

(١١) يُنۢبِتُ لَكُم بِهِ ٱلزَّرْعَ وَٱلزَّيْتُونَ وَٱلنَّخِيلَ وَٱلْأَعْنَٰبَ وَمِن كُلِّ ٱلثَّمَرَٰتِ إِنَّ فِى ذَٰلِكَ لَءَايَةً لِّقَوْمٍ يَتَفَكَّرُونَ

12. He has made subject to you
The Night and the Day;[2031]
The Sun and the Moon;
And the Stars are in subjection
By His Command: verily
In this are signs
For men who are wise.

(١٢) وَسَخَّرَ لَكُمُ ٱلَّيْلَ وَٱلنَّهَارَ وَٱلشَّمْسَ وَٱلْقَمَرَ وَٱلنُّجُومُ مُسَخَّرَٰتٌۢ بِأَمْرِهِۦٓ إِنَّ فِى ذَٰلِكَ لَءَايَٰتٍ لِّقَوْمٍ يَعْقِلُونَ

13. And the things on this earth
Which He has multiplied

(١٣) وَمَا ذَرَأَ لَكُمْ فِى ٱلْأَرْضِ

2030. The least thought and study of nature will show you Allah's wise and benign providence in making the processes of nature subserve man's use and refined life. A higher degree of intelligence and study is required ("men who are wise") to understand Allah's Signs to man in the process connected with the heavenly bodies (verse 12). And a still higher spiritual understanding ("men who celebrate His praises" with gratitude) to realise the marvellous gradation, colours, and nuances in the creatures on this little globe of ours (verse 13). Reason this out very carefully.

2031. The Night and Day are caused by astronomical rotations. What is important for man to note is how Allah has given intelligence to man to make use of this alternation for work and rest; how man can, as soon as he rises from the primitive stage, get over their inequalities by artificial illuminants, such as vegetable or mineral oils, coal, gas, or electricity, which ultimately are derived from the stored-up energy of the sun; how the sun's heat can be tempered by various artificial means and can be stored up for use by man as required; how man can be independent of the tides caused by the moon and the sun, which formerly controlled navigation, but which no longer stand in man's way, with his artificial harbours and great sea-going ships; how navigation was formerly subject to direct observation of the Polar Star and other stars but how the magnetic needle and charts have now completely altered the position, and man can calculate and to a certain extent control magnetic variations, etc. In such ways the sun, the moon, and the stars themselves become useful servants to him, all by Allah's gift and His Command, without which there would have been no laws governing them and no intelligence to make use of them.

In varying colours (and
qualities):[2032]
Verily in this is a Sign
For men who celebrate
The praises of Allah
(in gratitude).[2033]

مُخْتَلِفًا أَلْوَٰنُهُۥٓ
إِنَّ فِى ذَٰلِكَ لَءَايَةً
لِّقَوْمٍ يَذَّكَّرُونَ

14. It is He Who has made[2034]
The sea subject, that ye
May eat thereof flesh
That is fresh and tender,[2035]
And that ye may extract
Therefrom ornaments to wear,[2036]
And thou seest the ships
Therein that plough the waves,
That ye may seek (thus)
Of the bounty of Allah[2037]
And that ye may be grateful.

١٤ وَهُوَ ٱلَّذِى سَخَّرَ ٱلْبَحْرَ
لِتَأْكُلُوا۟ مِنْهُ لَحْمًا طَرِيًّا
وَتَسْتَخْرِجُوا۟ مِنْهُ حِلْيَةً تَلْبَسُونَهَا
وَتَرَى ٱلْفُلْكَ مَوَاخِرَ فِيهِ وَلِتَبْتَغُوا۟
مِن فَضْلِهِۦ وَلَعَلَّكُمْ تَشْكُرُونَ

15. And He has set up
On the earth mountains[2038]
Standing firm, lest it should

١٥ وَأَلْقَىٰ فِى ٱلْأَرْضِ رَوَٰسِىَ أَن

2032. Whose heart has not been moved by the glorious gradation of colours in the sunset clouds? The gradations are infinite, and it is only the eye of an artist that can express their collective beauty. They are but a type of the infinite variety and gradation of qualities in the spiritual sphere even in the little space of our own globe. The big things that can be measured and defined have been spoken of before. Here we have mention of the subtle nuances in the spiritual world which can only be perceived by men who are so high in spiritual insight that their only reaction is to "celebrate the praises of Allah" in gratitude for His infinite Mercies.

2033. Read again n. 2030 above, and see how subtly we are led up from the perception of the big to the perception of the subtle and delicate colours and qualities in the spiritual world.

2034. We have gone up in a climax of material things from the big to the subtle in the sky and the earth. Here we have another climax as regards the things of the sea. We get the delicate flesh of fishes and marine creatures of all kinds; we get the treasures of the deep: pearls, coral, amber, and things of that kind; and we have the stately ships ploughing the waves, for maritime commerce and intercourse, for unifying mankind, and for reaching the spiritual bounty of Allah which can best be expressed by the boundless ocean.

2035. Connoisseurs know the delicate flavours of sea fish, such as the pomfret of the Indian Ocean, the herring of the North Atlantic, the mullet of Marseilles, and many other kinds. *Ṭarī*, translated "fresh and tender," also refers to the soft moist nature of fresh fish. It is another wonder of Allah that salt water should produce flesh of such fresh, tender, and delicate flavour.

2036. Diving for pearls—in both the primitive and the more advanced form—is another instance of man's power over apparently inaccessible depths of the sea.

2037. After the material benefits which we get from the sea, we are asked to consider things of higher import to the spirit of man. There is the beautiful ship which stands as the symbol of international commerce and intercourse, things that may be of material benefit, but which have a higher aspect in unifying man and making his civilisation more universal. These are first steps in seeking of the "bounty of Allah" through the sea. But there are higher aspects. Navigation and international intercourse increase knowledge, which in its higher aspects should clean the mind and make it fitter to approach Allah. The salt water, which covers nearly 72 percent of the surface of the globe, is itself a purifying and sanitary agent, and is a good symbol of the higher bounties of Allah, which are as boundless as the ocean.

2038. *Cf.* 13:3 and 15:19. Here and elsewhere the earth is spoken of as a spacious carpet beneath our feet and the hills as a steadying agent to keep the carpet from rolling or shaking about. In 78:7 they are spoken of as pegs or stakes. (R).

Shake with you; and rivers
And roads; that ye
May guide yourselves,[2039]

تَمِيدَ بِكُمْ وَأَنْهَٰرًا وَسُبُلًا
لَّعَلَّكُمْ تَهْتَدُونَ

16. And marks and signposts;
And by the stars
(Men) guide themselves.[2040]

١٦ وَعَلَٰمَٰتٍ وَبِالنَّجْمِ هُمْ يَهْتَدُونَ

17. Is then He Who creates
Like one that creates not?
Will ye not receive admonition?[2041]

١٧ أَفَمَن يَخْلُقُ كَمَن لَّا يَخْلُقُ
أَفَلَا تَذَكَّرُونَ

18. If ye would count up
The favours of Allah,
Never would ye be able
To number them; for Allah
Is Oft-Forgiving, Most
Merciful.[2042]

١٨ وَإِن تَعُدُّوا نِعْمَةَ اللَّهِ لَا تُحْصُوهَآ
إِنَّ اللَّهَ لَغَفُورٌ رَّحِيمٌ

19. And Allah doth know
What ye conceal,
And what ye reveal.

١٩ وَاللَّهُ يَعْلَمُ مَا تُسِرُّونَ وَمَا تُعْلِنُونَ

20. Those whom they invoke
Besides Allah create nothing
And are themselves created.[2043]

٢٠ وَالَّذِينَ يَدْعُونَ مِن دُونِ اللَّهِ
لَا يَخْلُقُونَ شَيْـًٔا وَهُمْ يُخْلَقُونَ

2039. In this passage (16:15-16) we have the metaphor of the fixed mountains further allegorised. In these verses the key words are indicated by the symbols for man's guidance (*tahtadūn*). First, the physical symbols are indicated: the mountains that stand firm and do not change from day to day in the landscape, unlike shifting sand dunes, or the coastline of the sea, or rivers and streams, which frequently change their courses; then we have rivers and roads, which are more precise and therefore more useful, though less permanent; then we have *'alāmāt* (signposts), any kinds of signs erected by man, like direction posts, lighthouses or beacons, or provided in nature, as tall trees, etc.; and finally, we have the polestar, and now the magnetic needle, with its variations marked on navigation charts. All these are symbols for the higher Guidance which Allah provides for the spirit of man. See next note.

2040. See last note. Let us examine the completed allegory. As there are beacons, landmarks and signs to show the way to men on the earth, so in the spiritual world. And it is ultimately Allah Who provides them, and this is His crowning Mercy. Like the mountains, there are spiritual landmarks in the missions of the Great Teachers: they should guide us, or teach us to guide ourselves, and not shake hither and thither like a ship without a rudder or people without Faith. As rivers and streams mark out their channels, smoothing out levels, so we have wholesome laws and customs established, to help us in our lives. Then we have the example of Great Men as further signposts: "Lives of great men all remind us. We can make our lives sublime." In long distance travel, the polestar and the magnetic needle are our guides: so in our long distance journey to the other world, we have ultimately to look to heavenly guidance or its reflections in Allah's Revelations.

2041. The Supreme Majesty of Allah having been set out in His favours of all kinds, it will be seen at once that the worship of any other than Allah is meaningless and ridiculous. Shall we not take the hint and understand?

2042. Of all Allah's favours innumerable, His Mercy and Forgiveness in the spiritual plane are the greatest, and of eternal value to us in our future Lives.

2043. Allah is the only Creator and the Ultimate Reality. Everything else is created by Him, and reflects His glory. How foolish then to worship any other than Allah!

21. (They are things) dead,
Lifeless: nor do they know
When they will be raised up.[2044]

٢١ أَمْوَٰتٌ غَيْرُ أَحْيَآءٍ ۖ وَمَا يَشْعُرُونَ أَيَّانَ يُبْعَثُونَ

SECTION 3.

22. Your God is One God:
As to those who believe not
In the Hereafter, their hearts
Refuse to know, and they
Are arrogant.[2045]

٢٢ إِلَٰهُكُمْ إِلَٰهٌ وَٰحِدٌ ۚ فَٱلَّذِينَ لَا يُؤْمِنُونَ بِٱلْءَاخِرَةِ قُلُوبُهُم مُّنكِرَةٌ وَهُم مُّسْتَكْبِرُونَ

23. Undoubtedly, Allah doth know
What they conceal,
And what they reveal:[2046]
Verily He loveth not the arrogant.

٢٣ لَا جَرَمَ أَنَّ ٱللَّهَ يَعْلَمُ مَا يُسِرُّونَ وَمَا يُعْلِنُونَ ۚ إِنَّهُۥ لَا يُحِبُّ ٱلْمُسْتَكْبِرِينَ

24. When it is said to them,
"What is it that your Lord[2047]
Has revealed?" they say,
"Tales of the ancients!"

٢٤ وَإِذَا قِيلَ لَهُم مَّاذَآ أَنزَلَ رَبُّكُمْ ۙ قَالُوٓا۟ أَسَٰطِيرُ ٱلْأَوَّلِينَ

25. Let them bear, on the Day
Of Judgement, their own burdens
In full, and also (something)
Of the burdens of those
Without knowledge, whom they[2048]
Misled. Alas, how grievous
The burdens they will bear!

٢٥ لِيَحْمِلُوٓا۟ أَوْزَارَهُمْ كَامِلَةً يَوْمَ ٱلْقِيَٰمَةِ ۙ وَمِنْ أَوْزَارِ ٱلَّذِينَ يُضِلُّونَهُم بِغَيْرِ عِلْمٍ ۗ أَلَا سَآءَ مَا يَزِرُونَ

2044. Idols are dead wood or stone. If men worship stars, or heroes, or prophets, or great men, they too have no life except that which was given by Allah. In themselves, they are lifeless. If they worship figments of the imagination, they are reflections in a double degree, and have no life in themselves. All these things will be raised up on the Last Day, in order that false worhsippers may be confronted with them. But they themselves cannot tell when that Day will be.

2045. Everything points to Allah, the One True Eternal God. If so, there is a Hereafter, for He has declared it. Insofar as people do not believe this, the fault is in their Will: they do not wish to believe, and the motive behind is arrogance, the sin which brought about the fall of Iblīs: 2:34. (R).

2046. *Cf.* 16:19, where the same words refer to man generally. Whether he conceals or reveals what is in his heart, Allah knows it, and as Allah is Oft-Forgiving, Most Merciful, His grace is available as His highest favour if man will take it. Here the reference is to those who "refuse to know", who reject Allah's guidance out of arrogance. Allah "loveth not the arrogant". Such men deprive themselves of Allah's grace.

2047. When the arrogant Unbelievers are referred to some definite argument or illustration from Scripture, they dismiss it contemptuously with the remark, "Tales of the ancients!" In this, they are not only playing with their own conscience, but misleading others, with perhaps less knowledge than themselves.

2048. Their responsibility or crime is twofold: (1) that they rejected Allah's Message, and (2) that they misled others. Their Penalty will also be double. In 6:164, we are told that "no bearer of burdens can bear the burden of another". This is against the doctrine of vicarious atonement. Every man is responsible for his own sins: but the sin of misleading others is a sin of the misleader himself, and he must suffer the penalty for that also, without relieving those misled, of their responsibility.

C. 124.—(16:26-50.)
In all ages wicked men tried to plot
Against Allah's Way, but they never
Succeeded, and were covered with shame
In ways unexpected. The righteous
See good in Allah's Word, and their goal
Is the Good. Great Teachers were sent
To all nations, to warn against Evil
And guide to the Right. The penalty
For evil comes in many unexpected
Ways, for Evil is against Nature.
And all Nature proclaims Allah's Glory
And humbly serves Him, the Lord Supreme.

SECTION 4.

26. Those before them did also
Plot (against Allah's Way):
But Allah took their structures
From their foundations, and the roof
Fell down on them from above;
And the Wrath seized them
From directions they did not perceive.[2049]

٢٦ قَدْ مَكَرَ ٱلَّذِينَ مِن قَبْلِهِمْ
فَأَتَى ٱللَّهُ بُنْيَٰنَهُم مِّنَ ٱلْقَوَاعِدِ
فَخَرَّ عَلَيْهِمُ ٱلسَّقْفُ مِن فَوْقِهِمْ
وَأَتَىٰهُمُ ٱلْعَذَابُ مِنْ حَيْثُ لَا يَشْعُرُونَ

27. Then, on the Day of Judgement,
He will cover them
With shame, and say:
"Where are My 'partners'
Concerning whom ye used
To dispute (with the godly)?"
Those endued with knowledge[2050]
Will say: "This Day, indeed,
Are the Unbelievers covered
With Shame and Misery—

٢٧ ثُمَّ يَوْمَ ٱلْقِيَٰمَةِ يُخْزِيهِمْ وَيَقُولُ
أَيْنَ شُرَكَآءِىَ ٱلَّذِينَ
كُنتُمْ تُشَٰٓقُّونَ فِيهِمْ
قَالَ ٱلَّذِينَ أُوتُوا۟ ٱلْعِلْمَ إِنَّ
ٱلْخِزْىَ ٱلْيَوْمَ وَٱلسُّوٓءَ عَلَى ٱلْكَٰفِرِينَ

28. "(Namely) those whose lives the angels
Take in a state of wrongdoing

٢٨ ٱلَّذِينَ تَتَوَفَّىٰهُمُ ٱلْمَلَٰٓئِكَةُ ظَالِمِىٓ

2049. Evil will always devise plots against the Prophets of Allah. So was it with Al Muṣṭafā, and so was it with the Prophets before him. But the imposing structures which the ungodly build up (metaphorically) collapse at the Command of Allah, and they are often punished from quarters from which they least expected punishment. For example, the Quraysh were confident in their numbers, their organisation, and their superior equipment. But on the field of Badr they collapsed where they expected victory.

2050. The worshippers of false gods (the ungodly, the Unbelievers) will be unable to reply when brought before the Judgement Seat. The comment of those "endued with knowledge"—the Prophets and Teachers whom they had rejected—will be by way of indictment and explanation of the position of those before the Judgement Seat.

To their own souls.[2051]
Then would they offer submission
(With the pretence), 'We did[2052]
No evil (knowingly).'" (The angels
Will reply), "Nay, but verily
Allah knoweth all that ye did;

أَنفُسِهِمْ ۖ
فَأَلْقَوُا۟ ٱلسَّلَمَ مَا كُنَّا نَعْمَلُ مِن سُوٓءٍۭ ۚ
بَلَىٰٓ إِنَّ ٱللَّهَ عَلِيمٌۢ بِمَا كُنتُمْ تَعْمَلُونَ

29. "So enter the gates of Hell,
To dwell therein.
Thus evil indeed
Is the abode of the arrogant."

٢٩ فَٱدْخُلُوٓا۟ أَبْوَٰبَ جَهَنَّمَ خَٰلِدِينَ فِيهَا ۖ
فَلَبِئْسَ مَثْوَى ٱلْمُتَكَبِّرِينَ

30. To the righteous
(When) it is said, "What
Is it that your Lord[2053]
Has revealed?" they say,
"All that is good." To those
Who do good, there is good
In this world, and the Home
Of the Hereafter is even better[2054]
And excellent indeed is the Home
Of the righteous—

٣٠ وَقِيلَ لِلَّذِينَ ٱتَّقَوْا۟
مَاذَآ أَنزَلَ رَبُّكُمْ ۚ قَالُوا۟ خَيْرًا ۗ
لِّلَّذِينَ أَحْسَنُوا۟ فِى هَٰذِهِ ٱلدُّنْيَا حَسَنَةٌ ۚ
وَلَدَارُ ٱلْءَاخِرَةِ خَيْرٌ ۚ
وَلَنِعْمَ دَارُ ٱلْمُتَّقِينَ

31. Gardens of Eternity which they
Will enter: beneath them
Flow (pleasant) rivers: they
Will have therein all
That they wish: thus doth
Allah reward the righteous—

٣١ جَنَّٰتُ عَدْنٍ يَدْخُلُونَهَا تَجْرِى مِن تَحْتِهَا
ٱلْأَنْهَٰرُ ۖ لَهُمْ فِيهَا مَا يَشَآءُونَ ۚ
كَذَٰلِكَ يَجْزِى ٱللَّهُ ٱلْمُتَّقِينَ

32. (Namely) those whose lives
The angels take in a state[2055]
Of purity, saying (to them),
"Peace be on you; enter ye

٣٢ ٱلَّذِينَ تَتَوَفَّىٰهُمُ ٱلْمَلَٰٓئِكَةُ طَيِّبِينَ ۙ
يَقُولُونَ سَلَٰمٌ عَلَيْكُمُ ٱدْخُلُوا۟

2051. That is, those who died in a state of *kufr*, or rebellion against Allah, which was really wrongdoing against their own souls.

2052. The excuse is a mere pretence. At first they were too dazed to reply. When they reply, they cannot deny the facts, but resort to the sinner's excuse of saying that they sinned through ignorance, and that their motives were not wrong. Such a plea raises a question of hidden thoughts which are difficult to appraise before a human tribunal. But here they are before their Divine Author, Who knows every secret of their souls, and before Whom no false plea can be of any value. So they are concerned.

2053. The contrast and parallelism is with 16:24, where the ungodly in their levity and their deliberate rejection of guidance find no profit from Allah's revelation.

2054. Unlike the ungodly, the good find good everywhere—in this world and in the Hereafter; because they understand and are in accord with the truths around them.

2055. *In a state of purity*: from the evils of this world, from want of faith and want of grace. Purity from such evil is the mark of true Islam, and those who die in such purity will be received into Felicity with a salutation of Peace.

The Garden, because of (the good)
Which ye did (in the world)."

الْجَنَّةَ بِمَا كُنتُمْ تَعْمَلُونَ

33. Do the (ungodly) wait until
The angels come to them,
Or there comes the Command
Of thy Lord (for their doom)?[2056]
So did those who went
Before them. But Allah
Wronged them not: nay,
They wronged their own souls.

٣٣ هَلْ يَنظُرُونَ إِلَّا أَن تَأْتِيَهُمُ الْمَلَٰٓئِكَةُ
أَوْ يَأْتِيَ أَمْرُ رَبِّكَ كَذَٰلِكَ فَعَلَ الَّذِينَ مِن قَبْلِهِمْ
وَمَا ظَلَمَهُمُ اللَّهُ وَلَٰكِن كَانُوٓا۟
أَنفُسَهُمْ يَظْلِمُونَ

34. But the evil results
Of their deeds overtook them,
And that very (Wrath).
At which they had scoffed
Hemmed them in.

٣٤ فَأَصَابَهُمْ سَيِّئَاتُ مَا عَمِلُوا۟
وَحَاقَ بِهِم مَّا كَانُوا۟ بِهِۦ يَسْتَهْزِءُونَ

Section 5.

35. The worshippers of false gods
Say: "If Allah had so willed,
We should not have worshipped
Aught but Him—neither we[2057]
Nor our fathers—nor should
We have prescribed
prohibitions[2058]
Other than His." So did those
Who went before them.
But what is the mission
Of messengers but to preach
The Clear Message?[2059]

٣٥ وَقَالَ الَّذِينَ أَشْرَكُوا۟
لَوْ شَآءَ اللَّهُ مَا عَبَدْنَا مِن دُونِهِۦ مِن
شَىْءٍ نَّحْنُ وَلَآ ءَابَآؤُنَا وَلَا حَرَّمْنَا
مِن دُونِهِۦ مِن شَىْءٍ
كَذَٰلِكَ فَعَلَ الَّذِينَ مِن قَبْلِهِمْ
فَهَلْ عَلَى الرُّسُلِ إِلَّا الْبَلَٰغُ الْمُبِينُ

2056. That is, until death comes to them, or some Punishment in this life, itself, which precludes them from repentance and the Mercy of Allah.

2057. The age-old argument: if Allah is All-Powerful, why did He not force all persons to His Will? This ignores the limited free will granted to man, which is the whole basis of Ethics. Allah gives man every opportunity of knowing and understanding things, but He does not force him, for that would be against the whole Plan on which our present Life is constituted.

2058. The Pagan Arabs prescribed various arbitrary prohibitions in the matter of meat: see 6:143-145. These, of course, are not recognised by Islam, which also removed some of the restrictions of the Jewish Law: 6:146. The general meaning, however, is far wider. Men erect their own taboos and prohibitions, barriers and restrictions, and ascribe them to Religion. This is wrong, and more consonant with Pagan practice than with Islam.

2059. *Clear Message: Mubīn*: in three senses: (1) a Message clear and unambiguous; (2) one that makes all things clear to those who try to understand, because it accords with their own nature as created by Allah; (3) one preached openly and to everyone.

36. For We assuredly sent
Amongst every People a
messenger,[2060]
(With the Command), "Serve
Allah, and eschew Evil":
Of the poeple were some whom
Allah guided, and some
On whom Error became[2061]
Inevitably (established). So travel
Through the earth, and see
What was the end of those
Who denied (the Truth).

٣٦ وَلَقَدْ بَعَثْنَا فِي كُلِّ أُمَّةٍ رَّسُولًا
أَنِ ٱعْبُدُوا۟ ٱللَّهَ وَٱجْتَنِبُوا۟ ٱلطَّٰغُوتَ
فَمِنْهُم مَّنْ هَدَى ٱللَّهُ وَمِنْهُم
مَّنْ حَقَّتْ عَلَيْهِ ٱلضَّلَٰلَةُ
فَسِيرُوا۟ فِى ٱلْأَرْضِ فَٱنظُرُوا۟
كَيْفَ كَانَ عَٰقِبَةُ ٱلْمُكَذِّبِينَ

37. If thou art anxious
For their guidance, yet
Allah guideth not such
As He leaves to stray.[2062]
And there is none
To help them.

٣٧ إِن تَحْرِصْ عَلَىٰ هُدَىٰهُمْ
فَإِنَّ ٱللَّهَ لَا يَهْدِى مَن يُضِلُّ
وَمَا لَهُم مِّن نَّٰصِرِينَ

38. They swear their strongest
oath[2063]
By Allah, that Allah will not
Raise up those who die;[2064]
Nay, but it is a promise
(Binding) on Him in truth:
But most among mankind
Realise it not.

٣٨ وَأَقْسَمُوا۟ بِٱللَّهِ جَهْدَ أَيْمَٰنِهِمْ
لَا يَبْعَثُ ٱللَّهُ مَن يَمُوتُ
بَلَىٰ وَعْدًا عَلَيْهِ حَقًّا وَلَٰكِنَّ
أَكْثَرَ ٱلنَّاسِ لَا يَعْلَمُونَ

39. (They must be raised up),
In order that He may manifest

٣٩ لِيُبَيِّنَ

2060. Even though Allah's Signs are everywhere in Nature and in men's own conscience, yet in addition Allah has sent human Messengers to every People to call their attention to the Good and turn them from Evil. So they cannot pretend that Allah has abandoned them or that He does not care what they do. His divine Grace always invites their will to choose the right.

2061. While some people accept the guidance of the divine Grace, others so surrender themselves to Evil that it must necessarily follow that evil obtains a grip over them. They have only to travel through time or space to see the end of those who abandoned their lights and surrendered to Evil and error. For *ḥaqqah* and the meaning of *ḥaqq* in this connection *cf.* 15:64.

2062. When once Allah's Grace is rejected by anyone, such a person loses all help and guidance. Such persons are then outside Allah's Grace, and therefore they are outside guidance.

2063. The strongest oath of the Pagan Arabs would be by the Supreme Allah: less strong oaths would be by their subordinate deities, or their ancestors, or other things they valued or held sacred.

2064. The usual Pagan creed is: "If there is a God, it does not follow that He will raise us up: why should He?" The answer is twofold: (1) Allah has promised it, and Allah's promise is true, (2) He must finally manifest the Truth to them, convict them of their falsehood, and enforce their personal responsibility (16:39).

To them the truth of that
Wherein they differ, and that
The rejecters of Truth
May realise that they had
Indeed (surrendered to)
Falsehood.[2065]

لَهُمُ ٱلَّذِى يَخْتَلِفُونَ فِيهِ
وَلِيَعْلَمَ ٱلَّذِينَ كَفَرُوٓا۟ أَنَّهُمْ
كَانُوا۟ كَـٰذِبِينَ

40. For to anything which We
Have willed, We but say
The Word, "Be", and it is.[2066]

٤٠ إِنَّمَا قَوْلُنَا لِشَىْءٍ إِذَآ أَرَدْنَـٰهُ
أَن نَّقُولَ لَهُۥ كُن فَيَكُونُ

SECTION 6.

41. To those who leave
Their homes in the cause
Of Allah, after suffering
oppression —[2067]
We will assuredly give
A goodly home in this world:
But truly the reward
Of the Hereafter will be greater.
If they only realised (this)!

٤١ وَٱلَّذِينَ هَاجَرُوا۟
فِى ٱللَّهِ مِنۢ بَعْدِ مَا ظُلِمُوا۟
لَنُبَوِّئَنَّهُمْ فِى ٱلدُّنْيَا حَسَنَةً
وَلَأَجْرُ ٱلْـَٔاخِرَةِ أَكْبَرُ
لَوْ كَانُوا۟ يَعْلَمُونَ

42. (They are) those who persevere
In patience, and put
Their trust on their Lord.

٤٢ ٱلَّذِينَ صَبَرُوا۟
وَعَلَىٰ رَبِّهِمْ يَتَوَكَّلُونَ

43. And before thee also
The messengers We sent
Were but men,[2068] to whom
We granted inspiration: if ye

٤٣ وَمَآ أَرْسَلْنَا مِن قَبْلِكَ
إِلَّا رِجَالًا نُّوحِىٓ إِلَيْهِمْ

2065. See the last note.

2066. Allah's "Word" is in itself the Deed. Allah's Promise is in itself the Truth. There is no interposition of Time or Condition between His Will and its consequences, for He is the Ultimate Reality. He is independent of the proximate or material causes, for He Himself creates them and establishes their Laws as He pleases.

2067. There is no merit in suffering exile (*hijrah*) in itself. To have any merit, it must be: (1) in the cause of Allah, and (2) after such an oppression as forces the sufferer to choose between Allah and man. When these conditions are fulfilled, the exiles are entitled to the highest honour, as having made a great sacrifice in the cause of Allah. Such were the early Muslim exiles to Abyssinia; such were the later exiles to Madīnah, before the Prophet himself left his home in Makkah and went to Madīnah; and such were the exiles who went with the Prophet or followed him. At all these stages, his approval or advice was always obtained, either specifically or generally.

2068. Allah's prophets were always men, not angels; and their distinction was the inspiration they received.

Realise this not, ask of those
Who possess the Message.[2069]

فَسْـَٔلُوٓا۟ أَهْلَ ٱلذِّكْرِ إِن كُنتُمْ لَا تَعْلَمُونَ

44. (We sent them) with Clear Signs
And Scriptures[2070]
And We have sent down
Unto thee (also) the Message;
That thou mayest explain clearly
To men what is sent
For them, and that they
May give thought.

٤٤ بِٱلْبَيِّنَـٰتِ وَٱلزُّبُرِ ۗ
وَأَنزَلْنَآ إِلَيْكَ ٱلذِّكْرَ
لِتُبَيِّنَ لِلنَّاسِ مَا نُزِّلَ إِلَيْهِمْ
وَلَعَلَّهُمْ يَتَفَكَّرُونَ

45. Do then those who devise
Evil (plots) feel secure
That Allah will not cause
The earth to swallow them up,
Or that the Wrath will not
Seize them from directions
They little perceive?—[2071]

٤٥ أَفَأَمِنَ ٱلَّذِينَ مَكَرُوا۟ ٱلسَّيِّـَٔاتِ
أَن يَخْسِفَ ٱللَّهُ بِهِمُ ٱلْأَرْضَ أَوْ يَأْتِيَهُمُ
ٱلْعَذَابُ مِنْ حَيْثُ لَا يَشْعُرُونَ

46. Or that He may not
Call them to account
In the midst of their goings[2072]
To and fro, without a chance
Of their frustrating Him?—

٤٦ أَوْ يَأْخُذَهُمْ فِى تَقَلُّبِهِمْ
فَمَا هُم بِمُعْجِزِينَ

47. Or that He may not
Call them to account

٤٧ أَوْ يَأْخُذَهُمْ

2069. If the Pagan Arabs, who were ignorant of religious and other history, wondered how a man from among themselves could receive inspiration and bring a Message from Allah, let them ask the Jews, who had also received Allah's Message earlier through Moses, whether Moses was a man, or an angel, or a god. They would learn that Moses was a man like themselves, but inspired by Allah. "Those who possess the Message" may also mean any men of Wisdom, who were qualified to have an opinion in such matters.

2070. As the People of the Book had received "Clear Signs" and inspired Books before, so also Allah's Message came to the Prophet Muḥammad through the Qur'ān, which superseded the earlier revelations, already corrupted in the hands of their followers. (R).

2071. *Cf.* 16:26. The wicked plot against Prophets of Allah in secret, forgetting that every hidden thought of theirs is known to Allah, and that for every thought and action of theirs they will have to account to Allah. And Allah's punishment can seize them in various ways. Four are enumerated here. (1) They may be swallowed up in the earth like Qārūn, whose story is told in 28:76-81. He was swallowed up in the earth while he was arrogantly exulting on the score of his wealth. (2) It may be that, like Hāmān, the prime minister of Pharaoh, they are plotting against Allah, when they are themselves overwhelmed by some dreadful calamity: 40:36-38; 39:39-40. The case of Pharaoh is also in point. He was drowned while he was arrogantly hoping to frustrate Allah's plans for Israel: 10:90-92. For (3) and (4) see the next two notes. (R).

2072. (3) Or the punishment may come to people away from their homes and humble them in their pride. It so happened to Abū Jahl, who came exulting in his pride to the Battle of Badr (A.H.2). His army was three times the size of the Muslim army from Madīnah. But it suffered a crushing defeat, and he himself was ignominiously slain.

By a process of slow wastage—[2073]
For thy Lord is indeed
Full of kindness and mercy.

عَلَىٰ تَخَوُّفٍ فَإِنَّ رَبَّكُمْ لَرَءُوفٌ رَّحِيمٌ

48. Do they not look
At Allah's creation, (even)
Among (inanimate) things—[2074]
How their (very) shadows
Turn round, from the right
And the left, prostrating
Themselves to Allah, and that
In the humblest manner?

٤٨ أَوَلَمْ يَرَوْا إِلَىٰ مَا خَلَقَ ٱللَّهُ مِن شَىْءٍ
يَتَفَيَّؤُا ظِلَٰلُهُۥ عَنِ ٱلْيَمِينِ وَٱلشَّمَآئِلِ
سُجَّدًا لِّلَّهِ وَهُمْ دَٰخِرُونَ

49. And to Allah doth obeisance
All that is in the heavens
And on earth, whether
Moving (living) creatures[2075]
Or the angels: for none
Are arrogant (before their Lord).

٤٩ وَلِلَّهِ يَسْجُدُ مَا فِى ٱلسَّمَٰوَٰتِ
وَمَا فِى ٱلْأَرْضِ مِن دَآبَّةٍ وَٱلْمَلَٰٓئِكَةُ
وَهُمْ لَا يَسْتَكْبِرُونَ

50. They all revere their Lord,[2076]
High above them, and they do
All that they are commanded.

٥٠ يَخَافُونَ رَبَّهُم مِّن فَوْقِهِمْ
وَيَفْعَلُونَ مَا يُؤْمَرُونَ

C. 125.—There is but One God, He Who gives
(16:51-83.) All blessings to man and other creatures.
His greatest gift is that He reveals
Himself. But in many tangible ways
He cares for man and provides for his growth

2073. (4) Or, as often happens, the punishment comes slowly and imperceptibly, the power of the enemies of Allah being wasted gradually, until it is extinguished. This happened to the Makkans during the eight years of the Prophet's exile. The conquest of Makkah was bloodless, because the power of the enemy had gradually vanished. The Prophet was thus able to show the unexampled generosity and clemency which he showed on that occasion, for two of Allah's attributes are expressed in the titles "Full of kindness" (*Ra'ūf*) and "Full of mercy" *(Raḥīm)*.

2074. I take "things" here to be inanimate things, for the next verse speaks of living "moving creatures" and angels. By a metaphor even such inanimate things are spoken of as recognising Allah and humbly worshipping Him. Even their shadows turn around from right and left according to the light from above, and, they humbly prostrate themselves on the ground to celebrate the praises of Allah. The "shadows" suggest how all things in this life are mere shadows of the true Reality in heaven; and they should turn and move in accordance with the divine light, as the shadows of trees and buildings move in one direction or another, and lengthen or shorten according to the light from heaven.

2075. *Moving creatures, i.e.*, living creatures. "All that is in the heaven or earth," includes every created thing. And created things are mentioned in three classes: inanimate things, ordinary living things, and angels. Even the highest angels are not arrogant: they bow down and serve their Lord, and so does all Creation.

2076. Allah is so high above the highest of His creatures, that they all look up to him in awe and reverence. And they joyfully do their duty in serving him. This is the meaning of the "fear of the Lord."

And sustenance. In rain, in milk,
In fruits and honey, and in Nature and the life
Of man, with his opportunities
Of social, moral, and spiritual growth,
Are Signs for those who understand.
Why then does man show ingratitude
By going after false gods and forgetting Allah?

SECTION 7.

51. Allah has said: "Take not
(For worship) two gods:[2077]
For He is just One God:
Then fear Me (and Me alone)."

(٥١) وَقَالَ ٱللَّهُ لَا تَتَّخِذُوٓاْ إِلَٰهَيۡنِ ٱثۡنَيۡنِۖ إِنَّمَا هُوَ إِلَٰهٞ وَٰحِدٞ فَإِيَّٰيَ فَٱرۡهَبُونِ

52. To Him belongs whatever
Is in the heavens and on earth.
And to Him is duty due always:
Then will ye fear other[2078]
Than Allah?

(٥٢) وَلَهُۥ مَا فِي ٱلسَّمَٰوَٰتِ وَٱلۡأَرۡضِ وَلَهُ ٱلدِّينُ وَاصِبًاۚ أَفَغَيۡرَ ٱللَّهِ تَتَّقُونَ

53. And ye have no good thing
But is from Allah: and moreover,
When ye are touched by distress,
Unto Him ye cry with groans;[2079]

(٥٣) وَمَا بِكُم مِّن نِّعۡمَةٖ فَمِنَ ٱللَّهِۖ ثُمَّ إِذَا مَسَّكُمُ ٱلضُّرُّ فَإِلَيۡهِ تَجۡـَٔرُونَ

54. Yet, when He removes
The distress from you, behold!
Some of you turn to other gods
To join with their Lord—

(٥٤) ثُمَّ إِذَا كَشَفَ ٱلضُّرَّ عَنكُمۡ إِذَا فَرِيقٞ مِّنكُم بِرَبِّهِمۡ يُشۡرِكُونَ

55. (As if) to show their ingratitude
For the favours We have
Bestowed on them! Then enjoy
(Your brief day); but soon
Will ye know (your folly)!

(٥٥) لِيَكۡفُرُواْ بِمَآ ءَاتَيۡنَٰهُمۡۚ فَتَمَتَّعُواْ فَسَوۡفَ تَعۡلَمُونَ

2077. The ancient Persians believed in two powers in the Universe, one good and the other evil. The Pagan Arabs also had pairs of deities: *e.g.*, *Jibt* (Sorcery) and *Ṭāg͟hūt* (Evil), referred to in 4:51, n. 573, or the idols on Ṣafā and Marwah referred to in n. 160 to 2:158: their names were Isāf and Nayla.

2078. The Pagans might have a glimmering of the One True God, but they had also a haunting fear of malevolent Powers of Evil. They are told that such fears are groundless. Evil has no power over those who trust in Allah: 15:42. The only fear they should have is that of the Wrath of Allah. To the righteous all good things come from Allah, and they have no fear in their hearts.

2079. Which shows that the natural tendency of man is to seek Allah, the only Power which can truly relieve distress.

56. And they (even) assign,
To things they do not know,[2080]
A portion out of that
Which We have bestowed
For their sustenance![2081]
By Allah, ye shall certainly
Be called to account
For your false inventions.

٥٦ وَيَجْعَلُونَ لِمَا لَا يَعْلَمُونَ
نَصِيبًا مِّمَّا رَزَقْنَٰهُمْ ۗ
تَٱللَّهِ لَتُسْـَٔلُنَّ عَمَّا
كُنتُمْ تَفْتَرُونَ

57. And they assign daughters[2082]
For Allah!—Glory be to Him!—
And for themselves (sons—
The issue) they desire!

٥٧ وَيَجْعَلُونَ لِلَّهِ ٱلْبَنَٰتِ سُبْحَٰنَهُۥ ۙ
وَلَهُم مَّا يَشْتَهُونَ

58. When news is brought
To one of them, of (the birth
Of) a female (child), his face
Darkens, and he is filled
With inward grief!

٥٨ وَإِذَا بُشِّرَ أَحَدُهُم بِٱلْأُنثَىٰ
ظَلَّ وَجْهُهُۥ مُسْوَدًّا وَهُوَ كَظِيمٌ

59. With shame does he hide
Himself from his people,
Because of the bad news
He has had!
Shall he retain it[2083]
On (sufferance and) contempt,
Or bury it in the dust?[2084]
Ah! what an evil (choice)
They decide on?[2085]

٥٩ يَتَوَٰرَىٰ مِنَ ٱلْقَوْمِ
مِن سُوٓءِ مَا بُشِّرَ بِهِۦٓ ۚ
أَيُمْسِكُهُۥ عَلَىٰ هُونٍ
أَمْ يَدُسُّهُۥ فِى ٱلتُّرَابِ ۗ
أَلَا سَآءَ مَا يَحْكُمُونَ

2080. Idols and fictitious gods are certainly things of which they have no knowledge, idols being lifeless things of whose life or doings no knowledge is possible, and fictitious gods being but figments of their imagination.

2081. *Cf.* 6:136—140, 142-144, and 5:106. The Pagans, in assigning and dedicating some of their children, or some of their cattle, or some of the produce of their fields, to their false gods as shares with the true Supreme Allah, made themselves doubly ridiculous; first, because every good thing that they valued was given to them by Allah, and how could they patronisingly assign to Him a share of His own gifts?—and secondly, because they brought in other gods as shares, who had no existence whatever! Besides, the cattle and produce were given for their physical sustenance and the children for their social and spiritual sustenance, and how can they, poor creatures, give sustenance to Allah?

2082. Some of the Pagan Arabs called angels 'the daughters of Allah'. In their own life they hated to have daughters, as explained in the next two verses. They practised female infanticide. In their state of perpetual war, sons were a source of strength to them; daughters only made them subject to humiliating raids!

2083. "It," in this and the following clause, refers grammatically to the "news" (*mā bushshira bihi*). In meaning it refers to the "female child"—by the figure of speech known as metonymy.

2084. *Cf.* 81:8-9. The practice of female infanticide is condemned in scathing terms. Female children used to be buried alive by the Pagan Arabs.

2085. It was an evil choice to decide on. Either alternative—to keep the poor girl as a thing of sufferance and contempt, bringing disgrace on the family, or to get rid of it by burying it alive—was cruel and indefensible.

60. To those who believe not
In the Hereafter, applies
The similitude of evil:
To Allah applies the highest[2086]
Similitude: for He is
The Exalted in Power,
Full of Wisdom.

٦٠ لِلَّذِينَ لَا يُؤْمِنُونَ بِالْآخِرَةِ
مَثَلُ السَّوْءِ وَلِلَّهِ الْمَثَلُ الْأَعْلَىٰ
وَهُوَ الْعَزِيزُ الْحَكِيمُ

SECTION 8.

61. If Allah were to punish
Men for their wrongdoing,
He would not leave, on the (earth),
A single living creature:
But He gives them respite
For a stated Term:
When their Term expires,
They would not be able
To delay (the punishment)
For a single hour, just as
They would not be able
To anticipate it (for a single
hour).[2087]

٦١ وَلَوْ يُؤَاخِذُ اللَّهُ النَّاسَ بِظُلْمِهِم
مَّا تَرَكَ عَلَيْهَا مِن دَابَّةٍ وَلَٰكِن
يُؤَخِّرُهُمْ إِلَىٰ أَجَلٍ مُّسَمًّى
فَإِذَا جَاءَ أَجَلُهُمْ
لَا يَسْتَأْخِرُونَ سَاعَةً
وَلَا يَسْتَقْدِمُونَ

62. They attribute to Allah
What they hate (for
themselves).[2088]
And their tongues assert
The falsehood that all good
things[2089]
Are for themselves: without doubt
For them is the Fire, and they
Will be the first to be
Hastened on into it!

٦٢ وَيَجْعَلُونَ لِلَّهِ مَا يَكْرَهُونَ
وَتَصِفُ أَلْسِنَتُهُمُ الْكَذِبَ
أَنَّ لَهُمُ الْحُسْنَىٰ
لَا جَرَمَ أَنَّ لَهُمُ النَّارَ
وَأَنَّهُم مُّفْرَطُونَ

63. By Allah, We (also) sent
(Our prophets) to Peoples

٦٣ تَاللَّهِ لَقَدْ أَرْسَلْنَا إِلَىٰ أُمَمٍ

2086. The word *mathal* ordinarily denotes a similitude, but in the context of the present verse, especially with reference to Allah, it signifies His sublime attributes rather than a similitude. *Cf.* 30:27. (Eds.).

2087. Allah's decree works without fail. If He were to punish for every wrong or shortcoming, not a single living creature on earth would escape punishment. But in His infinite mercy and forgiveness, He gives respite: He provides time for repentance. If the repentance is forthcoming, Allah's Mercy is forthcoming without fail. If not, the punishment comes inevitably on the expiration of the Term. The sinner cannot anticipate it by an insolent challenge, nor can he delay it when the time arrives. Let him not think that the respite given him may mean that he can do what he likes, and that he can escape scot-free from the consequences.

2088. See above, 16:57-58 and notes.

2089. The philosophy of Pleasure (Hedonism) assumes that worldly enjoyment is good in itself and that there is nothing beyond. But it can be shown, even on its own ground, that every act has its inevitable consequences. No good can spring out of evil. For falsehood and wrong the agony of the Fire is waiting, and the boastful votaries of falsehood will be the first to fall into it.

Before thee: but Satan
Made, (to the wicked),
Their own acts seem alluring:
He is also their patron today,[2090]
But they shall have
A most grievous penalty.

مِن قَبْلِكَ فَزَيَّنَ لَهُمُ ٱلشَّيْطَٰنُ أَعْمَٰلَهُمْ
فَهُوَ وَلِيُّهُمُ ٱلْيَوْمَ
وَلَهُمْ عَذَابٌ أَلِيمٌ

64. And We sent down the Book
To thee for the express purpose,
That thou shouldst make clear
To them those things in which[2091]
They differ, and that it should be
A guide and a mercy
To those who believe.

(٦٤) وَمَآ أَنزَلْنَا عَلَيْكَ ٱلْكِتَٰبَ
إِلَّا لِتُبَيِّنَ لَهُمُ ٱلَّذِى ٱخْتَلَفُوا۟ فِيهِ ۙ
وَهُدًى وَرَحْمَةً لِّقَوْمٍ يُؤْمِنُونَ

65. And Allah sends down rain
From the skies, and gives therewith
Life to the earth after its death:
Verily in this is a Sign
For those who listen.[2092]

(٦٥) وَٱللَّهُ أَنزَلَ مِنَ ٱلسَّمَآءِ مَآءً
فَأَحْيَا بِهِ ٱلْأَرْضَ بَعْدَ مَوْتِهَآ ۚ
إِنَّ فِى ذَٰلِكَ لَءَايَةً لِّقَوْمٍ يَسْمَعُونَ

SECTION 9.

66. And verily in cattle (too)
Will ye find an instructive Sign.[2093]
From what is within their
bodies,[2094]

(٦٦) وَإِنَّ لَكُمْ فِى ٱلْأَنْعَٰمِ لَعِبْرَةً ۖ
نُّسْقِيكُم مِّمَّا فِى بُطُونِهِۦ

2090. In all ages and among all Peoples Allah sent His Messengers to teach the Truth and point the way to righteousness. But the allurements of Evil seemed always attractive, and many men preferred their own ways and the ways of their ancestors to the more difficult path of rectitude. This happened again in the time of Al Muṣṭafā, and will always happen as long as men succumb to Evil.

2091. But the path of duty before Allah's Messenger is clear. He is sent with the Revelation (the Qur'ān) for three express purposes: (1) that he should bring about unity among the jarring sects, for the Gospel of Unity, while preaching the One True God, leads also to the unity of mankind; (2) that the revelation should be a guide to right conduct; and (3) that it should show the path of repentance and salvation, and thus be the highest mercy to erring sinners.

2092. When the earth with all its vegetation is well-nigh dead, parched and shrivelled up, a vivifying shower of rain from above gives it new life. This natural phenomenon is a sign of Allah's infinite power, especially of His power to resurrect the dead, and thereafter muster them for Judgement. (Eds.).

2093. The spiritual sustenance which Allah gives is typified by the wonderful ways of sustenance in the physical world, which figure forth Allah's providence and loving care for His creation. And the wonderful transformation in the physical world, which all tend to the benefit of man, are also signs of His supreme wisdom. In the previous verse rain was mentioned, which gives new life to dead nature. In this and the following two verses our attention is drawn to milk, the products of the date and the vine, and honey.

2094. *Their*: in the Arabic, it is "its", in the singular number, for two reasons: (1) cattle is the generic plural, and may be treated as a singular noun; (2) the instructive sign is in cattle collectively, but the milk is the product of each single individual.

Between excretions and blood,[2095]
We produce, for your drink,
Milk, pure and agreeable
To those who drink it.

مِن بَيْنِ فَرْثٍ وَدَمٍ
لَّبَنًا خَالِصًا سَآئِغًا لِّلشَّـٰرِبِينَ

67. And from the fruit
Of the date palm and the vine,
Ye get out wholesome drink,[2096]
And food: behold, in this
Also is a Sign
For those who are wise.

٦٧ وَمِن ثَمَرَٰتِ ٱلنَّخِيلِ وَٱلْأَعْنَـٰبِ
تَتَّخِذُونَ مِنْهُ سَكَرًا وَرِزْقًا حَسَنًا
إِنَّ فِى ذَٰلِكَ لَـَٔايَةً لِّقَوْمٍ يَعْقِلُونَ

68. And thy Lord taught the Bee[2097]
To build its cells in hills,
On trees, and in (men's)
habitations;

٦٨ وَأَوْحَىٰ رَبُّكَ إِلَى ٱلنَّحْلِ أَنِ ٱتَّخِذِى
مِنَ ٱلْجِبَالِ بُيُوتًا وَمِنَ ٱلشَّجَرِ وَمِمَّا يَعْرِشُونَ

69. Then to eat of all
The produce (of the earth),[2098]
And find with skill the spacious[2099]
Paths of its Lord: there issues
From within their bodies
A drink of varying colours,
Wherein is healing for men:

٦٩ ثُمَّ كُلِى مِن كُلِّ ٱلثَّمَرَٰتِ فَٱسْلُكِى سُبُلَ
رَبِّكِ ذُلُلًا يَخْرُجُ مِنۢ بُطُونِهَا شَرَابٌ
مُّخْتَلِفٌ أَلْوَٰنُهُۥ فِيهِ شِفَآءٌ لِّلنَّاسِ

2095. Milk is a secretion in the female body, like other secretions, but more specialised. Is it not wonderful that the same food, eaten by males and females, produces in the latter, when they have young, the wholesome and complete food, known as milk? Then, when cattle are tamed and specially bred for milk, the supply of milk is vastly greater than is necessary for their young and lasts for a longer time than during the period they give suck to their young. And it is a wholesome and agreeable diet for man. It is pure, as typified by its whiteness. Yet it is a secretion like other secretions, between the excretions which the body rejects as worthless and the precious blood-stream which circulates within the body and is the symbol of life itself to the animal which produces it.

2096. There are wholesome drinks and foods that can be got out of the date palm and the vine: *e.g.*, non-alcoholic drinks from the date and the grape, vinegar, date sugar, grape sugar, and dates and grapes themselves for eating. If *sakar* is taken in the sense of fermented wine, it would refer to the time before intoxicants were prohibited, for this is a Makkan Sūrah and the prohibition came in Madīnah. In such a case it would imply a subtle disapproval of the use of intoxicants and mark the first of a series of steps that in time culminated in total prohibition. (R).

2097. *Awḥā: waḥyūn* ordinarily means inspiration, the Message put into the mind or heart by Allah. Here the Bee's instinct is referred to Allah's teaching, which it undoubtedly is. In 99:5, it is applied to the earth: we shall discuss the precise meaning when we come to that passage. The honeycomb, itself, with its hexagonal cells, geometrically perfect, is a wonderful structure, and is well called *buyūt*, homes. And the way the bee finds out inaccessible places, in the hills, in the trees, and even among the habitations of men, is one of the marvels of nature, *i.e.*, of Allah's working in His Creation.

2098. The bee assimilates the juice of various kinds of flowers and fruit, and forms within its body the honey which it stores in its cells of wax. The different kinds of food from which it makes its honey give different colours to the honey, *e.g.*, it is dark-brown, light-brown, yellow, white, and so on. The taste and flavour also varies, as in the case of heather honey, the honey formed from scented flowers, and so on. As food it is sweet and wholesome, and it is used in medicine. Note that while the instinctive individual acts are described in the singular number, the produce of "*their bodies*" is described in the plural, as the result of their collective effort.

2099. Dhululan: two meanings are possible: (1) ways easy and spacious, referring to the unerring way in which bees find their way from long distances to their combs; and (2) the idea of humility and obedience in them. From both we can derive a metaphorical and spiritual meaning.

Verily in this is a Sign
For those who give thought.

إِنَّ فِي ذَٰلِكَ لَآيَةً لِّقَوْمٍ يَتَفَكَّرُونَ

70. It is Allah Who creates you
And takes your souls at death;
And of you there are
Some who are sent back
To a feeble age, so that[2100]
They know nothing after
Having known (much):
For Allah is All-Knowing,[2101]
All-Powerful.

٧٠ وَاللَّهُ خَلَقَكُمْ ثُمَّ يَتَوَفَّاكُمْ
وَمِنكُم مَّن يُرَدُّ إِلَىٰ أَرْذَلِ الْعُمُرِ
لِكَيْ لَا يَعْلَمَ بَعْدَ عِلْمٍ شَيْئًا
إِنَّ اللَّهَ عَلِيمٌ قَدِيرٌ

SECTION 10.

71. Allah has bestowed His gifts
Of sustenance more freely on some
Of you than on others: those
More favoured are not going
To throw back their gifts
To those whom their right hands
Possess, so as to be equal
In that respect. Will they then
Deny the favours of Allah?[2102]

٧١ وَاللَّهُ فَضَّلَ بَعْضَكُمْ عَلَىٰ بَعْضٍ فِي الرِّزْقِ
فَمَا الَّذِينَ فُضِّلُوا بِرَادِّي رِزْقِهِمْ عَلَىٰ
مَا مَلَكَتْ أَيْمَانُهُمْ فَهُمْ فِيهِ سَوَاءٌ
أَفَبِنِعْمَةِ اللَّهِ يَجْحَدُونَ

72. And Allah has made for you
Mates (and Companions) of your
own nature,[2103]
And made for you, out of them,

٧٢ وَاللَّهُ جَعَلَ لَكُم مِّنْ أَنفُسِكُمْ أَزْوَاجًا
وَجَعَلَ لَكُم مِّنْ أَزْوَاجِكُم

2100. Besides the mystery and beauty of the many processes going on in the working of Allah's Creation, there is the wonderful life of man himself on this earth: how he is created as a child; how he grows in intelligence and knowledge; and how his soul is taken back and his body suffers dissolution. In some cases he lives so long that he falls into a feeble old age like a second childhood: he forgets what he learnt and seems almost to go back in Time. Is not all this wonderful, and evidence of the Knowledge and Power of Allah?

2101. Our attention having been called to the remarkable transformations in life and nature, by which the Knowledge and Power of Allah work out His beneficent Plan for His creatures, we are reminded that man at best is but a feeble creature, but for the grace of Allah. We then pass on in the next Section to the differences in the gifts which men themselves enjoy, distinguishing them into so many categories. How much greater is the difference between the created things and their Creator?

2102. Even in the little differences in gifts, which men enjoy from Allah, men with superior gifts are not going to abandon them so as to be equal with men of inferior gifts, whom, perhaps, they hold in subjection. They will never deny their own superiority. How then (as the argument is pursued in the two following verses), can they ignore the immense difference between the Creator and created things, and make the latter, in their thoughts, partners with Allah?

2103. *Of your nature*: or of yourselves. *Cf.* 4:1 and n. 504. Self, or Personality, or Soul, all imply a bundle of attributes, capacities, predilections, and dispositions, which we may sum up in the word *Nafs*, or nature. Woman was made to be (1) a mate or companion for man; (2) except for sex, of the same nature as man, and therefore with the same moral and religious rights and duties; and (3) she is not to be considered a source of all evil or sin, as the Christian monks characterised her but rather as a blessing, one of the favours, (*Ni'mah*) of Allah.

Sons and daughters and
grandchildren.[2104]
And provided for your sustenance
Of the best: will they
Then believe in vain things,
And be ungrateful for Allah's
favours?—

بَنِينَ وَحَفَدَةً
وَرَزَقَكُم مِّنَ الطَّيِّبَٰتِ
أَفَبِالْبَٰطِلِ يُؤْمِنُونَ وَبِنِعْمَتِ اللَّهِ هُمْ يَكْفُرُونَ

73. And worship others than Allah—
Such as have no power
Of providing them, for
sustenance,[2105]
With anything in the heavens or
earth,
And cannot possibly have such
power?

٧٣ وَيَعْبُدُونَ مِن دُونِ اللَّهِ
مَا لَا يَمْلِكُ لَهُمْ رِزْقًا مِّنَ السَّمَٰوَٰتِ
وَالْأَرْضِ شَيْـًٔا وَلَا يَسْتَطِيعُونَ

74. Invent not similitudes[2106]
For Allah: for Allah knoweth,
And ye know not.

٧٤ فَلَا تَضْرِبُوا لِلَّهِ الْأَمْثَالَ
إِنَّ اللَّهَ يَعْلَمُ وَأَنتُمْ لَا تَعْلَمُونَ

75. Allah sets forth the Parable
(Of two men: one) a slave
Under the dominion of
another;[2107]
He has no power of any sort;
And (the other) a man
On whom We have bestowed
Goodly favours from Ourselves.
And he spends thereof (freely),
Privately and publicly:
Are the two equal? (By no means;)

٧٥ ضَرَبَ اللَّهُ مَثَلًا عَبْدًا
مَّمْلُوكًا لَّا يَقْدِرُ عَلَىٰ شَيْءٍ
وَمَن رَّزَقْنَٰهُ مِنَّا رِزْقًا حَسَنًا
فَهُوَ يُنفِقُ مِنْهُ سِرًّا وَجَهْرًا
هَلْ يَسْتَوُۥنَ

2104. *Hafadah*: collective plural, daughters, grandchildren, and descendants. The root *hafada* also implies obedient service and ministration. Just as the sons (first mentioned) should be a source of strength, so daughters and grandchildren should serve and contribute to the happiness of fathers and grandparents, and are to be looked upon as further blessings.

2105. "Sustenance" (*rizq*) in all this passage (16:65-74), as elsewhere, implies all that is necesary for man's life and growth, physical, mental and spiritual. Milk, fruit, and honey are examples of physical gifts, with a metaphorical reference to mental and moral health; family life is an example of moral and social and (ultimately) spiritual opportunities in the life of man; and in 16:65 is an example of rain in the physical world as a type of Allah's revelation in the spiritual world.

2106. *Cf.* 16:60 above, and n. 2086. One instance of false similitudes is where Pagans say their gods are mere types or symbols, or where men pray to men as intercessors.

2107. The first parable is of two men, one of whom is a slave completely under the dominion of another, with no powers of any sort, and another a free man, who is gifted in every way, and is most generous in bestowing out of his opulent wealth (material as well as intangible), privately and publicly, without let or hindrance; for he is his own master and owes no account to anyone. The first is like the imaginary gods which men set up—whether powers of nature, which have no independent existence but are manifestations of Allah, or deified heroes or men, who can do nothing of their own authority but are subject to the Will and Power of Allah; the second describes in a faint way the position of Allah, the Self-Subsistent, to Whom belongs the dominion of all that is in heaven and earth, and Who bestows freely of His gifts on all His creatures.

Praise be to Allah. But
Most of them understand not.

الْحَمْدُ لِلَّهِ بَلْ أَكْثَرُهُمْ لَا يَعْلَمُونَ

76. Allah sets forth (another) Parable
Of two men: one of them
Dumb, with no power
Of any sort: a wearisome burden
Is he to his master;
Whichever way he directs him,
He brings no good:[2108]
Is such a man equal
With one who commands
Justice, and is on
A Straight Way?[2109]

٧٦ وَضَرَبَ اللَّهُ مَثَلًا رَجُلَيْنِ أَحَدُهُمَا
أَبْكَمُ لَا يَقْدِرُ عَلَىٰ شَيْءٍ وَهُوَ كَلٌّ عَلَىٰ
مَوْلَاهُ أَيْنَمَا يُوَجِّهْهُ لَا يَأْتِ بِخَيْرٍ
هَلْ يَسْتَوِي هُوَ وَمَنْ يَأْمُرُ بِالْعَدْلِ
وَهُوَ عَلَىٰ صِرَاطٍ مُسْتَقِيمٍ

SECTION 11.

77. To Allah belongeth the Mystery[2110]
Of the heavens and the earth.
And the Decision of the Hour[2111]
(Of Judgement) is as
The twinkling of any eye,
Or even quicker:
For Allah hath power
Over all things.

٧٧ وَلِلَّهِ غَيْبُ السَّمَاوَاتِ وَالْأَرْضِ
وَمَا أَمْرُ السَّاعَةِ إِلَّا كَلَمْحِ
الْبَصَرِ أَوْ هُوَ أَقْرَبُ
إِنَّ اللَّهَ عَلَىٰ كُلِّ شَيْءٍ قَدِيرٌ

78. It is He Who brought you
Forth from the wombs
Of your mothers when

٧٨ وَاللَّهُ أَخْرَجَكُمْ مِنْ بُطُونِ أُمَّهَاتِكُمْ

2108. In the second Parable, one man is dumb; he can explain nothing, and he can certainly do nothing; he is only a wearisome burden to his master, no matter what his master asks him to do; or perhaps he is really harmful instead of bringing any good; such are idols (literal and metaphorical) when taken as false gods. The other man is in a position to command, and he commands what is just and righteous; not only his commands but his doings also are on the path of righteousness. Such are the qualities of Allah.

2109. The gist of the argument is that those who deviate from the worship of Allah commit twofold treason: (1) They do not recognise the immense difference between the Creator and created things, although, in their own little selfish lives, they are tenacious of any little differences there may be between themselves and other fellow-creatures not so gifted. (2) They are guilty of gross ingratitude in forgetting that the source of goodness and power is Allah, to Whom alone they owe all the gifts they enjoy in life.

2110. The key to all things—not only those which we see and understand, but those which we do not see or of which we have no idea—is with Allah, Whose knowledge and power are supreme.

2111. Lures of this world and its fleeting pleasures often make man forget that the life of the hereafter is an imminent reality. Many of those who claim to believe in the life to come act and behave as if it belonged to a distant future, and had no relevance to their present activities and mode of living. The Qur'ān repeatedly reminds man that the Hour of Reckoning is not a distant possibility, but very close to man, and could come to pass any moment. The wisest course for man, therefore, is to be always alert and watchful and steer clear of all forms of sin and impiety, for when the Promised Hour comes it will come all of a sudden and without any prior notice. See also 10:45; 30:55, 45:32. (Eds.).

Ye knew nothing; and He
Gave you hearing and sight
And intelligence and affection:[2112]
That ye may give thanks
(To Allah).

لَا تَعْلَمُونَ شَيْـًٔا وَجَعَلَ لَكُمُ ٱلسَّمْعَ
وَٱلْأَبْصَٰرَ وَٱلْأَفْـِٔدَةَ لَعَلَّكُمْ تَشْكُرُونَ

79. Do they not look at
The birds, held poised
In the midst of (the air
And) the sky? Nothing
Holds them up but (the power[2113]
Of) Allah. Verily in this
Are Signs for those who believe.

٧٩ أَلَمْ يَرَوْا۟ إِلَى ٱلطَّيْرِ مُسَخَّرَٰتٍ
فِى جَوِّ ٱلسَّمَآءِ مَا يُمْسِكُهُنَّ إِلَّا ٱللَّهُ
إِنَّ فِى ذَٰلِكَ لَـَٔايَٰتٍ لِّقَوْمٍ يُؤْمِنُونَ

80. It is Allah Who made your habitations
Homes of rest and quiet[2114]
For you; and made for you,
Out of the skins of animals,
(Tents for) dwellings, which
Ye find so light (and handy)
When ye travel and when
Ye stop (in your travels),[2115]
And out of their wool,
And their soft fibres[2116]
(Between wool and hair),
And their hair, rich stuff
And articles of convenience
(To serve you) for a time.[2117]

٨٠ وَٱللَّهُ جَعَلَ لَكُم
مِّنۢ بُيُوتِكُمْ سَكَنًا
وَجَعَلَ لَكُم مِّن جُلُودِ ٱلْأَنْعَٰمِ بُيُوتًا
تَسْتَخِفُّونَهَا يَوْمَ ظَعْنِكُمْ
وَيَوْمَ إِقَامَتِكُمْ
وَمِنْ أَصْوَافِهَا وَأَوْبَارِهَا
وَأَشْعَارِهَآ أَثَٰثًا وَمَتَٰعًا إِلَىٰ حِينٍ

2112. Literally, 'hearts,' are considered the centres of the affections, and in Arabic idiom, of intelligence also. We should therefore give thanks to Allah, not to imaginary deities or powers or forces.

2113. All the wonderful things in creation are due to the artistry, power, and wisdom of Allah. Such as the flight of birds in midair. So also are the inventions and discoveries, due to man's intelligence, in the next verse; for man's intelligence is a gift direct from Allah.

2114. Man's social, intellectual, and spiritual gifts make, of his permanent dwellings, homes of rest and quiet, of refinement and the purer affections, which are the types, in this earthly life, of the highest spiritual Good, the Love of Allah. The pure home thus becomes the type of the highest spiritual destiny of man. And these capacities in man are the gifts of Allah.

2115. When man travels, he wants temporary dwellings, tents, which he can make of the skins of animals, or of the fabrics of vegetable fibres, similar to the skins of animals. These tents are easy to carry when moving, and easy to pitch during halts.

2116. *Ṣūf*, wool, is what we get from sheep. *Sha'r*, hair, is what we get from goats or similar animals, for weaving into fabrics. ***Wabar*** is the soft camel's hair of which, also, fabrics are woven: they may be considered intermediate between the other two: by extension and analogy the term may be applied to furs and such thing, by way of illustration.

2117. All such articles of refined luxury, and useful articles of comfort and convenience only last for awhile, but they must be considered Allah's gifts.

81. It is Allah Who made
Out of the things He created,
Some things to give you shade;[2118]
Of the hills He made some
For your shelter; He made you
Garments to protect you
From heat, and coats of mail
To protect you from
Your (mutual) violence.[2119]
Thus does He complete
His favours on you, that
Ye may bow to His Will[2120]
(In Islām).

٨١ وَٱللَّهُ جَعَلَ لَكُم مِّمَّا خَلَقَ ظِلَٰلًا
وَجَعَلَ لَكُم مِّنَ ٱلْجِبَالِ أَكْنَٰنًا
وَجَعَلَ لَكُمْ سَرَٰبِيلَ تَقِيكُمُ ٱلْحَرَّ
وَسَرَٰبِيلَ تَقِيكُم بَأْسَكُمْ
كَذَٰلِكَ يُتِمُّ نِعْمَتَهُۥ عَلَيْكُمْ
لَعَلَّكُمْ تُسْلِمُونَ

82. But if they turn away,
Thy duty is only to preach
The Clear Message.

٨٢ فَإِن تَوَلَّوْا۟ فَإِنَّمَا عَلَيْكَ
ٱلْبَلَٰغُ ٱلْمُبِينُ

83. They recognise the favours[2121]
Of Allah; then they deny them;
And most of them
Are (creatures) ungrateful.

٨٣ يَعْرِفُونَ نِعْمَتَ ٱللَّهِ ثُمَّ يُنكِرُونَهَا
وَأَكْثَرُهُمُ ٱلْكَٰفِرُونَ

C. 126.—Allah's Prophets, if rejected, will be witnesses
(16:84-100.) Against those who reject Allah's Truth!
And all false gods will disappear.
A life of justice and righteousness is enjoined
By Allah, and the strictest fidelity, in intent
And action. For Allah will judge us
By our faith and deeds, and no evil
Shall have power over those who believe
And put their trust in Allah their Lord.

2118. For example, trees, gardens, the roofs of houses; also from another point of view, the fact that the sun's rays at various times and in various parts of the earth, come obliquely, thus causing shadows along with sunshine. In the hills there are caves and grottoes.

2119. Our clothes protect us from heat and cold, just as our armour protects us from the hurt which we might otherwise receive in battle.

2120. All these blessings, which have both a physical and (by promoting the good of man) a spiritual purpose, should teach us to rally to Allah and tune our will with His Universal Will, which is another name for Islam.

2121. *'Arafa* is distinguished from *'alima* in implying a specific discernment (or recognition) of various qualities and uses. All mankind recognises the value of the blessings they enjoy, but in forgetting or disobeying their Author, the wicked show gross ingratitude: for in practice they deny their obligation to Him for those blessings.

Section 12.

84\. One day we shall raise
From all Peoples a Witness:[2122]
Then will no excuse be accepted
From Unbelievers, nor will they
Receive any favours.[2122-A]

(٨٤) وَيَوْمَ نَبْعَثُ مِن كُلِّ أُمَّةٍ شَهِيدًا ثُمَّ
لَا يُؤْذَنُ لِلَّذِينَ كَفَرُوا وَلَا هُمْ يُسْتَعْتَبُونَ

85\. When the wrongdoers
(Actually) see the Penalty,[2123]
Then will it in no way
Be mitigated, nor will they
Then receive respite.

(٨٥) وَإِذَا رَءَا الَّذِينَ ظَلَمُوا الْعَذَابَ
فَلَا يُخَفَّفُ عَنْهُمْ وَلَا هُمْ يُنظَرُونَ

86\. When those who gave partners
To Allah will see their "partners",
They will say: "Our Lord!
These are our 'partners', those
Whom we used to invoke[2124]
Besides Thee." But they will
Throw back their word at them
(And say): "Indeed ye are liars!"

(٨٦) وَإِذَا رَءَا الَّذِينَ أَشْرَكُوا شُرَكَاءَهُمْ
قَالُوا رَبَّنَا هَٰؤُلَاءِ شُرَكَاؤُنَا
الَّذِينَ كُنَّا نَدْعُوا مِن دُونِكَ فَأَلْقَوْا إِلَيْهِمُ
الْقَوْلَ إِنَّكُمْ لَكَاذِبُونَ

87\. That day shall they (openly) show[2125]
(Their) submission to Allah: and all
Their inventions shall leave
Them in the lurch.

(٨٧) وَأَلْقَوْا إِلَى اللَّهِ
يَوْمَئِذٍ السَّلَمَ
وَضَلَّ عَنْهُم مَّا كَانُوا يَفْتَرُونَ

88\. Those who reject Allah
And hinder (men) from the Path
Of Allah—for them
Will We add Penalty

(٨٨) الَّذِينَ كَفَرُوا وَصَدُّوا عَن
سَبِيلِ اللَّهِ زِدْنَاهُمْ عَذَابًا فَوْقَ

2122\. To each People is sent Allah's Messenger or Teacher, to point out the right way. There may be one, or there may be many. Such a Messenger (*Rasūl*) will be a witness that Allah's Truth was preached to all peoples in express terms, in addition to the Signs of Allah everywhere in nature. There will then be no room for excuses of any kind. Those who rejected Allah after repeated warnings cannot reasonably ask for more respite, as they had every kind of respite during their life of probation; nor can they now take refuge behind Allah's Grace, which they had repeatedly rejected.

2122-A. That is, they will not be allowed to seek grace by repentance. *Cf.* 30:57, 45:35. (Eds.).

2123\. When the terrible Penalty is actually on them, it is too late for repentance and for asking for Mercy. Justice must take its course.

2124\. The worshippers of false gods will try to shift the responsibility from their own shoulders to that of the false gods. They will suggest (though they will not have the courage for such a bare-faced lie) that they were misled by the false gods. But their lying suggestions will be contradicted and thrown back at them as explained in the next note.

2125\. Insofar as the false gods were real things, such as deified men or forces of nature, they will openly disclaim them and then (as always) show their submission to Allah. Insofar as the false gods were the inventions of the fancy of the idolators, they will leave their worshippers in the lurch, for they will be shown as non-existent.

To Penalty; for that they
Used to spread mischief.

الْعَذَابِ بِمَا كَانُوا يُفْسِدُونَ

89. One day We shall raise
From all Peoples a witness
Against them, from amongst themselves:[2126]
And We shall bring thee
As a witness against these
(Thy people): and We have sent down
To thee a Book explaining
All things, a Guide, a Mercy,
And Glad Tidings to Muslims.

٨٩ وَيَوْمَ نَبْعَثُ فِي كُلِّ أُمَّةٍ
شَهِيدًا عَلَيْهِم مِّنْ أَنفُسِهِمْ
وَجِئْنَا بِكَ شَهِيدًا عَلَىٰ هَٰؤُلَاءِ
وَنَزَّلْنَا عَلَيْكَ الْكِتَابَ تِبْيَانًا لِّكُلِّ شَيْءٍ
وَهُدًى وَرَحْمَةً وَبُشْرَىٰ لِلْمُسْلِمِينَ

SECTION 13.

90. Allah commands justice, the doing
Of good, and liberality to kith
And kin, and He forbids
All shameful deeds, and injustice
And rebellion: He instructs you,
That ye may receive admonition.[2127]

٩٠ إِنَّ اللَّهَ يَأْمُرُ بِالْعَدْلِ
وَالْإِحْسَانِ وَإِيتَاءِ ذِي الْقُرْبَىٰ
وَيَنْهَىٰ عَنِ الْفَحْشَاءِ وَالْمُنكَرِ وَالْبَغْيِ
يَعِظُكُمْ لَعَلَّكُمْ تَذَكَّرُونَ

91. Fulfil the Covenant of Allah
When ye have entered into it,
And break not your oaths
After ye have confirmed them:
Indeed ye have made[2128]

٩١ وَأَوْفُوا بِعَهْدِ اللَّهِ إِذَا عَاهَدتُّمْ
وَلَا تَنقُضُوا الْأَيْمَانَ بَعْدَ تَوْكِيدِهَا
وَقَدْ جَعَلْتُمُ

2126. To the thought expressed in 16:83 above, is added another detail here. Not only will there be witnesses from Peoples, but the witnesses will be men from amongst the Peoples themselves, men of their own kith and kin, who understood them and explained Allah's Message in their own language. The Prophet Muḥammad will be witness against all those who rejected the Message he brought. For those who believe in him (of all races and peoples), the Book which he brought will be an explanation, a guide, a mercy and a Gospel. (R).

2127. Justice is a comprehensive term, and may include all the virtues of cold philosophy. But religion asks for something warmer and more human, the doing of good deeds even where perhaps they are not strictly demanded by justice, such as returning good for ill, or obliging those who in worldly language "have no claim" on you; and of course *a fortiori* the fulfilling of the claims of those whose claims are recognised in social life. Similarly the opposites are to be avoided: everything that is recognised as shameful, and everything that is really unjust, and any inward rebellion against Allah's Law or our own conscience in its most sensitive form.

2128. The immediate reference may or may not be to the oath of fidelity to the Prophet taken at 'Aqabah fourteen months before the Hijrah and repeated a little later: see 5:8 and n. 705. But the general meaning is much wider. And this may be viewed in two aspects: (1) Every oath taken, or covenant made, is a Covenant before Allah, and should be faithfully observed. In this it approaches in meaning to 5:1. (2) In particular, every Muslim makes, by the profession of his Faith, a Covenant with Allah, and he confirms that Covenant every time he repeats that profession. He should therefore faithfully observe the duties taught to him by Islam.

Allah your surety; for Allah
Knoweth all that ye do.

اللَّهَ عَلَيْكُمْ كَفِيلًا إِنَّ اللَّهَ يَعْلَمُ مَا تَفْعَلُونَ

92. And be not like a woman
Who breaks into untwisted strands
The yarn she has spun
After it has become strong.[2129]
Nor[2130] take your oaths to practise
Deception between yourselves,
Lest one party should be
More numerous than another:[2131]
For Allah will test you by this;
And on the Day of Judgement
He will certainly make clear
To you (the truth of) that
Wherein ye disagree.[2132]

﴿٩٢﴾ وَلَا تَكُونُوا كَالَّتِي نَقَضَتْ غَزْلَهَا مِنْ
بَعْدِ قُوَّةٍ أَنكَاثًا تَتَّخِذُونَ أَيْمَانَكُمْ دَخَلًا
بَيْنَكُمْ أَن تَكُونَ أُمَّةٌ هِيَ أَرْبَىٰ مِنْ أُمَّةٍ
إِنَّمَا يَبْلُوكُمُ اللَّهُ بِهِ
وَلَيُبَيِّنَنَّ لَكُمْ يَوْمَ الْقِيَامَةِ
مَا كُنتُمْ فِيهِ تَخْتَلِفُونَ

93. If Allah so willed, He
Could make you all one People:
But He leaves straying[2133]
Whom He pleases, and He guides
Whom He pleases: but ye
Shall certainly be called to account
For all your actions.

﴿٩٣﴾ وَلَوْ شَاءَ اللَّهُ لَجَعَلَكُمْ أُمَّةً وَاحِدَةً
وَلَٰكِن يُضِلُّ مَن يَشَاءُ وَيَهْدِي مَن يَشَاءُ
وَلَتُسْأَلُنَّ عَمَّا كُنتُمْ تَعْمَلُونَ

94. And take not your oaths,
To practise deception between
yourselves,[2134]

﴿٩٤﴾ وَلَا تَتَّخِذُوا أَيْمَانَكُمْ دَخَلًا بَيْنَكُمْ

2129. The Covenant which binds us in the spiritual world makes us strong, like strands of fluffy cotton spun into a strong thread. It also gives us a sense of security against much evil in this world. It costs a woman much labour and skill to spin good strong yarn. She would be foolish indeed, after she has spun such yarn, to untwist its constituent strands and break them into flimsy pieces.

2130. *Nor*: I construe *tattakhidhūna* with *lā takūnū* in the previous clause.

2131. Do not make your religion merely a game of making your own party numerically strong by alliance cemented by oaths, which you readily break when a more numerous party offers you its alliance. The Quraysh were addicted to this vice, and in international politics at the present day, this seems to be almost a standard of national self-respect and international skill. Islam teaches nobler ethics for individuals and nations. A Covenant should be looked upon as a solemn thing, not to be entered into except with the sincerest intention of carrying it out; and it is binding even if large numbers are ranged against it.

2132. Disagreements need not necessarily cause conflict where the parties are sincere and honest and do not wish to take advantage of one another. In such cases they do not go by numbers, groupings, and alliances, but by just conduct as in the sight of Allah. Honest differences will be removed when all things are made clear in the Hereafter.

2133. *Cf.* 16:4 and n. 1875. Allah's Will and Plan, in allowing limited free will to man, is, not to force man's will, but to give all guidance, and leave alone those who reject that guidance, in case they should repent and come back into Grace. But in all cases, insofar as we are given the choice, we shall be called to account for all our actions. "Leaving to stray" does not mean that we can do what we please. Our personal responsibility remains.

2134. In 16:92, above, the motive for false and fraudulent covenants was pointed out with reprobation. Now are pointed out the consequences, *viz.*, (1) to others; if they had not been deceived, they might have walked firmly on the Path, but now they lose faith and perhaps commit like frauds for which you will be responsible; (2) to yourselves; you have not only gone wrong yourselves; but have set others on the wrong path; and deserve a double Penalty. Perhaps the "evil consequences" refer to this world, and the "Wrath" to the Hereafter.

With the result that someone's foot
May slip after it was
Firmly planted, and ye may
Have to taste the evil
(consequences)
Of having hindered (men)
From the Path of Allah,
And a mighty Wrath
Descend on you.

فَتَزِلَّ قَدَمٌۢ بَعۡدَ ثُبُوتِهَا
وَتَذُوقُواْ ٱلسُّوٓءَ بِمَا
صَدَدتُّمۡ عَن سَبِيلِ ٱللَّهِۖ
وَلَكُمۡ عَذَابٌ عَظِيمٞ

95. Nor sell the Covenant of Allah
For a miserable price:[2135]
For with Allah is (a prize)
Far better for you,
If ye only knew.

٩٥ وَلَا تَشۡتَرُواْ بِعَهۡدِ ٱللَّهِ ثَمَنٗا قَلِيلًاۚ
إِنَّمَا عِندَ ٱللَّهِ هُوَ خَيۡرٞ لَّكُمۡ
إِن كُنتُمۡ تَعۡلَمُونَ

96. What is with you must vanish:
What is with Allah will endure.
And We will certainly bestow,
On those who patiently persevere,
Their reward according to
The best of their actions.[2136]

٩٦ مَا عِندَكُمۡ يَنفَدُ وَمَا عِندَ ٱللَّهِ بَاقٖۗ
وَلَنَجۡزِيَنَّ ٱلَّذِينَ صَبَرُوٓاْ أَجۡرَهُم
بِأَحۡسَنِ مَا كَانُواْ يَعۡمَلُونَ

97. Whoever works righteousness,
Man or woman, and has Faith,
Verily, to him will We give
A new Life, and life[2137]
That is good and pure, and We
Will bestow on such their reward
According to the best
Of their actions.[2138]

٩٧ مَنۡ عَمِلَ صَٰلِحٗا مِّن ذَكَرٍ أَوۡ أُنثَىٰ
وَهُوَ مُؤۡمِنٞ فَلَنُحۡيِيَنَّهُۥ حَيَوٰةٗ طَيِّبَةٗۖ
وَلَنَجۡزِيَنَّهُمۡ أَجۡرَهُم بِأَحۡسَنِ
مَا كَانُواْ يَعۡمَلُونَ

98. When thou does read[2139]
The Qur'ān, seek Allah's
protection

٩٨ فَإِذَا قَرَأۡتَ ٱلۡقُرۡءَانَ فَٱسۡتَعِذۡ بِٱللَّهِ

2135. Any possible gain that you can make by breaking your Covenant and thus breaking Allah's Law must necessarily be miserable; while your own benefit is far greater in obeying Allah's Will and doing right.

2136. What comparison can there possibly be between spiritual Good, which will endure forever, and any temporal advantage which you may snatch in this world, which will fade and vanish in no time? And then, Allah's generosity is unbounded. He rewards you, not according to your merits, but according to the very best of your actions.

2137. Faith, if sincere, means right conduct. When these two confirm each other, Allah's grace transforms our life. Instead of being troubled and worried, we have peace and contentment: instead of being assailed at every turn by false alarms and the assaults of evil, we enjoy calm and attain purity. The transformation is visible in this life itself, but the "reward" in terms of the Hereafter will be far beyond our deserts.

2138. The same ending as in the previous verses deepens the overall effect of bringing home the message forcefully and beautifully. The argument is completed and rounded off. (R).

2139. Evil has no authority or influence on those who put their trust in Allah. It is good to express that trust in outward actions, and a formal expression of it—as in the formula, "I seek Allah's protection from Evil"—helps us. Reading or reciting the Qur'ān should be understood both literally and figuratively as the symbol of the earnest desire of the soul to know and understand Allah's Will and act in accordance therewith. Man is weak at best, and he should seek strength for his will in Allah's help and protection.

From Satan the Rejected One.

مِنَ ٱلشَّيْطَٰنِ ٱلرَّجِيمِ

99. No authority has he over those
Who believe and put their trust
In their Lord.

٩٩ إِنَّهُۥ لَيْسَ لَهُۥ سُلْطَٰنٌ عَلَى ٱلَّذِينَ ءَامَنُوا۟
وَعَلَىٰ رَبِّهِمْ يَتَوَكَّلُونَ

100. His authority is over those
Only, who take him as patron
And who join partners with Allah.

١٠٠ إِنَّمَا سُلْطَٰنُهُۥ عَلَى ٱلَّذِينَ يَتَوَلَّوْنَهُۥ
وَٱلَّذِينَ هُم بِهِۦ مُشْرِكُونَ

C. 127.—Allah's Truth may come in stages, but it gives
(16:101-128.) Strength, guidance, and glad tidings, and should
Be held fast when once received. Be not
Like those who get puffed up with pride
In worldly good, and scorn the Truth.
Enjoy the good things of life, but render
Thanks to Allah and obey His Law.
Be true in faith, and proclaim His Word
With gentle, patient wisdom: for Allah
Is with those who live in self-restraint
A pure, good, and righteous Life.

SECTION 14.

101. When We substitute one
revelation[2140]
For another—and Allah knows
best
What He reveals (in stages)—
They say, "Thou art but a forger":
But most of them understand not.

١٠١ وَإِذَا بَدَّلْنَآ ءَايَةً مَّكَانَ ءَايَةٍ
وَٱللَّهُ أَعْلَمُ بِمَا يُنَزِّلُ
قَالُوٓا۟ إِنَّمَآ أَنتَ مُفْتَرٍۭ
بَلْ أَكْثَرُهُمْ لَا يَعْلَمُونَ

102. Say, the Holy Spirit[2141] has brought
The revelation from thy Lord
In Truth, in order to strengthen
Those who believe,[2142] and as a
Guide
And Glad Tidings to Muslims.

١٠٢ قُلْ نَزَّلَهُۥ رُوحُ ٱلْقُدُسِ مِن رَّبِّكَ
بِٱلْحَقِّ لِيُثَبِّتَ ٱلَّذِينَ ءَامَنُوا۟
وَهُدًى وَبُشْرَىٰ لِلْمُسْلِمِينَ

2140. See 2:106, and n. 107. The doctrine of progressive revelation from age to age and time to time does not mean that Allah's fundamental Law changes. It is not fair to charge a Prophet of Allah with forgery because the Message, as revealed to him, is in a different form from that revealed before, when the core of the Truth is the same, for it comes from Allah.

2141. The title of the Angel Gabriel, through whom the revelation came down.

2142. The People of the Book, if they had true faith, were themselves strengthened in their faith and cleared of their doubts and difficulties by the revelations brought by Al Mustafā: and all whether People of the Book or not—who came within the fold of Islam, found the Qur'ān a Guide and a Gospel, *i.e.*, a substitute for the Mosaic Law and for the Christian Gospel, which had both been corrupted.

103. We know indeed that they
Say, "It is a man that
Teaches him." The tongue
Of him they wickedly point to
Is notably foreign, while this
Is Arabic, pure and clear.[2143]

١٠٣ وَلَقَدْ نَعْلَمُ أَنَّهُمْ يَقُولُونَ إِنَّمَا
يُعَلِّمُهُۥ بَشَرٌ لِّسَانُ الَّذِى يُلْحِدُونَ
إِلَيْهِ أَعْجَمِىٌّ وَهَٰذَا لِسَانٌ عَرَبِىٌّ مُّبِينٌ

104. Those who believe not
In the Signs of Allah—
Allah will not guide them,
And theirs will be
A grievous Penalty.

١٠٤ إِنَّ الَّذِينَ لَا يُؤْمِنُونَ بِـَٔايَٰتِ اللَّهِ
لَا يَهْدِيهِمُ اللَّهُ وَلَهُمْ عَذَابٌ أَلِيمٌ

105. It is those who believe not
In the Signs of Allah,
That forge falsehood:
It is they who lie![2144]

١٠٥ إِنَّمَا يَفْتَرِى الْكَذِبَ الَّذِينَ لَا يُؤْمِنُونَ
بِـَٔايَٰتِ اللَّهِ وَأُولَٰٓئِكَ هُمُ الْكَٰذِبُونَ

106. Anyone who, after accepting
Faith in Allah, utters
Unbelief—[2145]
Except under compulsion,
His heart remaining firm
In Faith—but such as
Open their breast to Unbelief—
On them is Wrath from Allah,
And theirs will be
A dreadful Penalty.

١٠٦ مَن كَفَرَ بِاللَّهِ مِنۢ بَعْدِ إِيمَٰنِهِۦٓ
إِلَّا مَنْ أُكْرِهَ وَقَلْبُهُۥ مُطْمَئِنٌّۢ بِالْإِيمَٰنِ
وَلَٰكِن مَّن شَرَحَ بِالْكُفْرِ صَدْرًا فَعَلَيْهِمْ
غَضَبٌ مِّنَ اللَّهِ وَلَهُمْ عَذَابٌ عَظِيمٌ

107. This because they love
The life of this world
Better than the Hereafter:
And Allah will not guide
Those who reject Faith.

١٠٧ ذَٰلِكَ بِأَنَّهُمُ اسْتَحَبُّوا الْحَيَوٰةَ الدُّنْيَا
عَلَى الْءَاخِرَةِ وَأَنَّ اللَّهَ لَا يَهْدِى
الْقَوْمَ الْكَٰفِرِينَ

2143. The wicked attribute to Prophets of Allah just such motives and springs of action as they themselves would be guilty of in such circumstances. The Pagans and those who were hostile to the revelation of Allah in Islam could not and cannot understand how such wonderful words could flow from the tongue of the Holy Prophet. They must postulate some human teacher. Unfortunately for their postulate, any possible human teacher they could think of would be poor in Arabic speech if he had all the knowledge that the Qur'ān reveals of previous revelations. Apart from that, even the most eloquent Arab could not, and cannot, produce anything of the eloquence, width, and depth of Quranic teaching, as is evident from every verse of the Book. (R).

2144. It is clearly those who raise the cry of forgery that are guilty of falsehood, as there is not the least basis or even plausibility in their suggestion.

2145. The exception refers to a case like that of 'Ammār, whose father Yāssir and mother Sumayya, were subjected to unspeakable tortures for their belief in Islam, but never recanted. 'Ammār, suffering under tortures himself and his mind acted on by the sufferings of his parents, uttered a word construed as recantation, though his heart never wavered and he came back at once to the Prophet, who consoled him for his pain and confirmed his faith. (R).

108. Those are they whose hearts,
Ears, and eyes Allah has
sealed up[2146]
And they take no heed.

١٠٨ أُولَٰٓئِكَ ٱلَّذِينَ طَبَعَ ٱللَّهُ عَلَىٰ قُلُوبِهِمْ
وَسَمْعِهِمْ وَأَبْصَٰرِهِمْ ۖ وَأُولَٰٓئِكَ هُمُ ٱلْغَٰفِلُونَ

109. Without doubt, in the Hereafter
They will perish.

١٠٩ لَا جَرَمَ أَنَّهُمْ فِى ٱلْءَاخِرَةِ
هُمُ ٱلْخَٰسِرُونَ

110. But verily thy Lord—
To those who leave their homes
After trials and persecutions—[2147]
And who thereafter strive
And fight for the Faith
And patiently persevere—
Thy Lord, after all this
Is Oft-Forgiving, Most Merciful.

١١٠ ثُمَّ إِنَّ رَبَّكَ لِلَّذِينَ هَاجَرُوا۟
مِنۢ بَعْدِ مَا فُتِنُوا۟ ثُمَّ جَٰهَدُوا۟ وَصَبَرُوٓا۟
إِنَّ رَبَّكَ مِنۢ بَعْدِهَا لَغَفُورٌ رَّحِيمٌ

SECTION 15.

111. One Day every soul
Will come up struggling[2148]
For itself, and every soul
Will be recompensed (fully)
For all its actions, and none
Will be unjustly dealt with.

١١١ يَوْمَ تَأْتِى كُلُّ نَفْسٍ تُجَٰدِلُ عَن
نَّفْسِهَا وَتُوَفَّىٰ كُلُّ نَفْسٍ مَّا عَمِلَتْ
وَهُمْ لَا يُظْلَمُونَ

112. Allah sets forth a Parable:
A city enjoying security[2149]
And quiet, abundantly supplied
With sustenance from every place:
Yet was it ungrateful
For the favours of Allah:
So Allah made it taste

١١٢ وَضَرَبَ ٱللَّهُ مَثَلًا قَرْيَةً كَانَتْ ءَامِنَةً
مُّطْمَئِنَّةً يَأْتِيهَا رِزْقُهَا رَغَدًا مِّن كُلِّ مَكَانٍ
فَكَفَرَتْ بِأَنْعُمِ ٱللَّهِ فَأَذَٰقَهَا ٱللَّهُ

2146. *Cf.* 2:7. On account of their iniquities and their want of Faith their hearts and their senses became impervious to Allah's grace, and they run headlong to perdition.

2147. I take this verse to refer to such men as were originally with the Pagans but afterwards joined Islam, suffered hardships and exile, and fought and struggled in the Cause, with patience and constancy. Their past would be blotted out and forgiven. Men like Khālid ibn Walid were numbered with the foremost heroes of Islam. In that case this verse would be a Madīnah verse, though the Sūrah as a whole is Makkan. Perhaps it would be better to read, with some Commentators, *fatanū* in the active voice rather than *futinū* in the passive voice, and translate "after inflicting trials and persecutions (on Muslims)." Notice the parallelism in construction between this verse and verse 119 below.

2148. When the Reckoning comes, each soul will stand on its own personal responsibility. No one else can help it. Full justice will be done, and all the seeming inequalities of this world will be redressed.

2149. The reference may be to any of the cities or populations in ancient or modern times, which were favoured with security and other blessings from Allah, but which rebelled from Allah's Law and tasted the inevitable penalty, even in the midst of their iniquities. Some commentators see here a reference to the city of Makkah under Pagan control. See next note.

Of hunger and terror (in extremes)
(Closing in on it) like a garment[2150]
(From every side), because
Of the (evil) which
(Its people) wrought.

لِبَاسَ ٱلْجُوعِ وَٱلْخَوْفِ
بِمَا كَانُوا۟ يَصْنَعُونَ

113. And there came to them
A Messenger from among
themselves,
But they falsely rejected him;
So the Wrath seized them
Even in the midst
Of their iniquities.

١١٣ وَلَقَدْ جَآءَهُمْ رَسُولٌ مِّنْهُمْ
فَكَذَّبُوهُ فَأَخَذَهُمُ ٱلْعَذَابُ
وَهُمْ ظَٰلِمُونَ

114. So eat of the sustenance
Which Allah has provided
For you, lawful and good;
And be grateful for the favours[2151]
Of Allah, if it is He
Whom ye serve.

١١٤ فَكُلُوا۟ مِمَّا رَزَقَكُمُ ٱللَّهُ
حَلَٰلًا طَيِّبًا وَٱشْكُرُوا۟ نِعْمَتَ ٱللَّهِ
إِن كُنتُمْ إِيَّاهُ تَعْبُدُونَ

115. He has only forbidden you[2152]
Dead meat, and blood,
And the flesh of swine,
And any (food) over which
The name of other than Allah
Has been invoked.
But if one is forced by necessity,
Without wilful disobedience,
Nor transgressing due limits—
Then Allah is Oft-Forgiving,
Most Merciful.

١١٥ إِنَّمَا حَرَّمَ عَلَيْكُمُ
ٱلْمَيْتَةَ وَٱلدَّمَ وَلَحْمَ ٱلْخِنزِيرِ
وَمَآ أُهِلَّ لِغَيْرِ ٱللَّهِ بِهِۦ
فَمَنِ ٱضْطُرَّ غَيْرَ بَاغٍ وَلَا عَادٍ
فَإِنَّ ٱللَّهَ غَفُورٌ رَّحِيمٌ

116. But say not—for any false thing[2153]
That your tongues may put
forth—
"This is lawful, and this

١١٦ وَلَا تَقُولُوا۟ لِمَا تَصِفُ أَلْسِنَتُكُمُ
ٱلْكَذِبَ هَٰذَا حَلَٰلٌ وَهَٰذَا

2150. There is a double metaphor: (1) the *tasting* of hunger and terror after the abundant supplies and the full security which it had enjoyed; and (2) the complete *enfolding* of the city as with a *garment*, by these two scourges, hunger and a state of subjective alarm. If the reference is to Makkah shortly before its fall to the Muslims, the "hunger" was the seven years' severe famine which afflicted it, and the alarm was the constant fear in the minds of the Pagans that their day was done. Peace and prosperity were restored after the re-entry of the Prophet.

2151. Ingratitude for Allah's sustenance (in the literal and figurative senses) may be shown in various ways: *e.g.*, (1) by forgetting or refusing to acknowledge the true source of the bounty, *viz.*, Allah, (2) by misusing or misapplying the bounty, as by committing excesses in things lawful, or refusing to share them with others of Allah's creatures when the need arises, or (3) by falsely ascribing to Allah any prohibition we may set up for ourselves for special reasons or because of our special idiosyncrasies.

2152. *Cf.* 2:173 and notes, 5:4-5 and 6:121 and 138-146.

2153. Men are apt to create taboos for themselves, out of superstition, and often for selfish ends, and enforce them in the name of religion. Nothing can be more reprehensible.

Is forbidden," so as to ascribe False things to Allah. For those Who ascribe false things To Allah, will never prosper.	حَرَامٌ لِّتَفْتَرُوا عَلَى ٱللَّهِ ٱلْكَذِبَ إِنَّ ٱلَّذِينَ يَفْتَرُونَ عَلَى ٱللَّهِ ٱلْكَذِبَ لَا يُفْلِحُونَ
117. In such falsehood Is but a paltry profit; But they will have A most grievous Penalty.	مَتَٰعٌ قَلِيلٌ ١١٧ وَلَهُمْ عَذَابٌ أَلِيمٌ
118. To the Jews We prohibited Such things as We have Mentioned to thee before:[2154] We did them no wrong, But they were used to Doing wrong to themselves.	وَعَلَى ٱلَّذِينَ هَادُوا حَرَّمْنَا ١١٨ مَا قَصَصْنَا عَلَيْكَ مِن قَبْلُ وَمَا ظَلَمْنَٰهُمْ وَلَٰكِن كَانُوٓا أَنفُسَهُمْ يَظْلِمُونَ
119. But verily thy Lord— To those who do wrong In ignorance, but who Thereafter repent and make amends— Thy Lord, after all this, Is Oft-Forgiving, Most Merciful.[2155]	ثُمَّ إِنَّ رَبَّكَ لِلَّذِينَ عَمِلُوا ٱلسُّوٓءَ ١١٩ بِجَهَٰلَةٍ ثُمَّ تَابُوا مِنۢ بَعْدِ ذَٰلِكَ وَأَصْلَحُوٓا إِنَّ رَبَّكَ مِنۢ بَعْدِهَا لَغَفُورٌ رَّحِيمٌ
SECTION 16.	
120. Abraham was indeed a model.[2156] Devoutly obedient to Allah, (And) true in faith, and he Joined not gods with Allah.[2157]	إِنَّ إِبْرَٰهِيمَ كَانَ أُمَّةً قَانِتًا لِّلَّهِ ١٢٠ حَنِيفًا وَلَمْ يَكُ مِنَ ٱلْمُشْرِكِينَ
121. He showed his gratitude For the favours of Allah, Who chose him, and guided him To a Straight Way.	شَاكِرًا لِّأَنْعُمِهِ ١٢١ ٱجْتَبَٰهُ وَهَدَىٰهُ إِلَىٰ صِرَٰطٍ مُّسْتَقِيمٍ

2154. See 6:146 and n. The further prohibitions to them were a punishment for their hardness of hearts, and not a favour.

2155. See above, 16:110 and n. 2147. The parallelism in construction confirms the suggestion of the alternative reading which is made in that note. The similarity of expression also rounds off the argument, as by a refrain in poetry. What follows now in this Sūrah is an exhortation to right conduct.

2156. *Ummah*: a model, pattern, example for imitation: but the idea that he was an Ummah in himself, standing alone against his world, should not be lost sight of. See next note.

2157. The Gospel of Unity has been the cornerstone of spiritual Truth for all time. In this respect Abraham is the model and fountainhead for the world of western Asia and its spirtual descendants all over the world. Abraham was among a people (the Chaldeans) who worshipped stars and had forsaken the Gospel of Unity. He was among them but not of them. He suffered persecution, and left his home and his people, and settled in the land of Canaan.

122. And We gave him Good
In this world, and he will be,
In the Hereafter, in the ranks
Of the Righteous.[2158]

123. So We have taught thee
The inspired (message),
"Follow the ways of Abraham
The True in Faith, and he
Joined not gods with Allah."

124. The Sabbath was only made[2159]
(Strict) for those who disagreed
(As to its observance);
But Allah will judge between them
On the Day of Judgement,
As to their differences.[2160]

125. Invite (all) to the Way
Of thy Lord with wisdom
And beautiful preaching;
And argue with them
In ways that are best
And most gracious:[2161]
For thy Lord knoweth best,
Who have strayed from His Path,
And who receive guidance.[2162]

(١٢٢) وَءَاتَيْنَٰهُ فِى ٱلدُّنْيَا حَسَنَةً
وَإِنَّهُۥ فِى ٱلْءَاخِرَةِ لَمِنَ ٱلصَّٰلِحِينَ

(١٢٣) ثُمَّ أَوْحَيْنَآ إِلَيْكَ أَنِ ٱتَّبِعْ مِلَّةَ
إِبْرَٰهِيمَ حَنِيفًا وَمَا كَانَ مِنَ ٱلْمُشْرِكِينَ

(١٢٤) إِنَّمَا جُعِلَ ٱلسَّبْتُ عَلَى ٱلَّذِينَ
ٱخْتَلَفُوا۟ فِيهِ وَإِنَّ رَبَّكَ لَيَحْكُمُ بَيْنَهُمْ يَوْمَ
ٱلْقِيَٰمَةِ فِيمَا كَانُوا۟ فِيهِ يَخْتَلِفُونَ

(١٢٥) ٱدْعُ إِلَىٰ سَبِيلِ رَبِّكَ بِٱلْحِكْمَةِ وَٱلْمَوْعِظَةِ
ٱلْحَسَنَةِ وَجَٰدِلْهُم بِٱلَّتِى هِىَ أَحْسَنُ
إِنَّ رَبَّكَ هُوَ أَعْلَمُ بِمَن ضَلَّ عَن سَبِيلِهِۦ
وَهُوَ أَعْلَمُ بِٱلْمُهْتَدِينَ

2158. *Cf.* 2:130.

2159. If Abraham's Way was the right way, the Jews were ready with the taunt, "Why don't you then observe the Sabbath?" The answer is twofold. (1) The Sabbath has nothing to do with Abraham. It was instituted with the Law of Moses because of Israel's hardness of heart (2:74); for they constantly disputed with their Prophet Moses (2:108), and there were constantly among them afterwards men who broke the Sabbath (2:65, and n. 79). (2) Which was the true Sabbath Day? The Jews observe Saturday. The Christians, who include the Old Testament in their inspired Scripture, observe Sunday, and a sect among them (the Seventh Day Adventists) disagree, and observe Saturday. So there is disagreement among the People of the Book. Let them dispute among themselves. Their dispute will not be settled till the Day of Judgement. Meanwhile, Muslims are emancipated from such stringent restriction. For them there is certainly the Day of United Prayer on Friday, but it is in no sense like the Jewish or the Scotch Sabbath!

2160. *Cf.* 2:113.

2161. In this wonderful passage are laid down principles of religious teaching, which are good for all time. But where are the Teachers with such qualifications? We must invite all to the Way of Allah, and expound His Universal Will; we must do it with wisdom and discretion, meeting people on their own ground and convincing them with illustrations from their own knowledge and experience, which may be very narrow, or very wide. Our preaching must be, not dogmatic, not self-regarding, not offensive, but gentle, considerate, and such as would attract their attention. Our manner and our arguments should not be acrimonious, but modelled on the most courteous and the most gracious example, so that the hearer may say to himself, "This man is not dealing merely with dialectics; he is not trying to get a rise out of me; he is sincerely expounding the faith that is in him, and his motive is the love of man and the love of Allah."

2162. It may be that the Preacher sometimes says to himself, "What is the use of teaching these people? They have made up their minds, or they are obstinate, or they are only trying to catch me out." Let him not yield to such a thought. Who knows how the seed of the Word of Allah may germinate in people's minds? It is not for man to look for results. Man's inner thoughts are known best to Allah.

126. And if ye do catch them out, Catch them out no worse Than they catch you out: But if ye show patience, That is indeed the best (course)[2163] For those who are patient.	١٢٦ وَإِنْ عَاقَبْتُمْ فَعَاقِبُوا۟ بِمِثْلِ مَا عُوقِبْتُم بِهِۦ ۖ وَلَئِن صَبَرْتُمْ لَهُوَ خَيْرٌ لِّلصَّـٰبِرِينَ
127. And do thou be patient,[2164] For thy patience is but From Allah; nor grieve over them: And distress not thyself Because of their plots.	١٢٧ وَٱصْبِرْ وَمَا صَبْرُكَ إِلَّا بِٱللَّهِ ۚ وَلَا تَحْزَنْ عَلَيْهِمْ وَلَا تَكُ فِى ضَيْقٍ مِّمَّا يَمْكُرُونَ
128. For Allah is with those[2165] Who restrain themselves, And those who do good.	١٢٨ إِنَّ ٱللَّهَ مَعَ ٱلَّذِينَ ٱتَّقَوا۟ وَّٱلَّذِينَ هُم مُّحْسِنُونَ

2163. In the context this passage refers to controversies and discussions, but the words are wide enough to cover all human struggles, disputes, and fights. In strictest equity you are not entitled to give a worse blow than is given to you. But those who have reached a higher spiritual standard do not even do that. They restrain themselves, and are patient. Lest you should think that such patience only gives an advantage to the adversary, you are told that the contrary is the case: the advantage is with the patient, the self-possessed, those who do not lose their temper or forget their own principles of conduct.

2164. In the previous verse are laid down the principles of conduct in controversy for all Muslims: 'if you catch them out, you are not entitled to strike a heavier blow that you received, but it is better to restrain yourself and be patient.' There patience was *recommended.* In this verse a command is directly addressed to the Prophet, 'Do thou be patient.' It is a *command*: his standard as the Great Teacher is much higher: and he carried it out in his life. His patience and self-restraint were under circumstances of extraordinary provocation. In his human wisdom it may sometimes have seemed questionable whether forbearance and self-restraint might not be human weakness: he had to defend his people as well as himself against the enemy's persecutions. He is told here that he need not entertain any such fears. Patience (with constancy) in those circumstances was in accordance with Allah's own command. Nor was he to grieve if they rejected Allah's Message: the Prophet had done his duty when he boldly and openly proclaimed it. Nor was his heart to be troubled if they hatched secret plots against himself and his people. Allah would protect them.

2165. And the Sūrah ends with the highest consolation which the righteous can receive: the assurance that Allah is with them. A double qualification is indicated for so high an honour—(1) that they should not yield to human passion or anger or impatience, and (2) that they should go on with constancy doing good all around them. To attain the Presence of Allah in the sense of "I am with you" is the culmination of the righteous man's aspiration.

INTRODUCTION TO SŪRAH 17—*AL ISRĀ'* OR *BANĪ ISRĀ'ĪL*

In the gradation of spiritual teaching (see Introduction to Sūrah 8), we saw that the first seven Sūrahs sketched the early spiritual history of man, and led up to the formation of the new Ummah of Islam. Sūrahs 8 to 16 formed another series dealing with the formation of the new Ummah and its consolidation, and Allah's dealing with man taken as an Ummah and considered in his social relations in organised commumities (see Introduction to Sūrahs 8, 10, and 16). We now come to a fresh series, (Sūrahs 17-29), which may be considered in three parts. Sūrahs 17-21 begin with an allusion to the *Mi'rāj* (of which more later), and proceed to spiritual history as touching individuals rather than nations. The old prophets and stories of the past are now referred to from this point of view. Sūrahs 22-25 refer to Hajj (pilgrimage), worship and prayer, chastity, privacy, etc., as related to a man's individual spiritual growth. Sūrahs 26-29 go back to the old prophets and stories of the past, as illustrating the growth of the individual soul in its reactions against the lives of the communities and the reactions of the communities to the lives of its great individual souls.

Let us now consider S. 17. by itself. It opens with the mystic Vision of the Ascension of the Holy Prophet: he was transported from the Sacred Mosque (of Makkah) to the Farthest Mosque (of Jerusalem) in a night and shown some of the Signs of Allah. The majority of Commentators take this Night Journey literally, but allow that there were other occasions on which a spiritual Journey or Vision occurred. Even on the supposition of a miraculous bodily Journey, it is conceded that the body was almost transformed into spiritual fineness. The Hadith literature gives details of this Journey and its study helps to elucidate its meaning. The Holy Prophet was first transported to the seat of the earlier relevations in Jerusalem, and then taken through the seven heavens even to the Sublime Throne, and initiated into the spiritual mysteries of the human soul struggling in Space and Time. The Spaniard, Miguiel Asin, Arabic Professor in the University of Madrid, has shown that this *Mi'rāj* literature had a great influence on the Mediaeval literature of Europe, and especially on the great Italian poem, the *Divine Comedy* (or Drama) of Dante, which towers like a landmark in mediaeval European literature.

The reference to this great mystic story of the *Mi'rāj* is a fitting prelude to the journey of the human soul in its spiritual growth in life. The first steps in such growth must be through moral conduct—the reciprocal rights of parents and children, kindness to our fellow-men, courage and firmness in the hour of danger, and sense of personal responsibility, and a sense of Allah's Presence through prayer and praise.

The *Mi'rāj* is usually dated to the 27th night of the month of Rajab (though other dates, *e.g.*, 17th of Rabī' I, are also given) in the year before the Hijrah. This fixes the date of the opening verse of the Sūrah, though portions of the Sūrah may have been a little earlier.

Summary—The spiritual experiences of the Prophets of Allah are given in order that Allah's Signs may be made clear to men: man is misled into evil, and must be guided to a sense of personal responsibility (17:1-22, and C. 128). (R).

Our service to Allah is shown also in our human relations, goodness to parents and kinsmen and strangers in want, as well as kindness to children, purity in sex relations, justice and respect for human life, protection of orphans, probity in all dealings, and avoidance of arrogance. (17:23-40, and C. 129).

Allah's glory is above all comparison, and the reception of His revelation marks off the man of faith from those who do not believe. But the Believers should speak fair and avoid dissensions, for Allah doth encompass all men (17:41-60, and C. 130).

Pride caused the fall of Iblīs, but the children of Adam have been raised in excellence above other Creation. They will be judged by their deeds. Prayer is good at stated times and at night, and the Qur'ān is offered as healing and mercy (17:61-84, and C. 131).

Inspiration (the Qur'ān) is a Sign of Allah's grace, and men should accept it without making carping excuses. Be humble in prayer and praise (17:85-111, and C. 132).

C. 128.—It is the privilege of the men of God
(17:1-22) To see the sublimest mysteries
Of the spiritual world and instruct men
In Righteousness; they warn and shield men
Against Evil. But nothing can lessen
Each soul's personal responsibility
For its own deeds. It carries its fate
Round its own neck. Allah's gifts
Are for all, but not all receive
The same gifts, nor are all gifts
Of equal dignity or excellence.

Sūrah 17.

Al Isrā' (The Night Journey), or
Banī Isrā'īl (The Children of Israel)

الجزء الخامس عشر سورة الإسراء

In the name of Allah, Most Gracious, Most Merciful.

بِسْمِ ٱللَّهِ ٱلرَّحْمَٰنِ ٱلرَّحِيمِ

1. Glory to (Allah)
Who did take His Servant
For a Journey by night[2166]
From the Sacred Mosque[2167]
To the Farthest Mosque,[2168]
Whose precincts We did
Bless—in order that We
Might show him some
Of Our Signs: for He
Is the One Who heareth
And seeth (all things).[2169]

١ سُبْحَٰنَ ٱلَّذِىٓ أَسْرَىٰ بِعَبْدِهِۦ لَيْلًا
مِّنَ ٱلْمَسْجِدِ ٱلْحَرَامِ
إِلَى ٱلْمَسْجِدِ ٱلْأَقْصَا ٱلَّذِى
بَٰرَكْنَا حَوْلَهُۥ لِنُرِيَهُۥ مِنْ ءَايَٰتِنَآ
إِنَّهُۥ هُوَ ٱلسَّمِيعُ ٱلْبَصِيرُ

2. We gave Moses the Book,[2170]
And made it a Guide

٢ وَءَاتَيْنَا مُوسَى ٱلْكِتَٰبَ وَجَعَلْنَٰهُ هُدًى

2166. The reference is to the *Mi'rāj* for which see the Introduction to this Sūrah.

2167. *Masjid* is a place of prayer: here it refers to the Ka'bah at Makkah. It had not yet been cleared of its idols and rededicated exclusively to the One True God. It was symbolical of the new Message which was being given to mankind.

2168. *The Farthest Mosque* must refer to the site of the Temple of Solomon in Jerusalem on the hill of Moriah, at or near which stands the Dome of the Rock. This and the Mosque known as the Farthest Mosque (*Masjid al Aqṣā*) were completed by the Amir 'Abd al Malik in A.H. 68. *Farthest*, because it was the place of worship farthest west which was known to the Arabs in the time of the Holy Prophet: it was a sacred place to both Jews and Christians, but the Christians then had the upper hand, as it was included in the Byzantine (Roman) Empire, which maintained a Patriarch at Jerusalem. The chief dates in connection with the Temple are: it was finished by Solomon about B.C. 1004; destroyed by the Babylonians under Nebuchadnezzar about 586 B.C.; rebuilt under Ezra and Nehemiah about 515 B.C.; turned into a heathen idol-temple by one of Alexander's successors, Antiochus Epiphanes, 167 B.C.; restored by Herod, B.C. 17 to A.C. 29; and completely razed to the ground by the Emperor Titus in A.C. 70. These ups and downs are among the greater Signs in religious history.

2169. Allah's knowledge comprehends all things, without any curtain of Time or any separation of Space. He can therefore see and hear all things, and the *Mi'rāj* was a reflection of this knowledge without Time or Space.

In this and the subsequent verses, the reference to Allah is generally in the first person and plural. But in the first and the last clause of this verse it is in the third person singular: "Glory to Allah, Who did take *His* Servant...", "He is the One...". In each of these two instances, the clause expresses the point of view of Allah's creatures, who glorify Him, and whose hearing and seeing are ordinarily so limited that they can do nothing but glorify Him when one of His creatures is raised up to hear and see the Mysteries. It is *they* who glorify Him. (R).

2170. *The Book*: the revelation that was given to Moses. It was there clearly laid down that those who followed Moses must consider Allah as all-in-all. "Thou shalt have no other gods before me; thou shalt not make unto thee any graven image...; thou shalt not bow down thyself to them nor serve them: for I the Lord thy God am a jealous God...;" etc. (Exod. xx. 3-5). These are the words of the English Bible. As a matter of fact the spirit of Mosaic teaching went further. It referred all things to the Providence of Allah: Allah is the Disposer of all affairs, and we are to look to none but Him. This is Islam, and the *Mi'rāj* showed that it was the teaching of Allah from the most ancient times, and yet it was violated by the very people who claimed to be its custodians.

لِّبَنِىٓ إِسْرَٰٓءِيلَ أَلَّا تَتَّخِذُوا۟ مِن دُونِى وَكِيلًا

To the Children of Israel,
(Commanding): "Take not
Other than Me[2171]
As Disposer of (your) affairs."

٣ ذُرِّيَّةَ مَنْ حَمَلْنَا مَعَ نُوحٍ إِنَّهُۥ كَانَ عَبْدًا شَكُورًا

3. O ye that are sprung
From those whom We carried
(In the Ark) with Noah![2172]
Verily he was a devotee
Most grateful.

٤ وَقَضَيْنَآ إِلَىٰ بَنِىٓ إِسْرَٰٓءِيلَ فِى ٱلْكِتَٰبِ لَتُفْسِدُنَّ فِى ٱلْأَرْضِ مَرَّتَيْنِ وَلَتَعْلُنَّ عُلُوًّا كَبِيرًا

4. And We gave (clear) warning
To the Children of Israel[2173]
In the Book, that twice[2174]
Would they do mischief
On the earth and be elated
With mighty arrogance
(And twice would they be
punished)!

٥ فَإِذَا جَآءَ وَعْدُ أُولَىٰهُمَا بَعَثْنَا عَلَيْكُمْ عِبَادًا لَّنَآ أُو۟لِى بَأْسٍ شَدِيدٍ فَجَاسُوا۟ خِلَٰلَ ٱلدِّيَارِ وَكَانَ وَعْدًا مَّفْعُولًا

5. When the first of the warnings
Came to pass, We sent
Against you Our servants
Given to terrible warfare.[2175]
They entered the very inmost
Parts of your homes;
And it was a warning
(Completely) fulfilled.

2171. Note the transition from "We" in the first clause to "Me" in the second clause. The first clause refers to the majesty of Allah as the Heavenly King: the second clause refers to His personal interest in all our affairs.

2172. After the Deluge of the time of Noah the only descendants of Noah were those who were saved in the Ark with him. They had special reason to celebrate the praise of Allah. But they relapsed into idolatry, sin, and abomination. They are reminded of the true and sincere devotion of Noah himself, as contrasted with the unworthiness of Noah's descendants, especially the Children of Israel.

2173. The Book is the revelation given to the Children of Israel. Here it seems to refer to the burning words of Prophets like Isaiah. For example, see Isaiah, chap. xxiv. or Isaiah v. 20-30, or Isaiah iii. 16-26.

2174. What are the two occasions referred to? It may be that "twice" is a figure of speech for "more than once", "often". Or it maybe that the two occasions refer to (1) the destruction of the Temple by the Babylonian Nebuchadnezzar in 586 B.C., when the Jews were carried off into captivity, and (2) the destruction of Jerusalem by Titus in A.C. 70, after which the Temple was never rebuilt. See n. 2168 above. On both occasions it was a judgement of Allah for the sins of the Jews, their backslidings, and their arrogance.

2175. A good description of the warlike Nebuchadnezzar and his Babylonians. They were servants of Allah in the sense that they were instruments through which the wrath of Allah was poured out on the Jews, for they penetrated through their lands, their Temple, and their homes, and carried away the Jews, men and women, into captivity. As regards "the daughters of Zion" see the scathing condemnation in Isaiah, iii. 16-26.

6. Then did we grant you
The Return as against them:[2176]
We gave you increase
In resources and sons,
And made you
The more numerous
In manpower.

٦ ثُمَّ رَدَدْنَا لَكُمُ الْكَرَّةَ عَلَيْهِمْ
وَأَمْدَدْنَٰكُم بِأَمْوَٰلٍ وَبَنِينَ
وَجَعَلْنَٰكُمْ أَكْثَرَ نَفِيرًا

7. If ye did well,
Ye did well for yourselves;
If ye did evil,
(Ye did it) against yourselves.[2177]
So when the second
Of the warnings came to pass,
(We permitted your enemies)
To disfigure your faces,[2178]
And to enter your Temple[2179]
As they had entered it before,
And to visit with destruction
All that fell into their power.[2180]

٧ إِنْ أَحْسَنتُمْ أَحْسَنتُمْ لِأَنفُسِكُمْ ۖ
وَإِنْ أَسَأْتُمْ فَلَهَا ۚ فَإِذَا جَآءَ وَعْدُ الْآخِرَةِ
لِيَسُۥٓـُٔوا۟ وُجُوهَكُمْ وَلِيَدْخُلُوا۟ الْمَسْجِدَ
كَمَا دَخَلُوهُ أَوَّلَ مَرَّةٍ
وَلِيُتَبِّرُوا۟ مَا عَلَوْا۟ تَتْبِيرًا

8. It may be that your Lord
May (yet) show Mercy[2181]
Unto you; but if ye

٨ عَسَىٰ رَبُّكُمْ أَن يَرْحَمَكُمْ ۚ وَإِنْ

2176. The return of the Jews from the Captivity was about 520 B.C. They started life afresh. They rebuilt the Temple. They carried out various reforms and built up a new Judaism in connection with Ezra. See Appendix II following S. 5. For a time they prospered. Meanwhile their old oppressors the Babylonians had been absorbed by Persia. Subsequently Persia was absorbed in Alexander's Empire. The whole of western Asia was Hellenized, and the new school of Jews was Hellenized also, and had a strong centre in Alexandria. But their footing in Palestine continued, and under the Asmonaean Dynasty (B.C. 167-63), they had a national revival, and the names of the Maccabees are remembered as those of heroes. Another dynasty, that of the Idumaeans, (B.C. 63 to B.C. 4), to which Herod belonged, also enjoyed some semi-independent power. The sceptre of Syria (including Palestine) passed to the Romans in B.C. 65, and Jewish feudatory Kings held power under them. But the Jews again showed a stiff-necked resistance to Allah's Messenger in the time of Jesus, and the inevitable doom followed in the complete and final destruction of the Temple under Titus in 70 A.C.

2177. This is a parenthetical sentence. If anyone follows Allah's Law, the benefit goes to himself: he does not bestow a favour on anyone else. Similarly evil brings its own recompense on the doer of evil.

2178. The second doom was due to the rejection of the Message of Jesus. "To disfigure your faces" means to destroy any credit or power you may have got: the face shows the personality of the man.

2179. Titus's destruction of Jerusalem in 70 A.C.. was complete. He was a son of the Roman Emperor Vespasian, and at the date of the destruction of Jerusalem, had the title of Caesar as heir to the throne. He ruled as Roman Emperor from 79 to 81 A.C..

2180. Merivale in his *Romans Under the Empire* gives a graphic account of the siege and final destruction (ed. 1890, 7:221-255). The population of Jerusalem was then 200,000. According to the Latin historian Tacitus it was as much as 600,000. There was a famine and there were massacres. There was much fanaticism. The judgement of Merivale is: "They" (the Jews) "were judicially abandoned to their own passions and the punishment which naturally awaited them." (7:221).

2181. Now we come to the time of our Holy Prophet. In spite of all the past, the Jews could still have obtained Allah's forgiveness if they had not obstinately rejected the greatest of the Prophets also. If they were to continue in their sins, Allah's punishment would also continue to visit them.

Revert (to your sins)
We shall revert
(To Our punishments):
And We have made Hell
A prison for those who
Reject (all Faith).[2182]

عُدتُّمْ عُدْنَا
وَجَعَلْنَا جَهَنَّمَ
لِلْكَٰفِرِينَ حَصِيرًا

9. Verily this Qur'ān
Doth guide to that
Which is most right (or stable),[2183]
And giveth the glad tidings
To the Believers who work
Deeds of righteousness,
That they shall have
A magnificent reward;

٩ إِنَّ هَٰذَا ٱلْقُرْءَانَ يَهْدِى
لِلَّتِى هِىَ أَقْوَمُ وَيُبَشِّرُ ٱلْمُؤْمِنِينَ
ٱلَّذِينَ يَعْمَلُونَ ٱلصَّٰلِحَٰتِ أَنَّ لَهُمْ أَجْرًا كَبِيرًا

10. And to those who believe not
In the Hereafter, (it announceth)
That We have prepared
For them a Penalty
Grievous (indeed).

١٠ وَأَنَّ ٱلَّذِينَ لَا يُؤْمِنُونَ بِٱلْءَاخِرَةِ
أَعْتَدْنَا لَهُمْ عَذَابًا أَلِيمًا

SECTION 2.

11. The prayer that man
Should make for good,
He maketh for evil;[2184]
For man is given to
Hasty (deeds).

١١ وَيَدْعُ ٱلْإِنسَٰنُ بِٱلشَّرِّ دُعَآءَهُۥ بِٱلْخَيْرِ
وَكَانَ ٱلْإِنسَٰنُ عَجُولًا

12. We have made the Night
And the Day as two[2185]

١٢ وَجَعَلْنَا ٱلَّيْلَ وَٱلنَّهَارَ ءَايَتَيْنِ

2182. There is such a thing as disgrace in this life, but the final disgrace is in the Hereafter, and that will be irretrievable.

Notice that the allegorical reference to Jewish history, when brought into relation with the true meaning of *Mi'rāj*, refers to the constant struggle of the individual soul against evil. It has its setbacks and its punishments. But if it is true to itself and is true to the Faith in Allah, Allah will give it strength and make it successful in its fight against evil. For Allah's Mercy is unbounded and comes to suffering humanity again and again. (R).

2183. The instability and crookedness of the Jewish soul having been mentioned, the healing balm which should have cured it is now pointed out. The Message of the Qur'ān is for all. Those who have Faith and show that Faith in their conduct must reap their spiritual reward. But those who reject Faith cannot escape punishment. Apart from what is past, apart from questions of national or racial history, there is a spiritual Hope—and a spiritual Danger—for every soul.

2184. Man in his ignorance or haste mistakes evil for good, and desires what he should not have. The wise and instructed soul has patience and does not put its own desires above the wisdom of Allah. He receives with contentment the favours of Allah, and prays to be rightly guided in his desires and petitions.

2185. If we were to cry when it is night, we shall look foolish when it is day; for the night is but a preparation for the day: perhaps, as the last verse says, we pray for the day when we want rest for the night. Both are Signs from Allah. Darkness and light stand for ignorance and knowledge. "Where ignorance is bliss, 'tis folly to be wise." Darkness and light may also stand for shadow and sunshine, sorrow and joy: both may be necessary for our development.

(Of Our) Signs: the Sign
Of the Night have We obscured,
While the Sign of the Day
We have made to enlighten
You; that ye may seek
Bounty from your Lord,[2186]
And that ye may know
The number and count
Of the years: all things
Have We explained in detail.

فَمَحَوْنَآ ءَايَةَ ٱلَّيْلِ وَجَعَلْنَآ ءَايَةَ ٱلنَّهَارِ
مُبْصِرَةً لِّتَبْتَغُوا۟ فَضْلًا مِّن رَّبِّكُمْ
وَلِتَعْلَمُوا۟ عَدَدَ ٱلسِّنِينَ وَٱلْحِسَابَ
وَكُلَّ شَىْءٍ فَصَّلْنَٰهُ تَفْصِيلًا

13. Every man's fate[2187]
We have fastened
On his own neck:
On the Day of Judgement
We shall bring out
For him a scroll,
Which he will see
Spread open.[2188]

١٣ وَكُلَّ إِنسَٰنٍ
أَلْزَمْنَٰهُ طَٰٓئِرَهُۥ فِى عُنُقِهِۦ
وَنُخْرِجُ لَهُۥ يَوْمَ ٱلْقِيَٰمَةِ كِتَٰبًا
يَلْقَىٰهُ مَنشُورًا

14. (It will be said to him:)
"Read thine (own) record;
Sufficient is thy soul
This day to make out
An account against thee."[2189]

١٤ ٱقْرَأْ كِتَٰبَكَ كَفَىٰ بِنَفْسِكَ
ٱلْيَوْمَ عَلَيْكَ حَسِيبًا

15. Who receiveth guidance,
Receiveth it for his own
Benefit: who goeth astray

١٥ مَّنِ ٱهْتَدَىٰ فَإِنَّمَا يَهْتَدِى لِنَفْسِهِۦ
وَمَن ضَلَّ

2186. By the physical light we see physical facts. And this physical gift of Allah is good for us in two ways: (1) we can arrange for our livelihood, or we can attain knowledge of the physical sciences and gain some control over the physical forces of nature; and (2) the daily rising and setting of the sun gives us the computation of days and years, for the physical natural year is the solar year. But there is spiritual light even more precious: by it we can similarly attain two objects, *viz*: (1) our spiritual livelihood and knowledge, and (2) our computation of the stages we reach in our spiritual years. Let us be patient and seek everything as from Allah—in joy and in sorrow, in knowledge and in want of knowledge of those things which are above us. Let us rejoice in what Allah has given us, and not be impatient about those things which He in His wisdom has thought fit to withhold from us. But all things should be sought and striven for under the guidance of the All-Knowing Allah.

2187. *Fate* : *Ṭā'ir,* literally a bird, hence an omen, an evil omen, fate. *Cf.* 36:19. The Arabs like the ancient Romans, sought to read the mysteries of human fate from the flight of birds. And many of us in our own day seek to read our future fortunes by similar superstitions. We read in the previous verse that there are Signs of Allah, but they are not meant to subserve the vulgar purpose of disclosing our future destiny in a worldly sense. They are meant for quite other purposes, as we have explained. Our real fate does not depend upon birds or omens or stars. It depends on our deeds, good or evil, and they hang round our necks. (R).

2188. These deeds, good or evil, will be embodied in a scroll which will be quite open to us in the light of the Day of Judgement, however much we may affect to be ignorant of it now or waste our energies in prying into mysteries that do not concern us.

2189. Our true accusers are our own deeds. Why not look to them instead of vainly prying into something superstitious which we call a book of fortune or a book of omens?

Doth so to his own loss:[2190]
No bearer of burdens
Can bear the burden[2191]
Of another: nor would We
Visit with Our Wrath
Until We had sent
A messenger (to give warning).

فَإِنَّمَا يَضِلُّ عَلَيْهَا
وَلَا تَزِرُ وَازِرَةٌ وِزْرَ أُخْرَىٰ
وَمَا كُنَّا مُعَذِّبِينَ حَتَّىٰ نَبْعَثَ رَسُولًا

16. When We decide to destroy
A population, We (first) send
A definite order to those
Among them who are given
The good things of this life[2192]
And yet transgress; so that
The word is proved true[2193]
Against them: then
We destroy them utterly.

١٦ وَإِذَا أَرَدْنَا أَن نُّهْلِكَ قَرْيَةً
أَمَرْنَا مُتْرَفِيهَا فَفَسَقُوا فِيهَا
فَحَقَّ عَلَيْهَا الْقَوْلُ
فَدَمَّرْنَاهَا تَدْمِيرًا

17. How many generations
Have We destroyed after Noah?[2194]
And enough is thy Lord
To note and see
The sins of His servants.[2195]

١٧ وَكَمْ أَهْلَكْنَا مِنَ الْقُرُونِ مِن بَعْدِ نُوحٍ
وَكَفَىٰ بِرَبِّكَ بِذُنُوبِ عِبَادِهِۦ خَبِيرًا بَصِيرًا

18. If any do wish
For the transitory things
(Of this life), We readily[2196]

١٨ مَّن كَانَ يُرِيدُ الْعَاجِلَةَ عَجَّلْنَا

2190. The doctrine of personal responsibility is insisted on, and the basis of ethics is shown to be our own good or evil as furthering or obstructing our highest development.

2191. The doctrine of vicarious atonement is condemned. Salvation for the wicked cannot be attained by the punishment of the innocent. One man cannot bear the burden of another: that would be unjust. Every man must bear his own personal responsibility. *Cf.* 6:164. But Allah never visits His wrath on anyone until due warning is conveyed to him through an accredited messenger.

2192. Allah's Mercy gives every chance to the wicked to repent. When wickedness gets so rampant that punishment becomes inevitable, even then Allah's Mercy and Justice act together. Those who are highly gifted from Allah—it may be with wealth or position or it may be with talents and opportunities—are expected to understand and obey. They are given a definite order and warning. If they still transgress there is no further room for argument. They cannot plead that they were ignorant. The command of the Lord is proved against them, and its application is called for beyond doubt. Then it is that their punishment is completed.

2193. *Qawl* here has the sense of word, order, law, charge framed against one under a definite law.

2194. Noah's Flood is taken as a new starting point in history. But even after that hundreds of empires, towns, and generations have perished for their wickedness.

2195. Let not the wicked think, because they are given a lease of life and luxury for a time, that their wickedness has escaped notice. Allah notes and sees all things, both open and secret. He knows the hidden motives and thoughts of men, and He has no need of any other evidence. His knowledge and sight are all-sufficient.

2196. An explanation is now given of how it is that prosperity sometimes seems to attend the wicked. The explanation is threefold: (1) the transitory things of this life are worth little in the eternal scheme of things; (2) even they are provided, not just because their recipients wish for them, but according to a definite Plan of Allah; and (3) in the end there is for the wicked the eternal misery and deprivation of grace—the Hell which is worse than destruction in the terms of this world.

Grant them—such things
As We will, to such persons
As We will: in the end
Have We provided Hell
For them: they will burn
Therein, disgraced and
rejected.[2197]

لَهُۥ فِيهَا مَا نَشَآءُ لِمَن نُّرِيدُ ثُمَّ
جَعَلْنَا لَهُۥ جَهَنَّمَ يَصْلَىٰهَا
مَذْمُومًا مَّدْحُورًا

19. Those who do wish
For the (things of) the
Hereafter,[2198]
And strive therefor
With all due striving,
And have Faith—[2199]
They are the ones
Whose striving is acceptable
(To Allah).

١٩ وَمَنْ أَرَادَ ٱلْـَٔاخِرَةَ
وَسَعَىٰ لَهَا سَعْيَهَا
وَهُوَ مُؤْمِنٌ فَأُو۟لَٰٓئِكَ
كَانَ سَعْيُهُم مَّشْكُورًا

20. Of the bounties of thy Lord
We bestow freely on all—
These as well as those:
The bounties of thy Lord
Are not closed (to anyone).[2200]

٢٠ كُلًّا نُّمِدُّ هَٰٓؤُلَآءِ وَهَٰٓؤُلَآءِ مِنْ عَطَآءِ
رَبِّكَ ۚ وَمَا كَانَ عَطَآءُ رَبِّكَ مَحْظُورًا

21. See how We have bestowed
More on some than on others;
But verily the Hereafter
Is more in rank and gradation
And more in excellence.[2201]

٢١ ٱنظُرْ كَيْفَ فَضَّلْنَا بَعْضَهُمْ عَلَىٰ بَعْضٍ ۚ
وَلَلْـَٔاخِرَةُ أَكْبَرُ دَرَجَٰتٍ وَأَكْبَرُ تَفْضِيلًا

22. Take not with Allah
Another object of worship;[2202]

٢٢ لَّا تَجْعَلْ مَعَ ٱللَّهِ إِلَٰهًا ءَاخَرَ

2197. All the pride and insolence will then be brought low. The disgrace and the exclusion from the "sight of the Face of Allah" will by themselves be punishments of which the magnitude cannot be measured in the terms of our present material life.

2198. This is in contrast to the last verse. Those who wish for mere earthly good sometimes get it and misuse it. Those whose eyes are fixed on the Hereafter, they too share in their Lord's bounty provided they fulfil the conditions explained in the next note; but their wishes and endeavours are more acceptable in the sight of Allah.

2199. A mere wish for moral and spiritual good is not enough. It must be backed up by hard endeavour and supported by a lively Faith. On those conditions the wishes are accepted by Allah.

2200. Allah's favours are showered on all—the just and the unjust, the deserving and the undeserving. But there is a difference as explained in the last two verses.

2201. Nor should man suppose that all gifts are of equal value. The spiritual ones rank far higher in dignity and real worth than the transitory ones. Therefore it is altogether wrong to compare the worldly prosperity of a wicked man with the apparent want of it to a man of spiritual worth. There is no comparison between them when measured by right standards.

2202. The seeming inequality of gifts to men might make short-sighted men impugn the impartiality of Allah. But the fault lies with such men's own want of knowledge and want of Faith. There is no excuse for them to seek other objects of worship than Allah. For there is none worthy of worship except Allah.

Or thou (O man!) wilt sit
In disgrace and destitution.[2203]

فَتَقْعُدَ مَذْمُومًا مَّخْذُولًا

C. 129.—(17:23-40.)

To be worthy of the service of the One True God,
We must love and serve His Creatures.
The parents who cherished us in childhood
Deserve our humble reverence and service: next
Come the rights of kinsmen, those in want,
And wayfaring strangers: to each
According to his need, not in spendthrift show.
And gentleness is needed to those whom we
Cannot help. Allah will provide. He has made
Life sacred and pure. Fulfil your trusts
For orphans and deal with all in strictest
Probity. Pry not into evil from curiousity,
And shun insolence: for Allah hates evil—
The One, the Good, the Universal Lord!

SECTION 3.

23. Thy Lord hath decreed
That ye worship none but Him,
And that ye be kind
To parents. Whether one
Or both of them attain
Old age in thy life,[2204]
Say not to them a word
Of contempt, nor repel them,
But address them
In terms of honour.

٢٣ وَقَضَىٰ رَبُّكَ أَلَّا تَعْبُدُوٓا
إِلَّآ إِيَّاهُ وَبِٱلْوَٰلِدَيْنِ إِحْسَٰنًا
إِمَّا يَبْلُغَنَّ عِندَكَ ٱلْكِبَرَ أَحَدُهُمَآ
أَوْ كِلَاهُمَا فَلَا تَقُل لَّهُمَآ أُفٍّ وَلَا تَنْهَرْهُمَا
وَقُل لَّهُمَا قَوْلًا كَرِيمًا

24. And, out of kindness,
Lower to them the wing[2205]
Of humility, and say:

٢٤ وَٱخْفِضْ لَهُمَا جَنَاحَ ٱلذُّلِّ
مِنَ ٱلرَّحْمَةِ وَقُل

2203. If foolish men turn to false objects of worship, they will not only be disappointed, but they will lose the respect of their own fellow-men, and spiritually they will be reduced to destitution. All their talents and their words will be of no avail.

2204. The spiritual and moral duties are now brought into juxtaposition. We are to worship none but Allah, because none but Allah is worthy of worship, not because "the Lord thy God is a jealous God, visiting the iniquity of the fathers upon the children unto the third and fourth generation of them that hate Me" (Exod. xx. 5).

Note that the act of worship may be collective as well as individual; hence the plural *ta'budū*. The kindness to parents is an individual act of piety; hence the singular *taqul, qul,* etc.

2205. *Cf.* 15:88 and n. 2011. The metaphor is that of a high-flying bird which lowers her wing out of tenderness to her offspring. There is a double aptness. (1) When the parent was strong and the child was helpless, parental affection was showered on the child: when the child grows up and is strong, and the parent is helpless, can he do less than bestow similar tender care on the parent? (2) But more: he must approach the matter with gentle humility; for does not parental love remind him of the love with which Allah cherished His creatures? There is something here more than simple human gratitude: it goes up into the highest spiritual region.

"My Lord! bestow on them
Thy Mercy even as they
Cherished me in childhood."[2206]

رَّبِّ ٱرْحَمْهُمَا كَمَا رَبَّيَانِى صَغِيرًا

25. Your Lord knoweth best
What is in your hearts:
If ye do deeds of righteousness,
Verily He is Most Forgiving
To those who turn to Him
Again and again
(in true penitence).[2207]

٢٥ رَّبُّكُمْ أَعْلَمُ بِمَا فِى نُفُوسِكُمْ ۚ
إِن تَكُونُوا۟ صَـٰلِحِينَ فَإِنَّهُۥ
كَانَ لِلْأَوَّٰبِينَ غَفُورًا

26. And render to the kindred
Their due rights, as (also)
To those in want,
And to the wayfarer:[2208]
But squander not (your wealth)
In the manner of a spendthrift.[2209]

٢٦ وَءَاتِ ذَا ٱلْقُرْبَىٰ حَقَّهُۥ
وَٱلْمِسْكِينَ وَٱبْنَ ٱلسَّبِيلِ
وَلَا تُبَذِّرْ تَبْذِيرًا

27. Verily spendthrifts are brothers
Of the Evil Ones
And the Evil One
Is to his Lord (Himself)
Ungrateful.[2210]

٢٧ إِنَّ ٱلْمُبَذِّرِينَ كَانُوٓا۟ إِخْوَٰنَ ٱلشَّيَـٰطِينِ ۖ
وَكَانَ ٱلشَّيْطَـٰنُ لِرَبِّهِۦ كَفُورًا

28. And even if thou hast
To turn away from them
In pursuit of the Mercy

٢٨ وَإِمَّا تُعْرِضَنَّ عَنْهُمُ ٱبْتِغَآءَ رَحْمَةٍ

2206. Note that we are asked to honour our father and mother, not "that thy days may be long upon the land which the Lord thy God giveth thee" (Exod. xx 12), but upon much higher and more universal grounds, such as befit a perfect revelation. In the first place, not merely respect, but cherishing kindness, and humility to parents, are commanded. In the second place this command is bracketed with the command to worship the One True God: Parental love should be to us a type of divine love: nothing that we can do can ever really compensate for that which we have received. In the third place (see next verse) our spiritual advancement is tested by this: we cannot expect Allah's forgiveness if we are rude or unkind to those who unselfishly brought us up.

2207. It is the heart, and its hidden and secret motives, by which we are judged: for Allah knows them all.

2208. In the Jewish Decalogue, which was given to a primitive and hard-hearted people, this refinement of kindness—to those in want and to wayfarers (*i.e.*, total strangers whom you come across) finds no place. Nor was there much danger of their wasting their substance out of exuberance. Even the command "to honour thy father and mother" comes after the ceremonial observance of the Sabbath. With us, the worship of Allah is linked up with kindness—to parents, kindred, those in want, those who are far from their homes though they may be total strangers to us. It is not mere verbal kindness. They have certain rights which must be fulfilled.

2209. All charity, kindness, and help are conditioned by our own resources. There is no merit if we merely spend out of bravado or for idle show. How many families are ruined by extravagant expenses at weddings, funerals, etc., or (as they may call it) to "oblige friends or relatives", or to give to able-bodied beggars? To no one was this command more necessary than it is to Muslims of the present day.

2210. Spendthrifts are not merely fools. They are of the same family as the Evil Ones. And the chief of the Evil Ones (notice the transition from the plural to the singular)—Satan himself—fell by his ingratitude to Allah. So those who misuse or squander Allah's gifts are also ungrateful to Allah.

From thy Lord which thou
Dost expect, yet speak
To them a word
Of easy kindness.[2211]

مِّن رَّبِّكَ تَرۡجُوهَا فَقُل
لَّهُمۡ قَوۡلٗا مَّيۡسُورٗا

29. Make not thy hand tied[2212]
(Like a niggard's) to thy neck,
Nor stretch it forth
To its utmost reach,
So that thou become
Blameworthy and destitute.

٢٩ وَلَا تَجۡعَلۡ يَدَكَ مَغۡلُولَةً إِلَىٰ عُنُقِكَ
وَلَا تَبۡسُطۡهَا كُلَّ ٱلۡبَسۡطِ
فَتَقۡعُدَ مَلُومٗا مَّحۡسُورًا

30. Verily thy Lord doth provide
Sustenance in abundance
For whom He pleaseth, and He
Provideth in a just measure,[2213]
For He doth know
And regard all His servants.

٣٠ إِنَّ رَبَّكَ يَبۡسُطُ ٱلرِّزۡقَ
لِمَن يَشَآءُ وَيَقۡدِرُ
إِنَّهُۥ كَانَ بِعِبَادِهِۦ خَبِيرَۢا بَصِيرٗا

SECTION 4.

31. Kill not your children[2214]
For fear of want: We shall
Provide sustenance for them
As well as for you.
Verily the killing of them
Is a great sin.

٣١ وَلَا تَقۡتُلُوٓاْ أَوۡلَٰدَكُمۡ
خَشۡيَةَ إِمۡلَٰقٖۖ نَّحۡنُ نَرۡزُقُهُمۡ وَإِيَّاكُمۡۚ
إِنَّ قَتۡلَهُمۡ كَانَ خِطۡـٔٗا كَبِيرٗا

32. Nor come nigh to adultery:
For it is a shameful (deed)

٣٢ وَلَا تَقۡرَبُواْ ٱلزِّنَىٰٓۖ إِنَّهُۥ كَانَ فَٰحِشَةٗ

2211. You may have to "turn away" from people for two reasons. (1) You may not have the wherewithal with which to entertain them and give them their rights; or (2) you may have to give them a wide berth because their thoughts are not as your thoughts. In either case there is no need to speak harshly to them. Your words should be those of "easy kindness", *i.e.*, the sort of kindness (not merely frigid politeness) which flows from pity and understanding and smooths over unnecessary difficulties in human intercourse.

2212. *Cf.* the phrase for niggardliness in 5:67. We are not to be so lavish as to make ourselves destitute and incur the just censure of wise men, nor is it becoming to keep back our resources from the just needs of those who have a right to our help. Even strangers have such a right, as we saw in 17:26 above. But we must keep a just measure between our capacity and other people's needs.

2213. If a foolish spendthrift pretends that his generosity, even if it ruins himself, is good for other people, he is reminded that Allah will take care of all. He knows every one's true needs and cares for them. He gives in abundance to some, but in all cases He gives in just measure. Who are we to pretend to greater generosity! (R).

2214. The Arabs were addicted to female infanticide. In a society perpetually at war a son was a source of strength whereas a daughter was a source of weakness. Even now infanticide is not unknown in other countries for economic reasons. This crime against children's lives is here characterised as one of the greatest of sins.

And an evil, opening the road[2215]
(To other evils).

وَسَآءَ سَبِيلًا

33. Nor take life—which Allah
Has made sacred—except
For just cause. And if
Anyone is slain wrongfully,
We have given his heir
Authority (to demand Qiṣāṣ[2216]
Or to forgive): but let him
Not exceed bounds in the matter
Of taking life: for he
Is helped (by the Law).

٣٣ وَلَا تَقْتُلُوا۟ ٱلنَّفْسَ
ٱلَّتِى حَرَّمَ ٱللَّهُ إِلَّا بِٱلْحَقِّ ۗ
وَمَن قُتِلَ مَظْلُومًا فَقَدْ جَعَلْنَا لِوَلِيِّهِۦ
سُلْطَـٰنًا فَلَا يُسْرِف فِّى ٱلْقَتْلِ ۖ
إِنَّهُۥ كَانَ مَنصُورًا

34. Come not nigh
To the orphan's property
Except to improve it,[2217]
Until he attains the age[2218]
Of full strength: and fulfil
(Every)[2219] engagement,
For (every) engagement
Will be enquired into
(On the Day of Reckoning).[2220]

٣٤ وَلَا تَقْرَبُوا۟ مَالَ ٱلْيَتِيمِ إِلَّا بِٱلَّتِى
هِىَ أَحْسَنُ حَتَّىٰ يَبْلُغَ أَشُدَّهُۥ ۚ
وَأَوْفُوا۟ بِٱلْعَهْدِ ۖ إِنَّ
ٱلْعَهْدَ كَانَ مَسْـُٔولًا

35. Give full measure when ye
Measure, and weigh

٣٥ وَأَوْفُوا۟ ٱلْكَيْلَ إِذَا كِلْتُمْ وَزِنُوا۟

2215. Literally, "it is evil as a road (or a way)." Adultery is not only shameful in itself and inconsistent with any self-respect or respect for others, but it opens the road to many evils. It destroys the basis of the family; it works against the interests of children born or to be born; it may cause murders and feuds and loss of reputation and property, and also loosens permanently the bonds of society. Not only should it be avoided as a sin, but any approach or temptation should be avoided.

2216. On the subject of Qiṣāṣ see 2:178 and the notes thereto. Under the strict limitations there laid down, a life may be taken for a life. The heir is given the right to demand the life; but he must not exceed due bounds, because he is helped by the Law. Some Commentators understand "he" in "he is helped (by the Law)" to refer to the heir of the person against whom Qiṣāṣ is sought. He too will be helped by the Law, if the heir of the first slain exceeds the bounds of Law.

2217. *Cf.* 6:152, and other passages relating to orphans, *e.g.*, 2:220. If an orphan's property is touched at all, it should be to improve it, or to give him something better than he had before—never to take a personal advantage for the benefit of the guardian. A bargain that may be quite fair as between two independent persons would be, under this verse, unfair as between a guardian and his orphan ward until the latter attains the full age of understanding.

2218. *Ashuddah* means the age when the orphan reaches his full maturity of strength and understanding, say between the ages of 18 and 30. The age of legal majority may be 18 (as for certain purposes in India) or 21 (as in England). For certain purposes in Muslim law it may be less than 18. In the orphan's interest a much stricter standard is required in his case.

2219. The definite article *al* has here a generic meaning, and is best translated "every".

2220. From the context the engagements referred to would relate to beneficial contracts connected with the orphan's property or promises or undertakings given by the guardian or implied in the terms of his appointment. But the words are general and may be interpreted in the general sense. Note that this sentence does not occur in the similar passage in 6:152, where there was a discussion of social laws: it is appropriate here, where the discussion is about the guardian's personal and individual responsibility in a spiritual sense.

With a balance that is straight:
That is the most fitting
And the most advantageous
In the final determination.[2221]

بِٱلْقِسْطَاسِ ٱلْمُسْتَقِيمِ
ذَٰلِكَ خَيْرٌ وَأَحْسَنُ تَأْوِيلًا

36. And pursue not that
Of which thou hast[2222]
No knowledge; for
Every act of hearing,
Or of seeing,
Or of (feeling in) the heart
Will be enquired into
(On the Day of Reckoning).

٣٦ وَلَا تَقْفُ مَا لَيْسَ لَكَ بِهِۦ عِلْمٌ
إِنَّ ٱلسَّمْعَ وَٱلْبَصَرَ وَٱلْفُؤَادَ كُلُّ
أُولَٰٓئِكَ كَانَ عَنْهُ مَسْـُٔولًا

37. Nor walk on the earth[2223]
With insolence: for thou
Canst not rend the earth
Asunder, nor reach
The mountains in height.

٣٧ وَلَا تَمْشِ فِي ٱلْأَرْضِ مَرَحًا
إِنَّكَ لَن تَخْرِقَ ٱلْأَرْضَ
وَلَن تَبْلُغَ ٱلْجِبَالَ طُولًا

38. Of all such things
The evil is hateful
In the sight of thy Lord.

٣٨ كُلُّ ذَٰلِكَ كَانَ سَيِّئُهُۥ عِندَ رَبِّكَ مَكْرُوهًا

39. These are among the (precepts
Of) wisdom, which thy Lord
Has revealed to thee.[2224]
Take not, with Allah,
Another object of worship,
Lest thou shouldst be thrown

٣٩ ذَٰلِكَ مِمَّآ أَوْحَىٰٓ
إِلَيْكَ رَبُّكَ مِنَ ٱلْحِكْمَةِ
وَلَا تَجْعَلْ مَعَ ٱللَّهِ إِلَٰهًا ءَاخَرَ فَتُلْقَىٰ

2221. Giving just measure and weight is not only right in itself but is ultimately to the best spiritual and material advantage of the person who gives it.

2222. Idle curiosity may lead us to nose into evil, through our ignorance that it is evil. We must guard against every such danger. We must only hear the things that are known to us to be of good report, and see things that are good and instructive and entertain in our hearts feelings or in our minds ideas that we have reason to expect will be spiritually profitable to us. We shall be called to account for the exercise of every faculty that has been given to us. This goes a little farther than a famous sculpture on a Japanese temple in which three monkeys are shown as putting their hands to their ears, eyes, and mouths, respectively, to show that they were not prepared to hear any evil, see any evil, or speak any evil. Here idle curiosity is condemned. Futility is to be avoided even if it does not reach the degree of positive evil.

2223. Insolence, or arrogance, or undue elation at our powers or capacities, is the first step to many evils. Besides, it is unjustified. All our gifts are from Allah.

2224. The moral law, as expounded in 17:23-39 is far in advance of the bare Decalogue in that it searches out motives, and draws pointed attention to the weak and helpless if we are to reach any spiritual understanding of Allah. It begins with a mention of the worship of Allah, the One True God and ends with a similar mention to close the argument, thus emphasizing the fact that the love of Allah embraces the love of man and practical help of our fellow-creatures. (R).

Into Hell, blameworthy and
rejected.[2225]

فِي جَهَنَّمَ مَلُومًا مَّدْحُورًا

40. Has then your Lord,
(O Pagans!) preferred for you
Sons, and taken for Himself
Daughters among the angels?[2226]
Truly ye utter
A most dreadful saying!

أَفَأَصْفَاكُمْ رَبُّكُم بِالْبَنِينَ ﴿٤٠﴾
وَاتَّخَذَ مِنَ الْمَلَائِكَةِ إِنَاثًا
إِنَّكُمْ لَتَقُولُونَ قَوْلًا عَظِيمًا

C. 130.—There is none like unto Allah. Exalted
(17:41-60.)
Beyond measure is He. All Creation
Declares His glory. His revelation
Is Truth, but is beyond comprehension
To those who believe not in the Hereafter.
Those who serve Him should beware
Lest words unseemly should escape them,
Whether to friend or foe. Avoid
Dissensions, and know that Allah's Wrath
When kindled is a terrible thing.
But we rejoice that He forbears and forgives.

SECTION 5.

41. We have explained (things)
In various (ways) in this Qur'ān,
In order that they may receive[2227]
Admonition, but it only increases
Their flight (from the Truth)!

وَلَقَدْ صَرَّفْنَا فِي هَٰذَا الْقُرْآنِ ﴿٤١﴾
لِيَذَّكَّرُوا وَمَا يَزِيدُهُمْ إِلَّا نُفُورًا

42. Say: if there had been
(Other) gods with Him—
As they say—behold,
They would certainly have
Sought out a way
To the Lord of the Throne![2228]

قُل لَّوْ كَانَ مَعَهُ آلِهَةٌ ﴿٤٢﴾
كَمَا يَقُولُونَ إِذًا لَّابْتَغَوْا إِلَىٰ
ذِي الْعَرْشِ سَبِيلًا

2225. "Blameworthy" carries us back by reminiscence to 17:29, between which and this verse there is mention of crimes committed out of covetousness and a selfish disregard of other people's rights. "Rejected" carries back our reminiscence to 17:18, from which to here we have a reference to crimes that lead to deprivation of Allah's grace. The latter is of course wider than the former. Note how subtly the two streams of thought are here conjoined.

2226. *Cf.* 16:57-59. Insistence on true worship means also exclusion of false worship or worship derogatory to Allah. In circles where daughters were despised and even their lives had to be protected by special legislation, what could have been more dreadful than ascribing daughters to Allah?

2227. Things are explained in the Qur'ān from all points of view, individual and national, by means of stories, parables, and figures of speech, and by way of categorical commands. But those who are evil, instead of profiting by such instruction, often go farther and farther away from the Truth.

2228. There is only One True God. But if, as polytheists say, there had been subsidiary gods, they would yet have had to go to the Throne of the Supreme God, for they could have done nothing without Him. Thus the Islamic idea of the unity of the Godhead is quite different from the polytheistic ideas of a supreme god, as in the Greek Pantheon, where Jupiter was often defied by the minor deities! But such ideas are absurd, as stated in the next verse.

43. Glory to Him! He is high
Above all that they say!—
Exalted and Great (beyond
measure)!

٤٣ سُبْحَٰنَهُۥ وَتَعَٰلَىٰ عَمَّا يَقُولُونَ
عُلُوًّا كَبِيرًا

44. The seven heavens and the earth,
And all beings therein,
Declare His glory:
There is not a thing
But celebrates His praise:
And yet ye understand not
How they declare His glory![2229]
Verily He is Oft-Forbearing,
Most Forgiving!

٤٤ تُسَبِّحُ لَهُ ٱلسَّمَٰوَٰتُ ٱلسَّبْعُ وَٱلْأَرْضُ وَمَن فِيهِنَّ
وَإِن مِّن شَىْءٍ إِلَّا يُسَبِّحُ بِحَمْدِهِۦ وَلَٰكِن
لَّا تَفْقَهُونَ تَسْبِيحَهُمْ
إِنَّهُۥ كَانَ حَلِيمًا غَفُورًا

45. When thou dost recite
The Qur'ān, We put,
Between thee and those who
Believe not in the Hereafter,
A veil invisible:[2230]

٤٥ وَإِذَا قَرَأْتَ ٱلْقُرْءَانَ جَعَلْنَا بَيْنَكَ وَبَيْنَ
ٱلَّذِينَ لَا يُؤْمِنُونَ بِٱلْءَاخِرَةِ حِجَابًا مَّسْتُورًا

46. And We put coverings
Over their hearts (and minds)
Lest they should understand
The Qur'ān, and deafness[2231]
Into their ears; when thou
Dost commemorate thy Lord—
And Him alone—in the Qur'ān,
They turn on their backs,
Fleeing (from the Truth).

٤٦ وَجَعَلْنَا عَلَىٰ قُلُوبِهِمْ أَكِنَّةً
أَن يَفْقَهُوهُ وَفِىٓ ءَاذَانِهِمْ وَقْرًا
وَإِذَا ذَكَرْتَ رَبَّكَ فِى ٱلْقُرْءَانِ وَحْدَهُۥ
وَلَّوْا۟ عَلَىٰٓ أَدْبَٰرِهِمْ نُفُورًا

2229. All Creation, animate and inanimate, sings Allah's praises and celebrates His glory—animate, with consciousness, and inanimate, in the evidence which it furnishes of the unity and glory of Allah. All Nature bears witness to His power, wisdom, and goodness. It is only "ye" *i.e.*, those who reject the whole trend of your nature and deny Faith simply because ye have been given a limited amount of choice and free will—it is only such as "ye" that understand not what every other creature understands and proclaims with joy and pride. What must be your degradation! And yet Allah bears with you and forgives you! Such is His goodness! (R).

2230. *Veil invisible*: Some Commentators understand *mastūr* here as equivalent to *sātir*: a veil that makes invisible, a thick or dark veil. But I think that the meaning of *mastūr* (in the passive voice) as "hidden or invisible" is more consonant with the whole passage. If all nature, external and within ourselves, declares Allah's glory, those unfortunates who cut themselves off from their better nature are isolated from the true servants of Allah and the revelation of Allah, because (1) they are unfit for being in their company, and (2) because the servants of Allah and the revelation of Allah must be protected from the pain which blasphemy or rebellion must cause to their unsullied nature. The veil is none the less real even though it is invisible. (R).

2231. The invisible veil being put against the ungodly on account of their deliberate rejection of Truth. The result is that their minds are fogged so that they cannot understand and their ears are clogged so that they cannot hear. In other words, the effects of Evil become cumulative in shutting out Allah's grace.

47. We know best why it is
They listen, when they listen[2232]
To thee; and when they
Meet in private conference,
Behold, the wicked say,
"Ye follow none other than
A man bewitched!"

٤٧ نَّحْنُ أَعْلَمُ بِمَا يَسْتَمِعُونَ بِهِۦٓ إِذْ يَسْتَمِعُونَ
إِلَيْكَ وَإِذْ هُمْ نَجْوَىٰٓ إِذْ يَقُولُ ٱلظَّـٰلِمُونَ
إِن تَتَّبِعُونَ إِلَّا رَجُلًا مَّسْحُورًا

48. See what similes they strike
For thee; but they have gone
Astray, and never can they
Find a way.[2233]

٤٨ ٱنظُرْ كَيْفَ ضَرَبُوا۟ لَكَ ٱلْأَمْثَالَ
فَضَلُّوا۟ فَلَا يَسْتَطِيعُونَ سَبِيلًا

49. They say: "What!
When we are reduced
To bones and dust,
Should we really be raised up
(To be) a new creation?"[2234]

٤٩ وَقَالُوٓا۟ أَءِذَا كُنَّا عِظَـٰمًا وَرُفَـٰتًا
أَءِنَّا لَمَبْعُوثُونَ خَلْقًا جَدِيدًا

50. Say: "(Nay!) be ye
Stones or iron,

٥٠ قُلْ كُونُوا۟ حِجَارَةً أَوْ حَدِيدًا

51. "Or created matter
Which, in your minds,
Is hardest (to be raised up)—
(Yet shall ye be raised up)!"
Then will they say:
"Who will cause us
To return?" Say: "He
Who created you first!"
Then will they wag

٥١ أَوْ خَلْقًا مِّمَّا يَكْبُرُ فِى صُدُورِكُمْ ۚ
فَسَيَقُولُونَ مَن يُعِيدُنَا ۖ
قُلِ ٱلَّذِى فَطَرَكُمْ أَوَّلَ مَرَّةٍ ۚ
فَسَيُنْغِضُونَ

2232. See last note. That being so, the only motive for the ungodly to listen to Allah's Truth is to scoff at it instead of to be instructed by it. They may make a show of listening, but when they meet together in private, they show themselves in their true colours. *Cf.* 2:14. They cannot help seeing that there is singular charm and attractiveness in Allah's Word, and that it consoles, helps, and elevates many people who receive it in the right spirit. So they pretend that they are superior to such people and laugh at them for listening to someone who is only under the influence of something which they call magic!

2233. Note that the word used is "Sabīlan" "a way", not "*the* way". In going astray they have lost the way; but never can they find *any* means of getting back to that way, or of justifying themselves or making good their wicked similes.

2234. They do not realise that Allah Who created them once out of nothing can create them again with memories of their past, in order to render to Him an account of how they used or misused the talents and opportunities which they were given. If it is to be a new Creation, what then? Bones and dust or ashes may yet retain something of the personality which was enshrined in them. But even if they were reduced to stones or iron or anything which their minds can conceive of as being most unlike them, yet there is nothing impossible to Allah! He has clearly sent a Message that we shall have to render an account of ourselves, and His Message is necessarily true. (R).

Their heads towards thee,[2235]
And say, "When will
That be?" Say, "Maybe
It will be quite soon!"

إِلَيْكَ رُءُوسَهُمْ وَيَقُولُونَ مَتَىٰ هُوَ
قُلْ عَسَىٰٓ أَن يَكُونَ قَرِيبًا

52. "It will be on a Day
When He will call you,
And ye will answer
(His call) with (words
Of) His praise, and ye[2236]
Will think that ye tarried
But a little while!"[2237]

٥٢ يَوْمَ يَدْعُوكُمْ
فَتَسْتَجِيبُونَ بِحَمْدِهِۦ
وَتَظُنُّونَ إِن لَّبِثْتُمْ إِلَّا قَلِيلًا

Section 6.

53. Say to My servants
That they should (only) say
Those things that are best:[2238]
For Satan doth sow
Dissensions among them:
For Satan is to man
An avowed enemy.

٥٣ وَقُل لِّعِبَادِى يَقُولُوا۟ ٱلَّتِى هِىَ
أَحْسَنُ إِنَّ ٱلشَّيْطَٰنَ يَنزَغُ بَيْنَهُمْ
إِنَّ ٱلشَّيْطَٰنَ كَانَ لِلْإِنسَٰنِ عَدُوًّا مُّبِينًا

54. It is your Lord
That knoweth you best;
If He please, He granteth[2239]

٥٤ رَّبُّكُمْ أَعْلَمُ بِكُمْ إِن يَشَأْ

2235. The sceptic shifts his ground when he is cornered in argument. It is no longer tenable for him to say that it cannot happen or that there is no one who can bring him back to life and memory. He now gets shaky, and says, "Well, when is that going to happen?" The actual time no man can tell. Indeed that event will be on a plane in which there will be no Time. Our relative ideas of time and place will have been completely overthrown, and it will appear to us then, not that it has been postponed too long, but that it has come too soon! See the next verse and note.

2236. It may be that this verse should not be in the inverted commas governed by the verb "say" in the last clause of the last verse. In that case, the answer to the sceptic would be finished in the last verse, and this verse would be a general statement applying also to the righteous, who will rise up celebrating the praises of Allah. But on the whole, I think it is better to take this verse as part of the answer to the sceptic referred to in the last verse.

2237. Whatever may have been your spiritual blindness in this life, the "new creation" will have opened your eyes to the Truth. No one will any longer be in any delusion as regards the Reality of Allah, and will be forced by their new circumstances, to recognise the Truth and sing Allah's praises. And all will be surprised at the seemingly short flight of time since they had their little ephemeral life on this earth. They will now appraise its true worth.

2238. This command refers to two situations. (1) Even to your enemies and the enemies of Allah you should speak fair: who are you to judge others? Judgement belongs to Allah alone, for He knows you (*i.e.*, all mankind) best, and your personal knowledge is at best imperfect. And Satan is always trying to divide mankind. (2) Amongst yourselves, also you should not entertain suspicions, but speak politely according to the best standards of human speech. A false or unkind word may destroy all your efforts at building up unity, because the forces of disruption are more numerous than the forces of unity.

2239. Man should never for a single moment entertain a thought that would imply that he was wiser than Allah. Allah's knowledge is all-embracing. If He grants mercy to some that you consider wicked or punishment to some that you consider righteous, it is your knowledge or your deductions that are at fault, not Allah's righteous Plan. Even Prophets of Allah are not sent to arrange or dispose of men's affairs, but only to teach Allah's Message. How much less can ordinary men presume to judge other men? The *Mashīyah*—Will and Plan of Allah—is above all human wisdom. (R).

You mercy, or if He please,
Punishment: We have not sent
Thee to be a disposer
Of their affairs for them.

يَرْحَمْكُمْ أَوْ إِن يَشَأْ يُعَذِّبْكُمْ
وَمَآ أَرْسَلْنَٰكَ عَلَيْهِمْ وَكِيلًا

55. And it is your Lord
That knoweth best all beings
That are in the heavens[2240]
And on earth: We
Did bestow on some Prophets
More (and other) gifts
Than on others: and We gave
To David (the gift
Of) the Psalms.[2241]

﴿٥٥﴾ وَرَبُّكَ أَعْلَمُ
بِمَن فِى ٱلسَّمَٰوَٰتِ وَٱلْأَرْضِ
وَلَقَدْ فَضَّلْنَا بَعْضَ ٱلنَّبِيِّۦنَ عَلَىٰ بَعْضٍ
وَءَاتَيْنَا دَاوُۥدَ زَبُورًا

56. Say: "Call on those—
Besides Him—whom ye fancy:
They have neither the power
To remove your troubles
From you nor to change them."[2242]

﴿٥٦﴾ قُلِ ٱدْعُوا۟ ٱلَّذِينَ زَعَمْتُم مِّن دُونِهِۦ فَلَا
يَمْلِكُونَ كَشْفَ ٱلضُّرِّ عَنكُمْ وَلَا تَحْوِيلًا

57. Those whom they call upon
Do desire (for themselves) means
Of access to their Lord—
Even those who are nearest:[2243]
They hope for His Mercy
And fear His Wrath:
For the Wrath of thy Lord
Is something to take heed of.

﴿٥٧﴾ أُو۟لَٰٓئِكَ ٱلَّذِينَ يَدْعُونَ
يَبْتَغُونَ إِلَىٰ رَبِّهِمُ ٱلْوَسِيلَةَ أَيُّهُمْ أَقْرَبُ
وَيَرْجُونَ رَحْمَتَهُۥ وَيَخَافُونَ عَذَابَهُۥٓ
إِنَّ عَذَابَ رَبِّكَ كَانَ مَحْذُورًا

2240. Not only are we not to judge other ordinary men and carp at them, we are not to set up false standards for judging the Prophets of Allah. If one was born of the unlearned Arab race, he yet was a mercy to all the worlds. If one spoke to Allah as *Kalīm Allah* or another's life as *Rūḥ Allah* begun with a spiritual miracle; it does not imply superiority. It only means that Allah's wisdom is more profound than we can fathom. (R).

2241. The spiritual gifts with which the prophets came may themselves take diffrent forms, according to the needs of the world and the times in which they lived, as judged by the wisdom of Allah. A striking example here given is the gift of song and music as given to David, but it implies no superiority of David over others. David was given the *Zabūr*, the Psalter or Psalms, intended to be sung for the worship of Allah and the celebration of Allah's praise. For the Book of Psalms, see the last part of n. 669 to 4:163, where exactly the same words are used about David.

2442. Men's suspicions of each or of the prophets have been condemned in the previous verses. We now have the strongest condemnation of all, that of imagining any other being as being equal or in the same category with One True God. Allah has all power: they have no power. They cannot remove men's troubles. They cannot even mitigate or change them so as to afford the least relief. Why indulge in false worship?

2443. Where men or heroes, or prophets or angels are worshipped, the worship is futile: because (1) even if they are good and holy, and ever so near to Allah, yet the nearest of them have need to seek means of access to Allah, and they do seek such means, *viz.*,: the hope of Allah's Grace: (2) though by their very nature it is impossible for us to suppose that they will incur the Wrath of Allah, yet they are but creatures and are subject to the law of personal responsibility.

58. There is not a population
But We shall destroy it
Before the Day of Judgement
Or punish it with
A dreadful Penalty:[2244]
That is written
In the (eternal) Record.

(٥٨) وَإِن مِّن قَرْيَةٍ إِلَّا نَحْنُ مُهْلِكُوهَا
قَبْلَ يَوْمِ ٱلْقِيَٰمَةِ أَوْ مُعَذِّبُوهَا عَذَابًا شَدِيدًا
كَانَ ذَٰلِكَ فِى ٱلْكِتَٰبِ مَسْطُورًا

59. And We refrain from sending
The Signs, only because
The men of former generations
Treated them as false:[2245]
We sent the She-camel[2246]
To the Thamūd to open
Their eyes, but they
Treated her wrongfully:
We only sent the Signs
By way of terror
(And warning from evil).[2247]

(٥٩) وَمَا مَنَعَنَآ أَن نُّرْسِلَ بِٱلْءَايَٰتِ
إِلَّآ أَن كَذَّبَ بِهَا ٱلْأَوَّلُونَ
وَءَاتَيْنَا ثَمُودَ ٱلنَّاقَةَ
مُبْصِرَةً فَظَلَمُوا۟ بِهَا
وَمَا نُرْسِلُ بِٱلْءَايَٰتِ إِلَّا تَخْوِيفًا

60. Behold! We told thee
That thy Lord doth encompass
Mankind round about:[2248]

(٦٠) وَإِذْ قُلْنَا لَكَ إِنَّ رَبَّكَ أَحَاطَ بِٱلنَّاسِ

2244. These verses are a commentary on the last clause of the last verse. "The Wrath of thy Lord is something to take heed of." The godless thoughtlessly challenge Allah's Wrath, but do they realise its nature? Even the best of us must be moved with terror when we think of its consequences, were it not for His unbounded Mercy. Those who deny the Hereafter fail to realise its terrible Portents. They ask for Portents and Miracles now, but do they realise that their coming means destruction and misery to those who reject faith? They will come soon enough. The whole world will be convulsed before the Day of Judgement. The part of the wise is to prepare for it.

2245. Past generations treated Signs and Portents with contempt or rebellion, and brought about their own undoing. It is only Allah's Mercy that gives them Grace for a time and prevents the coming of those Portents and Punishments which would overwhelm them if they were put to their trial at once.

2246. An example is cited from the story of Thamūd. A wonderful she-camel was sent among them as a Portent and a Symbol. In their wickedness they hamstrung her. So instead of her reclaiming them she was a cause of their destruction, as their sin and rebellion were laid bare. For the story of the she-camel and the reference to the passages in which she is mentioned, see n. 1044 to 7:73.

2247. Signs, Miracles, and Portents are sent by Allah as a warning, to strike terror into the hearts of evildoers and reclaim them to the right path. I have discussed Fear as a motive for reclaiming certain kinds of hard hearts, in my note 82 to 2:74. But some hearts are so hard that even this motive does not work. As they have a limited free will given by Allah, they are to that extent free to choose. But when they actually choose evil, Allah in His infinite Mercy delays their punishment and removes the occasion for their immediate self-destruction by withholding the Signs which might make them transgress all the more and compass their total destruction.

2248. The reference may be to 72:28, probably an earlier Makkan revelation. But the argument is independent of time. This verse falls naturally into three divisions. Warnings and Portents and Signs are sent or not sent according to Allah's All-Wise Plan or Mercy and Justice: this is in no wise inconsistent with the apparent freedom given to the wicked: because (1) in any case Allah is all around all His creatures, and His delay as a Sign of Mercy in no way diminishes His power; (2) the Visions of Truth vouchsafed to Prophets of Allah are themselves Signs by which they can warn the ungodly; and (3) sometimes it is more merciful to give them time by not immediately bringing the matter to judgement. (R).

We granted the Vision
Which We showed thee,[2249]
But as a trial for men—
As also the Cursed Tree[2250]
(Mentioned) in the Qur'ān:
We put terror (and warning)
Into them, but it only
Increases their inordinate
transgression!

وَمَا جَعَلْنَا الرُّءْيَا الَّتِي أَرَيْنَاكَ
إِلَّا فِتْنَةً لِّلنَّاسِ وَالشَّجَرَةَ الْمَلْعُونَةَ
فِي الْقُرْءَانِ وَنُخَوِّفُهُمْ
فَمَا يَزِيدُهُمْ إِلَّا طُغْيَانًا كَبِيرًا

C. 131.—Arrogance, jealousy, spite and hatred
(17:61-84.) Were the cause of the fall of Iblīs. Man
Was given pre-eminence above
Much of Allah's Creation, and owes
Higher responsibilities. He should give thanks
For Allah's mercies, and remember
To Day of Account. Not all the scheming
Of Evil will deflect Allah's righteous Plan
To protect His chosen ones. They should pray
Without ceasing, and seek His true Guidance;
For Truth will last, but Falsehood will perish.

SECTION 7.

61. Behold! We said to the angels:[2251]
"Bow down unto Adam":
They bowed down except Iblīs:
He said: "Shall I bow down
To one whom Thou didst create
From clay?"

٦١ وَإِذْ قُلْنَا لِلْمَلَٰٓئِكَةِ اسْجُدُوا لِآدَمَ
فَسَجَدُوٓا إِلَّآ إِبْلِيسَ
قَالَ ءَأَسْجُدُ لِمَنْ خَلَقْتَ طِينًا

62. He said: "Seest Thou? This is
The one whom Thou hast
honoured
Above me! If Thou wilt but
Respite me to the Day
Of Judgement, I will surely
Bring his descendants

٦٢ قَالَ أَرَءَيْتَكَ هَٰذَا الَّذِي
كَرَّمْتَ عَلَيَّ لَئِنْ أَخَّرْتَنِ
إِلَىٰ يَوْمِ الْقِيَٰمَةِ لَأَحْتَنِكَنَّ ذُرِّيَّتَهُ

2249. Some Commentators take this as referring to the *Mi'raj* (17:1) and others to other spiritual visions. Such visions are miracles, and become a stumbling block to unbelievers. They are an encouragement to men of faith. Thus they are "a trial for men".

2250. The tree of *Zaqqūm*, a bitter and pungent tree described as growing at the bottom of Hell, a type of all that is disagreeable. See 37:62-65; 44:43-46; and 56:52. All these are Sūrahs chronologically earlier than this Sūrah. The application of the name to a tree of the myrobalan kind in the region of Jericho is, I think, of post-Quranic date.

It is a trial for wrongdoers. See 37:63 and n. 4073.

2251. *Cf.* 7:11-18, which deals, as is the case here, with the temptation of the individual human soul, while 2:30-38 deals with the collective race of man through Adam. Arrogance, jealousy, spite, and hatred are the ingredients of the story of Iblīs.

Under my sway—
All but a few!"[2252]

إِلَّا قَلِيلًا

63. (Allah) said: "Go thy way;[2253]
If any of them follow thee,
Verily Hell will be
The recompense of you (all)—
An ample recompense.

قَالَ ٱذْهَبْ فَمَن تَبِعَكَ مِنْهُمْ فَإِنَّ جَهَنَّمَ جَزَآؤُكُمْ جَزَآءً مَّوْفُورًا ﴿٦٣﴾

64. "Lead to destruction those
Whom thou canst among
them,[2254]
With thy (seductive) voice,[2255]
Make assaults on them[2256]
With thy cavalry and thy
Infantry; mutually share
With them wealth and
children;[2257]
And make promises to them.
But Satan promises them
Nothing but deceit.[2258]

وَٱسْتَفْزِزْ مَنِ ٱسْتَطَعْتَ مِنْهُم بِصَوْتِكَ وَأَجْلِبْ عَلَيْهِم بِخَيْلِكَ وَرَجِلِكَ وَشَارِكْهُمْ فِى ٱلْأَمْوَٰلِ وَٱلْأَوْلَـٰدِ وَعِدْهُمْ ۚ وَمَا يَعِدُهُمُ ٱلشَّيْطَـٰنُ إِلَّا غُرُورًا ﴿٦٤﴾

65. "As for My servants,[2259]
No authority shalt thou
Have over them."
Enough is thy Lord
For a Disposer of affairs.[2260]

إِنَّ عِبَادِى لَيْسَ لَكَ عَلَيْهِمْ سُلْطَـٰنٌ ۚ وَكَفَىٰ بِرَبِّكَ وَكِيلًا ﴿٦٥﴾

66. Your Lord is He
That maketh the Ship

رَّبُّكُمُ ٱلَّذِى يُزْجِى لَكُمُ ٱلْفُلْكَ ﴿٦٦﴾

2252. The power of Evil over man is due to man's limited free will. In other words man hands himself to Evil. As to those who loyally worship and serve Allah, Evil has no power over them. This is expressly mentioned in verse 65 below, and in other places.

2253. The power of Evil is summarily dismissed, but not without a clear warning. "Do thy worst: if any of them misuse their limited free will and deliberately follow thee, they must take the consequences with thee: all of you must answer according to your personal responsibility."

2254. "Do thy worst; but ye are both warned that that path leads to destruction."

2255. Evil has many snares for mankind. The one that is put in the foreground is the voice—the seductive personal appeal, that "makes the worse appear the better part".

2256. The forcible assault of Evil is next mentioned under the metaphor of cavalry and infantry. It is when cajolery and tempting fair-seeming seem to fail that an attack is made in force with weapons of violence of all kinds, like the different arms in an organised army.

2257. If the first assaults are resisted, Evil has other weapons in its armoury. Tangible fruits are dangled before the eyes, ill-gotten gains and children of sin, that follow from certain very alluring methods of indulgence in passion. Or it may be children dedicated to sin or worldly gains, etc. And then there are all kinds of promises for the future.

2258. This is a parenthetical clause inserted to show up what the promises of the Evil One are worth.

2259. This verse should be read along with the two preceding ones to complete their meaning. Evil has no power except over those who yield to its solicitations.

2260. As Evil has no authority over the sincere servants of Allah, they should put their trust completely in Him. For He is All-Sufficient to carry out their affairs, and by His grace, to save them from all harm and danger.

Go smoothly for you
Through the sea, in order that
Ye may seek of His Bounty.[2261]
For He is unto you
Most Merciful.

فِي ٱلۡبَحۡرِ لِتَبۡتَغُواْ مِن فَضۡلِهِۦٓۚ
إِنَّهُۥ كَانَ بِكُمۡ رَحِيمٗا

67. When distress seizes you
At sea, those that ye
Call upon—besides Himself—
Leave you in the lurch!
But when He brings you back
Safe to land, ye turn
Away (from Him), Most
ungrateful[2262]
Is man!

﴿٦٧﴾ وَإِذَا مَسَّكُمُ ٱلضُّرُّ فِي ٱلۡبَحۡرِ
ضَلَّ مَن تَدۡعُونَ إِلَّآ إِيَّاهُۖ
فَلَمَّا نَجَّىٰكُمۡ إِلَى ٱلۡبَرِّ أَعۡرَضۡتُمۡۚ
وَكَانَ ٱلۡإِنسَٰنُ كَفُورًا

68. Do ye then feel secure
That He will not cause you
To be swallowed up
Beneath the earth[2263]
When ye are on land,
Or that He will not send
Against you a violent tornado
(With showers of stones)
So that ye shall find
No one to carry out
Your affairs for you?

﴿٦٨﴾ أَفَأَمِنتُمۡ أَن يَخۡسِفَ
بِكُمۡ جَانِبَ ٱلۡبَرِّ
أَوۡ يُرۡسِلَ
عَلَيۡكُمۡ حَاصِبٗا
ثُمَّ لَا تَجِدُواْ لَكُمۡ وَكِيلًا

69. Or do ye feel secure
That He will not send you
Back a second time
To sea and send against you
A heavy gale to drown you
Because of your ingratitude,[2264]
So that ye find no helper
Therein against Us?

﴿٦٩﴾ أَمۡ أَمِنتُمۡ أَن يُعِيدَكُمۡ فِيهِ تَارَةً أُخۡرَىٰ
فَيُرۡسِلَ عَلَيۡكُمۡ قَاصِفٗا مِّنَ ٱلرِّيحِ
فَيُغۡرِقَكُم بِمَا كَفَرۡتُمۡ
ثُمَّ لَا تَجِدُواْ لَكُمۡ عَلَيۡنَا بِهِۦ تَبِيعٗا

2261. This illustration of the sea, and the skill with which, by Allah's grace, men pass through it with ease in order to earn material gains by commerce, social gains by human intercourse, and spiritual gains by knowledge, is frequently used to enforce Allah's goodness to man. *Cf.* 2:164.

2262. Against Allah's gracious gifts and mercies is contrasted man's ingratitude. In danger he remembers Allah, the One True God, but relapses into his own fancies when the danger is past., *Cf.* also 10:22-23. (R).

2263. Man is safe neither on land nor at sea except by the grace and mercy of Allah. How forcibly this is brought home to us by the Quetta earthquake of 31st May 1935, when tens of thousands of men, women, and children, perished in a few moments, by night, buried in debris! The stories of violent destructive tornadoes in such areas as the southern United States are equally impressive. The destruction is so sudden that the victims have no time to arrange anything. They are simply wiped out.

2264. If a man flees from the Wrath of Allah, there is no place secure for him. He may flee from sea to land, and back again from land to sea. But his life depends on the Disposer of all affairs. He may go again and again to sea, and perhaps finally end by being drowned.

70. We have honoured the sons
Of Adam; provided them
With transport on land and sea;
Given them for sustenance things
Good and pure; and conferred
On them special favours,
Above a great part
Of Our Creation.[2265]

۞ وَلَقَدْ كَرَّمْنَا بَنِيٓ ءَادَمَ وَحَمَلْنَٰهُمْ فِى ٱلْبَرِّ وَٱلْبَحْرِ وَرَزَقْنَٰهُم مِّنَ ٱلطَّيِّبَٰتِ وَفَضَّلْنَٰهُمْ عَلَىٰ كَثِيرٍ مِّمَّنْ خَلَقْنَا تَفْضِيلًا ﴿٧٠﴾

SECTION 8.

71. One day We shall call
Together all human beings
With their (respective) Imāms:[2266]
Those who are given their record
In their right hand
Will read it (with pleasure),
And they will not be
Dealt with unjustly
In the least.[2267]

يَوْمَ نَدْعُوا۟ كُلَّ أُنَاسٍۭ بِإِمَٰمِهِمْ ۖ فَمَنْ أُوتِىَ كِتَٰبَهُۥ بِيَمِينِهِۦ فَأُو۟لَٰٓئِكَ يَقْرَءُونَ كِتَٰبَهُمْ وَلَا يُظْلَمُونَ فَتِيلًا ﴿٧١﴾

72. But those who were blind
In this world, will be
Blind in the Hereafter,[2268]
And most astray
From the Path.

وَمَن كَانَ فِى هَٰذِهِۦٓ أَعْمَىٰ فَهُوَ فِى ٱلْءَاخِرَةِ أَعْمَىٰ وَأَضَلُّ سَبِيلًا ﴿٧٢﴾

73. And their purpose was
To tempt thee away
From that which We
Had revealed unto thee,
To substitute in Our name

وَإِن كَادُوا۟ لَيَفْتِنُونَكَ عَنِ ٱلَّذِىٓ أَوْحَيْنَآ إِلَيْكَ لِتَفْتَرِىَ عَلَيْنَا ﴿٧٣﴾

2265. The distinction and honour conferred by Allah on man are recounted in order to enforce the corresponding duties and responsibilities of man. He is raised to a position of honour above the brute creation: he has been granted talents by which he can transport himself from place to place by land, sea, and now by air: all the means of the sustenance and growth of every part of his nature are provided by Allah, and his spiritual faculties (the greatest gift of Allah) raise him above the greater part of Allah's Creation. Should he not then realise his noble destiny and prepare for the real life in the Hereafter?

2266. I have discussed various meanings of *Imām* in 2:124, n. 1244. What is the meaning here? The Commentators are divided. Some understand the meaning to be that each People or Group will appear with its Leader, who will bear witness to its virtues or sins: *Cf.* 16:84. Another view is that the *Imām* is their revelation, their Book. A third is that the *Imām* is the record of deeds spoken of in the next clause. I prefer the first.

2267. Literally, by the value of a *fatīl*. a small skin in the cleft of a date stone: this has no value.

2268. On the Judgement Day the children of light will receive and peruse their record, and will render joyful thanks to Allah for His Mercies. What of the children of darkness? They had already been blind in this world's life, and they will not receive the light of Allah's Countenance then. On the contrary they will find that the longer the time they have travelled, the farther away they have gone from the Path. Notice the association of ideas—blindness, not seeing the light, going farther and farther away from the Path.

Something quite different:[2269]
(In that case), behold!
They would certainly have
Made thee (their) friend!

غَيْرَهُۥ
وَإِذًا لَّٱتَّخَذُوكَ خَلِيلًا

74. And had We not
Given thee strength
Thou wouldst nearly
Have inclined to them[2270]
A little.

وَلَوْلَآ أَن ثَبَّتْنَٰكَ لَقَدْ كِدتَّ ٧٤
تَرْكَنُ إِلَيْهِمْ شَيْـًٔا قَلِيلًا

75. In that case We should
Have made thee taste
An equal portion (of punishment)
In this life, and an equal
portion[2271]
In death: and moreover
Thou wouldst have found
None to help thee against Us![2272]

إِذًا لَّأَذَقْنَٰكَ ضِعْفَ ٧٥
ٱلْحَيَوٰةِ وَضِعْفَ ٱلْمَمَاتِ
ثُمَّ لَا تَجِدُ لَكَ عَلَيْنَا نَصِيرًا

76. Their purpose was to scare
Thee off the land,[2273]
In order to expel thee:
But in that case they
Would not have stayed
(Therein) after thee,
Except for a little while.

وَإِن كَادُوا۟ لَيَسْتَفِزُّونَكَ ٧٦
مِنَ ٱلْأَرْضِ لِيُخْرِجُوكَ مِنْهَا
وَإِذًا لَّا يَلْبَثُونَ خِلَٰفَكَ إِلَّا قَلِيلًا

77. (This was Our) way
With the messengers We sent

سُنَّةَ مَن قَدْ أَرْسَلْنَا قَبْلَكَ مِن رُّسُلِنَا ٧٧

2269. It happens with men of Allah, and it happened with the Holy Prophet, that they are tempted by the world with many things which appeal to the world generally, if they would make some small concession in their favour. The "small concession" may hold the key of the position, and neutralise the whole teaching sent by Allah. If the Prophet had accepted wealth and position among the Quraysh and "only respected" their idols! The Quraysh would have taken him into their inner circle! A dishonest liar like Musaylama would have jumped at the opportunity and been hailed as a friend and associate and made much of. But Prophets of Allah are made of sterner stuff. They are given special strength to resist all plausible deception. (R).

2270. From a purely human point of view it may seem policy to make a small "concession" to men's weakness in order to fulfil a divine mission. But the divine Messenger is given special strength to resist such temptations.

2271. If such a thing was possible for a true Messenger of Allah, *viz.*: a compromise with evil and a dereliction of his mission, he would be no exception to the law of personal responsibility. Indeed, as the power and the responsibility were greater, the punishment would have been greater too. It would have been double—an exposure in this life and the usual punishment in or after death for a desertion of the Truth.

2272. The motive held out by the world for a compromise with Truth is itself fallacious. The motive is that the compromise may bring influence, position, and opportunity, if not wealth and the other good things of life. But these in themselves (if attained) would not be of use or help if pitted against the command of Allah.

2273. As happened in the case of the Holy Prophet, the enemies try to frighten the Prophet of Allah away from their midst, so that, once away, they could expel him and keep him out. But they are counting without the Plan of Allah. If they persecute the righteous, they dig their own graves! (R).

Before thee: thou wilt find
No change in Our ways.[2274]

وَلَا تَجِدُ لِسُنَّتِنَا تَحْوِيلًا

SECTION 9.

78. Establish regular prayers—[2275]
At the sun's decline
Till the darkness of the night,
And the morning prayer
And reading: for the prayer
And reading in the morning
Carry their testimony.[2276]

٧٨ أَقِمِ ٱلصَّلَوٰةَ لِدُلُوكِ ٱلشَّمْسِ
إِلَىٰ غَسَقِ ٱلَّيْلِ وَقُرْءَانَ ٱلْفَجْرِ
إِنَّ قُرْءَانَ ٱلْفَجْرِ كَانَ مَشْهُودًا

79. And pray in the small watches
Of the morning: (it would be)[2277]
An additional prayer
(Or spiritual profit)
For thee: soon will thy Lord
Raise thee to a Station
Of Praise and Glory![2278]

٧٩ وَمِنَ ٱلَّيْلِ فَتَهَجَّدْ بِهِۦ
نَافِلَةً لَّكَ عَسَىٰٓ أَن يَبْعَثَكَ رَبُّكَ
مَقَامًا مَّحْمُودًا

80. Say: "O my Lord!
Let my entry be[2279]
By the Gate of Truth

٨٠ وَقُل رَّبِّ أَدْخِلْنِى مُدْخَلَ صِدْقٍ

2274. This was no new thing in history. Allah protects His own, and the ungodly cannot long enjoy the fruits of their unrighteousness even if their punishment be delayed a little while.

2275. The Commentators understand here the command for the five daily canonical prayers, *viz.*: the four from the declination of the sun from the zenith to the fullest darkness of the night, and the early morning prayers, Fajr, which is usually accompanied by a reading of the Holy Qur'ān. The four afternoon prayers are: Zuhr, immediately after the sun begins to decline in the afternoon; 'Aṣr, in the late afternoon; Maghrib, immediately after sunset; and Ishā, after the glow of sunset has disappeared and the full darkness of the night has set in. There is difference of opinion as to the meaning of particular words and phrases, but none as to the general effect of this passage.

2276. The morning prayer is specially singled out for separate mention, because the morning is a "Holy hour" and special spiritual influences act on the soul awaking from the night's rest. Special testimony is borne to the prayers of this hour by the angelic host.

2277. This was held to be addressed specially to the Holy Prophet who usually prayed more than the five canonical prayers. The *Tahajjud* was a prayer after midnight in the small watches of the morning.

2278. To the Prophet was to be assigned in the Hereafter the highest Post of Honour and Glory—the *Maqām Maḥmūd* implying his excellence above all other Prophets. The immediate reference may be to the hope that the Makkan persecution will soon be over and the glorious work in Madīnah will begin. (R).

2279. The entry and exit here referred to may be interpreted in four senses: (1) entry into death and exit at the resurrection for the righteous, who have purified their souls by prayer (last verse) and spiritual teaching from the Qur'ān (next verse), there is on each occasion a fuller and fuller realisation and enjoyment of truth and honour: for those who are estranged from Allah, the effect is the opposite: the truth becomes bitter and there is ignominy and exposure instead of honour; (2) entry for the Holy Prophet into the new life at Madīnah, which was still in the womb of futurity, and exit from the life of persecution and the milieu of falsehood, which surrounded him in his native city of Makkah still given up to idolatry; (3) referring to the impending Hijrah again, the prayer may mean, "Let it be from pure motives of truth and spiritual honour, and not from motives of anger against the city of Makkah or its persecutors, or of ambition or worldly power from the city of Madīnah, which was ready to lay everything at the Prophet's feet": (4) generally, entry and exit at every stage of life.

And Honour, and likewise
My exit by the Gate
Of Truth and Honour;
And grant me
From Thy Presence
An authority to aid (me)."2280

وَأَخْرِجْنِي مُخْرَجَ صِدْقٍ
وَاجْعَل لِّي مِن لَّدُنكَ
سُلْطَٰنًا نَّصِيرًا

81. And say: "Truth has (now)
Arrived, and Falsehood perished:
For Falsehood is (by its nature)
Bound to perish,"2281

٨١ وَقُلْ جَآءَ ٱلْحَقُّ وَزَهَقَ ٱلْبَٰطِلُ
إِنَّ ٱلْبَٰطِلَ كَانَ زَهُوقًا

82. We send down (stage by stage)
In the Qur'ān that which
Is a healing and a mercy
To those who believe:
To the unjust it causes
Nothing but loss after loss.2282

٨٢ وَنُنَزِّلُ مِنَ ٱلْقُرْءَانِ
مَا هُوَ شِفَآءٌ وَرَحْمَةٌ لِّلْمُؤْمِنِينَ
وَلَا يَزِيدُ ٱلظَّٰلِمِينَ إِلَّا خَسَارًا

83. Yet when We bestow
Our favours on man,
He turns away and becomes
Remote on his side (instead
Of coming to Us), and when
Evil siezes him he
Gives himself up to despair!2283

٨٣ وَإِذَآ أَنْعَمْنَا عَلَى ٱلْإِنسَٰنِ
أَعْرَضَ وَنَـَٔا بِجَانِبِهِۦ
وَإِذَا مَسَّهُ ٱلشَّرُّ كَانَ يَـُٔوسًا

84. Say: "Everyone acts
According to his own disposition:
But your Lord knows best
Who it is that is
Best guided on the Way."2284

٨٤ قُلْ كُلٌّ يَعْمَلُ عَلَىٰ شَاكِلَتِهِۦ
فَرَبُّكُمْ أَعْلَمُ بِمَنْ هُوَ أَهْدَىٰ سَبِيلًا

C. 132.—Who can define the Spirit of Inspiration?
(17:85-111.) Its gift is the highest of Allah's Mercies

2280. All prayer must be for Allah's aid and authority. However much we may plan, our success must depend on His aid. However nobler our motives, we have no right to imperil any lives unless there is authority in the Word of Allah. The Prophet only acts on Allah's commission and inspiration.

2281. From its nature falsehood must perish: for it is the opposite of Truth, and Truth must ever prevail.

2282. In Allah's revelation there is healing for our broken spirits, hope for our spiritual future, and joy in the forgiveness of our sins. All who work in faith will share in these privileges. It is only the rebels against Allah's Law who will suffer loss. The more they will oppose Truth, the deeper down will they go into the mire—the state of sin and Wrath, which is worse than destruction.

2283. Truth saves us from two extremes: when we are happy, we are saved from being puffed up, for we realise that everything comes from Allah; and when we suffer misfortunes, we are not in despair, for we know that Allah is our sure refuge and help.

2284. If the wicked go their own ways, there is nothing to discourage us. It is their nature. We must seek and hold fast to true guidance.

To man. The Qur'ān is divine, and no carpings
Can affect its greatness or the greatness
Of the Messenger who brought it to men.
Those who reject it will be called
To account on the Day of Judgment. Let not
Pride and Ignorance rush, like Pharaoh,
To the Punishment of the Hereafter.
The Qur'ān as revealed by stages teaches
The Truth: learn it and chant it, and praise
The Beautiful Names of Allah forever!

SECTION 10.

85. They ask thee concerning
The Spirit (of inspiration).[2285]
Say: "The Spirit (cometh)
By command of my Lord:
Of knowledge it is only
A little that is communicated
To you, (O men!)"

وَيَسْـَٔلُونَكَ عَنِ ٱلرُّوحِ ۖ ٨٥
قُلِ ٱلرُّوحُ مِنْ أَمْرِ رَبِّى
وَمَآ أُوتِيتُم مِّنَ ٱلْعِلْمِ إِلَّا قَلِيلًا

86. If it were Our Will,
We could take away
That which We have
Sent thee by inspiration:[2286]
Then wouldst thou find
None to plead thy affair
In that matter as against Us—

وَلَئِن شِئْنَا لَنَذْهَبَنَّ ٨٦
بِٱلَّذِىٓ أَوْحَيْنَآ إِلَيْكَ
ثُمَّ لَا تَجِدُ لَكَ بِهِۦ عَلَيْنَا وَكِيلًا

87. Except for Mercy from thy
Lord:[2287]
For His Bounty is
To thee (indeed) great.

إِلَّا رَحْمَةً مِّن رَّبِّكَ ۚ ٨٧
إِنَّ فَضْلَهُۥ كَانَ عَلَيْكَ كَبِيرًا

88. Say: 'If the whole
Of mankind and Jinns[2288]

قُل لَّئِنِ ٱجْتَمَعَتِ ٱلْإِنسُ وَٱلْجِنُّ ٨٨

2285. What is the nature of inspiration? Who brings it? Can it ask its Bringer questions? Can we ask anything which we wish? These are the sort of questions always asked when inspiration is called in question. The answer is given here. Inspiration is one of those high spiritual mysteries which cannot be explained in the terms of everyday human experience. It is spiritual. The Spirit (Gabriel) does not come of his own will. He comes by the command of Allah, and reveals what Allah commands him to reveal. Of the sum total of true spiritual knowledge what a small part it is that ordinary mortals can understand! They can be only given that which they can understand, however dimly. We are not in a position to ask anything that we wish. If we did so, it would only make us look foolish, for the guidance comes from Allah's Wisdom, not from our worldly knowledge.

2286. Even the spiritual knowledge that comes to us comes because of the favour and mercy of Allah. If He were to withhold it, who can call Him in question?

2287. In that case the only one who can plead for us is the Mercy of Allah. We can interpret the phrase in its widest abstract sense, as well as in the concrete sense of the title which is applied to the Holy Prophet Muḥammad, the Mercy of Allah. Thus we come from the abstract question to the concrete question of the Qur'ān, which is referred to by name in the verses that follow.

2288. For the meaning of "Jinns", see n. 929 to 6:100.

Were to gather together
To produce the like
Of this Qur'ān they
Could not produce
The like thereof, even if
They backed up each other
With help and support.[2289]

عَلَىٰٓ أَن يَأْتُوا۟ بِمِثْلِ هَٰذَا ٱلْقُرْءَانِ
لَا يَأْتُونَ بِمِثْلِهِۦ وَلَوْ كَانَ
بَعْضُهُمْ لِبَعْضٍ ظَهِيرًا

89. And We have explained
To man, in this Qur'ān,
Every kind of similitude:[2290]
Yet the greater part of men
Refuse (to receive it)
Except with ingratitude![2291]

٨٩ وَلَقَدْ صَرَّفْنَا لِلنَّاسِ فِى هَٰذَا ٱلْقُرْءَانِ
مِن كُلِّ مَثَلٍ فَأَبَىٰٓ أَكْثَرُ ٱلنَّاسِ
إِلَّا كُفُورًا

90. They say: 'We shall not
Believe in thee, until thou
Cause a spring to gush
Forth for us from the earth,[2292]

٩٠ وَقَالُوا۟ لَن نُّؤْمِنَ لَكَ
حَتَّىٰ تَفْجُرَ لَنَا مِنَ ٱلْأَرْضِ يَنۢبُوعًا

91. 'Or (until) thou hast
A garden of date trees
And vines, and causest rivers
To gush forth in their midst,
Carrying abundant water,[2293]

٩١ أَوْ تَكُونَ لَكَ جَنَّةٌ مِّن نَّخِيلٍ وَعِنَبٍ
فَتُفَجِّرَ ٱلْأَنْهَٰرَ خِلَٰلَهَا تَفْجِيرًا

92. 'Or thou causest the sky
To fall in pieces, as thou

٩٢ أَوْ تُسْقِطَ ٱلسَّمَآءَ كَمَا

2289. The proof of the Qur'ān is in its own beauty and nature, and the circumstances in which it was promulgated. The world is challenged to produce a Book like it and has not produced one. It is the only revealed Book whose text stands pure and uncorrupted today. *Cf.*, for a similar challenge, 2:23, 10:38, and 11:15.

2290. In the Qur'ān everything is explained in detail from various points of view, by commands, similitudes, examples, stories, parables, etc. It does not merely narrate stories or lay down vague abstract propositions. It gives very detailed help in outward and inner life.

2291. One form in which it can be received with ingratitude is to pay verbal tribute to it but not study it as it ought to be studied (2:121 *ḥaqqah tilāwatihi),* or to disobey its precepts or standards.

2292. *Cf.* 2:60.

2293. This ill-assorted and crude jumble of the sort of miracles which the Unbelievers wanted is in very appropriate contrast to the sober and reasoned argument which is begun in the last sentence of verse 93 and continued in sections 11 and 12, which close this Sūrah. It is throughout reminiscent of the materialistic imagination of the Jewish sceptics, which was mainly responsible for the fall of the Jewish nation (see verse 104 below). For a thirsty people sojourning in a dry land, the finding of a spring of water as in the story of Moses or of the well of Zamzam is an appropriate miracle. But miracles are not for the faithless crowds to gape at. A beautiful well-watered Garden is a symbol of Felicity; but a sceptic cannot order Allah to produce it for his pleasure. The same may be said about a house adorned with gold, except that its symbolism is even more materialistic. The fall of the sky or producing Allah face to face or climbing to the skies by a ladder, or bringing down a book of parchment which men could handle, are all irreverent suggestions that make no distinction between spiritual and material things.

Sayest (will happen), against us,[2294]
Or thou bring Allah
And the angels before (us)
Face to face;[2295]

زَعَمْتَ عَلَيْنَا كِسَفًا
أَوْ تَأْتِيَ بِاللَّهِ وَالْمَلَٰٓئِكَةِ قَبِيلًا

93. "Or thou have a house
Adorned with gold,
Or thou mount a ladder
Right into the skies.[2296]
No, we shall not even believe
In thy mounting until thou
Send down to us a book
That we can read."[2297]
Say: "Glory to my Lord!
Am I aught but a man—
A messenger?"[2298]

٩٣ أَوْ يَكُونَ لَكَ بَيْتٌ
مِّن زُخْرُفٍ أَوْ تَرْقَىٰ فِي السَّمَآءِ
وَلَن نُّؤْمِنَ لِرُقِيِّكَ حَتَّىٰ
تُنَزِّلَ عَلَيْنَا كِتَٰبًا نَّقْرَؤُهُۥ
قُلْ سُبْحَانَ رَبِّي هَلْ كُنتُ إِلَّا بَشَرًا رَّسُولًا

SECTION 11.

94. What kept men back
From Belief when Guidance
Came to them, was nothing
But this: they said.
"Has Allah sent a man[2299]
(Like us) to be (His) Messenger?"

٩٤ وَمَا مَنَعَ النَّاسَ أَن يُؤْمِنُوٓا۟
إِذْ جَآءَهُمُ الْهُدَىٰٓ إِلَّآ أَن قَالُوٓا۟
أَبَعَثَ اللَّهُ بَشَرًا رَّسُولًا

95. Say, "If there were settled,
On earth, angels walking about[2300]

٩٥ قُل لَّوْ كَانَ
فِي الْأَرْضِ مَلَٰٓئِكَةٌ يَمْشُونَ

2294. Contrast the sublime passages with 82:1, or that in 25:25, where the final breaking up of the firmaments as we know is referred to in the world's catastrophe, with the ridiculous demand that it should be done for the sport of the sceptics!

2295. *Cf.* 2:55 and 4:153 about the desire of the Israelites to see Allah face to face; and 6:8-9, about angels coming down to convince men.

2296. *Cf.* 6:35 about the ladder in the skies.

2297. *Cf.* 6:7 for the foolish idea of materialistic sceptics that a spiritual revelation could come down from the heavens on a piece of parchment that they can touch.

2298. A prophet or messenger of Allah is a man at the command of Allah, and not to satisfy the disingenuous whims and fancies of Unbelievers. Miracles greater than any that their foolish fancies could devise were before them. The Qur'ān was such a miracle, and it is a standing miracle that lasts through the ages. Why did they not believe? The real reason was spite and jealousy like that of Iblīs. See next verse.

2299. When a man is raised to honour and dignity, his brothers rejoice, for it is an honour that reflects its glory on them. But those with evil in their hearts are jealous like their prototype Iblīs, (17:61, n. 2251). To such men the mere fact that their own brother receives the grace of Allah is enough to turn them against that brother. Any other reasons they may devise are mere make-believe.

2300. The argument is that if the angels inhabited this earth, an angel from heaven could be sent down as a messenger to them, as they could mutually understand each other, and the Message of Allah could be explained without difficulty. But the earth is inhabited by men, and the men themselves are divided into races, or groups, or nations. To each group is sent a prophet from among their brethren: to 'Ād. *their brother* Hūd (11:50); to Thamūd, *their brother* Ṣāliḥ (11:61); and so on. As a matter of fact, with wicked men, constituted as they are, the appearance of an angel causes disturbance and an unseemly riot, as in the case of the angels that came to Lot (11:77-80). In any case they cannot carry out an effective mission among men (6:8-9).

In peace and quiet, We should
Certainly have sent them
Down from the heavens
An angel for a messenger."

مُطْمَئِنِّينَ لَنَزَّلْنَا عَلَيْهِم
مِّنَ ٱلسَّمَآءِ مَلَكًا رَّسُولًا

96. Say: "Enough is Allah
For a witness between me[2301]
And you: for He is
Well-acquainted with His servants,
And He sees (all things)."

٩٦ قُلْ كَفَىٰ بِٱللَّهِ شَهِيدًۢا بَيْنِى
وَبَيْنَكُمْ ۚ إِنَّهُۥ كَانَ بِعِبَادِهِۦ خَبِيرًۢا بَصِيرًا

97. It is he whom Allah guides,
That is on true guidance;
But he whom He leaves
Astray—for such wilt thou
Find no protector besides Him.[2302]
On the Day of Judgement
We shall gather them together,
Prone on their faces,
Blind, dumb, and deaf:
Their abode will be Hell:
Every time it shows abatement,
We shall increase for them
The fierceness of the Fire.[2303]

٩٧ وَمَن يَهْدِ ٱللَّهُ فَهُوَ ٱلْمُهْتَدِ ۖ
وَمَن يُضْلِلْ فَلَن تَجِدَ لَهُمْ أَوْلِيَآءَ مِن دُونِهِۦ ۖ
وَنَحْشُرُهُمْ يَوْمَ ٱلْقِيَٰمَةِ عَلَىٰ وُجُوهِهِمْ
عُمْيًا وَبُكْمًا وَصُمًّا ۖ
مَّأْوَىٰهُمْ جَهَنَّمُ ۖ
كُلَّمَا خَبَتْ زِدْنَٰهُمْ سَعِيرًا

98. That is their recompense,
Because they rejected Our Signs.
And said, "When we are reduced
To bones and broken dust,
Should we really be raised up
(To be) a new Creation?"[2304]

٩٨ ذَٰلِكَ جَزَآؤُهُم بِأَنَّهُمْ كَفَرُوا۟ بِـَٔايَٰتِنَا
وَقَالُوٓا۟ أَءِذَا كُنَّا عِظَٰمًا وَرُفَٰتًا
أَءِنَّا لَمَبْعُوثُونَ خَلْقًا جَدِيدًا

2301. 'If you want a real witness, it is not these sorts of fancy miracles, but the witness of the true ever-living God. Purify your hearts, and ask Him in true contrition and repentance, and He will guide you and show you the Way.' (R).

2302. 'All your insincere subtleties are of no use. The only real guidance is the guidance of Allah. If you do not seek His grace, you will be lost. Besides Him, there is no true friend or protector.'

2303. 'If you still persist in your evil ways, what is to be your evil end? You will become more and more identified with the company of Evil. You will come to shame and ignominy, like men thrown down prone on their faces. You will lose the use of all the faculties of judgement with which Allah had endowed you. Instead of seeing, you will be blind to Allah's Signs. Instead of having the power of seeking Him in prayer and rejoicing in His grace, you will be dumb. Instead of hearing the harmony and music of the spheres, as typified in the pure and harmonious lives of men, you will hear nothing or only hear dull or confused sounds like deaf men. The scorching fire of your punishment will not grow less, but grow more fierce as you go deeper into Hell.'

2304. This phrase is repeated from 17:49. The reminiscence rounds off the argument. After certain moral precepts to which Faith was linked, we have had a discussion of unfaith. Its various motives have been analysed, and its penalties have been allegorically shadowed forth. After this, the example of Pharaoh is held as a type of unfaith in the next section, and the Sūrah closed with an exhortation to faith and a declaration of the glory of Allah.

99. See they not that Allah,
Who created the heavens
And the earth, has power
To create the like of them[2305]
(Anew)? Only He has
Decreed a term appointed,
Of which there is no doubt.
But the unjust refuse
(To receive it) except
With ingratitude.[2306]

٩٩ أَوَلَمْ يَرَوْا أَنَّ اللَّهَ
الَّذِي خَلَقَ السَّمَٰوَٰتِ وَالْأَرْضَ
قَادِرٌ عَلَىٰٓ أَن يَخْلُقَ مِثْلَهُمْ
وَجَعَلَ لَهُمْ أَجَلًا لَّا رَيْبَ فِيهِ
فَأَبَى الظَّٰلِمُونَ إِلَّا كُفُورًا

100. Say: "If ye had
Control of the Treasures
Of the Mercy of my Lord,
Behold, ye would keep them
Back, for fear of spending
Them: for man
Is (ever) niggardly!"[2307]

١٠٠ قُل لَّوْ أَنتُمْ تَمْلِكُونَ خَزَآئِنَ
رَحْمَةِ رَبِّيٓ إِذًا لَّأَمْسَكْتُمْ خَشْيَةَ الْإِنفَاقِ ۚ
وَكَانَ الْإِنسَٰنُ قَتُورًا

SECTION 12

101. To Moses We did give
Nine Clear Signs:[2308]
Ask the Children of Israel:
When he came to them,[2309]
Pharaoh said to him:
"O Moses! I consider thee,

١٠١ وَلَقَدْ ءَاتَيْنَا مُوسَىٰ تِسْعَ ءَايَٰتٍۭ بَيِّنَٰتٍ ۖ
فَسْـَٔلْ بَنِيٓ إِسْرَٰٓءِيلَ إِذْ جَآءَهُمْ
فَقَالَ لَهُۥ فِرْعَوْنُ إِنِّي لَأَظُنُّكَ يَٰمُوسَىٰ

2305. Allah. Who created all that is in the heavens and on earth, has surely the power to receive the life of individual souls after their bodies have perished—and revive them with memories of their past life and for a continuation of their spiritual history. Only He has fixed a term for each stage of our existence, which we can neither prolong nor shorten.

2306. This phrase carries us back to 17:89. after we began the argument about the real motives for the rejection of the Qur'ān by sceptics. That argument is now closed in a sort of minor circle within the major circle sketched in n. 2304 above.

2307. A fresh argument is now addressed to those who confine Allah's revelations to a limited circle of men, such as they themselves belonged to. The reference was to the Jews, who could not understand how any Gentiles could receive revelations and guidance even superior to what they considered their own birthrigtht. But the tendancy is widespread in the human race. A particular race, or caste, or a particular kind of culture, claims to be the custodian of Allah's Message, whereas it is universal. Allah's Mercy is universal, and He scatters the priceless Treasures of His Mercy broadcast among His creatures. They are not exhausted by spending. It is only the misers who hoard their wealth for fear it should be used up by spending. 'Are you spiritual misers going to keep back Allah's holy Message from the multitude? Is that the reason why you deny the advent of the new Teacher, who comes as a Mercy to all men—to all Creation?'

2308. *Nine Clear Signs*: see 7:133, n. 1091. The story of Pharaoh (or a phase of it) is here told with a view to exhibiting the decline of a soul on account of pride in outward power and dignity.

2309. *To them: i.e.*, to Pharaoh, as sitting in his Council, with the Chiefs of his People. *Cf.* 7:103. The whole scene is described in some detail from the point of view of nations or Ummahs in 7:103-133.

Indeed, to have been
Worked upon by sorcery![2310]

مَسْحُورًا

102. Moses said, "Thou knowest
Well that these things
Have been sent down by none
But the Lord of the heavens
And the earth as eye-opening[2311]
Evidence: and I consider thee
Indeed, O Pharaoh, to be
One doomed to destruction!"

﴿١٠٢﴾ قَالَ لَقَدْ عَلِمْتَ مَآ أَنزَلَ هَٰٓؤُلَآءِ
إِلَّا رَبُّ ٱلسَّمَٰوَٰتِ وَٱلْأَرْضِ بَصَآئِرَ
وَإِنِّى لَأَظُنُّكَ يَٰفِرْعَوْنُ مَثْبُورًا

103. So he resolved to remove them[2312]
From the face of the earth:
But We did drown him
And all who were with him.

﴿١٠٣﴾ فَأَرَادَ أَن يَسْتَفِزَّهُم مِّنَ ٱلْأَرْضِ
فَأَغْرَقْنَٰهُ وَمَن مَّعَهُۥ جَمِيعًا

104. And We said thereafter
To The Children of Israel,
"Dwell securely in the land[2313]
(Of promise)": but when
The second of the warnings came
To pass, We gathered you
Together in a mingled crowd[2314]

﴿١٠٤﴾ وَقُلْنَا مِنۢ بَعْدِهِۦ لِبَنِىٓ إِسْرَٰٓءِيلَ
ٱسْكُنُوا۟ ٱلْأَرْضَ فَإِذَا جَآءَ وَعْدُ
ٱلْءَاخِرَةِ جِئْنَا بِكُمْ لَفِيفًا

105. We sent down the (Qur'ān)
In Truth, and in Truth[2315]
Has it descended: and We sent

﴿١٠٥﴾ وَبِٱلْحَقِّ أَنزَلْنَٰهُ وَبِٱلْحَقِّ نَزَلَ وَمَآ أَرْسَلْنَٰكَ

2310. At a different and later stage in the scene, Pharaoh's Chiefs call Moses a "sorcerer well-versed" (7:109). Here Moses, who had come with Nine Signs but had not yet shown them, is reproached with being the object of sorcery: he is practically told that he is mad!

2311. We can well suppose Moses to ask Pharaoh to recall all the past history of Moses, for Moses had been brought up in Pharaoh's palace in all the learning of the Egyptians. He could not therefore be mad, or a simpleton worked on by Egyptian magic. What he was going to show was something far greater; it was not the deceptive magic of Pharaoh's sorcerers, but true Signs that came from Allah, the Lord of all power. They were to open the eyes of his people, and if Pharaoh resisted faith, Moses warns him that Pharaoh in that case was doomed to destruction. This is the course of the soul that sinks down by Pride! (R).

2312. Pharaoh on this tries various subterfuges and plans for removing not only Moses but all his people by doing away with them. The detailed story is not told here but may be read in S. 7. But Allah's Wrath descended on Pharaoh and those who were with him in body and mind. The Egyptians who repented were subject to Pharaoh's wrath but were saved from the Wrath of Allah.

2313. The Israelites were taken to the Promised Land in Palestine, and they established their own kingdom there, but they forfeited Allah's favour by their sins and backslidings and will have to answer like all souls by the laws of personal responsibility at the Day of Judgement.

2314. The *second of the warnings*: the first was probably that mentioned above, in 17:5 and the second that mentioned in 17:7 (middle). When this second warning due to the rejection of Jesus came to pass, the Jews were gathered together in a mingled crowd. Some commentators understand the second warning to be the Day of Judgement, the Promise of the hereafter. (R).

2315. The Qur'ān was sent down by Allah in Truth: it was not forged by any mortal. It has descended in Truth: it was not falsified or corrupted in the process of being communicated to mankind.

Thee but to give Glad
Tidings and to warn (sinners).[2316]

إِلَّا مُبَشِّرًا وَنَذِيرًا

106. (It is) a Qur'ān
Which We have divided
(Into parts from time to time),
In order that thou mightest
Recite it to men
At intervals: We have
Revealed it by stages.[2317]

١٠٦ وَقُرْءَانًا فَرَقْنَٰهُ
لِتَقْرَأَهُۥ عَلَى ٱلنَّاسِ عَلَىٰ مُكْثٍ
وَنَزَّلْنَٰهُ تَنزِيلًا

107. Say: "Whether ye believe
In it or not, it is true
That those who were given[2318]
Knowledge beforehand, when
It is recited to them,
Fall down on their faces
In humble prostration,

١٠٧ قُلْ ءَامِنُوا۟ بِهِۦٓ أَوْ لَا تُؤْمِنُوٓا۟ۚ
إِنَّ ٱلَّذِينَ أُوتُوا۟ ٱلْعِلْمَ مِن قَبْلِهِۦٓ إِذَا يُتْلَىٰ
عَلَيْهِمْ يَخِرُّونَ لِلْأَذْقَانِ سُجَّدًا

108. And they say: "Glory
To our Lord! Truly
Has the promise of our Lord
Been fulfilled!"[2319]

١٠٨ وَيَقُولُونَ سُبْحَٰنَ رَبِّنَآ
إِن كَانَ وَعْدُ رَبِّنَا لَمَفْعُولًا

109. They fall down on their faces
In tears, and it increases
Their (earnest) humility.[2320]

١٠٩ وَيَخِرُّونَ لِلْأَذْقَانِ يَبْكُونَ
وَيَزِيدُهُمْ خُشُوعًا

2316. The part of the Prophet was that of a Messenger: he was not responsible if the ungodly rejected it. He fulfilled his mission in promulgating and explaining it and leaving it as a legacy to the world.

2317. The marvel is that these parts, revealed at different times and in different circumstances, should fit together so closely and consistently as they do. All revelation is progressive. The previous revelations were also progressive. Each of them marked a stage in the world's spiritual history. Man's mind does not take in more than his spiritual state will have prepared him for. Allah's revelation comes as a light to illuminate our difficulties and show us the way in actual situations that arise.

2318. No one's belief or unbelief affects the beauty or grandeur of Allah's revelation. But those endowed with spiritual knowledge or insight know at once when they hear Allah's Holy Word, and fall down and adore Allah. Those endowed with knowledge include those who had received previous revelations and had kept themselves free from corrupt ideas.

2319. Those who had received previous revelations find in the Qur'ān and in the Messenger who brought it, the promise of Allah fulfilled. Those who were spiritually prepared for it found in the same way the satisfaction of their spiritual yearnings: to them, also, Allah's promise was sent to be fulfilled.

2320. A feeling of earnest humility comes to the man who realises how, in spite of his own unworthiness, he is brought, by Allah's Mercy, into touch with the most sublime Truths. Such a man is touched with the deepest emotion, which finds its outlet in tears.

110\. Say: "Call upon Allah, or
Call upon Raḥmān:[2321]
By whatever name ye call
Upon Him, (it is well):
For to Him belong
The Most Beautiful Names.[2322]
Neither speak thy Prayer aloud,
Nor speak it in a low tone,[2323]
But seek a middle course
Between."

﴿١١٠﴾ قُلِ ٱدْعُوا۟ ٱللَّهَ أَوِ ٱدْعُوا۟ ٱلرَّحْمَٰنَ ۖ أَيًّا مَّا تَدْعُوا۟ فَلَهُ ٱلْأَسْمَآءُ ٱلْحُسْنَىٰ ۚ وَلَا تَجْهَرْ بِصَلَاتِكَ وَلَا تُخَافِتْ بِهَا وَٱبْتَغِ بَيْنَ ذَٰلِكَ سَبِيلًا

111\. Say: "Praise be to Allah,
Who begets no son,
And has no partner
In (His) dominion:
Nor (needs) He any
To protect Him from
humiliation:[2324]
Yea, magnify Him
For His greatness and glory!"

﴿١١١﴾ وَقُلِ ٱلْحَمْدُ لِلَّهِ ٱلَّذِى لَمْ يَتَّخِذْ وَلَدًا وَلَمْ يَكُن لَّهُۥ شَرِيكٌ فِى ٱلْمُلْكِ وَلَمْ يَكُن لَّهُۥ وَلِىٌّ مِّنَ ٱلذُّلِّ ۖ وَكَبِّرْهُ تَكْبِيرًۢا

2321\. *Cf.* 7:180. *Raḥmān* describes one of the attributes of Allah—His Grace and Mercy which come to the sinner even before he feels conscious of the need of it—the preventive Grace which saves Allah's servants from sin. See n. 19 to 1:1. Allah can be invoked, either by His simple name, which includes all attributes, or by one of the names implying the attributes by which we try to explain His nature to our limited understanding. The attribute of Mercy in *Rahmān* was particularly repugnant to the Pagan Arabs (see 25:60, and 21:36): that is why special stress is laid on it in the Qur'ān. (R).

2322\. These Beautiful Names of Allah are many. The Ḥadith related by Tirmidhi, accepted by some as authentic, mentions 99 names of Allah. Qāḍī Muḥammad Sulaimān has published an Urdu monograph on the subject, published by the Daftar Raḥmatun-lil-'Ālamīn, Patiala, India, 1930. Those who wish to see a poetic Commentary on the names in the form of stories in English may consult Sir Edwin Arnold's *Pearls of the Faith*. Sir Edwin's stories are of unequal merit, but a fine example is furnished by No. 4, *al-Malik*, "The King". (R).

2323\. *Cf.* 7:205. All prayer should be pronounced with earnestness and humilty, whether it is congregational prayer or the private outpouring of one's own soul. Such an attitude is not consistent with an over-loud pronunciation of the words, though in public prayers the standard of permissible loudness is naturally higher than in the case of private prayer. In public prayers, of course, the *adhān* or call to prayer will be in a loud voice to be heard near and far, but the chants from the Sacred Book should be neither so loud as to attract the hostile notice of those who do not believe nor so low in tone as not to be heard by the whole congregation.

2324\. A first step towards the understanding of Allah's attributes is to clear our mind from superstitions, such as that Allah begot a son, or that He has partners, or that He is dependent upon other beings to protect Him from harm and humiliation. We must realise that He is the One and Peerless. His greatness and glory are above anything we can conceive: but using our highest spiritual ideas, we must declare forth His greatness and glory.

The Sūrah began with singing the glory and praises of Allah: it ends in the same note, concluding the argument. The next Sūrah takes up the same theme from another point of view, and opens with the same note, "Praise be to Allah". (R).

INTRODUCTION TO SŪRAH 18—*AL KAHF*

It has been explained in the introduction to S. 17 how the five Sūrahs 17 to 21 develop the theme of the individual soul's spiritual history, and how they fit into the general scheme of exposition.

This particular Makkan Sūrah may be called a lesson in the brevity and mystery of Life. First there is the story of the Companions of the Cave who slept therein for a long period, and yet thought they had been there only a day or less. Then there is the story of the mysterious Teacher who shows Moses how Life itself is a parable. And further there is the story of D͟hu al Qarnayn, the two-horned one, the powerful ruler of west and east, who made an iron wall to protect the weak against the strong. The parables refer to the brevity, uncertainty, and vanity of this life; to the many paradoxes in it, which can only be understood by patience and the fulness of knowledge; and to the need of guarding our spiritual gains against the incursions of evil.

Summary—The Qur'ān is a direction and a warning. This life is brief and subject to vicissitudes. Our ideas of Time are defective, as shown in the story of the Companions of the Cave, who had faith, truth, patience, and other virtues. But their life was a mystery that can be fathomed but by few (18:1-22, and C. 133).

Knowledge is for Allah: be on your guard against idle conjectures and cocksure hopes. Learn from the Qur'ān the Parable of the man who is puffed up with this world's goods and is brought to nought (18:23-44, and C. 134.).

This life is uncertain and variable: goodness and virtue are better and more durable. For the Day of Reckoning will come, with its Mercy and its Wrath (18:45-59, and C. 135).

Moses in his thirst for knowledge forgot his limitations. Patience and faith were enjoined on him, and he understood when the paradoxes of Life were explained (18:60-82, and C. 136).

D͟hu al Qarnayn had a wide dominion: he punished the guilty and rewarded the good; he protected the weak from the lawless; but he had faith, and valued the guidance of Allah. Allah is One, and His service is righteousness (18:83-110, and C. 137).

C. 133.—The Book of Revelation gives straight
(18:1-22.) Directions to make our lives straight—
To warn us against Evil and guide us
To the Good everlasting. Teach the Truth.
But fret not about men rejecting it.
The Parable of the Companions of the Cave
Shows how Allah works wonders beyond
Our fathoming: how Faith is a sure
Refuge in ways we know not; how
Time itself works Allah's Plan
Before we know how it passes;
How He can give us rest, and raise
Us back to life against all odds;
And how futile it is to engage
In controversies about matters we know not.

Sūrah 18.

الجزء الخامس عشر سُورَةُ الكَهْفِ

Al Kahf **(The Cave)**

In the name of Allah, Most Gracious,
Most Merciful..

بِسْمِ ٱللَّهِ ٱلرَّحْمَـٰنِ ٱلرَّحِيمِ

1. Praise be to Allah,[2325]
Who hath sent to His Servant
The Book, and hath allowed
Therein no Crookedness:[2326]

١ ٱلْحَمْدُ لِلَّهِ ٱلَّذِىٓ أَنزَلَ عَلَىٰ عَبْدِهِ ٱلْكِتَـٰبَ وَلَمْ يَجْعَل لَّهُۥ عِوَجَا ۜ

2. (He hath made it) Straight[2327]
(And Clear) in order that
He may warn (the godless)
Of a terrible Punishment
From Him, and that He
May give Glad Tidings
To the Believers who work
Righteous deeds, that they
Shall have a goodly Reward.

٢ قَيِّمًا لِّيُنذِرَ بَأْسًا شَدِيدًا مِّن لَّدُنْهُ وَيُبَشِّرَ ٱلْمُؤْمِنِينَ ٱلَّذِينَ يَعْمَلُونَ ٱلصَّـٰلِحَـٰتِ أَنَّ لَهُمْ أَجْرًا حَسَنًا

3. Wherein they shall
Remain forever:[2328]

٣ مَّـٰكِثِينَ فِيهِ أَبَدًا

4. Further, that He may warn
Those (also) who say,
"Allah hath begotten a son":[2329]

٤ وَيُنذِرَ ٱلَّذِينَ قَالُوا۟ ٱتَّخَذَ ٱللَّهُ وَلَدًا

2325. See n. 2324 to 17:111. The theme of the last Sūrah, that Allah is good and worthy of all praise from His creatures, to whom He has granted a clear revelation, is continued in this Sūrah. The spirit of man makes gradual progress upwards, through the grace and mercy of Allah.

2326. Some people's idea of a Sacred Book is that it should be full of mysteries—dark corners, ambiguous expressions, words so far removed from human speech that they cover anything or nothing. Pagan oracles were couched in language which suggested one meaning to the hearer and claimed to have the very opposite meaning in the light of events which actually happened subsequently. They were distinctly crooked, not straight. In the next verse, the word "Straight" (*qayyim*) is used to characterise the Qur'ān, in contrast to this word "crooked" (*'iwaj*). See also 19:36, n. 2488.

2327. *Qayyim*: straight, that which has no bends and no corners to mystify people, that which speaks clearly and unambiguously, that which guides to the right path. *Cf.* 9:36. where the adjective is used for a straight usage, in contrast to usages, which tend to mystify and deceive people. The Qur'ān is above all things straight, clear, and perspicuous. Its directions are plain for everyone to understand. Any book that deals with the highest mysteries of spiritual life must necessarily have portions whose full meaning is clearer to some minds than to others not so well prepared. But here there is nowhere any mystification, any desire to wrap up things in dark sayings repugnant to human reason. Allah's purpose is to give clear warnings of spiritual dangers and lead up to the highest bliss.

2328. *Cf.* 4:122, 43:71, 65:11. 98:8.

2329. The warning is not only needed for those who deny Allah or deny His Message, but also for those whose false ideas of Allah degrade religion in supposing that Allah begot a son, for Allah is One and is High above any ideas of physical reproduction.

5. No knowledge have they
Of such a thing, nor
Had their fathers. It is
A grievous thing that issues
From their mouths as a saying.[2330]
What they say is nothing
But falsehood!

٥ مَّا لَهُم بِهِۦ مِنْ عِلْمٍ وَلَا لِآبَآئِهِمْ ۚ
كَبُرَتْ كَلِمَةً تَخْرُجُ مِنْ أَفْوَٰهِهِمْ ۚ
إِن يَقُولُونَ إِلَّا كَذِبًا

6. Thou wouldst only, perchance,
Fret thyself to death,
Following after them, in grief,[2331]
If they believe not
In this Message.

٦ فَلَعَلَّكَ بَٰخِعٌ نَّفْسَكَ عَلَىٰٓ ءَاثَٰرِهِمْ
إِن لَّمْ يُؤْمِنُوا۟ بِهَٰذَا ٱلْحَدِيثِ أَسَفًا

7. That which is on earth
We have made but as
A glittering show for the earth,[2332]
In order that We may test
Them—as to which of them
Are best in conduct.

٧ إِنَّا جَعَلْنَا مَا عَلَى ٱلْأَرْضِ
زِينَةً لَّهَا لِنَبْلُوَهُمْ
أَيُّهُمْ أَحْسَنُ عَمَلًا

8. Verily what is on earth
We shall make but as
Dust and dry soil
(Without growth or herbage).[2333]

٨ وَإِنَّا لَجَٰعِلُونَ مَا عَلَيْهَا
صَعِيدًا جُرُزًا

9. Or dost thou reflect[2334]

٩ أَمْ حَسِبْتَ

2330. The attribution of a son "begotten" to Allah has no basis in fact or in reason. It is only a "word" or "saying" that issues out of their mouths. It is not even a dogma that is reasoned out or can be explained in any way that is consistent with the sublime attributes of Allah. (R).

2331. In a reasonable world the preaching of a reasonable Faith like that of Islam would win universal acceptance. But the world is not altogether reasonable. It causes great distress to the unselfish Preacher of Islam that his Message met with so much opposition. He wanted to point the way to salvation. He only got, in the Makkan period, abuse from the chiefs of the Makkans—abuse and persecution, not only for himself but for the Truth which he was preaching. A heart less stout than his might have been appalled at what seemed the hopeless task of reclaiming the world from falsehood, superstition, selfishness, wrong, and oppression. He is here consoled, and told that he was not to fret himself to death: he was nobly doing his duty, and, as later events showed, the seed of Truth was already germinating, although this was not visible at the time. Besides, these "chiefs" and "leaders" were only strutting in false plumes: their glory was soon to fade forever.

2332. This world's goods—worldly power, glory, wealth, position, and all that men scramble for—are but a fleeting show. The possession or want of them does not betoken a man's real value or position in the spiritual world, the world which is to endure. Yet they have their uses. They test a man's sterling quality. He who becomes their slave loses rank in the spiritual world. He who uses them if he gets them, and does not fall into despair if he does not get them, shows his true mettle and quality. His conduct proclaims him.

2333. The fairest sights on the earth will become as dust and waste when this earth vanishes, and the spiritual values are restored.

2334. A wonderful story or allegory is now referred to. Its lessons are: (1) the relativity of Time, (2) the unreality of the position of oppressor and oppressed, persecutor and persecuted, on this earth, (3) the truth of the final Resurrection, when true values will be restored, and (4) the potency of Faith and Prayer to lead to the Right. Wonderful though such things may seem to be, they happen every day on Allah's earth!

That the Companions of the Cave[2335]
And of the Inscription[2336]
Were wonders among Our Signs?

أَنَّ أَصْحَٰبَ ٱلْكَهْفِ
وَٱلرَّقِيمِ كَانُوا۟ مِنْ ءَايَٰتِنَا عَجَبًا

10. Behold, the youths betook themselves[2337]
To the Cave: they said,
"Our Lord! bestow on us
Mercy from Thyself,
And dispose of our affair
For us in the right way![2338]

١٠ إِذْ أَوَى ٱلْفِتْيَةُ إِلَى ٱلْكَهْفِ
فَقَالُوا۟ رَبَّنَآ ءَاتِنَا مِن لَّدُنكَ رَحْمَةً
وَهَيِّئْ لَنَا مِنْ أَمْرِنَا رَشَدًا

11. Then We drew (a veil)[2339]
Over their ears, for a number

١١ فَضَرَبْنَا عَلَىٰٓ ءَاذَانِهِمْ

2335. The unbelieving Quraysh were in the habit of putting posers to the Holy Prophet—questions which they got from Christians and Jews, which they thought the Prophet would be unable to answer. In this way they hoped to discredit him. One of these questions was about the floating Christian legend of the Seven Sleepers of Ephesus. The Prophet not only told them the main story but pointed out the variations that were current, and rebuked men for disputing about such details (18:22). Most important, he treated the story (under inspiration) as a parable, pointing to spiritual lessons of the highest value. This is Revelation in the highest sense of the term. The story is recapitulated in n. 2337 below.

2336. *Raqīm* = Inscription. So interpreted by the Jalālayn, and the majority of Commentators agree. See. n. 2337, below. Others think it was the name of the dog: see 18:18, and n. 2330 below.

2337. The bare Christian story (without the spiritual lessons taught in the Qur'ān) is told in Gibbon's *Decline and Fall of the Roman Empire* (end of chapter 33). In the reign of a Roman Emperor who persecuted the Christians, seven Christian youths of Ephesus left the town and hid themselves in a cave in a mountain near by. They fell asleep,and remained asleep for some generations or centuries. When the wall which sealed up the cave was being demolished, the youths awoke. They still thought of the world in which they had previously lived. They had no idea of the duration of time. But when one of them went to the town to purchase provisions, he found that the whole world had changed. The Christian religion, instead of being persecuted was fashionable: in fact it was now the State religion. His dress and speech, and the money which he brought, seemed to belong to another world. This attracted attention. The great ones of the land visited the Cave, and verified the tale by questioning the man's Companions.

When the story became very popular and circulated throughout the Roman Empire, we may well suppose that an Inscription was put up at the mouth of the Cave. See verse 9 and n. 2336. This inscription was probably to be seen for many years afterwards, as Ephesus was a famous city on the west coast of Asia Minor, about forty to fifty miles south of Smyrna. Later on, the Khalīfah Wāthiq (842-846 A.C.) sent an expedition to examine and identify the locality, as he did about the Dhu al Qarnayn barrier in Central Asia (Appendix VI at the end of this Sūrah).

A popular story circulating from mouth to mouth would necessarily be vague as to dates and vary very much in details. Somewhere about the 6th century A.C. a Syriac writer reduced it to writing. He suggested that the youths were seven in number; that they went to sleep in the reign of the Emperor Decius (who reigned from 249-251 A.C., and who was a violent persecutor of Christians); and that they awoke in the reign of Theodosius II, who reigned from 408 to 450 A.C. In our literature Decius is known as Daqyānūs (from the adjectival Latin from Decianus), and the name stands as a symbol of injustice and oppression, and also of things old fashioned and out-of-date, as *res decianae* must have been two to three centuries after Decius.

2338. The youths hid in the cave, but they trusted in Allah, and made over their whole case to Him in prayer. Then they apparently fell alseep and knew nothing of what was happening in the world outside.

2339. *Drew (a veil) over their ears: i.e.,* sealed their ears so that they heard nothing. As they were in the Cave they saw nothing. So they were completely cut off from the outer world. It was as if they had died, with their knowledge and ideas remaining at the point of time when they entered the Cave. It is as if a watch stops at the exact moment of some accident, and any one taking it up afterwards can precisely fix the time of the accident.

Of years, in the Cave,
(So that they heard not):

فِي ٱلْكَهْفِ سِنِينَ عَدَدًا

12. Then We roused them,[2340]
In order to test which
Of the two parties was best[2341]
At calculating the term
Of years they had tarried!

١٢ ثُمَّ بَعَثْنَٰهُمْ لِنَعْلَمَ أَيُّ ٱلْحِزْبَيْنِ
أَحْصَىٰ لِمَا لَبِثُوٓا۟ أَمَدًا

SECTION 2.

13. We relate to thee their story
In truth: they were youths
Who believed in their Lord,
And We advanced them
In guidance:[2342]

١٣ نَّحْنُ نَقُصُّ عَلَيْكَ نَبَأَهُم بِٱلْحَقِّ
إِنَّهُمْ فِتْيَةٌ ءَامَنُوا۟ بِرَبِّهِمْ وَزِدْنَٰهُمْ هُدًى

14. We gave strength to their
hearts:[2343]
Behold, they stood up[2344]
And said: "Our Lord is
The Lord of the heavens
And of the earth: never
Shall we call upon any god
Other than Him: if we
Did, we should indeed
Have uttered an enormity!"

١٤ وَرَبَطْنَا عَلَىٰ قُلُوبِهِمْ إِذْ قَامُوا۟
فَقَالُوا۟ رَبُّنَا رَبُّ ٱلسَّمَٰوَٰتِ وَٱلْأَرْضِ
لَن نَّدْعُوَا۟ مِن دُونِهِۦٓ إِلَٰهًا
لَّقَدْ قُلْنَآ إِذًا شَطَطًا

15. "These our people have taken[2345]
For worship gods other

١٥ هَٰٓؤُلَآءِ قَوْمُنَا ٱتَّخَذُوا۟ مِن دُونِهِۦٓ ءَالِهَةً

2340. *Roused them*: or raised them up from their sleep or whatever condition they had fallen into (18:18), so that they began to perceive the things around them, but only with the memories of the time at which they had ceased to be in touch with the world.

2341. When they awoke to consciousness, they had lost all count of time. Though they had all entered together, and lain together on the same place for the same length of time, their impressions of the time that had passed were quite different. Time is thus related to our own internal experiences. We have to learn the lesson that men as good as ourselves may yet differ as to their reactions to certain facts, and that in such matters disputes are unseemly. It is best to say, "Allah knows best" (18:19).

2342. Their Faith carried them higher and higher on the road to Truth. Faith is cumulative. Each step leads higher and higher, by the grace and mercy of Allah.

2343. So that they were not afraid to speak out openly, and protest the truth of the Unity which they clearly saw in their own minds and hearts.

2344. We may suppose them to have taken their stand and made a public protest before they betook themselves to the Cave (18:16). The story really begins at 18:13, and the verses 18:9-12 may be considered as introductory. As the emphasis is on spiritual lessons, the facts stated in the introductory part are passed over lightly in the story.

2345. Besides the heathen gods, the cult of the Emperors also became fashionable in the Roman Empire in the first three centuries of the Christian Era. The statue of Diana (Artemis) at Ephesus had been one of the wonders of the ancient world. The city was a great seaport and the capital of Roman Asia. We may therefore imagine how the heathen cults must have flourished there. St. Paul spent three years preaching there, and was mobbed and assaulted, and compelled to leave (Acts, xix. 1-4).

Than Him: why do they
Not bring forward an authority
Clear (and convincing)
For what they do?
Who doth more wrong
Than such as invent
A falshood against Allah?

لَّوْلَا يَأْتُونَ
عَلَيْهِم بِسُلْطَٰنٍۭ بَيِّنٍ
فَمَنْ أَظْلَمُ مِمَّنِ ٱفْتَرَىٰ عَلَى ٱللَّهِ كَذِبًا

16. "When ye turn away
From them and the things
They worship other than Allah
Betake yourself to the Cave:
Your Lord will shower
His mercies on you
And dispose of your affair
Towards comfort and ease."[2346]

١٦ وَإِذِ ٱعْتَزَلْتُمُوهُمْ وَمَا يَعْبُدُونَ
إِلَّا ٱللَّهَ فَأْوُۥٓا۟ إِلَى ٱلْكَهْفِ
يَنشُرْ لَكُمْ رَبُّكُم مِّن رَّحْمَتِهِۦ
وَيُهَيِّئْ لَكُم مِّنْ أَمْرِكُم مِّرْفَقًا

17. Thou wouldst have seen
The sun, when it rose,
Declining to the right[2347]
From their Cave, and when
It set, turning away
From them to the left,
While they lay in the open
Space in the midst
Of the Cave. Such are
Among the signs of Allah:
He whom Allah guides[2348]
Is rightly guided; but he
Whom Allah leaves to stray—
For him wilt thou find
No protector to lead him
To the Right Way.

١٧ وَتَرَى ٱلشَّمْسَ إِذَا طَلَعَت
تَّزَٰوَرُ عَن كَهْفِهِمْ ذَاتَ ٱلْيَمِينِ
وَإِذَا غَرَبَت تَّقْرِضُهُمْ ذَاتَ ٱلشِّمَالِ
وَهُمْ فِى فَجْوَةٍ مِّنْهُ
ذَٰلِكَ مِنْ ءَايَٰتِ ٱللَّهِ
مَن يَهْدِ ٱللَّهُ فَهُوَ ٱلْمُهْتَدِ
وَمَن يُضْلِلْ فَلَن تَجِدَ
لَهُۥ وَلِيًّا مُّرْشِدًا

2346. That is, 'do not be afraid of anything; put your whole case in the hands of Allah; at present you are being persecuted; he will solve your difficulties and give you ease and comfort'. The public protest ends at verse 15. In verse 16 they are taking counsel among themselves. After they go into the Cave, verse 17 introduces us to the scene where they are lying in the midst of the Cave in tranquil confidence in Allah.

2347. In the latitude of Ephesus, 38° north, *i.e.* well above the sun's northern declination, a cave opening to the north, would never have the heat of the sun within it, as the sunny side would be the south. If the youths lay on their backs with their faces looking to the north, *i.e.* towards the entrace of the Cave, the sun would rise on their right side, declining to the south, and set on their left sides leaving them cool and comfortable.

2348. The youths, having faith and trust in Allah, found safety and refuge in the Cave. They were protected from the persecution and violence of the heathen. Their prayer (18:16) was heard.

Section 3.

18. Thou wouldst have deemed
them[2349]
Awake, whilst they were asleep,
And We turned them
On their right and on
Their left sides: their dog[2350]
Stretching forth his two forelegs
On the threshold: if thou
Hadst come up on to them,
Thou wouldst have certainly
Turned back from them in flight,
And wouldst certainly have been
Filled with terror of them.[2351]

19. Such (being their state),
We raised them up (from sleep).
That they might question[2352]
Each other. Said one of them,
"How long have ye stayed (here)?"
They said, "We have stayed
(Perhaps) a day, or part
Of a day." (At length)
They (all) said, "Allah (alone)
Knows best how long
Ye have stayed here. . .
Now send ye then one of you
With this money of yours[2353]
To the town: let him

١٨ وَتَحْسَبُهُمْ أَيْقَاظًا وَهُمْ رُقُودٌ ۚ
وَنُقَلِّبُهُمْ ذَاتَ الْيَمِينِ وَذَاتَ الشِّمَالِ ۖ
وَكَلْبُهُم بَاسِطٌ ذِرَاعَيْهِ بِالْوَصِيدِ ۚ
لَوِ اطَّلَعْتَ عَلَيْهِمْ
لَوَلَّيْتَ مِنْهُمْ فِرَارًا
وَلَمُلِئْتَ مِنْهُمْ رُعْبًا

١٩ وَكَذَٰلِكَ بَعَثْنَاهُمْ
لِيَتَسَاءَلُوا بَيْنَهُمْ ۚ
قَالَ قَائِلٌ مِّنْهُمْ كَمْ لَبِثْتُمْ ۖ
قَالُوا لَبِثْنَا يَوْمًا أَوْ بَعْضَ يَوْمٍ ۚ
قَالُوا رَبُّكُمْ أَعْلَمُ بِمَا لَبِثْتُمْ
فَابْعَثُوا أَحَدَكُم بِوَرِقِكُمْ هَٰذِهِ
إِلَى الْمَدِينَةِ

2349. Perhaps their eyes were open, even though their senses were sealed in sleep. They turned about on their sides as men do in sleep.

2350. The name of their dog is traditionally known as Qitmir, but see n. 2336 above.

2351. This graphic picture of the sleepers explains the human mechanism by which their saftey was ensured by Allah from their Pagan enemies.

2352. This is the point of the story. Their own human impressions were to be compared, each with the other. They were to be made to see that with the best goodwill and the most honest enquiry they might reach different conclusions; that they were not to waste their time in vain controversies, but to get on to the main business of life; and that Allah alone had full knowledge of the things that seem to us so strange, or inconsistent, or inexplicable, or that produce different impressions on different minds. If they entered the Cave in the morning and woke up in the afternoon, one of them might think they had been there only a few hours—only part of the day. This relative or fallacious impression of Time also gives us an inkling of the state when there will be no Time, of the Resurrection when all our little impressions of this life will be corrected by the final Reality. This mystery of time had puzzled many contemplative minds. *Cf.* "Dark time that haunts us with the briefness of our days" (Thomas Wolfe in "Of Time and the River").

2353. They now give up barren controversy and come to the practical business of life. But their thoughts are conditioned by the state of things that existed when they entered the Cave. The money they carried was the money coined in the reign of the monarch who persecuted the Religion of Unity and favoured the false cults of Paganism.

Find out which is the best[2354]
Food (to be had) and bring some
To you, that (ye may)
Satisfy your hunger therewith:
And let him behave
With care and courtesy,
And let him not inform
Any one about you.

فَلْيَنظُرْ أَيُّهَآ أَزْكَىٰ طَعَامًا
فَلْيَأْتِكُم بِرِزْقٍ مِّنْهُ وَلْيَتَلَطَّفْ
وَلَا يُشْعِرَنَّ بِكُمْ أَحَدًا

20. "For if they should
Come upon you, they would
Stone you or force you[2355]
To return to their cult,
And in that case ye would
Never attain prosperity."[2356]

٢٠ إِنَّهُمْ إِن يَظْهَرُوا۟ عَلَيْكُمْ يَرْجُمُوكُمْ
أَوْ يُعِيدُوكُمْ فِى مِلَّتِهِمْ
وَلَن تُفْلِحُوٓا۟ إِذًا أَبَدًا

21. Thus[2357] did We make
Their case known to the people,
That they might know
That the promise of Allah
Is true, and that there can
Be no doubt about the Hour
Of Judgement. Behold,
They dispute among themselves[2358]
As to their affair. (Some) said,
"Construct a building over them":

٢١ وَكَذَٰلِكَ أَعْثَرْنَا عَلَيْهِمْ
لِيَعْلَمُوٓا۟ أَنَّ وَعْدَ ٱللَّهِ حَقٌّ
وَأَنَّ ٱلسَّاعَةَ لَا رَيْبَ فِيهَآ
إِذْ يَتَنَٰزَعُونَ بَيْنَهُمْ أَمْرَهُمْ
فَقَالُوا۟ ٱبْنُوا۟ عَلَيْهِم بُنْيَٰنًا

2354. *Best food: i.e.*, purest, most wholesome, perhaps also most suitable for those who rejected idol worship, *i.e.*, not dedicated to idols. For they still imagined the world in the same state in which they had known it before they entered the Cave.

2355. They think that the world had not changed, and that the fierce persecution they knew was still raging, under which a man had to pay with his life for his religious faith, if he would not conform to Pagan worship.

2356. That is, never reap the spiritual good which your knowledge, instruction, and experience entitle you to attain. To become a renegade, to give up the Truth which you have won, simply on account of the fear of men, is the most despicable form of cowardice, and would rightly close the door of salvation if strict justice were to be done. But even then Allah's Mercy comes to the coward's aid so long as the door of repentance is open.

2357. *Thus*: in this way, by these means, *i.e.*, by the sending out of one of the Sleepers with the old money to the town to buy provisions. His old-fashioned dress, appearance, and speech, and the old uncurrent money which he brought, at once drew the attention of people to him. When they learnt his story, they realised that Allah, who can protect His servants thus and raise them up from sleep after such a long time, has power to raise up men for the Resurrection, and that His promise of goodness and mercy to those who serve Him is true and was exemplified in this striking way. On the other hand, to the men of the Cave themselves, it became clear that Allah can change the situation before we are aware, and our hope in Him is not futile, and that even when we are on the brink of despair, a revolution is surely working in the world before the world itself realises it.

2358. The perversity of man is such that as soon as ever a glimpse of truth becomes manifest, men fall into controversies about it. The Sleepers could not judge about the duration of their stay in the Cave, but they wisely left the matter and attended to the urgent business of their lives. The townsfolk could not agree as to the significance of the event: they fell to discussing immaterial details. What sort of a memorial should they raise?— a house or a place of worship or a tablet? The place of worship was built. But the real significance of the spiritual meaning was missed until explained in the Qur'ān.

Their Lord knows best About them: those who prevailed Over their affair said, "Let us surely build a place Of worship over them."	رَّبُّهُمْ أَعْلَمُ بِهِمْ قَالَ ٱلَّذِينَ غَلَبُواْ عَلَىٰٓ أَمْرِهِمْ لَنَتَّخِذَنَّ عَلَيْهِم مَّسْجِدًا
22. (Some) say they were three, The dog being the fourth Among them; (others) say They were five, the dog Being the sixth—doubtfully Guessing at the unknown;[2359] (Yet others) say they were Seven, the dog being the eighth. Say thou; "My Lord Knoweth best their number; It is but few that know[2360] Their (real case)." Enter not, Therefore, into controversies Concerning them, except On a matter that is clear,[2361] Nor consult any of them About (the affair of) the Sleepers.[2362]	٢٢ سَيَقُولُونَ ثَلَٰثَةٌ رَّابِعُهُمْ كَلْبُهُمْ وَيَقُولُونَ خَمْسَةٌ سَادِسُهُمْ كَلْبُهُمْ رَجْمًا بِٱلْغَيْبِ وَيَقُولُونَ سَبْعَةٌ وَثَامِنُهُمْ كَلْبُهُمْ قُل رَّبِّىٓ أَعْلَمُ بِعِدَّتِهِم مَّا يَعْلَمُهُمْ إِلَّا قَلِيلٌ فَلَا تُمَارِ فِيهِمْ إِلَّا مِرَآءً ظَٰهِرًا وَلَا تَسْتَفْتِ فِيهِم مِّنْهُمْ أَحَدًا

C. 134.—True knowledge is with Allah alone.
(18:23-44.) We are not to dispute on matters
Of conjecture, but to rely on the Truth
That comes from Allah, as in the Parable.
The man who piles up wealth
And is puffed up with this world's goods,
Despising those otherwise endowed,
Will come to an evil end,
For his hopes were not built on Allah.

2359. The controversy in later ages raged about the number of the Sleepers: were they three or five or seven? People answered, not from knowledge, but from conjecture. Gibbon's version, which has now become best known, makes the number of Sleepers seven. The point was immaterial: the real point was the spiritual lesson.

2360. The true significance of the story is known only to a few. Most men discuss futile details, which are not in their knowledge.

2361. It is unprofitable to enter such immaterial controversies, and many others that have been waged about Religion by shallow men from time immemorial. Yet, if there is a matter of clear knowledge from experience that matters, we must openly proclaim it, that the world may be brought to listen to Allah's Truth.

2362. Vulgar storymongers as such know little of the true significance of the stories and parables. We have a clear exposition in the Qur'ān. What need is there to go into details of the men in the Cave, or of the time they remained there?

SECTION 4.

23. Nor say of anything,
"I shall be sure to do
So and so tomorrow"—

٢٣ وَلَا تَقُولَنَّ لِشَاْيۡءٍ
إِنِّي فَاعِلٞ ذَٰلِكَ غَدًا

24. Without adding, "So please
Allah!"[2363]
And call thy Lord to mind
When thou forgetest, and say,
"I hope that my Lord
Will guide me ever closer
(Even) than this
To the right road."[2364]

٢٤ إِلَّآ أَن يَشَآءَ ٱللَّهُۚ
وَٱذۡكُر رَّبَّكَ إِذَا نَسِيتَ وَقُلۡ
عَسَىٰٓ أَن يَهۡدِيَنِ رَبِّي لِأَقۡرَبَ مِنۡ هَٰذَا رَشَدٗا

25. So they stayed in their Cave
Three hundred years, and (some)
Add nine (more).[2365]

٢٥ وَلَبِثُواْ فِي كَهۡفِهِمۡ ثَلَٰثَ مِاْئَةٖ سِنِينَ
وَٱزۡدَادُواْ تِسۡعٗا

26. Say: "Allah knows best
How long they stayed:
With Him is (the knowledge
Of) the secrets of the heavens
And the earth: how clearly
He sees, how finely He hears
(Everything)! They have no
protector[2366]

٢٦ قُلِ ٱللَّهُ أَعۡلَمُ بِمَا لَبِثُواْۖ
لَهُۥ غَيۡبُ ٱلسَّمَٰوَٰتِ وَٱلۡأَرۡضِۖ
أَبۡصِرۡ بِهِۦ وَأَسۡمِعۡۚ
مَا لَهُم مِّن دُونِهِۦ مِن وَلِيّٖ

2363. Verses 23 and 24 are parenthetical. We must never rely upon our own resources so much as to forget Allah. If by any chance we so forget, we must come back to Him and keep Him in remembrance, as did the Companions of the Cave.

2364. In geometry, the perfect circle is an ideal. Any given circle that we draw is not so perfect that we cannot draw one closer to the ideal. So in our life, there is always the hope of drawing closer and closer to Allah.

2365. This verse should be read with the next verse. In the floating oral tradition the duration of time in the Cave was given differently in different versions. When the tradition was reduced to writing, some Christian writers (*e.g.*, Simeon Metaphrates) named 372 years, some less. In round numbers, 300 years in the solar Calendar would amount to 309 in the lunar Calendar. But the next verse points out that all these are mere conjectures: the number is known to Allah alone.

The authority on which Gibbon relies mentions two definite reigns, that of Decius (249-252 A.C.) and that of Theodosius II (409-450 A.C.). Taking 250 and 450, we get an interval of 200 years. But the point of the story does not lie in the name of any given Emperor, but in the fact that the beginning of the period coincided with an Emperor who persecuted: the Emperor's name at the end of the period may be taken as approximately correct, because the story was recorded within two generations afterwards. One of the worst Emperors to persecute the Christians was Nero who reigned from 54 to 68. If we took the end of his reign (A.C. 68.) as the initial point, and (say) 440 A.C. as the final point, we get 372 years of Simeon Metaphrates. But none of these writers knew any more than we do. Our best course is to follow the Qur'ānic injunction, "Say, Allah knows best how long they stayed" (18:26). There is also a rebuke implied: 'do not imitate these men who love mischievous controversies!' After all, we are given the narrative more as a parable than as a story.

2366. Who are "they" in the sentence? They may be the Companions of the Cave, for they put themselves under the protection of Allah, and disowned all attribution of partners to Him. Or "they" may refer to the people in general who go wrong and become *"Mushriks", i.e.*, attribute imaginary partners to Allah.

Other than Him; nor does
He share His Command
With any person whatsoever.[2367]

وَلَا يُشْرِكُ فِي حُكْمِهِۦٓ أَحَدًا

27. And recite (and teach)
What has been revealed
To thee of the Book
Of thy Lord: none
Can change His Words,[2368]
And none wilt thou find
As a refuge other than Him.

٢٧ وَٱتْلُ مَآ أُوحِىَ إِلَيْكَ
مِن كِتَابِ رَبِّكَ
لَا مُبَدِّلَ لِكَلِمَٰتِهِۦ
وَلَن تَجِدَ مِن دُونِهِۦ مُلْتَحَدًا

28. And keep thy soul content
With those who call
On their Lord morning
And evening, seeking[2369]
His Face; and let not
Thine eyes pass beyond them,
Seeking the pomp and glitter
Of this Life; nor obey
Any whose heart We
Have permitted to neglect
The remembrance of Us,
One who follows his own
Desires, whose case has
Gone beyond all bounds.[2370]

٢٨ وَٱصْبِرْ نَفْسَكَ مَعَ ٱلَّذِينَ يَدْعُونَ
رَبَّهُم بِٱلْغَدَوٰةِ وَٱلْعَشِىِّ يُرِيدُونَ وَجْهَهُۥ
وَلَا تَعْدُ عَيْنَاكَ عَنْهُمْ
تُرِيدُ زِينَةَ ٱلْحَيَوٰةِ ٱلدُّنْيَا
وَلَا تُطِعْ مَنْ أَغْفَلْنَا قَلْبَهُۥ عَن ذِكْرِنَا
وَٱتَّبَعَ هَوَىٰهُ وَكَانَ أَمْرُهُۥ فُرُطًا

29. Say, "The Truth is
From your Lord":
Let him who will,
Believe, and let him
Who will, reject (it):[2371]

٢٩ وَقُلِ ٱلْحَقُّ مِن رَّبِّكُمْ
فَمَن شَآءَ فَلْيُؤْمِن وَمَن شَآءَ فَلْيَكْفُرْ

2367. *His Command: i.e.*, Allah's government of the world, or in His Judgement on the Day of Judgement.

2368. *His Words*: His Commands. Decrees. Orders.

2369. *Cf.* 6:52 and n. 870. The true servants of Allah are those whose hearts are turned to Him morning, noon, and night, and who seek not worldly gain, but Allah's Grace, Allah's own Self, His presence and nearness. "Face" is the symbol of Personality or Self. Even if they are poor in this world's goods, their society gives far more inward and spiritual satisfaction than worldly grandeur or worldly attraction.

2370. For those who stray from Allah's path, Allah's Grace is ever anxious: it seeks to reclaim them and bring them back to the path. If such a one resists, and follows his own lusts, a point is reached when his case becomes hopeless. Allah's Grace does not then reach him, and he is abandoned to his pride and insolence. Beware of following the example or advice of such a one or seeking his society, or hankering after his wretched idols.

2371. Our choice in our limited Free will involves a corresponding personal reponsibility. We are offered the Truth: again and again it is pressed on our attention. If we reject it, we must take all the terrible consequences which are prefigured in the Fire of Hell. Its flames and roof will completely enclose us like a tent. Ordinarily there is water to quench the heat of thirst: here the only drink will be like molten brass, thick, heavy, burning, sizzling. Before it reaches the mouth of the unfortunates, drops of it will scald their faces as it is poured out.

For the wrongdoers We
Have prepared a Fire
Whose (smoke and flames),
Like the walls and roof
Of a tent, will hem
Them in: if they implore
Relief they will be granted
Water like melted brass
That will scald their faces.
How dreadful the drink!
How uncomfortable a couch
To recline on!

إِنَّآ أَعْتَدْنَا لِلظَّٰلِمِينَ نَارًا
أَحَاطَ بِهِمْ سُرَادِقُهَا
وَإِن يَسْتَغِيثُوا۟ يُغَاثُوا۟
بِمَآءٍ كَٱلْمُهْلِ يَشْوِى ٱلْوُجُوهَ
بِئْسَ ٱلشَّرَابُ وَسَآءَتْ مُرْتَفَقًا

30. As to those who believe
And work righteousness,
Verily We shall not suffer
To perish the reward
Of any who do
A (single) righteous deed.[2372]

إِنَّ ٱلَّذِينَ ءَامَنُوا۟ وَعَمِلُوا۟ ﴿٣٠﴾
ٱلصَّٰلِحَٰتِ إِنَّا لَا نُضِيعُ
أَجْرَ مَنْ أَحْسَنَ عَمَلًا

31. For them will be Gardens
Of Eternity; beneath them
Rivers will flow: they will
Be adorned therein
With bracelets of gold,
And they will wear
Green garments[2373] of fine silk
And heavy brocade;
They will recline therein
On raised thrones.
How good the recompense!
How beautiful a couch
To recline on![2374]

أُو۟لَٰٓئِكَ لَهُمْ جَنَّٰتُ عَدْنٍ ﴿٣١﴾
تَجْرِى مِن تَحْتِهِمُ ٱلْأَنْهَٰرُ
يُحَلَّوْنَ فِيهَا مِنْ أَسَاوِرَ مِن ذَهَبٍ
وَيَلْبَسُونَ ثِيَابًا خُضْرًا مِّن سُندُسٍ وَإِسْتَبْرَقٍ
مُّتَّكِـِٔينَ فِيهَا عَلَى ٱلْأَرَآئِكِ
نِعْمَ ٱلثَّوَابُ وَحَسُنَتْ مُرْتَفَقًا

SECTION 5.

32. Set forth to them
The parable of two men:
For one of them We provided
Two gardens of grapevines

وَٱضْرِبْ لَهُم مَّثَلًا رَّجُلَيْنِ ﴿٣٢﴾
جَعَلْنَا لِأَحَدِهِمَا جَنَّتَيْنِ مِنْ أَعْنَٰبٍ

2372. The righteous will be rewarded, as has been said again and again, beyond their merits: 28:84; 30:39. Not a single good deed of theirs will lose its reward, and the mercy of Allah will blot out their sins.

2373. Heaven is figured by all the pictures of ease and comfort which we can imagine in our present state: Gardens: perpetual springs of crystal clear water, which we can see as in a landscape from above; the finest and most costly ornaments; the most beautiful clothes to wear; green is the colour mentioned, because it is the most refreshing to the eye, and fits in well with the Garden; the wearer takes the choice of fine silk or heavy brocade; and for rest and comfort, high thrones of dignity on which the blessed ones recline.

2374. This picture is in parallel contrast to the picture of Misery in the last verse.

And surrounded them
With date palms:
In between the two
We placed cornfields.[2375]

وَحَفَفْنَٰهُمَا بِنَخْلٍ
وَجَعَلْنَا بَيْنَهُمَا زَرْعًا

33. Each of those gardens
Brought forth its produce,
And failed not in the least
Therein: in the midst
Of them We caused
A river to flow.

٣٣ كِلْتَا ٱلْجَنَّتَيْنِ ءَاتَتْ أُكُلَهَا
وَلَمْ تَظْلِم مِّنْهُ شَيْـًٔا
وَفَجَّرْنَا خِلَٰلَهُمَا نَهَرًا

34. (Abundant) was the produce
This man had: he said
To his companion, in the course
Of a mutual argument:
"More wealth have I
Than you, and more honour
And power in (my following
Of) men."[2376]

٣٤ وَكَانَ لَهُۥ ثَمَرٌ فَقَالَ
لِصَٰحِبِهِۦ وَهُوَ يُحَاوِرُهُۥٓ
أَنَا۠ أَكْثَرُ مِنكَ مَالًا وَأَعَزُّ نَفَرًا

35. He went into his garden
In a state (of mind)
Unjust to his soul:[2377]
He said, "I deem not
That this will ever perish.

٣٥ وَدَخَلَ جَنَّتَهُۥ وَهُوَ ظَالِمٌ لِّنَفْسِهِۦ
قَالَ مَآ أَظُنُّ أَن تَبِيدَ هَٰذِهِۦٓ أَبَدًا

36. "Nor do I deem
That the Hour (of Judgement)
Will (ever) come:
Even if I am brought back
To my Lord, I shall
Surely find (there)
Something better in exchange.[2378]

٣٦ وَمَآ أَظُنُّ ٱلسَّاعَةَ قَآئِمَةً
وَلَئِن رُّدِدتُّ إِلَىٰ رَبِّى
لَأَجِدَنَّ خَيْرًا مِّنْهَا مُنقَلَبًا

2375. Here is a simple parable of the contrast between two men. One was purse-proud, and forgot that what he had was from Allah, by way of a trust and a trial in this life. The other boasted of nothing: his trust was in Allah. The worldly wealth of the first was destroyed, and he had nothing left. The second was the happier in the end.

2376. The two men began to compare notes. The arrogant one puffed up with his possessions, his income, and his large family and following, and thought in his self-complacency that it would last forever. He was also wrong in looking down on his Companion, who, though less affluent, was the better man of the two.

2377. It was not wealth that ruined him, but the attitude of his mind. He was unjust, not so much to his neighbour, as to his own soul. In his love of the material, he forgot or openly defied the spiritual. As verse 37 shows, he took his companion with him, to impress him with his own importance, but the companion was unmoved.

2378. Here comes out the grasping spirit of the materialist. In his mind "better" means more wealth and more power, of the kind he was enjoying in this life, although in reality, even what he had rested on hollow foundations and was doomed to perish and bring him down with it.

37. His companion said to him,
In the course of the argument
With him: "Dost thou deny
Him Who created thee
Out of the dust, then out of
A sperm-drop, then fashioned
Thee into a man?[2379]

٣٧ قَالَ لَهُۥ صَاحِبُهُۥ وَهُوَ يُحَاوِرُهُۥٓ
أَكَفَرْتَ بِٱلَّذِى خَلَقَكَ مِن تُرَابٍ
ثُمَّ مِن نُّطْفَةٍ ثُمَّ سَوَّىٰكَ رَجُلًا

38. "But (I think) for my part
That He is Allah,
My Lord, and none shall I
Associate with my Lord.

٣٨ لَّٰكِنَّا۠ هُوَ ٱللَّهُ رَبِّى
وَلَآ أُشْرِكُ بِرَبِّىٓ أَحَدًا

39. "Why didst thou not,
As thou goeth into
Thy garden, say: 'Allah's Will
(Be done)! There is no power
But with Allah!' If thou[2380]
Dost see me less than
Thee in wealth and sons,

٣٩ وَلَوْلَآ إِذْ دَخَلْتَ جَنَّتَكَ
قُلْتَ مَا شَآءَ ٱللَّهُ لَا قُوَّةَ إِلَّا بِٱللَّهِ
إِن تَرَنِ أَنَا۠ أَقَلَّ مِنكَ مَالًا وَوَلَدًا

40. "It may be that my Lord
Will give me something
Better than thy garden,
And that He will send
On thy garden thunderbolts
(By way of reckoning)
From heaven, making it
(But) slippery sand![2381] —

٤٠ فَعَسَىٰ رَبِّىٓ أَن يُؤْتِيَنِ خَيْرًا مِّن جَنَّتِكَ
وَيُرْسِلَ عَلَيْهَا حُسْبَانًا مِّنَ ٱلسَّمَآءِ
فَتُصْبِحَ صَعِيدًا زَلَقًا

41. "Or the water of the garden
Will run off underground
So that thou wilt never
Be able to find it.

٤١ أَوْ يُصْبِحَ مَآؤُهَا غَوْرًا
فَلَن تَسْتَطِيعَ لَهُۥ طَلَبًا

42. So his fruits (and enjoyment)
Were encompassed (with ruin),

٤٢ وَأُحِيطَ بِثَمَرِهِۦ

2379. Three stages of man's creation: first dust, or clay, itself created out of nothing and forming the physical basis for his body; then, out of the produce of the earth as incorporated in the parent's body, the sperm drop (with the corresponding receptive element); and then when the different elements were mixed in due proportion, and the soul was breathed into him, the fashioned man. *Cf.* 87:2. and 15:28-29.

2380. The companion's argument divides itself into five parts. (1) He remonstrates against the proud man denying Allah. (2) He, from his own spiritual experience, proclaims that Allah is One and that He is good. (3) He points out to him the better way of enjoying Allah's gift, with gratitude to Him. (4) He expresses contentment and satisfaction in Allah's dealings with him. (5) He gives warning of the fleeting nature of this world's goods and the certainty of Allah's punishment for inordinate vanity.

2381. The punishment was that of thunderbolts (*ḥusbānan*), but the general meaning of the word includes any punishment by way of a reckoning (*hisāb*), and I think that an earthquake is also implied, as it alters watercourses, diverts channels underground, throws up silt and sand, and covers large areas with ruin. (R).

And he remained twisting
And turning his hands
Over what he had spent[2382]
On his property, which had
(Now) tumbled to pieces
To its very foundations,
And he could only say,
"Woe is me! Would I had
Never ascribed partners
To my Lord and Cherisher!"[2383]

فَأَصْبَحَ يُقَلِّبُ كَفَّيْهِ
عَلَىٰ مَآ أَنفَقَ فِيهَا
وَهِىَ خَاوِيَةٌ عَلَىٰ عُرُوشِهَا وَيَقُولُ
يَٰلَيْتَنِى لَمْ أُشْرِكْ بِرَبِّىٓ أَحَدًا

43. Nor had he numbers
To help him against Allah,
Nor was he able
To deliver himself.[2384]

٤٣ وَلَمْ تَكُن لَّهُۥ فِئَةٌ يَنصُرُونَهُۥ
مِن دُونِ ٱللَّهِ وَمَا كَانَ مُنتَصِرًا

44. There, the (only) protection comes
From Allah, the True One.
He is the Best to reward,
And the Best to give success.[2385]

٤٤ هُنَالِكَ ٱلْوَلَٰيَةُ لِلَّهِ ٱلْحَقِّ
هُوَ خَيْرٌ ثَوَابًا وَخَيْرٌ عُقْبًا

C. 135.—The life of this world is ephemeral,
(18:45-59.) And its gains will not last. Good Deeds
Are the best of possessions in Allah's sight:
All will be levelled up on the Day
Of Judgement, and a new Order created
On the basis of Truth, according to the Book
Of Deeds. Pride is the root of Evil,
Rebellion, and wrong. Who will choose
Evil ones in preference to Allah? Let us accept
Truth, for though Falsehood may flourish
For a time, it must perish in the end.

SECTION 6.

45. Set forth to them
The similitude of the life
Of this world: it is like

٤٥ وَٱضْرِبْ لَهُم مَّثَلَ ٱلْحَيَوٰةِ ٱلدُّنْيَا

2382. "Fruits", "spent", "twisting of the hands", should all be understood in a wide metaphorical sense, as well as the literal sense. He had great income and satisfaction, which were all gone. What resources he had lavished on his property! His thoughts had been engrossed on it; his hopes had been built on it; it had become the absorbing passion of his life, if he had only looked to Allah, instead of to the ephemeral goods of this world!

2383. In this case, in his mind, there was his own Self and his Mammon as rivals to Allah!

2384. He had built up connections and obligated dependents, and was proud of having his "quiver full". But where were all things when the reckoning came? He could not help himself; how could others be expected to help him!

2385. All else is vanity, uncertainty, the sport of Time. The only hope or truth is from Allah. Other rewards, and other successes are illusory; the best Reward and the best Success come from Allah.

The rain which We send
Down from the skies:
The earth's vegetation absorbs it.
But soon it becomes
Dry stubble, which the winds[2386]
Do scatter: it is (only) Allah
Who prevails over all things.

كَمَآءٍ أَنزَلْنَٰهُ مِنَ ٱلسَّمَآءِ
فَٱخْتَلَطَ بِهِۦ نَبَاتُ ٱلْأَرْضِ فَأَصْبَحَ
هَشِيمًا تَذْرُوهُ ٱلرِّيَٰحُ وَكَانَ ٱللَّهُ عَلَىٰ كُلِّ شَىْءٍ مُّقْتَدِرًا

46. Wealth and sons are allurements
Of the life of this world:
But the things that endure,
Good Deeds, are best
In the sight of thy Lord,
As rewards, and best
As (the foundation for) hopes.[2387]

٤٦ ٱلْمَالُ وَٱلْبَنُونَ زِينَةُ ٱلْحَيَوٰةِ ٱلدُّنْيَا
وَٱلْبَٰقِيَٰتُ ٱلصَّٰلِحَٰتُ خَيْرٌ
عِندَ رَبِّكَ ثَوَابًا وَخَيْرٌ أَمَلًا

47. One Day We shall
Remove the mountains, and thou
Wilt see the earth
As a level stretch,[2388]
And We shall gather them,
All together, nor shall We
Leave out any one of them.

٤٧ وَيَوْمَ نُسَيِّرُ ٱلْجِبَالَ
وَتَرَى ٱلْأَرْضَ بَارِزَةً
وَحَشَرْنَٰهُمْ فَلَمْ نُغَادِرْ مِنْهُمْ أَحَدًا

48. And they will be marshalled
Before thy Lord in ranks,
(With the announcement),
"Now have ye come to Us
(Bare) as We created you[2389]
First: aye, ye thought
We shall not fulfil
The appointment made to you
To meet (Us)!":[2390]

٤٨ وَعُرِضُوا۟ عَلَىٰ رَبِّكَ صَفًّا
لَّقَدْ جِئْتُمُونَا كَمَا خَلَقْنَٰكُمْ أَوَّلَ مَرَّةٍۭ
بَلْ زَعَمْتُمْ أَلَّن نَّجْعَلَ
لَكُم مَّوْعِدًا

2386. Rainwater is a good thing in and of itself, but it does not last, and you can build no solid foundations on it. It is soon absorbed in the earth, and produces the flourishing appearance of grass and vegetation—for a time. Soon these decay, and become as dry stubble, which the least wind from any quarter will blow about like a thing of no importance. The water is gone, and so is the vegetation to which it lent a brave show of luxuriance temporarily. Such is the life of *this* world, contrasted with the inner and real Life, which looks to the Hereafter. Allah is the only enduring Power we can look to, supreme over all.

2387. Other things are fleeting: but Good Deeds have a lasting value in the sight of Allah. They are best as (or for) rewards in two ways: (1) they flow from us by the Grace of Allah, and are themselves rewards for our Faith; (2) they become the foundation of our hopes for the highest spiritual rewards in the Hereafter.

2388. On the Day of Judgement none of our present landmarks will remain.

2389. We shall stand as we were created, with none of the adventitious possessions that we collected in this life, which will all have vanished.

2390. The sceptics will now at length be convinced of the Reality which will be upon them.

49. And the Book (of Deeds)
Will be placed (before you);
And thou wilt see
The sinful in great terror
Because of what is (recorded)
Therein; they will say,
"Ah! woe to us!
What a book is this!
It leaves out nothing
Small or great, but
Takes account thereof!"
They will find all that they
Did, placed before them:
And not one will thy Lord
Treat with injustice.[2391]

(٤٩) وَوُضِعَ الْكِتَٰبُ فَتَرَى
الْمُجْرِمِينَ مُشْفِقِينَ مِمَّا فِيهِ
وَيَقُولُونَ يَٰوَيْلَتَنَا
مَالِ هَٰذَا الْكِتَٰبِ لَا يُغَادِرُ
صَغِيرَةً وَلَا كَبِيرَةً إِلَّآ أَحْصَىٰهَا
وَوَجَدُوا۟ مَا عَمِلُوا۟ حَاضِرًا
وَلَا يَظْلِمُ رَبُّكَ أَحَدًا

SECTION 7.

50. Behold! We said
To the angels, "Bow down[2392]
To Adam": they bowed down
Except Iblīs. He was
One of the Jinns,[2393] and he
Broke the Command
Of his Lord.
Will ye then take him
And his progeny[2394] as protectors
Rather than Me? And they
Are enemies to you!
Evil would be the exchange[2395]
For the wrongdoers!

(٥٠) وَإِذْ قُلْنَا لِلْمَلَٰٓئِكَةِ ٱسْجُدُوا۟
لِءَادَمَ فَسَجَدُوٓا۟ إِلَّآ إِبْلِيسَ
كَانَ مِنَ ٱلْجِنِّ فَفَسَقَ عَنْ أَمْرِ رَبِّهِۦٓ
أَفَتَتَّخِذُونَهُۥ وَذُرِّيَّتَهُۥٓ أَوْلِيَآءَ
مِن دُونِى وَهُمْ لَكُمْ عَدُوٌّۢ
بِئْسَ لِلظَّٰلِمِينَ بَدَلًا

51. I called them not
To witness the creation

(٥١) مَّآ أَشْهَدتُّهُمْ خَلْقَ

2391. Personal responsibility, for all deeds in this life, will then be enforced. But it will be done with perfect justice. Expressed in the forms of this world, it will amount to a clear statement of all we did in this life: the record will be put before us to convince us. As it will be a perfect record, with no omissions and no wrong entries, it will be perfectly convincing. Where there is punishment, it has been earned by the wrongdoer's own deeds, not imposed on him unjustly.

2392. *Cf.* 2:34, where the story is told of the fall of mankind through Adam. Here the point is referred to in order to bring home the individual responsibility of the erring soul. 'Iblis is your enemy: you have been told his history; will you prefer to go to him rather than to the merciful Allah, your Creator and Cherisher? What a false exchange you would make!'

2393. *Cf.* 6:100, n. 929.

2394. *Satan's progeny*: we need not take the epithet only in a literal sense. All his followers are also his progeny. (R).

2395. Out of the limited free-will that man has, if he were to choose Evil instead of Good, Satan instead of Allah, what a dreadful choice it would be! It would really be an evil exchange. For man is Allah's creature, cared for and cherished by Him. He abandons his Cherisher to become the slave of his enemy!

Of the heavens and the earth,
Nor (even) their own creation:
Nor is it for Me
To take as helpers
Such as lead (men) astray![2396]

ٱلسَّمَٰوَٰتِ وَٱلْأَرْضِ وَلَا خَلْقَ أَنفُسِهِمْ
وَمَا كُنتُ مُتَّخِذَ ٱلْمُضِلِّينَ عَضُدًا

52. One Day He will say,
"Call on those whom ye
Thought to be My partners,"
And they will call on them,
But they will not listen
To them; and We shall
Make for them a place
Of common perdition.[2397]

٥٢ وَيَوْمَ يَقُولُ نَادُوا۟ شُرَكَآءِىَ
ٱلَّذِينَ زَعَمْتُمْ فَدَعَوْهُمْ فَلَمْ يَسْتَجِيبُوا۟
لَهُمْ وَجَعَلْنَا بَيْنَهُم مَّوْبِقًا

53. And the Sinful shall see
The Fire and apprehend
That they have to fall
Therein: no means will they
Find to turn away therefrom.

٥٣ وَرَءَا ٱلْمُجْرِمُونَ ٱلنَّارَ فَظَنُّوٓا۟ أَنَّهُم
مُّوَاقِعُوهَا وَلَمْ يَجِدُوا۟ عَنْهَا مَصْرِفًا

SECTION 8.

54. We have explained
In detail in this Qur'ān,
For the benefit of mankind,
Every kind of similitude:
But man is, in most things,[2398]
Contentious.

٥٤ وَلَقَدْ صَرَّفْنَا فِى هَٰذَا ٱلْقُرْءَانِ
لِلنَّاسِ مِن كُلِّ مَثَلٍ
وَكَانَ ٱلْإِنسَٰنُ أَكْثَرَ شَىْءٍ جَدَلًا

55. And what is there
To keep back men
From believing, now that
Guidance has come to them,
Nor from praying for forgiveness
From their Lord, but that
(They ask that) the ways
Of the ancients be repeated[2399]
With them, or the Wrath

٥٥ وَمَا مَنَعَ ٱلنَّاسَ أَن يُؤْمِنُوٓا۟
إِذْ جَآءَهُمُ ٱلْهُدَىٰ
وَيَسْتَغْفِرُوا۟ رَبَّهُمْ
إِلَّآ أَن تَأْتِيَهُمْ سُنَّةُ ٱلْأَوَّلِينَ

2396. Allah wants man's good: how can He take Evil for His partner?

2397. Some Commentators construe: "And We shall make a partition between them": *i.e.*, the Evil ones will not even be seen by their misguided followers, much as the latter may go on calling on them.

2398. If men had not cultivated the habit of contention and obstinacy, they would have found that the parables and similitudes of Scripture had fully met their difficulties, and they would gladly have obeyed the call of Allah.

2399. But man's obstinacy or contrariness asks or calls for a repetition of what happened to the wicked and those who rejected Faith in ancient times. Out of curiosity, or by way of challenge, they seem to court the Punishment and ask that it be brought to pass at once. But it will come soon enough, and then they will think it too early! *Cf.* 13:6 and n. 1810.

Be brought to them
Face to face?

أَوْ يَأْتِيَهُمُ ٱلْعَذَابُ قُبُلًا

56. We only send the Messengers
To give glad tidings
And to give warnings:[2400]
But the Unbelievers dispute
With vain argument, in order
Therewith to weaken the truth,
And they treat My Signs
As a jest, as also the fact
That they are warned!

٥٦ وَمَا نُرْسِلُ ٱلْمُرْسَلِينَ إِلَّا مُبَشِّرِينَ
وَمُنذِرِينَ وَيُجَٰدِلُ ٱلَّذِينَ كَفَرُوا۟
بِٱلْبَٰطِلِ لِيُدْحِضُوا۟ بِهِ ٱلْحَقَّ
وَٱتَّخَذُوٓا۟ ءَايَٰتِى وَمَآ أُنذِرُوا۟ هُزُوًا

57. And who doth more wrong
Than one who is reminded
Of the Signs of his Lord,
But turns away from them,
Forgetting the (deeds) which his hands[2401]
Have sent forth? Verily We
Have set veils over their hearts
Lest they should understand this,
And over their ears, deafness.
If thou callest them
To guidance, even then
Will they never accept guidance.

٥٧ وَمَنْ أَظْلَمُ مِمَّن ذُكِّرَ بِـَٔايَٰتِ رَبِّهِۦ
فَأَعْرَضَ عَنْهَا وَنَسِىَ مَا قَدَّمَتْ يَدَاهُ
إِنَّا جَعَلْنَا عَلَىٰ قُلُوبِهِمْ أَكِنَّةً
أَن يَفْقَهُوهُ وَفِىٓ ءَاذَانِهِمْ وَقْرًا
وَإِن تَدْعُهُمْ إِلَى ٱلْهُدَىٰ
فَلَن يَهْتَدُوٓا۟ إِذًا أَبَدًا

58. But your Lord is Most Forgiving,
Full of Mercy. If He were
To call them (at once) to account
For what they have earned,
Then surely He would
Have hastened their Punishment:
But they have their appointed

٥٨ وَرَبُّكَ ٱلْغَفُورُ ذُو ٱلرَّحْمَةِ
لَوْ يُؤَاخِذُهُم بِمَا كَسَبُوا۟
لَعَجَّلَ لَهُمُ ٱلْعَذَابَ
بَل لَّهُم مَّوْعِدٌ

2400. The Prophets of Allah are not sent to humour us with dialectics or satisfy the vulgar curiosity for miracles of dark unusual things. There is no "crookedness" (18:1) in their preaching. They come to preach the Truth—not in an abstract way, but with special reference to our conduct. They give us the good news of salvation lest we despair in the presence of Sin, and to warn us clearly of the dangers of Evil. Vain controversies about words only weaken their mission, or turn it into ridicule. The ungodly have a trick also of treating the earnest preaching to them itself as a jest and ridicule it. (R).

2401. Considering the power of sin, and how it gets hold of the hearts of men, and considering all the wrongs that men have done, it is the height of folly and injustice on their part to turn away from warnings which are given expressly for their good. But a stage of callousness is reached, when, by their own choice, they have rendered themselves impervious to Allah's Grace. At that stage a veil is put over their hearts and they are left alone for a time, that they may commune with themselves and perhaps repent and seek Allah's Mercy again. If they do not, it is their own loss. See next verse.

Time, beyond which[2402] they
Will find no refuge.

لَّن يَجِدُوا۟ مِن دُونِهِۦ مَوْئِلًا

59. Such were the populations
We destroyed when they
Committed iniquities; but
We fixed an appointed time
For their destruction.[2403]

﴿٥٩﴾ وَتِلْكَ ٱلْقُرَىٰٓ أَهْلَكْنَـٰهُمْ
لَمَّا ظَلَمُوا۟ وَجَعَلْنَا لِمَهْلِكِهِم مَّوْعِدًا

C. 136.—Moses was up against mysteries
(18:60-82.)
Which he wanted to explore. He searched
Out a man endued with knowledge
Derived from the divine springs from which
Flow the paradoxes of life. He is shown
Three such paradoxes and how human
Impatience is inconsistent with their true
Understanding. The highest knowledge
Comes not except by divine gift,
And a constant, patient striving,
With Faith, to apprehend something
Of the purpose of the All-Wise Allah.

Section 9.

60. Behold, Moses said[2404]
To his attendant, "I will not
Give up until I reach
The junction of the two[2405]

﴿٦٠﴾ وَإِذْ قَالَ مُوسَىٰ لِفَتَىٰهُ
لَآ أَبْرَحُ حَتَّىٰٓ أَبْلُغَ مَجْمَعَ

2402. *Min dūni hī*: should we take the pronoun to refer to "the appointed time", or to "your Lord," mentioned at the beginning of the verse? Most Commentators take the former view, and I have translated accordingly. But I agree with those who take the latter view, and the better translation would be: "But they have their appointed time, and except with Allah, they will find no refuge." That means that even during the period allowed them, when they are left to wander astray as they have rejected Allah's Grace, Allah's Mercy is open to them if they will repent and return; but nothing but Allah's Mercy can save them.

2403. The instances of exemplary Punishment in former times were also subject to this rule, that Allah gives plenty of rope to the wicked, in case they might turn, repent, and obtain His Mercy.

2404. This episode in the story of Moses is meant to illustrate four points. (1) Moses was learned in all the wisdom of the Egyptians. Even so that wisdom did not comprehend everything, even as the whole stock of the knowledge of the present day, the sciences and the arts, and in literature, (if it could be supposed to be gathered in one individual), does not include all knowledge. Divine knowledge, as far as man is concerned, is unlimited. Even after Moses received his divine mission, his knowledge was not so perfect that it could not receive further additions. (2) Constant effort is necessary to keep our knowledge square with the march of time, and such effort Moses is shown to be making. (3) The mysterious man he meets (18:65 and n. 2411), to whom Tradition assigns the name of Khidr (literally, Green), is the type of that knowledge which is ever in contact with life as it is actually lived. (4) There are paradoxes in life: apparent loss may be real gain; apparent cruelty may be real mercy; returning good for evil may really be justice and not generosity (18:79-82). Allah's wisdom transcends all human calculation. (R).

2405. The most probable geographical location (if any is required in a story that is a parable) is where the two arms of the Red Sea join together, *viz.*, the Gulf of 'Aqabah and the Gulf of Suez. They enclose the Sinai Peninsula, in which Moses and the Israelites spent many years in their wanderings. There is also authority (see Bayḍāwī's note) for interpreting the two seas as the two great streams of knowledge, which were to meet in the persons of Moses and Khiḍr.

Seas or (until) I spend Years and years in travel."[2406]	ٱلْبَحْرَيْنِ أَوْ أَمْضِىَ حُقُبًا
61. But when they reached The Junction,[2407] they forgot (About) their Fish,[2408] which took Its course through the sea (Straight) as in a tunnel.	٦١ فَلَمَّا بَلَغَا مَجْمَعَ بَيْنِهِمَا نَسِيَا حُوتَهُمَا فَٱتَّخَذَ سَبِيلَهُۥ فِى ٱلْبَحْرِ سَرَبًا
62. When they had passed on (Some distance). Moses said To his attendant: "Bring us Our early meal; truly We have suffered much fatigue[2409] At this (stage of) our journey."	٦٢ فَلَمَّا جَاوَزَا قَالَ لِفَتَىٰهُ ءَاتِنَا غَدَآءَنَا لَقَدْ لَقِينَا مِن سَفَرِنَا هَـٰذَا نَصَبًا
63. He replied: "Sawest thou (What happened) when we Betook ourselves to the rock? I did indeed forget (About) the Fish: none but Satan made me forget To tell (you) about it:[2410] It took its course through The sea in a marvellous way!"	٦٣ قَالَ أَرَءَيْتَ إِذْ أَوَيْنَآ إِلَى ٱلصَّخْرَةِ فَإِنِّى نَسِيتُ ٱلْحُوتَ وَمَآ أَنسَىٰنِيهُ إِلَّا ٱلشَّيْطَـٰنُ أَنْ أَذْكُرَهُۥ وَٱتَّخَذَ سَبِيلَهُۥ فِى ٱلْبَحْرِ عَجَبًا
64. Moses said: "That was what We were seeking after:" So they went back	٦٤ قَالَ ذَٰلِكَ مَا كُنَّا نَبْغِ فَٱرْتَدَّا

2406. *Huqub* means a long but indefinite space of time. Sometimes it is limited to 80 years.

2407. Literally, 'the Junction of (the space) between the two,' *i.e.*, the point at which the two seas were united.

2408. Moses was to go and find a servant of Allah, who would instruct him in such knowledge as he had not already got. He was to take a fish with him. The place where he was to meet his mysterious Teacher would be indicated by the fact that the fish would disappear when he got to that place. The fish is the emblem of the fruit of secular knowledge, which merges itself in divine knowledge at the point where human intelligence is ready for the junction of the two. But the mere merger of secular knowledge does not in itself produce divine knowledge. The latter has to be sought patiently.

2409. When they came to the Junction of the Seas, Moses forgot about the fish, and his attendant forgot to tell him of the fact that he had seen the fish escaping into the sea in a marvellous way. They passed on, but the stages now became heavier and heavier, and more fatiguing to Moses. So when our old knowledge is exhausted, and we come to the brink of new knowledge, we have a feeling of strangeness, heaviness, and difficulty, especially when we want to pass the new knowledge by and do not make it our own. Some refreshment, even if it be in our old traditional way, is required to sustain us. But we must retrace our steps, and seek the accredited repository of the knowledge which is our quest. It is our business to seek him out. We shall not find him without effort.

2410. The attendant actually saw the fish swimming away in the sea, and yet "forgot" to tell his master. In his case the "forgetting" was more than forgetting. Inertia had made him refrain from telling the important news. In such matters inertia is almost as bad as active spite, the suggestion of Satan. So new knowledge or spiritual knowledge is not only passed by in ignorance, but sometimes by culpable negligence.

On their footsteps, following
(The path they had come).

عَلَىٰٓ ءَاثَارِهِمَا قَصَصًا

65. So they found one[2411]
Of Our servants,
On whom We had bestowed
Mercy from Ourselves
And whom We had taught
Knowledge from Our own[2412]
Presence.

٦٥ فَوَجَدَا عَبْدًا مِّنْ عِبَادِنَآ
ءَاتَيْنَٰهُ رَحْمَةً مِّنْ عِندِنَا
وَعَلَّمْنَٰهُ مِن لَّدُنَّا عِلْمًا

66. Moses said to him:
"May I follow thee,
On the footing that
Thou teach me something
Of the (Higher) Truth
Which thou hast been taught?"[2413]

٦٦ قَالَ لَهُۥ مُوسَىٰ
هَلْ أَتَّبِعُكَ عَلَىٰٓ أَن تُعَلِّمَنِ
مِمَّا عُلِّمْتَ رُشْدًا

67. (The other) said: "Verily
Thou wilt not be able
To have patience with me![2414]

٦٧ قَالَ إِنَّكَ لَن تَسْتَطِيعَ مَعِىَ صَبْرًا

68. "And how canst thou
Have patience about things
About which thy understanding
Is not complete?"[2415]

٦٨ وَكَيْفَ تَصْبِرُ عَلَىٰ
مَا لَمْ تُحِطْ بِهِۦ خُبْرًا

2411. *One of Our servants*: his name is not mentioned in the Qur'ān, but Tradition gives it as Khiḍr. Round him have gathered a number of picturesque folk tales, with which we are not here concerned. Khiḍr means "Green": his knowledge is fresh and green, and drawn out of the living sources of life for it is drawn from Allah's own Presence. He is a mysterious being, who had to be sought out. He has the secrets of the paradoxes of Life, which ordinary people do not understand, or understand in a wrong sense, as we shall see further on. The nearest equivalent figure in the literature of the People of the Book is Melchizedek or Melchisedek (the Greek form in the New Testament). In Gen. xiv. 18-20, he appears as king of Salem, priest of the Most High God: he blesses Abraham, and Abraham gives him tithes. St. Paul allegorises him in his Epistle to the Hebrews (v. 6-10; vii. 1-10): "he was without father, without mother, without descent, having neither beginning of days nor end of life". That is to say, he appeared mysteriously: neither his parentage nor his pedigree is known, and he seems to live for all time. These qualities are also attributed to Khiḍr in popular Muslim tradition. (R).

2412. Khiḍr had two special gifts from Allah: (1) Mercy from His own Presence, and (2) Knowledge from His own Presence. The first freed him from the ordinary incidents of daily human life, and the second entitled him to interpret the inner meaning and mystery of events, as we shall see further on. Much could be and has been written about this from the mystic point of view.

2413. Moses, not understanding the full import of what he was asking, makes a simple request. He wants to learn something of the special Knowledge which Allah bestowed on Khiḍr.

2414. Khiḍr smiles, and says that there will be many things which Moses will see with him, which Moses will not completely understand and which will make Moses impatient. The highest spiritual knowledge often seems paradoxical to those who have not the key to it.

2415. Khiḍr does not blame Moses. Each one of us can only follow out our own imperfect lights to the best of our judgement, but if we have Faith, we are saved many false steps.

69. Moses said: "Thou wilt
Find me, if Allah so will,
(Truly) patient: nor shall I
Disobey thee in aught."[2416]

٦٩ قَالَ سَتَجِدُنِيٓ إِن شَآءَ ٱللَّهُ
صَابِرًا وَلَآ أَعۡصِي لَكَ أَمۡرًا

70. The other said: "If then
Thou wouldst follow me,
Ask me no questions
About anything until I
Myself speak to thee
Concerning it."

٧٠ قَالَ فَإِنِ ٱتَّبَعۡتَنِي
فَلَا تَسۡـَٔلۡنِي عَن شَيۡءٍ حَتَّىٰٓ
أُحۡدِثَ لَكَ مِنۡهُ ذِكۡرًا

SECTION 10.

71. So they both proceeded:
Until, when they were
In the boat, he scuttled it.[2417]
Said Moses: "Hast thou
Scuttled it in order
To drown those in it?
Truly a strange thing
Hast thou done!"

٧١ فَٱنطَلَقَا حَتَّىٰٓ إِذَا
رَكِبَا فِي ٱلسَّفِينَةِ خَرَقَهَاۖ
قَالَ أَخَرَقۡتَهَا لِتُغۡرِقَ أَهۡلَهَا
لَقَدۡ جِئۡتَ شَيۡـًٔا إِمۡرًا

72. He answered: "Did I not
Tell thee that thou canst
Have no patience with me?"

٧٢ قَالَ أَلَمۡ أَقُلۡ إِنَّكَ
لَن تَسۡتَطِيعَ مَعِيَ صَبۡرًا

73. Moses said: "Rebuke me not
For forgetting, nor grieve me
By raising difficulties
In my case."

٧٣ قَالَ لَا تُؤَاخِذۡنِي بِمَا نَسِيتُ
وَلَا تُرۡهِقۡنِي مِنۡ أَمۡرِي عُسۡرًا

74. Then they proceeded:
Until, when they met
A young man, he slew him.[2418]
Moses said: "Hast thou
Slain an innocent person
Who had slain none?
Truly a foul (unheard-of) thing
Hast thou done!"

٧٤ فَٱنطَلَقَا حَتَّىٰٓ إِذَا
لَقِيَا غُلَٰمًا فَقَتَلَهُۥ
قَالَ أَقَتَلۡتَ نَفۡسًا زَكِيَّةَۢ بِغَيۡرِ نَفۡسٖ
لَّقَدۡ جِئۡتَ شَيۡـًٔا نُّكۡرًا

2416. Moses had Faith. He adopts the true attitude of the learner to the Teacher, and promises to obey in all things, with the help of Allah. The Teacher is doubtful, but permits him to follow him on condition that he asks no questions about anything until the Teacher himself mentions it first.

2417. The explanation follows in 18:79.

2418. The explanation follows in 18:80-81.

75. He answered: "Did I not
Tell thee that thou canst
Have no patience with me?"

قَالَ أَلَمْ أَقُل لَّكَ إِنَّكَ ﴿٧٥﴾
لَن تَسْتَطِيعَ مَعِىَ صَبْرًا

76. (Moses) said: "If ever I
Ask thee about anything
After this, keep me not
In thy company: then wouldst
Thou have received (full) excuse
From my side."

قَالَ إِن سَأَلْتُكَ عَن شَىْءٍۭ ﴿٧٦﴾
بَعْدَهَا فَلَا تُصَـٰحِبْنِى
قَدْ بَلَغْتَ مِن لَّدُنِّى عُذْرًا

77. Then they proceeded:
Until, when they came
To the inhabitants of a town,
They asked them for food,
But they refused them[2419]
Hospitality. They found there
A wall on the point of
Falling down, but he
Set it up straight.
(Moses) said: "If thou
Hadst wished, surely thou
Couldst have exacted some
Recompense for it!"[2420]

فَانطَلَقَا حَتَّىٰٓ إِذَآ أَتَيَآ ﴿٧٧﴾
أَهْلَ قَرْيَةٍ ٱسْتَطْعَمَآ أَهْلَهَا
فَأَبَوْا۟ أَن يُضَيِّفُوهُمَا
فَوَجَدَا فِيهَا جِدَارًا
يُرِيدُ أَن يَنقَضَّ فَأَقَامَهُۥ
قَالَ لَوْ شِئْتَ لَتَّخَذْتَ عَلَيْهِ أَجْرًا

78. He answered: "This is
The parting between me
And thee: now will I
Tell thee the interpretation
Of (those things) over which
Thou wast unable
To hold patience.[2421]

قَالَ هَـٰذَا فِرَاقُ بَيْنِى وَبَيْنِكَ ﴿٧٨﴾
سَأُنَبِّئُكَ بِتَأْوِيلِ مَا لَمْ
تَسْتَطِع عَّلَيْهِ صَبْرًا

79. As for the boat,
It belonged to certain
Men in dire want:
They plied on the water:
I but wished to render it

أَمَّا ٱلسَّفِينَةُ فَكَانَتْ ﴿٧٩﴾
لِمَسَـٰكِينَ يَعْمَلُونَ فِى ٱلْبَحْرِ فَأَرَدتُّ

2419. The inhabitants were churlish. They broke the universal Eastern rule of hospitality to strangers, and thus showed themselves beyond the pale of ordinary human courtesies. Note that they would have been expected to *offer* hospitality of themselves, unasked. Here Moses and his companion actually had to ask for hospitality and were refused point-blank.

2420. As they were refused hospitality, they should, as self-respecting men, have shaken the dust of the town off their feet, or shown their indignation in some way. Instead of that, Khidr actually goes and does a benevolent act. He rebuilds for them a falling wall, and never asks for any compensation for it. Perhaps he employed local workman for it and paid them wages, thus actually benefiting a town which had treated him and his companion so shabbily! Moses is naturally surprised and asks, "Could you not at least have asked for the cost?"

2421. The story and the interpretation are given with the greatest economy of words. It would repay us to search for the meaning in terms of our own inner and outer experience.

Unserviceable, for there was
After them a certain king
Who seized on every boat
By force.[2422]

أَنْ أَعِيبَهَا وَكَانَ وَرَآءَهُم مَّلِكٌ
يَأْخُذُ كُلَّ سَفِينَةٍ غَصْبًا

80. "As for the youth,
His parents were people
Of Faith, and we feared
That he would grieve them
By obstinate rebellion
And ingratitude (to Allah and
man).[2423]

٨٠ وَأَمَّا ٱلْغُلَٰمُ فَكَانَ أَبَوَاهُ مُؤْمِنَيْنِ
فَخَشِينَآ أَن يُرْهِقَهُمَا
طُغْيَٰنًا وَكُفْرًا

81. "So we desired that
Their Lord would give them
In exchange (a son)
Better in purity (of conduct)
And closer in affection.[2424]

٨١ فَأَرَدْنَآ أَن يُبْدِلَهُمَا رَبُّهُمَا
خَيْرًا مِّنْهُ زَكَوٰةً وَأَقْرَبَ رُحْمًا

82. "As for the wall,
It belonged to two youths,
Orphans, in the Town;
There was, beneath it,
A buried treasure, to which
They were entitled: their father
Had been a righteous man:[2425]

٨٢ وَأَمَّا ٱلْجِدَارُ فَكَانَ لِغُلَٰمَيْنِ
يَتِيمَيْنِ فِى ٱلْمَدِينَةِ وَكَانَ
تَحْتَهُۥ كَنزٌ لَّهُمَا وَكَانَ أَبُوهُمَا صَٰلِحًا

2422. They went on the boat, which was plying for hire. Its owners were not even ordinary men who plied for trade. They had been reduced to great poverty, perhaps from affluent circumstances, and deserved great commiseration, the more so as they preferred an honest calling to begging for charity. They did not know, but Khiḍr did, that the boat, perhaps a new one, had been marked down to be commandeered by an unjust king who seized on every boat he could get—it may have been, for warlike purposes. If this boat had been taken away from these self-respecting men, they would have been reduced to beggary, with no resources left them. By a simple act of making it unseaworthy, the boat was saved from seizure. The owners could repair it as soon as the danger was past. Khiḍr probably paid liberally in fares, and what seemed an unaccountably cruel act was the greatest act of kindness he could do in the circumstances.

2423. This seemed at first sight even a more cruel act than scuttling the boat. But the danger was also greater. Khiḍr knew that the youth was a potential parricide. His parents were worthy, pious people, who had brought him up with love. He had apparently gone wrong. Perhaps he had already been guilty of murders and robberies and had escaped the law by subtleties and fraud. See next note.

2424. The son was practically an outlaw—a danger to the public and a particular source of grief to his righteous parents. Even so, his summary capital punishment would have been unjustified if Khiḍr had been acting on his own. But Khiḍr was not acting on his own: see the latter part of the next verse. The plural "we" also implies that he was not acting on his own. He was acting on higher authority and removing a public scourge, who was also a source of extreme sorrow and humiliation to his parents. His parents are promised a better-behaved son who would love them and be a credit to them.

2425. The wall was in a ruinous state. If it had fallen, the treasure buried beneath it would have been exposed and would certainly have been looted, among so churlish and selfish a people. See n. 2419 above. The treasure had been collected and buried by a righteous man. It was not, in any sense of the word, ill-gotten gains: it was buried expressly in the interests of the orphans by their father before his death. It was intended that the orphans should grow up and safely take possession of their heritage. It was also expected that they would be righteous men like their father, and use the treasure in good works and in advancing righteousness among an otherwise wicked community. There was thus both public and private interests involved in all the three incidents. In the second incident Khiḍr uses the word "we", showing that he was associating in his act the public authorities of the place, who had been eluded by the outlaw.

So thy Lord desired that
They should attain their age[2426]
Of full strength and get out
Their treasure—a mercy
(And favour) from thy Lord.
I did it not of my own[2427]
Accord. Such is the interpretation
Of (those things) over which
Thou wast unable
To hold patience."

فَأَرَادَ رَبُّكَ أَن يَبْلُغَا أَشُدَّهُمَا
وَيَسْتَخْرِجَا كَنزَهُمَا رَحْمَةً مِّن رَّبِّكَ
وَمَا فَعَلْتُهُۥ عَنْ أَمْرِى ۚ ذَٰلِكَ تَأْوِيلُ
مَا لَمْ تَسْطِع عَّلَيْهِ صَبْرًا

C. 137.—Three episodes in the life of a great king.
(18:83-110.) Dhu al Qarnayn illustrated how power
And opportunities should be used in the service
Of Allah: he punished the guilty indeed,
But was kind to the righteous; he left
Primitive people their freedom of life;
And he protected industrious people from grasping
Neighbours. But he relied upon Allah, and made them
Remember the Day of Judgement, when all
Will see the Truth and receive the Punishments
And Rewards earned in their present Life.

SECTION 11.

83. They ask thee concerning
Dhu al Qarnayn.[2428] Say,
"I will rehearse to you
Something of his story."

٨٣ وَيَسْـَٔلُونَكَ عَن ذِى ٱلْقَرْنَيْنِ
قُلْ سَأَتْلُوا۟ عَلَيْكُم مِّنْهُ ذِكْرًا

84. Verily We established his power
On earth, and We gave him
The ways and the means
To all ends.[2429]

٨٤ إِنَّا مَكَّنَّا لَهُۥ فِى ٱلْأَرْضِ
وَءَاتَيْنَٰهُ مِن كُلِّ شَىْءٍ سَبَبًا

2426. *Age of full strength: Cf.* 17:34 and n. 2218.

2427. Those who act, not from a whim or a private impulse of their own, but from higher authority, have to bear the blame, with the vulgar crowd, for acts of the greater wisdom and utility. In human affairs many things are inexplicable, which are things of the highest wisdom in the Universal Plan.

2428. Literally, "the Two-horned One", the King with the Two Horns, or the Lord of the Two Epochs. Who was he? In what age, and where did he live? The Qur'ān gives us no material on which we can base a positive answer. Nor is it necessary to find an answer, as the story is treated as a Parable. Popular opinion identifies Dhu al Qarnayn with Alexander the Great. An alternative suggestion is an ancient Persian King, or a prehistoric Himyarite King. See a brief account of the controversy in Appendix VI printed at the end of this Sūrah.

Dhu al Qarnayn was a most powerful king, but it was Allah, Who, in His universal Plan, gave him power and provided him with the ways and means for his great work. His sway extended over East and West, and over people of diverse civilisations. He was just and righteous, not selfish or grasping. He protected the weak and punished the unlawful and the turbulent. Three of his expeditions are described in the text, each embodying a great ethical idea involved in the possession of kingship or power.

2429. Great was his power and great were his opportunities ("ways and means"), which he used for justice and righteousness. But he recognised that his power and opportunities were given to him as a trust by Allah. He had faith, and did not forget Allah.

85. One (such) way he followed, ٨٥ فَأَتْبَعَ سَبَبًا

86. Until, when he reached
The setting of the sun,[2430]
He found it set
In a spring of murky water:
Near it he found a People:
We said: "O Dhu al Qarnayn!
(Thou hast authority,) either
To punish them, or
To treat them with kindness."[2431]

٨٦ حَتَّىٰٓ إِذَا بَلَغَ مَغْرِبَ ٱلشَّمْسِ وَجَدَهَا تَغْرُبُ فِى عَيْنٍ حَمِئَةٍ وَوَجَدَ عِندَهَا قَوْمًا قُلْنَا يَٰذَا ٱلْقَرْنَيْنِ إِمَّآ أَن تُعَذِّبَ وَإِمَّآ أَن تَتَّخِذَ فِيهِمْ حُسْنًا

87. He said: "Whoever doth wrong,
Him shall we punish; then
Shall he be sent back[2432]
To his Lord; and He will
Punish him with a punishment
Unheard-of (before).

٨٧ قَالَ أَمَّا مَن ظَلَمَ فَسَوْفَ نُعَذِّبُهُۥ ثُمَّ يُرَدُّ إِلَىٰ رَبِّهِۦ فَيُعَذِّبُهُۥ عَذَابًا نُّكْرًا

88. "But whoever believes,
And works righteousness—
He shall have a goodly
Reward, and easy will be
His task as we order it
By our command."[2433]

٨٨ وَأَمَّا مَنْ ءَامَنَ وَعَمِلَ صَٰلِحًا فَلَهُۥ جَزَآءً ٱلْحُسْنَىٰ وَسَنَقُولُ لَهُۥ مِنْ أَمْرِنَا يُسْرًا

89. Then followed he (another) way. ٨٩ ثُمَّ أَتْبَعَ سَبَبًا

2430. This is the first of the three episodes here mentioned, his expedition to the west. "Reaching the setting of the sun" does not mean the extreme west, for there is no such thing. West and East are relative terms. It means a western expedition terminated by a "spring of murky water." This has puzzled Commentators, and they have understood this to mean the dark, tempestuous sea. If Dhu al Qarnayn is Alexander the Great, the reference is easily understood to be the Lychnitis (now Ochrida), west of Macedonia. It is fed entirely by underground springs in a limestone region, where the water is never very clear. (See Appendix VI at the end of the Sūrah).

2430. He had great power and great opportunity. He got authority over a turbulent and unruly people. Was he going to be severe with them and chastise them, or was he going to seek peace at any price, *i.e.*, to wink at violence and injustice so long as it did not affect his power? He chose the better course, as described in the next verse. To protect the weak and the innocent, he punished the guilty and the headstrong, but he remembered always that the true Punishment would come in the Hereaftear—the true and final justice before the throne of Allah.

2432. Through most powerful among kings, he remembered that his power was but human, and given by Allah. His punishments were but tentative, to preserve the balance of this life as he could appraise it. Even if his punishment was capital ("wrongdoer sent back to his Lord") it was nothing compared to the dire consequences of sin, in the final Justice of Allah.

2433. He never said like Pharaoh, "I am your Lord Most High!" (79:24). On the contrary, his punishments were humbly regulated as not being final, and he laid more stress on the good he could do to those who lived normal lives in faith and righteousness. His rule was easy to them: he imposed no heavy tasks because of his power, but gave every opportunity to rich and poor for the exercise of virtue and goodness. Such is the spiritual lesson to be learned from the first episode.

90. Until, when he came
To the rising of the sun,[2434]
He found it rising
On a people for whom
We had provided
No covering protection[2435]
Against the sun.

٩٠ حَتَّىٰٓ إِذَا بَلَغَ مَطْلِعَ ٱلشَّمْسِ
وَجَدَهَا تَطْلُعُ عَلَىٰ قَوْمٍ لَّمْ نَجْعَل
لَّهُم مِّن دُونِهَا سِتْرًا

91. (He left them) as they were:
We completely understood
What was before him.[2436]

٩١ كَذَٰلِكَ وَقَدْ أَحَطْنَا بِمَا لَدَيْهِ خُبْرًا

92. Then followed he (another) way,

٩٢ ثُمَّ أَتْبَعَ سَبَبًا

93. Until, when he reached
(A tract) between two
mountains,[2437]
He found, beneath them, a people
Who scarcely understood a
word.[2438]

٩٣ حَتَّىٰٓ إِذَا بَلَغَ بَيْنَ ٱلسَّدَّيْنِ
وَجَدَ مِن دُونِهِمَا قَوْمًا
لَّا يَكَادُونَ يَفْقَهُونَ قَوْلًا

94. They said: "O Dhu al Qarnayn!
The Gog and Magog (people)[2439]
Do great mischief on earth:
Shall we then render thee
Tribute in order that

٩٤ قَالُوا۟ يَٰذَا ٱلْقَرْنَيْنِ إِنَّ يَأْجُوجَ وَمَأْجُوجَ
مُفْسِدُونَ فِى ٱلْأَرْضِ فَهَلْ نَجْعَلُ لَكَ خَرْجًا

2434. We now come to the second episode. This is an expedition to the east. "Rising of the sun" has a meaning corresponding to "setting of the sun" in 18:86. as explained in n. 2430.

2435. The people here lived very simple lives. Perhaps the climate was hot, and they required neither roofs over their heads, nor much clothing to protect them from the sun. What did he do with them? See next note.

2436. They were a primitive people. He did not fuss over their primitiveness, but left them in the enjoyment of peace and tranquillity in their own way. In this he was wise. Power is apt to be intolerant and arrogant, and to interfere in everything that does not accord with its own glorification. Not so Dhu al Qarnayn. He recognised his own limitations in the sight of Allah: man never completely understands his own position, but if he devoutly looks to Allah, he will live and let live. This is the spiritual lesson from the second episode.

2437. The geography of the place (if geography is relevant in a parable story) is discussed in Appendix VI at the end of this Sūrah.

2438. It does not mean that they had no speech. It means that they did not understand the speech of the Conqueror. But they had parleys with him (through interpreters), as is evident from the verses following (18:94-98).

2439. Who were the Gog and Magog people? This question is connected with the question, who was Dhu al Qarnayn? Some discussion on the question will be found in Appendix VI at the end of this Sūrah.

What we are mainly concerned with is the spiritual interpretation. The Conqueror had now arrived among a people who were different in speech and race from him, but not quite primitive, for they were skilled in the working of metals, and could furnish blocks (or bricks) or iron, melt metals with bellows or blowpipes, and prepare molten lead (18:96). Apparently they were a peaceable and industrious race, much subject to incursions from wild tribes who are called Gog and Magog. Against these tribes they were willing to purchase immunity by paying the Conqueror tribute in return for protection. The permanent protection they wanted was the closing of a mountain gap through which the incursions were made.

Thou mightest erect a barrier
Between us and them?

عَلَىٰٓ أَن تَجْعَلَ بَيْنَنَا وَبَيْنَهُمْ سَدًّا

95. He said: "(The power) in which
My Lord had established me
Is better (than tribute):[2440]
Help me therefore with strength
(And labour): I will
Erect a stronger barrier
Between you and them:

٩٥ قَالَ مَا مَكَّنِّي فِيهِ رَبِّي خَيْرٌ فَأَعِينُونِي بِقُوَّةٍ أَجْعَلْ بَيْنَكُمْ وَبَيْنَهُمْ رَدْمًا

96. "Bring me blocks of iron."[2441]
At length, when he had
Filled up the space between
The two steep mountainsides,
He said, "Blow (with your bellows)"
Then, when he had made[2442]
It (red) as fire, he said:
"Bring me, that I may
Pour over it, molten lead."

٩٦ ءَاتُونِي زُبَرَ الْحَدِيدِ حَتَّىٰٓ إِذَا سَاوَىٰ بَيْنَ الصَّدَفَيْنِ قَالَ انفُخُوا حَتَّىٰٓ إِذَا جَعَلَهُۥ نَارًا قَالَ ءَاتُونِيٓ أُفْرِغْ عَلَيْهِ قِطْرًا

97. Thus were they made
Powerless to scale it
Or to dig through it.[2443]

٩٧ فَمَا اسْطَٰعُوٓا أَن يَظْهَرُوهُ وَمَا اسْتَطَٰعُوا لَهُۥ نَقْبًا

98. He said: "This is
A mercy from my Lord:[2444]
But when the promise

٩٨ قَالَ هَٰذَا رَحْمَةٌ مِّن رَّبِّي فَإِذَا جَآءَ وَعْدُ

2440. Dhu al Qarnayn was not greedy and did not want to impose a tribute to be carried away from an industrious population. He understood the power which Allah had given him, to involve duties and responsibilities on his part—the duty of protecting his subjects without imposing too heavy a taxation on them. He would provide the motive force and organising skill. Would they obey him and povide the material and labour, so that they could close the gap with a strong barrier, probably with well-secured gates? The word *radm*, translated "Barrier," does not necessarily mean a wall, but rather suggests a blocked door or entrance.

2441. I understand the defences erected to have been a strong barrier of iron, with iron Gates. The jambs of the Gates were constructed with blocks or bricks of iron, and the interstices filled up with molten lead, so as to form an impregnable mass of metal. It may be that there was a stone wall also, but that is not mentioned. There was none in the Iron Gate near Bukhārā; see Appendix VI at the end of his Sūrah.

2442. *Made it (red) as fire:* what does "it" refer to? Probably to the iron, either in sheets or blocks, to be welded with molten lead.

2443. The iron wall and gates and towers were sufficiently high to prevent their being scaled and sufficiently strong with welded metal to resist any attempt to dig through them.

2444. After all the effort which Dhu al Qarnayn has made for their protection, he claims no credit for himself beyond that of discharging his duty as a ruler. He turns their attention to Allah, Who has provided the ways and means by which they can be helped and protected. But all such human precautions are apt to become futile. The time must come when they will crumble into dust. Allah has said so in His Revelation; and His word is true.

And so the spiritual lesson from the third episode is: Take human precautions and do all in your power to protect yourselves from evil. But no protection is complete unless you seek the help and grace of Allah. The best of our precautions must crumble to dust when the appointed Day arrives.

Of my Lord comes to pass,
He will make it into dust;
And the promise of
My Lord is true."

رَبِّي جَعَلَهُۥ دَكَّآءَ
وَكَانَ وَعْدُ رَبِّي حَقًّا

99. On that day We shall
Leave them to surge
Like waves on one another;[2445]
The trumpet will be blown,
And We shall collect them
All together.

٩٩ وَتَرَكْنَا بَعْضَهُمْ
يَوْمَئِذٍ يَمُوجُ فِي بَعْضٍ
وَنُفِخَ فِي ٱلصُّورِ فَجَمَعْنَٰهُمْ جَمْعًا

100. And We shall present
Hell that day for Unbelievers
To see, all spread out—[2446]

١٠٠ وَعَرَضْنَا جَهَنَّمَ يَوْمَئِذٍ لِّلْكَٰفِرِينَ عَرْضًا

101. (Unbelievers) whose eyes
Had been under a veil
From Remembrance of Me,
And who had been unable
Even to hear.[2447]

١٠١ ٱلَّذِينَ كَانَتْ أَعْيُنُهُمْ فِي غِطَآءٍ
عَن ذِكْرِي وَكَانُوا۟ لَا يَسْتَطِيعُونَ سَمْعًا

SECTION 12.

102. Do the Unbelievers think
That they can take
My servants as protectors
Besides Me? Verily We
Have prepared Hell
For the Unbelievers
For (their) entertainment.

١٠٢ أَفَحَسِبَ ٱلَّذِينَ كَفَرُوٓا۟
أَن يَتَّخِذُوا۟ عِبَادِي مِن دُونِيٓ أَوْلِيَآءَ
إِنَّآ أَعْتَدْنَا جَهَنَّمَ لِلْكَٰفِرِينَ نُزُلًا

103. Say: "Shall we tell you
Of those who lose most
In respect of their deeds?—"[2448]

١٠٣ قُلْ هَلْ نُنَبِّئُكُم بِٱلْأَخْسَرِينَ أَعْمَٰلًا

104. "Those whose efforts have
Been wasted in this life.

١٠٤ ٱلَّذِينَ ضَلَّ سَعْيُهُمْ فِي ٱلْحَيَوٰةِ ٱلدُّنْيَا

2445. And so we pass on to the Last Days before the Great Summons comes from Allah. All human barriers will be swept away. There will be tumultuous rushes. The Trumpet will be blown, and the Judgement will be set on foot.

2446. If men had scoffed at Faith and the Hereafter, their eyes will be opened now, and they will see the terrible Reality.

2447. Those very men who refused to see the many Signs of Allah which in this world convey His Message and to hear the Word of the Lord when it came to them, will then see without any mistake the consequences fully brought up before them.

2448. That is, those who prided themselves on their works in this life, and now find that those works are of no avail. Their loss is all the greater because they had a misplaced confidence in their own deeds or in the assistance of false "protectors". Allah is the only Protector: no one else's protection is of any use.

While they thought that They were acquiring good By their works?"[2449]	وَهُمْ يَحْسَبُونَ أَنَّهُمْ يُحْسِنُونَ صُنْعًا
105. They are those who deny The Signs of their Lord And the fact of their Having to meet Him (In the Hereafter): vain Will be their works, Nor shall We, on the Day Of Judgement, give them Any Weight.[2450]	﴿١٠٥﴾ أُولَٰئِكَ الَّذِينَ كَفَرُوا بِآيَاتِ رَبِّهِمْ وَلِقَائِهِ فَحَبِطَتْ أَعْمَالُهُمْ فَلَا نُقِيمُ لَهُمْ يَوْمَ الْقِيَامَةِ وَزْنًا
106. That is their reward, Hell; because they rejected Faith, and took My Signs And My Messengers By way of jest.[2451]	﴿١٠٦﴾ ذَٰلِكَ جَزَاؤُهُمْ جَهَنَّمُ بِمَا كَفَرُوا وَاتَّخَذُوا آيَاتِي وَرُسُلِي هُزُوًا
107. As to those who believe And work righteous deeds, They have, for their entertainment, The Gardens of Paradise,[2452]	﴿١٠٧﴾ إِنَّ الَّذِينَ آمَنُوا وَعَمِلُوا الصَّالِحَاتِ كَانَتْ لَهُمْ جَنَّاتُ الْفِرْدَوْسِ نُزُلًا
108. Wherein they shall dwell (For aye): no change Will they wish for themselves.	﴿١٠٨﴾ خَالِدِينَ فِيهَا لَا يَبْغُونَ عَنْهَا حِوَلًا
109. Say:"If the ocean were Ink (wherewith to write out) The words of my Lord.[2453]	﴿١٠٩﴾ قُلْ لَوْ كَانَ الْبَحْرُ مِدَادًا لِكَلِمَاتِ رَبِّي

2449. Many people have such a smug sense of self-righteousness that while they go on doing wrong, they think that they are acquiring merit. So, in charity, all the elements that make for outward show or selfishness (as to get some worldly advantage) nullify the deed of charity. In the same way, hypocrites sometimes affect to be surprised that their declared effort for somebody's good is not appreciated, when they are really seeking some hidden gain or false glory for themselves. The sincere are only those who believe in their spiritual responsibility and act in Allah's sight.

2450. What weight can be attached to works behind which the motives are not pure, or are positively evil? They are either wasted or count against those who seek to pass them off as meritorious!

2451. False motives, pretence, deception, and hypocrisy, flourish because people do not take the higher life seriously. In effect they treat it as a jest. Signs and Messengers are sent as a special and personal Mercy from Allah, and for such things the first person singular is used as in this verse, even when it involves a sudden transition from the first person plural as in the last verse.

2452. *Firdaws* in Persian means an enclosed place, a park. In technical theological language the word is used for the inner circle of Heaven, or the highest Heaven, the destination of those who perfectly fulfil both requirements, *viz.*: a sound faith, and perfectly righteous conduct. Small faults in either respect are forgiven; the Mercy of Allah steps in. (R).

2453. The Words and Signs and Mercies of Allah are in all Creation, and can never be fully set out in human language, however extended our means may be imagined to be.

Sooner would the ocean be
Exhausted than would the words
Of my Lord, even if we
Added another ocean
Like it, for its aid."

لَنَفِدَ ٱلْبَحْرُ قَبْلَ أَن تَنفَدَ كَلِمَٰتُ
رَبِّى وَلَوْ جِئْنَا بِمِثْلِهِۦ مَدَدًا

110. Say: "I am but a man
Like yourselves, (but)
The inspiration has come
To me, that your God is
One God: whoever expects
To meet his Lord, let him
Work righteousness, and,
In the worship of his Lord,
Admit no one as partner."2454

قُلْ إِنَّمَآ أَنَا۠ بَشَرٌ مِّثْلُكُمْ ١١٠
يُوحَىٰٓ إِلَىَّ أَنَّمَآ إِلَٰهُكُمْ إِلَٰهٌ وَٰحِدٌ
فَمَن كَانَ يَرْجُوا۟ لِقَآءَ رَبِّهِۦ فَلْيَعْمَلْ
عَمَلًا صَٰلِحًا وَلَا يُشْرِكْ بِعِبَادَةِ رَبِّهِۦٓ أَحَدًۢا

2454. Righteousness and true respect for Allah—which excludes the worship of anything else, whether idols, or deified men, or forces of nature, or faculties of man, or Self—these are the criteria of true worship.

APPENDIX VI.

Who was D̲hu al Qarnayn?

(18:83-98.)

As stated in my n. 2428 to 18:83, I do not consider that historical or geographical considerations have much bearing on a story treated as a Parable, as D̲hu al Qarnayn's story is. Indeed all stories or narrations are referred to in the Qur'ān as Parables, for their spiritual meaning. Heated controversies or dogmatic assertions as to precise dates, personalities, or localities, seem to me to be out of place. But a great deal of literature has been piled up among our writers on the subject, and it seems desirable to set down a few notes as to the different views that have been expressed.

What is the meaning of the name or title *D̲hu al Qarnayn*— "Lord of two *Qarns*"? "*Qarn*" may mean: (1) a horn in the literal sense, as in the case of a ram or bull; (2) a horn in a metaphorical sense, as in English, the horns of a crescent, or by a further metaphor (not used in English), the horns of a kingdom or territory, two portions at opposite ends; (3) by another metaphor, a summit, a lock of hair, typifying strength, a crest such as Eastern kings wear on their diadems; (4) referring to time, an Epoch, an Age, a Generation. Meaning (1) is inapplicable to a man or a great King: but see the next paragraph about Alexander the Great. The other three meanings may be applicable, as implying: (2) Lord of East and West, Lord of wide territory or of two kingdoms; (3) Lord of two crests on his diadem, typifying two kingdoms, or a rank superior to that of an ordinary king; (4) Lord of more than one Epoch: one whose power and influence extend far beyond his lifetime.

If we accept the popular identification of D̲hu al Qarnayn with Alexander, all the three latter designations would be applicable to him, as he was lord of the West and the East, lord of the Greek States united for the first time (Hellenic Captain-General) and of the widely extended Persian Dominion which included all Western Asia, Egypt, Central Asia, Afghanistan, and the Punjab (at least portions). He is represented on his coins with two horns on his head: he considered himself a son of Jupiter Ammon (who had the two horns of a ram), with a divine mission. He revolutionised the history of Europe, Asia, and Africa (Eygpt), and his influence lasted for many generations after his death at the young age of 33. He lived from B.C. 356 to 323, but his name was one to conjure with for many centuries after him. It was not only on account of his political power, but his cultural influences. Through his conquests, Greek art gave the impulse to Gandhara art in Central Asia and Northwest India. The city of Alexandria which he founded in Egypt became the cultural centre, not only for Greece and Rome, but for Judaism and Christianity, and retained its supremacy till the sixth century of the Christian era. Justinian closed its schools of philosophy in 529. Its philosophic and scientific schools spread their influence over even a wider area than the Mediterranean basin.

Now the generality of the world of Islam have accepted Alexander the Great as the one meant by the epithet D̲hu al Qarnayn. But some of our 'Ulamā' have raised doubts about it and made other suggestions. One is that it was not the Macedonian Alexander the Great, but an earlier prehistoric king contemporary with Abraham; because, they say D̲hu al Qarnayn was a man of Faith (18:88,98), while Alexander the Great was a Pagan and believed in Grecian gods. An identification with a supposed prehistoric king, about whom nothing is known, is no identification at all. On the other hand, all that is known about Alexander the Great shows that he was a man of lofty ideals. He died over three centuries before the time of Jesus, but that does not mean he was not a man of Faith, for Allah revealed Himself to men of all nations in all ages. Alexander was a disciple of the philosopher Aristotle, noted for his pursuit of sound Truth in all departments of thought. Alexander's reference to Jupiter Ammon may have been no more than a playful reference to the superstitions of his time. Socrates spoke of the Grecian gods, and so did Aristotle and Plato;

but it would be wrong to call them idolaters or men without Faith. In the Ethiopic traditional stories of Alexander the Great, he is represented as a great prophet.

Another suggestion made is that D͟hu al Qarnayn was an ancient king of Persia. A king of Persia is referred to as a Ram with two horns in the Book of Daniel (8:3) in the Old Testament. But in the same Book, the Ram with the two horns was smitten, cast down to the ground, and stamped upon by a he-goat with one horn (8:7-8). There is nothing in our literature to suggest that D͟hu al Qarnayn came to any such ignominious end. Nor is the Book of Daniel an authority worth consideration. Its authenticity is very doubtful. There is no question that it is a patchwork, as parts of it are in the Aramaic (or Chaldee) language and parts in Hebrew, and there are in it a number of Greek words. The Septuagint version contained large additions. "Daniel"—whoever the writer or writers were—refers to historical Persian kings. If it is argued that it was some old prehistoric Persian king who built the Iron Gates (18:96) to keep out the Gog and Magog tribes (18:94), this is no identification at all. There is no unanimity about the identity of the Iron Wall, or the Gog and Magog tribes. Both these subjects will be referred to presently.

Another suggestion made is that he was some old prehistoric Himyarite king from Yemen, about whom nothing else is known. This, again, is no identification at all.

The question of Yājūj and Mājūj (Gog and Magog) and the iron Barrier built to keep them out is of some interest. It is practically agreed that they were the wild tribes of Central Asia which have made inroads on settled kingdoms and Empires at various stages of the world's history. The Chinese Empire suffered from their incursions and built the Great Wall of China to keep out the Manchus and Mongols. The Persian Empire suffered from them at various times and at various points. Their incursions into Europe in large hordes caused migrations and displacements of population on an enormous scale, and eventually broke up the Roman Empire. These tribes were known vaguely to the Greeks and Romans as "Scythians", but that term does not help us very much, either ethnically or geographically.

If we could locate the iron barrier or iron gates referred to in 18:96, we should have a closer idea of the tribes whom the barrier was meant to keep out. It is obvious that the Great Wall of China is out of the question. Begun in the third century B.C. and continued later, it covers the enormous length of 1,500 miles, and goes up the hills and down the valleys, with towers 40 feet high at intervals of 200 yards. Its average height is 20 to 30 feet. It is built of stone and earth. There is no particular point in it which can be identified with the iron barrier in the text. No one has suggested that D͟hu al Qarnayn was a Chinese Emperor, and none of the great Conquerors of Western Asia can be credited with the building of the Chinese Wall.

The Barrier in the text must have been more in the nature of iron gates than an iron wall. Two Iron Gates, geographically far apart, have been suggested in the alternative. Sometimes they have been mixed up by writers not strong in geography. Both of them have local associations with the name of Alexander the Great. Both are near a town Derbend, and have borne the name of Bāb al Ḥadīd (Arabic for "Iron Gate"). Let us examine the case of each in turn.

The best known in modern times is at the town and seaport of Derbend in the middle of the western coast of the Caspian Sea. It is now in Soviet territory, in the district of Daghistan. Before the southern expansion of Russia in 1813 it belonged to Persia. A spur of Mount Caucasus here comes up north, close to the sea. The Wall in question is 50 miles long, with an average height of 29 feet. As Azerbaijan (in Persia) is not far from this place, some writers have mixed up the Derbend Iron Gate with Azerbaijan, and some with the Caucasian town of K͟harz (Kars), which is to the south of the Caucasus. There are local traditions here, and in the Astrakhan region, at the mouth of the river Volga, higher up the Caspian, connecting this Caucasian Iron Gate with the name of Alexander, but there are good reasons why we should reject this as the site of the Iron Gate in the Quranic story. (1) This does not correspond exactly to the description in 18:96 ("the space between the steep mountain sites"); the gap is between the mountain and the sea. (2) Alexander the Great (assuming that D͟hu al Qarnayn is Alexander), is not known to have crossed the Caucasus. (3) There is an Iron Gate which corresponds exactly to the description, in a locality which we know Alexander to have visited. (4) In the early days, when Muslims spread to all parts of the world, local legends were started by ignorant people connecting the places they knew with places referred to in the Qur'ān.

We now come to the Iron Gate which corresponds exactly to the Quranic description, and has the best claim to be connected with Alexander's story. It is near another Derbend in Central Asia, Hissar District, about 150 miles southeast of Buk͟hārā. A very narrow defile, with overhanging rocks, occurs on the main route between Turkestan and India: latitude 38ºN; longitude 67ºE. It is now called in Turkish Buzghol-K͟hana (Goat-house), but was formerly known as the Iron Gate (Arabic, *Bāb al Ḥadīd*; Persian, *Dar-i-āhanī*; Chinese *T'ie-men-kuan*. There is no iron gate there now, but there was one in the seventh century, when the Chinese traveller Hiouen Tsiang saw it on his journey to India. He saw two folding gates cased with iron hung with bells. Nearby is a lake named Iskandar Kul, connecting the locality with Alexander the Great. We know from histroy that Alexander, after his conquest of Persia and before his journey to India, visited Sogdiana *(Buk͟hārā)* and Maracanda *(Samarqand)*. We also know from Muqaddasī, the Arab traveller and geographer, who wrote about A.H. 375 (A.C. 985-6) that the 'Abbāsī K͟halīfa Wāt͟hiq (842-846 A.C.) sent out a mission to Central Asia to report on this Iron Gate. They found the defile 150 yards wide: on two jambs, made with bricks of iron welded together with molten lead, were hung two huge gates, which were kept closed. Nothing could correspond more exactly with the description in 18:95-96.

If, then, the Barrier in 18:95-98 refers to the Iron Gate near Buk͟hārā, we are able to proceed to a consideration of the Gog-Magog people with some confidence. They were the Mongol tribes on the other side of the Barrier, while the industrious men who did not understand D͟hu al Qarnayn's language were the Turks, with their agglutinative language, so different from the languages then spoken in Western Asia. The Barrier served its purpose for the time being. But the warning that the time must come when it must crumble to dust has also come true. It has crumbled to dust. Long since, the Mongols pushed through on their westward journey, pushing the Turks before them, and the Turks became a European Power and still have a footing in Europe. We need not bother about the legends of the Gog and Magog people. They were reputed to be giants, and two tiny hills in flat Cambridgeshire are derisively called the Gog-Magog hills! Similarly the statues of Gog and Magog in the Guildhall in London, which M.M.A. takes so seriously, only remind us how legends are apt to grow and get transported to strange places. In the Alexander legends of medieval Europe, Gog and Magog are said to have come with 400,000 men to the help of Porus whom Alexander defeated, and to have fled after that defeat. They fled to the mountains, and Alexander built a wall with brass gates to prevent their irruptions. See Paul Meyer, *Alexandre le Grand dans la literature francaise du Moyen Age*: Paris, 1886; Vol. 2, pp. 386-389.

Personally, I have not the least doubt that D͟hu al Qarnayn is meant to be Alexander the Great, the historic Alexander, and not the legendary Alexander, of whom more presently. My first appointment after graduation was that of Lecturer in Greek history. I have studied the details of Alexander's extraordinary personality in Greek historians as well as in modern writers, and have since visited most of the localities connected with his brief but brilliant career. Few readers of Quranic literature have had the same privilege of studying the details of his career. It is one of the wonders of the Qur'ān, that, spoken through an *Ummī's* mouth, it should contain so many incidental details which are absolutely true. The more our knowledge increases, the more we feel this. There are little touches which need not have been mentioned. They come in incidentally like the incidental remarks of a person full of knowledge, who does not intend to put forward these points but whose fulness of knowledge brings them in inevitably.

One such point occurs in the mention of Alexander's westward journey (18:86). He saw the sun set in a piece of murky water which is described as a "Spring". Most Commentators have understood the "spring" to be the sea, and the "murky water" to be its dark-blue water. Niẓāmī, in his *Romance of Alexander*, takes Alexander right west along North Africa to Andalusia and the Atlantic Ocean. There is no historic proof that Alexander ever reached the Atlantic. But he was of course familiar with the deep-blue waters of the Mediterranean. The Mediterranean interpretation may pass if we had not a closer explanation. Alexander's first exploits were when he was a mere boy, in the reign of his father Phillip. The region of Illyricum was due west of Macedonia, and Macedonia's first expansion was in that direction. The town of Lychnis was annexed to Macedonia and thus the western frontier of Macedonia was secured. The northern frontier towards the Danube had already been secured, and the lesson he subsequently gave to Thebes secured him against attack from the Greek States to the south, and prepared the way for his great march east against the Persian Empire. To the west of the town of Lychnis is a lake 170 square miles in area, fed by underground springs that issue through limestone rocks and give out murky water. Both town and lake are now called Ochrida, about 50 miles west of Monastir. The water is so dark that the river which forms the outlet of the lake to the north is called the Black Drin. Looking at the sunset from the town, the observer would see the sun set in a pool of murky water (18:86). It was a question before the boy Alexander—the dreamy, impulsive, fearless rider—whether he would put the barbarous Illyricans to the sword or show them mercy. He showed true discrimination and statesmanship. He punished the guilty but showed kindness to the innocent, and thus consolidated his power in the west. This I construe to be the meaning of 18:86-87; otherwise these verses do not seem to be perfectly clear.

Another point may be noted. The three episodes mentioned are the journey to the west, the journey to the east, and the journey to the Iron Gate. The journey to the west I have just explained. The journey to the east was to the Persian Empire. Here he found a people who lived in the open and wore little clothing. This might apply to people who live in an inland place in the latitude of Persepolis or Multani. He left them alone as they were (18:91). He was not warring against populations: he was warring against proud but effete Persian Empire. He left them as they were, with their local institutions, and under their local chiefs. In feeling, he treated them as his own, not as aliens. In some things, he himself adopted their ways. His followers misunderstood him. But Allah understood, for He approves of all things that lead to Unity among mankind.

The direction of the third journey is not mentioned. The Commentators suggest the north, but they might with better reason have suggested the south, as Alexander visited Eygpt. But the visit to the Iron Gate was to the East—a continuation of his journey east. That is why the direction is not mentioned again. Here his mission was different. He had to protect a peaceful industrious population, whom perhaps the Persian Empire had failed to protect, against turbulent and restless invaders. He helped them to protect themselves, but warned them that all human precautions, though good and necessary, are vain without Allah's help.

Each of the episodes mentioned is historical. But the pomp and glitter of military conquest are not mentioned. On the contrary, spiritual motives are revealed and commended. We need not know or learn any history or geography or science or psychology or ethics to understand them. But the more real knowledge we have, the more completely shall we understand them and the lessons to be drawn from them. The earthly journeys are treated as mere symbols to show us the evolution of a great and noble soul which achieved so much in a short earthly life.

His career was so extraordinary that it impressed his contemporaries as a world event. It undoubtedly was one of the greatest world events in history. Legends began to grow up round his name. In many cases the legends overlaid the history. Today the world is thrilled by Sir Ayrel Stein's identification of Aornos, a very small geographical detail in a great career full of lessons, in political, ethical, and religious wisdom. But the generations immediately following Alexander's period wrote and transmitted all sorts of wonderful legends that passed current in East and West. The philosopher Kallisthenes had been with Alexander in Asia. Under his name was produced a Greek book in Alexandria some time before the second century of the Christian era. It was translated into Latin in the third century. Translations were subsequently made into most of the European languages. In Chaucer's time (1340-1400) these Alexander legends were known to every "wight that hath discrecion" (The Monk in *Cantebury Tales*).

Alexandria was a focus of Christian and Jewish learning for some centuries. The Christians also made Alexander a saint. The Jews carried the Alexander cycle into the East. Our Persian poet Jāmī (A.H. 535-599, A.C. 1141-1203) worked it up into his epic the *Iskandar-nāma*. He is careful to show the historical or semi-historical and the ethical parts separately. The one relates to action or exploits *(Iqbāl)* and the other to wisdom *(Khirad)*. He had the advantage of the Quranic story before him. That story mentions three historical episodes incidentally, but draws our attention to matters of the weightiest spiritual significance, and that is the chief thing to note in the story.

INTRODUCTION TO SŪRAH 19—*MARYAM*

The spiritual growth of man as an individual soul having been explained in S. 17. as beginning with the first principles of moral conduct and in S. 18. as being dependent upon our realisation of the brevity and mystery of this life and the true use of power as in the story of Dhu al Qarnayn, we now pass on the story of individual Messengers of Allah in their personal relations with their environment—Yaḥyā with his father Zakarīya, Jesus with his mother Mary; Abraham with his unbelieving father, Moses with his brother Aaron, Ismā'īl with his family, and Idrīs in the high station to which he was called. Seeing how these great ones fitted into the scheme of life, man is condemned for his want of faith, or for degrading his faith to superstition, and warned of the Hereafter.

In chronology, it was revealed before the first resort of the batch of Muslims to Abyssinia, say seven years before Hijrah.

***Summary*—Zakarīya was anxious to have an heir to carry on Allah's work in a world of unrighteousness, and Yaḥyā was given to him (19:1-15, and C. 138).**

Mary the mother of Jesus was maligned by her people, but Jesus comforted her and was good to her (19:16-40, and C. 139).

Abraham was persecuted for his Faith by his people, including his unbelieving father, but he withdrew from them, and was blessed; Moses was helped by his brother Aaron; Ismā'īl brought up his family in piety; and Idrīs was truthful and pious in a high station: they showed the way; yet men will not learn the good of life (19:41-65, and C. 140).

Man should not disbelieve in the Hereafter, nor sully his faith by false notions about Allah (19:68-98, and C. 141).

C. 138.—Men of God show their qualities
(19:1-15.) In their private relationships as much
As in their public ministry. Zakarīya
Was anxious, in a world of unrighteousness,
To find a successor to continue his godly
Errand. He was given a son, Yaḥyā,
Who heralded Jesus, and lived a life
Of wisdom, gentle love, and purity.

Sūrah 19.

الجزء السادس عشر سورة مريم

Maryam **(Mary)**

In the name of Allah, Most Gracious, Most Merciful.

بِسْمِ ٱللَّهِ ٱلرَّحْمَٰنِ ٱلرَّحِيمِ

1. Kāf Hā Yā ʻAyn Ṣād.[2455]

كٓهيعٓصٓ ﴿١﴾

2. (This is) a recital[2456]
Of the Mercy of thy Lord
To His Servant Zakarīya.

ذِكْرُ رَحْمَتِ رَبِّكَ عَبْدَهُۥ زَكَرِيَّآ ﴿٢﴾

3. Behold! he cried
To his Lord in secret,[2457]

إِذْ نَادَىٰ رَبَّهُۥ نِدَآءً خَفِيًّا ﴿٣﴾

4. Praying: "O my Lord!
Infirm indeed are my bones,
And the hair of my head
Doth glisten with grey:
But never am I unblest,
O my Lord, in my prayer[2458]
To Thee!

قَالَ رَبِّ إِنِّى وَهَنَ ٱلْعَظْمُ مِنِّى
وَٱشْتَعَلَ ٱلرَّأْسُ شَيْبًا
وَلَمْ أَكُنۢ بِدُعَآئِكَ
رَبِّ شَقِيًّا ﴿٤﴾

5. "Now I fear (what)
My relatives (and colleagues)

وَإِنِّى خِفْتُ ٱلْمَوَٰلِىَ ﴿٥﴾

2455. This is the only Sūrah which begins with these five Abbreviated Letters, *Kāf, Hā, Yā, ʻAyn, Ṣād.* For Abbreviated Letters generally, see Appendix I.

As stated in my note 25, such Letters are Symbols, of which the true meaning is known to Allah alone. We should not be dogmatic about any conjectures that we make. According to the interpretation of the last letter *Ṣād*, suggested in n. 989 to 7:1. I should be disposed to accept Ṣād with the meaning of *Qiṣaṣ, i.e.*, stories of the Prophets. The main figures referred to here are: Zakariya, Yaḥyā, Maryam, ʻĪsā, and Ibrāhim: the others are mentioned but incidentally. The strong letter in ZaKarīya is K; in IbraHīm. H; in YaḥYā and perhaps MarYam, Y; and in ʻĪsa—ʻA (*ʻAyn*). H also comes in Hārūn (Aaron), and the Arabic *Yā'* comes in all the names including Ismāʻīl and Idrīs.

I offer this suggestion with some diffidence. The suggestion of the *Tafsīr Kabīr* is that the letters stand for attributes of Allah: K. for *Kafī* (the One sufficient in Himself); H. for *Hādī* (He who guides); Y. for *Yad* (Hand as a symbol of Power and Authority; *Cf.* 48:10, "The Hand of Allah is above their hands"); ʻA. for *ʻAlīm* (the All-Knowing); and Ṣ for *Ṣādiq* (The True One).

2456. The Mercy of Allah to Zakarīya was shown in many ways: (1) in the acceptance of his prayer; (2) in bestowing a son like Yaḥyā; and (3) in the love between father and son, in addition to the work which Yaḥyā did as Allah's Messenger for the world. *Cf.* 3:38-41 and notes. There the public ministry was the point stressed; here the beautiful relations between the son and the father.

2457. *In secret*: because he feared that his own family and relatives were going wrong (19:5), and he wanted to keep the lamp of Allah burning bright. He could not very well mention the fear about his colleagues (who were his relations) in public.

2458. This preface shows the fervent faith of Zakarīya. Zakarīya was a priest of the Most High Allah. His office was the Temple, and his relatives were his colleagues. But he found in them no true spirit of the service of Allah and man. He was filled with anxiety as to who would uphold the godly ideas he had in mind, which were strange to his worldly colleagues.

(Will do) after me:
But my wife is barren:
So give me an heir[2459]
As from Thyself—

مِن وَرَآءِى وَكَانَتِ ٱمْرَأَتِى عَاقِرًا
فَهَبْ لِى مِن لَّدُنكَ وَلِيًّا

6. "(One that) will (truly)
Represent me, and represent[2460]
The posterity of Jacob;
And make him, O my Lord!
One with whom Thou art
Well-pleased!"

٦ يَرِثُنِى وَيَرِثُ
مِنْ ءَالِ يَعْقُوبَ
وَٱجْعَلْهُ رَبِّ رَضِيًّا

7. (His prayer was answered):
"O Zakariyyā We give thee
Good news of a son:
His name shall be Yaḥyā:
On none by that name
Have We conferred distinction
before."[2461]

٧ يَٰزَكَرِيَّآ
إِنَّا نُبَشِّرُكَ بِغُلَٰمٍ ٱسْمُهُۥ يَحْيَىٰ
لَمْ نَجْعَل لَّهُۥ مِن قَبْلُ سَمِيًّا

8. He said: "O my Lord!
How shall I have a son,
When my wife is barren
And I have grown quite decrepit
From old age?"

٨ قَالَ رَبِّ أَنَّىٰ يَكُونُ لِى غُلَٰمٌ
وَكَانَتِ ٱمْرَأَتِى عَاقِرًا
وَقَدْ بَلَغْتُ مِنَ ٱلْكِبَرِ عِتِيًّا

9. He said: "So (it will be):[2462]
Thy Lord saith, 'That is
Easy for Me: I did

٩ قَالَ كَذَٰلِكَ قَالَ رَبُّكَ هُوَ عَلَىَّ هَيِّنٌ

2459. His was not merely a vulgar desire for a son. If it had been, he would have prayed much earlier in his life, when he was a young man. He was too full of true piety to put merely selfish things into his prayers. But here was a public need, in the service of the Lord. He was too old, but could he perhaps adopt a child—who would be an heir "as from Allah?" (See n. 380 to 3:38).

2460. It is true that an heir inherits property, but his higher duty is to represent in everything the personality of him from whom he inherits. It is doubtful whether Zakariyyā had any worldly property. But he had character and virtue, as a man of God, and this he wanted to transmit to his heir as his most precious possession. It was almost the most precious possession of the posterity of Jacob. The people around him had fallen away from Allah's Message. Could his heir, like him, try and renew it?

2461. This was John the Baptist, the forerunner of Jesus. In accordance with his father's prayer he, and Jesus for whom he prepared the way, renewed the Message of Allah, which had been corrupted and lost among the Israelites. The Arabic form Yaḥyā suggests "Life". The Hebrew form is Johanan, which means "Jehovah has been Gracious". *Cf. Ḥanāna* in verse 13 below. It does not mean that the name was given for the first time, for we read of a Johanan the son of Careah in II Kings, xxv. 23, an otherwise obscure man. It means that Allah had, for the first time, called one of His elect by that name.

2462. Who is the "He" in this clause? As I have construed it, following the majority of Commentators, it means the angel who brought the message from Allah. *Cf.* 19:21 below. But some Commentators construe it to refer to Zakariyyā. In that case the meaning will be: Zakariyyā after a little reflection said (in his wonder) "So!", *i.e.* "Can it really be so? Can I really have a son in my old age?" The speech following, "Thy Lord saith," etc., will then be that of the angel-messenger.

Indeed create thee before,
When thou hadst been
nothing!'"[2463]

وَقَدْ خَلَقْتُكَ مِن قَبْلُ وَلَمْ تَكُ شَيْـًٔا

10. (Zakarīya) said: "O my Lord!
Give me a Sign."[2464]
"Thy Sign," was the answer,
"Shall be that thou
Shalt speak to no man
For three nights,[2465]
Although thou art not dumb."

١٠ قَالَ رَبِّ ٱجْعَل لِّيٓ ءَايَةً
قَالَ ءَايَتُكَ أَلَّا تُكَلِّمَ ٱلنَّاسَ
ثَلَٰثَ لَيَالٍ سَوِيًّا

11. So Zakarīya came out
To his people
From his chamber:
He told them by signs
To celebrate Allah's praises
In the morning
And in the evening.

١١ فَخَرَجَ عَلَىٰ قَوْمِهِۦ
مِنَ ٱلْمِحْرَابِ فَأَوْحَىٰٓ إِلَيْهِمْ
أَن سَبِّحُوا۟ بُكْرَةً وَعَشِيًّا

12. (To his son came the
command):[2466]
"O Yaḥyā! take hold
Of the Book with might":
And We gave him Wisdom[2467]
Even as a youth.

١٢ يَٰيَحْيَىٰ خُذِ
ٱلْكِتَٰبَ بِقُوَّةٍ
وَءَاتَيْنَٰهُ ٱلْحُكْمَ صَبِيًّا

2463. Every man was nothing just before he was created, *i.e.*, his personality was called into being by Allah. Even if there are material processes in forming the body, in accordance with the laws of nature, the real creative force is in Allah. But here there is a subtler meaning. John was the harbinger of Jesus, preparing the way for him: and this sentence also prepares us for the more wonderful birth of Jesus himself: see verse 21 below. Everything is possible with Allah.

2464. The "Sign", I understand, was not in order to convince Zakariya that the Lord's promise was true, for he had faith; but it was a symbol by which he was to show in his conduct that he was to conform to his new destiny as the father of Yaḥyā who was to come. Yaḥyā was to take up the work, and Zakariya was to be silent, although the latter was sound in body and there was nothing to prevent him from speaking.

2465. Compare this verse with 3:41. The variations are interesting. Here it is "for three nights": there it is "for three days". The meaning is the same, for a day is a period of 24 hours. But the point of view is different in each case. There it was from the point of view of the Ummah or Congregation, among whom he worked by day; here the point of view is that of his individual soul, which spent the nights in prayer and praise. Notice again that at the end of the next verse, we have here, "In the morning and in the evening", and at the end of 3:41, "In the evening and in the morning"—showing again that the point of view is reversed.

2466. Time passes. The son is born. In this section of the Sūrah the centre of interest is Yaḥyā, and the instruction is now given to him. 'Keep fast hold of Allah's revelation with all your might': for an unbelieving world had either corrupted or neglected it, and Yaḥyā (John the Baptist) was to prepare the way for Jesus, who was coming to renew and re-interpret it.

2467. *Ḥukm*, translated Wisdom, implies something more than Wisdom; it is the Wisdom or Judgement that is entitled to judge and command, as in the matter of denouncing sin.

13. And pity (for all creatures)
As from Us, and purity:[2468]
He was devout,

وَحَنَانًا مِّن لَّدُنَّا وَزَكَوٰةً وَكَانَ تَقِيًّا ﴿١٣﴾

14. And kind to his parents,
And he was not overbearing
Or rebellious.

وَبَرًّا بِوَٰلِدَيْهِ وَلَمْ يَكُن جَبَّارًا عَصِيًّا ﴿١٤﴾

15. So Peace on him
The day he was born
The day that he dies,
And the day that he
Will be raised up
To life (again)![2469]

وَسَلَٰمٌ عَلَيْهِ يَوْمَ وُلِدَ وَيَوْمَ يَمُوتُ وَيَوْمَ يُبْعَثُ حَيًّا ﴿١٥﴾

C. 139.—(19:16-40.) Next comes the story of Jesus and his mother
Mary. She gave birth, as a virgin, to Jesus.
But her people slandered and abused her
As a disgrace to her lineage. Her son
Did defend her and was kind to her. He
Was a servant of Allah, a true Prophet,
Blessed in the gifts of Prayer and Charity,
But no more than a man: to call him
The son of Allah is to derogate from Allah's
Majesty, for Allah is High above all
His Creatures, the Judge of the Last Day.

SECTION 2.

16. Relate in the Book
(The story of) Mary,[2470]
When she withdrew
From her family
To a place in the East.[2471]

وَٱذْكُرْ فِى ٱلْكِتَٰبِ مَرْيَمَ إِذِ ٱنتَبَذَتْ مِنْ أَهْلِهَا مَكَانًا شَرْقِيًّا ﴿١٦﴾

2468. John the Baptist did not live long. He was imprisoned by Herod, the tetrarch (provincial ruler under the Roman Empire), whom he had reproved for his sins, and eventually beheaded at the instigation of a woman with whom Herod was infatuated. But even in his young life, he was granted (1) wisdom by Allah, for he boldly denounced sin: (2) gentle pity and love for all Allah's creatures, for he moved among the humble and lowly, and despised "soft raiment": and (3) purity of life, for he renounced the world and lived in the wilderness. All his work he did in his youth. These things showed themselves in his conduct, for he was devout, showing love to Allah and to Allah's creatures, and more particularly to his parents (for we are considering that aspect of his life): this was also shown by the fact that he never used violence, from an attitude of arrogance, nor entertained a spirit of rebellion against divine Law. (R).

2469. This is spoken as in the lifetime of Yaḥyā. Peace and Allah's Blessings were on him when he was born; they continue when he is about to die an unjust death at the hands of a tyrant; and they will be specially manifest at the Day of Judgement.

2470. *Cf.* the story of Mary as related in 3:42-51. Here the whole theme is different: it is the personal side of the spiritual experiences of the worshippers of Allah in relation to their families or environment.

2471. To a private eastern chamber, perhaps in the Temple. She went into privacy, from her people and from people in general, for prayer and devotion. It was in this state of purity that the angel appeared to her in the shape of a man. She thought it *was* a man. She was frightened, and she adjured him not to invade her privacy.

17. She placed a screen
(To screen herself) from them;
Then We sent to her
Our angel, and he appeared
Before her as a man
In all respects.

(١٧) فَٱتَّخَذَتْ مِن دُونِهِمْ حِجَابًا
فَأَرْسَلْنَآ إِلَيْهَا رُوحَنَا
فَتَمَثَّلَ لَهَا بَشَرًا سَوِيًّا

18. She said: "I seek refuge
From thee to (Allah)
Most Gracious: (come not near)
If thou dost fear Allah."

(١٨) قَالَتْ إِنِّىٓ أَعُوذُ بِٱلرَّحْمَٰنِ
مِنكَ إِن كُنتَ تَقِيًّا

19. He said: "Nay, I am only
A messenger from thy Lord,
(To announce) to thee
The gift of a holy son."[2472]

(١٩) قَالَ إِنَّمَآ أَنَا۠ رَسُولُ رَبِّكِ
لِأَهَبَ لَكِ غُلَٰمًا زَكِيًّا

20. She said: "How shall I
Have a son, seeing that
No man has touched me,
And I am not unchaste?"

(٢٠) قَالَتْ أَنَّىٰ يَكُونُ لِى غُلَٰمٌ
وَلَمْ يَمْسَسْنِى بَشَرٌ وَلَمْ أَكُ بَغِيًّا

21. He said: "So (it will be):
Thy Lord saith, 'That is
Easy for Me: and (We
Wish) to appoint him
As a Sign unto men
And a Mercy from Us':[2473]
It is a matter
(So) decreed."[2474]

(٢١) قَالَ كَذَٰلِكِ
قَالَ رَبُّكِ هُوَ عَلَىَّ هَيِّنٌ
وَلِنَجْعَلَهُۥٓ ءَايَةً لِّلنَّاسِ وَرَحْمَةً مِّنَّا
وَكَانَ أَمْرًا مَّقْضِيًّا

22. So she conceived him,
And she retired with him
To a remote place.[2475]

(٢٢) فَحَمَلَتْهُ فَٱنتَبَذَتْ بِهِۦ مَكَانًا قَصِيًّا

2472. Allah had destined her to be the mother of the holy Prophet Jesus Christ, and now had come the time when this should be announced to her.

2473. The mission of Jesus is announced in two ways (1) he was to be a Sign to men; his wonderful birth and wonderful life were to turn an ungodly world back to Allah: and (2) his mission was to bring solace and salvation to the repentant. This, in some way or other, is the case with all prophets of Allah, and it was pre-eminently so in the case of the holy Prophet Muḥammad. But the point here is that the Israelites, to whom Jesus was sent, were a hardened race, for whom the message of Jesus was truly a gospel of Mercy.

2474. For anything that Allah wishes to create, He says "Be," and it is (*Cf.* 3:47). There is no interval between His decree and its accomplishment, except such as He imposes by His decree. Time may be only a projection of our own minds on this world of relativity.

2475. The annunciation and the conception, we may suppose, took place in Nazareth (of Galilee), say 65 miles north of Jerusalem. The delivery took place in Bethlehem about 6 miles south of Jerusalem. It was a remote place, not only with reference to the distance of 71 miles, but because in Bethlehem itself the birth was in an obscure corner under a palm tree, from which perhaps the babe was afterwards removed to a manger in a stable.

23\. And the pains of childbirth
Drove her to the trunk
Of a palm tree:
She cried (in her anguish):
"Ah! would that I had
Died before this! would that
I had been a thing
Forgotten and out of sight!"[2476]

٢٣ فَأَجَآءَهَا
ٱلْمَخَاضُ إِلَىٰ جِذْعِ ٱلنَّخْلَةِ
قَالَتْ يَٰلَيْتَنِى مِتُّ قَبْلَ هَٰذَا
وَكُنتُ نَسْيًا مَّنسِيًّا

24\. But (a voice) cried to her
From beneath the (palm tree):
"Grieve not! for thy Lord
Hath provided a rivulet
Beneath thee;

٢٤ فَنَادَىٰهَا مِن تَحْتِهَآ أَلَّا تَحْزَنِى
قَدْ جَعَلَ رَبُّكِ تَحْتَكِ سَرِيًّا

25\. "And shake towards thyself
The trunk of the palm tree;
It will let fall
Fresh ripe dates upon thee.[2477]

٢٥ وَهُزِّىٓ إِلَيْكِ بِجِذْعِ ٱلنَّخْلَةِ
تُسَٰقِطْ عَلَيْكِ رُطَبًا جَنِيًّا

26\. "So eat and drink
And cool (thine) eye.[2478]
And if thou dost see
Any man, say, 'I have
Vowed a fast to (Allah)
Most Gracious, and this day
Will I enter into no talk
With any human being'"[2479]

٢٦ فَكُلِى وَٱشْرَبِى وَقَرِّى عَيْنًا
فَإِمَّا تَرَيِنَّ مِنَ ٱلْبَشَرِ أَحَدًا فَقُولِىٓ
إِنِّى نَذَرْتُ لِلرَّحْمَٰنِ صَوْمًا
فَلَنْ أُكَلِّمَ ٱلْيَوْمَ إِنسِيًّا

27\. At length she brought
The (babe) to her people,
Carrying him (in her arms).
They said: "O Mary!

٢٧ فَأَتَتْ بِهِۦ قَوْمَهَا تَحْمِلُهُۥ
قَالُوا۟ يَٰمَرْيَمُ

2476\. She was but human, and suffered the pangs of an expectant mother, with no one to attend to her. The circumstances being peculiar, she had gotten far away from her people.

2477\. Unseen Providence had seen that she should not suffer from thirst or from hunger. The rivulet provided her with water also for ablutions.

2478\. *Cool thine eye*: An idiom for "comfort thyself and be glad". The literal meaning should not, however, be lost sight of. She was to cool her eyes (perhaps full of tears) with the fresh water of the rivulet and take comfort that a remarkable babe had been born to her. She was also to look around, and if any one came near, was to decline all conversation. It was quite true: she was under a vow, and could not talk to any one.

2479\. She was to decline all conversation with man or woman, on the plea of a vow to Allah. The "fast" here does not mean abstinence literally from eating and drinking. She had just been advised to eat the dates and drink of the stream. It means abstinence from the ordinary household meals, and indeed from human intercourse generally.

Truly an amazing thing
Hast thou brought![2480]

لَقَدْ جِئْتِ شَيْـًٔا فَرِيًّا

28. "O sister of Aaron![2481]
Thy father was not
A man of evil, nor thy
Mother a woman unchaste!"

٢٨ يَٰٓأُخْتَ هَٰرُونَ مَا كَانَ أَبُوكِ
ٱمْرَأَ سَوْءٍ وَمَا كَانَتْ أُمُّكِ بَغِيًّا

29. But she pointed to the babe.[2482]
They said: "How can we
Talk to one who is
A child in the cradle?"

٢٩ فَأَشَارَتْ إِلَيْهِ قَالُوا۟ كَيْفَ
نُكَلِّمُ مَن كَانَ فِى ٱلْمَهْدِ صَبِيًّا

30. He said: "I am indeed
A servant of Allah:
He hath given me
Revelation and made me
A prophet;

٣٠ قَالَ إِنِّى عَبْدُ ٱللَّهِ
ءَاتَىٰنِىَ ٱلْكِتَٰبَ وَجَعَلَنِى نَبِيًّا

31. "And He hath made me
Blessed wheresoever I be,
And hath enjoined on me
Prayer and Charity as long
As I live:[2483]

٣١ وَجَعَلَنِى مُبَارَكًا أَيْنَ مَا كُنتُ
وَأَوْصَٰنِى بِٱلصَّلَوٰةِ وَٱلزَّكَوٰةِ مَا دُمْتُ حَيًّا

32. "(He) hath made me kind
To my mother, and not
Overbearing or miserable;[2484]

٣٢ وَبَرًّۢا بِوَٰلِدَتِى
وَلَمْ يَجْعَلْنِى جَبَّارًا شَقِيًّا

2480. The amazement of the people knew no bounds. In any case they were ready to think the worst of her, as she disappeared from her kin for some time. But now she comes, shamelessly parading a babe in her arms! How she had disgraced the house of Aaron, the fountain of priesthood! We may suppose that the scene took place in the Temple in Jerusalem, or in Nazareth.

2481. Aaron, the brother of Moses, was the first in the line of Israelite priesthood. Mary and her cousin Elisabeth (mother of Yaḥyā) came of a priestly family, and were therefore "sisters of Aaron" or daughters of 'Imrān (who was Aaron's father). See n. 375 to 3:35. Mary is reminded of her high lineage and the unexceptionable morals of her father and mother. How, they said, she had fallen, and disgraced the name of her progenitors!

2482. What could Mary do! How could she explain? Would they, in their censorious mood, accept her explanation? All she could do was to point to the child, who, she knew, was no ordinary child. And the child came to her rescue. By a miracle he spoke, defended his mother, and preached—to an unbelieving audience. See 3:46, and n. 388.

2483. There is a parallelism throughout the accounts of Jesus and Yaḥyā, with some variations. Both the parallelisms and the variations are interesting. For instance Jesus declares at the very outset that he is a servant of Allah, thus negativing the false notion that he was Allah or the son of Allah. The greatness of Yaḥyā is described in 19:12-13 in terms that are not applied to Jesus, but the verses 19:14-15 as applied to Yaḥyā are in almost identical terms with those applied to Jesus here (19:32-33). Devotion in Prayer and Charity is a good description of the Church of Christ at its best, and pity, purity, and devotion in Yaḥyā are a good description of the ways leading to Prayer and Charity, just as John led to Jesus.

2484. Overbearing violence is not only unjust and harmful to those on whom it is practised; it is perhaps even more harmful to the person who practises it, for his soul becomes turbid, unsettled, and ultimately unhappy and wretched—the state of those in Hell. Here the negative qualities are "not overbearing or miserable." As applied to John they were "not overbearing or rebellious." John bore his punishment from the State without any protest or drawing back.

33. "So Peace is on me
The day I was born,
The day that I die,
And the Day that I
Shall be raised up
To life (again)"![2485]

وَالسَّلَٰمُ عَلَىَّ يَوْمَ وُلِدتُّ وَيَوْمَ أَمُوتُ وَيَوْمَ أُبْعَثُ حَيًّا ﴿٣٣﴾

34. Such (was) Jesus the son
Of Mary: (it is) a statement
Of truth, about which
They (vainly) dispute.[2486]

ذَٰلِكَ عِيسَى ٱبْنُ مَرْيَمَ قَوْلَ ٱلْحَقِّ ٱلَّذِى فِيهِ يَمْتَرُونَ ﴿٣٤﴾

35. It is not befitting
To (the majesty of) Allah
That He should beget
A son. Glory be to Him!
When He determines
A matter, He only says
To it, "Be," and it is.[2487]

مَا كَانَ لِلَّهِ أَن يَتَّخِذَ مِن وَلَدٍ سُبْحَٰنَهُۥٓ إِذَا قَضَىٰٓ أَمْرًا فَإِنَّمَا يَقُولُ لَهُۥ كُن فَيَكُونُ ﴿٣٥﴾

36. Verily Allah is my Lord
And your Lord: Him
Therefore serve ye: this is
A Way that is straight.[2488]

وَإِنَّ ٱللَّهَ رَبِّى وَرَبُّكُمْ فَٱعْبُدُوهُ هَٰذَا صِرَٰطٌ مُّسْتَقِيمٌ ﴿٣٦﴾

37. But the sects differ
Among themselves: and woe
To the Unbelievers because
Of the (coming) Judgement[2489]
Of a momentous Day!

فَٱخْتَلَفَ ٱلْأَحْزَابُ مِنۢ بَيْنِهِمْ فَوَيْلٌ لِّلَّذِينَ كَفَرُوا۟ مِن مَّشْهَدِ يَوْمٍ عَظِيمٍ ﴿٣٧﴾

38. How plainly will they see
And hear, the Day that
They will appear before Us!

أَسْمِعْ بِهِمْ وَأَبْصِرْ يَوْمَ يَأْتُونَنَا ﴿٣٨﴾

2485. *Cf.* 19:15, and n. 2469. Christ was not crucified (4:157). (R).

2486. The disputations about the nature of Jesus Christ were vain, but also persistent and sanguinary. The modern Christian churches have thrown them into the background, but they would do well to abandon irrational dogmas altogether.

2487. Begetting a son is a physical act depending on the needs of men's animal nature. Allah Most High is independent of all needs, and it is derogatory to Him to attribute such an act to Him. It is merely a relic of pagan and anthropomorphic materialist superstitions.

2488. As opposed to the crooked superstitions which take refuge in all sorts of metaphysical sophistries to prove three in one and one in three. In the Qur'ān there is no crookedness (18:1). Christ's teaching was simple, like his life, but the Chirstians have made it crooked.

2489. *Judgement*: the word in the original is *Mashhad*, which implies many things: (1) the time or place where evidence is taken, as in a Court of Judgement; (2) the time or place where people are produced (to be judged); and (3) the occasion for such production for the taking of evidence. A very expressive phrase for the Day of Judgement.

But the unjust today
Are in error manifest![2490]

لَٰكِنِ ٱلظَّٰلِمُونَ ٱلْيَوْمَ فِى ضَلَٰلٍ مُّبِينٍ

39. But warn them of the Day
Of Distress,[2491] when
The matter will be determined:
For (behold,) they are negligent
And they do not believe!

٣٩ وَأَنذِرْهُمْ يَوْمَ ٱلْحَسْرَةِ إِذْ قُضِىَ ٱلْأَمْرُ
وَهُمْ فِى غَفْلَةٍ وَهُمْ لَا يُؤْمِنُونَ

40. It is We Who will inherit[2492]
The earth, and all beings
Thereon: to Us will they
All be returned.

٤٠ إِنَّا نَحْنُ نَرِثُ ٱلْأَرْضَ وَمَنْ
عَلَيْهَا وَإِلَيْنَا يُرْجَعُونَ

C. 140.—Abraham pleaded with loving earnestness
(19:41-65.) With his father to accept the truth of Allah:
He was turned out, but he retained
His gentleness and was blessed. Moses
Asked for the aid of his brother Aaron
And was true to his people. Ismā'īl
Was loyal to his father and his God, and was
A willing and accepted sacrifice to Allah.
Idrīs in his highest station held fast
To truth and integrity. Thus are the righteous
Shown true in their personal environment,
And inherit the Bliss in which the salutation
Is Peace—perfect Peace, the reward of the Constant.

SECTION 3.

41. (Also) mention in the Book
(The story of) Abraham:
He was a man of Truth.
A prophet.

٤١ وَٱذْكُرْ فِى ٱلْكِتَٰبِ إِبْرَٰهِيمَ
إِنَّهُۥ كَانَ صِدِّيقًا نَّبِيًّا

42. Behold, he said to his father:[2493]
"O my father! why
Worship that which heareth not
And seeth not, and can
Profit thee nothing?

٤٢ إِذْ قَالَ لِأَبِيهِ يَٰٓأَبَتِ لِمَ تَعْبُدُ مَا
لَا يَسْمَعُ وَلَا يُبْصِرُ وَلَا يُغْنِى عَنكَ شَيْـًٔا

2490. *Cf.* 1:22, and that whole passage, where the Resurrection is described.

2491. *Ḥasrah*: Sighs, sighing, regrets, distress.

2492. *Cf.* 3:180, n. 485; 15:23 n. 1964. Material property passes from one to another: when one dies another inherits it. Allah gives life and death, and all that survives after physical death goes back to Allah, the original source of all things.

2493. The reference to Abraham here is in relation to his tender solicitude for his father, who had not received the light of Unity, and to whom Abraham wanted to be a guide and friend.

43. "O my father! to me
Hath come knowledge which
Hath not reached thee:[2494]
So follow me: I will guide
Thee to a Way that
Is even and straight.[2495]

٤٣ يا أبت إني قد جاءني
من العلم ما لم يأتك
فاتبعني أهدك صراطا سويا

44. "O my father! serve not
Satan: for Satan is
A rebel against (Allah)
Most Gracious.[2496]

٤٤ يا أبت لا تعبد الشيطان
إن الشيطان كان للرحمن عصيا

45. "O my father! I fear
Lest a Penalty afflict thee[2497]
From (Allah) Most Gracious,
So that thou become
To Satan a friend."

٤٥ يا أبت إني أخاف أن يمسك
عذاب من الرحمن فتكون للشيطان وليا

46. (The father) replied: "Dost thou
Hate my gods, O Abraham?
If thou forbear not, I will
Indeed stone thee:
Now get away from me
For a good long while!"[2498]

٤٦ قال أراغب أنت عن آلهتي يا إبراهيم
لئن لم تنته لأرجمنك
واهجرني مليا

47. Abraham said: "Peace be
On thee: I will pray
To my Lord for thy
forgiveness:[2499]

٤٧ قال سلام عليك
سأستغفر لك ربي

2494. Some are more receptive to Light than others. It is their duty and privilege to guide and point to the right Way.

2495. *Sawīyan*—right, smooth, even; complete, perfect; hence the derived meanings; in 19:10, 'in full possession of all the physical senses'; in that context, 'not dumb': in 19:17, when the angel appears in the form of a man, 'completely like' a man, a man 'in all respects.'

2496. The rebellion is all the more heinous and inexcusable, considering that Allah is Most Just, Most Merciful, Most Gracious.

2497. To entertain a feeling of friendliness, instead of aversion, to Evil, is in itself a degradation of our nature, a Penalty which Allah imposes on our deliberate rejection of the Truth. And the friendliness to Evil also implies the sharing of the outlawry of Evil.

2498. Note the gentle persuasive tone of Abraham in his speeches in 19:42-45 (for we may suppose those sentences to sum up a long course of arguments) and in 19:47-48, contrasted with the brusque and repellent tone of the father's reply in this verse. The one was the outcome of the true Light which had come to Abraham from Allah, as the other was the outcome of Pagan arrogance and the worship of brute force. The spiritual lesson from this episode of Abraham's life may be stated in four propositions: (1) the pious son is dutiful to his father and wishes him well in all things, material and spiritual; (2) if the father refuses Allah's Light, the son will do his utmost to bring such Light to the father; (3) having received the Light, the son will never renounce that Light, even if he has to forfeit his father's love and renounce his home; (4) even if the father repels him and turns him out, his answer will be a soft answer, full of love and forgiveness on the one hand, but firmness on behalf of Truth on the other.

2499. *Cf.* 9:114, where this promise of Abraham to pray for his father is referred to, and its limitations pointed out.

For He is to me
Most Gracious.

إِنَّهُۥ كَانَ بِى حَفِيًّا

48. "And I will turn away
From you (all) and from those
Whom ye invoke besides Allah:
I will call on my Lord:
Perhaps, by my prayer to my
Lord,
I shall be not unblest!"[2500]

٤٨ وَأَعْتَزِلُكُمْ وَمَا تَدْعُونَ
مِن دُونِ ٱللَّهِ وَأَدْعُوا رَبِّى عَسَىٰٓ
أَلَّآ أَكُونَ بِدُعَآءِ رَبِّى شَقِيًّا

49. When he had turned away
From them and from those
Whom they worshipped besides
Allah, We bestowed on him
Isaac and Jacob, and each one
Of them We made a
prophet.[2501]

٤٩ فَلَمَّا ٱعْتَزَلَهُمْ وَمَا يَعْبُدُونَ
مِن دُونِ ٱللَّهِ وَهَبْنَا لَهُۥٓ إِسْحَٰقَ وَيَعْقُوبَ
وَكُلًّا جَعَلْنَا نَبِيًّا

50. And We bestowed
Of Our Mercy on them,
And We granted them
Lofty honour on the tongue[2502]
Of truth.

٥٠ وَوَهَبْنَا لَهُم مِّن رَّحْمَتِنَا
وَجَعَلْنَا لَهُمْ لِسَانَ صِدْقٍ عَلِيًّا

SECTION 4.

51. Also mention in the Book
(The story of) Moses:
For he was specially chosen,
And he was a messenger
And a prophet.[2503]

٥١ وَٱذْكُرْ فِى ٱلْكِتَٰبِ مُوسَىٰٓ
إِنَّهُۥ كَانَ مُخْلَصًا وَكَانَ رَسُولًا نَّبِيًّا

2500. Abraham left his father and the home of his fathers (Ur of the Chaldees) and never returned. He left because he was turned out, and because it was not possible for him to make any compromise with what was false in religion. In return for abuse, he spoke gentle words. And he expressed his fervent hope that at least he (Abraham) would have Allah's blessing in reply to his prayers. Here was a prefigurement of another Hijrah many centuries later! In both cases the prayer was abundantly fulfilled.

2501. Isaac and Isaac's son Jacob are mentioned here as carrying on one line of Abraham's traditions. The other line was carried on by Ismā'īl, who is mentioned independently five verses lower down, as his line got special honour in the Holy Prophet of Islam. That is why his mention comes after that of Moses *Cf.* 21:72.

2502. Abraham and his son and grandson Isaac and Jacob, and their line, maintained the banner of Allah's spiritual truth for many generations, and they won deservedly high praise—the praise of truth—on the tongues of men. Abraham prayed that he should be praised by the tongue of truth among men to come in later ages: 26:84. Ordinary praise may mean nothing: it may be due to self-flattery on the part of others or artful management by the person praised. Praise on the tongue of sincere truth is praise indeed!

2503. Moses was (1) especially chosen, and therefore prepared and instructed in all the wisdom of the Egyptians, in order that he might free his people from Egyptian bondage; there may also be a reference to Moses's title of *Kalīm Allah,* the one to whom Allah spoke without the intervention of angels: see 4:164, and n. 670); (2) he was a prophet (*nabī*), in that he received inspiration; and (3) he was a messenger (*rasūl*) in that he had a Book of Revelation, and an Ummah or organised Community, for which he instituted laws. (R).

52. And We called him
From the right side[2504]
Of Mount (Sinai), and made
Him draw near to Us,
For mystic (converse).

﴿٥٢﴾ وَنَٰدَيۡنَٰهُ مِن جَانِبِ ٱلطُّورِ ٱلۡأَيۡمَنِ وَقَرَّبۡنَٰهُ نَجِيّٗا

53. And, out of Our Mercy,[2505]
We gave him his brother
Aaron, (also) a prophet.

﴿٥٣﴾ وَوَهَبۡنَا لَهُۥ مِن رَّحۡمَتِنَآ أَخَاهُ هَٰرُونَ نَبِيّٗا

54. Also mention in the Book
(The story of) Ismā'īl:
He was (strictly) true
To what he promised,[2506]
And he was a messenger
(And) a prophet.

﴿٥٤﴾ وَٱذۡكُرۡ فِي ٱلۡكِتَٰبِ إِسۡمَٰعِيلَۚ إِنَّهُۥ كَانَ صَادِقَ ٱلۡوَعۡدِ وَكَانَ رَسُولٗا نَّبِيّٗا

55. He used to enjoin
On his people Prayer
And Charity, and he was
Most acceptable in the sight
Of his Lord.[2507]

﴿٥٥﴾ وَكَانَ يَأۡمُرُ أَهۡلَهُۥ بِٱلصَّلَوٰةِ وَٱلزَّكَوٰةِ وَكَانَ عِندَ رَبِّهِۦ مَرۡضِيّٗا

56. Also mention in the Book
The case of Idrīs:[2508]

﴿٥٦﴾ وَٱذۡكُرۡ فِي ٱلۡكِتَٰبِ إِدۡرِيسَۚ

2504. The incident here I think refers to the incidents described more fully in 20:9-36; a reference may also be made to Exod. iii. 1-18 and iv. 1-17. The time is when Moses (with his family) was travelling and grazing the flocks of his father-in-law Jethro, just before he got his commission from Allah. The place is somewhere near Mount Sinai (*Jabal Mūsā*). Moses sees a Fire in the distance, but when he goes there, he hears a voice that tells him it is sacred ground. Allah asked him to put off his shoes and to draw near, and when he went near, great mysteries were revealed to him. He was given his commission, and his brother Aaron was given to him to go with him and aid him. It is after that that he and Aaron went and faced Pharaoh in Egypt, as narrated in 7:103-144, etc. The *right side* of the mountain may mean that Moses heard the voice from the right side of the mountain as he faced it: or it may have the figurative meaning of "right" in Arabic, *i.e.*, the side which was blessed or sacred ground. (R).

2505. Moses was diffident, and reluctant to go to Pharaoh as he had an impediment in his tongue, and he asked that his brother Aaron should be associated with him in his mission. Allah in His Mercy granted his request: 20:25-36.

2506. Ismā'īl was *Dhabīḥ Allah, i.e.*, the chosen sacrifice of Allah in Muslim tradition. When Abraham told him of the sacrifice, he voluntarily offered himself for it, and never flinched from his promise, until the sacrifice was redeemed by the substitution of a ram under Allah's commands. He was the fountainhead of the Arabian Ummah, and in his posterity came the Prophet of Allah. The Ummah and the Book of Islam reflect back the prophethood on Ismā'īl.

2507. An acceptable sacrifice: see last note.

2508. Idrīs is mentioned twice in the Qur'ān, *viz.*: here and in 21:85, where he is mentioned among those who patiently preserved His identification with the Biblical Enoch, who "walked with God" (Gen. v. 21-24), may or may not be correct. Nor are we justified in interpreting verse 57 here as meaning the same thing as in Gen. v. 24 ("God took him"), that he was taken up without passing through the portals of death. All we are told is that he was a man of truth and sincerity, and a prophet, and that he had a high position among his people. It is this point which brings him in the series of men just mentioned: he kept himself in touch with his people, and was honoured among them. Spiritual progress need not cut us off from our people, for we have to help and guide them. He kept to truth and piety in the highest station.

He was a man of truth
(And sincerity), (and) a prophet:

إِنَّهُۥ كَانَ صِدِّيقًا نَّبِيًّا

57. And We raised him
To a lofty station.

وَرَفَعْنَٰهُ مَكَانًا عَلِيًّا ٥٧

58. Those were some
Of the prophets on whom
Allah did bestow His Grace—
Of the posterity of Adam,
And of those whom We
Carried (in the Ark)
With Noah, and of
The posterity of Abraham[2509]
And Israel—of those
Whom We guided and chose;
Whenever the Signs
Of (Allah) Most Gracious
Were rehearsed to them,[2510]
They would fall down
In prostrate adoration
And in tears.

٥٨ أُولَٰٓئِكَ الَّذِينَ أَنْعَمَ اللَّهُ عَلَيْهِم
مِّنَ النَّبِيِّـۧنَ مِن ذُرِّيَّةِ ءَادَمَ
وَمِمَّنْ حَمَلْنَا مَعَ نُوحٍ
وَمِن ذُرِّيَّةِ إِبْرَٰهِيمَ وَإِسْرَٰٓءِيلَ
وَمِمَّنْ هَدَيْنَا وَاجْتَبَيْنَآ
إِذَا تُتْلَىٰ عَلَيْهِمْ ءَايَٰتُ الرَّحْمَٰنِ
خَرُّوا سُجَّدًا وَبُكِيًّا

59. But after them there followed
A posterity who missed
Prayers and followed after lusts:
Soon, then, will they
Face Destruction—[2511]

٥٩ فَخَلَفَ مِنۢ بَعْدِهِمْ خَلْفٌ أَضَاعُوا الصَّلَوٰةَ
وَاتَّبَعُوا الشَّهَوَٰتِ فَسَوْفَ يَلْقَوْنَ غَيًّا

60. Except those who repent
And believe, and work
Righteousness: for these
Will enter the Garden
And will not be wronged
In the least—

٦٠ إِلَّا مَن تَابَ وَءَامَنَ وَعَمِلَ
صَٰلِحًا فَأُولَٰٓئِكَ يَدْخُلُونَ الْجَنَّةَ
وَلَا يُظْلَمُونَ شَيْـًٔا

61. Gardens of Eternity, those
Which (Allah) Most Gracious
Has promised to His servants

٦١ جَنَّٰتِ عَدْنٍ الَّتِي وَعَدَ الرَّحْمَٰنُ عِبَادَهُۥ

2509. The earlier generations are grouped into three epochs from a spiritual point of view: (1) from Adam to Noah, (2) from Noah to Abraham, and (3) from Abraham to an indefinite time, say to the time when the Message of Allah was corrupted and the need arose for the final Messenger of Unity and Truth. Israel is another name for Jacob.

2510. The original is in the Aorist tense, implying that the "Posterity" alluded to includes not only the messengers but their worthy followers who are true to Allah and uphold His standard.

2511. This selfish godless posterity gains the upper hand at certain times but, even then there is always a minority who see the error of their ways, repent and believe, and live righteous lives. They are not penalised in the Hereafter because they were associated with the ungodly in time. They reap the full reward of their faith and righteousness.

In the Unseen: for His promise
Must (necessarily) come to pass.

بِٱلْغَيْبِ إِنَّهُۥ كَانَ وَعْدُهُۥ مَأْتِيًّا

62. They will not there hear
Any vain discourse, but
Only salutations of Peace:[2512]
And they will have therein
Their sustenance,[2313] morning
And evening.

٦٢ لَّا يَسْمَعُونَ فِيهَا لَغْوًا إِلَّا سَلَٰمًا
وَلَهُمْ رِزْقُهُمْ فِيهَا
بُكْرَةً وَعَشِيًّا

63. Such is the Garden which
We give as an inheritance
To those of Our Servants
Who guard against evil.

٦٣ تِلْكَ ٱلْجَنَّةُ ٱلَّتِى نُورِثُ مِنْ
عِبَادِنَا مَن كَانَ تَقِيًّا

64. (The angels say:)[2514]
"We descend not but
By command of thy Lord:
To Him belongeth what is
Before us, and what is
Behind us, and what is
Between: and thy Lord
Never doth forget"—

٦٤ وَمَا نَتَنَزَّلُ إِلَّا بِأَمْرِ رَبِّكَ
لَهُۥ مَا بَيْنَ أَيْدِينَا
وَمَا خَلْفَنَا وَمَا بَيْنَ ذَٰلِكَ
وَمَا كَانَ رَبُّكَ نَسِيًّا

65. "Lord of the heavens
And of the earth,
And of all that is
Between them: so worship Him,
And be constant and patient
In His worship: knowest thou
Of any who is worthy
Of the same Name as He?"[2515]

٦٥ رَّبُّ ٱلسَّمَٰوَٰتِ وَٱلْأَرْضِ
وَمَا بَيْنَهُمَا فَٱعْبُدْهُ
وَٱصْطَبِرْ لِعِبَٰدَتِهِۦ
هَلْ تَعْلَمُ لَهُۥ سَمِيًّا

2512. *Salām*, translated "Peace", has a much wider signification. It includes (1) a sense of security and permanence, which is unknown in this life; (2) soundness, freedom from defects, perfection, as in the word *salīm*; (3) preservation, salvation, deliverance, as in the word *sallama*; (4) salutation, accord with those around us; (5) resignation, in the sense that we are satisfied and not discontented; besides (6) the ordinary meaning of Peace, *i.e.*, freedom from any jarring element. All these shades of meaning are implied in the word *Islām*. (R).

2513. *Rizq*: literally sustenance or means of subsistence, the term covers all the means of perfect satisfaction of the body and soul. Morning and evening *i.e.*, early and late, all the time, always. (R).

2514. We are apt to be impatient of the evils we see around us. We may give of our best service to Allah, and yet see no results. In our human short-sightedness we may complain within ourselves. But we must not be impatient. The angels of Grace come not haphazardly, but by command of Allah according to His Universal Will and Purpose. Allah does not forget. If things are delayed, it is in accordance with a wise providence, which cares for all. Our plain duty is to be patient and constant in His service. (R).

2515. The more we taste of the truth and mystery of life, the more do we realise that there is no one to be mentioned in the same breath as Allah. He is above all names. But when we think of His beautiful qualities, and picture them to ourselves by names which give us some ideas of Him, we can search the whole wide world of our imagination, and we shall not find another to be compared with Him in name or quality. He is the One: praise be to Him!

C. 141. — Why should man disbelieve in the Hereafter?
(19:60-98.) We all must pass through the fire of temptation.
But Allah Most Gracious will save us
If we accept Him and do right. Sin
May have its respite, but must run
To its own destruction. We must not
Dishonour Allah by holding false
And monstrous ideas of Him. Glory
To Him that He cares for all His creatures!

SECTION 5.

66. Man says: "What!
When I am dead, shall I
Then be raised up alive?"

وَيَقُولُ ٱلْإِنسَٰنُ أَءِذَا مَا مِتُّ لَسَوْفَ أُخْرَجُ حَيًّا ﴿٦٦﴾

67. But does not man
Call to mind that We
Created him before
Out of nothing?

أَوَلَا يَذْكُرُ ٱلْإِنسَٰنُ أَنَّا خَلَقْنَٰهُ مِن قَبْلُ وَلَمْ يَكُ شَيْـًٔا ﴿٦٧﴾

68. So, by thy Lord,
Without doubt, We shall gather
Them together, and (also)
The Evil Ones (with them);[2516]
Then shall We bring them
Forth on their knees
Round about Hell;[2517]

فَوَرَبِّكَ لَنَحْشُرَنَّهُمْ وَٱلشَّيَٰطِينَ ثُمَّ لَنُحْضِرَنَّهُمْ حَوْلَ جَهَنَّمَ جِثِيًّا ﴿٦٨﴾

69. Then shall We certainly
Drag out from every sect
All those who were worst
In obstinate rebellion
Against (Allah) Most Gracious.

ثُمَّ لَنَنزِعَنَّ مِن كُلِّ شِيعَةٍ أَيُّهُمْ أَشَدُّ عَلَى ٱلرَّحْمَٰنِ عِتِيًّا ﴿٦٩﴾

70. And certainly We know best
Those who are most worthy
Of being burned therein.

ثُمَّ لَنَحْنُ أَعْلَمُ بِٱلَّذِينَ هُمْ أَوْلَىٰ بِهَا صِلِيًّا ﴿٧٠﴾

2516. The disbelief in a future state is not merely a philosophic doubt, but a warped will, a disingenuous obstinacy in face of our inner spiritual instincts and experiences. We were nothing before. Cannot the same Allah who created us out of nothing also continue our personality? But if we refuse to accept His light and guidance, our state will grow worse and worse. We shall be deprived of His grace. We shall be herded with the Evil Ones. In utter humiliation we shall be faced with all the consequences of our refusal of Truth.

2517 *Round about Hell*: There are many ways leading to evil, and people get to it from all round. Hence the mention of the seven Gates of Hell: see 15:44, and n. 1977. (R).

71. Not one of you but will[2518]
Pass over it: this is,
With thy Lord, a Decree
Which must be accomplished.

٧١ وَإِن مِّنكُمْ إِلَّا وَارِدُهَا ۚ كَانَ عَلَىٰ رَبِّكَ
حَتْمًا مَّقْضِيًّا

72. But We shall save those
Who guarded against evil,
And We shall leave
The wrongdoers therein,
(Humbled) to their knees.

٧٢ ثُمَّ نُنَجِّي الَّذِينَ اتَّقَوا
وَّنَذَرُ الظَّالِمِينَ فِيهَا جِثِيًّا

73. When Our Clear Signs
Are rehearsed to them,
The Unbelievers say to those
Who believe, "Which of the two
Sides is best in point of
Position? which makes the best
Show in Council?"[2519]

٧٣ وَإِذَا تُتْلَىٰ عَلَيْهِمْ آيَاتُنَا بَيِّنَاتٍ
قَالَ الَّذِينَ كَفَرُوا لِلَّذِينَ آمَنُوا أَيُّ الْفَرِيقَيْنِ
خَيْرٌ مَّقَامًا وَأَحْسَنُ نَدِيًّا

74. But how many (countless)
Generations before them
Have We destroyed,
Who were even better
In equipment and in glitter
To the eye?

٧٤ وَكَمْ أَهْلَكْنَا
قَبْلَهُم مِّن قَرْنٍ هُمْ
أَحْسَنُ أَثَاثًا وَرِئْيًا

75. Say: "If any man go
Astray, (Allah) Most Gracious
Extends (the rope) to them.
Until, when they see
The warning of Allah (being
Fulfilled)—either in punishment[2520]
Or in (the approach of)
The Hour—they will
At length realise who is

٧٥ قُلْ مَن كَانَ فِي الضَّلَالَةِ
فَلْيَمْدُدْ لَهُ الرَّحْمَٰنُ مَدًّا ۚ
حَتَّىٰ إِذَا رَأَوْا مَا يُوعَدُونَ إِمَّا الْعَذَابَ
وَإِمَّا السَّاعَةَ فَسَيَعْلَمُونَ مَنْ هُوَ

2518. Three interpretations are possible: (1) The general interpretation is that every soul must pass through or by or over the Fire. Those who have had *Taqwā* (see n. 26 to 2:2) will be saved by Allah's Mercy, while unrepentant sinners will suffer the torments in ignominy. (2) If we refer the pronoun "you" to those "in obstinate rebellion" in verse 69 above, both leaders and followers in sin, this verse only applies to the wicked. (3) Some refer this verse to the Bridge over Hell, the Bridge *Ṣirāṭ*, over which all must pass to their final Destiny. This Bridge is not mentioned in the Qur'ān. (R).

2519. The Unbelievers may, for a time, make a better show in worldly position, or in people's assemblages where things are judged by the counting of heads. But Truth must prevail even in this world, and ultimately the positions must be reversed.

2520. Allah's warning is that every evil deed must have its punishment, and that there will be a Hereafter, the Day of Judgement, or the Hour, as it is frequently called. The punishment of evil often begins in this very life. For instance, over-indulgence and excesses of all kinds bring on their Nemesis quite soon in this very life. But some subtler forms of selfishness and sin will be punished—as every evil will be punished—in its own good time, as the Hour approaches. In either case, the arrogant boasting sinners will realise that their taunt—who is best in position and in forces? (19:73)—is turned against themselves.

Worst in position, and (who)
Weaker in forces!

شَرٌّ مَّكَانًا وَأَضْعَفُ جُندًا

76. "And Allah doth advance
In guidance those who seek
Guidance: and the things
That endure. Good Deeds,[2521]
Are best in the sight
Of thy Lord, as rewards,
And best in respect of
(Their) eventual returns."

٧٦ وَيَزِيدُ ٱللَّهُ ٱلَّذِينَ ٱهْتَدَوْا۟ هُدًى ۗ
وَٱلْبَٰقِيَٰتُ ٱلصَّٰلِحَٰتُ خَيْرٌ
عِندَ رَبِّكَ ثَوَابًا وَخَيْرٌ مَّرَدًّا

77. Hast thou then seen
The (sort of) man who
Rejects Our Signs, yet
Says: "I shall certainly
Be given wealth and children?"[2522]

٧٧ أَفَرَءَيْتَ ٱلَّذِى كَفَرَ بِـَٔايَٰتِنَا
وَقَالَ لَأُوتَيَنَّ مَالًا وَوَلَدًا

78. Has he penetrated to
The Unseen, or has he
Taken a contract with
(Allah) Most Gracious?

٧٨ أَطَّلَعَ ٱلْغَيْبَ أَمِ ٱتَّخَذَ
عِندَ ٱلرَّحْمَٰنِ عَهْدًا

79. Nay! We shall record
What he says, and We
Shall add and add
To his punishment.[2523]

٧٩ كَلَّا ۚ سَنَكْتُبُ مَا يَقُولُ
وَنَمُدُّ لَهُۥ مِنَ ٱلْعَذَابِ مَدًّا

80. To Us shall return[2524]
All that he talks of,
And he shall appear
Before Us bare and alone.

٨٠ وَنَرِثُهُۥ مَا يَقُولُ
وَيَأْتِينَا فَرْدًا

81. And they have taken
(For worship) gods other than

٨١ وَٱتَّخَذُوا۟ مِن دُونِ ٱللَّهِ ءَالِهَةً

2521. These lines are the same as in 18:46 (second clause), (where see n. 2387), except that the word *maradda* (eventual returns) is here subsituted for *amal* (hope). The meaning is practically the same: but "hope" is more appropriate in the passage dealing with this world's goods, and "eventual returns" in the passage dealing with sinner's specific investments and commitments in worldly position and organised cliques.

2522. Besides the man who boasts of wealth and power in actual possession, there is a type of man who boasts of getting them in the future and builds his worldly hopes thereon. Is he sure? He denies Allah, and His goodness and Mercy. But all good is in the hands of Allah. Can such a man then bind Allah to bless him when he rejects faith in Allah? Or does he pretend that he has penetrated the mysteries of the future? For no man can tell what the future holds for him.

2523. Such a man deserves double punishment—for rejecting Allah, and for his blasphemies with His Holy Name.

2524. Literally, "We shall inherit", *Cf.* 19:40 and n. 2492. Even if the man had property and power, it must go back to the source of all things, and the man must appear before the Judgement Seat, alone and unaccompanied, stripped of all the things from which he expected so much!

Allah, to give them
Power and glory![2525]

لِيَكُونُوا لَهُمْ عِزًّا

82. Instead, they shall reject
Their worship, and become
Adversaries against them.[2526]

كَلَّا سَيَكْفُرُونَ بِعِبَادَتِهِمْ ﴿٨٢﴾
وَيَكُونُونَ عَلَيْهِمْ ضِدًّا

SECTION 6.

83. Seest thou not that We
Have set the Evil Ones on
Against the Unbelievers,
To incite them with fury?[2527]

أَلَمْ تَرَ أَنَّا أَرْسَلْنَا الشَّيَاطِينَ ﴿٨٣﴾
عَلَى الْكَافِرِينَ تَؤُزُّهُمْ أَزًّا

84. So make no haste
Against them, for We
But count out to them
A (limited) number (of days).

فَلَا تَعْجَلْ عَلَيْهِمْ ﴿٨٤﴾
إِنَّمَا نَعُدُّ لَهُمْ عَدًّا

85. The day We shall gather
The righteous to (Allah)
Most Gracious, like a band
Presented before a king for
honours.

يَوْمَ نَحْشُرُ الْمُتَّقِينَ ﴿٨٥﴾
إِلَى الرَّحْمَٰنِ وَفْدًا

86. And We shall drive
The sinners to hell,
Like thirsty cattle
Driven down to water—[2528]

وَنَسُوقُ الْمُجْرِمِينَ ﴿٨٦﴾
إِلَىٰ جَهَنَّمَ وِرْدًا

87. None shall have the power
Of intercession, but such a one
As has received permission
(or promise)
From (Allah) Most Gracious.

لَا يَمْلِكُونَ الشَّفَاعَةَ إِلَّا ﴿٨٧﴾
مَنِ اتَّخَذَ عِنْدَ الرَّحْمَٰنِ عَهْدًا

2525. *'Izza* = exalted rank, power, might, the ability to impose one's will or to carry out one's will.

2526. *Cf.* 10:28-30, where the idols deny that they knew anything of their worship, and leave their worshippers in the lurch; and 5:119, where Jesus denies that he asked for worship, and leaves his false worshippers to the punishment or the mercy of Allah.

2527. Under the laws instituted by Allah, when evil reaches a certain stage of rebellion and defiance, it is left to gather momentum and to rush with fury to its own destruction. It is given a certain amount of respite, as a last chance: but failing repentance, its days are numbered. The godly therefore should not worry themselves over the apparent worldly success of evil, but should get on with their own duties in a spirit of trust in Allah.

2528. Note the contrast between the saved and the doomed. The one march with dignity like honoured ones before a king, and the other rush in anguish to their punishment like a herd of cattle driven down by thirst to their watering place. Note the metaphor of the water. They rush madly for water but are plunged into the Fire!

88. They say: "(Allah) Most Gracious
Has begotten a son!

وَقَالُوا۟ ٱتَّخَذَ ٱلرَّحْمَٰنُ وَلَدًا ﴿٨٨﴾

89. Indeed ye have put forth
A thing most monstrous![2529]

لَّقَدْ جِئْتُمْ شَيْـًٔا إِدًّا ﴿٨٩﴾

90. As if the skies are ready
To burst, the earth
To split asunder, and
The mountains to fall down
In utter ruin.

تَكَادُ ٱلسَّمَٰوَٰتُ يَتَفَطَّرْنَ مِنْهُ وَتَنشَقُّ ٱلْأَرْضُ وَتَخِرُّ ٱلْجِبَالُ هَدًّا ﴿٩٠﴾

91. That they should invoke
A son for (Allah) Most Gracious.

أَن دَعَوْا۟ لِلرَّحْمَٰنِ وَلَدًا ﴿٩١﴾

92. For it is not consonant
With the majesty of (Allah)
Most Gracious that He
Should beget a son.[2530]

وَمَا يَنۢبَغِى لِلرَّحْمَٰنِ أَن يَتَّخِذَ وَلَدًا ﴿٩٢﴾

93. Not one of the beings
In the heavens and the earth
But must come to (Allah)
Most Gracious as a servant.

إِن كُلُّ مَن فِى ٱلسَّمَٰوَٰتِ وَٱلْأَرْضِ إِلَّآ ءَاتِى ٱلرَّحْمَٰنِ عَبْدًا ﴿٩٣﴾

94. He does take an account
Of them (all), and hath
Numbered them (all) exactly.[2531]

لَّقَدْ أَحْصَىٰهُمْ وَعَدَّهُمْ عَدًّا ﴿٩٤﴾

95. And every one of them
Will come to Him singly
On the day of Judgement.

وَكُلُّهُمْ ءَاتِيهِ يَوْمَ ٱلْقِيَٰمَةِ فَرْدًا ﴿٩٥﴾

96. On those who believe
And work deeds of righteousness,

إِنَّ ٱلَّذِينَ ءَامَنُوا۟ وَعَمِلُوا۟ ٱلصَّٰلِحَٰتِ ﴿٩٦﴾

2529. The belief in Allah begetting a son is not a question of words or of speculative thought. It is a stupendous blasphemy against Allah. It lowers Allah to the level of an animal. If combined with the doctrine of vicarious atonement, it amounts to a negation of Allah's justice and man's personal responsibility. It is destructive of all moral and spiritual order, and is condemned in the strongest possible terms.

2530. This basic principle was laid down early in the argument (19:35). It was illustrated by a reference to the personal history of many messengers, including Jesus himself, who behaved justly as men to their kith and kin and humbly served Allah. The evil results of such superstitions were pointed out in the case of many previous generations which went to their ruin by dishonouring Allah. And the argument is now rounded off towards the close of the Sūrah.

2531. Allah has no sons or favourites or parasites, such as we associate with human beings. On the other hand every creature of His gets His love,and His cherishing care. Every one of them, however humble, is individually marked before His Throne of Justice and Mercy, and will stand before Him on his own deserts.

Will (Allah) Most Gracious Bestow Love.[2532]	سَيَجۡعَلُ لَهُمُ ٱلرَّحۡمَٰنُ وُدّٗا
97. So have We made The (Qur'ān) easy In thine own tongue, That with it thou mayest give Glad tidings to the righteous, And warnings to people Given to contention.	٩٧ فَإِنَّمَا يَسَّرۡنَٰهُ بِلِسَانِكَ لِتُبَشِّرَ بِهِ ٱلۡمُتَّقِينَ وَتُنذِرَ بِهِۦ قَوۡمٗا لُّدّٗا
98. But how many (countless) Generations before them[2533] Have We destroyed? Canst thou Find a single one of them (Now) or hear (so much As) a whisper of them?	٩٨ وَكَمۡ أَهۡلَكۡنَا قَبۡلَهُم مِّن قَرۡنٍ هَلۡ تُحِسُّ مِنۡهُم مِّنۡ أَحَدٍ أَوۡ تَسۡمَعُ لَهُمۡ رِكۡزَۢا

2532. His own love, and the love for man's fellow creatures, in the world and in the Hereafter. Goodness breeds love and peace, and sin breeds hatred and contention.

2533. *Cf.* 19:74, from which this sentence is brought up as a reminiscence, showing the progress of sin, the Guidance which Allah gives to the good, the degradation of blasphemy, the respite granted, and the final End, when personal responsibility will be enforced.

INTRODUCTION TO SŪRAH 20—*ṬĀ HĀ*

The chronology of the Sūrah has some significance: it has some relation to the spiritual lessons which it teaches.

It was used with great effect in that remarkable scene which resulted in 'Umar's conversion, and which took place about the seventh year before the Hijrah.

The scene is described with dramatic details by Ibn Hishām. 'Umar had previously been one of the greatest enemies and persecutors of Islam. Like his blood-thirsty kinsmen the Quraysh, he meditated slaying the Prophet, when it was suggested to him that there were near relations of his that had embraced Islam. His sister Fāṭima and her husband Sa'īd were Muslims, but in those days of persecution they had kept their faith secret. When 'Umar went to their house, he heard them reciting this Sūrah from a written copy they had. For awhile they concealed the copy. 'Umar attacked his sister and her husband, but they bore the attack with exemplary patience, and declared their faith. 'Umar was so struck with their sincerity and fortitude that he asked to see the leaf from which they had been reading. It was given to him: his soul was touched, and he not only came into the Faith but became one of its strongest supporters and champions.

The leaf contained some portion of the Sūrah, perhaps the introductory portion. The mystic letters *Ṭā Hā* are prefixed to this Sūrah. What do they mean? The earliest tradition is that they denote a dialectical interjection meaning "O man!" If so, the title is particularly appropriate in two ways. (1) It was a direct and personal address to a man in a high state of excitement, tempted by his temper to do grievous wrong, but called by Allah's Grace, as by a personal appeal, to face the realities, for Allah knew his inmost secret thoughts (20:7): the revelation was sent by Allah, Most Gracious, out of His Grace and Mercy (20:5). (2) It takes up the story from the last Sūrah, of man as a spiritual being and illustrates it in further details. It tells the story of Moses in the crisis of his life when he received Allah's Commission and in his personal relation with his mother, and how he came to be brought up in the Pharaoh's house, to learn all the wisdom of the Egyptians, for use in Allah's service, and in his personal relations with Pharaoh, whom we take to be his adoptive father (28:9). It further tells the story of a fallen soul who misled the Israelites into idolatry, and recalls how man's Arch-enemy Satan caused his fall. Prayer and praise are necessary to man to cure his spiritual blindness and enable him to appreciate Allah's revelation. (R).

Summary—The revelation of Allah (the Qur'ān) is not an occasion of distress, but is a gift of mercy from Allah Most Gracious (20:1-8, and C. 142).

How Moses was first chosen, and led to his mission to Pharaoh with his brother Aaron (20:9-36, and C. 143).

How the mother of Moses was directed to cast the infant Moses into the river, to be brought up in Pharaoh's house under Allah's own supervision, in order to preach to Pharaoh and declare Allah's glory (20:37-76, and C. 144).

How Moses was directed to lead his people and quell their rebellious spirit, and how that spirit was stirred up by Sāmirī (20:77-104, and C. 145).

On the Day of Judgement personal responsibility will be enforced, and Allah's Truth acknowledged: man should guard against Adam's enemy, Satan, and should renounce vanities, purify himself with prayer and praise, and await the call to Allah (20:105-135, and C. 146).

C. 142.—Allah's revelation is not an occasion
(20:1-8.) For man's distress: it is a Message
To show that Allah the All-Knowing sits
On the throne of Mercy and guides all affairs.
There is no god but He; to Him
Belong all the Most Beautiful Names.

Sūrah 20.

Ṭā Hā[2534]

الجزء السادس عشر سورة طه

In the name of Allah, Most Gracious, Most Merciful.

بِسْمِ ٱللَّهِ ٱلرَّحْمَٰنِ ٱلرَّحِيمِ

1. Ṭā Hā.[2534]

طه ﴿١﴾

2. We have not sent down
The Qur'ān to thee to be
(An occasion) for thy distress,[2535]

مَآ أَنزَلْنَا عَلَيْكَ ٱلْقُرْءَانَ لِتَشْقَىٰٓ ﴿٢﴾

3. But only as an admonition
To those who fear (Allah)—

إِلَّا تَذْكِرَةً لِّمَن يَخْشَىٰ ﴿٣﴾

4. A revelation from Him
Who created the earth
And the heavens on high.

تَنزِيلًا مِّمَّنْ خَلَقَ ٱلْأَرْضَ وَٱلسَّمَٰوَٰتِ ٱلْعُلَى ﴿٤﴾

5. (Allah) Most Gracious[2536]
Is firmly established
On the throne (of authority).

ٱلرَّحْمَٰنُ عَلَى ٱلْعَرْشِ ٱسْتَوَىٰ ﴿٥﴾

6. To Him belongs what is
In the heavens and on earth,
And all between them,
And all beneath the soil.[2537]

لَهُۥ مَا فِى ٱلسَّمَٰوَٰتِ وَمَا فِى ٱلْأَرْضِ
وَمَا بَيْنَهُمَا وَمَا تَحْتَ ٱلثَّرَىٰ ﴿٦﴾

7. If thou pronounce the word
Aloud, (it is no matter):
For verily he knoweth

وَإِن تَجْهَرْ بِٱلْقَوْلِ فَإِنَّهُۥ يَعْلَمُ ﴿٧﴾

2534. For an explanation see the Introduction to this Sūrah. If the meaning is "O man!", that is itself a mystic meaning, as explained, but the letters form a word and would not be classified strictly as Abbreviated Letters: see n. 25 to 2:1. This, however, is a question of classification and does not affect the meaning. This is conjectural, and no one can be dogmatic about it.

2535. Allah's revelation may cause some human trouble for two reasons: (1) it checks man's selfishness and narrowness of view, and (2) it annoys the wicked and causes them to jeer and persecute. These are mere incidental things, due to man's own shortcomings. As far as the trouble is concerned, the revelation is meant to give a warning, so that persecutors may be reclaimed, (and of course for men of faith it is comfort and consolation, though that point does not arise in this context).

2536. *Cf.* 10:3, n. 1386. If things seem to be wrong in our imperfect vision on this earth, we must remember that Allah, Who encompasses all Creation and sits on the throne of Grace and Mercy, is in command, and our Faith tells us that all must be right. Allah's authority is not like an authority on earth, which may be questioned, or which may not last. His authority is "firmly established".

2537. An exhaustive definition of everything we can conceive of—what is in the heavens, on the earth, or between, or within the bowels of the earth.

What is secret and what
Is yet more hidden.[2538]

ٱلسِّرَّ وَأَخۡفَى

8. Allah! there is no god
But He! To Him belong
The Most Beautiful Names.[2539]

٨ ٱللَّهُ لَآ إِلَٰهَ إِلَّا هُوَۖ
لَهُ ٱلۡأَسۡمَآءُ ٱلۡحُسۡنَىٰ

C. 143.—The story of how Moses was chosen and told
(20:9-36.) Of his mission, has a high mystic meaning.
He was true to his family and solicitous
For their welfare. Encamped in the desert,
He saw a fire far off. Approaching,
He found it was holy ground. Allah
Did reveal Himself to him, so
That he saw life in things lifeless,
And light in his glorified Hand, that shone
White with light divine. Armed
With these Signs he was told to go forth
On his mission. But he thought of his brother
Aaron, and prayed that Allah might join him
In his mission, and his prayer was granted.

9. Has the story of Moses[2540]
Reached thee?

٩ وَهَلۡ أَتَىٰكَ حَدِيثُ مُوسَىٰٓ

10. Behold, he saw a fire:[2541]
So he said to his family,
"Tarry ye; I perceive
A fire; perhaps I can
Bring you some burning brand

١٠ إِذۡ رَءَا نَارٗا فَقَالَ لِأَهۡلِهِ ٱمۡكُثُوٓاْ إِنِّيٓ
ءَانَسۡتُ نَارٗا لَّعَلِّيٓ ءَاتِيكُم مِّنۡهَا بِقَبَسٍ

2538. There are two implications. (1) Whatever you profess, or say aloud, gives no information to Allah: He knows not only what is secret and perhaps unknown to others, but what people take special care to conceal. (2) It does you no good to make insincere professions: your hidden motives are known to Him, Who alone matters. (3) If you read the Word of Allah, or if you pray to Allah, it is not necessary to raise your voice: in either case, Allah will judge you by your inner thoughts which are like an open book to Him.

2539. *Cf.* 17:110 and n. 2322. Allah is all-in-all, and the most beautiful things we can think of are referable to Him. His names refer to His attributes which are like titles of Honour and Glory. (R).

2540. The story of Moses in its different incidents is told in many places in the Qur'ān, and in each case the phase most appropriate in the context is referred to or emphasised. In 2:49-61, it was a phase from the religious history of mankind; in 7:103-162, it was a phase from the story of the 'Ummah (or nation) of Israel, and the story was continued to the times after Moses; in 17:101-103, we have a picture of the decline of a soul in the arrogance of Pharaoh; here, in 20:9-24, we have a picture of the rise of a soul in the commission given to Moses from Allah; in 20:25-36, we have his spiritual relationship with his brother Aaron; in 20:37-40, we have his spiritual relation with his mother and sister, and his upbringing; in 20:41-76, we have his spiritual combat with Pharaoh; and in 20:77-98, we have his spiritual combat with his own people, the Israelites. For other incidents, consult the Index.

2541. *A fire*: It appeared like an ordinary fire, which always betokens the presence of men in a desert or a lonely place. Moses made for it alone, to fetch the wherewithal for making a fire for his family, and perhaps to find some direction as to the way, from the people he should meet there. But it was not an ordinary fire. It was a Burning Bush: a Sign of the Glory of Allah.

Therefrom, or find some guidance
At the fire."[2542]

أَوْ أَجِدُ عَلَى ٱلنَّارِ هُدًى

11. But when he came
To the fire, a voice
Was heard: "O Moses!

فَلَمَّآ أَتَىٰهَا نُودِيَ يَٰمُوسَىٰٓ ﴿١١﴾

12. "Verily I am thy Lord!
Therefore (in My presence)[2543]
Put off thy shoes: thou art
In the sacred valley Ṭuwā.[2544]

إِنِّىٓ أَنَا۠ رَبُّكَ فَٱخْلَعْ نَعْلَيْكَ ۖ
إِنَّكَ بِٱلْوَادِ ٱلْمُقَدَّسِ طُوًى ﴿١٢﴾

13. "I have chosen thee:
Listen, then to the inspiration
(Sent to thee).

وَأَنَا ٱخْتَرْتُكَ فَٱسْتَمِعْ لِمَا يُوحَىٰٓ ﴿١٣﴾

14. "Verily, I am Allah:
There is no god but I:
So serve thou Me (only),
And establish regular prayer
For celebrating My praise.

إِنَّنِىٓ أَنَا ٱللَّهُ لَآ إِلَٰهَ إِلَّآ أَنَا۠
فَٱعْبُدْنِى وَأَقِمِ ٱلصَّلَوٰةَ لِذِكْرِىٓ ﴿١٤﴾

15. "Verily the Hour is coming—[2545]
My design is to keep it
Hidden—[2546] for every soul
To receive its reward
By the measure of
Its Endeavour.

إِنَّ ٱلسَّاعَةَ ءَاتِيَةٌ
أَكَادُ أُخْفِيهَا لِتُجْزَىٰ
كُلُّ نَفْسٍۭ بِمَا تَسْعَىٰ ﴿١٥﴾

16. "Therefore let not such as
Believe not therein
But follow their own

فَلَا يَصُدَّنَّكَ عَنْهَا مَن لَّا يُؤْمِنُ بِهَا

2542. The spiritual history of Moses begins here. It was his spiritual birth. His physical life, infancy, and upbringing are referred to later on, to illustrate another point. Moses, when he grew up, left the palace of Pharaoh and went to the Midianite people, in the Sinai pennisula. He married among them, and was now travelling with his family and his flocks, when he was called to his mission by Allah. He went to look for a fire for comfort and guidance. He found a higher and holier comfort and guidance. The whole passage is full of portent meaning, which is reflected in the short rhymed verses in the original. (R).

2543. The shoes are to be put off as a mark of respect. Moses was now to put away his mere worldly interests, and anything of mere worldly utility, he having been chosen by Allah, the Most High. (R).

2544. This was the valley just below Mount Sinai, where subsequently he was to receive the Law. In the parallel mystic meaning, we are selected by trials in this humble life, whose valley is just as sacred and receives Allah's glory just as much as the heights of the Mount (*Ṭūr*) if we but have the insights to perceive it.

2545. The first need is to mend our lives and worship and serve Allah, as in the last verse. The next is to realise the meaning of the Hereafter, when every soul will get the meed of its conduct in this life.

2546. *Ukhfī* may mean either "keep it hidden", or "make it manifest", and the Commentators have taken, some one meaning and some the other. If the first is taken, it means that the exact hour or day when the Judgement comes is hidden from man; if the second, it means that the fact of the Judgement to come is made known, that man may remember and take warning. I think that both meanings are implied. (R).

Lusts, divert thee therefrom,[2547]
Lest thou perish!"

وَٱتَّبَعَ هَوَىٰهُ فَتَرْدَىٰ

17. "And what is that
In thy right hand,
O Moses?"

وَمَا تِلْكَ بِيَمِينِكَ يَٰمُوسَىٰ ﴿١٧﴾

18. He said, "It is[2548]
My rod: on it
I lean; with it
I beat down fodder
For my flocks; and
In it I find
Other uses."

قَالَ هِىَ عَصَاىَ أَتَوَكَّؤُا۟ عَلَيْهَا وَأَهُشُّ بِهَا عَلَىٰ غَنَمِى وَلِىَ فِيهَا مَـَٔارِبُ أُخْرَىٰ ﴿١٨﴾

19. (Allah) said, "Throw it,
O Moses!"

قَالَ أَلْقِهَا يَٰمُوسَىٰ ﴿١٩﴾

20. He threw it, and behold!
It was a snake,
Active in motion.[2549]

فَأَلْقَىٰهَا فَإِذَا هِىَ حَيَّةٌ تَسْعَىٰ ﴿٢٠﴾

21. (Allah) said, "Seize it
And fear not: We
Shall return it at once
To its former condition"...

قَالَ خُذْهَا وَلَا تَخَفْ سَنُعِيدُهَا سِيرَتَهَا ٱلْأُولَىٰ ﴿٢١﴾

22. "Now draw thy hand[2550]
Close to thy side:
It shall come forth white
(And shining), without harm
(Or stain)—as another Sign—

وَٱضْمُمْ يَدَكَ إِلَىٰ جَنَاحِكَ تَخْرُجْ بَيْضَآءَ مِنْ غَيْرِ سُوٓءٍ ءَايَةً أُخْرَىٰ ﴿٢٢﴾

2547. Moses had yet to meet the formidable opposition of the arrogant Pharaoh and his proud Egyptians, and later, the rebellion of his own people. In receiving his commission, he is warned of both dangers. This relates to man's own soul: when once the light reaches him let him hold fast to it, lest he perish. He will be beset with dangers of all kinds around him: the worst will be the danger of unbelieving people who seem to thrive on their selfishness and in following their own vain desires! (R).

2548. Now comes the miracle of the rod. First of all, the attention of Moses himself is drawn to it, and he thinks of the ordinary uses to which he puts it in his daily life. (R).

2549. *Cf.* 7:107, where a different word (*thu'bān* is used for *"snake"*, and the qualifying adjective is "plain (for all to see)". The scene there is before Pharaoh and his magicians and people: the object is to show the hollowness of their magic by a miracle: the rod appears before them as a long and creeping, writhing serpent. Here there is a symbol to present Allah's Mystery to Moses's mind and understanding: the rod becomes a *Hayy* (a *live* snake), and its *active* motion is what is most to be impressed on the mind of Moses, for there were no other spectators. So the highest spiritual mysteries can be grasped, with Allah's gift of insight, from the most ordinary things of daily use. Once they are grasped, there is no question of fear. They really are the virtues of this life lifted up to the glorious spiritual plane.

2550. The second of the greater Miracles shown to Moses was the "White (shining) Hand". Ordinarily, when the skin becomes white, it is a sign of disease, leprosy or something loathsome. Here there was no question of disease: on the contrary, the hand was glorified, and it shone as with a divine light. Such a miracle was beyond Egyptian or human magic. (R).

23. "In order that We
May show thee
(Two) of Our Greater Signs.

لِنُرِيَكَ مِنْ ءَايَٰتِنَا ٱلْكُبْرَى ٢٣

24. "Go thou to Pharaoh,[2551]
For he had indeed
Transgressed all bounds."

ٱذْهَبْ إِلَىٰ فِرْعَوْنَ إِنَّهُۥ طَغَىٰ ٢٤

SECTION 2.

25. (Moses) said: "O my Lord!
Expand me my breast;"[2552]

قَالَ رَبِّ ٱشْرَحْ لِى صَدْرِى ٢٥

26. "Ease my task for me;

وَيَسِّرْ لِىٓ أَمْرِى ٢٦

27. "And remove the impediment[2553]
From my speech.

وَٱحْلُلْ عُقْدَةً مِّن لِّسَانِى ٢٧

28. "So they may understand
What I say:

يَفْقَهُوا۟ قَوْلِى ٢٨

29. "And give me a Minister
From my family,

وَٱجْعَل لِّى وَزِيرًا مِّنْ أَهْلِى ٢٩

30. "Aaron, my brother;

هَٰرُونَ أَخِى ٣٠

31. "Add to my strength[2554]
Through him,

ٱشْدُدْ بِهِۦٓ أَزْرِى ٣١

32. "And make him share
My task:

وَأَشْرِكْهُ فِىٓ أَمْرِى ٣٢

33. "That we may celebrate[2555]
Thy praise without stint,

كَىْ نُسَبِّحَكَ كَثِيرًا ٣٣

2551. Moses, having been spiritually prepared now gets his definite commission to go to Pharaoh and point out the error of his ways. So inordinate was Pharaoh's vanity that he had it in his mind to say: "I am your Lord Most High!" (79:24).

2552. The breast is reputed to be the seat of knowledge and affections. The gift of the highest spiritual insight is what he prays for first. *Cf.* 94:1. This was the most urgent in point of time. There are three other things he also asks for: *viz.*, (1) Allah's help in his task, which at first appears difficult to him; (2) the gift of eloquence, and the removal of the impediment from his speech; and (3) the counsel and constant attendance with him of his brother Aaron, whom he loved and trusted, for he would otherwise be alone among the Egyptians.

2553. Literally, "Loosen a knot from my tongue".

2554. Literally, "Strengthen my back with him". A man's strength lies in his back and backbone so that he can stand erect and boldly face his tasks.

2555. The requests that Moses makes are inspired, not by earthly but by spiritual motives. The motive, expressed in the most general terms, is to glorify Allah, not in an occasional way, but systematically and continuously, "without stint." The clauses in this verse and the next, taken together, govern all the requests he makes, from verse 25 to verse 32.

34. "And remember Thee Without stint:	وَنَذْكُرَكَ كَثِيرًا ﴿٣٤﴾
35. "For Thou art He That (ever) regardeth us."[2556]	إِنَّكَ كُنتَ بِنَا بَصِيرًا ﴿٣٥﴾
36. (Allah) said: "Granted Is thy prayer, O Moses!"	قَالَ قَدْ أُوتِيتَ سُؤْلَكَ يَٰمُوسَىٰ ﴿٣٦﴾

C. 144.—From his birth was Moses prepared for his task.
(20:37-76.) His mother received guidance, so that
Allah's purpose might be fulfilled. Moses
Was brought up in Pharaoh's palace and trained
In all the learning of Egypt. Yet he drank
The Love of his people in his mother's milk.
Adventures and trials he had, including
His stay with the Midianites—until
He was called to his double mission: to preach
To Pharaoh and the Egyptians, and to free
His own people. So he and Aaron went
To Pharaoh, who rejected Allah and His Signs,
But appointed a trial of strength between
His magicians and Moses. Moses won;
And the Truth of Allah was accepted
By some Egyptains, but not by Pharaoh.

37. "And indeed We conferred A favour on thee Another time (before).	وَلَقَدْ مَنَنَّا عَلَيْكَ مَرَّةً أُخْرَىٰٓ ﴿٣٧﴾
38. "Behold! We sent[2557] To thy mother, by inspiration, The message:	إِذْ أَوْحَيْنَآ إِلَىٰٓ أُمِّكَ مَا يُوحَىٰٓ ﴿٣٨﴾
39. "'Throw (the child) Into the chest, and throw (The chest) into the river:	أَنِ ٱقْذِفِيهِ فِى ٱلتَّابُوتِ فَٱقْذِفِيهِ فِى ٱلْيَمِّ ﴿٣٩﴾

2556. The celebration of Allah's praise and rememberance is one form of showing gratitude on the part of Moses for the Grace which Allah had bestowed upon him.

2557. The story is not told, but only those salient points recapitulated which bear on the spiritual upbringing and work of Moses. Long after the age of Joseph, who had been a Wazīr to one of the Pharaohs, there came on the throne of Egypt a Pharaoh who hated the Israelites and wanted them annihilated. He ordered Israelite male children to be killed when they were born. Moses's mother hid him for a time, but when further concealment was impossible, a thought came into her mind that she should put her child into a chest and send the chest floating down the Nile. This was not merely a foolish fancy of hers. It was Allah's Plan to bring up Moses in all the learning of the Egyptians, in order that that learning itself should be used to expose what was wrong in it and to advance the glory of Allah. The chest was floated into the river Nile. It flowed on into a stream that passed through Pharaoh's Garden. It was picked up by Pharaoh's people and the child was adopted by Pharaoh's wife. See 28:4-13.

The river will cast him
Up on the bank, and he
Will be taken up by one
Who is an enemy to Me
And an enemy to him':2558
But I cast (the garment
Of) love over thee from Me:2559
And (this) in order that
Thou mayest be reared
Under Mine eye."2560

فَلْيُلْقِهِ ٱلْيَمُّ بِٱلسَّاحِلِ
يَأْخُذْهُ عَدُوٌّ لِّى وَعَدُوٌّ لَّهُۥ
وَأَلْقَيْتُ عَلَيْكَ مَحَبَّةً مِّنِّى
وَلِتُصْنَعَ عَلَىٰ عَيْنِىٓ

40. "Behold! thy sister goeth forth
And saith. 'Shall I show you
One who will nurse
And rear the (child)?'2561
So We brought thee back
To thy mother, that her eye2562
Might be cooled and she
Should not grieve.
Then thou didst slay2563
A man, but We saved thee
From trouble, and We tried
Thee in various ways.
Then didst thou tarry

إِذْ تَمْشِىٓ أُخْتُكَ ٤٠
فَتَقُولُ هَلْ أَدُلُّكُمْ عَلَىٰ مَن يَكْفُلُهُۥ
فَرَجَعْنَٰكَ إِلَىٰٓ أُمِّكَ
كَىْ تَقَرَّ عَيْنُهَا وَلَا تَحْزَنَ
وَقَتَلْتَ نَفْسًا فَنَجَّيْنَٰكَ مِنَ
ٱلْغَمِّ وَفَتَنَّٰكَ فُتُونًا فَلَبِثْتَ

2558. Pharaoh was an enemy to Allah, because he was puffed up and he blasphemed, claiming to be God himself. He was an enemy to the child Moses, because he hated the Israelites and wanted to have their male children killed; also because Moses stood for Allah's revelation to come.

2559. Allah made the child comely and lovable, and he attracted the love of the people who, on general grounds, would have killed him.

2560. See n. 2558 above. By making the child Moses so attractive as to be adopted into Pharaoh's household, not only was Moses brought up in the best way possible from and earthly point of view, but Allah's special Providence looked after him in bringing his mother to him, as stated in the next verse, and thus nourishing him on his mother's milk amd keeping in touch, in his inner growth, with the feelings and sentiments of his people Israel.

2561. We may suppose that the anxious mother, after the child was floated on the water, sent the child's sister to follow the chest from the bank and see where and by whom it was picked up. When it was picked up by Pharaoh's own family and they seemed to love the child, she appeared like a stranger before them, and said, "Shall I search out a good wet nurse for the child, that she may rear the child you are going to adopt?" That was exactly what they wanted. She ran home and told her mother. The mother was delighted to come and fold the infant in her arms again and feed it at her own breast, and all openly and without any concealment.

2562. The mother's eyes had, we may imagine, been sore with scalding tears at the separation from her baby. Now they were cooled: a phrase meaning that her heart was comforted.

2563. Years passed. The child grew up. In outward learning he was of the house of Pharaoh. In his inner soul and sympathy he was of Israel. One day, he went to the Israelite colony and saw all the Egyptian oppression under which Israel laboured. He saw an Egyptian smiting an Israelite, apparently with impunity. Moses felt brotherly sympathy and smote the Egyptian. He did not intend to kill him, but in fact the Egyptian died of the blow. When this became known, his position in Pharaoh's household became impossible. So he fled out of Egypt, and was only saved by Allah's grace. He fled to the Sinai Pennisula, to the land of the Midianites, and had various adventures. He marries one of the daughters of the Midianite chief, and lived with the Midianites for many years, as an Egyptian stranger. He had many trials and temptations, but he retained his integrity of character.

سِنِينَ فِيٓ أَهۡلِ مَدۡيَنَ
ثُمَّ جِئۡتَ عَلَىٰ قَدَرٖ يَٰمُوسَىٰ

A number of years
With the people of Midian.[2564]
Then didst thou come hither
As ordained, O Moses!

٤١ وَٱصۡطَنَعۡتُكَ لِنَفۡسِي

41. "And I have prepared thee
For Myself (for service)"...

٤٢ ٱذۡهَبۡ أَنتَ وَأَخُوكَ بِـَٔايَٰتِي
وَلَا تَنِيَا فِي ذِكۡرِي

42. "Go, thou and thy brother.[2565]
With My signs,
And slacken not,
Either of you, in keeping
Me in remembrance.

٤٣ ٱذۡهَبَآ إِلَىٰ فِرۡعَوۡنَ إِنَّهُۥ طَغَىٰ

43. "Go, both of you, to Pharaoh,[2566]
For he has indeed
Transgressed all bounds;[2567]

٤٤ فَقُولَا لَهُۥ قَوۡلٗا لَّيِّنٗا
لَّعَلَّهُۥ يَتَذَكَّرُ أَوۡ يَخۡشَىٰ

44. "But speak to him mildly;
Perchance he may take
Warning or fear (Allah)."[2568]

٤٥ قَالَا رَبَّنَآ إِنَّنَا نَخَافُ أَن يَفۡرُطَ عَلَيۡنَآ

45. They (Moses and Aaron) said:
"Our Lord! We fear lest
He hasten with insolence[2569]

2564. See last note. After many years spent in a quiet life, grazing his father-in-law's flocks, he came one day to the valley of Ṭuwā underneath the great mountain mass of Sinai, called Ṭūr (in Arabic). The peak on the Arabian side (where Moses was) was called Horeb by the Hebrews. Then was fulfilled Allah's Plan: he saw the fire in the distance, and when he went up, he was addressed by Allah and chosen to be Allah's Messenger for that age.

2565. We may suppose that Moses had fled alone to the land of Midian, and that he had now come alone (with his family but not with his brother) to Ṭuwā, as described in n. 2542 above. When he was honoured with his mission, and was granted his request that his brother Aaron should accompany him, we may suppose that he took steps to get Aaron to come to him, and their meeting was in Ṭuwā. Some time may be supposed to have elapsed before they were in Egypt, and then they prayed, and received these directions in their Egyptian home.

Aaron was either an elder or a younger brother—we are not told which. In either case he was born when the ban on Israelite new-born babes was not in operation. Moses had been out of touch with him, and it speaks greatly for his family affection that he remembered him and prayed for his comradeship in the most serious spiritual work of his life.

2566. Their mission was in the first instance to Pharaoh and to the Egyptians, and then to lead Israel out of Egypt.

2567. Compare the same phrase in 20:24. Having glanced at the early life of Moses we come back now to the time when Moses's actual ministry begins. The earlier personal story of Moses is rounded off.

2568. So far Pharaoh, in his inordinate vanity, had forgotten himself and forgotten how small a creature he was before Allah. This was to be brought to his recollection, so that he might perhaps repent and believe, or at least be deterred by fear from "transgressing all bounds". Some men eschew wrong from sincere love of Allah and understanding if their fellow-men, and some (of coarser minds) from the fear of consequences. Even the latter conduct may be a step to the former.

2569. They were now in Egypt (see n. 2565 above) and therefore in the power of the Pharaoh. The local atmosphere called for the greatest courage and firmness on their part to carry out the dangerous mission which had been entrusted to them.

Against us, or lest he
Transgress all bounds."

أَوْ أَن يَطْغَىٰ

46. He said: "Fear not:
For I am with you:
I hear and see (everything).

٤٦ قَالَ لَا تَخَافَا
إِنَّنِي مَعَكُمَا أَسْمَعُ وَأَرَىٰ

47. "So go ye both to him,
And say, 'Verily we are
Messengers sent by thy Lord:
Send forth, therefore, the Children
Of Israel with us, and
Afflict them not:[2570]
With a Sign, indeed,
Have we come from thy Lord!
And Peace to all
Who follow guidance![2571]

٤٧ فَأْتِيَاهُ فَقُولَا إِنَّا رَسُولَا رَبِّكَ
فَأَرْسِلْ مَعَنَا بَنِي إِسْرَاءِيلَ وَلَا تُعَذِّبْهُمْ
قَدْ جِئْنَاكَ بِآيَةٍ مِّن رَّبِّكَ
وَالسَّلَامُ عَلَىٰ مَنِ اتَّبَعَ الْهُدَىٰ

48. "'Verily it has been revealed
To us that the Penalty
(Awaits) those who reject
And turn away.'"

٤٨ إِنَّا قَدْ أُوحِيَ إِلَيْنَا أَنَّ الْعَذَابَ
عَلَىٰ مَن كَذَّبَ وَتَوَلَّىٰ

49. (When this message was delivered),
(Pharaoh) said: "Who then,
O Moses, is the Lord[2572]
Of you two?"

٤٩ قَالَ فَمَن
رَّبُّكُمَا يَا مُوسَىٰ

50. He said: "Our Lord is
He Who gave to each
(Created) thing its form
And nature, and further,
Gave (it) guidance."[2573]

٥٠ قَالَ رَبُّنَا الَّذِي أَعْطَىٰ
كُلَّ شَيْءٍ خَلْقَهُ ثُمَّ هَدَىٰ

2570. The Children of Israel were subjected to all sorts of oppression and indignities. They were given hard tasks; their leaders were unjustly beaten; they were forced to make bricks without straw; and they "groaned in bondage" (Exod. v. 6-19, vi. 5).

2571. Allah, in His infinite Mercy, always offers Peace to the most hardened sinners, even those who are warring against Him. But, as stated in the next verse, their defiance cannot go on with impunity indefinitely. The punishment must inevitably come for sin, whether the sinner is great or small.

2572. Notice how subtly Pharaoh rejects the implication in Moses's speech, in which Moses had referred to "thy Lord" (verse 47). Pharaoh implicitly repudiates the suggestion that the Allah who had sent Moses and Aaron could possibly be Pharaoh's Lord. He asks insolently, "Who is this Lord of yours, of Whom ye speak as having sent you?"

2573. The answer of Moses is straightforward, dignified, and illuminating. He will not dispute about "my Lord" or "your Lord", the God of Israel, or the God of Egypt. He and his brother were proud to serve "our Lord," but He was the universal Lord and Cherisher, the One and Only God, Who had created all beings and all things. It was from Him that each created thing derived its form and nature, including such free will and power as man had got. He, Pharaoh, was subject to the same condition. In order that the free will should be rightly exercised, Allah had given guidance through His Messengers, and His Signs. Moses and Aaron stood as such Messengers, with such Signs. Will Pharaoh now understand and do right?

51. (Pharaoh) said: "What then
Is the condition
Of previous generations?"[2574]

52. He replied: "The knowledge
Of that is with my Lord,[2575]
Duly recorded: my Lord
Never errs, nor forgets—

53. "He Who has made for you
The earth like a carpet
Spread out; has enabled you
To go about therein by roads[2576]
(And channels); and has sent
Down water from the sky."
With it have We produced[2577]
Diverse pairs of plants[2578]
Each separate from the others.

54. Eat (for yourselves) and pasture
Your cattle: verily, in this
Are Signs, for men
Endued with understanding.

SECTION 3.

55. From the (earth) did We
Create you, and into it
Shall We return you,

٥١ قَالَ فَمَا بَالُ ٱلْقُرُونِ ٱلْأُولَىٰ

٥٢ قَالَ عِلْمُهَا عِندَ رَبِّي فِي كِتَٰبٍ
لَّا يَضِلُّ رَبِّي وَلَا يَنسَى

٥٣ ٱلَّذِي جَعَلَ لَكُمُ ٱلْأَرْضَ مَهْدًا
وَسَلَكَ لَكُمْ فِيهَا سُبُلًا
وَأَنزَلَ مِنَ ٱلسَّمَآءِ مَآءً
فَأَخْرَجْنَا بِهِۦٓ أَزْوَٰجًا مِّن نَّبَاتٍ شَتَّىٰ

٥٤ كُلُوا۟ وَٱرْعَوْا۟ أَنْعَٰمَكُمْ
إِنَّ فِي ذَٰلِكَ لَءَايَٰتٍ لِّأُو۟لِي ٱلنُّهَىٰ

٥٥ مِنْهَا خَلَقْنَٰكُمْ وَفِيهَا نُعِيدُكُمْ

2574. But Pharaoh was not the man to accept teaching from the despised Israelite—one, too, who in his eyes was a renegade from the higher Egyptian civilisation. "If", he says in effect, "there is only one God, to Whom all things are referred, this is a new religion. What of the religion of our ancestors? Were they wrong in worshipping the Egyptian gods? And if they were wrong, are they in misery now? He wanted to trap Moses into scathing denunciations of his ancestors, which would at once have deprived him of the sympathy or the hearing of the Egyptian crowd.

2575. Moses did not fall into the trap. He remembered the injunction given to him to speak mildly (20:44). He speaks mildly, but does not in any way whittle down the truth. He said in effect: 'Allah's knowledge is perfect, as if, with men, it were a record. For men may make mistakes or may not remember, but Allah never makes mistakes and never forgets. But Allah is not only All-Knowing: He is also All-Good. Look around you: the whole earth is spread out like a carpet. Men go to and fro in it freely. He sends abundance of water from the skies, which comes down in Nile floods and fertilises the whole soil of Egypt, and feeds men and animals.'

2576. *Sabīl* means not only a road, but would include water-roads or channels, and in modern conditions, airways—in fact all means of communication.

2577. This seems to be outside the speech of Moses, and connects itself with the following verses 54-56, as part of the Word of Allah, expanding the speech of Moses and explaining the working of Allah's Providence in nature.

2578. *Azwāj*: we might translate here (as in 15:88) by "classes" instead of "pairs"; but as sex in plants seems to be referred to elsewhere (see 13:3, and n. 1804), I translate "pairs".

And from it shall We
Bring you out once again.[2579]

وَمِنْهَا نُخْرِجُكُمْ تَارَةً أُخْرَىٰ

56. And We showed Pharaoh
All Our Signs, but he
Did reject and refuse.[2580]

﴿٥٦﴾ وَلَقَدْ أَرَيْنَٰهُ ءَايَٰتِنَا كُلَّهَا
فَكَذَّبَ وَأَبَىٰ

57. He said: "Hast thou come
To drive us out
Of our land with thy magic[2581]
O Moses?

﴿٥٧﴾ قَالَ أَجِئْتَنَا لِتُخْرِجَنَا
مِنْ أَرْضِنَا بِسِحْرِكَ يَٰمُوسَىٰ

58. "But we can surely produce
Magic to match thine!
So make a tryst
Between us and thee,
Which we shall not fail
To keep—neither we nor thou—
In a place where both
Shall have even chances."[2582]

﴿٥٨﴾ فَلَنَأْتِيَنَّكَ بِسِحْرٍ مِّثْلِهِۦ
فَٱجْعَلْ بَيْنَنَا وَبَيْنَكَ
مَوْعِدًا لَّا نُخْلِفُهُۥ نَحْنُ
وَلَآ أَنتَ مَكَانًا سُوًى

59. Moses said: "Your tryst
Is the Day of the Festival,[2583]
And let the people be assembled
When the sun is well up."

﴿٥٩﴾ قَالَ مَوْعِدُكُمْ يَوْمُ ٱلزِّينَةِ
وَأَن يُحْشَرَ ٱلنَّاسُ ضُحًى

2579. This verse ought really to go into the last Section.

2580. This is a sort of general introduction to the confrontation between Moses and Pharaoh. The Signs are not only the countering of the fraudulent magic of Egypt with real miracles, but the subsequent Plagues (not mentioned here) and the Crossing of the Red Sea by Israel. (R).

2581. The Egyptians accused Moses of a design to deprive them of their land, and of exercising black magic. Both charges were palpably false. What Moses wanted to do was to free his people from bondage. The Egyptians had all the power in their possession; they wished to use the Israelites as untouchable helots; and anyone who wanted to mitigate this injustice was branded as a dreadful person who wished to deprive them of their lawful rights. As to magic, the Egyptians judged Moses by themselves. They practised sorcery to deceive the people. They accused the Prophet of Allah of doing the same, though both his outlook and the source of his strength were altogether different.

2582. *Suwan:* literally, 'equal, even.' It has been construed to mean: (1) a place equally distant for both sides, a central place, or (2) equally convenient to both sides, or (3) an open level plain, where the people can collect with ease. All these are possible meanings, but the one I have adopted is more comprehensive, and includes the others, *viz.:* (4) a place where both sides shall have even chances, "a fair place", as Palmer laconically translates it.

2583. A great day of a Temple Festival, when the temples and streets were decorated, and people were on holiday, free from work. Moses makes this appointment in order to collect as large a number as possible, for his first duty is to preach the Truth. And he apparently did it with some effect with some Egyptians (20:70, 72-76), though the Pharaoh and his high and mighty officers rejected the Truth and afterwards paid the Penalty.

60. So Pharaoh withdrew:
He concerted his plan,[2584]
And then came (back).

٦٠ فَتَوَلَّىٰ فِرْعَوْنُ
فَجَمَعَ كَيْدَهُۥ ثُمَّ أَتَىٰ

61. Moses said to them:
"Woe to you! Forge not
Ye a lie against Allah,
Lest He destroy you (at once)
Utterly by chastisement:
The forger must suffer[2585]
Frustration!"

٦١ قَالَ لَهُم مُّوسَىٰ وَيْلَكُمْ لَا تَفْتَرُوا۟
عَلَى ٱللَّهِ كَذِبًا فَيُسْحِتَكُم بِعَذَابٍ
وَقَدْ خَابَ مَنِ ٱفْتَرَىٰ

62. So they disputed, one with
Another, over their affair,
But they kept their talk secret.[2586]

٦٢ فَتَنَٰزَعُوٓا۟ أَمْرَهُم بَيْنَهُمْ
وَأَسَرُّوا۟ ٱلنَّجْوَىٰ

63. They said: "These two
Are certainly (expert) magicians:
Their object is to drive you
Out from your land
With their magic, and
To do away with your
Most cherished institutions.[2587]

٦٣ قَالُوٓا۟ إِنْ هَٰذَٰنِ لَسَٰحِرَٰنِ
يُرِيدَانِ أَن يُخْرِجَاكُم مِّنْ أَرْضِكُم
بِسِحْرِهِمَا وَيَذْهَبَا بِطَرِيقَتِكُمُ ٱلْمُثْلَىٰ

64. "Therefore concert your plan.
And then assemble
In (serried) ranks:
He wins (all along) today
Who gains the upper hand."[2588]

٦٤ فَأَجْمِعُوا۟ كَيْدَكُمْ ثُمَّ ٱئْتُوا۟ صَفًّا
وَقَدْ أَفْلَحَ ٱلْيَوْمَ مَنِ ٱسْتَعْلَىٰ

65. They said: "O Moses!
Whether wilt thou

٦٥ قَالُوا۟ يَٰمُوسَىٰٓ إِمَّآ

2584. Pharaoh was apparently taken aback at Moses appointing a solemn day of public Festival, when there would be a large concourse and there would sure to be some people not in the Court clique, who might be critical of Pharaoh's own sorcerers. But probably there was something more in their dark counsels, something unfair and wicked, to which Moses refers in his speech in the next verse.

2585. Moses had some idea of their trickery and deceit. They would palm off their fraudulent magic as coming from Allah or from their gods! He warns them that their tricks will stand exposed, and their hopes will be defeated.

2586. They knew that they had here to deal with no ordinary man, but a man with powers above what they could conceive of. But evil always thinks evil. Judging Moses and Aaron by their own standards, they thought that these two were also tricksters, with some tricks superior to their own. All they had to do was to stand together, and they must win. I construe 20:63-64 to be their private talk among themselves, followed by their open challenge to Moses in 20:65.

2587. *Cf.* 20:104. 'Your most cherished institutions,' *i.e.,* 'your ancestral and time-honoured religion and magic'. *Muthlā*, feminine of *Amthāl,* most distinguished, honoured, cherished. *Ṭarīqah* = way of life, institutions, conduct.

2588. Presumably Pharaoh was in this secret conference, and he promises the most lavish rewards to the magicians if they overcome Moses. See 7:114. That—but I think more than that—is implied. That day was to be the crisis: if they won then, they would win all along, and Moses and his people would be crushed.

That thou throw (first)
Or that we be the first
To throw?"

أَن تُلْقِيَ وَإِمَّآ أَن نَّكُونَ أَوَّلَ مَنْ أَلْقَىٰ

66. He said, "Nay, throw ye
First!" Then behold
Their ropes and their rods—[2589]
So it seemed to him
On account of their magic—
Began to be in lively motion!

٦٦ قَالَ بَلْ أَلْقُوا۟ ۖ
فَإِذَا حِبَالُهُمْ وَعِصِيُّهُمْ يُخَيَّلُ
إِلَيْهِ مِن سِحْرِهِمْ أَنَّهَا تَسْعَىٰ

67. So Moses conceived
In his mind
A (sort of) fear.[2590]

٦٧ فَأَوْجَسَ فِى نَفْسِهِۦ خِيفَةً مُّوسَىٰ

68. We said, "Fear not!
For thou hast indeed
The upper hand:

٦٨ قُلْنَا لَا تَخَفْ
إِنَّكَ أَنتَ ٱلْأَعْلَىٰ

69. "Throw that which is
In thy right hand:
Quickly will it swallow up
That which they have faked:
What they have faked
Is but a magician's trick:
And the magician thrives not,
(No matter) where he goes."[2591]

٦٩ وَأَلْقِ مَا فِى يَمِينِكَ
تَلْقَفْ مَا صَنَعُوٓا۟ ۖ
إِنَّمَا صَنَعُوا۟ كَيْدُ سَٰحِرٍ ۖ
وَلَا يُفْلِحُ ٱلسَّاحِرُ حَيْثُ أَتَىٰ

70. So the magicians were
Thrown down to prostration:
They said, "We believe
In the Lord of Aaron and
Moses".[2592]

٧٠ فَأُلْقِىَ ٱلسَّحَرَةُ سُجَّدًا
قَالُوٓا۟ ءَامَنَّا بِرَبِّ هَٰرُونَ وَمُوسَىٰ

71. (Pharaoh) said: "Believe ye
In Him before I give
You permission? Surely
This must be your leader,

٧١ قَالَ ءَامَنتُمْ لَهُۥ قَبْلَ أَنْ ءَاذَنَ لَكُمْ ۖ
إِنَّهُۥ لَكَبِيرُكُمُ

2589. Their bag of tricks was so clever that it imposed upon all beholders. Their ropes and their rods were thrown, and seemed to move about like snakes. So realistic was the effect that even Moses felt the least bit of doubt in his own mind. He of course had no tricks, and he relied entirely on Allah.

2590. The concerted attack of evil is sometimes so well-contrived from all points that falsehood appears and is acclaimed as the truth. The believer of truth is isolated, and a sort of moral dizziness creeps over his mind. But by Allah's grace Faith asserts itself, gives him confidence, and points out the specific truths which will dissipate and destroy the teeming brood of falsehood.

2591. The meaning may be either (1) that falsehood and trickery may have their day, but they cannot win everywhere, especially in the presence of Truth, or (2) that trickery and magic must come to an evil end.

2592. *Cf.* this passage with 7:120-126 and the notes thereon.

Who has taught you magic![2593]
Be sure I will cut off
Your hands and feet
On opposite sides, and I
Will have you crucified
On trunks of palm trees:
So shall ye know for certain
Which of us can give
The more severe and the more
Lasting Punishment!"

ٱلَّذِى عَلَّمَكُمُ ٱلسِّحْرَ
فَلَأُقَطِّعَنَّ أَيْدِيَكُمْ وَأَرْجُلَكُم مِّنْ خِلَٰفٍ
وَلَأُصَلِّبَنَّكُمْ فِى جُذُوعِ ٱلنَّخْلِ
وَلَتَعْلَمُنَّ أَيُّنَآ أَشَدُّ عَذَابًا وَأَبْقَىٰ

72. They said: "Never shall we
Regard thee as more than
The Clear Signs[2594] that have
Come to us or than
Him Who created us!
So decree whatever thou
Desirest to decree: for thou
Canst only decree (touching)
The life of this world.[2595]

٧٢ قَالُوا۟ لَن نُّؤْثِرَكَ عَلَىٰ مَا جَآءَنَا
مِنَ ٱلْبَيِّنَٰتِ وَٱلَّذِى فَطَرَنَا
فَٱقْضِ مَآ أَنتَ قَاضٍ
إِنَّمَا تَقْضِى هَٰذِهِ ٱلْحَيَوٰةَ ٱلدُّنْيَآ

73. "For us, we have believed
In our Lord: may He
Forgive us our faults,
And the magic to which
Thou didst compel us:[2596]
For Allah is Best
And Most Abiding."

٧٣ إِنَّآ ءَامَنَّا بِرَبِّنَا لِيَغْفِرَ لَنَا خَطَٰيَٰنَا
وَمَآ أَكْرَهْتَنَا عَلَيْهِ مِنَ ٱلسِّحْرِ
وَٱللَّهُ خَيْرٌ وَأَبْقَىٰٓ

74. Verily he who comes[2597]
To his Lord as a sinner
(At Judgement)—for him

٧٤ إِنَّهُۥ مَن يَأْتِ رَبَّهُۥ مُجْرِمًا فَإِنَّ لَهُۥ

2593. Pharaoh accuses his sorcerers who have been converted, of having been in league with Moses all the time, and in fact of having been led and taught by him! So arrogance and evil cannot conceive of Allah's worlds and worlds of beauty and truth beyond its own narrow vision! It is truly blind, and its very cleverness deludes it to wander far from the truth.

2594. *Clear Signs*: the miracles, the personality of the Messengers of Allah, the logic of events as they unfolded themselves, and the light of inner conviction in their own conscience. There are, in addition, the Signs and Proofs of Allah in nature, which are referred to in many places, *e.g.*, 20:53-54.

2595. Thus was the first part of the mission of Moses—that to the Egyptians—fulfilled. See n. 1083 to 7:126; also Appendix V.

2596. The magic, mummery, and deceptions which pertained to Egyptian Pagan religion became a creed, a State article of faith, to which all citizens were compelled to bow, and to which its priests were compelled actively to practise. And Pharaoh was at the head of the whole system—the high priest or the supreme god. With justice, therefore, do the converted magicians lay the blame on Pharaoh, effectively negativing Pharaoh's disingenuous charge that they had been in league with Moses.

These falsehoods and deceptions—combined in many cases with horrid cruelties, open and secret—were common to many Pagan systems. Some of them have been investigated in detail in Sir John G. Frazer's *Golden Bough*.

2597. The verses 20:74-76 are best construed as comments on the story of the converted Egyptians who had "purified themselves (from evil)". But some construe them as a continuation of their speech.

Is Hell; therein shall he
Neither die nor live.

جَهَنَّمَ لَا يَمُوتُ فِيهَا وَلَا يَحْيَىٰ

75. But such as comes
To Him as Believers
Who have worked righteous
deeds—
For them are ranks exalted—

﴿٧٥﴾ وَمَن يَأْتِهِۦ مُؤْمِنًا قَدْ عَمِلَ ٱلصَّٰلِحَٰتِ
فَأُو۟لَٰٓئِكَ لَهُمُ ٱلدَّرَجَٰتُ ٱلْعُلَىٰ

76. Gardens of Eternity,
Beneath which flow rivers:
They will dwell therein
For aye: such is the reward
Of those who purify
Themselves (from evil).[2598]

﴿٧٦﴾ جَنَّٰتُ عَدْنٍ تَجْرِى
مِن تَحْتِهَا ٱلْأَنْهَٰرُ خَٰلِدِينَ فِيهَا
وَذَٰلِكَ جَزَآءُ مَن تَزَكَّىٰ

C. 145.—(20:77-104.)
The people of Israel were rescued from bondage
And led on their way to the Promised Land.
Allah's Grace gave them light and guidance, but they
Rebelled under the leadership of one
Called the Sāmiri: he melted the gold
Of their jewels and made an idol—a calf
For their worship—a thing without life or power.
Moses destroyed the idol, and cursed
The man who led the people astray.

SECTION 4.

77. We sent an inspiration[2599]
To Moses: "Travel by night
With My servants, and strike
A dry path for them
Through the sea, without fear
Of being overtaken (by Pharaoh)
And without (any other) fear."

﴿٧٧﴾ وَلَقَدْ أَوْحَيْنَآ إِلَىٰ مُوسَىٰٓ أَنْ أَسْرِ بِعِبَادِى
فَٱضْرِبْ لَهُمْ طَرِيقًا فِى ٱلْبَحْرِ يَبَسًا
لَّا تَخَٰفُ دَرَكًا وَلَا تَخْشَىٰ

78. Then Pharaoh pursued them
With his forces, but
The waters completely
overwhelmed
Them and covered them up.

﴿٧٨﴾ فَأَتْبَعَهُمْ فِرْعَوْنُ بِجُنُودِهِۦ
فَغَشِيَهُم مِّنَ ٱلْيَمِّ مَا غَشِيَهُمْ

2598. As the Egyptian magicians had done when they confessed the One True God.

2599. Time passes and at last Moses is commanded to leave Egypt with his people by night. They were to cross the Red Sea into the Sinai Peninsula. They were told to have no fear of Pharaoh or of the sea or of the unknown desert country of Sinai into which they were going. They crossed dry-shod, while Pharaoh, who came in pursuit with his troops, was overwhelmed by the sea. He and his men all perished. There is no emphasis on this episode here. But the emphasis is laid on the hard task which Moses had with his own people after he had delivered them from the Egyptian bondage.

79. Pharaoh led his people astray
Instead of leading them aright.[2600]

وَأَضَلَّ فِرْعَوْنُ قَوْمَهُۥ وَمَا هَدَىٰ ﴿٧٩﴾

80. O ye Children of Israel!
We delivered you from
Your enemy, and We
Made a Covenant with you
On the right side of[2601]
Mount (Sinai), and We sent
Down to you Manna
And quails:

يَٰبَنِىٓ إِسْرَٰٓءِيلَ قَدْ أَنجَيْنَٰكُم مِّنْ عَدُوِّكُمْ وَوَٰعَدْنَٰكُمْ جَانِبَ ٱلطُّورِ ٱلْأَيْمَنَ وَنَزَّلْنَا عَلَيْكُمُ ٱلْمَنَّ وَٱلسَّلْوَىٰ ﴿٨٠﴾

81. (Saying): "Eat of the good[2602]
Things We have provided
For your sustenance, but
Commit no excess therein,
Lest My Wrath should justly
Descend on you: and those
On whom descends My Wrath
Do perish indeed![2603]

كُلُوا۟ مِن طَيِّبَٰتِ مَا رَزَقْنَٰكُمْ وَلَا تَطْغَوْا۟ فِيهِ فَيَحِلَّ عَلَيْكُمْ غَضَبِى ۖ وَمَن يَحْلِلْ عَلَيْهِ غَضَبِى فَقَدْ هَوَىٰ ﴿٨١﴾

82. "But, without doubt, I am
(Also) He that forgives
Again and again, to those
Who repent, believe,
And do right—who,
In fine, are ready to receive
True guidance."

وَإِنِّى لَغَفَّارٌ لِّمَن تَابَ وَءَامَنَ وَعَمِلَ صَٰلِحًا ثُمَّ ٱهْتَدَىٰ ﴿٨٢﴾

83. (When Moses was up on the
Mount,[2604]
Allah said): "What made thee
Hasten in advance of thy people,
O Moses?"

وَمَآ أَعْجَلَكَ عَن قَوْمِكَ يَٰمُوسَىٰ ﴿٨٣﴾

2600. It is the duty of kings and leaders to give the right lead to their people. Instead of that, the evil ones among them lead them astray, and are the cause of the whole of a people perishing.

2601. *Right side: Cf.* 19:52, and n. 2504, towards the end. The Arabian side of Sinai (Jabal Mūsā) was the place where Moses first received his commission before going to Egypt, and also where he received the Law after the Exodus from Egypt.

2602. *Cf.* 2:57 and n. 71; and 7:160. I should like to construe this not only literally but also metaphorically. 'Allah has looked after you and saved you. He has given you ethical and spiritual guidance. Enjoy the fruits of all this, but do not become puffed up and rebellious (another meaning in the root *Ṯaghā*): otherwise the Wrath of Allah is sure to descend on you.'

2603. This gives the keynote to Moses's constant tussle with his own people, and introduces immediately afterwards the incident of the golden calf.

2604. This was when Moses was up on the Mount for forty days and forty nights: 2:51 and n. 66. Moses had left the elders of Israel with Aaron behind him: Exod. xxiv. 14. While he was in a state of ecstatic honour on the Mount, his people were enacting strange scenes down below. They were tested and tried, and they failed in the trial. They made a golden image of a calf for worship, as described below. See also 7:148-150 and notes.

84. He replied: "Behold, they are Close on my footsteps: I hastened to Thee, O my Lord, To please Thee."	٨٤ قَالَ هُمْ أُولَآءِ عَلَىٰٓ أَثَرِى وَعَجِلْتُ إِلَيْكَ رَبِّ لِتَرْضَىٰ
85. (Allah) said: "We have tested Thy people in thy absence: The Sāmirī has led them[2605] Astray."	٨٥ قَالَ فَإِنَّا قَدْ فَتَنَّا قَوْمَكَ مِنۢ بَعْدِكَ وَأَضَلَّهُمُ ٱلسَّامِرِىُّ
86. So Moses returned to his people In a state of indignation And sorrow. He said: "O my people! did not Your Lord make a handsome[2606] Promise to you? Did then The promise seem to you Long (in coming)? Or did ye Desire that Wrath should Descend from your Lord on you, And so ye broke your promise To me?"	٨٦ فَرَجَعَ مُوسَىٰٓ إِلَىٰ قَوْمِهِۦ غَضْبَٰنَ أَسِفًا قَالَ يَٰقَوْمِ أَلَمْ يَعِدْكُمْ رَبُّكُمْ وَعْدًا حَسَنًا أَفَطَالَ عَلَيْكُمُ ٱلْعَهْدُ أَمْ أَرَدتُّمْ أَن يَحِلَّ عَلَيْكُمْ غَضَبٌ مِّن رَّبِّكُمْ فَأَخْلَفْتُم مَّوْعِدِى
87. They said: "We broke not The promise to thee, as far As lay in our power: But we were made to carry The weight of the ornaments[2607]	٨٧ قَالُوا۟ مَآ أَخْلَفْنَا مَوْعِدَكَ بِمَلْكِنَا وَلَٰكِنَّا حُمِّلْنَآ أَوْزَارًا مِّن زِينَةِ

2605. Who was this Sāmirī? If it was his personal name, it was sufficiently near the meaning of the original root word to have the definite article attached to it: *Cf.* the name of the khalīfah Mu'taṣim *(Al-Mu'taṣim).* What was the root for "Sāmirī"? If we look to old Egyptian, we have *Shemer* = A stranger, foreigner (Sir E. A. Wallis Budge's *Egyptian Hieroglyphic Dictionary.* 1920, p. 815 *b*). As the Israelites had just left Egypt, they might quite well have among them an Egyptianised Hebrew bearing that nickname. That the name *Shemer* was subsequently not unknown among the Hebrews is clear from the Old Testament. In I Kings, xvi. 24 we read that Omri, king of Israel, the northern portion of the divided kingdom, who reigned about 903-896 B.C., built a new city, Samaria, on a hill which he bought from Shemer, the owner of the hill, for two talents of silver. See also Renan: *History of Israel*, ii. 210. For a further discussion of the word, see n. 2608 below.

2606. There are two promises referred to in this verse, the promise of Allah and the promise of the people of Israel. They form one Covenant, which was entered into through their leader Moses. See 20:80, and 2:63, n. 78. Allah's promise was to protect them and lead them to the Promised Land, and their promise was to obey Allah's Law and His commandments.

2607. *Cf.* Exod. xii. 35-36: the Israelites, before they left Egypt, borrowed from the Egyptians "jewels of silver and jewels of gold, and raiment"; and "they spoiled the Egyptians" *i.e.*, stripped them of all their valuable jewelry. Note that the answer of the backsliders is disingenuous in various ways. (1) The Sāmirī was no doubt responsible for suggesting the making of the golden calf, but they could not on that account disclaim responsibility for themselves; the burden of the sin is on him who commits it, and he cannot pretend that he was powerless to avoid it. (2) At most the weight of the gold they carried could not have been heavy even if one or two men carried it, but would have been neglible if distributed. (3) Gold is valuable, and it is not likely that if they wanted to disburden themselves of it, they had any need to light a furnace, melt it, and cast it into the shape of a calf.

Of the (whole) people, and we
Threw them (into the fire),
And that was what
The Sāmirī suggested.[2608]

الْقَوْمِ فَقَذَفْنَٰهَا
فَكَذَٰلِكَ أَلْقَى السَّامِرِيُّ

88. "Then he brought out
(Of the fire) before the (people)
The image of a calf:[2609]
It seemed to low:[2610]
So they said: 'This is
Your god, and the god
Of Moses, but (Moses)
Has forgotten!'"[2611]

فَأَخْرَجَ لَهُمْ عِجْلًا جَسَدًا ٨٨
لَّهُۥ خُوَارٌ فَقَالُوا۟ هَٰذَآ إِلَٰهُكُمْ
وَإِلَٰهُ مُوسَىٰ فَنَسِىَ

89. Could they not see that
It could not return them
A word (for answer), and that
It had not power either
To harm them or
To do them good?[2612]

أَفَلَا يَرَوْنَ أَلَّا يَرْجِعُ ٨٩
إِلَيْهِمْ قَوْلًا وَلَا يَمْلِكُ
لَهُمْ ضَرًّا وَلَا نَفْعًا

SECTION 5.

90. Aaron had already, before this
Said to them: "O my people!
Ye are being tested in this:[2613]
For verily your Lord is (Allah)
Most Gracious: so follow me
And obey my command."[2614]

وَلَقَدْ قَالَ لَهُمْ هَٰرُونُ مِن قَبْلُ ٩٠
يَٰقَوْمِ إِنَّمَا فُتِنتُم بِهِۦ ۖ وَإِنَّ رَبَّكُمُ الرَّحْمَٰنُ
فَاتَّبِعُونِى وَأَطِيعُوٓا۟ أَمْرِى

91. They had said:[2615] "We will not
Abandon this cult, but we

قَالُوا۟ لَن نَّبْرَحَ عَلَيْهِ ٩١

2608. See n. 2605 about the Sāmirī. If the Egyptian origin of the root is not accepted, we have a Hebrew origin in "Shomer" a guard, watchman, sentinel; allied to the Arabic *Samara, yasmuru*, to keep awake by night, to converse by night: *samīr*, one who keeps awake by night. The Sāmirī may have been a watchman, in fact or by nickname.

2609. See n. 1113 to 7:148, where the same words are used and explained.

2610. See n. 1114 to 7:148.

2611. *Moses has forgotten: i.e.*, 'forgotten both us and his god. He has been gone for so many days. He is searching for a god on the Mount when his god is really here!' This is spoken by the Sāmirī and his partisans, but the people as a whole accepted it, and it therefore becomes their speech.

2612. This is a parenthetical comment. How blind the people were! They had seen Signs of the true living God, and yet they were willing to worship a dead image! The true living God had spoken in definite words of command, while this calf could only emit some sounds of lowing, which were themselves contrived by the fraud of the priests. This image could do neither good nor harm, while Allah was the Cherisher and Sustainer of the Universe, Whose Mercy was unbounded and Whose Wrath was terrible.

2613. "Resist this temptation: you are being tested in this. Do not follow after the semi-Egyptian Sāmiri, but obey me."

2614. The Bible story makes Aaron the culprit, which is inconsistent with his office as the high priest of Allah and the right hand of Moses. See n. 1116 to 7:150. Our version is more consistent, and explains, through the example of the Sāmirī, the lingering influences of the Egyptian cult of Osiris the bull-god.

2615. Obviously Aaron's speech in the last verse, and the rebels' defiance in this verse, were spoken before the return of Moses from the Mount.

Will devote ourselves to it
Until Moses returns to us."[2616]

عَٰكِفِينَ حَتَّىٰ يَرۡجِعَ إِلَيۡنَا مُوسَىٰ

92. (Moses) said: "O Aaron!
What kept thee back, when
Thou sawest them going wrong,

قَالَ يَٰهَٰرُونُ مَا مَنَعَكَ إِذۡ رَأَيۡتَهُمۡ ضَلُّوٓاْ ﴿٩٢﴾

93. "From following me? Didst thou
Then disobey my order?"[2617]

أَلَّا تَتَّبِعَنِۖ أَفَعَصَيۡتَ أَمۡرِي ﴿٩٣﴾

94. (Aaron) replied: "O son
Of my mother! Sieze (me) not
By my beard nor by
(The hair of) my head![2618]
Truly I feared lest thou
Shouldst say, 'Thou hast caused
A division among the Children
Of Israel, and thou didst not
Respect my word!'"[2619]

قَالَ يَبۡنَؤُمَّ لَا تَأۡخُذۡ
بِلِحۡيَتِي وَلَا بِرَأۡسِيٓۖ
إِنِّي خَشِيتُ أَن تَقُولَ
فَرَّقۡتَ بَيۡنَ بَنِيٓ إِسۡرَٰٓءِيلَ
وَلَمۡ تَرۡقُبۡ قَوۡلِي ﴿٩٤﴾

95. (Moses) said: "What then
Is thy case. O Sāmirī?"[2620]

قَالَ فَمَا خَطۡبُكَ يَٰسَٰمِرِيُّ ﴿٩٥﴾

96. He replied: "I saw what
They saw not, so I took
A handful (of dust) from
The footprint of the Messenger,
And threw it (into the calf):

قَالَ بَصُرۡتُ بِمَا لَمۡ يَبۡصُرُواْ بِهِۦ
فَقَبَضۡتُ قَبۡضَةٗ مِّنۡ أَثَرِ ٱلرَّسُولِ
فَنَبَذۡتُهَا ﴿٩٦﴾

2616. The rebels had so little faith that they had given Moses up for lost, and never expected to see him again.

2617. Moses, when he came back, was full of anger and grief. His speech to Aaron is one of rebuke, and he was also inclined to handle him roughly: see next verse. The order he refers to is that stated in 7:142. "Act for me amongst my people: do right, and follow not the way of those who do mischief."

2618. *Cf.* 7:150.

2619. This reply of Aaron's is in no way inconsistent with the reply as noted in 7:150. On the contrary, there is a dramatic aptness in the different points emphasised on each occasion. In S. 7 we were discussing the Ummah of Israel, and Aaron rightly says: "The people did indeed reckon me as naught, and went near to slay me!" In adding, "Let not the enemies rejoice over my misfortune" he is referring by implication to his brother's wish to maintain unity among the people. Here the unity is the chief point to emphasise: we are dealing with the Sāmirī as mischief-monger, and he could best be dealt with by Moses, who proceeds to do so.

2620. Moses now turns to the Sāmirī, and the Sāmirī's reply in the next verse sums up his character in a few wonderful strokes of character-painting. The lesson of the whole of this episode is the fall of a human soul that nominally comes to Allah's Truth in a humble position but makes mischief when and as it finds occasion. It is no less dangerous and culpable than the arrogant soul, typified by Pharaoh, which gets into high places and makes its leadership the cause of ruin of a whole nation.

Thus did my soul suggest
To me."[2621]

وَكَذَٰلِكَ سَوَّلَتْ لِى نَفْسِى

97. (Moses) said: "Get thee gone!
But thy (punishment) in this life
Will be that thou wilt say,[2622]
'Touch me not'; and moreover
(For a future penalty) thou hast
A promise that will not fail:[2623]
Now look at thy god,
Of whom thou hast become
A devoted worshipper:
We will certainly (melt) it
In a blazing fire and scatter
It broadcast in the sea!"[2624]

٩٧ قَالَ فَٱذْهَبْ فَإِنَّ
لَكَ فِى ٱلْحَيَوٰةِ أَن تَقُولَ لَا مِسَاسَ
وَإِنَّ لَكَ مَوْعِدًا لَّن تُخْلَفَهُۥ
وَٱنظُرْ إِلَىٰٓ إِلَٰهِكَ ٱلَّذِى ظَلْتَ عَلَيْهِ عَاكِفًا
لَّنُحَرِّقَنَّهُۥ ثُمَّ لَنَنسِفَنَّهُۥ فِى ٱلْيَمِّ نَسْفًا

98. But the God of you all
Is Allah: there is
No god but He: all things
He comprehends in His
knowledge.

٩٨ إِنَّمَآ إِلَٰهُكُمُ ٱللَّهُ ٱلَّذِى لَآ إِلَٰهَ إِلَّا هُوَ
وَسِعَ كُلَّ شَىْءٍ عِلْمًا

99. Thus do We relate to thee
Some stories of what happened
Before: for We have sent

٩٩ كَذَٰلِكَ نَقُصُّ عَلَيْكَ مِنْ أَنۢبَآءِ مَا قَدْ سَبَقَ
وَقَدْ ءَاتَيْنَٰكَ

2621. This answer of the Sāmirī is a fine example of unblushing effrontery, careful evasion of issues, and invented falsehoods. He takes upon himself to pretend that he had far more insight than anybody else: he saw what the vulgar crowd did not see. He saw something supernatural. "The Messenger" is construed by many Commentators to mean the angel Gabriel. *Rasūl* (plural, *rusul*) is used in several places for "angels" *e.g.*, in 11:69, 77; 19:19; and 35:1. But if we take it to mean the Messenger Moses, it means that the Sāmirī saw something sacred or supernatural in his footprints: perhaps he thinks a little flattery would make Moses forgive him. The dust became sacred, and his throwing it into the calf's image made the calf utter a lowing sound! As if that was the point at issue! He does not answer the charge of making an image for worship. But finally, with arrogant effrontery, he says, "Well, that is what my soul suggested to me, and that should be enough!"

2622. He and his kind were to become social lepers, untouchables; perhaps also sufficiently arrogant to hold others at arm's length, and say "*Noli me tangere*" (touch me not).

2623. Namely, the promised Wrath of Allah: see 20:81; 89:25.

2624. The cast effigy was re-melted and destroyed. Thus ends the Sāmirī's story, of which the lessons are indicated n. 2620 above. It may be interesting to pursue the transformations of the word Sāmirī in later times. For its origin see notes 2605 and 2608 above. Whether the root of Sāmirī was originally Egyptian or Hebrew does not affect the later history. Four facts may be noted. (1) There was a man bearing a name of that kind at the time of Moses, and he led a revolt againt Moses and was cursed by Moses. (2) In the time of King Omri (903-896 B.C.) of the northern kingdom of Israel, there was a man called Shemer, from whom, according to the Bible, was bought a hill on which was built the new capital of the kingdom, the town of Samaria. (3) The name of the hill was *Shomer* (= watchman, vigilant guardian), and that form of the name also appears as the name of a man (see II Kings xxii.21); some authorities think the town was called after the hill and not after the man (Hastings's *Encyclopedia of Relgions and Ethics*), but this is, for our present purposes, immaterial. (4) There was and is a dissenting community of Israelites called Samaritans, who have their own separate Pentateuch and Targum, who claim to be the true Children of Israel, and who hold the Orthodox Jews in contempt as the latter hold them in contempt: they claim to be the true guardians (*Shomerim*) of the Law, and that is probably the true origin of the name Samaritan, which may go further back in time than the foundation of the town of Samaria. I think it is probable that the schism originated from the time of Moses, and that the curse of Moses on the Sāmirī explains the position.

Thee a Message from
Our own Presence.[2625]

مِن لَّدُنَّا ذِكْرًا

100. If any do turn away
Therefrom, verily they will
Bear a burden
On the Day of Judgement;

(١٠٠) مَّنْ أَعْرَضَ عَنْهُ فَإِنَّهُۥ
يَحْمِلُ يَوْمَ ٱلْقِيَٰمَةِ وِزْرًا

101. They will abide in this (state):
And grievous will the burden[2626]
Be to them on that Day—

(١٠١) خَٰلِدِينَ فِيهِ
وَسَآءَ لَهُمْ يَوْمَ ٱلْقِيَٰمَةِ حِمْلًا

102. The Day when the Trumpet
Will be sounded: that Day,
We shall gather the sinful,
Blear-eyed (with terror),[2627]

(١٠٢) يَوْمَ يُنفَخُ فِى ٱلصُّورِ
وَنَحْشُرُ ٱلْمُجْرِمِينَ يَوْمَئِذٍ زُرْقًا

103. In whispers will they consult
Each other: "Ye tarried not
Longer than ten (Days);"[2628]

(١٠٣) يَتَخَٰفَتُونَ بَيْنَهُمْ
إِن لَّبِثْتُمْ إِلَّا عَشْرًا

104. We know best what they
Will say, when their leader[2629]
Most eminent in Conduct
Will say: "Ye tarried not
Longer than a day!"

(١٠٤) نَّحْنُ أَعْلَمُ بِمَا يَقُولُونَ إِذْ يَقُولُ
أَمْثَلُهُمْ طَرِيقَةً إِن لَّبِثْتُمْ إِلَّا يَوْمًا

C. 146.—(20:105-135.) Such is the lure of Evil: but high
And low will be levelled on the Day
Of Judgement, before the Eternal, the Gracious,
The King, the Truth, who sends the Qur'ān
To teach and to warn. Will man remember
How Adam's arch-enemy, Satan, caused
His fall, and will he yet be blind

2625. Thus superceding previous revelations; for this (the Qur'ān) is direct from Allah, and is not a second-hand exposition on other men's authority.

2626. *Cf.* 6:31. If people are so immersed in the evanescent falsehoods of this life to turn away from the True and the Eternal, they will have a rude awakening when the Judgement comes. These very things that they thought so enjoyable here—taking advantage of others, material self-indulgence, nursing grievances instead of doing good, etc., etc.—will be a grievous burden to them that day, which they will not be able to escape or lighten.

2627. *Zurqa* = having eyes different from normal colour, which in the East is black and white: having blue eyes, or eyes afflicted with dimness or blindness, or squint; hence metaphorically, blear-eyed (with terror).

2628. Faced with eternity, they will realise that their life on this earth, or the interval between their sin and their punishment, had a duration which practically amounted to nothing. They express this by the phrase "ten days", but their wiser heads think that even this is an over-estimate. It was but a brief day!

2629. *Cf.* 20:63 and n. 2587. Note that it is the shrewdest and most versed in Life who will say this, because they will be the first to see the true situation.

To the Signs of Allah? Nay—but let
Not Evil make you impatient: the Prize
Of the Hereafter is better than aught
Of the glitter of this life: wait in Faith,
And the End will show the triumph
Of Truth, Goodness, and Righteousness.

SECTION 6.

105. They ask thee concerning[2630]
The Mountains: say, "My Lord
Will uproot them and scatter
Them as dust;"[2631]

وَيَسْـَٔلُونَكَ عَنِ ٱلْجِبَالِ فَقُلْ يَنسِفُهَا رَبِّى نَسْفًا ﴿١٠٥﴾

106. "He will leave them as plains
Smooth and level;"

فَيَذَرُهَا قَاعًا صَفْصَفًا ﴿١٠٦﴾

107. "Nothing crooked or curved
Wilt thou see in their place."

لَّا تَرَىٰ فِيهَا عِوَجًا وَلَآ أَمْتًا ﴿١٠٧﴾

108. On that Day will they follow
The Caller[2632] (straight): no
crookedness
(Can they show) him: all sounds[2633]
Shall humble themselves in
The Presence of (Allah) Most
Gracious:
Nothing shalt thou hear
But the tramp of their feet
(As they march).

يَوْمَئِذٍ يَتَّبِعُونَ ٱلدَّاعِىَ لَا عِوَجَ لَهُۥ ۖ وَخَشَعَتِ ٱلْأَصْوَاتُ لِلرَّحْمَـٰنِ فَلَا تَسْمَعُ إِلَّا هَمْسًا ﴿١٠٨﴾

109. On that Day shall no
Intercession avail

يَوْمَئِذٍ لَّا تَنفَعُ ٱلشَّفَـٰعَةُ ﴿١٠٩﴾

2630. In the last verse, it was the deceptiveness and relativity of Time that was dealt with. Here we come to the question of space, solidity, bulk. The question was actually put to the Holy Prophet: what will become of the solid Mountains, or in the English phrase, "the eternal hills"? They are no more substantial than anything else in this temporal world. When the "new world", (13:5) of which Unbelievers doubted, is actually in being, the mountains will cease to exist. We can imagine the scene of judgement as a level plain, in which there are no ups and downs and no places of concealment. All is straight and level, without corners, mysteries, or lurking doubts.

2631. The one word *nasafa* carries the ideas of (1) tearing up by the roots, (2) scattering like chaff or dust, and (3) winnowing. Its twofold repetition here intensifies the meaning.

2632. *The Caller*: the angel whose voice will call and direct all souls. (R).

2633. A beautiful personification of hushed Sound. First there is the loud blast of the Trumpet. Then there is the stillness and hush of awe and reverence: only the tramp of the ranks marching along will be heard. (R).

Except for those for whom[2634]
Permission has been granted
By (Allah) Most Gracious
And whose word is
Acceptable to Him.

إِلَّا مَنْ أَذِنَ لَهُ ٱلرَّحْمَٰنُ
وَرَضِيَ لَهُۥ قَوْلًا

110. He knows what (appears
To His creatures as) before
Or after or behind them:[2635]
But they shall not compass it
With their knowledge.

١١٠ يَعْلَمُ مَا بَيْنَ أَيْدِيهِمْ وَمَا خَلْفَهُمْ
وَلَا يُحِيطُونَ بِهِۦ عِلْمًا

111. (All) faces shall be humbled
Before (Him)— the Living,
The Self-Subsisting, Eternal:
Hopeless indeed will be
The man that carries
Iniquity (on his back).[2636]

١١١ وَعَنَتِ ٱلْوُجُوهُ لِلْحَيِّ ٱلْقَيُّومِ
وَقَدْ خَابَ مَنْ
حَمَلَ ظُلْمًا

112. But he who works deeds
Of righteousness, and has faith,
Will have no fear of harm
Nor of any curtailment[2637]
(Of what is his due).

١١٢ وَمَن يَعْمَلْ مِنَ ٱلصَّٰلِحَٰتِ وَهُوَ مُؤْمِنٌ
فَلَا يَخَافُ ظُلْمًا وَلَا هَضْمًا

113. Thus have We sent this
Down—an Arabic Qur'ān—
And explained therein in detail
Some of the warnings,
In order that they may

١١٣ وَكَذَٰلِكَ أَنزَلْنَٰهُ قُرْءَانًا عَرَبِيًّا
وَصَرَّفْنَا فِيهِ مِنَ ٱلْوَعِيدِ لَعَلَّهُمْ

2634. *Cf.* 2:255 in the Verse of the Throne. Here *man* is in the accusative case governed by *tanfa'u*, and it is better to construe as I have done. That is, intercession will benefit no one except those for whom Allah has granted permission, and whose word (of repentance) is true and sincere, and therefore acceptable to Allah. Others construe: no intercession will avail, except by those to whom Allah has granted permission, and whose word (of intercession) is acceptable to Allah. In that case the two different clauses have no distinct meanings.

2635. *Cf.* 2:255 and n. 297. The slight difference in phraseology (which I have tried to preserve in the Translation) will be understood as beauty when we reflect that here our attention is directed to the Day of Judgement, and in 2:255 the wording is general, and applies to our present state also.

2636. The metaphor of the burden of sin which the unjust carry on their backs is referred to in 20:100-101 (see n. 2626), in 6:31, and in other passages. Note that *all* faces, those of the just as well as of the unjust, will be humbled before Allah: the best of us can claim no merit equal to Allah's Grace. But the just will have Hope: while the unjust, now that the curtain of Reality has risen, will be in absolute Despair!

2637. See the last note. Unlike the unjust, the righteous, who have come with Faith, will now find their Faith justified: not only will they be free from any fear of harm, but they will be rewarded to the full, or, as has been said in other passages, where His bounty rather than His justice is emphasised, they will get more than their due reward (3:27; 39:10).

يَتَّقُونَ أَوْ يُحْدِثُ لَهُمْ ذِكْرًا

Fear Allah, or that it may
Cause their remembrance
(of Him).[2638]

١١٤ فَتَعَٰلَى ٱللَّهُ ٱلْمَلِكُ ٱلْحَقُّ
وَلَا تَعْجَلْ بِٱلْقُرْءَانِ مِن قَبْلِ أَن
يُقْضَىٰٓ إِلَيْكَ وَحْيُهُۥ
وَقُل رَّبِّ زِدْنِى عِلْمًا

114. High above all is Allah,
The King, the Truth!
Be not in haste
With the Qur'ān before
Its revelation to thee[2639]
Is completed, but say,
"O my Lord! advance me
In knowledge

١١٥ وَلَقَدْ عَهِدْنَآ إِلَىٰٓ ءَادَمَ مِن قَبْلُ
فَنَسِىَ وَلَمْ نَجِدْ لَهُۥ عَزْمًا

115. We had already, beforehand,[2640]
Taken the covenant of Adam,
But he forgot: and We found
On his part no firm resolve.

SECTION 7.

١١٦ وَإِذْ قُلْنَا لِلْمَلَٰٓئِكَةِ ٱسْجُدُوا۟
لِءَادَمَ فَسَجَدُوٓا۟ إِلَّآ إِبْلِيسَ أَبَىٰ

116. When We said to the angels,
"Prostrate yourselves to Adam",
They prostrated themselves, but not
Iblīs: he refused.

١١٧ فَقُلْنَا يَٰٓـَٔادَمُ
إِنَّ هَٰذَا عَدُوٌّ لَّكَ وَلِزَوْجِكَ
فَلَا يُخْرِجَنَّكُمَا مِنَ ٱلْجَنَّةِ فَتَشْقَىٰٓ

117. Then We said: "O Adam!
Verily, this is an enemy
To thee and thy wife:
So let him not get you
Both out of the Garden,
So that thou art landed
In misery.[2641]

2638. The Qur'ān is in clear Arabic, so that even an unlearned people like the Arabs might understand and profit by its warnings, and the rest of the world may learn through them, as they did in the first few centuries of Islam and may do again when we Muslims show ourselves worthy to explain and exemplify its meaning. The evil are warned that they may repent: the good are confirmed in their Faith and strengthened by their remembrance of Him.

2639. Allah is above every human event or desire. His purpose is universal. But He is the Truth, the absolute Truth: and His kingdom is the true kingdom, that can carry out its will. That Truth unfolds itself gradually, as it did in the gradual revelation of the Qur'ān to the Holy Prophet. But even after it was completed in a volume, its true meaning and purpose only gradually unfold themselves to any given individual or nation. No one should be impatient about it. On the contrary, we should always pray for increase in our own knowledge, which can never at any given moment be complete.

2640. The spiritual fall of two individual souls, Pharaoh and the Sāmirī, having been referred to, the one through overweening arrogance, and the other through a spirit of mischief and false harking back to the past, our attention is now called to the prototype of Evil who tempted Adam, the original Man, and to the fact that though man was clearly warned that Evil is his enemy and will effect his ruin, he showed so little firmness that he succumbed to it at once at the first opportunity.

2641. See last note. The story is referred to, in order to draw attention to man's folly in rushing into the arms of Evil, though he had been clearly forewarned.

118. "There is therein (enough provision)
For thee not to go hungry[2642]
Nor to go naked,"

١١٨ إِنَّ لَكَ أَلَّا تَجُوعَ فِيهَا
وَلَا تَعْرَىٰ

119. "Nor to suffer from thirst,
Nor from the sun's heat."

١١٩ وَأَنَّكَ لَا تَظْمَؤُا۟ فِيهَا وَلَا تَضْحَىٰ

120. But Satan whispered evil
To him: he said, "O Adam!
Shall I lead thee to
The Tree of Eternity[2643]
And to a kingdom
That never decays?"

١٢٠ فَوَسْوَسَ إِلَيْهِ ٱلشَّيْطَـٰنُ
قَالَ يَـٰٓـَٔادَمُ هَلْ أَدُلُّكَ عَلَىٰ شَجَرَةِ
ٱلْخُلْدِ وَمُلْكٍ لَّا يَبْلَىٰ

121. In the result, they both
Ate of the tree, and so
Their nakedness appeared[2644]
To them: they began to sew
Together, for their covering,
Leaves from the Garden:
Thus did Adam disobey
His Lord, and allow himself[2645]
To be seduced.

١٢١ فَأَكَلَا مِنْهَا
فَبَدَتْ لَهُمَا سَوْءَٰتُهُمَا وَطَفِقَا
يَخْصِفَانِ عَلَيْهِمَا مِن وَرَقِ ٱلْجَنَّةِ ۚ
وَعَصَىٰٓ ءَادَمُ رَبَّهُۥ فَغَوَىٰ

122. But his Lord chose him
(For His Grace): He turned
To him, and gave him guidance.

١٢٢ ثُمَّ ٱجْتَبَـٰهُ رَبُّهُۥ
فَتَابَ عَلَيْهِ وَهَدَىٰ

123. He said: "Get ye down,
Both of you—all together,[2646]

١٢٣ قَالَ ٱهْبِطَا مِنْهَا جَمِيعًۢا

2642. Not only had the warning been given that Evil is an enemy to man and will effect his destruction, but it was clearly pointed out that all his needs were being met in the Garden of Happiness. Food and clothing, drink and shelter, were amply provided for.

2643. The suggestion of the Evil One is clever, as it always is: it is false, and at the same time plausible. It is false, because (1) that felicity was not temporary, like the life of this world, and (2) they were supreme in the Garden, and a "kingdom" such as was dangled before them would only add to their sorrows. It was plausible, because (1) nothing had been said to them about Eternity, as the opposite of Eternity was not yet known, and (2) the sweets of Power arise from the savour of Self, and Self is an alluring (if false) attraction that misleads the Will.

2644. Hitherto they were clothed in the garb of Innocence and knew no evil. Now, when disobedience to Allah had sullied their soul and torn off the garment of their Innocence, their sullied Self appeared to themselves in all its nakedness and ugliness, and they had to resort to external things (leaves of the Garden) to cover the shame of their self-consciousness.

2645. Adam had been given the will to choose, and he chose wrongly, and was about to be lost in the throng of the evil ones, when Allah's Grace came to his aid. His repentance was accepted, and Allah chose him for His Mercy, as stated in the next verse.

2646. The little variations between this passage and 2:38 are instructive, as showing how clearly the particular argument is followed in each case. Here *ihbiṭā* ('get ye down') is in the dual number, and refers to the two individual souls, our common ancestors: in 2:38 *ihbiṭū* is in the plural number, to include all mankind and Satan, for the argument is about the collective life of man. On the other hand, "all together" includes Satan, the spirit of evil, and the enmity "one to another" refers to the eternal feud between Man and Satan, between our better nature and Evil.

From the Garden, with enmity
One to another: but if,
As is sure, there comes to you
Guidance from Me, whosover
Follows My guidance, will not
Lose his way, nor fall[2647]
Into misery.

بَعْضُكُمْ لِبَعْضٍ عَدُوٌّ
فَإِمَّا يَأْتِيَنَّكُم مِّنِّى هُدًى
فَمَنِ ٱتَّبَعَ هُدَاىَ فَلَا يَضِلُّ وَلَا يَشْقَىٰ

124. "But whosoever turns away
From My Message, verily
For him is a life narrowed
Down, and We shall raise
Him up blind on the Day[2648]
Of Judgement."

١٢٤ وَمَنْ أَعْرَضَ عَن ذِكْرِى
فَإِنَّ لَهُۥ مَعِيشَةً ضَنكًا وَنَحْشُرُهُۥ
يَوْمَ ٱلْقِيَـٰمَةِ أَعْمَىٰ

125. He will say: "O my Lord!
Why hast thou raised me
Up blind, while I had
Sight (before)?"[2649]

١٢٥ قَالَ رَبِّ لِمَ حَشَرْتَنِىٓ
أَعْمَىٰ وَقَدْ كُنتُ بَصِيرًا

126. (Allah) will say: "Thus
Didst thou, when Our Signs
Came unto thee, disregard
Them: so wilt thou,
This day, be disregarded."[2650]

١٢٦ قَالَ كَذَٰلِكَ أَتَتْكَ ءَايَـٰتُنَا فَنَسِيتَهَا
وَكَذَٰلِكَ ٱلْيَوْمَ تُنسَىٰ

127. And thus do We recompense
Him who transgresses beyond bounds
And believes not in the Signs
Of his Lord: and the Penalty
Of the Hereafter is far more
Grievous and more enduring.[2651]

١٢٧ وَكَذَٰلِكَ نَجْزِى مَنْ أَسْرَفَ
وَلَمْ يُؤْمِنۢ بِـَٔايَـٰتِ رَبِّهِۦ
وَلَعَذَابُ ٱلْـَٔاخِرَةِ أَشَدُّ وَأَبْقَىٰٓ

2647. For the same reason as in the last note, we have the consequences of Guidance to the individual, *viz.*: being saved from going astray or from falling into misery and despair. In 2:38, the consequences expressed, though they apply to the individual, are also appropriate taken collectively: "on them shall be no fear, nor shall they grieve."

2648. Again, as in the last two verses, there is a variation from the previous passage (2:39). The consequences of the rejection of Allah's guidance are here expressed more individually: a life narrowed down, and a blindness that will persist beyond this life. "A life narrowed down" has many implications: (1) it is a life from which all the beneficent influences of Allah's wide world are excluded; (2) it is a life for Self, not for all; (3) in looking exclusively to the "good things" of this life, it misses the true Reality.

2649. Because Allah gave him physical sight in this life for trial, he thinks he should be favoured in the real world, the world that matters! He misused the physical sight and made himself blind for the other world.

2650. 'You were deliberately blind to Allah's Signs: now you will not see Allah's favours, and will be excluded from his Grace.'

2651. Blindness in the world of enduring Reality is far worse than physical blindness in the world of probation.

128. Is it not a warning to such
Men (to call to mind)
How many generations before
them
We destroyed, in whose haunts
They (now) move? Verily,
In this are Signs for men
Endued with understanding,[2652]

١٢٨ أَفَلَمْ يَهْدِ لَهُمْ كَمْ أَهْلَكْنَا قَبْلَهُم
مِّنَ ٱلْقُرُونِ يَمْشُونَ فِي مَسَٰكِنِهِمْ
إِنَّ فِي ذَٰلِكَ لَءَايَٰتٍ لِّأُوْلِي ٱلنُّهَىٰ

SECTION 8.

129. Had it not been
For a Word that went forth
Before from thy Lord,[2653]
(Their punishment) must
necessarily
Have come; but there is
A term appointed (for respite).

١٢٩ وَلَوْلَا كَلِمَةٌ سَبَقَتْ
مِن رَّبِّكَ لَكَانَ لِزَامًا
وَأَجَلٌ مُّسَمًّى

130. Therefore be patient with what
They say, and celebrate
(constantly)[2654]
The praises of thy Lord
Before the rising of the sun,
And before its setting;
Yea, celebrate them
For part of the hours
Of the night, and at the sides[2655]
Of the day: that thou
Mayest have (spiritual) joy.

١٣٠ فَٱصْبِرْ عَلَىٰ مَا يَقُولُونَ
وَسَبِّحْ بِحَمْدِ رَبِّكَ
قَبْلَ طُلُوعِ ٱلشَّمْسِ وَقَبْلَ غُرُوبِهَا
وَمِنْ ءَانَآيِٕ ٱلَّيْلِ فَسَبِّحْ
وَأَطْرَافَ ٱلنَّهَارِ لَعَلَّكَ تَرْضَىٰ

2652. *Cf.* 20:54. This phrase concluded the argument of Moses with Pharaoh about Pharaoh's blindness to Allah and the Signs of Allah. Now it concludes the more general argument about men, concerning whom the saying arose: 'none are so blind as those who *will* not see.'

2653. *Cf.* 10:19 and n. 1407: also 11:110. In Allah's Holy Plan and Purpose, there is a wise adjustment of all interests, and a merciful chance and respite given to all, the unjust as well as the just, and His decree or word abides. The most wicked have a term appointed for them for respite. Had it not been so, the punishment must necessarily have descended on them immediately for their evil deeds.

2654. All good men must be patient with what seems to them evil around them. That does not mean that they should sit still and do nothing to destroy evil; for the fight against evil is one of the cardinal points of Islam. What they are told is that they must not be impatient: they must pray to Allah and commune with Him, so that their patience and faith may be strengthened, and they may be able the better to grapple with evil. For they thus not only get strength but inward spiritual joy.

2655. *Ṭaraf,* plural *aṭrāf,* may mean sides, ends, extremities. If the day be compared to a tubular figure standing erect, the top and bottom are clearly marked, but the sides are not so clearly marked: they would be *aṭrāf* (plural), not *ṭarafayn* (dual). Now the prayer before sunrise is clearly *Fajr;* that before sunset is *'Aṣr:* "part of the hours of the night" would indicate *Maghrib* (early night, just after sunset), and *'Ishā*, before going to bed. There is left *Ẓuhr,* which is the indefinite side or middle of the day; it may be soon after the sun's decline from noon, but there is considerable latitude about the precise hour. The majority of Commentators interpret in favour of the five Canonical prayers, and some include optional prayers. But I think the words are even more comprehensive. A good man's life is all one sweet Song of Praise to Allah.

131. Nor strain thine eyes in longing
For the things We have given
For enjoyment to parties
Of them, the splendour
Of the life of this world,
Through which We test them:
But the provision of thy Lord[2656]
Is better and more enduring.

١٣١ وَلَا تَمُدَّنَّ عَيْنَيْكَ
إِلَىٰ مَا مَتَّعْنَا بِهِۦٓ أَزْوَٰجًا مِّنْهُمْ
زَهْرَةَ ٱلْحَيَوٰةِ ٱلدُّنْيَا لِنَفْتِنَهُمْ فِيهِ
وَرِزْقُ رَبِّكَ خَيْرٌ وَأَبْقَىٰ

132. Enjoin prayer on thy people,
And be constant therein.
We ask thee not to provide[2657]
Sustenance: We provide it
For thee. But the (fruit of)
The Hereafter is for Righteousness.

١٣٢ وَأْمُرْ أَهْلَكَ بِٱلصَّلَوٰةِ وَٱصْطَبِرْ عَلَيْهَا
لَا نَسْـَٔلُكَ رِزْقًا نَّحْنُ نَرْزُقُكَ
وَٱلْعَٰقِبَةُ لِلتَّقْوَىٰ

133. They say: "Why does he not[2658]
Bring us a Sign from
His Lord?" Has not
A Clear Sign come to them
Of all that was
In the former Books
Of revelation?

١٣٣ وَقَالُوا۟ لَوْلَا يَأْتِينَا بِـَٔايَةٍ مِّن رَّبِّهِۦٓ
أَوَلَمْ تَأْتِهِم بَيِّنَةُ مَا فِى
ٱلصُّحُفِ ٱلْأُولَىٰ

134. And if We had inflicted
On them a penalty before this,[2659]
They would have said:
"Our Lord! If only Thou
Hadst sent us a messenger,
We should certainly have followed
Thy Signs before we were
Humbled and put to shame."

١٣٤ وَلَوْ أَنَّآ أَهْلَكْنَٰهُم بِعَذَابٍ مِّن قَبْلِهِۦ
لَقَالُوا۟ رَبَّنَا لَوْلَآ أَرْسَلْتَ
إِلَيْنَا رَسُولًا فَنَتَّبِعَ ءَايَٰتِكَ مِن
قَبْلِ أَن نَّذِلَّ وَنَخْزَىٰ

2656. The good things of this life make a brave show, but they are as nothing compared with the good of the Hereafter. Both are provided by Allah, but the former are given to the just and the unjust as a test and trial, and in any case will pass away: while the latter come especially from Allah for his devoted servants, and are incomparably of more value and will last through eternity.

2657. Sustenance, in the sense of the ordinary needs of life, the man of Allah does not worry about. That is provided by Allah for all, the just and the unjust. But the special provision, the real Sustenance, the spiritual fruit, is for a righteous life in the sevice of Allah.

2658. The question or plea of the Unbelievers is disingenuous. Many Signs have come with this Revelation. But the one that should have appealed to those who believed in former revelations and should have convinced them was what was in their own books

2659. If the Signs mentioned in the last note did not convince them, it would mean that they were not true to their own faith. They were not straight with themselves. In justice they should have been punished for their falsehood. But they were given further respite. Or they would again have argued in a circle, and said: "If only Allah had sent us a living messenger we should have believed!" The living messenger they flout because they want a Sign. The Sign they wish to ignore, because they want a living messenger!

135. Say: "Each one (of us)
Is waiting: wait ye,
therefore,[2660]
And soon shall ye know
Who it is that is
On the straight and
even[2661]
Way, and who it is
That has received
guidance."

١٣٥ قُلْ كُلٌّ مُّتَرَبِّصٌ فَتَرَبَّصُوا۟
فَسَتَعْلَمُونَ مَنْ أَصْحَٰبُ
ٱلصِّرَٰطِ ٱلسَّوِىِّ
وَمَنِ ٱهْتَدَىٰ

2660. If people will not be true to their own lights, what further argument is left? The Prophet of Allah can only say: "Let us wait the issue; my faith tells me that Allah's Truth must prevail." *Cf.* 9:52. (R).

2661. *Cf.* 19:43. The straight and even Way must endure, and show that the man who follows it has received true guidance. All falsehood and crookedness must ultimately disappear.

INTRODUCTION TO SŪRAH 21—*AL ANBIYĀ'*

The last Sūrah dealt with the individual story (spiritual) of Moses and Aaron, and contrasted it with the growth of evil in individuals like the Pharaoh and the Sāmirī, and ended with a warning against Evil, and an exhortation to the purification of the soul with prayer and praise. This Sūrah begins with the external obstacles placed by Evil against such purification, and gives the assurance of Allah's power to defend men, illustrating this with reference to Abraham's fight against idolatry, Lot's fight against injustice and failure to proclaim Allah's glory by making full use of man's God-given faculties and powers, that of Job against impatience and want of self-confidence, that of Ismā'īl, Idrīs, and Dhul Kifl against want of steady perseverance, that of Dhā al Nūn against hasty anger, that of Zakarīya against spiritual isolation, and that of Mary against the lusts of this world. In each allusion there is a special point about the soul's purification. The common point is that the Prophets were not, as the vulgar suppose, just irresistible men. They had to win their ground inch by inch against all kinds of resistance from evil.

The chronology of this Sūrah has no significance. It probably dates from the middle of the Makkan period of inspiration.

Summary—Man treats, as he has always treated, the serious things of life with jest or contempt; but the Judgement must come, and Truth must triumph (21:1-29, and C. 147).

Unity of Design, and certainty of Allah's Promise: Allah's protection and mercy, and His justice (21:30-50, and C. 148).

How Abraham triumphed over idols, as did others among Allah's chosen ones over various forms of evil (21:51-93, and C. 149).

Work righteousness while it is yet time, for the Judgement will come, and only the righteous will inherit (21:94-112, and C. 150).

C. 147.—Men may lightly treat Allah's Signs
(21:1-29.) As jests, but the Judgement must come
Inevitably. His Message is true,
And delivered by Allah's Prophet, as from
Man to men. Truth must triumph
And all false gods and false worship
Must come to naught: for Allah is One,
And His Truth has been one throughout the ages.

Sūrah 21.

Al Anbiyā' (The Prophets)

In the Name of Allah, Most Gracious,
Most Merciful.

بِسْمِ اللَّهِ الرَّحْمَٰنِ الرَّحِيمِ

17
30

1. Closer and closer to mankind[2662]
Comes their Reckoning: yet they
Heed not and they turn away.

١ اقْتَرَبَ لِلنَّاسِ حِسَابُهُمْ
وَهُمْ فِي غَفْلَةٍ مُّعْرِضُونَ

2. Never comes (aught) to them
Of a renewed Message[2663]
From their Lord, but they
Listen to it as in jest—

٢ مَا يَأْتِيهِم مِّن ذِكْرٍ مِّن رَّبِّهِم مُّحْدَثٍ
إِلَّا اسْتَمَعُوهُ وَهُمْ يَلْعَبُونَ

3. Their hearts toying as with
Trifles. The wrongdoers conceal[2664]
Their private counsels, (saying),
"Is this (one) more than
A man like yourselves?
Will ye go to witchcraft
With your eyes open?"[2665]

٣ لَاهِيَةً قُلُوبُهُمْ وَأَسَرُّوا النَّجْوَى
الَّذِينَ ظَلَمُوا هَلْ هَٰذَا إِلَّا بَشَرٌ مِّثْلُكُمْ
أَفَتَأْتُونَ السِّحْرَ وَأَنتُمْ تُبْصِرُونَ

4. Say:[2666] "My Lord
Knoweth (every) word (spoken)[2667]
In the heavens and on earth:
He is the One that heareth
And knoweth (all things)."

٤ قَالَ رَبِّي يَعْلَمُ الْقَوْلَ فِي السَّمَاءِ وَالْأَرْضِ
وَهُوَ السَّمِيعُ الْعَلِيمُ

2662. Every minute sees them nearer to their doom, and yet they are sadly heedless, and even actively turn away from the Message that would save them.

2663. In each age, when the Message of Allah is renewed, the very people who should have known better and welcomed the renewal and the sweeping away of human cobwebs, either receive it with amused self-superiority, which later turns into active hostility, or with careless indifference.

2664. Allah's Message is free and open, in the full light of day. His enemies plot against it in secrecy, lest their own false motives be exposed. Their jealousy prevents them from accepting a "man like themselves" as a teacher or warner or guide.

2665. Literally, "in a state in which you (actually) see (that it is witchcraft)". When Allah's Messenger is proved to be above them in moral worth, in true insight, in earnestness and power of eloquence, they accuse him of witchcraft, a word which may mean nothing, or perhaps some mysterious deceitful arts.

2666. Notice that in the usual Arabic texts (that is, according to the *Qirā'ah* of *Hafs*) the word *qāla* is here and in 21:112 below, as well as in 23:112, spelt differently from the usual spelling of the word in other places (*e.g.*, in 20:125-126). *Qul* is the reading of the *Baṣrah Qirā'ah*, meaning, "Say thou" in the imperative. If we construe "he says", the pronoun refers to "this (one)" in the preceding verse, *viz.*: the Prophet. But more than one Commentator understands the meaning in the imperative, and I agree with them. The point is merely one of verbal construction. The meaning is the same in either case. See n. 2948 to 23:112. (R).

2667. Every word, whether whispered in secret (as in 21:3 above) or spoken openly, is known to Allah. Let not the wrongdoers imagine that their secret plots are secret to the Knower of all things.

5. "Nay," they say, "(these are)
Medleys of dreams!—Nay,
He forged it!—Nay,
He is (but) a poet![2668]
Let him then bring us
A Sign like the ones
That were sent to
(Prophets) of old!"

٥ بَلْ قَالُوٓا۟ أَضْغَٰثُ أَحْلَٰمٍۭ
بَلِ ٱفْتَرَىٰهُ بَلْ هُوَ شَاعِرٌ
فَلْيَأْتِنَا بِـَٔايَةٍ كَمَآ
أُرْسِلَ ٱلْأَوَّلُونَ

6. (As to those) before them,
Not one of the populations
Which We destroyed believed:
Will these believe?[2669]

٦ مَآ ءَامَنَتْ قَبْلَهُم مِّن
قَرْيَةٍ أَهْلَكْنَٰهَآ ۖ أَفَهُمْ يُؤْمِنُونَ

7. Before thee, also, the messengers
We sent were but men,
To whom We granted inspiration:
If ye realise this not, ask
Of those who possess the
Message.[2670]

٧ وَمَآ أَرْسَلْنَا قَبْلَكَ
إِلَّا رِجَالًا نُّوحِىٓ إِلَيْهِمْ ۖ
فَسْـَٔلُوٓا۟ أَهْلَ ٱلذِّكْرِ إِن كُنتُمْ لَا تَعْلَمُونَ

8. Nor did We give them
Bodies that ate no food,
Nor were they exempt from
death.[2671]

٨ وَمَا جَعَلْنَٰهُمْ جَسَدًا
لَّا يَأْكُلُونَ ٱلطَّعَامَ وَمَا كَانُوا۟ خَٰلِدِينَ

9. In the end We fulfilled
To them Our promise,
And We saved them
And those whom We pleased,
But We destroyed those
Who transgressed beyond
bounds.[2672]

٩ ثُمَّ صَدَقْنَٰهُمُ ٱلْوَعْدَ
فَأَنجَيْنَٰهُمْ وَمَن نَّشَآءُ
وَأَهْلَكْنَا ٱلْمُسْرِفِينَ

2668. The charges against Allah's inspired Messenger are heaped up "Magic!" says one: that means, "We don't understand it!" Says another, "Oh! but we know! he is a mere dreamer of confused dreams!" If the "dreams" fit in with real things and vital experience, another will suggest, "Oh yes! why drag in supernatural agencies? he is clever enough to forge it himself!" Or another suggests, "He is a poet! Poets can invent things and say them in beautiful words!" Another interposes, "What we should like to see is miracles, like those we read of in stories of the Prophets of old!"

2669. 'If such miracles as you read of failed to convince Unbelievers of old, what chance is there that these Unbelievers will believe? Miracles may come, but they are not cures for Unbelief.'

2670. See 16:43 and n. 2069. This answers the Unbelievers' taunt, "he is just a man like ourselves!" True, but all messengers sent by Allah were men, not angels or another kind of beings, who could not understand men or whom men could not understand.

2671. As men they were subject to the laws governing the physical bodies of men. They ate and drank, and their bodies perished in death.

2672. But, however difficult (or impossible) their mission may have appeared to them, or to the world at first, they won through eventually, even those who *seemed* to have been defeated. Examples are given in the latter part of this Sūrah, especially in 21:51-93. They were delivered from the Wrath which overtook the Unbelievers, as were those with them who accepted Allah's Message and placed themselves in conformity with His Will and Plan. That is the meaning of "whom We pleased".

10. We have revealed for you
(O men!) a book in which
Is a Message for you:
Will ye not then understand?

١٠ لَقَدْ أَنزَلْنَآ إِلَيْكُمْ كِتَـٰبًا فِيهِ ذِكْرُكُمْ
أَفَلَا تَعْقِلُونَ

Section 2.

11. How many were the populations
We utterly destroyed because
Of their iniquities, setting up
In their places other peoples?

١١ وَكَمْ قَصَمْنَا مِن قَرْيَةٍ كَانَتْ ظَالِمَةً
وَأَنشَأْنَا بَعْدَهَا قَوْمًا ءَاخَرِينَ

12. Yet, when they felt
Our Punishment (coming),
Behold, they (tried to) flee
From it.[2673]

١٢ فَلَمَّآ أَحَسُّوا۟ بَأْسَنَآ
إِذَا هُم مِّنْهَا يَرْكُضُونَ

13. Flee not, but return to
The good things of this life
Which were given you,
And to your homes,
In order that ye may
Be called to account.[2674]

١٣ لَا تَرْكُضُوا۟ وَٱرْجِعُوٓا۟
إِلَىٰ مَآ أُتْرِفْتُمْ فِيهِ وَمَسَـٰكِنِكُمْ
لَعَلَّكُمْ تُسْـَٔلُونَ

14. They said: "Ah! woe to us!
We were indeed wrongdoers!"

١٤ قَالُوا۟ يَـٰوَيْلَنَآ إِنَّا كُنَّا ظَـٰلِمِينَ

15. And that cry of theirs
Ceased not, till We made
Them as a field
That is mown, as ashes
Silent and quenched.[2675]

١٥ فَمَا زَالَت تِّلْكَ دَعْوَىٰهُمْ حَتَّىٰ
جَعَلْنَـٰهُمْ حَصِيدًا خَـٰمِدِينَ

2673. When they had every chance of repentance and reform, they rejected Allah's Message, and perhaps even put up an open defiance. When they actually began to feel the Wrath coming, they began to flee, but it was too late! Besides, where could they flee to from the Wrath of Allah? Hence the ironical appeal to them in the next verse: better go pack your luxuries and what you thought were your permanent homes! *Cf.* Christ's saying in the present Gospel of St. Matthew (iii. 7): "O generation of vipers, who hath warned you to flee from the Wrath to come?"

2674. See last note. 'You thought your homes so comfortable: why don't you go back to them? You will be called to account. Perhaps there may be rewards to be given you, who knows?' This irony is itself the beginning of the Punishment. but the ungodly now see how wrong they had been. But their sighs and regrets now avail them nothing. It is too late. They are lost, and nothing can save them.

2675. The two similies present two different aspects of the lamentations of the ungodly. When they really see the Wrath to come, there is a stampede, but where can they go to? Their lamentation is now the only mark of their life. But it dies away, as corn vanished from a field that is being mown, or as a dying fire is slowly extinguished! They do not die. They wish they were dead! (78:40).

16. Not for (idle) sport did We[2676]
Create the heavens and the earth
And all that is between!

١٦ وَمَا خَلَقْنَا ٱلسَّمَآءَ وَٱلْأَرْضَ
وَمَا بَيْنَهُمَا لَٰعِبِينَ

17. If it had been Our wish
To take (just) a pastime,
We should surely have taken
It from the things nearest
To Us, if We would
Do (such a thing)![2677]

١٧ لَوْ أَرَدْنَآ أَن نَّتَّخِذَ لَهْوًا
لَّٱتَّخَذْنَٰهُ مِن لَّدُنَّآ
إِن كُنَّا فَٰعِلِينَ

18. Nay, We hurl the Truth
Against falsehood, and it knocks
Out its brain, and behold,
Falsehood doth perish!
Ah! woe be to you
For the (false) things
Ye ascribe (to Us).[2678]

١٨ بَلْ نَقْذِفُ بِٱلْحَقِّ عَلَى ٱلْبَٰطِلِ
فَيَدْمَغُهُۥ فَإِذَا هُوَ زَاهِقٌ
وَلَكُمُ ٱلْوَيْلُ مِمَّا تَصِفُونَ

19. To Him belong all (creatures)
In the heavens and on earth:
Even those who are in His
(Very) Presence are not[2679]
Too proud to serve Him.
Nor are they (ever) weary
(Of His service):

١٩ وَلَهُۥ مَن فِى ٱلسَّمَٰوَٰتِ وَٱلْأَرْضِ
وَمَنْ عِندَهُۥ لَا يَسْتَكْبِرُونَ
عَنْ عِبَادَتِهِۦ وَلَا يَسْتَحْسِرُونَ

20. They celebrate His praises
Night and day, nor do they
Ever flag or intermit.

٢٠ يُسَبِّحُونَ ٱلَّيْلَ وَٱلنَّهَارَ
لَا يَفْتُرُونَ

21. Or have they taken
(For worship) gods from the
earth[2680]

٢١ أَمِ ٱتَّخَذُوٓا۟ ءَالِهَةً مِّنَ ٱلْأَرْضِ

2676. The Hindu doctrine of Līla, that all things were created for sport, is here negatived. But more: with Allah we must not associate any ideas but those of Truth. Righteousness, Mercy, Justice, and the other attributes implied in His Beautiful Names. He does not jest nor play with His creatures.

2677. If such an idea as that of play or pastime had been possible with regard to Allah, and if He had wished really to indulge in pastime, He would have done it with creatures of Light nearest to Him, not with the lowly material creation that we see around us.

2678. Such as that (1) Allah has partners (21:22), or (2) that He has gotten a son (21:26), or (3) has daughters (16:57), or any other superstitions derogatory to the dignity and glory of Allah.

2679. The pure angelic hosts, whom we imagine to be glorious creatures of light, high in the spiritual world, near the Throne of Allah Himself, are yet His creatures, and serve Him without ceasing, and are proud to do so. Such is the majesty of Allah Most High.

2680. The different kinds of false gods whom people raise from their imagination are now referred to. In verses 21-23, the reference is to the gods of the earth, whether idols or local godlings, or deified heroes, or animals or trees or forces of the nature around us, which men have from time to time worshipped. These, as deities, have not life except what their worshippers give them.

Who can raise (the dead)?[2681]

هُمْ يُنشِرُونَ

22. If there were, in the heavens
And the earth, other gods[2682]
Besides Allah, there would
Have been confusion in both!
But glory to Allah,
The Lord of the Throne:
(High is He) above
What they attribute to Him!

٢٢ لَوْ كَانَ فِيهِمَآ ءَالِهَةٌ
إِلَّا ٱللَّهُ لَفَسَدَتَا ۚ
فَسُبْحَـٰنَ ٱللَّهِ رَبِّ ٱلْعَرْشِ
عَمَّا يَصِفُونَ

23. He cannot be questioned
For His acts, but they[2683]
Will be questioned (for theirs).

٢٣ لَا يُسْـَٔلُ عَمَّا يَفْعَلُ
وَهُمْ يُسْـَٔلُونَ

24. Or have they taken
For worship (other) gods[2684]
Besides Him? Say, "Bring
Your convincing proof: this
Is the Message of those
With me and the Message
Of those before me."[2685]
But most of them know not
The Truth, and so turn away.

٢٤ أَمِ ٱتَّخَذُوا۟ مِن دُونِهِۦٓ ءَالِهَةً ۖ
قُلْ هَاتُوا۟ بُرْهَـٰنَكُمْ ۖ
هَـٰذَا ذِكْرُ مَن مَّعِىَ وَذِكْرُ مَن قَبْلِى ۗ
بَلْ أَكْثَرُهُمْ لَا يَعْلَمُونَ ٱلْحَقَّ ۖ فَهُم مُّعْرِضُونَ

25. Not a messenger did We
Send before thee without
This inspiration sent by Us
To him: that there is
No god but I; therefore
Worship and serve Me.

٢٥ وَمَآ أَرْسَلْنَا مِن قَبْلِكَ
مِن رَّسُولٍ إِلَّا نُوحِىٓ إِلَيْهِ
أَنَّهُۥ لَآ إِلَـٰهَ إِلَّآ أَنَا۠ فَٱعْبُدُونِ

2681. The answer of course is "no". No one but Allah can raise the dead to life. The miracle in the story of Jesus (3:49 and 5:113) was "by Allah's leave". It was a miracle of Allah, not one of Jesus by his own power or will.

2682. After the false gods of the earth (verse 21), are mentioned the false gods in the heavens and the earth, like those in the Greek Pantheon (verse 22), who quarrelled and fought and slandered each other and made their Olympus a perfect bear-garden!

2683. Allah is Self-Subsisting. All His creatures are responsible to Him and dependent on Him there is no other being to whom He can be responsible or on whom He can be dependent.

2684. See above, n. 2682, where two kinds of false worship are noted. Now we are warned against a third danger, the worship of false gods of any sort. Pagan man is prolific of creating abstract images for worship, including Self or abstract Intelligence or Power. In verse 26 below is mentioned a fourth kind of false worship, which imagines that Allah begets sons or daughters.

2685. This verse should be read with the next. All reason revolts against the idea of conflicting gods, and points to Unity in Creation and Unity in Godhead. This is not only the Message of Islam ("those with me") but the message of all prophets who came before the Holy Prophet Muḥammad ("those before me"), and the line of prophets was closed with him. The Message given to every prophet in all ages was that of Unity as the fundamental basis of Order and Design in the world, material, moral, and spiritual.

26. And they say: "(Allah)
Most Gracious has begotten[2686]
Offspring." Glory to Him!
They are (but) servants raised
To honour.

وَقَالُوا اتَّخَذَ الرَّحْمَٰنُ وَلَدًا ۗ سُبْحَانَهُ ۚ بَلْ عِبَادٌ مُّكْرَمُونَ ﴿٢٦﴾

27. They speak not before[2687]
He speaks, and they act
(In all things) by His command.

لَا يَسْبِقُونَهُ بِالْقَوْلِ وَهُم بِأَمْرِهِ يَعْمَلُونَ ﴿٢٧﴾

28. He knows what is before them,
And what is behind them,
And they offer no intercession
Except for those who are
Acceptable,[2688] and they[2689] stand
In awe and reverence
Of His (glory).

يَعْلَمُ مَا بَيْنَ أَيْدِيهِمْ وَمَا خَلْفَهُمْ وَلَا يَشْفَعُونَ إِلَّا لِمَنِ ارْتَضَىٰ وَهُم مِّنْ خَشْيَتِهِ مُشْفِقُونَ ﴿٢٨﴾

29. If any of them should say,
"I am a god besides Him",
Such a one We should
Reward with Hell: thus
Do We reward those
Who do wrong.

وَمَن يَقُلْ مِنْهُمْ إِنِّي إِلَٰهٌ مِّن دُونِهِ فَذَٰلِكَ نَجْزِيهِ جَهَنَّمَ ۚ كَذَٰلِكَ نَجْزِي الظَّالِمِينَ ﴿٢٩﴾

C. 148.—Look at Allah's Creation: contemplate
(21:30-50.) Its unity of Design and benevolence
Of Purpose. Death must come to all,
But life and faith are not objects of ridicule.
Truth will outlast all mockery: 'tis Allah
Who calls, because he cares for you,
And on His Judgement Seat will weigh
Each act, each thought, each motive, great
Or small, with perfect justice. Come,
Ye all, reject not His blessed Message.

2686. This refers both to the Trinitarian superstition that Allah has begotten a son, and to the Arab superstition that the angels were daughters of Allah. All such superstitions are derogatory to the glory of Allah. The prophets and angels are no more than servants of Allah: they are raised high in honour, and therefore they deserve our highest respect, but not our worship.

2687. They never say anything before they receive Allah's command to say it, and their acts are similarly conditioned. This is also the teaching of Jesus as reported in the Gospel of St. John (xii. 49-50): "For I have not spoken of myself: but the Father which sent me. He gave me a commandment, what I should say, and what I should speak. And I know that His commandment is life everlasting: whatsoever I speak therefore, even as the Father said unto me, so I speak." If rightly understood, "Father" has the same meaning as our "Rabb", Sustainer and Cherisher, not Begetter or Progenitor.

2688. *Cf.* 20:109. "Acceptable" means that they have conformed to the Will of Allah and obeyed His Law, thus winning the stamp of His approval.

2689. *They*: the usual interpretation refers the pronoun to the servants of Allah who intercede: it may also refer to those on whose behalf the intercession is made: they do not take it as a matter of course, but stand in due awe and reverence of Allah's great glory and mercy.

SECTION 3.

30. Do not the Unbelievers see
That the heavens and the earth
Were joined together (as one[2690]
Unit of Creation), before
We clove them asunder?
We made from water[2691]
Every living thing. Will they
Not then believe?

٣٠ أَوَلَمْ يَرَ الَّذِينَ كَفَرُوٓا أَنَّ السَّمَٰوَٰتِ
وَالْأَرْضَ كَانَتَا رَتْقًا فَفَتَقْنَٰهُمَا
وَجَعَلْنَا مِنَ الْمَآءِ كُلَّ شَيْءٍ حَيٍّ
أَفَلَا يُؤْمِنُونَ

31. And We have set on the earth
Mountains standing firm,[2692]
Lest it should shake with them,
And We have made therein
Broad highways (between mountains)
For them to pass through:
That they may receive guidance.[2693]

٣١ وَجَعَلْنَا فِي الْأَرْضِ
رَوَٰسِيَ أَن تَمِيدَ بِهِمْ
وَجَعَلْنَا فِيهَا فِجَاجًا سُبُلًا
لَّعَلَّهُمْ يَهْتَدُونَ

32. And We have made
The heavens as a canopy
Well guarded:[2694] yet do they

٣٢ وَجَعَلْنَا السَّمَآءَ سَقْفًا مَّحْفُوظًا

2690. The evolution of the ordered worlds as we see them is hinted at. As man's intellectual gaze over the physical world expands, he sees more and more how Unity is the dominating note in Allah's wonderful Universe. Taking the solar system alone, we know that the maximum intensity of sun-spots corresponds with the maximum intensity of magnetic storms on this earth. The universal law of gravitation seems to bind all mass together. Physical facts point to the throwing off of planets from vast quantities of diffused nebular matter, of which the central condensed core is a sun.

2691. About 72 percent of the surface of our Globe is still covered with water, and it has been estimated that if the inequalities of the surface were all levelled, the whole surface would be under water, as the mean elevation of land sphere-level would be 7,000-10,000 feet below the surface of the ocean. This shows the predominance of water on our Globe. That all life began in the water is also a conclusion to which our latest knowledge in biological science points. Apart from the fact that protoplasm, the original basis of living matter, is liquid or semi-liquid and in a state of constant flux and instability, there is the fact that land animals, like the higher vertebrates, including man, show, in their embryological history, organs like those of fishes, indicating the watery origin of their original habitat. The constitution of protoplasm is about 80 to 85 percent water.

2692. *Cf.* 16:15 and n. 2038. *Lest it should shake with them*: here "them" refers back to "they" at the end of the preceding verse, meaning "Unbelievers". It might be mankind in general, but the pointed address to those who do not realise and understand Allah's mercies is appropriate, to drive home to them the fact that it is Allah's well-ordered providence that protects them normally from cataclysms like earthquakes, but that they could for their iniquities be destroyed in an instant, as the 'Ād and the Thamūd were destroyed before them. As pointed out in n. 2691 above, if the surface of the earth were levelled up, it would all be under water, and therefore the firm mountains are a further source of security for life which has evolved in terrestrial forms. Though the mountains may seem impassable barriers, yet Allah's providence has provided broad passes between them to afford highways for human communications.

2693. In both the literal and the figurative sense. Literally, these natural mountain highways direct men in the way they should go. Figuratively, these wonderful instances of Allah's providence should turn men's thoughts to the true guidance of Allah in life and spiritual progress.

2694. *Canopy well-guarded*: the heavens form a canopy that is secure from falling down: they also form a sublime spectacle and a Mystery that man can only faintly reach. Perhaps also the mystery of spiritual life is metaphorically hinted at. *Cf.* also 15:17.

Turn away from the Signs
Which these things (point to)!

وَهُمْ عَنْ ءَايَـٰتِهَا مُعْرِضُونَ

33. It is He Who created
The Night and the Day,
And the sun and the moon:
All (the celestial bodies)
Swim along, each in its[2695]
Rounded course.

٣٣ وَهُوَ ٱلَّذِى خَلَقَ ٱلَّيْلَ وَٱلنَّهَارَ
وَٱلشَّمْسَ وَٱلْقَمَرَ ۖ
كُلٌّ فِى فَلَكٍ يَسْبَحُونَ

34. We granted not to any man
Before thee permanent life[2696]
(Here): if then thou shouldst die,
Would they live permanently?

٣٤ وَمَا جَعَلْنَا لِبَشَرٍ مِّن قَبْلِكَ ٱلْخُلْدَ ۖ
أَفَإِي۟ن مِّتَّ فَهُمُ ٱلْخَـٰلِدُونَ

35. Every soul shall have
A taste of death:[2697]
And We test you
By evil and by good
By way of trial.
To Us must ye return.

٣٥ كُلُّ نَفْسٍ ذَآئِقَةُ ٱلْمَوْتِ ۗ
وَنَبْلُوكُم بِٱلشَّرِّ وَٱلْخَيْرِ فِتْنَةً ۖ
وَإِلَيْنَا تُرْجَعُونَ

36. When the Unbelievers see thee,
They treat thee not except
With ridicule. "Is this,"
(They say), "The one who talks[2698]
Of your gods?" And they
Blaspheme at the mention
Of (Allah) Most Gracious!

٣٦ وَإِذَا رَءَاكَ ٱلَّذِينَ كَفَرُوٓا۟
إِن يَتَّخِذُونَكَ إِلَّا هُزُوًا أَهَـٰذَا ٱلَّذِى
يَذْكُرُ ءَالِهَتَكُمْ وَهُم بِذِكْرِ ٱلرَّحْمَـٰنِ
هُمْ كَـٰفِرُونَ

2695. I have indicated, unlike most translators, the metaphor of swimming implied in the original words: how beautiful it is to contemplate the heavenly bodies swimming through space (or ether) in their rounded courses before our gaze!

2696. Life on this planet without death has not been granted to any man. The Khiḍhr legends are popular tales. His life without death on this earth is nowhere mentioned in the Qur'ān. The taunt of the Unbelievers at the Holy Prophet was therefore futile. Could any of them live without death at some time or other? Could they name any one who did?

2697. *Cf.* 3:185, and n. 491. The soul does not die, but when it separates from the body at the death of the body, the soul gets a taste of death. In our life of probation on this earth, our virtue and faith are tested by many things: some are tested by calamities, and some by the good things of this life. If we prove our true mettle, we pass our probation with success. In any case all must return to Allah, and then will our life be appraised of its true value.

2698. To the godly man the issue between false worship and true worship is a very serious matter. To the sceptics and unbelievers it is only a joke. They take it lightly, and laugh at the godly ones. They not only laugh at him, but they blaspheme when the name of the One True God is mentioned. The reply to this is in the next verse.

37. Man is a creature of haste:[2699]
Soon (enough) will I show
You My Signs; then
Ye will not ask Me
To hasten them!

٣٧ خُلِقَ ٱلْإِنسَٰنُ مِنْ عَجَلٍ
سَأُو۟رِيكُمْ ءَايَٰتِى فَلَا تَسْتَعْجِلُونِ

38. They say: "When will this
Promise come to pass,
If ye are telling the truth?"

٣٨ وَيَقُولُونَ مَتَىٰ هَٰذَا ٱلْوَعْدُ
إِن كُنتُمْ صَٰدِقِينَ

39. If only the Unbelievers[2700]
Knew (the time) when they
Will not be able
To ward off the Fire
From their faces, nor yet
From their backs, and (when)
No help can reach them!

٣٩ لَوْ يَعْلَمُ ٱلَّذِينَ كَفَرُوا۟ حِينَ
لَا يَكُفُّونَ عَن وُجُوهِهِمُ ٱلنَّارَ
وَلَا عَن ظُهُورِهِمْ وَلَا هُمْ يُنصَرُونَ

40. Nay, it may come to them
All of a sudden and confound
Them: no power will they
Have then to avert it,
Nor will they (then)
Get respite.

٤٠ بَلْ تَأْتِيهِم بَغْتَةً
فَتَبْهَتُهُمْ فَلَا يَسْتَطِيعُونَ رَدَّهَا
وَلَا هُمْ يُنظَرُونَ

41. Mocked were (many)
Messengers before thee;
But their scoffers
Were hemmed in
By the thing that they mocked.[2701]

٤١ وَلَقَدِ ٱسْتُهْزِئَ بِرُسُلٍ مِّن قَبْلِكَ فَحَاقَ
بِٱلَّذِينَ سَخِرُوا۟ مِنْهُم مَّا كَانُوا۟ بِهِۦ يَسْتَهْزِءُونَ

SECTION 4.

42. Say: "Who can keep
You safe by night and by day
From (the Wrath of) (Allah)
Most Gracious?"[2702] Yet they

٤٢ قُلْ مَن يَكْلَؤُكُم بِٱلَّيْلِ
وَٱلنَّهَارِ مِنَ ٱلرَّحْمَٰنِ بَلْ هُمْ

2699. Haste is the very bone and marrow of man. If he is granted respite for his own sake, in order that he may have a further chance of repentance and coming back to Allah, he says impatiently and incredulously; "Bring on the Punishment quickly, that I may see if what you say is true!" Alas, it is too true! When the Punishment actually comes near and he sees it, he will not want it hastened. He will want more time and further delay! Poor creature of haste!

2700. They would not be so unreasonable if they only realised the terrible future for them! The Fire will envelop them on all sides, and no help will then be possible. Is it not best for them now to turn and repent? The Punishment may come too suddenly, as is said in the next verse.

2701. The same verse occurs at 6:10, where see n. 843. 'What they are mocking at now will be in a position to mock them in due time.'

2702. 'Allah is most Gracious: if, in spite of His great mercy, you are so rebellious and depraved as to incur His Wrath, who is there who can save you? His Wrath can descend on you at any time, by night or by day.'

Turn away from the mention
Of their Lord.

عَن ذِكۡرِ رَبِّهِم مُّعۡرِضُونَ

43. Or have they gods that
Can guard them from Us?
They have no power to aid
Themselves, nor can they
Be defended from us.[2703]

٤٣ أَمۡ لَهُمۡ ءَالِهَةٞ تَمۡنَعُهُم مِّن دُونِنَاۚ
لَا يَسۡتَطِيعُونَ نَصۡرَ أَنفُسِهِمۡ
وَلَا هُم مِّنَّا يُصۡحَبُونَ

44. Nay, We gave the good things
Of this life to these men
And their fathers until
The period[2704] grew long for them;
See they not that We[2705]
Gradually reduce the land
(In their control) from
Its outlying borders? Is it
Then they who will win?

٤٤ بَلۡ مَتَّعۡنَا هَٰٓؤُلَآءِ وَءَابَآءَهُمۡ حَتَّىٰ
طَالَ عَلَيۡهِمُ ٱلۡعُمُرُۗ أَفَلَا يَرَوۡنَ أَنَّا نَأۡتِي
ٱلۡأَرۡضَ نَنقُصُهَا مِنۡ أَطۡرَافِهَآۚ
أَفَهُمُ ٱلۡغَٰلِبُونَ

45. Say, "I do but warn you
According to revelation";
But the deaf will not hear
The call, (even) when
They are warned![2706]

٤٥ قُلۡ إِنَّمَآ أُنذِرُكُم بِٱلۡوَحۡيِۚ
وَلَا يَسۡمَعُ ٱلصُّمُّ ٱلدُّعَآءَ إِذَا مَا يُنذَرُونَ

46. If but a breath of the Wrath
Of thy Lord do touch them,
They will then say, "Woe
To us! we did wrong indeed!"

٤٦ وَلَئِن مَّسَّتۡهُمۡ نَفۡحَةٞ مِّنۡ عَذَابِ رَبِّكَ
لَيَقُولُنَّ يَٰوَيۡلَنَآ إِنَّا كُنَّا ظَٰلِمِينَ

47. We shall set up scales
Of justice for the day
Of Judgement, so that

٤٧ وَنَضَعُ ٱلۡمَوَٰزِينَ ٱلۡقِسۡطَ لِيَوۡمِ ٱلۡقِيَٰمَةِ

2703. *Aṣḥaba*: to join as a companion: with *'an* or *min* it has also the meaning of to defend or remove from someone. The full signification is best understood if paraphrased: 'they are not fit to be mentioned in the same breath with Us, nor can they be defended from Us.'

2704. *'Umr*, or *'Umur*: age, generation, period, time, life. Here "period" is most appropriate, as it covers many generations, "these men and their fathers."

2705. *Cf.* 13:41 and n. 1865. The particular signification is that Islam spread from the outer borders, social and geographical, gradually inwards. The social fringe was the humbler people, such as slaves and poor men. The geographical reference is to Madīnah and tribes away from the Makkah centre. The proud and ubelieving Quraysh were the last to come in when the circle was gradually drawn tighter and tighter around them. The general signification applies to all times. Allah's Truth makes its way first among the poor and the lowly, those whose minds are unsoiled by prejudices of false pride or false knowledge, but it gradually hems in the obstinate, until it prevails in the end.

2706. According to the English saying, "none is so deaf as those who will not hear". When they deliberately shut their ears to the warning from the Merciful Allah, meant for their own good, the responsibility is their own. But their cowardice is shown in the next verse by their behaviour when the first breath of the Wrath reaches them.

Not a soul will be dealt with
Unjustly in the least.
And if there be
(No more than) the weight
Of a mustard seed,[2707]
We will bring it (to account):
And enough are We
To take account.[2708]

فَلَا تُظْلَمُ نَفْسٌ شَيْئًا
وَإِن كَانَ مِثْقَالَ
حَبَّةٍ مِّنْ خَرْدَلٍ أَتَيْنَا بِهَا
وَكَفَىٰ بِنَا حَاسِبِينَ

48. In the past We granted
To Moses and Aaron
The Criterion (for judgement),[2709]
And a Light and a Message
For those who would do right—

٤٨ وَلَقَدْ آتَيْنَا مُوسَىٰ وَهَارُونَ
الْفُرْقَانَ وَضِيَاءً وَذِكْرًا لِّلْمُتَّقِينَ

49. Those who fear their Lord
In their most secret thoughts,
And who hold the Hour
(Of Judgement) in awe.[2710]

٤٩ الَّذِينَ يَخْشَوْنَ رَبَّهُم بِالْغَيْبِ
وَهُم مِّنَ السَّاعَةِ مُشْفِقُونَ

50. And this is a blessed
Message which We have
Sent down: will ye then
Reject it?[2711]

٥٠ وَهَٰذَا ذِكْرٌ مُّبَارَكٌ أَنزَلْنَاهُ
أَفَأَنتُمْ لَهُ مُنكِرُونَ

2707. Not the smallest action, word, thought, motive, or predilection but must come into the account of Allah. *Cf.* Browning (in *Rabbi Ben Ezra*): "But all, the world's coarse thumb and finger failed to plumb, So passed in making up the main account; All instincts immature, All purposes unsure, That weighed not as his work, yet swelled the man's account; Thoughts hardly to be packed Into a narrow act, Fancies that broke through language and escaped; All I could never be, All, men ignored in me, This, I was worth to God, Whose wheel the pitcher shaped."

2708. The literalism of Sale has here excelled itself: he translates, "and there will be sufficient accountants with us"! What is meant is that when Allah takes account, His accounting will be perfect: there will be no flaw in it, as there may be in earthly accountants, who require other people's help in some matters of account which they do not understand for want of knowledge of that particular department they are dealing with. Allah's knowledge is perfect, and therefore his justice will be perfect also; for He will not fail to take into account all the most intangible things that determine conduct and character. See last note. There is no contradiction between this and 18:104-105, where it is said that men of vain words, *i.e.*, shallow hypocritical deeds, will have no weight attached to their deeds. In fact the two correspond.

2709. *Cf.* 2:53 and n. 68, where the meaning of *Furqān* is discussed. Here three things are mentioned as given to Moses and Aaron: (1) The Criterion for judgement; this might well be the wonderful Proofs they saw of Allah's goodness and glory from which they could have no doubt as to Allah's will and command; (2) the Light; this was the inner enlightenment of their soul, such as comes from inspiration; and (3) the Message, the book, the original book of Moses, which Aaron as his lieutenant would also use as a guide for his people.

2710. Note the three kinds of fear mentioned in 21:48-49. *Taqwā* is the fear of running counter to the will of Allah; it is akin to the love of Him; for we fear to offend those we love; it results in right conduct, and those who entertain it are "those who would do right". Then there is Khashyah, the fear of Allah, lest the person who entertains it may be found, in his inmost thoughts, to be short of the standard which Allah wished for him; this is also righteous but in a less high degree than *Taqwā* which is akin to love. And thirdly, there is the fear of consequences on the Day of Judgement (*ishfaq);* this also may lead to righteousness, but is on a still lower plane. Perhaps the three correspond to the Criterion, the Light, and the Message (or Warning) of the last verse.

2711. Here is a Prophet and a Book, greater than Moses and his Book. Are you going to reject him and it? (R).

C. 149.—(21:51-93)

The great exemplars of virtue conquered
Evil, each according to his circumstances:
Abraham stood staunch in the fire
Of persecution, unhurt; Lūṭ was bold
In reproving abominations; Noah survived
The Flood by his faith, in a world of Unbelief;
David sought justice, and sang Allah's praises;
Solomon by wisdom subdued the refractory;
Job was patient in suffering; Ismā'īl,
Idrīs, and Dhu al Kifl were true in constancy
Amid temptation; Jonah turned to Allah
After a short misunderstanding: Zakarīyā
And his family were examplars of devoutness;
And Mary of chastity. All men and women
Of God form one united Brotherhood.

SECTION 5.

51. We bestowed aforetime
On Abraham his rectitude[2712]
Of conduct, and well were We
Acquainted with him.[2713]

وَلَقَدْ ءَاتَيْنَآ إِبْرَٰهِيمَ رُشْدَهُۥ مِن قَبْلُ وَكُنَّا بِهِۦ عَٰلِمِينَ ﴿٥١﴾

52. Behold! he said
To his father and his people[2714]
"What are these images,
To which ye are
(So assiduously) devoted?"

إِذْ قَالَ لِأَبِيهِ وَقَوْمِهِۦ مَا هَٰذِهِ ٱلتَّمَاثِيلُ ٱلَّتِىٓ أَنتُمْ لَهَا عَٰكِفُونَ ﴿٥٢﴾

53. They said, "We found
Our fathers worshipping them."

قَالُوا۟ وَجَدْنَآ ءَابَآءَنَا لَهَا عَٰبِدِينَ ﴿٥٣﴾

54. He said, "Indeed ye
Have been in manifest
Error—ye and your fathers."

قَالَ لَقَدْ كُنتُمْ أَنتُمْ وَءَابَآؤُكُمْ فِى ضَلَٰلٍ مُّبِينٍ ﴿٥٤﴾

55. They said, "Have you
Brought us the Truth,

قَالُوٓا۟ أَجِئْتَنَا بِٱلْحَقِّ ﴿٥٥﴾

2712. *Rushd*: right conduct, corresponding in action to the quality expressed in the epithet Ḥanif (sound or true in Faith) applied to Abraham in 2:135 and elsewhere.

2713. Hence Abraham's title "Friend of Allah" (*Khalīl Allah*): 4:125.

2714. Reference is made to Abraham in many places. In 19:42-49 it was with reference to his relations to his father: the problem was how a righteous man should deal with his father, when his duty to his father conflicts with his duty to Allah. Here the problem is: how a righteous man should deal with evil and overcome it; how he should fight against evil, and if he is subjected to the fire of persecution, how his firmness draws Allah's Mercy, and the very trouble he is placed in becomes his comfort and joy.

Or are you one
Of those who jest?"[2715]

أَمْ أَنتَ مِنَ ٱللَّـٰعِبِينَ

56. He said, "Nay, your Lord
Is the Lord of the heavens
And the earth. He Who
Created them (from nothing):[2716]
And I am a witness
To this (truth).

٥٦ قَالَ بَل رَّبُّكُمْ رَبُّ ٱلسَّمَـٰوَٰتِ
وَٱلْأَرْضِ ٱلَّذِى فَطَرَهُنَّ
وَأَنَا۠ عَلَىٰ ذَٰلِكُم مِّنَ ٱلشَّـٰهِدِينَ

57. "And by Allah, I have
A plan for your idols—
After ye go away
And turn your backs"...[2717]

٥٧ وَتَٱللَّهِ لَأَكِيدَنَّ أَصْنَـٰمَكُم
بَعْدَ أَن تُوَلُّوا۟ مُدْبِرِينَ

58. So he broke them to pieces,
(All) but the biggest of them,
That they might turn
(And address themselves) to it.[2718]

٥٨ فَجَعَلَهُمْ جُذَٰذًا إِلَّا كَبِيرًا لَّهُمْ
لَعَلَّهُمْ إِلَيْهِ يَرْجِعُونَ

59. They said, "Who has
Done this to our gods?
He must indeed be
Some man of impiety!"

٥٩ قَالُوا۟ مَن فَعَلَ هَـٰذَا بِـَٔالِهَتِنَآ
إِنَّهُۥ لَمِنَ ٱلظَّـٰلِمِينَ

60. They said, "We heard
A youth talk of them:[2719]
He is called Abraham."

٦٠ قَالُوا۟ سَمِعْنَا فَتًى يَذْكُرُهُمْ يُقَالُ لَهُۥٓ إِبْرَٰهِيمُ

61. They said, "Then bring him
Before the eyes of the people,
That they may bear witness:"

٦١ قَالُوا۟ فَأْتُوا۟ بِهِۦ عَلَىٰٓ أَعْيُنِ ٱلنَّاسِ
لَعَلَّهُمْ يَشْهَدُونَ

2715. Abraham looked at life with a serious eye, and his people took it light-heartedly. He was devoted to Truth, and they cared more for ancestral custom. In the conflict, he seemed to be in their power. But he was fearless, and he triumphed by Allah's Grace.

2716. For the various words for "creation" see n. 120 to 2:117, where *faṭara* is explained and differentiated from other words of similar meaning.

2717. He wants to convince them of the powerlessness of their idols. But he does not do it underhandedly. He tells them that he is going to do something when once they are gone and their backs are turned to the idols—as much as to say that the idols are dependent on their care and attention. Apparently the people are amused and want to see what he does. So they leave him to his own devices.

2718. He was enacting a scene, to make the people ashamed of worshipping senseless sticks and stones. He left the biggest idol untouched and broke the others to pieces, as if a fight had taken place between the idols, and the biggest has smashed the others. Would they turn to the surviving idol and ask him how it all happened?

2719. Different groups of people are speaking. Those who were not present at Abraham's speech in verse 57 ask, "who has done this?" Those who were, at once name him, whereupon a formal council of the people was held, and Abraham was arraigned.

62. They said, "Art thou
The one that did this
With our gods, O Abraham?"[2720]

(٦٢) قَالُوٓاْ ءَأَنتَ فَعَلْتَ
هَٰذَا بِـَٔالِهَتِنَا يَٰٓإِبْرَٰهِيمُ

63. He said: "Nay, this
Was done by—
This is their biggest one!
Ask them, if they
Can speak intelligently!"

(٦٣) قَالَ بَلْ فَعَلَهُۥ كَبِيرُهُمْ هَٰذَا
فَسْـَٔلُوهُمْ إِن كَانُواْ يَنطِقُونَ

64. So they turned to themselves
And said, "Surely ye
Are the ones in the wrong!"[2721]

(٦٤) فَرَجَعُوٓاْ إِلَىٰٓ أَنفُسِهِمْ فَقَالُوٓاْ
إِنَّكُمْ أَنتُمُ ٱلظَّٰلِمُونَ

65. Then were they confounded[2722]
With shame: (they said)
"Thou knowest full well that
These (idols) do not speak!"

(٦٥) ثُمَّ نُكِسُواْ عَلَىٰ رُءُوسِهِمْ
لَقَدْ عَلِمْتَ مَا هَٰٓؤُلَآءِ يَنطِقُونَ

66. (Abraham) said, "Do ye then
Worship, besides Allah,
Things that can neither
Be of any good to you
Nor do you harm?

(٦٦) قَالَ أَفَتَعْبُدُونَ مِن دُونِ ٱللَّهِ
مَا لَا يَنفَعُكُمْ شَيْـًٔا وَلَا يَضُرُّكُمْ

67. "Fie upon you, and upon[2723]
The things that ye worship
Besides Allah! Have ye
No sense?"..

(٦٧) أُفٍّ لَّكُمْ وَلِمَا تَعْبُدُونَ مِن دُونِ ٱللَّهِ
أَفَلَا تَعْقِلُونَ

2720. They asked him the formal question. There was no mystery about it. He had already openly threatened to do something to the idols, and people who had heard his threats were there. He now continues his ironic taunt to the idol-worshippers. 'You ask me! Why don't you ask the idols? Doesn't it look as if this big fellow has smashed the smaller ones in a quarrel?' If they do not ask the idols, they confess that the idols have not the intelligence enough to answer! This argument is developed in verses 64-67. Note that while the false worshipper laughed at his earnestness, he pays them back with a grim practical joke, which at the same time advances the cause of Truth.

2721. Abraham's biting irony cut them to the quick. What could they say? They turned to each other. Some among them thought he had the best of the argument. They were not keen on idolatry, and they told their fellows that it was useless arguing with Abraham. They all hung their heads in shame. But presently they thought they would face out Abraham, and take his words literally. They said, "You know quite well that idols do not speak!" This was precisely what Abraham wanted them to say, and he delivered his final blow! See n. 2723 below.

2722. Literally, "they were turned down on their heads" which may suggest a metaphorical somersault, *i.e.*, they recovered from their dawning shame for idolatry and were prepared to argue it out with the youth Abraham. But I think there is a better authority for the interpretation I have adopted.

2723. As soon as they admitted in so many words that the idols could not speak, Abraham delivered his final attack: 'Then why do you worship useless impotent creatures?' After that, there remains nothing but the argument of violence, which they proceed to exercise, being the party in power. 'Burn him at the stake' is an easy cry! But it was not Abraham that suffered: it was his persecutors (21:70).

68. **They said, "Burn him**
And protect your gods,
If ye do (anything at all)!"

قَالُواْ حَرِّقُوهُ وَٱنصُرُوٓاْ ءَالِهَتَكُمْ إِن كُنتُمْ فَٰعِلِينَ ﴿٦٨﴾

69. **We said, "O Fire![2724]**
Be thou cool,
And (a means of) safety
For Abraham!"[2725]

قُلْنَا يَٰنَارُ كُونِى بَرْدًا وَسَلَٰمًا عَلَىٰٓ إِبْرَٰهِيمَ ﴿٦٩﴾

70. **Then they sought a stratagem**
Against him: but We
Made them the ones
That lost most![2726]

وَأَرَادُواْ بِهِۦ كَيْدًا فَجَعَلْنَٰهُمُ ٱلْأَخْسَرِينَ ﴿٧٠﴾

71. **But We delivered him**
And (his nephew) Lūṭ
(And directed them) to the land[2727]
Which We have blessed
For the nations.

وَنَجَّيْنَٰهُ وَلُوطًا إِلَى ٱلْأَرْضِ ٱلَّتِى بَٰرَكْنَا فِيهَا لِلْعَٰلَمِينَ ﴿٧١﴾

2724. The nature of fire, by all the physical laws of matter, is to be hot. The supremacy of mind over matter is a phrase much used, but the supremacy of the spiritual over the material is not so commonly understood. And yet it is the greatest factor in the estimate of Reality. The material is ephemeral and relative. The spiritual is eternal and absolute. Through all the fire of persecution and hatred Abraham remained unhurt. The fire became cool, and a means of safety for Abraham.

2725. Can we form any idea of the place where he passed through the furnace, and the stage in his career at which this happened? He was born in Ur of the Chaldees, a place on the lower reaches of the Euphrates, not a hundred miles from the Persian Gulf. This was the cradle, or one of the cradles, of human civilisation. Astronomy was studied here in very ancient times, and the worship of the sun, moon, and stars was the prevailing form of religion. Abraham revolted against this quite early in life, and his argument is referred to in 6:74-82. They also had idols in their temples, probably idols representing heavenly bodies and celestial winged creatures. He was still a youth (21:60) when he broke the idols. This was stage No. 2. After this he was marked down as a rebel and persecuted. Perhaps some years passed before the incident of his being thrown into the Fire (21:68-69) took place, or the incident may be only allegorical. Traditionally the Fire incident is referred to a king called Nimrūd, about whom see n. 1565 to 11:69. If Nimrūd's capital was in Assyria, near Nineveh (site near modern Mosul), we may suppose either that the king's rule extended over the whole of Mesopotamia, or that Abraham wandered north through Babylonia to Assyria. Various stratagems were devised to get rid of him (21:70), but he was saved by the mercy of Allah. The final break came when he was probably a man of mature age and could speak to his father with some authority. This incident is referred to in 19:41-48. He now left his ancestral lands, and avoiding the Syrian desert, came to the fertile lands of Aram or Syria, and so south to Canaan, when the incident of 11:69-76 and the adventures of his nephew Lūṭ took place. It is some years after this that we may suppose he built the Ka'bah with Ismā'īl (2:124-29), and his prayer in 14:35-41 may be referred to the same time. His visit to Egypt (Gen. xii 10) is not referred to in the Qur'ān.

2726. As they could not get rid of him by open punishment, they tried secret plans, but were foiled throughout. It was not he that lost, but they. On the contrary, he left them and prospered and became the progenitor of great peoples.

2727. The land of Aram or Syria, which in its widest connotation includes Canaan or Palestine, Syria is a well-watered fertile land, with a Mediterranean sea-coast, on which the famous commercial cities of Tyre and Sidon were situated. Its population is very mixed, as it has been a bone of contention between all the great kingdoms and empires of Western Asia and Egypt, and European interest in it dates from the most ancient times. (R).

72. And We bestowed on him Isaac
And, as an additional gift,[2728]
(A grandson), Jacob, and We
Made righteous men of every one
(Of them).

وَوَهَبْنَا لَهُۥٓ إِسْحَٰقَ وَيَعْقُوبَ نَافِلَةً ۖ وَكُلًّا جَعَلْنَا صَٰلِحِينَ ﴿٧٢﴾

73. And We made them
Leaders, guiding (men) by
Our Command, and We
Sent them inspiration
To do good deeds,
To establish regular prayers,
And to practise regular charity;
And they constantly served
Us (and Us only).[2729]

وَجَعَلْنَٰهُمْ أَئِمَّةً يَهْدُونَ بِأَمْرِنَا وَأَوْحَيْنَآ إِلَيْهِمْ فِعْلَ ٱلْخَيْرَٰتِ وَإِقَامَ ٱلصَّلَوٰةِ وَإِيتَآءَ ٱلزَّكَوٰةِ ۖ وَكَانُوا۟ لَنَا عَٰبِدِينَ ﴿٧٣﴾

74. And to Lūṭ, too,
We gave Judgement and Knowledge,
And We saved him
From the town which practised
Abominations: truly they were
A people given to Evil,
A rebellious people.[2730]

وَلُوطًا ءَاتَيْنَٰهُ حُكْمًا وَعِلْمًا وَنَجَّيْنَٰهُ مِنَ ٱلْقَرْيَةِ ٱلَّتِى كَانَت تَّعْمَلُ ٱلْخَبَٰٓئِثَ ۗ إِنَّهُمْ كَانُوا۟ قَوْمَ سَوْءٍ فَٰسِقِينَ ﴿٧٤﴾

75. And We admitted him
To Our Mercy: for he
Was one of the Righteous.

وَأَدْخَلْنَٰهُ فِى رَحْمَتِنَآ ۖ إِنَّهُۥ مِنَ ٱلصَّٰلِحِينَ ﴿٧٥﴾

SECTION 6.

76. (Remember) Noah, when
He cried (to Us) aforetime:[2730-A]
We listened to his (prayer)

وَنُوحًا إِذْ نَادَىٰ مِن قَبْلُ فَٱسْتَجَبْنَا لَهُۥ ﴿٧٦﴾

2728. *Nāfilah* has many meanings: (1) booty; (2) extra work or prayer; (3) extra or additional gift; (4) grandson. The two last implications are implied here. Not only was Abraham given a son in his old age; he was given not only Isaac, but several sons, the chief being Ismā'īl and Isaac, who both joined in burying him (Gen. xxv. 9); and he also saw grandsons. Ismā'īl is specially mentioned later (21:85) apart from Isaac's line, on account of his special importance for Islam.

2729. The spiritual lesson from this passage may be recapitulated. The righteous man makes no compromise with evil. If the votaries of evil laugh at him he pays them in their own coin, but he stands firmly by his principles. His firmness causes some confusion among the followers of evil, and he openly declares the faith that is in him. They try, openly and secretly, to injure or kill him, but Allah protects him, while evil perished from its own excesses.

2730. Lot's people were given to unspeakable abominations. His mission was to preach to them. He withstood Evil, but they rejected him. They were punished, but he and his followers were saved. See 15:61-74, 11:77-82, and 7:80-84.

2730-A. The date of Noah was many centuries before that of Abraham. (R).

And delivered him and his
Family from great distress.[2731]

فَنَجَّيْنَٰهُ وَأَهْلَهُۥ مِنَ ٱلْكَرْبِ ٱلْعَظِيمِ

77. We helped him against
People who rejected Our Signs:
Truly they were a people
Given to Evil: so We
Drowned them (in the Flood)
All together.

٧٧ وَنَصَرْنَٰهُ مِنَ ٱلْقَوْمِ ٱلَّذِينَ كَذَّبُوا۟ بِـَٔايَٰتِنَآ ۚ
إِنَّهُمْ كَانُوا۟ قَوْمَ سَوْءٍ
فَأَغْرَقْنَٰهُمْ أَجْمَعِينَ

78. And remember David
And Solomon, when they
Give judgement in the matter
Of the field into which
The sheep of certain people
Had strayed by night:
We did witness their judgement.

٧٨ وَدَاوُۥدَ وَسُلَيْمَٰنَ إِذْ يَحْكُمَانِ فِى
ٱلْحَرْثِ إِذْ نَفَشَتْ فِيهِ غَنَمُ ٱلْقَوْمِ
وَكُنَّا لِحُكْمِهِمْ شَٰهِدِينَ

79. To Solomon We inspired[2732]
The (right) understanding
Of the matter: to each
(Of them) We gave Judgement
And Knowledge; it was
Our power that made
The hills and the birds
Celebrate Our praises.[2733]

٧٩ فَفَهَّمْنَٰهَا سُلَيْمَٰنَ ۚ
وَكُلًّا ءَاتَيْنَا حُكْمًا وَعِلْمًا ۚ
وَسَخَّرْنَا مَعَ دَاوُۥدَ
ٱلْجِبَالَ يُسَبِّحْنَ وَٱلطَّيْرَ ۚ

2731. The contemporaries of Noah were given to Unbelief, oppression of the poor, and vain disputations. He carried Allah's Message to them, and standing fast in faith, built the Ark, in which he was saved with his followers from the Flood, while the wicked were drowned. See 11:25-48.

2732. The sheep, on account of the negligence of the shepherd, got into a cultivated field (or vineyard) by night and ate up the young plants or their tender shoots, causing damage, to the extent of perhaps a whole year's crop. David was king, and in his seat of judgement he considered the matter so serious that he awarded the owner of the field the sheep themselves in compensation for his damage. The Roman Law of the Twelve Tables might have approved this decision, and on the same principle was built up the Deodand doctrine of English Law, now obsolete. His son Solomon, a mere boy of eleven, thought of a better decision, where the penalty would better fit the offence. The loss was the loss of the fruits or produce of the field or vineyard: the *corpus* of the property was not lost. Solomon's suggestion was that the owner of the field or vineyard should not take the sheep altogether but only detain them long enough to recoup his actual damage, from the milk, wool, and possibly young of the sheep, and then return the sheep to the shepherd. David's merit was that he accepted the suggestion, even though it came from a little boy: Solomon's merit was that he distinguished between the *corpus* and income, and though a boy, was not ashamed to put his case before his father. But in either case it was Allah Who inspired the true realisation of justice. He was present and witnessed the affair, as He is present everywhere.

2733. Whatever is in the heavens and the earth celebrates the praises of Allah: 17:44; 57:1; 16:48-50. Even the "thunder repeateth His praises"; 13:13. All nature ever sings the praises of Allah. David sang in his Psalms, cxlviii. 7-10: "Praise the Lord from the earth, ye. . .mountains and all hills. . .creeping things and flying fowl!" All nature sings to Allah's glory, in unison with David, and angels, and men of God. *Cf.* 34:10 and 38:18-19. (R).

With David: it was We
Who did (all these things).

وَكُنَّا فَٰعِلِينَ

80. It was We Who taught him[2734]
The making of coats of mail
For your benefit, to guard
You from each other's violence:
Will ye then be grateful?[2735]

٨٠ وَعَلَّمْنَٰهُ صَنْعَةَ لَبُوسٍ لَّكُمْ
لِتُحْصِنَكُم مِّنۢ بَأْسِكُمْ ۖ
فَهَلْ أَنتُمْ شَٰكِرُونَ

81. (It was Our power that
Made) the violent (unruly)
Wind flow (tamely) for
Solomon,[2736]
To his order, to the land[2737]
Which We had blessed:
For We do know all things.

٨١ وَلِسُلَيْمَٰنَ ٱلرِّيحَ عَاصِفَةً تَجْرِى بِأَمْرِهِۦٓ
إِلَى ٱلْأَرْضِ ٱلَّتِى بَٰرَكْنَا فِيهَا ۚ
وَكُنَّا بِكُلِّ شَىْءٍ عَٰلِمِينَ

82. And of the evil ones,
Were some who dived
For him, and did other work[2738]
Besides; and it was We
Who guarded them.

٨٢ وَمِنَ ٱلشَّيَٰطِينِ مَن يَغُوصُونَ لَهُۥ
وَيَعْمَلُونَ عَمَلًا دُونَ ذَٰلِكَ ۖ
وَكُنَّا لَهُمْ حَٰفِظِينَ

83. And (remember) Job, when
He cried to his Lord,

٨٣ وَأَيُّوبَ إِذْ نَادَىٰ رَبَّهُۥٓ

2734. The making of coats of mails is attributed to David. It is defensive armour, and therefore its discovery and supply is associated with deeds of righteousness in 34:10-11, in contrast with the deadly weapons which man invents for offensive purposes. Indeed, all fighting, unless in defence of righteousness is mere "violence."

2735. David's good work then was: (1) he was open to learn wisdom wherever it came from; (2) he sang the praises of Allah, in unison with all nature; (3) he made defensive armour. But all these things he did, because of the faculties which Allah had given him, and we must be grateful for this and for all things to Allah.

2736. *Cf.* 34:12, and 38:36-38. This has been interpreted to mean that Solomon had miraculous power over the winds, and could make them obey his order. Rationalists say that he had naval power on the Mediterranean, and through the Gulf of 'Aqaba on the Red Sea, and that he therefore figuratively commanded the winds, and we may say the same of airmen at the present day. In any case the power behind was, and is, from Allah, Who has granted man intelligence and the faculties by which he can tame the more unruly forces of nature.

2737. Evidently Palestine, in which was Solomon's capital, though his influence extended far north in Syria, and perhaps far south in Arabia and Ethiopia. In the Roman ruins of Baalbek, fifty miles north of Damascus, is still shown a quarry of huge stones supposed to have been cut for Solomon. I have seen them with my own eyes. This local tradition is interesting, even if invented.

2738. As in n. 2736, the literalists and the rationalists take different views. The former say that Solomon had power over supernatural beings of evil, whom he compelled to dive for pearls and do other hard tasks. Rationalists refer this to hostile unruly races whom he subjected to his sway. It was Allah's power ultimately, Who granted him wisdom. Solomon tamed evil with Wisdom.

"Truly distress has seized me.[2739]
But Thou are the Most
Merciful of those that are
Merciful."

أَنِّي مَسَّنِيَ ٱلضُّرُّ
وَأَنتَ أَرْحَمُ ٱلرَّٰحِمِينَ

84. So We listened to him:
We removed the distress
That was on him,
And We restored his people
To him, and doubled
Their number—as a Grace
From Ourselves, and a thing
For commemoration, for all
Who serve Us.[2740]

٨٤ فَٱسْتَجَبْنَا لَهُۥ
فَكَشَفْنَا مَا بِهِۦ مِن ضُرٍّ
وَءَاتَيْنَٰهُ أَهْلَهُۥ وَمِثْلَهُم مَّعَهُمْ رَحْمَةً
مِّنْ عِندِنَا وَذِكْرَىٰ لِلْعَٰبِدِينَ

85. And (remember) Ismā'īl,[2741]
Idrīs,[2742] and Dhu al Kifl,[2743] all

٨٥ وَإِسْمَٰعِيلَ وَإِدْرِيسَ وَذَا ٱلْكِفْلِ

2739. Job (*Ayūb*) was a prosperous man, with faith in Allah, living somewhere in the northeast corner of Arabia. He suffers from a number of calamities; his cattle are destroyed, his servants slain by the sword, and his family crushed under his roof. But he holds fast to his faith in Allah. As a further calamity he is covered with loathsome sores from head to foot. He loses his peace of mind, and he curses the day he was born. His false friends come and attribute his affliction to sin. These "Job's comforters" are no comforters at all, and he further loses his balance of mind, but Allah recalls to him all His mercies, and he resumes his humility and gives up self-justification. He is restored to prosperity, with twice as much as he had before; his brethren and friends come back to him; he had a new family of seven sons and three fair daughters. He lived to a good old age, and saw four generations of descendants. All this is recorded in the Book of Job in the Old Testament. Of all the Hebrew writings, the Hebrew of this Book comes nearest to Arabic. The account given in the Biblical sources and the image that it projects of Prophet Job is decidedly different from that found in the Qur'ān and the Hadīth, which present him as a prophet and a brilliant example of dignified patience becoming of a great Prophet of Allah ever trustful in Him and His promises. Nothing could be further from the truth than saying that he lost his peace of mind or resorted to curses during the period of his trial. (R).

2740. Job is the pattern of humility, patience, and faith in Allah. It was with these weapons that he fought and conquered evil.

2741. Ismā'īl is mentioned specially, apart from the line which descended through Isaac (21:72), as he was the founder of a separate and greater Ummah. His sufferings began in infancy (see n. 160 to 2:158); but his steady constancy and submission to the will of Allah were specially shown when he earned the title of "Sacrifice to Allah" (see n. 2506 to 19:54). That was the particular quality of his constancy and patience.

2742. For Idrīs see n. 2508 to 19:56. He was in a high station in life, but that did not spoil him. He was sincere and true, and that was the particular quality of his constancy and patience.

2743. *Dhu al Kifl* would literally mean "possessor of, or giving, a double requital or portion"; or else, "one who used a cloak of double thickness," that being one of the meanings of *Kifl*. The Commentators differ in opinion as to who is meant, why the title is applied to him, and the point of his being grouped with Ismā'īl and Idrīs for constancy and patience. I think the best suggestion is that afforded by Karsten Niebuhr in his *Reisebeschreibung nach Arabien*, Copenhagen, 1778, 2:264-266, as quoted in the *Encyclpaedia of Islam* under "Dhu al Kifl". He visited Meshed 'Alī in Irāq, and also the little town called Kefil, midway between Najaf and Hilla (Babylon). Kefil, he says, is the Arabic form of Ezekiel. The shrine of Ezekiel was there, and the Jews came to it on a pilgrimage.

If we accept "Dhu al Kifl" to be not an epithet, but an Arabicised form of "Ezekiel", it fits the context. Ezekiel was a prophet in Israel who was carried away to Babylon by Nebuchadnezzar after his second attack on Jerusalem (about B.C. 599). His Book is included in the English Bible (Old Testament). He was chained and bound, and put into prison, and for a time he was dumb (Ezekiel, iii. 25-26). He bore it all with patience and constancy, and continued to reprove boldly the evils in Israel. In a burning passage he denounces false leaders in words which are eternally true: "Woe be to the shepherds of Israel that do feed themselves! Should not the shepherds feed the flocks? Ye eat the fat, and ye clothe you with the wool, you kill them that are fed: but ye feed not the flock. The diseased have yet not strengthened, neither have ye healed that which was sick, neither have ye bound up that which was broken...", etc. (Ezekiel, xxxiv. 2-4).

Dhu al Kifl is again mentioned in 38:48 along with Ismā'īl and Elisha.

(Men) of constancy and patience;

كُلٌّ مِّنَ ٱلصَّٰبِرِينَ

86. We admitted them to
Our Mercy: for they
Were of the Righteous ones.

وَأَدْخَلْنَٰهُمْ فِى رَحْمَتِنَآ ۖ إِنَّهُم مِّنَ ٱلصَّٰلِحِينَ ﴿٨٦﴾

87. And remember Dhu al Nūn,[2744]
When he departed in wrath:
He imagined that We
Had no power over him!
But he cried through the depths
Of darkness, "There is
No god but Thou:
Glory to Thee: I was
Indeed wrong!"

وَذَا ٱلنُّونِ إِذ ذَّهَبَ مُغَٰضِبًا فَظَنَّ أَن لَّن نَّقْدِرَ عَلَيْهِ فَنَادَىٰ فِى ٱلظُّلُمَٰتِ أَن لَّآ إِلَٰهَ إِلَّآ أَنتَ سُبْحَٰنَكَ إِنِّى كُنتُ مِنَ ٱلظَّٰلِمِينَ ﴿٨٧﴾

88. So We listened to him:
And delivered him from
Distress: and thus do We
Deliver those who have faith.

فَٱسْتَجَبْنَا لَهُۥ وَنَجَّيْنَٰهُ مِنَ ٱلْغَمِّ ۚ وَكَذَٰلِكَ نُۨجِى ٱلْمُؤْمِنِينَ ﴿٨٨﴾

89. And (remember) Zakarīya,[2745]
When he cried to his Lord:
"O my Lord! leave me not
Without offspring, though Thou
Art the best of inheritors."[2746]

وَزَكَرِيَّآ إِذْ نَادَىٰ رَبَّهُۥ رَبِّ لَا تَذَرْنِى فَرْدًا وَأَنتَ خَيْرُ ٱلْوَٰرِثِينَ ﴿٨٩﴾

2744. *Dhū al Nūn*, "the man of the Fish or the Whale", is the title of Jonah (Yūnus), because he was swallowed by a large Fish or Whale. He was the prophet raised to warn the Assyrian capital Nineveh. For Nineveh see n. 1478 to 10:98. His story is told in 37:139-149. When his first warning was unheeded by the people, he denounced Allah's wrath on them. But they repented and Allah forgave them for the time being. Jonah, meanwhile, departed in wrath, discouraged at the apparent failure of his mission. He should have remained in the most discouraging circumstances, and relied on the power of Allah; for Allah had power both over Nineveh and over the Messenger He had sent to Nineveh. He went away to the sea and took a ship, but apparently the sailors threw him out as a man of bad omen in a storm. He was swallowed by a big Fish (or Whale), but in the depth of the darkness, he cried to Allah and confessed his weakness. The "darkness" may be interpreted both physically and spiritually; physically, as the darkness of the night and the storm and the Fish's body; spiritually as the darkness in his soul, his extreme distress in the situation which he had brought on himself. Allah Most Gracious forgave him. He was cast out ashore; he was given the shelter of a plant in his state of physical and mental lassitude. He was refreshed and strengthened, and the work of his mission prospered. Thus he overcame all his disappointment by repentance and Faith, and Allah accepted him.

2745. See 19:2-15, and 3:38-41. Zakariyā was a priest; both he and his wife were devout and punctilious in their duties. They were old, and they had no son. He was troubled in mind, not so much by the vulgar desire to have a son to carry on his line, but because he felt that his people were not unselfishly devout, and there would be no sincere work for Allah unless he could train some one himself. He was given a son Yaḥyā (John the Baptist), who added to the devout reputation of the family, for he is called "noble, chaste, and a prophet," (3:39). All three, father, mother, and son, were made worthy of each other, and they repelled evil by their devout emulation in virtue.

2746. 'It is not that I crave a personal heir to myself; all things go back to Thee, and Thou art the best of inheritors: but I see no one around me sincere enough to carry on my work for Thee; wilt Thou give me one whom I can train?'

90. So We listened to him: And We granted him Yaḥyā: We cured his wife's[2747] (Barrenness) for him. These (three) Were ever quick in emulation In good works; they used To call on Us with love And reverence, and humble themselves Before Us.	٩٠ فَاسْتَجَبْنَا لَهُۥ وَوَهَبْنَا لَهُۥ يَحْيَىٰ وَأَصْلَحْنَا لَهُۥ زَوْجَهُۥٓ إِنَّهُمْ كَانُوا۟ يُسَـٰرِعُونَ فِى ٱلْخَيْرَٰتِ وَيَدْعُونَنَا رَغَبًا وَرَهَبًا وَكَانُوا۟ لَنَا خَـٰشِعِينَ
91. And (remember) her who[2748] Guarded her chastity: We breathed into her Of Our Spirit, and We Made her and her son A Sign for all peoples.	٩١ وَٱلَّتِىٓ أَحْصَنَتْ فَرْجَهَا فَنَفَخْنَا فِيهَا مِن رُّوحِنَا وَجَعَلْنَـٰهَا وَٱبْنَهَآ ءَايَةً لِّلْعَـٰلَمِينَ
92. Verily, this Brotherhood Of yours is a single Brotherhood,[2749] And I am your Lord And Cherisher: therefore Serve Me (and no other).	٩٢ إِنَّ هَـٰذِهِۦٓ أُمَّتُكُمْ أُمَّةً وَٰحِدَةً وَأَنَا۠ رَبُّكُمْ فَٱعْبُدُونِ
93. But (later generations) cut off[2750] Their affairs (of unity), One from another: (yet) Will they all return to Us.	٩٣ وَتَقَطَّعُوٓا۟ أَمْرَهُم بَيْنَهُمْ كُلٌّ إِلَيْنَا رَٰجِعُونَ

C. 150.—(21:94-112.)

No good deed is fruitless: work
While yet there's time: for with Judgement
The door will be closed to repentance.
No false gods of fancy can help.
The Righteous will have no fear: for them
The angelic greetings will truly open

2747. *Aṣlaḥa* = to improve, to mend, to reform, to make better. Here, with reference to Zakarīya's wife, the signification is twofold: (1) that her barrenness would be removed, so that she could become a mother; and (2) her spiritual dignity should be raised in becoming the mother of John the Baptist; and by implication his also, in becoming the father of John.

2748. Mary, the mother of Jesus, chastity was her special virtue: with a son of virgin birth, she and Jesus became a miracle to all nations. That was the virtue with which they (both Mary and Jesus) resisted evil.

2749. *Ummah*: this is best translated by Brotherhood here. "Community", "race", and "nation", and "people" are words which import other ideas and do not quite correspond to "Ummah". "Religion" and "Way of Life" are derived meanings, which could be used in other passages, but are less appropriate here. Our attention has been drawn to people of very different temperaments and virtues, widely different in time, race, language, surroundings, history, and work to be performed, but forming the closest brotherhood as being men and women united in the highest service of Allah. They pre-figure the final and perfected Brotherhood of Islam.

2750. Allah's Message was and ever is one; and His Messengers treated it as one. It is people of narrower views who come later and trade on the earlier names, that break up the Message and the Brotherhood into jarring camps and sects.

A new world, which they will inherit.
This was Allah's Message of old, and the same
Is Allah's Message renewed: for Allah
Is one, and so is His Message, proclaimed
For all, freely and in loving Truth.

SECTION 7.

94. Whoever works any act
Of Righteousness and has Faith—
His endeavour will not
Be rejected: We shall
Record it in his favour.[2751]

٩٤ فَمَن يَعْمَلْ مِنَ ٱلصَّٰلِحَٰتِ
وَهُوَ مُؤْمِنٌ فَلَا كُفْرَانَ لِسَعْيِهِۦ
وَإِنَّا لَهُۥ كَٰتِبُونَ

95. But there is a ban
On any population which
We have destroyed: that they[2752]
Shall not return.

٩٥ وَحَرَٰمٌ عَلَىٰ قَرْيَةٍ أَهْلَكْنَٰهَآ
أَنَّهُمْ لَا يَرْجِعُونَ

96. Until the Gog and Magog
(people)[2753]
Are let through (their barrier),
And they swiftly swarm
From every hill.

٩٦ حَتَّىٰٓ إِذَا فُتِحَتْ يَأْجُوجُ وَمَأْجُوجُ
وَهُم مِّن كُلِّ حَدَبٍ يَنسِلُونَ

97. Then will the True Promise
Draw nigh (of fulfilment):
Then behold! the eyes
Of the Unbelievers will[2754]
Fixedly stare in horror: "Ah!
Woe to us! we were indeed
Heedless of this; nay; we
Truly did wrong!"

٩٧ وَٱقْتَرَبَ ٱلْوَعْدُ ٱلْحَقُّ
فَإِذَا هِىَ شَٰخِصَةٌ أَبْصَٰرُ ٱلَّذِينَ كَفَرُوا۟
يَٰوَيْلَنَا قَدْ كُنَّا فِى غَفْلَةٍ مِّنْ هَٰذَا
بَلْ كُنَّا ظَٰلِمِينَ

98. Verily ye, (Unbelievers),
And the (false) gods that
Ye worship besides Allah,
Are (but) fuel for Hell!
To it will ye (surely) come!

٩٨ إِنَّكُمْ وَمَا تَعْبُدُونَ مِن دُونِ
ٱللَّهِ حَصَبُ جَهَنَّمَ أَنتُمْ لَهَا وَٰرِدُونَ

2751. Allah gives credit for every act of righteousness, however small: when combined with sincere Faith in Allah, it becomes the stepping stone to higher and higher things. It is never lost.

2752. But when wickedness comes to such a pass that the Wrath of Allah descends, as it did on Sodom, the case becomes hopeless. The righteous were warned and delivered before the Wrath descended. But those destroyed will not get another chance, as they flouted all previous chances. They will only be raised at the approach of the Day of Judgement.

2753. For Gog and Magog see n. 2439 to 18:92. Their geographical position was discussed in Appendix VI. Here I do not think we are concerned with their geographical position. The name stands for wild and lawless tribes who will break their barriers and swarm through the earth. This will be one of the prognostications of the approaching Judgement.

2754. *Cf.* 14:42.

99. If these had been gods,
They would not have got
there![2755]
But each one will abide
Therein.

٩٩ لَوْ كَانَ هَٰٓؤُلَآءِ ءَالِهَةً مَّا وَرَدُوهَا
وَكُلٌّ فِيهَا خَٰلِدُونَ

100. There, sobbing will be
Their lot, nor will they
There hear (aught else).

١٠٠ لَهُمْ فِيهَا زَفِيرٌ
وَهُمْ فِيهَا لَا يَسْمَعُونَ

101. Those for whom
The Good (Record) from Us
Has gone before, will be
Removed far therefrom.[2756]

١٠١ إِنَّ ٱلَّذِينَ سَبَقَتْ لَهُم مِّنَّا ٱلْحُسْنَىٰٓ
أُو۟لَٰٓئِكَ عَنْهَا مُبْعَدُونَ

102. Not the slightest sound
Will they hear of Hell:
What their souls desired,
In that will they dwell.

١٠٢ لَا يَسْمَعُونَ حَسِيسَهَا
وَهُمْ فِى مَا ٱشْتَهَتْ أَنفُسُهُمْ خَٰلِدُونَ

103. The Great Terror will[2757]
Bring them no grief:
But the angels will meet them
(With mutual greetings):
"This is your Day—
(The Day) that ye were promised."

١٠٣ لَا يَحْزُنُهُمُ ٱلْفَزَعُ ٱلْأَكْبَرُ
وَتَتَلَقَّىٰهُمُ ٱلْمَلَٰٓئِكَةُ هَٰذَا يَوْمُكُمُ
ٱلَّذِى كُنتُمْ تُوعَدُونَ

104. The Day that We roll up
The heavens like a scroll
Rolled up for books
(completed)—
Even as We produced
The first Creation, so

١٠٤ يَوْمَ نَطْوِى ٱلسَّمَآءَ
كَطَىِّ ٱلسِّجِلِّ لِلْكُتُبِ
كَمَا بَدَأْنَآ أَوَّلَ خَلْقٍ

2755. The ultimate proof of Truth and Falsehood will be that Truth will endure and come to its own, while Falsehood will be destroyed. And so the men who worshipped Truth will come to their own, while those who worshipped Falsehood will be in a Fire of Punishment they could scarcely have imagined before. In that state there will be nothing but regrets and sighs and groans, and these evil sounds will drown everything else.

2756. In contrast to the misery of those who rejected Truth and Right, will be the happiness of those who accepted it. Their record does not lag behind: in fact it goes before. Our Deeds go before our journey in this life is completed. What then is Judgement? It is instantaneous: it will all be decided in the twinkling of an eye (16:77). The good will not hear the least sound of the groans of evil. Their true soul's desires will be fulfilled—not temporarily as in this world, but in a permanent form.

2757. The Judgement and balancing of accounts will be a mighty Terror to the evil doers. But it will cause, to the righteous, not grief or anxiety, but hope and happiness, for now they will be in a congenial atmosphere, and will see the fulfilment of their ideals in the meeting and greeting of the angels, preparatory to their enjoyment of the supreme Bliss—seeing the Face of Allah.

Shall We produce[2758]
A new one: a promise
We have undertaken:
Truly shall We fulfil it.

نُّعِيدُهُۥ وَعْدًا عَلَيْنَآ
إِنَّا كُنَّا فَٰعِلِينَ

105. Before this We wrote
In the Psalms,[2759] after the Message
(Given to Moses):[2760] "My servants,
The righteous, shall inherit
The earth."

١٠٥ وَلَقَدْ كَتَبْنَا فِى ٱلزَّبُورِ
مِنۢ بَعْدِ ٱلذِّكْرِ أَنَّ ٱلْأَرْضَ يَرِثُهَا
عِبَادِىَ ٱلصَّٰلِحُونَ

106. Verily in this (Qur'ān)
Is a Message for people
Who would (truly) worship Allah.[2761]

١٠٦ إِنَّ فِى هَٰذَا لَبَلَٰغًا
لِّقَوْمٍ عَٰبِدِينَ

107. We sent thee not, but
As a mercy for all creatures.[2762]

١٠٧ وَمَآ أَرْسَلْنَٰكَ إِلَّا رَحْمَةً لِّلْعَٰلَمِينَ

108. Say: "What has come to me
By inspiration is that
Your God is One God:
Will ye therefore bow
To His Will (in Islām)?"[2763]

١٠٨ قُلْ إِنَّمَا يُوحَىٰٓ إِلَىَّ أَنَّمَآ
إِلَٰهُكُمْ إِلَٰهٌ وَٰحِدٌ
فَهَلْ أَنتُم مُّسْلِمُونَ

109. But if they turn back,
Say: "I have proclaimed

١٠٩ فَإِن تَوَلَّوْا۟ فَقُلْ ءَاذَنتُكُمْ

2758. The world—the universe—as we know it, will be folded up like a scroll of parchment, for it will have done its work. If Allah created all this world out of nothing, He can create an entirely new heaven and a new earth, on a plane of which we can form no conception in our present life. And He will do so, for that is His promise.

Some Commentators understand *Sijill* to be the name of the Recording Angel who closes the Book of a man's Deeds after the man's death.

2759. *Zabūr:* the Book of the Psalms of David. The name of David is expressly mentioned in connection with the *Zabūr* in 4:163 and 17:55, although there the indefinite article is applied to the word as meaning a Book of Scripture. See Psalms xxv. 13, "his seed shall inherit the earth": xxxvii. 11, "the meek shall inherit the earth" (quoted by Jesus in Matt. v. 3); and xxxvii. 29, "the righteous shall inherit the land." (R).

2760. The same promise occurs in the Pentateuch, Exod. xxxii. 13, "they shall inherit it (the land) forever."

2761. The culmination of Allah's Revelation is in the Qur'ān, which confirms previous scriptures, corrects the errors which men introduced into them, and explains many points in detail for all who seek right worship and service to Allah—whether they inherit the previous Books ("People of the Book") or not. It is a universal Message.

2762. There is no question now of race or nation, of a "chosen people" or the "seed of Abraham"; or the "seed of David"; or of Hindu *Arya-varta;* of Jew or Gentile, Arab or *'Ajam* (Persian), Turk or *Tājik,* European or Asiatic, White or Coloured; Aryan, Semitic, Mongolian, or African; or American, Australian, or Polynesian. To all men and creatures other than men who have any spiritual responsibility, the principles universally apply.

2763. 'Not my God only, but also *your* God: for there is but One God, the Universal Lord, Who made and loves and cherishes all.'

The Message to you all alike
And in truth; but I
Know not whether that
Which ye are promised
Is near or far.[2764]

عَلَىٰ سَوَآءٍ وَإِنْ أَدْرِىٓ أَقَرِيبٌ أَم بَعِيدٌ مَّا تُوعَدُونَ

110. "It is He Who knows
What is open in speech
And what ye hide
(In your hearts).[2765]

إِنَّهُۥ يَعْلَمُ ٱلْجَهْرَ مِنَ ٱلْقَوْلِ وَيَعْلَمُ مَا تَكْتُمُونَ ١١٠

111. "I know not but that
It may be a trial
For you, and a grant
Of (worldly) livelihood
(To you) for a time."[2766]

وَإِنْ أَدْرِى لَعَلَّهُۥ فِتْنَةٌ لَّكُمْ وَمَتَٰعٌ إِلَىٰ حِينٍ ١١١

112. Say:[2767] "O my Lord!
Judge Thou in truth!"[2768]
"Our Lord Most Gracious
Is the One Whose assistance
Should be sought against
The blasphemies ye utter!"[2769]

قَٰلَ رَبِّ ٱحْكُم بِٱلْحَقِّ وَرَبُّنَا ٱلرَّحْمَٰنُ ٱلْمُسْتَعَانُ عَلَىٰ مَا تَصِفُونَ ١١٢

2764. 'If you do not realise the significance of the Message, I at least have done my duty. I have given the Good News for the Righteous and the Warning for the Unjust, without favour or partiality, and without abating one jot of the truth, openly and squarely for all. Do not ask me when the Good News and the Warning will be fulfilled. That is for Allah to decide, not for me or for you to know.'

2765. The Messenger of Allah freely and impartially teaches all how to carry out Allah's Will and live a good life. If some of them are hypocrites and come into the Ummah (Brotherhood) from baser motives and not the pure motives of the love of Allah, their motives and conduct will be judged by Allah and not by men.

2766. In the same way if men who come into the Brotherhood from pure motives and yet feel aggrieved that those outside are better off from a worldly point of view, they are wrong. It may be that the fleeting enjoyment of this world's goods is but a trial, and they should be grateful for being saved from temptation.

2767. See above, n. 2666 to 21:4. The beter reading is "Say" in the imperative, rather than "He (the Prophet) said (or says)" in the indicative mood. Note that, on that construction, there are three distinct things which the Prophet is asked to say: *viz.*: (1) the statement in verses 109-11, addressed to those who turn away from the Message; (2) the prayer addressed to Allah in the first part of verse 112; and (3) the advice given indirectly to the Believers, in the second part of verse 112. I have marked these divisions by means of inverted commas.

2768. That is, Allah's judgement as between the Teacher and those who refused the Message, or between the righteous and those who taunt them for their poverty, will be the true one, and both the Teacher and the Ummah must leave the judgement to Allah.

2769. Blasphemy is a dreadful sin. We must guard ourselves from it. But as regards others, if we cannot prevent it, we must pray to Allah for assistance and not rely upon carnal weapons.

INTRODUCTION TO SŪRAH 22—*AL ḤAJJ*

We now come to a new series of four Sūrahs, dealing with the environments and methods contributing to our spiritual progress, as the last five Sūrahs dealt with the Messengers who came in various ways to proclaim the Truth and conquer evil. See Introduction to S. 17.

The subject matter of this particular Sūrah is concerned mainly with the spiritual implications of the Sacred House, the Pilgrimage, the Sacrifice, Striving and Fighting in defence of Truth when attacked, and other acts that make for Unselfishness and uproot Falsehood.

On the chronology of this Sūrah, opinion is divided. Some parts were probably revealed in the latter Makkan period, and some in Madīnah. But the chronological question has no significance here.

Summary—Importance of the spiritual Future, and need of firmness in Faith: help for Truth and punishment for Evil (22:1-25, and C. 151).

Purity, Prayer, Humility, and Faith are implied in the Pilgrimage; in solemn Sacrifice we express our gratitude and reverence to Allah, and our desire to share food with our poorer brethren; Striving and Fighting in defence of Truth when attacked are necessary as tests of self-sacrifice (22:26-48, and C. 152).

The promptings of Evil may hinder the work of Allah's Prophet, but that work must triumph, and the Mercy and Truth of Allah must be established; therefore serve Allah humbly, and He will protect and help you (22:49-78, and C. 153).

C. 151.—Will not mankind take warning
(22:1-25.) From the dreadful consequences of Evil
Clearly proclaimed to them? Will they
Dispute about Allah and the Life of the Future?
They have only to look around and within them,
And they will see vestiges of the Plan
And Purpose of Allah. Let them not halt
Between Good and Evil: Allah's Message as well
As his Messenger must win against all
Obstacles. Only the evil will be brought
To shame and agony. The good—whose speech
Is pure and conduct worthy of praise—
Will have a meed of refinement, beauty, and bliss.

Sūrah 22.

Al Ḥajj (The Pilgrimage)

In the name of Allah, Most Gracious,
Most Merciful.

بِسْمِ ٱللَّهِ ٱلرَّحْمَٰنِ ٱلرَّحِيمِ

1. O mankind! Fear your Lord!
For the convulsion of the Hour
(Of Judgement) will be
A thing terrible![2770]

(١) يَٰٓأَيُّهَا ٱلنَّاسُ ٱتَّقُوا۟ رَبَّكُمْ
إِنَّ زَلْزَلَةَ ٱلسَّاعَةِ شَىْءٌ عَظِيمٌ

2. The Day ye shall see it,
Every mother giving suck
Shall forget her suckling babe,
And every pregnant female
Shall drop her load (unformed):
Thou shalt see mankind
As in a drunken riot,[2771]
Yet not drunk: but dreadful
Will be the Wrath of Allah.

(٢) يَوْمَ تَرَوْنَهَا تَذْهَلُ كُلُّ مُرْضِعَةٍ
عَمَّآ أَرْضَعَتْ وَتَضَعُ كُلُّ ذَاتِ حَمْلٍ
حَمْلَهَا وَتَرَى ٱلنَّاسَ سُكَٰرَىٰ وَمَا هُم
بِسُكَٰرَىٰ وَلَٰكِنَّ عَذَابَ ٱللَّهِ شَدِيدٌ

3. And yet among men
There are such as dispute
About Allah, without knowledge,
And follow every evil one
Obstinate in rebellion!

(٣) وَمِنَ ٱلنَّاسِ مَن يُجَٰدِلُ فِى ٱللَّهِ بِغَيْرِ عِلْمٍ
وَيَتَّبِعُ كُلَّ شَيْطَٰنٍ مَّرِيدٍ

4. About the (Evil One)
It is decreed that whoever
Turns to him for friendship,
Him will he lead astray,
And he will guide him
To the Penalty of the Fire.[2772]

(٤) كُتِبَ عَلَيْهِ أَنَّهُۥ
مَن تَوَلَّاهُ فَأَنَّهُۥ يُضِلُّهُۥ
وَيَهْدِيهِ إِلَىٰ عَذَابِ ٱلسَّعِيرِ

2770. As an introduction to the spiritual meaning of various symbolic acts in this life, the serious issues involved are indicated by showing how terrible the consequences will be for those who disobey Allah's Will. The terror will only be for those who rebel and disobey: the righteous will not suffer from it, but on the contrary will be greeted by angels with joy (21:103).

2771. Three metaphors are used for the extreme terror which the Awful Day will inspire. (1) No mother abandons the baby at her breast in the greatest danger; yet that will happen in this Dreadful Hour. (2) An expectant mother carries the young life within her with great pride and hope: "hope" is the actual word used in Urdu for this physical state; yet the terror will overpower the hope at this "Hour", and nature's working will be reversed. (3) Men ordinarily retain their self-possession except under intoxicants; here, without intoxication, they will be driven to frenzy with terror.

2772. Even after the warnings, there are men who are such fools as to turn away from Allah who created them and cherishes them with His love and care; they become outlaws in His Kingdom, making friends with Evil, which is a rebel in Allah's Kingdom.

5. O mankind! if ye have
A doubt about the
Resurrection,[2773]
(Consider) that We created you
Out of dust, then out of
Sperm, then out of a leech-like
Clot, then out of a morsel
Of flesh, partly formed[2774]
And partly unformed, in order
That We may manifest
(Our Power) to you;
And We cause whom We will[2775]
To rest in the wombs
For an appointed term,
Then do We bring you out
As babes, then (foster you)
That ye may reach your age
Of full strength; and some
Of you are called to die,
And some are sent back
To the feeblest old age,
So that they know nothing
After having known (much).[2776]
And (further), thou seest
The earth barren and lifeless,
But when We pour down
Rain on it, it is stirred
(To life), it swells,
And it puts forth every kind
Of beautiful growth in pairs.[2777]

٥ يَٰٓأَيُّهَا ٱلنَّاسُ
إِن كُنتُمْ فِى رَيْبٍ مِّنَ ٱلْبَعْثِ
فَإِنَّا خَلَقْنَٰكُم مِّن تُرَابٍ ثُمَّ مِن نُّطْفَةٍ
ثُمَّ مِنْ عَلَقَةٍ ثُمَّ مِن مُّضْغَةٍ
مُّخَلَّقَةٍ وَغَيْرِ مُخَلَّقَةٍ لِّنُبَيِّنَ لَكُمْ
وَنُقِرُّ فِى ٱلْأَرْحَامِ مَا نَشَآءُ
إِلَىٰٓ أَجَلٍ مُّسَمًّى ثُمَّ نُخْرِجُكُمْ طِفْلًا
ثُمَّ لِتَبْلُغُوٓا۟ أَشُدَّكُمْ
وَمِنكُم مَّن يُتَوَفَّىٰ
وَمِنكُم مَّن يُرَدُّ إِلَىٰٓ أَرْذَلِ ٱلْعُمُرِ
لِكَيْلَا يَعْلَمَ مِنۢ بَعْدِ عِلْمٍ شَيْـًٔا
وَتَرَى ٱلْأَرْضَ هَامِدَةً
فَإِذَآ أَنزَلْنَا عَلَيْهَا ٱلْمَآءَ ٱهْتَزَّتْ
وَرَبَتْ وَأَنۢبَتَتْ مِن كُلِّ زَوْجٍۭ بَهِيجٍ

2773. If they really have doubts in their minds about the life after death, they have only to turn their attention, either to their own nature, or to the nature around. How wonderful is their own physical growth, from lifeless matter, to seed, fertilised ovum, fetus, child, youth, age, and death! How can they doubt that the Author of all these wonderful stages in their life here can also give them another kind of life after the end of this life? Or, if they look at external nature, they see the earth dead and barren, and Allah's fertilising showers bring it to life, growth, and beauty in various forms. The Creator of this great pageant of Beauty can surely create yet another and a newer world.

2774. The stages of a man's physical growth from nothing till he completes the cycle of this life are described in words whose accuracy, beauty, and comprehensiveness can only be fully understood by biologists. Parallel to the physical growth, may be understood man's inner growth, also by stages and by Allah's creative artistry.

2775. That is, a male or a female child, a fair or an ugly child, a good or a rebellious child, etc., involving countless mysteries of genetics and heredity.

2776. *Cf.* 16:70. In that passage the mystery of our life was used to illustrate Allah's abundant mercies and favours to us. Here it is used to illustrate Allah's power in giving us a future Life of even greater promise.

2777. A beautiful nature passage so pregnant in meaning that the earnest student wonders what magic and truth have been conveyed in so few words. M. P.'s Egyptian colleague, Prof. Ghamrawi (see M. P.'s note on this passage) was but expressing the feelings of every careful student of the Qur'ān. The "subtlety and wealth of meaning" are indeed marvellous.

6. This is so, because Allah
Is the Reality: it is He
Who gives life to the dead,
And it is He Who has
Power over all things.[2778]

٦ ذَٰلِكَ بِأَنَّ ٱللَّهَ هُوَ ٱلْحَقُّ وَأَنَّهُۥ يُحْىِ ٱلْمَوْتَىٰ وَأَنَّهُۥ عَلَىٰ كُلِّ شَىْءٍ قَدِيرٌ

7. And verily the Hour will come:
There can be no doubt
About it, or about (the fact)
That Allah will raise up
All who are in the graves.

٧ وَأَنَّ ٱلسَّاعَةَ ءَاتِيَةٌ لَّا رَيْبَ فِيهَا وَأَنَّ ٱللَّهَ يَبْعَثُ مَن فِى ٱلْقُبُورِ

8. Yet there is among men
Such a one as disputes
About Allah, without knowledge,
Without guidance, and without
A Book of Enlightenment—[2779]

٨ وَمِنَ ٱلنَّاسِ مَن يُجَٰدِلُ فِى ٱللَّهِ بِغَيْرِ عِلْمٍ وَلَا هُدًى وَلَا كِتَٰبٍ مُّنِيرٍ

9. (Disdainfully) bending his side,
In order to lead (men) astray
From the Path of Allah:
For him there is disgrace[2780]
In this life, and on the Day
Of Judgement We shall
Make him taste the Penalty
Of burning (Fire).

٩ ثَانِىَ عِطْفِهِۦ لِيُضِلَّ عَن سَبِيلِ ٱللَّهِ لَهُۥ فِى ٱلدُّنْيَا خِزْىٌ وَنُذِيقُهُۥ يَوْمَ ٱلْقِيَٰمَةِ عَذَابَ ٱلْحَرِيقِ

10. (It will be said): "This is
Because of the deeds which
Thy hands sent forth,
For verily Allah is not
Unjust to His servants."[2781]

١٠ ذَٰلِكَ بِمَا قَدَّمَتْ يَدَاكَ وَأَنَّ ٱللَّهَ لَيْسَ بِظَلَّٰمٍ لِّلْعَبِيدِ

2778. All these beautiful and well-articulated pageants of life and nature point to the Reality behind them, *i.e.*, Allah. They will perish, but He is eternal. They are but shadows; the substance (if such a word may be used) is in Him. They are shifting and illusory, in the sense that they have neither permanency nor independent existence. But they have a sort of secondary reality in the sense in which a shadow is a real reflection from substance. No Power or Existence has any meaning except as a reflection of Allah's ineffable Glory.

2779. For "Book of Enlightenment" see 3:184 and n. 490. I understand "knowledge" to mean here their human knowledge or intelligence, "guidance" to mean divine guidance, such as comes from Allah or prophets of Allah or a revelation from Allah, and the "Book of Enlightenment" to mean the fundamental guide to good conduct, the clear rules laid down in all Dispensations to help men lead good lives. The "Book of Enlightenment" may mean a revealed Book in which case "Guidance" would refer to divine guidance through a prophet of Allah. (R).

2780. Some Commentators think this refers to Abū Jahl, but the words are perfectly general, and this type of man is common in all ages. The same may be said about verse 3 above: Commentators give the immediate reference to one Al Naḍr ibn Ḥārith.

2781. 'What you suffer is the consequence of your own sinful deeds; Allah is just; He is not unjust in the least to any of His creatures'. (R).

Section 2.

11. There are among men
Some who serve Allah,
As it were, on the verge:[2782]
If good befalls them, they are,
Therewith, well content; but
If a trial comes to them,
They turn on their faces:
They lose both this world
And the Hereafter: that
Is loss for all to see!

(١١) وَمِنَ النَّاسِ مَن يَعْبُدُ اللَّهَ
عَلَىٰ حَرْفٍ فَإِنْ أَصَابَهُۥ خَيْرٌ اطْمَأَنَّ بِهِۦ
وَإِنْ أَصَابَتْهُ فِتْنَةٌ انقَلَبَ عَلَىٰ وَجْهِهِۦ
خَسِرَ الدُّنْيَا وَالْآخِرَةَ
ذَٰلِكَ هُوَ الْخُسْرَانُ الْمُبِينُ

12. They call on such deities,[2783]
Besides Allah, as can neither
Hurt nor profit them:
That is straying far indeed
(From the Way)!

(١٢) يَدْعُوا مِن دُونِ اللَّهِ مَا لَا يَضُرُّهُۥ
وَمَا لَا يَنفَعُهُۥ ذَٰلِكَ هُوَ الضَّلَٰلُ الْبَعِيدُ

13. (Perhaps) they call on one
Whose hurt is nearer[2784]
Than his profit: evil, indeed,
Is the patron, and evil
The companion (for help)!

(١٣) يَدْعُوا لَمَن ضَرُّهُۥ أَقْرَبُ مِن نَّفْعِهِۦ
لَبِئْسَ الْمَوْلَىٰ وَلَبِئْسَ الْعَشِيرُ

14. Verily Allah will admit
Those who believe and work
Righteous deeds, to Gardens,
Beneath which rivers flow:
For Allah carries out
All that He plans.[2785]

(١٤) إِنَّ اللَّهَ يُدْخِلُ الَّذِينَ ءَامَنُوا وَعَمِلُوا
الصَّٰلِحَٰتِ جَنَّٰتٍ تَجْرِي مِن تَحْتِهَا
الْأَنْهَٰرُ إِنَّ اللَّهَ يَفْعَلُ مَا يُرِيدُ

15. If any think that Allah
Will not help him
(His Messenger) in this world

(١٥) مَن كَانَ يَظُنُّ أَن لَّن يَنصُرَهُ اللَّهُ فِي الدُّنْيَا

2782. They are men whose minds are not firm: they will have faith, if all goes well with them, but as soon as they are tried, they are found wanting. They differ from hypocrites. It is not fraud or double dealing that is their sin: it is a weak mind, petty standards of judging right by success, a selfishness that gives nothing but asks for all, a narrow-mindedness that does not go beyond petty mundane calculations—a "nicely calculated less or more" of the good things of this world. They fail in both worlds and their failure in this world is patent for every on-looker.

2783. To such minds religion does not mean high endeavour, self-sacrifice for noble ends, the recognition of Allah's infinite world, but just a small concession to formalism, perhaps a present to an idol (literal or figurative), perhaps attendance at worship if it can be done without trouble! It is false gods they worship, and the more they worship, the more they stray.

2784. Such false worship is not always neutral, bringing neither harm nor good. Perhaps the harm comes first, and there is no help from Allah. Such minds are themselves demoralised, and render themselves unfit for help!

2785. Allah is both true to His promise, and He has power to give full effect to His Will and Plan.

And the Hereafter, let him
Stretch out a rope
To the ceiling and cut (himself)[2786]
Off: then let him see
Whether his plan will remove
That which enrages (him)!

وَٱلْـَٔاخِرَةِ فَلْيَمْدُدْ بِسَبَبٍ إِلَى ٱلسَّمَآءِ
ثُمَّ لْيَقْطَعْ فَلْيَنظُرْ هَلْ يُذْهِبَنَّ
كَيْدُهُۥ مَا يَغِيظُ

16. Thus have We sent down[2787]
Clear Signs: and verily
Allah doth guide whom
He will!

١٦ وَكَذَٰلِكَ أَنزَلْنَٰهُ ءَايَٰتٍۭ بَيِّنَٰتٍ
وَأَنَّ ٱللَّهَ يَهْدِى مَن يُرِيدُ

17. Those who believe (in the Qur'ān),
Those who follow the Jewish
(scriptures),
And the Sabians,[2788] Christians,
Magians,[2789] and Polytheists—
Allah will judge between them
On the Day of Judgement:
For Allah is witness
Of all things.

١٧ إِنَّ ٱلَّذِينَ ءَامَنُوا۟ وَٱلَّذِينَ هَادُوا۟ وَٱلصَّٰبِـِٔينَ
وَٱلنَّصَٰرَىٰ وَٱلْمَجُوسَ وَٱلَّذِينَ أَشْرَكُوٓا۟
إِنَّ ٱللَّهَ يَفْصِلُ بَيْنَهُمْ يَوْمَ ٱلْقِيَٰمَةِ
إِنَّ ٱللَّهَ عَلَىٰ كُلِّ شَىْءٍ شَهِيدٌ

18. Seest thou not that
To Allah bow down in worship
All things that are
In the heavens and on earth—[2790]

١٨ أَلَمْ تَرَ أَنَّ ٱللَّهَ يَسْجُدُ لَهُۥ
مَن فِى ٱلسَّمَٰوَٰتِ وَمَن فِى ٱلْأَرْضِ

2786. There is some difference of opinion as to the interpretation of this verse. Most Commentators are agreed that the pronoun "him" in the second line ("will not help him") refers to the Holy Prophet, and that the "any" in the first line refers to his enemies, who wished to see him destroyed and removed from the scene of his labours. Ibn 'Abbās, whom I have followed here, and whom a great number of Commentators follow, construes the later clauses in the sense given in the text. Freely paraphrased, it means: if the enemies of Allah's Messenger are enraged at his successes, let them fix a rope to their ceiling and hang themselves. *Samā'* is thus rendered by the word "ceiling". If *Samā'* is rendered by the word "heaven" (the usual meaning), the paraphrase would be: if the enemies of Allah's Messenger are enraged at the help he gets from heavens, let them stretch a rope to heaven and see if they can cut off the help that way!—in other words, they are fools if they think they can intercept Allah's help by their petty devices!

2787. Instead of plotting against Allah's Messenger, the Unbelievers should observe the Clear Signs which he has brought and obey and follow the Guidance which comes from Allah according to the Laws which He has fixed by His Holy Will and Plan.

2788. For Sabians, see n. 76 to 2:62. They are also referred to in 5:72. In both those passages, the Muslims are mentioned with the Jews, Christians, and Sabians, as receiving Allah's protection and mercy. Here, besides the four religions, there is further mention of Magians and Polytheists: it is not said that they would receive Allah's Mercy, but only that Allah will judge between the various forms of faith. (R).

2789. This is the only place where the Magians (*Majūs*) are mentioned in the Qur'ān. Their cult is a very ancient one. They consider Fire as the purest and noblest element, and worship it as a fit emblem of Allah. Their location was the Persian and Median uplands and the Mesopotamian valleys, their religion was reformed by Zardusht (date uncertain, about B.C. 600?). Their scripture is the Zend-Avesta, the bible of the Pārsīs. They were "the Wise men of the East" mentioned in the Gospels. (R).

2790. *Cf.* 21:79, and n. 2733. All created things, animate and inanimate, depend on Allah for their existence, and this dependence can be construed as their *Sajda* or bowing down in worship. Their very existence proclaims their dependence. How can they be objects of worship? For *ḥaqqa* in this verse , *Cf.* 15:64, n. 1990.

The sun, the moon, the stars;
The hills, the trees, the animals;
And a great number among
Mankind? But a great number
Are (also) such as are
Fit for Punishment: and such
As Allah shall disgrace—
None can raise to honour:
For Allah carries out
All that He wills.[2791]

وَالشَّمْسُ وَالْقَمَرُ وَالنُّجُومُ وَالْجِبَالُ وَالشَّجَرُ
وَالدَّوَابُّ وَكَثِيرٌ مِّنَ النَّاسِ
وَكَثِيرٌ حَقَّ عَلَيْهِ الْعَذَابُ
وَمَن يُهِنِ اللَّهُ فَمَا لَهُ مِن مُّكْرِمٍ
إِنَّ اللَّهَ يَفْعَلُ مَا يَشَاءُ

19. These two antagonists dispute[2792]
With each other about their Lord:
But those who deny (their Lord)—
For them will be cut out
A garment of Fire:
Over their heads will be
Poured out boiling water.

١٩ هَٰذَانِ خَصْمَانِ اخْتَصَمُوا فِي رَبِّهِمْ
فَالَّذِينَ كَفَرُوا قُطِّعَتْ لَهُمْ ثِيَابٌ مِّن نَّارٍ
يُصَبُّ مِن فَوْقِ رُءُوسِهِمُ الْحَمِيمُ

20. With it will be scalded
What is within their bodies,
As well as (their) skins.[2793]

٢٠ يُصْهَرُ بِهِ مَا فِي بُطُونِهِمْ وَالْجُلُودُ

21. In addition there will be
Maces of iron (to punish) them.[2794]

٢١ وَلَهُم مَّقَامِعُ مِنْ حَدِيدٍ

22. Every time they wish
To get away therefrom,
From anguish, they will be
Forced back therein, and
(It will be said), "Taste ye
The Penalty of Burning!"

٢٢ كُلَّمَا أَرَادُوا أَن يَخْرُجُوا
مِنْهَا مِنْ غَمٍّ أُعِيدُوا فِيهَا
وَذُوقُوا عَذَابَ الْحَرِيقِ

Section 3.

23. Allah will admit those
Who believe and work righteous
deeds.

٢٣ إِنَّ اللَّهَ يُدْخِلُ الَّذِينَ
آمَنُوا وَعَمِلُوا الصَّالِحَاتِ

2791. *Cf.* 22:16. There the argument was that those who work in harmony with Allah's Law and Will will get their reward, for Allah always carries out His Plan. Here is the parallel argument: those who defy Allah's Will must suffer pain and disgrace, for Allah is well able to carry out His Will.

2792. *Two antagonists: i.e.*, parties of antagonists, *viz.*, Men of Faith, who confess their Lord and seek to carry out His Will, and Men who deny their Lord and defy His Will.

2793. The punishment, expressed in physical terms, will be all-pervading, not merely superficial.

2794. Read this with the next verse. There will be no escape from the final Punishment adjudged after the time of repentance is past.

To Gardens beneath which[2795]
Rivers flow: they shall be
Adorned therein with bracelets
Of gold and pearls; and
Their garments there
Will be of silk.

جَنَّٰتٍ تَجۡرِي مِن تَحۡتِهَا ٱلۡأَنۡهَٰرُ يُحَلَّوۡنَ
فِيهَا مِنۡ أَسَاوِرَ مِن ذَهَبٖ وَلُؤۡلُؤٗاۖ
وَلِبَاسُهُمۡ فِيهَا حَرِيرٞ

24. For they have been guided
(In this life) to the purest
Of speeches; they have been
Guided to the Path of Him
Who is Worthy of (all) Praise.

٢٤ وَهُدُوٓاْ إِلَى ٱلطَّيِّبِ مِنَ ٱلۡقَوۡلِ
وَهُدُوٓاْ إِلَىٰ صِرَٰطِ ٱلۡحَمِيدِ

25. As to those who have rejected
(Allah), and would keep back
(men)
From the Way of Allah, and
From the Sacred Mosque, which
We have made (open) to (all)
men—
Equal is the dweller there
And the visitor from the country—
And any whose purpose therein
Is profanity or wrongdoing—[2796]
Them will We cause to taste
Of a most grievous Penalty.

٢٥ إِنَّ ٱلَّذِينَ كَفَرُواْ وَيَصُدُّونَ
عَن سَبِيلِ ٱللَّهِ وَٱلۡمَسۡجِدِ ٱلۡحَرَامِ
ٱلَّذِي جَعَلۡنَٰهُ لِلنَّاسِ
سَوَآءً ٱلۡعَٰكِفُ فِيهِ وَٱلۡبَادِۚ
وَمَن يُرِدۡ فِيهِ بِإِلۡحَادِۭ بِظُلۡمٖ
نُّذِقۡهُ مِنۡ عَذَابٍ أَلِيمٖ

C. 152.—For our spiritual growth are provided
(22:26-48.) Symbols and means of expression in our ordinary
Lives. Such is the pilgrimage, meant
To gather men and women from far and near
To share in sacrifice, and prayer and praise,
In an age-old centre of worship. The sacrifices,
Too, are symbols of Piety of Heart,
A longing to share with fellow-men
In the bounties of Allah. In the Fight for Truth
Is tested our purity of motive, unselfishness
Of aim, and devotion to Right at the cost
Of Self. Fearless must we fight: for Truth
Has often been flouted, but must finally win.

2795. In 22:14 above, was described the meed of the Righteous as compared with the time-servers and those who worshipped false gods (*vv.* 10-13): here we have the case of those who were persecuted, abused, prevented from entering the Ka'bah and deprived of all that makes life smooth, agreeable, and comfortable. For them the meed is described in metaphors that negative all these afflictions: costly adornments (as against being stripped of home and property), purity of speech (as against the abuse they received), the Path of the Lord of Praise (as against the fierce and malignant persecution to which they were subjected).

2796. All these were enormities of which the Pagan clique in power in Makkah were guilty before and during the Hijrah.

SECTION 4.

26. Behold! We gave the site,[2797]
To Abraham, of the (Sacred)
House,
(Saying): "Associate not anything
(In worship) with Me;
And sanctify My House
For those who compass it
round,[2798]
Or stand up,
Or bow, or prostrate themselves
(Therein in prayer).

٢٦ وَإِذْ بَوَّأْنَا لِإِبْرَٰهِيمَ
مَكَانَ ٱلْبَيْتِ
أَن لَّا تُشْرِكْ بِى شَيْـًٔا
وَطَهِّرْ بَيْتِىَ لِلطَّآئِفِينَ
وَٱلْقَآئِمِينَ وَٱلرُّكَّعِ ٱلسُّجُودِ

27. "And proclaim the Pilgrimage
Among men: they will come
To thee on foot and (mounted)
On every kind of camel,
Lean on account of journeys
Through deep and distant
Mountain highways;[2799]

٢٧ وَأَذِّن فِى ٱلنَّاسِ بِٱلْحَجِّ
يَأْتُوكَ رِجَالًا وَعَلَىٰ كُلِّ ضَامِرٍ
يَأْتِينَ مِن كُلِّ فَجٍّ عَمِيقٍ

28. "That they may witness
The benefits (provided) for
them,[2800]
And celebrate the name
Of Allah, through the Days[2801]
Appointed, over the cattle[2802]
Which He has provided for them
(For sacrifice): then eat ye
Thereof and feed the distressed
Ones in want.

٢٨ لِّيَشْهَدُوا۟ مَنَٰفِعَ لَهُمْ
وَيَذْكُرُوا۟ ٱسْمَ ٱللَّهِ فِىٓ أَيَّامٍ مَّعْلُومَٰتٍ
عَلَىٰ مَا رَزَقَهُم مِّنۢ بَهِيمَةِ ٱلْأَنْعَٰمِ
فَكُلُوا۟ مِنْهَا وَأَطْعِمُوا۟
ٱلْبَآئِسَ ٱلْفَقِيرَ

2797. The site of Makkah was granted to Abraham (and his son Ismā'īl) for a place of worship that was to be pure (without idols, the worship being paid to Allah, the One True God) and universal, without being reserved (like Solomon's Temple of later times) to any one People or Race. (R).

2798. *Cf.* 2:125. Note that here the word *qā'imīn* (who stand up for prayer) occurs in place of *'ākifīn* (who use it as a retreat). In practice the meaning is the same. Those who go for a retreat to the Ka'bah stay there for the time being.

2799. When the Pilgrimage was proclaimed, people came to it from every quarter, near and far, on foot and mounted. The "lean camel" coming after a fatiguing journey through distant mountain roads typifies the difficulties of travel, which Pilgrims disregard on account of the temporal and spiritual benefits referred to in the next verse.

2800. There are benefits both for this our material life and for our spiritual life. Of the former kind are those associated with social intercourse which furthers trade and increases knowledge. Of the latter kind are the opportunities of realising some of our spiritual yearnings in sacred associations that go back to the most ancient times. Of both kinds may be considered the opportunities which the Pilgrimage provides for strengthening our international Brotherhood.

2801. The three special days of Ḥajj are the 8th, 9th, and 10th of the month of *Dhu al Hijjah,* and the two or three subsequent days of *Tashrīq*: see the rites explained in n. 217 to 2:197. But we may ordinarily include the first ten days of *Dhu al Ḥijjah* in the term.

2802. The great day of commemorative Sacrifice ('Id al Adḥā) is the 10th of *Dhu al Hijjah:* the meat then killed is meant to be eaten for food and distributed to the poor and needy. (R).

29. "Then let them complete
The rites prescribed[2803]
For them, perform their vows,[2804]
And (again) circumambulate
The Ancient House."

٢٩ ثُمَّ لْيَقْضُوا۟ تَفَثَهُمْ وَلْيُوفُوا۟ نُذُورَهُمْ وَلْيَطَّوَّفُوا۟ بِٱلْبَيْتِ ٱلْعَتِيقِ

30. Such (is the Pilgrimage):
Whoever honours the sacred
Rites of Allah, for him
It is good in the sight
Of his Lord. Lawful to you
(For food in Pilgrimage) are cattle,
Except those mentioned to you[2805]
(As exceptions): but shun
The abomination of idols,
And shun the word
That is false—

٣٠ ذَٰلِكَ وَمَن يُعَظِّمْ حُرُمَٰتِ ٱللَّهِ فَهُوَ خَيْرٌ لَّهُۥ عِندَ رَبِّهِۦ ۗ وَأُحِلَّتْ لَكُمُ ٱلْأَنْعَٰمُ إِلَّا مَا يُتْلَىٰ عَلَيْكُمْ ۖ فَٱجْتَنِبُوا۟ ٱلرِّجْسَ مِنَ ٱلْأَوْثَٰنِ وَٱجْتَنِبُوا۟ قَوْلَ ٱلزُّورِ

31. Being true in faith to Allah,
And never assigning partners
To Him: if anyone assigns
Partners to Allah, he is
As if he had fallen
From heaven and been snatched up
By birds, or the wind
Had swooped (like a bird
On its prey) and thrown him
Into a far-distant place.[2806]

٣١ حُنَفَآءَ لِلَّهِ غَيْرَ مُشْرِكِينَ بِهِۦ ۚ وَمَن يُشْرِكْ بِٱللَّهِ فَكَأَنَّمَا خَرَّ مِنَ ٱلسَّمَآءِ فَتَخْطَفُهُ ٱلطَّيْرُ أَوْ تَهْوِى بِهِ ٱلرِّيحُ فِى مَكَانٍ سَحِيقٍ

32. Such (is his state): and
Whoever holds in honour
The Symbols of Allah,[2807]

٣٢ ذَٰلِكَ وَمَن يُعَظِّمْ شَعَٰٓئِرَ ٱللَّهِ

2803. *Tafath*—the superfluous growth on one's body, such as nails, hair, etc., which is not permitted to remove in *Ihrām*. These may be removed on the 10th day, when the Ḥajj is completed: that is the rite of completion.

2804. The spirit of Pilgrimage is not completed by the performance of the outward rites. The Pilgrim should carry in mind some vow or spiritual service and endeavour to perform it. Then comes the final *Ṭawāf*.

2805. The general food prohibitions will be found in 2:173, 5:4-5, and 6:121, 138-146. They are meant for health and cleanliness, but the worst abominations to shun are those of false worship and false speech. Here the question is about food during Pilgrimage. Lawful meat but not game is allowed.

2806. A parable full of meaning. The man who falls from the worship of the One True God. is like a man who falls from heaven. His being taken up with false objects of worship is like the falling man being picked up in the air by birds of prey. But the false objects of worship cannot hold him permanently in their grip. A fierce blast of wind—the Wrath of Allah—comes and snatches him away and throws him into a place far, far away from any place he could have imagined—into the hell of those who defied Allah. (R).

2807. *Sha'ā'ir*, symbols, signs, marks by which something is known to belong to some particular body of men, such as flags. In 2:158 the word was applied to Ṣafā and Marwah: see n. 160 there. Here it seems to be applied to the rites of sacrifice. Such sacrifice is symbolic: it should betoken dedication and piety of heart. See below, 22:37.

(In the sacrifice of animals),
Such (honour) should come truly
From piety of heart.

فَإِنَّهَا مِن تَقْوَى ٱلْقُلُوبِ

33. In them[2808] ye have benefits
For a term appointed:
In the end their place
Of sacrifice is near[2809]
The Ancient House.

٣٣ لَكُمْ فِيهَا مَنَٰفِعُ إِلَىٰٓ أَجَلٍ مُّسَمًّى
ثُمَّ مَحِلُّهَآ إِلَى ٱلْبَيْتِ ٱلْعَتِيقِ

SECTION 5.

34. To every people did We
Appoint rites (of sacrifice),
That they might celebrate
The name of Allah over
The sustenance He gave them
From animals (fit for food),[2810]
But your God is One God:
Submit then your wills to Him
(In Islam): and give thou
The good news[2811] to those
Who humble themselves—

٣٤ وَلِكُلِّ أُمَّةٍ جَعَلْنَا
مَنسَكًا لِّيَذْكُرُوا۟ ٱسْمَ ٱللَّهِ
عَلَىٰ مَا رَزَقَهُم مِّنۢ بَهِيمَةِ ٱلْأَنْعَٰمِ ۗ
فَإِلَٰهُكُمْ إِلَٰهٌ وَٰحِدٌ فَلَهُۥٓ أَسْلِمُوا۟ ۗ
وَبَشِّرِ ٱلْمُخْبِتِينَ

35. To those whose hearts,
When Allah is mentioned,
Are filled with fear,
Who show patient perseverance
Over their afflictions, keep up
Regular prayer, and spend

٣٥ ٱلَّذِينَ إِذَا ذُكِرَ ٱللَّهُ وَجِلَتْ
قُلُوبُهُمْ وَٱلصَّٰبِرِينَ عَلَىٰ مَآ أَصَابَهُمْ
وَٱلْمُقِيمِى ٱلصَّلَوٰةِ

2808. *In them*: in cattle, or animals offered for sacrifice. It is quite true that they are useful in many ways to man, *e.g.*, camels in desert countries are useful as mounts or for carrying burdens, or for giving milk, and so for horses and oxen; and camels and oxen are also good for meat, and camel's hair can be woven into cloth; goats and sheep also yield milk and meat, and hair or wool. But if they are used for sacrifice, they become symbols by which men show that they are willing to give up some of their own benefits for the sake of satisfying the needs of their poorer brethren.

2809. *Ilā* = towards, near. The actual sacrifice is not performed in the Ka'bah, but at Minā, five or six miles off, where the Pilgrims encamp: see n. 217 to 2:197. *Thumma* = then, finally, in the end; *i.e.*, after all the rites have been performed, Ṭawāf, Ṣafā, and Marwah, and 'Arafāt.

2810. This is the true end of sacrifice, not propitiation of higher powers, for Allah is One, and He does not delight in flesh or blood (22:37), but a symbol of thanksgiving to Allah by sharing meat with fellow-men. The solemn pronouncement of Allah's name over the sacrifice is an essential part of the rite.

2811. *The good news: i.e.*, the Message of Allah, that He will accept in us the sacrifice of self for the benefit of our fellow-men.

(In charity) out of what
We have bestowed upon them.[2812]

وَمِمَّا رَزَقْنَٰهُمْ يُنفِقُونَ

36. The sacrificial camels
We have made for you
As among the Symbols from
Allah: in them is (much)
Good for you: then pronounce
The name of Allah over them
As they line up (for sacrifice):[2813]
When they are down
On their sides (after slaughter),
Eat ye thereof, and feed
Such as (beg not but)
Live in contentment,[2814]
And such as beg
With due humility: thus have
We made animals subject
To you, that ye
May be grateful.

٣٦ وَٱلْبُدْنَ جَعَلْنَٰهَا لَكُم
مِّن شَعَٰٓئِرِ ٱللَّهِ لَكُمْ فِيهَا خَيْرٌ
فَٱذْكُرُوا۟ ٱسْمَ ٱللَّهِ عَلَيْهَا صَوَآفَّ
فَإِذَا وَجَبَتْ جُنُوبُهَا
فَكُلُوا۟ مِنْهَا وَأَطْعِمُوا۟
ٱلْقَانِعَ وَٱلْمُعْتَرَّ
كَذَٰلِكَ سَخَّرْنَٰهَا لَكُمْ
لَعَلَّكُمْ تَشْكُرُونَ

37. It is not their meat
Nor their blood, that reaches
Allah: it is your piety
That reaches Him: He
Has thus made them subject
To you, that ye may glorify
Allah for His guidance to you:[2815]

٣٧ لَن يَنَالَ ٱللَّهَ لُحُومُهَا وَلَا دِمَآؤُهَا
وَلَٰكِن يَنَالُهُ ٱلتَّقْوَىٰ مِنكُمْ كَذَٰلِكَ سَخَّرَهَا لَكُمْ
لِتُكَبِّرُوا۟ ٱللَّهَ عَلَىٰ مَا هَدَىٰكُمْ

2812. Some qualities of Allah's devotees are mentioned here, in ascending order: (1) Humility before Allah makes them receptive, and prepares them to listen to Allah's Message; (2) fear of Allah, which is akin to love, touches their heart, and penetrates through their inmost being; (3) they are not afraid of anything in mortal life; they take their trials patiently, and they go on in a course of righteousness with constancy; (4) their prayer now is not a matter of form, but a real communion with Allah, with a sense of confidence such as a faithful servant feels in the presence of a kind and loving master; and (5) gratitude to Allah, as shown by practical acts of charity to all fellow-creatures.

2813. See n. 2808 to 22:33 above. What was expressed in general terms is applied here more particularly to camels, the most precious and useful animals of Arabia, whose mode of slaughter for sacrifice is different from that of smaller animals: the special word for such sacrifice is *Naḥr* (108:2).

2814. There are ethics in begging, as in charity. No approval is given to arrogant and insolent begging, though the relief of distress of all kinds, deserved and undeserved, is included in charity. But those who beg with humility and those who receive gifts with gratitude and contentment are both mentioned for special attention. Charity should not be given for show, or to get rid of importunate demands. It should find out real needs and meet them.

2815. The essence of sacrifice has been explained in n. 2810. No one should suppose that meat or blood is acceptable to the One True God. It was a Pagan fancy that Allah could be appeased by blood sacrifice. But Allah does accept the offering of our hearts, and as a symbol of such offer, some visible institution is necessary. He has given us power over the brute creation, and permitted us to eat meat, but only if we pronounce His name at the solemn act of taking life, for without this solemn invocation, we are apt to forget the sacredness of life. By the invocation we are reminded that wanton cruelty is not in our thoughts, but only the need of food. Now if we further deny ourselves the greater part of the food (some theologians fix the proportion at three-quarters or two-thirds) for the sake of our poorer brethren in solemn assembly in the precincts of the Ḥaram (sacred territory), our symbolic act finds practical expression in benevolence, and that is the virtue sought to be taught. We should be grateful to Allah for His guidance in this matter, in which many Peoples have gone wrong, and we should proclaim the true doctrine, so that virtue and charity may increase among men.

And proclaim the Good News
To all who do right.

وَبَشِّرِ ٱلْمُحْسِنِينَ

38. Verily Allah will defend
(From ill) those who believe:
Verily, Allah loveth not
Any that is a traitor
To faith, or shows ingratitude.

٣٨ إِنَّ ٱللَّهَ يُدَٰفِعُ عَنِ ٱلَّذِينَ ءَامَنُوٓا۟ ۗ
إِنَّ ٱللَّهَ لَا يُحِبُّ كُلَّ خَوَّانٍ كَفُورٍ

Section 6.

39. To those against whom[2816]
War is made, permission
Is given (to fight), because
They are wronged—and verily,
Allah is Most Powerful
For their aid—

٣٩ أُذِنَ لِلَّذِينَ يُقَٰتَلُونَ
بِأَنَّهُمْ ظُلِمُوا۟ ۚ وَإِنَّ ٱللَّهَ
عَلَىٰ نَصْرِهِمْ لَقَدِيرٌ

40. (They are) those who have
Been expelled from their homes
In defiance of right—
(For no cause) except
That they say, "Our Lord
Is Allah". Did not Allah
Check one set of people
By means of another[2817]
There would surely have been
Pulled down monasteries, churches,
Synagogues, and mosques, in which
The name of Allah is commemorated
In abundant measure. Allah will
Certainly aid those who
Aid His (cause)—for verily
Allah is Full of Strength,

٤٠ ٱلَّذِينَ أُخْرِجُوا۟ مِن دِيَٰرِهِم
بِغَيْرِ حَقٍّ إِلَّآ أَن
يَقُولُوا۟ رَبُّنَا ٱللَّهُ ۗ
وَلَوْلَا دَفْعُ ٱللَّهِ ٱلنَّاسَ بَعْضَهُم بِبَعْضٍ
لَّهُدِّمَتْ صَوَٰمِعُ وَبِيَعٌ وَصَلَوَٰتٌ
وَمَسَٰجِدُ يُذْكَرُ فِيهَا
ٱسْمُ ٱللَّهِ كَثِيرًا ۗ
وَلَيَنصُرَنَّ ٱللَّهُ مَن يَنصُرُهُۥٓ ۗ
إِنَّ ٱللَّهَ لَقَوِىٌّ

2816. Several translators have failed to notice that *yuqātalūna* (in the best-approved texts) is in the passive voice, "against whom war is made"—not "who take arms against the unbelievers" as Sale translates it. The clause "and verily. . .their aid" is parenthetical. Verse 40 connects on with "they are wronged". The wrong is indicated: 'driven by persecution from their home, for no other reason than that they worshipped the One True God'. This was the first occasion on which fighting—in self-defence—was permitted. This passage therefore undoubtedly dates from Madīnah.

2817. *Cf.* 2:251, where the expression is used in connection with David's fight against the Philistines. To allow a righteous people to fight against a ferocious and mischief-loving people was fully justified. But the justification was far greater here, when the little Muslim community was not only fighting for its own existence against the Makkan Quraysh, but for the very existence of the Faith in the One True God. They had as much right to be in Makkah and worship in the Ka'bah as the other Quraysh; yet they were exiled for their Faith. It affected not the faith of one particular people. The principle involved was that of all worship, Jewish or Christian as well as Muslim, and of all foundations built for pious uses.

Exalted in Might,[2818]
(Able to enforce His Will).

عَزِيزٌ

41. (They are) those who,
If We establish them
In the land, establish
Regular prayer and give
Regular charity, enjoin
The right and forbid wrong:[2819]
With Allah rests the end
(And decision) of (all) affairs.

ٱلَّذِينَ إِن مَّكَّنَّٰهُمْ فِى ٱلْأَرْضِ ﴿٤١﴾
أَقَامُوا۟ ٱلصَّلَوٰةَ وَءَاتَوُا۟ ٱلزَّكَوٰةَ
وَأَمَرُوا۟ بِٱلْمَعْرُوفِ وَنَهَوْا۟ عَنِ ٱلْمُنكَرِ
وَلِلَّهِ عَٰقِبَةُ ٱلْأُمُورِ

42. If they treat thy (mission)
As false, so did the Peoples
Before them (with their
Prophets)—[2820]
The People of Noah,
The 'Ād and Thamūd;

وَإِن يُكَذِّبُوكَ ﴿٤٢﴾
فَقَدْ كَذَّبَتْ قَبْلَهُمْ
قَوْمُ نُوحٍ وَعَادٌ وَثَمُودُ

43. Those of Abraham and Lūṭ;

وَقَوْمُ إِبْرَٰهِيمَ وَقَوْمُ لُوطٍ ﴿٤٣﴾

44. And the Companions[2821]
Of the Madyan people;
And Moses was rejected
(In the same way). But I
Granted respite to the Unbelievers,
And (only) after that
Did I punish them:
But how (terrible) was
My rejection (of them)![2822]

وَأَصْحَٰبُ مَدْيَنَ ﴿٤٤﴾
وَكُذِّبَ مُوسَىٰ فَأَمْلَيْتُ
لِلْكَٰفِرِينَ ثُمَّ أَخَذْتُهُمْ
فَكَيْفَ كَانَ نَكِيرِ

45. How many populations have We
Destroyed, which were given
To wrongdoing? They tumbled
down[2823]

فَكَأَيِّن مِّن قَرْيَةٍ أَهْلَكْنَٰهَا ﴿٤٥﴾
وَهِىَ ظَالِمَةٌ فَهِىَ خَاوِيَةٌ

2818. *'Azīz* means Exalted in power, rank, dignity; Incomparable; Full of might and majesty; Able to enforce His Will. The last signification is the one that predominates here.

2819. "Enjoining the right and forbidding the wrong" is an essential duty of the Muslim Ummah and one of the main purposes for which it has been raised. (See 3:104, 110; 9:71, 111-112,, 22:41). (Eds.).

2820. It is nothing new if the Prophet of Allah is accused of imposture. This was done in all ages: *e.g.*, Noah (7:64); Hūd the prophet of the 'Ād people (7:66); Ṣāliḥ the prophet of the Thamūd (7:76); Abraham (21:55); Lūṭ (7:82); Shu'aib the prophet of the Madyan people (7:85) and also of the Companions of the Wood (15:78). The case of Moses is mentioned apart, as his people survived to the time of our Prophet and survive to the present, and they frequently rebelled against Moses (2:49-61).

2821. Were they the same as the Companions of the Wood? See n. 2000 to 15:78.

2822. My Wrath on them, and the complete reversal of their fortune in consequence.

2823. The roofs fell in first, and the whole structure, walls and all, came tumbling after, as happens in ruins. The place was turned upside down.

On their roofs. And how many
Wells are lying idle and
neglected,[2824]
And castles lofty and well-built?

عَلَىٰ عُرُوشِهَا
وَبِئْرٍ مُّعَطَّلَةٍ وَقَصْرٍ مَّشِيدٍ

46. Do they not travel
Through the land, so that
Their hearts (and minds)[2825]
May thus learn wisdom
And their ears may
Thus learn to hear?
Truly it is not their eyes
That are blind, but their
Hearts which are
In their breasts.

٤٦ أَفَلَمْ يَسِيرُوا فِي الْأَرْضِ
فَتَكُونَ لَهُمْ قُلُوبٌ يَعْقِلُونَ بِهَا
أَوْ آذَانٌ يَسْمَعُونَ بِهَا
فَإِنَّهَا لَا تَعْمَى الْأَبْصَارُ
وَلَٰكِن تَعْمَى الْقُلُوبُ الَّتِي فِي الصُّدُورِ

47. Yet they ask thee
To hasten on the Punishment!
But Allah will not fail[2826]
In His promise. Verily
A Day in the sight of thy Lord
Is like a thousand years
Of your reckoning.

٤٧ وَيَسْتَعْجِلُونَكَ بِالْعَذَابِ
وَلَن يُخْلِفَ اللَّهُ وَعْدَهُ وَإِنَّ يَوْمًا
عِندَ رَبِّكَ كَأَلْفِ سَنَةٍ مِّمَّا تَعُدُّونَ

48. And to how many populations
Did I give respite, which[2827]
Were given to wrongdoing?
In the end I punished them.
To Me is the destination (of all).

٤٨ وَكَأَيِّن مِّن قَرْيَةٍ أَمْلَيْتُ لَهَا
وَهِيَ ظَالِمَةٌ ثُمَّ أَخَذْتُهَا وَإِلَيَّ الْمَصِيرُ

C. 153.—The power of Evil is in insidious suggestions:
(22:49-78.) They are only a trial to those whose hearts
Are inclined to evil, but Truth doth shine
The nobler for the Believers, by the grace

2824. In a dry country like Arabia, a well stands as a symbol for a living, flourishing population, and many place-names mean "the well of so-and-so" *e.g.*, Bīr 'Alī, a village just south of Madīnah, the quality of whose drinking water is famous, or Abyār Ibn Ḥassān, a noted stopping place on the road from Makkah to Madīnah, about 92 miles from Madīnah.

2825. The word for "heart" in Arabic speech imports both the seat of intelligent faculties and understanding as well as the seat of affections and emotions. Those who reject Allah's Message may have their physical eyes and ears, but their hearts are blind and deaf. If their faculties of understanding were active, would they not see the Signs of Allah's Providence and Allah's Wrath in nature around them and in the cities and ruins if they travel intelligently?

2826. If Allah gives respite, those to whom it is given have a real chance of repentance and amendment. He will not curtail His promise of respite. But on the other hand He has promised to call everyone to account for his deeds, and this involves justice and punishment for sin. This promise will also come true. It is foolish to try to hasten it. Time with Him is nothing. We keep count of time for our relative calculations. His existence is absolute, and not conditioned by Time or Place. What we call a thousand years may be nothing more than a day or a minute to Him.

2827. The argument begun in 22:45 is now rounded off and closed.

And guidance of Allah. Martyrs who give
Their all in the cause of Allah will find
A provision ample and eternal. The finest
And subtlest mysteries are but proofs of the goodness
Of Allah. Dispute not about rites and ceremonies:
Follow the Straight Way. Seek for worship
The Only True God, and strive in His service,
That ye may be witnesses among men
To Allah's Truth, as the Prophet is a witness to you.

SECTION 7.

49. Say: "O men! I am
(Sent) to you only to give
A clear warning:[2828]

قُلْ يَٰٓأَيُّهَا ٱلنَّاسُ إِنَّمَآ أَنَا۠ لَكُمْ نَذِيرٌ مُّبِينٌ ﴿٤٩﴾

50. "Those who believe and work
Righteousness, for them
Is forgiveness and a sustenance
Most generous.[2829]

فَٱلَّذِينَ ءَامَنُوا۟ وَعَمِلُوا۟ ٱلصَّٰلِحَٰتِ
لَهُم مَّغْفِرَةٌ وَرِزْقٌ كَرِيمٌ ﴿٥٠﴾

51. "But those who strive
Against Our Signs, to frustrate[2830]
Them—they will be
Companions of the Fire."

وَٱلَّذِينَ سَعَوْا۟ فِىٓ ءَايَٰتِنَا مُعَٰجِزِينَ
أُو۟لَٰٓئِكَ أَصْحَٰبُ ٱلْجَحِيمِ ﴿٥١﴾

52. Never did We send
A messenger or a prophet
Before thee, but, when he
Framed a desire, Satan
Threw some (vanity)[2831]
Into his desire: but Allah
Will cancel anything (vain)
That Satan throws in,

وَمَآ أَرْسَلْنَا مِن قَبْلِكَ
مِن رَّسُولٍ وَلَا نَبِىٍّ إِلَّآ إِذَا تَمَنَّىٰٓ
أَلْقَى ٱلشَّيْطَٰنُ فِىٓ أُمْنِيَّتِهِۦ
فَيَنسَخُ ٱللَّهُ مَا يُلْقِى ٱلشَّيْطَٰنُ

2828. It is the Messenger's duty to convey the warning in the clearest terms to the wicked. It is not part of his duty to coerce them or judge them, or bring on the Punishment for them. That only rests with Allah. But the warning itself is full of Mercy: for it gives the highest hope to the repentant sinner who turns and comes to Allah.

2829. The "sustenance" must be construed in the widest sense, spiritual as well as intellectual and physical. The reward of righteousness is far more generous than any merit there may be in the creature following the Will of his Creator.

2830. It will not be in their power to frustrate Allah's Plan; all they will do is to go further and further down in their spiritual state, deeper and deeper into their Hell.

2831. Prophets and messengers (the distinction is explained in n. 2503 to 19:51) are but human. Their actions are righteous and their motives pure, but in judging things from a human point of view, the suggestion may come to their mind (from Satan) that it would be good to have power or wealth or influence for furthering Allah's cause, or that it may be good to conciliate some faction which may be irreconcilable. In fact, in Allah's Plan, it may be the opposite. Allah, in His mercy and inspiration, will cancel any false or vain suggestions of this kind, and confirm and strengthen His own Commands and make known His Will in His Signs or revelations.

ثُمَّ يُحْكِمُ ٱللَّهُ ءَايَٰتِهِۦ ۗ
وَٱللَّهُ عَلِيمٌ حَكِيمٌ

And Allah will confirm
(And establish) His Signs:
For Allah is full of knoweldge
And wisdom:[2832]

٥٣ لِّيَجْعَلَ مَا يُلْقِى ٱلشَّيْطَٰنُ فِتْنَةً
لِّلَّذِينَ فِى قُلُوبِهِم مَّرَضٌ وَٱلْقَاسِيَةِ قُلُوبُهُمْ ۗ
وَإِنَّ ٱلظَّٰلِمِينَ لَفِى
شِقَاقٍۭ بَعِيدٍ

53. That He may make
The suggestions thrown in
By Satan, but a trial[2833]
For those in whose hearts
Is a disease and who are[2834]
Hardened of heart: verily
The wrongdoers are in a schism
Far (from the Truth):

٥٤ وَلِيَعْلَمَ ٱلَّذِينَ أُوتُوا۟ ٱلْعِلْمَ
أَنَّهُ ٱلْحَقُّ مِن رَّبِّكَ فَيُؤْمِنُوا۟ بِهِۦ
فَتُخْبِتَ لَهُۥ قُلُوبُهُمْ ۗ
وَإِنَّ ٱللَّهَ لَهَادِ ٱلَّذِينَ ءَامَنُوٓا۟
إِلَىٰ صِرَٰطٍ مُّسْتَقِيمٍ

54. And that those on whom[2835]
Knowledge has been bestowed
may learn
That the (Qur'ān) is the Truth
From thy Lord, and that they
May believe therein, and their
hearts
May be made humbly (open)
To it: for verily Allah is
The Guide of those who believe,
To the Straight Way.

٥٥ وَلَا يَزَالُ ٱلَّذِينَ كَفَرُوا۟
فِى مِرْيَةٍ مِّنْهُ حَتَّىٰ تَأْتِيَهُمُ ٱلسَّاعَةُ بَغْتَةً
أَوْ يَأْتِيَهُمْ عَذَابُ يَوْمٍ عَقِيمٍ

55. Those who reject Faith
Will not cease to be[2836]
In doubt concerning (Revelation)
Until the Hour (of Judgement)
Comes suddenly upon them,
Or there comes to them
The Penalty of a Day of Disaster.

2832. This clause and the similar clause at the end of the next verse are parenthetical.

2833. If any suggestion comes to the human mind that is not in accordance with Allah's Will and Plan, it has two opposite effects: to evil minds it is a trial and a temptation from the Evil One, but to the mind well-instructed in Faith, it stands self-condemned at once, and becomes a means of strengthening the Faith and stimulating redoubled efforts to conform to the Will of Allah.

2834. *Cf.* 2:10. I understand the "disease in the heart" to be an earlier state of curse, which leads in an intensified form to a complete "hardening of the heart".

2835. The last clause in the last verse was parenthetical. Treat this clause as parallel with the first clause in verse 53, "that he may make", etc. Both will then connect with "Allah will confirm (and establish) His Signs" in verse 52. See n. 2833 above.

2836. The penalty of deliberately rejecting Faith is that the person doing so closes the channels of Mercy that flow from Allah. He will always be subject to doubts and superstitions, until the time comes when all earthly scales fall from his spiritual eyes. But then there will be no time for Repentance: it will be too late to profit by the guidance of Allah given through Revelation.

56. On that Day the Dominion[2837]
Will be that of Allah:
He will judge between them:
So those who believe
And work righteous deeds will be
In Gardens of Delight.

٥٦ ٱلْمُلْكُ يَوْمَئِذٍ لِّلَّهِ يَحْكُمُ بَيْنَهُمْ ۚ
فَٱلَّذِينَ ءَامَنُوا۟ وَعَمِلُوا۟
ٱلصَّٰلِحَٰتِ فِى جَنَّٰتِ ٱلنَّعِيمِ

57. And for those who reject Faith
And deny Our Signs,
There will be a humiliating
Punishment.

٥٧ وَٱلَّذِينَ كَفَرُوا۟ وَكَذَّبُوا۟ بِـَٔايَٰتِنَا
فَأُو۟لَٰٓئِكَ لَهُمْ عَذَابٌ مُّهِينٌ

SECTION 8.

58. Those who leave their homes
In the cause of Allah,
And are then slain or die—
On them will Allah bestow verily
A goodly Provision:[2838]
Truly Allah is He Who
Bestows the best Provision.

٥٨ وَٱلَّذِينَ هَاجَرُوا۟ فِى سَبِيلِ ٱللَّهِ ثُمَّ
قُتِلُوٓا۟ أَوْ مَاتُوا۟ لَيَرْزُقَنَّهُمُ ٱللَّهُ رِزْقًا
حَسَنًا ۚ وَإِنَّ ٱللَّهَ لَهُوَ خَيْرُ ٱلرَّٰزِقِينَ

59. Verily He will admit them
To a place with which
They shall be well pleased:
For Allah is All-Knowing,
Most Forbearing.[2839]

٥٩ لَيُدْخِلَنَّهُم مُّدْخَلًا يَرْضَوْنَهُۥ ۗ
وَإِنَّ ٱللَّهَ لَعَلِيمٌ حَلِيمٌ

60. That (is so). And if one
Has retaliated to no greater
Extent than the injury he received,
And is again set upon
Inordinately, Allah will help
Him: for Allah is One

٦٠ ذَٰلِكَ وَمَنْ عَاقَبَ بِمِثْلِ مَا عُوقِبَ بِهِۦ
ثُمَّ بُغِىَ عَلَيْهِ لَيَنصُرَنَّهُ ٱللَّهُ ۚ
إِنَّ ٱللَّهَ

2837. Such power as Evil has over those who yield to it (17:62-64) will then be gone, as the respite granted to Satan will be over, and Allah's Kingdom will be established.

2838. *Rizq*: sustenance, provision. I have preferred the latter word here, because after death we can only think of *rizq* in a large metaphorical sense, *i.e.*, all the provision necessary to equip the person for a full and happy Future Life, and also, I think, a provision for his dependants and near and dear ones in this life. (R).

2839. Martyrdom is the sacrifice of life in the service of Allah. Its reward is therefore even greater than that of an ordinarily good life. The martyr's sins are forgiven by the very act of martyrdom, which implies service and self-surrender in the highest sense of the word. Allah knows all his past life but will forbear from calling him to account for things that should strictly come into his account.

That blots out (sins)
And forgives (again and again)[2840]

لَعَفُوٌّ غَفُورٌ

61. That is because Allah merges
Night into Day, and He
Merges Day into Night, and
Verily it is Allah Who hears
And sees (all things).[2841]

٦١ ذَٰلِكَ بِأَنَّ ٱللَّهَ يُولِجُ ٱلَّيْلَ فِى
ٱلنَّهَارِ وَيُولِجُ ٱلنَّهَارَ فِى ٱلَّيْلِ
وَأَنَّ ٱللَّهَ سَمِيعٌۢ بَصِيرٌ

62. That is because Allah—He[2842]
Is the Reality; and those
Besides Him whom they invoke—
They are but vain Falsehood:
Verily Allah is He, Most High,
Most Great.[2843]

٦٢ ذَٰلِكَ بِأَنَّ ٱللَّهَ هُوَ ٱلْحَقُّ
وَأَنَّ مَا يَدْعُونَ مِن دُونِهِۦ هُوَ ٱلْبَٰطِلُ
وَأَنَّ ٱللَّهَ هُوَ ٱلْعَلِىُّ ٱلْكَبِيرُ

63. Seest thou not that Allah
Sends down rain from the sky,
And forthwith the earth
Becomes clothed with green?
For Allah is He Who
understands[2844]
The finest mysteries, and
Is well-acquainted (with them).

٦٣ أَلَمْ تَرَ أَنَّ ٱللَّهَ أَنزَلَ مِنَ ٱلسَّمَآءِ مَآءً
فَتُصْبِحُ ٱلْأَرْضُ مُخْضَرَّةً
إِنَّ ٱللَّهَ لَطِيفٌ خَبِيرٌ

2840. Ordinarily Muslims are enjoined to bear injuries with patience and return good for evil (23:96). But there are occasions when human feelings get the better of our wise resolutions, or when, in a state of conflict or war, we return "as good as we get". In that case our retaliation is permissible, provided the injury we inflict is not greater than that we receive. After such retaliation, we are even, but if the other side again acts aggressively and goes beyond all bounds in attacking us, we are entitled to protection from Allah in spite of all our faults; for Allah is One that blots out our sins, and forgives again and again.

2841. To some it may appear strange or even irreconcilable that Allah should be both Merciful and Just: that He should both protect His devotees and yet ask for their self-sacrifice; that he should command them to return good for evil, and yet permit retaliation under certain restrictions. But such thoughts are short-sighted. Do they not see many inconsistencies in all Life, all Nature, and all Creation? Why, even in such simple phenomena as Night and Day, the one merges into the other, and no one can tell when precisely the one begins and the other ends. Yet we can see in a rough sort of way that the one gives rest and the other activity, that the one reveals the beauties of the starry heavens and the other the splendour of the sun. In countless ways we can see there the wisdom and the fine artistry of Allah. And there are subtle nuances and mergings in nature that our intelligence can hardly penetrate. Now human life and human relations are far more complicated, and it is Allah alone Who can see all the subtle distinctions and hear the cries of *all* His creatures, in a world which Tennyson described as "red in tooth and claw".

2842. The emphatic construction calls attention to the fact that Allah is the only abiding Reality. All else is like shadows that will pass away.

2843. See n. 2841 above Our vain imaginings, groundless doubts, foolish subtleties, and false worship should all give place to trust and faith in the one and only Reality.

2844. *Laṭīf*, as a name of Allah, is as difficult to define in words as the idea it seeks to represent is difficult to grasp in our minds. It implies: (1) fine, subtle (the basic meaning); (2) so fine and subtle as to be imperceptible to human sight; (3) so pure as to be incomprehensible; (4) with sight so perfect as to see and understand the finest subtleties and mysteries; (5) so kind and gracious as to bestow gifts of the most refined kind; extraordinarily gracious and understanding. No. 4 is the predominant meaning here and in 12:100; Nos. 2 and 3 in 6:103; and No. 5 in 42:19; but every shade of meaning must be borne in mind in each case, as a subsidiary factor in the spiritual melody.

64\. To Him belongs all that is
In the heavens and on earth:
For verily Allah—He is
Free of all wants,
Worthy of all praise.[2845]

٦٤ لَّهُۥ مَا فِى ٱلسَّمَـٰوَٰتِ وَمَا فِى ٱلْأَرْضِ ۗ
وَإِنَّ ٱللَّهَ لَهُوَ ٱلْغَنِىُّ ٱلْحَمِيدُ

SECTION 9.

65\. Seest thou not that Allah
Has made subject to you (men)
All that is on the earth,
And the ships that sail[2846]
Through the sea by His command?
He withholds the sky (rain)[2847]
From falling on the earth
Except by His leave:
For Allah is Most Kind
And Most Merciful to man.

٦٥ أَلَمْ تَرَ أَنَّ ٱللَّهَ سَخَّرَ لَكُم مَّا فِى ٱلْأَرْضِ
وَٱلْفُلْكَ تَجْرِى فِى ٱلْبَحْرِ بِأَمْرِهِۦ
وَيُمْسِكُ ٱلسَّمَآءَ أَن تَقَعَ
عَلَى ٱلْأَرْضِ إِلَّا بِإِذْنِهِۦٓ ۗ
إِنَّ ٱللَّهَ بِٱلنَّاسِ لَرَءُوفٌ رَّحِيمٌ

66\. It is He Who gave you life,
Will cause you to die,
And will again give you
Life: truly man is
A most ungrateful creature!

٦٦ وَهُوَ ٱلَّذِىٓ أَحْيَاكُمْ
ثُمَّ يُمِيتُكُمْ ثُمَّ يُحْيِيكُمْ ۗ
إِنَّ ٱلْإِنسَـٰنَ لَكَفُورٌ

67\. To every People have We
Appointed rites and ceremonies[2848]
Which they must follow:
Let them not then dispute
With thee on the matter,

٦٧ لِّكُلِّ أُمَّةٍ جَعَلْنَا مَنسَكًا هُمْ
نَاسِكُوهُ ۖ فَلَا يُنَـٰزِعُنَّكَ فِى ٱلْأَمْرِ ۚ

2845\. Each of the verses 22:61-63 mentioned two attributes of Allah with reference to the contents of that verse. This verse now sums up the whole argument, and the two attributes with which it closes sum up the idea by which we can understand Allah's goodness. Allah's loving kindness and mercies are not like those of human creatures who all depend upon one another, and often expect some kindness or recognition in return. Allah is above all wants and depends in no way whatever on His creatures. His mercies have therefore a special quality, which we cannot describe except by gratefully singing the praises of Allah. *Cf.* 2:267.

2846\. Land and sea have been made subject to man by Allah's command, so that man can develop his life freely on earth.

2847\. *Samā'* means (1) something high, (2) a roof, a ceiling, (3) the sky, the canopy of heaven, (4) cloud or rain. I understand the last meaning here, though most authorities seem to render it by some such word as "sky". If we understand rain here, we have a complete picture of the three elements in which man lives—land, air and sea. Rain is also appropriate for mention with Allah's kindness and mercy. He regulates the rain for man's benefit.

2848\. Rites and ceremonies may appear to be an unimportant matter compared with "weightier matters of the Law" and with the higher needs of man's spiritual nature. But they are necessary for social and religious organisation, and their effect on the individual himself is not to be despised. In any case, as they are visible external symbols, they give rise to the most heated controversies. Such controversies are to be deprecated. That does not mean that our rites and ceremonies are to be made light of. Those in Islam rest on the highest social and religious needs of man, and if we are convinced that we are on the Right Way, we should invite all to join us, without entering into controversies about such matters.

But do thou invite (them)
To thy Lord: for thou art
Assuredly on the Right Way.

وَٱدْعُ إِلَىٰ رَبِّكَ إِنَّكَ لَعَلَىٰ هُدًى مُّسْتَقِيمٍ

68. If they do wrangle with thee,
Say, "Allah knows best
What it is ye are doing."[2849]

٦٨ وَإِن جَٰدَلُوكَ فَقُلِ ٱللَّهُ أَعْلَمُ بِمَا تَعْمَلُونَ

69. "Allah will judge between you
On the Day of Judgement
Concerning the matters in which
Ye differ."[2850]

٦٩ ٱللَّهُ يَحْكُمُ بَيْنَكُمْ يَوْمَ ٱلْقِيَٰمَةِ
فِيمَا كُنتُمْ فِيهِ تَخْتَلِفُونَ

70. Knowest thou not that
Allah knows all that is
In heaven and on earth?
Indeed it is all
In a record, and that
Is easy for Allah.[2851]

٧٠ أَلَمْ تَعْلَمْ أَنَّ ٱللَّهَ يَعْلَمُ
مَا فِى ٱلسَّمَآءِ وَٱلْأَرْضِ
إِنَّ ذَٰلِكَ فِى كِتَٰبٍ إِنَّ ذَٰلِكَ عَلَى ٱللَّهِ يَسِيرٌ

71. Yet they worship, besides Allah,
Things for which no authority
Has been sent down to them,
And of which they have
(Really) no knowledge:
For those that do wrong
There is no helper.[2852]

٧١ وَيَعْبُدُونَ مِن دُونِ ٱللَّهِ مَا لَمْ يُنَزِّلْ بِهِۦ
سُلْطَٰنًا وَمَا لَيْسَ لَهُم بِهِۦ عِلْمٌ
وَمَا لِلظَّٰلِمِينَ مِن نَّصِيرٍ

72. When Our Clear Signs
Are rehearsed to them,
Thou wilt notice a denial[2853]
On the faces of the Unbelievers!
They nearly attack with violence
Those who rehearse Our Signs
To them. Say, "Shall I
Tell you of something

٧٢ وَإِذَا تُتْلَىٰ عَلَيْهِمْ ءَايَٰتُنَا بَيِّنَٰتٍ
تَعْرِفُ فِى وُجُوهِ ٱلَّذِينَ كَفَرُوا۟ ٱلْمُنكَرَ
يَكَادُونَ يَسْطُونَ بِٱلَّذِينَ يَتْلُونَ
عَلَيْهِمْ ءَايَٰتِنَا قُلْ أَفَأُنَبِّئُكُم

2849. 'You are only wrangling about matters about which you have no knowledge nor any deep religious feeling. The springs of your conduct are all open before Allah, and He will judge you.'

2850. 'You not only find fault with the very few and simple rites and ceremonies in Islam: you, outside Islam, have no rites and ceremonies which you are yourselves agreed upon, either as Christians or as Jews, or one compared with the other.'

2851. We human beings can only think of knowledge being accurately and permanently preserved by means of a record. Allah's knowledge has all the qualities of a perfect record, and it is moreover complete and comprehensive. This is not difficult for Him from whom flows all knowledge and intelligence.

2852. When plain common-sense shows the absurdity of false worship, behind which there is neither knowledge, intelligence, nor authority (quite the contrary), who or what can help the false misguided creatures who dishonour Allah by false worship?

2853. *Munkar*: (1) a refusal to accept something offered; (2) a denial of something stated or pointed out; (3) a feeling of disapproval or active aversion, or disgust.

(Far) worse than these Signs?[2854]
It is the Fire (of Hell)!
Allah has promised it
To the Unbelievers!
And evil is that destination!"

بِشَرٍّ مِّن ذَٰلِكُمُ
ٱلنَّارُ وَعَدَهَا ٱللَّهُ ٱلَّذِينَ كَفَرُوا۟
وَبِئْسَ ٱلْمَصِيرُ

SECTION 10.

73. O men! Here is
A parable set forth!
Listen to it! Those
On whom, besides Allah,
Ye call, cannot create
(Even) a fly, if they all
Met together for the purpose!
And if the fly should snatch
Away anything from them,
They would have no power
To release it from the fly.
Feeble are those who petition[2855]
And those whom they petition!

(٧٣) يَٰٓأَيُّهَا ٱلنَّاسُ
ضُرِبَ مَثَلٌ فَٱسْتَمِعُوا۟ لَهُۥٓ
إِنَّ ٱلَّذِينَ تَدْعُونَ مِن دُونِ ٱللَّهِ
لَن يَخْلُقُوا۟ ذُبَابًا وَلَوِ ٱجْتَمَعُوا۟ لَهُۥ
وَإِن يَسْلُبْهُمُ ٱلذُّبَابُ شَيْـًٔا لَّا يَسْتَنقِذُوهُ مِنْهُ
ضَعُفَ ٱلطَّالِبُ وَٱلْمَطْلُوبُ

74. No just estimate have they
Made of Allah: for Allah
Is He Who is strong
And able to carry out
His Will.[2856]

(٧٤) مَا قَدَرُوا۟ ٱللَّهَ حَقَّ قَدْرِهِۦٓ
إِنَّ ٱللَّهَ لَقَوِىٌّ عَزِيزٌ

75. Allah chooses Messengers[2857]
From angels and from men
For Allah is He Who hears
And sees (all things).[2858]

(٧٥) ٱللَّهُ يَصْطَفِى مِنَ ٱلْمَلَٰٓئِكَةِ
رُسُلًا وَمِنَ ٱلنَّاسِ إِنَّ ٱللَّهَ سَمِيعٌۢ بَصِيرٌ

76. He knows what is before them
And what is behind them:

(٧٦) يَعْلَمُ مَا بَيْنَ أَيْدِيهِمْ وَمَا خَلْفَهُمْ

2854. There is irony here. 'You think Allah's revelations and Signs are distasteful to you! There will be something far more distasteful to you if you do not repent! What do you say to the inevitable Punishment?'

2855. Both idols and their worshippers are poor, foolish, feeble creatures!

2856. No one who descends to the base forms of false worship can have a true idea of Allah. Allah has all power, and He is fully able to carry out every part of His Will and Plan. He is exalted above all in power and dignity. *Cf.* 22:40 and n. 2818 for the full meaning of *'Azīz*.

2857. Men are chosen as Messengers to ordinary men; for ordinary men will not be able to understand and be in communion with beings so refined as angels. But angels are sent as Messengers to Allah's chosen prophets, to convey the Message from time to time. In either case they are chosen by Allah, are subject to Allah's Will, and should not be worshipped as gods.

2858. As Allah regards the humblest of His creatures and hears their prayer, He sends men messengers out of their own brethren (see last note), and to such messengers He communicates the highest spiritual Truths through His angels.

And to Allah go back All questions (for decision).[2859]	وَإِلَى ٱللَّهِ تُرْجَعُ ٱلْأُمُورُ
77. O ye who believe! Bow down, prostrate yourselves, And adore your Lord; And do good; That ye may prosper.[2860]	يَٰٓأَيُّهَا ٱلَّذِينَ ءَامَنُوا۟ ٱرْكَعُوا۟ وَٱسْجُدُوا۟ وَٱعْبُدُوا۟ رَبَّكُمْ وَٱفْعَلُوا۟ ٱلْخَيْرَ لَعَلَّكُمْ تُفْلِحُونَ ﴿٧٧﴾
78. And strive in His cause As ye ought to strive, (With sincerity and under discipline).[2861] He has chosen you, and has Imposed no difficulties on you[2862] In religion; it is the cult Of your father Abraham. It is He Who has named You Muslims, both before[2863] And in this (Revelation); That the Messenger may be A witness for you, and ye Be witnesses for mankind![2864] So establish regular Prayer, Give regular Charity, And hold fast to Allah! He is your Protector— The best to protect And the Best to help!	﴿٧٨﴾ وَجَٰهِدُوا۟ فِى ٱللَّهِ حَقَّ جِهَادِهِۦ ۚ هُوَ ٱجْتَبَىٰكُمْ وَمَا جَعَلَ عَلَيْكُمْ فِى ٱلدِّينِ مِنْ حَرَجٍ ۚ مِّلَّةَ أَبِيكُمْ إِبْرَٰهِيمَ ۚ هُوَ سَمَّىٰكُمُ ٱلْمُسْلِمِينَ مِن قَبْلُ وَفِى هَٰذَا لِيَكُونَ ٱلرَّسُولُ شَهِيدًا عَلَيْكُمْ وَتَكُونُوا۟ شُهَدَآءَ عَلَى ٱلنَّاسِ ۚ فَأَقِيمُوا۟ ٱلصَّلَوٰةَ وَءَاتُوا۟ ٱلزَّكَوٰةَ وَٱعْتَصِمُوا۟ بِٱللَّهِ هُوَ مَوْلَىٰكُمْ ۖ فَنِعْمَ ٱلْمَوْلَىٰ وَنِعْمَ ٱلنَّصِيرُ

2859. Time, before or behind, may be of some importance to men. They may dispute as to what was the first Message, and what is the last Message. To Allah this question of priority and posteriority is of no consequence. All questions go back ultimately to him and are judged on their merits.

2860. *Prosper*: in a spiritual sense, both in this life and the Hereafter.

2861. As far as the striving is concerned with Jihād in the narrow sense, see the limitations in n. 204 to 2:190 and n. 205 to 2:191. But the words are perfectly general and apply to all true and unselfish striving for spiritual good.

2862. The Jews were hampered by many restrictions, and their religion was racial. Christianity, as originally preached, was a hermit religion: "sell whatsoever thou hast" (Mark x. 21): "take no thought for the morrow" (Matt. vi. 34). Islam, as originally preached, gives freedom and full play to man's faculties of every kind. It is universal, and claims to date from Adam: father Abraham is mentioned as the great Ancestor of those among whom Islam was first preached (Jews, Christians, and Arab Quraysh).

2863. *Before*: see Abraham's prayer in 2:128. *In this revelation*: in this very verse, as well as in other places.

2864. See 2:143, and notes 143 and 144. As the Prophet is a guide and exemplar among us, so Muslims ought to be exemplars amongst mankind. The best witness to Allah's Truth are those who show its light in their lives.

INTRODUCTION TO SŪRAH 23—*AL MU'MINŪN*

This Sūrah deals with the virtues which are the seed-bed of Faith, especially in an environment in which Truth is denied and its votaries insulted and persecuted. But Truth is One and must prevail. Those who do wrong will be filled with vain regrets when it is too late for repentance.

It belongs to the late Makkan period.

Summary.—Faith, coupled with humility in prayer, charity, abstinence from vanity and from indulgence in appetites, and strict probity, must lead to final success, even though people mock and accuse the righteous of false motives, as did the contemporaries of Noah, of Moses, and of Jesus (23:1-50, and C. 154).

The prophets of Allah and the righteous form one Brotherhood, but those who make schisms and refuse to believe have ample evidence pointing to Truth and the goodness and greatness of Allah (23:51-92, and C. 155).

Evil must be repelled by goodness and faith in Allah; for the future life is sure, and those who disbelieve will wish for another chance when it is too late (23:93-118, and C. 156).

C. 154.—Faith leads to humility, avoidance
(23:1-50.) Of vanity in word and deed, charity,
Continence, faithful observance
Of trusts and covenants, and devout
Approach to Allah—surest steps
To Bliss. Man carries in himself
Proofs of Allah's Providence; the same
Story is told if he looks at nature
Around him; and the long line of Teachers
Sent by Allah shows Allah's special care
Of humanity. What though they were
Rejected and scorned, maligned and persecuted?
Allah's Truth won through, as it always will.

Sūrah 23.

Al Mu'minūn (The Believers)

In the name of Allah, Most Gracious,
Most Merciful.

بِسْمِ اللَّهِ الرَّحْمَٰنِ الرَّحِيمِ

18/30

1. The Believers must
(Eventually) win through—[2865]

قَدْ أَفْلَحَ الْمُؤْمِنُونَ ١

2. Those who humble themselves[2866]
In their prayers;

الَّذِينَ هُمْ فِي صَلَاتِهِمْ خَاشِعُونَ ٢

3. Who avoid vain talk;

وَالَّذِينَ هُمْ عَنِ اللَّغْوِ مُعْرِضُونَ ٣

4. Who are active in deeds
Of charity;

وَالَّذِينَ هُمْ لِلزَّكَاةِ فَاعِلُونَ ٤

5. Who abstain from sex,[2867]

وَالَّذِينَ هُمْ لِفُرُوجِهِمْ حَافِظُونَ ٥

6. Except with those joined
To them in the marriage bond,
Or (the captives) whom
Their right hands possess—[2868]
For (in their case) they are
Free from blame,

إِلَّا عَلَىٰ أَزْوَاجِهِمْ ٦
أَوْ مَا مَلَكَتْ أَيْمَانُهُمْ
فَإِنَّهُمْ غَيْرُ مَلُومِينَ

7. But those whose desires exceed
Those limits are transgressors—

فَمَنِ ابْتَغَىٰ وَرَاءَ ذَٰلِكَ فَأُولَٰئِكَ هُمُ الْعَادُونَ ٧

2865. *Aflaḥa*: win through, prosper, succeed, achieve their aims or obtain salvation from sorrow and all evil. This verse connects on with verses 10 and 11 below. The success or victory may come in this world, but is certain and lasting in the world to come.

2866. Humility in prayer as regards (1) their estimate of their own worth in Allah's presence, (2) as regards their estimate of their own powers or strength unless they are helped by Allah, and (3) as regards the petitions they offer to Allah.

2867. The Muslim must guard himself against every kind of sex abuse or sex perversion. The new psychology associated with the name of Freud traces many of our hidden motives to sex, and it is common knowledge that our refinement or degradation may be measured by the hidden workings of our sex instincts. But even the natural and lawful exercise of sex is restricted to the marriage bond, under which the rights of both parties are duly regulated and maintained.

2868. This is further explained and amplified in 4:25. It will be seen there that the status of a captive when raised to freedom by marriage is the same as that of a free woman as regards her rights, but more lenient as regards the punishment to be inflicted if she falls from virtue.

8. Those who faithfully observe
Their trusts and covenants;[2869]

٨ وَٱلَّذِينَ هُمْ لِأَمَـٰنَـٰتِهِمْ وَعَهْدِهِمْ رَٰعُونَ

9. And who (strictly) guard[2870]
Their prayers—

٩ وَٱلَّذِينَ هُمْ عَلَىٰ صَلَوَٰتِهِمْ يُحَافِظُونَ

10. These will be the heirs,[2871]

١٠ أُوْلَـٰٓئِكَ هُمُ ٱلْوَٰرِثُونَ

11. Who will inherit Paradise:
They will dwell therein
(Forever).

١١ ٱلَّذِينَ يَرِثُونَ ٱلْفِرْدَوْسَ
هُمْ فِيهَا خَـٰلِدُونَ

12. Man We did create
From a quintessence (of clay);[2872]

١٢ وَلَقَدْ خَلَقْنَا ٱلْإِنسَـٰنَ مِن سُلَـٰلَةٍ مِّن طِينٍ

13. Then We placed him
As (a drop of) sperm
In a place of rest,[2873]
Firmly fixed;

١٣ ثُمَّ جَعَلْنَـٰهُ نُطْفَةً
فِي قَرَارٍ مَّكِينٍ

2869. Trusts may be express or implied. Express trusts are those where property is entrusted or duties are assigned by some one to some other whom he trusts, to carry out either immediately or in specified contingencies, such as death. Implied trusts arise out of power, or position, or opportunity; e.g., a king holds his kingdom on trust from Allah for his subjects: the Afghan official phrase for their kingdom used to be *Dawlat-i-Khudā-dād*('God-given kingdom'). The subject of covenants, express and implied, has been discussed in n. 682 to 5:1. Covenants create obligations, and express and implied trusts and covenants taken together cover the whole field of obligations.

2870. In verse 2 we were directed to the spirit of humility and earnestness in our prayers. Here we are told how necessary the habit of regular prayer is to our spiritual well-being and developement, as it brings us closer to Allah, and thus sums up the light of the seven jewels of our Faith, *viz.*: (1) humility, (2) avoidance of vanity, (3) charity, (4) sex purity, (5) fidelity to trusts, and (6) to covenants, and (7) an earnest desire to get closer to Allah.

2871. *Cf.* 21:105, where it is said that the righteous will inherit the earth. In the first verse of this Sūrah, the final success or victory is referred to. Truth will prevail even on this earth, but it may not be for any individual men of righteousness to see it: it may be in the time of their heirs and successors. But in the life to come, there is no doubt that every man will see the fruit of his life here, and the righteous will *inherit* heaven, in the sense that they will attain it after their death here.

2872. In this beautiful passage, Allah's creative work, as far as man is concerned, is recapitulated, in order to show man's real position in this life, and the certainty of the future: to which he was referred for his reward in verses 10-11 above. For the various stages of creation, see n. 120 to 2:117. Here we are not concerned with the earliest stage, the creation of primeval matter out of nothing. It is also a process of creation when inorganic matter becomes living matter. Thus inorganic constituents of the earth are absorbed into living matter by way of food and living matter reproduces itself by means of sperm. This is deposited in the ovum and fertilises it and rests for a time in security in the mother's womb. The first change in the fertilised ovum is the conversion into a sort of clot of thickly congealed blood; the zygote cells grow by segmentation; then the mass gradually assumes shape in its growth as a foetus. From the lump develop bones and flesh and organs and a nervous system. So far man's growth is like that of an animal, but a further process takes place which makes the infant animal into the infant man. This is the breathing of Allah's spirit into him (15:29): that process need not be precisely at a given point of time. It may be a continuous process parallel to that of physical growth. The child is born: it grows; it decays and dies; but after death another chapter opens for the individual, and it is to remind us of this most momentous chapter that the previous stages are recapitulated.

2873. The growth in the foetal stage is silent and unseen. The foetus is protected in the mother's womb like a king in a castle; it is firmly fixed, and gets the protection of the mother's body, on which it depends for its own growth until birth.

14. Then We made the sperm
Into a clot of congealed blood;
Then of that clot We made
A (foetus) lump; then We
Made out of that lump
Bones and clothed the bones
With flesh; then We developed
Out of it another creature.[2874]
So blessed be Allah,
The Best to create!

١٤ ثُمَّ خَلَقْنَا النُّطْفَةَ عَلَقَةً
فَخَلَقْنَا الْعَلَقَةَ مُضْغَةً فَخَلَقْنَا
الْمُضْغَةَ عِظَامًا فَكَسَوْنَا الْعِظَامَ
لَحْمًا ثُمَّ أَنشَأْنَاهُ خَلْقًا آخَرَ
فَتَبَارَكَ اللَّهُ أَحْسَنُ الْخَالِقِينَ

15. After that, at length
Ye will die.[2875]

١٥ ثُمَّ إِنَّكُم بَعْدَ ذَٰلِكَ لَمَيِّتُونَ

16. Again, on the Day
Of Judgement, will ye be
Raised up.

١٦ ثُمَّ إِنَّكُمْ يَوْمَ الْقِيَامَةِ تُبْعَثُونَ

17. And We have made, above you,
Seven tracts;[2876] and We
Are never unmindful
Of (Our) Creation.[2877]

١٧ وَلَقَدْ خَلَقْنَا فَوْقَكُمْ سَبْعَ طَرَائِقَ
وَمَا كُنَّا عَنِ الْخَلْقِ غَافِلِينَ

18. And We send down water
From the sky according to[2878]
(Due) measure, and We cause it

١٨ وَأَنزَلْنَا مِنَ السَّمَاءِ مَاءً بِقَدَرٍ

2874. From a mere animal, we now consider man as man. Is it not a Sign of wonder in itself that from dry dust (*turāb*, 22:5) or inorganic matter should be made protoplasm (moist clay or organic matter); from it should grow a new animal life; and out of it should grow human life, with all its capacities and responsibilities? Man carries within himself Signs of Allah's wisdom and power, and he can see them every day in the universe around him.

2875. Our physical death in this mortal life seems to make a break. But if it were the end of all, our life becomes meaningless. Our own instinct tells us that it cannot be so, and Allah assures us that there will be a resurrection for judgement.

2876. *Tarā'iq*: tracts, roads, orbits, or paths of motion in the visible heavens. These seven are regular and clearly marked to our eyes, in the immense space that we see around us. We must go to astronomy to form any plausible theories of these motions. But their simplest observation gives us a sublime view of beauty, order, and grandeur in the universe. The assurance given in the next clause, that Allah cares for us and all His Creation, calls our attention to Allah's goodness, which is further illustrated in the subsequent verses.

2877. Allah's care for His Creation is ceaseless. A few examples of His care for our physical well-being are given in verses 18-22, and for our spiritual well-being, in Sections 2 to 5.

2878. Normally the rain comes well distributed; it soaks into the soil; the moisture is retained for a long time in all high grounds; it soaks and penetrates through many layers of soil and forms the architecture of physical geography; the retentive powers of higher soil enable rivers to flow perennially even where, as in India, the rainfall is seasonal and confined to a few months in the year. Another form in which water comes down from the sky according to due measure is in snow and hail: these also have their place in the economy of air and soil. Were it not for snow and glaciers in the higher mountain regions, some of the rivers would fail in their abundant flow. As wonderful as the supply of water and moisture is its drainage. It returns to the sea and air in all sorts of ways, and the formation of mist and clouds repeats the cycle. Were it not for the drainage and the clearance of the waters, we should have floods and waterlogging, as happens when the normal processes of nature are temporarily obstructed. The same thing happens when the rain comes down in other than due measure. These abnormal conditions also have their value. But how grateful should man be for Allah's gifts in the ceaseless processes of nature on such an enormous scale!

To soak in the soil;
And We certainly are able
To drain it off (with ease).

فَأَسْكَنَّٰهُ فِى ٱلْأَرْضِ ۖ وَإِنَّا عَلَىٰ ذَهَابٍۭ بِهِۦ لَقَٰدِرُونَ

19. With it We grow for you
Gardens of date palms
And vines; in them have ye
Abundant fruits: and of them
Ye eat (and have enjoyment)—[2879]

١٩ فَأَنشَأْنَا لَكُم بِهِۦ جَنَّٰتٍ مِّن نَّخِيلٍ وَأَعْنَٰبٍ
لَّكُمْ فِيهَا فَوَٰكِهُ كَثِيرَةٌ وَمِنْهَا تَأْكُلُونَ

20. Also a tree springing
Out of Mount Sinai,[2880]
Which produces oil,
And relish for those
Who use it for food.

٢٠ وَشَجَرَةً تَخْرُجُ مِن طُورِ سَيْنَآءَ
تَنۢبُتُ بِٱلدُّهْنِ وَصِبْغٍ لِّلْءَاكِلِينَ

21. And in cattle (too) ye
Have an instructive example:[2881]
From within their bodies
We produce (milk) for you
To drink; there are, in them,
(Besides), numerous (other)
Benefits for you;
And of their (meat) ye eat;

٢١ وَإِنَّ لَكُمْ فِى ٱلْأَنْعَٰمِ لَعِبْرَةً ۖ
نُّسْقِيكُم مِّمَّا فِى بُطُونِهَا
وَلَكُمْ فِيهَا مَنَٰفِعُ كَثِيرَةٌ
وَمِنْهَا تَأْكُلُونَ

22. And on them, as well as
In ships, ye ride.

٢٢ وَعَلَيْهَا وَعَلَى ٱلْفُلْكِ تُحْمَلُونَ

SECTION 2

23. (Further, We sent a long line
Of prophets for your
instruction).[2882]
We sent Noah to his people:[2883]

٢٣ وَلَقَدْ أَرْسَلْنَا نُوحًا إِلَىٰ قَوْمِهِۦ

2879. *Cf.* 7:19 and n. 776 to 5:69.

2880. For Arabia the best olives grow round about Mount Sinai. The fig, the olive, Mount Sinai, and the sacred city of Makkah are mentioned together in association in 95:1-3, where we shall consider the mystic meaning. Olive oil is an ingredient in medicinal ointments and in ointments used for religious ceremonies such as the consecration of kings. It has thus a symbolic meaning. If used for food, the olive has a delicious flavour. *Cf.* also 24:35, where the olive is called a Blessed Tree, and n. 3000.

2881. *'Ibrah*: the root meaning of the verb is "to interpret, to expound, or instruct', as in 12:43; the noun means an interpretation, or example or Sign that instructs, as here and in 16:66, or gives a warning, as in 3:13. From cattle we get milk and meat; also from their skins we make leather for shoes, boots, straps, saddlery, and numerous other uses; from camel's hair and sheep's wool we weave cloth, hangings, carpets, etc.: from the horns of cattle we make cups and articles of ornament or use; and camels, horses, donkeys, mules, etc., are used for riding, carrying loads, or drawing vehicles.

2882. The material gifts having been mentioned, which we receive from a wise and kindly Providence, our attention is now directed to Allah's Providence in spiritual matters. He sent Teachers to instruct and guide us, and though they were mocked, rejected, and accused of falsehood and selfishness, they were protected by Allah, and Allah's Truth at length prevailed.

2883. "People" here is almost equivalent to "contemporaries".

He said, "O my people!
Worship Allah! Ye have
No other god but Him.
Will ye not hear (Him)?"[2884]

فَقَالَ يَٰقَوْمِ ٱعْبُدُوا۟ ٱللَّهَ
مَا لَكُم مِّنْ إِلَٰهٍ غَيْرُهُۥٓ ۚ أَفَلَا تَتَّقُونَ

24. The chiefs of the Unbelievers
Among his people said:
"He is no more than a man
Like yourselves: his wish is
To assert his superiority
Over you: if Allah had wished[2885]
(To send messengers),
He could have sent down
Angels: never did we hear
Such a thing (as he says),
Among our ancestors of old."

٢٤ فَقَالَ ٱلْمَلَؤُا۟ ٱلَّذِينَ كَفَرُوا۟
مِن قَوْمِهِۦ مَا هَٰذَآ إِلَّا بَشَرٌ مِّثْلُكُمْ
يُرِيدُ أَن يَتَفَضَّلَ عَلَيْكُمْ
وَلَوْ شَآءَ ٱللَّهُ لَأَنزَلَ مَلَٰٓئِكَةً
مَّا سَمِعْنَا بِهَٰذَا فِىٓ ءَابَآئِنَا ٱلْأَوَّلِينَ

25. (And some said): "He is [2878]
Only a man possessed:
Wait (and have patience)
With him for a time."

٢٥ إِنْ هُوَ إِلَّا رَجُلٌۢ بِهِۦ جِنَّةٌ
فَتَرَبَّصُوا۟ بِهِۦ حَتَّىٰ حِينٍ

26. (Noah) said: "O my Lord!
Help me; for that they
Accuse me of falsehood!"

٢٦ قَالَ رَبِّ ٱنصُرْنِى بِمَا كَذَّبُونِ

27. So We inspired him
(With this message); "Construct
The Ark within Our sight[2887]
And under Our guidance: then
When comes Our command,
And the fountains of the earth[2888]
Gush forth, take thou on board
Pairs of every species, male[2889]
And female, and thy family—

٢٧ فَأَوْحَيْنَآ إِلَيْهِ أَنِ ٱصْنَعِ ٱلْفُلْكَ
بِأَعْيُنِنَا وَوَحْيِنَا فَإِذَا جَآءَ أَمْرُنَا
وَفَارَ ٱلتَّنُّورُ ۙ فَٱسْلُكْ فِيهَا مِن
كُلٍّ زَوْجَيْنِ ٱثْنَيْنِ وَأَهْلَكَ

2884. *Cf.* 7:59. To fear Allah is to lead righteous lives and eschew evil.

2885. They attribute altogether wrong motives to him (such as they would have actuated themselves), in saying that he was trying to establish his own personal superiority over them by his preaching. Then they accuse him of falsehood in claiming to bring a message of Allah. "If", they say, "Allah had wished to send us messengers, He would have sent angels, not a man like ourselves and from among ourselves. Our ancestors did not worship One God: why should we?"

2886. I construe this to be a speech of another group among them. They thought he was mad, and best left alone. His madness would run out, or he would come to an evil end.

2887. *Cf.* this whole passage with 11:35-48, and notes thereon.

2888. See n. 1533 to 11:40, where the word *Tannūr* is explained.

2889. See n. 1534 to 11:40.

Except those of them
Against whom the Word
Has already gone forth;[2890]
And address Me not
In favour of the wrongdoers:
For they shall be drowned
(In the Flood).

إِلَّا مَن سَبَقَ عَلَيْهِ ٱلْقَوْلُ مِنْهُمْ
وَلَا تُخَٰطِبْنِى فِى ٱلَّذِينَ ظَلَمُوٓا۟
إِنَّهُم مُّغْرَقُونَ

28. And when thou hast embarked[2891]
On the Ark—thou and those
With thee—say: "Praise be
To Allah, Who has saved us
From the people who do wrong."

٢٨ فَإِذَا ٱسْتَوَيْتَ أَنتَ وَمَن مَّعَكَ عَلَى ٱلْفُلْكِ
فَقُلِ ٱلْحَمْدُ لِلَّهِ ٱلَّذِى نَجَّىٰنَا مِنَ ٱلْقَوْمِ ٱلظَّٰلِمِينَ

29. And say: "O my Lord![2892]
Enable me to disembark
With Thy blessing: for Thou
Art the Best to enable (us)
To disembark."

٢٩ وَقُل رَّبِّ أَنزِلْنِى مُنزَلًا مُّبَارَكًا
وَأَنتَ خَيْرُ ٱلْمُنزِلِينَ

30. Verily in this there are
Signs (for men to understand);
(Thus) do We try (men).[2893]

٣٠ إِنَّ فِى ذَٰلِكَ لَءَايَٰتٍ وَإِن كُنَّا لَمُبْتَلِينَ

31. Then We raised after them
Another generation.

٣١ ثُمَّ أَنشَأْنَا مِنۢ بَعْدِهِمْ قَرْنًا ءَاخَرِينَ

32. And We sent to them
A messenger from among
themselves,[2894]
(Saying), "Worship Allah!
Ye have no other god
But Him. Will ye not
Fear (Him)?"

٣٢ فَأَرْسَلْنَا فِيهِمْ رَسُولًا مِّنْهُمْ
أَنِ ٱعْبُدُوا۟ ٱللَّهَ مَا لَكُم مِّنْ إِلَٰهٍ غَيْرُهُۥٓ
أَفَلَا تَتَّقُونَ

2890. See n. 1535 to 11:40.

2891. For *istawā* see 1386 to 10:3. Here the meaning is: mounted on board, ascended, embarked.

2892. This second prayer was inspired when the Flood subsided, and the time came for disembarkation.

2893. Noah's contemporaries had all sorts of chances and warnings, but they refused to believe and perished. But Allah's Truth survived, and it went to the next and succeeding generations. Will not mankind understand?

2894. If this refers to any particular prophet, it must be Hūd whose mission was to the 'Ad people, or to Ṣāliḥ, whose mission was to the Thamūd people. That is the sequence after Noah in S. 11:50-60 and 61-68. But I think that as the name is not mentioned, we are to understand in general the type of post-Flood prophets until we come later on to Moses and Jesus. The object here is not to recount the stories, but to show that the resistance of the wicked made no difference to the triumph of Allah's Holy Truth.

SECTION 3.

33. And the chiefs
Of his people, who disbelieved
And denied the Meeting
In the Hereafter, and on whom
We had bestowed the good things
Of this life, said: "He is
No more than a man
Like yourselves: he eats
Of that of which ye eat,
And drinks of what ye drink.

٣٣ وَقَالَ ٱلْمَلَأُ مِن قَوْمِهِ
ٱلَّذِينَ كَفَرُوا۟ وَكَذَّبُوا۟ بِلِقَآءِ ٱلْءَاخِرَةِ
وَأَتْرَفْنَٰهُمْ فِى ٱلْحَيَوٰةِ ٱلدُّنْيَا
مَا هَٰذَآ إِلَّا بَشَرٌ مِّثْلُكُمْ يَأْكُلُ
مِمَّا تَأْكُلُونَ مِنْهُ وَيَشْرَبُ مِمَّا تَشْرَبُونَ

34. "If ye obey a man
Like yourselves, behold,
It is certain ye will be lost.[2895]

٣٤ وَلَئِنْ أَطَعْتُم بَشَرًا مِّثْلَكُمْ
إِنَّكُمْ إِذًا لَّخَٰسِرُونَ

35. "Does he promise that
When ye die and become dust
And bones, ye shall be
Brought forth (again)?

٣٥ أَيَعِدُكُمْ أَنَّكُمْ إِذَا مِتُّمْ وَكُنتُمْ تُرَابًا
وَعِظَٰمًا أَنَّكُم مُّخْرَجُونَ

36. "Far, very far is that
Which ye are promised!

٣٦ هَيْهَاتَ هَيْهَاتَ لِمَا تُوعَدُونَ

37. "There is nothing but
Our life in this world!
We shall die and we live![2896]
But we shall never
Be raised up again!

٣٧ إِنْ هِىَ إِلَّا حَيَاتُنَا ٱلدُّنْيَا
نَمُوتُ وَنَحْيَا وَمَا نَحْنُ بِمَبْعُوثِينَ

38. "He is only a man
Who invents a lie
Against Allah, but we
Are not the ones
To believe in him!"[2897]

٣٨ إِنْ هُوَ إِلَّا رَجُلٌ ٱفْتَرَىٰ عَلَى ٱللَّهِ
كَذِبًا وَمَا نَحْنُ لَهُۥ بِمُؤْمِنِينَ

39. (The prophet) said:
"O my Lord! help me:

٣٩ قَالَ رَبِّ ٱنصُرْنِى

2895. The type of the narrow Sybarite, who enjoys the good things of this life, denies a future life, and is jealous of any one who presumes to widen his horizon, is here described in a few masterly strokes. He is bored by any mention of the serious things beyond his ken. What good is it, he says, to talk about the future? Enjoy the present. The gain is all in the present: the loss is all in the future.

2896. They seem to say: "There is no future life: that we shall die is certain; that we have this life is certain: some die, some are born, some live; and so the cycle continues: but how can dead men be raised to life?"

2897. "He is only a fool, and invents things, and attributes them to Allah's inspiration! We are too wise to believe such things!"

For that they accuse me
Of falsehood."[2898]

بِمَا كَذَّبُونِ

40. (Allah) said: "In but
A little while, they
Are sure to be sorry!"[2899]

قَالَ عَمَّا قَلِيلٍ لَّيُصْبِحُنَّ نَٰدِمِينَ ﴿٤٠﴾

41. Then the Blast[2900] overtook them
With justice, and We made them
As rubbish of dead leaves[2901]
(Floating on the stream of Time)!
So away with the people
Who do wrong!

فَأَخَذَتْهُمُ ٱلصَّيْحَةُ بِٱلْحَقِّ
فَجَعَلْنَٰهُمْ غُثَآءً
فَبُعْدًا لِّلْقَوْمِ ٱلظَّٰلِمِينَ ﴿٤١﴾

42. Then We raised after them
Other generations.

ثُمَّ أَنشَأْنَا مِنۢ بَعْدِهِمْ قُرُونًا ءَاخَرِينَ ﴿٤٢﴾

43. No people can hasten
Their term, nor can they
Delay (it).

مَا تَسْبِقُ مِنْ أُمَّةٍ أَجَلَهَا وَمَا يَسْتَـْٔخِرُونَ ﴿٤٣﴾

44. Then sent We Our messengers
In succession: every time
There came to a people
Their messenger, they accused him
Of falsehood: so We made
Them follow each other
(In punishment): We made them
As a tale (that is told):[2902]
So away with a people
That will not believe!

ثُمَّ أَرْسَلْنَا رُسُلَنَا تَتْرَا
كُلَّ مَا جَآءَ أُمَّةً رَّسُولُهَا كَذَّبُوهُ
فَأَتْبَعْنَا بَعْضَهُم بَعْضًا وَجَعَلْنَٰهُمْ أَحَادِيثَ
فَبُعْدًا لِّقَوْمٍ لَّا يُؤْمِنُونَ ﴿٤٤﴾

45. Then We sent Moses
And his brother Aaron,
With Our Signs and
Authority manifest,[2903]

ثُمَّ أَرْسَلْنَا مُوسَىٰ وَأَخَاهُ هَٰرُونَ
بِـَٔايَٰتِنَا وَسُلْطَٰنٍ مُّبِينٍ ﴿٤٥﴾

2898. See above, 23:26. Every prophet is maligned and persecuted: it is always the same story with them, told in different ways.

2899. When the Punishment comes, they will be sorry for themselves, but it will be too late then.

2900. See 11:66, and notes 1563 and 1561.

2901. *Ghuthā'*: rubbish of dead leaves, or scum floating on a torrent.

2902. Their habitations and their organisation have been wiped out. What remains is merely a vague story of their existence, a tale that is told. Where their name remains, which is not always the case, it is only a byword, suggesting all that is unstable and ephemeral—"to point a moral and adorn a tale".

2903. Moses and Aaron had a twofold mission: (1) to Pharaoh and his Court, which failed because of Egyptian arrogance; (2) to the Israelites, for whom the Law was received on Mount Sinai, but they repeatedly rebelled against Allah. In both cases there were miracles ("Clear Signs") and other proofs which showed that they came at Allah's command and were inspired by His authority.

46. To Pharaoh and his Chiefs:
But these behaved insolently:
They were an arrogant people.

٤٦ إِلَىٰ فِرْعَوْنَ وَمَلَإِيْهِۦ فَٱسْتَكْبَرُوا۟ وَكَانُوا۟ قَوْمًا عَالِينَ

47. They said: "Shall we believe
In two men like ourselves?
And their people are subject[2904]
To us!"

٤٧ فَقَالُوٓا۟ أَنُؤْمِنُ لِبَشَرَيْنِ مِثْلِنَا وَقَوْمُهُمَا لَنَا عَٰبِدُونَ

48. So they accused them
Of falsehood, and they became
Of those who were destroyed.

٤٨ فَكَذَّبُوهُمَا فَكَانُوا۟ مِنَ ٱلْمُهْلَكِينَ

49. And We gave Moses
The Book, in order that
They might receive guidance.[2905]

٤٩ وَلَقَدْ ءَاتَيْنَا مُوسَى ٱلْكِتَٰبَ لَعَلَّهُمْ يَهْتَدُونَ

50. And We made
The son of Mary
And his mother
As a sign:[2906]
We gave them both
Shelter on high ground,
Affording rest and security
And furnished with springs.[2907]

٥٠ وَجَعَلْنَا ٱبْنَ مَرْيَمَ وَأُمَّهُۥٓ ءَايَةً وَءَاوَيْنَٰهُمَآ إِلَىٰ رَبْوَةٍ ذَاتِ قَرَارٍ وَمَعِينٍ

C. 155.—The Brotherhood of Truth is one in all ages:
(23:51-92.) It is narrow men who create sects.
Let them not think that the goods
Of this world can shield them from evil
Or its consequences. Allah's Truth and His Messenger
Can be known to all: for He in His Mercy
Has given us faculties and judgement, if we
Would but use them. The Message is not
New: all Creation proclaims it: High
Above all is the Lord of Glory Supreme!

2904. Racial arrogance made the Egyptians say, 'These men belong to a race which we hold in subjection as our slaves: how can we accept them as messengers of Allah?'

2905. Here the reference is to the second part of the mission of Moses, that to the Israelites, which the Israelites rendered ineffective by their want of faith. See n. 2903 above.

2906. The virgin birth of Jesus was a miracle both for him and his mother. She was falsely accused of unchastity, but the child Jesus triumphantly vindicated her by his own miracles (19:27-33), and showed by his life the meanness of the calumny against his mother.

2907. There is no need to look far for the place where mother and child were given secure shelter. It is described in 19:22-26. It was the place to which she withdrew to be delivered when the time drew near. There was a fruitful palm tree, evidently on high ground, for beneath it flowed a spring. She retired there in seclusion, and she and her child rested there until it was time for her to go to her people with her child.

SECTION 4.

51. O ye messengers! enjoy[2908]
(All) things good and pure,
And work righteousness;
For I am well-acquainted
With (all) that ye do.

٥١ يَٰٓأَيُّهَا ٱلرُّسُلُ كُلُوا۟ مِنَ ٱلطَّيِّبَٰتِ
وَٱعْمَلُوا۟ صَٰلِحًا ۖ إِنِّى بِمَا تَعْمَلُونَ عَلِيمٌ

52. And verily this Brotherhood
Of yours is a single
Brotherhood.[2909]
And I am your Lord
And Cherisher: therefore
Fear Me (and no other).

٥٢ وَإِنَّ هَٰذِهِۦٓ أُمَّتُكُمْ أُمَّةً وَٰحِدَةً
وَأَنَا۠ رَبُّكُمْ فَٱتَّقُونِ

53. But people have cut off
Their affair (of unity),
Between them, into sects:
Each party rejoices in that
Which is with itself.[2910]

٥٣ فَتَقَطَّعُوٓا۟ أَمْرَهُم بَيْنَهُمْ زُبُرًا ۖ
كُلُّ حِزْبٍۭ بِمَا لَدَيْهِمْ فَرِحُونَ

54. But leave them
In their confused ignorance
For a time.

٥٤ فَذَرْهُمْ فِى غَمْرَتِهِمْ حَتَّىٰ حِينٍ

55. Do they think that because
We have granted them abundance
Of wealth and sons,

٥٥ أَيَحْسَبُونَ أَنَّمَا نُمِدُّهُم بِهِۦ مِن مَّالٍ وَبَنِينَ

56. We would hasten them
On in every good? Nay
They do not understand.[2911]

٥٦ نُسَارِعُ لَهُمْ فِى ٱلْخَيْرَٰتِ ۚ بَل لَّا يَشْعُرُونَ

57. Verily those who live
In awe for fear of their Lord;

٥٧ إِنَّ ٱلَّذِينَ هُم مِّنْ خَشْيَةِ رَبِّهِم مُّشْفِقُونَ

58. Those who believe
In the Signs of their Lord;

٥٨ وَٱلَّذِينَ هُم بِـَٔايَٰتِ رَبِّهِمْ يُؤْمِنُونَ

2908. Literally, "eat". See n. 776 to 5:69. The prophets of Allah do not pose as ascetics, but receive gratefully all Allah's gifts, and show their gratitude by their righteous lives. (R).

2909. *Cf.* 21:92-93. All prophets form one Brotherhood: their Message is one, and their religion and teaching are one: they serve the One True God, Who loves and cherishes them; and they owe their duty to Him and Him alone.

2910. The people who began to trade on the names of the prophets cut off that unity and made sects; and each sect rejoices in its own narrow doctrine, instead of taking the universal teaching of Unity from Allah. But this sectarian confusion is of man's making. It will last for a time, but the rays of Truth and Unity will finally dissipate it.

2911. Worldly wealth, power, and influence may be but trials. Let not their possessors think that they are in themselves things that will necessarily bring them happiness.

59. Those who join not (in worship)
Partners with their Lord;

٥٩ وَٱلَّذِينَ هُم بِرَبِّهِمۡ لَا يُشۡرِكُونَ

60. And those who dispense
Their charity with their hearts[2912]
Full of fear, because
They will return to their Lord—

٦٠ وَٱلَّذِينَ يُؤۡتُونَ مَآ ءَاتَواْ وَّقُلُوبُهُمۡ
وَجِلَةٌ أَنَّهُمۡ إِلَىٰ رَبِّهِمۡ رَٰجِعُونَ

61. It is these who hasten
In every good work,
And these who are
Foremost in them.

٦١ أُوْلَٰٓئِكَ يُسَٰرِعُونَ فِي ٱلۡخَيۡرَٰتِ
وَهُمۡ لَهَا سَٰبِقُونَ

62. On no soul do We
Place a burden greater
Than it can bear:[2913]
Before Us is a record
Which clearly shows the truth.[2914]
They will never be wronged.

٦٢ وَلَا نُكَلِّفُ نَفۡسًا إِلَّا وُسۡعَهَاۖ
وَلَدَيۡنَا كِتَٰبٌ يَنطِقُ بِٱلۡحَقِّ
وَهُمۡ لَا يُظۡلَمُونَ

63. But their hearts are
In confused ignorance[2915]
Of this; and there are,
Besides that, deeds of theirs,[2916]
Which they will (continue)
To do—

٦٣ بَلۡ قُلُوبُهُمۡ فِي غَمۡرَةٍ مِّنۡ هَٰذَا
وَلَهُمۡ أَعۡمَٰلٌ مِّن دُونِ ذَٰلِكَ
هُمۡ لَهَا عَٰمِلُونَ

64. Until, when We seize
In Punishment those of them
Who received the good things
Of this world, behold,
They will groan in supplication!

٦٤ حَتَّىٰٓ إِذَآ أَخَذۡنَا مُتۡرَفِيهِم
بِٱلۡعَذَابِ إِذَا هُمۡ يَجۡـَٔرُونَ

65. (It will be said):
"Groan not in supplication
This day; for ye shall
Certainly not be helped by Us.

٦٥ لَا تَجۡـَٔرُواْ ٱلۡيَوۡمَۖ
إِنَّكُم مِّنَّا لَا تُنصَرُونَ

2912. Their hearts are full of reverence for Allah and fear lest their charity or their hearts be not good enough for acceptance before their Lord; for they have the certainty of a future life, in which they will stand before the Judgement Seat. They fear for their own worthiness, but they hope in Faith.

2913. *Cf.* 2:286 and n. 339.

2914. The record speaks clearly, and shows exactly what each soul has done and thought, and what is due to it in justice. The worst will receive full justice. The best will receive far more than their due: 28:84.

2915. This is said of the Unbelievers who rejected Faith and rejoiced in the vanities of this world. In spite of the proclamation of Truth, they are doubtful of the future Life and Judgement.

2916. In addition to their rejection of Faith, they have against them positive deeds of wrongdoing, from which, on account of their contempt of the Light from Allah, they will not desist until they are sharply pulled up for punishment: and then repentance will be too late!

66. "My Signs used to be
Rehearsed to you, but ye
Used to turn back
On your heels—

٦٦ قَدْ كَانَتْ ءَايَٰتِى تُتْلَىٰ عَلَيْكُمْ
فَكُنتُمْ عَلَىٰٓ أَعْقَٰبِكُمْ تَنكِصُونَ

67. "In arrogance: talking nonsense
About the (Qur'ān), like one
Telling fables by night."[2917]

٦٧ مُسْتَكْبِرِينَ بِهِۦ سَٰمِرًا تَهْجُرُونَ

68. Do they not ponder over
The Word (of Allah), or
Has anything (new) come
To them that did not
Come to their fathers of old?[2918]

٦٨ أَفَلَمْ يَدَّبَّرُوا۟ ٱلْقَوْلَ
أَمْ جَآءَهُم مَّا لَمْ يَأْتِ ءَابَآءَهُمُ ٱلْأَوَّلِينَ

69. Or do they not recognise
Their Messenger, that they
Deny him?

٦٩ أَمْ لَمْ يَعْرِفُوا۟ رَسُولَهُمْ فَهُمْ لَهُۥ مُنكِرُونَ

70. Or do they say, "he is
Possessed"? Nay, he has
Brought them the Truth,
But most of them
Hate the Truth.

٧٠ أَمْ يَقُولُونَ بِهِۦ جِنَّةٌۢ
بَلْ جَآءَهُم بِٱلْحَقِّ وَأَكْثَرُهُمْ لِلْحَقِّ كَٰرِهُونَ

71. If the Truth had been
In accord with their desires,
Truly the heavens and the earth,
And all beings therein
Would have been in confusion[2919]
And corruption! Nay, We
Have sent them their admonition,
But they turn away
From their admonition.

٧١ وَلَوِ ٱتَّبَعَ ٱلْحَقُّ أَهْوَآءَهُمْ
لَفَسَدَتِ ٱلسَّمَٰوَٰتُ وَٱلْأَرْضُ وَمَن فِيهِنَّ
بَلْ أَتَيْنَٰهُم بِذِكْرِهِمْ
فَهُمْ عَن ذِكْرِهِم مُّعْرِضُونَ

72. Or is it that thou
Askest them for some[2920]

٧٢ أَمْ تَسْـَٔلُهُمْ

2917. *Sāmir*: one who remains awake by night, one who passes the night in talk or in the recital of stories of romances, a favourite amusement in the Days of Ignorance.

2918. If they ponder over the matter, they will find that Allah's Message to humanity is as old as Adam. It is good for all ages. It never grows old, and it is never new.

2919. Allah is All-Wise and All-Good, and His architecture of the universe is on a perfect Plan. If these poor, low, selfish, ignorant creatures were to plan it according to their hearts' desires, it would be a dreadful world, full of confusion and corruption.

2920. This is the last of the questions, beginning with 23:68 above, showing the absurdity of the position taken up by the Unbelievers. (1) The Message of Allah is as old as humanity; why do they fight shy of it? (2) They have known their Prophet to be true and righteous: why do they deny him? (3) Is it madness to bring the bitter Truth before them? (4) Does the Prophet ask any worldly reward from them? If not, why do they reject his unselfish efforts for their own good?

Recompense? But the recompense
Of thy Lord is best:
He is the Best of those
Who give sustenance.

خَرْجًا فَخَرَاجُ رَبِّكَ خَيْرٌ
وَهُوَ خَيْرُ الرَّٰزِقِينَ

73. But verily thou callest them
To the Straight Way;

وَإِنَّكَ لَتَدْعُوهُمْ إِلَىٰ صِرَٰطٍ مُّسْتَقِيمٍ ٧٣

74. And verily those who
Believe not in the Hereafter
Are deviating from that Way.

وَإِنَّ الَّذِينَ لَا يُؤْمِنُونَ بِالْآخِرَةِ
عَنِ الصِّرَٰطِ لَنَٰكِبُونَ ٧٤

75. If We had mercy on them
And removed the distress[2921]
Which is on them, they
Would obstinately persist
In their transgression,
Wandering in distraction
To and fro.

وَلَوْ رَحِمْنَٰهُمْ
وَكَشَفْنَا مَا بِهِم مِّن ضُرٍّ
لَّلَجُّوا فِي طُغْيَٰنِهِمْ يَعْمَهُونَ ٧٥

76. We inflicted Punishment[2922]
On them, but they
Humbled not themselves
To their Lord, nor do they
Submissively entreat (Him)!—

وَلَقَدْ أَخَذْنَٰهُم بِالْعَذَابِ
فَمَا اسْتَكَانُوا لِرَبِّهِمْ وَمَا يَتَضَرَّعُونَ ٧٦

77. Until We open on them
A gate leading to
A severe Punishment: then
Lo! they will be plunged
In despair therein![2923]

حَتَّىٰ إِذَا فَتَحْنَا عَلَيْهِم بَابًا ذَا
عَذَابٍ شَدِيدٍ إِذَا هُمْ فِيهِ مُبْلِسُونَ ٧٧

SECTION 5.

78. It is He Who has created
For you (the faculties of)

وَهُوَ الَّذِي أَنشَأَ لَكُمُ ٧٨

2921. The reference is to a very severe famine felt in Makkah, which was attributed by the Unbelievers to the presence of the Holy Prophet among them and his preaching against their gods. As this is a Makkan Sūrah, the famine referred to must be that described by Ibn Kathīr as having occurred in the 8th year of the Mission, say about four years before the Hijrah. There was also a post-Hijrah famine, which is referred to by Bukhārī, but that was a later event.

2922. Some Commentators understand the battle of Badr to be meant here: if so, this particular verse would be of the Madīnah period. But it is better to understand it as referring to the same "distress" as in the preceding verse, or to punishments in general, which obstinate sinners refuse to take as warnings given to them to mend their ways and turn in repentance to Allah.

2923. *Cf.* 6:44. If the little trials in the present life will not open their eyes, will great trials do so? Unfortunately they only cause in the wicked a feeling of despair. In the final Punishment after the Judgement, it will be too late for them to repent, and despair will be their only lot.

Hearing, sight, feeling[2924]
And understanding: little thanks
It is ye give!

السَّمْعَ وَالْأَبْصَارَ وَالْأَفْئِدَةَ ۚ قَلِيلًا مَّا تَشْكُرُونَ

79. And He has multiplied you
Through the earth, and to Him
Shall ye be gathered back.

٧٩ وَهُوَ الَّذِي ذَرَأَكُمْ فِي الْأَرْضِ وَإِلَيْهِ تُحْشَرُونَ

80. It is He Who gives
Life and death, and to Him
(Is due) the alternation[2925]
Of Night and Day:
Will ye not then understand?

٨٠ وَهُوَ الَّذِي يُحْيِي وَيُمِيتُ وَلَهُ اخْتِلَافُ
اللَّيْلِ وَالنَّهَارِ ۚ أَفَلَا تَعْقِلُونَ

81. On the contrary they say
Things similar to what
The ancients said.[2926]

٨١ بَلْ قَالُوا مِثْلَ مَا قَالَ الْأَوَّلُونَ

82. They say: "What! When we
Die and become dust and bones,
Could we really be
Raised up again?

٨٢ قَالُوا أَإِذَا مِتْنَا وَكُنَّا تُرَابًا
وَعِظَامًا أَإِنَّا لَمَبْعُوثُونَ

83. "Such things have been promised
To us and to our fathers
Before! They are nothing
But tales of the ancients!"

٨٣ لَقَدْ وُعِدْنَا نَحْنُ وَآبَاؤُنَا هَٰذَا مِن قَبْلُ
إِنْ هَٰذَا إِلَّا أَسَاطِيرُ الْأَوَّلِينَ

84. Say: "To whom belong
The earth and all beings therein?
(Say) if ye know!"

٨٤ قُل لِّمَنِ الْأَرْضُ وَمَن فِيهَا
إِن كُنتُمْ تَعْلَمُونَ

85. They will say, "To Allah!"
Say: "Yet will ye not
Receive admonition?"[2927]

٨٥ سَيَقُولُونَ لِلَّهِ ۚ قُلْ أَفَلَا تَذَكَّرُونَ

2924. As elsewhere, "heart" is to be understood as the seat both of feeling and intelligence. 'All the means by which knowledge can be gathered, judgement formed, and goodness cultivated, are provided for you by Allah. If you were grateful, you would use those in His service, which is expressed in your service to your fellow men. But instead you ignore these gifts, question Allah's Providence, and blaspheme against Him!'

2925. The alternation of Night and Day stands here as a symbol for all the beneficent processes of Nature provided by Allah for the comfort and growth of man's outer and inner life.

2926. And they are the more culpable, as they have received a later and more complete revelation. Why should they now stand on the primitive ideas of their ancestors?

2927. If their argument is that such things about a future life cannot be known or proved, they are referred to the things which are actually before them. The tangible things of the earth—can they postulate their order or government except by a Power of Force or Energy outside them? They will admit that there is such a Power or Force or Energy. We call it Allah. Go a step further. We see a sublime Universe in the heavens above, stretching far, far beyond our ken. They will admit its existence and its grandeur. We ask them to entertain a feeling of reverence for the Power behind it, and to understand their own littleness and their dependence upon that Power.

86. Say: "Who is the Lord
Of the seven heavens,
And the Lord of the Throne
(Of Glory) Supreme?"2928

قُلْ مَن رَّبُّ ٱلسَّمَٰوَٰتِ ٱلسَّبْعِ وَرَبُّ ٱلْعَرْشِ ٱلْعَظِيمِ ﴿٨٦﴾

87. They will say, "(They belong)
To Allah." Say: "Will ye not
Then be filled with awe?"2929

سَيَقُولُونَ لِلَّهِ ۚ قُلْ أَفَلَا تَتَّقُونَ ﴿٨٧﴾

88. Say: "Who is it in whose
Hands is the governance
Of all things—Who protects
(All), but is not protected
(Of any)? (Say) if ye know."

قُلْ مَنۢ بِيَدِهِۦ مَلَكُوتُ كُلِّ شَىْءٍ وَهُوَ يُجِيرُ وَلَا يُجَارُ عَلَيْهِ إِن كُنتُمْ تَعْلَمُونَ ﴿٨٨﴾

89. They will say, "(It belongs)
To Allah," Say: "Then how
Are ye deluded?"2930

سَيَقُولُونَ لِلَّهِ ۚ قُلْ فَأَنَّىٰ تُسْحَرُونَ ﴿٨٩﴾

90. We have sent them the Truth:
But they indeed practise
Flasehood!

بَلْ أَتَيْنَٰهُم بِٱلْحَقِّ وَإِنَّهُمْ لَكَٰذِبُونَ ﴿٩٠﴾

91. No son did Allah beget,
Nor is there any god
Along with Him: (if there were
Many gods), behold, each god
Would have taken away
What he had created,
And some would have
Lorded it over others!2931
Glory to Allah! (He is free)
From the (sort of) things
They attribute to Him!

مَا ٱتَّخَذَ ٱللَّهُ مِن وَلَدٍ وَمَا كَانَ مَعَهُۥ مِنْ إِلَٰهٍ ۚ إِذًا لَّذَهَبَ كُلُّ إِلَٰهٍۭ بِمَا خَلَقَ وَلَعَلَا بَعْضُهُمْ عَلَىٰ بَعْضٍ ۚ سُبْحَٰنَ ٱللَّهِ عَمَّا يَصِفُونَ ﴿٩١﴾

92. He knows what is hidden
And what is open: too high
Is He for the partners
They attribute to Him!2932

عَٰلِمِ ٱلْغَيْبِ وَٱلشَّهَٰدَةِ فَتَعَٰلَىٰ عَمَّا يُشْرِكُونَ ﴿٩٢﴾

2928. *Cf.* 9:129.

2929. See n. 2927 above. 'If this great and glorious Universe inspires you with awe, surely the Power behind is more worthy of your awe, especially if you compare your dependence and its dependence upon Him.'

2930. The order and unity of purpose in the Universe argue unity of design and goodness in its Maker. Is it not then sheer madness for you to run after fancies and fail to understand and obey His Will? It is delusion in you to seek other than Allah.'

2931. *Cf.* 17:42. The multiplicity of gods is intellectually indefensible, considering the unity of Design and Purpose in His wonderful Universe.

2932. To suppose that Allah has a son or a family or partners or companions is to have a low idea of Allah, Who is high above all such relationships. He is the One True God, and there can be none to compare with Him.

C. 156.—(23:93-118.)

Let us eschew evil, but not
Pay back evil in its own coin,
However great the temptation: no chance
Will there be to retrieve our conduct,
Once death cuts us off. Then we shall only
Have to wait for Judgement: none can pass
That Barrier: our deeds will be weighed,
And happy those whose good weighs more
In the scale than ill. Only Faith and Goodness
Will prevail in the end: so glory to the Lord
Of the Throne exalted, of Mercy and Honour!

SECTION 6.

93. Say: "O my Lord!
If Thou wilt show me
(In my lifetime) that which
They are warned against—[2933]

٩٣ قُل رَّبِّ إِمَّا تُرِيَنِّي مَا يُوعَدُونَ

94. "Then, O my Lord! put me not
Amongst the people
Who do wrong!"

٩٤ رَبِّ فَلَا تَجْعَلْنِي فِي الْقَوْمِ الظَّٰلِمِينَ

95. And We are certainly able
To show thee (in fulfilment)
That against which they are
warned.

٩٥ وَإِنَّا عَلَىٰٓ أَن نُّرِيَكَ مَا نَعِدُهُمْ لَقَٰدِرُونَ

96. Repel evil with that[2934]
Which is best: We are
Well-acquainted with
The things they say.

٩٦ ادْفَعْ بِالَّتِي هِيَ أَحْسَنُ السَّيِّئَةَ ۚ نَحْنُ أَعْلَمُ بِمَا يَصِفُونَ

97. And say "O my Lord!
I seek refuge with Thee

٩٧ وَقُل رَّبِّ أَعُوذُ بِكَ

2933. In the first instance, this applied to the Holy Prophet. His subsequent Hijrah from Makkah and the eventual overthrow of the Makkan oligarchy amply prove the fulfilment of the prophecy. But in general meaning it applies to all. We are taught that evil will be visited with a terrible punishment, not only in a future life, but in this life when its cup is full and the time comes for punishment in Allah's Plan. If it has to come while we are still on the scene of this life, we are asked to pray that we may not be found in the company of those who draw such punishment on themselves. In other words we must eschew the society of evil ones.

2934. Whether people speak evil of you, in your presence or behind your back, or they do evil to you in either of those ways, all is known to Allah. It is not for you to punish. Your best course is not to do evil in your turn, but to do what will best repel the evil. Two evils do not make a good. *Cf.* 41:34, n. 4504.

From the suggestions
Of the Evil Ones.[2935]

مِن هَمَزَاتِ الشَّيَاطِينِ

98. "And I seek refuge with Thee
O my Lord! lest they
Should come near me."

وَأَعُوذُ بِكَ رَبِّ أَن يَحْضُرُونِ ﴿٩٨﴾

99. (In Falsehood will they be)[2936]
Until, when death comes
To one of them, he says:
"O my Lord! send me back[2937]
(To life)—

حَتَّىٰ إِذَا جَاءَ أَحَدَهُمُ الْمَوْتُ
قَالَ رَبِّ ارْجِعُونِ ﴿٩٩﴾

100. "In order that I may
Work righteousness in the
things[2938]
I neglected"—"By no means!
It is but a word he says"—[2939]
Before them is a Partition[2940]
Till the Day they are
Raised up.

لَعَلِّي أَعْمَلُ صَالِحًا فِيمَا تَرَكْتُ
كَلَّا إِنَّهَا كَلِمَةٌ هُوَ قَائِلُهَا
وَمِن وَرَائِهِم بَرْزَخٌ إِلَىٰ يَوْمِ يُبْعَثُونَ ﴿١٠٠﴾

101. Then when the Trumpet
Is blown, there will be
No more relationships
Between them that day,
Nor will one ask after another![2941]

فَإِذَا نُفِخَ فِي الصُّورِ فَلَا أَنسَابَ
بَيْنَهُمْ يَوْمَئِذٍ وَلَا يَتَسَاءَلُونَ ﴿١٠١﴾

2935. But in any case, shun evil for yourself, and you cannot do this without seeking the help and protection of Allah. Not only must you shun all promptings of evil, but you must shun its proximity. It may be that in retaliating on evil, or even in your curiosity to discover what evil is, you may fall into evil yourself. You should avoid going near it or anything which brings it near to you. And in this matter you should seek Allah's help.

2936. This verse I think connects on with 23:90 above. Though Allah proclaims His Truth everywhere, the wicked cling to Falsehood until they face the reality of Death.

2937. The verb for "send me back" is in the plural in Arabic, which is construed either (1) as an emphatic form, as if the singular were repeated, or (2) as a plural of respect, though such a plural is not ordinarily used in addressing Allah, or (3) as a plural addressed to the angels, after the address to Allah in "O my Lord!"

2938. The unrighteous will ask for another chance. But it will be too late then. The time for repentance will then have passed.

2939. Their request will mean nothing. It will be treated merely as an empty word of excuse. They had plenty of chances in this life. Not only did they reject them, but they did not even believe in Allah or ask for His assistance.

2940. *Barzakh*: a partition, a bar or barrier; the place or state in which people will be after death and before Judgement. *Cf.* 25:53 and 55:20. Behind them is the barrier of death, and in front of them is the *Barzakh*, partition, a quiescent state until the judgement comes.

2941. The old relationships of the world will then be dissovled. Each soul will stand on its merits.

102. Then those whose balance
(Of good deeds) is heavy—
They will attain salvation:[2942]

103. But those whose balance
Is light, will be those
Who have lost their souls;[2943]
In Hell will they abide.

104. The Fire will burn their faces,
And they will therein
Grin, with their lips displaced.[2944]

105. "Were not My Signs rehearsed
To you, and ye did but
Treat them as falsehoods?"

106. They will say: "Our Lord!
Our misfortune overwhelmed
us,[2945]
And we became a people
Astray!

107. "Our Lord! Bring us out
Of this: if ever we return
(To evil), then shall we be
Wrongdoers indeed!"

108. He will say: "Be ye
Driven into it (with ignominy)!
And speak ye not to Me![2946]

109. "A part of My servants
There was, who used to pray,
'Our Lord! we believe;
Then do Thou forgive us,
And have mercy upon us:

١٠٢ فَمَن ثَقُلَتْ مَوَٰزِينُهُۥ
فَأُولَٰٓئِكَ هُمُ ٱلْمُفْلِحُونَ

١٠٣ وَمَنْ خَفَّتْ مَوَٰزِينُهُۥ فَأُولَٰٓئِكَ
ٱلَّذِينَ خَسِرُوٓا۟ أَنفُسَهُمْ فِى جَهَنَّمَ خَٰلِدُونَ

١٠٤ تَلْفَحُ وُجُوهَهُمُ ٱلنَّارُ وَهُمْ فِيهَا كَٰلِحُونَ

١٠٥ أَلَمْ تَكُنْ ءَايَٰتِى تُتْلَىٰ عَلَيْكُمْ
فَكُنتُم بِهَا تُكَذِّبُونَ

١٠٦ قَالُوا۟ رَبَّنَا غَلَبَتْ عَلَيْنَا شِقْوَتُنَا
وَكُنَّا قَوْمًا ضَآلِّينَ

١٠٧ رَبَّنَآ أَخْرِجْنَا مِنْهَا
فَإِنْ عُدْنَا فَإِنَّا ظَٰلِمُونَ

١٠٨ قَالَ ٱخْسَـُٔوا۟ فِيهَا وَلَا تُكَلِّمُونِ

١٠٩ إِنَّهُۥ كَانَ فَرِيقٌ مِّنْ عِبَادِى يَقُولُونَ
رَبَّنَآ ءَامَنَّا فَٱغْفِرْ لَنَا وَٱرْحَمْنَا

2942. Good and evil deeds will be weighed against each other. If the good deeds prevail, the soul will attain falāḥ, *i.e.*, prosperity, well-being, bliss, or salvation; if the contrary, there will be the misery and anguish of Hell.

2943. The loss or perdition will not mean that they will die and feel no more: 14:17. The punishment will mean nothing, if there was no sensibility, but total annihilation.

2944. That is to say, their faces will be disfigured with anguish, and their lips will quiver and fall out of place, exposing their teeth.

2945. 'The evil in us conquered us; it was our misfortunes that we surrendered to evil, and went astray.' They forget that it was by their own deliberate choice that they surrendered to evil, and they are reminded in verses 109-110 of the ridicule with which they covered godly men in their life on earth.

2946. After their flouting of Allah's Signs and their mockery of godly men on earth, they have forfeited their right to plead for mercy before Allah's Throne.

For Thou art the Best
Of those who show mercy!'

وَأَنتَ خَيْرُ ٱلرَّٰحِمِينَ

110. "But ye treated them
With ridicule, so much so
That (ridicule of) them made
you[2947]
Forget My Message while
Ye were laughing at them!

فَٱتَّخَذْتُمُوهُمْ سِخْرِيًّا ﴿١١٠﴾
حَتَّىٰٓ أَنسَوْكُمْ ذِكْرِى
وَكُنتُم مِّنْهُمْ تَضْحَكُونَ

111. "I have rewarded them
This day for their patience
And constancy: they are indeed
The ones that have achieved
Bliss. . ."

إِنِّى جَزَيْتُهُمُ ٱلْيَوْمَ بِمَا صَبَرُوٓا۟ ﴿١١١﴾
أَنَّهُمْ هُمُ ٱلْفَآئِزُونَ

112. He will say:[2948] "What number
Of years did ye stay
On earth?"

قَٰلَ كَمْ لَبِثْتُمْ فِى ٱلْأَرْضِ عَدَدَ سِنِينَ ﴿١١٢﴾

113. They will say: "We stayed
A day or part of a day:[2949]
But ask those who
Keep account."

قَالُوا۟ لَبِثْنَا يَوْمًا أَوْ بَعْضَ يَوْمٍ ﴿١١٣﴾
فَسْـَٔلِ ٱلْعَآدِّينَ

114. He will say: "Ye stayed
Not but a little—
If ye had only known!

قَٰلَ إِن لَّبِثْتُمْ إِلَّا قَلِيلًا ﴿١١٤﴾
لَّوْ أَنَّكُمْ كُنتُمْ تَعْلَمُونَ

115. "Did ye then think
That We had created you
In jest, and that ye
Would not be brought back
To Us (for account)?"[2950]

أَفَحَسِبْتُمْ أَنَّمَا خَلَقْنَٰكُمْ عَبَثًا ﴿١١٥﴾
وَأَنَّكُمْ إِلَيْنَا لَا تُرْجَعُونَ

2947. Literally, 'they make you forget My Message'. The ungodly were so occupied in the backbiting and ridicule of the godly that the godly themselves became the unconscious cause of the ungodly forgetting the warnings declared by Allah against those who do not treat His Signs seriously. Thus evil often brings about its own ruin through the instrumentality of those whom it would make its victims.

2948. The Ḥafṣ reading is "Qāla", "He will say". This follows the Kūfah Qirā'ah. The Baṣrah Qirā'ah reads "*Qul*", "Say" (in the imperative). The point is only one of grammatical construction. See n. 2666 to 21:4. (R).

2949. The question and answer about Time imply two things. (1) The attention of the ungodly is drawn to the extremely short time of the life in this world, compared to the eternity which they face: they are made to see this, and to realise how mistaken they were in their comparative valuation of things spiritual and things material. (2) Time, as we know it now, will have faded away and appear as almost nothing. It is just a matter relative to this life of temporary probation. *Cf.* the experience of the Companions of the Cave: 18:19.

2950. Allah's Creation is not without a high serious purpose. It is not vain, or for mere play or sport. As far as man is concerned, the highest issues for him hang on his behaviour in this life. "Life is real, life is earnest, And the grave is not its goal", as Longfellow truly says. We must therefore earnestly search out Allah's Truth, encouraged by the fact that Allah's Truth is also, out of His unbounded mercy, searching us out and trying to reach us.

116. Therefore exalted be Allah,
The King, the Reality:
There is no god but He,
The Lord of the Throne
Of Honour!

١١٦ فَتَعَٰلَى ٱللَّهُ ٱلۡمَلِكُ ٱلۡحَقُّۖ
لَآ إِلَٰهَ إِلَّا هُوَ رَبُّ ٱلۡعَرۡشِ ٱلۡكَرِيمِ

117. If anyone invokes, besides Allah,
Any other god, he has
No authority therefor;
And his reckoning will be
Only with his Lord![2951]
And verily the Unbelievers
Will fail to win through![2952]

١١٧ وَمَن يَدۡعُ مَعَ ٱللَّهِ إِلَٰهًا ءَاخَرَ
لَا بُرۡهَٰنَ لَهُۥ بِهِۦ فَإِنَّمَا حِسَابُهُۥ عِندَ رَبِّهِۦٓۚ
إِنَّهُۥ لَا يُفۡلِحُ ٱلۡكَٰفِرُونَ

118. So say: "O my Lord!
Grant Thou forgiveness and mercy!
For Thou art the Best
Of those who show mercy!"

١١٨ وَقُل رَّبِّ ٱغۡفِرۡ وَٱرۡحَمۡ
وَأَنتَ خَيۡرُ ٱلرَّٰحِمِينَ

2951. Not with any one else whatever, as Allah is the Eternal Reality. If men, out of the figments of their imagination, fancy other gods, they will be rudely undeceived. And Allah is Lord, *i.e.*, our Cherisher as well as our Creator. In spite of all our shortcomings and our rebellions, He will forgive us if we go to Him not on our merits but on His grace. (R).

2952. See the same word used in describing the contrast with the Believers, in the first verse of this Sūrah. Righteousness must win and all opposition to it must fail. Thus the circle of the argument is completed.

INTRODUCTION TO SŪRAH 24—*AL NŪR*

The environmental and social influences which most frequently wreck our spiritual ideals have to do with sex and especially with its misuse, whether in the form of unregulated behaviour, or false charges or scandals, or breach of the refined conventions of personal or domestic privacy. Our complete conquest of all pitfalls in such matters enables us to rise to the higher regions of Light and of God-created Nature. This subject is continued in the next Sūrah. (R).

As the reprobation of false slanders about women (24:11-20) is connected with an incident that happened to 'Ā'ishah in A. H. 5-6 that fixes the chronological place of this Madīnah Sūrah.

Summary—Sex offences should be severely punished, but the strictest evidence should be required, and false slanderers are also worthy of punishment. Light talk about women is reprobated (24:1-26, and C. 157).

Privacy should be respected, and the utmost decorum should be observed in dress and manners (24:27-34, and C. 158).

Parable of Light and Darkness: order and obedience in Nature point to the spiritual duty of man (24:35-37, and C. 159).

Domestic manners and manners in public or collective life all contribute to the highest virtues, and are part of our spiritual duties leading up to Allah (24:58-64, and C. 160).

C. 157.—Chastity is a virtue, for men and women,
(24:1-26.) Whether joined in marriage, or single,
Or widowed. The punishment for offences
In such matters should be public. No less
Grave is the launching of false charges
Or rumours against the fair reputation
Of women, or the spreading of such
Slanders, or the facile belief in them.
Evil is ever spreading its net.
Good men and women should ever be
On their guard, and pray for Allah's grace and mercy.

Sūrah 24.

Al Nūr (The Light)

الجزء الثامن عشر سورة النور

In the name of Allah, Most Gracious,
Most Merciful.

بسم الله الرحمن الرحيم

1. A Sūrah which We
Have sent down and[2953]
Which We have ordained:
In it have We sent down
Clear Signs, in order that
Ye may receive admonition.

سُورَةٌ أَنزَلْنَاهَا وَفَرَضْنَاهَا وَأَنزَلْنَا فِيهَا آيَاتٍ بَيِّنَاتٍ لَّعَلَّكُمْ تَذَكَّرُونَ ﴿١﴾

2. The woman and the man
Guilty of adultery or
fornication—[2954]
Flog each of them
With a hundred stripes:[2955]
Let not compassion move you
In their case, in a matter
Prescribed by Allah, if ye believe
In Allah and the Last Day:
And let a party
Of the Believers
Witness their punishment.[2956]

الزَّانِيَةُ وَالزَّانِي فَاجْلِدُوا كُلَّ وَاحِدٍ مِّنْهُمَا مِائَةَ جَلْدَةٍ وَلَا تَأْخُذْكُم بِهِمَا رَأْفَةٌ فِي دِينِ اللَّهِ إِن كُنتُمْ تُؤْمِنُونَ بِاللَّهِ وَالْيَوْمِ الْآخِرِ وَلْيَشْهَدْ عَذَابَهُمَا طَائِفَةٌ مِّنَ الْمُؤْمِنِينَ ﴿٢﴾

3. Let no man guilty of
Adultery or fornication marry
Any but a woman
Similarly guilty, or an Unbeliever:
Nor let any but such a man
Or an Unbeliever
Marry such a woman:

الزَّانِي لَا يَنكِحُ إِلَّا زَانِيَةً أَوْ مُشْرِكَةً وَالزَّانِيَةُ لَا يَنكِحُهَا إِلَّا زَانٍ أَوْ مُشْرِكٌ ﴿٣﴾

2953. It must not be thought that the checking of sex offences or of minor improprieties, that relate to sex or privacy, are matters that do not affect spiritual life in the highest degree. These matters are intimately connected with spiritual teaching such as Allah has sent down in this Sūrah. The emphasis is on "We": these things are not mere matters of convenience, but Allah has ordained them for our observance in life.

2954. *Zinā* includes sexual intercourse between a man and a woman not married to each other. It therefore applies both to adultery (which implies that one or both of the parties are married to a person or persons other than the ones concerned) and to fornication, which, in its strict signification, implies that both parties are unmarried. The law of marriage and divorce is made easy in Islam, so that there may be less temptation for intercourse outside the well-defined incidents of marriage. This makes for greater self-respect for both man and woman. Other sex offences are also punishable, but this Section applies strictly to *Zinā* as above defined. [Although *Zinā* covers both fornication and adultery, in the opinion of Muslim jurists, the punishment laid down here applies only to un-married persons. As for married persons, their punishment, according to the *Sunnah* of the Prophet (peace be on him), is stoning to death. (Eds.).]

2955. *Cf.* 4:15, and n. 523.

2956. The punishment should be open, in order to be a deterrent.

To the Believers such a thing
Is forbidden.[2957]

وَحُرِّمَ ذَٰلِكَ عَلَى ٱلْمُؤْمِنِينَ

4. And those who launch
A charge against chaste women,
And produce not four witnesses
(To support their allegations)—
Flog them with eighty stripes;
And reject their evidence[2958]
Ever after: for such men
Are wicked transgressors—

٤ وَٱلَّذِينَ يَرْمُونَ ٱلْمُحْصَنَٰتِ
ثُمَّ لَمْ يَأْتُوا۟ بِأَرْبَعَةِ شُهَدَآءَ فَٱجْلِدُوهُمْ ثَمَٰنِينَ جَلْدَةً
وَلَا تَقْبَلُوا۟ لَهُمْ شَهَٰدَةً أَبَدًا ۚ
وَأُو۟لَٰٓئِكَ هُمُ ٱلْفَٰسِقُونَ

5. Unless they repent thereafter[2959]
And mend (their conduct);
For Allah is Oft-Forgiving,
Most Merciful.

٥ إِلَّا ٱلَّذِينَ تَابُوا۟ مِنۢ بَعْدِ ذَٰلِكَ وَأَصْلَحُوا۟
فَإِنَّ ٱللَّهَ غَفُورٌ رَّحِيمٌ

6. And for those who launch
A charge against their spouses,
And have (in support)
No evidence but their own—[2960]

٦ وَٱلَّذِينَ يَرْمُونَ أَزْوَٰجَهُمْ
وَلَمْ يَكُن لَّهُمْ شُهَدَآءُ إِلَّآ أَنفُسُهُمْ

2957. Islam commands sex purity, for men and for women, at all times—before marriage, during marriage, and after the dissolution of marriage. Those guilty of illicit practices are shut out of the marriage circle of chaste men and women.

2958. The most serious notice is taken of people who put forward slanders or scandalous suggestions about women without adequate evidence. If anything is said against a woman's chastity, it should be supported by evidence twice as strong as would ordinarily be required for business transactions, or even in murder cases. That is, four witnesses would be required instead of two. Failing such preponderating evidence, the slanderer should himself be treated as a wicked transgressor and punished with eighty stripes. Not only would he be subjected to this disgraceful form of punishment, but he would be deprived of the citizen's right of giving evidence in all matters all his life, unless he repents and reforms, in which case he can be readmitted to be a competent witness. (The verse lays down the punishment for slandering "*chaste women*", which by consensus of opinion also covers slandering chaste men. Chaste women have been specially mentioned, according to Commentators, because slandering them is more abhorrent. (Eds.).

2959. The punishment of stripes is inflicted in any case for unsupported slander. But the deprivation of the civic right of giving evidence can be cancelled by the man's subsequent conduct, if he repents, shows that he is sorry for what he did, and that he would not in future support by his statement anything for which he has not the fullest evidence. Secular courts do not enforce these principles, as their standards are lower than those which good Muslims set for themselves, but good Muslims must understand and act on the underlying principles, which protect the honour of womanhood. Abū Hanifa considers that neither the stripes nor the incompetence for giving future evidence is cancelled by repentance, but only the spiritual stigma of being "wicked transgressors". This of course is the more serious punishment, though it cannot be enforced in the Courts.

2960. The case of married persons is different from that of outsiders. If one of them accuses the other of unchastity, the accusation partly reflects on the accuser as well. Moreover, the link which unites married people even where differences supervene, is sure to act as a steadying influence against the concoction of false charges of unchastity particularly where divorce is allowed (as in Islam) for reasons other than unchastity. Suppose a husband catches a wife in adultery. In the nature of things four witnesses—or even one outside witness—would be impossible. Yet after such an experience it is against human nature that he can live a normal married life. The matter is then left to the honour of the two spouses. If the husband can solemnly swear four times to the fact, and in addition invoke a curse on himself if he lies, that is *prima facie* evidence of the wife's guilt. But if the wife swears similarly four times and similarly invokes a curse on herself, she is in law acquitted of the guilt. If she does not take this step, the charge is held proved and the punishment follows. In either case the marriage is dissolved, as it is against human nature that the parties can live together happily after such an incident.

Their solitary evidence
(Can be received) if they
Bear witness four times
(With an oath) by Allah
That they are solemnly
Telling the truth;

فَشَهَـٰدَةُ أَحَدِهِمْ
أَرْبَعُ شَهَـٰدَٰتٍۭ بِٱللَّهِ
إِنَّهُۥ لَمِنَ ٱلصَّـٰدِقِينَ

7. And the fifth (oath)
(Should be) that they solemnly
Invoke the curse of Allah
On themselves if they
Tell a lie.

٧ وَٱلْخَـٰمِسَةُ أَنَّ لَعْنَتَ ٱللَّهِ عَلَيْهِ
إِن كَانَ مِنَ ٱلْكَـٰذِبِينَ

8. But it would avert
The punishment from the wife,
If she bears witness
Four times (with an oath)
By Allah, that (her husband)
Is telling a lie;

٨ وَيَدْرَؤُا۟ عَنْهَا ٱلْعَذَابَ
أَن تَشْهَدَ أَرْبَعَ شَهَـٰدَٰتٍۭ بِٱللَّهِ
إِنَّهُۥ لَمِنَ ٱلْكَـٰذِبِينَ

9. And the fifth (oath)
Should be that she solemnly
Invokes the wrath of Allah
On herself if (her accuser)
Is telling the truth.

٩ وَٱلْخَـٰمِسَةَ أَنَّ غَضَبَ ٱللَّهِ عَلَيْهَآ
إِن كَانَ مِنَ ٱلصَّـٰدِقِينَ

10. If it were not
For Allah's grace and mercy
On you, and that Allah
Is Oft-Returning,
Full of Wisdom—
(Ye would be ruined indeed).[2961]

١٠ وَلَوْلَا فَضْلُ ٱللَّهِ
عَلَيْكُمْ وَرَحْمَتُهُۥ
وَأَنَّ ٱللَّهَ تَوَّابٌ حَكِيمٌ

SECTION 2.

11. Those who brought forward[2962]
The lie are a body

١١ إِنَّ ٱلَّذِينَ جَآءُو بِٱلْإِفْكِ عُصْبَةٌ

2961. *Cf.* 24:11-14, and n. 2962, which illustrates the matter by a concrete instance.

2962. The particular incident here referred to occurred on the return from the expedition to the Banū Muṣṭaliq, A.H. 5-6. When the march was ordered, 'Āishah was not in her tent, having gone to search for a valuable necklace she had dropped. As her litter was veiled, it was not noticed that she was not in it, until the army reached the next halt. Meanwhile, finding the camp had gone, she sat down to rest, hoping that some one would come back to fetch her when her absence was noticed. It was night, and she fell asleep. Next morning she was found by Ṣafwān, a Muhājir, who had been left behind in the camp expressly to pick up anything inadvertently left behind. He put her on his camel and brought her, leading the camel on foot. This gave occasion to enemies to raise a malicious scandal. The ringleader among them was the chief of the Madīnah Hypocrites, 'Abdullah ibn Ubayy, who is referred to in the last clause of this verse. He had other sins and enormities to his debit, and he was left to the spiritual punishment of an unrepentant sinner, for he died in that state. The minor tools were given the legal punishment of the law, and after penitence mended their lives. They made good.

Among yourselves: think it not
To be an evil to you;
On the contrary it is good[2963]
For you: to every man
Among them (will come
The punishment) of the sin
That he earned, and to him[2964]
Who took on himself the lead
Among them, will be
A Penalty grievous.

مِّنكُمْ لَا تَحْسَبُوهُ شَرًّا لَّكُم
بَلْ هُوَ خَيْرٌ لَّكُمْ لِكُلِّ امْرِئٍ
مِّنْهُم مَّا اكْتَسَبَ مِنَ الْإِثْمِ
وَالَّذِي تَوَلَّىٰ كِبْرَهُ مِنْهُمْ لَهُ عَذَابٌ عَظِيمٌ

12. Why did not the Believers—
Men and women[2965]—when ye
Heard of the affair—put
The best construction on it
In their own minds
And say, "This (charge)
Is an obvious lie"?

١٢ لَّوْلَا إِذْ سَمِعْتُمُوهُ ظَنَّ الْمُؤْمِنُونَ
وَالْمُؤْمِنَاتُ بِأَنفُسِهِمْ خَيْرًا
وَقَالُوا هَٰذَا إِفْكٌ مُّبِينٌ

13. Why did they not bring
Four witnesses to prove it?[2966]
When they have not brought
The witnesses, such men,
In the sight of Allah
(Stand forth) themselves as liars!

١٣ لَّوْلَا جَاءُوا عَلَيْهِ بِأَرْبَعَةِ شُهَدَاءَ
فَإِذْ لَمْ يَأْتُوا بِالشُّهَدَاءِ فَأُولَٰئِكَ
عِندَ اللَّهِ هُمُ الْكَاذِبُونَ

14. Were it not for the grace
And mercy of Allah on you,
In this world and the Hereafter,
A grievous penalty would have
Seized you in that ye rushed
Glibly into this affair.[2967]

١٤ وَلَوْلَا فَضْلُ اللَّهِ عَلَيْكُمْ وَرَحْمَتُهُ
فِي الدُّنْيَا وَالْآخِرَةِ لَمَسَّكُمْ فِي
مَا أَفَضْتُمْ فِيهِ عَذَابٌ عَظِيمٌ

15. Behold, ye received it
On your tongues.

١٥ إِذْ تَلَقَّوْنَهُ بِأَلْسِنَتِكُمْ

2963. It is the worse for a scandal to be whispered about with bated breath, than that is should be brought into the light of day and disproved.

2964. The ringleader: see n. 2962 above.

2965. Both men and women were involved in spreading the scandal. Their obvious duty was to put the best, not the worst, construction on the acts of one of the "mothers of the Believers".

2966. If any persons took it seriously, it was their duty to search for and produce the evidence, in the absence of which they themselves became guilty of slander.

2967. *Cf.* 24:10 above. It was Allah's mercy that saved them from many evil consequences, both in this life and in the Hereafter—in this life, because the Prophet's wise measures nipped in the bud any incipient estrangements between those nearest and dearest to him, and from a spiritual aspect in that the minor agents in spreading the scandal repented and were forgiven. No doubts and divisions, no mutual distrust, were allowed to remain in their hearts after the whole matter had been cleared up.

And said out of your mouths
Things of which ye had
No knowledge; and ye thought
It to be a light matter,
While it was most serious
In the sight of Allah.[2968]

وَتَقُولُونَ بِأَفْوَاهِكُم مَّا لَيْسَ
لَكُم بِهِۦ عِلْمٌ وَتَحْسَبُونَهُۥ هَيِّنًا
وَهُوَ عِندَ ٱللَّهِ عَظِيمٌ

16. And why did ye not
When ye heard it, say?—
"It is not right of us
To speak of this:
Glory to Thee (our Lord) this is
A most serious slander!"[2969]

(١٦) وَلَوْلَآ إِذْ سَمِعْتُمُوهُ قُلْتُم
مَّا يَكُونُ لَنَآ أَن نَّتَكَلَّمَ بِهَٰذَا
سُبْحَٰنَكَ هَٰذَا بُهْتَٰنٌ عَظِيمٌ

17. Allah doth admonish you,
That ye may never repeat
Such (conduct), if ye
Are (true) Believers.

(١٧) يَعِظُكُمُ ٱللَّهُ أَن تَعُودُوا۟
لِمِثْلِهِۦٓ أَبَدًا إِن كُنتُم مُّؤْمِنِينَ

18. And Allah makes the Signs
Plain to you: for Allah
Is full of knowledge and wisdom.

(١٨) وَيُبَيِّنُ ٱللَّهُ لَكُمُ ٱلْءَايَٰتِ
وَٱللَّهُ عَلِيمٌ حَكِيمٌ

19. Those who love (to see)
Scandal published broadcast
Among the Believers, will have
A grievous Penalty in this life
And in the Hereafter: Allah
Knows, and ye know not.[2970]

(١٩) إِنَّ ٱلَّذِينَ يُحِبُّونَ أَن تَشِيعَ ٱلْفَٰحِشَةُ فِى
ٱلَّذِينَ ءَامَنُوا۟ لَهُمْ عَذَابٌ أَلِيمٌ فِى ٱلدُّنْيَا وَٱلْءَاخِرَةِ
وَٱللَّهُ يَعْلَمُ وَأَنتُمْ لَا تَعْلَمُونَ

20. Were it not for the grace
And mercy of Allah on you,

(٢٠) وَلَوْلَا فَضْلُ ٱللَّهِ عَلَيْكُمْ وَرَحْمَتُهُۥ

2968. There are three things here reprobated by way of spiritual teaching: (1) if others speak an evil word, that is no reason why you should allow it to defile your tongue; (2) if you get a thought or suspicion which is not based on your certain knowledge, do not give it currency by giving it expression; and (3) others may think it is a small matter to speak lightly of something which blasts a person's character or reputation: in the eyes of Allah it is a most serious matter in any case, but specially when it involves the honour and reputation of pious women.

2969. The right course would have been to stop any further currency of false slanders by ignoring them and at least refusing to help in their circulation. The exclamation "*Subḥānaka*", "Praise to Thee (O Allah)", or "Glory to Allah!" is an exclamation of surprise and disavowal as much as to say, "We do not believe it! And we shall have nothing to do with you, O false slanderers!"

2970. What mischiefs can be planned by Evil to delude simple folk who mean no harm in their own minds but who by thoughtlessness are deluded step by step to become the instruments of Evil, may not be known to the most instructed of men, but it is all known to Allah. Man should therefore always be on his guard against the traps of Evil, and it is only Allah's grace that can save him.

And that Allah is
Full of kindness and mercy,
(Ye would be ruined indeed).[2971]

وَأَنَّ ٱللَّهَ رَءُوفٌ رَّحِيمٌ

SECTION 3.

21. O ye who believe!
Follow not Satan's footsteps:
If any will follow the footsteps
Of Satan, he will (but) command
What is shameful and wrong:
And were it not for the grace
And mercy of Allah on you,
Not one of you would ever[2972]
Have been pure: but Allah
Doth purify whom He pleases:[2973]
And Allah is One Who
Hears and knows (all things).

(٢١) يَٰٓأَيُّهَا ٱلَّذِينَ ءَامَنُوا۟
لَا تَتَّبِعُوا۟ خُطُوَٰتِ ٱلشَّيْطَٰنِ ۚ وَمَن يَتَّبِعْ
خُطُوَٰتِ ٱلشَّيْطَٰنِ فَإِنَّهُۥ يَأْمُرُ بِٱلْفَحْشَآءِ وَٱلْمُنكَرِ ۚ
وَلَوْلَا فَضْلُ ٱللَّهِ عَلَيْكُمْ وَرَحْمَتُهُۥ مَا زَكَىٰ مِنكُم
مِّنْ أَحَدٍ أَبَدًا وَلَٰكِنَّ ٱللَّهَ يُزَكِّى مَن يَشَآءُ ۗ
وَٱللَّهُ سَمِيعٌ عَلِيمٌ

22. Let not those among you
Who are endued with grace
And amplitude of means[2974]
Resolve by oath against helping
Their kinsmen, those in want,

(٢٢) وَلَا يَأْتَلِ أُو۟لُوا۟ ٱلْفَضْلِ مِنكُمْ وَٱلسَّعَةِ
أَن يُؤْتُوٓا۟ أُو۟لِى ٱلْقُرْبَىٰ وَٱلْمَسَٰكِينَ

2971. Note the refrain that comes four times in this passage, "Were it not for the grace and mercy of Allah. . ." Each time it has a different application. (1) In 24:10, it was in connection with the accusation of infidelity by one of the spouses against the other: they were both reminded of Allah's mercy and warned against suspicion and untruth. (2) In 24:14, the Believers were told to be wary of false rumours lest they should cause pain and division among themselves: it is Allah's grace that keeps them united. (3) Here is an admonition for the future: there may be conspiracies and snares laid by Evil against simple people: it is Allah's grace that protects them. (4) In 24:21, the general warning is directed to the observation of purity in act and in thought, concerning one's self and concerning others: it is only Allah's grace that can keep that purity spotless, for He hears prayers and knows of all the snares that are spread in the path of the good.

2972. See last note.

2973. Spotless purity in thought, word, and deed, includes the disposition to put the best construction on the motives of others, so that we ascribe no evil motive to the seeming indiscretions of virtuous people. Such a high standard can only come by the grace of Allah, Who hears all prayers and knows all the temptations to which human nature is subject. His Will and Plan make both for spiritual protection and spiritual peace, and we must place ourselves trustingly in His hands.

2974. The immediate reference was to Abū Bakr, the father of 'Ā'ishah. He was blessed both with spiritual grace from Allah and with ample means, which he always used in the service of Islam and of Muslims. One of the slanderers of 'Ā'ishah turned out to be Misṭah, a cousin of Abū Bakr, whom he had been in the habit of supporting. Naturally Abū Bakr wished to stop that aid, but according to the highest standards of Muslim ethics he was asked to forgive and forget, which he did, with the happiest results to the peace and unity of the Muslim community. But the general application holds good for all time. A generous patron should not, in personal anger, withdraw his support even for serious faults if the delinquent repents and mends his ways. If Allah forgives us, who are we to refuse forgiveness to our fellows?

And those who have left
Their homes in Allah's cause:
Let them forgive and overlook,
Do you not wish
That Allah should forgive you?
For Allah is Oft-Forgiving,
Most Merciful.

وَالْمُهَٰجِرِينَ فِي سَبِيلِ ٱللَّهِ ۖ
وَلْيَعْفُوا وَلْيَصْفَحُوٓا ۗ
أَلَا تُحِبُّونَ أَن يَغْفِرَ ٱللَّهُ لَكُمْ ۗ
وَٱللَّهُ غَفُورٌ رَّحِيمٌ

23. Those who slander chaste women,
Indiscreet but believing,[2975]
Are cursed in this life
And in the Hereafter:
For them is a grievous Penalty—

٢٣ إِنَّ ٱلَّذِينَ يَرْمُونَ ٱلْمُحْصَنَٰتِ ٱلْغَٰفِلَٰتِ
ٱلْمُؤْمِنَٰتِ لُعِنُوا فِي ٱلدُّنْيَا وَٱلْءَاخِرَةِ
وَلَهُمْ عَذَابٌ عَظِيمٌ

24. On the Day when their tongues,
Their hands, and their feet
Will bear witness against them[2976]
As to their actions.

٢٤ يَوْمَ تَشْهَدُ عَلَيْهِمْ أَلْسِنَتُهُمْ
وَأَيْدِيهِمْ وَأَرْجُلُهُم بِمَا كَانُوا يَعْمَلُونَ

25. On that Day Allah
Will pay them back
(All) their just dues,
And they will realise
That Allah is
The (very) Truth,
That makes all things manifest.[2977]

٢٥ يَوْمَئِذٍ يُوَفِّيهِمُ ٱللَّهُ
دِينَهُمُ ٱلْحَقَّ وَيَعْلَمُونَ
أَنَّ ٱللَّهَ هُوَ ٱلْحَقُّ ٱلْمُبِينُ

26. Women impure are for men
impure,
And men impure for women
impure,
And women of purity
Are for men of purity,
And men of purity

٢٦ ٱلْخَبِيثَٰتُ لِلْخَبِيثِينَ
وَٱلْخَبِيثُونَ لِلْخَبِيثَٰتِ ۖ
وَٱلطَّيِّبَٰتُ لِلطَّيِّبِينَ
وَٱلطَّيِّبُونَ

2975. Good women are sometimes indiscreet because they think of no evil. But even such innocent indiscretion lands them, and those who hold them dear, in difficulties. Such was the case with 'Ā'ishah, who was in extreme pain and anguish for a whole month because of the slanders spread about her. Her husband and her father were also placed in a most awkward predicament, considering their position and the great work in which they were engaged. But unprincipled people, who start false slanders, and their unthinking tools who help in spreading such slanders, are guilty of the gravest spiritual offence, and their worst punishment is the deprivation of Allah's grace, which is the meaning of a state of Curse.

2976. Our own limbs and faculties are the strongest witness against us if we misuse them for evil deeds instead of using them for the good deeds for which they were given to us.

2977. All that we thought of hiding will be clear as day before Allah's Judgement Seat, because He is the very essence of Truth and Reality. He is the true Light (24:35), of which all physical light is merely a type or reflection.

Are for women of purity:
These are not affected
By what people say:[2978]
For them there is forgiveness,
And a provision honourable.[2979]

لِلطَّيِّبَٰتِۚ أُوْلَٰٓئِكَ مُبَرَّءُونَ مِمَّا يَقُولُونَۖ
لَهُم مَّغْفِرَةٌ وَرِزْقٌ كَرِيمٌ

C. 158.—Privacy in the home is a nature of virtue:
(24:27-34.) Respect it with dignity and decorum. Guard
Your eyes and thoughts with rules of modesty
In dress and manners: and learn from these
To keep your spiritual gaze from straying
To any but Allah. True marriage should teach
Us charity and purity, and such
Are the virtues which lead us to the Light
Sublime which illuminates the world.

SECTION 4.

27. O ye who believe!
Enter not houses other than
Your own, until ye have
Asked permission and saluted
Those in them: that is
Best for you, in order that
Ye may heed (what is seemly).[2980]

٢٧ يَٰٓأَيُّهَا ٱلَّذِينَ ءَامَنُواْ لَا تَدْخُلُواْ بُيُوتًا
غَيْرَ بُيُوتِكُمْ حَتَّىٰ تَسْتَأْنِسُواْ وَتُسَلِّمُواْ
عَلَىٰٓ أَهْلِهَاۚ ذَٰلِكُمْ خَيْرٌ لَّكُمْ لَعَلَّكُمْ تَذَكَّرُونَ

28. If ye find no one[2981]
In the house, enter not
Until permission is given

٢٨ فَإِن لَّمْ تَجِدُواْ فِيهَآ أَحَدًا
فَلَا تَدْخُلُوهَا حَتَّىٰ يُؤْذَنَ لَكُمْۖ

2978. The pure consort with the pure, and the impure witht the impure. If the impure, out of the impurity of their thoughts, or imaginations, impute any evil to the pure, the pure are not affected by it, but they should avoid all occasions for random talk.

2979. *Forgiveness* for any indiscretion which they may have innocently committed, and spiritual provisions of protection against the assaults of Evil. It is also meant that the more evil ones attempt to defame or slander them, the more triumphantly will they be vindicated and provided with the physical and moral good which will advance their real life.

2980. The conventions of propriety and privacy are essential to a refined life of goodness and purity. The English saying that an Englishman's home is his castle, suggests a certain amount of exclusiveness and defiance. The Muslim principle of asking respectful permission and exchanging salutations ensures privacy without exclusiveness, and friendliness without undue familiarity.

2981. That is, if no one replies: there may be people in the house not in a presentable state. Or, even if the house is empty, you have no right to enter it until you obtain the owner's permission, wherever he may be. The fact of your not receiving a reply does not entitle you to enter without permission. You should wait, or knock twice or three times, and withdraw in case no permission is received. If you are actually asked to withdraw, as the inmates are not in a condition to receive you, you should *a fortiori* withdraw, either for a time, or altogether, as the inmates may wish you to do. Even if they are your friends, you have no right to take them by surprise or enter against their wishes. Your own purity of life and conduct as well as of motives is thus tested.

To you: if ye are asked
To go back, go back:
That makes for greater purity
For yourselves: and Allah
Knows well all that ye do.

وَإِن قِيلَ لَكُمُ ٱرْجِعُوا۟ فَٱرْجِعُوا۟
هُوَ أَزْكَىٰ لَكُمْ وَٱللَّهُ بِمَا تَعْمَلُونَ عَلِيمٌ

29. It is no fault on your part
To enter houses not used
For living in, which serve
Some (other) use for you:[2982]
And Allah has knowledge
Of what ye reveal
And what ye conceal.

٢٩ لَّيْسَ عَلَيْكُمْ جُنَاحٌ أَن تَدْخُلُوا۟ بُيُوتًا
غَيْرَ مَسْكُونَةٍ فِيهَا مَتَٰعٌ لَّكُمْ
وَٱللَّهُ يَعْلَمُ مَا تُبْدُونَ وَمَا تَكْتُمُونَ

30. Say to the believing men
That they should lower
Their gaze and guard[2983]
Their modesty: that will make
For greater purity for them:
And Allah is well acquainted
With all that they do.

٣٠ قُل لِّلْمُؤْمِنِينَ يَغُضُّوا۟ مِنْ أَبْصَٰرِهِمْ
وَيَحْفَظُوا۟ فُرُوجَهُمْ ذَٰلِكَ أَزْكَىٰ لَهُمْ
إِنَّ ٱللَّهَ خَبِيرٌۢ بِمَا يَصْنَعُونَ

31. And say to the believing women
That they should lower
Their gaze and guard[2984]
Their modesty; that they
Should not display their
Beauty and ornaments[2985] except
What (must ordinarily) appear
Thereof; that they should
Draw their veils over

٣١ وَقُل لِّلْمُؤْمِنَٰتِ يَغْضُضْنَ مِنْ أَبْصَٰرِهِنَّ
وَيَحْفَظْنَ فُرُوجَهُنَّ وَلَا يُبْدِينَ
زِينَتَهُنَّ إِلَّا مَا ظَهَرَ مِنْهَا
وَلْيَضْرِبْنَ بِخُمُرِهِنَّ عَلَىٰ

2982. The rule about dwelling houses is strict, because privacy is precious, and essential to a refined, decent, and well-ordered life. Such a rule of course does not apply to houses used for other useful purposes, such as an inn or caravanserai, or a shop, or a warehouse. But even here, of course, implied permission from the owner is necessary as a matter of common-sense. The question in this passage is that of refined privacy, not that of rights of ownership.

2983. The rule of modesty applies to men as well as women. A brazen stare by a man at a woman (or even at a man) is a breach of refined manners. Where sex is concerned, modesty is not only "good form": it is not only to guard the weaker sex, but also to guard the spiritual good of the stronger sex.

2984. The need for modesty is the same in both men and women. But on account of the differentiation of the sexes in nature, temperaments, and social life, a greater amount of privacy is required for women than for men, especially in the matter of dress and the uncovering of the bosom.

2985. *Zīnat* means both natural beauty and artificial ornaments. I think both are implied here, but chiefly the former. The woman is asked not to make a display of her figure or appear in undress except to the following classes of people: (1) her husband, (2) her near relatives who would be living in the same house, and with whom a certain amount of *negligé* is permissible: (3) her women, *i.e.*, her maid-servants, who would be constantly in attendance on her: some Commentators include all believing women; it is not good form in a Muslim household for women to meet other women, except when they are properly dressed; (4) slaves, male and female, as they would be in constant attendance; but this item would now be blank, with the abolition of slavery; (5) old or infirm men-servants; and (6) infants or small children before they get a sense of sex. *Cf.* also 33:59.

Their bosoms and not display
Their beauty except
To their husbands, their fathers,
Their husbands' fathers, their sons,
Their husbands' sons,
Their brothers or their brothers' sons,
Or their sisters' sons,
Or their women, or the slaves
Whom their right hands
Possess, or male servants
Free of physical needs,
Or small children who
Have no sense of the shame
Of sex; and that they
Should not strike their feet
In order to draw attention
To their hidden ornaments.[2986]
And O ye Believers!
Turn ye all together
Towards Allah, that ye
May attain Bliss.[2987]

جُيُوبِهِنَّ وَلَا يُبْدِينَ زِينَتَهُنَّ إِلَّا
لِبُعُولَتِهِنَّ أَوْ ءَابَآئِهِنَّ أَوْ ءَابَآءِ
بُعُولَتِهِنَّ أَوْ أَبْنَآئِهِنَّ أَوْ أَبْنَآءِ
بُعُولَتِهِنَّ أَوْ إِخْوَٰنِهِنَّ أَوْ بَنِىٓ إِخْوَٰنِهِنَّ
أَوْ بَنِىٓ أَخَوَٰتِهِنَّ أَوْ نِسَآئِهِنَّ أَوْ مَا مَلَكَتْ
أَيْمَٰنُهُنَّ أَوِ ٱلتَّٰبِعِينَ غَيْرِ أُو۟لِى ٱلْإِرْبَةِ مِنَ
ٱلرِّجَالِ أَوِ ٱلطِّفْلِ ٱلَّذِينَ لَمْ يَظْهَرُوا۟ عَلَىٰ
عَوْرَٰتِ ٱلنِّسَآءِ وَلَا يَضْرِبْنَ بِأَرْجُلِهِنَّ لِيُعْلَمَ
مَا يُخْفِينَ مِن زِينَتِهِنَّ وَتُوبُوٓا۟ إِلَى ٱللَّهِ جَمِيعًا
أَيُّهَ ٱلْمُؤْمِنُونَ لَعَلَّكُمْ تُفْلِحُونَ

32. Marry those among you
Who are single,[2988] or
The virtuous ones among
Your slaves, male or female:
If they are in poverty,
Allah will give them
Means out of His grace:
For Allah encompasseth all,[2989]
And He knoweth all things.

٣٢ وَأَنكِحُوا۟ ٱلْأَيَٰمَىٰ مِنكُمْ
وَٱلصَّٰلِحِينَ مِنْ عِبَادِكُمْ وَإِمَآئِكُمْ
إِن يَكُونُوا۟ فُقَرَآءَ يُغْنِهِمُ ٱللَّهُ مِن فَضْلِهِۦ
وَٱللَّهُ وَٰسِعٌ عَلِيمٌ

33. Let those who find not
The wherewithal for marriage
Keep themselves chaste, until

٣٣ وَلْيَسْتَعْفِفِ ٱلَّذِينَ لَا يَجِدُونَ نِكَاحًا حَتَّىٰ

2986. It is one of the tricks of showy or unchaste women to tinkle their ankle ornaments, to draw attention to themselves.

2987. While all these details of the purity and good form of domestic life are being brought to our attention, we are clearly reminded that the chief object we should hold in view is our spiritual welfare. All our brief life on this earth is a probation, and we must make our individual, domestic, and social life all contribute to our holiness, so that we can get the real success and bliss which is the aim of our spiritual endeavour. (R).

2988. The subject of sex ethics and manners brings us to the subject of marriage. "Single" (*ayāmā*, plural of *Ayyim*) here means any one not in the bond of wedlock, whether unmarried or lawfully divorced, or widowed. If we can, we must marry in our own circle, but if we have not the means, there is no harm if we choose from a lower circle, provided our choice is determined by virtue. Poverty in the other party does not matter if there is virtue and love. A happily married man has the best wealth in a virtuous wife, and his very happiness makes him a better potential earner of wealth. A slave becomes free by marriage.

2989. *Cf.* 10:57. Allah's mercy is for all: it is not confined to a class or grade of people.

Allah gives them means[2990]
Out of His grace.
And if any of your slaves
Ask for a deed in writing
(To enable them to earn
Their freedom for a certain sum),
Give them such a deed[2991]
If ye know any good
In them; yea, give them
Something yourselves
Out of the means which
Allah has given to you.
But force not your maids[2992]
To prostitution when[2993] they desire
Chastity, in order that ye
May make a gain
In the goods of this life.
But if anyone compels them,
Yet, after such compulsion,
Is Allah Oft-Forgiving,
Most Merciful (to them).[2994]

يُغْنِيَهُمُ ٱللَّهُ مِن فَضْلِهِۦ
وَٱلَّذِينَ يَبْتَغُونَ ٱلْكِتَٰبَ مِمَّا
مَلَكَتْ أَيْمَٰنُكُمْ فَكَاتِبُوهُمْ
إِنْ عَلِمْتُمْ فِيهِمْ خَيْرًا
وَءَاتُوهُم مِّن مَّالِ ٱللَّهِ ٱلَّذِىٓ ءَاتَىٰكُمْ
وَلَا تُكْرِهُوا۟ فَتَيَٰتِكُمْ عَلَى ٱلْبِغَآءِ إِنْ أَرَدْنَ
تَحَصُّنًا لِّتَبْتَغُوا۟ عَرَضَ ٱلْحَيَوٰةِ ٱلدُّنْيَا
وَمَن يُكْرِههُّنَّ فَإِنَّ ٱللَّهَ مِنۢ
بَعْدِ إِكْرَٰهِهِنَّ غَفُورٌ رَّحِيمٌ

34. We have already sent down
To you verses making things
Clear, an illustration from (the story
Of) people who passed away
Before you, and an admonition
For those who fear (Allah).[2995]

٣٤ وَلَقَدْ أَنزَلْنَآ إِلَيْكُمْ ءَايَٰتٍ
مُّبَيِّنَٰتٍ وَمَثَلًا مِّنَ ٱلَّذِينَ خَلَوْا۟
مِن قَبْلِكُمْ وَمَوْعِظَةً لِّلْمُتَّقِينَ

2990. A Muslim marriage requires some sort of a dower for the wife. If the man cannot afford that, he must wait and keep himself chaste. It is no excuse for him to say that the must satisfy his natural cravings within or outside marriage. It must be within marriage.

2991. The law of slavery in the legal sense of the term is now obsolete. While it had any meaning, Islam made the slave's lot as easy as possible. A slave, male or female, could ask for conditional manumission by a written deed fixing the amount required for manumission and allowing the slave meanwhile to earn money by lawful means and perhaps marry and bring up a family. Such a deed was not to be refused if the request was genuine and the slave had character. Not only that, but the master is directed to help with money out of his own resources in order to enable the slave to earn his or her own liberty.

2992. Where slavery was legal, what is now called the "white slave traffic" was carried on by wicked people like 'Abd Allah ibn Ubayy, the Hypocrite leader at Madīnah. This is absolutely condemned. While modern nations have abolished ordinary slavery, the "White Slave Traffic" is still a big social problem in individual States. Here it is absolutely condemned. No more despicable trade can be imagined. (R).

2993. I have translated "*in*" (literally, "if") by "when" because this is not a conditional clause but an explanatory clause, explaining the meaning of "force". "Forcing" a person necesarily means that it is against the wish or inclination of the person forced. Even if they were to give a formal consent, it is not valid because the persons concerned are in (legal, or now) economic slavery.

2994. The poor unfortunate girls, who are victims of such a nefarious trade, will yet find mercy from Allah, whose bounties extend to the lowest of His creatures.

2995. This prepares the way for the magnificent Verse of Light that follows, and its sublime meaning. (R).

C. 159. —Allah is the Light of the heavens and the earth.
(24:35-57.) High above our petty evanescent lives,
He illumines our souls with means that reach
Our inmost being. Universal is
His Light, so pure and so intense
That grosser beings need a veil
To take His rays: His elect are e'er
Absorbed in prayer and praise and deeds
Of love, unlike the children of Darkness,
Struggling in Depths profound of vanities
False. All Nature sings to the glory
Of Allah, and men of fraud and hypocrisy
Are but rebels in the Kingdom of Allah.

SECTION 5.

35. Allah is the Light[2996] Of the heavens and the earth.[2997] The parable of His Light Is as if there were a Niche And within it a Lamp: The Lamp enclosed in Glass;[2998] The glass as it were	٣٥ اللَّهُ نُورُ السَّمَاوَاتِ وَالْأَرْضِ مَثَلُ نُورِهِ كَمِشْكَاةٍ فِيهَا مِصْبَاحٌ الْمِصْبَاحُ فِي زُجَاجَةٍ الزُّجَاجَةُ كَأَنَّهَا

2996. Embedded within certains directions concerning a refined domestic and social life, comes this glorious parable of Light, which contains layer upon layer of transcendental truth about spiritual mysteries. No notes can do adequate justice to its full meaning. Volumes have been written on this subject, the most notable being Ghazālī's *Mishkāt al Anwār.* In these notes I propose to explain the simplest meaning of this passage. (R).

2997. The physical light is but a reflection of the true Light in the world of Reality, and that true Light is Allah. We can only think of Allah in terms of our phenomenal experience, and in the phenomenal world, light is the purest thing we know, but physical light has drawbacks incidental to its physical nature: *e.g.*, (1) it is dependent on some source external to itself: (2) it is a passing phenomenon: if we take it to be a form of motion or energy it is unstable, like all physical phenomena; (3) it is dependent on space and time; its speed is 186,000 miles per second, and there are stars whose light takes thousands (or millions or billions) of years before it reaches the earth. The perfect Light of Allah is free from any such defects. (R).

2998. The first three points in the Parable centre round the symbols of the Niche, the Lamp, and the Glass. (1) The Niche (*Mishkāt*) is the little shallow recess in the wall of an Eastern house, fairly high from the ground, in which a light (before the days of electricity) was usually placed. Its height enabled it to diffuse the light in the room and minimised the shadows. The background of the wall and the sides of the niche helped throw the light well into the room, and if the wall was white-washed, it also acted as a reflector: the opening in front made the way for the light. So with the spiritual Light: it is placed high above worldly things: it has a niche or habitation of its own, in Revelation and other Signs of Allah; its access to men is by a special Way, open to all, yet closed to those who refuse its rays. (2) The Lamp is the core of the spiritual Truth, which is the real illumination; the Niche is nothing without it; the Niche is actually made for it. (3) The Glass is the transparent medium through which the Light passes. On the one hand, it protects the light from moths and other forms of low life (lower motives in man) and from gusts of wind (passions), and on the other, it transmits the light through a medium which is made up of and akin to the grosser substances of the earth (such as sand, soda, potash, etc.), so arranged as to admit the subtle to the gross by its tranparency. So the spiritual Truth has to be filtered through human language or human intelligence to make it intelligible to mankind.

A brilliant star:[2999]
Lit from a blessed Tree,[3000]
An Olive, neither of the East
Nor of the West,[3001]
Whose Oil is well-nigh
Luminous,
Though fire scarce touched it:[3002]
Light upon Light!
Allah doth guide whom He will
To His light:[3003]
Allah doth set forth Parables
For men: and Allah
Doth know all things.

36. (Lit is such a light)[3004]
In houses, which Allah
Hath permitted to be raised[3005]
To honour; for the celebration,
In them, of His name:
In them is He glorified.

كَوْكَبٌ دُرِّيٌّ يُوقَدُ مِن شَجَرَةٍ
مُّبَٰرَكَةٍ زَيْتُونَةٍ لَّا شَرْقِيَّةٍ وَلَا غَرْبِيَّةٍ
يَكَادُ زَيْتُهَا يُضِىٓءُ وَلَوْ لَمْ تَمْسَسْهُ نَارٌ
نُّورٌ عَلَىٰ نُورٍ يَهْدِى ٱللَّهُ لِنُورِهِۦ مَن يَشَآءُ
وَيَضْرِبُ ٱللَّهُ ٱلْأَمْثَٰلَ لِلنَّاسِ
وَٱللَّهُ بِكُلِّ شَىْءٍ عَلِيمٌ
٣٦ فِى بُيُوتٍ أَذِنَ ٱللَّهُ أَن تُرْفَعَ
وَيُذْكَرَ فِيهَا ٱسْمُهُۥ
يُسَبِّحُ لَهُۥ فِيهَا

2999. The glass by itself does not shine. But when the light comes into it, it shines like a brilliant star. So men of God, who preach Allah's Truth, are themselves illuminated by Allah's Light and become like illuminating media through which that Light spreads and permeates human life.

3000. The olive tree is not a very impressive tree in its outward appearance. Its leaves have a dull greenish-brown colour, and in size it is inconspicuous. But its oil is used in sacred ceremonies and forms a wholesome ingredient of food. The fruit has a specially fine flavour. *Cf.* n. 2880 to 23:20. For the illuminating quality of its oil, see n. 3002 below.

3001. This mystic Olive is not localised. It is neither of the East nor the West. It is universal, for such is Allah's Light. As applied to the olive, there is also a more literal meaning, which can be allegorised in a different way. An olive tree with an eastern aspect gets only the rays of the morning sun; one with a western aspect, only the rays of the western sun. In the northern hemisphere the south aspect will give the sun's rays a great part of the day, while a north aspect will shut them out altogether, and *vice versa* in the southern hemisphere. But a tree in the open plain or on a hill will get perpetual sunshine by day: it will be more mature, and the fruit and oil will be of superior quality. So Allah's light is not localised or immature: it is perfect and universal.

3002. Pure olive oil is beautiful in colour, consistency, and illuminating power. The world has tried all kinds of illuminants, and for economic reasons or convenience, one replaces another. But for coolness, comfort to the eyes, and steadiness, vegetable oils are superior to electricity, mineral oils,and animal oils. And among vegetable oils, olive oil takes a high place and deserves its sacred associations. Its purity is almost like light itself: you may suppose it to be almost light before it is lit. So with spiritual Truth: it illuminates the mind and understanding imperceptibly, almost before the human mind and heart have been consciously touched by it.

3003. Glorious, illimitable Light, which cannot be described or measured. And there are grades and grades of it, passing transcendently into regions of spiritual height, which man's imagination can scarcely conceive of. The topmost pinnacle is the true prototypal Light, the real Light, of which all others were reflections; the Light of Allah. Hence the saying of the Holy Prophet about Allah's "Seventy thousand veils of Light".

3004. The punctuation of the Arabic text makes it necessary to carry back the adverbial clause, "in houses", to something in the last verse, say "Lit from a blessed Tree"—the intervening clause being treated as parenthetical.

3005. That is, in all places of pure worship; but some Commentators understand special Mosques, such as the Ka'bah in Makkah,or the Mosques in Madīnah or Jerusalem; for these are specially held in honour.

In the mornings and
In the evenings, (again and
again)—[3006]

بِالْغُدُوِّ وَالْآصَالِ

37. By men whom neither
Traffic nor merchandise
Can divert from the
Remembrance[3007]
Of Allah, nor from regular Prayer,
Nor from the practice
Of regular Charity:
Their (only) fear is
For the Day when
Hearts and eyes
Will be transformed[3008]
(In a world wholly new)—

٣٧ رِجَالٌ لَّا تُلْهِيهِمْ
تِجَٰرَةٌ وَلَا بَيْعٌ عَن ذِكْرِ ٱللَّهِ
وَإِقَامِ ٱلصَّلَوٰةِ وَإِيتَآءِ ٱلزَّكَوٰةِ
يَخَافُونَ يَوْمًا تَتَقَلَّبُ فِيهِ
ٱلْقُلُوبُ وَٱلْأَبْصَٰرُ

38. That Allah may reward them
According to the best[3009]
Of their deeds, and add
Even more for them
Out of His Grace:
For Allah doth provide
For those whom He will,
Without measure.

٣٨ لِيَجْزِيَهُمُ ٱللَّهُ أَحْسَنَ
مَا عَمِلُوا۟ وَيَزِيدَهُم مِّن فَضْلِهِۦ
وَٱللَّهُ يَرْزُقُ مَن يَشَآءُ بِغَيْرِ حِسَابٍ

39. But the Unbelievers—
Their deeds are like a mirage[3010]
In sandy deserts, which
The man parched with thirst
Mistakes for water; until
When he comes up to it,

٣٩ وَٱلَّذِينَ كَفَرُوٓا۟ أَعْمَٰلُهُمْ كَسَرَابٍۭ
بِقِيعَةٍ يَحْسَبُهُ ٱلظَّمْـَٔانُ مَآءً
حَتَّىٰٓ إِذَا جَآءَهُۥ

3006. *In the evenings*: the Arabic word is *Āṣāl*, a plural of a plural, to imply emphasis: I have rendered that shade of meaning by adding the words "again and again".

3007. "Remembrance of Allah" is wider than Prayer: it includes silent contemplation, and active service of Allah and His creatures. The regular Prayers and regular Charity are the social acts performed through the organised community.

3008. Some renderings suggest the effects of terror on the Day of Judgement. But here we are considering the case of the righteous, whose "fear" of Allah is akin to love and reverence and who (as the next verse shows) hope for the best reward from Allah. But the world they will meet will be a wholly changed one.

3009. The best of the righteous do not deserve the reward that they get: all their faults are forgiven, and only their best actions are considered in the reward that they get. Nay, more! Out of the unbounded Grace of Allah even more is added to them. For in giving rewards, Allah's bounty is boundless.

3010. We have had various metaphors to give us an idea of the beneficent Light of Allah in the spiritual world. Now we have contrasted metaphors to enable us to see those who deny or refuse that Light, and are overwhelmed in utter darkness. The Light (of Allah) is an absolute Reality, and is mentioned first, and the souls that follow that Light are a reflected reality and are mentioned after the Light. On the other hand the Darkness is not a reality in itself, but a negation of reality; the reflected existences that refuse the Light are mentioned, and then their state, which is Unreality. Two metaphors are given: a mirage, in this verse, and the depths of darkness in the sea, in the next.

He finds it to be nothing:[3011] But he finds Allah[3012] (Ever) with him, and Allah Will pay him his account: And Allah is swift In taking account.	لَمْ يَجِدْهُ شَيْـًٔا وَوَجَدَ ٱللَّهَ عِندَهُۥ فَوَفَّىٰهُ حِسَابَهُۥ وَٱللَّهُ سَرِيعُ ٱلْحِسَابِ
40. Or (the Unbelievers' state) Is like the depths of darkness In a vast deep ocean, Overwhelmed with billow Topped by billow, Topped by (dark) clouds:[3013] Depths of darkness, one[3014] Above another: if a man Stretches out his hand, He can hardly see it! For any to whom Allah Giveth not light, There is no light![3015]	٤٠ أَوْ كَظُلُمَٰتٍ فِى بَحْرٍ لُّجِّىٍّ يَغْشَىٰهُ مَوْجٌ مِّن فَوْقِهِۦ مَوْجٌ مِّن فَوْقِهِۦ سَحَابٌ ظُلُمَٰتٌۢ بَعْضُهَا فَوْقَ بَعْضٍ إِذَآ أَخْرَجَ يَدَهُۥ لَمْ يَكَدْ يَرَىٰهَا وَمَن لَّمْ يَجْعَلِ ٱللَّهُ لَهُۥ نُورًا فَمَا لَهُۥ مِن نُّورٍ
SECTION 6.	
41. Seest thou not that it is Allah Whose praises all beings In the heavens and on earth[3016] Do celebrate, and the birds (Of the air) with wings[3017] Outspread? Each one knows Its own (mode of) prayer	٤١ أَلَمْ تَرَ أَنَّ ٱللَّهَ يُسَبِّحُ لَهُۥ مَن فِى ٱلسَّمَٰوَٰتِ وَٱلْأَرْضِ وَٱلطَّيْرُ صَٰٓفَّٰتٍ كُلٌّ قَدْ عَلِمَ صَلَاتَهُۥ

3011. The mirage, of which I have seen several instances in the Arabian deserts and in Egypt, is a strange phenomenon of illusion. It is a trick of our vision. In the language of our Parable, it rejects the Light which shows us the Truth, and deceives us with Falsehood. A lonely traveller in a desert, nearly dying of thirst, sees a broad sheet of water. He goes in that direction, lured on and on, but finds nothing at all. He dies in protracted agony.

3012. The rebel against Allah finds himself like the man deluded by a mirage. The Truth which he rejected is always with him. The mirage which he accepted leads to his destruction.

3013. What a graphic picture of darkness is the depths of the Ocean, wave upon wave, and on top of all, dense dark clouds! There is so little light even in ordinary depths of the Ocean that fishes which live there lose their eyes as useless organs. For lines 4-5 I am indebted to Gardiner's Translation of Ghazālī's *Mishkāt*.

3014. A contrast to "Light upon Light" in 24:35 above.

3015. The true source of Light in the world of Reality is Allah, and anyone who cuts himself off from the Light is in utter darkness indeed, for it is the negation of the only true Light, and not merely relative darkness, like that which we see, say, in the shadows of moonlight.

3016. *Cf.* 21:19-20.

3017. All denizens of the heavens, such as angels, all denizens of the earth (including the waters) such as man, animals, insects, fishes, etc., and all denizens of the air, such as birds, celebrate the praises of Allah. Each has his own mode of prayer and praise. It is not necessarily with words, for language (as we know it) is peculiar to man. But actions and other modes of self-expression recognise and declare the Glory of Allah.

And praise. And Allah
Knows well all that they do.

وَتَسْبِيحَهُۥ وَٱللَّهُ عَلِيمٌۢ بِمَا يَفْعَلُونَ

42. Yea, to Allah belongs
The dominion of the heavens
And the earth; and to Allah
Is the final goal (of all).[3018]

٤٢ وَلِلَّهِ مُلْكُ ٱلسَّمَٰوَٰتِ وَٱلْأَرْضِ ۖ
وَإِلَى ٱللَّهِ ٱلْمَصِيرُ

43. Seest thou not that Allah
Makes the clouds move
Gently, then joins them
Together, then makes them
Into a heap?—then wilt thou
See rain issue forth[3019]
From their midst. And He
Sends down from the sky
Mountain masses (of clouds)
Wherein is hail: He strikes
Therewith whom He pleases
And He turns it away
From whom He pleases.
The vivid flash of His lightning
Well-nigh blinds the sight.

٤٣ أَلَمْ تَرَ أَنَّ ٱللَّهَ يُزْجِى سَحَابًا
ثُمَّ يُؤَلِّفُ بَيْنَهُۥ ثُمَّ يَجْعَلُهُۥ رُكَامًا
فَتَرَى ٱلْوَدْقَ يَخْرُجُ مِنْ خِلَٰلِهِۦ
وَيُنَزِّلُ مِنَ ٱلسَّمَآءِ مِن جِبَالٍ
فِيهَا مِنۢ بَرَدٍ فَيُصِيبُ بِهِۦ مَن يَشَآءُ
وَيَصْرِفُهُۥ عَن مَّن يَشَآءُ ۖ
يَكَادُ سَنَا بَرْقِهِۦ يَذْهَبُ بِٱلْأَبْصَٰرِ

44. Is it Allah Who alternates
The Night and the Day:[3020]
Verily in these things
Is an instructive example
For those who have vision!

٤٤ يُقَلِّبُ ٱللَّهُ ٱلَّيْلَ وَٱلنَّهَارَ ۚ
إِنَّ فِى ذَٰلِكَ لَعِبْرَةً لِّأُو۟لِى ٱلْأَبْصَٰرِ

45. And Allah has created
Every animal from water:[3021]
Of them there are some

٤٥ وَٱللَّهُ خَلَقَ كُلَّ دَآبَّةٍ مِّن مَّآءٍ ۖ فَمِنْهُم مَّن

3018. From Him we are; to Him we belong; and to Him we shall return. Not only we, but all Creation, proclaims this in the whole world.

3019. Artists, or lovers of nature, or observers of clouds will appreciate this description of cloud effects—thin clouds floating about in fantastic shapes, joining together and taking body and substance, then emerging as heavy clouds heaped up, which condense and pour forth their rain. Then the heavy dark clouds in the upper regions, that bring hail—how distinct and yet how similar! They are truly like mountain masses! And when the hailstones fall, how local their area! It hits some localities and leaves free others almost interlaced! And the lightning—how blinding flashes come from thunderous clouds! In this Book of Nature can we not see the hand of the powerful and beneficent Allah?

3020. His power, wisdom, and goodness are shown no less in the regular phenomena of nature like the succession of Day and Night, than in the seasonal or seeming irregular movements of clouds and rain and hail and lightning. Those who have the spiritual vision can read this Book of Allah with delight and instruction.

3021. *Cf.* 21:30 n. 2691. Protoplasm is the basis of all living matter, and "the vital power of protoplasm seems to depend on the constant presence of water" (Lowsons' Text-book of Botany, Indian Edition. London 1922, p. 23). Text books of Zoology are also clear on the point. For example, see T. J. Parker and W. A. Haswell, Textbook of Zoology, London, 1910, vol I. p. 15: "Living protoplasm always contains a large amount of water.

That creep on their bellies;
Some that walk on two legs;
And some that walk on four.[3022]
Allah creates what He wills;[3023]
For verily Allah has power
Over all things.

46. We have indeed sent down
Signs that make things manifest:
And Allah guides whom He wills
To a Way that is straight.

47. They[3024] say, "We believe
In Allah and in the Messenger,
And we obey": but
Even after that, some of them
Turn away: they are not
(Really) Believers.

48. When they are summoned
To Allah and His Messenger,
In order that He may judge
Between them, behold, some
Of them decline (to come).

49. But if the right is[3025]
On their side, they come
To him with all submission.

50. Is it that there is
A disease in their hearts?
Or do they doubt,
Or are they in fear,
That Allah and His Messenger
Will deal unjustly with them?

يَمْشِى عَلَىٰ بَطْنِهِۦ وَمِنْهُم مَّن يَمْشِى عَلَىٰ رِجْلَيْنِ
وَمِنْهُم مَّن يَمْشِى عَلَىٰٓ أَرْبَعٍ يَخْلُقُ ٱللَّهُ مَا يَشَآءُ
إِنَّ ٱللَّهَ عَلَىٰ كُلِّ شَىْءٍ قَدِيرٌ

﴿٤٦﴾ لَّقَدْ أَنزَلْنَآ ءَايَٰتٍ مُّبَيِّنَٰتٍ
وَٱللَّهُ يَهْدِى مَن يَشَآءُ إِلَىٰ صِرَٰطٍ مُّسْتَقِيمٍ

﴿٤٧﴾ وَيَقُولُونَ ءَامَنَّا بِٱللَّهِ وَبِٱلرَّسُولِ وَأَطَعْنَا
ثُمَّ يَتَوَلَّىٰ فَرِيقٌ مِّنْهُم مِّنۢ بَعْدِ ذَٰلِكَ
وَمَآ أُو۟لَٰٓئِكَ بِٱلْمُؤْمِنِينَ

﴿٤٨﴾ وَإِذَا دُعُوٓا۟ إِلَى ٱللَّهِ وَرَسُولِهِۦ لِيَحْكُمَ
بَيْنَهُمْ إِذَا فَرِيقٌ مِّنْهُم مُّعْرِضُونَ

﴿٤٩﴾ وَإِن يَكُن لَّهُمُ ٱلْحَقُّ يَأْتُوٓا۟ إِلَيْهِ مُذْعِنِينَ

﴿٥٠﴾ أَفِى قُلُوبِهِم مَّرَضٌ
أَمِ ٱرْتَابُوٓا۟ أَمْ يَخَافُونَ
أَن يَحِيفَ ٱللَّهُ عَلَيْهِمْ وَرَسُولُهُۥ

3022. The creeping things include worms and lowly forms of animal life as well as reptiles (like snakes), centipedes, spiders, and insects. Where these have legs they are small, and the description of creeping or crawling is more applicable to them than that of walking. Fishes and sea-animals generally cannot be said to walk: their swimming is like "creeping on their bellies". Two-legged animals include birds and man. Most of the mammals walk on four legs. This includes the whole of the animal world

3023. In Allah's Will and Plan, the variety of forms and habits among animals is adapted to their various modes of life and stages of biological evolution.

3024. The Hypocrites, far from profiting from Allah's Light and Revelation, or declaring their open hostility, play fast and loose according to their selfish worldly aims.

3025. The Hypocrites only wanted to go to the judge who they thought was likely to give judgement in their favour. If their case was incontestable, and justice was on their side, they readily came to the Prophet, knowing that he was just and would judge in their favour, even against his own adherents. But if they had done wrong, an impartial judge was not to their taste. They would rather go to some one who would tip the balance in their favour! This form of selfishness and iniquity was not confined to the Hypocrites of Madīnah: It is common in all ages, and should be suppressed.

Nay, it is they themselves
Who do wrong.[3026]

بَلْ أُولَٰئِكَ هُمُ الظَّالِمُونَ

SECTION 7.

51. The answer of the Believers,
When summoned to Allah
And His Messenger, in order
That he may judge between them,
Is no other than this:
They say, "We hear and we obey":[3027]
It is such as these
That will attain felicity.[3028]

(٥١) إِنَّمَا كَانَ قَوْلَ الْمُؤْمِنِينَ إِذَا دُعُوا
إِلَى اللَّهِ وَرَسُولِهِ لِيَحْكُمَ بَيْنَهُمْ
أَنْ يَقُولُوا سَمِعْنَا وَأَطَعْنَا ۚ
وَأُولَٰئِكَ هُمُ الْمُفْلِحُونَ

52. It is such as obey
Allah and His Messenger,
And fear Allah and do
Right, that will win
(In the end).

(٥٢) وَمَنْ يُطِعِ اللَّهَ وَرَسُولَهُ
وَيَخْشَ اللَّهَ وَيَتَّقْهِ فَأُولَٰئِكَ هُمُ الْفَائِزُونَ

53. They swear their strongest oaths
By Allah that, if only thou
Wouldst command them, they
Would leave (their homes).[3029]
Say: "Swear ye not;
Obedience is (more) reasonable;
Verily, Allah is well acquainted
With all that ye do."

(٥٣) وَأَقْسَمُوا بِاللَّهِ جَهْدَ
أَيْمَانِهِمْ لَئِنْ أَمَرْتَهُمْ لَيَخْرُجُنَّ ۖ
قُلْ لَا تُقْسِمُوا ۖ طَاعَةٌ مَعْرُوفَةٌ ۚ
إِنَّ اللَّهَ خَبِيرٌ بِمَا تَعْمَلُونَ

54. Say: "Obey Allah, and obey
The Messenger: but if ye turn
Away, he is only responsible
For the duty placed on him
And ye for that placed
On you. If ye obey him,
Ye shall be on right guidance.

(٥٤) قُلْ أَطِيعُوا اللَّهَ وَأَطِيعُوا الرَّسُولَ ۖ
فَإِنْ تَوَلَّوْا فَإِنَّمَا عَلَيْهِ مَا حُمِّلَ
وَعَلَيْكُمْ مَا حُمِّلْتُمْ ۖ وَإِنْ تُطِيعُوهُ تَهْتَدُوا

3026. The real fact is that their conscience smites them. They know their own iniquity, and do not wish to go before a just judge who would be open to no influence and would be sure to give a righteous decree.

3027. *Cf.* 2:285. Contrast with it the attitude of the Unbelievers or Hypocrites, who say aloud, "we hear", but intend in their hearts to disobey (2:93).

3028. True happiness, whether here or in the Hereafter, is not to be attained by fraud or duplicity: it is the privilege of those who listen attentively to good counsel and carry it out in their lives.

3029. Some people, especially hypocrites, give hyperbolic assurances, as did the Madīnah Hypocrites to the Holy Prophet, that they would do any bidding, even to the forsaking of their hearths and homes. To this they are ready to swear their strongest oaths, which mean nothing. They are asked to spare their oaths, and quietly do at least such unheroic duties as they are asked to do in everyday life. Idle words are not of the least value. Allah will judge by your actions, and He knows all, whether it is open or secret.

The Messenger's duty is only
To preach the clear (Message).[3030]

وَمَا عَلَى ٱلرَّسُولِ إِلَّا ٱلْبَلَٰغُ ٱلْمُبِينُ

55\. Allah has promised, to those
Among you who believe
And work righteous deeds, that He[3031]
Will, of a surety, grant them
In the land, inheritance
(Of power), as He granted it
To those before them; that
He will establish in authority
Their religion—the one
Which He has chosen for them;
And that He will change
(Their state), after the fear[3032]
In which they (lived), to one
Of security and peace:
'They will worship Me (alone)
And not associate aught with Me.'
If any do reject Faith
After this, they are
Rebellious and wicked.

٥٥ وَعَدَ ٱللَّهُ ٱلَّذِينَ ءَامَنُوا۟ مِنكُمْ وَعَمِلُوا۟
ٱلصَّٰلِحَٰتِ لَيَسْتَخْلِفَنَّهُمْ فِى ٱلْأَرْضِ
كَمَا ٱسْتَخْلَفَ ٱلَّذِينَ مِن قَبْلِهِمْ
وَلَيُمَكِّنَنَّ لَهُمْ دِينَهُمُ ٱلَّذِى ٱرْتَضَىٰ لَهُمْ
وَلَيُبَدِّلَنَّهُم مِّنۢ بَعْدِ خَوْفِهِمْ أَمْنًا ۚ
يَعْبُدُونَنِى لَا يُشْرِكُونَ بِى شَيْـًٔا ۚ
وَمَن كَفَرَ بَعْدَ ذَٰلِكَ
فَأُو۟لَٰٓئِكَ هُمُ ٱلْفَٰسِقُونَ

56\. So establish regular Prayer
And give regular Charity;
And obey the Messenger;
That ye may receive mercy.

٥٦ وَأَقِيمُوا۟ ٱلصَّلَوٰةَ وَءَاتُوا۟ ٱلزَّكَوٰةَ
وَأَطِيعُوا۟ ٱلرَّسُولَ لَعَلَّكُمْ تُرْحَمُونَ

57\. Never think thou
That the Unbelievers
Are going to frustrate
(Allah's Plan) on earth:
Their abode is the Fire—
And it is indeed
An evil refuge!

٥٧ لَا تَحْسَبَنَّ ٱلَّذِينَ كَفَرُوا۟
مُعْجِزِينَ فِى ٱلْأَرْضِ ۚ
وَمَأْوَىٰهُمُ ٱلنَّارُ ۖ وَلَبِئْسَ ٱلْمَصِيرُ

3030\. 'If you disobey Allah's commands as explained by His Prophet, you are not going to be forced. The Prophet's mission is to train your will and explain clearly all the implications of your conduct. The responsibility for your conduct rests entirely on yourselves.

3031\. Three things are promised here, to those who have Faith and obey Allah's Law: (1) that they will inherit power and authority on the land, not for any selfish purposes of theirs by way of favouritism, but in order that they may maintain Allah's Law; (2) that the Religion of Right, which Allah has chosen for them, will be openly established, and will suppress all wrong and oppression; (3) that the righteous will live in peace and security, instead of having to suffer persecution, or leave their hearths and homes for the cause of Allah, or practise the rites of their Faith in secret.

3032\. If this verse was revealed about the time of the Battle of the Ditch (*Khandaq*), also called the Battle of the Confederates (*Aḥzāb*), A.H. 4-5, we can imagine the comfort it gave to the Muslims who were besieged in Madīnah by a force ten times their number. The Muslims then lived in a state of great suspense and danger, and under arms for days on end. (See 33:9-20). The security and authority they were promised came to them subsequently in abundant measures.

C. 160.—(24:58-64.)

For a self-respecting life on earth, respect
For others' privacy is most essential,
In the home and abroad: but superstitions
Are not met in intercourse amongst kin
Or true friends. In public council never
Fail to observe the most punctilious
Form and order: your self-respect
Demands that ye should give your Leader
Sincere respect and all obedience.
Ye may not know but Allah doth know
The inwardness of things both great and small.

SECTION 8.

58. O ye who believe![3033]
Let those whom your right hands[3034]
Possess, and the (children) among you
Who have not come of age[3035]
Ask your permission (before
They come to your presence),
On three occasions: before
Morning prayer; the while
Ye doff your clothes
For the noonday heat;
And after the late-night prayer:
These are your three times[3036]
Of undress: outside these times
It is not wrong for you
Or for them to move about
Attending to each other:
Thus does Allah make clear

٥٨ يَٰٓأَيُّهَا ٱلَّذِينَ ءَامَنُوا۟
لِيَسْتَـْٔذِنكُمُ ٱلَّذِينَ مَلَكَتْ أَيْمَٰنُكُمْ
وَٱلَّذِينَ لَمْ يَبْلُغُوا۟ ٱلْحُلُمَ مِنكُمْ ثَلَٰثَ مَرَّٰتٍ
مِّن قَبْلِ صَلَوٰةِ ٱلْفَجْرِ وَحِينَ تَضَعُونَ ثِيَابَكُم
مِّنَ ٱلظَّهِيرَةِ وَمِنۢ بَعْدِ صَلَوٰةِ ٱلْعِشَآءِ
ثَلَٰثُ عَوْرَٰتٍ لَّكُمْ لَيْسَ
عَلَيْكُمْ وَلَا عَلَيْهِمْ جُنَاحٌۢ بَعْدَهُنَّ
طَوَّٰفُونَ عَلَيْكُم بَعْضُكُمْ عَلَىٰ
بَعْضٍ كَذَٰلِكَ يُبَيِّنُ ٱللَّهُ لَكُمُ

3033. We now come to rules of decorum within the family circle in refined society. Servants and children have rather more freedom of access, as they come and go at all hours, and there is less ceremony with them. But even in their case there are limitations. During the night, before morning prayer, *i.e.*, before dawn, they must discreetly ask for permission before they enter, partly because they must not unnecessarily disturb people asleep, and partly because the people are then undressed. The same applies to the time for the midday siesta, and again to the time after night prayers, when people usually undress and turn in to sleep. For grown-ups the rule is stricter: they must ask permission to come in at all times (24:59).

3034. This would mean slaves in a regime of slavery. But the principle applies to all personal servants, who have to render personal service to their masters or mistresses by day and by night.

3035. I have translated "come of age" euphemistically for "attain the age of puberty".

3036. It is mark of refinement for ladies and gentlemen not to be slipshod or vulgarly familiar, in dress, manners, or speech; and Islam aims at making every Muslim man or woman, however humble in station, a refined gentleman or lady, so that he or she can climb the ladder of spiritual development with humble confidence in Allah, and with the cooperation of his brothers and sisters in Islam. The principles here laid down apply, if they are interpreted with due elasticity, even if social and domestic habits change, with changes in climate or in racial and personal habits. Punctilious self-respect and respect for others, in small things as well as great, are the keynotes in the simple rules of etiquette.

The Signs to you: for Allah
Is full of knowledge and wisdom.

ٱلْأَيَـٰتِ ۗ وَٱللَّهُ عَلِيمٌ حَكِيمٌ

59. But when the children among you[3037]
Come of age, let them (also)
Ask for permission, as do those
Senior to them (in age):[3038]
Thus does Allah make clear
His Signs to you: for Allah
Is full of knowledge and wisdom.[3039]

٥٩ وَإِذَا بَلَغَ ٱلْأَطْفَـٰلُ مِنكُمُ ٱلْحُلُمَ
فَلْيَسْتَـْٔذِنُوا۟ كَمَا ٱسْتَـْٔذَنَ ٱلَّذِينَ مِن قَبْلِهِمْ ۚ
كَذَٰلِكَ يُبَيِّنُ ٱللَّهُ لَكُمْ ءَايَـٰتِهِۦ ۗ
وَٱللَّهُ عَلِيمٌ حَكِيمٌ

60. Such elderly women[3040] as are
Past the prospect of marriage—
There is no blame on them
If they lay aside
Their (outer) garments, provided
They make not a wanton display
Of their beauty: but
It is best for them
To be modest: and Allah
Is One Who sees and knows[3041]
All things.

٦٠ وَٱلْقَوَٰعِدُ مِنَ ٱلنِّسَآءِ ٱلَّـٰتِى لَا يَرْجُونَ
نِكَاحًا فَلَيْسَ عَلَيْهِنَّ جُنَاحٌ أَن يَضَعْنَ
ثِيَابَهُنَّ غَيْرَ مُتَبَرِّجَـٰتٍۭ بِزِينَةٍ ۖ
وَأَن يَسْتَعْفِفْنَ خَيْرٌ لَّهُنَّ ۗ
وَٱللَّهُ سَمِيعٌ عَلِيمٌ

61. It is no fault in the blind
Nor in one born lame, nor
In one afflicted with illness,[3042]

٦١ لَّيْسَ عَلَى ٱلْأَعْمَىٰ حَرَجٌ وَلَا عَلَى ٱلْأَعْرَجِ
حَرَجٌ وَلَا عَلَى ٱلْمَرِيضِ حَرَجٌ

3037. *Children among you: i.e.*, in your house, not necessarily your own children. All in the house, including the stranger within your gate, must conform to these wholesome rules.

3038. *Those senior to them*: literally, those before them, *i.e.*, those who have already become grown-up before these children attain their age. It is suggested that each generation as it grows up should follow the wholesome tradition of its predecessors. While they were children, they behaved like children: when they grow up, they must behave like grown-ups.

3039. The refrain connects up this verse with the last verse, whose meaning is completed here. The slight variation ("*His* Signs" here, against "*the* Signs" there) shows that this verse is more personal, as referring to children who have now become responsible men and women.

3040. For elderly women in the home the rules of dress and decorum are not so exacting as for younger women, but they are also enjoined to study modesty, both because it is good in itself, and as an example to the younger people.

3041. Another example of a refrain: see n. 3039 above. Verses 58 and 59 were closer connected: their refrain was practically identical. This verse, though ancillary, is less closely connected; its refrain comes in like a half note melody.

3042. There were various Arab superstitions and fancies which are combated and rejected here. (1) The blind, or the halt, or those afflicted with serious disease were supposed to be objects of divine displeasure, and as such not fit to be associated with us in meals in our houses: we are not to entertain such a thought, as we are not judges of the causes of people's misfortunes, which deserve our sympathy and kindness. (2) It was considered unbecoming to take meals in the houses of near relatives: this taboo is not approved. (3) A simple superstition about houses in our possession but not in our actual occupation is disapproved. (4) If people think they should not fall under obligation to casual friends, that does not apply to a sincere friend, in whose company a meal is not to be rejected, but welcomed. (5) If people make a superstition either that they should always eat separately, or that they must always eat in company, as some people weary of their own company think, either of them is wrong. Man is free and should regulate his life according to needs and circumstances. (R).

Nor in yourselves, that ye
Should eat in your own houses,
Or those of your fathers,
Or your mothers, or your brothers,
Or your sisters, or your father's
brothers
Or your father's sisters,
Or your mother's brothers,
Or your mother's sisters,
Or in houses of which
The keys are in your possession,
Or in the house of a sincere
Friend of yours: there is
No blame on you, whether
Ye eat in company or
Separately. But if ye
Enter houses, salute each other—
A greeting or blessing
And purity as from Allah,[3043]
Thus does Allah make clear
The Signs to you: that ye
May understand.[3044]

وَلَا عَلَىٰٓ أَنفُسِكُمْ أَن تَأْكُلُوا۟ مِنۢ بُيُوتِكُمْ
أَوْ بُيُوتِ ءَابَآئِكُمْ أَوْ بُيُوتِ أُمَّهَٰتِكُمْ
أَوْ بُيُوتِ إِخْوَٰنِكُمْ أَوْ بُيُوتِ أَخَوَٰتِكُمْ
أَوْ بُيُوتِ أَعْمَٰمِكُمْ أَوْ بُيُوتِ عَمَّٰتِكُمْ
أَوْ بُيُوتِ أَخْوَٰلِكُمْ أَوْ بُيُوتِ خَٰلَٰتِكُمْ
أَوْ مَا مَلَكْتُم مَّفَاتِحَهُۥٓ أَوْ صَدِيقِكُمْ
لَيْسَ عَلَيْكُمْ جُنَاحٌ أَن تَأْكُلُوا۟
جَمِيعًا أَوْ أَشْتَاتًا فَإِذَا دَخَلْتُم بُيُوتًا فَسَلِّمُوا۟
عَلَىٰٓ أَنفُسِكُمْ تَحِيَّةً مِّنْ عِندِ ٱللَّهِ مُبَٰرَكَةً
طَيِّبَةً كَذَٰلِكَ يُبَيِّنُ ٱللَّهُ لَكُمُ
ٱلْءَايَٰتِ لَعَلَّكُمْ تَعْقِلُونَ

SECTION 9.

62. Only those are Believers,
Who believe in Allah and
His Messenger: when they are
With him on a matter
Requiring collective action,[3045]
They do not depart until
They have asked for his leave:
Those who ask for thy leave
Are those who believe in Allah
And His Messenger; so when
They ask for thy leave,
For some business of theirs,
Give leave to those of them

٦٢ إِنَّمَا ٱلْمُؤْمِنُونَ ٱلَّذِينَ
ءَامَنُوا۟ بِٱللَّهِ وَرَسُولِهِۦ وَإِذَا كَانُوا۟ مَعَهُۥ
عَلَىٰٓ أَمْرٍ جَامِعٍ لَّمْ يَذْهَبُوا۟ حَتَّىٰ يَسْتَـْٔذِنُوهُ
إِنَّ ٱلَّذِينَ يَسْتَـْٔذِنُونَكَ أُو۟لَٰٓئِكَ
ٱلَّذِينَ يُؤْمِنُونَ بِٱللَّهِ وَرَسُولِهِۦ
فَإِذَا ٱسْتَـْٔذَنُوكَ لِبَعْضِ شَأْنِهِمْ فَأْذَن لِّمَن

3043. The shades of meaning in *Salām* are explained in n. 2512 to 19:62. Here, we were first told that we might accept hospitality and good fellowship in each other's houses. Now we are told what spirit should animate us in doing so. It should not be a spirit only of self-satisfaction in a worldly sense. It should rather be a spirit of good will in the highest spiritual sense of the term—purity of motives and purity of life, as in the sight of Allah. *Cf.* Dante in the *Paradiso* (iii. 85): "In His will is our Peace."

3044. See notes 3039 and 3041 above. The refrain comes again, in a different form, closing the argument from a different point of view.

3045. *Matter requiring collective action*: anything that affects the Community as a whole: *Jumu'ah* and *'Id* prayers are periodical occasions of this kind, but what is meant here is, I think, joint consultations with a view to joint undertakings, such as Jihād, or some kind of organisation in peace.

Whom thou wilt,[3046] and ask
Allah for their forgiveness:[3047]
For Allah is Oft-Forgiving,
Most Merciful.

شِئْتَ مِنْهُمْ وَٱسْتَغْفِرْ لَهُمُ ٱللَّهَ
إِنَّ ٱللَّهَ غَفُورٌ رَّحِيمٌ

63. Deem not the summons
Of the Messenger among
yourselves
Like the summons of one[3048]
Of you to another: Allah
Doth know those of you
Who slip away under shelter
Of some excuse: then
Let those beware who
Withstand the Messenger's order,
Lest some trial befall them,[3049]
Or a grievous Penalty
Be inflicted on them.

٦٣ لَّا تَجْعَلُوا۟ دُعَآءَ ٱلرَّسُولِ
بَيْنَكُمْ كَدُعَآءِ بَعْضِكُم بَعْضًا
قَدْ يَعْلَمُ ٱللَّهُ ٱلَّذِينَ
يَتَسَلَّلُونَ مِنكُمْ لِوَاذًا
فَلْيَحْذَرِ ٱلَّذِينَ يُخَالِفُونَ عَنْ أَمْرِهِۦٓ
أَن تُصِيبَهُمْ فِتْنَةٌ أَوْ يُصِيبَهُمْ عَذَابٌ أَلِيمٌ

64. Be quite sure that
To Allah doth belong
Whatever is in the heavens
And on earth. Well doth He
Know what ye are intent upon:[3050]
And one day they will be
Brought back to Him, and He
Will tell them the truth
Of what they did.[3051]
For Allah doth know
All things.

٦٤ أَلَآ إِنَّ لِلَّهِ
مَا فِى ٱلسَّمَٰوَٰتِ وَٱلْأَرْضِ
قَدْ يَعْلَمُ مَآ أَنتُمْ عَلَيْهِ
وَيَوْمَ يُرْجَعُونَ إِلَيْهِ
فَيُنَبِّئُهُم بِمَا عَمِلُوا۟
وَٱللَّهُ بِكُلِّ شَىْءٍ عَلِيمٌۢ

3046. That is, those to whom, in the exercise of your impartial discretion, you think it expedient to give leave. "Will", unless the context shows otherwise, means "right will", not a will without any definite principle behind it.

3047. In important matters of general consultation, even though leave of absense is given on sufficient excuse, it implies some defect in duty on the part of the person to whom the leave is given, and therefore the need of forgiveness from Him to Whom we owe duty in a perfect measure.

3048. Three significations are possible. One is that adopted in the Translation, which agrees with the view of most Commentators. Another would be: 'Do not think that the prayer of the Prophet of Allah is like your ordinary requests to another: the Prophet's prayer will be about serious matters and will be accepted by Allah.' A third interpretation would be: 'Do not address the Prophet familiarly as you would address one another: use proper terms of respect for him.'

3049. The "trial" is understood to be some misfortune in this life, and the "grievous Penalty" to be the punishment in the Hereafter.

3050. The condition or position you are in, the motives which actuate you, and the ends you have in view.

3051. Things misunderstood or maligned, falsely praised or held in honour, or fraudulently shown to be good when they are evil—everything will be revealed in its true light on the Day of Final Judgement.

INTRODUCTION TO SŪRAH 25—*AL FURQĀN*)

This Sūrah further develops the contrast between Light and Darkness, as symbolical of knowledge and ignorance, righteousness and sin, spiritual progress and degradation. It closes with a definition of the deeds by which the righteous are known in the environment of this world.

It is mainly an early Makkan Sūrah, but its date has no significance.

Summary—Allah's highest gift to man is that He has furnished a Criterion for judgement between right and wrong—in His revelation, which teaches us the true significance of our eternal Future (25:1-20, and C. 161).

Those who do not use that Criterion will be full of woe when the Judgement comes, for Allah gave full warning at all times (25:21-44, and C. 162).

In the contrasts of shade and sun, night and day, death and life, and the whole ordering of Allah's Creation, men may learn of Allah Most Gracious; and the virtues of the righteous respond to Allah's care for them (25:45-77, and C. 163).

C. 161. —Among the highest and greatest of the gifts of Allah
(25:1-20.) Is His Revelation, which is the Criterion
By which we may judge between right
And wrong—between false and true worship,
Between the Message that comes from Allah
And the forgeries of men, between the Real
In our eternal Future and the Fancies
By which we are misled. The Prophets of Allah
Come as men to live among men and guide them.

Sūrah 25.

Al Furqān (The Criterion)

الجزء الثامن عشر سورة الفرقان

In the name of Allah, Most Gracious,
Most Merciful.

بِسْمِ اللَّهِ الرَّحْمَٰنِ الرَّحِيمِ

1. Blessed[3052] is He Who
Sent down the Criterion[3053]
To His servant, that it[3054]
May be an admonition
To all creatures—

(١) تَبَارَكَ الَّذِي نَزَّلَ الْفُرْقَانَ عَلَىٰ عَبْدِهِ
لِيَكُونَ لِلْعَالَمِينَ نَذِيرًا

2. He to Whom belongs
The dominion of the heavens
And the earth: no son
Has He begotten, nor has He
A partner in His dominion:
It is He Who created
All things, and ordered them
In due proportions.[3055]

(٢) الَّذِي لَهُ مُلْكُ السَّمَاوَاتِ وَالْأَرْضِ
وَلَمْ يَتَّخِذْ وَلَدًا وَلَمْ يَكُن لَّهُ شَرِيكٌ فِي الْمُلْكِ
وَخَلَقَ كُلَّ شَيْءٍ فَقَدَّرَهُ تَقْدِيرًا

3. Yet have they taken,[3056]
Besides Him, gods that can
Create nothing but are themselves
Created; that have no control
Of hurt or good to themselves;
Nor can they control Death
Nor Life nor Resurrection.

(٣) وَاتَّخَذُوا مِن دُونِهِ آلِهَةً لَّا يَخْلُقُونَ
شَيْئًا وَهُمْ يُخْلَقُونَ وَلَا يَمْلِكُونَ لِأَنفُسِهِمْ
ضَرًّا وَلَا نَفْعًا وَلَا يَمْلِكُونَ مَوْتًا
وَلَا حَيَاةً وَلَا نُشُورًا

3052. *Tabāraka:* the root meaning is "increase" or "abundance." Here that aspect of Allah's dealing with His creatures is emphasised, which shows his abundant goodness to all His creatures, in that He sent the Revelation of His Will, not only in the unlimited Book of Nature, but in a definite Book in human language, which gives clear directions and admonitions to all. The English word "blessed" hardly conveys that meaning, but I can find no other without departing far from established usage. To emphasise the meaning I have explained, I have translated "Blessed is. . .", but "Blessed be. . ." is also admissible, as it brings out another shade of meaning, that we praise and bless His Holy Name.

3053. That by which we can judge clearly between right and wrong. Here the reference is to the Qur'ān, which has already been symbolised by Light. This symbol is continued here, and many contrasts are shown, in the midst of which we can distinguish between the true and false by Allah's Light, especially the contrast between righteousness and sin.

3054. The pronoun in *yakūna* may refer to *Furqān* (the Criterion) or the *'Abd* (the Holy Prophet). In either case the ultimate meaning is the same. The Qur'ān is the standing Criterion for judgement between right and wrong.

3055. The majesty of Allah and His independence of all wants or help are mentioned, to show how exceedingly great is His goodness in revealing His Will to us.

3056. This is the first great distinction taught by the Criterion: to know the attribute of the true God, as against the false fancies of men. (R).

4. But the Misbelievers say:
"Naught is this but a lie[3057]
Which he has forged,
And others have helped him
At it." In truth it is they
Who have put forward
An iniquity and a falsehood.

٤ وَقَالَ ٱلَّذِينَ كَفَرُوٓاْ إِنۡ هَٰذَآ إِلَّآ إِفۡكٌ
ٱفۡتَرَىٰهُ وَأَعَانَهُۥ عَلَيۡهِ قَوۡمٌ ءَاخَرُونَۖ
فَقَدۡ جَآءُو ظُلۡمٗا وَزُورٗا

5. And they say: "Tales of
The ancients, which he has caused
To be written: and they
Are dictated before him
Morning and evening."[3058]

٥ وَقَالُوٓاْ أَسَٰطِيرُ ٱلۡأَوَّلِينَ ٱكۡتَتَبَهَا
فَهِيَ تُمۡلَىٰ عَلَيۡهِ بُكۡرَةٗ وَأَصِيلٗا

6. Say: "The (Qur'ān) was sent down
By Him Who knows
The Mystery (that is) in the heavens[3059]
And the earth: verily He
Is Oft-Forgiving, Most Merciful."

٦ قُلۡ أَنزَلَهُ ٱلَّذِي يَعۡلَمُ ٱلسِّرَّ
فِي ٱلسَّمَٰوَٰتِ وَٱلۡأَرۡضِۚ
إِنَّهُۥ كَانَ غَفُورٗا رَّحِيمٗا

7. And they say: "What sort
Of a messenger is this,
Who eats foods, and walks
Through the streets? Why
Has not an angel
Been sent down to him
To give admonition with him?[3060]

٧ وَقَالُواْ مَالِ هَٰذَا ٱلرَّسُولِ
يَأۡكُلُ ٱلطَّعَامَ وَيَمۡشِي فِي ٱلۡأَسۡوَاقِ
لَوۡلَآ أُنزِلَ إِلَيۡهِ مَلَكٞ فَيَكُونَ مَعَهُۥ نَذِيرًا

3057. *Ifk*, which I have translated as a "lie" may be distinguished from *zūr* at the end of this verse, translated "falsehood". The "lie" which the enemies attributed to the Holy Prophet of Allah was supposed to be something which did not exist in reality, but was invented by him with the aid of other people: the implication was that (1) the Revelation was not a revelation but a forgery, and that (2) the things revealed *e.g.*, the news of the Hereafter, the Resurrection, the Judgement, the Bliss of the Righteous and the sufferings of the Evil, were fanciful and had no basis in fact. Delusion is also suggested. The reply is that, so far from that being the case, the facts were true and the charges were false (*zūr*)— the falsehood being due to the habits of iniquity for which the Misbelievers' whole mental and spiritual attitude was responsible. (R).

3058. In their misguided arrogance they say: 'We have heard such things before: they are pretty tales which have come down from ancient times; they are good for amusement, but who takes them seriously? When the beauty and power of the Revelation are pointed out, and its miracle as coming from an unlearned man, they again hint at other men who wrote them, though they could not produce any one who could write anything like it.

3059. The answer is that the Qur'ān teaches spiritual knowledge of what is ordinarily hidden from men's sight, and such knowledge can only come from Allah, to Whom alone is known the Mystery of the whole Creation. In spite of man's sin and shortcomings, He forgives, and He sends His most precious gift, *i.e.*, the revelation of His Will.

3060. This is another objection: 'He is only a man like us: why is not an angel sent down, if not by himself, at least with him?' The answer is: angels would be of no use to men as Messengers, as they and men would not understand each other, and if angels came, it might cause more confusion and wonder than understanding in men's minds. *Cf.* 21:7-8, 27:94-95. The office of an angel is different. A teacher for mankind is one who shares their nature, mingles in their life, is acquainted with their doings, and sympathises with their joys and sorrows.

8. "Or (why) has not a treasure
Been bestowed on him, or
Why has he (not) a garden
For enjoyment?"[3061] The wicked
Say: "Ye follow none other
Than a man bewitched."[3062]

٨ أَوْ يُلْقَىٰٓ إِلَيْهِ كَنزٌ أَوْ تَكُونُ لَهُۥ جَنَّةٌ
يَأْكُلُ مِنْهَا ۚ وَقَالَ ٱلظَّٰلِمُونَ
إِن تَتَّبِعُونَ إِلَّا رَجُلًا مَّسْحُورًا

9. See what kinds of companions
They make for thee!
But they have gone astray,
And never a way will they
Be able to find![3063]

٩ ٱنظُرْ كَيْفَ ضَرَبُوا۟ لَكَ ٱلْأَمْثَٰلَ
فَضَلُّوا۟ فَلَا يَسْتَطِيعُونَ سَبِيلًا

SECTION 2.

10. Blessed is He Who,[3064]
If that were His Will,
Could give thee better (things)
Than those—Gardens beneath
which[3065]
Rivers flow; and He could
Give thee Palaces (secure
To dwell in).

١٠ تَبَارَكَ ٱلَّذِىٓ إِن شَآءَ جَعَلَ لَكَ
خَيْرًا مِّن ذَٰلِكَ جَنَّٰتٍ تَجْرِى مِن تَحْتِهَا
ٱلْأَنْهَٰرُ وَيَجْعَل لَّكَ قُصُورًا

11. Nay, they deny the Hour
(Of the Judgement to come):[3066]
But We have prepared
A Blazing Fire for such
As deny the Hour:

١١ بَلْ كَذَّبُوا۟ بِٱلسَّاعَةِ ۖ
وَأَعْتَدْنَا لِمَن كَذَّبَ بِٱلسَّاعَةِ سَعِيرًا

3061. Literally, 'that he may eat out of it'. As shown in n. 775 to 5:69, *akala* (to eat) has a comprehensive meaning, implying enjoyment of all kinds, physical, social, mental and moral, and spiritual. Here the garden itself stands for a type of the amenities of life: its fruits would be available for eating, in coolness for rest and refreshment, its waters and its landscape for aesthetic delight.

3062. *Cf.* 17:47. This speech, of the wicked or the ungodly, is meant to be even more bitter than that of the Misbelievers. It makes out the Teacher to be a demented fool.

3063. The charges the enemies made against the Messenger of Allah recoiled on those who made them. The Messenger was vindicated, and went from strength to strength, for Allah's Truth will always prevail. The men who perversely leave the way of truth, righteousness, and sincerity, have not only missed *the* Way, but on account of their perversity they will never be able to find any way by which they can get back to Truth.

3064. *Cf.* above, 25:1 The reminiscent phrase shows that the first argument, about the Revelation and Prophethood, is completed, and we now pass on to the contrast, the fate of the rejecters of both.

3065. This phrase is usually symbolical of the Bliss in the Hereafter. If it were Allah's Plan, He could give his Messengers complete felicity and power in this life also. Instead of being persecuted, mocked, driven out of their homes, and having to exert their utmost powers of body, mind, and character to plant the flag of Truth in an unbelieving world, they could have lived in ease and security. But that would not have given the real lessons they came to teach struggling humanity by their example.

3066. Denying the Hour of Judgement means denying the power of Justice and Truth to triumph; it means asserting the dominion of Evil. But the Reality itself will punish them, as shown in the following verses.

12. When it sees them
From a place far off,
They will hear its fury
And its raging sigh.[3067]

(١٢) إِذَا رَأَتْهُم مِّن مَّكَانٍ بَعِيدٍ سَمِعُوا لَهَا تَغَيُّظًا وَزَفِيرًا

13. And when they are cast,
Bound together, into a
Constricted place therein, they
Will plead for destruction
There and then![3068]

(١٣) وَإِذَآ أُلْقُوا مِنْهَا مَكَانًا ضَيِّقًا مُّقَرَّنِينَ دَعَوْا هُنَالِكَ ثُبُورًا

14. "This day plead not
For a single destruction:
Plead for a destruction oft-
repeated!"

(١٤) لَّا تَدْعُوا الْيَوْمَ ثُبُورًا وَاحِدًا وَادْعُوا ثُبُورًا كَثِيرًا

15. Say: "Is that best, or
The eternal Garden, promised[3069]
To the righteous? For them,
That is a reward as well
As a goal (or attainment).[3070]

(١٥) قُلْ أَذَٰلِكَ خَيْرٌ أَمْ جَنَّةُ الْخُلْدِ الَّتِي وُعِدَ الْمُتَّقُونَ ۚ كَانَتْ لَهُمْ جَزَآءً وَمَصِيرًا

16. "For them there will be
Therein all that they wish for:
They will dwell (there) for aye:
A promise to be prayed for
From thy Lord."[3071]

(١٦) لَّهُمْ فِيهَا مَا يَشَآءُونَ خَالِدِينَ ۚ كَانَ عَلَىٰ رَبِّكَ وَعْدًا مَّسْئُولًا

17. The Day He will gather
Them together as well as
Those whom they worship
Besides Allah, He will ask[3072]
"Was it ye who led

(١٧) وَيَوْمَ يَحْشُرُهُمْ وَمَا يَعْبُدُونَ مِن دُونِ اللَّهِ فَيَقُولُ ءَأَنتُمْ أَضْلَلْتُمْ

3067. For *zafir*, a deep emission of breath or a sigh, see n. 1607 to 11:106. Here the Fire is personified. It is raging with hunger and fury, and as soon as it sees them from ever so far, it emits a sigh of desire. Till then they had not realised their full danger. Now, just as their heart begins to tremble with terror, they are bound together—like with like—and cast into the roaring flames!

3068. Anything—total annihilation—would be better than the anguish they will suffer. But no annihilation will be granted to them. One destruction will not be enough to wipe out the intensity of their anguish. They will have to ask for many destructions, but they will not get them!

3069. Shifting the scene back to this life, they may fairly be asked: "Here is the result of the two courses of conduct: which do you prefer?"

3070. To the righteous, the final Bliss will in one sense be a reward. But the word "reward" does not truly represent facts, for two reasons: (1) the Bliss will be greater than they deserved; and (2) righteousness is its own reward. The best way of expressing the result would be to say that their highest Wish will now have been attained; the goal will have been reached; they will be in Allah's Presence. That is salvation in the highest.

3071. That is the sort of thing—the Goal of Allah's Presence—to be prayed for from Allah, and not ephemeral things, even though they may be good. And that is the sort of thing that Allah has promised and undertaken to give.

3072. The question is as in a Court of Justice, to convince those who stand arraigned.

These My servants astray.
Or did they stray
From the Path themselves?"

عِبَادِى هَٰٓؤُلَآءِ أَمْ هُمْ ضَلُّوا۟ ٱلسَّبِيلَ

18. They will say: "Glory to Thee!
Not meet was it for us
That we should take
For protectors others besides
Thee:[3073]
But Thou didst bestow,
On them and their fathers,
Good things (in life), until
They forgot the Message:
For they were a people
(Worthless and) lost."

١٨ قَالُوا۟ سُبْحَٰنَكَ مَا كَانَ يَنۢبَغِى لَنَآ
أَن نَّتَّخِذَ مِن دُونِكَ مِنْ أَوْلِيَآءَ
وَلَٰكِن مَّتَّعْتَهُمْ وَءَابَآءَهُمْ
حَتَّىٰ نَسُوا۟ ٱلذِّكْرَ
وَكَانُوا۟ قَوْمًۢا بُورًا

19. (Allah will say): "Now
Have they proved you liars
In what ye say: so
Ye cannot avert (your penalty)[3074]
Nor (get) help." And whoever
Among you does wrong,
Him shall We cause to taste
Of a grievous Penalty.

١٩ فَقَدْ كَذَّبُوكُم بِمَا تَقُولُونَ
فَمَا تَسْتَطِيعُونَ صَرْفًا وَلَا نَصْرًا
وَمَن يَظْلِم مِّنكُمْ
نُذِقْهُ عَذَابًا كَبِيرًا

20. And the messengers whom We
Sent before thee were all
(Men) who ate food
And walked through the streets:[3075]
We have made some of you
As a trial for others:[3076]

٢٠ وَمَآ أَرْسَلْنَا قَبْلَكَ مِنَ ٱلْمُرْسَلِينَ
إِلَّآ إِنَّهُمْ لَيَأْكُلُونَ ٱلطَّعَامَ وَيَمْشُونَ
فِى ٱلْأَسْوَاقِ وَجَعَلْنَا بَعْضَكُمْ لِبَعْضٍ فِتْنَةً

3073. The creatures of Allah who were worshipped will prove that they never asked for worship: on the contrary they themselves worshipped Allah and sought the protection of Allah and of none but Allah. *Cf.* 46:5-6. They will go further and show that the false worshippers added ingratitude to their other sins: for Allah bestowed abundance on them, and they blasphemed against Allah. They were indeed "worthless and lost", for the word *būr* bears both significations.

3074. The argument is as in a court of justice. If the false worshippers plead that they were misled by those whom they falsely worshipped, the latter will be confronted with them and will prove that plea to be false. No help can be got from them, and the penalty cannot then be averted. After all these things are thus explained in detail beforehand, all ungodly men should repent and turn to Allah. False worship is here identified with sin, for sin is disobedience to Allah, and arises from a wrong appreciation of Allah's attributes and His goodness to His creatures. The sinful man refuses, in his conduct, to serve Allah: he serves other things than Allah. (R)

3075. *Cf.* above, 25:7.

3076. In Allah's universal Plan, each unit or thing serves a purpose. If some are rich, the poor should not envy them: it may be that the rich man's proximity is itself a trial of their value. If some are poor, the righteous rich should not despise or neglect them: it may be that their coming within their sight is a trial for the real feeling of charity or brotherly love in the rich. If *A* is bad-tempered or persecutes or ill-uses *B*, it may be an opportunity for *B* to show his patience or humility or his faith in the ultimate prevalence of justice and truth. Whatever our experiences with other human beings may be, we must make them subserve the ends of our spiritual improvement and perhaps theirs too.

Will ye have patience?
For Allah is One Who
Sees (all things).

أَتَصْبِرُونَ
وَكَانَ رَبُّكَ بَصِيرًا

C. 162.—Woe to the misbelievers who arrogantly
(25:21-44.) Demand to see Allah, yet reject
His Signs! The Judgement will come,
And then they will see, too late, how evil
Casts nothing but treacherous snares for man.
Slowly comes Allah's Revelation, in ways
Most conducive to man's enlightenment.
Men in their folly reject the most obvious
Signs of Allah. Let them mock! Soon
Will they know! Alas! men ruled by self-impulse
Are worse than brute beasts to guide or control!

SECTION 3.

19/30

21. Such as fear not
The meeting with Us[3077]
(For Judgement) say:
"Why are not the angels
Sent down to us, or
(Why) do we not see[3078]
Our Lord?" Indeed they
Have an arrogant conceit
Of themselves, and mighty
Is the insolence of their impiety!

٢١ وَقَالَ ٱلَّذِينَ لَا يَرْجُونَ لِقَآءَنَا
لَوْلَآ أُنزِلَ عَلَيْنَا ٱلْمَلَـٰٓئِكَةُ
أَوْ نَرَىٰ رَبَّنَا
لَقَدِ ٱسْتَكْبَرُوا۟ فِىٓ أَنفُسِهِمْ
وَعَتَوْ عُتُوًّا كَبِيرًا

22. The Day they see the angels—
No joy will there be
To the sinners that Day:
The (angels) will say:
"There is a barrier
Forbidden (to you) altogether!"[3079]

٢٢ يَوْمَ يَرَوْنَ ٱلْمَلَـٰٓئِكَةَ
لَا بُشْرَىٰ يَوْمَئِذٍ لِّلْمُجْرِمِينَ
وَيَقُولُونَ حِجْرًا مَّحْجُورًا

23. And We shall turn
To whatever deeds they did
(In this life), and We shall

٢٣ وَقَدِمْنَآ إِلَىٰ مَا عَمِلُوا۟ مِنْ عَمَلٍ

3077. The blasphemers who have given up all Faith and laugh at the Hereafter: nothing is sacred to them: their arrogance and insolence are beyond all bounds.

3078. *Cf.* 2:55. The Israelites in the time of Moses demanded to see Allah. But they were dazed with thunder and lightning even as they looked on. Indeed death would have been their fate, had it not been for the mercy of Allah.

3079. They will not be allowed to enjoy any of the felicity or peace which will be the normal state of the new world of Reality. Their own past will stand as a barrier to shut them off.

Make such deeds as floating dust Scattered about.[3080]	فَجَعَلْنَٰهُ هَبَآءً مَّنثُورًا
24. The Companions of the Garden Will be well, that Day, In their abode, and have The fairest of places for repose.[3081]	٢٤ أَصْحَٰبُ ٱلْجَنَّةِ يَوْمَئِذٍ خَيْرٌ مُّسْتَقَرًّا وَأَحْسَنُ مَقِيلًا
25. The Day the heaven shall be Rent asunder with clouds,[3082] And angels shall be sent down, Descending (in ranks)—	٢٥ وَيَوْمَ تَشَقَّقُ ٱلسَّمَآءُ بِٱلْغَمَٰمِ وَنُزِّلَ ٱلْمَلَٰٓئِكَةُ تَنزِيلًا
26. That Day, the dominion As of right and truth, Shall be (wholly) for (Allah)[3083] Most Merciful: it will be A Day for dire difficulty For the Misbelievers.	٢٦ ٱلْمُلْكُ يَوْمَئِذٍ ٱلْحَقُّ لِلرَّحْمَٰنِ وَكَانَ يَوْمًا عَلَى ٱلْكَٰفِرِينَ عَسِيرًا
27. The Day that the wrongdoer Will bite at his hands, He will say, "Oh! would that I had taken a (straight) path With the Messenger![3084]	٢٧ وَيَوْمَ يَعَضُّ ٱلظَّالِمُ عَلَىٰ يَدَيْهِ يَقُولُ يَٰلَيْتَنِى ٱتَّخَذْتُ مَعَ ٱلرَّسُولِ سَبِيلًا
28. "Ah! woe is me! Would that I had never Taken such a one For a friend!	٢٨ يَٰوَيْلَتَىٰ لَيْتَنِى لَمْ أَتَّخِذْ فُلَانًا خَلِيلًا
29. "He did lead me astray From the Message (of Allah) After it had come to me!	٢٩ لَّقَدْ أَضَلَّنِى عَنِ ٱلذِّكْرِ بَعْدَ إِذْ جَآءَنِى

3080. The false hopes they built on in this life, and the deeds they did under the shadow of such false hopes will be dissipated if they were dust flying about in the wind. They will have no value whatever.

3081. The barrier which will shut out the evil ones will not exist for the righteous, who will have an abode of bliss and repose, for they will be in the Garden of Allah's Good Pleasure.

3082. It will be a new world, and the symbolism to describe it must necessarily draw upon our present experience of the finest things in nature. The sky, which now appears remote and unpeopled will be rent asunder. There will appear clouds of glory—angels and spiritual Lights of all grades and ranks—and the true majesty and goodness of Allah will be visible as it should be in reality, and as it is not now, on account of "our muddy vesture of decay". (R).

3083. See last note.

3084. The words are general, and for us the interest is in a general sense. A man who actually receives the Truth and is on the right path is all the more culpable if he is diverted from that path by the machinations of a worldly friend. The particular person whom some Commentators mention in this connection was one 'Uqbah who received the light of Islam, but was misled afterwards by a worldly friend into apostasy and blasphemy. He came to an evil end afterwards.

Ah! the Evil One is But a traitor to man![3085]	وَكَانَ ٱلشَّيْطَٰنُ لِلْإِنسَٰنِ خَذُولًا
30. Then the Messenger will say: "O my Lord! Truly My people took this Qur'ān For just foolish nonsense."[3086]	﴿٣٠﴾ وَقَالَ ٱلرَّسُولُ يَٰرَبِّ إِنَّ قَوْمِى ٱتَّخَذُوا۟ هَٰذَا ٱلْقُرْءَانَ مَهْجُورًا
31. Thus have We made For every prophet an enemy Among the sinners: but enough Is thy Lord to guide And to help.[3087]	﴿٣١﴾ وَكَذَٰلِكَ جَعَلْنَا لِكُلِّ نَبِىٍّ عَدُوًّا مِّنَ ٱلْمُجْرِمِينَ وَكَفَىٰ بِرَبِّكَ هَادِيًا وَنَصِيرًا
32. Those who reject Faith Say: "Why is not the Qur'ān Revealed to him all at once? Thus (is it revealed), that We May strengthen thy heart[3088] Thereby, and We have Rehearsed it to thee in slow, Well-arranged stages, gradually.	﴿٣٢﴾ وَقَالَ ٱلَّذِينَ كَفَرُوا۟ لَوْلَا نُزِّلَ عَلَيْهِ ٱلْقُرْءَانُ جُمْلَةً وَٰحِدَةً كَذَٰلِكَ لِنُثَبِّتَ بِهِۦ فُؤَادَكَ وَرَتَّلْنَٰهُ تَرْتِيلًا
33. And no question do they Bring to thee but We Reveal to thee the truth And the best explanation (thereof).[3089]	﴿٣٣﴾ وَلَا يَأْتُونَكَ بِمَثَلٍ إِلَّا جِئْنَٰكَ بِٱلْحَقِّ وَأَحْسَنَ تَفْسِيرًا

3085. The seductive wiles of the Evil One are merely meant for snares. There is fraud and treachery in them. The deceived ones are left in the lurch after the way of escape is made impossible for them

3086. *"My people"* are of course the unbelieving Quraysh. They treated the Qur'ān as foolish nonsense *i.e.*, something to be discarded. But they were only a handful of people whose vested interests were touched by the beneficent reforms initiated by Islam. They soon passed away, and all Arabic-speaking or Arabic-understanding people have considered the Qur'ān as a treasury of Truths expressed in the most beautiful possible language, with a meaning that grows deeper with research. (R).

3087. It is the nature of sin to be hostile to truth and righteousness, but such hostility will not harm the righteous and need cause no misgiving because Allah will guide and help those who work in His cause. And what could be better or more effective than His guidance and help?

3088. Three reasons are given for the gradual revelation of the Qur'ān. (1) *"To strengthen thy heart"*: the tremendous task of winning the Arab nation, and, through them, the whole world, to Islam, required superhuman patience, constancy, and firmness, and these qualities were strengthened by the gradual promulgation of solutions to each difficulty as it arose. (2) *"Slow, well-arranged stages"*: though the stages were gradual, as the occasion demanded from time to time, in the course of twenty-three years, the whole emerged, when completed, as a well-arranged scheme of spiritual instruction, as we have seen in following the arrangement of the Sūrahs. (3) *Questions put and answers given*: see next note.

3089. Divine knowledge is a fathomless ocean. But glimpses of it can be obtained by any individuals sincerely searching for the Truth. Their progress will be in grades. If they ask questions, and answers are then furnished to them, they are more likely to apprehend the Truth, as they have already explored the part of the territory in which they are interested. In the same way, when concrete questions arise by the logic of events, and they are answered not only for the occasion, but from a general stand-point, the teaching has a far greater chance of penetrating the human intelligence and taking shape in practical conduct. And this is the usual way of instruction in the Qur'ān.

34. Those who will be gathered
To Hell (prone) on their
faces—[3090]
They will be in an evil
Plight, and as to Path,
Most astray.[3091]

٣٤ ٱلَّذِينَ يُحْشَرُونَ
عَلَىٰ وُجُوهِهِمْ إِلَىٰ جَهَنَّمَ
أُوْلَٰٓئِكَ شَرٌّ مَّكَانًا وَأَضَلُّ سَبِيلًا

SECTION 4.

35. (Before this), We sent Moses
The Book, and appointed
His brother Aaron with him
As Minister;[3092]

٣٥ وَلَقَدْ ءَاتَيْنَا مُوسَى ٱلْكِتَٰبَ
وَجَعَلْنَا مَعَهُۥٓ أَخَاهُ هَٰرُونَ وَزِيرًا

36. And We commanded: "Go ye
Both, to the people who
Have rejectd our Signs:"
And those (people) We destroyed
With utter destruction.

٣٦ فَقُلْنَا ٱذْهَبَآ إِلَى ٱلْقَوْمِ
ٱلَّذِينَ كَذَّبُوا۟ بِـَٔايَٰتِنَا فَدَمَّرْنَٰهُمْ تَدْمِيرًا

37. And the people of Noah—
When they rejected the
messengers,
We drowned them,
And We made them
As a Sign for mankind;[3093]
And We have prepared
For (all) wrongdoers
A grievous Penalty—

٣٧ وَقَوْمَ نُوحٍ لَّمَّا كَذَّبُوا۟
ٱلرُّسُلَ أَغْرَقْنَٰهُمْ
وَجَعَلْنَٰهُمْ لِلنَّاسِ ءَايَةً
وَأَعْتَدْنَا لِلظَّٰلِمِينَ عَذَابًا أَلِيمًا

38. And also 'Ād and Thamūd,
And the Companions[3094]

٣٨ وَعَادًا وَثَمُودَا۟ وَأَصْحَٰبَ

3090. That is, in ignominy.

3091. This verse may be compared and contrasted with 25:24 above. Here the argument is rounded off about the distinction between the Good and Evil in their final Destiny. The Good are to have "the fairest of places for repose", and in contrast, the Evil are, "as to Path, most astray". They have no repose, and their wanderings lead nowhere.

3092. *Cf.* 20:29, and the whole passage there, which is merely referred to here, to show how previous Prophets were treated, but how they stuck fast to the Criterion given, to distinguish between Good and Evil.

3093. The stories of Noah, of the prophets of 'Ād and Thamūd (and of other prophets), in the reactions of their communities to their teaching are told in 26:105-159, below. Here they are just mentioned to illustrate how little respect past ages had for their prophets and teachers of Truth. But Allah's Truth did not suffer: it was the blind rejecters of spiritual Truth who were wiped out.

3094. Commentators are not clear as to who the "Companions of the *Rass*" were. The root meaning of "*rass*" is an old well or shallow water-pit. Another root connects it with the burial of the dead. But it is probably the name of a town or place. The "Companions of the *Rass*" may well have been the people of Shu'ayb, as they are here mentioned with the 'Ād, the Thamūd, and Lot's people, and the people of Shu'ayb are mentioned in a similar connection in 26:176-190 and in 9:84-95. Shu'ayb was the prophet of the Madyan people in the northwest of Arabia, where many old wells are found. There is however, an oasis town *al Rass* in the district of Qasīm in Middle Najd, about thirty-five miles southwest of the town of 'Unayzah, reputed to be the central point of the Arabian Peninsula, and situated midway between Makkah and Baṣrah. See Doughty's *Arabia Deserta*, thin paper one-volume edition, London 1926, II. 435 and Map. Lat. 26ºN., and Long. 43ºE.

Of the *Rass*, and many
A generation between them.

ٱلرَّسِّ وَقُرُونًۢا بَيْنَ ذَٰلِكَ كَثِيرًا

39. To each one We set forth
Parables and examples;
And each one We broke
To utter annihilation
(For their sins).

٣٩ وَكُلًّا ضَرَبْنَا لَهُ ٱلْأَمْثَٰلَ
وَكُلًّا تَبَّرْنَا تَتْبِيرًا

40. And the (Unbelievers) must indeed
Have passed by the town
On which was rained[3095]
A shower of evil: did they not
Then see it (with their own
Eyes)? But they fear not
The Resurrection.

٤٠ وَلَقَدْ أَتَوْا عَلَى ٱلْقَرْيَةِ ٱلَّتِىٓ أُمْطِرَتْ
مَطَرَ ٱلسَّوْءِ ۚ أَفَلَمْ يَكُونُوا۟ يَرَوْنَهَا ۚ
بَلْ كَانُوا۟ لَا يَرْجُونَ نُشُورًا

41. When they see thee,
They treat thee no otherwise
Than in mockery: "Is this
The one whom Allah has sent
As a messenger?"

٤١ وَإِذَا رَأَوْكَ إِن يَتَّخِذُونَكَ إِلَّا هُزُوًا
أَهَٰذَا ٱلَّذِى بَعَثَ ٱللَّهُ رَسُولًا

42. "He indeed would well-nigh
Have misled us from
Our gods, had it not been
That we were constant
To them!"—Soon will they
Know, when they see
The Penalty, who it is
That is most misled
In Path![3096]

٤٢ إِن كَادَ لَيُضِلُّنَا عَنْ ءَالِهَتِنَا
لَوْلَآ أَن صَبَرْنَا عَلَيْهَا ۚ
وَسَوْفَ يَعْلَمُونَ حِينَ
يَرَوْنَ ٱلْعَذَابَ مَنْ أَضَلُّ سَبِيلًا

43. Seest thou such a one
As taketh for his god
His own passion (or impulse)?
Couldst thou be a disposer
Of affairs for him?[3097]

٤٣ أَرَءَيْتَ مَنِ ٱتَّخَذَ إِلَٰهَهُۥ هَوَىٰهُ
أَفَأَنتَ تَكُونُ عَلَيْهِ وَكِيلًا

3095. This refers to Lot's story and the destruction of Sodom and Gomorrah, the wicked cities of the plain near the Dead Sea, by a shower of brimstone. The site lies on the highway between Arabia and Syria. *Cf.* 15:74, 76, and n. 1998.

3096. "*Path*" (*Sabīl*) is almost equivalent here to conduct or way of life.

3097. The man who worships his own passions or impulses or desires is the most hopeless to teach or lead or guide. If it were anything else the matter with him, the Teacher could argue with him. But Reason cannot prevail over blind passion. It is vain to hope that such a man could be led, until his mad desires are killed. No one could undertake any responsibility for him, for he obeys no law and follows no advice. He is worse than brute beasts, which may not understand, but at least follow the wholesome instincts implanted in them by Allah. The lawless man has killed his instincts and is unwilling to submit to guidance.

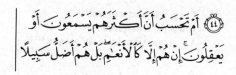

44. Or thinkest thou that most
Of them listen or understand?
They are only like cattle;—
Nay, they are worse astray
In Path.

٤٤ أَمْ تَحْسَبُ أَنَّ أَكْثَرَهُمْ يَسْمَعُونَ أَوْ يَعْقِلُونَ ۚ إِنْ هُمْ إِلَّا كَالْأَنْعَٰمِ ۖ بَلْ هُمْ أَضَلُّ سَبِيلًا

C. 163.—But the Signs of Allah are everywhere
(25:45-77.) In creation. The Sun and the Shadow,
The Day and the Night, the Wind and the Rain—
All things in nature are symbols, and point
To the Law Divine, and the destiny, good
Or ill, of man. Will he not learn
And put his trust in Him, the Merciful?
His true servants ever adore him
In humility and fear of wrong, in faith
And just moderation in life, in respect
For duties owed to Allah and men
And self, in avoidance of all that is false
Or futile, in strict and grateful attention
To Allah's Message, and in the wish
To put themselves and their families
In the van of those who love and honour Allah.

SECTION 5.

45. Hast thou not turned[3098]
Thy vision to thy Lord?—
How He doth prolong[3099]
The Shadow! If He willed,
He could make it stationary!
Then do We make
The sun its guide;[3100]

٤٥ أَلَمْ تَرَ إِلَىٰ رَبِّكَ كَيْفَ مَدَّ ٱلظِّلَّ وَلَوْ شَآءَ لَجَعَلَهُۥ سَاكِنًا ثُمَّ جَعَلْنَا ٱلشَّمْسَ عَلَيْهِ دَلِيلًا

3098. We saw in 24:35 that Allah is the Light of the heavens and the earth. We have now, another sublime passage, in which we are asked to contemplate the Glory of Allah by a parable of the subtle play of Light and Shade in Allah's creation. (R).

3099. In our artificial life and surroundings we fail to see some of the finest mysteries of Light and Shade. We praise, and rightly so, the wonderful colours of sunset. We see, particularly in climates more northerly than that of India, the subtle play of Light and Shade in the twilights succeeding sunsets. If we were as assiduous in seeing sunrises and the play of Light and Shade preceding them, we should see phenomena even more impressive, as the early morning seems to us more holy than any other time in the twenty-four hours of the sun's daily journey. There is the first false dawn, with its curious uncertain light and the curious long uncertain shadows which is casts. Then there are the streaks of black in the East, succeeded by the true dawn, with its delicate tones of colours, and light and shade. The light of this true or false Dawn is not given by the direct rays of the sun. In a sense it is not light, but the shadows or reflections of light. And they gradually merge into actual sunrise, with its more substantial or more defined shadows, which we can definitely connect with the sun.

3100. The morning shadows are long but more definite, and their length and direction are seen to be guided by the sun. But they change insensibly every second or fraction of a second.

46. Then We draw it in[3101]
Towards Ourselves—
A contraction by easy stages.[3102]

٤٦ ثُمَّ قَبَضْنَٰهُ إِلَيْنَا قَبْضًا يَسِيرًا

47. And He it is Who makes
The Night as a Robe
For you, and Sleep as Repose,
And makes the Day
(As it were) a Resurrection.[3103]

٤٧ وَهُوَ ٱلَّذِى جَعَلَ لَكُمُ ٱلَّيْلَ لِبَاسًا
وَٱلنَّوْمَ سُبَاتًا وَجَعَلَ ٱلنَّهَارَ نُشُورًا

48. And He it is Who sends
The Winds as heralds
Of glad tidings, going before[3104]
His Mercy, and We send down
Pure water from the sky—[3105]

٤٨ وَهُوَ ٱلَّذِىٓ أَرْسَلَ
ٱلرِّيَٰحَ بُشْرًۢا بَيْنَ يَدَىْ رَحْمَتِهِۦ ۚ
وَأَنزَلْنَا مِنَ ٱلسَّمَآءِ مَآءً طَهُورًا

49. That with it, We may give
Life to a dead land,
And slake the thirst
Of things We have created—[3106]
Cattle and men in great numbers.

٤٩ لِّنُحْۦِىَ بِهِۦ بَلْدَةً مَّيْتًا وَنُسْقِيَهُۥ
مِمَّا خَلَقْنَآ أَنْعَٰمًا وَأَنَاسِىَّ كَثِيرًا

3101. As the sun rises higher and higher, the shadows contract. In regions where the sun actually gets to the zenith at noon, there is no shadow left at that time. Where does it go? It was but a shadow cast by a substance and it gets absorbed by the substance which produced it. (R).

3102. Let us now reverently turn our vision (as far as we are able) to the symbolic meaning. Allah is the Light. All things in creation—whether concrete or abstract—are but shadows, depending on His Light. All shadows are not equal. He gives length or size of substance to such as He pleases. And some shadows almost become reflected lights, like the light of the false or the true Dawn. Such are holy men, in all kinds of gradations. The shadows are constantly in a state of flux; so are all things in Creation, all things we see or covet in this life. Allah, if He wills, can give some of them greater fixity or comparative stability. (R).

3103. Here the symbolism presents a fresh point of view. It is still a contrast between Light and Shade; but the shade of Night is as a Robe to cover and screen us and give us Repose from activity; and the Light of Day is for striving, work, activity. Or again, the Night is like Death, our temporary Death before Judgement, the time during which our senses are sealed in Sleep; and the Day is like the renewal of Life at the Resurrection.

3104. *Cf.* 7:57. The Winds are heralds of Joy, ushering in Rain, which is one form of Allah's Mercy. Again, the symbolism presents a fresh point of view. Heat (which is connected with light) sets up currents in the atmosphere, besides sucking up moisture from the seas, and distributing it by means of Winds over wide surfaces of the earth. In the physical world we know the beneficent action of heat on life, and by contrast, we also know how intolerable high temperatures may become, and how the cloud-bearing Winds come as welcome heralds of rain. (R).

3105. Rain water (in pure air) is not only pure water distilled in air and sky, but it is the best purifying and sanitating agent on the largest scale known to us.

3106. The whole cycle of water—sea, clouds, rain or hail or snow, rivers, and sea again—is a remarkable illustration of the processes of nature making Allah's providence visible to us. The salts of the sea sanitate and purify all the filth that pours into it. Water action, in the form of rain, frost, glaciers, rivers, lakes, etc., is responsible for the building up and configuration of the crust of the earth, and is the chief agent in physical geography. A parched desert quickly comes to life under the action of water. All drinking water, whether derived from rivers, canals, lakes, reservoirs, springs, wells, or waterworks of any kind, are ultimately traceable to rain. The connection of life with water is intimate. The physical basis of life itself, protoplasm, is, in great part, water: see 25:54 below.

50. And We have distributed
The (water) amongst them, in
order[3107]
That they may celebrate
(Our) praises, but most men
Are averse (to aught) but[3108]
(Rank) ingratitude.

وَلَقَدْ صَرَّفْنَٰهُ بَيْنَهُمْ لِيَذَّكَّرُوا۟ فَأَبَىٰٓ أَكْثَرُ ٱلنَّاسِ إِلَّا كُفُورًا ﴿٥٠﴾

51. Had it been Our Will,
We could have sent
A warner to every centre
Of population,[3109]

وَلَوْ شِئْنَا لَبَعَثْنَا فِى كُلِّ قَرْيَةٍ نَّذِيرًا ﴿٥١﴾

52. Therefore listen not
To the Unbelievers, but strive
Against them with the utmost
Strenuousness, with the
(Qur'ān).[3110]

فَلَا تُطِعِ ٱلْكَٰفِرِينَ وَجَٰهِدْهُم بِهِۦ جِهَادًا كَبِيرًا ﴿٥٢﴾

53. It is He Who has
Let free the two bodies
Of flowing water:[3111]
One palpable and sweet,
And the other salt and bitter;

وَهُوَ ٱلَّذِى مَرَجَ ٱلْبَحْرَيْنِ هَٰذَا عَذْبٌ فُرَاتٌ وَهَٰذَا مِلْحٌ أُجَاجٌ ﴿٥٣﴾

3107. The water is distributed all over the world, in order that all life may receive its support, according to its needs. In 25:48-50, we have the argument of contrasts stated in another way. Water is life, and is made available to sustain life all over the world: this is a physical fact which all can see. But water is also the symbol of spiritual life, whose sustaining principle is the Will of Allah as made known to us through Revelation. It sometimes comes to us in our inward or spiritual storms. Many violent unsettlements of the spirit are but heralds of the refreshing showers of spiritual understanding that come in their wake. They purify our souls, and produce spiritual Life even where there was a parched spiritual desert before. They continue to sustain us in our normal spiritual Life out of the reservoirs of Allah's Revelation, which are open to all, and well-distributed in time and space. The universality of distribution is again referred to in the following verse.

3108. In contrast to Allah's abounding Mercy is man's base ingratitude: another symbolic contrast between Light and Darkness, or Water and Drought.

3109. Allah's Message has been distributed to all nations. If it had been necessary, a Prophet could have been sent to every town and village. But Allah's Plan is different. He has sent His Light to every heart, through His Signs in man's conscience, in Nature, and in Revelation.

3110. The distribution of Allah's Signs being universal, the Prophet of Allah pays no heed to carping critics who reject Faith. He wages the biggest Jihād of all, with the weapon of Allah's Revelation. (R).

3111. *Maraja*: literally, let free or loose cattle for grazing. *Bahrayn*: two seas, or two bodies of flowing water: for *bahr* is applied both to the salt sea and to rivers. In the world taken as a whole, there are two bodies of water, *viz.*, (1) the great salt Ocean, and (2) the bodies of sweet water fed by rain, whether they are rivers, lakes, or underground springs: their source in rain makes them one, and their drainage, whether above ground or underground, eventually to the Ocean, also makes them one. They are free to mingle, and in a sense they do mingle, for there is a regular watercycle: see n. 3106 above: and the rivers flow constantly to the sea, and tidal rivers get sea water for several miles up their estuaries at high tide. Yet in spite of all this, the laws of gravitation are like a barrier or partition set by Allah, by which the two bodies of water as a whole are always kept apart and distinct. In the case of rivers carrying large quantities of water to the sea, like the Mississippi or the Yangtse-Kiang, the river water with its silt remains distinct from sea water for a long distance out to sea. But the wonderful Sign is that the two bodies of water, though they pass through each other, remain distinct bodies, with their distinct functions.

Yet has He
Made a barrier between them,
A partition that is forbidden
To be passed.[3112]

وَجَعَلَ بَيْنَهُمَا بَرْزَخًا
وَحِجْرًا مَّحْجُورًا

54. It is He Who has
Created man from water:[3113]
Then has He established
Relationships of lineage[3114]
And marriage: for thy Lord
Has power (over all things).

٥٤ وَهُوَ ٱلَّذِى خَلَقَ مِنَ ٱلْمَآءِ بَشَرًا
فَجَعَلَهُۥ نَسَبًا وَصِهْرًا
وَكَانَ رَبُّكَ قَدِيرًا

55. Yet do they worship,
Besides Allah, things that can
Neither profit them nor
Harm them: and the Misbeliever
Is a helper (of Evil),
Against his own Lord![3115]

٥٥ وَيَعْبُدُونَ مِن دُونِ ٱللَّهِ
مَا لَا يَنفَعُهُمْ وَلَا يَضُرُّهُمْ
وَكَانَ ٱلْكَافِرُ عَلَىٰ رَبِّهِۦ ظَهِيرًا

56. But thee We only sent
To give glad tidings
And admonition.

٥٦ وَمَآ أَرْسَلْنَـٰكَ إِلَّا مُبَشِّرًا وَنَذِيرًا

57. Say: "No reward do I
Ask of you for it but this:
That each one who will
May take a (straight) Path
To his Lord."

٥٧ قُلْ مَآ أَسْـَٔلُكُمْ عَلَيْهِ مِنْ أَجْرٍ
إِلَّا مَن شَآءَ أَن يَتَّخِذَ إِلَىٰ رَبِّهِۦ سَبِيلًا

3112. In Allah's overall scheme of things, bodies of salt and sweet water, which are adjoining and yet separate, have significant functions. Weaving a harmonious fabric out of these different fibres shows both Allah's power and wisdom. Incidentally, this verse points to a fact which has only recently been discovered by science. This fact relates to the oceans of the world: they meet and yet each remains separate for Allah has placed "a barrier, a partition" between them. (Eds.).

3113. The basis of all living matter in the physical world, protoplasm, is water: *Cf.* 24:45 and 21:30, and notes thereon.

3114. Water is a fluid, unstable thing: yet from it arises the highest form of life known to us in this world—man. And man has not only the functions and characteristics of the noblest animals, but his abstract relationships are also typical of his highest nature. He can trace lineage and pedigree, and thus remember and commemorate a long line of ancestors, to whom he is bound by ties of piety, which no mere animal can do. Further, there is the mystic union in marriage: it is not only like the physical union of animals, but it gives rise to relationships arising out of the sexes of individuals who were not otherwise related to each other. These are physical and social facts. But behind them, again, is the symbolic lesson of spiritual contrasts: as there is a long way to go between water and man, so there is a long way to go between an ordinary man and him who is lifted up to divine Light. As opposite sexes, though different in function, are one and contribute to each other's happiness, so persons of diverse talents may unite in the spiritual world for their own highest good and in the service of Allah.

3115. Here is the highest contrast of all—material things which are inert, and Allah, Whose goodness and power are supreme; Faith and Unfaith, meriting glad tidings and admonition; the selfish man who is self-centered, and the man of God, who works for others without reward.

58. And put thy trust
In Him Who lives
And dies not; and celebrate
His praise; and enough is He
To be acquainted with
The faults of His servants—[3116]

٥٨ وَتَوَكَّلْ عَلَى ٱلْحَىِّ
ٱلَّذِى لَا يَمُوتُ وَسَبِّحْ بِحَمْدِهِۦ
وَكَفَىٰ بِهِۦ بِذُنُوبِ عِبَادِهِۦ خَبِيرًا

59. He Who created the heavens
And the earth and all
That is between, in six days,[3117]
And is firmly established
On the Throne (of authority):[3118]
Allah, Most Gracious:
Ask thou, then, about Him
Of any acquainted (with such
things.[3119]

٥٩ ٱلَّذِى خَلَقَ ٱلسَّمَٰوَٰتِ وَٱلْأَرْضَ
وَمَا بَيْنَهُمَا فِى سِتَّةِ أَيَّامٍ
ثُمَّ ٱسْتَوَىٰ عَلَى ٱلْعَرْشِ
ٱلرَّحْمَٰنُ فَسْـَٔلْ بِهِۦ خَبِيرًا

60. When it is said to them,
"Adore ye (Allah) Most Gracious!",
They say, "And what is (Allah)
Most Gracious? Shall we adore
That which thou commandest us?"
And it increases their flight
(From the Truth).[3120]

٦٠ وَإِذَا قِيلَ لَهُمُ ٱسْجُدُوا۟ لِلرَّحْمَٰنِ
قَالُوا۟ وَمَا ٱلرَّحْمَٰنُ أَنَسْجُدُ لِمَا تَأْمُرُنَا
وَزَادَهُمْ نُفُورًا

SECTION 6.

61. Blessed is He Who made
Constellations in the skies,
And placed therein a Lamp[3121]
And a Moon giving light;

٦١ تَبَارَكَ ٱلَّذِى جَعَلَ فِى ٱلسَّمَآءِ بُرُوجًا
وَجَعَلَ فِيهَا سِرَٰجًا وَقَمَرًا مُّنِيرًا

3116. Allah knows our faults better than we or anyone else. It is no use hiding anything from Him. We must put our trust completely in Him. His care is for all, and He is Allah Most Gracious.

3117. *Cf.* 7:54 and n. 1031.

3118. See n. 1386 to 10:3.

3119. The argument is about the question, "in whom shall we put our trust?" Worldly men put their trust in worldly things: the righteous man only in Allah. The true distinction will be quite clear from a ray of divine knowledge. If you do not see it all clearly, ask of those who possess such knowledge.

3120. Those who have no spiritual Light cannot understand this precept about putting all our trust in Allah. It seems to them foolish. They have no faith, or but a superficial faith. They may possibly pronounce the name of Allah on their lips, but they cannot understand the full significance of His title of *Rahmān* (Most Gracious). Perhaps they are afraid on account of their sins; perhaps they do not see how unbounded is the mercy of Allah. Such men are contrasted against the true servants of Allah, who are described below in 25:63-75.

3121. The glorious Lamp of the skies is the Sun; and next to him is the Moon, which gives borrowed light. The Constellations of course, include the Signs of the Zodiac, which mark the path of the planets in the heavens.

62. And it is He Who made
The Night and the Day
To follow each other:
For such as have the will[3122]
To celebrate His praises
Or to show their gratitude.

٦٢ وَهُوَ ٱلَّذِى جَعَلَ ٱلَّيْلَ وَٱلنَّهَارَ
خِلْفَةً لِّمَنْ أَرَادَ أَن يَذَّكَّرَ
أَوْ أَرَادَ شُكُورًا

63. And the servants of (Allah)
Most Gracious are those
Who walk on the earth
In humility, and when the
ignorant[3123]
Address them, they say,
"Peace!";

٦٣ وَعِبَادُ ٱلرَّحْمَٰنِ ٱلَّذِينَ
يَمْشُونَ عَلَى ٱلْأَرْضِ هَوْنًا
وَإِذَا خَاطَبَهُمُ ٱلْجَٰهِلُونَ قَالُوا۟ سَلَٰمًا

64. Those who spend the night
In adoration of their Lord
Prostrate and standing;[3124]

٦٤ وَٱلَّذِينَ يَبِيتُونَ لِرَبِّهِمْ
سُجَّدًا وَقِيَٰمًا

65. Those who say: "Our Lord!
Avert from us the Wrath
Of Hell, for its Wrath
Is indeed an affliction
grievous—[3125]

٦٥ وَٱلَّذِينَ يَقُولُونَ رَبَّنَا
ٱصْرِفْ عَنَّا عَذَابَ جَهَنَّمَ
إِنَّ عَذَابَهَا كَانَ غَرَامًا

66. "Evil indeed is it
As an abode, and as
A place to rest in";[3126]

٦٦ إِنَّهَا سَآءَتْ مُسْتَقَرًّا وَمُقَامًا

67. Those who, when they spend,
Are not extravagant and not

٦٧ وَٱلَّذِينَ إِذَآ أَنفَقُوا۟ لَمْ يُسْرِفُوا۟ وَلَمْ

3122. The scenes of the phenomenal world are Signs of the Self-Revelation of Allah, for those who understand and who have the will to merge their wills with His. This they do (1) by praising Him, which means understanding something of His nature, and (2) by gratitude to Him, which means carrying out His Will, and doing good to their fellow creatures. These two attitudes of mind and heart give rise to various consequences in their lives, which are detailed in the following verse.

3123. *Ignorant*: in a spiritual sense. *Address*: in the aggressive sense. Their humility is shown in two ways: (1) to those in real search of knowledge, they give such knowledge as they have and as the recipients can assimilate; (2) to those who merely dispute, they do not speak harshly, but say "Peace!", as much as to say, "May it be well with you, may you repent and be better"; or "May Allah give me peace from such wrangling"; or "Peace, and Good-bye: let me leave you!".

3124. Humble prayer brings them nearer to Allah.

3125. This is a prayer of humility: such a person relies, not on any good works which he may have done, but on the Grace and Mercy of Allah: and he shows a lively sense of the Day of Judgement, when every action will weigh for or against a soul.

3126. The misery which results from sin is not only grievous to live in ("an abode") but also grievous "to rest in" or "to stand in", if it be only for a short time.

Niggardly, but hold a just
(balance)
Between those (extremes);[3127]

يَقْتُرُوا وَكَانَ بَيْنَ ذَٰلِكَ قَوَامًا

68. Those who invoke not,
With Allah, any other god,
Nor slay such life as Allah
Has made sacred, except
For just cause, nor commit[3128]
Fornication—and any that does
This (not only) meets punishment

٦٨ وَالَّذِينَ لَا يَدْعُونَ مَعَ اللَّهِ إِلَٰهًا آخَرَ
وَلَا يَقْتُلُونَ النَّفْسَ الَّتِي حَرَّمَ اللَّهُ إِلَّا بِالْحَقِّ
وَلَا يَزْنُونَ ۚ وَمَن يَفْعَلْ ذَٰلِكَ يَلْقَ أَثَامًا

69. (But) the Penalty on the Day
Of Judgement will be doubled
To him, and he will dwell
Therein in ignominy—[3129]

٦٩ يُضَاعَفْ لَهُ الْعَذَابُ يَوْمَ الْقِيَامَةِ
وَيَخْلُدْ فِيهِ مُهَانًا

70. Unless he repents, believes
And works righteous deeds,
For Allah will change
The evil of such persons
Into good, and Allah is
Oft-Forgiving, Most Merciful,[3130]

٧٠ إِلَّا مَن تَابَ وَآمَنَ وَعَمِلَ
عَمَلًا صَالِحًا فَأُولَٰئِكَ يُبَدِّلُ اللَّهُ
سَيِّئَاتِهِمْ حَسَنَاتٍ ۗ وَكَانَ اللَّهُ غَفُورًا رَّحِيمًا

71. And whoever repents and does
good
Has truly turned to Allah
With an (acceptable)
conversion—

٧١ وَمَن تَابَ وَعَمِلَ صَالِحًا
فَإِنَّهُ يَتُوبُ إِلَى اللَّهِ مَتَابًا

72. Those who witness no falsehood[3131]
And, if they pass by futility,[3132]

٧٢ وَالَّذِينَ لَا يَشْهَدُونَ الزُّورَ
وَإِذَا مَرُّوا بِاللَّغْوِ

3127. In ordinary spending, this is a wise rule. But even in charity, in which we give of our best, it is not expected that we should be extravagant, *i.e.*, that we should either do it for show (to impress other people), or do it thoughtlessly, which would be the case if we "rob Peter to pay Paul". We should certainly not be niggardly, but we should remember everyone's rights, including our own, and strike a perfectly just balance between them.

3128. Here three things are expressly condemned: (1) false worship, which is a crime against Allah; (2) the taking of life, which is a crime against our fellow creatures; and (3) fornication, which is a crime against our self-respect, against ourselves. Every crime is against Allah, His creatures, and ourselves, but some may be viewed more in relation to one than to another. The prohibition against taking life is qualified: "except for just cause": *e.g.*, in judicial punishment for murder, or in self-preservation, which may include not only self-defense in the legal sense, but also the clearing out of pests, and the provision of meat under conditions of *Halāl*: see n. 698 to 5:5. After this comes a long parenthesis, which ends with verse 71, below.

3129. The three crimes just mentioned are specially detestable and infamous, and as ignominy will be added to other punishments, the penalty will be double that of ordinary punishment.

3130. But even in the case of great crimes, if there is true repentance as tested by a changed life in conduct, Allah's Mercy is available, and it will transform the repentant's nature form evil to good.

3131. *Witness no falsehood* has two significations, both implied in this pasage: (1) those who give no evidence that is false; and (2) those who do not assist in anything which implies fraud or falsehood.

3132. There is not only condemnation of positive falsehood or of being mixed up with things implying falsehood, but futilities—vain random talk, unedifying jokes, useless show, etc.—are all condemned. If a good man finds himself in such an affair, he must withdraw from it in an honourable, dignified way, not in a fussy arrogant way.

They pass by it
With honourable (avoidance);

مَرُّوا كِرَامًا

73. Those who, when they are
Admonished with the Signs
Of their Lord, droop not down[3133]
At them as if they were
Deaf or blind;

٧٣ وَالَّذِينَ إِذَا ذُكِّرُوا بِآيَاتِ رَبِّهِمْ
لَمْ يَخِرُّوا عَلَيْهَا صُمًّا وَعُمْيَانًا

74. And those who pray,
"Our Lord! Grant unto us
Wives and offspring who will be
The comfort of our eyes,[3134]
And give us (the grace)
To lead the righteous."[3135]

٧٤ وَالَّذِينَ يَقُولُونَ رَبَّنَا هَبْ لَنَا
مِنْ أَزْوَاجِنَا وَذُرِّيَّاتِنَا قُرَّةَ أَعْيُنٍ
وَاجْعَلْنَا لِلْمُتَّقِينَ إِمَامًا

75. Those are the ones who
Will be rewarded with
The highest place in heaven,
Because of their patient constancy:
Therein shall they be met
With salutations and peace,

٧٥ أُولَٰئِكَ يُجْزَوْنَ
الْغُرْفَةَ بِمَا صَبَرُوا
وَيُلَقَّوْنَ فِيهَا تَحِيَّةً وَسَلَامًا

76. Dwelling therein—how beautiful
An abode and place of rest!

٧٦ خَالِدِينَ فِيهَا
حَسُنَتْ مُسْتَقَرًّا وَمُقَامًا

77. Say (to the Rejecters):
"My Lord is not uneasy
Because of you if ye call not on
Him:[3136]
But ye have indeed rejected
(Him), and soon will come
The inevitable (punishment)!"

٧٧ قُلْ مَا يَعْبَأُ بِكُمْ رَبِّي
لَوْلَا دُعَاؤُكُمْ
فَقَدْ كَذَّبْتُمْ فَسَوْفَ يَكُونُ لِزَامًا

3133. *Kharra* may mean: to fall down, to snore, to droop down as if the person were bored or inattentive, or did not wish to see or hear or pay attention.

3134. We must also pray for the maintenance of Allah's Law after us, through our wives and descendants: in our eyes they should not be mere accidents or play things, but a real comfort and fulfilment of our spiritual longings. Perhaps, through them, as well as through ourselves, we may, by Allah's grace, be able to give a lead for truth and righteousness.

3135. Let us recapitulate the virtues of the servants of Allah: (1) they are humble and forbearing to those below them in spiritual worth: (2) they are constantly, by adoration, in touch with Allah; (3) they always remember the Judgement in the Hereafter; (4) they are moderate in all things; (5) they avoid treason to Allah, to their fellow creatures, and to themselves; (6) they give a wide berth not only to falsehood but to futility; (7) they pay attention, both in mind and manner, to the Signs of their Lord; (8) their ambition is to bring up their families in righteousness and to lead in all good. A fine code of individual and social ethics, a ladder of spiritual development, open to all.

3136. Let not the wicked think that it causes Allah any annoyance or uneasiness if they do not serve or worship Him. He is high above all needs. But He turns in His Mercy to all who call on Him. For those who arrogantly reject Him, the evil consequences of their rejection are inevitable, and must soon come to pass. (R).

INTRODUCTION TO SŪRAH 26—*AL SHU'ARĀ'.*

This Sūrah begins a new series of four Sūrahs (26—29), which illustrate the contrast between the spirit of Prophecy and spiritual Light and the reactions to it in the communities among whom it appeared, by going back to old Prophets and the stories of the Past, as explained in the Introduction to S. 17.

In this particular Sūrah we have the story of Moses in his fight with Pharaoh and of Pharaoh's discomfiture. Other Prophets mentioned are Abraham, Noah, Hūd, Ṣāliḥ, Lūṭ, and Shu'ayb. The lesson is drawn that the Qur'ān is a continuation and fulfilment of previous Revelations, and is pure Truth, unlike poetry of vain poets.

Chronologically the Sūrah belongs to the middle Makkan period, when the contact of the Light of Prophecy with the milieu of Pagan Makkah was testing the Makkans in their most arrogant mood.

Summary—The conflict of Unbelief with Truth is vain: so was the conflict of Pharaoh with Moses: Pharaoh's magicians bowed to the Truth, and Pharaoh and his hosts were drowned (26:1-69, and C. 164).

Nor did Abraham's people gain anything by their resisting of the Truth he preached, and Noah's people perished by their Unbelief (26:70-122, and C. 165).

Hūd warned his people against reliance on their material strength and Sāliḥ against sacrilege, but in both cases the evil ones were brought low (26:123-159, and C. 166).

Lūṭ had to deal with unspeakable crimes, and Shu'ayb against dishonest dealings and mischief: their teaching was rejected, but the rejecters were wiped out (26:160-191, and C. 167).

So, when the spirit of Prophecy came to Makkah, it was resisted by the votaries of evil: but Truth is not like vain poetry, and must triumph at last (26:192-277, and C. 168).

C. 164.—Allah's Plan works unceasingly: His Light
(26:1-69.) Shines none the less brightly, because some
Reject it or mock at it. Moses was freed
From all fear when Allah gave him His Signs
And sent him to Pharaoh: he boldly
Proclaimed the Message, and won the wise ones
Of Egypt: the rejecters, with Pharaoh, perished,
And their heritage passed to worthier hands.

Sūrah 26.

Al Shu'arā' (The Poets)

In the name of Allah, Most Gracious, Most Merciful.

بِسْمِ ٱللَّهِ ٱلرَّحْمَٰنِ ٱلرَّحِيمِ

1. Ṭā' Sīn Mīm.[3137]

طسٓمٓ ﴿١﴾

2. These are Verses of the Book
That makes (things) clear.[3138]

تِلْكَ ءَايَٰتُ ٱلْكِتَٰبِ ٱلْمُبِينِ ﴿٢﴾

3. It may be thou frettest
Thy soul with grief, that they[3139]
Do not become Believers.

لَعَلَّكَ بَٰخِعٌ نَّفْسَكَ أَلَّا يَكُونُوا۟ مُؤْمِنِينَ ﴿٣﴾

4. If (such) were Our Will,[3140]
We could send down to them
From the sky a Sign,
To which they would bend
Their necks in humility.

إِن نَّشَأْ نُنَزِّلْ عَلَيْهِم مِّنَ ٱلسَّمَآءِ ءَايَةً فَظَلَّتْ أَعْنَٰقُهُمْ لَهَا خَٰضِعِينَ ﴿٤﴾

5. But there comes not
To them a newly-revealed
Message from (Allah) Most Gracious,
But they turn away therefrom.

وَمَا يَأْتِيهِم مِّن ذِكْرٍ مِّنَ ٱلرَّحْمَٰنِ مُحْدَثٍ إِلَّا كَانُوا۟ عَنْهُ مُعْرِضِينَ ﴿٥﴾

6. They have indeed rejected
(The Message):

فَقَدْ كَذَّبُوا۟ ﴿٦﴾

3137. This is a combination of three Abbreviated Letters, as to which, generally, see Appendix I, printed at the end of S. 2. This particular combination occurs here and at the head of S. 28, while the intervening Sūrah 27 has it in the syncopated form *Ṭā' Sīn*. None of the explanatory conjectures which I have seen carries conviction for me. If the letters stand for *Ṭur al Sīnīn* (Mount Sinai) and *Mūsā* (Moses), whose story fills a large part of this Sūrah, why is the letter *Mīm* omitted in S. 27. where the same meaning would apply? There is, however, one fact to which I should like to draw attention. There are eleven sections in this Sūrah, and eight of them end with the word *Raḥīm* (with the final *Mīm*). The three exceptions are sections 2 and 3, and section 11. But sections 2 and 3 are part of the story of Moses, which is completed in section 4, and that ends with "*Raḥīm*". The main argument in section 11 ends at verse 217, which ends with *Raḥīm*. We can say that the whole Sūrah is based on a refrain in the word "*Raḥīm*". Whether this has any bearing on our present enquiry I cannot say. My own position is that where we have material, we should pursue our researches, but we should never be dogmatic in such matters, as some Mysteries can never be solved by mere research.

3138. *Cf.* 5:17, and n. 716. The comparison of Allah's revelations with Light is continued.

3139. "They" are the Pagans of Makkah. From a human point of view it was a great disappointment to Allah's Messenger in the middle period of his Makkan ministry that the Makkans could not be brought to believe in the Truth.

3140. If it had been Allah's Will and Plan to force people's will, He could quite easily have forced the Makkans. But His Will and Plan work differently. His revelation is meant to train man's own will so that it conforms to Allah's beneficent purpose.

So they will know soon (enough)
the truth
Of what they mocked at![3141]

فَسَيَأْتِيهِمْ أَنۢبَٰٓؤُا۟ مَا كَانُوا۟ بِهِۦ يَسْتَهْزِءُونَ

7. Do they not look
At the earth—how many
Noble things of all kinds
We have produced therein?[3142]

٧ أَوَلَمْ يَرَوْا۟ إِلَى ٱلْأَرْضِ كَمْ أَنۢبَتْنَا فِيهَا مِن كُلِّ زَوْجٍ كَرِيمٍ

8. Verily, in this is a Sign:
But most of them
Do not believe.

٨ إِنَّ فِى ذَٰلِكَ لَءَايَةً ۖ وَمَا كَانَ أَكْثَرُهُم مُّؤْمِنِينَ

9. And verily, thy Lord
Is He, the Exalted in Might,[3143]
Most Merciful.

٩ وَإِنَّ رَبَّكَ لَهُوَ ٱلْعَزِيزُ ٱلرَّحِيمُ

SECTION 2.

10. Behold, thy Lord called[3144]
Moses: "Go to the people
Of iniquity—

١٠ وَإِذْ نَادَىٰ رَبُّكَ مُوسَىٰٓ أَنِ ٱئْتِ ٱلْقَوْمَ ٱلظَّٰلِمِينَ

11. "The people of Pharaoh:
Will they not fear Allah?"

١١ قَوْمَ فِرْعَوْنَ ۚ أَلَا يَتَّقُونَ

12. He said: "O my Lord!
I do fear that they
Will charge me with falsehood:

١٢ قَالَ رَبِّ إِنِّىٓ أَخَافُ أَن يُكَذِّبُونِ

13. "My breast will be straitened.[3145]
And my speech may not go
(Smoothly): so send unto Aaron.

١٣ وَيَضِيقُ صَدْرِى وَلَا يَنطَلِقُ لِسَانِى فَأَرْسِلْ إِلَىٰ هَٰرُونَ

3141. They may laugh at Allah's Message of righteousness, but they will soon see the power of Truth and realise the real significance of the movement which they opposed. Where were the Pagans of Makkah after Badr, and still more, after the bloodless surrender of Makkah? The meaning may be applied universally throughout history.

3142. If evil has a little run in this life, let them not run away with the notion that the world is for evil. They have only to look around at the physical and moral world around them, and they would be undeceived. But they are blind and without the Faith (the Light) which would open their eyes.

3143. One Who is able to carry out all His Will and Plans. See n. 2818 to 22:40.

3144. The part of the story of Moses told here is how Moses felt diffident about undertaking his commission; how Allah reassured him; how he went to Pharaoh with "the Signs"; how Pharaoh and his people rejected him; how their blasphemy recoiled on themselves, but the cause of Allah triumphed; in other words, the point here is the reaction of a wicked people to the Light that was held up to them, considered in its relation to the mind of Allah's Messenger.

3145. As we should say in English, "My heart would fail me, and my tongue cleave to my mouth." Moses had an impediment of speech, and his mission was risky: see next note. But Allah's Plan works in wondrous ways. Aaron was given to assist him in his mission, and Moses's shortcomings were transformed by Allah's grace into power, so that he became the most powerful leader of Israel.

14. And (further), they have
A charge of crime against me;[3146]
And I fear they may
Slay me."

١٤ وَلَهُمْ عَلَيَّ ذَنْبٌ فَأَخَافُ أَن يَقْتُلُونِ

15. Allah said: "By no means!
Proceed then, both of you,
With Our Signs; We
Are with you, and will
Listen (to your call).

١٥ قَالَ كَلَّا فَٱذْهَبَا بِـَٔايَٰتِنَآ إِنَّا مَعَكُم مُّسْتَمِعُونَ

16. "So go forth, both of you,
To Pharaoh, and say:
'We have been sent
By the Lord and Cherisher
Of the Worlds;

١٦ فَأْتِيَا فِرْعَوْنَ فَقُولَآ إِنَّا رَسُولُ رَبِّ ٱلْعَٰلَمِينَ

17. " 'Send thou with us
The Children of Israel.' "

١٧ أَنْ أَرْسِلْ مَعَنَا بَنِىٓ إِسْرَٰٓءِيلَ

18. (Pharaoh) said: "Did we not[3147]
Cherish thee as a child
Among us, and didst thou not
Stay in our midst
Many years of thy life?

١٨ قَالَ أَلَمْ نُرَبِّكَ فِينَا وَلِيدًا وَلَبِثْتَ فِينَا مِنْ عُمُرِكَ سِنِينَ

19. "And thou didst a deed
Of thine which (thou knowest)[3148]
Thou didst, and thou art
An ungrateful (wretch)!"

١٩ وَفَعَلْتَ فَعْلَتَكَ ٱلَّتِى فَعَلْتَ وَأَنتَ مِنَ ٱلْكَٰفِرِينَ

3146. Moses was brought up in the palace of Pharaoh, as narrated in his personal story in 20:39-40 and n. 2563. When he was grown-up he saw an Egyptian smiting an Israelite, and as the Israelites were being generally oppressed by the Egyptians, Moses's anger was roused, and he slew the Egyptian. He then fled to the Midianite country in the Sinai peninsula, where he received the divine commission. But the charge of slaying the Egyptian was hanging against him. He was also apparently irascible. But Allah's grace cured his temper and he became wise; his impediment in speech, for he stood up boldly to speak to Pharaoh; and his fear, for he dared the Egyptians with Allah's Signs, and they were afraid of him.

3147. There is a little play of wit here on the part of Pharaoh. When Moses speaks of the "Lord and Cherisher of the Worlds", Pharaoh says: "Who cherished you? Did we not bring you up as a child? Did you not grow up among us?" By implication Pharaoh suggests that he is the cherisher of Moses, and in any case Pharaoh laid claim to godhead himself.

3148. Further, Pharaoh reminds Moses of his having slain the Egyptian, and taunts him: "You are not only a murderer: you are an ungrateful wretch" (using *kāfir* again in a double sense) "to have killed one of the race that brought you up!"

20. Moses said: "I did it
Then, when I was
In error.[3149]

قَالَ فَعَلْتُهَآ إِذًا وَأَنَا۠ مِنَ ٱلضَّآلِّينَ ﴿٢٠﴾

21. "So I fled from you (all)
When I feared you;[3150]
But My Lord has (since)
Invested me with judgement
(And wisdom) and appointed me
As one of the messengers.

فَفَرَرْتُ مِنكُمْ لَمَّا خِفْتُكُمْ فَوَهَبَ لِى رَبِّى حُكْمًا وَجَعَلَنِى مِنَ ٱلْمُرْسَلِينَ ﴿٢١﴾

22. "And this is the favour[3151]
With which thou dost
Reproach me—that you
Hast enslaved the Children
Of Israel!"

وَتِلْكَ نِعْمَةٌ تَمُنُّهَا عَلَىَّ أَنْ عَبَّدتَّ بَنِىٓ إِسْرَٰٓءِيلَ ﴿٢٢﴾

23. Pharaoh said: "And what
Is the 'Lord and Cherisher
Of the Worlds?'"[3152]

قَالَ فِرْعَوْنُ وَمَا رَبُّ ٱلْعَٰلَمِينَ ﴿٢٣﴾

24. (Moses) said: "The Lord
And Cherisher of the heavens
And the earth, and all between—
If ye want to be
Quite sure."

قَالَ رَبُّ ٱلسَّمَٰوَٰتِ وَٱلْأَرْضِ وَمَا بَيْنَهُمَآ إِن كُنتُم مُّوقِنِينَ ﴿٢٤﴾

25. (Pharaoh) said to those
Around: "Do ye not listen
(To what he says)?"[3153]

قَالَ لِمَنْ حَوْلَهُۥٓ أَلَا تَسْتَمِعُونَ ﴿٢٥﴾

3149. What is Moses's reply? He is no longer afraid. He tells the whole truth, extenuating nothing in his own favour. "Yes I did it: but I did it under an error." There are three implications in this: "(1) I was wrong in doing it in a temper and in being hasty: (2) I was wrong in taking the law into my own hands, but I repented and asked for Allah's pardon (28:15-16): (3) that was a time when I was under your influence, but since then I am a changed man, as Allah has called me."

3150. He accounts for all his movements, much more than Pharaoh had asked for. He has nothing to hide. At that time, he was under the influence of fear, and he had fled from him. Now he is serving Allah, the Lord of the Worlds. He has no fear: he is a messenger.

3151. Pharaoh had called Moses ungrateful and reproached him with all the favours which Moses had received from the Egyptians. "What favours?" he says: "Do you count it also as a favour to me that you have enslaved my brethren the Children of Israel?" Moses was now speaking as a Prophet of Allah, not as an individual. Any individual favours he may have received were blotted out by the oppression of his people. (R).

3152. Moses having eliminated all personalities, the argument now comes up to the highest plane of all—the attributes of Allah and His mercies. Moses had put forward this before, as implied in verse 16 above, but Pharaoh had twisted it into personalities. Now we come back to the real issue. It may have been in the same sitting, or it may have been in a later sitting. (R).

3153. Moses had stirred up the wrath of Pharaoh, both by putting forward the name of the One True God as against Pharaoh's pretended godhead, and by suggesting that any man of judgement would understand Allah's majesty. While Pharaoh turns to his people in indignation, Moses drives the nail in further: "He is the God of the heavens and the earth and all between: therefore He is also *your* God, and the God of your fathers from the beginning. Any other pretensions are false!"

26. (Moses) said: "Your Lord
And the Lord of your fathers
From the beginning!"

قَالَ رَبُّكُمْ وَرَبُّ ءَابَآئِكُمُ ٱلْأَوَّلِينَ ٢٦

27. (Pharaoh) said: "Truly
Your messenger who has been
Sent to you is
A veritable madman!"[3154]

قَالَ إِنَّ رَسُولَكُمُ ٱلَّذِىٓ أُرْسِلَ إِلَيْكُمْ لَمَجْنُونٌ ٢٧

28. (Moses) said: "Lord of the East
And the West, and all between!
If ye only had sense!"

قَالَ رَبُّ ٱلْمَشْرِقِ وَٱلْمَغْرِبِ وَمَا بَيْنَهُمَآ إِن كُنتُمْ تَعْقِلُونَ ٢٨

29. (Pharaoh) said: "If thou
Dost put forward any god
Other than me, I will
Certainly put thee in prison!"[3155]

قَالَ لَئِنِ ٱتَّخَذْتَ إِلَٰهًا غَيْرِى لَأَجْعَلَنَّكَ مِنَ ٱلْمَسْجُونِينَ ٢٩

30. (Moses) said: "Even if I
Showed you something
Clear (and) convincing?"[3156]

قَالَ أَوَلَوْ جِئْتُكَ بِشَىْءٍ مُّبِينٍ ٣٠

31. (Pharaoh) said: "Show it then
If thou tellest the truth!"

قَالَ فَأْتِ بِهِۦٓ إِن كُنتَ مِنَ ٱلصَّٰدِقِينَ ٣١

32. So (Moses) threw his rod,
And behold, it was
A serpent, plain (for all to see)!

فَأَلْقَىٰ عَصَاهُ فَإِذَا هِىَ ثُعْبَانٌ مُّبِينٌ ٣٢

33. And he drew out his hand,
And behold, it was white
To all beholders![3157]

وَنَزَعَ يَدَهُۥ فَإِذَا هِىَ بَيْضَآءُ لِلنَّٰظِرِينَ ٣٣

3154. Pharaoh is further perturbed. In reply to Moses's statement that Allah, the One True God is also the God of the Egyptians and Pharaoh also, Pharaoh says sarcastically to his Court: "Look at this 'Messenger' of yours; he seems to be mad!" But Moses is not abashed. He boldly says what is the truth: "It is you who are mad! The God of Whom I preach is the universal Lord—of the East and of the West. He reigns wherever you go!" (R).

3155. Now we come to the crisis. Pharaoh threatens Moses with prison for treason. Moses remains calm and still argues: "What if I show you a miracle? Will it convince you that I am not mad, and that I have behind me the Lord of all the Worlds?"

3156. The Egyptians were addicted to magic and sorcery, which was mostly false. If a true miracle were shown to them, would they believe? Perhaps they would see the hollowness of their own magic. In fact this actually happened with the Egyptian sorcerers themselves and perhaps with the commonalty. But Pharaoh and his Court were too arrogant, and battened too much on frauds to yield to Truth.

3157. *Cf.* 7:107-8. See the whole passage there, and the notes thereon.

SECTION 3.

34. (Pharaoh) said to the Chiefs[3158]
Around him "This is indeed
A sorcerer well-versed:

٣٤ قَالَ لِلْمَلَإِ حَوْلَهُۥٓ إِنَّ هَٰذَا لَسَٰحِرٌ عَلِيمٌ

35. "His plan is to get you out
Of your land by his sorcery;
Then what is it ye counsel?"

٣٥ يُرِيدُ أَن يُخْرِجَكُم مِّنْ أَرْضِكُم بِسِحْرِهِۦ فَمَاذَا تَأْمُرُونَ

36. They said; "Keep him
And his brother in suspense
(For a while), and dispatch
To the Cities heralds to collect—

٣٦ قَالُوٓا۟ أَرْجِهْ وَأَخَاهُ وَٱبْعَثْ فِى ٱلْمَدَآئِنِ حَٰشِرِينَ

37. "And bring up to thee
All (our) sorcerers well-versed."

٣٧ يَأْتُوكَ بِكُلِّ سَحَّارٍ عَلِيمٍ

38. So the sorcerers were got
Together for the appointment
Of a day well-known,[3159]

٣٨ فَجُمِعَ ٱلسَّحَرَةُ لِمِيقَٰتِ يَوْمٍ مَّعْلُومٍ

39. And the people were told:
"Are ye (now) assembled?—

٣٩ وَقِيلَ لِلنَّاسِ هَلْ أَنتُم مُّجْتَمِعُونَ

40. "That we may follow[3160]
The sorcerers (in religion)
If they win?"

٤٠ لَعَلَّنَا نَتَّبِعُ ٱلسَّحَرَةَ إِن كَانُوا۟ هُمُ ٱلْغَٰلِبِينَ

41. So when the sorcerers arrived,
They said to Pharaoh:
"Of course—shall we have
A (suitable) reward[3161]
If we win?"

٤١ فَلَمَّا جَآءَ ٱلسَّحَرَةُ قَالُوا۟ لِفِرْعَوْنَ أَئِنَّ لَنَا لَأَجْرًا إِن كُنَّا نَحْنُ ٱلْغَٰلِبِينَ

42. He said: "Yea, (and more)—
For ye shall in that case

٤٢ قَالَ نَعَمْ وَإِنَّكُمْ إِذًا

3158. In 7:109 it is the Chiefs who say this. The fact is that it was a general consultation, and this was the general feeling, expressed in words by each to the others.

3159. *A day well-known*: a solemn day of festival: see 20:59. The object was to get together as large a concourse of people as possible. It was confidently expected that the Egyptian sorcerers with all their organisation would win with their tricks against these amateur Israelites, and so the State cult of the worship of Pharaoh would be fastened on the necks of the people more firmly than ever.

3160. See the last note. The people are to come and witness the triumph of the State religion, so that they may become the more obedient to Pharaoh and more compliant with the demands of the priests. The State religion included magic and the worship of Pharaoh.

3161. There was no such thing as pure loyalty to an exploiting ruler like this Pharaoh. The sorcerers, who were probably also priests, were venal, and they hoped to establish their own hold on both king and people by further enrichment of themselves and their order.

Be (raised to posts)
Nearest (to my person)."

لَمِنَ ٱلْمُقَرَّبِينَ

43. Moses said to them:
"Throw ye—that which
Ye are about to throw!"[3162]

قَالَ لَهُم مُّوسَىٰٓ أَلْقُواْ مَآ أَنتُم مُّلْقُونَ ﴿٤٣﴾

44. So they threw their ropes
And their rods, and said:
"By the might of Pharaoh,
It is we who will
Certainly win!"[3163]

فَأَلْقَوْاْ حِبَالَهُمْ وَعِصِيَّهُمْ
وَقَالُواْ بِعِزَّةِ فِرْعَوْنَ إِنَّا لَنَحْنُ ٱلْغَٰلِبُونَ ﴿٤٤﴾

45. Then Moses threw his rod,
When, behold, it straightway
Swallows up all
The falsehoods which they fake![3164]

فَأَلْقَىٰ مُوسَىٰ عَصَاهُ فَإِذَا
هِىَ تَلْقَفُ مَا يَأْفِكُونَ ﴿٤٥﴾

46. Then did the sorcerers
Fall down, prostrate in adoration,

فَأُلْقِىَ ٱلسَّحَرَةُ سَٰجِدِينَ ﴿٤٦﴾

47. Saying: "We believe
In the Lord of the Worlds,

قَالُوٓاْ ءَامَنَّا بِرَبِّ ٱلْعَٰلَمِينَ ﴿٤٧﴾

48. "The Lord of Moses and Aaron."

رَبِّ مُوسَىٰ وَهَٰرُونَ ﴿٤٨﴾

49. Said (Pharaoh): "Believe ye
In Him before I give
You permission? Surely he
Is your leader, who has
Taught you sorcery!
But soon shall ye know![3165]
"Be sure I will cut off
Your hands and your feet on
opposite sides,

قَالَ ءَامَنتُمْ لَهُۥ قَبْلَ أَنْ ءَاذَنَ لَكُمْ
إِنَّهُۥ لَكَبِيرُكُمُ ٱلَّذِى عَلَّمَكُمُ
ٱلسِّحْرَ فَلَسَوْفَ تَعْلَمُونَ
لَأُقَطِّعَنَّ أَيْدِيَكُمْ وَأَرْجُلَكُم مِّنْ خِلَٰفٍ ﴿٤٩﴾

3162. The euphemism implies a taunt, as if Moses had said: "I know about your tricks! You pretend to throw ropes and rods, and make people believe they are snakes. But now come on!"

3163. Though Pharaoh claimed to be a god, it is not likely that those nearest to him—his priests and sorcerers—believed such a thing! But it was a game of mutual pretence before the world. And so they appeal to his "divine" power.

3164. The sorceres' ropes and rods seemed to have become serpents, but the rod of Moses was mightier than all of them and quickly swallowed them up. So truth is more powerful than tricks and will expose and destroy them.

3165. The sorcerers knew that they had met something very different from their tricks. Allah's spirit worked on them and they professed the True God. As they represented the intelligence of the community, it may be presumed that they carried the intelligence of Eygpt with them and perhaps some of the commonalty, who were impressed by the dramatic scene! Hence Pharaoh's anger, but it is the begining of his decline!

And I
Will cause you all
To die on the cross!"

وَلَأُصَلِّبَنَّكُمْ أَجْمَعِينَ

50. They said: "No matter!
For us, we shall but
Return to our Lord!

قَالُوا لَا ضَيْرَ إِنَّا إِلَىٰ رَبِّنَا مُنقَلِبُونَ ﴿٥٠﴾

51. "Only, our desire is
That our Lord will
Forgive us our faults,
That we may become
Foremost among the Believers!"[3166]

إِنَّا نَطْمَعُ أَن يَغْفِرَ لَنَا رَبُّنَا خَطَايَانَا أَن كُنَّا أَوَّلَ الْمُؤْمِنِينَ ﴿٥١﴾

SECTION 4.

52. By inspiration We told Moses:
"Travel by night with
My servants; for surely
Ye shall be pursued."[3167]

وَأَوْحَيْنَا إِلَىٰ مُوسَىٰ أَنْ أَسْرِ بِعِبَادِي إِنَّكُم مُّتَّبَعُونَ ﴿٥٢﴾

53. Then Pharaoh sent heralds
To (all) the Cities,

فَأَرْسَلَ فِرْعَوْنُ فِي الْمَدَائِنِ حَاشِرِينَ ﴿٥٣﴾

54. (Saying): "These (Israelites)
Are but a small band,

إِنَّ هَٰؤُلَاءِ لَشِرْذِمَةٌ قَلِيلُونَ ﴿٥٤﴾

55. "And they are raging
Furiously against us;

وَإِنَّهُمْ لَنَا لَغَائِظُونَ ﴿٥٥﴾

56. "But we are a multitude
Amply forewarned."

وَإِنَّا لَجَمِيعٌ حَاذِرُونَ ﴿٥٦﴾

57. So We expelled them[3168]
From gardens, springs,

فَأَخْرَجْنَاهُم مِّن جَنَّاتٍ وَعُيُونٍ ﴿٥٧﴾

3166. This is the core of the lesson enforced on this passage. What was the reaction of the environment to the Light or Message of Allah? (1) It transformed Moses so that he became a fearless leader, one of the foremost in faith. (2) From men like Pharaoh and his corrupt court, it called forth obstinacy, spite, and all the tricks and snares of evil, but Evil was defeated on its own ground. (3) The very dupes of Evil were touched by the glorious Light of Allah, and they were ready to suffer tortures and death, their sole ambition (in their tranformed state) being to be foremost in Faith!

3167. The rest of the story—of the plagues of Egypt—is passed over as not germane to the present argument. We come now to the story of the Israelites leaving Egypt, pursued by Pharaoh. Here again there are three contrasts; (1) the blind arrogance of the Egyptians, against the development of Allah's Plan; (2) the Faith of Moses, against the fears of his people: and (3) the final deliverance of the seed of righteousness, against the destruction of the host of brute force.

3168. In deference to almost unanimous authority I have translated this passage (verses 58-60) as if it were a parenthetical statement of Allah's purpose. Personally I prefer another construction. According to that, verses 58-59 will be part of Pharaoh's proclamation: "We have dispossessed the Israelites from everything good in the land, and made them our slaves"; and verse 60 only will be parenthetical: "Poor ignorant men! You may oppress those who are helpless, but We (*i.e.* Allah) have declared that they shall inherit all these things", as they certainly did (for a time) in the Land of Promise, Palestine.

58. Treasures, and every kind
Of honourable position;

وَكُنُوزٍ وَمَقَامٍ كَرِيمٍ ﴿٥٨﴾

59. Thus it was, but
We made the Children
Of Israel inheritors[3169]
Of such things.

كَذَٰلِكَ وَأَوْرَثْنَٰهَا بَنِيٓ إِسْرَٰٓءِيلَ ﴿٥٩﴾

60. So they pursued them[3170]
At sunrise.

فَأَتْبَعُوهُم مُّشْرِقِينَ ﴿٦٠﴾

61. And when the two bodies
Saw each other, the people
Of Moses said: "We are
Sure to be overtaken."

فَلَمَّا تَرَٰٓءَا ٱلْجَمْعَانِ قَالَ أَصْحَٰبُ مُوسَىٰٓ إِنَّا لَمُدْرَكُونَ ﴿٦١﴾

62. (Moses) said: "By no means!
My Lord is with me!
Soon will He guide me!"[3171]

قَالَ كَلَّآ ۖ إِنَّ مَعِيَ رَبِّي سَيَهْدِينِ ﴿٦٢﴾

63. Then We told Moses
By inspiration: "Strike
The sea with thy rod."
So it divided, and each
Separate part became
Like the huge, firm mass
Of a mountain.

فَأَوْحَيْنَآ إِلَىٰ مُوسَىٰٓ أَنِ ٱضْرِب بِّعَصَاكَ ٱلْبَحْرَ ۖ فَٱنفَلَقَ فَكَانَ كُلُّ فِرْقٍ كَٱلطَّوْدِ ٱلْعَظِيمِ ﴿٦٣﴾

64. And We made the other
Party approach thither.[3172]

وَأَزْلَفْنَا ثَمَّ ٱلْءَاخَرِينَ ﴿٦٤﴾

65. We delivered Moses and all
Who were with him;

وَأَنجَيْنَا مُوسَىٰ وَمَن مَّعَهُۥٓ أَجْمَعِينَ ﴿٦٥﴾

66. But We drowned the others.

ثُمَّ أَغْرَقْنَا ٱلْءَاخَرِينَ ﴿٦٦﴾

3169. The Children of Israel certainly inherited the gardens, springs, treasures, and honourable positions in Palestine after many years' wanderings in the wilderness. But when they were false to Allah, they lost them again, and another people (the Muslims) inherited them when they were true in Faith. These latter not only inherited Palestine but also Egypt, and the old Pharaonic power and institutions were lost forever. *Of such things*: literally, "of them".

3170. The story is here resumed after the parenthesis of verses 58-60.

3171. *Guide me: i.e.*, show me some way of escape from danger. This actually happened, for Pharaoh's host was drowned. The faith of Moses stands in strong contrast to the fears of his people.

3172. The miracle was twofold: (1) Moses with his people passed safely through the sea; and (2) Pharaoh and his great host were drowned in the sea.

67. Verily in this is a Sign:
But most of them
Do not believe.[3173]

إِنَّ فِي ذَٰلِكَ لَآيَةً ﴿٦٧﴾
وَمَا كَانَ أَكْثَرُهُم مُّؤْمِنِينَ

68. And verily thy Lord
Is He, the Exalted in Might,
Most Merciful.[3174]

وَإِنَّ رَبَّكَ لَهُوَ الْعَزِيزُ الرَّحِيمُ ﴿٦٨﴾

C. 165.—Abraham patiently argued with his people
(26:70-122.) About Allah's Truth; prayed for wisdom
And righteousness, for himself, his father,
And future generations; and taught Truth
About the Hereafter. Noah preached
To a world of Unfaith, and would not reject
The humble and lowly: his arrogant rejecters
Were brought low: in him and his following
Were vindicated Allah's righteous Purpose and Mercy.

Section 5

69. And rehearse to them
(Something of) Abraham's
story.[3175]

وَاتْلُ عَلَيْهِمْ نَبَأَ إِبْرَاهِيمَ ﴿٦٩﴾

70. Behold, he said
To his father and his people:
"What worship ye?"

إِذْ قَالَ لِأَبِيهِ وَقَوْمِهِ مَا تَعْبُدُونَ ﴿٧٠﴾

71. They said: "We worship
Idols, and we remain constantly[3176]
In attendance on them."

قَالُوا نَعْبُدُ أَصْنَامًا فَنَظَلُّ لَهَا عَاكِفِينَ ﴿٧١﴾

72. He said: "Do they listen
To you when ye call (on them),

قَالَ هَلْ يَسْمَعُونَكُمْ إِذْ تَدْعُونَ ﴿٧٢﴾

73. Or do you good or harm?"

أَوْ يَنفَعُونَكُمْ أَوْ يَضُرُّونَ ﴿٧٣﴾

74. They said: "Nay, but we
Found our fathers doing
Thus (what we do)."

قَالُوا بَلْ وَجَدْنَا آبَاءَنَا كَذَٰلِكَ يَفْعَلُونَ ﴿٧٤﴾

3173. As it was then, so it is now. In spite of the obvious Signs of Allah, people who are blind in their obstinate resistance to Truth accomplish their own destruction, while humble, persecuted men of Faith are transformed by the Light of Allah, and obtain salvation.

3174. Nothing that the powers of Evil can do, will ever defeat the merciful Purpose of Allah. Evil, in resisting good, will effect its own destruction.

3175. For the argument of this Sūrah the incidents in Abraham's life are not relevant and are not mentioned. What is mentioned is: (1) the steps by which he taught about the sin of false worship, in the form of a Dialogue; (2) the aims of a righteous man not only for his individual life, but for his ancestors and posterity, in the form of a Prayer; and (3) a picture of the Future Judgement, in the form of a vision. (1) is covered by verses 70-82; (2) by 83-87; and (3) by 88-102.

3176. They want to show their true and assiduous devotion. But Abraham goes at once to the heart of the matter by asking: "To whom is your devotion paid? Is the object worthy of it?"

٧٥ قَالَ أَفَرَءَيْتُم مَّا كُنتُمْ تَعْبُدُونَ

75. He said: 'Do ye then
See whom ye have been
Worshipping—

٧٦ أَنتُمْ وَءَابَآؤُكُمُ ٱلْأَقْدَمُونَ

76. "Ye and your fathers before you?—

٧٧ فَإِنَّهُمْ عَدُوٌّ لِّيٓ إِلَّا رَبَّ ٱلْعَٰلَمِينَ

77. "For they are enemies to me;[3177]
Not so the Lord and Cherisher
Of the Worlds;

٧٨ ٱلَّذِى خَلَقَنِى فَهُوَ يَهْدِينِ

78. "Who created me, and
It is He who guides me;

٧٩ وَٱلَّذِى هُوَ يُطْعِمُنِى وَيَسْقِينِ

79. "Who gives me food and drink,

٨٠ وَإِذَا مَرِضْتُ فَهُوَ يَشْفِينِ

80. "And when I am ill,
It is He who cures me;

٨١ وَٱلَّذِى يُمِيتُنِى ثُمَّ يُحْيِينِ

81. "Who will cause me to die,
And then to live (again);

٨٢ وَٱلَّذِىٓ أَطْمَعُ أَن يَغْفِرَ لِى
خَطِيٓـَٔتِى يَوْمَ ٱلدِّينِ

82. "And who, I hope,
Will forgive me my faults
On the Day of Judgement...

٨٣ رَبِّ هَبْ لِى حُكْمًا
وَأَلْحِقْنِى بِٱلصَّٰلِحِينَ

83. "O my Lord! bestow wisdom[3178]
On me, and join me
With the righteous;

٨٤ وَٱجْعَل لِّى لِسَانَ صِدْقٍ فِى ٱلْءَاخِرِينَ

84. "Grant me honourable mention
On the tongue of truth[3179]
Among the latest (generations);

٨٥ وَٱجْعَلْنِى مِن وَرَثَةِ جَنَّةِ ٱلنَّعِيمِ

85. "Make me one of the inheritors
Of the Garden of Bliss;

3177. 'The things that you worship are enemies to mankind: let me testify from my own personal experience: they are enemies to me: they can do me no good, but would lead me astray. Contrast with their importance or their power of mischief the One True God Whom I worship: He created me and all the Worlds; He cherishes me and guides me; He takes care of me; and when I die, He will give me new life; He will forgive me and grant me final Salvation. Will you then come to this true worship? How can you doubt, after seeing the contrast of the one with the other? Is it not as the contrast between Light and Darkness?'

3178. Having shown clearly the distinction between the False and the True, Abraham now shows in the form of a Prayer what his inmost wishes are. (1) He wants his soul enlightened with divine wisdom, and (2) his heart and life filled with righteousness; (3) he will not be content with working for himself or his own generation; his view extends to all future generations; (4) and of course he wishes to attain the goal of the righteous, the Garden of the Bliss of the Divine Countenance; but he is not content with this; for (5) he wants his father and relatives to share in his spiritual joy, so that he can proudly see all whom he can reach, in an honourable station (contrasted with disgrace) on the Day of Judgement.

3179. *Cf.* 19:50. The whole of the passage about Abraham there may be compared with this passage.

86. "Forgive my father, for that
He is among those astray;

وَاغْفِرْ لِأَبِي إِنَّهُ كَانَ مِنَ الضَّالِّينَ ٨٦

87. "And let me not be
In disgrace on the Day
When (men) will be raised up—

وَلَا تُخْزِنِي يَوْمَ يُبْعَثُونَ ٨٧

88. "The Day whereon neither[3180]
Wealth nor sons will avail,

يَوْمَ لَا يَنفَعُ مَالٌ وَلَا بَنُونَ ٨٨

89. "But only he (will prosper)
That brings to Allah
A sound heart;

إِلَّا مَنْ أَتَى اللَّهَ بِقَلْبٍ سَلِيمٍ ٨٩

90. "To the righteous, the Garden
Will be brought near,[3181]

وَأُزْلِفَتِ الْجَنَّةُ لِلْمُتَّقِينَ ٩٠

91. "And to those straying in Evil,
The Fire will be placed
In full view;

وَبُرِّزَتِ الْجَحِيمُ لِلْغَاوِينَ ٩١

92. "And it shall be said
To them: 'Where are
The (gods) ye worshipped—

وَقِيلَ لَهُمْ أَيْنَ مَا كُنتُمْ تَعْبُدُونَ ٩٢

93. "Besides Allah? Can they
Help you or help themselves?'

مِن دُونِ اللَّهِ هَلْ يَنصُرُونَكُمْ أَوْ يَنتَصِرُونَ ٩٣

94. "Then they will be thrown
Headlong into the (Fire)—
They and those straying[3182]
In Evil,

فَكُبْكِبُوا فِيهَا هُمْ وَالْغَاوُونَ ٩٤

95. "And the whole hosts
Of Iblīs together.

وَجُنُودُ إِبْلِيسَ أَجْمَعُونَ ٩٥

96. "They will say there
In their mutual bickerings:

قَالُوا وَهُمْ فِيهَا يَخْتَصِمُونَ ٩٦

3180. Now we have a vision of the Day of Judgement. Nothing will then avail except a pure heart; all sorts of the so-called "good deeds" of this world, without the motive of purity, will be useless. The contrast of the Garden of Bliss with the Fire of Misery will be plainly visible. Evil will be shown in its true colours—isolated, helpless, cursing and despairing, and all chances will then have been lost.

3181. The Good will only see good (the Garden of Bliss), and the Evil will only see evil (the Fire of Hell). This type of contrast is shown to us in the world of our spiritual sense even in this life.

3182. The false gods, being devils or personified false fancies, will all be involved in the punishment of Hell, together with their worshippers, and the ultimate sources of evil, the hosts of Iblīs or Satan.

97. "'By Allah, we were truly
In an error manifest,[3183]

تَاللَّهِ إِن كُنَّا لَفِى ضَلَٰلٍ مُّبِينٍ ﴿٩٧﴾

98. "'When we held you as equals
With the Lord of the Worlds;

إِذْ نُسَوِّيكُم بِرَبِّ ٱلْعَٰلَمِينَ ﴿٩٨﴾

99. "'And our seducers were
Only those who were
Steeped in guilt.[3184]

وَمَآ أَضَلَّنَآ إِلَّا ٱلْمُجْرِمُونَ ﴿٩٩﴾

100. "'Now, then, we have none
To intercede (for us),

فَمَا لَنَا مِن شَٰفِعِينَ ﴿١٠٠﴾

101. "'Nor a single friend
To feel (for us).

وَلَا صَدِيقٍ حَمِيمٍ ﴿١٠١﴾

102. "'Now if we only had
A chance of return,
We shall truly be
Of those who believe!'"[3185]

فَلَوْ أَنَّ لَنَا كَرَّةً فَنَكُونَ مِنَ ٱلْمُؤْمِنِينَ ﴿١٠٢﴾

103. Verily in this is a Sign
But most of them
Do not believe.

إِنَّ فِى ذَٰلِكَ لَءَايَةً ۖ وَمَا كَانَ أَكْثَرُهُم مُّؤْمِنِينَ ﴿١٠٣﴾

104. And verily thy Lord
Is He, the Exalted in Might,
Most Merciful.

وَإِنَّ رَبَّكَ لَهُوَ ٱلْعَزِيزُ ٱلرَّحِيمُ ﴿١٠٤﴾

SECTION 6.

105. The people of Noah rejected
The messengers.

كَذَّبَتْ قَوْمُ نُوحٍ ٱلْمُرْسَلِينَ ﴿١٠٥﴾

3183. *Error manifest*: 'our error is now plainly manifest, but it should have been manifest to us before it was too late, because the Signs of Allah were always around us'. This will be said by the ungodly, whose eyes will then be fully opened.

3184. They now see that the people who seduced them were themselves evil and subject to the penalties of evil, and their seductions were frauds. They feel that they ought to have seen it before, for who would deliberately follow the paths of those condemned to misery and punishment? How simple they were not to see the true character of their seducers, though they had been warned again and again against them! It was their own folly that made them accept such obviously false guidance!

3185. This apparent longing for a chance of return is dishonest. If they were sent back, they would certainly return to their evil ways: 6:27-28. Besides, they have had numerous chances already in this life, and they have used them for mischief or evil.

106. Behold, their brother Noah[3186]
Said to them: "Will ye not
Fear (Allah)?

١٠٦ إِذْ قَالَ لَهُمْ أَخُوهُمْ نُوحٌ أَلَا تَتَّقُونَ

107. "I am to you a messenger
Worthy of all trust:[3187]

١٠٧ إِنِّي لَكُمْ رَسُولٌ أَمِينٌ

108. "So fear Allah, and obey me.

١٠٨ فَاتَّقُوا اللَّهَ وَأَطِيعُونِ

109. "No reward do I ask
Of you for it: my reward
Is only from the Lord
Of the Worlds:

١٠٩ وَمَا أَسْأَلُكُمْ عَلَيْهِ مِنْ أَجْرٍ
إِنْ أَجْرِيَ إِلَّا عَلَىٰ رَبِّ الْعَالَمِينَ

110. "So fear Allah, and obey me."[3188]

١١٠ فَاتَّقُوا اللَّهَ وَأَطِيعُونِ

111. They said: "Shall we
Believe in thee when it is
The meanest that follow thee?"[3189]

١١١ قَالُوا أَنُؤْمِنُ لَكَ وَاتَّبَعَكَ الْأَرْذَلُونَ

112. He said: "And what
Do I know as to
What they do?

١١٢ قَالَ وَمَا عِلْمِي بِمَا كَانُوا يَعْمَلُونَ

113. "Their account is only
With my Lord, if ye
Could (but) understand.

١١٣ إِنْ حِسَابُهُمْ إِلَّا عَلَىٰ رَبِّي
لَوْ تَشْعُرُونَ

114. "I am not one to drive away
Those who believe.[3190]

١١٤ وَمَا أَنَا بِطَارِدِ الْمُؤْمِنِينَ

3186. Noah's generation had lost all faith and abandoned themselves to evil. They had rejected the Message of messengers previously sent to the world. Noah was sent to them as one of themselves ("their brother"). His life was open before them: he had proved himself pure in heart and conduct (like the Holy Prophet of Arabia long after him), and worthy of every trust. Would they fear Allah and follow his advice? They could see that he had no ends of his own to serve. Would they not listen to him?

3187. *Amīn* = one to whom a trust had been given, with several shades of meaning implied: *e.g.*, (1) worthy of trust, (2) bound to deliver his trust, as a prophet is bound to deliver his Message, (3) bound to act entirely as directed by the trust, as a prophet is bound to give only the Message of Allah, and not add anything of his own, and (4) not seeking any interest of his own.

3188. Note the repetition rounds off the argument. See n. 3186 above.

3189. The leaders of the people are speaking, as the Quraysh leaders spoke in the time of the Holy Prophet. "We know that thou hast been trustworthy in thy life. But look at the 'rag tag and bob tail' that follow thee! Dost thou expect us to be like them or to be classed with them?" His answer was: "I know nothing against them; if they have done any wrong, or are only hypocrites, they are answerable to Allah; how can I drive them away from me, seeing that I am expressly sent to admonish all people?"

3190. *Cf.* 11:29. All people who have faith have the right to come and listen to Allah's Word and receive Allah's Mercy, whether they are publicans and sinners, "Harijans" and "low-caste" men, men of "superior" or "inferior" races. The Prophet of Allah welcomes them all, as His Message had to shine before the whole world. (R).

115. "I am sent only
To warn plainly in public."

إِنْ أَنَا۠ إِلَّا نَذِيرٌ مُّبِينٌ ١١٥

116. They said: "If thou
Desist not, O Noah!
Thou shalt be stoned
(to death)."[3191]

قَالُوا۟ لَئِن لَّمْ تَنتَهِ يَٰنُوحُ لَتَكُونَنَّ مِنَ ٱلْمَرْجُومِينَ ١١٦

117. He said: "O my Lord!
Truly my people have
Rejected me.

قَالَ رَبِّ إِنَّ قَوْمِى كَذَّبُونِ ١١٧

118. "Judge thou, then, between me
And them openly, and deliver
Me and those of the Believers
Who are with me."

فَٱفْتَحْ بَيْنِى وَبَيْنَهُمْ فَتْحًا وَنَجِّنِى وَمَن مَّعِىَ مِنَ ٱلْمُؤْمِنِينَ ١١٨

119. So We delivered him
And those with him,
In the Ark filled
(With all creatures).[3192]

فَأَنجَيْنَٰهُ وَمَن مَّعَهُۥ فِى ٱلْفُلْكِ ٱلْمَشْحُونِ ١١٩

120. Thereafter We drowned those
Who remained behind.

ثُمَّ أَغْرَقْنَا بَعْدُ ٱلْبَاقِينَ ١٢٠

121. Verily in this is a Sign:
But most of them
Do not believe.[3193]

إِنَّ فِى ذَٰلِكَ لَءَايَةً وَمَا كَانَ أَكْثَرُهُم مُّؤْمِنِينَ ١٢١

122. And verily thy Lord
Is He, the Exalted in Might,
Most Merciful.

وَإِنَّ رَبَّكَ لَهُوَ ٱلْعَزِيزُ ٱلرَّحِيمُ ١٢٢

C. 166.—The 'Ād were addicted to arrogance;
(26:123-159.) They exulted in material strength
And possessions, and had no faith but in force:
They were brought low, as were the Thamūd,
Who gave way to extravagance, and were guilty

3191. Two other cases occur to me where prophets of Allah were threatened with death by stoning: one was Abraham (19:46), and the other was Shu'ayb (11:91). In neither case did the threats deter them from carrying out their mission. On the contrary, the threats recoiled on those who threatened. So also did it happen in the case of Noah and the Holy Prophet.

3192. The story of Noah's Flood is told in 11:36-48. Here, the point emphasised is Noah's patience and constancy against threats, and the triumph and preservation of Allah's truth even though the world was ranged against it.

3193. This and the following verse run like a refrain throughout this Sūrah, and give the keynote to the subject matter: how the Message of Allah is preached, how it is rejected in all ages, and how it triumphs at last, through the Mercy of Allah. See 26:8-9, 68-69, 103-104, here (121-122), 139-140, 158-159, 174-175, and 190-191. (R).

Of sacrilage in destroying a symbol
Of justice and fair-dealing: their repentance
Was too late: they were blotted out
Of the earth for the mischief they had made.

SECTION 7.

123. The 'Ād (people) rejected[3194]
The messengers.

كَذَّبَتْ عَادٌ ٱلْمُرْسَلِينَ ﴿١٢٣﴾

124. Behold, their brother Hūd
Said to them: "Will ye not
Fear (Allah)?

إِذْ قَالَ لَهُمْ أَخُوهُمْ هُودٌ أَلَا تَتَّقُونَ ﴿١٢٤﴾

125. "I am to you a messenger
Worthy of all trust:[3195]

إِنِّي لَكُمْ رَسُولٌ أَمِينٌ ﴿١٢٥﴾

126. "So fear Allah and obey me.

فَٱتَّقُوا ٱللَّهَ وَأَطِيعُونِ ﴿١٢٦﴾

127. "No reward do I ask
Of you for it: my reward
Is only from the Lord
Of the Worlds.

وَمَآ أَسْـَٔلُكُمْ عَلَيْهِ مِنْ أَجْرٍ ۖ إِنْ أَجْرِيَ إِلَّا عَلَىٰ رَبِّ ٱلْعَٰلَمِينَ ﴿١٢٧﴾

128. "Do ye build a landmark
On every high place
To amuse yourselves?[3196]

أَتَبْنُونَ بِكُلِّ رِيعٍ ءَايَةً تَعْبَثُونَ ﴿١٢٨﴾

129. "And do ye get for yourselves
Fine buildings in the hope
Of living therein (forever)?

وَتَتَّخِذُونَ مَصَانِعَ لَعَلَّكُمْ تَخْلُدُونَ ﴿١٢٩﴾

130. "And when ye exert
Your strong hand,
Do ye do it like men
Of absolute power?[3197]

وَإِذَا بَطَشْتُم بَطَشْتُمْ جَبَّارِينَ ﴿١٣٠﴾

3194. See n. 1040 to 7:65 for the 'Ād people and their location. Here, the emphasis is on the fact that they were materialists believing in brute force, and felt secure in their fortresses and resources, but were found quite helpless when Allah's Message came and they rejected it.

3195. See n. 3187 to 26:107 above.

3196. Any merely material civilisation prides itself on show and parade. Its votaries scatter monuments for all sorts of things in conspicuous places—monuments which commemorate deeds and events which are forgotten in a few generations! *Cf.* Shelley's poem on Ozymandias: "I am Ozymandias. King of Kings! Look on my works, ye mighty, and despair!... Boundless and bare the lonely and level sands stretch far away!"

3197. "Without any responsibility or consideration for those who come within your power?"

131. "Now fear Allah, and obey me.[3198]	فَاتَّقُوا اللَّهَ وَأَطِيعُونِ ﴿١٣١﴾
132. "Yea, fear Him Who Has bestowed on you Freely all that ye know.[3199]	وَاتَّقُوا الَّذِي أَمَدَّكُم بِمَا تَعْلَمُونَ ﴿١٣٢﴾
133. "Freely has He bestowed On you cattle and sons—	أَمَدَّكُم بِأَنْعَامٍ وَبَنِينَ ﴿١٣٣﴾
134. "And Gardens and Springs.	وَجَنَّاتٍ وَعُيُونٍ ﴿١٣٤﴾
135. "Truly I fear for you The Penalty of a Great Day."[3200]	إِنِّي أَخَافُ عَلَيْكُمْ عَذَابَ يَوْمٍ عَظِيمٍ ﴿١٣٥﴾
136. They said: "It is the same To us whether thou Admonish us or be not Among (our) Admonishers![3201]	قَالُوا سَوَاءٌ عَلَيْنَا أَوَعَظْتَ أَمْ لَمْ تَكُن مِّنَ الْوَاعِظِينَ ﴿١٣٦﴾
137. "This is no other than A customary device Of the ancients,[3202]	إِنْ هَٰذَا إِلَّا خُلُقُ الْأَوَّلِينَ ﴿١٣٧﴾
138. "And we are not the ones To receive Pains and Penalties!"	وَمَا نَحْنُ بِمُعَذَّبِينَ ﴿١٣٨﴾
139. So they rejected him, And We destroyed them. Verily in this is a Sign: But most of them Do not believe.	فَكَذَّبُوهُ فَأَهْلَكْنَاهُمْ إِنَّ فِي ذَٰلِكَ لَآيَةً وَمَا كَانَ أَكْثَرُهُم مُّؤْمِنِينَ ﴿١٣٩﴾
140. And verily thy Lord Is He, the Exalted in Might, Most Merciful.	وَإِنَّ رَبَّكَ لَهُوَ الْعَزِيزُ الرَّحِيمُ ﴿١٤٠﴾

3198. See n. 3188 above.

3199. The gifts are described generally, immaterial and material. "All that ye know" includes not only material things, but knowledge and the faculties by which knowledge may be used for human well-being, all that makes life beautiful and refined. "Cattle" means wealth generally, and "sons" means population and man-power. "Gardens and Springs" are things that contribute to the delight and pleasure of man.

3200. "But you have misused all those gifts, and you will suffer the inevitable penalties for your misuse and for your ingratitude."

3201. "We are not going to attend to you whether you preach to us or not." The construction of the second clause, "or be not among our admonishers" is a rapier cut at Hūd, as if they had said: "Oh yes! we have heard plenty of admonishers like you!" See the next verse.

3202. They said, as many of our modern enemies of religion say, "you are only reviving an ancient superstition, a dope of the crowd; there is no such thing as a Hereafter, or the sort of punishments you announce!"

SECTION 8.

141. The Thamūd (people) rejected[3203]
The messengers.

كَذَّبَتْ ثَمُودُ ٱلْمُرْسَلِينَ ﴿١٤١﴾

142. Behold, their brother Ṣāliḥ
Said to them: "Will you not
Fear (Allah)?

إِذْ قَالَ لَهُمْ أَخُوهُمْ صَٰلِحٌ أَلَا تَتَّقُونَ ﴿١٤٢﴾

143. "I am to you a messenger
Worthy of all trust.

إِنِّي لَكُمْ رَسُولٌ أَمِينٌ ﴿١٤٣﴾

144. "So fear Allah, and obey me.

فَٱتَّقُوا۟ ٱللَّهَ وَأَطِيعُونِ ﴿١٤٤﴾

145. "No reward do I ask
Of you for it: my reward
Is only from the Lord
Of the Worlds.

وَمَآ أَسْـَٔلُكُمْ عَلَيْهِ مِنْ أَجْرٍ إِنْ أَجْرِىَ إِلَّا عَلَىٰ رَبِّ ٱلْعَٰلَمِينَ ﴿١٤٥﴾

146. "Will ye be left secure,
In (the enjoyment of) all
That ye have here?—

أَتُتْرَكُونَ فِى مَا هَٰهُنَآ ءَامِنِينَ ﴿١٤٦﴾

147. "Gardens and Springs,

فِى جَنَّٰتٍ وَعُيُونٍ ﴿١٤٧﴾

148. "And cornfields and date palms
With spathes near breaking[3204]
(With the weight of fruit)?

وَزُرُوعٍ وَنَخْلٍ طَلْعُهَا هَضِيمٌ ﴿١٤٨﴾

149. "And ye carve houses
Out of (rocky) mountains
With great skill.

وَتَنْحِتُونَ مِنَ ٱلْجِبَالِ بُيُوتًا فَٰرِهِينَ ﴿١٤٩﴾

150. "But fear Allah and obey me;

فَٱتَّقُوا۟ ٱللَّهَ وَأَطِيعُونِ ﴿١٥٠﴾

151. "And follow not the bidding
Of those who are extravagant—[3205]

وَلَا تُطِيعُوٓا۟ أَمْرَ ٱلْمُسْرِفِينَ ﴿١٥١﴾

3203. For the Thamūd people see n. 1043 to 7:73. They were great builders in stone and a people with agricultural wealth, but they were an exclusive people and oppressed the poor. The point emphasised here is: "How long will your wealth last, especially if you depress your own people and dishonour Allah's Signs by sacrilege?" The inscriptions on the Thamūd remains of rock-cut buildings in Al Ḥijr are described in Appendix VII at the end of this Sūrah.

3204. The date palm flowers on a long spathe: when the flowers develop into fruit, the heavy ones hang with the load of fruit. The Thamūd evidently were proud of their skill in producing corn and fruit and in hewing fine dwellings out of rocks, like the later dwellings of Roman times in the town of Petra.

3205. They are told: "All your skill is very well; but cultivate virtue and do not follow the ways of those who put forward extravagant claims for men's powers and material resources, or who lead lives of extravagance in luxury and self-indulgence; that makes mischief: but the door to repentance is open: will you repent?"

152. "Who make mischief in the land,
And mend not (their ways)."

١٥٢ ٱلَّذِينَ يُفْسِدُونَ فِى ٱلْأَرْضِ وَلَا يُصْلِحُونَ

153. They said: "Thou art only
One of those bewitched![3206]

١٥٣ قَالُوٓا۟ إِنَّمَآ أَنتَ مِنَ ٱلْمُسَحَّرِينَ

154. "Thou art no more than
A mortal like us:
Then bring us a Sign,
If thou tellest the truth!"

١٥٤ مَآ أَنتَ إِلَّا بَشَرٌ مِّثْلُنَا
فَأْتِ بِـَٔايَةٍ إِن كُنتَ مِنَ ٱلصَّـٰدِقِينَ

155. He said: "Here is
A she-camel: she has[3207]
A right of watering,
And ye have a right
Of watering, (severally)
On a day appointed.

١٥٥ قَالَ هَـٰذِهِۦ نَاقَةٌ
لَّهَا شِرْبٌ وَلَكُمْ شِرْبُ
يَوْمٍ مَّعْلُومٍ

156. "Touch her not with harm,
Lest the Penalty
Of a Great Day
Sieze you."

١٥٦ وَلَا تَمَسُّوهَا بِسُوٓءٍ
فَيَأْخُذَكُمْ عَذَابُ يَوْمٍ عَظِيمٍ

157. But they hamstrung her:
Then did they become
Full of regrets.[3208]

١٥٧ فَعَقَرُوهَا فَأَصْبَحُوا۟ نَـٰدِمِينَ

158. But the Penalty seized them.
Verily in this is a Sign:
But most of them
Did not believe.

١٥٨ فَأَخَذَهُمُ ٱلْعَذَابُ ۗ إِنَّ فِى ذَٰلِكَ لَـَٔايَةً
وَمَا كَانَ أَكْثَرُهُم مُّؤْمِنِينَ

159. And verily thy Lord
Is He, the Exalted in Might,
Most Merciful.

١٥٩ وَإِنَّ رَبَّكَ لَهُوَ ٱلْعَزِيزُ ٱلرَّحِيمُ

C. 167.—The task of Lot was a hard one: his mission
(26:160-191.) Was to people addicted to crimes abominable.
His reasoning with them was in vain: it only
Excited their wrath. They threatened to cast

3206. They think he is talking like a madman, and they say so.

3207. For this she-camel, see n. 1044 to 7:73. The she-camel was to be a Sign and a test case. Would they respect her rights of watering (and pasturage)?

3208. Their regrets were too late. They had themselves asked for a Sign. The Sign had been given them in the she-camel, which their prophet Ṣāliḥ had put forward as a test case. Would they, through that symbol, respect the law of equity by which all people had rights in water and in the gifts of nature? They refused to respect that law, and committed sacrilege by deliberately killing the she-camel. They themselves came to an evil end.

Him out, but were themselves overwhelmed
In disaster. Shu'ayb had to rebuke fraud
And commercial dishonesty: he met only
Ridicule, but the just and fair dealing
He preached was vindicated in the end.

SECTION 9.

160. The people of Lūṭ rejected[3209]
The messengers.

كَذَّبَتْ قَوْمُ لُوطٍ ٱلْمُرْسَلِينَ ﴿١٦٠﴾

161. Behold, their brother Lūṭ
Said to them: "Will ye not
Fear (Allah)?

إِذْ قَالَ لَهُمْ أَخُوهُمْ لُوطٌ أَلَا تَتَّقُونَ ﴿١٦١﴾

162. "I am to you a messenger
Worthy of all trust.

إِنِّي لَكُمْ رَسُولٌ أَمِينٌ ﴿١٦٢﴾

163. "So fear Allah and obey me.

فَٱتَّقُوا۟ ٱللَّهَ وَأَطِيعُونِ ﴿١٦٣﴾

164. "No reward do I ask
Of you for it: my reward
Is only from the Lord
Of the Worlds.

وَمَآ أَسْـَٔلُكُمْ عَلَيْهِ مِنْ أَجْرٍ ﴿١٦٤﴾
إِنْ أَجْرِيَ إِلَّا عَلَىٰ رَبِّ ٱلْعَٰلَمِينَ

165. "Of all the creatures
In the world, will ye
Approach males,

أَتَأْتُونَ ٱلذُّكْرَانَ مِنَ ٱلْعَٰلَمِينَ ﴿١٦٥﴾

166. "And leave those whom Allah
Has created for you
To be your mates?
Nay, ye are a people
Transgressing (all limits)!"

وَتَذَرُونَ مَا خَلَقَ لَكُمْ رَبُّكُم ﴿١٦٦﴾
مِّنْ أَزْوَٰجِكُم بَلْ أَنتُمْ قَوْمٌ عَادُونَ

167. They said. "If thou desist not
O Lūṭ! thou wilt assuredly
Be cast out!"[3210]

قَالُوا۟ لَئِن لَّمْ تَنتَهِ يَٰلُوطُ ﴿١٦٧﴾
لَتَكُونَنَّ مِنَ ٱلْمُخْرَجِينَ

3209. The story of Lūṭ (Lot) will be found in 7:80-84: see n. 1049. Here the point is that the people of the Cities of the Plain were shamelessly addicted to vice against nature, and Lūṭ's warning only exasperated them, until they were destroyed by a shower of brimstone.

3210. Their threat to cast him out has a grim significance in what actually happened. They were destroyed where they were, and he was glad to escape the dreadful Punishment according to the warning he had received.

168. He said: "I do detest[3211]
Your doings:"

قَالَ إِنِّي لِعَمَلِكُم مِّنَ ٱلْقَالِينَ ١٦٨

169. "O my Lord! deliver me
And my family from
Such things as they do!"

رَبِّ نَجِّنِي وَأَهْلِي مِمَّا يَعْمَلُونَ ١٦٩

170. So We delivered him
And his family—all

فَنَجَّيْنَٰهُ وَأَهْلَهُۥٓ أَجْمَعِينَ ١٧٠

171. Except an old woman[3212]
Who lingered behind.

إِلَّا عَجُوزًا فِي ٱلْغَٰبِرِينَ ١٧١

172. But the rest We destroyed
Utterly.

ثُمَّ دَمَّرْنَا ٱلْءَاخَرِينَ ١٧٢

173. We rained down on them
A shower (of brimstone):[3213]
And evil was the shower
On those who were admonished
(But heeded not)!

وَأَمْطَرْنَا عَلَيْهِم مَّطَرًا فَسَآءَ مَطَرُ ٱلْمُنذَرِينَ ١٧٣

174. Verily in this is a Sign:
But most of them
Do not believe.

إِنَّ فِي ذَٰلِكَ لَءَايَةً وَمَا كَانَ أَكْثَرُهُم مُّؤْمِنِينَ ١٧٤

175. And verily thy Lord
Is He, the Exalted in Might,
Most Merciful.

وَإِنَّ رَبَّكَ لَهُوَ ٱلْعَزِيزُ ٱلرَّحِيمُ ١٧٥

SECTION 10.

176. The Companions of the Wood[3214]
Rejected the messengers.

كَذَّبَ أَصْحَٰبُ لْـَٔيْكَةِ ٱلْمُرْسَلِينَ ١٧٦

177. Behold, Shu'ayb[3215] said to them:
"Will ye not fear (Allah)?

إِذْ قَالَ لَهُمْ شُعَيْبٌ أَلَا تَتَّقُونَ ١٧٧

178. "I am to you a messenger
Worthy of all trust.

إِنِّي لَكُمْ رَسُولٌ أَمِينٌ ١٧٨

3211. He was only among them from a stern sense of duty. The whole atmosphere there was detestable to him, and he was glad to escape when duty no longer demanded his presence there. He prayed for deliverance from such surroundings.

3212. This was Lūṭ's wife, who lingered behind and was among those who perished. See n. 1051 to 7:83.

3213. See n. 1052 to 7:84.

3214. See n. 2000 to 15:78.

3215. For Shu'ayb see n. 1054 to 7:85.

179. "So fear Allah and obey me.

فَاتَّقُوا اللَّهَ وَأَطِيعُونِ ﴿١٧٩﴾

180. "No reward do I ask
Of you for it: my reward
Is only from the Lord
Of the Worlds.

وَمَا أَسْأَلُكُمْ عَلَيْهِ مِنْ أَجْرٍ إِنْ أَجْرِيَ إِلَّا عَلَىٰ رَبِّ الْعَالَمِينَ ﴿١٨٠﴾

181. "Give just measure,[3216]
And cause no loss
(To others by fraud).

أَوْفُوا الْكَيْلَ وَلَا تَكُونُوا مِنَ الْمُخْسِرِينَ ﴿١٨١﴾

182. "And weigh with scales
True and upright.

وَزِنُوا بِالْقِسْطَاسِ الْمُسْتَقِيمِ ﴿١٨٢﴾

183. "And withhold not things
Justly due to men,
Nor do evil in the land,
Working mischief.

وَلَا تَبْخَسُوا النَّاسَ أَشْيَاءَهُمْ وَلَا تَعْثَوْا فِي الْأَرْضِ مُفْسِدِينَ ﴿١٨٣﴾

184. "And fear Him Who created
You and (Who created)
The generations before (you)"

وَاتَّقُوا الَّذِي خَلَقَكُمْ وَالْجِبِلَّةَ الْأَوَّلِينَ ﴿١٨٤﴾

185. They said: "Thou art only
One of those bewitched!

قَالُوا إِنَّمَا أَنْتَ مِنَ الْمُسَحَّرِينَ ﴿١٨٥﴾

186. "Thou art no more than
A mortal like us,
And indeed we think
Thou art a liar![3217]

وَمَا أَنْتَ إِلَّا بَشَرٌ مِثْلُنَا وَإِنْ نَظُنُّكَ لَمِنَ الْكَاذِبِينَ ﴿١٨٦﴾

187. "Now cause a piece
Of the sky to fall on us,
If thou art truthful!"[3218]

فَأَسْقِطْ عَلَيْنَا كِسَفًا مِنَ السَّمَاءِ إِنْ كُنْتَ مِنَ الصَّادِقِينَ ﴿١٨٧﴾

188. He said: "My Lord
Knows best what ye do."[3219]

قَالَ رَبِّي أَعْلَمُ بِمَا تَعْمَلُونَ ﴿١٨٨﴾

3216. They were a commercial people, but they were given to fraud, injustice, and wrongful mischief (by intermeddling with others). They are asked to fear Allah and follow His ways: it is He Who also created their predecessors among mankind, who never prospered by fraud and violent wrongdoing, but only justice and fair dealing.

3217. They deny that he is a prophet or that they are doing wrong, or that any former generations behaved differently. They think they are the true exponents of human nature, and that such as he—idealists—are mere madmen.

3218. 'If you really claim any real contact with Allah, let us see if you can bring down a piece of the sky to fall on us!'

3219. The challenge to bring down a piece of the sky was merely empty bravado, on the part of those who had called him a liar. But Shu'ayb does not insult them. He merely says: "Allah is the best judge of your conduct: what more can I say?" And Allah did punish them.

189. But they rejected him.
Then the punishment
Of a day of overshadowing
gloom[3220]
Seized them, and that was
The Penalty of a Great Day.[3221]

١٨٩ فَكَذَّبُوهُ فَأَخَذَهُمْ عَذَابُ يَوْمِ الظُّلَّةِ إِنَّهُ كَانَ عَذَابَ يَوْمٍ عَظِيمٍ

190. Verily in that is a Sign:
But most of them
Do not believe.

١٩٠ إِنَّ فِي ذَٰلِكَ لَآيَةً وَمَا كَانَ أَكْثَرُهُم مُّؤْمِنِينَ

191. And verily thy Lord
Is He, the Exalted in Might,
Most Merciful.[3222]

١٩١ وَإِنَّ رَبَّكَ لَهُوَ الْعَزِيزُ الرَّحِيمُ

C. 168.—Thus the Truth of Allah must win against folly
(26:192-227.) And falsehood. The Spirit of Inspiration
And Faith brought down the Qur'ān to the mind
Of the Holy Prophet, that he might teach
In noble Arabic speech, and through it
Reach the world. If obstinate rebels
Do resist the Message, their day is brief:
With humble, gentle kindness it must make
Its way to all, nearest and farthest.
It is not like the vain words of poets false,
Wandering without a goal: it is Truth,
That fills the heart which trusts in Allah.

SECTION 11.

192. Verily this is a Revelation[3223]
From the Lord of the Worlds:

١٩٢ وَإِنَّهُ لَتَنزِيلُ رَبِّ الْعَالَمِينَ

193. With it came down
The Spirit of Faith and Truth—[3224]

١٩٣ نَزَلَ بِهِ الرُّوحُ الْأَمِينُ

3220. Perhaps a shower of ashes and cinders accompanying a volcanic eruption. If these people were the same as the Midianites, there was also an earthquake. See 7:91 and n. 1063.

3221. It must have been a terrible day of wholesale destruction—earthquake, volcanic eruption, lava, cinders and ashes and rumbling noises to frighten those whose death was not instantaneous.

3222. See above, n. 3193 to 26:121.

3223. The hostile reception of some of the previous Messengers having been mentioned, the special characteristics of the Qur'ān are now referred to, to show (1) that it is true, and (2) that its rejection by the Makkan Pagans was of a piece with the previous experience in the history of man: vested interests resist Truth, but it conquers.

3224. *Rūḥ al Amīn*, the epithet of Gabriel, who came with the inspired Messages to the Holy Prophet, is difficult to render in a single epithet in translation. In n. 3187 to 26:107 I have described some of the various shades of meaning attached to the adjective *Amīn* as applied to a Prophet. A further signification as attached to the Spirit of Inspiration is that it is the very quintessence of Faith and Truth, unlike the lying spirits which delude men with falsehood. On the whole, I think "the Spirit of Faith and Truth" will best represent the original here.

194. To thy heart and mind,[3225]
That thou mayest admonish

١٩٤ عَلَىٰ قَلْبِكَ لِتَكُونَ مِنَ ٱلْمُنذِرِينَ

195. In the perspicuous
Arabic tongue.

١٩٥ بِلِسَانٍ عَرَبِيٍّ مُّبِينٍ

196. Without doubt it is (announced)
In the revealed Books[3226]
Of former peoples.

١٩٦ وَإِنَّهُۥ لَفِى زُبُرِ ٱلْأَوَّلِينَ

197. Is it not a Sign
To them that the Learned
Of the Children of Israel
Knew it (as true)?[3227]

١٩٧ أَوَلَمْ يَكُن لَّهُمْ ءَايَةً أَن يَعْلَمَهُۥ
عُلَمَٰٓؤُا۟ بَنِىٓ إِسْرَٰٓءِيلَ

198. Had We revealed it
To any of the non-Arabs,

١٩٨ وَلَوْ نَزَّلْنَٰهُ عَلَىٰ بَعْضِ ٱلْأَعْجَمِينَ

199. And had he recited it
To them, they would not
Have believed in it.[3228]

١٩٩ فَقَرَأَهُۥ عَلَيْهِم مَّا كَانُوا۟ بِهِۦ مُؤْمِنِينَ

200. Thus have We caused it
To enter the hearts
Of the Sinners.[3229]

٢٠٠ كَذَٰلِكَ سَلَكْنَٰهُ فِى قُلُوبِ ٱلْمُجْرِمِينَ

201. They will not believe
In it until they see
The grievous Penalty;

٢٠١ لَا يُؤْمِنُونَ بِهِۦ حَتَّىٰ يَرَوُا۟ ٱلْعَذَابَ ٱلْأَلِيمَ

3225. *Qalb* (Heart) signifies not only the seat of the affections, but also the seat of the memory and understanding. The process of inspiration is indicated by the impression of the divine Message on the inspired one's heart, memory, and understanding, from which it was promulgated in human speech to the world. In this case the human speech was the perspicuous Arabic tongue, which would be plainly intelligible to the audience who would immediately hear it and be through them transmitted to all the world.

3226. The word *Zubur,* used here, is plural of *Zabūr,* which is mentioned in the Qur'ān as the Book revealed to the Prophet Dāwūd. It has also been used in the Qur'ān in the generic sense of "Book" (54:52). Here the word refers to the earlier Revelations. (Eds.).

3227. Many of the Jewish Doctors recognised the Holy Prophet's Message as a Message from Allah, *e.g.,* 'Abdullāh ibn Salām and Mukhayrīq. The latter was a man of property, which he left for Islam. (There were also Christian monks and learned men who recognised the Prophet's mission.)

3228. The turn of Arabia having come for receiving Allah's Revelation, as was foretold in previous Revelations, it was inevitable that it should be in the Arab tongue through the mouth of an Arab. Otherwise it would have been unintelligible, and the Arabs could not have received the Faith and become the vehicles for its promulgation as actually happened in history.

3229. "Thus" I think means through the medium of the Arabic language and the Arab people. The Qur'ān penetrated through their language and their hearts. If the hardhearted among them did not believe, they will see when the Penalty comes, how grievous a mistake they made. For the Penalty must come; even when they least expected it. They will be caught saying or thinking, "There is plenty of time; we can get another respite," when already it will have become too late for them to turn over a new leaf.

202. But the (Penalty) will come
To them of a sudden,
While they perceive it not;

فَيَأْتِيَهُم بَغْتَةً وَهُمْ لَا يَشْعُرُونَ ٢٠٢

203. Then they will say:
"Shall we be respited?"

فَيَقُولُوا هَلْ نَحْنُ مُنظَرُونَ ٢٠٣

204. Do they then ask
For Our Penalty to be
Hastened on?[3230]

أَفَبِعَذَابِنَا يَسْتَعْجِلُونَ ٢٠٤

205. Seest thou? If We do
Let them enjoy (this life)
For a few years,

أَفَرَءَيْتَ إِن مَّتَّعْنَاهُمْ سِنِينَ ٢٠٥

206. Yet there comes to them
At length the (Punishment)
Which they were promised!

ثُمَّ جَاءَهُم مَّا كَانُوا يُوعَدُونَ ٢٠٦

207. It will profit them not
That they enjoyed (this life)!

مَا أَغْنَىٰ عَنْهُم مَّا كَانُوا يُمَتَّعُونَ ٢٠٧

208. Never did We destroy
A population, but had
Its warners—

وَمَا أَهْلَكْنَا مِن قَرْيَةٍ إِلَّا لَهَا مُنذِرُونَ ٢٠٨

209. By way of reminder;
And We never are unjust.[3231]

ذِكْرَىٰ وَمَا كُنَّا ظَالِمِينَ ٢٠٩

210. No evil ones have brought[3232]
Down this (Revelation):

وَمَا تَنَزَّلَتْ بِهِ الشَّيَاطِينُ ٢١٠

211. It would neither suit them
Nor would they be able
(To produce it).

وَمَا يَنبَغِي لَهُمْ وَمَا يَسْتَطِيعُونَ ٢١١

3230. While some sinners out of negligence postpone the day of repentance till it is too late, others more bold actually ask out of bravado that Allah's Punishment should be brought down on them at once, as they do not believe in Allah or His Punishment! The answer to them is: It will come soon enough—too soon, they will think, when it comes! *Cf.* 22:47 and notes.

3231. Allah will grant much respite to sinners, for He is Most Gracious and Merciful. But all this respite will profit them nothing if they are merely immersed in the vanities of this world. Again and again, in spite of their rebellion and their rejection, does Allah send warnings and warners before the final Punishment of Justice. For Allah knows human weakness, and He will never be unjust in the least.

3232. When anything extraordinary happens, there are always people desirous of putting the worst construction on it, and saying that it is the work of the evil ones, the devils. So when the Qur'ān came with its Message in wondrous Arabic, its enemies could only account for its power by attributing it to evil spirits! Such a beneficient message can never suit the purposes of the evil ones, nor would it be in their power to produce it. In fact Good and Evil are poles asunder, and Evil cannot even hear words of Good, of tender Pity for sinners and Forgiveness for the penitent!

212. Indeed they have been removed
Far from even (a chance of)
Hearing it.

إِنَّهُمْ عَنِ ٱلسَّمْعِ لَمَعْزُولُونَ ٢١٢

213. So call not on any
Other god with Allah,
Or thou wilt be among
Those under the Penalty.

فَلَا تَدْعُ مَعَ ٱللَّهِ إِلَٰهًا ءَاخَرَ ٢١٣
فَتَكُونَ مِنَ ٱلْمُعَذَّبِينَ

214. And admonish thy nearest
Kinsmen,

وَأَنذِرْ عَشِيرَتَكَ ٱلْأَقْرَبِينَ ٢١٤

215. And lower thy wing[3233]
To the Believers who
Follow thee.

وَٱخْفِضْ جَنَاحَكَ ٢١٥
لِمَنِ ٱتَّبَعَكَ مِنَ ٱلْمُؤْمِنِينَ

216. Then if they disobey thee,
Say: "I am free (of responsibility)
For what ye do!"[3234]

فَإِنْ عَصَوْكَ فَقُلْ إِنِّى بَرِىٓءٌ مِّمَّا تَعْمَلُونَ ٢١٦

217. And put thy trust
On the Exalted in Might,
The Merciful—

وَتَوَكَّلْ عَلَى ٱلْعَزِيزِ ٱلرَّحِيمِ ٢١٧

218. Who seeth thee standing
Forth (in prayer),

ٱلَّذِى يَرَىٰكَ حِينَ تَقُومُ ٢١٨

219. And thy movements among
Those who prostrate themselves.[3235]

وَتَقَلُّبَكَ فِى ٱلسَّٰجِدِينَ ٢١٩

220. For it is He
Who heareth and knoweth
All things.

إِنَّهُۥ هُوَ ٱلسَّمِيعُ ٱلْعَلِيمُ ٢٢٠

3233. That is, be kind, gentle, and considerate with them, as a highflying bird is when she lowers her wing to her offspring. *Cf.* 17:24 and n. 2205, and 15:88 and n. 2011.

3234. "Disobey thee" implied that they did something wrong, for the Holy Prophet commanded what was right and forbade what was wrong. If, then, any of his flock did wrong the responsibility was not his, for he, like a good shepherd, tried to keep them right. What was he then to do? He would continue his teaching. But if any of them went so far wrong as to try to injure their own Teacher, Leader and guide, there was nothing for him to fear. His trust was only in Allah and Allah sees and appraises all men's actions at their true worth.

3235. Literally, the standing and prostration are postures of Muslim prayer: the Holy Prophet was equally earnest, sincere, and zealous in prayer for himself and for all his people. The Prophet's behaviour was exemplary in all the turns of fortune, and however foolish men may cavil, his purity and uprightness are fully known to Allah. (R).

221. Shall I inform you,
(O people!), on whom it is
That the evil ones descend?[3236]

هَلْ أُنَبِّئُكُمْ عَلَىٰ مَن تَنَزَّلُ ٱلشَّيَٰطِينُ ﴿٢٢١﴾

222. They descend on every
Lying, wicked person,

تَنَزَّلُ عَلَىٰ كُلِّ أَفَّاكٍ أَثِيمٍ ﴿٢٢٢﴾

223. (Into whose ears) they pour
Hearsay vanities, and most
Of them are liars.

يُلْقُونَ ٱلسَّمْعَ وَأَكْثَرُهُمْ كَٰذِبُونَ ﴿٢٢٣﴾

224. And the Poets—[3237]
It is those straying in Evil,
Who follow them:

وَٱلشُّعَرَآءُ يَتَّبِعُهُمُ ٱلْغَاوُۥنَ ﴿٢٢٤﴾

225. Seest thou not that they
Wander distractedly in every
Valley?—

أَلَمْ تَرَ أَنَّهُمْ فِى كُلِّ وَادٍ يَهِيمُونَ ﴿٢٢٥﴾

226. And that they say
What they practise not?—

وَأَنَّهُمْ يَقُولُونَ مَا لَا يَفْعَلُونَ ﴿٢٢٦﴾

227. Except those who believe,[3238]
Work righteousness, engage much
In the remembrance of Allah,
And defend themselves only after
They are unjustly attacked.
And soon will the unjust[3239]
Assailants know what vicissitudes
Their affairs will take!

إِلَّا ٱلَّذِينَ ءَامَنُوا۟ وَعَمِلُوا۟ ٱلصَّٰلِحَٰتِ ﴿٢٢٧﴾
وَذَكَرُوا۟ ٱللَّهَ كَثِيرًا وَٱنتَصَرُوا۟ مِنۢ بَعْدِ مَا ظُلِمُوا۟
وَسَيَعْلَمُ ٱلَّذِينَ ظَلَمُوٓا۟
أَىَّ مُنقَلَبٍ يَنقَلِبُونَ

3236. To people who maliciously suggested that the Holy Prophet was possessed or inspired by evil spirits (26:210 above) the reply had already been made, but it is now declared that the suggestion is itself the work of Evil. Behind such suggestions are lying and wickedness, or at best some half-truths caught up in hearsay and twisted so as to show Allah in an evil light.

3237. *The Poets*: to be read along with the exceptions mentioned in verse 227 below. Poetry and other arts are not in themselves evil, but may, on the contrary, be used in the service of religion and righteousness. But there is a danger that they may be prostituted for base purposes. If they are insincere ("they say what they do not") or are divorced from actual life or its goodness or its serious purpose, they may become instruments of evil or futility. They then wander about without any set purpose, and seek the depths (valleys) of human folly rather than the heights of divine light.

3238. Poetry and the fine arts which are to be commended are those which emanante from minds steeped in the Faith, which try to carry out in life the fine sentiments they express in their artistic work, aim at the glory of Allah rather than at self-glorification or the fulsome praise of men with feet of clay, and do not (as in Jihād) attack anything except aggressive evil. In this sense a perfect artist should be a perfect man. Perfection may not be attainable in this life, but it should be the aim of every man, and especially of one who wishes to become a supreme artist, not only in technique but in spirit and essentials. Among the commendable poets contemporary with the Holy Prophet may be mentioned Ḥassān and Labīd: the latter had the honour of being one of the seven whose poems were selected for "hanging" (the *Mu'allaqāt*) in the Days of Ignorance.

3239. These were the scurrilous rhymsters, who were doomed to come to an evil end.

APPENDIX VII.

Thamūd Inscriptions at al Ḥijr (26:141-159; 15:80-84; and 7:73-79).

Mr. C.M. Doughty travelled in Northwestern Arabia and Najd in the 1880's, and his book *Arabia Deserta* forms one of the most notable of Arabian travel books. It was first published in two volumes by the Cambridge University Press in 1888, and has recently gone through several editions. The edition I have used is the unabridged one-volume edition printed in London in 1926. The references in this Appendix should be understood to refer to that edition.

Doughty travelled on the old Pilgrim Caravan from Damascus as far as Madā'in Ṣāliḥ, and then parted company with the Pilgrims and turned into Najd. Madā'in Ṣāliḥ (the Cities of Ṣāliḥ), is one of the stations on the Syrian Pilgrim route, about 180 miles north of Madīnah. Tabūk, to which the Holy Prophet led an expedition in A.H. 9 (see Introduction to S. 9.), is about 170 miles farther to the northwest, and Ma'ān Junction about 150 miles still farther. Madā'in Ṣāliḥ's was also an important station on the prehistoric gold and frankincense (*bakhūr*) route between Yemen and Egypt or Syria. In sacred history it marks the ruined site of the Thamūd people to whom the prophet Ṣāliḥ was sent, whose she-camel was a symbolic Sign and is connected with Ṣāliḥ's history. See n. 3208 to 26:155-157. To the west and northwest of Madā'in Ṣāliḥ are three *Ḥarrāt* or tracts of volcanic land covered with lava, stretching as far as Tabūk.

This is how Doughty describes his first view of Madā'in Ṣāliḥ, approaching from the northwest. "At length in the dim morning twilight, as we journeyed, we were come to a sandy brow and a straight descending place betwixt cliffs of sandstones. There was some shouting in the forward, and Aswad bid me look up, 'this was a famous place, *Mabrak al Nāqah*'" (the kneeling place of the she-camel of Ṣāliḥ. "It is short, at first steep, and issues upon the plain of *Al Ḥijr,* which is Madā'in Ṣāliḥ; where the sun coming up showed the singular landscape of this valley plain, encompassed with might sandstone precipices (which here resemble ranges of city walls, fantastic towers, and castle buildings), and upon them lie high shouldering sand drifts. The bottom is sand, with much growth of desert bushes; and I perceived some thin sprinkled volcanic drift. Westward is seen the immense mountain blackness, terrible and lowering, of the *Ḥarrāt*." (*Arabia Deserta,* p. 83, vol. I.)

Doughty took some rubbings of some of the Inscriptions which were accessible to him and they were studied by the great Semitic scholar M. Ernest Renan and published by the Academie des Inscriptions et Belles-Lettres. Renan's Report in French is printed as an Appendix to Chapters IV, V and VI of *Arabia Deserta* (pp. 180-187, vol. I) and M. le Marquis de Vofgue's Note (also in French) on the Nabataean sculptured Architecture at Madā'in Ṣāliḥ at pp. 620-623, vol. I.

The general result of these studies may be summarised. The sculpture and architecture are found to be of the same kind as the Nabataean monuments at Petra (for which see n. 1043 to 7:73). At Petra there are no dated Inscriptions preserved, but at Madā'in Ṣāliḥ we have several. There are at Madā'in Ṣāliḥ perhaps 100 sepulchral rock-hewn chambers, in some of which are found human bones and remains, showing that the Nabataeans knew the art of embalming, and used linen of the same kind as was used in ancient Egypt. The tombs are dedicated in perpetuity to named families, and the named Nabataean kings have, each, the epithet "loving his people". There are flat side-pilasters, and the figures of four-footed beasts, eagles, and other birds are discernible. Besides the sepulchral chambers, there is a great Hall or Council Chamber (*Dīwān*), 25ft. x 27ft. x 13ft. This may have been a Temple. The gods worshipped there were those whose names we know from other Nabataean sources—Dusares, Martaba, Allāt, Manāt, Ka'īs, and Hubal. Allāt, Manāt, and Hubal are also known to us in connection with the idols of the Pagan Quraysh of the Times of Ignorance. It is interesting to find the word *Mesjeda* (Arabic *Masjid*) already used here for "place of worship". Triads of stones were worshipped as gods.

The Inscriptions have dates from 3 B.C. to 79 A.C. Within this short period of 82 years we can see something of the development of Semitic palaeography. The writing becomes more and more cursive with the years. We have here a central point between Old Armenian, Square Hebrew, Palmyran, Sinaitic, Kūfī and Naskh.

We may treat the Nabataeans as historical, as we have established dates. The Thamūd were prehistoric, and occupied sites which were afterwards occupied by the Nabataeans and others. The kneeling place of Ṣaliḥ's she-camel (*Mabrak al Nāqah*) and the well of the she-camel (*Bīru al Nāqah*), and a number of local names keep alive the race memory of an ancient Arabic people and their prophet Ṣāliḥ.

INTRODUCTION TO SŪRAH 27–*AL NAML*

This Sūrah is cognate in subject to the one preceding it and the two following it. Its chronological place is also in the same group of four, in the middle Makkan period.

Here there is much mystic symbolism. Wonders in the physical world are types of greater wonders in the spiritual world. The Fire, the White Hand, and the Rod, in the story of Moses; the speech of birds, the crowds of Jinns and men pitted against a humble ant, and the Hoopoe and the Queen of Sheba, in Solomon's story; the defeat of the plot of the nine wicked men in the story of Ṣāliḥ; and the crime of sin with open eyes in the story of Lūṭ—lead up to the lessons of true and false worship and the miracles of Allah's grace and revelation.

Summary—Wonderful in Revelation, like the Fire which Moses saw, which was a glimpse of Allah's Glory, and His Miracles, which searched out those who refused Faith in spite of the light they had received (27:1-14, and C. 169).

Solomon knew the speech of Birds and had hosts of Jinns and men; yet the wise ant had ample defence against them: the Hoopoe who was absent at his muster, was yet serving him: the Queen of Sheba had a kingdom, but it submitted with conviction to the Wisdom of Solomon and the Kingdom of Allah (27:15-44, and C. 170).

Fools ascribe ill-luck to godliness as in Ṣāliḥ's story, or fall into the lusts with their eyes open, as in Lūṭ's story; but their plots and their rage will be foiled by Allah (27:45-58, and C. 171).

Allah's glory and goodness are supreme over all Creation: Unfaith will yield to Faith in the final adjustment of values: so follow Revelation, serve Allah, and trust in Him, (27:59-93, and C. 172).

C. 169.—Revelation shows us a glimpse of the spiritual
(27:1-14.) World, guides us in this life, and gives us
The Hope of eternal Bliss in the Hereafter.
It works a complete transformation in us,
As it did with Moses when he saw
The mystic Fire and was given the Signs
With which to reclaim a people lost
In superstition and sin, and proud of sin.

Sūrah 27.

Al Naml (The Ants)

الجزء التاسع عشر سورة النمل

In the Name of Allah, Most Gracious, Most Merciful.

بِسْمِ ٱللَّهِ ٱلرَّحْمَٰنِ ٱلرَّحِيمِ

1. Ṭā Sīn.[3240]
These are verses
Of the Qur'ān—A Book
That makes (things) clear;

طسٓ ۚ تِلْكَ ءَايَٰتُ ٱلْقُرْءَانِ وَكِتَابٍ مُّبِينٍ ﴿١﴾

2. A Guide; and Glad Tidings
For the Believers—[3241]

هُدًى وَبُشْرَىٰ لِلْمُؤْمِنِينَ ﴿٢﴾

3. Those who establish regular prayers
And give in regular charity,
And also have (full) assurance
Of the Hereafter.

ٱلَّذِينَ يُقِيمُونَ ٱلصَّلَوٰةَ وَيُؤْتُونَ ٱلزَّكَوٰةَ وَهُم بِٱلْءَاخِرَةِ هُمْ يُوقِنُونَ ﴿٣﴾

4. As to those who believe not
In the Hereafter, We have
Made their deeds pleasing[3242]
In their eyes; and so they
Wander about in distraction.

إِنَّ ٱلَّذِينَ لَا يُؤْمِنُونَ بِٱلْءَاخِرَةِ زَيَّنَّا لَهُمْ أَعْمَٰلَهُمْ فَهُمْ يَعْمَهُونَ ﴿٤﴾

5. Such are they for whom
A grievous Penalty is (waiting):
And in the Hereafter theirs
Will be the greatest loss.[3243]

أُو۟لَٰٓئِكَ ٱلَّذِينَ لَهُمْ سُوٓءُ ٱلْعَذَابِ وَهُمْ فِى ٱلْءَاخِرَةِ هُمُ ٱلْأَخْسَرُونَ ﴿٥﴾

6. As to thee, the Qur'ān
Is bestowed upon thee
From the presence of One
Who is Wise and All-Knowing.

وَإِنَّكَ لَتُلَقَّى ٱلْقُرْءَانَ مِن لَّدُنْ حَكِيمٍ عَلِيمٍ ﴿٦﴾

3240. See n. 3137 to 26:1.

3241. Revelation is here presented in three aspects: (1) it explains things, the attributes of Allah, our own position, and the spiritual world around; (2) it directs us to right conduct and keeps us from evil; and (3) to those who have Faith and accept its guidance, it gives the good news of forgiveness, purification, and the achievement of salvation. (R).

3242. Those who reject Allah and follow Evil have a good conceit of themselves. Their deeds are pleasing to no one else. As they have rejected Allah's guidance, they are allowed to embrace their own self-conceit, and given further respite for repentance. But they follow their own whims and wander about in distraction, as they have no standards such as guide the godly.

3243. The account will then be made up, and they will be found to be terribly in loss. They will be the worst in loss, for all their self-complacency.

7. Behold! Moses said[3244]
To his family: "I perceive
A fire; soon will I bring you
From there some information,
Or I will bring you
A burning brand to light
Our fuel, that ye may
Warm yourselves.

(٧) إِذْ قَالَ مُوسَىٰ لِأَهْلِهِۦٓ
إِنِّىٓ ءَانَسْتُ نَارًا سَـَٔاتِيكُم مِّنْهَا بِخَبَرٍ
أَوْ ءَاتِيكُم بِشِهَابٍ قَبَسٍ
لَّعَلَّكُمْ تَصْطَلُونَ

8. But when he came
To the (Fire), a voice
Was heard: "Blessed are those[3245]
In the Fire and those around:
And Glory to Allah,
The Lord of the Worlds.

(٨) فَلَمَّا جَآءَهَا نُودِىَ أَنۢ
بُورِكَ مَن فِى ٱلنَّارِ وَمَنْ حَوْلَهَا
وَسُبْحَـٰنَ ٱللَّهِ رَبِّ ٱلْعَـٰلَمِينَ

9. "O Moses! Verily,
I am Allah, the Exalted
In Might, the Wise!...

(٩) يَـٰمُوسَىٰٓ إِنَّهُۥٓ أَنَا ٱللَّهُ ٱلْعَزِيزُ ٱلْحَكِيمُ

10. "Now do thou throw they rod!"[3246]
But when he saw it
Moving (of its own accord)
As if it had been a snake,
He turned back in retreat,
And retraced not his steps:
"O Moses!" (it was said)
"Fear not: truly, in My presence,
Those called as messengers
Have no fear—[3247]

(١٠) وَأَلْقِ عَصَاكَ
فَلَمَّا رَءَاهَا تَهْتَزُّ كَأَنَّهَا جَآنٌّ
وَلَّىٰ مُدْبِرًا وَلَمْ يُعَقِّبْ
يَـٰمُوسَىٰ لَا تَخَفْ إِنِّى لَا يَخَافُ
لَدَىَّ ٱلْمُرْسَلُونَ

3244. *Cf.* 20:9-24. Both there and here there is a reference to the dawn of Revelation in the heart of Moses. The points there emphasised will be found in the notes to that passage. Here the emphasis is on the wonderful nature of the Fire and the wonderful way in which Moses was transformed at the touch of spiritual Light. He was travelling in the Sinai desert with his family. Seeking ordinary light, he came upon a Light which took him to the highest mysteries of Allah. No doubt all his inner history had prepared him for his great destiny. It is the inner history that matters, and not the place of the position of a man in the eyes of his ordinary fellows.

3245. *Those*: in the original the pronoun is in the singular, "*man*", which is often used with a plural meaning. The Commentators usually construe it to mean that this was not a physical fire, but it was the glory of the Angels, a reflection of the Glory of Allah. Hence the exclamation at the end of the verse.

3246. Moses was now transported into an entirely new world. What he had taken to be an ordinary fire was a dream of the spiritual world—rays from the angels of light. The desert in which he had been was the lower life stripped of its ornaments, leading to the divine light of Sinai. Through that Light he heard the Voice of the Source of Wisdom and Power. His own rod or staff was no longer the dead piece of wood that had hitherto supported him. It became instinct with life, a life that moved, and had the power of offence and defence in it, as all living Good must have in its fight with Evil. His own transformation is described in the next note.

3247. In this great, new, wonderful world, that was opening out to Moses, he had to get his vision adjusted to his new surroundings, as an ordinary man has to adjust his sight before he can see into any very strong light that is new to him. The staff which had become alive as a snake frightened him: yet it was to be his own instrument of work in his new mission. All fear was to be cast out of his mind, as befitted a man chosen by Allah.

11. "But if any have done wrong
And have thereafter substituted
Good to take the place of evil,[3248]
Truly, I am Oft-Forgiving,
Most Merciful.

إِلَّا مَن ظَلَمَ ثُمَّ بَدَّلَ حُسْنًا بَعْدَ سُوٓءٍ
فَإِنِّي غَفُورٌ رَّحِيمٌ ١١

12. "Now put thy hand into
Thy bosom, and it will
Come forth white without stain[3249]
(Or harm): (these are) among
The nine Signs (thou wilt take)[3250]
To Pharaoh and his people:
For they are a people
Rebellious in transgression."

وَأَدْخِلْ يَدَكَ فِي جَيْبِكَ
تَخْرُجْ بَيْضَآءَ مِنْ غَيْرِ سُوٓءٍ
فِي تِسْعِ ءَايَٰتٍ إِلَىٰ فِرْعَوْنَ وَقَوْمِهِۦٓ
إِنَّهُمْ كَانُوا۟ قَوْمًا فَٰسِقِينَ ١٢

13. But when Our Signs came
To them, that should have[3251]
Opened their eyes, they said:
"This is sorcery manifest!"

فَلَمَّا جَآءَتْهُمْ ءَايَٰتُنَا مُبْصِرَةً
قَالُوا۟ هَٰذَا سِحْرٌ مُّبِينٌ ١٣

14. And they rejected those Signs
In iniquity and arrogance,
Though their souls were convinced
Thereof: so see what was
The end of those
Who acted corruptly!

وَجَحَدُوا۟ بِهَا
وَٱسْتَيْقَنَتْهَآ أَنفُسُهُمْ ظُلْمًا وَعُلُوًّا
فَٱنظُرْ كَيْفَ كَانَ عَٰقِبَةُ ٱلْمُفْسِدِينَ ١٤

C. 170. (27:15-44.) — No less were David and Solomon versed
In knowledge and mystic wisdom. Even
Solomon could appreciate the wisdom
Of the humble Ant. He used all his power
And resources in extending the Kingdom
Of Allah. In wonderful ways did he lead
The Queen of Sheba to the Light of the Faith
Of Unity, and confirmed her in pure
Worship, the worship of the Lord of the Worlds.

3248. His slaying the Egyptian (n. 3146 to 26:14), however defensible from certain aspects, was yet something from his past that had to be washed off, and Allah, Oft-Forgiving, Most Merciful, did it out of His abounding Grace. Nay, more; he was given a pure, Radiant Hand, as a Sign of his personal transformation, as stated in the next verse.

3249. *Cf.* 20:22. There the expression is: "Draw thy hand close to thy side." As far as the physical act is concerned, the expressions there and here mean the same thing. Moses had a loose-fitting robe. If he put his hand within the folds of the robe, it would go to his bosom on the side of his body opposite to that from which the hand came: *i.e.*, if it was his right hand it would go to the left side of his bosom. But the difference of expression has little spiritual significance. The bosom here stands for his innermost being, which was being so transformed with divine light as to lend the radiance to his hand also, his instrument of action. The hand comes out white and radiant without a stain. Ordinarily if the skin becomes white it is a sign of disease or leprosy. Here it was the opposite. It was a sign of radiance and glory from the higher Light.

3250. *The nine Signs*: see n. 1091 to 7:133.

3251. The Signs should have clearly opened the eyes of any persons who honestly examined them and thought about them. Those who rejected them were perverse and were going against their own light and inner conviction. That was the aggravating feature of their sin.

SECTION 2.

15. We gave (in the past)
Knowledge to David and
Solomon:[3252]
And they both said:
"Praise be to Allah, Who
Has favoured us above many
Of His servants who believe!"[3253]

١٥ وَلَقَدْ ءَاتَيْنَا دَاوُۥدَ وَسُلَيْمَـٰنَ عِلْمًا
وَقَالَا ٱلْحَمْدُ لِلَّهِ ٱلَّذِى فَضَّلَنَا
عَلَىٰ كَثِيرٍ مِّنْ عِبَادِهِ ٱلْمُؤْمِنِينَ

16. And Solomon was David's heir.[3254]
He said: "O ye people!
We have been taught the speech[3255]
Of Birds, and on us
Has been bestowed (a little)
Of all things: this is
Indeed Grace manifest (from
Allah.)"[3256]

١٦ وَوَرِثَ سُلَيْمَـٰنُ دَاوُۥدَ
وَقَالَ يَـٰٓأَيُّهَا ٱلنَّاسُ عُلِّمْنَا مَنطِقَ
ٱلطَّيْرِ وَأُوتِينَا مِن كُلِّ شَىْءٍ
إِنَّ هَـٰذَا لَهُوَ ٱلْفَضْلُ ٱلْمُبِينُ

17. And before Solomon were
marshalled
His hosts—of Jinns and men

١٧ وَحُشِرَ لِسُلَيْمَـٰنَ جُنُودُهُۥ
مِنَ ٱلْجِنِّ وَٱلْإِنسِ

3252. *Cf.* 21:78-82. "Knowledge" means such knowledge as leads up to the higher things in life, the Wisdom that was shown in their decisions and judgements, and the understanding that enabled them to fulfil their mission in life. They were both just men and prophets of Allah. The Bible, as we have it, is inconsistent: on the one hand it calls David "a man after God's own heart" (I Samuel, xiii. 14, and Acts xiii. 22); and the Christians acclaim Christ as a son of David; but on the other hand, horrible crimes are ascribed to him, which, if he had committed them, would make him a monster of cruelty and injustice. About Solomon, too, while he is described as a glorious king, there are stories of his lapses into sin and idolatry. The Muslim teaching considers them both to be men of piety and wisdom, and high in spiritual knowledge.

3253. They ascribed, as was proper, their knowledge, wisdom, and power to the only true Source of all good, Allah.

3254. The point is that Solomon not only inherited his father's kingdom but his spiritual insight and the prophetic office, which do not necessarily go from father to son.

3255. *Speech of Birds.* The spoken word in human speech is different from the means of communication which birds and animals have between each other. But no man can doubt that they have means of communication with each other, if he only observes the orderly flight of migratory birds or the regulated behaviour of ants, bees, and other creatures who live in communities. The wisdom of Solomon and others like him (he speaks of "we") consisted in understanding these things—in the animal world and in the lower fringes of human intelligence.

3256. *A little of all things*: Solomon was a king of power and authority; outside his kingdom he had influence among many neighbouring peoples: he had knowledge of birds, and beasts and plants: he was just and wise, and understood men: and above all, he had spiritual insight, which brought him near to Allah. Thus he had something of all kinds of desirable gifts. And with true gratitude he referred them to Allah, the Giver of all gifts.

And birds, and they were all
Kept in order and ranks.[3257]

وَٱلطَّيْرِ فَهُمْ يُوزَعُونَ

18. At length, when they came
To a (lowly) valley of ants,
One of the ants said:
"O ye ants, get into
Your habitations, lest Solomon
And his hosts crush you
(Under foot) without knowing
it."[3258]

١٨ حَتَّىٰٓ إِذَآ أَتَوْا۟ عَلَىٰ وَادِ ٱلنَّمْلِ
قَالَتْ نَمْلَةٌ يَـٰٓأَيُّهَا ٱلنَّمْلُ ٱدْخُلُوا۟
مَسَـٰكِنَكُمْ لَا يَحْطِمَنَّكُمْ
سُلَيْمَـٰنُ وَجُنُودُهُۥ وَهُمْ لَا يَشْعُرُونَ

19. So he smiled, amused
At its speech; and he said:
"O my Lord! so order me
That I may be grateful
For Thy favours, which Thou
Hast bestowed on me and[3259]
On my parents, and that
I may work the righteousness
That will please Thee:[3260]
And admit me, by Thy Grace,
To the ranks of Thy
Righteous Servants."[3261]

١٩ فَتَبَسَّمَ ضَاحِكًا مِّن قَوْلِهَا
وَقَالَ رَبِّ أَوْزِعْنِىٓ أَنْ أَشْكُرَ نِعْمَتَكَ
ٱلَّتِىٓ أَنْعَمْتَ عَلَىَّ وَعَلَىٰ وَٰلِدَىَّ
وَأَنْ أَعْمَلَ صَـٰلِحًا تَرْضَىٰهُ
وَأَدْخِلْنِى بِرَحْمَتِكَ
فِى عِبَادِكَ ٱلصَّـٰلِحِينَ

20. And he took a muster
Of the Birds; and he said:

٢٠ وَتَفَقَّدَ ٱلطَّيْرَ فَقَالَ

3257. Besides the literal meaning, there are two symbolical meanings. (1) All his subjects of varying grades of intelligence, taste, and civilisation, were kept in due order and cooperation by his discipline, justice, and good government. (2) The gifts of various kinds, which he possessed (see last note), he used in proper order and coordination, as they were a well disciplined army, thus getting the best possible results from them.

3258. This verse and the next, read together, suggest the symbolical meaning as predominant. The ant, to outward appearances, is a very small and humble creature. In the great pomp and circumstances of the world, it may be neglected or even trampled on by a people who mean it no harm. Yet, by its wisdom, it carries on its own life within its own sphere ("habitations") unmolested, and makes a useful contribution to the economy of the world. So there is room for the humblest people in the spiritual world.

3259. The counterpart to the position of the humble ant is the position of a great king like Solomon. He prays that his power and wisdom and other gifts may be used for righteousness and for the benefit of all around him. The ant being in his thoughts, we may suppose that he means particularly in his prayer that he may not even unwittingly tread on humble beings in his preoccupation with the great things of the world.

3260. The righteousness which pleases the world is often very different from the righteousness which pleases Allah. Solomon prays that he may always take Allah's Will as his standard, rather than the standards of men.

3261. In the Kingdom of Allah, righteousness is the badge of citizenship. And although there are great and noble grades (see n. 586 to 4:69), the base of that citizenship is the universal brotherhood of righteousness. The greatest in that Kingdom are glad and proud to pray for that essential badge.

"Why is it I see not
The Hoopoe? Or is he
Among the absentees?[3262]

21. "I will certainly punish him
With a severe penalty,
Or execute him, unless
He bring me a clear reason
(For absence)."

22. But the Hoopoe tarried not
Far: he (came up and) said:
"I have compassed (territory)
Which thou hast not compassed,
And I have come to thee
From Sabā'[3263] with tidings true.

23. "I found (there) a woman[3264]
Ruling over them and provided[3265]
With every requisite; and she
Has a magnificent throne.

24. "I found her and her people

مَالِيَ لَآ أَرَى ٱلْهُدْهُدَ
أَمْ كَانَ مِنَ ٱلْغَآئِبِينَ

٢١ لَأُعَذِّبَنَّهُۥ عَذَابًا شَدِيدًا أَوْ لَأَا۟ذْبَحَنَّهُۥٓ
أَوْ لَيَأْتِيَنِّى بِسُلْطَٰنٍ مُّبِينٍ

٢٢ فَمَكَثَ غَيْرَ بَعِيدٍ فَقَالَ
أَحَطتُ بِمَا لَمْ تُحِطْ بِهِۦ
وَجِئْتُكَ مِن سَبَإٍۭ بِنَبَإٍ يَقِينٍ

٢٣ إِنِّى وَجَدتُّ ٱمْرَأَةً تَمْلِكُهُمْ
وَأُوتِيَتْ مِن كُلِّ شَىْءٍ وَلَهَا عَرْشٌ عَظِيمٌ

٢٤ وَجَدتُّهَا وَقَوْمَهَا

3262. Solomon was no idle or easy-going king. He kept all his organisation strictly up to the mark, both his armies literally and his forces (metaphorically). His most mobile arm was the Birds, who were light on the wing and flew and saw everything like efficient scouts. One day he missed the Hoopoe in his muster. The hoopoe is a light, graceful creature, with elegant plumage of many colours, and a beautiful yellow crest on his head, which entitles him to be called a royal bird.

3263. Sabā' may reasonably be identified as the Biblical Sheba (1 Kings x. 1-10). It is further referred to in the Sūrah called after its name: 34:15-20. It was a city in Yemen, said to have been three days' journey (say 50 miles) from the city of Ṣan'ā. A recent German explorer, Dr. Ham Helfritz, claims to have located it in what is now Ḥadhramawt territory. The famous dam of Ma'rib made the country very prosperous, and enabled it to attain a high degree of civilisation ("provided with every requisite" in the next verse). The Queen of Sheba therefore rightly held up her head high until she saw the glories of Solomon.

3264. The Queen of Sheba (by name Bilqīs in Arabian tradition) came apparently from Yemen, but she had affinities with Abyssinia and possibly ruled over Abyssinia also. The Ḥabasha tribe (after whom Abyssinia was named) came from Yemen. Between the southern coast of Yemen and the northeastern coast of Abyssinia there are only the Straits of Bāb al Mandab, barely twenty miles across. In the 10th or 11 century B.C. there were frequent invasions of Abyssinia from Arabia, and Solomon's reign of 40 years is usually synchronised with B.C. 992 to 952. The Sabaean and Ḥimyarite alphabets in which we find the south Arabian pre-Islamic inscriptions, passed into Ethiopic, the language of Abyssinia. The Abyssinians possess a traditional history called "The Book of the Glory of Kings" (*Kebra Negast*), which has been translated from Ethiopic into English by Sir E.A. Wallis Budge (Oxford, 1932). It gives an account of the Queen of Sheba and her only son Menyelek I, as founders of the Abyssinian dynasty. (R).

3265. *Provided with every requisite*: I take this to refer not only to the abundance of spices and gems and gold in her country, but to sciences and arts, and perhaps the spiritual possibilities which made her accept the religion of Unity and Truth (27:44).

Worshipping the sun besides
Allah:[3266]
Satan has made their deeds
Seem pleasing to their eyes,
And has kept them away
From the Path—so
They receive no guidance—

يَسْجُدُونَ لِلشَّمْسِ مِن دُونِ ٱللَّهِ
وَزَيَّنَ لَهُمُ ٱلشَّيْطَٰنُ أَعْمَٰلَهُمْ
فَصَدَّهُمْ عَنِ ٱلسَّبِيلِ فَهُمْ لَا يَهْتَدُونَ

25. "(Kept them away from the Path),
That they should not worship
Allah, Who brings to light[3267]
What is hidden in the heavens
And the earth, and knows
What ye hide and what
Ye reveal.

٢٥ أَلَّا يَسْجُدُوا۟ لِلَّهِ ٱلَّذِى يُخْرِجُ ٱلْخَبْءَ
فِى ٱلسَّمَٰوَٰتِ وَٱلْأَرْضِ وَيَعْلَمُ
مَا تُخْفُونَ وَمَا تُعْلِنُونَ

26. "Allah!—there is no god
But He!—Lord of the Throne[3268]
Supreme!"

٢٦ ٱللَّهُ لَآ إِلَٰهَ إِلَّا هُوَ
رَبُّ ٱلْعَرْشِ ٱلْعَظِيمِ

27. (Solomon) said: "Soon shall we
See whether thou hast told
The truth or lied![3269]

٢٧ قَالَ سَنَنظُرُ أَصَدَقْتَ
أَمْ كُنتَ مِنَ ٱلْكَٰذِبِينَ

28. "Go thou, with this letter
Of mine, and deliver it
To them: then draw back

٢٨ ٱذْهَب بِّكِتَٰبِى هَٰذَا
فَأَلْقِهْ إِلَيْهِمْ ثُمَّ تَوَلَّ

3266. The ancient religions of the people of Sabā' (the Ḥimyar or Sabaeans) consisted in the worship of the heavenly bodies, the sun, the planets, and the stars. Possibly the cult was connected with that of Chaldea, the homeland of Abraham: see 6:75-79 and notes thereon. Yemen had easy access to Mesopotamia and the Persian Gulf by way of the sea, as well as with Abyssinia. That accounts for the Christians of Najrān and the Jewish dynasty of kings (*e.g.*, Dhu Nuwās, d. 525 A.C.) who persecuted them in the century before Islam—also for the Christian Abyssinian Governor Abrahah and his discomfiture in the year of the Prophet's birth (S. 105), say 570 A.C. Jewish-Christian influences were powerful in Arabia in the sixth century of the Christian era.

The religion of these Sabaeans (written in Arabic with a *Sīn*) should not be confounded with that of the Ṣabians (with a *Ṣād*), as to whom see n. 76 to 2:62.

3267. The false worship of the Sabaeans is here exposed in three ways: (1) that they were self-satisfied with their own human achievements, instead of looking up to Allah; and (2) that the light of the heavenly bodies which they worshipped was only dependent on the true Light of Allah, which extends over heaven and earth; the Creator should be worshipped rather than His Creation; and (3) Allah knows the hidden secrets of men's minds as well as the objects which they openly profess: are false worshippers really only worshipping their own selves or the "sins they have a mind to" and are therefore afraid to go to Allah, Who knows all?

3268. The messenger (Hoopoe) is a pious bird, as befits a messenger of Solomon. After mentioning the false worship of the Sabaeans, he pronounces the Creed of Unity, and emphasises Allah's attribute as Lord of the Throne of Glory supreme, in order to make it clear that whatever may be the magnificence of a human throne such as he has described (in verse 25), he is not in any way misled from his loyalty to Solomon, the exponent of the true Religion of Liberty.

3269. Solomon does not doubt his messenger's pleas that he has scouted a new country, but wants to test whether he has loosened the rein of imagination in describing its splendours or its worship.

From them, and (wait to) see
What answer they return"...

عَنْهُمْ فَانظُرْ مَاذَا يَرْجِعُونَ

29. (The Queen) said: "Ye chiefs!
Here is—delivered to me—
A letter worthy of respect.

٢٩ قَالَتْ يَٰٓأَيُّهَا ٱلْمَلَؤُا۟ إِنِّىٓ أُلْقِىَ إِلَىَّ كِتَٰبٌ كَرِيمٌ

30. "It is from Solomon, and is
(As follows): 'In the name[3270]
Of Allah, Most Gracious
Most Merciful:

٣٠ إِنَّهُۥ مِن سُلَيْمَٰنَ وَإِنَّهُۥ بِسْمِ ٱللَّهِ ٱلرَّحْمَٰنِ ٱلرَّحِيمِ

31. " 'Be ye not arrogant
Against me, but come
To me in submission
(To the true Religion).' "

٣١ أَلَّا تَعْلُوا۟ عَلَىَّ وَأْتُونِى مُسْلِمِينَ

SECTION 3.

32. She said: "Ye chiefs!
Advise me in (this)
My affair: no affair
Have I decided
Except in your presence."

٣٢ قَالَتْ يَٰٓأَيُّهَا ٱلْمَلَؤُا۟ أَفْتُونِى فِىٓ أَمْرِى مَا كُنتُ قَاطِعَةً أَمْرًا حَتَّىٰ تَشْهَدُونِ

33. They said: "We are endued
With strength, and given
To vehement war:
But the command is
With thee; so consider
What thou wilt command."

٣٣ قَالُوا۟ نَحْنُ أُو۟لُوا۟ قُوَّةٍ وَأُو۟لُوا۟ بَأْسٍ شَدِيدٍ وَٱلْأَمْرُ إِلَيْكِ فَٱنظُرِى مَاذَا تَأْمُرِينَ

34. She said: "Kings, when they[3271]
Enter a country, despoil it,
And make the noblest
Of its people its meanest
Thus do they behave.

٣٤ قَالَتْ إِنَّ ٱلْمُلُوكَ إِذَا دَخَلُوا۟ قَرْيَةً أَفْسَدُوهَا وَجَعَلُوٓا۟ أَعِزَّةَ أَهْلِهَآ أَذِلَّةً ۖ وَكَذَٰلِكَ يَفْعَلُونَ

3270. Solomon expressly begins his letter with the formula of the true and universal Religion of Unity, and he invites to the true Faith the new people with whom he establishes honourable relations, not for worldly conquest but for the spreading of the Light of Allah.

3271. The character of Queen Bilqīs, as disclosed here, is that of a ruler enjoying great wealth and dignity, and the full confidence of her subjects. She does nothing without consulting her Council, and her Council are ready to carry out her commands in all things. Her people are manly, loyal, and contented, and ready to take the field against any enemy in their country. But their queen is prudent in policy, and is not willing to embroil her country in war. She has the discrimination to see that Solomon is not like ordinary kings who conquer by violence. Perhaps in her heart she has a ray of divine light already, though her people are yet Pagans. She wishes to carry her people with her in whatever she does, because she is as loyal to them as they are to her. An exchange of presents would probably establish better relations between the two kingdoms. And perhaps she anticipates some spiritual understanding also, a hope which was afterwards realised. In Bilqīs we have a picture of womanhood, gentle, prudent, and able tame the wilder passions of her subjects. (R).

35. "But I am going to send
Him a present, and (wait)
To see with what (answer)
Return (my) ambassadors."

٣٥ وَإِنِّي مُرْسِلَةٌ إِلَيْهِم بِهَدِيَّةٍ
فَنَاظِرَةٌۢ بِمَ يَرْجِعُ ٱلْمُرْسَلُونَ

36. Now when (the embassy) came
To Solomon, he said:
"Will ye give me abundance
In wealth? But that which
Allah has given me is better
Than that which He has
Given you! Nay it is ye
Who rejoice in your gift![3272]

٣٦ فَلَمَّا جَآءَ سُلَيْمَٰنَ قَالَ
أَتُمِدُّونَنِ بِمَالٍ فَمَآ ءَاتَىٰنِۦَ ٱللَّهُ
خَيْرٌ مِّمَّآ ءَاتَىٰكُم بَلْ أَنتُم
بِهَدِيَّتِكُمْ تَفْرَحُونَ

37. "Go back to them, and be sure
We shall come to them
With such hosts as they
Will never be able to meet:
We shall expel them
From there in disgrace,
And they will feel
Humbled (indeed)."

٣٧ ٱرْجِعْ إِلَيْهِمْ
فَلَنَأْتِيَنَّهُم بِجُنُودٍ لَّا قِبَلَ لَهُم بِهَا
وَلَنُخْرِجَنَّهُم مِّنْهَآ أَذِلَّةً
وَهُمْ صَٰغِرُونَ

38. He said (to his own men):
"Ye Chiefs! which of you
Can bring me her throne[3273]
Before they come to me
In submission?"

٣٨ قَالَ يَٰٓأَيُّهَا ٱلْمَلَؤُا۟ أَيُّكُمْ يَأْتِينِى بِعَرْشِهَا
قَبْلَ أَن يَأْتُونِى مُسْلِمِينَ

39. Said an 'Ifrīt,[3274] of the Jinns:
"I will bring it to thee
Before thou rise from thy
Council: indeed I have
Full strength for the purpose,
And may be trusted."

٣٩ قَالَ عِفْرِيتٌ مِّنَ ٱلْجِنِّ
أَنَا۠ ءَاتِيكَ بِهِۦ قَبْلَ أَن تَقُومَ مِن مَّقَامِكَ ۖ
وَإِنِّى عَلَيْهِ لَقَوِىٌّ أَمِينٌ

3272. Poor Bilqis! she thought she had arranged with womanly tact to conciliate Solomon, and at the same time pacify her warlike subjects! But the effect of the embassy with presents was the very opposite. Solomon took it as an insult that she should send her presents instead of her submission to the true Religion! He flung back the presents at her, as much as to say, "Let these baubles delight your own hearts! Allah has blessed me with plenty of worldly goods, and something infinitely better, *viz.*: His Light and Guidance! Why do you say nothing about that? Will you only understand the argument of armies and violence?" Or perhaps his speech was only meant for the Sabaean crowd. For when she actually came, he treated her kindly, and she accepted the religion of Unity.

3273. The throne is symbolical of power and dignity. So far her throne was based on material wealth: Solomon is going to alter it to a basis of Faith and the Religion of Unity.

3274. *'Ifrīt*: a large, powerful jinn, reputed to be wicked and crafty: hence he is anxious to be recognised as one that "could be trusted".

40. Said one who had knowledge[3275]
Of the Book: "I will
Bring it to thee within
The twinkling of any eye!"
Then when (Solomon) saw it
Placed firmly before him,
He said: "This is
By the grace of my Lord!—[3276]
To test me whether I am
Grateful or ungrateful!
And if any is grateful,
Truly his gratitude is (a gain)
For his own soul; but if
Any is ungrateful, truly
My Lord is Free of All Needs,
Supreme in Honour!"[3277]

٤٠ قَالَ الَّذِي عِندَهُۥ عِلْمٌ مِّنَ الْكِتَٰبِ
أَنَا۠ ءَاتِيكَ بِهِۦ قَبْلَ أَن يَرْتَدَّ إِلَيْكَ طَرْفُكَ
فَلَمَّا رَءَاهُ مُسْتَقِرًّا عِندَهُۥ
قَالَ هَٰذَا مِن فَضْلِ رَبِّي
لِيَبْلُوَنِي ءَأَشْكُرُ أَمْ أَكْفُرُ
وَمَن شَكَرَ فَإِنَّمَا يَشْكُرُ لِنَفْسِهِۦ
وَمَن كَفَرَ فَإِنَّ رَبِّي غَنِيٌّ كَرِيمٌ

41. He said: "Transform her throne
Out of all recognition by her:
Let us see whether she
Is guided (to the truth)[3278]
Or is one of those who
Receive no guidance."

٤١ قَالَ نَكِّرُوا لَهَا عَرْشَهَا
نَنظُرْ أَتَهْتَدِي أَمْ تَكُونُ
مِنَ الَّذِينَ لَا يَهْتَدُونَ

42. So when she arrived,
She was asked, "Is this
Thy throne?" She said,

٤٢ فَلَمَّا جَآءَتْ قِيلَ أَهَٰكَذَا عَرْشُكِ
قَالَتْ

3275. The symbolic meaning still continues. The big 'Ifrīt had boasted of his brute strength, and his reliability. But this is not enough to transform a power (throne) based on materialism into one based on inward knowledge, knowledge of the heart and spirit, the sort of knowledge that comes from the Book of the Grace of Allah, the spirit of truth and benevolence which is the invisible magic of Prophets of Allah. Even if worldly power and common honesty may be able to effect some good, it will take a comparatively long time, while the magic of spiritual love acts instantaneously. Solomon was thankful to Allah for he had men endowed with such power, and he had the throne of Bilqīs transported to his Court and transformed as he desired, without Bilqīs even knowing it. (R).

3276. If Solomon had been ungrateful to Allah, *i.e.*, if he had worked for his own selfish or worldly ends, he could have used the brute strength of 'Ifrīt to add to his worldly strength and glory. Instead, he uses the higher magic of the Book—or the Spirit—to transform the throne of Bilqīs for her highest good, which means also the highest good for her subjects, by the divine Light. He had the two alternatives, and he chooses the better, and he thus shows his gratitude to Allah for the Grace He had given him.

3277. Man's gratitude to Allah is not a thing that benefits Allah for Allah is high above all needs; it benefits a man's soul and gives him higher rank in the spiritual world. *Per contra*, man's ingratitude will not detract from Allah's Glory and Honour or the value of Allah's generous gifts to man: for Allah is supreme in honour, glory and generosity. *Karīm* in Arabic involved all three significations.

3278. The throne having been transformed, it will be a test to see whether Bilqīs recognises it as her own and accepts it of her own free will as her own, or rejects it as something alien to her, something she will not accommodate herself to. So in our life. We get used to certain habits and customs and certain ways of thought. Allah's message comes to transform us and set us on a different kind of throne, with our own active and willing consent. If we are wise, we feel honoured and grateful. If we are "obstinately rebellious", we reject it as not our own, and pine for the old slavery, as the Israelites pined for Egypt when they were under Allah's guidance in the wilderness.

It was just like this;[3279]
And knowledge was bestowed
On us in advance of this,
And we have submitted
To Allah (in Islam)."

كَأَنَّهُۥ هُوَ
وَأُوتِينَا ٱلْعِلْمَ مِن قَبْلِهَا وَكُنَّا مُسْلِمِينَ

43. And he diverted her[3280]
From the worship of others
Besides Allah: for she was
(Sprung) of a people
That had no faith.

٤٣ وَصَدَّهَا مَا كَانَت تَّعْبُدُ مِن دُونِ ٱللَّهِ
إِنَّهَا كَانَتْ مِن قَوْمٍ كَٰفِرِينَ

44. She was asked to enter[3281]
The lofty Palace: but
When she saw it, she
Thought it was a lake
Of water, and she (tucked up)
Her skirts), uncovering her legs.
He said: "This is
But a palace paved
Smooth with slabs of glass."
She said: "O my Lord!
I have indeed wronged[3282]
My soul: I do (now)
Submit (in Islam), with Solomon,
To the Lord of the Worlds."

٤٤ قِيلَ لَهَا ٱدْخُلِى ٱلصَّرْحَ
فَلَمَّا رَأَتْهُ حَسِبَتْهُ لُجَّةً
وَكَشَفَتْ عَن سَاقَيْهَا
قَالَ إِنَّهُۥ صَرْحٌ مُّمَرَّدٌ مِّن قَوَارِيرَ
قَالَتْ رَبِّ إِنِّى ظَلَمْتُ نَفْسِى
وَأَسْلَمْتُ مَعَ سُلَيْمَٰنَ لِلَّهِ رَبِّ ٱلْعَٰلَمِينَ

C. 171.—In Ṣāliḥ's pure preaching the evil Thamūd
(27:45-58.) Found omens of ill to themselves: in secret
They plotted to take his life, and like cowards

3279. Bilqīs stands the test. She knows it was her throne, yet not exactly the same, for it was now much better. And she is proud of her good fortune, and acknowledges, for herself and her people, with gratitude, the light which was given to them by Allah, by which they recognised Allah's prophet in Solomon and received the true Religion with all their will and heart and soul.

3280. Some Commentators and Translators adopt an alternative construction for the last clause of the last verse and the first clause of this verse. They understand the former to be spoken by Solomon and to mean, 'we had knowledge of Allah's Message and accepted it before her.' They understand the latter to mean, 'the worship of others besides Allah diverted her (from the true Religion).' If we accept the construction adopted in this Translation, the visit to Solomon confirmed the true Faith of Bilqīs and prevented her from lapsing into her ancestral false worship.

3281. Bilqīs, having been received with honour on her arrival, and having accepted the transformation of her throne, placed presumably in an outer building of the Palace, is asked to enter the great Palace itself. Its floor was made of slabs of smooth polished glass, that glistened like water. She thought it was water, and tucked up her clothes to pass through it, showing her bare feet and ankles. This was a very undignified position for a woman, especially one of the position of a Queen. Solomon immediately undeceived her, and told her the real facts, when she felt grateful, and joined herself with Solomon in praising Allah.

3282. In symbolic language, a new entrant into the Palace of divine knowledge, may yet carry in his mind many of the illusions of the lower world. the transparent crystal of Truth he may yet mistake for the unstable water of worldly vanity, which soils the vestments of those who paddle in it. This leads to many undignified positions and mistakes. But a gentle leader points out the truth. Instead of resenting it, the new entrant is grateful, acknowledges his own mistake freely and frankly, and heartily joins with the Teacher in the worship of Allah, the Source of all truth and knowledge.

They made a league to cover their crime
With lies. Lo! on themselves recoiled
The plot: they perished in utter ruin.
The men admonished by Lūṭ were false
To themselves: they insulted the nature given
Them by Allah, and mocked the Message of Purity.
Lo! they were buried in a shower of brimstone!

SECTION 4.

45. We sent (aforetime),
To the Thamūd, their brother[3283]
Ṣāliḥ, saying: "Serve Allah";
But behold, they became
Two factions quarrelling
With each other.

وَلَقَدْ أَرْسَلْنَا إِلَىٰ ثَمُودَ ﴿٤٥﴾
أَخَاهُمْ صَٰلِحًا أَنِ ٱعْبُدُوا۟ ٱللَّهَ
فَإِذَا هُمْ فَرِيقَانِ يَخْتَصِمُونَ

46. He said: "O my people!
Why ask ye to hasten on
The evil in preference to the good?[3284]
If only ye ask Allah for forgiveness,
Ye may hope to receive mercy."

قَالَ يَٰقَوْمِ لِمَ تَسْتَعْجِلُونَ بِٱلسَّيِّئَةِ ﴿٤٦﴾
قَبْلَ ٱلْحَسَنَةِ ۖ لَوْلَا تَسْتَغْفِرُونَ ٱللَّهَ
لَعَلَّكُمْ تُرْحَمُونَ

47. They said: "Ill omen
Do we augur from thee
And those that are with thee".
He said: "Your ill omen
Is with Allah, yea, ye are
A people under trial."[3285]

قَالُوا۟ ٱطَّيَّرْنَا بِكَ وَبِمَن مَّعَكَ ۚ ﴿٤٧﴾
قَالَ طَٰٓئِرُكُمْ عِندَ ٱللَّهِ ۖ
بَلْ أَنتُمْ قَوْمٌ تُفْتَنُونَ

48. There were in the City
Nine men of a family
Who made mischief in the land,
And would not reform.[3286]

وَكَانَ فِى ٱلْمَدِينَةِ تِسْعَةُ رَهْطٍ ﴿٤٨﴾
يُفْسِدُونَ فِى ٱلْأَرْضِ وَلَا يُصْلِحُونَ

3283. The main story of the Thamūd, who were broken into two factions, the rich oppressing the poor and keeping them out of the good things of life and the test case of the She-camel, will be found in 26:141-159 and the notes thereon. The point here is the secret plot of the nine men against the Prophet of Allah, whose teaching, they thought, brought them ill-luck; but what they called ill-luck was the just punishment from Allah for their own ill-deeds. Their plot was foiled, and the whole community, which was involved in evil, was destroyed. (R).

3284. *Cf.* 13:6. The evildoers were really hastening on their own punishment by their feuds against the poor. The advocates of justice were not bringing ill-luck to them. They were showing the way to ward it off. Their own injustice was bringing on them disaster.

3285. All evil unpunished is not evil condoned, but evil given a chance for reform. They are on trial, by the mercy of Allah. What they call "ill omen" is really the just punishment for their ill-deeds, and that punishment rests with Allah.

3286. They had made up their minds to wage a relentless war against justice. They did not destroy justice, but justice destroyed them.

49. They said: "Swear
A mutual oath by Allah
That we shall make
A secret night attack
On him and his people,[3287]
And that we shall then
Say to his heir (when he
Seeks vengeance): 'We were not
Present at the slaughter
Of his people, and we are
Positively telling the truth.' "

٤٩ قَالُوا تَقَاسَمُوا بِاللَّهِ
لَنُبَيِّتَنَّهُ وَأَهْلَهُ
ثُمَّ لَنَقُولَنَّ لِوَلِيِّهِ
مَا شَهِدْنَا مَهْلِكَ أَهْلِهِ
وَإِنَّا لَصَادِقُونَ

50. They plotted and planned,[3288]
But We too planned,
Even while they perceived it not.

٥٠ وَمَكَرُوا مَكْرًا
وَمَكَرْنَا مَكْرًا وَهُمْ لَا يَشْعُرُونَ

51. Then see what was the end
Of their plot!—this,
That We destroyed them
And their people, all (of them).

٥١ فَانظُرْ كَيْفَ كَانَ عَاقِبَةُ
مَكْرِهِمْ أَنَّا دَمَّرْنَاهُمْ وَقَوْمَهُمْ أَجْمَعِينَ

52. Now such were their houses—
In utter ruin—because
They practised wrongdoing.
Verily in this is a Sign
For people of knowledge.

٥٢ فَتِلْكَ بُيُوتُهُمْ خَاوِيَةً بِمَا ظَلَمُوا
إِنَّ فِي ذَٰلِكَ لَآيَةً لِقَوْمٍ يَعْلَمُونَ

53. And We saved those
Who believed and practised
Righteousness.

٥٣ وَأَنجَيْنَا الَّذِينَ آمَنُوا
وَكَانُوا يَتَّقُونَ

54. (We also sent) Lūṭ[3289]
(As a messenger): behold,
He said to his people,
"Do ye do what is shameful
Though ye see (its iniquity)?

٥٤ وَلُوطًا إِذْ قَالَ لِقَوْمِهِ
أَتَأْتُونَ الْفَاحِشَةَ وَأَنتُمْ تُبْصِرُونَ

3287. A most dastardly plot, because (1) it was to be secret, (2) by night, (3) taking their victims unawares, and (4) because careful provision was made that they should all tell lies together, saying that they knew nothing about it, in order to evade the vengeance which Ṣāliḥ's heirs (if any were left) or his tribe might want to exact! And yet such were exactly the plots laid against the Holy Prophet himself.

3288. *Cf.* 3:54. Their secret plotting is all known to Allah, but of Allah's just and beneficient plans they know nothing. And the wicked must come to an evil end.

3289. The story of Lūṭ is referred to elsewhere. The passages to which reference may be made here are: 26:160-175, and 7:80-84. But the point emphasised here is that the crime of the Cities of the Plain was against their own nature, and they saw its enormity, and yet they indulged in it. Can degradation go further? His wife was not apparently a Believer. Her previous sympathy with the sinful people "destined her" (verse 57 below) to a miserable end, as she lagged behind and shared in the destruction of her kinsfolk.

55. Would ye really approach men
In your lusts rather than
Women? Nay, ye are
A people (grossly) ignorant![3290]

٥٥ أَئِنَّكُمْ لَتَأْتُونَ الرِّجَالَ شَهْوَةً
مِّن دُونِ النِّسَاءِ ۚ بَلْ أَنتُمْ قَوْمٌ تَجْهَلُونَ

20
30

56. But his people gave
No other answer but this:
They said, "Drive out
The followers of Lūṭ from
Your city: these are
Indeed men who want
To be clean and pure!"[3291]

٥٦ فَمَا كَانَ جَوَابَ قَوْمِهِ
إِلَّا أَن قَالُوا أَخْرِجُوا
آلَ لُوطٍ مِّن قَرْيَتِكُمْ ۖ
إِنَّهُمْ أُنَاسٌ يَتَطَهَّرُونَ

57. But We saved him
And his family, except
His wife: her We destined
To be of those
Who lagged behind.

٥٧ فَأَنجَيْنَاهُ وَأَهْلَهُ إِلَّا امْرَأَتَهُ
قَدَّرْنَاهَا مِنَ الْغَابِرِينَ

58. And We rained down on them
A shower (of brimstone):
And evil was the shower
On those who were admonished
(But heeded not)!

٥٨ وَأَمْطَرْنَا عَلَيْهِم مَّطَرًا ۖ
فَسَاءَ مَطَرُ الْمُنذَرِينَ

C. 172.—Allah's goodness and mercy are manifest
(27:59-93.) Through all nature and in the heart and conscience
Of man. He alone knows all: our knowledge
Can at best be partial. Yet we can travel
Through space and time and see how Evil
Never prospered. Allah teaches us good,
But how can we see if we make ourselves blind?
At the end of all things shall we know how small
Is our state, but for Allah's Grace: let us bow
To His Will and accept His true guidance:
Let us praise Him and trust Him—now and forever!

3290. The ignorance referred to here is the spiritual ignorance, the ignorance of how grossness and sins that bring shame on their own physical and moral nature are doomed to destroy them: it is their own loss. That they knew the iniquity of their sins has already been stated in the last verse. That knowledge makes their spiritual ignorance all the more culpable, just as a man consciously deceiving people by half-truths is a greater liar than a man who tells lies inadvertantly.

3291. *Cf.* 7:82-84. Instead of being ashamed on account of the consciousness of their own guilt, they attack the pure ones with their sarcasm, as if not they but the pure ones were in the wrong, trying to set them on the right way.

SECTION 5.

59. Say: Praise be to Allah,
And Peace on His servants[3292]
Whom He has chosen
(For His Message). (Who)
Is better?—Allah or
The false gods they associate
(With Him)?

٥٩ قُلِ ٱلْحَمْدُ لِلَّهِ وَسَلَٰمٌ
عَلَىٰ عِبَادِهِ ٱلَّذِينَ ٱصْطَفَىٰٓ
ءَآللَّهُ خَيْرٌ أَمَّا يُشْرِكُونَ

60. Or, who has created[3293]
The heavens and the earth,
And who sends you down
Rain from the sky?
Yea, with it We cause
To grow well-planted orchards
Full of beauty and delight:
It is not in your power
To cause the growth[3294]
Of the trees in them. (Can there be
Another) god besides Allah?
Nay, they are a people
Who swerve from justice.

٦٠ أَمَّنْ خَلَقَ ٱلسَّمَٰوَٰتِ وَٱلْأَرْضَ
وَأَنزَلَ لَكُم مِّنَ ٱلسَّمَآءِ مَآءً
فَأَنۢبَتْنَا بِهِۦ حَدَآئِقَ ذَاتَ بَهْجَةٍ
مَّا كَانَ لَكُمْ أَن تُنۢبِتُوا۟ شَجَرَهَآ
أَءِلَٰهٌ مَّعَ ٱللَّهِ
بَلْ هُمْ قَوْمٌ يَعْدِلُونَ

61. Or, who has made the earth
Firm to live in; made
Rivers in its midst; set
Thereon mountains
immovable,[3295]

٦١ أَمَّن جَعَلَ ٱلْأَرْضَ قَرَارًا وَجَعَلَ
خِلَٰلَهَآ أَنْهَٰرًا وَجَعَلَ لَهَا رَوَٰسِىَ

3292. Allah's revelation having been described as Light, Guidance, and Mercy, we ought all to be grateful to Allah for vouchsafing His revelation. We ought also to appreciate the services of Allah's Messengers, who are chosen to deliver His Message: we ought to send salutations of Peace on them, instead of plotting, as the wicked do, for their removal or persecution, or banishment or death, for these Prophets of Allah undergo every kind of hardship and forego every kind of advantage or pleasure in life for serving mankind. And Allah is truth and goodness, and all our fancies of false worship are falshoods and evils. Shall we prefer falsehood and evil to truth and goodness? (R).

3293. The order, beauty, and grandeur of the universe are appealed to. They show unity of design and purpose. How can unjust, ignorant, foolish, heedless, false men think of a multiplicity of gods, or of any god besides the One True God?

3294. To make a single seed germinate and grow into a tree is beyond man's power. When it comes to a great well-laid-out garden of beauty and delight, no one would think it grew up of itself without a gardener's consummate art. And the orchard is more than the trees in it: there is design and beauty in their arrangement; proper spaces have to be left between them for the growth of their roots, for the aeration of the soil beneath them, and for the penetration of air and sunlight between their branches. How can anyone then think of the wonderful universe as a whole, without thinking of the far higher Unity of Design, the evidence of the One True Allah? (R).

3295. *Cf.* 16:15 and notes 2038 and 2039. The *terra firma*, the flowing water, and the cycle of water circulation—sea, vapour, clouds, rain, rivers, and sea again—all one and yet all distinct, with a sort of wonderful barrier between salt water and fresh water: can man see all this and yet be ignorant of Allah?

And made a separating bar Between the two bodies[3296] Of flowing water? (Can there be another) god Besides Allah? Nay, most Of them know not.	وَجَعَلَ بَيْنَ ٱلْبَحْرَيْنِ حَاجِزًا ۗ أَءِلَٰهٌ مَّعَ ٱللَّهِ ۚ بَلْ أَكْثَرُهُمْ لَا يَعْلَمُونَ
62. Or, who listens to the (soul) Distressed when it calls On Him, and who relieves[3297] Its suffering, and makes you (Mankind) inheritors of the earth?[3298] (Can there be another) god Besides Allah? Little it is That ye heed!	أَمَّن يُجِيبُ ٱلْمُضْطَرَّ إِذَا دَعَاهُ وَيَكْشِفُ ٱلسُّوٓءَ وَيَجْعَلُكُمْ خُلَفَآءَ ٱلْأَرْضِ ۗ أَءِلَٰهٌ مَّعَ ٱللَّهِ ۚ قَلِيلًا مَّا تَذَكَّرُونَ ﴿٦٢﴾
63. Or, who guides you Through the depths of darkness On land and sea, and who Sends the winds as heralds[3299] Of glad tidings, going before His mercy? (Can there be Another) god besides Allah?— High is Allah above what They associate with Him!	أَمَّن يَهْدِيكُمْ فِى ظُلُمَٰتِ ٱلْبَرِّ وَٱلْبَحْرِ وَمَن يُرْسِلُ ٱلرِّيَٰحَ بُشْرًۢا بَيْنَ يَدَىْ رَحْمَتِهِۦٓ ۗ أَءِلَٰهٌ مَّعَ ٱللَّهِ ۚ تَعَٰلَى ٱللَّهُ عَمَّا يُشْرِكُونَ ﴿٦٣﴾
64. Or, who originates Creation, Then repeats it,[3300] And who gives you sustenance From heaven and earth?[3301] (Can there be another) god Besides Allah? Say, "Bring forth Your argument, if ye Are telling the truth!"[3302]	أَمَّن يَبْدَؤُا۟ ٱلْخَلْقَ ثُمَّ يُعِيدُهُۥ وَمَن يَرْزُقُكُم مِّنَ ٱلسَّمَآءِ وَٱلْأَرْضِ ۗ أَءِلَٰهٌ مَّعَ ٱللَّهِ ۚ قُلْ هَاتُوا۟ بُرْهَٰنَكُمْ إِن كُنتُمْ صَٰدِقِينَ ﴿٦٤﴾

3296. *Cf.* 25:53 and notes 3111 aand 3112.

3297. Besides the evidence of external nature, there is still more intimate evidence in man's inner conscience and heart. Allah listens to man's cry of agony and relieves his suffering, and He has given him superiority over other creation on this earth, through his mind and soul. Is man then going to run after inferior beings and forget Allah?

3298. *Cf.* 6:165, n. 988.

3299. *Cf.* 25:48, n. 3104. After external nature, our attention was drawn to our inner consciousness; after that, it is drawn here to our social and collective life, in which we use the forces of nature for international intercourse, trade, agriculture, production, and economic well-being generally. In the next verse, we are asked to contemplate creation from its primeval stages, through its intermediate processes, to the final Destiny in a new creation—a new heaven and a new earth.

3300. *Cf.* 10:34, and n. 1428.

3301. *Sustenance*: of course in the spiritual as well as the material sense.

3302. All the arguments point to the Unity of Allah: there is none whatever against it.

65. Say: None in the heavens Or on earth, except Allah, Knows what is hidden:[3303] Nor can they perceive When they shall be raised Up (for Judgement).	قُل لَّا يَعْلَمُ مَن فِي السَّمَٰوَاتِ وَالْأَرْضِ الْغَيْبَ إِلَّا اللَّهُ وَمَا يَشْعُرُونَ أَيَّانَ يُبْعَثُونَ ﴿٦٥﴾
66. Still less can their knowledge Comprehend the Hereafter: nay, They are in doubt and uncertainty Thereanent; nay, they are blind Thereunto![3304]	بَلِ ادَّارَكَ عِلْمُهُمْ فِي الْآخِرَةِ بَلْ هُمْ فِي شَكٍّ مِّنْهَا بَلْ هُم مِّنْهَا عَمُونَ ﴿٦٦﴾
SECTION 6.	
67. The Unbelievers say: "What! When we become dust— We and our fathers—shall we Really be raised (from the dead)?	وَقَالَ الَّذِينَ كَفَرُوا أَإِذَا كُنَّا تُرَابًا وَآبَاؤُنَا أَئِنَّا لَمُخْرَجُونَ ﴿٦٧﴾
68. "It is true we were promised This—we and our fathers Before (us): these are nothing But tales of the ancients."	لَقَدْ وُعِدْنَا هَٰذَا نَحْنُ وَآبَاؤُنَا مِن قَبْلُ إِنْ هَٰذَا إِلَّا أَسَاطِيرُ الْأَوَّلِينَ ﴿٦٨﴾
69. Say: "Go ye through the earth And see what has been The end of those guilty (Of sin)."[3305]	قُلْ سِيرُوا فِي الْأَرْضِ فَانظُرُوا كَيْفَ كَانَ عَاقِبَةُ الْمُجْرِمِينَ ﴿٦٩﴾
70. But grieve not over them, Nor distress thyself Because of their plots.[3306]	وَلَا تَحْزَنْ عَلَيْهِمْ وَلَا تَكُن فِي ضَيْقٍ مِّمَّا يَمْكُرُونَ ﴿٧٠﴾
71. They also say: "When will This promise (come to pass)? (Say) if ye are truthful."	وَيَقُولُونَ مَتَىٰ هَٰذَا الْوَعْدُ إِن كُنتُمْ صَادِقِينَ ﴿٧١﴾

3303. The existence of Allah is certain. But nothing else can be known with certainty to our knowledge. He has told us of the Hereafter, and therefore we know it is true. But those who do not believe in Allah—what knowledge or certainty can they have? Even when it is actually coming, they will not have the sense to perceive it.

3304. The Unbelievers are generally materialists, who cannot go beyond the evidence of their physical senses. As to a spiritual vision of the future, their physical senses would only leave them in doubt and uncertainty, while their rejection of the spiritual Light makes them blind altogether to the spiritual world.

3305. Even if the Unbelievers are willing to take any mystic doctrine, they have only to observe what has actually happened on the earth, and they will see that evil always came to an evil end, and that Truth and righteousness ultimately won.

3306. *Cf.* 16:127, and n. 2164. The righteous need not worry over the unjust. The plots of the unjust can never defeat or deflect the purpose of Allah.

72. Say: "It may be that Some of the events which Ye wish to hasten on May be (close) in your pursuit!"[3307]	قُلْ عَسَىٰٓ أَن يَكُونَ رَدِفَ لَكُم بَعْضُ ٱلَّذِى تَسْتَعْجِلُونَ ﴿٧٢﴾
73. But verily thy Lord is Full of grace to mankind: Yet most of them are ungrateful.	وَإِنَّ رَبَّكَ لَذُو فَضْلٍ عَلَى ٱلنَّاسِ وَلَٰكِنَّ أَكْثَرَهُمْ لَا يَشْكُرُونَ ﴿٧٣﴾
74. And verily thy Lord knoweth All that their hearts do hide, As well as all that They reveal.	وَإِنَّ رَبَّكَ لَيَعْلَمُ مَا تُكِنُّ صُدُورُهُمْ وَمَا يُعْلِنُونَ ﴿٧٤﴾
75. Nor is there aught Of the Unseen, in heaven Or earth, but is (recorded)[3308] In a clear record.	وَمَا مِنْ غَآئِبَةٍ فِى ٱلسَّمَآءِ وَٱلْأَرْضِ إِلَّا فِى كِتَٰبٍ مُّبِينٍ ﴿٧٥﴾
76. Verily this Qur'ān doth explain To the Children of Israel Most of the matters In which they disagree.[3309]	إِنَّ هَٰذَا ٱلْقُرْءَانَ يَقُصُّ عَلَىٰ بَنِىٓ إِسْرَٰٓءِيلَ أَكْثَرَ ٱلَّذِى هُمْ فِيهِ يَخْتَلِفُونَ ﴿٧٦﴾
77. And it certainly is A Guide and a Mercy To those who believe.	وَإِنَّهُۥ لَهُدًى وَرَحْمَةٌ لِّلْمُؤْمِنِينَ ﴿٧٧﴾
78. Verily, thy Lord will decide Between them by His Decree:[3310] And He is Exalted in Might, All-Knowing.	إِنَّ رَبَّكَ يَقْضِى بَيْنَهُم بِحُكْمِهِۦ وَهُوَ ٱلْعَزِيزُ ٱلْعَلِيمُ ﴿٧٨﴾

3307. The Unbelievers—or even men of halfhearted faith—may say, "Why worry over distant future events? Take the day as it comes!" But that is a fallacy. Judgement is certain, and it may be that this very hour may be the hour of doom for any given individual. This is the hour of repentance and amendment. For Allah wishes well to all mankind in spite of their ingratitude.

3308. *Cf.* 22:70, 36:12, 57:22. [Eds.].

3309. The Jews had numerous sects. Some were altogether out of the pale, *e.g.*, the Samaritans, who had a separate Tawrah of their own: they hated the other Jews and were hated by them. But even in the orthodox body, there were several sects, of which the following may be mentioned: (1) the Pharisees, who were literalists, formalists, and fatalists, and had a large body of traditional literature, with which they overlaid the Law of Moses; (2) the Sadducees, who were rationalists, and seemed to have doubted the doctrine of the Resurrection or of a Hereafter; (3) the Essenes, who practised a sort of Communism and Asceticism and prohibited marriage. About many of their doctrines they had bitter disputes, which were settled by the Qur'ān, which supplemented and perfected the Law of Moses. It also explained clearly the attributes of Allah and the nature of Revelation, and the doctrine of the Hereafter.

3310. 'Decree': *ḥukm*: the disputes between rival sects can only be settled by the Decree of Allah—(1) in the form of a Revelation, as was done by the Qur'ān, or (2) by the logic of events, for hundreds of sects have been extinguished and forgotten in the course of time, and (3) in the Decree of Judgement in the Hereafter, when all warring sects will at length see their errors.

79. So put thy trust in Allah:
For thou art on (the Path
Of) manifest Truth.

فَتَوَكَّلْ عَلَى ٱللَّهِ إِنَّكَ عَلَى ٱلْحَقِّ ٱلْمُبِينِ ٧٩

80. Truly thou canst not cause
The Dead to listen, nor
Canst thou cause the Deaf
To hear the call,
(Especially) when they
Turn back in retreat.[3311]

إِنَّكَ لَا تُسْمِعُ ٱلْمَوْتَىٰ ٨٠
وَلَا تُسْمِعُ ٱلصُّمَّ ٱلدُّعَآءَ
إِذَا وَلَّوْا۟ مُدْبِرِينَ

81. Nor canst thou be a guide
To the Blind, (to prevent them)
From straying: only those
Wilt thou get to listen
Who believe in Our Signs,
And they will bow in Islam.

وَمَآ أَنتَ بِهَٰدِى ٱلْعُمْىِ عَن ضَلَٰلَتِهِمْ ٨١
إِن تُسْمِعُ إِلَّا مَن يُؤْمِنُ بِـَٔايَٰتِنَا
فَهُم مُّسْلِمُونَ

82. And when the Word is[3312]
Fulfilled against them (the unjust),
We shall produce from the earth
A Beast to (face) them:[3313]
He will speak to them,
For that mankind did not
Believe with assurance
In our Signs.

وَإِذَا وَقَعَ ٱلْقَوْلُ عَلَيْهِمْ ٨٢
أَخْرَجْنَا لَهُمْ دَآبَّةً مِّنَ ٱلْأَرْضِ تُكَلِّمُهُمْ أَنَّ
ٱلنَّاسَ كَانُوا۟ بِـَٔايَٰتِنَا لَا يُوقِنُونَ

SECTION 7.

83. One Day We shall gather
Together from every people
A troop of those who reject
Our Signs, and they shall
Be kept in ranks—

وَيَوْمَ نَحْشُرُ مِن كُلِّ أُمَّةٍ ٨٣
فَوْجًا مِّمَّن يُكَذِّبُ بِـَٔايَٰتِنَا فَهُمْ يُوزَعُونَ

3311. The Prophet's responsibility was to preach and show the way. Men and women of good will had faith and accepted the Message. But he was not responsible for the obstinacy and perversity of men who turned away from Allah's Signs and rejected the Truth.

3312. *The Word*: the Decree or Sentence, the Decision to end the respite and restore the true values of right and wrong in a new world: their cup of iniquity will then have been full.

3313. The Beast will be one of the Signs of the Last Day to come, before the present World passes away and the new World is brought into being. In symbolic language it would represent gross Materialism. It will be the embodiment of fat worldly triumph, which will appeal to a misguided and degenerate world, because such a corrupt world will have no assured belief in the Signs of Allah or in spiritual Light. It will itself be a Sign or Portent, closing the door or repentance. I do not know whether this Beast has any reference to the symbolism in chapter xii of the Book of Revelation, which closes the New Testament. If *taklimuhum* is read instead of *tukallimuhum*, it would mean that the Beast would wound them, symbolically, that Materialism would produce its own Nemesis.

84. Until, when they come
(Before the Judgement Seat),
(Allah) will say: "Did ye
Reject My Signs, though ye[3314]
Comprehended them not
In knowledge, or what
Was it ye did?"

٨٤ حَتَّىٰٓ إِذَا جَآءُو قَالَ
أَكَذَّبْتُم بِـَٔايَٰتِى وَلَمْ تُحِيطُوا۟ بِهَا عِلْمًا
أَمَّاذَا كُنتُمْ تَعْمَلُونَ

85. And the Word will be[3315]
Fulfilled against them, because
Of their wrongdoing, and they
Will be unable to speak
(In plea).

٨٥ وَوَقَعَ ٱلْقَوْلُ عَلَيْهِم بِمَا ظَلَمُوا۟
فَهُمْ لَا يَنطِقُونَ

86. See they not that We
Have made the Night
For them to rest in
And the Day to give[3316]
Them light? Verily in this
Are Signs for any people
That believe!

٨٦ أَلَمْ يَرَوْا۟ أَنَّا جَعَلْنَا
ٱلَّيْلَ لِيَسْكُنُوا۟ فِيهِ وَٱلنَّهَارَ مُبْصِرًا ۚ
إِنَّ فِى ذَٰلِكَ لَـَٔايَٰتٍ لِّقَوْمٍ يُؤْمِنُونَ

87. And the Day that the Trumpet
Will be sounded—then will be
Smitten with terror those
Who are in the heavens,
And those who are on earth,
Except such as Allah will please
(To exempt): and all shall come
To His (Presence) as beings
Conscious of their lowliness.[3317]

٨٧ وَيَوْمَ يُنفَخُ فِى ٱلصُّورِ
فَفَزِعَ مَن فِى ٱلسَّمَٰوَٰتِ وَمَن فِى ٱلْأَرْضِ
إِلَّا مَن شَآءَ ٱللَّهُ ۚ
وَكُلٌّ أَتَوْهُ دَٰخِرِينَ

88. Thou seest the mountains
And thinkest them firmly fixed:[3318]

٨٨ وَتَرَى ٱلْجِبَالَ تَحْسَبُهَا جَامِدَةً

3314. The charge against them will be: 'You had no knowledge, and yet you arrogantly rejected My Signs: is that true, or have you any plea in your defence?'

3315. There will be no plea, because the charge will be only too true. The Decree will be passed and executed.

3316. *Night, Day, Rest,* and *Light*: both in the literal and the symbolic sense. Any one with a scrap of faith or spiritual insight could see that the Night is a blessing when used for rest and a curse when used to cover ignorance or sin; and that the Day is for work and enlightenment, and its misuse is gross ingratitude to Allah. Or, understand Truth and practise Righteousness while it is yet Light and the Message of Allah is here to guide you: for there comes the Night when Endeavour will cease and there will be no room for Repentance.

3317. Arrogance will flee with Ignorance, and Self will see itself in its true place—that of humility and lowliness—when the scales of ignorance fall from its eyes.

3318. This is so in the present phase of phenomenal things, both literally and figuratively. There seems nothing more firm or fixed or permanent than the "eternal hills": yet when the new order of things comes and the new World is brought into being, they will be as flimsy and insubstantial as clouds. So, in the revelation of things in the spiritual World, persons or things or ideas that seem so great and so firmly established now will pass away like mere fancies and give way to the Reality of Allah.

But they shall pass away
As the clouds pass away:
(Such is) the artistry of Allah,
Who disposes of all things[3319]
In perfect order: for He is
Well acquainted with all that ye
do.

وَهِيَ تَمُرُّ مَرَّ السَّحَابِ
صُنْعَ اللَّهِ الَّذِي أَتْقَنَ كُلَّ شَيْءٍ
إِنَّهُ خَبِيرٌ بِمَا تَفْعَلُونَ

89. If any do good, good will
(Accrue) to them therefrom;
And they will be secure
From terror that Day.

٨٩ مَن جَاءَ بِالْحَسَنَةِ فَلَهُ خَيْرٌ مِّنْهَا
وَهُم مِّن فَزَعٍ يَوْمَئِذٍ آمِنُونَ

90. And if any do evil,
Their faces will be thrown
Headlong into the Fire:[3320]
"Do ye receive a reward
Other than that which ye
Have earned by your deeds?"[3321]

٩٠ وَمَن جَاءَ بِالسَّيِّئَةِ
فَكُبَّتْ وُجُوهُهُمْ فِي النَّارِ
هَلْ تُجْزَوْنَ إِلَّا مَا كُنتُمْ تَعْمَلُونَ

91. For me, I have been
Commanded to serve the Lord[3322]
Of this City, Him Who has
Sactified it and to Whom
(Belong) all things:
And I am commanded
To be of those who bow
In Islam to Allah's Will—

٩١ إِنَّمَا أُمِرْتُ أَنْ أَعْبُدَ
رَبَّ هَٰذِهِ الْبَلْدَةِ الَّذِي
حَرَّمَهَا وَلَهُ كُلُّ شَيْءٍ
وَأُمِرْتُ أَنْ أَكُونَ مِنَ الْمُسْلِمِينَ

92. And to rehearse the Qur'ān:[3323]
And if any accept guidance,

٩٢ وَأَنْ أَتْلُوَ الْقُرْآنَ فَمَنِ اهْتَدَىٰ

3319. *Atqana*: to arrange or dispose of things with art, or so as to obtain the most perfect results. The present phenomenal world and the Future that is to be, all have a definite object and purpose in the Plan of Allah, Who knows perfectly what we are, what we do, what we think, and what we need. Who can praise His artistry enough?

3320. *Headlong*: it may be that the very things of which we were proudest, which we considered foremost in our present order of the world, will be the first to go into the Fire, as they are but the window-dressing (*i.e.,* faces) of Evil.

3321. There will be no punishment except such as has been deserved by actual conduct in the present life of probation.

3322. *The Lord of this City.* This was spoken in Makkah, say about the 5th year before the Hijrah, when the Holy Prophet and his adherents were being persecuted as enemies to the cult of Makkah. So far from being against the true spirit of the Holy City of Makkah, it was actually in furtherance of that spirit, which had been overlaid by the idolatries and abominations of the Pagan Quraysh. They are told that the new Teaching is from the Lord of Makkah itself, the One True God, Who had sanctified it in the time of Abraham. Lest they should think that it was a local or tribal or narrow cult, it is added that He is not only Lord of this city, but Lord of the Worlds, "to Whom belong all things". It is a universal message: but how sad it would be if the Makkans, among whom it came first, were to reject it?

3323. The duty of the Prophet and his adherents was, first, to accept Islam and become themselves shining examples of Allah's grace and mercy, as they in fact were, and secondly to preach that message and spread that Light to all around. It was not for them to force it on unwilling people: for any who rejected it would find their own spiritual loss in such rejection. But they must clearly warn them of the consequences.

They do it for the good
Of their own souls,
And if any stray, say:
"I am only a Warner".

فَإِنَّمَا يَهْتَدِى لِنَفْسِهِۦ
وَمَن ضَلَّ فَقُلْ إِنَّمَآ أَنَا۠ مِنَ ٱلْمُنذِرِينَ

93. And say: "Praise be to Allah,
Who will soon show you[3324]
His Signs, so that ye
Shall know them"; and thy Lord
Is not unmindful
Of all that ye do.[3325]

وَقُلِ ٱلْحَمْدُ لِلَّهِ ٩٣
سَيُرِيكُمْ ءَايَٰتِهِۦ فَتَعْرِفُونَهَا
وَمَا رَبُّكَ بِغَٰفِلٍ عَمَّا تَعْمَلُونَ

3324. In a few years after that, many wonderful things happened that removed the doubts of the doubters and confirmed the faith of the Believers. They showed how the logic of events proved the true mission of the holy Prophet. Other things some minds may not be able to grasp. But the logic of events is for all to see.

3325. Trials and tribulations, persecution and exile, and the patient endurance and constancy with which they were met by the Believers—all are known to Allah and will be credited to their spiritual account.

INTRODUCTION TO SŪRAH 28—*AL QAṢAṢ*

This Sūrah continues the subject of Revelation and its reception by those to whom it is sent. But it emphasises new points: how the recipient of inspiration is prepared for his high destiny, even in the growth of his ordinary life, and how the rejection of Allah's Message by groups of men or by individuals is caused by overweening arrogance or avarice. The plight of those who reject the Truth is contrasted with the reward of the righteous.

With the possible exception of a few verses, it belongs to the late Makkan period, just preceding the Hijrah.

Summary—Pharaoh was arrogant and unjust, but Allah's Plan was to strengthen the weak: in infancy Moses was prepared for his mission; in youth he trusted in the Lord and was guided; in his exile he found help and love; and when he was called, he was supported by Allah (28:1-42, and C. 173).

So was the Holy Prophet Muḥammad fed spiritually by Allah's Grace, and his Revelation was recognised by those who knew the earlier Revelations: it came to an old and sacred Centre, to warn those seduced by this world's life (28:43-60, and C. 174).

The Future is with those who repent, have faith, and do good: for all Mercy and Truth are with Allah (28:61-75, and C. 175).

But men puffed up with wealth, like Qārūn, will come to an evil end, while the lowly and the righteous will attain Allah's Mercy (28:76-88, C. 176).

C. 173.—Allah's Messengers are men, and win through good life
(28:1-42.) By Allah's Grace and their Faith. So Moses
Was saved from the Tyrant's wrath in infancy,
And reared in the Tyrant's own den, but gently
In a mother's love. In youth was he endowed
With wisdom and knowledge; strength and the will
To do right. In sorrow or misfortune
He trusted on Allah and opened his heart
To Him. On self-imposed exile he won
Love by his chivalry and confidence by Truth.
In his mission he triumphed over arrogant
Wrong by his meekness, patience, and Faith.
So good follows good, and Evil must fall.
Cursed, loathed, disgraced, and despised.

Sūrah 28.

Al Qaṣaṣ (The Narrations)

In the name of Allah, Most Gracious,
Most Merciful.

1. Ṭā Sīn Mīm.[3326]

2. These are Verses of the Book
That makes (things) clear.[3327]

3. We rehearse to thee some
Of the story of Moses
And Pharaoh in Truth,
For people who believe.[3328]

4. Truly Pharaoh elated himself
In the land and broke up
Its people into sections,[3329]
Depressing a small group
Among them: their sons he slew,
But he kept alive their females:
For he was indeed
A maker of mischief.

5. And We wished to be
Gracious to those who were
Being depressed on the land.[3330]

بِسْمِ ٱللَّهِ ٱلرَّحْمَٰنِ ٱلرَّحِيمِ

١ طسٓمٓ

٢ تِلْكَ ءَايَٰتُ ٱلْكِتَٰبِ ٱلْمُبِينِ

٣ نَتْلُوا۟ عَلَيْكَ مِن نَّبَإِ مُوسَىٰ وَفِرْعَوْنَ
بِٱلْحَقِّ لِقَوْمٍ يُؤْمِنُونَ

٤ إِنَّ فِرْعَوْنَ عَلَا فِى ٱلْأَرْضِ وَجَعَلَ
أَهْلَهَا شِيَعًا يَسْتَضْعِفُ طَآئِفَةً مِّنْهُمْ
يُذَبِّحُ أَبْنَآءَهُمْ وَيَسْتَحْىِۦ نِسَآءَهُمْ
إِنَّهُۥ كَانَ مِنَ ٱلْمُفْسِدِينَ

٥ وَنُرِيدُ أَن نَّمُنَّ عَلَى ٱلَّذِينَ
ٱسْتُضْعِفُوا۟ فِى ٱلْأَرْضِ

3326. See n. 3137 to 26:1.

3327. See n. 3138 to 26:2.

3328. The part of the story of Moses told here is how Moses and his mother were guided in the child's infancy, that even as he grew up, he might be prepared for his high destiny; how in youth he trusted Allah in the most awkward situations and sought his help; how he fled into exile, and yet found love and support because of his welldoing; and how, when he was called to his mission, he received Allah's favour, which defeated all the plots of his enemies. Thus Allah's Plan works continuously in the web of events. Those who have faith will thus see the hand of Allah in everything and welcome the light that comes to them by Revelation. With such a Faith there is no room for Chance or blind Fate. (R).

3329. For a king or ruler to make invidious distinctions between his subjects, and specially to depress or oppress any particular class of his subjects, is a dereliction of his kingly duties, for which he is responsible to Allah. Pharaoh and his clique were intoxicated with pride of race and pride of material civilisation, and grievously oppressed the Israelites. Pharaoh decreed that all sons born to his Israelite subjects should be killed, and the females kept alive for the pleasure of the Egyptians. Moses was saved in a wonderful way, as related further.

3330. What Pharaoh wished was to crush them. But Allah's Plan was to protect them as they were weak, and indeed to make them custodians and leaders in His Faith, and to give them in inheritance a land "flowing with milk and honey". Here they were established in authority for such time as they followed Allah's Law. As regards Pharaoh and his ministers and hosts, they were to be shown that they would suffer, at the hands of the Israelites, the very calamities against which they were so confidently taking precautions for themselves.

To make them leaders (in faith)
And make them heirs,

وَنَجْعَلَهُمْ أَيِمَّةً وَنَجْعَلَهُمُ ٱلْوَٰرِثِينَ

6. To establish a firm place
For them in the land,
And to show Pharaoh, Hāmān,[3331]
And their hosts, at their hands,
The very things against which
They were taking precautions.[3332]

٦ وَنُمَكِّنَ لَهُمْ فِي ٱلْأَرْضِ
وَنُرِيَ فِرْعَوْنَ وَهَٰمَٰنَ وَجُنُودَهُمَا
مِنْهُم مَّا كَانُوا۟ يَحْذَرُونَ

7. So We sent this inspiration
To the mother of Moses:
"Suckle (thy child), but when
Thou hast fears about him,
Cast him into the river,[3333]
But fear not nor grieve:
For We shall restore him
To thee, and We shall make
Him one of Our messengers."

٧ وَأَوْحَيْنَآ إِلَىٰٓ أُمِّ مُوسَىٰٓ أَنْ أَرْضِعِيهِ
فَإِذَا خِفْتِ عَلَيْهِ فَأَلْقِيهِ فِي ٱلْيَمِّ
وَلَا تَخَافِي وَلَا تَحْزَنِيٓ
إِنَّا رَآدُّوهُ إِلَيْكِ وَجَاعِلُوهُ مِنَ ٱلْمُرْسَلِينَ

8. Then the people of Pharaoh
Picked him up (from the river):
(It was intended) that (Moses)
Should be to them an adversary
And a cause of sorrow:[3334]
For Pharaoh and Hāmān
And (all) their hosts were
Men of sin.

٨ فَٱلْتَقَطَهُۥٓ ءَالُ فِرْعَوْنَ
لِيَكُونَ لَهُمْ عَدُوًّا وَحَزَنًا
إِنَّ فِرْعَوْنَ وَهَٰمَٰنَ وَجُنُودَهُمَا
كَانُوا۟ خَٰطِـِٔينَ

9. The wife of Pharaoh said:
"(Here is) a joy of the eye,[3335]

٩ وَقَالَتِ ٱمْرَأَتُ فِرْعَوْنَ قُرَّتُ عَيْنٍ

3331. Hāmān was evidently Pharaoh's minister, not to be confounded with a Hāmān who is mentioned in the Old Testament (Esther iii. 1), as a minister of Ahasuerus (Xerxes) King of Persia, the same who invaded Greece, and ruled from B.C. 485 to 464.

3332. Pharaoh was trying to kill the Israelites. Instead, the Plagues of Egypt, invoked by Moses, killed thousands of Egyptains (7:133, and notes 1091-92), because "they were steeped in arrogance,—a people given to sin." In pursuing the Israelites in their fight, Pharaoh and his army were themselves overwhelmed in the sea.

3333. The Egyptian midwives had orders to kill Israelite babies. Moses was saved from them, and his mother nursed the infant at her breast herself. But when the danger of discovery was imminent, she put him into a chest or basket, and floated him on the river Nile. It flowed by the King's palace, and the chest with the baby was picked up, as related further on. The mother had no cause to fear or grieve afterwards, as the child grew up under her tender care and became afterwards one of the Prophets of Allah.

3334. This was the Plan of Providence; that the wicked might cast a net round themselves by fostering the man who was to bring them to naught and be the instrument of their punishment—or (looking at it from the other side) that Moses might learn all the wisdom of the Egyptians in order to expose all that was hollow and wicked in it.

3335. He was a darling to look at, and Pharaoh had apparently no son, but only a daughter, who afterwards shared his throne. This is on the supposition that the Pharaoh was Thothmes I (see Appendix IV, S. 7).

For me and for thee:
Slay him not. It may be
That he will be of use
To us, or we may adopt
Him as a son." And they
Perceived not (what they
Were doing)![3336]

لِي وَلَكَ ۖ لَا تَقْتُلُوهُ عَسَىٰٓ أَن يَنفَعَنَآ أَوْ نَتَّخِذَهُۥ وَلَدًا وَهُمْ لَا يَشْعُرُونَ

10. But there came to be
A void in the heart
Of the mother of Moses:
She was going almost to
Disclose his (case), had We
Not strengthened her heart
(With faith), so that she
Might remain a (firm) believer.[3337]

١٠ وَأَصْبَحَ فُؤَادُ أُمِّ مُوسَىٰ فَٰرِغًا ۖ إِن كَادَتْ لَتُبْدِى بِهِۦ لَوْلَآ أَن رَّبَطْنَا عَلَىٰ قَلْبِهَا لِتَكُونَ مِنَ ٱلْمُؤْمِنِينَ

11. And she said to the sister
Of (Moses), "Follow him",
So she (the sister) watched him
In the character of a stranger.
And they knew not.

١١ وَقَالَتْ لِأُخْتِهِۦ قُصِّيهِ ۖ فَبَصُرَتْ بِهِۦ عَن جُنُبٍ وَهُمْ لَا يَشْعُرُونَ

12. And We ordained that he
Refused suck at first, until
(His sister came up
And) said: "Shall I
Point out to you the people
Of a house that will nourish
And bring him up for you[3338]
And be sincerely attached
To him?"..

١٢ وَحَرَّمْنَا عَلَيْهِ ٱلْمَرَاضِعَ مِن قَبْلُ فَقَالَتْ هَلْ أَدُلُّكُمْ عَلَىٰٓ أَهْلِ بَيْتٍ يَكْفُلُونَهُۥ لَكُمْ وَهُمْ لَهُۥ نَٰصِحُونَ

13. Thus did We restore him
To his mother, that her eye
Might be comforted, that she
Might not grieve, and that
She might know that the promise

١٣ فَرَدَدْنَٰهُ إِلَىٰٓ أُمِّهِۦ كَىْ تَقَرَّ عَيْنُهَا وَلَا تَحْزَنَ وَلِتَعْلَمَ أَنَّ وَعْدَ

3336. In all life Providence so orders things that Evil is defeated by its own weapons. Not only is it defeated, but it actually, though unwittingly, advances the cause of Good! In non-religious language this is called the work of the Ironic Fates. If Thomas Hardy had not made Napoleon the Puppet of Fate in his "Dynasts", he could well have taken Pharaoh as an illustration of the Irony of Fate, or, as we should prefer to call it, the working of the Universal Plan of Allah. (R).

3337. The mother's heart felt the gaping void at parting from her son; but her Faith in Allah's Providence kept her from betraying herself.

3338. *For you: i.e.*, on your behalf. Thus Moses got the benefit of his mother's milk (symbolical of all the traditions and spiritual heritage of his ancestry and his people) as well as the prestige and the opportunities of being brought up in the royal family, with the best of teachers to teach him Egyptian wisdom. In addition, there was the comfort to his mother.

Of Allah is true; but
Most of this do not
understand.[3339]

ٱللَّهِ حَقٌّ وَلَٰكِنَّ أَكْثَرَهُمْ لَا يَعْلَمُونَ

SECTION 2.

14. When he reached full age,
And was firmly established[3340]
(In life), We bestowed on him
Wisdom and knowledge: for thus
Do We reward those
Who do good.

١٤ وَلَمَّا بَلَغَ أَشُدَّهُۥ
وَٱسْتَوَىٰٓ ءَاتَيْنَٰهُ حُكْمًا وَعِلْمًا ۚ
وَكَذَٰلِكَ نَجْزِى ٱلْمُحْسِنِينَ

15. And he entered the City
At a time when its people[3341]
Were not watching: and he
Found there two men fighting—
One of his own people,
And the other, of his foes.
Now the man of his own
People appealed to him
Against his foe, and Moses
Struck him with his fist[3342]
And made an end of him.
He said: "This is a work
Of Evil (Satan): for he is
An enemy that manifestly
Misleads!"

١٥ وَدَخَلَ ٱلْمَدِينَةَ عَلَىٰ حِينِ غَفْلَةٍ مِّنْ
أَهْلِهَا فَوَجَدَ فِيهَا رَجُلَيْنِ يَقْتَتِلَانِ
هَٰذَا مِن شِيعَتِهِۦ وَهَٰذَا مِنْ عَدُوِّهِۦ ۖ
فَٱسْتَغَٰثَهُ ٱلَّذِى مِن شِيعَتِهِۦ عَلَى ٱلَّذِى
مِنْ عَدُوِّهِۦ فَوَكَزَهُۥ مُوسَىٰ فَقَضَىٰ عَلَيْهِ ۖ
قَالَ هَٰذَا مِنْ عَمَلِ ٱلشَّيْطَٰنِ ۖ
إِنَّهُۥ عَدُوٌّ مُّضِلٌّ مُّبِينٌ

16. He prayed: "O my Lord!
I have indeed wronged my soul!
Do Thou then forgive me!"

١٦ قَالَ رَبِّ إِنِّى ظَلَمْتُ نَفْسِى فَٱغْفِرْ لِى

3339. Allah's promise is always true, but short-sighted people, if they are a little thwarted in their plan, do not understand that Allah's wisdom, power, and goodness are far more comprehensive than any little plans which they may form.

3340. *Full age* may be taken to be mature youth, say between 18 and 30 years of age. By that time a person is fully estabilshed in life: his physical build is completed, and his mental and moral habits are formed. In this case, as Moses was good at heart, true and loyal to his people, and obedient and just to those among whom he lived, he was granted wisdom and knowledge from on high, to be used for the times of conflict which were coming for him. His internal development being complete, he now goes out into the outer world, where he is again tried and proved, until he gets his divine commission.

3341. That may have been either the time of the noontide siesta, when all business is suspended even now in Egypt, or the time of night, when people are usually asleep. The latter is more probable, in view of verse 18 below. But there is also another suggestion. A guest in a Palace is not free to wander about at will in the plebeian quarters of the City at all sorts of hours, and this applies even more to an inmate of the Palace brought up as a son. Moses was therefore visiting the City privately and eluding the guards. His object may have been to see for himself how things were going on; perhaps he had heard that his people were being oppressed, as we may suppose that he had retained contact with his mother.

3342. His object was apparently to strike him so as to release the Israelite, not to kill the Egyptian. In fact he killed the Egyptian. This was unfortunate in more ways than one. His visit to the City was clandestine; he had taken the side of the weaker and despised party; and he had taken the life of an Egyptian. He was full of regrets and repentance, and he prayed to Allah, and obtained Allah's forgiveness.

So (Allah) forgave him: For He
Is the Oft-Forgiving, Most
Merciful.

فَغَفَرَ لَهُۥٓ إِنَّهُۥ هُوَ ٱلْغَفُورُ ٱلرَّحِيمُ

17. He said: "O my Lord!
For that Thou hast bestowed
Thy Grace on me, never
Shall I be a help
To those who sin!"[3343]

قَالَ رَبِّ بِمَآ أَنْعَمْتَ عَلَىَّ ﴿١٧﴾
فَلَنْ أَكُونَ ظَهِيرًا لِّلْمُجْرِمِينَ

18. So he saw the morning
In the City, looking about,
In a state of fear, when
Behold, the man who had,
The day before, sought his help
Called aloud for his help
(Again). Moses said to him:
"Thou art truly, it is clear,
A quarrelsome fellow!"[3344]

فَأَصْبَحَ فِى ٱلْمَدِينَةِ خَآئِفًا ﴿١٨﴾
يَتَرَقَّبُ فَإِذَا ٱلَّذِى ٱسْتَنصَرَهُۥ
بِٱلْأَمْسِ يَسْتَصْرِخُهُۥ
قَالَ لَهُۥ مُوسَىٰٓ إِنَّكَ لَغَوِىٌّ مُّبِينٌ

19. Then, when he decided to lay
Hold of the man who was[3345]
An enemy to both of them,
That man said: "O Moses!
Is it thy intention to slay me
As thou slewest a man
Yesterday? Thy intention is
None other than to become
A powerful violent man
In the land, and not to be
One who sets things right!"[3346]

فَلَمَّآ أَنْ أَرَادَ أَن يَبْطِشَ بِٱلَّذِى ﴿١٩﴾
هُوَ عَدُوٌّ لَّهُمَا قَالَ يَٰمُوسَىٰٓ أَتُرِيدُ أَن
تَقْتُلَنِى كَمَا قَتَلْتَ نَفْسًۢا بِٱلْأَمْسِ
إِن تُرِيدُ إِلَّآ أَن تَكُونَ جَبَّارًا فِى ٱلْأَرْضِ
وَمَا تُرِيدُ أَن تَكُونَ مِنَ ٱلْمُصْلِحِينَ

3343. He takes a conscious and solemn vow to dedicate himself to Allah, and to do nothing that may in any way assist those who were doing wrong. This was his general idea, but no plan had yet shaped itself in his mind, until a second catastrophe brought matters to a head, and he was plunged in adventure.

3344. The man was an Israelite. But Moses was himself in a distracted mood, for the reasons given in n. 3342 above, and he was exasperated at this public appeal to him again.

3345. When Moses considered further that the Egyptian was unjust and that the Egyptian was an enemy to Israel generally (including both Moses and the man assaulted), he was going to intervene again, when he recieved a double warning, one from the Egyptian who was fighting, and the other from some man (Israelite or Egyptian) who was friendly to him, as explained below. We may suppose that after the first day's fight, there had been a great deal of talk in the bazaars, both among Israelites and Egyptians. Probably the Israelites were elated at finding a champion—perhaps more elated than they should have been, and in a provocative mood, which deserved Moses' rebuke. Probably the Egyptians had discussed who this new champion was, and had already appraised the Palace, to which Moses had not dared to return.

3346. The Egyptian saw the tactical advantage of his position. In effect he said: 'We have found out all about you. You live in the Palace, and yet you come clandestinely and kill our Egyptians. Are you going to do the same with me? You are nothing but a bully! And you talk of setting things right! That is what you should do if you were true to your salt!'

20. And there came a man,
Running, from the furthest end[3347]
Of the City. He said:
"O Moses! the Chiefs
Are taking counsel together
About thee, to slay thee
So get thee away, for I
Do give thee sincere advice."

٢٠ وَجَآءَ رَجُلٌ مِّنْ
أَقْصَا ٱلْمَدِينَةِ يَسْعَىٰ قَالَ يَـٰمُوسَىٰٓ
إِنَّ ٱلْمَلَأَ يَأْتَمِرُونَ بِكَ لِيَقْتُلُوكَ
فَٱخْرُجْ إِنِّى لَكَ مِنَ ٱلنَّـٰصِحِينَ

21. He therefore got away
therefrom,[3348]
Looking about, in a state
Of fear. He prayed:
"O my Lord! save me
From people given to wrong-
doing."

٢١ فَخَرَجَ مِنْهَا خَآئِفًا يَتَرَقَّبُ
قَالَ رَبِّ نَجِّنِى مِنَ
ٱلْقَوْمِ ٱلظَّـٰلِمِينَ

SECTION 3.

22. Then, when he turned his face
Towards (the land of) Madyan,[3349]
He said: "I do hope
That my Lord will show me
The smooth and straight Path."

٢٢ وَلَمَّا تَوَجَّهَ تِلْقَآءَ مَدْيَنَ قَالَ
عَسَىٰ رَبِّىٓ أَن يَهْدِيَنِى سَوَآءَ ٱلسَّبِيلِ

23. And when he arrived at
The watering (place) in
Madyan,[3350]
He found there a group
Of men watering (their flocks),
And besides them he found
Two women who were keeping
Back (their flocks). He said:

٢٣ وَلَمَّا وَرَدَ مَآءَ مَدْيَنَ
وَجَدَ عَلَيْهِ أُمَّةً مِّنَ ٱلنَّاسِ يَسْقُونَ
وَوَجَدَ مِن دُونِهِمُ ٱمْرَأَتَيْنِ تَذُودَانِ
قَالَ

3347. Apparently rumours had reached the Palace, a Council had been held, and the death of Moses had been decreed!

3348. Moses saw that his position was now untenable, both in the Palace and in the City, and indeed anywhere in Pharaoh's territory. So he suffered voluntary exile. But he did not know where to go to. His mind was in a state of agitation. But he turned to Allah and prayed. He got consolation, and felt that after all it was no hardship to leave Egypt, where there was so much injustice and oppression.

3349. East of Lower Egypt, for about 300 miles, runs the Sinai Peninsula, bounded on the south by the Gulf of Suez, and on the north by what was the Isthmus of Suez, now cut by the Suez Canal. Over the Isthmus ran the highroad to Palestine and Syria, but a fugitive could not well take that road, as the Egyptains were after him. If he could, after crossing the Isthmus, plunge into the Sinai desert, east or southeast, he would be in the Midianite territory, where the people would be Arabs and not Egyptians. He turned thither, and again prayed to Allah for guidance.

3350. The first thing that a wanderer in a desert would make for would be an oasis where he could get water from a spring or well, the shade of trees against the scorching sun, and some human company. The Midianite watering place was probably a deep well, as surface springs are rare in sandy desert, where the water level is low, unless there was a hill from which issued a spring.

"What is the matter with you?"
They said: "We cannot water
(Our flocks) until the shepherds
Take back (their flocks):
And our father is
A very old man."[3351]

مَا خَطْبُكُمَا
قَالَتَا لَا نَسْقِي حَتَّىٰ يُصْدِرَ ٱلرِّعَآءُ
وَأَبُونَا شَيْخٌ كَبِيرٌ

24. So he watered (their flocks)
For them; then he turned back
To the shade, and said:
"O my Lord!
Truly am I
In (desperate) need
Of any good
That Thou dost send me!"...[3352]

(٢٤) فَسَقَىٰ لَهُمَا
ثُمَّ تَوَلَّىٰٓ إِلَى ٱلظِّلِّ
فَقَالَ رَبِّ إِنِّي لِمَآ أَنزَلْتَ
إِلَيَّ مِنْ خَيْرٍ فَقِيرٌ

25. Afterwards one of the (damsels)
Came (back) to him, walking
Bashfully. She said: "My father
Invites thee that he may
Reward thee for having watered[3353]
(Our flocks) for us." So when
He came to him and narrated
The story, he said:
"Fear thou not: (well) hast thou

(٢٥) فَجَآءَتْهُ إِحْدَىٰهُمَا تَمْشِي عَلَى
ٱسْتِحْيَآءٍ قَالَتْ إِنَّ أَبِي يَدْعُوكَ
لِيَجْزِيَكَ أَجْرَ مَا سَقَيْتَ لَنَا
فَلَمَّا جَآءَهُۥ وَقَصَّ عَلَيْهِ ٱلْقَصَصَ قَالَ
لَا تَخَفْ

3351. Here is a pretty little idyll, told in the fewest and most beautiful words possible. Moses arrives at an oasis in the desert, weary and travel-worn, with his mind full of anxiety and uncertainty owing to his recent experiences in Egypt. He was thirsty and would naturally seek water. At the well or spring he found shepherds (or perhaps goat-herds) watering their flocks. As a stranger it was not for him to thrust himself among them. He waited under the shade of a tree until they should finish. He noticed two damsels, also waiting, with their flocks, which they had come to water. His chivalry was roused. He went at once among the goat-herds, made a place for the flocks of the damsels, gave them water, and then resumed his place in the shade. They were modest maidens, and had given him in three Arabic words the key of the whole situation. *'Abūnā shaykhun kabīrun*: our father is very old man, and therefore cannot come to water the flocks; we therefore do the work; we could not very well trust ourselves among these men.'

3352. The maidens are gone, with smiles on their lips and gratitude in their hearts. What were the reflections of Moses as he returned to the shade of the tree? He returned thanks to Allah for the bright little vision which he had just seen. Had he done a good deed? Precious was the opportunity he had had. He had slaked his thirst. But he was a homeless wanderer and had a longing in his soul, which he dared not put into words. Those shepherds were no company for him. He was truly like a beggar in desperate need. For any little good that came his way, he was grateful. But what was this?—this vision of a comfortable household, presided over by an old man rich in flocks and herds, and richer still in two daughters, as modest as they were beautiful? Perhaps he would never see them again! But Providence was preparing another surprise for him.

3353. Scarcely had he rested, when one of the damsels came back, walking with bashful grace! Modestly she gave her message, 'My father is grateful for what you did for us. He invites you, that he may thank you personally, and at least give some return for your kindness.'

Escaped from unjust people."[3354]

نَجَوْتَ مِنَ الْقَوْمِ الظَّٰلِمِينَ

26. Said one of the (damsels):
"O my (dear) father! engage[3355]
Him on wages: truly the best
Of men for thee to employ is
The (man) who is strong and
trusty" . . .[3356]

٢٦ قَالَتْ إِحْدَىٰهُمَا يَٰٓأَبَتِ ٱسْتَـْٔجِرْهُ
إِنَّ خَيْرَ مَنِ ٱسْتَـْٔجَرْتَ
ٱلْقَوِىُّ ٱلْأَمِينُ

27. He said: "I intend to wed
One of these my daughters
To thee, on condition that
Thou serve me for eight years;[3357]
But if thou complete ten years,
It will be (grace) from thee.
But I intend not to place
Thee under a difficulty:
Thou wilt find me,
Indeed, if Allah wills,
One of the righteous."

٢٧ قَالَ إِنِّىٓ أُرِيدُ أَنْ أُنكِحَكَ إِحْدَى
ٱبْنَتَىَّ هَٰتَيْنِ عَلَىٰٓ أَن تَأْجُرَنِى ثَمَٰنِىَ حِجَجٍ
فَإِنْ أَتْمَمْتَ عَشْرًا فَمِنْ عِندِكَ
وَمَآ أُرِيدُ أَنْ أَشُقَّ عَلَيْكَ
سَتَجِدُنِىٓ إِن شَآءَ ٱللَّهُ مِنَ
ٱلصَّٰلِحِينَ

3354. Nothing could have been more welcome than such a message, and through such a messenger. Moses went of course, and saw the old man. He found such a well-ordered patriarchal household. The old man was happy with his daughters and they with him. There was mutual confidence. They had evidently described the stranger to him in terms which made his welcome a foregone conclusion. On the other hand Moses had allowed his imagination to paint the father in something of the glorious colours in which his daughters had appeared to him like an angelic vision. The two men got to be friends at once. Moses told the old man his story—who he was, how he was brought up, and what misfortunes had made him quit Egypt. Perhaps the whole household, including the daughters, listened breathlessly to his tale. Perhaps their wonder and admiration were mingled with a certain amount of pity—perhaps with some more tender feeling in the case of the girl who had been to fetch him. Perhaps the enchantment which Desdemona felt in Othello's story was working on her. In any case the stranger had won his place in their hearts. The old man, the head of the household, assured him of hospitality and safety under his roof. As one with a long experience of life he congratulated him on his escape. 'Who would live among unjust people? It is as well you are free of them!'

3355. A little time passes. A guest after all cannot stay forever. They all felt that it would be good to have him with them permanently. The girl who had given her heart to him had spoken their unspoken thoughts. Why not employ him to tend the flocks? The father was old, and a young man was wanted to look after the flocks. And—there may be other possibilities.

3356. *Strong and trusty*: Moses had proved himself to be both, and these were the very qualities which a woman most admires in the man she loves.

3357. A little time passed, and at length the father broached the subject of marriage. It was not for the fugutive to suggest a permanent tie, especially when, in the wealth of this world, the girl's family was superior, and they had an established position, while he was a mere wanderer. The father asked if he would marry one of the daughters and stay with them for at least eight years, or if he liked, ten years, but the longer term was at his option. If he brought no dower, his service for that period was more than sufficient in lieu of dower. The particular girl intended was no doubt tacitly settled long before, by the mutual attraction of the young hearts themselves. Moses was glad of the proposal, and accepted it. They ratified it in the most solemn manner, by appealing to Allah. The old man, knowing the worth of his son-in-law, solemnly assured him that in any event he would not take advantage of his position to be a hard task-master or to insist on anything inconsistent with Moses's interests, should a new future open out to him. And a new and glorious future was awaiting him after his apprenticeship.

28. He said: 'Be that (the agreement)
Between me and thee:
Whichever of the two terms
I fulfil, let there be
No ill-will to me.
Be Allah a witness
To what we say.'[3358]

٢٨ قَالَ ذَٰلِكَ بَيْنِي وَبَيْنَكَ ۖ أَيَّمَا ٱلْأَجَلَيْنِ قَضَيْتُ فَلَا عُدْوَٰنَ عَلَيَّ ۖ وَٱللَّهُ عَلَىٰ مَا نَقُولُ وَكِيلٌ

SECTION 4.

29. Now when Moses had fulfilled
The term, and was travelling[3359]
With his family, he perceived
A fire in the direction
Of Mount Ṭūr. He said
To his family: "Tarry ye;
I perceive a fire; I hope
To bring you from there
Some information, or a burning
Firebrand, that ye may
Warm yourselves."[3360]

٢٩ فَلَمَّا قَضَىٰ مُوسَى ٱلْأَجَلَ وَسَارَ بِأَهْلِهِۦٓ ءَانَسَ مِن جَانِبِ ٱلطُّورِ نَارًا قَالَ لِأَهْلِهِ ٱمْكُثُوٓا۟ إِنِّىٓ ءَانَسْتُ نَارًا لَّعَلِّىٓ ءَاتِيكُم مِّنْهَا بِخَبَرٍ أَوْ جَذْوَةٍ مِّنَ ٱلنَّارِ لَعَلَّكُمْ تَصْطَلُونَ

30. But when he came
To the (Fire), a voice
Was heard from the right bank
Of the valley, from a tree[3361]
In hallowed ground:
"O Moses! Verily
I am Allah, the Lord
Of the Worlds. . .

٣٠ فَلَمَّآ أَتَىٰهَا نُودِىَ مِن شَٰطِئِ ٱلْوَادِ ٱلْأَيْمَنِ فِى ٱلْبُقْعَةِ ٱلْمُبَٰرَكَةِ مِنَ ٱلشَّجَرَةِ أَن يَٰمُوسَىٰٓ إِنِّىٓ أَنَا ٱللَّهُ رَبُّ ٱلْعَٰلَمِينَ

3358. In patriarchal society it was not uncommon to have a marriage bargain of this kind conditional on a certain term of service. In this case the episode conveys two lessons. (1) A man destined to be a messenger of Allah is yet a man, and must pass through the ups and downs of life like any other man: only he will do it with more grace and distinction than other men. (2) The beautiful relations in love and marriage may themselves be a preparation for the highest spiritual destiny that may await a Messenger of Allah. A woman need not necessarily be a snare and a temptation: she may be the understanding help-mate that the Lady Khadījah was to the Holy Prophet.

3359. The episode in the desert, full of human interest, now closes, and we come to the threshold of the sacred Call to the divine ministry of Moses. Here we may compare this passage with that in 27:7-14 and previous passages. In this passage we are told, after reference to Moses's preparation for his high destiny, of the particular sin of Arrogance and Sacrilege of which Pharaoh was guilty (28:38-39, how it was punished, and with what instruments in the hands of Moses and Pharaoh. The notes on the earlier passage should be read, as explanations already given need not now be repeated. (R).

3360. Note how the transition is effected from the happy earthly life of Moses (with its previous earthly storm and stress) to the new spiritual storm and stress of his prophetic mission.

3361. We are to suppose the appearance of a bush burning but not consumed (Exod. iii 2), a device adopted by the Scottish Church in its armorial bearings. Scotland apparently took that emblem and motto (Nes tamen consumebatur, 'nevertheless it was not consumed') from the Synod of the Reformed Church of France, which had adopted it in 1583. (I am indebted for this information to the Rev. D.Y. Robertson, Chaplain of the Church of Scotland in Simla, India). The real explanation of the Burning Bush will be found in 27:8. n. 3245: it was not a fire, but a reflection of the Glory of God.

31. "Now do thou throw thy rod!"
But when he saw it
Moving (of its own accord)
As if it had been a snake,
He turned back in retreat,
And retraced not his steps:
"O Moses!" (it was said),
"Draw near, and fear not:
For thou art of those
Who are secure.[3362]

(٣١) وَأَنْ أَلْقِ عَصَاكَ
فَلَمَّا رَءَاهَا تَهْتَزُّ كَأَنَّهَا جَآنٌّ
وَلَّىٰ مُدْبِرًا وَلَمْ يُعَقِّبْ
يَٰمُوسَىٰٓ أَقْبِلْ وَلَا تَخَفْ
إِنَّكَ مِنَ ٱلْءَامِنِينَ

32. "Move thy hand into
Thy bosom, and it will
Come forth white without stain
(Or harm), and draw thy hand
Close to thy side
(To guard) against fear.[3363]
Those are the two credentials
From thy Lord to Pharaoh
And his Chiefs: for truly
They are a people
Rebellious and wicked."

(٣٢) ٱسْلُكْ يَدَكَ فِى جَيْبِكَ تَخْرُجْ بَيْضَآءَ مِنْ غَيْرِ
سُوٓءٍ وَٱضْمُمْ إِلَيْكَ جَنَاحَكَ مِنَ ٱلرَّهْبِ
فَذَٰنِكَ بُرْهَٰنَانِ مِن رَّبِّكَ
إِلَىٰ فِرْعَوْنَ وَمَلَإِي۟هِۦٓ
إِنَّهُمْ كَانُوا۟ قَوْمًا فَٰسِقِينَ

33. He said: "O my Lord!
I have slain a man
Among them, and I fear[3364]
Lest they slay me.

(٣٣) قَالَ رَبِّ إِنِّى قَتَلْتُ مِنْهُمْ نَفْسًا
فَأَخَافُ أَن يَقْتُلُونِ

34. "And my brother Aaron—
He is more eloquent in speech
Than I: so send him
With me as a helper,
To confirm (and strengthen) me:
For I fear that they may
Accuse me of falsehood."

(٣٤) وَأَخِى هَٰرُونُ هُوَ أَفْصَحُ مِنِّى لِسَانًا
فَأَرْسِلْهُ مَعِىَ رِدْءًا يُصَدِّقُنِىٓ
إِنِّىٓ أَخَافُ أَن يُكَذِّبُونِ

3362. The verbal meaning is: "you have nothing to fear from what appears to be a snake: it is a snake, not for you, but for Pharaoh." But there is a deeper meaning besides. Moses had now been called to a higher and spiritual mission. He had to meet the hatred of the Egyptians and circumvent their trickery and magic. He had now the security of Faith: in all dangers and difficulties Allah would guide and protect him, for he was actually in Allah's service, one of the Elect.

3363. Literally, "draw thy wing close to thy side, (away) from fear". When a bird is frightened, it ruffles its wings and prepares to fly away, but when it is calm and composed, it sits with its wings drawn close to its sides, showing a mind secure from danger: *Cf.*also n. 2550 to 20:22.

3364. It is not that Moses is not reassured from all fear on account of the apparent snake which his rod had become, or from the sacred and unfamiliar surroundings in which he found himself. On this point his heart had been completely assured. But he is still new to his mission, and the future is obscure to his mind. Pharaoh was after him, to take his life, and apparently with good cause, because one of Pharaoh's men had been slain at his hands. And now he is commanded to go to Pharaoh and rebuke him and his Chiefs. The inner doubts and difficulties of his human mind he frankly lays before his Lord, and asks for a little human and visible support, which is granted him at once, *viz.*: the help of his brother Aaron.

35. He said: "We will certainly
Strengthen thy arm through
Thy brother, and invest you both
With authority, so they
Shall not be able to[3365]
Touch you: with Our Signs
Shall ye triumph—you two
As well as those
Who follow you."[3366]

قَالَ سَنَشُدُّ عَضُدَكَ بِأَخِيكَ ٣٥
وَنَجْعَلُ لَكُمَا سُلْطَٰنًا
فَلَا يَصِلُونَ إِلَيْكُمَا
بِـَٔايَٰتِنَآ أَنتُمَا وَمَنِ ٱتَّبَعَكُمَا ٱلْغَٰلِبُونَ

36. When Moses came to them
With Our Clear Signs, they said;
"This is nothing but sorcery[3367]
Faked up: never did we
Hear the like among our fathers
Of old!"[3368]

فَلَمَّا جَآءَهُم مُّوسَىٰ بِـَٔايَٰتِنَا ٣٦
بَيِّنَٰتٍ قَالُوا۟ مَا هَٰذَآ إِلَّا سِحْرٌ مُّفْتَرًى
وَمَا سَمِعْنَا بِهَٰذَا فِىٓ ءَابَآئِنَا ٱلْأَوَّلِينَ

37. Moses said: "My Lord
Knows best who it is
That comes with guidance
From Him and whose End
Will be best in the Hereafter:
Certain it is that
The wrongdoers will not
prosper."[3369]

وَقَالَ مُوسَىٰ رَبِّىٓ أَعْلَمُ ٣٧
بِمَن جَآءَ بِٱلْهُدَىٰ مِنْ عِندِهِۦ
وَمَن تَكُونُ لَهُۥ عَٰقِبَةُ ٱلدَّارِ
إِنَّهُۥ لَا يُفْلِحُ ٱلظَّٰلِمُونَ

38. Pharaoh said: "O Chiefs!
No god do I know for you[3370]
But myself: therefore,
O Hāmān! light me a (kiln
To bake bricks) out of clay,

وَقَالَ فِرْعَوْنُ يَٰٓأَيُّهَا ٱلْمَلَأُ ٣٨
مَا عَلِمْتُ لَكُم مِّنْ إِلَٰهٍ غَيْرِى
فَأَوْقِدْ لِى يَٰهَٰمَٰنُ عَلَى ٱلطِّينِ

3365. *To touch you*: to approach you anywhere near, in the wonders and Signs that you will show them under the divine authority with which you are invested.

3366. The potency of Allah's Light is such that its divine rays reach the humblest of those who seek after Him. The Prophets can certainly work wonders, but their sincere followers in Faith can do so also in their own spheres. Wonders may appeal to people, but they are not the highest Signs of Allah's workings and they are around us every day in our lives.

3367. This is what Moses was thinking of when he had said: "They may accuse me of falsehood". To accuse the purest Truth of lying is a favourite trick of those whose chief stock in trade is deception and sorcery and catching the attention of the vulgar by arts adapted to their ignorant minds!

3368. 'As to this higher talk of the worship of the One true God, why, our ancestors have worshipped power and patronage, as concentrated in Pharaoh, from the most ancient times!'

3369. *Cf.* 6:135. The only argument in such a case is an appeal to Allah and to the ultimate Future. Both of these appeals require Faith. But even if you do not rely on anything so high, you can see that Falsehood or evils crystallised in ancestral customs are not going to do any one any good.

3370. Pharaoh claimed, himself, to be God—not only one god among many, but the only god: "I am your Lord Most High": 79:24. At any rate he did not see why his people should worship any one but him.

And build me a lofty[3371]
Palace, that I may mount up
To the god of Moses:
But as far as I am concerned,
I think (Moses) is a liar!"

فَٱجْعَل لِّي صَرْحًا
لَّعَلِّيٓ أَطَّلِعُ إِلَىٰٓ إِلَٰهِ مُوسَىٰ
وَإِنِّي لَأَظُنُّهُۥ مِنَ ٱلْكَٰذِبِينَ

39. And he was arrogant and insolent
In the land, beyond reason—
He and his hosts: they thought
That they would not have
To return to Us![3372]

٣٩ وَٱسْتَكْبَرَ هُوَ وَجُنُودُهُۥ
فِي ٱلْأَرْضِ بِغَيْرِ ٱلْحَقِّ
وَظَنُّوٓا۟ أَنَّهُمْ إِلَيْنَا لَا يُرْجَعُونَ

40. So We seized him
And his hosts, and We
Flung them into the sea:[3373]
Now behold what was the End
Of those who did wrong!

٤٠ فَأَخَذْنَٰهُ وَجُنُودَهُۥ
فَنَبَذْنَٰهُمْ فِي ٱلْيَمِّ فَٱنظُرْ كَيْفَ
كَانَ عَٰقِبَةُ ٱلظَّٰلِمِينَ

41. And We made them (but)
Leaders inviting to the Fire;
And on the Day of Judgement
No help shall they find.

٤١ وَجَعَلْنَٰهُمْ أَئِمَّةً يَدْعُونَ
إِلَى ٱلنَّارِ وَيَوْمَ ٱلْقِيَٰمَةِ لَا يُنصَرُونَ

42. In this world We made
A Curse to follow them:[3374]
And on the Day of Judgement
They will be among
The loathed (and despised).

٤٢ وَأَتْبَعْنَٰهُمْ فِي هَٰذِهِ ٱلدُّنْيَا لَعْنَةً
وَيَوْمَ ٱلْقِيَٰمَةِ هُم مِّنَ ٱلْمَقْبُوحِينَ

C. 174.—As with Moses, so with the Prophet Muḥammad:
(28:43-60.) Revelation was given to him, by which
He knew and understood, and led men and was kind.
He was a Mercy to men, sent by Allah, to warn
Those in sin, and, by precept and example,
To bring the Light to their very doors.

3371. I understand his speech to his minister Hāmān to be sarcastic. But some Commentators have taken it very seriously and imagined that he actually thought of reaching the heavens by building lofty towers.

3372. They did not believe in the Hereafter. They did not understand that every deed must have its inevitable consequence, good, or evil, unless the Grace of Allah intervenes to save us from ourselves!

3373. Pharaoh and his hosts were drowned in the sea in their pursuit of the Israelites: see 7:130-136. They are the type of men who lead—only to Destruction. They invite, not to Peace and Happiness, but to the Fire of Wrath, mutual Envy, and Hatred.

3374. Power and patronage may be lauded by sycophants and selfish place-hunters; but when they are misused, and when their exposure causes their fall, they suffer ignominy even in this life. If they manage to escape exposure while alive, it often happens that they are found out after their death, and the curses of many generations follow those whose oppressions and wrongdoing spoiled the fair face of Allah's earth. But even this is nothing to the true Punishment that will come in the Hereafter. There, true values will be restored, and some of the highest and mightiest will be in the lowest depths of degradation.

Those who had spiritual eyes rejoiced.
And walked in Allah's ancient Way, now reopened,
Valuing the things of the Spirit as Allah's
Own gifts, to be their possession forever!

SECTION 5.

43. We did reveal to Moses
The Book after We had
Destroyed the earlier generations,
(To give) Insight to men,
And Guidance and Mercy,
That they might receive
admonition.[3375]

وَلَقَدْ ءَاتَيْنَا مُوسَى ٱلْكِتَٰبَ ﴿٤٣﴾
مِنۢ بَعْدِ مَآ أَهْلَكْنَا ٱلْقُرُونَ ٱلْأُولَىٰ بَصَآئِرَ
لِلنَّاسِ وَهُدًى وَرَحْمَةً لَّعَلَّهُمْ يَتَذَكَّرُونَ

44. Thou wast not on the Western[3376]
Side when We decreed
The commission to Moses,
Nor wast thou a witness
(Of those events).

وَمَا كُنتَ بِجَانِبِ ٱلْغَرْبِىِّ إِذْ قَضَيْنَآ ﴿٤٤﴾
إِلَىٰ مُوسَى ٱلْأَمْرَ وَمَا كُنتَ مِنَ ٱلشَّٰهِدِينَ

45. But We raised up (new)
Generations, and long were the
ages[3377]
That passed over them;
But thou wast not a dweller
Among the people of Madyan,
Rehearsing Our Signs to them;
But it is We Who send
Messengers (with inspiration).[3378]

وَلَٰكِنَّآ أَنشَأْنَا قُرُونًا ﴿٤٥﴾
فَتَطَاوَلَ عَلَيْهِمُ ٱلْعُمُرُ
وَمَا كُنتَ ثَاوِيًا فِىٓ أَهْلِ مَدْيَنَ تَتْلُوا۟
عَلَيْهِمْ ءَايَٰتِنَا وَلَٰكِنَّا كُنَّا مُرْسِلِينَ

3375. After the destruction of the Pharaonic Tyranny and other similar Tyrannies before them, Allah began a new age of Revelation, the age of Moses and his Book. Humanity began as it were with a clean slate again. It was a full Revelation (or *Sharī'ah*) which may be looked at from three points of view: (1) as Light or Insight for men, so that they should not grope in darkness; (2) as a Guide to show them the Way, so that they should not be misled into wrong Paths; and (3) as a Mercy from Allah, so that by following the Way they may receive Allah's Forgiveness and Grace. In 6:91, we have a reference to Light and Guidance in connection with the Revelation of Moses, and in 6:154 we have a reference to Guidance and Mercy in the same connection. Here all three are combined, with the substitution of *Baṣā'ir* for *Nūr. Baṣā'ir* is the plural of *Baṣīrah*, and also be translated Proofs, as I have done in 6:104 *Cf.* also 7:203, n. 1175, where the word is translated "Lights".

3376. The Sinai Peninsula is in the northwest corner of Arabia. But the reference here is, I think, to the western side of the valley of Ṭuwā. Mount Ṭūr, where Moses received his prophetic commission, is on the western side of the valley.

3377. That is, there were many generations that passed between Moses and the holy Prophet. Yet he knew by inspiration of the events of those times. Even if he had lived then, he could not have known the events that took place among the Midianites, except by inspiration, as he did not dwell among them.

3378 'Though thou wast not among the Midianites, Our inspiration has told thee of the momentous events that took place among them when Moses was with them. This is itself a Sign that should make thy people understand.'

46. Nor wast thou at the side
Of (the Mountain of) Ṭūr
When We called (to Moses).
Yet (art thou sent)
As a Mercy from thy Lord,
To give warning to a people[3379]
To whom no warner had come
Before thee: in order that
They may receive admonition.

وَمَا كُنتَ بِجَانِبِ ٱلطُّورِ إِذْ نَادَيْنَا وَلَٰكِن رَّحْمَةً مِّن رَّبِّكَ لِتُنذِرَ قَوْمًا مَّآ أَتَىٰهُم مِّن نَّذِيرٍ مِّن قَبْلِكَ لَعَلَّهُمْ يَتَذَكَّرُونَ ﴿٤٦﴾

47. If (We had) not (sent thee
To the Quraysh)—in case
A calamity should seize them
For (the deeds) that their hands
Have sent forth, they might say:
"Our Lord! why didst Thou not[3380]
Send us a messenger? We
Should then have followed
The Signs and been amongst
Those who believe!"

وَلَوْلَآ أَن تُصِيبَهُم مُّصِيبَةٌۢ بِمَا قَدَّمَتْ أَيْدِيهِمْ فَيَقُولُوا۟ رَبَّنَا لَوْلَآ أَرْسَلْتَ إِلَيْنَا رَسُولًا فَنَتَّبِعَ ءَايَٰتِكَ وَنَكُونَ مِنَ ٱلْمُؤْمِنِينَ ﴿٤٧﴾

48. But (now), when the Truth
Has come to them from Ourselves,
They say, "Why are not
(Signs) sent to him, like
Those which were sent to
Moses?"[3381]
Do they not then reject
(The Signs) which were formerly
Sent to Moses? They say:
"Two kinds of sorcery,
Each assisting the other?"[3382]

فَلَمَّا جَآءَهُمُ ٱلْحَقُّ مِنْ عِندِنَا قَالُوا۟ لَوْلَآ أُوتِىَ مِثْلَ مَآ أُوتِىَ مُوسَىٰٓ ۚ أَوَلَمْ يَكْفُرُوا۟ بِمَآ أُوتِىَ مُوسَىٰ مِن قَبْلُ ۖ قَالُوا۟ سِحْرَانِ تَظَٰهَرَا ﴿٤٨﴾

3379. This people was the Quraysh. 'Though thou didst not see how Moses was invested with the prophetic office at Mount Ṭūr, thou hast had similar experience thyself, and We have sent thee to the Quraysh to warn them of all their sins, and to repent and come into the Faith'.

3380. Now that a warner has come among them with all the authority that previous Messengers possessed and with all the knowledge which can only come by divine inspiration, they have no excuse left whatever. They cannot say, "No warner came to us." If any evil comes to them, as the inevitable result of their ill-deeds, they cannot blame Allah and say that they were not warned. *Cf.* 20:134.

3381. When a Revelation is sent to them, in the Qur'ān, adapted to all their needs and the needs of the time they live in, they hark back to antiquity. The Holy Prophet was in many respects like Moses, but the times in which he lived were different from the times of Moses, and his age did not suffer from the deceptions of sorcery, like that of Moses. The remedies which his age and future ages required (for his Message was universal) were different. His miracle of the Qur'ān was different and most permanent than the Rod and the Radiant-White Hand of Moses. But supposing that the Quraysh had been humoured in their insincere demands, would they have believed? Did they believe in Moses? They were only put up by the Jews to make objections which they themselves did not believe in.

3382. Moses was called a sorcerer by the Egyptians, and the wonderful words of the Qur'ān were called sorcery by the Quraysh. As the Qur'ān confirmed the Message of Moses, the Quraysh objectors said that they were in collusion. The Quraysh did not believe in Allah's Revelation at all.

And they say: "For us,
We reject all (such things)!"

وَقَالُوٓا۟ إِنَّا بِكُلٍّ كَٰفِرُونَ

49. Say: "Then bring ye
A Book from Allah,
Which is a better Guide
Than either of them,
That I may follow it!
(Do), if ye are truthful!"

(٤٩) قُلْ فَأْتُوا۟ بِكِتَٰبٍ
مِّنْ عِندِ ٱللَّهِ هُوَ أَهْدَىٰ مِنْهُمَآ
أَتَّبِعْهُ إِن كُنتُمْ صَٰدِقِينَ

50. But if they hearken not[3383]
To thee, know that they
Only follow their own lusts:
And who is more astray
Than one who follows his own
Lusts, devoid of guidance
From Allah? For Allah guides not
People given to wrongdoing.

(٥٠) فَإِن لَّمْ يَسْتَجِيبُوا۟ لَكَ فَٱعْلَمْ
أَنَّمَا يَتَّبِعُونَ أَهْوَآءَهُمْ ۚ وَمَنْ أَضَلُّ مِمَّنِ
ٱتَّبَعَ هَوَىٰهُ بِغَيْرِ هُدًى مِّنَ ٱللَّهِ ۚ
إِنَّ ٱللَّهَ لَا يَهْدِى ٱلْقَوْمَ ٱلظَّٰلِمِينَ

SECTION 6.

51. Now have We caused
The Word to reach them
Themselves, in order that
They may receive admonition[3384]

(٥١) وَلَقَدْ وَصَّلْنَا لَهُمُ ٱلْقَوْلَ
لَعَلَّهُمْ يَتَذَكَّرُونَ

52. Those to whom We sent
The Book before this—they
Do believe in this (Revelation);

(٥٢) ٱلَّذِينَ ءَاتَيْنَٰهُمُ ٱلْكِتَٰبَ
مِن قَبْلِهِۦ هُم بِهِۦ يُؤْمِنُونَ

53. And when it is recited
To them, they say: "We
Believe therein, for it is
The Truth from our Lord:
Indeed we have been Muslims
(Bowing to Allah's Will)
From before this.[3385]

(٥٣) وَإِذَا يُتْلَىٰ عَلَيْهِمْ قَالُوٓا۟
ءَامَنَّا بِهِۦٓ إِنَّهُ ٱلْحَقُّ مِن رَّبِّنَآ
إِنَّا كُنَّا مِن قَبْلِهِۦ مُسْلِمِينَ

3383. They were challenged to produce something better, to be a guide in life. But as they could not, it was evident that their objections were fractious. They were only following their own selfish lusts of power, monopoly, and exploitation of the poor and ignorant. How can such people receive guidance?

3384. Before this the Quraysh might have said that the Word of Allah had come to the Hebrews in their tongue or in Greek, which was used by the Hebrews in the time of Jesus. Now that Word is brought to their own doors, in their own Arabic tongue, by a man of their own race and family. Surely they have no excuse now for remaining strangers to the higher moral and spiritual law.

3385. There were Christians and Jews who recognised that Islam was a logical and natural development of Allah's revelations as given in earlier ages, and they not only welcomed and accepted Islam, but claimed, and rightly, that they had always been Muslims. In that sense Adam, Noah, Abraham, Moses, and Jesus had all been Muslims. (R).

54. Twice will they be given[3386]
Their reward, for that they
Have persevered, that they avert
Evil with Good, and that
They spend (in charity) out of
What We have given them.

٥٤ أُوْلَٰٓئِكَ يُؤْتَوْنَ أَجْرَهُم مَّرَّتَيْنِ بِمَا صَبَرُواْ
وَيَدْرَءُونَ بِٱلْحَسَنَةِ ٱلسَّيِّئَةَ
وَمِمَّا رَزَقْنَٰهُمْ يُنفِقُونَ

55. And when they hear vain talk,
They turn away therefrom
And say: "To us our deeds,
And to you yours;[3387]
Peace be to you: we
Seek not the ignorant."

٥٥ وَإِذَا سَمِعُواْ ٱللَّغْوَ أَعْرَضُواْ عَنْهُ
وَقَالُواْ لَنَآ أَعْمَٰلُنَا وَلَكُمْ أَعْمَٰلُكُمْ
سَلَٰمٌ عَلَيْكُمْ لَا نَبْتَغِى ٱلْجَٰهِلِينَ

56. It is true thou wilt not
Be able to guide every one[3388]
Whom thou lovest; but Allah
Guides those whom He will
And He knows best those
Who receive guidance.

٥٦ إِنَّكَ لَا تَهْدِى مَنْ أَحْبَبْتَ
وَلَٰكِنَّ ٱللَّهَ يَهْدِى مَن يَشَآءُ
وَهُوَ أَعْلَمُ بِٱلْمُهْتَدِينَ

57. They say: "If we were
To follow the guidance with thee,
We should be snatched away[3389]
From our land." Have We not
Established for them a secure
Sanctuary, to which are brought
As tribute fruits of all kinds—
A provision from Ourselves?
But most of them understand not.

٥٧ وَقَالُوٓاْ إِن نَّتَّبِعِ ٱلْهُدَىٰ مَعَكَ
نُتَخَطَّفْ مِنْ أَرْضِنَآ أَوَلَمْ نُمَكِّن لَّهُمْ حَرَمًا
ءَامِنًا يُجْبَىٰٓ إِلَيْهِ ثَمَرَٰتُ كُلِّ شَىْءٍ رِّزْقًا مِّن لَّدُنَّا
وَلَٰكِنَّ أَكْثَرَهُمْ لَا يَعْلَمُونَ

3386. Their credit is twofold, in that before they knew Islam, they followed the earliest Law in truth and sincerity, and when they were offered Islam, they readily recognised and accepted it, suffered in patient perseverance for its sake, and brought forth the fruits of righteousness.

3387. The righteous do not encourage idle talk or foolish arguments about things sacred. If they find themselves in some company in which such things are fashionable, they leave politely. Their only rejoinder is: "We are responsible for our deeds, and you for yours; we have no ill-will against you; we wish you well and that is why we wish you to know of the knowledge we have received; after that knowledge you cannot expect us to go back to the Ignorance which we have left."

3388. The immediate occasion for this was the death of Abū Ṭālib, an uncle whom the Holy Prophet loved dearly and who had befriended and protected him. The Prophet was naturally anxious that he should die in the profession of the true Faith, but the pagan Quraysh leaders persuaded him to remain true to the faith of his fathers. This was an occasion of disappointment and grief to the Prophet. We are told that in such circumstances we should not grieve. All whom we love do not necessarily share our views or beliefs. We must not judge. Allah will guide whom He pleases and as He pleases. He alone knows the true inwardness of things.

3389. Some Quraysh said: "We see the truth of Islam, but if we abandon our people, we shall lose our hold on the land, and other people will dispossess us." The answer is twofold, one literal and the other of deeper import. (1) 'Your land? Why, the sanctuary of Makkah is sacred and secure because Allah has made it so, If you obey Allah's Word, you will be strengthened, not weakened.' (2) 'Makkah is the symbol of the Fortress of Spiritual Well-being. The Fruit of every Deed comes or should come as a tribute to Spiritual Well-being. What are you afraid of? It is Allah's Fortress. The more you seek Allah, the stronger you are in the Fortress.'

58. And how many populations
We destroyed, which exulted
In their life (of ease and plenty)!
Now those habitations of theirs,
After them, are deserted—
All but a (miserable) few!
And We are their heirs![3390]

﴿٥٨﴾ وَكَمْ أَهْلَكْنَا مِن قَرْيَةٍ بَطِرَتْ
مَعِيشَتَهَا فَتِلْكَ مَسَٰكِنُهُمْ لَمْ تُسْكَن
مِّنۢ بَعْدِهِمْ إِلَّا قَلِيلًا وَكُنَّا نَحْنُ ٱلْوَٰرِثِينَ

59. Nor was thy Lord the one
To destroy a population until
He had sent to its Centre
A messenger, rehearsing to them
Our Signs: nor are We
Going to destroy a population
Except when its members
Practise iniquity.

﴿٥٩﴾ وَمَا كَانَ رَبُّكَ مُهْلِكَ ٱلْقُرَىٰ حَتَّىٰ
يَبْعَثَ فِىٓ أُمِّهَا رَسُولًا يَتْلُوا۟ عَلَيْهِمْ ءَايَٰتِنَا
وَمَا كُنَّا مُهْلِكِى ٱلْقُرَىٰٓ
إِلَّا وَأَهْلُهَا ظَٰلِمُونَ

60. The (material) things which
Ye are given are but
The conveniences of this life
And the glitter thereof;[3391]
But that which is with Allah
Is better and more enduring:
Will ye not then be wise?

﴿٦٠﴾ وَمَآ أُوتِيتُم مِّن شَىْءٍ
فَمَتَٰعُ ٱلْحَيَوٰةِ ٱلدُّنْيَا وَزِينَتُهَا
وَمَا عِندَ ٱللَّهِ خَيْرٌ وَأَبْقَىٰٓ أَفَلَا تَعْقِلُونَ

C. 175.—Material good is nothing compared
(28:61-75.) To the spiritual. In the Hereafter
No plea 'that others misled' will avail.
Each soul must answer for itself.
Whether it honoured Allah alone
Or worshipped something else,
And whether it received or rejected
The Teachers sent by Allah. The Wisdom
And Plan of Allah are beyond all praise:
And mercy and truth proceed from Him,
And there is no other—none—besides Him.

3390. A life of ease and plenty is nothing to boast of. Yet people or cities or civilisations grow insolently proud of such things. There were many such in the past, which are now mere names! Their very sites are deserted in most cases, or buried in the debris of ages. Indo-Pakistan subcontinent is full of such sites nearly everywhere. The sites of Harappa and Mohenjo Daro are the most ancient hitherto unearthed in Pakistan, and they are themselves in layers covering centuries of time! And how many more there may be, of which we do not know even names! Fatehpur-Sikri was a magnificent ruin within a single generation. And there are thousands of Qaṣbas once flourishing and now reduced to small villages or altogether deserted. But Allah is merciful and just. He does not destroy or degrade a people until they have had full opportunities of turning in repentance to Him and they have deliberately rejected His Law and continued in the practice of iniquity.

3391. The good things in this life have their uses and serve their convenience. But they are fleeting and their value is infinitely lower than that of Truth and Justice and Spiritual Well-being, the gifts which come as it were from the very Presence of Allah. No wise soul will be absorbed in the one and neglect the other, or will hesitate for a moment if it comes to a choice between them.

SECTION 7.

61. Are (these two) alike?—
One to whom We have made
A goodly promise, and who
Is going to reach its (fulfilment).[3392]
And one to whom We have
Given the good things of this
Life, but who, on the Day
Of Judgement, is to be among
Those brought up (for
punishment)?

٦١ أَفَمَن وَعَدْنَٰهُ
وَعْدًا حَسَنًا فَهُوَ لَٰقِيهِ
كَمَن مَّتَّعْنَٰهُ مَتَٰعَ ٱلْحَيَوٰةِ ٱلدُّنْيَا
ثُمَّ هُوَ يَوْمَ ٱلْقِيَٰمَةِ مِنَ ٱلْمُحْضَرِينَ

62. That Day (Allah) will
Call to them, and say:
"Where are My 'partners'?—
Whom ye imagined (to be such)?"

٦٢ وَيَوْمَ يُنَادِيهِمْ فَيَقُولُ
أَيْنَ شُرَكَآءِىَ ٱلَّذِينَ كُنتُمْ تَزْعُمُونَ

63. Those against whom the charge[3393]
Will be proved, will say:
"Our Lord! These are the ones
Whom we led astray:
We led them astray, as we
Were astray ourselves: we free
Ourselves (from them) in Thy
presence:
It was not us they worshipped."[3394]

٦٣ قَالَ ٱلَّذِينَ حَقَّ عَلَيْهِمُ ٱلْقَوْلُ
رَبَّنَا هَٰٓؤُلَآءِ ٱلَّذِينَ أَغْوَيْنَآ
أَغْوَيْنَٰهُمْ كَمَا غَوَيْنَا تَبَرَّأْنَآ إِلَيْكَ
مَا كَانُوٓا۟ إِيَّانَا يَعْبُدُونَ

64. It will be said (to them):
"Call upon your 'partners'
(For help)": they will call
Upon them, but they will not
Listen to them; and they
Will see the Penalty (before them);
(How they will wish)

٦٤ وَقِيلَ ٱدْعُوا۟ شُرَكَآءَكُمْ
فَدَعَوْهُمْ فَلَمْ يَسْتَجِيبُوا۟ لَهُمْ
وَرَأَوُا۟ ٱلْعَذَابَ ۚ

3392. The two classes of people are: (1) those who have faith in the goodly promise of Allah to the righteous, and who are doing everything in life to reach the fulfilment of that promise, *i.e.*, those who believe and work righteousness, and (2) those who are ungrateful for such good things in this life as Allah has bestowed on them, by worshipping wealth or power or other symbols or idols of their fancy, *i.e.*, those who reject Faith and lead evil lives, for which they will have to answer in the Hereafter. The two classes are poles asunder, and their future is described below.

3393. This and the next verse are concerned with the examination of those who neglected truth and righteousness and went after the worship of false gods, *viz.*, their own lusts. These were the "partners" they associated with Allah. Insofar as they were embodied in false or wicked leaders, the leaders will disown responsibility for them. 'We ourselves went wrong, and they followed our example, because it suited them: they worshipped, not us, but their own lusts.'

3394. *Cf.* 10:28. False worship often names others, but really it is the worship of the Self. The others whom they name will have nothing to do with them when the awful Penalty stands in the sight of both. Then each wrongdoer will have to look to his own case. The wicked will then realise the gravity of the situation and wish that they had accepted the true guidance of Allah's Messengers.

'If only they had been
Open to guidance!'

لَوْ أَنَّهُمْ كَانُوا يَهْتَدُونَ

65. That Day (Allah) will[3395]
Call to them, and say:
"What was the answer
Ye gave to the messengers?"

٦٥ وَيَوْمَ يُنَادِيهِمْ فَيَقُولُ
مَاذَآ أَجَبْتُمُ ٱلْمُرْسَلِينَ

66. Then the (whole) story that day
Will seem obscure to them[3396]
(Like light to the blind)
And they will not be able
(Even) to question each other.

٦٦ فَعَمِيَتْ عَلَيْهِمُ ٱلْأَنۢبَآءُ يَوْمَئِذٍ
فَهُمْ لَا يَتَسَآءَلُونَ

67. But any that (in this life)
Had repented, believed, and worked
Righteousness, will have hopes
To be among those who
Achieve salvation.

٦٧ فَأَمَّا مَن تَابَ وَءَامَنَ وَعَمِلَ
صَٰلِحًا فَعَسَىٰٓ أَن يَكُونَ
مِنَ ٱلْمُفْلِحِينَ

68. Thy Lord does create and choose
As He pleases:[3397] no choice
Have they (in the matter):
Glory to Allah! and far
Is He above the partners
They ascribe (to Him)!

٦٨ وَرَبُّكَ يَخْلُقُ مَا يَشَآءُ وَيَخْتَارُ
مَا كَانَ لَهُمُ ٱلْخِيَرَةُ سُبْحَٰنَ ٱللَّهِ
وَتَعَٰلَىٰ عَمَّا يُشْرِكُونَ

69. And thy Lord knows all
That their hearts conceal
And all that they reveal.[3398]

٦٩ وَرَبُّكَ يَعْلَمُ مَا تُكِنُّ
صُدُورُهُمْ وَمَا يُعْلِنُونَ

70. And He is Allah: there is
No god but He. To Him
Be praise, at the first
And at the last:

٧٠ وَهُوَ ٱللَّهُ لَآ إِلَٰهَ إِلَّا هُوَ
لَهُ ٱلْحَمْدُ فِى ٱلْأُولَىٰ وَٱلْءَاخِرَةِ

3395. Now we come to the examination of those who rejected or persecuted Allah's Messengers on the earth. It may be the same men as those mentioned in 28:62-64, but this is a different count in the charge.

3396. In their utter confusion and despair their minds will be blank. The past will seem to them unreal, and the present unintelligible, and they will not even be able to consult each other, as every one's state will be the same.

3397. *As He pleases*: according to His own Will and Plan. Allah is not dependent on other people for advice or help. He has no partners. All creation is an act of His Will, and no one can direct Him how or why certain things should be, because He is supreme in wisdom and knowledge. He chooses His messengers also by His own unfettered choice. Inspiration or spiritual knowledge and dignity cannot be judged by our relative or temporary standards. Worldly greatness or even wisdom do not necessarily go with spiritual insight.

3398. Men may form all sorts of vain wishes or conceal their designs. But Allah's Will is supreme, and nothing can withstand its fulfilment.

For Him is the Command,
And to Him shall ye
(All) be brought back.

وَلَهُ ٱلْحُكْمُ وَإِلَيْهِ تُرْجَعُونَ

71. Say: See ye? If Allah
Were to make the Night[3399]
Perpetual over you to the Day
Of Judgement, what god
Is there other than Allah,
Who can give you enlightenment?
Will ye not then hearken?

(٧١) قُلْ أَرَءَيْتُمْ إِن جَعَلَ ٱللَّهُ عَلَيْكُمُ ٱلَّيْلَ سَرْمَدًا إِلَىٰ يَوْمِ ٱلْقِيَٰمَةِ مَنْ إِلَٰهٌ غَيْرُ ٱللَّهِ يَأْتِيكُم بِضِيَآءٍ أَفَلَا تَسْمَعُونَ

72. Say: See ye: If Allah
Were to make the Day
Perpetual over you to the Day
Of Judgement, what god
Is there other than Allah
Who can give you a Night
In which ye can rest?
Will ye not then see?[3400]

(٧٢) قُلْ أَرَءَيْتُمْ إِن جَعَلَ ٱللَّهُ عَلَيْكُمُ ٱلنَّهَارَ سَرْمَدًا إِلَىٰ يَوْمِ ٱلْقِيَٰمَةِ مَنْ إِلَٰهٌ غَيْرُ ٱللَّهِ يَأْتِيكُم بِلَيْلٍ تَسْكُنُونَ فِيهِ أَفَلَا تُبْصِرُونَ

73. It is out of His Mercy
That He has made for you
Night and Day—that ye
May rest therein, and that
Ye may seek of His Grace—
And in order that ye
May be grateful.

(٧٣) وَمِن رَّحْمَتِهِۦ جَعَلَ لَكُمُ ٱلَّيْلَ وَٱلنَّهَارَ لِتَسْكُنُوا۟ فِيهِ وَلِتَبْتَغُوا۟ مِن فَضْلِهِۦ وَلَعَلَّكُمْ تَشْكُرُونَ

74. The Day that He will[3401]
Call on them, He will say:

(٧٤) وَيَوْمَ يُنَادِيهِمْ فَيَقُولُ

3399. In the physical world the Night and Day are both blessings, the one for rest and the other for work, and the alternation itself is one of the mercies of Allah, and none but He can give us these blessings. If we were perpetually resting, or screened from the light, our faculties would be blunted and we should be worse than dead. If we were perpetually working, we should be tired, and we should also be dead in another way. This daily miracle keeps us alive and prepares us, in this our probationary life, for our final destiny in the Hereafter. So in the spiritual world. Some kinds of ignorance—such as ignorance of what is coming in the future—are necessary to conserve our powers and give rest to our minds and spirits, but if we were to remain ignorant perpetually, we should be spiritually dead. In the same way our spiritual strivings require periodical alternations to rest in the form of attention to our temporal concerns: hence the justification of a good and pure life on the plane of this earth also. Also, in the world's history, there are periods when a living messenger stimulates intense spiritual activity, and periods when it is comparatively quiescent (the so-called Dark Ages); but both are examples of the working of Allah's Plan of wisdom and mercy. But this applies only up to the Day of Judgement. After that we shall be on another plane altogether.

3400. In verse 71 was mentioned a "perpetual Night," for which the faculty of "hearkening" was appropriate, as all light was shut out. In this verse a perpetual Day is mentioned, for which the faculty of "seeing" is appropriate. Through many doors can the higher knowledge enter our souls. Shall we not use each of them as the occasion demands?

3401. *Cf.* 28:62 above. The reminiscence of the words closes and rounds off the argument of this Section.

"Where are my partners?
Whom ye imagined (to be such)?"

أَيْنَ شُرَكَآءِيَ ٱلَّذِينَ كُنتُمْ تَزْعُمُونَ

75. And from each people
Shall We draw a witness,[3402]
And We shall say: "Produce
Your Proof": then shall they
Know that the Truth is in
Allah (alone), and the (lies)
Which they invented will
Leave them in the lurch.[3403]

٧٥ وَنَزَعْنَا مِن كُلِّ أُمَّةٍ شَهِيدًا فَقُلْنَا
هَاتُوا۟ بُرْهَـٰنَكُمْ فَعَلِمُوٓا۟ أَنَّ ٱلْحَقَّ لِلَّهِ
وَضَلَّ عَنْهُم مَّا كَانُوا۟ يَفْتَرُونَ

C. 176.—Men puffed up with wealth, like Qārūn,
(28:76-88.) Are not pleasing to Allah: for wealth
Is for service, not for hoarding or show
In the midst of his pride was Qārūn
Swallowed up in the earth, and the earth
Knew him no more! It is the righteous
That attain a happy End. Let nothing
Keep your eyes back from that End:
Then, and only then, shall ye reach
The Eternal Reality, the glorious Reality,
Which is Allah, Who endureth forever! (R).

SECTION 8.

76. Qārūn was doubtless,[3404]
Of the people of Moses; but
He acted insolently towards them:
Such were the treasures We[3405]
Had bestowed on him, that
Their very keys would
Have been a burden to

٧٦ إِنَّ قَـٰرُونَ كَانَ
مِن قَوْمِ مُوسَىٰ فَبَغَىٰ عَلَيْهِمْ
وَءَاتَيْنَـٰهُ مِنَ ٱلْكُنُوزِ مَآ إِنَّ مَفَاتِحَهُۥ لَتَنُوٓأُ

3402. *Cf.* 4:41. The Prophet from each People or Nation will bear testimony that he preached the true gospel of Unity, and the People who rejected him will be asked to show the Proof or authority on which they rejected him: *Cf.* 2:111.

3403. In that new world, Allah will be the only Truth or Reality, and all the fancies or lies, which had been invented in this world of reflected or relative truths mixed with illusions, will have vanished, and left those who relied on them in the lurch. *Cf.* 6:24.

3404. Qārūn is identified with the Korah of the English Bible. His story is told in Num. xvi. 1-35. He and his followers, numbering 250 men, rose in rebellion against Moses and Aaron, on the ground that their position and fame in the congregation entitled them to equality in spiritual matters with the Priests—that they were as holy as any, and they claimed to burn incense at the sacred Altar reserved for the Priests. They had an exemplary punishment: "the earth opened her mouth, and swallowed them up, and their houses, and all the men that appertained unto Korah, and all their goods: they, and all that appertained to them, went down alive into the pit, and the earth closed upon them: and they perished from among the congregation."

3405. Qārūn's boundless wealth is described in the Midrashim, or the Jewish compilations based on the oral teachings of the Synagogues, which however exaggerate the weight of the keys to be the equivalent of the load of 300 mules!

A body of strong men:[3406]
Behold, his people said to him:
"Exult not, for Allah loveth not
Those who exult (in riches).

بِٱلْعُصْبَةِ أُو۟لِى ٱلْقُوَّةِ إِذْ قَالَ لَهُۥ قَوْمُهُۥ
لَا تَفْرَحْ ۖ إِنَّ ٱللَّهَ لَا يُحِبُّ ٱلْفَرِحِينَ

77. "But seek, with the (wealth)
Which Allah has bestowed on thee,
The Home of the Hereafter,[3407]
Nor forget thy portion in this
World: but do thou good,
As Allah has been good
To thee, and seek not
(Occasions for) mischief in the land:
For Allah loves not those
Who do mischief."

(٧٧) وَٱبْتَغِ فِيمَآ ءَاتَىٰكَ ٱللَّهُ ٱلدَّارَ ٱلْءَاخِرَةَ ۖ
وَلَا تَنسَ نَصِيبَكَ مِنَ ٱلدُّنْيَا ۖ
وَأَحْسِن كَمَآ أَحْسَنَ ٱللَّهُ إِلَيْكَ ۖ
وَلَا تَبْغِ ٱلْفَسَادَ فِى ٱلْأَرْضِ ۖ
إِنَّ ٱللَّهَ لَا يُحِبُّ ٱلْمُفْسِدِينَ

78. He said: "This has been given
To me because of a certain
Knowledge which I have."[3408]
Did he not know that Allah
Had destroyed, before him
(Whole) generations—which were
Superior to him in strength
And greater in amount
(Of riches) they had collected?
But the wicked are not
Called (immediately) to account[3409]
For their sins.

(٧٨) قَالَ إِنَّمَآ أُوتِيتُهُۥ عَلَىٰ عِلْمٍ عِندِىٓ ۚ
أَوَلَمْ يَعْلَمْ أَنَّ ٱللَّهَ قَدْ أَهْلَكَ
مِن قَبْلِهِۦ مِنَ ٱلْقُرُونِ مَنْ
هُوَ أَشَدُّ مِنْهُ قُوَّةً وَأَكْثَرُ جَمْعًا ۚ
وَلَا يُسْـَٔلُ عَن ذُنُوبِهِمُ
ٱلْمُجْرِمُونَ

79. So he went forth among
His people in the (pride
Of his worldly) glitter.
Said those whose aim is

(٧٩) فَخَرَجَ عَلَىٰ قَوْمِهِۦ فِى زِينَتِهِۦ ۖ
قَالَ ٱلَّذِينَ يُرِيدُونَ

3406. *'Uṣbah*: a body of men, here used indefinitely. It usually implies a body of 10 to 40 men. The old-fashioned keys were big and heavy, and if there were hundreds of treasure chests, the keys must have been a great weight. As they were travelling in the desert, the treasures were presumably left behind in Egypt, and only the keys were carried. The disloyal Qārūn had left his heart in Egypt, with his treasures.

3407. That is, 'spend your wealth in charity and good works. It is Allah Who has given it to you, and you should spend it in Allah's cause. Nor should you forget the legitimate needs of this life, as misers do, and most people become misers who think too exclusively of their wealth. If wealth is not used properly, there are three evils that follow: (1) its possessor may be a miser and forget all claims due to himself and those about him; (2) he may forget the higher needs of the poor and needy, or the good causes which require support; and (3) he may even misspend on occasions and cause a great deal of harm and mischief.' Apparently Qārūn had all three vices.

3408. He was so blind and arrogant that he thought that his own merit, knowledge, and skill or cleverness had earned him his wealth, and that now, on account of it, he was superior to everybody else and was entitled to ride rough-shod over them. Fool!—he was soon pulled up by Allah.

3409. Even Qārūn was given a long run of enjoyment with his fabulous wealth before he had to be removed for the mischief he was doing.

The Life of this World:
"Oh! that we had the like
Of what Qārūn has got!
For he is truly a lord
Of mighty good fortune!"[3410]

ٱلْحَيَوٰةَ ٱلدُّنْيَا يَٰلَيْتَ لَنَا مِثْلَ مَآ أُوتِيَ قَٰرُونُ إِنَّهُۥ لَذُو حَظٍّ عَظِيمٍ

80. But those who had been granted
(True) knowledge said: "Alas
For you! The reward of Allah
(In the Hereafter) is best
For those who believe
And work righteousness: but this
None shall attain, save those
Who steadfastly presevere
(in good)."

وَقَالَ ٱلَّذِينَ أُوتُوا۟ ٱلْعِلْمَ وَيْلَكُمْ ثَوَابُ ٱللَّهِ خَيْرٌ لِّمَنْ ءَامَنَ وَعَمِلَ صَٰلِحًا وَلَا يُلَقَّىٰهَآ إِلَّا ٱلصَّٰبِرُونَ ﴿٨٠﴾

81. Then We caused the earth[3411]
To swallow him up and
His house; and he had not
(The least little) party
To help him against Allah,
Nor could he defend himself.

فَخَسَفْنَا بِهِۦ وَبِدَارِهِ ٱلْأَرْضَ فَمَا كَانَ لَهُۥ مِن فِئَةٍ يَنصُرُونَهُۥ مِن دُونِ ٱللَّهِ وَمَا كَانَ مِنَ ٱلْمُنتَصِرِينَ ﴿٨١﴾

82. And those who had envied
His position the day before
Began to say on the morrow:
"Ah! It is indeed Allah
Who enlarges the provision[3412]
Or restricts it, to any
Of His servants He pleases!
Had it not been that Allah

وَأَصْبَحَ ٱلَّذِينَ تَمَنَّوْا۟ مَكَانَهُۥ بِٱلْأَمْسِ يَقُولُونَ وَيْكَأَنَّ ٱللَّهَ يَبْسُطُ ٱلرِّزْقَ لِمَن يَشَآءُ مِنْ عِبَادِهِۦ وَيَقْدِرُ لَوْلَآ أَن مَّنَّ ٱللَّهُ ﴿٨٢﴾

3410. When he was in the hey-day of his glory, worldly people envied him and thought how happy they would be if they were in his place. Not so the people of wisdom and discernment. They knew a more precious and lasting wealth, which is described in the next verse.

3411. See n. 3404 above. *Cf.* also 16:45 and n. 2071. Besides the obvious moral in the literal interpretation of the story, that material wealth is fleeting and may be a temptation and a cause of fall, there are some metaphorical implications that occur to me. (1) Qārūn was with Israel in the wilderness, even his material wealth was of no use to him there; he had the mere empty keys; material wealth has no value in itself, but only a relative and local value. (2) In body he was with Israel in the wilderness, but his heart was in Egypt with its fertility and its slavery. Such is the case of many hypocrites, who like to be seen in righteous company but whose thoughts, longings, and doings are inconsistent with such company. (3) There is no good in this life but comes from Allah. To think otherwise is to set up a false god besides Allah. Our own merits are so small that they should never be the object of our idolatry. (4) If Qārūn on account of his wealth was setting himself up in rivalry with Moses and Aaron, he was blind to the fact that spiritual knowledge is far above any little cleverness in worldly affairs. Mob-leaders have no position before spiritual guides.

3412. *Provision* or Sustenance, both literally and figuratively: wealth and material things in life as well as the things that sustain our higher and spiritual faculties. The rabble, that admired Qārūn's wealth when he was in worldly prosperity, now sees the other side of the question and understands that there are other gifts more precious and desirable, and that these may actually be withheld from men who enjoy wealth and worldly prosperity. In fact it is false prosperity, or no prosperity in the real sense of the word, which is without spiritual well-being.

Was gracious to us, He
Could have caused the earth
To swallow us up! Ah!
Those who reject Allah
Will assuredly never prosper."

عَلَيْنَا لَخَسَفَ بِنَا
وَيْكَأَنَّهُۥ لَا يُفْلِحُ ٱلْكَٰفِرُونَ

SECTION 9.

83. That House of the Hereafter
We shall give to those
Who intend not high-handedness
Or mischief on earth:[3413]
And the End is (best)
For the righteous.

٨٣ تِلْكَ ٱلدَّارُ ٱلْءَاخِرَةُ نَجْعَلُهَا
لِلَّذِينَ لَا يُرِيدُونَ عُلُوًّا فِى ٱلْأَرْضِ وَلَا فَسَادًا
وَٱلْعَٰقِبَةُ لِلْمُتَّقِينَ

84. If any does good, the reward
To him is better than
His deed; but if any
Does evil, the doers of evil
Are only punished (to the extent)
Of their deeds.[3414]

٨٤ مَن جَآءَ بِٱلْحَسَنَةِ فَلَهُۥ خَيْرٌ مِّنْهَا
وَمَن جَآءَ بِٱلسَّيِّئَةِ فَلَا يُجْزَى ٱلَّذِينَ
عَمِلُوا۟ ٱلسَّيِّـَٔاتِ إِلَّا مَا كَانُوا۟ يَعْمَلُونَ

85. Verily He Who ordained[3415]
The Qur'ān for thee, will bring
Thee back to the Place[3416]
Of Return. Say: "My Lord
Knows best who it is
That brings true guidance.
And who is in manifest error."[3417]

٨٥ إِنَّ ٱلَّذِى فَرَضَ عَلَيْكَ ٱلْقُرْءَانَ
لَرَآدُّكَ إِلَىٰ مَعَادٍ قُل رَّبِّىٓ أَعْلَمُ مَن جَآءَ
بِٱلْهُدَىٰ وَمَنْ هُوَ فِى ضَلَٰلٍ مُّبِينٍ

86. And thou hadst not expected

٨٦ وَمَا كُنتَ تَرْجُوٓا۟

3413. *High-handedness* or arrogance, as opposed to submission to the Will of Allah, Islam. *Mischief*, as opposed to doing good, bringing forth fruits of righteousness. It is the righteous who will win in the end.

3414. A good deed has its sure reward, and that reward will be better than the merits of the doer. An evil deed may be forgiven by repentance, but in any case will not be punished with severer penalty than justice demands.

3415. That is: order in His wisdom and mercy that the Qur'ān should be revealed, containing guidance for conduct in this life and the next, and further ordered that it should be read out and taught and its principles observed in practice. It is because of this teaching and preaching that the Holy Prophet was persecuted, but as Allah sent the Qur'ān, He will see that those who follow it will not eventually suffer, but be restored to happiness in the Place of Return, for which see next note.

3416. *Place of Return*: (1) a title of Makkah; (2) the occasion when we shall be restored to the Presence of our Lord. It is said that this verse was revealed at *Juhfa*, on the road from Makkah to Madīnah, a short distance from Makkah, on the Hijrah journey. The Prophet was sad at heart, and this was given as consolation to him. If this was the particular occasion, the general meaning would refer the Place of Return to the occasion of the Resurrection, when all true values will be restored, however they may be disturbed by the temporary interference of Evil in this life.

3417. Allah knows the true from the false, and if we are persecuted for our Faith and attacked or spoken ill of because we dare to do right, our surest refuge is an appeal to Allah rather than to men.

That the Book would be
Sent to thee except as
A Mercy from thy Lord:[3418]
Therefore lend not thou support
In any way to those
Who reject (Allah's Message).[3419]

أَن يُلْقَىٰٓ إِلَيْكَ
ٱلْكِتَـٰبُ إِلَّا رَحْمَةً مِّن رَّبِّكَ
فَلَا تَكُونَنَّ ظَهِيرًا لِّلْكَـٰفِرِينَ

87. And let nothing keep thee
Back from the Signs of Allah
After they have been revealed
To thee: and invite (men)
To thy Lord, and be not
Of the company of those
Who join gods with Allah.[3420]

٨٧ وَلَا يَصُدُّنَّكَ عَنْ ءَايَـٰتِ ٱللَّهِ بَعْدَ
إِذْ أُنزِلَتْ إِلَيْكَ وَٱدْعُ إِلَىٰ رَبِّكَ
وَلَا تَكُونَنَّ مِنَ ٱلْمُشْرِكِينَ

88. And call not, besides Allah,
On another god. There is
No god but He. Everything
(That exists) will perish
Except His own Face.[3421]
To Him belongs the Command,
And to Him will ye
(All) be brought back.

٨٨ وَلَا تَدْعُ مَعَ ٱللَّهِ إِلَـٰهًا ءَاخَرَ
لَآ إِلَـٰهَ إِلَّا هُوَ كُلُّ شَىْءٍ هَالِكٌ إِلَّا وَجْهَهُۥ
لَهُ ٱلْحُكْمُ وَإِلَيْهِ
تُرْجَعُونَ

3418. Revelation and the preaching of Truth may in the beginning bring persecution, conflict, and sorrow in its train; but in reality it is the truest mercy from Allah, which comes even without our expecting it, as it came to the Prophets without their consciously asking for it. This is proved in the history of Moses related in this Sūrah, and the history of the Holy Prophet which it is meant to illustrate.

3419. If Allah's Message is unpalatable to Evil and is rejected by it, those who accept it may (in their natural human feelings) sometimes wonder that such should be the case, and whether it is really Allah's Will that the conflict which ensues should be pursued. Any such hesitation would lend unconscious support to the aggressions of evil and should be discarded. The servant of Allah stands forth boldly as his *Mujāhid* (fighter of the good fight), daring all, and knowing that Allah is behind him.

3420. The soldier of Allah, having taken up the fight against Evil, and knowing that he is in touch with the true Light, never yields an inch of ground. He is always to the fore in inviting others to his own ranks, but he himself refuses to be with those who worship anything else but Allah.

3421. This sums up the lesson of the whole Sūrah. The only Eternal Reality is Allah. The whole phenomenal world is subject to flux and change and will pass away, but He will endure forever. (R).

INTRODUCTION TO SŪRAH 29—*AL 'ANKABŪT*

This Sūrah is the last of the series begun with S. 17, in which the growth of the spiritual man as an individual is considered, especially illustrated by the way in which the great Prophets were prepared for their work and received their mission, and the nature of Revelation in relation to the environments in which it was promulgated. (See Introduction to S. 17). It also closes the sub-series beginning with S. 26, which is concerned with the spiritual Light, and the reactions to it at certain periods of spiritual history. (See Introduction to S. 26.)

The last Sūrah closed with a reference to the doctrine of the *Ma'ād*, or final Return of Man to Allah. This theme is further developed here, and as it is continued in the subsequent three Sūrahs all bearing the Abbreviated Letters, "Alif Lām Mīm", it forms a connecting link between the present series and those three Sūrahs.

In particular, emphasis is laid here on the necessity of linking actual conduct with the reception of Allah's revelation, and reference is again made to the stories of Noah, Abraham, and Lot among the Prophets, and the stories of Madyan, 'Ād, Thamūd, and Pharaoh among the rejecters of Allah's Message. This world's life is contrasted with the real Life of the Hereafter.

Chronologically the main Sūrah belongs to the late Middle Makkan period, but the chronology has no significance except as showing how clearly the vision of the Future was revealed long before the Hijrah, to the struggling Brotherhood of Islam.

Summary—Belief is tested by trial in life and practical conduct: though Noah lived 950 years, his people refused Faith, and Abraham's generation threatened to burn Abraham (29:1-27, and C. 177).

Lot's people not only rejected Allah's Message but publicly defied him in sin: the 'Ād and the Thamūd had intelligence but misused it, and Qārūn, Pharaoh, and Hāmān perished for their overweening arrogance: they found their worldly power as frail as a spider's web (29:28-44, and C. 178).

The Qur'ān as a revelation stands on its own merits and is a Sign: it teaches the distinction between Right and Wrong, and shows the importance and excellence of the Hereafter (29:45-69, and C. 179).

C. 177.—Faith must be tested in the conflicts
(29:1-27.) Of practical life, but Good can never
Be submerged. On the contrary, Allah
Will wash off all stains from those
Who strive, and admit them to the Fellowship
Of the Righteous. Not so are the hypocrites
And those who reject Faith. Their hearts
Are diseased, and they will not accept
The right though a Noah preached it to them
For a thousand years, or an Abraham
Reasoned with them on Allah's most wonderful
Providence. But the true will ever search out
The Truth, and Truth will always prevail.

Sūrah 29

Al 'Ankabūt (The Spider)

الجزء العشرون سورة العنكبوت

In the name of Allah, Most Gracious Most Merciful.

بِسْمِ ٱللَّهِ ٱلرَّحْمَٰنِ ٱلرَّحِيمِ

1. Alif Lām Mīm.[3422]

الٓمٓ ١

2. Do men think that
They will be left alone
On saying, "We believe",[3423]
And that they will not
Be tested?

أَحَسِبَ ٱلنَّاسُ أَن يُتْرَكُوٓا۟ أَن يَقُولُوٓا۟ ءَامَنَّا وَهُمْ لَا يُفْتَنُونَ ٢

3. We did test those
Before them, and Allah will
Certainly know[3424] those who are
True from those who are false.

وَلَقَدْ فَتَنَّا ٱلَّذِينَ مِن قَبْلِهِمْ ۖ فَلَيَعْلَمَنَّ ٱللَّهُ ٱلَّذِينَ صَدَقُوا۟ وَلَيَعْلَمَنَّ ٱلْكَٰذِبِينَ ٣

4. Do those who practise
Evil think that they
Will get the better of Us?
Evil is their judgement![3425]

أَمْ حَسِبَ ٱلَّذِينَ يَعْمَلُونَ ٱلسَّيِّـَٔاتِ أَن يَسْبِقُونَا ۚ سَآءَ مَا يَحْكُمُونَ ٤

5. For those whose hopes are
In the meeting with Allah[3426]
(In the Hereafter, let them strive);
For the Term (appointed)

مَن كَانَ يَرْجُوا۟ لِقَآءَ ٱللَّهِ فَإِنَّ أَجَلَ ٥

3422. For these Abbreviated Letters see n. 25 to 2:1. We are asked to contrast, in our present life the real inner life against the outer life, and learn from the past about the struggles of the soul which uphold Allah's Truth, against the environment of evil which resists it, and to turn our thoughts to the *Ma'ād,* or man's future destiny in the Hereafter.

3423. Mere lip profession of Faith is not enough. It must be tried and tested in the real turmoil of life. The test will be applied in all kinds of circumstances, in individual life and in relation to the environment around us, to see whether we can strive constantly and put Allah above Self. Much pain, sorrow, and self-sacrifice may be necessary, not because they are good in themselves, but because they will purify us, like fire applied to a goldsmith's crucible to burn out the dross.

3424. The word "know" is used here more in the sense of testing than of acquiring knowledge. Allah is All-Knowing: He needs no test to increase His own knowledge, but the test is to burn out the dross within ourselves, as explained in the last note.

3425. If the enemies of Truth imagine that they will "be first" by destroying Truth before it takes root, they are sadly at fault, for their own persecution may help to plant Allah's Truth more firmly in men's hearts.

3426. The men of Faith look forward to Allah. Their quest is Allah, and the object of their hopes is the meeting with Allah. They should strive with might and main to serve Him in this life, for this life is short, and the Term appointed for their probation will soon be over.

By Allah is surely coming:[3427]
And He hears and knows
(All things).

ٱللَّهِ لَءَاتٍۚ وَهُوَ ٱلسَّمِيعُ ٱلْعَلِيمُ

6. And if any strive (with might
And main), they do so
For their own souls:[3428]
For Allah is free of all
Needs from all creation.

وَمَن جَـٰهَدَ فَإِنَّمَا يُجَـٰهِدُ لِنَفْسِهِۦٓۚ
إِنَّ ٱللَّهَ لَغَنِىٌّ عَنِ ٱلْعَـٰلَمِينَ ٦

7. Those who believe and work
Righteous deeds—from them
Shall We blot out all evil
(That may be) in them,[3429]
And We shall reward
Them according to
The best of their deeds.

وَٱلَّذِينَ ءَامَنُوا۟ وَعَمِلُوا۟ ٱلصَّـٰلِحَـٰتِ
لَنُكَفِّرَنَّ عَنْهُمْ سَيِّـَٔاتِهِمْ وَلَنَجْزِيَنَّهُمْ
أَحْسَنَ ٱلَّذِى كَانُوا۟ يَعْمَلُونَ ٧

8. We have enjoined on man
Kindness to parents: but if
They (either of them) strive
(To force) thee to join
With Me (in worship)
Anything of which thou hast
No knowledge,[3430] obey them not.
Ye have (all) to return
To Me, and I will
Tell you (the truth)
Of all that ye did.[3431]

وَوَصَّيْنَا ٱلْإِنسَـٰنَ بِوَٰلِدَيْهِ حُسْنًا ۖ
وَإِن جَـٰهَدَاكَ لِتُشْرِكَ بِى مَا لَيْسَ
لَكَ بِهِۦ عِلْمٌ فَلَا تُطِعْهُمَآ ۚ
إِلَىَّ مَرْجِعُكُمْ فَأُنَبِّئُكُم
بِمَا كُنتُمْ تَعْمَلُونَ ٨

3427. The Term (*ajal*) may signify: (1) the time appointed for death, which ends the probation of this life; (2) the time appointed for this life, so that we can prepare for the Hereafter; the limit will soon expire. In either case the ultimate meaning is the same. We must strive *now* and not postpone anything for the future. And we must realise and remember that every prayer we make to Allah is heard by Him, and that every unspoken wish or motive of our heart, good or bad, is known to Him, and goes to swell our spiritual account.

3428. All our striving enures to our own spiritual benefit. When we speak of serving Allah, it is not that we confer any benefit on Him. For He has no needs, and is independent of all His Creation. In conforming to His Will, we are seeking our own good, as in yielding to evil we are doing harm to ourselves.

3429. In striving to purify our Faith and Life, we are enabled to avoid the consequences of our misdeeds for Allah will forgive any evil in our past, purify any tendencies towards evil which we may have inherited from that past, and help to the attainment of a Future based on the best of what we have done rather than on the poor average of our own merits. The atonement or expiation is by Allah's Mercy, not by our merits or the merits or sacrifices of anyone else. (R).

3430. That is, no certainty, in virtue of the spiritual light. In matters of faith and worship, even parents have no right to force their children. They cannot and must not hold up before them any worship but that of the One True God.

3431. Children and parents must all remember that they all have to go before Allah's tribunal, and answer, each for his own deeds. In cases where one set of people have lawful authority over another set of people (as in the case of parents and children), and the two differ in important matters like that of Faith, the latter are justified in rejecting authority: the apparent conflict will be solved when the whole truth is revealed to all eyes in the Final Judgement.

9. And those who believe
And work righteous deeds—
Them shall We admit
To the company of the
Righteous.[3432]

﴿٩﴾ وَالَّذِينَ ءَامَنُوا وَعَمِلُوا الصَّلِحَتِ
لَنُدْخِلَنَّهُمْ فِي الصَّلِحِينَ

10. Then there are among men
Such as say: "We believe
In Allah"; but when they suffer
Affliction in (the cause of) Allah,
They treat men's oppression
As if it were the Wrath
Of Allah! And if help
Comes (to thee) from thy Lord,
They are sure to say,[3433]
"We have (always) been
With you!" Does not Allah
Know best all that is
In the hearts of all Creation?!

﴿١٠﴾ وَمِنَ النَّاسِ مَن يَقُولُ ءَامَنَّا بِاللَّهِ
فَإِذَا أُوذِيَ فِي اللَّهِ جَعَلَ فِتْنَةَ النَّاسِ
كَعَذَابِ اللَّهِ وَلَئِن جَاءَ نَصْرٌ مِّن رَّبِّكَ
لَيَقُولُنَّ إِنَّا كُنَّا مَعَكُمْ
أَوَلَيْسَ اللَّهُ بِأَعْلَمَ بِمَا
فِي صُدُورِ الْعَلَمِينَ

11. And Allah most certainly knows
Those who believe, and as
certainly
Those who are Hypocrites.[3434]

﴿١١﴾ وَلَيَعْلَمَنَّ اللَّهُ الَّذِينَ ءَامَنُوا
وَلَيَعْلَمَنَّ الْمُنَفِقِينَ

12. And the Unbelievers say
To those who believe:
"Follow our path, and we
Will bear (the consequences)[3435]
Of your faults." Never
In the least will they
Bear their faults: in fact
They are liars!

﴿١٢﴾ وَقَالَ الَّذِينَ كَفَرُوا لِلَّذِينَ ءَامَنُوا
اتَّبِعُوا سَبِيلَنَا وَلْنَحْمِلْ خَطَيَكُمْ وَمَا هُم
بِحَمِلِينَ مِنْ خَطَيَهُم مِّن شَيْءٍ
إِنَّهُمْ لَكَذِبُونَ

3432. The picking up again of the words which began verse 7 above shows that the same subject is now pursued from another aspect. The expiation or reward which was first spoken of is not so much a tangible thing as a restoration of status. The striving in righteous deeds will restore fallen man to the society of the Righteous—the ideal Fellowship described in 4:69 and n. 586.

3433. *Cf.* 9:56, and other passages where the cunning of the Hypocrites is exposed. The man who turns away from Faith in adversity and only claims the friendship of the Faithful when there is something to be gained by it, is worthy of a double condemnation: first because he rejected Faith and Truth, and secondly because he falsely pretended to be one of those whom he feared or hated in his heart. But nothing in all Creation is concealed from Allah.

3434. *Cf.* 29:3 above. The general opposition between Truth and Falsehood is now brought down to the specific case of the Hypocrites, who are against the Faith militant but swear friendship with it when it seems to be gaining ground. The argument is rounded off with the next two verses.

3435. Besides the hypocrite there is another type of man who openly scoffs at Faith. 'Take life as we take it,' he says: 'we shall bear your sins.' As if they could! Each soul bears its own burdens, and no one else can bear them. The principle also applies to the type of man who preaches vicarious atonement, for, if followed to its logical conclusion, it means both injustice and irresponsibility, and puts quite a different complexion on the nature of sin.

13. They will bear their own
Burdens, and (other) burdens
Along with their own,[3436]
And on the Day of Judgement
They will be called to account
For their falsehoods.

١٣ وَلَيَحۡمِلُنَّ أَثۡقَالَهُمۡ وَأَثۡقَالٗا
مَّعَ أَثۡقَالِهِمۡۖ وَلَيُسۡـَٔلُنَّ يَوۡمَ ٱلۡقِيَٰمَةِ
عَمَّا كَانُواْ يَفۡتَرُونَ

Section 2.

14. We (once) sent Noah
To his people, and he tarried
Among them a thousand years[3437]
Less fifty: but the Deluge
Overwhelmed them while they
(Persisted in) sin.

١٤ وَلَقَدۡ أَرۡسَلۡنَا نُوحًا إِلَىٰ قَوۡمِهِۦ
فَلَبِثَ فِيهِمۡ أَلۡفَ سَنَةٍ إِلَّا خَمۡسِينَ عَامٗا
فَأَخَذَهُمُ ٱلطُّوفَانُ وَهُمۡ ظَٰلِمُونَ

15. But We saved him
And the Companions
Of the Ark, and We made
The (Ark) a Sign
For all Peoples!

١٥ فَأَنجَيۡنَٰهُ وَأَصۡحَٰبَ ٱلسَّفِينَةِ
وَجَعَلۡنَٰهَآ ءَايَةٗ لِّلۡعَٰلَمِينَ

16. And (We also saved)
Abraham: behold, he said[3438]
To his people: "Serve Allah
And fear Him: that
Will be best for you—
If ye understand!

١٦ وَإِبۡرَٰهِيمَ إِذۡ قَالَ
لِقَوۡمِهِ ٱعۡبُدُواْ ٱللَّهَ وَٱتَّقُوهُۖ
ذَٰلِكُمۡ خَيۡرٞ لَّكُمۡ إِن كُنتُمۡ تَعۡلَمُونَ

17. "For ye do worship idols
Besides Allah, and ye invent
Falsehood. The things that ye
Worship besides Allah have
No power to give you sustenance:

١٧ إِنَّمَا تَعۡبُدُونَ مِن دُونِ ٱللَّهِ أَوۡثَٰنٗا
وَتَخۡلُقُونَ إِفۡكًاۚ إِنَّ ٱلَّذِينَ تَعۡبُدُونَ مِن
دُونِ ٱللَّهِ لَا يَمۡلِكُونَ لَكُمۡ رِزۡقٗا

3436. Besides the burdens of their own infidelity, they will bear the burden of deluding others with falsehood.

3437. The story of Noah and his Flood is not told here. It is told in other places: *e.g.*, see 11:25-48 or 26:105-22. It is only referred to here to point out that Noah's period lasted a long time, 950 years. (*Cf.* Gen. ix. 28-29, where his whole age is declared to have been 950 years, of which 350 years were after the Flood). In spite of this long period, his contemporaries failed to listen, and they were destroyed. but the story of the Ark remains an everlasting Sign and Warning to mankind—a Sign of deliverance to the righteous and of destruction to the wicked.

3438. The story of Abraham has been told in various phases in different passages. The ones most germane to the present passage are: 21:51-72 (his being cast into the fire and being saved from it); and 19:41-49 (his voluntary exile from the home of his fathers). Here the story is not told but is referred to in order to stress the following points; (1) Abraham's people only responded to his preaching by threatening to burn him (29:16-18, 24); (2) evil consorts with evil but will have a rude awakening (29:25); (3) the good adhere to the good, and are blessed (29:26-27). Note that the passage 29:19-23 is a parenthetical comment, though some Commentators treat a portion of it as part of Abraham's speech.

Then seek ye sustenance[3439]
From Allah, serve Him,
And be grateful to Him:
To Him will be your return.

فَٱبْتَغُوا۟ عِندَ ٱللَّهِ ٱلرِّزْقَ وَٱعْبُدُوهُ وَٱشْكُرُوا۟ لَهُۥٓ ۖ إِلَيْهِ تُرْجَعُونَ

18. "And if ye reject (the Message),
So did generations before you:
And the duty of the messenger
Is only to preach publicly
(And clearly)."

١٨ وَإِن تُكَذِّبُوا۟ فَقَدْ كَذَّبَ أُمَمٌ مِّن قَبْلِكُمْ ۖ وَمَا عَلَى ٱلرَّسُولِ إِلَّا ٱلْبَلَـٰغُ ٱلْمُبِينُ

19. See they not how Allah
Originates creation, then[3440]
Repeats it: truly that
Is easy for Allah.

١٩ أَوَلَمْ يَرَوْا۟ كَيْفَ يُبْدِئُ ٱللَّهُ ٱلْخَلْقَ ثُمَّ يُعِيدُهُۥٓ ۚ إِنَّ ذَٰلِكَ عَلَى ٱللَّهِ يَسِيرٌ

20. Say: "Travel through the earth[3441]
And see how Allah did
Originate creation; so will
Allah produce a later creation:
For Allah has power
Over all things.

٢٠ قُلْ سِيرُوا۟ فِى ٱلْأَرْضِ فَٱنظُرُوا۟ كَيْفَ بَدَأَ ٱلْخَلْقَ ۚ ثُمَّ ٱللَّهُ يُنشِئُ ٱلنَّشْأَةَ ٱلْـَٔاخِرَةَ ۚ إِنَّ ٱللَّهَ عَلَىٰ كُلِّ شَىْءٍ قَدِيرٌ

21. "He punishes whom He pleases,
And He grants mercy to whom
He pleases, and towards Him
Are ye turned.[3442]

٢١ يُعَذِّبُ مَن يَشَآءُ وَيَرْحَمُ مَن يَشَآءُ ۖ وَإِلَيْهِ تُقْلَبُونَ

3439. *Sustenance*: in the symbolic as well as the literal sense. Seek from Allah all that is necessary for your upkeep and development, and for preparing you for your future Destiny. Lay all your hopes in Him and in no one else. Dedicate yourselves to His worship. He will give you all that is necessary for your growth and well being, and you should show your gratitude to Him by conforming your will entirely to His.

3440. The originating of creation is the creation of primeval matter. The repetition of the process of creation goes on constantly, for at every moment new processes are being called into being by the creative power of Allah, and according to His Laws. And the final creation as far as man is concerned will be in the *Ma'ād*, when the whole world as man sees it will be entirely newly created on a different plane. As far as Allah is concerned, there is nothing final—no first and last, for He is infinite. He was before our First and will be after our Last, and if there is any meaning in these relative terms, He is the real First and the real Last.

3441. *Travel through the earth*: again, literally as well as symbolically. If we actually go through this wide earth, we shall see the wonderful things in His Creation—the Grand Canyon and the Niagaras in North America, beautiful harbours like that at Sydney in Australia, mountains like Fujiyama, the Himalayas, and Elburz in Asia, the Nile with its wonderful cataracts in Africa, the Fiords of Norway, the Geysers of Iceland, the city of the midnight sun in Tromsoe, and innumerable wonders everywhere. But wonders upon wonders are disclosed in the constitution of matter itself, the atom, and the forces of energy, as also in the instincts of animals, and the minds and capacities of man. And there is no limit to these things. Worlds upon worlds are created and transformed every moment, within and presumably beyond man's vision. From what we know we can judge of the unknown.

3442. I think *ilayhi tuqlabūn* is better translated "towards Him are ye turned" than "towards Him will be your return", as it implies not only the return of man to Allah in the Hereafter (*turja'un* in verse 17 above) but also the fact explained in verse 22 that man's needs are always to be obtained from Allah: man cannot frustrate Allah's designs, and can have no help or protection except from Allah: man has always to face Allah, whether man obeys Allah or tries to ignore Allah. Man will never be able to defeat Allah's Plan. According to His wise Will and Plan, He will grant His grace or withhold it from man.

22. "Not on earth nor in heaven
Will ye be able (fleeing)
To frustrate (His Plan),
Nor have ye, besides Allah,
Any protector or helper."

٢٢ وَمَآ أَنتُم بِمُعْجِزِينَ فِى ٱلْأَرْضِ
وَلَا فِى ٱلسَّمَآءِ ۖ وَمَا لَكُم مِّن دُونِ ٱللَّهِ
مِن وَلِىٍّ وَلَا نَصِيرٍ

SECTION 3.

23. Those who reject the Signs
Of Allah and the Meeting
With Him (in the Hereafter)—
It is they who shall despair
Of My mercy: it is they[3343]
Who will (suffer)
A most grievous Penalty.

٢٣ وَٱلَّذِينَ كَفَرُوا۟
بِـَٔايَٰتِ ٱللَّهِ وَلِقَآئِهِۦٓ
أُو۟لَٰٓئِكَ يَئِسُوا۟ مِن رَّحْمَتِى
وَأُو۟لَٰٓئِكَ لَهُمْ عَذَابٌ أَلِيمٌ

24. So naught was the answer
Of (Abraham's) people except
That they said: "Slay him
Or burn him." But Allah
Did save him from the Fire.[3444]
Verily in this are Signs
For people who believe.

٢٤ فَمَا كَانَ جَوَابَ قَوْمِهِۦٓ
إِلَّآ أَن قَالُوا۟ ٱقْتُلُوهُ أَوْ حَرِّقُوهُ
فَأَنجَىٰهُ ٱللَّهُ مِنَ ٱلنَّارِ
إِنَّ فِى ذَٰلِكَ لَءَايَٰتٍ لِّقَوْمٍ يُؤْمِنُونَ

25. And he said: "For you,
Ye have taken (for worship)
Idols besides Allah, out of
Mutual love and regard[3445]
Between yourselves in this life;
But on the Day of Judgement
Ye shall disown each other
And curse each other:
And your abode will be

٢٥ وَقَالَ إِنَّمَا ٱتَّخَذْتُم مِّن دُونِ ٱللَّهِ
أَوْثَٰنًا مَّوَدَّةَ بَيْنِكُمْ فِى ٱلْحَيَوٰةِ ٱلدُّنْيَا ۖ
ثُمَّ يَوْمَ ٱلْقِيَٰمَةِ يَكْفُرُ بَعْضُكُم بِبَعْضٍ
وَيَلْعَنُ بَعْضُكُم بَعْضًا
وَمَأْوَىٰكُمُ

3443. The emphasis is on "*they*" (*ūlā'ika*). It is only the people who ignore or reject Allah's Signs and reject a Hereafter, that will find themselves in despair and suffering. Allah's mercy is open to all, but if any reject His Mercy, they must suffer.

3444. See 21:66-70. Abraham was cast into the fire, but he was unhurt, by the grace of Allah. So righteous people suffer no harm from the plots of the wicked. But they must leave the environment of evil even if they have to forsake their ancestral home, as Abraham did.

3445. In sin and wickedness there is as much log-rolling as in politics. Evil men humour each other and support each other; they call each other's vice by high-sounding names. They call it mutual regard or friendship or love; at the lowest, they call it toleration. Perhaps they flourish in this life by such arts. But they deceive themselves, and they deceive each other. What will be their relations in the Hereafter? They will disown each other when each has to answer on the principle of personal responsibility. Each will accuse the others of misleading him, and they will curse each other. But there will then be no help, and they must suffer in the Fire.

The Fire, and ye shall have
None to help."

ٱلنَّارُ وَمَا لَكُم مِّن نَّٰصِرِينَ

26. But Lūṭ had faith in him:[3446]
He said: "I will leave
Home for the sake of
My Lord: for He is
Exalted in Might, and Wise."

۞٢٦ فَـَٔامَنَ لَهُۥ لُوطٌ
وَقَالَ إِنِّى مُهَاجِرٌ إِلَىٰ رَبِّىٓ
إِنَّهُۥ هُوَ ٱلْعَزِيزُ ٱلْحَكِيمُ

27. And We gave (Abraham)
Isaac and Jacob, and ordained
Among his progeny
Prophethood[3447]
And Revelation, and We
Granted him his reward
In this life; and he was
In the Hereafter (of the company)
Of the Righteous.[3448]

۞٢٧ وَوَهَبْنَا لَهُۥٓ إِسْحَٰقَ وَيَعْقُوبَ
وَجَعَلْنَا فِى ذُرِّيَّتِهِ ٱلنُّبُوَّةَ وَٱلْكِتَٰبَ
وَءَاتَيْنَٰهُ أَجْرَهُۥ فِى ٱلدُّنْيَا
وَإِنَّهُۥ فِى ٱلْءَاخِرَةِ
لَمِنَ ٱلصَّٰلِحِينَ

C. 178. — Worldly power cannot through sin
(29:28-44.) Defy the right, as was proved in the ministry
Of Lūṭ; nor can Intelligence misused
Stand in the place of Allah's Light; nor
Can boastful insolence do aught
But dig its own grave. The strength
And skill, the beauty and power, of this world's
Life are no more than a Spider's Web,
Flimsy before the force of the eternal
Verities that flow from Allah Supreme!

28. And (remember) Lūṭ: behold,
He said to his people:
"Ye do commit lewdness,
Such as no people in Creation[3349]
(Ever) committed before you.

۞٢٨ وَلُوطًا إِذْ قَالَ لِقَوْمِهِۦٓ إِنَّكُمْ
لَتَأْتُونَ ٱلْفَٰحِشَةَ مَا سَبَقَكُم
بِهَا مِنْ أَحَدٍ مِّنَ ٱلْعَٰلَمِينَ

3446. Lūṭ was a nephew of Abraham. He adhered to Abraham's teaching and faith and accepted voluntary exile with him, for Abraham left the home of his fathers in Chaldaea and migrated to Syria and Palestine, where Allah gave him increase and prosperity, and a numerous family, who upheld the flag of Unity and the Light of Allah.

3447. Isaac was Abraham's son and Jacob his grandson, and among his progeny was included Ismā'īl the eldest son of Abraham. Each of these became a fountainhead of Prophecy and Revelation. Isaac and Jacob through Moses, and Ismā'īl through the Holy Prophet Muḥammad. Jacob got the name of "Israel" at Bethel: Gen. 32; 28; 35:10; and his progeny got the title of "The Children of Israel".

3448. *Cf.* 29:9, and 4:69, n.586.

3449. *Cf.* 7:80. A discreet reference is made to their unspeakable crimes, which were against the laws of nature.

29. "Do ye indeed approach men,
And cut off the highway?—[3450]
And practise wickedness
(Even) in your councils?"
But his people gave no answer
But this: they said:
"Bring us the Wrath of Allah
If thou tellest the truth."[3451]

﴿٢٩﴾ أَيِنَّكُمْ لَتَأْتُونَ ٱلرِّجَالَ وَتَقْطَعُونَ
ٱلسَّبِيلَ وَتَأْتُونَ فِى نَادِيكُمُ ٱلْمُنكَرَ ۖ
فَمَا كَانَ جَوَابَ قَوْمِهِۦٓ إِلَّآ أَن قَالُوا۟ ٱئْتِنَا
بِعَذَابِ ٱللَّهِ إِن كُنتَ مِنَ ٱلصَّٰدِقِينَ

30. He said: "O my Lord!
Help Thou me against people
Who do mischief!"

﴿٣٠﴾ قَالَ رَبِّ ٱنصُرْنِى
عَلَى ٱلْقَوْمِ ٱلْمُفْسِدِينَ

SECTION 4.

31. When Our Messengers came
To Abraham with the good
news,[3452]
They said: "We are indeed
Going to destroy the people
Of this township:[3453] for truly
They are (addicted to) crime."

﴿٣١﴾ وَلَمَّا جَآءَتْ رُسُلُنَآ إِبْرَٰهِيمَ بِٱلْبُشْرَىٰ
قَالُوٓا۟ إِنَّا مُهْلِكُوٓا۟ أَهْلِ هَٰذِهِ ٱلْقَرْيَةِ ۖ
إِنَّ أَهْلَهَا كَانُوا۟ ظَٰلِمِينَ

32. He said: "But there is
Lūṭ there." They said:
"Well do we know who
Is there: we will certainly
Save him and his following—
Except his wife: she is
Of those who lag behind!"[3454]

﴿٣٢﴾ قَالَ إِنَّ فِيهَا لُوطًا ۚ
قَالُوا۟ نَحْنُ أَعْلَمُ بِمَن فِيهَا ۖ
لَنُنَجِّيَنَّهُۥ وَأَهْلَهُۥٓ إِلَّا ٱمْرَأَتَهُۥ
كَانَتْ مِنَ ٱلْغَٰبِرِينَ

3450. They infested highways and committed their horrible crimes not only secretly, but openly and publicly, even in their assemblies. Some Commentators understand "cutting off the highway" to refer to highway robberies; this is possible, and it is also possible that the crimes in their assemblies may have been injustice, rowdiness, etc. But the context seems to refer to their own special horrible crime, and the point here seems to be that they were not ashamed of it and that they practised it publicly. Degradation could go no further.

3451. This is another instance of their effrontery, in addition to that mentioned in 7:82: the two supplement each other. Here the point emphasised is that they did not believe in Allah or His Punishment, and dared Allah's Prophet Lūṭ to bring about the Punishment if he could. And it did come and destroy them.

3452. See 11:69-76. The angels, who were coming on the mission to destroy the people who were polluting the earth with their crimes, called on their way on Abraham to give the good news of the birth of a son to him in his old age. When they told him their destination, he feared for his nephew who he knew was there. They reassured him and then came on to Lūṭ.

3453. By translating "township" I imply the two neighbouring populations of Sodom and Gomorrah, who had already gone too far in their crime, their shamelessness, and their defiance, to profit by any mercy from Allah.

3454. She was not loyal to her husband. Tradition says that she belonged to the wicked people, and was not prepared to leave them. She had no faith in the mission either of her husband or of the angels who had come as his guests.

33. And when Our Messengers
Came to Lūṭ, he was
Grieved on their account,
And felt himself powerless[3455]
(To protect) them: but they said:
"Fear thou not, nor grieve:
We are (here) to save thee
And thy following, except
Thy wife: she is
Of those who lag behind.

٣٣ وَلَمَّآ أَن جَآءَتۡ رُسُلُنَا لُوطٗا
سِيٓءَ بِهِمۡ وَضَاقَ بِهِمۡ ذَرۡعٗا
وَقَالُواْ لَا تَخَفۡ وَلَا تَحۡزَنۡ
إِنَّا مُنَجُّوكَ وَأَهۡلَكَ إِلَّا ٱمۡرَأَتَكَ
كَانَتۡ مِنَ ٱلۡغَٰبِرِينَ

34. "For we are going to
Bring down on the people
Of this township a Punishment[3456]
From heaven, because they
Have been wickedly rebellious."

٣٤ إِنَّا مُنزِلُونَ عَلَىٰٓ أَهۡلِ هَٰذِهِ ٱلۡقَرۡيَةِ
رِجۡزٗا مِّنَ ٱلسَّمَآءِ بِمَا كَانُواْ يَفۡسُقُونَ

35. And We have left thereof
An evident Sign,[3457]
For any people who
(Care to) understand.

٣٥ وَلَقَد تَّرَكۡنَا مِنۡهَآ ءَايَةَۢ
بَيِّنَةٗ لِّقَوۡمٖ يَعۡقِلُونَ

36. To the Madyan (people)
(We sent) their brother Shu'ayb.
Then he said: "O my people!
Serve Allah, and fear the Last
Day: nor commit evil
On the earth, with intent
To do mischief."

٣٦ وَإِلَىٰ مَدۡيَنَ أَخَاهُمۡ شُعَيۡبٗا فَقَالَ
يَٰقَوۡمِ ٱعۡبُدُواْ ٱللَّهَ وَٱرۡجُواْ ٱلۡيَوۡمَ ٱلۡأٓخِرَ
وَلَا تَعۡثَوۡاْ فِي ٱلۡأَرۡضِ مُفۡسِدِينَ

37. But they rejected him:
Then the mighty Blast[3458]
Seized them, and they lay
Prostrate in their homes
By the morning.

٣٧ فَكَذَّبُوهُ فَأَخَذَتۡهُمُ ٱلرَّجۡفَةُ
فَأَصۡبَحُواْ فِي دَارِهِمۡ جَٰثِمِينَ

3455. This part of the story may be read in greater detail in 11:77-83.

3456. The Punishment was a rain of brimstone, which completely overwhelmed the Cities, with possibly an earthquake and a volcanic eruption (see 11:82).

3457. The whole tract on the east side of the Dead Sea (where the Cities were situated) is covered with sulphurous salts and is deadly to animal and plant life. The Dead Sea itself is called in Arabic the Baḥr Lūṭ (the sea of Lot). It is a scene of utter desolation, that should stand as a Symbol of the Destruction that awaits Sin.

3458. The story of Shu'ayb and the Madyan people is only referred to here. It is told in 11:84-95. Their besetting sin was fraud and commercial immorality. Their punishment was a mighty Blast, such as accompanies volcanic eruptions. The point of the reference here is that they went about doing mischief on the earth, and never thought of the *Ma'ād* or the Hereafter, the particular theme of this Sūrah. The same point is made by the brief references in the following two verses to the 'Ād and the Thamūd, and to Qārūn, Pharaoh, and Hāmān, though the besetting sin in each case was different. The Midianites were a commercial people and trafficked from land to land; their frauds are well described as spreading "mischief on the earth".

38. (Remember also) the 'Ād
And the T̲hamūd (people):[3459]
Clearly will appear to you
From (the traces) of their buildings
(Their fate): the Evil One
Made their deeds alluring[3460]
To them, and kept them back
From the Path, though they
Were gifted with Intelligence
And Skill.

وَعَادًا وَثَمُودَا۟ وَقَد ﴿٣٨﴾
تَّبَيَّنَ لَكُم مِّن مَّسَٰكِنِهِمْ ۖ
وَزَيَّنَ لَهُمُ ٱلشَّيْطَٰنُ أَعْمَٰلَهُمْ
فَصَدَّهُمْ عَنِ ٱلسَّبِيلِ وَكَانُوا۟ مُسْتَبْصِرِينَ

39. (Remember also) Qārūn,[3461]
Pharaoh, and Hāmān: there came
To them Moses with Clear Signs,
But they behaved with insolence
On the earth; yet they
Could not overreach (Us).

وَقَٰرُونَ وَفِرْعَوْنَ وَهَٰمَٰنَ ۖ ﴿٣٩﴾
وَلَقَدْ جَآءَهُم مُّوسَىٰ بِٱلْبَيِّنَٰتِ
فَٱسْتَكْبَرُوا۟ فِى ٱلْأَرْضِ وَمَا كَانُوا۟ سَٰبِقِينَ

40. Each one of them We seized
For his crime: of them,
Against some We sent
A violent tornado (with showers[3462]
Of stones); some were caught
By a (mighty) Blast;[3463] some
We caused the earth[3464]
To swallow up; and some
We drowned (in the waters):[3465]
It was not Allah Who
Injured (or oppressed) them:

فَكُلًّا أَخَذْنَا بِذَنۢبِهِۦ ۖ ﴿٤٠﴾
فَمِنْهُم مَّنْ أَرْسَلْنَا عَلَيْهِ حَاصِبًا
وَمِنْهُم مَّنْ أَخَذَتْهُ ٱلصَّيْحَةُ وَمِنْهُم مَّنْ
خَسَفْنَا بِهِ ٱلْأَرْضَ وَمِنْهُم مَّنْ أَغْرَقْنَا ۚ
وَمَا كَانَ ٱللَّهُ لِيَظْلِمَهُمْ

3459. For the 'Ād people see 7:65-72, and n. 1040, and for the T̲hamūd, 7:73-79, and n.1043. The remains of their buildings show (1) that they were gifted with great intelligence and skill; (2) that they were proud of their material civilisation; and (3) their destruction argues how the greatest material civilisation and resources cannot save a People who disobey Allah's moral law.

3460. They were so arrogant and self-satisfied, that they missed the higher purpose of life, and strayed clean away from the Path of Allah. Though their intelligence should have kept them straight, Evil made them crooked and led them and kept them astray.

3461. For Qārūn see 28:76-82; Pharaoh is mentioned frequently in the Qur'ān, but he is mentioned in association with Hāmān in 28:6; for their blasphemous arrogance and defiance of Allah see 28:38. They thought such a lot of themselves, but they came to an evil end.

3462. For *ḥāṣib* (violent tornado with showers of stones), see 17:68: this punishment as inflicted on the Cities of the Plain, to which Lot preached (54:34). Some Commentators think that this also applied to the 'Ād, but their punishment is described as by a violent and unseasonable cold wind (41:16; 54:19 and 69:6), such as blows in sand storms in the Aḥqāf, the region of shifting sands which was in their territory.

3463. For *ṣayḥah* (Blast) see 11:67 and n. 1561, as also n. 1047 to 7:78 and n. 1996 to 15:73. This word is used in describing the fate of (1) the T̲hamūd (11:67); Madyan (11:94); the population to which Lūṭ preached (15:73); and the *Al Ḥijr* (15:3), part of the territory of the T̲hamūd; also in the Parable of the City to which came the three Prophets, who found a single believer (36:29).

3464. This was the fate of Qārūn: see 28:81. *Cf.* also 16:45 and n. 2071.

3465. This was the fate of the hosts of Pharaoh and Hāmān (28:40) as well as the wicked generation of Noah (26:120).

They injured (and oppressed)
Their own souls.

وَلَٰكِن كَانُوٓا۟ أَنفُسَهُمْ يَظْلِمُونَ

41. The parable of those who
Take protectors other than Allah
Is that of the Spider,
Who builds (to itself)
A house; but truly
The flimsiest of houses[3466]
Is the Spider's house—[3467]
If they but knew.

٤١ مَثَلُ ٱلَّذِينَ ٱتَّخَذُوا۟ مِن دُونِ ٱللَّهِ
أَوْلِيَآءَ كَمَثَلِ ٱلْعَنكَبُوتِ ٱتَّخَذَتْ بَيْتًا ۖ
وَإِنَّ أَوْهَنَ ٱلْبُيُوتِ لَبَيْتُ ٱلْعَنكَبُوتِ ۖ
لَوْ كَانُوا۟ يَعْلَمُونَ

42. Verily Allah doth know
Of (every thing) whatever[3468]
That they call upon
Besides Him: and He is
Exalted (in power), Wise.

٤٢ إِنَّ ٱللَّهَ يَعْلَمُ مَا يَدْعُونَ
مِن دُونِهِۦ مِن شَىْءٍ ۚ
وَهُوَ ٱلْعَزِيزُ ٱلْحَكِيمُ

43. And such are the Parables
We set forth for mankind,
But only those understand them
Who have Knowledge.[3469]

٤٣ وَتِلْكَ ٱلْأَمْثَٰلُ نَضْرِبُهَا لِلنَّاسِ ۖ
وَمَا يَعْقِلُهَآ إِلَّا ٱلْعَٰلِمُونَ

3466. The Spider's house is one of the wonderful Signs of Allah's creation. It is made up of fine silk threads spun out of silk glands in the spider's body. There are many kinds of spiders and many kinds of spider houses. Two main types of houses may be mentioned. There is the tubular nest or web, a silk-lined house or burrow with one or two trap doors. This may be called his residential or family mansion. Then there is what is ordinarily called a spider's web, consisting of a central point with radiating threads running in all directions and acting as tie-beams to the quasi-circular concentric threads that form the body of the web. This is his hunting box. The whole structure exemplifies economy in time, material, and strength. If an insect is caught in the net, the vibration set up in the radiating threads is at once communicated to the spider, who can come and kill his prey. In case the prey is powerful, the spider is furnished with poison glands with which to kill his prey. The spider sits either in the centre of the web or hides on the underside of a leaf or in some crevice, but he always has a single thread connecting him with his web, to keep him in telephonic communication. The female spider is much bigger than the male, and in Arabic the generic gender of *'Ankabūt* is feminine.

3467. Most of the facts in the last note can be read into the Parable. For their thickness, the spider's threads are very strong from the point of view of relativity, but in our actual world they are flimsy, especially the threads of the gossamer spider floating in the air. So is the house and strength of the man who relies on material resources however fine or beautiful relatively; before the eternal Reality they are as nothing. The spider's most cunning architecture cannot stand against a wave of man's hand. His poison glands are like the hidden poison in our beautiful worldly plants which may take various shapes but have seeds of death in them.

3468. The last verse told us that men, out of spiritual ignorance, build their hopes on flimsy unsubstantial things (like the spider's web) which are broken by a thousand chance attacks of wind and weather or the actions of animals or men. If they cannot fully grasp their own good, they should seek His Light. To Him everything is known—men's frailty, their false hopes, their questionable motives, the false gods whom they enthrone in their midst, the mischief done by the neglect of Truth, and the way out for those who have entangled themselves in the snares of Evil. He is All-Wise and is able to carry out all He wills, and they should turn to Him.

3469. Parables seem simple things, but their profound meaning and application can only be understood by those who seek knowledge and by Allah's grace attain it.

44. Allah created the heavens
And the earth in true
(proportions):[3470]
Verily in that is a Sign
For those who believe.

٤٤ خَلَقَ ٱللَّهُ ٱلسَّمَٰوَٰتِ وَٱلْأَرْضَ بِٱلْحَقِّ
إِنَّ فِى ذَٰلِكَ لَءَايَةً لِّلْمُؤْمِنِينَ

C. 179.—Proclaim the Message of Allah, and pray
(29:45-69.) To Him for purity and guidance.
Allah's Revelation carries its own
Proofs and is recognised by men
Of wisdom. Its rejecters but lose
Their own chances of profiting
By the Truth, and attaining the Paths
That lead to Allah's own gracious Presence!

SECTION 5.

45. Recite what is sent[3471]
Of the Book by inspiration
To thee, and establish
Regular Prayer: for Prayer
Restrains from shameful
And unjust deeds;
And remembrance of Allah
Is the greatest (thing in life)
Without doubt. And Allah knows
The (deeds) that ye do.

٤٥ ٱتْلُ مَآ أُوحِىَ إِلَيْكَ مِنَ ٱلْكِتَٰبِ
وَأَقِمِ ٱلصَّلَوٰةَ إِنَّ ٱلصَّلَوٰةَ تَنْهَىٰ
عَنِ ٱلْفَحْشَآءِ وَٱلْمُنكَرِ
وَلَذِكْرُ ٱللَّهِ أَكْبَرُ
وَٱللَّهُ يَعْلَمُ مَا تَصْنَعُونَ

21/30

46. And dispute ye not
With the People of the Book,
Except with means better[3472]
(Than mere disputation), unless
It be with those of them

٤٦ وَلَا تُجَٰدِلُوٓا۟ أَهْلَ ٱلْكِتَٰبِ
إِلَّا بِٱلَّتِى هِىَ أَحْسَنُ إِلَّا ٱلَّذِينَ

3470. *Cf.* 6:73 and n. 896. In all Allah's Creation, not only is there evidence of intelligent Purpose, fitting all parts together with wisdom, but also of supreme Goodness and cherishing Care, by which all needs are satisfied and all the highest and truest cravings fulfilled. These are like beckoning signals to lead on those who pray and search in Faith, those who with the most intense desire of their soul can pray, as in Cardinal Newman's Hymn, "Lead, kindly Light! Amid the encircling gloom, lead Thou me on!"

3471. The *tilāwat* of the Qur'ān implies: (1) rehearsing or reciting it, and publishing it abroad to the world; (2) reading it to ourselves; (3) studying it to understand it as it should be studied and understood (2:121); (4) meditating on it so as to accord our knowledge and life and desires with it. When this is done, it merges into real Prayer, and Prayer purges us of anything (act, plan, thought, motive, words) of which we should be ashamed or which would work injustice to others. Such Prayer passes into our inmost life and being, for then we realise the Presence of Allah, and that is true *dhikr* (or remembrance), for remembrance is the bringing to mind of things as present to us which might otherwise be absent to us. And that is the greatest thing in life. It is subjective to us: it fills our consciousness with Allah. For Allah is in any case always present and knows all.

3472. Mere disputations are futile. In order to achieve our purpose as true standard-bearers for Allah, we shall have to find true common grounds of belief, as stated in the latter part of this verse, and also to show by our urbanity, kindness, sincerity, truth, and genuine anxiety, for the good of others, that we are not cranks or merely seeking selfish or questionable aims.

Who inflict wrong (and injury);[3473]
But say, "We believe
In the Revelation which has
Come down to us and in that
Which came down to you;
Our God and your God
Is One; and it is to Him
We bow (in Islam)."[3474]

ظَلَمُوا۟ مِنْهُمْ ۖ
وَقُولُوٓا۟ ءَامَنَّا بِٱلَّذِىٓ أُنزِلَ إِلَيْنَا وَأُنزِلَ
إِلَيْكُمْ وَإِلَـٰهُنَا وَإِلَـٰهُكُمْ وَٰحِدٌ
وَنَحْنُ لَهُۥ مُسْلِمُونَ

47. And thus[3475] (it is) that We
Have sent down the Book
To thee. So the People
Of the Book believe therein,[3476]
As also do some of these[3477]
(Pagan Arabs): and none
But Unbelievers reject Our Signs.

(٤٧) وَكَذَٰلِكَ أَنزَلْنَآ إِلَيْكَ ٱلْكِتَـٰبَ ۚ
فَٱلَّذِينَ ءَاتَيْنَـٰهُمُ ٱلْكِتَـٰبَ يُؤْمِنُونَ بِهِۦ ۖ
وَمِنْ هَـٰٓؤُلَآءِ مَن يُؤْمِنُ بِهِۦ ۚ وَمَا يَجْحَدُ
بِـَٔايَـٰتِنَآ إِلَّا ٱلْكَـٰفِرُونَ

48. And thou wast not (able)
To recite a Book before
This (Book came), nor art thou
(Able) to transcribe it

(٤٨) وَمَا كُنتَ تَتْلُوا۟
مِن قَبْلِهِۦ مِن كِتَـٰبٍ وَلَا تَخُطُّهُۥ

3473. Of course those who are deliberately trying to wrong or injure others will have to be treated firmly, as we are guardians of each other. With them, there is little question of finding common ground or exercising patience, until the injury is prevented or stopped.

3474. That is, the religion of all true and sincere men of Faith is, or should be, one; and that is the ideal of Islam.

3475. It is in this spirit that all true Revelation comes from Allah. Allah is One, and His Message cannot come in one place or at one time to contradict His Message in another place or at another time in spirit, though there may be local variations according to the needs or understanding of men at any given time or place.

3476. The sincere Jews and Christians found in the Holy Prophet a fulfillment of their own religion. For the names of some Jews who recognised and embraced Islam, see n. 3227 to 26:197. Among the Christians, too, the Faith slowly won ground. Embassies were sent by the Holy Prophet in the 6th and 7th years of the Hijrah to all the principal countries around Arabia, *viz.*, the capital of the Byzantine Empire (Constantinople), the capital of the Persian Empire (Madā'in), the Sāsānian capital known to the West by the Greek name of Ctesiphon, (about thirty miles south of modern Baghdād), Syria, Abyssinia, and Egypt. All these (except Persia) were Christian countries. In the same connection, an embassy was also sent to Yamāmah in Arabia itself (east of the Ḥijāz) where the Banū Ḥanīfah tribe was Christian, like the Ḥārith tribe of Najrān who voluntarily sent an embassy to Madīnah. All these countries except Abyssinia eventually became Muslim, and Abyssinia itself has a considerable Muslim population now and sent some Muslim converts to Madīnah in the time of the Prophet himself. As a generalisation, it is true that the Jewish and the Christian peoples as they existed in the seventh century of the Christian era have been mainly absorbed by Islam, as well as the lands in which they predominated. Remnants of them built up new nuclei. The Roman Catholic Church conquered new lands among the northern (Germanic) Pagans and the Byzantine Church among the eastern (Slavonic) Pagans, and the Protestantism of the 16th century gave a fresh stimulus to the main ideas for which Islam stands, *viz.*, the abolition of priestcraft, the right of private judgement, the simplification of ritual, and the insistence upon the simple, practical, everyday duties of life.

3477. The Pagan Arabs also gradually came in until they were all absorbed in Islam.

With thy right hand:[3478]
In that case, indeed, would
The talkers of vanities
Have doubted.

بِيَمِينِكَ
إِذًا لَّارْتَابَ الْمُبْطِلُونَ

49. Nay, here are Signs
Self-evident in the hearts
Of those endowed with
knowledge:[3479]
And none but the unjust
Rejects Our Signs.[3480]

٤٩ بَلْ هُوَ ءَايَٰتٌۢ بَيِّنَٰتٌ
فِي صُدُورِ الَّذِينَ أُوتُوا الْعِلْمَ
وَمَا يَجْحَدُ بِـَٔايَٰتِنَآ إِلَّا الظَّٰلِمُونَ

50. Yet they say: "Why
Are not Signs sent down
To him from his Lord?"
Say: "The Signs are indeed
With Allah: and I am
Indeed a clear Warner."[3481]

٥٠ وَقَالُوا لَوْلَآ أُنزِلَ عَلَيْهِ ءَايَٰتٌ مِّن رَّبِّهِۦ
قُلْ إِنَّمَا الْـَٔايَٰتُ عِندَ اللَّهِ
وَإِنَّمَآ أَنَا۠ نَذِيرٌ مُّبِينٌ

51. And is it not enough
For them that We have
Sent down to thee
The Book which is rehearsed
To them? Verily, in it
Is Mercy and a Reminder
To those who believe.[3482]

٥١ أَوَلَمْ يَكْفِهِمْ أَنَّآ أَنزَلْنَا
عَلَيْكَ الْكِتَٰبَ يُتْلَىٰ عَلَيْهِمْ
إِنَّ فِي ذَٰلِكَ لَرَحْمَةً وَذِكْرَىٰ
لِقَوْمٍ يُؤْمِنُونَ

3478. The Holy Prophet was not a learned man. Before the Qur'ān was revealed to him, he never claimed to proclaim a Message from Allah. He was not in the habit of preaching eloquent truths as from a Book, before he received his Revelations, nor was he able to write or transcribe with his own hand. If he had had these worldly gifts, there would have been some plausibility in the charge of the talkers of vanities that he spoke not from inspiration but from other people's books, or that he composed the beautiful verses of the Qur'ān himself and committed them to memory in order to recite them to people. The circumstance in which the Qur'ān came bear their own testimony to its truth as from Allah.

3479. "Knowledge" (*'ilm*) means both power of judgement in discerning the value of truth and acquaintance with previous revelations. It implies both literary and spiritual insight. To men so endowed, Allah's revelations and Signs are self-evident. They commend themselves to their hearts, minds, and understandings, which are typified in Arabic by the word *ṣadr*, "breast".

3480. *Cf.* the last clause of verse 47 above. There the argument was that the rejection of the Qur'ān was a mark of Unbelief. Now the argument is carried a stage farther. Such rejection is also a mark of injustice, a deliberate perversity in going against obvious Signs, which should convince all honest men.

3481. See last note. In the Qur'ān, as said in verse 49, are Signs which should carry conviction to all honest hearts. And yet the Unbelievers ask for Signs! They mean some special kinds of Signs or Miracles, such as their own foolish minds dictate. Everything is possible for Allah, but Allah is not going to humour the follies of men or listen to their disingenuous demands. He has sent a Messenger to explain His Signs clearly, and to warn them of the consequences of rejections. Is it not enough?

3482. The perspicuous Qur'ān, as explained in detail by Allah's Messenger, in conjunction with Allah's Signs in nature and in the hearts of men, should be enough for all. It is mere fractious opposition to demand vaguely something more. *Cf.* also 6:124, and n. 946.

SECTION 6.

52. Say: "Enough is Allah
For a Witness between me
And you: He knows
What is in the heavens[3483]
And on earth. And it is
Those who believe in vanities
And reject Allah, that
Will perish (in the end).[3484]

٥٢ قُلْ كَفَىٰ بِٱللَّهِ بَيْنِى وَبَيْنَكُمْ شَهِيدًا ۖ
يَعْلَمُ مَا فِى ٱلسَّمَٰوَٰتِ وَٱلْأَرْضِ ۗ
وَٱلَّذِينَ ءَامَنُوا۟ بِٱلْبَٰطِلِ وَكَفَرُوا۟ بِٱللَّهِ
أُو۟لَٰٓئِكَ هُمُ ٱلْخَٰسِرُونَ

53. They ask thee
To hasten on the Punishment[3485]
(For them): had it not been
For a term (of respite)
Appointed, the Punishment
Would certainly have come
To them: and it will
Certainly reach them—
Of a sudden, while they
Perceive not!

٥٣ وَيَسْتَعْجِلُونَكَ بِٱلْعَذَابِ ۚ
وَلَوْلَآ أَجَلٌ مُّسَمًّى
لَّجَآءَهُمُ ٱلْعَذَابُ
وَلَيَأْتِيَنَّهُم بَغْتَةً
وَهُمْ لَا يَشْعُرُونَ

54. They ask thee
To hasten on the Punishment:[3486]
But, of a surety,
Hell will encompass
The rejecters of Faith!—

٥٤ يَسْتَعْجِلُونَكَ بِٱلْعَذَابِ
وَإِنَّ جَهَنَّمَ لَمُحِيطَةٌۢ بِٱلْكَٰفِرِينَ

55. On the Day that
The Punishment shall cover them
From above them and
From below them,[3487]
And (a Voice) shall say:

٥٥ يَوْمَ يَغْشَىٰهُمُ ٱلْعَذَابُ
مِن فَوْقِهِمْ وَمِن تَحْتِ أَرْجُلِهِمْ وَيَقُولُ

3483. The test of a Revelation is whether it comes from Allah or not. This is made clear by the life and teachings of the Messenger who brings it. No fraud or falsehood can for a moment stand before Allah. All the most hidden things in heaven and earth are open before him.

3484. If Truth is rejected, Truth does not suffer. It is the rejecters who suffer and perish in the end.

3485. *Cf.* 22:47 and n. 2826. The rejecters of Faith throw out a challenge out of bravado: "Let us see if you can hasten the punishment on us!" This is a vain taunt. Allah's Plan will take its course, and it can neither be delayed nor hastened. It is out of His Mercy that He gives respite to sinners—in order that they may have a chance of repentance. If they do not repent, the Punishment must certainly come to them—and on a sudden, before they perceive that it is coming! And then it will be too late for repentance.

3486. The challenge of the wicked for Punishment was answered in the last verse by reference to Allah's merciful Respite, to give chances of repentance. It is answered in this verse by an assurance that if no repentance is forthcoming, the Punishment will be certain and of an all-pervasive kind. Hell will surround them on all sides, and above them and below them.

3487. *Cf.* a similar phrase in 6:65.

"Taste ye (the fruits)
Of your deeds!"[3488]

ذُوقُواْ مَا كُنتُمْ تَعْمَلُونَ

56. O My servants who believe!
Truly, spacious is My Earth:[3489]
Therefore serve ye Me—
(And Me alone)!

(٥٦) يَٰعِبَادِيَ ٱلَّذِينَ ءَامَنُوٓاْ
إِنَّ أَرْضِي وَٰسِعَةٌ فَإِيَّٰيَ فَٱعْبُدُونِ

57. Every soul shall have
A taste of death:[3490]
In the end to Us
Shall ye be brought back.

(٥٧) كُلُّ نَفْسٍ ذَآئِقَةُ ٱلْمَوْتِ
ثُمَّ إِلَيْنَا تُرْجَعُونَ

58. But those who believe
And work deeds of righteousness—
To them shall We give
A Home in Heaven—[3491]
Lofty mansions beneath which
Flow rivers—to dwell therein
For aye—an excellent reward
For those who do (good)!—

(٥٨) وَٱلَّذِينَ ءَامَنُواْ وَعَمِلُواْ ٱلصَّٰلِحَٰتِ
لَنُبَوِّئَنَّهُم مِّنَ ٱلْجَنَّةِ غُرَفًا تَجْرِي
مِن تَحْتِهَا ٱلْأَنْهَٰرُ خَٰلِدِينَ فِيهَا
نِعْمَ أَجْرُ ٱلْعَٰمِلِينَ

59. Those who persevere in patience,
And put their trust
In their Lord and Cherisher,

(٥٩) ٱلَّذِينَ صَبَرُواْ وَعَلَىٰ رَبِّهِمْ يَتَوَكَّلُونَ

60. How many are the creatures
That carry not their own[3492]

(٦٠) وَكَأَيِّن مِّن دَآبَّةٍ لَّا تَحْمِلُ

3488. This is not merely a reproach, but a justification of the Punishment. "It is you who brought it on yourselves by your evil deeds: blame none but yourselves. Allah's Mercy gave you many chances: His Justice has now overtaken you."

3489. There is no excuse for any one to plead that he could not do good or was forced to evil by his circumstances and surroundings, or by the fact that he lived in evil times. We must shun evil and seek good, and Allah's Creation is wide enough to enable us to do that, provided we have the will, the patience, and the constancy to do it. It may be that we have to change our village or city or country; or that we have to change our neighbours or associates; or to change our habits or our hours, our position in life or our human relationships, or our callings. Our integrity before Allah is more important than any of these things, and we must be prepared for exile (or *Hijrah*) in all these senses. For the means with which Allah provides us for His service are ample, and it is our fault if we fail.

3490. *Cf.* 3:185, n. 451, and 21:35 and n. 2697. Death is the separation of the soul from the body when the latter perishes. We should not be afraid of death, for it only brings us back to Allah. The various kinds of *hijrah* or exile, physical and spiritual, mentioned in the last note, are also modes of death in a sense: what is there to fear in them?

3491. The goodly homes mentioned in 16:41 referred to this life, but it was stated there that the reward of the Hereafter would be greater. Here the simile of the Home is referred to Heaven: it will be beautiful: it will be picturesque, with the sight and sound of softly murmuring streams: it will be lofty or sublime: and it will be eternal.

3492. If we look at the animal creation, we see that many creatures seem almost helpless to find their own food or sustain their full life, being surrounded by many enemies. Yet in the Plan of Allah they find full sustenance and protection. So does man. Man's needs—as well as helplessness—are by many degrees greater. Yet Allah provides for him as for all His creatures. Allah listens to the wish and cry of all His creatures and He knows their needs and how to provide for them all. Man should not therefore hesitate to suffer exile or persecution in Allah's Cause.

Sustenance? It is Allah
Who feeds (both) them and you,
For He hears and knows
(All things).

رِزْقَهَا ٱللَّهُ يَرْزُقُهَا وَإِيَّاكُمْ
وَهُوَ ٱلسَّمِيعُ ٱلْعَلِيمُ

61. If indeed thou ask them[3493]
Who has created the heavens
And the earth and subjected[3494]
The sun and the moon
(To His Law), they will
Certainly reply, "Allah".
How are they then deluded
Away (from the truth)?

٦١ وَلَئِن سَأَلْتَهُم مَّنْ خَلَقَ ٱلسَّمَٰوَٰتِ
وَٱلْأَرْضَ وَسَخَّرَ ٱلشَّمْسَ وَٱلْقَمَرَ
لَيَقُولُنَّ ٱللَّهُ
فَأَنَّىٰ يُؤْفَكُونَ

62. Allah enlarges the sustenance
(Which He gives) to whichever
Of His servants He pleases:[3495]
And He (similarly) grants
By (strict) measure, (as He pleases):
For Allah has full knowledge
Of all things.

٦٢ ٱللَّهُ يَبْسُطُ ٱلرِّزْقَ لِمَن
يَشَآءُ مِنْ عِبَادِهِۦ وَيَقْدِرُ لَهُۥٓ
إِنَّ ٱللَّهَ بِكُلِّ شَيْءٍ عَلِيمٌ

63. And if indeed thou ask them[3496]
Who it is that sends down
Rain from the sky,
And gives life therewith
To the earth after its death,
They will certainly reply,
"Allah!" Say, "Praise be
To Allah!" but most
Of them understand not.

٦٣ وَلَئِن سَأَلْتَهُم مَّن نَّزَّلَ مِنَ ٱلسَّمَآءِ
مَآءً فَأَحْيَا بِهِ ٱلْأَرْضَ مِنۢ بَعْدِ مَوْتِهَا
لَيَقُولُنَّ ٱللَّهُ قُلِ ٱلْحَمْدُ لِلَّهِ
بَلْ أَكْثَرُهُمْ لَا يَعْقِلُونَ

3493. *Cf.* 23:84-89. "Them" in both passages refers to the sort of inconsistent men who acknowledge the power of Allah, but are deluded by false notions into disobedience of Allah's Law and disregard of Allah's Message.

3494. *Cf.* 13:2, and 23:85. The perfect order and law of Allah's universe should be Signs to man's intelligence to get his own will into tune with Allah's Will; for only so can he hope to attain his full development.

3495. *Cf.* 13:26. Unequal gifts are not a sign of chaos in Allah's universe. Allah provides for all according to their real needs and their most suitable requirement, according to His perfect knowledge and understanding of His creatures.

3496. In 29:61 above, the point was that there is a certain type of man that realises the power of Allah, but yet goes after false ideas and false worship. Here the point is that there is another type of man to whom the goodness of Allah is made clear by rain and the gifts of nature and who realises the daily, seasonal, and secular changes which evidence Allah's goodness in giving us life (physical and spiritual) and reviving us after we seem to die,—and who yet fails to draw the right conclusion from it and to make his own life true and beautiful, so that when his period of probation in this transitory life is ended, he can enter into his eternal heritage. Having come so far such men fail at the crucial stage. At that stage they ought to have praised and glorified Allah, and accepted His Grace and Light, but they show their want of true understanding by failing to profit by Allah's gifts.

SECTION 7.

64. What is the life of this world
But amusement and play?[3497]
But verily the Home
In the Hereafter—that is
Life indeed, if they but knew.

٦٤ وَمَا هَٰذِهِ ٱلْحَيَوٰةُ ٱلدُّنْيَآ إِلَّا لَهْوٌ وَلَعِبٌ ۚ
وَإِنَّ ٱلدَّارَ ٱلْءَاخِرَةَ لَهِىَ ٱلْحَيَوَانُ ۚ
لَوْ كَانُوا۟ يَعْلَمُونَ

65. Now, if they embark
On a boat, they call
On Allah, making their devotion
Sincerely (and exclusively) to
Him;[3498]
But when He has delivered
Them safely to (dry) land,
Behold, they give a share
(Of their worship to others)!—

٦٥ فَإِذَا رَكِبُوا۟ فِى ٱلْفُلْكِ
دَعَوُا۟ ٱللَّهَ مُخْلِصِينَ لَهُ ٱلدِّينَ
فَلَمَّا نَجَّىٰهُمْ إِلَى ٱلْبَرِّ
إِذَا هُمْ يُشْرِكُونَ

66. Disdaining ungratefully Our gifts,
And giving themselves up[3499]
To (worldly) enjoyment! But soon
Will they know.

٦٦ لِيَكْفُرُوا۟ بِمَآ ءَاتَيْنَٰهُمْ وَلِيَتَمَتَّعُوا۟ ۖ
فَسَوْفَ يَعْلَمُونَ

67. Do they not then see
That We have made
A Sanctuary secure, and that
Men are being snatched away
From all around them[3500]
Then, do they believe in that
Which is vain, and reject
The Grace of Allah!

٦٧ أَوَلَمْ يَرَوْا۟ أَنَّا جَعَلْنَا حَرَمًا ءَامِنًا
وَيُتَخَطَّفُ ٱلنَّاسُ مِنْ حَوْلِهِمْ ۚ
أَفَبِٱلْبَٰطِلِ يُؤْمِنُونَ
وَبِنِعْمَةِ ٱللَّهِ يَكْفُرُونَ

3497. *Cf.* 6:32. Amusement and play have no lasting significance except as preparing us for the serious work of life. So this life is but an interlude, a preparation for the real Life, which is in the Hereafter. This world's vanities are therefore to be taken for what they are worth; but they are not to be allowed to deflect our minds from the requirements of the inner life that really matters.

3498. *Cf.* 7:29, where I have slightly varied the English phrase according to the context.

It was shown in the last verse that the life of this world is fleeting, and that the true life—that which matters—is the Life in the Hereafter. In contrast with this inner reality is now shown the shortsighted folly of man. When he faces the physical dangers of the sea, which are but an incident in the phenomenal world, he actually and sincerely seeks the help of Allah; but when he is safely back on land, he forgets the Realities, plunges into the pleasures and vanities of fleeting phenomena, and his devotion, which should be given exclusively to Allah, is shared by idols and vanities of his own imagination. (R).

3499. Such folly results in the virtual rejection (even though it may not be express) of Allah and His Grace. It plunges man into the pleasures and vanities that merely delude and are bound to pass away. This delusion, however, will come to an end when the true Reality of the Hereafter will shine forth in all its splendour.

3500. If they want evidences of their folly in the phenomenal world itself, they will see sacred Sanctuaries where Allah's Truth abides safely in the midst of the Deluge of broken hopes, disappointed ambitions and unfulfilled plans in the world around. The immediate reference was to the Sanctuary of Makkah and the gradual progress of Islam in the districts surrounding the Quraysh in the midst of the trying Makkan period. But the general application holds good for all times and places.

68. And who does more wrong[3501]
Than he who invents
A lie against Allah
Or rejects the Truth
When it reaches him?
Is there not a home
In Hell for those who
Reject Faith?

٦٨ وَمَنْ أَظْلَمُ مِمَّنِ
افْتَرَىٰ عَلَى اللَّهِ كَذِبًا
أَوْ كَذَّبَ بِالْحَقِّ لَمَّا جَاءَهُۥٓ
أَلَيْسَ فِي جَهَنَّمَ مَثْوًى لِّلْكَٰفِرِينَ

69. And those who strive[3502]
In Our (Cause)—We will
Certainly guide them
To Our Paths:[3503]
For verily Allah
Is with those
Who do right.

٦٩ وَالَّذِينَ جَٰهَدُوا فِينَا
لَنَهْدِيَنَّهُمْ سُبُلَنَا
وَإِنَّ اللَّهَ لَمَعَ الْمُحْسِنِينَ

3501. *Cf.* 6:21. Even from a worldly point of view those who reject Allah's Truth are at a disadvantage. But those who deliberately invent lies and set up false gods for worship—what punishment can we imagine for them except a permanent deprivation of Allah's grace, and a home in Hell? (R).

3502. *Strive in Our Cause.* All that man can do is to strive in Allah's Cause. As soon as he strives with might and main, with constancy and determination, the Light and Mercy of Allah come to meet him. They cure his defects and shortcomings. They provide him with the means by which he can raise himself above himself. They point out the Way, and all the Paths leading up to it. See next note.

3503. The Way of Allah (*ṣirāṭ al Mustaqīm*) is a Straight Way. But men have strayed from it in all directions. And there are numerous Paths by which they can get back to the Right Way, the way in which the purity of their own nature, and the Will and Mercy of Allah, require them to walk. All these numerous Paths become open to them once they give their hearts in keeping to Allah and work in right Endeavour (*Jihād*) with all their mind and soul and resources. Thus will they get out of the Spider's web of this frail world and attain to eternal Bliss in the fulfilment of their true Destiny.

INTRODUCTION TO SŪRAH 30—*AL RŪM*

This Sūrah, as remarked in the Introduction to the last Sūrah, deals with the question of *Ma'ād* or the Final End of Things, from various points of view. In the last Sūrah, we saw that Revelation was linked up with Life and Conduct, and Time (looking backwards and forwards) figured forth the frailty of this Life. In this Sūrah the Time theme and its mystery are brought into relation with human history in the foreground and the evolution of the world in all its aspects in the background. The corruption introduced by man is cleared away by Allah, Whose Universal Plan points to the Hereafter. We shall see that the next two Sūrahs (31 and 32) present the theme in other aspects. All four are introduced with the Abbreviated Letters Alif, Lām, Mīm, which (without being dogmatic) I have suggested as symbolical of the Past, Present and Future.

The chronology of this Sūrah is significant. It was revealed about the 7th or 6th year *before* the Hijrah, corresponding to 615-16 of the Christian era, when the tide of Persian conquest over the Roman Empire was running strong, as explained in Appendix VIII (to follow this Sūrah). The Christian Empire of Rome had lost Jerusalem to the Persians, and Christianity had been humbled in the dust. At that time it seemed outside the bounds of human possibility, even to one intimately acquainted with the inner resources and conditions of the Persian and Roman armies and empires, that the tables would be turned and the position reversed within the space of eight or nine years. The pro-Persian Pagan Quraysh rejoiced exceedingly, and redoubled their taunts and persecution against the Holy Prophet, whose Message was a renewal of the Message of Christ preached in Jerusalem. Then was this passage 30:1-6 revealed, clearly foreshadowing the final defeat of Persia (Appendix VIII, 14-16) as a prelude to the destruction of the Persian Empire. There is no doubt about the prophecy and its fulfilment. For the exulting Pagans of Makkah laid a heavy wager against the fulfilment of the prophecy with Abū Bakr, and they lost it on its fulfilment.

But the rise and fall even of such mighty empires as the Persian and Roman Empires, were but small events on the chequerboard of Time, compared to a mightier movement that was taking birth in the promulgation of Islam. In the seventh or sixth year *before* the Hijrah, and for a year or two after the Hijrah, Islam was struggling in the world like the still small voice in the conscience of humanity. It was scarcely heeded, and when it sought to insist upon its divine claim, it was insulted, assaulted, persecuted, boycotted, and (as it seemed) suppressed. The agony of Ṭā'if (two years before the Hijrah) and the murder-plot on the eve of the Hijrah were yet to come. But the purpose of Allah is not to be thwarted. Badr (A.H. 2 = A.C. 624), rightly called the critical Day of Decision, began to redress the balance of outward events in early Islam, in the same year in which Issus (Appendix VIII, 16) began to redress the balance of outward events in Perso-Roman relations. Mightier events were yet to come. A new inner World was being created through Islam. The spiritual Revolution was an infinitely greater moment in world history. The toppling down of priestcraft and false worship, the restoration of simplicity in faith and life, the rehabilitation of this life as the first step to the understanding of the Hereafter, the displacement of superstition and hair-splitting theology by a spirit of rational enquiry and knowledge, and the recognition of the divine as covering not merely an isolated thing called "Religion" but the whole way of Life, Thought, and Feeling—this was and is the true Message of Islam and its mission. Its struggle—its fight—continues, but it is not without effect, as may be seen in the march of centuries in world history.

Summary.—The ebb and flow of worldly power—as symbolised in the conflict of the Persian and Roman Empires—are but outward events: the deeper meaning is in the working of Allah's Universe—how Good and Evil reach their final End (30:1-19, and C. 180).

The changes and changing variety in Allah's Creation, physical, moral, and spiritual, yet point to Unity in Nature and Religion: man should not break away from that Unity, but glorify Him, the One, for there is none like unto Him (30:20-40, and C. 181).

The hands of men have wrought corruption and mischief: but Allah purifies the moral world as He does the world of physical nature, strengthening the weak and pulling down the mighty in due season: wait therefore in patience and constancy, and be not depressed (30:41-60, and c. 182).

C. 180.—(30:1-19.)

Great Empires rise and fall, conquer
And are conquered, as happened
To Rome and Persia: but the true Decision
Is with Allah, Who will make the righteous
Rejoice. Men may see but the outward
Crust of things, but in truth the End
Of things is all-in-all. In His own
Good time He will separate good from evil:
Praise and glory to Him forever!

Sūrah 30.

Al Rūm (The Romans)

In the name of Allah, Most Gracious,
Most Merciful.

بِسْمِ ٱللَّهِ ٱلرَّحْمَٰنِ ٱلرَّحِيمِ

1. Alif Lām Mīm.[3504]

الٓمٓ ﴿١﴾

2. The Roman Empire[3505]
Has been defeated—

غُلِبَتِ ٱلرُّومُ ﴿٢﴾

3. In a land close by:
But they, (even) after
(This) defeat of theirs,
Will soon be victorious—[3506]

فِىٓ أَدْنَى ٱلْأَرْضِ وَهُم مِّنۢ بَعْدِ غَلَبِهِمْ سَيَغْلِبُونَ ﴿٣﴾

4. Within a few years.[3507]
With Allah is the Decision.
In the Past
And in the Future:
On that Day shall
The Believers rejoice—[3508]

فِى بِضْعِ سِنِينَ ۗ لِلَّهِ ٱلْأَمْرُ مِن قَبْلُ وَمِنۢ بَعْدُ ۚ وَيَوْمَئِذٍ يَفْرَحُ ٱلْمُؤْمِنُونَ ﴿٤﴾

5. With the help of Allah.
He helps whom He will,[3509]
And He is Exalted in Might,
Most Merciful.

بِنَصْرِ ٱللَّهِ ۚ يَنصُرُ مَن يَشَآءُ ۖ وَهُوَ ٱلْعَزِيزُ ٱلرَّحِيمُ ﴿٥﴾

3504. See n. 25 to 2:1 and Introduction to this Sūrah.

3505. The remarkable defeats of the Roman Empire under Heraclius and the straits to which it was reduced are reviewed in Appendix VIII (to follow this Sūrah). It was not merely isolated defeats; the Roman Empire lost most of its Asiatic territory and was hemmed in on all sides at its capital, Constantinople. The defeat, "in a land close by" must refer to Syria and Palestine. Jerusalem was lost in 614-15 A.C., shortly before this Sūrah was revealed.

3506. The Pagan Quraysh of Makkah rejoiced at the overthrow of Rome by Persia. They were pro-Persian, and in their heart of hearts they hoped that the nascent movement of Islam, which at that time was, from a worldly point of view, very weak and helpless, would also collapse under their persecution. But they misread the true Signs of the times. They are told here that they would soon be disillusioned in both their calculations, and it actually so happened at the battle of Issus in 622 (the year of Hijrah) and in 624, when Heraclius carried his campaign into the heart of Persia (see Appendix VIII) and the Makkan Quraysh were beaten off at Badr.

3507. *Biḍ'un* in the text means a short period—a period of from three to nine years. The period between the loss of Jerusalem (614-15) by the Romans and their victory at Issus (622) was seven years, and that to the penetration of Persia by Heraclius was nine years. See last note.

3508. See n. 3506 and Appendix VIII. The battle of Badr (2 A.H. = 624 A.C.) was a real time of rejoicing for the Believers and a time of disillusionment for the arrogant Quraysh, who thought that they could crush the whole movememt of Islam in Madīnah as they had tried to do in Makkah, but they were signally repulsed. See n. 352 to 3:13.

3509. *Whom He will.* As explained elsewhere, Allah's Will or Plan is not arbitrary: it is full of the highest wisdom. His Plan is formed in mercy, so as to safeguard the interests of *all* his creatures, against the selfish aggrandizement of any section against them. And He is able to carry out His Plan in full, and there is no power that can stop or delay His Plan.

6. (It is) the promise of Allah.[3510]
Never does Allah depart
From His promise:
But most men understand not.

٦ وَعْدَ ٱللَّهِ ۖ لَا يُخْلِفُ ٱللَّهُ وَعْدَهُۥ
وَلَٰكِنَّ أَكْثَرَ ٱلنَّاسِ لَا يَعْلَمُونَ

7. They know but the outer[3511]
(Things) in the life
Of this world: but
Of the End of things[3512]
They are heedless.

٧ يَعْلَمُونَ ظَٰهِرًا مِّنَ ٱلْحَيَوٰةِ ٱلدُّنْيَا
وَهُمْ عَنِ ٱلْءَاخِرَةِ هُمْ غَٰفِلُونَ

8. Do they not reflect
In their own minds?
Not but for just ends[3513]
And for a term appointed,
Did Allah create the heavens
And the earth, and all
Between them: yet are there
Truly many among men
Who deny their meeting[3514]
With their Lord
(At the Resurrection)!

٨ أَوَلَمْ يَتَفَكَّرُوا۟ فِىٓ أَنفُسِهِم ۗ
مَّا خَلَقَ ٱللَّهُ ٱلسَّمَٰوَٰتِ وَٱلْأَرْضَ
وَمَا بَيْنَهُمَآ إِلَّا بِٱلْحَقِّ وَأَجَلٍ مُّسَمًّى ۗ
وَإِنَّ كَثِيرًا مِّنَ ٱلنَّاسِ
بِلِقَآئِ رَبِّهِمْ لَكَٰفِرُونَ

9. Do they not travel
Through the earth, and see
What was the End
Of those before them?
They were superior to them
In strength: they tilled
The soil and populated it
In greater numbers than these
Have done: there came to them

٩ أَوَلَمْ يَسِيرُوا۟ فِى ٱلْأَرْضِ فَيَنظُرُوا۟
كَيْفَ كَانَ عَٰقِبَةُ ٱلَّذِينَ مِن قَبْلِهِمْ ۚ
كَانُوٓا۟ أَشَدَّ مِنْهُمْ قُوَّةً وَأَثَارُوا۟ ٱلْأَرْضَ
وَعَمَرُوهَآ أَكْثَرَ مِمَّا عَمَرُوهَا وَجَآءَتْهُمْ

3510. The promise refers to the Decision of all things by the Command of Allah, Who will remove all troubles and difficulties from the path of His righteous Believers, and help them to rejoice over the success of their righteous Cause. This refers to all times and all situations. The righteous should not despair in their darkest moments, for Allah's help will come. Ordinarily men are puffed up if they score a seeming temporary success against the righteous, and do not realise that Allah's Will can never be thwarted.

3511. Men are misled by the outward show of things, though the inner reality may be quite different. Many seeming disasters are really godsends if we only understood.

3512. *Ākhirah*: I have usually translated "Hereafter". Here the context is perfectly general, and refers to the End of things or enterprises in history as well as the Hereafter in the technical theological sense.

3513. *Cf.* 15:85. Here the argument is about the ebb and flow of worldly power, and the next clause is appropriately added, "and for a term appointed". Let not any one who is granted worldly power or advantage run away with the notion that it is permanent. It is definitely limited in the high Purpose of Allah, which is just and true. And an account will have to be given of it afterwards on the basis of strict personal responsibility.

3514. It is therefore all the more strange that there should be men who not only forget themselves but even deny that there is a return to Allah or an End or Hereafter, when a full reckoning will be due for this period of probation. They are asked to study past history, as in the next verse.

Their messengers with Clear
(Signs).[3515]
(Which they rejected, to their
Own destruction): it was not
Allah who wronged them, but
They wronged their own souls.

رُسُلُهُم بِٱلْبَيِّنَٰتِ
فَمَا كَانَ ٱللَّهُ لِيَظْلِمَهُمْ
وَلَٰكِن كَانُوٓا۟ أَنفُسَهُمْ يَظْلِمُونَ

10. In the long run
Evil in the extreme[3516]
Will be the End of those
Who do evil; for that
They rejected the Signs
Of Allah, and held them up
To ridicule.

(١٠) ثُمَّ كَانَ عَٰقِبَةَ ٱلَّذِينَ أَسَٰٓـُٔوا۟
ٱلسُّوٓأَىٰٓ أَن كَذَّبُوا۟ بِـَٔايَٰتِ ٱللَّهِ
وَكَانُوا۟ بِهَا يَسْتَهْزِءُونَ

Section 2.

11. It is Allah Who begins
(The process of) creation;[3517]
Then repeats it; then
Shall ye be brought back
To Him.

(١١) ٱللَّهُ يَبْدَؤُا۟ ٱلْخَلْقَ
ثُمَّ يُعِيدُهُۥ ثُمَّ إِلَيْهِ تُرْجَعُونَ

12. On the Day that
The Hour will be established,[3518]
The guilty will be
Struck dumb with despair.

(١٢) وَيَوْمَ تَقُومُ ٱلسَّاعَةُ
يُبْلِسُ ٱلْمُجْرِمُونَ

3515. Let not any generation think that it is superior to all that went before it. We may be "heirs to all the ages, in the foremost files of times." That is no reason for arrogance, but on the contrary adds to our responsibility. When we realise what flourishing cities and kingdoms existed before, how they flourished in numbers and prosperity, what chances they were given, and how they perished when they disobeyed the law of Allah, we shall feel a sense of humility, and see that it was rebellion and self-will that brought them down. Allah was more than just. He was also merciful. But they brought about their own ruin.

3516. The Arabic superlative feminine, referring to the feminine noun *'Āqibah*, I have translated by "Evil in the extreme". In this life good and evil may seem to be mixed up, and it may be that some things or persons that are evil get what seem to be good rewards or blessings, while the opposite happens to the good. But this is only a temporary appearance. In the long run Evil will have its own evil consequences, multiplied cumulatively. And this, because Evil not only rejected Allah's Message of Good but laughed at Good and misled others.

3517. Nothing exists of its own accord or fortuitously. It is Allah Who originates all creation. What appears to be death may be only transformation; for Allah can and does recreate. And His creative activity is continuous. Our death is but a phenomenal event. What we become after death is the result of a process of recreation by Allah, Who is both the source and the goal of all things. When we are brought back to him, it will be as conscious and responsible beings, to receive the consequences of our brief life on this earth.

3518. *The Hour will be established*: in due time the Hour will come when Judgement will be established, and the seeming disturbance of balance in this world will be redressed. Then the Good will rejoice, and the Guilty, faced with the Realities, will lose all their illusions and be struck dumb with despair.

13. No intercessor will they have
Among their "Partners",[3519]
And they will (themselves)
Reject their "Partners".

14. On the Day that
The Hour will be established—
That Day shall (all men)[3520]
Be sorted out.

15. Then those who have believed
And worked righteous deeds,
Shall be made happy
In a Mead of Delight.

16. And those who have rejected
Faith and falsely denied
Our Signs and the meeting
Of the Hereafter—such
Shall be brought forth to
Punishment.

17. So (give) glory to Allah,
When ye reach eventide[3521]
And when ye rise
In the morning;

18. Yea, to Him be praise,
In the heavens and on earth;
And in the late afternoon
And when the day
Begins to decline.

19. It is He Who brings out
The living from the dead,

١٣ وَلَمْ يَكُن لَّهُم مِّن شُرَكَآئِهِمْ شُفَعَـٰٓؤُا۟
وَكَانُوا۟ بِشُرَكَآئِهِمْ كَـٰفِرِينَ

١٤ وَيَوْمَ تَقُومُ ٱلسَّاعَةُ
يَوْمَئِذٍ يَتَفَرَّقُونَ

١٥ فَأَمَّا ٱلَّذِينَ ءَامَنُوا۟ وَعَمِلُوا۟
ٱلصَّـٰلِحَـٰتِ فَهُمْ فِى رَوْضَةٍ يُحْبَرُونَ

١٦ وَأَمَّا ٱلَّذِينَ كَفَرُوا۟
وَكَذَّبُوا۟ بِـَٔايَـٰتِنَا وَلِقَآئِ ٱلْـَٔاخِرَةِ
فَأُو۟لَـٰٓئِكَ فِى ٱلْعَذَابِ مُحْضَرُونَ

١٧ فَسُبْحَـٰنَ ٱللَّهِ حِينَ
تُمْسُونَ وَحِينَ تُصْبِحُونَ

١٨ وَلَهُ ٱلْحَمْدُ فِى
ٱلسَّمَـٰوَٰتِ وَٱلْأَرْضِ
وَعَشِيًّا وَحِينَ تُظْهِرُونَ

١٩ يُخْرِجُ ٱلْحَىَّ مِنَ ٱلْمَيِّتِ

3519. False worship will then appear in its true colours. Anything to which we offered the worship due to Allah alone, will vanish instead of being of any help. Indeed the deluded false worshippers, whose eyes will now be opened, will themselves reject their falsehoods, as the Truth will now shine with unquestioned splendour.

3520. In the fullness of time good and evil will all be sorted out and separated. The good will reach their destination of felicity in rich and luscious, well-watered meadows, which stand as the type of all that is fair to see and pleasant to feel. The evil will no longer imagine that they are enjoying good fortune, for the testing time will be over, and the grim reality will stare them in the face. They will receive their just Punishment. (R).

3521. The special times for Allah's remembrance are so described as to include all our activites in life—when we rise early in the morning, and when we go to rest in the evening; when we are in the midst of our work, at the decline of the sun, and in the late afternoon. It may be noted that these are all striking stages in the passage of the sun through our terrestrial day, as well as stages in our daily working lives. On this are based the hours of the five canonical prayers afterwards prescibed in Madīnah; *viz.*, (1) early morning before sunrise (*Fajr*); (2) when the day begins to decline, just after noon (*Zuhr*); (3) in the late afternoon, say midway between noon and sunset (*'Aṣr*); and (4) and (5) the two evening prayers, one just after sunset (*Maghrib*), and the other after the evening twilight has all faded from the horizon, the hour indicated for rest and sleep (*'Ishā'*). *Cf.* 11:114, nn. 1616-17; 17:78-79, n. 2275; 20:130, n. 2655.

And brings out the dead[3522]
From the living, and Who
Gives life to the earth[3523]
After it is dead:
And thus shall ye be
Brought out (from the dead).

وَيُخْرِجُ ٱلْمَيِّتَ مِنَ ٱلْحَيِّ
وَيُحْىِ ٱلْأَرْضَ بَعْدَ مَوْتِهَا
وَكَذَٰلِكَ تُخْرَجُونَ

C. 181.— (30:20-40.) Allah's Signs are many, and so are His mysteries:
Yet each does point to His Unity, Goodness,
Power, and Mercy. There is none like
Unto Him. His teaching is one, and men
That split up His standard Religion
Are but following their own lusts. Ungrateful
Are they to give part-worship to others,
When all worship and praise and glory
Are due to Him and Him alone,
In Whom we have our life and being!

SECTION 3.

20. Among His Signs is this,
That He created you[3524]
From dust; and then—
Behold, ye are men
Scattered (far and wide)!

٢٠ وَمِنْ ءَايَٰتِهِۦٓ أَنْ خَلَقَكُم مِّن تُرَابٍ
ثُمَّ إِذَآ أَنتُم بَشَرٌ تَنتَشِرُونَ

21. And among His Signs
Is this, that He created
For you mates from among[3525]
Yourselves, that ye may
Dwell in tranquillity with them,[3526]

٢١ وَمِنْ ءَايَٰتِهِۦٓ أَنْ خَلَقَ لَكُم
مِّنْ أَنفُسِكُمْ أَزْوَٰجًا لِّتَسْكُنُوٓا۟ إِلَيْهَا

3522. *Cf.* 10:31. From dead matter Allah's creative act produces life and living matter, and even science has not yet been able to explain the mystery of life. Life and living matter again seem to reach maturity and again die, as we see every day. No material thing seems to have perpetual life. But again we see the creative process of Allah constantly at work, and the cycle of life and death seems to go on.

3523. *Cf.* 2:164. The earth itself, seemingly so inert, produces vegetable life at once from a single shower of rain, and in various ways sustains animal life. Normally it seems to die in the winter in northern climates, and in a drought everywhere, and the spring revives it in all its glory. Metaphorically many movements, institutions, organisations, seem to die and then to live again, all under the wonderful dispensation of Allah. So will our personality be revived when we apparently die on this earth, in order to reap the fruit of this, our probationary life.

3524. *Cf.* 18:37 and n. 2379. In spite of the lowly origin of man's body, Allah has given him a mind and soul by which he can almost compass the farthest reaches of Time and Space. Is this not enough for a miracle or Sign? From a physical point of view, see how man, a creature of dust, scatters himself over the farthest corners of the earth!

3525. This refers to the wonderful mystery of sex. Children arise out of the union of the sexes. And it is always the female sex that brings forth the offspring, whether female or male. And the father is as necessary as the mother for bringing forth daughters.

3526. *Cf.* 7:189. Unregenerate man is pugnacious in the male sex, but rest and tranquillity are found in the normal relations of a father and mother dwelling together and bringing up a family. A man's chivalry to the opposite sex is natural and God-given. The friendship of two men between each other is quite different in quality and temper from the feeling which unspoilt nature expects as between men and women. There is a special kind of love and tenderness between them. And as woman is the weaker vessel, that tenderness may from a certain aspect be likened to mercy, the protecting kindness which the strong should give to the weak.

And He has put love
And mercy between your (hearts):
Verily in that are Signs
For those who reflect.

وَجَعَلَ بَيْنَكُم مَّوَدَّةً وَرَحْمَةً
إِنَّ فِي ذَٰلِكَ لَآيَاتٍ لِّقَوْمٍ يَتَفَكَّرُونَ

22. And among His Signs
Is the creation of the heavens
And the earth, and the
variations[3527]
In your languages
And your colours; verily
In that are Signs
For those who know.

٢٢ وَمِنْ آيَاتِهِ خَلْقُ
السَّمَاوَاتِ وَالْأَرْضِ
وَاخْتِلَافُ أَلْسِنَتِكُمْ وَأَلْوَانِكُمْ
إِنَّ فِي ذَٰلِكَ لَآيَاتٍ لِّلْعَالِمِينَ

23. And among His Signs
Is the sleep that ye take
By night and by day,[3528]
And the quest that ye
(Make for livelihood)
Out of His Bounty: verily
In that are Signs
For those who hearken.[3529]

٢٣ وَمِنْ آيَاتِهِ مَنَامُكُم بِاللَّيْلِ
وَالنَّهَارِ وَابْتِغَاؤُكُم مِّن فَضْلِهِ
إِنَّ فِي ذَٰلِكَ لَآيَاتٍ
لِّقَوْمٍ يَسْمَعُونَ

3527. The variations in languages and colours may be viewed from the geographical aspect or from the aspect of periods of time. All mankind was created of a single pair of parents; yet they have spread to different countries and climates and developed different languages and different shades of complexions. And yet their basic unity remains unaltered. They feel in the same way, and are all equally under Allah's care. Then there are the variations in time. Old languages die out and new ones are evolved. New conditions of life and thought are constantly evolving new words and expressions, new syntactical structures, and new modes of pronunciation. Even old races die, and new races are born.

3528. If we consider deeply, sleep and dreams, the refreshment we get from sleep to wakefulness as well as from wakefulness to sleep, as also the state of our thoughts and feelings and subconscious self in these conditions, are both wonderful and mysterious. Normally, we sleep by night and do our ordinary work "in quest of the Bounty of Allah" by day. But sleep and rest may come and be necessary by day, and we may have to work by night. And our work for our livelihood may pass by insensible transitions to our work or thought or service of a higher and spiritual kind. These processes suggest a background of things which we know but vaguely, but which are as much miracles as other Signs of Allah.

3529. From verse 20 to verse 25 are mentioned a series of Signs or Miracles, which should awaken our souls and lead us to true Reality if we try to understand Allah. (1) There is our own origin and destiny, which must necessarily be our subjective starting-point: "I think; therefore I am": no particular exertion of our being is here necessary (30:20). (2) The first beginnings of social life arise through sex and love: see 4:1, and n. 506; to understand this in all its bearing, we must "reflect" (30:21). (3) The next point is to understand our diversities in speech, colour, etc., arising from differences of climate and external conditions; yet there is unity beneath that diversity, which we shall realise by extended knowledge (30:22). (4) Next we turn to our psychological conditions, sleep, rest, visions, insight, etc.; here we want teaching and guidance, to which we must hearken (20:23). (5) Next, we must approach the higher reaches of spiritual hopes and fears, as symbolised by such subtle forces of nature as lightning and electricity, which may kill the foolish or bring prosperity in its train by rain and abundant harvests; to understand the highest spiritual hopes and fears so symbolised, we want the highest wisdom (30:24). (6) And lastly, we may become so transformed that we rise above all petty, worldly, ephemeral things: Allah calls to us and we rise, as from our dead selves to a Height which we can only describe as the Heaven of stability: here no human processes serve, for the Call of Allah Himself has come (30:25-27).

24. And among His Signs,
He shows you the lightning,
By way both of fear[3530]
And of hope, and He sends
Down rain from the sky
And with it gives life to
The earth after it is dead:
Verily in that are Signs
For those who are wise.

٢٤ وَمِنْ ءَايَٰتِهِۦ يُرِيكُمُ ٱلْبَرْقَ
خَوْفًا وَطَمَعًا وَيُنَزِّلُ مِنَ ٱلسَّمَآءِ مَآءً
فَيُحْىِۦ بِهِ ٱلْأَرْضَ بَعْدَ مَوْتِهَآ ۚ
إِنَّ فِى ذَٰلِكَ لَءَايَٰتٍ لِّقَوْمٍ يَعْقِلُونَ

25. And among His Signs is this,
That heaven and earth
Stand by His Command:[3531]
Then when He calls you,
By a single call, from the earth,
Behold, ye (straightway) come forth.

٢٥ وَمِنْ ءَايَٰتِهِۦٓ أَن تَقُومَ
ٱلسَّمَآءُ وَٱلْأَرْضُ بِأَمْرِهِۦ ۚ ثُمَّ إِذَا دَعَاكُمْ
دَعْوَةً مِّنَ ٱلْأَرْضِ إِذَآ أَنتُمْ تَخْرُجُونَ

26. To Him belongs every being
That is in the heavens
And on earth: all are[3532]
Devoutly obedient to Him.

٢٦ وَلَهُۥ مَن فِى ٱلسَّمَٰوَٰتِ وَٱلْأَرْضِ ۖ
كُلٌّ لَّهُۥ قَٰنِتُونَ

27. It is He Who begins
(The process of) creation;[3533]
Then repeats it; and
For Him it is most easy.
To Him belongs the loftiest[3534]

٢٧ وَهُوَ ٱلَّذِى يَبْدَؤُا۟ ٱلْخَلْقَ
ثُمَّ يُعِيدُهُۥ وَهُوَ أَهْوَنُ عَلَيْهِ ۚ
وَلَهُ ٱلْمَثَلُ ٱلْأَعْلَىٰ

3530. See last note, item (5). *Cf.* 13:12. To cowards lightning and thunder appear as terrible forces of nature: lightning seems to kill and destroy where its irresistible progress is not assisted by proper lightning-conductors. But lightning is also a herald of rain-bearing clouds and showers that bring fertility and prosperity in their train. This double aspect is also symbolical of spiritual fears and hopes—fears lest we may not be found receptive or worthy of the irresistible perspicuous Message of Allah, and hopes that we may receive in the right spirit and be blessed by its mighty power of transformation to achieve spiritual well-being. Note that the repetition of the phrase "gives life to the earth after it is dead" connects this verse with verse 19 above: in other words, the Revelation, which we must receive with wisdom and understanding, is a Sign of Allah's own power and mercy, and is vouchsafed in order to safeguard our own final Future.

3531. In the physical world, the sky and the earth, as we see them, stand unsupported, by the artistry of Allah. They bear witness to Allah, and in—that our physical life depends on them—the earth for its produce and the sky for rain, the heat of the sun, and other phenomena of nature—they call to our mind our relation to Allah Who made them and us. How can we then be so dense as not to realise that our higher Future—our *Ma'ād*—is bound up with the call and the mercy of Allah!

3532. All nature in Creation not only obeys Allah, but devoutly obeys Him, *i.e.*, glories in its privilege of service and obedience. Why should we not do likewise? It is part of our original unspoilt nature, and we must respond to it, as all beings do, by their very nature.

3533. *Cf.* 30:11 above, where the same phrase began the argument about the beginning and end of all things being with Allah. This has been illustrated by reference to various Signs in Creation, and now the argument is rounded off with the same phrase.

3534. Allah's glory and Allah's attributes are above any names we can give them. Human language is not adequate to express them. We can only form some idea of them at our present stage by means of Similitudes and Parables. But even so, the highest we can think of falls short of the true Reality. For Allah is higher and wiser than the highest and wisest we can think of.

Similitude (we can think of)
In the heavens and the earth:
For He is Exalted in Might,
Full of wisdom.

SECTION 4.

28. He does propound
To you a similitude
From your own (experience):[3535]
Do ye have partners
Among those whom your right hands
Possess, to share as equals
In the wealth We have[3536]
Bestowed on you? Do ye
Fear them as ye fear[3537]
Each other? Thus do We
Explain the Signs in detail
To a people that understand.[3538]

29. Nay, the wrongdoers (merely)
Follow their own lusts,
Being devoid of knowledge
But who will guide those
Whom Allah leaves astray?[3539]
To them there will be
No helpers.

30. So set thou thy face
Steadily and truly to the Faith:[3540]

فِي ٱلسَّمَٰوَٰتِ وَٱلۡأَرۡضِۚ
وَهُوَ ٱلۡعَزِيزُ ٱلۡحَكِيمُ

٢٨ ضَرَبَ لَكُم مَّثَلٗا مِّنۡ أَنفُسِكُمۡۖ
هَل لَّكُم مِّن مَّا مَلَكَتۡ أَيۡمَٰنُكُم
مِّن شُرَكَآءَ فِي مَا رَزَقۡنَٰكُمۡ
فَأَنتُمۡ فِيهِ سَوَآءٞ تَخَافُونَهُمۡ كَخِيفَتِكُمۡ
أَنفُسَكُمۡۚ كَذَٰلِكَ نُفَصِّلُ ٱلۡأٓيَٰتِ
لِقَوۡمٖ يَعۡقِلُونَ

٢٩ بَلِ ٱتَّبَعَ ٱلَّذِينَ
ظَلَمُوٓاْ أَهۡوَآءَهُم بِغَيۡرِ عِلۡمٖۖ
فَمَن يَهۡدِي مَنۡ أَضَلَّ ٱللَّهُۖ
وَمَا لَهُم مِّن نَّٰصِرِينَ

٣٠ فَأَقِمۡ وَجۡهَكَ لِلدِّينِ حَنِيفٗاۚ

3535. One way in which we can get some idea of the things higher than our own plane is to think of Parables and Similitudes drawn from our own lives and experience. And such a Similitude or Parable is offered to us now about false worship. See next note.

3536. Allah is far higher above His Creation than any, the highest, of His creatures can be above any, the lowest, of His creatures. And yet would a man share his wealth on equal terms with his dependents? Even what he calls his wealth is not really his own, but given by Allah. It is "his" in common speech by reason merely of certain accidental circumstances. How then can men raise Allah's creatures to equality with Allah in worship?

3537. Men fear each other as equals in a state of society at perpetual warfare. To remove this fear they appoint an authority among themselves—a King or sovereign authority whom they consider just—to preserve them from this fear and give them an established order. But they must obey and revere this authority and depend upon this authority for their own tranquillity and security. Even with their equals there is always the fear of public opinion. But men do not fear, or obey, or revere those who are their slaves or dependents. Man is dependent on Allah. And Allah is the Sovereign authority in an infinitely higher sense. He is in no sense dependent on us, but we must honour and revere Him and fear to disobey His Will or His Law. "The fear of Allah is the beginning of wisdom."

3538. *Cf.* 6:55, and 7:32, 174, etc.

3539. The wrongdoers—those who deliberately reject Allah's guidance and break Allah's Law—have put themselves out of the region of Allah's mercy. In this they have put themselves outside the pale of the knowledge of what is for their own good. In such a case they must suffer the consequences of the personal responsibility which flows from the grant of a limited free will. Who can then guide them or help them?

3540. For *Hanīf* see n. 134 to 2:135. Here "true" is used in the sense in which we say, "the magnetic needle is true to the north." Those who have been privileged to receive the Truth should never hesitate or swerve, but remain constant, as men who know.

(Establish) Allah's handiwork
according
To the pattern on which
He has made mankind:
No change (let there be)
In the work (wrought)[3541]
By Allah: that is
The standard Religion:[3542]
But most among mankind
Understand not.

31. Turn ye back in repentance[3543]
To Him, and fear Him:
Establish regular prayers,
And be not ye among those
Who join gods with Allah—

32. Those who split up
Their Religion, and become
(Mere) Sects—each party
Rejoicing in that which[3544]
Is with itself!

33. When trouble touches men,
They cry to their Lord,[3545]
Turning back to Him
In repentance: but when
He gives them a taste

فِطْرَتَ ٱللَّهِ
ٱلَّتِى فَطَرَ ٱلنَّاسَ عَلَيْهَا
لَا تَبْدِيلَ لِخَلْقِ ٱللَّهِ
ذَٰلِكَ ٱلدِّينُ ٱلْقَيِّمُ وَلَٰكِنَّ
أَكْثَرَ ٱلنَّاسِ لَا يَعْلَمُونَ
٣١ مُنِيبِينَ إِلَيْهِ وَٱتَّقُوهُ وَأَقِيمُوا۟ ٱلصَّلَوٰةَ
وَلَا تَكُونُوا۟ مِنَ ٱلْمُشْرِكِينَ
٣٢ مِنَ ٱلَّذِينَ فَرَّقُوا۟
دِينَهُمْ وَكَانُوا۟ شِيَعًا
كُلُّ حِزْبٍۭ بِمَا لَدَيْهِمْ فَرِحُونَ
٣٣ وَإِذَا مَسَّ ٱلنَّاسَ ضُرٌّ دَعَوْا۟ رَبَّهُم
مُنِيبِينَ إِلَيْهِ ثُمَّ إِذَآ أَذَاقَهُم

3541. As turned out from the creative hand of Allah, man is innocent, pure, true, free, inclined to right and virtue, and endued with true understanding about his own position in the Universe and about Allah's goodness, wisdom, and power. That is his true nature, just as the nature of a lamb is to be gentle and of a horse is to be swift. But man is caught in the meshes of customs, superstitions, selfish desires, and false teaching. This may make him pugnacious, unclean, false, slavish, hankering after what is wrong or forbidden, and deflected from the love of his fellow-men and the pure worship of the One True God. The problem before spiritual Teachers is to cure this crookedness, and to restore human nature to what it should be under the Will of Allah.

3542. In 9:36, I translated *Dīn qayyim* as "straight usage." Here the menaing is wider, as it includes the whole life, thoughts and desires of man. The "standard Religion," or the Straight Way is thus contrasted with the various human systems that conflict with each other and call themselves separate "religions" or "sects" (see verse 32 below). Allah's standard Religion is one, as God is One.

3543. "Repentance" does not mean sackcloth and ashes, or putting on a gloomy pessimism. It means giving up disease for health, crookedness (which is abnormal) for the Straight Way, the restoration of our nature as Allah created it from the falsity introduced by the enticements of Evil. To revert to the simile of the magnetic needle (n. 3540 above), if the needle is held back by obstructions, we must restore its freedom, so that it points true again to the magnetic pole.

3544. A good description of self-satisfied sectarianism as against real Religion. See n. 3542 above.

3545. *Cf.* 10:12. It is trouble, distress, or adversity that makes men realise their helplessness and turns their attention back to the true Source of all goodness and happiness. But when they are shown special Mercy—often more than they deserve—they forget themselves and attribute it to their own cleverness, or to the stars, or to some false ideas to which they pay court and worship, either to the exclusion of Allah or in addition to the lip-worship which they pay to Allah. Their action in any case amounts to gross ingratitude; but in the circumstances it looks as if they had gone out of their way to show ingratitude.

Of Mercy as from Himself.
Behold, some of them
Pay part-worship to
Other gods besides their Lord—

مِّنْهُ رَحْمَةً إِذَا فَرِيقٌ
مِّنْهُم بِرَبِّهِمْ يُشْرِكُونَ

34. (As if) to show their ingratitude
For the (favours) We have
Bestowed on them! Then enjoy
(Your brief day); but soon
Will ye know (your folly).[3546]

٣٤ لِيَكْفُرُوا بِمَا آتَيْنَاهُمْ ۚ
فَتَمَتَّعُوا فَسَوْفَ تَعْلَمُونَ

35. Or have We sent down
Authority to them, which
Points out to them[3547]
The things to which
They pay part-worship?

٣٥ أَمْ أَنزَلْنَا عَلَيْهِمْ سُلْطَانًا
فَهُوَ يَتَكَلَّمُ بِمَا كَانُوا بِهِ يُشْرِكُونَ

36. When We give men
A taste of Mercy,[3548]
They exult thereat:
And when some evil
Afflicts them because of
What their (own) hands
Have sent forth, behold,
They are in despair!

٣٦ وَإِذَا أَذَقْنَا
النَّاسَ رَحْمَةً فَرِحُوا بِهَا ۖ
وَإِن تُصِبْهُمْ سَيِّئَةٌ بِمَا قَدَّمَتْ
أَيْدِيهِمْ إِذَا هُمْ يَقْنَطُونَ

37. See they not that Allah
Enlarges the provision and
Restricts it, to whomsoever[3549]
He pleases? Verily in that
Are Signs for those who believe.

٣٧ أَوَلَمْ يَرَوْا أَنَّ اللَّهَ يَبْسُطُ
الرِّزْقَ لِمَن يَشَاءُ وَيَقْدِرُ ۚ
إِنَّ فِي ذَٰلِكَ لَآيَاتٍ لِّقَوْمٍ يُؤْمِنُونَ

3546. *Cf.* 16:54. They are welcome to their fancies and false worship, and to the enjoyment of the pleasures of this Life, but they will soon be disillusioned. Then they will realise the true values of the things they neglected and the things they cultivated.

3547. Their behaviour is exactly as if they were satisfied within themselves that they were entitled or given a licence to worship God and Mammon. In fact the whole thing is their own invention or delusion.

3548. *Cf.* 30:33. In that passage the unreasonable behaviour of men in sorrow and in affluence is considered with reference to their attitude to Allah: in distress they turn to Him, but in prosperity they turn to other things. Here the contrast in the two situations is considered with reference to men's inner psychology: in affluence they are puffed up and unduly elated, and in adversity they lose all heart. Both attitudes are wrong. In prosperity men should realise that it is not their merits that deserve all the Bounty of Allah, but that it is given out of Allah's abundant generosity; in adversity they should remember that their suffering is brought on by their own folly and sin, and humbly pray for Allah's grace and mercy, in order that they may be set on their feet again. For, as the next verse points out, Allah gives opportunities, gifts, and the good things of life to every one, but in greater or lesser measure, and at some time or other, according to His All-Wise Plan, which is the expression of His Holy and benevolent Will.

3549. *Cf.* 28:82 and n. 3412. Also see last note. Allah's grant of certain gifts to some, as well as His withholding of certain gifts from others, are themselves Signs (trial or warnings) to men of faith and understanding.

38. So give what is due
To kindred, the needy,
And the wayfarer.
That is best for those
Who seek the Countenance,[3550]
Of Allah, and it is they
Who will prosper.[3551]

فَـَٔاتِ ذَا ٱلْقُرْبَىٰ حَقَّهُۥ وَٱلْمِسْكِينَ وَٱبْنَ ٱلسَّبِيلِ ۚ ذَٰلِكَ خَيْرٌ لِّلَّذِينَ يُرِيدُونَ وَجْهَ ٱللَّهِ ۖ وَأُو۟لَـٰٓئِكَ هُمُ ٱلْمُفْلِحُونَ ﴿٣٨﴾

39. That which ye lay out
For increase through the property
Of (other) people, will have[3552]
No increase with Allah:
But that which ye lay out
For charity, seeking
The Countenance of Allah,[3553]
(Will increase): it is
These who will get
A recompense multiplied.

وَمَآ ءَاتَيْتُم مِّن رِّبًا لِّيَرْبُوَا۟ فِىٓ أَمْوَٰلِ ٱلنَّاسِ فَلَا يَرْبُوا۟ عِندَ ٱللَّهِ ۖ وَمَآ ءَاتَيْتُم مِّن زَكَوٰةٍ تُرِيدُونَ وَجْهَ ٱللَّهِ فَأُو۟لَـٰٓئِكَ هُمُ ٱلْمُضْعِفُونَ ﴿٣٩﴾

40. It is Allah who has
Created you: further, He has
Provided for your sustenance;
Then He will cause you
To die; and again He will
Give you life. Are there
Any of your (false) "Partners"[3554]
Who can do any single
One of these things?
Glory to Him! and High
Is He above the partners[3555]
They attribute (to Him)!

ٱللَّهُ ٱلَّذِى خَلَقَكُمْ ثُمَّ رَزَقَكُمْ ثُمَّ يُمِيتُكُمْ ثُمَّ يُحْيِيكُمْ ۖ هَلْ مِن شُرَكَآئِكُم مَّن يَفْعَلُ مِن ذَٰلِكُم مِّن شَىْءٍ ۚ سُبْحَـٰنَهُۥ وَتَعَـٰلَىٰ عَمَّا يُشْرِكُونَ ﴿٤٠﴾

3550. For *Wajh* (Face, Countenance), see n. 114 to 2:112. Also see 6:52.

3551. In both this life and the next. See n. 29 to 2:5.

3552. *Ribā'* (literally 'usury' or 'interest') is prohibited, for the principle is that any profit which we should seek should be through our own exertions and at our own expense, not through exploiting other people or at their expense, however we may wrap up the process in the spacious phraseology of high finance or City jargon. But we are asked to go beyond this negative precept of avoiding what is wrong. We should show our active love for our neighbourhood by spending our own substance or resources or the utilisation of our own talents and opportunities in the service of those who need them. Then our reward or recompense will not be merely what we deserve. It will be multiplied to many times more than our strict account. According to Commentators this verse specially applies to those who give to others, whether gifts or services, in order to receive from them greater benefits in return. Such seemingly good acts are void of any merit and deserve no reward from Allah since He knows the real intention behind such ostensibily good deeds. (R).

3553. Seeking the "Face" or "Countenance" of Allah, *i.e.*, out of our pure love for the true vision of Allah's own Self. See also n. 3550 above.

3554. The person or thing or ideas to which we give part-worship, while our whole and exclusive worship is due to Allah, are the "Partners" we set up. Do we owe our existence to them? Do they sustain our being? Can they take or give back to us? Certainly not. Then how foolish of us to give them part-worship!

3555. *Cf.* 10:8 and similar passages.

C. 182.—(30:41-60.)
The result of Evil is Evil. So
Mischief spreads, but Allah will restore
The balance in the End. He did create
All things pure, and will purge and purify,
As He does the physical world with Winds.
Destruction awaits those that break
His Harmony and Law: it will come when least
Expected. Let the righteous wait and endure
With constancy, for Evil is shaky,
With no faith in itself and no roots,
And is doomed to perish utterly.

SECTION 5.

41. Mischief has appeared
On land and sea because
Of (the meed) that the hands
Of men have earned.[3556]
That (Allah) may give them
A taste of some of their
Deeds: in order that they[3557]
May turn back (from Evil).

٤١ ظَهَرَ ٱلْفَسَادُ فِى ٱلْبَرِّ وَٱلْبَحْرِ
بِمَا كَسَبَتْ أَيْدِى ٱلنَّاسِ
لِيُذِيقَهُم بَعْضَ ٱلَّذِى عَمِلُوا۟
لَعَلَّهُمْ يَرْجِعُونَ

42. Say: "Travel through the earth
And see what was the End
Of those before (you):
Most of them worshipped[3558]
Others besides Allah."

٤٢ قُلْ سِيرُوا۟ فِى ٱلْأَرْضِ فَٱنظُرُوا۟
كَيْفَ كَانَ عَٰقِبَةُ ٱلَّذِينَ مِن قَبْلُ
كَانَ أَكْثَرُهُم مُّشْرِكِينَ

43. But set thou thy face
To the right Religion,
Before there comes from Allah
The Day which there is[3559]

٤٣ فَأَقِمْ وَجْهَكَ لِلدِّينِ ٱلْقَيِّمِ
مِن قَبْلِ أَن يَأْتِىَ يَوْمٌ

3556. Allah's Creation was pure and good in itself. All the mischief or corruption was introduced by Evil, *viz.*, arrogance, selfishness, etc. See n. 3541 to 30:30 above. As soon as the mischief has come in, Allah's mercy and goodness step in to stop it. The consequences of Evil must be evil, and this should be shown in such partial punishment as "the hands of men have earned," so that it may be a warning for the future and an invitation to enter the door of repentance.

3557. The ultimate object of Allah's justice and punishment is to reclaim man fro..n Evil, and to restore him to the pristine purity and innocence in which he was created. The Evil introduced by his possession of a limited free will should be eliminated by the education and purification of man's own will. For, with his will and motives purified, he is capable of much greater heights than a creature not endowed with any free will.

3558. If you contemplate history and past experience (including spiritual experience), you will find that evil and corruption tended to destroy themselves, because they had false idols for worship, false standards of conduct, and false goals of desire.

3559. We should recover the balance of what has been upset by Evil and Falsehood before it is too late. For a Day will surely come when true values will be restored and all falsehood and evil will be destroyed. Nothing but repentance and amendment can avert the consequences of Evil. When the Day actually comes, repentance will be too late: for the impassable barrier between Evil and Good will have been fixed, and the chance of return to Allah's pattern will have been lost.

No chance of averting:
On that Day shall men
Be divided (in two).[3560]

لَا مَرَدَّ لَهُۥ مِنَ ٱللَّهِ
يَوْمَئِذٍ يَصَّدَّعُونَ

44. Those who reject Faith
Will suffer from that rejection:
And those who work righteousness
Will spread their couch
(Of repose) for themselves
(In heaven):

٤٤ مَن كَفَرَ فَعَلَيْهِ كُفْرُهُۥ
وَمَنْ عَمِلَ صَٰلِحًا
فَلِأَنفُسِهِمْ يَمْهَدُونَ

45. That He may reward those
Who believe and work righteous
Deeds, out of His Bounty.[3561]
For He loves not those
Who reject Faith.[3562]

٤٥ لِيَجْزِىَ ٱلَّذِينَ ءَامَنُوا۟
وَعَمِلُوا۟ ٱلصَّٰلِحَٰتِ مِن فَضْلِهِۦٓ
إِنَّهُۥ لَا يُحِبُّ ٱلْكَٰفِرِينَ

46. Among His Signs is this,[3563]
That He sends the Winds,
As heralds of Glad Tidings,
Giving you a taste
Of His (Grace and) Mercy—[3564]
That the ships may sail
(Majestically) by His Command
And that ye may seek[3565]
Of His Bounty: in order
That ye may be grateful.

٤٦ وَمِنْ ءَايَٰتِهِۦٓ أَن يُرْسِلَ
ٱلرِّيَاحَ مُبَشِّرَٰتٍ وَلِيُذِيقَكُم مِّن رَّحْمَتِهِۦ
وَلِتَجْرِىَ ٱلْفُلْكُ بِأَمْرِهِۦ
وَلِتَبْتَغُوا۟ مِن فَضْلِهِۦ
وَلَعَلَّكُمْ تَشْكُرُونَ

3560. The sharp division will then have been accomplished between the unfortunate ones who rejected Truth and Faith and will suffer for their rejection, and the righteous ones who will attain Peace and Salvation: see next verse. Note that the state of the Blessed will not merely be a passive state. They will actively earn and contribute to their own happiness: "they will spread their couch of repose for themselves."

3561. Though the repose and bliss will have been won by the righteous by their own efforts, it must not be supposed that their own merits were equal to the reward they will earn. What they will get will be due to the infinte Grace and Bounty of Allah.

3562. In form this clause is (there as elsewhere) negative, but it has a positive meaning: Allah loves those who have faith and trust in Him, and will, out of His Grace and Bounty, reward them in abundant measure.

3563. The theme of Allah's artistry in the physical and the spiritual world was placed before us above in 30:20-27. Then, in verse 28-40, we were shown how man and nature were pure as they came out of the hand of Allah, and how we must restore this purity in order to fulfil the Will and Plan of Allah. Now we are told how the restorative and purifying agencies were sent by Allah Himself—in both the physical and the spiritual world.

3564. *Cf.* 7:57 and n. 1036 and 25:48 and n. 3104.

3565. In the physical world, the winds not only cool and purify the air, and bring the blessings of rain, which fertilises the soil, but they help international commerce and intercourse among men through seaways and now by airways. Those who know how to take advantage of these blessings of Allah prosper and rejoice, while those who ignore or fail to understand these Signs perish in storms. So in the spiritual world: heralds of glad tidings were sent by Allah in the shape of Messengers: those who profited by their Message prospered in spiritual gain, and those who ignored or opposed the Clear Sign perished spriritually: see next verse.

47. We did indeed send,
Before thee, messengers
To their (respective) peoples,
And they came to them
With Clear Signs: then,
To those who transgressed,
We meted out Retribution:
And it was due from Us
To aid those who believed.

٤٧ وَلَقَدۡ أَرۡسَلۡنَا
مِن قَبۡلِكَ رُسُلًا إِلَىٰ قَوۡمِهِمۡ
فَجَآءُوهُم بِٱلۡبَيِّنَٰتِ
فَٱنتَقَمۡنَا مِنَ ٱلَّذِينَ أَجۡرَمُواْۖ
وَكَانَ حَقًّا عَلَيۡنَا نَصۡرُ ٱلۡمُؤۡمِنِينَ

48. It is Allah Who sends
The Winds, and they raise[3566]
The Clouds: then does He
Spread them in the sky
As He wills, and break them
Into fragments, until thou seest
Raindrops issue from the midst
Thereof: then when He has
Made them reach such[3567]
Of His servants as He wills,
Behold, they do rejoice!—

٤٨ ٱللَّهُ ٱلَّذِي يُرۡسِلُ ٱلرِّيَٰحَ
فَتُثِيرُ سَحَابًا فَيَبۡسُطُهُۥ
فِي ٱلسَّمَآءِ كَيۡفَ يَشَآءُ وَيَجۡعَلُهُۥ
كِسَفًا فَتَرَى ٱلۡوَدۡقَ يَخۡرُجُ مِنۡ خِلَٰلِهِۦۖ
فَإِذَآ أَصَابَ بِهِۦ مَن يَشَآءُ مِنۡ عِبَادِهِۦٓ
إِذَا هُمۡ يَسۡتَبۡشِرُونَ

49. Even though, before they received
(The rain)—just before this—
They were dumb with despair!

٤٩ وَإِن كَانُواْ مِن قَبۡلِ أَن يُنَزَّلَ
عَلَيۡهِم مِّن قَبۡلِهِۦ لَمُبۡلِسِينَ

50. Then contemplate (O man!)
The memorials of Allah's Mercy!—
How He gives life[3568]
To the earth after
Its death: verily the Same
Will give life to the men
Who are dead: for He
Has power over all things.

٥٠ فَٱنظُرۡ إِلَىٰٓ ءَاثَٰرِ رَحۡمَتِ ٱللَّهِ
كَيۡفَ يُحۡيِ ٱلۡأَرۡضَ بَعۡدَ مَوۡتِهَآۚ
إِنَّ ذَٰلِكَ لَمُحۡيِ ٱلۡمَوۡتَىٰۖ
وَهُوَ عَلَىٰ كُلِّ شَيۡءٖ قَدِيرٞ

3566. Again the Parable of the Winds is presented from another aspect, both physical and spiritual. In the physical world, see their play with the Clouds; how they suck up the moisture from terrestrial water, carry it about in dark clouds as needed, and break it up with rain as needed. So Allah's wonderful Grace draws up men's spiritual aspirations from the most unlikely places and suspends them as dark mysteries according to His Holy Will and Plan; and when His Message reaches the hearts of men even in the smallest fragments, how its recipients rejoice, even though before it, they were in utter despair!

3567. See last note.

3568. After the two Parables about the purifying action of the Winds and their fertilising action, we now have the Parable of the earth that dies in winter or drought and lives again in spring or rain, by Allah's Grace: so in the spiritual sphere, man may be dead and may live again by the Breath of Allah and His Mercy if he will only place himself in Allah's hands.

51. And if We (but) send
A Wind from which[3569]
They see (their tilth)
Turn yellow—behold,
They become, thereafter,
Ungrateful (Unbelievers)!

٥١ وَلَئِنْ أَرْسَلْنَا رِيحًا
فَرَأَوْهُ مُصْفَرًّا لَّظَلُّوا
مِنۢ بَعْدِهِۦ يَكْفُرُونَ

52. So verily thou canst not
Make the dead to hear,[3570]
Nor canst thou make
The deaf to hear
The call, when they show
Their backs and turn away.

٥٢ فَإِنَّكَ لَا تُسْمِعُ ٱلْمَوْتَىٰ
وَلَا تُسْمِعُ ٱلصُّمَّ ٱلدُّعَآءَ
إِذَا وَلَّوْا۟ مُدْبِرِينَ

53. Nor canst thou lead back
The blind from their straying:[3571]
Only those wilt thou make
To hear, who believe
In Our Signs and submit
(Their wills in Islam).

٥٣ وَمَآ أَنتَ بِهَٰدِ ٱلْعُمْىِ عَن ضَلَٰلَتِهِمْ
إِن تُسْمِعُ إِلَّا مَن يُؤْمِنُ بِـَٔايَٰتِنَا
فَهُم مُّسْلِمُونَ

Section 6.

54. It is Allah Who
Created you in a state
Of (helpless) weakness, then
Gave (you) strength after weakness,
Then, after strength, gave (you)
Weakness and a hoary head:[3572]

٥٤ ٱللَّهُ ٱلَّذِى خَلَقَكُم
مِّن ضَعْفٍ ثُمَّ جَعَلَ مِنۢ بَعْدِ ضَعْفٍ قُوَّةً
ثُمَّ جَعَلَ مِنۢ بَعْدِ قُوَّةٍ ضَعْفًا وَشَيْبَةً

3569. Another Parable from the forces of nature. We saw how the Winds gladdened, vivified, and enriched those who utilised them in the right spirit. But a wind might be destructive to tilth in certain circumstances: so the blessings of Allah may—by the wrongdoers resisting and blaspheming—bring punishment to the wrongdoers. Instead of taking the punishment in the right spirit—in the spirit in which Believers of Allah take their misfortunes—the Unbelievers curse and deepen their sin!

3570. The marvels of Allah's creation can be realised in a general way by every one who has a disposition to allow such knowledge to penetrate his mind. But if men, out of perversity, kill the very faculties which Allah has given them, how can they then understand? Besides the men who deaden their spiritual sense, there are men who may be likened to the deaf, who lack one faculty but to whom an appeal can be made through other faculties, such as the sense of sight: but if they turn their backs and refuse to be instructed at all, how can the Truth reach them?

3571. See last note. Then there is the case of men about whom the saying holds true, that none are so blind as those who *will* not see. They *prefer* to stray in the paths of wrong and of sensory pleasures. How can they be guided in any way? The only persons who gain by spiritual teaching are those who bring a mind to it—who believe and submit their wills to Allah's Will. This is the central doctrine of Islam.

3572. What was said before about the people who make Allah's teaching "of none effect" does not mean that Evil will defeat Allah. On the contrary, we are asked to contemplate the mysteries of Allah's wisdom with another Parable. In our physical life we see how strength is evolved out of weakness and weakness out of strength. The helpless babe becomes a lusty man in the pride of manhood, and then sinks to a feeble old age: and yet there is wisdom in all these stages in the Universal Plan. So Allah carries out His Plan in the spiritual world "as He wills", *i.e.*, according to His Will and Plan, and none can gainsay it. And His Plan is wise and can never be frustrated.

He creates as He wills,
And it is He Who has
All knowledge and power.

يَخۡلُقُ مَا يَشَآءُۖ
وَهُوَ ٱلۡعَلِيمُ ٱلۡقَدِيرُ

55. On the Day that
The Hour (of reckoning)
Will be established,[3573]
The transgressors will swear
That they tarried not
But an hour: thus were
They used to being deluded!

٥٥ وَيَوۡمَ تَقُومُ ٱلسَّاعَةُ يُقۡسِمُ
ٱلۡمُجۡرِمُونَ مَا لَبِثُواْ غَيۡرَ سَاعَةٖۚ
كَذَٰلِكَ كَانُواْ يُؤۡفَكُونَ

56. But those endued with knowledge
And faith will say:
"Indeed ye did tarry,
Within Allah's Decree,
To the Day of Resurrection,
And this is the Day[3574]
Of Resurrection: but ye—
Ye were not aware!"

٥٦ وَقَالَ ٱلَّذِينَ أُوتُواْ ٱلۡعِلۡمَ وَٱلۡإِيمَٰنَ
لَقَدۡ لَبِثۡتُمۡ فِي كِتَٰبِ ٱللَّهِ إِلَىٰ يَوۡمِ ٱلۡبَعۡثِۖ
فَهَٰذَا يَوۡمُ ٱلۡبَعۡثِ وَلَٰكِنَّكُمۡ
كُنتُمۡ لَا تَعۡلَمُونَ

57. So on that Day no excuse
Of theirs will
Avail the Transgressors,[3575]
Nor will they be invited (then)
To seek grace (by repentance).

٥٧ فَيَوۡمَئِذٖ لَّا يَنفَعُ ٱلَّذِينَ ظَلَمُواْ
مَعۡذِرَتُهُمۡ وَلَا هُمۡ يُسۡتَعۡتَبُونَ

58. Verily We have propounded
For men, in this Qur'ān,
Every kind of Parable:
But if thou bring to them
Any Sign, the Unbelievers[3576]

٥٨ وَلَقَدۡ ضَرَبۡنَا لِلنَّاسِ
فِي هَٰذَا ٱلۡقُرۡءَانِ مِن كُلِّ مَثَلٖۚ
وَلَئِن جِئۡتَهُم بِـَٔايَةٖ لَّيَقُولَنَّ ٱلَّذِينَ كَفَرُوٓاْ

3573. Whatever the seeming inequalities may be now—when the good appear to be weak and the strong seem to oppress—will be removed when the balance will be finally redressed. That will happen in good time—indeed so quickly that the Transgressors will be taken by surprise. They were deluded by the fact that what they took to be their triumph or their freedom to do what they liked was only a reprieve, a "Term Appointed", in which they could repent and amend and get Allah's Mercy. Failing this, they will then be up against the Penalties which they thought they had evaded or defied.

3574. The men of knowledge and faith knew all along of the true values—of the things of this ephemeral life and the things that will endure and face them at the End—unlike the wrongdoers who were content with falsehoods and were taken by surprise, like ignorant men, when they faced the Realities.

3575. It will be no use for those who deliberately rejected the clearest warnings in Allah's Message to say: "Oh we did not realise this!" The excuse will be false, and it would be unreasonable to suppose that they would then be asked to seek Grace by repentance. It will then be too late.

3576. Things of the highest moment have been explained in the Qur'ān from various points of view, as in this Sūrah itself, by means of parables and similitudes drawn from nature and from our ordinary daily life. But whatever the explanation, however convincing it may be to men who earnestly seek after Truth, those who deliberately turn their backs to Truth can find nothing convincing. In their eyes the explanations are mere "vain talk" or false arguments.

Are sure to say, "Ye
Do nothing but talk vanities."

إِنْ أَنتُمْ إِلَّا مُبْطِلُونَ

59. Thus does Allah seal up[3577]
The hearts of those
Who understand not.

٥٩ كَذَٰلِكَ يَطْبَعُ ٱللَّهُ عَلَىٰ
قُلُوبِ ٱلَّذِينَ لَا يَعْلَمُونَ

60. So patiently persevere: for
Verily the promise of Allah
Is true: nor let those[3578]
Shake thy firmness, who have
(Themselves) no certainty of faith.

٦٠ فَٱصْبِرْ إِنَّ وَعْدَ ٱللَّهِ حَقٌّ
وَلَا يَسْتَخِفَّنَّكَ ٱلَّذِينَ لَا يُوقِنُونَ

3577. When an attitude of obstinate resistance to Truth is adopted, the natural consequence (by Allah's Law) is that the heart and mind get more and more hardened with every act of deliberate rejection. It becomes more and more impervious to the reception of Truth, just as a sealed envelope is unable to receive any further letter or message after it is sealed. *Cf.* also 2:7 and n. 31.

3578. The Prophet of Allah does not slacken in his efforts or feel discouraged because the Unbelievers laugh at him or persecute him or even seem to succeed in blocking his Message. He has firm faith, and he knows that Allah will finally establish His Truth. He goes on in his divinely entrusted task, with patience and perseverance, which must win against the levity of his opponents, who have no faith or certainty at all to sustain them. (R).

APPENDIX VIII.

FIRST CONTACT OF ISLAM WITH WORLD MOVEMENTS

The contemporary Roman and Persian Empires (see 30:2-7 and notes)

The conflict between the Byzantine Emperor Heraclius and the Persian King Khasrau Parwīz (Chosroes II) is referred to in Sūrah 30. (*Al Rūm*). It will therefore be convenient now to review very briefly the relations of those two great empires and the way in which they gradually decayed before the rising sun of Islam. The story has not only a political significance, but a deep spiritual significance in world history.

2. If we take the Byzantine Empire as a continuation of the Empire that grew out of the Roman Republic, the first conflict took place in B.C. 53, when the Consul Crassus (famous for his riches) was defeated in his fight with the Parthians. If we go back further, to the time of the Greek City-States, we can refer back to the invasion of Greece by Xerxes in B.C. 480-479 and the effective repulse of that invasion by sea and land by the united cooperation of the Greek States. The Persian Empire in those days extended to the western (Mediterranean) coast of Asia Minor. But as it included the Greek cities of Asia Minor, there was constant intercourse in war and peace between Persia and the Hellenic (Greek) world. The cities in Greece proper had their own rivalries and jealousies, and Greek cities or parties often invoked the aid of the Great King (Shahinshah of Persia) against their opponents. By the Peace of Antalcidas, B.C. 387, Persia became practically the suzerain power of Greece. This was under the Achaemenian Dynasty of Persia.

3. Then came the rise of Macedonia and Alexander's conquest of the Persian Empire (B.C. 330). This spread the Hellenic influence as far east as Central Asia, and as far south as Syria (including Palestine), Egypt, and Northern Africa generally. Rome in its expansion westwards reached the Atlantic, and in its expansion eastwards absorbed the territories of Alexander's successors, and became the mistress of all countries with a Mediterranean seacoast. The nations of the Roman Empire "insensibly melted away into the Roman name and people" (Gibbon, chap. ii).

4. Meanwhile there were native forces in Persia which asserted themselves and established (A.C. 10) the Dynasty of the Arsacids (*Ashkāniān*). This was mainly the outcome of a revolt against Hellenism, and its spearpoint was in Parthia. The Arsacids won back Persia proper, and established the western boundary of Persia in a line drawn roughly from the eastern end of the Black Sea southwards to the Euphrates at a point northeast of Palmyra. This would include the region of the Caucasus (excluding the Black Sea coast) and Armenia and Lower Mesopotamia, in the Persian Empire. This was the normal boundary between Persia and the Roman Empire until the Islamic Empire wiped out the old Monarchy of Persia and a great part of the Byzantine Empire, and annexed Egypt, Palestine, Syria, and gradually Asia Minor, finally extinguishing the whole of the Byzantine Empire.

5. Another stage in Persian history was reached when the Arsacids were overthrown and the Sāsānians came into power under Ardshir I, A.C. 225. The Sāsānian Empire was, in a sense, a continuation of the Achaemenian Empire, and was a reaction against the corruptions of the Zoroastrian religion which had crept in under the Parthian Dynasty of the Arsacids. But the religious reforms were only partial. There was some interaction between Christianity and the Zoroastrian religion. For example, the great mystic Mānī, who was a painter as well as a religious leader, founded

the sect of Manichaeism. He flourished in the reign of Shāpūr I (A.C. 241-272) and seems to have preached a form of Gnostic faith, in which Alexandrian philosophy was mixed with Christian doctrine and the old Persian belief in the dual principle of Good and Evil. The Sāsānians failed to purify religion and only adhered to fire-worship in arrogance, luxury, sensuality, and monopoly of power and privilege, which it is the office of Religion to denounce and root out. That office was performed by Islam.

6. When the seat of the Roman Empire was transferred to Constantinople (Byzantium) in the time of Constantine (A.C. 330), the conflict between Rome and Persia became more and more frequent. The true Peninsula of Arabia was never conquered either by Rome or by Persia, although its outlying parts were absorbed in either the one or the other at various times. It is interesting to notice that the Roman Emperor Philip (A.C. 244-249) was a born Arab and that the architecture of the Nabataeans in the city of Petra and in Ḥijr shows a mixture of Roman, Greek, Egyptian, and indigenous Arab cultures.

7. Arabia received the cultural influences of Persia and the Byzantine Empire, but was a silent spectator of their conflicts until Islam was brought into the main currents of world politics.

8. The Yemen coast of Arabia, which was easily accessible by sea to Persia, was the battle-ground between the Persian Empire and the Abyssinian Empire just across the Red Sea. Abyssinia and Arabia had had cultural and political relations for many centuries. Amharic, the ruling language of Abyssinia, is closely allied with Arabic, and the Amharic people went as colonists and conquerors from Arabia through Yemen. Shortly before the birth of the Holy Prophet, Abyssinia had been in occupation of Yemen for some time, having displaced a Jewish dynasty. The Abyssinians professed the Christian religion, and although their Church was doctrinally separate from the Byzantine Church, there was a great deal of sympathy between the Byzantines and the Abyssinians on account of their common Christian religion. One of the Abyssinian viceroys in Yemen was Abrahah, who conceived the design of destroying the Temple at Makkah. He led an expedition, in which elephants formed a conspicuous feature, to invade Makkah and destroy the Ka'bah. He met a disastrous repulse, which is referred to in the Qur'ān (Sūrah 105). This event was in the year of the Prophet's birth, and marks the beginning of the great conflict which enabled Arabia eventually to obtain a leading place among the nations of the world. The year usually given for the Prophet's birth is 570 A.C., though the date must be taken as only approximate, being the middle figure between 569 and 571, the extreme possible limits. The Abyssinians having been overthrown, the Persians were established in Yemen, and their power lasted there until about the 7th year of the Hijrah (approximately 628 A.C.), when Yemen accepted Islam.

9. The outstanding event in Byzantine history in the 6th century was the reign of Justinian (527-565) and in Persian history the reign of Anawshīrwān (531-579). Justinian is well-known for his great victories in Africa and for the great Digest he made of Roman Law and Jurisprudence. In spite of the scandalous life of his queen Theodora, he occupies an honourable place in the history of the Roman Empire. Anawshīrwān is known in Persian history as the "Just King". They were contemporary rulers for a period of 34 years. In their time the Roman and Persian Empires were in close contact during peace and war. Anawshīrwān just missed being adopted by the Roman Emperor. If the adoption had come off, he would have become one of the claimants to the Byzantine throne. He invaded Syria and destroyed the important Christian city of Antioch in 540-541. It was only the able defence of Belisarius, the Roman general, which saved the Roman Empire from further disasters in the east. On the other hand the Turanian Avars, driven in front of the Turks, had begun the invasion of Constantinople from the western side. Justinian made an alliance with the Abyssinians as a Christian nation, and the Abyssinians and the Persians came to conflict in Yemen. Thus world conditions were hemming in Arabia on all sides. It was Islam that not only saved Arabia but enabled it to expand and to play a prominent part in world history after the annihilation of the Persian Empire and the partial destruction of the Byzantine Empire.

10. The sixth century of the Christian era and the first half of the seventh century were indeed a marvellous period in the world's history. Great events and transformations were taking place throughout the then known world. We have referred to the Roman Empire and the Persian Empire which dominated the civilised portions of Europe, Africa and Western Asia. The only two other countries of note in history in those days were India and China. In India there was the glorious period of Harsha Vardhana (606-647 A.C.), in which art, science, and literature flourished, political power was on a healthy basis, and religious enquiry was bringing India and China into closer relationship. The famous Chinese Buddhist traveller Yuang-Chwang (or Yuang-Tsang or Hsuan-Tsang) performed his pious pilgrimage to India in 629-45. In China, the glorious T'ang Dynasty was established in 618. The Chinese art of that Dynasty led the world. In political power, China extended from the Pacific in the east to the Persian Gulf on the west. There was unity and peace, and China—hitherto more or less isolated—received ambassadors from Persia, Constantinople, Magadha, and Nepal, in 643. But all this pomp and glitter had in it the seeds of decay. Persia and Byzantium collapsed in the next generation. India was in chaos after Harsha's death. The Chinese Empire could not long remain free from the "Barbarians": the Great Wall, begun in the the third century B.C., was soon to be out of date. By about 683 the Khitans from the northwest and the Tibetans from the south were molesting China. The Germans, the Goths and the Vandals were pressing further and further into the Roman Empire. From Asia, the Avars and the Turks were pressing both on the Romans and the Persians, and sometimes playing off the one against the other. The simpler and less sophisticated nations, with their ruder but more genuine virtues, were gaining ground. Into all that welter came the Message of Islam, to show up, as by galvanic action, the false from the truth, the empty from the eternal, the decrepit and corrupt from the vigorous and pure. The ground of History was being prepared for the New Birth in Religion.

11. Anawshīrwān was succeeded on the Persian throne by an unworthy son Hurmuz (579-590). Had it not been for the talents of his able General Bahrām, his Empire would have been ruined by the invasions of the Turks on one side and the Romans on the other. Eventually Bahrām rebelled, and Hurmuz was deposed and killed. His son Khusraw Parwīz (Chosroes II) took refuge with the Byzantine Emperor Maurice, who practically adopted him as a son and restored him to the Persian throne with Roman arms. Khusraw reigned over Persia from 590 to 628. It was to him that the Holy Prophet addressed one of his letters, inviting him to Islam towards the end of his life. It is not certain whether the letter was actually delivered to him or to his successor, as it is not easy to calculate precisely synchronous dates of the Christian era with those of the earliest years of the Hijrah era.

12. In Arabic and Persian records the term Kisrā refers usually to Khusraw Parwīz (Chosroes II) and sometimes to Khusraw Anawshīrwān (Chosroes I), while the term Khusraw is usually treated as generic—as the title of the Kings of Persia generally. But this is by no means always the case. "Kisrā" is an Arabic form of "Khusraw". The name of Anawshīrwān has been shortened from the time of Firdawsī onwards to Nūshīrwān. The Pehlevi form is Anoshek-ruwān, "of immortal soul".

13. The Roman Emperor Maurice (582-602) had a mutiny in his army, and his capital revolted against him. The army chose a simple centurion called Phocas as Emperor and executed Maurice himself. The usurper Phocas ruled from 602 to 610, but his tyranny soon disgusted the Empire. Heraclius, the governor (exarch) of a distant province in Africa, raised the standard of rebellion, and his young son, also called Heraclius, was sent to Constantinople to depose Phocas and assume the reins of power. It was this younger Heraclius, who ascended the throne of Constantinople in 610 and ruled till 642, who figures in Muslim history as *Hiraql*.

14. Khusraw Parwīz called himself the son of the Emperor Maurice. During his refuge at Constantinople he had married a Byzantine wife. In Nizāmī's Romance she is known as Maryam. According to some historians she was a daughter of the Emperor Maurice, but Gibbon throws doubt on that relationship. In any case, he used the resources of the Persian Empire to fight the usurper Phocas. He invaded the Byzantine Empire in 603. The war between the Persians and the Romans became a national war and continued after the fall of Phocas in 610. The Persians

had sweeping victories, and conquered Aleppo, Antioch, and the chief Syrian cities, including Damascus in 611. Jerusalem fell to their arms in 614-615, just 8 to 7 years before the sacred Hijrah. The city was burnt and pillaged, the Christians were massacred, the churches were burnt, the burial place of Christ was itself insulted, and many relics, including the "true Cross" on which the Christians believed that Christ had been crucified, were carried away to Persia. The priests of the Persian religion celebrated an exultant triumph over the priests of Christ. In this pillage and massacre the Persians were assisted by crowds of Jews, who were discontented with the Christian domination, and the Pagan Arabs to whom any opportunity of plunder and destruction was in itself welcome. It is probably this striking event—this victory of the Persians over the Roman Empire—which is referred to in Sūrah 30 (*Al Rūm*) of the Qur'ān. The Pagan Arabs naturally sided with the Persians in their destructive zeal, and thought that the destruction of the Christian power of Rome would also mean a setback to the Message of the Prophet, the true successor of Jesus. For our Holy Prophet had already begun his mission and the promulgation of Allah's Revelation in A.C. 610. While the whole world believed that the Roman Empire was being killed by Persia, it was revealed to him that the Persian victory was short-lived and that within a period of a few years the Romans would conquer again and deal a deadly blow to the Persians. The Pagan Arabs, who were then persecuting the Holy Prophet in Makkah, hoped that their persecution would destroy the Holy Prophet's new Revelation. In fact both their persecution and the deadly blows aimed by the Persians and the Romans at each other were instruments in Allah's hands for producing those conditions which made Islam thrive and increase until it became the predominant power in the world.

15. The Persian flood of conquest did not stop with the conquest of Jerusalem. It went on to Egypt, which was also conquered and annexed to the Persian Empire in 616. The Persian occupation reached as far as Tripoli in North Africa. At the same time another Persian army ravaged Asia Minor and reached right up to the gates of Constantinople. Not only the Jews and Pagan Arabs, but the various Christian sects which had been persecuted as heretics by the Romans, joined in the fray and helped the Persians. The condition of Heraclius became indeed pitiable. With all these calamities, he had to deal with the Avars who were attacking from the other side of Constantinople, which was practically in a state of siege. Famine and pestilence added to the horrors of the situation.

16. In these desperate circumstances Heraclius conceived a brilliant plan. He knew that the Persians were weak in sea-power. He used his sea-power to attack them in the rear in 622 (the year of the Hijrah). He transported his army by sea through the Aegean Sea to the bay just south of the Taurus Mountains. He fought a decisive battle with the Persians at Issus, in the same plain in which Alexander the Great had defeated the Persians of his day in his famous march to Syria and Egypt. The Persians were taken by surprise and routed. But they had still a large force in Asia Minor, which they could have brought into play against the Romans if Heraclius had not made another and equally unexpected dash by sea from the north. He returned to Constantinople by sea, made a treaty with the Avars, and with their help kept the Persians at bay around the capital. Then he led three campaigns, in 623, 624 and 625, along the southern shore of the Black Sea and took the Persians again in the rear in the region round Trebizond and Kars. Through Armenia, he penetrated into Persia and got into Mesopotamia. He was now in a position to strike at the very heart of the Persian Empire. A decisive battle was fought on the Tigris near the city of Mosul in December 627. Before this battle, however, he had taken care to get the alliance of the Turks and with their help to relieve Constantinople in 626 against the Persians and the treacherous Avars who had then joined the Persians.

17. Heraclius celebrated his triumph in Constantinople in March 628. Peace was then made between the two Empires on the basis of the *status quo ante*. Heraclius, in pursuance of a vow he had made, went south in the autumn to Emessa (Ḥimiṣ) and from there marched on foot to Jerusalem to celebrate his victories, and restore to its place the Holy Cross which had been carried away by the Persians and was returned to the Emperor as a condition of peace. Heraclius's route

was strewn with costly carpets, and he thought that the final deliverance had come for his people and his empire. Either on the way, or in Jerusalem, he met a messenger from the Holy Prophet, carrying a letter inviting him to the True Faith as renewed in the living Messenger of the age. He apparently received the message with courtesy. But he did not realise the full import of the new World which was being shaped according to Allah's plans, and the future that was opening through the new Revelation. Perhaps in his heart he felt impressed by the story which he had heard from the Arabs about the Holy Prophet, but the apparent grandeur of his empire and the pride of his people prevented him from openly accepting the renewed Message of Allah. He caused a search to be made for any Arab who was sufficiently acquainted with the Prophet to tell him something about him. Abū Sufyān was then trading in a caravan in Syria. He was a cousin of the Prophet, and belonged to the Umayyah branch of the family. He was sent for to Jerusalem (Aelia Capitolina).

18. When Abū Sufyān was called to the presence of Heraclius, the Emperor questioned him closely about this new Prophet. Abū Sufyān himself was at that time outside Islam and really an enemy of the Prophet and his Message. Yet the story he told—of the truth and sincerity of the Holy Prophet, of the way in which the poor and the lowly flocked to him, of the wonderful increase of his power and spiritual influence, and the way in which people who had once received the Light never got disillusioned or went back to their life of ignorance, and above all the integrity with which he kept all his covenants—made a favourable impression on the mind of Heraclius. That story is told in dramatic detail by Bukhārī and other Arabian writers.

19. The relations of the Persian Monarch with Islam were different. He—either Khusraw Parwīz or his successor—received the Holy Prophet's messenger with contumely and tore up his letter. "So will his kingdom be torn up," said the Holy Prophet when the news reached him. The Persian Monarch ordered his Governor in Yemen to go and arrest the man who had so far forgotten himself as to address the grandson of Anawshīrwān on equal terms. When the Persian Governor tried to carry out his Monarch's command, the result was quite different from what the great Persian King of Kings had expected. His agent accepted the truth of Islam, and Yemen was lost as a province to the Persian Empire and became a portion of the new Muslim State. Khusraw Parwīz died in February 628. He had been deposed and imprisoned by his own cruel and undutiful son, who reigned only for a year and a half. There were nine candidates for the Persian throne in the remaining four years. Anarchy reigned supreme in the Sāsānian Empire, until the dynasty was extinguished by the Muslim victory at the battle of Madā'in in 637. The great and glorious Persian monarchy, full of pride and ambition, came to an ignominious end, and a new chapter opened for Persia under the banner of Islam.

20. The Roman Empire itself began to shrink gradually, losing its territory, not to Persia, but to the new Muslim Power which absorbed both the ancient Empires. This Power arose in its vigour to proclaim a new and purified creed to the whole world. Already in the last seven years of Heraclius's reign (635-642) several of the provinces nearest to Arabia had been annexed to the Muslim Empire. The Muslim Empire continued to spread on, in Asia Minor to the north and Egypt to the south. The Eastern Roman Empire became a mere shadow with a small bit of territory round its capital. Constantinople eventually surrendered to the Muslims in 1453.

21. That was the real end of the Roman Empire. But in the wonderful century in which the Prophet lived, another momentous Revolution was taking place. The Roman Pontificate of Gregory the Great (590-604) was creating a new Christianity as the old Christianity of the East was slowly dying out. The Patriarch of Constantinople had claimed to be the Universal Bishop, with jurisdiction over all the other bishops of Christendom. This had been silently but gradually questioned by the Popes of Rome. They had been building up a liturgy, a church organisation and a body of discipline for the clergy, different from those of the Holy Orthodox Church. They had been extending their spiritual authority in the Barbarian provinces of Gaul and Spain. They had been amassing estates and endowments. They had been accumulating secular authority in their own hands. Pope Gregory the Great converted the Anglo-Saxon invaders of Great Britain

to his form of Christianity. He protected Italy from the ravages of the Franks and Lombards and raised the See of Rome to the position of a Power which exercised ample jurisdiction over the Western world. He was preparing the way for the time when one of his successors would crown under his authority the Frankish Charlemagne as Emperor of Rome and of the West (A.C. 800), and another of his successors would finally break away from the Orthodox Church of Constantinople in 1054 by the Pope's excommunication of the Patriarch of Constantinople and the Greeks. (See the last paragraph in Appendix V.)

References: Among Western writers, the chief authority is Gibbon's *Decline and Fall of the Roman Empire*: mainly chapters 40-42, and 45-46; I have given references to other chapters in the body of this Appendix: his delineation of the characters of Heraclius and Chosroes II is brief but masterly. L. Drapeyron's French monograph, *L'Empereur Heraclius* (Paris, 1869) throws further light on an interesting personality. A.J. Butler's *Arab Conquest of Egypt* (Oxford, 1902) gives a good account of Heraclius. The famous French dramatist Corneille has left a play of Heraclius, but it turns more on an intricate and imaginary plot in the early life of Heraclius than on the character of Heraclius as Emperor. Niẓāmī, in his Khusraw-o-Shīrīn (571 H.= 1175-66 A.D.) makes a reference at the end of his Romance to the Holy Prophet's letter to the Persian King, and does attempt in the course of the Romance a picture of the King's character. He is a sort of wild Prince Hal before he comes to the throne. Shīrīn is an Armenian princess in love with Khusraw; she marries Khusraw after the death of his first wife Maryam, daughter of the Roman Emperor, and mother of the undutiful son who killed Khusraw and seized his throne. Among the other Eastern writers, we find a detailed description of the interview of Abū Sufyān in Bukhārī's *Ṣaḥīḥ* (book on the beginning of Inspiration): the notes in the excellent English translation of Muḥammad Asad (Leopold Weiss) are helpful. Ṭabarī's History is as usual valuable. Mīrkhond's (Khāwind-Shāh') *Rawḍah al Ṣafā' (translated by Rehatsek)* will give English readers a summary (at second hand) of the various Arabic authorities. Mawlāna Shiblī's otherwise excellent *Sīrah al Nabī* is in this respect disappointing. Mawlāna Ẓafar 'Alī's *Ghalaba-i-Rūm* (Urdu, Lahore, 1926) is interesting for its comments.

A note on the Persian capitals may be interesting. So long as Persia was under the influence of the Semitic Elamites, the chief residence of the rulers was at Sūsa, near the modern Dizful, about 50 miles northeast of Shustar. In the Medic or Median period (say B.C. 700 to 550) the capital was, as we should expect, in the highlands of Media, in Ecbatana, the site of the modern city of Hamadān, 180 miles west of modern Ṭihrān. Ecbatana remained even in Sāsānian times the summer capital of Persia. With the Achaemenians (B.C. 550 to 330) we come to a period of full national and imperial life. Sūsa was the chief Achaemenian capital from the time of Darius I onwards, though Persepolis (Istakhr) in the mountain region near modern Shīrāz, and about 40 miles northeast of Shīrāz, was used as the city of royal burial. Alexander himself, as Ruler in Persia, died in Babylon. Later, when the centre of gravity moved north and northeast, other sites were selected. The Arsacids (*Ashkāniān*) or Parthians were a tribal power, fitly called in Arabic the *mulūk al Tawā'if*, and had probably no fixed or centralised capital. The Sāsānian took over a site where there were a number of cities, among which were Ctesiphon and Seleucia on opposite banks of the river Tigris. This site is about 45 miles north of the old site of Babylon and 25 miles below the later city of Baghdād. Ctesiphon and Seleucia were Greek cities founded by one of Alexander's successors. Seleucia being named after Seleucus.

This complex of seven cities was afterwards called by the Arabic name of Madā'in ("the Cities"). The Takht-i-Kisrā (or Arch of Ctesiphon) still stands in a ruinous condition on this site. This seems to have been the chief capital of the Sāsānians at the Arab conquest, which may be dated either from the battle of *Qādisīyah* or that of Madā'in (both fought in 637 A.D.), after which Persia which then included 'Iraq came into the Muslim Empire. The 'Abbāsī Empire built Baghdad for its capital under Manṣūr in 762 A.D. When that Empire was broken up in 1258 A.D., there was some confusion for two centuries. Then a national Persian Empire, the Ṣafawī (1499-1736) arose, and Shāh Salīm established his capital in the northwest corner in Ṭabrīz. Shāh 'Abbās the Great (1587-1628) had his capital at the more central city of Iṣpahān (or Iṣfahān). After the Ṣafawī dynasty confusion reigned again for about four decades, when the Afghans were in the ascendant. When the Qāchār (or Qājār) dynasty (1795-1925) was firmly established under Agha Muḥammad Khān. Ṭihrān (Tehran), near the Caspian, where his family originated, became the capital, and it still remains the capital under the modern Pehlevi Dynasty.

APPENDIX IX.

COMPARATIVE CHRONOLOGY OF THE EARLY YEARS OF ISLAM

(See paras. 8 and 11 of Appendix VIII.)

The dates after the Hijrah, when given according to the Arabian Calendar, can usually be calculated exactly according to other Calendars, but it is not possible to synchronise exactly the earliest dates of the Arabian Calendar with the dates of the Christian Calendar, and for two reasons. In the first place, there seems to have been some discrepancy between the Calendars in Madīnah and in Makkah. In the second place, the Arabian Calendar was roughly luni-solar, before the years of the Farewell Pilgrimage (Dhu al Ḥijjah, 10 H.= March 632). The Pagan Arabs were in the habit of counting months by the appearance of the moon, but irregularly intercalating a month once in about three years to bring the calendar up into conformity with the seasons. They did not do it on any astronomical calculations or on any system, but just as it suited their own selfish purposes, thus often upsetting all the old-established conventions about the months of peace and security from war and thus getting an unfair advantage for the clique in power in Makkah over their enemies (see my n. 1295 to 9:36). Unless exact mathematical calculations are applied and reduced to a well-established system, there is apt to be confusion, and this can well be taken advantage of by arbitrary cliques in power. After the Holy Prophet's adoption of the purely lunar calendar for ecclesiastical purposes, there is no confusion. Every date after A.H. 10 is exactly convertible into a corresponding date in any other accurate calendar. Wustenfeld's and other Comparative Tables of Muslim and Christian dates may therefore be relied upon for dates after A.H. 10, but much caution is necessary in synchronisation for earlier dates.

Mawlānā Shiblī, in his *Sīrah al Nabī,* Vol. I, p. 124 (edition of 1336 H., 1918 C.), adopts for the Prophet's Birthday the date 20th April 571, following Maḥmūd Pāshā. They go on the basis of an astronomical event, the total eclipse of the sun that was visible in Madīnah on the day that the Prophet's son Ibrāhīm was taken to the mercy of Allah. But there is no agreement among the authorities as to the exact date *either* by the Christian or the Arabian Calendar. Shiblī, following Maḥmūd Pāshā, takes the date of the eclipse to be the 7th November 632. Muir (*Life,* ed. 1923, p. 429), assumes some date in June or July 631. L. Caetani (*Chronographica Islamica,* A.H. 10) gives the date of the eclipse as 4th or 5th July 631, which he synchronises with the 28th or 29th of Rabī' 1, A.H. 10, but he quotes authorities for the death of Ibrāhīm as on the 16th June 631, synchronising it with the 10th of Rabī' 1, A.H. 10. There is something wrong here, as the death and the eclipse occurred on the same day. Wāqidī gives the month as Rabī' 1, A.H. 10, and gives Ibrāhīm a life of 15 months. But if Abū Dāwūd and Bayhaqī are correct, Ibrāhīm lived only 2 months and 10 days, and as his date of birth is given in Dhu al Hijjah A.H. 8, the date of death according to these authorities would be in Rabī' 1, A.H. 9. On a review of all the authorities I feel inclined to accept the date for the eclipse and death of Ibrāhīm as 28th or 29th of Rabī' 1, A.H. 10= 4th or 5th July 631. But this cannot be asserted with certainty. The French work of reference, *L'art de verifier les dates,* Paris 1818 (Vol. I, p. 310), gives the date of the solar eclipse as the 3rd of August 631, 2:30 P.M. and according to the system adopted in that book, the corresponding Hijrah date would be the 28th Rabī' 2, A.H. 10.

Even if this particular date was certain and exact, a certain amount of uncertainty remains in counting dates backwards. Most authorities assume a purely lunar year of 354 days for working backwards. Probably the Muslims in Madīnah counted in this way even before the lunar year was fixed exactly in A.H. 10. But the mass of Pagan Arabs in Makkah and elsewhere probably were all the time intercalating a month roughly once in three years, as has been stated before, until their power was utterly destroyed by the conquest of Makkah; and therefore precise exactitude in pre-Conquest date or in the counting of people's ages in years before 8-10 A.H. is unattainable. See a note on this subject in Margoliouth's Life of the Prophet (p. xix. of the 3rd edition) and in Muir's Life (p. x. of the 1923 edition).

The date of the actual Hijrah as given in Caetani may be accepted as Sept.-Oct. 622, being in the month of Rabī' 1. If the ninth of that month would be accepted as the date of departure from the cave of Thawr, the best synchronised date would be the 22nd of September 622 C. But as the first month of the Arab year was (and is) Muḥarram, the Hijrah year 1 is counted as beginning on the 15th or 16th July 622 (= 1 Muḥarram A.H. 1). The formal adoption of the Hijrah era in official documents date from the Khilāfah of 'Umar—from the year 17-18 H. according to Ṭabarī.

Sir Wolseley Haig's *Comparative Tables of Muḥammadan and Christian Dates* (London, Luzac, 1932), gives in a handy form three comparative Tables which enable the synchronisation of Hijrah years from A.H. 1 to A.H. 1421. The main table for these years was printed earlier at the end of S. Haīm's *New English-Persian Dictionary,* Tehran, 1931. The exact title of Wustenfeld's German Tables is: *Wustenfeld-Mahler, Vergleichungs-Tabellen*, Leipzig, 1926 (2nd edition).

INTRODUCTION TO SŪRAH 31—*LUQMĀN*

The argument of the Final End of Things is here continued from another point of view. What is Wisdom? Where shall it be found? Will it solve the mysteries of Time and Nature, and that world higher than physical Nature, which brings us nearer to Allah? "Yes," is the answer: "if, as in the advice of Luqmān the Wise, human wisdom looks to Allah in true worship, ennobles every act of life with true kindness, but avoids the false indulgence that infringes the divine law—and in short follows the golden mean of virtue." And this is indicated by every Sign in nature.

The chronology of this Sūrah has no significance. In the main, it belongs to the late Makkan period.

Summary—The earnest seekers after righteousness receive guidance, unlike the seekers after vanity, who perish: all Creation bears witness to this: Wisdom, as expounded by Luqmān the Wise, is true service to Allah, and consists in moderation (31:1-19, and C. 183).

True Wisdom is firm and enduring, and discerns Allah's Law in the working of His Creation: it looks to the Final End of Things, whose mystery is only known to Allah (31:20-34, and C. 184).

C. 183.—What is the Book of Wisdom? It is
(31:1-19.) A Guide and a Mercy to men, and teaches
Them how to attain Bliss. Allah's Mercies
Are infinite: how can man deny them?
Luqmān the Wise taught grateful worship
Of the One True God, and the service of men.
Beginning with Parents; every good deed
Is known to Allah and is brought to account.
So walk in the Golden Mean, and serve
Him with constancy and firmness of purpose.

Sūrah 31.

Luqmān

In the name of Allah, Most Gracious,
Most Merciful.

بِسْمِ ٱللَّهِ ٱلرَّحْمَٰنِ ٱلرَّحِيمِ

1. Alif Lām Mīm.[3579]

١ الٓمٓ

2. These are Verses
Of the Wise Book—[3580]

٢ تِلْكَ ءَايَٰتُ ٱلْكِتَٰبِ ٱلْحَكِيمِ

3. A Guide and a Mercy
To the Doers of Good—[3581]

٣ هُدًى وَرَحْمَةً لِّلْمُحْسِنِينَ

4. Those who establish regular Prayer,
And give regular Charity,
And have (in their hearts)
The assurance of the Hereafter.[3582]

٤ ٱلَّذِينَ يُقِيمُونَ ٱلصَّلَوٰةَ
وَيُؤْتُونَ ٱلزَّكَوٰةَ وَهُم
بِٱلْءَاخِرَةِ هُمْ يُوقِنُونَ

5. These are on (true) guidance[3583]
From their Lord; and these
Are the ones who will prosper.

٥ أُوْلَٰٓئِكَ عَلَىٰ هُدًى مِّن رَّبِّهِمْ
وَأُوْلَٰٓئِكَ هُمُ ٱلْمُفْلِحُونَ

6. But there are, among men,
Those who purchase idle tales,[3584]
Without knowledge (or meaning),
To mislead (men) from the Path
Of Allah and throw ridicule
(On the Path): for such
There will be a humiliating
Penalty.

٦ وَمِنَ ٱلنَّاسِ مَن يَشْتَرِى
لَهْوَ ٱلْحَدِيثِ لِيُضِلَّ عَن سَبِيلِ
ٱللَّهِ بِغَيْرِ عِلْمٍ وَيَتَّخِذَهَا هُزُوًا
أُوْلَٰٓئِكَ لَهُمْ عَذَابٌ مُّهِينٌ

3579. See n. 25 to 2:1 and Introduction to S. 30.

3580. This Sūrah relates to Wisdom and the Qur'ān is appropriately called the Wise Book, or the Book of Wisdom. In verse 12 below there is a reference to Luqmān the Wise. "Wise" in this sense (*Ḥakīm*) means not only a man versed in knowledge human and divine, but one carrying out in practical conduct (*'amal*) the right course in life to the utmost of his power. His knowledge is correct and practical, but not necessarily complete: for no man is perfect. Such an ideal involves the conception of a man of heroic action as well as of deep and workman-like knowledge of nature and human nature—not merely dreams or speculation. That ideal was fulfilled in a most remarkable degree in the Holy Prophet, and in the sacred Book which was revealed through him. "The Wise Book" (*al kitāb al ḥakīm*) is one of the titles of the Qur'ān.

3581. A guide to all, and, to those who accept its guidance, a source of mercy leading them to Salvation.

3582. The righteous are distinguished here by three marks, which are summed up in the phrase "doers of good", *viz.*: (1) they yearn towards Allah in duty, love and prayer, (2) they love and serve their fellow-men in charity, (3) they win peace and rest for themselves in the assured hope of the Future.

3583. They get the blessings because they submit their will to Allah's Will and receive His guidance. They will do well in this life (from the highest standpoint) and will reach their true Goal in the Future.

3584. Life is taken seriously by men who realise the issues that hang upon it. But there are men of a frivolous turn of mind who prefer idle tales to true Realities and they are justly rebuked here. In the time of the Holy Prophet there was a pagan Naḍr ibn al Ḥārith who preferred Persian romance to the Message of Allah, and turned away ignorant men from the preaching of Allah's Word.

7. When Our Signs are rehearsed
To such a one, he turns[3585]
Away in arrogance, as if
He heard them not, as if
There were deafness in both
His ears: announce to him
A grievous Penalty.

٧ وَإِذَا تُتْلَىٰ عَلَيْهِ ءَايَٰتُنَا وَلَّىٰ مُسْتَكْبِرًا
كَأَن لَّمْ يَسْمَعْهَا كَأَنَّ فِىٓ أُذُنَيْهِ وَقْرًا
فَبَشِّرْهُ بِعَذَابٍ أَلِيمٍ

8. For those who believe
And work righteous deeds,
There will be Gardens
Of Bliss—

٨ إِنَّ ٱلَّذِينَ ءَامَنُوا۟ وَعَمِلُوا۟
ٱلصَّٰلِحَٰتِ لَهُمْ جَنَّٰتُ ٱلنَّعِيمِ

9. To dwell therein. The promise
Of Allah is true: and He
Is Exalted in power,[3586] Wise.

٩ خَٰلِدِينَ فِيهَا وَعْدَ ٱللَّهِ حَقًّا
وَهُوَ ٱلْعَزِيزُ ٱلْحَكِيمُ

10. He created the heavens
Without any pillars that ye[3587]
Can see; He set
On the earth mountains[3588]
Standing firm, lest it
Should shake with you;
And He scattered through it
Beasts of all kinds.[3589]
We send down rain[3590]
From the sky, and produce
On the earth every kind
Of noble creature, in pairs.[3591]

١٠ خَلَقَ ٱلسَّمَٰوَٰتِ بِغَيْرِ عَمَدٍ تَرَوْنَهَا
وَأَلْقَىٰ فِى ٱلْأَرْضِ رَوَٰسِىَ أَن تَمِيدَ بِكُمْ
وَبَثَّ فِيهَا مِن كُلِّ دَآبَّةٍ
وَأَنزَلْنَا مِنَ ٱلسَّمَآءِ مَآءً
فَأَنۢبَتْنَا فِيهَا مِن كُلِّ
زَوْجٍ كَرِيمٍ

3585. Such men behave as if they had heard nothing of serious import, or laugh at serious teaching. The loss will be their own. They will miss the higher things of life and be left out of Allah's blessings. Ignorance and arrogance are in most cases the causes of their fall.

3586. He is Exalted in power, and can carry out His Will, and nothing can stop the carrying out of His promise. He is also infinitely Wise: His promise is therefore full of meaning: it is not merely without purpose; it has a place in the Universal Plan.

3587. *Cf.* 13:2 and n. 1800.

3588. *Cf.* 16:15 and n. 2038.

3589. *Cf.* 2:164 and n. 166.

3590. Note the change of the pronoun at this stage in the verse. Before this, Allah was spoken of in the third person. "He", and the acts of Creation referred to were acts that, in the main, were completed when the universe as we see it came into being, though its slow age-long evolution continues. After this, Allah speaks in the first person "We"—the plural of honour, as explained before (see n. 56 to 2:38); and the processes spoken of are those that go on continually before us, as in the case of rain and the growth of the vegetable kingdom. In some way the creation of the heavens and the earth and animal life on it may be considered impersonal to man, while the processes of rain and vegetation may be considered in special personal relationship to him.

3591. I think that sex life in plants is referred to, as in 13:3, where see n. 1804, though the pairs here may refer to animals also. "Noble" (*karīm*) may refer to the more beneficent plants and trees (and animals), which Allah has created for man's use.

11. Such is the Creation of Allah:
Now show Me[3592] what is there
That others besides Him
Have created; nay, but
The Transgressors are
In manifest error.

(١١) هَٰذَا خَلْقُ ٱللَّهِ فَأَرُونِى
مَاذَا خَلَقَ ٱلَّذِينَ مِن دُونِهِۦ ۚ
بَلِ ٱلظَّٰلِمُونَ فِى ضَلَٰلٍ مُّبِينٍ

SECTION 2.

12. We bestowed (in the past)
Wisdom on Luqmān:[3593]
"Show (thy) gratitude to Allah."
Any who is (so) grateful
Does so to the profit
Of his own soul; but if
Any is ungrateful, verily[3594]
Allah is free of all wants,
Worthy of all praise.

(١٢) وَلَقَدْ ءَاتَيْنَا لُقْمَٰنَ
ٱلْحِكْمَةَ أَنِ ٱشْكُرْ لِلَّهِ ۚ
وَمَن يَشْكُرْ فَإِنَّمَا يَشْكُرُ لِنَفْسِهِۦ ۖ
وَمَن كَفَرَ فَإِنَّ ٱللَّهَ غَنِىٌّ حَمِيدٌ

13. Behold, Luqmān said[3595]
To his son by way of
Instruction: "O my son!
Join not in worship
(Others) with Allah: for
False worship is indeed
The highest wrongdoing."

(١٣) وَإِذْ قَالَ لُقْمَٰنُ لِٱبْنِهِۦ
وَهُوَ يَعِظُهُۥ يَٰبُنَىَّ لَا تُشْرِكْ بِٱللَّهِ ۖ
إِنَّ ٱلشِّرْكَ لَظُلْمٌ عَظِيمٌ

14. And We have enjoined on man
(To be good) to his parents:
In travail upon travail
Did his mother bear him,

(١٤) وَوَصَّيْنَا ٱلْإِنسَٰنَ بِوَٰلِدَيْهِ
حَمَلَتْهُ أُمُّهُۥ وَهْنًا عَلَىٰ وَهْنٍ

3592. The transition from "We" in the last verse to "Me" in this verse means a still more personal relation to Allah; (see n. 56 to 2:38): as we are now asked about the true worship of Allah, as against the false worship of others besides Allah.

3593. The sage Luqmān, after whom this Sūrah is called, belongs to Arab tradition. Very little is known of his life. He is usually associated with a long life, and his title is *Mu'ammar* (the long-lived). He is referred by some to the age of the 'Ād people, for whom see n. 1040 to 7:65. He is the type of perfect wisdom. It is said that he belonged to a humble station in life, being a slave or a carpenter, and that he refused worldly power and a kingdom. Many instructive apologues are credited to him, similar to Aesop's Fables in Greek tradition. The identification of Luqmān and Aesop has no historical foundation, though it is true that the traditions about them influenced each other.

3594. *Cf.* 14:7. The basis of moral Law is man's own good, and not any benefit to Allah, for Allah is above all needs, and "worthy of all praise"; *i.e.*, even in praising Him, we do not advance His glory. When we obey His Will, we bring our position into conformity with our own nature as made by Him.

3595. Luqmān is held up as a pattern of wisdom, because he realised the best in a wise life in this world, as based upon the highest Hope in the inner life. To him, as in Islam, true human wisdom is also divine widsom; the two cannot be separated. The beginning of all wisdom, therefore, is conformity with the Will of Allah (31:12). That means that we must understand our relations to Him and worship Him aright (31:13). Then we must be good to mankind, beginning with our own parents (31:14). For the two duties are not diverse, but one. Where they appear to conflict, there is something wrong with the human will (see n. 3597).

And in years twain[3596]
Was his weaning: (hear
The command), "Show gratitude
To Me and to thy parents:
To Me is (thy final) Goal.

وَفِصَٰلُهُۥ فِى عَامَيْنِ
أَنِ ٱشْكُرْ لِى وَلِوَٰلِدَيْكَ
إِلَىَّ ٱلْمَصِيرُ

15. "But if they strive[3597]
To make thee join
In worship with Me
Things of which thou hast
No knowledge, obey them not;
Yet bear them company
In this life with justice
(And consideration), and follow
The way of those who
Turn to Me (in love):[3598]
In the End the return
Of you all is to Me,
And I will tell you
The truth (and meaning)[3599]
Of all that ye did."

١٥ وَإِن جَٰهَدَاكَ
عَلَىٰٓ أَن تُشْرِكَ بِى مَا لَيْسَ
لَكَ بِهِۦ عِلْمٌ فَلَا تُطِعْهُمَا ۖ
وَصَاحِبْهُمَا فِى ٱلدُّنْيَا مَعْرُوفًا ۖ
وَٱتَّبِعْ سَبِيلَ مَنْ أَنَابَ إِلَىَّ ۚ
ثُمَّ إِلَىَّ مَرْجِعُكُمْ فَأُنَبِّئُكُم
بِمَا كُنتُمْ تَعْمَلُونَ

16. "O my son!" (said Luqmān),[3600]
"If there be (but) the weight
Of a mustard seed and
It were (hidden) in a rock,[3601]

١٦ يَٰبُنَىَّ إِنَّهَآ إِن تَكُ مِثْقَالَ
حَبَّةٍ مِّنْ خَرْدَلٍ فَتَكُن فِى صَخْرَةٍ

3596. The set of milk teeth in a human child is completed at the age of two years, which is therefore the natural extreme limit for breast-feeding. In our artificial life the duration is much less.

3597. Where the duty to man conflicts with the duty to Allah, it means that there is something wrong with the human will, and we should obey Allah rather than man. But even here, it does not mean that we should be arrogant or insolent. To parents and those in authority, we must be kind, considerate, and courteous, even where they command things which we should not do and therefore disobedience becomes our highest duty.

The worship of things other than Allah is the worship of false things, things which are alien to our true knowledge, things that go against our own pure nature as created by Allah.

3598. In any apparent conflict of duties our standard should be Allah's Will, as declared to us by His command. That is the way of those who love Allah and their motive in disobedience to parents or human authority where disobedience is necessary by Allah's Law, is not self-willed rebellion or defiance, but love of Allah, which means the true love of man in the highest sense of the word. And the reason we should give is, "Both you and I have to return to Allah: therefore not only must I follow Allah's Will, but you must command nothing against Allah's will."

3599. These conflicts may appear to us strange and puzzling in this life. But in Allah's Presence we shall see their real meaning and significance. It may be that that was one way in which our true mettle could be tested: for it is not easy to disobey and love man at the same time.

3600. Verses 14-15 are not the direct speech of Luqmān but flow by way of commentary on his teaching. He was speaking as a father to his son, and he could not very well urge respect for himself and draw the son's attention to the limitations of that obedience. These verses may be supposed to be general directions flowing from Luqmān's teaching to men, and not directed to his son, though in either case, as Luqmān received wisdom from Allah, it is divine principles that are enunciated.

3601. The mustard seed is proverbially a small, minute thing, that people may ordinarily pass by. Not so Allah. Further emphasis is laid by supposing the mustard seed to be hidden beneath a rock or in the cleft of a rock, or to be lost in the spaciousness of the earth or the heavens. To Allah everything is known, and He will bring it forth; *i.e.*, take account of it.

Or (anywhere) in the heavens or
On earth. Allah will bring it
Forth: for Allah understands[3602]
The finer mysteries, (and)
Is well-acquainted (with them).

أَوْ فِى ٱلسَّمَٰوَٰتِ أَوْ فِى
ٱلْأَرْضِ يَأْتِ بِهَا ٱللَّهُ
إِنَّ ٱللَّهَ لَطِيفٌ خَبِيرٌ

17. "O my son! establish
Regular prayer, enjoin what is
Just, and forbid what is wrong;
And bear with patient constancy
Whate'er betide thee; for this
Is firmness (of purpose)
In (the conduct of) affairs.

١٧ يَٰبُنَىَّ أَقِمِ ٱلصَّلَوٰةَ وَأْمُرْ بِٱلْمَعْرُوفِ
وَٱنْهَ عَنِ ٱلْمُنكَرِ وَٱصْبِرْ عَلَىٰ مَآ أَصَابَكَ
إِنَّ ذَٰلِكَ مِنْ عَزْمِ ٱلْأُمُورِ

18. "And swell not thy cheek[3603]
(For pride) at men,
Nor walk in insolence
Through the earth:
For Allah loveth not
Any arrogant boaster.

١٨ وَلَا تُصَعِّرْ خَدَّكَ لِلنَّاسِ
وَلَا تَمْشِ فِى ٱلْأَرْضِ مَرَحًا
إِنَّ ٱللَّهَ لَا يُحِبُّ كُلَّ مُخْتَالٍ فَخُورٍ

19. "And be moderate
In thy pace, and lower[3604]
Thy voice; for the harshest
Of sounds without doubt
Is the braying of the ass."

١٩ وَٱقْصِدْ فِى مَشْيِكَ وَٱغْضُضْ مِن صَوْتِكَ
إِنَّ أَنكَرَ ٱلْأَصْوَٰتِ لَصَوْتُ ٱلْحَمِيرِ

C. 184. — True Wisdom sees Allah's boundless Bounties
(31:20-34.) To man, and how all nature is made
To serve man's ends. It is due from us
To know our place, discern the limits
Of our knowledge, and see how far above us
Is Allah's Wisdom, and His Law. Let us not
Deceive ourselves. The end of all things
Will come, but the When and the How are known
To Allah alone, to Whom be all Praise!

3602. For *Latif* as a title applied to Allah, see n. 2844 to 22:63.

3603. The word "cheek" in English, too, means arrogance or effrontery, with a slightly different shade added, *viz.*: effrontery from one in an inferior position to one in a superior position. The Arabic usage is wider, and includes smug self-satisfaction and a sense of lofty superiority.

3604. The "Golden Mean" is the pivot of the philosophy of Luqmān as it is the philosophy of Aristotle and indeed of Islam. And it flows naturally from a true understanding of our relation to Allah and His universe and to you fellow-creatures, especially man. In all things be moderate. Do not go the pace, and, do not stand stationary or slow. Do not be talkative and do not be silent. Do not be loud and do not be timid or half-hearted. Do not be too confident, and do not be cowed down. If you have patience, it is to give you constancy and determination, that you may bravely carry on the struggle of life. If you have humility, it is to save you from unseemly swagger, not to curb your right spirit and your reasoned determination.

SECTION 3.

20. Do ye not see
That Allah has subjected[3605]
To your (use) all things
In the heavens and on earth,
And has made His bounties
Flow to you in exceeding
Measure, (both) seen and
unseen?[3606]
Yet there are among men
Those who dispute about Allah,
Without knowledge and without
Guidance, and without a Book.[3607]
To enlighten them!

٢٠ أَلَمْ تَرَوْا أَنَّ ٱللَّهَ سَخَّرَ لَكُم
مَّا فِى ٱلسَّمَـٰوَٰتِ وَمَا فِى ٱلْأَرْضِ
وَأَسْبَغَ عَلَيْكُمْ نِعَمَهُۥ ظَـٰهِرَةً وَبَاطِنَةً ۗ
وَمِنَ ٱلنَّاسِ مَن يُجَـٰدِلُ فِى ٱللَّهِ
بِغَيْرِ عِلْمٍ وَلَا هُدًى
وَلَا كِتَـٰبٍ مُّنِيرٍ

21. When they are told to follow
The (Revelation) that Allah
Has sent down, they say:
"Nay, we shall follow
The ways that we found
Our fathers (following)."[3608]
What! even if it is
Satan beckoning them
To the Penalty
Of the (Blazing) Fire?

٢١ وَإِذَا قِيلَ لَهُمُ ٱتَّبِعُوا۟
مَآ أَنزَلَ ٱللَّهُ قَالُوا۟ بَلْ نَتَّبِعُ
مَا وَجَدْنَا عَلَيْهِ ءَابَآءَنَآ ۚ
أَوَلَوْ كَانَ ٱلشَّيْطَـٰنُ
يَدْعُوهُمْ إِلَىٰ عَذَابِ ٱلسَّعِيرِ

22. Whoever submits
His whole self to Allah,
And is a doer of good,
Has grasped indeed
The most trustworthy handhold;[3609]
And with Allah rests the End[3610]
And Decision of (all) affairs.

٢٢ وَمَن يُسْلِمْ وَجْهَهُۥٓ إِلَى ٱللَّهِ
وَهُوَ مُحْسِنٌ فَقَدِ ٱسْتَمْسَكَ بِٱلْعُرْوَةِ ٱلْوُثْقَىٰ ۗ
وَإِلَى ٱللَّهِ عَـٰقِبَةُ ٱلْأُمُورِ

3605. Allah's Creation is independent of man. But Allah, in His infinte mercy, has given man the faculty to subdue the forces of nature and to penetrate through high mysteries with his powers of reason and insight. But this is not merely a question of power. For in His Universal Plan, all are safeguarded. But man's destiny, as far as we can see, is noble to the highest degree.

3606 Allah's grace and bounties work for us at all times. Sometimes we see them, and sometimes we do not. In things which we can apprehend with our senses, we can see Allah's grace, but even in them, sometimes it works beyond the sphere of our knowledge. In the inner or spiritual world, sometimes, when our vision is clear, we can see it working, and often we are not conscious of it, but it works all the same.

3607. Such men lack knowledge, as they make no use of their intellects but are swayed by their passions; they lack guidance, as they are impatient of control; and the fruits of revelation, or spiritual insight, do not reach them, as they reject Faith and Revelation.

3608. They do not realise that in the spiritual world, as in the physical world, there is constant progress for the live ones: they are spiritually dead, as they are content to stand on ancestral ways, many of them evil, and leading to perdition.

3609. *Cf.* 2:256 and n. 301.

3610. *Cf.* 22:41. Everything goes back to Allah. He is our final Goal, as He is the final Goal of all things.

23. But if any reject Faith,
Let not his rejection
Grieve thee: to Us[3611]
Is their Return, and We
Shall tell them the truth
Of their deeds: for Allah
Knows well all that is
In (men's) hearts.

٢٣ وَمَن كَفَرَ فَلَا يَحْزُنكَ كُفْرُهُۥٓ ۚ
إِلَيْنَا مَرْجِعُهُمْ فَنُنَبِّئُهُم بِمَا عَمِلُوٓا۟ ۚ
إِنَّ ٱللَّهَ عَلِيمٌۢ بِذَاتِ ٱلصُّدُورِ

24. We grant them their pleasure
For a little while:[3612]
In the end shall We
Drive them to
A chastisement unrelenting.

٢٤ نُمَتِّعُهُمْ قَلِيلًا
ثُمَّ نَضْطَرُّهُمْ
إِلَىٰ عَذَابٍ غَلِيظٍ

25. If thou ask them,
Who it is that created
The heavens and the earth,[3613]
They will certainly say,
"Allah". Say: "Praise be to
Allah."[3614]
But most of them
Understand not.

٢٥ وَلَئِن سَأَلْتَهُم مَّنْ خَلَقَ
ٱلسَّمَٰوَٰتِ وَٱلْأَرْضَ لَيَقُولُنَّ ٱللَّهُ ۚ
قُلِ ٱلْحَمْدُ لِلَّهِ ۚ
بَلْ أَكْثَرُهُمْ لَا يَعْلَمُونَ

26. To Allah belong all things
In heaven and earth: verily
Allah is He (that is)
Free of all wants,
Worthy of all praise.[3615]

٢٦ لِلَّهِ مَا فِى ٱلسَّمَٰوَٰتِ وَٱلْأَرْضِ ۚ
إِنَّ ٱللَّهَ هُوَ ٱلْغَنِىُّ ٱلْحَمِيدُ

3611. The man of God should not grieve because people reject Faith. He should do his duty and leave the rest to Allah. Every soul must return to Allah for his reckoning. Allah knows everything, and his Universal Plan is full of wisdom.

3612. *Cf.* 2:126. The respite in this life is of short duration. The ultimate Penalty of Evil is such as cannot be quenched. *Cf.* 14:17. It will be too late then to repent.

3613. *Cf.* 23:84-89, and 29:61 and n. 3493. Men will acknowledge that Allah created the heavens and the earth, and yet fail to understand the love and goodness of Allah in continuing to cherish and maintain them with His gifts. Even if they allow this, they sometimes yet fall short of the corollary, that He is the only One to be worshipped, and run after their own false gods in the shapes of their fancies and lusts. They do not do the duties which, if they rightly understood their own nature and position, they should take a delight in doing.

3614. This ejaculation expresses our satisfaction that at least this is recognised—that the Creator of the whole world is Allah. It is a pity that they do not go further and recognise other facts and duties (see the last note).

3615. *Cf.* above, 31:12. There was begun the argument about showing gratitude to Allah, introducing Luqmān's teaching and philosophy. Such gratitude is shown by our understanding His love and doing our duty to Him by serving our fellow-men. For Allah Himself is Free from all wants and is in no way dependent on our service. That argument has been illustrated in various ways. But now we are told that it can never be completed, for no human tongue or human resources can be adequate either to praise him or to expound His Word.

27. And if all the trees
On earth were pens
And the Ocean (were ink),
With seven Oceans behind it
To add to its (supply),
Yet would not the Words[3616]
Of Allah be exhausted
(In the writing): for Allah
Is Exalted in power,
Full of Wisdom.

٢٧ وَلَوْ أَنَّمَا فِي الْأَرْضِ
مِن شَجَرَةٍ أَقْلَامٌ وَالْبَحْرُ يَمُدُّهُ
مِن بَعْدِهِ سَبْعَةُ أَبْحُرٍ
مَّا نَفِدَتْ كَلِمَاتُ اللَّهِ
إِنَّ اللَّهَ عَزِيزٌ حَكِيمٌ

28. And your creation
Or your resurrection
Is in no wise but
As an individual soul:[3617]
For Allah is He Who
Hears and sees (all things).

٢٨ مَّا خَلْقُكُمْ وَلَا بَعْثُكُمْ
إِلَّا كَنَفْسٍ وَاحِدَةٍ
إِنَّ اللَّهَ سَمِيعٌ بَصِيرٌ

29. Seest thou not that
Allah merges Night into Day[3618]
And He merges Day into Night;
That He has subjected the sun
And the moon (to His Law),
Each running its course
For a term appointed; and
That Allah is well acquainted
With all that ye do?

٢٩ أَلَمْ تَرَ أَنَّ اللَّهَ يُولِجُ اللَّيْلَ فِي النَّهَارِ
وَيُولِجُ النَّهَارَ فِي اللَّيْلِ وَسَخَّرَ الشَّمْسَ
وَالْقَمَرَ كُلٌّ يَجْرِي إِلَىٰ أَجَلٍ مُّسَمًّى
وَأَنَّ اللَّهَ بِمَا تَعْمَلُونَ خَبِيرٌ

30. That is because Allah is
The (only) Reality, and because
Whatever else they invoke[3619]

٣٠ ذَٰلِكَ بِأَنَّ اللَّهَ هُوَ الْحَقُّ
وَأَنَّ مَا يَدْعُونَ

3616. *Words of Allah*: His wonderful Signs and Commandments are infinite and cannot be expressed if all the trees were made into pens, and all the wide Ocean, multiplied seven times, were made into ink. Any Book of His Revelation would deal with matters which man can understand and use in his life: there are mysteries beyond mysteries that man can never fathom. Nor would any praise that we could write with infinite resources be adequate to describe His power, glory, and wisdom.

3617. Allah's greatness and infinitude are such that He can create and cherish not only a whole mass, but each individual soul, and He can follow its history and doings until the final Judgement. This shows not only Allah's glory and omniscience and omnipotence: it also shows the value of each individual soul in His eyes, and lifts individual responsibility right up into relations with Him.

3618. *Cf.* 22:61 and n. 2841. Even when we can form a conception of Allah's infinitude by His dealings with each individual in His Creation as in verse 28 above, it is still inadequate. What is an individual himself? What is his relation to the universal Laws of Allah? In outer nature we can see that there is no clear-cut line between night and day: each merges into the other. Yet the sun and the moon obey definite laws. Though they seem to go on forever. Yet their existence and duration themselves are but an atom in Allah's great universe. How much more "merging" and imperceptible gradation there is in the inner and spiritual world? Our actions themselves cannot be classified and ticketed and labelled when examined in relation to motives and circumstances. Yet they are like an open book before Allah.

3619. *Cf.* 22:62 and note 2842 and 2843. All the wonderful complexities, gradations, and nuances, that we find in Creation, are yet blended in one harmonious whole, that obeys Law and exemplifies Order. They therefore point to the One True God. He is the only Eternal Reality. Anything put up in competition or equality with Him is only Falsehood, for He is higher and greater than anything we can imagine. (R).

Besides Him is Falsehood;
And because Allah—He is
The Most High, Most Great.

مِن دُونِهِ ٱلْبَٰطِلُ
وَأَنَّ ٱللَّهَ هُوَ ٱلْعَلِيُّ ٱلْكَبِيرُ

SECTION 4.

31. Seest thou not that
The ships sail through
The Ocean by the grace
Of Allah?—that He may
Show you of His Signs?
Verily in this are Signs
For all who constantly persevere[3620]
And give thanks.

٣١ أَلَمْ تَرَ أَنَّ ٱلْفُلْكَ تَجْرِى فِى
ٱلْبَحْرِ بِنِعْمَتِ ٱللَّهِ لِيُرِيَكُم مِّنْ ءَايَٰتِهِۦٓ
إِنَّ فِى ذَٰلِكَ لَءَايَٰتٍ
لِّكُلِّ صَبَّارٍ شَكُورٍ

32. When a wave covers them
Like the canopy (of clouds),
They call to Allah,
Offering Him sincere devotion,[3621]
But when He has delivered them
Safely to land, there are
Among them those that halt[3622]
Between (right and wrong).
But none reject Our Signs
Except only a perfidious
Ungrateful (wretch)!

٣٢ وَإِذَا غَشِيَهُم مَّوْجٌ
كَٱلظُّلَلِ دَعَوُا۟ ٱللَّهَ مُخْلِصِينَ لَهُ ٱلدِّينَ
فَلَمَّا نَجَّىٰهُمْ إِلَى ٱلْبَرِّ فَمِنْهُم مُّقْتَصِدٌ
وَمَا يَجْحَدُ بِـَٔايَٰتِنَآ
إِلَّا كُلُّ خَتَّارٍ كَفُورٍ

33. O mankind! do your duty
To your Lord, and fear
(The coming of) a Day
When no father can avail
Aught for his son, nor
A son avail aught
For his father.[3623]
Verily, the promise of Allah

٣٣ يَٰٓأَيُّهَا ٱلنَّاسُ ٱتَّقُوا۟ رَبَّكُمْ
وَٱخْشَوْا۟ يَوْمًا لَّا يَجْزِى وَالِدٌ عَن وَلَدِهِۦ
وَلَا مَوْلُودٌ هُوَ جَازٍ عَن وَالِدِهِۦ شَيْـًٔا
إِنَّ وَعْدَ ٱللَّهِ حَقٌّ

3620. Even the things that man makes are, as using the forces of Nature, evidence of the grace of Allah, Who has subdued these wonderful forces to the use of man. But this gift of mastery can only be understood and appreciated by constant perseverance, combined with a recognition of the divine gifts ("giving thanks"). *Ṣabbār* is an intensive form of *ṣabr* and I have indicated it by the adverb "constantly".

3621. *Cf.* 7:29. Unlike the people mentioned in the last verse, who constantly seek Allah's help and give thanks for His mercies by using them aright and doing their duty, there is a class of men whose worship is merely inspired by terror. When they are in physical danger—the only kind of danger they appreciate—*e.g.*, in a storm at sea, they genuinely think of Allah. But once the danger is past, they become indifferent or wish to appear good while dallying with evil. See next verse.

3622. They halt between two opinions. They are not against good, but they will not eschew evil. They are a contrast to those who "constantly persevere and give thanks". But such an attitude amounts really to "perfidious ingratitude".

3623. On the Day of Reckoning no one can help another. The most loving father cannot help his son or be a substitute for him, and *vice versa*. Each will have his own personal responsibilities.

Is true: let not then This present life deceive you, Nor let the Chief Deceiver[3624] Deceive you about Allah.	فَلَا تَغُرَّنَّكُمُ ٱلْحَيَوٰةُ ٱلدُّنْيَا وَلَا يَغُرَّنَّكُم بِٱللَّهِ ٱلْغَرُورُ
34. Verily the knowledge Of the Hour is With Allah (alone). It is He Who sends down Rain, and He Who knows What is in the wombs.[3625] Nor does anyone know What it is that he will Earn on the morrow;[3626] Nor does anyone know In what land he is To die. Verily with Allah Is full knowledge and He Is acquainted (with all things).[3627]	٣٤ إِنَّ ٱللَّهَ عِندَهُۥ عِلْمُ ٱلسَّاعَةِ وَيُنَزِّلُ ٱلْغَيْثَ وَيَعْلَمُ مَا فِى ٱلْأَرْحَامِ وَمَا تَدْرِى نَفْسٌ مَّاذَا تَكْسِبُ غَدًا وَمَا تَدْرِى نَفْسٌۢ بِأَىِّ أَرْضٍ تَمُوتُ إِنَّ ٱللَّهَ عَلِيمٌ خَبِيرٌۢ

3624. The Chief Deceiver is the Power of Evil. It may make us forget that Time is fleeting and delude us by suggesting that the Reckoning may not come, whereas it is certain to come, because Allah's promise is true. We must not play with Time nor be deceived by appearances. The Day may come today or tomorrow or when we least expect it.

3625. The question of Knowledge or Mystery governs both clauses here, *viz.*: Rain and Wombs. In fact it governs all the five things mentioned in this verse: *viz.* (1) The Hour; (2) Rain; (3) the Birth of a new Life (Wombs); (4) our Physical Life from day to day; (5) our Death. See n. 3627 below. As regards Rain we are asked to contemplate how and when it is sent down. The moisture may be sucked up by the sun's heat in the Arabian Sea or the Red Sea or the Indian Ocean near East Africa, or in the Lake Region in Central Africa. The winds drive it hither and thither across thousands of miles, or it may be, only short distances. "The wind bloweth where it listeth." No doubt it obeys certain physical Laws established by Allah, but how these Laws are interlocked, one with another! Meteorology, gravity, hydrostatics and dynamics, climatology, hygrometry, and a dozen other sciences are involved, and no man can completely master all of them, and yet this relates to only one of the millions of facts in physical nature, which are governed by Allah's Knowledge and Law. The whole vegetable kingdom is primarily affected by Rain. The mention of Wombs brings in the mystery of animal life, embryology, sex, and a thousand other things. Who can tell—to take man alone—whether the child conceived is male or female, how long it will remain in the womb, whether it will be born alive, what sort of new individual it will be—a blessing or a curse to its parents, or to Society?

3526. "Earn" here, as elsewhere, means not only "earn one's livelihood" in a physical sense but also to reap the consequences (good or ill) of one's conduct generally. The whole sentence practically means: "no man knows what the morrow may bring forth."

3627. See the five Mysteries summed up in n. 3625 above. The Argument is about the mystery of Time and Knowledge. We are supposed to know things in ordinary life. But what does that knowledge amount to in reality? Only a superficial acquaintance with things. And Time is even more uncertain. In the case of rain, which causes vegetable life to spring up, or in the case of new animal life, can we answer with precision questions as to When or How or Wherefore? So about questions of our life from day to day or of our death. These are great Mysteries, and full knowledge is with Allah only. How much more so in the case of the *Ma'ād*, the Final House, when all true values will be restored and the balance redressed? It is certain, but the When and the How are known to Allah alone.

INTRODUCTION TO SŪRAH 32—*AL SAJDAH*

This short Sūrah closes the series of four Alif, Lām, Mīm Sūrahs, which began with the 29th. Its theme is the mystery of Creation, the mystery of Time and the mystery of the *Ma'ād* (the Final End) as viewed through the light of Allah's revelation. The contemplation of these mysteries should lead to Faith and the adoration of Allah. In chronology it belongs to the middle Makkan period and is therefore a little earlier than the last, but its chronology has no significance.

Summary—The mystery of Creation, the mystery of Time, and the mystery of the End of Things are but known by external symbols to man: Revelation brings faith and humble adoration, and is a blessing like Rain, which brings life to dead soil (32:1-30, and C. 185).

C. 185.—How can Unbelievers realise the Mystery
(32:1-30.) Of Revelation? They do not even
See the marvel and Mystery of Time
And Allah's Creation, and how they were themselves
Created! If they could but see how the End
Will shape itself—how the Good will be sorted out
From Evil! The two are not equal in Goal.
Clear are the Signs and the Revelation of Allah—
In nature, history, and the Message of His living
Prophets. If they learn not now, alas!
It will be too late when Time's wings are furled.

Sūrah 32.

Al Sajdah (The Prostration)

In the name of Allah, Most Gracious,
Most Merciful.

بِسۡمِ ٱللَّهِ ٱلرَّحۡمَٰنِ ٱلرَّحِيمِ

1. Alif Lām Mīm.[3628]

١ الٓمٓ

2. (This is) the revelation
Of the Book in which
There is no doubt —[3629]
From the Lord of the Worlds.

٢ تَنزِيلُ ٱلۡكِتَٰبِ لَا رَيۡبَ
فِيهِ مِن رَّبِّ ٱلۡعَٰلَمِينَ

3. Or[3630] do they say,
"He has forged it"?
Nay, it is the Truth
From thy Lord, that thou
Mayest admonish a people
To whom no warner
Has come before thee:
In order that they
May receive guidance.[3631]

٣ أَمۡ يَقُولُونَ ٱفۡتَرَىٰهُۚ
بَلۡ هُوَ ٱلۡحَقُّ مِن رَّبِّكَ لِتُنذِرَ قَوۡمٗا
مَّآ أَتَىٰهُم مِّن نَّذِيرٖ مِّن قَبۡلِكَ
لَعَلَّهُمۡ يَهۡتَدُونَ

4. It is Allah Who has
Created the heavens
And the earth, and all
Between them, in six Days,[3632]
Then He established Himself

٤ ٱللَّهُ ٱلَّذِي خَلَقَ ٱلسَّمَٰوَٰتِ
وَٱلۡأَرۡضَ وَمَا بَيۡنَهُمَا فِي سِتَّةِ أَيَّامٖ
ثُمَّ ٱسۡتَوَىٰ

3628. See 1:25 to 2:1, and Introduction to S. 30.

3629. By the time of the Holy Prophet the earlier Book of Revelation had been corrupted by human ignorance or selfishness or fraud, or misinterpreted or lost altogether. There were sects violently disputing with each other as to their true meaning. Such doubts had to be set at rest and they were set at rest by the revelation of the Qur'ān. The Quranic inspiration came directly from Allah, the Lord of the Worlds, and did not consist merely of human conjecture or a reconstructed philosophy, in which there is always room for doubt or dispute. *Cf.* also 2:2.

3630. The force of "or" (*am* in Arabic) is that the only alternative to the acceptance of the Book as a divine revelation is the supposition that it was a forgery by the Holy Prophet. But this supposition is absurd on the face of it because (1) the Quraysh, his critics, knew him to be an honest and truthful man; (2) he was unlettered, and such a Book would have been beyond his powers as a simple unlettered Arab, unless Allah inspired it; and (3) there was a definite reason for its coming as it did, because the Arabs had received no Messenger before him and Allah has sent Messengers to every nation.

3631. The Arabs very much needed guidance for themselves, and the advent of a World Prophet through them was what might have been expected in view of the past course of Allah's Revelations.

3632. *Six Days*: see n. 1031, to 7:54. The "Day" does not mean a day as we reckon it, *viz.*: one apparent course of the sun round the earth, for it refers to conditions which began before the earth and the sun were created. In verse 5 below, a Day is compared to a thousand years of our reckoning, and in 70:4 to 50,000 years. These figures "as we reckon" have no relation to "timeless Time", and must be taken to mean very long Periods, or Ages, or Aeons. See further 41:9-12, and notes.

On the Throne (of authority);[3633]
Ye have none, besides Him,
To protect or intercede (for you):
Will ye not then
Receive admonition?

عَلَى ٱلْعَرْشِ مَا لَكُم مِّن دُونِهِۦ مِن وَلِىٍّ وَلَا شَفِيعٍ أَفَلَا تَتَذَكَّرُونَ

5. He rules (all) affairs
From the heavens
To the earth: in the end
Will (all affairs) go up[3634]
To Him, on a Day,
The space whereof will be
(As) a thousand years
Of your reckoning.

٥ يُدَبِّرُ ٱلْأَمْرَ مِنَ ٱلسَّمَآءِ إِلَى ٱلْأَرْضِ ثُمَّ يَعْرُجُ إِلَيْهِ فِى يَوْمٍ كَانَ مِقْدَارُهُۥٓ أَلْفَ سَنَةٍ مِّمَّا تَعُدُّونَ

6. Such is He, the Knower
Of all things, hidden
And open, the Exalted
(In power), the Merciful—[3635]

٦ ذَٰلِكَ عَٰلِمُ ٱلْغَيْبِ وَٱلشَّهَٰدَةِ ٱلْعَزِيزُ ٱلرَّحِيمُ

7. He Who has made
Everything which He has
created[3636]
Most Good: He began
The creation of man
With (nothing more than) clay,[3637]

٧ ٱلَّذِىٓ أَحْسَنَ كُلَّ شَىْءٍ خَلَقَهُۥ وَبَدَأَ خَلْقَ ٱلْإِنسَٰنِ مِن طِينٍ

8. And made his progeny
From a quintessence

٨ ثُمَّ جَعَلَ نَسْلَهُۥ مِن سُلَٰلَةٍ

3633. *Cf.* 3:3, n. 1386. Allah created the World as we see it in six great Stages. But after the initial creation, He is still in authority and directs and controls all affairs. He has not delegated His powers to others, and Himself retired. Also see 7:54.

3634. How could the immense mystery of Time behind our ideas of it be enforced on our minds better? Our Day may be a thousand or fifty thousand years, and our years in proportion. In the immense Past was Allah's act of creation: it still continues, for He guides, rules, and controls all affairs: and in the immense Future all affairs will go up to Him, for He will be the Judge, and His restoration of all values will be as a Day or an Hour or the Twinkling of an eye; and yet to our idea it will be a thousand years!

3635. Allah's attributes, then, may be summed up with reference to knowledge, Power, and Mercy. Where our knowledge is partial and uncertain, His is complete and certain. Where our power often falls short of the carrying out of our will, or needs the help of Time, His is complete and counters ours with His Will. Where our mercy seems to be bounded by or opposed to justice, His is absolute and unconditioned.

3636. Allah's creation in itself is good; it is beautiful in proper proportions, and adapted for the functions it has to perform. There is no evil or disorder in it. Such evil or disorder as creeps in is due to man's will (as far as the world of man is concerned), and spiritual Teaching is directed to train and cure that will and bring it into conformity with the Universal Order and Plan.

3637. Man is asked to contemplate his own humble beginning. His material body (apart from life) is a piece of earth or clay, which is another term for primeval matter. Matter is therefore the first stage, but even matter was not self-created. It was created by Allah.

Of the nature of
A fluid despised:[3638]

مِن مَّآءٍ مَّهِينٍ

9. But He fashioned him
In due proportion, and breathed
Into him something of[3639]
His spirit. And He gave
You (the faculties of) hearing
And sight and feeling[3640]
(And understanding):
Little thanks do ye give!

٩ ثُمَّ سَوَّىٰهُ وَنَفَخَ فِيهِ
مِن رُّوحِهِۦ وَجَعَلَ لَكُمُ ٱلسَّمْعَ
وَٱلْأَبْصَٰرَ وَٱلْأَفْـِٔدَةَ
قَلِيلًا مَّا تَشْكُرُونَ

10. And they say: "What!
When we lie, hidden
And lost, in the earth,
Shall we indeed be
In a Creation renewed?"[3641]
Nay, they deny the Meeting
With their Lord!

١٠ وَقَالُوٓا۟ أَءِذَا ضَلَلْنَا
فِى ٱلْأَرْضِ أَءِنَّا لَفِى خَلْقٍ جَدِيدٍۭ
بَلْ هُم بِلِقَآءِ رَبِّهِمْ كَٰفِرُونَ

11. Say: "The Angel of Death,
Put in charge of you,
Will (duly) take your souls[3642]
Then shall ye be brought
Back to your Lord."

١١ قُلْ يَتَوَفَّىٰكُم مَّلَكُ ٱلْمَوْتِ
ٱلَّذِى وُكِّلَ بِكُمْ ثُمَّ إِلَىٰ رَبِّكُمْ تُرْجَعُونَ

3638. Then comes life and the reproduction of life. We are still looking at the purely physcial aspect, but it is now a stage higher; it is an animal. Its reproduction is through the sperm or semen, which is a quintessence of every part of the body of man. Yet it issues from the same part of his body as the urine, and is therefore despicable in man's sight. It is a living cell or cells, summing up so much ancestral life-history. *Cf.* 23:12, and n. 2872.

3639. The third stage is indicated by "fashioned him in due proportion". *Cf.* 15:29. After the fertilisation of the ovum by the sperm, an individual life comes into existence, and it is gradually fashioned into shape; its limbs are formed; its animal life begins to function; all the beautiful adaptations come into play. The fourth stage here mentioned is that of distinctive Man, into whom Allah's spirit is breathed. Then he rises higher than animals.

3640. As a complete man he gets the higher faculties. The five animal senses I understand to be included in the third stage. But in the fourth stage he rises higher and is addressed in the second person, "you," instead of the third person "him". He has now the spiritual counterpart of hearing (*i.e.*, the capacity to hear Allah's Message) and seeing (i.e., the inner vision), and feeling the nobler heights of love and understanding the bearings of the inner life (both typified by the Heart). Yet with all these gifts, what thanks does unregenerate or corrupted man give to Allah?

3641. *Cf.* 13:5. It has been the cry of Materialists and Sceptics through the ages not only to bound their horizon with this brief life, but to deny dogmatically that there can be a future life. Though this is against the professed principles of Sceptics, in practice they take up that attitude. Here "they" refers to those "who give little thanks" to Allah, mentioned in the last verse. The argument used against them is: if Allah can produce such a wonderful creation the first time, why can He not make it again? That points to the possibility: our own general inner hope and expectation of a future life, coupled with Faith in Allah's work, is the ground of our certainty.

3642. If death is certain, as it is, and this life by itself in no way satisfies our instincts and expectations, we may be sure that the agency which separates our soul from our bodies will bring us into the new world. If we believe in a soul at all—the very foundation of Religion—we must believe in a Future, without which the soul has no meaning.

SECTION 2.

12. If only thou couldst see
When the guilty ones
Will bend low their heads
Before their Lord, (saying:)
"Our Lord! We have seen
And we have heard:[3643]
Now then send us back
(To the world): we will
Work righteousness: for we
Do indeed (now) believe."

وَلَوْ تَرَىٰٓ إِذِ ٱلْمُجْرِمُونَ نَاكِسُوا۟ رُءُوسِهِمْ عِندَ رَبِّهِمْ رَبَّنَآ أَبْصَرْنَا وَسَمِعْنَا فَٱرْجِعْنَا نَعْمَلْ صَـٰلِحًا إِنَّا مُوقِنُونَ ﴿١٢﴾

13. If We had so willed,[3644]
We could certainly have brought
Every soul its true guidance:
But the Word from Me[3645]
Will come true, "I will
Fill Hell with Jinns
And men all together."

وَلَوْ شِئْنَا لَـَٔاتَيْنَا كُلَّ نَفْسٍ هُدَىٰهَا وَلَـٰكِنْ حَقَّ ٱلْقَوْلُ مِنِّى لَأَمْلَأَنَّ جَهَنَّمَ مِنَ ٱلْجِنَّةِ وَٱلنَّاسِ أَجْمَعِينَ ﴿١٣﴾

14. "Taste ye then—for ye
Forgot the Meeting[3646]
Of this Day of yours.
And We too will
Forget you—taste ye
The penalty of Eternity
For your (evil) deeds!"

فَذُوقُوا۟ بِمَا نَسِيتُمْ لِقَآءَ يَوْمِكُمْ هَـٰذَآ إِنَّا نَسِينَـٰكُمْ وَذُوقُوا۟ عَذَابَ ٱلْخُلْدِ بِمَا كُنتُمْ تَعْمَلُونَ ﴿١٤﴾

15. Only those believe
In Our Signs, who, when
They are recited to them

إِنَّمَا يُؤْمِنُ بِـَٔايَـٰتِنَا ٱلَّذِينَ إِذَا ذُكِّرُوا۟ بِهَا ﴿١٥﴾

3643. In life on the new plane, there will be no room for deception or self-deception. The most hardened sinner will see the truth and the justice of the Day of Account. He will wish he could be sent back, but it will be too late. The world as we know it will have already passed away.

3644. Could evil have been averted? Certainly everything is in Allah's power. If it had been His Will and Plan, He could have created a world in which there would have been no choice or will in any of His creatures. But that was not His Will and Plan. In the world as we see it, man has a certain amount of choice and free will. That being so, He has provided Signs and means of instruction for man, in order that man's will may be straight and pure. A necessary corollary will be Punishment for the infractions of His Law. That Punishment must come to pass, for Allah's Word is true and must be fulfilled.

3645. *Cf.* 11:119, n. 1623, and 7:18, and see last note. Jinns are the evil spirits that tempt men, and the men who will suffer punishment will be those who have succumbed to their temptations.

3646. *Cf.* n. 1029 to 7:51. "Forget" here is in the sense of "to ignore deliberately, to reject with scorn". In the sense of mistake or defect of knowledge it is inapplicable to the All-Perfect Being, for we are expressly told, "My Lord never errs, nor forgets": 20:52.

Fall down in adoration,[3647]
And celebrate the praises
Of their Lord, nor are they
(Ever) puffed up with pride.

16. Their limbs do forsake[3648]
Their beds of sleep, the while
They call on their Lord,
In Fear and Hope:[3649]
And they spend (in charity)
Out of the sustenance which
We have bestowed on them.

17. Now no person knows
What delights of the eye[3650]
Are kept hidden (in reserve)
For them—as a reward
For their (good) Deeds.

18. Is then the man
Who believes no better
Than the man who is
Rebellious and wicked?[3651]
Not equal are they.

19. For those who believe
And do righteous deeds,
Are Gardens as hospitable[3652]
Homes, for their (good) deeds.

20. As to those who are
Rebellious and wicked, their
abode

خَرُّوا سُجَّدًا وَسَبَّحُوا بِحَمْدِ
رَبِّهِمْ وَهُمْ لَا يَسْتَكْبِرُونَ

(١٦) تَتَجَافَىٰ جُنُوبُهُمْ عَنِ الْمَضَاجِعِ
يَدْعُونَ رَبَّهُمْ خَوْفًا وَطَمَعًا
وَمِمَّا رَزَقْنَاهُمْ يُنفِقُونَ

(١٧) فَلَا تَعْلَمُ نَفْسٌ
مَّا أُخْفِيَ لَهُم مِّن قُرَّةِ أَعْيُنٍ
جَزَاءً بِمَا كَانُوا يَعْمَلُونَ

(١٨) أَفَمَن كَانَ مُؤْمِنًا
كَمَن كَانَ فَاسِقًا
لَّا يَسْتَوُونَ

(١٩) أَمَّا الَّذِينَ آمَنُوا وَعَمِلُوا الصَّالِحَاتِ
فَلَهُمْ جَنَّاتُ الْمَأْوَىٰ نُزُلًا بِمَا كَانُوا يَعْمَلُونَ

(٢٠) وَأَمَّا الَّذِينَ فَسَقُوا فَمَأْوَاهُمُ النَّارُ

3647. *In adoration*: *Sujjadan*, or in a posture of prostration, expressive of deep humility and faith. This is the keyword of the Sūrah, which bears the title of *Al Sajdah*. All the Signs of Allah lead our thoughts upwards towards Him, and when they are expounded, our attitude should be one of humble gratitude to Allah. At this passage it is usual to make a prostration. (R).

3648. *Junūb*: sides, on which men sleep and turn in their sleep: I have translated this "limbs" for shortness. Holy men and women "breathless with adoration" shun soft, comfortable beds, and luxurious sleep. Their limbs are better exercised in offices of devotion and prayer, especially by night. Commentators specially refer this to Prayers called *Tahajjud*, which are offered after midnight in the small hours of the morning, in twelve *Rak'at*.

3649. *In Fear and Hope*: in spiritual fear lest their dedication to Allah should not be sufficiently worthy to be accepted, and a spiritual longing or hope that their shortcomings will be overlooked by the Mercy of Allah. And their adoration is not shown only in Prayer, but also in practical Service and Charity, out of whatever gifts they may have received from Allah.

3650. *Delights of the eye*: an idiom for that which pleases most and gives most satisfaction. In our present state we can scarcely imagine the real Bliss that will come to us in the Future.

3651. The Future of the two classes—the Blessed and the Wicked—is described in verses 19:22.

3652. A home brings before our minds a picture of peace and happiness. When to it are added honour and hospitality, it adds further to the idea of happiness.

Will be the Fire: every time[3653]
They wish to get away
Therefrom, they will be forced
Thereinto, and it will be said
To them: "Taste ye
The Penalty of the Fire,
The which ye were wont
To reject as false."

كُلَّمَآ أَرَادُوٓاْ أَن يَخْرُجُواْ مِنْهَآ
أُعِيدُواْ فِيهَا وَقِيلَ لَهُمْ
ذُوقُواْ عَذَابَ ٱلنَّارِ ٱلَّذِى
كُنتُم بِهِۦ تُكَذِّبُونَ

21. And indeed We will make
Them taste of the Penalty
Of this (life) prior to[3654]
The supreme Penalty, in order
That they may (repent and)
return.

٢١ وَلَنُذِيقَنَّهُم مِّنَ ٱلْعَذَابِ
ٱلْأَدْنَىٰ دُونَ ٱلْعَذَابِ ٱلْأَكْبَرِ
لَعَلَّهُمْ يَرْجِعُونَ

22. And who does more wrong
Than one to whom are recited
The Signs of his Lord
And who then turns away[3655]
Therefrom? Verily from those
Who transgress We shall exact
(Due) Retribution.

٢٢ وَمَنْ أَظْلَمُ مِمَّن
ذُكِّرَ بِـَٔايَٰتِ رَبِّهِۦ ثُمَّ أَعْرَضَ عَنْهَآ
إِنَّا مِنَ ٱلْمُجْرِمِينَ مُنتَقِمُونَ

SECTION 3.

23. We did indeed aforetime
Give the Book to Moses:[3656]
Be not then in doubt
Of its reaching (thee):[3657]

٢٣ وَلَقَدْ ءَاتَيْنَا مُوسَى ٱلْكِتَٰبَ
فَلَا تَكُن فِى مِرْيَةٍ مِّن لِّقَآئِهِۦ

3653. *Cf.* 22:22. Just as the Garden is a type of Bliss, so is the Fire a type of Penalty and suffering. There will be no getting away from it. What will be the thoughts of those who had earned it? "We used to reject the idea of the Consequences as mere chimera: and now we find it to be true!" What will be their feelings then? How will they like it!

3654. The final Penalty is to come in the Hereafter. There is no doubt about it. But before it comes, a minor Penalty comes in this very life. It may be in some kind of misfortune, or it may be in the pangs of a tortured conscience or secret sorrow. But this minor Penalty may be really a mercy, as it gives them a chance of repentance and amendment.

3655. The worst and most hardened sinner is the man to whom Allah's Signs are actually brought home and who yet prefers Evil and turns away from the Light of Allah. The Signs may be in the words and guidance of a great Teacher or in some minor sorrow or warning, which he disregards with contumely. Or it may be a catastrophic blow to his conscience, which should open his eyes, but from which he deliberately refuses to profit. The penalty—the Nemesis—must necessarily come eventually.

3656. *The Book* is not here co-extensive with Revelation. Moses had, revealed to him, a Law, a *sharī'ah*, which was to guide his people in all the practical affairs of their life. Jesus, after him, was also inspired by Allah: but his *Injīl* or Gospel contained only general principles and not a Code or *sharī'ah*. The Holy Prophet was the next one to have a *sharī'ah* or "Book" in that sense: for the Qur'ān contains both a Code and general principles. This Sūrah is a Makkan Sūrah. The Code came later in Madīnah. But he is given the assurance that will also have a Code, to supersede the earlier Law, and complete the Revelation of Allah.

3657. *Its reaching (thee): liqā'ihī*. Commentators differ as to the construction of the pronoun *hi*, which may be translated either "its" or "his". I construe it to refer to "the Book", as that gives the most natural meaning, as explained in the last note.

And We made it
A guide to the Children
Of Israel.

وَجَعَلْنَٰهُ هُدًى لِّبَنِىٓ إِسْرَٰٓءِيلَ

24. And We appointed, from among
Them, Leaders, giving
guidance[3658]
Under Our command, so long
As they persevered with patience
And continued to have faith
In Our Signs.

٢٤ وَجَعَلْنَا مِنْهُمْ أَئِمَّةً
يَهْدُونَ بِأَمْرِنَا لَمَّا صَبَرُوا۟ ۖ
وَكَانُوا۟ بِـَٔايَٰتِنَا يُوقِنُونَ

25. Verily thy Lord will judge
Between them on the Day
Of Judgement, in the matters
Wherein they differ
(among themselves)[3659]

٢٥ إِنَّ رَبَّكَ هُوَ يَفْصِلُ بَيْنَهُمْ يَوْمَ
ٱلْقِيَٰمَةِ فِيمَا كَانُوا۟ فِيهِ يَخْتَلِفُونَ

26. Does it not teach them
A lesson, how many generations
We destroyed before them,
In whose dwellings they
(Now) go to and fro?[3660]
Verily in that are Signs:
Do they not then listen?[3661]

٢٦ أَوَلَمْ يَهْدِ لَهُمْ كَمْ أَهْلَكْنَا
مِن قَبْلِهِم مِّنَ ٱلْقُرُونِ يَمْشُونَ فِى مَسَٰكِنِهِمْ ۚ
إِنَّ فِى ذَٰلِكَ لَءَايَٰتٍ ۖ أَفَلَا يَسْمَعُونَ

27. And do they not see
That We do drive Rain[3662]
To parched soil (bare
Of herbage), and produce
therewith
Crops, providing food

٢٧ أَوَلَمْ يَرَوْا۟ أَنَّا نَسُوقُ ٱلْمَآءَ
إِلَى ٱلْأَرْضِ ٱلْجُرُزِ فَنُخْرِجُ
بِهِۦ زَرْعًا تَأْكُلُ مِنْهُ

3658. The series of Judges, Prophets, and Kings in Israel continued to give good guidance, in accordance with Allah's Law, as long as the people continued in Faith and Constancy (persevering patience). When that condition ceased, Allah's grace was withdrawn and the people broke up into wrangling sects and practically suffered national annihilation.

3659. These wrangles and disputes among them will continue until the Day of Judgement, but meantime a new *Ummah* (that of Islam) will arise and take its place, with a universal and unified Message for mankind.

3660. If a nation gone astray could only learn from the history of earlier nations that were destroyed for their evil! They could see vestiges of them in their daily goings to and fro: the Jews could see vestiges of the Philistines, Amalekites, etc. in Palestine, and the pagan Arabs, of the 'Ād and Thamūd in Arabia.

3661. *Listen: i.e.*, listen to the warnings conveyed in Allah's Signs. Notice how naturally the transition is effected from the physical to the spiritual—from the ruined physical vestiges of ungodly nations on this earth to the more intangible signs conveyed by History and Revelation. Here the sense of Hearing is mentioned, both in its physical and its metaphysical or spiritual aspect. In the next verse the sense of Sight is mentioned in both aspects.

3662. Again, as in the last verse, there is an easy transition from the phsyical to the spiritual. In physical nature there may be parched soil, which is to all intents and purposes dead. Allah sends rain, and the dead soil is converted into living land producing rich crops of fodder and corn, nuts and fruits, to satisfy the hunger of man and beast. So in the spiritual world. The dead man is revivified by Allah's grace and mercy through His Revelation. He becomes not only an asset to himself but to his dependents and those around him.

For their cattle and themselves?
Have they not the vision?[3663]

28. They say: "When will
This Decision be, if ye[3664]
Are telling the truth?"

29. Say: "On the Day
Of Decision, no profit
Will it be to Unbelievers
If they (then) believe!
Nor will they be granted
A respite."

30. So turn away from them,
And wait: they too[3665]
Are waiting.

أَنْعَٰمُهُمْ وَأَنفُسُهُمْ ۖ أَفَلَا يُبْصِرُونَ

وَيَقُولُونَ مَتَىٰ هَٰذَا ٱلْفَتْحُ إِن كُنتُمْ صَٰدِقِينَ ﴿٢٨﴾

قُلْ يَوْمَ ٱلْفَتْحِ لَا يَنفَعُ ٱلَّذِينَ كَفَرُوٓا۟ إِيمَٰنُهُمْ وَلَا هُمْ يُنظَرُونَ ﴿٢٩﴾

فَأَعْرِضْ عَنْهُمْ وَٱنتَظِرْ إِنَّهُم مُّنتَظِرُونَ ﴿٣٠﴾

3663. The verse begins with "do they not *see*?" (*a wa lam yaraw*), a physical act. It ends with "have they not the *vision*?" (*afalā yubṣirūn*), a matter of spiritual insight. This is parallel to the two kinds of "hearing" or "listening", explained in n. 3661 above.

3664. The Unbelievers may say: "If all this which you say is true, tell us when this final restoration of Realities, Life and true Values will come about." The answer is: "If you mean that you will postpone your repentance and reform till then, it will be no use: it will be too late for repentance, and no respite will be granted *then*: this is the Respite, and this is your chance."

3665. Read 6:158 and n. 984 as commentary on this. There it is said to the Unbelievers: "Wait ye: we too are waiting." Here the Righteous one is told: "Wait (thou): they too are waiting." The reversal of the order is appropriate: in each case the person (or persons) addressed is mentioned first. *Cf.* also 7:71.

INTRODUCTION TO SŪRAH 33—*AL AḤZĀB*

The series of mystic Sūrahs beginning with S. 26 having been closed with the last Sūrah, we now come back to the hard facts of this life. Two questions are mainly considered here, *viz.*, (1) the attempt by violence and brute force to crush the truth, and (2) the attempt by slander or unseemly conduct, to poison the relations of women with men.

As regards the first, the story of Al Aḥzāb or the Confederates, who tried to surround and annihilate the Muslim community in Madīnah, is full of underhand intrigues on the part of such diverse enemies as the Pagan Quraysh, the Jews (Banū Naḍīr) who had been already expelled from Madīnah for their treachery, the Ghaṭfān tribe of Bedouin Arabs from the interior, and the Jewish tribe of Banū Quraẓah in Madīnah. This was the unholy Confederacy against Islam. But though they caused a great deal of anxiety and suffering to the beleaguered Muslims, Islam came triumphantly out of the trial and became more firmly established than ever.

The Quraysh in Makkah had tried all sorts of persecution, boycott, insult, and bodily injuries to the Muslims, leading to their partial hijrah to Abyssinia and their Hijrah as a body to Madīnah. The first armed conflict between them and the Muslims took place at Badr in Ramaḍān A.H. 2, when the Quraysh were signally defeated. (See n. 352 to 3:13). Next year (Shawwāl A.H. 3) they came to take revenge on Madīnah. The battle was fought at Uḥud, and though the Muslims suffered severely, Madīnah was saved and the Makkans had to return to Makkah with their object frustrated. Then they began to make a network of intrigues and alliances, and besieged Madīnah with a force of 10,000 men in Shawwāl and Dhu al Qa'dah A.H. 5. This is the siege of the Confederates referred to in 33:9-27, which lasted over two weeks: some accounts give 27 days. It caused much suffering, from hunger, cold, an unceasing shower of arrows, and constant general or concentrated assaults. But it ended in the discomfiture of the Confederates, and established Islam firmer than ever. It was a well-organised and formidable attack, but the Muslims had made preparations to meet it. One of the preparations, which took the enemy by surprise, was the Trench (*Khandaq*) dug round Madīnah by the Prophets' order and under the supervision of Salmān the Persian. The siege and battle are therefore known as the Battle of the Trench or the Battle of the Confederates.

As regards the position and dignity of the ladies of the Prophet's Household and the Muslim women generally, salutary principles are laid down to safeguard their homes and protect them from slander and insult. The ladies of the Household interested themselves in social work and work of instruction for the Muslim women, and Muslim women were being trained more and more in community service. Two of them (the two Zaynabs) devoted themselves to the poor. The nursing of the wounded on or by the battlefield was specially necessary in those days of warfare. The Prophet's daughter Fāṭimah, then aged about 19 to 20, lovingly nursed her father's wounds at Uḥud (A.H. 3): Rufaydah nursed Sa'd ibn Mu'ādh wounds at the Siege of Madīnah by the Confederates (A.H. 5): and in the Khaybar expedition (A.H. 7) Muslim women went out from Madīnah for nursing service.

A portion of this Sūrah sums up the lessons of the Battle of the Trench and must have been revealed some time after that Battle (Shawwāl A.H. 5). The marriage with Zaynab referred to in verse 37 also took place in the same year. Some portions (*e.g.*, verse 27, see n. 3705) were probably revealed in A.H. 7 after the Khaybar settlement.

Summary—The pagan customs in human relationships should be abandoned, and men and women should be held in honour according to natural relationships and spiritual positions (33:1-8, and C. 186).

The Battle of the Trench and its lessons: hypocrites and their fears: Truth and noble examples to be followed (33:9-27, and C. 187).

High position and seemly conduct for the Prophet's wives: unhappy marriages (like Zaynab's) not to be perpetuated on false scruples: Prophet's wives to be treated kindly and gently (33:28-52, and C. 188).

Respect due to Prophet and his family: slander to be avoided and punished: guard your words and your responsibilities (33:53-73, and C. 189).

C. 186.—The issue of all things depends
(33:1-8.) On Allah alone: we must put our trust
On Him as the Guardian of all things, both great
And small: call things by their right names.
If false relationships by custom or superstition
Do harm to men or women, shun them.
The spiritual Guide is more than Father:
The ladies of his household are Mothers
To the Believers—in rank, dignity, and duty.
The Guide will have to give an account
In the Hereafter, and how the Truth was received
Which he was charged to proclaim to men.

Sūrah 33.

الجزء الحادي والعشرون سورة الأحزاب

Al Aḥzāb (The Confederates)

In the Name of Allah, Most Gracious,
Most Merciful.

بِسْمِ اللَّهِ الرَّحْمَٰنِ الرَّحِيمِ

1. O Prophet! Fear Allah,
And hearken not
To the Unbelievers[3666]
And the Hypocrites:
Verily Allah is full
Of knowledge and wisdom.

يَٰٓأَيُّهَا ٱلنَّبِىُّ ٱتَّقِ ٱللَّهَ وَلَا تُطِعِ ٱلْكَٰفِرِينَ وَٱلْمُنَٰفِقِينَ ۗ إِنَّ ٱللَّهَ كَانَ عَلِيمًا حَكِيمًا ﴿١﴾

2. But follow that which
Comes to thee by inspiration
From thy Lord: for Allah
Is well acquainted[3667]
With (all) that ye do.

وَٱتَّبِعْ مَا يُوحَىٰٓ إِلَيْكَ مِن رَّبِّكَ ۚ إِنَّ ٱللَّهَ كَانَ بِمَا تَعْمَلُونَ خَبِيرًا ﴿٢﴾

3. And put thy trust
In Allah, and enough is
Allah[3668]
As a Disposer of affairs.

وَتَوَكَّلْ عَلَى ٱللَّهِ ۚ وَكَفَىٰ بِٱللَّهِ وَكِيلًا ﴿٣﴾

4. Allah has not made
For any man two hearts[3669]
In his (one) body: nor has

مَّا جَعَلَ ٱللَّهُ لِرَجُلٍ مِّن قَلْبَيْنِ فِى جَوْفِهِۦ ۚ وَمَا ﴿٤﴾

3666. The fifth year A.H. was a critical year in the external history of early Islam, and this Sūrah must be read in the light of the events that then took place. As explained in the Introduction, the Grand Confederacy against Islam came and invested Madīnah and failed utterly. It consisted of the Makkan Unbelievers, the desert Arabs of Central Arabia, the Jews previously expelled for treachery from Madīnah, the Jews remaining in Madīnah, and the Hypocrites led by 'Abd Allah ibn Ubayy, who have already been described in 9:43-110. Their bond of union was the common hatred of Islam and it snapped under the reserves they met. It is important to note three points. (1) The Jews as a body now lost their last chance of bearing the standard of Islam: the best of them had already accepted the renewal of Allah's Message. (2) A definite status was given to the Prophet's household, after the slanders on 'Āishah had been stilled (24:11-26), and the true position of the Mothers of the Believers had been cleared. (3) A further exposition of the purity of sexual relations was given, based on the story of Zaynab, the "Mother of the Poor". These points will be referred to in later notes.

3667. In the most adverse circumstances, in the midst of the assaults of Evil, the plots of treason and hypocrisy, the darts of slander and false charges, and stupid superstitions and taboos, the Prophet of Allah should steer his course steadily according to Allah's Law and not fear human evil, in whatever form it appears. Men may misjudge, but Allah knows all. Men may try to overthrow Good, but Wisdom is with Allah. (R).

3668. We must wholly trust Allah: He is the true and efficient Guardian of all interests. *Cf.* 4:81, and n. 600.

3669. *Two hearts in his (one) breast*: two inconsistent attitudes: such as serving Allah and Mammon; or subscribing to both Truth and Superstition; or hypocritically pretending one thing and intending another. Such a thing is against Allah's Law and Will. Apart from the condemnation of general hypocrisy, two pagan customs of the Times of Ignorance are mentioned, and their iniquity pointed out. See the notes 3670 and 3671. Nor can a man love two women with equal love; hence the injustice of marrying more than one wife; see the second clause in 4:3. (R).

He made your wives whom
Ye divorce by Ẓihār[3670]
Your mothers: nor has He
Made your adopted sons[3671]
Your sons. Such is (only)
Your (manner of) speech
By your mouths. But Allah
Tells (you) the Truth, and He
Shows the (right) Way.

جَعَلَ أَزْوَٰجَكُمُ
ٱلَّٰٓـِٔى تُظَٰهِرُونَ مِنْهُنَّ أُمَّهَٰتِكُمْ
وَمَا جَعَلَ أَدْعِيَآءَكُمْ أَبْنَآءَكُمْ ذَٰلِكُمْ قَوْلُكُم
بِأَفْوَٰهِكُمْ وَٱللَّهُ يَقُولُ ٱلْحَقَّ وَهُوَ يَهْدِى ٱلسَّبِيلَ

5. Call them by (the names
Of) their fathers: that is
Juster in the sight of Allah.
But if ye know not[3672]
Their father's (names, call
Them) your Brothers in faith,
Or your *Mawlās*.
But there is no blame
On ye if ye make[3673]
A mistake therein:
(What counts is)
The intention of your hearts:
And Allah is Oft-Forgiving,
Most Merciful.

٥ ٱدْعُوهُمْ لِءَابَآئِهِمْ هُوَ أَقْسَطُ عِندَ ٱللَّهِ
فَإِن لَّمْ تَعْلَمُوٓا۟ ءَابَآءَهُمْ
فَإِخْوَٰنُكُمْ فِى ٱلدِّينِ وَمَوَٰلِيكُمْ
وَلَيْسَ عَلَيْكُمْ جُنَاحٌ فِيمَآ أَخْطَأْتُم بِهِۦ
وَلَٰكِن مَّا تَعَمَّدَتْ قُلُوبُكُمْ
وَكَانَ ٱللَّهُ غَفُورًا رَّحِيمًا

6. The Prophet is closer
To the Believers than

٦ ٱلنَّبِىُّ أَوْلَىٰ بِٱلْمُؤْمِنِينَ مِنْ

3670. This was an evil Arab custom, by which the husband selfishly deprived his wife of her conjugal rights and yet kept her to himself like a slave without her being free to remarry. He pronounced words importing that she was like his mother. After that she could not demand conjugal rights but was not free from his control and could not contract another marriage. See also 58:1-5, where this is condemned in the strongest terms and punishment is promised for it. A man sometimes said such words in a fit of anger: they did not affect him, but they degraded her position.

3671. If a man called another's son "his son", it might create complications with natural and normal relationships if taken too literally. It is pointed out that it is not only a *facon de parler* in men's mouths, and should not be taken literally. The truth is the truth and cannot be altered by men's adopting "sons". "Adoption" in the technical sense is not allowed in Muslim Law. Those who have been "wives of your sons proceeding from your loins" are within the Prohibited Degrees of marriage; 4:23; but this does not apply to "adopted" sons.

3672. Freedmen were often called after their master's name as the "son of so and so". When they were slaves, perhaps their fathers' names were lost altogether. It is more correct to speak of them as the *Mawlā* of so and so. But *Mawlā* in Arabic might also imply a close relationship of friendship: in that case, too, it is better to use the right term instead of the term "son". "Brother" is not objectionable because "Brotherhood" is used in a wider sense than "fatherhood", and is not likely to be misunderstood.

3673. What is aimed at is to destroy the superstition of erecting false relationships to the detriment or loss of true blood relations. It is not intended to penalise an unintentional slip in the matter, and indeed even if a man deliberately calls another his son or father, who is not his son or father, out of politeness or affections, 'Allah is Oft-Forgiving, Most Merciful". It is the action of mischievous parties which is chiefly reprehended, if they intend false insinuations. A mere mistake on their part does not matter. (R).

Their own selves,[3674]
And his wives are[3675]
Their mothers. Blood-relations
Among each other have
Closer personal ties,
In the Decree of Allah,
Than (the Brotherhood of)
Believers and Muhājirs:[3676]
Nevertheless do ye
What is just to your
Closest friends: such is
The writing of the Decree
(Of Allah).

أَنفُسِهِمْ وَأَزْوَٰجُهُۥٓ أُمَّهَٰتُهُمْ
وَأُولُوا۟ ٱلْأَرْحَامِ بَعْضُهُمْ أَوْلَىٰ
بِبَعْضٍ فِى كِتَٰبِ ٱللَّهِ
مِنَ ٱلْمُؤْمِنِينَ وَٱلْمُهَٰجِرِينَ
إِلَّآ أَن تَفْعَلُوٓا۟ إِلَىٰٓ أَوْلِيَآئِكُم مَّعْرُوفًا
كَانَ ذَٰلِكَ فِى ٱلْكِتَٰبِ مَسْطُورًا

7. And remember We took
From the Prophets their
Covenant:[3677]
As (We did) from thee:
From Noah, Abraham, Moses,
And Jesus the son of Mary:
We took from them
A solemn Covenant:

٧ وَإِذْ أَخَذْنَا مِنَ ٱلنَّبِيِّـۧنَ مِيثَٰقَهُمْ
وَمِنكَ وَمِن نُّوحٍ وَإِبْرَٰهِيمَ
وَمُوسَىٰ وَعِيسَى ٱبْنِ مَرْيَمَ
وَأَخَذْنَا مِنْهُم مِّيثَٰقًا غَلِيظًا

8. That (Allah) may question
The (Custodians) of Truth
concerning

٨ لِّيَسْـَٔلَ ٱلصَّٰدِقِينَ عَن

3674. In spiritual relationships the Prophet is entitled to more respect and consideration than blood-relations. The Believers should follow him rather than their fathers or mothers or brothers, where there is conflict of duties. He is even nearer—closer to our real interests—than our own selves. In some Qirā'ahs, like that of Ubayy ibn Ka'ab, occur also the words "and he is a father of them", which imply his spiritual relationship and connect on with the words "and his wives are their mothers". Thus his spiritual fatherhood would be contrasted pointedly with the repudiation of the vulgar superstition of calling any one like Zayd ibn Ḥārthah by the appellation Zayd ibn Muḥammad (33:40): such an application is really disrespectful of the Prophet.

3675. See last note. This Sūrah establishes the dignity and position of the Holy Prophet's wives, who had a special mission and responsibility as Mothers of the Believers. They were not to be like ordinary women: they had to instruct women in spiritual matters, visit and minister to those who were ill or in distress, and do other kindly offices in aid of the Prophet's mission.

3676. No man should deprive his blood-relations of such rights of maintenance and property as they might have. The community of Believers, inhabitants of Madīnah and those who had migrated to Madīnah from Makkah, also had their mutual rights, but they were not to be put forward as an excuse to defeat the prior rights of natural relationships. In the early Madīnah days, Anṣār were allowed to inherit from Muhājirs whose natural relations had not emigrated, but this practice was discontinued when normal relations were reestablished between Makkah and Madīnah.

3677. *Cf.* 3:81. There is an implied covenant on all created things to follow Allah's Law, which is the law of their being: see 5:1. But there is a special implied covenant with all Prophets, strict and solemn, that they shall carry out their mission, proclaim Allah's Truth without fear or favour, and be ever ready in His service in all circumstances. That gives them their position and dignity as explained in the last verse, and their tremendous responsibilities in respect of the people whom they come to instruct and lead to the right Path.

The Truth they (were charged with)[3678]
And He has prepared
For the Unbelievers
A grievous Penalty.

صِدْقِهِمْۚ
وَأَعَدَّ لِلْكَٰفِرِينَ عَذَابًا أَلِيمًا

C. 187.—When the formidable forces of a whole Confederacy
(33:9-27.) Bent on destroying Islam burst
Upon Madīnah, it was Allah's grace that saved
The Muslims. The enemies and the Hypocrites
Did their best to defeat the purpose of Allah,
But they were foiled. In the Prophet was found
The ideal Leader for the men of God,
Who became heirs to the heritage: misused
By enemies to Faith and the Laws of Allah.

SECTION 2,

9. O ye who believe!
Remember the Grace of Allah,
(Bestowed) on you, when
There came down on you
Hosts (to overwhelm you):[3679]
But We sent against them[3680]
A hurricane and forces
That ye saw not:
But Allah sees (clearly)[3681]
All that ye do.

٩ يَٰٓأَيُّهَا ٱلَّذِينَ ءَامَنُوا۟
ٱذْكُرُوا۟ نِعْمَةَ ٱللَّهِ عَلَيْكُمْ
إِذْ جَآءَتْكُمْ جُنُودٌ فَأَرْسَلْنَا
عَلَيْهِمْ رِيحًا وَجُنُودًا لَّمْ تَرَوْهَاۚ
وَكَانَ ٱللَّهُ بِمَا تَعْمَلُونَ بَصِيرًا

3678. The men to whom Allah's Truth has been committed for promulgation will be asked in the Hereafter how the Truth fared in the world—how it was received, who opposed it, and who assisted it. Like all trustees, they will have to give a full account of their trust. Allah knows all, and it will not add to His information. But it will be evidence for and against those to whom it was preached, so that the responsibility of those who dishonoured it may be duly enforced. The primary custodians of spiritual Truth are the Prophets, but in descending degrees all men to whom Allah's Message comes are included.

3679. In this verse is summed up the beginning and the end of the fateful struggle of the Siege of Madīnah in A.H. 5. The composition of the unhallowed Confederacy that came to destroy Islam is referred to in the Introduction. They came with a force of ten to twelve thousand fighting men, an unprecedented army for that time and country. The battle is known as the Battle of the Trench.

3680. After a close investment of two to four weeks, during which the enemy were disheartened by their ill success, there was a piercing blast of the cold east wind. It was a severe winter, and February can be a very cold month in Madīnah, which is about 3,000 feet above the sea level. The enemy's tents were torn up, their fires were extinguished, the sand and rain beat in their faces, and they were terrified by the portents against them. They had already well nigh fallen out amongst themselves, and beating a hasty retreat, they melted away. The Madīnah fighting strength was no more than 3,000, and the Jewish tribe of the Banū Qurayẓah who were in their midst was a source of weakness as they were treacherously intriguing with the enemy. And further there were the Hypocrites: see n. 3666 above. But there were hidden forces that helped the Muslims. Besides the forces of nature there were moral forces—mutual distrust and bickering in the enemy camp, and on the other side, perfect discipline among the real Muslims, and the superb leadership of the Holy Prophet.

3681. Allah sees everything. Therefore we may conclude that the discipline and moral fervour of the Muslims, as well as the enemy's insincerities, intrigues, and reliance on brute force, were all contributory causes to his repulse, under Allah's dispensation. There were many hidden causes which neither party saw clearly.

10. Behold! they came on you
From above you and from
Below you, and behold,
The eyes became dim
And the hearts gaped[3682]
Up to the throats,
And ye imagined various
(Vain) thoughts about Allah!

(١٠) إِذْ جَآءُوكُم مِّن فَوْقِكُمْ
وَمِنْ أَسْفَلَ مِنكُمْ وَإِذْ زَاغَتِ ٱلْأَبْصَٰرُ
وَبَلَغَتِ ٱلْقُلُوبُ ٱلْحَنَاجِرَ
وَتَظُنُّونَ بِٱللَّهِ ٱلظُّنُونَا۠

11. In that situation
Were the Believers tried:
They were shaken as by
A tremendous shaking.

(١١) هُنَالِكَ ٱبْتُلِىَ ٱلْمُؤْمِنُونَ
وَزُلْزِلُوا۟ زِلْزَالًا شَدِيدًا

12. And behold! The Hypocrites
And those in whose hearts
Is a disease (even) say: "Allah
And His Messenger promised us
Nothing but delusions!"[3683]

(١٢) وَإِذْ يَقُولُ ٱلْمُنَٰفِقُونَ
وَٱلَّذِينَ فِى قُلُوبِهِم مَّرَضٌ
مَّا وَعَدَنَا ٱللَّهُ وَرَسُولُهُۥٓ إِلَّا غُرُورًا

13. Behold! A party among them
Said: "Ye men of Yat͟hrib!
Ye cannot stand (the attack)!
Therefore go back!"
And a band of them
Ask for leave of the Prophet
Saying, "Truly our houses[3684]
Are bare and exposed," though
They were not exposed:
They intended nothing but
To run away.

(١٣) وَإِذْ قَالَت طَّآئِفَةٌ مِّنْهُمْ
يَٰٓأَهْلَ يَثْرِبَ لَا مُقَامَ لَكُمْ فَٱرْجِعُوا۟ ۚ
وَيَسْتَـْٔذِنُ فَرِيقٌ مِّنْهُمُ
ٱلنَّبِىَّ يَقُولُونَ إِنَّ بُيُوتَنَا
عَوْرَةٌ وَمَا هِىَ بِعَوْرَةٍ ۖ
إِن يُرِيدُونَ إِلَّا فِرَارًا

3682. The psychology of the combatants is described with matchless vigour in the Holy Test. The onrush of the enemy was really tremendous. The Trench round Madīnah was between the defenders and the huge attacking force, which had some high ground behind them "above you": when any of them came through the valley or over the Trench they seemed to come from below. The showers of arrows and stone on both sides must also have seemed to come from the air.

3683. Before this year's mass attack on Madīnah, the Muslims had successfully reached the Syrian border on the north, and there were hopes of reaching Yemen in the south. The Holy Prophet had seen signs of expansion and victory for the Muslims. Now that they were shut within the Trench on the defensive, the Hypocrites taunted them with having indulged in delusive hopes. But the event showed that the hopes were *not* delusive. They were realised beyond expectations in a few years.

3684. All the fighting men of Madīnah had come out of the City and camped in the open space between the City and the Trench that had been dug all round. The disaffected Hypocrites sowed defeatist rumours and pretended to withdraw for the defence of their homes, though their homes were not exposed, and were fully covered by the vigilant defensive forces inside the Trench.

14. And if an entry had
Been effected to them[3685]
From the sides of the (City),
And they had been
Incited to sedition,
They would certainly have
Brought it to pass, with
None but a brief delay!

﴿١٤﴾ وَلَوْ دُخِلَتْ عَلَيْهِم مِّنْ أَقْطَارِهَا
ثُمَّ سُئِلُوا الْفِتْنَةَ لَآتَوْهَا
وَمَا تَلَبَّثُوا بِهَا إِلَّا يَسِيرًا

15. And yet they had already
Covenanted with Allah not to turn
Their backs, and a covenant[3686]
With Allah must (surely)
Be answered for.

﴿١٥﴾ وَلَقَدْ كَانُوا عَاهَدُوا اللَّهَ مِن قَبْلُ
لَا يُوَلُّونَ الْأَدْبَارَ وَكَانَ عَهْدُ اللَّهِ مَسْئُولًا

16. Say: "Running away will not
Profit you if ye are
Running away from death[3687]
Or slaughter: and even if
(Ye do escape), no more
Than a brief (respite)
Will ye be allowed to enjoy!"

﴿١٦﴾ قُل لَّن يَنفَعَكُمُ الْفِرَارُ
إِن فَرَرْتُم مِّنَ الْمَوْتِ أَوِ الْقَتْلِ
وَإِذًا لَّا تُمَتَّعُونَ إِلَّا قَلِيلًا

17. Say: "Who is it that can
Screen you from Allah
If it be His wish
To give you Punishment
Or to give you Mercy?"[3688]
Nor will they find for themselves,
Besides Allah, any protector
Or helper.

﴿١٧﴾ قُلْ مَن ذَا الَّذِي يَعْصِمُكُم مِّنَ اللَّهِ إِنْ
أَرَادَ بِكُمْ سُوءًا أَوْ أَرَادَ بِكُمْ رَحْمَةً
وَلَا يَجِدُونَ لَهُم مِّن دُونِ اللَّهِ
وَلِيًّا وَلَا نَصِيرًا

18. Verily Allah knows those
Among you who keep back

﴿١٨﴾ قَدْ يَعْلَمُ اللَّهُ الْمُعَوِّقِينَ مِنكُمْ

3685. The brunt of all the fighting was on the north side, but the whole Trench was guarded. At one or two points enemy warriors did break within the circuit of the Trench, but they were soon disposed of. 'Ali particularly distinguished himself in many fights, wearing the Prophet's own sword and armour. If any of the enemy had been able to penetrate into the City, the disaffected element, which was only sitting on the fence, would have risen against the Muslims at once—with no delay except what might have been necessary to put on their armour and arms.

3686. Apparently, after the battle of Uḥud, certain men who had then shown cowardice were forgiven on undertaking that they would behave better next time. A solemn promise made to the Messenger of Allah is a promise to Allah, and it cannot be broken with impunity.

3687. The coward in a fight does not usually save himself from death. He is subject, after desertion, to the fury both of the enemy and of his own side for cowardice and desertion. Assuming that he did escape with his life, where could he go to? The brand of cowardice will be on him, and he will be subject to the vengeance of his own people. In any case, his life would be in ignominy and would be brief, and he would have lost irretrievably the meed of valour.

3688. It is still worse if the cowardice or desertion is shown in a Cause, which because of the high issues of truth and justice, may be called the Cause of Allah. How can anyone escape Allah's Punishment? And in the same way, how can anyone prevent another from obtaining Allah's mercy by repentance and amendment? The better path, therefore, is to stand firm in Allah's Way, and if you fail through human weakness, to repent and seek Allah's Mercy. *Cf.* 33:24, and n. 3698 below.

(Men) and those who say
To their brethren, "Come along
To us", but come not
To the fight except
For just a little while,

وَٱلْقَآئِلِينَ لِإِخْوَٰنِهِمْ هَلُمَّ إِلَيْنَا
وَلَا يَأْتُونَ ٱلْبَأْسَ إِلَّا قَلِيلًا

19. Covetous over you.[3689]
Then when fear comes,
Thou wilt see them looking
To thee, their eyes revolving,
Like (those of) one over whom
Hovers death: but when
The fear is past,
They will smite you
With sharp tongues, covetous[3690]
Of goods. Such men have
No faith, and so Allah
Has made their deeds[3691]
Of none effect: and that
Is easy for Allah.[3692]

(١٩) أَشِحَّةً عَلَيْكُمْ
فَإِذَا جَآءَ ٱلْخَوْفُ رَأَيْتَهُمْ يَنظُرُونَ إِلَيْكَ
تَدُورُ أَعْيُنُهُمْ كَٱلَّذِى يُغْشَىٰ عَلَيْهِ مِنَ ٱلْمَوْتِ
فَإِذَا ذَهَبَ ٱلْخَوْفُ سَلَقُوكُم
بِأَلْسِنَةٍ حِدَادٍ أَشِحَّةً عَلَى ٱلْخَيْرِ
أُو۟لَٰٓئِكَ لَمْ يُؤْمِنُوا۟ فَأَحْبَطَ ٱللَّهُ أَعْمَٰلَهُمْ
وَكَانَ ذَٰلِكَ عَلَى ٱللَّهِ يَسِيرًا

20. They think that the Confederates
Have not withdrawn; and if
The Confederates should come
(again),
They would wish they were
In the deserts (wandering)
Among the Bedouins, and[3693]

(٢٠) يَحْسَبُونَ ٱلْأَحْزَابَ لَمْ يَذْهَبُوا۟
وَإِن يَأْتِ ٱلْأَحْزَابُ يَوَدُّوا۟
لَوْ أَنَّهُم بَادُونَ فِى ٱلْأَعْرَابِ

3689. *Ashiḥḥatan*: covetous, grasping, niggardly. Here the meaning is twofold: (1) they spare themselves in the fight as compared with you; they are niggardly with themselves as against you; they contribute little either in personal effort or with their money and resources; and (2) they covet any gains made or booty won, on the part of the real fighters.

3690. In time of danger, they would look to the Holy Prophet for protection, and keep themselves snugly from the fight. When the danger is past, they will come and brag and wrangle and show their covetousness or greed for gain though they gave of themselves but sparingly.

3691. Even any good they may have done becomes vain because of their motives of envy, greed, and covetousness and their cowardice.

3692. It is not surprising that men's deeds fall as it were dead because there is no pure motive behind them. For men it may be difficult to probe motives, but it is easy for Allah, Whom hypocrisy or false show can never deceive.

3693. This completes the picture of the psychology of the Hypocrites, begun in verse 12. Let us analyse it. (1) When they first saw the enemy they were already in a defeatist mood, and thought all was over (verse 12). (2) Not content with disloyalty themselves, they tried to infect others, who made paltry excuses to withdraw from the fight (verse 13). (3) They were ready to betray the City to the enemy if the enemy had gained entrance (verse 14). (4) They forgot all the promises of fidelity which they had previously sworn (verse 15). (5) In their paltry calculations they forgot that cowardice in war does not pay (verses 16-17). (6) Without taking much part in the actual defence, they were ready to talk glibly and claim a lion's share in the fruits of the victory (verses 18-19). (7) Even when the enemy had withdrawn, their cowardly minds were still afraid that the enemy would return, and were alreay meditating what they would do in that case; perhaps they would dwell in the deserts and spy on Madīnah from a safe distance: and if caught in Madīnah they would fight little and intrigue much.

It was a miracle that with such men in their midst, the Holy Prophet and his band won through.

Seeking news about you
(From a safe distance);
And if they were
In your midst, they
Would fight but little.

يَسْـَٔلُونَ عَنْ أَنۢبَآئِكُمْ
وَلَوْ كَانُوا۟ فِيكُم مَّا قَٰتَلُوٓا۟ إِلَّا قَلِيلًا

Section 3.

21. Ye have indeed
In the Messenger of Allah
A beautiful pattern (of
conduct)
For any one whose hope is[3694]
In Allah and the Final Day,
And who engages much[3695]
In the praise of Allah.

٢١ لَّقَدْ كَانَ لَكُمْ
فِى رَسُولِ ٱللَّهِ أُسْوَةٌ حَسَنَةٌ
لِّمَن كَانَ يَرْجُوا۟ ٱللَّهَ وَٱلْيَوْمَ ٱلْـَٔاخِرَ
وَذَكَرَ ٱللَّهَ كَثِيرًا

22. When the Believers saw
The Confederate forces
They said: "This is
What Allah and His
Messenger[3696]
Had promised us, and Allah
And His Messenger told us
What was true." And it
Only added to their faith
And their zeal in obedience.

٢٢ وَلَمَّا رَءَا ٱلْمُؤْمِنُونَ ٱلْأَحْزَابَ
قَالُوا۟ هَٰذَا مَا وَعَدَنَا ٱللَّهُ وَرَسُولُهُۥ
وَصَدَقَ ٱللَّهُ وَرَسُولُهُۥ
وَمَا زَادَهُمْ إِلَّآ إِيمَٰنًا
وَتَسْلِيمًا

23. Among the Believers are men
Who have been true to
Their Covenant with Allah:
Of them some have
completed[3697]
Their vow (to the extreme),
And some (still) wait:
But they have never changed
(Their determination) in the
least:

٢٣ مِّنَ ٱلْمُؤْمِنِينَ رِجَالٌ
صَدَقُوا۟ مَا عَٰهَدُوا۟ ٱللَّهَ عَلَيْهِ
فَمِنْهُم مَّن قَضَىٰ نَحْبَهُۥ
وَمِنْهُم مَّن يَنتَظِرُ
وَمَا بَدَّلُوا۟ تَبْدِيلًا

3694. We now have the psychology of the Believers—God-fearing men, led by that pattern of men and of leaders, Muḥammad.

3695. *Cf.* 26:227: see especially the last clause of that verse in a Makkan Sūrah, which was amply fulfilled in Madīnah.

3696. This is in contrast to what the Hypocrites said in verse 12 above. The divine promise of help and success is contingent upon our striving and faith. Nothing comes to the poltroon and the sceptical idler. Dangers and difficulties, and conflict with Evil, are foretold us, and we must meet them with fortitude and courage.

3697. In the fight for Truth were (and are) many who sacrificed their all—resources, knowledge, influence, life itself—in the Cause, and never wavered. If they won the crown of martyrdom, they were blessed. Such a one was Sa'ad ibn Mu'ādh, the chief of the Aws tribe, the intrepid standard-bearer of Islam, who died of a wound he had received in the Battle of the Trench. Other heroes fought valiantly and lived, always ready to lay down their lives. Both classes were staunch, they never changed or wavered.

24. That Allah may reward
The men of Truth for
Their Truth, and punish
The Hypocrites if that be[3698]
His Will, or turn to them
In Mercy: for Allah is
Oft-Forgiving, Most Merciful.

﴿٢٤﴾ لِّيَجْزِىَ ٱللَّهُ ٱلصَّـٰدِقِينَ بِصِدْقِهِمْ
وَيُعَذِّبَ ٱلْمُنَـٰفِقِينَ إِن شَآءَ أَوْ يَتُوبَ عَلَيْهِمْ ۚ
إِنَّ ٱللَّهَ كَانَ غَفُورًا رَّحِيمًا

25. And Allah turned back
The Unbelievers for (all)
Their fury: no advantage[3699]
Did they gain: and enough
Is Allah for the Believers
In their fight. And Allah
Is full of Strength, Able
To enforce His Will.[3700]

﴿٢٥﴾ وَرَدَّ ٱللَّهُ ٱلَّذِينَ
كَفَرُوا۟ بِغَيْظِهِمْ لَمْ يَنَالُوا۟ خَيْرًا ۚ
وَكَفَى ٱللَّهُ ٱلْمُؤْمِنِينَ ٱلْقِتَالَ ۚ
وَكَانَ ٱللَّهُ قَوِيًّا عَزِيزًا

26. And those of the people[3701]
Of the Book who aided
Them—Allah did take them
Down from their strongholds[3702]
And cast terror into
Their hearts, (so that)[3703]

﴿٢٦﴾ وَأَنزَلَ ٱلَّذِينَ ظَـٰهَرُوهُم مِّنْ
أَهْلِ ٱلْكِتَـٰبِ مِن صَيَاصِيهِمْ
وَقَذَفَ فِى قُلُوبِهِمُ ٱلرُّعْبَ

3698. Before the Throne of Allah's Mercy there is always room for repentance and forgiveness, even after treason and crime: but the forgiveness will be according to Allah's Will and Plan, which will judge the penitent's sincerity and capacity for good to the nicest degree in his favour. *Cf.* also 33:17 above.

3699. In spite of the mighty preparations and the great forces which the Makkans, in concert with the Central Arabian Bedouins, the discontented Jews, and the treacherous Hypocrites, brought to the siege of Madīnah, all their plans were frustrated. Their fury availed them nothing. They departed in hot haste. This was the last and dying effort. The initiative thereafter lay with the forces of Islam.

3700. For the meaning of *'Azīz*, see n. 2818 to 22:40.

3701. The reference is to the Jewish tribe of the Banū Qurayẓah. They counted among the citizens of Madīnah and were bound by solemn engagements to help in the defence of the city. But on the occasion of the Confederate siege by the Quraysh and their allies, they intrigued with the enemies and treacherously aided them. Immediately after the siege was raised and the Confederates had fled in hot haste, the Prophet turned his attention to the treacherous "friends" who had betrayed his City in the hour of danger.

3702. The Banū Qurayẓah (see last note) were filled with terror and dismay when Madīnah was free from the Quraysh danger. They shut themselves up in their castles about three or four miles to the east (or north east) of Madīnah, and sustained a siege of 25 days, after which they surrendered, stipulating that they would abide by the decision of their fate at the hands of Sa'ad ibn Mu'ādh, chief of the Aws tribe, with which they had been in alliance.

3703. Sa'ad applied to them the Jewish Law of the Old Testament, not as strictly as the case warranted. In Deut. xx 10-18, the treatment of a city "which is very far off from thee" is prescribed to be comparatively more lenient than the treatment of a city "of the people, which the Lord thy God does give thee for an inheritance," *i.e.*, which is near enough to corrupt the religion of the Jewish people. The punishment for these is total annihilation: "thou shall save alive nothing that breatheth" (Deut. xx. 16). The more lenient treatment for faroff cities is described in the next note. According to the Jewish standard, then, the Banū Qurayẓah deserved total extermination—of men, women, and children. They were in the territory of Madīnah itself, and further they had broken their engagements and helped the enemy.

Some ye slew, and some[3704]
Ye made prisoners.

فَرِيقًا تَقْتُلُونَ وَتَأْسِرُونَ فَرِيقًا

27. And He made you heirs
Of their lands, their houses,
And their goods,
And of a land which[3705]
Ye had not frequented
(Before). And Allah has
Power over all things.

﴿٢٧﴾ وَأَوْرَثَكُمْ أَرْضَهُمْ وَدِيَٰرَهُمْ
وَأَمْوَٰلَهُمْ وَأَرْضًا لَّمْ تَطَـُٔوهَا
وَكَانَ ٱللَّهُ عَلَىٰ كُلِّ شَىْءٍ قَدِيرًا

C. 188.—The Prophet's household is not for worldly
(33:28-52.) Ends: his consorts have a place
And dignity beyond ordinary women
They must recite and proclaim the Signs
Of Allah. For women have spiritual virtues
And duties like unto men. Allah decrees,
No unhappy wedlock: fear not
To dissolve such and provide what is right
And fitting for the service of Allah. High
Is the Prophet's positions, and he must order
His household as best befits his work
And duties. Allah doth watch all things.

SECTION 4.

28. O Prophet! say
To thy Consorts:
"If it be that ye desire
The life of this world,

﴿٢٨﴾ يَٰٓأَيُّهَا ٱلنَّبِىُّ قُل لِّأَزْوَٰجِكَ
إِن كُنتُنَّ تُرِدْنَ ٱلْحَيَوٰةَ ٱلدُّنْيَا

3704. Sa'ad adjudged them the mildest treatment of the "far-off" cities which is thus described in the Jewish Law: "Thou shalt smite every male thereof with the edge of the sword: but the women and the little ones, and the cattle, and all that is in the city, even all the spoil thereof, shalt thou take unto thyself, and thou shalt eat the spoil of thine enemies, which the Lord thy God hath given thee" (Deut. xx. 13-14). The men of the Qurayẓah were slain: the women were sold as captives of war: and their lands and properties were divided among the Muhājirs.

3705. If this part of the Sūrah was revealed after the autumn of the Hijrah year 7, it refers to the result of the K͟haybar expedition of that autumn. K͟haybar is a Ḥarrah or volcanic tract, well-watered with many springs issuing from its basaltic rocks. It has a good irrigation system and produces good harvests of grain and dates in its wet valleys, while the outcrop of rocks in the high ground affords sites for numerous fortresses. At present it is inhabited chiefly by men of the race of Bilāl (the Abyssinian) who played a prominent part in the expedition. It is a sort of island in the deserts on the outskirts of Najd. In the Holy Prophet's time there were Jewish colonies settled here, but they were a source of constant trouble, especially after the Siege of Madīnah. It became a nest of all the hostile Jewish elements expelled for their treachery from elsewhere. Its capital, K͟haybar, is about 90 miles due north of Madīnah. Its inhabitants offered some resistance, and 'Ali, though he had just risen from a bed of illness, performed prodigies of valour. After its surrender, a land settlement was made, which retained the cultivators of the soil on the land, but brought them under control, so that no further focus of active hostility should remain near Madīnah. The terms of the settlement will be found in Wāqidī.

And its glitter,—then come![3706]
I will provide for your
Enjoyment and set you free
In a handsome manner."

وَزِينَتَهَا فَتَعَالَيْنَ
أُمَتِّعْكُنَّ وَأُسَرِّحْكُنَّ سَرَاحًا جَمِيلًا

29. But if ye seek Allah
And His Messenger, and
The Home of the Hereafter,
Verily Allah has prepared
For the well-doers amongst
you[3707]
A great reward.

٢٩ وَإِن كُنتُنَّ تُرِدْنَ ٱللَّهَ
وَرَسُولَهُۥ وَٱلدَّارَ ٱلْءَاخِرَةَ فَإِنَّ ٱللَّهَ أَعَدَّ
لِلْمُحْسِنَٰتِ مِنكُنَّ أَجْرًا عَظِيمًا

30. O Consorts of the Prophet
If any of you were guilty
Of evident unseemly
conduct,[3708]
The Punishment would be
Doubled to her, and that
Is easy for Allah.[3709]

٣٠ يَٰنِسَآءَ ٱلنَّبِيِّ مَن يَأْتِ مِنكُنَّ بِفَٰحِشَةٍ
مُّبَيِّنَةٍ يُضَٰعَفْ لَهَا ٱلْعَذَابُ ضِعْفَيْنِ
وَكَانَ ذَٰلِكَ عَلَى ٱللَّهِ يَسِيرًا

3706. We now come to the subject of the position of the Consorts of Purity (*azwāj muṭahharāt*), the wives of the Holy Prophet. Their position was not like that of ordinary women or ordinary wives. They had special duties and responsibilities. The only youthful marriage of the Holy Prophet was his first marriage—that with Khadījah, the best of women and the best of wives. He married her fifteen years before he received the call to Prophethood; the married life lasted for twenty-five years, and their mutal devotion was of the noblest, judged by spiritual as well as social standards. During her life he had no other wife, which was unusual for a man of his standing among his people. When she died, his age was 50, and but for two considerations, he would probably never have married again, as he was most abstemious in his physical life. The two considerations which governed his later marriages were: (1) compassion and clemency, as when he wanted to provide for suffering widows, who could not be provided for in any other way in that stage of society; some of them, like Sawdā', had issue by their former marriage, requiring protection; (2) help in his duties of leadership, with women, who had to be instructed and kept together in the large Muslim family, where women and men had similar social rights. 'Ā'ishah, daughter of Abū Bakr, was clever and learned, and in Ḥadīth she is an important authority on the life of the Prophet. Zaynab, daughter of Khuzaymah, was specially devoted to the poor: she was called the "Mother of the Poor". The other Zaynab, daughter of Jaḥsh, also worked for the poor, for whom she provided from the proceeds of her manual work, as she was skilled in leather work. But all the Consorts in their high position had to work and assist as Mothers of the Ummah. Theirs were not idle lives, like those of Odalisques, either for their own pleasure or the pleasure of their husband. They are told here that they had no place in the sacred Household if they merely wished for ease or worldly glitter. If such were the case, they could be divorced and amply provided for.

3707. They were all well-doers. But being in their exalted position, they had extra responsibility, and they had to be specially careful to discharge it. In the same way, their reward would be "great", for higher services bring higher spiritual satisfaction, though they were asked to deny themselves some of the ordinary indulgences of life.

3708. *Evident unseemly conduct: i.e.*, proved misconduct, as opposed to false slanders from enemies. Such slanders were of no account, but if any of them had behaved in an unseemly manner, it would have been a worse offence than in the case of ordinary women, on account of their special position. Of course none of them were in the least guilty.

3709. *Cf.* 33:19 and n. 3692. The punishment in this life for a married woman's unchastity is very severe: for adultery, public flogging with a hundred stripes, under 24:2; or for lewdness (see 4:15) imprisonment; or stoning to death for adultery, according to certain precedents established in Canon Law. But here the question is not about this kind of punishment or this kind of offence. Even minor indiscretions, in the case of women who were patterns of decorum, would have been reprehensible; and the punishment in the Hereafter is on a higher plane, which we can scarcely understand. But Allah can appreciate every shade of motive in us. More or less is possible there, which might not be possible in the rough and ready law which we administer here.

22
30

31. But any of you that is
Devout in the service of
Allah and His Messenger,
And works righteousness—
To her shall We grant
Her reward twice[3710]: and We
Have prepared for her
A generous Sustenance.[3711]

٣١ وَمَن يَقْنُتْ مِنكُنَّ لِلَّهِ وَرَسُولِهِۦ
وَتَعْمَلْ صَٰلِحًا نُّؤْتِهَآ أَجْرَهَا مَرَّتَيْنِ
وَأَعْتَدْنَا لَهَا رِزْقًا كَرِيمًا

32. O Consorts of the Prophet!
Ye are not like any
Of the (other) women:[3712]
If ye do fear (Allah),
Be not too complaisant
Of speech, lest one
In whose heart is
A disease should be moved
With desire: but speak ye
A speech (that is) just.[3713]

٣٢ يَٰنِسَآءَ ٱلنَّبِيِّ لَسْتُنَّ كَأَحَدٍ مِّنَ ٱلنِّسَآءِ
إِنِ ٱتَّقَيْتُنَّ فَلَا تَخْضَعْنَ بِٱلْقَوْلِ
فَيَطْمَعَ ٱلَّذِى فِى قَلْبِهِۦ مَرَضٌ
وَقُلْنَ قَوْلًا مَّعْرُوفًا

33. And stay quietly in
Your houses, and make not
A dazzling display, like
That of the former Times
Of Ignorance: and establish
Regular Prayer, and give
Regular Charity; and obey[3714]
Allah and His Messenger.
And Allah only wishes
To remove all abomination
From you, ye Members[3715]

٣٣ وَقَرْنَ فِى بُيُوتِكُنَّ
وَلَا تَبَرَّجْنَ تَبَرُّجَ ٱلْجَٰهِلِيَّةِ ٱلْأُولَىٰ
وَأَقِمْنَ ٱلصَّلَوٰةَ وَءَاتِينَ ٱلزَّكَوٰةَ
وَأَطِعْنَ ٱللَّهَ وَرَسُولَهُۥٓ إِنَّمَا يُرِيدُ ٱللَّهُ
لِيُذْهِبَ عَنكُمُ ٱلرِّجْسَ أَهْلَ

3710. *Twice, i.e.,* once as a righteous woman and again as a Mother of the Believers, serving the believing women and thus showing her devotion to Allah and His Prophet.

3711. *Sustenance*: in the spiritual sense: all that is necessary to sustain her in happiness in her future life.

3712. This is the core of the whole passage. The Prophet's Consorts were not like ordinary women, nor was their marriage an ordinary marriage, in which only personal or social considerations enter. They had a special position and special responsibilities, in the matter of guiding and instructing women who came into the fold of Islam. Islam is a Way of Life, and the Muslims are a family: women have as much place in Islam as men, and their intimate instruction must obviously be through women.

3713. While they were to be kind and gentle to all, they were to be guarded on account of their special position lest people might misunderstand or take advantage of their kindness. They were to make no vulgar worldly displays as in the times of Paganism.

3714. Obedience to Allah's Law sums up all duties. Regular Prayer (seeking nearness to Allah) and Regular Charity (doing good to fellow-creatures) are mentioned as specially symbolical of our Religion.

3715. Notice the transition in this clause to the masculine gender, while before this the verbs and pronouns were in the feminine gender as referring to the Consorts. The statement in this clause is now more general including (besides the Consorts) the whole family, namely Fāṭimah the daughter, 'Alī the son-in-law, and their sons Ḥasan and Ḥusayn, the beloved grandsons of the Prophet. The masculine gender is used generally, in speaking of a mixed assembly of men and women.

Of the Family, and to make
You pure and spotless.

الْبَيْتِ وَيُطَهِّرَكُمْ تَطْهِيرًا

34. And recite[3716] what is
Rehearsed to you in your
Homes, of the Signs of Allah
And His Wisdom:
For Allah understands
The finest mysteries and
Is well-acquainted (with them).[3717]

(٣٤) وَاذْكُرْنَ مَا يُتْلَىٰ فِي
بُيُوتِكُنَّ مِنْ آيَاتِ اللَّهِ وَالْحِكْمَةِ ۚ
إِنَّ اللَّهَ كَانَ لَطِيفًا خَبِيرًا

SECTION 5.

35. For Muslim men and
women—[3718]
For believing men and women,
For devout men and women,
For true men and women,
For men and women who are
Patient and constant, for men
And women who humble
themselves,
For men and women who give[3719]
In charity, for men and women
Who fast (and deny themselves),
For men and women who
Guard their chastity, and
For men and women who
Engage much in Allah's
praise—[3720]
For them has Allah prepared
Forgiveness and great reward.

(٣٥) إِنَّ الْمُسْلِمِينَ وَالْمُسْلِمَاتِ
وَالْمُؤْمِنِينَ وَالْمُؤْمِنَاتِ وَالْقَانِتِينَ
وَالْقَانِتَاتِ وَالصَّادِقِينَ وَالصَّادِقَاتِ وَالصَّابِرِينَ
وَالصَّابِرَاتِ وَالْخَاشِعِينَ وَالْخَاشِعَاتِ
وَالْمُتَصَدِّقِينَ وَالْمُتَصَدِّقَاتِ وَالصَّائِمِينَ
وَالصَّائِمَاتِ وَالْحَافِظِينَ فُرُوجَهُمْ
وَالْحَافِظَاتِ وَالذَّاكِرِينَ
اللَّهَ كَثِيرًا وَالذَّاكِرَاتِ
أَعَدَّ اللَّهُ لَهُم مَّغْفِرَةً وَأَجْرًا عَظِيمًا

3716. The verb is *udhkurna*, feminine gender, as referring to the *Azwāj* again. It means not only "remember" but "recite", "teach", "make known", "publish", the Message which ye learn at home from the Holy Prophet, the fountain of spiritual knowledge. The "Signs of Allah" refer specifically to the verses of the Qur'ān, and Wisdom to the resulting instruction derived therefrom.

3617. *Cf.* 22:63 and n. 2844. Allah's understanding is perfect in every detail, however minute. Therefore use His Revelation for every phase of life.

3618. Islam, or submitting our will to Allah's Will, includes all the virtues, as particularly specified in this verse. See n. 3720.

3619. A number of Muslim virtues are specified here, but the chief stress is laid on the fact that these virtues are as necessary to women as to men. Both sexes have spiritual as well as human rights and duties in an equal degree, and the future "reward" of the Hereafter, *viz.*, Spiritual Bliss, is provided for the one as for the other.

3720. The virtues referred to are: (1) Faith, hope, and trust in Allah, and in His benevolent government of the world; (2) devotion and service in practical life; (3) love and practice of truth, in thought and intention, word and deed; (4) patience and constancy, in suffering and in right endeavour; (5) humility, the avoidance of an attitude of arrogance and superiority; (6) charity, *i.e.*, help to the poor and unfortunate ones in life, a special virtue arising out of the general duty of service (No. 2); (7) self-denial, typically in food, but generally in all appetites; (8) chastity, purity in sex life, purity in motive, thought, word, and deed; and (9) constant attention to Allah's Message, and cultivation of the desire to get nearer to Allah.

36. It is not fitting
For a Believer, man or woman,
When a matter has been decided
By Allah and His Messenger,
To have any option
About their decision:[3721]
If anyone disobeys Allah
And His Messenger, he is indeed
On a clearly wrong Path.

٣٦ وَمَا كَانَ لِمُؤْمِنٍ وَلَا مُؤْمِنَةٍ
إِذَا قَضَى ٱللَّهُ وَرَسُولُهُۥٓ أَمْرًا
أَن يَكُونَ لَهُمُ ٱلْخِيَرَةُ مِنْ أَمْرِهِمْ ۗ
وَمَن يَعْصِ ٱللَّهَ وَرَسُولَهُۥ فَقَدْ ضَلَّ ضَلَٰلًا مُّبِينًا

37. Behold! thou didst say
To one who had received
The grace of Allah[3722]
And thy favour: "Retain thou
(In wedlock) thy wife,
And fear Allah." But thou
Didst hide in thy heart[3723]
That which Allah was about
To make manifest: thou didst
Fear the people, but it is
More fitting that thou
shouldst[3724]
Fear Allah. Then when Zayd
Had dissolved (his marriage)
With her, with the necessary[3725]
(Formality), We joined her
In marriage to thee:
In order that (in future)
There may be no difficulty
To the Believers in (the matter

٣٧ وَإِذْ تَقُولُ لِلَّذِىٓ
أَنْعَمَ ٱللَّهُ عَلَيْهِ وَأَنْعَمْتَ عَلَيْهِ
أَمْسِكْ عَلَيْكَ زَوْجَكَ وَٱتَّقِ ٱللَّهَ
وَتُخْفِى فِى نَفْسِكَ مَا ٱللَّهُ
مُبْدِيهِ وَتَخْشَى ٱلنَّاسَ وَٱللَّهُ
أَحَقُّ أَن تَخْشَىٰهُ ۖ
فَلَمَّا قَضَىٰ زَيْدٌ مِّنْهَا وَطَرًا
زَوَّجْنَٰكَهَا لِكَىْ لَا يَكُونَ
عَلَى ٱلْمُؤْمِنِينَ حَرَجٌ

3721. We must not put our own wisdom in competition with Allah's wisdom. Allah's decree is often known to us by the logic of facts. We must accept it loyally, and do the best we can to help in our own way to carry it out. We must make our will consonant to the Allah's Will. (R).

3722. This was Zayd, son of Ḥārithah, one of the first to accept the faith of Islam. He was freedman of the Holy Prophet, who loved him as a son and gave him in marriage to his own cousin Zaynab. The marriage however turned out unhappy. See next note.

3723. Zayd's marriage with the Prophet's cousin Zaynab, daughter of Jaḥsh, did not turn out happy. Zaynab the high-born looked down upon Zayd the freedman who had been a slave. And he was not comely to look at. Both were good people in their own ways, and both loved the Prophet, but there was mutual incompatibility, and this is fatal to married life. Zayd wished to divorce her, but the Prophet asked him to hold his hand, and he obeyed. She was closely related to the Prophet; he had given a handsome marriage gift on her marriage to Zayd; and people would certainly talk if such a marriage was broken off. But marriages are made on earth, not in heaven, and it is no part of Allah's Plan to torture people in a bond which should be a source of happiness but actually is a source of misery. Zayd's wish—indeed the mutual wish of the couple—was for the time being put away, but it became eventually an established fact, and everybody came to know of it. (R).

3724. All actual facts are referred to Allah. When the marriage is unhappy, Islam permits the bond to be dissolved, provided that all interests concerned are safeguarded. Apparently there was no issue here to be considered. Zaynab had to be considered, and she obtained the dearest wish of her heart in being raised to be a Mother of the Believers, with all the dignity and responsibility of that position. See n. 3706 to 33:28 above.

3725. The *'Iddah* or period of waiting after divorce (2:28, and n. 254) was duly completed.

Of) marriage with the wives[3726]
Of their adopted sons, when
The latter have dissolved
With the necessary (formality)
(Their marriage) with them.
And Allah's command must
Be fulfilled.

فِىٓ أَزْوَٰجِ أَدْعِيَآئِهِمْ
إِذَا قَضَوْا۟ مِنْهُنَّ وَطَرًا
وَكَانَ أَمْرُ ٱللَّهِ مَفْعُولًا

38. There can be no difficulty
To the Prophet in what
Allah has indicated to him[3727]
As a duty: It was
The practice (approved) of Allah
Amongst those of old
That have passed away,[3728]
And the command of Allah
Is a decree determined.[3729]

٣٨ مَّا كَانَ عَلَى ٱلنَّبِىِّ
مِنْ حَرَجٍ فِيمَا فَرَضَ ٱللَّهُ لَهُۥ
سُنَّةَ ٱللَّهِ فِى ٱلَّذِينَ خَلَوْا۟ مِن قَبْلُ
وَكَانَ أَمْرُ ٱللَّهِ قَدَرًا مَّقْدُورًا

39. (It is the practice of those)
Who preach the Messages
Of Allah, and fear Him,
And fear none but Allah.
And enough is Allah
To call (men) to account.[3730]

٣٩ ٱلَّذِينَ يُبَلِّغُونَ رِسَٰلَٰتِ ٱللَّهِ
وَيَخْشَوْنَهُۥ وَلَا يَخْشَوْنَ أَحَدًا إِلَّا ٱللَّهَ
وَكَفَىٰ بِٱللَّهِ حَسِيبًا

40. Muḥammad is not
The father of any
Of your men, but (he is)
The Messenger of Allah,
And the Seal of the Prophets:[3731]
And Allah has full knowledge
Of all things.

٤٠ مَّا كَانَ مُحَمَّدٌ أَبَآ أَحَدٍ مِّن رِّجَالِكُمْ
وَلَٰكِن رَّسُولَ ٱللَّهِ وَخَاتَمَ ٱلنَّبِيِّـۧنَ
وَكَانَ ٱللَّهُ بِكُلِّ شَىْءٍ عَلِيمًا

3726. The Pagan superstition and taboo about adopted sons had to be destroyed. See 33:4-5 and notes 3671-3672 above.

3727. See n. 3724 above.

3728. The next clause is parenthetical. Those words then connect on with verse 39. Among the people of the Book there was no taboo about adopted sons, as there was in Pagan Arabia.

3729. Allah's ordering of the world is always full of wisdom. Even our unhappiness and misery may actually have a great meaning for ourselves or others or both. If our first Plan seems to fail, we must not murmur and repine, but retrieve the position by adopting a course which appears to be the best position in the light of our duties as indicated by Allah. For Allah's Plan is framed on universal principles that cannot be altered by human action.

3730. Our responsibility is to Allah, not to men. Men's opinions may have a bearing in our own interpretation of duty, but when that duty is clear, our only course is to obey Allah rather than men.

3731. When a document is sealed, it is complete, and there can be no further addition. The Holy Prophet Muḥammad closed the long line of Messengers. Allah's teaching is and will always be continuous, but there has been and will be no Prophet after Muḥammad. The later ages will want thinkers and reformers, not Prophets. This is not an arbitrary matter. It is a decree full of knowledge and wisdom, "for Allah has full knowledge of all things."

SECTION 6.

41. O ye who believe!
Celebrate the praises of Allah,
And do so often;

يَـٰٓأَيُّهَا ٱلَّذِينَ ءَامَنُوا۟ ٱذْكُرُوا۟ ٱللَّهَ ذِكْرًا كَثِيرًا ﴿٤١﴾

42. And glorify Him
Morning and evening.

وَسَبِّحُوهُ بُكْرَةً وَأَصِيلًا ﴿٤٢﴾

43. He it is Who sends[3732]
Blessings on you, as do
His angels, that He may
Bring you out from the depths
Of Darkness into Light:
And He is Full of Mercy
To the Believers.[3733]

هُوَ ٱلَّذِى يُصَلِّى عَلَيْكُمْ وَمَلَـٰٓئِكَتُهُۥ
لِيُخْرِجَكُم مِّنَ ٱلظُّلُمَـٰتِ إِلَى ٱلنُّورِ
وَكَانَ بِٱلْمُؤْمِنِينَ رَحِيمًا ﴿٤٣﴾

44. Their salutation on the Day
They meet Him will be
"Peace!": and He has
Prepared for them
A generous Reward.

تَحِيَّتُهُمْ يَوْمَ يَلْقَوْنَهُۥ سَلَـٰمٌ
وَأَعَدَّ لَهُمْ أَجْرًا كَرِيمًا ﴿٤٤﴾

45. O Prophet! Truly We
Have sent thee as
A Witness, a Bearer[3734]
Of Glad Tidings,
And a Warner—

يَـٰٓأَيُّهَا ٱلنَّبِىُّ إِنَّآ أَرْسَلْنَـٰكَ
شَـٰهِدًا وَمُبَشِّرًا وَنَذِيرًا ﴿٤٥﴾

46. And as one who invites
To Allah's (Grace) by His leave,[3735]

وَدَاعِيًا إِلَى ٱللَّهِ بِإِذْنِهِۦ ﴿٤٦﴾

3732. *Blessings*: good wishes and mercies. Allah wishes well to all His creatures, and His angels carry out His work, for their will is in all things His Will. His chief and everlasting blessing is that He gives us a knowledge of the spiritual world, and helps us towards its attainment. For the symbolic meaning of Light and Darkness, see 24:35-40, and notes.

3733. His Mercies are for all His creatures, but for those who believe and trust in Him, there are special mercies, "a generous Reward" as in the next verse.

3734. The Prophet was sent by Allah in five capacities. Three are mentioned in this verse, and the other two in the verse following. (1) He comes as a *Witness* to all men about the spiritual truths which had been obscured by ignorance or superstition, or by the dust of sectarian controversy. He did not come to establish a new religion or sect. He came to teach Religion. He is also a witness to Allah about men's doings and how they receive Allah's Message; see 4:41 and n. 560. (2) He comes as a Bearer of the *Glad Tidings* of the Mercy of Allah. No matter how far men may have transgressed, they have hope if they believe, repent, and live a good life. (3) He also comes as a *Warner* to those who are heedless. This life will not last. There is a Future Life, and that is all-important. See next note.

3735. See last note. The two other capacities in which the Prophet was sent are here specified. (4) He comes as one who has a right to *invite* all men to repentance and the forgiveness of sins; but he does this, not of his own authority, but by the permission and authority given to him by Allah. This is said lest people may deny the Prophet as they did with other Prophets before him. The personal responsibility of each individual remains, but the Prophet can lead him on to the Right and help him. (5) The Prophet also comes as a *Light* of a Lamp (*Sirāj*) to illuminate the whole world. In 71:16 and elsewhere the same word (*Sirāj*) is used for the sun. The comparison is apt. When the sun appears, all the lesser lights pale before his light. And the Message of Islam, *i.e.*, of the Universal Religion, is to diffuse Light everywhere.

And as a Lamp
Spreading Light.

وَسِرَاجًا مُّنِيرًا

47. Then give the glad tidings
To the Believers, that
They shall have from Allah
A very great Bounty.[3736]

٤٧ وَبَشِّرِ ٱلْمُؤْمِنِينَ بِأَنَّ لَهُم
مِّنَ ٱللَّهِ فَضْلًا كَبِيرًا

48. And obey not (the behests)
Of the Unbelievers
And the Hypocrites,
And heed not their
annoyances,[3737]
But put thy trust in Allah.
For enough is Allah
As a Disposer of affairs.

٤٨ وَلَا تُطِعِ ٱلْكَـٰفِرِينَ وَٱلْمُنَـٰفِقِينَ
وَدَعْ أَذَىٰهُمْ وَتَوَكَّلْ عَلَى ٱللَّهِ
وَكَفَىٰ بِٱللَّهِ وَكِيلًا

49. O ye who believe!
When ye marry believing
women,
And then divorce them
Before ye have touched them,
No period of *'Iddah*[3738]
Have ye to count
In respect of them:
So give them a present,[3739]
And set them free
In a handsome manner.[3740]

٤٩ يَـٰٓأَيُّهَا ٱلَّذِينَ ءَامَنُوٓا۟
إِذَا نَكَحْتُمُ ٱلْمُؤْمِنَـٰتِ ثُمَّ طَلَّقْتُمُوهُنَّ
مِن قَبْلِ أَن تَمَسُّوهُنَّ فَمَا لَكُمْ
عَلَيْهِنَّ مِنْ عِدَّةٍ تَعْتَدُّونَهَا
فَمَتِّعُوهُنَّ وَسَرِّحُوهُنَّ سَرَاحًا جَمِيلًا

50. O Prophet! We have
Made lawful to thee[3741]
Thy wives to whom thou

٥٠ يَـٰٓأَيُّهَا ٱلنَّبِىُّ إِنَّآ
أَحْلَلْنَا لَكَ أَزْوَٰجَكَ ٱلَّـٰتِىٓ

3736. The light of Islam is the Biggest Bounty possible and if they truly understand it, they should glory in it.

3737. Men of little or no Faith will often lay down the law and tell better men than themselves what to do. In case of refusal they shower insults and injuries. No attention is to be paid to them. It is their way. All will be right under the government of Allah.

3738. See n. 254 to 2:228. The *'Iddah* counts for three monthly courses, or if there are no courses, for three months; see 65:4.

3739. This present is held, by some, to be in addition to the half dower due to them under 2:237. If the dower had not been fixed, the gift would presumably be larger, and it would absorb the gift prescribed in 2:236.

3740. The gift should be given with good grace, and the freedom of the woman should not be interfered with in any way. If she chooses to marry again immediately, no obstacle should be placed in her path. On no pretext should she be allowed to remain doubtful about her freedom.

3741. This introduces no new exemption or privilege. Verses 50-52 merely declare the points in which, on account of the special circumstances (see n. 3706 above), the Prophet's marriages differed from those of ordinary Muslims. This is considered under four heads, which we shall examine in the four notes following.

Hast paid their dowers;[3742]	ءَاتَيْتَ أُجُورَهُنَّ
And those whom thy	
Right hand possesses out of	وَمَا مَلَكَتْ يَمِينُكَ
The prisoners of war whom[3743]	
Allah has assigned to thee;	مِمَّآ أَفَآءَ ٱللَّهُ عَلَيْكَ
And daughters of thy paternal	
Uncles and aunts, and daughters	وَبَنَاتِ عَمِّكَ وَبَنَاتِ عَمَّـٰتِكَ
Of thy maternal uncles	وَبَنَاتِ خَالِكَ وَبَنَاتِ
And aunts, who migrated[3744]	
(From Makkah) with thee;	خَـٰلَـٰتِكَ ٱلَّـٰتِى هَاجَرْنَ مَعَكَ
And any believing woman	
Who dedicates her soul	وَٱمْرَأَةً مُّؤْمِنَةً إِن وَهَبَتْ نَفْسَهَا
To the Prophet if the Prophet[3745]	لِلنَّبِىِّ إِنْ أَرَادَ ٱلنَّبِىُّ أَن يَسْتَنكِحَهَا
Wishes to wed her—this	
Only for thee, and not	خَالِصَةً لَّكَ مِن دُونِ ٱلْمُؤْمِنِينَ
For the Believers (at large):	
We know what We have	قَدْ عَلِمْنَا مَا فَرَضْنَا عَلَيْهِمْ فِىٓ
Appointed for them as to[3746]	
Their wives and the captives	أَزْوَٰجِهِمْ وَمَا مَلَكَتْ
Whom their right hands	أَيْمَـٰنُهُمْ لِكَيْلَا
Possess—in order that[3747]	
There should be no difficulty	يَكُونَ عَلَيْكَ حَرَجٌ

3742. Head 1. Marriage with dower (4:4): this is the universal Muslim marriage. The difference in the Prophet's case was that there was no limitation to the number of four (4:3), and women of the People of the Book (5:6) were not among his wives, but only Believers. These points are not expressly mentioned here, but are inferred by his actual practice. Obviously women who are expected to instruct other women in Islam must be Muslims.

3743. Head 2. Women Prisoners of War: the same remark as the last note. The point does not now arise, as the whole condition and incidents of war have been altered and slavery has been abolished by international agreement.

3744. Head 3. These are first cousins, and not within the Prohibited Degrees of Marriage (see 4:23-24). These are specially mentioned here by way of limitation. None of them could marry the Prophet unless she had performed the Hijrah with him. If she had not so performed it in spite of her close relationship, she could not be credited with any great fervour for Islam, or be considered suitable for instructing other women in Islam.

3745. Head 4. A believing woman who dedicates her soul to the Prophet: obviously this case, like the last, is only applicable to the Prophet, and is hedged around with the limitations that the Prophet considers it a suitable and proper case of true service to the community, and not merely a sentimental woman's freak. Some Commentators think there was no such case. But others, with whom I agree, think that this applies to Zaynab bint Khuzaymah, who had dedicated herself to the poor and was called the Mother of the Poor (*Umm al masākīn*). Similarly, the last head might possibly refer to Zaynab bint Jaḥsh, who was a daughter of the Prophet's paternal aunt, herself a daughter of 'Abd al Muṭṭalib.

3746. The ordinary law of Muslim marriage will be found chiefly in 2:221-235, 4:19-25, 4:34-35, and 5:6.

3747. The words "this only for thee. . .right hands possess" are parenthetical, and the words "in order that. . ." connect on with the previous clauses beginning with "O Prophet, We have made lawful. . .wishes to wed her."

For Thee. And Allah is
Oft-Forgiving, Most Merciful.[3748]

وَكَانَ ٱللَّهُ غَفُورًا رَّحِيمًا

51. Thou mayest defer (the turn[3749]
Of) any of them that thou
Pleasest, and thou mayest receive
Any thou pleasest: and there
Is no blame on thee if
Thou invite one whose (turn)[3750]
Thou hadst set aside.
This were nigher to
The cooling of the eyes,[3751]
The prevention of their grief,
And their satisfaction—
That of all of them—
With that which thou
Hast to give them:[3752]
And Allah knows (all)
That is in your hearts:[3753]
And Allah is All-Knowing,
Most Forbearing.

٥١ تُرْجِى مَن تَشَآءُ مِنْهُنَّ
وَتُـْٔوِىٓ إِلَيْكَ مَن تَشَآءُ ۖ وَمَنِ ٱبْتَغَيْتَ
مِمَّنْ عَزَلْتَ فَلَا جُنَاحَ عَلَيْكَ ۚ
ذَٰلِكَ أَدْنَىٰٓ أَن تَقَرَّ أَعْيُنُهُنَّ
وَلَا يَحْزَنَّ وَيَرْضَيْنَ
بِمَآ ءَاتَيْتَهُنَّ كُلُّهُنَّ ۚ
وَٱللَّهُ يَعْلَمُ مَا فِى قُلُوبِكُمْ ۚ
وَكَانَ ٱللَّهُ عَلِيمًا حَلِيمًا

3748. Marriage is an important relationship not only in our physical life, but in our moral and spiritual life, and its effects extend not only to the parties themselves but to children and future generations. A number of special problems arise according to special circumstances. Every man and woman must seriously consider all sides of the question and must do the best in his or her power to temper instincts and inclinations with wisdom and guidance from Allah. Allah wishes to make every one's path easy, for He is indeed "Oft-Forgiving, Most Merciful".

3749. In 4:3 it is laid down that more than one wife is not permissible "If ye fear that ye shall not be able to deal justly with them". In a Muslim household there is no room for a "favourite wife" in the sense that such a wife is recipient of favours denied to other wives. In the special circumstances of the Prophet there were more than one, and he usually observed the rule of equality with them, in other things as well as in the rotation of conjugal rights. But considering that his marriages, after he was invested with the Prophetic office, were mainly dictated by other than conjugal or personal considerations (see n. 3706, 33:28), the rotation could not always be observed, though he observed it as much as possible. This verse absolved him from absolute adherence to a fixed rotation. There are other interpretations, but I agree with most of the Commentators in the view I have explained. (R).

3750. Where the rotation was, for some reason, interfered with, it was permissible, by another interference with the usual rotation, to bring satisfaction to one who had been previously set aside. This was not only permitted, but commended, as tending to remove dissatisfaction and cheer and comfort the eyes and hearts of those who were disappointed in their turn.

3751. *Cooling the eyes*: an Arabic idiom for cheering and comforting eyes which yearn to see those they love. A verse of Zeb al Nisā', daughter of the Mughal Emperor Awrangzeb, may be rendered thus:

"My heart is glad whenever lover-wise
I dwell upon thy beauties and thy grace!
But how can I content my hungry eyes,
That ask continually to see thy face?"

3752. There was not much in the way of worldly goods or satisfaction that the Prophet could give them: see 33:28 above. But he was kind, just, and true—the best of men to his family, and they all clung to him.

3753. Our human hearts, however good on the whole, may yet, in their motives, have possibly some baser admixture. The feminine hearts are not more immune in this respect than the masculine. But everthing is known and understood by Allah, Who will in His Mercy make allowances for our human weaknesses. His title of "Most Forgiving" (*Ḥalīm*) also gives His devoted worshippers the cue: why should we not also forbear with the faults and weaknesses of our neighbours and fellow-creatures?

52. It is not lawful for thee
(To marry more) women[3754]
After this, nor to change
Them for (other) wives,
Even though their beauty
Attract thee, except any
Thy right hand should
Possess (as handmaidens):
And Allah doth watch
Over all things.

﴿٥٢﴾ لَا يَحِلُّ لَكَ ٱلنِّسَآءُ مِنۢ بَعْدُ
وَلَآ أَن تَبَدَّلَ بِهِنَّ مِنْ أَزْوَٰجٍ
وَلَوْ أَعْجَبَكَ حُسْنُهُنَّ
إِلَّا مَا مَلَكَتْ يَمِينُكَ ۗ
وَكَانَ ٱللَّهُ عَلَىٰ كُلِّ شَىْءٍ رَّقِيبًا

C. 189.—Believers should cultivate refined respect
(33:53-73.) In social and spiritual life. And the Mothers
Of the Faithful have to uphold their dignity,
So should all women protect their honour
And uphold their dignity. The Hour
Will come when all Evil will be punished.
Fear Allah, and always speak the word
That leads to Right. Arduous is the Quest
Of Mankind's high and noble Destiny—
Beyond the reach of other creatures:
Let man but strive in Faith, and fulfil
Allah's Trust—by the grace and mercy of Allah.

SECTION 7.

53. O ye who Believe!
Enter not the Prophet's
houses—
Until leave is given you—[3755]
For a meal, (and then)
Not (so early as) to wait
For its preparation: but when
Ye are invited, enter;
And when ye have taken
Your meal, disperse,
Without seeking familiar talk.

﴿٥٣﴾ يَٰٓأَيُّهَا ٱلَّذِينَ ءَامَنُوا۟ لَا تَدْخُلُوا۟
بُيُوتَ ٱلنَّبِىِّ إِلَّآ أَن يُؤْذَنَ لَكُمْ إِلَىٰ طَعَامٍ
غَيْرَ نَٰظِرِينَ إِنَىٰهُ وَلَٰكِنْ إِذَا دُعِيتُمْ
فَٱدْخُلُوا۟ فَإِذَا طَعِمْتُمْ فَٱنتَشِرُوا۟
وَلَا مُسْتَـْٔنِسِينَ لِحَدِيثٍ

3754. This was revealed in A.H. 7. After that the Prophet did not marry again, except the handmaiden, Mary the Copt, who was sent as a present by the Christian Muqawqas of Egypt. She became the mother of Ibrāhīm, who died in his infancy.

3755. The rules of refined social ethics are as necessary to teach today as it was with the rude Arabs whom the Holy Prophet had to teach in his day. Those mentioned in this verse may be briefly recapitulated thus: (1) Enter not a friend's house without permission; (2) if invited to dine, don't go too early; you are asked to dine, not to wait for the preparation of the food; (3) be there at the time appointed, so that you enter when you are expected and invited; (4) after the meal, don't get familiar with your host, especially if there is a great distance between him and you; (5) don't waste time in tittle-tattle, causing inconvenience and perhaps annoyance to your host; (6) understand what is proper behaviour for you, he may be too polite to ask you to depart. All this has a spiritual as well as a social bearing: respect and delicate consideration for others are among the highest virtues.

Such (behaviour) annoys
The Prophet: he is ashamed
To dismiss you, but
Allah is not ashamed
(To tell you) the truth.

إِنَّ ذَٰلِكُمْ كَانَ يُؤْذِى ٱلنَّبِىَّ
فَيَسْتَحْيِۦ مِنكُمْ
وَٱللَّهُ لَا يَسْتَحْيِۦ مِنَ ٱلْحَقِّ

And when ye
Ask (his ladies)[3756]
For anything ye want
Ask them from before
A screen: that makes
For greater purity for
Your hearts and for theirs.

وَإِذَا سَأَلْتُمُوهُنَّ مَتَٰعًا
فَسْـَٔلُوهُنَّ مِن وَرَآءِ حِجَابٍ
ذَٰلِكُمْ أَطْهَرُ
لِقُلُوبِكُمْ وَقُلُوبِهِنَّ

Nor is it right for you[3757]
That ye should annoy[3758]
Allah's Messenger, or that
Ye should marry his widows
After him at any time.
Truly such a thing is
In Allah's sight an enormity.

وَمَا كَانَ لَكُمْ أَن تُؤْذُوا۟
رَسُولَ ٱللَّهِ وَلَآ أَن تَنكِحُوٓا۟
أَزْوَٰجَهُۥ مِنۢ بَعْدِهِۦٓ أَبَدًا
إِنَّ ذَٰلِكُمْ كَانَ عِندَ ٱللَّهِ عَظِيمًا

54. Whether ye reveal anything[3759]
Or conceal it, verily
Allah has full knowledge
Of all things.

٥٤ إِن تُبْدُوا۟ شَيْـًٔا أَوْ تُخْفُوهُ
فَإِنَّ ٱللَّهَ كَانَ بِكُلِّ شَىْءٍ عَلِيمًا

55. There is no blame
(On those ladies if they

٥٥ لَّا جُنَاحَ عَلَيْهِنَّ فِىٓ

3756. The actual manner of showing respect to ladies may be different in different circumstances. But it is an essential principle of good society to show the greatest deference to them. To the "Mothers of the Believers" this respect was due in an exceptional degree.

3757. Considering his position, the Holy Prophet deserved to be respected before all other men and nothing should be done to cause him the least harm and annoyance. This applied not only during his lifetime, but it applies now, because his teaching and personality are alive to us. It was not fitting that his widows, both for their own position and for the position of the Prophet, should be married by other men after him. And this mark of respect was duly observed in history.

3758. "Annoy": *Adha'* may equally mean to vex, to cause hurt or injury, to insult, to ill-treat by slander or unseemly conduct, or hurt the feelings of (someone). The Prophet came with a divine mission to teach and reclaim the world, and he is entitled to the respect of all, even of those who do not consciously acknowledge his mission, for his mission works constantly like the forces of nature. In a minor degree the "Mothers of the Believers" are also entitled to respect.

3759. Respect or opposition may be shown overtly or in devious hidden ways. All good and evil are open before Allah, and He will take due account of everything.

Appear) before their fathers[3760]
Or their sons, their brothers,
Or their brothers' sons,
Or their sisters' sons,
Or their women,
Or the (slaves) whom
Their right hands possess.
And, (ladies), fear Allah;
For Allah is Witness
To all things.

ءَابَآئِهِنَّ وَلَآ أَبْنَآئِهِنَّ
وَلَآ إِخْوَٰنِهِنَّ وَلَآ أَبْنَآءِ إِخْوَٰنِهِنَّ
وَلَآ أَبْنَآءِ أَخَوَٰتِهِنَّ وَلَا نِسَآئِهِنَّ
وَلَا مَا مَلَكَتْ أَيْمَٰنُهُنَّ وَٱتَّقِينَ ٱللَّهَ
إِنَّ ٱللَّهَ كَانَ عَلَىٰ كُلِّ شَىْءٍ شَهِيدًا

56. Allah and His Angels
Send blessings on the Prophet:[3761]
O ye that believe!
Send ye blessings on him,
And salute him
With all respect.

٥٦ إِنَّ ٱللَّهَ وَمَلَٰٓئِكَتَهُۥ يُصَلُّونَ عَلَى ٱلنَّبِىِّ
يَٰٓأَيُّهَا ٱلَّذِينَ ءَامَنُوا۟ صَلُّوا۟ عَلَيْهِ
وَسَلِّمُوا۟ تَسْلِيمًا

57. Those who annoy[3762]
Allah and His Messenger—
Allah has cursed them
In this world and
In the Hereafter,
And has prepared for them
A humiliating Punishment.

٥٧ إِنَّ ٱلَّذِينَ يُؤْذُونَ ٱللَّهَ وَرَسُولَهُۥ
لَعَنَهُمُ ٱللَّهُ فِى ٱلدُّنْيَا وَٱلْءَاخِرَةِ
وَأَعَدَّ لَهُمْ عَذَابًا مُّهِينًا

58. And those who annoy
Believing men and women
Undeservedly, bear (on
themselves)[3763]
A calumny and a glaring sin.

٥٨ وَٱلَّذِينَ يُؤْذُونَ ٱلْمُؤْمِنِينَ
وَٱلْمُؤْمِنَٰتِ بِغَيْرِ مَا ٱكْتَسَبُوا۟
فَقَدِ ٱحْتَمَلُوا۟ بُهْتَٰنًا وَإِثْمًا مُّبِينًا

3760. This refers back to the *Ḥijāb* (screen) portion of verse 53 above. The list of those before whom the Prophet's wives could appear informally without a screen is their fathers, sons, brothers, brothers' or sisters' sons, serving women, and household slaves or servants. Commentators include uncles (paternal and maternal) under the heading of "fathers". *Their women* is held to mean all women who belonged to the Muslim community: other women were in the position of strangers, whom they received not so intimately, but with the formality of a screen as in the case of men. Compare with this list and the wording here the list and the wording in 24:31, which applies to all Muslim women. In the list here, husbands and husbands' relatives are not necessary to be mentioned, as we are speaking of a single household, that of the central figure in Islam, nor men-servants nor children, as there were none. In the wording note that for Muslim women generally, no screen or *Ḥijāb* (Pardah) is mentioned, but only a veil to cover the bosom, and modesty in dress. The screen was a special feature of honour for the Prophet's household, introduced about five or six years before his death.

3761. Allah and His angels honour and bless the Holy Prophet as the greatest of men. We are asked to honour and bless him all the more because he took upon himself to suffer the sorrow and afflictions of this life in order to guide us to Allah's Mercy and the highest inner Life.

3762. *Cf.* n. 3758 above.

3763. *Cf.* 4:112. In that passage we were told that anyone who was himself guilty but accused an innocent man of his guilt, was obviously placing himself in double jeopardy; first, for his own original guilt, and secondly for the guilt of a false accusation. Here we take two classes of men instead of two individuals. The men and women of faith (if they deserve the name) and doing all they can to serve Allah and humanity. If they are insulted, hurt, or annoyed by those whose sins they denounce, the latter suffer the penalites of a double guilt, *viz.*, their sins to start with, and the insults or injuries they offer to those who correct them. Instead of resenting the preaching of Truth, they should welcome it and profit by it.

SECTION 8.

59\. O Prophet! Tell
Thy wives and daughters,
And the believing women,[3764]
That they should cast
Their outer garments over[3765]
Their persons (when abroad):
That is most convenient,
That they should be known[3766]
(As such) and not molested.
And Allah is Oft-Forgiving,[3767]
Most Merciful.

٥٩ يَـٰٓأَيُّهَا ٱلنَّبِىُّ قُل لِّأَزْوَٰجِكَ
وَبَنَاتِكَ وَنِسَآءِ ٱلْمُؤْمِنِينَ
يُدْنِينَ عَلَيْهِنَّ مِن جَلَـٰبِيبِهِنَّ
ذَٰلِكَ أَدْنَىٰٓ أَن يُعْرَفْنَ فَلَا يُؤْذَيْنَ
وَكَانَ ٱللَّهُ غَفُورًا رَّحِيمًا

60\. Truly, if the Hypocrites,
And those in whose hearts
Is a disease, and those who
Stir up sedition in the City,[3768]
Desist not, We shall certainly
Stir thee up against them:
Then will they not be
Able to stay in it
As thy neighbours
For any length of time:

٦٠ لَّئِن لَّمْ يَنتَهِ ٱلْمُنَـٰفِقُونَ
وَٱلَّذِينَ فِى قُلُوبِهِم مَّرَضٌ
وَٱلْمُرْجِفُونَ فِى ٱلْمَدِينَةِ
لَنُغْرِيَنَّكَ بِهِمْ ثُمَّ لَا يُجَاوِرُونَكَ
فِيهَآ إِلَّا قَلِيلًا

61\. They shall have a curse[3769]
On them: wherever they
Are found, they shall be

٦١ مَّلْعُونِينَ أَيْنَمَا ثُقِفُوٓا۟

3764\. This is for all Muslim women, those of the Prophet's household, as well as the others. They were asked to cover themselves with outer garments when walking around. (R).

3765\. *Jilbāb*, plural *Jalābīb*: an outer garment: a long gown covering the whole body, or a cloak covering the neck and bosom.

3766\. The object was not to restrict the liberty of women but to protect them from harm and molestation. In the East and the West a distinctive public dress of some sort or another has always been a badge of honour or distinction, both among men and women. This can be traced back to the earliest civilisations. Assyrian Law in its palmiest days (say, 7th century B.C.), enjoined the veiling of married women and forbade the veiling of slaves and women of ill fame: see *Cambridge Ancient History*, III, 107.

3767\. That is, if a Muslim woman sincerely tries to observe this rule, but owing to human weakness falls short of the ideal, then "Allah is Oft-Forgiving, Most Merciful". (R).

3768\. It was necessary to put down all kinds of unseemly conduct in the Prophet's City. And here is the warning in the plainest terms. And the warning had its effect. The "Hypocrites" were men who pretended to be in Islam but whose manners and morals were anti-Islamic. Those "with diseased hearts" may have been the ones that molested innocent women. "Those who stirred up sedition" put false rumours in circulation to excite the crowd. Alas! we must ask ourselves the question: "Are these conditions present among us today?"

3769\. They will be deprived of the blessing and guidance of Allah. They sought to cause disorder in Allah's world—moral as well as material, but they will themselves be destroyed. Those who become outlaws, rebels against the Law, will themselves be destroyed by the Law. Capital punishment is the only adequate punishment for treason and crimes of sustained concerted violence—for the protection of the hearths and homes of innocent citizens and the honour of their women.

Seized and slain
(Without mercy).

أُخِذُوا وَقُتِّلُوا تَقْتِيلًا

62. (Such was) the practice
(Approved) of Allah among those[3770]
Who lived aforetime:
No change wilt thou find
In the practice (approved)
Of Allah.

٦٢ سُنَّةَ ٱللَّهِ فِي
ٱلَّذِينَ خَلَوْا مِن قَبْلُ
وَلَن تَجِدَ لِسُنَّةِ ٱللَّهِ تَبْدِيلًا

63. Men ask thee concerning
The Hour: say, "The knowledge[3771]
Thereof is with Allah (alone)":
And what will make thee
Understand?—perchance
The Hour is nigh!

٦٣ يَسْـَٔلُكَ ٱلنَّاسُ عَنِ ٱلسَّاعَةِ
قُلْ إِنَّمَا عِلْمُهَا عِندَ ٱللَّهِ
وَمَا يُدْرِيكَ لَعَلَّ ٱلسَّاعَةَ تَكُونُ قَرِيبًا

64. Verily Allah has cursed
The Unbelievers and prepared
For them a Blazing Fire—

٦٤ إِنَّ ٱللَّهَ لَعَنَ ٱلْكَٰفِرِينَ
وَأَعَدَّ لَهُمْ سَعِيرًا

65. To dwell therein forever:
No protector will they find,
Nor helper.

٦٥ خَٰلِدِينَ فِيهَآ أَبَدًا
لَّا يَجِدُونَ وَلِيًّا وَلَا نَصِيرًا

66. The Day that their faces
Will be turned upside down[3772]
In the Fire, they will say:
"Woe to us! would that
We had obeyed Allah
And obeyed the Messenger!

٦٦ يَوْمَ تُقَلَّبُ وُجُوهُهُمْ فِي ٱلنَّارِ
يَقُولُونَ يَٰلَيْتَنَآ أَطَعْنَا ٱللَّهَ
وَأَطَعْنَا ٱلرَّسُولَا

67. And they would say:
"Our Lord! We obeyed

٦٧ وَقَالُوا رَبَّنَآ إِنَّآ أَطَعْنَا

3770. The Jewish Law was much more severe: see notes 3703 and 3704 to 33:26. That severity is mitigated in Islam. But it is a universal principle that any element which deliberatley refuses to obey law and aggressively tries to subvert all order in society, secretly and openly, must be effectively suppressed, for the preservation of the life and health of the general community.

3771. *Cf.* 7:187 and n. 1159, where the idea is further explained. The knowledge of the Final Hour is with Allah alone. The fact of its coming is certain: the exact time when it will come has not been revealed. If it were, it would disturb our thoughts and life. "Heavy were its burden through the heavens and the earth." But at any given moment it cannot be far distant. In theological language, each individual's death is a Final Hour, a *Qiyāmah Ṣughrā* (Lesser Day of Judgement). In that sense it is not the same for all individuals, and is certainly always near. "In the midst of life we are in death", as the Anglican Prayer-Book says in its Burial Service.

3772. The face is the expression of their Personality, their Self; and turning upside down is a sign of degradation and ignominy. When the Retribution comes, the evil ones will be humiliated, and they will wish that they had followed right guidance when they had the chance. They will then fall to accusing their leaders who misled them. But they forget their own personal responsibility.

Our chiefs and our great ones,
And they misled us
As to the (right) path.

سَادَتَنَا وَكُبَرَآءَنَا فَأَضَلُّونَا ٱلسَّبِيلَا۠

68. "Our Lord! Give them
Double Penalty[3773]
And curse them
With a very great Curse!"

رَبَّنَآ ءَاتِهِمْ ضِعْفَيْنِ مِنَ ٱلْعَذَابِ وَٱلْعَنْهُمْ لَعْنًا كَبِيرًا ﴿٦٨﴾

SECTION 9.

69. O ye who believe!
Be ye not like those
Who vexed and insulted Moses,[3774]
But Allah cleared him
Of the (calumnies) they
Had uttered: and he
Was honourable in Allah's sight.

يَٰٓأَيُّهَا ٱلَّذِينَ ءَامَنُوا۟ لَا تَكُونُوا۟ كَٱلَّذِينَ ءَاذَوْا۟ مُوسَىٰ فَبَرَّأَهُ ٱللَّهُ مِمَّا قَالُوا۟ ۚ وَكَانَ عِندَ ٱللَّهِ وَجِيهًا ﴿٦٩﴾

70. O ye who believe!
Fear Allah, and (always) say
A word directed to the Right:[3775]

يَٰٓأَيُّهَا ٱلَّذِينَ ءَامَنُوا۟ ٱتَّقُوا۟ ٱللَّهَ وَقُولُوا۟ قَوْلًا سَدِيدًا ﴿٧٠﴾

71. That He may make
Your conduct whole and sound
Anf forgive you your sins:
He that obeys Allah
And His Messenger, has already

يُصْلِحْ لَكُمْ أَعْمَٰلَكُمْ وَيَغْفِرْ لَكُمْ ذُنُوبَكُمْ ۗ وَمَن يُطِعِ ٱللَّهَ وَرَسُولَهُۥ فَقَدْ ﴿٧١﴾

3773. *Cf.* 25:69 and n. 3129, and 11:20 and n. 1515. The double Penalty invoked will be because (1) they went wrong themselves and (2) they misled others.

3374. The people of Moses often vexed him and rebelled against him and against Allah's Law. Here the reference seems to be to Num. xii. 1-13. It is there said that Moses's own sister Miriam and his brother Aaron spoke against Moses because Moses had married an Ethiopian woman. Allah cleared Moses of the charge of having done anything wrong: "My servant Moses is not so, who is faithful in all mine house." Miriam was afflicted with leprosy for seven days as a punishment, after which she was forgiven, as also was Aaron. This is the Old Testament story. The Holy Prophet was also attacked because of his marriage with Zaynab bint Jahsh, but not by his own circle; his motives were of the highest and were completely vindicated as we have seen above.

3775. We must not only speak the truth as far as we know it, but we must always try to hit the right point; *i.e.*, we must not speak unseasonably, and when we do speak, we must not beat about the bush, but go straight to that which is right, in deed as well as in word. Then Allah will make our conduct right and cure any defects that there may be in our knowledge and character. With our endeavour directed straight to the goal, we shall be forgiven our errors, shortcomings, faults, and sins of the past.

Attained the highest
Achievement.[3376]

فَازَ فَوْزًا عَظِيمًا

72. We did indeed offer
The Trust[3777] To the Heavens
And the Earth
And the Mountains;[3778]
But they refused[3779]
To undertake it,[3780]

(٧٢) إِنَّا عَرَضْنَا ٱلْأَمَانَةَ
عَلَى ٱلسَّمَٰوَٰتِ وَٱلْأَرْضِ وَٱلْجِبَالِ
فَأَبَيْنَ أَن يَحْمِلْنَهَا

3776. This is salvation, the attainment of our real spiritual desire or ambition, as we are on the highway to nearness to Allah.

3777. The Trust is something given to a person, over which he has a power of disposition: he is expected to use it as directed or expected, but he has the power to use it otherwise. There is no trust if the trustee has no power, and the trust implies that the giver of the trust believes and expects that the trustee would use it according to the wish of the creator of the trust, and not otherwise.

3778. What is the meaning of the offer of the Trust to the Heavens, the Earth, and the Mountains? *Cf.* 59:21, where the hypothetical sending down of the Qur'ān to the Mountains is mentioned, and it is mentioned that such Parables are put forth in order to aid men to reflection. We may therefore take the Mountains, the Earth, and the Heavens as symbolical. The mountains stand for firmness and stability: they have been created for this quality, and they are always true to that quality. An earthquake or a volcano has to do with movements within the earth's crust: it has nothing to do with the Mountain's will. In fact it has no free will of any kind: there is no question of any Trust here. If we take the Earth as a whole, as a part of the solar system or a compendium of the terrestrial Nature we see around us, it obeys the fixed laws of Allah, and there is no Will or Trust. If we take the Heavens either as celestial space, or as symbolical of the Angels, they absolutely obey Allah's Will and law: they have no will of their own.

3779. The Heavens, the Earth, and the Mountains, *i.e.*, other creatures of Allah, besides man, refused to undertake a Trust or a responsibility, and may be imagined as happy without a choice of good or evil being given through their will. In saying that they refused, we imply a will, but we limit it by the statement that they did not undertake to be given a choice between good and evil. They preferred to submit their will entirely to Allah's Will, which is All-Wise and Perfect, and which would give them far more happiness than a faculty of choice, with their imperfect knowledge. Man was too audacious and ignorant to realise this, and the result has been that man as a race has been disrupted: the evil ones have betrayed the trust and brought Punishment on themselves, though the good have been able to rise far above other Creation, to be the *muqarrabīn*, the nearest ones to Allah: 56:11 and 56:88. What can be higher than this for any creature?

It follows incidentally from this that the Heavens and the Earth were created before man was created, and this is in accordance with what we know of the physical world in science: man came on the scene at a comparatively late stage.

3780. *Ḥamala*: to undertake, bear, carry (the Trust or responsibility), to be equal to it. This is the ordinary meaning, and the majority of Commentators construe so. But some understand it to mean "to carry away, run away with, to embezzle (the thing entrusted); hence to be false to the Trust, to betray the Trust." In that case the sense of verses 72-73 would be: "Allah offered the Trust to other creatures, but they refused, lest they should betray it, being afraid from that point of view: but man was less fair to himself: in his ignorance he accepted and betrayed the trust, with the result that some of his race became Hypocrites and Unbelievers and were punished, though others were faithful to the Trust and received Allah's Mercy." The resulting conclusion is the same under both interpretations.

Being afraid thereof: But man undertook it—[3781] He was indeed unjust[3782] And foolish—	وَأَشْفَقْنَ مِنْهَا وَحَمَلَهَا ٱلْإِنسَٰنُ إِنَّهُۥ كَانَ ظَلُومًا جَهُولًا
73. (With the result) that Allah has to punish[3783] The Hypocrites, men and women, And the Unbelievers, men And women, and Allah turns In Mercy to the Believers,[3784] Men and women: for Allah Is Oft-Forgiving, Most Merciful.	لِّيُعَذِّبَ ٱللَّهُ ٱلْمُنَٰفِقِينَ وَٱلْمُنَٰفِقَٰتِ ﴿٧٣﴾ وَٱلْمُشْرِكِينَ وَٱلْمُشْرِكَٰتِ وَيَتُوبَ ٱللَّهُ عَلَى ٱلْمُؤْمِنِينَ وَٱلْمُؤْمِنَٰتِ وَكَانَ ٱللَّهُ غَفُورًا رَّحِيمًا

3781. See 2:30-34 and notes. Allah intended a very high destiny for man, and placed him in his uncorrupted state even above the angels, but in his corruption he made himself even lower than the beasts. What was it that made man so high and noble? The differentiating quality which Allah gave man was that Allah breathed something of His own spirit into man (32:9; 15:29 and n. 1968; and other passages). This meant that man was given a limited choice of good and evil, and that he was made capable of Forbearance, Love, and Mercy. And in himself man summed up Allah's great world: man is in himself a microcosm.

3782. That man should undertake the God-like attributes (in however small a degree) of Will, Forbearance, Love, and Mercy, brought him nearer to Allah than was possible for any other creature of Allah. This was part of Allah's Will and Plan, but little did man realise then what a tremendous task he was undertaking or question himself whether he would be equal to it. *Ẓalūm* (translated "unjust") and *Jahūl* (ignorant) are both in the Arabic intensive form; as much as to say, 'man *signally* failed to measure his own powers or his own knowledge'. But Allah's Grace came to his assistance. Where man did his best, he won through by Allah's Grace, even though man's Best was but a poor Good.

How did man generically undertake this great Responsibility, which made him Vicegerent of Allah (2:30)? Here comes in the mystic doctrine of a Covenant, expressed or implied, between Allah and Humanity. See 7:172-73 and notes 1146-1148, also 5:1 and n. 682. A Covenant (*Mīthāq*) necessarily implies Trust, and its breach necessarily implies Punishment.

3783. Man's generic Covenant, which flowed from his exercising the option given him, choosing Will, Forbearance, Love, and Mercy, made it necessary that breach of it should carry its own punishment. Breach of it is here classed under two heads: those who betray their Trust act either as Hypocrites or as Unbelievers. Hypocrites are those who profess Faith but bring not forth the fruits of Faith. Unbelievers are those who openly defy Faith, and from whom therefore no fruits of Faith are to be expected.

3784. Those who remain firm to their Faith and their Covenant (see notes 3781-82) will receive the aid of Allah's Grace; their faults and weaknesses will be cured: and they will be made worthy of their exalted Destiny. For Allah is Oft-Returning and Most Merciful.

So ends a Sūrah which deals with the greatest complications and misunderstandngs in our throbbing life here below, and points upwards to the Great Achievement, the highest Salvation.

INTRODUCTION TO SŪRAH 34—*SABA'*

Now we begin a series of Sūrahs S. 34 to S. 39 which recapitulate some of the features of the spiritual world. This Sūrah leads off with emphasis on Allah's Mercy and Power and Truth. Then (in S. 35.) we are told how angels manifest the Power of Allah, and how different is Good from Evil and Truth from Falsehood. S. 36 is devoted to the Holy Prophet and the Qur'ān that came through him. In S. 37 the emphasis is on the snares of the Evil One; in S. 38, on the conquest of evil by wisdom and power as in the case of David and Solomon, and by Patience and Constancy as in the case of Job; and in S. 39, on the Final Judgement, which will sort out Faith from Unfaith and give to each its due.

The chronology has here no significance. This Sūrah belongs to the early Makkan period.

Summary—No Good or Truth is ever lost: Human Power and Prosperity are fleeting; but Allah's Power and Justice endure, and will enforce personal responsibility on man on the Last Day (34:1-30, and C. 190).

Faith and Unfaith will eventually find their true places and true values; Falsehood has no power; Truth is with Allah (34:31-54, and C. 191).

C. 190. —Allah's Mercy and Power endure forever:
(34:1-30.) Man should understand and not resist
Allah's Revelation. Human wisdom and Power,
As given to David, were only for establishing
Righteousness. Human glory, like Solomon's
Rested on slender foundations. Saba'
But enjoyed her fair and prosperous state
As long as she obeyed the Law
Of Allah, but perished for unrighteousness.
Learn, then, that the Mercy and Power, Wisdom
And Justice, of Allah are beyond all comparison.
Do right and prepare for the Final Day.

Sūrah 34.

Saba' (Sheba)[3784-A]

In the name of Allah, Most Gracious,
Most Merciful.

1. Praise be to Allah,[3785]
To Whom belong all things
In the heavens and on earth:
To Him be Praise
In the Hereafter:
And He is Full of Wisdom,
Acquainted with all things.

2. He knows all that goes[3786]
Into the earth, and all that
Comes out thereof: all that
Comes down from the sky[3787]
And all that ascends thereto
And He is the Most Merciful,
The Oft-Forgiving.

3. The Unbelievers say,[3788]
"Never to us will come
The Hour": say, "Nay!

الجزء الثاني والعشرون سُورَةُ سَبَإٍ

بِسْمِ اللَّهِ الرَّحْمَٰنِ الرَّحِيمِ

(١) الْحَمْدُ لِلَّهِ الَّذِي لَهُ مَا فِي السَّمَاوَاتِ
وَمَا فِي الْأَرْضِ وَلَهُ الْحَمْدُ فِي الْآخِرَةِ
وَهُوَ الْحَكِيمُ الْخَبِيرُ

(٢) يَعْلَمُ مَا يَلِجُ فِي الْأَرْضِ وَمَا يَخْرُجُ مِنْهَا
وَمَا يَنزِلُ مِنَ السَّمَاءِ وَمَا يَعْرُجُ فِيهَا
وَهُوَ الرَّحِيمُ الْغَفُورُ

(٣) وَقَالَ الَّذِينَ كَفَرُوا
لَا تَأْتِينَا السَّاعَةُ قُلْ بَلَىٰ

3784-A. *Saba'*: see S. 34:15.

3785. All Creation declares His Praises, *i.e.*, manifests His Mercy and Power, Goodness and Truth—all the sublime attributes summed up in His Most Beautiful Names (7:180 and 17:110 and notes). For man, to contemplate these is in itself a Revelation. This sentiment opens five Sūrahs of the Qur'ān evenly distributed, *viz.*, 1, 4., 18, 34, and 35. Here the point most emphasised is that His wisdom and mercy comprehend all things, extended in space or in time—here and everywhere, now and evermore. (R).

3786. An ignorant man may think that water absorbed in the soil or seed sown beneath the sod is lost, but it replenishes numerous rills and streams, and feeds and sustains numerous roots and forms of life, and throws up all kinds of vegetable life. So with things that come out of the earth who can count the myriad forms of herbs and trees that grow and perish, and yet sustain a continuous life for ages and ages? Yet these are symbolical of other things or entities beyond time or space, and beyond physical form. We see the birth and death of the animal part of man: when he is buried beneath the soil, the ignorant man thinks there is an end of him. But what countless stages still lie before him for his inner and spiritual life? And so with the Platonic Forms of Things: Goodness, Virtue, Mercy, and the various functions of the soul. They are never lost, but go up to Allah.

3787. The vapours that rise from the earth and ascend to the sky descend again as rain and snow and as symbols of Allah's Mercy. So are the prayers of the devout and the call of those in agony for help and light, answered by the descent of mercy and guidance, help and light from the Throne of Majesty. The imagery indicated in the last note can be worked out to moral and spiritual forces, and they all centre in Allah. Do not forget that, just as there is the element of Mercy, so there is an element of Justice and Punishment—in the physical forces as well as in the moral and spiritual forces, all centering in Allah.

3788. The last two verses prepared us to realise the positions of Unbelievers in Allah's great Universe. They are the discord in the universal harmony of Prayer and Praise. Their existence is due to the grant of a limited free will, the Trust which the Unbelievers have betrayed (see 33:72 and notes). But they must and will be eliminated: see verse 5 below. For there is nothing more certain in the world, physical, moral and spiritual, than that every cause, great or small, must have it corresponding consequences.

But most surely,
By my Lord,[3789] it will come
Upon you—by Him
Who knows the unseen—
From Whom is not hidden
The least little atom
In the Heavens or on earth:
Nor is there anything less
Than that, or greater, but
Is in the Record Perspicuous:[3790]

وَرَبِّي لَتَأْتِيَنَّكُمْ عَٰلِمِ ٱلْغَيْبِ
لَا يَعْزُبُ عَنْهُ مِثْقَالُ ذَرَّةٍ
فِي ٱلسَّمَٰوَٰتِ وَلَا فِي ٱلْأَرْضِ
وَلَآ أَصْغَرُ مِن ذَٰلِكَ وَلَآ أَكْبَرُ
إِلَّا فِي كِتَٰبٍ مُّبِينٍ

4. That He may reward
Those who believe and work
Deeds of righteousness: for such
Is Forgiveness and a Sustenance[3791]
Most Generous."

٤ لِّيَجْزِيَ ٱلَّذِينَ
ءَامَنُوا۟ وَعَمِلُوا۟ ٱلصَّٰلِحَٰتِ
أُو۟لَٰٓئِكَ لَهُم مَّغْفِرَةٌ وَرِزْقٌ كَرِيمٌ

5. But those who strive
Against Our Signs, to frustrate[3792]
Them—for such will be
A Penalty—a Punishment
Most humiliating.

٥ وَٱلَّذِينَ سَعَوْ فِيٓ ءَايَٰتِنَا مُعَٰجِزِينَ
أُو۟لَٰٓئِكَ لَهُمْ عَذَابٌ مِّن رِّجْزٍ أَلِيمٌ

6. And those to whom[3793]
Knowledge has come see
That the (Revelation) sent down
To thee from thy Lord—
That is the Truth,
And that it guides
To the Path of the Exalted
(In Might), Worthy
Of all praise.

٦ وَيَرَى ٱلَّذِينَ أُوتُوا۟ ٱلْعِلْمَ
ٱلَّذِيٓ أُنزِلَ إِلَيْكَ
مِن رَّبِّكَ هُوَ ٱلْحَقَّ
وَيَهْدِيٓ إِلَىٰ صِرَٰطِ
ٱلْعَزِيزِ ٱلْحَمِيدِ

3789. The strongest emphasis and the most perfect assurance of certainty are indicated by reference to the authority of Allah Himself, the Ruler of the Day of Judgement.

3790. In the symbolical language of our own human experiences, a record is more enduring than memory: in fact (if properly preserved) it is perpetual. If, further, it is expressed in clear language, without any obscurity, it can always be read with perfect precision and without any doubt whatever. Apply these qualities, free from human defects, to Allah's laws and decrees. They are unerring and enduring. Everything, greater or small, will receive due recognition—a Reward for Good and Punishment for Evil.

3791. *Sustenance*: Spiritual in things spiritual, and physical in things physical. It implies not only the satisfaction of desire, but the provision of means for sustaining the ground won and for winning more ground in the march of progress.

3792. *Cf.* 22:51. Allah's Plan cannot be frustrated. It is those who work against it, who will be eliminated and destroyed.

3793. Against the doubts and vain imaginings of the Ignorant is the certainty of knowledge of the Enlightened: that Allah reveals Himself, and that His Revelation is true and leads to the Path of true Guidance. That Path is the Path of Allah, Who, in His infinite love and Mercy, is Worthy of all Praise.

It is possible to connect this with the "Record Perspicuous" in verse 3 above: "it is perspicuous.. for the Enlightened do see.."

7. The Unbelievers say
(In ridicule): "Shall we
Point out to you a man[3794]
That will tell you,
When ye are all scattered
To pieces in disintegration,
That ye shall (then be
Raised) in a New Creation?

٧ وَقَالَ ٱلَّذِينَ كَفَرُوا۟
هَلْ نَدُلُّكُمْ عَلَىٰ رَجُلٍ يُنَبِّئُكُمْ
إِذَا مُزِّقْتُمْ كُلَّ مُمَزَّقٍ
إِنَّكُمْ لَفِى خَلْقٍ جَدِيدٍ

8. "Has he invented a falsehood
Against Allah, or has
A spirit (seized) him?"—[3795]
Nay, it is those who
Believe not in the Hereafter,
That are in (real) Penalty,
And in farthest Error.

٨ أَفْتَرَىٰ عَلَى ٱللَّهِ كَذِبًا أَم بِهِۦ جِنَّةٌۢ
بَلِ ٱلَّذِينَ لَا يُؤْمِنُونَ بِٱلْءَاخِرَةِ
فِى ٱلْعَذَابِ وَٱلضَّلَـٰلِ ٱلْبَعِيدِ

9. See they not what is
Before them and behind them,
Of the sky and the earth?[3796]
If We wished, We could
Cause the earth to swallow[3797]
Them up, or cause a piece
Of the sky to fall upon
them.[3798]
Verily in this is a Sign
For every devotee that
Turns to Allah (in repentance).

٩ أَفَلَمْ يَرَوْا۟ إِلَىٰ مَا بَيْنَ أَيْدِيهِمْ
وَمَا خَلْفَهُم مِّنَ ٱلسَّمَآءِ وَٱلْأَرْضِ
إِن نَّشَأْ نَخْسِفْ بِهِمُ ٱلْأَرْضَ
أَوْ نُسْقِطْ عَلَيْهِمْ كِسَفًا مِّنَ ٱلسَّمَآءِ
إِنَّ فِى ذَٰلِكَ لَءَايَةً لِّكُلِّ عَبْدٍ مُّنِيبٍ

10. We bestowed Grace aforetime
On David from Ourselves:[3799]

١٠ وَلَقَدْ ءَاتَيْنَا دَاوُۥدَ مِنَّا فَضْلًا

3794. This is a taunt against the Holy Prophet, and it is applicable to all who preach the doctrine of a Future Life. How is it possible, say the Unbelievers, that when a man's body is reduced to dust and scattered about, the man should rise again and become a new Creation? They add that such a preacher is inventing a deliberate falsehood or is demented.

3795. The answer is: the Future Life is the truest of all Truths; so far is the man who teaches it from being demented, that it is those who deny it, that lack knowledge and are in real jeopardy for their souls; for they persecute Truth and must not only suffer defeat, but go farther and farther from Realities and thus suffer the worst hallucinations about the spiritual world.

3796. The men who walk in spiritual darkness and laugh at a Hereafter have but to observe the Power of Allah in the nature around them. He Who created the heavens and the earth and sustains them can surely make a new Creation! And the cosmic Laws which are so just and inevitable should surely give them an idea of the inexorable Justice that must redress all balance.

3797. *Cf.* 16:45, and n. 2071. Who are these puny creatures—sceptics that question the might and majesty of Allah?

3798. *Cf.* 26:187. this was actually a challenge hurled at Shu'ayb and a shower of ashes and cinders came from above and overwhelmed the challengers!

3799. *Cf.* 21:79-80, and notes 2733-34. David had the gift of song and sacred music, and this is shown in his Psalms. All nature—hills and birds—sing and echo back the Praise of Allah.

"O ye Mountains! sing ye
Back the Praises of Allah
With him! and ye birds
(Also)! And We made
The iron soft for him—[3800]

11. (Commanding), "Make thou
Coats of mail, balancing well[3801]
The rings of chain armour,
And work ye righteousness;[3802]
For be sure I see
(Clearly) all that ye do."

12. And to Solomon (We
Made) the Wind (obedient):[3803]
Its early morning (stride)
Was a month's (journey),
And its evening (stride)
Was a month's (journey);
And We made a Font[3804]
Of molten brass to flow
For him; and there were
Jinns that worked in front[3805]
Of him, by the leave
Of his Lord, and if any
Of them turned aside
From Our command, We
Made him taste

يَٰجِبَالُ أَوِّبِي مَعَهُۥ وَٱلطَّيْرَ
وَأَلَنَّا لَهُ ٱلْحَدِيدَ
١١ أَنِ ٱعْمَلْ سَٰبِغَٰتٍ
وَقَدِّرْ فِي ٱلسَّرْدِ وَٱعْمَلُوا۟ صَٰلِحًا
إِنِّي بِمَا تَعْمَلُونَ بَصِيرٌ
١٢ وَلِسُلَيْمَٰنَ ٱلرِّيحَ
غُدُوُّهَا شَهْرٌ وَرَوَاحُهَا شَهْرٌ
وَأَسَلْنَا لَهُۥ عَيْنَ ٱلْقِطْرِ
وَمِنَ ٱلْجِنِّ مَن يَعْمَلُ
بَيْنَ يَدَيْهِ بِإِذْنِ رَبِّهِۦ
وَمَن يَزِغْ مِنْهُمْ عَنْ أَمْرِنَا
نُذِقْهُ

3800. Iron or steel is hard stuff: but in the hands of a craftsman it becomes soft and pliable, and with it can be made instruments for the defence of righteousness. These, in the literal sense, are coats of mail, and defensive armour, and the manufacture of them is traditionally attributed to David. (R).

3801. Coats of chain armour have to be made with cunning art, if the chains are to fit into each other and the whole garment is to be worn in comfort in fierce warfare.

3802. Note the transition from the singular, "make them coats of mail", to the plural "and work ye righteousness". The first is addressed to David, who was the artificer of defensive armour: and the second is addressed to him and his whole people. He made the armour, but it was to be worn not only by him but all the warriors. But he and his people were to be careful to see that they did not deviate from the paths of righteousness. Fighting is a dangerous weapon and may well degenerate (as it so often does) into mere violence. They were to see that this should not happen, and they were told that Allah was watching over them all with personal solicitude implied in the singular pronoun "I".

3803. *Cf.* 21:81-82, n. 2736, and 38:36-38. See also 27:38-39. The winds are swift and can cover in a short morning's or evening's flight the distance it takes a whole month to cover on foot or by bullock cart. In our own day, with air speeds of 400 miles and more per hour, this seems a moderate statement.

3804. In the Old Testament, II. Chronicles, Chapters iii., and iv., are described the various costly materials with which Solomon's Temple was built, and it was furnished with vessels, candlesticks, lamps, censers, etc. "Solomon made all these vessels in great abundance: for the weight of the brass could not be found out" (II. Chronicles, iv. 18). "Also he made a molten sea of ten cubits from brim to brim, round in compass, and five cubits the height thereof: and a line of thirty cubits did compass it round about" (II. Chronicles, iv. 2). The receptacle or "sea" or Font was made of molten brass: presumably it contained flowing water for washing with.

3805. See 27:17, and n. 3257. (R).

Of the Penalty
Of the Blazing Fire.

مِنْ عَذَابِ ٱلسَّعِيرِ

13. They worked for him
As he desired, (making)
Arches,[3806]
Images, Basins,
As large as Reservoirs,
And (cooking) Cauldrons fixed
(In their places): "Work ye,[3807]
Sons of David, with thanks!
But few of My servants
Are grateful!"

١٣ يَعْمَلُونَ لَهُۥ مَا يَشَآءُ
مِن مَّحَٰرِيبَ وَتَمَٰثِيلَ وَجِفَانٍ
كَٱلْجَوَابِ وَقُدُورٍ رَّاسِيَٰتٍ
ٱعْمَلُوٓاْ ءَالَ دَاوُۥدَ شُكْرًا
وَقَلِيلٌ مِّنْ عِبَادِىَ ٱلشَّكُورُ

14. Then, when We decreed
(Solomon's) death, nothing
showed them
His death except a little[3808]
Worm of the earth, which
Kept (slowly) gnawing away
At his staff: so when he
Fell down, the Jinns saw[3809]
Plainly that if they had
Known the unseen, they
Would not have tarried

١٤ فَلَمَّا قَضَيْنَا عَلَيْهِ ٱلْمَوْتَ
مَا دَلَّهُمْ عَلَىٰ مَوْتِهِۦٓ إِلَّا دَآبَّةُ
ٱلْأَرْضِ تَأْكُلُ مِنسَأَتَهُۥ
فَلَمَّا خَرَّ تَبَيَّنَتِ ٱلْجِنُّ أَن لَّوْ كَانُواْ
يَعْلَمُونَ ٱلْغَيْبَ مَا لَبِثُواْ

3806. *Miḥrāb* (Plural *Maḥārib*), translated "arch", may be applied to any fine, elevated, spacious architectural structure. As the reference here is to the Temple of Solomon, the word "arches" is I think most appropriate. "Arches" would be structure Ornaments in the Temple. Images would be like the images of oxen and Cherubim mentioned in II. Chronicles, iv. 3 and iii. 14; the Basons (II. Chronicles iv. 22) were perhaps huge dishes round which many men could sit together and eat, according to ancient Eastern custom, while the cooking Cauldrons or Pots (II. Chronicles, iv. 16), were fixed in one place, being so large in capacity that they could not be moved about. Indian readers will get some idea of them from the huge cooking *Degs*, which they use in the 'Urs at Ajmir Sharif.

3807. The building of the Temple was a great event in Israelite history. The motto here given is "Work!": for only that would justify the maintenance of the Kingdom of David, which reached its zenith under Solomon. Without work, both literally, and figuratively for "righteous deeds", all that glory and power would be out of place, and it fell away in a few generations, with the decline of the moral spirit which was at its back.

3808. This allegory illustrates three points: (1) however great and glorious human power and grandeur may be, it is only for a time, and it may fade away even before people know of its decline; (2) the most remarkable events may be brought to light, not by a flourish of trumpets, but by a humble individual, unknown and unseen, who works imperceptibly and undermines even so strong a thing as a staff, on which a great man may lean; (3) work done by men merely on the basis of brute strength or fear, as in the case of the Jinns, will not endure. This is brought up in strong contrast against the Power and Majesty of Allah, which will endure, which cannot be sapped, and which can only be fully appreciated by a training of the will and heart. In the same way, in David's story above, his mighty strength as a warrior (see 2:251) and his skill in making armour are only to be valued when used, as it was used, in the service of Allah, in righteous works (34:11).

3809. The Jinns looked upon their work as a Penalty, and so it became to them. The people who worked at the Temple of Solomon as the People of David worked and gloried in their work as a thanksgiving to Allah, and their work became sanctified. The Jinns knew nothing of hidden secrets; they only saw the obvious, and had not even the significance of the little worm that slowly gnawed away Solomon's staff.

In the humiliating Penalty (Of their Task).	فِي ٱلْعَذَابِ ٱلْمُهِينِ
15. There was, for Saba',[3810] Aforetime, a Sign in their Homeland—two Gardens To the right and to the left. Eat of the Sustenance (provided) By your Lord, and be grateful To Him: a territory fair and happy, And a Lord Oft-Forgiving![3811]	لَقَدْ كَانَ لِسَبَإٍ فِي مَسْكَنِهِمْ ءَايَةٌ ۖ (١٥) جَنَّتَانِ عَن يَمِينٍ وَشِمَالٍ ۖ كُلُوا۟ مِن رِّزْقِ رَبِّكُمْ وَٱشْكُرُوا۟ لَهُۥ ۚ بَلْدَةٌ طَيِّبَةٌ وَرَبٌّ غَفُورٌ
16. But they turned away (From Allah), and We sent Against them the flood[3812] (Released) from the Dams,[3813] And We converted their two Garden (rows) into "gardens" Producing bitter fruit, And tamarisks, and some few (Stunted) Lote trees.[3814]	فَأَعْرَضُوا۟ فَأَرْسَلْنَا عَلَيْهِمْ (١٦) سَيْلَ ٱلْعَرِمِ وَبَدَّلْنَٰهُم بِجَنَّتَيْهِمْ جَنَّتَيْنِ ذَوَاتَىْ أُكُلٍ خَمْطٍ وَأَثْلٍ وَشَىْءٍ مِّن سِدْرٍ قَلِيلٍ

3810. This is the same city and territory in Yemen as is mentioned in 27:22: see note there as to its location. There the period was the time of Solomon and Queen Bilqīs. Here it is some centuries later. It was still a happy and prosperous country, amply irrigated from the Ma'ārib dam. Its road or perhaps its canals, were skirted by gardens on both sides, right and left: at any given point you always saw two gardens. It produced fruit, spices, and frankincense, and got the name of Araby the Blest for that part of the country.

3811. The land was fair to look upon: the people happy and prosperous: and they enjoyed the blessings of Allah, Who is Gracious and does not punish small human faults or weaknesses.

3812. Into that happy Garden of Eden in Arabia Felix (Araby the Blest) came the insidious snake of Unfaith and Wrongdoing. Perhaps the people became arrogant of their prosperity, or of their science, or of their skill in irrigation engineering, in respect of the wonderful works of the Dam which their ancestors had constructed. Perhaps they got broken up into rich and poor, privileged and unprivileged, high-caste and low-caste, disregarding the gifts and closing the opportunities given by Allah to all His creatures. Perhaps they broke the laws of the very Nature which fed and sustained them. The Nemesis came. It may have come suddenly, or it may have come slowly. The pent-up waters of the eastern side of the Yemen highlands were collected in a high lake confined by the Dam of Ma'ārib. A mighty flood came: the dam burst: and it has never been repaired since. This was a spectacular crisis: it may have been preceded and followed by slow dessication of the country.

3813. "*'Arim*" (= Dams or Embankments) may have been a proper noun, or may simply mean the great earthworks lined with stone, which formed the Ma'ārib dam, of which traces still exist. The French traveller T.J. Arnaud saw the town and ruins of the Dam of Ma'ārib in 1843, and described its gigantic works and its inscriptions: See *Journal Asiatique* for January 1874: the account is in French. For a secondary account in English, see W.B. Harris, *Journey Through Yemen*, Edinburgh, 1893. The dam as measured by Arnaud was two miles long and 120 ft. high. The date of its destruction was somewhere about 120 A.C., though some authorities put it much later.

3814. The flourishing "Garden of Arabia" was converted into a waste. The luscious fruit trees became wild, or gave place to wild plants with bitter fruit. The feathery leaved tamarisk, which is only good for twigs and wattle-work, replaced the fragrant plants and flowers. Wild and stunted kinds of thorny bushes, like the wild Lote tree, which were good for neither fruit nor shade, grew in place of the pomegranates, the date palms, and the grapevines. The lote tree belongs to the family Rhamnaceae, *Zizyphus Spina Christi*. of which (it is supposed) Christ's crown of thorns was made, allied to the *Zizyphus Jujuba*, or *ber* tree of India. Wild, it is shrubby, thorny and useless. In cultivation it bears good fruit, and some shade, and can be thornless, thus becoming a symbol of heavenly bliss: 56:28.

17. That was the Requital
We gave them because
They ungratefully rejected
Faith:[3815]
And never do We give
(Such) requital except to such
As are ungrateful rejecters.

18. Between them and the Cities[3816]
On which We had poured
Our blessings, We had placed
Cities in prominent positions,
And between them We had
Appointed stages of journey
In due proportion: "Travel therein,
Secure, by night and by day."

19. But they said:[3717] "Our Lord!
Place longer distances
Between our journey-stages":[3818]
But they wronged themselves
(therein)
At length We made them
As a tale (that is told),[3819]

(١٧) ذَٰلِكَ جَزَيْنَٰهُم بِمَا كَفَرُوا۟ۖ
وَهَلْ نُجَٰزِىٓ
إِلَّا ٱلْكَفُورَ

(١٨) وَجَعَلْنَا بَيْنَهُمْ
وَبَيْنَ ٱلْقُرَى ٱلَّتِى بَٰرَكْنَا فِيهَا
قُرًى ظَٰهِرَةً وَقَدَّرْنَا فِيهَا ٱلسَّيْرَۖ
سِيرُوا۟ فِيهَا لَيَالِىَ وَأَيَّامًا ءَامِنِينَ

(١٩) فَقَالُوا۟ رَبَّنَا بَٰعِدْ بَيْنَ أَسْفَارِنَا
وَظَلَمُوٓا۟ أَنفُسَهُمْ
فَجَعَلْنَٰهُمْ أَحَادِيثَ

3815. *Kafūr*: intensive form: "those who deliberately and continuously reject Allah and are ungrateful for His Mercies, as shown by their constant wrongdoing.

3816. An instance is now given of the sort of covetousness on the part of the people of Saba', which ruined their prosperity and trade and cut their own throats. The old Frankincense route was the great Highway (*imām mubīn* 15:79; *sabīl muqīm*, 15:76) between Arabia and Syria. Through Syria it connected with the great and flourishing Kingdoms of the Euphrates and Tigris valleys on the one hand and Egypt on the other, and with the great Roman Empire round the Mediterranean. At the other end, through the Yemen Coast, the road connected, by sea transport, with India, Malaya, and China. The Yemen-Syria road was much frequented, and Madā'in Ṣāliḥ was one of the stations on that route, and afterwards on the Pilgrim route: see Appendix VII to S. 26. Syria was the land on which Allah "had poured his blessings", being a rich fertile country, where Abraham had lived: it includes the Holy Land of Palestine. The route was studded in the days of its prosperity with many stations (cities) close to each other, on which merchants could travel with ease and safety, "by night and by day". The close proximity of stations prevented the inroads of highwaymen.

3817. *Said*: in this and other places in the Qur'ān, "language" is used for thought or deed. The Commentators call it the "Language of actual facts" (*zabān hāl*) as opposed to the "language of words" (*zabān qāl*).

3818. The covetous Saba' people, in order to get more profit from travellers' supplies by concentrating them on a few stations which they could monopolise, tended to choke off traffic and ruin the big trade. Selfishness often runs counter to true self-interest. It is a historical fact that the great Yemen-Syria route in Arabia declined with the decline of Yemen. There were no doubt physical causes, but supreme above all were the moral causes, the grasping nature of the people, and their departure from the highest standards of righteousness.

3819. The people of Saba' were given every chance. They had prosperity, skill, trade and commerce, and a healthy and beautiful country. They also had, apparently, great virtues, and as long as they remained true to their virtues, *i.e.*, to the Law of Allah, they remained happy and contented. But when they became covetous and selfish, and became jealous of other people's prosperity instead of rejoicing in it, they fell from grace and declined. It may be that the climate changed, the rainfall became scantier, perhaps on account of the cutting down of hill forests: trade routes changed, on account of the people falling off in the virtues that make men popular: behind all the physical causes was the root-cause, that they began to worship mammon, self, greed, or materialism. They fell into the snare of Satan. They gradually passed out of history, and became only a name in a story. Moral: it is only Allah's Mercy that can give true happiness or prosperity, and happiness or prosperity is only a snare unless used for the highest service of Allah and man.

And We dispersed them
All in scattered fragments.
Verily in this are Signs
For every (soul that is)
Patiently constant and grateful.

20. And on them did Satan
Prove true his idea,[3720]
And they followed him, all
But a Party that believed.

21. But he had no authority
Over them—except that We
Might test the man who[3821]
Believes in the Hereafter
From him who is in doubt
Concerning it: and thy Lord
Doth watch over all things.

SECTION 3.

22. Say: "Call upon other (gods)[3822]
Whom ye fancy, besides Allah:
They have no power—
Not the weight of an atom—
In the heavens or on earth:[3823]
No (sort of) share have they
Therein, nor is any of them
A helper to Allah.

23. "No intercession can avail
In His Presence, except for
those[3824]

وَمَزَّقْنَٰهُمْ كُلَّ مُمَزَّقٍ ۚ
إِنَّ فِى ذَٰلِكَ لَءَايَٰتٍ لِّكُلِّ صَبَّارٍ شَكُورٍ

٢٠ وَلَقَدْ صَدَّقَ عَلَيْهِمْ إِبْلِيسُ ظَنَّهُۥ
فَٱتَّبَعُوهُ إِلَّا فَرِيقًا مِّنَ ٱلْمُؤْمِنِينَ

٢١ وَمَا كَانَ لَهُۥ عَلَيْهِم مِّن سُلْطَٰنٍ إِلَّا
لِنَعْلَمَ مَن يُؤْمِنُ بِٱلْءَاخِرَةِ مِمَّنْ هُوَ مِنْهَا فِى شَكٍّ ۗ
وَرَبُّكَ عَلَىٰ كُلِّ شَىْءٍ حَفِيظٌ

٢٢ قُلِ ٱدْعُوا۟ ٱلَّذِينَ زَعَمْتُم مِّن دُونِ ٱللَّهِ ۖ
لَا يَمْلِكُونَ مِثْقَالَ ذَرَّةٍ فِى
ٱلسَّمَٰوَٰتِ وَلَا فِى ٱلْأَرْضِ وَمَا لَهُمْ
فِيهِمَا مِن شِرْكٍ وَمَا لَهُۥ مِنْهُم مِّن ظَهِيرٍ

٢٣ وَلَا تَنفَعُ ٱلشَّفَٰعَةُ عِندَهُۥٓ

3820. *Cf.* 17:62, Satan out of arrogance had said, when he asked for respite from the Most High: "I will bring (Adam's) descendants under my sway, all but a few." This was now proved true on the Saba' people. He had no power to force them. It was their own will that went wrong and put them into his power.

3821. *Might test*: the word in the original is *might know.* It is not that Allah does not know all. Why does He want to test? It is in order to help us subjectively, to train our will, to put us definitely the question, "Will you obey Allah or other than Allah?" *Cf.* n. 467 to 3:154.

3822. Other objects of worship, such as Self, or Money, or Power, or things we imagine will bring us luck or prosperity, though they can do nothing of the kind.

3823. The false gods have no power whatever either in heaven or on earth, either in influencing our spiritual life or our ordinary worldly life. To suppose that they have some share, or that they can give some help to Allah, even though Allah is Supreme, is both false and blasphemous. Allah is One and Supreme, without sharer, helper, or equal.

3824. *Cf.* 20:109, n. 2634, where I have explained the two possible modes of interpretation. Each soul is individually and personally responsible. And if there is any intercession, it can only be by Allah's gracious permission. For the Day of Judgement will be a terrible Day, or Day of Wrath (*Dies irae*) according to the Latin hymn, when the purest souls will be stupefied at the manifestation of Allah's Power. See next note.

For whom He has granted
Permission. So far (is this
The case) that, when terror
Is removed from their hearts[3825]
(At the Day of Judgement, then)
Will they say, 'What is it
That your Lord
commanded?'[3826]
They will say: 'That which is
True and just; and He is
The Most High, Most Great'."

إِلَّا لِمَنْ أَذِنَ لَهُۥ
حَتَّىٰٓ إِذَا فُزِّعَ عَن قُلُوبِهِمْ
قَالُوا۟ مَاذَا قَالَ رَبُّكُمْ
قَالُوا۟ ٱلْحَقَّ
وَهُوَ ٱلْعَلِىُّ ٱلْكَبِيرُ

24. Say: "Who gives you[3827]
Sustenance, from the heavens
And the earth?" Say:
"It is Allah; and certain it is
That either we or ye[3828]
Are on right guidance
Or in manifest error!"

﴿٢٤﴾ قُلْ مَن يَرْزُقُكُم مِّنَ ٱلسَّمَٰوَٰتِ
وَٱلْأَرْضِ قُلِ ٱللَّهُ وَإِنَّآ أَوْ إِيَّاكُمْ
لَعَلَىٰ هُدًى أَوْ فِى ضَلَٰلٍ مُّبِينٍ

25. Say: "Ye shall not be
Questioned as to our sins,[3829]
Nor shall we be questioned
As to what ye do."

﴿٢٥﴾ قُل لَّا تُسْـَٔلُونَ عَمَّآ أَجْرَمْنَا
وَلَا نُسْـَٔلُ عَمَّا تَعْمَلُونَ

26. Say: "Our Lord will gather us
Together and will in the end
Decide the matter between us
(And you) in truth and
justice:[3830]

﴿٢٦﴾ قُلْ يَجْمَعُ بَيْنَنَا رَبُّنَا
ثُمَّ يَفْتَحُ بَيْنَنَا بِٱلْحَقِّ

3825. "Their hearts": the pronoun "their" refers to the angels nearest to Allah. On the Day of Judgement there will be such an irresistible manifestation of Power that even they will be silent for a while, and will scarcely realise what is happening. They will question each other, and only thus will they regain their bearings. Or "their" may refer to those who seek intercession.

3826. In their mutual questionings they will realise that Allah's Judgement, as always, is right and just. Does this mean that no sort of intercession is required?

3827. There are six propositions introduced here with the word "Say", at verses 22, 24, 25, 26, 27, and 30. They clearly explain the doctrine of Unity (verse 22), the Mercy of Allah (verse 23), man's Personal Responsibility (verse 25), the Final Justice of Allah (verse 26), Allah's Power and Wisdom (verse 27), and the Inevitability of the Judgement, by which the true values will be restored (verse 30).

3828. Right and Wrong, Good and Evil, are incompatible, one with another. In this matter we can make no compromise. It is true that in men there may be various degrees of good or evil mixed together, and we have to tolerate men as our fellow-creatures, with all their faults and shortcomings. But this does not mean that we can worship Allah and Mammon together. Wrong is the negation of Right as light is of darkness. Though there may be apparently varying depths of darkness, this is only due to the imperfection of our vision: it is varying strengths of light as perceived by our relative powers of sight. So we may perceive the Light of Allah in varying degrees according to our spiritual vision. But in simple questions of Right and Wrong, we are faced by the Categorical Imperative.

3829. Therefore do not prosecute us, or bring personal animus to bear on us. We must do our duty in declaring the universal Message, which is for you as much as for us.

3830. Human controversies are vain and inconclusive. If you put your trust in Allah and we put our trust in Allah, we belong to one Brotherhood, and we shall see the perfect Truth finally when the Time comes.

And He is the One to decide,
The One Who knows all."

وَهُوَ ٱلْفَتَّاحُ ٱلْعَلِيمُ

27. Say: "Show me those whom
Ye have joined with Him
As partners: by no means
(Can ye). Nay, He is Allah[3831]
The Exalted in Power,
The Wise."

قُلْ أَرُونِيَ ٱلَّذِينَ أَلْحَقْتُم بِهِۦ شُرَكَآءَ ۖ كَلَّا ۚ بَلْ هُوَ ٱللَّهُ ٱلْعَزِيزُ ٱلْحَكِيمُ ﴿٢٧﴾

28. We have not sent thee
But as a universal
(Messenger)[3832]
To men, giving them
Glad tidings, and warning them
(Against sin), but most men
Understand not.

وَمَآ أَرْسَلْنَٰكَ إِلَّا كَآفَّةً لِّلنَّاسِ بَشِيرًا وَنَذِيرًا وَلَٰكِنَّ أَكْثَرَ ٱلنَّاسِ لَا يَعْلَمُونَ ﴿٢٨﴾

29. They say: "When will this
Promise (come to pass)
If ye are telling the truth?"

وَيَقُولُونَ مَتَىٰ هَٰذَا ٱلْوَعْدُ إِن كُنتُمْ صَٰدِقِينَ ﴿٢٩﴾

30. Say: "The appointment to you
Is for a Day, which ye
Cannot put back for an hour[3833]
Nor put forward."

قُل لَّكُم مِّيعَادُ يَوْمٍ لَّا تَسْتَـْٔخِرُونَ عَنْهُ سَاعَةً وَلَا تَسْتَقْدِمُونَ ﴿٣٠﴾

C. 191.—Unfaith has no stable foundations to rest on:
(34:31-54.) Misleaders and misled will all be responsible
For their deeds. True values are not to be judged
By the seeming good of this Life: true Good
Will come to its own in the End, however
Derided and scorned in the period of Trial.
Revelation and the Mission of the men of Allah
Will stand every test. Allah's Truth will endure,
While Falsehood will perish, and its votaries find
The door of Repentance closed in the End.

3831. Wisdom and Power only belong to Allah. If you put your trust in other things, they will fail you, because they do not exist—as objects of worship. All else that you set your hearts upon will and must fail you, because they cannot in any wise be brought in to rivalry with Allah.

3832. Allah's Revelation, through the Holy Prophet, was not meant for one faith or tribe, one race or set of people. It was meant for all mankind, to whom, if they turn to Allah, it is a Message of the glad tidings of His Mercy, and if they do not turn to Him, it is a warning against sin and the inevitable Punishment. That the Punishment does not come immediately (as far as they perceive) is no reason for doubting it. It has been declared in clear and unequivocal terms, and nothing can be more certain. Why delay? Why ask carping questions? Why not profit by the Message, turn to Allah in repentance, and bring forth the fruits of righteousness?

3833. When that Day actually arrives, your period of probation will have passed. It will be too late. Now is the time for action and spiritual profit.

SECTION 4.

31. The Unbelievers say:
"We shall neither believe
In this scripture nor in (any)
That (came) before it."[3834]
Couldst thou but see when
The wrongdoers will be made
To stand before their Lord,
Throwing back the word
(of blame)[3835]
On one another! Those who
Had been despised will say
To the arrogant ones:[3836]
"Had it not been for you,
We should certainly
Have been believers!"

(٣١) وَقَالَ ٱلَّذِينَ كَفَرُوا۟ لَن نُّؤْمِنَ
بِهَٰذَا ٱلْقُرْءَانِ وَلَا بِٱلَّذِى بَيْنَ يَدَيْهِ ۗ
وَلَوْ تَرَىٰٓ إِذِ ٱلظَّٰلِمُونَ مَوْقُوفُونَ عِندَ
رَبِّهِمْ يَرْجِعُ بَعْضُهُمْ إِلَىٰ بَعْضٍ ٱلْقَوْلَ
يَقُولُ ٱلَّذِينَ ٱسْتُضْعِفُوا۟
لِلَّذِينَ ٱسْتَكْبَرُوا۟
لَوْلَآ أَنتُمْ لَكُنَّا مُؤْمِنِينَ

32. The arrogant ones will say
To those who had been
despised:
"Was it we who kept you
Back from Guidance after
It reached you? Nay, rather,
It was ye who transgressed."[3837]

(٣٢) قَالَ ٱلَّذِينَ ٱسْتَكْبَرُوا۟ لِلَّذِينَ ٱسْتُضْعِفُوٓا۟
أَنَحْنُ صَدَدْنَٰكُمْ عَنِ ٱلْهُدَىٰ بَعْدَ إِذْ جَآءَكُم ۖ
بَلْ كُنتُم مُّجْرِمِينَ

33. Those who had been despised
Will say to the arrogant ones:
"Nay! it was a plot
(Of yours) by day and by
night:[3838]
Behold! ye (constantly) ordered
us
To be ungrateful to Allah

(٣٣) وَقَالَ ٱلَّذِينَ
ٱسْتُضْعِفُوا۟ لِلَّذِينَ ٱسْتَكْبَرُوا۟
بَلْ مَكْرُ ٱلَّيْلِ وَٱلنَّهَارِ إِذْ
تَأْمُرُونَنَآ أَن نَّكْفُرَ بِٱللَّهِ

3834. To the Pagans all scriptures are taboo, whether it be the Qur'ān or any Revelation that came before it. The people of the Book despised the Pagans, but in their arrogant assumption of superiority, prevented them, by their example, from accepting the latest and most universal Scripture when it came in the form of the Qur'ān. This relative position of men who fancy themselves on their knowledge, and men whom they despise but exploit and mislead, always exists on this earth. I have mentioned the people of the Book and the Pagan Arabs merely by way of illustration.

3835. One disbelief is as bad as another. There is little to choose between them. But when the final account will be taken, there will be mutual recriminations between the one and the other.

3836. The Pagans will naturally say to the people of the Book: "You misled us; you had previous Revelations, and you should have known how Allah sent His Messengers; had it not been for your bad example, we should have received Allah's Revelation and become Believers." Or the humble followers will say this to their leaders, or those less gifted will say to those by whom they were misled and exploited. The dichotomy is between such as pretentiously held their heads high in the world and such as they profited by but held in contempt.

3837. In the mutual reproaches between the misleaders and the misled ones, there will be a grain of truth on both sides, and yet both were guilty in not realising their own personal responsiblity.

3638. The more intelligent ones who exploit the weaker ones are constantly plotting night and day to keep the latter ignorant and under their thumb. They show them the ways of Evil, because by that means they are more in their power.

And to attribute equals to
Him!"[3839]

وَنَجْعَلَ لَهُۥٓ أَندَادًا

They will declare (their)
repentance[3840]
When they see the Penalty:
We shall put yokes
On the necks of the
Unbelievers:
It would only be a requital
For their (ill) Deeds.

وَأَسَرُّواْ ٱلنَّدَامَةَ لَمَّا رَأَوُاْ ٱلْعَذَابَ
وَجَعَلْنَا ٱلْأَغْلَٰلَ فِىٓ أَعْنَاقِ ٱلَّذِينَ كَفَرُواْ
هَلْ يُجْزَوْنَ إِلَّا مَا كَانُواْ يَعْمَلُونَ

34. Never did We send
A Warner to a population,
But the wealthy ones among
them[3841]
Said: "We believe not
In the (Message) with which
Ye have been sent."

٣٤ وَمَآ أَرْسَلْنَا فِى قَرْيَةٍ
مِّن نَّذِيرٍ إِلَّا قَالَ مُتْرَفُوهَآ
إِنَّا بِمَآ أُرْسِلْتُم بِهِۦ كَٰفِرُونَ

35. They said: "We have more
In wealth and in sons,[3842]
And we cannot be punished."

٣٥ وَقَالُواْ نَحْنُ أَكْثَرُ أَمْوَٰلًا
وَأَوْلَٰدًا وَمَا نَحْنُ بِمُعَذَّبِينَ

36. Say: "Verily my Lord enlarges
And restricts the Provision[3843]
To whom He pleases, but
Most men understand not."

٣٦ قُلْ إِنَّ رَبِّى يَبْسُطُ ٱلرِّزْقَ لِمَن يَشَآءُ
وَيَقْدِرُ وَلَٰكِنَّ أَكْثَرَ ٱلنَّاسِ لَا يَعْلَمُونَ

SECTION 5.

37. It is not your wealth
Nor your sons, that will
Bring you nearer to Us[3844]

٣٧ وَمَآ أَمْوَٰلُكُمْ وَلَآ
أَوْلَٰدُكُم بِٱلَّتِى تُقَرِّبُكُمْ عِندَنَا

3839. If all men worshipped the true God, and none but Him, they could not on the one hand be trampled upon, and on the other hand they could not be unjust. It is in the worship of false ideals or false gods that alluring structures of fraud and injustice are built up.

3940. *Cf.* 10:54, and n. 1445. All these mutual recriminations would be swallowed up in the general realisation of the Truth by both sides in the Hereafter. They would be prepared openly to declare their repentance, but it would be too late. The yoke of slavery to Evil will be on their necks. Allah's justice put it there, but what else could it do? Their own sins will cry out against them and hold them under their yokes.

3841. Whenever the Message of Allah comes, the vested interests range themselves against it. Worldly power has made them arrogant: worldly pleasures have deadened their sensibility to Truth. They reject the Message because it attacks their false position.

3842. Their arrogance is openly based on their worldly power and position, their family influence, and the strength of their man-power. Turn back again to the contrast drawn between the arrogant ones and those whom they despised, in verses 31-33.

3843. *Provision* (or Sustenance): good things of all kinds in this life, material goods as well as power, opportunities, influence, mental gifts, etc. These do not necessarily all go to the good, nor is their denial to be interpreted to mean that it is a withdrawal of Allah's favour. Very often the contrary is the case. Their distribution is in accordance with the Universal Plan and Purpose, which is All-Wise and All-Good. but ignorant people cannot understand this.

3844. The true test of progress in spiritual life is to be measured by other things than material wealth and influence. What we have to ask ourselves is: are we the least bit nearer to Allah?

In degree: but only
Those who believe and work
Righteousness—these are
The ones for whom there is
A multiplied Reward[3845]
For their deeds, while
Secure they (reside)
In the dwellings on high![3846]

زُلْفَىٰٓ إِلَّا مَنْ ءَامَنَ وَعَمِلَ صَٰلِحًا فَأُو۟لَٰٓئِكَ لَهُمْ جَزَآءُ ٱلضِّعْفِ بِمَا عَمِلُوا۟ وَهُمْ فِى ٱلْغُرُفَٰتِ ءَامِنُونَ

38. Those who strive against
Our Signs, to frustrate them,[3847]
Will be given over
Into Punishment.

٣٨ وَٱلَّذِينَ يَسْعَوْنَ فِىٓ ءَايَٰتِنَا مُعَٰجِزِينَ أُو۟لَٰٓئِكَ فِى ٱلْعَذَابِ مُحْضَرُونَ

39. Say: "Verily my Lord enlarges
And restricts the Sustenance[3848]
To such of His servants
As He pleases: and nothing
Do ye spend in the least
(In His Cause) but He
Replaces it: for He is[3849]
The Best of those who
Grant Sustenance.

٣٩ قُلْ إِنَّ رَبِّى يَبْسُطُ ٱلرِّزْقَ لِمَن يَشَآءُ مِنْ عِبَادِهِۦ وَيَقْدِرُ لَهُۥ وَمَآ أَنفَقْتُم مِّن شَىْءٍ فَهُوَ يُخْلِفُهُۥ وَهُوَ خَيْرُ ٱلرَّٰزِقِينَ

40. One Day He will
Gather them all together,
And say to the angels,[3850]
"Was it you that these
Men used to worship?"

٤٠ وَيَوْمَ يَحْشُرُهُمْ جَمِيعًا ثُمَّ يَقُولُ لِلْمَلَٰٓئِكَةِ أَهَٰٓؤُلَآءِ إِيَّاكُمْ كَانُوا۟ يَعْبُدُونَ

41. They will say, "Glory to Thee!
Our (tie) is with Thee—

٤١ قَالُوا۟ سُبْحَٰنَكَ أَنتَ وَلِيُّنَا

3845. *Cf.* 30:39. All worldly goods are but a shadow that will pass away. Its intrinsic and eternal value is small. But those who work righteousness in Faith are on the true path of self-development. The rewards they will get will be intimately more than their merits entitle them to. For they will partake of the boundless Bounties of Allah.

3846. Their happiness will not only be great in quantity ("multiplied"), but it will be of a specially sublime quality ("dwellings on high"), and it will endure without any chance of its loss or diminution ("secure they reside").

3847. *Cf.* 34:3, where the argument was urged that human efforts to defeat Allah's Plan will only bring humiliation to those who indulge in them. Here the argument is rounded off by the statement that such efforts, besides their failures, will land them in an abyss of punishment contrasted with the "dwellings on high" of the blessed ones.

3848. *Cf.* 34:36, above, and n. 3843.

3849. Even in the seeming inequality of distribution of the good things of life, Allah has a wise and merciful purpose: for nothing arises by chance. He is the best to give us, now and evermore, just those things which subserve our real needs and advance our inner development.

3850. Here we have the case of the worship of angels or supposed Powers of Allah, or supposed beneficent spirits that men turn to instead of worshipping the true God. In fact these are mere names to the false worshippers. It is not the Good that they worship but the Evil, which leads them astray.

As Protector[3851]—not with them.
Nay, but they worshipped
The Jinns:[3852] most of them
Believed in them."

مِن دُونِهِم بَلْ كَانُوا يَعْبُدُونَ الْجِنَّ
أَكْثَرُهُم بِهِم مُّؤْمِنُونَ

42. So on that Day
No power shall they have
Over each other, for profit
Or harm: and We shall
Say to the wrongdoers,
"Taste ye the Penalty[3853]
Of the Fire—the which
Ye were wont to deny!"

(٤٢) فَالْيَوْمَ لَا يَمْلِكُ
بَعْضُكُمْ لِبَعْضٍ نَّفْعًا وَلَا ضَرًّا
وَنَقُولُ لِلَّذِينَ ظَلَمُوا ذُوقُوا عَذَابَ
النَّارِ الَّتِي كُنتُم بِهَا تُكَذِّبُونَ

43. When Our Clear Signs
Are rehearsed to them,
They say, "This is only
A man who wishes
To hinder you from the
(worship)[3854]
Which your fathers practised."
And they say,: "This is
Only a falsehood invented!"
And the Unbelievers say
Of the Truth when it comes
To them. "This is nothing
But evident magic!"

(٤٣) وَإِذَا تُتْلَىٰ عَلَيْهِمْ آيَاتُنَا بَيِّنَاتٍ
قَالُوا مَا هَٰذَا إِلَّا رَجُلٌ يُرِيدُ
أَن يَصُدَّكُمْ عَمَّا كَانَ يَعْبُدُ آبَاؤُكُمْ
وَقَالُوا مَا هَٰذَا إِلَّا إِفْكٌ مُّفْتَرًى
وَقَالَ الَّذِينَ كَفَرُوا لِلْحَقِّ لَمَّا
جَاءَهُمْ إِنْ هَٰذَا إِلَّا سِحْرٌ مُّبِينٌ

3851. *Walī* in Arabic may mean Friend either in the sense of Protector and Benefactor or in the sense of the Beloved. The tie of benevolence, confidence, and friendship is implied, either active or passive. The angels first proclaim their dependence on Allah and their need of His protection, and then disclaim any idea of their having protected or encouraged the false worshippers to worship beings other than Allah. They go further, and suggest that when men pretended to worship angels, they worshipped, not angels, but Jinns. See next note.

3852. *Jinns*: see 6:100 and n. 929. The false worshippers pretended to worship the bright and radiant angels of good, but in reality worshipped the dark and hidden forces of evil—the devils hidden within themselves or in the life around them. They trusted and believed in such forces of evil, although such forces of evil had really no power.

3853. The supposed "rivals" of Allah—the false things whereon men set their hopes and fears—will have no power whatever when true values are restored; and the Fire—the Penalty—which they doubted or derided, will become the dominating thing in their experience.

3854. Apart from the worship of Evil in the guise of the Powers of Light, there is another form of false worship, which depends on ancestral tradition. "Why" it is said "should we not do as our fathers did?" They reject a new prophet of Truth simply because his teaching does not agree with the ways of their ancestors. The answer to this is given in verse 44 below. But meanwhile the rejectors' objection to new Truth is stated in three forms: (1) our ancestors knew nothing of this: (2) The story of inspiration is false; it is merely an invention; we do not believe in inspiration: (3) when in some particular points, the new Truth does work wonders in men's hearts, they account for it by saying it is magic. The third objection is merely traditional. What is magic? If it is merely deception by the fact that the Messenger who comes with new spiritual Truth is acknowledged to be truthful in other relations of life: why should he be false where his preaching brings him no gain but much sorrow and persecution? For the ancestral objection see next note.

44. But We had not given
Them Books which they could
Study, nor sent messengers[3855]
To them before thee
As Warners.

٤٤ وَمَآ ءَاتَيْنَٰهُم مِّن كُتُبٍ يَدْرُسُونَهَا ۖ
وَمَآ أَرْسَلْنَآ إِلَيْهِمْ قَبْلَكَ مِن نَّذِيرٍ

45. And their predecessors rejected
(The Truth); these have
Not received a tenth
Of what We had granted[3856]
To those: yet when they
rejected
My messengers, how (terrible)
Was My rejection (of them)!

٤٥ وَكَذَّبَ ٱلَّذِينَ مِن قَبْلِهِمْ
وَمَا بَلَغُوا۟ مِعْشَارَ مَآ ءَاتَيْنَٰهُمْ
فَكَذَّبُوا۟ رُسُلِى ۖ
فَكَيْفَ كَانَ نَكِيرِ

SECTION 6.

46. Say: "I do admonish you
On one point: that ye
Do stand up before Allah—
(It may be) in pairs,[3857]
Or (it may be) singly—
And reflect (within yourselves):
Your Companion is not[3858]
Possessed: he is no less
Than a Warner to you,
In face of a terrible
Penalty."

٤٦ قُلْ إِنَّمَآ أَعِظُكُم بِوَٰحِدَةٍ ۖ
أَن تَقُومُوا۟ لِلَّهِ مَثْنَىٰ وَفُرَٰدَىٰ
ثُمَّ تَتَفَكَّرُوا۟ ۚ مَا بِصَاحِبِكُم مِّن جِنَّةٍ ۚ
إِنْ هُوَ إِلَّا نَذِيرٌ لَّكُم
بَيْنَ يَدَىْ عَذَابٍ شَدِيدٍ

47. Say: "No reward do I
Ask of you: it is (all)
In your interest: my reward[3859]

٤٧ قُلْ مَا سَأَلْتُكُم مِّنْ أَجْرٍ فَهُوَ لَكُمْ ۖ
إِنْ أَجْرِىَ

3855. The ancestors (as in the case of the Arabs of the Times of Ignorance) had received no revelation of the clear kind which a messenger and a Book bring them. This is a reason for welcoming, not for rejecting, new Truth.

3856. Passing to Peoples before the immediate ancestors, the People of the Book, or the People of Saba' and 'Ād and Thamūd, had received favours and gifts, power and wealth, ten times more than were enjoyed by the Pagan Quraysh. Yet when they turned away from them, and what terrible consequences descended on them when they lost Allah's Grace! This should make everyone humble, not least the posterity of Muhammad the Messenger if they forsake Allah's Truths! For they have received a higher Teaching!

3857. A crowd mentality is not the best for the perception of the final spiritual truths. For these, it is necessary that each soul should commune within itself with earnest sincerity as before Allah: if it requires a Teacher, let it seek out one, or it may be that it wants the strengthening of the inner convictions that dawn on it, by the support of a sympathiser or friend. But careful and heartfelt reflection is necessary to appraise the higher Truths.

3858. Note that in verses 46, 47, 48 , 49 and 50, arguments are suggested to the Prophet, by which he can convince any right-thinking man of his sincerity and truth. Here the argument is that he is not possessed or out of his mind. If he is different from ordinary men, it is because he had to give a warning of a terrible spiritual danger to the men whom he loves but who will not understand his Message.

3859. *Cf.* 10:72. The second argument is that he has nothing to gain from them. His message is for their own good. He is willing to suffer persecution and insult, because he has to fulfil his mission from Allah.

Is only due from Allah:
And He is Witness
To all things."

إِلَّا عَلَى ٱللَّهِ وَهُوَ عَلَىٰ كُلِّ شَىْءٍ شَهِيدٌ

48. Say: "Verily my Lord
Doth cast the (mantle
Of) Truth (over His servants)—[3860]
He that has full knowledge
Of (all) that is hidden."

٤٨ قُلْ إِنَّ رَبِّى يَقْذِفُ بِٱلْحَقِّ
عَلَّٰمُ ٱلْغُيُوبِ

49. Say: "The Truth has arrived,
And Falsehood neither creates[3861]
Anything new, nor restores
Anything."

٤٩ قُلْ جَآءَ ٱلْحَقُّ
وَمَا يُبْدِئُ ٱلْبَٰطِلُ وَمَا يُعِيدُ

50. Say: "If I am astray,
I only stray to the loss
Of my own soul: but if
I receive guidance, it is [3862]
Because of the inspiration
Of my Lord to me:
It is He Who hears
All things, and is (ever) near."

٥٠ قُلْ إِن ضَلَلْتُ
فَإِنَّمَآ أَضِلُّ عَلَىٰ نَفْسِى
وَإِنِ ٱهْتَدَيْتُ فَبِمَا يُوحِىٓ إِلَىَّ رَبِّىٓ
إِنَّهُۥ سَمِيعٌ قَرِيبٌ

51. If thou couldst but see
When they will quake
With terror; but then
There will be no escape[3863]
(For them), and they will be
Seized from a position
(Quite) near.

٥١ وَلَوْ تَرَىٰٓ إِذْ فَزِعُوا۟
فَلَا فَوْتَ وَأُخِذُوا۟ مِن
مَّكَانٍ قَرِيبٍ

3860. Allah's Truth is so vast that no man in this life can compass the whole of it. But Allah in His mercy selects His servants on whom it is cast like a mantle. They see enough to be able to teach their fellow men. It is through that mantle—that mission received from Allah—that a messenger can speak with authority to men. He cannot explain the exact mystery of inspiration, but he *knows* it is from Allah, and this is his third argument.

3861. The fourth argument is that the Truth is final: it does not come and go: it creates new situations and new developments, and if by chance it *seems* to be defeated for a time, it comes back and restores the true balance—unlike Falsehood, which by its very nature is doomed to perish: 17:81. The Prophet's credentials are known by the test of Time. This was already becoming apparent to discerning eyes when this Sūrah was revealed in Makkah, but it became clear to the whole world with the story of Islām's progress in Madīnah.

3862. If it could possibly be supposed that the Prophet was a self-deceived visionary, it would affect him only, and could not fail to appear in his personality. But in fact he was steady in his constancy and Faith, and he not only went from strength to strength, but won the enduring and wholehearted love and devotion of his nearest and dearest and of those who most came into contact with him. How was this possible, unless he had the Truth and the inspiration of Allah behind him? This is the fifth and last argument in this passage.

3863. After the arguments for the reality and triumph of Truth, we are asked to contemplate the position of the opposers of Truth when Truth is established. They will be struck with terror: For Truth is all-compelling. They will wish they could get away from that position, but that would be impossible. They will not be able to move far; they will be held fast to the consequences of their own earlier conduct. They will be caught quite close to the point of their departure from Truth.

52. And they will say, "We do believe (now) In the (Truth)"; but how[3864] Could they receive (Faith) From a position (so) far off—	وَقَالُوٓاْ ءَامَنَّا بِهِۦ ﴿٥٢﴾ وَأَنَّىٰ لَهُمُ ٱلتَّنَاوُشُ مِن مَّكَانٍۭ بَعِيدٍ
53. Seeing that they did reject Faith (entirely) before, and That they (continually) cast[3865] (Slanders) on the Unseen From a position far off?	وَقَدْ كَفَرُواْ بِهِۦ مِن قَبْلُ ﴿٥٣﴾ وَيَقْذِفُونَ بِٱلْغَيْبِ مِن مَّكَانٍۭ بَعِيدٍ
54. And between them And their desires, Is placed a barrier,[3866] As was done in the past With their partisans:[3867] For they were indeed In suspicious (disquieting) doubt.[3868]	وَحِيلَ بَيْنَهُمْ وَبَيْنَ مَا يَشْتَهُونَ ﴿٥٤﴾ كَمَا فُعِلَ بِأَشْيَاعِهِم مِّن قَبْلُ إِنَّهُمْ كَانُواْ فِي شَكٍّ مُّرِيبٍۭ

3864. They will now profess their faith in Truth, but of what value will such a profession be? Faith is a belief in things unseen: now everything is plain and open before them. The position in which they could have received Faith is left far off behind them, when Truth was struggling and asked for help or asylum, and they cruelly, arrogantly, insultingly repudiated Truth.

3865. Not only did they reject the Truth of the Unseen (the true Reality), but they spread all sorts of false and malicious insinuations at the preachers of Truth, calling them dishonest men, liars, hypocrites, and so on. They did it like a coward taking up a sneaking position far from the fight and speeding arrows at a distant target.

3866. What they desire is to suppress Truth and to indulge in the satisfaction of their own evil, selfish motives. They will be baulked in both, and that itself will be their anguish and punishment. That had always been the law in the eternal struggle between Right and Wrong. *Cf.* Shakespeare, (Trolius and Cressida. i. 3. 116). "Right and wrong. Between whose endless jar justice resides." All partisans of such cliques have always suffered the same fate.

3867. Note that verses 51-54 are a powerful description of the conflict between right and wrong, and may be understood in many meanings. (1) The description applies to the position in the final Hereafter, as compared with the position in this life. (2) It applies to the position of triumphant Islam in Madīnah and later, as compared with the position of persecuted Islam in its early days in Makkah. (3) It applies to the reversal of the position of right and wrong at various phases of the world's history, or of (4) individual history.

3868. *Cf.* 14:9, and see n. 1884.

INTRODUCTION TO SŪRAH 35—*FĀṬIR*

See Introduction to the last Sūrah.

This Sūrah deals with the mystery of Creation and its maintenance, with various forces typified by the wings of Angels. Whether we look to outer nature or to man, Allah's Grace proclaims His Glory, and protects His votaries from Evil.

It is an early Makkan Sūrah, but its chronology has no significance.

Summary—The forces which maintain Creation, as typified by angels, were themselves created by Allah, to Whom alone all praise is due: all else is naught (35:1-26, and C. 192).

All good is from Allah: who then will choose Evil, and reach the doom that goes with Evil? (35:27-45, and C. 193).

C. 192.—Allah is the source of all things: all Power,
(35:1-26.) Wisdom, Beauty, and Truth flow from Him.
It is Evil that deceives and plots in the dark.
All knowledge is with Allah. The things
That are good and pure and true are not
As the things that are evil, deceitful, and false.
Allah is free of all needs: it is we
That need Him: let us seek His love and live.
His Message will save us from wrong, while dark
Is the fate of those who reject Him.
Praise and glory to Him, the Cherisher of all!

Sūrah 35.

Fāṭir (The Originator of Creation)

In the name of Allah, Most Gracious,
Most Merciful.

بسم الله الرحمن الرحيم

1. Praise be to Allah,[3869]
Who created (out of nothing)[3870]
The heavens and the earth,
Who made the angels[3871]
Messengers with wings—
Two, or three, or four (Pairs):
He adds to Creation[3872]
As He pleases: for Allah
Has power over all things.

(١) الحمد لله فاطر السموت والأرض
جاعل الملئكة رسلا أولي
أجنحة مثنى وثلث وربع
يزيد في الخلق ما يشاء
إن الله على كل شيء قدير

2. What Allah out of His Mercy
Doth bestow on mankind
There is none can withhold:
What He doth withhold,
There is none can grant,[3873]
Apart from Him:

(٢) ما يفتح الله للناس
من رحمة فلا ممسك لها
وما يمسك فلا مرسل له من بعده

3869. See n. 3785 to 34:1. When we praise Allah, it means that we understand and bring to mind that His glory and power are exercised for the good of His Creation, and this is the subject matter of the Sūrah.

3870. As man's knowledge of the processes of nature advances, he sees how complex is the evolution of matter itself, leaving out the question of Life and the spiritual forces, which are beyond the ken of experimental science. But this knowledge itself becomes a sort of "veil of Light"; man becomes so conscious of the proximate causes, that he is apt, in his pride, to forget the primal Cause, the Cause of Causes, the ultimate Hand of Allah in Creation. And then, Creation is such a complex process; see some of the ideas involved explained by different words in n. 120 to 2:117. The word *faṭara* here used means the creation of primeval matter, to which further creative processes have to be added by the Hand of Allah, or Allah "adds to His Creation as He pleases", not only in quantity, but in qualities, function, relations, and variations in infinite ways.

3871. The grosser ideas which men have of angels must be dismissed from our minds. They are beings expressive of qualities or powers, which may be typified by "wings". We need not suppose that angelic "wings" have muscles and feathers, like the wings of birds. If they had, how could there be three, or any odd number? We may suppose "two, three, or four" to refer to pairs of wings. But we must not suppose "two, three, or four" to express precise numbers, for in sacred literature we find mention of angels with six hundred wings. And we can imagine angels with just one pair of wings. They are Messengers or Instruments of Allah's Will, and may have a few or numerous Errands entrusted to them. *Cf.* the description of the Spirit of Inspiration in 26:193, and of the spirits or angels for executing the Commands of Allah in 79:1-5.

3872. See n. 3870 above, where the complexities of the creative processes is referred to. Allah's creation did not stop at some past time: it continues, for He has all power, and His mercies are ever poured forth without stint.

3873. As Allah is the Creator and Sustainer of all beings and things, so does His Kindness extend to all Creatures. No one can intercept Allah's mercies and gifts. Whatever is His Will and Plan and Purpose He can and does carry out. And if from any creature He withholds any particular gifts, there is no other person or power that can give those gifts. But such withholding is not arbitrary. He is full of wisdom and goodness, and every act of His, whether He withholds or gives, is full of kindness and mercy to His creatures.

And He is the Exalted
In Power, Full of Wisdom.

وَهُوَ الْعَزِيزُ الْحَكِيمُ

3. O men! call to mind
The grace of Allah unto you!
Is there a Creator, other[3874]
Than Allah, to give you
Sustenance from heaven
Or earth? There is
No god but He: how
Then are ye deluded
Away from the Truth?

٣ يَا أَيُّهَا النَّاسُ اذْكُرُوا نِعْمَتَ اللَّهِ عَلَيْكُمْ
هَلْ مِنْ خَالِقٍ غَيْرُ اللَّهِ يَرْزُقُكُمْ
مِنَ السَّمَاءِ وَالْأَرْضِ لَا إِلَٰهَ إِلَّا هُوَ
فَأَنَّىٰ تُؤْفَكُونَ

4. And if they reject thee,
So were messengers rejected[3875]
Before thee: to Allah
Go back for decision
All affairs.

٤ وَإِنْ يُكَذِّبُوكَ فَقَدْ كُذِّبَتْ رُسُلٌ مِنْ قَبْلِكَ
وَإِلَى اللَّهِ تُرْجَعُ الْأُمُورُ

5. O men! certainly
The promise of Allah[3876]
Is true. Let not then
This present life deceive you,[3877]
Nor let the Chief Deceiver
Deceive you about Allah.

٥ يَا أَيُّهَا النَّاسُ إِنَّ وَعْدَ اللَّهِ حَقٌّ
فَلَا تَغُرَّنَّكُمُ الْحَيَاةُ الدُّنْيَا
وَلَا يَغُرَّنَّكُمْ بِاللَّهِ الْغَرُورُ

6. Verily Satan is an enemy
To you: so treat him[3878]
As an enemy. He only
Invites his adherents,
That they may become
Companions of the Blazing Fire.

٦ إِنَّ الشَّيْطَانَ لَكُمْ عَدُوٌّ فَاتَّخِذُوهُ عَدُوًّا
إِنَّمَا يَدْعُو حِزْبَهُ لِيَكُونُوا
مِنْ أَصْحَابِ السَّعِيرِ

3874. As the primal Cause of all things is Allah, an appeal is made to man to turn to Allah instead of running after false fancies. Allah is not only the source, but the centre of all life and activity, and all affairs return to Him. The world is sustained, and human life is sustained, by Allah's grace and providence. "Sustenance" is to be taken, in Quranic language, for all that helps to maintain and develop every aspect of life, physical and spiritual. It would be the height of folly, then, for man to ignore Allah's gracious Message, as explained in His Revelation.

3875. And yet there will be human perversity which will reject the True and accept the False. The Prophet of Allah is not discouraged by this, as everything ultimately returns to Allah, and we must trust His Wisdom in His Universal Plan. (R).

3876. In verse 3 above the appeal was on the basis of the Past and the Present; now the appeal is on the basis of the Future. Allah's grace has promised us the Garden of Bliss; His justice has promised us the Fire of Suffering. Both promises are certain to be fulfilled. On which side shall we range ourselves?

3877. *Cf.* 31:33 and n. 3624. The deception of Evil takes two forms. (1) The seductive temptations of this world may deceive us into forgetting the Hereafter. (2) The Arch-Enemy himself may so blind our spiritual vision that we may say with him, "Evil! be thou my good!" We may be misled be easy stages. Are we on our guard?

3878. Evil is our enemy and should be treated as such. It is really foreign to our nature, however much it may disguise itself to deceive us as our friend, or a part of our nature. Personifying the Spirit of Evil, we may say that he wants us to share in his own damnation. Shall we allow ourselves to fall into his snare?

7\. For those who reject Allah,[3879]
Is a terrible Penalty: but
For those who believe
And work righteous deeds,
Is Forgiveness, and
A magnificent Reward.

(٧) ٱلَّذِينَ كَفَرُوا۟ لَهُمْ عَذَابٌ شَدِيدٌ ۖ
وَٱلَّذِينَ ءَامَنُوا۟ وَعَمِلُوا۟ ٱلصَّـٰلِحَـٰتِ
لَهُم مَّغْفِرَةٌ وَأَجْرٌ كَبِيرٌ

SECTION 2.

8\. Is he, then, to whom
The evil of his conduct
Is made alluring, so
That he looks upon it[3880]
As good, (equal to one
Who is rightly guided)?
For Allah leaves to stray
Whom He wills, and guides
Whom He wills. So
Let not thy soul go out
In (vainly) sighing after them:
For Allah knows well
All that they do!

(٨) أَفَمَن زُيِّنَ لَهُۥ سُوٓءُ
عَمَلِهِۦ فَرَءَاهُ حَسَنًا ۖ
فَإِنَّ ٱللَّهَ يُضِلُّ مَن
يَشَآءُ وَيَهْدِى مَن يَشَآءُ ۖ
فَلَا تَذْهَبْ نَفْسُكَ عَلَيْهِمْ حَسَرَٰتٍ ۚ
إِنَّ ٱللَّهَ عَلِيمٌۢ بِمَا يَصْنَعُونَ

9\. It is Allah Who sends
Forth the Winds, so that
They raise up the Clouds,[3881]
And We drive them
To a Land that is dead,
And revive the earth therewith
After its death: even so
(Will be) the Resurrection!

(٩) وَٱللَّهُ ٱلَّذِىٓ أَرْسَلَ ٱلرِّيَـٰحَ
فَتُثِيرُ سَحَابًا فَسُقْنَـٰهُ إِلَىٰ بَلَدٍ مَّيِّتٍ
فَأَحْيَيْنَا بِهِ ٱلْأَرْضَ بَعْدَ مَوْتِهَا ۚ
كَذَٰلِكَ ٱلنُّشُورُ

3879\. To reject Allah is to reject all the good which He has implanted in our nature. Are we going to be false to the true Pattern according to which He created us, and suffer the consequences? Or are we going to be true to that Pattern and achieve the high and noble Destiny intended for us?

3880\. *Cf.* n. 3877 above. When a stage is reached at which a man accepts Evil as his Good, his case is hopeless. Can such a man profit by preaching or guidance? He has himself deliberately rejected all guidance. Such a man is best left to stray. Perhaps, even in the paths in which he is straying, some sudden flash of light may come to him! That may be as Allah wills in His holy and wise Purpose and Plan. But the man of God is not to worry or feel disheartened by such men's attitude. He must go on tilling the soil that is open to him. For Allah's Plan may work in all sorts of unexpected ways, as in the allegory in the next verse. (R).

3881\. The allegory here is double. (1) Dry, unpromising soil may seem, to all intents and purposes, dead; there is no source of water near; moisture is sucked up by the sun's heat in a far-off ocean, and clouds are formed; winds arise; it seems as if the wind "bloweth as it listeth", but it is really Allah's Providence that drives it to the dead land; the rain falls, and behold! there is life and motion and beauty everywhere! So in the spiritual world. Allah's Revelation is His Mercy and His Rain; there may be the individual resurrection (*Nushūr*) or unfolding of a soul. (2) So again, may be the general Resurrection (*Nushūr*), the unfolding of a new World in the Hereafter, out of an old World that is folded up and dead (*Takwīr*, S. 81).

10. If any do seek
For glory and power—[3882]
To Allah belong
All glory and power.
To Him mount up
(All) Words of Purity:
It is He Who exalts
Each Deed of Righteousness.
Those that lay Plots[3883]
Of Evil—for them
Is a Penalty terrible;
And the plotting of such
Will be void (of result).

١٠ مَن كَانَ يُرِيدُ ٱلْعِزَّةَ فَلِلَّهِ ٱلْعِزَّةُ جَمِيعًا
إِلَيْهِ يَصْعَدُ ٱلْكَلِمُ ٱلطَّيِّبُ
وَٱلْعَمَلُ ٱلصَّٰلِحُ يَرْفَعُهُۥ
وَٱلَّذِينَ يَمْكُرُونَ ٱلسَّيِّـَٔاتِ
لَهُمْ عَذَابٌ شَدِيدٌ
وَمَكْرُ أُوْلَٰٓئِكَ هُوَ يَبُورُ

11. And Allah did create[3884]
You from dust;
Then[3885] from a sperm drop;
Then He made you
In pairs. And no female
Conceives, or lays down
(Her load), but with His
Knowledge. Nor is a man
Long-lived granted length
Of days, nor is a part
Cut off from his life,
But is in a Decree[3886]
(Ordained). All this
Is easy for Allah.[3887]

١١ وَٱللَّهُ خَلَقَكُم مِّن تُرَابٍ
ثُمَّ مِن نُّطْفَةٍ ثُمَّ جَعَلَكُمْ أَزْوَٰجًا
وَمَا تَحْمِلُ مِنْ أُنثَىٰ
وَلَا تَضَعُ إِلَّا بِعِلْمِهِۦ
وَمَا يُعَمَّرُ مِن مُّعَمَّرٍ وَلَا يُنقَصُ
مِنْ عُمُرِهِۦٓ إِلَّا فِى كِتَٰبٍ
إِنَّ ذَٰلِكَ عَلَى ٱللَّهِ يَسِيرٌ

3882. Good and Evil are to be distinguished sharply. No good is ever lost: it goes up to the Throne of Allah. The humblest Good, in word or deed, is exalted to high rank. If man seeks for mere glory and power, there is no such thing apart from Allah. But seeking Allah, we attain to the highest glory and power.

3883. It is the nature of Evil to work underground, to hide from the Light, to plot against Righteousness: but Evil inevitably carries its own punishment. Its plots must fail miserably. And eventually Evil itself is to be blotted out.

3884. *Cf.* 18:37 and n. 2379; 22:5 and n. 2773; and 30:20 and n. 3524. Here the argument is that man's physical origin is lowly; his physical body is but dust; his life-sperm issues from a part of his body which he hides and considers as a place of shame; and the mystery of sex shows that no one individual among mankind is sufficient for himself. Glory and power and knowledge are not in him, but in Allah, from Whom alone he derives any glory, or power, or knowledge that he possesses.

3885. "Then" in this and the following clause refers, not to stages of time, but to stages in the argument. It is almost equivalent to "further", "also", and "in addition".

3886. Things that appear most secret and mysterious to man are all known and ordained by Allah. They are all subject to Allah's Laws and Decrees. The mystery of human birth (see n. 3625 to 31:34), the mystery of sex, the mystery of Life and Death and many other things, seem to man inexplicable. But they are all ordained by Allah, and their reasons are fully known to Him.

3887. Man's knowledge may be acquired laboriously and may be a burden to him. Allah's knowledge is different; it is no task or burden to Him. *Cf.* 33:19 and 30.

12. Nor are the two bodies[3888]
Of flowing water alike—
The one palatable, sweet,
And pleasant to drink,
And the other, salty
And bitter. Yet from each
(Kind of water) do ye
Eat flesh fresh and tender,[3889]
And ye extract ornaments[3890]
To wear; and thou seest
The ships therein that plough
The waves, that ye may
Seek (thus) of the Bounty
Of Allah that ye
May be grateful.

١٢ وَمَا يَسْتَوِي الْبَحْرَانِ
هَٰذَا عَذْبٌ فُرَاتٌ سَائِغٌ شَرَابُهُ
وَهَٰذَا مِلْحٌ أُجَاجٌ
وَمِن كُلٍّ تَأْكُلُونَ لَحْمًا طَرِيًّا
وَتَسْتَخْرِجُونَ حِلْيَةً تَلْبَسُونَهَا
وَتَرَى الْفُلْكَ فِيهِ مَوَاخِرَ لِتَبْتَغُوا مِن فَضْلِهِ
وَلَعَلَّكُمْ تَشْكُرُونَ

13. He merges Night into Day,[3891]
And He merges Day
Into Night, and He has
Subjected the sun and
The moon (to His Law):[3892]
Each one runs its course
For a term appointed.
Such is Allah your Lord:[3893]
To Him belongs all Dominion.
And those whom ye invoke

١٣ يُولِجُ اللَّيْلَ فِي النَّهَارِ وَيُولِجُ النَّهَارَ
فِي اللَّيْلِ وَسَخَّرَ الشَّمْسَ وَالْقَمَرَ
كُلٌّ يَجْرِي لِأَجَلٍ مُّسَمًّى
ذَٰلِكُمُ اللَّهُ رَبُّكُمْ لَهُ الْمُلْكُ
وَالَّذِينَ تَدْعُونَ

3888. See 25:53 and notes 3111 and 3112. The great salt Ocean with its seas and gulfs is all one; and the great masses of sweet water in rivers, lakes, ponds, and underground springs are also one; and each is connected with the other by the constant circulation going on, which sucks up vapours, carries them about in clouds or atmospheric moisture, and again brings them condensed into water or snow or hail to mingle with rivers and streams and get back into the Ocean.

3889. For this whole passage see 26:14 and notes 2034 and 2035. Both from the sea and from rivers and lakes we get fish, of which some kinds have a flesh particularly fresh and tender, and of a most delicate flavour.

3890. Such as pearls and coral from the sea, and such delicately tinted stones as the *'Aqīq* (carnelian), the agate, the goldstone, or other varieties of quartz pebbles found in riverbeds, and considered as gems. Many such are found in the Ken river in Banda District (in India). Some river sands also yield minute quantities of gold. In large navigable rivers and big lakes like those of North America, as well as in the sea, there are highways for shipping and commerce. (R).

3891. *Cf.* 22:61. The phases of Light in nature may have other uses. But for man they mark periods of rest and activity, and have great influence on his physical, moral, and spiritual life.

3892. *Cf.* 13:2. The sun and the moon mark phases of light, and serve man during the periods of the day and night. The sun marks the seasons, and is the source of heat and energy and physical life for the whole solar system. The sun and the moon run according to fixed laws, and they will continue to do so, not forever, but for the period appointed for their duration by Allah.

3893. Allah's might and majesty, and Allah's goodness and wisdom, having been shown by a few examples, it follows that it is folly to seek or worship any other power but Allah. It only throws off man into false paths, and takes him farther and farther away from the Truth.

Besides Him have not
The least power.[3894]

مِن دُونِهِۦ مَا يَمۡلِكُونَ مِن قِطۡمِيرٍ

14. If ye invoke them,
They will not listen
To your call, and if[3895]
They were to listen,
They cannot answer
Your (prayer). On the Day
Of Judgement they will reject[3896]
Your "Partnership". And none,
(O man!) can tell thee[3897]
(The Truth) like the One
Who is acquainted with all things.

١٤ إِن تَدۡعُوهُمۡ لَا يَسۡمَعُواْ دُعَآءَكُمۡ
وَلَوۡ سَمِعُواْ مَا ٱسۡتَجَابُواْ لَكُمۡۖ
وَيَوۡمَ ٱلۡقِيَٰمَةِ يَكۡفُرُونَ
بِشِرۡكِكُمۡۚ
وَلَا يُنَبِّئُكَ مِثۡلُ خَبِيرٖ

SECTION 3.

15. O ye men! It is
Ye that have need
Of Allah: but Allah is[3898]
The One Free of all wants,
Worthy of all praise.

١٥ يَٰٓأَيُّهَا ٱلنَّاسُ أَنتُمُ ٱلۡفُقَرَآءُ إِلَى ٱللَّهِۖ
وَٱللَّهُ هُوَ ٱلۡغَنِيُّ ٱلۡحَمِيدُ

16. If He so pleased, He
Could blot you out
And bring in
A New Creation

١٦ إِن يَشَأۡ يُذۡهِبۡكُمۡ
وَيَأۡتِ بِخَلۡقٖ جَدِيدٖ

17. Nor is that (at all)
Difficult for Allah.[3899]

١٧ وَمَا ذَٰلِكَ عَلَى ٱللَّهِ بِعَزِيزٖ

3894. *Qiṭmīr*: the thin, white skin that covers the date stone. It has neither strength nor texture, and has no value whatever. Any one relying on any power other than that of Allah relies on nothing whatever. The *Qiṭmīr* is worse than the proverbial "broken reed", *Cf.* 4:53 and 4:124, where the word *naqīr*, 'the groove in a date stone', is used similarly for a thing of no value or significance.

3895. False or imaginary objects of worship serve no purpose whatever. They cannot hear; if they could hear, they could not grant prayers or petitions. In fact, if they are real creatures, such as angels or deified human beings, they will very rightly repudiate any such worship as brings them into competition or "partnership" with Allah. See next note.

3896. *Cf.* 10:28 and n. 1418; also 34:40-41. No false ideas or false impressions will remain when true values are restored. Why not then accept the Truth now in this life, and get on to the true path of Grace?

3897. None can tell you the Truth better than He Who is All-Wise and All-Knowing. Why not accept His Message and receive His guidance?

3898. What is man that Allah should care for him, instruct him, and send him special messengers to warn him of danger and harm? It is man that depends on Allah and has need of Him every moment of his life. Allah has no need of him, but He bestows His Grace on him as on all His creatures, out of His unbounded Mercy and loving kindness. If it were Allah's Will, He could blot out man for his rebellion and create an entirely new world.

3899. There is no limit to Allah's creative power, nor is His creative energy anything rare or unusual. This is the force of the word *'azīz* here. Allah's creative energy is exercised every moment, and it is the normal condition in the universe.

18. Nor can a bearer[3900] of burdens
Bear another's burden.
If one heavily laden should
Call another to (bear) his load,
Not the least portion of it
Can be carried (by the other),
Even though he be nearly[3901]
Related. Thou canst but
Admonish such as fear
Their Lord unseen[3902]
And establish regular Prayer.[3903]
And whoever purifies himself
Does so for the benefit
Of his own soul; and
The destination (of all)
Is to Allah.

﴿١٨﴾ وَلَا تَزِرُ وَازِرَةٌ وِزْرَ أُخْرَىٰ ۚ
وَإِن تَدْعُ مُثْقَلَةٌ إِلَىٰ حِمْلِهَا
لَا يُحْمَلْ مِنْهُ شَيْءٌ
وَلَوْ كَانَ ذَا قُرْبَىٰٓ ۗ
إِنَّمَا تُنذِرُ ٱلَّذِينَ يَخْشَوْنَ
رَبَّهُم بِٱلْغَيْبِ وَأَقَامُوا۟ ٱلصَّلَوٰةَ ۚ
وَمَن تَزَكَّىٰ فَإِنَّمَا يَتَزَكَّىٰ لِنَفْسِهِۦ ۚ
وَإِلَى ٱللَّهِ ٱلْمَصِيرُ

19. The blind and the seeing
Are not alike;[3904]

﴿١٩﴾ وَمَا يَسْتَوِى ٱلْأَعْمَىٰ وَٱلْبَصِيرُ

20. Nor are the depths
Of Darkness and the Light;

﴿٢٠﴾ وَلَا ٱلظُّلُمَٰتُ وَلَا ٱلنُّورُ

21. Nor are the (chilly) shade
And the (genial) heat of the sun:

﴿٢١﴾ وَلَا ٱلظِّلُّ وَلَا ٱلْحَرُورُ

3900. Bearer: *ḥāmilatun*: feminine in Arabic, as referring to the soul (*nafs*), as in 6:164.

3901. Natural relationship may be considered as a reasonable cause or opportunity for bearing each other's burdens. For example, a mother or a father might offer to die for her or his child, and *vice versa*. But this does not apply to spiritual matters. There the responsibility is strictly personal and cannot be transferred to another. In 29:13 we are told that the misleaders "will bear other burdens along with their own": but the context shows that the "other" burdens are the burdens of deluding the others with their falsehoods. Both sins are their own, *viz.*, their original sin, and the sin of deluding the others. But the responsibility will be doubled.

3902. *Bil ghayb:* unseen in the adverbial sense. The man, who, though he does not see Allah, so realises Allah's Presence in himself as if he saw Him, is the man of genuine Faith, and for him Allah's Revelation comes through many channels and is always fruitful.

3903. Prayer is one of the means of purifying ourselves of lower motives in life, for in prayer we seek the Presence of Allah; but the purity which we seek is for our own souls: we confer no favour on Allah or on any Power in the spiritual world, as some imagine who make "gifts" to Allah. In any case the destination of all is to Allah.

3904. Now we are offered some contrasts between those who obey Allah's Law and are thus citizens of Allah's Kingdom and those who are rebels against Allah's Kingdom and are thus outlaws. How can they be considered alike? The godly are like those who see, as contrasted with those who are blind; and their motives and actions are like the purest and highest Light, contrasted with the depths of darkness; or, to take another metaphor, their lives are like the genial and warmth-giving heat of the sun, which benefits all who come within its influence, contrasted with the chilly shadows of gloom in which no vegetation flourishes. (R).

22. Nor are alike those[3905]
That are living and those
That are dead. Allah can
Make any that He wills
To hear; but thou
Canst not make those
To hear who are
(Buried) in graves.

٢٢ وَمَا يَسْتَوِي الْأَحْيَاءُ وَلَا الْأَمْوَاتُ
إِنَّ اللَّهَ يُسْمِعُ مَن يَشَاءُ
وَمَا أَنتَ بِمُسْمِعٍ
مَّن فِي الْقُبُورِ

23. Thou art no other
Than a warner.[3906]

٢٣ إِنْ أَنتَ إِلَّا نَذِيرٌ

24. Verily We have sent thee
In truth, as a bearer
Of glad tidings,[3907]
And as a warner:
And there never was
A people, without a warner
Having lived among them
(In the past).

٢٤ إِنَّا أَرْسَلْنَاكَ
بِالْحَقِّ بَشِيرًا وَنَذِيرًا
وَإِن مِّنْ أُمَّةٍ إِلَّا خَلَا فِيهَا نَذِيرٌ

25. And if they reject thee,
So did their predecessors,
To whom came their messengers
With Clear Signs,
Scriptures[3908]
And the Book
Of Enlightenment.

٢٥ وَإِن يُكَذِّبُوكَ فَقَدْ كَذَّبَ الَّذِينَ
مِن قَبْلِهِمْ جَاءَتْهُمْ رُسُلُهُم بِالْبَيِّنَاتِ
وَبِالزُّبُرِ وَبِالْكِتَابِ الْمُنِيرِ

26. In the end did I
Punish those who rejected
Faith: and how (terrible)[3909]
Was My rejection (of them)!

٢٦ ثُمَّ أَخَذْتُ الَّذِينَ كَفَرُوا
فَكَيْفَ كَانَ نَكِيرِ

3905. The final contrast between the Living and the Dead; those whose future has in it the promise of growth and fulfilment, and those who are inert and on the road to perish. With Allah everything is possible: He can give Life to the Dead. But the human Teacher should not expect that people who are (spiritually) dead and buried will by any chance hear his call.

3906. The function of a Prophet is to preach Allah's Truth, to point out the right Way, to show men the need of repentance, and to warn them against the dangers which they incur by living a life of evil. He cannot compel them to accept the Truth or listen to the Message.

3907. It is Allah Who sends the Revelation. While there is warning in it for the heedless, there is good news (in Christian terms, the gospel) for those who listen and repent. The warning always came to all peoples before punishment.

3908. The three things here mentioned are also mentioned in 3:184, where I have explained the meaning in n. 490. All spiritual teaching centres round the evidences of Allah in our lives, the sublime teaching of men of God, and the rules and laws which guide holy living. (R).

3909. *Cf.* 22:44 and 34:45. The rejecters of Allah hardly realise the terrible consequences to them individually and collectively, if Allah's grace is withdrawn from them and they are left to perish in their own sins and wrongdoing.

C. 193.—(35:27-45.)

Man can see by his own experience
What infinite shades and grades of colour
There are in nature. So are there grades
In the spiritual world. The Good and the True
Understand Allah, Who knows and watches
Over all His creatures. The Good will reach
Eternal Bliss, while the Evil will find
No helper. Arrogance and plotting will be
The undoing of Evil: its doom
Is sure, if it fails to profit by the respite
Granted by the All-Merciful Allah.

SECTION 4.

27. Seest thou not that
Allah sends down rain
From the sky? With it
We then bring out produce
Of various colours.[3910]
And in the mountains
Are tracts white and red,[3911]
Of various shades of colour,
And black intense in hue.

٢٧ أَلَمْ تَرَ أَنَّ ٱللَّهَ أَنزَلَ مِنَ ٱلسَّمَآءِ مَآءً
فَأَخْرَجْنَا بِهِۦ ثَمَرَٰتٍ مُّخْتَلِفًا أَلْوَٰنُهَا ۚ
وَمِنَ ٱلْجِبَالِ جُدَدٌۢ بِيضٌ وَحُمْرٌ
مُّخْتَلِفٌ أَلْوَٰنُهَا وَغَرَابِيبُ سُودٌ

28. And so amongst men
And crawling creatures and cattle,
Are they of various colours.[3912]
Those truly fear Allah,
Among His Servants,
Who have knowledge:[3913]

٢٨ وَمِنَ ٱلنَّاسِ وَٱلدَّوَآبِّ
وَٱلْأَنْعَٰمِ مُخْتَلِفٌ أَلْوَٰنُهُۥ كَذَٰلِكَ ۗ
إِنَّمَا يَخْشَى ٱللَّهَ مِنْ عِبَادِهِ ٱلْعُلَمَٰٓؤُا۟ ۗ

3910. Everyone can see how Allah's artistry produces from rain the wonderful variety of crops and fruits—golden, green, red, yellow, and showing all the most beautiful tints we can think of. And each undergoes in nature the gradual shading off in its transformation from the raw stage to the stage of maturity.

3911. These wonderful colours and shades of colours are to be found not only in vegetation but in rocks and mineral products. There are the white veins of marble and quartz or of chalk, the red laterite, the blue basaltic rocks, the ink-black flints, and all the variety, shade, and gradation of colours. Speaking of mountains, we think of their "azure hue" from a distance, due to atmospheric effects, and these atmospheric effects lead our thoughts to the glories of clouds, sunsets, the zodiacal lights, the *aurora borealis,* and all kinds of Nature's gorgeous pageantry.

3912. In the physical shapes of human and animal life, also, we see variations in shades and gradations of colours of all kinds. But these variations and gradations, marvellous though they be, are as nothing compared with variations and differences in the inner or spiritual world. See next note.

3913. In outer nature we can, through colours, understand and appreciate the finest shades and gradations. But in the spiritual world that variation or gradation is even more subtle and more comprehensive. Who can truly understand it? Only Allah's servants, *who know, i.e.*, who have the inner knowledge which comes through their acquaintance with the spiritual world—it is such people who truly appreciate the inner world, and it is they who know that the fear of Allah is the beginning of wisdom. For such fear is akin to appreciation and love—appreciation of all the marvellous beauties of Allah's outer and inner world ("Allah is Exalted in Might") and love because of his Grace and Kindness ("Oft-Forgiving"). But Allah's forgiveness extends to many who do not truly understand Him.

For Allah is Exalted in Might,
Oft-Forgiving.

إِنَّ ٱللَّهَ عَزِيزٌ غَفُورٌ

29. Those who rehearse the Book
Of Allah, establish regular
Prayer,
And send (in Charity)[3914]
Out of what We have provided
For them, secretly and openly,
Hope for a Commerce[3915]
That will never fail:

(٢٩) إِنَّ ٱلَّذِينَ يَتْلُونَ كِتَٰبَ ٱللَّهِ
وَأَقَامُوا۟ ٱلصَّلَوٰةَ وَأَنفَقُوا۟ مِمَّا
رَزَقْنَٰهُمْ سِرًّا وَعَلَانِيَةً
يَرْجُونَ تِجَٰرَةً لَّن تَبُورَ

30. For He will pay them
Their meed, nay, He will
Give them (even) more
Out of His Bounty:
For He is Oft-Forgiving,[3916]
Most Ready to appreciate
(service).[3917]

(٣٠) لِيُوَفِّيَهُمْ أُجُورَهُمْ
وَيَزِيدَهُم مِّن فَضْلِهِۦٓ
إِنَّهُۥ غَفُورٌ شَكُورٌ

31. That which We have revealed
To thee of the Book
Is the Truth—confirming
What was (revealed) before it:
For Allah is assuredly—
With respect to His servants—
Well acquainted and[3918]
Fully-Observant.

(٣١) وَٱلَّذِىٓ أَوْحَيْنَآ إِلَيْكَ مِنَ ٱلْكِتَٰبِ
هُوَ ٱلْحَقُّ مُصَدِّقًا لِّمَا بَيْنَ يَدَيْهِ
إِنَّ ٱللَّهَ بِعِبَادِهِۦ
لَخَبِيرٌۢ بَصِيرٌ

3914. The man of God takes Allah's Revelation ("the Book") to heart, ever seeks to get closer and closer to Allah ("regular Prayer"), and in doing so, is moved more and more to practical Charity for his fellow-creatures. He is not ashamed of his Charity ("openly"), but he does not do it to be seen of men ("secretly"): he just does what is necessary for his fellow-creatures, whether people talk about it or not.

3915. Here is a metaphor from commerce. The good man's Charity comes not merely out of superfluities, but out of "what Allah has provided" for him. He therefore recognises two things: (1) that his wealth (literal and metaphorical) is not his absolutely, but that it is given to him by Allah: and (2) that he must deny himself the use of some of it, as a merchant puts by some of his wealth to invest as capital. Only, the godly man's Commerce will never fail or fluctuate; because Allah guarantees him the return, and even adds something to the return out of His own Bounty. That is, Allah gives more than ever our merits deserve.

3916. No man is perfect. Everyone has his faults. But when a man tries his best in the service of Allah, his faults are blotted out, and he is treated as if he had committed no faults: "for Allah is Oft-Forgiving, and ready to appreciate service".

3917. *Cf.* 14:5, and n. 2877 for *shakūr.* Allah is ready to recognise, appreciate, and reward the smallest service, without regard to the defects in that service. His gracious acceptance is compared to "gratitude" among men.

3918. All Revelation is one. The Qur'ān therefore confirms the main and uncorrupted features of previous revelations. It must be so, because Allah is fully cognisant of the needs of every age and people; and therefore His Message, while it meets those needs, must in essence be the same. His Messengers did not meet each other as men; but their contact with Allah through inspiration unified their Message. And He cares for and watches over all men, and He knows fully what their needs are, even better than they know themselves.

32. Then[3919] We have given
The Book for inheritance
To such of Our servants
As We have chosen:
But there are among them[3920]
Some who wrong their own
Souls; some who follow
A middle course; and some
Who are, by Allah's leave,
Foremost in good deeds;
That is the highest Grace.

٣٢ ثُمَّ أَوْرَثْنَا ٱلْكِتَٰبَ
ٱلَّذِينَ ٱصْطَفَيْنَا مِنْ عِبَادِنَا
فَمِنْهُمْ ظَالِمٌ لِّنَفْسِهِۦ وَمِنْهُم مُّقْتَصِدٌ
وَمِنْهُمْ سَابِقٌۢ بِٱلْخَيْرَٰتِ بِإِذْنِ ٱللَّهِ
ذَٰلِكَ هُوَ ٱلْفَضْلُ ٱلْكَبِيرُ

33. Gardens of Eternity will they[3921]
Enter: therein will they
Be adorned with bracelets[3922]
Of gold and pearls;
And their garments there
Will be of silk.

٣٣ جَنَّٰتُ عَدْنٍ يَدْخُلُونَهَا يُحَلَّوْنَ
فِيهَا مِنْ أَسَاوِرَ مِن ذَهَبٍ وَلُؤْلُؤًا
وَلِبَاسُهُمْ فِيهَا حَرِيرٌ

34. And they will say:
"Praise be to Allah,
Who has removed from us
(All) sorrow: for our Lord
Is indeed Oft-Forgiving
Ready to appreciate (service):[3923]

٣٤ وَقَالُوا۟ ٱلْحَمْدُ لِلَّهِ
ٱلَّذِىٓ أَذْهَبَ عَنَّا ٱلْحَزَنَ
إِنَّ رَبَّنَا لَغَفُورٌ شَكُورٌ

3919. The force of "then" is that of finality. The Qur'ān is the last Book revealed. Or it may be here to point the contrast between "to thee" in the last verse, *i.e.*, the Holy Prophet, in contradistinction to the People of Islam, who inherited the Book after him.

3920. The custodians of the Qur'ān after the Holy Prophet were the People of Islam. They were chosen for the Book, not in any narrow sense, but in the sense that the Book was given for their age and they were charged to obey it and preserve and propagate it, so that all mankind should receive the Message. But it does not follow that they are all true and faithful to their charge, as indeed we see too painfully around us today. Just as mankind was chosen collectively to be Vicegerents for Allah, and yet some among mankind fell into evil—even so, some in the house of Islam fail to follow the Light given to them, and thus "wrong their own souls". But some follow a middle course; in their case "the spirit is indeed willing, but the flesh is weak": their intentions are good, but they have much to learn yet of the true Muslim life and Muslim virtues. Then there is a third class: they may not indeed be perfect, but both their intentions and their conduct are sound, and they form an example to other men: they are "foremost" in every good deed. They are so, not by their own merits, but by the Grace of Allah. And they have reached the highest Achievement—the salvation, which is typified by the various metaphors that follow.

3921. "The Garden" signifies their environment: all they see about them will give them comfort, rest, and satisfaction, and a feeling of beauty and dignity. The jewels and clothes signify their personal external state: here, again, everything will give them a sense of beauty and dignity, comfort, rest, and satisfaction. And finally, most important of all, comes their internal state, where again they will have the same sense of beauty, dignity, comfort, rest, and satisfaction: this is indicated by their words of Praise (verses 34-35).

3922. *Cf.* 18:31 and 22:23.

3923. *Cf.* above, 35:30. Note how beautifully the argument is rounded off. In verse 30 they were told that "Allah is Oft-Forgiving, Most Ready to appreciate service". Now they have reached the Goal, and they have found the Promise profoundly true. All their hopes are fulfilled, and their sorrows ended.

35. "Who has, out of His Bounty,
Settled us in a Home
That will last: no toil
Nor sense of weariness[3924]
Shall touch us therein."

٣٥ ٱلَّذِىٓ أَحَلَّنَا دَارَ ٱلْمُقَامَةِ مِن فَضْلِهِۦ
لَا يَمَسُّنَا فِيهَا نَصَبٌ وَلَا يَمَسُّنَا فِيهَا لُغُوبٌ

36. But those who reject (Allah)—
For them will be
The Fire of Hell:[3925]
No term shall be determined
For them, so they should die,
Nor shall its Penalty
Be lightened for them.
Thus do We reward
Every ungrateful one!

٣٦ وَٱلَّذِينَ كَفَرُوا۟ لَهُمْ
نَارُ جَهَنَّمَ لَا يُقْضَىٰ عَلَيْهِمْ فَيَمُوتُوا۟
وَلَا يُخَفَّفُ عَنْهُم مِّنْ عَذَابِهَا
كَذَٰلِكَ نَجْزِى كُلَّ كَفُورٍ

37. Therein will they cry
Aloud (for assistance):
"Our Lord! Bring us out:[3926]
We shall work righteousness,[3927]
Not the (deeds) we used
To do!"—"Did We not
Give you long enough life
So that he that would
Should receive admonition?
And (moreover) the warner
Came to you. So taste ye[3928]
(The fruits of your deeds):
For the Wrongdoers
Their is no helper."

٣٧ وَهُمْ يَصْطَرِخُونَ فِيهَا
رَبَّنَآ أَخْرِجْنَا نَعْمَلْ صَٰلِحًا
غَيْرَ ٱلَّذِى كُنَّا نَعْمَلُ
أَوَلَمْ نُعَمِّرْكُم مَّا يَتَذَكَّرُ فِيهِ
مَن تَذَكَّرَ وَجَآءَكُمُ ٱلنَّذِيرُ
فَذُوقُوا۟ فَمَا لِلظَّٰلِمِينَ مِن نَّصِيرٍ

SECTION 5.

38. Verily Allah knows
(All) the hidden things

٣٨ إِنَّ ٱللَّهَ عَٰلِمُ غَيْبِ

3924. In case it should be thought that perpetual happiness might cloy or be dull, as would be the case in this life, it is added—as the experience of those who attain that state—that it is not so on that plane of existence. Not only is there Joy, but it remains fresh and leads to no weariness.

3925. The "Fire" is the opposite of the "Garden". Instead of there being comfort, rest, and satisfaction in their environment, there will be pain, suffering and anguish. Instead of there being dignity there will be humiliation. And there will be no hope of its termination or abatement, not even a hope of annihilation.

3926. *Cf.* 23:107. Not only will their surroundings be the opposite of those in Heaven: their internal state will be one of humiliation, of piteous and fruitless appeals, of vain regrets for a past that cannot be recalled, and vain sighs for a future whose gates they have themselves barred. If they were sent back, they would relapse to their sins. *Cf.* 6:28.

3927. *Cf.* 7:53. Their hankering after another chance, after having deliberately rejected all chances, will have no basis of reason in it.

3928. They had a long enough respite for repentance and amendment. And moreover, besides all the other sources, in nature, history, and their own hearts, by which they could learn of the Right, they had the actual teaching and warning of a messenger whose words spoke directly to them. In the circumstances the Penalty is only the fruit of their own conduct.

Of the heavens and the
earth:[3929]
Verily He has full knowledge
Of all that is
In (men's) hearts.

ٱلسَّمَٰوَٰتِ وَٱلۡأَرۡضِۚ
إِنَّهُۥ عَلِيمُۢ بِذَاتِ ٱلصُّدُورِ

39. He it is that has made
You inheritors in the earth:[3930]
If, then, any do reject
(Allah), their rejection (works)
Against themselves: their
rejection[3931]
But adds to the odium
For the Unbelievers
In the sight of their Lord:
Their rejection but adds
To (their own) undoing.

٣٩ هُوَ ٱلَّذِي جَعَلَكُمۡ خَلَٰٓئِفَ فِي ٱلۡأَرۡضِۚ
فَمَن كَفَرَ فَعَلَيۡهِ كُفۡرُهُۥۖ
وَلَا يَزِيدُ ٱلۡكَٰفِرِينَ
كُفۡرُهُمۡ عِندَ رَبِّهِمۡ إِلَّا مَقۡتٗاۖ
وَلَا يَزِيدُ ٱلۡكَٰفِرِينَ كُفۡرُهُمۡ إِلَّا خَسَارٗا

40. Say: "Have ye seen[3932]
(These) 'Partners' of yours
Whom ye call upon
Besides Allah? Show me
What it is they have created
In the (wide) earth.
Or have they a share
In the heavens? Or
Have We given them a Book
From which they (can derive)
Clear (evidence)?—Nay,
The wrongdoers promise
Each other nothing but
delusions.

٤٠ قُلۡ أَرَءَيۡتُمۡ شُرَكَآءَكُمُ
ٱلَّذِينَ تَدۡعُونَ مِن دُونِ ٱللَّهِ
أَرُونِي مَاذَا خَلَقُواْ مِنَ ٱلۡأَرۡضِ
أَمۡ لَهُمۡ شِرۡكٞ فِي ٱلسَّمَٰوَٰتِ أَمۡ ءَاتَيۡنَٰهُمۡ
كِتَٰبٗا فَهُمۡ عَلَىٰ بَيِّنَتٖ مِّنۡهُۚ
بَلۡ إِن يَعِدُ ٱلظَّٰلِمُونَ
بَعۡضُهُم بَعۡضًا إِلَّا غُرُورًا

3929. Everything that exists is known to Allah: not only concrete things, but feelings, motives, plans, and acts of the will in the human breast.

3930. Inheritors: *khalā'if*. In two senses: (1) as Vicegerents of Allah on earth, and (2) as successors to previous people who forfeited their rights by wrongdoing. The honour and dignity of (1) and the examples of the past in (2) should have kept them straight and made them truly grateful. See also 6:165 and n. 988

3931. Their rejection and ingratitude only causes injury to themselves. They lose all honour and incur odium in the sight of Allah, and they complete their own undoing.

3932. The people who enthrone in their hearts for worship anything besides Allah may well be asked a few questions. Some of such questions are indicated in the text with terse precision: (1) Have you seen these gods of yours? Do they exist? "Seeing" of course does not necessarily mean physical sight. We do not see the air, but no one doubts that it exists. And the air is a physical substance. There are forces that we know exist, but we do not see them. To us, who have Faith, Allah is a truer Reality than anything else that we know, including ourselves. Can the false worshippers say that of any of their false gods? (2) Have your gods created or originated anything on earth? You may worship power or wealth, but that is a scramble for things as between selfish men. Power or wealth does not create new men or new worlds. (3) Have they a share in the ordering of the heavens? "The heavens" may mean what you see in the physical universe of astronomy, or the still subtler inner life. Obviously your false gods fail there. (4) Or have these false gods a book or revelation from the Supreme God, with clear evidence, to give them authority to teach men? The Prophets or Messengers of Allah have such authority, and they bring evidence of the One True God. The fact is that falsehood is falsehood, however much one form of it may support another by delusions.

41. It is Allah Who sustains
The heavens and the earth,[3933]
Lest they cease (to function):
And if they should fail,
There is none—not one—
Can sustain them thereafter:
Verily He is Most Forbearing,[3934]
Oft-Forgiving.

(٤١) إِنَّ ٱللَّهَ يُمْسِكُ
ٱلسَّمَٰوَٰتِ وَٱلْأَرْضَ أَن تَزُولَا
وَلَئِن زَالَتَآ إِنْ أَمْسَكَهُمَا مِنْ أَحَدٍ مِّنۢ بَعْدِهِۦٓ
إِنَّهُۥ كَانَ حَلِيمًا غَفُورًا

42. They swore their strongest oaths
By Allah that if a warner
Came to them, they would
Follow his guidance better[3935]
Than any (other) of the Peoples:
But when a warner came
To them, it has only
Increased their flight
(From righteousness)—

(٤٢) وَأَقْسَمُوا۟ بِٱللَّهِ جَهْدَ
أَيْمَٰنِهِمْ لَئِن جَآءَهُمْ نَذِيرٌ
لَّيَكُونُنَّ أَهْدَىٰ مِنْ إِحْدَى ٱلْأُمَمِ
فَلَمَّا جَآءَهُمْ نَذِيرٌ
مَّا زَادَهُمْ إِلَّا نُفُورًا

43. On account of their arrogance
In the land and their
Plotting of Evil.[3936]
But the plotting of Evil
Will hem in only
The authors thereof. Now
Are they but looking for
The way the ancients[3937]
Were dealt with? But

(٤٣) ٱسْتِكْبَارًا فِى
ٱلْأَرْضِ وَمَكْرَ ٱلسَّيِّئِ
وَلَا يَحِيقُ ٱلْمَكْرُ ٱلسَّيِّئُ إِلَّا بِأَهْلِهِۦ
فَهَلْ يَنظُرُونَ إِلَّا سُنَّتَ ٱلْأَوَّلِينَ

3933. The universe, as we know it, shows not only evidence of initial designs, but also the working of an intelligent Providence, which constantly sustains it. That is Allah. If you could imagine that removed, what is there to keep it going? There would only be chaos.

3934. Allah's world goes on according to the laws and decrees established by Him. There are occasional lapses and deviations on the part of His creatures. But He does not punish every petty fault. One of His merciful qualities is that of repeated forbearance and forgiveness.

3935. *Cf.* 6:157. In the first instance this referred to the Quraysh. Their attitude to the People of the Book had been one of lofty superiority or of insincere excuses. They twitted the Jews and Christians with deviating from their own lights and their own revelations; and for themselves, they said they had received no direct revelation from Allah, or they would have shown themselves the most amenable to discipline, the most ready to follow Allah's Law. This was before the Holy Prophet received his mission from Allah. When he received it and announced it, they turned away from it. They fled from it and put a greater and greater distance between it and themselves. But this is the way of all sinners. They find much to carp at in others, and much to excuse in themselves. But when all grounds for excuse are removed, they will be found, not nearer, but farther and farther away from truth and righteousness.

3936. Two causes are mentioned why the Truth is refused acceptance. (1) Unregenerate man is arrogant, and Truth and Righteousness expose all his pretences. (2) He hopes, by underhanded plots, to undermine Truth and destroy it; but he is caught in his own snares, while Truth marches forward triumphant.

3937. In all history, men who followed evil were dealt with in three stages by Allah: (1) He was forbearing and merciful, and gave them respite; (2) He sent them admonition through his messengers, or His Signs, or His revelation; (3) He dealt out justice and punishment. At any given moment, those given to iniquity may well be asked:"Are you going to wait through all these stages or are you going at once to repent, obtain forgiveness, and walk in the ways of righteousness?"

No change wilt thou find
In Allah's way (of dealing):[3938]
No turning off wilt thou
Find in Allah's way (of dealing).

فَلَن تَجِدَ لِسُنَّتِ ٱللَّهِ تَبْدِيلًا ۖ
وَلَن تَجِدَ لِسُنَّتِ ٱللَّهِ تَحْوِيلًا

44. Do they not travel
Through the earth, and see[3939]
What was the End
Of those before them—
Though they were superior
To them in strength?
Nor is Allah to be frustrated
By anything whatever
In the heavens
Or on earth: for He
Is All-Knowing, All-Powerful.

٤٤ أَوَلَمْ يَسِيرُوا۟ فِى ٱلْأَرْضِ
فَيَنظُرُوا۟ كَيْفَ كَانَ عَٰقِبَةُ ٱلَّذِينَ مِن
قَبْلِهِمْ وَكَانُوٓا۟ أَشَدَّ مِنْهُمْ قُوَّةً ۚ
وَمَا كَانَ ٱللَّهُ لِيُعْجِزَهُۥ مِن شَىْءٍ
فِى ٱلسَّمَٰوَٰتِ وَلَا فِى ٱلْأَرْضِ ۚ
إِنَّهُۥ كَانَ عَلِيمًا قَدِيرًا

45. If Allah were to punish[3940]
Men according to what
They deserve, He would not
Leave on the back
Of the (earth) a single[3941]
Living creature: but He
Gives them respite
For a stated Term:
When their Term expires,
Verily Allah has in His sight[3942]
All His servants.

٤٥ وَلَوْ يُؤَاخِذُ ٱللَّهُ ٱلنَّاسَ
بِمَا كَسَبُوا۟ مَا تَرَكَ
عَلَىٰ ظَهْرِهَا مِن دَآبَّةٍ
وَلَٰكِن يُؤَخِّرُهُمْ إِلَىٰٓ أَجَلٍ مُّسَمًّى ۖ
فَإِذَا جَآءَ أَجَلُهُمْ فَإِنَّ ٱللَّهَ
كَانَ بِعِبَادِهِۦ بَصِيرًۢا

3938. Allah's Laws are fixed, and His ways of dealing with those who follow iniquity are the same in all ages. Our human will may falter or turn away from its course, but Allah's Will ever follows its course and cannot be turned away by any cause whatever.

3939. *Cf.* 30:9. If no other argument will convince men who follow evil, let them travel through space or time, and learn from the experience of others. Evil always came to an evil end. Let not any one individual or generation think that it could escape by some special trick or power. Far wiser and more powerful men were personally brought to account for their iniquities.

3940. *Cf.* 16:61. There would be no salvation for any of us if we went merely on our deserts. It is Allah's mercy that saves us and helps us to a better and better life until we attain the goal of our existence.

3941. *A single living creature.* This may refer to man, the living crawling creature, with so many possibilities and yet so many weaknesses. But it may mean all creatures literally, as the life of this planet more or less centres round the life of man. He has been given dominion on this earth, and in his state of purity he is Allah's vicegerent.

3942. *Has in His sight all creatures: i.e.*, to deal with, according to His Laws of Forbearance, Mercy and Justice: see n. 3937 above. The respite does not mean that any one escapes His vigilant eye. All will be dealt with according to their deeds, with justice tempered with mercy.

INTRODUCTION TO SŪRAH 36—*YĀ SĪN*

See Introduction to S. 34. This particular Sūrah is devoted to the Holy Prophet and the Revelation which he brought. The Abbreviated Letters *Yā Sīn* are usually construed as a title of the Holy Prophet. But it is not permissible to be dogmatic about the meaning of Abbreviated Letters. See Appendix I after S. 2. This Sūrah is considered to be "the heart of the Qur'ān", as it concerns the central figure in the teaching of Islam and the central doctrine of Revelation and the Hereafter. As referring to the Hereafter, it is appropriately read in solemn ceremonies after death.

In chronology it belongs to the middle or early Makkan period.

In S. 37:130 (a cognate Sūrah) occurs the word *Ilyāsīn*: see n. 4115-A.

Summary—The Qur'ān is full of wisdom, and those are unfortunate who cannot profit by it: Parable of the City that defied—all but one—the Messengers of Grace and Mercy (36:1-32, and C. 194).

Various Signs of Allah in nature and Revelation (36:33-50, and C. 195).

The Resurrection and the Hereafter (36:51-83, and C. 195).

C. 194.—The wisdom of Revelation—the Qur'ān received
(36:1-32.) Through the Holy Prophet—is a guide
To the Straight Path, and a warning against
The terrible state in which the yokes
Of Sin enslave us. The righteous receive it
With joy, for they believe in the Hereafter.
Behold, there was once a City, to which
Came two righteous men with the Gospel of Truth,
But they were rejected and persecuted: they were joined
By a third. But the City refused to believe
Or to turn from iniquity. Only one man was found
In its outskirts, to bear witness to Truth,
Faith, and Righteousness, and he did suffer
Martyrdom. He attained Peace, but mourned
For his people, in that they shut the gates
Of Salvation and Allah's Mercy on themselves.
Alas for man's short-sighted folly in defying
The Grace that would shield and deliver him!

Sūrah 36.

Yā Sīn

In the name of Allah, Most Gracious, Most Merciful

1. Yā Sīn.[3943]

2. By the Qur'ān,[3944]
Full of Wisdom—

3. Thou art indeed
One of the messengers,

4. On a Straight Way.

5. It is a Revelation[3945]
Sent down by (Him),
The Exalted in Might,
Most Merciful,

6. In order that thou mayest
Admonish a people,
Whose fathers had received[3946]
No admonition, and who
Therefore remained heedless
(Of the Signs of Allah).

7. The Word is proved true[3947]
Against the greater part of
them;
For they do not believe.

الجزء الثاني والعشرون سُورَةُ يسٓ

بِسْمِ ٱللَّهِ ٱلرَّحْمَٰنِ ٱلرَّحِيمِ

يسٓ ﴿١﴾

وَٱلْقُرْءَانِ ٱلْحَكِيمِ ﴿٢﴾

إِنَّكَ لَمِنَ ٱلْمُرْسَلِينَ ﴿٣﴾

عَلَىٰ صِرَٰطٍ مُّسْتَقِيمٍ ﴿٤﴾

تَنزِيلَ
ٱلْعَزِيزِ ٱلرَّحِيمِ ﴿٥﴾

لِتُنذِرَ قَوْمًا
مَّآ أُنذِرَ ءَابَآؤُهُمْ
فَهُمْ غَٰفِلُونَ ﴿٦﴾

لَقَدْ حَقَّ ٱلْقَوْلُ عَلَىٰٓ
أَكْثَرِهِمْ فَهُمْ لَا يُؤْمِنُونَ ﴿٧﴾

3943. Some Commentators take *Yā* to be the vocative article, and *Sīn* to be the abbreviation of *Insān*, *Sīn* being the only "Firm Letter" in the word. In that case it would be an address to man. "O man!" But "man" in this connection is understood to mean the Leader of man, the noblest of mankind, Muḥammad, the Prophet of Allah. For this Sūrah deals mainly with the Holy Prophet and his Message. But no dogmatic assertion can be made about the Abbreviated Letters, for which see Appendix I, following S. 2. *Yā Sīn* is usually treated as a title of the Holy Prophet.

3944. The best credentials of the Holy Prophet are: (1) the revelation which he brought ("the Qur'ān"), and the heroic unselfish life which he led ("on a Straight Way"). The appeal is therefore made on the testimony of these two facts.

3945. The Revelation again is characterised by two attributes which we find most helpful in contemplating about Allah. It has force and power: for Allah is Exalted in Might and able to enforce His Will. And it brings a Message of hope and mercy; for Allah is Most Merciful. By its characteristics we know that the Qur'ān is from Allah. (R).

3946. The Quraysh had received no Prophet before, and therefore one of themselves was made the vehicle for the universal Message to the whole world. See C. 12-15.

3947. *Cf.* 7:30, and n. 1012; also 17:16, and n. 2193. If people deliberately and obstinately refuse "to believe", *i.e.*, to receive guidance and admonition, the result must be that Allah's grace and mercy are withdrawn from them. Their own perversity inevitably blocks up all channels for their correction.

8. We have put yokes[3948]
Round their necks
Right up to their chins,
So that their heads are
Forced up (and they cannot
see).

٨ إِنَّا جَعَلْنَا فِىٓ أَعْنَـٰقِهِمْ أَغْلَـٰلًا فَهِىَ إِلَى ٱلْأَذْقَانِ فَهُم مُّقْمَحُونَ

9. And We have put
A bar in front of them[3949]
And a bar behind them,
And further, We have
Covered them up; so that
They cannot see.

٩ وَجَعَلْنَا مِنۢ بَيْنِ أَيْدِيهِمْ سَدًّا وَمِنْ خَلْفِهِمْ سَدًّا فَأَغْشَيْنَـٰهُمْ فَهُمْ لَا يُبْصِرُونَ

10. The same is it to them[3950]
Whether thou admonish them
Or thou do not admonish
Them: they will not believe.

١٠ وَسَوَآءٌ عَلَيْهِمْ ءَأَنذَرْتَهُمْ أَمْ لَمْ تُنذِرْهُمْ لَا يُؤْمِنُونَ

11. Thou canst but admonish[3951]
Such a one as follows
The Message and fears
The (Lord) Most Gracious,
unseen:[3952]
Give such a one, therefore,[3953]

١١ إِنَّمَا تُنذِرُ مَنِ ٱتَّبَعَ ٱلذِّكْرَ وَخَشِىَ ٱلرَّحْمَـٰنَ بِٱلْغَيْبِ ۖ فَبَشِّرْهُ

3948. Man's misdeeds inevitably call forth the operation of Allah's Law, and therefore the result is in Quranic language attributed to Allah. The result of man's willful disobedience is now described in a series of metaphors. (1) Refusal of Allah's Light means less and less freedom of action for man: the yoke of sin is fastened round man's neck, and it gets more and more tightened, right up to the chin. (2) The head is forced up and kept in a stiff position, so that the mind becomes befogged. Moral obliquity taints the intellect. According to the Sanskrit proverb, "When destruction comes near, understanding is turned upside down." According to the Latin proverb, "Whom God wishes to destroy, He first makes demented." In other words, iniquity not only is folly, but leads deeper and deeper into folly, narrowness of vision, and blindness to the finer things of life. (3) This state of deprivation of Grace leads to such a decline in spriritual vitality that the victim can neither progress nor turn back, as explained in the next verse.

3949. Their retreat is cut off and their progress is impossible. Further the Light that should come from above is cut off, so that they become totally devoid of any hope, and the last gleam of any spiritual understanding is extinguished in them.

3950. When the stage just described is reached, revelation or spiritual teaching ceases to have any value for them. Why then preach? The answer is given in the verses following.

3951. *Cf.* 35:18. As far as those are concerned, who have obstinately delivered themselves to evil, the preaching of Allah's Message has no appeal, because their own will shuts them out. But there are others who are anxious to hear Allah's Message and receive Allah's grace. They love Allah and fear to offend against His Holy Law, and their fear is not merely superficial but deep-seated: for while they do not yet see Allah, nor do other people see them, they have the same sense of Allah's presence as if they saw Him, and their religion is not a mere pose, 'to be seen of men'.

3952. See n. 3902 to 35:18. *Unseen* is here adverbial: their reverence for Allah is unaffected by the fact that they do not see him, or that other people do not observe them, because their attitude arises out of a genuine love for Allah.

3953. To such persons the Messenger of Allah comes as a gospel or good news: because it shows them the way of forgiveness for anything wrong in their past, and it gives them the promise of a full reward in the future—generous beyond any deserts of their own, but arising out of Allah's unbounded Bounty.

Good tidings, of Forgiveness
And a Reward most generous.

بِمَغْفِرَةٍ وَأَجْرٍ كَرِيمٍ

12. Verily We shall give life[3954]
To the dead, and We record
That which they sent before
And that which they leave[3955]
Behind, and of all things
Have We taken account
In a clear Book[3956]
(Of evidence).

١٢ إِنَّا نَحْنُ نُحْيِ الْمَوْتَىٰ
وَنَكْتُبُ مَا قَدَّمُوا وَآثَارَهُمْ
وَكُلَّ شَيْءٍ أَحْصَيْنَاهُ
فِي إِمَامٍ مُبِينٍ

SECTION 2.

13. Set forth to them,
By way of a parable,
The (story of) the Companions[3957]
Of the City. Behold,
There came messengers to it.

١٣ وَاضْرِبْ لَهُمْ مَثَلًا
أَصْحَابَ الْقَرْيَةِ إِذْ جَاءَهَا الْمُرْسَلُونَ

14. When We (first) sent
To them two messengers,
They rejected them:
But We strengthened them[3958]
With a third: they said,
"Truly, we have been sent
On a mission to you."

١٤ إِذْ أَرْسَلْنَا إِلَيْهِمُ اثْنَيْنِ
فَكَذَّبُوهُمَا فَعَزَّزْنَا بِثَالِثٍ
فَقَالُوا إِنَّا إِلَيْكُمْ مُرْسَلُونَ

3954. All this is possible, because there is the assurance of a Hereafter, in which Allah will be all-in-all, and evil will no longer bestride the world, as the term of its respite will have expired.

3955. Our deeds, good and bad, go to Allah's Judgement Seat before us. They will of course be brought to our account; but our account will also be swelled by the example we left behind us and the consequences of our deeds, that will come into play or continue to operate after our earthly life had ceased. Our moral and spiritual responsibility is therefore much wider than as affects our own person.

3956. *Cf.* 2:124, and n. 124. All our account will be exactly preserved as in a book of record.

3957. Many of the classical Commentators have supposed that the City referred to was Antioch. Now Antioch was one of the most important cities in North Syria in the first century of the Christian era. It was a Greek city founded by Selecus Nicator, one of the successors of Alexander, about 300 B.C. in memory of his father Antiochus. It was close to the sea, and had its seaport at Seleucia. Soon after Christ his disciples successfully preached there, and they "were called Christians first in Antioch", Acts, xi. 26. It afterwards became the seat of a most important Bishopric of the Christian Church. In the story told here "by way of a parable", the City rejected the Message, and the City was destroyed: 36:29. Following Ibn Kathīr, I reject the identification with Antioch decisively. No name, or period, or place is mentioned in the text. The significance of the story is in the lessons to be derived from it as a parable, for which see the next note. That is independent of name, time, or place.

3958. Allah sends His messengers or teachers of Truth by ones and twos, and where the opposition is great and He considers it necessary, he supports them with others. Their mission is divine, but they do not claim to be more than men. This is used by the unjust and the ungodly as if it were a reproach, whereas it should commmend them to men, for mankind is glorified by such commisssion and by Allah's Self-revelation. The Message is clearly expressed in human language, but because it exposes all evil, men think it unlucky, as it checks their selfishness. It is often the poorest and most despised of mankind, from the outskirts or "farthest parts of the City", that accept the Message and are willing to work and die for it. The stiff-necked resist and accomplish their own destruction.

15. The (people) said: "Ye are
Only men like ourselves;[3959]
And (Allah) Most Gracious
Sends no sort of revelation:[3960]
Ye do nothing but lie."

١٥ قَالُوا۟ مَآ أَنتُمْ إِلَّا بَشَرٌ مِّثْلُنَا
وَمَآ أَنزَلَ ٱلرَّحْمَٰنُ مِن شَىْءٍ إِنْ أَنتُمْ إِلَّا تَكْذِبُونَ

16. They said: "Our Lord doth
Know that we have beeen sent
On a mission to you:[3961]

١٦ قَالُوا۟ رَبُّنَا يَعْلَمُ إِنَّآ إِلَيْكُمْ لَمُرْسَلُونَ

17. "And our duty is only
To proclaim the clear
Message."[3962]

١٧ وَمَا عَلَيْنَآ إِلَّا ٱلْبَلَٰغُ ٱلْمُبِينُ

18. The (people) said "For us,
We augur an evil omen[3963]
From you: if ye desist not,
We will certainly stone you,
And a grievous punishment
Indeed will be inflicted
On you by us."

١٨ قَالُوٓا۟ إِنَّا تَطَيَّرْنَا بِكُمْ
لَئِن لَّمْ تَنتَهُوا۟ لَنَرْجُمَنَّكُمْ
وَلَيَمَسَّنَّكُم مِّنَّا عَذَابٌ أَلِيمٌ

19. They said: "Your evil omens
Are with yourselves:[3964]
(Deem ye this an evil omen),
If ye are admonished?
Nay, but ye are a people
Transgressing all bounds!"[3965]

١٩ قَالُوا۟ طَٰٓئِرُكُم مَّعَكُمْ
أَئِن ذُكِّرْتُم
بَلْ أَنتُمْ قَوْمٌ مُّسْرِفُونَ

3959. *Cf.* Acts, xiv. 15, where Paul and Barnabas say, in the city of Lystra near the modern Konia, "We also are men with like passions with you, and preach unto you that ye should turn from these vanities. . ."

3960. They not only reject the mission of the particular messengers, but they deny the possibility of Allah's sending such mission. Note how they convict themselves of inconsistency by using Allah's name "Most Gracious", even though they may mean it ironically!

3961. Just as a Messenger whose credentials are doubted can refer to the authority granted by his Principal, as the highest proof of his mission, so these messengers of Allah invoke the authority of Allah in proof of their mission. In effect they say: "The knowledge of Allah is perfect, and He knows that our mission is from Him; if you do not, it is your own misfortune." (R).

3962. Then they proceed to explain what their mission is. It is not to force them but to convince them. It is to proclaim openly and clearly Allah's Law, which they were breaking—to denounce their sins and to show them the better path. If they were obstinate, it was their own loss. If they were rebellious against Allah, the punishment rested with Allah.

3963. *Ṭā'ir* means a bird. Like the Roman augurs, the Arabs had a superstition about deriving omens from birds. *Cf.* the English word *auspcious*, from the Latin *avis*, a bird, and *specio*, I see. From *Ṭā'ir* (bird) came *taṭayyara*, or *iṭṭayyara*, to draw evil omens. Because the prophets of Allah denounced evil, the evildoers thought that they brought ill-luck to them. As a matter of fact any evil that happened to them was the result of their own ill-deeds. *Cf.* 7:131, where the Egyptians ascribed their calamities to the ill-luck brought by Moses: and 27:47, where the Thamūd ascribed ill-luck to the preaching of Ṣāliḥ.

3964. 'What ye call omens arise from your own ill-deeds. Do you suppose that a man who comes to warn you and teach you the better way brings you ill-luck? Fie upon you!

3965. To call Good evil and accuse of falsehood men of truth who come unselfishly to bring the message of the beneficent Mercy of Allah, is the very height of extravagance and transgression.

20. Then there came running,
From the farthest part
Of the City, a man,[3966]
Saying, "O my People
Obey the messengers:

٢٠ وَجَآءَ مِنْ أَقْصَا ٱلْمَدِينَةِ رَجُلٌ
يَسْعَىٰ قَالَ يَٰقَوْمِ ٱتَّبِعُوا۟ ٱلْمُرْسَلِينَ

21. "Obey those who ask
No reward of you
(For themselves), and who have
Themselves received Guidance.[3967]

٢١ ٱتَّبِعُوا۟ مَن لَّا يَسْـَٔلُكُمْ
أَجْرًا وَهُم مُّهْتَدُونَ

22. "It would not be reasonable
In me if I did not
Serve Him Who created me,[3968]
And to Whom ye shall
(All) be brought back.

٢٢ وَمَا لِىَ لَآ أَعْبُدُ ٱلَّذِى
فَطَرَنِى وَإِلَيْهِ تُرْجَعُونَ

23. "Shall I take (other) gods
Besides Him? If (Allah)
Most Gracious should
Intend some adversity for me,[3969]
Of no use whatever
Will be their intercession
For me, nor can they
Deliver me.

٢٣ ءَأَتَّخِذُ مِن دُونِهِۦٓ ءَالِهَةً
إِن يُرِدْنِ ٱلرَّحْمَٰنُ بِضُرٍّ
لَّا تُغْنِ عَنِّى شَفَٰعَتُهُمْ شَيْـًٔا
وَلَا يُنقِذُونِ

24. "I would indeed,
If I were to do so,
Be in manifest Error.

٢٤ إِنِّىٓ إِذًا لَّفِى ضَلَٰلٍ مُّبِينٍ

3966. While the wealthy, influential, and fashionable men in the City were doubtful of Allah's providence and superstitiously believed in Chance and evil omens, the Truth was seen by a man in the outskirts of the City, a man held in low esteem by the arrogant. He had believed, and he wanted his City to believe. So, in Arabia, when the arrogant chiefs of the Quraysh exiled the Holy Prophet, it was men from Madīnah and from the outskirts, who welcomed him, believed in him, and supported his mission in every way.

3967. Prophets do not seek their own advantage. They serve Allah and humanity. Their hope lies in the good pleasure of Allah, to Whose service they are devoted. *Cf.* 10:72; 12:104; etc.

3968. The argument throughout is that of intense personal conviction for the individual himself, coupled with an appeal to his people to follow that conviction and get the benefit of the spiritual satisfaction which he has himself achieved. He says in effect: 'how is it possible for me to do otherwise than to serve and adore my Maker? I shall return to Him, and so will you, and all this applies to you as much as to me.' Note how effective is the transition from the personal experience to the collective appeal.

3969. The next plea is that for exclusive service to Allah. 'Suppose it were proper to worship other gods—Mammon, Self, or imaginary deities set up as idols—yet of what benefit would that be? All power is in Allah. In His universal Plan, He may think fit to give me some sorrow or punishment: would these subordinate deities be able to help me or intercede for me with Him? Not at all. What use would they be? In fact I should obviously be going astray—wandering from the true Path.'

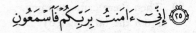

25. "For me, I have faith
In the Lord of you (all):[3970]
Listen, then, to me!"

إِنِّىٓ ءَامَنتُ بِرَبِّكُمْ فَٱسْمَعُونِ ﴿٢٥﴾

26. It was said: "Enter thou[3971]
The Garden." He said:
"Ah me! Would that
My People knew (what I know)!—

قِيلَ ٱدْخُلِ ٱلْجَنَّةَ ۖ قَالَ يَـٰلَيْتَ قَوْمِى يَعْلَمُونَ ﴿٢٦﴾

27. "For that my Lord[3972]
Has granted me Forgiveness
And has enrolled me
Among those held in honour!"

بِمَا غَفَرَ لِى رَبِّى وَجَعَلَنِى مِنَ ٱلْمُكْرَمِينَ ﴿٢٧﴾

23/30

28. And We sent not down
Against his People, after him,
Any hosts from heaven,
Nor was it needful
For Us so to do.

وَمَآ أَنزَلْنَا عَلَىٰ قَوْمِهِۦ مِنۢ بَعْدِهِۦ مِن جُندٍ مِّنَ ٱلسَّمَآءِ وَمَا كُنَّا مُنزِلِينَ ﴿٢٨﴾

29. It was no more than
A single mighty Blast,[3973]
And behold! they were
(like ashes)[3974]
Quenched and silent.

إِن كَانَتْ إِلَّا صَيْحَةً وَٰحِدَةً فَإِذَا هُمْ خَـٰمِدُونَ ﴿٢٩﴾

3970. Again a transition from the assured personal conviction to the appeal to all to profit by the speaker's experience. 'I have found the fullest satisfaction for my soul in Allah. He is my God, but He is your God also. My experience can be yours also. Will you not follow my advice, and prove for yourselves that the Lord is indeed good?'

3971. This godly and righteous man entered into the Peace of Allah, typified by the Garden of Rest and Beauty. Perhaps it is implied that he suffered martyrdom. But even then his thoughts were always with his People. He regretted their obstinacy and want of understanding, and wished even then that they might repent and obtain salvation, but they were obdurate and suffered for their sins as we learn from verses 28-29 below.

3972. This man was just a simple honest soul, but he heard and obeyed the call of the prophets and obtained his spiritual desire for himself and did his best to obtain salvation for his people. For he loved his people and respected his ancestral traditions as far as they were good, but had no hesitation in accepting the new Light when it came to him. All his past was forgiven him and he was raised to dignity and honour in the Kingdom of Heaven.

3973. Allah's Justice or Punishment does not necessarily come with pomp and circumstance, nor have the forces of human evil or wickedness the power to require the exertion of mighty spiritual forces to subdue them. A single mighty Blast—either the rumbling of an earthquake, or a great and violent wind—was sufficient in this case. *Cf.* 11:67 and n. 1561 (which describes the fate of the Thamūd; also,n. 3463 to 29:40.

3974. *Cf.* 21:15. They had made a great deal of noise in their time, but they were reduced to silence, like spent ashes.

30. Ah! alas for (My) servants!
There comes not a messenger
To them but they mock him![3975]

٣٠ يَـٰحَسۡرَةً عَلَى ٱلۡعِبَادِۚ مَا يَأۡتِيهِم
مِّن رَّسُولٍ إِلَّا كَانُواْ بِهِۦ يَسۡتَهۡزِءُونَ

31. See they not how many
Generations before them
We destroyed? Not to them[3976]
Will they return:

٣١ أَلَمۡ يَرَوۡاْ كَمۡ أَهۡلَكۡنَا قَبۡلَهُم
مِّنَ ٱلۡقُرُونِ أَنَّهُمۡ إِلَيۡهِمۡ لَا يَرۡجِعُونَ

32. But each one of them
All—will be brought
Before Us (for judgement).

٣٢ وَإِن كُلّٞ لَّمَّا جَمِيعٞ لَّدَيۡنَا مُحۡضَرُونَ

C. 195.—Are there not Signs enough around you
(36:33-50.) To bear witness to Allah, and His saving Grace?
The earth dies and revives; there are mysteries
Of Life and Sex, of Light and the Stars
And Planets in heaven, that follow
Their orbits by Law and in harmony!
There are the ships and the modes of transport
By which man can conquer the forces
Around him with God-given Gifts!
Learn the Law of Goodness from them
And believe in the Hereafter; it will come
When least expected. Be prepared for Allah!

SECTION 3.

33. A Sign for them
Is the earth that is dead:[3977]
We do give it life,
And produce grain therefrom,
Of which ye do eat.

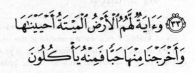

٣٣ وَءَايَةٞ لَّهُمُ ٱلۡأَرۡضُ ٱلۡمَيۡتَةُ أَحۡيَيۡنَٰهَا
وَأَخۡرَجۡنَا مِنۡهَا حَبّٗا فَمِنۡهُ يَأۡكُلُونَ

3975. *Cf.* 6:10 and many other passages of similar import. Ignorant men mock at Allah's prophets, or anyone who takes Religion seriously. But they do not reflect that such levity reacts on themselves. Their own lives are ruined and they cease to count. If they study history, they will see that countless generations were destroyed before them because they did not take Truth seriously and undermined the very basis of their individual and collective existence.

My servants is here equivalent to "men". Allah regrets the folly of men, especially as He cherishes them as His own servants.

3976. *Not to them will they return.* What do the pronouns *them* and *they* refer to? Commentators and translators have construed them differently, and some of them evade the question. To my mind the best construction seems to be: the generations which we have destroyed before the people addressed ('do *they* not see?') will not be restored to the people addressed; *generations* (*qurn*) standing for the periods of prosperity and good fortune enjoyed by the ancestors. They have all been wiped out; they will never be restored, but all people will be brought before the Judgement Seat for giving an account of their deeds.

3977. . Lest anyone should say, 'if they are destroyed, how can they be brought before the Judgement Seat' a symbol is pointed to. The earth is to all intents and purposes dead in the winter, but Allah revives it in the spring. *Cf.* 2:164, 30:19, and many other passages to that effect.

34. And We produce therein
Orchards with date palms[3978]
And Vines, and We cause
Springs to gush forth therein:

٣٤ وَجَعَلْنَا فِيهَا جَنَّٰتٍ مِّن نَّخِيلٍ
وَأَعْنَٰبٍ وَفَجَّرْنَا فِيهَا مِنَ ٱلْعُيُونِ

35. That they may enjoy[3979]
The fruits of this (artistry):
It was not their hands[3980]
That made this:
Will they not then give thanks?

٣٥ لِيَأْكُلُوا۟ مِن ثَمَرِهِۦ
وَمَا عَمِلَتْهُ أَيْدِيهِمْ ۖ
أَفَلَا يَشْكُرُونَ

36. Glory to Allah, Who created
In pairs all things that[3981]
The earth produces, as well as
Their own (human) kind
And (other) things of which
They have no knowledge.

٣٦ سُبْحَٰنَ ٱلَّذِى خَلَقَ ٱلْأَزْوَٰجَ كُلَّهَا
مِمَّا تُنۢبِتُ ٱلْأَرْضُ وَمِنْ أَنفُسِهِمْ
وَمِمَّا لَا يَعْلَمُونَ

37. And a Sign for them
Is the Night: We withdraw[3982]
Therefrom the Day, and behold
They are plunged in darkness;

٣٧ وَءَايَةٌ لَّهُمُ ٱلَّيْلُ نَسْلَخُ
مِنْهُ ٱلنَّهَارَ فَإِذَا هُم مُّظْلِمُونَ

38. And the Sun
Runs its course
For a period determined[3983]
For it; that is

٣٨ وَٱلشَّمْسُ تَجْرِى
لِمُسْتَقَرٍّ لَّهَا

3978 Date palms and vines stand as symbols for fruit trees of all kinds, these being the characteristic fruits of Arabia. Grain was mentioned in the last verse; fruit is mentioned now. All that is necessary for food and the satisfaction of the choicest palate is produced from what looks like inert soil, fertilised by rain and springs. Here is wonderful evidence of the artistry and providence of Allah.

3979. Literally, *eat (akala)*. *Cf.* 7:19. n. 1004 and 5:69, n. 776. The same wide meaning of profit, satisfaction, and enjoyment may be attached to the word "eat" in verse 33 above.

3980. Man may till the soil and sow the seed, but the productive forces of nature were not made by man's hands. They are the handiwork and artistry of Allah, and are evidence of Allah's providence for His creatures. See n. 3978 above.

3981. The mystery of sex runs through all creation—in man, in animal life, in vegetable life and possibly in other things of which we have no knowledge. Then there are pairs of opposite forces in nature, *e.g.*, positive and negative electricity, etc. The atom itself consists of a positively charged nucleus of proton, surrounded by negatively charged electrons. The constitution of matter itself is thus referred to pairs of opposite energies.

3982. *Withdrawing the Day from the Night:* is a striking phrase and very apt. The Day or the Light is the positive thing. The Night or Darkness is merely negative. We cannot withdraw the negative. But if we withdraw the real thing, the positive, which filled the void, nothing is left but the void. The whole of this section deals with Signs and Symbols—things in the physical world around us, from which we can learn the deepest spiritual truths if we earnestly apply ourselves to them.

3983. *Mustaqarr* may mean: (1) a limit of time, a period determined, as in 6:67, or (2) a place of rest or quiescence; or (3) a dwelling place, as in 2:36. I think the first meaning is best applicable here; but some Commentators take the second meaning. In that case the simile would be that of the sun running a race while it is visible to us, and taking a rest during the night to prepare itself to renew its race the following day. Its stay with the antipodes appears to us as its period of rest.

The decree of (Him),
The exalted in Might,
The All-Knowing.

ذَٰلِكَ تَقْدِيرُ ٱلْعَزِيزِ ٱلْعَلِيمِ

39. And the Moon—
We have measured for it[3984]
Mansions (to traverse)
Till it returns
Like the old (and withered)
Lower part of a date stalk[3985]

٣٩ وَٱلْقَمَرَ قَدَّرْنَٰهُ
مَنَازِلَ حَتَّىٰ عَادَ
كَٱلْعُرْجُونِ ٱلْقَدِيمِ

40. It is not permitted
To the Sun to catch up[3986]
The Moon, nor can
The Night outstrip the Day:
Each (just) swims along[3987]
In (its own) orbit
(According to Law).

٤٠ لَا ٱلشَّمْسُ يَنۢبَغِي لَهَآ أَن تُدْرِكَ
ٱلْقَمَرَ وَلَا ٱلَّيْلُ سَابِقُ ٱلنَّهَارِ
وَكُلٌّ فِي فَلَكٍ يَسْبَحُونَ

41. And a Sign for them
Is that We bore[3988]
Their race (through the Flood)
In the loaded Ark;

٤١ وَءَايَةٌ لَّهُمْ أَنَّا حَمَلْنَا ذُرِّيَّتَهُمْ
فِي ٱلْفُلْكِ ٱلْمَشْحُونِ

42. And We have created
For them similar (vessels)[3989]
On which they ride.

٤٢ وَخَلَقْنَا لَهُم مِّن مِّثْلِهِۦ مَا يَرْكَبُونَ

3984. The lunar mansions are the 28 divisions of the Zodiac, which are supposed to make the daily course of the moon in the heavens from the time of the new moon to the time when the moon fades away in its "inter-lunar swoon", an expressive phrase coined by the poet Shelley.

3985. *'Urjūn*; a raceme of dates or of a date palm; or the base or lower part of the raceme. When it becomes old, it becomes yellow, dry, and withered, and curves up like a sickle. Hence the comparison with the sickle-like appearance of the new moon. The moon runs through all its phases, increasing and decreasing, until it disappears, and then reappears as a little thin curve.

3986. Though the sun and the moon both traverse the belt of the Zodiac, and their motions are different, they never catch up each other. When the sun and the moon are on the same side and on a line with the earth there is a solar eclipse, and when on opposite sides in a line, there is a lunar eclipse, but there is no clash. Their Laws are fixed by Allah, and form the subject of study in astronomy. Similarly Night and Day follow each other, but being opposites cannot coincide, a fit emblem of the opposition of Good and Evil, Truth and Falsehood: see also n. 3982 above.

3987. *Cf.* 21:33, and n. 2695. How beautifully the rounded courses of the planets and heavenly bodies are described, "swimming" through space, with perfectly smooth motion! As Shakespeare expresses it, each "in his motion like an angel sings, Still quiring to the young-eyed cherubims!"

3988. Besides the beauty of the Night, with the stars and the planets "swimming" in their rounded courses according to perfect Law, suggesting both symmetry and harmony, there are other Signs touching closely the life of man himself, projected through Time, in the past history of his race and in his own personal experience. The past history of his race takes us to the story of the Flood, which is symbolical of the deliverance of man from the forces of nature. Noah's Ark is the symbol of that deliverance. But the symbol still remains as a memorial: the Ark was a "Sign to all Peoples"; 29:15. Man's own personal experience is appealed to in every ship afloat; see next note.

3989. The stately ships sailing through the seas, heavier than air, yet carrying man and his goods safely and smoothly across the waters, are another Sign for man. Ships are not mentioned, but (vessels) like the Ark: they would cover all kinds of seacraft, but also the modern aircraft, which "swims" through air instead of through water.

43. If it were Our Will,[3990]
We could drown them:
Then would there be
No helper (to hear
Their cry), nor could
They be delivered

44. Except by way of Mercy
From Us, and by way
Of (worldly) convenience
(To serve them) for a time.[3991]

45. When they are told,
"Fear ye that which is[3992]
Before you and that which
Will be after you, in order
That ye may receive Mercy,"
(They turn back).

46. Not a Sign come to them
From among the Signs[3993]
Of their Lord, but they
Turn away therefrom.

47. And when they are told,
"Spend ye of (the bounties)[3994]
With which Allah
Has provided you." the Unbelievers
Say to those who believe:
"Shall we then feed those

٤٣ وَإِن نَّشَأْ نُغْرِقْهُمْ
فَلَا صَرِيخَ لَهُمْ
وَلَا هُمْ يُنقَذُونَ

٤٤ إِلَّا رَحْمَةً مِّنَّا
وَمَتَاعًا إِلَىٰ حِينٍ

٤٥ وَإِذَا قِيلَ لَهُمُ اتَّقُوا
مَا بَيْنَ أَيْدِيكُمْ وَمَا خَلْفَكُمْ
لَعَلَّكُمْ تُرْحَمُونَ

٤٦ وَمَا تَأْتِيهِم مِّنْ آيَةٍ مِّنْ آيَاتِ
رَبِّهِمْ إِلَّا كَانُوا عَنْهَا مُعْرِضِينَ

٤٧ وَإِذَا قِيلَ لَهُمْ أَنفِقُوا مِمَّا
رَزَقَكُمُ اللَّهُ قَالَ الَّذِينَ كَفَرُوا
لِلَّذِينَ آمَنُوا أَنُطْعِمُ

3990. Were it not that Allah gives man the intelligence and ingenuity to construct and manage seacraft and aircraft, the natural laws of gravity would lead to the destruction of any who attempted to pass through sea or air. It is the gift (mercy) of Allah that saves him.

3991. *Cf.* 16:80. Allah has given man all these wonderful things in nature and utilities produced by the skill and intelligence which Allah has given to man. Had it not been for these gifts, man's life would have been precarious on sea or land or in the air. It is only Allah's Mercy that saves man from destruction for man's own follies, and that saving or the enjoyment of these utilities and conveniences he should not consider as eternal: they are only given for a time, in this life of probation.

3992. Man should consider and beware of the consequences of his past, and guard against the consequences in his future. The present is only a fleeting moment poised between the past and the future, and gone even while it is being mentioned or thought about. Man should review his whole life and prepare for the Hereafter. If he does so, Allah is Merciful: He will forgive, and give strength for a better and higher life in the future. But this kind of teaching does not suit those steeped in this ephemeral life. They are bored, and turn away from it, to their own loss.

3993. The Signs of Allah are many, in His great world—in nature, in the heart of man, and in the Revelation sent through His messengers. They turn away from all of them, as a man who has ruined his eyesight turns away from the light.

3994. To selfish men, the good may make an appeal, and say: "Look Allah has given you wealth, or influence, or knowledge, or talent. Why not spend some of it in charity, *i.e.*, for the good of your fellow-creatures?" But the selfish only think of themselves and laugh such teaching to scorn.

Whom, if Allah had so willed,[3995]
He would have fed, (Himself)?—
Ye are in nothing
But manifest error."

مَن لَّوْ يَشَآءُ ٱللَّهُ أَطْعَمَهُۥٓ
إِنْ أَنتُمْ إِلَّا فِى ضَلَٰلٍ مُّبِينٍ

48. Further, they say, "When
Will this promise (come to
pass),[3996]
If what ye say is true?"

٤٨ وَيَقُولُونَ مَتَىٰ هَٰذَا ٱلْوَعْدُ
إِن كُنتُمْ صَٰدِقِينَ

49. They will not (have
To) wait for aught
But a single Blast:
It will seize them while
They are yet disputing
Among themselves!

٤٩ مَا يَنظُرُونَ إِلَّا صَيْحَةً
وَٰحِدَةً تَأْخُذُهُمْ
وَهُمْ يَخِصِّمُونَ

50. No (chance) will they then
Have, by will, to dispose
(Of their affairs), nor
To return to their own people!

٥٠ فَلَا يَسْتَطِيعُونَ تَوْصِيَةً
وَلَآ إِلَىٰٓ أَهْلِهِمْ يَرْجِعُونَ

C. 196.—(36:51-83.)

When the Day comes, men will be taken
Aback. The Judgement Seat will be established.
Blessed will be those who attain Salvation:
Their Joy, Satisfaction, and Peace will be crowned
With nearness to their Lord!
Alas for the Sinful, who deliberately
Followed Evil: their own nature
And actions will speak against them:
They will face the realities of Punishment!
Both Revelation and Nature are eloquent
In instructing man for his own good
In the Hereafter, which will come
As a certainty. Praise and Glory to Allah!

3995. They are too full of themselves to have a corner in their hearts for others. "If," they say, "Allah gave them nothing, why should we?" There is arrogance in this as well as blasphemy: arrogance in thinking that they are favoured because of their merits, and blasphemy in laying the blame of other people's misfortunes on Allah. They further try to turn the tables on the Believers by pretending that the Believers are entirely on the wrong track. They forget that all men are on probation and trial: they hold their gifts on trust; those apparently less favoured, in that they have fewer of this world's goods, may be really more fortunate, because they are learning patience, self-reliance, and the true value of things ephemeral which is apt to be very much exaggerated in men's eyes.

3996. In addition to the arrogance and blasphemy referred to in the last note, they not only refuse Faith, but they taunt the men of Faith as if the man of Faith were dealing in falsehood: "If there is a Hereafter, tell us when it will be!" The answer is: "It will come sooner than you expect; you will yet be disputing about things of Faith and neglecting your opportunities in Life, when the Hour will sound, and you will have not time even to make your disposition in this life: you will be cut off from everyone whom you thought to be near and dear to you, or able to help you!"

SECTION 4.

51. The trumpet shall be[3997]
Sounded, when behold!
From the sepulchres (men)
Will rush forth
To their Lord!

٥١ وَنُفِخَ فِي ٱلصُّورِ فَإِذَا هُم
مِّنَ ٱلْأَجْدَاثِ إِلَىٰ رَبِّهِمْ يَنسِلُونَ

52. They will say: "Ah!
Woe unto us! Who
Hath raised us up
From our beds of repose?"..[3998]
(A voice will say:)
"This is what (Allah)
Most Gracious had promised,
And true was the word
Of the messengers!"

٥٢ قَالُوا يَٰوَيْلَنَا
مَنۢ بَعَثَنَا مِن مَّرْقَدِنَا ۜ
هَٰذَا مَا وَعَدَ ٱلرَّحْمَٰنُ
وَصَدَقَ ٱلْمُرْسَلُونَ

53. It will be no more
Than a single Blast,[3999]
When lo! they will all
Be brought up before Us!

٥٣ إِن كَانَتْ إِلَّا صَيْحَةً وَٰحِدَةً
فَإِذَا هُمْ جَمِيعٌ لَّدَيْنَا مُحْضَرُونَ

54. Then, on that Day,
Not a soul will be
Wronged in the least,[4000]
And ye shall but
Be repaid the meeds
Of your past Deeds.

٥٤ فَٱلْيَوْمَ لَا تُظْلَمُ
نَفْسٌ شَيْـًٔا وَلَا تُجْزَوْنَ
إِلَّا مَا كُنتُمْ تَعْمَلُونَ

55. Verily the Companions[4001]
Of the Garden shall

٥٥ إِنَّ أَصْحَٰبَ ٱلْجَنَّةِ

3997. Traditionally, the angel who will sound the Trumpet is Isrāfīl, but the name does not occur in the Qur'ān. The Trumpet is mentioned in many places: *e.g.*, 6:73; 78:18, etc.

3998. The dead will rise as in a stupor, and they will be confused in the new conditions! They will gradually regain their memory and their personality. They will be reminded that Allah in His grace and mercy had already announced the Hereafter in their probationary lives, and the word of Allah's messengers, which then seemed so strange and remote, was true and was now being fulfilled!

3999. Time and Space, as we know them here, will be no more. The whole gathering will be as in the twinkling of an eye. *Cf.* 36:49 above.

4000. The Judgement will be on the highest standard of Justice and Grace. Not the least merit will go unrewarded, though the reward will be for the righteous far more than their deserts. No penalty will be extracted but that which the doer himself by his past deeds brought on himself. *Cf.* 28:84.

4001. We now have the symbolism for the indescribable Bliss of the Hereafter, in the four verses, 55-58. Notice the subtle gradation in the description. First, in this verse, we have the nature of the *mise en scene* and the nature of the joy therein. It will be a Garden *i.e.*, everything agreeable to see and hear and feel and taste and smell; our bodily senses will have been transformed, but we can imagine something corresponding to them in our spiritual being: delightfully green lawns and meadows, trees and shrubs: the murmur of streams and the songs of birds: the delicate texture of flowers and leaves and the shapes of beauty in clouds and mist; the flavours of fruits; and the perfumes of flowers and scents. The joy in the Garden will be an active joy, without fatigue: whatever we do in it, every employment in which we engage there, will be a source of joy without alloy.

That Day have joy
In all that they do;

ٱلْيَوْمَ فِى شُغُلٍ فَٰكِهُونَ

56. They and their associates[4002]
Will be in groves
Of (cool) shade, reclining
On Thrones (of dignity);

٥٦ هُمْ وَأَزْوَٰجُهُمْ فِى ظِلَٰلٍ
عَلَى ٱلْأَرَآئِكِ مُتَّكِـُٔونَ

57. (Every) fruit (enjoyment)[4003]
Will be there for them;
They shall have whatever
They call for;

٥٧ لَهُمْ فِيهَا فَٰكِهَةٌ
وَلَهُم مَّا يَدَّعُونَ

58. "Peace!"—a Word[4004]
(Of salutation) from a Lord
Most Merciful!

٥٨ سَلَٰمٌ قَوْلًا مِّن رَّبٍّ رَّحِيمٍ

59. "And O ye in sin![4005]
Get ye apart this Day!

٥٩ وَٱمْتَٰزُوا۟ ٱلْيَوْمَ أَيُّهَا ٱلْمُجْرِمُونَ

60. "Did I not enjoin[4006]
On you, O ye children
Of Adam, that ye
Should not worship Satan;

٦٠ أَلَمْ أَعْهَدْ إِلَيْكُمْ يَٰبَنِىٓ ءَادَمَ
أَن لَّا تَعْبُدُوا۟ ٱلشَّيْطَٰنَ

4002. Secondly, the joy or happiness is figured to be, not solitary, but shared—shared by associates like those whom we imagine in spiritual Love or Marriage; in whose fair faces "some ray divine reflected shines" (Jāmī): whose society is enjoyed in homes of happiness, situated in soothing shade, and furnished with thrones of dignity and peace.

4003. Thirdly, besides any external conditions of Bliss, the Bliss in the Hereafter has an inner quality, expressed by the word *fākihatun*. The root *fakihah* means 'to rejoice greatly', to be full of merriment'. The ordinary meaning of 'fruit' attached to *fākihah* is derived from the idea that the flavour of choice, ripe fruit, delights the heart of man. Just as *akala* (to eat) is used for 'enjoyment', (5:69, n. 776 and 13:35, n. 1854), so *fākihah*, 'fruit', stands here for that specially choice enjoyment, which goes with a fastidious and well-cultivated taste. In other words, it suggests that highest kind of joy which depends upon the inner faculty rather than any outward circumstance. This is further emphasised by the second clause: "they shall have whatever they call for". Again using the language of this life, the musician's heaven will be full of music; the mathematician's will be full of mathematical symmetry and perfection; the artist's will be full of beauty of form, and so on.

4004. Fourthly, we reach the highest grade of bliss, the mystic salutation "Peace!" from Allah Most Merciful. *Cf.* 10:10. That Word sums up the attainment of the final Goal. For it explains the nature of the Most High—He is not only a Lord and Cherisher, but a Lord Whose supreme glory is Mercy, Peace, and Harmony!

4005. Notice how this finely balanced passage, after reaching the summit of sublimity in describing the state of the Blessed, in the word Salām, gradually takes us down to contemplate the state of the Sinners in a graduated descent.

In the first place, it refers to their negative state, their state of isolation. From this Day of Judgement, they will no longer have the chance of being with the Blessed and perhaps of profiting spiritually by that proximity. The first feature of the Day of Judgement is that it is a Day of Separation—of sorting out. Each soul now finds its own true level, as the period of probation is over.

4006. Secondly, there is a gentle reproach to the wrongdoers, more in sorrow than in anger. They are addressed as "children of Adam", to emphasise two facts, (1) that they have disgraced their ancestry, for Adam after his Fall repented and was forgiven, and the high Destiny of mankind has been the prize open to all his descendants, and (2) that Allah Most Merciful has throughout the ages continued to warn mankind against the snares laid by Satan, the avowed enemy of man, and that Allah's Grace was ever on the watch to help all to freedom from those snares.

For that he was to you
An enemy avowed?—

إِنَّهُۥ لَكُمْ عَدُوٌّ مُّبِينٌ

61. "And that ye should[4007]
Worship Me, (for that) this
Was the Straight Way?

وَأَنِ ٱعْبُدُونِى هَٰذَا صِرَٰطٌ مُّسْتَقِيمٌ ٦١

62. "But he did lead astray
A great multitude of you.
Did ye not, then, understand?[4008]

وَلَقَدْ أَضَلَّ مِنكُمْ جِبِلًّا كَثِيرًا ۖ
أَفَلَمْ تَكُونُوا۟ تَعْقِلُونَ ٦٢

63. "This is the Hell[4009]
Of which ye were
(Repeatedly) warned!

هَٰذِهِۦ جَهَنَّمُ ٱلَّتِى كُنتُمْ تُوعَدُونَ ٦٣

64. "Embrace ye the (Fire)[4010]
This Day, for that ye
(Persistently) rejected (Truth)."

ٱصْلَوْهَا ٱلْيَوْمَ بِمَا كُنتُمْ تَكْفُرُونَ ٦٤

65. That Day shall We set
A seal on their mouths.[4011]
But their hands will speak
To Us, and their feet
Bear witness, to all
That they did.

ٱلْيَوْمَ نَخْتِمُ عَلَىٰٓ أَفْوَٰهِهِمْ
وَتُكَلِّمُنَآ أَيْدِيهِمْ وَتَشْهَدُ أَرْجُلُهُم
بِمَا كَانُوا۟ يَكْسِبُونَ ٦٥

66. If it had been Our Will,[4012]
We could surely have
Blotted out their eyes;

وَلَوْ نَشَآءُ لَطَمَسْنَا عَلَىٰٓ أَعْيُنِهِمْ ٦٦

4007. Thirdly, besides the negative warning, a positive Way was shown to them—the Straight Way, the Ways of those who receive Allah's Grace and attain to Bliss, the Rope which would save them from shipwreck, the Shield which would save them from assault, the key to the door of proximity to Allah.

4008. Fourthly, it is pointed out that they were given Understanding (*'aql*), so that by their own faculties they could have judged their own best interests, and yet they betrayed or misused those faculties, and deliberately threw away their chance! And not only a few, but so many! They went gregariously to ruin in spite of the individual care which their Lord and Cherisher bestowed on them!

4009. Fifthly, the naked fact is now placed before them—the Hell—the state of damnation, which they could so easily have avoided!

4010. As they deliberately and persistently rejected all teaching, guidance, and warnings, they are now told to experience the Fire of Punishment, for it is but the consequence of their own acts.

4011. The ungodly will now be dumbfounded. They will be unable to speak or offer any defence. (The consequences of all acts, which follow according to Allah's Law, are, in Quranic language, attributed to Allah). But their silence will not matter. Their own hands and feet will speak against them. "Hands and feet" in this connection are symbolical of all the instruments for action which they were given in this life, including their faculties and opportunities. The same extended meaning is to be understood for "eyes" in the following verse. *Cf.* also 41:2021, where eyes, ears, and skins are all mentioned as bearing witness against such as misused them.

4012. *If it had been Our Will: i.e.*, if such had been the Will and Plan of Allah. If Allah had not intended to give man his limited free will, or power of choice, the case would have been different: there would have been no moral responsibility which could have been enforced. They could have had no sight or intelligence, and they could not have been blamed for not seeing or understanding. But such is not the case.

Then should they have
Run about groping for the Path,
But how could they have seen?

فَٱسْتَبَقُوا۟ ٱلصِّرَٰطَ فَأَنَّىٰ يُبْصِرُونَ

67. And if it had been
Our Will, We could
Have transformed them
(To remain) in their places;[4013]
Then should they have been
Unable to move about,
Nor could they have returned
(After error).

٦٧ وَلَوْ نَشَآءُ لَمَسَخْنَٰهُمْ
عَلَىٰ مَكَانَتِهِمْ فَمَا
ٱسْتَطَٰعُوا۟ مُضِيًّا
وَلَا يَرْجِعُونَ

Section 5.

68. If We grant long life
To any, We cause him
To be reversed in nature:[4014]
Will they not then understand?

٦٨ وَمَن نُّعَمِّرْهُ نُنَكِّسْهُ
فِى ٱلْخَلْقِ أَفَلَا يَعْقِلُونَ

69. We have not instructed
The (Prophet) in Poetry,[4015]
Nor is it meet for him:
This is no less than
A Message and a Qur'ān
Making things clear:

٦٩ وَمَا عَلَّمْنَٰهُ
ٱلشِّعْرَ وَمَا يَنۢبَغِى لَهُۥٓ
إِنْ هُوَ إِلَّا ذِكْرٌ وَقُرْءَانٌ مُّبِينٌ

70. That it may give admonition
To any (who are) alive,[4016]

٧٠ لِّيُنذِرَ مَن كَانَ حَيًّا

4013. If Allah's Plan had been to grant no limited freedom of choice or will to men, He could have created them quite different, or could have transformed them into stationary creatures, either in physical form as in the case of trees, or in moral or spiritual qualities, where there was no possibility either of progress or deterioration. Man would then have been unable to reach the heights of grandeur which are now open to him, or, if he goes wrong, to return through the door of repentance and mercy, and still pursue his path of ascent. But it was Allah's Plan to give man all these privileges, and man must shoulder all the responsibilities that go with them.

4014. This connects on with the last verse. Everything is possible with Allah. If you doubt how man can be transformed from his present nature, contemplate the transformations he already undergoes in his present nature at different ages. As a child, his powers of mind and body are still undeveloped. As he grows, they grow, and certain moral qualities, such as courage, daring, the will to conquer, unfold themselves. In extreme old age these are again obscured, and a second childhood supervenes. The back of the man who walked proudly straight and erect is now bent. If the transformations take place even in his present nature and constitution, how much easier was it for Allah to cast him in an immobile mould? But Allah granted him instead the high possibilities and responsibilities referred to in the last note.

4015. *Cf.* 26:224 and n. 3237. Here "Poetry" is used as connoting fairy tales, imaginary descriptions, things futile, false, or obscure, such as decadent Poetry is, whereas the Qur'ān is a practical guide, true and clear.

4016. "Alive", both in English and Arabic, means not only "having physical life", but having all the active qualities which we associate with life. In religious language, those who are not responsive to the realities of the spiritual world are no better than those who are dead. The Message of Allah penetrates the hearts of those who are alive in the spiritual sense.

And that the charge[4017]
May be proved against those
Who reject (Truth).

وَيَحِقَّ ٱلْقَوْلُ عَلَى ٱلْكَٰفِرِينَ

71. See they not that it is
We Who have created
For them—among other things
Which our hands have
fashioned—
Cattle, which are under[4018]
Their dominion?—

٧١ أَوَلَمْ يَرَوْا۟ أَنَّا خَلَقْنَا لَهُم
مِّمَّا عَمِلَتْ أَيْدِينَآ أَنْعَٰمًا
فَهُمْ لَهَا مَٰلِكُونَ

72. And that We have
Subjected them to their (use)?
Of them some do carry them
And some they eat:

٧٢ وَذَلَّلْنَٰهَا لَهُمْ
فَمِنْهَا رَكُوبُهُمْ وَمِنْهَا يَأْكُلُونَ

73. And they have (other) profits[4019]
From them (besides), and they
Get (milk) to drink.
Will they not then
Be grateful?[4020]

٧٣ وَلَهُمْ فِيهَا مَنَٰفِعُ وَمَشَارِبُ ۖ
أَفَلَا يَشْكُرُونَ

74. Yet they take (for worship)
Gods other than Allah,
(Hoping) that they might
Be helped!

٧٤ وَٱتَّخَذُوا۟ مِن دُونِ ٱللَّهِ ءَالِهَةً
لَّعَلَّهُمْ يُنصَرُونَ

75. They have not the power
To help them: but they
Will be brought up

٧٥ لَا يَسْتَطِيعُونَ نَصْرَهُمْ وَهُمْ لَهُمْ

4017. *Cf.* 28:63. If people reject Truth and Faith after they have been admonished and warned, the charge against them, of willful rebellion, is proved. They cannot then plead either ignorance or inadvertence.

4018. If they are blind to other Signs of Allah, they can at least see the simple homely things of life in which they receive so many benefits from Allah's mercy. How is it that wild animals can be domesticated, and in domestication can be so useful to man? Man can use them for riding or for draught; he can use their flesh for food and drink their milk; he can use their hair or wool. *Cf.* 16:66, 80; and 23:21-22.

4019. Such as skins for leather, furs for warmth, sheep's wool or camel's hair for blankets or textiles, musk for perfume, and so on.

4020. The whole argument turns on this. 'Our teaching is for your own benefit. We confer all these blessings on you, and yet ye turn away from the Giver of all, and run after your own vain imagination!'

(Before Our Judgement Seat) As a troop (to be condemned).[4021]	جُندٌ مُّحۡضَرُونَ
76. Let not their speech, then,[4022] Grieve thee. Verily We know What they hide as well as What they disclose.	٧٦ فَلَا يَحۡزُنكَ قَوۡلُهُمۡۘ إِنَّا نَعۡلَمُ مَا يُسِرُّونَ وَمَا يُعۡلِنُونَ
77. Doth not man see That it is We Who Created him from sperm?[4023] Yet behold! he (stands forth) As an open adversary!	٧٧ أَوَلَمۡ يَرَ ٱلۡإِنسَٰنُ أَنَّا خَلَقۡنَٰهُ مِن نُّطۡفَةٖ فَإِذَا هُوَ خَصِيمٞ مُّبِينٞ
78. And he makes comparisons[4024] For Us, and forgets his own (Origin and) Creation: He says, "Who can give Life to (dry) bones And decomposed ones (at that)?"	٧٨ وَضَرَبَ لَنَا مَثَلٗا وَنَسِيَ خَلۡقَهُۥۖ قَالَ مَن يُحۡيِ ٱلۡعِظَٰمَ وَهِيَ رَمِيمٞ
79. Say, "He will give them Life Who created them For the first time![4025]	٧٩ قُلۡ يُحۡيِيهَا ٱلَّذِيٓ أَنشَأَهَآ أَوَّلَ مَرَّةٖۖ

4021. There is some difference of opinion among Commentators as to the exact meaning to be attached to this clause. As I understand it, the meaning seems to be this. Man is apt to forget or turn away from the true God, the source of all the good which he enjoys, and to go after imaginary powers in the shape of gods; heroes, men, or abstract things like Science or Nature or Philosophy, or superstitious things like Magic, or Good Fortune or Ill-Fortune, or embodiments of his own selfish desires. He thinks that they might help him in this Life or in the Hereafter (if he believes in a Hereafter). But they cannot help him: on the contrary all things that are false will be brought up and condemned before Allah's Judgement Seat, and the worshippers of the Falsehoods will also be treated as a troop favouring the Falsehoods and therefore worthy of condemnation. The Falsehoods, therefore, instead of helping them, will contribute to their condemnation.

4022. If men are so foolish as to reject Allah, let not the men of Allah grieve over it. They should do their duty, and leave the rest to Allah. Allah knows all the open and secret motives that sway the wicked and His Plan must ultimately prevail, however much appearances may be against it at any given time.

4023. Man's disobedience and folly are all the more surprising, seeing that—apart from Allah's greatness and mercy—man is himself such a puny creature, created out of something that is less than a drop in the vast ocean of Existence. Yet man has the hardihood to stand out and dispute with his Maker, and institute idle comparisons as in the next verse!

4024. That is, man thinks that Allah is like His creatures, who at best have very limited powers, or man draws idle parallels like that mentioned at the end of this verse. 'Who can give life to dry bones, and decomposed ones at that?' Man certainly cannot, and no power in nature can do that. But why compare the powers and capacities of Allah's creatures with the powers and capacities of the Creator? The first creation—out of nothing—is far more difficult for us to imagine than a second or subsequent process for which there is already a basis. And Allah has power over all things.

4025. Allah's creative artistry is evident in every phase of nature, and it works every minute or second. The more man understands himself and the things within his reach, the more he realises this. How foolish, then, for anyone to set imaginary limits to Allah's power? There are more ways of creation than are dreamt of in man's imagination.

For He is well-versed
In every kind of creation!—

وَهُوَ بِكُلِّ خَلْقٍ عَلِيمٌ

80. "The same Who produces
For you fire out of[4026]
The green tree, when behold!
Ye kindle therewith
(Your own fires)!

٨٠ ٱلَّذِى جَعَلَ لَكُم مِّنَ ٱلشَّجَرِ
ٱلْأَخْضَرِ نَارًا فَإِذَآ أَنتُم مِّنْهُ تُوقِدُونَ

81. "Is not He Who created
The heavens and the earth
Able to create the like[4027]
Thereof?"—Yea, indeed!
For He is the Creator Supreme,
Of skill and knowledge (infinite)!

٨١ أَوَلَيْسَ ٱلَّذِى خَلَقَ ٱلسَّمَٰوَٰتِ وَٱلْأَرْضَ
بِقَٰدِرٍ عَلَىٰٓ أَن يَخْلُقَ مِثْلَهُمۚ
بَلَىٰ وَهُوَ ٱلْخَلَّٰقُ ٱلْعَلِيمُ

82. Verily, when He intends[4028]
A thing, His Command is,
"Be", and it is!

٨٢ إِنَّمَآ أَمْرُهُۥٓ إِذَآ أَرَادَ شَيْـًٔا
أَن يَقُولَ لَهُۥ كُن فَيَكُونُ

83. So glory to Him
In Whose hands is
The dominion of all things:
And to Him will ye[4029]
Be all brought back.

٨٣ فَسُبْحَٰنَ ٱلَّذِى بِيَدِهِۦ
مَلَكُوتُ كُلِّ شَىْءٍ وَإِلَيْهِ تُرْجَعُونَ

4026. Even older and more primitive than the method of striking fire against steel and flint is the method of using twigs of trees for the purpose. In the *E.B.*, 14th edition, 9:262, will be found a picture of British Guyana boys making a fire by rotating a stick in a round hole in a piece of wood lying on the ground. The Arab method was to use a wooden instrument called the *Zinād*. It consisted of two pieces to be rubbed together. The upper was called the *'Afār* or *Zand*, and the lower the *Markh*. The *markh* is a twig from a kind of spreading tree, the *Cynanchuin viminale*, of which the branches are bare, without leaves or thorns. When they are tangled together, and a wind blows, they get ignited and strike fire (Lane's Arabic Lexicon). In modern Arabic *Zand* is by analogy applied to the flint piece used for striking fire with steel.

4027. *Cf.* 89:27. Which is the more difficult to create—man, or the heavens and the earth, with all creatures? Allah created the heavens and the earth, with all creatures, and He can create worlds and worlds like these in infinity. To him it is small matter to raise you up for the Hereafter!

4028. And His creation is not dependent on time, on instruments or means, or any conditions whatsoever. Existence waits on His Will, or Plan, or Intention. The moment He wills a thing, it becomes His Word or Command, and the thing forthwith comes into existence. *Cf.* 2:177; 16:40, n. 2066; etc.

4029. All things were created by Allah; are maintained by Him; and will go back to Him. But the point of special interest to man is that man will also be brought back to Allah and is answerable to Him, and to Him alone. This Message is the core of Revelation; it explains the meaning of the Hereafter; and it fitly closes a Sūrah specially connected with the name (*Yā Sīn*) of the Holy Prophet.

INTRODUCTION TO SŪRAH 37—*AL ṢĀFFĀT*

As explained in the Introduction to S. 34, this is the fourth of a series of Sūrahs in which the mysteries of the spiritual world are manifested in different ways, tending to the defeat and final extirpation of Evil. The defeat of Evil is throughout connected with Revelation, and here the ranged fight is illustrated by a reference to the angels in heaven and to the earlier Prophets in our earthly history, from Noah to Jonah. In chronology, this Sūrah belongs to the early middle Makkan period.

Summary—Through all the mysteries of the heavens and the earth, there is a sorting out of the evil against the good: their final destinations contrasted (37:1-74, and C. 197).

Peace and victory came to Noah, Abraham, Moses and Aaron, Ilyās and Lūṭ, in their conflict with Evil (37:75-138, and C. 198).

So was it with Jonah when he glorified Allah. But men will ascribe to Allah what is unworthy of Him: Allah's Prophets strive for His glory, and shall be victorious (37:139-182, and C. 199).

C. 197.—Allah is One, the Source and Centre
(37:1-74.) Of all affairs, and we must work
In discipline, harmony, and unity
To put down Evil. The Hereafter
Is sure, when personal responsibility
Will be enforced. For the true
And sincere servants of Allah,
There will be the highest Bliss,
Unmixed and everlasting:
For those who defy Allah's Law
There will be the deepest enduring
Misery. Which will men choose?

Sūrah 37.

Al Ṣāffāt (Those Ranged in Ranks)

الجزء الثالث والعشرون سُورَةُ الصَّافَّاتِ

In the name of Allah, Most Gracious,
Most Merciful.

بِسْمِ اللَّهِ الرَّحْمَٰنِ الرَّحِيمِ

1. By[4030] those who range
Themselves in ranks,[4031]

وَالصَّٰٓفَّٰتِ صَفًّا ﴿١﴾

2. And so are strong
In repelling (evil),[4032]

فَالزَّٰجِرَٰتِ زَجْرًا ﴿٢﴾

3. And thus proclaim
The Message (of Allah)!

فَالتَّٰلِيَٰتِ ذِكْرًا ﴿٣﴾

4. Verily, verily, your God
Is One!—[4033]

إِنَّ إِلَٰهَكُمْ لَوَٰحِدٌ ﴿٤﴾

5. Lord of the heavens
And of the earth,
And all between them,

رَّبُّ السَّمَٰوَٰتِ وَالْأَرْضِ وَمَا بَيْنَهُمَا ﴿٥﴾

4030. At a later stage, we shall study the general meaning of the adjurations in the Qur'ān indicated by the particle *wa*. See App. XI. Here we may note that the last Sūrah (*Yā Sīn*) practically began with the adjuration "by the Qur'ān, full of wisdom", emphasising the fact that Revelation was the evidence by which we could learn the highest wisdom of the spiritual world. Here our attention is called in three verses or clauses, to three definite attitudes which illustrate the triumph of Good and the frustration of Evil. See the notes following.

4031. Two questions arise: (1) are the doers of the three things noted in verses 1-3 the same persons, whose actions or qualities are differently described, or are they three distinct sets of persons? (2) in either case, who are they? As to (1) the most authoritative view is that the three clauses describe the same set of persons in different aspects. As to (2) some take them to refer to angels, and others understand by them the good men, the men of God, who strive and range themselves in Allah's service. The words are perfectly general, and I interpret them to refer to both classes. The feminine form is grammatically used in Arabic idiom for the indefinite plural. In 37:165 below, the word *ṣāffūn* is used in the definite plural, and seems to be spoken by these beings, angels or men of God or both, according to how we interpret this verse.

4032. The three acts in verses 1-3 are consecutive, as shown by the particle *fa*. I understand them to mean that angels and good men (1) are ever ready to range themselves in ranks in the service of Allah and work in perfect discipline and accord at all times; (2) that they check and frustrate evil wherever they find it and they are strengthened in doing so by their discipline and their ranging themselves in ranks; and (3) that this service furthers the Kingdom of Allah and proclaims His Message and His glory to all creation.

4033. That divine Message is summed up in the gospel of Divine Unity, on which the greatest emphasis is laid: "verily, verily your God is One". It is a fact intimately connected with our own life and destiny. '*Your* Lord is one Who cares for you and cherishes you; you are dear to Him. And He is *One*: it is only He that you have to look to, the source of all goodness, love, and power. You are not the sport of many contending forces or blind chances. There is complete harmony and unity in heaven and you have to put yourselves into unison with it—by discipline in ranks, by unity of plan and purpose in repelling evil, and by concerted action in promoting the Kingdom of God.' Here is the mystery of the manifold variety of creation pointing to the absolute Unity of the Creator.

And Lord of every point
At the rising of the sun![4034]

وَرَبُّ ٱلْمَشَٰرِقِ

6. We have indeed decked
The lower heaven[4035] with beauty
(In) the stars—[4036]

إِنَّا زَيَّنَّا ٱلسَّمَآءَ ٱلدُّنْيَا بِزِينَةٍ ٱلْكَوَاكِبِ ﴿٦﴾

7. (For beauty) and for guard[4037]
Against all obstinate
Rebellious evil spirits,

وَحِفْظًا مِّن كُلِّ شَيْطَٰنٍ مَّارِدٍ ﴿٧﴾

8. (So) they should not strain
Their ears in the direction
Of the Exalted Assembly[4038]
But be cast away
From every side,

لَّا يَسَّمَّعُونَ إِلَى ٱلْمَلَإِ ٱلْأَعْلَىٰ
وَيُقْذَفُونَ مِن كُلِّ جَانِبٍ ﴿٨﴾

9. Repulsed, for they are
Under a perpetual penalty,

دُحُورًا ۖ وَلَهُمْ عَذَابٌ وَاصِبٌ ﴿٩﴾

10. Except such as snatch away
Something by stealth, and they
Are pursued by a flaming[4039]
Fire, of piercing brightness.

إِلَّا مَنْ خَطِفَ ٱلْخَطْفَةَ
فَأَتْبَعَهُۥ شِهَابٌ ثَاقِبٌ ﴿١٠﴾

4034. Allah is the Lord of everything that exists—'the heavens and the earth, and all between them'. He is the Lord of the *Mashāriq*—of every point at the rising of the sun. As the Commentators tell us, there are in the solar year only two equinoctial days, when the sun rises due east: on every other the sun rises at a shifting point either north or south of due east. In 7:137 we have *mashāriq al arḍi wa maghāribahā*, where the plural of the words for East and West is negligible, as the conjunction of the two embraces all points. The same may be said of 70:40, where Allah is called "Lord of all points in the East and the West". If we are speaking of longitudes, they may embrace all latitudes. In 55:17 Allah is called "Lord of the *two* Easts and the *two* Wests", referring to the extreme points in either case. A cursory reader may ask, why is only the East referred to here? The reply is that it is not so much the East as the rising of the sun, on which stress is laid. The Arabic *mashriq* or *mashāriq* is close enough to the root word *sharaqa*, to suggest, not so much the East as the rising of the sun, especially when the plural form is used. The glorious sun rises from different points, as seen by us, but it illuminates the whole heaven and earth. It is an emblem of Unity.

4035. *Cf.* 67:8-9. [Eds.].

4036. 'Stars' may be taken here in the popular sense, as referring to fixed stars, planets, comets, shooting stars, etc. On a clear night the beauty of the starry heavens is proverbial. Here they are meant to illustrate two points: (1) their marvellous beauty and their groupings and motions (apparent or real) manifest and typify the Design and Harmony of the One true Creator: and (2) the power and glory behind them typify that there is a guard against the assaults of Evil (see verse 7 below).

4037. Verses 7-11 seem to refer to shooting stars. *Cf.* 15:17-18, and notes 1951-53. The heavens typify not only beauty but power. The Good in Allah's world is guarded and protected against every assault of Evil. The Evil is not part of the heavenly system: it is a thing in outlawry, merely a self-willed rebellion—"cast away on every side, repulsed under a perpetual penalty" (verses 8-9).

4038. We can form a mental picture of the Court of the Most High, in the highest heaven, conforming to the highest idea we can form of goodness, beauty, purity, and grandeur. The Exalted Assembly of angels is given some knowledge of the Plan and Will of Allah. Evil is altogether foreign to such an atmosphere, but is actuated by feelings of jealousy and curiosity. It tries to approach by stealth and overhear something from the august Assembly. It is repulsed and pursued by a flaming fire, of which we can form some idea in our physical world by the piercing trail of a shooting star.

4039. See last note and *Cf.* 15:18 and notes 1953-54.

11. Just ask their[4040] opinion:
Are they the more difficult
To create, or the (other) beings
We have created?
Them have We created
Out of a sticky clay![4041]

فَٱسْتَفْتِهِمْ أَهُمْ أَشَدُّ خَلْقًا أَم مَّنْ خَلَقْنَآ إِنَّا خَلَقْنَٰهُم مِّن طِينٍ لَّازِبٍ ﴿١١﴾

12. Truly dost thou marvel,[4042]
While they ridicule,

بَلْ عَجِبْتَ وَيَسْخَرُونَ ﴿١٢﴾

13. And, when they are
Admonished, pay no heed—

وَإِذَا ذُكِّرُوا۟ لَا يَذْكُرُونَ ﴿١٣﴾

14. And, when they see
A Sign, turn it
To mockery,

وَإِذَا رَأَوْا۟ ءَايَةً يَسْتَسْخِرُونَ ﴿١٤﴾

15. And say, "This is nothing
But evident sorcery!

وَقَالُوٓا۟ إِنْ هَٰذَآ إِلَّا سِحْرٌ مُّبِينٌ ﴿١٥﴾

16. "What! when we die,
And become dust and bones,
Shall we (then) be
Raised up (again)?

أَءِذَا مِتْنَا وَكُنَّا تُرَابًا وَعِظَٰمًا أَءِنَّا لَمَبْعُوثُونَ ﴿١٦﴾

17. "And also our fathers[4043]
Of old?"

أَوَءَابَآؤُنَا ٱلْأَوَّلُونَ ﴿١٧﴾

18. Say thou: "Yea, and ye shall
Then be humiliated
(On account of your evil)."[4044]

قُلْ نَعَمْ وَأَنتُمْ دَٰخِرُونَ ﴿١٨﴾

4040. *Their:* "they" are the doubters, the evil ones, the deniers of Allah's grace and mercy, who laugh at Revelation and disbelieve in a Hereafter. Are they more important or more difficult to create than the wonderful variety of beings in Allah's spacious Creation? Do they forget their own lowly state, as having been created from muddy clay?

4041. *Cf.* 6:2; 7:12; 32:7; etc.

4042. It is indeed strange that unregenerate man should forget, on the one hand, his lowly origin, and on the other hand, his high Destiny, as conferred upon him by the grace and mercy of Allah. The indictment of him here comprises four counts: (1) they ridicule the teaching of Truth; (2) instead of profiting by admonition, they pay no heed; (3) when Allah's Signs are brought home to them, they ridicule them as much as they ridiculed the teaching of Truth: and (4) when they have to acknowledge incontestable facts, they give them false names like "sorcery", which imply fraud or something which has no relation to their life, although the facts touch the inner springs of their life intimately.

4043. Although the Hereafter, and the spiritual life of which it is a corollary, are the most solid facts in our intelligent existence, materialists deny them. They cannot believe that they could have any existence beyond the grave—still less their ancestors who died ages and ages ago: how could they ever come to life again?

4044. They are assured that the future life is a solid fact, but that it will be in very different conditions from those they know now. All their present arrogance will have been humbled in the dust. There will be another plane, in which souls will have experiences quite different from those in their probationary life here. In that life the virtues they lacked will count, and the arrogance they hugged will be brought low.

19. Then it will be a single
(Compelling) cry;[4045]
And behold, they will
Begin to see![4046]

فَإِنَّمَا هِيَ زَجْرَةٌ وَٰحِدَةٌ فَإِذَا هُمْ يَنظُرُونَ ﴿١٩﴾

20. They will say, "Ah!
Woe to us! this is
The Day of Judgement!"

وَقَالُوا۟ يَٰوَيْلَنَا هَٰذَا يَوْمُ ٱلدِّينِ ﴿٢٠﴾

21. (A voice will say,)
"This is the Day[4047]
Of Sorting Out, whose
Truth ye (once) denied!"

هَٰذَا يَوْمُ ٱلْفَصْلِ ٱلَّذِى كُنتُم بِهِۦ تُكَذِّبُونَ ﴿٢١﴾

SECTION 2.

22. "Bring ye up",
It shall be said,
"The wrongdoers
And their wives,[4048]
And the things they worshipped—

ٱحْشُرُوا۟ ٱلَّذِينَ ظَلَمُوا۟ وَأَزْوَٰجَهُمْ وَمَا كَانُوا۟ يَعْبُدُونَ ﴿٢٢﴾

23. "Besides Allah,
And lead them to the Way
To the (Fierce) Fire!

مِن دُونِ ٱللَّهِ فَٱهْدُوهُمْ إِلَىٰ صِرَٰطِ ٱلْجَحِيمِ ﴿٢٣﴾

24. "But stop them,[4049]
For they must be asked:

وَقِفُوهُمْ إِنَّهُم مَّسْـُٔولُونَ ﴿٢٤﴾

25. "What is the matter
With you that ye
Help not each other?"[4050]

مَا لَكُمْ لَا تَنَاصَرُونَ ﴿٢٥﴾

4045. *Cf.* 36:29, 49, and 53.

4046. Their spiritual blindness will then leave them. But they will be surprised at the suddenness of their disillusion.

4047. The Day of Judgement is the day of sorting out. *Cf.* 36:59. Good and evil will finally be separated, unlike the apparently inexplicable conditions in the present probationary life, when they seem to be mixed together.

4048. That is, if their wives were also wrongdoers. They are separately mentioned, because the Arabic phrase for "wrongdoers" is of the masculine gender. All the associates in wrongdoing will be marshalled together. There will be personal responsibility: neither husband nor wife can lay the blame on the other.

4049. The scene here is after judgement. As, in an earthly tribunal, the prisoner or his advocate is asked why sentence should not be pronounced upon him, so here those who are proved to have been guilty of wrong are allowed to consider if anything or anyone can help them. Then comes the exposure of the misleaders.

4050. Obviously no one can stand and intercede, for it is a question of personal responsibility for each soul. No one can help another.

26. Nay, but that day they
Shall submit (to Judgement);[4051]

٢٦ بَلْ هُمُ ٱلْيَوْمَ مُسْتَسْلِمُونَ

27. And they will turn to
One another, and question
One another.

٢٧ وَأَقْبَلَ بَعْضُهُمْ عَلَىٰ بَعْضٍ يَتَسَآءَلُونَ

28. They will say: "It was ye
Who used to come to us
From the right hand
(Of power and authority)!"[4052]

٢٨ قَالُوٓا۟ إِنَّكُمْ كُنتُمْ
تَأْتُونَنَا عَنِ ٱلْيَمِينِ

29. They will reply: "Nay, ye
Yourselves had no Faith![4053]

٢٩ قَالُوا۟ بَل لَّمْ تَكُونُوا۟ مُؤْمِنِينَ

30. "Nor had we any authority
Over you. Nay, it was
Ye who were a people
In obstinate rebellion!

٣٠ وَمَا كَانَ لَنَا عَلَيْكُم مِّن سُلْطَٰنٍۭ
بَلْ كُنتُمْ قَوْمًا طَٰغِينَ

31. "So now has been proved true,[4054]
Against us, the Word
Of our Lord that we
Shall indeed (have to) taste
(The punishment of our sins):

٣١ فَحَقَّ عَلَيْنَا قَوْلُ رَبِّنَآ
إِنَّا لَذَآئِقُونَ

32. "We led you astray: for truly[4055]
We were ourselves astray."

٣٢ فَأَغْوَيْنَٰكُمْ إِنَّا كُنَّا غَٰوِينَ

4051. All the previous arrogance of this life will be gone, but they will face each other, and those who were given a false lead, as in the story of Pharaoh (*Cf.* 20:79), will question their misleaders as in the following verses.

4052. This is the mutual recrimination of the sinners—those who sinned, against those whose instigation or evil example led them into sin. The misleaders in the life here below often used their power and influence to spread evil. The "right hand" is the hand of power and authority. Instead of using it for righteous purposes, they used it for evil,—selfishly for their own advantage, and mischievously for the degradation of others.

4053. But the fact that others mislead, or that evil example is before us, does not justify us in falling from right conduct. Faith should save us from the fall. But if we have ourselves no Faith—in righteousness, or a future life, or the reality of Allah's Law, how can we blame others? The misleaders can well say, "You will be judged according to your misdeeds!" The responsibility is personal, and cannot be shifted on the other. The others may get a double punishment,—for their own evil, and for misleading their weaker brethren. But the weaker brethren cannot go free from responsibilty of their own deeds; for evil means a personal rebellion against Allah, if we believe in a personal God. Evil has no authority over us, except insofar as we deliberately choose it.

4054. Allah's decree of justice requires that every soul should taste the consequences of its own sins, and that decree must be fulfilled. No excuses can serve. It is only Allah's mercy that can save.

4055. Further, the misleaders can well urge against those who reproach them for misleading them: "How could you expect anything better from us? You were warned by Allah's Message that we were astray."

33. Truly, that Day, they will
(All) share in the Penalty.

34. Verily that is how We
Shall deal with Sinners.

35. For they, when they were
Told that there is
No god except Allah, would
Puff themselves up with Pride,[4056]

36. And say: "What! Shall we
Give up our gods
For the sake of
A Poet possessed?"[4057]

37. Nay! he has come
With the (very) Truth,
And he confirms (the Message
Of) the messengers (before
him).[4058]

38. Ye shall indeed taste
Of the Grievous Penalty—

39. But it will be no more
Than the retribution[4059]
Of (the Evil) that ye
Have wrought—

40. But the sincere (and devoted)
Servants of Allah—

41. For them is a Sustenance[4060]
Determined,[4061]

٣٣ فَإِنَّهُمْ يَوْمَئِذٍ فِي ٱلْعَذَابِ مُشْتَرِكُونَ

٣٤ إِنَّا كَذَٰلِكَ نَفْعَلُ بِٱلْمُجْرِمِينَ

٣٥ إِنَّهُمْ كَانُوٓا۟ إِذَا قِيلَ لَهُمْ
لَآ إِلَٰهَ إِلَّا ٱللَّهُ يَسْتَكْبِرُونَ

٣٦ وَيَقُولُونَ أَئِنَّا لَتَارِكُوٓا۟
ءَالِهَتِنَا لِشَاعِرٍ مَّجْنُونٍۭ

٣٧ بَلْ جَآءَ بِٱلْحَقِّ
وَصَدَّقَ ٱلْمُرْسَلِينَ

٣٨ إِنَّكُمْ لَذَآئِقُوا۟ ٱلْعَذَابِ ٱلْأَلِيمِ

٣٩ وَمَا تُجْزَوْنَ إِلَّا
مَا كُنتُمْ تَعْمَلُونَ

٤٠ إِلَّا عِبَادَ ٱللَّهِ ٱلْمُخْلَصِينَ

٤١ أُو۟لَٰٓئِكَ لَهُمْ رِزْقٌ مَّعْلُومٌ

4056. Selfish arrogance was the seed of sin and rebellion: 2:34 (of Satan): 27:39 (of Pharaoh); etc. It is that kind of arrogance which prevents man from mending his life and conduct. When he speaks of ancestral ways, or public opinion, or national honour, he is usually thinking of himself or of a small clique which thrives on injustice. The recognition of Allah, the one true God, as the only standard of life and conduct, the Eternal Reality, cuts out Self, and is therefore disagreeable to Sin. If false gods are imagined, who themselves would have weaknesses that fit in with sin, they give countenance to evils, and it becomes difficult to give them up, unless Allah's grace comes to our assistance. (R).

4057. Possessed of an evil spirit, or mad. Such was the charge which the Unbelievers sometimes levelled at the Holy Prophet in the early stages of his preaching.

4058. The message of Islam, so far from being "mad" or in any way peculiar, is eminently conformable to reason and the true facts of nature as created by Allah. It is the Truth in the purest sense of the term, and confirms the Message of all true Messengers that ever lived.

4059. Justice demands that those who sow evil should reap the fruit, but the punishment is due to their own conduct and not to anything external to themselves.

4060. *Sustenance:* metaphorical sense, correlated with the Fruits mentioned below: see next verse.

4061. *Determined: Ma'lūm*: the reward of the Blessed will not be a chance or a fleeting thing. It will follow a firm Decree of Allah, on principles that can be known and understood.

42. Fruits (Delights);[4062] and they
(Shall enjoy) honour and dignity,

فَوَٰكِهُ وَهُم مُّكْرَمُونَ ﴿٤٢﴾

43. In Gardens of Felicity,

فِي جَنَّٰتِ ٱلنَّعِيمِ ﴿٤٣﴾

44. Facing each other
On Thrones (of dignity):

عَلَىٰ سُرُرٍ مُّتَقَٰبِلِينَ ﴿٤٤﴾

45. Round will be passed
To them a Cup
From a clear-flowing fountain,

يُطَافُ عَلَيْهِم بِكَأْسٍ مِّن مَّعِينٍ ﴿٤٥﴾

46. Crystal-white, of a taste
Delicious to those
Who drink (thereof),

بَيْضَآءَ لَذَّةٍ لِّلشَّٰرِبِينَ ﴿٤٦﴾

47. Free from headiness;[4063]
Nor will they suffer
Intoxication therefrom.

لَا فِيهَا غَوْلٌ وَلَا هُمْ عَنْهَا يُنزَفُونَ ﴿٤٧﴾

48. And besides them will be
Chaste women; restraining
Their glances, with big eyes [4064]
(Of wonder and beauty).

وَعِندَهُمْ قَٰصِرَٰتُ ٱلطَّرْفِ عِينٌ ﴿٤٨﴾

49. As if they were [4065]
(Delicate) eggs closely guarded.

كَأَنَّهُنَّ بَيْضٌ مَّكْنُونٌ ﴿٤٩﴾

50. Then they will turn to
One another and question
One another.[4066]

فَأَقْبَلَ بَعْضُهُمْ عَلَىٰ بَعْضٍ يَتَسَآءَلُونَ ﴿٥٠﴾

4062. *Fruits: Cf.* 36:57, and n. 4003. The spiritual Delights are figured forth from parallel experiences in our present life, and follow an ascending order: Food and Fruits; Gardens of Bliss, (with all their charm, design, greenery, birds' songs, fountains, etc.); the Home of Happiness and Dignity, with congenial company seated on Thrones; Delicious Drinks from crystal Springs, for social pleasure; and the society of Companions of the opposite sex, with beauty and charm but none of the grossness too often incidental to such companionship in this life.

4063. The passing round of the social cup, as in the case of other pleasures, is without any of the drawbacks and evil accompaniments of the pleasures of this world, which are taken as types. In drink there is no intoxication: in fruit there is no satiety. *Cf.* Dante: "The bread of Angels upon which One liveth here and grows not sated by it." (*Paradiso,* Canto II., Longfellow's translation.)

4064. In the emblem used here, again, the pure type of chaste womanhood is figured. They are chaste, not bold with their glances: but their eyes are big with wonder and beauty, prefiguring grace, innocence, and a refined capacity of appreciation and admiration.

4065. This is usually understood to refer to the delicate complexion of a beautiful woman, which is compared to the transparent shell of eggs in the nest, closely guarded by the mother-bird; the shell is warm and free from stain. In 55:58 the phrase used is "like rubies and coral", referring to the red or pink of a beautiful complexion.

4066. *Cf.* above, 37:27, where the same phrase is used in the reverse conditions. In each case there is a going back to the earlier memories or experiences of this life.

51. One of them will start The talk and say: "I had an intimate Companion (on the earth),[4067]	قَالَ قَآئِلٌ مِّنْهُمْ إِنِّي كَانَ لِي قَرِينٌ ﴿٥١﴾
52. "Who used to say, 'What! art thou amongst those Who bear witness to The truth (of the Message)?	يَقُولُ أَءِنَّكَ لَمِنَ ٱلْمُصَدِّقِينَ ﴿٥٢﴾
53. "'When we die and become Dust and bones, shall we Indeed receive rewards And punishments?'"	أَءِذَا مِتْنَا وَكُنَّا تُرَابًا وَعِظَٰمًا أَءِنَّا لَمَدِينُونَ ﴿٥٣﴾
54. (A voice) said: "Would ye Like to look down?"	قَالَ هَلْ أَنتُم مُّطَّلِعُونَ ﴿٥٤﴾
55. He looked down And saw him In the midst of the Fire.[4068]	فَٱطَّلَعَ فَرَءَاهُ فِي سَوَآءِ ٱلْجَحِيمِ ﴿٥٥﴾
56. He said: "By Allah! Thou wast little short Of bringing me to perdition!	قَالَ تَٱللَّهِ إِن كِدتَّ لَتُرْدِينِ ﴿٥٦﴾
57. "Had it not been for The Grace of my Lord,[4069] I should certainly have been Among those brought (there)!	وَلَوْلَا نِعْمَةُ رَبِّي لَكُنتُ مِنَ ٱلْمُحْضَرِينَ ﴿٥٧﴾
58. "Is it (the case) that We shall not die,	أَفَمَا نَحْنُ بِمَيِّتِينَ ﴿٥٨﴾
59. "Except our first death, And that *we*[4070] Shall not be punished?"	إِلَّا مَوْتَتَنَا ٱلْأُولَىٰ وَمَا نَحْنُ بِمُعَذَّبِينَ ﴿٥٩﴾

4067. This companion was a sceptic, who laughed at Religion and a Hereafter. How the tables are now turned! The devout man backed up his Faith with a good life and is now in Bliss: the other was a cynic and made a mess of his life, and is now burning in the Fire.(R)

4068. He is allowed a peep into the state which he so narrowly escaped by the grace of Allah.

4069. And he gratefully acknowledges his shortcomings: "I should have been a sinner just like this, but for the grace of Allah!" He sees that if he had erred it would have been no excuse to plead the other man's example. He had Faith and was saved, to walk in the path of righteousness.

4070. After he realises the great danger from which he narrowly escaped, his joy is so great that he can hardly believe it! Is the danger altogether past now? Are the portals of death closed forever? Is he safe now from the temptations which will bring him to ruin and punishment?

60. Verily this is
The supreme achievement![4071]

إِنَّ هَٰذَا لَهُوَ ٱلْفَوْزُ ٱلْعَظِيمُ ٦٠

61. For the like of this
Let all strive,
Who wish to strive.

لِمِثْلِ هَٰذَا فَلْيَعْمَلِ ٱلْعَٰمِلُونَ ٦١

62. Is that the better entertainment
Or the Tree of Zaqqūm?[4072]

أَذَٰلِكَ خَيْرٌ نُّزُلًا أَمْ شَجَرَةُ ٱلزَّقُّومِ ٦٢

63. For We have truly
Made it (as) a trial[4073]
For the wrongdoers.

إِنَّا جَعَلْنَٰهَا فِتْنَةً لِّلظَّٰلِمِينَ ٦٣

64. For it is a tree
That springs out
Of the bottom of Hellfire:

إِنَّهَا شَجَرَةٌ تَخْرُجُ فِىٓ أَصْلِ ٱلْجَحِيمِ ٦٤

65. The shoots of its fruit-stalks
Are like the heads
Of devils:

طَلْعُهَا كَأَنَّهُۥ رُءُوسُ ٱلشَّيَٰطِينِ ٦٥

66. Truly they will eat thereof[4074]
And fill their bellies therewith.

فَإِنَّهُمْ لَءَاكِلُونَ مِنْهَا فَمَالِـُٔونَ مِنْهَا ٱلْبُطُونَ ٦٦

67. Then on top of that
They will be given
A mixture made of
Boiling water.

ثُمَّ إِنَّ لَهُمْ عَلَيْهَا لَشَوْبًا مِّنْ حَمِيمٍ ٦٧

4071. The answer is: Yes. "Beyond the flight of Time, Beyond the realm of Death. There surely is some blessed clime, Where Life is not a breath!" In the words of Longfellow this was an aspiration on this earth. In the Hereafter it is a realisation!

Some interpret verses 60-62 as a continuation of the speech of the man in heaven. The meaning would in that case be the same.

4072. *Cf.* 17:60, n. 2250. This bitter tree of Hell is a symbol of the contrast with the beautiful Garden of heaven with its delicious fruits.

4073. This dreadful bitter Tree of Hell is truly a trial to the wrongdoers. (1) It grows at the bottom of Hell; (2) even its fruit-stalks, which should have been tender, are like the heads of devils; (3) its produce is eaten voraciously; (4) on top of it is a boiling mixture to cut up their entrails (see next note); and (5) every time they complete this round of orgies they return to the same game. A truly lurid picture, but more lurid in reality are the stages in spiritual Evil. (1) It takes its rise in the lowest depths of corrupted human nature; (2) its tenderest affections are degraded to envy and hate: (3) the appetite for Evil grows with what it feeds on;(4) its "cures" serve but to aggravate the disease; and (5) the chain of evil is unending; one round is followed by another in interminable succession.

4074. The parable of fruits and drinks in the contrasted fortunes of the Good and the Evil is further elaborated in 47:15, where the boiling water given to the evil ones cuts up their entrails.

68. Then shall their return[4075]
Be to the (Blazing) Fire.

ثُمَّ إِنَّ مَرْجِعَهُمْ لَإِلَى الْجَحِيمِ ﴿٦٨﴾

69. Truly they found their fathers
On the wrong Path;

إِنَّهُمْ أَلْفَوْا آبَاءَهُمْ ضَالِّينَ ﴿٦٩﴾

70. So they (too) were rushed[4076]
Down on their footsteps!

فَهُمْ عَلَىٰ آثَارِهِمْ يُهْرَعُونَ ﴿٧٠﴾

71. And truly before them,
Many of the ancients
Went astray—

وَلَقَدْ ضَلَّ قَبْلَهُمْ أَكْثَرُ الْأَوَّلِينَ ﴿٧١﴾

72. But We sent aforetime,[4077]
Among them, (messengers)
To admonish them—

وَلَقَدْ أَرْسَلْنَا فِيهِمْ مُنْذِرِينَ ﴿٧٢﴾

73. Then see what was
The End of those who[4078]
Were admonished
(but heeded not)—

فَانْظُرْ كَيْفَ كَانَ عَاقِبَةُ الْمُنْذَرِينَ ﴿٧٣﴾

74. Except the sincere (and
devoted)[4079]
Servants of Allah.

إِلَّا عِبَادَ اللَّهِ الْمُخْلَصِينَ ﴿٧٤﴾

C. 198.—The Prophets of Allah formed a series
(37:75-138.) That worked in Allah's service to instruct
Their fellow-men. In case of distress
Allah helped and delivered them. Men did flout
And persecute them, but they carried out
Their mission with constancy; and Allah's Purpose
Always won, to the destruction of Evil.
So was it in the story of Noah and the Flood,

4075. When they eat of the *zaqqūm* in the lowest depths of hell, they are apparently brought up to drink of the mixture as a further punishment, after which they go back to repeat the round.

4076. A grim reproach. 'You found your fathers doing wrong; and you must rush headlong in their footsteps to perdition!'

4077. It is human to err. The error is forgiven if there is repentance and amendment. The point is that Allah in His mercy at all times in history sent messengers and teachers to give His Message, and men deliberately rejected that Message.

4078. It is on the reception or rejection of Allah's teachings and guidance that judgement will come. In this world itself, see what is the teaching of history. Unrighteousness and wrongdoing never prosper in the long run.

4079. But there is always a band of sincere and devoted men who serve Allah, and the highest spiritual life is open to them.

Note that this verse occurs at 37:40 above, where the argument of the difference betweeen the fates of the righteous and the unrighteous was begun. Here it is rounded off with the same phrase, and now we proceed to take illustrations from the early Prophets.

Of Abraham the True, of Ismā'īl
Ready for self-sacrifice, of Isaac
The righteous, of Moses and Aaron, of Elias
And Lot: all men of Faith, who receive
The blessings of posterity and Peace
And Salutation from Allah Most Gracious.

SECTION 3.

75. (In the days of old),
Noah cried to Us,[4080]
And We are the Best
To hear prayer.

وَلَقَدْ نَادَىٰنَا نُوحٌ فَلَنِعْمَ ٱلْمُجِيبُونَ ﴿٧٥﴾

76. And We delivered him
And his people from
The Great Calamity,[4081]

وَنَجَّيْنَٰهُ وَأَهْلَهُۥ مِنَ ٱلْكَرْبِ ٱلْعَظِيمِ ﴿٧٦﴾

77. And made his progeny
To endure (on this earth);[4082]

وَجَعَلْنَا ذُرِّيَّتَهُۥ هُمُ ٱلْبَاقِينَ ﴿٧٧﴾

78. And We left (this blessing)
For him among generations[4083]
To come in later times:

وَتَرَكْنَا عَلَيْهِ فِى ٱلْءَاخِرِينَ ﴿٧٨﴾

79. "Peace and salutation to Noah
Among the nations!"[4084]

سَلَٰمٌ عَلَىٰ نُوحٍ فِى ٱلْعَٰلَمِينَ ﴿٧٩﴾

80. Thus indeed do We reward
Those who do right.

إِنَّا كَذَٰلِكَ نَجْزِى ٱلْمُحْسِنِينَ ﴿٨٠﴾

81. For he was one
Of Our believing Servants.

إِنَّهُۥ مِنْ عِبَادِنَا ٱلْمُؤْمِنِينَ ﴿٨١﴾

4080. *Cf.* 21:76-77. The story of Noah occurs in many places; here the point is that when men gird themselves against evil, Allah protects them, and Evil cannot triumph against Allah's Plan.

4081. The Deluge, the Flood of Noah. The main story will be found in 11:25-48.

4082. Noah's posterity survived the Flood in the Ark, while the rest perished.

4083. His name is remembered forever, commencing a new era in religious history. Note that the words in verses 78-81, with slight modifications, form a sort of refrain to the following paragraphs about Abraham, Moses, and Elias, but not about Lot and Jonah. Lot was a nephew of Abraham, and may be supposed to belong to the story of Abraham. Jonah's career nearly ended in a tragedy for himself, and his people got a further lease of power "for a time" (37:148). And both Lot and Jonah belong to a limited local tradition.

4084. The story of the Flood is found in some form or other among all nations, and not only among those who follow the Mosaic tradition. In Greek tradition the hero of the flood is Deukalion, with his wife Pyrrha; in Hindu tradition (*Shatapatha Brāhmana* and *Mahābhārata)* it is the sage Manū and the Fish. The Chinese tradition of a great Flood is recorded in *Shū-King*. Among American Indians the tradition was common to many tribes.

82. Then the rest We overwhelmed
In the Flood.

ثُمَّ أَغْرَقْنَا ٱلْـَٔاخَرِينَ ﴿٨٢﴾

83. Verily among those
Who followed his Way
Was Abraham.[4085]

وَإِنَّ مِن شِيعَتِهِۦ لَإِبْرَٰهِيمَ ﴿٨٣﴾

84. Behold, he approached his Lord
With a sound heart.[4086]

إِذْ جَآءَ رَبَّهُۥ بِقَلْبٍ سَلِيمٍ ﴿٨٤﴾

85. Behold, he said to his father
And to his people, "What
Is that which ye worship?

إِذْ قَالَ لِأَبِيهِ وَقَوْمِهِۦ مَاذَا تَعْبُدُونَ ﴿٨٥﴾

86. "Is it a Falsehood—
Gods other than Allah
That ye desire?[4087]

أَئِفْكًا ءَالِهَةً دُونَ ٱللَّهِ تُرِيدُونَ ﴿٨٦﴾

87. "Then what is your idea
About the Lord of the Worlds?"[4088]

فَمَا ظَنُّكُم بِرَبِّ ٱلْعَٰلَمِينَ ﴿٨٧﴾

88. Then did he cast
A glance at the Stars,

فَنَظَرَ نَظْرَةً فِى ٱلنُّجُومِ ﴿٨٨﴾

89. And he said, "I am
Indeed sick (at heart)!"[4089]

فَقَالَ إِنِّى سَقِيمٌ ﴿٨٩﴾

90. So they turned away
From him, and departed.

فَتَوَلَّوْا۟ عَنْهُ مُدْبِرِينَ ﴿٩٠﴾

91. Then did he turn
To their gods and said,

فَرَاغَ إِلَىٰٓ ءَالِهَتِهِمْ فَقَالَ ﴿٩١﴾

4085. The main story will be found in 21:51-73; but the episode about his readiness and that of his son to submit to the most extreme form of self-sacrifice under trial (in verses 102-107 below) is told here for the first time, as this Sūrah deals with the theme, "Not my will, but Thine be done!" In "followed his way", the pronoun "his" refers to Noah, "he", of verse 81 above.

4086. "A sound heart"; *qalb salīm*: a heart that is pure, and unaffected by the diseases that afflict others, As the heart in Arabic is taken to be not only the seat of feelings and affections, but also of intelligence and resulting action, it implies the whole character. *Cf.* Abraham's title of *Ḥanīf* (the True); 2:135 and n. 134. *Cf.* also 26:89: "only he will prosper who brings to Allah a sound heart."

4087. False worship—worship of idols or stars or symbols, or Mammon or Self—is due either to false and degrading conceptions of Allah, or to a sort of make-believe, where practice is inconsistent with knowledge or ignores the inner promptings of Conscience. Abraham's challenge to his people is : 'Are you fools or hypocrites?'

4088. 'Do you not realise that the real Creator is One—above all the forms and superstitions that you associate with Him?'

4089. The grief was really preying on his mind and soul, that he should be associated with such falsehoods. His father himself was among the chief supporters of such falsehoods, and his people were given up wholly to them. He could not possibly share in their mummeries, and they left him in disgust. Then he made his practical protest in the manner narrated in 21:56-64.

"Will ye not eat
(Of the offerings before you)?...

أَلَا تَأْكُلُونَ

92. "What is the matter
With you that ye
Speak not (intelligently)?"

٩٢ مَا لَكُمْ لَا تَنطِقُونَ

93. Then did he turn
Upon them, striking (them)[4090]
With the right hand.[4091]

٩٣ فَرَاغَ عَلَيْهِمْ ضَرْبًا بِالْيَمِينِ

94. Then came (the worshippers)
With hurried steps,
And faced (him).

٩٤ فَأَقْبَلُوا إِلَيْهِ يَزِفُّونَ

95. He said: "Worship ye
That which ye have
(Yourselves) carved?[4092]

٩٥ قَالَ أَتَعْبُدُونَ مَا تَنْحِتُونَ

96. "But Allah has created you
And your handiwork!"

٩٦ وَاللَّهُ خَلَقَكُمْ وَمَا تَعْمَلُونَ

97. They said, "Build him
A furnace, and throw him[4093]
Into the blazing fire!"

٩٧ قَالُوا ابْنُوا لَهُ بُنْيَانًا فَأَلْقُوهُ فِي الْجَحِيمِ

98. (This failing), they then
Sought a stratagem against
him,[4094]
But We made them the ones
Most humiliated!

٩٨ فَأَرَادُوا بِهِ كَيْدًا فَجَعَلْنَاهُمُ الْأَسْفَلِينَ

99. He said: "I will go
To my Lord! He

٩٩ وَقَالَ إِنِّي ذَاهِبٌ إِلَىٰ رَبِّي

4090. See the reference in the last note.

4091. *With the right hand*: as the right hand is the hand of power, the phrase means that he struck them with might and main and broke them.

4092. His action was a challenge, and he drives home the challenge now with argument. 'Do you worship your own handiwork? Surely worship is due to Him Who made you and made possible your handiwork!'

4093. The argument of Abraham was so sound that it could not be met by argument. In such cases Evil resorts to violence, or secret plotting. Here there was both violence and secret plotting. The violence consisted in throwing him into a blazing Furnace. But by the mercy of Allah the fire did not harm him (21:69), and so they resorted to plotting. But the plotting, as the next verse (37:98) shows, was a boomerang that recoiled on their own heads.

4094. *Cf.* 21:71. Their plot against the righteous Abraham failed. Abraham migrated from the country (Chaldea, Babylon, and Assyria) and prospered in Syria and Palestine. It was his persecutors that suffered humiliation.

Will surely guide me![4095]

سَيَهْدِينِ

100. "O my Lord! grant me
A righteous (son)!"

١٠٠ رَبِّ هَبْ لِى مِنَ ٱلصَّٰلِحِينَ

101. So We gave him
The good news[4096]
Of a boy ready
To suffer and forbear.[4097]

١٠١ فَبَشَّرْنَٰهُ بِغُلَٰمٍ حَلِيمٍ

102. Then, when (the son)
Reached (the age of)
(Serious) work with him,
He said: "O my son!
I see in vision[4098]
That I offer thee in sacrifice:[4099]
Now see what is
Thy view!" (The son) said:
"O my father! Do
As thou art commanded:
Thou wilt find me,
If Allah so wills one
Practising Patience and
Constancy!"

١٠٢ فَلَمَّا بَلَغَ مَعَهُ ٱلسَّعْىَ
قَالَ يَٰبُنَىَّ إِنِّىٓ أَرَىٰ فِى ٱلْمَنَامِ
أَنِّىٓ أَذْبَحُكَ فَٱنظُرْ مَاذَا تَرَىٰ ۚ
قَالَ يَٰٓأَبَتِ ٱفْعَلْ مَا تُؤْمَرُ ۖ
سَتَجِدُنِىٓ إِن شَآءَ ٱللَّهُ
مِنَ ٱلصَّٰبِرِينَ

103. So when they had both[4100]
Submitted their wills (to Allah),
And he had laid him

١٠٣ فَلَمَّآ أَسْلَمَا وَتَلَّهُۥ

4095. This was the Hijrah of Abraham. He left his people and his land, because the Truth was dearer to him than the ancestral falsehoods of his people. He trusted himself to Allah, and under Allah's guidance he laid the foundations of great peoples. See n. 2725 to 21:69.

4096. This was in the fertile land of Syria and Palestine. The boy thus born was, according to Muslim tradition, (which however is not unanimous on this point), the first-born son of Abraham, *viz.*, Ismāʿīl. The name itself is from the root *Samiʿa,* to hear, because Allah had heard Abraham's prayer (verse 100). Abraham's age when Ismāʿīl was born was 86 (Gen. xvi. 16).

4097. The boy's character was to be *Ḥalīm,* which I have translated "ready to suffer and forbear". This title is also applied to Abraham (in 9:114 and 11:75). It refers to the patient way in which both father and son cheerfully offered to suffer any self-sacrifice in order to obey the Command of Allah. See next verse.

4098. Where did this vision occur? The Muslim view is that it was in or near Makkah. Some would identify it with the valley of Minā, six miles north of Makkah, where a commemoration sacrifice is annually celebrated as a rite of the *Hajj* on the tenth of *Dhu al Hijjah,* the *ʿId* of Sacrifice, in memory of this Sacrifice of Abraham and Ismāʿīl (see n. 217 to 2:197). Others say that the original place of sacrifice was near the hill of Marwah (the companion hill to Safā, 2:158), which is associated with the infancy of Ismāʿīl.

4099. At what stage in Abraham's history did this occur? See n. 2725 to 21:69. It was obviously after his arrival in the land of Cannan and after Ismāʿīl had grown up to years of discretion. Was it before or after the building of the Kaʿbah (2:127)? There are no data on which this question can be answered. But we may suppose it was before that event, and that event may itself have been commemorative.

4100. Note that the sacrifice was demanded of *both* Abraham and Ismāʿīl. It was a trial of the will of the father and the son. By way of trial the father had the command conveyed to him in a vision. He consulted the son. The son readily consented, and offered to stand true to his promise if his self-sacrifice was really required. The whole thing is symbolical. Allah does not require the flesh and blood of animals (22:37), much less of human beings. But he does require the giving of our whole being to Allah, the symbol of which is that we should give up something very dear to us, if Duty requires that sacrifice. (R).

Prostrate on his forehead
(For sacrifice),[4101]

لِلْجَبِينِ

104. We called out to him,[4102]
"O Abraham!

وَنَٰدَيْنَٰهُ أَن يَٰٓإِبْرَٰهِيمُ ١٠٤

105. "Thou hast already fulfilled
The vision!"—thus indeed
Do We reward
Those who do right.

قَدْ صَدَّقْتَ ٱلرُّءْيَآ إِنَّا كَذَٰلِكَ نَجْزِى ٱلْمُحْسِنِينَ ١٠٥

106. For this was obviously
A trial—

إِنَّ هَٰذَا لَهُوَ ٱلْبَلَٰٓؤُا۟ ٱلْمُبِينُ ١٠٦

107. And We ransomed him
With a momentous sacrifice:[4103]

وَفَدَيْنَٰهُ بِذِبْحٍ عَظِيمٍ ١٠٧

108. And We left (this blessing)[4104]
For him among generations
(To come) in later times:

وَتَرَكْنَا عَلَيْهِ فِى ٱلْءَاخِرِينَ ١٠٨

109. "Peace and salutation
To Abraham!"

سَلَٰمٌ عَلَىٰٓ إِبْرَٰهِيمَ ١٠٩

110. Thus indeed do We reward
Those who do right

كَذَٰلِكَ نَجْزِى ٱلْمُحْسِنِينَ ١١٠

4101. Our version may be compared with the Jewish-Christian version of the present Old Testament. The Jewish tradition, in order to glorify the younger branch of the family, descended from Isaac, ancestor of the Jews, as against the elder branch, descended from Ismā'īl, ancestor of the Arabs, refers this sacrifice to Isaac (Gen. xxii. 1-18). Now Isaac was born when Abraham was 100 years old (Gen. xxi. 5), while Ismā'īl was born to Abraham when Abraham was 86 years old (Gen.xvi. 16). Ismā'īl was therefore 14 years older than Isaac. During his first 14 years Ismā'īl was the *only* son of Abraham; at no time was Isaac the *only* son of Abraham. Yet, in speaking of the sacrifice, the Old Testament says (Gen. xxii. 2): 'And He said, Take now thy son, thine *only* son Issac, whom thou lovest, and get thee into the land of Moriah: and offer him there for a burnt offering...." This slip shows at any rate which was the older version, and how it was overlaid, like the present Jewish records, in the interests of a tribal religion. The "land of Moriah" is not clear: it was three days' journey from Abraham's place (Gen.xxii.4). There is less warrant for identifying it with the hill of Moriah on which Jerusalem was afterwards built than with the hill of Marwah which is identified with the Arab tradition about Ismā'īl.

4102. In the Biblical version Isaac's consent is not taken: in fact Isaac asks, 'where is the lamb for sacrifice?' and is told that 'God would provide it'. It is a complete human sacrifice like those to Moloch. In our version it is as much a sacrifice by the will of Ismā'īl as by that of Abraham. And in any case it is symbolic: "this was obviously a trial"; "thou hast already fulfilled thy vision": etc.

4103. The adjective qualifying "sacrifice" here, *'aẓīm*, (great, momentous) may be understood both in a literal and a figurative sense. In a literal sense it implies that a fine sheep or ram was substituted symbolically. The figurative sense is even more important. It was indeed a great and momentous occasion, when two men, with concerted will, "ranged themselves in the ranks" of those to whom self-sacrifice in the service of Allah was the supreme thing in life. In this sense, said Jesus, "he that loseth his life for my sake shall find it", (Matt. x. 39). (R).

4104. *Cf.* above, 37:78-81 and n. 4083.

111. For he was one
Of Our believing Servants.

إِنَّهُۥ مِنْ عِبَادِنَا ٱلْمُؤْمِنِينَ ﴿١١١﴾

112. And We gave him[4105]
The good news
Of Isaac—a prophet—
One of the Righteous.

وَبَشَّرْنَٰهُ بِإِسْحَٰقَ نَبِيًّا مِّنَ ٱلصَّٰلِحِينَ ﴿١١٢﴾

113. We blessed him and Isaac:
But of their progeny
Are (some) that do right,
And (some) that obviously[4106]
Do wrong, to their own souls.

وَبَٰرَكْنَا عَلَيْهِ وَعَلَىٰٓ إِسْحَٰقَ ۚ وَمِن ذُرِّيَّتِهِمَا مُحْسِنٌ وَظَالِمٌ لِّنَفْسِهِۦ مُبِينٌ ﴿١١٣﴾

SECTION 4.

114. Again, (of old,)
We bestowed Our favour
On Moses and Aaron,[4107]

وَلَقَدْ مَنَنَّا عَلَىٰ مُوسَىٰ وَهَٰرُونَ ﴿١١٤﴾

115. And We delivered them
And their people from
(Their) Great Calamity;[4108]

وَنَجَّيْنَٰهُمَا وَقَوْمَهُمَا مِنَ ٱلْكَرْبِ ٱلْعَظِيمِ ﴿١١٥﴾

116. And We helped them,
So they overcame (their
troubles);[4109]

وَنَصَرْنَٰهُمْ فَكَانُوا۟ هُمُ ٱلْغَٰلِبِينَ ﴿١١٦﴾

117. And We gave them
The Book which helps[4110]
To make things clear;

وَءَاتَيْنَٰهُمَا ٱلْكِتَٰبَ ٱلْمُسْتَبِينَ ﴿١١٧﴾

4105. Isaac was Abraham's second son, born of Sarah, when Abraham was 100 years of age. See n. 4101. He was also blessed and became the ancestor of the Jewish people. See next note.

4106. So long as the Children of Israel upheld the righteous banner of Allah, they enjoyed Allah's blessing and their history is a portion of sacred history. When they fell from grace, they did not stop Allah's Plan: they injured their own souls.

4107. The story of Moses is told in numerous passages of the Qur'ān. The passages most illustrative of the present passage will be found in 28:4 (oppression of the Israelites in Egypt) and 20:77-79 (the Israelites triumphant over their enemies when the latter were drowned in the Red Sea).

4108. What could have been a greater calamity to them than that they should have been held in slavery by the Egyptians, that their male children should have been killed and their female children should have been saved alive for the Egyptians?

4109. The Israelites were delivered by three steps mentioned in verses 114, 115, and 116 respectively; but the consummation of Allah's favour on them was (verses 117-118) the Revelation given to them, which guided them on the Straight Way, so long as they preserved the Revelation intact and followed its precepts. The three steps were: (1) the divine commission to Moses and Aaron: (2) the deliverance from bondage; and (3) the triumphant crossing of the Red Sea and the destruction of Pharaoh's army.

4110. *Mustabīn* has a slightly different force from *Mubīn*. I have translated the former by "which *helps* to make things clear", and the latter by "which makes things clear"—apt descriptions as applied to the Tawrāh and the Qur'ān.

118. And We guided them
To the Straight Way.

وَهَدَيْنَٰهُمَا ٱلصِّرَٰطَ ٱلْمُسْتَقِيمَ ﴿١١٨﴾

119. And We left (this blessing)[4111]
For them among generations
(To come) in later times:

وَتَرَكْنَا عَلَيْهِمَا فِى ٱلْءَاخِرِينَ ﴿١١٩﴾

120. "Peace and salutation
To Moses and Aaron!"

سَلَٰمٌ عَلَىٰ مُوسَىٰ وَهَٰرُونَ ﴿١٢٠﴾

121. Thus indeed do We reward
Those who do right.

إِنَّا كَذَٰلِكَ نَجْزِى ٱلْمُحْسِنِينَ ﴿١٢١﴾

122. For they were two
Of Our believing Servants.

إِنَّهُمَا مِنْ عِبَادِنَا ٱلْمُؤْمِنِينَ ﴿١٢٢﴾

123. So also was Elias[4112]
Among those sent (by Us).

وَإِنَّ إِلْيَاسَ لَمِنَ ٱلْمُرْسَلِينَ ﴿١٢٣﴾

124. Behold, he said
To his people,
"Will ye not fear (Allah)?

إِذْ قَالَ لِقَوْمِهِۦٓ أَلَا تَتَّقُونَ ﴿١٢٤﴾

125. "Will ye call upon Ba'l[4113]
And forsake the Best
Of Creators—

أَتَدْعُونَ بَعْلًا وَتَذَرُونَ أَحْسَنَ ٱلْخَٰلِقِينَ ﴿١٢٥﴾

126. "Allah, your Lord and Cherisher
And the Lord and Cherisher
Of your fathers of old?"

ٱللَّهَ رَبَّكُمْ وَرَبَّ ءَابَآئِكُمُ ٱلْأَوَّلِينَ ﴿١٢٦﴾

127. But they rejected him,[4114]
And they will certainly
Be called up (for punishment)—

فَكَذَّبُوهُ فَإِنَّهُمْ لَمُحْضَرُونَ ﴿١٢٧﴾

4111. See above, 37:78-81 and n. 4083.

4112. See n. 905 to 6:85. Elias is the same as Elijah, whose story will be found in the Old Testament in 1 Kings xvii-xix. and 2 Kings i-ii. Elijah lived in the reign of Ahab (B.C. 896-874) and Ahaziah (B.C. 874-872), kings of the (northern) kingdom of Israel or Samaria. He was a prophet of the desert, like John the Baptist—unlike our Holy Prophet, who took part in, controlled, and guided all the affairs of his people. Both Ahab and Ahaziah were prone to lapse into the worship of Ba'l, the sun-god worshipped in Syria. That worship also included the worship of nature-powers and procreative powers, as in the Hindu worship of the Lingam, and led to many abuses. King Ahab had married a princess of Sidon, Jezebel, a wicked woman who led her husband to forsake Allah and adopt Ba'l-worship. Elijah denounced all Ahab's sins as well as the sins of Ahaziah and had to flee for his life. Eventually, according to the Old Testament (2 Kings, ii-11) he was taken up in a whirlwind to heaven in a chariot of fire after he had left his mantle with Elisha the prophet. (R).

4113. For Ba'l-worship see last note.

4114. They persecuted him and he had to flee for his life. Eventually he disappeared mysteriously; see n. 4112.

128. Except the sincere and devoted
Servants of Allah (among them).

إِلَّا عِبَادَ ٱللَّهِ ٱلْمُخْلَصِينَ ﴿١٢٨﴾

129. And We left (this blessing)[4115]
For him among generations
(To come) in later times:

وَتَرَكْنَا عَلَيْهِ فِي ٱلْآخِرِينَ ﴿١٢٩﴾

130. "Peace and salutation
To such as Elias!"[4115-A]

سَلَٰمٌ عَلَىٰٓ إِلْ يَاسِينَ ﴿١٣٠﴾

131. Thus indeed do We reward
Those who do right.

إِنَّا كَذَٰلِكَ نَجْزِي ٱلْمُحْسِنِينَ ﴿١٣١﴾

132. For he was one
Of Our believing Servants.

إِنَّهُۥ مِنْ عِبَادِنَا ٱلْمُؤْمِنِينَ ﴿١٣٢﴾

133. So also was Lūṭ[4116]
Among those sent (by Us).

وَإِنَّ لُوطًا لَّمِنَ ٱلْمُرْسَلِينَ ﴿١٣٣﴾

134. Behold, We delivered him
And his adherents, all

إِذْ نَجَّيْنَٰهُ وَأَهْلَهُۥٓ أَجْمَعِينَ ﴿١٣٤﴾

135. Except an old woman
Who was among those
Who lagged behind:[4117]

إِلَّا عَجُوزًا فِي ٱلْغَٰبِرِينَ ﴿١٣٥﴾

136. Then We destroyed
The rest.

ثُمَّ دَمَّرْنَا ٱلْآخَرِينَ ﴿١٣٦﴾

137. Verily, ye pass[4118]
By their (sites),
By day—

وَإِنَّكُمْ لَتَمُرُّونَ عَلَيْهِم مُّصْبِحِينَ ﴿١٣٧﴾

138. And by night:
Will ye not understand?

وَبِٱلَّيْلِ أَفَلَا تَعْقِلُونَ ﴿١٣٨﴾

4115. See above, 37:78-81, and n. 4083.

4115-A. *Ilyāsīn* may be an alternative form of *Ilyās: Cf. Saynā'a* (23:20) and *Sīnīn* (95:2). Or it may be the plural of *Ilyās,* meaning "such people as Ilyās".

4116. The best illustration of this passage about Lūṭ will be found in 7:80-84. He was a prophet sent to Sodom and Gomorrah, Cities of the Plain, by the Dead Sea. The inhabitants were given over to abominable crimes, against which he preached. They insulted him and threatened to expel him. But Allah in His mercy saved him and his family, with one exception, (see the following note), and then destroyed the Cities.

4117. *Cf.* 7:83, and n. 1051. Lot's wife had no faith: she lagged behind, and perished in the general ruin.

4118. *Cf.* 15:76, and 1998. The tract where they lay is situated on the highway to Syria where the Arab caravans travelled regularly, "by day and by night". Could not future generations learn wisdom from the destruction of those who did wrong?

C. 199.—So was it also with Jonah; he had
(37:139-182.) His trials, but Allah had mercy on him.
And his mission was successful. How
Can men ascribe to Allah qualities
And relations derogatory to His nature?
High is He above all creatures.
The ranks of angels and messengers stand firm
In His service. Evil is sure to be overcome.
So Praise and Glory to Allah, the Lord
Of Honour and Power, and Peace to His messengers!

SECTION 5.

139. So also was Jonah[4119]
Among those sent (by Us).

وَإِنَّ يُونُسَ لَمِنَ ٱلْمُرْسَلِينَ ﴿١٣٩﴾

140. When he ran away
(Like a slave from captivity)[4120]
To the ship (fully) laden,

إِذْ أَبَقَ إِلَى ٱلْفُلْكِ ٱلْمَشْحُونِ ﴿١٤٠﴾

141. He (agreed to) cast lots,[4121]
And he was condemned:

فَسَاهَمَ فَكَانَ مِنَ ٱلْمُدْحَضِينَ ﴿١٤١﴾

142. Then the big Fish[4122]
Did swallow him,
And he had done[4123]
Acts worthy of blame.

فَٱلْتَقَمَهُ ٱلْحُوتُ وَهُوَ مُلِيمٌ ﴿١٤٢﴾

143. Had it not been
That he (repented and)
Glorified Allah,[4124]

فَلَوْلَآ أَنَّهُۥ كَانَ مِنَ ٱلْمُسَبِّحِينَ ﴿١٤٣﴾

4119. For illustrative passages, see 21:87-88, n. 2744, and 67:48-50. Jonah's mission was to the city of Nineveh, then steeped in wickedness. He was rejected and he denounced Allah's wrath on them, but they repented and obtained Allah's forgiveness. But Jonah "departed in wrath" (21:87), forgetting that Allah has Mercy as well as forgiveness. See the notes following, *Cf.* 10:98, n. 1478.

4120. Jonah ran away from Nineveh like a slave from captivity. He should have stuck to his post and merged his own will in Allah's Will. He was hasty, and went off to take a ship. As if he could escape from Allah's Plan!

4121. The ship was fully laden and met foul weather. The sailors, according to their superstition, wanted to find out who was responsible for the ill-luck: a fugitive slave would cause such ill-luck. The lot fell on Jonah, and he was cast off.

4122. The rivers of Mesopotamia have some huge fishes. The word used here is *Hūt,* which may be a fish or perhaps a crocodile. If it were in an open northern sea, it might be a whale. The locality is not mentioned: in the Old Testament he is said to have taken ship in the port of Joppa (now Jaffa) in the Mediterranean (Jonah. i. 3), which would be not less than 600 miles from Nineveh. The Tigris river, mentioned by some of our Commentators, is more likely, and it contains some fishes of extraordinary size.

4123. See n. 4120.

4124. "But he cried through the depths of darkness, 'There is no god but Thee; glory to Thee! I was indeed wrong!" (21:87).

144. He would certainly have
Remained inside the Fish[4125]
Till the Day of Resurrection.

١٤٤ لَلَبِثَ فِى بَطْنِهِۦٓ إِلَىٰ يَوْمِ يُبْعَثُونَ

145. But We cast him forth
On the naked shore
In a state of sickness,[4126]

١٤٥ فَنَبَذْنَـٰهُ بِٱلْعَرَآءِ وَهُوَ سَقِيمٌ

146. And We caused to grow,
Over him, a spreading plant
Of the Gourd kind,

١٤٦ وَأَنۢبَتْنَا عَلَيْهِ شَجَرَةً مِّن يَقْطِينٍ

147. And We sent him
(On a mission)
To a hundred thousand[4127]
(Men) or more.

١٤٧ وَأَرْسَلْنَـٰهُ إِلَىٰ مِائَةِ أَلْفٍ أَوْ يَزِيدُونَ

148. And they believed;
So We permitted them
To enjoy (their life)[4128]
For a while.

١٤٨ فَـَٔامَنُوا۟ فَمَتَّعْنَـٰهُمْ إِلَىٰ حِينٍ

149. Now ask them their opinion:[4129]
Is it that thy Lord
Has (only) daughters, and they
Have sons?—

١٤٩ فَٱسْتَفْتِهِمْ أَلِرَبِّكَ ٱلْبَنَاتُ
وَلَهُمُ ٱلْبَنُونَ

150. Or that We created
The angels female, and they
Are witnesses (thereto)?

١٥٠ أَمْ خَلَقْنَا ٱلْمَلَـٰٓئِكَةَ
إِنَـٰثًا وَهُمْ شَـٰهِدُونَ

4125. This is just the idiom. This was to be the burial and the grave of Jonah. If he had not repented, he could not have got out of the body of the creature that had swallowed him, until the Day of Resurrection, when all the dead would be raised up.

4126. *Cf.* 37:89 above. His strange situation might well have caused him to be ill. He wanted fresh air and solitude. He got both in the open plain, and the abundantly shady Gourd Plant or some fruitful tree like it gave him both shade and sustenance. The Gourd is a creeper that can spread over any roof or ruined structure.

4127. The city of Nineveh was a very large city. The Old Testament says: "Nineveh was an exceeding great city of three days' journey" (Jonah, iii. 3); "wherein are more than six score thousand persons" (Jonah, iv. 11). In other words its circuit was about 45 miles, and its population was over a hundred and twenty thousand inhabitants.

4128. They repented and believed, and Nineveh got a new lease of life. For the dates to which Jonah may be referred, and the vicissitudes of the City's history as the seat of the Assyrian Empire, see notes 1478-79 to 10:98.

The lessons from Jonah's story are: (1) that no man should take upon himself to judge of Allah's wrath or Allah's mercy; (2) that nevertheless Allah forgives true repentance, whether in a righteous man, or in a wicked city; and (3) that Allah's Plan will always prevail, and can never be defeated.

4129. We begin a new argument here. The Pagan Arabs called angels daughters of Allah. They themselves were ashamed of having daughters, and preferred to have sons, to add to their power and dignity. See 16:57-59, and n. 2082. Yet they invented daughters for Allah!

151. Is it not that they Say, from their own invention,	أَلَآ إِنَّهُم مِّنْ إِفْكِهِمْ لَيَقُولُونَ ﴿١٥١﴾
152. "Allah has begotten children"?[4130] But they are liars!	وَلَدَ ٱللَّهُ وَإِنَّهُمْ لَكَٰذِبُونَ ﴿١٥٢﴾
153. Did He (then) choose[4131] Daughters rather than sons?	أَصْطَفَى ٱلْبَنَاتِ عَلَى ٱلْبَنِينَ ﴿١٥٣﴾
154. What is the matter With you? How judge ye?	مَا لَكُمْ كَيْفَ تَحْكُمُونَ ﴿١٥٤﴾
155. Will ye not then Receive admonition?	أَفَلَا تَذَكَّرُونَ ﴿١٥٥﴾
156. Or have ye An authority manifest?	أَمْ لَكُمْ سُلْطَٰنٌ مُّبِينٌ ﴿١٥٦﴾
157. Then bring ye your Book (Of authority) if ye be Truthful!	فَأْتُوا۟ بِكِتَٰبِكُمْ إِن كُنتُمْ صَٰدِقِينَ ﴿١٥٧﴾
158. And they have invented A blood-relationship[4132] Between Him and the Jinns: But the Jinns know (Quite well) that they Have indeed to appear (Before His Judgement Seat)!	وَجَعَلُوا۟ بَيْنَهُۥ وَبَيْنَ ٱلْجِنَّةِ نَسَبًا ﴿١٥٨﴾ وَلَقَدْ عَلِمَتِ ٱلْجِنَّةُ إِنَّهُمْ لَمُحْضَرُونَ
159. Glory to Allah! (He is free) From the things they ascribe (To Him)!	سُبْحَٰنَ ٱللَّهِ عَمَّا يَصِفُونَ ﴿١٥٩﴾
160. Not (so do) the Servants Of Allah, sincere and devoted.[4133]	إِلَّا عِبَادَ ٱللَّهِ ٱلْمُخْلَصِينَ ﴿١٦٠﴾

4130. Any attribution to Allah of ideas derogatory to His Oneness and His supreme height above all creatures is likely to degrade our own conception of Allah's Universal Plan, and is condemned in the strongest terms.

4131. There is the strongest irony in this passage.

4132. The angels are at least pure beings engaged in the service of Allah. But the Pagan superstitions not only connect them with Allah as daughters but even connect Allah by relationship with all kinds of spirits, good or evil! In some mythologies the most evil powers are gods or goddesses as if they belonged to the family of Allah the Creator and had some semblance of equality with Him! This, too, is repudiated in the strongest terms. For Jinns see n. 929 to 6:100.

4133. Those sincere in devotion to Allah never ascribe such degrading ideas to Allah.

161. For, verily, neither ye
Nor those ye worship—

فَإِنَّكُمْ وَمَا تَعْبُدُونَ ﴿١٦١﴾

162. Can lead (any)[4134]
Into temptation
Concerning Allah,

مَآ أَنتُمْ عَلَيْهِ بِفَٰتِنِينَ ﴿١٦٢﴾

163. Except such as are
(Themselves) going to
The blazing Fire!

إِلَّا مَنْ هُوَ صَالِ ٱلْجَحِيمِ ﴿١٦٣﴾

164. (Those ranged in ranks say):[4135]
"Not one of us but has
A place appointed;

وَمَا مِنَّآ إِلَّا لَهُۥ مَقَامٌ مَّعْلُومٌ ﴿١٦٤﴾

165. "And we are verily
Ranged in ranks (for service);

وَإِنَّا لَنَحْنُ ٱلصَّآفُّونَ ﴿١٦٥﴾

166. "And we are verily those
Who declare (Allah's) glory!"

وَإِنَّا لَنَحْنُ ٱلْمُسَبِّحُونَ ﴿١٦٦﴾

167. And there were those[4136]
Who said,

وَإِن كَانُوا۟ لَيَقُولُونَ ﴿١٦٧﴾

168. "If only we had had
Before us a Message
From those of old,

لَوْ أَنَّ عِندَنَا ذِكْرًا مِّنَ ٱلْأَوَّلِينَ ﴿١٦٨﴾

169. "We should certainly have
Been Servants of Allah,[4137]
Sincere (and devoted)!"

لَكُنَّا عِبَادَ ٱللَّهِ ٱلْمُخْلَصِينَ ﴿١٦٩﴾

4134. Evil has no power over faith, truth, and sincerity. Such power as it has is over those who deliberately put themselves in the way of Destruction. It is their own will that leads them astray. If they were fortified against Evil by Faith, Patience, and Constancy, Evil would have no power to hurt them. Allah would protect them.

4135. To round off the argument of the Sūrah we go back to the idea with which it began. Those who range themselves in ranks for the united service of Allah (see above, 37:1 and n. 4031)—whether angels or men of God—are content to keep their ranks and do whatever service is assigned to them. It is not for them to question Allah's Plan, because they know that it is good and that it will ultimately triumph. Any seeming delays or defeats do not worry them. Nor do they ever break their ranks.

4136. There were the sceptics or Unbelievers—primarily the Pagan Arabs, but in a more extended sense, all who doubt Allah's providence or revelation.

4137. Such men take refuge in ancestral tradition. 'If our forefathers had had an inkling of Revelation or miracles, or had worshipped as we are now taught to worship, we should gladly have accepted. Or if they had had anything of the miracles which other nations of old are said to have received, we could then have accepted.' But now stronger and more convincing proofs have come to them in the Qur'ān in their own tongue, and they doubt and reject it.

170. But (now that the Qur'ān
Has come), they reject it;
But soon will they know![4138]

(١٧٠) فَكَفَرُوا۟ بِهِۦ ۖ فَسَوْفَ يَعْلَمُونَ

171. Already has Our Word
Been passed before (this)
To Our Servants sent (by Us),

(١٧١) وَلَقَدْ سَبَقَتْ كَلِمَتُنَا لِعِبَادِنَا ٱلْمُرْسَلِينَ

172. That they would certainly
Be assisted,

(١٧٢) إِنَّهُمْ لَهُمُ ٱلْمَنصُورُونَ

173. And that Our forces—[4139]
They surely must conquer.

(١٧٣) وَإِنَّ جُندَنَا لَهُمُ ٱلْغَٰلِبُونَ

174. So turn thou away[4140]
From them for a little while,

(١٧٤) فَتَوَلَّ عَنْهُمْ حَتَّىٰ حِينٍ

175. And watch them (how[4141]
They fare), and they soon
Shall see (how thou farest)!

(١٧٥) وَأَبْصِرْهُمْ فَسَوْفَ يُبْصِرُونَ

176. Do they wish (indeed)[4142]
To hurry on our Punishment?

(١٧٦) أَفَبِعَذَابِنَا يَسْتَعْجِلُونَ

177. But when it descends
Into the open space[4143]
Before them, evil will be
The morning for those who
Were warned (and heeded not)!

(١٧٧) فَإِذَا نَزَلَ بِسَاحَتِهِمْ
فَسَآءَ صَبَاحُ ٱلْمُنذَرِينَ

4138. Allah's Truth will manifest itself against all odds, and the whole world will see.

4139. The victory will be the victory of Allah's Truth by the forces of Allah, but every soldier in the army of Truth, who has done his duty, will be entitled to claim a share in the victory.

4140. Addressed in the first instance to the Holy Prophet, but good for all time. He was not to be discouraged by his initial failures. Soon came victory to him from Allah. So is it always in the struggles of truth and righteousness. The righteous can afford to ignore opposition, confident in the strength which comes from the Grace of Allah.

4141. Watch and wait, for the Right must come to its own.

4142. The last verse enjoined Patience under the attacks of Evil, in the knowledge that evil must be conquered at last. Evil may perhaps turn back scoffingly and say. 'If a punishment is to come, why not bring it on now? Why indeed? The answer is: when it comes, it will come like a rush by night when the enemy is overpowered, when he least expects it: when the day dawns, it is a sorry plight in which the enemy finds himself. *Cf.* 22:47, and n. 2826: and 26:204, n. 3230.

4143. See last note. The parable is that of an enemy camp in a plain, which is surprised and destroyed by a night attack from the hills. Evil is the plight of any survivors in the morning. Their regrets will be all the more poignant if they had had some sort of a warning before hand and had paid no heed to it!

178. So turn thou away[4144]
From them for a little while,

وَتَوَلَّ عَنْهُمْ حَتَّىٰ حِينٍ ﴿١٧٨﴾

179. And watch (how they fare)
And they soon shall see
(How thou farest)!

وَأَبْصِرْ فَسَوْفَ يُبْصِرُونَ ﴿١٧٩﴾

180. Glory to thy Lord,[4145]
The Lord of Honour
And Power! (He is free)
From what they ascribe
(To Him)!

سُبْحَٰنَ رَبِّكَ رَبِّ ٱلْعِزَّةِ عَمَّا يَصِفُونَ ﴿١٨٠﴾

181. And Peace on the Messengers

وَسَلَٰمٌ عَلَى ٱلْمُرْسَلِينَ ﴿١٨١﴾

182. And Praise to Allah,
The Lord and Cherisher
Of the Worlds.

وَٱلْحَمْدُ لِلَّهِ رَبِّ ٱلْعَٰلَمِينَ ﴿١٨٢﴾

4144. This and the following verse repeat verses 174-75 (with a slight verbal alteration). The argument in verses 176-77 brought in a new point. When that is finished, the repetition carries us back to the main argument, and rounds off the whole Sūrah.

4145. This and the following two verses recapitulate: (1) Glory, Honour, and Power belong to Allah; (2) No one is equal to Him; (3) He sends Messengers and revelations, and His aid will overcome all obstacles; for (4) He loves and cherishes all His Creation.

INTRODUCTION TO SŪRAH 38—*ṢĀD*

For the place of this Sūrah in the series of six, dealing with some of the mysteries of the spiritual world, see Introduction to S. 34.

This Sūrah, both in chronology and subject matter, is cognate to S. 37, and carries forward the same argument. But here the emphasis is laid on the working of earthly power when combined with spiritual power, and it is pointed out how much more significant (and real) spiritual power is. For this reason the illustrative stories are mainly those of David and Solomon who were kings as well as prophets, and a parallel is suggested with the unfolding public life of our Holy Prophet.

Summary—Worldly and evil men are surprised at the renewal of Truth and Righteousness: but righteousness has more power than worldly strength, as is seen in the story of kings like David, who had both (38:1-26, and C. 201).

So also Solomon loved the Lord more than worldly power, which may be good but may be misused by evil men; so also Job and other men of power and insight, chose the path of final bliss rather than final misery (38:27-64, and C. 201).

So also in the case of the final Messenger; his Gospel of Unity must triumph over all Jealousy and Arrogance in God's good time (38:65-88, and C. 202).

C. 200.—Self-glory and Separatism, these
(38:1-26.) Are among the roots of Evil, also Envy
And Suspicion. Not all the combinations
Of Evil can for a moment reverse
Allah's Purpose or His Justice. David,
Endowed with worldly Power and the Virtues
Had yet to purge himself of the thought
Of Self-glory, which he did; and thus
He became one of those nearest to Allah.

Sūrah 38.

Ṣād

In the name of God, Most Gracious,
Most Merciful.

بِسْمِ اللَّهِ الرَّحْمَٰنِ الرَّحِيمِ

1. Ṣād:[4146]
By the Qur'ān,
Full of Admonition:[4147]
(This is the Truth).

(١) ص ۚ
وَالْقُرْآنِ ذِي الذِّكْرِ

2. But the Unbelievers
(Are steeped) in Self-glory[4119]
And Separatism.

(٢) بَلِ الَّذِينَ كَفَرُوا فِي عِزَّةٍ وَشِقَاقٍ

3. How many generations
Before them did We destroy?
In the end they cried[4149]
(For mercy)—when
There was no longer time
For being saved!

(٣) كَمْ أَهْلَكْنَا
مِنْ قَبْلِهِمْ مِنْ قَرْنٍ فَنَادَوْا
وَلَاتَ حِينَ مَنَاصٍ

4. So they wonder
That a Warner has come

(٤) وَعَجِبُوا أَنْ جَاءَهُمْ مُنْذِرٌ

4146. Ṣād is a letter of the Arabic alphabet. It is used here as an Abbreviated Letter, for which see Appendix I (at the end of Sūrah 2:). See also the second para. of n. 989 to 7:1 for this particular letter. No dogmatism is permissible in trying to interpret Abbreviated Letters. But it is suggested that it may stand for *Qasaṣ* ("Stories"), in which the dominant consonant is *ṣ*. For this Sūrah is concerned mainly with the stories of David and Solomon as illustrative of the relative positions of spiritual and worldly power. Sale's note: "It may stand for Solomon": is a real howler: for in Arabic the letter *Ṣād* does not occur at all in the name of Solomon.

4147. *Full of admonition*: the word dhikr is far more comprehensive than any single word or phrase that I can think of in English: it implies (1) remembrance in a spirit of reverence; (2) recital, celebrating the praises of God; (3) teaching, admonition, warning; (4) Message, Revelation, as in *Ahl al dhikr,* "those who possess the Message" 16:43, and n. 2069). In Sūfī phraseology it implies mystical enlightenment, both the aspiration and the attainment, for in the highest spiritual atmosphere, the two are one. Devotional exercises are also called *dhikr,* with reference to meaning (2) above.

4148. The great root of Evil and Unbelief is Self-glory or Arrogance, as is pointed out in several places with regard to Satan: *cf,* below, 38:74-76. This leads to Envy and Separatism, or a desire to start a peculiar doctrine or sect of one's own, instead of a desire to find common grounds of belief and life, which lead to the Religion of Unity in Allah. This teaching of Unity was what the Pagans objected to in the Holy Prophet (verse 5 below)!

4149. Teaching, Warning, Signs have been given by Allah to all nations and at all times, and yet nations have rebelled and gone wrong and suffered destruction. If only later generations could learn that wrongdoing results in self-destruction! For the justice of Allah merely carries out the result of their own choice and actions. At any time during their probation they could repent and obtain mercy, but their "Self-glory and Separatism" stand in the way. Ultimately they do cry for a way of escape, but it is then too late.

To them from among
themselves![4150]
And the Unbelievers say,
"This is a sorcerer
Telling lies!

منهم
وقال الكفرون هذا سحر كذّاب

5. "Has he made the gods[4151]
(All) into one God?
Truly this is
A wonderful thing!"

٥ أجعل الالهة الها وحدا
إن هذا لشيء عجاب

6. And the leaders among them
Go away (impatiently),
(saying),[4152]
"Walk ye away, and remain
Constant to your gods!
For this is truly
A thing designed (against you)!

٦ وانطلق الملأ منهم
أن امشوا واصبروا على ءالهتكم
إن هذا لشيء يراد

7. "We never heard (the like)
Of this among the people
Of these latter days:[4153]
This is nothing but
A made-up tale!"

٧ ما سمعنا بهذا في الملة الاخرة
إن هذا إلا اختلق

8. "What! Has the Message
Been sent to him—[4154]
(Of all persons) among us?"...
But they are in doubt

٨ أءنزل عليه الذكر من بيننا
بل هم في شك

4150. Their wonder is only stimulated. They are full of envy and spite against one of themselves who has been chosen by Allah to be His Messenger, and they vent their spite by making all sorts of false accusations. The man who was pre-eminent for truth and conscientious consideration, they call "a sorcerer and a liar"!

4151. And what is the offence of the Messenger of Unity? That he has made all their fantastic gods disappear: that in place of chaos he has brought harmony; that in place of conflict he brings peace! It is a wonderful thing, but not in the sarcastic sense in which the Unbelievers scoff at it!

4152. When the message of Islam was being preached in its infancy, and the Preacher and his followers were being persecuted by the Pagans, one of the devices adopted by the Pagan leaders was to get the Prophet's uncle Abū Ṭālib to denounce or renounce his beloved nephew. A conference was held with Abū Ṭālib for this purpose. On its failure the leaders walked away, and began to discredit the great movement by falsely giving out that it was designed against their personal influence, and to throw power into the hands of the Prophet. 'Umar's conversion occurred in the sixth year of the Mission (seventh year before the Hijrah). The circumstances connected with it (see Introduction to S. 20) greatly alarmed the Quraysh chiefs, who, greedy of autocracy themselves, confused the issue by accusing the righteous Preacher of plotting against their power.

4153. 'Whatever may have been the case in the past', they said, 'our own immediate ancestors worshipped these idols in Makkah, and why should we give them up? Self-complacency was stronger with them than Truth; and so they call Truth "a made-up tale"! Some Commentators interpret *millat akhirah* to refer to the last religion preached before Islam, *viz*. Christianity, which had itself departed from Monotheism to Trinity. (R).

4154. Here comes in envy. 'If a Message had to come, why should it come to him, the orphan son of 'Abd Allah, and not to one of our own great men?'

Concerning My (own) Message![4155]
Nay, they have not yet
Tasted My Punishment!

مِن ذِكْرِي بَل لَّمَّا يَذُوقُوا عَذَابِ

9. Or have they the Treasures
Of the Mercy of thy Lord—[4156]
The Exalted in Power,
The Grantor of Bounties
Without measure?

٩ أَمْ عِندَهُمْ خَزَائِنُ رَحْمَةِ رَبِّكَ الْعَزِيزِ الْوَهَّابِ

10. Or have they the dominion
Of the heavens and the earth
And all between? If so,
Let them mount up[4157]
With the ropes and means
(To reach that end)!

١٠ أَمْ لَهُم مُّلْكُ السَّمَاوَاتِ وَالْأَرْضِ وَمَا بَيْنَهُمَا فَلْيَرْتَقُوا فِي الْأَسْبَابِ

11. But there—will be[4158]
Put to flight even a host
Of confederates.

١١ جُندٌ مَّا هُنَالِكَ مَهْزُومٌ مِّنَ الْأَحْزَابِ

12. Before them (were many
Who) rejected messengers—[4159]
The People of Noah,
And 'Ād, and Pharaoh
The Lord of Stakes,[4160]

١٢ كَذَّبَتْ قَبْلَهُمْ قَوْمُ نُوحٍ وَعَادٌ وَفِرْعَوْنُ ذُو الْأَوْتَادِ

13. And Thamūd, and the People
Of Lūṭ, and the Companions[4161]

١٣ وَثَمُودُ وَقَوْمُ لُوطٍ وَأَصْحَابُ

4155. They have no clear idea of how Allah's Message comes! It is not a worldly thing to be given to anyone. It is a divine thing requiring spiritual preparation. If they close their eyes to it now, it will be brought home to them when they taste the consequences of their folly!

4156. If they set themselves to judge Allah, have they anything to show comparable to Allah's Mercy and Power! He has both in infinite measure. Who are they to question the grant of His Mercy and Revelation to His own Chosen One?

4157. Weak and puny creatures though they are, they dare to raise their heads against the Omnipotent, as if they had dominion over Creation and not He! If they had any power, let them mount up to heaven and use all the means they have to that end, and see how they can frustrate Allah's Purpose!

4158. Of course they cannot frustrate Allah's Purpose. In that world—the spiritual world—they will be ignominiously routed, even if they form the strongest confederacy of the Powers of Evil that ever could combine. *Cf.* the last clause of verse 13 below.

4159. In their day, Noah's contemporaries, or the 'Ād and the Thamūd, so frequently mentioned, or Pharaoh the mighty king of Egypt, or the people to whom Lot was sent (*Cf.* 37:85-82; 7:65-73; 7:103-137; 7:80-84) were examples of arrogance and rebellion against Allah: they rejected the divine Message brought by their messengers, and they all came to an evil end. Will not their posterity learn their lesson?

4160. The title of Pharaoh, "Lord of the Stakes", denotes power and arrogance, in all or any of the following ways: (1) the stake makes a tent firm and stable, and is a symbol of firmness and stability; (2) many stakes mean a large camp and a numerous army to fight; (3) impaling with stakes was a cruel punishment resorted to by the Pharaohs in arrogant pride of power.

4161. *Companions of the Wood*: see 15:78, and n. 2000.

Of the Wood— such were The Confederates.[4162]	لَـْٔيكَةِ أُوْلَـٰٓئِكَ ٱلْأَحْزَابُ
14. Not one (of them) but Rejected the messengers, But My Punishment Came justly and inevitably[4163] (On them).	﴿١٤﴾ إِن كُلٌّ إِلَّا كَذَّبَ ٱلرُّسُلَ فَحَقَّ عِقَابِ
SECTION 2.	
15. These (today) only wait For a single mighty Blast,[4164] Which (when it comes) Will brook no delay.[4165]	﴿١٥﴾ وَمَا يَنظُرُ هَـٰٓؤُلَآءِ إِلَّا صَيْحَةً وَٰحِدَةً مَّا لَهَا مِن فَوَاقٍ
16. They say: "Our Lord! Hasten to us our sentence[4166] (Even) before the Day Of Account!"	﴿١٦﴾ وَقَالُوا۟ رَبَّنَا عَجِّل لَّنَا قِطَّنَا قَبْلَ يَوْمِ ٱلْحِسَابِ
17. Have patience at what they Say, and remember Our Servant David, the man of strength:[4167] For he ever turned (to Allah).	﴿١٧﴾ ٱصْبِرْ عَلَىٰ مَا يَقُولُونَ وَٱذْكُرْ عَبْدَنَا دَاوُۥدَ ذَا ٱلْأَيْدِ إِنَّهُۥٓ أَوَّابٌ
18. It was We that made The hills declare,[4168] In unison with him,	﴿١٨﴾ إِنَّا سَخَّرْنَا ٱلْجِبَالَ مَعَهُۥ

4162. *Cf.* above, verse 11, and n. 4258.

4163. *Cf.* 15:64, n. 1990; and 22:18.

4164. *Cf.* 36:29, n. 3973.

4165. *Fawāq*: delay, the interval between one milking of a she-camel, and another, either to give her a breathing space or to give her young time to suck—or perhaps the milker to adjust his fingers. Such an internal will be quite short. The derived meaning is that when the inevitable punishment for sin arrives, it will not tarry, but do its work without delay.

4166. *Cf.* 26:204 and n. 3230. Those who do not believe in the Hereafter say ironically: "Let us have our punishment and sentence now: why delay it?" The last verse and the next verse supply the commentary. As to those who mock, they will find out the truth soon enough, when it is too late for repentance or mercy. As to the prophets of Allah, who are mocked, they must wait patiently for Allah to fulfil His Plan: even men who had worldly strength and power, like David, had to exercise infinite patience when mocked by their contemporaries.

4167. David was a man of exceptional strength, for even as a raw youth, he slew the Philistine giant Goliath. See 2:249-252, and notes 286-87. Before that fight, he was mocked by his enemies and chidden even by his own elder brother. But he relied upon Allah, and won through, and afterwards became king.

4168. See n. 2733 to 21:79. All nature sings in unison and celebrates the praises of Allah. David was given the gift of music and psalmody, and therefore the hills and birds are expressed as singing Allah's praises in unison with him. The special hours when the hills and groves echo the songs of birds are in the evening and at dawn, when also the birds gather together, for those are respectively their roosting hours and the hours of their concerted flight for the day.

Our Praises, at eventide
And at break of day,

يُسَبِّحْنَ بِالْعَشِيِّ وَالْإِشْرَاقِ

19. And the birds gathered
(In assemblies): all with him
Did turn (to Allah).[4169]

﴿١٩﴾ وَالطَّيْرَ مَحْشُورَةً كُلٌّ لَهُ أَوَّابٌ

20. We strengthened his kingdom,
And gave him wisdom
And sound judgement[4170]
In speech and decision.

﴿٢٠﴾ وَشَدَدْنَا مُلْكَهُ وَآتَيْنَاهُ الْحِكْمَةَ
وَفَصْلَ الْخِطَابِ

21. Has the Story of
The Disputants reached thee?[4171]
Behold, they climbed over
The wall of the private chamber;

﴿٢١﴾ وَهَلْ أَتَاكَ نَبَأُ الْخَصْمِ
إِذْ تَسَوَّرُوا الْمِحْرَابَ

22. When they entered
The presence of David,[4172]
And he was terrified
Of them, they said:
"Fear not: we are two
Disputants, one of whom
Has wronged the other:
Decide now between us
With truth, and treat us not
With injustice, but guide us
To the even Path.

﴿٢٢﴾ إِذْ دَخَلُوا عَلَىٰ دَاوُودَ
فَفَزِعَ مِنْهُمْ قَالُوا لَا تَخَفْ
خَصْمَانِ بَغَىٰ بَعْضُنَا عَلَىٰ بَعْضٍ
فَاحْكُمْ بَيْنَنَا بِالْحَقِّ وَلَا تُشْطِطْ
وَاهْدِنَا إِلَىٰ سَوَاءِ الصِّرَاطِ

23. "This man is my brother:[4173]
He has nine and ninety
Ewes, and I have (but) one:
Yet he says, 'Commit her

﴿٢٣﴾ إِنَّ هَٰذَا أَخِي لَهُ تِسْعٌ وَتِسْعُونَ نَعْجَةً
وَلِيَ نَعْجَةٌ وَاحِدَةٌ فَقَالَ

4169. Note the mutual echo between this verse and verse 17 above. The Arabic *awwāb* is common to both, and it furnishes the rhyme or rhythm of the greater part of this Sūrah, thus echoing the main theme: 'Turn to Allah in Prayer and Praise, for that is more than any worldly power or wisdom.'

4170. *Cf.* n. 2732 to 21:79 for David's sound judgement in decisions; he could also express himself aptly, as his Psalms bear witness.

4171. This story or Parable is not found in the Bible, unless the vision here described be considered as equivalent to Nathan's parable in II Samuel, 11 and 12. Bayḍāwī would seem to favour that view, but other Commentators reject it. David was a pious man, and he had a well-guarded private chamber (*miḥrāb*) for Prayer and Praise.

4172. David was used to retiring to his private chamber at stated times for his devotions. One day, suddenly, his privacy was invaded by two men, who had obtained access by climbing over a wall. David was frightened at the apparition. But they said: "We have come to seek thy justice as king: we are brothers, and we have a quarrel, which we wish thee to decide."

4173. The brother who was most aggrieved said: "This my brother has a flock of ninety-nine sheep, and I have but one; yet he wants me to give up my one sheep to his keeping; and moreover he is not even fair-spoken. He talks like one meditating mischief, and he has not even the grace to ask as an equal, of one sharing in a business or inheritance. What shall I do?"

To my care,' and is (moreover)
Harsh to me in speech."

أَكْفِلْنِيهَا وَعَزَّنِى فِى ٱلْخِطَابِ

24. (David) said: "He has
Undoubtedly wronged thee[4174]
In demanding thy (single) ewe
To be added to his (flock
Of) ewes; truly many
Are the Partners (in business)[4175]
Who wrong each other:
Not so do those who believe
And work deeds of righteousness,
And how few are they?"...
And David gathered that We
Had tried him: he asked
Forgiveness of his Lord,[4176]
Fell down, bowing
(In prostration), and turned
(To Allah in repentance)[4176-A].

(٢٤) قَالَ لَقَدْ ظَلَمَكَ
بِسُؤَالِ نَعْجَتِكَ إِلَىٰ نِعَاجِهِۦ ۖ
وَإِنَّ كَثِيرًا مِّنَ ٱلْخُلَطَآءِ لَيَبْغِى
بَعْضُهُمْ عَلَىٰ بَعْضٍ إِلَّا ٱلَّذِينَ ءَامَنُوا۟
وَعَمِلُوا۟ ٱلصَّٰلِحَٰتِ وَقَلِيلٌ مَّا هُمْ ۗ
وَظَنَّ دَاوُۥدُ أَنَّمَا فَتَنَّٰهُ فَٱسْتَغْفَرَ رَبَّهُۥ
وَخَرَّ رَاكِعًا وَأَنَابَ

25. So We forgave him
This (lapse): he enjoyed,
Indeed, a Near Approach to Us,
And a beautiful Place
Of (final) Return.

(٢٥) فَغَفَرْنَا لَهُۥ ذَٰلِكَ ۖ
وَإِنَّ لَهُۥ عِندَنَا لَزُلْفَىٰ وَحُسْنَ مَـَٔابٍ

26. O David! We did indeed
Make thee a vicegerent[4177]
On earth: so judge thou
Between men in truth (and
justice):

(٢٦) يَٰدَاوُۥدُ إِنَّا جَعَلْنَٰكَ خَلِيفَةً
فِى ٱلْأَرْضِ فَٱحْكُم بَيْنَ ٱلنَّاسِ بِٱلْحَقِّ

4174. The circumstances were mysterious, the accusation was novel; it was not clear why the unjust brother should also have come with the complainant, risking his life in climbing the wall to evade the guard, and he certainly said nothing. David took them literally, and began to preach about the falsehood and the fraud of men, who should be content with what they have, but who always covet more. (R).

4175. Especially, said David, is it wrong for brothers or men in partnership to take advantage of each other; but how few are the men who are righteous? He had in mind his own devotions and justice. But lo and behold! the men disappeared as mysteriously as they had come. It was then that David realised that his visions had been a trial or temptation—a test of his moral or spiritual fibre! Great though he was as a king, and just though he was as a judge, the moment that he thought of these things in self-pride, his merit vanished. In himself he was as other men; it was Allah's grace that gave him wisdom and justice, and he should have been humble in the sight of Allah.

4176. Judged by ordinary standards, David had done no wrong; he was a good and just king. Judged by the hightest standard of those nearest to Allah (*Muqarrabūn*, 56:11), the thought of self-pride and self-righteousness had to be washed off from him by his own act of self-realisation and repentance. This was freely accepted by Allah, as the next verse shows.

4176-A. Some commentators say that David's fault here was his hastiness in judging before hearing the case of the other party. When he realised his lapse, he fell down in repentance. [Eds.].

4177. *Cf.* 2:30, and n. 47. David's kingly power, and the gifts of wisdom, justice, psalmody, and prophethood were bestowed on him as a trust. These great gifts were not to be a matter of self-glory.

Nor follow thou the lusts
(Of thy heart), for they will
Mislead thee from the Path[4178]
Of Allah: for those who
Wander astray from the Path
Of Allah, is a Penalty Grievous,
For that they forget
The Day of Account.

ولا تتبع الهوى
فيضلك عن سبيل الله
إن الذين يضلون عن سبيل الله
لهم عذاب شديد بما نسوا يوم الحساب

C. 201.—For just ends was the world created.
(38:27-64.) Solomon, in the midst of his worldly power
And glory, never forgot Allah, nor Job
In the midst of afflictions; nor other men
Of Power and Vision, whose patience and constancy
Brought them nearer to Allah. So should
All the righteous strive to win
The final Bliss, for truly grievous
Are the woes of Evil in the final Account.

SECTION 3.

27. Not without purpose did We[4179]
Create heaven and earth
And all between! That
Were the thought of Unbelievers!
But woe to the Unbelievers
Because of the Fire (of Hell)!

٢٧ وما خلقنا السماء والأرض
وما بينهما باطلا ذلك ظن الذين كفروا
فويل للذين كفروا من النار

28. Shall We treat those
Who believe and work deeds[4180]
Of righteousness, the same
As those who do mischief
On earth? Shall We treat

٢٨ أم نجعل الذين ءامنوا وعملوا
الصالحات كالمفسدين في الأرض أم نجعل

4178. As stated in 4171 above, this vision and its moral are nowhere to be found in the Bible. Those who think they see a resemblance to the Parable of the prophet Nathan (2 Samuel, xii. 1-17) have nothing to go upon but the mention of the "one ewe" here and the "one little ewe-lamb" in Nathan's Parable. The whole story is here different, and the whole atmosphere is different. The Biblical title given to David, "a man after God's own heart" is refuted by the Bible itself in the scandalous tale of heinous crimes attributed to David in chapters xi. and xii. of 2 Samuel, *viz.*, adultery, fraudulent dealing with one of his own servants, and the contriving of his murder. Further, in chapter xiii, we have the story of rapes, incest, and fratricide in David's own household! The fact is that passages like these are mere *chroniques scandaleuses, i.e.*, narratives of scandalous crimes of the grossest character. The Muslim idea of David is that of a man just and upright, endowed with all the virtues, in whom even the least thought of self-elation has to be washed off by repentance and forgiveness. (R).

4179. *Cf.* 3:191. Unbelief is the subjective negation of a belief in Order, Beauty, Purpose, and Eternal Life. Unbelief is to Faith as Chaos is to Cosmos, as the Fire of Misery is to the Garden of Bliss.

4180. The reference to the Hereafter at the end of verse 26 above is of a piece with the whole tenor of this Sūrah, which deals with the superiority of the spiritual kingdom and the Hereafter. If there were no Hereafter, how could you reconcile the inequalities of this world? Would not the Unbelievers be right in acting as if all Creation and all life were futile? But there is a Hereafter and Allah will not treat the Good and Evil alike. He is just and will fully restore the balance disturbed in this life.

Those who guard against evil,
The same as those who
Turn aside from the right?

ٱلْمُتَّقِينَ كَٱلْفُجَّارِ

29. (Here is) a Book which
We have sent down
Unto thee, full of blessings,[4181]
That they may meditate
On its Signs, and that
Men of understanding may
Receive admonition.

٢٩ كِتَٰبٌ أَنزَلْنَٰهُ إِلَيْكَ
مُبَٰرَكٌ لِّيَدَّبَّرُوٓا۟ ءَايَٰتِهِۦ
وَلِيَتَذَكَّرَ أُو۟لُوا۟ ٱلْأَلْبَٰبِ

30. To David We gave
Solomon (for a son)—[4182]
How excellent in Our service!
Ever did he turn (to Us)!

٣٠ وَوَهَبْنَا لِدَاوُۥدَ سُلَيْمَٰنَ ۚ
نِعْمَ ٱلْعَبْدُ ۖ إِنَّهُۥٓ أَوَّابٌ

31. Behold, there were brought[4183]
Before him, at eventide,
Coursers of The highest breeding,[4184]
And swift of foot;

٣١ إِذْ عُرِضَ عَلَيْهِ بِٱلْعَشِىِّ
ٱلصَّٰفِنَٰتُ ٱلْجِيَادُ

32. And he said, "Truly
Do I love the love[4185]
Of Good, with a view
To the glory of my Lord"—

٣٢ فَقَالَ إِنِّىٓ أَحْبَبْتُ
حُبَّ ٱلْخَيْرِ عَن ذِكْرِ رَبِّى

4181. Revelation is not a mere chance or haphazard thing. It is a real blessing—among the greatest that Allah has bestowed on man. By meditation on it in an earnest spirit man may learn of himself, and his relation to nature around him and to Allah the Author of all. Men of understanding may, by its help, resolve all genuine doubts that there may be in their minds, and learn the true lessons of spiritual life.

4182. The greatest in this life have yet need of this spiritual blessing: without it all worldly good is futile. Referring back to the story of David, we are now introduced to Solomon, who was a great king but greater still because he served Allah and turned to Him. The Qur'ān, unlike the Old Testament, represents Solomon as a righteous king, not as an idolator, doing "evil in the sight of the Lord" (1 Kings, xi. 6).

4183. The passages about David and Solomon have been variously interpreted by the Commentators. The versions which I have suggested have good authority behind them, though I have followed my own judgement in filling in the details.

4184. *Ṣāfināt*: literally, horses that stand, when at ease, on three legs, firmly planted, with the hoof of the fourth leg resting lightly on the ground. This would imply breeding and a steady temper, to match with the quality of swiftness mentioned in the next clause.

4185. The story is not found in the Old Testament. I interpret it to mean that, like his father David, Solomon was also most meticulous in not allowing the least motive of self to be mixed up with his spiritual virtues. He was fond of horses: he had great armies and wealth; but he used them all in Allah's service. *Cf.* 27:19, n. 3259; 27:40, n. 3276, etc. His battles were not fought for lust of blood, but as *Jihād* in the cause of righteousness. His love of horses was not like that of a mere race-goer or of a warrior: there was a spiritual element in it. He loved by a kind of love which was spiritual—the love of the highest Good.

Some commentators interpret this verse saying that Solomon, peace be upon him, was so engrossed in the inspection of his fine horses that he completely forgot to say his 'Asr prayer before the sunset. In the light of this interpretation the verse may be translated: "And he said, Truly did I prefer the good things (of this world) to the remembrance of my Lord". (R).

Until (the sun) was hidden
In the veil (of Night):[4186]

حَتَّىٰ تَوَارَتْ بِالْحِجَابِ

33. "Bring them back to me."
Then began he to pass[4187]
His hand over (their) legs
And their necks.

رُدُّوهَا عَلَيَّ ۖ ٣٣
فَطَفِقَ مَسْحًا بِالسُّوقِ وَالْأَعْنَاقِ

34. And We did try[4188]
Solomon: We placed
On his throne a body[4189]
(Without life): but he did turn
(To Us in true devotion):

وَلَقَدْ فَتَنَّا سُلَيْمَانَ ٣٤
وَأَلْقَيْنَا عَلَىٰ كُرْسِيِّهِ جَسَدًا ثُمَّ أَنَابَ

35. He said: "O my Lord!
Forgive me,[4190] and grant me[4191]
A Kingdom which,
(It may be), suits not
Another after me:
For Thou art the Grantor[4192]
Of Bounties (without measure).

قَالَ رَبِّ اغْفِرْ لِي وَهَبْ لِي ٣٥
مُلْكًا لَا يَنْبَغِي لِأَحَدٍ مِنْ بَعْدِي ۖ
إِنَّكَ أَنْتَ الْوَهَّابُ

4186. His review of his fine horses was interrupted by his evening devotion, but he resumed it after his devotions.

4187. Like all lovers of horses, he patted them on their necks and passed his hand over their forelegs and was proud of having them—not as vanities but as a "lover of Good". In the light of the alternative interpretation this verse would mean that upon missing 'Asr prayer, Solomon, peace be upon him, was so upset and sorry that he asked for the horses to be brought back to him and then "he fell to slashing with his sword their legs and necks", that is, he slaughtered them in expiation of his lapse seeking the forgiveness and pleasure of Allah. (R).

4188. What was the trial of Solomon? All the power, wealth, and glory, which were given to him were a spiritual trial to him. They might have turned another man's head, but he was staunch and true, and while he enjoyed and used all the power he had—over spirits, men, and the forces of nature, (see below), he kept his mind steady to the service of Allah *Cf.* 8:28, where "your possessions and your progeny" are declared to be "but a trial".

4189. *The body (without life) on his throne* has been variously interpreted. The interpretation that appeals to me most is that his earthly power, great as it was, was like a body without a soul, unless it was vivified by Allah's spirit. But Solomon did turn to Allah in true devotion, and his real power lay there. He did his best to root out idolatry, and he completed the Temple in Jerusalem for the worship of the One True God. *Cf.* his conversion of Bilqīs the Queen of Sheba, 27:40, n. 3276. See also 7:148, where the same word *jasad* is used in connection with the image of a calf which the Israelites had set up for worship in the absence of Moses. Men may worship worldly Power as they may worship an idol, and there is great temptation in such Power, though Solomon withstood such temptation.

I do not think that a reference to 34:14 (n. 3808) will fit the context here. (R).

4190. The seeking of worldly Power, even if intended to be used for Allah's service, has a little of Self in it. It may be quite legitimate and even meritorious in ordinary men, but even the thought of it in a Prophet is to be apologised for. See a similar idea in the case of David explained in n. 4176 to 37:24 above.

4191. He asked for a Power that *he* would not misuse, though others might not be able to refrain from misusing it—such as power over forces of nature or forces of violence (see the next three verses).

4192. *Cf.* 38:9, above.

36. Then We subjected the Wind[4193]
To his power, to flow
Gently to his order,
Whithersoever he willed—

٣٦ فَسَخَّرۡنَا لَهُ ٱلرِّيحَ
تَجۡرِي بِأَمۡرِهِۦ رُخَآءً حَيۡثُ أَصَابَ

37. As also the evil ones,[4194]
(Including) every kind
Of builder and diver—

٣٧ وَٱلشَّيَٰطِينَ كُلَّ بَنَّآءٖ وَغَوَّاصٖ

38. As also others bound[4195]
Together in fetters.

٣٨ وَءَاخَرِينَ مُقَرَّنِينَ فِي ٱلۡأَصۡفَادِ

39. "Such are Our Bounties:
Whether thou bestow them[4196]
(On others) or withhold them,
No account will be asked."

٣٩ هَٰذَا عَطَآؤُنَا
فَٱمۡنُنۡ أَوۡ أَمۡسِكۡ بِغَيۡرِ حِسَابٖ

40. And he enjoyed, indeed,[4197]
A Near Approach to Us,
And a beautiful Place
Of (final) Return.

٤٠ وَإِنَّ لَهُۥ عِندَنَا لَزُلۡفَىٰ
وَحُسۡنَ مَـَٔابٖ

SECTION 4.

41. Commemorate Our Servant
Job.[4198]
Behold he cried to his Lord:
"The Evil One has afflicted
Me with distress[4199] and suffering!"

٤١ وَٱذۡكُرۡ عَبۡدَنَآ أَيُّوبَ إِذۡ نَادَىٰ رَبَّهُۥٓ
أَنِّي مَسَّنِيَ ٱلشَّيۡطَٰنُ بِنُصۡبٖ وَعَذَابٍ

4193. *Cf.* 21:81, and n. 2736.

4194. *Cf.* 21:82, and n. 2738. *Cf.* also 34:12-13 and notes there: in the latter passage the spirits mentioned are called Jinns. The divers were probably those employed in pearl fisheries.

4195. *Cf.* 14:49, where the same expression "bound together in fetters" is applied to Sinners on the Day of Judgement.

4196. Allah bestowed such abundant powers and bounties on Solomon that they could not be counted or measured: and he was free to give away anything he liked or keep anything he liked. In this was great temptation for an ordinary man. Solomon as a prophet withstood it and asked to be forgiven for power and such a kingdom as others might not be able to use lawfully. His earthly kingdom went to pieces after his death. But his name and fame endure. And what is more, he obtained a place among the Nearest Ones to Allah. See next verse.

4197. The same words are used of David in 38:25 above, thus symmetrically closing the argument about the two greatest kings in Israel.

4198. For this passage, verses 41-44, *Cf.* 21:83-84.

4199. The distress was of many kinds, physical, mental, and spiritual. See n. 2739 to 21:83. He suffered from loathsome sores; he lost his home, his possessions, and his family; and almost his balance of mind. But he did not lose Faith but turned to Allah (see verse 44 below), and the recuperative process began.

42. (The command was given:)
"Strike with thy foot:[4200]
Here is (water) wherein
To wash, cool and refreshing
And (water) to drink."

٤٢ ٱرْكُضْ بِرِجْلِكَ
هَٰذَا مُغْتَسَلٌۢ بَارِدٌ وَشَرَابٌ

43. And We gave him (back)
His people and doubled
Their number—as a Grace[4201]
From Ourselves, and a thing
For commemoration, for all
Who have Understanding.

٤٣ وَوَهَبْنَا لَهُۥٓ أَهْلَهُۥ
وَمِثْلَهُم مَّعَهُمْ رَحْمَةً مِّنَّا
وَذِكْرَىٰ لِأُو۟لِى ٱلْأَلْبَٰبِ

44. "And take in thy hand
A little grass, and strike[4202]
Therewith: and break not
(Thy oath)." Truly We found
Him full of patience and
constancy,
How excellent in Our service![4203]
Ever did he turn (to Us)!

٤٤ وَخُذْ بِيَدِكَ ضِغْثًا
فَٱضْرِب بِّهِۦ وَلَا تَحْنَثْ
إِنَّا وَجَدْنَٰهُ صَابِرًا
نِّعْمَ ٱلْعَبْدُ إِنَّهُۥٓ أَوَّابٌ

45. And commemorate Our Servants
Abraham, Isaac, and Jacob,
Possessors of Power and Vision.[4204]

٤٥ وَٱذْكُرْ عِبَٰدَنَآ إِبْرَٰهِيمَ وَإِسْحَٰقَ وَيَعْقُوبَ
أُو۟لِى ٱلْأَيْدِى وَٱلْأَبْصَٰرِ

46. Verily We did choose them
For a special (purpose)—
Proclaiming the Message
Of the Hereafter.

٤٦ إِنَّآ أَخْلَصْنَٰهُم بِخَالِصَةٍ
ذِكْرَى ٱلدَّارِ

4200. The recuperative process having begun, he was commanded to strike the earth or a rock with his foot, and a fountain or fountains gushed forth—to give him a bath and clean his body, to refresh his spirits, and to give him drink and rest. This is a fresh touch, not mentioned in S. 21 or in the Book of Job, but adding beautifully to our realisation of the picture.

4201. *Cf.* 21:84, and notes 2739-2740.

4202. In his worst distress Job was patient and constant in faith, but apparently his wife was not. According to the book of Job (ii. 9-10), "Then said his wife unto him, dost thou still retain thine integrity? Curse God, and die. But he said unto her, thou speakest as one of the foolish women speaketh. What? Shall we receive good at the hand of God, and shall we not receive evil? In all this did not Job sin with his lips." He must have said in his haste to the woman that he would beat her: he is asked now to correct her with only a wisp of grass, to show that he was gentle and humble as well as patient and constant.

4203. *Cf.* 38:30 above, where similar words are spoken of Solomon. Patience and constancy are also a form of service, if our attitude is due to an *active* faith in Allah, and not mere passivity. So Milton in his Sonnet: "They also serve who only stand and wait."

4204. In the last Sūrah (37:83-113), Abraham and Isaac (and by implication Jacob) were mentioned as resisting Evil and winning through. Here they are mentioned as men with spiritual power and vision, Israelite patriarchs, who bore witness to the Gospel of the Hereafter, and were therefore a blessing to their people, for they taught the Truth.

47. They were, in Our sight,
Truly, of the company
Of the Elect and the Good.

٤٧ وَإِنَّهُمْ عِندَنَا لَمِنَ الْمُصْطَفَيْنَ الْأَخْيَارِ

48. And commemorate Ismā'īl,[4205]
Elisha, and Dhu al Kifl:
Each of them was
Of the company of the Good.

٤٨ وَاذْكُرْ إِسْمَٰعِيلَ وَالْيَسَعَ وَذَا الْكِفْلِ
وَكُلٌّ مِّنَ الْأَخْيَارِ

49. This is a Message
(Of admonition): and verily,
For the Righteous,[4206]
Is a beautiful place
Of (final) Return—

٤٩ هَٰذَا ذِكْرٌ
وَإِنَّ لِلْمُتَّقِينَ لَحُسْنَ مَـَٔابٍ

50. Gardens of Eternity,
Whose doors will (ever)
Be open to them;[4207]

٥٠ جَنَّٰتِ عَدْنٍ مُّفَتَّحَةً لَّهُمُ الْأَبْوَٰبُ

51. Therein will they
Recline (at ease):
Therein can they
Call (at pleasure)
For fruit in abundance,[4208]
And (delicious) drink;

٥١ مُتَّكِـِٔينَ فِيهَا
يَدْعُونَ فِيهَا بِفَٰكِهَةٍ
كَثِيرَةٍ وَشَرَابٍ

52. And beside them will be
Chaste women restraining[4209]
Their glances, (companions)
Of equal age.[4210]

٥٢ وَعِندَهُمْ قَٰصِرَٰتُ
الطَّرْفِ أَتْرَابٌ

4205. Ismā'īl, the Patriarch of the Arab race, was also mentioned (37:101-107) as a pattern of self-sacrifice, now he is mentioned in the company of the Good, *i.e.*, of those who were a blessing to their people. Here he is bracketed with Elisha (for whom see n. 906 to 6:86), and Dhu al Kifl (for whom see n. 2743 to 21:85). All these three were examples of constancy and patience under suffering.

4206. Some of the pre-eminent examples of the Elect and the Good having been mentioned, we have now a reference to the Righteous as a body (rank and file as well as leaders) and their future in the Hereafter as won by victory over Evil.

4207. The Final bliss will not be a hole-and-corner thing, a pale reflection of some Palace or Retreat, where mystery reigns behind closed doors. Its doors will be open, and its inmates will be free to go in and out as they will, because their wills will be purified and brought into accord with the Universal Law.

4208. See n. 4003 to 36:57. The free Gardens are types of satisfaction in external surroundings: the comfortable reclining thrones, the fruit and the drink are types of the soul's individual satisfaction; and the society of pure-minded companions, of equal ages, in the type of a soul's social satisfaction.

4209. *Cf.* 37:48 and n. 4064, and 36:56, n. 4002. As we conceive happiness in this life, it is not complete if it is only solitary. How we hanker after some one who can share in our highest joy! That feeling is also figured here.

4210. To make the metaphor of social happiness complete, we want companionship of equal age. Age and youth cannot be happy together. It is not suggested that in the Timeless state figured here, there will be old age; but if it is possible to conceive of temperamental differences then, the company will be so arranged that it will be congenial. Or we can accept the type of youth and freshness as common to all in that happy state.

53. Such is the Promise
Made to you
For the Day of Account!

هَٰذَا مَا تُوعَدُونَ لِيَوْمِ الْحِسَابِ ﴿٥٣﴾

54. Truly such will be
Our Bounty (to you);
It will never fail—

إِنَّ هَٰذَا لَرِزْقُنَا مَا لَهُ مِن نَّفَادٍ ﴿٥٤﴾

55. Yea, such! But—
For the wrongdoers
Will be an evil place[4211]
Of (final) Return!

هَٰذَا ۚ وَإِنَّ لِلطَّاغِينَ لَشَرَّ مَآبٍ ﴿٥٥﴾

56. Hell!—they will burn
Therein—an evil bed
(Indeed to lie on)!—[4212]

جَهَنَّمَ يَصْلَوْنَهَا فَبِئْسَ الْمِهَادُ ﴿٥٦﴾

57. Yea, such!—Then
Shall they taste it—
A boiling fluid, and a fluid[4213]
Dark, murky, intensely cold!—

هَٰذَا فَلْيَذُوقُوهُ حَمِيمٌ وَغَسَّاقٌ ﴿٥٧﴾

58. And other Penalties
Of a similar kind,
To match them!

وَآخَرُ مِن شَكْلِهِ أَزْوَاجٌ ﴿٥٨﴾

59. Here is a troop
Rushing headlong with you![4214]
No welcome for them!
Truly, they shall burn
In the Fire!

هَٰذَا فَوْجٌ مُّقْتَحِمٌ مَّعَكُمْ ۖ لَا مَرْحَبًا بِهِمْ ۚ إِنَّهُمْ صَالُو النَّارِ ﴿٥٩﴾

60. (The followers shall cry
To the misleaders:)
"Nay, ye (too)! No welcome
For you! It is ye who
Have brought this upon us![4215]

قَالُوا بَلْ أَنتُمْ لَا مَرْحَبًا بِكُمْ ۖ أَنتُمْ قَدَّمْتُمُوهُ لَنَا ﴿٦٠﴾

4211. This is in parallel contrast to the state of the Blessed in 38:49 above.

4212. *Cf.* 14:29. This continues the parallel contrast to the state of the Blessed already described.

4213. *Cf.* 10:4, and n. 1390. The conjunction of the boiling fluid with the dark, murky, intensely cold fluid heightens the effect of the Penalty. In place of harmony, there is the discord of extreme opposites. And the discord is not confined to this. It runs through the whole idea of Hell. See the next verse.

4214. The wonder is that so many people should embrace Evil, and in so much hurry and eagerness! Here they may be welcomed by the leaders of Evil, but in the final state it will be the opposite of welcome. They will be followed with reproaches and curses.

4215. It is the nature of Evil to shift the blame to others. The followers will reproach the leaders, but none can escape personal responsibility for his own acts and deeds!

Now evil is (this) place
To stay in!"

فَبِئْسَ ٱلْقَرَارُ

61. They will say: "Our Lord!
Whoever brought this upon us—
Add to him a double[4216]
Penalty in the Fire!"

٦١ قَالُوا۟ رَبَّنَا مَن قَدَّمَ لَنَا هَٰذَا
فَزِدْهُ عَذَابًا ضِعْفًا فِى ٱلنَّارِ

62. And they will say:
"What has happened to us
That we see not men
Whom we used to number
Among the bad ones?"[4217]

٦٢ وَقَالُوا۟ مَا لَنَا لَا نَرَىٰ رِجَالًا
كُنَّا نَعُدُّهُم مِّنَ ٱلْأَشْرَارِ

63. "Did we treat them
(As such) in ridicule,
Or have (our) eyes
Failed to perceive them?"

٦٣ أَتَّخَذْنَٰهُمْ سِخْرِيًّا
أَمْ زَاغَتْ عَنْهُمُ ٱلْأَبْصَٰرُ

64. Truly that is just and fitting—[4218]
The mutual recriminations
Of the People of the Fire!

٦٤ إِنَّ ذَٰلِكَ لَحَقٌّ تَخَاصُمُ أَهْلِ ٱلنَّارِ

C. 202.—(38:65-88.)
The Gospel of Unity is the true cure
For Evil: for it gives the good news
Of Allah's Power Supreme, and His Mercy
And Forgiveness again and again. It warns
Us to aviod Evil, for Evil arose
From selfish Pride and Rebellion. No power
Has it over Allah's servants, sincere
And true: while Revelation comes
As a gift free to all Allah's Creation.

SECTION 5.

65. Say: "Truly am I
A Warner: no god
Is there but the One

٦٥ قُلْ إِنَّمَآ أَنَا۠ مُنذِرٌ ۖ وَمَا مِنْ إِلَٰهٍ إِلَّا

4216. *Cf.* 7:38, and n. 1019. See also 11:20. The evil ones now vent their spite on others. Here they ask for a double penalty for their misleaders, but they forget their own personal responsibility. In the next verse, they express their surprise that others have escaped the torments, which they themselves have earned.

4217. *The bad ones: i.e.*, the ones whom they (evil ones) ridiculed as fools sure to come to an evil end, because they refused to join in with the evil ones on their plots. The values are now reversed. The good ones are among the Blessed, and are to be seen in the 'Bed of Misery'. The ridicule is now against the evil ones.

4218. The mutual recriminations and spite are themselves a part of the Penalty, for such feelings increase their unhappiness.

God, Supreme and
Irresistible—[4219]

اللَّهُ الْوَاحِدُ الْقَهَّارُ

66, "The Lord of the heavens
And the earth, and all
Between—Exalted in Might,
Able to enforce His Will,[4220]
Forgiving again and again."[4221]

رَبُّ السَّمَاوَاتِ وَالْأَرْضِ وَمَا بَيْنَهُمَا الْعَزِيزُ الْغَفَّارُ ﴿٦٦﴾

67. Say: "That is a Message
Supreme (above all)—

قُلْ هُوَ نَبَأٌ عَظِيمٌ ﴿٦٧﴾

68. "From which ye
Do turn away![4222]

أَنْتُمْ عَنْهُ مُعْرِضُونَ ﴿٦٨﴾

69. "No knowledge have I
Of the Chiefs on high,
When they discuss
(Matters) among themselves.[4223]

مَا كَانَ لِيَ مِنْ عِلْمٍ بِالْمَلَإِ الْأَعْلَىٰ إِذْ يَخْتَصِمُونَ ﴿٦٩﴾

70. "Only this has been revealed
To me: that I am
To give warning
Plainly and publicly."[4224]

إِنْ يُوحَىٰ إِلَيَّ إِلَّا أَنَّمَا أَنَا نَذِيرٌ مُبِينٌ ﴿٧٠﴾

71. Behold, thy Lord said[4225]

إِذْ قَالَ رَبُّكَ ﴿٧١﴾

4219. *Cf.* 12:39, where Joseph preaches to the men in prison. The one supreme Message of importance to mankind was (and is) the Unity of Allah: that He is the Creator and Sustainer of all: that His Will is supreme: that He can carry out His Will without question, and no powers of Evil can defeat it; and that He forgives by His grace again and again. This Message the Holy Prophet came to deliver, and he delivered it.

4220. In n. 2818 to 22:40, I have explained the full import of *'Azīz* as a title applied to Allah, and I have expressed two of the leading ideas involved, in the two lines here. The argument in this Sūrah turns upon the contrast between earthly Power and the Divine Power: the one is impotent and the other is supreme.

4221. *Ghaffār* is the emphatic intensive form, and I have accordingly translated it as "Forgiving again and again". *Cf.* 20:82.

4222. The Message which is of supreme import to mankind—from that they turn away. Instead of profiting by it, they turn away to side issues, or unprofitable speculation: such as: what is the origin of Evil; when will Judgement come? etc.

4223. The hierarchy in Heaven, under Allah's command, discuss questions of high import in the Universe. Those are not necessarily revealed to men, except insofar as it is good for men to know, as in verses 71-85 below. But the chief thing for man is to know that Allah is Most Merciful, that He forgives again and again, and that Evil has no power over those who trust in Allah.

4224. Two things are implied in *Mubīn*: (1) that the warning should be clear and perspicuous; there should be no mincing of matters, no ambiguity, no compromise with evil, 7:184; (2) that the warning should be delivered publicly, before all people, in spite of opposition and persecution, 26:115. Both these ideas I have tried to express in this passage.

4225. Two passages may be compared with this: *viz.*: (1) 2:30-39, where merely the first stages of the Rebellion against Allah and its consequences to mankind are mentioned, and (2) 15:29-40, where the further intrusion of evil in man's life here below is referred to, and an assurance is given that Evil will have no power except over those who yield to it. The latter is the passage most relevant here, as we are now dealing with the power of Revelation to defeat the machinations of Evil.

To the angels: "I am
About to create man
From clay:[4226]

لِلْمَلَٰٓئِكَةِ إِنِّى خَٰلِقٌۢ بَشَرًا مِّن طِينٍ

72. "When I have fashioned him
(In due proportion) and breathed
Into him of My spirit,[4227]
Fall ye down in obeisance
Unto him."

٧٢ فَإِذَا سَوَّيْتُهُۥ
وَنَفَخْتُ فِيهِ مِن رُّوحِى
فَقَعُوا۟ لَهُۥ سَٰجِدِينَ

73. So the angels prostrated themselves,
All of them together:

٧٣ فَسَجَدَ ٱلْمَلَٰٓئِكَةُ كُلُّهُمْ أَجْمَعُونَ

74. Not so Iblīs: he
Was haughty, and became[4228]
One of those who reject Faith.

٧٤ إِلَّآ إِبْلِيسَ ٱسْتَكْبَرَ وَكَانَ مِنَ ٱلْكَٰفِرِينَ

75. (Allah) said: "O Iblīs!
What prevents thee from
Prostrating thyself to one
Whom I have created
With My hands?[4229]
Art thou haughty?
Or art thou one[4230]
Of the high (and mighty) ones?"

٧٥ قَالَ يَٰٓإِبْلِيسُ مَا مَنَعَكَ
أَن تَسْجُدَ لِمَا خَلَقْتُ بِيَدَىَّ
أَسْتَكْبَرْتَ أَمْ كُنتَ
مِنَ ٱلْعَالِينَ

76. (Iblīs) said: "I am better
Than he: Thou createdst
Me from fire, and him
Thou createdst from clay."

٧٦ قَالَ أَنَا۠ خَيْرٌ مِّنْهُ
خَلَقْتَنِى مِن نَّارٍ وَخَلَقْتَهُۥ مِن طِينٍ

77. (Allah) said: "Then get thee
Out from here: for thou
Art rejected, accursed.

٧٧ قَالَ فَٱخْرُجْ مِنْهَا فَإِنَّكَ رَجِيمٌ

4226. This shows that the material world round us was created by Allah before Allah fashioned man and breathed of His soul into him. Geology also shows that man came on the scene at a very late stage in the history of this planet.

4227. See n. 1968 to 15:29, where the spiritual significance of this is explained.

4228. Arrogance (self-love) is thus the root of Evil and of Unfaith.

4229. Man, as typified by Adam, is in himself nothing but frail clay. But as fashioned by Allah's creative power into something with Allah's spirit breathed into him, his dignity is raised above that of the highest creatures.

4230. If, then, Satan refuses, it is a rebellion against Allah. It arises from arrogance or haughtiness, an exaggerated idea of Self. Or, it is asked, are you really sufficiently high in rank to dispute with the Almighty? Of course he was not.

78. "And My Curse shall be
On thee till the Day[4231]
Of Judgement."

وَإِنَّ عَلَيْكَ لَعْنَتِىٓ إِلَىٰ يَوْمِ ٱلدِّينِ ﴿٧٨﴾

79. (Iblīs) said: "O my Lord!
Give me then respite[4232]
Till the Day
The (dead) are raised."

قَالَ رَبِّ فَأَنظِرْنِىٓ ﴿٧٩﴾
إِلَىٰ يَوْمِ يُبْعَثُونَ

80. (Allah) said: "Respite then
Is granted thee—

قَالَ فَإِنَّكَ مِنَ ٱلْمُنظَرِينَ ﴿٨٠﴾

81. "Till the Day
Of the Time Appointed."[4233]

إِلَىٰ يَوْمِ ٱلْوَقْتِ ٱلْمَعْلُومِ ﴿٨١﴾

82. (Iblīs) said: "Then,
By Thy Power,[4234] I will
Put them all in the wrong—[4235]

قَالَ فَبِعِزَّتِكَ لَأُغْوِيَنَّهُمْ أَجْمَعِينَ ﴿٨٢﴾

83. "Except Thy Servants
Amongst them, sincere
And purified (by Thy grace)."

إِلَّا عِبَادَكَ مِنْهُمُ ٱلْمُخْلَصِينَ ﴿٨٣﴾

84. (Allah) said: "Then
It is just and fitting—[4236]
And I say what is
Just and fitting—

قَالَ فَٱلْحَقُّ ﴿٨٤﴾
وَٱلْحَقَّ أَقُولُ

85. "That I will certainly fill[4237]
Hell with thee
And those who follow thee—
Every one."

لَأَمْلَأَنَّ جَهَنَّمَ مِنكَ ﴿٨٥﴾
وَمِمَّن تَبِعَكَ مِنْهُمْ أَجْمَعِينَ

4231. See n. 1972 to 15:35, where it is explained why the respite is to the Day of Judgement. The whole of that passage in S. 15 forms a good commentary on this.

4232. For the significance of the respite see n. 1973 to 15:36.

4233. It is not an indefinite respite. It is for a period definitely limited, while this our Probation lasts in this world. It is part of the test as to how we use our limited free will. After that, our whole existence will be on a different plane. The good will have been sorted out, the chain of consequences of the present world will be broken, and "a new Creation" will have taken the place of the present World.

4234. This phrase, this oath of Satan, is a fresh point introduced in this passage, because here we are dealing with Power—the Power of Good contrasted with Evil—the spiritual Power of Allah as contrasted with the power that we see in our earthly affairs. Satan acknowledges that even his power, such as it is , has no reality except insofar as it is permitted to operate by Allah in Allah's wise and universal Plan, and that it cannot harm the true and sincere worshippers of Allah.

4235. See n. 1974 to 15:39.

4236. *Cf.* n. 1990 to 15:64.

4237. *Cf.* 7:18; 7:179, and 11:119. n. 1623. The punishment of defiance, and rebellion is inevitable and just, and the followers who chose to identify themselves with the disobedience must suffer as well as the leaders. *Cf.* 10:33

86. Say: "No reward do I ask[4238]
Of you for this (Qur'ān),
Nor am I a pretender.[4239]

قُلْ مَآ أَسْـَٔلُكُمْ عَلَيْهِ مِنْ أَجْرٍ وَمَآ أَنَا۠ مِنَ ٱلْمُتَكَلِّفِينَ ﴿٨٦﴾

87. "This is no less than
A Message to (all)[4240]
The Worlds.

إِنْ هُوَ إِلَّا ذِكْرٌ لِّلْعَٰلَمِينَ ﴿٨٧﴾

88. "And ye shall certainly
Know the truth of it (all)[4241]
After a while."

وَلَتَعْلَمُنَّ نَبَأَهُۥ بَعْدَ حِينٍۭ ﴿٨٨﴾

4238. *Cf.* 25:57; 26:109; and many other passages. The prophet of Allah neither seeks nor expects any reward from men. On the contrary he suffers much at their hands. He is unselfish and offers his services under Allah's inspiration. He is satisfied with the hope "that each one who will may take a straight Path to his Lord." That is his reward. And the reward he hopes for from Allah is similarly unselfish. He earnestly hopes to win His Good Pleasure—or, to use another metaphor, "to see His Face."

4239. *Mutakallif*: a man who pretends to things that are not true, or declares as facts things that do not exist, one who takes upon himself tasks to which he is not equal. True prophets are not people of that kind.

4240. So far from there being any false or selfish motive in the Message proclaimed in Revelation, it is a healing mercy to all mankind. More, it is in accord with all parts of Allah's Creation, and makes us kin with all Creation, the handiwork of the One True God.

4241. There may be many things which we in our "muddy vesture of decay" may not fully understand or take in. If we only follow the right Path, we shall arrive at the Goal in the Hereafter, and then everything will be clear to us.

INTRODUCION TO SŪRAH 39—*AL ZUMAR*

This is the last of the series of six Sūrahs beginning with S. 34, which deal with the mysteries of the spiritual world, as leading up to the *Ma'ād,* or the Hereafter. See Introduction to S. 34.

Its subject matter is how Creation in its great variety is yet sorted out in Groups or Classes, all governed by one Plan, and created and sustained by One God, Who will separate Good from Evil at the last Day. The word *zumar* occurs in verses 71 and 73.

Its chronology has no significance. It belongs to the later Makkan period.

Summary—The variety in Creation yet points to the unity of Plan: there is only One God: to Him is due all worship and from Him flow all Justice and Grace (39:1-21, and C. 203).

There is unity in Revelation, and guidance comes from Allah alone: turn to Him only, for all else is false (39:22-52, and C. 204). God's Mercy is all-embracing: despair not: seek it before it is too late: for Judgement and Justice will come for certain (39:53-75, and C. 205).

C. 203.—To Allah is due sincere devotion, and to Him
(39:1-21.) Alone: there is none like unto Him.
All nature obeys His laws, and our own
Growth and life proclaim Him Lord
And Cherisher. How can we blaspheme?
We must serve Him, the One, the True,
With sincere devotion, and follow His Law
In its highest meaning: or else the loss
Is our own. All nature proclaims
Aloud His Grace and Loving-kindness.

Sūrah 39.

Al Zumar (Crowds)

In the name of Allah, Most Gracious,
Most Merciful.

بِسْمِ ٱللَّهِ ٱلرَّحْمَٰنِ ٱلرَّحِيمِ

1. The revelation
Of this Book
Is from Allah,[4242]
The Exalted in Power,
Full of Wisdom.

١ تَنزِيلُ ٱلْكِتَٰبِ
مِنَ ٱللَّهِ ٱلْعَزِيزِ ٱلْحَكِيمِ

2. Verily it is We Who have
Revealed the Book to thee
In Truth: so serve Allah,
Offering Him sincere devotion.

٢ إِنَّآ أَنزَلْنَآ إِلَيْكَ ٱلْكِتَٰبَ
بِٱلْحَقِّ فَٱعْبُدِ ٱللَّهَ مُخْلِصًا لَّهُ ٱلدِّينَ

3. Is it not to Allah[4243]
That sincere devotion
Is due? But those who
Take for protectors others
Than Allah (say): "We only
Serve them in order that
They may bring us nearer[4244]
To Allah." Truly Allah
Will judge between them
In that wherein they differ.[4245]
But Allah guides not
Such as are false
And ungrateful.

٣ أَلَا لِلَّهِ ٱلدِّينُ ٱلْخَالِصُ ۚ
وَٱلَّذِينَ ٱتَّخَذُوا۟ مِن دُونِهِۦٓ أَوْلِيَآءَ
مَا نَعْبُدُهُمْ إِلَّا لِيُقَرِّبُونَآ إِلَى ٱللَّهِ زُلْفَىٰٓ
إِنَّ ٱللَّهَ يَحْكُمُ بَيْنَهُمْ
فِى مَا هُمْ فِيهِ يَخْتَلِفُونَ ۗ
إِنَّ ٱللَّهَ لَا يَهْدِى مَنْ هُوَ كَٰذِبٌ كَفَّارٌ

4. Had Allah wished
To take to Himself

٤ لَّوْ أَرَادَ ٱللَّهُ أَن يَتَّخِذَ

4242. In connection with Revelation two qualities of Allah are mentioned: (1) that He is All-Powerful and can carry out His Will in spite of all opposition; and (2) that He is full of knowledge and wisdom. The first answers those who question how Allah can send Revelation to man; the second explains that true wisdom consists in carrying out Allah's Will as revealed to us.

4243. In many Signs in Creation as described below, there yet is a clear indication of the unity of Plan, pointing to the Unity of the Creator. Worship of service is due to none but Him. And He wants exclusive and sincere devotion.

4244. Worshippers of Idols or of deities other than Allah, *e.g.*, saints or perhaps Wealth and Power, Science or Selfish Desire, may pretend that these are symbols that may get them nearer to their self-development, nearer to the goal of their life, nearer to Allah, but they are altogether on the wrong track.

4245. This departure of theirs from true worship, this divergence from the right way, produces endless disputations and sects. Allah will judge between them. But if they are determined to go after falsehoods and forget the gratitude and service which they owe to Allah, and Allah alone, they are putting themselves on a Path where they will get no guidance. They are cutting themselves off from revealed Truth.

A son, He could have
Chosen whom He pleased
Out of those whom He[4246]
Doth create: but Glory
Be to Him! (He is above
Such things.) He is Allah,
The One, the Irresistible.

وَلَدًا لَّاصْطَفَىٰ مِمَّا
يَخْلُقُ مَا يَشَاءُ سُبْحَانَهُ
هُوَ اللَّهُ الْوَاحِدُ الْقَهَّارُ

5. He created the heavens
And the earth
In true (proportions):[4247]
He makes the Night
Overlap the Day, and the Day
Overlap the Night:
He has subjected
The sun and the moon
(To His law):
Each one follows a course
For a time appointed.
Is not He the Exalted
In Power—He Who forgives[4248]
Again and again?

٥ خَلَقَ السَّمَاوَاتِ
وَالْأَرْضَ بِالْحَقِّ
يُكَوِّرُ اللَّيْلَ عَلَى النَّهَارِ
وَيُكَوِّرُ النَّهَارَ عَلَى اللَّيْلِ
وَسَخَّرَ الشَّمْسَ وَالْقَمَرَ
كُلٌّ يَجْرِي لِأَجَلٍ مُّسَمًّى
أَلَا هُوَ الْعَزِيزُ الْغَفَّارُ

6. He created you (all)
From a single Person:[4249]
Then created, of like nature,
His mate; and He
Sent down for you eight
head[4250]
Of cattle in pairs:
He makes you,
In the wombs
Of your mothers,

٦ خَلَقَكُم مِّن نَّفْسٍ وَاحِدَةٍ
ثُمَّ جَعَلَ مِنْهَا زَوْجَهَا وَأَنزَلَ
لَكُم مِّنَ الْأَنْعَامِ ثَمَانِيَةَ أَزْوَاجٍ
يَخْلُقُكُمْ فِي بُطُونِ أُمَّهَاتِكُمْ

4246. It is blasphemy to say that Allah begot a son. If that were true, He should have had a wife (6:101), and His son would have been of the same kind as Himself; whereas Allah is One, with no one else like unto Him (112:4). Begetting is an animal act which goes with sex. How can it be consistent with our conception of One who is above all Creatures? If such a blasphemous thought were possible, as that Allah wanted some one else to help Him, He could have chosen the best of His creatures instead of lowering Himself to an animal act. But glory to Allah! He is above such things! His Unity is the first thing that we have to learn about Him. As He is Omnipotent, He requires no creatures to help Him or bring other creatures to Him.

4247. *Cf.* 6:73, and n. 896.

4248. His Power is equalled by His Mercy. Who can there be like unto Him?

4249. *Cf.* 4:1, and n. 504.

4250. See 6:143-4, where four kinds of cattle are mentioned in pairs in connection with certain Arab superstitions which are there condemned. Here the same four kinds are mentioned as representative of domesticated cattle given by Allah as useful to man. These are sheep, goats, camels, and oxen. In Arab idiom the horse is not included among "cattle".

For the wisdom and goodness of Allah in granting man dominion over cattle, see 36:71-73.

In stages, one after another,[4251]
In three veils of darkness.[4252]
Such is Allah, your Lord
And Cherisher: to Him belongs
(All) dominion. There is
No god but He: then
How are ye turned away[4253]
(From your true Centre)?

خَلْقًا مِّنۢ بَعْدِ خَلْقٍ فِى ظُلُمَٰتٍ ثَلَٰثٍ ۚ
ذَٰلِكُمُ ٱللَّهُ رَبُّكُمْ لَهُ ٱلْمُلْكُ ۖ
لَآ إِلَٰهَ إِلَّا هُوَ ۖ
فَأَنَّىٰ تُصْرَفُونَ

7. If ye reject (Allah),
Truly Allah hath no need
Of you; but He liketh not[4254]
Ingratitude from His servants:
If ye are grateful, He
Is pleased with you.
No bearer of burdens[4255]
Can bear the burden
Of another. In the End,
To your Lord is your Return,
When He will tell you
The truth of all
That ye did (in this life).
For He knoweth well
All that is in (men's) hearts.

٧ إِن تَكْفُرُوا۟ فَإِنَّ ٱللَّهَ غَنِىٌّ عَنكُمْ ۖ
وَلَا يَرْضَىٰ لِعِبَادِهِ ٱلْكُفْرَ ۖ
وَإِن تَشْكُرُوا۟ يَرْضَهُ لَكُمْ ۗ
وَلَا تَزِرُ وَازِرَةٌ وِزْرَ أُخْرَىٰ ۗ
ثُمَّ إِلَىٰ رَبِّكُم مَّرْجِعُكُمْ
فَيُنَبِّئُكُم بِمَا كُنتُمْ تَعْمَلُونَ ۚ
إِنَّهُۥ عَلِيمٌۢ بِذَاتِ ٱلصُّدُورِ

8. When some trouble toucheth man,[4256]
He crieth unto his Lord,
Turning to Him in repentance:

٨ وَإِذَا مَسَّ ٱلْإِنسَٰنَ ضُرٌّ
دَعَا رَبَّهُۥ مُنِيبًا إِلَيْهِ

4251. See 22:5, where the gradual physical growth of man in several successive stages is mentioned as one of the Signs of Allah's creative Power and cherishing care.

4252. The three veils of darkness which cover the unborn child are: the caul or membrane, the womb, and the hollow in which the womb is enclosed. But we might understand "three" in a cumulative rather than a numerical sense.

4253. It is clear that you owe your very existence and your maintenance, growth, and preservation, to Allah; how is it that you are turned away by chance things from Him? (R).

4254. Allah is independent of all wants, and therefore man's ingratitude does not affect Allah. But Allah cares for man, and therefore man's gratitude and service earn Allah's Good Pleasure, and man's ingratitude and rebellion are displeasing to Allah.

4255. *Cf.* 6:164. The account is between you and Allah. No one else can take your burdens or carry your sins. Vicarious atonement would be unjust. You have to return to Allah in the Hereafter. You will find that He knows all that you did in this life, and its full significance. He will explain to you even better than you can understand yourself, because all your secret hidden motives which you sometimes tried to ignore yourself, are fully known to Him.

4256. *Cf.* 10:12. Trouble and adversity often bring a man to his bearings. But if He is not firm and constant, he forgets the lessons which life is meant to teach him. As soon as he gets a little prosperity, he forgets that it is from Allah, and attributes it to something which may only be a secondary cause, *e.g.*, his own efforts or the Powers of Nature, or something which he has invented and made into a god, *e.g.*, idols or fate. Allah is the Ultimate Cause of all things. To set up rivals to Him in this way is not only wrong and degrading to the false worshipper himself, but misleads countless ignorant people, who may not be able to make allowances for the figures of speech or the symbolism by which subtler minds can explain away falsehoods.

But when He bestoweth
A favour upon him
As from Himself, (man)
Doth forget what he cried
And prayed for before,
And he doth set up
Rivals unto Allah,
Thus misleading others
From Allah's Path.
Say, "Enjoy thy blasphemy[4257]
For a little while:
Verily thou art (one)
Of the Companions of the Fire!"

ثُمَّ إِذَا خَوَّلَهُۥ نِعْمَةً مِّنْهُ
نَسِىَ مَا كَانَ يَدْعُوٓا۟ إِلَيْهِ مِن قَبْلُ
وَجَعَلَ لِلَّهِ أَندَادًا
لِّيُضِلَّ عَن سَبِيلِهِۦ
قُلْ تَمَتَّعْ بِكُفْرِكَ قَلِيلًا
إِنَّكَ مِنْ أَصْحَٰبِ ٱلنَّارِ

9. Is one who worships devoutly
During the hours of the night[4258]
Prostrating himself or standing
(In adoration), who takes heed
Of the Hereafter, and who
Places his hope in the Mercy
Of his Lord—(like one
Who does not)? Say:
"Are those equal, those who know
And those who do not know?
It is those who are
Endued with understanding
That receive admonition."[4259]

٩ أَمَّنْ هُوَ قَٰنِتٌ ءَانَآءَ ٱلَّيْلِ
سَاجِدًا وَقَآئِمًا يَحْذَرُ
ٱلْءَاخِرَةَ وَيَرْجُوا۟ رَحْمَةَ رَبِّهِۦ
قُلْ هَلْ يَسْتَوِى ٱلَّذِينَ
يَعْلَمُونَ وَٱلَّذِينَ لَا يَعْلَمُونَ
إِنَّمَا يَتَذَكَّرُ أُو۟لُوا۟ ٱلْأَلْبَٰبِ

SECTION 2.

10. Say: "O ye
My servants who believe!
Fear your Lord.[4260]
Good is (the reward)
For those who do good
In this world.

١٠ قُلْ يَٰعِبَادِ
ٱلَّذِينَ ءَامَنُوا۟ ٱتَّقُوا۟ رَبَّكُمْ
لِلَّذِينَ أَحْسَنُوا۟ فِى هَٰذِهِ ٱلدُّنْيَا حَسَنَةٌ

4257. Those who practise and those who teach evil and blasphemy may seem to flourish in this world. But their satisfaction will be of very short duration. They are treading all the while the Path that leads to the Fire of Perdition.

4258. *Cf.* 3:113-117. It is a great thing when a man gets into the attitude of humble devotion to Allah. To him the Hereafter is a real thing, and he prepares for it with good works. He does not build his hopes on the vanities of this world, but on Allah's Grace and Mercy. Such a man is "endued with understanding" and receives Allah's Message with fervour and alacrity. He is not to be compared with the cynic or the unbeliever, who knows nothing of the real value of the inner life.

4259. *Cf.* 3:19.

4260. The "fear of Allah" (*Taqwā*) is explained in n. 26 to 2:2. See also n. 2912 to 23:60. The fear of Allah is akin to love, for it means that we are afraid to displease Him.

Spacious is Allah's earth![4261]
Those who patiently persevere
Will truly receive
A reward without measure!"

وَأَرْضُ ٱللَّهِ وَٰسِعَةٌ
إِنَّمَا يُوَفَّى ٱلصَّٰبِرُونَ أَجْرَهُم بِغَيْرِ حِسَابٍ

11. Say: "Verily, I am commanded
To serve Allah
With sincere devotion;

قُلْ إِنِّىٓ أُمِرْتُ أَنْ أَعْبُدَ ٱللَّهَ مُخْلِصًا لَّهُ ٱلدِّينَ ﴿١١﴾

12. "And I am commanded
To be the first[4262]
Of those who bow
To Allah in Islam."

وَأُمِرْتُ لِأَنْ أَكُونَ أَوَّلَ ٱلْمُسْلِمِينَ ﴿١٢﴾

13. Say: "I would, if I[4263]
Disobeyed my Lord,
Indeed have fear
Of the Penalty
Of a Mighty Day."

قُلْ إِنِّىٓ أَخَافُ إِنْ عَصَيْتُ رَبِّى عَذَابَ يَوْمٍ عَظِيمٍ ﴿١٣﴾

14. Say: "It is Allah I serve,
With my sincere
(And exclusive) devotion:

قُلِ ٱللَّهَ أَعْبُدُ مُخْلِصًا لَّهُۥ دِينِى ﴿١٤﴾

15. "Serve ye what ye will[4264]
Besides Him." Say:
"Truly, those in loss
Are those who lose
Their own souls
And their People[4265]
On the Day of Judgement:
Ah! that is indeed
The (real and) evident Loss!"

فَٱعْبُدُوا۟ مَا شِئْتُم مِّن دُونِهِۦ ۗ
قُلْ إِنَّ ٱلْخَٰسِرِينَ ٱلَّذِينَ خَسِرُوٓا۟
أَنفُسَهُمْ وَأَهْلِيهِمْ يَوْمَ ٱلْقِيَٰمَةِ ۗ
أَلَا ذَٰلِكَ هُوَ ٱلْخُسْرَانُ ٱلْمُبِينُ ﴿١٥﴾

4261. *Cf.* 29:56 and n. 3489. We must always do right. We cannot plead that the circumstances in which we find ourselves force our hands. If our home conditions do not allow us to act according to the Faith that is in us, we must be prepared to suffer ostracism or even exile.

4262. *Cf.* 6:14. "The first" need not necessarily be chronological: it may also refer to the first rank in zeal, and in readiness to suffer for the Cause.

4263. *Cf.* 6:15. The worst penalty in a spiritual sense is the Displeasure of Allah, just as the highest achievement, the fulfilment of all desire, is the attainment of Allah's Good Pleasure: 6:16.

4264. This is not a command or permission but a reproach and warning. The address of the Prophet of Allah may be paraphrased thus: 'Whatever happens I will follow the command of Allah. He has revealed Himself, and I know that He is One, supreme over all creatures. Him alone will I serve. Is there any so ignorant as to seek anyone else? Let him do so and see the results. The loss will be his own. For he falls from Grace into Evil.' (R).

4265. The cult of Evil results in the destruction of all that is best and most valuable in us, as well as poisons all the affections which link us to our families, and people, in the Final Adjustment, which we call the Day of Judgement.

16. They shall have Layers[4266]
Of Fire above them,
And Layers (of Fire)
Below them: with this
Doth Allah warn off[4267]
His Servants: "O My Servants!
Then fear ye Me!"

(١٦) لَهُم مِّن فَوْقِهِمْ ظُلَلٌ مِّنَ النَّارِ
وَمِن تَحْتِهِمْ ظُلَلٌ ذَٰلِكَ يُخَوِّفُ اللَّهُ بِهِۦ عِبَادَهُۥ
يَٰعِبَادِ فَاتَّقُونِ

17. Those who eschew Evil—
And fall not into[4268]
Its worship—and turn
To Allah (in repentance)—
For them is Good News:
So announce the Good News
To My Servants—

(١٧) وَالَّذِينَ اجْتَنَبُوا الطَّٰغُوتَ
أَن يَعْبُدُوهَا وَأَنَابُوٓا إِلَى اللَّهِ لَهُمُ الْبُشْرَىٰ
فَبَشِّرْ عِبَادِ

18. Those who listen
To the Word,
And follow
The best (meaning) in it:[4269]
Those are the ones
Whom Allah has guided, and those
Are the ones endued
With understanding.

(١٨) الَّذِينَ يَسْتَمِعُونَ الْقَوْلَ
فَيَتَّبِعُونَ أَحْسَنَهُۥٓ
أُولَٰٓئِكَ الَّذِينَ هَدَىٰهُمُ اللَّهُ
وَأُولَٰٓئِكَ هُمْ أُولُوا الْأَلْبَٰبِ

19. Is, then, one against whom
The decree of Punishment
Is justly due (equal
To one who eschews evil)?[4270]

(١٩) أَفَمَنْ حَقَّ عَلَيْهِ
كَلِمَةُ الْعَذَابِ

4266. The consequences of Sin when Judgement comes are aptly figured by Layers upon Layers of Fire, which hem in the sinners above and below. It is also suggested that the Layers, though of Fire, have something dark in them—the scorching quality of Sin.

4267. But Allah does not leave mankind without warning. Man has been granted a limited amount of free will, and in order to help him in its right use, all the consequences of his action are clearly explained to him. To those who will listen to Reason are given arguments which can be apprehended by their own intelligence; to those who are swayed by affections and emotions, an appeal is made in the name of the Love of Allah; to those who understand nothing but fear, the warning is conveyed by a portrayal of the dreadful consequences of wrongdoing.

4268. There is always the danger that Evil may seize us even if we approach it out of mere curiosity. If we take an interest in it we may become its worshippers or slaves. The wise man eschews it altogether, and so he enrols among the Servants of Allah, and gets the good news of His Mercy and Good Pleasure.

4269. The Commentators construe this clause in two alternative ways. (1) If "word" be taken as any word, the clause would mean that good men listen to all that is said and choose the best of it. (2) If "word" be taken to mean Allah's Word, it would mean that they should listen reverently to it, and where permissive and alternative courses are allowed for those who are not strong enough to follow the higher course, those "endued with understanding" should prefer to attempt the higher course of conduct. For example, it is permitted (within limits) to punish those who wrong us, but the nobler course is to repel evil with good (23:96), we should try to follow the nobler course. I prefer the latter construction: it accords better with my interpretation of the last verse: see n. 4268.

4270. If a man is already steeped in sin and has rejected Allah's Grace, how can we expect Revelation to work in his soul?

Wouldst thou, then, deliver
One (who is) in the Fire?

أَفَأَنتَ تُنقِذُ مَن فِي ٱلنَّارِ

20. But it is for those
Who fear their Lord,
That lofty mansions,[4271]
One above another,
Have been built:
Beneath them flow
Rivers (of delight): (such is)
The Promise of Allah:
Never doth Allah fail in
(His) promise.[4272]

٢٠ لَٰكِنِ ٱلَّذِينَ ٱتَّقَوْا۟ رَبَّهُمْ
لَهُمْ غُرَفٌ مِّن فَوْقِهَا غُرَفٌ مَّبْنِيَّةٌ
تَجْرِى مِن تَحْتِهَا ٱلْأَنْهَٰرُ وَعْدَ ٱللَّهِ
لَا يُخْلِفُ ٱللَّهُ ٱلْمِيعَادَ

21. Seest thou not that Allah
Sends down rain from
The sky, and leads it
Through springs in the earth?[4273]
Then He causes to grow,
Therewith, produce of various
Colours: then it withers;
Thou wilt see it grow yellow;
Then He makes it
Dry up and crumble away.
Truly, in this, is
A Message of remembrance to
Men of understanding.

٢١ أَلَمْ تَرَ أَنَّ ٱللَّهَ أَنزَلَ مِنَ ٱلسَّمَآءِ
مَآءً فَسَلَكَهُۥ يَنَٰبِيعَ فِى ٱلْأَرْضِ
ثُمَّ يُخْرِجُ بِهِۦ زَرْعًا مُّخْتَلِفًا أَلْوَٰنُهُۥ
ثُمَّ يَهِيجُ فَتَرَىٰهُ مُصْفَرًّا
ثُمَّ يَجْعَلُهُۥ حُطَٰمًا
إِنَّ فِى ذَٰلِكَ لَذِكْرَىٰ
لِأُو۟لِى ٱلْأَلْبَٰبِ

C. 204. — What distance separates the man
(39:22-52.) Whose heart is melted by the Message
Of Allah and enlightened by His Light,
And him who rejects Revelation! Allah
Teaches men by Parables: straight
Is His Word and clear. Any doubts in the minds
Of men will be resolved after Death:
Even now, Allah's Signs are enough: no other
Can guide. Death and his twin brother,

4271. *Cf.* 29:58, and 34:37. The idea of heaven here is that of a Home of sublimity and beauty, with a picturesque outlook, such as we would describe in this life by the type of a palace by gently-flowing streams. The mansions will also suggest generous space and architectural beauty, tiers upon tiers piled one upon another.

4272. *Mī'ād*: the time, place and manner of the fulfilment of a Promise. Allah's promise will be fulfilled in all particulars better than we can possibly imagine.

4273. The circuit of water, by which the rain falls from the clouds, is absorbed through the earth, and flows through rivers or underground streams to the sea, where it again rises as vapour and forms clouds, was explained in notes 311-12 to 25:53. Here our attention is drawn to one portion of the process. The rain fructifies the soil and the seeds. Produce of various kinds is raised. The harvest ripens and is gathered in. The plants wither, dry up, and crumble away. Men and animals are fed. And the circuit starts again in another season. Here is a Sign of the Grace and Goodness of Allah, clear to those who understand.

Sleep, are in the hands of Allah: to Him
Is our Goal. He will judge in the End.
His Will is all-in-all. No other thing
Can be of any account before His Law.

SECTION 3.

22. Is one whose heart
Allah has opened to Islam,[4274]
So that he has received
Enlightenment from Allah,
(No better than one
hardhearted)?
Woe to those whose hearts
Are hardened against
celebrating[4275]
The praises of Allah! They
Are manifestly wandering
(In error)!

٢٢ أَفَمَن شَرَحَ
ٱللَّهُ صَدْرَهُۥ لِلْإِسْلَٰمِ
فَهُوَ عَلَىٰ نُورٍ مِّن رَّبِّهِۦ
فَوَيْلٌ لِّلْقَٰسِيَةِ
قُلُوبُهُم مِّن ذِكْرِ ٱللَّهِ
أُو۟لَٰٓئِكَ فِى ضَلَٰلٍ مُّبِينٍ

23. Allah has revealed
(From time to time)
The most beautiful Message
In the form of a Book,
Consistent with itself,[4276]
(Yet) repeating (its teaching
In various aspects):[4277]
The skins of those who
Fear their Lord tremble[4278]
Thereat: then their skins

٢٣ ٱللَّهُ نَزَّلَ
أَحْسَنَ ٱلْحَدِيثِ
كِتَٰبًا مُّتَشَٰبِهًا مَّثَانِىَ
تَقْشَعِرُّ مِنْهُ جُلُودُ ٱلَّذِينَ
يَخْشَوْنَ رَبَّهُمْ ثُمَّ تَلِينُ جُلُودُهُمْ

4274. Those who listen to Allah's Message find at each stage Allah's Grace helping them more and more to expand their spiritual understanding and to receive Allah's light, so that they travel farther and farther to their Goal in the Path of Truth and Righteousness. They are not to be compared to those who shut out Allah's Light from their hearts. See next note.

4275. Just as there is spiritual progress for those who seek Allah, so there is more and more spiritual retrogression for those who close their hearts to Allah. Their hearts get hardened, and they allow less and less Allah's Grace to penetrate within. But it is obvious that they flounder on the Way, and cannot walk with the firm steps of those of assured Faith.

4276. Is *Mutashābih* here to be understood in the same sense as in 3:7? See n. 347. The better opinion is that there is a slightly different shade of meaning here, as suggested by the context. In the earlier passages, it was opposed to *Muḥkam*: here it is contrasted or compared to *Mathānī*. The root meaning is: 'having something similar; working by analogy or allegory, or parable; having its parts consistent with each other'. The last meaning I adopt here. The Qur'ān was revealed in parts at different times. And yet its parts all conform to each other. There is no contradiction or inconsistency anywhere. (R).

4277. *Mathānī*: *Cf.* 15:87, where we have translated "oft-repeated": "The seven *oft-repeated* (verses)". See n. 2008 to that passage. Here the meaning is similar, but the context gives a different colour to it, as is seen in the translation.

4278. The skin is the outer integument of the body. It receives the first shock from the impact of anything unusual, and it trembles and its hair stands on end under excitement. So in spiritual matters the first stimulation from Allah's Message is external. Those who receive Faith do it as it were with tremor and not with apathy. But the next stage is that it penetrates their outer nature and goes right into their hearts. Their whole nature is "softened" to receive the beneficent Message, and it transforms them through and through.

And their hearts do soften To the celebration of Allah's praises. Such is The guidance of Allah: He guides therewith Whom He pleases,[4279] but such As Allah leaves to stray, Can have none to guide.	وَقُلُوبُهُمْ إِلَىٰ ذِكْرِ ٱللَّهِ ذَٰلِكَ هُدَى ٱللَّهِ يَهْدِى بِهِۦ مَن يَشَآءُ وَمَن يُضْلِلِ ٱللَّهُ فَمَا لَهُۥ مِنْ هَادٍ
24. Is, then, one who Has to fear the brunt Of the Penalty on the Day Of Judgement (and receive it) On his face,[4280] (like one Guarded therefrom)? It will Be said to the wrongdoers: "Taste ye (the fruits Of) what ye earned!"[4281]	٢٤ أَفَمَن يَتَّقِى بِوَجْهِهِۦ سُوٓءَ ٱلْعَذَابِ يَوْمَ ٱلْقِيَٰمَةِ وَقِيلَ لِلظَّٰلِمِينَ ذُوقُوا۟ مَا كُنتُمْ تَكْسِبُونَ
25. Those before them (also) Rejected (revelation), and so The Punishment came to them From directions they did not Perceive.[4282]	٢٥ كَذَّبَ ٱلَّذِينَ مِن قَبْلِهِمْ فَأَتَىٰهُمُ ٱلْعَذَابُ مِنْ حَيْثُ لَا يَشْعُرُونَ
26. So Allah gave them A taste of humiliation In the present life,[4283] But greater is the Punishment Of the Hereafter, If they only knew!	٢٦ فَأَذَاقَهُمُ ٱللَّهُ ٱلْخِزْىَ فِى ٱلْحَيَوٰةِ ٱلدُّنْيَا وَلَعَذَابُ ٱلْءَاخِرَةِ أَكْبَرُ لَوْ كَانُوا۟ يَعْلَمُونَ

4279. "Whom He pleases" and "leaves to stray" are explained fully in n. 2133 to 16:93. See also 16:4 and n. 1875.

4280. The unrepentant Sinners will receive the full Penalty on the Day of Judgement. They will receive it full in the face, *i.e.*, their whole being will be affected by it. Their hands (figuratively) will be tied, and they cannot therefore use their hands to ward off the Penalty of the Fire: in any case their hands will not have the power to ward it off. Are such helpless people to be compared for a moment with people who have received Grace and are therefore guarded from all harm and danger? Certainly not. To the evil the fruit of their deed, and to the good the grace of their Lord!

4281. That is, of all their misdeeds, all the evil which they did in the world.

4282. *Cf.* 16:26. They will be punished from quarters or in ways they do not perceive. From their Unbelief and Rebellion they think they derive great advantages, but they suddenly find out, when too late, that that which they exulted in was the cause of their undoing.

4283. *Cf.* 2:114. Sin often brings disgrace and humiliation in this life, but the greater and truer punishment is in the Hereafter. But men often do not know the inwardness of this matter. If they flourish here for a time, they think they will escape the real consequences in the Hereafter. Or if they suffer little harm here, they think that will make up the Penalty, and they will escape the Hereafter. Both ideas are wrong.

27. We have put forth
For men, in this Qur'ān
Every kind of Parable,[4284]
In order that they
May receive admonition.

٢٧ وَلَقَدْ ضَرَبْنَا لِلنَّاسِ فِي هَٰذَا
ٱلْقُرْءَانِ مِن كُلِّ مَثَلٍ لَّعَلَّهُمْ يَتَذَكَّرُونَ

28. (It is) a Qur'ān
In Arabic,[4285] without any
Crookedness (therein):[4286]
In order that they
May guard against Evil.

٢٨ قُرْءَانًا عَرَبِيًّا غَيْرَ ذِى
عِوَجٍ لَّعَلَّهُمْ يَتَّقُونَ

29. Allah puts forth a Parable—
A man belonging to many[4287]
Partners at variance with each
other,
And a man belonging entirely
To one master: are those two
Equal in comparison?
Praise be to Allah![4288]
But most of them
Have no knowledge.

٢٩ ضَرَبَ ٱللَّهُ مَثَلًا
رَّجُلًا فِيهِ شُرَكَآءُ مُتَشَٰكِسُونَ
وَرَجُلًا سَلَمًا لِّرَجُلٍ
هَلْ يَسْتَوِيَانِ مَثَلًا
ٱلْحَمْدُ لِلَّهِ بَلْ أَكْثَرُهُمْ لَا يَعْلَمُونَ

30. Truly thou wilt die[4289]
(One day), and truly they
(Too) will die (one day).

٣٠ إِنَّكَ مَيِّتٌ وَإِنَّهُم مَّيِّتُونَ

31. In the End will ye
(All), on the Day
Of Judgement, settle your
disputes[4290]
In the presence of your Lord.

٣١ ثُمَّ إِنَّكُمْ يَوْمَ ٱلْقِيَٰمَةِ
عِندَ رَبِّكُمْ تَخْتَصِمُونَ

4284. Men can only understand high spiritual truths by parables and similitudes and these are given abundantly in the Qur'ān. The object is, not merely to tell stories, but to teach lessons of spiritual wisdom.

4285. Previous revelations had been in other languages. Now the revelation was given in Arabia in Arabic itself, the language of the country which all could understand. And it is a beautiful language, straight and flexible, and fit to be the vehicle of sublime truths. *Cf.* C. 12.

4286. See 18:1 and n. 2326. *Cf.* also 7:45, n. 1024; and 19:36, n. 2488.

4287. The difference between the creed of Polytheism and the Gospel of Unity is explained by the analogy of two men. One belongs to many masters; the masters disagree among themselves, and the poor man of many masters has to suffer from the quarrel of his many masters: it is an impossible and unnatural position. The other serves only one master, his master is good, and does all he can for his servant; the servant can concentrate his attention on his service; he is happy himself and his service is efficiently performed. Can there be any doubt as to (1) which of them is the happier, and (2) which of them is in a more natural position? No man can serve two, still less, numerous masters.

4288. Allah is praised that He has put us, not under gods many and lords many, but has, out of His infinite Mercy, allowed us direct approach to Him, the One, the True, the Eternal.

4289. Even the prophets are not exempt from bodily death, much less the righteous, but they live in their beneficent work and the memories they leave behind them. All men have to die, good and alike. But there is a life after death, and in that life all the unexplained things about which people dispute in this world will be made clear in the presence of Allah.

4290. See last note.

SECTION 4.

32. Who, then, doth more wrong
Than one who utters
24 A lie concerning Allah,[4291]
30 And rejects the Truth
When it comes to him!
Is there not in Hell[4292]
An abode for blasphemers?

٣٢ فَمَنْ أَظْلَمُ مِمَّن كَذَبَ
عَلَى ٱللَّهِ وَكَذَّبَ بِٱلصِّدْقِ إِذْ جَآءَهُۥٓ ۚ
أَلَيْسَ فِى جَهَنَّمَ مَثْوًى لِّلْكَٰفِرِينَ

33. And he who brings the Truth
And he who confirms[4293]
(And supports) it—such are
The men who do right.

٣٣ وَٱلَّذِى جَآءَ بِٱلصِّدْقِ وَصَدَّقَ بِهِۦٓ ۙ
أُو۟لَٰٓئِكَ هُمُ ٱلْمُتَّقُونَ

34. They shall have all
That they wish for,[4294]
In the presence of their Lord:
Such is the reward
Of those who do good:

٣٤ لَهُم مَّا يَشَآءُونَ عِندَ رَبِّهِمْ ۚ
ذَٰلِكَ جَزَآءُ ٱلْمُحْسِنِينَ

35. So that Allah will
Turn off from them
(Even) the worst in their
deeds[4295]
And give them their reward
According to the best
Of what they have done.

٣٥ لِيُكَفِّرَ ٱللَّهُ عَنْهُمْ
أَسْوَأَ ٱلَّذِى عَمِلُوا۟ وَيَجْزِيَهُمْ أَجْرَهُم
بِأَحْسَنِ ٱلَّذِى كَانُوا۟ يَعْمَلُونَ

4291. When the creature deliberately adopts and utters falsehoods against his own Creator, in spite of the Truth being brought, as it were, to his very door by Allah's Signs, what offence can we imagine more heinous than this? In Christian theology this is the blasphemy "against the Holy Ghost" spoken of in Matt. xii. 31-32: "whosoever speaketh a word against the Son of man", (Christ), "it shall be forgiven him; but whosoever speaketh against the Holy Ghost, it shall not be forgiven him, neither in this world, neither in the world to come".

4292. *Cf.* 2:151; 16:29 [Eds.].

4293. This is true of the Prophet, and all men of God and all righteous persons. Anyone who preaches the Truth and brings home Allah's Signs to men is performing the duty of a right and noble life. In this he confirms the teaching of all previous men of God. Anyone who supports and confirms such a teacher is also doing his duty and on the right way. (R).

4294. At that stage their wills will have been purified, and they could wish for nothing that they could not or should not have. And it will be as "in the presence of their Lord". If an earthly king gives a decoration, how much greater is the honour when the investiture takes place by the king himself personally?

4295. The conjunction (*Lām* in Arabic, translated "so that") indicates here the results, not the purpose. Allah's Reward is so bounteous, that if we truly and sincerely put our will into His keeping, He will remove the consequences not only of our minor faults but of the worst of our sins, and judge us according to the very best of our deeds.

36. Is not Allah enough[4296]
For His servant? But
They try to frighten thee
With other (gods) besides Him!
For such as Allah leaves
To stray, there can be
No guide.

٣٦ أَلَيْسَ ٱللَّهُ بِكَافٍ عَبْدَهُۥ ۖ
وَيُخَوِّفُونَكَ بِٱلَّذِينَ مِن دُونِهِۦ ۚ
وَمَن يُضْلِلِ ٱللَّهُ فَمَا لَهُۥ مِنْ هَادٍ

37. And such as Allah doth[4297]
Guide there can be
None to lead astray.
Is not Allah Exalted
In Power, (Able to enforce
His Will), Lord of
Retribution?[4298]

٣٧ وَمَن يَهْدِ ٱللَّهُ
فَمَا لَهُۥ مِن مُّضِلٍّ ۗ
أَلَيْسَ ٱللَّهُ بِعَزِيزٍ ذِى ٱنتِقَامٍ

38. If indeed thou ask them
Who it is that created[4299]
The heavens and the earth,
They would be sure to say,
"Allah". Say: "See ye then?"
The things that ye invoke
Besides Allah—can they,
If Allah wills some Penalty
For me, remove His Penalty?—
Or if He wills some Grace
For me, can they keep back[4300]
His Grace?" Say: "Sufficient
Is Allah for me!

٣٨ وَلَئِن سَأَلْتَهُم مَّنْ خَلَقَ
ٱلسَّمَٰوَٰتِ وَٱلْأَرْضَ لَيَقُولُنَّ ٱللَّهُ ۚ
قُلْ أَفَرَءَيْتُم مَّا تَدْعُونَ مِن دُونِ ٱللَّهِ إِنْ أَرَادَنِىَ
ٱللَّهُ بِضُرٍّ هَلْ هُنَّ كَٰشِفَٰتُ ضُرِّهِۦٓ أَوْ أَرَادَنِى
بِرَحْمَةٍ هَلْ هُنَّ مُمْسِكَٰتُ رَحْمَتِهِۦ ۚ
قُلْ حَسْبِىَ ٱللَّهُ ۖ

4296. The righteous man will find Allah enough for all the protection he needs, all the rest and peace he craves for, and all the happiness he can imagine. If the evil ones wish to frighten him with false gods, he knows that that is mere superstition. In the case of idols to whom worship is paid, this is easily intelligble. But there are other false gods which men worship—wealth, power, science, selfish desire, and so on. The idea may occur to them: "this is the right course, but what will men say?" or "shall I lose my case if I tell the truth?" or "will it ruin my chances if I denounce sin in high places?" All such false gods will only mislead and leave their victims in the lurch. The worship of them will lose them the Grace of Allah, which wants to guide and comfort all who seek Allah.

4297. On the other hand if anyone holds fast to Allah's Truth, nothing can mislead or betray him.

4298. Allah's Power can protect, and will defeat all plots against His Will, as well as punish Evil when it gets beyond bounds.

4299. *Cf.* 29:61; also n. 2927 to 23:85. Most worshippers of false gods are neither atheists nor sceptics. They admit the existence of Allah as an abstract proposition, but it has not come into their hearts and souls: it has not been translated into their lives. They run after false worship on account of ancestral custom or on account of their thoughtlessness or false environment, or on account of their own selfish desires or limited outlook. To them is addressed the argument: 'Ultimately your false gods can do nothing for you: why not turn to the One True God, on Whom you depend, and Who can give you Grace and Mercy, Justice and Punishment?'

4300. *Cf.* 33:17.

In Him trust those
Who put their trust."[4301]

عَلَيۡهِ يَتَوَكَّلُ ٱلۡمُتَوَكِّلُونَ

39. Say: "O my people!
Do whatever ye can:
I will do (my part):[4302]
But soon will ye know—

٣٩ قُلۡ يَٰقَوۡمِ ٱعۡمَلُواْ عَلَىٰ مَكَانَتِكُمۡ
إِنِّي عَٰمِلٞۖ فَسَوۡفَ تَعۡلَمُونَ

40. "Who it is to whom
Comes a Penalty[4303]
Of ignominy, and on whom
Descends a Penalty that abides."

٤٠ مَن يَأۡتِيهِ عَذَابٞ يُخۡزِيهِ
وَيَحِلُّ عَلَيۡهِ عَذَابٞ مُّقِيمٌ

41. Verily We have revealed
The Book to thee
In Truth, for (instructing)
mankind.[4304]
He, then, that receives guidance
Benefits his own soul:
But he that strays
Injures his own soul.
Nor art thou set[4305]
Over them to dispose
Of their affairs.

٤١ إِنَّآ أَنزَلۡنَا عَلَيۡكَ
ٱلۡكِتَٰبَ لِلنَّاسِ بِٱلۡحَقِّۖ
فَمَنِ ٱهۡتَدَىٰ فَلِنَفۡسِهِۦۖ
وَمَن ضَلَّ فَإِنَّمَا يَضِلُّ عَلَيۡهَاۖ
وَمَآ أَنتَ عَلَيۡهِم بِوَكِيلٍ

SECTION 5.

42. It is Allah that takes
The souls (of men) at death;[4306]
And those that die not

٤٢ ٱللَّهُ يَتَوَفَّى ٱلۡأَنفُسَ حِينَ
مَوۡتِهَا وَٱلَّتِي لَمۡ تَمُتۡ

4301. *Cf.* 12:67, and 14:12. Allah alone is He Who will and can discharge any trust put in Him. All other things will fail. Therefore those who put their trust in anything should put their trust in Allah.

4302. *Cf.* 11:121 and n. 1624-A.

4303. *Cf.* 11:93. The two clauses, about those who suffer a Penalty of ignominy and those on whom descends a lasting Penalty, apparently refer to the same person in two different aspects: (1) they suffer shame, and (2) their punishment endures.

4304. Revelation is sent by Allah through His messenger, but it is for all. It is given in order that men and women may be taught Righteousness. It is given in Truth: there is no pretence about it. It is for their own good. If they reject it and follow Evil, the loss is their own.

4305. Allah's messengers do all they can to teach mankind. But they cannot force men's wills. If men reject their teaching, the account of the rejecters is with Allah. *Cf.* 6:107, and n. 935.

4306. The mystery of life and death, sleep and dreams, is a fascinating enigma, of which the solution is perhaps beyond the ken of man. A vast mass of superstition as well as imaginative and psychological literature has grown up about it. But the simplest and truest religious doctrine is laid down here in a few words. In death we surrender our physical life, but our soul does not die; it goes back to a plane of existence in which it is more conscious of the realities of the spiritual world: "Allah takes the soul".

(He takes) during their
sleep:[4307]
Those on whom He
Has passed the decree
Of death, He keeps back[4308]
(From returning to life),
But the rest He sends
(To their bodies)
For a term appointed.
Verily in this are Signs[4309]
For those who reflect.

فِي مَنَامِهَا
فَيُمْسِكُ ٱلَّتِي قَضَىٰ
عَلَيْهَا ٱلْمَوْتَ وَيُرْسِلُ
ٱلْأُخْرَىٰٓ إِلَىٰٓ أَجَلٍ مُّسَمًّى
إِنَّ فِي ذَٰلِكَ لَآيَٰتٍ لِّقَوْمٍ يَتَفَكَّرُونَ

43. What! Do they take
For intercessors others[4310]
Besides Allah? Say: "Even if
They have no power whatever
And no intelligence?"

٤٣ أَمِ ٱتَّخَذُوا۟ مِن دُونِ ٱللَّهِ شُفَعَآءَ
قُلْ أَوَلَوْ كَانُوا۟ لَا يَمْلِكُونَ
شَيْـًٔا وَلَا يَعْقِلُونَ

44. Say: "To Allah belongs
Exclusively (the right)
To grant) Intercession:[4311]
To Him belongs the dominion

٤٤ قُل لِّلَّهِ ٱلشَّفَٰعَةُ جَمِيعًا
لَّهُۥ مُلْكُ

4307. *Cf.* 6:60. What is sleep? As far as animal life is concerned, it is the cessation of the working of the nervous system, though other animal functions, such as digestion, growth, and the circulation of the blood, continue, possibly at a different pace. It is the repose of the nervous system, and in this respect it is common to man and animals, and perhaps even to plants, if, as is probable, plants have a nervous system. The mentai processes (and certainly volition) are also suspended in sleep, except that in ordinary dreams there is a medley of recollections, which often present vividly to our consciousness things that do not or cannot happen in nature as we know it in our coordinated minds. But there is another kind of dream which is rarer—one in which the dreamer sees things as they actually happen, backwards or forwards in time, or in which gifted individuals see spiritual truths otherwise imperceptible to them. How can we explain this? It is suggested that our soul or personaltiy—that something which is above our animal life—is then in a plane of spiritual existence akin to physical death (see last note), when we are nearer to Allah. In poetic imagery, Sleep is "twin-brother to Death".

4308. Sleep being twin-brother to Death, our souls are for the time being released from the bondage of the flesh. Allah takes them for the time being. If, as some do, we are to die peacefully in sleep, our soul does not come back to the physical body, and the latter decays and dies. If we still have some period of life to fulfil according to Allah's decree, our soul comes back to the body, and we resume our functions in this life.

4309. If we contemplate these things, we can see more clearly many spiritual truths: *e.g.* (1) that our bodily life and death are not the whole story of our existence; (2) that in our bodily life we may be dead to the spiritual world, and in our bodily death, may be our awakening to the spiritual world; (3) that our nightly Sleep, besides performing the function of rest to our physical life, gives us a foretaste of what we call death, which does not end our personality; and (4) that the Resurrection is not more wonderful than our daily rising from Sleep, "twin-brother to Death".

4310. Let alone worship, men should not rely upon any power or person other than Allah to help them out or intercede for them. When it is idols, they are poor lifeless things which have obviously neither power nor intelligence. But even prophets or saints or heroes have no power to intercede except as Allah wills and permits. See next note.

4311. For *Shafā'ah* (Intercession, Advocacy) see 2:255; 10:3; 20:109, n. 2634; and 21:28, n. 2688. It follows that no one can intercede with Allah, except (1) by Allah's permission, and (2) for those who have prepared themselves by penitence for Allah's acceptance. Even in earthly Courts, Advocacy is not permitted to anyone; the Advocate must be granted the position of Advocate before he can plead before the judge. Nor can it be supposed that a plea for forgiveness or mercy can be put forward except on grounds recognised by equity and jutice.

Of the heavens and the earth:
In the End, it is to Him[4312]
That ye shall be
Brought back."

ٱلسَّمَٰوَٰتِ وَٱلْأَرْضِ
ثُمَّ إِلَيْهِ تُرْجَعُونَ

45. When Allah, the One and Only,
Is mentioned, the hearts
Of those who believe not
In the Hereafter are filled
With disgust and horror;[4313]
But when (gods) other than He
Are mentioned, behold
They are filled with joy!

٤٥ وَإِذَا ذُكِرَ ٱللَّهُ وَحْدَهُ ٱشْمَأَزَّتْ
قُلُوبُ ٱلَّذِينَ لَا يُؤْمِنُونَ بِٱلْءَاخِرَةِ
وَإِذَا ذُكِرَ ٱلَّذِينَ مِن دُونِهِۦٓ
إِذَا هُمْ يَسْتَبْشِرُونَ

46. Say: "O Allah!
Creator of the heavens
And the earth!
Knower of all that is
Hidden and open![4314]
It is Thou that wilt
Judge between Thy Servants
In those matters about which
They have differed."

٤٦ قُلِ ٱللَّهُمَّ فَاطِرَ ٱلسَّمَٰوَٰتِ
وَٱلْأَرْضِ عَٰلِمَ ٱلْغَيْبِ وَٱلشَّهَٰدَةِ
أَنتَ تَحْكُمُ بَيْنَ عِبَادِكَ
فِى مَا كَانُوا۟ فِيهِ يَخْتَلِفُونَ

47. Even if the wrongdoers
Had all that there is
On earth, and as much more,[4315]
(In vain) would they offer it
For ransom from the pain
Of the Penalty on the Day
Of Judgement: but something
Will confront them from Allah,
Which they could never
Have counted upon![4316]

٤٧ وَلَوْ أَنَّ لِلَّذِينَ ظَلَمُوا۟
مَا فِى ٱلْأَرْضِ جَمِيعًا وَمِثْلَهُۥ مَعَهُۥ
لَٱفْتَدَوْا۟ بِهِۦ مِن سُوٓءِ ٱلْعَذَابِ يَوْمَ ٱلْقِيَٰمَةِ
وَبَدَا لَهُم مِّنَ ٱللَّهِ مَا لَمْ
يَكُونُوا۟ يَحْتَسِبُونَ

4312. At all times, including our present life, all dominion belongs to Allah. At the End of the present plane of existence, we shall be placed before Allah for Judgement. *Cf.* 10:4.

4313. To evil ones, the mention of the exclusive service of Good is hateful: they only rejoice when other motives are added, *e.g.*, personal indulgence, ancestral custom, and numerous things in life which compete with Allah's Law in this world.

4314. The mysteries of life and death, of worship and spiritual growth, are matters of high moment, which it may be difficult for us to apprehend in this present life. It is no use arguing about them and plunging in endless controversies. The proper attitude is to appeal to Allah humbly to accept our purified hearts and Faith, in the firm hope that everything which is now vague to us will be cleared up in the Hereafter, and to pray to Him for His guidance and mercy.

4315. *Cf.* 13:18. Those who reject Allah's Message must realise that the time will come when they will wish they had sacrificed everything in the cause of Truth and Righteousness. It will be too late then. Why not examine the matter seriously now and accept Allah's Grace and Light?

4316. This something will be beyond anything they can conceive of in this life. Just as the righteous will then attain a bliss which no human imagination can conceive of now, so the unrighteous will be in a misery of which they can form no conception now. See next note.

48. For the evils of their Deeds
Will confront them,
And they will be (completely)[4317]
Encircled by that which
They used to mock at!

٤٨ وَبَدَا لَهُمْ سَيِّـَٔاتُ مَا كَسَبُوا۟
وَحَاقَ بِهِم مَّا كَانُوا۟ بِهِۦ يَسْتَهْزِءُونَ

49. Now, when trouble touches man,
He cries to Us:[4318]
But when We bestow
A favour upon him[4319]
As from Ourselves,
He says, "This has been
Given to me because of
A certain knowledge (I have)!"[4320]
Nay, but this is
But a trial, but most
Of them understand not!

٤٩ فَإِذَا مَسَّ ٱلْإِنسَـٰنَ ضُرٌّ دَعَانَا
ثُمَّ إِذَا خَوَّلْنَـٰهُ نِعْمَةً مِّنَّا
قَالَ إِنَّمَآ أُوتِيتُهُۥ عَلَىٰ عِلْمٍۭ ۚ
بَلْ هِىَ فِتْنَةٌ وَلَـٰكِنَّ
أَكْثَرَهُمْ لَا يَعْلَمُونَ

50. Thus did the (generations)
Before them say! But
All that they did
Was of no profit to them.

٥٠ قَدْ قَالَهَا ٱلَّذِينَ مِن قَبْلِهِمْ
فَمَآ أَغْنَىٰ عَنْهُم مَّا كَانُوا۟ يَكْسِبُونَ

51. Nay, the evil results
Of their deeds overtook them.[4321]
And the wrongdoers
Of this (generation)—
The evil results of their deeds
Will soon overtake them (too),[4322]
And they will never be
Able to frustrate (Our Plan)!

٥١ فَأَصَابَهُمْ سَيِّـَٔاتُ مَا كَسَبُوا۟ ۚ
وَٱلَّذِينَ ظَلَمُوا۟ مِنْ هَـٰٓؤُلَآءِ
سَيُصِيبُهُمْ سَيِّـَٔاتُ مَا كَسَبُوا۟
وَمَا هُم بِمُعْجِزِينَ

52. Know they not that
Allah enlarges the provision[4323]

٥٢ أَوَلَمْ يَعْلَمُوٓا۟ أَنَّ ٱللَّهَ يَبْسُطُ ٱلرِّزْقَ

4317. How humiliating it will be for them to realise that the things they used to mock at are realities all around them, and the things they were so eager to pursue are mere falsehoods or vanities!

4318. *Cf.* 30:33 and n. 3545.

4319. *Cf.* 39:8 above.

4320. *Cf.* 38:78, and n. 3408. Prosperity may be a trial as much as adversity.

4321. *Cf.* 16:34.

4322. It is the same story through the ages. People laugh at Truth, persecute Truth, and try to destroy Truth. But Allah's Plan is never to be frustrated. It will be carried out, and only the enemies of Truth will accomplish their own undoing. So it happened in Arabia: so will it happen always and everywhere.

4323. *Cf.* 28:82. Allah's gifts are given to all men—to some in a greater degree than to others. But it is all done according to His wise Plan, for His Will is just and looks to the good of all creatures, No one should therefore be puffed up in prosperity or cast down in adversity. Prosperity does not necessarily mean merit on man's part, nor adversity the reverse. Thinking men bear in mind the large Plan—which is visible in all Allah's Signs.

Or restricts it, for any
He pleases? Verily, in this are
Signs for those who believe!

لِمَن يَشَآءُ وَيَقۡدِرُۚ
إِنَّ فِي ذَٰلِكَ لَأٓيَٰتٖ لِّقَوۡمٖ يُؤۡمِنُونَ

C. 205.—(39:53-75.)
But no soul need be in despair because
Of its sin: Allah's Forgiveness and Mercy are
Unbounded. Turn to Allah in repentance
Now, for at Judgement it will be too late.
Unity in worhip and life is commanded
By Allah. Go not astray. When Judgement
Comes, it will be a new World.
In perfect justice will the followers
Of Evil be sorted out from the Good.
And the righteous will rejoice, singing
Praises to Allah with the angels on high.

SECTION 6.

53. Say: "O my Servants who
Have transgressed against their
souls!
Despair not of the Mercy
Of Allah: for Allah forgives[4324]
All sins for He is
Oft-Forgiving, Most Merciful.

۞ قُلۡ يَٰعِبَادِيَ ٱلَّذِينَ أَسۡرَفُواْ عَلَىٰٓ
أَنفُسِهِمۡ لَا تَقۡنَطُواْ مِن رَّحۡمَةِ ٱللَّهِۚ
إِنَّ ٱللَّهَ يَغۡفِرُ ٱلذُّنُوبَ جَمِيعًاۚ
إِنَّهُۥ هُوَ ٱلۡغَفُورُ ٱلرَّحِيمُ ٥٣

54. "Turn ye to your Lord
(In repentance) and bow
To His (Will), before[4325]
The Penalty comes on you:
After that ye shall not
Be helped.

وَأَنِيبُوٓاْ إِلَىٰ رَبِّكُمۡ
وَأَسۡلِمُواْ لَهُۥ مِن قَبۡلِ أَن يَأۡتِيَكُمُ
ٱلۡعَذَابُ ثُمَّ لَا تُنصَرُونَ ٥٤

55. "And follow the Best[4326]
Of (the courses) revealed
To you from your Lord,
Before the Penalty comes
On you—of a sudden,
While ye perceive not!—

وَٱتَّبِعُوٓاْ أَحۡسَنَ مَآ أُنزِلَ إِلَيۡكُم
مِّن رَّبِّكُم مِّن قَبۡلِ أَن يَأۡتِيَكُمُ
ٱلۡعَذَابُ بَغۡتَةٗ وَأَنتُمۡ لَا تَشۡعُرُونَ ٥٥

4324. *Forgives all sins*: *i.e.*, on sincere repentance and amendment of conduct.

4325. The exhortation in brief is: 'Repent and work righteousness, before it becomes too late'. No help will come to you when the Judgement is actually established and you stand before the Judgement Seat.

4326. *Cf.* 39:18, and n. 4269. Allah's Command meets the weakness of His weakest servants, and only asks that His servants should surrender their selfish will to Allah's Will. In divine compassion, therefore, we are allowed to do just what we can, even though our standard should fall short of the highest assistance. But we must do so in this life—and at once, as soon as the Word penetrates our mind or understanding. We must not delay a moment, for the Judgement may come at any time, suddenly, before we even perceive where we are.

56. "Lest the soul should (then)
Say: 'Ah! woe is me!—[4327]
In that I neglected
(My Duty) towards Allah,
And was but among those
Who mocked!'—

٥٦ أَن تَقُولَ نَفْسٌ يَٰحَسْرَتَىٰ
عَلَىٰ مَا فَرَّطتُ فِى جَنۢبِ ٱللَّهِ
وَإِن كُنتُ لَمِنَ ٱلسَّٰخِرِينَ

57. "Or (lest) it should say:[4328]
'If only Allah had guided
Me, I should certainly
Have been among the righteous!'—

٥٧ أَوْ تَقُولَ لَوْ أَنَّ ٱللَّهَ هَدَىٰنِى
لَكُنتُ مِنَ ٱلْمُتَّقِينَ

58. "Or (lest) it should say[4329]
When it (actually) sees
The Penalty: 'If only
I had another chance,
I should certainly be
Among those who do good!'

٥٨ أَوْ تَقُولَ حِينَ تَرَى ٱلْعَذَابَ
لَوْ أَنَّ لِى كَرَّةً فَأَكُونَ
مِنَ ٱلْمُحْسِنِينَ

59. "(The reply will be:) 'Nay,[4330]
But there came to thee
My Signs, and thou didst
Reject them: thou wast
Haughty, and became one
Of those who reject Faith!'"[4331]

٥٩ بَلَىٰ قَدْ جَآءَتْكَ ءَايَٰتِى
فَكَذَّبْتَ بِهَا وَٱسْتَكْبَرْتَ
وَكُنتَ مِنَ ٱلْكَٰفِرِينَ

60. On the Day of Judgement
Wilt thou see those
Who told lies against Allah—
Their faces will be turned[4332]
Black; is there not

٦٠ وَيَوْمَ ٱلْقِيَٰمَةِ تَرَى ٱلَّذِينَ
كَذَبُوا۟ عَلَى ٱللَّهِ وُجُوهُهُم مُّسْوَدَّةٌ

4327. Many kinds of sighs and regrets will then assail us. In the first place, we shall see our shortcomings: we were negligent when we should have been serious: we mocked when we should have tried to learn and understand. But it will be too late then to retrieve our position.

4328. In the second place, we might be inclined to say, 'I wish I had received warning or guidance'. But this would not be true, because the warning and guidance are being conveyed in the clearest manner in Allah's Revelation. That is the force of 'lest it should say'. It could have said so, had it not seen that the objection is clearly anticipated in the call to repent and in the warning about the Hereafter.

4329. In the third place, when we stand face to face with the Penalty of our own deeds, we might say, 'I wish I had another chance'. But not one, but many, chances are being given, especially when we are told (verse 53 above): 'Despair not of the Mercy of Allah: for Allah forgives all sins: for He is Oft-Forgiving, Most Merciful'. The force of 'lest it should say' here is the same as explained in the last note.

4330. The reply explains how all such pleas have been anticipated and met. It was deliberate rejection that will deserve and meet its consequences. It is further explained that the motive of sin, as with Satan, was haughtiness and Self. (R).

4331. *Cf.* 2:34. The example of the arch-sinner illustrates what happens, to a minor degree, to every kind of sinner.

4332. As spotless white is the symbol of purity, honour and truth, so black is the symbol of evil, disgrace, and falsehood. Perhaps "black" in connection with Hell also refers to the scorching punishment of the Fire.

In Hell an abode[4333]
For the Haughty?

أَلَيْسَ فِى جَهَنَّمَ مَثْوًى لِّلْمُتَكَبِّرِينَ

61. But Allah will deliver
The righteous to their place[4334]
Of salvation: no evil
Shall touch them,
Nor shall they grieve.

﴿٦١﴾ وَيُنَجِّى ٱللَّهُ ٱلَّذِينَ ٱتَّقَوْا۟ بِمَفَازَتِهِمْ
لَا يَمَسُّهُمُ ٱلسُّوٓءُ وَلَا هُمْ يَحْزَنُونَ

62. Allah is the Creator
Of all things, and He
Is the Guardian and Disposer[4335]
Of all affairs.

﴿٦٢﴾ ٱللَّهُ خَٰلِقُ كُلِّ شَىْءٍ ۖ
وَهُوَ عَلَىٰ كُلِّ شَىْءٍ وَكِيلٌ

63. To Him belong the keys
Of the heavens
And the earth:
And those who reject
The Signs of Allah—
It is they who will[4336]
Be in loss.

﴿٦٣﴾ لَّهُۥ مَقَالِيدُ ٱلسَّمَٰوَٰتِ وَٱلْأَرْضِ ۗ
وَٱلَّذِينَ كَفَرُوا۟ بِـَٔايَٰتِ ٱللَّهِ
أُو۟لَٰٓئِكَ هُمُ ٱلْخَٰسِرُونَ

SECTION 7.

64. Say: "Is it
Someone other than Allah
That ye order me[4337]
To worship, O ye
Ignorant ones?"

﴿٦٤﴾ قُلْ أَفَغَيْرَ ٱللَّهِ تَأْمُرُوٓنِّىٓ
أَعْبُدُ أَيُّهَا ٱلْجَٰهِلُونَ

65. But it has already
Been revealed to thee—[4338]
As it was to those
Before thee—"If thou

﴿٦٥﴾ وَلَقَدْ أُوحِىَ إِلَيْكَ
وَإِلَى ٱلَّذِينَ مِن قَبْلِكَ لَئِنْ

4333. *Cf.* above, 39:32, and n. 4292, where the subtle implication of the interrogative form is explained.

4334. *Mafāzah:* place or state of safety or salvation, place or state of victory or achievement; accomplishment of wish or desire. This is contrasted against the frustration, failure, and perdition of the children of evil—what may be called damnation in theological phraseology.

4335. Allah has not only created all the Worlds, but He maintains them and cares for them. He does not sit apart from His world. Everything depends upon Him.

4336. Allah has nothing to lose by the rebellion or disobedience of His creatures. It is they who lose, because they go counter to their own nature, the beautiful mould in which Allah created them.

4337. *Order me:* there is great irony here. The Prophet of Allah turns to his critics and says: "You arrogate to yourselves the right to *order* me how to worship! But who are you? You are only ignorant men! My commission is from Allah. It is the same as came to Prophets of Allah before me in all ages, *viz.*, (1) that the only Truth is in the Gospel of Unity; and (2) that if you worship other things and turn away from Allah, your life will be wasted and all your probation will have been of no account. (R).

4338. The Message of Unity, renewed in Islam, has been the Message of Allah since the world began.

Wert to join (gods
With Allah), truly fruitless[4339]
Will be thy work (in life),
And thou wilt surely
Be in the ranks of those
Who lose (all spiritual good)".

أَشْرَكْتَ
لَيَحْبَطَنَّ عَمَلُكَ
وَلَتَكُونَنَّ مِنَ الْخَٰسِرِينَ

66. Nay, but worship Allah,
And be of those who
Give thanks.[4340]

٦٦ بَلِ اللَّهَ فَاعْبُدْ
وَكُن مِّنَ الشَّٰكِرِينَ

67. No just estimate
Have they made of Allah,[4341]
Such as is due to Him:
On the Day of Judgement
The whole of the earth
Will be but His handful,[4342]
And the heavens will be
Rolled up in His right hand:
Glory to Him!
High is He above
The Partners they attribute
To Him!

٦٧ وَمَا قَدَرُوا اللَّهَ حَقَّ قَدْرِهِۦ
وَالْأَرْضُ جَمِيعًا
قَبْضَتُهُۥ يَوْمَ الْقِيَٰمَةِ
وَالسَّمَٰوَٰتُ مَطْوِيَّٰتٌۢ بِيَمِينِهِۦ
سُبْحَٰنَهُۥ وَتَعَٰلَىٰ عَمَّا يُشْرِكُونَ

68. The Trumpet will (just)
Be sounded, when all
That are in the heavens
And on earth will swoon,[4343]
Except such as it will
Please Allah (to exempt).
Then will a second one
Be sounded, when, behold,
They will be standing
And looking on!

٦٨ وَنُفِخَ فِي الصُّورِ
فَصَعِقَ مَن فِي السَّمَٰوَٰتِ
وَمَن فِي الْأَرْضِ إِلَّا مَن شَاءَ اللَّهُ
ثُمَّ نُفِخَ فِيهِ أُخْرَىٰ
فَإِذَا هُمْ قِيَامٌ يَنظُرُونَ

4339. *Cf.* 5:6. False worship means that we run after fruitless things, and the main purpose of our spiritual lives is lost.

4340. To "give thanks" is to show by our conduct that we esteem the gifts of Allah and will use them in His service.

4341. *Cf.* 6:91, and n. 909; and 22:74. In running after false gods or the powers of nature they have forgotten that all creatures are as nothing before Allah.

4342. See last note. The whole earth will be no more to Allah than a thing that a man might enclose in the hollow of his hand, nor will the heavens with their vast expanse be more than a scroll, which a man might roll up with his right hand, the hand of power and action. *Cf.* 21:104, and 81:1.

4343. *Ṣa'iqa* implies the idea of a swoon, or loss of all consciousness of being; it implies a cessation of the normal functioning of the usual powers of life or feeling. With the first Trumpet of the Ressurrection, the whole world will cease to be in the form and the relations which we see now: there will be a new heaven and a new earth, see 14:48, n. 1925; human souls will for the time being be dazed and lose all memory or consciousness of time or place or personality. With the second one, they will stand in a new world; they will see with clearer vision than ever before; and judgement will proceed. (R).

69. And the Earth will shine
With the glory of its Lord:[4344]
The Record (of Deeds)
Will be placed (open);
The prophets and the witnesses
Will be brought forward;
And a just decision[4345]
Pronounced between them;
And they will not
Be wronged (in the least).

٦٩ وَأَشْرَقَتِ ٱلْأَرْضُ
بِنُورِ رَبِّهَا وَوُضِعَ ٱلْكِتَٰبُ
وَجِاىٓءَ بِٱلنَّبِيِّـۧنَ وَٱلشُّهَدَآءِ
وَقُضِىَ بَيْنَهُم بِٱلْحَقِّ
وَهُمْ لَا يُظْلَمُونَ

70. And to every soul will be
Paid in full (the fruit)
Of its deeds; and (Allah)
Knoweth best all that[4346]
They do.

٧٠ وَوُفِّيَتْ كُلُّ نَفْسٍ مَّا عَمِلَتْ
وَهُوَ أَعْلَمُ بِمَا يَفْعَلُونَ

SECTION 8.

71. The Unbelievers will be
Led to Hell in crowd:[4347]
Until, when they arrive there,
Its gates will be opened.
And its Keepers will say,[4348]
"Did not messengers come
To you from among yourselves,
Rehearsing to you the Signs
Of your Lord, and warning you
Of the Meeting of this Day
Of yours?" The answer
Will be: "True: but

٧١ وَسِيقَ ٱلَّذِينَ كَفَرُوٓا۟ إِلَىٰ جَهَنَّمَ زُمَرًا
حَتَّىٰٓ إِذَا جَآءُوهَا فُتِحَتْ أَبْوَٰبُهَا وَقَالَ
لَهُمْ خَزَنَتُهَآ أَلَمْ يَأْتِكُمْ رُسُلٌ مِّنكُمْ
يَتْلُونَ عَلَيْكُمْ ءَايَٰتِ رَبِّكُمْ
وَيُنذِرُونَكُمْ لِقَآءَ يَوْمِكُمْ هَٰذَا
قَالُوا۟ بَلَىٰ وَلَٰكِنْ

4344. It will be a new Earth. All traces of injustice or inequality, darkness or evil, will have gone. There will be the one universal Light, the Glory of Allah, which will now illuminate all. Falsehood, pretence, and illusion will have disappeared. Everything will be seen in its true light.

4345. It is in such a scene of Reality that Judgement will be held. Before the Throne of Allah, the book of each man's deeds and motives will be placed wide open, which all may see; the Prophets and Preachers of Truth and the martyrs who gave their lives or made their real sacrifices in the cause of Truth, will be in the Court, to give evidence; and the decision pronounced will be absolutely just, for the Judge will not only be just, but He will know every fact and circumstance, and His wisdom will give due weight to everything, great or small. (R).

4346. In an earthly court, a decision may possibly go wrong because the judge is deceived; here no deceit or mistake will be possible, for Allah knows all, and knows it better than anyone else can. (R).

4347. *Crowds:* this is the word which gives the keynote to the Sūrah. If the soul does not stand to its own convictions or search out the Truth by itself, it will be classed with the crowds that go to Perdition!

4348. The Keepers may be supposed to be angels, who know nothing of the conditions of evil on this earth, and are surprised at such crowds coming to the "Evil Abode." (R).

The Decree of Punishment
Has been proved true[4349]
Against the Unbelievers!"

حقت كلمة العذاب على الكافرين

72. (To them) will be said:
"Enter ye the gates of Hell,
To dwell therein:
And evil is (this)
Abode of the arrogant!"[4350]

(٧٢) قيل ادخلوا أبواب جهنم خالدين فيها
فبئس مثوى المتكبرين

73. And those who feared
Their Lord will be led
To the Garden in crowds:[4351]
Until behold, they arrive there;
Its gates will be opened;
And its Keepers will say:
"Peace be upon you!
Well have ye done![4352]
Enter ye here,
To dwell therein."

(٧٣) وسيق الذين اتقوا
ربهم إلى الجنة زمرا
حتى إذا جاءوها وفتحت أبوابها
وقال لهم خزنتها سلام عليكم
طبتم فادخلوها خالدين

74. They will say: "Praise be[4353]
To Allah, Who has
Truly fulfilled His promise
To us, and has given us
(This) land in heritage:[4354]
We can dwell in the Garden
As we will: how excellent
A reward for those
Who work (righteousness)!"

(٧٤) وقالوا الحمد لله
الذي صدقنا وعده وأورثنا الأرض
نتبوأ من الجنة حيث نشاء
فنعم أجر العاملين

75. And thou wilt see
The angels surrounding
The Throne (Divine)
On all sides, singing Glory
And Praise to their Lord.

(٧٥) وترى الملائكة حافين من حول
العرش يسبحون بحمد ربهم

4349. *Cf.* 10:33. The answer is perhaps given by other angels: 'yes; messengers were sent to them from among themselves, to warn them and proclaim to them Mercy through repentance; but the decree of Allah, which warned them of punishment, has now come true against them, for they rebelled and were haughty; they rejected Truth, Faith, and Mercy!'

4350. As elsewhere, the root of Evil is pointed out to be in self-love and arrogance. *Cf.* 2:34, etc.

4351. The righteous ones will also go in crowds, and not be alone. There is now a true sorting out. Verses 73-75 are parallel in contrast to verses 71-72 above.

4352. The angels in heaven are not surprised at the advent of the good and righteous souls. They are glad; they greet them with the salutation of Peace; they congratulate them; and they welcome them in.

4353. This is said by the new arrivals in heaven. As is right, they begin with the Praises of Allah, which shows at once their satisfaction and their gratitude.

4354. *In heritage: i.e.* as our Portion. *Cf.* 3:180, and n. 485; 6:165, and n. 988. There is no question here of their passing on any property to heirs. They are the final possessors of Heaven for eternity, by the grace of Allah.

The Decision between them
(At Judgement) will be
In (perfect) justice,
And the cry (on all sides)
Will be, "Praise be to Allah,[4355]
The Lord of the Worlds!"

وَقُضِيَ بَيْنَهُم بِٱلْحَقِّ
وَقِيلَ ٱلْحَمْدُ لِلَّهِ
رَبِّ ٱلْعَٰلَمِينَ ٠

4355. These are the opening words of the first Sūrah, and they describe the atmosphere of the final Bliss in Heaven, in the Light of the Countenance of their Lord, The Universal Lord of all!

INTRODUCTION TO SŪRAH 40—*GHĀFIR* or *AL MU'MIN*

This Sūrah is called Ghāfir (Forgiver, see verse 3). It is also called "The Believer" *(Mu'min)* from the story of the individual Believer among the people of Pharaoh, who declares his faith and looks to the Future (verses 28-45). In S. 23, called *The Believers (Mu'minūn)*, the argument was about the collective force of Faith and virtue. Here it is about the Individual's witness to Faith and Virtue, and his triumph in the End.

We now begin a series of seven Sūrahs (40-46) to which are affixed the Abbreviated Letters *Ḥā Mīm*. Chronologically they all belong to the same period, the later Makkan Period, and they immediately follow the last Sūrah in time. About the Abbreviated Letters generally, see Appendix I at the end of S. 2. As to the precise meaning of *Ḥā Mīm* no authoritative explanation is available. If *Mīm* here has a signification similar to *Mīm* in *Alif, Lām, Mīm* (see n. 25 to 2), it means the End of things, the Last Day, and all these Sūrahs direct our special attention to that *Ḥā*, the emphatic guttural, in contrast with the softer breathing of *Alif*, may be meant to suggest that the Beginning (see n. 25 to 2:1, last paragraph) is only for the End, the Present for the Future, and to emphasise the eschatological element in Faith. But this is mere conjecture, and should be taken for no more than it is worth.

The general theme of the whole series is the relation of Faith to Unfaith, Revelation to Rejection, Goodness to Evil, Truth to Falsehood. It is shown that the first in each of these pairs is the real friend, helper, and protector of man, while the second is his enemy. The very word *Ḥamīm* in that sense is used in Sūrahs 40 and 41 (40:18 and 41:34), while in the other Sūrahs we have words of equivalent import, *e.g. walī* or *naṣīr* (42:8 and 31); *qarīn* (43:36, 38); *mawlā* (44:41); *awliyā'* or *nāṣirīn* (45:19, 34); and *awliyā'* (46:32). Is it permissible to connect the Abbreviated Letters *Ḥā Mīm* with these ideas as expressed in the word *Ḥamīm?*

Another suggestion worthy of consideration is that *Ḥā* stands for *Ḥayy*, and *Mīm* for *Qayyūm*. These are two attributes of Allah, meaning, (1) the Living, and (2) the Self-Subsisting, Eternal. The one points to Life, and Revelation, and the other to the Hereafter and Eternity; and both these matters are specially dealt with in the seven *Ḥā Mīm* Sūrahs. The first letter of *Ḥayy (Ḥā)* is appropriate for life, and the last letter of *Qayyūm* is appropriate for the Last Days, the *Ma'ād*, the Hereafter. Again, this is mere conjecture, and should not be taken for more than it is worth.

Summary—Faith is ever justified, for Allah forgives: but evil deeds must have evil fruits, for Allah knows and is just (40:1-20 and C. 206).

In all history Evil came to evil; the protest of Faith, in the midst of Evil, may be ignored; but Faith is protected by Allah, while Evil perishes (40:21-50, and C. 207).

No doubt is there of the Future Judgement; the Power, Goodness, and Justice of God are manifest; will man dispute, or will he accept the Signs before it is too late? (40:51-85, and C. 208).

C. 106.—Believe in God. For He is Perfect
(40:1-20.) In Knowledge and Power, forgives Sin
And accepts Repentance, and justly
Enforces His Law. Those who reject Him

Are but in deceit: His glory is sung
By the highest and purest. Give all devotion
To Him alone. The Day of Requital
Is ever drawing near, when Falsehood
Will vanish, and Allah's Truth and Justice
Will be established for all Eternity.

Sūrah 40.

Ghāfir (Forgiver) or ***Al Mu'min*** (The Believer)

In the name of Allah, Most Gracious, Most Merciful

1. Ḥā Mīm.[4356]

2. The revelation
Of this Book
Is from Allah,
Exalted in Power,
Full of Knowledge—[4357]

3. Who forgiveth Sin,
Accepteth Repentance,[4358]
Is Strict in Punishment,
And hath a Long Reach
(In all things).
There is no god
But He: to Him
Is the Final Goal.

4. None can dispute
About the Signs of Allah[4359]
But the Unbelievers.
Let not, then
Their strutting about[4360]
Through the land
Deceive thee!

5. But (there were people) before them,
Who denied (the Signs)—
The People of Noah,

الجزء الرابع والعشرون سورة غافر

بسم الله الرحمن الرحيم

حم ١

تنزيل الكتب ٢
من الله العزيز العليم

غافر الذنب وقابل التوب ٣
شديد العقاب ذي الطول
لا إله إلا هو
إليه المصير

ما يجدل في ءايت الله ٤
إلا الذين كفروا فلا يغررك
تقلبهم في البلد

كذبت قبلهم ٥
قوم نوح

4356. See paragraphs 2-4 of the Introduction to this Sūrah.

4357. This verse is the same as 39:1, except for the last words describing the attribute of Allah. In S. 39:1, it was "Full of Wisdom", because stress was laid on the wisdom of Allah's Plan in ordering His World. In this Sūrah the stress is laid on Allah's Knowledge, before which the shallow knowledge of men is vain (40:83).

4358. Allah's knowledge is supreme and all-reaching. But there are other attributes of His, which concern us even more intimately; *e.g.*, He forgives sin and accepts our repentance when it is sincere and results in our change of heart and life: but He is also just, and strict in punishment; and so no loophole will be left for Evil except in repentance. And further, all His attributes reach forward to everything: His Mercy, as well as His Knowledge and Justice; His Bounties as well as His Punishments.

4359. Allah's knowledge and attributes are perfect, and everything around us proclaims this. We are surrounded by His Signs. It is only want of Faith that will make people dispute about them.

4360. *Cf.* 3:196. Their strutting about shows how little they can read the Signs.

And the Confederates[4361]
(Of Evil) after them;
And every People plotted
Against their prophet,
To seize him, and disputed
By means of vanities,[4362]
Therewith to condemn
The Truth: but it was I
That seized them!
And how (terrible)[4363]
Was My Requital!

وَالْأَحْزَابُ مِن بَعْدِهِمْ
وَهَمَّتْ كُلُّ أُمَّةٍ بِرَسُولِهِمْ لِيَأْخُذُوهُ
وَجَادَلُوا بِالْبَاطِلِ لِيُدْحِضُوا
بِهِ الْحَقَّ فَأَخَذْتُهُمْ
فَكَيْفَ كَانَ عِقَابِ

6. Thus was the Decree
Of thy Lord proved true
Against the Unbelievers;[4364]
That truly they are
Companions of the Fire!

(٦) وَكَذَٰلِكَ حَقَّتْ كَلِمَتُ رَبِّكَ عَلَى
الَّذِينَ كَفَرُوا أَنَّهُمْ أَصْحَابُ النَّارِ

7. Those who sustain[4365]
The Throne (of Allah)
And those around it
Sing Glory and Praise
To their Lord; believe
In Him; and implore Forgiveness
For those who believe:
"Our Lord! Thy Reach[4366]
Is over all things,
In Mercy and Knowledge.
Forgive, then, those who
Turn in Repentance, and follow
Thy Path; and preserve them
From the Penalty
Of the Blazing Fire!

(٧) الَّذِينَ يَحْمِلُونَ الْعَرْشَ
وَمَنْ حَوْلَهُ يُسَبِّحُونَ
بِحَمْدِ رَبِّهِمْ وَيُؤْمِنُونَ بِهِ
وَيَسْتَغْفِرُونَ لِلَّذِينَ آمَنُوا رَبَّنَا
وَسِعْتَ كُلَّ شَيْءٍ رَّحْمَةً وَعِلْمًا
فَاغْفِرْ لِلَّذِينَ تَابُوا وَاتَّبَعُوا سَبِيلَكَ
وَقِهِمْ عَذَابَ الْجَحِيمِ

4361. *Cf.* 38:11-13, and n. 4158. All the hosts of wickedness collected together from history will have no power against Allah's Truth, or the Messenger of that Truth, or Allah's Holy Plan for all His Creation.

4362. Whenever a great or vital Truth is proclaimed and renewed, there are always shallow minds that are ready to dispute about it! And what petty and vain arguments they advance! They think they can discredit or condemn the Truth in this way, or render "of none effect" Allah's Plan. But they are mistaken. If they seem to succeed for a time, that is merely their trial. They may try to plan and plot against Allah's men. But their plots will fail in the long run. They will themselves be caught in their own snares. And then, how terrible will be their Punishment!

4363. *Cf.* 13:32.

4364. *Cf.* 39:71. The Decree, or Word, of Allah, by which Evil was to be judged and condemned, was proved true against these men. They are "Companions of the Fire": in other words, they are fit to live only in the environment of Evil!

4365. *Cf.* 39:75. (R).

4366. *Cf.* verse 3 above.

8. "And grant, our Lord!
That they enter
The Gardens of Eternity,
Which Thou hast promised
To them, and to the righteous
Among their fathers,[4367]
Their wives, and their posterity!
For Thou art (He),
The Exalted in Might,
Full of Wisdom.

٨ رَبَّنَا وَأَدْخِلْهُمْ
جَنَّٰتِ عَدْنٍ ٱلَّتِي وَعَدتَّهُمْ
وَمَن صَلَحَ مِنْ ءَابَآئِهِمْ
وَأَزْوَٰجِهِمْ وَذُرِّيَّٰتِهِمْ
إِنَّكَ أَنتَ ٱلْعَزِيزُ ٱلْحَكِيمُ

9. "And preserve them
From (all) ills;
And any whom Thou
Dost preserve from ills[4368]
That Day—on them
Wilt Thou have bestowed
Mercy indeed: and that
Will be truly (for them)
The highest Achievement."[4369]

٩ وَقِهِمُ ٱلسَّيِّـَٔاتِ
وَمَن تَقِ ٱلسَّيِّـَٔاتِ
يَوْمَئِذٍ فَقَدْ رَحِمْتَهُۥ
وَذَٰلِكَ هُوَ ٱلْفَوْزُ ٱلْعَظِيمُ

SECTION 2.

10. The Unbelievers will be
Addressed: "Greater was
The aversion of Allah to you[4370]
Than (is) your aversion
To yourselves, seeing that ye
Were called to the Faith
And ye used to refuse."

١٠ إِنَّ ٱلَّذِينَ كَفَرُوا۟ يُنَادَوْنَ
لَمَقْتُ ٱللَّهِ أَكْبَرُ مِن مَّقْتِكُمْ أَنفُسَكُمْ
إِذْ تُدْعَوْنَ إِلَى ٱلْإِيمَٰنِ فَتَكْفُرُونَ

11. They will say: "Our Lord!
Twice hast Thou made us[4371]

١١ قَالُوا۟ رَبَّنَآ أَمَتَّنَا ٱثْنَتَيْنِ

4367. There is nothing selfish in prayer. We pray for all who are true and sincere. But just as Evil is catching, so Goodness is catching in another sense. The associates of the Good and those near and dear to them also share in their goodness and happiness, if only they try to walk in the same Way. And the Grace of Allah is working for all, all the time.

4368. That is the final Judgement, and any who is saved from the evil consequences of their deeds in this life will truly have been saved by Allah's Mercy, and for them it is the highest achievement they could have, the attainment of all their wishes, the fulfilment of their destiny and the noblest purpose of their Life, the supreme Salvation and Felicity.

4369. Muslim Salvation, then, is more positive than mere safety from dangers or evils: it is the complete fulfilment of the noble destiny of man in the attainment of the fullest Grace.

4370. The Unbelievers having rejected Allah's Signs, they now see how they are shut out from Grace, and they feel disgusted with themselves. How much greater was Allah's displeasure with them, when He showered mercy upon mercy on them and they yet rebelled! How could they now hope for Grace!

4371. *Cf.* 2:28:"How can ye reject the faith in Allah?—seeing that ye were without life, and He gave you life; then will He cause you to die, and will again bring you to life; and again to Him will ye return." Nonexistence, or existence as clay without life was equivalent to death. Then came true Life on this earth; then came physical death or the cessation of our physical life; and now at the Resurrection, is the second life.

Without life, and twice
Hast Thou given us Life!
Now have we recognised
Our sins: is there
Any way out (of this)?"

وَأَحْيَيْتَنَا ٱثْنَتَيْنِ فَٱعْتَرَفْنَا بِذُنُوبِنَا
فَهَلْ إِلَىٰ خُرُوجٍ مِّن سَبِيلٍ

12. (The answer will be:)
"This is because, when
Allah was invoked as
The Only (object of worship),[4372]
Ye did reject Faith,
But when partners were
Joined to Him, ye believed!
The Command is with Allah,[4373]
Most High, Most Great!"

ذَٰلِكُم بِأَنَّهُۥٓ إِذَا دُعِىَ ﴿١٢﴾
ٱللَّهُ وَحْدَهُۥ كَفَرْتُمْ
وَإِن يُشْرَكْ بِهِۦ تُؤْمِنُوا۟
فَٱلْحُكْمُ لِلَّهِ ٱلْعَلِىِّ ٱلْكَبِيرِ

13. He it is Who showeth
You His Signs, and sendeth
Down Sustenance for you[4374]
From the sky: but only
Those receive admonition
Who turn (to Allah).

هُوَ ٱلَّذِى يُرِيكُمْ ءَايَٰتِهِۦ ﴿١٣﴾
وَيُنَزِّلُ لَكُم مِّنَ ٱلسَّمَآءِ رِزْقًا
وَمَا يَتَذَكَّرُ إِلَّا مَن يُنِيبُ

14. Call ye, then, upon Allah
With sincere devotion to Him,
Even though the Unbelievers[4375]
May detest it.

فَٱدْعُوا۟ ٱللَّهَ مُخْلِصِينَ لَهُ ﴿١٤﴾
ٱلدِّينَ وَلَوْ كَرِهَ ٱلْكَٰفِرُونَ

15. Raised high above ranks
(Or degrees),[4376]
(He is) the Lord
Of the Throne (of authority):
By His Command doth He
Send the spirit (of inspiration)

رَفِيعُ ٱلدَّرَجَٰتِ ﴿١٥﴾
ذُو ٱلْعَرْشِ
يُلْقِى ٱلرُّوحَ مِنْ أَمْرِهِۦ

4372. *Cf.* 39:45, and n. 4313. When exclusive devotion is not rendered to Allah, there is no true understanding, in the mind of a creature, of his own true position, or of the working of the Divine Will and Purpose. How can he then hope to achieve the purpose of his life, or obtain Allah's Mercy, which is the only way to obtain release from the consequences of Sin?

4373. At the Judgement, the matter will have passed out of the stage at which further chances could have been hoped for. But in any case Allah is High above all things, Great above all that we can conceive of, both in Mercy and in Justice. The Decision will be with Him, and Him alone.

4374. Lest it should be thought that Allah's Grace did not meet the Sinner again and again and offer Allah's Mercy again and again, it is pointed out that Allah's Signs were freely vouchsafed everywhere and continuously, and that every kind of means was provided for man's "Sustenance" or growth and development, physical, mental, and spiritual. But only those could take advantage of it who turned their attention to Allah, who submitted their will to Him.

4375. *Cf.* 9:33.

4376. He is raised far above any rank or degree which we can imagine. It is possible also to treat *Rafī'*, as equivalent to *Rāfi'*, meaning that He can raise His creatures to the highest ranks and degrees in His spiritual kingdom, for He is the fountain of all honour.

To any of His servants[4377]
He pleases, that it may
Warn (men) of the Day
Of Mutual Meeting—[4378]

عَلَىٰ مَن يَشَآءُ مِنْ عِبَادِهِۦ
لِيُنذِرَ يَوْمَ ٱلتَّلَاقِ

16. The Day whereon
They will (all) come forth:
Not a single thing
Concerning them is hidden
From Allah. Whose will be
The Dominion that Day?[4379]
That of Allah, the One,
The Irresistible!

١٦ يَوْمَ هُم بَٰرِزُونَ
لَا يَخْفَىٰ عَلَى ٱللَّهِ مِنْهُمْ شَىْءٌ
لِّمَنِ ٱلْمُلْكُ ٱلْيَوْمَ
لِلَّهِ ٱلْوَٰحِدِ ٱلْقَهَّارِ

17. That Day will every soul
Be requited for what
It earned; no injustice
Will there be that Day,
For Allah is Swift[4380]
In taking account.

١٧ ٱلْيَوْمَ تُجْزَىٰ كُلُّ نَفْسٍۭ
بِمَا كَسَبَتْ لَا ظُلْمَ ٱلْيَوْمَ
إِنَّ ٱللَّهَ سَرِيعُ ٱلْحِسَابِ

18. Warn them of the Day
That is (ever) drawing near,
When the Hearts will
(Come) right up to the
Throats[4381]
To choke (them);
No intimate friend[4382]

١٨ وَأَنذِرْهُمْ يَوْمَ
ٱلْءَازِفَةِ إِذِ ٱلْقُلُوبُ
لَدَى ٱلْحَنَاجِرِ كَٰظِمِينَ

4377. The choosing of a man to be the recipient of inspiration—to be the standard bearer of Allah's Truth—is the highest honour possible in the spiritual Kingdom. And Allah bestows that honour according to His own most perfect Will and Plan, which no one can question, for He is the fountain of all honour, dignity, and authority.

4378. All men will meet together and meet their Lord at the Resurrection, no matter how far scattered they may have been in life or in death.

4379. The Kingdom of Allah—of Justice, Truth, and Righteousness—will then be fully established. Evil can then no more come into competition with Good, even in the subjective consciousness of man.

4380. *Swift* in several senses: (1) the time of the present life or of the interval before Judgement, *i.e.*, before the restoration of true values, is so short as compared to Eternity, that it may be counted as negligible: in the next verse the Day is characterised as "(ever) drawing near"; (2) in spite of the great concourse of souls to be judged, the process of Judgement will be almost instantaneous, "in the twinkling of an eye" (16:77), because everything is already known to Allah; and yet not the least injustice will be done.

4381. *Hearts will come right up to the Throats to choke them:* an idiom implying that the whole of their life-functions will be choked up with terror. But a more subtle meaning emerges from further analysis. The heart (or the breast) is the seat of affection, emotion, and every kind of feeling, such as terror, pain, despair, etc. These things will as it were overflow right up to the throat and choke it. The throat is the vehicle for the voice; their voice will be choked, and they will be able to say nothing. The throat is the channel for food, which goes to the stomach and maintains a healthy functioning of life; the choking means that the healthy functioning will stop, and there will be nothing but woe.

4382. In that enforcement of personal responsiblity, what sympathy or intercession can the wrongdoers get? Is *Ḥamīm* in any way connected with the Abbreviated Letters *Ḥā Mīm* attached to this Sūrah? See Introduction.

Nor intercessor will the wrongdoers
Have, who could be
Listened to.

مَا لِلظَّٰلِمِينَ مِنْ حَمِيمٍ وَلَا شَفِيعٍ يُطَاعُ

19. (Allah) knows of (the tricks)
That deceive with the eyes,[4383]
And all that the hearts
(Of men) conceal.[4384]

١٩ يَعْلَمُ خَآئِنَةَ ٱلْأَعْيُنِ وَمَا تُخْفِى ٱلصُّدُورُ

20. And Allah will judge
With (Justice and) Truth:
But those whom (men)
Invoke besides Him, will
Not (be in a position)
To judge at all.
Verily it is Allah (alone)
Who hear and sees[4385]
(All things).

٢٠ وَٱللَّهُ يَقْضِى بِٱلْحَقِّ وَٱلَّذِينَ يَدْعُونَ مِن دُونِهِۦ لَا يَقْضُونَ بِشَىْءٍ إِنَّ ٱللَّهَ هُوَ ٱلسَّمِيعُ ٱلْبَصِيرُ

C. 207.—(40:21-50.)
Travel in space and time, and you
Will see that Evil came to nothing
But evil. Mighty men of old
In arrogance plotted against Allah's Truth,
But were brought low. A humble Believer
In Pharaoh's Court stood up for Truth,
And counselled his People to obey the Right:
In earnest humility did he address them.
They heard him not. But he was saved,
And they were engulfed in the Wrath of Allah.

SECTION 3.

21. Do they not travel
Through the earth and see
What was the End
Of those before them?[4386]

٢١ أَوَلَمْ يَسِيرُوا۟ فِى ٱلْأَرْضِ فَيَنظُرُوا۟ كَيْفَ كَانَ عَٰقِبَةُ ٱلَّذِينَ كَانُوا۟ مِن قَبْلِهِمْ

4383. Men may be taken in by tricks that deceive with the eyes, but Allah's perfect knowledge penetrates through all mysteries. "Deceive with the eyes" may mean several things: (1) a sleight of hand (literally or figuratively) may deceive in respect of the eyes of beholders, for the things that they see do not actually happen; (2) it may be the deceiver's own eyes that play false, because, for example, they show love when hatred is meant; or (3) it may be that the eyes of the beholder play him false, in that he sees things that he should not see, and thus sins with his eyes.

4384. Here we come into the region of evil motives and thoughts which may be concealed in the hearts, breast, or mind, but which are all perfectly known to Allah.

4385. If men build their hopes or their faith in anything except the Divine Grace, they will find themselves deserted. Any pretences that they make will be known to Allah. On the other hand every single good act, or word, or motive, or aspiration of their will, will reach Allah's Throne of Mercy.

4386. *Cf.* 30:9. and several other similar passages.

They were even superior
To them in strength,
And in the traces (they[4387]
Have left) in the land:
But Allah did call them
To account for their sins,
And none had they
To defend them against Allah.

كَانُوا هُمْ أَشَدَّ مِنْهُمْ قُوَّةً
وَءَاثَارًا فِي الْأَرْضِ
فَأَخَذَهُمُ اللَّهُ بِذُنُوبِهِمْ
وَمَا كَانَ لَهُم مِّنَ اللَّهِ مِن وَاقٍ

22. That was because there came
To them their messengers[4388]
With Clear (Signs),
But they rejected them:
So Allah called them
To account: for He is
Full of Strength,
Strict in Punishment.

٢٢ ذَٰلِكَ بِأَنَّهُمْ كَانَت
تَّأْتِيهِمْ رُسُلُهُم بِالْبَيِّنَٰتِ
فَكَفَرُوا فَأَخَذَهُمُ اللَّهُ
إِنَّهُۥ قَوِيٌّ شَدِيدُ الْعِقَابِ

23. Of old We sent Moses,[4389]
With Our Signs
And an Authority manifest,

٢٣ وَلَقَدْ أَرْسَلْنَا مُوسَىٰ بِـَٔايَٰتِنَا
وَسُلْطَٰنٍ مُّبِينٍ

24. To Pharaoh, Hāmān,[4390]
And Qārūn; but they
Called (him) "a sorcerer
Telling lies!"...

٢٤ إِلَىٰ فِرْعَوْنَ وَهَٰمَٰنَ وَقَٰرُونَ
فَقَالُوا سَٰحِرٌ كَذَّابٌ

4387. See n. 3515 to 30:9. We can learn from the history of previous nations. Many of them were more powerful, or have left finer and more imposing monuments and made a deeper impression on the world around them than any particular generation addressed. "Traces" in the text may be taken in that extended sense. And yet all this did not save them from the consequences of their sins. They were called to account and punished. None of the power or pomp or skill of which they boasted could for a moment ward off the punishment when it came in Allah's good time.

4388. But Allah in His Mercy always sends a Message of warning and good news through his messengers, and He gives His messengers Clear Signs and an authority that can be recognised. Among the Clear Signs are: (1) the pure and unselfish lives of the messengers; (2) the revelation of truth which they bring; (3) their influence on the course of events in their own and succeeding generations; etc. Some of these may be so remarkable that they merit the name of Miracles.

4389. This is not the story of Moses himself, so much as an introduction to the story of the one just man who believed, in the court of Pharaoh: see verse 28 below. This Sūrah's alternate title ("The Believer") refers to him.

4390. Here are three types of Unfaith, each showing a different phase, and yet all united in opposition to the Truth and Mission of Moses. (1) Pharaoh is the type of arrogance, cruelty, and reliance on brute force; *cf.* 28:38-39. (2) Hāmān was Pharaoh's minister (n. 3331 to 28:6; also 28:38): he was the type of a sycophant who would pander to the vanity of any man in power. (3) Qārūn excelled in his wealth, was selfish in its use, and overbearing to the poor (28:76-81, and n. 3404). They all came to an evil end eventually.

25. Now, when he came to them[4391]
In Truth, from Us,
They said, "Slay the sons
Of those who believe[4392]
With him, and keep alive
Their females," but the plots
Of Unbelievers (end) in nothing
But errors (and delusions)!...

٢٥ فَلَمَّا جَآءَهُم بِٱلْحَقِّ مِنْ عِندِنَا
قَالُوا۟ ٱقْتُلُوٓا۟ أَبْنَآءَ ٱلَّذِينَ ءَامَنُوا۟
مَعَهُۥ وَٱسْتَحْيُوا۟ نِسَآءَهُمْ ۚ
وَمَا كَيْدُ ٱلْكَٰفِرِينَ إِلَّا فِى ضَلَٰلٍ

26. Said Pharaoh: "Leave me
To slay Moses; and let him
Call on his Lord![4393]
What I fear is lest
He should change your
religion,[4394]
Or lest he should cause
Mischief to appear
In the land!"

٢٦ وَقَالَ فِرْعَوْنُ ذَرُونِىٓ
أَقْتُلْ مُوسَىٰ وَلْيَدْعُ رَبَّهُۥٓ ۖ
إِنِّىٓ أَخَافُ أَن يُبَدِّلَ دِينَكُمْ
أَوْ أَن يُظْهِرَ فِى ٱلْأَرْضِ ٱلْفَسَادَ

27. Moses said: "I have indeed
Called upon my Lord
And your Lord[4395]
(For protection) from every
Arrogant one who believes not
In the Day of Account!"

٢٧ وَقَالَ مُوسَىٰٓ إِنِّى عُذْتُ
بِرَبِّى وَرَبِّكُم مِّن كُلِّ مُتَكَبِّرٍ
لَّا يُؤْمِنُ بِيَوْمِ ٱلْحِسَابِ

4391. Verse 24 described the opposition of three types of Unfaith, which opposed Faith, in different ways, as described in the last note. Qārūn, in his overweening insolence, may well have called Moses and Aaron "sorcerers telling lies" in the Sinai desert, as he despised priests and men of God, and might cast the Egyptian reproach in their teeth as a reminiscence. Here, in verse 25, we have an episode about the time of the birth of Moses: "them" and "they" refer to Pharaoh and his Court; the "coming" of Moses here refers to the time of his birth. On that construction, "with him", lower down in their speech would be elliptical, referring to "slay the sons", as if they had said, "Kill all Israelite male children: the unknown Prophet to be born would be amongst them: so kill them all with him." In verse 26 we again skip some years and recall an episode when Moses, having got his mission, stood in Pharaoh's Court, and some of the Egyptian Commonalty were almost ready to believe in him.

4392. That is, the Israelites, for they were the custodians of Allah's Faith then. For the slaughter of Israelite children by Pharaoh, see 27:4-6, and notes.

4393. This is an episode that occurs when Moses, invested with his mission, confronts Pharaoh in his Court and preaches to him: see 20:49 and following verses; also 20:57, 63.

4394. Some of Pharaoh's people did afterwards give up the worship of Pharaoh and of the Egyptian gods and believed "in the Lord of Aaron and Moses" and in fact suffered martyrdom for the Faith of Unity: 20:70-73.

4395. The whole point of the Gospel of Unity which Moses preached was that the God of Moses and the God of Pharaoh, of Israel and Egypt, the Lord of all the Worlds, was One—Allah, the only True God See 20:49-50 and notes 2572 and 2573. (R).

SECTION 4.

28. A Believer, a man[4396]
From among the people
Of Pharaoh, who had
concealed
His faith, said: "Will ye
Slay a man because he
Says, 'My Lord is Allah'?—
When he has indeed come
To you with Clear (Signs)
From your Lord? And if
He be a liar, on him
Is (the sin of) his lie;
But, if he is telling[4397]
The Truth, then will
Fall on you something
Of the (calamity) of which
He warns you: truly
Allah guides not one[4398]
Who transgresses and lies!

٢٨ وَقَالَ رَجُلٌ مُّؤْمِنٌ
مِّنْ ءَالِ فِرْعَوْنَ يَكْتُمُ إِيمَٰنَهُۥٓ
أَتَقْتُلُونَ رَجُلًا أَن يَقُولَ رَبِّىَ ٱللَّهُ
وَقَدْ جَآءَكُم بِٱلْبَيِّنَٰتِ مِن رَّبِّكُمْ
وَإِن يَكُ كَٰذِبًا فَعَلَيْهِ كَذِبُهُۥ
وَإِن يَكُ صَادِقًا يُصِبْكُم
بَعْضُ ٱلَّذِى يَعِدُكُمْ
إِنَّ ٱللَّهَ لَا يَهْدِى مَنْ
هُوَ مُسْرِفٌ كَذَّابٌ

29. "O my People! yours
Is the dominion this day:
Ye have the upper hand[4399]
In the land: but who
Will help us from
The Punishment of Allah,
Should it befall us?"
Pharaoh said: "I but
Point out to you that
Which I see (myself);[4400]

٢٩ يَٰقَوْمِ لَكُمُ ٱلْمُلْكُ ٱلْيَوْمَ
ظَٰهِرِينَ فِى ٱلْأَرْضِ فَمَن
يَنصُرُنَا مِنۢ بَأْسِ ٱللَّهِ إِن جَآءَنَا
قَالَ فِرْعَوْنُ مَآ أُرِيكُمْ
إِلَّا مَآ أَرَىٰ

4396. There is nothing to justify the identification of this man with the man mentioned in 28:20, who warned Moses long before Moses had received his mission. On the contrary, in this passage, the man is evidently speaking after Moses had received his mission, preached to Pharaoh, and got a certain amount of success, for which Pharaoh and his people were trying to seek his life. Moses had evidently already brought his Clear Signs.

4397. A commonsense view is put before them by an Egyptian who loves his own people and does not wish them to perish in sin. "Will you kill this man for calling on Allah? Have you not seen his character and behaviour? Do you not see the 'Clear Signs' about him that bespeak his credentials? Suppose for a moment that he is a liar and pretender: he will suffer for his falsehood, but why should you turn against Allah? But suppose that he is really inspired by Allah to tell you the truth and warn you against evil, what will be your fate when Allah's Wrath descends? For it must descend if he is a true Messenger sent by Allah."

4398. This is with reference to the "Clear Signs". 'They are Signs of Allah's guidance, for Allah would never guide a man who exceeds the bounds of truth and tells you lies! Such a man is bound to be found out!'

4399. 'Do not be puffed up with arrogance because the power is in your hands at present! Do you deserve it? Will it last? If you are sinning and drawing upon yourselves Allah's Punishment, is there anything that can shield you from it?'

4400. Pharaoh's egotism and arrogance come out. 'I can see and understand everything. As I see things, so do I direct you. The Path which I see must be right, and you must follow it.'

Nor do I guide you
But to the Path of Right!"

وَمَآ أَهۡدِيكُمۡ إِلَّا سَبِيلَ ٱلرَّشَادِ

30. Then said the man
Who believed: "O my People!
Truly I do fear
For you something like[4401]
The Day (of disaster)
Of the Confederates (in sin)!—[4402]

٣٠ وَقَالَ ٱلَّذِيٓ ءَامَنَ
يَٰقَوۡمِ إِنِّيٓ أَخَافُ عَلَيۡكُم
مِّثۡلَ يَوۡمِ ٱلۡأَحۡزَابِ

31. "Something like the fate
Of the People of Noah,
The 'Ād, and the Thamūd,
And those who came
After them: but Allah
Never wishes injustice[4403]
To His Servants.

٣١ مِثۡلَ دَأۡبِ قَوۡمِ نُوحٖ
وَعَادٖ وَثَمُودَ وَٱلَّذِينَ مِنۢ بَعۡدِهِمۡۚ
وَمَا ٱللَّهُ يُرِيدُ ظُلۡمٗا لِّلۡعِبَادِ

32. "And O my People!
I fear for you a Day[4404]
When there will be
Mutual calling (and wailing)—

٣٢ وَيَٰقَوۡمِ إِنِّيٓ أَخَافُ
عَلَيۡكُمۡ يَوۡمَ ٱلتَّنَادِ

33. "A Day when ye
Shall turn your backs
And flee: no defender
Shall ye have from Allah:
Any whom Allah leaves
To stray, there is none
To guide. . .

٣٣ يَوۡمَ تُوَلُّونَ مُدۡبِرِينَ
مَا لَكُم مِّنَ ٱللَّهِ مِنۡ عَاصِمٖۗ
وَمَن يُضۡلِلِ ٱللَّهُ فَمَا لَهُۥ مِنۡ هَادٖ

4401. He appeals to past history. "Have you not heard of people who lived before you?—like the generations of Noah, the 'Ād, the Thamūd, and many more—who held together in sin against Allah's Preachers, but were wiped out for their sins?"

4402. *Cf.* 38:11-13, and n. 4158, also 40:5, and n. 4361.

4403. 'All these disasters happened in history, and they will happen again to you if you do not give up evil. Do not for a moment think that Allah is unjust. It is you who are deliberately preparing the disasters by your conduct.'

4404. This Day may refer to the Day of Judgement, of which three features are here referred to. (1) People may wail and call to each other, but no one can help another: each one will have his own judgement to face; (2) the wicked will then be driven to Hell from the Judgement Seat; and (3) there will be no one to help, guide, or intercede, because the grace and guidance of Allah had already been rejected. But the words are perfectly general, and are applicable to all stages at which the Wrath of Allah is manifest.

34. "And to you there came
Joseph in times gone by,[4405]
With Clear Signs, but
Ye ceased not to doubt
Of the (mission) for which
He had come: at length,
When he died, ye said:
'No Messenger will Allah send[4406]
After him.' Thus doth Allah
Leave to stray such as
Transgress and live in doubt

٣٤ وَلَقَدْ جَآءَكُمْ يُوسُفُ مِن قَبْلُ
بِٱلْبَيِّنَٰتِ فَمَا زِلْتُمْ فِى شَكٍّ مِّمَّا جَآءَكُم بِهِۦ
حَتَّىٰٓ إِذَا هَلَكَ قُلْتُمْ لَن يَبْعَثَ
ٱللَّهُ مِنۢ بَعْدِهِۦ رَسُولًا
كَذَٰلِكَ يُضِلُّ ٱللَّهُ مَنْ
هُوَ مُسْرِفٌ مُّرْتَابٌ

35. "(Such) as dispute about
The Signs of Allah,
Without any authority
That hath reached them.
Grievous and odious
(In such conduct)
In the sight of Allah
And of the Believers.
Thus doth Allah seal up[4407]
Every heart—of arrogant
And obstinate transgressors."

٣٥ ٱلَّذِينَ يُجَٰدِلُونَ
فِىٓ ءَايَٰتِ ٱللَّهِ بِغَيْرِ سُلْطَٰنٍ أَتَىٰهُمْ
كَبُرَ مَقْتًا عِندَ ٱللَّهِ وَعِندَ ٱلَّذِينَ ءَامَنُوا۟
كَذَٰلِكَ يَطْبَعُ ٱللَّهُ عَلَىٰ كُلِّ
قَلْبِ مُتَكَبِّرٍ جَبَّارٍ

36. Pharaoh said: "O Hāmān!
Build me a lofty palace,[4408]
That I may attain
The ways and means—

٣٦ وَقَالَ فِرْعَوْنُ يَٰهَٰمَٰنُ ٱبْنِ لِى
صَرْحًا لَّعَلِّىٓ أَبْلُغُ ٱلْأَسْبَٰبَ

4405. So far he has been speaking of general religious tradition. Now, as an Egyptian, addressing Egyptians, he refers to the mission of Joseph in Egypt. Joseph was not born in Egypt, nor was he an Egyptian. With what wonderful incidents he came into Egypt! What difficulties did he not surmount among his own brothers first, and in the Egyptian family which afterwards adopted him! How injustice, spite, and forgetfulness on the part of others, yet wove a spell round him and made him a ruler and saviour of Egypt in times of famine! How he preached to prisoners in prison, to Zulaykhā in her household, to the Egyptian ladies in their banquet, and to the Court of Pharaoh generally! The Egyptians profited by the material gains which came to them through him, but as a nation remained sceptical of his spiritual truths for many generations after him.

4406. See Appendix IV, p. 406, for a discussion of the interval between Joseph and Moses. Perhaps the interval was about one to three centuries, a very short period for the memory of a learned nation like the Egyptians. And yet they as a nation ignored his spiritual work, and afterwards even persecuted Israel in Egypt until Moses delivered them. They actually saw the benefits conferred by Joseph, but did not realise that Allah's Kingdom works continuously even though men ignore it. See Appendix V, pp. 408-13; for a sketch of Religion in Egypt. For such men how could the Grace and Guidance of Allah be effective in their hearts?

4407. See the last note. The arrogant transgressors having closed their hearts to the Message of Allah and to every appeal made to them, it followed by Allah's Law that their hearts were sealed up to any fresh influences for good. *Cf.* 7:100; also 2:7, and n. 31.

4408. *Cf.* 28:38, and n. 3371. There are two points to be noted here. (1) Pharaoh, in the arrogance of his materialism, thinks of the Kingdom of Heaven like a kingdom on earth; he thinks of spiritual things in terms of palaces and ladders: notice that the word *asbāb* (ways and means) is emphasised by repetition. (2) His sarcasm turns Moses and Allah to ridicule. Really he does not believe in anything spiritual, and he frankly states that 'for his part he thinks Moses is a liar', though other men less lofty than he (Pharaoh) may be deceived by the Clear Signs of Moses.

37. "The ways and means
Of (reaching) the heavens,
And that I may mount up
To the God of Moses:
But as far as I am concerned,
I think (Moses) is a liar!"
Thus was made alluring,[4409]
In Pharaoh's eyes,
The evil of his deeds,
And he was hindered
From the Path; and the plot[4410]
Of Pharaoh led to nothing
But perdition (for him).

٣٧ أَسۡبَٰبَ ٱلسَّمَٰوَٰتِ
فَأَطَّلِعَ إِلَىٰٓ إِلَٰهِ مُوسَىٰ
وَإِنِّي لَأَظُنُّهُۥ كَٰذِبٗاۚ
وَكَذَٰلِكَ زُيِّنَ لِفِرۡعَوۡنَ
سُوٓءُ عَمَلِهِۦ وَصُدَّ عَنِ ٱلسَّبِيلِۚ
وَمَا كَيۡدُ فِرۡعَوۡنَ إِلَّا فِي تَبَابٖ

Section 5.

38. The man who believed said
Further: "O my People!
Follow me: I will lead
You to the Path of Right.[4411]

٣٨ وَقَالَ ٱلَّذِيٓ ءَامَنَ يَٰقَوۡمِ
ٱتَّبِعُونِ أَهۡدِكُمۡ سَبِيلَ ٱلرَّشَادِ

39. "O my People! This life
Of the present is nothing
But (temporary) convenience:
It is the Hereafter
That is the Home
That will last.[4412]

٣٩ يَٰقَوۡمِ إِنَّمَا هَٰذِهِ
ٱلۡحَيَوٰةُ ٱلدُّنۡيَا مَتَٰعٞ
وَإِنَّ ٱلۡأٓخِرَةَ هِيَ دَارُ ٱلۡقَرَارِ

40. "He that works evil
Will not be requited
But by the like thereof:
And he that works
A righteous deed—whether
Man or woman—and is
A Believer—such will enter
The Garden (of Bliss): therein

٤٠ مَنۡ عَمِلَ سَيِّئَةٗ فَلَا يُجۡزَىٰٓ إِلَّا مِثۡلَهَاۖ
وَمَنۡ عَمِلَ صَٰلِحٗا مِّن ذَكَرٍ
أَوۡ أُنثَىٰ وَهُوَ مُؤۡمِنٞ
فَأُوْلَٰٓئِكَ يَدۡخُلُونَ ٱلۡجَنَّةَ

4409. Pharaoh's speech shows how his own egotism and haughty arrogance brought him to this pass, that even the evil which he did seemed alluring in his own eyes! His heart was indeed sealed, and his arrogance prevented him from seeing the right path. (With the Kūfī Qirā'ah I read *sudda* in the passive voice).

4410. Pharaoh had plotted to slay Moses (40:26) and to kill the Children of Israel (40:25). The plot recoiled on his own head and on the head of his people who joined in the plot; for they were all drowned in the Red Sea.

4411. Note the contrast between the earnest beseeching tone of the Believer here and the hectoring tone of Pharaoh in using similar words in 40:29 above.

4412. Faith makes him see the contrast between vanities, even though they may glitter temporarily, and the eternal Good that is destined for man.

Will they have abundance[4413] Without measure.	يُرْزَقُونَ فِيهَا بِغَيْرِ حِسَابٍ
41. "And O my People! How (strange) it is[4414] For me to call you To Salvation while ye Call me to the Fire!	٤١ وَيَٰقَوْمِ مَا لِيٓ أَدْعُوكُمْ إِلَى ٱلنَّجَوٰةِ وَتَدْعُونَنِيٓ إِلَى ٱلنَّارِ
42. "Ye do call upon me To blaspheme against Allah,[4415] And to join with Him Partners of whom I have No knowledge; and I Call you to the Exalted In Power, Who forgives Again and again!"	٤٢ تَدْعُونَنِي لِأَكْفُرَ بِٱللَّهِ وَأُشْرِكَ بِهِۦ مَا لَيْسَ لِي بِهِۦ عِلْمٌ وَأَنَا۠ أَدْعُوكُمْ إِلَى ٱلْعَزِيزِ ٱلْغَفَّٰرِ
43. "Without doubt ye do call Me to one who is not Fit to be called to,[4416] Whether in this world, Or in the Hereafter; Our Return will be To Allah; and the Transgressors Will be Companions Of the Fire!	٤٣ لَا جَرَمَ أَنَّمَا تَدْعُونَنِيٓ إِلَيْهِ لَيْسَ لَهُۥ دَعْوَةٌ فِي ٱلدُّنْيَا وَلَا فِي ٱلْءَاخِرَةِ وَأَنَّ مَرَدَّنَآ إِلَى ٱللَّهِ وَأَنَّ ٱلْمُسْرِفِينَ هُمْ أَصْحَٰبُ ٱلنَّارِ
44. "Soon will ye remember What I say to you (now).[4417] My (own) affair I commit	٤٤ فَسَتَذْكُرُونَ مَآ أَقُولُ لَكُمْ وَأُفَوِّضُ أَمْرِيٓ

4413. *Cf.* 2:212. The spiritual Good will not only last. It will be a most liberal reward, far above any merits of the recipient.

4414. It may seem strange according to the laws of this world that he should be seeking their Good while they are seeking his damnation! But that is the merit of Faith. Its mission is to rescue its enemies and Allah's enemies, as far as their will will consent!

4415. The worship of Pharaoh was but typical of Egyptian blasphemy, but it had many sides, including the worship of heroes, animals, powers of good and evil in nature, and idols of all kinds. It is this comprehensive cult which required forgiveness again and again, but Allah is Exalted in Power, and gives such forgiveness on repentance.

4416. Faith is not content with its own inner vision and conviction. It can give ample arguments. Three are mentioned here: (1) nothing but Allah is worthy of worship, either in this world of sense or in the spiritual world; (2) our Return will be to Allah, the Eternal Reality; and (3) the worship of Falsehood must necessarily lead to the Penalty of Falsehood, unless Allah's Mercy intervenes and forgives on our sincere repentance. (R).

4417. The wording suggests as if there was a plot to kill him, but he was saved, as the next verse shows. His thought to the last is with his People. 'No matter what you do to me: you will have cause to remember my admonition, when perhaps it is too late for you to repent. For my part I commit myself to the care of Allah, and my Faith tells me that all will be right.'

To Allah: for Allah (ever) Watches over His Servants."	إِلَى ٱللَّهِۚ إِنَّ ٱللَّهَ بَصِيرٌۢ بِٱلْعِبَادِ
45. Then Allah saved him From (every) ill that they Plotted (against him), But the brunt of the Penalty[4418] Encompassed on all sides The People of Pharaoh.	٤٥ فَوَقَىٰهُ ٱللَّهُ سَيِّـَٔاتِ مَا مَكَرُوا۟ۖ وَحَاقَ بِـَٔالِ فِرْعَوْنَ سُوٓءُ ٱلْعَذَابِ
46. In front of the Fire Will they be brought, Morning and evening:[4419] And (the Sentence will be) On the Day that Judgement will be established: "Cast ye the People Of Pharaoh into The severest Penalty!"	٤٦ ٱلنَّارُ يُعْرَضُونَ عَلَيْهَا غُدُوًّا وَعَشِيًّاۖ وَيَوْمَ تَقُومُ ٱلسَّاعَةُ أَدْخِلُوٓا۟ ءَالَ فِرْعَوْنَ أَشَدَّ ٱلْعَذَابِ
47. Behold, they will dispute With each other in the Fire![4420] The weak ones (who followed) Will say to those who Had been arrogant, "We but Followed you: can ye then Take (on yourselves) from us Some share of the Fire?"	٤٧ وَإِذْ يَتَحَآجُّونَ فِى ٱلنَّارِ فَيَقُولُ ٱلضُّعَفَـٰٓؤُا۟ لِلَّذِينَ ٱسْتَكْبَرُوٓا۟ إِنَّا كُنَّا لَكُمْ تَبَعًا فَهَلْ أَنتُم مُّغْنُونَ عَنَّا نَصِيبًا مِّنَ ٱلنَّارِ
48. Those who had been arrogant Will say: "We are all[4421] In this (Fire)! Truly, Allah has judged Between (His) Servants!"	٤٨ قَالَ ٱلَّذِينَ ٱسْتَكْبَرُوٓا۟ إِنَّا كُلٌّ فِيهَآ إِنَّ ٱللَّهَ قَدْ حَكَمَ بَيْنَ ٱلْعِبَادِ

4418. The Pharaoh of the time of Moses, and his people, suffered many calamities in this world: 7:130-136. But those were nothing to the spiritual Penalties mentioned in the next verse.

4419. When the Judgement really comes, it is not like an ordinary physical disaster. The Fire of Punishment is ever present—morning and evening—*i.e.*, at all times. The sentence becomes final and there is no mitigation.

4420. Just as Unity, Harmony, and Peace are symbols of Truth, Bliss, and Salvation, so Reproaches, Disputes, and Disorders are symbols of Hell.

4421. Note the evasion and cynicism of the answer, befitting the character of spiritual misleaders! 'What! are we not suffering with you in the same Fire! Pray to Allah if you like! He has pronounced His Judgement!' *Cf.* 14:21-22.

49. Those in the Fire will say
To the Keepers of Hell:[4422]
"Pray to your Lord
To lighten us the Penalty
For a Day (at least)!"

٤٩ وَقَالَ ٱلَّذِينَ فِى ٱلنَّارِ لِخَزَنَةِ جَهَنَّمَ
ٱدْعُوا۟ رَبَّكُمْ يُخَفِّفْ عَنَّا يَوْمًا مِّنَ ٱلْعَذَابِ

50. They will say: "Did there
Not come to you
Your messengers with Clear
Signs?"
They will say: "Yes".
They will reply, "Then[4423]
Pray (as ye like)! But
The Prayer of those
Without Faith is nothing
But (futile wandering)
In (mazes of) error!"

٥٠ قَالُوٓا۟ أَوَلَمْ تَكُ
تَأْتِيكُمْ رُسُلُكُم بِٱلْبَيِّنَٰتِ
قَالُوا۟ بَلَىٰ قَالُوا۟ فَٱدْعُوا۟
وَمَا دُعَٰٓؤُا۟ ٱلْكَٰفِرِينَ
إِلَّا فِى ضَلَٰلٍ

C. 208.—Allah's grace and help are ever ready
(40:51-58.) For His servants who patiently persevere.
Let not arrogance blind the souls
Of men: the Hour of Judgement is bound
To come. The keys of Life and Death
Are in the hands of Allah. Dispute not
The Signs of Allah, but learn from History
And the world around you. Science and skill
Avail you not if the soul is dead.

SECTION 6.

51. We will, without doubt,
Help Our messengers and those
Who believe, (both)
In this world's life
And on the Day
When the Witnesses[4424]
Will stand forth—

٥١ إِنَّا لَنَنصُرُ رُسُلَنَا
وَٱلَّذِينَ ءَامَنُوا۟ فِى ٱلْحَيَوٰةِ ٱلدُّنْيَا
وَيَوْمَ يَقُومُ ٱلْأَشْهَٰدُ

4422. *Cf.* 39:71. The poor misguided ones will turn to the angels who are their Keepers, asking them to pray and intercede for them. But the angels are set there to watch over them, not to intercede for them. In their innocence they ask, 'Did you have no warnings from messengers, men like yourselves, in your past life?'

4423. The answer being in the affirmative, they will have to tell the dreadful truth: 'This is neither the time nor the place for prayer, for mercy! And in any case, Prayer without Faith is Delusion, and must miss its mark.' *Cf.* 13:14.

4424. The Day of Judgement is described as "the Day when Witnesses will stand forth". This description implies two things: (1) that there man will be judged justly; his past actions and his faculties and opportunities will be witnesses as to the use he made of them (34:24); in fact he will himself be a witness against himself (6:130); and the prophets and just men will bear witness to the fact that they preached and warned men (39:69; 2:133).

52. The Day when no profit
Will it be to Wrongdoers
To present their excuses,[4425]
But they will (only) have
The Curse and the Home
Of Misery.

٥٢ يَوْمَ لَا يَنفَعُ ٱلظَّٰلِمِينَ مَعْذِرَتُهُمْ
وَلَهُمُ ٱللَّعْنَةُ وَلَهُمْ
سُوٓءُ ٱلدَّارِ

53. We did aforetime give Moses
The (Book of) Guidance,[4426]
And We gave the Book
In inheritance to the Children
Of Israel—

٥٣ وَلَقَدْ ءَاتَيْنَا مُوسَى ٱلْهُدَىٰ
وَأَوْرَثْنَا بَنِىٓ إِسْرَٰٓءِيلَ ٱلْكِتَٰبَ

54. A Guide and a Message
To men of understanding.

٥٤ هُدًى وَذِكْرَىٰ لِأُو۟لِى ٱلْأَلْبَٰبِ

55. Patiently, then, persevere:[4427]
For the Promise of Allah
Is true: and ask forgiveness[4428]
For thy fault, and celebrate
The Praises of thy Lord
In the evening
And in the morning.[4429]

٥٥ فَٱصْبِرْ إِنَّ وَعْدَ ٱللَّهِ حَقٌّ
وَٱسْتَغْفِرْ لِذَنۢبِكَ وَسَبِّحْ
بِحَمْدِ رَبِّكَ بِٱلْعَشِىِّ وَٱلْإِبْكَٰرِ

56. Those who dispute
About the Signs of Allah
Without any authority
Bestowed on them—there is[4430]
Nothing in their breasts

٥٦ إِنَّ ٱلَّذِينَ يُجَٰدِلُونَ فِىٓ
ءَايَٰتِ ٱللَّهِ بِغَيْرِ سُلْطَٰنٍ أَتَىٰهُمْ
إِن فِى صُدُورِهِمْ

4425. After the testimony mentioned in the last note, there will be no room for excuses, and if any were made, they could serve no purpose, unlike the state of matters in this world, where there is much make-believe, and Falsehood often masquerades as Truth and is accepted as such even by those who should know better.

4426. Moses was given a Revelation, and it was given in heritage to the Children of Israel, to preserve it, guide their conduct by, and hold aloft its Message; but they failed in all these particulars.

4427. The Israelites corrupted or lost their Book: they disobeyed Allah's Law; and failed to proclaim and exemplify Allah's Message. That is why the new Revelation came to the Holy Prophet. If, in the beginning, it was rejected and persecuted, there was no cause for discouragement; on the contrary, there was all the greater need for patience and perseverance.

4428. Every mortal according to his nature and degree of spiritual enlightenment falls short of the perfect standard of Allah (16:61), and should therefore ask Allah for forgiveness. What is merit in an ordinary man may be a human shortcoming in one nearest to Allah: see 38:24-25, and notes 4175-76. Prophets have a further responsibility for their People or their Ummah, and they ask in a representative capacity.

4429. *Cf.* 3:41. Evening and morning are the best times for contemplation and spiritual effort. But the phrase "evening and morning" may mean "at all times". (R).

4430. The Disputes are actuated by nothing but the desire for self-glory and self-aggrandizement. Their desire is not likely to receive fruition, but others should take warning from it.

But (the quest of) greatness,
Which they shall never
Attain to: seek refuge,
Then, in Allah: it is He
Who hears and sees (all things).

إِلَّا كِبْرٌ مَّا هُم بِبَٰلِغِيهِ ۚ
فَٱسْتَعِذْ بِٱللَّهِ ۖ إِنَّهُۥ هُوَ
ٱلسَّمِيعُ ٱلْبَصِيرُ

57. Assuredly the creation[4431]
Of the heavens
And the earth
Is a greater (matter)
Than the creation of men:
Yet most men understand not.

٥٧ لَخَلْقُ ٱلسَّمَٰوَٰتِ وَٱلْأَرْضِ
أَكْبَرُ مِنْ خَلْقِ ٱلنَّاسِ وَلَٰكِنَّ
أَكْثَرَ ٱلنَّاسِ لَا يَعْلَمُونَ

58. Not equal are the blind
And those who (clearly) see:[4432]
Nor are (equal) those
Who believe and work
Deeds of righteousness, and
Those who do evil.
Little do ye learn
By admonition!

٥٨ وَمَا يَسْتَوِى ٱلْأَعْمَىٰ
وَٱلْبَصِيرُ وَٱلَّذِينَ ءَامَنُوا۟ وَعَمِلُوا۟
ٱلصَّٰلِحَٰتِ وَلَا ٱلْمُسِىٓءُ ۚ
قَلِيلًا مَّا تَتَذَكَّرُونَ

59. The Hour will certainly come:[4433]
Therein is no doubt:
Yet most men believe not.

٥٩ إِنَّ ٱلسَّاعَةَ لَءَاتِيَةٌ لَّا رَيْبَ فِيهَا
وَلَٰكِنَّ أَكْثَرَ ٱلنَّاسِ لَا يُؤْمِنُونَ

60. And your Lord says:
"Call on Me; I
Will answer your (Prayer):[4434]
But those who are
Too arrogant to serve Me
Will surely find themselves
In Hell—in humiliation!"

٦٠ وَقَالَ رَبُّكُمُ ٱدْعُونِىٓ أَسْتَجِبْ لَكُمْ ۚ
إِنَّ ٱلَّذِينَ يَسْتَكْبِرُونَ عَنْ عِبَادَتِى
سَيَدْخُلُونَ جَهَنَّمَ دَاخِرِينَ

4431. The heavens and the earth include mankind and all other creatures and millions of stars. Man is himself but a tiny part of creation. Why should he be so egocentric? The whole is greater than a tiny part of it. And Allah Who created the whole of the Worlds is able to do much more wonderful things than can enter the imagination of man. Why should man be arrogant and doubt the Resurrection, and take upon himself to doubt the possibility of Allah's Revelation? It is only because he has made himself blind. See next verse.

4432. The man of Faith who backs his faith by righteous conduct is like the man of clear vision, who sees things in their true perspective and walks with firm steps in the Way of Allah. The man who does evil is like a blind man: the Light of Allah is all around him, but the man has made himself blind, and he can see nothing. He has rejected Faith and cannot even learn by other people's admonition.

4433. "The Hour" is the crown and consummation of man's life on this earth—the gateway to the Hereafter.

4434. As this life is not the end of all things, and we are to have its fulfillment in the Hereafter, we have only to pray to the Lord of the Present and the Hereafter, and He will hear us, forgive us, guide us, and make our Path smooth. But Pride will have its fall—and its humiliating Punishment. *Cf.* 37:18.

SECTION 7.

61. It is Allah Who has[4435]
Made the Night for you,
That ye may rest therein,
And the Day, as that
Which helps (you) to see.
Verily Allah is Full of
Grace and Bounty to men:
Yet most men give
No thanks.

٦١ ٱللَّهُ ٱلَّذِى جَعَلَ لَكُمُ ٱلَّيْلَ لِتَسْكُنُوا۟ فِيهِ وَٱلنَّهَارَ مُبْصِرًا ۚ إِنَّ ٱللَّهَ لَذُو فَضْلٍ عَلَى ٱلنَّاسِ وَلَٰكِنَّ أَكْثَرَ ٱلنَّاسِ لَا يَشْكُرُونَ

62. Such is Allah, your Lord,
The Creator of all things.
There is no god but He:
Then how ye are deluded[4436]
Away from the Truth!

٦٢ ذَٰلِكُمُ ٱللَّهُ رَبُّكُمْ خَٰلِقُ كُلِّ شَىْءٍ لَّآ إِلَٰهَ إِلَّا هُوَ ۖ فَأَنَّىٰ تُؤْفَكُونَ

63. Thus are deluded those[4437]
Who are wont to reject
The Signs of Allah.

٦٣ كَذَٰلِكَ يُؤْفَكُ ٱلَّذِينَ كَانُوا۟ بِـَٔايَٰتِ ٱللَّهِ يَجْحَدُونَ

64. It is Allah Who has[4438]
Made for you the earth
As a resting place,[4439]
And the sky as a canopy,
And has given you shape—[4440]
And made your shapes
Beautiful—and has provided
For you Sustenance.[4441]

٦٤ ٱللَّهُ ٱلَّذِى جَعَلَ لَكُمُ ٱلْأَرْضَ قَرَارًا وَٱلسَّمَآءَ بِنَآءً وَصَوَّرَكُمْ فَأَحْسَنَ صُوَرَكُمْ وَرَزَقَكُم

4435. The succession of Day and Night in our physical life is frequently appealed to, as a symbol to draw our attention to the Mercy and Bounty of Allah. If we viewed these things aright, we should serve Allah and seek Light from Him and Rest from Him, and celebrate His praises with gratitude.

4436. If we worship false gods, *i.e.*, go after vanities, what is it that deludes us and leads us astray? What could it be but our rank ingratitude and failure to use the understanding which Allah has given us?

4437. See the last two notes. If men are deluded by Falsehoods, it is because they reject Revelation and refuse to learn from the Signs of Allah all around them.

4438. The argument in the last two verses was from man's personal experience of his physical life. In this and the next verse a parallel argument is addressed to man on a much higher plane: 'look at the spacious earth and the canopy of the sky; look at the special position you occupy above other animals that you know, in shape and form, and moral and spiritual capacities; consider your refinements in food and fruits and the higher spiritual Sustenance of which your physical food is a type; would you not indeed say that the Lord is good, and would you not glorify His Holy Name?'

4439. *A resting place:* I understand this to imply a temporary place of rest or sojourn, a period of probation, to be followed by the eternal Home.

4440. *Cf.* 7:11 and n. 996. The shape and form refer to the physical form as well as to the inborn moral and spiritual capacities of man. As regards physical form, *Cf.* Milton's description of Adam and Eve, "Two of far noble shape, erect and tall" *(Paradise Lost*, 4:288). As regards moral and spiritual capacities, they are typified by the breathing of Allah's spirit into man: 15:29.

4441. *"Sustenance"* all that is necessary for growth and development, physical, moral, and spiritual. *Cf.* n. 2105 and 16:73.

Of things pure and good—
Such is Allah your Lord.
So Glory to Allah,
The Lord of the Worlds!

مِّنَ ٱلطَّيِّبَٰتِ ذَٰلِكُمُ ٱللَّهُ رَبُّكُمْ
فَتَبَارَكَ ٱللَّهُ رَبُّ ٱلْعَٰلَمِينَ

65. He is the Living (One):[4442]
There is no god but He:
Call upon Him, giving Him
Sincere devotion. Praise be
To Allah, Lord of the Worlds!

(٦٥) هُوَ ٱلْحَىُّ لَآ إِلَٰهَ إِلَّا هُوَ
فَٱدْعُوهُ مُخْلِصِينَ لَهُ ٱلدِّينَ
ٱلْحَمْدُ لِلَّهِ رَبِّ ٱلْعَٰلَمِينَ

66. Say: "I have been forbidden[4443]
To invoke those whom ye
Invoke besides Allah—seeing that
The Clear Signs have come
To me from my Lord;
And I have been commanded
To bow (in Islām)
To the Lord of the Worlds."

(٦٦) قُلْ إِنِّى نُهِيتُ أَنْ أَعْبُدَ
ٱلَّذِينَ تَدْعُونَ مِن دُونِ ٱللَّهِ
لَمَّا جَآءَنِىَ ٱلْبَيِّنَٰتُ مِن رَّبِّى
وَأُمِرْتُ أَنْ أُسْلِمَ لِرَبِّ ٱلْعَٰلَمِينَ

67. It is He Who has[4444]
Created you from dust,
Then from a sperm-drop,
Then from a leech-like clot;
Then does He get you
Out (into the light)
As a child; then lets you
(Grow and) reach your age
Of full strength; then
Lets you become old—
Though of you there are
Some who die before—
And lets you reach
A Term appointed;
In order that ye
May learn wisdom.

(٦٧) هُوَ ٱلَّذِى خَلَقَكُم مِّن تُرَابٍ
ثُمَّ مِن نُّطْفَةٍ ثُمَّ مِنْ عَلَقَةٍ
ثُمَّ يُخْرِجُكُمْ طِفْلًا
ثُمَّ لِتَبْلُغُوٓا۟ أَشُدَّكُمْ
ثُمَّ لِتَكُونُوا۟ شُيُوخًا
وَمِنكُم مَّن يُتَوَفَّىٰ مِن قَبْلُ
وَلِتَبْلُغُوٓا۟ أَجَلًا مُّسَمًّى
وَلَعَلَّكُمْ تَعْقِلُونَ

4442. The real, self-subsisting Life is only in Him. *Cf.* 2:255, and n. 296. All other forms of life are but shadows compared to His perfect Light.

4443. All objects of worship besides Allah are mere delusions. To anyone who sees this clearly, through Allah's Self-revelations, the only possible course is to give up everything else, which his own inner experience as well as outer Revelation tell him is false or of a temporary nature, and to bring his own will and actions into complete unison with Allah's Will: for that is the meaning of Islam, bowing to the Will of Allah. When we bow to the Real and Everlasting, we are automatically saved from falling victims to the False and Evanescent. (R).

4444. *Cf.* this passage with 22:5 and notes 2773 and 2774. The various stages of man's physical life are: (1) first, simple matter (dust); (2) the sperm-drop in the father; (3) the fertilised ovum in the mother's womb; (4) out into the light, as a human child; (5) youth and full maturity; (6) decay; and (7) death. In some cases the late stages are curtailed or cut off; but in any case, a Term appointed is reached, so that the higher purpose of Allah's Will and Plan may be fulfilled in each given case, that man "may learn wisdom".

68. It is He Who gives Life [4445]
And Death; and when He
Decides upon an affair,
He says to it, "Be",
And it is.

٦٨ هُوَ ٱلَّذِى يُحْىِۦ وَيُمِيتُ ۖ
فَإِذَا قَضَىٰٓ أَمْرًا فَإِنَّمَا يَقُولُ لَهُۥ كُن فَيَكُونُ

SECTION 8.

69. Seest thou not those
That dispute concerning
The Signs of Allah?
How are they turned away[4446]
(From Reality)?—

٦٩ أَلَمْ تَرَ إِلَى ٱلَّذِينَ يُجَٰدِلُونَ
فِىٓ ءَايَٰتِ ٱللَّهِ أَنَّىٰ يُصْرَفُونَ

70. Those who reject the Book[4447]
And the (revelations) with which
We sent Our messengers:
But soon shall they know—

٧٠ ٱلَّذِينَ كَذَّبُوا۟ بِٱلْكِتَٰبِ
وَبِمَآ أَرْسَلْنَا بِهِۦ رُسُلَنَا ۖ
فَسَوْفَ يَعْلَمُونَ

71. When the yokes (shall be)[4448]
Round their necks,
And the chains;
They shall be dragged along—

٧١ إِذِ ٱلْأَغْلَٰلُ فِىٓ أَعْنَٰقِهِمْ
وَٱلسَّلَٰسِلُ يُسْحَبُونَ

72. In the boiling fetid fluid;[4449]
Then in the Fire
Shall they be burned;

٧٢ فِى ٱلْحَمِيمِ ثُمَّ فِى ٱلنَّارِ يُسْجَرُونَ

73. Then shall it be said
To them: "Where are
The (deities) to which
Ye gave part-worship—

٧٣ ثُمَّ قِيلَ لَهُمْ أَيْنَ
مَا كُنتُمْ تُشْرِكُونَ

4445. The keys of life and death are in Allah's hands. But He is not dependent on time or place or instruments or materials. All that He has to do is to say "Be", and it comes into existence. *Cf.* 16:40, and n. 2066; 36:82, and n. 4029. Conversely, His Will or Command is sufficient to annihilate Existence into Non-Existence (Life into Death) or determine the limits or conditions of Existence or Non-Existence.

4446. Those who dispute about the Signs of Allah which are clear to all who care to see, are merely in the mists of Unreality: *Cf.* 10:32.

4447. "The Book" may refer to the Holy Qur'ān or to the fundamental Revelation, the "Mother of the Book" (13:39), while the Books revealed to the messengers are the definite Revelations that came down to men from time to time.

4448. The rejection of Allah's Message, however brought, carries its own penalty. The yoke of spiritual slavery to Sin and Evil is fastened more and more firmly round the rejecter's neck, because there is no one to safeguard his freedom, and the chains of superstitions and the ugly consequences of evil restrict his freedom and the limited faculty of choice which was given by Allah to man. This process receives its climax at the Hour of Judgement.

4449. The sinner gets dragged further and further in the disgusting consequences of his evil actions, until the fire of destruction closes in upon him.

74. "In derogation of Allah?"
They will reply: "They have[4450]
Left us in the lurch:
Nay, we invoked not,
Of old, anything (that had
Real existence)." Thus
Does Allah leave
The Unbelievers to stray.

٧٤ مِن دُونِ ٱللَّهِ ۖ
قَالُوا۟ ضَلُّوا۟ عَنَّا بَل لَّمْ
نَكُن نَّدْعُوا۟ مِن قَبْلُ شَيْـًٔا ۚ
كَذَٰلِكَ يُضِلُّ ٱللَّهُ ٱلْكَٰفِرِينَ

75. "That was because[4451]
Ye were wont to rejoice
On the earth in things
Other than the Truth,
And that ye were wont
To be insolent.

٧٥ ذَٰلِكُم بِمَا كُنتُمْ تَفْرَحُونَ
فِى ٱلْأَرْضِ بِغَيْرِ ٱلْحَقِّ
وَبِمَا كُنتُمْ تَمْرَحُونَ

76. "Enter ye the gates[4452]
Of Hell, to dwell therein:
And evil is (this) abode
Of the arrogant!"

٧٦ ٱدْخُلُوٓا۟ أَبْوَٰبَ جَهَنَّمَ خَٰلِدِينَ فِيهَا ۖ
فَبِئْسَ مَثْوَى ٱلْمُتَكَبِّرِينَ

77. So persevere in patience;
For the Promise of Allah
Is true: and whether[4453]
We show thee (in this life)
Some part of what We
Promise them — or We
Take thy soul (to Our Mercy)
(Before that) — (in any case)
It is to Us that
They shall (all) return.

٧٧ فَٱصْبِرْ إِنَّ
وَعْدَ ٱللَّهِ حَقٌّ ۚ
فَإِمَّا نُرِيَنَّكَ بَعْضَ
ٱلَّذِى نَعِدُهُمْ أَوْ نَتَوَفَّيَنَّكَ
فَإِلَيْنَا يُرْجَعُونَ

78. We did aforetime send
Messengers before thee: of
them[4454]
There are some whose story
We have related to thee,

٧٨ وَلَقَدْ أَرْسَلْنَا رُسُلًا مِّن قَبْلِكَ
مِنْهُم مَّن قَصَصْنَا عَلَيْكَ

4450. All falsehood will vanish: *Cf.* 7:36. The only Reality will be fully manifest even to those to whom Evil was made to seem alluring in the lower life. They will feel in their inmost souls that they had been pursuing mere shadows, things of no real existence. This was the result of their rejecting the Light and the Grace of Allah: they got entangled in the mazes of error.

4451. Allah does not withdraw His grace from any unless (1) they actively and deliberately take a delight in things that are vain or false, and (2) they insolently reject the things that are true — in other words, unless men are deliberately false to their own lights, as illuminated by the Light of Allah.

4452. *Cf.* 39:72.

4453. *Cf.* 10:46, and n. 1438. As the eventual justice and readjustment of values must take place, when every soul returns to the Judgement Seat of Allah, it makes no difference if good and evil meet their deserts in this very life or not. *Cf.* also 13:40.

4454. *Cf.* 4:164. Allah sent Messengers of His Truth to every people. There are some whose names are known to us through the Holy Qur'ān, but there are a large number whose names are not made known to us through that medium. We must recognise the Truth wherever we find it.

And some whose story
We have not related
To thee. It was not
(Possible) for any messenger
To bring a Sign except
By the leave of Allah:
But when the Command[4455]
Of Allah issued,
The matter was decided
In truth and justice,
And there perished,
There and then, those
Who stood on Falsehoods.

وَمِنْهُم مَّن لَّمْ نَقْصُصْ عَلَيْكَ
وَمَا كَانَ لِرَسُولٍ أَن يَأْتِيَ
بِـَٔايَةٍ إِلَّا بِإِذْنِ ٱللَّهِ
فَإِذَا جَآءَ أَمْرُ ٱللَّهِ
قُضِىَ بِٱلْحَقِّ وَخَسِرَ
هُنَالِكَ ٱلْمُبْطِلُونَ

Section 9.

79. It is Allah who made[4456]
Cattle for you, that ye
May use some for riding
And some for food;

٧٩ ٱللَّهُ ٱلَّذِى جَعَلَ لَكُمُ ٱلْأَنْعَٰمَ
لِتَرْكَبُوا۟ مِنْهَا وَمِنْهَا تَأْكُلُونَ

80. And there are (other) advantages
In them for you (besides);
That ye may through them
Attain to any need
(There may be) in your hearts;
And on them and on ships
Ye are carried.

٨٠ وَلَكُمْ فِيهَا مَنَٰفِعُ
وَلِتَبْلُغُوا۟ عَلَيْهَا حَاجَةً
فِى صُدُورِكُمْ وَعَلَيْهَا
وَعَلَى ٱلْفُلْكِ تُحْمَلُونَ

81. And He shows you (always)[4457]
His Signs: then which
Of the Signs of Allah
Will ye deny?

٨١ وَيُرِيكُمْ ءَايَٰتِهِۦ
فَأَىَّ ءَايَٰتِ ٱللَّهِ تُنكِرُونَ

4455. The Signs of Allah are everywhere, and can be seen by the discerning eye at all times. But if any extraordinary Signs are demanded by cynics or Unbelievers, they will not be granted merely because they are demanded. It is Allah's Will that issues them, not merely the desire of human beings, even if he be a Messenger of Allah. But when an extraordinary Sign does issue by the Command of Allah, it means that the cup of the iniquitous is full; that their case is decided, and their time of respite is past; and that Justice takes the place of Mercy, and evil is blotted out.

4456. *Cf.* 16:5-8. The fact that beasts, which in their wild state are so noxious, are, when domesticated, so useful to man, is itself one of the great and standing Signs of Allah's care for man. The great usefulness of cattle is very instructive. They serve for riding, and many of them for food; further, they are used for the plough, and they produce milk, or wool or hair; and from their carcases man derives bones and horns for many industrial uses; but passing on to the higher aspects of life, they further social, moral, and spiritual uses as draught-animals, in that transport serves one of the fundamental purposes of civilisation, being in this respect like ships for international commerce: 30:46, and n. 3565. It is by means of human intercourse through transport that we can carry out the highest needs of our culture, "any need there may be in our hearts", *i.e.*, in our inner being.

4457. The Signs of Allah's goodness and mercy are so numerous that it is impossible to enumerate them. Which of them can any mortal deny? This is the theme of that highly poetical Sūrah, *Al Raḥmān* (S. 55).

82. Do they not travel through
The earth and see what
Was the End of those
Before them? They were
More numerous than these
And superior in strength[4458]
And in the traces
(They have left) in the land:
Yet all that they accomplished
Was of no profit to them.

٨٢ أَفَلَمْ يَسِيرُوا۟ فِى ٱلْأَرْضِ فَيَنظُرُوا۟ كَيْفَ
كَانَ عَٰقِبَةُ ٱلَّذِينَ مِن قَبْلِهِمْ
كَانُوٓا۟ أَكْثَرَ مِنْهُمْ وَأَشَدَّ
قُوَّةً وَءَاثَارًا فِى ٱلْأَرْضِ
فَمَآ أَغْنَىٰ عَنْهُم مَّا كَانُوا۟ يَكْسِبُونَ

83. For when their messengers
Came to them
With Clear Signs, they exulted[4459]
In such knowledge (and skill)
As they had; but
That very (Wrath) at which[4460]
They were wont to scoff
Hemmed them in.

٨٣ فَلَمَّا جَآءَتْهُمْ
رُسُلُهُم بِٱلْبَيِّنَٰتِ
فَرِحُوا۟ بِمَا عِندَهُم مِّنَ ٱلْعِلْمِ
وَحَاقَ بِهِم مَّا كَانُوا۟ بِهِۦ يَسْتَهْزِءُونَ

84. But when they saw
Our Punishment, they said:
"We believe in Allah—
The One God—and we
Reject the partners we used
To join with Him."

٨٤ فَلَمَّا رَأَوْا۟ بَأْسَنَا
قَالُوٓا۟ ءَامَنَّا بِٱللَّهِ وَحْدَهُۥ
وَكَفَرْنَا بِمَا كُنَّا بِهِۦ مُشْرِكِينَ

85. But their professing the Faith[4461]
When they (actually) saw
Our Punishment was not going
To profit them.
(Such has been) Allah's way

٨٥ فَلَمْ يَكُ يَنفَعُهُمْ
إِيمَٰنُهُمْ لَمَّا رَأَوْا۟ بَأْسَنَا
سُنَّتَ ٱللَّهِ

4458. *Cf.* 9:69. For any generation to take inordinate pride in its own single achievements in science or skill becomes ridiculous if we consider the broad stream of history. In the first place, men will find that a great deal of what they attribute to their own merits only became possible owing to the earlier work of their predecessors. Secondly, many of their predecessors were more numerous and mightier in power than they, although the perspective of time may have reduced the apparent depth of their influence, and the monuments which they have left behind may have suffered from the destroying hand of Time. Thirdly, and most important of all, when they forgot Allah and His inexorable Law, nothing of their own handiwork profited them: they perished in the common ruin as all vanities must perish. *Cf.* also 40:21 above, and n. 4387. See how the recapitulation rounds off the argument.

4459. Arrogance and an exaggerated idea of Self were at the bottom of the Evil to which they succumbed.

4460. *Cf.* 16:34. Nothing could stop the Justice of Allah punishing Evil. What they had ridiculed came as an inexorable fact. None of their grandeur or art or science or skill was of any use when they lost their souls!

4461. Again and again were they given chances, and again and again did they reject them. When it was too late, and in fact when it had no meaning, they offered to profess Faith. That was of no use. Allah does not accept unmeaning things of that kind. He wants to train and purify our will. For their disobedience and rebellion they perished utterly.

Of dealing with His servants
(From the most ancient times).
And even thus did
The rejecters of Allah
Perish (utterly)!

ٱلَّتِي قَدْ خَلَتْ فِي عِبَادِهِۦۖ
وَخَسِرَ هُنَالِكَ ٱلْكَٰفِرُونَ

INTRODUCTION TO SŪRAH 41—*FUṢṢILAT* or *ḤA MĪM*

This is the second of the series of seven Sūrahs bearing the Abbreviated Letters *Ḥā Mīm*, as explained in the Introduction to S. 40. To prevent confusion with other Sūrahs of the *Ḥā Mīm* series, the word *Sajdah* is sometimes added to the title, making it *Ḥā Mīm al Sajdah*, the double title being necessary as there is another Sūrah called Sajdah (S. 32). To avoid the double title, it is sometimes called *Fuṣṣilat*, from the occurrence of the word in verse 3.

The meaning of *Ḥā Mīm* has been explained in the Introduction to S. 40., where will also be found a note on the chronology and general theme of the seven *Ḥa Mīm* Sūrahs.

For this particular Sūrah the theme is that the basis of Faith and Revelation is Allah's Power and Goodness, and the fruit of both is man's righteousness and healing.

Summary.—What is Revelation and Faith, and what is man's attitude to both, and what are its consequences? (41:1-32, and C. 209).

The fruits of Faith and Unfaith, Truth and Falsehood, (41:33-54, and C. 210).

C. 209.—Revelation explains, and makes things clear;
(41:1-32.) It gives the message of hope and mercy,
And it warns men against the snares
Of Evil. Deny not Allah, the Lord
Of the Worlds, Whose glory and power
Are shown in Creation, and His Mercy
In Revelation. Learn from the fate
Of the Peoples of old! Learn from the warnings
Of your own nature: your very limbs
And faculties, if misused, bear witness
Against you. Repent ere it be too late.

Fuṣṣilat (Expounded), or *Ḥā Mīm*

الجزء الرابع والعشرون سورة فصلت

In the name of Allah, Most Gracious, Most Merciful.

بِسْمِ اللَّهِ الرَّحْمَٰنِ الرَّحِيمِ

1. Ḥā Mīm.[4462]

حمٓ ﴿١﴾

2. A revelation from (Allah),[4463]
Most Gracious, Most
Merciful—

تَنزِيلٌ مِّنَ الرَّحْمَٰنِ الرَّحِيمِ ﴿٢﴾

3. A Book, whereof the verses
Are explained in detail—
A Qur'ān in Arabic,
For people who understand—

كِتَٰبٌ فُصِّلَتْ ءَايَٰتُهُۥ قُرْءَانًا عَرَبِيًّا لِّقَوْمٍ يَعْلَمُونَ ﴿٣﴾

4. Giving Good News
And Admonition: yet most[4464]
Of them turn away,
And so they hear not.

بَشِيرًا وَنَذِيرًا فَأَعْرَضَ أَكْثَرُهُمْ فَهُمْ لَا يَسْمَعُونَ ﴿٤﴾

5. They say: "Our hearts are[4465]
Under veils, (concealed)
From that to which thou
Dost invite us, and
In our ears is a deafness,
And between us and thee

وَقَالُوا۟ قُلُوبُنَا فِىٓ أَكِنَّةٍ مِّمَّا تَدْعُونَآ إِلَيْهِ وَفِىٓ ءَاذَانِنَا وَقْرٌ وَمِنۢ بَيْنِنَا وَبَيْنِكَ ﴿٥﴾

4462. Abbreviated Letters: See Introduction to S. 40. See also n. 4382 to 40:8, and n. 4505 to 41:34.

4463. In the last Sūrah (40:2-3) the revelation was described with reference to some of the qualities of Allah from Whom it came. Here it is described mainly with reference to its subject matter. (1) It brings the Message of Grace and Mercy; (2) it is not merely a book of Dark Sayings, but everything is explained clearly and from various points of view; (3) it is in Arabic, the language of the people among whom it was first promulgated, and therefore easily intelligible to them if they take the trouble to understand; and (4) it opens the way to Forgiveness through Repentance and gives warning of all spiritual Dangers.

4464. With all the qualities mentioned in the last note, if men do not profit by its blessings, the fault lies in their will: they turn away, and thus fail to hear the voice that calls to them.

4465. The consequence of their wilful rejection is that a distance is created between Revelation and those for whom it is meant; their ears become deaf, so that the voice falls fainter and fainter on their ears: they feel a bar between themselves and the Messenger who comes to teach them. *Cf.* 7:25.

Is a screen: so do[4466] Thou (what thou wilt); For us, we shall do (What we will!)"	حِجَابٌ فَاعْمَلْ إِنَّنَا عَامِلُونَ
6. Say thou: "I am But a man like you:[4467] It is revealed to me By inspiration, that your God Is One God: so stand True to Him, and ask For His forgiveness."[4468] And woe to those who Join gods with Allah—	٦ قُلْ إِنَّمَا أَنَا بَشَرٌ مِّثْلُكُمْ يُوحَىٰ إِلَيَّ أَنَّمَا إِلَٰهُكُمْ إِلَٰهٌ وَاحِدٌ فَاسْتَقِيمُوا إِلَيْهِ وَاسْتَغْفِرُوهُ وَوَيْلٌ لِّلْمُشْرِكِينَ
7. Those who practise not Regular Charity, and who Even deny the Hereafter.	٧ الَّذِينَ لَا يُؤْتُونَ الزَّكَوٰةَ وَهُم بِالْآخِرَةِ هُمْ كَافِرُونَ
8. For those who believe[4469] And work deeds of righteousness Is a reward that will Never fail.	٨ إِنَّ الَّذِينَ آمَنُوا وَعَمِلُوا الصَّالِحَاتِ لَهُمْ أَجْرٌ غَيْرُ مَمْنُونٍ

SECTION 2.

9. Say: Is it that ye Deny Him Who created The earth in two Days?[4470]	٩ قُلْ أَئِنَّكُمْ لَتَكْفُرُونَ بِالَّذِي خَلَقَ الْأَرْضَ فِي يَوْمَيْنِ

4466. This is either a superiority complex adopting the sarcastic tone of an inferiority complex, or it expresses calculated indifference to spiritual teaching. In effect it says: "Our hearts and minds are not intelligent enough to understand your noble ideas, nor our ears sufficiently acute to hear their exposition: you and we are quite different; there is a gulf between us. Why worry about us? You go your way, and we shall go ours!"

4467. The reply is in effect: that the bringer of the Message is not an angel nor a god, and so there can and ought to be no barrier between him and his hearers; but he has been chosen to bring a Message of Truth and Hope to them; they should accept the Gospel of Unity, and by Repentance obtain Allah's Grace and Forgiveness.

4468. There is nothing but pity for those who reject Truth, run after false worship, have no sympathy or charity for their fellow-men, and even deny that there is any future Life.

4469. But blessed are those who have Faith. They will have a Future and a Bliss that will never fail.

4470. This is a difficult passage, describing the primal creation of our physical earth and the physical heavens around us. If we count the two Days mentioned in this verse, the four Days, mentioned in verse 10, and the two Days mentioned in verse 12, we get a total of eight Days, while in many passages the creation is stated to have taken place in six Days: see 7:54, n. 1031; and 32:4, n. 3632. The Commentators understand the "four Days" in verse 10 to include the two Days in verse 9, so that the total for the universe comes to six Days. This is reasonable, because the processess described in verses 9 and 10 form really one series. In the one case it is the creation of the formless matter of the earth; in the other case it is the gradual evolution of the form of the earth, its mountains and seas, and its animal and vegetable life, with the "nourishment in due proportion", proper to each. *Cf.* also 15:19-20.

And do ye join equals With Him? He is The Lord of (all) The Worlds.	وَتَجْعَلُونَ لَهُۥٓ أَندَادًاۚ ذَٰلِكَ رَبُّ ٱلْعَٰلَمِينَ
10. He set on the (earth). Mountains standing firm,[4471] High above it, And bestowed blessings on The earth, and measured therein All things to give them Nourishment in due proportion, In four Days,[4472] in accordance With (the needs of) Those who seek (sustenance).[4473]	١٠ وَجَعَلَ فِيهَا رَوَٰسِيَ مِن فَوْقِهَا وَبَٰرَكَ فِيهَا وَقَدَّرَ فِيهَآ أَقْوَٰتَهَا فِيٓ أَرْبَعَةِ أَيَّامٍ سَوَآءً لِّلسَّآئِلِينَ
11. Moreover, He Comprehended[4474] In His design the sky,[4475] And it had been (as) smoke: He said to it And to the earth: "Come ye together,[4476] Willingly or unwillingly." They said: "We do come (Together), in willing obedience."	١١ ثُمَّ ٱسْتَوَىٰٓ إِلَى ٱلسَّمَآءِ وَهِيَ دُخَانٌ فَقَالَ لَهَا وَلِلْأَرْضِ ٱئْتِيَا طَوْعًا أَوْ كَرْهًا قَالَتَآ أَتَيْنَا طَآئِعِينَ
12. So He completed them As seven firmaments	١٢ فَقَضَىٰهُنَّ سَبْعَ سَمَٰوَاتٍ

4471. *Cf.* 13:3 and 16:15, n. 2038. *High above it:* the highest mountains are 29,000 feet above sea level, and the lowest depths of the bottom of the ocean are 31,600 feet below sea level, so that the vertical difference between the highest and lowest points on the solid crust of the earth is about 11.5 miles. The highland areas are the main sources of the water supply in all the regions of the earth, and vegetable and animal life depends on water supply.

4472. See n. 4470 above.

4473. *Sā'ilīn* may mean either (1) those who seek, or (2) those who ask or enquire. If the former meaning is adopted, the clause means that everything is apportioned to the needs and appetites of Allah's creatures. If the latter, it means that the needs of enquirers are sufficiently met by what is stated here.

4474. For *istawā* see n. 1386 to 10:3. *CF.* also 2:29.

4475. From 79:30 it would appear as if the earth was spread out after the sky was made. In the present passage the creation of the earth and the evolution of life on our globe are mentioned first; and the making of the sky into the seven firmaments is mentioned last. The two statements are not inconsistent. It is stated here that when the sky was made into seven firmaments, it had existed previously as smoke, or vapour, or steam. The idea I derive from a collation of the relevant Quranic passages is that Allah first created primeval matter, which was as yet without order, shape, or symmetry. This state is called Chaos as opposed to Cosmos in Greek Cosmogony. The next stage would be the condensation of this primeval matter, into gases, liquids, or solids: on this subject no precise information is given us: it belongs to the realm of Physics. About the earth we are told of four stages or Days, and about the heavens, of two stages or Days. For Days seen n. 4477 below. If these stages proceeded or proceed together in time, it is obvious that each stage as we know it on earth is half as long as each stage in the heavens. But these are questions of Physics, Astronomy, or Geology, not questions of Religion.

4476. I take this to mean that Allah's design in creation was not to keep heaven and earth separate, but together, as we indeed are, being part of the solar system, and travellers through space, crossing the path of several comets. And all matter created by Allah willingly obeys the laws laid down for it.

In two Days[4477] and He
Assigned to each heaven
Its duty and command.
And We adorned
The lower heaven
With lights, and (provided it)[4478]
With guard. Such
Is the Decree of (Him)
The Exalted in Might,
Full of knowledge.

فِي يَوْمَيْنِ وَأَوْحَىٰ
فِي كُلِّ سَمَاءٍ أَمْرَهَا
وَزَيَّنَّا السَّمَاءَ الدُّنْيَا
بِمَصَابِيحَ وَحِفْظًا
ذَٰلِكَ تَقْدِيرُ الْعَزِيزِ الْعَلِيمِ

13\. But if they turn away,
Say thou: "I have warned
You of a stunning Punishment
(As of thunder and lightning)[4479]
Like that which (overtook)
The 'Ād and the Thamūd!"

١٣ فَإِنْ أَعْرَضُوا
فَقُلْ أَنذَرْتُكُمْ صَاعِقَةً
مِّثْلَ صَاعِقَةِ عَادٍ وَثَمُودَ

14\. Behold, the messengers came
To them, from before them[4480]
And behind them, (preaching):
"Serve none but Allah."
They said, "If our Lord
Had so pleased, He would
Certainly have sent down angels[4481]
(To preach): now we reject
Your mission (altogether)."

١٤ إِذْ جَاءَتْهُمُ الرُّسُلُ مِنْ بَيْنِ أَيْدِيهِمْ
وَمِنْ خَلْفِهِمْ أَلَّا تَعْبُدُوا إِلَّا اللَّهَ
قَالُوا لَوْ شَاءَ رَبُّنَا لَأَنزَلَ مَلَائِكَةً
فَإِنَّا بِمَا أُرْسِلْتُم بِهِ كَافِرُونَ

4477\. For *"Days"*, which may include thousands of years, see 7:54, and n. 1031. They refer to stages in the evolution of physical nature. In the Biblical cosmogony, (Gen. i, and ii. 1-7), which reflects old Babylonian cosmogony, the scheme is apparently to be taken literally as to days and is as follows: the first day Allah created light; the second, the firmament; the third, the earth and vegetation; the fourth, the stars and plants; the fifth, fish and fowl from the sea; and the sixth, cattle, creeping things, beasts on land, and man; on the seventh day He ended His work and rested. Our scheme is wholly different. (1) Allah did not rest, and never rests. "His Throne doth extend over the heavens and the earth, and He feeleth no fatigue in guarding and preserving them"; (2) Allah's work has not ended; His activity still goes on 32:5; 7:54; (3) man in our scheme does not come in with land animals; his advent is much later; (4) our stages are not sharply divided from each other, as in the above scheme, where the stars and planets having been created on the fourth day, it is not intelligible how the first three days were counted, nor how vegetation grew on the third day. Our stages for earth and heavens are not in sequence of time for the heavens and the earth. Our six stages are broadly speaking, (1) the throwing off of our planet from cosmic matter; (2) its cooling and condensing; (3) and (4) the growth of vegetable and animal life; (5) and (6) the parallel growth of the starry realm and our solar system.

4478\. *Cf.* 15:17, and n. 1951; also 37:609. The transition from the third person ("He completed," etc.) to the first person ("We adorned,"etc.) may be noted. The act of creation is an impersonal act: the act of adornment and guarding is a personal favour to Allah's creatures.

4479\. See verse 17. below.

4480\. *"From before them and behind them": i.e.*, from every side. They were warned from every point of view.

4481\. *Cf.* 15:7, n. 1941; 6:8-9, n. 841-42. The 'Ād had more power and material civilisation than the Pagan Arabs contemporary with the Holy Prophet. But the greater the material civilisation, the greater the arrogance as the besetting sin.

15. Now the 'Ād behaved
Arrogantly through the land,
Against (all) truth and reason,[4482]
And said: "Who is superior
To us in strength?" What!
Did they not see that
Allah, Who created them,
Was superior to them
In strength? But they
Continued to reject Our Signs!

(١٥) فَأَمَّا عَادٌ فَٱسْتَكْبَرُوا۟ فِى ٱلْأَرْضِ بِغَيْرِ ٱلْحَقِّ وَقَالُوا۟ مَنْ أَشَدُّ مِنَّا قُوَّةً ۖ أَوَلَمْ يَرَوْا۟ أَنَّ ٱللَّهَ ٱلَّذِى خَلَقَهُمْ هُوَ أَشَدُّ مِنْهُمْ قُوَّةً ۖ وَكَانُوا۟ بِـَٔايَـٰتِنَا يَجْحَدُونَ

16. So We sent against them
A furious Wind through days[4483]
Of disaster, that We might
Give them a taste
Of a Penalty of humiliation
In this Life; but the Penalty
Of the Hereafter will be
More humiliating still:
And they will find
No help.

(١٦) فَأَرْسَلْنَا عَلَيْهِمْ رِيحًا صَرْصَرًا فِىٓ أَيَّامٍ نَّحِسَاتٍ لِّنُذِيقَهُمْ عَذَابَ ٱلْخِزْىِ فِى ٱلْحَيَوٰةِ ٱلدُّنْيَا ۖ وَلَعَذَابُ ٱلْـَٔاخِرَةِ أَخْزَىٰ ۖ وَهُمْ لَا يُنصَرُونَ

17. As to the Thamūd,[4484]
We gave them guidance,
But they preferred blindness
(Of heart) to Guidance:
So the stunning Punishment[4485]
Of humiliation seized them,
Because of what they had earned.

(١٧) وَأَمَّا ثَمُودُ فَهَدَيْنَـٰهُمْ فَٱسْتَحَبُّوا۟ ٱلْعَمَىٰ عَلَى ٱلْهُدَىٰ فَأَخَذَتْهُمْ صَـٰعِقَةُ ٱلْعَذَابِ ٱلْهُونِ بِمَا كَانُوا۟ يَكْسِبُونَ

18. But We delivered those
Who believed and practised
righteousness.

(١٨) وَنَجَّيْنَا ٱلَّذِينَ ءَامَنُوا۟ وَكَانُوا۟ يَتَّقُونَ

SECTION 3.

19. On the Day that
The enemies of Allah
Will be gathered together

(١٩) وَيَوْمَ يُحْشَرُ أَعْدَآءُ ٱللَّهِ

4482. *Against (all) truth and reason: Cf.* 7:33. Their estimate of their own strength was greater than was justified by facts, but if they had all the strength which they arrogated to themselves, yet how could they stand before Allah?

4483. The detailed story of the 'Ād and their besetting sin, and the preaching of their Prophet Hūd to them will be found in 26:123-140; also 7:62-72, and n. 1040. For the furious Wind, *Cf.* 54:19.

4484. The story of the Thamūd usually goes with that of the 'Ād. *CF.* 36:140-59; also 7:73-79, and n. 1043.

4485. *"The stunning Punishment"*: *i.e.*, deafening noises like those of thunder and lightning; or the rumbling of a terrible earthquake. In 7:78, an earthquake is suggested: see n. 1047 to that verse. *Cf.* also above, 41:13.

To the Fire, they will
Be marched in ranks.[4486]

إِلَى ٱلنَّارِ فَهُمْ يُوزَعُونَ

20. At length, when they reach
The (Fire), their hearing,
Their sight, and their skins[4487]
Will bear witness against them,
As to (all) their deeds.

٢٠ حَتَّىٰٓ إِذَا مَا جَآءُوهَا شَهِدَ عَلَيْهِمْ
سَمْعُهُمْ وَأَبْصَٰرُهُمْ وَجُلُودُهُم بِمَا كَانُوا۟ يَعْمَلُونَ

21. They will say to their skins:[4488]
"Why bear ye witness
Against us?" They will say:
"Allah hath given us speech—
(He) Who giveth speech
To everything: He created
You for the first time,
And unto Him were ye
To return.

٢١ وَقَالُوا۟ لِجُلُودِهِمْ لِمَ
شَهِدتُّمْ عَلَيْنَا ۖ قَالُوٓا۟ أَنطَقَنَا ٱللَّهُ ٱلَّذِىٓ
أَنطَقَ كُلَّ شَىْءٍ وَهُوَ خَلَقَكُمْ
أَوَّلَ مَرَّةٍ وَإِلَيْهِ تُرْجَعُونَ

22. "Ye did not seek[4489]
To hide yourselves, lest
Your hearing, your sight,
And your skins should bear
Witness against you! But
Ye did think that Allah
Knew not many of the things
That ye used to do!

٢٢ وَمَا كُنتُمْ تَسْتَتِرُونَ
أَن يَشْهَدَ عَلَيْكُمْ سَمْعُكُمْ وَلَآ أَبْصَٰرُكُمْ
وَلَا جُلُودُكُمْ وَلَٰكِن ظَنَنتُمْ أَنَّ ٱللَّهَ
لَا يَعْلَمُ كَثِيرًا مِّمَّا تَعْمَلُونَ

23. "But this thought of yours[4490]
Which ye did entertain
Concerning your Lord, hath
Brought you to destruction,

٢٣ وَذَٰلِكُمْ ظَنُّكُمُ ٱلَّذِى
ظَنَنتُم بِرَبِّكُمْ أَرْدَىٰكُمْ

4486. "*Marched in ranks*": to show their further humiliation; for they will be like prisoners going to Punishment.

4487. All the members of their bodies and the faculties of their minds, which they misused, will bear witness against them. Similarly, in 36:65, their hands and their feet bear witness against them. The "skin" not only includes the sense of touch (which is so often misused in sex), but also the sense of taste and the sense of smell. which are specialised forms of the organ of touch. All the sensory organs, and all their intellectual and emotional counterparts advance us by their use and pull us down by their misuse. They become tell-tale witnesses against us if abused.

4488. A new phase of their existence will now dawn on them. They used to think that if they concealed their evil deeds from the rest of the world, nothing would happen to them! But Allah can give "tongues to trees", and can make every fact in life, known and unknown to the world, contribute to the elucidation of truth and justice. "Speech" on behalf of their senses and faculties should of course be understood figuratively. When we succumb to evil, our limbs and faculties betray us.

4489. The limbs and faculties will say: "You did not seek to hide your evil from us: in fact you used us for your evil, because we were in your power. Did you not know that Allah knew everything and that our knowledge would be evidence against you?"

4490. "You now see the situation! We were given for your use and service. You misused us, to your own utter and irretrievable destruction!"

And (now) have ye become
Of those utterly lost!"

فَأَصْبَحْتُم مِّنَ ٱلْخَٰسِرِينَ

24. If, then, they have patience,[4491]
The Fire will be
A Home for them!
And if they beg
To be received into favour
Into favour will they not
(Then) be received

فَإِن يَصْبِرُوا۟ فَٱلنَّارُ مَثْوًى لَّهُمْ ۖ وَإِن يَسْتَعْتِبُوا۟ فَمَا هُم مِّنَ ٱلْمُعْتَبِينَ ﴿٢٤﴾

25. And We have destined
For them intimate companions[4492]
(Of like nature), who made
Alluring to them what was
Before them and behind them;[4493]
And the sentence among
The previous generations of
Jinns[4494]
And men, who have passed away,
Is proved against them;
For they are utterly lost.[4495]

وَقَيَّضْنَا لَهُمْ قُرَنَآءَ فَزَيَّنُوا۟ لَهُم مَّا بَيْنَ أَيْدِيهِمْ وَمَا خَلْفَهُمْ وَحَقَّ عَلَيْهِمُ ٱلْقَوْلُ فِىٓ أُمَمٍ قَدْ خَلَتْ مِن قَبْلِهِم مِّنَ ٱلْجِنِّ وَٱلْإِنسِ ۖ إِنَّهُمْ كَانُوا۟ خَٰسِرِينَ ﴿٢٥﴾

SECTION 4.

26. The Unbelievers say;
"Listen not to this Qur'ān,[4496]
But talk at random
In the midst
Of its (reading), that ye
May gain the upper hand!"

وَقَالَ ٱلَّذِينَ كَفَرُوا۟ لَا تَسْمَعُوا۟ لِهَٰذَا ٱلْقُرْءَانِ وَٱلْغَوْا۟ فِيهِ لَعَلَّكُمْ تَغْلِبُونَ ﴿٢٦﴾

4491. *If they have patience:* there is sarcasm in the meaning. "Let them not be impatient; they will soon find a home in the Fire of Hell! If they ask for grace and forgiveness then, it will be too late."

4492. Just as the idea of happiness in heaven is expressed, not only by individual satisfaction, but by congenial society, so the idea of Punishment in hell is deepened by the fact that Evil will be made to meet evil: those who made sin fair-seeming in this life will be there to share in the regrets and mutual recriminations which will make life a burden. In fact, in these *Ḥā Mīm* verses, the idea of fit companionship for the Good and uncongenial company for the Evil, runs like a thread throughout. See instruction to S. 11.

4493. They painted in glowing colours the pleasures of sin in the past and the pleasure of sin in the future, thus practising a double deception, which will now be found out.

4494. *Jinns:* see n. 929 to 6:100. All spirits of wickedness and all men who submitted to them, in the past, were under one common sentence; and future generations who embrace evil will also join them. *Cf.* 6:128.

4495. The echo here of verse 23 above completes the argument from another point of view.

4496. A favourite trick of those who wish to dishonour Revelation is, not only not to listen to it themselves, but to talk loudly and insolently when it is being read, so that even the true listeners may not be able to perform their devotions. They think that they are drowning the voice of Allah: in fact they are piling up misery for themselves in the future. For Allah's voice can never be silenced.

27. But We will certainly
Give the Unbelievers a taste
Of a severe Penalty,
And We will require them
For the worst of their deeds.[4497]

٢٧ فَلَنُذِيقَنَّ ٱلَّذِينَ كَفَرُوا۟ عَذَابًا
شَدِيدًا وَلَنَجْزِيَنَّهُمْ أَسْوَأَ ٱلَّذِى كَانُوا۟ يَعْمَلُونَ

28. Such is the requital
Of the enemies of Allah—
The Fire: therein will be
For them the Eternal Home:
A (fit) requital, for
That they were wont
To reject Our Signs.

٢٨ ذَٰلِكَ جَزَآءُ أَعْدَآءِ ٱللَّهِ ٱلنَّارُ ۖ
لَهُمْ فِيهَا دَارُ ٱلْخُلْدِ ۖ
جَزَآءًۢ بِمَا كَانُوا۟ بِـَٔايَٰتِنَا يَجْحَدُونَ

29. And the Unbelievers will say:
"Our Lord! Show us those,[4498]
Among Jinns and men,
Who misled us: we shall
Crush them beneath our feet,
So that they become
The vilest (before all)."

٢٩ وَقَالَ ٱلَّذِينَ كَفَرُوا۟ رَبَّنَآ أَرِنَا
ٱلَّذَيْنِ أَضَلَّانَا مِنَ ٱلْجِنِّ وَٱلْإِنسِ نَجْعَلْهُمَا
تَحْتَ أَقْدَامِنَا لِيَكُونَا مِنَ ٱلْأَسْفَلِينَ

30. In the case of those
Who say, "Our Lord
Is Allah", and, further,[4499]
Stand straight and steadfast,
The angels descend on them
(From time to time):
"Fear ye not!" (they suggest),
"Nor grieve! But receive
The Glad Tidings
Of the Garden (of Bliss),
That which ye were promised!

٣٠ إِنَّ ٱلَّذِينَ قَالُوا۟ رَبُّنَا ٱللَّهُ
ثُمَّ ٱسْتَقَٰمُوا۟ تَتَنَزَّلُ عَلَيْهِمُ
ٱلْمَلَٰٓئِكَةُ أَلَّا تَخَافُوا۟
وَلَا تَحْزَنُوا۟ وَأَبْشِرُوا۟ بِٱلْجَنَّةِ
ٱلَّتِى كُنتُمْ تُوعَدُونَ

31. "We are your protectors[4500]
In this life and
In the Hereafter:

٣١ نَحْنُ أَوْلِيَآؤُكُمْ فِى ٱلْحَيَوٰةِ
ٱلدُّنْيَا وَفِى ٱلْءَاخِرَةِ ۖ

4497. Nothing that they can do, however outrageous, will escape its fit punishment. And to reject Allah's Signs is to shut the very door to His Grace and Mercy.

4498. It is one of the qualities of sin and all evil, that it wishes to drag down others in its own camp, and rejoices to see them humiliated and disgraced, just as, in the opposite case, the good rejoice to help and honour others and make them happy wherever they can. *Cf.* 6:112-113.

4499. The people who succeed in eternal Life are those who recognise and understand the one and only Eternal Reality, that is Allah, and further shape their probationary Life firmly and steadfastly on the principles of that Truth and Reality. They will have their friends and protectors in the good angels, in contrast to the evil ones, who will have no friendship or protection, but only the reproaches of the Evil Ones.

4500. *"Protectors"*: a key-thought for the *Ḥā Mīm* Sūrahs *Cf.* n. 4492 to 41:25 above, and n. 4505 to 41:34 below.

Therein shall ye have
All that your souls[4501]
Shall desire; therein
Shall ye have all
That ye ask for!—

وَلَكُمْ فِيهَا مَا تَشْتَهِىٓ أَنفُسُكُمْ
وَلَكُمْ فِيهَا مَا تَدَّعُونَ

32. "A hospitable gift from One[4502]
Oft-Forgiving, Most Merciful!"

نُزُلًا مِّنْ غَفُورٍ رَّحِيمٍ ﴿٣٢﴾

C. 210.—(41:33-54.)

The best of men is the man of Faith,
Who calls all men to share his Faith,
Whose life is pure, and whose law of life
Is the Will of Allah. Eschew all evil,
And adore Allah, and Him alone.
His Signs are everywhere, and His Message
Is the same through all the ages, a guide
And a healing to those who believe.
Dispute not, but live righteousness.
Knowledge belongs to Allah, but Falsehood
Deprives man of hope, humility,
And clear sight, and drives him to
Hypocrisy. So turn to Truth, and live.

SECTION 5.

33. Who is better in speech[4503]
Than one who calls (men)
To Allah, works righteousness,
And says, "I am of those
Who bow in Islam"?

وَمَنْ أَحْسَنُ قَوْلًا مِّمَّن دَعَآ إِلَى ٱللَّهِ
وَعَمِلَ صَٰلِحًا وَقَالَ إِنَّنِى مِنَ ٱلْمُسْلِمِينَ ﴿٣٣﴾

34. Nor can Goodness and Evil[4504]
Be equal. Repel (Evil)
With what is better:
Then will he between whom

وَلَا تَسْتَوِى ٱلْحَسَنَةُ وَلَا ٱلسَّيِّئَةُ ﴿٣٤﴾
ٱدْفَعْ بِٱلَّتِى هِىَ أَحْسَنُ فَإِذَا ٱلَّذِى بَيْنَكَ وَبَيْنَهُۥ

4501. *Cf.* 21:102, 43:71, 52:22. [Eds.].

4502. *Cf.* 3:198. Through Allah's infinite Mercy and Forgiveness, they will now be in the position of guests to Host, and will receive unnumbered gifts out of all proportion to their own merits.

4503. *Better in speech: i.e.*, speaks better counsel; or is more worthy of being listened to. That his word reaches the highest mark of human speech is evidenced by three facts: (1) that he calls all to the Truth of Allah, showing that his thoughts are not centered on himself; (2) every deed of his is righteousness, showing that there is no divergence between his preaching and his conduct; and (3) he completely associates himself with the Will of Allah, showing that he is the full embodiment of Islam. What a fine description of the Holy Prophet!

4504. You do not *return* good for evil, for there is no equality or comparison between the two. You repel or destroy evil with something which is far better, just as an antidote is better than poison. You foil hatred with love. You repel ignorance with knowledge, folly and wickedness with the friendly message of Revelation. The man who was in the bondage of sin, you not only liberate from sin, but make him your greatest friend and helper in the cause of Allah! Such is the alchemy of the Word of Allah! *Cf.* 23:96; 28:54

And thee was hatred
Become as it were
Thy friend and intimate![4505]

عَدَٰوَةٌ كَأَنَّهُۥ وَلِيٌّ حَمِيمٌ

35. And no one will be [4506]
Granted such goodness
Except those who exercise
Patience and self-restraint—
None but persons of
The greatest good fortune.

٣٥ وَمَا يُلَقَّىٰهَآ
إِلَّا ٱلَّذِينَ صَبَرُواْ
وَمَا يُلَقَّىٰهَآ إِلَّا ذُو حَظٍّ عَظِيمٍ

36. And if (at any time)
An incitement to discord[4507]
Is made to thee
By the Evil One,
Seek refuge in Allah.
He is the One
Who hears and knows
All things.

٣٦ وَإِمَّا يَنزَغَنَّكَ
مِنَ ٱلشَّيْطَٰنِ نَزْغٌ
فَٱسْتَعِذْ بِٱللَّهِ
إِنَّهُۥ هُوَ ٱلسَّمِيعُ ٱلْعَلِيمُ

37. Among His Signs are[4508]
The Night and the Day,
And the Sun and the Moon.
Adore not the sun
And the moon, but adore
Allah, Who created them,
If it is Him ye wish
To serve.

٣٧ وَمِنْ ءَايَٰتِهِ ٱلَّيْلُ
وَٱلنَّهَارُ وَٱلشَّمْسُ وَٱلْقَمَرُ
لَا تَسْجُدُواْ لِلشَّمْسِ وَلَا لِلْقَمَرِ وَٱسْجُدُواْ لِلَّهِ
ٱلَّذِى خَلَقَهُنَّ إِن كُنتُمْ إِيَّاهُ تَعْبُدُونَ

38. But if the (Unbelievers)
Are arrogant, (no matter):[4509]

٣٨ فَإِنِ ٱسْتَكْبَرُواْ

4505. *Ḥamīm:* the keyword of the *Ḥā Mīm* Sūrahs. See n. 4500 above, and Introduction to S. 40.

4506. The moral standard referred to in the last verse can only be reached by the exercise of the highest patience and self-restraint. All sorts of human weaknesses and counsels of pseudo-wisdom and "self-respect" will keep breaking in, but resist them as suggestions of Evil (see next verse). If you reach anywhere near that high standard, you will be indeed most fortunate in a spiritual sense, for Allah's Revelation will have made you great and free.

4507. *Nazagha* has in it the idea of discord, slander, disharmony, as well as incitements to such disturbances in the soul. They can only proceed from evil, and should be resisted with the help of Allah. See also last note.

4508. Night and Day are opposites, and yet, by the alchemy of Allah, they can both subserve the purpose of human good, because the Night can give rest while the Day can promote activity. The Sun and the Moon are similarly complementary. So, in moral and spiritual affairs, seeming opposites may by Allah's alchemy be made to subserve the purposes of Good. They are but instruments: Allah is the Cause. Adore Allah, and not the things which He has created. Use the things which He has created, but do not adore them.

4509. It does not in any way affect Allah if men rebel against Him. It is men's own loss. Allah's glory is being celebrated night and day by angels and men who receive the privilege of approaching His presence. To them it is a delight and an honour to be in the sunshine of Truth and Happiness.

For in the presence
Of thy Lord are those
Who celebrate His praises
By night and by day.
And they never flag
(Nor feel themselves
Above it).

فَٱلَّذِينَ عِندَ رَبِّكَ
يُسَبِّحُونَ لَهُۥ بِٱلَّيْلِ وَٱلنَّهَارِ
وَهُمْ لَا يَسْـَٔمُونَ

39. And among His Signs
Is this: thou seest
The earth barren and desolate;[4510]
But when We send down
Rain to it, it is stirred
To life and yields increase.
Truly, He Who gives life[4511]
To the (dead) earth
Can surely give life
To (men) who are dead.
For He has power
Over all things.

٣٩ وَمِنْ ءَايَٰتِهِۦٓ أَنَّكَ
تَرَى ٱلْأَرْضَ خَٰشِعَةً فَإِذَآ أَنزَلْنَا
عَلَيْهَا ٱلْمَآءَ ٱهْتَزَّتْ وَرَبَتْ ۚ
إِنَّ ٱلَّذِىٓ أَحْيَاهَا لَمُحْىِ ٱلْمَوْتَىٰٓ ۚ
إِنَّهُۥ عَلَىٰ كُلِّ شَىْءٍ قَدِيرٌ

40. Those who pervert[4512]
The Truth in Our Signs
Are not hidden from Us.
Which is better?—he that
Is cast into the Fire,
Or he that comes safe through,
On the Day of Judgement?
Do what ye will:
Verily He seeth (clearly)
All that ye do.

٤٠ إِنَّ ٱلَّذِينَ يُلْحِدُونَ
فِىٓ ءَايَٰتِنَا لَا يَخْفَوْنَ عَلَيْنَآ ۗ
أَفَمَن يُلْقَىٰ فِى ٱلنَّارِ خَيْرٌ
أَم مَّن يَأْتِىٓ ءَامِنًا يَوْمَ ٱلْقِيَٰمَةِ ۚ
ٱعْمَلُوا۟ مَا شِئْتُمْ ۖ إِنَّهُۥ بِمَا تَعْمَلُونَ بَصِيرٌ

41. Those who reject the Message[4513]
When it comes to them
(Are not hidden from Us).
And indeed it is a Book
Of exalted power.

٤١ إِنَّ ٱلَّذِينَ كَفَرُوا۟
بِٱلذِّكْرِ لَمَّا جَآءَهُمْ ۖ
وَإِنَّهُۥ لَكِتَٰبٌ عَزِيزٌ

4510. Evil makes of the souls of men what drought makes of land: it kills life, beauty, and fruitfulness. Allah's Word in the spiritual world has the same wonderful effect as rain has on barren land; it gives life, beauty, and fruitfulness. And the effect of Allah's Word is also seen through the lives of men who repel evil with what is better. They also convert dead souls (which harbour spite and hatred) into living souls, which come into the main current of spiritual life, and help in carrying out Allah's beneficent Purpose.

4511. Why should we wonder then at the potency of Allah's Word, whether in our probationary lives here, or in the eternal life of the Hereafter.

4512. *Pervert the Truth in Our Signs:* either by corrupting the scriptures or turning them to false and selfish uses; or by neglecting the Signs of Allah in nature around them, or silencing His voice in their own conscience. Everything is known to Allah. Why not work for true salvation at the final Judgement?

4513. Mere rejection by men will not silence the Signs of Allah, which will work unintermittently and with the fullest potency.

42. No falsehood can approach it
From before or behind it:[4514]
It is sent down
By One Full of Wisdom,
Worthy of all Praise.

٤٢ لَّا يَأْتِيهِ ٱلْبَـٰطِلُ
مِنۢ بَيْنِ يَدَيْهِ وَلَا مِنْ خَلْفِهِۦ
تَنزِيلٌ مِّنْ حَكِيمٍ حَمِيدٍ

43. Nothing is said to thee
That was not said
To the messengers before thee:[4515]
That thy Lord has
At His command (all) Forgiveness
As well as a most
Grievous Penalty.

٤٣ مَّا يُقَالُ لَكَ إِلَّا مَا
قَدْ قِيلَ لِلرُّسُلِ مِن قَبْلِكَ
إِنَّ رَبَّكَ لَذُو مَغْفِرَةٍ وَذُو عِقَابٍ أَلِيمٍ

44. Had We sent this as
A Qur'ān (in a language)[4516]
Other than Arabic, they would
Have said: "Why are not
Its verses explained in detail?
What! (a Book) not in Arabic?
And (a Messenger) an Arab?"
Say: "It is a guide
And a healing to those
Who believe; and for those
Who believe not, there is
A deafness in their ears,[4517]
And it is blindness in their (eyes):
They are (as it were)
Being called from a place
Far distant!"

٤٤ وَلَوْ جَعَلْنَـٰهُ قُرْءَانًا أَعْجَمِيًّا
لَّقَالُوا۟ لَوْلَا فُصِّلَتْ ءَايَـٰتُهُۥٓ
ءَا۬عْجَمِىٌّ وَعَرَبِىٌّ قُلْ هُوَ
لِلَّذِينَ ءَامَنُوا۟ هُدًى وَشِفَآءٌ
وَٱلَّذِينَ لَا يُؤْمِنُونَ فِىٓ ءَاذَانِهِمْ
وَقْرٌ وَهُوَ عَلَيْهِمْ عَمًى
أُو۟لَـٰٓئِكَ يُنَادَوْنَ
مِن مَّكَانٍۭ بَعِيدٍ

SECTION 6.

45. We certainly gave Moses
The Book aforetime: but disputes
Arose herein. Had it not

٤٥ وَلَقَدْ ءَاتَيْنَا مُوسَى ٱلْكِتَـٰبَ
فَٱخْتُلِفَ فِيهِ وَلَوْلَا

4514. Allah's Truth is fully guarded on all sides. No one can get the better of it by attacking it from before or behind it, openly or secretly, or in any way whatever.

4515. The gist of Allah's Message, now, before, and for ever, is the same: Mercy to the erring and repentant; just punishment to those who wilfully rebel against Allah.

4516. *Cf.* 16:103-105; 12:2; etc. It was most natural and reasonable that the Messenger being Arab, the Message should be in his own tongue, that he might explain it in every detail, with the greatest power and eloquence. Even though it was to be for the whole world, its initial exposition was thus to be in Arabic. But if people had no faith and were spiritually deaf or blind, it would not matter in what language it came.

4517. *Cf.* 41:5, and 6:25. They pretended that it was too deep for them, when they meant that they were superior to it! The fact was that by putting themselves in an artificially false position, they rendered themselves impervious to the Message. The voice of Revelation or the voice of conscience sounded to them as if it came from a far-off place! They themselves made themselves strangers to it.

Been for a Word[4518]
That went forth before
From thy Lord, (their differences)
Would have been settled
Between them: but they
Remained in suspicious
Disquieting doubt thereon.

كَلِمَةٌ سَبَقَتْ
مِن رَّبِّكَ لَقُضِيَ بَيْنَهُمْ
وَإِنَّهُمْ لَفِي شَكٍّ مِّنْهُ مُرِيبٍ

46. Whoever works righteousness
Benefits his own soul;
Whoever works evil, it is
Against his own soul:
Nor is thy Lord ever
Unjust (in the least)
To His servants.

(٤٦) مَّنْ عَمِلَ صَٰلِحًا فَلِنَفْسِهِۦ
وَمَنْ أَسَآءَ فَعَلَيْهَا
وَمَا رَبُّكَ بِظَلَّٰمٍ لِّلْعَبِيدِ

25/30

47. To Him is referred[4519]
The Knowledge of the Hour
(Of Judgement: He knows all):
No date-fruit comes out
Of its sheath, nor does
A female conceive (within
Her womb) nor bring forth
(Young), but by His Knowledge,
The Day that (Allah) will propound
To them the (question),[4520]
"Where are the Partners
(Ye attributed) to Me?"
They will say, "We do
Assure Thee not one
Of us can bear witness!"

(٤٧) إِلَيْهِ يُرَدُّ عِلْمُ ٱلسَّاعَةِ
وَمَا تَخْرُجُ مِن ثَمَرَٰتٍ مِّنْ
أَكْمَامِهَا وَمَا تَحْمِلُ مِنْ أُنثَىٰ
وَلَا تَضَعُ إِلَّا بِعِلْمِهِۦ
وَيَوْمَ يُنَادِيهِمْ أَيْنَ
شُرَكَآءِى
قَالُوٓا۟ ءَاذَنَّٰكَ
مَا مِنَّا مِن شَهِيدٍ

48. The (deities) they used to invoke
Aforetime will leave them
In the lurch, and they

(٤٨) وَضَلَّ عَنْهُم
مَّا كَانُوا۟ يَدْعُونَ مِن قَبْلُ

4518. Callousness and self-sufficiency in religion are often illustrated by sects like the Pharisees and Sadducees among the Jews. Where there are honest differences of opinion, they can, in Allah's Plan, lead to greater enquiry and emulation. Where the differences are fractious, there is often even then time left for repentance. In any case the Word or Decree of Allah is for the best good of all, and should not disturb Faith. *Cf.* 10:19. A good life, of faith and truth, is in our own interests, and the opposite against our own interests. Allah is never unjust.

4519. There are profound mysteries which the knowledge of man cannot fathom but which are all open knowledge to Allah, because He plans, guides and controls all things. The precise time of the Hour of Judgement is one of these. We are not to dispute about matters like these, which are matters of speculation as far as human intelligence is concerned. Such speculations ruined the Ummah of Moses, and set them on the arid path of doubts and controversies. Our task is to do our duty and love Allah and man (see the last two verses). *Cf.* also 21:4.

4520. When the final restoration of true values comes, all falsehood will be exposed openly and publicly. The false gods will vanish, and their falsehood will be acknowledged by those who had lapsed from true worship. But it will be too late then for repentance.

Will preceive that they
Have no way of escape.

وَظَنُّوا مَا لَهُم مِّن مَّحِيصٍ

49. **M**an does not weary[4521]
Of asking for good (things),
But if ill touches him,
He gives up all hope
(And) is lost in despair.

٤٩ لَّا يَسْـَٔمُ الْإِنسَٰنُ مِن دُعَآءِ الْخَيْرِ
وَإِن مَّسَّهُ الشَّرُّ فَيَـُٔوسٌ قَنُوطٌ

50. When We give him a taste[4522]
Of some mercy from Ourselves
After some adversity has
Touched him, he is sure
To say, "This is due
To my (merit): I think not
That the Hour (of Judgement)
Will (ever) be established;
But if I am brought back
To my Lord, I have
(Much) good (stored) in His sight!"
But We will show
The Unbelievers the truth
Of all that they did,
And We shall give them
The taste of a severe
Penalty.

٥٠ وَلَئِنْ أَذَقْنَٰهُ
رَحْمَةً مِّنَّا مِنۢ بَعْدِ ضَرَّآءَ
مَسَّتْهُ لَيَقُولَنَّ هَٰذَا لِى
وَمَآ أَظُنُّ السَّاعَةَ قَآئِمَةً
وَلَئِن رُّجِعْتُ إِلَىٰ رَبِّىٓ
إِنَّ لِى عِندَهُۥ لَلْحُسْنَىٰ
فَلَنُنَبِّئَنَّ الَّذِينَ كَفَرُوا بِمَا عَمِلُوا
وَلَنُذِيقَنَّهُم مِّنْ عَذَابٍ غَلِيظٍ

51. **W**hen We bestow favours[4523]
On man, he turns away,
And gets himself remote
On his side (instead of[4524]
Coming to Us); and when

٥١ وَإِذَآ أَنْعَمْنَا عَلَى الْإِنسَٰنِ
أَعْرَضَ وَنَـَٔا بِجَانِبِهِۦ

4521. Not only is man prone to doubts and speculations in matters beyond his ken, thus disturbing the even tenor of his spiritual life: he is apt to run into opposite extremes in his daily experiences in this life. He is always hankering after the good things of this life. They are not all good for him. If he receives a little check, even though it may be to bring him to his bearings and turn his thoughts to higher things, he is apt to fall into despair.

4522. When men entertain false ideas of values in life, there are two or three possible attitudes they may adopt in reaction to their experiences. In the first place, their desire may be inordinate for the good things of this life, and any little check brings them into a mood of despair. See last note. In the second place, if their desire is granted, they are puffed up, and think that everything is due to their own cleverness or merit, and they forget Allah. Not only that, but they go a step further, and begin to doubt a Hereafter at all! If by chance they have a faint glimmering of the Hereafter, which they cannot help recognising, they think themselves "favoured of Heaven", because of some small favours given to them in this life by way of trial. Thus they turn all things, good or evil, away from their real purpose, because they are devoted to falsehood.

4523. The last verse and note dealt with men's distortion of the values of life. Here we come to men's ingratitude and hypocrisy. If they receive good, they go farther away from Allah, instead of coming nearer to him. If they suffer ill, they call on Allah and offer prolonged prayers, but it is not sincere devotion and therefore worthless.

4524. *Cf.* 18:83.

Evil seizes him, (he comes)
Full of prolonged prayer!

وَإِذَا مَسَّهُ ٱلشَّرُّ فَذُو دُعَآءٍ عَرِيضٍ

52. Say: "See ye if[4524-A]
The (Revelation) is (really)
From Allah, and yet do ye
Reject it? Who is more
Astray than one who
Is in a schism[4524-B]
Far (from any purpose)?"

٥٢ قُلْ أَرَءَيْتُمْ إِن كَانَ
مِنْ عِندِ ٱللَّهِ ثُمَّ كَفَرْتُم بِهِۦ
مَنْ أَضَلُّ مِمَّنْ هُوَ فِى
شِقَاقٍۭ بَعِيدٍ

53. Soon will We show them
Our Signs in the (furthest)
Regions (of the earth), and[4524-C]
In their own souls, until
It becomes manifest to them
That this is the Truth.
Is it not enough that
Thy Lord doth witness
All things?

٥٣ سَنُرِيهِمْ ءَايَٰتِنَا
فِى ٱلْءَافَاقِ وَفِىٓ أَنفُسِهِمْ
حَتَّىٰ يَتَبَيَّنَ لَهُمْ أَنَّهُ ٱلْحَقُّ
أَوَلَمْ يَكْفِ بِرَبِّكَ أَنَّهُۥ
عَلَىٰ كُلِّ شَىْءٍ شَهِيدٌ

54. Ah indeed! are they
In doubt concerning
The Meeting with their Lord?[4525]
Ah indeed! it is He
That doth encompass
All things!

٥٤ أَلَآ إِنَّهُمْ
فِى مِرْيَةٍ مِّن لِّقَآءِ رَبِّهِمْ
أَلَآ إِنَّهُۥ بِكُلِّ شَىْءٍ مُّحِيطٌۢ

4524-A. An argument is now addressed, of a most searching nature. Examine your own souls. See if you do not really find something unusual in Allah's Revelation! If you do, and yet you reject it, what a terrible responsibility fastens itself on you? Could anything be more foolish or more misguided than to reject a Message which is transforming the whole world?

4524-B. 'If you resist the convictions of the whole world, you are only forming a Cave or a narrow obscure sect or schism, which serves no purpose, and is unfit to live in the broad light of Universal Religion.' *Cf.* 2:176, n. 176.

4524-C. Allah's Truth always spreads, in its own good time, across to the uttermost ends of the earth, as it did in the case of Islam. But its intensive spread in the hearts and souls of people is even more remarkable than its extensive spread over large areas. Men like the four Companions of the Prophet—and many more—became leaders of men and arbiters of the world's fate. Madīnah, from being a focus of jarring tribes and factions that hated each other, became the seat of heroic actions and plans and the nursery of great and noble heroic deeds that resounded throughout the world. It makes no difference what men may say or do. Allah's Truth must prevail, and He knows who obstruct and who help.

4525. Short-sighted people may like to think that there may be no Judgement. But Judgement is inevitable and cannot be escaped, for Allah "doth encompass all things."

INTRODUCTION TO SŪRAH 42—*AL SHŪRĀ*

This is the third Sūrah of the *Ḥā Mīm* series of seven Sūrahs, for which see the Introduction to S. 40.

The theme is how evil and blasphemy can be cured by the Mercy and Guidance of Allah, which come through His Revelation. Men are asked to settle their differences in patience by mutual Consultation (42:38); which explains the title of the Sūrah.

Summary—The Contrast of blasphemy and disputation against Revelation, Unity, and Faith, as relying on the Signs and the Mercy of Allah (42:1-29, and C. 211).

Evil comes through men's own deeds, of which they cannot avoid the consequences, but Guidance comes through Allah's Mercy and Revelation (42:30-53, and C. 212).

C. 211.—Inspiration is part of the Glory and Goodness
(42:1-29.) Of Allah. His Unity is shown
In His Creation; yet man will turn
To false gods, and dispute about Religion.
Faith has been one at all times,
But sects and divisions rose through selfish
Contumacy. Let all contention cease,
And conduct weighed by the just balance
Of Allah's Word. The just and the unjust
Will all be brought before Allah, Whose Mercy
And Bounty are writ large in the Signs
In His marvellous Creation—one, yet diverse!

Sūrah 42.

***Al Shūrā* (Consultation)**

In the name of Allah, Most Gracious, Most Merciful.

بِسْمِ ٱللَّهِ ٱلرَّحْمَٰنِ ٱلرَّحِيمِ

1. Ḥā Mīm;[4526]

حمٓ ﴿١﴾

2. 'Ain Sīn Qāf.[4527]

عٓسٓقٓ ﴿٢﴾

3. Thus doth (He) send
Inspiration to thee
As (He did) to those before
thee—[4528]
Allah, Exalted in Power,
Full of Wisdom.

كَذَٰلِكَ يُوحِىٓ إِلَيْكَ وَإِلَى ٱلَّذِينَ مِن قَبْلِكَ ٱللَّهُ ٱلْعَزِيزُ ٱلْحَكِيمُ ﴿٣﴾

4. To Him belongs all
That is in the heavens
And on earth: and He
Is Most High, Most Great.[4529]

لَهُۥ مَا فِى ٱلسَّمَٰوَٰتِ وَمَا فِى ٱلْأَرْضِ ۖ وَهُوَ ٱلْعَلِىُّ ٱلْعَظِيمُ ﴿٤﴾

5. The heavens are almost
Rent asunder from above them[4530]
(By His Glory):
And the angels celebrate
The Praises of their Lord,
And pray for forgiveness
For All beings on earth:[4531]
Behold! Verily Allah is He,
The Oft-Forgiving,
Most Merciful.

تَكَادُ ٱلسَّمَٰوَٰتُ يَتَفَطَّرْنَ مِن فَوْقِهِنَّ ۚ وَٱلْمَلَٰٓئِكَةُ يُسَبِّحُونَ بِحَمْدِ رَبِّهِمْ وَيَسْتَغْفِرُونَ لِمَن فِى ٱلْأَرْضِ ۗ أَلَآ إِنَّ ٱللَّهَ هُوَ ٱلْغَفُورُ ٱلرَّحِيمُ ﴿٥﴾

4526. See Introduction to S. 40, paragraphs 2-24.

4527. This Sūrah has a double set of Abbreviated Letters, one in the first verse, and one in this second verse. No authoritative explanation of this second set is available, and I refrain from speculation. See Appendix I.

4528. Inspiration is full of Power and Wisdom, and both these qualities are derived from the Power and Wisdom of Allah. Unlike human power, this Power is necessarily good and merciful; unlike human wisdom, this Wisdom is necessarily complete and indisputable.

4529. We cannot conceive the distance which separates the Most High from the highest of His creatures. Allah Most Great from the greatest of the beings that we can imagine. The highest heavens are mentioned in the next verse, as well as the noblest creatures that we can imagine, the angels.

4530. How can we conceive of sublimity and greatness in a higher degree than this, that the highest heavens are almost ready to burst asunder by His Glory, which is higher than all?

4531. The angels are the noblest and purest beings of whom we can conceive. They reflect on the one side Allah's Glory and Praise, and on the other, two other attributes of Allah, that look towards His erring creatures, *viz.*: Forgiveness and Mercy. The two sets of attributes are complementary. They thus proclaim in their own being and in their prayers the Greatness and unbounded Goodness of Allah.

6. And those who take As protectors others besides Him—[4532] Allah doth watch over them; And thou art not The disposer of their affairs.	٦ وَٱلَّذِينَ ٱتَّخَذُوا۟ مِن دُونِهِۦٓ أَوْلِيَآءَ ٱللَّهُ حَفِيظٌ عَلَيْهِمْ وَمَآ أَنتَ عَلَيْهِم بِوَكِيلٍ
7. Thus have We sent By inspiration to thee An Arabic Qur'ān:[4533] That thou mayest warn The Mother of Cities[4534] And all around her— And warn (them) of The Day of Assembly, Of which there is no doubt: (When) some will be[4535] In the Garden, and some In the Blazing Fire.	٧ وَكَذَٰلِكَ أَوْحَيْنَآ إِلَيْكَ قُرْءَانًا عَرَبِيًّا لِّتُنذِرَ أُمَّ ٱلْقُرَىٰ وَمَنْ حَوْلَهَا وَتُنذِرَ يَوْمَ ٱلْجَمْعِ لَا رَيْبَ فِيهِ فَرِيقٌ فِى ٱلْجَنَّةِ وَفَرِيقٌ فِى ٱلسَّعِيرِ
8. If Allah had so willed,[4536] He could have made them A single people: but He Admits whom He will To His Mercy: And the wrongdoers Will have no protector Nor helper.	٨ وَلَوْ شَآءَ ٱللَّهُ لَجَعَلَهُمْ أُمَّةً وَٰحِدَةً وَلَٰكِن يُدْخِلُ مَن يَشَآءُ فِى رَحْمَتِهِۦ وَٱلظَّٰلِمُونَ مَا لَهُم مِّن وَلِىٍّ وَلَا نَصِيرٍ
9. What! Have they taken (For worship) protectors Besides Him? But it is Allah—He is the Protector,[4537] And it is He Who Gives life to the dead:	٩ أَمِ ٱتَّخَذُوا۟ مِن دُونِهِۦٓ أَوْلِيَآءَ فَٱللَّهُ هُوَ ٱلْوَلِىُّ وَهُوَ يُحْىِ ٱلْمَوْتَىٰ

4532. We now come to the contrast, the folly and ingratitude of man. But that cannot escape its final doom in the Universal Plan of Allah. Only Judgement rests with Allah. A Prophet is not responsible for the conduct of men, in a system which permits some limited free will and personal responsibility.

4533. The point of the Qur'ān being in Arabic is that it is plain and intelligible to the people through whom and among whom it was promulgated; see next clause.

4534. The City of Makkah. See n. 913 to 6:92. This is undoubtedly a Makkan verse. Even apart from the Qiblah, Makkah is the centre of Islam, and "all around her" is the whole world.

4535. The contrast is again emphasised, as explained in the Summary.

4536. *Cf.* 5:51, and n. 761. It is one of the Signs of Allah that He has made us different, that we may be tried in the exercise of our will, and that we may reach, through righteousness and Faith, our highest development, and enjoy His gifts of Mercy and Grace. But we must not become contentious, and fall into evil: we must understand our own limitations. Otherwise we shall lose His grace and protection.

4537. There can be no greater ingratitude or blasphemy than to worship false gods, or to seek protection from things that have no power, when Allah—Who has power over all things—is always seeking to protect and cherish His creatures, and placing in their way all the means for attaining the best in them.

It is He Who has power
Over all things.

وَهُوَ عَلَىٰ كُلِّ شَيْءٍ قَدِيرٌ

SECTION 2.

10. Whatever it be wherein
Ye differ, the decision
Thereof is with Allah:[4538]
Such is Allah my Lord:
In Him I trust,
And to Him I turn.

(١٠) وَمَا اخْتَلَفْتُمْ فِيهِ
مِن شَيْءٍ فَحُكْمُهُ إِلَى اللَّهِ
ذَٰلِكُمُ اللَّهُ رَبِّي عَلَيْهِ تَوَكَّلْتُ وَإِلَيْهِ أُنِيبُ

11. (He is) the Creator
Of the heavens and
The earth: He has made
For you pairs
From among yourselves,
And pairs among cattle:[4539]
By this means does He
Multiply you: there is nothing
Whatever like unto Him,
And He is the One
That hears and sees (all things).

(١١) فَاطِرُ السَّمَاوَاتِ وَالْأَرْضِ
جَعَلَ لَكُم مِّنْ أَنفُسِكُمْ أَزْوَاجًا
وَمِنَ الْأَنْعَامِ أَزْوَاجًا يَذْرَؤُكُمْ فِيهِ
لَيْسَ كَمِثْلِهِ شَيْءٌ
وَهُوَ السَّمِيعُ الْبَصِيرُ

12. To Him belongs the keys
Of the heavens and the earth:
He enlarges and restricts[4540]
The Sustenance to whom
He will: for He knows
Full well all things.

(١٢) لَهُ مَقَالِيدُ السَّمَاوَاتِ وَالْأَرْضِ
يَبْسُطُ الرِّزْقَ لِمَن يَشَاءُ وَيَقْدِرُ
إِنَّهُ بِكُلِّ شَيْءٍ عَلِيمٌ

13. The same religion has He
Established for you as that

(١٣) شَرَعَ لَكُم مِّنَ الدِّينِ

4538. In the highest issues of life men may see things differently. If their differences arise merely from selfish motives, or narrowness of vision, they are sinning against their own souls. If their differences arise from sincere but mistaken notions, their proper course is not to form divisions and sects, or to increase contention and hatred among men, but to leave all things to Allah, trusting in Him and turning to Him in all difficulties. The final decision in all things is with Him.

4539. The mystery of sex has not only its physical aspects, but its moral and spiritual aspects, and therefore mankind is in this respect differentiated from the lower animals, and among mankind the grades and qualities are suggested by the phrase *"from among yourselves"*. As regards cattle, they are specially mentioned among the animals, as having special relations with man and specially subserving his needs, not only in the physical sphere, but also in the matter of transport, which is the key to all civilisation and culture: *Cf.* 36:71-73; also 23:21-22, where they are compared to ships, the symbol of international intercourse.

4540. *"Sustenance"*, here as elsewhere, stands for all things that support every phase of life, physical, social, intellectual, or spiritual. *Cf.* 10:59, n. 1447. The source of all gifts is Allah; His bounty is inexhaustible, and He gives to all; but He does not give to all in the same measure, because, out of the fullness of His knowledge and wisdom, He can judge best what is best for any of His creatures.

Which He enjoined on
Noah—[4541]
That which We have sent
By inspiration to thee—
And that which We enjoined
On Abraham, Moses, and
Jesus:
Namely, that ye should remain
Steadfast in Religion, and make
No divisions therein:[4542]
To those who worship
Other things than Allah,
Hard is the (way)
To which thou callest them.[4543]
Allah chooses to Himself
Those whom He pleases,
And guides to Himself
Those who turn (to Him).

14. And they became divided[4544]
Only after knowledge
Reached them—through selfish
Envy as between themselves.
Had it not been
For a Word that
Went forth before[4545]
From thy Lord,
(Tending) to a Term appointed,
The matter would have
Been settled between them:
But truly those who have
Inherited the Book after them

مَا وَصَّىٰ بِهِۦ نُوحًا
وَالَّذِىٓ أَوْحَيْنَآ إِلَيْكَ
وَمَا وَصَّيْنَا بِهِۦٓ إِبْرَٰهِيمَ
وَمُوسَىٰ وَعِيسَىٰٓ
أَنْ أَقِيمُوا۟ الدِّينَ وَلَا تَتَفَرَّقُوا۟ فِيهِ
كَبُرَ عَلَى الْمُشْرِكِينَ
مَا تَدْعُوهُمْ إِلَيْهِ
اللَّهُ يَجْتَبِىٓ إِلَيْهِ مَن يَشَآءُ
وَيَهْدِىٓ إِلَيْهِ مَن يُنِيبُ
١٤ وَمَا تَفَرَّقُوٓا۟ إِلَّا مِنۢ
بَعْدِ مَا جَآءَهُمُ الْعِلْمُ بَغْيًۢا بَيْنَهُمْ
وَلَوْلَا كَلِمَةٌ سَبَقَتْ مِن
رَّبِّكَ إِلَىٰٓ أَجَلٍ مُّسَمًّى
لَّقُضِىَ بَيْنَهُمْ
وَإِنَّ الَّذِينَ أُورِثُوا۟
الْكِتَٰبَ مِنۢ بَعْدِهِمْ

4541. Allah's Religion is the same in essence, whether given, for example, to Noah, Abraham, Moses, or Jesus, or to our Holy Prophet. The source of unity is the revelation from Allah. In Islam it is "established" as an institution, and does not remain merely a vague suggestion.

4542. Faith, Duty, or Religion, is not a matter to dispute about. The formation of sects is against the very principle of Religion and Unity. What we should strive for is steadfastness in duty and faith, and unity among mankind.

4543. Unity, unselfishness, love for Allah and man—these things are inconsistent with selfish aggrandizement, unjust suppression of our fellow-creatures, false worship, and false conduct to our brethren. Hence the Gospel of Unity, though it is in complete accord with the pure pattern after which Allah made us, is yet hard to those who love self and falsehood. But Grace is free to all, and in His wise Plan. He will specially select Teachers to show the Way to humanity, and no one who turns to Him will lack guidance.

4544. *Cf.* 2:213. If you reject Truth after it has reached you, it can only be through selfish contumacy or envy.

4545. *Cf.* 10:19, and n. 1407. Allah's decree has allowed a certain Term during which a sinner has the chance of repentance and forgiveness. Were it not so, sin would be punished at once, and the matter would be decided straightway: So also, when people reject Truth from selfish or contumacious motives, they get rope: perchance they may repent.

Are in suspicious (disquieting)[4546]
Doubt concerning it.

لَفِى شَكٍّ مِّنْهُ مُرِيبٍ

15. Now then, for that (reason),[4547]
Call (them to the Faith),
And stand steadfast
As thou art commanded,
Nor follow thou their vain
Desires; but say: "I believe
In the Book which
Allah has sent down;
And I am commanded
To judge justly between you.
Allah is our Lord[4548]
And your Lord: For us
(Is the reponsibility for)
Our deeds, and for you
For your deeds. There is
No contention between us
And you. Allah will
Bring us together,
And to Him is
(Our) final goal."

١٥ فَلِذَٰلِكَ فَادْعُ
وَاسْتَقِمْ كَمَآ أُمِرْتَ
وَلَا تَتَّبِعْ أَهْوَآءَهُمْ
وَقُلْ ءَامَنتُ بِمَآ أَنزَلَ
ٱللَّهُ مِن كِتَٰبٍ
وَأُمِرْتُ لِأَعْدِلَ بَيْنَكُمُ
ٱللَّهُ رَبُّنَا وَرَبُّكُمْ
لَنَآ أَعْمَٰلُنَا وَلَكُمْ أَعْمَٰلُكُمْ
لَا حُجَّةَ بَيْنَنَا وَبَيْنَكُمُ
ٱللَّهُ يَجْمَعُ بَيْنَنَا وَإِلَيْهِ ٱلْمَصِيرُ

16. But those who dispute
Concerning Allah after He
Had been accepted—[4549]
Futile is their dispute
In the sight of
Their Lord: on them

١٦ وَٱلَّذِينَ يُحَآجُّونَ فِى ٱللَّهِ
مِنۢ بَعْدِ مَا ٱسْتُجِيبَ لَهُۥ حُجَّتُهُمْ
دَاحِضَةٌ عِندَ رَبِّهِمْ وَعَلَيْهِمْ

4546. *Cf.* 14:9 and n. 1884. "Those who have inherited the Book" are the People of the Book, of the ages since the Book or Revelation came to them. Referring to the Jews and Christians contemporary with our Prophet, how true it is that they were broken up into hostile sects which hated and persecuted each other! Islam came to unite them, and it did. For the present phases of Christianity and Judaism are of later growth.

4547. How beautifully the mission of Islam is commended in this verse! (1) the more sectarianism and division there is in the world, the more need is there for the Gospel of Unity. (2) It must steadfastly pursue its way. (3) It must not be deflected by wordly or political motives. (4) Its faith must be directly in Allah and in Allah's Revelation. "The Book", mentioned here, covers all the revelations sent by Allah to His prophets. (5) It must judge justly between warring factions, as the Religion of Peace and Unity.

4548. The mission of Islam is further described. (6) The God whom it preaches is not an exclusive God: He is the Lord of the Worlds: to any given person, of whatever faith, 'He is your Allah, as well as mine' (7) Our faith is not a question of words; it is deeds which decide; each one of us has personal reponsibility for his own conduct. (8) There is no cause of contention whatever, when we preach Unity, Truth, and the Hereafter. (9) If you have doubts, the final arbiter is Allah, and His Throne is our Goal.

4549. *After He has been accepted.* The disputants are the Unbelievers who pugnaciously assault the minds of Believers after the Believers have by conviction accepted Faith in Allah as leading to spiritual Light. Such disputation is futile. An inner spiritual experience can never be shaken by dialectical assaults. On the contrary such disputations recoil on the heads of those who indulge in them. Allah's Wrath is on them in this life, and the terrible Penalty of the Hereafter must inevitably follow their evil plots against Truth.

Is Wrath, and for them
Will be a Penalty
Terrible.

غضب ولهم عذاب شديد

17. It is Allah Who has
Sent down the Book in truth,
And the Balance[4550]
(By which to weigh conduct).
And what will make thee
Realise that perhaps the Hour
Is close at hand?

١٧ الله الذي أنزل
الكتب بالحق والميزان
وما يدريك لعل الساعة قريب

18. Only those wish to[4551]
Hasten it who believe not
In it: those who believe
Hold it in awe,
And know that it is
The Truth. Behold, verily
Those that dispute concerning
The Hour are far astray.

١٨ يستعجل بها الذين لا يؤمنون بها
والذين ءامنوا مشفقون منها ويعلمون
أنها الحق ألا إن الذين يمارون
في الساعة لفي ضلل بعيد

19. Gracious is Allah[4552]
To His servants:[4553]
He gives Sustenance[4554]
To whom He pleases:
And He has Power
And can carry out
His Will.

١٩ الله لطيف بعباده
يرزق من يشاء
وهو القوي العزيز

SECTION 3.

20. To any that desires
The tilth of the Hereafter,
We give increase

٢٠ من كان يريد حرث الآخرة نزد له

4550. Revelation is like a balance, an instrument placed by Allah in our hands, by which we can weigh all moral issues, all questions of right and wrong in conduct. We must do so constantly. For the Judgement in any given case may come at any time: it may be quite near, and we must always be prepared. The Balance may also refer to the God-given faculty by which man can judge between right and wrong.

4551. The Unbelievers do not believe in Judgement and laugh at it. They say defiantly, "If there is to be a punishment, let it come at once!" The threefold answer to this will be found in n. 1810 to 13:6. With those who believe, the case is different. They know that the Hereafter is an awful Reality, and prepare for it. They see clearly on what a wrong track the scoffers are!

4552. *Laṭīf:* so kind, gracious, and understanding, as to bestow gifts finely suited to the needs of the recipients. For the various meaning of *Laṭīf*, see n. 2844 to 22:63. *Cf.* also 12:100.

4553. "Servants" here seems to include all men, just and unjust, for Allah provided for them all.

4554. *Sustenance, i.e.*, provision for all needs, physical, moral, spiritual, etc. *"To whom He pleases"* is not restrictive, but modal. 'Allah provides for all, but His provision is according to His wise Will and Plan, and not according to people's extravagant demands.' He can provide for all, because He has complete power and can carry out His Will. A further commment will be found in the next verse.

In his tilth; and to any
That desires the tilth
Of this world, We grant
Somewhat thereof, but he[4555]
Has no share or lot
In the Hereafter.

فِي حَرْثِهِۦ ۖ
وَمَن كَانَ يُرِيدُ حَرْثَ ٱلدُّنْيَا
نُؤْتِهِۦ مِنْهَا وَمَا لَهُۥ فِي ٱلْأَخِرَةِ مِن نَّصِيبٍ

21. What! Have they partners[4556]
(In godhead), who have
Established for them some
Religion without the permission
Of Allah? Had it not
Been for the Decree
Of Judgement, the matter
Would have been decided
Between them (at once).
But verily the wrongdoers
Will have a grievous Penalty.

٢١ أَمْ لَهُمْ شُرَكَـٰٓؤُا۟
شَرَعُوا۟ لَهُم مِّنَ ٱلدِّينِ
مَا لَمْ يَأْذَنۢ بِهِ ٱللَّهُ ۚ
وَلَوْلَا كَلِمَةُ ٱلْفَصْلِ لَقُضِيَ بَيْنَهُمْ ۗ
وَإِنَّ ٱلظَّـٰلِمِينَ لَهُمْ عَذَابٌ أَلِيمٌ

22. Thou wilt see the wrongdoers[4557]
In fear on account of what
They have earned, and (the burden
Of) that must (necessarily)
Fall on them. But those
Who believe and work
Righteous deeds will be
In the luxuriant meads[4558]
Of the Gardens: they shall
Have, before their Lord,
All that they wish for.
That will indeed be
The magnificent Bounty
(Of Allah).

٢٢ تَرَى ٱلظَّـٰلِمِينَ
مُشْفِقِينَ مِمَّا
كَسَبُوا۟ وَهُوَ وَاقِعٌۢ بِهِمْ ۗ
وَٱلَّذِينَ ءَامَنُوا۟ وَعَمِلُوا۟ ٱلصَّـٰلِحَـٰتِ
فِي رَوْضَاتِ ٱلْجَنَّاتِ ۖ
لَهُم مَّا يَشَآءُونَ عِندَ رَبِّهِمْ ۚ
ذَٰلِكَ هُوَ ٱلْفَضْلُ ٱلْكَبِيرُ

4555. The parable is from the efforts of the husbandman, who ploughs and prepares the soil, sows the seed, weeds in due season, and reaps the harvest. You reap as you sow. But Allah will add manifold advantages for spiritual tilth. To those who are only engrossed in the vanities of this world, something may accrue in this world, but the spiritual world is closed to them.

4556. Nothing can exist without the permission of Allah. Can people, who indulge in false worship say: "Why does Allah permit it?" The answer is: "a certain latitude is allowed with the grant of a limited form of free will. When the time for Judgement comes, the Punishment is sure." See n. 1810 to 13:6. *Decree (or Word) of Judgement:* See n. 1407 to 10:19.

4557. The chief feature of the punishment of wrongdoing is that the minds of the wrongdoers are haunted with terror on account of their own guilty conscience. They cannot possibly escape the weight of that terror.

4558. In contrast with the withering terror of the wrongdoers is the ease and rational happiness of those who do good. "On them shall be no fear, nor shall they grieve" (2:38). Their wills will have been purified, and they shall have all that they shall desire, "before their Lord". That is, their highest Bliss will be the sight of their Lord. No higher Bounty can they wish for.

23. That is (the Bounty) whereof[4559]
Allah gives Glad Tidings
To His Servants who
Believe and do righteous deeds.
Say: "No reward do I
Ask of you for this
Except the love
Of those near of kin."[4560]
And if anyone earns
Any good, We shall give
Him an increase of good
In respect thereof: for Allah
Is Oft-Forgiving, Most Ready[4561]
To appreciate (service).

(٢٣) ذَٰلِكَ ٱلَّذِي يُبَشِّرُ ٱللَّهُ عِبَادَهُ
ٱلَّذِينَ ءَامَنُواْ وَعَمِلُواْ ٱلصَّٰلِحَٰتِ
قُل لَّآ أَسۡـَٔلُكُمۡ عَلَيۡهِ أَجۡرًا
إِلَّا ٱلۡمَوَدَّةَ فِي ٱلۡقُرۡبَىٰ
وَمَن يَقۡتَرِفۡ حَسَنَةً نَّزِدۡ لَهُۥ فِيهَا حُسۡنًاۚ
إِنَّ ٱللَّهَ غَفُورٞ شَكُورٌ

24. What! Do they say,
"He has forged a falsehood
Against Allah?" But if Allah
Willed, He could seal up[4562]
Thy heart. And Allah
Blots out Vanity, and proves
The Truth by His Words.
For He knows well
The secrets of all hearts.

(٢٤) أَمۡ يَقُولُونَ ٱفۡتَرَىٰ عَلَى ٱللَّهِ كَذِبٗاۖ
فَإِن يَشَإِ ٱللَّهُ يَخۡتِمۡ عَلَىٰ قَلۡبِكَۗ
وَيَمۡحُ ٱللَّهُ ٱلۡبَٰطِلَ وَيُحِقُّ ٱلۡحَقَّ بِكَلِمَٰتِهِۦٓۚ
إِنَّهُۥ عَلِيمُۢ بِذَاتِ ٱلصُّدُورِ

25. He is the One that accepts[4563]
Repentance from His Servants
And forgives sins:
And He knows all
That ye do.

(٢٥) وَهُوَ ٱلَّذِي يَقۡبَلُ ٱلتَّوۡبَةَ عَنۡ عِبَادِهِۦ
وَيَعۡفُواْ عَنِ ٱلسَّيِّـَٔاتِ وَيَعۡلَمُ مَا تَفۡعَلُونَ

26. And He listens to[24564]
Those who believe and

(٢٦) وَيَسۡتَجِيبُ ٱلَّذِينَ ءَامَنُواْ

4559. Heaven may be pictured to our minds in various forms. This is one of the highest, and Allah announces it freely to the righteous.

4560. No sort of tangible reward does the man of God ask for proclaiming the Glad Tidings of Allah. But at least he has the right to ask that his kith and kin should not persecute him and put all sorts of obstacles in his way, as did the Quraysh against the Holy Prophet. The love of kindred may be extended to mean the love of our common humanity, for all mankind are brothers descended from Adam. Everyone can understand the ordinary love of kindred. (R).

4561. *Cf.* 35:29-30, and notes 3915 (for increase) and 3917 (for Allah's appreciation of service).

4562. If anyone has a doubt about a prophet's mission, let him look at the prophet's life, at his work, at his character. Allah loves Truth, not Falsehood. Allah's aid goes with Truth, not with Falsehood. The beauty and power of Allah's Word cannot be found in Falsehood. The false man's heart would be sealed, not expanded to new heights, as is that of the Message-bearer of Allah.

4563. Whatever the sin. Allah's Mercy is open to sincere Repentance, at all times, until the decree of condemnation issues.

4564. To the prayers of the righteous He listens, and He gives them of His Bounty beyond their deserts. Every time they do a little good, they are increased in their goodness. Every right impulse or aspiration is strenghtened and leads to progressive spiritual advancement.

Do deeds of righteousness,
And gives them increase
Of His Bounty: but
For the Unbelievers there is
A terrible Penalty.

وَعَمِلُوا۟ ٱلصَّٰلِحَٰتِ وَيَزِيدُهُم مِّن فَضْلِهِۦ ۚ
وَٱلْكَٰفِرُونَ لَهُمْ عَذَابٌ شَدِيدٌ

27. If Allah were to enlarge[4565]
The provision for His Servants,
They would indeed transgress
Beyond all bounds
Through the earth;
But He sends (it) down
In due measure
As He pleases.[4566]
For He is with His Servants
Well-Acquainted, Watchful.

٢٧ وَلَوْ بَسَطَ ٱللَّهُ ٱلرِّزْقَ
لِعِبَادِهِۦ لَبَغَوْا۟ فِى ٱلْأَرْضِ
وَلَٰكِن يُنَزِّلُ بِقَدَرٍ مَّا يَشَآءُ ۚ
إِنَّهُۥ بِعِبَادِهِۦ خَبِيرٌۢ بَصِيرٌ

28. He is the One that sends down
Rain (even) after (men) have
Given up all hope,[4567]
And scatters His Mercy
(Far and wide). And He
Is the Protector, Worthy
Of all Praise.

٢٨ وَهُوَ ٱلَّذِى يُنَزِّلُ ٱلْغَيْثَ
مِنۢ بَعْدِ مَا قَنَطُوا۟ وَيَنشُرُ رَحْمَتَهُۥ ۚ
وَهُوَ ٱلْوَلِىُّ ٱلْحَمِيدُ

29. And among His Signs
Is the creation of
The heavens and the earth,
And the living creatures[4568]
That He has scattered
Through them:[4569] and He

٢٩ وَمِنْ ءَايَٰتِهِۦ خَلْقُ ٱلسَّمَٰوَٰتِ
وَٱلْأَرْضِ وَمَا بَثَّ فِيهِمَا مِن دَآبَّةٍ ۚ
وَهُوَ

4565. It may be objected that all prayers, even of good people, are not answered. The reply is: (1) that even everyone who is good does not necessarily know what is best for him, for the values in this life are curiously distorted; and (2) on account of their want of knowledge, if everyone got all he asked for, there would be chaos and confusion, and "transgression beyond bounds through the earth", for the different interests are so intermingled and balanced that some measure must be observed in granting people's wishes. This measure is best supplied by the watchful care of Allah and His perfect knowledge of all our real needs.

4566. *As He pleases* is here almost equivalent to *as He thinks best.*

4567. That men should get such a blessing as rain when they expect it according to ordinary calculations of probabilities does not impress them, as it is a daily occurrence. But Allah's mercy is more than this. It comes to our aid even when all hope is lost, and gives us new chances and new openings where we least expect them. His quality of cherishing and protecting His creatures is always active, and what higher praise can we give?

4568. *Dābbatun:* beasts, living, crawling creatures of all kinds: see n. 166 to 2:164. Similarly in 24. 45, and other passages, the word is used for living creatures of all kinds, life generally, whose material basis is the mysterious thing which science calls protoplasm. The more our biological knowledge increases, the more do we marvel at the unity of Life on the one hand, and its diversity on the other.

4569. Life is not confined to our one little Planet. It is a very old speculation to imagine some life like human life on the planet Mars. Though no scientific demonstration is possible, it is reasonable to suppose that Life in some form or other is scattered through some of the millions of heavenly bodies scattered through space. What a wonderful Sign of Allah! the Almighty Who created such countless beings has surely the power to bring them together.

Has Power to gather them
Together when He wills.

عَلَىٰ جَمْعِهِمْ إِذَا يَشَآءُ قَدِيرٌ

C. 212.—What we call the ills of life is due
(42:30-53.) To our own ill-deeds, and many of them
Are forgiven by Allah. His Plan can never
Be frustrated. This Life is but a stage
Of convenience: live true and resist
All wrong, but learn the best way to do so.
On Allah rely; else no protector
Will you find. Allah's Revelation
Comes as a Guide and Mercy: it shows
The Sraight Way, the Way of Allah All-Wise.

SECTION 4.

30. Whatever misfortune
Happens to you, is because
Of the things your hands[4570]
Have wrought, and for many
(Of them) He grants forgiveness.

٣٠ وَمَآ أَصَٰبَكُم مِّن مُّصِيبَةٍ فَبِمَا كَسَبَتْ أَيْدِيكُمْ وَيَعْفُوا۟ عَن كَثِيرٍ

31. Nor can ye frustrate (aught),
(Fleeing) through the earth;[4571]
Nor have ye, besides Allah,
Anyone to protect
Or to help.

٣١ وَمَآ أَنتُم بِمُعْجِزِينَ فِى ٱلْأَرْضِ ۖ وَمَا لَكُم مِّن دُونِ ٱللَّهِ مِن وَلِىٍّ وَلَا نَصِيرٍ

32. And among His Signs
Are the ships, smooth-running[4572]
Through the ocean, (tall)
As mountains.

٣٢ وَمِنْ ءَايَٰتِهِ ٱلْجَوَارِ فِى ٱلْبَحْرِ كَٱلْأَعْلَٰمِ

33. If it be His Will,
He can still the Wind:
Then would they become
Motionless on the back

٣٣ إِن يَشَأْ يُسْكِنِ ٱلرِّيحَ فَيَظْلَلْنَ رَوَاكِدَ عَلَىٰ ظَهْرِهِۦٓ ۚ

4570. All evil, all sorrow, all pain and affliction, are things not normal, things twisted from the pure and holy nature as created by Allah's hands. As far as man is concerned, his misfortunes are but the consequences of the things he has done, He must bear personal reponsibility for them and not throw the blame on others.

4571. Every evil deed or word or thought must have its evil consequences: but if Allah forgives anything—and He forgives much—let no one imagine that he has defeated—or can defeat—Allah's Will or Plan. The only help or protection that is possible is from Allah. *Cf.* 29:22.

4572. The great and stately ships are appealed to again and again as being among the Signs of Allah, from many aspects. The aspect referred to here is how the great sailing ship runs prosperously as long as "the breath of heaven fill the sail", and what a miserable helpless creature she becomes when she once becomes becalmed. Students of English literature will remember the striking picture which Coleridge draws in his "Rime of the Ancient Mariner." The becalmed ship is as it were in the grip of Death because of the crime which the sailor had committed, and his mind feels psychologically the full force of the Sign. By analogy we can apply this to other craft: the steamer is not free from other dangers of the sea, nor aircraft from numerous dangers of the air.

Of the (ocean). Verily
In this are Signs
For everyone who patiently[4573]
Perseveres and is grateful.

إِنَّ فِي ذَٰلِكَ لَآيَٰتٖ
لِّكُلِّ صَبَّارٖ شَكُورٍ

34. Or He can cause them
To perish because of
The (evil) which (of men)
Have earned; but much
Doth He forgive.

٣٤ أَوۡ يُوبِقۡهُنَّ بِمَا كَسَبُواْ
وَيَعۡفُ عَن كَثِيرٖ

35. But let those know, who[4574]
Dispute about Our Signs,
That there is for them
No way of escape.

٣٥ وَيَعۡلَمَ ٱلَّذِينَ يُجَٰدِلُونَ فِيٓ ءَايَٰتِنَا
مَا لَهُم مِّن مَّحِيصٖ

36. Whatever ye are given (here)
Is (but) a convenience[4575]
Of this Life: but that
Which is with Allah
Is better and more lasting:
(It is) for those who believe[4576]
And put their trust
In their Lord;

٣٦ فَمَآ أُوتِيتُم مِّن شَيۡءٖ
فَمَتَٰعُ ٱلۡحَيَوٰةِ ٱلدُّنۡيَاۖ
وَمَا عِندَ ٱللَّهِ خَيۡرٞ وَأَبۡقَىٰ لِلَّذِينَ
ءَامَنُواْ وَعَلَىٰ رَبِّهِمۡ يَتَوَكَّلُونَ

37. Those who aviod the greater[4577]
Crimes and shameful deeds,
And, when they are angry
Even then forgive;

٣٧ وَٱلَّذِينَ يَجۡتَنِبُونَ كَبَٰٓئِرَ ٱلۡإِثۡمِ
وَٱلۡفَوَٰحِشَ وَإِذَا مَا غَضِبُواْ هُمۡ يَغۡفِرُونَ

4573. If we study such Signs in the right spirit, we learn the highest lessons for our spiritual life: on the one hand, patient perseverance with reliance on Allah, and on the other a feeling or attitude of grateful thanks to Allah, that He enables us to achieve so much in spite of our shortcomings, and forgives in us so much that deserves punishment and disaster.

4574. If we treat Allah's Signs in the wrong spirit, *i.e.*, contumaciously reject them or constantly dispute about them instead of trying to understand them, we are told that such tactics will avail us nothing: we cannot escape the consequences of our sins. The only way to escape is by repentance on our part and the grant of mercy by Allah.

4575. Any good (or ill) which is our lot is only a temporary phase to serve the convenience of this life, But there is a higher good, which comes from Allah's own Presence. Such good is both superior in quality, and more permanent. In the same way, any ills that we may suffer in this life, have reference only to the conditions of this our life of probation. The ills that we "earn" in our spititual Life—such as deprivation of Allah's Grace—are far more momentous and permanent.

4576. The higher and more permanent gifts which come from Allah's Presence are for those who truly worship and serve Allah. These are described by nine of their characteristics: *viz.* (1) they have Faith: and it follows that (2) they trust in Allah, instead of running after false standards or values: (3) they eschew the more serious offences against Allah's Law, and of course keep clear of any offences against sex ("shameful deeds"); (4) while knowing that they are not themselves perfect, they are ready to forgive others, even though they are sorely tried with anger and provocation; for the rest see n. 4578.

4577. Here we are speaking of the ordinary man or woman who tries to follow Allah's Law: he or she is not perfect, but at least eschews the major breaches of conduct. For those higher in spiritual degree there is of course a stricter standard. But all are entitled to the blessing of Islam, whatever their degree.

38. Those who harken[4578]
To their Lord, and establish
Regular prayer; who (conduct)
Their affairs by mutual
Consultation;[4579]
Who spend out of what
We bestow on them
For Sustenance;

39. And those who, when
An oppressive wrong is inflicted
On them, (are not cowed
But) help and defend
themselves.[4580]

40. The recompense for an injury
Is an injury equal thereto[4581]

٣٨ وَالَّذِينَ اسْتَجَابُوا
لِرَبِّهِمْ وَأَقَامُوا الصَّلَوٰةَ
وَأَمْرُهُمْ شُورَىٰ بَيْنَهُمْ
وَمِمَّا رَزَقْنَٰهُمْ يُنفِقُونَ

٣٩ وَالَّذِينَ إِذَا أَصَابَهُمُ
الْبَغْيُ هُمْ يَنتَصِرُونَ

٤٠ وَجَزَٰٓؤُا سَيِّئَةٍ سَيِّئَةٌ مِّثْلُهَا

4578. Continuing the enumeration of the characteristics described in n. 4576. above, we have the following further qualities in those who wish to serve Allah. (5) They are ready at all times to hearken to Allah's Signs, or to listen to the admonitions of prophets of Allah, and to follow the true Path, as they understand it: (6) they keep personal contact with Allah, by habits of Prayer and Praise; (7) their conduct in life is open and determined by mutual Consultation between those who are entitled to a voice, *e.g.*, in private domestic affairs, as between husband and wife, or other responsible members of the household: in affairs of business, as between partners or parties interested: and in State affairs, as between rulers and ruled, or as between different departments of administration, to reserve the unity of administration: (8) they do not forget Charity, or the help due to their weaker brethren, out of the wealth or gifts or talents or opportunities, which Allah had provided for themselves: and (9) when other people use them despitefully, they are not cowed down or terrorised into submission and acceptance of evil, but stand up for their rights within the limits mentioned in verse 40. (R).

4579. *Consultation.* This is the keyword of the Sūrah, and suggests the ideal way in which a good man should conduct his affiars, so that, on the one hand, he may not become too egotistical, and, on the other, he may not lightly abandon the responsibilities which devolve on him as a Personality whose development counts in the sight of Allah. See the points in head (7) under n. 4578 above. This principle was applied to its fullest extent by the Holy Prophet in his private and public life, and was fully acted upon by the early rulers of Islam. Modern representative government is an attempt—by no means perfect—to apply this principle in State affairs. See my *Religion Polity of Islam.*

4580. This follows from the high value attached to an individual soul's Personality in Islam. *Cf.* last note. There are four possible situations that may arise: an individual may have to stand up against an oppressor (1) for his own trampled rights, or (2) for the rights of other within his ken; or (3) a community may have similarly to stand up for its own rights collectively; or (4) for the rights of others. Nos. 2, 3. and 4 are considered highly meritorious for all, though few have the courage or the spirit to rise to so high a standard. No. 1 is specially liable to abuse on account of man's selfishness; Nos. 2, 3 and 4 are also abused by men pretending to motives of public good when they are serving their own personal interests or idiosyncracies; hence the qualifications mentioned in the next four verses and the notes thereto.

4581. See last note. When you stand up for rights, either on private or public grounds, it may be through processes of law, or by way of private defence insofar as the law permits private action. but in all cases you must not seek a compensation greater than the injury suffered. The most you can do is to demand equal redress. *i.e.* a harm equivalent to the harm done to you. Even this may serve to curb your unregenerate soul, or a community bent on revenge. But the ideal mode is not to slake your thirst for vengeance, but to follow better ways leading to the reform of the offender or his reconciliation. See 41:34, and 23:96. You can take steps to prevent repetition, by physical or moral means; the best moral means would be to turn hatred into friendship by forgiveness and love. In that case the compensation or reward (if we must use such terms) is infinitely greater, for it wins the good pleasure of Allah.

But this active righting of wrongs, whether by physical or by moral or spiritual means, which are commended as better, is an antithesis to the monkish doctrine, when you are smitten on one cheek, to turn the other also. This would not suppress, but encourage wrongdoing. It is practised by none but poltroons, and is preached only by hypocrites, or men who want to make slaves or others by depriving them of the power of self-defence. It occurs in two of the four canonical Gospels (Matt. v. 39, and Luke vi. 29), but we need not therefore assume that it was preached by Jesus.

(In degree): but if a person
Forgives and makes reconciliation,
His reward is due[4582]
From Allah: for (Allah)
Loveth not those who
Do wrong.[4583]

فَمَنْ عَفَا وَأَصْلَحَ
فَأَجْرُهُۥ عَلَى ٱللَّهِ
إِنَّهُۥ لَا يُحِبُّ ٱلظَّٰلِمِينَ

41. But indeed if any do help
And defend themselves
After a wrong (done)
To them, against such[4584]
There is no cause
Of blame.

٤١ وَلَمَنِ ٱنتَصَرَ بَعْدَ ظُلْمِهِۦ
فَأُو۟لَٰٓئِكَ مَا عَلَيْهِم
مِّن سَبِيلٍ

42. The blame is only[4585]
Against those who oppress
Men with wrongdoing
And insolently transgress
Beyond bounds through the land,
Defying right and justice:
For such there will be
A Penalty grievous.

٤٢ إِنَّمَا ٱلسَّبِيلُ عَلَى ٱلَّذِينَ
يَظْلِمُونَ ٱلنَّاسَ وَيَبْغُونَ
فِى ٱلْأَرْضِ بِغَيْرِ ٱلْحَقِّ
أُو۟لَٰٓئِكَ لَهُمْ عَذَابٌ أَلِيمٌ

43. But indeed if any
Show patience and forgive,[4586]
That would truly be
An exercise of courageous will
And resolution in the conduct
Of affairs.

٤٣ وَلَمَن صَبَرَ
وَغَفَرَ إِنَّ ذَٰلِكَ
لَمِنْ عَزْمِ ٱلْأُمُورِ

SECTION 5.

44. For any whom Allah
Leaves astray, there is

٤٤ وَمَن يُضْلِلِ ٱللَّهُ

4582. To love Allah is the highest motive of our conduct, for it leads to the love of Allah's creatures; to win the approbation and love of Allah, is the highest reward, far transcending any compensation or satisfaction we can obtain in this life.

4583. Allah does not love those who do wrong. If, therefore, we tolerate wrong, or encourage wrong by allowing it to run rampant when we can prevent it, we fail in our duty to Allah.

4584. Such people are not to be blamed, though they are following the lower law. The blame is on those who arrogantly ride roughshod over the land, oppressing people with grievous wrong. See next verse.

4585. The fact that men seek the lower rather than the higher Law is itself a result of arrogant wrongdoing of which the type was the Pharaoh who claimed to be "your Lord Most High" and oppressed the Israelites, and kept his own people under slavery and subjection, and the false glamour of magic and deception.

4586. It is harder to be patient and forgive, and yet to get wrongs righted, as was done by the Holy Prophet, than to bluster about and "punish the guilty" or "teach them lessons". It may look like futility or lack of purpose, but in reality it is the highest and noblest form of courage and resolution. And it may carry out the purpose of reform and the suppression of evil even better than stern punishment. The gentleness of innocence often "persuades where stronger measures fail." But of course circumstances alter cases, and there is some allowance also to be made for the personal equation of the men you have to deal with: in some cases severity may be called for, but it should be from a strict judicial motive, and not merely from personal anger or spite or lower motive in disguise.

No protector thereafter.
And thou wilt see
The wrongdoers, when
In sight of the Penalty,
Say: "Is there any way[4587]
(To effect) a return?"

فَمَا لَهُۥ مِن وَلِيٍّ مِّنۢ بَعۡدِهِۦۗ
وَتَرَى ٱلظَّٰلِمِينَ لَمَّا رَأَوُاْ ٱلۡعَذَابَ
يَقُولُونَ هَلۡ إِلَىٰ مَرَدّٖ مِّن سَبِيلٖ

45. And thou wilt see them
Brought forward to the (Penalty),
In a humble frame of mind
Because of (their) disgrace,[4588]
(And) looking with a stealthy
Glance. And the Believers
Will say: "Those are indeed[4589]
In loss who have given
To perdition their own selves
And those belonging to them
On the Day of Judgement.
Behold! Truly the wrongdoers
Are in a lasting Penalty!"

٤٥ وَتَرَىٰهُمۡ يُعۡرَضُونَ
عَلَيۡهَا خَٰشِعِينَ مِنَ ٱلذُّلِّ
يَنظُرُونَ مِن طَرۡفٍ خَفِيّٖۗ
وَقَالَ ٱلَّذِينَ ءَامَنُوٓاْ إِنَّ ٱلۡخَٰسِرِينَ ٱلَّذِينَ
خَسِرُوٓاْ أَنفُسَهُمۡ وَأَهۡلِيهِمۡ يَوۡمَ ٱلۡقِيَٰمَةِۗ
أَلَآ إِنَّ ٱلظَّٰلِمِينَ فِي عَذَابٖ مُّقِيمٖ

46. And no protectors have they[4590]
To help them,
Other than Allah.
And for any whom Allah
Leaves to stray, there is
No way (to the Goal).

٤٦ وَمَا كَانَ لَهُم مِّنۡ
أَوۡلِيَآءَ يَنصُرُونَهُم مِّن دُونِ ٱللَّهِۗ
وَمَن يُضۡلِلِ ٱللَّهُ فَمَا لَهُۥ مِن سَبِيلٍ

47. Hearken ye to your Lord,
Before there come a Day
Which there will be
No putting back, because[4591]

٤٧ ٱسۡتَجِيبُواْ لِرَبِّكُم
مِّن قَبۡلِ أَن يَأۡتِيَ يَوۡمٞ لَّا مَرَدَّ لَهُۥ

4587. When the actual consequences of evil are in sight, the foolish sinner wishes that it were possible to get back to the life of probation. But he neglected or abused it and rejected Allah's Grace all the time. How can he then be restored to a closed chapter of his life?

4588. They were very arrogant in their probationary life. Now will they be humbled to the dust. And they will be in utter despair and misery. They will not be able to see the favours and good things of the other life *(Cf.* 20:124-126). Even their misery, which will face them as a terrible Reality, they will only be able to look at askance, so thoroughly cowed will be their spirit.

4589. This will be their thought, and their realised experience: 'after all, any troubles and sorrows, any persecutions and taunts which they suffered in the life of probation from the enemies of truth, were of no consequence; the real loss was that revealed at the Judgement at the restoration of true values; the wicked and the arrogant have lost their own souls, and have brought to perdition all who attached themselves to them and followed their evil ways; and this Penalty is one that will endure! How much more real it is!'

4590. The argument begun in verse 44 above is here rounded off. 'If once men finally cut themselves off from Allah's guidance and care, they will have no protection whatever. All their false objects of worship will only mislead them further and further. How they will wish the fact blotted out when they are in sight of Judgement, and vainly wish for time to be reversed! They will be in the Fire, while the men whom they despised and rejected will have reached the final Goal! For them there will be no such way!'

4591. The Day of Judgement is inevitable. Allah has ordained it, and it cannot in any way be put back.

Of (the ordainment of) Allah!
That Day there will be
For you no place of refuge
Nor will there be for you
Any room for denial[4592]
(Of your sins)!

مِنَ ٱللَّهِۚ مَا لَكُم
مِّن مَّلۡجَإٖ يَوۡمَئِذٖ
وَمَا لَكُم مِّن نَّكِيرٖ

48. If then they turn away,
We have not sent thee
As a guard over them.[4593]
Thy duty is but to convey
(The Message). And truly,
When We give man
A taste of a Mercy[4594]
From ourselves, he doth
Exult thereat, but
When some ill happens
To him, on account
Of the deeds which
His hands have sent forth,
Truly then is man ungrateful!

٤٨ فَإِنۡ أَعۡرَضُواْ فَمَآ
أَرۡسَلۡنَٰكَ عَلَيۡهِمۡ حَفِيظًاۖ
إِنۡ عَلَيۡكَ إِلَّا ٱلۡبَلَٰغُۗ
وَإِنَّآ إِذَآ أَذَقۡنَا ٱلۡإِنسَٰنَ
مِنَّا رَحۡمَةٗ فَرِحَ بِهَاۖ
وَإِن تُصِبۡهُمۡ سَيِّئَةُۢ بِمَا قَدَّمَتۡ
أَيۡدِيهِمۡ فَإِنَّ ٱلۡإِنسَٰنَ كَفُورٞ

49. To Allah belongs the dominion
Of the heavens and the earth.
He creates what He wills[4595]
(And plans). He bestows
(Children) male or female
According to His Will (and Plan),

٤٩ لِّلَّهِ مُلۡكُ ٱلسَّمَٰوَٰتِ وَٱلۡأَرۡضِۚ
يَخۡلُقُ مَا يَشَآءُۚ يَهَبُ لِمَنۡ يَشَآءُ إِنَٰثٗا
وَيَهَبُ لِمَن يَشَآءُ ٱلذُّكُورَ

4592. At Judgement no one can escape the consequences of his crimes or deeds. And no one can disavow them or deny them, or by any chance pretend that they do not apply to him.

4593. The warning is now given, that men may repent and do good, and pray for Allah's Mercy and Grace. If the warning is not heeded or is rejected, the prophet of Allah is not responsible for bringing about the Penalty or for forcing people to come to the right Path. He is not a guard set over them to free them from the need of exercising their limited free will. (R).

4594. *Cf.* 30:36. It is a sad reflection that men, when they receive some gift out of Allah's Mercy, exult in their good fortune and attribute it to some merit in themselves, instead of to the Grace and Mercy of Allah, thus missing the real lesson of Life. On the other hand, when they are in trouble, due to their own errors and shortcomings, they fall into despair and blame Allah, instead of blaming themselves. This is rank ingratitude. So they miss the true lesson of Life in the case also.

4595. Verses 49-50 deal, in their ordinary meaning, with Allah's creative power replete with knowledge and continued purpose, contrasted with man's instincts and gropings after knowledge. The mystery of sex and parenthood is referred to in a new light. With reference to children, a parent is often spoken of as the "author" of their being. The growth of population and the proportion of males and females in it have various sociological and psychological implications; yet how little do parents really know about them? The knowledge of science as regards the determination of sex in the embryo is practically nothing. Even if advancing knowledge threw light on what may be called the mechanical aspects of the question, the profounder problems touched by it are beyond the reach of man. Yet they are not governed by chance. Allah has a meaning and purpose in all things, and His power is complete to carry out His purpose.

50. Or He bestows both males[4596]
And females, and He leaves
Barren whom He will:
For He is full
Of knowledge and power.

أَوْ يُزَوِّجُهُمْ ذُكْرَانًا وَإِنَاثًا ۖ وَيَجْعَلُ مَن يَشَاءُ عَقِيمًا ۚ إِنَّهُۥ عَلِيمٌ قَدِيرٌ ﴿٥٠﴾

51. It is not fitting[4597]
For a man that Allah
Should speak to him
Except by inspiration,[4598]
Or from behind a veil,[4599]
Or by the sending
Of a Messenger[4600]
To reveal, with Allah's permission,
What Allah wills: for He
Is Most High, Most Wise.

وَمَا كَانَ لِبَشَرٍ أَن يُكَلِّمَهُ ٱللَّهُ إِلَّا وَحْيًا أَوْ مِن وَرَآئِ حِجَابٍ أَوْ يُرْسِلَ رَسُولًا فَيُوحِيَ بِإِذْنِهِۦ مَا يَشَآءُ ۚ إِنَّهُۥ عَلِيٌّ حَكِيمٌ ﴿٥١﴾

52. And thus have We,
By Our command, sent
Inspiration to thee:
Thou knewest not (before)[4601]

وَكَذَٰلِكَ أَوْحَيْنَآ إِلَيْكَ رُوحًا مِّنْ أَمْرِنَا ۚ مَا كُنتَ تَدْرِى ﴿٥٢﴾

4596. To parents themselves it is a mystery why a male or female child is given at any birth, or how the balance of the two sexes is made up in a family or in large groups of mankind, or why in some cases the womb is barren and the would-be parents are denied the joys and responsibilities of parenthood. But each individual human soul is precious in the Plan of Allah, and all these variations, besides their reactions on parents and on society, have a purpose to fulfil in the large Plan of Allah.

4597. This leads us on to the higher spiritual meaning of verses 49-50, as leading up to verses 51-53. Man is but a speck in Allah's creation. His growth and family relationships are not by any means comparable to Allah's creative acts, whose various stages are referred to in n. 120 to 2:117, n. 916 to 6:94, and n. 923 to 6:98. That being so in the mysteries of man's daily life, how much more profound is the contrast between man and Allah in the apprehension of the higher spiritual problems concerned with Revelation? How can man be fit to speak to Allah? He is not fit. But there are three ways in which Allah, in His infinite Mercy, communicates with man, as described in verses 51-53.

4598. Allah is Most High, Most Wise: man is, in spite of his high destiny, often the lowest of the low (95:5). Yet Allah, out of His infinite Mercy and Grace, has bestowed His Revelation on man. How does it come about? Three ways are mentioned: (1) *Wahyun*, Inspiration: (2) from behind a veil; and (3) by the sending of a Messenger: see the notes following.

Wahyun, Inspiration, is interpreted to be of two kinds: (1) a suggestion thrown by Allah into the heart or mind of man, by which man understands the substance of the Message, whether it is a command or prohibition, or an explanation of a great truth; and (2) verbal or literal inspiration, by which the actual words of Allah are conveyed in human language. (R).

4599. *Behind a veil:* not of course a material veil, but the mystic veil of Light. (R).

Ṣaḥiḥ Muslim relates a tradition that the Prophet said: "His veil is Light: were He to withdraw it, then would the august splendors of His countenance surely consume everything that comes within His Sight." (R).

4600. *Messenger: Rasūl:* the angel Gabriel, through whom the revelations were given to the Holy Prophet. These spiritual visions, conveying the message of Revelation, are the basis of the Qur'ān.

4601. Before the receipt of his mission in his fortieth year, the Holy Prophet, though a man of steadfast virtue and purity and unflinching in his search for Truth (see C. 22-23), was yet unacquainted with Revelation in the highest sense of the term and with the certainty that comes from perfected Faith, or realised nearness to Allah. *Rūḥ*, which I have here translated Inspiration has also been understood by some Commentators to refer to the angel Gabriel, the vehicle of Revelation. The Light of the Qur'ān made all things clear to man, and to the world.

What was Revelation, and
What was Faith; but We
Have made the (Qur'ān)
A Light, wherewith We
Guide such of Our servants
As We will; and verily
Thou dost guide (men)[4602]
To the Straight Way—

مَا الْكِتَٰبُ وَلَا الْإِيمَٰنُ
وَلَٰكِن جَعَلْنَٰهُ نُورًا
نَّهْدِى بِهِۦ مَن نَّشَآءُ مِنْ عِبَادِنَا ۚ
وَإِنَّكَ لَتَهْدِىٓ إِلَىٰ صِرَٰطٍ مُّسْتَقِيمٍ

53. The Way of Allah,[4603]
To Whom belongs
Whatever is in the heavens
And whatever is on earth.
Behold (how) all affairs
Tend towards Allah!

٥٣ صِرَٰطِ اللَّهِ الَّذِى لَهُۥ
مَا فِى السَّمَٰوَٰتِ وَمَا فِى الْأَرْضِ ۗ
أَلَآ إِلَى اللَّهِ تَصِيرُ الْأُمُورُ

4602. The Qur'ān and the inspired Prophet who proclaimed it, are here identified. They were a Guide to men, showing the Straight Way. This Way is described in various ways: for example, see 1:6, and n. 22; 18:1-2, and notes 2326-27; and 90:11-18.

4603. The most comprehensive description of the Straight Way is that it is the Way of Allah, the Way of the Universal Law; for Allah is the source, centre, and goal of all things in heaven and earth. Everything goes back to Him. According to our own understanding we make our own laws, our own standards, and our own institutions. But the ultimate test of their validity or authority is Allah's Will, as revealed to us by His Revelation.

INTRODUCTION TO SŪRAH 43—*AL ZUKHRUF*

This is the fourth Sūrah of the *Ḥā Mīm* series of seven Sūrahs. For their chronology and general theme see the Introduction to S. 40.

This Sūrah deals with the contrasts between the real glory of Truth and Revelation and the false glitter of what people like to believe and worship. It cites the examples of Abraham, Moses, and Jesus, as exposing the False and holding up the Truth. The keyword *(Zukhruf*, Gold Adornments) occurs in verse 38, but the idea occurs all through the Sūrah.

Summary—The Book of Revelation makes things clear, even though the ignorant and foolish mock at it and ignore Allah's Signs: it will last, while its rejecters will perish (43:1-25, and C. 213.).

Abraham exposed the falsehood of traditional worship: the glitter and adornments of this world will not last: what was the end of Pharaoh in his arrogant fight with Moses? (43:26-56, and C. 214).

Jesus was a servant of Allah, but his sectarian followers raised false disputations about him: all is known to Allah, Whose Truth will shine, in spite of unfaith (43:57-89, and C. 215).

C. 213.—Revelation makes everlasting Truths
(43:1-25.) Clear: those who mock merely undo themselves.
Consider the Signs of Allah's gracious kindness
Around you, and glorify Him: attribute not
Unworthy qualities nor any companions
To the One True God. Seek Truth in worship
More than mere ancestral ways,
And shut not out Revelation's Light.

Sūrah 43.

Al Zukhruf (The Gold Adornments)

الجزء الخامس والعشرون سورة الزخرف

In the name of Allah, Most Gracious,
Most Merciful.

بِسۡمِ ٱللَّهِ ٱلرَّحۡمَٰنِ ٱلرَّحِيمِ

1. Ḥā Mīm.[4604]

حمٓ ١

2. By the Book that
Makes things clear—

وَٱلۡكِتَٰبِ ٱلۡمُبِينِ ٢

3. We have made it
A Qur'ān in Arabic,[4605]
That ye may be able
To understand (and learn
wisdom).

إِنَّا جَعَلۡنَٰهُ قُرۡءَٰنًا عَرَبِيّٗا ٣
لَّعَلَّكُمۡ تَعۡقِلُونَ

4. And verily, it is
In the Mother of the Book,[4606]
In Our Presence, high
(In dignity), full of wisdom.

وَإِنَّهُۥ فِيٓ أُمِّ ٱلۡكِتَٰبِ ٤
لَدَيۡنَا لَعَلِيٌّ حَكِيمٌ

5. Shall We then[4607]
Take away the Message
From you and repel (you),
For that ye are a people
Transgressing beyond bounds?

أَفَنَضۡرِبُ عَنكُمُ ٥
ٱلذِّكۡرَ صَفۡحًا
أَن كُنتُمۡ قَوۡمٗا مُّسۡرِفِينَ

6. But how many were[4608]
The prophets We sent
Amongst the peoples of old?

وَكَمۡ أَرۡسَلۡنَا مِن نَّبِيّٖ فِي ٱلۡأَوَّلِينَ ٦

4604. Abbreviated Letters: see Introduction to S. 40, paragraphs 2-4.

4605. *Cf.* 42:7, n. 4533.

4606. *Cf.* 3:7, n. 347; and 13:39, n. 1864. The Mother of the Book, the Foundation of Revelation, the Preserved Tablet *(Lawḥ Maḥfūẓ*, 85:22), is the core or essence of Revelation, the original principle or fountainhead of Allah's Eternal and Universal Law. From this fountainhead are derived all streams of knowledge and wisdom, that flow through Time and feed the intelligence of created minds. The Mother of the Book is in Allah's own Presence, and its dignity and wisdom are more than all we can think of in the spiritual world.

4607. In vouchsafing Revelation, what an inestimable Mercy has Allah conferred on mankind! Yet so many deluded souls are ungrateful, and ignore or oppose its teaching. If it were not for His attributes of Forgiveness and Forbearing He would be justified in withdrawing that Light, but He continues to shed it, that all who will may come and be blessed by it.

4608. In spite of, or because of, man's obstinate and rebellious nature, Allah sent prophet after prophet to the peoples of old, but there was among them always a party that ridiculed them and treated Allah's Signs as naught.

7. And never came there
A prophet to them
But they mocked him.

٧ وَمَا يَأْتِيهِم مِّن نَّبِيٍّ
إِلَّا كَانُوا۟ بِهِۦ يَسْتَهْزِءُونَ

8. So We destroyed (them)—
Stronger in power than these—
And (thus) has passed on[4609]
The Parable of the peoples
Of old.

٨ فَأَهْلَكْنَآ أَشَدَّ مِنْهُم بَطْشًا
وَمَضَىٰ مَثَلُ ٱلْأَوَّلِينَ

9. If thou wert
To question them, 'Who created
The heavens and the earth?'[4610]
They would be sure to reply,
'They were created by (Him),
The Exalted in Power,
Full of Knowledge'—[4611]

٩ وَلَئِن سَأَلْتَهُم
مَّنْ خَلَقَ ٱلسَّمَٰوَٰتِ وَٱلْأَرْضَ
لَيَقُولُنَّ خَلَقَهُنَّ ٱلْعَزِيزُ ٱلْعَلِيمُ

10. (Yea, the same that)[4612]
Has made for you
The earth (like a carpet)[4613]
Spread out, and has made
For you roads (and channels)
Therein, in order that ye
May find guidance (on the way);

١٠ ٱلَّذِى جَعَلَ لَكُمُ ٱلْأَرْضَ
مَهْدًا وَجَعَلَ لَكُمْ فِيهَا سُبُلًا
لَّعَلَّكُمْ تَهْتَدُونَ

11. That sends down
(From time to time)
Rain from the sky
In due measure—[4614]
And We raise to life

١١ وَٱلَّذِى نَزَّلَ مِنَ ٱلسَّمَآءِ
مَآءًۢ بِقَدَرٍ فَأَنشَرْنَا بِهِۦ

4609. The result of rebellion was destruction. And the pagan Makkan generation contemporary with the Prophet are reminded that the peoples of old who were destroyed were, many of them, more powerful than they, and that they, in disobeying Allah's Law, were inviting the same fate for themselves. The events of the past have become Parables for the present and the future.

4610. *Cf.* 29:61 and n. 3493; and 31:25 and n. 3613. This class of men acknowledge Allah's Power and Allah's Knowledge or Wisdom, but do not realise Allah's infinite Mercy and care for His creatures.

4611. Note the beautiful rhetorical figure of speech here. The reply of the inconsistent men who do not follow Allah's Law is turned against themselves. When they acknowledge Allah's Power and Knowledge, their speech is interrupted, and the concomitant qualities of Allah's Mercy and care of His creatures, with pointed reference to the inconsistent ones themselves, is set out in eloquent terms, as completing what they themselves had said, and the right course of conduct is pointed out to them (verses 10-14).

4612. See last note.

4613. *Cf.* 20:53 and n. 2576. *Mihad.* a carpet or bed spread out, implies not only freedom of movement but rest also. The 'roads and channels' carry out the idea of communications and include land routes, sea routes, and airways.

4614. *In due measure: i.e.*, according to needs, as measured by local as well as universal considerations. This applies to normal rainfall: floods and droughts are abnormal conditions, and may be called unusual manifestations of His power, fulfilling some special purpose that we may or may not understand.

Therewith a land that is Dead; even so will ye Be raised (from the dead)—[4615]	بَلْدَةً مَّيْتًا كَذَٰلِكَ تُخْرَجُونَ
12. That has created pairs[4616] In all things, and has made For you ships and cattle[4617] On which ye ride,	﴿١٢﴾ وَالَّذِي خَلَقَ الْأَزْوَاجَ كُلَّهَا وَجَعَلَ لَكُم مِّنَ الْفُلْكِ وَالْأَنْعَامِ مَا تَرْكَبُونَ
13. In order that ye may Sit firm and square On their backs, and when So seated, ye may Celebrate the (kind) favour[4618] Of your Lord, and say, "Glory to Him Who Has subjected these To our (use), for we Could never have accomplished This (by ourselves)".	﴿١٣﴾ لِتَسْتَوُوا عَلَىٰ ظُهُورِهِ ثُمَّ تَذْكُرُوا نِعْمَةَ رَبِّكُمْ إِذَا اسْتَوَيْتُمْ عَلَيْهِ وَتَقُولُوا سُبْحَانَ الَّذِي سَخَّرَ لَنَا هَٰذَا وَمَا كُنَّا لَهُ مُقْرِنِينَ
14. "And to our Lord, surely,[4619] Must we turn back!"	﴿١٤﴾ وَإِنَّا إِلَىٰ رَبِّنَا لَمُنقَلِبُونَ
15. Yet they attribute[4620] To some of His servants A share with Him (In His godhead)! Truly is man a blasphemous Ingrate avowed!	﴿١٥﴾ وَجَعَلُوا لَهُ مِنْ عِبَادِهِ جُزْءًا إِنَّ الْإِنسَانَ لَكَفُورٌ مُّبِينٌ

4615. The clause 'And We raise. . .(from the dead)' is parenthetical. *Cf.* 35:9, n. 3881. Note the transition from the third to the first person, to mark the Resurrection as a special act of Allah as distinguished from the ordinary processes of nature ordained by Allah.

4616. *Cf.* n. 2578 to 20:53. Also see 36:36, n. 3981.

4617. By analogy all means of transport, including horses, camels, ships, steamers, railways, aeroplanes, airships, etc. The domestication of animals as well as the invention of mechanical means of transport require a skill and ingenuity in man, which are referred to Allah as His gifts or endowments to man.

4618. See last note. People of understanding attribute all good to its true and original source *viz.*: Allah.

4619. Men of understanding, every time they take a journey on earth, are reminded of that more momentous journey which they are taking of the back of Time to Eternity. Have they tamed Time to their lawful use, or do they allow Time to run away with them wildly to where they know not? Their goal is Allah, and their thoughts are ever with Allah.

4620. As a contrast to the men of true understanding are the ungrateful blasphemous creatures, who offer a share in godhead to others besides Allah! They imagine sons and daughters to Allah, and forget the true lesson of the whole of Creation, which points to the Unity of Allah. This theme is further developed in the following Section.

SECTION 2.

16. What! Has He taken[4621]
Daughters out of what He
Himself creates, and granted
To you sons for choice?

١٦ أَمِ اتَّخَذَ مِمَّا يَخْلُقُ بَنَاتٍ
وَأَصْفَىٰكُم بِالْبَنِينَ

17. When news is brought[4622]
To one of them of (the birth
Of) what he sets up
As a likeness to (Allah)
Most Gracious, his face
Darkens, and he is filled
With inward grief!

١٧ وَإِذَا بُشِّرَ أَحَدُهُم
بِمَا ضَرَبَ لِلرَّحْمَٰنِ مَثَلًا
ظَلَّ وَجْهُهُۥ مُسْوَدًّا وَهُوَ كَظِيمٌ

18. Is then one brought up[4623]
Among trinkets, and unable
To give a clear account
In a dispute (to be
Associated with Allah)?

١٨ أَوَمَن يُنَشَّؤُا فِي الْحِلْيَةِ
وَهُوَ فِي الْخِصَامِ غَيْرُ مُبِينٍ

19. And they make into females
Angels who themselves serve[4624]
Allah. Did they witness
Their creation? Their evidence
Will be recorded, and they
Will be called to account!

١٩ وَجَعَلُوا الْمَلَٰٓئِكَةَ الَّذِينَ هُمْ
عِبَٰدُ الرَّحْمَٰنِ إِنَٰثًا ۚ أَشَهِدُوا خَلْقَهُمْ ۚ
سَتُكْتَبُ شَهَٰدَتُهُمْ وَيُسْـَٔلُونَ

20. ("Ah!") they say, "If
It had been the Will[4625]
Of (Allah) Most Gracious,

٢٠ وَقَالُوا لَوْ شَآءَ الرَّحْمَٰنُ

4621. To imagine goddesses (female gods) or mothers or daughters to Allah was particularly blasphemous in the mouths of people who held the female sex in contempt. Such were the pagan Arabs, and such (it is to be feared) are some of the moderns. They wince when a daughter is born to them and hanker after sons. With that mentality, how can they attribute daughters to Allah?

4622. *Cf.* 16:57-59 and notes. With scathing irony it is pointed out that what they hate and are ashamed of for themselves they attribute to Allah!

4623. The softer sex is usually brought up among trinkets and ornaments, and, on account of the retiring modesty which for the sex is a virtue, is unable to stand up boldly in a fight and give clear indications of the will to win. Is that the sort of quality to be associated with Allah?

4624. Angels for grace and purity may be compared to the most graceful and purest forms we know. But it is wrong to attribute sex to them. They are servants and messengers of Allah and so far from being rivals seeking worship, are always engaged in devotion and service. If any persons invent blasphemies about Allah, such blasphemies will form a big blot in their Book of Deeds, and they will be called to account for them.

4625. Worsted in argument they resort to a dishonest sarcasm. 'We worship these deities: if Allah does not wish us to do so, why does He not prevent us?" In throwing the responsibility on Allah, they ignore the limited free will on which their whole life is based. They are really playing with truth. They are arguing against their own knowledge. They have no authority in any scripture, and indeed they are so slippery that they hold fast to no scripture at all.

We should not have
Worshipped such (deities)!"
Of that they have
No knowledge! they
Do nothing but lie![4626]

مَا عَبَدْنَٰهُم مَّا لَهُم بِذَٰلِكَ مِنْ عِلْمٍ
إِنْ هُمْ إِلَّا يَخْرُصُونَ

21. What! have We given them
A Book before this,
To which they are
Holding fast?

أَمْ ءَاتَيْنَٰهُمْ كِتَٰبًا مِّن قَبْلِهِۦ (٢١)
فَهُم بِهِۦ مُسْتَمْسِكُونَ

22. Nay! they say: "We found[4627]
Our fathers following
A certain religion,
And we do guide ourselves
By their footsteps."

بَلْ قَالُوٓا۟ إِنَّا وَجَدْنَآ ءَابَآءَنَا (٢٢)
عَلَىٰٓ أُمَّةٍ وَإِنَّا عَلَىٰٓ ءَاثَٰرِهِم مُّهْتَدُونَ

23. Just in the same way,
Whenever We sent a Warner
Before thee to any people,
The wealthy ones among
them[4628]
Said: "We found our fathers
Following a certain religion,
And we will certainly
Follow in their footsteps."

وَكَذَٰلِكَ مَآ أَرْسَلْنَا مِن قَبْلِكَ (٢٣)
فِى قَرْيَةٍ مِّن نَّذِيرٍ إِلَّا قَالَ مُتْرَفُوهَآ
إِنَّا وَجَدْنَآ ءَابَآءَنَا عَلَىٰٓ أُمَّةٍ
وَإِنَّا عَلَىٰٓ ءَاثَٰرِهِم مُّقْتَدُونَ

24. He said: "What![4629]
Even if I brought you
Better guidance than that
Which ye found
Your fathers following?"
They said: "For us,
We deny that ye (prophets)
Are sent (on a mission
At all)."

قَٰلَ أَوَلَوْ جِئْتُكُم بِأَهْدَىٰ (٢٤)
مِمَّا وَجَدتُّمْ عَلَيْهِ ءَابَآءَكُمْ
قَالُوٓا۟ إِنَّا بِمَآ أُرْسِلْتُم بِهِۦ
كَٰفِرُونَ

25. So We extracted retribution
From them: now see

فَٱنتَقَمْنَا مِنْهُمْ فَٱنظُرْ (٢٥)

4626. *Cf.* 6:116.

4627. Then comes the argument about ancestral custom, which was repudiated by Abraham (see verses 26-28 below). Indeed a good reply to ancestral custom in the case of the Arabs was the example of Abraham, the True in Faith, for Abraham was the common ancestor of the Arabs and the Israelites.

4628. It is some privileged position, and not ancestral custom, which is really at the bottom of much falsehood and hypocrisy in the world. This has been again and again in religious history.

4629. The Warner or messenger pointed out the merits and the truth of his teaching, and how superior it was to what they called their ancestral customs. But they denied his mission itself or the validity of any such mission. In other words they did not believe in inspiration or revelation, and went on in their evil ways, with the inevitable result that they brought themselves to destruction.

What was the end
Of those who rejected (Truth)!

كَيْفَ كَانَ عَٰقِبَةُ ٱلْمُكَذِّبِينَ

C. 214.—(43:26-56.) If the Arabs hark back to ancestry, why not
Accept the Faith of Abraham the True?
He joined not gods with Allah. Spiritual
Worth is measured by other things
Than gold or silver or the adornments
Of this world. These are but things of the hour.
The lasting gifts are those of the Hereafter.
If Israel goes back to Moses, how he
Was mocked by Pharaoh in his pride
Of power! Yet Pharaoh and his deluded
People perished: so ends the pomp
And power and vanity of this world!

SECTION 3.

26. Behold! Abraham said[4630]
To his father and his people:
"I do indeed clear myself
Of what ye worship:"

٢٦ وَإِذْ قَالَ إِبْرَٰهِيمُ لِأَبِيهِ وَقَوْمِهِۦٓ
إِنَّنِى بَرَآءٌ مِّمَّا تَعْبُدُونَ

27. "(I worship) only Him
Who made me, and He
Will certainly guide me."

٢٧ إِلَّا ٱلَّذِى فَطَرَنِى فَإِنَّهُۥ سَيَهْدِينِ

28. And he left it
As a Word[4631]
To endure among those
Who came after him,
That they may turn back
(To Allah).

٢٨ وَجَعَلَهَا كَلِمَةًۢ
بَاقِيَةً فِى عَقِبِهِۦ
لَعَلَّهُمْ يَرْجِعُونَ

29. Yea, I have given[4632]
The good things of this life
To these (men) and

٢٩ بَلْ مَتَّعْتُ هَٰٓؤُلَآءِ

4630. The plea of ancestral ways is refuted by the example of Abraham, in two ways: (1) he gave up the ancestral cults followed by his father and his people, and followed the true Way, even at some sacrifice to himself; and (2) he was an ancestor of the Arabs, and if the Arabs stood on ancestral ways, why should they not follow their good ancestor Abraham, rather than their bad ancestors who fell into evil? See n. 4627 above. The incident in Abraham's story referred to here will be found in 21:51-70.

4631. *A Word: i.e.*, the Gospel of Unity, *viz.*,: "I worship only Him Who made me", as in verse 27. This was his teaching, and this was his legacy to those who followed him. He hoped that they would keep it sacred, and uphold the standard of Unity. *Cf.* C. 7-8. *Cf.* also 37:108-111.

4632. Note the first person singular, as showing Allah's personal solicitude and care for the descendants of Abraham in both branches. The context here refers to the prosperity enjoyed by Makkah and the Makkans until they rejected the truth of Islam when it was preached in their midst by a messenger whose Message was as clear as the light of the sun.

Their fathers, until the Truth
Has come to them,
And a Messenger
Making things clear.

وَءَابَآءَهُمْ حَتَّىٰ
جَآءَهُمُ ٱلْحَقُّ وَرَسُولٌ مُّبِينٌ

30. But when the Truth came
To them, they said:
"This is sorcery, and we[4633]
Do reject it."

٣٠ وَلَمَّا جَآءَهُمُ ٱلْحَقُّ قَالُوا۟
هَٰذَا سِحْرٌ وَإِنَّا بِهِۦ كَٰفِرُونَ

31. Also, they say: "Why
Is not this Qur'ān sent
Down to some leading man
In either of the two[4634]
(Chief) cities?"

٣١ وَقَالُوا۟ لَوْلَا نُزِّلَ هَٰذَا ٱلْقُرْءَانُ
عَلَىٰ رَجُلٍ مِّنَ ٱلْقَرْيَتَيْنِ عَظِيمٍ

32. Is it they who would portion out
The Mercy of thy Lord?[4635]
It is We Who portion out
Between them their livelihood
In the life of this world:
And We raise some of them
Above others in ranks,
So that some may command
Work from others.
But the Mercy of thy Lord
Is better than the (wealth)
Which they amass.

٣٢ أَهُمْ يَقْسِمُونَ رَحْمَتَ رَبِّكَ ۚ
نَحْنُ قَسَمْنَا بَيْنَهُم مَّعِيشَتَهُمْ فِى ٱلْحَيَوٰةِ ٱلدُّنْيَا ۚ
وَرَفَعْنَا بَعْضَهُمْ فَوْقَ بَعْضٍ دَرَجَٰتٍ
لِّيَتَّخِذَ بَعْضُهُم بَعْضًا سُخْرِيًّا ۗ
وَرَحْمَتُ رَبِّكَ خَيْرٌ مِّمَّا يَجْمَعُونَ

33. And were it not that[4636]
(All) men might become

٣٣ وَلَوْلَآ أَن يَكُونَ ٱلنَّاسُ

4633. When the pagan Makkans could not understand the wonderful power and authority with which the Holy Prophet preached, they called his God-given influence sorcery!

4634. The world judges by its own low standards. From a worldly point of view, the Holy Prophet was poor and an orphan. Why, they thought, should he be so richly endowed in spiritual knowledge and power? If such a gift had to come to a man among them, it was the right (they foolishly said) of one of the chiefs in either the sacred city of Makkah, or the fertile garden city of Ṭa'if!

4635. That is, spiritual gifts, those connected with Revelation. What audacity or folly in them to claim to divide or distribute them among themselves? They may think they are distributing the good things of this world among themselves. In a sense that may be true, but even here, their own power and initiative are very limited. Even here it is Allah's Will on which all depends. In His wisdom Allah allows some to grow in power or riches, and command work from others, and various relative gradations are established. Men scramble for these good things of this world, but they are of no value compared to the spiritual gifts.

4636. So little value is attached in the spiritual world to silver or gold, or worldly ranks or adornments, that they would freely be at the disposal of everyone who denied or blasphemed Allah, were it not that in that case there would be too great temptation placed in the way of men, for they might all scramble to sell their spiritual life for wealth! They might have silver roofs and stairways, silver doors and thrones, and all kinds of adornments of gold. But Allah does not allow too great a temptation to be placed in the path of men. He distributes these things differently, some to unjust men, and some to just men, in various degrees, so that the possession of these is no test either of an unjust or a just life. His wisdom searches out motives far more subtle and delicate than any we are even aware of.

Of one (evil) way of life,
We would provide,
For everyone that blasphemes
Against (Allah) Most Gracious,
Silver roofs for their houses,
And (silver) stairways
On which to go up,

أمة وحدة لجعلنا
لمن يكفر بالرحمن لبيوتهم سقفا
من فضة ومعارج عليها يظهرون

34. And (silver) doors
To their houses, and thrones
(Of silver) on which
They could recline,

٣٤ ولبيوتهم أبوابا
وسررا عليها يتكئون

35. And also adornments[4637]
Of gold. But all this
Were nothing but conveniences
Of the present life:
The Hereafter, in the sight
Of thy Lord, is
For the Righteous.

٣٥ وزخرفا وإن كل
ذلك لما متع الحيوة الدنيا
والآخرة عند ربك للمتقين

SECTION 4.

36. If anyone withdraws himself[4638]
From remembrance
Of (Allah) Most Gracious,
We appoint for him
An evil one, to be
An intimate companion to him.

٣٦ ومن يعش عن ذكر
الرحمن نقيض له شيطنا
فهو له قرين

37. Such (evil ones) really
Hinder them from the Path,[4639]
But they think that they
Are being guided aright!

٣٧ وإنهم ليصدونهم عن السبيل
ويحسبون أنهم مهتدون

38. At length, when (such a one)[4640]
Comes to Us, he says

٣٨ حتى إذا جاءنا قال

4637. *Adornments of gold:* the keyword to this Sūrah. All false glitter and adornments of this world are as naught. They more often hinder than help.

4638. If men deliberately put away the remembrance of Allah from their minds, the natural consequence, under Allah's decree, is that they join on with evil. Like consorts with like. We can generalise evil in the abstract, but it takes concrete shape in our life companions.

4639. The downward course in evil is rapid. But the most tragic consequence is that evil persuades its victims to believe that they are pursuing good. They think evil to be their good. They go deeper and deeper into the mire, and become more and more callous. *Them* and *they* represent the generic plural of anyone who "withdraws himself from... Allah" (see last verse).

4640. If ever the presence of Allah is felt, or at the time of Judgement, a glimmering of truth comes to the deceived soul, and it cries to its evil companions in its agony, "Would that I had never come across thee! Would that we were separated poles apart!" But it cannot shake off evil. By deliberate choice it had put itself in its snare.

(To his evil companion):
"Would that between me
And thee were the distance
Of East and West!"[4641] Ah!
Evil is the companion (indeed)!

يَٰلَيْتَ بَيْنِى وَبَيْنَكَ
بُعْدَ ٱلْمَشْرِقَيْنِ فَبِئْسَ ٱلْقَرِينُ

39. When ye have done wrong,[4642]
It will avail you nothing,
That day, that ye shall be
Partners in punishment!

٣٩ وَلَن يَنفَعَكُمُ ٱلْيَوْمَ
إِذ ظَّلَمْتُمْ أَنَّكُمْ فِى ٱلْعَذَابِ مُشْتَرِكُونَ

40. Canst thou then make[4643]
The deaf to hear, or give
Direction to the blind
Or to such as (wander)
In manifest error?[4644]

٤٠ أَفَأَنتَ تُسْمِعُ ٱلصُّمَّ أَوْ تَهْدِى
ٱلْعُمْىَ وَمَن كَانَ فِى ضَلَٰلٍ مُّبِينٍ

41. Even if We take thee[4645]
Away, We shall be sure
To exact retribution from them,

٤١ فَإِمَّا نَذْهَبَنَّ بِكَ فَإِنَّا مِنْهُم مُّنتَقِمُونَ

42. Or We shall show thee
That (accomplished) which We
Have promised them:
For verily We shall
Prevail over them.

٤٢ أَوْ نُرِيَنَّكَ ٱلَّذِى وَعَدْنَٰهُمْ
فَإِنَّا عَلَيْهِم مُّقْتَدِرُونَ

43. So hold thou fast[4646]
To the Revelation sent down
To thee: verily thou
Art on a Straight Way.

٤٣ فَٱسْتَمْسِكْ بِٱلَّذِىٓ أُوحِىَ إِلَيْكَ
إِنَّكَ عَلَىٰ صِرَٰطٍ مُّسْتَقِيمٍ

4641. *Distance of East and West:* literally, 'distance of the two Easts'. Most Commentators understand in this sense, but some construe the phrase as meaning the distance of the extreme points of the rising of the sun, between the summer solstice and the winter solstice. *Cf.* n. 4034 to 37:5. A good equivalent idiom in English would be "poles apart", for they could never meet.

4642. All partners in evil will certainly share in the punishment, but that is no consolation to any individual soul. Evil desires the evil of others, but that does not diminish its own torment, or get rid of the personal responsibility of each individual soul.

4643. *Cf.* 30:52-53. The evil go headlong into sin, and sink deeper and deeper until their spiritual faculties are deadened, and no outside help can bring them back. Allah's grace they have rejected.

4644. There is hope for a person who wanders in quest of truth, and even for one who wanders through mistake or by weakness of will. But there is none for one who, by deliberate choice, plunges into "manifest error", *i.e.*, error which anyone can see.

4645. *Cf.* 8:30: "how the Unbelievers plotted against thee, to keep thee in bonds, or slay thee, or get thee out (of thy home)." They were always plotting against the Holy Prophet in his Makkan period. But even if their plots had succeeded against human beings, they could not defeat Allah's Plan, nor escape the just punishment of their deeds. *Cf.* also 10:46, and n. 1438.

4646. Let the wicked rage, say what they like, or do their worst: the Prophet of Allah is encouraged to go forward steadfastly in the Light given him, for he is on a Path that leads straight to Allah. (R).

44. The (Qur'an) is indeed
The Message,[4647] for thee
And for thy people;
And soon shall ye
(All) be brought to account.

وَإِنَّهُۥ لَذِكْرٌ لَّكَ وَلِقَوْمِكَ ۖ ﴿٤٤﴾
وَسَوْفَ تُسْـَٔلُونَ

45. And question thou our
messengers[4648]
Whom We sent before thee;
Did We appoint any deities
Other than (Allah) Most Gracious,
To be worshipped?

وَسْـَٔلْ مَنْ أَرْسَلْنَا مِن قَبْلِكَ ﴿٤٥﴾
مِن رُّسُلِنَآ أَجَعَلْنَا مِن دُونِ ٱلرَّحْمَٰنِ
ءَالِهَةً يُعْبَدُونَ

SECTION 5.

46. We did send Moses[4649]
Aforetime, with Our Signs,
To Pharaoh and his Chiefs:
He said, "I am a messenger
Of the Lord of the Worlds."

وَلَقَدْ أَرْسَلْنَا مُوسَىٰ بِـَٔايَٰتِنَآ ﴿٤٦﴾
إِلَىٰ فِرْعَوْنَ وَمَلَإِي۟هِۦ
فَقَالَ إِنِّى رَسُولُ رَبِّ ٱلْعَٰلَمِينَ

47. But when he came to them
With Our Signs, behold,
They ridiculed them.[4650]

فَلَمَّا جَآءَهُم بِـَٔايَٰتِنَآ إِذَا هُم مِّنْهَا يَضْحَكُونَ ﴿٤٧﴾

48. We showed them Sign[4651]
After Sign, each greater
Than its fellow, and We
Seized them with Punishment,
In order that they
Might turn (to Us).

وَمَا نُرِيهِم مِّنْ ءَايَةٍ ﴿٤٨﴾
إِلَّا هِىَ أَكْبَرُ مِنْ أُخْتِهَا ۖ
وَأَخَذْنَٰهُم بِٱلْعَذَابِ لَعَلَّهُمْ يَرْجِعُونَ

49. And they said, "O thou[4652]
Sorcerer! Invoke thy Lord

وَقَالُوا۟ يَٰٓأَيُّهَ ٱلسَّاحِرُ ٱدْعُ لَنَا رَبَّكَ ﴿٤٩﴾

4647. *Dhikrun:* Message, Remembrance, Cause of remembrance, Memorial, Title for remembrance to posterity. Thus two meanings emerge, not necessarily mutually exclusive. (1) The Qur'an brings a Message of Truth and Guidance to the Prophet, and his people; (2) the Revelation of the Qur'an raises the rank of the Prophet, and the people among whom, and in whose language, it was promulgated, making them worthy of remembrance in the world's history for all time. But the honour also carried its responsibilities. All who hear it must give an account of how far they profit by it spiritually.

4648. That is, by examining their Message, and asking the learned among their real followers. It will be found that no Religion really teaches the worship of other than Allah.

4649. For the story of Moses in detail, see 7:103-137, but especially 7:104, 130-136.

4650. For the mockery of Moses and his Signs see 17:101; also below, 43:49, 52-53.

4651. Moses showed them nine Clear Signs: see n. 1091 to 7:133; also 17:101. Each one of them in its own setting and circumstances was greater than any of its "sister" Signs. The object was if possible to reclaim as many Egyptians as possible from their defiance of Allah.

4652. This speech is half a mockery, and half a ruse. In spite of their unbelief, they had fear in their minds, and in order to stop the plagues, one after another, they promised to obey Allah, and when the particular plague was removed, they again became obdurate. See 7:133-135.

For us according to
His covenant with thee;
For we shall truly
Accept guidance."

بِمَا عَهِدَ عِندَكَ إِنَّنَا لَمُهْتَدُونَ

50. But when We removed
The Penalty from them,
Behold, they broke their word.

٥٠ فَلَمَّا كَشَفْنَا عَنْهُمُ الْعَذَابَ إِذَا هُمْ يَنكُثُونَ

51. And Pharaoh proclaimed
Among his people, saying:
"O my people! Does not
The dominion of Egypt
Belong to me, (witness)[4653]
These streams flowing
Underneath my (palace)? What!
See ye not then?

٥١ وَنَادَىٰ فِرْعَوْنُ فِي قَوْمِهِ قَالَ يَٰقَوْمِ أَلَيْسَ لِي مُلْكُ مِصْرَ وَهَٰذِهِ الْأَنْهَٰرُ تَجْرِي مِن تَحْتِيٓ أَفَلَا تُبْصِرُونَ

52. "Am I not better
Than this (Moses), who
Is a contemptible wretch[4654]
And can scarcely
Express himself clearly?

٥٢ أَمْ أَنَا۠ خَيْرٌ مِّنْ هَٰذَا الَّذِي هُوَ مَهِينٌ وَلَا يَكَادُ يُبِينُ

53. "Then why are not[4655]
Gold bracelets bestowed
On him, or (why)
Come (not) with him
Angels accompanying him
In procession?"

٥٣ فَلَوْلَآ أُلْقِيَ عَلَيْهِ أَسْوِرَةٌ مِّن ذَهَبٍ أَوْ جَآءَ مَعَهُ الْمَلَٰٓئِكَةُ مُقْتَرِنِينَ

54. Thus did he make
Fools of his people,
And they obeyed him:
Truly were they a people
Rebellious (against Allah).

٥٤ فَاسْتَخَفَّ قَوْمَهُۥ فَأَطَاعُوهُ إِنَّهُمْ كَانُوا۟ قَوْمًا فَٰسِقِينَ

4653. The *wāw* here in Arabic is the *Wāw ḥāliyah:* the abundant streams from the Nile flowing beneath his palace being evidence of his power, prosperity, and sovereignty. The Nile made (and makes) Egypt, and the myth of the god Osiris was a compound of the myths of the Nile and the sun. The Pharaoh, therefore, as commanding the Nile, commanded the gods who personified Egypt. He boasted of water, and he perished in water,—a fitting punishment!

4654. Being a despised Israelite in any case, and having further an impediment in his speech. See 20:27, and notes 2552-53.

4655. Gold bracelets and gold chains were possibly among the insignia of royalty. In any case they betokened wealth, and the materialists judge a man's worth by his wealth and his following and equipage. So Pharaoh wanted to see Moses, if he had any position in the spiritual kingdom, invested with gold bracelets, and followed by a great train of angels as his Knight-companions! The same kind of proofs were demanded by the materialistic Quraysh of our Holy Prophet. These were puerilities, but such puerilities go down with the crowd. Barring a few Egyptians who believed in Allah and in the Message of Moses, the rest of Pharaoh's entourage followed Pharaoh in his pursuit of revenge, and were drowned in the Red Sea.

55. When at length they[4656]
Provoked Us, We exacted
Retribution from them, and
We drowned them all.[4657]

﴿٥٥﴾ فَلَمَّآ ءَاسَفُونَا ٱنتَقَمْنَا مِنْهُمْ فَأَغْرَقْنَٰهُمْ أَجْمَعِينَ

56. And We made them
(A people) of the Past[4658]
And an Example
To later ages.

﴿٥٦﴾ فَجَعَلْنَٰهُمْ سَلَفًا وَمَثَلًا لِّلْءَاخِرِينَ

C. 215. — If Christians go back to Jesus, he
(43:57-89.) Was but a man and a servant of Allah:
He came to still the jarring sects,
Not to create a new one. He preached
The One True God, his Lord. So give up
Disputing, and join in devotion to Allah.
That is the Way to the Garden of Bliss,
But the opposite leads to the Fire. Beware!
The Truth has come, and Allah knows how you
Receive it. He is the Lord of power and mercy.
The Truth must prevail: resist it not.

SECTION 6.

57. When (Jesus) the son[4659]
Of Mary is held up
As an example, behold
Thy people raise a clamour
Thereat (in ridicule)!

﴿٥٧﴾ وَلَمَّا ضُرِبَ ٱبْنُ مَرْيَمَ مَثَلًا إِذَا قَوْمُكَ مِنْهُ يَصِدُّونَ

58. And they say, "Are
Our gods best, or he?"
This they set forth
To thee, only by way

﴿٥٨﴾ وَقَالُوٓا۟ ءَأَٰلِهَتُنَا خَيْرٌ أَمْ هُوَ ۚ مَا ضَرَبُوهُ لَكَ

4656. Allah is long-suffering, and gives many and many opportunities to the most hardened sinners for repentance. But at length comes a time when His justice is provoked, and the inevitable punishment follows.

4657. *Cf.* 7:136.

4658. Pharaoh and his hosts were blotted out, and became as a tale of the past. Their story is an instructive warning and example to future generations. The later course of Egyptian religion after the Exodus is referred to in Appendix V.

4659. Jesus was a man, and a prophet to the Children of Israel, "though his own received him not". Some of the churches that were founded after him worshipped him as "God" and as "the son of God", as do the Trinitarian churches to the present day. The orthodox churches did so in the time of the Holy Prophet. When the doctrine of Unity was renewed, and the false worship of others besides Allah was strictly prohibited, all false gods were condemned, *e.g.*, at 21:98. The pagan Arabs looked upon Jesus as being in the same category as their false gods, and could not see why a foreign cult, or a foreign god, as they viewed him, should be considered better than their own gods or idols. There was no substance in this, but mere mockery, and verbal quibbling. Jesus was one of the greater prophets: he was not a god, nor was he responsible for the quibbling subtleties of the Athanasian Creed.

Of disputation: yea, they
Are a contentious people.

إِلَّا جَدَلًا بَلْ هُمْ قَوْمٌ خَصِمُونَ

59. He was no more than
A servant: We granted
Our favour to him,
And We made him
An example to the Children[4660]
Of Israel.

٥٩ إِنْ هُوَ إِلَّا عَبْدٌ
أَنْعَمْنَا عَلَيْهِ وَجَعَلْنَٰهُ مَثَلًا
لِّبَنِىٓ إِسْرَٰٓءِيلَ

60. And if it were Our Will,[4661]
We could make angels
From amongst you, succeeding
Each other on the earth.

٦٠ وَلَوْ نَشَآءُ لَجَعَلْنَا مِنكُم
مَّلَٰٓئِكَةً فِى ٱلْأَرْضِ يَخْلُفُونَ

61. And (Jesus) shall be[4662]
A Sign (for the coming
Of) the Hour (of Judgement):
Therefore have no doubt
About the (Hour), but
Follow ye Me: this
Is a Straight Way.

٦١ وَإِنَّهُۥ لَعِلْمٌ لِّلسَّاعَةِ
فَلَا تَمْتَرُنَّ بِهَا وَٱتَّبِعُونِ
هَٰذَا صِرَٰطٌ مُّسْتَقِيمٌ

62. Let not the Evil One
Hinder you: for he is
To you an enemy avowed.

٦٢ وَلَا يَصُدَّنَّكُمُ ٱلشَّيْطَٰنُ
إِنَّهُۥ لَكُمْ عَدُوٌّ مُّبِينٌ

63. When Jesus came
With Clear Signs, he said:
"Now have I come
To you with Wisdom,[4663]
And in order to make
Clear to you some
Of the (points) on which
Ye dispute: therefore fear Allah
And obey me.

٦٣ وَلَمَّا جَآءَ عِيسَىٰ بِٱلْبَيِّنَٰتِ
قَالَ قَدْ جِئْتُكُم بِٱلْحِكْمَةِ وَلِأُبَيِّنَ
لَكُم بَعْضَ ٱلَّذِى تَخْتَلِفُونَ فِيهِ
فَٱتَّقُوا۟ ٱللَّهَ وَأَطِيعُونِ

4660. A reference to the limited mission of the prophet Jesus, whose Gospel to the Jews only survives in uncertain fragmentary forms.

4661. If it were said that the birth of Jesus without a father sets him above other prophets, the creation of angels without either father or mother would set them still higher, especially as angels do not eat and drink and are not subject to physical laws. But angels are not higher.

4662. This is understood to refer to the second coming of Jesus in the Last Days before the Resurrection, when he will destroy the false doctrines that pass under his name, and prepare the way for the universal acceptance of Islam, the Gospel of Unity and Peace, the Straight Way of the Qur'an.

4663. True wisdom consists in understanding the unity of the Divine purpose and the Unity of the Divine Personality. The man Jesus came to reconcile the jarring sects in Israel, and his true teaching was just the same as that which was expounded in a wider form by Islam. He did not claim to be God; why should not the Christians follow the doctrine of Unity rather than what has become their ancestral and traditional custom?

64. "For Allah, He is my Lord[4664]
And your Lord: so worship
Ye Him: this is
A Straight Way."

إِنَّ ٱللَّهَ هُوَ رَبِّى وَرَبُّكُمْ فَٱعْبُدُوهُ هَٰذَا صِرَٰطٌ مُّسْتَقِيمٌ ﴿٦٤﴾

65. But sects from among
Themselves fell into disagreement:
Then woe to the wrongdoers,
From the Penalty
Of a Grievous Day!

فَٱخْتَلَفَ ٱلْأَحْزَابُ مِنۢ بَيْنِهِمْ فَوَيْلٌ لِّلَّذِينَ ظَلَمُوا۟ مِنْ عَذَابِ يَوْمٍ أَلِيمٍ ﴿٦٥﴾

66. Do they only wait[4665]
For the Hour—that it
Should come on them
All of a sudden,
While they perceive not?

هَلْ يَنظُرُونَ إِلَّا ٱلسَّاعَةَ أَن تَأْتِيَهُم بَغْتَةً وَهُمْ لَا يَشْعُرُونَ ﴿٦٦﴾

67. Friends on that Day[4666]
Will be foes, one
To another—except
The Righteous.

ٱلْأَخِلَّآءُ يَوْمَئِذٍۭ بَعْضُهُمْ لِبَعْضٍ عَدُوٌّ إِلَّا ٱلْمُتَّقِينَ ﴿٦٧﴾

SECTION 7.

68. My devotees![4667]
No fear shall be
On you that Day,
Nor shall ye grieve—

يَٰعِبَادِ لَا خَوْفٌ عَلَيْكُمُ ٱلْيَوْمَ وَلَآ أَنتُمْ تَحْزَنُونَ ﴿٦٨﴾

69. (Being) those who have believed
In Our Signs and bowed
(Their wills to Ours) in Islam.

ٱلَّذِينَ ءَامَنُوا۟ بِـَٔايَٰتِنَا وَكَانُوا۟ مُسْلِمِينَ ﴿٦٩﴾

4664. In verses 26-28 an appeal is made to the pagan Arabs, that Islam is their own religion, the religion of Abraham their ancestor; in verses 46-54, an appeal is made to the Jews that Islam is the same religion as was taught by Moses, and that they should not allow their leaders to make fools of them; in verses 57-65 an appeal is made to the Christians that Islam is the same religion as was taught by Jesus, and that they should give up their sectarian attitude and follow the universal religion, which shows the Straight Way.

4665. *Cf.* 12:107. What is there to wait for? The Hour of Judgement may come at any moment. It will come all of a sudden before they realise that it is on them. They should make up their minds to give up misleading disputations and come to the Straight Path.

4666. The hatred and spite, which are associated with evil, will be felt with peculiar intensity in that period of agony. That itself would be a punishment, from which the righteous will be free. The righteous will have passed all perils of falling into wrong frames of mind.

4667. The devotion and service to Allah result in the soul being made free from all fear and sorrow, as regards the past, present, and future, if we may take an analogy from Time for a timeless state. Such devotion and service are shown by (1) believing in Allah's Signs, which means understanding and accepting His Will, and (2) by merging our will completely in His universal Will, which means being in tune with the Infinite, and acting in all things to further His Kingdom.

70. Enter ye the Garden,[4668]
Ye and your wives,
In (beauty and) rejoicing.

٧٠ ٱدْخُلُوا۟ ٱلْجَنَّةَ أَنتُمْ
وَأَزْوَٰجُكُمْ تُحْبَرُونَ

71. To them will be passed[4669]
Round, dishes and goblets
Of gold: there will be
There all that the souls
Could desire, all that
The eyes could delight in:
And ye shall abide
Therein (for aye).

٧١ يُطَافُ عَلَيْهِم
بِصِحَافٍ مِّن ذَهَبٍ وَأَكْوَابٍ ۖ
وَفِيهَا مَا تَشْتَهِيهِ ٱلْأَنفُسُ وَتَلَذُّ ٱلْأَعْيُنُ ۖ
وَأَنتُمْ فِيهَا خَٰلِدُونَ

72. Such will be the Garden
Of which ye are made[4670]
Heirs for your (good) deeds
(In life).

٧٢ وَتِلْكَ ٱلْجَنَّةُ ٱلَّتِىٓ
أُورِثْتُمُوهَا بِمَا كُنتُمْ تَعْمَلُونَ

73. Ye shall have therein
Abundance of fruit,[4671] from which
Ye shall have satisfaction.[4672]

٧٣ لَكُمْ فِيهَا فَٰكِهَةٌ
كَثِيرَةٌ مِّنْهَا تَأْكُلُونَ

74. The sinners will be
In the Punishment of Hell,
To dwell therein (for aye):

٧٤ إِنَّ ٱلْمُجْرِمِينَ فِى عَذَابِ جَهَنَّمَ خَٰلِدُونَ

75. Nowise will the (punishment)
Be lightened for them,
And in despair will they
Be there overwhelmed.

٧٥ لَا يُفَتَّرُ عَنْهُمْ وَهُمْ
فِيهِ مُبْلِسُونَ

4668. The Garden is the type of all that is beautiful to eye, mind, and soul; all that is restful and in tune, a complete state of bliss, such as we can scarcely conceive of in this troubled world. Several metaphors indicate how we can try to picture that bliss to ourselves in "this muddy vesture of decay."

4669. We shall have all our near and dear ones ("wives") with us: perfected Love will not be content with Self, but like a note of music will find its melody in communion with others. The richest and most beautiful vessels will minister to our purified desires, and give complete and eternal satisfaction to our souls in every way.

4670. We shall be there, not as strangers, or temporary guests, but as heirs—made heirs in eternity because of the good lives we had led on earth.

4671. The "fruit" here links on with the last words in the last verse (72): "ye are made heirs for your (good) deeds (in life)". It is not a doctrine of "rewards", strictly so called. A reward is measured by merit, but here the bliss is beyond all merits or deserts. It is a doctrine of works and their fruits: every deed must have its inevitable consequences. At first sight it may be compared to the doctrine of "Karma", but it differs from it in postulating Allah's unbounded Mercy, and the efficacy of Repentance. (R).

4672. Literally, "shall eat". But the word *akala* is used in many places in the comprehensive sense of "enjoy", "have satisfaction". For example, see n. 776 to 5:69. *Cf.* also 7:19 and n. 1004.

76. Nowise shall We[4673]
Be unjust to them:
But it is they who
Have been unjust themselves.

(٧٦) وَمَا ظَلَمْنَٰهُمْ
وَلَٰكِن كَانُوا۟ هُمُ ٱلظَّٰلِمِينَ

77. They will cry: "O Mālik![4674]
Would that thy Lord
Put an end to us!"
He will say, "Nay, but
Ye shall abide!"[4675]

(٧٧) وَنَادَوْا۟ يَٰمَٰلِكُ لِيَقْضِ عَلَيْنَا رَبُّكَ
قَالَ إِنَّكُم مَّٰكِثُونَ

78. Verily We have brought[4676]
The Truth to you:
But most of you
Have a hatred for Truth.

(٧٨) لَقَدْ جِئْنَٰكُم بِٱلْحَقِّ
وَلَٰكِنَّ أَكْثَرَكُمْ لِلْحَقِّ كَٰرِهُونَ

79. What! Have they settled[4677]
Some Plan (among themselves)?
But it is We Who
Settle things.

(٧٩) أَمْ أَبْرَمُوٓا۟ أَمْرًا
فَإِنَّا مُبْرِمُونَ

80. Or do they think[4678]
That We hear not
Their secrets and their
Private counsels? Indeed
(We do), and Our Messengers
Are by them, to record.

(٨٠) أَمْ يَحْسَبُونَ أَنَّا
لَا نَسْمَعُ سِرَّهُمْ وَنَجْوَىٰهُم
بَلَىٰ وَرُسُلُنَا لَدَيْهِمْ يَكْتُبُونَ

81. Say: "If (Allah) Most Gracious
Had a son, I would[4679]
Be the first to worship."

(٨١) قُلْ إِن كَانَ لِلرَّحْمَٰنِ وَلَدٌ
فَأَنَا۠ أَوَّلُ ٱلْعَٰبِدِينَ

4673. The wrongdoers suffer not because Allah is unjust or cruel, nor as a deterrent to others, for the probationary period will then have passed, but because their evil deeds must bear their inevitable fruit. Allah's Grace was ever ready to offer opportunities for Repentance and Forgiveness. But they rejected them. They were unjust to themselves. This is complementary to the doctrine of works and their fruits, as explained in n. 4671 above.

4674. *Mālik:* one who is lord or possessor; one who is in charge; applied to the Angel in charge of Hell.

4675. *Cf.* 20:74. Annihilation is better than agony. But wrongdoers cannot destroy the "fruits" of their actions, by asking for annihilation.

4676. We come back now to the Present—primarily to the time when Islam was being preached in Makkah, but by analogy the present time or any time. Truth is often bitter to the taste of those who live on Falsehoods and Shams and profit by them. They hate the Truth, and plot against it. But will they succeed? See next verse and note.

4677. Men cannot settle the high affairs of the universe. If they plot against the Truth, the Truth will destroy them, just as, if they accept the Truth, the Truth will make them free. It is Allah Who disposes of affairs.

4678. However secretly men may plot, everything is known to Allah. His recording Angels are by, at all times and in all places, to prepare a Record of their Deeds for their own conviction when the time comes for Judgement.

4679. The prophet of Allah does not object to true worship in any form. But it must be true: it must not superstitiously attribute derogatory things to Allah, or foster false ideas.

82. Glory to the Lord
Of the heavens and the earth,
The Lord of the Throne[4680]
(Of Authority)! (He is
Free) from the things
They attribute (to Him)!

سُبْحَٰنَ رَبِّ ٨٢
ٱلسَّمَٰوَٰتِ وَٱلْأَرْضِ رَبِّ ٱلْعَرْشِ
عَمَّا يَصِفُونَ

83. So leave them to babble
And play (with vanities)
Until they meet that Day[4681]
Of theirs, which they
Have been promised.

فَذَرْهُمْ يَخُوضُوا۟ وَيَلْعَبُوا۟ ٨٣
حَتَّىٰ يُلَٰقُوا۟ يَوْمَهُمُ ٱلَّذِى يُوعَدُونَ

84. It is He Who is God
In heaven and God on earth;
And He is Full
Of Wisdom and Knowledge.

وَهُوَ ٱلَّذِى فِى ٱلسَّمَآءِ إِلَٰهٌ ٨٤
وَفِى ٱلْأَرْضِ إِلَٰهٌ وَهُوَ ٱلْحَكِيمُ ٱلْعَلِيمُ

85. And blessed is He[4682]
To Whom belongs the dominion
Of the heavens and the earth,
And all between them:
With Him is the knowledge
Of the Hour (of Judgement):
And to Him shall ye
Be brought back.

وَتَبَارَكَ ٱلَّذِى لَهُۥ مُلْكُ ٨٥
ٱلسَّمَٰوَٰتِ وَٱلْأَرْضِ وَمَا بَيْنَهُمَا
وَعِندَهُۥ عِلْمُ ٱلسَّاعَةِ
وَإِلَيْهِ تُرْجَعُونَ

86. And those whom they invoke
Besides Allah have no power
Of intercession—only he[4683]
Who bears witness to the Truth,
And they know (him).

وَلَا يَمْلِكُ ٱلَّذِينَ ٨٦
يَدْعُونَ مِن دُونِهِ ٱلشَّفَٰعَةَ
إِلَّا مَن شَهِدَ بِٱلْحَقِّ وَهُمْ يَعْلَمُونَ

4680. *Cf.* 7:54 and n. 1032. All Power, Authority, Knowledge, and Truth are with Allah. He neither begets nor is begotten. Glory to Him!

4681. *That Day of theirs:* they had their Day on earth; they will have a different sort of Day in the Hereafter, according to the promise of Allah about the Resurrection and Judgement, or perhaps about Retribution in this very life! So leave them to play about with their fancies and vanities. Truth must eventually prevail!

4682. We glorify Allah, and we call His name blessed, because He has not only supreme power and authority, but because we shall return to Him and see "the Light of His Countenance" (30:38).

4683. The classical Commentators construe this clause differently. According to their construction, the clause would be translated, "except those who bear witness to the Truth, and with full knowledge." "Truth" they would construe to be the Gospel of Unity. According to them, while idols and false gods have no power of intercession, persons like Jesus, who is falsely worshipped by his misguided followers, but who himself preached the Gospel of Unity with full understanding, will have the power of intercession. This implies that we construe the singular *man shahida* to refer to the same person or persons as the plural *hum ya'lamūn*. This difficulty is removed if we construe as I have translated it. In that case "he who bears witness to the Truth" is the Holy Prophet, who came to renew the Gospel of Unity, and "they know (him)" would refer to the Quraysh, amongst whom he was brought up and among whom he earned the reputation of being a man of probity *(Amīn)*.

87. If thou ask them, Who[4684]
Created them, they will
Certainly say, Allah: how
Then are they deluded
Away (from the Truth)?

وَلَئِن سَأَلْتَهُم مَّنْ خَلَقَهُمْ لَيَقُولُنَّ ٱللَّهُ فَأَنَّىٰ يُؤْفَكُونَ ﴿٨٧﴾

88. (Allah has knowledge)[4685]
Of the (Prophet's) cry,
"O my Lord! Truly
These are a people
Who will not believe!"[4686]

وَقِيلِهِۦ يَٰرَبِّ إِنَّ هَٰٓؤُلَآءِ قَوْمٌ لَّا يُؤْمِنُونَ ﴿٨٨﴾

89. But turn away from them,
And say "Peace!"[4687]
But soon shall they know!

فَٱصْفَحْ عَنْهُمْ وَقُلْ سَلَٰمٌ ۚ فَسَوْفَ يَعْلَمُونَ ﴿٨٩﴾

4684. *Cf.* 31:25, and n. 3613; and 39:38, and n. 4299.

4685. Commentators are divided in opinion as to the construction. The best opinion is that which I have adopted, referring back *qīlihī* genitive governed by *'ilm* in verse 85. An alternative construction is to construe the *wāw* here as the *wāw qasamiyah:* in that case we should have to suppose some other clause as understood, in order to complete the sense.

4686. The Prophet was much troubled in mind by the Unfaith of the Quraysh: 18:6. He is here told to leave them alone for a time, for the Truth must soon prevail.

4867. *Cf.* 25:63, and n. 3123.

INTRODUCTION TO SŪRAH 44—*AL DUKHĀN*

For the chronology and the general theme of the Sūrahs of the *Ḥā Mīm* series of which this is the fifth, see the Introduction to S. 40.

The theme of this particular Sūrah is how wordly pride and power are humbled in the dust if they resist spiritual forces, and how Evil and Good find their true setting in the Hereafter.

The title word *Dukhān* occurs in verse 10. It means smoke or mist, and may refer to a drought or famine, as explained in the notes to that verse.

Summary—Revelation explains clearly how wordly pride and arrogance may come to naught, even at long odds, against spiritual truths (44:1-29, and C. 216).

A people may be given all blessings and may fail in its trust, as did Israel: will the Quraysh learn the lesson of Good and Evil? (44:30-59, and C. 217).

C. 216.—Blest is the night in which Allah's Message
(44:1-29.) Comes down, as a Mercy to men, to warn them
Against Evil. How fractious of men to ignore
Or suppress such warnings? Proud Pharaoh
And his Chiefs did resist Allah's authority,
But their sins rebounded on themselves:
They were swallowed up by the sea; and their tilth,
Their gardens, their noble fanes and buildings,
And all the advantages of which they boasted
Passed to other hands. Not a tear
Was shed over them in heaven or earth.
Thus ends the tale of power misused.

Sūrah 44.

Al Dukhān (The Smoke)

In the name of Allah, Most Gracious,
Most Merciful.

بِسْمِ ٱللَّهِ ٱلرَّحْمَٰنِ ٱلرَّحِيمِ

1. Ḥā Mīm.[4688]

حمٓ ①

2. By the Book that[4689]
Makes things clear—

وَٱلْكِتَٰبِ ٱلْمُبِينِ ②

3. We sent it down
During a blessed night:[4690]
For We (ever) wish
To warn (against Evil).

إِنَّآ أَنزَلْنَٰهُ فِى لَيْلَةٍ مُّبَٰرَكَةٍ ۚ ③
إِنَّا كُنَّا مُنذِرِينَ

4. In that (night) is made
Distinct every affair
Of wisdom,[4691]

فِيهَا يُفْرَقُ كُلُّ أَمْرٍ حَكِيمٍ ④

5. By command, from Our
Presence. For We (ever)
Send (revelations),

أَمْرًا مِّنْ عِندِنَآ ۚ إِنَّا كُنَّا مُرْسِلِينَ ⑤

6. As a Mercy
From thy Lord:
For He hears and knows[4692]
(All things);

رَحْمَةً مِّن رَّبِّكَ ۚ ⑥
إِنَّهُۥ هُوَ ٱلسَّمِيعُ ٱلْعَلِيمُ

7. The Lord of the heavens
And the earth and all

رَبِّ ٱلسَّمَٰوَٰتِ وَٱلْأَرْضِ ⑦

4688. These Abbreviated Letters are discussed in the Introduction to S. 40, paragraphs 2-4.

4689. The Qur'an is its own evidence. In the last Sūrah (53:3) stress was laid on the fact that everyone could understand it. Here the stress is on the fact that it is a Message of Mercy from Allah in that it warns mankind against evil.

4690. Usually taken to be a night in the month of Ramaḍān, say the 23rd, 25th, or 27th night of that month. It is referred to as the Night of Power in 97:1-2. See also 2:185. But perhaps we need not fix it literally by the calendar. The night that a Message descends from Allah is indeed a blessed night like a day of rain for a parched land.

4691. Such an occasion is one on which divine Wisdom places before us, through Revelation, the solution of spiritual problems of the highest import to mankind.

4692. It is because Allah is the friend of the friendless and the help of the helpless that He hears all sincere prayers, and as His knowledge embraces all things, He grants to us whatever is best for us, not as we see it, but as He knows it in His perfect knowledge.

Between them, if ye (but)
Have an assured faith.[4693]

وَمَا بَيْنَهُمَآ إِن كُنتُم مُّوقِنِينَ

8. There is no god but He:
It is He Who gives life
And gives death—
The Lord and Cherisher
To you and your earliest
Ancestors.

٨ لَآ إِلَٰهَ إِلَّا هُوَ يُحْيِۦ وَيُمِيتُ
رَبُّكُمْ وَرَبُّ ءَابَآئِكُمُ ٱلْأَوَّلِينَ

9. Yet they play about[4694]
In doubt.

٩ بَلْ هُمْ فِى شَكٍّ يَلْعَبُونَ

10. Then watch thou
For the Day[4695]
That the sky will
Bring forth a kind
Of smoke (or mist)[4696]
Plainly visible,

١٠ فَٱرْتَقِبْ يَوْمَ تَأْتِى
ٱلسَّمَآءُ بِدُخَانٍ مُّبِينٍ

11. Enveloping the people:
This will be a Penalty
Grievous.

١١ يَغْشَى ٱلنَّاسَ هَٰذَا عَذَابٌ أَلِيمٌ

12. (They will say:)
"Our Lord! Remove

١٢ رَّبَّنَا ٱكْشِفْ

4693. *Cf.* 2:4. They cannot fully realise what a tremendous thing it is that Allah is their own Lord and Cherisher (next verse), as He is the Lord and Cherisher of the whole Universe, until they firmly believe—until their Faith amounts to a certainty, secure and unshakable.

4694. The story is mainly about the Quraysh. But there is a wider meaning behind it, applicable to men generally, and at all times. As a body the Quraysh, especially in the earlier stages of the preaching of Islam, before they started persecution, received the Message with more amusement than hatred. They played about with it, and expressed doubts about it, whereas the Preacher was most earnest about it, with all his heart and soul in it, as he loved his people and wished to save them from their wickedness and folly.

4695. What Day is this? It obviously refers to a great calamity, and from the wording it is to be a great calamity in the future, seen with the prophetic eye. The word *yaghshā* in verse 11 may be compared to *ghāshiyah* in 88:1, which obviously refers to the final Day of Judgement. But verse 15 below ("We shall remove the Penalty for a while") shows that it is not the final Judgement referred to here, but some calamity that was to happen soon afterwards. Perhaps it was a famine, about which see the next note.

4696. The "smoke" or "mist" is interpreted on good authority to refer to a severe famine in Makkah, in which men were so pinched with hunger that they saw mist before their eyes when they looked at the sky. Ibn Kathīr in his *Tārīkh* mentions two famines in Makkah, one in the 8th year of the Mission, say the fourth year before the Hijrah, and another about the 8th year after the Hijrah. But as either or both of these famines lasted as many as seven years, the dates are to be taken very roughly. It is even possible that the two famines were continuous, of varying severity from year to year. Bukhārī mentions only the post-Hijrah famine, which was apparently so severe that men began to eat bones and carrion. Abū Sufyān (about 8 A.H.) approached the Holy Prophet to intercede and pray for the removal of the famine, as the Pagans attributed it to the curse of the Prophet. Sūrah 23, which is also Makkan, but of later date than the present Sūrah, also refers to a famine: see 23:75, and n. 2921. As Sūrahs were not all revealed entire, but many came piecemeal, it is possible that particular verses in a given Sūrah may be of different dates from the Sūrah as a whole.

The Penalty from us,
For we do really believe!"

عَنَّا الْعَذَابَ إِنَّا مُؤْمِنُونَ

13. How shall the Message
Be (effectual) for them,[4697]
Seeing that a Messenger
Explaining things clearly
Has (already) come to them—

أَنَّىٰ لَهُمُ الذِّكْرَىٰ ﴿١٣﴾ وَقَدْ جَاءَهُمْ رَسُولٌ مُّبِينٌ

14. Yet they turn away
From him and say: "Tutored
(By others), a man possessed!"[4698]

ثُمَّ تَوَلَّوْا عَنْهُ وَقَالُوا مُعَلَّمٌ مَّجْنُونٌ ﴿١٤﴾

15. We shall indeed remove[4699]
The Penalty for a while,
(But) truly ye will revert
(To your ways).

إِنَّا كَاشِفُوا الْعَذَابِ قَلِيلًا ۚ إِنَّكُمْ عَائِدُونَ ﴿١٥﴾

16. One day We shall seize
You with a mighty onslaught:
We will indeed (then)
Exact Retribution!

يَوْمَ نَبْطِشُ الْبَطْشَةَ الْكُبْرَىٰ إِنَّا مُنتَقِمُونَ ﴿١٦﴾

17. We did, before them,
Try the people of Pharoah:[4700]
There came to them
A messenger most honourable,[4701]

وَلَقَدْ فَتَنَّا قَبْلَهُمْ قَوْمَ فِرْعَوْنَ وَجَاءَهُمْ رَسُولٌ كَرِيمٌ ﴿١٧﴾

4697. The Quraysh had before them a prophet whose purity of life was openly known to them; they themselves called him *Al Amīn* (worthy of all trust); he preached in their own language in words of burning eloquence and transparent clearness; yet they turned away from him and called him a madman, or one whose Message was not inspired by Allah, but written by some hidden hand (see next note)! How will the teaching of spiritual Truth make way among such unreasonable people?

4698. *Tutored:* see 16:103, and n. 2143.

Possessed: see 15:6, and n. 1940.

4699. Allah gives every chance to all His creatures, however rebellious. He gives them a little trial, perhaps personal, perhaps economic, to see if that would bring them to their bearings, and train their will in the right direction. Some are thus reclaimed, and some do not learn. Perhaps, for the latter, he gives them a chance by removing the trial; some are reclaimed, and some still remain obdurate. And so, in His wisdom, He allows His grace to work, again and again, until, at the last, Judgement must sieze the last and irreclaimable remnant "with a mighty onslaught".

Such working of Allah's Providence is clearly visible in the story of the Quraysh. It is a pity that the economic conditions of Makkah have not been studied in detail in any of the standard biographies of the Prophet. The so-called biographies by non-Muslims, *e.g.*, Muir's *Life*, do not even mention any Makkan famine or its reactions on the Quraysh mind!

4700. This reference is to the pride of Pharaoh and his Egyptians, and their fall, rather than to the story of Moses himself; just as in 44:30-33 the reference is to the blessings bestowed on Israel, contrasted with their pride, unbelief, and fall; and in 44:37, to the ancient Himyar kingdom in Yemen, which similarly fell for its sins.

4701. *Most honourable:* this epithet is specially applied to Moses here, as expressing the truth, in contrast to the Pharoah's false characterisation of him as "a contemptible wretch"(43:52).

18. Saying: "Restore to me[4702]
The servants of Allah:
I am to you a messenger
Worthy of all trust;[4703]

١٨ أَنْ أَدُّوٓا۟ إِلَىَّ عِبَادَ ٱللَّهِ ۖ إِنِّى لَكُمْ رَسُولٌ أَمِينٌ

19. "And be not arrogant
As against Allah:
For I come to you
With authority manifest.

١٩ وَأَن لَّا تَعْلُوا۟ عَلَى ٱللَّهِ ۖ إِنِّىٓ ءَاتِيكُم بِسُلْطَٰنٍ مُّبِينٍ

20. "For me, I have sought[4704]
Safety with my Lord
And your Lord, against
Your injuring me.[4705]

٢٠ وَإِنِّى عُذْتُ بِرَبِّى وَرَبِّكُمْ أَن تَرْجُمُونِ

21. "If ye believe me not,[4706]
At least keep yourselves
Away from me."

٢١ وَإِن لَّمْ تُؤْمِنُوا۟ لِى فَٱعْتَزِلُونِ

22. (But they were aggressive:)[4707]
Then he cried
To his Lord:
"These are indeed
A people given to sin."

٢٢ فَدَعَا رَبَّهُۥٓ أَنَّ هَٰٓؤُلَآءِ قَوْمٌ مُّجْرِمُونَ

23. (The reply came:)
"March forth with my servants
By night: for ye are
Sure to be pursued.

٢٣ فَأَسْرِ بِعِبَادِى لَيْلًا إِنَّكُم مُّتَّبَعُونَ

4702. The argument of Moses and his "authority manifest" will be found at 7:104-108, 120-126, 130-137. Notice how fully he assumes the authority of his office here. He claims all "servants of Allah", *i.e.*, true worshippers, as under his protection, for his mission was both to the Egyptians and the Israelites; he asks that they should be restored to *him;* and he boldly denounces the Pharaoh's arrogance "as against Allah".

4703. "Worthy of all trust": *Amīn*, a title that applied to prophets in S. 26, *e.g.*, see 26:107. As the Holy Prophet had historically earned that title among his own people, the reminiscences of the story of Moses apply to him in his relations with the arrogant Quraysh.

4704. It is no use their plotting his death or his vilification; for his safety is in Allah. As he truly says, "Allah is not only *my* Lord, but *your* Lord also; your responsibility arises apart from my preaching, but I preach in order to remind you of it."

4705. "*Injuring me*": literally "stoning me". "Stoning may be here symbolical of any injury or vilification.

4706. If you do not believe me, at least go your ways; do not add to your sins by trying to suppress me and the Message of Truth which I bring: keep out of my way.

4707. They would not even leave him alone to do his duty. So he cried to Allah, not indeed to destroy them, for a Prophet does not judge, but only Allah judges; he justified himself in prayer, that he had done his best, but they were obdurate in sin, and they were trying to oppress and injure the believers. Then came the order to march. They were to march under the cover of night, because the enemy was sure to pursue. They were to march with all believers, presumably believing Egyptians (such as were not martyred) as well as Israelites, for some Egyptians had believed: 7:121.

24. "And leave the sea
As a furrow (divided):[4708]
For they are a host
(Destined) to be drowned."

٢٤ وَٱتۡرُكِ ٱلۡبَحۡرَ رَهۡوًاۖ إِنَّهُمۡ جُندٞ مُّغۡرَقُونَ

25. How many were the gardens[4709]
And springs they left behind,

٢٥ كَمۡ تَرَكُواْ مِن جَنَّٰتٖ وَعُيُونٖ

26. And cornfields
And noble buildings,

٢٦ وَزُرُوعٖ وَمَقَامٖ كَرِيمٖ

27. And wealth (and conveniences
Of life), wherein they
Had taken such delight!

٢٧ وَنَعۡمَةٖ كَانُواْ فِيهَا فَٰكِهِينَ

28. Thus (was their end)!
And We make other people
Inherit (those things)!

٢٨ كَذَٰلِكَۖ وَأَوۡرَثۡنَٰهَا قَوۡمًا ءَاخَرِينَ

29. And neither heaven[4710]
Nor earth shed a tear
Over them: nor were
They given a respite (again).

٢٩ فَمَا بَكَتۡ عَلَيۡهِمُ ٱلسَّمَآءُ وَٱلۡأَرۡضُ وَمَا كَانُواْ مُنظَرِينَ

C. 217.—(44:30-59.)
So with the Children of Israel:
Granted gifts and favours, they became
Arrogant and fell. Can the Quraysh
Escape the doom for sin? We created
The world for just ends. The Day
Will come when good and evil will be
Sorted out: each will meet
The fruits of its own deeds. Give good heed
To the Message revealed, and wait and watch.

SECTION 2.

30. We did deliver aforetime
The Children of Israel
From humiliating Punishment,[4711]

٣٠ وَلَقَدۡ نَجَّيۡنَا بَنِيٓ إِسۡرَٰٓءِيلَ مِنَ ٱلۡعَذَابِ ٱلۡمُهِينِ

4708. For the passage of Moses and his following, the sea had divided: they were to pass through the gap or furrow and leave it alone, to lure on the Egyptian host, on which the sea afterwards closed in, totally destroying them.

4709. There follows a wordpicture of all the fine and enjoyable things which the ruling caste had monopolised. Now these proud monopolists were drowned in the sea, and the inheritance went to other hands.

4710. They died, "unwept, unhonoured, and unsung". They were too inordinate to be given another chance. Pharaoh had claimed to be their supreme god; and they had followed him!

4711. The Israelites were held in bondage prior to the Exodus. Their hard taskmaster placed every indignity on them, and by Pharaoh's decree their male children were to be killed, and their females were to be kept alive for the Egyptians.

31. Inflicted by Pharaoh, for he
Was arrogant (even) among
Inordinate transgressors.

٣١ مِن فِرْعَوْنَ ۚ
إِنَّهُۥ كَانَ عَالِيًا مِّنَ ٱلْمُسْرِفِينَ

32. And We chose them aforetime
Above the nations, knowingly,[4712]

٣٢ وَلَقَدِ ٱخْتَرْنَٰهُمْ عَلَىٰ عِلْمٍ عَلَى ٱلْعَٰلَمِينَ

33. And granted them Signs[4713]
In which there was
A manifest trial.

٣٣ وَءَاتَيْنَٰهُم مِّنَ ٱلْءَايَٰتِ
مَا فِيهِ بَلَٰٓؤٌا۟ مُّبِينٌ

34. As to these (Quraysh),[4714]
They say forsooth:

٣٤ إِنَّ هَٰٓؤُلَآءِ لَيَقُولُونَ

35. "There is nothing beyond
Our first death,
And we shall not
Be raised again.

٣٥ إِنْ هِىَ إِلَّا مَوْتَتُنَا ٱلْأُولَىٰ
وَمَا نَحْنُ بِمُنشَرِينَ

36. "Then bring (back)
Our forefathers, if what
Ye say is true!"

٣٦ فَأْتُوا۟ بِـَٔابَآئِنَآ إِن كُنتُمْ صَٰدِقِينَ

37. What! are they better
Than the people of Tubba'[4715]
And those who were
Before them? We destroyed

٣٧ أَهُمْ خَيْرٌ أَمْ قَوْمُ تُبَّعٍ وَٱلَّذِينَ مِن قَبْلِهِمْ ۚ
أَهْلَكْنَٰهُمْ

4712. From degrading servitude, Israel was delivered, and taken, in spite of many rebellions and backslidings on the way, to "a land flowing with milk and honey", where later they established the glorious kingdom of David and Solomon. This was not merely fortuitous. In Allah's prescience it was to be a link in furthering the great universal Plan. But their being chosen did not mean that they could do what they liked. In that sense there is no "chosen race" before Allah. But Allah gives every race and every individual a chance, and when the race or individual fails to live up to it, he or it must fall and give place to others.

4713. Among the "Signs" given to Israel were their own Revelation under Moses, their prosperous land of Canaan, their flourishing Kingdom under David and Solomon, their prophets and teachers of Truth, and the advent of Jesus to reclaim the lost ones among them. All these were trials. When they failed in the trials, they were left to wander desolate and suffer.

4714. The cases of the Egyptians and the Israelites having been cited as great nations which fell through inordinate vanity and wrongdoing, the case is now pressed home against the Quraysh leaders in their arrogance to the Holy Prophet himself. They deny Revelation; they deny a future life, as the Sadducees did among the Jews before them; they persecute the Prophet of Allah, and those who believe in him: and they mockingly demand that their ancestors should be brought back to life, if it is true that there is a future life. They are reminded that better men than they lived in their own country of Arabia, men who had knowledge of Allah's revelation under the earliest Dispensation. See next note. They perished because of their unbelief and wrongdoing. What chance have they unless they turn and repent?

4715. *Tubba'* is understood to be a title or family name of Ḥimyar kings in Yemen, of the tribe of Hamdān. The Ḥimyar were an ancient race. At one time they seem to have extended their hegemony over all Arabia and perhaps beyond, to the East African Coast. Their earliest religion seems to have been Sabianism, or the worship of the heavenly bodies. They seem at different times, later on, to have professed the Jewish and the Christian religion. Among the Embassies sent by the Holy Prophet in A.H. 9-10 was one to the Ḥimyar of Yemen, which led to their coming into Islam. This was of course much later than the date of this Sūrah.

Them because they were
Guilty of sin.[4716]

إِنَّهُمْ كَانُوا۟ مُجْرِمِينَ

38. We created not
The heavens, the earth,
And all between them,
Merely in (idle) sport;[4717]

وَمَا خَلَقْنَا ٱلسَّمَـٰوَٰتِ وَٱلْأَرْضَ وَمَا بَيْنَهُمَا لَـٰعِبِينَ ﴿٣٨﴾

39. We created them not
Except for just ends:
But most of them
Do not understand.

مَا خَلَقْنَـٰهُمَآ إِلَّا بِٱلْحَقِّ وَلَـٰكِنَّ أَكْثَرَهُمْ لَا يَعْلَمُونَ ﴿٣٩﴾

40. Verily the Day of[4718]
Sorting Out is the time
Appointed for all of them—

إِنَّ يَوْمَ ٱلْفَصْلِ مِيقَـٰتُهُمْ أَجْمَعِينَ ﴿٤٠﴾

41. The Day when no protector[4719]
Can avail his client
In aught, and no help
Can they receive,

يَوْمَ لَا يُغْنِى مَوْلًى عَن مَّوْلًى شَيْـًٔا وَلَا هُمْ يُنصَرُونَ ﴿٤١﴾

42. Except such as receive[4720]
Allah's Mercy: for He is
Exalted in Might, Most Merciful.

إِلَّا مَن رَّحِمَ ٱللَّهُ ۚ إِنَّهُۥ هُوَ ٱلْعَزِيزُ ٱلرَّحِيمُ ﴿٤٢﴾

SECTION 3.

43. Verily the tree[4721]
Of Zaqqūm[4722]

إِنَّ شَجَرَتَ ٱلزَّقُّومِ ﴿٤٣﴾

4716. In prehistoric times the Ḥimyar and Yemen seem to have played a large part in Arabia and even beyond: see last note. But when they were intoxicated with power, they fell into sin, and gradually they ceased to count, not only in Arabia but even in Yemen.

4717. *Cf.* 21:16, and n. 2676. All creation is for a wise and just purpose. But men usually do not realise or understand it, because they are steeped in their own ignorance, folly, or passions.

4718. Day of Sorting Out, or the Day of Decision. *Cf.* 37:21, and n. 4047. Ignorance, prejudice, passion, spite, and selfishness, seem sometimes to flourish in this probationary life. In any case they are mixed up with knowledge, justice, common sense, love and regard for others. But the good and the evil will be sorted out and separated at the Day of Judgement. There is a time appointed for it. In Allah's good time all will come right.

4719. When that Day comes, the strictest justice will prevail. No man, however prominently he may have walked on the world's stage, can help another. He himself will need help, not the sort of logrolling help which high and low render to each other in this life, but which in the conditions of reality will be of no avail. The only things which will help will be the Mercy of Allah.

4720. Allah's Mercy will be the only thing of any efficacy: for He is both *able* to help ("Exalted in Might") and *willing* to forgive ("Most Merciful").

4721. Now follows a wordpicture of the horrors to which Evil must lead us. What human language and what figures of speech can adequately describe them?

4722. The opposite of "delicious Fruits" is the terrible tree of *Zaqqūm*, which is further described in 37:62-68, where see n. 4073. Also see 17:60, n. 2250.

44. Will be the food
Of the Sinful—

طَعَامُ ٱلۡأَثِيمِ ﴿٤٤﴾

45. Like molten brass;
It will boil
In their insides,

كَٱلۡمُهۡلِ يَغۡلِي فِي ٱلۡبُطُونِ ﴿٤٥﴾

46. Like the boiling
Of scalding water.

كَغَلۡيِ ٱلۡحَمِيمِ ﴿٤٦﴾

47. (A voice will cry:
"Seize ye him
And drag him
Into the midst
Of the Blazing Fire!"

خُذُوهُ فَٱعۡتِلُوهُ إِلَىٰ سَوَآءِ ٱلۡجَحِيمِ ﴿٤٧﴾

48. "Then pour over his head
The Penalty of Boiling Water.

ثُمَّ صُبُّواْ فَوۡقَ رَأۡسِهِۦ مِنۡ عَذَابِ ٱلۡحَمِيمِ ﴿٤٨﴾

49. "Taste thou (this)!
Truly wast thou
Mighty, full of honour!"[4723]

ذُقۡ إِنَّكَ أَنتَ ٱلۡعَزِيزُ ٱلۡكَرِيمُ ﴿٤٩﴾

50. "Truly this is what
Ye used to doubt!"[4724]

إِنَّ هَٰذَا مَا كُنتُم بِهِۦ تَمۡتَرُونَ ﴿٥٠﴾

51. As to the Righteous
(They will be) in
A position of Security.[4725]

إِنَّ ٱلۡمُتَّقِينَ فِي مَقَامٍ أَمِينٖ ﴿٥١﴾

52. Among Gardens and Springs;

فِي جَنَّٰتٖ وَعُيُونٖ ﴿٥٢﴾

53. Dressed in fine silk[4726]
And in rich brocade,
They will face each other;[4727]

يَلۡبَسُونَ مِن سُندُسٖ وَإِسۡتَبۡرَقٖ مُّتَقَٰبِلِينَ ﴿٥٣﴾

4723. In this particular Sūrah the besetting sin we are considering is the arrogance born of place or power, wealth or honour, as understood in this world. The punishment of ignominy looks back to the kind of sin which is to be punished.

4724. When the Punishment becomes a realised fact, how foolish will those look who doubted whether there would be a Hereafter?

4725. There will be no uncertainty, as on this earth; no danger of discontinuance; no possibility of their satisfaction being terminated?

4726. *Cf.* 18:31, and n. 2373.

4727. Everything will be open and in social companionship: for all the petty feelings of jealousy or exclusiveness will have passed away.

54. Moreover, We shall
Join them to Companions[4728]
With beautiful, big,
And lustrous eyes.[4729]

كَذَٰلِكَ وَزَوَّجْنَٰهُم بِحُورٍ عِينٍ ﴿٥٤﴾

55. There can they call
For every kind of fruit[4730]
In peace and security;

يَدْعُونَ فِيهَا بِكُلِّ فَٰكِهَةٍ ءَامِنِينَ ﴿٥٥﴾

56. Nor will they there
Taste Death, except the first[4731]
Death; and He will preserve
Them from the Penalty
Of the Blazing Fire—[4732]

لَا يَذُوقُونَ فِيهَا ٱلْمَوْتَ إِلَّا ٱلْمَوْتَةَ ٱلْأُولَىٰ وَوَقَىٰهُمْ عَذَابَ ٱلْجَحِيمِ ﴿٥٦﴾

57. As a Bounty from thy Lord!
That will be
The supreme achievement![4733]

فَضْلًا مِّن رَّبِّكَ ذَٰلِكَ هُوَ ٱلْفَوْزُ ٱلْعَظِيمُ ﴿٥٧﴾

58. Verily, We have made
This (Qur'an) easy,[4734]
In thy tongue,
In order that they
May give heed.

فَإِنَّمَا يَسَّرْنَٰهُ بِلِسَانِكَ لَعَلَّهُمْ يَتَذَكَّرُونَ ﴿٥٨﴾

59. So wait thou and watch;
For they (too) are waiting.

فَٱرْتَقِبْ إِنَّهُم مُّرْتَقِبُونَ ﴿٥٩﴾

4728. The Companions, like the scene, the dress, the outlook, and the fruit, will be beautiful. There will be life, but free from all earthly grossness. The women as well as the men of this life will attain to this indescribable bliss. (R).

4729. *Ḥūr* implies the following ideas: (1) purity; possibly the word *Ḥawariyūn*, as applied to the first Disciples of Jesus, is connected with this root; (2) beauty, especially of eyes, where the intense white of the eyeballs stands out against the intense black of the pupil, thus giving the appearance of lustre, and intense feeling: as opposed to dullness or want of expression; and (3) truth and good will.

4730. The metaphorical signification is explained in n. 4671 to 43:73.

4731. *First Death:* the ordinary natural death from this life, which brought them to the Garden of Felicity: there will be no further death after that. *Cf.* 37:59, and n. 4071.

4732. In Islam we are taught that salvation is not possible of our unaided efforts. Certainly, striving on our part is an indispensable condition: but it is the Mercy of Allah which comes to our help and keeps us from the Fire of final Punishment. This is mentioned last as the foundation on which is built our eternal felicity and our positive spiritual joys. (R).

4733. This is our idea of Salvation: the negative avoidance of all the consequences of evil, and the positive attainment of all—and more than all—that our hearts could possibly desire. For Allah's Bounty outstrips anything that our eyes have seen, or our ears have heard of, or our imagination can conceive.

4734. *Easy:* not only to understand, being in the Arabic tongue; but mellifluous, whose rhythm carries off our spirits to a higher spiritual plane. In another sense, it is difficult; for to get its deepest meaning, we shall have to strive hard, as the contents of this Sūrah alone will show.

INTRODUCTION TO SŪRAH 45—*AL JĀTHIYAH*

This is the sixth of the *Hā Mīm* series: for their general theme and chronology, see the Introdution to S. 40.

Summary—The title, *Al Jāthiyah* ('The Kneeling Down', or 'Bowing the knee'), taken from verse 28, expresses the leading idea in the Sūrah. In this life, in spite of the Signs of Allah, and the evidences of His goodness all around, men go about in Unfaith, and mocking at Faith; but the End will bring them all to their knees.

C. 218.—The Signs of Allah are everywhere:
(45:1-37.) His power, wisdom, and goodness are shown
Through all Creation and in Revelation.
How can man be so ungrateful
As to reject true Guidance, reaping thus
The fruits of Evil? But men of Faith
Have patience and forgive their weaker
Brethren, and trust in the final justice
Of Allah. Form no sects, as was done
Aforetime, nor make your lusts your gods:
The future is sure, and in the hands
Of Allah, to Whom all will bend the knee,
When Truth will shine in all its glory.
So praise and glory to Allah, the Lord
And Cherisher of all the worlds!

Sūrah 45.

Al Jāthiyah (The Kneeling Down)

In the name of Allah, Most Gracious, Most Merciful.

بِسْمِ ٱللَّهِ ٱلرَّحْمَٰنِ ٱلرَّحِيمِ

1. Ḥā Mīm.[4735]

حمٓ ﴿١﴾

2. The revelation[4736]
Of the Book
Is from Allah
The Exalted in Power,
Full of Wisdom.

تَنزِيلُ ٱلْكِتَٰبِ مِنَ ٱللَّهِ ٱلْعَزِيزِ ٱلْحَكِيمِ ﴿٢﴾

3. Verily in the heavens[4737]
And the earth, are Signs
For those who believe.

إِنَّ فِى ٱلسَّمَٰوَٰتِ وَٱلْأَرْضِ لَءَايَٰتٍ لِّلْمُؤْمِنِينَ ﴿٣﴾

4. And in the creation[4738]
Of yourselves and the fact
That animals are scattered
(Through the earth), are Signs
For those of assured Faith.

وَفِى خَلْقِكُمْ وَمَا يَبُثُّ مِن دَآبَّةٍ ءَايَٰتٌ لِّقَوْمٍ يُوقِنُونَ ﴿٤﴾

5. And in the alternation[4739]
Of Night and Day,
And the fact that Allah
Sends down Sustenance[4740] from
The sky, and revives therewith
The earth after its death,

وَٱخْتِلَٰفِ ٱلَّيْلِ وَٱلنَّهَارِ وَمَآ أَنزَلَ ٱللَّهُ مِنَ ٱلسَّمَآءِ مِن رِّزْقٍ فَأَحْيَا بِهِ ٱلْأَرْضَ بَعْدَ مَوْتِهَا

4735. See Introduction to S. 40, paragraphs 2-4.

4736. This verse is the same as 40:2. except that "wisdom" is here substituted in the last line for "Knowledge". This is appropriate, as in this Sūrah we are dealing with the folly of those who reject Allah and His Signs, while S. 40 dealt with the individual soul's witness to Faith and Virtue.

4737. Verses 3-5 deal with some of the points in the noble argument in 2:164, but again there are differences on account of the different context. Note that here the argument is divided into three parts, one in each verse. (1) In verse 3 we are dealing with big Signs external to ourselves, some of which are far beyond our personal experiences: for them we require Faith: they are Signs "for those who believe." For the other two see the next two notes.

4738. (2) These Signs are in our own nature and in the animals we meet with every day; here we have certainty within human limits: these are "for those of assured Faith."

4739. (3) These are our daily experiences from external things, but they affect us and our lives intimately: here are questions of deductions "for those that are wise."

4740. "Sustenance" is almost equivalent here to "rain" itself, and its revival of a dead earth, which refer symbolically to Revelation and its putting new life into a dead soul. Similarly the alternation of Night and Day, and the change of the winds, besides being Signs as wonderful phenomena of Nature, refer to spiritual ignorance and knowledge, rest and activity, and the constant beneficent changes that are going on in the world, making for the spread of the blessing of Allah's Revelation.

And in the change
Of the winds—are Signs
For those that are wise.

وَتَصۡرِيفِ ٱلرِّيَٰحِ ءَايَٰتٞ لِّقَوۡمٖ يَعۡقِلُونَ

6. Such are Signs[4741]
Of Allah, which We rehearse to thee
In truth: then in what
Exposition will they believe
After (rejecting) Allah
And His Signs?

٦ تِلۡكَ ءَايَٰتُ ٱللَّهِ
نَتۡلُوهَا عَلَيۡكَ بِٱلۡحَقِّۖ
فَبِأَيِّ حَدِيثِۭ بَعۡدَ ٱللَّهِ وَءَايَٰتِهِۦ يُؤۡمِنُونَ

7. Woe to each sinful
Dealer in Falsehoods:[4742]

٧ وَيۡلٞ لِّكُلِّ أَفَّاكٍ أَثِيمٖ

8. He hears the Signs
Of Allah rehearsed to him,
Yet is obstinate and lofty,
As if he had not
Heard them: then announce
To him a Penalty Grievous!

٨ يَسۡمَعُ ءَايَٰتِ ٱللَّهِ تُتۡلَىٰ عَلَيۡهِ
ثُمَّ يُصِرُّ مُسۡتَكۡبِرٗا كَأَن لَّمۡ يَسۡمَعۡهَاۖ
فَبَشِّرۡهُ بِعَذَابٍ أَلِيمٖ

9. And when he learns
Sonmething of Our Signs,
He takes them in jest:
For such there will be
A humiliating Penalty.[4743]

٩ وَإِذَا عَلِمَ مِنۡ ءَايَٰتِنَا شَيۡـًٔا ٱتَّخَذَهَا هُزُوًاۚ
أُوْلَٰٓئِكَ لَهُمۡ عَذَابٞ مُّهِينٞ

10. In front of them is
Hell: and of no profit
To them is anything
They may have earned,
Nor any protectors they
May have taken to themselves
Besides Allah: for them
Is a tremendous Penalty.[4744]

١٠ مِّن وَرَآئِهِمۡ جَهَنَّمُۖ
وَلَا يُغۡنِي عَنۡهُم مَّا كَسَبُواْ شَيۡـٔٗا
وَلَا مَا ٱتَّخَذُواْ مِن دُونِ ٱللَّهِ أَوۡلِيَآءَۖ
وَلَهُمۡ عَذَابٌ عَظِيمٌ

4741. If there are any to whom the Signs from Nature, from within their own heart and conscience, and from the voice of Revelation, are not enough to convince them, what possible kind of exposition will they accept?

2742. A soul so dead, as described in the last note, is indeed wretched. It will resort to falsehoods, in worship, in conduct, and in its attitude towards Allah. It will be obstinate, and pretend to be "above such things'. It will hear the most beautiful Message but not profit by it. The loss or punishment is its own, and grievous it is!

4743. Note that in each of the verses 8-11 the Penalty is characterised by a certain description, which accords with the crime. (1) In verse 8, the man is arrogant about the Signs of Allah's love and care all around him, and his Penalty is "grievous". (2) In verse 9, he ridicules Allah's Signs, and his Penalty is "humiliating": he makes himself a ridiculous fool. (3) and (4) are described in the two following notes.

4744. (3) In verse 10 the sinner has piled up all the good things of this life, and thinks he has got plenty of helpers and protectors but all these things are of no use. On the contrary, his Penalty will be "tremendous", to correspond with the great pains which he has taken to multiply the gods of his worship.

11. This is (true) Guidance:
And for those who reject
The Signs of their Lord,
Is a grievous Penalty
Of abomination.[4745]

(١١) هَٰذَا هُدًى
وَالَّذِينَ كَفَرُوا بِآيَاتِ رَبِّهِمْ لَهُمْ
عَذَابٌ مِّن رِّجْزٍ أَلِيمٌ

SECTION 2.

12. It is Allah Who has
Subjected the sea to you,[4746]
That ship may sail
Through it by His command,
That ye may seek
Of His Bounty, and that
Ye may be gateful.

(١٢) اللَّهُ الَّذِي سَخَّرَ لَكُمُ الْبَحْرَ لِتَجْرِيَ
الْفُلْكُ فِيهِ بِأَمْرِهِ وَلِتَبْتَغُوا مِن فَضْلِهِ
وَلَعَلَّكُمْ تَشْكُرُونَ

13. And He has subjected
To you, as from Him,
All that is in the heavens[4747]
And on earth: behold,
In that are Signs indeed
For those who reflect.

(١٣) وَسَخَّرَ لَكُم مَّا فِي السَّمَاوَاتِ
وَمَا فِي الْأَرْضِ جَمِيعًا مِّنْهُ
إِنَّ فِي ذَٰلِكَ لَآيَاتٍ لِّقَوْمٍ يَتَفَكَّرُونَ

14. Tell those who believe,
To forgive those who
Do not look forward
To the Days of Allah:[4748]
It is for Him to recompense[4749]

(١٤) قُل لِّلَّذِينَ آمَنُوا يَغْفِرُوا
لِلَّذِينَ لَا يَرْجُونَ أَيَّامَ اللَّهِ لِيَجْزِيَ

4745. (4) In verse 11, he has flouted and rejected the specific guidance that came to him from the Word of Allah, or from the admonition of a Prophet of Allah. His Penalty is a penalty of abomination: he earns unspeakable horror and abomination from all the Righteous, and is an unclean object in the Kingdom of Heaven.

4746. *Cf.* 16:14 and notes thereon, especially n. 2037. The one encircling ocean of our globe is one of the most significant facts in our physical geography. Its salt water is an agent of global sanitation. The salubrious effects of sea air, with its ozone, are well known to everyone who has recouped his health by its means. Thanks to ships, the sea unites rather than divides: communications are, and have always been, more active between seacoast towns then further inland. They thus further human intercourse, and help us to seek the "Bounty of Allah", not only in a commercial but in an intellectual and spiritual sense. All this is through "Allah's command" *i.e.*, by His beneficent ordering of the universe, and we should be grateful.

4747. *Cf.* 31:20, and n. 3605. The sea was only one example of Allah's cherishing care in making all things in nature available for the use of man, through the genius and faculties which He has given to man. Man should never forget that it is all "as from Him". *i.e.*, from Allah. For is not man Allah's vicegerent on earth (2:30)?

4748. *Cf.* 7:54, n. 1031. The *Days of Allah* I interpret to mean not periods of twenty-four hours, but the stages through which Allah's Purpose works in us on bringing home to us a sense of sin and a sense of Allah's Mercy. We must be patient with those who have not yet aquired that sense. "Days of Allah" may also mean the Days of the Kingdom of Allah, when evil will be destroyed and Allah's authority will reign unquestioned.

4749. Allah will give due recompense for good or evil according to His own full Knowledge and righteous Plan, and in His own good time. (R).

(For good or ill) each People[4750]
According to what
They have earned.

قَوْمًا بِمَا كَانُوا يَكْسِبُونَ

15. If anyone does[4751]
A righteous deed,
It enures to the benefit
Of his own soul;
If he does evil,
It works against
(His own soul).
In the end will ye
(All) be brought back
To your Lord.

١٥ مَنْ عَمِلَ صَٰلِحًا فَلِنَفْسِهِۦ ۖ
وَمَنْ أَسَآءَ فَعَلَيْهَا ۖ
ثُمَّ إِلَىٰ رَبِّكُمْ
تُرْجَعُونَ

16. We did aforetime
Grant to the Children[4752]
Of Israel the Book,
The Power of Command,
And Prophethood; We gave
Them, for Sustenance, things[4753]
Good and pure; and We
Favoured them above the nations.

١٦ وَلَقَدْ ءَاتَيْنَا بَنِىٓ إِسْرَٰٓءِيلَ
ٱلْكِتَٰبَ وَٱلْحُكْمَ وَٱلنُّبُوَّةَ
وَرَزَقْنَٰهُم مِّنَ ٱلطَّيِّبَٰتِ
وَفَضَّلْنَٰهُمْ عَلَى ٱلْعَٰلَمِينَ

17. And We granted them
Clear Signs in affairs
(Of Religion): it was only[4754]
After knowledge had been
Granted to them that they
Fell into schisms, through
Insolent envy[5755] among themselves
Verily thy Lord will judge
Between then on the Day

١٧ وَءَاتَيْنَٰهُم بَيِّنَٰتٍ مِّنَ ٱلْأَمْرِ ۖ
فَمَا ٱخْتَلَفُوٓا۟ إِلَّا مِنۢ بَعْدِ
مَا جَآءَهُمُ ٱلْعِلْمُ بَغْيًۢا بَيْنَهُمْ ۚ
إِنَّ رَبَّكَ يَقْضِى بَيْنَهُمْ يَوْمَ

4750. "People" here may be taken to be a group of common characteristics, *e.g.*, the righteous in contrast with the unrighteous, the oppressed in contrast with the oppressors, and so on.

4751. Ordinarily good and evil come to their own even in this world; but in any case there is the final Judgement before Allah.

4752. The argument here is similar to that in 44:32-33 but; it is more particularised here. Israel had the Revelation given through Moses, the power of judgement and command through the Kingdom of David and Solomon, and numerous prophetic warnings through such men as Isaiah and Jeremiah.

4753. "Sustenance", here as elsewhere is to be understood both in a physical and metaphorical sense. The Mosaic Law laid down rules of diet, excluding things unclean, and it laid down rules for a pure and honourable life. In this way Israel became the standard-bearer of Allah's law, thus "favoured above the nations."

4754. *Cf.* 10:93. The Jews were the more to blame that they fell from Grace after all the divine favours which they had enjoyed. Their schisms and differences arose from mutual envy, which was rebellious insolence against Allah. As the next verse shows, some of them (not all) rejected the mission of the Holy Prophet, also through envy that a Prophet had come among the Arabians.

4755. *Cf.* 2:90, and that whole passage, with its notes.

Of Judgement as to those
Matters in which they
Set up differences.

الْقِيَـٰمَةِ فِيمَا كَانُوا فِيهِ يَخْتَلِفُونَ

18. Then We put thee
On the (right) Way[4756]
Of Religion: so follow
Thou that (Way),
And follow not the desires
Of those who know not.

١٨ ثُمَّ جَعَلْنَـٰكَ عَلَىٰ
شَرِيعَةٍ مِّنَ الْأَمْرِ فَاتَّبِعْهَا
وَلَا تَتَّبِعْ أَهْوَآءَ الَّذِينَ لَا يَعْلَمُونَ

19. They will be of no
Use to thee in the sight[4757]
Of Allah: it is only
Wrongdoers (that stand as)
Protectors, one to another:
But Allah is the Protector
Of the Righteous.

١٩ إِنَّهُمْ لَن يُغْنُوا عَنكَ مِنَ اللَّهِ شَيْـًٔا
وَإِنَّ الظَّـٰلِمِينَ بَعْضُهُمْ أَوْلِيَآءُ بَعْضٍ
وَاللَّهُ وَلِيُّ الْمُتَّقِينَ

20. These are clear evidences[4758]
To men, and a Guidance
And Mercy to those
Of assured Faith.

٢٠ هَـٰذَا بَصَـٰٓئِرُ لِلنَّاسِ
وَهُدًى وَرَحْمَةٌ لِّقَوْمٍ يُوقِنُونَ

21. What! do those who
Seek after evil ways
Think that We shall
Hold them equal with[4759]
Those who believe and
Do righteous deeds—that
Equal will be their
Life and their death?

٢١ أَمْ حَسِبَ الَّذِينَ اجْتَرَحُوا
السَّيِّـَٔاتِ أَن نَّجْعَلَهُمْ كَالَّذِينَ
ءَامَنُوا وَعَمِلُوا الصَّـٰلِحَـٰتِ
سَوَآءً مَّحْيَاهُمْ وَمَمَاتُهُمْ

4756. Sharī'ah is best translated the "right Way of Religion", which is wider than the mere formal rites and legal provisions, which mostly came in the Madīnah period, long after this Makkan verse had been revealed.

4757. That is, in thy service of Allah. Ignorant and contentious men are of no use or service to any Cause. The more you seek their help, the more do their ignorance and their contentiousness increase their own importance in their own eyes. Evil protects (or thinks it protects) evil: it has really no power of protection at all, for itself or for others. The righteous seek the protection of Allah, Who can and will protect them.

4758. The evidences of Allah's Signs should be clear to all men: to men of Faith, who accept Allah's Grace, they are a Guide and a Mercy.

4759. Three meanings can be deduced. (1) The evil ones are not in Allah's sight like the righteous ones; neither in life nor in death are they equal; in life the righteous are guided by Allah and receive His Grace, and after death His Mercy, while the others reject His Grace, and after death receive condemnation. (2) Neither are the two the same in this life and in the afterlife; if the wicked flourish here, they will be condemned in the Hereafter; if the good are in suffering or sorrow here, they will receive comfort and consolation in the Hereafter; (3) The real life of the righteous—for they have received spiritual life—is not like the nominal life of the wicked, which is really death; nor is the physical death of the righteous, which will bring them into eternal life, like the terrible death of the wicked which will bring them to eternal misery.

Ill is the judgement
That they make.

سَآءَ مَا يَحْكُمُونَ

SECTION 3.

22. Allah created the heavens[4760]
And the earth for
Just ends, and in order
That each soul may find
The recompense of what
It has earned, and none
Of them be wronged.

(٢٢) وَخَلَقَ ٱللَّهُ ٱلسَّمَٰوَٰتِ وَٱلْأَرْضَ بِٱلْحَقِّ
وَلِتُجْزَىٰ كُلُّ نَفْسٍ بِمَا كَسَبَتْ
وَهُمْ لَا يُظْلَمُونَ

23. Then seest thou such[4761]
A one as takes
As his god his own
Vain desire? Allah has,
Knowing (him as such),
Left him astray, and sealed[4762]
His hearing and his heart
(And understanding), and put
A cover on his sight.
Who, then, will guide him
After Allah (has withdrawn
Guidance)? Will ye not
Then receive admonition?

(٢٣) أَفَرَءَيْتَ مَنِ ٱتَّخَذَ
إِلَٰهَهُۥ هَوَىٰهُ وَأَضَلَّهُ ٱللَّهُ عَلَىٰ عِلْمٍ
وَخَتَمَ عَلَىٰ سَمْعِهِۦ وَقَلْبِهِۦ
وَجَعَلَ عَلَىٰ بَصَرِهِۦ غِشَٰوَةً
فَمَن يَهْدِيهِ مِنۢ بَعْدِ ٱللَّهِ
أَفَلَا تَذَكَّرُونَ

24. And they say: "What is
There but our life
In this world?
We shall die and we live,[4763]
And nothing but Time
Can destroy us." But
Of that they have no
Knowledge: they merely
conjecture:

(٢٤) وَقَالُوا۟ مَا هِىَ إِلَّا حَيَاتُنَا ٱلدُّنْيَا
نَمُوتُ وَنَحْيَا وَمَا يُهْلِكُنَآ إِلَّا ٱلدَّهْرُ
وَمَا لَهُم بِذَٰلِكَ مِنْ عِلْمٍ
إِنْ هُمْ إِلَّا يَظُنُّونَ

4760 *Cf.* 44:38-39, and n. 4717. The government of the world is so ordered that each soul gets every chance for its full development, and it reaps the fruit of all its activities. If it breaks away from Allah's Grace, it suffers, but no injustice is done to anyone: on the contrary Allah's Bounty is always beyond man's deserts.

4761. If a man follows, not the laws of Allah, which are also the laws of his own pure nature as made by Allah, but the desires of his own distorted self, as shaped by the rebellion of his will, the inevitable consequence will be the withdrawal of Allah's grace and guidance. All his faculties will then be debased, and there will be nothing to guide him, unless he turns in repentance again to Allah.

4762. *Cf.* 2:7 and notes.

4763. *Cf.* 23:37, and n. 2896. The additional touch here, "And nothing but Time can destroy us", suggests the materialist philosophy that Matter and Time are eternal backwards and forwards; and possibly also that though each individual perishes, the race lasts till Time destroys it. This is not knowledge but conjecture. Why not accept light from Him Who knows all.

25. And when Our Clear
Signs are rehearsed to them,
Their argument is nothing
But this: they say, "Bring[4764]
(Back) our forefathers, if
What ye say is true!"

(٢٥) وَإِذَا تُتْلَىٰ عَلَيْهِمْ ءَايَٰتُنَا بَيِّنَٰتٍ
مَّا كَانَ حُجَّتَهُمْ إِلَّآ أَن قَالُوا۟ ٱئْتُوا۟
بِـَٔابَآئِنَآ إِن كُنتُمْ صَٰدِقِينَ

26. Say:"It is Allah Who
Gives you life, then
Gives you death; then
He will gather you together
For the Day of Judgement
About which there is
No doubt": but most
Men do not understand.

(٢٦) قُلِ ٱللَّهُ يُحْيِيكُمْ ثُمَّ يُمِيتُكُمْ
ثُمَّ يَجْمَعُكُمْ إِلَىٰ يَوْمِ ٱلْقِيَٰمَةِ لَا رَيْبَ فِيهِ
وَلَٰكِنَّ أَكْثَرَ ٱلنَّاسِ لَا يَعْلَمُونَ

SECTION 4.

27. To Allah belongs
The dominion of the heavens
And the earth, and
The Day that the Hour
Of Judgement is established—
That Day will the dealers[4765]
In Falsehood perish!

(٢٧) وَلِلَّهِ مُلْكُ ٱلسَّمَٰوَٰتِ وَٱلْأَرْضِ ۚ
وَيَوْمَ تَقُومُ ٱلسَّاعَةُ يَوْمَئِذٍ
يَخْسَرُ ٱلْمُبْطِلُونَ

28. And thou wilt see
Every sect bowing the knee:[4766]
Every sect will be called
To its Record: "This Day
Shall ye be recompensed
For all that ye did!

(٢٨) وَتَرَىٰ كُلَّ أُمَّةٍ جَاثِيَةً ۚ
كُلُّ أُمَّةٍ تُدْعَىٰٓ إِلَىٰ كِتَٰبِهَا
ٱلْيَوْمَ تُجْزَوْنَ مَا كُنتُمْ تَعْمَلُونَ

29. "This Our Record speaks
About you with truth:
For We were wont[4767]

(٢٩) هَٰذَا كِتَٰبُنَا يَنطِقُ
عَلَيْكُم بِٱلْحَقِّ ۚ إِنَّا كُنَّا

4764. *Cf.* 44:36. It is no argument to say, "If there is a future life, bring back our forefathers and let us see them here and now!" It is not for a man to raise the dead when and where he pleases. It is for Allah to command. And His promise is about the general Resurrection for the Day of Judgement. In His hands are the keys of life and death.

4765. These vain wranglers about the future life and deniers of the Truth may have a run in this fleeting world; but the moment the world of Reality is established, they will see what they now deny. The facts will destroy their fancies, and they themselves will find themselves humiliated and lost, for having deliberately ignored Allah's Signs and acted in opposition to His Holy Will.

4766. *Bowing the knee:* the key phrase of the Sūrah, and its title, *Cf.* 19:72. Whatever the arrogance of the wicked may be in this life, whatever exclusive sects and divisions they may form in this life, the time will come when they will humbly submit and bow the knee of the Truth. Before the Judgement Seat, when their Record is produced, they must necessarily be dumb.

4767. *Cf.* 44:80. Nothing misses the Recording Angel, and whatever is said in the Record is true.

To put on record
All that ye did."

نَسْتَنسِخُ مَا كُنتُمْ تَعْمَلُونَ

30. Then, as to those who
Believed and did righteous
Deeds, their Lord will
Admit them to His Mercy:
That will be the Achievement[4768]
For all to see.

٣٠ فَأَمَّا ٱلَّذِينَ ءَامَنُوا۟ وَعَمِلُوا۟ ٱلصَّٰلِحَٰتِ
فَيُدْخِلُهُمْ رَبُّهُمْ فِى رَحْمَتِهِۦ
ذَٰلِكَ هُوَ ٱلْفَوْزُ ٱلْمُبِينُ

31. But as to those who
Rejected Allah, (to them
Will be said): "Were not
Our Signs rehearsed to you?
But ye were arrogant,
And were a people
Given to sin!

٣١ وَأَمَّا ٱلَّذِينَ كَفَرُوٓا۟
أَفَلَمْ تَكُنْ ءَايَٰتِى تُتْلَىٰ عَلَيْكُمْ
فَٱسْتَكْبَرْتُمْ وَكُنتُمْ قَوْمًا مُّجْرِمِينَ

32. "And when it was said
That the promise of Allah
Was true, and that the Hour—
There was no doubt
About its (coming), ye
Used to say, 'We
Know not what is[4769]
The Hour: we only think
It is an idea, and we
Have no firm assurance.'"

٣٢ وَإِذَا قِيلَ إِنَّ وَعْدَ ٱللَّهِ حَقٌّ
وَٱلسَّاعَةُ لَا رَيْبَ فِيهَا
قُلْتُم مَّا نَدْرِى مَا ٱلسَّاعَةُ
إِن نَّظُنُّ إِلَّا ظَنًّا
وَمَا نَحْنُ بِمُسْتَيْقِنِينَ

33. Then will appear to them
The evil (fruits) of what
They did, and they will be[4770]
Completely encircled by that
Which they used to mock at!

٣٣ وَبَدَا لَهُمْ سَيِّـَٔاتُ مَا عَمِلُوا۟
وَحَاقَ بِهِم مَّا كَانُوا۟ بِهِۦ يَسْتَهْزِءُونَ

34. It will also be said:
"This Day We will forget[4771]
You as ye forgot
The meeting of this Day
Of yours! And your

٣٤ وَقِيلَ ٱلْيَوْمَ نَنسَىٰكُمْ
كَمَا نَسِيتُمْ لِقَآءَ يَوْمِكُمْ هَٰذَا

4768. The attainment and satisfaction of all hopes and desires; the reaching of the final goal of Bliss. *Cf.* 44:57, and n. 4733.

4769. There is arrogance as well as untruth in this pretence. The coming of Judgement has been proclaimed times out of number by every Prophet of Allah. They cannot dismiss it as a mere idea or superstition. Their object is merely an ostentatious and lofty rejection of Faith.

4770. *Cf.* 11:8. Their mockery will be turned against themselves, for they will be hemmed in by the very Realities which they had ignored or doubted or laughed at.

4771. *Cf.* 7:51 and n. 1029. "Forget" is of course metaphorical for "deliberately to ignore".

Abode is the Fire, and
No helpers have ye!

وَمَأْوَىٰكُمُ ٱلنَّارُ وَمَا لَكُم مِّن نَّٰصِرِينَ

35. "This, because ye used
To take the Signs of Allah
In jest, and the life
Of the world deceived you:"[4772]
(From) that Day, therefore,
They shall not be taken out
Thence, nor shall they be
Received into Grace.

٣٥ ذَٰلِكُم بِأَنَّكُمُ ٱتَّخَذْتُمْ ءَايَٰتِ ٱللَّهِ هُزُوًا
وَغَرَّتْكُمُ ٱلْحَيَوٰةُ ٱلدُّنْيَا
فَٱلْيَوْمَ لَا يُخْرَجُونَ مِنْهَا
وَلَا هُمْ يُسْتَعْتَبُونَ

36. Then Praise be to Allah,[4773]
Lord of the heavens
And Lord of the earth—
Lord and Cherisher
Of all the worlds!

٣٦ فَلِلَّهِ ٱلْحَمْدُ رَبِّ ٱلسَّمَٰوَٰتِ
وَرَبِّ ٱلْأَرْضِ رَبِّ ٱلْعَٰلَمِينَ

37. To Him be Glory
Throughout the heavens
And the earth: and He
Is Exalted in Power,
Full of Wisdom!

٣٧ وَلَهُ ٱلْكِبْرِيَآءُ فِى ٱلسَّمَٰوَٰتِ وَٱلْأَرْضِ
وَهُوَ ٱلْعَزِيزُ ٱلْحَكِيمُ

4772. It is implied that 'you deliberately allowed yourselves to be deceived by the vanities of this world', or 'that you put yourselves into a position where you were deceived, for you were expressly warned against Evil'.

4773. The argument having been completed about the fruits of this life being reaped in the *Ma'ād*, or the Hereafter, when perfect balance will be restored and perfect Justice will reign supreme, the Sūrah closes with praise and glory to Allah, Who is not only Omnipotent but is full of Wisdom, and cherishes and cares for all His creation. We began with the remembrance of His Revelation and Mercy, and we close with the celebration of His goodness, power, and wisdom. Note how the argument is rounded off by the reminiscence of the last clause of the second verse of this Sūrah.

INTRODUCTION TO SŪRAH 46—*AL AḤQĀF*

This is the seventh and last Sūrah of the *Ḥā Mīm* series. For the general theme and chronological place of these Sūrahs see the Introduction to S. 40.

The *Aḥqāf* (mentioned in verse 21) are the long and winding crooked tracts of sandhills, characteristic of the country of the 'Ād people, adjoining Ḥaḍramawt and Yemen: see 7:65, n. 1040. These people had, at that time, probably a fertile irrigated country, but their sins brought on the calamity mentioned in 46:24-25. The lesson of this Sūrah is that if the Truth is challenged, the challenge will be duly answered, and Truth vindicated.

Summary—All Creation has a Purpose behind it: Truth and Revelation will be vindicated, and those who question it will be undone by the very means by which they set such store: the righteous should wait in patience and constancy (46:1-35, and C. 219).

C. 219.—Creation is for just ends, and Falsehood
(46:1-35) Is but straying from the Path:
Say what people may
Truth carries its own vindication:
Follow it firmly. Let age think of youth,
And youth not turn rebellious. There are fine
Gradations in the kingdom of Allah: then strive
For the best. Let not pride and arrogance
Undo you: the humble are often the best
Recipients of Truth. All will come right
In good time: so persevere with patient firmness
Of purpose. Justice that seems to tarry
Comes really on swiftest foot but sure.

Sūrah 46.

Al Aḥqāf [4773-A] (Winding Sand-tracts)

In the name of Allah, Most Gracious, Most Merciful.

1. Ḥā Mīm.[4774]

2. The revelation[4775]
Of the Book
Is from Allah
The Exalted in Power,
Full of Wisdom.

3. We created not[4776]
The heavens and the earth
And all between them
But for just ends, and
For a term appointed:
But those who reject Faith
Turn away from that
Whereof they are warned.

4. Say: "Do ye see[4777]
What it is ye invoke
Besides Allah? Show me
What it is they
Have created on earth,
Or have they a share
In the heavens?
Bring me a Book[4778]
(Revealed) before this,

الجزء السادس والعشرون سورة الأحقاف

بِسْمِ ٱللَّهِ ٱلرَّحْمَٰنِ ٱلرَّحِيمِ

حمٓ ﴿١﴾

تَنزِيلُ ٱلْكِتَٰبِ مِنَ
ٱللَّهِ ٱلْعَزِيزِ ٱلْحَكِيمِ ﴿٢﴾

مَا خَلَقْنَا ٱلسَّمَٰوَٰتِ
وَٱلْأَرْضَ وَمَا بَيْنَهُمَآ
إِلَّا بِٱلْحَقِّ وَأَجَلٍ مُّسَمًّى
وَٱلَّذِينَ كَفَرُوا۟ عَمَّآ أُنذِرُوا۟ مُعْرِضُونَ ﴿٣﴾

قُلْ أَرَءَيْتُم مَّا تَدْعُونَ مِن
دُونِ ٱللَّهِ أَرُونِى مَاذَا خَلَقُوا۟ مِنَ ٱلْأَرْضِ
أَمْ لَهُمْ شِرْكٌ فِى ٱلسَّمَٰوَٰتِ
ٱئْتُونِى بِكِتَٰبٍ مِّن قَبْلِ هَٰذَآ ﴿٤﴾

4773-A. See introduction to S. 46, paragraph 2.

4774. See introduction to S. 40, paragraphs 2-4.

4775. This verse is the same as the second verse of the last Sūrah, but the theme is worked out differently in the two Sūrahs. In S. 45 was shown how deniers of Revelation will at last be humbled until they can no longer deny its truth and power. In this Sūrah is shown how Truth and Revelation will be vindicated by patience and constancy (46:35).

4776. *Cf.* 45:22. Many things may appear to us in the present world as strange and inexplicable. But everything made by Allah has a just purpose which must be fulfilled. Nothing in this world is permanent: everything is for an appointed term. The Word of Allah alone abides. All else will pass away after it has fulfilled its purpose. But Unbelievers refuse to face the danger of which they are warned.

4777. Some people may rush thoughtlessly into false worship, because it is the fashion or an ancestral custom, etc. They are asked to pause and see for themselves. Have the false gods or falsehood created anything? (They destroy much). Or have they any share or lot in the things we associate with the heavens—spiritual well-being, etc.?

4778. Or is there any warrant for you from any earlier revelation, assuming that you do not believe in this Revelation? Or can you point to the least scrap or remnant of real knowledge on which you can base what we condemn as your false life? No, you cannot.

Or any remnant of knowledge
(Ye may have), if ye
Are telling the truth!

أَوْ أَثَـٰرَةٍ مِّنْ عِلْمٍ إِن كُنتُمْ صَـٰدِقِينَ

5. And who is more astray[4779]
Than one who invokes,
Besides Allah, such as will
Not answer him to the Day
Of Judgement, and who
(In fact) are unconscious
Of their call (to them)?

٥ وَمَنْ أَضَلُّ مِمَّن يَدْعُوا۟ مِن
دُونِ ٱللَّهِ مَن لَّا يَسْتَجِيبُ لَهُۥٓ إِلَىٰ يَوْمِ ٱلْقِيَـٰمَةِ
وَهُمْ عَن دُعَآئِهِمْ غَـٰفِلُونَ

6. And when mankind
Are gathered together
(At the Resurrection),
They will be hostile
To them and reject
Their worship (altogether)!

٦ وَإِذَا حُشِرَ ٱلنَّاسُ
كَانُوا۟ لَهُمْ أَعْدَآءً
وَكَانُوا۟ بِعِبَادَتِهِمْ كَـٰفِرِينَ

7. When Our Clear Signs
Are rehearsed to them,
The Unbelievers say,
Of the Truth
When it comes to them:[4780]
"This is evident sorcery!"

٧ وَإِذَا تُتْلَىٰ عَلَيْهِمْ ءَايَـٰتُنَا بَيِّنَـٰتٍ
قَالَ ٱلَّذِينَ كَفَرُوا۟ لِلْحَقِّ لَمَّا جَآءَهُمْ
هَـٰذَا سِحْرٌ مُّبِينٌ

8. Or do they say,
"He has forged it"?
Say: "Had I forged it,
Then can ye obtain[4781]
No single (blessing) for me
From Allah. He knows best
Of that whereof ye talk
(So glibly)! Enough is He
For a witness between me

٨ أَمْ يَقُولُونَ ٱفْتَرَىٰهُ ۖ
قُلْ إِنِ ٱفْتَرَيْتُهُۥ فَلَا تَمْلِكُونَ لِى مِنَ ٱللَّهِ شَيْـًٔا ۖ
هُوَ أَعْلَمُ بِمَا تُفِيضُونَ فِيهِ ۖ
كَفَىٰ بِهِۦ شَهِيدًۢا بَيْنِى

4779. As there is no argument at all in favour of your sham worship, what sense is there in it? Either your false gods are senseless stocks and stones which will never answer you to the end of Time, being themselves devoid of understanding, or they are real objects which will disown you at the last. If you worshipped Self, your own misused faculties will witness against you at the last (41:20-23). If you worshipped good men or prophets, like Jesus, they will disown you (5:119). Similarly, if you worshipped angels, they will disown you (34:40-41).

4780. When the truth is actually brought to their doors, they call it sorcery! *Cf.* 37:12-15, and n. 4042.

4781. 'If I forged a message from myself as one purporting to come from Allah, you would not be able to see me enjoy any of the blessings from Allah which I enjoy: you would not see me calm and relying on Allah, nor would you see me bear the reputation of being a trustworthy man. A liar comes to an evil end. But what about those who talk so glibly and freely about things which they know not? Allah knows all, and He is my witness! But even against your false accusations, I pray for His forgiveness and mercy to you, for He is Oft-Forgiving, Most Merciful!'

And you! And He is Oft-Forgiving, Most Merciful."	وَبَيْنَكُمْ وَهُوَ الْغَفُورُ الرَّحِيمُ
9. Say: "I am no bringer[4782] Of new-fangled doctrine Among the messengers, nor Do I know what will Be done with me or With you. I follow But that which is revealed To me by inspiration: I am but a Warner Open and clear."	٩ قُلْ مَا كُنتُ بِدْعًا مِّنَ الرُّسُلِ وَمَا أَدْرِي مَا يُفْعَلُ بِي وَلَا بِكُمْ إِنْ أَتَّبِعُ إِلَّا مَا يُوحَىٰ إِلَيَّ وَمَا أَنَا إِلَّا نَذِيرٌ مُّبِينٌ
10. Say: "See ye?[4783] If (this teaching) be From Allah, and ye reject it, And a witness from among The Children of Israel testifies To its similarity[4784] (With earlier scripture), And has believed While ye are arrogant, (How unjust ye are!) Truly, Allah guides not A people unjust."	١٠ قُلْ أَرَءَيْتُمْ إِن كَانَ مِنْ عِندِ اللَّهِ وَكَفَرْتُم بِهِۦ وَشَهِدَ شَاهِدٌ مِّنۢ بَنِىٓ إِسْرَٰٓءِيلَ عَلَىٰ مِثْلِهِۦ فَـَٔامَنَ وَاسْتَكْبَرْتُمْ إِنَّ اللَّهَ لَا يَهْدِى الْقَوْمَ الظَّٰلِمِينَ
SECTION 2.	
11. The Unbelievers say Of those who believe: "If (this Message) were[4785]	١١ وَقَالَ الَّذِينَ كَفَرُوا لِلَّذِينَ ءَامَنُوا لَوْ كَانَ

4782. 'What is there to forge? All prophets have taught the Unity of Allah and our duty to mankind. I bring no new-fangled doctrine, but eternal truths that have been known to good men through the ages. It is to reclaim you that I have come. I do not know what will be your fate for all this callousness, nor what you will do to me. But this I know, that I am preaching truth and righteousness as inspired by Allah. My duty is only to proclaim aloud and clearly the Message entrusted to me by Allah. The rest I leave to Allah.'

4783. Another side of the argument is now presented, 'You pagan Arabs! You are puffed up with pride, though you are an ignorant nation. Among Israel there are men who understand the previous scriptures, and who find the Qur'ān and its Preacher a true confirmation of the previous scriptures. They accept Islam as a fulfillment of the revelation of Moses himself! (See Deut. xviii. 18-19). And yet you hold back, though the Qur'ān has come in your own language, in order to help you to understand. How unjust and how shameful! In that case, with what face can you seek guidance from Allah?'

4784. There were learned Jews (and Christians) who saw in the Holy Prophet the Messenger of Allah foreshadowed in previous Revelations, and accepted Islam. As this is a Makkan Sūrah we need not construe this as a reference to 'Abd Allāh ibn Salām, whose conversion was in Madīnah only two years before the Prophet's death, unless we accept this particular verse to be so late in date. The sincere Jews were in a position to understand how this Revelation fitted in with all they had learnt about Revelation.

4785. A great many of the early Muslims were in humble positions, and were despised by the Quraysh leaders. 'If such men could see any good in Islam,' they said, 'there could be no good in it: if there had been any good in it, we should have been the first to see it!' The spiritually blind have such a good conceit of themselves! As they reject it, and as the Revelation is proved to have historic foundations, they can only call it "an old, old falsehood"!

A good thing, (such men)
Would not have gone
To it first, before us!"
And seeing that they
Guide not themselves thereby,
They will say, "This is
An (old), old falsehood!"

خَيْرًا مَّا سَبَقُونَآ إِلَيْهِ
وَإِذْ لَمْ يَهْتَدُوا۟ بِهِۦ
فَسَيَقُولُونَ هَٰذَآ إِفْكٌ قَدِيمٌ

12. And before this, was[4786]
The Book of Moses
As a guide and a mercy:
And this Book confirms (it)
In the Arabic tongue;
To admonish the unjust,
And as Glad Tidings
To those who do right.

١٢ وَمِن قَبْلِهِۦ كِتَٰبُ مُوسَىٰٓ إِمَامًا وَرَحْمَةً
وَهَٰذَا كِتَٰبٌ مُّصَدِّقٌ لِّسَانًا عَرَبِيًّا
لِّيُنذِرَ ٱلَّذِينَ ظَلَمُوا۟
وَبُشْرَىٰ لِلْمُحْسِنِينَ

13. Verily those who say,[4787]
"Our Lord is Allah,"
And remain firm
(On that Path)—
On them shall be no fear,[4788]
Nor shall they grieve.

١٣ إِنَّ ٱلَّذِينَ قَالُوا۟ رَبُّنَا ٱللَّهُ
ثُمَّ ٱسْتَقَٰمُوا۟ فَلَا خَوْفٌ عَلَيْهِمْ
وَلَا هُمْ يَحْزَنُونَ

14. Such shall be Companions
Of the Garden, dwelling
Therein (for aye): a recompense
For their (good) deeds.

١٤ أُو۟لَٰٓئِكَ أَصْحَٰبُ ٱلْجَنَّةِ
خَٰلِدِينَ فِيهَا جَزَآءًۢ بِمَا كَانُوا۟ يَعْمَلُونَ

15. We have enjoined on man[4789]
Kindness to his parents:
In pain did his mother

١٥ وَوَصَّيْنَا ٱلْإِنسَٰنَ بِوَٰلِدَيْهِ إِحْسَٰنًا
حَمَلَتْهُ أُمُّهُۥ كُرْهًا

4786. The last revealed Book which was a Code of Life *(Sharī'ah)* was the Book of Moses: for that of Jesus was not such a Code, but merely moral precepts to sweep away the corruptions that had crept in. The Qur'ān has the same attitude to it as the teaching of Jesus had to the Law. Jesus said (Matt. v. 17): "Think not that I am come to destroy the Law or the prophets; I am not come to destroy, but to fulfil." But the corruptions took new forms in Christian Churches: an entirely new *Sharī'ah* became necessary, and this was provided in Islam.

4787. To say, "Our Lord is Allah" is to acknowledge that we owe no service to any creature, and shall render none: Allah shall have our exclusive devotion. "To remain firm on that Path" is shown by our conduct: we prove that we love Allah and all His creatures, and will unflinchingly do our duty in all circumstances.

4788. *Cf.* 2:38. The phrase occurs in numerous other places, with a new application on each occasion. Here, if our claim is true that 'our Lord is Allah', what fear can possibly come to us, or what calamity can there be to cause us grief? For our Lord is our Cherisher, Defender, and Helper, our Hope and our Comfort, which can never fail.

4789. *Cf.* 29:8 and 31:14.

Bear him, and in pain
Did she give him birth.
The carrying of the (child)
To his weaning is
(A period of) thirty months.[4790]
At length, when he reaches
The age of full strength[4791]
And attains forty years,
He says, "O my Lord!
Grant me that I may be
Grateful for Thy favour
Which Thou hast bestowed
Upon me, and upon both
My parents, and that I
May work righteousness
Such as Thou mayest approve;
And be gracious to me
In my issue. Truly
Have I turned to Thee
And truly do I bow
(To Thee) in Islam."

وَوَضَعَتْهُ كُرْهًا
وَحَمْلُهُۥ وَفِصَٰلُهُۥ ثَلَٰثُونَ شَهْرًا
حَتَّىٰٓ إِذَا بَلَغَ أَشُدَّهُۥ
وَبَلَغَ أَرْبَعِينَ سَنَةً
قَالَ رَبِّ أَوْزِعْنِىٓ أَنْ
أَشْكُرَ نِعْمَتَكَ ٱلَّتِىٓ
أَنْعَمْتَ عَلَىَّ وَعَلَىٰ وَٰلِدَىَّ
وَأَنْ أَعْمَلَ صَٰلِحًا تَرْضَىٰهُ
وَأَصْلِحْ لِى فِى ذُرِّيَّتِىٓ
إِنِّى تُبْتُ إِلَيْكَ وَإِنِّى
مِنَ ٱلْمُسْلِمِينَ

16. Such are they from whom
We shall accept the best[4792]
Of their deeds and pass by
Their ill deeds: (they shall
Be) among the Companions
Of the Garden: a promise
Of truth, which was
Made to them
(In this life).

(١٦) أُو۟لَٰٓئِكَ ٱلَّذِينَ
نَتَقَبَّلُ عَنْهُمْ أَحْسَنَ مَا عَمِلُوا۟
وَنَتَجَاوَزُ عَن سَيِّـَٔاتِهِمْ فِىٓ أَصْحَٰبِ ٱلْجَنَّةِ
وَعْدَ ٱلصِّدْقِ ٱلَّذِى
كَانُوا۟ يُوعَدُونَ

4790. In 31:14 the time of weaning was stated to be at the age of two years, *i.e.*, 24 months. See also 2:233. That leaves six months as the *minimum* period of human gestation after which the child is known to be viable. This is in accordance with the latest ascertained scientific facts. The *average* period is 280 days, or ten times the inter-menstrual period, and of course the average period of weaning is much less than 24 months.

The maximum period of breast-feeding (2 years) is again in accordance with the time that the first dentition is ordinarily completed in a human child. The lower milk incisors in the centre come out between the 6th and 9th months; then come out the milk teeth at intervals, until the canines appear. The second molars come out at about 24 months, and with them the child has a complete apparatus of milk teeth. Nature now expects him to chew and masticate and be independent of his mother's milk completely. On the other hand it hurts the mother to feed from the breast after the child has a complete set of milk teeth. The permanent teeth begin at the sixth year, and the second molars come at 12 years. The third molars are the wisdom teeth, which may appear at 18 to 20 years, or not at all.

4791. The age of full strength *(ashudd)* is held to be between 18 and 30 or 32. Between 30 and 40 the man is in his best manhood. After that he begins to look to his growing issue, and rightly commends the new generation to Allah. Perhaps his spiritual faculties also gain the upper hand after 40.

4792. *Cf.* 29:7 and n. 3429.

17. But (there is one)[4793]
Who says to his parents,
"Fie on you! Do ye
Hold out the promise
To me that I
Shall be raised up,
Even though generations
Have passed before me
(Without rising again)?"
And they two seek
Allah's aid, (and rebuke
The son): "Woe to thee!
Have Faith! For the promise
Of Allah is true."
But he says, "This is
Nothing but tales
Of the ancients!"

١٧ وَٱلَّذِى قَالَ
لِوَٰلِدَيْهِ أُفٍّ لَّكُمَآ
أَتَعِدَانِنِىٓ أَنْ أُخْرَجَ
وَقَدْ خَلَتِ ٱلْقُرُونُ مِن قَبْلِى
وَهُمَا يَسْتَغِيثَانِ ٱللَّهَ وَيْلَكَ
ءَامِنْ إِنَّ وَعْدَ ٱللَّهِ حَقٌّ
فَيَقُولُ مَا هَٰذَآ إِلَّآ
أَسَٰطِيرُ ٱلْأَوَّلِينَ

18. Such are they against whom[4794]
Is proved the Sentence
Among the previous generations
Of Jinns and men, that have
Passed away; for they will
Be (utterly) lost.

١٨ أُو۟لَٰٓئِكَ ٱلَّذِينَ حَقَّ عَلَيْهِمُ ٱلْقَوْلُ
فِىٓ أُمَمٍ قَدْ خَلَتْ مِن قَبْلِهِم مِّنَ ٱلْجِنِّ وَٱلْإِنسِ
إِنَّهُمْ كَانُوا۟ خَٰسِرِينَ

19. And to all[4795]
Are (assigned) degrees
According to the deeds
Which they (have done),
And in order that (Allah)
May recompense their deeds,
And no injustice be done
To them.

١٩ وَلِكُلٍّ دَرَجَٰتٌ مِّمَّا عَمِلُوا۟
وَلِيُوَفِّيَهُمْ أَعْمَٰلَهُمْ
وَهُمْ لَا يُظْلَمُونَ

4793. A godly man often has an ungodly son, who flouts all that the father held sacred, and looks upon his father himself as old-fashioned and unworthy of respect or regard. The contrast in an individual family may be matched by the contrast in the passing and the rising generations of mankind. All this happens as a passing phase in the normal evolution of mankind, and there is nothing in this to be despondent about. What we have to do is for the mature generations to bring up their successors in godly ways, and for the younger generations to realise that age and experience count for something, especially in the understanding of spiritual matters and other matters of the highest moment to man.

4794. *Cf.* 41:25 and n. 4494. Each individual, each generation, and each people is responsible for its own good deeds or misdeeds. The law of actions and their fruits applies: you cannot blame one for another. The only remedy lies in seeking for Allah's Grace and Mercy, not only for ourselves but for others in brotherly or fatherly love.

This verse is in balanced contrast to verse 16 above.

4795. There is fine grading in the spiritual Kingdom. Every deed, good or bad, is judged and weighed to the minutest degree, with its motives, intentions, results, and relevant circumstances. It is not a mere rough classification. The fruits of evil will be exactly according to the degree of evil. But, as stated in other passages (*e.g.*, 28:84), the reward of good deeds will be far beyond their merits, on account of the Mercy and unbounded Bounty of Allah.

20. And on the Day that
The Unbelievers will be
Placed before the Fire,
(It will be said to them):
"Ye received your good
things[4796]
In the life of the world,
And ye took your pleasure
Out of them: but today
Shall ye be recompensed[4797]
With a Penalty of humiliation:
For that ye were arrogant
On earth without just cause,
And that ye (ever) transgressed."

وَيَوْمَ يُعْرَضُ ٱلَّذِينَ كَفَرُوا۟ عَلَى ٱلنَّارِ أَذْهَبْتُمْ طَيِّبَٰتِكُمْ فِى حَيَاتِكُمُ ٱلدُّنْيَا وَٱسْتَمْتَعْتُم بِهَا فَٱلْيَوْمَ تُجْزَوْنَ عَذَابَ ٱلْهُونِ بِمَا كُنتُمْ تَسْتَكْبِرُونَ فِى ٱلْأَرْضِ بِغَيْرِ ٱلْحَقِّ وَبِمَا كُنتُمْ تَفْسُقُونَ ﴿٢٠﴾

SECTION 3.

21. Mention (Hūd)
One of 'Ād's (own) brethren:[4798]
Behold, he warned his people
About the winding Sand-tracts:[4799]
But there have been Warners
Before him and after him:
"Worship ye none other
Than Allah: truly I fear
For you the Penalty
Of a Mighty Day."

وَٱذْكُرْ أَخَا عَادٍ إِذْ أَنذَرَ قَوْمَهُۥ بِٱلْأَحْقَافِ وَقَدْ خَلَتِ ٱلنُّذُرُ مِنۢ بَيْنِ يَدَيْهِ وَمِنْ خَلْفِهِۦٓ أَلَّا تَعْبُدُوٓا۟ إِلَّا ٱللَّهَ إِنِّىٓ أَخَافُ عَلَيْكُمْ عَذَابَ يَوْمٍ عَظِيمٍ ﴿٢١﴾

22. They said: "Hast thou come[4800]
In order to turn us aside
From our gods? Then bring
Upon us the (calamity)
With which thou dost
Threaten us, if thou
Art telling the truth!"

قَالُوٓا۟ أَجِئْتَنَا لِتَأْفِكَنَا عَنْ ءَالِهَتِنَا فَأْتِنَا بِمَا تَعِدُنَآ إِن كُنتَ مِنَ ٱلصَّٰدِقِينَ ﴿٢٢﴾

4796. *Received your good things* implies (in Arabic) grabbing at them, being greedy of them, seeking them as fleeting pleasures rather than the most serious things of life, sacrificing the spiritual for the material.

4797. They will be told: 'You took your choice, and you must pay the price. You did wrong in a rebellious spirit, and prided yourselves on your wrongdoing, not occasionally, but of set purpose and constantly. Now will you be humbled in the dust, as a fitting punishment.'

4798. *Cf.* 7:65, and note 1040. The point is that the Warner who was raised among the 'Ād people—as among other peoples—was not a stranger, but one of their own brethren, even as the Holy Prophet began his preaching with a call to his own brethren the Quraysh.

4799. *Winding Sand-tracts: Aḥqāf:* see Introduction to this Sūrah. The very things, which, under irrigation and with Allah's Grace, gave them prosperity and power, were to be their undoing when they broke Allah's Law and defied His Grace. See verses 24-26 below.

4800. They were too much wedded to their evil ways—to the false gods that they worshipped—to appreciate the sincere advice of the Prophet of Allah. They defied him and defied Allah Who had sent him. Mockingly they challenged him to bring on the threatened punishment! For they did not believe a word of what he said.

23. He said: "The Knowledge[4801]
(Of when it will come)
Is only with Allah: I
Proclaim to you the mission
On which I have been sent:
But I see that ye
Are a people in ignorance!"...

٢٣ قَالَ إِنَّمَا الْعِلْمُ عِندَ اللَّهِ
وَأُبَلِّغُكُم مَّا أُرْسِلْتُ بِهِ
وَلَٰكِنِّي أَرَاكُمْ قَوْمًا تَجْهَلُونَ

24. Then, when they saw[4802]
The (Penalty in the shape of)
A cloud traversing the sky,
Coming to meet their valleys,
They said, "This cloud
Will give us rain!"
"Nay, it is the (calamity)
Ye were asking to be
Hastened!—a wind
Wherein is a Grievous Penalty!

٢٤ فَلَمَّا رَأَوْهُ عَارِضًا مُّسْتَقْبِلَ
أَوْدِيَتِهِمْ قَالُوا هَٰذَا عَارِضٌ مُّمْطِرُنَا
بَلْ هُوَ مَا اسْتَعْجَلْتُم بِهِ
رِيحٌ فِيهَا عَذَابٌ أَلِيمٌ

25. "Everything will it destroy
By the command of its Lord!"
Then by the morning
they—[4803]
Nothing was to be seen
But (the ruins of) their houses!
Thus do We recompense
Those given to sin!

٢٥ تُدَمِّرُ كُلَّ شَيْءٍ بِأَمْرِ رَبِّهَا
فَأَصْبَحُوا لَا يُرَىٰ
إِلَّا مَسَاكِنُهُمْ
كَذَٰلِكَ نَجْزِي الْقَوْمَ الْمُجْرِمِينَ

26. And We had firmly established
Them in a (prosperity and)
power
Which We have not given
To you (ye Quraysh!)
And We had endowed them

٢٦ وَلَقَدْ مَكَّنَّاهُمْ
فِيمَا إِن مَّكَّنَّاكُمْ فِيهِ
وَجَعَلْنَا لَهُمْ

4801. The coming of the Punishment for evil was (and is always) certain. At what particular time it would come he could not tell. It is not for the prophet, but for Allah, to bring on the Penalty. But he saw that it was useless to appeal to them on account of the ignorance in which they were content to dwell.

4802. The Punishment came suddenly, and when they least expected it. They wanted rain, and they saw a cloud and rejoiced. Behold, it was coming towards their own tracts, winding through the hills. Their irrigation channels would be full, their fields would be green, and their season would be fruitful. But no! What is this? It is a tremendous hurricane, carrying destruction on its wings! A violent blast, with dust and sand! Its fury destroys everything in its wake! Lives lost! Fields covered with sandhills! The morning dawns on a scene of desolation! Where were the men who boasted and defied their Lord! There are only the ruins of their houses to witness to the past!

4803. Here is the figure of speech known in rhetoric as aposiopesis, to heighten the effect of the suddenness and completeness of the calamity. In the Arabic text, the verb *aṣbaḥū*, in the third person plural, leads us to expect that we shall be told what they were doing in the morning. But no! They had been wiped out, and any small remnant had fled (see n. 1040 to 7:65). Nothing was to be seen but the ruins of their houses.

With (faculties of)[4804]
Hearing, seeing, heart and
intellect:
But of no profit to them
Were their (faculties of)
Hearing, sight, and heart
And intellect, when they
Went on rejecting the Signs[4805]
Of Allah: and they were
(Completely) encircled[4806]
By that which they
Used to mock at!

سَمْعًا وَأَبْصَٰرًا وَأَفْـِٔدَةً
فَمَآ أَغْنَىٰ عَنْهُمْ سَمْعُهُمْ
وَلَآ أَبْصَٰرُهُمْ وَلَآ أَفْـِٔدَتُهُم مِّن شَىْءٍ
إِذْ كَانُوا۟ يَجْحَدُونَ بِـَٔايَٰتِ ٱللَّهِ
وَحَاقَ بِهِم مَّا كَانُوا۟ بِهِۦ
يَسْتَهْزِءُونَ

SECTION 4.

27. We destroyed aforetime
Populations round about you;[4807]
And We have shown
The Signs in various ways,
That they may turn (to Us).

٢٧ وَلَقَدْ أَهْلَكْنَا مَا حَوْلَكُم مِّنَ ٱلْقُرَىٰ
وَصَرَّفْنَا ٱلْـَٔايَٰتِ لَعَلَّهُمْ يَرْجِعُونَ

28. Why then was no help
Forthcoming to them from those
Whom they worshipped as gods,
Besides Allah, as a means
Of access (to Allah)? Nay,
They left them in the lurch:
But that was their
Falsehood and their invention.[4808]

٢٨ فَلَوْلَا نَصَرَهُمُ ٱلَّذِينَ ٱتَّخَذُوا۟
مِن دُونِ ٱللَّهِ قُرْبَانًا ءَالِهَةًۢ
بَلْ ضَلُّوا۟ عَنْهُمْ
وَذَٰلِكَ إِفْكُهُمْ وَمَا كَانُوا۟ يَفْتَرُونَ

29. Behold, We turned
Towards thee a company[4809]

٢٩ وَإِذْ صَرَفْنَآ إِلَيْكَ نَفَرًا

4804. The 'Ād and their successors the Thamūd were more richly endowed with the faculties of the arts, sciences, and culture than ever were the Quraysh before Islam. "Hearing and seeing" refer to the experimental faculties; the word "heart" in Arabic includes intellect, or the rational faculties, as well as the instruments of feeling and emotion, the aesthetic faculties. The Second 'Ād, or the Thamūd, have left interesting traces of their architecture in the country round the Ḥijr: see n. 1043 to 7:73, and notes 2002-2003 to 15:80-82.

4805. The highest talents and faculties of this world are useless in the spiritual world if we reject the laws of the spiritual world and thus become outlaws there.

4806. See n. 4770 to 45:33. They used to mock at Allah's Signs, but those were the very things which hemmed them in, and showed that they had more power and effectiveness than anything else.

4807. In Arabian history and tradition alone, to say nothing of Allah's Signs elsewhere, sin inevitably suffered its Punishment, and in various ways. Would not the later people take warning?

4808. The false things that they worshipped were figments of their imagination. If they had had any existence in fact, it was not of the kind they imagined.

4809. *A company of Jinns. Nafar* (company) may mean a group of from three to ten persons. For *Jinns*, see n. 929 to 6:100. They listened to the reading of the Qur'ān with great respect. The next verse shows that they had heard of the Jewish religion, but they were impressed with the Message of Islam, and they seem to have gone back to their people to share the Good News with them. (R).

Of Jinns (quietly) listening
To the Qur'ān: when they
Stood in the presence
Thereof, they said, "Listen
In silence!" When the (reading)
Was finished, they returned
To their people, to warn
(Them of their sins).

مِنَ ٱلْجِنِّ يَسْتَمِعُونَ ٱلْقُرْءَانَ
فَلَمَّا حَضَرُوهُ قَالُوٓا۟ أَنصِتُوا۟ ۖ
فَلَمَّا قُضِىَ وَلَّوْا۟ إِلَىٰ
قَوْمِهِم مُّنذِرِينَ

30. They said, "O our people!
We have heard a Book
Revealed after Moses,
Confirming what came
Before it: it guides (men)
To the Truth and
To a Straight Path.

٣٠ قَالُوا۟ يَٰقَوْمَنَآ إِنَّا سَمِعْنَا كِتَٰبًا
أُنزِلَ مِنۢ بَعْدِ مُوسَىٰ مُصَدِّقًا لِّمَا بَيْنَ يَدَيْهِ
يَهْدِىٓ إِلَى ٱلْحَقِّ وَإِلَىٰ طَرِيقٍ مُّسْتَقِيمٍ

31. "O our people, hearken
To the one who invites[4810]
(You) to Allah, and believe
In him: He will forgive
You your faults,
And deliver you from
A Penalty Grievous.

٣١ يَٰقَوْمَنَآ أَجِيبُوا۟ دَاعِىَ ٱللَّهِ
وَءَامِنُوا۟ بِهِۦ يَغْفِرْ لَكُم مِّن ذُنُوبِكُمْ
وَيُجِرْكُم مِّنْ عَذَابٍ أَلِيمٍ

32. "If any does not hearken
To the one who invites
(Us) to Allah, he cannot[4811]
Frustrate (Allah's Plan) on earth,
And no protectors can he have
Besides Allah: such men
(Wander) in manifest error."

٣٢ وَمَن لَّا يُجِبْ دَاعِىَ ٱللَّهِ فَلَيْسَ
بِمُعْجِزٍ فِى ٱلْأَرْضِ وَلَيْسَ لَهُۥ مِن دُونِهِۦٓ أَوْلِيَآءُ ۚ
أُو۟لَٰٓئِكَ فِى ضَلَٰلٍ مُّبِينٍ

33. See they not that
Allah, Who created the heavens
And the earth, and never
Wearied with their creation,[4812]
Is able to give life

٣٣ أَوَلَمْ يَرَوْا۟ أَنَّ ٱللَّهَ ٱلَّذِى خَلَقَ ٱلسَّمَٰوَٰتِ
وَٱلْأَرْضَ وَلَمْ يَعْىَ بِخَلْقِهِنَّ بِقَٰدِرٍ عَلَىٰٓ أَن يُحْۦِىَ

4810. The one who invites all to Allah is the Holy Prophet. He invites us to Allah: if we believe in Allah and His Prophet, Allah will forgive us our sins on our repentance and amendment of our lives, and save us the Penalty of the future life.

4811. If a person refuses to believe the Truth, or opposses it, it has not the least effect on Allah's Holy Plan, which will go on to its completion; but it will deprive such a person of Grace and of any protection whatever; he will wander about as an outlaw in manifest helplessness.

4812. *Cf.* 2:255 (Verse of the Throne): "His Throne doth extend over the heavens and the earth, and He feeleth no fatigue in guarding and preserving them." He Whose power is constant and unwearied in creating and preserving all things in heavens and earth can surely give life to the dead at the Resurrection.

To the dead? Yea, verily
He has power over all things.

ٱلْمَوْتَىٰ ۚ بَلَىٰٓ إِنَّهُۥ عَلَىٰ كُلِّ شَىْءٍ قَدِيرٌ

34. And on the Day that[4813]
The Unbelievers will be
Placed before the Fire,
(They will be asked,)
"Is this not the Truth?"
They will say, "Yea,
By our Lord!"
(One will say:)
"Then taste ye[4814]
The Penalty, for that ye
Were wont to deny (Truth)!"

٣٤ وَيَوْمَ يُعْرَضُ
ٱلَّذِينَ كَفَرُوا۟ عَلَى ٱلنَّارِ
أَلَيْسَ هَٰذَا بِٱلْحَقِّ ۖ
قَالُوا۟ بَلَىٰ وَرَبِّنَا ۚ
قَالَ فَذُوقُوا۟ ٱلْعَذَابَ
بِمَا كُنتُمْ تَكْفُرُونَ

35. Therefore patiently persevere,
As did (all) messengers
Of inflexible purpose;
And be in no haste
About the (Unbelievers). On the Day
That they see the (Punishment)[4815]
Promised them, (it will be)
As if they had not
Tarried more than an hour
In a single day. (Thine
But) to proclaim the Message:[4816]
But shall any be destroyed
Except those who transgress?

٣٥ فَٱصْبِرْ كَمَا صَبَرَ
أُو۟لُوا۟ ٱلْعَزْمِ مِنَ ٱلرُّسُلِ
وَلَا تَسْتَعْجِل لَّهُمْ ۚ
كَأَنَّهُمْ يَوْمَ يَرَوْنَ
مَا يُوعَدُونَ لَمْ يَلْبَثُوٓا۟
إِلَّا سَاعَةً مِّن نَّهَارٍۭ ۚ
بَلَٰغٌ ۚ
فَهَلْ يُهْلَكُ
إِلَّا ٱلْقَوْمُ ٱلْفَٰسِقُونَ

4813. *Cf.* 46:20, where the argument was closed about the undutiful son of a good father. After that the example of the 'Ād and of the believing Jinns was cited, and now is closed that argument in similar terms.

4814. The Truth which they denied is now all too clear to them. They are out of the Light of Truth, out of the Light of Allah's Countenance. And that in itself is a terrible Penalty.

4815. All spiritual work proceeds in its own good time. We should never be impatient either about its success or about the punishment which is bound to come for those who oppose it or wish to suppress it. The inevitable punishment is spoken of as the *Punishment promised*. It will come so soon and so suddenly that it will appear as if there was not the delay of a single hour in a single day! Time is a great factor in our affairs in this world, but it hardly counts in the spiritual Kingdom.

4816. The Preacher's duty is to proclaim the Message in unmistakable terms. If any human beings come in the way, it will be to their own destruction; but none but rebellious transgressor will be punished. There is always hope and forgiveness for repentance and amendment.

INTRODUCTION TO SŪRAH 47—*MUḤAMMAD*

We have examined and followed the current arrangement of the Sūrahs according to subject matter and independently of chronology, and we have found that a logical thread runs through them. We have now finished more than five-sixths of the Qur'ān. The remaining sixth consists of short Sūrahs, but these are again grouped according to subject matter.

We begin the first of such groups with a group of three Sūrahs (47 to 49), which deal with the organisation of the Muslim Ummah or community both for external defence and in internal relations. The present Sūrah deals with the necessity of defence against external foes by courage and strenuous fighting, and dates from about the first year of the Hijrah, when the Muslims were under threat of extinction by invasion from Makkah.

Summary—Aggressive hostility to Faith and Truth should be fought firmly, and Allah will guide (47:1-19 and C. 220).

Faint-heartedness condemned; those who strive and those who turn away will be sorted out (47:20-38 and C. 221).

C. 220. No plots against Truth or Faith will succeed:
(47:1-19.) But those who follow both will be strengthened.
Be firm in the fight, and Allah will guide.
Rebellion against Allah is destruction: fidelity
Will cool the mind and feed the heart;
It will warm the affections and sweeten life.
Hypocrisy carries its own doom.

Sūrah 47.

الجزء السادس والعشرون سورة محمد

Muḥammad

In the name of Allah, Most Gracious,
Most Merciful.

بسم الله الرحمن الرحيم

1. Those who reject Allah
And hinder (men) from
The Path of Allah—
Their deeds will Allah
Render astray[4817]
(From their mark).

(١) الَّذِينَ كَفَرُوا
وَصَدُّوا عَن سَبِيلِ اللَّهِ
أَضَلَّ أَعْمَالَهُمْ

2. But those who believe
And work deeds of
Righteousness, and believe
In the (Revelation) sent down
To Muḥammad—for it is
The Truth from their Lord—
He will remove from them
Their ills and improve
Their condition.[4818]

(٢) وَالَّذِينَ آمَنُوا وَعَمِلُوا الصَّالِحَاتِ
وَآمَنُوا بِمَا نُزِّلَ عَلَىٰ مُحَمَّدٍ
وَهُوَ الْحَقُّ مِن رَّبِّهِمْ ۙ
كَفَّرَ عَنْهُمْ سَيِّئَاتِهِمْ وَأَصْلَحَ بَالَهُمْ

3. This because those who
Reject Allah follow vanities,
While those who believe follow
The Truth from their Lord:
Thus does Allah set forth[4819]
For men their lessons
By similitudes.

(٣) ذَٰلِكَ بِأَنَّ الَّذِينَ كَفَرُوا اتَّبَعُوا الْبَاطِلَ
وَأَنَّ الَّذِينَ آمَنُوا اتَّبَعُوا الْحَقَّ مِن رَّبِّهِمْ ۚ
كَذَٰلِكَ يَضْرِبُ اللَّهُ لِلنَّاسِ أَمْثَالَهُمْ

4. Therefore, when ye meet[4820]
The Unbelievers (in fight),
Smite at their necks;
At length, when ye have

(٤) فَإِذَا لَقِيتُمُ الَّذِينَ كَفَرُوا
فَضَرْبَ الرِّقَابِ حَتَّىٰ

4817. Whatever they do will miss its mark, because Allah is the source of all energy and life. If the wicked try to persecute men or seduce them from the Truth, the result will be the opposite of what they intend.

4818. *Bāl* means state or condition, whether external, or of the heart and mind. Both meanings apply here. The more the wicked rage, the better will be the position of the righteous, and Allah will make it easier and easier for the righteous to love and follow the Truth.

4819. We learn the greatest spiritual lessons by parables and similitudes from things that happen in the outer world. If a man goes after a mirage or a thing that has no real existence, he can never reach his goal, while the man that follows the kindly Light from Allah that leads him on must be happier in mind, sounder in heart, and firmer in life, generally for every moment that he lives.

4820. When once the fight *(Jihād)* is entered upon, carry it out with the utmost vigour, and strike home your blows at the most vital points *(smite at their necks)*, both literally and figuratively. You cannot wage war with kid gloves.

Thoroughly subdued them,
Bind a bond[4821]
Firmly (on them): thereafter
(Is the time for) either
Generosity or ransom:[4822]
Until the war lays down
Its burdens. Thus (are ye
Commanded): but if it
Had been Allah's Will,
He could certainly have exacted
Retribution from them (Himself);
But (He lets you fight)
In order to test you,[4823]
Some with others.
But those who are slain[4824]
In the way of Allah—
He will never let
Their deeds be lost.

5. Soon will He guide them[4825]
And improve their condition,

6. And admit them to
The Garden which He[4826]
Has announced for them.

7. O ye who believe!
If ye will aid
(The cause of) Allah,
He will aid you,
And plant your feet firmly.

إِذَآ أَثْخَنتُمُوهُمْ فَشُدُّوا۟ ٱلْوَثَاقَ
فَإِمَّا مَنًّۢا بَعْدُ وَإِمَّا فِدَآءً
حَتَّىٰ تَضَعَ ٱلْحَرْبُ أَوْزَارَهَا ۚ
ذَٰلِكَ وَلَوْ يَشَآءُ ٱللَّهُ
لَٱنتَصَرَ مِنْهُمْ
وَلَٰكِن لِّيَبْلُوَا۟
بَعْضَكُم بِبَعْضٍ ۗ
وَٱلَّذِينَ قُتِلُوا۟ فِى سَبِيلِ ٱللَّهِ
فَلَن يُضِلَّ أَعْمَٰلَهُمْ
٥ سَيَهْدِيهِمْ وَيُصْلِحُ بَالَهُمْ
٦ وَيُدْخِلُهُمُ ٱلْجَنَّةَ عَرَّفَهَا لَهُمْ
٧ يَٰٓأَيُّهَا ٱلَّذِينَ ءَامَنُوٓا۟ إِن تَنصُرُوا۟ ٱللَّهَ
يَنصُرْكُمْ وَيُثَبِّتْ أَقْدَامَكُمْ

4821. In the first onset there must necessarily be great loss of life; but when the enemy is fairly beaten, which means, in a Jihād, that he is not likely to seek again the persecution of Truth, firm arrangements should be made to bring him under control. I thus construe the words "bind a bond firmly (on them)", but other have construed the words to mean, "after the enemy's numbers are fairly thinned down, prisoners may be taken". With this passage may be compared 8:67, and n. 1234.

4822. When once the enemy is brought under control, generosity *(i.e.,* the release of prisoners without ransom) or ransom is recommended.

4823. The Believers are tested in Faith by the extent to which they are willing to make sacrifices, even to the laying down of their lives; and the enemies are tested as to whether they would repent and let the righteous live in freedom and security.

4824. There are two alternative readings, (1) *qātalū*, "those who fight", and (2) *qutilū*, "those who are slain". The meaning under the first reading is wider, and includes that under the second. I have translated on the basis of the second reading, which is an accordance with the text of the Royal Egyptian edition.

4825. If we read "who are slain" in the last clause but one of verse 4, (see last note), "guide" would mean "guide them in their spiritual journey after death". *Improve their condition:* see n. 4818 above. If after death, their minds and hearts will be more and more settled and at rest, and their spiritual satisfaction greater.

4826. *The Garden which He has announced for them*: the state of Bliss which is declared in Revelation to be destined for those who serve Allah.

8. But those who reject (Allah—
For them is destruction,
And (Allah) will render
Their deeds astray[4827]
(From their mark).

٨ وَالَّذِينَ كَفَرُوا فَتَعْسًا لَّهُمْ
وَأَضَلَّ أَعْمَالَهُمْ

9. That is because they
Hate the Revelation of Allah;
So He has made
Their deeds fruitless.[4828]

٩ ذَٰلِكَ بِأَنَّهُمْ كَرِهُوا مَا أَنزَلَ اللَّهُ
فَأَحْبَطَ أَعْمَالَهُمْ

10. Do they not travel[4829]
Through the earth, and see
What was the End
Of those before them
(Who did evil)?
Allah brought utter destruction
On them, and similar
(Fates await) those who
Reject Allah.

١٠ أَفَلَمْ يَسِيرُوا فِي الْأَرْضِ فَيَنظُرُوا كَيْفَ
كَانَ عَاقِبَةُ الَّذِينَ مِن قَبْلِهِمْ
دَمَّرَ اللَّهُ عَلَيْهِمْ
وَلِلْكَافِرِينَ أَمْثَالُهَا

11. That is because Allah
Is the Protector of those
Who believe, but
Those who reject Allah
Have no protector.

١١ ذَٰلِكَ بِأَنَّ اللَّهَ مَوْلَى الَّذِينَ آمَنُوا
وَأَنَّ الْكَافِرِينَ لَا مَوْلَىٰ لَهُمْ

SECTION 2.

12. Verily Allah will admit
Those who believe and do
Righteous deeds, to Gardens
Beneath which rivers flow;
While those who reject Allah
Will enjoy (this world)[4830]
And eat as cattle eat;
And the Fire will
Be their abode.

١٢ إِنَّ اللَّهَ يُدْخِلُ الَّذِينَ آمَنُوا وَعَمِلُوا
الصَّالِحَاتِ جَنَّاتٍ تَجْرِي مِن تَحْتِهَا الْأَنْهَارُ
وَالَّذِينَ كَفَرُوا يَتَمَتَّعُونَ
وَيَأْكُلُونَ كَمَا تَأْكُلُ الْأَنْعَامُ
وَالنَّارُ مَثْوًى لَّهُمْ

4827. See above, 47:1 and n. 4817.

4828. Their deeds are *fruitless* in the sense that they are in vain; they do not produce the results intended by their doers. But they will not be exempt from producing the natural consequences of evil, *viz.*, further degradation and misery for the soul.

4829. The end of evil is evil. All past history and tradition shows that. Will not men of every generation learn that lesson? Allah helps His servants, but those who rebel against Allah have no one to help them.

4830. An apt simile. Beasts of the field eat their fill, but have no higher interests. Men who worship the world exclusively are no better: their pleasures and enjoyments rise no higher than those of the beasts of the field. They have no inkling of spiritual happiness. On the contrary, as they were endowed with spiritual faculties which they misused, they will not escape the Fire of Punishment, the Penalty of Sin.

13. And how many cities,
With more power than
Thy city which has
Driven thee out,[4831]
Have We destroyed
(For their sins)?
And there was none
To aid them.

١٣ وَكَأَيِّن مِّن قَرْيَةٍ هِيَ أَشَدُّ قُوَّةً
مِّن قَرْيَتِكَ ٱلَّتِىٓ أَخْرَجَتْكَ
أَهْلَكْنَٰهُمْ فَلَا نَاصِرَ لَهُمْ

14. Is then one who is
On a clear[4832] (Path)
From his Lord,
No better than one
To whom the evil
Of his conduct seems pleasing,
And such as follow
Their own lusts?

١٤ أَفَمَن كَانَ عَلَىٰ بَيِّنَةٍ مِّن رَّبِّهِۦ
كَمَن زُيِّنَ لَهُۥ سُوٓءُ عَمَلِهِۦ
وَٱتَّبَعُوٓا۟ أَهْوَآءَهُم

15. (Here is) a Parable
Of the Garden which
The righteous are promised:
In it are rivers
Of water incorruptible;[4833]
Rivers of milk
Of which the taste
Never changes; rivers
Of wine, a joy
To those who drink;
And rivers of honey
Pure and clear. In it
There are for them
All kinds of fruits;[4834]
And Grace from their Lord.[4835]
(Can those in such Bliss)
Be compared to such as

١٥ مَّثَلُ ٱلْجَنَّةِ ٱلَّتِى وُعِدَ ٱلْمُتَّقُونَ
فِيهَآ أَنْهَٰرٌ مِّن مَّآءٍ غَيْرِ ءَاسِنٍ
وَأَنْهَٰرٌ مِّن لَّبَنٍ لَّمْ يَتَغَيَّرْ طَعْمُهُۥ
وَأَنْهَٰرٌ مِّنْ خَمْرٍ لَّذَّةٍ لِّلشَّٰرِبِينَ
وَأَنْهَٰرٌ مِّنْ عَسَلٍ مُّصَفًّى
وَلَهُمْ فِيهَا مِن كُلِّ ٱلثَّمَرَٰتِ
وَمَغْفِرَةٌ مِّن رَّبِّهِمْ
كَمَنْ هُوَ

4831. A reference to Pagan Makkah, which drove out the Holy Prophet because of his righteousness and because he preached Repentance. The date of this Sūrah must therefore be after the Hijrah.

4832. *Clear*, or enlightened; a Path on which shines the Light of Allah.

4833. In this symbolism there are four kinds of drinks and all kinds of fruits; and the summing up of all spiritual delights in the "Grace from their Lord". The four kinds of drinks are: (1) delicious, cool, pure water, not like earthly water, for it never suffers corruption; (2) milk which never turns sour, whose taste is like that of fresh warm milk drawn from the udder; (3) wine, not like any wine on earth, for it leaves no headaches behind, and causes no intoxication, which is a kind of madness or poison, but is ever a joy to drink; and (4) honey, pure and clear, with no admixture of wax or any foreign substance. These drinks, again speaking metaphorically, will cool the spirit, feed the heart, warm the affections, and sweeten life. (R).

4834. See n. 4671 to 43:73. (Eds.).

4835. *Grace from their Lord:* that is the covering up or blotting out of sin and all that was sad or unsatisfactory in the lower life; the pure Light from the Countenance of Allah Most High: 92:20.

Shall dwell forever
In the Fire, and be given,
To drink, boiling water,
So that it cuts up[4836]
Their bowels (to pieces)?

خَٰلِدٌ فِي ٱلنَّارِ وَسُقُوا۟ مَآءً
حَمِيمًا فَقَطَّعَ أَمْعَآءَهُمْ

16. And among them are men
Who listen to thee,
But in the end, when they
Go out from thee,[4837]
They say to those who
Have received Knowledge,
"What is it he said
Just then?" Such are
Men whose hearts Allah
Has sealed, and who
Follow their own lusts.

١٦ وَمِنْهُم مَّن يَسْتَمِعُ إِلَيْكَ
حَتَّىٰٓ إِذَا خَرَجُوا۟ مِنْ عِندِكَ
قَالُوا۟ لِلَّذِينَ أُوتُوا۟ ٱلْعِلْمَ مَاذَا قَالَ ءَانِفًا
أُو۟لَٰٓئِكَ ٱلَّذِينَ طَبَعَ ٱللَّهُ عَلَىٰ قُلُوبِهِمْ
وَٱتَّبَعُوٓا۟ أَهْوَآءَهُمْ

17. But to those who receive[4838]
Guidance, He increases
The (light of) Guidance,
And bestows on them
Their Piety and Restraint
(From evil).

١٧ وَٱلَّذِينَ ٱهْتَدَوْا۟
زَادَهُمْ هُدًى
وَءَاتَىٰهُمْ تَقْوَىٰهُمْ

18. Do they then only wait[4839]
For the Hour—that it
Should come on them
Of a sudden? But already
Have come some tokens[4840]
Thereof, and when it
(Actually) is on them,

١٨ فَهَلْ يَنظُرُونَ إِلَّا ٱلسَّاعَةَ أَن تَأْتِيَهُم بَغْتَةً
فَقَدْ جَآءَ أَشْرَاطُهَا
فَأَنَّىٰ لَهُمْ

4836. *Cf.* 37:66-67, and n. 4074. Just as the Bliss of the Blessed will penetrate their being through and through, so the agony of the condemned ones will penetrate their being through and through. "Bowels" besides meaning their inmost being, also suggests the seat of their feelings and affections.

4837. *Cf.* 10:42, and n. 1434; also 6:25, 36, and n. 857. The case here referred to is that of the Hypocrites who came to the assemblies of Islam in Madīnah and pretended to listen to the Prophet's teaching and preaching. But their heart and mind were not in learning righteousness, but in carping at things they saw and heard. When they got out, they knew nothing of the teaching, but on the contrary asked foolish and ignorant questions, such as might raise doubts.

4838. Spiritual advancement is progressive: each step makes the next ones easier and more complete.

4839. *Cf.* 43:66, and n. 4665.

4840. The sands of time are always running, and when a wrong is done, the time for its punishment is approaching every moment. No one should therefore wait. The time for repentance is *Now* at any given time. When the punishment comes, it is too late for repentance, and all admonition would be useless.

Looking to the particular time when this Sūrah was revealed, *viz.*, about a year after the Hijrah, already there were Signs that the plans of the Pagans to crush Islam were crumbling to pieces. The Hijrah showed how much good will there was in Madīnah for the Holy Prophet of Allah, and how many people from Makkah adhered to him. The battle of Badr showed that they could hold their own against odds of three to one.

How can they benefit
Then by their admonition?

إذا جاءتهم ذكرىهم

19. Know, therefore, that
There is no god
But Allah, and ask
Forgiveness for thy fault,[4841]
And for the men
And women who believe:
For Allah knows how ye[4842]
Move about and how
Ye dwell in your homes.

(١٩) فاعلم أنه لا إله إلا الله
واستغفر لذنبك
وللمؤمنين والمؤمنات
والله يعلم متقلبكم ومثوىكم

C. 221.—Those eager for service want the call for service;
(47:20-38.) But the hypocrites blanch at such call.
If it were not obeyed, and evil should get
The upper hand, will it not stalk arrogant
Over the land, and trample under foot
All claims of right and kinship? Fight it,
And fail not in the test of your mettle. Be bold
And establish the Flag of Righteousness
In the highest places. Thus comes Peace,
For which due sacrifice must be made.

SECTION 3.

20. Those who believe say,[4843]
"Why is not a Sūrah
Sent down (for us)?"
But when a Sūrah
Of basic or categorical[4844]
Meaning is revealed,
And fighting is mentioned
Therein, thou wilt see those
In whose hearts is a disease[4845]
Looking at thee with a look

(٢٠) ويقول الذين ءامنوا لولا نزلت سورة
فإذا أنزلت سورة محكمة
وذكر فيها القتال
رأيت الذين في قلوبهم مرض
ينظرون إليك نظر

4841. *Cf.* 40:55, and n. 4428.

4842. The time and manner of our conducting ourselves at home and when we move about on our business are all material to the judgement of our conduct, and for every nuance in our moral and spiritual progress, we must seek Allah's help and guidance.

4843. The men of faith and loyalty are eager and anxious to get a command to serve the Cause even if it be at the sacrifice of their lives. Not so the Hypocrites, "those in whose hearts is a disease". They are mortally afraid as mentioned below.

4844. *Cf.* 3:7, and n. 347. The defence of truth and righteousness at all sacrifice, when a definite and categorical command issues from the Amīr al Mu'minīn is a fundamental condition of enlistment in the cause of Allah. It is true that Punishment and Judgement belong to Allah alone; but our mettle and fidelity have to be tested, (see verse 4 above), and Allah uses human agency in human affairs. (R).

4845. *Cf.* 2:10. The disease is hypocrisy, disloyalty to the Cause, want of courage and of the spirit of self-sacrifice, want of true understanding.

Of one in swoon at
The approach of death.
But more fitting for them—

21. Were it to obey
And say what is just,
And when a matter[4846]
Is resolved on, it were
Best for them if they
Were true to Allah.

22. Then, is it[4847]
To be expected of you,
If ye were put in authority,
That ye will do mischief,
In the land, and break
Your ties of kith and kin?

23. Such are the men
Whom Allah has cursed[4848]
For He has made them
Deaf and blinded their sight.

24. Do they not then
Earnestly seek to understand
The Qur'ān, or are
Their hearts locked up
By them?

25. Those who turn back[4849]
As apostates after Guidance
Was clearly shown to them—
The Evil One has instigated
Them and buoyed them up
With false hopes.

ٱلْمَغْشِيِّ عَلَيْهِ مِنَ ٱلْمَوْتِ
فَأَوْلَىٰ لَهُمْ
(٢١) طَاعَةٌ وَقَوْلٌ مَّعْرُوفٌ
فَإِذَا عَزَمَ ٱلْأَمْرُ فَلَوْ صَدَقُوا۟ ٱللَّهَ
لَكَانَ خَيْرًا لَّهُمْ
(٢٢) فَهَلْ عَسَيْتُمْ إِن تَوَلَّيْتُمْ
أَن تُفْسِدُوا۟ فِى ٱلْأَرْضِ
وَتُقَطِّعُوٓا۟ أَرْحَامَكُمْ
(٢٣) أُو۟لَـٰٓئِكَ ٱلَّذِينَ لَعَنَهُمُ ٱللَّهُ
فَأَصَمَّهُمْ وَأَعْمَىٰٓ أَبْصَـٰرَهُمْ
(٢٤) أَفَلَا يَتَدَبَّرُونَ ٱلْقُرْءَانَ
أَمْ عَلَىٰ قُلُوبٍ أَقْفَالُهَآ
(٢٥) إِنَّ ٱلَّذِينَ ٱرْتَدُّوا۟ عَلَىٰٓ أَدْبَـٰرِهِم
مِّنۢ بَعْدِ مَا تَبَيَّنَ لَهُمُ ٱلْهُدَى
ٱلشَّيْطَـٰنُ سَوَّلَ لَهُمْ وَأَمْلَىٰ لَهُمْ

4846. The resolution is not taken except under guidance from Allah. Those, therefore, who fail to implement it by their own effort and sacrifice, are not true to Allah. And such disloyalty or cowardice is not even good for them from a worldly point of view. With what face can they meet their friends after their disgraceful conduct?

4847. It is no use to say, as the Quraysh said, that it is not seemly to fight against kith and kin. From one point of view the stand against sin brings "not peace, but a sword". It is a case of either subduing evil or being subdued by evil. If evil gets the upper hand, it is not likely to respect ties of kith and kin. It did not in the case of the Holy Prophet and his adherents, and had to be suppressed, to bring about the conditions necessary for peace.

4848. *Cursed: i.e.*, deprived of His Grace: left them straying, because they deliberately rejected His guidance. The result is that what they hear is as if they had not heard, and what they see is as if they had not seen. They have no desire to understand Allah's Will or Allah's Revelation—or is it that they have themselves locked and bolted their hearts and minds, so that nothing can penetrate them?

4849. Such men are entirely in the hands of Evil. They follow its suggestions, and their hopes are built on its deceptions.

26. This, because they said[4850]
To those who hate what
Allah has revealed, "We
Will obey you in part
Of (this) matter"; but Allah
Knows their (inner) secrets.

٢٦ ذَٰلِكَ بِأَنَّهُمْ قَالُواْ لِلَّذِينَ كَرِهُواْ مَا
نَزَّلَ ٱللَّهُ سَنُطِيعُكُمْ فِي بَعْضِ ٱلْأَمْرِ
وَٱللَّهُ يَعْلَمُ إِسْرَارَهُمْ

27. But how (will it be)[4851]
When the angels take
Their souls at death,
And smite their faces[4852]
And their backs?

٢٧ فَكَيْفَ إِذَا تَوَفَّتْهُمُ ٱلْمَلَٰٓئِكَةُ
يَضْرِبُونَ وُجُوهَهُمْ وَأَدْبَٰرَهُمْ

28. This because they followed
That which called forth
The Wrath of Allah, and
They hated Allah's good pleasure;
So He made their deeds
Of no effect.

٢٨ ذَٰلِكَ بِأَنَّهُمُ ٱتَّبَعُواْ مَآ أَسْخَطَ ٱللَّهَ
وَكَرِهُواْ رِضْوَٰنَهُۥ
فَأَحْبَطَ أَعْمَٰلَهُمْ

SECTION 4.

29. Or do those in whose[4853]
Hearts is a disease, think
That Allah will not bring
To light all their rancour?

٢٩ أَمْ حَسِبَ ٱلَّذِينَ فِي قُلُوبِهِم مَّرَضٌ
أَن لَّن يُخْرِجَ ٱللَّهُ أَضْغَٰنَهُمْ

30. Had We so willed,
We could have shown them
Up to thee, and thou
Shouldst have known them[4854]
By their marks: but surely
Thou wilt know them

٣٠ وَلَوْ نَشَآءُ لَأَرَيْنَٰكَهُمْ
فَلَعَرَفْتَهُم بِسِيمَٰهُمْ
وَلَتَعْرِفَنَّهُمْ فِي

4850. They have become so impervious to facts and truths, because, without the courage to oppose Allah's Cause openly, they secretly intrigue with Allah's enemies, and say that they will follow them part of the way, and by remaining partly in the other camp, they will be far more useful as spies and half-hearted doubters than by going over altogether. If they think that this game will be successful, they are mistaken. All the inner secrets and motives of their hearts are known to Allah. *Cf.* 59:11.

4851. It is all very well for them to practise hypocrisy in this life. How will they feel at death, when they find that the angels know all, and touch the very spots they had taken such care to conceal?

4852. *Their faces and their backs:* there is a subtle metaphor. The *face* is what looks to the front, the side you present to the outer world; the *back* is what is not shown, what is hidden from the world. The hypocrites will be hit at both points. Or, the *face* is what they boast of, what they are proud of; the back is the skeleton in the cupboard, the things they dare not utter, but which yet haunt them. The hypocrites are hit on every side. *Cf.* 8:50.

4853. *Cf.* verse 20 above, and n. 4845. Being diseased at the very core of their being, they do not understand the simplest facts of spiritual life.

4854. Evil is not always necessarily branded in this life with a distinguishing mark or brand. But the discerning ones know. Evil is betrayed by its speech and behaviour.

By the tone of their speech!
And Allah knows
All that ye do.

لَحۡنِ ٱلۡقَوۡلِۚ
وَٱللَّهُ يَعۡلَمُ أَعۡمَٰلَكُمۡ

31. And We shall try you[4855]
Until We test those
Among you who strive
Their utmost and persevere
In patience; and We shall
Try your reported (mettle).[4856]

٣١ وَلَنَبۡلُوَنَّكُمۡ حَتَّىٰ نَعۡلَمَ
ٱلۡمُجَٰهِدِينَ مِنكُمۡ وَٱلصَّٰبِرِينَ
وَنَبۡلُوَاْ أَخۡبَارَكُمۡ

32. Those who reject Allah,
Hinder (men) from
The Path of Allah, and resist
The Messenger, after Guidance
Has been clearly shown to
them,[4857]
Will not injure Allah
In the least, but He
Will make their deeds
Of no effect.

٣٢ إِنَّ ٱلَّذِينَ كَفَرُواْ
وَصَدُّواْ عَن سَبِيلِ ٱللَّهِ وَشَآقُّواْ ٱلرَّسُولَ
مِنۢ بَعۡدِ مَا تَبَيَّنَ لَهُمُ ٱلۡهُدَىٰ
لَن يَضُرُّواْ ٱللَّهَ شَيۡـٔٗا
وَسَيُحۡبِطُ أَعۡمَٰلَهُمۡ

33. O ye who believe!
Obey Allah, and obey
The Messenger, and make
Not vain your deeds!

٣٣ يَٰٓأَيُّهَا ٱلَّذِينَ ءَامَنُوٓاْ أَطِيعُواْ ٱللَّهَ
وَأَطِيعُواْ ٱلرَّسُولَ وَلَا تُبۡطِلُوٓاْ أَعۡمَٰلَكُمۡ

34. Those who reject Allah,[4858]
And hinder (men) from the Path
Of Allah, then die rejecting
Allah—
Allah will not forgive them.

٣٤ إِنَّ ٱلَّذِينَ كَفَرُواْ وَصَدُّواْ عَن سَبِيلِ ٱللَّهِ
ثُمَّ مَاتُواْ وَهُمۡ كُفَّارٞ فَلَن يَغۡفِرَ ٱللَّهُ لَهُمۡ

35. Be not weary and
Fainthearted, crying for peace,
When ye should be[4859]

٣٥ فَلَا تَهِنُواْ وَتَدۡعُوٓاْ إِلَى ٱلسَّلۡمِ وَأَنتُمُ

4855. *Cf.* 34:21, and n. 3821. The test and trial is for our own psychological development, to help in the exercise of such choice as has been given to us in our free will. *Cf.* also 3:154, and n. 467.

4856. *Akhbār:* the things reported of you; reputation for courage and constancy, which has to be brought to the test of facts and experience. In an epigram of Tacitus we are told of a Roman Emperor that he would have been considered in every way to have been worthy of being a ruler if only he had never ruled! So in life people may think us courageous, true, noble, and self-sacrificing; and we may consider ourselves as possessing all such virtues; but it is actual experience that will bring them to the test.

4857. *Cf.* verse 25 above, and verse 34 below; in verse 25 was shown the source of the evil, *viz.*, yielding to the deceptions of the Evil One; in this verse are shown the proximate consequences of such yielding to evil, *viz.*, failure of all we do; and in verse 34 below are shown the eternal consequences, *viz.*, our deprivation of Allah's Grace and Mercy.

4858. See last note.

4859. To those who are trying to root out evil, and *have authority* to do so, the question is not of peace or conflict, but of whether Good or Evil is to prevail. They must remember the Good must ultimately prevail, and Allah's help is with those who, as far as men can, are trying to further the universal Plan. *Cf.* n. 4847 to verse 22 above.

Uppermost: for Allah is
With you, and will never
Put you in loss
For your (good) deeds.

ٱلْأَعْلَوْنَ وَٱللَّهُ مَعَكُمْ
وَلَن يَتِرَكُمْ أَعْمَـٰلَكُمْ

36. The life of this world
Is but play and amusement:[4860]
And if ye believe
And guard against evil,
He will grant you
Your recompense, and will not
Ask you (to give up)
your possessions.[4861]

٣٦ إِنَّمَا ٱلْحَيَوٰةُ ٱلدُّنْيَا لَعِبٌ وَلَهْوٌ
وَإِن تُؤْمِنُوا۟ وَتَتَّقُوا۟ يُؤْتِكُمْ أُجُورَكُمْ
وَلَا يَسْـَٔلْكُمْ أَمْوَٰلَكُمْ

37. If He were to ask you
For all of them, and
Press you, ye would
Covetously withhold, and He would[4862]
Bring out all your ill-feeling.[4863]

٣٧ إِن يَسْـَٔلْكُمُوهَا
فَيُحْفِكُمْ تَبْخَلُوا۟
وَيُخْرِجْ أَضْغَـٰنَكُمْ

38. Behold, ye are those[4864]
Invited to spend
(Of your substance)
In the Way of Allah:
But among you are some
That are niggardly. But any
Who are niggardly are so
At the expense of
Their own souls.

٣٨ هَـٰٓأَنتُمْ هَـٰٓؤُلَآءِ تُدْعَوْنَ
لِتُنفِقُوا۟ فِى سَبِيلِ ٱللَّهِ
فَمِنكُم مَّن يَبْخَلُ
وَمَن يَبْخَلْ فَإِنَّمَا يَبْخَلُ عَن نَّفْسِهِۦ

4860. *Cf.* 6:32, and n. 855; and 29:64, and n. 3497. Amusement and play are not bad things in themselves. As preparations for the more serious life, they have their value. But if we concentrate on them, and neglect the business of life, we cannot prosper. So we must use our life in this world as a preparation for our spiritual or inner life.

4861. Complete self-sacrifice, if voluntarily offered, has a meaning: it means that the person's devotion is exclusively and completely for the Cause. But no law or rule can *demand* it. And a mere offer to kill yourself has no meaning. You should be ready to take risks to your life in fighting for the Cause, but you should aim at life, not death. If you live, you should be ready to place your substance and your acquisitions at the disposal of the Cause. But it is not reasonable to pauperise yourself and become a hanger-on for the Cause. Moreover, the inborn tendency to self-preservation in an average man would lead to concealment and niggardliness if *all* were asked for the Cause, by Law, and there would further be a feeling of bitterness and rebellion.

4862. *Cf.* 3:180.

4863. *Cf.* above, verse 29. Rancour or ill-feeling, or any desire but that of devotion, should never be given a handle in a wise Law.

4864. Here the cases of the special devotee and of the average man with his human foibles are distinguished. Stinginess is not a virtue: it hurts more the finer nature of the individual practising it than it hurts the Cause. Allah is free of all wants and independent of any need that we can meet. His Cause is similarly independent of human aid. But it uses human agency for our own human advancement. The need to be able to serve Allah's cause is ours. We are the needy beggars who should claim the privilege before the Lord of Bounties unbounded. (R).

وَاللَّهُ الْغَنِيُّ وَأَنتُمُ الْفُقَرَاءُ
وَإِن تَتَوَلَّوْا يَسْتَبْدِلْ قَوْمًا غَيْرَكُمْ
ثُمَّ لَا يَكُونُوا أَمْثَالَكُم

But Allah is free
Of all wants,
And it is ye that are needy.
If ye turn back[4865]
(From the Path), He will
Substitute in your stead
Another people; then they
Would not be like you!

4865. If we desert the Cause, the Cause will not fail. Better men than we will uphold the flag. But we should fall, and others will take our place, who are not so timid, half-hearted, or stingy. In Wordsworth's words, "High Heaven rejects the lore of nicely calculated less or more."

INTRODUCTION TO SŪRAH 48—*AL FATḤ*

1. This is the second of the group of three Madīnah Sūrahs described in the Introduction to S. 47. Its date is fixed by the mention of the Treaty of Ḥudaybīyah, Dhu al Qa'dah A.H. 6 = Feb. 628 (see n. 1261 to 9:13).

2. Ḥudaybīyah is a plain, a short day's march to the north of Makkah, a little to the west of the Madīnah-Makkah road, as used in the Prophet's time. Six years had passed since the Prophet had left his beloved City, and it has been in the hands of the Pagan autocracy. But Islam had grown during these six years. Its Qiblah was towards the Ka'bah. The Pagans had tried to attack Islam at various times and had been foiled. By Arab custom every Arab was entitled to visit the Sacred Enclosure unarmed, and fighting of any kind was prohibited during the Sacred Months (see n. 209 to 2:194), which included the month of *Dhu al Qa'dah*. In *Dhu al Qa'dah* A.H. 6, therefore, the Prophet desired to perform the 'Umrah or lesser pilgrimage (n. 212 to 2:196), unarmed, but accompanied with his followers. A large following joined him, to the number of fourteen to fifteen hundred.

3. This was not to the liking of the Pagan autocracy at Makkah, which took alarm, and in breach of all Arab tradition and usage, prepared to prevent the peaceful party from performing the rites of pilgrimage. They marched out to fight the unarmed party. The Prophet turned a little to the west of the road, and encamped at Ḥudaybīyah, where negotiations took place. On the one hand, the Prophet was unwilling to give the Quraysh any pretended excuse for violence in the Sacred Territory; on the other, the Quraysh had learnt, by six years' bitter experience, that their power was crumbling on all sides, and Islam was growing with its moral and spiritual forces, which were also reflected in its powers of organisation and resistance. The enthusiasm with which the Covenant of Fealty was entered into under a tree in Ḥudaybīyah (48:18) by that great multitude united in devotion to their great leader, was evidence of the great power which he commanded even in a worldly sense if the Quraysh had chosen to try conclusions with him.

4. A peaceful Treaty was therefore concluded, known as the Treaty of Ḥudaybīyah. It stipulated: (1) that there was to be peace between the parties for ten years; (2) that any tribe or person was free to join either party or make an alliance with it; (3) that if a Quraysh person from Makkah, under guardianship, should join the Prophet without the guardian's permission, he (or she) should be sent back to the guardian, but in the contrary case, they should not be sent back; and (4) that the Prophet and his party were not to enter Makkah that year, but that they could enter unarmed the following year.

5. Item 3, not being reciprocal, was objected to in the Muslim camp, but it really was of little importance. Muslims under guardianship, sent back to Makkah, were not likely to renounce the blessings of Islam; on the other hand Muslims going to Makkah would be centres of influence for Islam, and it was more important that they should be allowed to remain there than that they should be sent back to Madīnah. It was impossible to think that there would be apostates or renegades to Paganism! "Look on this picture, and on that!"

6. The Muslims faithfully observed the terms of the Treaty. The following year (A.H. 7) they performed the lesser Pilgrimage in great state for three days. It is true that the Makkans later on broke the Peace in the attack which one of their allied tribes (the Banū Bakr) made on the Muslim Banū Khuzā'ah (who were in alliance with the Prophet), but this led to the conquest of Makkah and the sweeping away of the autocracy. Meanwhile Ḥudaybīyah was a great victory, morally and socially, as well as politically, and its lessons are expounded in this Sūrah, as the lessons of Badr were expounded in 8:42-48, and of Uḥud in 3:121-129, 149-180.

Summary—Victory comes from cool courage, devotion, faith, and patience, as shown at Ḥudaybīyah; therefore remember Allah, and follow His Prophet (48:1-29, and C. 222).

C. 222.—Victory and Help go with calmness of mind,
(48:1-29) Faith, fidelity, zeal, and earnestness,
Not with greed, lukewarmness, or timidity.
Discipline and obedience are essential
For service. The rewards for service are not
To be measured by immediate results,
But accrue in countless hidden ways
For Patience and Restraint. Be strong
Against Evil, but kind and gentle amongst
Yourselves: the seed will grow and become
Strong, to your wonder and delight.

Sūrah 48.

الجزء السادس والعشرون سورة الفتح

Al Fatḥ (The Victory)

In the name of Allah, Most Gracious,
Most Merciful.

بِسْمِ اللَّهِ الرَّحْمَٰنِ الرَّحِيمِ

1. Verily We have granted
Thee a manifest Victory:[4866]

إِنَّا فَتَحْنَا لَكَ فَتْحًا مُّبِينًا ١

2. That Allah may forgive thee[4867]
Thy faults of the past
And those to follow;
Fulfil His favour to thee;
And guide thee
On the Straight Way;

لِّيَغْفِرَ لَكَ اللَّهُ مَا تَقَدَّمَ مِن ذَنۢبِكَ ٢
وَمَا تَأَخَّرَ وَيُتِمَّ نِعْمَتَهُۥ عَلَيْكَ
وَيَهْدِيَكَ صِرَٰطًا مُّسْتَقِيمًا

3. And that Allah may help[4868]
Thee with powerful help.

وَيَنصُرَكَ اللَّهُ نَصْرًا عَزِيزًا ٣

4. It is He Who sent
Down Tranquillity[4869]
Into the hearts of
The Believers, that they may
Add Faith to their Faith—[4870]
For to Allah belong
The Forces of the heavens[48671]

هُوَ الَّذِىٓ أَنزَلَ السَّكِينَةَ فِى قُلُوبِ ٤
الْمُؤْمِنِينَ لِيَزْدَادُوٓا إِيمَٰنًا مَّعَ إِيمَٰنِهِمْ
وَلِلَّهِ جُنُودُ السَّمَٰوَٰتِ

4866. This is best referred to the Treaty of Ḥudaybīyah, for which see the Introduction to this Sūrah. By this Treaty the Makkan Quraysh, after many years of unrelenting conflict with Islam, at length recognised Islam as (what they thought) an equal power with themselves. In reality the door was then opened for the free spread of Islam throughout Arabia and thence through the world.

4867. See n. 4428 to 40:55, and *Cf.* 47:19. Any mistakes of the past were now rectified, and any future ones prevented by the free scope now offered, by the act of the Quraysh Pagans themselves, to the recognition and free promulgation of Islam.

4868. Three objects or results of the Treaty are mentioned: (1) forgiveness, which is equivalent to Mercy, (2) fulfilment of the dignity of Prophethood with the dignity of an effective and recognised position in Arabia; (3) opening up a straight way leading to Islam, by access to Makkah from next year, Makkah being the symbolic centre of Islam. These three are summed up in the comprehensive phrase "powerful (or effective) help".

4869. The results were achieved by tranquillity, calmness, and cool courage among the 1400 to 1500 unarmed men who accompanied the Prophet to Ḥudaybīyah and who were threatened with violence by the excited Quraysh leaders of Makkah.

4870. It is a casuistical question to ask, are there degrees in Faith? The plain meaning is that Believers will see one Sign of Allah after another, and with each their Faith is confirmed. During all the long years of persecution and conflict they had Faith, but when they see their old enemies actually coming out to negotiate with them, their Faith is justified, fulfilled, and confirmed: and they turn in gratitude to Allah.

4871. There are visible forces which you see in the physical world. Men fight with armed forces, and the Muslims had to defend themselves with arms also, and not without success. But social, moral, and spiritual forces were fighting for them under Allah's command, and they were the real forces that established the Message of Islam and the position of its Leader and Preacher.

And the earth; and Allah is
Full of Knowledge and Wisdom—

وَالْأَرْضِ وَكَانَ اللَّهُ عَلِيمًا حَكِيمًا

5. That He may admit[4872]
The men and women
Who believe, to Gardens
Beneath which rivers flow,
To dwell therein for aye,
And remove their ills
From them—and that is,
In the sight of Allah,
The highest achievement
(For man)—

٥ لِيُدْخِلَ الْمُؤْمِنِينَ وَالْمُؤْمِنَاتِ
جَنَّاتٍ تَجْرِي مِن تَحْتِهَا الْأَنْهَارُ خَالِدِينَ فِيهَا
وَيُكَفِّرَ عَنْهُمْ سَيِّئَاتِهِمْ
وَكَانَ ذَٰلِكَ عِندَ اللَّهِ فَوْزًا عَظِيمًا

6. And that He may punish
The Hypocrites, men and
Women, and the Polytheists,
Men and women, who imagine
An evil opinion of Allah.
On them is a round[4873]
Of Evil: the Wrath of Allah
Is on them: He has cursed[4874]
Them and got Hell ready
For them: and evil
Is it for a destination.

٦ وَيُعَذِّبَ الْمُنَافِقِينَ وَالْمُنَافِقَاتِ
وَالْمُشْرِكِينَ وَالْمُشْرِكَاتِ الظَّانِّينَ
بِاللَّهِ ظَنَّ السَّوْءِ عَلَيْهِمْ دَائِرَةُ السَّوْءِ
وَغَضِبَ اللَّهُ عَلَيْهِمْ وَلَعَنَهُمْ وَأَعَدَّ لَهُمْ جَهَنَّمَ
وَسَاءَتْ مَصِيرًا

7. For to Allah belong[4875]
The Forces of the heavens
And the earth; and Allah is
Exalted in Power,
Full of Wisdom.

٧ وَلِلَّهِ جُنُودُ السَّمَاوَاتِ وَالْأَرْضِ
وَكَانَ اللَّهُ عَزِيزًا حَكِيمًا

8. We have truly sent thee[4876]
As a witness, as a

٨ إِنَّا أَرْسَلْنَاكَ شَاهِدًا

4872. This clause is coordinated to the previous clause, "That they may add Faith to their Faith". The intervening words, "For to Allah...and Wisdom" are parenthetical. The third co-ordinate clause comes in the next verse, "And that He may punish..." The skeleton construction will be, "Allah sends down calm courage to Believers in order that they may be confirmed in their Faith; that they may qualify for the Bliss of Heaven; and that the evil ones may receive the punishment they deserve."

4873. They will be encircled (or hemmed in) by Evil.

4874. That is, deprived them of His Grace, on account of their continued rejection of it.

4875. These words are repeated (with a slight change) from the parenthetical clause in verse 4, to emphasize the assertion as a substantive proposition, that fighting and visible forces in the physical world are not the only forces with which Allah works out His Plan. The invisible forces are more important as they were at Ḥudaybīyah. The slight difference is instructive; in the parenthetical clause, Allah's Knowledge was emphasized, and in the substantive clause it is Allah's Power. Knowledge plans, and Power executes.

4876. The Prophet came in order to establish Faith in Allah and true worship. We can view him in three capacities: (1) as a witness to help the weak if they were oppressed and check the strong if they did wrong; (2) as a giver of the Glad Tidings of Allah's Grace and Mercy to those who repented and lived good lives; and (3) as one who warned sinners of the consequences of their sin.

Bringer of Glad Tidings,
And as a Warner:

وَمُبَشِّرًا وَنَذِيرًا

9. In order that ye
(O men) may believe
In Allah and His Messenger,
That ye may assist
And honour Him,[4876-A]
And celebrate His praises
Morning and evening.

٩ لِّتُؤْمِنُوا بِاللَّهِ وَرَسُولِهِۦ
وَتُعَزِّرُوهُ وَتُوَقِّرُوهُ وَتُسَبِّحُوهُ
بُكْرَةً وَأَصِيلًا

10. Verily those who plight[4877]
Their fealty to thee
Do no less than plight
Their fealty to Allah:
The Hand of Allah is
Over their hands:
Then anyone who violates
His oath, does so
To the harm of his own
Soul, and anyone who
Fulfils what he has
Covenanted with Allah—
Allah will soon grant him
A great Reward.

١٠ إِنَّ الَّذِينَ يُبَايِعُونَكَ
إِنَّمَا يُبَايِعُونَ اللَّهَ
يَدُ اللَّهِ فَوْقَ أَيْدِيهِمْ ۚ
فَمَن نَّكَثَ فَإِنَّمَا يَنكُثُ عَلَىٰ نَفْسِهِۦ ۖ
وَمَنْ أَوْفَىٰ بِمَا عَاهَدَ عَلَيْهُ اللَّهَ
فَسَيُؤْتِيهِ أَجْرًا عَظِيمًا

SECTION 2.

11. The desert Arabs who[4878]
Lagged behind will
Say to thee:
"We were engaged in
(Looking after) our flocks
And herds, and our families:

١١ سَيَقُولُ لَكَ
الْمُخَلَّفُونَ مِنَ الْأَعْرَابِ
شَغَلَتْنَا أَمْوَالُنَا وَأَهْلُونَا

4876-A. *Assist and honour Him:* most commentators agree that the pronoun 'Him' refers to Allah, while a few believe it refers to the Holy Prophet. [Eds.].

4877. In the Ḥudaybīyah negotiations, when it was uncertain whether the Quraysh would treat well or ill the Prophet's delegate to Makkah, there was a great wave of feeling in the Muslim camp of 1400 to 1500 men. They came with great enthusiasm and swore their fealty to the Prophet, by placing hand on hand according to the Arab custom: see paragraph 3 of the Introduction to this Sūrah. This in itself was wonderful demonstration of moral and material strength, a true Victory; it is called *Bay'ah al Riḍwān* (Fealty of Allah's Good Pleasure) in Islamic History. They placed their hands on the Prophet's hand, but the Hand of Allah was above them, and He accepted their Fealty.

'Alayhu is an archaic form for *'Alayhi*.

4878. When the Prophet started from Madīnah on the Makkah journey which ended in Ḥudaybīyah, he asked all Muslims to join him in the pious undertaking, and he had a splendid response. But some of the desert tribes hung back and made excuses. Their faith was but lukewarm, and they did not want to share in any trouble which the Makkans might give to the unarmed Muslims on pilgrimage. Their excuse that they were engaged in looking after their flocks and herds and their families was an afterthought, and in any case made after the return of the Prophet and his party with enhanced prestige to Madīnah

Do thou then ask
Forgiveness for us,"[4879]
They say with their tongues
What is not in their hearts.
Say: "Who then has
Any power at all
(To intervene) on your behalf
With Allah, if His Will
Is to give you some loss[4880]
Or to give you some profit?
But Allah is well acquainted
With all that ye do.

فَاسْتَغْفِرْ لَنَا
يَقُولُونَ بِأَلْسِنَتِهِم
مَّا لَيْسَ فِي قُلُوبِهِمْ
قُلْ فَمَن يَمْلِكُ لَكُم مِّنَ اللَّهِ شَيْئًا
إِنْ أَرَادَ بِكُمْ ضَرًّا أَوْ أَرَادَ بِكُمْ نَفْعًا
بَلْ كَانَ اللَّهُ بِمَا تَعْمَلُونَ خَبِيرًا

12. "Nay, ye thought that
The Messenger and the Believers
Would never return to
Their families; this seemed
Pleasing in your hearts,[4881]
and
Ye conceived an evil thought,
For ye are a people
Lost (in wickedness)."

١٢ بَلْ ظَنَنتُمْ أَن لَّن يَنقَلِبَ
الرَّسُولُ وَالْمُؤْمِنُونَ إِلَىٰ أَهْلِيهِمْ أَبَدًا
وَزُيِّنَ ذَٰلِكَ فِي قُلُوبِكُمْ وَظَنَنتُمْ
ظَنَّ السَّوْءِ وَكُنتُمْ قَوْمًا بُورًا

13. And if any believe not
In Allah and His Messenger,
We have prepared,
For those who reject Allah,
A Blazing Fire!

١٣ وَمَن لَّمْ يُؤْمِن بِاللَّهِ وَرَسُولِهِ
فَإِنَّا أَعْتَدْنَا لِلْكَافِرِينَ سَعِيرًا

14. To Allah belongs the dominion
Of the heavens and the earth:
He forgives whom He
wills,[4882]
And He punishes whom He
Wills: but Allah is
Oft-Forgiving, Most Merciful.

١٤ وَلِلَّهِ مُلْكُ السَّمَاوَاتِ وَالْأَرْضِ
يَغْفِرُ لِمَن يَشَاءُ وَيُعَذِّبُ مَن يَشَاءُ
وَكَانَ اللَّهُ غَفُورًا رَّحِيمًا

4879. They said this with their tongues, but no thought of piety was in their hearts.

4880. Their false excuse was based on a calculation of worldly profit and loss. But what about the spiritual loss in detaching themselves from the Holy Prophet or spiritual profit in joining in the splendidly loyal feelings of service and obedience which were demonstrated at Ḥudaybīyah? And in any case they need not think that all their real and secret motives were not known to Allah.

4881. Their faith was so shaky that they thought the worst would happen, and that the Makkan Quraysh would destroy the unarmed band. In their heart of hearts they would not have been sorry, because they were steeped in wickedness and rejoiced in the sufferings of others. But such persons will burn in the fire of their own disappointment.

4882. Evil must inevitably have its punishment, but there is one way of escape, *viz.*, through repentance and the Mercy of Allah. Allah's Justice will punish, but Allah's Mercy will forgive; and the Mercy is the predominant feature in Allah's universe: "He is Oft-Forgiving, Most Merciful."

15. Those who lagged behind[4883]
(Will say), when ye (are
Free to) march and take
Booty (in war): "Permit us
To follow you." They wish
To change Allah's decree:
Say: "Not thus[4884]
Will ye follow us:
Allah has already declared[4885]
(This) beforehand": then they
Will say, "But ye are[4886]
Jealous of us." Nay,
But little do they understand
(Such things).

١٥ سَيَقُولُ ٱلْمُخَلَّفُونَ إِذَا ٱنطَلَقْتُمْ
إِلَىٰ مَغَانِمَ لِتَأْخُذُوهَا ذَرُونَا نَتَّبِعْكُمْ
يُرِيدُونَ أَن يُبَدِّلُوا۟ كَلَٰمَ ٱللَّهِ
قُل لَّن تَتَّبِعُونَا كَذَٰلِكُمْ قَالَ ٱللَّهُ
مِن قَبْلُ فَسَيَقُولُونَ بَلْ تَحْسُدُونَنَا
بَلْ كَانُوا۟ لَا يَفْقَهُونَ إِلَّا قَلِيلًا

16. Say to the desert Arabs[4887]
Who lagged behind: "Ye
Shall be summoned (to fight)
Against a people given to[4888]
Vehement war: then shall ye
Fight, or they shall submit.[4889]
Then if ye show obedience,
Allah will grant you
A goodly reward, but if
Ye turn back as ye
Did before, He will punish
You with a grievous Penalty."

١٦ قُل لِّلْمُخَلَّفِينَ مِنَ ٱلْأَعْرَابِ
سَتُدْعَوْنَ إِلَىٰ قَوْمٍ أُو۟لِى بَأْسٍ
شَدِيدٍ تُقَٰتِلُونَهُمْ أَوْ يُسْلِمُونَ
فَإِن تُطِيعُوا۟ يُؤْتِكُمُ ٱللَّهُ أَجْرًا حَسَنًا
وَإِن تَتَوَلَّوْا۟ كَمَا تَوَلَّيْتُم مِّن قَبْلُ
يُعَذِّبْكُمْ عَذَابًا أَلِيمًا

17. No blame is there
On the blind, nor is
There blame on the lame,
Nor on one ill (if he

١٧ لَّيْسَ عَلَى ٱلْأَعْمَىٰ حَرَجٌ
وَلَا عَلَى ٱلْأَعْرَجِ حَرَجٌ وَلَا عَلَى ٱلْمَرِيضِ حَرَجٌ

4883. Now comes out another motive behind the minds of the laggards. The journey for pilgrimage had no promise of war booty. If at any future time there should be a promise of booty they would come! But that is to reverse Allah's law and decree. Jihād is not for personal gain or booty: see S. 8 and Introduction to S. 8, paragraph 2. On the contrary Jihād is hard striving, in war and peace, in the Cause of Allah.

4884. *Not thus: i.e.*, not on those terms; not if your object is only to gain booty.

4885. See 8:1, and n. 1179.

4886. The desert Arabs loved fighting and plunder, and understood such motives for war. The higher motives seemed to be beyond them. Like ignorant men they attributed petty motives or motives of jealousy if they were kept out of the vulgar circle of fighting for plunder. But they had to be schooled, and they were schooled to higher ideas of discipline, self-sacrifice, and striving hard for a Cause.

4887. While they are reproached for their supineness in the march which led to Ḥudaybīyah, where there was danger but no prospect of booty, they are promised, if they learn discipline, to be allowed to follow the Banner of Islam where (as happened later in the Persian and Byzantine Wars) there was real fighting with formidable and well-organised armies.

4888. *Cf.* 27:33.

4889. That is, you shall go forth to war if you learn discipline, not for booty, but for a great and noble Cause. For if your opponents submit to the Cause, there will be no fighting and no booty.

Joins not the war):
But he that obeys Allah[4890]
And His Messenger—(Allah)
Will admit him to Gardens
Beneath which rivers flow;
And he who turns back,
(Allah) will punish him
With a grievous Penalty.

وَمَن يُطِعِ ٱللَّهَ وَرَسُولَهُۥ يُدْخِلْهُ
جَنَّٰتٍ تَجْرِى مِن تَحْتِهَا ٱلْأَنْهَٰرُ ۖ
وَمَن يَتَوَلَّ يُعَذِّبْهُ عَذَابًا أَلِيمًا

SECTION 3.

18. Allah's Good Pleasure[4891]
Was on the Believers
When they swore Fealty
To thee under the Tree:[4892]
He knew[4893] what was
In their hearts, and He
Sent down Tranquillity[4894]
To them; and He rewarded
Them with a speedy Victory;[4895]

١٨ لَّقَدْ رَضِىَ ٱللَّهُ عَنِ
ٱلْمُؤْمِنِينَ إِذْ يُبَايِعُونَكَ تَحْتَ ٱلشَّجَرَةِ
فَعَلِمَ مَا فِى قُلُوبِهِمْ فَأَنزَلَ ٱلسَّكِينَةَ عَلَيْهِمْ
وَأَثَٰبَهُمْ فَتْحًا قَرِيبًا

19. And many gains will they
Acquire (besides): and Allah
Is Exalted in Power,
Full of Wisdom.

١٩ وَمَغَانِمَ كَثِيرَةً يَأْخُذُونَهَا ۗ
وَكَانَ ٱللَّهُ عَزِيزًا حَكِيمًا

20. Allah has promised you
Many gains that ye shall[4896]
Acquire, and He has given[4897]

٢٠ وَعَدَكُمُ ٱللَّهُ مَغَانِمَ كَثِيرَةً
تَأْخُذُونَهَا فَعَجَّلَ لَكُمْ

4890. There may be neither fighting nor booty. But all who obey the righteous Imām's call to Jihād with perfect discipline will get the Rewards of the Hereafter. The blind, the maimed, and the infirm will of course be exempted from active compliance with the Call, but they can render such services as are within their power, and then they will not be excluded from the reward.

4891. The noun from the very *raḍiya* is *riḍwān* (Good Pleasure); hence the name of this *Bay'ah, Bay'ah al Riḍwān*, the Fealty of Allah's Good Pleasure: see n. 4877 to 48:10.

4892. The great ceremony of the Fealty of Allah's Good Pleasure took place while the Holy Prophet sat under a tree in the plain of Ḥudaybīyah. (R).

4893. Or tested: see n. 4855 to 47:31.

4894. *Sakīnah* = Peace, calm, sense of security and confidence, tranquillity. *Cf.* above 48:4, and n. 4869. The same word is used in connection with the battle of Ḥunayn in 9:26, and in connection with the Cave of Thawr at an early stage in the Hijrah: 9:40.

4895. The Treaty of Ḥudaybīyah itself was a "speedy Victory": it followed immediately after the *Bay'ah*.

4896. The gains so far seen from the *Bay'ah* and their calm and disciplined behaviour were certainly great; but greater still were to follow in the spiritual sense, in the rapid spread of Islam, in the clearance from the Sacred House of the idolatrous autocracy, and in the universal acceptance of the Message of Allah in Arabia.

4897. The first fruits of the *Bay'ah* were the victory or treaty of Ḥudaybīyah, the cessation for the time being of the hostility of the Makkan Quraysh, and the opening out of the way to Makkah. These things are implied in the phrase. "He has restrained the hands of men from you."

You these beforehand; and
He has restrained the hands
Of men from you; that it
May be a Sign for[4898]
The Believers, and that
He may guide you
To a Straight Path;

هَٰذِهِۦ وَكَفَّ أَيْدِىَ ٱلنَّاسِ عَنكُمْ
وَلِتَكُونَ ءَايَةً لِّلْمُؤْمِنِينَ وَيَهْدِيَكُمْ
صِرَٰطًا مُّسْتَقِيمًا

21. And other gains (there are),
Which are not within[4899]
Your power, but which
Allah has compassed: and Allah
Has power over all things.

٢١ وَأُخْرَىٰ لَمْ تَقْدِرُوا۟ عَلَيْهَا قَدْ أَحَاطَ ٱللَّهُ بِهَا ۚ
وَكَانَ ٱللَّهُ عَلَىٰ كُلِّ شَىْءٍ قَدِيرًا

22. If the Unbelievers
Should fight you, they would[4900]
Certainly turn their backs;
Then would they find
Neither protector nor helper.

٢٢ وَلَوْ قَٰتَلَكُمُ ٱلَّذِينَ كَفَرُوا۟ لَوَلَّوُا۟ ٱلْأَدْبَٰرَ
ثُمَّ لَا يَجِدُونَ وَلِيًّا وَلَا نَصِيرًا

23. (Such has been) the practice[4901]
(Approved) of Allah already
In the past: no change
Wilt thou find in
The practice (approved) of Allah.

٢٣ سُنَّةَ ٱللَّهِ ٱلَّتِى قَدْ خَلَتْ مِن قَبْلُ ۖ
وَلَن تَجِدَ لِسُنَّةِ ٱللَّهِ تَبْدِيلًا

24. And it is He Who
Has restrained their hands
From you and your hands
From them in the midst[4902]
Of Makkah, after that He
Gave you the victory
Over them. And Allah sees
Well all that ye do.

٢٤ وَهُوَ ٱلَّذِى كَفَّ أَيْدِيَهُمْ عَنكُمْ
وَأَيْدِيَكُمْ عَنْهُم بِبَطْنِ مَكَّةَ
مِنۢ بَعْدِ أَنْ أَظْفَرَكُمْ عَلَيْهِمْ ۚ
وَكَانَ ٱللَّهُ بِمَا تَعْمَلُونَ بَصِيرًا

4898. Ḥudaybīyah (in both the *Bay'ah* and the Treaty) was truly a sign post for the Believers: it showed the solidarity of Islam, and the position which the Muslims had won in the Arab world.

4899. *Other gains:* these are usually referred to the later victories of Islam, but we must view them not merely in their political or material aspect, but chiefly in the rise of Islam as a world power morally and spiritually.

4900. Their morale was not truly broken.

4901. *Cf.* 33:62.

4902. Little incidents had taken place that might have plunged the Quraysh and the Muslims from Madīnah into a fight. On the one hand, the Quraysh were determined to keep out the Muslims, which they had no right to do: and on the other hand, the Muslims, though unarmed, had sworn to stand together, and if they had counter-attacked they could have forced their entrance to the Ka'bah, the centre of Makkah. But Allah restrained both sides from anything that would have violated the Peace of the Sanctuary, and after the Treaty was signed, all danger was past.

25. They are the ones who
Denied revelation and hindered
you
From the Sacred Mosque
And the sacrificial
animals,[4903]
Detained from reaching their
Place of sacrifice. Had there
Not been believing men
And believing women whom
Ye did not know that[4904]
Ye were trampling down
And on whose account
A crime would have accrued
To you without (your)
knowledge,
(Allah would have allowed you
To force your way, but
He held back your hands)
That He may admit
To His Mercy whom He
will.[4905]
If they had been[4906]
Apart, We should
Certainly have punished
The Unbelievers among them
With a grievous punishment.

٢٥ هُمُ ٱلَّذِينَ كَفَرُوا۟
وَصَدُّوكُمْ عَنِ ٱلْمَسْجِدِ ٱلْحَرَامِ
وَٱلْهَدْىَ مَعْكُوفًا أَن يَبْلُغَ مَحِلَّهُۥ ۚ
وَلَوْلَا رِجَالٌ مُّؤْمِنُونَ
وَنِسَآءٌ مُّؤْمِنَٰتٌ لَّمْ تَعْلَمُوهُمْ
أَن تَطَـُٔوهُمْ فَتُصِيبَكُم
مِّنْهُم مَّعَرَّةٌۢ بِغَيْرِ عِلْمٍ ۖ
لِّيُدْخِلَ ٱللَّهُ فِى
رَحْمَتِهِۦ مَن يَشَآءُ ۚ
لَوْ تَزَيَّلُوا۟ لَعَذَّبْنَا ٱلَّذِينَ
كَفَرُوا۟ مِنْهُمْ
عَذَابًا أَلِيمًا

26. While the Unbelievers
Got up in their hearts
Heat and cant—the heat[4907]
And cant of Ignorance—

٢٦ إِذْ جَعَلَ ٱلَّذِينَ كَفَرُوا۟
فِى قُلُوبِهِمُ ٱلْحَمِيَّةَ حَمِيَّةَ ٱلْجَٰهِلِيَّةِ

4903. The Muslims from Madīnah had brought the animals for sacrifice with them, and had put on the *Iḥrām* or pilgrim's garb (see n. 217 to 2:197), but they were not only prevented from entering Makkah, but were also prevented from sending the sacrificial animals to the place of sacrifice in Makkah, as they could have done under 2:196. The sacrifice was therefore actually offered at Ḥudaybīyah.

4904. There were at the time in Makkah believing Muslims, men and women, and the faith of some of them was unknown to their brethren from Madīnah. Had a fight taken place in Makkah, even though the Muslims had been successful, they would unwittingly have killed some of these unknown Muslims, and thus would unwittingly have been guilty of shedding Muslim blood. This was prevented by the Treaty.

4905. Allah works according to His wise and Holy Will and Plan, and not according to what seems to us, in the excitement of human life, to be the obvious course of things. By preventing a fight He saved many valuable lives, not only of Muslims but also of some who became Muslims afterwards and served Islam. He grants His Mercy on far higher standards than man in his limited horizon can see.

4906. If the party from Madīnah could have distinguished Muslims from non-Muslims among the Makkans, they might have been allowed to enter and punish the pagan Quraysh for their inordinate vanity and gross breach of the unwritten law of the land. But in the actual circumstances the best solution was the Treaty of Ḥudaybīyah.

4907. While the Unbelievers were blustering and excited, and meticulously objected to introductory words such as "In the name of Allah, Most Gracious, Most Merciful, from Muḥammad, the Prophet of Allah" (they did not like the titles), the Prophet remained calm and collected, and got the substance of their demands embodied in the Treaty without worrying about words. Even though the terms of the Treaty appeared to the companions, at first, to be unfair to Muslims, they remained faithful to their Leader and showed trust in his better judgement, a trust that was vindicated by the events that followed. (R).

Allah sent down His
Tranquillity[4908]
To his Messenger and to
The Believers, and made them
Stick close to the command
Of self-restraint; and well
Were they entitled to it[4909]
And worthy of it.
And Allah has full knowledge
Of all things.

فَأَنزَلَ ٱللَّهُ سَكِينَتَهُۥ
عَلَىٰ رَسُولِهِۦ وَعَلَى ٱلْمُؤْمِنِينَ
وَأَلْزَمَهُمْ كَلِمَةَ ٱلتَّقْوَىٰ
وَكَانُوٓا۟ أَحَقَّ بِهَا وَأَهْلَهَا
وَكَانَ ٱللَّهُ بِكُلِّ شَىْءٍ عَلِيمًا

SECTION 4.

27. Truly did Allah fulfil
The vision for His Messenger:[4910]
Ye shall enter the Sacred
Mosque, if Allah wills,
With minds secure, heads shaved,
Hair cut short, and without fear.
For He knew what ye
Knew not, and He granted,
Besides this, a speedy victory.[4911]

٢٧ لَّقَدْ صَدَقَ ٱللَّهُ رَسُولَهُ ٱلرُّءْيَا بِٱلْحَقِّ
لَتَدْخُلُنَّ ٱلْمَسْجِدَ ٱلْحَرَامَ إِن شَآءَ ٱللَّهُ ءَامِنِينَ
مُحَلِّقِينَ رُءُوسَكُمْ وَمُقَصِّرِينَ لَا تَخَافُونَ
فَعَلِمَ مَا لَمْ تَعْلَمُوا۟ فَجَعَلَ مِن دُونِ ذَٰلِكَ
فَتْحًا قَرِيبًا

28. It is He Who has sent
His Messenger with Guidance
And the Religion of Truth,
To proclaim it over
All religion: and enough
Is Allah for a Witness.[4912]

٢٨ هُوَ ٱلَّذِىٓ أَرْسَلَ رَسُولَهُۥ بِٱلْهُدَىٰ
وَدِينِ ٱلْحَقِّ لِيُظْهِرَهُۥ عَلَى ٱلدِّينِ كُلِّهِۦ
وَكَفَىٰ بِٱللَّهِ شَهِيدًا

29. Muḥammad is the Messenger
Of Allah; and those who are
With him are strong
Against Unbelievers, (but)
Compassionate amongst each
other.[4913]

٢٩ مُّحَمَّدٌ رَّسُولُ ٱللَّهِ
وَٱلَّذِينَ مَعَهُۥٓ أَشِدَّآءُ عَلَى ٱلْكُفَّارِ
رُحَمَآءُ بَيْنَهُمْ

4908. *Cf.* above 48:18, and n. 4894.

4909. *It* = Tranquillity. Their calmness amid much provocation was a gift of Allah; they had earned a right to it by their obedience and discipline, and showed themselves well worthy of it.

4910. The Prophet had had a dream that he had entered the Sacred Mosque at Makkah, just before he decided on the journey which resulted in the Treaty of Ḥudaybīyah. By it he and his people could enter next year without the least molestation and in the full customary garb, with head shaved or hair cut short, and all the customary minor rites of pilgrimage.

4911. See above, 48:18, and n. 4895.

4912. The divine disposition of events in the coming of Islam and its promulgation by the Holy Prophet are themselves evidence of the truth of Islam and its all-reaching character; for there is nothing which it has not influenced. See also 61:9, n. 5442.

4913. *Cf.* 9:128. The devotees of Allah wage unceasing war against evil, for themselves, and for others; but to their own brethren in faith—especially the weaker ones—they are mild and compassionate: they seek out every opportunity to sympathise with them and help them.

Thou wilt see them bow
And prostrate themselves
(In prayer), seeking Grace
From Allah and (His) Good
Pleasure.[4914]
On their faces are their
Marks, (being) the traces[4915]
Of their prostration.
This is their similitude
In the Tawrāh;[4916]
And their similitude
In the Gospel is[4917]
Like a seed which sends
Forth its blade, then
Makes it strong; it then
Becomes thick, and it stands
On its own stem, (filling)
The sowers with wonder
And delight. As a result,[4918]
It fills the Unbelievers
With rage at them.
Allah has promised those
Among them who believe
And do righteous deeds
Forgiveness,
And a great Reward.

تَرَىٰهُمْ رُكَّعًا سُجَّدًا
يَبْتَغُونَ فَضْلًا مِّنَ ٱللَّهِ وَرِضْوَٰنًا
سِيمَاهُمْ فِى وُجُوهِهِم
مِّنْ أَثَرِ ٱلسُّجُودِ
ذَٰلِكَ مَثَلُهُمْ فِى ٱلتَّوْرَىٰةِ
وَمَثَلُهُمْ فِى ٱلْإِنجِيلِ
كَزَرْعٍ أَخْرَجَ شَطْـَٔهُۥ فَـَٔازَرَهُۥ
فَٱسْتَغْلَظَ فَٱسْتَوَىٰ
عَلَىٰ سُوقِهِۦ يُعْجِبُ ٱلزُّرَّاعَ
لِيَغِيظَ بِهِمُ ٱلْكُفَّارَ
وَعَدَ ٱللَّهُ ٱلَّذِينَ ءَامَنُوا۟
وَعَمِلُوا۟ ٱلصَّٰلِحَٰتِ مِنْهُم
مَّغْفِرَةً وَأَجْرًا عَظِيمًۢا

4914. Their humility is before Allah and His Prophet and all who have authority from Allah, but they yield no power or pomp, nor do they worship worldly show or glitter. Nor is their humility before Allah a mere show for men.

4915. The traces of their earnestness and humility are engraved on their faces, *i.e.*, penetrate their inmost being, the face being the outward sign of the inner man. If we take it in its literal sense, the traces might mean the marks left by repeated prostration on their foreheads. Moreover, a good man's face alone shows in him the grace and light of Allah; he is gentle, kind and forbearing, ever helpful, relying on Allah and possessing 'a blessed Peace and Calmness' (*i.e., sakīnah: cf.* 48:26; 48:18, n. 4894) that can come from no other source. (R).

4916. In the Book of Moses, which is now found in a corrupt form in the Pentateuch, the posture of humility in prayer is indicated by prostration: *e.g.*, Moses and Aaron "fell upon their faces", Num. xvi. 22.

4917. The similitude in the Gospel is about how the good seed is sown and grows gradually, even beyond the expectation of the sower: "the seed should spring and grow up, he knoweth now how; for the earth bringeth forth fruit of herself; first the blade, then the ear, after that the full corn in the ear"; Mark, iv. 27-28. Thus Islam was preached by the Holy Prophet; the seed seemed to human eyes lost in the ground; but it put forth its shoot, and grew, and became strong, until it was able to stand on its own legs, and its worst enemies recognised its existence and its right to live. Note how much more complete the parable is in the Qur'ān. The mentality of the sowers of the seed is expressed in beautiful terms: its growth and strength filled them "with wonder and delight."

4918. I construe the particle *"li"* as expressing not the object, but the result. The result of the wonderful growth of Islam in numbers and strength was that its enemies were confounded, and raged furiously within their own minds, a contrast to the satisfaction, wonder, and delight of the Prophet and his Companions. The pronoun in "rage at *them*" of course refers to the Prophet and his Companions, and goes back to the earlier words, "on *their* faces" etc.

INTRODUCTION TO SŪRAH 49—*AL ḤUJURĀT*

This is the third of the group of three Madīnah Sūrahs, which began with S. 47. See the Introduction to that Sūrah.

Its subject matter is the manners to be observed by the members of the rapidly-growing Muslim community, among themselves and towards its Leader. The keyword *"Ḥujurāt"* (Chambers) occurs in verse 4.

Its date is referred to the Year of Deputations, A.H. 9, when a large number of deputations of all kinds visited Madīnah to offer their allegiance to Islam.

Summary—A community must show its respect to its Leader in all forms of behaviour; quarrels are unseemly and should be composed; manners spring from morals; and mutual respect and confidence are a duty and a privilege in Islam (49:1-18, and C. 223).

C. 223.—Respectful behaviour to the Leader, in manner,
(49:1-18) Voice, and demeanour, are the bonds and cement
Of an organised community. The whispers
Of rumours should be tested, and selfish impatience
Should be curbed to discipline. All quarrels
Should be composed, if necessary by the force
Of the community, but with perfect
Fairness and justice. Ridicule, taunts,
And biting words, should be avoided,
In presence or in absence. Suspicion
And spying are unworthy of men who believe.
All men are descended from one pair:
Their honour depends, not on race, but
On righteousness. Faith is not a matter
Of words, but of accepting Allah's Will
And striving in His Cause. The coming
Into Islam confers no favour on others,
But is itself a favour and a privilege,
A guidance for those who are true and sincere.

Sūrah 49.

Al Ḥujurāt (The Chambers)

الجزء السادس والعشرون سورة الحجرات

In the name of Allah, Most Gracious,
Most Merciful.

بسم الله الرحمن الرحيم

1. O ye who believe!
Put not yourselves forward[4919]
Before Allah and His Messenger;
But fear Allah: for Allah
Is He Who hears
And knows all things.

١ يَا أَيُّهَا الَّذِينَ آمَنُوا لَا تُقَدِّمُوا
بَيْنَ يَدَيِ اللَّهِ وَرَسُولِهِ وَاتَّقُوا اللَّهَ
إِنَّ اللَّهَ سَمِيعٌ عَلِيمٌ

2. O ye who believe!
Raise not your voices[4920]
Above the voice of the Prophet,
Nor speak aloud to him
In talk, as ye may
Speak aloud to one another,
Lest your deeds become[4921]
Vain and ye perceive not.

٢ يَا أَيُّهَا الَّذِينَ آمَنُوا
لَا تَرْفَعُوا أَصْوَاتَكُمْ فَوْقَ صَوْتِ النَّبِيِّ
وَلَا تَجْهَرُوا لَهُ بِالْقَوْلِ كَجَهْرِ بَعْضِكُمْ
لِبَعْضٍ أَنْ تَحْبَطَ أَعْمَالُكُمْ وَأَنْتُمْ لَا تَشْعُرُونَ

3. Those that lower their voice
In the presence of
Allah's Messenger—their hearts
Has Allah tested for piety:[4922]
For them is Forgiveness
And a great Reward.

٣ إِنَّ الَّذِينَ يَغُضُّونَ أَصْوَاتَهُمْ عِنْدَ رَسُولِ اللَّهِ
أُولَٰئِكَ الَّذِينَ امْتَحَنَ اللَّهُ قُلُوبَهُمْ لِلتَّقْوَىٰ
لَهُمْ مَغْفِرَةٌ وَأَجْرٌ عَظِيمٌ

4. Those who shout out[4923]
To thee from without

٤ إِنَّ الَّذِينَ يُنَادُونَكَ

4919. Several shades of meaning are implied: (1) do not make yourselves conspicuous in word or deed when in the presence of Allah *(e.g.* in a Mosque, or at Prayers or religious assemblies); (2) do not anticipate in word or deed what your Leader (Allah's Messenger) may say or do; (3) do not be impatient, trying to hasten things before the time is ripe, of which the best Judge is Allah, Who speaks through His Messenger. Be reverent in all things, as in the presence of Allah: for He hears and sees all things. (4) Look to the Qur'ān and the Sunnah of the Prophet (peace be on him) for guidance and let nothing else take precedence over them. (R).

4920. It is bad manners to talk loudly before your Leader. Some ill-mannered people so raise their voices as to drown the voice of their Leader, in conversation or in Council.

4921. Such rudeness may even destroy the value of such services as they may otherwise have been able to render, and all this without their even realising the harm they were doing to the Cause.

4922. The essence of good manners arises from the heart. The man who really and sincerely respects his Leader has true piety in his heart, just as the man who does the opposite may undo the work of years by weakening the Leader's authority.

4923. To shout aloud to your Leader from outside his Chambers shows disrespect both for his person, his time, and his engagements. Only ignorant fools would be guilty of such unseemly behaviour. It is more seemly of them to wait and bide their time until he is free to come out and attend to them. But, in the Court of a spiritual King, much is forgiven that is due to lack of knowledge and understanding. In the earthly Court, ignorance of the Law excuseth no man. If a man behaved in that way to the General of an army or the Governor of a Province, not to speak of an earthly King, he would be laid hands on by the Guard, and could never gain the access he desires.

The Inner Apartments[4923-A] —
Most of them lack understanding.

مِن وَرَآءِ ٱلْحُجُرَٰتِ أَكْثَرُهُمْ لَا يَعْقِلُونَ

5. If only they had patience
Until thou couldst
Come out to them,
It would be best
For them: but Allah is
Oft-Forgiving, Most Merciful.

(٥) وَلَوْ أَنَّهُمْ صَبَرُوا۟ حَتَّىٰ
تَخْرُجَ إِلَيْهِمْ لَكَانَ خَيْرًا لَّهُمْ
وَٱللَّهُ غَفُورٌ رَّحِيمٌ

6. O ye who believe!
If a wicked person comes[4924]
To you with any news,
Ascertain the truth, lest
Ye harm people unwittingly,
And afterwards become
Full of repentance for
What ye have done.

(٦) يَٰٓأَيُّهَا ٱلَّذِينَ ءَامَنُوٓا۟
إِن جَآءَكُمْ فَاسِقٌۢ بِنَبَإٍ فَتَبَيَّنُوٓا۟
أَن تُصِيبُوا۟ قَوْمًۢا بِجَهَٰلَةٍ فَتُصْبِحُوا۟
عَلَىٰ مَا فَعَلْتُمْ نَٰدِمِينَ

7. And know that among you[4925]
Is Allah's Messenger: were he,
In many matters, to follow
Your (wishes), ye would
Certainly fall into misfortune:
But Allah has endeared[4926]
The Faith to you, and
Has made it beautiful
In your hearts, and He
Has made hateful to you
Unbelief, wickedness, and
Rebellion: such indeed are
Those who walk in righteousness —

(٧) وَٱعْلَمُوٓا۟ أَنَّ فِيكُمْ رَسُولَ ٱللَّهِ
لَوْ يُطِيعُكُمْ فِى كَثِيرٍ مِّنَ ٱلْأَمْرِ لَعَنِتُّمْ
وَلَٰكِنَّ ٱللَّهَ حَبَّبَ إِلَيْكُمُ ٱلْإِيمَٰنَ
وَزَيَّنَهُۥ فِى قُلُوبِكُمْ وَكَرَّهَ إِلَيْكُمُ
ٱلْكُفْرَ وَٱلْفُسُوقَ وَٱلْعِصْيَانَ
أُو۟لَٰٓئِكَ هُمُ ٱلرَّٰشِدُونَ

8. A grace and favour
From Allah; and Allah
Is full of Knowledge
And Wisdom,

(٨) فَضْلًا مِّنَ ٱللَّهِ وَنِعْمَةً
وَٱللَّهُ عَلِيمٌ حَكِيمٌ

4923-A. *Al Ḥujurāt:* "The Inner Apartments" or "The Chambers."

4924. All tittle-tattle or reports — especially if emanating from persons you do not know — are to be tested, and the truth ascertained. If they were believed and passed on, much harm may be done, of which you may have cause afterwards to repent heartily. Scandal or slander of all kinds is here condemned. That about women is specially denounced: 24:11-20; 23-26.

4925. The messenger of Allah, if he consults his friends and associates, should not be expected to follow their advice in all matters. The judgement and responsibility are his: he sees farther than the rest, and he is not swayed by personal feeling as others may be. (R).

4926. Fortunate indeed was the generation among whom the Prophet of Allah walked in his daily life. His example was inspiring. Their inner Faith was dear to them; it was a thing to be proud of in their innermost hearts; and they loved discipline, obedience, and righteousness. No wonder all their other disadvantages were neutralised, and they went from strength to strength. Nothing but the Grace of Allah could have brought about such a result.

9. If two parties among[4927]
The Believers fall into
A quarrel, make ye peace
Between them: but if
One of them transgresses
Beyond bounds against the other,
Then fight ye (all) against
The one that transgresses
Until it complies with
The command of Allah;
But if it complies, then
Make peace between them
With justice, and be fair:
For Allah loves those
Who are fair (and just).

٩ وَإِن طَآئِفَتَانِ مِنَ ٱلْمُؤْمِنِينَ
ٱقْتَتَلُوا۟ فَأَصْلِحُوا۟ بَيْنَهُمَا
فَإِنۢ بَغَتْ إِحْدَىٰهُمَا عَلَى ٱلْأُخْرَىٰ
فَقَٰتِلُوا۟ ٱلَّتِى تَبْغِى حَتَّىٰ تَفِىٓءَ إِلَىٰٓ أَمْرِ ٱللَّهِ
فَإِن فَآءَتْ فَأَصْلِحُوا۟
بَيْنَهُمَا بِٱلْعَدْلِ وَأَقْسِطُوٓا۟
إِنَّ ٱللَّهَ يُحِبُّ ٱلْمُقْسِطِينَ

10. The Believers are but
A single Brotherhood:[4928]
So make peace and
Reconciliation between your
Two (contending) brothers;
And fear Allah, that ye
May receive Mercy.

١٠ إِنَّمَا ٱلْمُؤْمِنُونَ إِخْوَةٌ
فَأَصْلِحُوا۟ بَيْنَ أَخَوَيْكُمْ
وَٱتَّقُوا۟ ٱللَّهَ لَعَلَّكُمْ تُرْحَمُونَ

SECTION 2.

11. O ye who believe!
Let not some men
Among you laugh at others:[4929]
It may be that
The (latter) are better
Than the (former):
Nor let some women
Laugh at others:
It may be that
The (latter) are better
Than the (former):

١١ يَٰٓأَيُّهَا ٱلَّذِينَ ءَامَنُوا۟
لَا يَسْخَرْ قَوْمٌ مِّن قَوْمٍ
عَسَىٰٓ أَن يَكُونُوا۟ خَيْرًا مِّنْهُمْ
وَلَا نِسَآءٌ مِّن نِّسَآءٍ عَسَىٰٓ أَن
يَكُنَّ خَيْرًا مِّنْهُنَّ

4927. Individual quarrels are easier to compose than group quarrels, or, in the modern world, national quarrels. But the collective community of Islam should be supreme over groups or nations. It would be expected to act justly and try to compose the quarrel, for peace is better than fighting. But if one party is determined to be the aggressor, the whole force of the community is brought to bear on it. The essential condition of course is that there should be perfect fairness and justice and respect for the highest principles; for Islam takes account of every just and legitimate interest without separating spiritual from temporal matters. The League of Nations failed because these essentials were absent and today the United Nations fails for the same reason. (R).

4928. The enforcement of the Muslim Brotherhood is the greatest social ideal of Islam. On it was based the Prophet's Sermon at his last pilgrimage, and Islam cannot be completely realised until this ideal is achieved.

4929. Mutual ridicule ceases to be fun when there is arrogance or selfishness or malice behind it. We may laugh *with* people, to share in the happiness of life: we must never laugh *at* people in contempt or ridicule. In many things they may be better than ourselves!

Nor defame nor be[4930]
Sarcastic to each other,
Nor call each other
By (offensive) nicknames:
Ill-seeming is a name
Connoting wickedness,
(To be used of one)
After he has believed:
And those who
Do not desist are
(Indeed) doing wrong.

وَلَا تَلْمِزُوٓا۟ أَنفُسَكُمْ
وَلَا تَنَابَزُوا۟ بِٱلْأَلْقَٰبِ ۖ
بِئْسَ ٱلِٱسْمُ ٱلْفُسُوقُ بَعْدَ ٱلْإِيمَٰنِ ۚ
وَمَن لَّمْ يَتُبْ فَأُو۟لَٰٓئِكَ
هُمُ ٱلظَّٰلِمُونَ

12. O ye who believe!
Avoid suspicion as much[4931]
(As possible): for suspicion
In some cases is a sin:
And spy not on each other,
Nor speak ill of each other
Behind their backs. Would any
Of you like to eat
The flesh of his dead[4932]
Brother? Nay, ye would
Abhor it... But fear Allah:
For Allah is Oft-Returning,
Most Merciful.

١٢ يَٰٓأَيُّهَا ٱلَّذِينَ ءَامَنُوا۟ ٱجْتَنِبُوا۟
كَثِيرًا مِّنَ ٱلظَّنِّ إِنَّ بَعْضَ ٱلظَّنِّ إِثْمٌ ۖ
وَلَا تَجَسَّسُوا۟ وَلَا يَغْتَب بَّعْضُكُم بَعْضًا ۚ
أَيُحِبُّ أَحَدُكُمْ أَن يَأْكُلَ
لَحْمَ أَخِيهِ مَيْتًا فَكَرِهْتُمُوهُ ۚ
وَٱتَّقُوا۟ ٱللَّهَ ۚ إِنَّ ٱللَّهَ تَوَّابٌ رَّحِيمٌ

13. O mankind! We created[4933]
You from a single (pair)
Of a male and a female,
And made you into

١٣ يَٰٓأَيُّهَا ٱلنَّاسُ إِنَّا خَلَقْنَٰكُم
مِّن ذَكَرٍ وَأُنثَىٰ وَجَعَلْنَٰكُمْ

4930. Defamation may consist in speaking ill of others by the spoken or written word, or in acting in such a way as to suggest a charge against some person whom we are not in a position to judge. A cutting, biting remark or taunt of sarcasm is included in the word *lamaza*. An offensive nickname may amount to defamation, but in any case there is no point in using offensive nicknames, or names that suggest some real or fancied defect. They ill accord with the serious purpose which Muslims should have in life. For example, even if a man is lame, it is wrong to address him as "O lame one!" It causes him pain, and it is bad manners. So in the case of the rude remark, "the black man".

4931. Most kinds of suspicion are baseless and to be avoided, and some are crimes in themselves: for they do cruel injustice to innocent men and women. Spying, or enquiring too curiously into other people's affairs, means either idle curiosity, and is therefore futile, or suspicion carried a stage further, which almost amounts to sin. Back-biting also is a brood of the same genus. It may be either futile but all the same mischievous, or it may be poisoned with malice, in which case it is a sin added to sin.

4932. No one would like even to think of such an abomination as eating the flesh of his brother. But when the brother is dead, and the flesh is carrion, abomination is added to abomination. In the same way we are asked to refrain from hurting people's feelings when they are present; how much worse is it when we say things, true or false, when they are absent!

4933. This is addressed to all mankind and not only to the Muslim brotherhood, though it is understood that in a perfected world the two would be synonymous. As it is, mankind is descended from one pair of parents. Their tribes, races, and nations are convenient labels by which we may know certain differing characteristics. Before Allah they are all one, and he gets most honour who is most righteous.

Nations and tribes, that
Ye may know each other
(Not that ye may despise
(Each other). Verily
The most honoured of you
In the sight of Allah
Is (he who is) the most
Righteous of you.
And Allah has full knowledge
And is well-acquainted
(With all things).

شُعُوبًا وَقَبَآئِلَ لِتَعَارَفُوٓا۟ ۚ
إِنَّ أَكْرَمَكُمْ
عِندَ ٱللَّهِ أَتْقَىٰكُمْ ۚ
إِنَّ ٱللَّهَ عَلِيمٌ خَبِيرٌ

14. The desert Arabs say,[4934]
"We believe." Say, "Ye
Have no faith; but ye
(Only) say, 'We have submitted[4935]
Our wills to Allah,'
For not yet has Faith
Entered your hearts.
But if ye obey Allah
And His Messenger, He
Will not belittle aught
Of your deeds: for Allah
Is Oft-Forgiving, Most Merciful."

(١٤) قَالَتِ ٱلْأَعْرَابُ ءَامَنَّا ۖ
قُل لَّمْ تُؤْمِنُوا۟ وَلَٰكِن قُولُوٓا۟ أَسْلَمْنَا
وَلَمَّا يَدْخُلِ ٱلْإِيمَٰنُ فِى قُلُوبِكُمْ ۖ
وَإِن تُطِيعُوا۟ ٱللَّهَ وَرَسُولَهُۥ لَا يَلِتْكُم
مِّنْ أَعْمَٰلِكُمْ شَيْـًٔا ۚ
إِنَّ ٱللَّهَ غَفُورٌ رَّحِيمٌ

15. Only those are Believers
Who have believed in Allah
And His Messenger, and have
Never since doubted, but
Have striven with their
Belongings and their persons
In the Cause of Allah:
Such are the sincere ones.

(١٥) إِنَّمَا ٱلْمُؤْمِنُونَ ٱلَّذِينَ
ءَامَنُوا۟ بِٱللَّهِ وَرَسُولِهِۦ ثُمَّ لَمْ يَرْتَابُوا۟
وَجَٰهَدُوا۟ بِأَمْوَٰلِهِمْ وَأَنفُسِهِمْ فِى سَبِيلِ ٱللَّهِ ۚ
أُو۟لَٰٓئِكَ هُمُ ٱلصَّٰدِقُونَ

16. Say: "What! Will ye[4936]
Instruct Allah about your
Religion? But Allah knows
All that is in the heavens

(١٦) قُلْ أَتُعَلِّمُونَ ٱللَّهَ بِدِينِكُمْ
وَٱللَّهُ يَعْلَمُ مَا فِى ٱلسَّمَٰوَٰتِ

4934. The desert Arabs were somewhat shaky in their faith. Their hearts and minds were petty, and they thought of petty things, while Islam requires the complete submission of one's being to Allah. See next verse. Some of the failings of the desert Arabs are described in 48:11-15. But the reference here is said to be to the Banū Asad, who came to profess Islam in order to get charity during a famine.

4935. 'This is what ye ought to prove if your faith has any meaning, but ye only say it with your tongues.'

4936. 'You say (or perhaps even think) that you are Muslims, but where are the fruits of your Faith? Allah knows the innermost motives and secrets of your heart, and you cannot deceive Him by attaching a certain label to yourselves.' Alas! that this answer to the desert Arabs is true of so many others in our own times!

And on earth: He has
Full knowledge of all things.

وَمَا فِي ٱلْأَرْضِ وَٱللَّهُ بِكُلِّ شَيْءٍ عَلِيمٌ

17. They impress on thee[4937]
As a favour that they
Have embraced Islam.
Say, "Count not your Islam
As a favour upon me:
Nay, Allah has conferred
A favour upon you
That He has guided you
To the Faith, if ye
Be true and sincere.

﴿١٧﴾ يَمُنُّونَ عَلَيْكَ أَنْ أَسْلَمُوا۟ قُل لَّا تَمُنُّوا۟ عَلَيَّ إِسْلَٰمَكُم بَلِ ٱللَّهُ يَمُنُّ عَلَيْكُمْ أَنْ هَدَىٰكُمْ لِلْإِيمَٰنِ إِن كُنتُمْ صَٰدِقِينَ

18. "Verily Allah Knows[4938]
The secrets of the heavens
And the earth: and Allah
Sees well all
That ye do."

﴿١٨﴾ إِنَّ ٱللَّهَ يَعْلَمُ غَيْبَ ٱلسَّمَٰوَٰتِ وَٱلْأَرْضِ وَٱللَّهُ بَصِيرٌۢ بِمَا تَعْمَلُونَ

4937. Islam in itself is a precious privilege. By accepting it we confer no favour on its preacher or on any community. If the acceptance is from the heart, it is a great favour done to those who accept, that the Light of Allah has entered their hearts and they have received guidance.

4938. This does not mean that we should seek petty motives in newcomers into the House of Islam. That would indeed be harbouring suspicions or allowing curiosity to spy out motives, which would be a crime under 49:12. We should be true, sincere, and devoted ourselves, and leave the case of others to Allah, from Whose eyes nothing is hidden.

INTRODUCTION TO SŪRAH 50—*QĀF*

We now come to a group of seven Makkan Sūrahs (50-56), dealing with Allah's revelation through nature, through history, and through the mouths of the Prophets, and pointing to the Hereafter. We saw that the last group of three (47—49) dealt with the external and internal relations of the Ummah when formed. In the present group our attention is more particularly directed to aspects eschatological—the Future before us when this life is done.

This particular Sūrah belongs to the early Makkan period. After an appeal to nature and to the fate of wicked peoples in history, it removes as it were the veil (verse 22) from the Future after death.

Summary—Sceptics can look up to the heavens above and to Nature around them, as well as to the fate of sin in the history of the past: will they doubt Allah's Revelation when the veil is lifted? (59:1-29, and C. 224).

A vision of the Day of Recompense and the Day of Reality (50:30-45, and C. 225).

C. 224.—The Prophet's credentials are the Revelation
(50:1-29.) He brings. Let them not wonder at the Message
Or at the News of the Hereafter. They have but
To look at the starry heavens and at Nature
Around them to see Allah's goodness and His power
To bring life out of the dead, and to punish
All wrong. Every deed, word, and thought are in
The eternal Record. Death will open
Your eyes and make you see Realities.
Then will every action bear
Its due fruit, and no soul can shift
Its responsibility on to another.

Sūrah 50.

Qāf [4939]

الجزء السادس والعشرون — سورة ق

In the name of Allah, Most Gracious,
Most Merciful.

بسم الله الرحمن الرحيم

1. Qāf: [4939]
By the Glorious [4940] Qur'ān
(Thou art Allah's Messenger).

ق ۚ وَالْقُرْءَانِ الْمَجِيدِ ﴿١﴾

2. But they wonder that [4941]
There has come to them
A Warner from among
Themselves.
So the Unbelievers say:
"This is a wonderful thing!

بَلْ عَجِبُوٓا أَن جَآءَهُم مُّنذِرٌ مِّنْهُمْ فَقَالَ الْكَٰفِرُونَ هَٰذَا شَىْءٌ عَجِيبٌ ﴿٢﴾

3. "What! When we die [4942]
And become dust, (shall we
Live again?) That is
A (sort of) Return
Far (from our understanding)."

أَءِذَا مِتْنَا وَكُنَّا تُرَابًا ۖ ذَٰلِكَ رَجْعٌ بَعِيدٌ ﴿٣﴾

4. We already know
How much of them [4943]
The earth takes away:
With Us is a Record
Guarding (the full account).

قَدْ عَلِمْنَا مَا تَنقُصُ الْأَرْضُ مِنْهُمْ ۖ وَعِندَنَا كِتَٰبٌ حَفِيظٌ ﴿٤﴾

5. But they deny the truth
When it comes to them:

بَلْ كَذَّبُوا بِالْحَقِّ لَمَّا جَآءَهُمْ ﴿٥﴾

4939. This is an Abbreviated Letter. For Abbreviated Letters generally, see Appendix I. This particular Abbreviated Letter *Qāf* occurs only here as a single letter, and in combination at the beginning of S. 42, where I was unable to explain the full combination. Here the Qāf is taken by several Commentators to represent *Quḍiyah al Amr*, "the matter has been decreed," with reference to the eschatological trend of the Sūrah. Allah knows best.

4940. *Majīd* (translated "Glorious") is one of the beautiful appellations of the Qur'ān. Its glory is that of the rising sun: the more it rises on your mental and spiritual horizon, the more you are lost in admiration of its glory. Its meanings are manifest and inexhaustible. The greater your experience, the more light is your spiritual eye able to bear. And in that glory is a beauty that none can tell who has not experienced it in his soul. It is in itself the proof of the mission of the Holy Prophet.

4941. In a sense their wonder is natural: do we wonder at the glorious sun? In another sense it is unnatural: what should we say of a man who fails to see in broad daylight?

4942. Cf 37:16.

4943. The earth only corrupts and takes away the body when they are dead; it has no power over the soul. The full account of the soul's doings is in Allah's Record.

So they are in
A confused state.[4944]

فَهُمْ فِىٓ أَمْرٍ مَّرِيجٍ

6. Do they not look
At the sky above them?—
How We have made it[4945]
And adorned it,
And there are no
Flaws in it?

٦ أَفَلَمْ يَنظُرُوٓا۟ إِلَى ٱلسَّمَآءِ
فَوْقَهُمْ كَيْفَ بَنَيْنَٰهَا وَزَيَّنَّٰهَا
وَمَا لَهَا مِن فُرُوجٍ

7. And the earth—
We have spread it out,[4946]
And set thereon mountains
Standing firm, and produced
Therein every kind of
Beautiful growth (in pairs)—[4947]

٧ وَٱلْأَرْضَ مَدَدْنَٰهَا
وَأَلْقَيْنَا فِيهَا رَوَٰسِىَ وَأَنۢبَتْنَا فِيهَا
مِن كُلِّ زَوْجٍۭ بَهِيجٍ

8. To be observed
And commemorated
By every devotee[4948]
Turning (to Allah).

٨ تَبْصِرَةً وَذِكْرَىٰ
لِكُلِّ عَبْدٍ مُّنِيبٍ

9. And We send down
From the sky Rain
Charged with blessing,
And We produce therewith
Gardens and Grain for harvests;

٩ وَنَزَّلْنَا مِنَ ٱلسَّمَآءِ مَآءً مُّبَٰرَكًا
فَأَنۢبَتْنَا بِهِۦ جَنَّٰتٍ وَحَبَّ ٱلْحَصِيدِ

10. And tall (and stately)[4949]
Palm trees, with shoots
Of fruit stalks, piled
One over another—

١٠ وَٱلنَّخْلَ بَاسِقَٰتٍ
لَّهَا طَلْعٌ نَّضِيدٌ

4944. If they deny what has been made clear to them, their minds must necessarily get into confusion. All nature declares the glory and goodness of Allah. Revelation explains the inequalities of this life and how they will be redressed in the Hereafter. If they do not accept this, they are not in a logical position. They cannot reconcile the known with the unknown.

4945. The greatest philosophers have found a difficulty in understanding the sceptical position when they contemplate the wonder and mystery of the skies with all the countless beautiful stars and planets and lights in them, and laws of order, motion, and symmetry, that respond to the highest mathematical abstractions without a flaw. Can blind Chance give rise to such conditions?

4946. *Cf.* 13:3; and 15:19 and n. 1955. The earth is round, and yet it appears stretched out as a vast expanse, like a carpet kept steady with the weight of the mountains.

4947. *Cf.* 22:5, and n. 2777. Sex in plants may be hinted at : see n. 1804 to 13:3.

4948. For all these things go into his very heart and soul. He loves to contemplate them, to remember them for himself as evidence of Allah's goodness and glory, and to mention and proclaim them, in the form of Psalms, Hymns, or Ẓikrs. (R)

4949. A beautiful nature passage. How graphic and unforgettable to anyone who has seen a spring and summer in an Arabian oasis!

11. As sustenance for
(Allah's) Servants—
And We give (new) life
Therewith to land that is
Dead: thus will be
The Resurrection.

(١١) رِّزْقًا لِّلْعِبَادِ ۖ
وَأَحْيَيْنَا بِهِۦ بَلْدَةً مَّيْتًا ۚ
كَذَٰلِكَ ٱلْخُرُوجُ

12. Before them was denied
(The Hereafter) by the People[4950]
Of Noah, the Companions
Of the Rass, the Thamūd,

(١٢) كَذَّبَتْ قَبْلَهُمْ قَوْمُ نُوحٍ
وَأَصْحَٰبُ ٱلرَّسِّ وَثَمُودُ

13. The ʻĀd, Pharaoh,
The Brethren of Lūṭ,

(١٣) وَعَادٌ وَفِرْعَوْنُ وَإِخْوَٰنُ لُوطٍ

14. The Companions of the Wood,
And the People of Tubbaʻ;
Each one (of them) rejected
The messengers, and My warning
Was duly fulfilled (in them).

(١٤) وَأَصْحَٰبُ ٱلْأَيْكَةِ وَقَوْمُ تُبَّعٍ ۚ
كُلٌّ كَذَّبَ ٱلرُّسُلَ فَحَقَّ وَعِيدِ

15. Were We then weary
With the first Creation,
That they should be
In confused doubt[4951]
About a new Creation?

(١٥) أَفَعَيِينَا بِٱلْخَلْقِ ٱلْأَوَّلِ ۚ
بَلْ هُمْ فِى لَبْسٍ مِّنْ خَلْقٍ جَدِيدٍ

SECTION 2.

16. It was We Who
Created man, and We know
What dark suggestions his soul[4952]
Makes to him: for We
Are nearer to him
Than (his) jugular vein.

(١٦) وَلَقَدْ خَلَقْنَا ٱلْإِنسَٰنَ
وَنَعْلَمُ مَا تُوَسْوِسُ بِهِۦ نَفْسُهُۥ ۖ
وَنَحْنُ أَقْرَبُ إِلَيْهِ مِنْ حَبْلِ ٱلْوَرِيدِ

4950. Just the names of the peoples of Arabian tradition who were punished for their sins are mentioned; their stories will be found elsewhere. For the *People of Noah*, see 11:25-48 and other passages. For the *Companions of the Rass*, see 25:38 and n. 3094; for the *ʻĀd* and the *Thamūd*, see 26:123-158, and other passages; for *Pharaoh* and his People, see 2:49-50 and other passages: for the *Brethren of Lūṭ*, see 7:80-84, and other passages; for the *Companions of the Wood*, see 15:78-79, and n. 2000; and for the *People of Tubbaʻ*, see 44:37 and n. 4715.

4951. *Cf.* 46:33, and n. 4912.

4952. Allah created man, and gave him his limited free will. Allah knows inmost desires and motives of man even better than man does himself. He is nearer to a man than the man's own jugular vein. The jugular vein is the big trunk vein, one on each side of the neck, which brings the blood back from the head to the heart. The two jugular veins correspond to the two carotid arteries which carry the blood from heart to the head. As the blood-stream is the vehicle of life and consciousness, the phrase "nearer than the jugular vein" implies that Allah knows more truly the innermost state of our feeling and consciousness than does our own ego.

17. Behold, two (guardian angels)[4953]
Appointed to learn (his doings)
Learn (and note them),
One sitting on the right
And one on the left.

إِذْ يَتَلَقَّى ٱلْمُتَلَقِّيَانِ عَنِ ٱلْيَمِينِ وَعَنِ ٱلشِّمَالِ قَعِيدٌ ﴿١٧﴾

18. Not a word does he[4954]
Utter but there is
A sentinel by him,
Ready (to note it).

مَّا يَلْفِظُ مِن قَوْلٍ إِلَّا لَدَيْهِ رَقِيبٌ عَتِيدٌ ﴿١٨﴾

19. And the stupor of death[4955]
Will bring truth (before
His eyes): "This was
The thing which thou
Wast trying to escape!"

وَجَآءَتْ سَكْرَةُ ٱلْمَوْتِ بِٱلْحَقِّ ذَٰلِكَ مَا كُنتَ مِنْهُ تَحِيدُ ﴿١٩﴾

20. And the Trumpet[4956]
Shall be blown:
That will be the Day
Whereof Warning (had been
given).

وَنُفِخَ فِي ٱلصُّورِ ذَٰلِكَ يَوْمُ ٱلْوَعِيدِ ﴿٢٠﴾

21. And there will come forth
Every soul: with each
Will be an (angel) to drive,[4957]
And an (angel) to
Bear witness.

وَجَآءَتْ كُلُّ نَفْسٍ مَّعَهَا سَآئِقٌ وَشَهِيدٌ ﴿٢١﴾

4953. Two angels are constantly by him to note his thoughts, words, and actions. One sits on the right side and notes his good deeds and the other on the left, to note his bad deeds; corresponding to the Companions of the Right and the Companions of the Left mentioned in 46:27 and 41. (R).

4954. Then each "word" spoken is taken down by a "sentinel" *(raqīb)*. This has been construed to mean that the sentinel only records words, not thoughts which are not uttered. Thoughts may be forgiven if not uttered, and still more if they do not issue in action. At the stage at which we clothe a thought in words, we have already done an action. The Recorders mentioned in the last verse make a complete Record, in order to supply motives and springs of action, which will affect the degrees or status in the spiritual Hereafter. The three together, individuals or kinds, make the honourable Recorders, *Kirāman Kātibīn*, (plural, not dual number) mentioned in 72:11.

4955. What is stupor or unconsciousness to this probationary life will be the opening of the eyes to the spiritual world: for Death is the Gateway between the two. Once through that Gateway man will realise how the things which he neglected or looked upon as remote are the intimate Realities, and the things which seemed to loom large in his eyes in this world were shadows that have fled. The things we wanted to avoid are the things that have really come to pass. Both Good and Evil will realise the Truth now in its intensity.

4956. The next stage will be the Judgement, heralded with the blowing of the Trumpet. Every soul will then come forth.

4957. Several interpretations are possible, leading to the same truth, that the Judgement will be set up; the Record will be produced; the good and bad deeds will speak for and against; and complete justice will be done, each act leading to its own due fruit. (1) The (angel) to drive and the (angel) to bear witness may be the Recording Angels of the left and the right (verse 17); or (2) it may not be angels, but the evil deeds will drive like task-masters, and the good deeds will bear witness for the soul on trial; or (3) his misused limbs and faculties will drive him to his doom, while his well-used limbs and faculties will witness for him.

22. (It will be said:)
"Thou wast heedless
Of this; now have We
Removed thy veil,
And sharp is thy sight[4958]
This Day!"

٢٢ لَقَدْ كُنتَ فِى غَفْلَةٍ مِّنْ هَٰذَا
فَكَشَفْنَا عَنكَ غِطَآءَكَ
فَبَصَرُكَ ٱلْيَوْمَ حَدِيدٌ

23. And his Companion[4959] will say:
"Here is (his record) ready
With me!"

٢٣ وَقَالَ قَرِينُهُۥ هَٰذَا مَا لَدَىَّ عَتِيدٌ

24. (The sentence will be:)
"Throw, throw[4960] into Hell
Every contumacious Rejecter,
(Of Allah)!—

٢٤ أَلْقِيَا فِى جَهَنَّمَ كُلَّ
كَفَّارٍ عَنِيدٍ

25. "Who forbade what was good,
Transgressed all bounds,
Cast doubts and suspicions;

٢٥ مَّنَّاعٍ لِّلْخَيْرِ مُعْتَدٍ مُّرِيبٍ

26. "Who set up another god
Beside Allah: throw him
Into a severe Penalty."

٢٦ ٱلَّذِى جَعَلَ مَعَ ٱللَّهِ إِلَٰهًا
ءَاخَرَ فَأَلْقِيَاهُ فِى ٱلْعَذَابِ ٱلشَّدِيدِ

27. His Companion[4961] will say:
"Our[4962] Lord! I did not
Make him transgress,[4963]
But he was (himself)
Far astray."

٢٧ قَالَ قَرِينُهُۥ رَبَّنَا مَآ أَطْغَيْتُهُۥ
وَلَٰكِن كَانَ فِى ضَلَٰلٍ بَعِيدٍ

4958. The clearness of vision will now be even greater: see n. 4955 above.

4959. *Qarīn:* Companion. If we take No. 1 of the constructions suggested in n. 4957, the Companion will be one of the Recording Angels mentioned above, in verse 21, perhaps the one that drives; or perhaps the third one mentioned in verse 18, for he has the Record ready with him. If we take any of the other constructions mentioned in n. 4957, it will be the evil deeds or the misused faculties. In any case it will be the factors on whose testimony his conviction will be based.

4960. The original for "throw", here and in verse 26 below, is in the dual number, which some Commentators explain by saying that the dual form is used for emphasis, as if the verb ("throw, throw") were twice repeated. Examples of this are found in Arabic. But is it possible that the dual refers to the two angels mentioned in verses 17 and 21? In that case the Companions in verse 27 will be the third one mentioned in verses 18 and 23. In any case the third one will be the one on whose Record the sentence will be passed.

4961. See last note. But some people understand by "Companion" here an evil associate in the world, an evil one who misled.

4962. *Our Lord.* One man speaks: "I did not", etc. Yet he uses the plural pronoun in saying, "Our Lord". This is beautifully appropriate, as he is speaking so as to include the person to be judged: as if he were to say, "Thou art my Lord, or the Lord of us angels or of all Creation, but Thou art his Lord also, for Thou didst cherish him and warn him, and he owed duties to Thee."

4963. Neither the Recording Angels nor the misused limbs and faculties, nor anything else whatever was responsible for the Evil: it was the personal responsibility of the Doer himself, with his free will.

28. He will say: 'Dispute not[4964]
With each other
In My Presence:
I had already in advance
Sent you[4965] Warning.

۝٢٨ قَالَ لَا تَخْتَصِمُوا لَدَيَّ
وَقَدْ قَدَّمْتُ إِلَيْكُم بِالْوَعِيدِ

29. "The Word changes not
Before Me, and I do not
The least injustice
To My Servants."[4966]

۝٢٩ مَا يُبَدَّلُ الْقَوْلُ لَدَيَّ
وَمَا أَنَا بِظَلَّامٍ لِّلْعَبِيدِ

C. 225.—As Goodness has possibilities unlimited,
(50:30-45.) So has Evil in the opposite direction.
To those who bring a heart unsullied
And to Allah devoted, will be Peace,
Security, and Eternal Life—the Rays
From Allah's own Presence. Adore ye Allah
And pay no heed to whispers of Doubt
And Evil: these must vanish at Judgement,
When Truth and Justice reign supreme.

SECTION 3.

30. One Day We will
Ask Hell, "Art thou
Filled to the full?"[4967]
It will say, "Are there
Any more (to come)?"

۝٣٠ يَوْمَ نَقُولُ لِجَهَنَّمَ هَلِ امْتَلَأْتِ
وَتَقُولُ هَلْ مِن مَّزِيدٍ

31. And the Garden[4968]
Will be brought nigh

۝٣١ وَأُزْلِفَتِ الْجَنَّةُ

4964. It is suggested that sinners whose Record is black, driven into a corner, accuse others of misleading them: the others may be Recorders, or their faculties or opportunities or surroundings or their associates in the world, or anything but themselves. Such recriminations are not allowed in the Court of Judgement.

4965. Besides, personal responsibility had already been clearly preached to them in Allah's Message, and they had been warned of the consequences. "You" is in the plural number: 'all of you who are before the Judgement Seat had clear warning of the consequences of your conduct.'

4966. *'Abd* has two plurals: (1) *'Abīd*, as here, means all Servants of Allah, *i.e.*, all his creatures; (2) *'Ibād* has the further connotation of Servants of Allah, devoted to his service; I have translated it in many cases by the word "devotees". The Sentence before the Judgement Seat is pronounced with perfect justice: it does not change, and requires no change; the inevitable consequences of sin must follow; the time for Mercy is past.

4967. As the capacity of Good is unlimited, so is the capacity of Evil—unlimited. Hell is personified and asked, "Art thou sated to the full?" It replies, "If there are more to come, let them come." It is not satisfied.

4968. In this life, the ideals of the spirit, the accomplishments of the things in our hearts and our hopes, seem to be ever so far, seem even to recede as we think we come nearer. Not so in the Hereafter. The fruits of righteousness will no longer be in the distance. They will be realised. They will seem themselves to approach the Righteous.

To the Righteous—no more A thing distant.	لِلْمُتَّقِينَ غَيْرَ بَعِيدٍ
32. (A voice will say:) "This is what was Promised for you— For everyone who turned[4969] (To Allah) in sincere repentance, Who kept (His Law),	هَٰذَا مَا تُوعَدُونَ ﴿٣٢﴾ لِكُلِّ أَوَّابٍ حَفِيظٍ
33. "Who feared (Allah) Most Gracious unseen,[4970] And brought a heart Turned in devotion (to Him):	﴿٣٣﴾ مَّنْ خَشِيَ الرَّحْمَٰنَ بِالْغَيْبِ وَجَاءَ بِقَلْبٍ مُّنِيبٍ
34. "Enter ye therein In Peace and Security;[4971] This is a Day Of Eternal Life!"	﴿٣٤﴾ ادْخُلُوهَا بِسَلَامٍ ذَٰلِكَ يَوْمُ الْخُلُودِ
35. There will be for them Therein all that they wish— And more besides In Our Presence.[4972]	﴿٣٥﴾ لَهُم مَّا يَشَاءُونَ فِيهَا وَلَدَيْنَا مَزِيدٌ
36. But how many Generations before them Did We destroy (for their Sins)—stronger in power[4973] Than they? Then did they Wander through the land: Was there any place Of escape (for them)?	﴿٣٦﴾ وَكَمْ أَهْلَكْنَا قَبْلَهُم مِّن قَرْنٍ هُمْ أَشَدُّ مِنْهُم بَطْشًا فَنَقَّبُوا فِي الْبِلَادِ هَلْ مِن مَّحِيصٍ

4969. The description of the Righteous is given in four masterly clauses: (1) those who turned away from Evil in sincere repentance; (2) those whose new life was good and righteous; (3) those who in their innermost hearts and in their most secret doings were actuated by God-fearing love, the fear that is akin to love in remembering Allah under His title of "Most Gracious"; and (4) who gave up their whole heart and being to Him.

4970. *Cf.* 36:11 and n. 3952; and 35:18, and n. 3902.

4971. The true meaning of Islam: peace, security, salutation, and accord with Allah's Plan in all Eternity.

4972. To get all that our purified wishes and desires comprehend may seem to sum up final Bliss; but there is something still wanting, which is supplied by the Presence of Allah, the Light of His Countenance.

4973. While virtue and righteousness will accomplish their final goal, what will be the End of Sin? Let the past tell its story. Many powerful and arrogant generations were swept away, to stray in the paths of misery, without any way of escape from the consequences of their sin. This was already seen in the life of this world. In the world to come, it will be worse, as already stated in verses 24-26 above.

37. Verily in this[4974]
Is a Message
For any that has
A heart and understanding
Or who gives ear and
Earnestly witnesses (the truth).

٣٧ إِنَّ فِي ذَٰلِكَ لَذِكْرَىٰ لِمَن كَانَ لَهُۥ قَلْبٌ أَوْ أَلْقَى ٱلسَّمْعَ وَهُوَ شَهِيدٌ

38. We created the heavens[4975]
And the earth and all
Between them in Six Days,[4976]
Nor did any sense
Of weariness touch Us.[4977]

٣٨ وَلَقَدْ خَلَقْنَا ٱلسَّمَٰوَٰتِ وَٱلْأَرْضَ وَمَا بَيْنَهُمَا فِي سِتَّةِ أَيَّامٍ وَمَا مَسَّنَا مِن لُّغُوبٍ

39. Bear, then, with patience,
All that they say,
And celebrate the praises
Of thy Lord, before[4978]
The rising of the sun
And before (its) setting,

٣٩ فَٱصْبِرْ عَلَىٰ مَا يَقُولُونَ وَسَبِّحْ بِحَمْدِ رَبِّكَ قَبْلَ طُلُوعِ ٱلشَّمْسِ وَقَبْلَ ٱلْغُرُوبِ

40. And during part
Of the night, (also,)
Celebrate His praises
And (so likewise)
After the postures[4979]
Of adoration.

٤٠ وَمِنَ ٱلَّيْلِ فَسَبِّحْهُ وَأَدْبَٰرَ ٱلسُّجُودِ

4974. As Christ said (Matt. xi 15), "he that hath ears to hear, let him hear". These are matters of high moment. Many spiritual lessons can be learnt from these things by anyone who has the heart and understanding to apply to Allah's teaching and can give genuine thought to what he sees, as a witness does who has to swear to the facts on his oath.

4975. Allah's creation of the heavens and the earth in long stages or periods of time, as we count time, shows how things evolve in their own good time. We must therefore be patient if God does not *seem* to come to its own according to *our* ideas. Our will should merge itself in Allah's Will, and we should praise Him, realising that He is All-Good and that all adjustments will be in the Hereafter.

4976. *Cf.* 7:54, n. 1031; and 41:12. n. 4477.

4977. *Cf.* 35:35.

4978. Allah should be remembered at all times. But the best time for individual adoration is early in the morning before sunrise, late in the day before sunset, and a portion of the night, when there is stillness in the air, and man's spirit loves to commune with things spiritual. Those who would connect this with the five canonical prayers, instituted at a later stage in Madīnah, would take the *Fajr* for the prayer before sunrise, the *Ẓuhr* and the *'Aṣr* for the afternoon prayers before sunset and the *Maghrib* and the *'Ishā'* for the night prayers.

4979. The general meaning of *after the postures of adoration* would be the contemplation and remembrance of Allah after prayers. Those who would connect this passage with the five canonical prayers understand these further prayers "following the *sujūd* or postures of adoration" to mean the extra or supernumerary prayers known as *nafl,* also the use of the Rosary or the fingers in remembering the Names of Allah.

41. And listen for the Day[4980]
When the Caller will call
Out from a place
Quite near—[4981]

وَٱسْتَمِعْ يَوْمَ يُنَادِ ٱلْمُنَادِ ﴿٤١﴾
مِن مَّكَانٍ قَرِيبٍ

42. The Day when they will
Hear a (mighty) Blast[4982]
In (very) truth: that
Will be the Day
Of Resurrection.

يَوْمَ يَسْمَعُونَ ٱلصَّيْحَةَ بِٱلْحَقِّ ﴿٤٢﴾
ذَٰلِكَ يَوْمُ ٱلْخُرُوجِ

43. Verily it is We Who
Give Life and Death;
And to Us is
The Final Goal—

إِنَّا نَحْنُ نُحْيِۦ وَنُمِيتُ ﴿٤٣﴾
وَإِلَيْنَا ٱلْمَصِيرُ

44. The Day when
The Earth will be[4983]
Rent asunder, from (men)
Hurrying out: that will be
A gathering together—
Quite easy for Us.[4984]

يَوْمَ تَشَقَّقُ ﴿٤٤﴾
ٱلْأَرْضُ عَنْهُمْ سِرَاعًا
ذَٰلِكَ حَشْرٌ عَلَيْنَا يَسِيرٌ

45. We know best what they[4985]
Say; and thou art not
One to overawe them
By force. So admonish
With the Qur'an such
As fear My Warning!

نَّحْنُ أَعْلَمُ بِمَا يَقُولُونَ ﴿٤٥﴾
وَمَآ أَنتَ عَلَيْهِم بِجَبَّارٍ
فَذَكِّرْ بِٱلْقُرْءَانِ مَن يَخَافُ وَعِيدِ

4980. The Day of Resurrection, when the Call to the souls to arise and come to the Judgement Seat will be immediately answered, and they will arise and come forth. *Cf.* 36:49-53, and notes 3997 and 3999.

4981. In the life of this world it seemed all so remote. In the new life at the Resurrection it will all be so near; for there will be neither time nor space as we know them here.

4982. The word *Al Ṣayḥatūn* (mighty Blast) is used for the Resurrection (as here) or for the sudden punishment of the guilty on this earth, as in 11:67, where see further references.

4983. Men will hurry out from all corners of the earth to answer the call, and the earth itself will be rent asunder. In 25:25 the imagery used was the heaven being rent asunder, and angels coming out in ranks: see n. 3082 Cf. also 84:1-4.

4984. It may seem to our material imaginations a difficult task to collect together the souls of all sorts of men, who died in all sorts of conditions at different times, but it will be a different kind of world and creation altogether, and to Allah all things are not only possible but easy.

4985. People may throw all sorts of doubts about the Judgement and the Hereafter. The Prophet's task is not to force them to accept anything. His task is to deliver the Message of the Qur'ān, and admonish those who are spiritually fit and ready to receive admonition and to prepare themselves for the new and higher life destined for man.

INTRODUCTION TO SŪRAH 51—*AL DHĀRIYĀT*

This is an early Makkan Sūrah, the second of the seven Sūrahs forming a group dealing with Revelation and the Hereafter. See Introduction to S. 50. This Sūrah deals with the varying ways in which Truth prevails irresistibly even against all human probabilities. (R).

Summary—The winds may blow and scatter, lift and rush, or divide in all directions; but the Truth and Promise of Allah are sure and stable, whereof you may see Signs both around and within you (51:1-23, and C. 226).

Past events and what you see before you point to the unfailing consequences of all you do: Allah, of His Grace, sends you a Reminder: the loss is your own if you reject and deny (51:24-60, and C. 227).

C. 226.—Various are the ways of working we see
(51:1-23.) In Allah's world—strong and gentle, scattering
And uniting: through it all runs a Purpose
True and stable, which we all shall see fulfilled
On the Day of Judgement and Justice, which
Must inevitably come to pass: give up
False doctrines, which agree not among themselves
Or with facts. For evil must end in evil,
And good in joy and felicity. The good
Worship Allah and serve Allah's creatures:
Those needing help are ever in their thoughts.
They see Signs of Allah in all things in heaven
And earth, and in their own hearts and minds.

Sūrah 51.

Al Dhāriyāt (The Winds That Scatter)

الجزء السادس والعشرون سورة الذاريات

*In the name of Allah, Most Gracious,
Most Merciful.*

بِسْمِ اللَّهِ الرَّحْمَٰنِ الرَّحِيمِ

1. By the (Winds)[4986]
That scatter broadcast;[4987]

وَالذَّارِيَاتِ ذَرْوًا ﴿١﴾

2. And those that[4988]
Lift and bear away
Heavy weights;

فَالْحَامِلَاتِ وِقْرًا ﴿٢﴾

3. And those that[4989]
Flow with ease
And gentleness;

فَالْجَارِيَاتِ يُسْرًا ﴿٣﴾

4. And those that[4900]
Distribute and apportion
By Command—

فَالْمُقَسِّمَاتِ أَمْرًا ﴿٤﴾

5. Verily that which ye[4901]
Are promised is true;

إِنَّمَا تُوعَدُونَ لَصَادِقٌ ﴿٥﴾

4986. Four agencies are mentioned in verses 1 to 4 as evidences or types or symbols of the certainty and unity of a Truth described in verses 5-6. What these agencies are is described by certain adjectival participles, the noun understood being usually taken to be "Winds": the word for Wind *(Rīḥ)* being feminine in Arabic. Some Commentators however understand other nouns as being implied, *e.g.*, angels in all four verses, or different things in each of the four verses. Whatever the agencies are, their different modes of working are evidence of the power and goodness of Allah, the Unity of His Plan, and the certainty of Good and Evil reaching their own destined ends, when Judgement and Justice will have given each one his due. (R).

4987. Winds may blow strong, and scatter particles of dust far and wide; but they do not diminish by one jot the substance of Allah's material creation; on the contrary they help to readjust things. They reshape the configuration of the earth; in the vegetable kingdom they carry seeds about and plant new seeds in old soils; in the region of air they produce mighty changes in temperature and pressure that affect animal and vegetable life; they carry the moisture of equatorial Africa to the parched plains of India; and so on. Yet they are just one little agency showing Allah's working in the material world. So in the spiritual world. Revelation works mighty changes; it may be resisted, but the resistance will be swept away; it ever points to the one Great Final Event, "to which the whole Creation moves".

4988. The things that lift and bear away heavy weights may be the Winds that carry the heavy rain clouds or that sweep off every resistance from their path, or it may be the heavy moisture-laden clouds themselves. So works Revelation: it lifts and sweeps away the burdens of custom, superstition, or man's inertia, and ever leads onwards to the destined End.

4989. These may be Winds that fill the sails of ships with gentle and favourable breezes, that carry men and merchandise to their destinations. Or they may be the ships themselves, whose smooth motion through the waters is described in many places by the verb *jarā*, "to flow", *e.g.*, *cf.* 2:164.

4990. These may be Winds (or other agencies) that distribute and apportion moisture or rain or atmospheric pressure to other blessings of Allah—not haphazard but by fixed laws, *i.e.*, according to the Command of their Lord. So with Revelation. Its blessings are distributed all around, and it produces its marvelous effects sometimes in the most unlikely places and ways.

4991. *That which ye are promised:* the Promise of Allah about Mercy and Forgiveness to the Penitent, and Justice and Penalty to the Rebellious; the promise of the Hereafter; the promise that all does not end here, but that there is a truer and more lasting world to come, for which this is but a preparation.

6. And verily Judgement[4992] And Justice must Indeed come to pass.	وَإِنَّ ٱلدِّينَ لَوَٰقِعٌ ﴿٦﴾
7. By the Sky With (its) numerous Paths,[4993]	وَٱلسَّمَآءِ ذَاتِ ٱلْحُبُكِ ﴿٧﴾
8. Truly ye are in A doctrine discordant,[4994]	إِنَّكُمْ لَفِى قَوْلٍ مُّخْتَلِفٍ ﴿٨﴾
9. Through which are deluded (away From the Truth) such As would be deluded.[4995]	يُؤْفَكُ عَنْهُ مَنْ أُفِكَ ﴿٩﴾
10. Woe to the falsehood-mongers—	قُتِلَ ٱلْخَرَّٰصُونَ ﴿١٠﴾
11. Those who (flounder) heedless[4996] In a flood of confusion:	ٱلَّذِينَ هُمْ فِى غَمْرَةٍ سَاهُونَ ﴿١١﴾
12. They ask, "When will be The Day of Judgement And Justice?"	يَسْـَٔلُونَ أَيَّانَ يَوْمُ ٱلدِّينِ ﴿١٢﴾
13. (It will be) a Day When they will be tried (And tested) over the Fire!	يَوْمَ هُمْ عَلَى ٱلنَّارِ يُفْتَنُونَ ﴿١٣﴾
14. "Taste ye your trial! This is what ye used To ask to be hastened!"[4997]	ذُوقُوا۟ فِتْنَتَكُمْ هَٰذَا ٱلَّذِى كُنتُم بِهِۦ تَسْتَعْجِلُونَ ﴿١٤﴾

4992. *Dīn* = the giving to each person his precise and just due; this is implied in Judgement and Justice. All the inequalities of this life are to be redressed.

4993. The study of the numerous regular orbits of the planets and irregularly regular orbits of comets, and the various motions, visible or invisible, of the fixed stars or revolving stars, form in themselves a network of knowledge or science, of a highly technical nature; the highest astronomy or mathematics can only barely reach its fringe. But these have all a fixed Plan and Purpose under Allah's Dispensation. In them variety leads to Unity. In contrast look at the confused medley of doctrines, views, and dicta put forward by the Sceptics, as described in the next verse.

4994. *Qawl* = saying, word, theory, doctrine. *Mukhtalif* = differing, various, inconsistant with itself, discordant. No theory or doctrine based on a denial of a Hereafter can be consistant with spiritual facts as we know them, or with Allah's Goodness, Justice, and Mercy.

4995. Some Commentators draw from this a rigid doctrine of Calvinistic Predestination or Determinism, which I do not think is fairly deducible from the words. *"Yu'fak"* should I think be translated *"will* be or *would* be deluded", meaning "have the wish or desire to be", and not "must necessarily be deluded by eternal predestination". The word occurs in many places in the Qur'ān: *e.g., Cf.* 5:78, or 9:30.

4996. They are in great spiritual danger: yet they care not.

4997. They used to say scoffingly, "if there is to be punishment for our sins, let it come at once!" When it comes, they will know what a terrible thing it is! Cf. 26:204 n. 3230.

15. As to the Righteous,
They will be in the midst
Of Gardens and Springs,[4998]

إِنَّ ٱلْمُتَّقِينَ فِى جَنَّٰتٍ وَعُيُونٍ ١٥

16. Taking joy in the things
Which their Lord gives them,
Because, before then, they
Lived a good life.

ءَاخِذِينَ مَآ ءَاتَىٰهُمْ رَبُّهُمْ ۚ ١٦
إِنَّهُمْ كَانُوا۟ قَبْلَ ذَٰلِكَ مُحْسِنِينَ

17. They were in the habit[4999]
Of sleeping but little
By night,

كَانُوا۟ قَلِيلًا مِّنَ ٱلَّيْلِ مَا يَهْجَعُونَ ١٧

18. And in the hours
Of early dawn,
They (were found) praying
For Forgiveness;[5000]

وَبِٱلْأَسْحَارِ هُمْ يَسْتَغْفِرُونَ ١٨

19. And in their wealth
And possessions (was remembered)
The right of the (needy),
Him who asked, and him
Who (for some reason) was[5001]
Prevented (from asking).

وَفِىٓ أَمْوَٰلِهِمْ حَقٌّ ١٩
لِّلسَّآئِلِ وَٱلْمَحْرُومِ

20. On the earth
Are Signs for those
Of assured Faith,

وَفِى ٱلْأَرْضِ ءَايَٰتٌ لِّلْمُوقِنِينَ ٢٠

21. As also in your own[5002]
Selves: will ye not
Then see?

وَفِىٓ أَنفُسِكُمْ ۚ أَفَلَا تُبْصِرُونَ ٢١

4998. Gardens and Springs are the two most frequent symbols for the highest satisfaction and bliss.

4999. They were engaged most of the night in worship and in the planning of good deeds. They preferred activity to idleness, the service of Allah and His creatures to the indulgence of Self.

5000. They were up early before dawn, ready for their devotions. The praying for Forgiveness and Mercy does not necessarily imply that they had committed fresh sins. Indeed they *began* the day with such devotions, showing their great humility before Allah and their anxious care for others, for whom they prayed as much as for themselves. See the last sentence of n. 21 to 1:5.

5001. True charity remembers not only those in need who ask, but also those who are prevented by some reason from asking. The man of true charity seeks out the latter. There may be various reasons which prevent a man from asking for help: (1) he may be ashamed to ask, or his sense of honour may prevent him from asking; (2) he may be so engrossed in some great ideal that he may not think of asking; (3) he may even not know that he is in need, especially when we think of wealth and possessions in a spiritual sense, as including spiritual gifts and talents; (4) he may not know that you possess the things that can supply his needs; and (5) he may be a dumb and helpless creature, whether a human being or a dumb animal, or any creature within your ken or power. Charity in the higher sense includes all help, from one better endowed to one less well endowed. *Cf.* n. 179 to 2:177; also 2:273-274, and notes 322 and 323.

5002. The Signs and Evidence of Allah are in all nature and within the body and soul of man, if man has but the spiritual eyes to see. *Cf.* 41:53.

22. And in heaven is[5003]
Your Sustenance, as (also)
That which ye are promised.

وَفِي السَّمَاءِ رِزْقُكُمْ وَمَا تُوعَدُونَ ﴿٢٢﴾

23. Then, by the Lord[5004]
Of heaven and earth,
This is the very Truth,
As much as the fact
That ye can speak
Intelligently to each other.

فَوَرَبِّ السَّمَاءِ وَالْأَرْضِ إِنَّهُ لَحَقٌّ مِّثْلَ مَا أَنَّكُمْ تَنطِقُونَ ﴿٢٣﴾

C. 227.—Even Abraham the True had need to be told
(51:24-60) Before he could realise the purpose of Allah.
Clear Signs were sent for warning, as, of old,
To Pharaoh, the 'Ād, the Thamūd, and the people
Of Noah, and the warning inevitably came
To pass. Our Signs are for your instruction.
Heed them and learn by them. Those who believe
Find profit in their lives: those who reject
Or deny—alas! they learn not from the past.
Woe unto them! The loss is their own!

SECTION 2.

24. Has the story[5005]
Reached thee, of the honoured
Guests of Abraham?

هَلْ أَتَاكَ حَدِيثُ ضَيْفِ إِبْرَاهِيمَ الْمُكْرَمِينَ ﴿٢٤﴾

25. Behold, they entered[5006]
His presence, and said:
"Peace!" He said, "Peace!"
(And thought, "These seem)
Unusual people."[5007]

إِذْ دَخَلُوا عَلَيْهِ فَقَالُوا سَلَامًا قَالَ سَلَامٌ قَوْمٌ مُّنكَرُونَ ﴿٢٥﴾

5003. "Sustenance", here as elsewhere, includes physical sustenance, as well as spiritual sustenance. Similarly heaven or sky has both the physical and the spiritual meaning. The physical sustenance grows from rain from the sky; the spiritual sustenance comes from divine aid, grace, and mercy, and includes the Good News and the Warning which come from Revelation about the Hereafter.

5004. Attention having been called to the Signs or Evidences of Allah's working on the earth, within ourselves, and in the heavens, in verses 20-22, an appeal is made to our own inner conscience, in the name of the Lord of heaven and earth, to acknowledge and act up to the truth of Revelation, and turn to the spiritual Realities. For they are as real as our own conscious and self-intelligent existence, on which is based all our knowledge. As a philosopher (Descartes) has said: "I think; therefore I am."

5005. *Cf.* 11:69-73 and notes, where further details of the story will be found. *Cf.* also 15:51-56.

5006. They were angels, who appeared suddenly before him at his tent door in the guise of men, and saluted him with the salutation of peace. He returned the salutation, but felt, from their appearance and their manner, that they were unusual, not ordinary, strangers.

5007. *Munkar:* unknown, uncommon, unusual, not customary, (hence by derived meaning, not applicable here, not fair or just): opposite in both primary and secondary meanings to *ma'rūf*, well-known, usual, customary, just. *Cf.* 15:62.

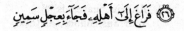

26. Then he turned quickly[5008]
To his household, brought
Out a fatted calf,

فَرَاغَ إِلَىٰٓ أَهْلِهِۦ فَجَآءَ بِعِجْلٍ سَمِينٍ ٢٦

27. And placed it before them...
He said, "Will ye not
Eat?"

فَقَرَّبَهُۥٓ إِلَيْهِمْ قَالَ أَلَا تَأْكُلُونَ ٢٧

28. (When they did not eat).
He conceived a fear of them.
They said, "Fear not,"
And they gave him
Glad tidings of a son
Endowed with knowledge.

فَأَوْجَسَ مِنْهُمْ خِيفَةً ۖ
قَالُوا۟ لَا تَخَفْ ۖ
وَبَشَّرُوهُ بِغُلَٰمٍ عَلِيمٍ ٢٨

29. But his wife came forward[5009]
(Laughing) aloud: she smote
Her forehead and said:
"A barren old woman!"

فَأَقْبَلَتِ ٱمْرَأَتُهُۥ فِى صَرَّةٍ
فَصَكَّتْ وَجْهَهَا وَقَالَتْ عَجُوزٌ عَقِيمٌ ٢٩

30. They said, "Even so[5010]
Has thy Lord spoken:
And He is full
Of Wisdom and Knowledge."

قَالُوا۟ كَذَٰلِكِ قَالَ رَبُّكِ ۖ
إِنَّهُۥ هُوَ ٱلْحَكِيمُ ٱلْعَلِيمُ ٣٠

27/30

31. (Abraham) said: "And what,
O ye Messengers,
Is your errand (now)?"

قَالَ فَمَا خَطْبُكُمْ أَيُّهَا ٱلْمُرْسَلُونَ ٣١

32. They said, "We have
Been sent to a people
(Deep) in sin—

قَالُوٓا۟ إِنَّآ أُرْسِلْنَآ إِلَىٰ قَوْمٍ مُّجْرِمِينَ ٣٢

5008. They seemed unusual strangers, but he said nothing and quietly proceeded to perform the rites of hospitality. He brought a roast fatted calf and placed it before them to eat. But the strangers did not eat (11:70). This disconcerted him. According to the laws of hospitality, a stranger under your roof is under your protection, but if he refuses to eat, he refuses your hospitality and keeps himself free from any ties of guest and host. "What were their designs?" thought Abraham, and he felt some distrust. But they were angels and could not eat. They declared themselves, and announced the birth to Abraham of a son endowed with wisdom—in other words that Abraham was to be the head of a long line of Prophets! (15:53).

5009. Abraham's wife Sarah was old and barren. This news seemed to her too good to be true. She came forward, laughed aloud (11:71), struck her forehead with her hands, indicative of her amusement and incredulity as "a barren old woman": 11:72.

5010. The angels said: "What may sound improbable to human beings will yet come to pass if Allah commands. And Allah thy Lord has spoken. So shall it be. For all His promises are full of wisdom and knowledge." So the angels on that occasion. But the application is for all time and to all human affairs. Never despair. However much Truth may be in the shade, it will shine with full splendour. And the Judgement will come, when good will come to its own!

33. "To bring on, on them,
(A shower of) stones
Of clay (brimstone),[5011]

٣٣ لِنُرْسِلَ عَلَيْهِمْ حِجَارَةً مِّن طِينٍ

34. "Marked as from thy Lord[5012]
For those who trespass
Beyond bounds."

٣٤ مُّسَوَّمَةً عِندَ رَبِّكَ لِلْمُسْرِفِينَ

35. Then we evacuated[5013]
Those of the Believers
Who were there,

٣٥ فَأَخْرَجْنَا مَن كَانَ فِيهَا مِنَ ٱلْمُؤْمِنِينَ

36. But We found not there
Any just (Muslim) persons
Except in one house:[5014]

٣٦ فَمَا وَجَدْنَا فِيهَا غَيْرَ بَيْتٍ مِّنَ ٱلْمُسْلِمِينَ

37. And We left there
A Sign for such as
Fear the Grievous Penalty.[5015]

٣٧ وَتَرَكْنَا فِيهَآ ءَايَةً لِّلَّذِينَ
يَخَافُونَ ٱلْعَذَابَ ٱلْأَلِيمَ

38. And in Moses[5016]
(Was another Sign):
Behold, We sent him
To Pharaoh, with authority
Manifest.

٣٨ وَفِى مُوسَىٰٓ إِذْ أَرْسَلْنَٰهُ إِلَىٰ
فِرْعَوْنَ بِسُلْطَٰنٍ مُّبِينٍ

39. But (Pharaoh) turned back
With his Chiefs, and said,
"A sorcerer, or
One possessed!"

٣٩ فَتَوَلَّىٰ بِرُكْنِهِۦ وَقَالَ
سَٰحِرٌ أَوْ مَجْنُونٌ

5011. *Cf.* 11:82, and n. 1052 to 7:84. The angels' errand of mercy to Abraham (to announce the succession of godly men in his line) was coupled with their errand of justice and punishment to the people of Lūṭ, the people of Sodom and Gomorrah, who were deep in the most abominable and unnatural sins. So Allah's Mercy and Justice go hand in hand in all human affairs. Faith has nothing to fear, and wickedness has only to turn and repent, to obtain Allah's Mercy.

5012. *Cf.* 11:83, and n. 1580. Every crime has its due punishment as marked out in the decrees of Allah.

5013. The only just or righteous persons found in Sodom and Gomorrah (Cities of the Plain by the Dead Sea) were in the house of Lūṭ, who was the Prophet sent to call them to repentance. He and his believing family and adherents were told to leave in due time, and the wicked were destroyed in a shower of brimstone.

5014. That was the house of Lūṭ; and even there, his wife had no faith: she disobeyed the Command and perished: 11:81, n. 1577.

5015. *The Grievous Penalty:* that is, the Final Judgement. The destruction of Sodom and Gomorrah in this life is taken as the type of the Final Judgement. The vestiges can be seen—as a Sign and a Warning—in the sulphury plain round the Dead Sea: *Cf.* 15:79.

5016. *Cf.* 44:127-31. The story of Moses and Pharaoh is here just referred to. The points emphasised here are: (1) that Moses had manifest authority, yet Pharaoh doubted; (2) that Pharaoh's reliance was on his Chiefs and his forces, but they could not help when his doom came; and (3) that in the most extraordinary and incredible ways (judged by ordinary human standards), his arrogance and his reliance on his Chiefs and forces were his undoing.

40. So We took him
And his forces, and
Threw them into the sea:
And his was the blame.[5017]

﴿٤٠﴾ فَأَخَذْنَٰهُ وَجُنُودَهُۥ
فَنَبَذْنَٰهُمْ فِى ٱلْيَمِّ وَهُوَ مُلِيمٌ

41. And in the ʻĀd (people)[5018]
(Was another Sign):
Behold, We sent against them
The devastating Wind:

﴿٤١﴾ وَفِى عَادٍ إِذْ أَرْسَلْنَا
عَلَيْهِمُ ٱلرِّيحَ ٱلْعَقِيمَ

42. It left nothing whatever
That it came up against,
But reduced it to ruin
And rottenness.

﴿٤٢﴾ مَا تَذَرُ مِن شَىْءٍ أَتَتْ عَلَيْهِ
إِلَّا جَعَلَتْهُ كَٱلرَّمِيمِ

43. And in the Thamūd[5019]
(Was another Sign):
Behold, they were told,
"Enjoy (your brief day)[5020]
For a little while!"

﴿٤٣﴾ وَفِى ثَمُودَ إِذْ قِيلَ لَهُمْ
تَمَتَّعُوا۟ حَتَّىٰ حِينٍ

44. But they insolently defied[5021]
The Command of their Lord:
So the stunning noise[5022]
(Of an earthquake) seized
Them, even while they
Were looking on.

﴿٤٤﴾ فَعَتَوْا۟ عَنْ أَمْرِ رَبِّهِمْ
فَأَخَذَتْهُمُ ٱلصَّٰعِقَةُ
وَهُمْ يَنظُرُونَ

45. Then they could not
Even stand (on their feet),[5023]
Nor could they help themselves.

﴿٤٥﴾ فَمَا ٱسْتَطَٰعُوا۟ مِن قِيَامٍ
وَمَا كَانُوا۟ مُنتَصِرِينَ

5017. The ungodly Egyptians were all destroyed, but the chief blame lay on Pharaoh for misleading them. Pharaoh's punishment was just. He could not blame anyone else. And certainly no one can blame the course of Allah's Justice, for Allah was long-suffering, and gave him many chances to repent.

5018. *Cf.* 46:21-26. The point here is that the ʻAd were a gifted people: Allah had given them talents and material wealth: but when they defied Allah, they and all their belongings were destroyed in a night, by a hurricane which they thought was bringing them the rain to which they were looking forward. How marvelously Allah's Providence works, to help the good and destroy the wicked!

5019. See the story of the Thamūd and their prophet Ṣāliḥ in 7:73-79. Here the point is the suddenness of their punishment and its unexpected nature.

5020. Ṣāliḥ, their prophet, gave them three days' clear warning for repentance (11:65). But they heeded him not. On the contrary they flouted him and continued in their evil courses.

5021. They had already defied the order to preserve the She-camel, which was symbolical of the grazing rights of the common people: see 11:64-65 and n. 1560. They continued to flout the warnings of the prophet until the earthquake came on them with a stunning noise and buried them where they were: 7:78; and 11:67.

5022. *Ṣāʻiqah:* a stunning sound like that of thunder and lightning (2:55); such a sound often accompanies an earthquake (see 41:17, n. 4485, and 7:78 and n. 1047).

5023. They were swept off in the earthquake.

46. So were the People[5024]
Of Noah before them:
For they wickedly transgressed.

وَقَوْمَ نُوحٍ مِّن قَبْلُ إِنَّهُمْ كَانُوا قَوْمًا فَاسِقِينَ ﴿٤٦﴾

SECTION 3.

47. With the power and skill[5025]
Did We construct
The Firmament:
For it is We Who create
The vastness of Space.

وَالسَّمَاءَ بَنَيْنَاهَا بِأَيْدٍ وَإِنَّا لَمُوسِعُونَ ﴿٤٧﴾

48. And We have spread out
The (spacious) earth:
How excellently
We do spread out!

وَالْأَرْضَ فَرَشْنَاهَا فَنِعْمَ الْمَاهِدُونَ ﴿٤٨﴾

49. And of everything
We have created pairs:[5026]
That ye may receive
Instruction.

وَمِن كُلِّ شَيْءٍ خَلَقْنَا زَوْجَيْنِ لَعَلَّكُمْ تَذَكَّرُونَ ﴿٤٩﴾

50. Hasten ye then (at once)[5027]
To Allah: I am from Him
A Warner to you,
Clear and open!

فَفِرُّوا إِلَى اللَّهِ إِنِّي لَكُم مِّنْهُ نَذِيرٌ مُّبِينٌ ﴿٥٠﴾

5024. The generation of Noah was swept away in the Flood for their sins: 7:59-64. The point is that such a flood seemed so unlikely to them that they thought Noah was "wandering in his mind" when he delivered Allah's Message: 7:60.

5025. If you do not wish to go back to the wonderful things of the past, which show the power and goodness of Allah, and His justice supreme over all wrongdoing, look at the wonderful things unfolding themselves before your very eyes! (1) The space in the heavens above! Who can comprehend it but He Who made it and sustains it? (2) The globe of the earth under your feet! How great its expanse seems over sea and land, and spread out for you like a wonderful carpet or bed of rest! (3) All things are in twos: sex in plants and animals, by which one individual is complementary to another; in the subtle forces of nature, Day and Night, positive and negative electricity, forces of attraction and repulsion: and numerous other opposites, each fulfilling its purpose, and contributing to the working of Allah's Universe: and in the moral and spiritual world, Love and Aversion, Mercy and Justice, Striving and Rest, and so on—all fulfilling their functions according to the Artistry and wonderful Purpose of Allah. Everything has its counterpart, or pair, or complement. Allah alone is One, with none like Him, or needed to complement Him. These are noble things to contemplate. And they lead us to a true understanding of Allah's Purpose and Message.

5026. See (3) in the last note. *Cf.* 36:36, n. 3981.

5027. If you understand Nature and yourselves aright, you will know that Allah is all-in-all, and you will fly at once to Him. This is the teaching which the Prophet of Allah has come to give you, in clear terms and openly to all.

51. And make not another[5028]
An object of worship
With Allah:
I am from Him
A Warner to you,
Clear and open!

٥١ وَلَا تَجۡعَلُواْ
مَعَ ٱللَّهِ إِلَٰهًا ءَاخَرَۖ
إِنِّي لَكُم مِّنۡهُ نَذِيرٞ مُّبِينٞ

52. Similarly, no messenger came
To the Peoples before them,
But they said (of him)
In like manner,
"A sorcerer, or
One possessed"![5029]

٥٢ كَذَٰلِكَ مَآ أَتَى
ٱلَّذِينَ مِن قَبۡلِهِم مِّن رَّسُولٍ
إِلَّا قَالُواْ سَاحِرٌ أَوۡ مَجۡنُونٌ

53. Is this the legacy[5030]
They have transmitted,
One to another?
Nay, they are themselves
A people transgressing
Beyond bounds!

٥٣ أَتَوَاصَوۡاْ بِهِۦۚ
بَلۡ هُمۡ قَوۡمٞ
طَاغُونَ

54. So turn away[5031]
From them: not thine
Is the blame.

٥٤ فَتَوَلَّ عَنۡهُمۡ
فَمَآ أَنتَ بِمَلُومٖ

55. But teach (thy Message):
For teaching benefits
The Believers.

٥٥ وَذَكِّرۡ فَإِنَّ ٱلذِّكۡرَىٰ
تَنفَعُ ٱلۡمُؤۡمِنِينَ

56. I have only created[5032]
Jinns and men, that
They may serve Me.

٥٦ وَمَا خَلَقۡتُ ٱلۡجِنَّ
وَٱلۡإِنسَ إِلَّا لِيَعۡبُدُونِ

5028. Verses 50 and 51, ending with the same clause to emphasise the connection between the two, should be read together. The Prophet's mission was (and is): (1) to show us the urgent need for repentance; and (2) to wean us from the precipice of false worship. The one convinces us of sin and opens the door to the Mercy of Allah; the other cures us of the madness of paying court to idle or worthless objects of desire: for in the worship of Allah, the One True God, is included the best service to ourselves and our fellow-creatures. If fully understood, this sums up the whole duty of man: for it leads us by the right Path to the love of Allah and the love of man and of all creatures.

5029. They said this of Moses: 51:39. And they said this of the Holy Prophet: 38:4; 44:14.

5030. There is a tradition of Evil as there is a tradition of Good. The ways of Evil in dealing with the teachers of Truth are similar in all ages. But such evil traditions would have no effect, were it not that the generation following them is itself ungodly, "transgressing beyond bounds."

5031. When the Prophet freely proclaims his Message, it is not his fault if obstinate wickedness refuses to listen. He can leave them alone, but he should continue to teach for the benefit of those who have Faith.

5032. Creation is not for idle sport or play: 21:16. Allah has a serious Purpose behind it, which, in our imperfect state, we can only express by saying that each creature is given the chance of development and progress towards the Goal, which is Allah. Allah is the source and centre of all power and all goodness, and our progress depends upon our putting ourselves into accord with His Will. This is His service. It is not of any benefit to Him: (see the next two verses)—it is for our own benefit.

57. No Sustenance do I require[5033]
Of them, nor do I
Require that they should
Feed Me.

﴿٥٧﴾ مَآ أُرِيدُ مِنْهُم مِّن رِّزْقٍ وَمَآ أُرِيدُ أَن يُطْعِمُونِ

58. For Allah is He Who
Gives (all) Sustenance—
Lord of Power—[5034]
Steadfast (forever).

﴿٥٨﴾ إِنَّ ٱللَّهَ هُوَ ٱلرَّزَّاقُ ذُو ٱلْقُوَّةِ ٱلْمَتِينُ

59. For the wrongdoers,
Their portion is like
Unto the portion of their[5035]
Fellows (of earlier generations):
Then let them not ask Me
To hasten (that portion)!

﴿٥٩﴾ فَإِنَّ لِلَّذِينَ ظَلَمُوا۟ ذَنُوبًا مِّثْلَ ذَنُوبِ أَصْحَٰبِهِمْ فَلَا يَسْتَعْجِلُونِ

60. Woe, then, to the Unbelievers,
On account of that Day[5036]
Of theirs which they
Have been promised!

﴿٦٠﴾ فَوَيْلٌ لِّلَّذِينَ كَفَرُوا۟ مِن يَوْمِهِمُ ٱلَّذِى يُوعَدُونَ

5033. *Sustenance:* in both the literal and the figurative sense: so also "Feed Me" at the end of the verse. Allah is independent of all needs. It is therefore absurd to suppose that He should require *any* Sustenance, and still more absurd to suppose that *we* can feed Him! The gifts, the Sustenance, the goodness, all come from His side.

5034. Allah commands all power; therefore any power we seek must be from Him. And His power is steadfast, the same today as yesterday, and forever. Therefore His help is always sure.

5035. Each generation, that acts like any of its predecessors, must meet a similar fate. If the wicked came to an evil end in the past, the same results will follow in the present and the future. The punishment will come suddenly enough: let them not in mockery ask that it should be hastened.

5036. That is, their eternal Punishment in the Hereafter, as well as any punishment that may come to them in this life.

INTRODUCTION TO SŪRAH 52—*AL ṬŪR*

This is the third of the group of seven Makkan Sūrahs described in the Introduction to S. 50.

It is, like its predecessor, an early Makkan Sūrah. The points here emphasised are: that Revelation is in accord with all Allah's Signs, including previous Revelations, and that the Hereafter is inevitable, and we must prepare for it.

Summary—All Signs of Allah, including previous Revelations, point to the inevitable consequences of ill-deeds and good deeds: how can people deny or ignore the Message of Revelation? (52:1-49, and C. 228).

C. 228.—By the sacred Symbols—of the Mount
(52:1-49.) Sublime, the Eternal Record on an open
Scroll, the House of Worship thronged
With men, the Canopy blue of unfathomed
Heights, and the boundless Ocean with
Its resistless tidal Swell—all acts
Of men must have their inevitable fruits.
New worlds will be born with the Day of Doom:
New values established by Allah's Decree.
Consumed will be Evil in the fire of Reality:
And Good will come to its own—in personal
And social Bliss, but most in the full
Realisation that Allah is good, the Beneficent,
The Merciful...Proclaim, then, the praises
Of the Lord, nor heed the slanders of Ignorance
Or Spite: for the Lord Who created will cherish;
His plan will overthrow the puny plots
Of men. Hold firm with patience in Faith
In the Hereafter, and sing His praises
Even in the busy marts of this world,
But chiefly in the stillness of the Night
And the holy hour of Dawn as the Stars
Retreat, singing glory to the Maker
Of their own most glorious Sun.

Sūrah 52.

Al Ṭūr (The Mount)

الجزء السابع والعشرون سورة الطور

In the name of Allah, Most Gracious, Most Merciful.

بِسْمِ اللَّهِ الرَّحْمَٰنِ الرَّحِيمِ

1. By the Mount (of Revelation);[5037]
وَالطُّورِ ١

2. By a Decree Inscribed[5038]
وَكِتَابٍ مَسْطُورٍ ٢

3. In a Scroll unfolded;
فِي رَقٍّ مَنْشُورٍ ٣

4. By the much-frequented Fane;[5039]
وَالْبَيْتِ الْمَعْمُورِ ٤

5. By the Canopy Raised High;[5040]
وَالسَّقْفِ الْمَرْفُوعِ ٥

6. And by the Ocean[5041]
وَالْبَحْرِ ٦

5037. The adjuration is by five things which we shall presently explain. An appeal is made to these five Signs in verses 1 to 6, and the certainty of future events is asserted in the most emphatic terms in verses 7 to 28, in three parts, *viz.*, the coming of judgement and the passing away of this phenomenal world (verses 7-10); the future ill consequences of ill-deeds done (verses 11-16); and future attainment of bliss and complete realisation of Allah's love and mercy (verses 17-28).

5038. See last note. The five Signs to which appeal is made are: (1) the Mount (of Revelation), verse 1; (2) the Decree Inscribed, verses 2-3; (3) The Much-frequented Fane, verse 4; (4) the Canopy Raised High, verse 5; and (5) the Ocean filled with Swell, verse 6.

Let us examine these in detail. Each of them has a figurative and a mystic meaning. (1) The Mount is the sublime world of Revelation. In the case of Moses it is typified by Mount Sinai: *Cf.* 95:2, where it is mentioned in juxtaposition to the sacred territory of Makkah, 95:3. In the case of Jesus it is the Mount of Olives: *Cf.* 95:1, and also Matt. xxiv. 3-51, where Jesus made his striking pronouncement about the Judgement to come. In the case of Muḥammad, it is the Mountain of Light, where the divine inspiration made him one with the spiritual world: *Cf.* C. 31, and n. 11 (2). The Decree Inscribed is Allah's Eternal Decree. When it becomes Revelation to man, it is further described as "inscribed", reduced to writing; and as it is made clear to the intelligence of man, it is further described as "in a scroll unfolded", that is, spread out so that everyone who has the will can seek its guidance.

5039. See the last two notes. (3) "The much-frequented Fane" (or House) is usually understood to mean the Ka'bah, but in view of the parallelism noted in the last note, it may be taken generally to mean any Temple of House of Worship dedicated to the true God. It would then include the Tabernacle of the Israelites in the wilderness, the Temple of Solomon, the Temple in which Jesus worshipped, and the Ka'bah which the Holy Prophet purified and rededicated to true worship. These would be only illustrations. Other concrete places of worship would be included, and in a more abstract meaning, the heart of man, which craves, with burning desire, to find and worship Allah. The Fane is "much-frequented" as there is a universal desire in the heart of man to worship Allah, and his sacred Temples draw large crowds of devotees.

5040. (4) "The Canopy Raised High" is the canopy of heaven, to whose height or sublimity no limit can be assigned by the mind of man. It is Nature's Temple, in which all Creation worships Allah—the Symbol in which the material and the visible merges into the spiritual and the intuitional.

5041. (5) The Ocean—the vast, limitless, all encircling Ocean—is the material symbol of the universal, unlimited, comprehensive nature of the invisible spiritual world. It is expressed to be *masjūr*, full of a mighty swell, boiling over, poured forth all over the earth, as if overwhelming all landmarks; *Cf.* 81:6—a fitting description of the final disappearance of our temporal world in the supreme establishment of the Reality behind it.

Filled with Swell—[5042]

ٱلْمَسْجُورِ

7. Verily, the Doom of thy Lord
Will indeed come to pass—

إِنَّ عَذَابَ رَبِّكَ لَوَٰقِعٌ ٧

8. There is none
Can avert it—

مَّا لَهُۥ مِن دَافِعٍ ٨

9. On the Day when[5043]
The firmament will be
In dreadful commotion.

يَوْمَ تَمُورُ ٱلسَّمَآءُ مَوْرًا ٩

10. And the mountains will fly
Hither and thither.[5044]

وَتَسِيرُ ٱلْجِبَالُ سَيْرًا ١٠

11. Then woe that Day
To those that treat
(Truth) as Falsehood—[5045]

فَوَيْلٌ يَوْمَئِذٍ لِّلْمُكَذِّبِينَ ١١

12. That play (and paddle)
In shallow trifles.

ٱلَّذِينَ هُمْ فِى خَوْضٍ يَلْعَبُونَ ١٢

13. That Day shall they be
Thrust down to the Fire
Of Hell, irresistibly.

يَوْمَ يُدَعُّونَ إِلَىٰ نَارِ جَهَنَّمَ دَعًّا ١٣

14. "This", it will be said,[5046]
"Is the Fire—which ye
Were wont to deny!

هَٰذِهِ ٱلنَّارُ ٱلَّتِى كُنتُم بِهَا تُكَذِّبُونَ ١٤

5042. This completes the five Signs or Symbols by which man may know for certain of the Judgement to come. Note that they are in a descending order—the highest, or most remote from man's consciousness, being mentioned first, and that nearest to man's consciousness being mentioned last. The truth of Revelation; its embodiment in a Prophet's Message given in human language; the universal appeal of divine worship; the starry world above; and the encircling Ocean, full of life and motion below—all are evidences that the Day of Allah will finally come, and nothing can avert it. (R).

5043. The Day of Judgement is typified by two figures. (1) "The firmament will be in dreadful commotion." The heavens as we see them suggest to us peace and tranquillity, and the power of fixed laws which all the heavenly bodies obey. This will all be shaken in the rise of the new spiritual world. *Cf.* Matt. xxvi. 29: "Immediately after the tribulation of those days. . . the powers of the heavens shall be shaken." For (2) see next note.

5044. (2) The mountains are a type of firmness and stability. But things that we think of as firm and stable in this material life will be shaken to pieces, and will be no more substantial than a mirage in a desert. *Cf.* 78:20.

5045. That Day will be a Day of Woe to the wrongdoers described in two aspects, the rebels against Allah and Allah's Truth, just as it will be a Day of Joy and Thanksgiving to the Righteous, who are described in three aspects in verses 17 to 28. The rebels are here described as being those who openly defied Truth and plunged into wrongdoing, or who trifled with truth, who jested with serious matter, who had not the courage to plunge openly into wrongdoing but who secretly took profit out of it, who wasted their life in doubts and petty quibbles. It is difficult to say which attitude did more harm to themselves and to others. Both are aspects of deep-seated sin and rebellion. But the mercy of Allah was open to all if they had repented and amended their lives.

5046. In face of the Realities, it will be borne in on them how wrong it was for them in this life to deny or forget that every wicked thought or deed had its own retributive chain of consequences.

15. "Is this then a fake,[5047]
Or is it ye that
Do not see?

١٥ أَفَسِحْرٌ هَٰذَآ أَمْ أَنتُمْ لَا تُبْصِرُونَ

16. "Burn ye therein:
The same is it to you
Whether ye bear it
With patience, or not:[5048]
Ye but receive the recompense
Of your (own) deeds."

١٦ ٱصْلَوْهَا فَٱصْبِرُوٓا۟
أَوْ لَا تَصْبِرُوا۟ سَوَآءٌ عَلَيْكُمْ ۖ
إِنَّمَا تُجْزَوْنَ مَا كُنتُمْ تَعْمَلُونَ

17. As to the Righteous,[5049]
They will be in Gardens,
And in Happiness—

١٧ إِنَّ ٱلْمُتَّقِينَ فِى جَنَّٰتٍ وَنَعِيمٍ

18. Enjoying the (Bliss) which
Their Lord hath bestowed
On them, and their Lord
Shall deliver them from
The Penalty of the Fire.

١٨ فَٰكِهِينَ بِمَآ ءَاتَىٰهُمْ رَبُّهُمْ
وَوَقَىٰهُمْ رَبُّهُمْ عَذَابَ ٱلْجَحِيمِ

19. (To them will be said:)[5050]
"Eat and drink ye,
With profit and health,[5051]
Because of your (good) deeds."

١٩ كُلُوا۟ وَٱشْرَبُوا۟ هَنِيٓـًٔۢا
بِمَا كُنتُمْ تَعْمَلُونَ

20. They will recline (with ease)
On Thrones (of dignity)
Arranged in ranks;[5052]

٢٠ مُتَّكِـِٔينَ عَلَىٰ سُرُرٍ مَّصْفُوفَةٍ ۖ

5047. Perhaps they had said that the Hereafter was a fake, mere old wives' tales! If they had given serious thought to the Signs of Allah, they would have been saved from that serious spiritual blindness: then they will see that the fault was their own, and that the warnings of the messengers of Truth were nothing but pure Truth.

5048. At that stage they will have no justification for anger or impatience; for their whole position will have been due to their own conduct and their rejection of Allah's Grace. Nor will there be time for patience or repentance, for their period of probation will then have been over.

5049. The Righteous will be in Bliss far beyond their merits: their sins and faults will be forgiven by the grace of Allah, which will save them from the penalties which they may have incurred from human frailty. It will be their own effort or striving which will win them Allah's grace: see verse 19 below. But the fruits will be greater than they could strictly have earned.

5050. The bliss of the Righteous is described in three aspects: (1) their individual bliss, verses 17-20; (2) their social bliss, verses 21-24; and (3) their satisfaction in the dissipation of past shadows, and their full understanding of the goodness of Allah, verses 25-28.

5051. Individual satisfaction is expressed in three types or figures of speech. (1) eating and drinking. (2) thrones of dignity, and (3) the joy of individual companionship. But the eating and drinking will not be like the physical acts, which are subject to drawbacks, such as excess, aftereffects and satiety: here there will be pure health, profit, and enjoyment. So about the other two: see the notes following.

Cf. with this the symbolical description of heaven in 37:40-49: while the general account is the same, special phases are brought out in two passages to correspond with the context.

5052. Every one will have a Throne of dignity, but it does not follow that the dignity will be the same. Every one's Personality will be purified but it will not be merged into one general sameness.

And We shall join them
To Companions, with beautiful
Big and lustrous eyes.[5053]

وَزَوَّجْنَٰهُم بِحُورٍ عِينٍ

21. And those who believe
And whose families[5054] follow
Them in Faith—to them
Shall We join their families:
Nor shall We deprive them
(Of the fruit) of aught
Of their works:
(Yet) is each individual
In pledge for his deeds.[5055]

٢١ وَٱلَّذِينَ ءَامَنُوا۟ وَٱتَّبَعَتْهُمْ
ذُرِّيَّتُهُم بِإِيمَٰنٍ أَلْحَقْنَا بِهِمْ ذُرِّيَّتَهُمْ
وَمَآ أَلَتْنَٰهُم مِّنْ عَمَلِهِم مِّن شَىْءٍ
كُلُّ ٱمْرِئٍۭ بِمَا كَسَبَ رَهِينٌ

22. And We shall bestow
On them, of fruit and meat,[5056]
Anything they shall desire.

٢٢ وَأَمْدَدْنَٰهُم بِفَٰكِهَةٍ وَلَحْمٍ مِّمَّا يَشْتَهُونَ

23. They shall there exchange,
One with another,
A (loving) cup
Free of frivolity,[5057]
Free of all taint
Of ill.

٢٣ يَتَنَٰزَعُونَ فِيهَا كَأْسًا
لَّا لَغْوٌ فِيهَا
وَلَا تَأْثِيمٌ

24. Round about them will serve,
(Devoted) to them,

٢٤ وَيَطُوفُ عَلَيْهِمْ غِلْمَانٌ لَّهُمْ

5053. *Cf.* 44:54, and notes 4728 and 4729, where the meaning of *Ḥūr* is fully explained. This is the special sharing of individual Bliss one with another. The next verse refers to the general social satisfaction shared with all whom we lived in this earthly life.

5054. *D͟hurriyyah:* literally, progeny, offspring, family: applied by extension to mean all near and dear ones whether related or not. Love is unselfish, and works not merely, or chiefly, for Self, but for others; provided the others have Faith and respond according to their capacities or degrees, they will be joined on to the Head of the Group, even though on individual merits their rank might be less. This applies specially to a Prophet and his *Ummah* (or following).

5055. As already explained in the last note, though the love poured out by Prophets, ancestors, decendants, friends, or good men and women, will secure for their loved ones the enjoyment of their society, it is an indispensable condidtion that the loved ones should also, according to their lights, have shown their faith and their goodness in deeds. Each individual is responsible for his conduct. In the kingdom of heaven there is no boasting of ancestors or friends. But it is part of the satisfaction of the good ones who poured out their love that those who were in any way worthy to receive their love should also be admitted to their society, and this satisfaction shall in no wise be diminished to them.

5056. Note that this verse is embedded in the midst of the description of *social* bliss; the individual bliss figured by meat and drink has already been mentioned in verse 19 above. The social pleasure will be of any kind or quantity they shall desire, but their desires will then be purified, just as their pleasures will be on a different plane. (R).

5057. Drinking or loving cups, in our life on this earth, are apt to be misused in two ways: (1) they may be occasions for mere frivolity or the wasting of time; (2) they may lead to evil thoughts, evil suggestions, evil talk, or evil deeds. (R).

Youths (handsome) as Pearls[5058]
Well-guarded.

كَأَنَّهُمْ لُؤْلُؤٌ مَّكْنُونٌ

25. They will advance[5059]
To each other, engaging
In mutual enquiry.

وَأَقْبَلَ بَعْضُهُمْ عَلَىٰ بَعْضٍ يَتَسَآءَلُونَ ﴿٢٥﴾

26. They will say: "Aforetime,
We were not without fear
For the sake of our people.[5060]

قَالُوٓا۟ إِنَّا كُنَّا قَبْلُ فِىٓ أَهْلِنَا مُشْفِقِينَ ﴿٢٦﴾

27. "But Allah has been good
To us, and has delivered us
From the Penalty
Of the Scorching Wind.[5061]

فَمَنَّ ٱللَّهُ عَلَيْنَا
وَوَقَىٰنَا عَذَابَ ٱلسَّمُومِ ﴿٢٧﴾

28. "Truly, we did call
Unto Him from of old:
Truly it is He,
The Beneficent, the Merciful!"[5062]

إِنَّا كُنَّا مِن قَبْلُ نَدْعُوهُ
إِنَّهُۥ هُوَ ٱلْبَرُّ ٱلرَّحِيمُ ﴿٢٨﴾

SECTION 2.

29. Therefore proclaim thou[5063]
The praises (of thy Lord):
For by the Grace
Of thy Lord, thou art
No (vulgar) soothsayer, nor
Art thou one possessed.

فَذَكِّرْ فَمَآ أَنتَ
بِنِعْمَتِ رَبِّكَ بِكَاهِنٍ
وَلَا مَجْنُونٍ ﴿٢٩﴾

5058. *Maknūn:* well-guarded, kept close, concealed from exposure: the beautiful nacreous lustre of Pearls is disfigured by exposure to gases, vapours, or acids; when not actually in use they are best kept in closed caskets, guarded from deteriorating agencies. (R).

5059. The third—and the highest—stage of Bliss, after individual Bliss and social Bliss, is the satisfaction of looking to the Past without its shadows and realising to the full in the Present the goodness of Allah. See n. 5050. This, again, is shared in mutual converse and confidence.

5060. A man may be good, and may with limits have found goodness in his own spiritual life, but may have anxieties about his family or friends whom he loves. All such shadows are removed in heaven by the Grace of Allah, and he is free to dwell in it in this confidential converse with other men similarly circumstanced.

5061. "Us" includes the good man or woman and all whom he or she cared for. This would be an ever-expanding circle, until it includes all mankind through Teachers like the Chosen One. The "Scorching Wind" is the type of haste, arrogance, and fire, such as entered into the composition of Jinns: 15:27. The destiny of man is to attain to calm, peace, security, the Garden of Bliss.

5062. 'Before this, we called upon Him, in faith that He is good: now we know in our inmost souls that He is indeed good—the Beneficent, the Merciful.' This is the climax of the description of Heaven.

5063. The greatest of the Prophets was called a soothsayer, *i.e.*, one who tells fortunes by divination, or a madman possessed of some evil spirit, or a poet singing spiteful satires. Much more may lesser men be called by such names because they proclaim the Truth. They should go on in spite of it all. (R).

30. Or do they say—
"A Poet! we await
For him some calamity[5064]
(Hatched) by Time!"

٣٠ أَمْ يَقُولُونَ شَاعِرٌ نَّتَرَبَّصُ بِهِۦ رَيْبَ ٱلْمَنُونِ

31. Say thou: "Await ye!—
I too will wait[5065]
Along with you!"

٣١ قُلْ تَرَبَّصُوا۟ فَإِنِّى مَعَكُم مِّنَ ٱلْمُتَرَبِّصِينَ

32. Is it that their faculties
Of understanding urge them[5066]
To this, or are they
But a people transgressing[5067]
Beyond bounds?

٣٢ أَمْ تَأْمُرُهُمْ أَحْلَٰمُهُم بِهَٰذَآ أَمْ هُمْ قَوْمٌ طَاغُونَ

33. Or do they say,
"He fabricated the (Message)"?[5068]
Nay, they have no faith!

٣٣ أَمْ يَقُولُونَ تَقَوَّلَهُۥ بَل لَّا يُؤْمِنُونَ

34. Let them then produce
A recital like unto it—
If (it be) they speak
The Truth!

٣٤ فَلْيَأْتُوا۟ بِحَدِيثٍ مِّثْلِهِۦٓ إِن كَانُوا۟ صَٰدِقِينَ

35. Were they created of nothing,[5069]
Or were they themselves
The creators?

٣٥ أَمْ خُلِقُوا۟ مِنْ غَيْرِ شَىْءٍ أَمْ هُمُ ٱلْخَٰلِقُونَ

5064. If a spiteful poet foretells evil calamities for men, men can afford to laugh at him, hoping that Time will bring about its revenge, and spite will come to an evil end. For the various meanings of *Rayb*, see n. 1884 to 14:9. Some Commentators suggest Death as the Calamity hatched by Time.

5065. *Cf.* 9:52. If the wicked wait or look for some calamity to befall the preacher of Truth, the preacher of Truth can with far more justice await the decision of the issue between him and his persecutors. For he stands for right, and Allah will support the right.

5066. It may be that the persecutors of Truth are ignorant, and their deficient faculties of understanding mislead them, but it is more often the case that they are perverse rebels against the law of Allah, defending their own selfish interests, and preventing those whom they oppress, from getting justice.

5067. *Cf.* 51:53.

5068. As an alternative to the charges of being a soothsayer or a madman or a disgruntled poet, there is the charge of a forger or fabricator applied to the Prophet of Allah when he produces his Message. This implies that there can be no revelation or inspiration from Allah. Such an attitude negatives Faith altogether. But if this is so can they produce a work of man that can compare with the inspired Word of Allah? They cannot. *Cf.* 10:37-39, and 17:88.

5069. *Were they created of nothing?* Three possible alternative meanings are suggested by the Commentators, according to the meaning we give to the Arabic preposition *min* = of, by, with, for. (1) 'Were they created by nothing? Did they come into existence of themselves? Was it a mere chance that they came into being? (2) Were they created as men out of nothing? Was there not a wonderful seed, from which their material growth can be traced, as the handiwork of a wise and wonderful Creator? Must they not then seek His Will? (3) Were they created for nothing, to no purpose? If they *were* created for a purpose, must they not try to learn that purpose by understanding Allah's Revelation?

36. Or did they create The heavens and the earth? Nay, they have No firm belief.[5070]	٣٦ أَمْ خَلَقُوا۟ ٱلسَّمَٰوَٰتِ وَٱلْأَرْضَ بَل لَّا يُوقِنُونَ
37. Or are the Treasures Of thy Lord with them,[5071] Or are they managers (Of affairs)?	٣٧ أَمْ عِندَهُمْ خَزَآئِنُ رَبِّكَ أَمْ هُمُ ٱلْمُصَيْطِرُونَ
38. Or have they a ladder,[5072] By which they can (climb Up to heaven and) listen (To its secrets)? Then let (Such a) listener of theirs Produce a manifest proof.	٣٨ أَمْ لَهُمْ سُلَّمٌ يَسْتَمِعُونَ فِيهِ فَلْيَأْتِ مُسْتَمِعُهُم بِسُلْطَٰنٍ مُّبِينٍ
39. Or has He only daughters[5073] And ye have sons?	٣٩ أَمْ لَهُ ٱلْبَنَٰتُ وَلَكُمُ ٱلْبَنُونَ
40. Or is it that thou Dost ask for a reward,[5074] So that they are burdened With a load of debt?—	٤٠ أَمْ تَسْـَٔلُهُمْ أَجْرًا فَهُم مِّن مَّغْرَمٍ مُّثْقَلُونَ
41. Or that the Unseen[5075] Is in their hands, And they write it down?	٤١ أَمْ عِندَهُمُ ٱلْغَيْبُ فَهُمْ يَكْتُبُونَ
42. Or do they intend A plot (against thee)?[5076]	٤٢ أَمْ يُرِيدُونَ كَيْدًا

5070. They obviously did not create the wonders of the starry heavens and the fruitful globe of the earth. But they can assign no definite cause to explain it, as they have no firm belief on the subject themselves.

5071. *Cf.* 6:50, and n. 867. The Treasures of Allah's Knowledge are infinite. But the doubters and unbelievers have no access to them, much less can the doubters and unbelievers manage the wonders of this world. Must they not therefore seek grace and revelation from Allah?

5072. *Cf.* 6:35: a reference to the Pagan belief that by means of a material ladder a man might climb up to heaven and learn its secrets!

5073. *Cf.* 16:57-59, and n. 2082. To the gospel of Unity it is repugnant to assign begotten sons or daughters to Allah. But the Arab superstition about angels being the daughters of Allah was particularly blasphemous as the Pagan Arabs hated to have daughters themselves and considered it a mark of humiliation!

5074. The Prophets of Allah ask for no reward to preach the Message of Allah and direct men to the right Path. Why then do men shun them and persecute those who seek to bring blessings to them?

5075. The Unseen in the spiritual world is a subject of Revelation, though it works through the common everyday life of man. The men who reject Revelation simply because it is outside their own experience ought on the contrary to try to learn about it and seek to understand it.

5076. Shallow men who plot against Good are themselves the willing victims of insidious plots laid by Evil.

But those who defy Allah
Are themselves involved
In a Plot!

فَٱلَّذِينَ كَفَرُواْ هُمُ ٱلْمَكِيدُونَ

43. Or have they a god[5077]
Other than Allah?
Exalted is Allah
Far above the things
They associate with Him!

٤٣ أَمْ لَهُمْ إِلَٰهٌ غَيْرُ ٱللَّهِ
سُبْحَٰنَ ٱللَّهِ عَمَّا يُشْرِكُونَ

44. Were they to see
A piece of the sky[5078]
Falling (on them), they
Would (only) say: "Clouds
Gathered in heaps!"

٤٤ وَإِن يَرَوْاْ كِسْفًا مِّنَ ٱلسَّمَآءِ سَاقِطًا
يَقُولُواْ سَحَابٌ مَّرْكُومٌ

45. So leave them alone
Until they encounter
That Day of theirs,
Wherein they shall (perforce)
Swoon (with terror)—[5079]

٤٥ فَذَرْهُمْ حَتَّىٰ يُلَٰقُواْ
يَوْمَهُمُ ٱلَّذِى فِيهِ يُصْعَقُونَ

46. The Day when their plotting
Will avail them nothing
And no help shall be
Given them.

٤٦ يَوْمَ لَا يُغْنِى عَنْهُمْ كَيْدُهُمْ شَيْـًٔا
وَلَا هُمْ يُنصَرُونَ

47. And verily, for those
Who do wrong, there is
Another punishment besides
this:[5080]
But most of them
Understand not.

٤٧ وَإِنَّ لِلَّذِينَ ظَلَمُواْ
عَذَابًا دُونَ ذَٰلِكَ
وَلَٰكِنَّ أَكْثَرَهُمْ لَا يَعْلَمُونَ

48. Now await in patience
The command of thy Lord:

٤٨ وَٱصْبِرْ لِحُكْمِ رَبِّكَ

5077. This is the final and decisive question: Is there really any god other than Allah the One True God? Every argument points to the negative. A series of questions has been asked pointing to the negative of the superstitions of the godless. The gospel of Unity, Revelation, and the Hereafter had thus been preached by a searching examination of the position of the Unbelievers. And the Sūrah ends with an exhortation to leave alone those who will not believe because they wish not to believe, and to let Time work out the web and pattern of Allah's Plan.

5078. In 26:187, Shu'ayb, the Prophet of Allah, is challenged by the Companions of the Wood "to cause a piece of sky to fall on us, if thou art truthful." Such a challenge, in some form or other, is addressed to all Prophets of Allah. It is mere defiance. It has no meaning. If a piece of the sky were to fall on them, it would not convince them, for they would only say: "These are only clouds gathered in heaps." They do not wish to believe. Otherwise there are ample Signs and Evidences of Allah's Plan in Creation and in man's own heart.

5079. That is, the Day of Judgement. *Cf.* 39:68, and n. 4343.

5080. The final Judgement is for all. But in addition, wrongdoers have to fear a retribution or punishment in this very life, an open punishment through external events or, at least the bitter pangs of conscience within.

For verily thou art
In Our eyes:[5081]
And celebrate the praises
Of thy Lord the while
Thou standest forth,[5082]

فَإِنَّكَ بِأَعْيُنِنَا
وَسَبِّحْ بِحَمْدِ رَبِّكَ حِينَ تَقُومُ

49. And for part of the night[5083]
Also praise thou Him—
And at the retreat[5084]
Of the stars!

وَمِنَ الَّيْلِ فَسَبِّحْهُ ﴿٤٩﴾
وَإِدْبَرَ النُّجُومِ

5081. The messenger of Allah must strive his utmost to proclaim the Message of Allah: as for results, it is not for him to command them. He must wait patiently, in the knowledge that he is not forgotten by Allah, but is constantly under Allah's eyes—under His loving care and protection. And he must glorify Allah's name, as he is a standard-bearer of Allah's Truth.

5082. The translators and Commentators nearly all understand *taqūmu* in the sense of rising up from sleep. But the rendering I have given is consistent with Quranic usage. In 26:218, we have the same two words *ḥīna taqūmu*, meaning "standing forth (in prayer)". In 57:25, we have *liyaqūma al nāsu bilqisṭi*, which obviously means "that men may stand forth in justice," *i.e.*, do all their business in justice. In 78:38, we have *yaqūmu* used for the angels standing forth in ranks.

On my rendering the meaning will be: 'celebrate Allah's praises when you stand forth in prayer, or at all times when you go about your business; but also for part of the night and at early dawn when worldly life is at a standstill.'

5083. It is not necessary to understand this for any particular canonical prayers. It is good to spend a part of the night in prayer and praise: *Cf.* 23:6. And the Dawn is a daily recurring miracle of nature, full of spiritual influences and "testimony": *Cf.* 17:78-79.

5084. *Idbār al nujūm:* the retreat of the stars: the glorious hour of early dawn. In 113:1, we seek Allah's protection as "Lord of the Dawn".

INTRODUCTION TO SŪRAH 53—*AL NAJM*

This is an early Makkan Sūrah, and is the fourth of the series of seven which were described in the Introduction to S. 50.

The particular theme of this Sūrah is that Revelation is not an illusion: the illusion is in the minds of those who doubt and have false ideas of Allah: Allah is the source and goal of all things.

In some Sūrahs the consecutive arrangement is shown or suggested by a cue-word. Here the cue-word is "star", corresponding to "stars" in the last verse of the last Sūrah. So in 46:1, the words: "Exalted in Power, Full of Wisdom": are carried forward from the last verse of S. 45, and indeed the same words occur in the first verse of S. 45. So, again the words: "Most Merciful, Oft-Forgiving"; in 34:2, refer back to the words: "Oft-Forgiving, Most Merciful": in the last line of S. 33. In S. 54:1, the nearness of Judgement recalls the same idea at the end of the previous Sūrah (53:57). Other examples will also be found.

Summary—The impression received by the Prophet in revelation is neither error on his part nor deception by others, nor does he speak from selfish motives: it comes clearly from Allah, Who is not what the vain imaginations of men conceive: He is All-in-All, First and Last, Lord of all, Ample in forgiveness (53:10-32, and C. 229).

Those who turn away are petty and ignorant, not knowing that Allah is the source and goal of all things—in men, in nature, and in the events of history: therefore serve ye Him (53:33-62, and C. 230).

C. 229.—True revelation is not a process
(53:1-32.) Either of error or deception, nor does
The Prophet speak from himself as he desires.
It is Allah's inspiration, true, without doubt.
It is reality—the inner reality
Of heaven as far as knowledge can reach,
Not the false ideas and idols that men
Construct for themselves, names without truth
Behind them. The goal of all things is Allah,
As He is the One from Whom starts Reality.
No other can e'er intercede except
As He wills. He made us, and knows all
That we are. It is not for us to justify
Ourselves, but to offer ourselves as we are.

Sūrah 53.

Al Najm (The Star)

*In the name of Allah, Most Gracious,
Most Merciful.*

بِسْمِ اللَّهِ الرَّحْمَٰنِ الرَّحِيمِ

1. By the Star[5085]
When it goes down—

وَالنَّجْمِ إِذَا هَوَىٰ ١

2. Your Companion is neither[5086]
Astray nor being misled,

مَا ضَلَّ صَاحِبُكُمْ وَمَا غَوَىٰ ٢

3. Nor does he say (aught)
Of (his own) Desire.

وَمَا يَنطِقُ عَنِ الْهَوَىٰ ٣

4. It is no less than
Inspiration sent down to him:

إِنْ هُوَ إِلَّا وَحْيٌ يُوحَىٰ ٤

5. He was taught by one[5087]
Mighty in Power,

عَلَّمَهُ شَدِيدُ الْقُوَىٰ ٥

6. Endued with Wisdom:
For he appeared
(In stately form)

ذُو مِرَّةٍ فَاسْتَوَىٰ ٦

7. While he was in
The highest part[5088]
Of the horizon:

وَهُوَ بِالْأُفُقِ الْأَعْلَىٰ ٧

5085. *Najm* is interpreted in various ways. As most commonly accepted, it means either a Star generically, or the close cluster of seven stars known as the Pleiades in the Constellation Taurus, which the sun enters about the 21st of April every year. In mid-April, or a little later, the beautiful cluster would set just after the sun, after having gradually ascended the sky in the winter months. In late May, or a little later, it would rise just before the sun. In its western aspects, it might be considered a spring constellation. To open-air nations (including the Arabs) whose climate usually presents starry skies, this is an object of great interest, and many folklore tales gather round it. When so glorious a cluster is content to bow down in the horizon and merge its light in the greater light created by Allah (see the last three lines of C. 228), it becomes a symbol of humility in beauty and power before the Most High, Whose revelation discloses the summit of beauty, power and wisdom.

Hawā in the text may mean either "goes down (or sets)" or "rises". Whichever meaning we take, it makes no difference to the symbolic interpretation given above.

5086. "Your Companion" is the Holy Prophet Muḥammad, who had lived among the Quraysh all his life. He is defended from three kinds of charges that the Unbelievers brought against him: (1) that he was going astray, either through defect of intelligence or through carelessness; (2) that he was being misled or deceived by evil spirits; and (3) that he spoke out of a whim or impulse, or from a selfish desire to impress his own personality. None of these charges were true. On the contrary he had direct inspiration from Allah.

5087. This is referred by the Commentators to the angel Gabriel, through whom the inspiration came. *Cf.* 81:20.

5088. Gabriel appeared in stately form, perhaps towering above the Mountain of Light (see C. 31). *Istawā* in verse 6, translated "appeared", means literally "mounted" or "ascended", or "set himself to execute a design": see n. 1386 to 10:3.

8. Then he approached
And came closer,

ثُمَّ دَنَا فَتَدَلَّىٰ ﴿٨﴾

9. And was at a distance
Of but two bow-lengths[5089]
Or (even) nearer;

فَكَانَ قَابَ قَوْسَيْنِ أَوْ أَدْنَىٰ ﴿٩﴾

10. So did (Allah) convey[5090]
The inspiration to His Servant—
(Conveyed) what He (meant)
To convey.

فَأَوْحَىٰٓ إِلَىٰ عَبْدِهِۦ مَآ أَوْحَىٰ ﴿١٠﴾

11. The (Prophet's) (mind and) heart
In no way falsified[5091]
That which he saw.

مَا كَذَبَ ٱلْفُؤَادُ مَا رَأَىٰٓ ﴿١١﴾

12. Will ye then dispute
With him concerning
What he saw?

أَفَتُمَٰرُونَهُۥ عَلَىٰ مَا يَرَىٰ ﴿١٢﴾

13. For indeed he saw him
At a second descent,[5092]

وَلَقَدْ رَءَاهُ نَزْلَةً أُخْرَىٰ ﴿١٣﴾

14. Near the Lote-tree[5093]
Beyind which none may pass:

عِندَ سِدْرَةِ ٱلْمُنتَهَىٰ ﴿١٤﴾

15. Near it is the Garden
Of Abode.[5094]

عِندَهَا جَنَّةُ ٱلْمَأْوَىٰٓ ﴿١٥﴾

16. Behold, the Lote-tree
Was shrouded
(In mystery unspeakable!)

إِذْ يَغْشَى ٱلسِّدْرَةَ مَا يَغْشَىٰ ﴿١٦﴾

17. (His) sight never swerved,
Nor did it go wrong!

مَا زَاغَ ٱلْبَصَرُ وَمَا طَغَىٰ ﴿١٧﴾

5089. Two bow-shots (counting 100 to 150 yards to a bow-shot) would be a clearly visible distance. (R).

5090. Gabriel would be just a messenger, to do no more than convey Allah's Message to Allah's Messenger.

5091. "Heart" in Arabic includes the faculty of intelligence as well as the faculty of feeling. The impression conveyed was pure truth; there was no illusion in it.

5092. The first occasion when Gabriel appeared in a visible form was at the Mountain of Light, when he brought his first revelation beginning with *Iqra':* see C. 29-35. The second was at the Prophet's *Mi'rāj* or Ascension: see Introduction to S. 17, paras. 2-4. These were the only two occasions when Gabriel appeared in visible form. (R).

5093. For the Lote-tree in its literal meaning, see n. 3814 to 24:16. The wild Lote is thorny; under cultivation it yields good fruit and shade, and is symbolic of heavenly bliss, as here and in 56:28.

5094. The "Garden of Abode" *(Jannah al Ma'wa)* lies close to the Lote-tree and, in the opinion of some authorities, is so called because the souls of believers will find their abode therein. [Eds.].

18. For truly did he see,
Of the signs of his Lord,
The Greatest!

لَقَدْ رَأَىٰ مِنْ ءَايَٰتِ رَبِّهِ ٱلْكُبْرَىٰٓ ١٨

19. Have ye seen[5095]
Lāt, and 'Uzzā,

أَفَرَءَيْتُمُ ٱللَّٰتَ وَٱلْعُزَّىٰ ١٩

20. And another,
The Third (goddess), Manāt?

وَمَنَوٰةَ ٱلثَّالِثَةَ ٱلْأُخْرَىٰٓ ٢٠

21. What! For you[5096]
The male sex,
And for Him, the female?

أَلَكُمُ ٱلذَّكَرُ وَلَهُ ٱلْأُنثَىٰ ٢١

22. Behold, such would be
Indeed a division
Most unfair!

تِلْكَ إِذًا قِسْمَةٌ ضِيزَىٰٓ ٢٢

23. These are nothing but names
Which ye have devised—[5097]
Ye and your fathers—
For which Allah has sent
Down no authority (whatever).
They follow nothing but[5098]
Conjecture and what
Their own souls desire!—
Even though there has already
Come to them Guidance
From their Lord!

إِنْ هِىَ إِلَّآ أَسْمَآءٌ
سَمَّيْتُمُوهَآ أَنتُمْ وَءَابَآؤُكُم
مَّآ أَنزَلَ ٱللَّهُ بِهَا مِن سُلْطَٰنٍ
إِن يَتَّبِعُونَ إِلَّا ٱلظَّنَّ وَمَا تَهْوَى ٱلْأَنفُسُ
وَلَقَدْ جَآءَهُم مِّن رَّبِّهِمُ ٱلْهُدَىٰٓ ٢٣

24. Nay, shall man have (just)
Anything he hankers after?[5099]

أَمْ لِلْإِنسَٰنِ مَا تَمَنَّىٰ ٢٤

5095. From the heights of divine Glory, we come back again to this sorry earth, with its base idolatries. We are asked to "look at this picture, and at that!" The three principal idols of Pagan Arab Idolatry were the goddesses Lāt, 'Uzzā, and Manāt. Opinions differ as to their exact forms: one version is that Lāt was in human shape, 'Uzzā had its origin in a sacred tree, and Manāt in a white stone. (R).

5096. To show Allah in human shape, or imagine sons or daughters of Allah, as if Allah were flesh, was in any case a derogation from the supreme glory of Allah, high above all creatures, even if the human shapes were invested with great beauty and majesty as in the Greek Pantheon. But when we consider in what low opinion Pagan Arabia held the female sex, it was particularly degrading to show Allah, or so-called daughters of Allah, in female shapes. *Cf.* 16:57-59, and n. 2082; also 52:39, and n. 5073.

5097. *Cf.* 7:71; 12:40, n. 1693. The divine names which they give to stocks and stones, or to heroes living or dead, or even to prophets and men of God, are but the creatures of their own fancy. Whatever they were, they were not gods.

5098. *Cf.* 6:116. Conjecture is a dangerous thing in speaking of divine things. It follows lines which reflect the lusts of men's own hearts. Why not follow the divine guidance which comes through the prophets of Allah?

5099. The unpurified desires of men's hearts often lead to destruction, for they are dictated by Evil. The true source of guidance and light is Allah, just as He is also the goal to which all persons and things—all existence—returns.

25. But it is to Allah
That the End and
The Beginning (of all things)
Belong.

فَلِلَّهِ ٱلْـَٔاخِرَةُ وَٱلْأُولَىٰ ٢٥

SECTION 2.

26. How many so ever be
The angels in the heavens,[5100]
Their intercession will avail
nothing
Except after Allah has given[5101]
Leave for whom He pleases
And that he is acceptable
To Him.

وَكَم مِّن مَّلَكٍ فِى ٱلسَّمَٰوَٰتِ ٢٦
لَا تُغْنِى شَفَٰعَتُهُمْ شَيْـًٔا
إِلَّا مِنۢ بَعْدِ أَن يَأْذَنَ ٱللَّهُ
لِمَن يَشَآءُ وَيَرْضَىٰٓ

27. Those who believe not
In the Hereafter, name
The angels with female names.[5102]

إِنَّ ٱلَّذِينَ لَا يُؤْمِنُونَ بِٱلْـَٔاخِرَةِ ٢٧
لَيُسَمُّونَ ٱلْمَلَٰٓئِكَةَ تَسْمِيَةَ ٱلْأُنثَىٰ

28. But they have no knowledge
Therein. They follow nothing
But conjecture; and conjecture[5103]
Avails nothing against Truth.

وَمَا لَهُم بِهِۦ مِنْ عِلْمٍ إِن يَتَّبِعُونَ إِلَّا ٱلظَّنَّ ٢٨
وَإِنَّ ٱلظَّنَّ لَا يُغْنِى مِنَ ٱلْحَقِّ شَيْـًٔا

29. Therefore shun those who
Turn away from Our Message
And desire nothing but
The life of this world.

فَأَعْرِضْ عَن مَّن تَوَلَّىٰ عَن ذِكْرِنَا ٢٩
وَلَمْ يُرِدْ إِلَّا ٱلْحَيَوٰةَ ٱلدُّنْيَا

30. That is as far as[5104]
Knowledge will reach them.
Verily thy Lord knoweth best
Those who stray from

ذَٰلِكَ مَبْلَغُهُم مِّنَ ٱلْعِلْمِ ٣٠
إِنَّ رَبَّكَ هُوَ أَعْلَمُ بِمَن ضَلَّ عَن

5100. We are apt to imagine the angelic host of heaven as beings of immense power. But their power is all derived from Allah. Men, when they attain to the highest spiritual dignities, may have even more power and position than angels in the sight of Allah, as is typified by angels bidden to bow down to Adam: 2:34. The Quraysh superstition about angels being intermediaries and intercessors for man with Allah is condemned.

5101. *Cf.* 20:109 and 21:28. No one can intercede except with the permission of Allah, and that permission will only be given for one who is acceptable to Allah. For a possible different shade of meaning, see n. 2643 to 20:109.

5102. *Cf.* 53:21 above, and n. 5096. The Pagan Quraysh had no firm belief in the Hereafter. Their prayers for intercession to angels and deities was on account of their worldly affairs.

5103. *Cf.* 53:23 above, and n. 5098.

5104. Men with a materialist turn of mind, whose desires are bounded by sex and material things, will not go beyond those things. Their knowledge will be limited to the narrow circle in which their thoughts move. The spiritual world is beyond their ken. While persons with a spiritual outlook, even though they may fail again and again in attaining their full ideals, are on the right Path. They are willing to receive guidance and Allah's Grace will find them out and help them.

His Path, and He knoweth
Best those who receive guidance.

سَبِيلِهِۦ وَهُوَ أَعْلَمُ بِمَنِ ٱهْتَدَىٰ

31. Yea, to Allah belongs all
That is in the heavens
And on earth: so that
He rewards those who do[5105]
Evil, according to their deeds,
And He rewards those who
Do good, with what is best.

٣١ وَلِلَّهِ مَا فِى ٱلسَّمَٰوَٰتِ وَمَا
فِى ٱلْأَرْضِ لِيَجْزِىَ ٱلَّذِينَ أَسَٰٓـُٔوا۟ بِمَا عَمِلُوا۟
وَيَجْزِىَ ٱلَّذِينَ أَحْسَنُوا۟ بِٱلْحُسْنَى

32. Those who aviod
Great sins and shameful deeds,
Only (falling into) small faults—
Verily thy Lord is ample[5106]
In forgiveness. He knows
You well when He brings
You out of the earth,
And when ye are hidden
In your mothers' wombs.
Therefore justify not yourselves:[5107]
He knows best who it is
That guards against evil.

٣٢ ٱلَّذِينَ يَجْتَنِبُونَ كَبَٰٓئِرَ
ٱلْإِثْمِ وَٱلْفَوَٰحِشَ إِلَّا ٱللَّمَمَ
إِنَّ رَبَّكَ وَٰسِعُ ٱلْمَغْفِرَةِ
هُوَ أَعْلَمُ بِكُمْ إِذْ أَنشَأَكُم مِّنَ ٱلْأَرْضِ
وَإِذْ أَنتُمْ أَجِنَّةٌ فِى بُطُونِ أُمَّهَٰتِكُمْ
فَلَا تُزَكُّوٓا۟ أَنفُسَكُمْ هُوَ أَعْلَمُ بِمَنِ ٱتَّقَىٰٓ

C. 230.—(53:33-62.)
When once in Allah's Way, turn not away,
Nor check your generous impulse to give
Your all to Allah. The spiritual world
Unseen is above all worldly bargains.
Each soul must bear its own responsibility.
It must strive its utmost and attain its end.
The final Goal of all is Allah:
In His hands are Laughter and Tears, Life
And Death, the mystery of Birth and Creation,
And the Hereafter. He controls our Bliss
And inner satisfaction. He is Lord
Of the highest and noblest in Nature. His hand

5105. All deeds have their consequences, good or ill. But this is not an iron law, as the Determinists in philosophy, or the preachers of bare Karma, would have us believe. Allah does not sit apart. He governs the world. And Mercy as well as Justice are His attributes. In His Justice every deed or word or thought of evil has its consequence for the doer or speaker or thinker. But there is always in this life room for repentance and amendment. As soon as this is forthcoming, Allah's Mercy comes into action. It can blot out our evil, and the "reward" which it gives is nearly always greater than our merits.

5106. Allah's attributes of Mercy and Forgiveness are unlimited. They come into action without our asking, but on our bringing our will as offerings to Him. Our asking or prayer helps us to bring our minds and wills as offering to Him. That is necessary to frame our own psychological preparedness. It informs Allah of nothing for He knows all.

5107. As Allah knows our inmost being, it is absurd for us to justify ourselves either by pretending that we are better than we are or by finding excuses for our conduct. We must offer ourselves unreservedly such as we are: it is His Mercy and Grace that will cleanse us. If we try, out of love for Him, to guard against evil, our striving is all that He asks for.

Traces the course of History. Learn,
Oh learn from His Revelation and
Adore the Lord of your inmost Soul!

SECTION 3.

33. Seest thou one[5108]
Who turns back,

أَفَرَءَيْتَ ٱلَّذِى تَوَلَّىٰ ﴿٣٣﴾

34. Gives a little,
Then hardens (his heart)?

وَأَعْطَىٰ قَلِيلًا وَأَكْدَىٰٓ ﴿٣٤﴾

35. What! Has he knowledge
Of the Unseen
So that he can see?[5109]

أَعِندَهُۥ عِلْمُ ٱلْغَيْبِ فَهُوَ يَرَىٰٓ ﴿٣٥﴾

36. Nay, is he not acquainted
With what is in the books[5110]
Of Moses—

أَمْ لَمْ يُنَبَّأْ بِمَا فِى صُحُفِ مُوسَىٰ ﴿٣٦﴾

37. And of Abraham[5111]
Who fulfilled his
engagements—[5112]

وَإِبْرَٰهِيمَ ٱلَّذِى وَفَّىٰٓ ﴿٣٧﴾

38. Namely, that no bearer[5113]
Of burdens can bear
The burden of another;

أَلَّا تَزِرُ وَازِرَةٌ وِزْرَ أُخْرَىٰ ﴿٣٨﴾

39. That man can have nothing
But what he strives for;

وَأَن لَّيْسَ لِلْإِنسَٰنِ إِلَّا مَا سَعَىٰ ﴿٣٩﴾

5108. The particular reference in this passage, according to Bayḍāwī is to Walīd ibn Mughayrah, who bargained with a Quraysh Pagan for a certain sum if the latter would take upon himself the sins of Walīd. He paid a part of the sum but withheld the rest. The general application that concerns us is threefold: (1) if we accept Islam, we must accept it whole-heartedly and not look back to Pagan superstitions; (2) we cannot play fast and loose with our promises and (3) no man can bargain about spiritual matters for he cannot see what his end will be unless he follows the law of Allah, which is the law of righteousness.

5109. 'So that he can see what will happen in the Hereafter': for no bargains can be struck about matters unknown.

5110. *Books of Moses:* apparently not the Pentateuch, in the *Tawrāh*, but some other book or books now lost. For example, the Book of the Wars of Jehovah is referred to in the Old Testament (Num. xxi. 14) but is now lost. The present Pentateuch has no clear message at all of a Life to come.

5111. No original *Book of Abraham* is now extant. But a book called "The Testament of Abraham" has come down to us which seems to be a Greek translation of a Hebrew original. See n. 6094 to 87:19, where the Books of Moses and Abraham are again mentioned together.

5112. One of the titles of Abraham is *Ḥanif*, the True in Faith: *Cf.* 16:120, 123.

5113. Here follows a series of eleven aphorisms of ancient wisdom apparently incorporated in current Semitic folklore. The first is that a man's spiritual burden—the responsibility for his sin—must be borne by himself and not by another: *Cf.* 6:164. There can be no vicarious atonement.

40. That (the fruit of) his striving[5114]
Will soon come in sight;

وَأَنَّ سَعْيَهُۥ سَوْفَ يُرَىٰ ﴿٤٠﴾

41. Then will he be rewarded
With a reward complete;

ثُمَّ يُجْزَىٰهُ ٱلْجَزَآءَ ٱلْأَوْفَىٰ ﴿٤١﴾

42. That to thy Lord
Is the final Goal;[5115]

وَأَنَّ إِلَىٰ رَبِّكَ ٱلْمُنتَهَىٰ ﴿٤٢﴾

43. That it is He Who
Granteth Laughter and Tears;

وَأَنَّهُۥ هُوَ أَضْحَكَ وَأَبْكَىٰ ﴿٤٣﴾

44. That it is He Who
Granteth Death and Life;

وَأَنَّهُۥ هُوَ أَمَاتَ وَأَحْيَا ﴿٤٤﴾

45. That He did create
In pairs—male and female,[5116]

وَأَنَّهُۥ خَلَقَ ٱلزَّوْجَيْنِ ٱلذَّكَرَ وَٱلْأُنثَىٰ ﴿٤٥﴾

46. From a seed when lodged
(In its place);

مِن نُّطْفَةٍ إِذَا تُمْنَىٰ ﴿٤٦﴾

47. That He hath promised
A Second Creation
(Raising of the Dead);[5117]

وَأَنَّ عَلَيْهِ ٱلنَّشْأَةَ ٱلْأُخْرَىٰ ﴿٤٧﴾

48. That it is He Who
Giveth wealth and satisfaction;[5118]

وَأَنَّهُۥ هُوَ أَغْنَىٰ وَأَقْنَىٰ ﴿٤٨﴾

49. That He is the Lord
Of Sirius (the Mighty Star);[5119]

وَأَنَّهُۥ هُوَ رَبُّ ٱلشِّعْرَىٰ ﴿٤٩﴾

5114. The second and third aphorisms are that man must strive, or he will gain nothing; and that if he strives, the result must soon appear in sight and he will find his reward in full measure.

5115. The fourth, fifth, and sixth aphorisms are that all things return to Allah; that all our hope should be in Him and we should fear none but Him; and that He alone can give Life and Death.

5116. The seventh aphorism relates to the mystery of sex: all things are created in pairs: each sex performs its proper function, and yet its wonderful working is part of the creative process of Allah: the living seed fructifies, but contains within itself all the factors disclosed in its later development and life.

5117. No less wonderful is the promise He has made about the raising of the dead, and a new life in the Hereafter, and this is the subject of the eighth aphorism.

5118. Wealth and material gain are sought by most men, in the hope that they will be a source of enjoyment and satisfaction. But this hope is not always fulfilled. There is a psychical and spiritual side to it. But both the material and the spiritual side depend upon the working of Allah's Plan. This is referred to in the ninth aphorism.

5119. The tenth aphorism refers to a mighty phenomenon of nature, the magnificent star Sirius, which is such a prominent object in the skies, in the early part of the solar year, say, from January to April. It is the brightest star in the firmament, and its bluish light causes wonder and terror in Pagan minds. The Pagan Arabs worshipped it as a divinity. But Allah is the Lord, Creator and Cherisher, of the most magnificent part of Creation, and worship is due to Him alone.

50. And that it is He
Who destroyed the (powerful)
Ancient 'Ād (people),[5120]

وَأَنَّهُۥٓ أَهْلَكَ عَادًا ٱلْأُولَىٰ ﴿٥٠﴾

51. And the Thamūd,
Nor gave them a lease
Of perpetual life.

وَثَمُودَا۟ فَمَآ أَبْقَىٰ ﴿٥١﴾

52. And before them,
The people of Noah,
For that they were (all)
Most unjust
And most insolent transgressors,

وَقَوْمَ نُوحٍ مِّن قَبْلُ ۖ إِنَّهُمْ كَانُوا۟ هُمْ أَظْلَمَ وَأَطْغَىٰ ﴿٥٢﴾

53. And He destroyed
The Overthrown Cities[5121]
(Of Sodom and Gomorrah),

وَٱلْمُؤْتَفِكَةَ أَهْوَىٰ ﴿٥٣﴾

54. So that (ruins unknown)
Have covered them up.

فَغَشَّىٰهَا مَا غَشَّىٰ ﴿٥٤﴾

55. Then which of the gifts[5122]
Of thy Lord, (O man,)
Wilt thou dispute about?

فَبِأَىِّ ءَالَآءِ رَبِّكَ تَتَمَارَىٰ ﴿٥٥﴾

56. This is a Warner,[5123]
Of the (series of) Warners
Of old!

هَٰذَا نَذِيرٌ مِّنَ ٱلنُّذُرِ ٱلْأُولَىٰٓ ﴿٥٦﴾

57. The (Judgement) ever
approaching
Draws nigh:

أَزِفَتِ ٱلْءَازِفَةُ ﴿٥٧﴾

5120. The eleventh and last aphorism refers to the punishment of the most powerful ancient peoples for their sins. For the 'Ād people, see n. 1040 to 7:65, and for the Thamūd, see n. 1043 to 7:73. They were strong; and they were talented: but their strength and their talents did not save them from being destroyed for their sins. The same may be said about the earlier generation of Noah, who were destroyed in the Flood: they "rejected Our Signs: they were indeed a blind people" (7:64); see also n. 1039 to 7:59; and 11:25-49.

Ancient 'Ād (people): some Commentators construe, *First 'Ād people,* distinguishing them from the later 'Ād people, a remnant that had their day and passed away.

5121. Verses 53-60 may be construed as a commentary on the aphorisms. The story of the Overthrown Cities, to which Lot was sent for a warning, will be found in 11:74-83 and the notes thereon. This story may well be treated as separate from the aphorisms as it refers to events that happened in the later life of Abraham.

5122. With a slight modification this forms the refrain of the next Sūrah but one, the highly poetical Sūrah of *Al Raḥmān.* In S. 54. 15, 17 etc., there is a similar refrain in different words. Every gift and benefit you have is from Allah, and to save you from the just punishment of your sins, Allah at all times sends revelations and Messengers to warn you. Why not accept Allah's Grace instead of disputing about it?

5123. The Prophet before the Quraysh (and before us) continues the line of messengers of Allah who have come to teach mankind and lead men into unity and righteousness. Shall we not listen to his voice? Every day that passes, the Judgement approaches nearer and nearer. But Allah alone can say at what precise hour it will come to any of us. It is certain, and yet it is a mystery, which Allah alone can lay bare.

58. No (soul) but Allah
Can lay it bare.

﴿٥٨﴾ لَيْسَ لَهَا مِن دُونِ ٱللَّهِ كَاشِفَةٌ

59. Do ye then wonder[5124]
At this recital?

﴿٥٩﴾ أَفَمِنْ هَٰذَا ٱلْحَدِيثِ تَعْجَبُونَ

60. And will ye laugh[5125]
And not weep,—

﴿٦٠﴾ وَتَضْحَكُونَ وَلَا تَبْكُونَ

61. Wasting your time
In vanities?

﴿٦١﴾ وَأَنتُمْ سَٰمِدُونَ

62. But fall ye down in prostration
To Allah and adore (Him)![5126]

﴿٦٢﴾ فَٱسْجُدُوا۟ لِلَّهِ وَٱعْبُدُوا۟

5124. Mere wondering will not do, even if it is the wonder of admiration. Each soul must strive and act, and Allah's Mercy will take it under its wings.

5125. The higher issues of Life and the Hereafter are serious, and therefore all that we do in this life is serious and important. We must shun inanities and frivolities. It is no laughing time. If we only realised our own shortcomings, we should weep, with our good angels who weep for us. But weeping by itself will not help. We must try and understand Allah and adore Him. Thus shall we be able to understand ourselves and our fellow-men.

5126. And so we are invited to prostrate ourselves and adore Him. For this is the true end of Revelation and the true attitude when we understand the world, Nature, History and the working of Allah's Plan.

INTRODUCTION TO SŪRAH 54—*AL QAMAR*

This is an early Makkan Sūrah, the fifth in the series dealing with Judgement, and the truth of Revelation, as explained in the Introduction to S. 50.

The theme of the Sūrah is explained by the refrain: "Is there any that will receive admonition?" which occurs six times, at the end of each reference to a past story of sin and rejection of warnings and in the appeal to the simplicity of the Qur'ān (verses 15, 17, 22, 32, 40, and 51). There is an invitation to listen to the Message and turn to Truth and Righteousness.

Summary—The Hour of Judgement is nigh, but men forget or reject the Message, as did the people of Noah, of 'Ād, of Thamūd, of Lot, and of Pharaoh. Is there any that will receive admonition? (54:1-55, and C. 231).

C. 231.—With every breath of our life, comes nearer
(54:1-55.) And nearer the Hour of Judgement: the proud
Will be brought low: the lovers of ease
Will find themselves in hardship. Come!
Is there any that will truly receive admonition?
So said Noah, but his people rejected
The warning and perished. We have made
Our Revelation easy to understand and follow.
Is there any that will truly receive admonition?
So said the prophets of 'Ād and Thamūd;
So said the prophets deputed to the People
Of Luṭ and the Pharaoh: but the wicked continued
In sin and defiance and perished. Will the present
Generation learn wisdom by warning? Alas!
Is there any that will truly receive admonition?
The Righteous will dwell in their Gardens of Bliss—
In joyful Assembly of realised Truth,
In the Presence of their Sovereign Most High!

Sūrah 54.

Al Qamar (The Moon)

الجزء السابع والعشرون — سورة القمر

In the name of Allah, Most Gracious,
Most Merciful.

بِسۡمِ ٱللَّهِ ٱلرَّحۡمَٰنِ ٱلرَّحِيمِ

1. The Hour (of Judgement)[5127]
Is nigh, and the moon
Is cleft asunder.[5128]

ٱقۡتَرَبَتِ ٱلسَّاعَةُ وَٱنشَقَّ ٱلۡقَمَرُ ١

2. But if they see
A Sign, they turn away,
And say, "This is
(But) transient magic."[5129]

وَإِن يَرَوۡاْ ءَايَةً يُعۡرِضُواْ
وَيَقُولُواْ سِحۡرٌ مُّسۡتَمِرٌّ ٢

3. They reject (the warning)
And follow their (own) lusts
But every matter has[5130]
Its appointed time.

وَكَذَّبُواْ وَٱتَّبَعُوٓاْ أَهۡوَآءَهُمۡۚ
وَكُلُّ أَمۡرٍ مُّسۡتَقِرٌّ ٣

4. There have already come
To them Recitals wherein[5131]
There is (enough) to check (them),

وَلَقَدۡ جَآءَهُم مِّنَ ٱلۡأَنۢبَآءِ
مَا فِيهِ مُزۡدَجَرٌ ٤

5. Mature wisdom—but
(The preaching of) Warners
Profits them not.

حِكۡمَةُۢ بَٰلِغَةٞۖ فَمَا تُغۡنِ ٱلنُّذُرُ ٥

6. Therefore, (O Prophet)[5132]
Turn away from them.

فَتَوَلَّ عَنۡهُمۡۘ ٦

5127. See paragraph 2 of the Introduction to S. 53. The idea of the Judgement being nigh at the beginning of this Sūrah connects it with the same idea at the end of the last Sūrah (verse 57), though the actual words used in the two cases are different.

5128. Three explanations are given in the *Mufradāt*, and perhaps all three apply here: (1) that the moon once appeared cleft asunder in the valley of Makkah within sight of the Prophet, his Companions, and some Unbelievers; (2) that the prophetic past tense indicates the future, the cleaving asunder of the moon being a Sign of the Judgement approaching; and (3) that the phrase is metaphorical, meaning that the matter has become clear as the moon. That the first was noticed by contemporaries, including Unbelievers, is clear from verse 2. The second is an incident of the disruption of the solar system at the New Creation: *Cf.* 75:8-9. And the third might well be implied as in eastern allegory, based on the other two.

5129. *Mustamirr:* transient, or powerful: either meaning will apply. The Unbelievers acknowledge the unusual appearance, but call it magic. They do not therefore profit by the spiritual lesson.

5130. The prevalence of sin and the persecution of truth may have its day, but it must end at last.

5131. The stories of the sins of past generations having been visited with exemplary punishments were already in their possession, and should, if they had been wise, have opened their eyes and checked them in their mad career of sin. Five of these stories are again referred to later in this Sūrah by way of illustration.

5132. For a time godlessness seems to triumph, but the triumph is short-lived. And in any case there is the great Reckoning of the Day of Judgement.

The Day that the Caller[5133]
Will call (them)
To a terrible affair,

يَوْمَ يَدْعُ ٱلدَّاعِ إِلَىٰ شَيْءٍ نُّكُرٍ

7. They will come forth—
Their eyes humbled—
From (their) graves, (torpid)[5134]
Like locusts scattered abroad,

خُشَّعًا أَبْصَٰرُهُمْ يَخْرُجُونَ ﴿٧﴾
مِنَ ٱلْأَجْدَاثِ كَأَنَّهُمْ جَرَادٌ مُّنتَشِرٌ

8. Hastening, with eyes transfixed,
Towards the Caller!—
"Hard is this Day!"
The Unbelievers will say.

مُّهْطِعِينَ إِلَى ٱلدَّاعِ ﴿٨﴾
يَقُولُ ٱلْكَٰفِرُونَ هَٰذَا يَوْمٌ عَسِرٌ

9. Before them the People
Of Noah rejected (their
messenger):
They rejected Our servant,[5135]
And said, "Here is
One possessed!", and he
Was driven out.

كَذَّبَتْ قَبْلَهُمْ قَوْمُ نُوحٍ ﴿٩﴾
فَكَذَّبُوا۟ عَبْدَنَا وَقَالُوا۟
مَجْنُونٌ وَٱزْدُجِرَ

10. Then he called on his Lord:
"I am one overcome:
Do Thou then help (me)!"[5136]

فَدَعَا رَبَّهُۥٓ أَنِّى مَغْلُوبٌ فَٱنتَصِرْ ﴿١٠﴾

11. So We opened the gates
Of heaven, with water
Pouring forth.

فَفَتَحْنَآ أَبْوَٰبَ ٱلسَّمَآءِ بِمَآءٍ مُّنْهَمِرٍ ﴿١١﴾

12. And We caused the earth
To gush forth with springs.
So the waters met (and rose)[5137]
To the extent decreed.

وَفَجَّرْنَا ٱلْأَرْضَ عُيُونًا ﴿١٢﴾
فَٱلْتَقَى ٱلْمَآءُ عَلَىٰٓ أَمْرٍ قَدْ قُدِرَ

5133. The angel whose voice will call at the Resurrection and direct all souls. *Cf.* 20:108-111.

5134. At one stage in the invasion of locust swarms, the locusts are torpid and are scattered abroad all over the ground. I have seen them on railway tracks in 'Irāq, crushed to death in hundreds by passing trains. The simile is apt for the stunned beings who will rise up in swarms from their graves and say, 'Ah! woe unto us! who had raised us up?" (36:52).

5135. The story of Noah and the Flood is frequently referred to in the Qur'ān. The passage which best illustrates this passage will be found in 11:25-48. Note in that passage how they first insult and abuse him arrogantly; how he humbly argues with them; how they laugh him to scorn, as much as to say that he was a madman possessed of some evil spirit; and how the Flood comes and he is saved in the Ark, and the wicked are doomed to destruction.

5136. He did not call down punishment. He merely asked for help in his mission, as he felt himself overpowered by brute force and cast out, which prevented the fulfilment of his mission. But the wicked generation were past all repentance, and they were wiped out.

5137. The torrents of rain from above combined with the gush of waters from underground springs, and caused a huge Flood which inundated the country.

13. But We bore him
On an (Ark) made of
Broad planks and caulked[5138]
With palm-fibre:

وَحَمَلْنَٰهُ عَلَىٰ ذَاتِ أَلْوَٰحٍ وَدُسُرٍ ﴿١٣﴾

14. She floats under Our eyes
(And care): a recompense[5139]
To one who had been
Rejected (with scorn)!

تَجْرِى بِأَعْيُنِنَا جَزَآءً لِّمَن كَانَ كُفِرَ ﴿١٤﴾

15. And We have left
This as a Sign[5140]
(For all time): then
Is there any that will
Receive admonition?[5141]

وَلَقَد تَّرَكْنَٰهَآ ءَايَةً فَهَلْ مِن مُّدَّكِرٍ ﴿١٥﴾

16. But how (terrible) was[5142]
My Penalty and My Warning?

فَكَيْفَ كَانَ عَذَابِى وَنُذُرِ ﴿١٦﴾

17. And We have indeed
Made the Qur'ān easy[5143]
To understand and remember:
Then is there any that
Will receive admonition?

وَلَقَدْ يَسَّرْنَا ٱلْقُرْءَانَ لِلذِّكْرِ فَهَلْ مِن مُّدَّكِرٍ ﴿١٧﴾

18. The 'Ād (people) (too)
Rejected (Truth): then
How terrible was
My Penalty and My Warning?

كَذَّبَتْ عَادٌ فَكَيْفَ كَانَ عَذَابِى وَنُذُرِ ﴿١٨﴾

19. For We sent against them[5144]

إِنَّآ أَرْسَلْنَا عَلَيْهِمْ ﴿١٩﴾

5138. *Dusur,* plural of *disār,* which means the palm fibre with which boats are caulked: from *dasara,* to ram in, to spear. A derived meaning is "nails", (which are driven into planks): this latter meaning also applies, and is preferred by translators not familiar with the construction of simple boats.

5139. As usual, Allah's Mercy in saving His faithful servants takes precedence of His Wrath and Penalty. And He helps and rewards those whom the world rejects and despises!

5140. *Cf.* 29:15, where the Ark (with the salvation it brought to the righteous) is mentioned as a Sign for all Peoples. So also in 25:37 and 26:121, it is a Sign for men. Similarly the saving of Lot, with the destruction of the wicked Cities of the Plain, is mentioned as a Sign left for those who would understand: 29, 35, and 51:37.

5141. A refrain that occurs six times in this Sūrah: see Introduction.

5142. While the Mercy of Allah is always prominently mentioned, we must not forget or minimise the existence of Evil, and the terrible Penalty it incurs if the Grace of Allah and His Warning are deliberately rejected.

5143. While the Qur'ān sums up the highest philosophy of the inner life, its simple directions for conduct are plain and easy to understand and act upon. Is this not in itself a part of the Grace of Allah? And what excuse is there for anyone to fail in receiving admonition?

5144. *Cf.* 41:16. How graphic is the description of the tornado that uprooted them! It must indeed be a dreadful tornado that plucks up the palm trees by their tap-roots. The "Day" is an indefinite period of time. The wind that destroyed the 'Ād people lasted seven nights and eight days: 69:7.

A furious wind, on a Day
Of violent Disaster,

رِيحًا صَرْصَرًا فِي يَوْمِ نَحْسٍ مُّسْتَمِرٍّ

20. Plucking out men as if
They were roots of palm-trees
Torn up (from the ground).

تَنزِعُ النَّاسَ كَأَنَّهُمْ أَعْجَازُ نَخْلٍ مُّنقَعِرٍ ٢٠

21. Yea, how (terrible) was
My Penalty and My Warning![5145]

فَكَيْفَ كَانَ عَذَابِي وَنُذُرِ ٢١

22. But We have indeed
Made the Qur'ān easy
To understand and remember:
Then is there any that
Will receive admonition?

وَلَقَدْ يَسَّرْنَا الْقُرْآنَ لِلذِّكْرِ فَهَلْ مِن مُّدَّكِرٍ ٢٢

SECTION 2.

23. The Thamūd (also)
Rejected (their) Warners.

كَذَّبَتْ ثَمُودُ بِالنُّذُرِ ٢٣

24. For they said: "What![5146]
A man! A solitary one
From among ourselves!
Shall we follow such a one?[5147]
Truly should we then be
Straying in mind, and mad!

فَقَالُوا أَبَشَرًا مِّنَّا وَاحِدًا نَّتَّبِعُهُ إِنَّا إِذًا لَّفِي ضَلَالٍ وَسُعُرٍ ٢٤

25. "Is it that the Message
Is sent to *him*,
Of all people amongst us?
Nay, he is a liar
An insolent one!"[5148]

أَأُلْقِيَ الذِّكْرُ عَلَيْهِ مِن بَيْنِنَا بَلْ هُوَ كَذَّابٌ أَشِرٌ ٢٥

26. Ah! they will know
On the morrow, which is
The liar, the insolent one!

سَيَعْلَمُونَ غَدًا مَّنِ الْكَذَّابُ الْأَشِرُ ٢٦

5145. Repeated from verse 18 to heighten the description of the sin, the penalty, and the criminal negligence of the sinners in refusing the warnings on account of their self-complacent confidence in their own strength and stability! It is repeated again as a secondary refrain in 54:30 and (with slight modification) in 54:32 and 39.

5146. The psychology of the Thamūd is more searchingly analysed here than in 41:17, to show up the contrast between shallow men's ideas about Revelation, and the real sanity, humanism, social value, and truth of Revelation. To them the Revelation was brought by Ṣāliḥ.

5147. Because the Preacher is one among so many, and different from them, although brought up among themselves, it is made a cause of reproach against him, when it should have been an index leading to a searching of their hearts and an examination of their ways.

5148. Pure abuse, as a contrast to Ṣāliḥ's expostulation! See 26:141-158, and notes.

27. For We will send
The she-camel[5149]
By way of trial for them.
So watch them, (O Ṣāliḥ),
And possess thyself in patience!

إِنَّا مُرۡسِلُواْ ٱلنَّاقَةِ (٢٧)
فِتۡنَةٗ لَّهُمۡ فَٱرۡتَقِبۡهُمۡ وَٱصۡطَبِرۡ

28. And tell them that
The water is to be
Divided between them:[5150]
Each one's right to drink
Being brought forward
(By suitable turns).

وَنَبِّئۡهُمۡ أَنَّ (٢٨)
ٱلۡمَآءَ قِسۡمَةُۢ بَيۡنَهُمۡۖ
كُلُّ شِرۡبٖ مُّحۡتَضَرٞ

29. But they called
To their companion,
And he took a sword
In hand, and hamstrung (her).

فَنَادَوۡاْ صَاحِبَهُمۡ (٢٩)
فَتَعَاطَىٰ فَعَقَرَ

30. Ah! how (terrible) was
My Penalty and My Warning!

فَكَيۡفَ كَانَ عَذَابِي وَنُذُرِ (٣٠)

31. For We sent against them[5151]
A single Mighty Blast,
And they became
Like the dry stubble used
By one who pens cattle.[5152]

إِنَّآ أَرۡسَلۡنَا عَلَيۡهِمۡ صَيۡحَةٗ وَٰحِدَةٗ (٣١)
فَكَانُواْ كَهَشِيمِ ٱلۡمُحۡتَظِرِ

32. And We have indeed
Made the Qur'ān easy
To understand and remember:
Then is there any that
Will receive admonition?

وَلَقَدۡ يَسَّرۡنَا ٱلۡقُرۡءَانَ (٣٢)
لِلذِّكۡرِ فَهَلۡ مِن مُّدَّكِرٖ

33. The People of Lūṭ[5153]
Rejected (his) Warning.

كَذَّبَتۡ قَوۡمُ لُوطِۭ بِٱلنُّذُرِ (٣٣)

34. We sent against them
A violent tornado

إِنَّآ أَرۡسَلۡنَا عَلَيۡهِمۡ حَاصِبًا (٣٤)

5149. See n. 1044 to 7:73, for the she-camel as a trial or test among selfish people who tried to monopolise water and pasture as against the poor.

5150. See 26:155-56. All were to have water in due turn. It was to be no one's monopoly. And certainly the gates were not to be shut against the poor or their cattle.

5151. See n. 1047 to 7:78, and *Cf.* the same phrase "single Blast" used for the signal for the Resurrection in 36:53. In the case of the Thamūd, the destruction seems to have been by a severe earthquake accompanied with a terrible rumbling noise.

5152. They became like dry sticks such as are used by herdsmen in making pens or enclosures for their cattle.

5153. The story of Lot (Lūṭ) and the Cities of the Plain has been frequently referred to. See 11:74-83.

With showers of stones,[5154]
(Which destroyed them), except
Lūṭ's household: them We
Delivered by early Dawn—

إِلَّآ ءَالَ لُوطٍ
نَّجَّيْنَٰهُم بِسَحَرٍ

35. As a Grace from Us:
Thus do We reward
Those who give thanks.[5155]

٣٥ نِّعْمَةً مِّنْ عِندِنَا
كَذَٰلِكَ نَجْزِى مَن شَكَرَ

36. And (Lūṭ) did warn them[5156]
Of Our Punishment, but
They disputed about the
Warning.

٣٦ وَلَقَدْ أَنذَرَهُم بَطْشَتَنَا
فَتَمَارَوْا بِالنُّذُرِ

37. And they even sought
To snatch away his guests[5157]
From him, but We blinded
Their eyes. (They heard:)
"Now taste ye My Wrath
And My Warning."

٣٧ وَلَقَدْ رَٰوَدُوهُ عَن ضَيْفِهِۦ
فَطَمَسْنَآ أَعْيُنَهُمْ فَذُوقُوا
عَذَابِى وَنُذُرِ

38. Early on the morrow
An abiding Punishment
Seized them:

٣٨ وَلَقَدْ صَبَّحَهُم بُكْرَةً
عَذَابٌ مُّسْتَقِرٌّ

39. "So taste ye My Wrath
And My Warning."

٣٩ فَذُوقُوا عَذَابِى وَنُذُرِ

40. And We have indeed
Made the Qur'ān easy
To understand and remember:
Then is there any that
Will receive admonition?

٤٠ وَلَقَدْ يَسَّرْنَا الْقُرْءَانَ لِلذِّكْرِ
فَهَلْ مِن مُّدَّكِرٍ

5154. *Ḥāṣib:* a violent tornado bringing a shower of stones. The word occurs here; in 17:68 (without reference to any particular place); in 29:40 (where it seems to refer to Lot's Cities, see n. 3462); and in 67:17 (where again there is no reference to a particular place). In Lot's Cities the shower was of brimstone: see 11:82.

5155. "Giving thanks" to Allah in Quranic phrase is to obey Allah's Law, to do His Will, to practise righteousness, to use all gifts in His service.

5156. *Cf.* 11:78-79.

5157. Lot had been preaching to them some time against their iniquities. The crisis of their fate came when the two angels came to Lot in the guise of handsome young men. The men of the whole City came in an uproar, assaulted his house, and tried to snatch away the two handsome men. Lot tried to prevent them, but was powerless. Darkness fell on their eyes, as the first stage in their punishment, and before next morning the wicked cities were buried under a shower of brimstone. Lot and his believing household were saved.

SECTION 3.

41. To the People[5158]
Of Pharaoh, too, aforetime,
Came Warners (from Allah).

وَلَقَدْ جَآءَ ءَالَ فِرْعَوْنَ ٱلنُّذُرُ ﴿٤١﴾

42. The (people) rejected all
Our Signs; but We
Seized them with such Penalty
(As comes) from One
Exalted in Power,
Able to carry out His Will.

كَذَّبُوا۟ بِـَٔايَـٰتِنَا كُلِّهَا فَأَخَذْنَـٰهُمْ أَخْذَ عَزِيزٍ مُّقْتَدِرٍ ﴿٤٢﴾

43. Are your Unbelievers,
(O Quraysh), better than they?[5159]
Or have ye an immunity
In the Sacred Books?

أَكُفَّارُكُمْ خَيْرٌ مِّنْ أُو۟لَـٰٓئِكُمْ أَمْ لَكُم بَرَآءَةٌ فِى ٱلزُّبُرِ ﴿٤٣﴾

44. Or do they say:
"We acting together
Can defend ourselves"?

أَمْ يَقُولُونَ نَحْنُ جَمِيعٌ مُّنتَصِرٌ ﴿٤٤﴾

45. Soon will their multitude
Be put to flight,
And they will show
Their backs.

سَيُهْزَمُ ٱلْجَمْعُ وَيُوَلُّونَ ٱلدُّبُرَ ﴿٤٥﴾

46. Nay, the Hour (of Judgement)
Is the time promised them
(For their full recompense):[5160]
And that Hour will be
Most grievous and most bitter.

بَلِ ٱلسَّاعَةُ مَوْعِدُهُمْ وَٱلسَّاعَةُ أَدْهَىٰ وَأَمَرُّ ﴿٤٦﴾

5158. The Egyptian people of old are the last people mentioned in this Sūrah as an example of iniquity meeting with punishment. And the moral is driven home to the Pagan Quraysh, to warn them of their fate if they persisted in their evil lives. The Egyptians had many Signs given them. They were gifted people and had made much progress in the sciences and the arts. They could have learnt from history that when the highest virtues disappear, the nation must fall. Moses was brought up among them and commissioned to give Allah's Message to them. But they were arrogant; they were unjust to Allah's creatures; they followed debasing forms of worship; they mocked at Truth; and were at last punished with destruction in the Red Sea for their arrogant leaders and army. See 10:75-90 for a narrative.

5159. If the Egyptains with all their power and science were unable to resist the punishment of their sins, the Pagan Quraysh are asked: how will you fare when you come to a trial of strength against Allah's Truth? You are not specially favoured so as to be immune from Allah's Law. And if you rely on your numbers, they will be a broken reed when the trial comes, as indeed happened at the Battle of Badr.

5160. The calculations of unjust men—on their science, their resources, their numbers, etc.—will in many cases be falsified even in this world, as stated in the last two verses, but their real Punishment will come with Judgement, *i.e.*, when they find their real place in the spiritual world at the restoration of true values. It will then be a most grievous and bitter experience for them, throwing into the shade any calamities they may suffer in this life.

47. Truly those in sin
Are the ones
Straying in mind, and mad.[5161]

إِنَّ ٱلْمُجْرِمِينَ فِي ضَلَٰلٍ وَسُعُرٍ ﴿٤٧﴾

48. The Day they will be
Dragged through the Fire
On their faces,[5162] (they
Will hear:) "Taste ye
The touch of Hell!"

يَوْمَ يُسْحَبُونَ فِي ٱلنَّارِ عَلَىٰ وُجُوهِهِمْ ذُوقُوا۟ مَسَّ سَقَرَ ﴿٤٨﴾

49. Verily, all things
Have We created
In proportion and measure.[5163]

إِنَّا كُلَّ شَيْءٍ خَلَقْنَٰهُ بِقَدَرٍ ﴿٤٩﴾

50. And Our Command
Is but a single (Act)—[5164]
Like the twinkling
Of an eye.

وَمَآ أَمْرُنَآ إِلَّا وَٰحِدَةٌ كَلَمْحٍۭ بِٱلْبَصَرِ ﴿٥٠﴾

51. And (oft) in the past,
Have We destroyed gangs[5165]
Like unto you: then

وَلَقَدْ أَهْلَكْنَآ أَشْيَاعَكُمْ ﴿٥١﴾

5161. *Cf.* liv. 24 above. Note how the tables are turned in the argument by the repetition. The unjust think that the godly are wandering in mind and mad. They will find that it is really they who were wandering in mind, and mad, even when they were in the plenitude of their power and in the enjoyment of all the good things of this life. These minor echoes heighten the effect of the major refrain mentioned in the Introduction.

5162. *On their faces:* the Face is the symbol of Personality. Their whole Personality will be subverted and degraded—in the midst of the Fire of Suffering.

5163. Allah's Creation is not haphazard. Everything goes by law, proportion, and measure. Everything has its appointed time, place, and occasion, as also its definite limitation. Nothing happens but according to His Plan, and every deed, word, and thought of man has its fullest consequences, except insofar as the Grace and Mercy of Allah intervenes, and that is according to law and plan.

5164. While in the life of created things there is "proportion and measure", and a lag of time or distance or circumstance, in Allah's Command, the Design, the Word, the Execution, and the Consequences are but a single Act. The simile given is that of the twinkling of an eye, which is the shortest time that a simple man can think of: the cause which occasions the twinkling, the movement of the muscles connected with it, the closing of the eyelids, and their reopening, are all almost like a simultaneous act. By way of contrast take an illustration life that of a man writing a book. He must form the design in his mind; he must prepare himself by research, collection of knowledge, or of personal experience; he must use or acquire the art of writing; he must collect the material for writing, *viz.*, paper, ink, pen, etc., and this will connect with a chain of manufacturing processes in which he is dependent upon other people's work and experience; then his book may have to be printed or lithographed or bound, and sold, or taken to a library, or presented to a friend, which will bring into play numerous other chains of proceses, and dependence upon other people's work or skill; and the lag of Time, Space, and Circumstance will occur at numerous stages. In Allah's Command, the word "Be" *(kun)* includes everything, without the intervention, of or dependence upon any other being or thing whatever. And this is also another phase of the philosophy of Unity.

5165. *Ashyā'akum:* 'gangs or parties or collection of men like you'—addressed to wicked men who arrogantly rely upon their own strength or combination, neither of which can stand for a moment against the Will of Allah.

Is there any that
Will receive admonition?[5166]

فَهَلْ مِن مُّدَّكِرٍ

52. All that they do
Is noted in (their)
Books (of Deeds):[5167]

وَكُلُّ شَيْءٍ فَعَلُوهُ فِي الزُّبُرِ ﴿٥٢﴾

53. Every matter, small and great,
Is a record.

وَكُلُّ صَغِيرٍ وَكَبِيرٍ مُّسْتَطَرٌ ﴿٥٣﴾

54. As to the Righteous,
They will be in the midst
Of Gardens and Rivers,[5168]

إِنَّ الْمُتَّقِينَ فِي جَنَّاتٍ وَنَهَرٍ ﴿٥٤﴾

55. In an Assembly to Truth,[5169]
In the Presence of[5170]
A Sovereign Omnipotent.[5171]

فِي مَقْعَدِ صِدْقٍ عِندَ مَلِيكٍ مُّقْتَدِرٍ ﴿٥٥﴾

5166. The cases of Pharaoh's men of old and the Pagan Quraysh are considered as parallel, and an appeal is addressed to the latter from the experience of the former: 'will ye not learn and repent?'

5167. The point is that nothing which men do is lost—good or evil. Everything gives rise to an inevitable chain of consequences, from which a release is only obtained by the intervention of Allah's Grace acting on an act, a striving of the human will to repent and turn to Allah. (R).

5168. The record, in the case of those who dishonoured and violated Truth, will lead to their undoing; but in the case of those who honoured the Truth and adopted it so as to shine in their righteous lives, the result is expressed by four metaphors, in an ascending degree of sublimity: (1) they will be in the midst of Gardens where rivers flow; (2) they will be in an Assembly of Truth; (3) in the Presence of Allah; (4) Whose sovereignty is omnipotent.

"Gardens" with Rivers (flowing beneath): this has been explained more than once already: *Cf.* n. 4668 to 43:70. The Garden suggests all the Bliss we can imagine through our senses. (R).

5169. While we possess our bodily senses, the best conceptions we can form are through our sense-perceptions, and the Garden is a good symbol from that point of view. The next higher understanding of spiritual truth is through our intellect and social satisfaction. This is best symbolised by the Assembly of Truth—the gathering in which we sit with our fellows and enjoy the realisation of Truth and the dissipation of falsehoods and half-truths.

5170. But there is a higher conception still, something so intensely spiritual that it can only be expressed by reference to the Presence of Allah. (R).

5171. *Muqtadir,* which is translated Omnipotent, implies something more: the eighth-declension form denotes not only complete mastery, but the further idea that the mastery arises form Allah's own nature, and depends on nothing else whatever. (R).

INTRODUCTION TO SŪRAH 55—*AL RAḤMĀN*

The majority of Commentators consider this an early Makkan Sūrah, though some consider at least a part of it as dating from Madīnah. The greater part of it is undoubtedly early Makkan.

It is highly poetical and most sublime, and the refrain "Then which of the favours of your Lord will ye deny?" is interspersed 31 times among its 78 verses. (R).

It is the sixth of the series of seven dealing with Revelation, the favours of Allah, and the Hereafter: see Introduction to S. 1.

Here the special theme is indicated by the refrain. The rhyme in most cases is in the Dual grammatical form, and the Argument implies that though things are created in pairs, there is an underlying Unity, through the Creator, in the favours which He bestows, and in the goal to which they are marching.

Summary—Allah Most Gracious has sent Revelation, one of His greatest favours to man; His creation is in pairs, well-balanced; all created things receive His favours, but they will all pass away, and only Allah will endure through the ages (55:1-34, and C. 232).

Ultimately all evil shall return to its destination, as well as all Good, but ever blessed is the name of Allah, Lord of Glory, Honour and Bounty (55:35-78, and C. 233).

C. 232.—Allah's creatures! Which favours of Allah will ye deny?
(55:1-34.) Most Gracious is Allah, Who reveals Himself
In the Qur'ān, in man's Intelligence,
And in the nature around man.
Balance and Justice, Goodness and Care,
Are the Laws of His Worlds. Created
From clay, man can yet comprehend
The Lord of the Easts and the Wests, Him
Who sustains all His creatures, Him
Who bestows the Jewels of Life and Faith,
Him Who abides when all else perisheth,
Him Whose Eternity is the Hope
Of man's Future, the Lord Everlasting
Of Justice and Glory and Bounty and Honour!
Which, then, of the favours of your Lord will ye deny?

Sūrah 55.

Al Raḥmān (The Most Gracious)

In the name of Allah, Most Gracious, Most Merciful.

بِسْمِ ٱللَّهِ ٱلرَّحْمَٰنِ ٱلرَّحِيمِ

1. (Allah) Most Gracious!

ٱلرَّحْمَٰنُ ١

2. It is He Who has[5172]
Taught the Qur'ān.

عَلَّمَ ٱلْقُرْءَانَ ٢

3. He has created man:

خَلَقَ ٱلْإِنسَٰنَ ٣

4. He has taught him speech[5173]
(And Intelligence).

عَلَّمَهُ ٱلْبَيَانَ ٤

5. The sun and the moon
Follow courses (exactly)
computed;[5174]

ٱلشَّمْسُ وَٱلْقَمَرُ بِحُسْبَانٍ ٥

6. And the herbs[5175] and the trees—
Both (alike) bow in adoration.[5176]

وَٱلنَّجْمُ وَٱلشَّجَرُ يَسْجُدَانِ ٦

7. And the Firmament has He
Raised high, and He has set up
The Balance (of Justice),[5177]

وَٱلسَّمَآءَ رَفَعَهَا وَوَضَعَ ٱلْمِيزَانَ ٧

8. In order that ye may
Not transgress (due) balance.

أَلَّا تَطْغَوْا۟ فِى ٱلْمِيزَانِ ٨

5172. The Revelation comes from Allah Most Gracious, and it is one of the greatest Signs of His grace and favour. He is the source of all Light, and His light is diffused throughout the universe.

5173. *Bayān:* intelligent speech: power of expression: capacity to understand clearly the relation of things and to explain them. Allah has given this to man, and besides this revelation in man's own heart, has aided him with revelation in nature and revelation through prophets and messengers.

5174. In the great astronomical universe there are exact mathematical laws, which bear witness to Allah's Wisdom and also to His favours to His creatures; for we all profit by the heat and light, the seasons, and the numerous changes in the tides and the atmosphere, on which the constitution of our globe and the maintenance of life depend.

5175. *Najm:* may mean stars collectively, or herbs collectively; perhaps both meanings are implied.

5176. All nature adores Allah. *Cf.* 22:18, and n. 2790; 13:15; and 16:48-49.

5177. The "balance of justice" in this verse is connected with "the Balance" in the next two verses, that men may act justly to each other and observe due balance in all their actions, following the golden mean and not transgressing due bounds in anything. But the Balance is also connected figuratively with the heavens above in three symbols: (1) Justice is a heavenly virtue; (2) the heavens themselves are sustained by mathematical balance; and (3) the constellation Libra (the Balance) is entered by the sun at the middle of the zodiacal year.

9. So establish weight with justice[5178]
And fall not short
In the balance.

٩ وَأَقِيمُوا۟ ٱلْوَزْنَ بِٱلْقِسْطِ
وَلَا تُخْسِرُوا۟ ٱلْمِيزَانَ

10. It is He Who has
Spread out the earth[5179]
For (His) creatures:

١٠ وَٱلْأَرْضَ وَضَعَهَا لِلْأَنَامِ

11. Therein is fruit
And date palms, producing
Spathes (enclosing dates):

١١ فِيهَا فَٰكِهَةٌ وَٱلنَّخْلُ ذَاتُ ٱلْأَكْمَامِ

12. Also corn, with (its)
Leaves and stalk for fodder,
And sweet-smelling plants.

١٢ وَٱلْحَبُّ ذُو ٱلْعَصْفِ وَٱلرَّيْحَانُ

13. Then which of the favours[5180]
Of your Lord will ye deny?

١٣ فَبِأَىِّ ءَالَآءِ رَبِّكُمَا تُكَذِّبَانِ

14. He created man
From sounding clay[5181]
Like unto pottery,

١٤ خَلَقَ ٱلْإِنسَٰنَ مِن
صَلْصَٰلٍ كَٱلْفَخَّارِ

15. And He created Jinns[5182]
From fire free of smoke:

١٥ وَخَلَقَ ٱلْجَآنَّ مِن مَّارِجٍ مِّن نَّارٍ

5178. To be taken both literally and figuratively. A man should be honest and straight in every daily matter, such as weighing out things which he is selling: and he should be straight, just and honest, in all the highest dealings, not only with other people, but with himself and in his obedience to Allah's Law. Not many do either the one or the other when they have an opportunity of deceit. Justice is the central virtue, and the aviodance of both excess and defect in conduct keeps the human world balanced just as the heavenly world is kept balanced by mathematical order.

5179. How can Allah's favours be counted? Look at the earth alone. Life and the conditions here are mutually balanced for Allah's creatures. The vegetable world produces fruit of various kinds and corn or grain of various kinds for human food. The grain harvest yields with it fodder for animals in the shape of leaves and straw, as well as food for men in the shape of grain. The plants not only supply food but sweet-smelling herbs and flowers. *Rayḥān* is the sweet basil, but is here used in the generic sense, for agreeable produce in the vegetable world, to match the useful produce already mentioned.

5180. Both the pronoun "your" and the verb "will ye deny" are in the Arabic in the Dual Number. The whole Sūrah is a symphony of Duality, which leads up to Unity, as explained in the Introduction. All creation is in pairs: 51:49, and notes 5025-26; 36:36, n. 3981. Justice is the conciliation of two opposites to unity, the settlement of the unending feud between Right and Wrong. The things and concepts mentioned in this Sūrah are in pairs: man and outer nature; sun and moon; herbs and trees; heavens and earth; fruit and corn; human food and fodder for cattle; things nourishing and things sweet-smelling; and so on throughout the Sūrah. Then there is man and Jinn, for which see n. 5182 below.

Will ye deny? that is, fail to acknowledge either in word or thought or in your conduct. If you misuse Allah's gifts or ignore them, that is equivalent to ingratitude or denial or refusal to profit by Allah's infinite Grace.

5181. See n. 1966 to 15:26. The creation of men and Jinns is contrasted. Man was made of sounding clay, dry and brittle like pottery. The Jinn (see next note) was made from a clear flame of fire. Yet each has capacities and possibilities which only Allah's Grace bestows on them. How can they deny Allah's favours?

5182. For the meaning of Jinn. see n. 929 to 6:100. They are spirits, and therefore subtle like a flame of fire. Their being free from smoke implies that they are free from grossness, for smoke is the grosser accompaniment of fire. (R).

16. Then which of the favours
Of your Lord will ye deny?[5183]

فَبِأَيِّ ءَالَآءِ رَبِّكُمَا تُكَذِّبَانِ ﴿١٦﴾

17. (He is) Lord
Of the two Easts[5184]
And Lord
Of the two Wests:

رَبُّ ٱلْمَشْرِقَيْنِ وَرَبُّ ٱلْمَغْرِبَيْنِ ﴿١٧﴾

18. Then which of the favours
Of your Lord will ye deny?

فَبِأَيِّ ءَالَآءِ رَبِّكُمَا تُكَذِّبَانِ ﴿١٨﴾

19. He has let free[5185]
The two bodies
Of flowing water,
Meeting together:

مَرَجَ ٱلْبَحْرَيْنِ يَلْتَقِيَانِ ﴿١٩﴾

20. Between them is a Barrier
Which they do not transgress:

بَيْنَهُمَا بَرْزَخٌ لَّا يَبْغِيَانِ ﴿٢٠﴾

21. Then which of the favours
Of your Lord will ye deny?

فَبِأَيِّ ءَالَآءِ رَبِّكُمَا تُكَذِّبَانِ ﴿٢١﴾

22. Out of them come
Pearls and Coral:[5186]

يَخْرُجُ مِنْهُمَا ٱللُّؤْلُؤُ وَٱلْمَرْجَانُ ﴿٢٢﴾

23. Then which of the favours
Of your Lord will ye deny?

فَبِأَيِّ ءَالَآءِ رَبِّكُمَا تُكَذِّبَانِ ﴿٢٣﴾

5183. Part of the idea of this refrain will be found in 16:71, 72; 40:81: and 53:55 (where see n. 5122).

5184. *The two Easts* are the two extreme points where the sun rises during the year, and includes all the points between. Similarly the two Wests include the two extreme points of the sun's setting and all the points between. The Dual Number fits in with the general atmosphere of Duality in this Sūrah. Allah is Lord of every region of the earth and sky, and He scatters His bounties everywhere. See also n. 4641 to 43:38, and n. 4034 to 37:5.

5185. See 25:53. and n. 3111, where it is explained how the two bodies of water, salt and sweet, meet together, yet keep separate, as if there was a barrier or partition between them. This is also one of the favours of Allah. Sea water is a sanitating agent, while fresh water is sweet and palatable to drink. For the allegorical interpretation, see notes 2404-5 to 18:60; also n. 5186 (end) below.

5186. Pearls are produced by the oyster and coral by the polyp, a minute marine creature which, working in millions, has by its secretions produced the reefs, islands, and banks in and on both sides of the Red Sea and in other parts of the world. The pearl has a translucent lustre, usually white, but sometimes pink or black. Coral is usually opaque, red or pink, but often white, and is seen in beautiful branching or cup-like shapes as visitors to Port Sudan will recall. Both are used as gems and stand here for gems generally. Mineral gems, such as agate and cornelian, are found in river-beds. Pearl oysters are also found in some rivers.

Taken allegorically, the two kinds of gems would denote the jewels of this life and the jewels of the spiritual world. The jewels of this world—like coral—are hard, widely spread over the world, comparatively cheap, and less absorptive of the light from above. The spiritual jewels—like pearls—are soft, rare, costly, and translucent, absorbent of light and showing the more lustre the more they are in light. The analogy can be carried further to the two seas—the two bodies of flowing water—mentioned in verses 19-20 above. They are the two kinds of knowledge—human and divine—referred to in the story of Moses and Khiḍr: see notes 2404-5 to 18:60..

24. And His are the Ships[5187]
Sailing smoothly through the seas,
Lofty as mountains:[5188]

٢٤ وَلَهُ ٱلْجَوَارِ ٱلْمُنشَـَٔاتُ فِى ٱلْبَحْرِ كَٱلْأَعْلَـٰمِ

25. Then which of the favours
Of your Lord will ye deny?

٢٥ فَبِأَىِّ ءَالَآءِ رَبِّكُمَا تُكَذِّبَانِ

SECTION 2.

26. All that is on earth
Will perish:

٢٦ كُلُّ مَنْ عَلَيْهَا فَانٍ

27. But will abide (forever)
The Face of thy Lord—[5189]
Full of Majesty,
Bounty and Honour.[5190]

٢٧ وَيَبْقَىٰ وَجْهُ رَبِّكَ
ذُو ٱلْجَلَـٰلِ وَٱلْإِكْرَامِ

28. Then which of the favours
Of your Lord will ye deny?

٢٨ فَبِأَىِّ ءَالَآءِ رَبِّكُمَا تُكَذِّبَانِ

29. Of Him seeks (its need)[5191]
Every creature in the heavens
And on earth:
Every day in (new) Splendour[5192]
Doth He (shine)!

٢٩ يَسْـَٔلُهُۥ مَن فِى ٱلسَّمَـٰوَٰتِ وَٱلْأَرْضِ
كُلَّ يَوْمٍ هُوَ فِى شَأْنٍ

30. Then which of the favours
Of your Lord will ye deny?

٣٠ فَبِأَىِّ ءَالَآءِ رَبِّكُمَا تُكَذِّبَانِ

5187. The Ships—sailing ships and steamers, and by extension of the analogy, aeroplanes and airships majestically navigating the air—are made by man, but the intelligence and science which made them possible are given by man's Creator; and therefore the Ships also are the gifts of Allah.

5188. *Lofty as mountains:* both in respect of the high sails, or masts, and in respect of the height to which the top of the ship towers above the surface of the sea. The 'Queen Mary'—the biggest ship afloat in 1936—has a height, from the keel to the top of the superstructure, of 135 ft. and from keel to the masthead, of 234 ft.

5189. The most magnificent works of man—such as they are—are but fleeting. Ships, Empires, the Wonders of Science and Art, the splendours of human glory or intellect, will all pass away. The most magnificent objects in outer Nature—the mountains and valleys, the sun and moon, the Constellation Orion and the star Sirius—will also pass away in their appointed time. But the only One that will endure forever is the "Face" of Allah. "Face" expresses Personality, Glory, Majesty, Inner Being, Essence, Self—all the noble qualities which we associate with the Beautiful Names of Allah. See n. 114 to 2:112; also n. 1154 to 7:180, and n. 2322 to 17:110.

5190. *Ikrām:* two ideas are prominent in the word. (1) the idea of generosity, as proceeding from the person whose attribute it is, and (2) the idea of honour, as given by others to the person whose attribute it is. Both these ideas are summed up in "nobility". To make the meaning quite clear, I have employed in the translation the two words "Bounty and Honour" for the single word *Ikrām*. The same attributes recur in the last verse of this Sūrah. In the Fact of Allah's Eternity is the Hope of our Future.

5191. Every single creature depends on Allah for its needs: of all of them the Cherisher and Sustainer is Allah. *Seek (its needs):* does not necessarily mean 'seek them in words': what is meant is the dependence: the allusion is to the Source of supply.

5192. *Sha'n:* state, splendour; aim, work, business, momentous affair. Allah's is still the directing hand in all affairs. He does not sit apart, careless of mankind or of any of His creatures. But His working shows new Splendour every day, every hour, every moment.

31. Soon shall We
Settle your affairs,
O both ye worlds![5193]

سَنَفْرُغُ لَكُمْ أَيُّهَ ٱلثَّقَلَانِ ﴿٣١﴾

32. Then which of the favours
Of your Lord will ye deny?

فَبِأَيِّ ءَالَآءِ رَبِّكُمَا تُكَذِّبَانِ ﴿٣٢﴾

33. O ye assembly of Jinns[5194]
And men! If it be
Ye can pass beyond
The zones of the heavens
And the earth, pass ye!
Not without authority
Shall ye be able to pass!

يَٰمَعْشَرَ ٱلْجِنِّ وَٱلْإِنسِ إِنِ ٱسْتَطَعْتُمْ أَن تَنفُذُوا۟ مِنْ أَقْطَارِ ٱلسَّمَٰوَٰتِ وَٱلْأَرْضِ فَٱنفُذُوا۟ ۚ لَا تَنفُذُونَ إِلَّا بِسُلْطَٰنٍ ﴿٣٣﴾

34. Then which of the favours[5195]
Of your Lord will ye deny?

فَبِأَيِّ ءَالَآءِ رَبِّكُمَا تُكَذِّبَانِ ﴿٣٤﴾

C. 233.—Let not Evil think that it will escape
(55:35-78.) Justice: its telltale Mark is on those
Who follow it, and it must meet its Reward
In the final adjustment. But the Good,
The Righteous, must reach their Fulfilment
In the Gardens of Bliss, where every Delight
Will be theirs in Beauty and Dignity.
How can such Delights be pictured in words?
In symbols subjective let each take his choice.
For Good can there ever be any Reward
Other than Good? Beautiful sights
And sounds, delicious fruits to nourish
The soul, and Companionship where Grace
Is mingled with Love, may figure forth our Bliss.

5193. *Thaqal:* weight, something weighty, something weighed with something else. The two *thaqals* are Jinns and men who are burdened with responsiblity or, as some commentators hold, with sin. They are both before Allah, and the affairs of both are conducted under His Command. If there are inequalities or apparent disturbances of balance, that is only for a season. Allah gives to both good and evil men a chance in this period of probation; but this period will soon be over, and Judgement will be established. To give you this chance, this probation, this warning, is itself a favour, by which you should profit, and for which you should be grateful. (R).

5194. *Cf.* 6:130, where the Jinns and men are addressed collectively. That whole passage, 6:130-134, should be read as a commentary on this verse. 'If you think that because you do things in secret, or because some of your sins do not *seem* to meet their inevitable punishment or some of your good deeds seem to go unnoticed, do not be deceived. Judgement will soon come. You cannot possibly escape out of the zones in which your lives have been cast, without authority from Allah. Be grateful to Allah for the chances He has given you'. All that hath been promised unto you will come to pass: nor can ye frustrate it in the least bit" (6:134).

5195. Note how gradually we have been led up in the Argument. 'The Signs of Allah are all about you, in revelation, in your intelligence, and in nature around you. Your creation; the mystic light and heat typified by the sun in all directions; the cycle of waters in the physical earth and of Knowledge in the world of Intelligence; the help and cherishing care of Allah Himself—all these things should teach you the Truth and warn you about the Future, which is more particularly referred to in the remainder of the Sūrah.

Blessed be Allah, full of Majesty and Bounty.
Allah's creatures! What favours of Allah will ye
deny?

35. On you will be sent
(O ye evil ones twain!)[5196]
A flame of fire (to burn)
And a smoke (to choke):[5197]
No defence will ye have:

يُرْسَلُ عَلَيْكُمَا شُوَاظٌ مِّن نَّارٍ وَنُحَاسٌ فَلَا تَنتَصِرَانِ ٣٥

36. Then which of the favours[5198]
Of your Lord will ye deny?

فَبِأَيِّ ءَالَآءِ رَبِّكُمَا تُكَذِّبَانِ ٣٦

37. When the sky is rent
Asunder, and it becomes red
Like ointment:[5199]

فَإِذَا ٱنشَقَّتِ ٱلسَّمَآءُ فَكَانَتْ وَرْدَةً كَٱلدِّهَانِ ٣٧

38. Then which of the favours
Of your Lord will ye deny?

فَبِأَيِّ ءَالَآءِ رَبِّكُمَا تُكَذِّبَانِ ٣٨

39. On that Day
No question will be asked[5200]
Of man or Jinn
As to his sin,

فَيَوْمَئِذٍ لَّا يُسْـَٔلُ عَن ذَنۢبِهِۦٓ إِنسٌ وَلَا جَآنٌّ ٣٩

40. Then which of the favours
Of your Lord will ye deny?

فَبِأَيِّ ءَالَآءِ رَبِّكُمَا تُكَذِّبَانِ ٤٠

41. (For) the sinners will be
Known by their Marks:[5201]
And they will be seized
By their forelocks and
Their feet.

يُعْرَفُ ٱلْمُجْرِمُونَ بِسِيمَٰهُمْ فَيُؤْخَذُ بِٱلنَّوَٰصِى وَٱلْأَقْدَامِ ٤١

5196. The Dual is with reference to the two worlds explained above in n. 5193.

5197. We now come to the terrors of the Judgement on the evil ones.

5198. Here and in some of the verses that follow, (verses 40, 42, and 45 below), the refrain applies with an ironical meaning. It is as if it was said: 'You used to laugh at Revelation, and at the warnings which were given for your own benefit in order to draw you to repentance and Allah's Mercy; what do you find now? Is not all that was said to you true?' To reject Allah's Law is in itself to deny Allah's Mercies.

5199. Melting away like grease or ointment. The red colour will be due to the flames and the heat. The whole of the world as we know it now will dissolve.

5200. This does not of course mean that they will not be called to account for their sin. They will certainly be called to account for all their deeds: 15:92. The meaning of this whole passage is that their personal responsibility will be enforced. But their own tongues and hands and feet will bear witness against them as to their actions: 24:24. Every man will bear marks on his person, showing his classification in the Final Account: 7:48. After these Marks are affixed, everyone's position and status in the Final Account will be known to everyone. As to the Judge on the Throne of Judgement. He will of course know all before Judgement is set up. But to give every chance to the accused, his record will be produced and shown to him (49:19,25; 18:49), and he will be given a chance to plead (7:53), but if a sinner, he will be in confusion (28:66).

5201. *By their Marks:* see last note.

42. Then which of the favours Of your Lord will ye deny?	﴿٤٢﴾ فَبِأَيِّ ءَالَآءِ رَبِّكُمَا تُكَذِّبَانِ
43. This is the Hell which The Sinners deny:[5202]	﴿٤٣﴾ هَٰذِهِۦ جَهَنَّمُ ٱلَّتِى يُكَذِّبُ بِهَا ٱلْمُجْرِمُونَ
44. In its midst And in the midst Of boiling hot water Will they wander round![5203]	﴿٤٤﴾ يَطُوفُونَ بَيْنَهَا وَبَيْنَ حَمِيمٍ ءَانٍ
45. Then which of the favours Of your Lord will ye deny?	﴿٤٥﴾ فَبِأَيِّ ءَالَآءِ رَبِّكُمَا تُكَذِّبَانِ

SECTION 3.

46. But for such as fear The time when they will Stand before (the Judgement Seat[5204] Of) their Lord, There will be two Gardens—[5205]	﴿٤٦﴾ وَلِمَنْ خَافَ مَقَامَ رَبِّهِۦ جَنَّتَانِ
47. Then which of the favours Of your Lord will ye deny?	﴿٤٧﴾ فَبِأَيِّ ءَالَآءِ رَبِّكُمَا تُكَذِّبَانِ
48. Containing all kinds (Of trees and delights)—	﴿٤٨﴾ ذَوَاتَآ أَفْنَانٍ
49. Then which of the favours Of your Lord will ye deny?	﴿٤٩﴾ فَبِأَيِّ ءَالَآءِ رَبِّكُمَا تُكَذِّبَانِ
50. In them (each) will be Two Springs flowing (free);[5206]	﴿٥٠﴾ فِيهِمَا عَيْنَانِ تَجْرِيَانِ
51. Then which of the favours Of your Lord will ye deny?	﴿٥١﴾ فَبِأَيِّ ءَالَآءِ رَبِّكُمَا تُكَذِّبَانِ

5202. It will then become too real to them. "Oh! that this too, too solid flesh would melt", as Hamlet said to his Queen-Mother (*Hamlet*, i. 2. 129).

5203. They will apparently have no rest. The fire will burn but not consume them, and their drink will be only boiling water.

5204. The reference to the Punishment of Sin having been dismissed in a few short lines, we now come to a description of the state of the Blessed. (R).

5205. Here two Gardens are mentioned, and indeed four, counting the other two mentioned in 55:62-76. Opinions are divided about this, but the best opinion is that the two mentioned in verses 46-61 are for the degree of those Nearest to Allah *(Muqarrabūn)*, and those in verses 62-76 for the Companions of the Right Hand: Why two for *each?* The Duality is to express variety, and the whole scheme of the Sūrah runs in twos. There will be no dullness of uniformity: as our minds can conceive it now, there will be freshness in change, but it will be from Bliss to Bliss, and there will be Unity. (R).

5206. *Two* Springs, for the same reasons as there will be two Gardens. See last note.

52. In them will be Fruits
Of every kind, two and two.[5207]

فِيهِمَا مِن كُلِّ فَٰكِهَةٍ زَوْجَانِ ٥٢

53. Then which of the favours
Of your Lord will ye deny?

فَبِأَيِّ ءَالَآءِ رَبِّكُمَا تُكَذِّبَانِ ٥٣

54. They will recline on Carpets,
Whose inner linings will be
Of rich brocade: the Fruit
Of the Gardens will be
Near (and easy of reach).[5208]

مُتَّكِـِٔينَ عَلَىٰ فُرُشٍۭ بَطَآئِنُهَا مِنْ إِسْتَبْرَقٍ ۚ وَجَنَى ٱلْجَنَّتَيْنِ دَانٍ ٥٤

55. Then which of the favours
Of your Lord will ye deny?

فَبِأَيِّ ءَالَآءِ رَبِّكُمَا تُكَذِّبَانِ ٥٥

56. In them will be (Maidens),[5209]
Chaste, restraining their
glances,[5210]
Whom no man or Jinn
Before them has touched—

فِيهِنَّ قَٰصِرَٰتُ ٱلطَّرْفِ لَمْ يَطْمِثْهُنَّ إِنسٌ قَبْلَهُمْ وَلَا جَآنٌّ ٥٦

57. Then which of the favours
Of your Lord will ye deny?

فَبِأَيِّ ءَالَآءِ رَبِّكُمَا تُكَذِّبَانِ ٥٧

58. Like unto rubies and coral.[5211]

كَأَنَّهُنَّ ٱلْيَاقُوتُ وَٱلْمَرْجَانُ ٥٨

59. Then which of the favours
Of your Lord will ye deny?

فَبِأَيِّ ءَالَآءِ رَبِّكُمَا تُكَذِّبَانِ ٥٩

60. Is there any Reward
For Good—other than Good?[5212]

هَلْ جَزَآءُ ٱلْإِحْسَٰنِ إِلَّا ٱلْإِحْسَٰنُ ٦٠

61. Then which of the favours
Of your Lord will ye deny?

فَبِأَيِّ ءَالَآءِ رَبِّكُمَا تُكَذِّبَانِ ٦١

62. And besides these two,
There are two other Gardens—[5213]

وَمِن دُونِهِمَا جَنَّتَانِ ٦٢

5207. The Duality of Fruits is for the same reason as the Duality of the Gardens. See n. 5205.

5208. The toil and fatigue of this life will be over: *Cf.* 35:35.

5209. See notes 4728-29 to 44:54. (R).

5210. *Cf.* 37:48 and n. 4064. Their purity is the feature chiefly symbolised.

5211. Delicate pink, with reference to their complexions and their beauty of form. The gems also indicate their worth and dignity.

5212. This is the summing up of all the symbolism used to express the Fruit of Goodness or Good. The symbolism must necessarily resort to comparative terms, to subjective ideas of Bliss. But the fullest expression can only be given in abstract terms: "Is there any reward for Good—other than Good?" Can anything express it better?

5213. See n. 5205 above.

63\. Then which of the favours
Of your Lord will ye deny?

فَبِأَيِّ ءَالَآءِ رَبِّكُمَا تُكَذِّبَانِ ﴿٦٣﴾

64\. Dark green in colour[5214]
(From plentiful watering).

مُدْهَآمَّتَانِ ﴿٦٤﴾

65\. Then which of the favours
Of your Lord will ye deny?

فَبِأَيِّ ءَالَآءِ رَبِّكُمَا تُكَذِّبَانِ ﴿٦٥﴾

66\. In them (each) will be
Two Springs pouring forth
water[5215]
In continuous abundance:

فِيهِمَا عَيْنَانِ نَضَّاخَتَانِ ﴿٦٦﴾

67\. Then which of the favours
Of your Lord will ye deny?

فَبِأَيِّ ءَالَآءِ رَبِّكُمَا تُكَذِّبَانِ ﴿٦٧﴾

68\. In them will be Fruits,
And dates and pomegranates:[5216]

فِيهِمَا فَٰكِهَةٌ وَنَخْلٌ وَرُمَّانٌ ﴿٦٨﴾

69\. Then which of the favours
Of your Lord will ye deny?

فَبِأَيِّ ءَالَآءِ رَبِّكُمَا تُكَذِّبَانِ ﴿٦٩﴾

70\. In them will be
Fair (Companions), good,
beautiful —[5217]

فِيهِنَّ خَيْرَٰتٌ حِسَانٌ ﴿٧٠﴾

71\. Then which of the favours
Of your Lord will ye deny?

فَبِأَيِّ ءَالَآءِ رَبِّكُمَا تُكَذِّبَانِ ﴿٧١﴾

72\. Companions restrained (as to[5218]
Their glances), in (goodly)
pavilions —[5219]

حُورٌ مَّقْصُورَٰتٌ فِى ٱلْخِيَامِ ﴿٧٢﴾

73\. Then which of the favours
Of your Lord will ye deny?

فَبِأَيِّ ءَالَآءِ رَبِّكُمَا تُكَذِّبَانِ ﴿٧٣﴾

5214\. *Dark green in colour"*; these Gardens will also be fruitful and flourishing, and watered plentifully; but their aspect and characteristics will be different, corresponding to the subjective differences in the ideas of Bliss among those who would respectively enjoy the two sets of Gardens.

5215\. In comparison with the Springs in the other two Gardens, described in 55:50 above, these Springs would seem to irrigate crops of vegetables and fruits requiring a constant supply of abundant water.

5216\. See last note. *Cf.* also with 55:52 above, where "fruits of every kind" are mentioned.

5217\. see n. 5209 above. Goodness and Beauty are specially feminine attributes.

5218\. *Maqṣūrāt* here is the passive participle of the same verb as the active participle *Qāṣirāt* in 55:56, 37:48 and 38:52. As I have translated *Qāṣirāt* by the phrase "restraining (their glances)", I think I am right in translating the passive *Maqṣūrāt* by "restrained (as to their glances)". This is the only place in the Qur'ān where the passive form occurs.

5219\. The Pavilions seem to add dignity to their status. In the other Gardens (55:58), the description "like rubies and corals" is perhaps an indication of higher dignity.

74. Whom no man or Jinn
Before them has touched—

لَمْ يَطْمِثْهُنَّ إِنْسٌ قَبْلَهُمْ وَلَا جَانٌّ ﴿٧٤﴾

75. Then which of the favours
Of your Lord will ye deny?

فَبِأَيِّ آلَاءِ رَبِّكُمَا تُكَذِّبَانِ ﴿٧٥﴾

76. Reclining on green Cushions[5220]
And rich Carpets of beauty.

مُتَّكِئِينَ عَلَىٰ رَفْرَفٍ خُضْرٍ وَعَبْقَرِيٍّ حِسَانٍ ﴿٧٦﴾

77. Then which of the favours
Of your Lord will ye deny?

فَبِأَيِّ آلَاءِ رَبِّكُمَا تُكَذِّبَانِ ﴿٧٧﴾

78. Blessed be the name
Of thy Lord,
Full of Majesty,
Bounty and Honour.[5221]

تَبَارَكَ اسْمُ رَبِّكَ ذِي الْجَلَالِ وَالْإِكْرَامِ ﴿٧٨﴾

5220. *Cf.* the parallel words for the other two Gardens, in 55:54 above, which suggest perhaps a higher dignity.

Rafraf is usually translated by Cushions or Pillows, and I have followed this meaning in view of the word "reclining". But another interpretation is "Meadows", in view of the adjective "green"—*abqarī:* carpets richly figured and dyed, and skillfully worked.

5221. *Cf.* 55:27 and n. 5190. This minor echo completes the symmetry of the two leading Ideas of this Sūrah—the Bounty and Majesty of Allah, and the Duty of man to make himself worthy of nearness to Allah.

INTRODUCTION TO SŪRAH 56—*AL WĀQI'AH*

This is the seventh and last Sūrah of the series devoted to Revelation and the Hereafter, as explained in the Introduction to S. 50.

It belongs to the early Makkan period, with the possible exception of one or two verses.

The theme is the certainty of the Day of Judgement and its adjustment of true Values (56:1-56); Allah's Power, Goodness and Glory (56:57-74); and the truth of Revelation (56:75-96).

Summary—When the Day of Judgement comes, the world as we know it will be shaken to its foundations, and men shall be sorted out into three sorts: Those nearest to Allah, in exalted Bliss; the Companions of the Right Hand, in Bliss; and the Companions of the Left Hand, in Misery (56:1-56, and C. 234).

Surely the Power and Goodness of Allah, of which Revelation is a Sign, should lead man to accept the Message and glorify Him (56:57-96. and C. 235).

C. 234.—The Event Inevitable is the Day
(56:1-56) Of Judgement: the world as we know it
Will be shaken to its depths, and its place
Will be taken by a world made new,
Where Good will be sorted out from Evil.
In Dignity and Bliss will the Good find Fulfilment:
Both those Nearest to the Throne of Allah,
And those who earned, by faith and good life,
The title, Companions of the Right Hand.
Who can tell of the Misery in which
The Companions of the Left Hand will live?
They will be as it were in a fierce blast
Of Fire; their drink but boiling water;
Their shade that of Black Smoke that chokes
Their lungs—ever burning with hunger and thirst,
And never satisfied: fit emblems
Of the Life in Death to which Evil leads.

Sūrah 56.

Al Wāqi'ah (The Inevitable)

الجزء السابع والعشرون سورة الواقعة

In the name of Allah, Most Gracious, Most Merciful.

بِسْمِ اللَّهِ الرَّحْمَٰنِ الرَّحِيمِ

1. When the Event Inevitable[5222]
Cometh to pass,

إِذَا وَقَعَتِ الْوَاقِعَةُ ①

2. Then will no (soul)
Entertain falsehood
Concerning its coming.

لَيْسَ لِوَقْعَتِهَا كَاذِبَةٌ ②

3. (Many) will it bring low;[5223]
(Many) will it exalt;

خَافِضَةٌ رَّافِعَةٌ ③

4. When the earth shall be
Shaken to its depths,

إِذَا رُجَّتِ الْأَرْضُ رَجًّا ④

5. And the mountains shall
Be crumbled to atoms,[5224]

وَبُسَّتِ الْجِبَالُ بَسًّا ⑤

6. Becoming dust scattered abroad,

فَكَانَتْ هَبَاءً مُّنۢبَثًّا ⑥

7. And ye shall be sorted out
Into three classes.[5225]

وَكُنتُمْ أَزْوَاجًا ثَلَٰثَةً ⑦

8. Then (there will be)
The Companions of
The Right Hand—
What will be
The Companions of
The Right Hand?

فَأَصْحَٰبُ الْمَيْمَنَةِ مَآ أَصْحَٰبُ الْمَيْمَنَةِ ⑧

5222. The Event Inevitable is the Hour of Judgement. People may doubt now whether it will come. But when it comes, as it will come, suddenly upon them, it will come with such tremendous reality that it will be burnt deep into the experience of every soul. No one can then be deceived or entertain false notions about it.

5223. There will be a sorting out of Good and Evil. Or rather, (verse 7 below), there will be three main classes. Among the Good there will be the specially exalted class, those nearest to Allah *(muqarrabūn*, 56:11-26), and the righteous people generally, called the Companions of the Right Hand *(Aṣḥāb al maymanah*, 56:27-40). And there will be those in agony, the Companions of the Left Hand *(Aṣḥāb al mash'amah*. 56:41-56). Many who were high and mighty in this life will be brought low for their sins, and many who were lowly but virtuous will be exalted to various ranks and degrees. The old landmarks will be lost in the inner world, as they will be in the outer world.

5224. The old physical world will disappear in the New Creation.

5225. See n. 5223 above.

9. And the Companions of
The Left Hand—
What will be
The Companions of
The Left Hand?

وَأَصْحَٰبُ ٱلْمَشْـَٔمَةِ مَآ أَصْحَٰبُ ٱلْمَشْـَٔمَةِ ﴿٩﴾

10. And those Foremost
(In Faith) will be
Foremost (in the Hereafter).[5226]

وَٱلسَّٰبِقُونَ ٱلسَّٰبِقُونَ ﴿١٠﴾

11. These will be
Those Nearest to Allah:[5227]

أُو۟لَٰٓئِكَ ٱلْمُقَرَّبُونَ ﴿١١﴾

12. In Gardens of Bliss:

فِى جَنَّٰتِ ٱلنَّعِيمِ ﴿١٢﴾

13. A number of people
From those of old,[5228]

ثُلَّةٌ مِّنَ ٱلْأَوَّلِينَ ﴿١٣﴾

14. And a few from those
Of later times.

وَقَلِيلٌ مِّنَ ٱلْءَاخِرِينَ ﴿١٤﴾

15. (They will be) on Thrones[5229]
Encrusted (with gold
And precious stones),

عَلَىٰ سُرُرٍ مَّوْضُونَةٍ ﴿١٥﴾

16. Reclining on them,
Facing each other.[5230]

مُّتَّكِـِٔينَ عَلَيْهَا مُتَقَٰبِلِينَ ﴿١٦﴾

17. Round about them will (serve)[5231]
Youths of perpetual (freshness),

يَطُوفُ عَلَيْهِمْ وِلْدَٰنٌ مُّخَلَّدُونَ ﴿١٧﴾

5226. *Foremost (in Faith)*: There are two meanings, and both are implied. (1) Those who have reached the highest degree in spiritual understanding, such as the great prophets and teachers of mankind, will also take precedence in the Hereafter. (2) Those who are the first in time—the quickest and readiest—to accept Allah's Message—will have the first place in the Kingdom of Heaven. Verses 8,9 and 10 mention the three main categories or classifications after Judgement. In the subsequent verses their happiness or misery are symbolised. This category, Foremost in Faith, is nearest to Allah.

5227. See n. 5223 above. Nearness to Allah is the test of the highest Bliss. (R).

5228. Of great Prophets and Teachers there were many before the time of the Holy Prophet Muḥammad. As he was the last of the Prophets, he and the great Teachers under his Dispensation will be comparatively fewer in number, but their teaching is the sum and flower of all mankind's spiritual experience.

5229. *Cf.* 15:47; 37:44, 52:20, and 48:13. [Eds.].

5230. But they will not be separate each in his own corner. They will face each other. For they are all one, and their mutual society will be part of their Bliss.

5231. *Cf.* 52:24, and n. 5058. The youth and freshness with which the attendants will serve is a symbol of true service such as we may expect in the spiritual world. That freshness will be perpetual and not subject to any moods, or chances, or changes.

18. With goblets, (shining) beakers,
And cups (filled) out of
Clear-flowing fountains:

١٨ بِأَكْوَابٍ وَأَبَارِيقَ وَكَأْسٍ مِّن مَّعِينٍ

19. No after-ache will they
Receive therefrom, nor will they
Suffer intoxication:[5232]

١٩ لَّا يُصَدَّعُونَ عَنْهَا وَلَا يُنزِفُونَ

20. And with fruits,
Any that they may select;

٢٠ وَفَٰكِهَةٍ مِّمَّا يَتَخَيَّرُونَ

21. And the flesh of fowls,
Any that they may desire.

٢١ وَلَحْمِ طَيْرٍ مِّمَّا يَشْتَهُونَ

22. And (there will be) Companions
With beautiful, big,
And lustrous eyes—[5233]

٢٢ وَحُورٌ عِينٌ

23. Like unto Pearls[5234]
Well-guarded.

٢٣ كَأَمْثَٰلِ ٱللُّؤْلُوِ ٱلْمَكْنُونِ

24. A Reward for the Deeds
Of their past (Life).

٢٤ جَزَآءًۢ بِمَا كَانُوا۟ يَعْمَلُونَ

25. No frivolity will they[5235]
Hear therein, nor any
Taint of ill—

٢٥ لَا يَسْمَعُونَ فِيهَا لَغْوًا وَلَا تَأْثِيمًا

26. Only the saying,[5236]
"Peace! Peace".

٢٦ إِلَّا قِيلًا سَلَٰمًا سَلَٰمًا

27. The Companions of
The Right Hand—
What will be

٢٧ وَأَصْحَٰبُ ٱلْيَمِينِ مَآ

5232. The Feast of Reason and the Flow of Soul are typified by all that is best in the feasts in this imperfect world, but there will be none of the disadvantages incident to such feasts in this world, such as satiety, aches, excess, a sense of exhaustion, or loss of senses, etc. *Cf.* 37:47, and n. 4063. A goblet is a bowl without handles; a beaker has a "lip" and a stem; "cup" is a general term.

5233. *Cf.* 44:54, and n. 4729. The companionship of Beauty and Grace is one of the highest pleasures of life. In this bodily life it takes bodily form. In the higher life it takes a higher form. (R).

5234. *Cf.* 52:24, where this description is applied to the youths who serve. See also n. 5058 there. In 56:78 below the adjective *maknūn* is applied to the Qur'ān, "the well-guarded Book".

5235. *Cf.* 52:23. Apart from the physical ills, worldly feasts or delights are apt to suffer from vain or frivolous discourse, idle boasting, foolish flattery, or phrases pointed with secret venom or moral mischief. The negation of these from spiritual Bliss follows as a matter of course, but it is specially insisted on to guard against the perversities of human nature, which likes to read ill into the best that can be put in words.

5236. *Qīl* is best translated "saying", rather than "word". For the saying is an act, a thought, a fact, which may be embodied in a word, but which goes far beyond the word. The "Peace of Allah" is an atmosphere which sums up Heaven even better than "Bliss".

The Companions of
The Right Hand!

أَصْحَٰبُ ٱلْيَمِينِ

28. (They will be) among[5237]
Lote trees without thorns,

٢٨ فِى سِدْرٍ مَّخْضُودٍ

29. Among Ṭalḥ trees[5238]
With flowers (or fruits)
Piled one above another—

٢٩ وَطَلْحٍ مَّنضُودٍ

30. In shade long-extended,

٣٠ وَظِلٍّ مَّمْدُودٍ

31. By water flowing constantly,

٣١ وَمَآءٍ مَّسْكُوبٍ

32. And fruit in abundance,

٣٢ وَفَٰكِهَةٍ كَثِيرَةٍ

33. Whose season is not limited,
Nor (supply) forbidden,[5239]

٣٣ لَّا مَقْطُوعَةٍ وَلَا مَمْنُوعَةٍ

34. And on Thrones (of Dignity),
Raised high.

٣٤ وَفُرُشٍ مَّرْفُوعَةٍ

35. We have created
(their Companions)[5240]
Of special creation,

٣٥ إِنَّآ أَنشَأْنَٰهُنَّ إِنشَآءً

36. And made them
Virgin-pure (and undefiled)—

٣٦ فَجَعَلْنَٰهُنَّ أَبْكَارًا

37. Beloved (by nature),
Equal in age—

٣٧ عُرُبًا أَتْرَابًا

38. For the Companions
Of the Right Hand.

٣٨ لِّأَصْحَٰبِ ٱلْيَمِينِ

5237. *Lote trees:* see 34:16 n. 3814. (R).

5238. *Ṭalḥ:* some understand by this the plantain or banana tree, of which the fruit is borne in bunches, one tier above another; but the banana tree does not grow in Arabia and its ordinary Arabic name is Mawz; perhaps it is better to understand a special kind of Acacia tree, which flowers profusely, the flowers appearing in tiers one above another.

5239. As it is not like earthly fruit, its season is not limited, nor is there any prohibition by law or custom or circumstance as to when or how it is to be consumed. (R).

5240. The pronoun in Arabic is in the feminine gender, but lest grosser ideas of sex should intrude, it is made clear that these Companions for heavenly society will be of special creation—of virginal purity, grace, and beauty inspiring and inspired by love, with the question of time and age eliminated. Thus every person among the Righteous will have the Bliss of Heaven and the Peace of Allah.

SECTION 2.

39. A (goodly) number
From those of old,[5241]

ثُلَّةٌ مِّنَ ٱلْأَوَّلِينَ ﴿٣٩﴾

40. And a (goodly) number
From those of later times.

وَثُلَّةٌ مِّنَ ٱلْآخِرِينَ ﴿٤٠﴾

41. The Companions of
The Left Hand—
What will be
The Companions of
The Left Hand?

وَأَصْحَـٰبُ ٱلشِّمَالِ مَآ أَصْحَـٰبُ ٱلشِّمَالِ ﴿٤١﴾

42. (They will be) in the midst
Of a fierce Blast of Fire[5242]
And in Boiling Water,

فِى سَمُومٍ وَحَمِيمٍ ﴿٤٢﴾

43. And in the shades
Of Black Smoke:[5243]

وَظِلٍّ مِّن يَحْمُومٍ ﴿٤٣﴾

44. Nothing (will there be)
To refresh, nor to please:

لَّا بَارِدٍ وَلَا كَرِيمٍ ﴿٤٤﴾

45. For that they were wont
To be indulged, before that,
In wealth (and luxury),[5244]

إِنَّهُمْ كَانُوا۟ قَبْلَ ذَٰلِكَ مُتْرَفِينَ ﴿٤٥﴾

46. And persisted obstinately
In wickedness supreme![5244-A]

وَكَانُوا۟ يُصِرُّونَ عَلَى ٱلْحِنثِ ٱلْعَظِيمِ ﴿٤٦﴾

47. And they used to say,
"What! when we die
And become dust and bones,[5245]

وَكَانُوا۟ يَقُولُونَ أَئِذَا مِتْنَا وَكُنَّا تُرَابًا وَعِظَـٰمًا ﴿٤٧﴾

5241. This class—the righteous—will be a large company in Heaven, belonging to all the ages of the world. *Cf.* n. 5228 to 56:13 above. Such is the unbounded Bounty of Allah. These verses 39-40 should really be in the last Section.

5242. Notice the parallelism in the contrast between those in Bliss and those in Misery. The allegory in each case pursues the idea of contrast, and the allegories about Misery lose nothing by their terse brevity. The fierce Blast of Fire and the Boiling Water are in contrast to the happy Lote tree and the flowers and fruits in verses 28-29 above.

5243. Even the Shades get a different quality in the Abode of Misery: shades of black smoke in contrast to the cool and refreshing long extended shades of trees by brooks in verses 30-31 above.

5244. *Cf.* 34:34, and 43:23. We must read verses 45-46 together. They had wealth and the good things of life, but they used them in self-indulgence and shameless crime, and now they are in humiliation.

5244-A. Wickedness supreme: *i.e.* their associating others with Allah in His divinity. [Eds.].

5245. Their want of belief and ridicule of Allah's Message contrasts with the stern reality which they see around them now.

Shall we then indeed
Be raised up again?—

أَءِنَّا لَمَبْعُوثُونَ

48. "(We) and our fathers of old?"

أَوَءَابَآؤُنَا ٱلْأَوَّلُونَ ﴿٤٨﴾

49. Say: "Yea, those of old
And those of later times,

قُلْ إِنَّ ٱلْأَوَّلِينَ وَٱلْءَاخِرِينَ ﴿٤٩﴾

50. "All will certainly be
Gathered together for the meeting
Appointed for a Day
Well-known.[5246]

لَمَجْمُوعُونَ إِلَىٰ مِيقَٰتِ يَوْمٍ مَّعْلُومٍ ﴿٥٠﴾

51. "Then will ye truly—
O ye that go wrong,
And treat (Truth) as Falsehood!—

ثُمَّ إِنَّكُمْ أَيُّهَا ٱلضَّآلُّونَ ٱلْمُكَذِّبُونَ ﴿٥١﴾

52. "Ye will surely taste
Of the Tree of Zaqqūm.[5247]

لَءَاكِلُونَ مِن شَجَرٍ مِّن زَقُّومٍ ﴿٥٢﴾

53. "Then will ye fill
Your insides therewith,

فَمَالِـُٔونَ مِنْهَا ٱلْبُطُونَ ﴿٥٣﴾

54. "And drink Boiling Water
On top of it:

فَشَٰرِبُونَ عَلَيْهِ مِنَ ٱلْحَمِيمِ ﴿٥٤﴾

55. "Indeed ye shall drink
Like diseased camels
Raging with thirst!"[5248]

فَشَٰرِبُونَ شُرْبَ ٱلْهِيمِ ﴿٥٥﴾

56. Such will be their entertainment
On the Day of Requital!

هَٰذَا نُزُلُهُمْ يَوْمَ ٱلدِّينِ ﴿٥٦﴾

C. 235.—Learn ye then to witness the Truth in your lives.
(56:57-96.) Your own creation and growth, the seeds
That ye sow in the ground, the Circuit of Water
Through streams, rivers, and seas, to vapour,
Clouds, and rain that feeds the streams,
The Fire that stands as an emblem of Life
And Light—all point to your Lord Supreme.

5246. In 26:38 (see n. 3159) the phrase *a day well-known* is used for a solemn day of festival, when the multitude of people gather together. The Day of Judgement is such a day in the supreme sense of the word.

5247. This is the Cursed Tree mentioned in 17:60, where see n. 2250. *Cf.* also 37:62, n. 4072; and 44:43-46 and n. 4722.

5248. A terrible picture of Misery in contrast to the Companionship of the Good, the True, and the Beautiful, on Thrones of Dignity, for the Companions of the Right Hand, in verses 34-38 above.

His Revelation conveys the same Message
To the pure in heart. Will ye receive it
And live, assured of the truth of the Hereafter?
Glory and Praise to Allah the Beneficent,
Supreme to Justice, Mercy, and Truth!

57. It is We Who have
Created you: why will ye[5249]
Not witness the Truth?

نَحْنُ خَلَقْنَٰكُمْ فَلَوْلَا تُصَدِّقُونَ ﴿٥٧﴾

58. Do ye then see?—
The (human Seed) that
Ye throw out,—

أَفَرَءَيْتُم مَّا تُمْنُونَ ﴿٥٨﴾

59. Is it ye who create it,
Or are We the Creators?

ءَأَنتُمْ تَخْلُقُونَهُۥٓ أَمْ نَحْنُ ٱلْخَٰلِقُونَ ﴿٥٩﴾

60. We have decreed Death
To be your common lot,[5250]
And We are not
To be frustrated

نَحْنُ قَدَّرْنَا بَيْنَكُمُ ٱلْمَوْتَ وَمَا نَحْنُ بِمَسْبُوقِينَ ﴿٦٠﴾

61. From changing your Forms
And creating you (again)
In (Forms) that ye know not.

عَلَىٰٓ أَن نُّبَدِّلَ أَمْثَٰلَكُمْ وَنُنشِئَكُمْ فِى مَا لَا تَعْلَمُونَ ﴿٦١﴾

62. And ye certainly know already
The first form of creation:
Why then do ye not
Celebrate His praises?

وَلَقَدْ عَلِمْتُمُ ٱلنَّشْأَةَ ٱلْأُولَىٰ فَلَوْلَا تَذَكَّرُونَ ﴿٦٢﴾

63. See ye the seed that[5251]
Ye sow in the ground?

أَفَرَءَيْتُم مَّا تَحْرُثُونَ ﴿٦٣﴾

64. Is it ye that cause it
To grow, or are We
The Cause?

ءَأَنتُمْ تَزْرَعُونَهُۥٓ أَمْ نَحْنُ ٱلزَّٰرِعُونَ ﴿٦٤﴾

5249. Man is apt to forget his Creator, and even the fact that he, man, is a created being. The seed of his body, out of which his physical life starts, is not created by man, but by Allah in the process of the unfoldment of the world. Why will not man recognise and bear witness of this fact by a life of obedience to Allah's Law?

5250. Just as Allah has created this life that we see, so He has decreed that Death should be the common lot of all of us. Surely, if He can thus give life and death, as we see it, why should we refuse to believe that He can give us other forms when this life is over? The Future Life, though indicated by what we know now, is to be on a wholly different plane. (R).

5251. Having appealed to our own nature within us, He appeals now to the external nature around us, which should be evidence to us (1) of His loving care for us, and (2) of its being due to causes other than those which we produce and control. Three examples are given: (1) the seed which we sow in the soil; it is Allah's processes in nature, which make it grow; (2) the water which we drink; it is Allah's processes in nature, that send it down from the clouds as rain, and distribute it through springs and rivers; (3) the fire which we strike; it is again a proof of Allah's Plan and Wisdom in nature.

65. Were it Our Will,
We could crumble it
To dry powder, and ye would
Be left in wonderment,

﴿٦٥﴾ لَوْ نَشَآءُ لَجَعَلْنَٰهُ حُطَٰمًا فَظَلْتُمْ تَفَكَّهُونَ

66. (Saying), "We are indeed
Left with debts (for nothing):[5252]

﴿٦٦﴾ إِنَّا لَمُغْرَمُونَ

67. "Indeed are we shut out
(Of the fruits of our labour)".

﴿٦٧﴾ بَلْ نَحْنُ مَحْرُومُونَ

68. See ye the water
Which ye drink?

﴿٦٨﴾ أَفَرَءَيْتُمُ ٱلْمَآءَ ٱلَّذِى تَشْرَبُونَ

69. Do ye bring it Down
(In rain) from the Cloud
Or do We?

﴿٦٩﴾ ءَأَنتُمْ أَنزَلْتُمُوهُ مِنَ ٱلْمُزْنِ أَمْ نَحْنُ ٱلْمُنزِلُونَ

70. Were it Our Will,
We could make it
Salt (and unpalatable):[5253]
Then why do ye not
Give thanks?

﴿٧٠﴾ لَوْ نَشَآءُ جَعَلْنَٰهُ أُجَاجًا فَلَوْلَا تَشْكُرُونَ

71. See ye the Fire
Which ye kindle?

﴿٧١﴾ أَفَرَءَيْتُمُ ٱلنَّارَ ٱلَّتِى تُورُونَ

72. Is it ye who grow
The tree which feeds[5254]
The fire, or do We
Grow it?

﴿٧٢﴾ ءَأَنتُمْ أَنشَأْتُمْ شَجَرَتَهَآ أَمْ نَحْنُ ٱلْمُنشِـُٔونَ

73. We have made it
A memorial (of Our
handiwork),[5255]

﴿٧٣﴾ نَحْنُ جَعَلْنَٰهَا تَذْكِرَةً

5252. The cultivator contracts debts for seed and gives labour for ploughing, sowing, watering, and weeding, in the hope of reaping a harvest. Should he not give thanks to Allah when his harvest is in?

5253. The mystery of the two streams of water, one sweet and the other salt, constantly mingling, and yet always separate, is referred to more than once. The never-ending circuit is established by streams and rivers mingling with the ocean, the ocean sending forth mists and steam through a process of evaporation which forms clouds, and the clouds by condensation pouring forth rain to feed the streams and rivers again: see notes 3111-2 to 25:53, and n. 5185 to 55:19, and the further references given there.

5254. The relation of Fire to Trees is intimate. In nearly all the fire that we burn, the fuel is derived from the wood of trees. Even mineral coal is nothing but the wood of prehistoric forests petrified under the earth through geological ages. Fire produced out of green trees is referred to in 36:80; and n. 4026 there gives instances.

5255. Fire is a fit memorial of Allah's handiwork in nature. It is also an emblem of man's earliest civilisation. It can stand as a symbol of physical comfort and convenience to man, of the source of spiritual light, and also of the warning to Evil about its destruction. In the same way the sower's seed has a symbolical meaning in the preaching of the Message: see 48:29, and n. 4917: and the Rain and the Streams of Water have a symbolical meaning: see notes 2404-5 to 18:60.

And an article of comfort
And convenience for
The denizens of deserts.[5256]

وَمَتَـٰعًا لِّلْمُقْوِينَ

74. Then celebrate with praises[5257]
The name of thy Lord,
The Supreme!

فَسَبِّحْ بِٱسْمِ رَبِّكَ ٱلْعَظِيمِ ٧٤

SECTION 3.

75. Furthermore I call
To witness the setting[5258]
Of the Stars—

فَلَآ أُقْسِمُ بِمَوَٰقِعِ ٱلنُّجُومِ ٧٥

76. And that is indeed
A mighty adjuration[5259]
If ye but knew—

وَإِنَّهُۥ لَقَسَمٌ لَّوْ تَعْلَمُونَ عَظِيمٌ ٧٦

77. That this is indeed
A Qur'ān most honourable,[5260]

إِنَّهُۥ لَقُرْءَانٌ كَرِيمٌ ٧٧

78. In a Book well-guarded,

فِى كِتَـٰبٍ مَّكْنُونٍ ٧٨

79. Which none shall touch
But those who are clean:

لَّا يَمَسُّهُۥٓ إِلَّا ٱلْمُطَهَّرُونَ ٧٩

5256. *Cf.* 20:10, and n. 2541, where the mystic meaning of the Fire which Moses saw in the desert is explained. Even ordinarily, a fire in a desert is a sign of human habitation; by following it you may get human society and human comfort. A fire, or light, or beacon in many places directs a traveller on the way. Lighthouses at sea and beacons in modern aerodromes serve the same purpose for mariners and airmen.

Another parable about fire will be found in 2:17-18, and n. 38.

5257. Seeing all these Signs in nature and their symbolical meaning in the spiritual world, man must turn to Allah and do His Will.

5258. *The setting of the Stars:* a number of mystic meanings are attached. Here are three. (1) *Cf.* 43:1 and n. 5085; the setting of a glorious star is a symbol of humility before the power, beauty, and goodness of Allah. (2) It may refer to the extinction of the stars at the Day of Judgement, betokening the establishment of Allah's Justice and the Truth of His Revelation. (3) What is bright or beautiful to our senses may disappear from our ken within a few hours, even though its own existence may continue. All light is relative except the Light of Allah.

5259. The glory of the firmament as it exists, and the wonder of its passing away, are both evidence, to the discerning mind, of the Future which Allah has prepared, but this evidence can only be effective if men "but knew", *i.e.*, turned their earnest attention to it.

5260. Your attention is drawn to the momentous issues of the Future by the Qur'ān. It is a Revelation described by four characteristics. (1) It is most honourable, *karīm*, which implies, besides the fact that it is worthy of receiving honour, that it confers great favours on those who receive it. (2) It is well-guarded, *maknūn;* precious in itself, and well-preserved in its purity; see n. 5234 to 56:23; see also 15:9, and n. 1944. (3) None but the clean shall touch it—clean in body, mind, thought, intention, and soul; only such can achieve real contact with its full meaning. (4) It is a Revelation from the Lord of the Worlds, and therefore universal for all.

80. A Revelation from the Lord
Of the Worlds.

٨٠ تَنزِيلٌ مِّن رَّبِّ ٱلْعَٰلَمِينَ

81. Is it such a Message
That ye would hold[5261]
In light esteem?

٨١ أَفَبِهَٰذَا ٱلْحَدِيثِ أَنتُم مُّدْهِنُونَ

82. And have ye made it[5262]
Your livelihood that ye
Should declare it false?

٨٢ وَتَجْعَلُونَ رِزْقَكُمْ أَنَّكُمْ تُكَذِّبُونَ

83. Then why do ye not[5263]
(Intervene) when (the soul
Of the dying man)
Reaches the throat—

٨٣ فَلَوْلَآ إِذَا بَلَغَتِ ٱلْحُلْقُومَ

84. And ye the while
(Sit) looking on—[5264]

٨٤ وَأَنتُمْ حِينَئِذٍ تَنظُرُونَ

85. But We are nearer
To him than ye,
And yet see not—

٨٥ وَنَحْنُ أَقْرَبُ إِلَيْهِ مِنكُمْ وَلَٰكِن لَّا تُبْصِرُونَ

86. Then why do ye not—[5265]
If you are exempt
From (future) account—

٨٦ فَلَوْلَآ إِن كُنتُمْ غَيْرَ مَدِينِينَ

87. Call back the soul,[5266]
If ye are true
(In your claim of Independence)?

٨٧ تَرْجِعُونَهَآ إِن كُنتُمْ صَٰدِقِينَ

5261. The Message being such as is described in the last note, how can anyone ignore it or treat it with contempt or refuse to allow it to improve his life?

5262. The worst indictment of an enemy of Revelation would be that he should make Falsehood a source of filthy lucre for himself, or that he should let his precious life be corrupted by such unholy occupation.

5263. There is a hiatus after *why do ye not?*—and two parenthetical clauses—after which the clause *why do ye not?* is resumed again in verse 86 below, with its complement in verse 87. It is permissible to the translator to add some such word as *intervene* here, to make the translation run smoothly.

5264. The dying man's friends, relatives and companions may be sitting round him and quite close to him in his last moments, but Allah is nearer still at all times for He is nearer than the man's own jugular vein (1:16), and one of Allah's own titles is "Ever Near" (34:50).

5265. These words resume the sentence begun at verse 83 above and interrupted by the two parenthetical clauses in verses 84 and 85. See n. 5263 above.

5266. The sentence may now be briefly paraphrased. 'If you disbelieve in Revelation and a future Judgement, and claim to do what you like and be independent of Allah, how is it you cannot call back a dying man's soul to his body when all of you congregate round him at his death-bed? But you are not independent of Judgement. There *is* a Day of Account, when you will have to be judged by your deeds in this life.'

88. Thus, then, if he Be of those Nearest to Allah,[5267]	فَأَمَّآ إِن كَانَ مِنَ ٱلْمُقَرَّبِينَ ﴿٨٨﴾
89. (There is for him) Rest And Satisfaction,[5268] and A Garden of Delights.	فَرَوْحٌ وَرَيْحَانٌ وَجَنَّتُ نَعِيمٍ ﴿٨٩﴾
90. And if he be Of the Companions of The Right Hand,[5269]	وَأَمَّآ إِن كَانَ مِنْ أَصْحَٰبِ ٱلْيَمِينِ ﴿٩٠﴾
91. (For him is the salutation), "Peace be unto thee,"[5270] From the Companions Of the Right Hand.	فَسَلَٰمٌ لَّكَ مِنْ أَصْحَٰبِ ٱلْيَمِينِ ﴿٩١﴾
92. And if he be Of those who treat (Truth) as Falsehood,[5271] Who go wrong,	وَأَمَّآ إِن كَانَ مِنَ ٱلْمُكَذِّبِينَ ٱلضَّآلِّينَ ﴿٩٢﴾
93. For him is Entertainment With Boiling Water,	فَنُزُلٌ مِّنْ حَمِيمٍ ﴿٩٣﴾
94. And burning in Hell-Fire.	وَتَصْلِيَةُ جَحِيمٍ ﴿٩٤﴾
95. Verily, this is The very Truth And Certainty.[5272]	إِنَّ هَٰذَا لَهُوَ حَقُّ ٱلْيَقِينِ ﴿٩٥﴾
96. So celebrate with praises[5273] The name of thy Lord, The Supreme.	فَسَبِّحْ بِٱسْمِ رَبِّكَ ٱلْعَظِيمِ ﴿٩٦﴾

5267. See above, 56:11-26 and notes.

5268. *Rayḥān:* sweet-smelling plants, as in 55:12. Here used as symbolical of complete Satisfaction and Delight.

5269. See above, 56:27-38 and notes.

5270. In 56:26 above the salutation of "Peace, Peace!" is addressed to those Nearest to Allah. Here we learn that it is also addressed to the Companions of the Right Hand. Both are in Gardens of Bliss: only the former have a higher Dignity than the latter.

5271. *Cf.* above 56:51-55.

5272. "The assurance of the Hereafter" is one of the strongest features of Faith. For without it the apparent inequalities and injustices of this Life cannot be satisfactorily explained.

5273. *Cf.* 56:74 above. That was the conclusion of the argument about the Future from the examples of Allah's goodness in nature. Now we have the conclusion of the same argument from Allah's revelation through His inspired Messengers.

INTRODUCTION TO SŪRAH 57—*AL ḤADĪD*

We have now studied the contents of nearly nine-tenths of the Qur'ān. We have found that the arrangement of the Sūrahs in the present Text is not haphazard, but that they follow a distinct logical order more helpful for study than the chronological order. The comprehensive scheme of building up the new *Ummah* or Brotherhood and its spiritual implications is now complete. The remaining tenth of the Qur'ān may be roughly considered in two parts. The first contains ten Sūrahs (S. 57 to S. 66), all revealed in Madīnah, and each dealing with some special point which needs emphasis in the social life of the Ummah. The second (S. 67 to 94.) contains short Makkan lyrics, each dealing with some aspect of spiritual life, expressed in language of great mystic beauty.

The present Madīnah Sūrah is chiefly concerned with spiritual humility and the avoidance of arrogance, and a warning that retirement from the world may not be the best way of seeking the good pleasure of Allah. Its probable date is after the Conquest of Makkah, A. H. 8.

Summary—Allah's Power and Knowledge extend to all things: follow His Light direct, without doubt or fear or half-heartedness, but with humility, generous charity, and faith, and not in a life of isolation from the world. (57:1-29, and C. 236).

C. 236.—Allah is All-in-All: follow His Law
(57:1-29.) And His Light, and obey His Prophet, who invites
You to deeds of goodness and charity.
Strive and spend your resources and yourselves
In the Cause of Allah: He will grant you a Light
To go before you and guide you to your Eternal
Goal, where no Evil can enter. When success
Crowns your efforts, even then is the time
To humble yourselves before Allah, in sincere
Witness to His Love. The pleasures here below
Are deceptive: be foremost in seeking Allah
And His Good Pleasure: trust Him: be not
Like those who mistook mere renunciation
Of the world for Allah's service. Allah's Grace
Is for all: be your love and your service for all.

Sūrah 57.

Al Ḥadīd (Iron)[5274]

In the name of Allah, Most Gracious, Most Merciful.

بِسْمِ ٱللَّهِ ٱلرَّحْمَٰنِ ٱلرَّحِيمِ

1. Whatever is in
The heavens and on earth—
Let it declare
The Praises and Glory of Allah:[5275]
For He is the Exalted
In Might, the Wise.

سَبَّحَ لِلَّهِ مَا فِي ٱلسَّمَٰوَٰتِ وَٱلْأَرْضِ ۖ وَهُوَ ٱلْعَزِيزُ ٱلْحَكِيمُ ١

2. To Him belongs the dominion
Of the heavens and the earth:
It is He Who gives
Life and Death; and He
Has Power over all things.

لَهُۥ مُلْكُ ٱلسَّمَٰوَٰتِ وَٱلْأَرْضِ ۖ يُحْيِۦ وَيُمِيتُ ۖ وَهُوَ عَلَىٰ كُلِّ شَيْءٍ قَدِيرٌ ٢

3. He is the First
And the Last,
The Evident
And the Hidden:[5276]
And He has full knowledge
Of all things.

هُوَ ٱلْأَوَّلُ وَٱلْءَاخِرُ وَٱلظَّٰهِرُ وَٱلْبَاطِنُ ۖ وَهُوَ بِكُلِّ شَيْءٍ عَلِيمٌ ٣

4. He it is Who created
The heavens and the earth
In six Days,[5277] and is moreover
Firmly established on the
Throne
(Of authority),[5278] He knows

هُوَ ٱلَّذِي خَلَقَ ٱلسَّمَٰوَٰتِ وَٱلْأَرْضَ فِي سِتَّةِ أَيَّامٍ ثُمَّ ٱسْتَوَىٰ عَلَى ٱلْعَرْشِ ۚ يَعْلَمُ ٤

5274. Iron is the type and emblem of strength and reliability, on which depend the real virtues expounded in this Sūrah, such as real humility, whole-heartedness, and charity, as opposed to Monasticism, Loadiceanism, and Niggardliness. See 57:25. below.

5275. A connecting thought between this and the last Sūrah, of which see verse 96. See also paragrah 3 of the Introduction to S. 53.

5276. Allah is Evident insofar as there is ample evidence of His existence and providence all around us. On the other hand, Allah is Hidden insofar as intellect cannot grasp His essence nor can He be seen in the present world. The following tradition in Ṣaḥiḥ Muslim is also significant for an understanding of this verse. The Prophet (peace be on him) said: "Thou art the First, so that there was nothing before Thee; and Thou art the Last, so that there is nothing after Thee; and Thou art Evident, (or Ascendant) so that there is nothing above Thee, and Thou art the Hidden, the Knower of hidden things, so that there is nothing hidden from Thee." [Eds.].

5277. *In six Days:* see 41:9-12, and notes; also more briefly, n. 1031 to 7:54.

5278. *Cf.* 10:3, and n. 1386. It is not that Allah completed His Creation in six days and rested on the seventh day, or rests now. Certain external forms of the universe were by Allah's Command completed in six periods of evolution. But His creative process still goes on, and He is still, and will always be, in full control, knowing all and guiding all affairs. (R).

What enters within the earth
And what comes forth out
Of it, what comes down
From heaven and what mounts
Up to it. And He is
With you wheresoever ye[5279]
May be. And Allah sees
Well all that ye do.

مَا يَلِجُ فِي ٱلْأَرْضِ وَمَا يَخْرُجُ مِنْهَا
وَمَا يَنزِلُ مِنَ ٱلسَّمَآءِ وَمَا يَعْرُجُ فِيهَا
وَهُوَ مَعَكُمْ أَيْنَ مَا كُنتُمْ
وَٱللَّهُ بِمَا تَعْمَلُونَ بَصِيرٌ

5. To Him belongs the dominion
Of the heavens and the earth:[5280]
And all affairs are
Referred back to Allah.

٥ لَهُۥ مُلْكُ ٱلسَّمَٰوَٰتِ وَٱلْأَرْضِ
وَإِلَى ٱللَّهِ تُرْجَعُ ٱلْأُمُورُ

6. He merges Night into Day,
And He merges Day into Night;
And He has full knowledge
Of the secrets of (all) hearts.

٦ يُولِجُ ٱلَّيْلَ فِي ٱلنَّهَارِ وَيُولِجُ ٱلنَّهَارَ فِي ٱلَّيْلِ
وَهُوَ عَلِيمٌۢ بِذَاتِ ٱلصُّدُورِ

7. Believe in Allah
And His Messenger,
And spend (in charity)
Out of the (substance)
Whereof He has made you[5281]
Heirs. For, those of you
Who believe and spend
(In charity)—for them
Is a great Reward.

٧ ءَامِنُوا۟ بِٱللَّهِ وَرَسُولِهِۦ
وَأَنفِقُوا۟ مِمَّا جَعَلَكُم مُّسْتَخْلَفِينَ فِيهِ
فَٱلَّذِينَ ءَامَنُوا۟ مِنكُمْ
وَأَنفَقُوا۟ لَهُمْ أَجْرٌ كَبِيرٌ

8. What cause have ye[5282]
Why ye should not believe
In Allah?—And the Messenger
Invites you to believe

٨ وَمَا لَكُمْ لَا تُؤْمِنُونَ بِٱللَّهِ
وَٱلرَّسُولُ يَدْعُوكُمْ لِتُؤْمِنُوا۟

5279. Allah watches over man and observes his deeds. His knowledge comprehends all, the earth, heavens, what is in them or above them or whatever is in between them, comes out of them or goes into them, for "not a leaf doth fall but with His knowledge", and "there is not a grain in the darkness (or depths) of the earth, nor anything fresh of dry (green or withered), but is inscribed in a Record". (6:59). [Eds.].

5280. See 57:2 above, where this phrase referred to Allah's complete authority over the whole of the external universe: the same phrase now refers to His complete authority over the abstract world—of thoughts and affairs. Every affair must finally go back to Him, whether it comes out here from Darkness into Light, or hides itself from Light into Darkness. Allah's knowledge penetrates into the inmost recesses of all Hearts.

5281. Whenever power or wealth or influence or any good thing is transferred from one person or group of persons to another, it involves added responsibilities to the persons receiving these advantages. They must be the more zealous in real charity and all good works, for that is a part of the evidence which they give of their faith and gratitude. And, besides, their good deeds, under the general law in the spiritual world, carry their own reward.

5282. *What cause have ye why should not. . .?* A figure of speech implying a far wider meaning than the words express. It is equivalent to saying: "There is every reason why ye *should* believe in Allah", etc. The same construction applies to verse 10 below.

In your Lord, and has
Indeed taken your Covenant,[5283]
If ye are men of faith.

بِرَبِّكُمْ وَقَدْ أَخَذَ مِيثَٰقَكُمْ إِن كُنتُم مُّؤْمِنِينَ

9. He is the One Who
Sends to His Servant[5284]
Manifest Signs, that He
May lead you from
The depths of Darkness
Into the Light. And verily,
Allah is to you
Most Kind and Merciful.

(٩) هُوَ ٱلَّذِى يُنَزِّلُ عَلَىٰ عَبْدِهِۦٓ
ءَايَٰتٍۭ بَيِّنَٰتٍ لِّيُخْرِجَكُم
مِّنَ ٱلظُّلُمَٰتِ إِلَى ٱلنُّورِ
وَإِنَّ ٱللَّهَ بِكُمْ لَرَءُوفٌ رَّحِيمٌ

10. And what cause have ye
Why ye should not spend
In the cause of Allah?—
For to Allah belongs[5285]
The heritage of the heavens
And the earth.
Not equal among you
Are those who spent (freely)
And fought, before the
Victory,[5286]
(With those who did so later).
Those are higher in rank
Than those who spent (freely)
And fought afterwards.
But to all has Allah promised
A goodly (reward). And Allah
Is well-acquainted
With all that ye do.

(١٠) وَمَا لَكُمْ أَلَّا تُنفِقُوا۟
فِى سَبِيلِ ٱللَّهِ وَلِلَّهِ مِيرَٰثُ
ٱلسَّمَٰوَٰتِ وَٱلْأَرْضِ
لَا يَسْتَوِى مِنكُم مَّنْ أَنفَقَ
مِن قَبْلِ ٱلْفَتْحِ وَقَٰتَلَ
أُو۟لَٰٓئِكَ أَعْظَمُ دَرَجَةً مِّنَ
ٱلَّذِينَ أَنفَقُوا۟ مِنۢ بَعْدُ وَقَٰتَلُوا۟
وَكُلًّا وَعَدَ ٱللَّهُ ٱلْحُسْنَىٰ
وَٱللَّهُ بِمَا تَعْمَلُونَ خَبِيرٌ

5283. There are two shades of meaning. (1) There is the implied Convenant in a man who accepts the Gospel of Unity that he will bring forth all the fruits of that Gospel, *i.e.*, believe in Allah, and serve Allah and humanity. See n. 682 to 5:1. (2) There were at various times express Covenants entered into by the Muslims to serve Allah and be true to the Prophet, comparable to the Covenants of the Jewish nation about the Message of Moses; *e.g.*, the two Covenants of 'Aqabah (5:8, and n. 705) and the Pledge of Ḥudaybīyah (48:10, n. 4877). For the Covenant with Israel at Mount Sinai, see 2:63, n. 78.

5284. The Holy Prophet Muḥammad. The Signs sent to him were: (1) The Āyahs of the Qur'ān, and (2) his life and work, in which Allah's Plan and Purpose were unfolded.

5285. *To Allah belongs the heritage of. . .*: see n. 485 to 3:180; also n. 988 to 6:165; and n. 1964 to 15:23.

5286. This is usually understood to refer to the Conquest of Makkah, after which the Muslims succeeded to the power and position which the Pagan Quraysh had so misused at Makkah. Thereafter the Muslims had the hegemony of Arabia, and in a few centuries, for a time, the hegemony of the world. But the words are perfectly general, and we must understand the general meaning also: that the people who fight and struggle in Allah's Cause and give of their best to it at any time are worthy of praise: but those are worthy of special distinction who do it when the Cause is being persecuted and in most need of assistance, before victory comes.

SECTION 2.

11. Who is he that will
Loan to Allah a beautiful[5287]
Loan? For (Allah) will
Increase it manifold
To his credit,
And he will have (besides)
A liberal reward.

﴿١١﴾ مَن ذَا ٱلَّذِى يُقْرِضُ ٱللَّهَ
قَرْضًا حَسَنًا فَيُضَٰعِفَهُۥ لَهُۥ
وَلَهُۥٓ أَجْرٌ كَرِيمٌ

12. One Day shalt thou see
The believing men and
The believing women—
How their Light runs[5288]
Forward before them
And by their right hands:
(Their greeting will be):
"Good News for you this Day!
Gardens beneath which flow rivers!
To dwell therein for aye!
This is indeed
The highest Achievement!"[5289]

﴿١٢﴾ يَوْمَ تَرَى ٱلْمُؤْمِنِينَ
وَٱلْمُؤْمِنَٰتِ يَسْعَىٰ نُورُهُم
بَيْنَ أَيْدِيهِمْ وَبِأَيْمَٰنِهِم
بُشْرَىٰكُمُ ٱلْيَوْمَ جَنَّٰتٌ تَجْرِى
مِن تَحْتِهَا ٱلْأَنْهَٰرُ خَٰلِدِينَ فِيهَا
ذَٰلِكَ هُوَ ٱلْفَوْزُ ٱلْعَظِيمُ

13. One Day will the Hypocrites—
Men and women—say
To the Believers: "Wait
For us! Let us borrow
(A light) from your Light!"[5290]
It will be said: "Turn
Ye back to your rear!
Then seek a light (where
Ye can)!" So a wall[5291]
Will be put up betwixt them,
With a gate therein.

﴿١٣﴾ يَوْمَ يَقُولُ ٱلْمُنَٰفِقُونَ
وَٱلْمُنَٰفِقَٰتُ لِلَّذِينَ ءَامَنُوا۟
ٱنظُرُونَا نَقْتَبِسْ مِن نُّورِكُمْ
قِيلَ ٱرْجِعُوا۟ وَرَآءَكُمْ فَٱلْتَمِسُوا۟ نُورًا
فَضُرِبَ بَيْنَهُم بِسُورٍ لَّهُۥ بَابٌۢ

5287. *Cf.* 2:245, n. 276.

5288. In the Darkness of the Day of Judgement there will be a Light to guide the righteous to their Destination. This will be the Light of their Faith and their Good Works. Perhaps the Light of the Right Hand mentioned here is the Light of their Good Works: for the Blessed will receive their Record in their right hand (69:19-24).

5289. The highest Achievement, the highest felicity, the attainment of Salvation, the fulfillment of all desires. See n. 4733 to 44:57.

5290. Watchful preparation in Life, and the light of Faith, which reflects the divine Light, are matters of personal Life, and cannot be borrowed from another. So, in Christ's parable of the Ten Virgins (Matt. xv. 1-13), when the foolish ones had let their lamps go out for want of oil, they asked to borrow oil from the wise ones, but the wise ones answered and said, "Not so;. . . but go ye rather to them that sell, and buy for yourselves".

5291. The wall of Personality, or Record of Deeds, will divide the Good from the Evil. But the Gateway in it will show that communication will not be cut off. Evil must realise that Good—*i.e.*, Mercy and Felicity—had been within its reach, and that the Wrath which envelops it is due to its own rejection of Mercy.

Within it will be Mercy
Throughout, and without it,
All alongside, will be
(Wrath and) Punishment!

بَاطِنُهُۥ فِيهِ ٱلرَّحْمَةُ
وَظَٰهِرُهُۥ مِن قِبَلِهِ ٱلْعَذَابُ

14. (Those without) will call out,
"Were we not with you?"[5292]
(The others) will reply, "True!
But ye led yourselves
Into temptation; ye looked forward
(To our ruin); ye doubted
(Allah's Promise); and (your false)
Desires deceived you; until
There issued the Command
Of Allah. And the Deceiver
Deceived you in respect of
Allah.[5293]

١٤ يُنَادُونَهُمْ أَلَمْ نَكُن مَّعَكُمْ
قَالُوا۟ بَلَىٰ وَلَٰكِنَّكُمْ فَتَنتُمْ أَنفُسَكُمْ
وَتَرَبَّصْتُمْ وَٱرْتَبْتُمْ وَغَرَّتْكُمُ
ٱلْأَمَانِىُّ حَتَّىٰ جَآءَ أَمْرُ ٱللَّهِ
وَغَرَّكُم بِٱللَّهِ ٱلْغَرُورُ

15. "This Day shall no ransom
Be accepted of you, nor
Of those who rejected Allah[5294]
Your abode is the Fire:
That is the proper place
To claim you: and an evil
Refuge it is!"

١٥ فَٱلْيَوْمَ لَا يُؤْخَذُ مِنكُمْ فِدْيَةٌ وَلَا
مِنَ ٱلَّذِينَ كَفَرُوا۟ مَأْوَىٰكُمُ ٱلنَّارُ
هِىَ مَوْلَىٰكُمْ وَبِئْسَ ٱلْمَصِيرُ

16. Has not the time arrived[5295]
For the Believers that
Their hearts in all humility
Should engage in the
remembrance
Of Allah and of the Truth
Which has been revealed (to
them),
And that they should not
Become like those to whom

١٦ أَلَمْ يَأْنِ لِلَّذِينَ ءَامَنُوٓا۟
أَن تَخْشَعَ قُلُوبُهُمْ لِذِكْرِ
ٱللَّهِ وَمَا نَزَلَ مِنَ ٱلْحَقِّ
وَلَا يَكُونُوا۟ كَٱلَّذِينَ

5292. The evil will now claim some right of kinship or association or proximity with the good in earthly life; but in fact they had been arrogant and had selfishly despised them before. The reply will be: (1) you yourselves chose temptation and evil; (2) when you had power in your earthly life, you hoped for ruin to the good, and perhaps plotted for it; (3) you were warned by prophets of Allah, but you doubted Allah's very existence and certainly His Mercy and Justice, and the Hereafter; (4) you followed your own lusts and neglected Reason and Truth; (5) you were given plenty of rope, but you followed your mad career, until Judgement came upon you, and now it is too late for repentance.

5293. The Arch-Deceiver (Satan) deceived you in respect of Allah in many ways: for example, he made you oblivious of Allah's Mercy and loving-kindness; he made you reject His Grace; he made you think that Allah's Justice may not overtake you; etc.

5294. In personal responsibility there is no room for vicarious ransom or for ransom by payments of gold or silver or by sacrifice of possessions. Nor can the crime be expiated for *after* Judgement 'You' and 'those who rejected Allah' are two ways of looking at the same persons. 'You are rejected because you rejected Allah.'

5295. Humility and the remembrance of Allah and His Message are never more necesssary than in the hour of victory and prosperity.

Was given Revelation
aforetime,[5296]
But long ages passed over them
And their hearts grew hard?
For many among them
Are rebellious transgressors.

17. Know ye (all) that
Allah giveth life
To the earth after its death![5297]
Already have We shown
The Signs plainly to you,
That ye may learn wisdom.

18. For those who give
In Charity, men and women,
And loan to Allah[5298]
A Beautiful Loan,
It shall be increased manifold
(To their credit),
And they shall have (besides)
A liberal reward.

19. And those who believe
In Allah and His messengers—
They are the Sincere[5299]
(Lovers of Truth), and
The Witnesses (who testify),[5300]
In the eyes of their Lord:
They shall have their Reward
And their Light.[5301]

أُوتُوا۟ ٱلْكِتَـٰبَ مِن قَبْلُ
فَطَالَ عَلَيْهِمُ ٱلْأَمَدُ فَقَسَتْ قُلُوبُهُمْ
وَكَثِيرٌ مِّنْهُمْ فَـٰسِقُونَ

١٧ ٱعْلَمُوٓا۟ أَنَّ ٱللَّهَ يُحْىِ ٱلْأَرْضَ بَعْدَ مَوْتِهَا
قَدْ بَيَّنَّا لَكُمُ ٱلْـَٔايَـٰتِ
لَعَلَّكُمْ تَعْقِلُونَ

١٨ إِنَّ ٱلْمُصَّدِّقِينَ وَٱلْمُصَّدِّقَـٰتِ
وَأَقْرَضُوا۟ ٱللَّهَ قَرْضًا حَسَنًا
يُضَـٰعَفُ لَهُمْ
وَلَهُمْ أَجْرٌ كَرِيمٌ

١٩ وَٱلَّذِينَ ءَامَنُوا۟ بِٱللَّهِ وَرُسُلِهِۦٓ
أُو۟لَـٰٓئِكَ هُمُ ٱلصِّدِّيقُونَ
وَٱلشُّهَدَآءُ عِندَ رَبِّهِمْ
لَهُمْ أَجْرُهُمْ وَنُورُهُمْ

5296. The men immediately referred to are the contemporary Jews and Christians. To each of these Ummahs was given Allah's Revelation, but as time passed, they corrupted it, became arrogant and hard-hearted, and subverted justice, truth, and the purity of Life. But the general lesson is far wider. No one is favoured by Allah except on the score of righteousness. Except on that score, there is no chosen individual or race. There is no blind good fortune or ill fortune. All happens according to the just laws and Will of Allah. But at no time is humility or righteousness more necessary than in the hour of victory or triumph.

5297. As the dead earth is revived after the refreshing showers of rain, so is it with the spirit of man, whether as an individual or a race or Ummah. There is no cause for dispair. Allah's Truth will revive the Spiritual faculties if it is accepted with humility and zeal.

5298. *Cf.* 57:11; also see 2:245, n. 276.

5299. *Cf.* 4:69, and n. 586. The four categories there mentioned as constituting the beautiful Fellowship of Faith are: the Prophets who teach, the Sincere Lovers of Truth, the Witnesses who testify, and the Righteous who do good. Of these, the prophets or messengers have already been mentioned in this verse. The Righteous who do good are mentioned as the men and women given over to deeds of charity in verse 18.

5300. The Witnesses are not only Martyrs, but all those who carry the Banner of Truth against all odds and in all positions of danger, whether by pen or speech, or deed or counsel.

5301. Note that these two are specially high degrees in the spiritual kingdom, just short of Prophethood. For they have not only their reward in the spiritual Kingdom of Allah, like those who practise charity (verse 18 above), but they themselves become sources of light and leading.

But those who reject Allah
And deny Our Signs—
They are the Companions
Of Hell-Fire.

وَٱلَّذِينَ كَفَرُوا۟ وَكَذَّبُوا۟ بِـَٔايَٰتِنَآ
أُو۟لَٰٓئِكَ أَصْحَٰبُ ٱلْجَحِيمِ

SECTION 3.

20. Know ye (all), that
The life of this world
Is but play and amusement,[5302]
Pomp and mutual boasting
And multiplying, (in rivalry)
Among yourselves, riches
And children.
Here is a similitude;[5303]
How rain and the growth
Which it brings forth, delight
(The hearts of) the tillers;[5304]
Soon it withers; thou
Wilt see it grow yellow;
Then it becomes dry
And crumbles away.
But in the Hereafter
Is a Penalty severe
(For the devotees of wrong).
And Forgiveness from Allah
And (His) Good Pleasure
(For the devotees of Allah).
And what is the life
Of this world, but
Goods and chattels
Of deception?[5305]

٢٠ ٱعْلَمُوٓا۟ أَنَّمَا ٱلْحَيَوٰةُ
ٱلدُّنْيَا لَعِبٌ وَلَهْوٌ وَزِينَةٌ
وَتَفَاخُرٌۢ بَيْنَكُمْ وَتَكَاثُرٌ
فِى ٱلْأَمْوَٰلِ وَٱلْأَوْلَٰدِ
كَمَثَلِ غَيْثٍ أَعْجَبَ ٱلْكُفَّارَ
نَبَاتُهُۥ ثُمَّ يَهِيجُ فَتَرَىٰهُ
مُصْفَرًّا ثُمَّ يَكُونُ حُطَٰمًا
وَفِى ٱلْـَٔاخِرَةِ عَذَابٌ شَدِيدٌ
وَمَغْفِرَةٌ مِّنَ ٱللَّهِ وَرِضْوَٰنٌ
وَمَا ٱلْحَيَوٰةُ ٱلدُّنْيَآ
إِلَّا مَتَٰعُ ٱلْغُرُورِ

21. Be ye foremost (in seeking)
Forgiveness from your Lord,
And a Garden (of Bliss),

٢١ سَابِقُوٓا۟ إِلَىٰ مَغْفِرَةٍ
مِّن رَّبِّكُمْ وَجَنَّةٍ

5302. *Cf.* 6:32, and n. 855. In the present passage the idea is further amplified. In this life people not only play and amuse themselves and each other, but they show off, and boast, and pile up riches and man-power and influence, in rivalry with each other.

5303. *Cf.* 39:21, and n. 4273. Here the Parable is meant to teach a slightly different lesson. Allah's mercies are free and open to all, like His rain. But how do men make use of them? The good men take the real spiritual harvest and store the spiritual grain. The men who are in love with the ephemeral are delighted with the green of the tares and the grass; but such things give no real nourishment; they soon wither, become dry, and crumble to pieces, like the worldly pleasures and pomps, boastings and tumults, possessions and friends.

5304. *Kuffār* is here used in the unusual sense of 'tillers or husbandmen', because they sow the seed and cover it up with soil. But the ordinary meaning, 'Rejectors of Truth', is not absent. The allegory refers to such men.

5305. *Cf.* 3:185, and n. 492. Many of the attractive vanities of this world are but nets set by the Evil One to deceive men. The only thing real and lasting is the Good Life lived in the Light of Allah.

The width whereof is
As the width of
Heaven and earth,[5306]
Prepared for those who believe
In Allah and His messengers:
That is the Grace of Allah,
Which He bestows on whom[5307]
He pleases: and Allah is
The Lord of Grace abounding.

عَرْضُهَا كَعَرْضِ ٱلسَّمَآءِ وَٱلْأَرْضِ
أُعِدَّتْ لِلَّذِينَ ءَامَنُوا۟ بِٱللَّهِ وَرُسُلِهِۦ
ذَٰلِكَ فَضْلُ ٱللَّهِ يُؤْتِيهِ مَن يَشَآءُ
وَٱللَّهُ ذُو ٱلْفَضْلِ ٱلْعَظِيمِ

22. No misfortune can happen
On earth or in your souls[5308]
But is recorded in
A decree before We bring[5309]
It into existence:
That is truly easy for Allah:

(٢٢) مَآ أَصَابَ مِن مُّصِيبَةٍ فِى ٱلْأَرْضِ وَلَا فِىٓ
أَنفُسِكُمْ إِلَّا فِى كِتَٰبٍ مِّن قَبْلِ أَن نَّبْرَأَهَآ
إِنَّ ذَٰلِكَ عَلَى ٱللَّهِ يَسِيرٌ

23. In order that ye may
Not despair over matters
That pass you by,
Nor exult over favours
Bestowed upon you.
For Allah loveth not
Any vainglorious boaster—[5310]

(٢٣) لِّكَيْلَا تَأْسَوْا۟ عَلَىٰ مَا فَاتَكُمْ
وَلَا تَفْرَحُوا۟ بِمَآ ءَاتَىٰكُمْ
وَٱللَّهُ لَا يُحِبُّ كُلَّ مُخْتَالٍ فَخُورٍ

24. Such persons as are[5311]
Covetous and commend
Covetousness to men,
And if any turn back[5312]

(٢٤) ٱلَّذِينَ يَبْخَلُونَ وَيَأْمُرُونَ
ٱلنَّاسَ بِٱلْبُخْلِ وَمَن يَتَوَلَّ

5306. *Cf.* 3:133, and n. 452.

5307. *Bestows on whom He Pleases:* that is, such grace and favour is beyond anyone's own merits. It is bestowed by Allah according to His Holy Will and Plan, which is just, merciful, and righteous.

5308. External disasters or misfortunes may strike people's eye or imagination, but there are worse crises and misfortunes in the spiritual world, which are of equal or greater importance to man's future. All this happens according to the Will and Plan of Allah. Even where we are allowed the exercise of our own wills, the consequences that follow are in accordance with the laws and Plan decreed by Allah beforehand.

5309. For *bara'a*, 'to bring into existence', and other words denoting Allah's creative energy, see n. 120 to 2:117; n. 916 to 6:94; and n. 923 to 6:98.

5310. In the external world, what people may consider misfortune or good fortune may both turn out to be illusory—in Kipling's words, "both imposters just the same". The righteous man does not grumble if some one else has possessions, nor exult if he has them. He does not covet and he does not boast. If he has any advantages, he shares them with other people, as he considers them not due to his own merits, but as gifts from Allah. (R).

5311. Neither the Covetous nor the Boasters have any place in the Good Pleasure of Allah. The Covetous are particularly insidious, as their avarice and niggardliness not only keep back the gifts of Allah from men, but their pernicious example dries up the streams of Charity in others.

5312. It is Charity in Allah's Way that is specially in view here. If people are selfish and withhold their hand, they only injure themselves. They do not hurt Allah's Cause, for He is independent of all needs, and He will find other means of assisting His more meagrely endowed servants; He is worthy of all praise in His care for His creatures.

(From Allah's Way), verily
Allah is free of all needs,
Worthy of all praise.

25. We sent aforetime
Our messengers with Clear Signs
And sent down with them
The Book and the Balance[5313]
(Of Right and Wrong), that men
May stand forth in justice;
And We sent down[5314] Iron,[5315]
In which is (material for)
Mighty war, as well as
Many benefits for mankind,
That Allah may test who
It is that will help,
Unseen,[5316] Him and His
messengers:[5317]
For Allah is Full of Strength,
Exalted in Might[5318]
(And able to enforce His Will).

SECTION 4.

26. And We sent Noah
And Abraham, and established
In their line Prophethood
And Revelation: and some of
them[5319]

فَإِنَّ ٱللَّهَ هُوَ ٱلْغَنِيُّ ٱلْحَمِيدُ

(٢٥) لَقَدْ أَرْسَلْنَا رُسُلَنَا
بِٱلْبَيِّنَٰتِ وَأَنزَلْنَا مَعَهُمُ ٱلْكِتَٰبَ
وَٱلْمِيزَانَ لِيَقُومَ ٱلنَّاسُ بِٱلْقِسْطِ
وَأَنزَلْنَا ٱلْحَدِيدَ فِيهِ بَأْسٌ شَدِيدٌ
وَمَنَٰفِعُ لِلنَّاسِ وَلِيَعْلَمَ ٱللَّهُ
مَن يَنصُرُهُۥ وَرُسُلَهُۥ بِٱلْغَيْبِ
إِنَّ ٱللَّهَ قَوِيٌّ عَزِيزٌ

(٢٦) وَلَقَدْ أَرْسَلْنَا نُوحًا
وَإِبْرَٰهِيمَ وَجَعَلْنَا فِى ذُرِّيَّتِهِمَا
ٱلنُّبُوَّةَ وَٱلْكِتَٰبَ فَمِنْهُم

5313. Three things are mentioned as gifts of Allah. In concrete terms they are the Book, the Balance, and Iron, which stand as emblems of three things which hold society together, *viz.*, Revelation, which commands Good and forbids Evil; Justice, which gives to each person his due; and the strong arm of the Law, which maintains sanctions for evildoers. For *Balance*, see also 42:17, and n. 4550.

5314. *Sent down: anzala;* in the sense of revealed to man the use of certain things, created in him the capacity of understanding and using them: *Cf.* 39:6: "sent down for you eight head of cattle in pairs".

5315. *Iron:* the most useful metal known to man. Out of it is made steel, and from steel and iron are made implements of war, such as swords, spears, guns, etc., as well as instruments of peace, such as ploughshares, bricklayers' trowels, architects' and engineers' instruments, etc. Iron stands as the emblem of Strength, Power, Discipline, Law's sanctions, etc. Iron and steel industries have also been the foundation of the prosperity and power of modern manufacturing nations. (R).

5316. In 21:49, I have translated "in their most secret thoughts" for the more literal "unseen" *(bil ghayb)*. Perhaps the more literal "unseen" may do if understood in the adverbial sense as explained in 35:18, n. 3902. The sincere man will help the Cause, whether he is seen or brought under notice or not.

5317. To help Allah and His messengers is to help their Cause. It is to give men an opportunity of striving and fighting for His Cause and proving their true mettle, for thus is their spirit tested. As explained in the next line, Allah in Himself is Full of Strength, Exalted in Power, and Able to enforce His Will, and He has no need of others' assistance.

5318. *Cf.* 22:40 and n. 2818. "Strength" is specific; Power or Might is more abstract, the ability to enforce what is willed.

5319. *Some of them: i.e.*, of their line, or posterity, or Ummah. When the Book that was given to them became corrupted, many of them followed their own fancies and became transgressors.

Were on right guidance,
But many of them
Became rebellious transgressors.

مُّهْتَدٍ وَكَثِيرٌ مِّنْهُمْ فَٰسِقُونَ

27. Then, in their wake,
We followed them up
With (others of) Our mesengers:
We sent after them
Jesus the son of Mary,
And bestowed on him
The Gospel; and We ordained
In the hearts of those
Who followed him
Compassion and Mercy,[5320]
But the Monasticism
Which they invented
For themselves, We did not
Prescribe for them:[5321]
(We commanded) only
The seeking for the Good
Pleasure of Allah; but that
They did not foster[5322]
As they should have done.
Yet We bestowed, on those
Among them who believed,[5323]
Their (due) reward, but
Many of them are
Rebellious transgressors.[5324]

(٢٧) ثُمَّ قَفَّيْنَا عَلَىٰٓ
ءَاثَٰرِهِم بِرُسُلِنَا
وَقَفَّيْنَا بِعِيسَى ٱبْنِ مَرْيَمَ
وَءَاتَيْنَٰهُ ٱلْإِنجِيلَ
وَجَعَلْنَا فِى قُلُوبِ ٱلَّذِينَ
ٱتَّبَعُوهُ رَأْفَةً وَرَحْمَةً وَرَهْبَانِيَّةً
ٱبْتَدَعُوهَا مَا كَتَبْنَٰهَا عَلَيْهِمْ
إِلَّا ٱبْتِغَآءَ رِضْوَٰنِ ٱللَّهِ فَمَا
رَعَوْهَا حَقَّ رِعَايَتِهَا
فَـَٔاتَيْنَا ٱلَّذِينَ ءَامَنُوا۟
مِنْهُمْ أَجْرَهُمْ
وَكَثِيرٌ مِّنْهُمْ فَٰسِقُونَ

5320. The chief characteristic of the teaching in the Gospels is humility and other-worldliness. The first blessings in the Sermon on the Mount are on "the poor in spirit", "they that mourn", and they that are "meek" (Matt. v. 3-5). Christ's disciples were enjoined to "take no thought for the morrow", and told: "Sufficient unto the day is the evil thereof" (Matt. vi. 34). They were also commanded "that ye resist not evil; but whosoever shall smite thee on thy right cheek, turn to him the other also" (Matt. v. 39). These are fragmentary presentments of an imperfect philosophy as seen through monastic eyes. Insofar as they represent pity, sympathy with suffering, and deeds of mercy, they represent the spirit of Christ.

5321. But Allah's Kingdom requires also courage, resistance to evil, the firmness, law, and discipline which will enforce justice among men. It requires to mingle with men, so that they can uphold the standard of Truth, against odds if necessary. These were lost sight of in Monasticism, which was not prescribed by Allah.

5322. Allah certainly requires that men shall renounce the idle pleasures of this world, and turn to the Path which leads to Allah's Good Pleasure. But that does not mean gloomy lives, ("they that mourn"), nor perpetual and formal prayers in isolation. Allah's service is done through pure lives in the turmoil of this world. This spirit was lost, or at least not fostered by monastic institutions. On the contrary, a great part of the "struggle and striving" for noble lives was suppressed.

5323. Many of them lost true Faith, or had their Faith corrupted by superstitions. But those who continued firm in Faith saw the natural development of Religion in Islam. Their previous belief was not a disadvantage to them, but helped them, because they kept it free from false and selfish prejudices. These are the ones who are further addressed at the beginning of verse 28 below.

5324. The corruptions in the Christian Church, the hair-splitting disputes, and mutual strife and hatred of sects had become a scandal by the time that the light of Islam came into the world. The pages of Gibbon's great History bear witness. Not only had the religion become void of grace, but the lives of the people, priests and laity, had fallen into great depths of degradation. See remarks in my Appendix V, and the general picture in Kingsley's *Hypatia*.

28. O ye that believe![5325]
Fear, Allah, and believe
In His Messenger, and He will
Bestow on you a double[5326]
Portion of His Mercy:
He will provide for you
A Light by which ye[5327]
Shall walk (straight
In your path), and He
Will forgive you (your past);[5328]
For Allah is Oft-Forgiving,
Most Merciful:

٢٨ يَٰٓأَيُّهَا ٱلَّذِينَ ءَامَنُوا۟
ٱتَّقُوا۟ ٱللَّهَ وَءَامِنُوا۟ بِرَسُولِهِۦ
يُؤْتِكُمْ كِفْلَيْنِ مِن رَّحْمَتِهِۦ وَيَجْعَل
لَّكُمْ نُورًا تَمْشُونَ بِهِۦ وَيَغْفِرْ لَكُمْ ۚ
وَٱللَّهُ غَفُورٌ رَّحِيمٌ

29. That the People of
The Book may know
That they have no power[5329]
Whatever over the Grace
Of Allah, that (His) Grace
Is (entirely) in His Hand,
To bestow it on
Whomsoever He wills.
For Allah is the Lord
Of Grace abounding.

٢٩ لِّئَلَّا يَعْلَمَ أَهْلُ
ٱلْكِتَٰبِ أَلَّا يَقْدِرُونَ
عَلَىٰ شَىْءٍ مِّن فَضْلِ ٱللَّهِ ۙ
وَأَنَّ ٱلْفَضْلَ بِيَدِ ٱللَّهِ يُؤْتِيهِ مَن يَشَآءُ ۚ
وَٱللَّهُ ذُو ٱلْفَضْلِ ٱلْعَظِيمِ

5325. From the context before (see n. 5323 above) and after (see next note), this is held to refer to the Christians and People of the Book who kept their Faith true and undefiled.

5326. The double portion refers to the past and the future. As noted in the last note, this passage is addressed to the Christians and the People of the Book, who, when honestly facing the question of the new Revelation in Islam, find in it the fulfilment of previous revelations, and therefore believe in Allah's Messenger Muḥammad, and walk by the new Light. Their previous merits will be duly recognised, and they will be treated on fully equal terms in the new Ummah. This is their double share, not necessarily more in quantity than that of their brethren in Islam who passed through no other gate, but having a twofold aspect.

5327. As this refers to the Christians and the People of the Book, the following saying of Christ in his last days may interest them: "Yet a little while is the light with you. Walk while ye have the light, lest darkness come upon you. . .While ye have the light, believe in the light, that ye may be the children of light. These things spake Jesus, and departed, and did hide himself from them". (John, xii. 35-36). The light of Christ's Gospel soon departed; his Church was enveloped in darkness; then came the light again, in the fuller light of Islam. And they are asked to believe in the Light, and to walk in it. *Cf.* also 57:12, and n. 5288 above.

5328. Any wrongs they may have committed through ignorance or misconceptions in their previous religion will be forgiven them, as they have seen the new Light and walk by it.

5329. Let not any race, or people, or community, or group, believe that they have exclusive possession of Allah's Grace, or that they can influence its grant or its withholding. Allah's Grace is free, and entirely controlled by Him, independently of any priests and privileged people. He dispenses it according to His own wise and Holy Will and Plan; and to His Grace there is no limit.

INTRODUCTION TO SŪRAH 58—*AL MUJĀDILAH*

This is the second of the ten Madīnah Sūrahs referred to in the Introduction to the last Sūrah, Its subject matter is the acceptance of a woman's Plea on behalf of herself and her children (see n. 5330 to 58:1 below), and a condemnation of all secret counsels and intrigues in the Muslim Brotherhood.

The date is somewhat close to that of S. 33, say between A. H. 5 and A. H. 7.

Summary—All false pretences, especially those that degrade a woman's position, are condemned—as well as secret consultations between men and intrigues with falsehood, mischief, and sedition. (58:1-22, and C. 237).

C. 237.—Let not false pretences or superstitions
(58:1-22) Degrade the position of women. Eschew
Secret plottings and secret counsels.
Observe order and decorum in public assemblies,
And seek not in selfish pride to engage
Your Leader's private attention. It is wrong
To turn to the enemies of Allah for friendship:
They make their oaths a cloak for wrongdoing,
And keep back men from the Right. But none
Can resist the Power or the Judgement of Allah.
The righteous seek only His Good Pleasure,
And rejoice therein as their highest Achievement.

Sūrah 58.

Al Mujādilah (The Woman Who Pleads)

الجزء الثامن والعشرون — سورة المجادلة

In the name of Allah, Most Gracious, Most Merciful.

بِسْمِ اللَّهِ الرَّحْمَٰنِ الرَّحِيمِ

28/30

1. Allah has indeed
Heard (and accepted) the statement
Of the woman who pleads[5330]
With thee concerning her husband
And carries her complaint
(In prayer) to Allah:
And Allah (always) hears
The arguments between both[5331]
Sides among you: for Allah
Hears and sees (all things).

(١) قَدْ سَمِعَ ٱللَّهُ قَوْلَ
ٱلَّتِي تُجَٰدِلُكَ فِي زَوْجِهَا
وَتَشْتَكِيٓ إِلَى ٱللَّهِ
وَٱللَّهُ يَسْمَعُ تَحَاوُرَكُمَآ
إِنَّ ٱللَّهَ سَمِيعٌۢ بَصِيرٌ

2. If any men among you
Divorce their wives by Zihār[5332]
(Calling them mothers),
They cannot be their mothers:
None can be their mothers
Except those who gave them
Birth. And in fact
They use words (both) iniquitous[5333]
And false: but truly
Allah is One that blots out[5334]
(Sins), and forgives
(Again and again).

(٢) ٱلَّذِينَ يُظَٰهِرُونَ مِنكُم
مِّن نِّسَآئِهِم مَّا هُنَّ أُمَّهَٰتِهِمْ
إِنْ أُمَّهَٰتُهُمْ إِلَّا ٱلَّٰٓـِٔي وَلَدْنَهُمْ
وَإِنَّهُمْ لَيَقُولُونَ
مُنكَرًا مِّنَ ٱلْقَوْلِ وَزُورًا
وَإِنَّ ٱللَّهَ لَعَفُوٌّ غَفُورٌ

5330. The immediate occasion was what happened to Khawlah bint Tha'labah, wife of Aws son of Ṣāmit. Though in Islam, he divorced her by an old Pagan custom: the formula was known as Ẓihār, and consisted of the words "Thou art to me as the back of my mother". This was held by Pagan custom to imply a divorce and freed the husband from any responsibility for conjugal duties, but did not leave the wife free to leave the husband's home, or to contract a second marriage. Such a custom was in any case degrading to a woman. It was particularly hard on Khawlah, for she loved her husband and pleaded that she had little children who she had no resources herself to support and whom under *Ẓihār* her husband was not bound to support. She urged her plea to the Prophet and in prayer to Allah. Her just plea was accepted, and this iniquitous custom, based on false words, was abolished. See also n. 3670 to 33:4.

5331. For He is a just God, and will not allow human customs or pretences to trample on the just rights of the weakest of His creatures.

5332. See n. 5330 above.

5333. Such words are false in fact and iniquitous, inasmuch as they are unfair to the wife and unseemly in decent society.

5334. *Cf.* 4:99 and 22:60. Were it not that Allah in His Mercy makes allowances for our weaknesses and the various grades of motives that actuate us, such conduct would be inexpiable. But He prescribes expiation as in the next verse, because He wishes to blot out what is wrong and give us a chance to reform by His forgiveness.

3. But those who divorce
Their wives by Ẓihār,
Then wish to go back[5335]
On the words they uttered—
(It is ordained that
Such a one)
Should free a slave
Before they touch each other:
This are ye admonished
To perform: and Allah is
Well-acquainted with (all)
That ye do.

وَٱلَّذِينَ يُظَٰهِرُونَ مِن نِّسَآئِهِمْ ثُمَّ يَعُودُونَ لِمَا قَالُوا۟ فَتَحْرِيرُ رَقَبَةٍ مِّن قَبْلِ أَن يَتَمَآسَّا ۚ ذَٰلِكُمْ تُوعَظُونَ بِهِۦ ۚ وَٱللَّهُ بِمَا تَعْمَلُونَ خَبِيرٌ ٣

4. And if any has not
(The wherewithal),[5336]
He should fast for
Two months consecutively
Before they touch each other.
But if any is unable
To do so, he should feed
Sixty indigent ones.[5337]
This, that ye may show
Your faith in Allah[5338]
And His Messenger,
Those are limits (set
By) Allah. For those who
Reject (Him), there is
A grievous Penalty.[5339]

فَمَن لَّمْ يَجِدْ فَصِيَامُ شَهْرَيْنِ مُتَتَابِعَيْنِ مِن قَبْلِ أَن يَتَمَآسَّا ۖ فَمَن لَّمْ يَسْتَطِعْ فَإِطْعَامُ سِتِّينَ مِسْكِينًا ۚ ذَٰلِكَ لِتُؤْمِنُوا۟ بِٱللَّهِ وَرَسُولِهِۦ ۚ وَتِلْكَ حُدُودُ ٱللَّهِ ۗ وَلِلْكَٰفِرِينَ عَذَابٌ أَلِيمٌ ٤

5335. If *Ẓihār* were to be ignored as if the words were never uttered, it would mean that men may foolishly resort to it without penalty. It is therefore recognised in respect of the penalty which the man incurs, but safeguards the woman's rights. She can sue for maintenance for herself and her children, but her husband could not claim his conjugal rights. If it was a hasty act and he repented of it, he could not claim his conjugal rights until after the performance of his penalty as provided below. If she loved him, as in Khawlah's case, she could also herself sue for conjugal rights in the legal sense of the term and compel her husband to perform the penalty and resume marital relations.

5336. *Cf.* 4:92. The penalty is: to get a slave his freedom, whether it is your own slave or you purchase his freedom from another; if that is not possible, to fast for two months consecutively (in the manner of the *Ramaḍān* fast); if that is not possible, to feed sixty poor. See next note.

5337. There is a great deal of learned argument among the jurists as to the precise requirements of Canon Law under the term "feeding" the indigent. For example, it is laid down that half a *Ṣā'* of wheat or a full *Ṣā'* of dates or their equivalent in money would fulfil the requirements, a *Ṣā'* being a measure corresponding roughly to about 9 lbs. of wheat in weight. Others hold that a *Mudd* measure equivalent to about 2¼ lbs. would be sufficient. This would certainly be nearer the daily ration of a man. It is better to take the spirit of the text in its plain simplicity, and say that an indigent man should be given enough to eat for two meals a day. The sixty indigent ones fed for a day would be equivalent to a single individual fed for sixty days, or two for thirty days, and so on. But there is no need to go into minutiae in such matters.

5338. These penalties in the alternative are prescribed, that we may show our repentance and Faith and our renunciation of "iniquity and falsehood" (verse 2 above), whatever our circumstances may be.

5339. It would seem that this refers to the spiritual Penalty in the Hereafter for not complying with the small penalty here prescribed. The next verse would then refer to the bigger "humiliating Penalty" for "resistance" to Allah's Law generally.

5. Those who resist Allah
And His Messenger will be
Humbled to dust, as were
Those before them: for We
Have already sent down
Clear Signs. And the
Unbelievers
(Will have) a humiliating
Penalty,

٥ إِنَّ ٱلَّذِينَ يُحَآدُّونَ ٱللَّهَ وَرَسُولَهُۥ
كُبِتُوا۟ كَمَا كُبِتَ ٱلَّذِينَ مِن قَبْلِهِمْ ۚ
وَقَدْ أَنزَلْنَآ ءَايَـٰتٍۭ بَيِّنَـٰتٍ ۚ
وَلِلْكَـٰفِرِينَ عَذَابٌ مُّهِينٌ

6. On the Day that
Allah will raise them
All up (again) and show
Them the truth (and
meaning)[5340]
Of their conduct. Allah has
Reckoned its (value), though
They may have forgotten it,
For Allah is Witness
To all things.

٦ يَوْمَ يَبْعَثُهُمُ ٱللَّهُ جَمِيعًا
فَيُنَبِّئُهُم بِمَا عَمِلُوٓا۟ ۚ
أَحْصَىٰهُ ٱللَّهُ وَنَسُوهُ ۚ
وَٱللَّهُ عَلَىٰ كُلِّ شَىْءٍ شَهِيدٌ

SECTION 2.

7. Seest thou not that
Allah doth know (all) that is
In the heavens and
On earth? There is not
A secret consultation
Between three, but He
Makes the fourth among
them—[5341]
Nor between five but
He makes the sixth—
Nor between fewer nor more,
But He is with them,
Wheresoever they be:
In the end will He
Tell them the truth
Of their conduct, on the Day
Of Judgement. For Allah
Has full knowledge
Of all things.

٧ أَلَمْ تَرَ أَنَّ ٱللَّهَ يَعْلَمُ
مَا فِى ٱلسَّمَـٰوَٰتِ وَمَا فِى ٱلْأَرْضِ ۖ
مَا يَكُونُ مِن نَّجْوَىٰ ثَلَـٰثَةٍ
إِلَّا هُوَ رَابِعُهُمْ وَلَا خَمْسَةٍ
إِلَّا هُوَ سَادِسُهُمْ
وَلَآ أَدْنَىٰ مِن ذَٰلِكَ وَلَآ
أَكْثَرَ إِلَّا هُوَ مَعَهُمْ أَيْنَ مَا كَانُوا۟ ۖ
ثُمَّ يُنَبِّئُهُم بِمَا عَمِلُوا۟ يَوْمَ ٱلْقِيَـٰمَةِ ۚ
إِنَّ ٱللَّهَ بِكُلِّ شَىْءٍ عَلِيمٌ

5340. This phrase, "Allah will tell them the truth of their deeds (or their doings or their conduct)" occurs frequently. See 5:51, n. 762; 5:108, n. 811; 6:60; 9:94; etc. In this life there is a certain mist or illusion in our spiritual sight. We see things from different angles and dispute about them; we hide real motives, and pretend to virtues which we do not possess; others may attribute such virtues to us, and we may come to believe it ourselves; we conceive likes and hatreds on insufficient grounds; we forget what we should remember, and remember what we should forget. Our vision is narrow, and our values are false. On the Day of Account all this will be remedied. Not only will true values be restored. but we shall ourselves see the inwardness of things in our own lives, which we never saw before.

5341. Secrecy is a relative and limited term among ourselves. There is nothing hidden or unknown to Allah. Usually secrecy implies fear or distrust, plotting or wrongdoing. But all is open before Allah's sight.

8. Turnest thou not thy sight
Towards those who were
Forbidden secret counsels[5342]
Yet revert to that which
They were forbidden (to do)?
And they hold secret counsels
Among themselves for iniquity
And hostility, and disobedience
To the Messenger. And when
They come to thee,
They salute thee,[5343]
Not as Allah salutes thee,
(But in crooked ways):
And they say to themselves,
"Why does not Allah
Punish us for our words?"[5344]
Enough for them is Hell:
In it will they burn,
And evil is that destination!

٨ أَلَمْ تَرَ إِلَى ٱلَّذِينَ نُهُوا۟ عَنِ
ٱلنَّجْوَىٰ ثُمَّ يَعُودُونَ لِمَا نُهُوا۟ عَنْهُ
وَيَتَنَٰجَوْنَ بِٱلْإِثْمِ وَٱلْعُدْوَٰنِ
وَمَعْصِيَتِ ٱلرَّسُولِ
وَإِذَا جَآءُوكَ حَيَّوْكَ
بِمَا لَمْ يُحَيِّكَ بِهِ ٱللَّهُ
وَيَقُولُونَ فِىٓ أَنفُسِهِمْ
لَوْلَا يُعَذِّبُنَا ٱللَّهُ بِمَا نَقُولُ
حَسْبُهُمْ جَهَنَّمُ يَصْلَوْنَهَا
فَبِئْسَ ٱلْمَصِيرُ

9. O ye who believe!
When ye hold secret counsel,
Do it not for iniquity
And hostility, and disobedience
To the Messenger; but do it
For righteousness and self-restraint;[5345]
And fear Allah, to Whom
Ye shall be brought back.

٩ يَٰٓأَيُّهَا ٱلَّذِينَ ءَامَنُوٓا۟ إِذَا تَنَٰجَيْتُمْ
فَلَا تَتَنَٰجَوْا۟ بِٱلْإِثْمِ وَٱلْعُدْوَٰنِ وَمَعْصِيَتِ
ٱلرَّسُولِ وَتَنَٰجَوْا۟ بِٱلْبِرِّ وَٱلتَّقْوَىٰ
وَٱتَّقُوا۟ ٱللَّهَ ٱلَّذِىٓ إِلَيْهِ تُحْشَرُونَ

10. Secret counsels are only
(Inspired) by the Evil One,

١٠ إِنَّمَا ٱلنَّجْوَىٰ مِنَ ٱلشَّيْطَٰنِ

5342. When the Muslim Brotherhood was acquiring strength in Madīnah, and the forces of disruption were being discomfited in open fight against the Messenger of Righteousness, the wicked resorted to duplicity and secret intrigues, in which the ringleaders were the disaffected Jews and the Hypocrites, whose machinations have been frequently referred to in the Qur'ān. *E.g.*, see 2:8-16; and 4:142-145.

5343. The salutation of Allah was (and is) "Peace!" But the enemies, who had not the courage to fight openly often twisted the words, and by using a word like *Sām*, which meant "Death!" or "Destruction!" instead of *Salām!* (Peace!), they thought they were secretly venting their spite and yet apparently using a polite form of salutation. *Cf.* 2:106, and n. 107, where another similar trick is exposed.

5344. The enemies derisively enjoyed their trick (see last note) according to their own perverted mentality. They asked blasphemously, "Why does not Allah punish us?" The answer is given; there *is* a Punishment, far greater than they imagine; it will come in good time; it will be the final Punishment after Judgement: it is delayed in order to give them a chance of repentance and reformation.

5345. Ordinarily secrecy implies deeds of darkness, something which men have to hide; see the next verse. But there are good deeds which may be concerted and done in secret: *e.g.*, charity, or the prevention of mishcief, or the defeat of the dark plots of evil. The determining factor is the motive. Is the man doing some wrong or venting his spite, or trying to disobey a lawful command? Or is he doing some good, which out of modesty or self-renuncuiation he does not want known, or is he in a righteous cause defeating the machinations of Evil, which may involve great sacrifice of himself?

In order that he may
Cause grief to the Believers;
But he cannot harm them
In the least, except as[5346]
Allah permits; and on Allah
Let the Believers
Put their trust.

لِيَحْزُنَ ٱلَّذِينَ ءَامَنُوا۟
وَلَيْسَ بِضَآرِّهِمْ شَيْـًٔا إِلَّا بِإِذْنِ ٱللَّهِ ۚ
وَعَلَى ٱللَّهِ فَلْيَتَوَكَّلِ ٱلْمُؤْمِنُونَ

11. O ye who believe!
When ye are told
To make room
In the assemblies,[5347]
(Spread out and) make room:
(Ample) room will Allah provide
For you. And when
Ye are told to rise up,[5348]
Rise up: Allah will
Raise up, to (suitable) ranks
(And degrees), those of you
Who believe and who have
Been granted Knowledge.[5349]
And Allah is well-acquainted
With all ye do.

١١ يَـٰٓأَيُّهَا ٱلَّذِينَ ءَامَنُوٓا۟ إِذَا قِيلَ
لَكُمْ تَفَسَّحُوا۟ فِى ٱلْمَجَـٰلِسِ
فَٱفْسَحُوا۟ يَفْسَحِ ٱللَّهُ لَكُمْ ۖ
وَإِذَا قِيلَ ٱنشُزُوا۟ فَٱنشُزُوا۟
يَرْفَعِ ٱللَّهُ ٱلَّذِينَ ءَامَنُوا۟ مِنكُمْ
وَٱلَّذِينَ أُوتُوا۟ ٱلْعِلْمَ دَرَجَـٰتٍ ۚ
وَٱللَّهُ بِمَا تَعْمَلُونَ خَبِيرٌ

12. O ye who believe!
When ye consult
The Messenger in private,[5350]
Spend something in charity

١٢ يَـٰٓأَيُّهَا ٱلَّذِينَ ءَامَنُوٓا۟
إِذَا نَـٰجَيْتُمُ ٱلرَّسُولَ فَقَدِّمُوا۟

5346. Evil can harm no one who is good, except insofar as (1) there is some question of trial in Allah's Universal Plan, or (2) what appears to be harm may be real good. Nothing happens without Allah's will and permission. And we must always trust Him, and not our cleverness or any adventitious circumstances that draw us the least bit from the path of rectitude.

5347. Even when a great man or a Leader comes into an Assembly, we are not to press forward without discipline, as it causes inconvenience to him and detriment to public business. Nor are we to shut out other people who have equal rights to be in the Assembly. We must spread out, for Allah's earth is spacious, and so are our opportunities.

5348. Rising up is a mark of respect. Just as those who obey soon become worthy of command, so those who honour where honour is due, become themselves worthy of honour, in various degrees according to their capacities. "Rise up" may also here imply: 'when the Assembly is dismissed, do not loiter about'.

5349. Faith makes all people equal in the Kingdom of Allah, as regards the essentials of citzenship in the Kingdom. But there is leadership, and rank and degree, joined with greater or less responsibility, and that depends on true knowledge and insight. (R).

5350. In the Kingdom of Allah all instruction or consultation is open and free. But human nature is weak. And people want special instruction or private consultation with the Teacher from one of several motives: (1) they may have, or think they have, a special case, which they are not willing to disclose to their brethren in general; (2) they may have some sense of delicacy or dignity, which can only be satisfied by a private interview; (3) they may even be selfish enough to want to monopolise the Teacher's time. These motives are, in an ascending order, worth discouraging; and yet, considering the weakness of human nature, they cannot be reprobated to the extent of shutting out their victims from chances of improvement. It is therefore recommended that they spend something in charity for the good of their poorer brethern before they indulge in such weaknesses.

Before your private consultation.
That will be best for you,
And most conducive
To purity (of conduct).[5351]
But if ye find not
(The wherewithal), Allah is
Oft-Forgiving, Most Merciful.

بَيْنَ يَدَىْ نَجْوَىٰكُمْ صَدَقَةً
ذَٰلِكَ خَيْرٌ لَّكُمْ وَأَطْهَرُ
فَإِن لَّمْ تَجِدُوا فَإِنَّ ٱللَّهَ غَفُورٌ رَّحِيمٌ

13. Is it that ye are
Afraid of spending sums[5352]
In charity before your
Private consultation (with him)?
If, then, ye do not so,
And Allah forgives you,
Then (at least) establish
Regular prayer; practise[5353]
Regular charity; and obey
Allah and His Messenger.
And Allah is well-acquainted
With all that ye do.

١٣ ءَأَشْفَقْتُمْ أَن تُقَدِّمُوا
بَيْنَ يَدَىْ نَجْوَىٰكُمْ صَدَقَٰتٍ
فَإِذْ لَمْ تَفْعَلُوا وَتَابَ ٱللَّهُ عَلَيْكُمْ
فَأَقِيمُوا ٱلصَّلَوٰةَ وَءَاتُوا ٱلزَّكَوٰةَ
وَأَطِيعُوا ٱللَّهَ وَرَسُولَهُ
وَٱللَّهُ خَبِيرٌۢ بِمَا تَعْمَلُونَ

SECTION 3.

14. Turnest thou not
Thy attention to those[5354]
Who turn (in friendship)
To such as have the Wrath
Of Allah upon them?[5355]
They are neither of you
Nor of them, and they
Swear to falsehood knowingly.[5356]

١٤ أَلَمْ تَرَ إِلَى ٱلَّذِينَ تَوَلَّوْا
قَوْمًا غَضِبَ ٱللَّهُ عَلَيْهِم
مَّا هُم مِّنكُمْ وَلَا مِنْهُمْ
وَيَحْلِفُونَ عَلَى ٱلْكَذِبِ وَهُمْ يَعْلَمُونَ

5351. The charity is a sort of expiation for their pardonable weakness. Having made some monetary sacrifice for their poorer brethren they could face them with less shame, and the charity would direct their attention to the need for purifying their motives and conduct. At the same time, this special charity is not made obligatory, lest such persons should be shut out altogether from chances of the higher teaching on account of their pardonable foibles.

5352. Note the plural here, *Ṣadaqāt,* instead of the singular, *Ṣadaqah* in verse 12 above. While people with the foibles described in n. 5350 may be willing to spend "something" (small) in charity for a special consultation occaionally, they may be frightened of spending large sums when their needs for consultation may be numerous. What is to be done then? Are they to be shut out altogether? No. They are asked to be punctilious in the discharge of their normal duties of at least normal regular prayers and regular charity, "if Allah forgives you", *i.e.*, if Allah's Messenger relieves them of further special contributions such as those noted in verse 12. This condition, "if Allah forgives you", provides the safeguard against the abuse of the privilege. The messenger would know in each case what is best for the individual and for the community.

5353. *Zakāh,* which I have translated "regular charity", was instituted about A.H. 2.

5354. This refers to the Hypocrites of Madīnah who pretended to be in Islam but intrigued with the Jews. See references as given in n. 5342 above.

5355. By this time the Jews of Madīnah and the Jewish tribes around had become actively hostile to Islam, and were being sharply called to account for their treachery.

5356. They knew that as Muslims their duty was to refrain from the intrigues of the enemies of Islam and to assist Islam against them.

15. Allah has prepared for them
A severe Penalty: evil
Indeed are their deeds.

(١٥) أَعَدَّ ٱللَّهُ لَهُمْ عَذَابًا شَدِيدًا ۖ
إِنَّهُمْ سَآءَ مَا كَانُوا۟ يَعْمَلُونَ

16. They have made their oaths
A screen (for their misdeeds):
Thus they obstruct (men)[5357]
From the Path of Allah:
Therefore shall they have
A humiliating Penalty.

(١٦) ٱتَّخَذُوٓا۟ أَيْمَٰنَهُمْ جُنَّةً
فَصَدُّوا۟ عَن سَبِيلِ ٱللَّهِ
فَلَهُمْ عَذَابٌ مُّهِينٌ

17. Of no profit whatever
To them, against Allah,
Will be their riches[5358]
Nor their sons:
They will be Companions
Of the Fire, to dwell
Therein (for aye)!

(١٧) لَّن تُغْنِىَ عَنْهُمْ أَمْوَٰلُهُمْ
وَلَآ أَوْلَٰدُهُم مِّنَ ٱللَّهِ شَيْـًٔا ۚ
أُو۟لَٰٓئِكَ أَصْحَٰبُ ٱلنَّارِ ۖ هُمْ فِيهَا خَٰلِدُونَ

18. One Day will Allah
Raise them all up
(For Judgement): then
Will they swear to Him[5359]
As they swear to you:
And they think that they
Have something (to stand upon).
No, indeed! they are
But liars!

(١٨) يَوْمَ يَبْعَثُهُمُ ٱللَّهُ جَمِيعًا
فَيَحْلِفُونَ لَهُۥ كَمَا يَحْلِفُونَ لَكُمْ ۖ
وَيَحْسَبُونَ أَنَّهُمْ عَلَىٰ شَىْءٍ ۚ
أَلَآ إِنَّهُمْ هُمُ ٱلْكَٰذِبُونَ

19. The Evil One has
Got the better of them:[5360]
So he has made them
Lose the remembrance
Of Allah. They are the Party
Of the Evil One. Truly,
It is the Party

(١٩) ٱسْتَحْوَذَ عَلَيْهِمُ ٱلشَّيْطَٰنُ
فَأَنسَىٰهُمْ ذِكْرَ ٱللَّهِ ۚ أُو۟لَٰٓئِكَ حِزْبُ ٱلشَّيْطَٰنِ ۚ
أَلَآ إِنَّ حِزْبَ

5357. A false man, by swearing that he is true, makes his falsehood all the more heinous. He stands in the way of other people accepting Truth. He gives a handle to the cynics and the sceptics.

5358. They may arrogantly boast of riches and alliances and followers in manpower. But what are such worldly advantages before the Throne of the Disposer of all events? They must come to utter misery.

5359. When Judgement is established, and before they realise the Truth, they may think (as now) that some oaths or excuses will save them. But they have not now—much less will they have then—any footing to stand upon. Falsehood is falsehood, and must perish. They must learn the worthlessness of their falsehood.

5360. Man's original nature as created by Allah is good (30:30, and n. 3541). It is because man, in spite of the warnings he has received, allows Evil to get the mastery over him, that man forgets Allah and the divine qualities which Allah gave him. The result of the perversion is that man becomes a partisan of Evil, and as such dooms himself to perdition.

Of the Evil One
That will Perish!

ٱلشَّيْطَٰنِ هُمُ ٱلْخَٰسِرُونَ

20. Those who resist
Allah and His Messenger
Will be among those
Most humiliated.[5361]

٢٠ إِنَّ ٱلَّذِينَ يُحَآدُّونَ ٱللَّهَ وَرَسُولَهُۥٓ
أُو۟لَٰٓئِكَ فِى ٱلْأَذَلِّينَ

21. Allah has decreed:
"It is I and My messengers
Who must prevail":
For Allah is One
Full of strength,
Able to enforce His Will.[5362]

٢١ كَتَبَ ٱللَّهُ
لَأَغْلِبَنَّ أَنَا۠ وَرُسُلِىٓ ۚ
إِنَّ ٱللَّهَ قَوِىٌّ عَزِيزٌ

22. Thou wilt not find
Any people who believe
In Allah and the Last Day,
Loving those who resist
Allah and His Messenger,
Even though they were
Their fathers or their sons,[5363]
Or their brothers, or
Their kindred. For such
He has written Faith[5364]
In their hearts, and strengthened
Them with a spirit[5365]
From Himself. And He
Will admit them to Gardens
Beneath which Rivers flow,
To dwell therein (forever).
Allah will be well pleased

٢٢ لَّا تَجِدُ قَوْمًا يُؤْمِنُونَ
بِٱللَّهِ وَٱلْيَوْمِ ٱلْءَاخِرِ يُوَآدُّونَ مَنْ
حَآدَّ ٱللَّهَ وَرَسُولَهُۥ وَلَوْ كَانُوٓا۟
ءَابَآءَهُمْ أَوْ أَبْنَآءَهُمْ
أَوْ إِخْوَٰنَهُمْ أَوْ عَشِيرَتَهُمْ ۚ
أُو۟لَٰٓئِكَ كَتَبَ فِى قُلُوبِهِمُ
ٱلْإِيمَٰنَ وَأَيَّدَهُم بِرُوحٍ مِّنْهُ ۖ
وَيُدْخِلُهُمْ جَنَّٰتٍ تَجْرِى مِن تَحْتِهَا
ٱلْأَنْهَٰرُ خَٰلِدِينَ فِيهَا ۚ
رَضِىَ ٱللَّهُ

5361. There are various degrees of humiliation in the final state in the spiritual world. But the worst is the humiliation of being numbered among those who ignominiously attempted to resist the Irresistible.

5362. For the meaning of *'Azīz,* see n. 2818 to 22:40.

5363. If anyone believes in Allah and His goodness and justice, and in the Hereafter, in which all true values will be restored he will never love evil or wrongdoing or rebellion against Allah, even if these things are found in his nearest kith and kin.

5364. Faith in Allah is indelibly written on the tablets of their hearts and they can never be false to Allah.

5365. *Cf.* 2:87 and 253, where it is said that Allah strengthened the Prophet Jesus with the Holy Spirit. Here we learn that all good and righteous men are strengthened by Allah with the Holy Spirit. If anything, the phrase used here is stronger, "a spirit from Himself". Whenever anyone offers his heart in faith and purity to Allah, Allah accepts it, engraves that Faith on the seeker's heart, and further fortifies him with the divine spirit, which we can no more define adequately than we can define in human language the nature and attributes of Allah.

With them, and they with Him.[5366]
They are the Party[5367]
Of Allah. Truly it is
The Party of Allah that
Will achieve Felicity.

عَنۡهُمۡ وَرَضُواْ عَنۡهُۚ
أُوْلَٰٓئِكَ حِزۡبُ ٱللَّهِۚ
أَلَآ إِنَّ حِزۡبَ ٱللَّهِ هُمُ ٱلۡمُفۡلِحُونَ

5366. Again we have the doctrine of Allah's Good Pleasure as the highest goal of man, the spiritual heaven which he achieves by a life of purity and faith. He not only attains Allah's Good Pleasure as the crown of his felicity, but his own nature is so far transformed to the pattern of Allah's original creation that his own good pleasure is in nothing but in Allah's Good Pleasure. The mutual good pleasure shows the heights to which man can attain. (R).

5367. This is in antithesis to the Party of the Evil One, mentioned in verse 19 above. That Party of Evil will perish, but while it has its run in the scheme of the present world, the Party of Truth and Reality may be figuratively called the Party of Allah, even though all Creation is Allah's in another sense.

INTRODUCTION TO SŪRAH 59—*AL HASHR*

This is the third of the series of ten short Madīnah Sūrahs, dealing each with a special point in the life of the Ummah: see Introduction to S. 57. The special theme here is how treachery to the Ummah on the part of its enemies recoils on the enemies themselves, while it strengthens the bond between the different sections of the Ummah itself, and this is illustrated by the story of the expulsion of the Jewish tribe of the Banū Naḍīr in *Rabī' al Awwal*, 4 A.H.

This fixes the date of the Sūrah.

Summary—The expulsion of the treacherous Jews from the neighbourhood of Madīnah was smoothly accomplished: their reliance on their fortified positions and on the faith of their allies in treachery proved futile. But the internal bonds in the Ummah were strengthened. Such is the wisdom of Allah, Lord of the Most Beautiful Names. (59:1-24, and C. 238).

C. 238.—Allah's wisdom foils the treachery of men,
(59:1-24.) And makes the path smooth for Believers who strive
Even against odds. Against Allah's decrees
All resistance is vain. In property taken
From the enemy, let those in need have a share,
And those who sacrifice their all for the Cause.
But those who lend a helping hand
In the hour of need do it for love
And crave no reward, nor feel the least
Envy or jealousy. They all rejoice
That the Brotherhood should thrive. Not so
The Hypocrites: they are false even among
Themselves. Perdition is the end
Of all evil. But the Good and Faithful
Will achieve felicity. Such is the power
Of Truth and Allah's Revelation. Allah!
There is no god but He!—the Good,
The Glorious, the Irresistible!
All Creation sings His praise—
The Exalted in Might, the Wise!

Sūrah 59.

Al Ḥashr (The Mustering)

In the name of Allah, Most Gracious,
Most Merciful.

بِسۡمِ ٱللَّهِ ٱلرَّحۡمَٰنِ ٱلرَّحِيمِ

1. Whatever is
In the heavens and
On earth, let it declare
The Praises and Glory[5368]
Of Allah: for He is
The Exalted in Might,
The Wise.

١ سَبَّحَ لِلَّهِ مَا فِي
ٱلسَّمَٰوَٰتِ وَمَا فِي ٱلۡأَرۡضِ
وَهُوَ ٱلۡعَزِيزُ ٱلۡحَكِيمُ

2. It is He Who got out
The Unbelievers among
The People of the Book[5369]
From their homes
At the first gathering
(Of the forces).
Little did ye think
That they would get out:[5370]
And they thought
That their fortresses
Would defend them from Allah!
But the (Wrath of) Allah
Came to them from quarters[5371]

٢ هُوَ ٱلَّذِيٓ أَخۡرَجَ
ٱلَّذِينَ كَفَرُواْ مِنۡ أَهۡلِ ٱلۡكِتَٰبِ
مِن دِيَٰرِهِمۡ لِأَوَّلِ ٱلۡحَشۡرِ
مَا ظَنَنتُمۡ أَن يَخۡرُجُواْ
وَظَنُّوٓاْ أَنَّهُم مَّانِعَتُهُمۡ حُصُونُهُم
مِّنَ ٱللَّهِ فَأَتَىٰهُمُ ٱللَّهُ مِنۡ حَيۡثُ

5368. This verse, introducing the Sūrah is identical with 57:1, introducing S. 57. The theme of both is the wonderful working of Allah's Plan and Providence. In the one case it referred to the conquest of Makkah and taught the lesson of humility. In this case it refers to the dislodgement of the treacherous Banū Naḍīr from their nest of intrigue in the neighbourhood of Madīnah, practically without a blow. See next note.

5369. This refers to the Jewish tribe of the Banū Naḍīr whose intrigues and treachery nearly undid the Muslim cause during the perilous days of the battle of Uḥud in *Shawwāl*, A.H. 3. Four months after, in *Rabī' al Awwal*, A.H. 4, steps were taken against them. They were asked to leave the strategic position which they occupied, about three miles south of Madīnah, endangering the very existence of the Ummah in Madīnah. At first they demurred, relying on their fortresses and on their secret alliances with the Pagans of Makkah and the Hypocrites of Madīnah. But when the Muslim army was gathered to punish them and actually besieged them for some days, their allies stirred not a finger in their aid, and they were wise enough to leave. Most of them joined their brethren in Syria, which they were permitted to do, after being disarmed. Some of them joined their brethren in Khaybar: see n. 3705 to 33:27. The Banū Naḍīr richly deserved punishment, but their lives were spared, and they were allowed to carry away their goods and chattels.

5370. That is, without actual hostilities, and the shedding of precious Muslim blood.

5371. They had played a double game. Originally they were sworn allies of the Madīnah Muslims under the Holy Prophet, but they secretly intrigued with the Makkah Pagans under Abū Sufyān and the Madīnah Hypocrites. They even tried treacherously to take the life of the Prophet while he was on a visit to them, breaking both the laws of hospitality and their own sworn alliance. They thought the Pagan Quraysh of Makkah and the Hypocrites of Madīnah would help them, but they did not help them. On the contrary the eleven day siege showed them their own helplessness. Their supplies were cut off: the exigencies of the siege necessitated the destruction of their outlying palm trees; and the unexpected turn in their fortunes disheartened them. Their hearts were struck with terror and they capitulated. But they laid waste their homes before they left: see next note.

From which they little
Expected (it), and cast
Terror into their hearts,
So that they destroyed
Their dwellings by their own[5372]
Hands and the hands
Of the Believers.
Take warning, then,
O ye with eyes (to see)!

لَمْ يَحْتَسِبُوا
وَقَذَفَ فِي قُلُوبِهِمُ الرُّعْبَ
يُخْرِبُونَ بُيُوتَهُم بِأَيْدِيهِمْ وَأَيْدِي الْمُؤْمِنِينَ
فَاعْتَبِرُوا يَا أُولِي الْأَبْصَارِ

3. And had it not been
That Allah had decreed
Banishment for them,[5373]
He would certainly have
Punished them in this world:
And in the Hereafter
They shall (certainly) have
The Punishment of the Fire.

(٣) وَلَوْلَا أَن كَتَبَ
اللَّهُ عَلَيْهِمُ الْجَلَاءَ
لَعَذَّبَهُمْ فِي الدُّنْيَا
وَلَهُمْ فِي الْآخِرَةِ عَذَابُ النَّارِ

4. That is because they
Resisted Allah and His Messenger:
And if anyone resists Allah,[5374]
Verily Allah is severe
In Punishment.

(٤) ذَٰلِكَ بِأَنَّهُمْ شَاقُّوا اللَّهَ وَرَسُولَهُ
وَمَن يُشَاقِّ اللَّهَ فَإِنَّ اللَّهَ شَدِيدُ الْعِقَابِ

5. Whether ye cut down
(O ye Muslims!)
The tender palm trees,
Or ye left them standing
On their roots, it was[5375]
By leave of Allah, and
In order that He might[5376]

(٥) مَا قَطَعْتُم مِّن لِّينَةٍ
أَوْ تَرَكْتُمُوهَا قَائِمَةً
عَلَىٰ أُصُولِهَا فَبِإِذْنِ اللَّهِ

5372. Their lives were spared, and they were allowed ten days in which to remove themselves, their families, and such goods as they could carry. In order to leave no habitations for the Muslims they demolished their own houses and laid waste their property, to complete the destruction which the operations of war had already caused at the hands of the besieging force of the Muslims.

5373. Banishment was a comparatively mild punishment for them, but the Providence of Allah had decreed that a chance should be given to them even though they were a treacherous foe. Within two years, their brethren the Banū Qurayẓah showed that they had not profited by their example, and had to be dealt with in another way: see 33:26 and notes.

5374. The punishment of the Banū Naḍīr was because in breaking their plighted word with the Messenger and in actively resisting Allah's Message and supporting the enemies of that Message, they rebelled against His Holy Will. For such treason and rebellion the punishment is severe, and yet in this case it was seasoned with Mercy.

5375. The unnecessary cutting down of fruit trees or destruction of crops, or any wanton destruction whatever in war, is forbidden by the law and practice of Islam. But some destruction may be necessary for putting pressure on the enemy, and to that extent it is allowed. But as far as possible, consistently with that objective of military operations, such trees should not be cut down. Both these principles are in accordance with the Divine Will, and were followed by the Muslims in their expedition.

5376. The arrogance of the Banū Naḍīr had to be humbled, and their power for mischief destroyed.

Cover with shame
The rebellious transgressors.

وَلِيُخْزِيَ ٱلْفَٰسِقِينَ

6. What Allah has bestowed
On His Messenger (and taken
Away) from them — for this
Ye made no expedition
With either cavalry or camelry:[5377]
But Allah gives power
To His messengers over
Any He pleases: and Allah[5378]
Has power over all things.

٦ وَمَآ أَفَآءَ ٱللَّهُ عَلَىٰ رَسُولِهِۦ مِنْهُمْ فَمَآ أَوْجَفْتُمْ عَلَيْهِ مِنْ خَيْلٍ وَلَا رِكَابٍ وَلَٰكِنَّ ٱللَّهَ يُسَلِّطُ رُسُلَهُۥ عَلَىٰ مَن يَشَآءُ ۚ وَٱللَّهُ عَلَىٰ كُلِّ شَىْءٍ قَدِيرٌ

7. What Allah has bestowed[5379]
On His Messenger (and taken
Away) from the people[5380]
Of the townships — belongs
To Allah — to His Messenger[5381]
And to kindred and orphans,
The needy and the wayfarer;
In order that it may not
(Merely) make a circuit
Between the wealthy among you.
So take what the Messenger
Assigns to you, and deny
Yourselves that which he
Withholds from you.[5381-A]
And fear Allah; for Allah
Is strict in Punishment.

٧ مَّآ أَفَآءَ ٱللَّهُ عَلَىٰ رَسُولِهِۦ مِنْ أَهْلِ ٱلْقُرَىٰ فَلِلَّهِ وَلِلرَّسُولِ وَلِذِى ٱلْقُرْبَىٰ وَٱلْيَتَٰمَىٰ وَٱلْمَسَٰكِينِ وَٱبْنِ ٱلسَّبِيلِ كَىْ لَا يَكُونَ دُولَةًۢ بَيْنَ ٱلْأَغْنِيَآءِ مِنكُمْ ۚ وَمَآ ءَاتَىٰكُمُ ٱلرَّسُولُ فَخُذُوهُ وَمَا نَهَىٰكُمْ عَنْهُ فَٱنتَهُوا۟ ۚ وَٱتَّقُوا۟ ٱللَّهَ ۖ إِنَّ ٱللَّهَ شَدِيدُ ٱلْعِقَابِ

5377. Neither cavalry nor troops mounted on camels were employed in the siege. In fact the enemy surrendered at the first onset. See 59:2, and n. 5369 above.

5378. Allah accomplishes His Purpose in various ways, according to His Wise and Holy Will and Plan. In some cases a fight is necessary. In some cases the godly attain their objective and overawe the forces of evil without actual fighting.

5379. The Jews had originally come from outside Arabia, and seized on the land near Madīnah. They refused to adapt themselves to the people of Arabia, and were in fact a thorn in the side of the genuine Arabs of Madīnah. Their dispossession is therefore a restoration of the land to its original people. But the word *Fā'* is here understood in a technical sense, as meaning property abandoned by the enemy or taken from him without a formal war. In that sense it is distinguished from *Anfāl*, or spoils, taken after actual fighting, about which see 8:1 and 41.

5380. *The people of the townships:* the townships were the Jewish settlements round Madīnah, of the Banū Naḍīr, and possibly of other tribes. *Cf.* the "townships" mentioned in 59:14 below. The reference cannot be to the Wādī al Qurā (Valley of Towns), now Madā'in Ṣāliḥ, which was subjugated after Khaybar and Fadak in A.H. 7, unless this verse is later than the rest of the Sūrah.

5381. *Belongs to Allah: i.e.*, to Allah's Cause; and the beneficiaries are further detailed. No shares are fixed; they depend upon circumstances, and are left to the judgement of the Leader. Compare a similar list of those entitled to Charity, in 2:177, but the two lists refer to different circumstances and have different beneficiaries in addition to the portion common to both.

5381-A. Alternatively these words may be translated: "So take what the Messenger gives you, and refrain from what he prohibits you". [Eds.].

8. (Some part is due)
To the indigent Muhājirs,[5382]
Those who were expelled
From their homes and their property,
While seeking Grace from Allah
And (His) Good Pleasure,
And aiding Allah and His Messenger:
Such are indeed
The sincere ones—

٨ لِلْفُقَرَآءِ ٱلْمُهَٰجِرِينَ ٱلَّذِينَ
أُخْرِجُوا۟ مِن دِيَٰرِهِمْ وَأَمْوَٰلِهِمْ
يَبْتَغُونَ فَضْلًا مِّنَ ٱللَّهِ وَرِضْوَٰنًا
وَيَنصُرُونَ ٱللَّهَ وَرَسُولَهُۥٓ
أُو۟لَٰٓئِكَ هُمُ ٱلصَّٰدِقُونَ

9. But those who
Before them, had homes[5383]
(In Madīnah)
And had adopted the Faith—
Show their affection to such
As came to them for refuge,
And entertain no desire
In their hearts for things
Given to the (latter),
But give them preference
Over themselves, even though
Poverty was their (own lot).
And those saved from
The covetousness of their own
Souls—they are the ones
That achieve prosperity.

٩ وَٱلَّذِينَ تَبَوَّءُو ٱلدَّارَ
وَٱلْإِيمَٰنَ مِن قَبْلِهِمْ
يُحِبُّونَ مَنْ هَاجَرَ إِلَيْهِمْ وَلَا يَجِدُونَ فِى
صُدُورِهِمْ حَاجَةً مِّمَّآ أُوتُوا۟ وَيُؤْثِرُونَ
عَلَىٰٓ أَنفُسِهِمْ وَلَوْ كَانَ بِهِمْ خَصَاصَةٌ
وَمَن يُوقَ شُحَّ نَفْسِهِۦ
فَأُو۟لَٰٓئِكَ هُمُ ٱلْمُفْلِحُونَ

10. And those who came[5384]
After them say: "Our Lord!
Forgive us, and our brethren
Who came before us

١٠ وَٱلَّذِينَ جَآءُو مِنۢ بَعْدِهِمْ يَقُولُونَ
رَبَّنَا ٱغْفِرْ لَنَا وَلِإِخْوَٰنِنَا ٱلَّذِينَ سَبَقُونَا

5382. The *Muhājir* are those who forsook their homes and property in Makkah in order to assist the Holy Prophet in his migration to Madīnah *(Hijrah)*. Their devotion and sincerity were proved beyond doubt by their self-denial, and they were now to be rewarded.

5383. This refers to the *Anṣār* (the Helpers), the people of Madīnah, who accepted Islam when it was persecuted in Makkah, and who invited the Holy Prophet to join them and become their Leader in Madīnah. The Hijrah was possible because of their good will and their generous hospitality. They entertained the Prophet and all the refugees *(Muhājirs)* who came with him. The most remarkable ties of full brotherhood were established between individual members of the one group and the other. Until the Ummah got its own resources, the Helpers regularly gave and the Refugees regularly received. The Helpers counted it a privilege to entertain the Refugees, and even the poor vied with the rich in their spirit of self-sacrifice. When the confiscated land and property of the Banū Naḍīr was divided, and the major portion was assigned to the refugees, there was not the least jealousy on the part of the Helpers. They rejoiced in the good fortune of their brethren. And incidentally they were themselves relieved of anxiety and responsibility on their behalf.

5384. *Those that came after them:* the immediate meaning would refer to later arrivals in Madīnah or later accessions to Islam, compared with the early *Muhājirs.* But the general meaning would include all future comers into the House of Islam. They pray, not only for themselves, but for all their brethren, and above all, they pray that their hearts may be purified of any desire or tendency to disparage the work or virtues of other Muslims or to feel any jealousy on account of their successes or good fortune.

Into the Faith,
And leave not,
In our hearts,
Rancour (or sense of injury)[5385]
Against those who have believed.
Our Lord! Thou art
Indeed Full of Kindness,
Most Merciful."

بِٱلْإِيمَٰنِ
وَلَا تَجْعَلْ فِى قُلُوبِنَا
غِلًّا لِّلَّذِينَ ءَامَنُوا۟
رَبَّنَآ إِنَّكَ رَءُوفٌ رَّحِيمٌ

SECTION 2.

11. Hast thou not observed
The Hypocrites say
To their misbelieving brethren
Among the People of the
Book?—[5386]
"If ye are expelled,
We too will go out
With you, and we will
Never hearken to any one
In your affair; and if
Ye are attacked (in fight)
We will help you".
But Allah is witness[5387]
That they are indeed liars.

١١ أَلَمْ تَرَ إِلَى ٱلَّذِينَ نَافَقُوا۟ يَقُولُونَ
لِإِخْوَٰنِهِمُ ٱلَّذِينَ كَفَرُوا۟ مِنْ أَهْلِ ٱلْكِتَٰبِ
لَئِنْ أُخْرِجْتُمْ لَنَخْرُجَنَّ مَعَكُمْ
وَلَا نُطِيعُ فِيكُمْ أَحَدًا أَبَدًا
وَإِن قُوتِلْتُمْ لَنَنصُرَنَّكُمْ
وَٱللَّهُ يَشْهَدُ إِنَّهُمْ لَكَٰذِبُونَ

12. If they are expelled,
Never will they go out
With them; and if they
Are attacked (in fight),
They will never help them;
And if they do help them,
They will turn their backs;
So they will receive no help.[53288]

١٢ لَئِنْ أُخْرِجُوا۟ لَا يَخْرُجُونَ
مَعَهُمْ وَلَئِن قُوتِلُوا۟ لَا يَنصُرُونَهُمْ
وَلَئِن نَّصَرُوهُمْ لَيُوَلُّنَّ ٱلْأَدْبَٰرَ
ثُمَّ لَا يُنصَرُونَ

13. Of a truth ye are
Stronger (than they)

١٣ لَأَنتُمْ أَشَدُّ

5385. *Cf.* 7:43, and n. 1021.

5386. The Jews of the Banū Naḍīr had been assured by the Hypocrites of Madīnah of their support to their cause. They had thought that their defection from the Prophet's Cause would so weaken that cause that they would save their friends. But they never intended to undertake any act involving self-sacrifice on their part; if they had helped their Jewish friends, it was not likely that they would have succeeded; and if they had actually gone to the fight, they had neither valour nor fervour to support them, and they would have fled ignominiously before the discipline, earnestness, and Faith of the men of Islam.

5387. For this actually happened. They never stirred a finger for the Jews, and they never intended to do so. And Allah knows all their motives and secrets: *cf.* 47:26, n. 4850.

5388. All hopes founded on iniquity and treachery are vain and illusory. There may be honour among thieves. But there is no honour as between dishonest intriguers, and they are not likely to get any real help from any quarter.

Because of the terror[5389]
In their hearts,
(Sent) by Allah.
This is because they are
Men devoid of understanding.

رَهْبَةً فِي صُدُورِهِم مِّنَ ٱللَّهِ
ذَٰلِكَ بِأَنَّهُمْ قَوْمٌ لَّا يَفْقَهُونَ

14. They will not fight you
(Even) together, except
In fortified townships,
Or from behind walls.[5390]
Strong is their fighting (spirit)
Amongst themselves:
Thou wouldst think
They were united,
But their hearts are divided:[5391]
That is because they
Are a people devoid
Of wisdom.

(١٤) لَا يُقَٰتِلُونَكُمْ جَمِيعًا
إِلَّا فِي قُرًى مُّحَصَّنَةٍ أَوْ مِن وَرَآءِ جُدُرٍ
بَأْسُهُم بَيْنَهُمْ شَدِيدٌ
تَحْسَبُهُمْ جَمِيعًا وَقُلُوبُهُمْ شَتَّىٰ
ذَٰلِكَ بِأَنَّهُمْ قَوْمٌ
لَّا يَعْقِلُونَ

15. Like those who lately[5392]
Preceded them, they have
Tasted the evil result
Of their conduct; and
(In the Hereafter there is)
For them a grievous Penalty—

(١٥) كَمَثَلِ ٱلَّذِينَ مِن قَبْلِهِمْ قَرِيبًا
ذَاقُوا۟ وَبَالَ أَمْرِهِمْ
وَلَهُمْ عَذَابٌ أَلِيمٌ

16. (Their allies deceived them),
Like the Evil One,
When he says to man,

(١٦) كَمَثَلِ ٱلشَّيْطَٰنِ إِذْ قَالَ لِلْإِنسَٰنِ

5389. As construed here, the meaning is: "Ye Muslims, even if ye are weak numerically, or they may have other seeming advantages, ye are really stronger than they are, because they have a wholesome fear in their minds, and Allah sends such fear into the hearts of wrongdoers!" An alternative construction would yield the meaning: Being Unbelievers they fear you more than they fear Allah, because your valour they see, but in Allah they do not believe.

5390. They have not sufficient self-confidence or *élan* to sustain them in a fight except under material advantages or defences. Even if they join forces, they have not sufficient trust in each other to expose themselves to open fighting.

5391. 'It may be that they have a strong fighting spirit among themselves, but they have no Cause to fight for and no common objective to achieve. The Makkan Pagans want to keep their own unjust autocracy; the Madīnah Hypocrites wish for their own domination in Madīnah; and the Jews want their racial superiority established over the Arabs, of whose growing union and power they are jealous.' Their pretended alliance could not stand the strain of either a defeat or a victory. If they had been wise, they would have accepted the Cause of Unity, Faith, and Truth.

5392. The immediate reference was probably to the Jewish goldsmith tribe of the Qaynuqā', who were also settled in a fortified township near Madīnah. They were also punished and banished for their treachery, about a month after the battle of Badr, in which the Makkan Pagans had suffered a signal defeat, in *Shawwāl*, A. H. 2. The Naḍīr evidently did not take that lesson to heart. The general meaning is that we must learn to be on our guard against the consequences of treachery and sin. No fortuitous alliances with other men of iniquity will save us.

"Deny Allah": but when[5393]
(Man) denies Allah,
(The Evil One) says,
"I am free of thee:
I do fear Allah,
The Lord of the Worlds!"

اكْفُرْ فَلَمَّا كَفَرَ
قَالَ إِنِّي بَرِيٓءٌ مِّنكَ
إِنِّيٓ أَخَافُ ٱللَّهَ رَبَّ ٱلْعَٰلَمِينَ

17. The end of both will be
That they will go
Into the Fire, dwelling
Therein forever.
Such is the reward
Of the wrongdoers.

فَكَانَ عَٰقِبَتَهُمَآ ﴿١٧﴾
أَنَّهُمَا فِي ٱلنَّارِ خَٰلِدَيْنِ فِيهَا
وَذَٰلِكَ جَزَٰٓؤُاْ ٱلظَّٰلِمِينَ

SECTION 3.

18. O ye who believe!
Fear Allah,[5394]
And let every soul look
To what (provision) he has[5395]
Sent forth for the morrow.
Yea, fear Allah:[5395-A]
For Allah is well-acquainted
With (all) that ye do.

يَٰٓأَيُّهَا ٱلَّذِينَ ءَامَنُواْ ﴿١٨﴾
ٱتَّقُواْ ٱللَّهَ وَلْتَنظُرْ نَفْسٌ
مَّا قَدَّمَتْ لِغَدٍ وَٱتَّقُواْ ٱللَّهَ
إِنَّ ٱللَّهَ خَبِيرٌۢ بِمَا تَعْمَلُونَ

19. And be ye not like
Those who forgot Allah;[5396]
And He made them forget
Their own souls! Such
Are the rebellious transgressors!

وَلَا تَكُونُواْ كَٱلَّذِينَ ﴿١٩﴾
نَسُواْ ٱللَّهَ فَأَنسَىٰهُمْ أَنفُسَهُمْ
أُوْلَٰٓئِكَ هُمُ ٱلْفَٰسِقُونَ

5393. An apt simile. Evil tempts man in all sorts of ways, and presents seductive promises and alliances to delude him into the belief that he will be saved from the consequences. The Evil One says, "Deny Allah": which means not merely denial in words, but denial in acts—disobedience of Allah's Law, deviation from the path of rectitude. When the sinner gets well into the mire, the Evil One says cynically: "How can I help you against Allah? Don't you see I am afraid of Him? All our alliances and understandings were moonshine. You must bear the consequences of your own folly."

5394. The "fear of Allah" is akin to love; for it means the fear of offending Him or doing anything wrong that will forfeit His Good Pleasure. This is *Taqwā*, which implies self-restraint, guarding ourselves from all sin, wrong, and injustice, and the positive doing of good. See 2:2, and n. 26.

5395. The positive side of *Taqwā* or "fear of Allah" (see last note) is here emphasised. It is not merely a feeling or an emotion: it is an act, a doing of things which become a preparation and provision for the Hereafter—the next life, which may be described as "the morrow" in relation to the present Life, which is "today".

5395-A. The repetition emphasises both sides of *Taqwā:* "let your soul fear to do wrong and let it do every act of righteousness; for Allah observes both your inner motives and your acts, and in His scheme of things everything will have its due consequences."

5396. To forget Allah is to forget the only Eternal Reality. As we are only reflected realities, how can we understand or do justice to or remember ourselves, when we forget the very source of our being? (R).

20. Not equal are
The Companions of the Fire
And the Companions
Of the Garden:
It is the Companions
Of the Garden,
That will achieve Felicity.[5397]

٢٠ لَا يَسْتَوِىٓ أَصْحَٰبُ
ٱلنَّارِ وَأَصْحَٰبُ ٱلْجَنَّةِ ۚ
أَصْحَٰبُ ٱلْجَنَّةِ هُمُ ٱلْفَآئِزُونَ

21. Had We sent down
This Qur'ān on a mountain,[5398]
Verily, thou wouldst have seen
It humble itself and cleave[5399]
Asunder for fear of Allah.
Such are the similitudes
Which We propound to men,
That they may reflect.

٢١ لَوْ أَنزَلْنَا هَٰذَا ٱلْقُرْءَانَ عَلَىٰ جَبَلٍ لَّرَأَيْتَهُۥ
خَٰشِعًا مُّتَصَدِّعًا مِّنْ خَشْيَةِ ٱللَّهِ ۚ
وَتِلْكَ ٱلْأَمْثَٰلُ نَضْرِبُهَا لِلنَّاسِ
لَعَلَّهُمْ يَتَفَكَّرُونَ

22. Allah is He, than Whom
There is no other god—[5400]
Who knows (all things)
Both secret and open;
He, Most Gracious,
Most Merciful.

٢٢ هُوَ ٱللَّهُ ٱلَّذِى لَآ إِلَٰهَ إِلَّا هُوَ ۖ
عَٰلِمُ ٱلْغَيْبِ وَٱلشَّهَٰدَةِ ۖ
هُوَ ٱلرَّحْمَٰنُ ٱلرَّحِيمُ

23. Allah is He, than Whom
There is no other god—[5401]
The Sovereign, the Holy One,
The Source of Peace
(and Perfection),

٢٣ هُوَ ٱللَّهُ ٱلَّذِى لَآ إِلَٰهَ إِلَّا هُوَ
ٱلْمَلِكُ ٱلْقُدُّوسُ ٱلسَّلَٰمُ

5397. The others, the Companions of the Fire, will find their lives wasted and nullified. Their capacities will be rendered inert and their wishes will end in futility.

5398. There are two ideas associated in men's minds with a mountain: one is its height, and the other that it is rocky, stony, hard. Now comes the metaphor. The Revelation of Allah is so sublime that even the highest mountains humble themselves before it. The Revelation is so powerful and convincing that even the hard rock splits asunder under it. Will man then be so arrogant as to consider himself superior to it, or so hardhearted as not to be affected by its powerful Message? The answer is "No" for unspoilt man; "Yes" for man when degraded by sin to be the vilest of creatures.

5399. *Cf.* 7:143, and n. 1103, where, in the story of Moses, the Mount became as dust "when the Lord manifested His Glory". Also *cf.* 33:72, and n. 3778, where the mountains are mentioned as an emblem of stability, but as refusing to accept the Trust *(Amānah)* because they felt themselves to be too humble to be equal to such a tremendous Trust. (R).

5400. Here follows a passage of great sublimity, summing up the attributes of Allah. In this verse, we have the general attributes, which give us the fundamental basis on which we can form some idea of Allah. We start with the proposition that there is nothing else like Him. We think of His Unity; all the varying and conflicting forces in Creation are controlled by Him and look to Him, and we can never get a true idea of Him unless we understand the meaning of Unity. His knowledge extends to everything seen and unseen, present and future, near and far, in being and not in being: in fact these contrasts, which apply to our knowledge, do not apply to Him. His Grace and His Mercy are unbounded: see 1:1, and n. 19; and unless we realise these, we can have no true conception of our position in the working of His Will and Plan. (R).

5401. This phrase is repeated from the last verse in order to lead us to the contemplation of some other attributes of Allah, after we have realised those which form our fundamental conceptions of Allah. See the preceding and the following note.

The Guardian of Faith,
The Preserver of Safety,[5402]
The Exalted in Might,
The Irresistible, the Supreme:[5403]
Glory to Allah!
(High is He)
Above the partners[5404]
They attribute to Him.

ٱلْمُؤْمِنُ ٱلْمُهَيْمِنُ ٱلْعَزِيزُ
ٱلْجَبَّارُ ٱلْمُتَكَبِّرُ
سُبْحَٰنَ ٱللَّهِ
عَمَّا يُشْرِكُونَ

24. He is Allah, the Creator,[5405]
The Evolver,
The Bestower of Forms[5406]
(Or Colours).
To Him belong[5407]
The Most Beautiful Names:
Whatever is in
The heavens and on earth,
Doth declare[5408]
His Praises and Glory;
And He is the Exalted
In Might, the Wise.

﴿٢٤﴾ هُوَ ٱللَّهُ ٱلْخَٰلِقُ
ٱلْبَارِئُ ٱلْمُصَوِّرُ
لَهُ ٱلْأَسْمَآءُ ٱلْحُسْنَىٰ
يُسَبِّحُ لَهُۥ مَا فِى
ٱلسَّمَٰوَٰتِ وَٱلْأَرْضِ
وَهُوَ ٱلْعَزِيزُ ٱلْحَكِيمُ

5402. How can a translator reproduce the sublimity and the comprehensiveness of the magnificient Arabic words, which mean so much in a single symbol? (1) "The Sovereign" in our human language implies the one undisputed authority which is entitled to give commands and to receive obedience, and which in fact receives obedience; the power which enforces law and justice. (2) Human authority may be misused, but in the title "the Holy One", we postulate a Being free from all stain or evil, and replete with the highest Purity. (3) "*Salām*" has not only the idea of Peace as opposed to Conflict, but wholeness as opposed to defects: hence our paraphrase "Source of Peace and Perfection". (4) *Mū'min*, one who entertains Faith, who gives Faith to others, who is never false to the Faith that others place in him; hence our paraphrase "Guardian of Faith". (5) "Preserver of Safety": guarding all from danger, corruption, loss, etc.: the word is used for the Qur'ān in 5:51. These are the attributes of kindness and benevolence: in the next note are described the attributes of power.

5403. See last note. (6) Allah is not only good, but He can carry out His Will. (7) And if anything resists or opposes Him, His Will prevails. (8) For He is Supreme, above all things and creatures. Thus we come back to the Unity with which we began in verse 22.

5404. Such being Allah's attributes of Goodness and Power, how foolish is it of men to worship anything else but Him? Who can approach His glory and goodness?

5405. Allah's attributes of Goodness and Power having been referred to, we are now told of His creative energy, of which three aspects are here mentioned, as explained in the following note. The point is emphasised that He does not merely create and leave alone; He goes on fashioning, evolving new forms and colours, and sustaining all the energies and capacities which he has put into His Creation, according to various laws which He has established.

5406. The act or acts of creation have various aspects, and the various words used in this connection are summarised in n. 120 to 2:117, as supplemented by n. 916 to 6:94 and n. 923 to 6:98. Kh*alaqa* is the general term for creation, and the Author of all Creation is *Khāliq*. *Bara'a* implies a process of evolving from previously created matter or state: the Author of this process is *Bāri'*, the Evolver. *Ṣawwara* implies giving definite form or colour, so as to make a thing exactly suited to a given end or object: hence the title *Musawwir*, Bestower of Forms or Colours: for this shows the completion of the visible stage of creation.

5407. *Cf.* 7:180. n. 1154; and 17:110, n. 2322.

5408. Thus the argument of the Sūrah is rounded off on the same note as was struck at the beginning, 59:1. The first verse and the last verse of the Sūrah are the same, except as regards the tense of the verb *sabbaḥa*. In the first verse it is the optative form of the preterite *sabbaḥa*: 'let everything declare the Glory of Allah'. After the illustrations given, the declaratory form of the aorist is appropriate, *yusabbiḥu*: "everything doth declare the Glory of Allah".

INTRODUCTION TO SŪRAH 60—*AL MUMTAḤINAH*

This is the fourth of the ten Madīnah Sūrahs, each dealing with a special point in the life of the Ummah.

Here the point is: what social relations are possible with the Unbelievers? A distinction is made between those who persecute you for your Faith and want to destroy you and your Faith, and those who have shown no such rancour. For the latter there is hope of mercy and forgiveness. The question of women and cross-marriages is equitably dealt with.

The date is after the Pagans had broken the treaty of Ḥudaybīyah, for which see Introduction to S. 47—say about A. H. 8, not long before the conquest of Makkah.

Summary—The enemies of your Faith, who would exterminate you and your Faith, are not fit objects of your love: follow Abraham's example: but with those Unbelievers who show no rancour, you should deal with kindness and justice: marriages between Believers and Unbelievers. (60:1-13, and C. 239).

C. 239.—What social relations should you hold
(60:1-13.) With men whose hearts are filled with rancour—
Who hate both Allah and men of God?
Surely you cannot offer love and friendship
To such as seek to destroy your Faith,
And you. Seek protection for you and yours
From Allah and not from Allah's sworn enemies.
But deal kindly and justly with all: it may be
That those who hate you now may love you:
For Allah can order all things. But look not
For protection to those who are bent on driving
You out. Let not believing women
Be handed over to Unbelievers:
No marriage tie is lawful between them.
When women wish to join your society,
Take their assurance that they yield not
To sin or unbeseeming conduct.
Take every care to keep your society
Free and pure, and self-contained.

Sūrah 60.

Al Mumtaḥinah (That Which Examines)

In the name of Allah, Most Gracious, Most Merciful.

بِسْمِ ٱللَّهِ ٱلرَّحْمَـٰنِ ٱلرَّحِيمِ

1. O ye who believe!
Take not My enemies
And yours as friends
(Or protectors)—offering them[5409]
(Your) love, even though
They have rejected the Truth
That has come to you,
And have (on the contrary)
Driven out the Messenger
And yourselves (from your homes),
(Simply) because ye believe
In Allah your Lord![5410]
If ye have come out
To strive in My Way
And to seek My Good Pleasure,
(Take them not as friends),
Holding secret converse
Of love (and friendship)
With them: for I know
Full well all that ye
Conceal and all that ye
Reveal. And any of you
That does this has strayed
From the Straight Path.

١ يَـٰٓأَيُّهَا ٱلَّذِينَ ءَامَنُوا۟
لَا تَتَّخِذُوا۟ عَدُوِّى وَعَدُوَّكُمْ أَوْلِيَآءَ
تُلْقُونَ إِلَيْهِم بِٱلْمَوَدَّةِ
وَقَدْ كَفَرُوا۟ بِمَا جَآءَكُم مِّنَ ٱلْحَقِّ
يُخْرِجُونَ ٱلرَّسُولَ وَإِيَّاكُمْ ۙ
أَن تُؤْمِنُوا۟ بِٱللَّهِ رَبِّكُمْ
إِن كُنتُمْ خَرَجْتُمْ جِهَـٰدًا
فِى سَبِيلِى وَٱبْتِغَآءَ مَرْضَاتِى ۚ
تُسِرُّونَ إِلَيْهِم بِٱلْمَوَدَّةِ وَأَنَا۠ أَعْلَمُ
بِمَآ أَخْفَيْتُمْ وَمَآ أَعْلَنتُمْ ۚ
وَمَن يَفْعَلْهُ مِنكُمْ فَقَدْ
ضَلَّ سَوَآءَ ٱلسَّبِيلِ

2. If they were to get[5411]
The better of you,

٢ إِن يَثْقَفُوكُمْ

5409. The immediate occasion for this was a secret letter sent by one Ḥāṭib, a *Muhājir,* from Madīnah, to the Pagans at Makkah, in most friendly terms, seeking for their protection on behalf of his children and relatives left behind in Makkah. The letter was intercepted, and he confessed the truth. He was forgiven as he told the truth and his motive did not appear to be heinous, but this instruction was given for future guidance. This was shortly before the conquest of Makkah, but the principle is of universal application. You cannot be on terms of secret intimacy with the enemies of your Faith and people, who are persecuting your Faith and seeking to destroy your Faith and you. You may not do so even for the sake of your relatives as it compromises the life and existence of your whole community.

5410. Such was the position of the Muslim community in Madīnah after the Hijrah and before the conquest of Makkah.

5411. Besides the question of your fidelity to your own people, even your own selfish interests require you to beware of secret intrigues with the enemies. They will welcome you as cat's paws. But what will happen when they have used you and got the better of you and your people? Then they will show you their hand. And a heavy hand it will be! Not only will they injure you with their hands but with their tongues! The only words they will use for you will be "Traitors to their own"! If they intrigue with you now, it is to pervert you from the Path of Truth and righteousness and to win you over to their evil ways.

They would behave to you
As enemies, and stretch forth
Their hands and their tongues
Against you for evil;
And they desire that ye
Should reject the Truth.

3. Of no profit to you[5412]
Will be your relatives
And your children
On the Day of Judgement:
He will judge between you:
For Allah sees well
All that ye do.

4. There is for you
An excellent example (to follow)
In Abraham and those with
him,[5413]
When they said
To their people:
"We are clear of you
And of whatever ye worship
Besides Allah: we have rejected
You, and there has arisen,
Between us and you, enmity[5414]
And hatred forever—unless
Ye believe in Allah
And Him alone":
But not when Abraham
Said to his father:
"I will pray for forgiveness[5415]
For thee, though I have
No power (to get) aught
On thy behalf from Allah."

يَكُونُوا لَكُمْ أَعْدَاءً
وَيَبْسُطُوا إِلَيْكُمْ أَيْدِيَهُمْ وَأَلْسِنَتَهُم
بِالسُّوءِ وَوَدُّوا لَوْ تَكْفُرُونَ

٣ لَن تَنفَعَكُمْ أَرْحَامُكُمْ وَلَا أَوْلَادُكُمْ
يَوْمَ الْقِيَامَةِ يَفْصِلُ بَيْنَكُمْ
وَاللَّهُ بِمَا تَعْمَلُونَ بَصِيرٌ

٤ قَدْ كَانَتْ لَكُمْ أُسْوَةٌ
حَسَنَةٌ فِي إِبْرَاهِيمَ وَالَّذِينَ مَعَهُ
إِذْ قَالُوا لِقَوْمِهِمْ إِنَّا بُرَآءُ مِنكُمْ
وَمِمَّا تَعْبُدُونَ مِن دُونِ اللَّهِ
كَفَرْنَا بِكُمْ وَبَدَا بَيْنَنَا وَبَيْنَكُمُ
الْعَدَاوَةُ وَالْبَغْضَاءُ أَبَدًا
حَتَّىٰ تُؤْمِنُوا بِاللَّهِ وَحْدَهُ
إِلَّا قَوْلَ إِبْرَاهِيمَ لِأَبِيهِ
لَأَسْتَغْفِرَنَّ لَكَ وَمَا أَمْلِكُ
لَكَ مِنَ اللَّهِ مِن شَيْءٍ

5412. The plea of children and relatives (see n. 5409 above) will be no excuse for treachery when the Day of Judgement comes. Your children and family will not save you. The Judgement will be in the hands of Allah, and He has full knowledge of all your overt and hidden acts and motives.

5413. See 9:114. Abraham was tender-hearted, and loyal to his father and his people. He warned them against idolatry and sin, and prayed for his father, but when his father and his people became open enemies of Allah. Abraham entirely dissociated himself from them, and left his home, his father, his people, and his country. *Those with him* were his believing wife and nephew Lūṭ and any other Believers that went into exile with him.

5414. The enemies of Allah are enemies of the righteous, and they hate the righteous. Therefore the righteous must cut themselves off eternally from them, unless they repent and come back to Allah. In that case they receive Allah's mercy and are entitled to all the rights of love and brotherhood. This shows that our detestation is for evil, not for men as such so long as there is a chance for repentance. See also verse 7 below. But we must give no chance to Evil for working evil on our Brotherhood at any time.

5415. Refer again to 9:114. n. 1365: and n. 5413 above. Abraham's conduct is not condemned: it was a special case, and is not to be imitated by weaker men, who may fall into sin by thinking too much of sinners.

(They prayed): "Our Lord![5416]
In Thee do we trust,
And to Thee do we turn
In repentance: to Thee
Is (our) final Goal.

رَّبَّنَا عَلَيْكَ تَوَكَّلْنَا
وَإِلَيْكَ أَنَبْنَا
وَإِلَيْكَ الْمَصِيرُ

5. "Our Lord! Make us not
A (test and) trial[5417]
For the Unbelievers,
But forgive us, our Lord!
For Thou are the Exalted
In Might, the Wise."

٥ رَبَّنَا لَا تَجْعَلْنَا فِتْنَةً
لِّلَّذِينَ كَفَرُوا وَاغْفِرْ لَنَا رَبَّنَا
إِنَّكَ أَنتَ الْعَزِيزُ الْحَكِيمُ

6. There was indeed in them[5418]
An excellent example for you
To follow—for those
Whose hope is in Allah
And in the Last Day.
But if any turn away,
Truly Allah is Free of all[5419]
Wants, Worthy of all Praise.

٦ لَقَدْ كَانَ لَكُمْ فِيهِمْ أُسْوَةٌ حَسَنَةٌ
لِّمَن كَانَ يَرْجُوا اللَّهَ وَالْيَوْمَ الْآخِرَ
وَمَن يَتَوَلَّ فَإِنَّ اللَّهَ هُوَ الْغَنِيُّ الْحَمِيدُ

SECTION 2.

7. It may be that Allah
Will grant love (and friendship)[5420]
Between you and those whom
Ye (now) hold as enemies.
For Allah has power
(Over all things); And Allah is
Oft-Forgiving, Most Merciful.

٧ عَسَى اللَّهُ أَن يَجْعَلَ بَيْنَكُمْ
وَبَيْنَ الَّذِينَ عَادَيْتُم مِّنْهُم مَّوَدَّةً
وَاللَّهُ قَدِيرٌ وَاللَّهُ غَفُورٌ رَّحِيمٌ

8. Allah forbids you not,
With regard to those who
Fight you not for (your) Faith

٨ لَّا يَنْهَاكُمُ اللَّهُ عَنِ
الَّذِينَ لَمْ يُقَاتِلُوكُمْ فِي الدِّينِ

5416. This prayer indicates what our attitude should be. We must trust to Allah, and not to Allah's enemies to protect and befriend ourselves, our families, or those near and dear to us.

5417. In n. 1198 to 8:25, I have explained the shades of meaning in the word *Fitnah.* In 2:102 Hārūt and Mārūt were a trial to test the righteous who trusted in Allah from the unrighteous who resorted to evil and superstition. Here the prayer to Allah is that we should be saved from becoming so weak as to tempt the Unbelievers to try to attack and destroy us.

5418. *In them: i.e.*, in their attitude of prayer and reliance on Allah, and of dissociation from evil.

5419. If anyone rejects Allah's Message or Law, the loss is his own. It is not Allah Who needs him or his worship or his sacrifice or his praise. Allah is independent of all wants, and His attributes are inherently deserving of all praise, whether the wicked give such praise or not, in word or deed.

5420. Apparent religious hatred or enmity or persecution may be due to ignorance or over-zeal in a soul, which Allah will forgive and use eventually in His service, as happened in the case of 'Umar, who was a different man before and after his conversion. As stated in n. 5414 above, we should hate evil, but not men as such.

Nor drive you out
Of your homes,
From dealing kindly and
justly[5421]
With them: For Allah loveth
Those who are just.

وَلَمْ يُخْرِجُوكُم مِّن دِيَٰرِكُمْ
أَن تَبَرُّوهُمْ وَتُقْسِطُوٓا۟ إِلَيْهِمْ ۚ
إِنَّ ٱللَّهَ يُحِبُّ ٱلْمُقْسِطِينَ

9. Allah only forbids you,
With regard to those who
Fight you for (your) Faith,
And drive you out,
Of your homes, and support
(Others) in driving you out,
From turning to them
(For friendship and protection).
It is such as turn to them
(In these circumstances),
That do wrong.

٩ إِنَّمَا يَنْهَىٰكُمُ ٱللَّهُ عَنِ
ٱلَّذِينَ قَٰتَلُوكُمْ فِى ٱلدِّينِ
وَأَخْرَجُوكُم مِّن دِيَٰرِكُمْ
وَظَٰهَرُوا۟ عَلَىٰٓ إِخْرَاجِكُمْ أَن تَوَلَّوْهُمْ ۚ
وَمَن يَتَوَلَّهُمْ فَأُو۟لَٰٓئِكَ هُمُ ٱلظَّٰلِمُونَ

10. O ye who believe!
When there come to you
Believing women refugees,[5422]
Examine (and test) them:
Allah knows best as to
Their Faith: if ye ascertain[5423]
That they are Believers,
Then send them not back
To the Unbelievers.
They are not lawful (wives)
For the Unbelievers, nor are
The (Unbelievers) lawful
(husbands)
For them. But pay
The Unbelievers what they

١٠ يَٰٓأَيُّهَا ٱلَّذِينَ ءَامَنُوٓا۟ إِذَا جَآءَكُمُ
ٱلْمُؤْمِنَٰتُ مُهَٰجِرَٰتٍ فَٱمْتَحِنُوهُنَّ ۖ
ٱللَّهُ أَعْلَمُ بِإِيمَٰنِهِنَّ ۖ
فَإِنْ عَلِمْتُمُوهُنَّ مُؤْمِنَٰتٍ
فَلَا تَرْجِعُوهُنَّ إِلَى ٱلْكُفَّارِ ۖ
لَا هُنَّ حِلٌّ لَّهُمْ وَلَا هُمْ يَحِلُّونَ لَهُنَّ ۖ
وَءَاتُوهُم

5421. Even with Unbelievers, unless they are rampant and out to destroy us and our Faith, we should deal kindly and equitably, as is shown by our Holy Prophet's own example.

5422. Under the treaty of Ḥudaybīyah [see Introduction to S. 48, paragraph 4, condition (3)], women under guardianship (including married women), who fled from the Quraysh in Makkah to the Prophet's protection at Madīnah were to be sent back. But before this Āyah was issued, the Quraysh had already broken the treaty, and some instruction was necessary as to what the Madīnah Muslims should do in those circumstances. Muslim women married to Pagan husbands in Makkah were oppressed for their Faith, and some of them came to Madīnah as refugees. After this, they were not to be returned to the custody of their Pagan husbands at Makkah, as the marriage of believing women with non-Muslims was held to be dissolved if the husbands did not accept Islam. But in order to give no suspicion to the Pagans that they were badly treated as they lost the dower they had given on marraige, that dower was to be repaid to the husbands. Thus helpless women refugees were to be protected at the cost of the Muslims.

5423. The condition was that they should be Muslim women. How were the Muslims to know? A non-Muslim woman, in order to escape from her lawful guardians in Makkah, might pretend that she was a Muslim. The true state of her mind and heart would be known to Allah alone. But if the Muslims, on an examination of the woman, found that she professed Islam, she was to have protection. The examination would be directed (among other things) to the points mentioned in verse 12 below.

Have spent (on their dower).
And there will be no blame
On you if ye marry them[5424]
On payment of their dower
To them. But hold not
To the guardianship of[5425]
Unbelieving women: ask
For what ye have spent
On their dowers, and let
The (Unbelievers) ask for
What they have spent
(On the dowers of women
Who come over to you).
Such is the command
Of Allah: He judges
(With justice) between you.
And Allah is Full of
Knowledge and Wisdom.

مَآ أَنفَقُوا۟
وَلَا جُنَاحَ عَلَيْكُمْ أَن تَنكِحُوهُنَّ
إِذَآ ءَاتَيْتُمُوهُنَّ أُجُورَهُنَّ
وَلَا تُمْسِكُوا۟ بِعِصَمِ ٱلْكَوَافِرِ
وَسْـَٔلُوا۟ مَآ أَنفَقْتُمْ
وَلْيَسْـَٔلُوا۟ مَآ أَنفَقُوا۟
ذَٰلِكُمْ حُكْمُ ٱللَّهِ
يَحْكُمُ بَيْنَكُمْ
وَٱللَّهُ عَلِيمٌ حَكِيمٌ

11. And if any
Of your wives deserts you
To the Unbelievers,[5426]
And ye have an accession
(By the coming over of
A woman from the other side),
Then pay to those
Whose wives have deserted
The equivalent of what they
Had spent (on their dower).
And fear Allah,
In Whom ye believe.

(١١) وَإِن فَاتَكُمْ شَىْءٌ مِّنْ
أَزْوَٰجِكُمْ إِلَى ٱلْكُفَّارِ فَعَاقَبْتُمْ
فَـَٔاتُوا۟ ٱلَّذِينَ ذَهَبَتْ
أَزْوَٰجُهُم مِّثْلَ مَآ أَنفَقُوا۟
وَٱتَّقُوا۟ ٱللَّهَ ٱلَّذِىٓ
أَنتُم بِهِۦ مُؤْمِنُونَ

5424. As the marriage was held to be dissolved (see n. 5422 above), there was no bar to the remarriage of the refugee Muslim woman with a Muslim man on the payment of the usual dower to her.

5425. Unbelieving women in a Muslim society would only be a clog and a handicap. There would be neither happiness for them, nor could they conduce in any way to the healthy life of the society in which they lived as aliens. They were to be sent away, as their marriage was held to be dissolved; and the dowers paid to them were to be demanded from the guardians to whom they were sent back, just as in the contrary case the dowers of believing women were to be paid back to their Pagan ex-husbands (n. 5422 above).

5426. A very unlikely contingency, considering how much better position the women occupied in Islam than under Pagan custom. But all contingencies have to be provided for equitably in legislation. If a woman went over to the Pagans, her dower would be recoverable from the Pagans and payable to the deserted husband. If a woman came over from the Pagans, her dower would be payable to the Pagans. Assuming that the two dowers were equal, the one would be set off against the other as between the two communities; but within the communities the deserted individual would be compensated by the individual who gains a wife. If the dowers were unequal, the balance would be recoverable as between the communities, and the adjustment would then be made as between the individuals. In practice the common Fund compensated the deserted husband in anticipation of any necessary adjustments.

12. O Prophet![5427]
When believing women come
To thee to take the oath
Of fealty to thee, that they
Will not associate in worship
Any other thing whatever
With Allah, that they
Will not steal, that they
Will not commit adultery
(Or fornication), that they
Will not kill their children,
That they will not utter
Slander, intentionally forging
Falsehood,[5427-A] and that they
Will not disobey thee
In any just matter—
Then do thou receive
Their fealty, and pray to Allah[5428]
For the forgiveness (of
Their sins): for Allah is
Oft-Forgiving, Most Merciful.

١٢ يَٰٓأَيُّهَا ٱلنَّبِىُّ
إِذَا جَآءَكَ ٱلْمُؤْمِنَٰتُ يُبَايِعْنَكَ
عَلَىٰٓ أَن لَّا يُشْرِكْنَ بِٱللَّهِ شَيْـًٔا
وَلَا يَسْرِقْنَ وَلَا يَزْنِينَ
وَلَا يَقْتُلْنَ أَوْلَٰدَهُنَّ
وَلَا يَأْتِينَ بِبُهْتَٰنٍ يَفْتَرِينَهُۥ
بَيْنَ أَيْدِيهِنَّ وَأَرْجُلِهِنَّ
وَلَا يَعْصِينَكَ فِى مَعْرُوفٍ
فَبَايِعْهُنَّ وَٱسْتَغْفِرْ لَهُنَّ ٱللَّهَ
إِنَّ ٱللَّهَ غَفُورٌ رَّحِيمٌ

13. O ye who believe!
Turn not (for friendship)
To people on whom
Is the Wrath of Allah.[5429]
Of the Hereafter they are
Already in despair, just as

١٣ يَٰٓأَيُّهَا ٱلَّذِينَ ءَامَنُوا۟
لَا تَتَوَلَّوْا۟ قَوْمًا غَضِبَ ٱللَّهُ عَلَيْهِمْ
قَدْ يَئِسُوا۟ مِنَ ٱلْـَٔاخِرَةِ كَمَا

5427. Now come directions as to the points on which women entering Islam should pledge themselves. Similar points apply to men, but here the question is about women, and especially such as were likely, in those early days of Islam, to come from Pagan society into Muslim society in the conditions discussed in notes 5422 and 5423 above. A pledge on these points would search out their real motives; (1) to worship none but Allah; (2) not to steal; (3) not to indulge in sex outside the marriage tie; (4) not to commit infanticide; (the Pagan Arabs were prone to female infanticide); (5) not to indulge in slander or scandal; and (6) generally, to obey loyally the law and principles of Islam. The last was a comprehensive and sufficient phrase, but it was good to indicate also the special points to which attention was to be directed in those special circumstances. Obedience was, of course, to be in all things just and reasonable: Islam requires strict discipline but not slavishness. (R).

5427-A. "That they will not utter slander, intentionally forging falsehood": Literally, "...nor produce any lie that they have devised between their hands and feet". These words mean that they should not falsely attribute the paternity of their illegitimate children to their lawful husbands thereby adding to the monstrosity of their original sin of infidelity. [Eds.].

5428. If pledges are sincerely given for future conduct, admission to Islam is open. If there is anything in the past, for which there is evidence of sincere repentance, forgiveness is to be prayed for. Allah forgives in such cases: how can man refuse to give such cases a real chance?

5429. So we come back to the theme with which we started in this Sūrah: that we should not turn for friendship and intimacy to those who break Allah's Law and are outlaws in Allah's Kingdom. The various phrases of this question, and the legitimate qualifications, have already been mentioned, and the argument is here rounded off. *Cf.* also 57:14.

The Unbelievers are
In despair about those
(Buried) in graves.[5430]

يَئِسَ الْكُفَّارُ مِنْ أَصْحَٰبِ الْقُبُورِ

5430. The Unbelievers, who do not believe in a Future Life, can therefore have no hope beyond this life. Miserable indeed is this life to them; for the ills of this life are real to them, and they can have no hope of redress. But such is also the state of others—People of the Book or not—who wallow in sin and incur the divine Wrath. Even if they believe in a Future Life, it can only be to them a life of horror, punishment, and despair. For those of Faith the prospect is different. They may suffer in this life, but this life to them is only a fleeting shadow that will soon pass away. The Reality is beyond; there will be full redress in the Beyond, and Achievement and Felicity such as they can scarcely conceive of in the terms of this life.

INTRODUCTION TO SŪRAH 61—*AL ṢAFF*

This is the fifth Sūrah of the series of short Madīnah Sūrahs beginning with S. 57. Its subject matter is the need of discipline, practical work, and self-sacrifice in the cause of the Ummah. Its date is uncertain, but it was probably shortly after the battle of Uḥud, which was fought in *Shawwāl*, A. H. 3.

Summary—Allah's Glory shines through all Creation: but what discipline can you show to back your words with action? What lessons can you learn from the stories of Moses and Jesus? Help the Cause, and Allah's help will come with glorious results (61:1-14, and C. 240).

C. 240.—Allah's glory shines through all the universe.
(61:1-14.) What deeds of unity and discipline,
Of love and righteousness, have *you*
To show in conduct? Or do you
Only mock and insult the messengers
As they did of old? Nay, trust in Allah
And strive your utmost in His Cause.
Little have you to give, but glorious
Is the reward that Allah will give you—
Now and in the Eternal Life to come!

Sūrah 61.

Al Ṣaff (The Battle Array)

In the name of Allah, Most Gracious,
Most Merciful.

بِسْمِ ٱللَّهِ ٱلرَّحْمَٰنِ ٱلرَّحِيمِ

1. Whatever is[5431]
In the heavens and
On earth, let it declare
The Praises and Glory
Of Allah: for He is
The Exalted in Might,
The Wise.

١ سَبَّحَ لِلَّهِ مَا فِي
ٱلسَّمَٰوَٰتِ وَمَا فِي ٱلْأَرْضِ
وَهُوَ ٱلْعَزِيزُ ٱلْحَكِيمُ

2. O ye who believe!
Why say ye that
Which ye do not?[5432]

٢ يَٰٓأَيُّهَا ٱلَّذِينَ ءَامَنُوا۟
لِمَ تَقُولُونَ مَا لَا تَفْعَلُونَ

3. Grievously odious is it
In the sight of Allah
That ye say that
Which ye do not.

٣ كَبُرَ مَقْتًا عِندَ ٱللَّهِ
أَن تَقُولُوا۟ مَا لَا تَفْعَلُونَ

4. Truly Allah loves those
Who fight in His Cause
In battle array, as if[5433]
They were a solid
Cemented structure.

٤ إِنَّ ٱللَّهَ يُحِبُّ ٱلَّذِينَ يُقَٰتِلُونَ
فِي سَبِيلِهِۦ صَفًّا كَأَنَّهُم بُنْيَٰنٌ مَّرْصُوصٌ

5. And remember, Moses said[5434]
To his people: "O my people!
Why do ye vex and insult
Me, though ye know

٥ وَإِذْ قَالَ مُوسَىٰ لِقَوْمِهِۦ
يَٰقَوْمِ لِمَ تُؤْذُونَنِي وَقَد تَّعْلَمُونَ

5431. This verse is identical with 59:1. The latter illustrated the theme of the wonderful working of Allah's providence in defeating the wiles of His enemies. Here the same theme is illustrated by showing the need of unshaken discipline if we are to receive the help of Allah.

5432. At Uḥud there was some disobedience and therefore breach of discipline. People had talked much, but had failed to back up their resolution in words with firmness in action. See n. 442 to 3:121. But on all occasions when men's deeds are not commensurate with their words, their conduct is odious in the sight of Allah, and it is only due to Allah's Mercy if they are saved from disaster.

5433. A battle array, in which a large number of men stand, march, or hold together against assault as if they were a solid wall, is a striking example of order, discipline, cohesion, and courage. *A solid cemented structure* is even a better simile than the usual "solid wall" as the "structure" or building implies a more diversified organisation held together in unity and strength, each part contributing strength in its own way, and the whole held together not like a mass but like a living organism. *Cf.* also 37:1 and n. 4031.

5434. The people of Moses often rebelled against him, vexed his spirit, and insulted him. See 33:69. n. 3774, and (in the Old Testament) Num xii. 1-13. They did it not through ignorance, but from a selfish, perverse, and rebellious spirit, for which they received punishment. The Ummah of Islam should remember and take note of it, and should avoid any deviation from the Law and Will of Allah.

That I am the messenger
Of Allah (sent) to you?"
Then when they went wrong,[5435]
Allah let their hearts go wrong.
For Allah guides not those
Who are rebellious transgressors.

أَنِّي رَسُولُ ٱللَّهِ إِلَيْكُمْ
فَلَمَّا زَاغُوٓا۟ أَزَاغَ ٱللَّهُ قُلُوبَهُمْ
وَٱللَّهُ لَا يَهْدِى ٱلْقَوْمَ ٱلْفَٰسِقِينَ

6. And remember, Jesus,
The son of Mary, said:
"O Children of Israel!
I am the messenger of Allah
(Sent) to you,[5436] confirming[5437]
The Law (which came)
Before me, and giving
Glad Tidings of a Messenger
To come after me,
Whose name shall be Aḥmad."[5438]
But when he came to them
With Clear Signs,[5439]
They said, "This is
Evident sorcery!"

٦ وَإِذْ قَالَ عِيسَى ٱبْنُ مَرْيَمَ
يَٰبَنِىٓ إِسْرَٰٓءِيلَ إِنِّى رَسُولُ ٱللَّهِ إِلَيْكُم
مُّصَدِّقًا لِّمَا بَيْنَ يَدَىَّ مِنَ ٱلتَّوْرَىٰةِ
وَمُبَشِّرًۢا بِرَسُولٍ يَأْتِى مِنۢ
بَعْدِى ٱسْمُهُۥٓ أَحْمَدُ
فَلَمَّا جَآءَهُم بِٱلْبَيِّنَٰتِ
قَالُوا۟ هَٰذَا سِحْرٌ مُّبِينٌ

7. Who doth greater wrong
Than one who invents
Falsehood against Allah,
Even as he is being invited[5440]

٧ وَمَنْ أَظْلَمُ مِمَّنِ ٱفْتَرَىٰ
عَلَى ٱللَّهِ ٱلْكَذِبَ وَهُوَ يُدْعَىٰٓ

5435. The sinner's own will deviates, *i.e.*, goes off from the right way, and he does wrong. That means that he shuts off Allah's grace. Allah then, after the sinner's repeated rebellion, withdraws the protecting Grace from him, and the sinner's heart is tainted: there is " a disease in his heart", which is the centre of his being: his spiritual state is ruined. Allah's guidance is withdrawn from him.

5436. The mission of Jesus was to his own people, the Jews. *Cf.* Matt. x 5-6. See also Matt. xv. 24: "I am not sent but to the lost sheep of Israel;" also Matt. xv. 26: "It is not meet to take the children's bread, and to cast it to the dogs."

5437. *Cf.* Matt v. 17.

5438. "Aḥmad", or "Muḥammad", the Praised One, is almost a translation of the Greek word *Periclytos.* In the present Gospel of John, xiv. 16, xv. 26, and xvi. 7, the word "Comforter" in the English version is for the Greek word "Paracletos", which means "Advocate", "one called to the help of another, a kind friend", rather than "Comforter". Our doctors contend that Paracletos is a corrupt reading for Periclytos, and that in their original saying of Jesus there was a prophecy of our Holy Prophet *Aḥmad* by name. Even if we read Paracelete, it would apply to the Holy Prophet, who is "a Mercy for all creatures" (21:107) and "most kind and merciful to the Believers" (9:128). See also n. 416 to 3:81.

5439. Our Holy Prophet was foretold in many ways; and when he came, he showed forth many Clear Signs, for his whole life from beginning to end was one vast miracle. He fought and won against odds. Without learning from men he taught the highest wisdom. He melted hearts that were hard, and he strengthened hearts that were tender and required support. In all his sayings and doings men of discernment could see the working of Allah's hand; yet the ignorant Unbelievers called it all Sorcery!—called that unreal which became the most solid fact of human history!

5440. It is wrong in any case to uphold falsehoods and debasing superstitions, but it is doubly wrong when these are put forward in rivalry or opposition to the light of eternal Unity and Harmony which is Islam. See C. 7-11. Allah sends His guidance freely, but withdraws His Grace from those who wilfully do wrong.

To Islam? And Allah
Guides not those
Who do wrong.

إِلَى ٱلْإِسْلَٰمِ
وَٱللَّهُ لَا يَهْدِى ٱلْقَوْمَ ٱلظَّٰلِمِينَ

8. Their intention is
To extinguish Allah's Light
(By blowing) with their mouths:[5441]
But Allah will complete
(The revelation of) His Light,
Even though the Unbelievers
May detest (it).

٨ يُرِيدُونَ لِيُطْفِـُٔوا۟ نُورَ ٱللَّهِ
بِأَفْوَٰهِهِمْ وَٱللَّهُ مُتِمُّ نُورِهِۦ
وَلَوْ كَرِهَ ٱلْكَٰفِرُونَ

9. It is He Who has sent
His Messenger with Guidance
And the Religion of Truth,
That he may proclaim it
Over all religion,[5442]
Even though the Pagans
May detest (it).

٩ هُوَ ٱلَّذِىٓ أَرْسَلَ رَسُولَهُۥ بِٱلْهُدَىٰ
وَدِينِ ٱلْحَقِّ لِيُظْهِرَهُۥ عَلَى ٱلدِّينِ كُلِّهِۦ
وَلَوْ كَرِهَ ٱلْمُشْرِكُونَ

SECTION 2.

10. O ye who believe!
Shall I lead you
To a bargain[5443] that will
Save you from
A grievous Penalty?—

١٠ يَٰٓأَيُّهَا ٱلَّذِينَ ءَامَنُوا۟ هَلْ أَدُلُّكُمْ
عَلَىٰ تِجَٰرَةٍ تُنجِيكُم مِّنْ عَذَابٍ أَلِيمٍ

11. That ye believe in Allah
And His Messenger, and that
Ye strive (your utmost)
In the Cause of Allah,
With your property
And your persons:

١١ تُؤْمِنُونَ بِٱللَّهِ وَرَسُولِهِۦ
وَتُجَٰهِدُونَ فِى سَبِيلِ ٱللَّهِ
بِأَمْوَٰلِكُمْ وَأَنفُسِكُمْ

5441. Allah's Light is unquenchable. A foolish, ignorant person who thinks of extinguishing it is like a rustic who wants to blow out electric light as he might blow out a rush candle! *With their mouths* also implies the babble and cackle of Ignorance aganist Allah's Truth. The more the foolish ones try to quench Allah's Light, the clearer it shines, to shame them!

5442. *Over all religion*: in the singular: not over all other religions, in the plural. There is really only one true Religion, the Message of Allah, submission to the Will of Allah: this is called Islam. It was the religion preached by Moses and Jesus; it was the religion of Abraham, Noah, and all the prophets, by whatever name it may be called. If people corrupt that pure light, and call their religions by different names, we must bear with them, and we may allow the names for convenience. But Truth must prevail over all. See also 9:33, n. 1290, and 68:28, n. 4912.

5443. *Tijārah:* bargain, trade, traffic, transaction: something given or done, in return for something which we desire to get. What we give or do on our part is described in verse 11 below, and what we get is described in verse 12. It is truly a wonderful bargain: what we are asked to give is so little; what we are promised in return is so much. There comes Allah's unbounded Bounty and Munificence. *Cf.* also 9:111, where the bargain is stated in another way.

That will be best for you,
If ye but knew![5444]

ذَٰلِكُمْ خَيْرٌ لَّكُمْ إِن كُنتُمْ تَعْلَمُونَ

12. He will forgive you
Your sins, and admit you
To Gardens beneath which
Rivers flow, and to beautiful
Mansions in Gardens
Of Eternity: that is indeed
The supreme Achievement.

يَغْفِرْ لَكُمْ ذُنُوبَكُمْ وَيُدْخِلْكُمْ جَنَّٰتٍ تَجْرِي مِن تَحْتِهَا ٱلْأَنْهَٰرُ وَمَسَٰكِنَ طَيِّبَةً فِي جَنَّٰتِ عَدْنٍ ذَٰلِكَ ٱلْفَوْزُ ٱلْعَظِيمُ ﴿١٢﴾

13. And another (favour
Will He bestow), which ye[5445]
Do love—help from Allah
And a speedy victory.
So give the Glad Tidings
To the Believers.

وَأُخْرَىٰ تُحِبُّونَهَا نَصْرٌ مِّنَ ٱللَّهِ وَفَتْحٌ قَرِيبٌ وَبَشِّرِ ٱلْمُؤْمِنِينَ ﴿١٣﴾

14. O ye who believe!
Be ye helpers of Allah:[5446]
As said Jesus, the son of Mary,[5447]
To the Disciples, "Who will be
My helpers to (the work
Of) Allah?" Said the Disciples,
"We are Allah's helpers!"
Then a portion of the Children
Of Israel believed, and
A portion disbeleived:
But We gave power
To those who believed
Against their enemies,

يَٰٓأَيُّهَا ٱلَّذِينَ ءَامَنُوا۟ كُونُوٓا۟ أَنصَارَ ٱللَّهِ كَمَا قَالَ عِيسَى ٱبْنُ مَرْيَمَ لِلْحَوَارِيِّـۧنَ مَنْ أَنصَارِيٓ إِلَى ٱللَّهِ قَالَ ٱلْحَوَارِيُّونَ نَحْنُ أَنصَارُ ٱللَّهِ فَـَٔامَنَت طَّآئِفَةٌ مِّنۢ بَنِيٓ إِسْرَٰٓءِيلَ وَكَفَرَت طَّآئِفَةٌ فَأَيَّدْنَا ٱلَّذِينَ ءَامَنُوا۟ عَلَىٰ عَدُوِّهِمْ ﴿١٤﴾

5444. It would indeed be a great and wonderful bargain to give so little and get so much, if we only knew and understood the comparative value of things—the sacrifice of our fleeting advantages for forgiveness, the love of Allah, and eternal bliss.

5445. The supreme Achievement has already been mentioned, *viz.:* the Gardens of Eternity in the Presence of Allah. But lest that seem too remote or abstract for the understanding of men not spiritually advanced, another type or symbol or metaphor is mentioned which the men who first heard this Message could at once understand and appreciate—"which ye do love": *viz.:* Help and Victory. For all striving in a righteous Cause we get Allah's help: and however much the odds against us may be, we are sure of victory with Allah's help. But all life is a striving or struggle—the spiritual life even more than any other; and the final victory there is the same as the Garden of Eternity.

5446. If we seek Allah's help, we must first help Allah's Cause, *i.e.*, dedicate ourselves to Him entirely and without reserve. This was also the teaching of Jesus, as mentioned in this verse. As found in the New Testament, the metaphor used is that of the Cross. "Then said Jesus to his disciples, if any man will come after me, let him deny himself, and take up his cross, and follow me." (Matt. xvi. 24).

5447. See 3:52, and n. 392; and for the Biblical reference, see the last note. The names of the twelve Disciples will be found in Matt. x. 2-4.

And they became
The ones that prevailed.[5448]

فَأَصْبَحُوا ظَٰهِرِينَ

5448. A portion of the Children of Israel—the one that really cared for the Truth—believed in Jesus and followed his guidance. But the greater portion of them were hard hearted, and remained in their beaten track of formalism and false racial pride. The majority *seemed* at first to have the upper hand when they thought they had crucified Jesus and killed his Message. But they were soon brought to their senses. Jerusalem was destroyed by Titus in A.C. 70 and the Jews have been scattered ever since. "The Wandering Jew" has become a byword in many literatures. On the other hand, those who followed Jesus permeated the Roman Empire, brought many new races within their circle, and through the Roman Empire, Christianity became the predominant religion of the world until the advent of Islam. So is it promised to the people of Islam: they must prevail if they adhere to the Truth. Badr (A.H. 2) was a landmark against Pagan Arabia: Qādisīyah (A.H. 14) and Madā'in (A.H. 16) against the might of Persia: Yarmūk (A.H. 15) against the might of the Byzantine Empire in Christian Syria; and Heliopolis (A.H. 19) against the same Empire in Christian Egypt and Africa. These were symbols in external events. The moral and spiritual landmarks are less tangible, and more gradual, but none the less real. Mark how the arrogance and power of Priesthood have been quelled; how superstition and belief in blind Fate have been checked; how the freedom of human individuals has been reconciled with the sanctity of marriage in the Law of Divorce, how the civil position of women has been raised; how temperance and sobriety have been identified with religion; what impetus has been given to knowledge and experimental science; and how economic reconstruction has been pioneered by rational schemes for the expenditure and distribution of wealth.

INTRODUCTION TO SŪRAH 62—*AL JUMU'AH*

This is the sixth Sūrah in the Madīnah series of short Sūrahs which began with S. 57.

The special theme here is the need for mutual contact in the Community for worship and understanding: for the spirit of the Message is for all, ignorant and learned, in order that they may be purified and may learn wisdom.

The date has no special significance: it may be placed in the early Madīnah period, say between A.H. 2 and 3.

Summary—The Revelation has come among unlearned men, to teach purity and wisdom not only to them but to others, including those who may have an older Message but do not understand it: meet solemnly for the Assembly (Friday) Prayer, and let not worldly interests deflect you therefrom. (62:1-11, and C. 241).

C. 241.—Allah's care for His creatures is universal.
(62:1-11) His Revelation is for all—ignorant
And lowly as well as learned and high-placed—
Now and forever. None can arrogantly
Claim exclusive possession of Allah's gifts:
If they do, search their hearts within, and you
Will find them afraid of Death and Judgement.
Men of Faith! On the Day of Assembly,
When you hear the call, hasten earnestly
To answer it: leave off business, and join
In common worship and devotion. Then
You may disperse about your ordinary business,
But remember the Praises of Allah always:
It is He alone that can provide
For you every need, and *His* gifts are best.

Sūrah 62.

Al Jumu'ah (Friday)

In the name of Allah, Most Gracious,
Most Merciful.

بِسْمِ ٱللَّهِ ٱلرَّحْمَٰنِ ٱلرَّحِيمِ

1. Whatever is
In the heavens and
On earth, doth declare[5449]
The Praises and Glory
Of Allah—the Sovereign,[5450]
The Holy One, the Exalted
In Might, the Wise.

١ يُسَبِّحُ لِلَّهِ مَا فِي
ٱلسَّمَٰوَٰتِ وَمَا فِي ٱلْأَرْضِ
ٱلْمَلِكِ ٱلْقُدُّوسِ ٱلْعَزِيزِ ٱلْحَكِيمِ

2. It is He Who has sent
Amongst the Unlettered[5451]
A messenger from among
Themselves, to rehearse
To them His Signs,[5452]
To sanctify them, and
To instruct them in Scripture[5453]
And Wisdom—although[5454]
They had been, before,
In manifest error—

٢ هُوَ ٱلَّذِي بَعَثَ
فِي ٱلْأُمِّيِّـۧنَ رَسُولًا مِّنْهُمْ
يَتْلُوا۟ عَلَيْهِمْ ءَايَٰتِهِۦ وَيُزَكِّيهِمْ
وَيُعَلِّمُهُمُ ٱلْكِتَٰبَ وَٱلْحِكْمَةَ
وَإِن كَانُوا۟ مِن قَبْلُ لَفِي ضَلَٰلٍ مُّبِينٍ

5449. See n. 5408 to 59:24, where I have explained the difference in signification between *sabbaḥa* and *yusabbiḥu*. The latter form is used here to express an actual fact. 'Everything declares the Praises and Glory of Allah, because Allah's mercies extend to all His creatures: He sends His Revelation for the benefit of the ignorant and unlettered as well as for those who have learning in their midst, especially as the latter are apt, by the very weight of their ponderous learning, to miss the real point and spirit of Allah's Message.'

5450. See 59:23, and n. 5402. Here we have two of the divine attributes repeated from 59:23 and two from the end of 59:24, implying a reminiscence of all the beautiful divine attributes mentioned in that passage.

5451. *The Unlettered:* as applied to a people, it refers to the Arabs, in comparison with the People of the Book, who had a longer tradition of learning, but whose failure is referred to in verse 5 below. As applied to individuals, it means that Allah's Revelation is for the benefit of all men, whether they have worldly learning or not.

5452. *His Signs:* Allah's wonderful Signs in His Creation and in His ordering of the world. It may include the Verses of the Qur'ān, but they are more specifically referred to as "Scripture" in the next line but one.

5453. *Cf.* 2:129, and n. 129. Read again the attributes in the last verse. Allah is full Sovereign, and therefore cares for all His subjects, including the meanest and most ignorant, and sends His prophets or messengers to them. He is the Holy One, and therefore purifies and sanctifies those who were steeped in superstition and wickedness. He is Exalted in Power, and therefore He can confer all these blessings on the most unlikely people (verse 3), and no one can stay His hand. He is wise, and therefore He instructs in wisdom, both through written Scriptures, and in other ways, *e.g.*, by means of a knowledge of life and its laws, and an understanding of His wonderful universe.

5454. Previous ignorance or error is no bar to a person or nation receiving the blessings of Allah's revelation, provided such person or nation has the will to come to Allah and the capacity to bear His Message. For an instance of incapacity through arrogance, see verse 6 below. For some remarks on the Arabs as vehicles of the new Light, see. C. 12-15.

3. As well as (to confer All these benefits upon) Others of them,[5455] who Have not already joined them: And He is Exalted In Might, Wise.	وَءَاخَرِينَ مِنْهُمْ ﴿٣﴾ لَمَّا يَلْحَقُوا بِهِمْ وَهُوَ الْعَزِيزُ الْحَكِيمُ
4. Such is the Bounty of Allah, Which He bestows On whom He will:[5456] And Allah is the Lord Of the highest bounty.	ذَٰلِكَ فَضْلُ اللَّهِ يُؤْتِيهِ مَن يَشَاءُ ﴿٤﴾ وَاللَّهُ ذُو الْفَضْلِ الْعَظِيمِ
5. The similitude of those Who were charged With the (obligations Of the) Mosaic Law, But who subsequently failed In those (obligations), is That of a donkey[5457] Which carries huge tomes (But understands them not). Evil is the similitude Of people who falsify The Signs of Allah: And Allah guides not People who do wrong.	مَثَلُ الَّذِينَ ﴿٥﴾ حُمِّلُوا التَّوْرَاةَ ثُمَّ لَمْ يَحْمِلُوهَا كَمَثَلِ الْحِمَارِ يَحْمِلُ أَسْفَارًا بِئْسَ مَثَلُ الْقَوْمِ الَّذِينَ كَذَّبُوا بِآيَاتِ اللَّهِ وَاللَّهُ لَا يَهْدِي الْقَوْمَ الظَّالِمِينَ
6. Say: "O ye that Stand on Judaism![5458] If ye think that ye Are friends to Allah, To the exclusion of (Other) men, then express	قُلْ يَا أَيُّهَا الَّذِينَ ﴿٦﴾ هَادُوا إِن زَعَمْتُمْ أَنَّكُمْ أَوْلِيَاءُ لِلَّهِ مِن دُونِ النَّاسِ

5455. *Others of them:* refers to other persons or peoples who may be ignorant, *i.e.*, others than those among whom the Holy Prophet came as a messenger. In other words his Message is for his Arab people and his non-Arab contemporaries as well as those who live in other ages, and have no personal contact with him or his Companions.

5456. That is, according to His wise Will and Plan, and also as a result of His unbounded generosity to all.

5457. The Children of Israel were chosen as special vehicles for Allah's Message early in history. When their descendants corrupted the Message and became guilty of all abominations against which prophets like Isaiah inveighed with such zeal and fire, they merely became like beasts of burden that carry learning and wisdom on their backs but do not understand or profit by it.

5458. *Standing on Judaism* is a very different thing from following the Law and Will of Allah. An arrogant claim to be a chosen people, to be the exclusive possessors of divine teaching, to be exempt from any punishment for breaches of the divine law, (*cf.* 2:88), is presumptuous blasphemy. It may be Judaism, but it is not in the spirit of Moses.

Your desire for Death,
If ye are truthful!"[5459]

فَتَمَنَّوُا۟ ٱلْمَوْتَ إِن كُنتُمْ صَٰدِقِينَ

7. But never will they
Express their desire
(For Death), because of
The (deeds) their hands
Have sent on before them!
And Allah knows well
Those that do wrong!

وَلَا يَتَمَنَّوْنَهُۥٓ أَبَدًۢا بِمَا قَدَّمَتْ أَيْدِيهِمْ ۚ وَٱللَّهُ عَلِيمٌۢ بِٱلظَّٰلِمِينَ ﴿٧﴾

8. Say: "The Death from which
Ye flee will truly
Overtake you: then will
Ye be sent back
To the Knower of things
Secret and open: and He
Will tell you (the truth[5460]
Of) the things that ye did!"

قُلْ إِنَّ ٱلْمَوْتَ ٱلَّذِى تَفِرُّونَ مِنْهُ فَإِنَّهُۥ مُلَٰقِيكُمْ ۖ ثُمَّ تُرَدُّونَ إِلَىٰ عَٰلِمِ ٱلْغَيْبِ وَٱلشَّهَٰدَةِ فَيُنَبِّئُكُم بِمَا كُنتُمْ تَعْمَلُونَ ﴿٨﴾

SECTION 2.

9. O ye who believe!
When the call is proclaimed
To prayer on Friday[5461]
(The Day of Assembly),
Hasten earnestly to the
Remembrance
Of Allah, and leave off

يَٰٓأَيُّهَا ٱلَّذِينَ ءَامَنُوٓا۟ إِذَا نُودِىَ لِلصَّلَوٰةِ مِن يَوْمِ ٱلْجُمُعَةِ فَٱسْعَوْا۟ إِلَىٰ ذِكْرِ ٱللَّهِ وَذَرُوا۟ ﴿٩﴾

5459. *Cf.* 2:94-96. If they claimed to be special friends of Allah, why do they not eagerly desire death, which would bring them nearer to Allah? But of all people, they are the most tenacious of this life and the good things of this life! And they know that their grasping selfish lives have run up a score of sin against them, which will meet its recompense.

5460. Before Allah's Judgement Seat, when Judgement is established, we shall see the full inwardness of all deeds in this world. The veil of illusion and delusion will be torn off. All our secret motives will be laid bare. The results of all our little plots and plans and their reactions on our spiritual and eternal welfare will be clearly visible to us. All make-believe will disappear.

5461. Friday, is primarily the Day of Assembly, the weekly meeting of the Congregation, when we show our unity by sharing in common public worship, preceded by a *Khuṭbah,* in which the Imām (or Leader) reviews the week's spiritual life of the Community and offers advice and exhortation on holy living. Notice the gradations of social contact for Muslims if they followed the wise ordinances of their Faith. (1) Each individual remembers Allah for himself or herself five or more times eveyday in the home or place of business, or local mosque, or open air, as the case may be. (2) On Friday in every week there is a local meeting in the central mosque of each local centre—it may be a village, or town, or ward of a big city. (3) At the two 'Īds every year, there is a large local area meeting in one centre. (4) Once at least in a lifetime, where possible, a Muslim shares in the vast international assemblage of the world, in the centre of Islam, at the Makkan Pilgrimage. A happy combination of decentralisation and centralisation, of individual liberty and collective meeting, and contact at various stages or grades. The mechanical part of this ordinance is easy to carry out. Are we carrying out the more difficult part?—the spirit of unity, brotherhood, mutual consultation, and collective understanding and action? (R).

Business (and traffic):[5462]
That is best for you
If ye but knew![5463]

ٱلْبَيْعَ ذَٰلِكُمْ خَيْرٌ لَّكُمْ إِن كُنتُمْ تَعْلَمُونَ

10. And when the Prayer
Is finished, then may ye
Disperse through the land,
And seek of the Bounty
Of Allah: and celebrate
The Praises of Allah
Often (and without stint):
That ye may prosper.[5464]

١٠ فَإِذَا قُضِيَتِ ٱلصَّلَوٰةُ
فَٱنتَشِرُوا فِى ٱلْأَرْضِ وَٱبْتَغُوا مِن
فَضْلِ ٱللَّهِ وَٱذْكُرُوا ٱللَّهَ كَثِيرًا
لَّعَلَّكُمْ تُفْلِحُونَ

11. But when they see
Some bargain or some
Amusement, they disperse
Headlong to it, and leave
Thee standing. Say:
"The (blessing) from the Presence
Of Allah is better than
Any amusement or bargain!
And Allah is the Best
To provide (for all needs)."[5465]

١١ وَإِذَا رَأَوْا تِجَٰرَةً أَوْ لَهْوًا
ٱنفَضُّوٓا إِلَيْهَا وَتَرَكُوكَ قَآئِمًا
قُلْ مَا عِندَ ٱللَّهِ خَيْرٌ
مِّنَ ٱللَّهْوِ وَمِنَ ٱلتِّجَٰرَةِ
وَٱللَّهُ خَيْرُ ٱلرَّٰزِقِينَ

5462. The idea behind the Muslim weekly "Day of Assembly" is different from that behind the Jewish Sabbath (Saturday) or the Christian Sunday. The Jewish Sabbath is primarily a commemoration of Allah's ending His work and resting on the seventh day (Gen. ii. 2; Exod. xx. 11): we are taught that Allah needs no rest, nor does He feel fatigue (2:255). The Jewish command forbids work on that day but says nothing about worship or prayer (Exod. xx.10); our ordinance lays chief stress on the remembrance of Allah. Jewish formalism went so far as to kill the spirit of the sabbath, and call forth the protest of Jesus: "the sabbath was made for man, and not man for the sabbath" (Mark, ii. 27). But the Christian Church, although it has changed the day from Saturday to Sunday, has inherited the Jewish spirit: witness the Scottish Sabbath; except insofar as it has been secularised. Our teaching says: 'When the time for *Jumu'ah* Prayer comes, close your business and answer the summons loyally and earnestly, meet earnestly, pray, consult and learn by social contact: when the meeting is over, scatter and go about your business'.

5463. The immediate and temporal worldly gain may be the ultimate and spiritual loss, and *vice versa.*

5464. Prosperity is not to be measured by wealth or worldly gains. There is a higher prosperity—the health of the mind and the spirit.

5465. Do not be distracted by the craze for amusement or gain. If you lead a righteous and sober life, Allah will provide for you in all senses, better than any provision you can possibly think of.

INTRODUCTION TO SŪRAH 63—*AL MUNĀFIQŪN*

This is the seventh of the ten short Madīnah Sūrahs dealing with a special feature in the social life of the Brotherhood.

The special feature here dealt with is the wiles and mischief of the Hypocrite element in any community, and the need of guarding against it and against the temptation it throws in the way of the Believers.

The battle of Uḥud (*Shawwāl* A.H. 3) unmasked the Hypocrites in Madīnah: see 3:167, and n. 476. This Sūrah may be referred to some time after that event, say about 4 A.H. or possibly 5 A.H. if the words reported in verse 8 were uttered in the expedition against the Banū Muṣṭaliq, A.H. 5. (See n. 5475 below).

Summary—False are the oaths of the Hypocrites: they only seek selfish ends: Believers should beware of their wiles and strive devotedly always for the Cause (63:1-11, and C. 242).

C. 242.—The oaths of Hypocrites are a screen
(63:1-11.) For their misdeeds. They think they deceive
With their fair exteriors and plausible talk,
But their minds are impervious to the real Truth.
They may plot to withhold from men of God
Such things of this world as they may command;
They may plot to expel and persecute the righteous;
They may call them ill names and slight them.
But to Allah belong the treasures of the heavens
And the earth, and He will bestow according
To His wise and universal Plan. Let not
The world's foolish craze divert the Believers
From the service of Allah—from good deeds and Charity.
Now is the time: all vain will be
Your pleas and your regrets when the shadow
Of Death cuts off your last chance of Repentance!

Sūrah 63.

الجزء الثامن والعشرون — سورة المنافقون

Al Munāfiqūn (The Hypocrites)

In the name of Allah, Most Gracious,
Most Merciful.

بِسْمِ ٱللَّهِ ٱلرَّحْمَٰنِ ٱلرَّحِيمِ

1. When the Hypocrites[5466]
Come to thee, they say,
"We bear witness that thou
Art indeed the Messenger
Of Allah." Yea, Allah
Knoweth that thou art
Indeed His Messenger,
And Allah beareth witness
That the Hypocrites are
Indeed liars.

(١) إِذَا جَآءَكَ ٱلْمُنَٰفِقُونَ قَالُوا۟
نَشْهَدُ إِنَّكَ لَرَسُولُ ٱللَّهِ
وَٱللَّهُ يَعْلَمُ إِنَّكَ لَرَسُولُهُۥ
وَٱللَّهُ يَشْهَدُ إِنَّ ٱلْمُنَٰفِقِينَ
لَكَٰذِبُونَ

2. They have made their oaths[5467]
A screen (for their misdeeds):
Thus they obstruct (men)
From the Path of Allah:
Truly evil are their deeds.

(٢) ٱتَّخَذُوٓا۟ أَيْمَٰنَهُمْ جُنَّةً
فَصَدُّوا۟ عَن سَبِيلِ ٱللَّهِ
إِنَّهُمْ سَآءَ مَا كَانُوا۟ يَعْمَلُونَ

3. That is because they believed,
Then they rejected Faith:
So a seal was set[5468]
On their hearts: therefore
They understand not.

(٣) ذَٰلِكَ بِأَنَّهُمْ ءَامَنُوا۟ ثُمَّ كَفَرُوا۟
فَطُبِعَ عَلَىٰ قُلُوبِهِمْ
فَهُمْ لَا يَفْقَهُونَ

4. When thou lookest
At them, their exteriors[5469]

(٤) وَإِذَا رَأَيْتَهُمْ تُعْجِبُكَ أَجْسَامُهُمْ

5466. The hypocrite element, if one exists in any society, is a source of weakness and a danger to its health and its very existence. When the Holy Prophet came to Madīnah in *Hijrah*, his arrival was welcome to all the patriotic citizens: it not only united them in common life and healed their old differences, but it brought honour and light to them in the person of the greatest living Teacher of Truth. But there were some baser elements filled with envy. Such hopes as they had entertained of attaining power and leadership by playing on the animosities of the factions were now dashed to the ground. They now began to work underground. For fear of the majority they dared not oppose the new growing Brotherhood of Righteousness. They tried to undermine it by intriguing secretly with its enemies and swearing openly its loyalty to the Holy Prophet. They were thoroughly unmasked and discredited at the battle of Uhud. See 3:167, and n. 476.

5467. *Cf.* 58:16 and n. 5358. When they say that Muhammad is the Prophet of Allah, it is Allah's own truth: but what is in their hearts? Nothing but falsehood.

5468. *Cf.* 2:7. Their double-dealing has fogged their understanding. In Arabic the heart is taken to be the seat of understanding as well as of affection.

5469. The Hypocrites at all times are plausible people, and so were the Hypocrites of Madīnah. They present a fine exterior; they dress well; they can usually afford fine equipages; they try to win the confidence of everyone, as they have no scruples in telling lies, and apparently expressing agreement with everyone. Their words are fair-spoken, and as truth does not check their tongues, their flattery and deception know no bounds. But all this is on the outside. As they have no sincerity, nothing that they say or do is worth anything.

Please thee; and when
They speak, thou listenest
To their words. They are
As (worthless as hollow)
Pieces of timber propped up,[5470]
(Unable to stand on their own).
They think that every
Cry is against them.[5471]
They are the enemies;
So beware of them.
The curse of Allah be
On them! How are they
Deluded (away from the Truth)!

5. And when it is said
To them, "Come, the Messenger
Of Allah will pray for your[5472]
Forgiveness", they turn aside
Their heads, and thou wouldst
See them turning away
Their faces in arrogance.

6. It is equal to them
Whether thou pray for
Their forgiveness or not.[5473]
Allah will not forgive them.
Truly Allah guides not
Rebellious transgressors.

7. They are the ones who say,
"Spend nothing on those
Who are with Allah's
Messenger,[5474]
To the end that they

وَإِن يَقُولُوا تَسْمَعْ لِقَوْلِهِمْ
كَأَنَّهُمْ خُشُبٌ مُّسَنَّدَةٌ
يَحْسَبُونَ كُلَّ صَيْحَةٍ عَلَيْهِمْ
هُمُ الْعَدُوُّ فَاحْذَرْهُمْ
قَاتَلَهُمُ اللَّهُ
أَنَّىٰ يُؤْفَكُونَ

٥ وَإِذَا قِيلَ لَهُمْ تَعَالَوْا
يَسْتَغْفِرْ لَكُمْ رَسُولُ اللَّهِ لَوَّوْا رُءُوسَهُمْ
وَرَأَيْتَهُمْ يَصُدُّونَ وَهُم مُّسْتَكْبِرُونَ

٦ سَوَاءٌ عَلَيْهِمْ أَسْتَغْفَرْتَ لَهُمْ
أَمْ لَمْ تَسْتَغْفِرْ لَهُمْ لَن يَغْفِرَ اللَّهُ لَهُمْ
إِنَّ اللَّهَ لَا يَهْدِي الْقَوْمَ الْفَاسِقِينَ

٧ هُمُ الَّذِينَ يَقُولُونَ لَا تُنفِقُوا
عَلَىٰ مَنْ عِندَ رَسُولِ اللَّهِ حَتَّىٰ

5470. Good timber is strong in itself and can support roofs and buildings. Hollow timber is useless, and has to be propped up against other things. The Hypocrites are like rotten timber. They have no firm character themselves, and for others they are unsafe props to rely upon.

5471. Their conscience always troubles them. If any cry is raised, they immediately get alarmed, and think it is against themselves. Such men are worse than open enemies.

5472. Even hypocrisy like other sins can be forgiven by repentance and amendment, provided there is a will and earnest desire to turn from evil and seek the Grace of Allah. In this case there was none.

5473. The stiff-necked rejecters of Allah's Truth have made a wide gulf between themselves and Allah's Grace. No prayer for them will help them. In the attitude of rebellion and transgression they cannot obtain Allah's forgiveness.

5474. The *Muhājirūn*, who had come to be with the Holy Prophet in Madīnah in exile, were received, helped, entertained by the *Anṣār* (Helpers). The Hypocrites in Madīnah did not like this, and tried in underhand ways to dissuade the good folk of Madīnah from doing all they could for the exiles. But their tricks did not succeed. The small Muslim community grew from strength to strength until they were able to stand on their own resources and greatly to augment the resources of their hosts as well. It is goodness that produces strength and prosperity, and Allah holds the keys of the treasures of man's well-being. It is not for Allah's enemies to dole out or withhold the unbounded treasures of Allah.

May disperse (and quit
Madīnah)."
But to Allah belong
The treasures of the heavens
And the earth; but
The Hypocrites understand not.

يَنفَضُّوا ۗ
وَلِلَّهِ خَزَائِنُ السَّمَاوَاتِ وَالْأَرْضِ
وَلَٰكِنَّ الْمُنَافِقِينَ لَا يَفْقَهُونَ

8. They say, "If we[5475]
Return to Madīnah, surely
The more honourable (element)
Will expel therefrom the meaner".
But honour belongs to Allah
And His Messenger, and
To the Believers; but
The Hypocrites know not.

﴿٨﴾ يَقُولُونَ لَئِن رَّجَعْنَا إِلَى الْمَدِينَةِ
لَيُخْرِجَنَّ الْأَعَزُّ مِنْهَا الْأَذَلَّ ۚ
وَلِلَّهِ الْعِزَّةُ وَلِرَسُولِهِ وَلِلْمُؤْمِنِينَ
وَلَٰكِنَّ الْمُنَافِقِينَ لَا يَعْلَمُونَ

SECTION 2.

9. O ye who believe!
Let not your riches
Or your children divert you
From the remembrance of Allah.
If any act thus,
The loss is their own.[5476]

﴿٩﴾ يَا أَيُّهَا الَّذِينَ آمَنُوا لَا تُلْهِكُمْ أَمْوَالُكُمْ
وَلَا أَوْلَادُكُمْ عَن ذِكْرِ اللَّهِ ۚ
وَمَن يَفْعَلْ ذَٰلِكَ فَأُولَٰئِكَ هُمُ الْخَاسِرُونَ

10. And spend something (in charity)
Out of the substance[5477]
Which We have bestowed
On you, before Death
Should come to any of you
And he should say,
"O my Lord! Why didst
Thou not give me
Respite for a little while?
I should then have given
(Largely) in charity, and I

﴿١٠﴾ وَأَنفِقُوا مِن مَّا رَزَقْنَاكُم
مِّن قَبْلِ أَن يَأْتِيَ
أَحَدَكُمُ الْمَوْتُ فَيَقُولَ
رَبِّ لَوْلَا أَخَّرْتَنِي إِلَىٰ أَجَلٍ قَرِيبٍ
فَأَصَّدَّقَ

5475. Words of this import were spoken by 'Abd Allah Ibn Ubayy, the leader of the Madīnah Hypocrites to or about the Exiles, in the course of the expedition against the Banū Muṣṭaliq in the fourth or fifth year of the Hijrah. He had hopes of leadership which were disappointed by the coming to Madīnah of a man far greater than he. So he arrogated to himself and his clique the title of "the more honourable (element)" and slightingly spoke of the Emigrants as the "meaner" element that had intruded from outside.

5476. Riches and human resources of all kinds are but fleeting sources of enjoyment. They should not turn away the good man from his devotion to Allah. "Remembrance of Allah" includes every act of service and goodness, every kind thought and kind deed, for this is the service and sacrifice which Allah requires of us. If we fail in this, the loss is our own, not anyone else's: for it stunts our own spiritual growth.

5477. "Substance" or "Sustenance", in every sense, literal and metaphorical. Whatever good we enjoy comes from Allah, and it is our duty to use some of it in the service of others, for that is Charity and the service of Allah. Every unselfish act is Charity. And we must not postpone our good resolutions to the future. Death may come suddenly on us, and we cannot *then* be allowed to plead for more time. Every present moment calls urgently for its good deed.

Should have been one
Of the doers of good".

وَأَكُن مِّنَ ٱلصَّـٰلِحِينَ

11. But to no soul
Will Allah grant respite[5478]
When the time appointed
(For it) has come; and Allah
Is well-acquainted
With (all) that ye do.

وَلَن يُؤَخِّرَ ٱللَّهُ نَفْسًا إِذَا جَآءَ أَجَلُهَا ۚ وَٱللَّهُ خَبِيرٌۢ بِمَا تَعْمَلُونَ ﴿١١﴾

5478. When our limited period of probation is over, we cannot justly ask for more time, nor will more time be given to us then. Procrastination is itself a fault, and Allah knows every hidden thought and motive in our minds.

INTRODUCTION TO SŪRAH 64—*AL TAGHĀBUN*

This is the eighth of the short Madīnah Sūrahs, each dealing with a special aspect of the life of the Community.

The special aspect spoken of here is the mutual gain and loss of Good and Evil, contrasted in this life and in the Hereafter.

It is an early Madīnah Sūrah, of the year 1 of the Hijrah or possibly even of the Makkan period just before the Hijrah. (See n. 5494 below).

Summary—Both the Unbelievers and the Believers were created by the One True God, Who created all and knows all: why should Unbelief and Evil exult in worldly gain when their loss will be as manifest in the Hereafter as will be the gains of the Believers? (64:1-18, and C. 243).

C. 243.—The self-same God created all men.
(64:1-18.) If some do good and others evil,
And ye wonder how the good do suffer
And the evil thrive, remember the Final
Goal, when true adjustments will
Be made. The Gainers here will be
The Losers there, and the Losers Gainers.
Some of this exchange you will see
Even here, in this life, for Unbelievers
Who deny the Hereafter; but in the Hereafter,
Full account and true adjustment
Of good and ill will follow before
The Judgement Seat: nay, Good will get
More than its full reward: for Allah
Is Bounteous, Merciful, Mighty, Wise.

Sūrah 64.

Al Taghābun (The Mutual Loss and Gain)

In the name of Allah, Most Gracious,
Most Merciful.

بِسْمِ ٱللَّهِ ٱلرَّحْمَٰنِ ٱلرَّحِيمِ

1. Whatever is
In the heavens and
On earth, doth declare[5479]
The Praises and Glory
Of Allah: to Him belongs
Dominion, and to Him belongs
Praise: and He has power
Over all things.

١ يُسَبِّحُ لِلَّهِ مَا فِي
ٱلسَّمَٰوَٰتِ وَمَا فِي ٱلْأَرْضِ
لَهُ ٱلْمُلْكُ وَلَهُ ٱلْحَمْدُ
وَهُوَ عَلَىٰ كُلِّ شَيْءٍ قَدِيرٌ

2. It is He Who has
Created you; and of you
Are some that are
Unbelievers, and some[5480]
That are Believers:
And Allah sees well
All that ye do.

٢ هُوَ ٱلَّذِي خَلَقَكُمْ
فَمِنكُمْ كَافِرٌ وَمِنكُم مُّؤْمِنٌ
وَٱللَّهُ بِمَا تَعْمَلُونَ بَصِيرٌ

3. He has created the heavens
And the earth
In just proportions,
And has given you shape,[5481]
And made your shapes
Beautiful: and to Him
Is the final Goal.[5482]

٣ خَلَقَ ٱلسَّمَٰوَٰتِ وَٱلْأَرْضَ
بِٱلْحَقِّ وَصَوَّرَكُمْ فَأَحْسَنَ صُوَرَكُمْ
وَإِلَيْهِ ٱلْمَصِيرُ

4. He knows what is
In the heavens
And on earth;

٤ يَعْلَمُ مَا فِي ٱلسَّمَٰوَٰتِ وَٱلْأَرْضِ

5479. *Cf.* 62:1, and n. 5449. All things by their very existence proclaim the Glory and the Praises of Allah. He has dominion over all things, but He uses His dominion for just and praiseworthy ends. He has power over all things: therefore He can combine justice with mercy, and His Plan and Purpose cannot be frustrated by the existence of Evil along with Good in His Kingdom.

5480. It is not that He does not see Rebellion and Evil, nor that He cannot punish them. He created all things pure and good, and if evil crept in by the grant of a limited free will by Him, it is not unforeseen; it is in His wise and universal Plan, for giving man a chance of rising higher and ever higher.

5481. *Cf.* 40:64, and n. 4440: also 7:11 and n. 996. In addition to the beauty and grandeur of all God's Creation, He has endowed man with special aptitudes, faculties and capacities, and special excellencies which raise him at his best to the position of Allah's vicegerent on earth. "Beautiful" also includes the idea of "adapted to the ends for which they were created".

5482. *The final Goal*: not only of mankind, but of all things created, whether material or in the realm of ideas and events. All things return to Allah: as they derive their origin from Him, so is the return or destination of all of them to Allah.

And He knows what[5483]
Ye conceal and what
Ye reveal: yea, Allah
Knows well the (secrets)
Of (all) hearts.

وَيَعْلَمُ مَا تُسِرُّونَ وَمَا تُعْلِنُونَ ۚ
وَاللَّهُ عَلِيمٌ بِذَاتِ الصُّدُورِ

5. Has not the story
Reached you, of those
Who rejected Faith aforetime?
So they tasted the evil
Result of their conduct;[5484]
And they had
A grievous Penalty.

٥ أَلَمْ يَأْتِكُمْ نَبَؤُا
الَّذِينَ كَفَرُوا مِن قَبْلُ
فَذَاقُوا وَبَالَ أَمْرِهِمْ وَلَهُمْ عَذَابٌ أَلِيمٌ

6. That was because there
Came to them messengers
With Clear Signs,
But they said:
"Shall (mere) human beings[5485]
Direct us?" So they rejected
(The Message) and turned away.
But Allah can do without (them):
And Allah is[5486]
Free of all needs,
Worthy of all praise.

٦ ذَٰلِكَ بِأَنَّهُ كَانَت
تَّأْتِيهِمْ رُسُلُهُم بِالْبَيِّنَاتِ
فَقَالُوا أَبَشَرٌ يَهْدُونَنَا
فَكَفَرُوا وَتَوَلَّوا ۚ
وَّاسْتَغْنَى اللَّهُ ۚ
وَاللَّهُ غَنِيٌّ حَمِيدٌ

7. The Unbelievers think
That they will not be
Raised up (for Judgement).[5487]
Say: "Yea, by my Lord,
Ye shall surely be

٧ زَعَمَ الَّذِينَ كَفَرُوا أَن لَّن يُبْعَثُوا ۚ
قُلْ بَلَىٰ وَرَبِّي

5483. Not only does He create and develop and sustain all things; but all thoughts, motives, feelings, ideas, and events are known to Him. Therefore we must not imagine that, if some evil seems to go unpunished, it is not known to Him or has escaped His notice. His Plan is wise and good in its fullest compass: sometimes we do not see its wisdom and goodness because we see only a broken fragment of it, as our own intelligence is narrow.

5484. "The evil result of their conduct" begins to manifest itself in this very life, either in external events, or in internal restlessness and agonies of conscience. But its culminating force will be seen in the "grievous Penalty" of the Hereafter.

5485. This is referred to in a more expanded form in 14:9-11.

5486. Their obedience is not necessary to Allah, nor will their rejection of Truth affect the validity of Truth or injure the progress of Truth. Allah is free of all needs or dependence on any circumstance whatever. He sends His Message for the good of mankind, and it is man who suffers by ignoring, rejecting, or opposing it.

5487. In other words, they think that there is no future life, and no responsibility for our actions beyond what we see in the present life. If that were true, all the profits of fraud and roguery, which remain unpunished in this world—and many do remain unpunished in this world—will remain with the wicked; and all the losses and pain suffered by integrity and righteousness, if they find no compensation in this life, will never find any compensation. This would be an odd result in a world of justice. We are taught that this is not true—that it is certain that the balance will be redressed in a better future world; that there will be a resurrection of what we call the dead; and that on that occasion the full import of all we did will be made plain to us, and our moral and spiritual responsibility will be fully enforced.

Raised up: then shall ye
Be told (the truth) of
All that ye did.
And that is easy for Allah."

لَتُبْعَثُنَّ ثُمَّ لَتُنَبَّؤُنَّ بِمَا عَمِلْتُمْ
وَذَٰلِكَ عَلَى ٱللَّهِ يَسِيرٌ

8. Believe, therefore, in Allah
And His Messenger, and
In the Light which We[5488]
Have sent down. And Allah
Is well-acquainted
With all that ye do.

٨ فَـَٔامِنُوا۟ بِٱللَّهِ وَرَسُولِهِۦ
وَٱلنُّورِ ٱلَّذِىٓ أَنزَلْنَا
وَٱللَّهُ بِمَا تَعْمَلُونَ خَبِيرٌ

9. The Day that He assembles
You (all) for a Day
Of Assembly—that will be
A day of mutual loss[5489]
And gain (among you).
And those who believe
In Allah and work righeousness—
He will remove from them[5490]
Their ill, and He will admit
Them to gardens beneath which[5491]
Rivers flow, to dwell therein
Forever: that will be
The Supreme Achievement.

٩ يَوْمَ يَجْمَعُكُمْ لِيَوْمِ ٱلْجَمْعِ
ذَٰلِكَ يَوْمُ ٱلتَّغَابُنِ
وَمَن يُؤْمِنۢ بِٱللَّهِ وَيَعْمَلْ
صَٰلِحًا يُكَفِّرْ عَنْهُ سَيِّـَٔاتِهِۦ
وَيُدْخِلْهُ جَنَّٰتٍ تَجْرِى مِن تَحْتِهَا
ٱلْأَنْهَٰرُ خَٰلِدِينَ فِيهَآ أَبَدًا
ذَٰلِكَ ٱلْفَوْزُ ٱلْعَظِيمُ

10. But those who reject Faith
And treat Our Signs
As falsehoods, they will be
Companions of the Fire,
To dwell therein for aye:
And evil is that Goal.

١٠ وَٱلَّذِينَ كَفَرُوا۟ وَكَذَّبُوا۟
بِـَٔايَٰتِنَآ أُو۟لَٰٓئِكَ أَصْحَٰبُ
ٱلنَّارِ خَٰلِدِينَ فِيهَا ۖ وَبِئْسَ ٱلْمَصِيرُ

5488. *The Light which We have sent down*: *i.e.*, the light of Revelation, the light of conscience, the light of reason, and every kind of true light by which we may know Allah and His Will. If we play false with any such lights, it is fully known to Allah.

5489. The Day of Judgement will truly be "a Day of Mutual Loss and Gain", as the title of this Sūrah indicates. Men who thought they were laying up riches will find themselves paupers in the Kingdom of Heaven. Men who thought they were acquiring good by wrongdoing will find their efforts were wasted; 28:104. On the other hand the meek and lowly of this life will acquire greater dignity and honour in the next; the despised ones doing good here will be the accepted ones there; the persecuted righteous will be in eternal happiness. The two classes will as it were change their relative positions.

5490. *Remove from them their ills.* The ills may be sins, faults, mistakes, or evil tendencies; Allah will of His grace cover them up, and blot out the account against them; or they may be sorrows, sufferings, or disappointements: Allah may even change the evil of such persons into good, their apparent calamities into opportunities for spiritual advancement; 25:70. This is because of their sincere Faith as evidenced by their repentance and amendment.

5491. "Gardens" the symbol of the highest Bliss, see 2:25, n. 44; 13:35; 47:15. (R).

SECTION 2.

11. No kind of calamity Can occur, except By the leave of Allah: And if anyone believes[5492] In Allah, (Allah) guides his Heart (aright): for Allah Knows all things.	مَآ أَصَابَ مِن مُّصِيبَةٍ إِلَّا بِإِذْنِ ٱللَّهِ وَمَن يُؤْمِنۢ بِٱللَّهِ يَهْدِ قَلْبَهُۥ وَٱللَّهُ بِكُلِّ شَىْءٍ عَلِيمٌ ﴿١١﴾
12. So obey Allah, and obey His Messenger: but if Ye turn back, the duty Of Our Messenger is but To proclaim (the Message)[5493] Clearly and openly.	وَأَطِيعُوا۟ ٱللَّهَ وَأَطِيعُوا۟ ٱلرَّسُولَ فَإِن تَوَلَّيْتُمْ فَإِنَّمَا عَلَىٰ رَسُولِنَا ٱلْبَلَٰغُ ٱلْمُبِينُ ﴿١٢﴾
13. Allah! There is no god But He: and on Allah, Therefore, let the Believers Put their trust.	ٱللَّهُ لَآ إِلَٰهَ إِلَّا هُوَ وَعَلَى ٱللَّهِ فَلْيَتَوَكَّلِ ٱلْمُؤْمِنُونَ ﴿١٣﴾
14. O ye who believe! Truly, among your wives And your children are (some That are) enemies to[5494] Yourselves: so beware Of them! But if ye Forgive and overlook,[5495] And cover up (their faults), Verily Allah is Oft-Forgiving, Most Merciful.	يَٰٓأَيُّهَا ٱلَّذِينَ ءَامَنُوٓا۟ إِنَّ مِنْ أَزْوَٰجِكُمْ وَأَوْلَٰدِكُمْ عَدُوًّا لَّكُمْ فَٱحْذَرُوهُمْ وَإِن تَعْفُوا۟ وَتَصْفَحُوا۟ وَتَغْفِرُوا۟ فَإِنَّ ٱللَّهَ غَفُورٌ رَّحِيمٌ ﴿١٤﴾

5492. What we consider calamities may be blessings in disguise. Pain in the body is often a signal of something wrong, which we can cure by remedial measures. So in the moral and spiritual world, we should in all circumstances hold firmly to the faith that nothing happens without Allah's knowledge and leave; and therefore there must be some justice and wisdom according to His great universal Plan. Our duty is to find out our own shortcomings and remedy them. If we try to do so in all sincerity of heart, Allah will give us guidance.

5493. The Messenger comes to guide and teach, not to force and compel. The Messenger's teaching is clear and unambiguous, and it is open and free to all. *Cf.* also 5:95.

5494. In some cases the demand of families, *i.e.*, wife and children may conflict with a man's moral and spiritual convictions and duties. In such cases he must guard against the abandonment of his convictions, duties, and ideals to their requests or desires. But he must not treat them harshly. He must make reasonable provision for them, and if they persist in opposing his clear duties and convictions, he must forgive them and not expose them to shame or ridicule, while at the same time holding on to his clear duty. Such cases occurred when godly men undertook exile from their native city of Makkah to follow the Faith in Madīnah. In some cases their families murmured, but all came right in the end.

5495. For the different words for "forgiveness" see n. 110 to 2:109.

15. Your riches and your children
May be but a trial:[5496]
But in the Presence of Allah
Is the highest Reward.

(١٥) إِنَّمَآ أَمْوَٰلُكُمْ وَأَوْلَٰدُكُمْ فِتْنَةٌ ۚ
وَٱللَّهُ عِندَهُۥٓ أَجْرٌ عَظِيمٌ

16. So fear Allah[5497]
As much as ye can;
Listen and obey;
And spend in charity
For the benefit of
Your own souls.[5498]
And those saved from
The covetousness of their own
Souls—they are the ones
That achieve prosperity.[5499]

(١٦) فَٱتَّقُوا۟ ٱللَّهَ مَا ٱسْتَطَعْتُمْ
وَٱسْمَعُوا۟ وَأَطِيعُوا۟ وَأَنفِقُوا۟
خَيْرًا لِّأَنفُسِكُمْ ۗ
وَمَن يُوقَ شُحَّ نَفْسِهِۦ
فَأُو۟لَٰٓئِكَ هُمُ ٱلْمُفْلِحُونَ

17. If ye loan to Allah[5500]
A beautiful loan, He
Will double it to
Your (credit), and He
Will grant you Forgiveness:
For Allah is most Ready
To appreciate (service),[5501]
Most Forbearing—

(١٧) إِن تُقْرِضُوا۟
ٱللَّهَ قَرْضًا حَسَنًا
يُضَٰعِفْهُ لَكُمْ وَيَغْفِرْ لَكُمْ ۚ
وَٱللَّهُ شَكُورٌ حَلِيمٌ

18. Knower of what is hidden
And what is open,

(١٨) عَٰلِمُ ٱلْغَيْبِ وَٱلشَّهَٰدَةِ

5496. Children may be a *trial* in many senses: (1) their different ways of looking at things may cause you to reflect, and to turn to the highest things of eternal importance; (2) their relationship with you and with each other may confront you with problems far more complicated than those in separate individual lives, and thus become a test of your own strength of character and sense of responsibility; (3) their conflict with your ideals (see n. 5494 above) may vex your spirit, but may at the same time search out your fidelity to Allah; and (4) their affection for you and your affection for them, may be a source of strength for you if it is pure, just as it may be a danger if it is based on selfish or unworthy motives. So also riches and worldly goods have their advantages as well as dangers.

5497. *Fear Allah* combined with *as much as you can* obviously means: "lead lives of self-restraint and righteousness": the usual meaning of *Taqwā:* see n. 26 to 2:2.

5498. Charity is meant to help and do good to other people who need it. But it has the highest subjective value for the person who gives it. Like mercy "it blesseth him that gives and him that takes". It purifies the giver's soul: the affection that he pours out is for his own spiritual benefit and progress. *Cf.* Coleridge: "He prayeth best who loveth all things both great and small, for the Great God Who loveth us, Who made and loveth all".

5499. *Cf.* 59:9. Our worst enemy is within ourselves—the grasping selfishness which would deprive others of their just rights or seize things which do not properly belong to it. If we can get over this covetous selfishness, we achieve real Prosperity in justice and truth.

5500. *Cf.* 2:245 and n. 276. Our Charity or Love is called a loan to Allah, which not only increases our credit account manifold, but obtains for us the forgiveness of our sins, and the capacity for increased service in the future.

5501. *Cf.* 14:5, n. 1877; and 35:30, n. 3917. Allah's appreciation of our service or our love goes far deeper than its intrinsic merits or its specific expression on our side. His reward is beyond our deserts, and passes over our defects. He judges by our motives, which He can read through and through; see next verse.

Exalted in Might,
Full of Wisdom.[5502]

ٱلْعَزِيزُ ٱلْحَكِيمُ

5502. Allah's Appreciation and Forbearing Kindness can reach so far beyond our merits, because (1) His universal knowledge comprehends hidden motives, which others cannot see in us; (2) His power is so great that He can afford to reward even the unworthy; and (3) His Wisdom is so great that He can turn even our weakness into our strength.

INTRODUCTION TO SŪRAH 65—*AL ṬALĀQ*

This is the ninth of the ten short Madīnah Sūrahs dealing with the social life of the Community. The aspect dealt with here is Divorce, and the necessity of precautions to guard against its abuse. The relations of the sexes are an important factor in the social life of the Community, and this and the following Sūrah deal with certain aspects of it. "Of all things permitted by Law", said the Prophet, "divorce is the most hateful in the sight of Allah". (Abū Dāwūd, *Sunan*, xiii. 3). While the sanctity of marriage is the essential basis of family life, the incompatibility of individuals and the weaknesses of human nature require certain outlets and safeguards if that sanctity is not to be made into a fetish at the expense of human life. That is why the question of Divorce is in this Sūrah linked with the question of insolent impiety and its punishment.

The date is somewhere about A.H. 6, but the chronology has no significance.

Summary—Provision to be made for women in case of Divorce; insolent impiety always leads to punishment (65:1-12, and C. 244).

C. 244.—Guard well your truth and pure integrity
(65:1-12.) In sex relations. Keep the tie
Of marriage sacred; but where it must
Be dissolved, use all precautions to ensure
Justice to the weaker party and protect
The interests of unborn or newborn lives
As well as social decency; and close not
To the last the door of reconciliation.
Allah's Laws must be obeyed; 'tis man's
Own loss if he is deaf to the Voice
Which teaches him, or blind to the Light
Which guides him. Allah's universe
Of beauty and wonder stands strong in wisdom:
Let man but tune himself thereto.

Sūrah 65.

Al Ṭalāq **(Divorce)**

In the name of Allah, Most Gracious,
Most Merciful.

بِسْمِ ٱللَّهِ ٱلرَّحْمَٰنِ ٱلرَّحِيمِ

1. O Prophet![5503] When ye
Do divorce women,[5504]
Divorce them at their
Prescribed periods,[5505]
And count (accurately)
Their prescribed periods:
And fear Allah your Lord:[5506]
And turn them not out
Of their houses, nor shall
They (themselves) leave,[5507]
Except in case they are
Guilty of some open lewdness,
Those are limits
Set by Allah: and any
Who transgresses the limits
Of Allah, does verily
Wrong his (own) soul:
Thou knowest not if
Perchance Allah will

١ يَٰٓأَيُّهَا ٱلنَّبِيُّ إِذَا طَلَّقْتُمُ ٱلنِّسَآءَ
فَطَلِّقُوهُنَّ لِعِدَّتِهِنَّ وَأَحْصُوا۟ ٱلْعِدَّةَ
وَٱتَّقُوا۟ ٱللَّهَ رَبَّكُمْ
لَا تُخْرِجُوهُنَّ مِنۢ بُيُوتِهِنَّ
وَلَا يَخْرُجْنَ إِلَّآ أَن
يَأْتِينَ بِفَٰحِشَةٍ مُّبَيِّنَةٍ
وَتِلْكَ حُدُودُ ٱللَّهِ
وَمَن يَتَعَدَّ حُدُودَ ٱللَّهِ
فَقَدْ ظَلَمَ نَفْسَهُۥ
لَا تَدْرِى لَعَلَّ ٱللَّهَ

5503. Note that in the first instance the Prophet is himself addressed individually, as the Teacher and representative of the Community. Then the actual directions: "when ye...": are addressed to the Community collectively.

5504. "Of all things permitted by law, Divorce is the most hateful in the sight of Allah": see Introduction to this Sūrah. The general directions and limitations of Divorce may be studied in 2:228-232, 236-237, 241, and notes; also 4:35.

5505. *'Iddah*, as a technical term in divorce law, is explained in n. 254 to 2:228. Its general meaning is "a prescribed period": in that general sense it is used in 2:185 for a prescribed period of fasting.

5506. The prescribed period (see last note) is in the interests of the wife, of the husband, of an unborn child (if there is any), and of sex laws in nature, and therefore the elementary dictates of refined human society. In English Law the six months interval between the decree *nisi* and the decree absolute in divorce attains the same purpose in a round-about way. The Commentators suggest that the divorce should not be pronounced during the courses. Read with 2:222, this implies that any incipient differences between husband and wife should not be forced to an issue at a time when sex is least attractive and almost repulsive. Everything should be done to strengthen the social and spiritual aspects of marriage and keep down stray impulses of animal instinct. The parties are to think seriously in a mood of piety, keeping the fear of Allah in their minds.

5507. As Islam treats the married woman as a full juristic personality in every sense of the term, a married woman has a right, in the married state, to a house or apartment of her own. And a house or apartment implies the reasonable expenses for its upkeep and for her own and her children's maintenance. And this is obligatory not only in the married state, but during the *'iddah*, which is necessarily a most trying period for the woman. During this period she must not only not be turned out, but it is not decent for her to leave of her own accord, lest the chances of reconciliation should be diminished: see the next note.

Bring about thereafter
Some new situation.[5508]

يُحْدِثُ بَعْدَ ذَٰلِكَ أَمْرًا

2. Thus when they fulfil
Their term appointed,
Either take them back
On equitable terms[5509]
Or part with them
On equitable terms;
And take for witness
Two persons from among you,
Endued with justice,
And establish the evidence[5510]
(As) before Allah. Such
Is the admonition given
To him who believes
In Allah and the Last Day.
And for those who fear
Allah, He (ever) prepares[5511]
A way out,

٢ فَإِذَا بَلَغْنَ أَجَلَهُنَّ
فَأَمْسِكُوهُنَّ بِمَعْرُوفٍ
أَوْ فَارِقُوهُنَّ بِمَعْرُوفٍ
وَأَشْهِدُوا ذَوَىْ عَدْلٍ مِّنكُمْ
وَأَقِيمُوا الشَّهَادَةَ لِلَّهِ
ذَٰلِكُمْ يُوعَظُ بِهِ مَن كَانَ
يُؤْمِنُ بِاللَّهِ وَالْيَوْمِ الْآخِرِ
وَمَن يَتَّقِ اللَّهَ يَجْعَل لَّهُ مَخْرَجًا

3. And He provides for him
From (sources) he never
Could imagine. And if
Anyone puts his trust
In Allah, sufficient is (Allah)
For him. For Allah will
Surely accomplish His purpose:[5512]

٣ وَيَرْزُقْهُ مِنْ حَيْثُ لَا يَحْتَسِبُ
وَمَن يَتَوَكَّلْ عَلَى اللَّهِ فَهُوَ حَسْبُهُ
إِنَّ اللَّهَ بَالِغُ أَمْرِهِ

5508. A reconciliation is possible, and is indeed recommended at every stage. The first serious differences between the parties are to be submitted to a family council on which both sides are represented (4:35); divorce is not to be pronounced when mutual physical attraction is at an ebb (n. 5506); when it is pronounced, there should be a period of probationary waiting; dower has to be paid and due provision has to be made for many things on equitable terms; every facility has to be given for reconciliation till the last moment, and impediments are provided against hasty impulse leading to rupture. *Thou knowest not if perchance Allah will bring about thereafter some new situation.*

5509. *Cf.* 2:231. Everything should be done fairly and squarely, and all interests should be safeguarded.

5510. Publicity and the establishment of proper evidence ensure that no one will act unjustly or selfishly. All should remember that these are matters of serious import, affecting our most intimate lives, and therefore our position in the spiritual kingdom.

5511. In these very delicate and difficult matters, the wisdom of jurists provides a less satisfactory solution than a sincere desire to be just and true, which is described as the "fear of Allah". Where such a desire exists, Allah often provides a solution in the most unexpected ways or from the most unexpected quarters; *e.g.*, the worst enemies may be reconciled, or the cry or the smile of an infant baby may heal seemingly irreparable injuries or unite hearts seemingly alienated forever. And Faith is followed at once by a psychological feeling of rest for the troubled spirit.

5512. Our anger and our impatience have to be curbed. Our friends and our mates or associates may seem to us ever so weak and unreasonable, and the circumstances may be ever so disheartening; yet we must trust in Allah. How can we measure our own weakness or perhaps blindness? He knows all. His universal Purpose is always good. His Will must be accomplished, and we should wish for its accomplishment. His ordering of the universe observes a due, just, and perfect proportion.

Verily, for all things
Has Allah appointed
A due proportion.

قَدْ جَعَلَ ٱللَّهُ لِكُلِّ شَىْءٍ قَدْرًا

4. Such of your women
As have passed the age
Of monthly courses, for them
The prescribed period, if ye
Have any doubts, is
Three months, and for those
Who have no courses
(It is the same):[5513]
For those who carry
(Life within their wombs),
Their period is until
They deliver their burdens:
And for those who
Fear Allah, He will
Make their path easy.[5514]

٤ وَٱلَّـٰٓـِٔى يَئِسْنَ مِنَ ٱلْمَحِيضِ
مِن نِّسَآئِكُمْ إِنِ ٱرْتَبْتُمْ فَعِدَّتُهُنَّ
ثَلَـٰثَةُ أَشْهُرٍ وَٱلَّـٰٓـِٔى لَمْ يَحِضْنَ
وَأُو۟لَـٰتُ ٱلْأَحْمَالِ أَجَلُهُنَّ
أَن يَضَعْنَ حَمْلَهُنَّ
وَمَن يَتَّقِ ٱللَّهَ يَجْعَل لَّهُۥ
مِنْ أَمْرِهِۦ يُسْرًا

5. That is the Command
Of Allah, which He
Has sent down to you:
And if anyone fears Allah,
He will remove his ills[5515]
From him, and will enlarge
His reward.

٥ ذَٰلِكَ أَمْرُ ٱللَّهِ أَنزَلَهُۥٓ إِلَيْكُمْ
وَمَن يَتَّقِ ٱللَّهَ يُكَفِّرْ عَنْهُ سَيِّـَٔاتِهِۦ
وَيُعْظِمْ لَهُۥٓ أَجْرًا

6. Let the women live
(In *'iddah)* in the same
Style as ye live,
According to your means:
Annoy them not, so as
To restrict them.[5516]
And if they carry (life

٦ أَسْكِنُوهُنَّ مِنْ حَيْثُ سَكَنتُم مِّن وُجْدِكُمْ
وَلَا تُضَآرُّوهُنَّ لِتُضَيِّقُوا۟ عَلَيْهِنَّ
وَإِن كُنَّ أُو۟لَـٰتِ حَمْلٍ

5513. *Cf.* 2:228. For normal women, the *'iddah* is the three monthly courses after separation: if there are no courses or if the courses are in doubt, it is three calendar months. By that time it will be clear whether there is pregnancy: if there is, the waiting period is still after delivery.

5514. *Cf.* n. 5511 above. If there is a true and sincere desire to obey the Will of Allah and do right the difficulties will vanish, and these delicate matters will be settled for the greatest happiness of all.

5515. Allah's ordinance is nothing arbitrary. It is to help us, and to lead us on to our highest good, temporal and spiritual. If we obey Allah, His wisdom will not only solve our difficulties, but it will remove other ills that we may have, subjective and objective. Like a good shepherd, he will lead us on to more and more luscious pastures. With each step higher, our position becomes more and more sure and our reward more and more precious.

5516. *Cf.* n. 5507 above. A selfish man, because he has divorced his wife, may, in the probationary period before the divorce becomes absolute, treat her with contumely, and while giving her residence and maintenance, may so restrict it as to make her life miserable. This is forbidden. She must be provided on the same scale as he is, according to his status in life. There is still hope of reconciliation, and if not, yet the parting must be honourable.

In their wombs), then[5517]
Spend (your substance) on them
Until they deliver
Their burden: and if
They suckle your (offspring),
Give them their recompense:
And take mutual counsel
Together, according to
What is just and reasonable.
And if ye find yourselves[5518]
In difficulties, let another
Woman suckle (the child)
On the (father's) behalf.[5519]

7. Let the man of means
Spend according to
His means: and the man
Whose resources are restricted,
Let him spend according
To what Allah has given him.
Allah puts no burden
On any person beyond
What He has given him.
After a difficulty, Allah
Will soon grant relief.[5520]

SECTION 2.

8. How many populations
That insolently opposed[5521]
The command of their Lord

فَأَنفِقُواْ عَلَيْهِنَّ
حَتَّىٰ يَضَعْنَ حَمْلَهُنَّۚ
فَإِنْ أَرْضَعْنَ لَكُمْ فَـَٔاتُوهُنَّ أُجُورَهُنَّۖ
وَأْتَمِرُواْ بَيْنَكُم بِمَعْرُوفٍۖ
وَإِن تَعَاسَرْتُمْ فَسَتُرْضِعُ
لَهُۥٓ أُخْرَىٰ

٧ لِيُنفِقْ ذُو سَعَةٍ مِّن سَعَتِهِۦۖ
وَمَن قُدِرَ عَلَيْهِ رِزْقُهُۥ
فَلْيُنفِقْ مِمَّآ ءَاتَىٰهُ ٱللَّهُۚ
لَا يُكَلِّفُ ٱللَّهُ نَفْسًا إِلَّا مَآ ءَاتَىٰهَاۚ
سَيَجْعَلُ ٱللَّهُ بَعْدَ عُسْرٍ يُسْرًا

٨ وَكَأَيِّن مِّن قَرْيَةٍ
عَتَتْ عَنْ أَمْرِ رَبِّهَا

5517. If there is a pregnancy, a sacred third life comes on the scene, for which there is added responsibility (perhaps added hope for reconciliation) for both parents. In any case no separation is possible until after the child is born. Even after birth, if no reconciliation between parents is possible, yet for the nursing of the child and for its welfare the care of the mother remains the duty of the father, and there must be mutual counsel between him and the mother in all truth and sincerity.

5518. *If ye find yourselves in difficulties*: *e.g.*, if the mother's milk fails, or if her health fails, or if any circumstance arises which bars the natural course of the mother nursing her own child. There may be psychological difficulties also.

5519. That is, the father must stand all expenses, without cutting down the reasonable allowance to which the mother is entitled.

5520. We must trust in Allah, and do whatever is possible for us in the interests of the young life for which we are responsible. We must not be frightened by difficulties. Allah will give us relief and provide a solution if we act with honest integrity. *Cf.* 96:5-6.

5521. Insolent impiety consists not only in the breach of the rites of religion. Even more vital is the defiance of the laws of nature which Allah has made for us. These laws, for us human beings include those which relate to our fellow-beings in society to whom kindness and consideration form the basis of our social duties. Our duties to our families and our children in intimate matters such as were spoken of in the last Section, are as important as any in our spiritual life. Peoples who forgot the moral law in marriage or family life perished in this world and will have no future in the Hereafter. The lessons apply not only to individuals but to whole nations or social groups.

And of His messengers,
Did We not then
Call to account—
To severe account?—
And We imposed on them
An exemplary Punishment.[5522]

وَرُسُلِهِۦ
فَحَاسَبْنَٰهَا حِسَابًا شَدِيدًا
وَعَذَّبْنَٰهَا عَذَابًا نُّكْرًا

9. Then did they taste
The evil result of
Their conduct, and the End
Of their conduct
Was Perdition.

٩ فَذَاقَتْ وَبَالَ أَمْرِهَا
وَكَانَ عَٰقِبَةُ أَمْرِهَا خُسْرًا

10. Allah has prepared for them
A severe Punishment[5523]
(In the Hereafter).
Therefore fear Allah,
O ye men of understanding—
Who have believed!—
For Allah hath indeed
Sent down to you
A Message—[5524]

١٠ أَعَدَّ ٱللَّهُ لَهُمْ عَذَابًا شَدِيدًا
فَٱتَّقُوا۟ ٱللَّهَ يَٰٓأُو۟لِى
ٱلْأَلْبَٰبِ ٱلَّذِينَ ءَامَنُوا۟
قَدْ أَنزَلَ ٱللَّهُ إِلَيْكُمْ ذِكْرًا

11. A Messenger, who rehearses
To you the Signs of Allah
Containing clear explanations,
That he may lead forth
Those who believe
And do righteous deeds
From the depths of Darkness[5525]
Into Light. And those who
Believe in Allah and work
Righteousness, He will admit
To Gardens beneath which rivers
Flow, to dwell therein
Forever: Allah has indeed
Granted for them
A most excellent provision.

١١ رَّسُولًا يَتْلُوا۟ عَلَيْكُمْ ءَايَٰتِ ٱللَّهِ
مُبَيِّنَٰتٍ لِّيُخْرِجَ ٱلَّذِينَ ءَامَنُوا۟ وَعَمِلُوا۟
ٱلصَّٰلِحَٰتِ مِنَ ٱلظُّلُمَٰتِ إِلَى ٱلنُّورِ
وَمَن يُؤْمِنۢ بِٱللَّهِ وَيَعْمَلْ صَٰلِحًا
يُدْخِلْهُ جَنَّٰتٍ تَجْرِى مِن تَحْتِهَا
ٱلْأَنْهَٰرُ خَٰلِدِينَ فِيهَآ أَبَدًا
قَدْ أَحْسَنَ ٱللَّهُ لَهُۥ رِزْقًا

5522. This refers to the present life: apparently the Hereafter is implied in verse 10 below.

5523. See last note.

5524. There is no excuse for us to go astray, seeing that Allah in His infinite Mercy has explained to us His Message by His many Signs around us and clearly by means of the human Teachers and Messengers whom He has sent for our instruction: see next verse.

5525. *Cf.* 24:40: the unbelievers' state is "like the depths of darkness in a vast deep ocean, overwhelmed with billow topped by billow, topped by dark clouds; depths of darkness, one above another." *Cf.* 2:257: "Allah is the Protector of those who have Faith: from the depths of darkness He will lead them forth into light."

12. Allah is He Who
Created seven Firmaments[5526]
And of the earth
A similar number.[5527]
Through the midst
Of them (all) descends[5528]
His Command: that ye may
Know that Allah has power
Over all things, and that
Allah comprehends all things
In (His) Knowledge.

ٱللَّهُ ٱلَّذِى خَلَقَ ﴿١٢﴾
سَبْعَ سَمَٰوَٰتٍ وَمِنَ ٱلْأَرْضِ مِثْلَهُنَّ
يَتَنَزَّلُ ٱلْأَمْرُ بَيْنَهُنَّ لِتَعْلَمُوٓا۟ أَنَّ
ٱللَّهَ عَلَىٰ كُلِّ شَىْءٍ قَدِيرٌ وَأَنَّ ٱللَّهَ
قَدْ أَحَاطَ بِكُلِّ شَىْءٍ عِلْمًۢا

5526. "Seven Firmaments." (*Cf.* 2:29; 17:44; 23:86; and 51:12.) [Eds.].

5527. As there are grades one above the other in the spiritual kingdom, there are similar grades in our life on this earth. If we take the literal meaning—just as we see the heavenly spheres one above another, over our heads, so we can see that the crust of the earth is built up of geological strata one above another. (R).

5528. But in all spheres of life and Creation, whatever conception we are able to form of them, it is certain that the Command or Law of Allah runs through them all, for His knowledge and power extend through all things.

INTRODUCTION TO SŪRAH 66—*AL TAHRĪM*

This is the tenth and last of the series of short Madīnah Sūrahs which began with S. 57: see Introduction to that Sūrah. The point dealt with here is: how far the turning away from sex or the opposition of one sex against another or a want of harmony between the sexes may injure the higher interests of society.

The date may be taken to be somewhere about A.H. 7.

Summary—The failings of the weaker sex should not turn away men from normal social life: harmony and mutual confidence should be taught and enforced, and Allah's blessing will descend on the virtuous even if their lot is cast with the wicked (66:1-12, and C. 245).

C. 245.—The relations between the sexes are embittered
(66:1-12.) By misunderstandings and conflicts that produce
Unhappiness and misery, personal and social.
Harmony and confidence are due between
The sexes, not disgust or isolation, which may
Please some but cause injustice to others.
Respect each other's confidence, and if
You fail, repent and make amends.
The good man seeks virtue for himself
And his family. If Evil is yoked to Good,
It must take the fruit of its own deeds;
The worldly tie will profit naught;
But Good should firmly make a stand
And will be saved, for Allah doth care
For all His true devoted Servants.

Sūrah 66.

الجزء الثامن والعشرون سورة التحريم

Al Taḥrīm (Prohibition)

In the name of Allah, Most Gracious,
Most Merciful.

بِسْمِ ٱللَّهِ ٱلرَّحْمَـٰنِ ٱلرَّحِيمِ

1. O Prophet! Why
Holdest thou to be forbidden
That which Allah has[5529]
Made lawful to thee?
Thou seekest to please[5530]
Thy consorts. But Allah
Is Oft-Forgiving, Most Merciful.

١ يَـٰٓأَيُّهَا ٱلنَّبِيُّ
لِمَ تُحَرِّمُ مَآ أَحَلَّ ٱللَّهُ لَكَ
تَبْتَغِى مَرْضَاتَ أَزْوَٰجِكَ
وَٱللَّهُ غَفُورٌ رَّحِيمٌ

2. Allah has already ordained[5531]
For you, (O men),
The dissolution of your oaths
(In some cases): and Allah
Is your Protector, and He
Is Full of Knowledge
And Wisdom.

٢ قَدْ فَرَضَ ٱللَّهُ
لَكُمْ تَحِلَّةَ أَيْمَـٰنِكُمْ
وَٱللَّهُ مَوْلَىٰكُمْ
وَهُوَ ٱلْعَلِيمُ ٱلْحَكِيمُ

5529. The Prophet's household was not like other households. The Consorts of Purity were expected to hold a higher standard in behaviour and reticence than ordinary women, as they had higher work to perform. See n. 3706 to 33:28. But they were human beings after all, and were subject to the weaknesses of their sex, and they sometimes failed. The imprudence of 'Ā'ishah (see n. 2962 to 24:11) once caused serious difficulties: the Holy Prophet's mind was sore distressed, and he renounced the society of his wives for some time. This renunciation seems to be referred to here. The situation was none the less difficult for him because she was a daughter of Abū Bakr, one of the truest and most in. imate of his Companions and lieutenants. The commentators usually cite the following incident in connection with the revelation of these verses. It is narrated from 'Ā'ishah, the wife of the Holy Prophet (peace be on him) by Bukhārī, Muslim, Nasa'i, Abu Dawūd and others that the Holy Prophet usually visited his wives daily after *'Aṣr* Prayer. Once it so happened that he stayed longer than usual at the quarters of Zaynab bint Jaḥsh, for she had received from somewhere some honey which the Holy Prophet liked very much. "At this", says 'Ā'ishah, "I felt jealous, and I, Ḥafṣah, Sawda and Ṣafiyah agreed among ourselves that when he visits us each of us would tell him that a peculiar odour came from his mouth as a result of what he had eaten, for we knew that he was particularly sensitive to offensive smells". So when his wives hinted at it, he vowed that he would never again use honey. Thereupon these verses were revealed reminding him that he should not declare to himself unlawful that which Allah had made lawful to him. The important point to bear in mind is that he was at once rectified by revelation, which reinforces the fact that the prophets are always under divine protection, and even the slightest lapse on their part is never left uncorrected. (R).

5530. The tender words of admonition addressed to the Consorts in 33:28-34 explain the situation far better than any comments can express. If the Holy Prophet had been a mere husband in the ordinary sense of the term, he could not have held the balance even between his private feelings and his public duties. But he was not an ordinary husband, and he abandoned his renunciation on his realisation of the higher duties with which he was charged, and which required conciliation with firmness.

5531. *Cf.* 2:224. If your vows prevent you from doing good, or acting rightly, or making peace between persons, you should expiate the vow, but not refrain from your good deed.

3. When the Prophet disclosed
A matter of confidence[5532]
To one of his consorts,
And she then divulged it
(To another), and Allah made it
Known to him, he confirmed[5533]
Part thereof and repudiated
A part. Then when he
Told her thereof, she said,
"Who told thee this?"
He said, "He told me
Who knows and is well-acquainted
(With all things)"

٣ وَإِذْ أَسَرَّ ٱلنَّبِيُّ
إِلَىٰ بَعْضِ أَزْوَٰجِهِۦ حَدِيثًا
فَلَمَّا نَبَّأَتْ بِهِۦ وَأَظْهَرَهُ ٱللَّهُ عَلَيْهِ
عَرَّفَ بَعْضَهُۥ وَأَعْرَضَ عَنۢ بَعْضٍ
فَلَمَّا نَبَّأَهَا بِهِۦ قَالَتْ مَنْ أَنۢبَأَكَ هَٰذَا
قَالَ نَبَّأَنِىَ ٱلْعَلِيمُ ٱلْخَبِيرُ

4. If ye two turn in repentance[5534]
To Him, your hearts
Are indeed so inclined;
But if ye back up
Each other against him,
Truly Allah is his Protector,
And Gabriel, and (every)
Righteous one among those
Who believe—and
furthermore,[5535]
The angels—will back (him) up.

٤ إِن تَتُوبَآ إِلَى ٱللَّهِ
فَقَدْ صَغَتْ قُلُوبُكُمَا
وَإِن تَظَٰهَرَا عَلَيْهِ
فَإِنَّ ٱللَّهَ هُوَ مَوْلَىٰهُ
وَجِبْرِيلُ وَصَٰلِحُ ٱلْمُؤْمِنِينَ
وَٱلْمَلَٰٓئِكَةُ بَعْدَ ذَٰلِكَ ظَهِيرٌ

5532. Who these two consorts were, and what was the matter in confidence which was disclosed, we are not expressly told, but the facts mentioned in n. 5529 above will help us to understand this passage. The sacred words imply that the matter was of great importance to the principle involved, but that the details were not of sufficient importance for permanent record. For the lessons to be drawn, see the notes following.

5533. The moral we have to draw is manifold. (1) If anything is told to us in confidence, especially by one at the head of affairs, we must not divulge it to our closest friend. (2) If such divulgence is made in the most secret whispers, Allah's Plan is such that it will come to light and expose those guilty of breach of confidence. (3) When the whispered version is compared with the true version and the actual facts, it will be found that the whispered version is in great part untrue, due to the misunderstanding and exaggeration inevitable in the circumstances. (4) The breach of confidence must inevitably redound to the shame of the guilty party, whose surprise only covers a sense of humiliation. See next note.

5534. There are further lessons. (5) Both the party betraying confidence and that encouraging the betrayal must purge their conduct by repentance. (6) Frank repentance would be what their hearts and conscience themselves would dictate and they must not resist such amends on account of selfish obstinacy. (7) If they were to resist frank repentance and amends, they are only abetting each other's wrong, and they cannot prevail against all the spiritual forces which will be ranged on the side of the right.

5535. Do not forget the dual meaning: immediate, in application to the Holy Prophet, and general, being the lesson which we ought all to learn. The Holy Prophet could not be injured by any persons doing anything against him even though they might unconsciously put him in greater jeopardy: for Allah, the Angel Gabriel, (who was the Messenger to him), and the whole Community, would protect him,—to say nothing of the army of angels or hidden spiritual forces that always guarded him. *Cf.* 33:56. The general lesson for us is that the good man's protection is that of the spiritual forces around him; it is divine protection, against which human weakness or folly will have no power.

5. It may be, if he
Divorced you (all),[5536]
That Allah will give him
In exchange Consorts
Better than you—
Who submit (their wills),
Who believe, who are devout,
Who turn to Allah in repentance,
Who worship (in humility),
Who travel (for Faith) and
fast—[5537]
Previously married or virgins.

٥ عَسَىٰ رَبُّهُۥٓ إِن طَلَّقَكُنَّ
أَن يُبْدِلَهُۥٓ أَزْوَٰجًا خَيْرًا مِّنكُنَّ
مُسْلِمَٰتٍ مُّؤْمِنَٰتٍ
قَٰنِتَٰتٍ تَٰٓئِبَٰتٍ
عَٰبِدَٰتٍ سَٰٓئِحَٰتٍ
ثَيِّبَٰتٍ وَأَبْكَارًا

6. O ye who believe![5538]
Save yourselves and your
Families from a Fire
Whose fuel is Men[5539]
And Stones, over which
Are (appointed) angels
Stern (and) severe,[5540]
Who flinch not (from
Executing) the Commands
They receive from Allah,
But do (precisely) what
They are commanded.

٦ يَٰٓأَيُّهَا ٱلَّذِينَ ءَامَنُوا۟
قُوٓا۟ أَنفُسَكُمْ وَأَهْلِيكُمْ
نَارًا وَقُودُهَا ٱلنَّاسُ وَٱلْحِجَارَةُ
عَلَيْهَا مَلَٰٓئِكَةٌ غِلَاظٌ شِدَادٌ
لَّا يَعْصُونَ ٱللَّهَ مَآ أَمَرَهُمْ
وَيَفْعَلُونَ مَا يُؤْمَرُونَ

7. (They will say),
"O ye Unbelievers!

٧ يَٰٓأَيُّهَا ٱلَّذِينَ كَفَرُوا۟

5536. From the case of two in verse 4, we now come to the case of all the Consorts generally, in verse 5. *Cf.* 33:28-30. Their duties and responsibilities were higher than those of other women, and therefore their failure would also be more serious. This is only hypothetical, in order to show us the virtues expected of them: faith and devotion, worship and service, readiness for travel or *hijrah*, whether they were young or old, new to married life or otherwise. From them again the more general application follows—to all women in Islam.

5537. *Sā'iḥāt:* literally, those who travel about for the Faith, renouncing hearth and home: hence those who go on pilgrimage, who fast, who deny themselves the ordinary pleasures of life. Note that the spiritual virtues are named, in the descending order: submitting their wills (Islam), faith and devotion, turning ever to worship and faith, and performing other rites, or perhaps being content with asceticism. And this applies to all women, maiden girls or women of mature experience who were widows or separated from previous husbands by divorce.

5538. Note how we have been gradually led up in admonition from two Consorts to all consorts, to all women, to all Believers, and to all men and women including Unbelievers. We must carefully guard not only our own conduct, but the conduct of our families, and of all who are near and dear to us. For the issues are most serious, and the consequences of a fall are most terrible.

5539. *A Fire whose fuel is Men and Stones. Cf.* 2:24. This is a terrible Fire: not merely like the physical fire which burns wood or charcoal or substances like that, and consumes them. This spiritaul Fire will have for its fuel men who do wrong and are as hardhearted as stones, or stone Idols as symbolical of all the unbending Falsehoods in life.

5540. *Cf.* 74:31. We think of angelic nature as gentle and beautiful, but in another aspect perfection includes justice, fidelity, discipline, and the firm execution of duty according to lawful Commands. So, in the attributes of Allah Himself, Justice and Mercy, Kindness and Correction are not contradictory but complementary. An earthly ruler will be unkind to his loyal subjects if he does not punish evildoers.

Make no excuses This Day! Ye are being[5541] But requited for All that ye did!"	لَا تَعْتَذِرُوا الْيَوْمَ إِنَّمَا تُجْزَوْنَ مَا كُنتُمْ تَعْمَلُونَ

SECTION 2.

8. O ye who believe![5542] Turn to Allah With sincere repentance: In the hope that Your Lord will remove[5543] From you your ills And admit you to Gardens Beneath which Rivers flow— The Day that Allah Will not permit To be humiliated The Prophet and those Who believe with him. Their Light will run[5544] Forward before them And by their right hands, While they say, "Our Lord! Perfect our Light for us, And grant us Forgiveness: For Thou hast power Over all things."	٨ يَا أَيُّهَا الَّذِينَ آمَنُوا تُوبُوا إِلَى اللَّهِ تَوْبَةً نَّصُوحًا عَسَىٰ رَبُّكُمْ أَن يُكَفِّرَ عَنكُمْ سَيِّئَاتِكُمْ وَيُدْخِلَكُمْ جَنَّاتٍ تَجْرِي مِن تَحْتِهَا الْأَنْهَارُ يَوْمَ لَا يُخْزِي اللَّهُ النَّبِيَّ وَالَّذِينَ آمَنُوا مَعَهُ نُورُهُمْ يَسْعَىٰ بَيْنَ أَيْدِيهِمْ وَبِأَيْمَانِهِمْ يَقُولُونَ رَبَّنَا أَتْمِمْ لَنَا نُورَنَا وَاغْفِرْ لَنَا إِنَّكَ عَلَىٰ كُلِّ شَيْءٍ قَدِيرٌ
9. O Prophet! Strive hard[5545] Against the Unbelievers	٩ يَا أَيُّهَا النَّبِيُّ جَاهِدِ الْكُفَّارَ

5541. 'This is no hardship or injustice imposed on you. It is all but the fruit of your own deeds; the result of your own deliberate choice.'

5542. The opposition of sex against sex, individual or concerted, having been condemned, we are now exhorted to turn to the Light, and to realise that the good and righteous can retain their integrity even though their own mates, in spite of their example and precept, remain in evil and sin.

5543. Whatever may have been the faults of the past, unite in good deeds, and abandon petty sectional jealousies, and Allah will remove your difficulties and distresses, and all the evils from which you suffer. Indeeed He will grant you the Bliss of Heaven and save you from any humiliation which you may have brought on yourselves by your conduct and on the revered Prophet and Teacher whose name you professed to take.

5544. See 57:12, and n. 5288. The darkness of evil will be dispelled, and the Light of Allah will be realised by them more and more. But even so they will not be content: for they will pray for the least taint of evil to be removed from them, and perfection to be granted to them. In that exalted state they will be within reach of perfection—not by their own merits, but by the infinite Mercy and Power of Allah.

5545. See 9:73, where the same words introduce the argument against the Hypocrites. Here they introduce the argument against wickedness, which, though given the privilege of association with goodness and piety, persisted in wicked deeds, and in favour of those noble souls, which, though tied to wickedness, retained their purity and integrity. Two examples of each kind are given—of women, as this Sūrah is mainly concerned with women.

And the Hypocrites,
And be firm against them.
Their abode is Hell—
An evil refuge (indeed).

وَالْمُنَٰفِقِينَ وَاغْلُظْ عَلَيْهِمْ ۚ
وَمَأْوَىٰهُمْ جَهَنَّمُ ۖ وَبِئْسَ الْمَصِيرُ

10. Allah sets forth,
For an example
To the Unbelievers,
The wife of Noah[5546]
And the wife of Lūṭ:[5547]
They were (respectively)
Under two of our righteous
Servants, but they were
False to their (husbands),[5548]
And they profited nothing
Before Allah on their account,
But were told: "Enter ye
The Fire along with
(Others) that enter!"

(١٠) ضَرَبَ اللَّهُ مَثَلًا لِّلَّذِينَ
كَفَرُوا امْرَأَتَ نُوحٍ وَامْرَأَتَ لُوطٍ ۖ
كَانَتَا تَحْتَ عَبْدَيْنِ مِنْ عِبَادِنَا
صَٰلِحَيْنِ فَخَانَتَاهُمَا فَلَمْ يُغْنِيَا
عَنْهُمَا مِنَ اللَّهِ شَيْـًٔا
وَقِيلَ ادْخُلَا النَّارَ
مَعَ الدَّٰخِلِينَ

11. And Allah sets forth,
As an example
To those who believe,
The wife of Pharaoh:[5549]
Behold she said:
"O my Lord! build
For me, in nearness[5550]

(١١) وَضَرَبَ اللَّهُ مَثَلًا
لِّلَّذِينَ ءَامَنُوا امْرَأَتَ فِرْعَوْنَ
إِذْ قَالَتْ رَبِّ ابْنِ لِي عِندَكَ

5546. Read Noah's story in 11:36-48. Evidently his contemporary world had got so corrupt that it needed a great Flood to purge it. "None of the people will believe except those who have believed already. So grieve no longer over their evil deeds." But there were evil ones in his own family. A foolish and undutiful son is mentioned in 11:42-46. Poor Noah tried to save him and pray for him as one "of his family"; but the answer came: "he is not of thy family; for his conduct is unrighteous". We might expect such a son to have a mother like him, and here we are told that it was so. Noah's wife was also false to the standards of her husband, and perished in this world and the Hereafter.

5547. The wife of Lūṭ has already been mentioned more than once. See 11:81, and n. 1577; 7:83, and n. 1051; etc. The world around her was wicked and she sympathised with and followed that wicked world, rather than her righteous husband. She suffered the fate of her wicked world.

5548. *False to their husbands*: not necessarily in sex, but in the vital spiritual matters of truth and conduct. They had the high privilege of the most intimate relationship with the noblest spirits of their age: but if they failed to rise to the height of their dignity, their relationship did not save them. They could not plead that they were the wives of pious husbands. They had to enter Hell like any other wicked women. There is personal responsibility before Allah. One soul cannot claim the merits of another, any more than one pure soul can be injured by association with a corrupt soul. The pure one should keep its purity intact. See the next two examples.

5549. Traditionally, she is known as 'Āsiyah, one of the four perfect women, the other three being Mary the mother of Jesus, Khadījah the wife of the Holy Prophet, and Fāṭimah his daughter. Pharaoh is the type of arrogance, godlessness, and wickedness. For his wife to have preserved her Faith, her humility, and her righteousness was indeed a great spiritual triumph. She was probably the same who saved the life of the infant Moses: 28:9.

5550. Her spiritual vision was directed to Allah, rather than to the worldly grandeur of Pharaoh's court. It is probable that her prayer implies a desire for martyrdom, and it may be that she attained her crown of martyrdom.

To Thee, a mansion
In the Garden,
And save me from Pharaoh
And his doings,
And save me from
Those that do wrong";

بَيْتًا فِي ٱلْجَنَّةِ
وَنَجِّنِي مِن فِرْعَوْنَ وَعَمَلِهِۦ
وَنَجِّنِي مِنَ ٱلْقَوْمِ ٱلظَّٰلِمِينَ

12. And Mary the daughter[5551]
Of 'Imrān, who guarded
Her chastity; and We
Breathed into (her body)[5552]
Of Our spirit; and she
Testified to the truth
Of the words of her Lord
And of his Revelations,
And was one of the
Devout (Servants).[5553]

١٢ وَمَرْيَمَ ٱبْنَتَ عِمْرَٰنَ
ٱلَّتِىٓ أَحْصَنَتْ فَرْجَهَا
فَنَفَخْنَا فِيهِ مِن رُّوحِنَا
وَصَدَّقَتْ بِكَلِمَٰتِ رَبِّهَا وَكُتُبِهِۦ
وَكَانَتْ مِنَ ٱلْقَٰنِتِينَ

5551. 'Imrān was traditionally the name of the father of Mary the mother of Jesus: see n. 375 to 3:35. She was herself one of the purest of women, though the Jews accused her falsely of unchastity: *Cf.* 19:27-28.

5552. *Cf.* 21:91. As a virgin she gave birth to Jesus: 19:16-29. In 32:9, it is said of Adam's progeny, man, that Allah "fashioned him in due proportion, and breathed into him something of His spirit". In 15:29, similar words are used with reference to Adam. The virgin birth should not therefore be supposed to imply that Allah was the father of Jesus in the sense in which Greek mythology makes Zeus the father of Apollo by Latona or of Minos by Europa. And yet that is the doctrine to which the Christian idea of "the only begotten Son of God" leads.

5553. Mary had true faith and testified her faith in the Prophet Jesus and in his revelation as well as in the revelations which he came to confirm (and to foreshadow). She was of the company of the Devout of all ages. The fact that *Qānitīn* (devout) is not here in the feminine gender implies that the highest spiritual dignity is independent of sex. And so we close the lesson of this Sūrah, that while sex is a fact of our physical existence, the sexes should act in harmony and cooperation for in the highest spiritual matters we are all one. "We made her and her son a Sign for all peoples. Verily this Brotherhood of yours is a single Brotherhood, and I am your Lord and Cherisher: therefore serve Me and no other" (21:91-92).

INTRODUCTION TO SŪRAH 67—*AL MULK*

We have now done fourteen-fifteenths of the Qur'ān, and have followed step by step the development of its argument establishing the *Ummah* or Brotherhood of Islam.

There is a logical break here. The remaining fifteenth consists of short spiritual Lyrics, mostly of the Makkan period, dealing mainly with the inner life of man, and in its individual aspects. They may be compared to Hymns or Psalms in other religious literature. But these short Quranic Sūrahs have a grandeur, a beauty, a mystic meaning, and a force of earnestness under persecution, all their own. With their sources in the sublimest regions of heaven; their light penetrates into the darkest recesses of Life, into the concrete facts which are often mistaken for the whole of Reality, though they are but an insignificant portion and on the surface and fleeting. There is much symbolism in language and thought, in describing the spiritual in terms of the things we see and understand.

It is the contrast between the shadows of Reality here and the eternal Reality, between the surface world and the profound inner World, that is urged on our attention here.

This Sūrah of 30 verses belongs to the Middle Makkan period, just before S. 69 and S. 70. Allah is mentioned here by the name *Raḥmān* (Most Gracious), as He is mentioned by the names of *Rabb* (Lord and Cherisher) and *Raḥmān* (Most Gracious) in S. 19.

C. 246.—Lordship in right and in fact belongs
(67:1-30.) To Allah Most Gracious, Whose Goodness
And Glory and Power are writ large
On all His Creation. The beauty and order
Of the Heavens above us proclaim Him.
Then who can reject His call but those
In pitiful delusion? And who can fail
To accept, that truly knows himself
And the mighty Reality behind him?
The earth and the good things thereof are prepared
For man by his Gracious Lord, Who guards
Him from hourly dangers. Who sustains
The wonderful flight of the Birds in midair?
Above, and below, and in midair can we see
His boundless Signs. We know that His Promise
Of the Hereafter is true. The spring and source
Of the goodness of things is in Him, and will
Appear triumphant when the Hour is established.

Sūrah 67.

Al Mulk (The Dominion)

In the name of Allah, Most Gracious,
Most Merciful.

29
30

1. Blessed[5554] be He
In Whose hands
Is Dominion;[5555]
And He over all things
Hath Power—

2. He Who created Death[5556]
And Life, that He
May try which of you
Is best in deed;[5557]
And He is the Exalted[5558]
In Might, Oft-Forgiving—

3. He Who created
The seven heavens[5559]

الجزء التاسع والعشرون سورة الملك

بِسْمِ ٱللَّهِ ٱلرَّحْمَـٰنِ ٱلرَّحِيمِ

تَبَـٰرَكَ ٱلَّذِى بِيَدِهِ ٱلْمُلْكُ وَهُوَ عَلَىٰ كُلِّ شَىْءٍ قَدِيرٌ ﴿١﴾

ٱلَّذِى خَلَقَ ٱلْمَوْتَ وَٱلْحَيَوٰةَ لِيَبْلُوَكُمْ أَيُّكُمْ أَحْسَنُ عَمَلًا ۚ وَهُوَ ٱلْعَزِيزُ ٱلْغَفُورُ ﴿٢﴾

ٱلَّذِى خَلَقَ سَبْعَ سَمَـٰوَٰتٍ ﴿٣﴾

5554. What do we mean when we bless the name of Allah, or proclaim (in the optative mood) that the whole Creation should bless the name of the Lord? We mean that we recognise and proclaim His beneficence to us; for all increase and happiness is through Him, "in His hands"—in the hands of Him Who also holds Dominion or Power. In our human affairs we sometimes see the separation of Dominion or Power from Goodness or Beneficence: in the divine nature we recognise that there is no separation or antithesis.

5555. *Mulk:* Dominion, Lordship, Sovereignty, the Right to carry out His Will, or to do all that He wills. *Power* (in the clause following) is the Capacity to carry out His Will, so that nothing can resist or neutralise it. Here is beneficence completely identified with Lordship and Power; and it is exemplified in the verses following. Note that *Mulk* here has a different shade of meaning from *Malakūt* in 36:83. Both words are from the same root, and I have translated both by the word "Dominion". But *Malakūt* refers to Lordship in the invisible World, while *Mulk* to Lordship in the visible World. Allah is Lord of both.

5556. *Created Death and Life.* Death is here put before Life, and it is created. Death is therefore not merely a negative state. In 2:28 we read "Seeing that ye were without life (literally, *dead),* and He gave you life; then will He cause you to die, and will again bring you to life; and again to Him will ye return." In 53:44, again, Death is put before Life. Death then is: (1) the state before life began, which may be non-existence or existence in some other form; (2) the state in which Life as we know it ceases, but existence does not cease; a state of *Barzakh* (23:100), or Barrier or Partition, after our visible Death and before Judgement; after that will be the new Life, which we conceive of under the term Eternity.

5557. Creation, therefore, is not in mere sport, or without a purpose with reference to man. The state before our present Life, or the state after, we can scarcely understand. But our present Life is clearly given to enable us to strive by good deeds to reach a nobler state.

5558. All this is possible, because Allah is so Exalted in Might that He can perfectly carry out His Will and Purpose, and that Purpose is Love, Mercy, and Goodness to His creatures.

5559. *Cf.* 45:12, and n. 5526-27. The heavens as they appear to our sight seem to be arranged in layers one above another, and ancient astronomy accounted for the motions of the heavenly bodies in an elaborate scheme of spheres. What we are concerned with here is the order and beauty of the vast spaces and the marvellous bodies that follow regular laws of motion in those enormous spaces in the visible world. From these we are to form some conception of the vastly greater Invisible World, for which we want special spiritual vision.

One above another:
No want of proportion
Wilt thou see
In the Creation
Of (Allah) Most Gracious.
So turn thy vision again:
Seest thou any flaw?

طِبَاقًا
مَّا تَرَىٰ فِي خَلْقِ الرَّحْمَٰنِ مِن تَفَاوُتٍ
فَارْجِعِ الْبَصَرَ هَلْ تَرَىٰ مِن فُطُورٍ

4. Again turn thy vision[5560]
A second time: (thy) vision
Will come back to thee
Dull and discomfited,
In a state worn out.

﴿٤﴾ ثُمَّ ارْجِعِ الْبَصَرَ كَرَّتَيْنِ
يَنقَلِبْ إِلَيْكَ الْبَصَرُ خَاسِئًا وَهُوَ حَسِيرٌ

5. And We have,
(From of old),
Adorned the lowest heaven[5561]
With Lamps, and We
Have made such (Lamps)
(As) missiles to drive[5562]
Away the Evil Ones,
And have prepared for them
The Penalty
Of the Blazing Fire.

﴿٥﴾ وَلَقَدْ زَيَّنَّا
السَّمَاءَ الدُّنْيَا
بِمَصَابِيحَ وَجَعَلْنَاهَا
رُجُومًا لِّلشَّيَاطِينِ
وَأَعْتَدْنَا لَهُمْ عَذَابَ السَّعِيرِ

6. For those who reject
Their Lord (and Cherisher)[5563]
Is the Penalty of Hell:
And evil is (such) destination.

﴿٦﴾ وَلِلَّذِينَ كَفَرُوا بِرَبِّهِمْ عَذَابُ جَهَنَّمَ
وَبِئْسَ الْمَصِيرُ

7. When they are cast therein,
They will hear

﴿٧﴾ إِذَا أُلْقُوا فِيهَا سَمِعُوا

5560. Reverting to the symbolism of the external or visible world, we are asked to observe and study it again and again, and as minutely as our powers will allow. However closely we observe it, we shall find no flaw in it. Indeed the region of enquiry is so vast and stretches so far beyond our ken, that our eyes, aided with the most powerful telescopes, will confess themselves defeated in trying to penetrate to the ultimate mysteries. We shall find no defect in Allah's handiwork: it is our own powers that we shall find fail to go beyond a certain compass.

5561. *Lowest* (or, *nearest) heaven:* see n. 4035 to 37:6.

5562. The phenomenon of the shooting stars has been explained in 15:16-18, notes 1951-54; and in 37. 6-10 and notes thereon. (R).

5563. We have seen how the fire in the stars can suggest the beauty and order of the external world; and yet, when it meets with resistance and disharmony, it can burn and destroy. So in the moral and spiritual world. What can be a greater sign of evil, disharmony, and rebellion than to reject the Cherisher and Sustainer, on Whom our life depends, and from Whom we receive nothing but goodness? The Punishment, then, is Fire in its fiercest intensity, as typified in the next two verses.

The (terrible) drawing in[5564] Of its breath Even as it blazes forth,	لَهَا شَهِيقًا وَهِيَ تَفُورُ
8. Almost bursting with fury: Every time a Group Is cast therein, its Keepers[5565] Will ask, "Did no Warner Come to you?"	تَكَادُ تَمَيَّزُ مِنَ الْغَيْظِ ۖ كُلَّمَا أُلْقِيَ فِيهَا فَوْجٌ سَأَلَهُمْ خَزَنَتُهَا أَلَمْ يَأْتِكُمْ نَذِيرٌ ﴿٨﴾
9. They will say: "Yes indeed; A Warner did come to us, But we rejected him And said, 'Allah never Sent down any (Message): Ye are in nothing but An egregious delusion!'"[5566]	قَالُوا بَلَىٰ قَدْ جَاءَنَا نَذِيرٌ فَكَذَّبْنَا وَقُلْنَا مَا نَزَّلَ اللَّهُ مِن شَيْءٍ إِنْ أَنتُمْ إِلَّا فِي ضَلَالٍ كَبِيرٍ ﴿٩﴾
10. They will further say: "Had we but listened Or used our intelligence,[5567] We should not (now) Be among the Companions Of the Blazing Fire!"	وَقَالُوا لَوْ كُنَّا نَسْمَعُ أَوْ نَعْقِلُ مَا كُنَّا فِي أَصْحَابِ السَّعِيرِ ﴿١٠﴾
11. They will then confess[5568] Their sins: but far	فَاعْتَرَفُوا بِذَنبِهِمْ ﴿١١﴾

5564. For *shahīq* see n. 1607 to 11:106. There *shahīq* (sobs) was contrasted with *zafīr* (sighs): in the one case it is the drawing in of breath, and in the other the emission of a deep breath. Here the latter process is represented by the verb *fāra*, to swell, to blaze forth, to gush forth. In 11:40, the verb *fāra* was applied to the gushing forth of the waters of the Flood: here the verb is applied to the blazing forth of the Fire of Punishment. Fire is personified: in its intake it has a fierce appetite: in the flames which it throws out, it has a fierce aggressiveness. And yet in ultimate result evil meets the same fate, whether typified by water or fire.

5565. *Cf.* 39:71, n. 4348. *Every time:* it may not be the same angels who are guarding the gates of Hell every time new inmates come in. The pure, innocent angel nature does not know the crookedness of human evil, and is surprised at so many human beings coming in for punishment: it wonders if no warning was conveyed to men, whereas in fact men have a warning in Clear Signs during all the period of their probation. The Clear Signs come from Revelation, from their own conscience, and from all nature around them.

5566. Allah's Signs were not only rejected or defied, but their very existence was denied. Nay, more, even their possibility was denied, and alas! righteous people and spiritual Teachers were persecuted or mocked (36:30). They were called fools or madmen, or men under a delusion!

5567. Man has himself the power given to him to distinguish good from evil, and he is further helped by the teachings of the great Messengers or World Teachers. Where such Teachers do not come into personal contact with an individual or a generation, the true meaning of their teaching can be understood by means of the Reason which Allah has given to every human soul to judge by. It is failure to follow a man's own lights sincerely that leads to his degradation and destruction.

5568. They will then have passed through the fire of Judgement and will now be in the fire of Punishment. The Reality will not only now be clear to them, but after the questionings of the angels they cannot even pretend to make any excuses. They will freely confess, but that is not repentance, for repentance implies amendment, and the time for repentance and amendment will have long been past.

Will be (Forgiveness)
From the Companions
Of the Blazing Fire!

فَسُحْقًا لِّأَصْحَـٰبِ ٱلسَّعِيرِ

12. As for those who
Fear their Lord unseen,[5569]
For them is Forgiveness
And a great Reward.

١٢ إِنَّ ٱلَّذِينَ يَخْشَوْنَ رَبَّهُم بِٱلْغَيْبِ
لَهُم مَّغْفِرَةٌ وَأَجْرٌ كَبِيرٌ

13. And whether ye hide
Your word or publish it,
He certainly has (full) knowledge,
Of the secrets of (all) hearts.

١٣ وَأَسِرُّوا۟ قَوْلَكُمْ أَوِ ٱجْهَرُوا۟ بِهِۦٓ
إِنَّهُۥ عَلِيمٌۢ بِذَاتِ ٱلصُّدُورِ

14. Should He not know—
He that created?[5570]
And He is the One
That understands the finest
Mysteries (and) is
Well-acquainted (with them).

١٤ أَلَا يَعْلَمُ مَنْ خَلَقَ
وَهُوَ ٱللَّطِيفُ ٱلْخَبِيرُ

SECTION 2.

15. It is He Who has
Made the earth manageable[5571]
For you, so traverse
Ye through its tracts
And enjoy of the Sustenance
Which He furnishes: but
Unto Him is the Resurrection.[5572]

١٥ هُوَ ٱلَّذِى جَعَلَ لَكُمُ
ٱلْأَرْضَ ذَلُولًا فَٱمْشُوا۟ فِى
مَنَاكِبِهَا وَكُلُوا۟ مِن رِّزْقِهِۦ
وَإِلَيْهِ ٱلنُّشُورُ

5569. See n. 3902 to 35:18. Read "unseen" adverbially. To fear the Lord is to love Him so intensely that you fear to do anything which is against His Will, and you do it because you realise Him intensely in your hearts, though you do not see Him with your bodily senses. Nor is it of any consequence whether other people see your love or the consequences that flow from your love, for your good deeds are for the love of Allah and not for show in the eyes of men. Such intensity of love obtains forgiveness for any past, and is indeed rewarded with Allah's love, which is immeasurably precious beyond any merits you may possess.

5570. He Who creates must necessarily know His own handiwork. But lest we should measure His knowledge by such imperfect knowledge as we possess. His knowledge is further characterised as understanding the finest mysteries and being well-acquainted with them *(Laṭīf* and *Khabīr)*: see 22:63, n. 2844.

5571. *Dhalūl* is used in 2:71 for an animal trained and tractable; here it is used to qualify the earth, and I have translated 'manageable'. Man has managed to make paths through deserts and over mountains; through rivers and seas by means of ships; through the air by means of airways; he has made bridges and tunnels and other means of communication. But this he has only been able to do because Allah has given him the necessary intelligence and has made the earth tractable to that intelligence.

5572. In describing Allah's gifts and mercies and watchful care in this our temporary sojourn on this earth, it is made clear that the ultimate end is the Hereafter. The real Beyond, which is the goal, is the life after the Resurrection.

16. Do ye feel secure that
He Who is in Heaven
Will not cause you
To be swallowed up[5573]
By the earth when it
Shakes (as in an earthquake)?

١٦ ءَأَمِنتُم مَّن فِى ٱلسَّمَآءِ
أَن يَخْسِفَ بِكُمُ ٱلْأَرْضَ
فَإِذَا هِىَ تَمُورُ

17. Or do ye feel secure
That He Who is in Heaven
Will not send against you
A violent tornado[5574]
(With showers of stones),
So that ye shall
Know how (terrible)
Was My warning?

١٧ أَمْ أَمِنتُم مَّن فِى ٱلسَّمَآءِ
أَن يُرْسِلَ عَلَيْكُمْ حَاصِبًا
فَسَتَعْلَمُونَ كَيْفَ نَذِيرِ

18. But indeed men before them
Rejected (My warning):
Then how (terrible) was
My rejection (of them)?[5575]

١٨ وَلَقَدْ كَذَّبَ ٱلَّذِينَ مِن قَبْلِهِمْ
فَكَيْفَ كَانَ نَكِيرِ

19. Do they not observe
The birds above them,[5576]
Spreading their wings
And folding them in?[5577]
None can uphold them
Except (Allah) Most Gracious:
Truly it is He
That watches over all things.

١٩ أَوَلَمْ يَرَوْا۟ إِلَى ٱلطَّيْرِ
فَوْقَهُمْ صَٰٓفَّٰتٍ وَيَقْبِضْنَ
مَا يُمْسِكُهُنَّ إِلَّا ٱلرَّحْمَٰنُ
إِنَّهُۥ بِكُلِّ شَىْءٍۭ بَصِيرٌ

5573. *Cf.* 17:68 and n. 2263. Also *Cf.* the story of Qārūn in 28:76-82. If we feel safe on land, it is because Allah has made this earth amenable, manageable and serviceable to us (verse 15 above). But if we defy Allah and break His Law, have we any security, that even this comparatively unimportant safety in a fleeting world will last? Looking at it from a purely physical point of view, have there not been dreadful earthquakes, typhoons, and tornadoes?

5574. *Cf.* 17:68; and 29:40, n. 3462. Such a violent wind destroyed the wicked Cities which defied Lūṭ's warning.

5575. *Cf.* 22:42-44, and n. 2822.

5576. The flight of birds is one of the most beautiful and wonderful things in nature. The make and arrangement of their feathers and bones, and their streamlined shapes, from beak to tail, are instances of purposive adaptation. They soar with outstretched wings; they dart about with folded wings; their motions upwards and downwards, as well as their stabilisation in the air, and when they rest on their feet, have given many ideas to man in the science and art of aeronautics. But who taught or gave to birds this wonderful adaptation? None but Allah, Whose infinite Mercy provides for every creature just those conditions which are best adapted for its life.

5577. In the Arabic, there is an artistic touch which it is not possible to reproduce in the translation. *Ṣāffāt* (spreading their wings) is in the form of the active participle, suggesting the continuous soaring on outspread wings; while *yaqbiḍna* (folding them in) is in the Aorist form, suggesting the spasmodic flapping of wings.

20. Nay, who is there
That can help you,
(Even as) an army,[5578]
Besides (Allah) Most Merciful?
In nothing but delusion
Are the Unbelievers.

٢٠ أَمَّنْ هَٰذَا ٱلَّذِى هُوَ جُندٌ
لَّكُمْ يَنصُرُكُم مِّن دُونِ ٱلرَّحْمَٰنِ ۚ
إِنِ ٱلْكَٰفِرُونَ إِلَّا فِى غُرُورٍ

21. Or who is there
That can provide you[5579]
With Sustenance if He
Were to withhold His provision?
Nay, they obstinately persist
In insolent impiety
And flight (from the Truth).

٢١ أَمَّنْ هَٰذَا ٱلَّذِى
يَرْزُقُكُمْ إِنْ أَمْسَكَ رِزْقَهُۥ ۚ
بَل لَّجُّوا۟ فِى عُتُوٍّ وَنُفُورٍ

22. Is then one who
Walks headlong, with his face[5580]
Grovelling, better guided—
Or one who walks[5581]
Evenly on a Straight Way?

٢٢ أَفَمَن يَمْشِى مُكِبًّا عَلَىٰ وَجْهِهِۦٓ أَهْدَىٰٓ
أَمَّن يَمْشِى سَوِيًّا عَلَىٰ صِرَٰطٍ مُّسْتَقِيمٍ

23. Say: "It is He Who[5582]
Has created you (and made[5583]
You grow), and made
For you the faculties
Of hearing, seeing,
Feeling and understanding:
Little thanks it is ye give.

٢٣ قُلْ هُوَ ٱلَّذِىٓ أَنشَأَكُمْ وَجَعَلَ
لَكُمُ ٱلسَّمْعَ وَٱلْأَبْصَٰرَ وَٱلْأَفْـِٔدَةَ ۖ
قَلِيلًا مَّا تَشْكُرُونَ

24. Say: "It is He Who
Has multiplied you

٢٤ قُلْ هُوَ ٱلَّذِى ذَرَأَكُمْ

5578. Not the greatest army that man can muster is of any use against the Wrath of Allah: while the constant watchful care of Allah is all-in-all to us, and we can never do without it. If the godless wander about in search for blessings otherwise than in the Mercy and Grace of Allah, they are wandering in vain delusions.

5579. "Sustenance" here, as elsewhere, (*e.g.*, in 16:73, n. 2105), refers to all that is necessary to sustain and develop life in all its phases, spiritual and mental, as well as physical. Allah Most Gracious is the Source of all our Sustenance, and if we persist in looking to Vanities for our Sustenance, we are pursuing a mirage, and, if we examine the matter, we are only following obstinate impulses of rebellion and impiety.

5580. *Cf.* 27:90, and n. 3320. The man of probity is the man who walks evenly on a Straight Way, his feet guided by Allah's Light and his heart sustained by Allah's Mercy. The man who chooses evil grovels, with his face down, in paths of Darkness, stumbling on the way, and in constant distrust and fear, the fear of Evil. The two kinds of men are poles apart, although they live on the same earth, see the same Signs, and are fed with the same Mercies from Allah.

5581. Like Abraham trying to guide his unbelieving father: *Cf.* 19:43.

5582. The Teacher is asked to draw constant attention to Allah, the source of all growth and development, the Giver of the faculties by which we can judge and attain to higher and higher spiritual dignity. And yet, such is our self-will, we use our faculties for wrong purposes and thus show our ingratitude to Allah.

5583. For *anshā'* see n. 923 to 6:98.

Through the earth,[5584]
And to Him shall ye
Be gathered together."

فِي ٱلْأَرْضِ وَإِلَيْهِ تُحْشَرُونَ

25. They ask: When will
This promise be (fulfilled)?
If ye are telling[5585]
The truth.

٢٥ وَيَقُولُونَ مَتَىٰ هَٰذَا ٱلْوَعْدُ
إِن كُنتُمْ صَٰدِقِينَ

26. Say: "As to the knowledge
Of the time, it is
With Allah alone:[5586]
I am (sent) only
To warn plainly in public."

٢٦ قُلْ إِنَّمَا ٱلْعِلْمُ عِندَ ٱللَّهِ
وَإِنَّمَآ أَنَا۠ نَذِيرٌ مُّبِينٌ

27. At length, when they
See it close at hand,[5587]
Grieved will be the faces
Of the Unbelievers,
And it will be said
(To them): "This is
(The promise fulfilled),[5588]
Which ye were calling for!"

٢٧ فَلَمَّا رَأَوْهُ زُلْفَةً
سِيٓـَٔتْ وُجُوهُ ٱلَّذِينَ كَفَرُوا۟
وَقِيلَ هَٰذَا ٱلَّذِى
كُنتُم بِهِۦ تَدَّعُونَ

28. Say: "See ye?—
If Allah were
To destroy me,
And those with me,[5589]
Or if He bestows
His mercy on us—
Yet who can deliver

٢٨ قُلْ أَرَءَيْتُمْ إِنْ
أَهْلَكَنِىَ ٱللَّهُ وَمَن مَّعِىَ
أَوْ رَحِمَنَا فَمَن يُجِيرُ

5584. Mankind, from one set of parents, has been multiplied and scattered through the earth. Men have not only multiplied in numbers, but they have developed different languages and characteristics, inner and outer. But they will all be gathered together at the End of Things, when the mischief created by the wrong exercise of man's will will be cancelled, and the Truth of Allah will reign universally.

5585. The Unbelievers are sceptical, but they are answered in the next two verses.

5586. The Judgement is certain to come. But when it will exactly come, is known to Allah alone. The Prophet's duty is to proclaim that fact openly and clearly. It is not for him to punish or to hasten the punishment of evil. *Cf.* 22:47-49.

5587. "It", i.e., the fulfilment of the promise, the Day of Judgement. When it is actually in sight, then the Unbelievers realise that those whom they used to laugh at for their Faith were in the right, and that they themselves, the sceptics, were terribly in the wrong.

5588. They had defiantly asked for it. Now that it has come near, and it is too late for repentance, there is "weeping and gnashing of teeth".

5589. The sceptics might say and do say to the righteous: "Ah well! if calamities come, they involve the good with the bad, just as you say that Allah showers His mercies on both good and evil!" The answer is: "Don't you worry about us: even supposing we are destroyed, with all who believe with us, is that any consolation to you? Your sins must bring on you suffering, and nothing can ward it off. If we get any sorrows or sufferings, we take them as a mere trial to make us better, for we believe in Allah's goodness and we put our trust in Him." See next verse.

The Unbelievers from
A grievous Penalty?"

ٱلْكَٰفِرِينَ مِنْ عَذَابٍ أَلِيمٍ

29. Say: "He is (Allah)
Most Gracious: we have
Believed in Him,
And on Him have we
Put our trust:
So, soon will ye know[5590]
Which (of us) it is
That is in manifest error."

قُلْ هُوَ ٱلرَّحْمَٰنُ ءَامَنَّا بِهِۦ وَعَلَيْهِ تَوَكَّلْنَا فَسَتَعْلَمُونَ مَنْ هُوَ فِى ضَلَٰلٍ مُّبِينٍ ﴿٢٩﴾

30. Say: "See ye?–
If your stream be
Some morning lost[5591]
(In the underground earth),
Who then can supply you
With clear-flowing water?"

قُلْ أَرَءَيْتُمْ إِنْ أَصْبَحَ مَآؤُكُمْ غَوْرًا فَمَن يَأْتِيكُم بِمَآءٍ مَّعِينٍۭ ﴿٣٠﴾

5590. See the end of the last note. "Our Faith tells us that Allah will deliver us from all harm if we sincerely repent and lead righteous lives. You, Unbelievers, have no such hope. When the real adjustment of values is established, you will soon see whether we were in the wrong or you!"

5591. The Sūrah is closed with a parable, taken from a vital fact of our physical life, and leading up to the understanding of our spiritual life. In our daily life, what would happen if we woke up some fine morning to find that the sources and springs of our water supply had disappeared and gone down into the hollows of the earth? Nothing could save our life. Without water we cannot live, and water cannot rise above its level, but always seeks a lower level. So in spiritual life. Its sources and springs are in the divine wisdom that flows from on high. Allah is the real source of that life, as He is of all forms of life. We must seek His Grace and Mercy. We cannot find grace or mercy or blessing from anything lower. His Wisdom and Mercy are like fresh clear-flowing spring water, not like the muddy murky wisdom and goodness of this lower world which is only relative, and which often hampers life rather than advances it.

INTRODUCTION AND SUMMARY: SŪRAH 68—*AL QALAM*

This is a very early Makkan revelation. The general opinion of Muslim Commentary is that a great part of it was second in order of revelation, the first being S. 96: *(Iqra')*, verses 1-5: see *Itqān*. Chapter 7.

The last Sūrah having defined the true Reality in contrast with the false standards set up by men, this illustrates the theme by an actual historical example. Our Holy Prophet was the sanest and wisest of men: those who could not understand him called him mad or possessed. So, in every age, it is the habit of the world to call Truth Falsehood and Wisdom Madness, and, on the other hand, to exalt Selfishness as Planning, and Arrogance as Power. The contrast is shown up between the two kinds of men and their real inner worth.

Summary—Let the good carry on their work, in spite of the abuse of the Companions of Evil: let all remember Allah, before Whom all men are on trial (68:1-33, and C. 247).

True Judgement comes from Allah, and not from the false standards of men (68:34-52, and C. 248).

C. 247.—The Pen is the symbol of the permanent Record,
(68:1-33.) The written Decree, the perfect Order
In the government of the world. And by that token,
The man of Allah comes with a Plan
And Guidance that must win against
All detraction. Truth is high above Slander.
But men must be tried against selfishness
And overweening confidence in themselves
Such as would lead them to forget Allah
And His providence—like the brothers who built
Castles in the air about their garden
And found it desolate in one night's storm.
But repentance brought them forgiveness:
Thus work the Wrath and the Mercy of Allah.

Sūrah 68.

Al Qalam (The Pen), or **Nūn**[5592]

الجزء التاسع والعشرون سورة القلم

In the name of Allah, Most Gracious,
Most Merciful.

بِسْمِ اللَّهِ الرَّحْمَٰنِ الرَّحِيمِ

1. Nūn.[5592-A] By the Pen[5593]
And by the (Record)
Which (men) write—

نٓ وَٱلْقَلَمِ وَمَا يَسْطُرُونَ ﴿١﴾

2. Thou art not,
By the grace of thy Lord,
Mad or possessed.[5594]

مَآ أَنتَ بِنِعْمَةِ رَبِّكَ بِمَجْنُونٍ ﴿٢﴾

3. Nay, verily for thee
Is a Reward unfailing:[5595]

وَإِنَّ لَكَ لَأَجْرًا غَيْرَ مَمْنُونٍ ﴿٣﴾

4. And thou (standest)
On an exalted standard
Of character.

وَإِنَّكَ لَعَلَىٰ خُلُقٍ عَظِيمٍ ﴿٤﴾

5. Soon wilt thou see,[5596]
And they will see,

فَسَتُبْصِرُ وَيُبْصِرُونَ ﴿٥﴾

6. Which of you is
Afflicted with madness.

بِأَييِّكُمُ ٱلْمَفْتُونُ ﴿٦﴾

5592. *Nūn* is an Abbreviated Letter: see Appendix I at the end of S. 2.

Nūn may mean a fish, or an ink holder, or it may be just the Arabic letter of the alphabet, N. In the last case, it may refer to either or both of the other meanings. Note also that the Arabic rhyme in this Sūrah ends in N. The reference to ink would be an appropriate link with the Pen in verse 1. The reference to the fish would be appropriate with reference to the story of Jonah in verses 48-50. Jonah's title is "the Companion of the Fish", (Ḏhu al Nūn, 21:87), as he was, in the story, swallowed by the Fish. The letter N could also symbolically represent Jonah in the Arabic form Yūnus, where the characteristic "Firm Letter" is N. (R).

5592-A. See note above.

5593. The Pen and the Record are the symbolical foundations of the Revelation to man. The adjuration by the Pen disposes of the flippant charge that Allah's Messenger was mad or possessed. For he spoke words of power, not incoherent, but full of meaning, and through the Record of the Pen, that meaning unfolds itself, in innumerable aspects to countless generations. Muḥammad was the living Grace and Mercy of Allah, and his very nature exalted him above abuse and persecution. (R).

5594. People usually call anyone mad whose standards are different from their own. And madness is believed by superstitious people to be due to demoniacal possession, an idea distinctly in the minds of the New Testament writers: for Luke speaks of a man from whom the "devils" were cast out, as being then "clothed, and in his right mind." (Luke, viii. 35). (R).

5595. Instead of being out of his right mind, the Prophet of Allah had been raised to a great spiritual dignity, a reward that was not like an earthly reward that passes away, but one that was in the very core of his being, and would never fail him in any circumstances. He was really granted a nature and character far above the shafts of grief or suffering, slander or persecution.

5596. Though Al Muṣṭafā's nature raised him above the petty spite of his contemporaries, an appeal is made to their reason and to the logic of events. Was it not his accusers that were really mad? What happened to Walīd ibn Mughayrah, or Abū Jahl, or Abū Lahab?—and to Allah's Messenger and those who followed his guidance? The world's history gives the answer. And the appeal is not only to his contemporaries, but for all time.

7. Verily it is thy Lord
That knoweth best,
Which (among men)
Hath strayed from His Path:
And He knoweth best[5597]
Those who receive
(True) Guidance.

إِنَّ رَبَّكَ هُوَ
أَعْلَمُ بِمَن ضَلَّ عَن سَبِيلِهِۦ
وَهُوَ أَعْلَمُ بِٱلْمُهْتَدِينَ ﴿٧﴾

8. So hearken not
To those who
Deny (the Truth).[5598]

فَلَا تُطِعِ ٱلْمُكَذِّبِينَ ﴿٨﴾

9. Their desire is that
Thou shouldst be pliant:
So would they be pliant.

وَدُّوا۟ لَوْ تُدْهِنُ فَيُدْهِنُونَ ﴿٩﴾

10. Heed not the type
Of despicable man—[5599]
Ready with oaths,[5600]

وَلَا تُطِعْ كُلَّ حَلَّافٍ مَّهِينٍ ﴿١٠﴾

11. A slanderer, going about
With calumnies,

هَمَّازٍ مَّشَّآءٍۭ بِنَمِيمٍ ﴿١١﴾

12. (Habitually) hindering (all) good,
Transgressing beyond bounds,
Deep in sin,

مَّنَّاعٍ لِّلْخَيْرِ مُعْتَدٍ أَثِيمٍ ﴿١٢﴾

13. Violent (and cruel)—[5601]
With all that, base-born—

عُتُلٍّۭ بَعْدَ ذَٰلِكَ زَنِيمٍ ﴿١٣﴾

5597. Men set up false standards of judgement. The right standard is that of Allah. For His Knowledge is complete and all-embracing; He reads hidden motives as well as things that appear before men's sight; and He knows the past history in which the roots of present actions are embedded, as well as the future consequences of present actions.

5598. The enemies of Allah's truth are sometimes self-deceived. But quite often they have a glimmering of the truth in spite of their desire to shut their eyes. Then they compromise, and they would like the preachers of inconvenient truths to compromise with them. On those terms there would be mutual laudation. This easy path of making the best of both worlds is a real danger or temptation to the best of us, and we must be on our guard against it if we would really enter into the company of the Righteous who submit their wills to the Will of Allah. Abū Jahl freely offered impossible compromises to the Holy Prophet.

5599. The type of each of these hateful qualities is not uncommon, though the combination of all in one man makes him peculiarly despicable, as was Al Walīd ibn Al Mughīrah, who was a ringleader in calumniating our Prophet and who came to an evil end not long after the battle of Badr, in which he received injuries.

5600. It is only liars who swear on all occasions, small or great, because their ordinary word is not believed in. The true man's word, according to the proverb, is as good as his bond.

5601. Besides the self-deceiver and the easy-going man, there is a third type, even more degraded. He has no idea of truth or sincerity. He is ready to swear friendship with everyone and fidelity to every cause. But at the same moment he will slander and backbite, and cause mischief even between good but credulous persons. Evil seems to be his good, and good his evil. He will not only pursue evil courses himself but prevent other people from doing right. When checked, he resorts to violence. In any case, he will intrude where he has no right, claiming relationship or power or consideration in circles which would gladly disown him. He is vain of his wealth or because he has a large following at his beck and call. Religion is to him merely old-fashioned superstition.

14. Because[5602] he possesses
Wealth and (numerous) sons.

أَن كَانَ ذَا مَالٍ وَبَنِينَ ⑭

15. When to him are rehearsed
Our Signs,[5603]
"Tales of the Ancients",[5604]
He cries!

إِذَا تُتْلَىٰ عَلَيْهِ ءَايَٰتُنَا قَالَ أَسَٰطِيرُ ٱلْأَوَّلِينَ ⑮

16. Soon shall We brand
(The beast) on the snout![5605]

سَنَسِمُهُۥ عَلَى ٱلْخُرْطُومِ ⑯

17. Verily We have tried them
As We tried the People
Of the Garden,[5606]
When they resolved to gather
The fruits of the (garden)
In the morning,

إِنَّا بَلَوْنَٰهُمْ كَمَا بَلَوْنَآ أَصْحَٰبَ ٱلْجَنَّةِ إِذْ أَقْسَمُوا۟ لَيَصْرِمُنَّهَا مُصْبِحِينَ ⑰

18. But made no reservation,
("If it be Allah's Will").[5607]

وَلَا يَسْتَثْنُونَ ⑱

19. Then there came
On the (garden)

فَطَافَ عَلَيْهَا ⑲

5602. *Because* may connect with *heed not* in verse 10, or with *violent and cruel* in verse 13. In the former case, we construe: 'Pay no attention to despicable men of the character described, simply because they happen to have wealth or influence, or much backing in manpower'. In the latter case, we construe: the fellow is violent and cruel, because he is puffed up with his wealth or riches or backing in manpower'. In the eyes of Allah such a man is in any case branded and marked out as a sinner.

5603. Allah's Signs, by which He calls us, are everywhere—in nature and in our very heart and soul. In Revelation, every verse is a Sign, for it stands symbolically for far more than it says. "Sign" *(Āyah)* thus becomes a technical term for a verse of the Qur'ān.

5604. *Cf.* 6:25.

5605. Literally, proboscis, the most sensitive limb of the elephant. The sinner makes himself a beast and can only be controlled by his snout.

5606. "Why do the wicked flourish?" is a question asked in all ages. The answer is not simple. It must refer to (1) the choice left to man's will, (2) his moral responsibility, (3) the need of his tuning his will to Allah's Will, (4) the long-suffering quality of Allah, which allows the widest possible chance for the operation of (5) His Mercy, and (6) in the last resort, to the nature of spiritual Punishment, which is not a merely abrupt or arbitrary act, but a long, gradual process, in which there is room for repentance at every stage. All these points are illustrated in the remarkable Parable of the People of the Garden, which also illustrates the greed, selfishness, and heedlessness of man, as well as his tendency to throw the blame on others if he can but think of a scapegoat. All these foibles are shown, but the Mercy of Allah is boundless, and even after the worst sins and punishments, there may be hope of an even better orchard than the one lost, if only the repentance is true, and there is complete surrender to Allah's Will. But if, in spite of all this, there is no surrender of the will, then, indeed, the punishment in the Hereafter is something incomparably greater than the little calamities in the Parable.

5607. We must always remember, in all our plans, that they depend for their success on how far they accord with Allah's Will and Plan. His universal Will is supreme over all affairs. These foolish men had a secret plan to defraud the poor of their just rights, but they were put into a position where they could not do so. In trying to frustrate others, they were themselves frustrated.

A visitation from thy Lord,[5608] (Which swept away) all around, While they were asleep.	طَآئِفٌ مِّن رَّبِّكَ وَهُمْ نَآئِمُونَ
20. So the (garden) became, By the morning, like A dark and desolate spot, (Whose fruit had been gathered).	فَأَصْبَحَتْ كَٱلصَّرِيمِ ٢٠
21. As the morning broke, They called out, One to another—	فَتَنَادَوْا۟ مُصْبِحِينَ ٢١
22. "Go ye to your tilth (Betimes) in the morning,[5609] If ye would gather The fruits."	أَنِ ٱغْدُوا۟ عَلَىٰ حَرْثِكُمْ إِن كُنتُمْ صَٰرِمِينَ ٢٢
23. So they departed, conversing In secret low tones, (saying)—	فَٱنطَلَقُوا۟ وَهُمْ يَتَخَٰفَتُونَ ٢٣
24. "Let not a single indigent[5610] Person break in upon you Into the (garden) this day."	أَن لَّا يَدْخُلَنَّهَا ٱلْيَوْمَ عَلَيْكُم مِّسْكِينٌ ٢٤
25. And they opened the morning, Strong in an (unjust) resolve.	وَغَدَوْا۟ عَلَىٰ حَرْدٍ قَٰدِرِينَ ٢٥
26. But when they saw The (garden), they said: "We have surely lost our way:[5611]	فَلَمَّا رَأَوْهَا قَالُوٓا۟ إِنَّا لَضَآلُّونَ ٢٦
27. "Indeed we are shut out (Of the fruits of our labour)!"[5612]	بَلْ نَحْنُ مَحْرُومُونَ ٢٧

5608. It was a terrible storm that blew down and destroyed the fruits and the trees. The whole place was changed out of all recognition.

5609. Awakening from sleep, they were not aware that the garden had been destroyed by the storm overnight. They were in their own selfish dreams: by going very early, they thought they could cheat the poor of their share. See next note.

5610. The poor man has a right in the harvest—whether as a gleaner or as an artisan or a menial in an Eastern village. The rich owners of the orchard in the Parable wanted to steal a march at an early hour and defeat this right, but their greed was punished, so that it led to a greater loss to themselves. They wanted to cheat but had not the courage to face those they cheated, and by being in the field before anyone was up they wanted to make it appear to the world that they were unconscious of any rights they were trampling on.

5611. Their fond dreams were dispelled when they found that the garden had been changed out of all recognition. It was as if they had come to some place other then their own smiling garden. Where they had expected to reap a rich harvest, there was only a howling wilderness. They reflected. Their first thought was of their own personal loss, the loss of their labour and the loss of their capital. They had plotted to keep out others from the fruits: now, as it happened, the loss was their own.

5612. *Cf.* 56:67. Also see last note.

28. Said one of them,
More just (than the rest):[5613]
"Did I not say to you,
'Why not glorify (Allah)?'"

٢٨ قَالَ أَوْسَطُهُمْ أَلَمْ أَقُل لَّكُمْ لَوْلَا تُسَبِّحُونَ

29. They said: "Glory
To our Lord! Verily we
Have been doing wrong!"

٢٩ قَالُوا سُبْحَانَ رَبِّنَا إِنَّا كُنَّا ظَالِمِينَ

30. Then they turned, one
Against another, in reproach.[5614]

٣٠ فَأَقْبَلَ بَعْضُهُمْ عَلَىٰ بَعْضٍ يَتَلَاوَمُونَ

31. They said: "Alas for us!
We have indeed transgressed!

٣١ قَالُوا يَا وَيْلَنَا إِنَّا كُنَّا طَاغِينَ

32. "It may be that our Lord
Will give us in exchange
A better (garden) than this:
For we do turn to Him
(In repentance)!"[5615]

٣٢ عَسَىٰ رَبُّنَا أَن يُبْدِلَنَا خَيْرًا مِّنْهَا إِنَّا إِلَىٰ رَبِّنَا رَاغِبُونَ

33. Such is the Punishment
(In this life); but greater
Is the Punishment[5616]
In the Hereafter—
If only they knew!

٣٣ كَذَٰلِكَ الْعَذَابُ وَلَعَذَابُ الْآخِرَةِ أَكْبَرُ لَوْ كَانُوا يَعْلَمُونَ

C. 248.—To evil and good there can never be the same
(68:34-52.) End: no authority can the unjust produce
For their false imaginings. In shame
Will they realise this on the Day when all
Illusions will vanish and they find that the time
For repentance is past. The good man should wait

5613. This was not necessarily a righteous man, but there are degrees in guilt. He had warned them, but he had joined in their unjust design.

5614. When greed or injustice is punished people are ready to throw the blame on others. In this case, one particular individual may have seen the moral guilt of defying the Will of Allah and the right of man, but if he shared in the enterprise in the hope of profit, he could not get out of all responsibility.

5615. If the repentance was true, there was hope. For Allah often turns a great evil to our good. If not true, they only added hypocrisy to their other sins.

The Parable presupposes that the garden came into the possession of selfish men, who were so puffed up with their good fortune that they forgot Allah. That meant that they also became harsh to their fellow-creatures. In their arrogance they plotted to get up early and defeat the claims of the poor at harvest time. They found their garden destroyed by a storm. Some reproached others, but those who sincerely repented obtained mercy. The "better garden" may have been the same garden, flourishing in a future season under Allah's gift of abundance.

5616. Even in this life the punishment for heedless or selfish arrogance and sin comes suddenly when we least expect it. But there is always room for Allah's Mercy if we sincerely repent. If the Punishment in this life seems to us so stupefying, how much worse will it be in the Hereafter, when the Punishment will not be only for a limited time, and the time for repentance will have passed?

And should never lose patience, even though
Things go dead against him. Jonah suffered
In agony, but his sincere repentance
Brought him the grace of his Lord, and he
Joined the company of the Righteous:
For Truth is firm and unshaken, is calm
And works good, through all Allah's Creation.

SECTION 2.

34. Verily, for the Righteous,
Are Gardens of Delight,[5617]
In the Presence
Of their Lord.

إِنَّ لِلْمُتَّقِينَ عِندَ رَبِّهِمْ جَنَّٰتِ ٱلنَّعِيمِ ﴿٣٤﴾

35. Shall We then treat
The People of Faith
Like the People of Sin?[5618]

أَفَنَجْعَلُ ٱلْمُسْلِمِينَ كَٱلْمُجْرِمِينَ ﴿٣٥﴾

36. What is the matter
With you? How judge ye?

مَا لَكُمْ كَيْفَ تَحْكُمُونَ ﴿٣٦﴾

37. Or have ye a Book
Through which ye learn—

أَمْ لَكُمْ كِتَٰبٌ فِيهِ تَدْرُسُونَ ﴿٣٧﴾

38. That ye shall have,
Through it whatever
Ye choose?[5619]

إِنَّ لَكُمْ فِيهِ لَمَا تَخَيَّرُونَ ﴿٣٨﴾

39. Or have ye Covenants
With Us on oath,[5620]

أَمْ لَكُمْ أَيْمَٰنٌ عَلَيْنَا ﴿٣٩﴾

5617. All symbols of delight, expressed in terms of sense, are spiritualized by their being referred to the presence of Allah. The Garden is a joy, but the joy of this spiritual Garden is the sense of nearness to Allah. (R).

5618. The spiritual arrogance which rejects faith in Allah is perhaps the worst Sin, because it makes itself impervious to the Mercy of Allah, as a bed of clay is impervious to the absorption of water. It sets up its own standards and its own will, but how can it measure or bind the Will of Allah? It sets up its own fetishes—idols, priests, gods, or godlings. The fetishes may be even God-given gifts or faculties. Intellect or Science, if pushed up to the position of idols. If they are made rivals to Allah, question them: Will they solve Allah's mysteries, or even the mysteries of Life and Soul?

5619. It is clearly against both logic and justice that men of righteousness should have the same End as men of sin. Even in this life, man cannot command whatever he chooses, though he is allowed a limited freedom of choice. How can he expect such a thing under a reign of perfect Justice and Truth?

5620. Nor can the Pagans plead that they have any special Covenants with Allah which give them a favoured position above other morals. The "Chosen Race" idea of the Jews is also condemned. It is quite true that a certain race or group, on account of special aptitude may be chosen by Allah to uphold His truth and preach it. But this is conditional on their following Allah's Law. As soon as they become arrogant and selfish, they lose that position. They cannot have a perpetual and unconditional lease till the Day of Judgement.

Reaching to the Day
Of Judgement, (providing)
That ye shall have
Whatever ye shall demand?

بَٰلِغَةٌ إِلَىٰ يَوْمِ ٱلْقِيَٰمَةِ ۙ
إِنَّ لَكُمْ لَمَا تَحْكُمُونَ

40\. Ask thou of them,
Which of them will stand
Surety for that!

٤٠ سَلْهُمْ أَيُّهُم بِذَٰلِكَ زَعِيمٌ

41\. Or have they some
"Partners" (in Godhead)?[5621]
Then let them produce
Their "partners"
If they are truthful!

٤١ أَمْ لَهُمْ شُرَكَآءُ
فَلْيَأْتُوا۟ بِشُرَكَآئِهِمْ إِن كَانُوا۟ صَٰدِقِينَ

42\. The Day that the Shin[5622]
Shall be laid bare,
And they shall be summoned
To bow in adoration,
But they shall not be able—

٤٢ يَوْمَ يُكْشَفُ عَن سَاقٍ
وَيُدْعَوْنَ إِلَى ٱلسُّجُودِ فَلَا يَسْتَطِيعُونَ

43\. Their eyes will be[5623]
Cast down—ignominy will
Cover them; seeing that
They had been summoned
Aforetime to bow in adoration,
While they were whole,[5624]
(And had refused).

٤٣ خَٰشِعَةً أَبْصَٰرُهُمْ تَرْهَقُهُمْ ذِلَّةٌ ۖ
وَقَدْ كَانُوا۟ يُدْعَوْنَ إِلَى ٱلسُّجُودِ
وَهُمْ سَٰلِمُونَ

44\. Then leave Me[5625] alone
With such as reject
This Message: by degrees
Shall We punish them

٤٤ فَذَرْنِى وَمَن يُكَذِّبُ بِهَٰذَا ٱلْحَدِيثِ ۖ
سَنَسْتَدْرِجُهُم

5621\. *"Partners" in Godhead:* as in the doctrine of the Trinity, or indeed in any form of polytheism. Such a doctrine destroys the cardinal doctrine of the Unity of Allah.

5622\. *The Day that the Shin shall be laid bare*, that is, when men are confronted with the stark reality of the Day of Judgement. On that occasion men will be summoned to adoration, not necessarily in words, but by the logic of facts, when the Reality will be fully manifest: the Glory will be too dazzling for the Unbelievers, whose past deliberate refusal, when they had freedom to choose, and yet rejected, will stand in their way. (R).

5623\. Their past memories, combined with their present position, will then fill them with a sense of the deepest dismay and humilation. See last note.

5624\. *Sālimūn:* whole, in full possession of the power of judgement and will; not constrained, as they now will be, by the Punishment staring them full in the face.

5625\. Notice the transition between "Me" and "We" in this verse, and again to "I" and "My" in the next verse. The first person plural ordinarily used in the Holy Qur'ān as Allah's Word, is the plural of respect. In Royal decrees the first person plural is similarly used. When the first person singular is used, it marks some special personal relation, either of Mercy or favours (as in 2:38 or 2:150) or of punishment, as here. (*Cf.* n. 56 to 2:38).

From directions they perceive
not.[5626]

مِنْ حَيْثُ لَا يَعْلَمُونَ

45. A (long) respite will I
Grant them: truly
Powerful is My Plan.

٤٥ وَأُمْلِي لَهُمْ إِنَّ كَيْدِي مَتِينٌ

46. Or is it that thou dost
Ask them for a reward,[5627]
So that they are burdened
With a load of debt?—

٤٦ أَمْ تَسْأَلُهُمْ أَجْرًا فَهُم
مِّن مَّغْرَمٍ مُّثْقَلُونَ

47. Or that the Unseen[5628]
Is in their hands, so that
They can write it down?

٤٧ أَمْ عِندَهُمُ الْغَيْبُ فَهُمْ يَكْتُبُونَ

48. So wait with patience
For the Command
Of thy Lord, and be not
Like the Companion[5629]
Of the Fish—when he
Cried out in agony.

٤٨ فَاصْبِرْ لِحُكْمِ رَبِّكَ
وَلَا تَكُن كَصَاحِبِ الْحُوتِ
إِذْ نَادَىٰ وَهُوَ مَكْظُومٌ

49. Had not Grace
From His Lord
Reached him, he
Would indeed have been
Cast off on the naked[5630]
Shore, in disgrace.

٤٩ لَّوْلَا أَن تَدَارَكَهُ
نِعْمَةٌ مِّن رَّبِّهِ لَنُبِذَ بِالْعَرَاءِ
وَهُوَ مَذْمُومٌ

5626. *Cf.* 7:182. and n. 1154-A. We must not be impatient if we see the wicked flourish. It may be that the very appearance of flourishing here may be a part of the Punishment. There may be an eventual punishment by a sort of Cataclysm; but evolutionary punishment is gradual and sure. Allah may punish wicked people by granting them respite and providing them worldly benefits in abundance, which encourages them in sin and transgression. So when they are finally seized by the Wrath of Allah they are caught suddenly and utterly unprepared, as it were, red-handed while engrossed in disbelief, a life of impiety and open revolt against their Lord! (R).

5627. *Cf.* 52:40 n. 5074. It costs the Unbelievers nothing to hear the Preacher, for the Preacher asks for no reward, and indeed suffers for their benefit. The Preacher need not look even for appreciation or conversions. Al Muṣṭafā is addressed in the first instance, but there is always a universal interpretation. The righteous man asks for no reward for his preaching or example: if he did, the value would be too great for the world to pay for. The Unbelievers behave as if they had the secret of the Unseen, but they are empty triflers, for, if they only tried to formulate spiritual laws, they would fail.

5628. *Cf.* 52:41, n. 5075. The Unseen is certainly not within their knowledge or control. If it were, they could clearly write it down for their own guidance or the guidance of others. They should listen to the words of inspiration, sent by the Knower of all things.

5629. This was Dhu al Nūn, or Jonah, for whom see n. 2744 to 21:87-88. *Cf.* also 37:139-148 and the notes there. Jonah was asked to preach to the people of Nineveh, a wicked city. He met with hostility and persecution, fled from his enemies, and took a boat. He was caught in a storm and thrown into the sea. He was swallowed by a fish or whale, but he repented in his living prison, and was forgiven. But the people of Nineveh were also forgiven, for they, too, repented. Here is a double allegory of Allah's mercy and forgiveness, and a command to patience, and complete and joyful submission to the Will of Allah.

5630. *Cf.* 37:145-146, and n. 4126.

50\. Thus did his Lord[5631]
Choose him and make him
Of the company
Of the Righteous.[5632]

٥٠ فَٱجۡتَبَٰهُ رَبُّهُۥ فَجَعَلَهُۥ مِنَ ٱلصَّٰلِحِينَ

51\. And the Unbelievers
Would almost trip thee up[5633]
With their eyes when they
Hear the Message; and they
Say: "Surely he is possessed!"

٥١ وَإِن يَكَادُ ٱلَّذِينَ كَفَرُواْ لَيُزۡلِقُونَكَ بِأَبۡصَٰرِهِمۡ لَمَّا سَمِعُواْ ٱلذِّكۡرَ وَيَقُولُونَ إِنَّهُۥ لَمَجۡنُونٞ

52\. But it is nothing less
Than a Message[5634]
To all the worlds.

٥٢ وَمَا هُوَ إِلَّا ذِكۡرٞ لِّلۡعَٰلَمِينَ

5631\. Jonah was chosen by Allah's Grace and Mercy to be Allah's Prophet to Nineveh. If in his human frailty he lost a little patience, he suffered his punishment, but his true and sincere repentance and recognition of Allah's goodness and mercy restored him from his physical and mental distress, and from the obscuration of the spiritual Light in him.

5632\. *Cf.* 4:69, n. 586. In the beautiful Fellowship of the Righteous there is room for all, of every grade of spiritual advancement, from the highest to the most ordinary. But, as in democratic politics every citizen's rights and status have complete recognition, so, in the spiritual Fellowship, the badge of Righteousness is the bond, even though there may be higher degrees of knowledge or experience.

5633\. The eyes of evil men look at a good man as if they would "eat him up", or trip him up or disturb him from his position of stability or firmness. They use all sorts of terms of abuse—"madman" or "one possessed by an evil spirit", and so on. *Cf.* 68:2 above, and n. 5594. But the good man is unmoved, and takes his even course. The Message of Allah is true and will endure, and it is a Message to all Creation.

5634\. This is the extreme antithesis to madness or demoniacal possession. So far from the Holy Prophet uttering words disjointed or likely to harm people, he was bringing the Message of true Reality, which was to be cure of all evil, in every kind of world. For the different kinds of worlds see n. 20 to 1:2.

INTRODUCTION AND SUMMARY: SŪRAH 69—*AL HĀQQAH*

This Sūrah belongs to the early middle period of Makkan Revelation. The eschatological argument is pressed home: 'the absolute Truth cannot fail; it must prevail; therefore be not lured by false appearances in this life; it is Revelation that points to the sure and certain Reality.

C. 249.—In this fleeting world few things are what
(69:1-52.) They seem. What then is sure Reality?
Nations and men in the past assumed
Arrogance and perished because they were unjust,
But that destruction was but a foretaste
Of the Doom to come in the Hereafter, when all
Creation will be on a new plane, and true values
Will be fully established: to the Righteous
Will be Bliss, and to Evil, Punishment.
The Word of Revelation is not a Poet's
Imagination or a Soothsayer's groping
Into the future. It is Allah's own Message,
Of Mercy to the Righteous, and warning
To those who reject the Truth. Praise
And Glory to the name of Allah Most High!

Sūrah 69.

الجزء التاسع والعشرون سورة الحاقة

Al Ḥāqqah (The Sure Reality)

In the Name of Allah, Most Gracious Most Merciful.

بِسْمِ ٱللَّهِ ٱلرَّحْمَٰنِ ٱلرَّحِيمِ

1. The Sure Reality![5635]

(١) ٱلْحَآقَّةُ

2. What is the Sure Reality?

(٢) مَا ٱلْحَآقَّةُ

3. And what will make
Thee realise what
The Sure Reality is?

(٣) وَمَآ أَدْرَىٰكَ مَا ٱلْحَآقَّةُ

4. The Thamūd[5636]
And the 'Ad people
(Branded) as false
The Stunning Calamity![5637]

(٤) كَذَّبَتْ ثَمُودُ وَعَادٌۢ بِٱلْقَارِعَةِ

5. But the Thamūd—
They were destroyed
By a terrible Storm[5638]
Of thunder and lightning!

(٥) فَأَمَّا ثَمُودُ فَأُهْلِكُوا۟ بِٱلطَّاغِيَةِ

6. And the 'Ad—[5639]
They were destroyed
By a furious Wind,
Exceedingly violent;

(٦) وَأَمَّا عَادٌ فَأُهْلِكُوا۟ بِرِيحٍ صَرْصَرٍ عَاتِيَةٍ

7. He made it rage
Against them seven nights
And eight days in succession:

(٧) سَخَّرَهَا عَلَيْهِمْ سَبْعَ لَيَالٍ وَثَمَٰنِيَةَ أَيَّامٍ حُسُومًا

5635. *Al Ḥāqqah:* the sure Truth: the Event that must inevitably come to pass; the state in which all falsehood and pretence will vanish, and the absolute Truth will be laid bare. The question in the three verses raise an air of mystery. The solution is suggested in what happened to the Thamūd and the 'Ād, and other people of antiquity, who disregarded the Truth of Allah and came to violent end, even in this life—symbolically suggesting the great Cataclysm of the Hereafter, the Day of Doom.

5636. For these two peoples of antiquity, see n. 1043 to 7:73, and n. 1040 to 7:65.

5637. Another description of the terrible Day of Judgement. This word *Qāri'ah* also occurs as the title of S. 101.

5638. The Thamūd were addicted to class arrogance. They oppressed the poor. The prophet Ṣāliḥ preached to them, and put forward a wonderful she-camel as symbol of the rights of the poor, but they hamstrung her. See n. 1044 to 7:73. They were destroyed in a mighty calamity, an earthquake accompanying a terrible thunderstorm.

5639. The 'Ād were an unjust people spoilt by their prosperity. The prophet Hūd preached to them in vain. They were apparently destroyed by a terrible blast of wind. See n. 1040 to 7:65. See also 41:15-16, n. 4483, and 54:19, n. 5144.

So that thou couldst see
The (whole) people lying
Prostrate in its (path),
As if they had been
Roots of hollow palm trees[5640]
Tumbled down!

فَتَرَى ٱلْقَوْمَ فِيهَا صَرْعَىٰ
كَأَنَّهُمْ أَعْجَازُ نَخْلٍ خَاوِيَةٍ

8. Then seest thou any
Of them left surviving?[5641]

فَهَلْ تَرَىٰ لَهُم مِّنۢ بَاقِيَةٍ ﴿٨﴾

9. And Pharaoh,[5642]
And those before him,[5643]
And the Cities Overthrown,[5644]
Committed habitual Sin,

وَجَآءَ فِرْعَوْنُ وَمَن قَبْلَهُۥ ﴿٩﴾
وَٱلْمُؤْتَفِكَٰتُ بِٱلْخَاطِئَةِ

10. And disobeyed (each)
The messenger of their Lord;
So He punished them
With an abundant Penalty.

فَعَصَوْا رَسُولَ رَبِّهِمْ ﴿١٠﴾
فَأَخَذَهُمْ أَخْذَةً رَّابِيَةً

11. We, when the water
(Of Noah's Flood) overflowed
Beyond its limits,[5645]
Carried you (mankind),
In the floating (Ark),

إِنَّا لَمَّا طَغَا ٱلْمَآءُ ﴿١١﴾
حَمَلْنَٰكُمْ فِى ٱلْجَارِيَةِ

12. That We might
Make it a Message[5646]

لِنَجْعَلَهَا لَكُمْ تَذْكِرَةً ﴿١٢﴾

5640. A graphic simile. Dead men all lying about like hollow trunks of palm trees with their roots exposed! The 'Ād were reputed to be of a tall stature.

5641. The calamity was thorough. The 'Ād were destroyed, and then the Thamūd, and only the tradition of them was left behind. See the references in n. 5636.

5642. Pharaoh's Messenger was Moses. See the story in 7:103-137 and the notes there. Pharaoh was inordinately proud, and his fall was proportionately great: it gradually extended to his dynasty and his people: See Appendix V of S. 7.

5643. If we follow the sequence of peoples whose sins destroyed them, as mentioned in 7:59-158, we begin with Noah, then have the 'Ād, and the Thamūd, then the Cities of the Plain, then Midian, then the people whose prophet was Moses (who occupies a central place in the canvas), and then the Pagan Quraysh, to whom came the last and the greatest of the prophets, our holy Prophet Muḥammad. This is the chronological sequence. Here there is no detail, nor even complete mention. But Noah is alluded to last, and the 'Ād and the Thamūd mentioned first, because the latter two belong to Arab tradition, and this is specially addressed to the Pagans of Makkah. Pharaoh is mentioned rather than Moses for the same reason, and any others are "those before Pharaoh".

5644. *The Cities Overthrown:* Sodom and Gomorrah, Cities of the Plain, to whom Lot preached see 9:70, n. 1330; and 7:80-84, n. 1049.

5645. It was a widespread Flood. *Cf.* 7:59-64; also 11:25-49. Noah was ridiculed for his preparations for the Flood: see 11:38, n. 1531. But Allah had commanded him to build an Ark, in order that mankind should be saved from perishing in the Flood. But only those of Faith got into the Ark and were saved. As the Ark was built to Allah's command, Allah "carried you (mankind) in the floating (Ark)". (R).

5646. It was a memorial for all time, to show that evil meets with its punishment, but the good are saved by the mercy of Allah.

Unto you, and that ears
(That should hear the tale
And) retain its memory
Should bear its (lessons)
In remembrance.[5647]

وَتَعِيَهَآ أُذُنٌ وَٰعِيَةٌ

13. Then, when one
Blast is sounded
On the Trumpet,[5648]

فَإِذَا نُفِخَ فِي ٱلصُّورِ نَفْخَةٌ وَٰحِدَةٌ ﴿١٣﴾

14. And the earth is moved,
And its mountains,[5649]
And they are crushed to powder
At one stroke—

وَحُمِلَتِ ٱلْأَرْضُ وَٱلْجِبَالُ فَدُكَّتَا دَكَّةً وَٰحِدَةً ﴿١٤﴾

15. On that Day
Shall the (Great) Event
Come to pass,

فَيَوْمَئِذٍ وَقَعَتِ ٱلْوَاقِعَةُ ﴿١٥﴾

16. And the sky will be
Rent asunder, for it will
That Day be flimsy,

وَٱنشَقَّتِ ٱلسَّمَآءُ فَهِيَ يَوْمَئِذٍ وَاهِيَةٌ ﴿١٦﴾

17. And the angels will be
On its sides,[5650]
And eight will, that Day,
Bear the Throne[5651]
Of thy Lord above them.

وَٱلْمَلَكُ عَلَىٰٓ أَرْجَآئِهَا ۚ وَيَحْمِلُ عَرْشَ رَبِّكَ فَوْقَهُمْ يَوْمَئِذٍ ثَمَٰنِيَةٌ ﴿١٧﴾

18. That Day shall ye be
Brought to Judgement:

يَوْمَئِذٍ تُعْرَضُونَ ﴿١٨﴾

5647. *Cf.* the biblical phrase, "He that hath ears to hear, let him hear" (Matt. xi. 15). But the phrase used here has a more complicated import. An ear may hear, but for want of will in the hearer the hearer may not wish, for the future or for all time, to retain the memory of the lessons he has heard, even though for the time being he was impressed by it. The penetration of the Truth has to be far deeper and subtler, and this is desired here.

5648. We now come to the Inevitable Event, the Day of Judgement, the theme of this Sūrah. This is the first Blast referred to in 39:65, n. 4343.

5649. The whole of our visible world, as we now know it, will pass away. and a new world will come into being. The mountains are specially mentioned, because they stand as a type of hardness, size, and durability. They will be "crushed to powder", *i.e.*, lose their form and being at one stroke.

5650. The whole picture is painted in graphic poetical images, to indicate that which cannot be adequately described in words, and which indeed our human faculites with their present limited powers are not ready to comprehend. The angels will be on all sides, arrayed in ranks upon ranks, and the Throne of the Lord on high will be borne by eight angels (or eight rows of angels). That will be the Day when Justice will be fully established and man be mustered to his Lord for reckoning. (R).

5651. The number eight has perhaps no special significance, unless it be with reference to the shape of the Throne or the number of the angels. The Oriental Throne is often octagonal, and its bearers would be one at each corner. (R).

Not an act of yours
That ye hide will be hidden.

لا تخفى منكم خافية

19. Then he that will be
Given his Record
In his right hand[5652]
Will say: "Ah here!
Read ye my Record!

١٩ فأما من أوتي كتبه بيمينه
فيقول هاؤم اقرءوا كتبيه

20. "I did really understand[5653]
That my Account would
(One Day) reach me!"

٢٠ إني ظننت أني ملق حسابيه

21. And he will be
In a life of Bliss,

٢١ فهو في عيشة راضية

22. In a Garden on high,

٢٢ في جنة عالية

23. The Fruits whereof[5654]
(Will hang in bunches)
Low and near.

٢٣ قطوفها دانية

24. "Eat ye and drink ye,
With full satisfaction;
Because of the (good)
That ye sent before you,[5655]
In the days that are gone!"[5656]

٢٤ كلوا واشربوا هنيئا
بما أسلفتم في الأيام الخالية

25. And he that will
Be given his Record
In his left hand,[5657]

٢٥ وأما من أوتي كتبه بشماله

5652. *Cf.* 18:71, where the righteous are described as those who are given their record in their right hand at Judgement. In 56:27, 38, and other passages, the righteous are called "Companions of the Right Hand".

5653. The righteous one rejoices that the faith he had during this world's life was fully justified, and is now actually realised before him. He quite understood and believed that good and evil must meet with their due consequences in the Hereafter, however much appearances may have been against it in the life in the lower world, "in the days that are gone."

5654. The symbolism is that of ripe, luscious grapes, hanging low in heavy bunches, so near that they could be gathered and enjoyed in dignified ease. *Cf.* also 6:54; 76:14.

5655. *Cf.* 2:110: "Whatever good ye send forth for your souls before you, ye shall find it with Allah: for Allah sees well all that ye do."

5656. It will be a wholly new world, a new earth and a new heaven, when the blessed might well think with calm relief of "the days that are gone". *Cf.* 14:48, and n. 1925. Even Time and Space will be no more, so that any ideas that we may form here will be found to have become wholly obsolete by them.

5657. This is in contrast to the righteous ones who will receive their record in their right hand. *Cf.* 69:19, n. 5652. The righteous are glad when they remember their past: their memory is itself a precious possession. The unjust are in agony when they remember their past. Their memory is itself a grievous punishment.

Will say: "Ah! would
That my record had not
Been given to me!

فَيَقُولُ يَٰلَيۡتَنِي لَمۡ أُوتَ كِتَٰبِيَهۡ

26. "And that I had never
Realised how
My account (stood)!

وَلَمۡ أَدۡرِ مَا حِسَابِيَهۡ ٢٦

27. "Ah! would that (Death)[5658]
Had made an end of me!

يَٰلَيۡتَهَا كَانَتِ ٱلۡقَاضِيَةَ ٢٧

28. "Of no profit to me
Has been my wealth!

مَآ أَغۡنَىٰ عَنِّي مَالِيَهۡۜ ٢٨

29. "My power has
Perished from me!"...[5659]

هَلَكَ عَنِّي سُلۡطَٰنِيَهۡ ٢٩

30. (The stern command will say):
"Seize ye him,
And bind ye him,[5660]

خُذُوهُ فَغُلُّوهُ ٣٠

31. "And burn ye him
In the Blazing Fire.

ثُمَّ ٱلۡجَحِيمَ صَلُّوهُ ٣١

32. "Further, make him march
In a chain, whereof[5661]
The length is seventy cubits!

ثُمَّ فِي سِلۡسِلَةٖ ذَرۡعُهَا
سَبۡعُونَ ذِرَاعٗا فَٱسۡلُكُوهُ ٣٢

33. "This was he that
Would not believe[5662]
In Allah Most High,

إِنَّهُۥ كَانَ لَا يُؤۡمِنُ بِٱللَّهِ ٱلۡعَظِيمِ ٣٣

5658. The death as from this life was but a transition into a new world. They would wish that that death had been the end of all things, but it will not be.

5659. The intensest agony is when the soul loses power over itself, when the personality tries to realise itself in new conditions and cannot: this is life in death.

5660. Perhaps the word for 'bind' should be construed: 'bind his hands round his neck, to remind him that his hands when they were free were closed to all acts of charity and mercy': *Cf.* 17:29.

5661. The sinful men who will be given their record on the Day of Judgement in their left hands will be in utter despair. Their power and authority which they misused to perpetrate injustice and oppression will be gone. The wealth that had made them turn a deaf ear to the call of truth will be no more. They will cry out in agony, "O would that we were never raised again! O would that death had obliterated us once for all". But these cries will be of no avail. They will be seized, bound in chains and thrown into the Blazing Fire for their crimes against Allah and man. [Eds.].

5662. The grip of sin was fastened on sinners because they forsook Allah. They ran after their own lusts and worshipped them or they ran after Allah's creatures, ignoring Him Who is the cause and source of all good.

34. "And would not encourage[5663]
The feeding of the indigent!

وَلَا يَحُضُّ عَلَىٰ طَعَامِ ٱلْمِسْكِينِ ﴿٣٤﴾

35. "So no friend hath he
Here this Day.

فَلَيْسَ لَهُ ٱلْيَوْمَ هَٰهُنَا حَمِيمٌ ﴿٣٥﴾

36. "Nor hath he any food
Except the corruption[5664]
From the washing of wounds,

وَلَا طَعَامٌ إِلَّا مِنْ غِسْلِينٍ ﴿٣٦﴾

37. "Which none do eat
But those in sin."

لَّا يَأْكُلُهُۥٓ إِلَّا ٱلْخَٰطِـُٔونَ ﴿٣٧﴾

SECTION 2.

38. So I do
Call to witness[5665]
What ye see

فَلَآ أُقْسِمُ بِمَا تُبْصِرُونَ ﴿٣٨﴾

39. And what ye see not,

وَمَا لَا تُبْصِرُونَ ﴿٣٩﴾

40. That this is
Verily the word
Of an honoured messenger;[5666]

إِنَّهُۥ لَقَوْلُ رَسُولٍ كَرِيمٍ ﴿٤٠﴾

41. It is not the word
Of a poet:[5667]
Little it is
Ye believe!

وَمَا هُوَ بِقَوْلِ شَاعِرٍ ۚ قَلِيلًا مَّا تُؤْمِنُونَ ﴿٤١﴾

5663. *Cf.* 107:3; 89:18. The practical result of their rebellion against the God of Mercy was that their sympathies dried up. Not only did they not help or feed those in need, but they hindered others from doing so. And they have neither friend nor sympathy (food) in the Hereafter.

5664. They wounded many people by their cruelty and injustice in this life, and it is befitting that they should have no food other than "the corruption from the washing of wounds". (R).

5665. This is an adjuration in the same form as that which occurs in 56:75, 70:40, 90:1, and elsewhere. Allah's Word is the quintessence of Truth. But what if someone doubts whether a particular Messenger is Allah's Word communicated through His Messenger, or merely an imaginary tale presented by a poet, or a soothsayer's vain prophecy? Then we have to examine it in the light of our highest spiritual faculties. The witness to that Word is what we know in the visible world, in which falsehood in the long run gives place to truth, and what we know in the invisible world, through our highest spiritual faculties. We are asked to examine and test it in both these ways.

5666. *Honoured messenger:* one that is worthy of honour on account of the purity of his life, and may be relied upon not to invent things but to give the true inner experiences of his soul in Revelation.

5667. A poet draws upon his imagination, and the subjective factor is so strong that though we may learn much from him, we cannot believe as facts the wonderful tales he has to tell. And the poet who is not a Seer is merely a vulgar votary of exaggerations and falsehoods.

42. Nor is it the word
Of a soothsayer:[5668]
Little admonition it is
Ye receive.

٤٢ وَلَا بِقَوْلِ كَاهِنٍ قَلِيلًا مَّا تَذَكَّرُونَ

43. (This is) a Message
Sent down from the Lord
Of the Worlds.

٤٣ تَنزِيلٌ مِّن رَّبِّ ٱلْعَٰلَمِينَ

44. And if the messenger
Were to invent
Any sayings in Our name,

٤٤ وَلَوْ تَقَوَّلَ عَلَيْنَا بَعْضَ ٱلْأَقَاوِيلِ

45. We should certainly seize him
By his right hand,[5669]

٤٥ لَأَخَذْنَا مِنْهُ بِٱلْيَمِينِ

46. And We should certainly
Then cut off the artery
Of his heart:[5670]

٤٦ ثُمَّ لَقَطَعْنَا مِنْهُ ٱلْوَتِينَ

47. Nor could any of you
Withhold him[5671]
(From Our wrath).

٤٧ فَمَا مِنكُم مِّنْ أَحَدٍ عَنْهُ حَٰجِزِينَ

48. But verily this
Is a Message for
The God-fearing.

٤٨ وَإِنَّهُۥ لَتَذْكِرَةٌ لِّلْمُتَّقِينَ

49. And We certainly know
That there are amongst you
Those that reject (it).

٤٩ وَإِنَّا لَنَعْلَمُ أَنَّ مِنكُم مُّكَذِّبِينَ

50. But truly (Revelation)
Is a cause of sorrow[5672]
For the Unbelievers.

٥٠ وَإِنَّهُۥ لَحَسْرَةٌ عَلَى ٱلْكَٰفِرِينَ

5668. A soothsayer merely pretends to foretell future events of no profound spiritual consequence. Most of his prophecies are frauds, and none of them is meant to teach lessons of real admonition. Such admonition is the work of an honoured prophet.

5669. The right hand is the hand of power and action. Anyone who is seized by his right hand is prevented from acting as he wishes or carrying out his purpose. The argument is that if an imposter were to arise, he would soon be found out. He could not carry out his fraud indefinitely. But the prophets of Allah, however much they are persecuted, gain more and more power every day, as did the Holy Prophet, whose truth, earnestness, sincerity, and love for all, were recognised as his life unfolded itself. (R).

5670. This would effectually stop the functioning of his life.

5671. The protection which the prophets of Allah enjoy in circumstances of danger and difficulty would not be available for imposters. (R).

5672. The Message of Allah is glad tidings for those who believe in Him and follow His Law, for it is a message of Mercy and Forgiveness through repentance and amendment. But in the case of the wicked it is a cause of sorrow, for it denounces sin and proclaims the punishment of those who do not turn from evil.

51. But verily it is Truth[5673]
Of assured certainty.

٥١ وَإِنَّهُۥ لَحَقُّ ٱلْيَقِينِ

52. So glorify the name[5674]
Of thy Lord Most High.

٥٢ فَسَبِّحْ بِٱسْمِ رَبِّكَ ٱلْعَظِيمِ

5673. All Truth is in itself certain. But as received by men, and understood with reference to men's psychology, certainty may have certain degrees. There is the probability or certainty resulting from the application of man's power of judgement and his appraisement of evidence. This is *'ilm al yaqīn*, certainty by reasoning or inference. Then there is the certainty of seeing something with our own eyes. "Seeing is believing." This is *'ain al yaqīn*, certainty by personal inspection. See 102:5, 7. Then, as here, there is the absolute Truth, with no possibility of error of judgement or error of the eye, (which stands for any instrument of sense-perception and any ancillary aids, such as microscopes, etc.). This absolute Truth is the *ḥaqq al yaqīn* spoken of here.

5674. As Allah has given us this absolute Truth through His Revelation, it behooves us to understand it and be grateful to Him. We must celebrate His praises in thought, word and deed.

INTRODUCTION AND SUMMARY: SŪRAH 70—*MA'ĀRIJ*

This is another eschatological Sūrah closely connected in subject matter with the last one. Patience and the mystery of Time will show the ways that climb to Heaven. Sin and Goodness must each eventually come to its own.

Chronologically it belongs to the late early or early middle Makkan period, possibly soon after S. 49.

C. 250.—Man can ascend to the Presence of Allah,
(70:1-44.) But by gradual Ways and in process of Time.
But what is Time? A Day is as fifty
Thousand years, on two different planes.
What seems near is far, and what seems far is near.
So will be Judgement, when things as we know them
Will be transformed completely in a world
All new. Evil will come to its own,
Whatever its masks in this transitory world,
And good will surely reach its goal.
The good life is patient, in prayer
And well-doing, Faith and the earnest search
For the Good Pleasure of Allah, purity and probity.
These are the paths to the Heights and the Gardens
Of Bliss. No evil can enter there:
For the evil are other ways, leading
By steep descent to dark Ignominy!

Sūrah 70.

الجزء التاسع والعشرون سورة المعارج

Al Maʿārij (The Ways of Ascent)

In the name of Allah, Most Gracious,
Most Merciful.

بِسْمِ ٱللَّهِ ٱلرَّحْمَٰنِ ٱلرَّحِيمِ

1. A questioner asked[5675]
About a Penalty
To befall—

سَأَلَ سَآئِلٌۢ بِعَذَابٍ وَاقِعٍ ١

2. The Unbelievers,
The which there is none
To ward off—

لِّلْكَٰفِرِينَ لَيْسَ لَهُۥ دَافِعٌ ٢

3. (A Penalty) from Allah,
Lord of the Ways
Of Ascent.[5676]

مِّنَ ٱللَّهِ ذِى ٱلْمَعَارِجِ ٣

4. The angels and
The Spirit[5677] ascend
Unto Him in a Day[5678]
The measure whereof
Is (as) fifty thousand years:

تَعْرُجُ ٱلْمَلَٰٓئِكَةُ وَٱلرُّوحُ إِلَيْهِ فِى
يَوْمٍ كَانَ مِقْدَارُهُۥ خَمْسِينَ أَلْفَ سَنَةٍ ٤

5. Therefore do thou hold
Patience—a Patience
Of beautiful (contentment).[5679]

فَٱصْبِرْ صَبْرًا جَمِيلًا ٥

5675. Any one might ask. When will Judgement come? That question usually implies doubt. The answer is: the mystery of Time is beyond man's comprehension. But there is something which touches him closely and concerns his conduct and his future welfare; and that is explained in four propositions: (1) Judgement is sure to come, and none can ward it off; (2) it will exact a dreadful Penalty from Unbelievers, but the righteous have nothing to fear; (3) it will be a Penalty from Allah, the Lord of both Justice and Mercy, it will not be merely a blind calamity of fate; and (4) further we are reminded of another title of Allah. "Lord of the Ways of Ascent"; which means that though He sits high on His Throne of Glory, He is not inaccessible, but in His infinite Mercy has provided ways of ascent to Him; see next note.

5676. *Maʿārij:* stairways, ways of ascent. In 43:33, the word is used in its literal sense: "silver stairways on which to go up". Here there is a profound spiritual meaning. Can we reach up to Allah Most High? In His infinite grace He gives that privilege to angels and spiritual beings, man being such in his highest aspect. But the way is not easy, nor can it be travelled in a day. See the next two notes.

5677. *Rūḥ:* "The Spirit", *Cf.* 78:38, "the Spirit and the angels"; and 97:4, "the angels and the Spirit". In 16:2, we have translated *Rūḥ* by *"inspiration"*. Some Commentators understand the angel Gabriel by "the Spirit". But I think a more general meaning is possible, and fits the context better. (R).

5678. *Cf.* 32:4-5, and notes 3632 and 3634.

5679. The prophet of Allah, persecuted and in trouble with the world, should yet hold Patience—not the sort of patience which goes with complaints expressed or suppressed, but the sort of patience that is *content* with the ordering of Allah's world, for he believes and knows it to be good, as did the holy Prophet Muḥammad. Such a patience is akin to Good Pleasure, for it arises from the purest faith and trust in Allah. (R).

6. They see the (Day) indeed As a far-off (event):	إِنَّهُمْ يَرَوْنَهُۥ بَعِيدًا ⦗٦⦘
7. But We see it (Quite) near.[5680]	وَنَرَىٰهُ قَرِيبًا ⦗٧⦘
8. The Day that The sky will be like Molten brass,[5681]	يَوْمَ تَكُونُ ٱلسَّمَآءُ كَٱلْمُهْلِ ⦗٨⦘
9. And the mountians will be Like wool,[5682]	وَتَكُونُ ٱلْجِبَالُ كَٱلْعِهْنِ ⦗٩⦘
10. And no friend will ask After a friend,[5683]	وَلَا يَسْـَٔلُ حَمِيمٌ حَمِيمًا ⦗١٠⦘
11. Though they will be put In sight of each other— The sinner's desire will be: Would that he could Redeem himself from The Penalty of that Day[5684] By (sacrificing) his children,	يُبَصَّرُونَهُمْ ⦗١١⦘ يَوَدُّ ٱلْمُجْرِمُ لَوْ يَفْتَدِى مِنْ عَذَابِ يَوْمِئِذٍۭ بِبَنِيهِ
12. His wife and his brother,	وَصَٰحِبَتِهِۦ وَأَخِيهِ ⦗١٢⦘
13. His kindred who sheltered him.	وَفَصِيلَتِهِ ٱلَّتِى تُـْٔوِيهِ ⦗١٣⦘

5680. The men of evil may see the just retribution for their sins so far off that they doubt whether it would ever come. But in Allah's sight, and on the scale of the Universal Plan, it is quite near; for time as we know it hardly exists in the spiritual world. It may come even in this life: but it is bound to come eventually.

5681. *Cf.* 18:29 (where the wrongdoer will have a drink like melted brass in Hell); and 44:45, (where his food will be like molten brass). Here the appearance of the sky is compared to molten brass, or, as some understand it, like the dregs of oil. What is conveyed by the metaphor is that the beautiful blue sky will melt away.

5682. *Cf.* 101:5, where the metaphor of carded wool is used. The mountains which seem so solid will be like flakes of wool driven by the carder's hand.

5683. The world as we know it will have so completely passed away that the landmarks in the heavens and on earth will also have vanished. Not only that, but the human relationships of mind and heart will have been transformed by sin into something ugly and dreadful. The sinners will be so overcome with terror at the realisation of their personal responsiblity that they will desert their most intimate friends, and indeed their very sight of each other will add to their agony.

5684. The sinner will offer his children, his family, his kinsmen, who had sheltered and protected him—in fact everything on earth that he could—as a ransom for himself. Such would be his selfishness and his agony.

14. And all, all that is
On earth—so it could
Deliver him:[5685]

وَمَن فِي ٱلْأَرْضِ جَمِيعًا ثُمَّ يُنجِيهِ ﴿١٤﴾

15. By no means!
For it would be
The Fire of Hell!—

كَلَّآ إِنَّهَا لَظَىٰ ﴿١٥﴾

16. Plucking out (his being)
Right to the skull!—[5686]

نَزَّاعَةً لِّلشَّوَىٰ ﴿١٦﴾

17. Inviting (all) such
As turn their backs[5687]
And turn away their faces
(From the Right),

تَدْعُوا۟ مَنْ أَدْبَرَ وَتَوَلَّىٰ ﴿١٧﴾

18. And collect (wealth)
And hide it (from use)!

وَجَمَعَ فَأَوْعَىٰ ﴿١٨﴾

19. Truly man was created
Very impatient—[5688]

إِنَّ ٱلْإِنسَٰنَ خُلِقَ هَلُوعًا ﴿١٩﴾

20. Fretful when evil
Touches him;

إِذَا مَسَّهُ ٱلشَّرُّ جَزُوعًا ﴿٢٠﴾

21. And niggardly when
Good reaches him—[5689]

وَإِذَا مَسَّهُ ٱلْخَيْرُ مَنُوعًا ﴿٢١﴾

5685. What would not the sinner give for his own deliverance! But nothing could save him. The Fire of Hell would be roaring for him!

5686. It would be a Fire not only burning his body, but reaching right up to his brains and his understanding and—as is said in 104:7—his heart and affections also. In other words the Penalty typified by the Fire will burn into his inmost being.

5687. The analysis of sin is given in four masterstrokes, of which the first two refer to the will or psychology of the sinner, and the last two to the use he makes of the good things of this life. (1) Sin begins with turning your back to the Right, refusing to face it squarely, running away from it whether from cowardice or indifference. (2) But Conscience and the sense of Right will try to prevent the flight; the Grace of Allah will meet the sinner at all corners and try to reclaim him; the hardened sinner will deliberately turn away his face from it, insult it, and reject it. (3) The result of this psychology will be that he will abandon himself to greed, to the collection of riches, and the acquisition of material advantages to which he is not entitled; this may involve hypocrisy, fraud, and crime. (4) Having acquired the material advantages, the next step will be to keep others out of them, to prevent hoarded wealth from fructifying by circulation, to conceal it from envy or spite. This is the spiritual Rake's Progress.

5688. Man, according to the Plan of Allah, was to be in the best of moulds (95:4). But in order to fulfil his high destiny he was given free will to a limited extent. The wrong use of this free will makes his nature weak (4:28), or hasty (17:11), or impatient, as here. That becomes his nature by his own act, but he is spoken of as so created because of the capacities given to him in his creation.

5689. In adversity he complains and gets into despair. In prosperity he becomes arrogant and forgets other people's rights and his own shortcomings. *Cf.* 41:49-50.

22. Not so those devoted
To Prayer—[5690]

٢٢ إلا المصلين

23. Those who remain steadfast
To their prayer;

٢٣ الذين هم على صلاتهم دائمون

24. And those in whose wealth
Is a recognised right

٢٤ والذين في أموالهم حق معلوم

25. For the (needy) who asks
And him who is prevented
(For some reason from asking);[5691]

٢٥ للسائل والمحروم

26. And those who hold
To the truth of the Day
Of Judgement;

٢٦ والذين يصدقون بيوم الدين

27. And those who fear[5692]
The displeasure of their Lord—

٢٧ والذين هم من عذاب ربهم مشفقون

28. For their Lord's displeasure
Is the opposite of Peace
And Tranquility—[5693]

٢٨ إن عذاب ربهم غير مأمون

29. And those who guard
Their chastity,

٢٩ والذين هم لفروجهم حافظون

30. Except with their wives
And the (captives) whom[5694]

٣٠ إلا على أزواجهم أو ما ملكت

5690. The description of those devoted to Prayer is given in a number of clauses that follow, introduced by the words "Those who. . .". "Devoted to Prayer" is here but another aspect of what is described elsewhere as the Faithful and the Righteous. Devotion to prayer does not mean merely a certain number of formal rites or prostrations. It means a complete surrender of one's being to Allah. This means an earnest approach to and realisation of Allah's Presence ("steadfastness in Prayer"); acts of practical and real charity; and attempt to read this life in terms of the Hereafter; the seeking of the Peace of Allah and avoidance of His displeasure; chastity; probity; true and firm witness; and guarding the sacredness of the Presence (verse 34).

5691. See n. 5001 to 51:19. True charity consists in finding out those in real need, whether they ask or not. Most frequently those who ask are idle men who insolently wish to live upon others. But all cases of those who ask should be duly investigated, in case a little timely help may set the erring on the way. But the man with wealth or talent or opportunity has the further responsibility of searching out those in need of his assistance, in order to show that he holds all gifts in trust for the service of his fellow creatures.

5692. A true fear of Allah is the fear of offending against His Holy Will and Law, and is therefore akin to the love of Allah. It proceeds from the realisation that all true peace and tranquility comes from attuning our will to the Universal Will, and that sin causes discord, disharmony, and displeasure—another name for the Wrath of Allah.

5693. Some would construe this verse: "And their Lord's displeasure is one against which there is no security"; meaning that the punishment of sin may come suddenly at any time, when you least expect it.

5694. Captives of war may be married as such: see 4:25: but their status is inferior to that of free wives until they are free. This institution of the captives of war is now obsolete. Such inferiority of status as there was, was in the status of captivity, not in the status of marriage as such, in which there are no degrees except by local customs, which Islam does not recognise.

Their right hands possess—
For (then) they are not
To be blamed,

أَيْمَٰنُهُمْ فَإِنَّهُمْ غَيْرُ مَلُومِينَ

31. But those who trespass
Beyond this are transgressors—

فَمَنِ ٱبْتَغَىٰ وَرَآءَ ذَٰلِكَ فَأُو۟لَٰٓئِكَ هُمُ ٱلْعَادُونَ ٣١

32. And those who respect
Their trusts and covenants;[5695]

وَٱلَّذِينَ هُمْ لِأَمَٰنَٰتِهِمْ وَعَهْدِهِمْ رَٰعُونَ ٣٢

33. And those who stand firm
In their testimonies;[5696]

وَٱلَّذِينَ هُم بِشَهَٰدَٰتِهِمْ قَآئِمُونَ ٣٣

34. And those who guard
(The sacredness) of their
worship—[5697]

وَٱلَّذِينَ هُمْ عَلَىٰ صَلَاتِهِمْ يُحَافِظُونَ ٣٤

35. Such will be
The honoured ones
In the Gardens (of Bliss).

أُو۟لَٰٓئِكَ فِى جَنَّٰتٍ مُّكْرَمُونَ ٣٥

SECTION 2.

36. Now what is
The matter with the Unbelievers
That they rush madly
Before thee—[5698]

فَمَالِ ٱلَّذِينَ كَفَرُوا۟ قِبَلَكَ مُهْطِعِينَ ٣٦

37. From the right
And from the left,
In crowds?

عَنِ ٱلْيَمِينِ وَعَنِ ٱلشِّمَالِ عِزِينَ ٣٧

38. Does every man of them
Long to enter
The Garden of Bliss?

أَيَطْمَعُ كُلُّ ٱمْرِئٍ مِّنْهُمْ
أَن يُدْخَلَ جَنَّةَ نَعِيمٍ ٣٨

5695. For obligations of trusts and covenants, express or implied, see n. 682 to 5:1. They are just as sacred in ordinary everyday life as they are in special spiritual relationships. In addition, our life itself, and such reason and talents as we possess, as well as our wealth and possessions are trusts, of which we must fulfil the duties punctiliously.

5696. If we know any truth of any kind, to that we must bear witness, as affecting the lives or interests of our fellow beings—firmly, not half-heartedly, without fear or favour, even if it causes loss or trouble to us, or if it loses us friends or associates.

5697. Worship or prayer includes honest work, charity, and every good deed. To guard the sacredness of this ideal is to sum up the whole duty of man. We began with "steadfastness in prayer" in verse 23 above, and after a review of various aspects of the good man's life, close with the sacredness of worship, *i.e.*, living as in the sight of Allah.

5698. *Before thee.* The Unbelievers did not believe in a Hereafter. When the Bliss of the Hereafter was described, as in the last verse, they ridiculed it and pretended to be running in for it as in a race. They are here rebuked in the same tone of sarcasm.

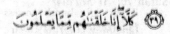

39. By no means!
For We have created them
Out of the (base matter)
They know![5699]

كَلَّآ إِنَّا خَلَقْنَٰهُم مِّمَّا يَعْلَمُونَ ﴿٣٩﴾

40. Now I do
Call to witness[5700]
The Lord of all points
In the East and the West[5701]
That We can certainly—[5702]

فَلَآ أُقْسِمُ بِرَبِّ ٱلْمَشَٰرِقِ
وَٱلْمَغَٰرِبِ إِنَّا لَقَٰدِرُونَ ﴿٤٠﴾

41. Substitute for them
Better (men) than they;
And We are not
To be defeated
(In Our Plan).

عَلَىٰٓ أَن نُّبَدِّلَ خَيْرًا مِّنْهُمْ
وَمَا نَحْنُ بِمَسْبُوقِينَ ﴿٤١﴾

42. So leave them
To plunge in vain talk
And play about,[5703]
Until they encounter
That Day of theirs which
They have been promised!—

فَذَرْهُمْ يَخُوضُوا۟
وَيَلْعَبُوا۟ حَتَّىٰ يُلَٰقُوا۟
يَوْمَهُمُ ٱلَّذِى يُوعَدُونَ ﴿٤٢﴾

43. The Day whereon
They will issue
From their sepulchres
In sudden haste
As if they were
Rushing to a goalpost
(Fixed for them)—[5704]

يَوْمَ يَخْرُجُونَ
مِنَ ٱلْأَجْدَاثِ سِرَاعًا كَأَنَّهُمْ
إِلَىٰ نُصُبٍ يُوفِضُونَ ﴿٤٣﴾

44. Their eyes lowered
In dejection—

خَٰشِعَةً أَبْصَٰرُهُمْ ﴿٤٤﴾

5699. The animal part of man is nothing to be proud of, and they know it. It is by spiritual effort, and long preparation through a good life that a man can rise above the mere animal part of him to his high dignity as a spiritual being, and his noble destiny in the Hereafter.

5700. For the form of adjuration, *Cf.* 69:38, n. 5665; also 56:75. Here the witness placed before us by Allah is His own power and glory manifested in the splendour of sunrise and sunset at different points through the solar year.

5701. See n. 4034 to 37:5. If Allah has such power in the wonderful phenomena of the rising of the sun at varying points, repeated year after year, can you not see that He can easily substitute better men than you Unbelievers and blasphemers?

5702. The transition from the singular "I" to the plural "We" may be noted. See n. 56 to 2:38

5703. Their talk, their scepticism, is vain, because all spiritual evidence is against it, it is like the foolish play of people who do not think seriously. But the tremendous Day of Judgement and Reality will come, as described in the next two verses.

5704. Now there will be a definite Goalpost or Banner or Standard of Truth fixed, which all must acknowledge. But they will acknowledge it in shame and dejection. For the time for their repentance and amendment will then have passed.

Ignominy covering them
(All over)!
Such is the Day
The which they
Are promised!

تَرْهَقُهُمْ ذِلَّةٌ
ذَٰلِكَ الْيَوْمُ الَّذِي كَانُوا يُوعَدُونَ

INTRODUCTION AND SUMMARY TO SŪRAH 71—*NŪḤ*

This is another early Makkan Sūrah, of which the date has no significance. The theme is that while Good must uphold the standard of Truth and Righteousness, a stage is reached when it must definitely part company with Evil, lest Evil should spread its corruption. The story of Noah's agony is almost a Parable for the Holy Prophet's persecution in the Makkan period.

C. 251.—The Prophet's Message, as was that of Noah,
(71:1-28.) Is a warning against sin, and the Good News of Mercy
Through the door of Repentance: for Allah is loving
And long-suffering, and His Signs are within us
And around us. But the sinners are obstinate:
They plot against Righteousness, and place their trust
In futile falsehoods. They will be swept away,
And the earth will be purged of Evil. Let us
Pray for Mercy and Grace for ourselves,
For those nearest and dearest to us,
And for all who turn in faith to Allah.
In all ages and all countries,
And amongst all Peoples.

Sūrah 71.

Nūḥ (Noah)

In the name of Allah, Most Gracious,
Most Merciful.

بِسۡمِ ٱللَّهِ ٱلرَّحۡمَٰنِ ٱلرَّحِيمِ

1. We sent Noah[5705]
To his People
(With the Command):
"Do thou warn thy People
Before there comes to them
A grievous Penalty."

(١) إِنَّآ أَرۡسَلۡنَا نُوحًا إِلَىٰ قَوۡمِهِۦٓ
أَنۡ أَنذِرۡ قَوۡمَكَ مِن قَبۡلِ أَن يَأۡتِيَهُمۡ
عَذَابٌ أَلِيمٞ

2. He said: "O my People!
I am to you
A Warner, clear and open:[5706]

(٢) قَالَ يَٰقَوۡمِ إِنِّي لَكُمۡ نَذِيرٞ مُّبِينٌ

3. "That ye should worship
Allah, fear Him,
and obey me:[5707]

(٣) أَنِ ٱعۡبُدُواْ ٱللَّهَ وَٱتَّقُوهُ وَأَطِيعُونِ

4. "So He may forgive you
Your sins and give you
Respite for a stated Term:
For when the Term given
By Allah is accomplished,
It cannot be put forward:[5708]
If ye only knew."

(٤) يَغۡفِرۡ لَكُم مِّن ذُنُوبِكُمۡ
وَيُؤَخِّرۡكُمۡ إِلَىٰٓ أَجَلٖ مُّسَمًّىۚ
إِنَّ أَجَلَ ٱللَّهِ إِذَا جَآءَ لَا يُؤَخَّرُۚ
لَوۡ كُنتُمۡ تَعۡلَمُونَ

5. He said: "O my Lord!
I have called to my People
Night and day:

(٥) قَالَ رَبِّ إِنِّي دَعَوۡتُ قَوۡمِي لَيۡلٗا وَنَهَارٗا

5705. Noah's mission is referred to in many places. See specially 11:25-49 and notes. His contemporaries had completely abandoned the moral law. A purge had to be made, and the great Flood made it. This gives a new starting point in history for Noah's People—*i.e.*, for the remnant saved in the Ark.

5706. His Warning was to be both clear *(i.e.*, unambigous) and open *(i.e.*, publicly proclaimed). Both these meanings are implied in *Mubīn. Cf.* 67:26. The meaning of the Warning was obviously that if they had repented, they would have obtained mercy.

5707. Three aspects of man's duty are emphasised: (1) true worship with heart and soul; (2) God-fearing recognition that all evil must lead to self-deterioration and Judgement; (3) hence repentance and amendment of life, and obedience to good men's counsels.

5708. Allah gives respite freely; but it is for Him to give it. His command is definite and final; neither man nor any other authority can alter or in any way modify it. If we could only realise this to the full in our inmost soul, it would be best for us and lead to our happiness.

6. "But my call only
Increases (their) flight
(From the Right."[5709]

فَلَمْ يَزِدْهُمْ دُعَآءِىٓ إِلَّا فِرَارًا ٦

7. "And every time I have
Called to them, that Thou
Mightest forgive them,
They have (only) thrust
Their fingers into their ears,
Covered themselves up with[5710]
Their garments, grown obstinate,
And given themselves up
To arrogance.

وَإِنِّى كُلَّمَا دَعَوْتُهُمْ ٧
لِتَغْفِرَ لَهُمْ جَعَلُوٓا۟ أَصَٰبِعَهُمْ فِىٓ ءَاذَانِهِمْ
وَٱسْتَغْشَوْا۟ ثِيَابَهُمْ وَأَصَرُّوا۟
وَٱسْتَكْبَرُوا۟ ٱسْتِكْبَارًا

8. "So I have called to them
Aloud;"

ثُمَّ إِنِّى دَعَوْتُهُمْ جِهَارًا ٨

9. "Further I have spoken
To them in public[5711]
And secretly in private,"

ثُمَّ إِنِّىٓ أَعْلَنتُ لَهُمْ وَأَسْرَرْتُ لَهُمْ إِسْرَارًا ٩

10. "Saying. 'Ask forgiveness
From your Lord;
For He is Oft-Forgiving;'"

فَقُلْتُ ٱسْتَغْفِرُوا۟ رَبَّكُمْ إِنَّهُۥ كَانَ غَفَّارًا ١٠

11. "'He will send rain[5712]
To you in abundance;

يُرْسِلِ ٱلسَّمَآءَ عَلَيْكُم مِّدْرَارًا ١١

12. "'Give you increase
In wealth and sons;
And bestow on you

وَيُمْدِدْكُم بِأَمْوَٰلٍ وَبَنِينَ وَيَجْعَل لَّكُمْ ١٢

5709. When convincing arguments and warnings are placed before sinners, there are two kinds of reactions. Those who are wise receive admonition, repent, and bring forth fruits of repentance, *i.e.*, amend their lives and turn to Allah. On the other hand, those who are callous to any advice take it up as a reproach, fly farther and farther from righteousness, and shut out more and more the channels through which Allah's healing Grace can reach them and work for them.

5710. The literal meaning would be that, just as they thrust their fingers into their ears to prevent the voice of the admonisher reaching them, so they covered their bodies with their garments that the light of truth should not penetrate to them and that they should not even be seen by the Preacher. But there is a further symbolic meaning."Their garments" are the adornments of vanities, their evil habits, customs, and traditions, and their ephemeral interests and standards. They drew them closer round them to prevent the higher Light reaching them. They grew obstinate and gave themselves up to the grossest form of selfish arrogance.

5711. Noah used all the resources of the earnest preacher: he dinned the Message of Allah into their ears; he spoke in public places; and he took individuals into his confidence and appealed to them; but all in vain.

5712. They had perhaps been suffering from drought or famine. If they had taken the message in the right way, the rain would have been a blessing to them. They took it in the wrong way, and the rain was a curse to them, for it flooded the country and drowned the wicked generation. In the larger Plan, it was a blessing all the same; for it purged the world, and gave it a new start, morally and spiritually.

Gardens and bestow on you
Rivers (of flowing water).[5713]

جَنَّٰتٍ وَيَجْعَل لَّكُمْ أَنْهَٰرًا

13. "'What is the matter
With you, that ye
Place not your hope
For kindness and long-suffering
In Allah—[5713-A]

مَّا لَكُمْ لَا تَرْجُونَ لِلَّهِ وَقَارًا ١٣

14. "'Seeing that it is He
That has created you
In diverse stages?[5714]

وَقَدْ خَلَقَكُمْ أَطْوَارًا ١٤

15. "'See ye not
How Allah has created
The seven heavens
One above another,[5715]

أَلَمْ تَرَوْا كَيْفَ خَلَقَ ٱللَّهُ
سَبْعَ سَمَٰوَٰتٍ طِبَاقًا ١٥

16. "'And made the moon
A light in their midst,
and made the sun
As a (Glorious) Lamp?[5716]

وَجَعَلَ ٱلْقَمَرَ فِيهِنَّ نُورًا
وَجَعَلَ ٱلشَّمْسَ سِرَاجًا ١٦

17. "'And Allah has produced
You from the earth,
Growing (gradually),[5717]

وَٱللَّهُ أَنۢبَتَكُم مِّنَ ٱلْأَرْضِ نَبَاتًا ١٧

18. "'And in the End
He will return you
Into the (earth),

ثُمَّ يُعِيدُكُمْ فِيهَا ١٨

5713. Each of these blessings—rain and crops, wealth and manpower, flourishing gardens, and perennial streams—are indications of prosperity, and have not only a material but also a spiritual meaning. Note the last point, "rivers of flowing water". The perennial springs make the prosperity as it were permanent; they indicate a settled population, honest and contented, and enjoying their blessings here on earth as the foretaste of the eternal joys of heaven.

5713-A. An alternative translation would be "...that ye fear Allah's Message", *i.e.*, why don't you fear Allah's Majesty. His greatness and consequent punishment for your sinfulness and hope for His mercy, kindness and reward for your faith and good deeds. The words of the verse contain the twin strands—fear and hope—simultaneously.

5714. *Cf.* 22:5, and notes 2773-2777; also 23:12-17, and notes 2872-2875. The meaning here may be even wider. Man in his various states exhibits various wonderful qualities or capacities, mental and spiritual, that may be compared with the wonderful workings of nature on the earth and in the heavens. Will he not then be grateful for these Mercies and turn to Allah. Who created all these marvels?

5715. See n. 5559 to 67:3.

5716. *Cf.* 25:61, where the sun is referred to as the glorious Lamp of the heavens: "Blessed is He Who made the Constellations in the skies, and placed therein a lamp, and a moon giving light."

5717. *Cf.* 3:37, where the growth of the child Mary the Mother of Jesus is described by the same word *nabāt*, ordinarily denoting the growth of plants and trees. The simile is that if a seed sown, that germinates, grows, and dies, and goes back to the earth. In man, there is the further process of the Resurrection *Cf.* also 20:55.

And raise you forth
(Again at the Resurrection)?

وَيُخْرِجُكُمْ إِخْرَاجًا

19. "'And Allah has made
The earth for you
As a carpet (spread out),[5718]

وَاللَّهُ جَعَلَ لَكُمُ الْأَرْضَ بِسَاطًا ﴿١٩﴾

20. "'That ye may go about
Therein, in spacious roads.'"[5719]

لِتَسْلُكُوا مِنْهَا سُبُلًا فِجَاجًا ﴿٢٠﴾

SECTION 2.

21. Noah said: "O my Lord!
They have disobeyed me,
But they follow (men)[5719-A]
Whose wealth and children
Give them no Increase
But only Loss.

قَالَ نُوحٌ رَبِّ إِنَّهُمْ عَصَوْنِي ﴿٢١﴾
وَاتَّبَعُوا مَنْ لَمْ يَزِدْهُ مَالُهُ وَوَلَدُهُ
إِلَّا خَسَارًا

22. "And they have devised
A tremendous Plot.[5720]

وَمَكَرُوا مَكْرًا كُبَّارًا ﴿٢٢﴾

23. "And they have said
(To each other),
'Abandon not your gods:[5721]
Abandon neither Wadd
Nor Suwā', neither
Yaghūth nor Ya'ūq,
Nor Nasr—

وَقَالُوا لَا تَذَرُنَّ آلِهَتَكُمْ ﴿٢٣﴾
وَلَا تَذَرُنَّ وَدًّا وَلَا سُوَاعًا
وَلَا يَغُوثَ وَيَعُوقَ وَنَسْرًا

24. "They have already
Misled many, and
Grant Thou no increase

وَقَدْ أَضَلُّوا كَثِيرًا وَلَا تَزِدِ ﴿٢٤﴾

5718. *Cf.* 22:53.

5719. *Fijāj* implies valley roads or passes between mountains. Though there are mountain chains on the earth, Allah's artistry has provided even in such regions, valleys and channels by which men may go about. Mountain roads usually follow the valleys.

5719-A. Sinners always resent it as a reproach that righteous men should speak to them for their own good. They prefer smooth flatterers, and they worship power even though the depositories of power are selfish men, who neither profit themselves nor profit others by the wealth and manpower that they collect round themselves. They forget that mere material things may be a delusion and a snare unless the moral and spiritual factor behind them sanctifies them.

5720. Having got material resources the wicked devise plots to get rid of the righteous whose presence is a reproach to them. For a time their plots may seem tremendous and have the appearance of success, but they can never defeat Allah's Purpose.

5721. For an account of how these Pagan gods and superstitions connected with them originated, and how they became adopted into the Arabian Pagan Pantheon, see Appendix X at the end of this Sūrah.

To the wrongdoers but in
Staying (from their mark)."[5722]

ٱلظَّٰلِمِينَ إِلَّا ضَلَٰلًا

25. Because of their sins
They were drowned
(In the flood),[5723]
And were made to enter
The Fire (of Punishment);
And they found—
In lieu of Allah—
None to help them.

﴿٢٥﴾ مِّمَّا خَطِيٓـَٰٔتِهِمْ أُغْرِقُوا۟
فَأُدْخِلُوا۟ نَارًا فَلَمْ يَجِدُوا۟ لَهُم
مِّن دُونِ ٱللَّهِ أَنصَارًا

26. And Noah said:
"O my Lord! Leave not
Of the Unbelievers,
A single one on earth![5724]

﴿٢٦﴾ وَقَالَ نُوحٌ رَّبِّ لَا تَذَرْ عَلَى
ٱلْأَرْضِ مِنَ ٱلْكَٰفِرِينَ دَيَّارًا

27. "For, if Thou dost leave
(Any of) them, they will
But mislead Thy devotees,
And they will breed none
But wicked ungrateful ones.

﴿٢٧﴾ إِنَّكَ إِن تَذَرْهُمْ يُضِلُّوا۟ عِبَادَكَ
وَلَا يَلِدُوٓا۟ إِلَّا فَاجِرًا كَفَّارًا

28. "O my Lord! Forgive me,
My parents, all who
Enter my house in Faith,
And (all) believing men
And believing women:[5725]
And to the wrongdoers
Grant Thou no increase
But in Perdition!"[5726]

﴿٢٨﴾ رَّبِّ ٱغْفِرْ لِى وَلِوَٰلِدَىَّ
وَلِمَن دَخَلَ بَيْتِىَ مُؤْمِنًا
وَلِلْمُؤْمِنِينَ وَٱلْمُؤْمِنَٰتِ
وَلَا تَزِدِ ٱلظَّٰلِمِينَ إِلَّا تَبَارًۢا

5722. Such Pagan superstitions and cults do not add to human knowledge or human well-being. They only increase error and wrongdoing. For example, how much lewdness resulted from the Greek and Roman Saturnalia! And how much lewdness results from ribald Holy songs! This is the natural result, and Noah in his bitterness of spirit prays that Allah's grace may be cut off from men who hug them to their hearts. They mislead others: let them miss their own mark! See also verse 28 below.

5723. The Punishment of sin seizes the soul from every side and in every form. Water (drowning) indicates death by suffocation, through the nose, ears, eyes, mouth, throat, and lungs. Fire has the opposite effects; it burns the skin, the limbs, the flesh, the brains, the bones, and every part of the body. So the destruction wrought by sin is complete from all points of view. And yet it is not death (20:74); for death would be a merciful release from the Penalty, and the soul steeped in sin has closed the gates of Allah's Mercy on itself. There they will abide, unless and "except as Allah willeth" (6:128). For time and eternity, as we conceive them now, have no meaning in the wholly new world which the soul enters after death or Judgement.

5724. The Flood was sent in order to purge all sin. The prayer of Noah is not vindictive. It simply means, "Cut off all the roots of sin". See next note.

5725. Indeed he prays for himself, his parents, his guests, and all who in earnest faith turn to Allah, in all ages and in all places. Praying for their forgiveness is also praying for the destruction of sin.

5726. This is slightly different in form from verse 24 above, where see n. 5722. See also last note.

APPENDIX X.

Ancient Forms of Pagan Worship (see 71:23, n. 5721)

From prehistoric times man has sought to worship powers of nature, or symbols representing those powers, or idols representing those symbols. In vulgar minds they become debased superstitions, and seem to come into competition with the worship of the one True God.

2. The five names mentioned in 71:23 represent some of the oldest Pagan cults, before the Flood as well as after the Flood, though the names themselves are in the form in which they were worshipped by local Arab tribes. The names of the tribes have been preserved to us by the Commentators, but they are of no more than archaeological interest to us now. But the names of the false gods are interesting to us from the point of view of comparative religion, as, under one form or another, such cults still exist in countries which have not accepted the Gospel of Unity, as they have always existed since man turned from his Maker and Sustainer to the worship of created things or invented fancies.

3. The names of the five false gods and the symbols under which they were represented were as follows:

Pagan god	**Shape**	**Quality represented**
1. Wadd	Man	Manly Power
2. Suwā'	Woman	Mutability, Beauty
3. Yaghūth	Lion (or Bull)	Brute Strength
4. Ya'ūq	Horse	Swiftness
5. Nasr	Eagle, or Vulture, or Falcon	Sharp Sight, Insight

It is not clear whether these names are to be connected with true Arabic verbal roots or are merely Arabicised forms of names derived from foreign cults, such as those of Babylonia or Assyria, the region of Noah's Flood. The latter supposition is probable. Even in the case of *Wadd* (Affection, Love) and *Nasr* (Eagle), which are good Arabic words, it is doubtful whether they are not, in this connection, translations or corruptions of words denoting foreign cults.

4. In studying ancient comparative mythologies we must never forget the following facts. (1) Men's ideas of God always tend to be anthropomorphic. The qualities which they admire they transfer to their godhead. (2) But fear in primitive man also leads to the transfer of anything mysterious or imagined to be injurious, to the Pantheon. Such things have to be placated in order that they may not injure man. Thus, in popular Hinduism the goddess of smallpox, which causes terror over an ignorant countryside, has to be worshipped, placated, or appeased with sacrifice. (3) This leads to the worship of animals noxious to man, such as serpent worship, which has prevailed and still prevails in many primitive areas. In ancient Egyptian mythology the Crocodile (so common in the Nile), the Dog, the Bull, and the Ibis were worshipped both literally and symbolically. See Appendix V. (4) But as men's knowledge grows, and they observe the wonderful heavenly bodies and their motions, they begin to feel their sublimity, beauty and mystery, and they transfer their worship to the heavenly bodies. The first great astronomers in the ancient world were the Babylonians

and Chaldaeans. Among them was Abraham's homeland. The allegory of Abraham (6:74-82 and notes) points to the importance of the cult of the worship of heavenly bodies and the fallacy in them. "It is those who believe, and confuse not their beliefs with wrong—that are truly in security, for they are on right guidance" (6:82). The Sabaean worship of heavenly bodies in Arabia had probably its source in Chaldaea (see last paragraph of n. 76 to 2:62). (5) A further refined step in Paganism is to worship abstractions, to treat concrete things as symbols of abstact qualities which they represent. For example, the planet Saturn with its slow motion was treated as phlegmatic and evil. The planet Mars with its fiery red light was treated as betokening war and havoc and evil, and so on. Jupiter, with its magnificent golden light, was treated as lucky and benignant to any who came under its influence. Venus became the symbol and the goddess of carnal love. The Pagan Arabs erected Time *(Dahr)* into a deity, existing from eternity to eternity, and dispensing good and ill fortune to man. The ancient Aegean religion treated the vital principle in the same way, as spontaneous and eternal, and traces of this are found in many religions, ancient and modern. (6) The next step was to reincarnate as it were these qualities in beings of flesh and blood, with lives, feelings, and passions like those of ordinary men and women, and to fill up a confused Pantheon with gods and goddesses that quarrelled, hated, loved, were jealous, and suffered or enjoyed life like human beings. In such a Pantheon there was room for demi-gods and real human heroes that were worshipped as gods. The Greek poets and artists were past masters in carrying out this process, under cover of which they discussed profound human problems with great power. They made religion dramatic. While they gained in humanism, they lost the purer spiritual conceptions which lift the divine world far above the futilities and crimes of this life. Hierarchical Christianity has suffered from this inheritance of the Greek tradition. (7) Where there was a commingling of peoples and cultures, several of these ideas and processes got mixed up together. Gods and goddesses of different origins were identified with one another, *e.g.* Artemis, the chaste virgin huntress goddesss of the Greek Pantheon, was identified with Diana of the Romans, Diana of the Ephesians (representing the teeming like of nature), and Selene the cold moon-goddess. Similarly Diana was identified with the Egyptian Isis, and Diana's twin brother Apollo (the sun) with the Egyptian Osiris. Forces of nature, animals, trees, qualities, astronomical bodies, and various other factors got mixed up together, and formed a shapeless medley of superstitions, which are all condemned by Islam.

5. To revert to the worship of the heavenly bodies. The countless fixed stars in the firmament occupied always the same relative positions in the heavens, and did not impress the imagination of the ancients like the objects which stood out vividly with mysterious laws of relative motion. A few individual stars did attract the worshippers' attention: *e.g.*, Sirius the Dog star, the brightest fixed star in the heavens, with a bluish tinge in its light, and Algol the variable star, being Beta of the constellation Perseus, whose variation can be perceived by the naked eye in two or three nights, became connected with many legends, myths, and superstitions. It is probably Sirius that is referred to as the fixed star in the Parable of Abraham (6:76). With regard to the fixed stars in their myriads, the astronomers turned their fancy to devising Groups or Constellations. But the moving "stars", or planets, each with its own individual laws of motion, stood out to them personified, each with a motion and therefore will or influence of its own. As they knew and understood them, they were seven in number, *viz.*: (1) and (2) the moon and the sun, the two objects which most closely and indubitably influence the tides, the temperatures, and the life on our planet: (3) and (4) the two inner planets, Mercury and Venus, which are morning and evening stars, and never travel far from the sun; and (5), (6) and (7) Mars, Jupiter, and Saturn, the outer planets, whose elongations from the sun on the ecliptic can be as wide as possible. The number seven became itself a mystic number, as explained in n. 5526 to 65:12.

6. It will be noticed that the sun and the moon and the five planets got identified each with a living deity, god or goddess, with characteristics and qualities of its own. The solar myth was a myth of very fruitful vitality, and got mixed up with many other myths and ideas. In late Roman religion it appears in the story of Apollo, the sun-god of light and learning and of manly

beauty, twin brother to Diana the moon-goddess. In ancient Egypt it appears in the myth of Horus, the falcon-eyed, or Ra or Re, the Eye, which sees all things. Further, the eagle, or falcon, or hawk, became itself identified with the sun, with its piercing light. The sun myth mixes itself up with the myth of the Nile and with the cycle of legends connected with Isis and Osiris, who were subsequently identified with the moon and the sun divinities. In Babylon the name Shamash (Arabic, *Shams)* proclaims the glory of the sun-god corresponding to the old Sumerian Utu of Babbar, while the hymns to Sūrya (the sun) in the Rig-Veda and the cult of Mithra in Persia proclaim the dominance of sun-worship.

7. Moon-worship was equally popular in various forms. I have already referred to the classical legends of Apollo and Diana, twin brother and sister, representing the sun and the moon. The Egyptain Khonsu, traversing the sky in a boat, referred to the moon, and the moon legends also got mixed up with those about the god of magic, Thoth, and the Ibis. In the Vedic religion of India the moon-god was Soma, the lord of the planets, and the name was also applied to the juice which was the drink of the gods. It may be noted that the moon was a male divinity in ancient India; it was also a male divinity in ancient Semitic religion, and the Arabic word for the moon *(qamar)* is of the masculine gender. On the other hand, the Arabic word for the sun *(shams)* is of the feminine gender. The Pagan Arabs evidently looked upon the sun as a goddess and the moon as a god.

8. Of the five planets, perhaps Venus as the evening star and the morning star alternately impressed itself most on the imagination of astro-mythology. This planet was in different places considered both male and female. In the Bible (Isaiah, xiv. 12), the words "How art thou fallen, O Lucifer, son of the morning!" are understood to refer to the Morning Star in the first instance, and by analogy to the King of Babylon. The Fathers of the Christian Church, on the other hand, transferred the name Lucifer to Satan, the power of evil. Mercury is a less conspicuous planet, and was looked upon as a child in the family, the father and mother being the moon and the sun, or the sun and the moon (according to the sex attributed to these divinities), or else either the sun or moon was the father and Venus the mother (the sexes being inter-changeable in the myths). Of the three outer planets. Jupiter is the most conspicuous: indeed, after the sun and the moon, it is the most conspicuous object in the heavens, and was reputed to be beneficent and to bestow good fortune. The sun and the moon being considered in a class apart, Jupiter was considered the father of the planets, and possibly his worship got occasionally mixed up with that of the sun. Mars and Saturn, as has already been stated, were considered malevolent planets, to be feared for the mischief that they might do; for the Pagan Pantheons worshipped powers both of good and evil.

9. It is remarkable that the days of the week are named after the seven planets of geocentric astronomy, and if we take them in alternate sequence they indicate the order in which their heavens were arranged with reference to proximity to the earth. The following table represents this grouping:—

Planet	**Presiding god or goddess**	**Day of the week in alternate sequence**
Moon	Diana	Sunday
Mercury	Mercury	Tuesday
Venus	Venus	Thursday
The Sun	Apollo	Saturday
Mars	Mars	Monday
Jupiter	Jupiter	Wednesday
Saturn	Saturn	Friday

This alternate sequence is carried into a circle, as the total number is seven, itself a mystic number.

10. These cross-currents and mixtures of nature-worship, astral-worship, heroworship, worship of abstract qualities, etc., resulted in a medley of debasing superstitions which are summed up in the five names, Wadd, Suwā', Yaghūth, Ya'ūq, and Nasr, as noted in paragraph 3 above. The time of Noah is taken to be the peak of superstition and false worship, and the most ancient cults may thus be symbolically brought under these heads. If wadd and Suwā' represented Man and Woman, they might well represent human self-glorification, the worship of Self as against Allah, or they might represent the worship of Manly Power and Female Beauty, or other abstract qualities of that kind. On the other hand, it is possible that the worship of Jupiter and Venus itself not mixed up with the worship of the sun-moon pair. One pair being identified with another pair in a Septet, the number seven was reduced to five, and the five (itself a mystic number) might itself represent the seven planets as then worshipped. Further, it may be that Nasr (the vulture, falcon, hawk, or eagle, the Egyptian Horus) also represents a solar myth, mixed up with the cult of the planets. These cross-currents of astro-myuthological mixtures of cults are well-known to students of ancient popular religions. If the five names, from another angle of vision, represent qualities, the Wadd-Suwā' pair (Sun-Moon, Jupiter-Venus) would represent manly power and womanly beauty or mutability respectively, and the three remaining ones (paragraph 3) might represent Brute Strength, like that of a Bull or a Lion; Swiftness like that of a Horse or sharpness (of sight or intelligence) like that of a vulture, hawk, or eagle.

11. It may be noted that the five names of deities mentioned here to a represent very ancient religious cults are well-chosen. They are not the names of the deities best known in Makkah, but rather those which survived as fragments of very ancient cults among the outlying tribes of Arabia, which were influenced by the cults of Mesopotamia (Noah's country). The Pagan deities best known in the Ka'bah and round about Makkah were Lāt, 'Uzzā, and Manāt. (Manāt was also known round Yathrib, which afterwards became Madīnah.) See 53:19-20. They were all female goddesses. Lāt almost certainly represents another wave of sun-worship: the sun being feminine in Arabic and in Semitic languages generally. "Lāt" may be the original of the Greek "Leto", the mother of Apollo the sun-god (*Encyclopcedia of Islam,* I, p. 380). If so, the name was brought in prehistoric times from South Arabia by the great Incense Route (n. 3816 to 34:18) to the Mediterranean. 'Uzzā probably represents the planet venus. The origin of Manāt is not quite clear, but it would not be surprising if it also turned out to be astral. The 350 idols established by the Pagans in the Ka'bah probably represented the 360 days of an inaccurate solar yar. This was the actual "modern" Pagan worship as known to the Quraysh contemporary with our Prophet. In sharp contrast to this is mentioned the ancient antediluvian worship under five heads, of which fragments persisted in outlying places, as they still persist in different forms and under different names in all parts of the world where the pure worship of Allah in unity and truth is not firmly established in the minds and hearts of men.

References: The classical work on Arabian idol-worship is Ibn al Kalbī's *Kitāb al aṣnām*, of the late second century of the Hijrah. The book is not easily accessible. Our doctors of religion have evinced no interest in the study of ancient cults, or in comparative religion, and most of them had not before them the results of modern archaeology. But a modern school of Egyptian archaeologists is arising, which takes a great deal of interest in the antiquities of their own country. For astral worship consult Hastings' *Encyclopaedia of Religion and Ethics*, articles on "Sun, Moon, and Stars," as worshipped in different countries. Consult also Sir E.A. Wallis Budge, *Gods of the Egyptians*, London 1904; A.H. Sayce, *Religions of Ancient Egypt* and *Babylonia*, Gifford Lectures, Edinburgh 1902: M. Jastrow, *Religion of Babylonia and Assyria*, Boston 1898: E.W. Hopkins, *Religions of India*, London 1896; G.A. Barton, *Sketches of Semitic Origins*, New York 1902. Any Classical Dictionary would give the details of Greek and Roman Mythology. It is curious that the Indus Civilization, which resembles the Second Pre-diluvian Culture of Elam and Mesopotamia, does not clearly disclose any signs of astral worship. But this study is still in its tentative stage. There is tree and animal worship, phallic worship, and the worship of the great Mother-goddess. Animal worship regards strength, courage virility, or swiftness, as in the Pagan Arabian deities we have been considering. See Sir John Marshall, *Mohenjo Daro and the Indus Civilization*, 3 vols. London 1931.

Sir J.G. Frazer, in his *Adonis, Attis,* and *Osiris* (4th ed. London 1914, Vol. i, pp. 8-9) refers to *Allatu* or Eresh-Kigal as "the stern queen of the internal regions" in Babylonian religion: she was the goddess of the nether regions, of darkness and desolation, as her counterpart Ishtar was the chief goddess of the upper regions, or reproduction and fertility, associated with the planet Venus.

INTRODUCITON AND SUMMARY: SŪRAH 72—*AL JINN*

This is a late Makkan Sūrah, of which we can be tolerably certain of the date. It was two years before the Hijrah, when the Prophet, despised and rejected in his native city of Makkah, went to evangelise the lordly men of Ṭā'if. They maltreated him and nearly killed him; what caused him even greater pain was the maltreatment of the humble and lowly men who went with him. Ṭabarī has handed down that memorable Prayer of faith and humility which he offered in the midst of his suffering. On his return journey to Makkah, a glorious vision was revealed to him—hidden spiritual forces working for him—people not known to him accepting his mission while his own people were still rejecting him. Within two months some strangers from Madīnah had privately met him and laid the foundations of that Hijrah which was to change the fate of Arabia and the course of world history.

C. 252.—Spiritual Truth finds its lodgement
(72:1-28.) In all sorts of unexpected places, and in all sorts
Of unexpected ways. The man of God,
When most depressed by the buffets of a world
Steeped in selfishness, sees a glorious vision:
Hidden spiritual forces work for him,
Make known the truth in marvellous ways,
And proclaim the Goodness and Judgement of Allah.
They reject all Error and lead others to purify
Their wills and come to Allah. Behold!
Every place and time, every gift
Is meet for the service of Allah, the One,
The True, Whose Word the righteous one
Proclaims and must proclaim at all cost.
Man's Duty is plain, but in the Kingdom
Of Allah, through Allah's chosen ones,
We rise to higher and higher Mysteries,
As may be expedient for us. Yet when
Or how our End may be, is not given
To man to know: let him but take
The Treasures well-guarded, that come to him,
And praise the Lord of all Knowledge and Wisdom!

Sūrah 72.

الجزء التاسع والعشرون — سورة الجن

Al Jinn (The Spirits)

In the name of Allah, Most Gracious,
Most Merciful.

بسم الله الرحمن الرحيم

1. Say: It has been
Revealed[5727] to me that
A company of Jinns[5728]
Listened (to the Qur'ān).
They said, 'We have
Really heard a wonderful
Recital![5729]

١ قُلْ أُوحِيَ إِلَيَّ أَنَّهُ اسْتَمَعَ نَفَرٌ مِّنَ الْجِنِّ فَقَالُوا إِنَّا سَمِعْنَا قُرْآنًا عَجَبًا

2. 'It gives guidance
To the Right,
And we have believed therein:
We shall not join (in worship)
Any (gods) with our Lord.

٢ يَهْدِي إِلَى الرُّشْدِ فَآمَنَّا بِهِ وَلَن نُّشْرِكَ بِرَبِّنَا أَحَدًا

3. 'And exalted is the Majesty
Of our Lord: He has
Taken neither a wife
Nor a son.[5730]

٣ وَأَنَّهُ تَعَالَىٰ جَدُّ رَبِّنَا مَا اتَّخَذَ صَاحِبَةً وَلَا وَلَدًا

4. 'There were some foolish ones
Among us, who used
To utter extravagant lies
Against Allah;

٤ وَأَنَّهُ كَانَ يَقُولُ سَفِيهُنَا عَلَى اللَّهِ شَطَطًا

5. 'But we do think
That no man or spirit
Should say aught that is
Untrue against Allah.[5731]

٥ وَأَنَّا ظَنَنَّا أَن لَّن تَقُولَ الْإِنسُ وَالْجِنُّ عَلَى اللَّهِ كَذِبًا

5727. Revelation may be through various channels, and one of the channels may be a vision, by which the Prophet sees and hears events clearly passing before him. This particular vision may be the same as that referred to more briefly in 46:29-32, where see n. 4809. The Jinns had evidently heard of previous revelations, that of Moses (46:30), and the error of Trinitarian Christianity (72:3). The people from whom they come have all sorts of good and bad persons, but they are determined to preach the good Message of Unity which they have heard and believed in.

5728. For Jinns, see n. 929 to 6:100. (R).

5729. The Holy Qur'ān would be to them a wonderful Recital—both in subject matter and in the circumstance that it had come in Arabia among a pagan and ignorant nation.

5730. They abjure paganism and also the doctrine of a son begotten by Allah, which would also imply a wife of whom he was begotten. *Cf.* 6:101.

5731. No one ought to entertain false notions about Allah. For by joining false gods in our ideas of worship, we degrade our conception of ourselves and the duty we owe to our Creator and Cherisher, to Whom we have to give a final account of life and conduct. If we worship idols or heavenly bodies, or human beings, or any creature, or false fancies born of self or foolish abstractions, or the lusts and desires of our own hearts, we are not only doing violence to Truth, but we are causing discord in the harmony of the world.

6. 'True, there were persons
Among mankind who took shelter
With persons among the Jinns,
But they increased them
In folly.[5732]

(٦) وَأَنَّهُۥ كَانَ رِجَالٌ مِّنَ ٱلْإِنسِ يَعُوذُونَ
بِرِجَالٍ مِّنَ ٱلْجِنِّ فَزَادُوهُمْ رَهَقًا

7. 'And they (came to) think
As ye thought, that Allah
Would not raise up
Any one (to Judgement).

(٧) وَأَنَّهُمْ ظَنُّوا۟ كَمَا ظَنَنتُمْ
أَن لَّن يَبْعَثَ ٱللَّهُ أَحَدًا

8. 'And we pried into
the secrets of heaven;
But we found it filled
With stern guards
And flaming fires.[5733]

(٨) وَأَنَّا لَمَسْنَا ٱلسَّمَآءَ فَوَجَدْنَٰهَا
مُلِئَتْ حَرَسًا شَدِيدًا وَشُهُبًا

9. 'We used, indeed, to sit there
In (hidden) stations, to (steal)
A hearing; but any
Who listens now[5734]
Will find a flaming fire
Watching him in ambush.

(٩) وَأَنَّا كُنَّا نَقْعُدُ مِنْهَا مَقَٰعِدَ لِلسَّمْعِ ۖ
فَمَن يَسْتَمِعِ ٱلْـَٔانَ يَجِدْ لَهُۥ
شِهَابًا رَّصَدًا

10. 'And we understand not
Whether ill is intended
To those on earth,[5735]
Or whether their Lord
(Really) intends to guide
Them to right conduct.

(١٠) وَأَنَّا لَا نَدْرِىٓ أَشَرٌّ
أُرِيدَ بِمَن فِى ٱلْأَرْضِ
أَمْ أَرَادَ بِهِمْ رَبُّهُمْ رَشَدًا

5732. If human beings think that by a resort to some myterious spirits they can shelter themselves from the struggles and actualities of their own lives, they are sadly mistaken. They must "dree their own weird", as the Scots would say. It is folly to try to escape from the duties which they can understand in their own natural surroundings, or to try to avoid the consequences of their own acts. Only such persons do so as do not realise that they will ultimately have to answer at the Judgement Seat of Allah, whose first outpost is in their own conscience.

5733. See notes 1951, 1953, and 1954 to 15:17-18. See also n. 5562 to 67:5. The speakers here have repented of sin and evil; but they recognise that there are evil ones among them, who love stealth and prying, but their dark plots will be defeated by vigilant guardians of the Right, whose repulse of the attacks of evil is figured by the shafts of meteoric light in the heavens.

5734. What is the force of "now"? It refers to the early Makkan period of Revelation. It means that whatever excuse there may have been before, for people to try to seek out the hidden truths of the Unseen World through spirits, there was none now, as the perspicuous Qur'ān had restored the Message of Unity and cleared religion of all the cobwebs, mysteries, and falsehoods with which priestcraft and pious fraud had overlaid it. The result is that such seekers after false hidden knowledge will find themselves confronted now by the flaming fire of the Qur'ān, which, like the shafts of meteoric light (see last note), will lie in wait for and nip such priestcraft and black magic in the bud.

5735. To these spirits this revolutionary gospel is yet new, and appears like a flaming sword which destroys falsehood while it protects Truth. They frankly confess that they do not clearly understand whether on the whole it will be a mercy to mankind or a punishment for mankind forsaking the paths of Allah. But they rightly feel that it must be a blessing if all seek right Guidance.

11. 'There are among us
Some that are righteous,
And some the contrary:
We follow divergent paths.

وَأَنَّا مِنَّا الصَّٰلِحُونَ وَمِنَّا دُونَ ذَٰلِكَ ۖ كُنَّا طَرَآئِقَ قِدَدًا ١١

12. 'But we think that we
Can by no means frustrate
Allah throughout the earth,
Nor can we frustrate Him
By flight.[5736]

وَأَنَّا ظَنَنَّآ أَن لَّن نُّعْجِزَ ٱللَّهَ فِى ٱلْأَرْضِ وَلَن نُّعْجِزَهُۥ هَرَبًا ١٢

13. 'And as for us,
Since we have listened
To the Guidance, we have
Accepted it: and any
Who believes in his Lord
Has no fear, either[5737]
Of a short (account)
Or of any injustice.

وَأَنَّا لَمَّا سَمِعْنَا ٱلْهُدَىٰٓ ءَامَنَّا بِهِۦ ۖ فَمَن يُؤْمِنۢ بِرَبِّهِۦ فَلَا يَخَافُ بَخْسًا وَلَا رَهَقًا ١٣

14. 'Amongst us are some
That submit their wills
(To Allah), and some
That swerve from justice.
Now those who submit
Their wills—they have[5738]
Sought out (the path)
Of right conduct:

وَأَنَّا مِنَّا ٱلْمُسْلِمُونَ وَمِنَّا ٱلْقَٰسِطُونَ ۖ فَمَنْ أَسْلَمَ فَأُو۟لَٰٓئِكَ تَحَرَّوْا۟ رَشَدًا ١٤

15. 'But those who swerve—
They are (but) fuel
For Hell-fire'—[5739]

وَأَمَّا ٱلْقَٰسِطُونَ فَكَانُوا۟ لِجَهَنَّمَ حَطَبًا ١٥

16. (And Allah's Message is):
"If they (the Pagans)
Had (only) remained

وَأَلَّوِ ٱسْتَقَٰمُوا۟ ١٦

5736. See last note. In any case, they know that Allah's Truth and Allah's Plan must prevail, and no one can frustrate Allah's Purpose, or escape from it. Why not then bring the human will into conformity with it, and find Peace, as they have found, by the acceptance of Faith?

5737. Possibly, from this world's standards, it may be that a man suffers for his Faith. He may be laughed at, persecuted, and actually hurt, "in mind, body, or estate". But he is not perturbed. he takes it all cheerfully, because he knows that when his full account is made up—real gain against apparent loss—he is a gainer rather than a loser. And his Faith tells him that Allah is a just God, and will never allow him to suffer any injustice, or permit the account of his merit to appear one whit shorter than it is.

5738. Any one who responds to true Guidance, and submits his will to Allah, finds that he makes rapid progress in the path of right conduct and right life. He gets more and more assurance that his destination is the Garden of Bliss.

5739. An unjust life carries its own condemnation. It does no good to itself or to anyone else. It bears no fruit. It becomes merely fuel for the Fire of Punishment.

On the (right) Way,
We should certainly have
Bestowed on them Rain[5740]
In abundance.

عَلَى ٱلطَّرِيقَةِ
لَأَسْقَيْنَٰهُم مَّآءً غَدَقًا

17. "That We might try them
By that (means).
But if any turns away
From the remembrance[5741]
Of his Lord, He will
Cause him to undergo
A severe Penalty.

١٧ لِّنَفْتِنَهُمْ فِيهِ
وَمَن يُعْرِضْ عَن ذِكْرِ رَبِّهِۦ
يَسْلُكْهُ عَذَابًا صَعَدًا

18. "And the places of worship[5742]
Are for Allah (alone):
So invoke not anyone
Along with Allah;

١٨ وَأَنَّ ٱلْمَسَٰجِدَ لِلَّهِ
فَلَا تَدْعُوا۟ مَعَ ٱللَّهِ أَحَدًا

19. "Yet when the Devotee[5743]
Of Allah stands forth
To invoke Him, they[5744] just
Make round him a dense crowd."

١٩ وَأَنَّهُۥ لَمَّا قَامَ عَبْدُ ٱللَّهِ يَدْعُوهُ
كَادُوا۟ يَكُونُونَ عَلَيْهِ لِبَدًا

SECTION 2.

20. Say: "I do
No more than invoke

٢٠ قُلْ إِنَّمَآ أَدْعُوا۟

5740. *Rain:* literally, water: stands for all kinds of blessings, material, moral, and spiritual. Among the spiritual blessings, is the insight into higher things, which results from our will and endeavour to stand firm on the right Way, the natural, moral, and spiritual Law established by Allah. All blessings come by way of trial: the more we have, the more is expected of us. A man of gifts, talents, or insight is expected to show a higher standard of love and unselfishness than one less gifted, just as a rich man is expected to give more in charity than a poor man.

5741. To remember Allah is to realise His presence, acknowledge His Goodness, and accept His guidance. If we fail to do so, by deliberately turning away, He will withdraw His Grace, and that will be a severe Penalty indeed.

5742. This is a Makkan Sūrah, and *Masjid* must be understood, not in the later technical sense of a Mosque, but in the root meaning, of any place, or occasion of worship or humble prostration in the service of Allah, or any limbs of faculties or accessories used in such worship, *e.g.*, hands and feet, lips and voice, understanding or organisation. A number of meanings therefore follow: (1) No place of worship whatever should be used for the worship of any other but Allah the true God. The Ka'bah was then full of idols, but the idols and their votaries were usurpers. (2) Worship should not be mixed up with vain objects, but should be reserved for the sincere service of Allah. (3) All our gifts are for Allah's service, which includes the service of His creatures, and not for our vainglory. (R).

5743. *The Devotee of Allah:* the Holy Prophet Muḥammad.

5744. *They.* The immediate reference was to the Pagan Quaryṣh who were then in possession of the Ka'bah and who put all sorts of obstacles and indignities in the way of Holy Prophet for preaching the One True God and denouncing idol-worship. They used to surround him and mob him and to treat him as if he was guilty of some dreadful crime. But the wider application refers to the habit of the world to make a marked man of any who diverges from the beaten paths of their favourite sins and who pleads earnestly for the cause of truth and righteousness. They ridicule him; they surround him with jeers and obloquy; and they try to make the physical condition of his life as difficult for him as possible.

My Lord, and I join not With Him any (false god)."	رَبِّي وَلَآ أُشۡرِكُ بِهِۦٓ أَحَدٗا
21. Say: "It is not In my power to cause[5745] You harm, or to bring You to right conduct."	٢١ قُلۡ إِنِّي لَآ أَمۡلِكُ لَكُمۡ ضَرّٗا وَلَا رَشَدٗا
22. Say: "No one can Deliver me from Allah[5746] (If I were to disobey Him), Nor should I find refuge Except in Him.	٢٢ قُلۡ إِنِّي لَن يُجِيرَنِي مِنَ ٱللَّهِ أَحَدٞ وَلَنۡ أَجِدَ مِن دُونِهِۦ مُلۡتَحَدًا
23. "Unless I procliam what I receive from Allah And His Messages: For any that disobey Allah And His Messenger—for them Is Hell: they shall dwell Therein forever."	٢٣ إِلَّا بَلَٰغٗا مِّنَ ٱللَّهِ وَرِسَٰلَٰتِهِۦۚ وَمَن يَعۡصِ ٱللَّهَ وَرَسُولَهُۥ فَإِنَّ لَهُۥ نَارَ جَهَنَّمَ خَٰلِدِينَ فِيهَآ أَبَدًا
24. At length, when they See (with their own eyes) That which they are promised—[5747] Then will they know Who it is that is Weakest in (his) helper And least important In point of numbers.	٢٤ حَتَّىٰٓ إِذَا رَأَوۡاْ مَا يُوعَدُونَ فَسَيَعۡلَمُونَ مَنۡ أَضۡعَفُ نَاصِرٗا وَأَقَلُّ عَدَدٗا
25. Say: "I know not whether The (Punishment) which ye Are promised is near,[5748]	٢٥ قُلۡ إِنۡ أَدۡرِيٓ أَقَرِيبٞ مَّا تُوعَدُونَ

5745. 'Do not suppose that I am going to harm you individually or socially; the very opposite is my wish; but I cannot force you to right conduct; that must depend upon the purification of your own faith and will.'

5746. 'My mission is from Allah. I cannot choose but obey. He has charged me to deliver the Message, and if I were to disobey him, I would myself be worthy of His punishment, and no one can save me. From every kind of trouble and difficulty my only refuge is in Him. I must proclaim His Message: otherwise I am false to the mission He has entrusted to me.'

5747. When the Hereafter arrives, and true values are restored, they will see clearly that the Promise of Allah was true, and that death on this earth was not the end of all things. Then they will see that those who were accounted weak on this earth will, in the realm of Reality, be strong ones; those who seemed to have no following here will have, there, all the great and true ones with them, to help them and welcome them to their own ranks.

5748. The coming of Judgement is certain. But the exact time, relatively to our standards on this earth, no one can tell. Allah alone knows it. Even a Prophet of Allah, as such, does not know the Mysteries of the Unseen World, except insofar as they have been revealed to him by Allah's Revelation. *Cf.* 6:50, and notes 867-68.

Or whether my Lord
Will appoint for it
A distant term.

أَمْ يَجْعَلُ لَهُۥ رَبِّىٓ أَمَدًا

26. "He (alone) knows the Unseen,
Nor does He make anyone
Acquainted with His
Mysteries—[5749]

عَٰلِمُ ٱلْغَيْبِ فَلَا ﴿٢٦﴾
يُظْهِرُ عَلَىٰ غَيْبِهِۦٓ أَحَدًا

27. "Except a messenger[5750]
Whom He has chosen:
And then he makes
A band of watchers[5751]
March before him
And behind him,

إِلَّا مَنِ ٱرْتَضَىٰ مِن رَّسُولٍ ﴿٢٧﴾
فَإِنَّهُۥ يَسْلُكُ مِنۢ بَيْنِ يَدَيْهِ
وَمِنْ خَلْفِهِۦ رَصَدًا

28. "That he may know
That they have (truly)[5751-A]
Brought and delivered
The Messages of their Lord:
And He surrounds[5752]
(All the mysteries) that are
With them, and takes account
Of every single thing."[5753]

لِّيَعْلَمَ أَن قَدْ أَبْلَغُوا۟ ﴿٢٨﴾
رِسَٰلَٰتِ رَبِّهِمْ
وَأَحَاطَ بِمَا لَدَيْهِمْ
وَأَحْصَىٰ كُلَّ شَىْءٍ عَدَدًۢا

5749. *Mystery,* or the Unseen, has two aspects. The relative Unseen is so with reference to a particular person, because of the intervention of Time, Space, or particular circumstances. For example: I cannot see today a house which I saw last year, because it has since been pulled down; or I cannot in Lahore see the "Gateway of India" in Bombay, although anyone in Bombay can see it; or I cannot see the satellites of Jupiter with the naked eye, though I can through a telescope; but the Absolute Unseen, the Absolute Mystery, or Allah's Mystery, is something which no creature can know or see, except insofar as Allah reveals it to him; and Allah reveals such things to the extent that is good for men, through His chosen messengers, among whom the greatest is Muḥammad. The exact time of the Hour of Judgement has not been so shown, because we must not wait for it, but live as if it is to be at this minute. See last note and next note, and the references there.

5750. *Cf.* 3:179, and n. 482. See also last note.

5751. Revelation is not a mechanical or material thing. It has to be safeguarded from being distorted or corrupted by ignorance, selfishness, or the powers of evil. How can its precious and subtle worth and the spiritual safeguards against its misuse by human folly or the perversity of evil be expressed in plain human words? We can imagine a very great treasure, which has to be transmitted. To guard it against evilly-disposed persons, a strong escort is required, to march in front and behind, so as to protect it from all sides. When it reaches its destination, the escort presents its credentials and an Invoice showing the Treasure being transmitted. Then the destined receiver knows that it has come intact and feels satisfied. So, about spiritual Revelation, the spiritual man recognises the credentials and checks the contents on the tablets of his own heart and insight. He has then no doubt that it is a true Message from Allah, and that those who bring it are the true messengers "of their Lord". (R).

5751-A. *They:* the band of watchers. In "he may know" it is better to construe "he" to refer to the Prophet who receives the Message from the "watchers".

5752. *Aḥāṭa:* surrounds, encompasses, encloses, guards on all sides, keeps under his own possession and control, and does not allow to be corrupted or debased. See last not but one.

5753. In the spiritual Kingdom—as indeed, in all things—Allah's knowledge, wisdom, and Plan comprehend all things, great and small. There is nothing which we do, nothing which happens that is outside His account.

INTRODUCTION AND SUMMARY TO SŪRAH 73—*AL MUZZAMMIL*

This is one of the earliest Sūrahs to have been revealed. The first was S. 96:1-5 *(Iqra')*, in the fortieth year of the Prophet's life, say about 12 years before the Hijrah. Then there was an interruption *(Fatrah)*, of which the duration cannot be exactly ascertained, as there was no external history connected with it. The usual estimate puts it at about six months, but it may have been a year or two years. The years were then counted by the luni-solar calendar: see Appendix IX. The second Sūrah in chronological order was probably a great portion of S. 68. *(Al Qalam)*, which came after the *Fatrah* was over. About the same time came this Sūrah (say third) and S. 74, which follows (say fourth), and the remainder of S. 96. We may roughly put the date of this Sūrah at about 11 to 10 years before the Hijrah.

The subject matter is the significance of Prayer and Humility in spiritual life and the terrible fate of those who reject Faith and Revelation.

C. 253.—Devote yourself to the service of Allah
(73:1-20.) In the stillness of the night, but not
All night. In the world's persecution rely
On Allah, Who will deal with His enemies fittingly.
Let not Allah's service be a matter
Of difficulty to you: do all your duties
In whole-hearted remembrance of Allah.
And ever seek His bountiful Grace.

Sūrah 73.

Al Muzzammil (The Enfolded One)

الجزء التاسع والعشرون سورة المزمل

In the name of Allah, Most Gracious, Most Merciful.

بِسْمِ ٱللَّهِ ٱلرَّحْمَٰنِ ٱلرَّحِيمِ

1. O thou folded
In garments![5754]

يَٰٓأَيُّهَا ٱلْمُزَّمِّلُ ﴿١﴾

2. Stand (to prayer) by night,
But not all night—[5755]

قُمِ ٱلَّيْلَ إِلَّا قَلِيلًا ﴿٢﴾

3. Half of it—
Or a little less,

نِّصْفَهُۥٓ أَوِ ٱنقُصْ مِنْهُ قَلِيلًا ﴿٣﴾

4. Or a little more;
And recite the Qur'ān[5756]
In slow, measured rhythmic tones.

أَوْ زِدْ عَلَيْهِ وَرَتِّلِ ٱلْقُرْءَانَ تَرْتِيلًا ﴿٤﴾

5. Soon shall We send down
To thee a weighty Message.[5757]

إِنَّا سَنُلْقِى عَلَيْكَ قَوْلًا ثَقِيلًا ﴿٥﴾

6. Truly the rising by night
Is most potent for governing
(The soul), and most suitable
For (framing) the Word[5758]
(Of Prayer and Praise).

إِنَّ نَاشِئَةَ ٱلَّيْلِ هِىَ أَشَدُّ وَطْـًٔا وَأَقْوَمُ قِيلًا ﴿٦﴾

7. True, there is for thee
By day prolonged occupation

إِنَّ لَكَ فِى ٱلنَّهَارِ ﴿٧﴾

5754. *Muzzammil:* Some Commentators understand by this, "properly dressed for prayer", or "folded" in a sheet, as one renouncing the vanities of this world. *Muzzammil* is one of the titles of our Holy Prophet. But there is a deeper mystic meaning in this and the address "Thou wrapped up" of the next Sūrah. Human nature requires warm garments and wrappings to protect the body from cold or heat or rain. But in the spiritual world these wrappings are useless; the soul must stand bare and open before Allah, in the silence of the night, but not too austerely, as the following verses show.

5755. The Prophet was prone to austerities in the cave of Ḥirā', both before and after he received his mission, spending days and nights in prayer and contemplation. See C. 29. Midnight and after-midnight prayers have technically received the name of *Tahajjud.* See also verse 20 below; also 17:79. (R).

5756. At this time there was only S. 96, S. 68, and possibly S. 74, and the opening Sūrah *(Al Ḥamd)*; but the heart of the Messenger had received enlightenment, and that Light was gradually finding expression in the verse of the Qur'ān. For us, now, with the whole of the Qur'ān before us, the injunction is specially necessary. The words of the Qur'ān must not be read hastily, merely to get through so much reading. They must be studied, and their deep meaning pondered over. They are themselves so beautiful that they must be lovingly pronounced in tones of rhythmic music.

5757. The Qur'ān as completed by degrees, after the *Fatrah* (see Introduction to this Sūrah).

5758. For contemplation, prayer, and praise, what time can be so suitable as the night, when calm and silence prevail, the voices of the marketplace are still, and the silent stars pour forth their eloquence to the discerning soul.

With ordinary duties:[5759]

سَبۡحًا طَوِيلٗا

8. But keep in remembrance
The name of thy Lord
And devote thyself
To Him wholeheartedly.

٨ وَٱذۡكُرِ ٱسۡمَ رَبِّكَ
وَتَبَتَّلۡ إِلَيۡهِ تَبۡتِيلٗا

9. (He is) Lord of the East
And the West: there is
No god but He:
Take Him therefore
For (thy) Disposer of Affairs.[5760]

٩ رَّبُّ ٱلۡمَشۡرِقِ وَٱلۡمَغۡرِبِ
لَآ إِلَٰهَ إِلَّا هُوَ فَٱتَّخِذۡهُ وَكِيلٗا

10. And have patience with what
They say, and leave them
With noble (dignity).

١٠ وَٱصۡبِرۡ عَلَىٰ مَا يَقُولُونَ
وَٱهۡجُرۡهُمۡ هَجۡرٗا جَمِيلٗا

11. And leave Me
(Alone to deal with)
Those in possession of
The good things of life,[5761]
Who (yet) deny the Truth;
And bear with them
For a little while.

١١ وَذَرۡنِي وَٱلۡمُكَذِّبِينَ
أُوْلِي ٱلنَّعۡمَةِ
وَمَهِّلۡهُمۡ قَلِيلًا

12. With Us are Fetters[5762]
(To bind them), and a Fire[5763]
(To burn them),

١٢ إِنَّ لَدَيۡنَآ أَنكَالٗا وَجَحِيمٗا

13. And a Food that chokes,[5764]

١٣ وَطَعَامٗا ذَا غُصَّةٖ

5759. A prophet of Allah, as a man, a member of a family, or a citizen, has many ordinary duties to perform; and his work may be made difficult and irksome in protecting those who listen to his preaching and are therefore molested and persecuted by the world. But while discharging all his ordinary duties, he should work as in the presence of Allah, and in all matters and at all times retain the sense of Allah's nearness. His work may be on earth, but his heart is in Heaven.

5760. Allah is all-in-all-. He is Lord of all places. He rules the world. Therefore be not discouraged by the plots or enmity of wicked men. Leave all things to Allah; trust Him; He is just and will do justice. Only turn away from the unjust, but in a worthy, noble way; *i.e.*, to show them clearly that you do not fear them, but that you leave all affairs in Allah's hands. If we divide the world into hemispheres from the north to south, "East and West" will cover all directions.

5761. Men who enjoy the good things of life have special cause for gratitude to Allah. Who bestowed them. When they are in the ranks of Allah's enemies, none but Allah can adequately deal with them.

5762. *Cf.* 13:5; 34:33; 40:71 and 69:30-32. [Eds.].

5763. *Cf.* 44:47 and 56:94. [Eds.].

5764. *Cf.* 44:43; lvi. 52; 69:36-37, and 88:6. [Eds.].

And a Penalty Grievous.[5765]

وَعَذَابًا أَلِيمًا

14. One Day the earth
And the mountains
Will be in violent commotion.
And the mountains will be
As a heap of sand
Poured out and flowing down.[5766]

(١٤) يَوْمَ تَرْجُفُ
ٱلْأَرْضُ وَٱلْجِبَالُ
وَكَانَتِ ٱلْجِبَالُ كَثِيبًا مَّهِيلًا

15. We have sent to you,
(O men!) a messenger,
To be a witness concerning you,[5767]
Even as We sent
A messenger to Pharaoh.

(١٥) إِنَّآ أَرْسَلْنَآ إِلَيْكُمْ رَسُولًا
شَٰهِدًا عَلَيْكُمْ كَمَآ أَرْسَلْنَآ إِلَىٰ فِرْعَوْنَ رَسُولًا

16. But Pharaoh disobeyed[5768]
The messenger; so We
Seized him with
A heavy Punishment.

(١٦) فَعَصَىٰ فِرْعَوْنُ ٱلرَّسُولَ
فَأَخَذْنَٰهُ أَخْذًا وَبِيلًا

17. Then how shall ye,
If ye deny (Allah)
Guard yourselves against

(١٧) فَكَيْفَ تَتَّقُونَ إِن كَفَرْتُمْ

5765. In general terms, the Penalty of sin may be described as a Penalty Grievous, an Agony. It may come in this very life, but that in the Hereafter is certain! See next verse.

We can also consider punishments from another aspect. The first object of punishment is to protect the innocent from the depredations of the criminal; we have to bind him. The next object is to produce in his heart the fire of repentance, to consume his evil proclivities and to light his conscience. Where that is not enough, a more drastic punishment for the callous is something which causes him pain in things which ordinarily cause him pleasure, such as food, drink, and the satisfaction of physical needs. People in whom the higher spiritual faculties are dead may perchance be awakened through the lower physical features of their life, which appeal to them. Where this also fails, there is finally the complete Agony, a type or symbol too terrible to contemplate,

5766. The Judgement is described as a violent commotion which will change the whole face of nature as we know it. Even the hard rock of mountains will be like loose sand running without any cohesion.

5767. Our Holy Prophet has to warn his age, *i.e.*, the present age, reclaim it from sin, and be a witness for the righteous and against evil, as Moses did his office in his age. For Pharaoh, his arrogance, and his punishment, see 10:75-92.

5768. Pharaoh the earthly king faces Moses the Prophet of Allah. In earthly eyes it was Moses who disobeyed Pharaoh. In spiritual relations, it was Pharaoh who disobeyed Moses. Pharaoh represented an ancient and mighty kingdom, with a long history behind it, and a pride in its learning and science, art, organisation, and power. Moses led a depressed people, hewers of wood and drawers of water. But the might of Allah was behind him. What became of the wisdom, power, and armies of Pharaoh? They were rent asunder when the day came, and the terror and surprise must have been the same as if the heavens had been rent asunder, and children's hair had turned grey! But formidable revolutions turn children grey-haired in another way. Nations that were as children became wise before they in their turn decayed, and from similar disobedience to the laws of Allah. For Allah's law must stand and be fulfilled when all else is swept away.

A Day that will make
Children hoary-headed?—[5769]

يَوْمًا يَجْعَلُ الْوِلْدَانَ شِيبًا

18. Whereon the sky will be
Cleft asunder?
His Promise needs must
Be accomplished.

السَّمَاءُ مُنفَطِرٌ بِهِۦ ١٨
كَانَ وَعْدُهُۥ مَفْعُولًا

19. Verily this is an Admonition;[5770]
Therefore, whoso will, let him
Take a (straight) path
To his Lord!

إِنَّ هَٰذِهِۦ تَذْكِرَةٌ ١٩
فَمَن شَاءَ اتَّخَذَ إِلَىٰ رَبِّهِۦ سَبِيلًا

SECTION 2.

20. Thy Lord doth know
That thou standest forth
(To prayer) nigh two-thirds
Of the night, or half
The night, or a third[5771]
Of the night, and so doth
A party of those with thee.
But Allah doth appoint Night
And Day in due measure.
He knoweth that ye are
Unable to keep count therof.[5772]
So He hath turned to you
(In mercy): read ye,

إِنَّ رَبَّكَ يَعْلَمُ أَنَّكَ تَقُومُ ٢٠
أَدْنَىٰ مِن ثُلُثَيِ اللَّيْلِ وَنِصْفَهُۥ وَثُلُثَهُۥ
وَطَائِفَةٌ مِّنَ الَّذِينَ مَعَكَ
وَاللَّهُ يُقَدِّرُ اللَّيْلَ وَالنَّهَارَ
عَلِمَ أَن لَّن تُحْصُوهُ فَتَابَ عَلَيْكُمْ
فَاقْرَءُوا

5769. If already you deny and disobey Allah in this life of probation, how can you stand up to the Day of Judgement, the Day of the terrible Reality? That Day is described in two metaphors; (1) It will be a time of such stress that even children will become like hoary-headed men; (2) What we look upon as the eternal sky, ever the same, will be cleft asunder; *cf.* 82:1. In other words, the shape of things will be completely altered, both within man and in outer nature, and all true values will be restored. For the Promise of Allah, in this as in all other respects, cannot but be fulfilled.

5770. This is no empty threat. It is an admonition for your good. If you have the will, you can at once come for the Grace and Mercy of Allah, and obtain it. For Repentance and Amendment are the straight Way to the nearness of Allah.

5771. *Cf.*, above, 73:2-4. The Prophet, and a zealous band of his disciples, were often up, two-thirds of the night, or a half, or a third, rejecting sleep and giving themselves up to Prayer and Praise and the reading of the Qur'ān. They are told that this was too severe a tax on them, especially if their health was affected, or they were on a journey, or they were striving, with might and main, in other ways, for the cause of Allah. See the lines following.

5772. The usual meaning taken is that the counting of the exact hours of night and day may not be possible for ordinary people, in order to determine exactly the half, or the third, or the two-thirds of a night. The length of the night and day varies everyday of the solar year, and the precise hour of midnight can only be determined by exact observation in clear skies or by chronometers, which is not possible for everyone. But I understand it in a wider meaning. Allah fixes night and day in due proportions; for rest and work, and according to seasonal variations. For prayer and praise no meticulous observations of that kind are necessary or possible. Allah's service can be done in many ways as detailed below. But we must give some time to devotion, as may be most easy and convenient to us, in various circumstances of health, travel, and the performance of various duties.

Therefore, of the Qur'ān[5773]
As much as may be
Easy for you. He knoweth
That there may be (some)
Among you in ill-health;
Others travelling through the land,
Seeking of Allah's bounty;
Yet others fighting[5774]
In Allah's Cause. Read ye,
Therefore, as much of the Qur'ān
As may be easy (for you);
And establish regular Prayer
And give regular Charity;
And loan to Allah
A Beautiful Loan.[5775]
And whatever good
Ye send forth
For your souls,[5776]
Ye shall find it
In Allah's Presence—
Yea, better and
Greater, in Reward,
And seek ye the Grace
Of Allah: for Allah is[5777]
Oft-Forgiving, Most Merciful.

مَا تَيَسَّرَ مِنَ ٱلْقُرْءَانِ
عَلِمَ أَن سَيَكُونُ مِنكُم مَّرْضَىٰ
وَءَاخَرُونَ يَضْرِبُونَ فِى ٱلْأَرْضِ
يَبْتَغُونَ مِن فَضْلِ ٱللَّهِ
وَءَاخَرُونَ يُقَٰتِلُونَ فِى سَبِيلِ ٱللَّهِ
فَٱقْرَءُوا۟ مَا تَيَسَّرَ مِنْهُ
وَأَقِيمُوا۟ ٱلصَّلَوٰةَ وَءَاتُوا۟ ٱلزَّكَوٰةَ
وَأَقْرِضُوا۟ ٱللَّهَ قَرْضًا حَسَنًا
وَمَا تُقَدِّمُوا۟ لِأَنفُسِكُم مِّنْ خَيْرٍ تَجِدُوهُ
عِندَ ٱللَّهِ هُوَ خَيْرًا وَأَعْظَمَ أَجْرًا
وَٱسْتَغْفِرُوا۟ ٱللَّهَ
إِنَّ ٱللَّهَ غَفُورٌ رَّحِيمٌۢ

5773. The reading of the Qur'ān here is a part of Prayer and religious devotion. This is not to be made into an obsession or a burden. *Cf.* 20:2: "We have not sent down the Qur'ān to thee to be an occasion for thy distress." We must do it whole-mindedly, but not by formal mechanical computations.

5774. This refers to *Jihād.* The better opinion is that this particular verse was revealed in Madinah, long after the greater part of the Sūrah. The reference, further on, to canonical Prayers and regular Charity *(Zakāh)*, points to the same conclusion.

5775. *Cf.* 2:245, and n. 276, where the meaning of "a Beautiful Loan" is explained. See also 57:18. The "Beautiful Loan" should be that of our own souls. We should expect no returns in kind, for that is not possible. But the reward we shall find with Allah will be infinitely greater and nobler. *Cf.* the biblical phrase, "Lay up for yourselves treasures in heaven" (Matt. vi. 20).

5776. Any good that we do raises our own spiritual status and dignity. We must not think that when we speak of Allah's service or Allah's Cause, we are doing anything for His benefit: He is independent of all needs whatsoever.

5777. This emphasises the need of Allah's Grace. Whatever good we do, our own merits are comparatively small. Allah's Grace must lift us up and blot out our shortcomings. Even in piety there may be an arrogance which may become a sin. We should always seek Allah's Mercy in all humility.

INTRODUCTION AND SUMMARY TO SŪRAH 74—*AL MUDDATHTHIR*

This Sūrah dates from about the same time as the last one. Its subject matter is also similar: Prayer and Praise, and the need of patience in a period of great spiritual stress: the unjust who cause sorrow and suffering now will themselves experience agony in the Hereafter.

C. 254.—The Seer, by devotion and contemplation,
(74:1-56.) Prepares himself for the duties of Guide
And Leader to mankind: but when there comes
The clear Call, he must stand forth
And proclaim the Message—in purity,
Unselfish devotion, and patience long-suffering—
To save men from the Distress of the Final Day.
For many there be who glory in a life
Of ease and plenty, arrogant splendour,
And the applause of men, who scorn Allah's Truth
And reject the divine. How will they fare
When the Judgement comes, and the Penalty?
Every Fact of Life's grand Pageant
Is but a Portent for the Future.
Every soul is in pledge and must
Redeem itself by Faith and Prayer,
By Charity and earnest care for the Realities
Of Life. Bring but the will, and Allah
Will guide—the Lord of Righteousness,
The Lord of Mercy and Forgiveness!

Sūrah 74.

الجزء التاسع والعشرون سورة المدثر

Al Muddaththir (The One Wrapped Up)

In the name of Allah, Most Gracious, Most Merciful.

بسم الله الرحمن الرحيم

1. O thou wrapped up[5778]
(In a mantle)!

يَـٰٓأَيُّهَا ٱلْمُدَّثِّرُ ١

2. Arise and deliver thy warning!

قُمْ فَأَنذِرْ ٢

3. And thy Lord
Do thou magnify!

وَرَبَّكَ فَكَبِّرْ ٣

4. And thy garments[5779]
Keep free from stain!

وَثِيَابَكَ فَطَهِّرْ ٤

5. And all abomination shun![5780]

وَٱلرُّجْزَ فَٱهْجُرْ ٥

6. Nor expect, in giving,
Any increase (for thyself)![5781]

وَلَا تَمْنُن تَسْتَكْثِرُ ٦

7. But, for thy Lord's (Cause)[5782]
Be patient and constant!

وَلِرَبِّكَ فَٱصْبِرْ ٧

8. Finally, when the Trumpet
Is sounded,

فَإِذَا نُقِرَ فِى ٱلنَّاقُورِ ٨

5778. In these wonderful early mystic verses there is a double thread of thought; (1) A particular occasion or person is referred to; (2) a general spiritual lesson is taught. As to (1), the Prophet was now past the stage of personal contemplation, lying down or sitting in his mantle; he was now to go forth; boldly to deliver his Message and publicly proclaim the Lord; his heart had always been purified, but now all his outward doings must be dedicated to Allah, and conventional respect for ancestral customs or worship must be thrown aside; his work as a Messenger was the most generous gift that could flow from his personality, but no reward or appreciation was to be expected from his people, but quite the contrary; there would be much call on his patience, but his contentment would arise from the good pleasure of Allah. As to (2), similar stages arise in a minor degree in the life of every good man, for which the Prophet's life is to be a universal pattern. (R).

5779. Possibly, in its immediate application, there is a reference to the dirt and filth which the Pagans used to throw at the Prophet to insult and persecute him.

5780. *Rujz* or *Rijz:* abomination: usually understood to refer to idolatry. It is even possible that there was an idol called *Rujz.* But it has a wider signification, as including a mental state opposed to true worship a state of doubt or indecision.

5781. The legal and commercial formula is that you give in order to receive. And usually you expect to receive what is worth to *you* a little more than you give. The spiritual consideration is that you give, but expect nothing from the receiver. You serve Allah and Allah's creatures.

5782. Our zeal for Allah's Cause itself requires that we should not be impatient, and that we should show constancy in our efforts for His Cause. For we have faith, and we know that He is All-Good, All-Wise, and All-Powerful, and everything will ultimately be right.

9. That will be—that Day—
A Day of Distress—[5783]

فَذَٰلِكَ يَوْمَئِذٍ يَوْمٌ عَسِيرٌ ﴿٩﴾

10. Far from easy
For those without Faith.

عَلَى ٱلْكَٰفِرِينَ غَيْرُ يَسِيرٍ ﴿١٠﴾

11. Leave Me alone, (to deal)[5784]
With the (creature) whom
I created (bare and) alone!—[5785]

ذَرْنِى وَمَنْ خَلَقْتُ وَحِيدًا ﴿١١﴾

12. To whom I granted
Resources in abundance,

وَجَعَلْتُ لَهُۥ مَالًا مَّمْدُودًا ﴿١٢﴾

13. And sons to be
By his side!—[5786]

وَبَنِينَ شُهُودًا ﴿١٣﴾

14. To whom I made
(Life) smooth and comfortable!

وَمَهَّدتُّ لَهُۥ تَمْهِيدًا ﴿١٤﴾

15. Yet is he greedy—
That I should add
(Yet more)—[5787]

ثُمَّ يَطْمَعُ أَنْ أَزِيدَ ﴿١٥﴾

16. By no means!
For to Our Signs
He has been refractory!

كَلَّآ إِنَّهُۥ كَانَ لِءَايَٰتِنَا عَنِيدًا ﴿١٦﴾

17. Soon will I visit him
With a mount of calamities![5788]

سَأُرْهِقُهُۥ صَعُودًا ﴿١٧﴾

18. For he thought
And he plotted—

إِنَّهُۥ فَكَّرَ وَقَدَّرَ ﴿١٨﴾

19. And woe to him![5789]
How he plotted!—

فَقُتِلَ كَيْفَ قَدَّرَ ﴿١٩﴾

5783. The Sinner's course is now shown in contrast to the Seeker's. The Sinner may be self-complacent now; but what will be his position when the Reckoning comes? Not easy; indeed a Day of Distress!

5784. The question of Justice and Punishment to men is for Allah alone. For man at his best can see only one side of truth, and only Allah is All-Knowing. He alone can judge the limits of Justice and Mercy.

5785. Man's adventitious advantages—wealth, power, position, talents—are not due to his own merits. They are gifts from Allah, Who created him. In himself he came bare and alone.

5786. The great ones of the earth may have wealth, a large following, sons by their side to defend them and do their bidding and manpower to help them in their battles. Life may be smooth and agreeable to them. But their responsibility is to Allah.

5787. The Sinner takes Allah's gifts as if they were his right. The more he gets, the more is he greedy. Yet to Allah's Signs and revelations he is willfully deaf or even openly rebellious. But he is only preparing the way for his own undoing.

5788. "A mount of calamities" or disasters: may be understood as a phrase for cumulative disasters. (R).

5789. *Cf.* 51:10; "Woe to the falsehood mongers!"

20. Yea, woe to him; How he plotted!—	ثُمَّ قُتِلَ كَيْفَ قَدَّرَ ﴿٢٠﴾
21. Then he looked round;	ثُمَّ نَظَرَ ﴿٢١﴾
22. Then he frowned And he scowled;	ثُمَّ عَبَسَ وَبَسَرَ ﴿٢٢﴾
23. Then he turned back And was haughty;	ثُمَّ أَدْبَرَ وَٱسْتَكْبَرَ ﴿٢٣﴾
24. Then said he:[5790] "This is nothing but magic, Derived from of old;"	فَقَالَ إِنْ هَٰذَآ إِلَّا سِحْرٌ يُؤْثَرُ ﴿٢٤﴾
25. "This is nothing but The word of a mortal!"	إِنْ هَٰذَآ إِلَّا قَوْلُ ٱلْبَشَرِ ﴿٢٥﴾
26. Soon will I Cast him into Hell-Fire![5791]	سَأُصْلِيهِ سَقَرَ ﴿٢٦﴾
27. And what will explain To thee what Hell-Fire is?	وَمَآ أَدْرَىٰكَ مَا سَقَرُ ﴿٢٧﴾
28. Naught doth it permit To endure, and naught[5792] Doth it leave alone!—	لَا تُبْقِى وَلَا تَذَرُ ﴿٢٨﴾
29. Darkening and changing The colour of man!	لَوَّاحَةٌ لِّلْبَشَرِ ﴿٢٩﴾
30. Over it are Nineteen.[5793]	عَلَيْهَا تِسْعَةَ عَشَرَ ﴿٣٠﴾

5790. The Commentators understand the reference to be to Walīd ibn Mughayrah, who was a wealthy Sybarite, Pagan to the core, and an inveterate enemy to the Holy Prophet. He and Ābu̲ Jahl did all they could, from the beginning of the preaching of Islam, to abuse and persecute the Preacher, to run down his doctrine, and to injure those who believed in it. But the meaning for us is much wider. There are Walīds in all ages. They cannot understand divine inspiration, and seek to explain its wonderful influence over the lives of men by some such unmeaning formula as "magic". The eternal Hope is to them mere human delusion!

5791. The Sinner's perversity can only end in the Fire of Punishment. It enters his very being. See next note.

5792. He is in a state in which he neither lives nor dies (87:13). Looked at in another way, the things that in a good man are meant to last and grow, are for the sinner destroyed, and no part of his nature is left untouched. The brightness of his very manhood is darkened and extinguished by sin.

5793. The figure nineteen refers to angels appointed to guard Hell. See verse 31 below and the corresponding note. [Eds.].

31. And We have set none[5794]
But angels as guardians
Of the Fire; and We
Have fixed their number[5795]
Only as a trial
For Unbelievers—in order
That the People of the Book
May arrive at certainty,
And the Believers may increase
In Faith—and that no doubts
May be left for the People
Of the Book and the Believers,
And that those in whose hearts
Is a disease and the Unbelievers
May say, "What symbol
Doth Allah intend by this?"[5796]
Thus doth Allah leave to stray
Whom He pleaseth, and guide
Whom He pleaseth; and none
Can know the forces
Of thy Lord, except He.[5797]

٣١ وَمَا جَعَلْنَآ أَصْحَٰبَ ٱلنَّارِ إِلَّا مَلَٰٓئِكَةً ۙ
وَمَا جَعَلْنَا عِدَّتَهُمْ إِلَّا فِتْنَةً لِّلَّذِينَ كَفَرُوا۟
لِيَسْتَيْقِنَ ٱلَّذِينَ أُوتُوا۟ ٱلْكِتَٰبَ
وَيَزْدَادَ ٱلَّذِينَ ءَامَنُوٓا۟ إِيمَٰنًا ۙ
وَلَا يَرْتَابَ ٱلَّذِينَ أُوتُوا۟ ٱلْكِتَٰبَ وَٱلْمُؤْمِنُونَ ۙ
وَلِيَقُولَ ٱلَّذِينَ فِى قُلُوبِهِم مَّرَضٌ
وَٱلْكَٰفِرُونَ مَاذَآ أَرَادَ ٱللَّهُ بِهَٰذَا مَثَلًا ۚ
كَذَٰلِكَ يُضِلُّ ٱللَّهُ مَن يَشَآءُ
وَيَهْدِى مَن يَشَآءُ ۚ
وَمَا يَعْلَمُ جُنُودَ رَبِّكَ إِلَّا هُوَ

5794. *Cf.* 66:6, and n. 5540.

There was a great volume of angelology in the religious literature of the People of the Book (*i.e.*. the Jews and Christians) to whom (among others) an appeal is made in this verse. The Essenes, a Jewish brotherhood with highly spiritual ideas, to which perhaps the Prophet Jesus himself belonged, had an extensive literature of angelology. In the Midrash also, which was a Jewish school of exegesis and mystical interpretation, there was much said about angels. The Eastern Christian sects contemporary with the birth of Islam had borrowed and developed many of these ideas, and their mystics owed much to the Gnostics and the Persian apocalyptic systems. In the New Testament the relation of the angels with Fire is referred to more than once. In Rev. ix. 11 we have "the angel of the bottomless pit, whose name in the Hebrew tongue is Abaddon, but in the Greek tongue hath his name Apollyon". In Rev. xiv. 18 there is an "angel which had power over fire", and in Rev. xvi. 8 and angel has "power. . .given unto him to scorch men with fire". In the Old Testament (Daniel vii. 9-10) the essence of all angels is fire: thousands of them issued as a firey stream from before the Ancient of Days, whose "throne was like the fiery flame, and His wheels as burning fire".

5795. The mystic significance of numbers is a favourite theme with some writers, but I lay no stress on it. In Christian theology the number of the Beast, 666, in Rev. xiii. 18 has given rise to much controversy, and may refer only to the numerical value of the letters in the name of the Roman Emperor Nero. In our own literature I think that we ought to avoid too much insistence on speculative conjectures. (R).

5796. There are four classes of people mentioned here: (1) the Muslims will have their faith increased, because they believe that all revelation is from Allah Most Merciful, and all His forces will work in their favour; (2) the People of the Book, those who had received previous revelations of an analogous character, the Jews and Christians, had numerous sects disputing with each other on minute points of doctrine; but they will now, if they believe, find rest from controversies in a broad understanding of scripture; (3) those in whose hearts is a disease (see 2:8-10, notes 33-34), the insincere ones, the hypocrites, will only be mystified, because they believe nothing and have rejected the grace and mercy of Allah; (4) the Unbelievers have frankly done the same and must suffer similar consequences. (R).

5797. It is a necessary consequence of moral responsibility and freedom of choice in man, that he should be left free to stray if he chooses to do so, in spite of all the warning and the instruction he receives. Allah's channels of warning and instruction—His spiritual forces—are infinite, as are His powers. No man can know them. But this warning or reminder is addressed to all mankind.

All things are referred to Allah. But we must not attribute evil to Him. In 4:79 we are expressly told that the good comes from Allah, and the evil from ourselves.

And this is no other than
A warning to mankind.

وَمَا هِيَ إِلَّا ذِكْرَىٰ لِلْبَشَرِ

SECTION 2.

32. Nay, verily:
By the Moon,[5798]

كَلَّا وَالْقَمَرِ ﴿٣٢﴾

33. And by the Night[5799]
As it retreateth,

وَاللَّيْلِ إِذْ أَدْبَرَ ﴿٣٣﴾

34. And by the Dawn
As it shineth forth—

وَالصُّبْحِ إِذَا أَسْفَرَ ﴿٣٤﴾

35. This is but one[5800]
Of the mighty (Portents),

إِنَّهَا لَإِحْدَى الْكُبَرِ ﴿٣٥﴾

36. A warning to mankind—

نَذِيرًا لِلْبَشَرِ ﴿٣٦﴾

37. To any of you that
Chooses to press forward,
Or to follow behind—[5801]

لِمَنْ شَاءَ مِنْكُمْ أَنْ يَتَقَدَّمَ أَوْ يَتَأَخَّرَ ﴿٣٧﴾

5798. An oath in human speech calls in evidence something sacred in the heart of man. In Allah's Message, also, when delivered in human language, solemn emphasis is indicated by an appeal to something striking among the Signs of Allah, which will go straight to the human heart which is addressed. In each case the symbol of the appeal has reference to the particular point enforced in the argument. Here we are asked to contemplate three wonderful phenomena, and they lead up to the conclusion in verse 38. (1) The moon, next after the sun, is the most striking luminary to our sight. Its reflected light has for us even a greater mystery than the direct light of the sun, which looks to us like pure fire. The moon was worshipped as a deity in times of darkness. But in reality, though she rules the night, her rays are only reflections, and are wanting in warmth and vitality. So every soul which looks up to a mere creature of Allah for a sort of vicarious salvation is in spiritual darkness of error; for the true source of spiritual light and life is Allah, and Allah alone. For (2) the Night and (3) the Dawn, see the following note.

5799. (2) The Night when it is illuminated by the Moon is light in a sense, but it is really dark and must give place to (3) the Dawn when it comes, as the harbinger of the Sun. So in spiritual matters, when every soul realises its own responsibility, it will look less and less to reflected lights, and through the beauty of a dawn-like awakening, will be prepared more and more for the splendour of the light of Allah Himself, the goal of the Heaven of our dreams.

5800. *This is but one, etc.* There are numerous Signs of Allah, of which Judgement is one, and one of the mightiest portents. Or the reference may be to the waning of the Moon, the decline of the night, and the glorious sunrise, as tokens or symbols of the world renewed when the present transitory world passes away. According to some commentators "This" here refers to Hell. (R).

5801. Three interpretations are possible. (1) Those pressing forward may be the Righteous, and those following behind may be the laggards, the Unbelievers, who reject Allah's love, care, and mercy. (2) Men of two kinds of temperament may be referred to; those who are always in the van and those who are always in the rear. Allah's Message is open to both. But there may be a danger to both; in the one case, overconfidence, or hope in wrong things; in the other case missing great opportunities so that their spiritual lives may be "bound in shallows and in miseries". Extremes should be avoided. (3) Or it may mean that the warning is effective only for those willing to move forwards or backwards, as the case may be, but is lost in some cases we have to retreat from false positions. The hopeless case is that of the obstinate man, whose heart is so dead that he dares not advance to the right or withdraw from the wrong.

38. Every soul will be (held)
In pledge for its deeds.[5802]

٣٨ كل نفس بما كسبت رهينة

39. Except the Companions
Of the Right Hand,[5803]

٣٩ إلا أصحاب اليمين

40. (They will be) in Gardens
(Of Delight); they will
Question each other,

٤٠ في جنات يتساءلون

41. And (ask) of the Sinners:

٤١ عن المجرمين

42. "What led you
Into Hell-Fire?"

٤٢ ما سلككم في سقر

43. They will say;
"We were not of those
Who prayed;"

٤٣ قالوا لم نك من المصلين

44. "Nor were we of those
Who fed the indigent;"

٤٤ ولم نك نطعم المسكين

45. "But we used to talk
Vanities with vain talkers;"

٤٥ وكنا نخوض مع الخائضين

46. "And we used to deny
The Day of Judgement,"

٤٦ وكنا نكذب بيوم الدين

47. "Until there came to us
(The Hour) that is certain."[5804]

٤٧ حتى أتانا اليقين

48. Then will no intercession
Of (any) intercessors
Profit them.

٤٨ فما تنفعهم شفاعة الشافعين

49. Then what is
The matter with them

٤٩ فما لهم عن

5802. *Cf.* 52:21. Man cannot shift his responsibility to vicarious saviours or saints. His redemption depends upon the grace of Allah, for which he should constantly and wholeheartedly strive by means of right conduct. If he does so he will be redeemed and he will join the Companions of the Right Hand.

5803. *Cf.* n. 5223 to 56:3, and see 56:27-38. The Companions of the Right Hand will be the Righteous or the Blessed in the Hereafter. Their grounds of merit will be Prayer, Charity, Earnestness, and Faith in Allah's just Judgement; all which are within the reach of the humblest Seeker. They are not separate acts of virtues, but are all interconnected. At Judgement, the pledge of their soul will be redeemed by Allah's Grace at the Taking of the Account.

5804. *Cf.* 15:99, and n. 2018. The Hour that is Certain is usually taken to be Death. (R).

That they turn away
From admonition?—[5805]

التَّذْكِرَةِ مُعْرِضِينَ

50. As if they were
Affrighted asses,

كَأَنَّهُمْ حُمُرٌ مُّسْتَنفِرَةٌ ﴿٥٠﴾

51. Fleeing from a lion!

فَرَّتْ مِن قَسْوَرَةٍ ﴿٥١﴾

52. Forsooth, each one of them
Wants to be given[5806]
Scrolls (of revelation) spread out!

بَلْ يُرِيدُ كُلُّ امْرِئٍ مِّنْهُمْ أَن يُؤْتَىٰ صُحُفًا مُّنَشَّرَةً ﴿٥٢﴾

53. By no means! But
They fear not the Hereafter,

كَلَّا ۖ بَل لَّا يَخَافُونَ الْآخِرَةَ ﴿٥٣﴾

54. Nay, this surely
Is an admonition:

كَلَّا إِنَّهُ تَذْكِرَةٌ ﴿٥٤﴾

55. Let any who will,[5807]
Keep it in remembrance!

فَمَن شَاءَ ذَكَرَهُ ﴿٥٥﴾

56. But none will keep it
In rememberance except
As Allah wills: He[5808]
Is the Lord of Righteousness,
And the Lord of Forgiveness.

وَمَا يَذْكُرُونَ إِلَّا أَن يَشَاءَ اللَّهُ ۚ هُوَ أَهْلُ التَّقْوَىٰ وَأَهْلُ الْمَغْفِرَةِ ﴿٥٦﴾

5805. If the Day of Judgement is inevitable, it is strange that men should not heed a plain warning, but go on as if they were thoughtless and obstinate asses stampeding from a lion. Instead of heeding the warning, they try to avoid it. They are frightened at Allah's Word.

5806. *Cf.* 17:93: "Until thou send down to us a book, that we could not read". The Unbelievers pretend in ridicule that they would believe if a special message written on open scrolls and addressed to them severally were brought to them by a miracle! There is a disease in their hearts and understandings. The Teacher's warning is plain, and enough for any reasonable man who has the will to seek Allah.

5807. The Qur'ān it self is the admonition—the latest among the revealed Books of Allah. If man has the will to learn, he will keep the Message always before Him, and Allah's grace will help him to carry out in his conduct.

5808. Righteousness as well as Forgiveness have their source in Allah's Will Man's Righteousness has no meaning except in relation to the Universal Will. For *Taqwā* see n. 26 to 2:2. If we take the word here in the sense of "the fear of Allah", the translation would be: "He alone is worthy to be feared, and He alone is entitled to grant Forgiveness."

INTRODUCTION AND SUMMARY TO SŪRAH 75—*AL QIYĀMAH*

This Sūrah belongs to the early Makkan period, but comes chronologically a good deal later that the last Sūrahs.

Its subject matter is the Resurrection, viewed from the point of view of Man, especially unregenerate Man, as he is now, and as he will be then—his inner and psychological history.

C. 255.—Eschew all Evil: for man was not created
(75:1-40.) Without purpose or without responsibility.
The Day of Account will come, and his own
Conscience bears witness that he
Must walk straight; for he must face
That Day's Realities. With patience await
The unfoldment of Allah's view. The faces
Of the Blest will beam with brightness and beauty.
For the others, Death will be a terror—
For duties neglected and sins committed.
Woe unto man that he thinks not now
Of Allah's Purpose and the noble Destiny
For which Allah gave him Life and its Gifts.

Sūrah 75.

Al Qiyāmah (The Resurrection)

الجزء التاسع والعشرون سورة القيامة

In the name of Allah, Most Gracious, Most Merciful.

بِسْمِ اللَّهِ الرَّحْمَٰنِ الرَّحِيمِ

1. I do call to witness[5809]
The Resurrection Day;

لَا أُقْسِمُ بِيَوْمِ الْقِيَامَةِ ١

2. And I do call to witness
The self-reproaching spirit;[5810]
(Eschew Evil).

وَلَا أُقْسِمُ بِالنَّفْسِ اللَّوَّامَةِ ٢

3. Does man think that We
Cannot assemble his bones?[5811]

أَيَحْسَبُ الْإِنسَانُ أَلَّن نَّجْمَعَ عِظَامَهُ ٣

4. Nay, We are able to put
Together in perfect order
The very tips of his fingers.[5812]

بَلَىٰ قَادِرِينَ عَلَىٰ أَن نُّسَوِّيَ بَنَانَهُ ٤

5. But man wishes to do
Wrong (even) in the time
In front of him.[5813]

بَلْ يُرِيدُ الْإِنسَانُ لِيَفْجُرَ أَمَامَهُ ٥

6. He questions: "When[5814]
Is the Day of Resurrection?"

يَسْأَلُ أَيَّانَ يَوْمُ الْقِيَامَةِ ٦

7. At length, when
The Sight is dazed,[5815]

فَإِذَا بَرِقَ الْبَصَرُ ٧

5809. *Cf.* 70:40, and n. 5700. Here the point to be enforced is understood: I have added it in brackets; "eschew Evil". The appeal is made to two considerations: (1) That every act has to be accounted for, and evil must have its recompense at the Resurrection; and (2) that man's own spirit has a conscience which would reproach him of sin, if he did not suppress that inner voice.

5810. Our doctors postulate three states or stages of the development of the human soul; (1) *Ammārah* (12:53), which is prone to evil, and, if not checked and controlled, will lead to perdition; (2) *Lawwāmah*, as here, which feels conscious of evil, and resists it, asks for Allah's grace and pardon after repentance and tries to amend; it hopes to reach salvation; (3) *Muṭma'innah* (89:27), the highest stage of all, when it achieves full rest and satisfaction. Our second stage may be compared to Conscience, except that in English usage Conscience is a faculty and not a stage in spiritual development.

5811. The Unbelievers' usual cry is: "What! when we are reduced to bones and dust, how can our personality be called to account?" (17:49). The answer is: Allah has said so, and He will do it; for the death here is not the end of all things.

5812. An idiom for the most delicate parts of the body.

5813. It is bad enough not to repent of past sins. But the evildoer who rejects a Day of Reckoning and has no conscience wants to go on in his career of sin and jeopardise his future also.

5814. The question is sceptical or derisive. He does not believe that there is any chain of consequences in the Hereafter. He does not believe in a Hereafter.

5815. At the Hour of Judgement the full light and glory of the Lord will shine, and the effulgence will daze man's eyes. For the world as we knew it will go to pieces and a new World will come into being.

8. And the moon is
Buried in darkness.[5816]

وَخَسَفَ ٱلْقَمَرُ ﴿٨﴾

9. And the sun and moon
Are joined together—[5817]

وَجُمِعَ ٱلشَّمْسُ وَٱلْقَمَرُ ﴿٩﴾

10. That Day will Man say;
"Where is the refuge?"

يَقُولُ ٱلْإِنسَٰنُ يَوْمَئِذٍ أَيْنَ ٱلْمَفَرُّ ﴿١٠﴾

11. By no means!
No place of safety!

كَلَّا لَا وَزَرَ ﴿١١﴾

12. Before thy Lord (alone),
That Day will be
The place of rest.

إِلَىٰ رَبِّكَ يَوْمَئِذٍ ٱلْمُسْتَقَرُّ ﴿١٢﴾

13. That Day will Man
Be told (all) that he
Put forward, and all
That he put back.[5818]

يُنَبَّؤُا۟ ٱلْإِنسَٰنُ يَوْمَئِذٍۭ بِمَا قَدَّمَ وَأَخَّرَ ﴿١٣﴾

14. Nay, man will be
Evidence against himself,[5819]

بَلِ ٱلْإِنسَٰنُ عَلَىٰ نَفْسِهِۦ بَصِيرَةٌ ﴿١٤﴾

15. Even though he were
To put up his excuses.

وَلَوْ أَلْقَىٰ مَعَاذِيرَهُۥ ﴿١٥﴾

16. Move not thy tongue
Concerning the (Qur'ān)
To make haste therewith.[5820]

لَا تُحَرِّكْ بِهِۦ لِسَانَكَ لِتَعْجَلَ بِهِۦٓ ﴿١٦﴾

5816. Not only will man's sight be dazed, but the great luminaries themselves will lose their light. The moon with its present reflected light will then cease to shine. All reflected or relative truth or goodness will sink into nothing before the true and Eternal Reality. (R).

5817. To the moon the sun is the original light, but the sun itself is a created light, and it will sink into nothingness along with the moon. Both will be like empty shells "whose lights are fled, whose glories dead", because the Prototype of all Light now shines in full splendour in a new World. See n. 4344 to 39:69.

5818. All good and bad deeds, positive and negative, *i.e.*, all sins of commission and ommission, and all the good that a man did and all the evil that he omitted, all the influence that he radiated before him and all that he left behind him.

5819. *Cf.* 24:24, and n. 2976: "On the Day when their tongues, their heads, and their feet will bear witness against them as to their actions." It is not what a man says about himself, or what others say of him, that determines judgement about him. It is what he is in himself. His own personality betrays him or commends him.

5820. *Cf.* 20. 114, and n. 2639: "Be not in haste with the Qur'ān before its revelation to thee is completed." S. 75. is an earlier revelation, and the shade of meaning is slightly different. The immediate meaning was that the Holy Prophet was to allow the revelation conveyed to him to sink into his mind and heart and not to be impatient about it; Allah would certainly complete it according to His Plan, and see that it was collected and preserved for men, and not lost; that the inspired one was to follow it and recite it as the inspiration was conveyed to him; and that it carries its own explanation according to the faculties bestowed by Allah on man. The general meaning follows the same lines; we must not be impatient about the inspired Word; we must follow it as made clear to us by the faculties given to us by Allah.

17. It is for Us to collect it
And to promulgate it:

إِنَّ عَلَيْنَا جَمْعَهُۥ وَقُرْءَانَهُۥ ﴿١٧﴾

18. But when We have
Promulgated it, follow thou
Its recital (as promulgated):

فَإِذَا قَرَأْنَٰهُ فَٱتَّبِعْ قُرْءَانَهُۥ ﴿١٨﴾

19. Nay more, it is
For us to explain it
(And make it clear):

ثُمَّ إِنَّ عَلَيْنَا بَيَانَهُۥ ﴿١٩﴾

20. Nay, (ye men!)
But ye love
The fleeting life,[5821]

كَلَّا بَلْ تُحِبُّونَ ٱلْعَاجِلَةَ ﴿٢٠﴾

21. And leave alone
The Hereafter.

وَتَذَرُونَ ٱلْءَاخِرَةَ ﴿٢١﴾

22. Some faces, that Day,[5822]
Will beam (in brightness
And beauty)—

وُجُوهٌ يَوْمَئِذٍ نَّاضِرَةٌ ﴿٢٢﴾

23. Looking towards their Lord;

إِلَىٰ رَبِّهَا نَاظِرَةٌ ﴿٢٣﴾

24. And some faces, that Day,
Will be sad and dismal,

وَوُجُوهٌ يَوْمَئِذٍۭ بَاسِرَةٌ ﴿٢٤﴾

25. In the thought that some
Backbreaking calamity was about
To be inflicted on them;

تَظُنُّ أَن يُفْعَلَ بِهَا فَاقِرَةٌ ﴿٢٥﴾

26. Yea, when (the soul)[5823]
Reaches to the collarbone
(In its exit),

كَلَّآ إِذَا بَلَغَتِ ٱلتَّرَاقِىَ ﴿٢٦﴾

5821. *Cf.* 21:37. Man loves haste and things of haste. For that reason he pins his faith on transitory things that come and go, and neglects the things of lasting moment, which come slowly, and whose true import will only be fully seen in the Hereafter.

5822. This passage (especially with reference to verses 26-28) would seem to refer to what our Doctors call the Lesser Judgement *(Qiyāmah al Ṣughrā)*, which takes place immediately after death, and not to the Greater or General Judgement, which may be supposed to be referred to in such passages as occur in S. 56. There are other passages referring to the Lesser Judgement immediately after death; *e.g.*, 7:37 etc. If I understand aright, the punishment of sin takes place in three ways; (1) it may take place in this very life, but this may be deferred, to give the sinner respite; (2) it may be an agony immediately after death, with the Partition or *Barzakh* (23:100) separating the sinner from the final Resurrection; and (3) in the final Resurrection, when the whole of the present order gives place to a wholly new World: 14:48.

5823. A symbolic picture of the agony of death.

27. And there will be a cry,
"Who is a magician
(To restore him)?"

وَقِيلَ مَنْۜ رَاقٍ ﴿٢٧﴾

28. And he[5824] will conclude
That it was (the Time)
Of Parting;

وَظَنَّ أَنَّهُ ٱلْفِرَاقُ ﴿٢٨﴾

29. And one leg will be[5825]
Joined with another:

وَٱلْتَفَّتِ ٱلسَّاقُ بِٱلسَّاقِ ﴿٢٩﴾

30. That Day the Drive
Will be (all) to thy Lord!

إِلَىٰ رَبِّكَ يَوْمَئِذٍ ٱلْمَسَاقُ ﴿٣٠﴾

SECTION 2.

31. So he gave nothing
In charity, nor
Did he pray!—[5826]

فَلَا صَدَّقَ وَلَا صَلَّىٰ ﴿٣١﴾

32. But on the contrary,
He rejected Truth
And turned away!

وَلَٰكِن كَذَّبَ وَتَوَلَّىٰ ﴿٣٢﴾

33. Then did he stalk
To his family
In full conceit![5827]

ثُمَّ ذَهَبَ إِلَىٰٓ أَهْلِهِۦ يَتَمَطَّىٰٓ ﴿٣٣﴾

34. Woe to thee,
(O man!), yea, woe!

أَوْلَىٰ لَكَ فَأَوْلَىٰ ﴿٣٤﴾

35. Again, woe to thee,
(O man!), yea, woe!

ثُمَّ أَوْلَىٰ لَكَ فَأَوْلَىٰٓ ﴿٣٥﴾

5824. 'He' = the dying man, whose soul is referred to in verse 26 above.

5825. When the soul has departed, the legs of the dead body are placed together in position, in preparation for the rites preliminary to the burial. *Sāq* (literally, leg) may also be taken metaphorically to mean a calamity: calamity will be joined to calamity for the poor departed sinner's soul, as his life story in this world is now done. Willy-nilly, he will now have to go before the Throne of Judgement.

5826. His indictment in this and the succeeding verse consists of four counts: (1) he neglected prayer; (2) he neglected charity; (3) he rejected Truth; and (4) he turned away. In 74:43-46, the four counts are: (1) neglecting prayer; (2) neglecting charity; (3) talking vanities; (4) denying the Day of Judgement; see n. 5803, Nos. (1) and (2) are identical in both places, and Nos. (3) and (4) are analogous. Rejecting the truth is equivalent to talking vanities and making an alliance with falsehoods. Denying the Day of Judgement means behaving as if no account was to be given of our actions. *i.e.*, turning away from right conduct. An additional touch is found here in verse 33. See next note.

5827. Conceit or arrogance is the root cause of most Evil. By that cause fell Iblīs: see 2:34.

36. Does Man think
That he will be left
Uncontrolled, (without
purpose)?[5828]

أَيَحْسَبُ ٱلْإِنسَٰنُ أَن يُتْرَكَ سُدًى ﴿٣٦﴾

37. Was he not a drop
Of sperm emitted
(In lowly form)?[5829]

أَلَمْ يَكُ نُطْفَةً مِّن مَّنِيٍّ يُمْنَىٰ ﴿٣٧﴾

38. Then did he become
A clinging clot;
Then did (Allah) make
And fashion (him)
In due proportion.

ثُمَّ كَانَ عَلَقَةً فَخَلَقَ فَسَوَّىٰ ﴿٣٨﴾

39. And of him He made
Two sexes, male
And female.

فَجَعَلَ مِنْهُ ٱلزَّوْجَيْنِ ٱلذَّكَرَ وَٱلْأُنثَىٰٓ ﴿٣٩﴾

40. Has not He, (the same),
The power to give life
To the dead?

أَلَيْسَ ذَٰلِكَ بِقَٰدِرٍ عَلَىٰٓ أَن يُحْـِۧىَ ٱلْمَوْتَىٰ ﴿٤٠﴾

5828. *Suda:* has many implications; (1) uncontrolled, free to do what he likes; (2) without any moral responsibility; not accountable for his actions; (3) without a purpose, useless; (4) forsaken.

5829. *Cf.* 22:5, where the argument is developed in greater detail. The briefer argument here may be stated thus. His lowly animal origin makes him no higher than a brute; his foetal development is still that of a brute animal; then at some stage come human limbs and shape; the divine spirit is poured into him, and he is fashioned in due proportion for his higher destiny. In spite of that the mystery of sex remains in his nature: we are living souls, yet men and women. Allah Who creates these wonders—has He not the power to bring the dead to life at the Resurrection?

INTRODUCTION AND SUMMARY TO SŪRAH 76—*AL INSĀN* or *AL DAHR*

The revelation of this Sūrah was probably in the early Makkan period, with the possible exception of some verses, but its date has no particular significance

Its theme is the contrast between the two classes of men, those who choose good and those who choose evil, with special reference to the former.

The title of the Sūrah recalls a Pagan Arab idea, which personified Time as existing spontaneously from eternity to eternity and responsible for the misery or the happiness of mankind. In 45:24 we read: "They say. . 'nothing but Time can destroy us.'" This attitude is of course wrong. Time is a created thing: it has its mysteries, but it is no more eternal than matter. It is also relative to our conceptions and not absolute, as Einstein has proved. It is only Allah Who is Self-Subsisting, Eternal from the beginning and Eternal to the end, the absolute Existence and Reality. We must not transfer His attributes to any figments of our imagination.

This deification of Time *(Dahr)* as against a living personal God has given rise to the term *dahrīyah*, as applied to an atheist or a materialist.

The whole of the Sūrah is full of the highest symbolism, as is generally the case with Makkan Sūrahs, and this should always be remembered in their interpretation.

C. 256.—Man was evolved out of nothing, and through low
(76:1-31) Beginnings; but he was given Insight
And Understanding. Allah showed him the Way;
And if man doth willfully reject the Right,
Man but chooses Chains and Yokes and a Blazing
Fire within his own soul. Not so
The Devotees of Right: they attain
The Mystic Fountain of *Kāfūr:*
For, purely out of love for Allah,
They do good to Allah's Creatures, and serve them.
The Light of Beauty and Joy will be
On them. In full felicity and honour
Will they live in the garden of Delights, and share
In the Banquet—the Presence and Glory Divine!

* * * *

The Righteous are patient in Constant Devotion:
Allah's Way is open to all: whosoever
Has the Will, may attain to the Perfect Goal.

Sūrah 76.

Al Insān (Man), or ***Al Dahr*** (The Time)

In the name of Allah, Most Gracious,
Most Merciful.

بِسْمِ ٱللَّهِ ٱلرَّحْمَٰنِ ٱلرَّحِيمِ

1. Has there not been[5830]
Over Man a long period
Of Time,[5831] when he was
Nothing—(not even) mentioned?

هَلْ أَتَىٰ عَلَى ٱلْإِنسَٰنِ حِينٌ ﴿١﴾
مِّنَ ٱلدَّهْرِ لَمْ يَكُن شَيْـًٔا مَّذْكُورًا

2. Verily We created
Man from a drop
Of mingled sperm,[5832]
In order to try him:
So We gave him (the gifts),
Of Hearing and Sight.

إِنَّا خَلَقْنَا ٱلْإِنسَٰنَ ﴿٢﴾
مِن نُّطْفَةٍ أَمْشَاجٍ نَّبْتَلِيهِ
فَجَعَلْنَٰهُ سَمِيعًۢا بَصِيرًا

3. We showed him the Way:
Whether he be grateful
Or ungrateful (rests[5833]
On his will).

إِنَّا هَدَيْنَٰهُ ٱلسَّبِيلَ ﴿٣﴾
إِمَّا شَاكِرًا وَإِمَّا كَفُورًا

4. For the Rejecters
We have prepared
Chains, Yokes, and
A Blazing Fire.[5834]

إِنَّآ أَعْتَدْنَا لِلْكَٰفِرِينَ ﴿٤﴾
سَلَٰسِلَا۟ وَأَغْلَٰلًا وَسَعِيرًا

5. As to the Righteous.
They shall drink

إِنَّ ٱلْأَبْرَارَ يَشْرَبُونَ ﴿٥﴾

5830. The undoubted fact is mentioned in the form of a question, to get the assent of man. It is certain that the physical world existed long before man was ever heard of or mentioned, as geological records prove. It is also true that the spiritual world existed long before man came on the scene: see 2:30-31. Man is here taken in a generic sense.

5831. *Dahr* is Time as a whole, or for a long period. Time used to be deified by the Pagan Arabs, as explained in the Introduction to this Sūrah. An analogy can be found in the Greek ideas connected with Chronos or Kronos, themselves a blend of different myths. Kronos (or Time), they said, was the father of Zeus himself.

5832. *Mingled:* the female ovum has to be fertilised with the male sperm before a new animal can be born. Man as an animal has this humble origin. But he has been given the gift of certain faculties of receiving instruction (typified by Hearing) and of intellectual and spiritual insight (typified by Sight). His life has therefore a meaning: with a certain amount of free will, he is to be Allah's vicegerent on earth (2:30). But he must be trained and tried, and that is the whole problem of human life.

5833. Besides the gift of the faculties, Man has been shown the Way by means of Revelation, through men of the highest spiritual standing. If he is grateful, he will accept Guidance, be of the Righteous, and join the company of the Blessed. If not, he puts chains round himself, thus burdening himself with sin, and gets into the Blazing Fire of Punishment. See next verse. His choice rests on his will. (R).

5834. *Cf.* 13:5; 34:33 and 40:71. [Eds.].

Of a Cup (of Wine)
Mixed with *Kāfūr*—[5835]

مِن كَأْسٍ كَانَ مِزَاجُهَا كَافُورًا

6. A Fountain where
The Devotees of Allah
Do drink, making it
Flow in unstinted abundance.

عَيْنًا يَشْرَبُ بِهَا عِبَادُ ٱللَّهِ يُفَجِّرُونَهَا تَفْجِيرًا ﴿٦﴾

7. They[5836] perform (their) vows,[5837]
And they fear a Day
Whose evil flies far and wide.[5838]

يُوفُونَ بِٱلنَّذْرِ وَيَخَافُونَ يَوْمًا كَانَ شَرُّهُۥ مُسْتَطِيرًا ﴿٧﴾

8. And they feed, for the love
Of Allah, the indigent,
The orphan, and the captive—[5839]

وَيُطْعِمُونَ ٱلطَّعَامَ عَلَىٰ حُبِّهِۦ مِسْكِينًا وَيَتِيمًا وَأَسِيرًا ﴿٨﴾

9. (Saying), "We feed you
For the sake of Allah alone:
No reward do we desire
From you, nor thanks."[5840]

إِنَّمَا نُطْعِمُكُمْ لِوَجْهِ ٱللَّهِ لَا نُرِيدُ مِنكُمْ جَزَآءً وَلَا شُكُورًا ﴿٩﴾

10. "We only fear a Day
Of distressful Wrath
From the side of our Lord."[5841]

إِنَّا نَخَافُ مِن رَّبِّنَا يَوْمًا عَبُوسًا قَمْطَرِيرًا ﴿١٠﴾

5835. *Kāfūr* is literally Camphor. It is a fountain in the Realms of Bliss. It is a seasoning added to the Cup of pure, beatific Wine, which causes no intoxication (56:18-19), but stands for all that is wholesome, agreeable, and refreshing. Camphor is cool and refreshing, and is given as a soothing tonic in Eastern medicine. In minute doses its odour and flavour are also agreeable. (R).

5836. *They: i.e.,* the Righteous: they are known in the present life by the virtues symbolically described in verses 7-10, and in the life of the Hereafter they will enjoy the Bliss symbolically described in verses 11-22.

5837. *Cf.* 22:29. The vows must be vows of spiritual service, which of course includes service to humanity, such as is mentioned in the next verse. They are Devotees of Allah, and they must perform all vows and contracts (5:1 and n. 682). Vows of the Pagan sort, savouring of a sort of "bribe" to the Deity, are not approved.

5838. That is, they prepare for the Judgement to come, where the effects of Sin will not be transitory but far-reaching.

5839. *The captive:* when taken literally, it refers to the old state of things when captives of war had to earn their own food, or their own redemption; even ordinary prisoners in jail for criminal offences often starved unless food was provided for them by private friends or from their own earnings. But there is a further symbolic meaning, which applies to the indigent, the orphans, and the captives, *viz.* those who are so in a spiritual sense: those have no mental or moral resources, or have no one to look after them, or are held down in social or moral or economic captivity. They hunger for spiritual food, or perhaps their appetite is deadened, but the Righteous understand and supply their real needs. It has also been held that "captives" include dumb animals who are under subjection to man; they must be properly fed, housed, and looked after; and the righteous man does not forget them.

5840. These words need not be actually uttered. They express the true motives of pious and unpretentious Charity.

5841. It is a Day of Wrath for sin and evil. But the truly righteous are not self-righteous. They have the fear of Allah in their minds: they know they are human, and they fear lest they should be found wanting in the sight of Allah. But Allah in His Mercy gives them a bountiful Reward.

11. But Allah will deliver
Them from the evil
Of that Day, and will
Shed over them a Light[5842]
Of Beauty and
A (blissful) Joy.

١١ فَوَقَىٰهُمُ ٱللَّهُ
شَرَّ ذَٰلِكَ ٱلْيَوْمِ
وَلَقَّىٰهُمْ نَضْرَةً وَسُرُورًا

12. And because they were
Patient and constant, He will
Reward them with a Garden
And (garments of) silk.[5843]

١٢ وَجَزَىٰهُم بِمَا صَبَرُوا۟
جَنَّةً وَحَرِيرًا

13. Reclining in the (Garden)
On raised thrones,[5844]
They will see there neither
The sun's (excessive heat)
Nor (the moon's) excessive cold.[5845]

١٣ مُّتَّكِـِٔينَ فِيهَا عَلَى ٱلْأَرَآئِكِ
لَا يَرَوْنَ فِيهَا شَمْسًا وَلَا زَمْهَرِيرًا

14. And the shades of the (Garden)
Will come low over them,
And the bunches (of fruit),
There, will hang low
In humility.[5846]

١٤ وَدَانِيَةً عَلَيْهِمْ ظِلَـٰلُهَا
وَذُلِّلَتْ قُطُوفُهَا تَذْلِيلًا

15. And amongst them will be
Passed round vessels of silver[5847]
And goblets of crystal—

١٥ وَيُطَافُ عَلَيْهِم بِـَٔانِيَةٍ
مِّن فِضَّةٍ وَأَكْوَابٍ كَانَتْ قَوَارِيرَا۠

16. Crystal-clear, made of silver:[5848]
They will determine
The measure thereof
(According to their wishes).

١٦ قَوَارِيرَا۟ مِن فِضَّةٍ
قَدَّرُوهَا تَقْدِيرًا

5842. *Cf.* 75:22-23.

5843. *Cf.* 22:23.

5844. *Cf.* 18:31.

5845. The sun and the moon as we know them will be no longer there. It will be a new world on a different plane. But to give us an idea of comfort we recall the excessive heat of the sun especially in tropical climates, and the excessive cold of the moon especially in northern climates, and we negative them both. That is, the temperature will be just that delightful one that is most agreeable to our sensations as we know them now. The moon is not mentioned, but *Zamharīr* (excessive cold) is sometimes used for the moon. (R).

5846. Without sun and moon there will of course be no shade in the literal sense of the word. But for full comfort, there will be sheltering shade for rest and change from whatever light there be. But the whole idea here is that of humility. Even the shadows show humility: *cf.* 13:15. So does the fruit in hanging low for man. Man has now reached the height of his dignity. (R).

5847. *Cf.* 43:71, where "dishes and goblets of gold" are mentioned. The idea conveyed is that of rarity, preciousness, and spotless splendour. (R).

5848. That is, silver polished and white, and shining like crystal.

17. And they will be given
To drink there of a Cup
(Of Wine) mixed[5849]
With *Zanjabīl*—

18. A fountain there,
Called *Salsabīl*.[5850]

19. And round about them
Will (serve) youths
Of perpetual (freshness):[5851]
If thou seest them,
Thou wouldst think them
Scattered Pearls.[5852]

20. And when thou lookest,
It is there thou wilt see
A Bliss and
A Realm Magnificent.

21. Upon them will be
Green Garments of fine silk
And heavy brocade,
And they will be adorned
With Bracelets of silver;[5853]
And their Lord will
Give to them to drink
Of a Wine
Pure and Holy.[5854]

(١٧) وَيُسْقَوْنَ فِيهَا كَأْسًا كَانَ
مِزَاجُهَا زَنجَبِيلًا

(١٨) عَيْنًا فِيهَا تُسَمَّىٰ سَلْسَبِيلًا

(١٩) وَيَطُوفُ عَلَيْهِمْ
وِلْدَانٌ مُّخَلَّدُونَ إِذَا رَأَيْتَهُمْ
حَسِبْتَهُمْ لُؤْلُؤًا مَّنثُورًا

(٢٠) وَإِذَا رَأَيْتَ ثَمَّ رَأَيْتَ
نَعِيمًا وَمُلْكًا كَبِيرًا

(٢١) عَالِيَهُمْ ثِيَابُ سُندُسٍ
خُضْرٌ وَإِسْتَبْرَقٌ
وَحُلُّوا أَسَاوِرَ مِن فِضَّةٍ
وَسَقَاهُمْ رَبُّهُمْ شَرَابًا طَهُورًا

5849. *Cf.* above, 76:5-6, and n. 5835, where the Cup of *Kāfūr* (Camphor) was mentioned for coolness and refreshment to the Righteous, who had just passed the great Event of Judgement. The second stage is symbolised by verses 12-14, when they enter the Garden in Garments of Silk, and find that their former humility in the probationary life is rewarded with high honour in the new world they have entered. The third stage is in verses 15-21, where they settle down in Bliss, with Garments of fine silk and heavy brocades, with Ornaments and Jewels, with an ordered Feast of set service, and the Cup of *Zanjabīl*. This literally means Ginger. In Eastern medicine Ginger is administered to give warmth to the body and zest to the taste; this is appropriate for the Royal Feast which is now figured forth. (R).

5850. *Salsabīl* literally means: "Seek the Way". The Way is now open to the presence of the Most High. The Banquet is spread. Get thyself ready. It is a "Realm Magnificent" (verse 20) in a new spiritual world. (R).

5851. *Cf.* 56:17 and n. 5231.

5852. *Pearls* for beauty and splendour: *scattered*, because they are moving to and fro all round the Banquet.

5853. *Cf.* 17:31. The bracelets are there said to be of gold.

5854. This would seem to be the culmination of the honour which the Blessed receive at the Royal and Divine Banquet. The words in the next verse express the sort of speech which will make the Guest a denizen of Heaven. (R).

22. "Verily this is a Reward
For you, and your Endeavour
Is accepted and recognised."

٢٢ إِنَّ هَٰذَا كَانَ لَكُمْ جَزَآءً
وَكَانَ سَعْيُكُم مَّشْكُورًا

SECTION 2.

23. It is We Who
Have sent down the Qur'ān
To thee by stages.[5855]

٢٣ إِنَّا نَحْنُ نَزَّلْنَا عَلَيْكَ
ٱلْقُرْءَانَ تَنزِيلًا

24. Therefore be patient
With constancy to the Command
Of thy Lord, and hearken not
To the sinner or the ingrate
Among them.

٢٤ فَٱصْبِرْ لِحُكْمِ رَبِّكَ وَلَا تُطِعْ
مِنْهُمْ ءَاثِمًا أَوْ كَفُورًا

25. And celebrate the name[5856]
Of thy Lord morning
And evening,

٢٥ وَٱذْكُرِ ٱسْمَ رَبِّكَ بُكْرَةً وَأَصِيلًا

26. And part of the night,
Prostrate thyself to Him;
And glorify Him[5857]
A long night through.

٢٦ وَمِنَ ٱلَّيْلِ فَٱسْجُدْ لَهُۥ
وَسَبِّحْهُ لَيْلًا طَوِيلًا

27. As to these, they love
The fleeting life,
And put away behind them[5858]
A Day (that will be) hard.

٢٧ إِنَّ هَٰٓؤُلَآءِ يُحِبُّونَ ٱلْعَاجِلَةَ
وَيَذَرُونَ وَرَآءَهُمْ يَوْمًا ثَقِيلًا

5855. The Qur'ān was being revealed stage by stage as the occasion demanded and at the date of this Sūrah it was still one of the earlier stages. Persecution, abuse, and false charges were being levelled against the man of Allah, but he is bidden to stand firm and do his duty. In a minor degree this applies to all of us who suffer in the cause of Truth.

5856. Three methods of Prayer and Devotion are mentioned: (1) to remember and celebrate the Holy Name of Allah always; (2) to spend a part of the night in humble prostration; and (3) to glorify Him in the long hours of a weary night of waiting and watching. As to (1), "morning and evening" means all the waking hours of our life, but in the special hours of morning and evening the physical world without us, and the inner world within us, combine to make us specially receptive of spiritual influences. The "name" of Allah includes His attributes, as a locked golden casket might include priceless jewels. Anyone may carry the casket, even though he may not be worthy to handle the jewels. If he carries the casket, he is in potential possession of the jewels, and he hopes some time to get the key which opens the jewels to him. So the tyro, who celebrates the Holy Name of Allah, hopes some day to see the "Face" of Allah and be blessed with the privilege of proximity to His Person. For (2) and (3) see next note. (R).

5857. See last note. (2) Humble *prostration* to Allah means some visible mode or symbol of dedication. That is best done at night, when the soul, free from worldly occupations, is alone with its God. (3) The weary hours of a long night are no longer weary, but become full of meaning when we join in concert with the whole Creation, which glorifies Allah: 57:1.

5858. *Fleeting life: Cf.* 75:20. *They:* the immediate reference was to the Pagan Quraysh; the general reference is to the Unbelievers of all ages. They reject, or at least put away the thought of, a Hereafter, a Day that will be hard, for the easy pleasures of a fleeting life.

28. It is We Who created
Them, and We have made
Their joints strong;[5859]
But, when We will,
We can substitute
The like of them[5860]
By a complete change.

٢٨ نَحْنُ خَلَقْنَٰهُمْ
وَشَدَدْنَآ أَسْرَهُمْ ۖ
وَإِذَا شِئْنَا بَدَّلْنَآ أَمْثَٰلَهُمْ تَبْدِيلًا

29. This is an admonition:
Whosoever will, let him
Take a (straight) Path
To his Lord.

٢٩ إِنَّ هَٰذِهِۦ تَذْكِرَةٌ ۖ
فَمَن شَآءَ ٱتَّخَذَ إِلَىٰ رَبِّهِۦ سَبِيلًا

30. But ye will not,
Except as Allah wills:[5861]
For Allah is full of
Knowledge and Wisdom.

٣٠ وَمَا تَشَآءُونَ إِلَّآ أَن يَشَآءَ ٱللَّهُ ۚ
إِنَّ ٱللَّهَ كَانَ عَلِيمًا حَكِيمًا

31. He will admit
To His Mercy Whom He will;[5862]
But the wrongdoers—
For them has He prepared
A grievous Penalty.

٣١ يُدْخِلُ مَن يَشَآءُ فِى رَحْمَتِهِۦ ۚ
وَٱلظَّٰلِمِينَ أَعَدَّ لَهُمْ عَذَابًا أَلِيمًۢا

5859. Allah has not only created men, but "made their joints strong", *i.e.*, given them the power and strength to withstand the temptations of Evil and stand firmly in the Path of Right.

5860. If, in spite of Allah's loving care, any particular men or group of men, misuse their powers or wilfully disobey Allah's Law, Allah will set them aside, and substitute others in their place, with like powers. Allah's gifts are free, but let no one think that he can monopolise them or misuse them without being called to answer for the trust. And the man of Allah must not be discouraged by the whole world being at some moment completely against him. Allah can in a moment make a complete change. Either the same men that fought against him will be his zealous adherents, or another generation will spring up, which will carry the flag of Righteousness to victory. Allah's Will and Plan work in their own good time.

5861. Man in himself is weak; he must seek Allah's Grace; without it he can do nothing; with it he can do all. For Allah knows all things, and His wisdom comprehends the good of all.

5862. That is according to His just and wise Plan. If the will is right, it obtains Allah's Grace and Mercy. If the will of man rejects Allah, man must suffer the Penalty.

INTRODUCTION AND SUMMARY TO SŪRAH 77—*AL MURSALĀT*

This Sūrah belongs to the early Makkan period, somewhere near to S. 75. *(Al Qiyāmah)*. The theme is somewhat similar. It denounces the horrors of the Hereafter, for those who rejected Truth. The refrain, "Ah woe, that Day, to the Rejecters of Truth!" which occurs ten times in its fifty verses, or, on an average, once in every five verses, indicates the *leitmotif*.

C. 257.—The winds in the world of nature are types
(77:1-50.) Of Allah's Bounty and Power: they gently bring
The beneficent rain, and when roused to wrath,
They clean the world and wipe out Infection.
So works Allah's Revelation, in sunshine
And storm. It will root out Evil, and restore
True values at Judgement. Truly terrible
Will be that Day for the evil ones.
It will be a Day of Sorting out:
Ah woe, that Day, to the Rejecters of Truth!
Will man not learn from his own little story,
Or from nature around him? The Blazing Fire
Will be indeed an enveloping Punishment.
How dreadful the contrast with the Bliss of the Righteous!
Learn, ye, therefore, Humility, and approach
Allah's Throne in Repentance and Earnest Endeavour.

Sūrah 77.

Al Mursalāt (Those Sent Forth)

الجزء التاسع والعشرون سورة المرسلات

In the name of Allah, Most Gracious, Most Merciful.

بِسْمِ اللَّهِ الرَّحْمَٰنِ الرَّحِيمِ

1. By the (Winds) Sent Forth[5863]
One after another
(To man's profit);[5864]

وَالْمُرْسَلَاتِ عُرْفًا ①

2. Which then blow violently
In tempestuous Gusts,[5865]

فَالْعَاصِفَاتِ عَصْفًا ②

3. And scatter (things)
Far and wide;

وَالنَّاشِرَاتِ نَشْرًا ③

4. Then separate them,
One from another,

فَالْفَارِقَاتِ فَرْقًا ④

5. Then spread abroad
A Message,[5866]

فَالْمُلْقِيَاتِ ذِكْرًا ⑤

5863. This Sūrah begins with an appeal to five things, as pointing to the substantive statement in verse 7, that the Day of Justice and Judgement is bound to come, and we must prepare for it. It is difficult to translate, but easy to understand, if we remember that a triple thread of allegory runs through this passage (verses 1-7). The five things or phases, which will be presently considered in detail, refer to (a) Winds in the physical world, (b) Angels in the spiritual world, and (c) Prophets in the human world, connecting it with the spiritual world.

5864. Understanding the reference to Winds, we can see that they are powerful factors in the government of the physical world. (1) They come gently as harbingers of the blessings of rain and fertility (15:22, 30:48); but (2) they can come as violent tornadoes, uprooting and destroying (51:41-42); (3) they can scatter seeds far and wide, and (4) they can separate chaff from grain, or clear the air from epidemics; and (5) they literally carry sound, and therefore Messages, and metaphorically they are instrumental in making Allah's Revelation accessible to hearers, whether by way of justification or repentance for the Penitent, or warning for unrepentant Sinners. All these things point to the power and goodness of Allah, and we are asked to believe that His promise of Mercy and Justice in the Hereafter is indeed true.

Cf. this passage with 51:1-6 *(Al Dhāriyāt)* with which it has many affinities.

5865. If we understand the reference to be, not to Winds, but to Angels, they are agencies in the spiritual world, which carry out similar functions, changing and revolutionising the face of the world. (1) They come softly, on beneficent errands of Mercy; (2) they are charged with the mission of punishment and destruction for sin as in the case of the two angels who came to Lūṭ (15:57-66); (3) they distribute Allah's Mercies as the Winds distribute good seeds; (4) they sort out the good from the evil among men; and (5) they are the agency through which Allah's Messages and Revelations are conveyed to the Prophets (see No. 5 in the last note).

5866. If we understand the reference to Prophets or Messengers of Allah, or the verses of Revelation which would be particularly appropriate for verses 5-6, we also get a satisfactory solution of the Allegory. (1) The Prophets have followed one another in a series: the verses of the Qur'ān came, one after another as needed; in both cases it was for man's spiritual profit; (2) they caused great disturbance in a spiritually decadent world; they pulled down evil institutions root and branch, and substituted new ones; (3) they proclaimed their truths far and wide, without fear and without favour; (4) through them were sorted out men of Faith and rebels against Allah's Law; and (5) they gave a Message, through which just men were justified through repentance, and evil men were warned of their sins.

Some Commentators take one or other of these allegories, and some apply one allegory to a few of these verses, and another to another few. In my opinion the Allegory is wide enough to comprehend all the meanings which I have sketched. I wish a translation could do justice to those marvellously terse sentences in the original.

6. Whether of Justification
Or of Warning—

عُذْرًا أَوْ نُذْرًا ﴿٦﴾

7. Assuredly, what ye are
Promised must come to pass.

إِنَّمَا تُوعَدُونَ لَوَٰقِعٌ ﴿٧﴾

8. Then when the stars
Become dim;[5867]

فَإِذَا ٱلنُّجُومُ طُمِسَتْ ﴿٨﴾

9. When the heaven
Is cleft asunder;

وَإِذَا ٱلسَّمَآءُ فُرِجَتْ ﴿٩﴾

10. When the mountains are
Scattered (to the winds) as dust;

وَإِذَا ٱلْجِبَالُ نُسِفَتْ ﴿١٠﴾

11. And when the messengers
Are (all) appointed a time
(To collect)—[5868]

وَإِذَا ٱلرُّسُلُ أُقِّتَتْ ﴿١١﴾

12. For what Day are these
(Portents) deferred?

لِأَيِّ يَوْمٍ أُجِّلَتْ ﴿١٢﴾

13. For the Day of Sorting out.[5869]

لِيَوْمِ ٱلْفَصْلِ ﴿١٣﴾

14. And what will explain
To thee what is
The Day of Sorting out?

وَمَآ أَدْرَىٰكَ مَا يَوْمُ ٱلْفَصْلِ ﴿١٤﴾

15. Ah woe, that Day,
To the Rejecters of Truth!

وَيْلٌ يَوْمَئِذٍ لِّلْمُكَذِّبِينَ ﴿١٥﴾

16. Did We not destroy
The men of old[5870]
(For their evil)?

أَلَمْ نُهْلِكِ ٱلْأَوَّلِينَ ﴿١٦﴾

5867. The lustre of the stars will become dim; in fact they will disappear: *cf.* 81:2, and 82:2. The heaven's canopy will be torn asunder: *cf.* 82:1, and 73:18. The mountains will be uprooted and fly about like dust: *cf.* 69:14, 81:3, etc. All the old landmarks of the physical world as we know them will be swept away. (R).

5868. The Resurrection will be established. In the world which will then have passed away, inspired Prophets had been sent in succession at different times to all nations. Now they will be gathered together in one place before the Judgement Seat to bear witness as to the righteous or the evil ones within their respective spheres of work. *Cf.* 39:69.

5869. *Cf.* 37:21 and n. 4047; also 44:40, and n. 4718. That will be the Day of Judgement or Day of Decision. Good will then be completely separated from Evil. And the men who rejected Truth and flourished on Falsehood will find that in the world of Realities they will be absolutely nowhere. Hence the refrain of this Sūrah, "Ah woe, that Day, to the Rejecters of Truth!". It sounds like a dirge on Sin.

5870. Allah's Law is always the same. Sin or corruption prepares its own destruction. It was so with the generation of Noah. In Arab tradition it was so with the 'Ād and the Thamūd. In our own day we see relics of prehistoric civilisations, in Egypt, Mesopotamia, the Indus Valley, and the Aegean: these were men of wonderful skill and resource, but they went under. If our generations, which pride themselves on their science and skill, desert Allah's Law, they will be certain to meet the same fate.

17. So shall We make
Later (generations)
Follow them.

ثُمَّ نُتْبِعُهُمُ ٱلْآخِرِينَ ﴿١٧﴾

18. Thus do We deal
With men of sin.

كَذَٰلِكَ نَفْعَلُ بِٱلْمُجْرِمِينَ ﴿١٨﴾

19. Ah woe, that Day,
To the Rejecters of Truth!

وَيْلٌ يَوْمَئِذٍ لِّلْمُكَذِّبِينَ ﴿١٩﴾

20. Have We not created
You from a fluid
(Held) despicable?—[5871]

أَلَمْ نَخْلُقكُّم مِّن مَّآءٍ مَّهِينٍ ﴿٢٠﴾

21. The which We placed
In a place of rest,
Firmly fixed,[5872]

فَجَعَلْنَٰهُ فِى قَرَارٍ مَّكِينٍ ﴿٢١﴾

22. For a period (of gestation),
Determined (according to
need)?[5873]

إِلَىٰ قَدَرٍ مَّعْلُومٍ ﴿٢٢﴾

23. For We do determine
(According to need); for We[5874]
Are the Best to determine (things).

فَقَدَرْنَا فَنِعْمَ ٱلْقَٰدِرُونَ ﴿٢٣﴾

24. Ah woe, that Day!
To the Rejecters of Truth!

وَيْلٌ يَوْمَئِذٍ لِّلْمُكَذِّبِينَ ﴿٢٤﴾

25. Have We not made
The earth (as a place)
To draw together

أَلَمْ نَجْعَلِ ٱلْأَرْضَ كِفَاتًا ﴿٢٥﴾

26. The living and the dead,[5875]

أَحْيَآءً وَأَمْوَٰتًا ﴿٢٦﴾

5871. *Cf.* 32:8, n. 3638. Man is ashamed of the process of physical creation, by which he comes into being. Yet he is arrogant in life and neglectful of the Future.

5872. See n. 2873 to 23:13. The silent growth in the mother's womb, and the protection and sustenance which the growing life receives from the life of the mother, are themselves wonders of creation.

5873. The period roughly of nine months and ten days is subject to many adjustments. In fact throughout our prenatal as well as postnatal life there are wonderful and nicely-balanced adjustments of which we are ourselves unconscious. Should we not turn in love and gratitude to Allah our Creator?

5874. Perhaps the life in the womb, in relation to the life after birth, is an allegory for our probationary life on earth in relation to the eternal Life to come. Perhaps, also, our state when we are buried in the tomb suggests an allegory to the life in the womb, in relation to the life in the Hereafter.

5875. What a wonderful parable! The earth is a place where death and life, decay and growth and decay, green grass, stubble, and fuel, corruption and purification jostle together—one often leading to the other. The drama which we see with our own eyes in this world should enable us to appreciate the wonders in the spiritual world where the despised and rejected receive the highest honour. Lazarus rests in Abraham's bosom, and the Pharaoh is led in chains for his arrogance and his sin.

27. And made therein
Mountains standing firm,[5876]
Lofty (in stature);
And provided for you
Water sweet (and wholesome)?

وَجَعَلْنَا فِيهَا رَوَاسِيَ شَامِخَاتٍ وَأَسْقَيْنَاكُم مَّاءً فُرَاتًا ﴿٢٧﴾

28. Ah woe, that Day,
To the Rejecters of Truth!

وَيْلٌ يَوْمَئِذٍ لِّلْمُكَذِّبِينَ ﴿٢٨﴾

29. (It will be said:)
"Depart ye to that
Which ye used to reject
As false!"

انطَلِقُوا إِلَىٰ مَا كُنتُم بِهِ تُكَذِّبُونَ ﴿٢٩﴾

30. "Depart ye to a Shadow[5877]
(Of smoke ascending)
In three columns,

انطَلِقُوا إِلَىٰ ظِلٍّ ذِي ثَلَاثِ شُعَبٍ ﴿٣٠﴾

31. "(Which yields) no shade
Of coolness, and is
Of no use against
The fierce Blaze.

لَّا ظَلِيلٍ وَلَا يُغْنِي مِنَ اللَّهَبِ ﴿٣١﴾

32. "Indeed it throws about
Sparks (huge) as Forts,[5878]

إِنَّهَا تَرْمِي بِشَرَرٍ كَالْقَصْرِ ﴿٣٢﴾

33. "As if there were
(A string of) yellow camels
(Marching swiftly)."[5879]

كَأَنَّهُ جِمَالَتٌ صُفْرٌ ﴿٣٣﴾

34. Ah woe, that Day,
To the Rejecters of Truth!

وَيْلٌ يَوْمَئِذٍ لِّلْمُكَذِّبِينَ ﴿٣٤﴾

5876. See n. 2038 to 16:15. The solid mountains are frequently referred to: *cf.* 13:3. The parable here is that the mountains are hard, solid rock, and yet they act as sponges to collect, store up, and filter sweet and wholesome water, which on account of their altitude they are able to distribute by gravity to the lower, dry land by means of rivers or springs. Anyone who has seen the parched Makkan valleys and the delicious springs in the mountains around, or the Zubaydah Canal, which is the main source of Makkah's water supply, will appreciate the aptness of the metaphor, but it applies to any country, though not to so striking a degree. If the wisdom and power of Allah can do such things before your eyes, how can you reject His teaching of a still more wonderful future Life?

5877. The Sinners, instead of reposing in cool shades, will only see the blazing Fire. The only shadow they will see will be that of Smoke, ascending in three columns, right, left, and above, *i.e.*, completely enveloping them. But it will give no comfort or coolness. On the contrary, it will contain huge sparks. (R).

5878. *Qaṣr:* Fort, big building, palace. An alternative reading is *Qaṣar,* plural of *Qaṣarat (-un),* meaning bundles of wood used for fuel: Ibn 'Abbās *apud* Bukhārī. I almost prefer this latter reading.

5879. The yellow sparks flying swiftly one after another suggest a string of camels marching swiftly, such as the Arabs of Nejd and central Arabia are so proud of. There is a double allegory. It refers not only to the colour and the rapid succession of sparks, but to the vanity of worldly pride, as much as to say: "your fine yellow camels in which you took such pride in the world are but sparks that fly away and even sting you in the Hereafter!" Smoke with sparks may also assume fantastic shapes like long-necked camels.

35. That will be a Day
When they shall not
Be able to speak,[5880]

هَٰذَا يَوْمُ لَا يَنطِقُونَ ٣٥

36. Nor will it be
Open to them
To put forth pleas.

وَلَا يُؤْذَنُ لَهُمْ فَيَعْتَذِرُونَ ٣٦

37. Ah woe, that Day,
To the Rejecters of Truth!

وَيْلٌ يَوْمَئِذٍ لِّلْمُكَذِّبِينَ ٣٧

38. That will be a Day
Of Sorting out! We shall
Gather you together
And those before (you)![5881]

هَٰذَا يَوْمُ الْفَصْلِ ۖ جَمَعْنَاكُمْ وَالْأَوَّلِينَ ٣٨

39. Now, if ye have
A trick (or plot),
Use it against Me![5882]

فَإِن كَانَ لَكُمْ كَيْدٌ فَكِيدُونِ ٣٩

40. Ah woe, that Day,
To the Rejecters of Truth!

وَيْلٌ يَوْمَئِذٍ لِّلْمُكَذِّبِينَ ٤٠

SECTION 2.

41. As to the Righteous,
They shall be amidst
(Cool) shades and springs
(Of water).[5883]

إِنَّ الْمُتَّقِينَ فِي ظِلَالٍ وَعُيُونٍ ٤١

42. And (they shall have)
Fruits—all they desire.[5884]

وَفَوَاكِهَ مِمَّا يَشْتَهُونَ ٤٢

5880. They will be dumbfounded; *i.e.*, (when read with the next verse), they will not be in a position to put forward any valid defence or plea. Facts will speak too plainly against them. They might perversely try to deny false worship: 6:23; but their own tongues and limbs will bear witness against them: 24:24. Nor does the fighting out or settling of doctrinal disputes in the Hereafter (39:31) amount to putting forward pleas in defence.

5881. We may suppose this as spoken primarily to the Quraysh who were plotting against the Prophet. You may use all your wisdom and that of your ancestors, but you will not be able to defeat Allah or His Plan. See next verse.

5882. The plots against the Holy Prophet were plots against Allah's Truth, and therefore against Allah. Can anyone hope to profit by such plots? Can anyone defeat Allah's Plan and Purpose? Let them try. They will only ruin themselves, as the Pagan leaders did. There can only be pity for such men. What will be their state in the Hereafter? "Ah woe, that Day, to the Rejecters of Allah's Truth!"

5883. This is in contrast to the triple shade of smoke and sin for the sinners, which neither gives them coolness nor protects them from the Blazing Fire. The Shade, *i.e.*, Covering, of Allah's Good Pleasure, will be the greatest Boon of all, and the Spring of Allah's Love will be inexhaustible. (R).

5884. *Fruits:* see n. 4671 to 43:73. (R).

43. Eat ye and drink ye
To your heart's content:
For that ye worked
(Righteousness).[5885]

كُلُوا وَاشْرَبُوا هَنِيٓـًٔا ٤٣
بِمَا كُنتُمْ تَعْمَلُونَ

44. Thus do We certainly
Reward the Doers of Good.

إِنَّا كَذَٰلِكَ نَجْزِى ٱلْمُحْسِنِينَ ٤٤

45. Ah woe, that Day,
To the Rejecters of Truth!

وَيْلٌ يَوْمَئِذٍ لِّلْمُكَذِّبِينَ ٤٥

46. (O ye Unjust!)
Eat ye and enjoy yourselves
(But) a little while,[5886]
For that ye are Sinners.

كُلُوا وَتَمَتَّعُوا قَلِيلًا ٤٦
إِنَّكُم مُّجْرِمُونَ

47. Ah woe, that Day,
To the Rejecters of Truth!

وَيْلٌ يَوْمَئِذٍ لِّلْمُكَذِّبِينَ ٤٧

48. And when it is said
To them, "Prostrate yourselves!"
They do not so.[5887]

وَإِذَا قِيلَ لَهُمُ ٱرْكَعُوا لَا يَرْكَعُونَ ٤٨

49. Ah woe, that Day,
To the Rejecters of Truth!

وَيْلٌ يَوْمَئِذٍ لِّلْمُكَذِّبِينَ ٤٩

50. Then what Message,
After that,[5888]
Will they believe in?

فَبِأَيِّ حَدِيثٍ بَعْدَهُۥ يُؤْمِنُونَ ٥٠

5885. The fruits of righteousness are contentment in this life and the supreme Bliss in the next.

5886. "Eat" is symbolical of having the good things of life in this world. It may be that they are only given for a trial. Because their minds and wishes run to wrong things, the opportunities for wrong are multiplied, as the impetus for good or for evil increases progressively. They are to believe and repent. But if they do not, they are to be pitied, even for the good things of this life, for they will come to an evil End in the Hereafter.

5887. Prostration is a symbol of humility and a desire to get nearer to Allah by Prayer and a good life. Those who refuse to adopt this Path are to be pitied: how will they fare at Judgement?

5888. *That* may refer to verse 48: they were given plain and clear Guidance, and they refused to accept it: after that what kind of Message will they accept? The Guidance referred to is obviously that of Islam or the Qur'ān.

INTRODUCTION AND SUMMARY TO SŪRAH 78—*AL NABA'*

This beautiful Makkan Sūrah is not quite so early as the last (S. 77) nor quite so late as S. 76, but nearer in time to the later.

It sets forth Allah's loving care in a fine nature passage, and deduces from it the Promise of the Future, when Evil will be destroyed and Good will come to its own; and invites all who have the will, to seek refuge with their Lord.

C. 258.—The Great News for man, in his spiritual Destiny,
(78:1-40.) Is the Judgement to come, the Day of Sorting Out.
Do not the Power, the Goodness, and the Justice
Of Allah reveal themselves in all nature?
The Panorama around us, the voice in our souls,
And the harmony between heaven and earth?
That Day is sure to arrive at its time
Appointed, when behold! the present order
Will pass away. Then will the Fruits
Of Evil appear, and the Fruits of Righteousness.
Allah's blessings will be more than the merits of men;
But who can argue with the Fountain of Grace?
And who can prevent the course of Justice?
Let us then, before it becomes too late,
Betake ourselves to our Lord Most Gracious!

Sūrah 78.

الجزء الثلاثون سورة النبأ

Al Naba' (The Great News)

In the name of Allah, Most Gracious, Most Merciful.

بِسْمِ اللَّهِ الرَّحْمَٰنِ الرَّحِيمِ

30/30

1. Concerning what
Are they disputing?

عَمَّ يَتَسَاءَلُونَ ①

2. Concerning the Great News,[5889]

عَنِ النَّبَإِ الْعَظِيمِ ②

3. About which they
Cannot agree.

الَّذِي هُمْ فِيهِ مُخْتَلِفُونَ ③

4. Verily, they shall soon
(Come to) know!

كَلَّا سَيَعْلَمُونَ ④

5. Verily, verily they shall
Soon (come to) know!

ثُمَّ كَلَّا سَيَعْلَمُونَ ⑤

6. Have We not made
The earth as a wide[5890]
Expanse,

أَلَمْ نَجْعَلِ الْأَرْضَ مِهَادًا ⑥

7. And the mountains as pegs?

وَالْجِبَالَ أَوْتَادًا ⑦

8. And (have We not) created
you in pairs,

وَخَلَقْنَاكُمْ أَزْوَاجًا ⑧

9. And made your sleep
For rest,

وَجَعَلْنَا نَوْمَكُمْ سُبَاتًا ⑨

5889. *Great News:* usually understood to mean the News or Message of the Resurrection or the Hereafter, about which there are various schools of thought among the Jews and Christians and other nations. There is practically nothing about the Resurrection in the Old Testament, and the Jewish sect of Sadducees even in the time of Christ denied the Resurrection altogether. The Pagan ideas of a future life—if any—varied from place to place and from time to time. Even in the early Christian Church, as we learn from Paul's First Epistle to the Corinthians, there were contentions in that little community (I. Corinthians, i. 11), and some definitely denied the resurrection of the dead *(ib.*, xv. 12).

Great News may also be translated *Great Message* or a *Message Supreme* as I have translated at 38:67. In that case it would refer to the Qur'ān, or the Message of Revelation, or the Message of the Holy Prophet, about which there was great contention in those days. As this Message also lays great stress on the Day of Judgement and the Resurrection, the practical result by either mode of interpretation amounts to the same.

5890. See n. 2038 to 16:15. *Cf.* also 13:3 and 15:19. The spacious expanse of the earth may be compared to a carpet, to which the mountains act as pegs. The Signs of Allah are thus enumerated: the great panorama of outer nature (verses 6-7); the creation of Man in pairs, with the succession of rest and work fitting in with the succession of night and day (verses 8-11); the firmaments above, with their splendid lights (verses 12-13); and the clouds and rain and abundant harvests, which knit sky and earth and man together (verses 14-16). These point to Allah, and Allah's Message points to the Future Life.

10. And made the night As a covering,[5891]	وَجَعَلْنَا ٱلَّيْلَ لِبَاسًا ﴿١٠﴾
11. And made the day As a means of subsistence?[5892]	وَجَعَلْنَا ٱلنَّهَارَ مَعَاشًا ﴿١١﴾
12. And (have We not) Built over you The seven firmaments,[5893]	وَبَنَيْنَا فَوْقَكُمْ سَبْعًا شِدَادًا ﴿١٢﴾
13. And placed (therein) A Light of Splendour?[5894]	وَجَعَلْنَا سِرَاجًا وَهَّاجًا ﴿١٣﴾
14. And do We not send down From the clouds water In abundance,[5895]	وَأَنزَلْنَا مِنَ ٱلْمُعْصِرَٰتِ مَآءً ثَجَّاجًا ﴿١٤﴾
15. That We may produce Therewith corn and vegetables,	لِّنُخْرِجَ بِهِۦ حَبًّا وَنَبَاتًا ﴿١٥﴾
16. And gardens of luxurious growth?	وَجَنَّٰتٍ أَلْفَافًا ﴿١٦﴾
17. Verily the Day Of Sorting Out[5896] Is a thing appointed—	إِنَّ يَوْمَ ٱلْفَصْلِ كَانَ مِيقَٰتًا ﴿١٧﴾
18. The Day that the Trumpet[5897] Shall be sounded, and ye Shall come forth in crowds;	يَوْمَ يُنفَخُ فِى ٱلصُّورِ فَتَأْتُونَ أَفْوَاجًا ﴿١٨﴾

5891. The darkness of the night is as a covering. Just as a covering protects us from exposure to cold or heat, so this covering gives us spiritual respite from the buffets of the material world, and from the tiring activities of our own inner exertions. The rest in sleep (in verse 9) is supplemented by the covering of the night with which we are provided by Allah.

5892. *Subsistence* in English only partly covers the idea of *ma'āsh*, which includes every kind of life activity. The Day is specially illuminated, so runs the figure of speech, in order that these life activities of all kinds may be fully exercised.

5893. See n. 5526 to 65:12 and n. 2876 to 23:17, also 37:6 and notes there.

5894. That is, the sun. *Cf.* 25:61; 38:46 (where it is used metaphorically for the Holy Prophet); and 71:16.

5895. Note how the evidences of Allah and His beneficence are set out in four groups. (1) Look to external nature on the earth around you (verses 6-7); (2) your own nature, physical, mental and spiritual (verses 8-11); (3) the starry heavens, and the glory of the sun (verses 12-13); and (4) the interdependence of earth, air, and sky in the cycle of water, clouds, rain, corn and gardens, all serving in their several ways to further the whole plan of the World as it affects us. Can you not then believe that a Creator who does this will sort out Good and Evil on an appointed Day with real justice and power?

5896. *Cf.* 37:21, n. 4047, and 36:59, n. 4005 (end). The Day of Judgement is the Day of Sorting Out, as between Good and Evil.

5897. The angel charged with the sounding of the Trumpet is Isrāfīl. It will herald Judgement, *Cf.* 1:20: also 39:68, and n. 4343; and 69:13, n. 5648.

19. And the heavens
Shall be opened
As if there were doors,[5898]

وَفُتِحَتِ ٱلسَّمَآءُ فَكَانَتْ أَبْوَٰبًا ١٩

20. And the mountains
Shall vanish, as if
They were a mirage.

وَسُيِّرَتِ ٱلْجِبَالُ فَكَانَتْ سَرَابًا ٢٠

21. Truly Hell is
As a place of ambush—[5899]

إِنَّ جَهَنَّمَ كَانَتْ مِرْصَادًا ٢١

22. For the transgressors
A place of destination:

لِّلطَّٰغِينَ مَـَٔابًا ٢٢

23. They will dwell therein
For ages.

لَّٰبِثِينَ فِيهَآ أَحْقَابًا ٢٣

24. Nothing cool shall they taste
Therein, nor any drink,

لَّا يَذُوقُونَ فِيهَا بَرْدًا وَلَا شَرَابًا ٢٤

25. Save a boiling fluid
And a fluid, dark, murky,
Intensely cold—[5900]

إِلَّا حَمِيمًا وَغَسَّاقًا ٢٥

26. A fitting recompense
(For them).[5901]

جَزَآءً وِفَاقًا ٢٦

27. For that they used not
To fear any account
(For their deeds),[5902]

إِنَّهُمْ كَانُوا۟ لَا يَرْجُونَ حِسَابًا ٢٧

5898. A sign that the present order of things will have ceased to exist, and a new world will have come into being. Such a figure applies to the heavens in this verse and to the earth in the next verse. The mystery of what is beyond the heavens will have vanished through the doors which will then be opened. The solid mountains, as we suppose them to be, will have vanished like an unsubstantial mirage.

5899. Hell, the embodiment of evil, is lying in wait like an ambush for everyone. We should be on our guard. For the transgressors, those who have wilfully rebelled against Allah, it will be a definite destination, from which there is no return, except, it may be, after ages *i.e.*, unless Allah so wills: *Cf.* 6:128, and n. 951.

5900. *Cf.* 10:4, and n. 1390; also 38:57, and n. 4213.

5901. Their transgressions go on progressively as they refuse to repent and turn to Allah. The fire of misery begins to blaze forth more and more fiercely, and there is nothing to cool that blaze; their food and drink themselves are tainted with the disorder of contradictory elements—boiling hot drink, with intensely cold, murky, and disgusting fluids. These are fitting punishments for their crimes, which are inconsistent with the pure and gentle mould in which Allah had originally cast their nature.

5902. It was not isolated acts, but a continued course of evil conduct; they repudiated the moral and spiritual responsibility for their lives; and they impudently called Truth itself by false names and disdained Allah's Signs, which were vouchsafed for their instruction. These are not mere impressions; these are hard facts "preserved on record", so that every deed can have its due weight in making up the account.

28. But they (impudently) treated
Our Signs as false.

وَكَذَّبُوا بِآيَاتِنَا كِذَّابًا ﴿٢٨﴾

29. And all things have We
Preserved on record.

وَكُلَّ شَيْءٍ أَحْصَيْنَاهُ كِتَابًا ﴿٢٩﴾

30. "So taste ye (the fruits
Of your deeds);
For no increase[5903]
Shall We grant you,
Except in Punishment."

فَذُوقُوا فَلَن نَّزِيدَكُمْ إِلَّا عَذَابًا ﴿٣٠﴾

SECTION 2.

31. Verily for the Righteous
There will be
A fulfilment of
(The Heart's) desires;[5904]

إِنَّ لِلْمُتَّقِينَ مَفَازًا ﴿٣١﴾

32. Gardens enclosed, and
Grapevines;[5905]

حَدَائِقَ وَأَعْنَابًا ﴿٣٢﴾

33. Companions of Equal Age;[5906]

وَكَوَاعِبَ أَتْرَابًا ﴿٣٣﴾

34. And a Cup full
(To the Brim).[5907]

وَكَأْسًا دِهَاقًا ﴿٣٤﴾

35. No Vanity shall they hear
Therein, not Untruth—[5908]

لَّا يَسْمَعُونَ فِيهَا لَغْوًا وَلَا كِذَّابًا ﴿٣٥﴾

5903. Just as there is a progressive deterioration in the sinner's soul when he surrenders himself to evil, so there is a progressive increase in the Penalty which he suffers.

5904. This is true Salvation. It is not only safety and felicity, but the attainment of the final Goal, the supreme Achievement, the Fulfilment of the highest in human nature, the satisfaction of the true and pure desires of the heart—seeing the "Face of Allah". See n. 4733 to 44:57.

5905. The supreme Achievement, or the Fulfilment of the Heart's Desires, spoken of in the last verse, is now described in three symbols (verses 32-34), as further explained by two negatives (verse 35). The first symbol is the enclosed Fruit Garden, and the symbol taken for the fruit is the Grape. The Garden in its many aspects is the most frequent symbol adopted for Bliss. Here the symbolism is further particularised. The most carefully-tended Garden is a Fruit Garden, with walls all round to protect it, and the most characteristic fruit mentioned here is the luscious Grape. (R).

5906. The second symbol is Companions of Equal Age. Maidens or Virgins, symbols of purity, grace, beauty, innocence, truth, and sympathy. (R).

5907. The third symbol, the Cup, takes us partly to the Grapes mentioned in verse 32 and partly to the Springs or Rivers mentioned with the Garden in so many places. *Full to the brim* brings to our mind the unbounded Bounty of Allah.

5908. The explanation of the three symbols is made further clear by the two negatives. (1) There will be no talk of vanities, such as are usully associated on this earth with pleasant Gardens, Companions of equal age, or generous Cups flowing in Assemblies. (2) There will be no Untruth or Falsehood. Insincerity or Hollowness there. Everything will be on a plane of absolute Truth and Reality.

36. Recompense from thy Lord,
A Gift, (amply) sufficient[5909]—

٣٦ جَزَآءً مِّن رَّبِّكَ عَطَآءً حِسَابًا

37. (From) the Lord
Of the heavens
And the earth,
And all between—
(Allah) Most Gracious:
None shall have power
To argue with Him.[5910]

٣٧ رَّبِّ ٱلسَّمَٰوَٰتِ وَٱلْأَرْضِ
وَمَا بَيْنَهُمَا ٱلرَّحْمَٰنِ
لَا يَمْلِكُونَ مِنْهُ خِطَابًا

38. The Day that
The Spirit[5911] and the angels
Will stand forth in ranks,
None shall speak
Except any who is
Permitted by (Allah) Most Gracious,
And he will say
What is right.[5912]

٣٨ يَوْمَ يَقُومُ ٱلرُّوحُ
وَٱلْمَلَٰٓئِكَةُ صَفًّا
لَّا يَتَكَلَّمُونَ إِلَّا مَنْ أَذِنَ
لَهُ ٱلرَّحْمَٰنُ وَقَالَ صَوَابًا

39. That Day will be
The sure Reality:[5913]
Therefore, whoso will, let him
Take a (straight) Return
To his Lord!

٣٩ ذَٰلِكَ ٱلْيَوْمُ ٱلْحَقُّ
فَمَن شَآءَ ٱتَّخَذَ
إِلَىٰ رَبِّهِۦ مَـَٔابًا

5909. The Recompense is not exactly a Reward in proportion to merit, but is rather a Gift or a Bounty from the Merciful—a Gift most amply sufficient to satisfy all desire on that plane of purity. *A Gift (amply) sufficient* might almost be translated: a liberal and bountiful gift. *Cf.* the phrase, *A'ṭā fa aḥsana* = he gave generously, or bountifully. (R).

5910. No one has the right or the power to argue with Allah about the Gifts which He may bestow on His devotees beyond their deserts, (verse 36 above) or about the Penalty which His justice may inflict for sin or wrongdoing. He is high above all Creation. But He is also Most Gracious. Therefore He may permit special Dignitaries, of honour in His eyes, to plead for sinners, but they will only plead in truth and righteousness: see verse 38 below.

5911. *The Spirit:* see n. 5677 to 70:4. Some Commentators understand by "the Spirit" the angel Gabriel as he is charged specially with bringing Messages to human prophets: see 21:193. n. 3224. (R).

5912. See n. 5910 above. No one has the right to speak before the Judgement Seat; but certain great Dignitaries may be given permission to plead for mercy for sinners, and they will only so plead if the mercy is not negatory of Allah's universal justice.

5913. *Cf.* 69:1 and n. 5635. Judgement is sure to come, and Truth will then be free from all veils. Why should not man, therefore, now in this life of probation, turn back to Allah, and understand and do His Will?

40. Verily, We have warned you
Of a Penalty near—[5914]
The Day when man will
See (the Deeds) which
His hands have sent forth,
And the Unbeliever will say,
"Woe unto me! Would that
I were (mere) dust!"[5915]

إِنَّآ أَنذَرْنَٰكُمْ عَذَابًا قَرِيبًا ﴿٤٠﴾
يَوْمَ يَنظُرُ ٱلْمَرْءُ مَا قَدَّمَتْ يَدَاهُ
وَيَقُولُ ٱلْكَافِرُ يَٰلَيْتَنِى
كُنتُ تُرَٰبًۢا

5914. Is Judgement very near? Yes. There are three stages of Judgement. (1) Many of our sins and wrongdoings find their penalty in this very life. It may not be an open or striking event, but it corrodes the soul and conscience all the time. Let us therefore turn back to Allah in repentance and ask for forgiveness (2) Where the Penalty is not actually perceived or is not visible in this life, Death is considered the Lesser Judgement for each individual soul: see n. 5822 to 75:22. Death may come to anyone at any time, and we must all be ready for it. (3) Then there is the final Judgement, when the whole of the present order passes away, and there is a New World. Time as we know it will not exist. Fifty thousand years as we reckon now will be but as a Day; 70:4. According to those standards even this Final Judgement is quite near, and we must prepare for it. For it will be too late then for repentance.

5915. The Unbeliever, the Rejecter of Allah, will then find himself in a world of absolute Reality, in which there will be no place for him. He will neither live nor die: 20:74. He will wish that he could be reduced to nothingness, but even that would not be possible.

INTRODUCTION AND SUMMARY TO SŪRAH 79—*AL NĀZI'ĀT*

This is also an early Makkan Sūrah, of about the same date as the last, and deals with the theme of Judgement from the point of view of Pride and its Fall. The parable of Pharaoh occupies a central place in the argument: for he said, "I am your Lord Most High", and perished with his followers.

C. 259.—Never can Evil escape Allah's order
(79:1-46.) And law: His angels are ever present
To bring the wicked to their bearings
And they ever strive and press forward to bring
Comfort, succour, and Allah's Mercy to those
Who seek it. Then will come the Day
When the proud shall be humbled, though they
Deny the coming Judgement. What happened
To Pharaoh? He flouted Allah's Message specially
Sent to Him, and arrogantly proclaimed:
"I am your Lord Most High!" He perished
In this life and will answer for his deeds in the next.

* * * *

But can ye not see, O men, the mighty
Works of Allah in the heavens and on earth?—
The darksome splendour of the Night with its Stars.
And the daylight splendour of the Sun?—
How the earth, with its spacious expanse and its mountains,
Yields moisture and pasture, and feeds and sustains
Men and cattle, through Allah's wise Providence?
Ah! transgress not all bounds and earn not the Fire
Or Punishment, but fear Allah and His Judgement,
And prepare for the Garden of Perpetual Bliss.
Delay not! The Judgement is sure, and it's nigh!

Sūrah 79.

Al Nāzi'āt (Those Who Tear Out)

الجزء الثلاثون سورة النازعات

In the name of Allah, Most Gracious,
Most Merciful.

بسم الله الرحمن الرحيم

1. By the (angels)[5916]
Who tear out
(The souls of the wicked)
With violence;[5917]

وَالنَّٰزِعَٰتِ غَرْقًا ١

2. By those who gently
Draw out (the souls
Of the blessed);[5918]

وَالنَّٰشِطَٰتِ نَشْطًا ٢

3. And by those who glide
Along (on errands of mercy),[5919]

وَالسَّٰبِحَٰتِ سَبْحًا ٣

4. Then press forward
As in a race,

فَالسَّٰبِقَٰتِ سَبْقًا ٤

5. Then arrange to do
(The Commands of their
Lord)—

فَالْمُدَبِّرَٰتِ أَمْرًا ٥

5916. The beginning of this Sūrah may be compared with the beginning of S. 77. A translator's task in such passages is extremely difficult. He has to contend, again and again, with verities of a realm beyond man's normal range of experience expressed in elliptical language and he has to render them in another language with words of precision intelligible to readers. It is therefore necessary for him to put in part of the Commentary in the Translation in such cases. (R).

The evidence of five things is here invoked in verses 1-5, in order to lead to the conclusion in verse 6 and those following. Or, if we treat verses 3-5 as three stages of the same thing, there are three things to be considered in five stages. What are they? And what is the conclusion? See the following notes.

5917. There is much difference of opinion among the Commentators as to the five things or beings mentioned in these verses. I follow the general opinion in my interpretation, which is that angels are referred to as the agency which in their dealings with mankind show clearly Allah's Justice, Power, and Mercy, which again point to the Judgement to come, as a certainty which none can evade. The first point, referred to in this verse, is that the souls of the wicked are loath to part with their material body at death, but their will will not count: their souls will be wrenched out into another world. Who will then deny Resurrection and Judgement?

5918. The second point is that in contrast with the wicked, the souls of the blessed will be drawn out gently to their new life. They will be ready for it. In fact death for them will be a release from the grosser incidents of bodily sense. To them the approach of Judgement will be welcome.

5919. At all times are errands of mercy and blessings and errands of justice, which the angels are prompt to execute by order of Allah. There are three features of this, thus giving the third, fourth, and fifth points. (3) Their movement is compared to that of gliding or swimming *(sabḫan)*. In 21:33 this verb is applied to the motion of the celestial bodies: they all "swim along, each in its rounded course". *Cf.* Shakespeare, *Merchant of Venice:* "There's not an orb which thou behold'st, But in his motion life and angel sings, Still quiring to the young-eyed cherubims". (4) In hurrying on their errands angels press forth as in a race. (5) And thus they promptly execute the orders of their Lord.

6. One Day everything that
Can be in commotion will
Be in violent commotion,[5920]

٦ يَوْمَ تَرْجُفُ الرَّاجِفَةُ

7. Followed by oft-repeated
(Commotions):[5921]

٧ تَتْبَعُهَا الرَّادِفَةُ

8. Hearts that Day[5922]
Will be in agitation;

٨ قُلُوبٌ يَوْمَئِذٍ وَاجِفَةٌ

9. Cast down will be[5923]
(Their owners') eyes.

٩ أَبْصَٰرُهَا خَٰشِعَةٌ

10. They say (now): "What!
Shall we indeed be[5924]
Returned to (our) former state?"—

١٠ يَقُولُونَ أَءِنَّا لَمَرْدُودُونَ فِي الْحَافِرَةِ

11. "What!—when we shall
Have become rotten bones?"

١١ أَءِذَا كُنَّا عِظَٰمًا نَّخِرَةً

12. They say: "It would,
In that case, be
A return with loss!"

١٢ قَالُوا۟ تِلْكَ إِذًا كَرَّةٌ خَاسِرَةٌ

13. But verily, it will
Be but a single
(Compelling) Cry,[5925]

١٣ فَإِنَّمَا هِيَ زَجْرَةٌ وَٰحِدَةٌ

5920. The evidence of the wonderful working of the spiritual world having been invoked in the first five verses, the conclusion is now drawn and stated. It is certain that one great Day (to be taken in a spiritual sense as the Day of Account), the whole world as we now see it in our life will be in violent revolution. It will be like an earthquake destroying all landmarks. But that will affect only things subject to change: they will suffer violent convulsions as a preliminary to their disappearance. But Allah and His divine order will not change: his "Face" abideth forever, full of Majesty, Bounty, and Honour (55:27).

5921. The Commotion will be repeated again and again in the transitory world, to make way for the new world that will then come into being.

5922. All hearts will be in agitation: those of the blessed ones to see the beginning of the fulfilment of their Lord's Promise; those of the Rejecters of Allah for fear of His just Judgement.

5923. Similarly all eyes will be cast down: those of the blessed ones to see the beginning of the fulfilment of the Rejecters of Allah, in utter humiliation, sorrow, and shame, for their arrogance and insolence in their probationary life.

5924. The Unbelievers say now, in their arrogance, insolence, and mocking defiance: "Surly death here is the end of all things! When we are dead and buried, and our bones are rotten, how can we be restored again?" They add, "If that were so, then we should indeed be in a turn of dreadful luck! Instead of gaining by the Resurrection, we should be in terrible loss (with our rotten bones)!" They mean this in biting mockery. But there will indeed be an Account taken, and they will indeed be in a terrible loss, for they will go to perdition!

5925. Judgement will be inaugurated with a single compelling Cry. *Cf.* 37:19. See also 36:29 and 49, where the single mighty Blast seems to refer to the sinners being cut off in this life and plunged into the other world where they will be further judged, and 36:53, where the final Judgement is referred to.

14. When, behold, they
Will be in the (full)
Awakening (to Judgement).[5926]

فَإِذَا هُم بِالسَّاهِرَةِ ﴿١٤﴾

15. Has the story[5927]
Of Moses reached thee?

هَلْ أَتَاكَ حَدِيثُ مُوسَىٰ ﴿١٥﴾

16. Behold, thy Lord did call
To him in the sacred valley
Of Ṭuwā—[5928]

إِذْ نَادَاهُ رَبُّهُ بِالْوَادِ الْمُقَدَّسِ طُوًى ﴿١٦﴾

17. "Go thou to Pharaoh,
For he had indeed
Transgressed all bounds.[5929]

اذْهَبْ إِلَىٰ فِرْعَوْنَ إِنَّهُ طَغَىٰ ﴿١٧﴾

18. "And say to him,
'Wouldst thou that thou
Shouldst be purified
(From sin)?—

فَقُلْ هَل لَّكَ إِلَىٰ أَن تَزَكَّىٰ ﴿١٨﴾

19. "'And that I guide thee
To thy Lord, so thou[5930]
Shouldst fear Him?'"

وَأَهْدِيَكَ إِلَىٰ رَبِّكَ فَتَخْشَىٰ ﴿١٩﴾

20. Then did (Moses) show him
The Great Sign.[5931]

فَأَرَاهُ الْآيَةَ الْكُبْرَىٰ ﴿٢٠﴾

21. But (Pharaoh) rejected it
And disobeyed (guidance);

فَكَذَّبَ وَعَصَىٰ ﴿٢١﴾

5926. They will have been more or less dormant before the Great Judgement, as contrasted with the Lesser Judgement (n. 5914 to 78:40, and n. 5822 to 75:22). When the resurrection comes, they will come fully into the new world, the old heaven and earth having then completely passed away, not only for them but absolutely.

5927. This is just a reference to the story of Moses told more fully in S. 20:9-76. The lessons drawn are: (1) That even to an arrogant blasphemer and rebel against Allah's Law, like Pharaoh, Allah's grace was offered through a major prophet Moses; (2) that this rejection brought about his signal downfall even in this world; and (3) that his humiliaiton and punishment will be completed in the Hereafter at Judgement.

5928. *Cf.* 20:12.

5929. *Cf.* 20:24.

5930. Even for such a one as Pharaoh, intoxicated with his own power and greatness, guidance and grace were offered through Moses.

5931. What was the Great Sign? Some Commentators understand by it the "White Shining Hand": see n. 2550 to 20:22-23. Others think it was the miracle of the rod that became a "snake active in motion": see 20:20, n. 2549. These were among the Greater Signs: 20:23. In 17:101 there is a reference to nine clear Signs given to Moses, and these are specified in detail in n. 1091 to 7:133. the fact is, there were many Signs given, "openly self-explained," but Pharaoh and his men "were steeped in arrogance—a people given to sin" (7:133). the pre-eminently Great Sign was therefore the fact of Moses being sent to Pharaoh, which subsequently converted the magicians and the more learned Egyptians to the true God (20:70-73), though Pharaoh and his Chiefs resisted and suffered for their sins. (R).

22. Further, he turned his back,
Striving hard (against Allah).

ثُمَّ أَدْبَرَ يَسْعَىٰ ﴿٢٢﴾

23. Then he collected (his men)
And made a proclamation,

فَحَشَرَ فَنَادَىٰ ﴿٢٣﴾

24. Saying, "I am your Lord,
Most High".

فَقَالَ أَنَا رَبُّكُمُ الْأَعْلَىٰ ﴿٢٤﴾

25. But Allah did punish him
(And made an) example
Of him—in the Hereafter,
As in this life.[5932]

فَأَخَذَهُ اللَّهُ نَكَالَ الْآخِرَةِ وَالْأُولَىٰ ﴿٢٥﴾

26. Verily in this is
An instructive warning[5933]
For whosoever feareth (Allah):

إِنَّ فِي ذَٰلِكَ لَعِبْرَةً لِّمَن يَخْشَىٰ ﴿٢٦﴾

SECTION 2.

27. What! Are ye the more
Difficult to create
Of the heaven (above)?[5934]
(Allah) hath constructed it:

ءَأَنتُمْ أَشَدُّ خَلْقًا أَمِ السَّمَاءُ بَنَاهَا ﴿٢٧﴾

28. On high hath He raised
Its canopy, and He hath
Given it order and perfection.[5935]

رَفَعَ سَمْكَهَا فَسَوَّاهَا ﴿٢٨﴾

29. Its night doth He
Endow with darkness,
And its splendour doth He
Bring out (with light).[5936]

وَأَغْطَشَ لَيْلَهَا وَأَخْرَجَ ضُحَاهَا ﴿٢٩﴾

5932. See 20:78-79, also 7:135-137.

5933. *Cf.* 24:44.

5934. If man grows arrogant or forgets his accountability to Allah, in his ignorance or thoughtlessness, he is reminded that he is only an insignificant speck in Allah's spacious Creation. All the excellence that man acquires is the gift of Allah. Who had bestowed on him a high Destiny if he fulfils the purpose of his creation: 2:30-39. Then follows a nature passage, pointing to the glory of the heavens and the earth, and how they are both made to subserve the life of man.

5935. *Cf.* 2:29. The mystery of the heavens with their countless stars and the planets obeying the laws of motion, and the sun and moon influencing the temperature and climates of the earth from thousands or millions of miles, illustrate the order and perfection which Allah has given to His Creation. Can man then remain exempt from his reponsibility for his deeds, endowed as he is with a will, or deny the Day of Sorting Out, which is the Day of Judgement?

5936. *Its* of course refers to the starry heaven. Both the Night and the Day have each its own beauty and its utility for man, as has been frequently pointed out in the Qur'an. The night is a period of darkness, but it has also its splendours of light in the moon, or the planets Jupiter or Venus, or stars like Sirius or the Milky Way. These countless lights of night have their own beauty, and by day there is splendour of the sun for us, which in Creation as a whole, is just one of countless stars.

30. And the earth, moreoever,[5937]
Hath He extended
(To a wide expanse);

وَالْأَرْضَ بَعْدَ ذَٰلِكَ دَحَاهَا ﴿٣٠﴾

31. He draweth out
Therefrom its moisture
And its pasture;[5938]

أَخْرَجَ مِنْهَا مَاءَهَا وَمَرْعَاهَا ﴿٣١﴾

32. And the mountians
Hath He firmly fixed—[5939]

وَالْجِبَالَ أَرْسَاهَا ﴿٣٢﴾

33. For use and convenience[5940]
To you and your cattle.

مَتَاعًا لَّكُمْ وَلِأَنْعَامِكُمْ ﴿٣٣﴾

34. Therefore, when there comes
The great, overwhelming
(Event)—[5941]

فَإِذَا جَاءَتِ الطَّامَّةُ الْكُبْرَىٰ ﴿٣٤﴾

35. The Day when Man
Shall remember (all)
That he strove for,[5942]

يَوْمَ يَتَذَكَّرُ الْإِنسَانُ مَا سَعَىٰ ﴿٣٥﴾

36. And Hell-Fire shall be
Placed in full view[5943]
For (all) to see—

وَبُرِّزَتِ الْجَحِيمُ لِمَن يَرَىٰ ﴿٣٦﴾

37. Then, for such as had
Transgressed all bounds,

فَأَمَّا مَن طَغَىٰ ﴿٣٧﴾

5937. *Moreover:* or, more literally, *after that*. See n. 4475 to 41:11.

5938. The underground springs and wells as well as rivers and glaciers in northern climates are due to the different levels of highlands not lowlands. They spread the moisture evenly as wanted, and give corn, fruits, and vegetables to man, and pastures and feeding grounds to beasts of the fields. For the wonderful circuit or cycle of water between heaven and earth, see notes 3106 (25:49) and 3111 (25:53).

5939. See n. 2038 to 16:15. the "eternal hills" are the main reservoirs for the storage and gradual distribution of water, the very basis of the life of man and beast.

5940. This clause I construe to apply to verses 30, 31, and 32 above. Everything on earth has, by Allah's bountiful providence, been arranged to subserve the use and convenience of man and the lower life which depends upon him. The intermediary between Allah's providence and the actual use made for Allah's other gifts is man's own intelligence and initiative, which are also gifts of Allah.

5941. The Judgement, the time for sorting out all things according to their true, intrinsic, and eternal values.

5942. The Judgement will be not only for his acts but for his motives, "all he strove for", In this life he may forget his ill-deeds, but in the new conditions he will not only remember them, but the Fire of Punishment will be plainly visible to him, and not only to him, but it will be "for all to see". This will add to the sinner's humiliation.

5943. *Cf.* 26:91.

38. And had preferred[5944]
The life of this world,

وَءَاثَرَ ٱلْحَيَوٰةَ ٱلدُّنْيَا ٣٨

39. The Abode will be Hell-Fire;

فَإِنَّ ٱلْجَحِيمَ هِيَ ٱلْمَأْوَىٰ ٣٩

40. And for such as had
Entertained the fear
Of standing before[5945]
Their Lord's (tribunal)
And had restrained
(Their) souls from lower Desires,

وَأَمَّا مَنْ خَافَ
مَقَامَ رَبِّهِۦ وَنَهَى
ٱلنَّفْسَ عَنِ ٱلْهَوَىٰ ٤٠

41. Their Abode will be
The Garden.

فَإِنَّ ٱلْجَنَّةَ هِيَ ٱلْمَأْوَىٰ ٤١

42. They ask thee[5946]
About the Hour—'When
Will be its appointed time?'

يَسْـَٔلُونَكَ عَنِ ٱلسَّاعَةِ أَيَّانَ مُرْسَىٰهَا ٤٢

43. Wherein art thou (concerned)
With the declaration thereof?

فِيمَ أَنتَ مِن ذِكْرَىٰهَآ ٤٣

44. With thy Lord is
The Limit[5947] fixed therefor.

إِلَىٰ رَبِّكَ مُنتَهَىٰهَآ ٤٤

45. Thou art but a Warner
For such as fear it.[5948]

إِنَّمَآ أَنتَ مُنذِرُ مَن يَخْشَىٰهَا ٤٥

46. The Day they see it,
(It will be) as if they
Had tarried but a single

كَأَنَّهُمْ يَوْمَ يَرَوْنَهَا لَمْ يَلْبَثُوٓا۟ إِلَّا ٤٦

5944. The abiding Punishment will be for those who had willfully and persistently rebelled against Allah, "transgressing all bounds", and had given themselves up to the vanities and lusts of this lower life. This Punishment will not touch those who had repented and been forgiven, nor those guilty, through human frailty, of minor sins, whose deeds will be weighed in the balance against their good deeds: 101:6-9.

5945. The contrast is complete and parallel: the persistent rebels against Allah's Law, who preferred the lower life, are to dwell in the Fire of Punishment, while those who humbly feared the punishment of sin and believing in their Lord's warnings restrained their lower desires, will dwell in the Garden. See last note.

5946. *Cf.* 7:187 and n. 1159. Only Allah can reveal it. But were it known, "heavy were its burden through the heavens and the earth".

5947. Our time has no sort of comparison with the timeless state in the new spiritual World in which the final Judgement will take place. Nor can its limits—how long it will last—be set except in the Will of Almighty Allah, Lord of Supreme Wisdom, Justice, and Goodness: 11:107-108. But it is near, in the sense explained in n. 5914 to 78:40.

5948. The warning is only effective for those who believe in Allah and in the Final Account. Such men immediately turn in repentance to Allah, and it is to lead such men and help them, that Prophets are sent.

Evening, or (at most 'till)
The following morn![5949]

عَشِيَّةً أَوْ ضُحَاهَا

5949. *Cf.* 10:45, where the expression used is: "it will be as if they had tarried but an hour of a day." Here the metaphor used is "a single evening, or at most, 'till the following morn". Death is like sleep, and may be compared to the evening of life. In sleep we do not know how the time passes. When we wake up from the sleep of Death at the Resurrection, we shall not know whether it was the following moment or the following hour after we slept, but we shall feel that it is morning, for we shall be conscious of all that goes on, as one awakened in the morning.

INTRODUCTION AND SUMMARY TO SŪRAH 80—'*ABASA*

This is an early Makkan Sūrah, and is connected with an incident which reflects the highest honour on the Prophet's sincerity in the Revelations that were vouchsafed to him even if they seemed to reprove him for some natural and human zeal that led him to a false step in his mission according to his own high standards.

He was once deeply and earnestly engaged in trying to explain the Holy Qur'ān to Pagan Quraysh leaders, when he was interrupted by a blind man, 'Abd Allah ibn Umm Maktūm, one who was also poor, so that no one took any notice of him. He wanted to learn the Qur'ān. The Holy Prophet naturally disliked the interruption and showed impatience. Perhaps the poor man's feelings were hurt. But he whose gentle heart ever sympathised with the poor and the afflicted, got new Light from above, and without the least hesitation published this revelation, which forms part of the sacred scripture of Islam, as described in verses 13-16. And the Prophet always afterwards held the man in high honour.

The incident was only a passing incident, but after explaining the eternal principles of revelation, the Sūrah recapitulates the Mercies of Allah to man, and the consequences of a good or a wicked life here, as seen in the spiritual world to come, in the Hereafter.

C. 260.—Men not blest with the good things of this life
(80:1-42.) May yet be earnest seekers of Truth
And Purity, and deserve as much attention as those
Who seem to wield some influence, yet who
In their pride are self-sufficient. Allah's Message
Is universal: all have a right
To hear it. Held high in honour, kept
Pure and holy, it should be writ
By none but good and honourable men.

* * * *

Allah's Grace is showered on man not less
For his inner growth than in his outward
Life. There must be a final Reckoning,
When each soul must stand on its own past Record:
The faces, then, of the Blest will beam
With Joy and Light, while the Doers of Iniquity
Will hide in Dust and Shame and Darkness.

Sūrah 80.

الجزء الثلاثون سورة عبس

'Abasa (He Frowned)

In the name of Allah, Most Gracious,
Most Merciful.

بسم الله الرحمن الرحيم

1. (The Prophet) frowned
And turned away,[5950]

عبس وتولى ١

2. Because there came to him
The blind man (interrupting).

أن جاءه الأعمى ٢

3. But what could tell thee
But that perchance he might
Grow (in spiritual understanding)?

وما يدريك لعله يزكى ٣

4. Or that he might receive
Admonition, and the teaching
Might profit him?[5951]

أو يذكر فتنفعه الذكرى ٤

5. As to one who regards
Himself as self-sufficient,[5952]

أما من استغنى ٥

6. To him dost thou attend;

فأنت له تصدى ٦

7. Though it is no blame
On thee if he grow not[5953]
(In spiritual understanding).

وما عليك ألا يزكى ٧

8. But as to him who came
To thee striving earnestly,

وأما من جاءك يسعى ٨

5950. See the Introduction to this Sūrah for the incident to which this refers. The lesson is that neither spiritual worth nor the prospect of effective spiritual guidance is to be measured by a man's position in life. The poor, or the blind, the halt, or the maimed, may be more susceptible to the teaching of Allah's Word than men who are apparently gifted, but who suffer from arrogance and self-sufficiency.

5951. It may be that the poor blind man might, on account of his will to learn, be more likely to grow in his own spiritual development or to profit by any lessons taught to him even in reproof than a self-sufficient leader. In fact it was so. For the blind man became a true and sincere Muslim and lived to become a governor of Madīnah.

5952. Such a one would be a Pagan Quraysh leader, whom the Holy Prophet was anxious to get into his fold, in order that the work of preaching Allah's Message might be facilitated. But such a Message works first amongst the simple and lowly, the poor and despised folk, and the mighty ones of the earth only come in when the stream rushes in with irresistible force.

5953. Allah's Message is for all, but if the great ones arrogantly keep back from it, it is no fault of the Preacher, so long as he has proclaimed the Message. He should attend to all, and specially to the humble and lowly.

9. And with fear
(In his heart),[5954]
وَهُوَ يَخۡشَىٰ ﴿٩﴾

10. Of him wast thou unmindful.
فَأَنتَ عَنۡهُ تَلَهَّىٰ ﴿١٠﴾

11. By no means
(Should it be so)!
For it is indeed
A Message of instruction:[5955]
كَلَّآ إِنَّهَا تَذۡكِرَةٞ ﴿١١﴾

12. Therefore let whoso will,
Keep it in remembrance.
فَمَن شَآءَ ذَكَرَهُۥ ﴿١٢﴾

13. (It[5956] is) in Books
Held (greatly) in honour,
فِي صُحُفٖ مُّكَرَّمَةٖ ﴿١٣﴾

14. Exalted (in dignity),
Kept pure and holy,
مَّرۡفُوعَةٖ مُّطَهَّرَةِۭ ﴿١٤﴾

15. (Written) by the hands
Of scribes—
بِأَيۡدِي سَفَرَةٖ ﴿١٥﴾

16. Honourable and
Pious and Just.
كِرَامِۭ بَرَرَةٖ ﴿١٦﴾

17. Woe to man!
What hath made him
Reject Allah?
قُتِلَ ٱلۡإِنسَٰنُ مَآ أَكۡفَرَهُۥ ﴿١٧﴾

18. From what stuff
Hath He created him?
مِنۡ أَيِّ شَيۡءٍ خَلَقَهُۥ ﴿١٨﴾

5954. The fear in the blind man's heart may have been twofold. (1) He was humble and God-fearing, not arrogant and self-sufficient: (2) being poor and blind, he feared to intrude: yet his earnest desire to learn the Qur'ān made him bold, and he came, perhaps unseasonably, but was yet worthy of encouragement, because of the purity of his heart.

5955. Allah's Message is a universal Message, from which no one is to be excluded—rich or poor, old or young, great or lowly, learned or ignorant. If anyone had the spiritual craving that needed satisfaction, he was to be given precedence if there was to be any question of precedence at all.

5956. At the time this Sūrah was revealed, there were perhaps only about 42 or 45 Sūrahs in the hands of the Muslims. But it was a sufficient body of Revelation of high spiritual value, to which the description given here could be applied. It was held in the highest honour; its place in the hearts of Muslims was more exalted than that of anything else: as Allah's Word, it was pure and sacred; and those who transcribed it were men who were honourable, just and pious. The legend that the early Sūrahs were not carefully written down and preserved in books is a pure invention. The recensions made later in the time of the first and the third Khalīfahs were merely to preserve the purity and safeguard the arrangement of the text at a time when the expansion of Islam among non-Arabic-speaking peoples made such precautions necessary.

19. From a sperm drop:[5957]
He hath created him, and then
Mouldeth him in due proportions;

١٩ مِن نُّطْفَةٍ خَلَقَهُۥ فَقَدَّرَهُۥ

20. Then doth He make
His path smooth for him;

٢٠ ثُمَّ ٱلسَّبِيلَ يَسَّرَهُۥ

21. Then He causeth him to die,
And putteth him in his Grave;[5958]

٢١ ثُمَّ أَمَاتَهُۥ فَأَقْبَرَهُۥ

22. Then, when it is
His Will, He will
Raise him up (again).

٢٢ ثُمَّ إِذَا شَآءَ أَنشَرَهُۥ

23. By no means hath he
Fulfilled what Allah
Hath commanded him.[5959]

٢٣ كَلَّا لَمَّا يَقْضِ مَآ أَمَرَهُۥ

24. Then let man look
At his Food,[5960]
(And how We provide it):

٢٤ فَلْيَنظُرِ ٱلْإِنسَٰنُ إِلَىٰ طَعَامِهِۦٓ

25. For that We pour forth
Water in abundance,

٢٥ أَنَّا صَبَبْنَا ٱلْمَآءَ صَبًّا

26. And We split the earth
In fragments,[5961]

٢٦ ثُمَّ شَقَقْنَا ٱلْأَرْضَ شَقًّا

5957. *Cf.* 76:2, and n. 5832. The origin of man as an animal is lowly indeed. But what further faculties and capacities has not Allah granted to men? Besides his animal body, in which also he shares in all the blessings which Allah has bestowed on the rest of His Creation, man has been granted divine gifts which entitle him to be called Vicegerent of Allah on earth: 2:30. He has a will; he has spiritual perception; he is capable of divine love; he can control nature within certain limits, and subject nature's forces to his own use. And he has been given the power of judgement, so that he can avoid excess and defect, and follow the middle path. And that path, as well as all that is necessary for his life in its manifold aspects, has been made easy for him.

5958. *Cf.* 20:55. Death is an inevitable event after the brief life on this earth, but it is also in a sense a blessing—a release from the imperfections of this world, a close of the probationary period, after which will dawn the full Reality. *The Grave* may be understood to be the period between physical death and immortal Life, whatever may be the mode of diposal of the dead body. This intermediate period is the *Barzakh* or Partition: see n. 2940 to 23:101.

5959. Though all these blessings and stages have been provided by Allah's Grace for the good of man, yet unregenerate man fails in carrying out the purpose of his creation and life.

5960. After a reference to man's inner history, there is now a reference to just one item in his daily outer life, his food: and it is shown how the forces of heaven and earth unite by Allah's Command to serve man and his dependants, "for use and convenience to you and your cattle" (verse 32 below). If that is the case with just one item, food, how much more comprehensive is Allah's beneficence when the whole of man's needs are considered!

5961. The water comes from the clouds in plentiful abundance; the earth is ploughed, and the soil is broken up in fragments, and yields an abundant harvest of cereals (Corn), trellised fruit (Grapes), and vegetable food (nutritious Plants), as well as fruit that can keep for long periods and serve many uses, like olives and dates.

27. And produce therein[5962] Corn,

فَأَنۢبَتۡنَا فِيهَا حَبّٗا ﴿٢٧﴾

28. And Grapes and nutritious Plants,

وَعِنَبٗا وَقَضۡبٗا ﴿٢٨﴾

29. And Olives and Dates,

وَزَيۡتُونٗا وَنَخۡلٗا ﴿٢٩﴾

30. And enclosed Gardens,[5963]
Dense with lofty trees,

وَحَدَآئِقَ غُلۡبٗا ﴿٣٠﴾

31. And Fruits and Fodder—

وَفَٰكِهَةٗ وَأَبّٗا ﴿٣١﴾

32. For use and convenience
To you and your cattle.[5964]

مَّتَٰعٗا لَّكُمۡ وَلِأَنۡعَٰمِكُمۡ ﴿٣٢﴾

33. At length, when there
Comes the Deafening Noise—[5965]

فَإِذَا جَآءَتِ ٱلصَّآخَّةُ ﴿٣٣﴾

34. That Day shall a man
Flee from his own brother,

يَوۡمَ يَفِرُّ ٱلۡمَرۡءُ مِنۡ أَخِيهِ ﴿٣٤﴾

35. And from his mother
And his father,

وَأُمِّهِۦ وَأَبِيهِ ﴿٣٥﴾

36. And from his wife
And his children.[5966]

وَصَٰحِبَتِهِۦ وَبَنِيهِ ﴿٣٦﴾

37. Each one of them,
That Day, will have
Enough concern (of his own)
To make him indifferent
To the others.[5967]

لِكُلِّ ٱمۡرِيٕٖ مِّنۡهُمۡ
يَوۡمَئِذٖ شَأۡنٞ يُغۡنِيهِ ﴿٣٧﴾

5962. *Therein: i.e.*, from within the earth or the soil.

5963. We not only get field crops such as were mentioned in n. 5961 above, but we have the more highly cultivated garden crops, both in the way of lofty trees, and in the way of carefully tended fruits like the fig; and then we have grass and all kinds of fodder.

5964. The same verse occurs at 79:33, where n. 5940 explains the wider meaning in that context.

5965. Preliminary to the establishment of the Final Judgement.

5966. Even those who were nearest and dearest in this life will not be able or willing to help each other on that awful Day. On the contrary, if they have to receive a sentence for their sins, they will be anxious to avoid even sharing each other's sorrows or witnessing each other's humiliation; for each will have enough of his own troubles to occupy him. On the other hand, the Righteous will be united with their righteous families: 52:21; and their faces will be "beaming, laughing, rejoicing" (80:38-39).

5967. *Cf.* 70:10-14. No friend will ask after a friend That Day. On the contrary the sinner will desire to save himself at the expense even of his own family and benefactors.

38. Some Faces that Day
Will be beaming,

وُجُوهٌ يَوْمَئِذٍ مُّسْفِرَةٌ ﴿٣٨﴾

39. Laughing, rejoicing.

ضَاحِكَةٌ مُّسْتَبْشِرَةٌ ﴿٣٩﴾

40. And other faces that Day
Will be dust stained;[5968]

وَوُجُوهٌ يَوْمَئِذٍ عَلَيْهَا غَبَرَةٌ ﴿٤٠﴾

41. Blackness will cover them:

تَرْهَقُهَا قَتَرَةٌ ﴿٤١﴾

42. Such will be
The Rejecters of Allah,
The Doers of Iniquity.

أُولَٰئِكَ هُمُ الْكَفَرَةُ الْفَجَرَةُ ﴿٤٢﴾

5968. The dust on the faces of the sinners will be in contrast to the beaming light on the faces of the righteous; and the blackness in contrast to the "laughing, rejoicing" faces of the righteous. But the dust also suggests that being Rejecters of Allah, their faces and eyes and faculties were choked in dust, and the blackness suggests that being Doers of Iniquity they had no part or lot in purity or Light. Another contrast may possibly be deduced: the humble and lowly may be "in the dust" in this life, and the arrogant sinners in sunshine, but the roles will be reversed at Judgement.

INTRODUCTION TO SŪRAH 81—*AL TAKWĪR*

This is quite an early Makkan Sūrah, perhaps the sixth or seventh in chronological order. It opens with a series of highly graphic images portraying the break-up of the world as we know it (verses 1-13) and the enforcement of complete personal responsibility for each soul (verse 14). This is followed by a passage showing how the Quranic Revelation was true, and revealed through the angel Gabriel, and not merely a rhapsody from one possessed. Revelation is given for man's spiritual guidance (verses 14-29). (R).

Comparable with this Sūrah are Sūrahs 82 and 84 which may be read with this.

C. 261.—How can the soul's self-conviction be fitly
(81:1-29.) Expressed, except by types of tremendous
Cataclysms in nature, and still more by tremendous
Searchings in the heart of man? These want
Deep pondering. When once the spiritual Dawn
Has "breathed away" the Darkness of the Night,
The Vision Glorious clears all doubts,
And brings us face to face with Truth.
The highest Archangel in heaven is sent
By Allah to bring these truths to men
Through their Prophet. Allah's Grace flows freely:
We have but to tune our Will to His—
The ever-loving Righteous God.

Sūrah 81.

الجزء الثلاثون سُورَةُ التَّكْوِيرِ

Al Takwīr (The Folding Up)

In the name of Allah, Most Gracious, Most Merciful.

بِسْمِ اللَّهِ الرَّحْمَٰنِ الرَّحِيمِ

1. When the sun[5969]
(With its spacious light)
Is folded up;[5970]

إِذَا ٱلشَّمْسُ كُوِّرَتْ ١

2. When the stars[5971]
Fall, losing their lustre;

وَإِذَا ٱلنُّجُومُ ٱنكَدَرَتْ ٢

3. When the mountains vanish
(Like a mirage);[5972]

وَإِذَا ٱلْجِبَالُ سُيِّرَتْ ٣

4. When the she-camels,
Ten months with young,
Are left untended;[5973]

وَإِذَا ٱلْعِشَارُ عُطِّلَتْ ٤

5. When the wild beasts
Are herded together
(In human habitations);[5974]

وَإِذَا ٱلْوُحُوشُ حُشِرَتْ ٥

5969. Verses 1 to 13 are conditional clauses, and the substantive clause is in verse 14. The time will come when nature's processes as we know them will cease to function, and the soul will only then know by self-conviction the results of its actions. With reference to an individual soul, its resurrection is its supreme crisis: the whole world of sense, and even of imagination and reason, melts away, and its whole spiritual scroll is laid bare before it.

5970. The conditional clauses are twelve, in two groups of six. The first six affect the outer or physical life of man; the last six, his inmost spiritual life. Let us take them one by one. (1) The biggest factor affecting us in the external physical World is the light, heat, and perhaps electric or magnetic energy of the sun. The sun is the source of all the light, heat, and energy, and indeed the source and support of all physical life that we know. It is the biggest factor and yet most remote from us in our solar system. Yet the sources of our inner spiritual life will be greater and more lasting, for they will survive it. The sun as the centre of our solar system also stands as a symbol of the present order of things. The physical forces, as defined in Newton's laws of Matter and Attraction, will also break up with the break-up of the sun.
Is folded up: is folded up, or twisted up, like a sheet or garment.

5971. (2) Next after the sun, we can derive faint lights from the innumerable stars in the firmament. For all the ages of which we have any record, these stars have remained fixed. Nothing can be more fixed: yet they can and will fail.

5972. *Cf.* 78:20. (3) On our own earth the mountains—the "eternal hills"—seem the most striking examples of stability; yet they will be swept away like a mirage, as if they had never existed.

5973. (4) The type of Arab property, as well as the type of the Arab pet, was the camel, and the most precious camel was the she-camel just about to be delivered of her young. She would in normal times be most sedulously cared for. But when all our landmarks of this life vanish, even she would be left untended. Nothing would then be as it is now.

5974. (5) In the present world, the wild animals fear each other, and they all fear man and normally keep away from human habitations. But when this order passes away, there will be scarcely any differentiation between human habitations and the wilds of the forests.

6. When the oceans[5975]
Boil over with a swell;

٦ وَإِذَا ٱلْبِحَارُ سُجِّرَتْ

7. When the souls
Are sorted out,[5976]
(Being joined, like with like);

٧ وَإِذَا ٱلنُّفُوسُ زُوِّجَتْ

8. When the female (infant),
Buried alive, is questioned—

٨ وَإِذَا ٱلْمَوْءُۥدَةُ سُئِلَتْ

9. For what crime
She was killed;[5977]

٩ بِأَيِّ ذَنۢبٍ قُتِلَتْ

10. When the Scrolls
Are laid open;[5978]

١٠ وَإِذَا ٱلصُّحُفُ نُشِرَتْ

11. When the World on High[5979]
Is unveiled;

١١ وَإِذَا ٱلسَّمَآءُ كُشِطَتْ

12. When the Blazing Fire[5980]
Is kindled to fierce heat;

١٢ وَإِذَا ٱلْجَحِيمُ سُعِّرَتْ

5975. See 52:6 and n. 5041. (6) The oceans, which now keep their bounds, will surge and boil over, and overwhelm all landmarks. At present the waters seem to have reached their fixed and normal levels, but the whole equilibrium will then be disturbed. Such will be the complete wreck of this transitory world, at the approach of the dawn of the permanent Reality. But these are physical symbols, relating to the outer nature surrounding the physical nature of man. The remaining six, *viz.*: the 7th to the 12th, describe the ordering of the new spiritual World, from which all present seeming incongruities will be removed.

5976. *Cf.* 56:7, where the sorting out into three classes is mentioned, *viz.*: Those Nearest to Allah, the Companions of the Right Hand, and the Companions of the Left Hand. That was a sort of broad general division. The meaning in this passage is wider. (7) Whereas in this world of probation, good is mixed with evil, knowledge with ignorance, power with arrogance, and so on—in the new world of Reality, all true values will be restored, and like will consort with like, for it will be a world of perfect Peace, Harmony, and Justice.

5977. (8) In this world of sin and sorrow, much unjust suffering is caused, and innocent lives sacrificed, without a trace being left, by which offenders can be brought to justice. A striking example before the Quraysh was female infanticide: *cf.* 16:58-59, and n. 2084. The crime was committed in the guise of social plausibility in secret collusion, and no question was asked here. But in the spiritual world of Justice, full questions will be asked, and the victim herself—dumb here—will be able to give evidence, for she had committed no crime herself. The proofs will be drawn from the very means used for concealment.

5978. (9) The Scrolls recording the deeds of men, good or bad, will then be laid open before all. *Cf.* 50:17-18, n. 4954; also 82:11-12. In the present phenomenal world, things may be concealed; but in the spiritual world of absolute Reality, every secret is opened out, good or bad. The whole tale of acts, omissions, motives, imponderable spiritual hurt, neglect, or help will be laid bare.

5979. *The World on High:* literally, the Sky, or Heaven as standing for both the Blazing Fire and the Garden, the Home of the Hereafter. (10) The soul's spiritual Sky—the things it held high or sacred—will be stripped of the thin blue that gave rest—and partly illusion—to its spiritual eye in the world of illusions. Just as when an animal is skinned, its real flesh and blood and inner organs become visible, without any outer coating to hold them together, so the inmost state of the spiritual world will then become plain.

5980. (11) Then will burn the *Blazing Fire of the Hell,* worse than the fiercest fire. (R).

13. And when the Garden[5981]
Is brought near—[5982]

وَإِذَا الْجَنَّةُ أُزْلِفَتْ ﴿١٣﴾

14. (Then) shall each soul know
What it has put forward.[5983]

عَلِمَتْ نَفْسٌ مَّا أَحْضَرَتْ ﴿١٤﴾

15. So verily I call[5984]
To witness the Planets—[5985]
That recede,

فَلَا أُقْسِمُ بِالْخُنَّسِ ﴿١٥﴾

16. Go straight, or hide;

الْجَوَارِ الْكُنَّسِ ﴿١٦﴾

17. And the Night
As it dissipates;[5986]

وَاللَّيْلِ إِذَا عَسْعَسَ ﴿١٧﴾

18. And the Dawn
As it breathes away
The darkness—[5987]

وَالصُّبْحِ إِذَا تَنَفَّسَ ﴿١٨﴾

19. Verily this is the word
Of a most honourable
Messenger,[5988]

إِنَّهُ لَقَوْلُ رَسُولٍ كَرِيمٍ ﴿١٩﴾

5981. (12) The last of the Metaphors, the Garden of Bliss—the Light of Allah's Face (92:20)—will come in sight—not yet attained, but visible, or "brought near". For the scales have fallen from the eyes, and the soul knows itself.

5982. See 75:22, n. 5822; 78:40, n. 5914; and 79:14, n. 5926. [Eds.].

5983. This is the conclusion. It is only on such conditions that the soul reaches its full realisation. *Put forward: cf.* "the Deeds which his hands have sent forth" in 78:40.

5984. *Cf.* 76:75, n. 5258, for the witness that the heavenly bodies bear symbolically to the power, beauty, and goodness of Allah, in sending His Revelation. See n. 5798 to 74:32, for the significance of an adjuration in the Qur'ān.

5985. The appeal here is made to three things, the Planets, the Night, and the Dawn. (1) The Planets have a retrograde and a forward motion, and during occultation, hide or disappear behind the sun or moon, or are otherwise invisible or appear stationary. They behave differently from the millions of stars around them. Yet they are not mere erratic bodies, but obey definite laws, and evidence the power and wisdom of Allah.

5986. How the Night gradually declines after its height at midnight! It seems gradually to steal away, and as Dawn approaches, to merge into Day. So a soul in spiritual darkness gradually awakes to its spiritual Dawn through Revelation.

5987. The slow "breathing out" of the darkness by the Dawn, shown us, by beautiful imagery, that these mysterious operations, of which people in their ignorance are frightened if they have to do with darkness, are really beneficient operations of Allah. They have nothing to do with evil spirits, or witches, or magic. For three questions were actually raised about the Holy Prophet's Ministry by the ignorant. (1) Did his wonderful works come from himself and not from Allah? (2) Was he possessed of an evil spirit? In other words, was he mad? For that was the theory of madness, then current. (3) Was he a soothsayer, or necromancer, or magician? For he had virtues, powers, and eloquence, so extraordinary that they could not understand him.

5988. They are told here that all their three theories were foolish. The Revelation was really from Allah. Their wonder should cease if they observe the daily miracles worked round them in nature. The bringer of Allah's Message was the angel Gabriel, and not an evil spirit.

20. Endued with Power, With rank before The Lord of the Throne,[5989]	ذِي قُوَّةٍ عِندَ ذِي ٱلْعَرْشِ مَكِينٍ ﴿٢٠﴾
21. With authority there, (And) faithful to his trust.	مُّطَاعٍ ثَمَّ أَمِينٍ ﴿٢١﴾
22. And (O people)! Your Companion is not One possessed;[5990]	وَمَا صَاحِبُكُم بِمَجْنُونٍ ﴿٢٢﴾
23. And without doubt he saw him In the clear horizon.[5991]	وَلَقَدْ رَءَاهُ بِٱلْأُفُقِ ٱلْمُبِينِ ﴿٢٣﴾
24. Neither doth he withhold Grudgingly a knowledge Of the Unseen.[5992]	وَمَا هُوَ عَلَى ٱلْغَيْبِ بِضَنِينٍ ﴿٢٤﴾
25. Nor is it the word Of an evil spirit accursed.[5993]	وَمَا هُوَ بِقَوْلِ شَيْطَٰنٍ رَّجِيمٍ ﴿٢٥﴾
26. Then whither go ye?[5994]	فَأَيْنَ تَذْهَبُونَ ﴿٢٦﴾
27. Verily this is no less Than a Message To (all) the Worlds:[5995]	إِنْ هُوَ إِلَّا ذِكْرٌ لِّلْعَٰلَمِينَ ﴿٢٧﴾

5989. Not only was the bringer of the Revelation, Gabriel, an honourable Messenger, incapable of deceit, but he had, in the angelic kingdom, rank and authority before Allah's Throne, and he could convey an authoritative divine Message. He was, like the Holy Prophet, faithful to his trust; and therefore there could be no question of the Message being delivered in any other way than exactly according to the divine Will and Purpose. These epithets could apply to the Prophet himself, but in veiw of verse 23 below, it is best to understand them of Gabriel.

5990. After describing the credentials of the Archangel Gabriel, the Text now appeals to the people to consider their own "Companion", the Prophet, who had been born among them and had lived with them, and was known to be an honourable, truthful, and trustworthy man. If Gabriel was the one who brought the Message to him, then there was no question of demoniacal possession. And the Prophet had seen him in his inspired vision "in the clear horizon".

5991. Read along with this the whole passage in 53:1-18 and notes there; specially n. 5092, where the two occasions are mentioned when there was a vision of inspiration: "For truly did he see, of the Signs of his Lord, the Greatest" (53:18).

5992. Such would be the words of a soothsayer, guarded, ambiguous, and misleading. Here everything was clear, sane, true, and under divine inspiration.

5993. Such as evil suggestions of envy, spite, greed, selfishness, or other vices. On the contrary, the teaching of the Qur'ān is beneficient, pointing to the Right Way, and Way of Allah. *Rajīm:* literally, driven away with stones, rejected with complete ignominy. *Cf.* 15:17. The rite of throwing stones in the valley of Minā at the close of the Makkan Pilgrimage [see n. 217 (6) to 2:197] suggests symbolically that the Pilgrim emphatically, definitely, and finally rejects all Evil.

5994. It has been shown that this is no word of a mortal, but that it is full of divine wisdom: that its teaching is not that of a madman, but sane to the core and in accordance with human needs: that it freely and clearly directs you to the right Path and forbids you the Path of evil. Why then hesitate? Accept the divine Grace; repent of your sins; and come to the higher Life.

5995. It is not meant for one class or race; it is universal, and is addressed to all the Worlds. For the meaning of "Worlds", see n. 20 to 1:2.

28. (With profit) to whoever
Among you wills
To go straight:[5996]

٢٨ لِمَن شَاءَ مِنكُمْ أَن يَسْتَقِيمَ

29. But ye shall not will
Except as Allah wills—
The Cherisher of the Worlds.

٢٩ وَمَا تَشَاءُونَ إِلَّا أَن يَشَاءَ اللَّهُ رَبُّ الْعَالَمِينَ

5996. *Cf.* 74:55-56. Allah is the Cherisher of the Worlds, Lord of Grace and Mercy, and His guidance is open to all who have the will to profit by it. But that will must be exercised in conformity with Allah's Will (verse 29). Such conformity is Islam. Verse 28 points to human free will and responsibility; verse 29 to its limitations. Both extremes, *viz.*: cast-iron Determination and an idea of chaotic Free Will, are condemned.

INTRODUCTION TO SŪRAH 82—*AL INFIṬĀR*

In subject matter this Sūrah is cognate to the last, though the best authorities consider it a good deal later in chronology in the early Makkan Period.

Its argument is subject to the threefold interpretation mentioned in n. 5982 to 81:13, *viz.*, as referring (1) to the final Day of Judgement, (2) to the Lesser Judgement, on an individual's death, and (3) to the awakening of the Inner Light in the soul at any time, that being considered as Death to the Falsities of this life and a Rebirth to the true spiritual Reality.

C. 262.—How fixed is the order holding together
(82:1-19.) This material universe above and below us?
Yet it must give way before the vast
Unfathomed Truth in which man will see
His past and his future in true perspective.
To Allah he owes his life and all
Its blessings: will he not see
That the Future depends on Right and Justice?
Righteousness must come to its own,
And so must Discord and Rebellion.
The Day must come when Discord
Must finally cease, and the Peace of Allah
And His Command are all-in-all.

Sūrah 82.

الجزء الثلاثون سُورَةُ الانفِطَار

Al Infiṭār (The Cleaving Asunder)

In the Name of Allah, Most Gracious, Most Merciful

بِسْمِ اللَّهِ الرَّحْمَٰنِ الرَّحِيمِ

1. When[5997] the Sky
Is cleft asunder;[5998]

إِذَا السَّمَاءُ انفَطَرَتْ ١

2. When the Stars
Are scattered;[5999]

وَإِذَا الْكَوَاكِبُ انتَثَرَتْ ٢

3. When the Oceans
Are suffered to burst forth;[6000]

وَإِذَا الْبِحَارُ فُجِّرَتْ ٣

4. And when the Graves
Are turned upside down—[6001]

وَإِذَا الْقُبُورُ بُعْثِرَتْ ٤

5. (Then) shall each soul know
What it hath sent forward[6002]
And (what it hath) kept back.

عَلِمَتْ نَفْسٌ مَّا قَدَّمَتْ وَأَخَّرَتْ ٥

5997. *Cf.* the passage 81:1-14 and notes. For the three parallel interpretations, see the Introduction to this Sūrah. There are four conditional clauses here, and the substantive clause is in verse 5. In S. 81. there were 12 conditional clauses, and the conclusion was similar, but not expressed in precisely the same terms. See 72:5, n. 6002 below. The physical world as we see it now will be destroyed before the final Day of Judgement, establishing the true spiritual Reality. In the following four clauses we have a reference to the Lesser Judgement, the individual dawn of the true Reality at Death. (R).

5998. *Cf.* 73:18, n. 5869. The beautiful blue sky overhead, which we take for granted in sunshine and storm, will be shattered to pieces before the New World is established. The partition which seems at present to divide things divine from the phenomenal world has to be shattered before each soul knows the reality about itself. (R).

5999. *Cf.* 81:2, where the word for "stars" *(Nujūm)* is different, and the verb is different. *Najm* has reference to brightness, and the verb "losing their lustre" was appropriate there, to show the opposite. *Kawkab* (used here) has more the meaning of a star as fixed in a constellation; and the opposite of a fixed and definite order is "scattered", the verb used here. In fact, throughout this passage, the dominating idea is the disturbance of order and symmetry. The metaphor behind the scattering of the constellations is that in the present order of things we see many things associated together, *e.g.*, rank with honour, wealth with comfort, etc. In the New World this will be seen to have been merely fortuitous. (R).

6000. *Cf.* 81:6, "when the oceans boil over with a swell". Here, "are suffered to burst forth" expresses the end of the present order of things. This may be in two ways: (1) The barrier, which keeps within their respective bounds the various streams.of salt and fresh water (55:20, n. 5185), will be removed; (2) the Ocean will overwhelm the whole Globe. (R).

6001. This item is not mentioned in 81:1-14. Here it is introduced to show that the whole order of things will be so reversed that even Death will not be Death. We think there is tranquillity in Death, but there will be no tranquillity. Literally, and figuratively, Death will be the beginning of a new Life. What we think to be Death will bring forth Life.

6002. *Sent Forward and kept back:* may mean: the deeds of commission and omission in this life. Or the Arabic words may also be translated: *sent forward and left behind: i.e.*, the spiritual possibilities which it sent forward for its other life, and the physical things on which it prided itself in this life, but which it had to leave behind in this life. Or else, the things it put first and the things it put last in importance may change places in the new world of Reality. "The first shall be last and the last shall be first".

6. O man! what has
Seduced thee from
Thy Lord Most Beneficient?—

يَٰٓأَيُّهَا ٱلْإِنسَٰنُ مَا غَرَّكَ بِرَبِّكَ ٱلْكَرِيمِ ﴿٦﴾

7. Him Who created thee,
Fashioned thee in due
proportion,[6003]
And gave thee a just bias;[6004]

ٱلَّذِى خَلَقَكَ فَسَوَّىٰكَ فَعَدَلَكَ ﴿٧﴾

8. In whatever Form[6005] He wills,
Does He put thee together.

فِىٓ أَىِّ صُورَةٍ مَّا شَآءَ رَكَّبَكَ ﴿٨﴾

9. Nay! but ye do
Reject Right and Judgement![6006]

كَلَّا بَلْ تُكَذِّبُونَ بِٱلدِّينِ ﴿٩﴾

10. But verily over you
(Are appointed angels)[6007]
To protect you—

وَإِنَّ عَلَيْكُمْ لَحَٰفِظِينَ ﴿١٠﴾

11. Kind and honourable—
Writing down (your deeds):

كِرَامًا كَٰتِبِينَ ﴿١١﴾

12. They know (and understand)
All that ye do.

يَعْلَمُونَ مَا تَفْعَلُونَ ﴿١٢﴾

13. As for the Righteous,
They will be in Bliss;

إِنَّ ٱلْأَبْرَارَ لَفِى نَعِيمٍ ﴿١٣﴾

14. And the Wicked—
They will be in the Fire,

وَإِنَّ ٱلْفُجَّارَ لَفِى جَحِيمٍ ﴿١٤﴾

6003. *Cf.* 15:29. Allah not only created man, but fashioned him in due proportions, giving him extraordinary capacities, and the means wherewith he can fulfil his high destiny.

6004. See n. 834 to 6:1. Having given a limited free will, He gave us a just bias through our reason and our spiritual faculties. If we err, it is our will that is at fault.

6005. By "Form" *(Sūrah)* here I understand the general shape of things in which any given personality is placed, including his physical and social environments, his gifts of mind and spirit, and all that goes to make up his outer and inner life. The Grace of Allah is shown in all these things, for His Will is formed from perfect knowledge, wisdom, and goodness.

6006. The goodness and mercies of Allah, and His constant watchful care of all His creatures should make men grateful, instead of which they turn away from the Right and deny the Day of Sorting Out, the Day when every action performed here will find its fulfilment in just reward or punishment.

6007. Besides the faculties given to man to guide him, and the Form and Personality through which he can rise by stages to the Presence of Allah, there are spiritual agencies around him to help and protect him, and to note down his Record, so that perfect justice may be done to him at the end. For these Guardian Angels, see 50:17-18, and n. 4954.

15. Which they will enter[6008]
On the Day of Judgement,

يَصْلَوْنَهَا يَوْمَ الدِّينِ ﴿١٥﴾

16. And they will not be
Able to keep away therefrom.

وَمَا هُمْ عَنْهَا بِغَآئِبِينَ ﴿١٦﴾

17. And what will explain
To thee what the Day
Of Judgement is?

وَمَآ أَدْرَىٰكَ مَا يَوْمُ الدِّينِ ﴿١٧﴾

18. Again, what will explain
To thee what the Day
Of Judgement is?[6009]

ثُمَّ مَآ أَدْرَىٰكَ مَا يَوْمُ الدِّينِ ﴿١٨﴾

19. (It will be) the Day
When no soul shall have
Power (to do) aught
For another:[6010]
For the Command, that Day,
Will be (wholly) with Allah.

يَوْمَ لَا تَمْلِكُ نَفْسٌ لِّنَفْسٍ شَيْـًٔا وَٱلْأَمْرُ يَوْمَئِذٍ لِّلَّهِ ﴿١٩﴾

6008. I understand this relative clause to govern "the Fire", *i.e.*, the Punishment. It will be postponed as long as possible, to give the Sinner every chance of repentance and amendment. But once the period of probation is past, it will be irrevocable. There will be no going back from it. By inference, the Righteous may individually reach some stage of Bliss at once, possibly in this life, possibly after death, though the Final Judgement will be the general and complete cessation of this fleeting world and the creation of the world of Eternity.

6009. We can speak of Rewards and Punishments, the Fruits of Actions, the Resurrection and the Tribunal, the Restoration of True Values, the Elimination of all Wrong, and a hundred other phrases. They might serve to introduce our minds vaguely to a new World, of which they cannot possibly form any adequate conception under present conditions. The question is repeated in verses 17-18 to emphasise this difficulty, and a simple answer is suggested, as explained in the next note.

6010. The answer is suggested by a negative proposition: 'No soul shall have power to do aught for another'. This is full of meaning. Personal responsibility will be fully enforced. In this world we all depend on one another proximately, though our ultimate dependence is always on Allah, now and forever. But here a father helps a son forward; husband and wife influence each other's destinies; human laws and institutions may hold large masses of mankind under their grip; falsehood and evil may seem to flourish for a time, because a certain amount of limited free will has been granted to man. This period will be all over then. The good and the pure will have been separated from the evil and the rebellious; the latter will have been rendered inert, and the former will have been so perfected that their wills will be in complete consonance with Allah's Universal Will. The Command, thenceforward, will be wholly with Allah.

INTRODUCTION TO SŪRAH 83—*AL MUṬAFFIFĪN*

This Sūrah is close in time to the last one and the next one.

It condemns all fraud—in daily dealings, as well as and especially in matters of Religion and higher spiritual Life.

C. 263.—Shun Fraud in all things: in little
(83:1-36.) Things of daily life, but specially
In those subtler forms of higher life,
Which will be exposed to view at Judgement,
However hidden they may be
In this life. Give everyone his due
For the Record of ill deeds and good
Is fully kept, and the stains of sin
Corrupt the soul. Reject not the Real
Now, nor mock: for the time will come
When the True will come to its own, and then
The mighty arrogant will be abased!

Sūrah 83. الجزء الثلاثون سورة المطففين

Al Muṭaffifīn (The Dealers in Fraud)

In the name of Allah, Most Gracious, Most Merciful.

بِسْمِ ٱللَّهِ ٱلرَّحْمَٰنِ ٱلرَّحِيمِ

1. Woe to those
That deal in fraud—[6011]

وَيْلٌ لِّلْمُطَفِّفِينَ ١

2. Those who, when they
Have to receive by measure
From men, exact full measure,

ٱلَّذِينَ إِذَا ٱكْتَالُوا۟ عَلَى ٱلنَّاسِ يَسْتَوْفُونَ ٢

3. But when they have
To give by measure
Or weight to men,
Give less than due.

وَإِذَا كَالُوهُمْ أَو وَّزَنُوهُمْ يُخْسِرُونَ ٣

4. Do they not think
That they will be called
To account?—[6012]

أَلَا يَظُنُّ أُو۟لَٰٓئِكَ أَنَّهُم مَّبْعُوثُونَ ٤

5. On a Mighty Day,

لِيَوْمٍ عَظِيمٍ ٥

6. A Day when (all) mankind
Will stand before
The Lord of the Worlds?

يَوْمَ يَقُومُ ٱلنَّاسُ لِرَبِّ ٱلْعَٰلَمِينَ ٦

7. Nay! Surely the Record
Of the Wicked is
(Preserved) in *Sijjīn*.[6013]

كَلَّآ إِنَّ كِتَٰبَ ٱلْفُجَّارِ لَفِى سِجِّينٍ ٧

6011. "Fraud" must here be taken in a widely general sense. It covers giving short measure or short weight, but it covers much more than that. The next two verses make it clear that it is the spirit of injustice that is condemned—giving too little and asking too much. This may be shown in commercial dealings, where a man exacts a higher standard in his own favour than he is willing to concede as against him. In domestic or social matters an individual or group may ask for honour, or respect, or services which he or they are not willing to give on their side in similar circumstances. It is worse than one-sided selfishness: for it is double injustice. But it is worst of all in religion or spiritual life: with what face can a man ask for Mercy or Love from Allah when he is unwilling to give it to his fellow-men? In one aspect this is a statement of the Golden Rule. 'Do as you would be done by'. But it is more completely expressed. You must give in full what is due from you, whether you expect or wish to receive full consideration from the other side or not.

6012. Legal and social sanctions against Fraud depend for their efficacy on whether there is a chance of being found out. Moral and religious sanctions are of a different kind. 'Do you wish to degrade your own nature?' 'Do you not consider that there is a Day of Account before a Judge Who knows all, and Who safeguards all interests, for He is the Lord and Cherisher of the Worlds? Whether other people know anything about your wrong or not, you are guilty before Allah.'

6013. This is a word from the same root as *Sijn*, a Prison. It rhymes with and is contrasted with *'Illīyīn* in verse 18 below. It is therefore understood by many Commentators to be a place, a Prison or a Dungeon in which the Wicked are confined pending their appearance before the Judgement Seat. The mention of the Inscribed Register in verse 9 below may imply that *Sijjīn* is the name of the Register of Black Deeds, though verse 9 may be elliptical and may only describe the place by the significance of its contents.

8. And what will explain
To thee what *Sijjīn* is?

وَمَآ أَدْرَىٰكَ مَا سِجِّينٌ ﴿٨﴾

9. (There is) a Register
(Fully) inscribed.[6014]

كِتَٰبٌ مَّرْقُومٌ ﴿٩﴾

10. Woe, that Day, to those
That deny—

وَيْلٌ يَوْمَئِذٍ لِّلْمُكَذِّبِينَ ﴿١٠﴾

11. Those that deny
The Day of Judgement.[6015]

ٱلَّذِينَ يُكَذِّبُونَ بِيَوْمِ ٱلدِّينِ ﴿١١﴾

12. And none can deny it
But the Transgressor
Beyond bounds,
The Sinner!

وَمَا يُكَذِّبُ بِهِۦٓ إِلَّا كُلُّ مُعْتَدٍ أَثِيمٍ ﴿١٢﴾

13. When Our Signs are rehearsed
To him, he says,
"Tales of the Ancients!"[6016]

إِذَا تُتْلَىٰ عَلَيْهِ ءَايَٰتُنَا قَالَ أَسَٰطِيرُ ٱلْأَوَّلِينَ ﴿١٣﴾

14. By no means!
But on their hearts
Is the stain of the (ill)
Which they do![6017]

كَلَّا ۖ بَلْ ۜ رَانَ عَلَىٰ قُلُوبِهِم مَّا كَانُوا۟ يَكْسِبُونَ ﴿١٤﴾

15. Verily, from (the Light
Of) their Lord, that Day,
Will they be veiled.[6018]

كَلَّآ إِنَّهُمْ عَن رَّبِّهِمْ يَوْمَئِذٍ لَّمَحْجُوبُونَ ﴿١٥﴾

16. Further, they will enter
The Fire of Hell.

ثُمَّ إِنَّهُمْ لَصَالُوا۟ ٱلْجَحِيمِ ﴿١٦﴾

6014. If we take *Sijjīn* to be the Register itself, and not the place where it is kept, the Register itself is a sort of Prison for those who do wrong. It is inscribed fully: *i.e.*, no one is omitted who ought to be there, and for every entry there is a complete record, so that there is no escape for the sinner. (R).

6015. The fact of Personal Responsibility for each soul is so undoubted that people who deny it are to be pitied, and will indeed be in a most pitiable condition on the Day of Reckoning, and none but the most abandoned sinner can deny it, and he only denies it by playing with Falsehoods.

6016. *Cf.* 6:25; 68:15; etc. They scorn Truth and pretend that it is Falsehood.

6017. The heart of a man, as created by Allah, is pure and unsullied. Every time that a man does an ill deed, it marks a stain or rust on his heart. But on repentance and forgiveness, such stain is washed off. If there is no repentance and forgiveness, the stains deepen and spread more and more, until the heart is sealed (2:7), and eventually the man dies a spiritual death. It is such stains that stand in the way of his perceiving Truths which are obvious to others. That is why he mocks at Truth and hugs Falsehood to his bosom.

6018. The stain of evil deeds on their hearts sullies the mirror of their hearts, so that it does not receive the light. At Judgement the true Light, the Glory of the Lord, the joy of the Righteous, will be hidden by veils from the eyes of the Sinful. Instead, the Fire of Punishment will be to them the only reality which they will perceive.

17. Further, it will be said
To them: "This is
The (reality) which ye
Rejected as false!

ثُمَّ يُقَالُ هَٰذَا ٱلَّذِى كُنتُم بِهِۦ تُكَذِّبُونَ ﴿١٧﴾

18. Nay, verily the Record
Of the Righteous is
(Preserved) in *'Illīyīn*.[6019]

كَلَّآ إِنَّ كِتَٰبَ ٱلْأَبْرَارِ لَفِى عِلِّيِّينَ ﴿١٨﴾

19. And what will explain
To thee what *'Illīyūn* is?

وَمَآ أَدْرَىٰكَ مَا عِلِّيُّونَ ﴿١٩﴾

20. (There is) a Register
(Fully) inscribed,[6020]

كِتَٰبٌ مَّرْقُومٌ ﴿٢٠﴾

21. To which bear witness
Those Nearest (to Allah).[6021]

يَشْهَدُهُ ٱلْمُقَرَّبُونَ ﴿٢١﴾

22. Truly the Righteous
Will be in Bliss:

إِنَّ ٱلْأَبْرَارَ لَفِى نَعِيمٍ ﴿٢٢﴾

23. On Thrones (of Dignity)[6022]
Will they command a sight
(Of all things):

عَلَى ٱلْأَرَآئِكِ يَنظُرُونَ ﴿٢٣﴾

24. Thou wilt recognise
In their Faces[6023]
The beaming brightness of Bliss.

تَعْرِفُ فِى وُجُوهِهِمْ نَضْرَةَ ٱلنَّعِيمِ ﴿٢٤﴾

25. Their thirst will be slaked
With Pure Wine sealed:[6024]

يُسْقَوْنَ مِن رَّحِيقٍ مَّخْتُومٍ ﴿٢٥﴾

6019. *'Illīyīn:* the oblique form of the nominative *'Illīyūn*, which occurs in the next verse. It is in contrast to the *Sijjīn* which occurs in verse 7 above, where see n. 6013. Literally, it means the 'High Places', but it is probably not the same as the 'Heights' *(A'rāf)* mentioned in 7:46. Nor need we necessarily identify it with the "dwellings on high" *(ghurufāt)* mentioned in 34:37. Applying the reasoning parallel to that which we applied to *Sijjīn*, we may interpret it as the Place where is kept the Register of the Righteous.

6020. This repeats verse 9 above, where see n. 6014. But the Register is of the opposite kind, that of the Righteous. It contains every detail of the Righteous. (R).

6021. See 56:11, n. 5227; also n. 5223. Those Nearest to Allah will be witnesses to this Righteous Record; or as it may also be rendered, they will be present at the Record, and watch this Record. Metaphorically, the hightest spiritual dignitaries are always helping and assisting at the piling up of the good record of every soul that strives for good, however humble in rank that soul may be.

6022. *Cf.* 36:56.

6023. *Cf.* 75:22, and 76:11.

6024. The Wine will be of the utmost purity and flavour, so precious that it will be protected with a seal, and the seal itself will be of the costly material of musk, which is most highly esteemed in the East for its perfume. Perhaps a better interpretation of the "seal" is to take it as implying the final effect of the drink: just as a seal closes a document, so the seal of the drink will be the final effect of the delicious perfume and flavour of musk, heightening the enjoyment and helping in the digestion. (R).

26. The seal thereof will be
Musk: and for this
Let those aspire,
Who have aspirations:[6025]

٢٦ خِتَٰمُهُۥ مِسْكٌ ۚ وَفِى ذَٰلِكَ فَلْيَتَنَافَسِ ٱلْمُتَنَٰفِسُونَ

27. With it will be (given)
A mixture of *Tasnīm*:[6026]

٢٧ وَمِزَاجُهُۥ مِن تَسْنِيمٍ

28. A spring, from (the waters)
Whereof drink
Those Nearest to Allah.

٢٨ عَيْنًا يَشْرَبُ بِهَا ٱلْمُقَرَّبُونَ

29. Those in sin used
To laugh at those
Who believed,

٢٩ إِنَّ ٱلَّذِينَ أَجْرَمُوا۟ كَانُوا۟ مِنَ ٱلَّذِينَ ءَامَنُوا۟ يَضْحَكُونَ

30. And whenever they passed
By them, used to wink
At each other (in mockery);

٣٠ وَإِذَا مَرُّوا۟ بِهِمْ يَتَغَامَزُونَ

31. And when they returned
To their own people,
They would return jesting;

٣١ وَإِذَا ٱنقَلَبُوٓا۟ إِلَىٰٓ أَهْلِهِمُ ٱنقَلَبُوا۟ فَكِهِينَ

32. And whenever they saw them,
They would say, "Behold!
These are the people
Truly astray!"[6027]

٣٢ وَإِذَا رَأَوْهُمْ قَالُوٓا۟ إِنَّ هَٰٓؤُلَآءِ لَضَآلُّونَ

33. But they had not been
Sent as Keepers over them![6028]

٣٣ وَمَآ أُرْسِلُوا۟ عَلَيْهِمْ حَٰفِظِينَ

6025. If you understand true and lasting values, this is the kind of pure Bliss to aspire for, and not the fleeting enjoyments of this world, which always leave a sting behind.

6026. *Tasnīm* literally indicates height, fulness, opulence. Here it is the name of a heavenly Fountain, whose drink is superior to that of the Purest Wine. It is the nectar drunk by Those Nearest to Allah (n. 5227 to 56:11), the highest in spiritual dignity; but a flavour of it will be given to all, according to their spiritual capacity. See n. 5835 to 76:5 *(Kāfūr* fountain), and n. 5849 to 76:17-28 *(Salsabīl)*, (R).

6027. The wicked laugh at the righteous in this world in many ways. (1) They inwardly laugh at their Faith, because they feel themselves so superior. (2) In public places, when the righteous pass, they wink at each other and insult them. (3) In their own houses they run them down. (4) Whenever and wherever they see them, they reproach them with being fools who have lost their way, when the boot is really on the other leg. In the Hereafter all these tricks and falsehoods will be shown for what they are, and the tables will be reversed.

6028. But the wicked critics of the Righteous have no call in any case to sit in judgement over them. Who set them as Keepers or guardians over the Righteous? Let them look to their own condition and future first.

34. But on this Day
The Believers will laugh
At the Unbelievers:[6029]

فَٱلْيَوْمَ ٱلَّذِينَ ءَامَنُوا۟ مِنَ ٱلْكُفَّارِ يَضْحَكُونَ ٣٤

35. On Thrones (of Dignity)
They will command (a sight)
(Of all things).[6030]

عَلَى ٱلْأَرَآئِكِ يَنظُرُونَ ٣٥

36. Will not the Unbelievers
Have been paid back
For what they did?

هَلْ ثُوِّبَ ٱلْكُفَّارُ مَا كَانُوا۟ يَفْعَلُونَ ٣٦

6029. The tables will then be reversed, and he laughs best who laughs last.

6030. A repetition of verse 23 above, but with a different shade of meaning. The Righteous on their Thrones of Dignity will be able to see all the true values restored in their own favour: but they will also see something else: they will also see the arrogant braggarts brought low, who brought about their own downfall by their own actions.

INTRODUCTION TO SŪRAH 84—*AL INSHIQĀQ*

Chronologically this Sūrah is closely connected with the last one. In subject matter it resembles more S. 82 and 81, with which it may be compared.

The Sūrah, which opens with a mention of some cataclysmic events, shows that the present phenomenal order will not last, and Allah's full Judgement will certainly be established: man should therefore strive for that World of Eternity and True Values. (R).

C. 264.—All mysteries, fair or shrouded in gloom,
(84:1-25.) Will vanish when the full Reality
Stands revealed. If this Life is but Painful
Toil, there's the Hope of the Meeting with the Lord!
That will be Bliss indeed for the Righteous,
But woe to the arrogant dealers in sin!
Like the sunset Glow or the shades of Night,
Or the Moon's ever-changing light, man's life
Never rests here below, but travels ever onwards
Stage by stage. Grasp then Allah's Message
And reach the Heights, to reap a Reward
That will never fail through all eternity!

Sūrah 84.

Al Inshiqāq (The Rending Asunder)

الجزء الثلاثون سورة الانشقاق

In the name of Allah, Most Gracious, Most Merciful.

بِسْمِ ٱللَّهِ ٱلرَّحْمَٰنِ ٱلرَّحِيمِ

1. When the Sky is
Rent asunder,[6031]

إِذَا ٱلسَّمَآءُ ٱنشَقَّتْ ﴿١﴾

2. And hearkens to[6032]
(The Command of) its Lord—
And it must needs
(Do so)—

وَأَذِنَتْ لِرَبِّهَا وَحُقَّتْ ﴿٢﴾

3. And when the Earth
Is flattened out,[6033]

وَإِذَا ٱلْأَرْضُ مُدَّتْ ﴿٣﴾

4. And casts forth
What is within it
And becomes (clean) empty,

وَأَلْقَتْ مَا فِيهَا وَتَخَلَّتْ ﴿٤﴾

5. And hearkens to[6034]
(The Command of) its Lord—
And it must needs
(Do so)—(then will come
Home the full Reality).[6035]

وَأَذِنَتْ لِرَبِّهَا وَحُقَّتْ ﴿٥﴾

6. O thou man!
Verily thou art ever

يَٰٓأَيُّهَا ٱلْإِنسَٰنُ إِنَّكَ ﴿٦﴾

6031. The passing away of this world of sense to make way for a new World of Reality is here indicated by two Facts, which are themselves Symbols for a complete revolution in our whole knowledge and experience. At the beginning of S. 82 and S. 81, other Symbols were used, to lead up to the arguments there advanced. Here the Symbols are: (1) the Sky being rent asunder and giving up its secrets, and (2) the Earth being flattened out from the globe it is, and giving up its secrets. See the following notes.

6032. We may think that the heavens we see above us—high and sacred, seemingly vast and limitless, eternal and timeless—are not created matter. But they are. And they remain just so long as Allah wills it so, and not a moment longer. As soon as His Command issues for their dissolution, they will obey and vanish, and all their mystery will be emptied out. And it must necessarily be so; their very nature as created beings requires that they must hearken to the voice of their Creator, even to the extent of their own extinction.

6033. The Earth is a globe, enclosing within it many secrets and mysteries—gold and diamonds in its mines, heat and magnetic forces in its entrails, and the bodies of countless generations of men buried within its soil. At its dissolution all these contents will be disgorged: it will lose its shape as a globe, and cease to exist.

A more mystic meaning lies behind the ordinary meaning of the vanishing of the heavens and the earth as we see them. Our ideas of them—their subjective contents with reference to ourselves will also lose all shape and form and vanish before the eternal verities.

6034. See n. 6032. We think the earth so solid and real. All our perishable things dissolve into the earth. But the earth itself will dissolve into a truer Reality.

6035. The substantive clause, to follow the two conditional clauses preceding, may be filled up from the suggestion contained in 82:5.

Toiling on towards thy Lord—[6036]
Painfully toiling—but thou
Shalt meet Him.

كَادِحٌ إِلَىٰ رَبِّكَ كَدْحًا فَمُلَٰقِيهِ

7. Then he who is given
His Record in his
Right hand,[6037]

فَأَمَّا مَنْ أُوتِيَ كِتَٰبَهُۥ بِيَمِينِهِۦ ﴿٧﴾

8. Soon will his account
Be taken by an easy reckoning,

فَسَوْفَ يُحَاسَبُ حِسَابًا يَسِيرًا ﴿٨﴾

9. And he will turn
To his people,[6038] rejoicing!

وَيَنقَلِبُ إِلَىٰٓ أَهْلِهِۦ مَسْرُورًا ﴿٩﴾

10. But he who is given
His Record behind his back—[6039]

وَأَمَّا مَنْ أُوتِيَ كِتَٰبَهُۥ وَرَآءَ ظَهْرِهِۦ ﴿١٠﴾

11. Soon will he cry
For Perdition,[6040]

فَسَوْفَ يَدْعُوا۟ ثُبُورًا ﴿١١﴾

12. And he will enter
A Blazing Fire.

وَيَصْلَىٰ سَعِيرًا ﴿١٢﴾

13. Truly, did he go about
Among his people, rejoicing![6041]

إِنَّهُۥ كَانَ فِىٓ أَهْلِهِۦ مَسْرُورًا ﴿١٣﴾

14. Truly, did he think
That he would not

إِنَّهُۥ ظَنَّ أَن لَّن ﴿١٤﴾

6036. This life is ever full of toil and misery, if looked at as empty of the Eternal Hope which Revelation gives us. Hence the literature of pessimism in poetry and philosophy, which thinking minds have poured forth in all ages, when that Hope was obscured to them. "Our sweetest songs are those that tell of saddest thought." "To each his suffering; all are men condemned alike to groan!" It is the noblest men that have to "scorn delights and live laborious days" in this life. The good suffer on account of their very goodness: the evil on account of their Evil. But the balance will be set right in the end. Those that wept shall be made to rejoice, and those that went about thoughtlessly rejoicing, shall be made to weep for their folly. They will all go to their account with Allah and meet Him before His Throne of Judgement.

6037. *Right Hand: Cf.* 17:71. These will be the fortunate ones, who spent their lives in goodness and truth: for them the account will be made easy; for even after the balancing, they will receive more than their merits deserve, on account of the infinite grace and mercy of Allah.

6038. *His people:* should be understood in a large sense, including all righteous persons of his category, (including of course all those nearest and dearest to him), who are spiritually of his family, whether before him or after him in time.

6039. In 69:24, the wicked are given the Record in their left hand. But their hands will not be free. Sin will have tied their hands behind their back: and thus they can only receive their Records in their left hand, behind their back.

6040. The wicked will cry for death and annihilation: but they will neither live nor die: 20:74.

6041. The tables are now turned. His self-complacence and self-conceit in his lower life will now give place to weeping and gnashing of teeth! *Cf.* n. 6036 above.

Have to return (to Us)![6042]

يَحُورَ

15. Nay, nay! for his Lord
Was (ever) watchful of him!

بَلَىٰٓ إِنَّ رَبَّهُۥ كَانَ بِهِۦ بَصِيرًا ١٥

16. So I do call[6043]
To witness the ruddy glow
Of Sunset;[6044]

فَلَآ أُقْسِمُ بِٱلشَّفَقِ ١٦

17. The Night and its Homing;[6045]

وَٱلَّيْلِ وَمَا وَسَقَ ١٧

18. And the Moon
In her Fulness:[6046]

وَٱلْقَمَرِ إِذَا ٱتَّسَقَ ١٨

19. Ye shall surely travel
From stage to stage.[6047]

لَتَرْكَبُنَّ طَبَقًا عَن طَبَقٍ ١٩

20. What then is the matter
With them, that they
Believe not?—[6048]

فَمَا لَهُمْ لَا يُؤْمِنُونَ ٢٠

6042. Most of the Evil in this world is due to the false idea that man is irresponsible, or to a mad and thoughtless indulgence of self. Man is not irresponsible. He is responsible for every deed, word, and thought of his, to his Maker, to Whom he has to return, to give an account of himself. To remember this and act accordingly is to achieve salvation; to forget or flout that responsibility is to get into the Fire of self-deception and misery.

6043. The same form of adjuration as in 69:37. The substantive statement is in verse 19 below: "Ye shall surely travel from stage to stage". Nothing in this life is fixed, or will last. Three things are mentioned which on the one hand have remained from age to age for as far back as the memory of man can go, and yet each of them is but a short phase, gone as it were in the twinkling of an eye. See the following notes: So our life here is but a fleeting show. Its completion is to be looked for elsewhere.

6044. (1) The sun seems such a great reality that people worshipped it as a divinity. The beautiful glow it leaves when it sets is but momentary: it changes every moment and vanishes with the twilight.

6045. (2) The Night is a phenomenon you see during almost half of every twenty-four hours in ordinary latitudes. At nightfall, all the wandering flocks and herds come home. The men scattered abroad for their livelihood return home to rest and sleep. The Night collects them in their homes, and yet this phase of Homing lasts but a little while. Presently all is silent and still. So will it be with our souls when this life is ended with our death. We shall be collected in a newer and larger Homing.

6046. (3) The astronomical Full Moon does not last a moment. The moment the moon is full, she begins to decline, and the moment she is in her "inter-lunar swoon", she begins her career anew as a growing New Moon. So is man's life here below. It is not fixed or permanent, either in its physical phases, or even more strikingly, in its finer phases, intellectual, emotional, or spiritual.

6047. Man travels and ascends stage by stage. In 67:3 the same word in the form *ṭibāqa* was used of the heavens, as if they were in layers one above another. Man's spiritual life may similarly be compared to an ascent from one heaven to another.

6048. Considering man's high destiny, and the fact that this life is but a stage or a sojourn for him, it might be expected that he would eagerly embrace every opportunity of welcoming Allah's Revelation and ascending by Faith to heights of spiritual wisdom. There is something wrong with his will if he does not do so. Notice the transition from the second person in verse 19, where there is a direct appeal to Allah's votaries, to the third person in verses 20-21, where men who are rebels against Allah's Kingdom are spoken of as if they were alien.

21. And when the Qur'ān
Is read to them, they
Fall not prostrate,[6049]

وَإِذَا قُرِئَ عَلَيْهِمُ ٱلْقُرْءَانُ لَا يَسْجُدُونَ ۩ ﴿٢١﴾

22. But on the contrary
The Unbelievers reject (it).

بَلِ ٱلَّذِينَ كَفَرُوا۟ يُكَذِّبُونَ ﴿٢٢﴾

23. But Allah has full Knowledge
Of what they secrete
(In their breasts).

وَٱللَّهُ أَعْلَمُ بِمَا يُوعُونَ ﴿٢٣﴾

24. So announce to them
A Penalty Grievous,

فَبَشِّرْهُم بِعَذَابٍ أَلِيمٍ ﴿٢٤﴾

25. Except to those who believe
And work righteous deeds:
For them is a Reward
That will never fail.[6050]

إِلَّا ٱلَّذِينَ ءَامَنُوا۟ وَعَمِلُوا۟ ٱلصَّٰلِحَٰتِ لَهُمْ أَجْرٌ غَيْرُ مَمْنُونٍۭ ﴿٢٥﴾

6049. *Prostrate:* out of respect and humble gratitude to Allah.

6050. *Cf.* 41:8.

INTRODUCTION AND SUMMARY TO SŪRAH 85—*AL BURŪJ*

This is one of the earlier Makkan Sūrahs, chronologically cognate with S. 91. The subject matter is the persecution of Allah's votaries. Allah watches over His own, and will deal with the enemies of Truth as He dealt with them in the past.

C. 265.—Woe to those who persecute Truth!
(85:1-22.) They are being watched by mighty Eyes;
They will have to answer when the Judgement comes;
And a clear Record will witness against them.
Are they cruel to men because of their Faith?
The Fire they use will be turned against them.
For Allah is strong, and will subdue
The mightiest foes. Be warned, and learn
From His gracious Message, preserved through all Time!

Sūrah 85.

الجزء الثلاثون سورة البروج

Al Burūj (The Constellations)

In the name of Allah, Most Gracious, Most Merciful.

بِسْمِ اللَّهِ الرَّحْمَٰنِ الرَّحِيمِ

1. By the Sky, (displaying)[6051]
The Zodiacal Signs;[6052]

وَالسَّمَاءِ ذَاتِ الْبُرُوجِ ١

2. By the promised Day
(Of Judgement);[6053]

وَالْيَوْمِ الْمَوْعُودِ ٢

3. By one that witnesses,
And the subject of the witness—[6054]

وَشَاهِدٍ وَمَشْهُودٍ ٣

4. Woe to the makers
Of the pit (of fire),[6055]

قُتِلَ أَصْحَابُ الْأُخْدُودِ ٤

5. Fire supplied (abundantly)
With Fuel:

النَّارِ ذَاتِ الْوَقُودِ ٥

6051. Here is an appeal to three symbols in verses 1-3, and the substantive proposition is in verses 4-8, a denunciation of wicked persecutors of the votaries of Allah, persecutors who burnt righteous men for their Faith. The three Symbols are: (1) the Glorious Sky, with the broad belt of the Constellations marking the twelve Signs of the Zodiac; (2) the Day of Judgement, when all evil will be punished; and (3) certain Persons that will be witnesses, and certain Persons or things that will be the subjects of the witness. See the notes following.

6052. See n. 1950 to 15:16. The Stars of the Zodiac as well as of other Constellations are like the eyes of the Night. It may be that crimes are committed in the darkness of night (literally or metaphorically). But countless eyes (metaphorically) are watching all the time, and every author of evil will be brought to book.

6053. The Day of Judgement, when the Sinner will have to give an account of every deed, open or hidden, is not merely a matter of speculation. It is definitely promised in revelation, and will inevitably come to pass. Woe then to the Sinners for their crimes.

6054. The literal meaning is clear, but its metaphorical application has been explained in a variety of ways by different Commentators. The words are fairly comprehensive, and should, I think, be understood in connection with Judgement. There the Witnesses may be: (1) the Prophets (3:81); Allah Himself (3:81, and 10:61); the Recording Angels (50:21); the Sinner's own misused limbs (24:24); his record of deeds (17:14); or the Sinner himself (17:14). The subject of the witness may be the deed or crime, or the Sinner against whom the testimony cries out. The appeal to these things means that the Sinner cannot possibly escape the consequences of his crime. He should repent, seek Allah's Mercy, and amend his life.

6055. Who were the makers of the pit of fire in which they burnt people for their Faith? The words are perfectly general, and we need not search for particular names, except by way of illustration. In ancient history, and in Mediaeval Europe, many lives were sacrificed at the stake because the victims did not conform to the established religion. In Arab tradition there is the story of Abraham: Nimrūd tries to burn him to death, but on account of Abraham's Faith, the fire became "a means of safety for Abraham": 21:69, and n. 2725. Another case cited is that of Dhu Nuwās, the last Ḥimyarite King of Yemen, by religion a Jew, who persecuted the Christians of Najrān and is said to have burnt them to death. He seems to have lived in the latter half of the sixth Christian century, in the generation immediately preceding the Prophet's birth in 570 A.D. While the words are perfectly general, a reference is suggested to the persecution to which the early Muslims were subjected by the Pagan Quraysh. Among other cruelties, they were stripped, and their skins were exposed to the burning rays of the Arabian summer sun. (R).

6. Behold! They sat[6056]
Over against the (fire),

إِذْ هُمْ عَلَيْهَا قُعُودٌ ﴿٦﴾

7. And they witnessed
(All) that they were doing
Against the Believers.

وَهُمْ عَلَىٰ مَا يَفْعَلُونَ بِالْمُؤْمِنِينَ شُهُودٌ ﴿٧﴾

8. And they ill-treated them
For no other reason than
That they believed in Allah,
Exalted in Power,
Worthy of all Praise!—

وَمَا نَقَمُوا مِنْهُمْ إِلَّا أَنْ
يُؤْمِنُوا بِاللَّهِ الْعَزِيزِ الْحَمِيدِ ﴿٨﴾

9. Him to Whom belongs
The dominion of the heavens
And the earth!
And Allah is Witness
To all things.[6057]

الَّذِي لَهُ مُلْكُ السَّمَاوَاتِ وَالْأَرْضِ ۚ
وَاللَّهُ عَلَىٰ كُلِّ شَيْءٍ شَهِيدٌ ﴿٩﴾

10. Those who persecute (or draw
into temptation)
The Believers, men and women,
And do not turn
In repentance, will have
The Penalty of Hell:
They will have the Penalty
Of the Burning Fire.[6058]

إِنَّ الَّذِينَ فَتَنُوا
الْمُؤْمِنِينَ وَالْمُؤْمِنَاتِ ثُمَّ لَمْ يَتُوبُوا
فَلَهُمْ عَذَابُ جَهَنَّمَ
وَلَهُمْ عَذَابُ الْحَرِيقِ ﴿١٠﴾

11. For those who believe
And do righteous deeds,
Will be Gardens,[6059]
Beneath which Rivers flow:
That is the great Salvation,
(The fulfilment of all desires),[6060]

إِنَّ الَّذِينَ آمَنُوا وَعَمِلُوا الصَّالِحَاتِ
لَهُمْ جَنَّاتٌ تَجْرِي مِنْ تَحْتِهَا الْأَنْهَارُ ۚ
ذَٰلِكَ الْفَوْزُ الْكَبِيرُ ﴿١١﴾

12. Truly strong is the Grip
(And Power) of thy Lord.

إِنَّ بَطْشَ رَبِّكَ لَشَدِيدٌ ﴿١٢﴾

6056. The persecutors sat calmly to gloat over the agonies of their victims in the well-fed fire.

6057. It is suggested that the persecutors will richly deserve to be punished in the Fire of Hell. That Punishment will be far more real and lasting than the undeserved cruelty which they inflicted on men for their Faith in the One True God.

6058. The "Penalty of the Burning Fire" has been mentioned here in addition to the "Penalty of Hell". This assumes a special significance in the background of the cruel burning of the Faithful by the "makers of the pit". These criminals would be duly retributed by being subjected to a similar kind of suffering that they had caused their innocent victims. [Eds.].

6059. *Cf.* 5:122; 9:72 and 22:19. [Eds.].

6060. *Cf.* 5:122, n. 833.

13. It is He Who Creates From the very beginning,[6061] And He can restore (life).	إِنَّهُۥ هُوَ يُبْدِئُ وَيُعِيدُ ﴿١٣﴾
14. And He is the Oft-Forgiving, Full of loving-kindness,	وَهُوَ ٱلْغَفُورُ ٱلْوَدُودُ ﴿١٤﴾
15. Lord of the Throne of Glory,	ذُو ٱلْعَرْشِ ٱلْمَجِيدُ ﴿١٥﴾
16. Doer (without let)[6062] Of all that He intends.	فَعَّالٌ لِّمَا يُرِيدُ ﴿١٦﴾
17. Has the story Reached thee, Of the Forces—[6063]	هَلْ أَتَىٰكَ حَدِيثُ ٱلْجُنُودِ ﴿١٧﴾
18. Of Pharaoh And the Thamūd?	فِرْعَوْنَ وَثَمُودَ ﴿١٨﴾
19. And yet the Unbelievers (Persist) in rejecting (The Truth)![6064]	بَلِ ٱلَّذِينَ كَفَرُوا۟ فِى تَكْذِيبٍ ﴿١٩﴾
20. But Allah doth Encompass them From behind![6065]	وَٱللَّهُ مِن وَرَآئِهِم مُّحِيطٌۢ ﴿٢٠﴾
21. Nay, this is A Glorious Qur'ān	بَلْ هُوَ قُرْءَانٌ مَّجِيدٌ ﴿٢١﴾

6061. For the various words for "Creation" and the ideas implied in them, see n. 120 to 2:117.

6062. Allah's Will is itself the Word and the Deed. There is no interval between them. He does not change His mind. No circumstances whatever can come between His Will and the execution thereof. Such are His Power and His Glory. Compare it with that of men, described in the next two verses.

6063. In contrast to the real, all-embracing, and eternal power of Allah, what are the forces of man at their best? Two examples are mentioned. (1) Pharaoh was a proud monarch of a powerful kingdom, with resources and organisation, material, moral, and intellectual, as good as any in the world. When he pitted himself against Allah's Prophet, he and his forces were destroyed. See 79:15-26. (2) The Thamūd were great builders, and had a high standard of material civilisation. But they defied the law of Allah and perished. See 7:73-79, and n. 1043.

6064. In spite of the great examples of the past, by which human might and skill were shown to have availed nothing when the law of Allah was broken, the unbelievers persist (in all ages) in defying that law. But Allah will know how to deal with them.

6065. Allah encompasses everything. But the wicked will find themselves defeated not only in conditions that they foresee, but from all sorts of unexpected directions, perhaps from behind them, *i.e.*, from the very people or circumstances which in their blindness they despised or thought of as helping them.

22. (Inscribed) in
A Tablet Preserved![6066]

فِى لَوۡحٍ مَّحۡفُوظٍۭ ﴿٢٢﴾

6066. *Inscribed in a Table Preserved, i.e.*, Allah's Message is not ephemeral. It is eternal. The "Tablet" is "preserved" or guarded from corruption: 15:9: for Allah's Message must endure forever. That Message is the "Mother of the book": see n. 347 to 3:7. (R).

INTRODUCTION AND SUMMARY TO SŪRAH 86—*AL ṬĀRIQ*

This Sūrah also belongs to the early Makkan period, perhaps not far removed from the last Sūrah.

Its subject matter is the protection afforded to every soul in the darkest period of its spiritual history. The physical nature of man may be insignificant, but the soul given to him by Allah must win a glorious Future in the end.

C. 266.—Through the darkest night comes the penetrating light
(86:1-17.) Of a glorious Star. Such is the power
Of Revelation: it protects and guides the erring.
For what is man? But a creature of flesh
And bones! But Allah by His Power doth raise
Man's state to a Life Beyond!—when lo!
All things hidden will be made plain.
Man's help will then be but the Word
Of Allah, which none can thwart. So wait
With gentle patience—for His Decision.

Sūrah 86.

Al Ṭāriq (The Night Star)

الجزء الثلاثون سورة الطارق

In the name of Allah, Most Gracious, Most Merciful.

بِسْمِ اللَّهِ الرَّحْمَٰنِ الرَّحِيمِ

1. By the Sky[6067]
And the Night-Visitant[6068]
(Therein)—

وَالسَّمَاءِ وَالطَّارِقِ ﴿١﴾

2. And what will explain to thee
What the Night-Visitant is?—

وَمَا أَدْرَاكَ مَا الطَّارِقُ ﴿٢﴾

3. (It is) the Star
Of piercing brightness—

النَّجْمُ الثَّاقِبُ ﴿٣﴾

4. There is no soul but has
A protector over it.[6069]

إِن كُلُّ نَفْسٍ لَّمَّا عَلَيْهَا حَافِظٌ ﴿٤﴾

5. Now let man but think
From what he is created!

فَلْيَنظُرِ الْإِنسَانُ مِمَّ خُلِقَ ﴿٥﴾

6. He is created from
A drop emitted—[6070]

خُلِقَ مِن مَّاءٍ دَافِقٍ ﴿٦﴾

7. Proceeding from between
The backbone and the ribs:[6071]

يَخْرُجُ مِن بَيْنِ الصُّلْبِ وَالتَّرَائِبِ ﴿٧﴾

6067. The appeal here is to a single mystic Symbol, *viz.:* the Sky with its Night-Visitant: and the substantive proposition is in verse 4: "There is no soul but has a protector over it". In the last Sūrah we considered the persecution of Allah's votaries, and how Allah protects them. Here the same theme is presented in another aspect. In the darkest sky shines out most brilliantly the light of the most brilliant star. So in the night of spiritual darkness—whether through ignorance or distress—shines the glorious star of Allah's revelation. By the same token the man of Faith and Truth has nothing to fear. Allah will protect His own.

6068. This is explained in verse 3 below. The "Star of piercing brightness" is understood by some to be the Morning Star, by others to be the planet Saturn, by others again to be Sirius, or the Pleiades or shooting stars. I think it is best to take the "Star" in the collective or generic sense, for stars shine on every night in the year, and their piercing brightness is most noticeable on the darkest night.

6069. If man has a true spiritual understanding, he has nothing to be afraid of. He is protected by Allah in many ways that he does not even know. He may be an insignificant creature as a mere animal, but his soul raises him to a dignity above other creation. And all sorts of divine forces guard and protect him.

6070. See n. 5832 to 76:2. See also last note.

6071. A man's seed is the quintessence of his body. It is therefore said metaphorically to proceed from his loins, *i.e.*, from his back between the hipbones and his ribs. His backbone is the source and symbol of his strength and personality. In the spinal cord and in the brain is the directive energy of the central nervous system, and this directs all action, organic and psychic. The spinal cord is continuous with the Medulla Oblongata in the brain.

8. Surely (Allah) is able
To bring him back
(To life)![6072]

إِنَّهُۥ عَلَىٰ رَجْعِهِۦ لَقَادِرٌ ﴿٨﴾

9. The Day that
(All) things secret
Will be tested,

يَوْمَ تُبْلَى ٱلسَّرَآئِرُ ﴿٩﴾

10. (Man) will have
No power,
And no helper[6073]

فَمَا لَهُۥ مِن قُوَّةٍ وَلَا نَاصِرٍ ﴿١٠﴾

11. By the Firmament[6074]
Which returns (in its round),

وَٱلسَّمَآءِ ذَاتِ ٱلرَّجْعِ ﴿١١﴾

12. And by the Earth
Which opens out[6075]
(For the gushing of springs
Or the sprouting of vegetation)—

وَٱلْأَرْضِ ذَاتِ ٱلصَّدْعِ ﴿١٢﴾

13. Behold this is the Word
That distinguishes (Good
From Evil):[6076]

إِنَّهُۥ لَقَوْلٌ فَصْلٌ ﴿١٣﴾

14. It is not a thing
For amusement.

وَمَا هُوَ بِٱلْهَزْلِ ﴿١٤﴾

15. As for them,[6077] they
Are but plotting a scheme,

إِنَّهُمْ يَكِيدُونَ كَيْدًا ﴿١٥﴾

6072. The Creator who can mingle the forces of psychic and physical muscular action in the creation of man, as explained in the last note, can surely give a new life after physical death here, and restore man's personality in the new world that will open out in the Hereafter.

6073. In that new world, all our actions, motives, thoughts, and imaginings of this life, however secret, will be brought into the open, and tested by the standards of absolute Truth, and not by false standards of custom, prejudice, or partiality. In that severe test, any adventitious advantages of this life will have no strength or force whatever, and cannot help in any way.

6074. The Firmament above is always the same, and yet it performs its diurnal round, smoothly and punctually. So does Allah's Revelation show forth the Truth, which like a circle is ever true to its centre—which is ever the same, though it revolves through the changing circumstances of our present life.

6075. The earth seems hard, but springs can gush forth and vegetables sprout through it and make it green and soft. So is Truth: hard perhaps to mortals, but through the fertilising agency of Revelation, it allows our inner personality to sprout and blossom forth.

6076. See the last two notes. Revelation—Allah's Truth—can pierce through the hardest crusts, and ever lead us back to the centre and goal of our spiritual life: for it separates Good from Evil definitely. It is not mere play or amusement, any more than the Sky or the Earth is. It helps us in the highest issues of our life.

6077. Though Allah in His Mercy has provided a piercing light to penetrate our spiritual darkness, and made our beings responsive to the growth of spiritual understanding, just as the hard earth is responsive to the sprouting of a seed or the gushing of a stream, yet there are evil, unregenerate men who plot and scheme against the beneficent purpose of Allah. But their plots will be of no avail, and Allah's Purpose will prevail. It happened so with the Quraysh who wanted to thwart the growth of Islam. It will be so in all ages.

16. And I am planning
A scheme.[6078]

وَأَكِيدُ كَيْدًا ﴿١٦﴾

17. Therefore grant a delay
To the unbelievers:
Give respite to them
Gently (for awhile).[6079]

فَمَهِّلِ ٱلْكَٰفِرِينَ أَمْهِلْهُمْ رُوَيْدًۢا ﴿١٧﴾

6078. *Makara* is applied both to plotting with an evil purpose and planning with a good purpose. *Cf.* 3:54, and n. "And the unbelievers plotted and planned, and Allah too planned, and the best of planners is Allah."

6079. Gentle forbearance with Evil shows our trust in Allah and Allah's Plan: for it can never be frustrated. This does not mean that we should assist or compromise with evil, or fail to put it down where we have the power. It means patience and humility where we have no visible power to prevent Evil.

INTRODUCTION AND SUMMARY TO SŪRAH 87—*AL A'LĀ*

This is one of the earliest of the Makkan Sūrahs, being usually placed eighth in chronological order, and immediately after S. 81.

The argument is that Allah has made man capable of progress by ordered steps, and by His Revelation will lead him still higher to purification and perfection.

C. 267.—Wonderful are the ways of Allah
(87:1-19.) In creation, and the love with which
He guides His creatures' destinies,
Gives them the means by which to strive
For maturity by ordered steps, and reach
The end most fitted for their natures.
His Law is just and easy, and His Grace
Is ever ready to help: let us look
To the Eternal Goal, with hearts and souls
Of Purity, and glorify His name:
For in this changing, fleeting world,
His Word is always true, and will remain,
Through all the ages, ever the same.

Sūrah 87.

Al A'la (The Most High)

الجزء الثلاثون سُورَةُ الأَعْلَى

In the name of Allah, Most Gracious, Most Merciful.

بِسْمِ اللَّهِ الرَّحْمَٰنِ الرَّحِيمِ

1. Glorify the name
Of thy Guardian-Lord[6080]
Most High,

سَبِّحِ اسْمَ رَبِّكَ الْأَعْلَى ﴿١﴾

2. Who hath created,[6081]
And further, given
Order and proportion;

الَّذِي خَلَقَ فَسَوَّىٰ ﴿٢﴾

3. Who hath ordained laws.[6082]
And granted guidance;

وَالَّذِي قَدَّرَ فَهَدَىٰ ﴿٣﴾

4. And Who bringth out[6083]
The (green and luscious) pasture,

وَالَّذِي أَخْرَجَ الْمَرْعَىٰ ﴿٤﴾

5. And then doth make it
(But) swarthy stubble.

فَجَعَلَهُ غُثَاءً أَحْوَىٰ ﴿٥﴾

6. By degrees shall We
Teach thee to declare[6084]

سَنُقْرِئُكَ ﴿٦﴾

6080. The word "Lord" by itself is an inadequate rendering here for *Rabb.* For it implies cherishing, guarding from harm, sustaining, granting all the means and opportunities of development. See n. 20 to 1:2. For shortness, perhaps "Guardian-Lord" will be sufficient in the Text.

6081. The story of Creation is wonderful and continuous. There are several processes which we contemplate in glorifying Allah's name. First, He brings us into being. Secondly, He endows us with forms and faculties exactly suited to what is expected of us, and to the environments in which our life will be cast, giving to everything due order and proportion.

6082. Thirdly, He has ordained laws and decrees, by which we can develop ourselves and fit ourselves into His whole scheme of evolution for all His Creation. He has measured exactly the needs of all, and given us instincts and physical and psychic predispositions which fit into His decrees. Fourthly,.He gives us guidance, so that we are not the sport of mechanical laws. Our reason and our will are exercised, that we may reach the higher destiny of man.

6083. Fifthly, after maturity comes decay. But even in that decay, as when green pasture turns to stubble, we subserve other ends. Insofar as we are animals, we share these processes with other forms of material. Creation, animal, vegetable, and even mineral, which all have their appointed laws of growth and decay. But man's higher destiny is referred to in subsequent verses.

6084. The soul, as it reaches the Light of Allah, makes gradual progress, like a man going from darkness into light. So the Qur'ān was revealed by stages. So all revelation from Allah comes by stages.

As usual, there are two parallel meanings: (1) that connected with the occasion of direct inspiration to the Holy Prophet; and (2) the more general Message to mankind for all time. Everyone who understands the Message must declare it, in words, and still more, in his conduct.

(The Message), so thou
Shalt not forget,[6085]

فَلَا تَنسَىٰٓ

7. Except as Allah wills:[6086]
For He knoweth
What is manifest
And what is hidden.

إِلَّا مَا شَآءَ ٱللَّهُ ۚ إِنَّهُۥ يَعْلَمُ ٱلْجَهْرَ وَمَا يَخْفَىٰ ﴿٧﴾

8. And We will make it
Easy for thee (to follow)
The simple (Path).[6087]

وَنُيَسِّرُكَ لِلْيُسْرَىٰ ﴿٨﴾

9. Therefore give admonition
In case the admonition[6088]
Profits (the hearer).

فَذَكِّرْ إِن نَّفَعَتِ ٱلذِّكْرَىٰ ﴿٩﴾

10. The admonition will be received
By those who fear (Allah):

سَيَذَّكَّرُ مَن يَخْشَىٰ ﴿١٠﴾

11. But it will be avoided
By those most unfortunate ones,

وَيَتَجَنَّبُهَا ٱلْأَشْقَى ﴿١١﴾

12. Who will enter
The Great Fire,[6089]

ٱلَّذِى يَصْلَى ٱلنَّارَ ٱلْكُبْرَىٰ ﴿١٢﴾

6085. The particular occasion was an assurance to the Prophet, that though he was unlettered, the Message given to him would be preserved in his heart and in the hearts of men. The more general sense is that mankind, having once seized great spiritual truths, will hold fast to them, except as qualified in the following verse.

6086. There can be no question of this having any reference to the abrogation of any verses of the Qur'ān, for this Sūrah is one of the earliest revealed, being placed about eighth according to the most accepted chronological order. While the basic principles of Allah's Law remain the same, its form, expression, and application have varied from time to time, *e.g.*, from Moses to Jesus, and from Jesus to Muḥammad. It is one of the beneficent mercies of Allah that we should forget some things of the past, lest our minds become confused and our development is retarded. Besides, Allah knows what is manifest and what is hidden, and His Will and Plan work with supreme wisdom and goodness.

6087. The path of Islam is simple and easy. It depends on no abstruse mysteries or self-mortifications, but on straight and manly conduct in accordance with the laws of man's nature as implanted in him by Allah (30:30). On the other hand, spiritual perfection may be most difficult, for it involves complete surrender on our part of Allah in all our affairs, thoughts, and desires: but after that surrender Allah's Grace will make our path easy.

6088. This is not so strong as the Biblical phrase, "Cast not pearls before swine" (Matt. vii. 6) The cases where admonition does produce spiritual profit and where it does not, are mentioned below in verses 10 and 11-13 respectively. Allah's Message should be proclaimed to all; but particular and personal admonitions are also due to those who attend and in whose hearts is the fear of Allah; in the case of those who run away from it and dishonour it, such particular and personal admonition is useless. They are the unfortunate ones who prepare their own ruin.

6089. The Great Fire is the final Penalty or Disaster in the Hereafter, as contrasted with the minor Penalties or Disasters from which all evil suffers from within in this very life.

13. In which they will then
Neither die nor live.6090

ثُمَّ لَا يَمُوتُ فِيهَا وَلَا يَحْيَىٰ ١٣

14. But those will prosper6091
Who purify themselves,6092

قَدْ أَفْلَحَ مَن تَزَكَّىٰ ١٤

15. And glorify the name
Of their Guardian-Lord,
And (lift their hearts)
In Prayer.

وَذَكَرَ ٱسْمَ رَبِّهِۦ فَصَلَّىٰ ١٥

16. Nay (behold), ye prefer
The life of this world;

بَلْ تُؤْثِرُونَ ٱلْحَيَوٰةَ ٱلدُّنْيَا ١٦

17. But the Hereafter
Is better and more enduring.

وَٱلْءَاخِرَةُ خَيْرٌ وَأَبْقَىٰٓ ١٧

18. And this is
In the Books
Of the earliest (Revelations)—6093

إِنَّ هَٰذَا لَفِى ٱلصُّحُفِ ٱلْأُولَىٰ ١٨

19. The Books of
Abraham6094 and Moses.6095

صُحُفِ إِبْرَٰهِيمَ وَمُوسَىٰ ١٩

6090. A terrible picture of those who ruin their whole future by evil lives here below. They introduce a discord into Creation, while life should be one great universal concord. And their past clings to them as part of their own will. They are not even like the dry swarthy stubble mentioned in verse 5 above, which grew naturally out of the luscious pasture, for they have grown harmful, in defiance of their own nature. *"Neither die nor live"*; *Cf.* 20:74.

6091. *Prosper:* in the highest and spiritual sense; attain to Bliss or Salvation: as opposed to "enter the Fire".

6092. The first process in godliness is to cleanse ourselves in body, mind, and soul. Then we shall be in a fit state to see and proclaim the Glory of Allah. That leads us to our actual absorption in Praise and Prayer.

6093. The law of righteousness and godliness is not a new law, nor are the vanity and short duration of this world preached here for the first time. But spiritual truths have to be renewed and reiterated again and again.

6094. No Book of Abraham has come down to us. But the Old Testament recognises that Abraham was a prophet (Gen. xx. 7). There is a book in Greek, which has been translated by Mr. G.H. Box, called the Testament of Abraham (published by the Society for the Promotion of Christian Knowledge, London, 1927). It seems to be a Greek translation of a Hebrew original. The Greek Text was probably written in the second Christian century, in Egypt, but in its present form it probably goes back only to the 9th or 10th Century. It was popular among the Christians. Perhaps the Jewish Midrash also refers to a Testament of Abraham.

6095. The original Revelation of Moses, of which the Present Pentateuch is a surviving recension. See Appendix II., p. 288-290.

The present Gospels do not come under the definition of the "earliest" Books. Nor could they be called "Books of Jesus"; they were written not by him, but about him, and long after his death.

INTRODUCTION AND SUMMARY TO SŪRAH 88—*AL GHĀSHIYAH*

This is a late Sūrah of the early Makkan period, perhaps close in date to S. 53. Its subject matter is the contrast between the destinies of the Good and the Evil in the Hereafter—on the Day when the true balance will be restored: the Signs of Allah even in this life should remind us of the Day of Account, for Allah is good and just, and His creation is for a just Purpose.

C. 268.—Have you heard of that Tremendous Day
(88:1-26.) When the Good from the Evil will be separated?

There will be Souls that Day will burn
And grovel in the blazing Fire of Wrath!
No Food can fill their Hunger: no Drink,
Alas, can slake their fierce Thirst!

There will be Souls that Day will shout
With Joy to the glory of their Lord!
Their past Endeavour will now be Achievement.
Raised high on Thrones of Dignity they
Will be Guests at the sumptuous Feast of Bliss.

Let man but look at his dominion o'er
The beasts of the field, or his glorious Canopy
Of stars, or the Eternal Hills that feed
His streams, or the wide expanse of Mother
Earth that nurtures him, and he
Will see the ordered Plan of Allah.
To Him must he return and give account!
Let him, then, learn his Lesson and live!

Sūrah 88.

Al Ghāshiyah (The Overwhelming Event) الجزء الثلاثون سُورَةُ الغَاشِيَةِ

In the name of Allah, Most Gracious,
Most Merciful.

بِسْمِ اللَّهِ الرَّحْمَٰنِ الرَّحِيمِ

1. Has the story Reached thee, of The Overwhelming (Event)?[6096]	هَلْ أَتَىٰكَ حَدِيثُ ٱلْغَٰشِيَةِ ①
2. Some faces, that Day,[6097] Will be humiliated,	وُجُوهٌ يَوْمَئِذٍ خَٰشِعَةٌ ②
3. Labouring (hard), weary—[6098]	عَامِلَةٌ نَّاصِبَةٌ ③
4. The while they enter The Blazing Fire—	تَصْلَىٰ نَارًا حَامِيَةً ④
5. The while they are given To drink, of a boiling hot spring,	تُسْقَىٰ مِنْ عَيْنٍ ءَانِيَةٍ ⑤
6. No food will there be For them but a bitter *Darī'*[6099]	لَّيْسَ لَهُمْ طَعَامٌ إِلَّا مِن ضَرِيعٍ ⑥
7. Which will neither nourish Nor satisfy hunger.	لَّا يُسْمِنُ وَلَا يُغْنِى مِن جُوعٍ ⑦
8. (Other) faces that Day Will be joyful,	وُجُوهٌ يَوْمَئِذٍ نَّاعِمَةٌ ⑧
9. Pleased with their Striving—[6100]	لِّسَعْيِهَا رَاضِيَةٌ ⑨

6096. *Ghāshiyah:* the thing or event that overshadows or overwhelms, that covers over or makes people lose their senses. In 12:107, it is described as the "covering veil of the Wrath of Allah"; where see n. 1790. The Day of Judgement is indicated, as the Event of overwhelming importance in which all our petty differences of this imperfect world are covered over and overwhelmed in a new world of perfect justice and truth.

6097. *Cf.* 75:22, 24.

6098. On the faces of the wicked will appear the hard labour and consequent fatigue of the task they will have in battling against the fierce Fire which their own Deeds will have kindled.

6099. The root meaning implies again the idea of humiliation. It is a plant, bitter and thorny, loathsome in smell and appearance, which will neither give fattening nourishment to the body nor in any way satisfy the burning pangs of hunger—a fit plant for Hell, like *Zaqqūm* (56:52; or 17:60, n. 2250).

6100. Notice the parallelism in contrast, between the fate of the Wicked and that of the Righteous. In the one case there was humiliation in their faces; in the other, there is joy; where there was labour and weariness in warding off the Fire, there is instead a healthy Striving, which is itself pleasurable—a Striving which is a pleasant consequence of the spiritual Endeavour in the earthly life, which may have brought trouble or persecution from without, but which brought inward peace and satisfaction.

10. In a Garden on high,[6101]	فِي جَنَّةٍ عَالِيَةٍ ١٠
11. Where they shall hear No (word) of vanity:	لَّا تَسْمَعُ فِيهَا لَٰغِيَةً ١١
12. Therein will be A bubbling spring:[6102]	فِيهَا عَيْنٌ جَارِيَةٌ ١٢
13. Therein will be Thrones (Of dignity), raised on high,	فِيهَا سُرُرٌ مَّرْفُوعَةٌ ١٣
14. Goblets placed (ready),	وَأَكْوَابٌ مَّوْضُوعَةٌ ١٤
15. And Cushions set in rows,	وَنَمَارِقُ مَصْفُوفَةٌ ١٥
16. And rich carpets (All) spread out.	وَزَرَابِيُّ مَبْثُوثَةٌ ١٦
17. Do they not look At the Camels,[6103] How they are made?—	أَفَلَا يَنظُرُونَ إِلَى ٱلْإِبِلِ كَيْفَ خُلِقَتْ ١٧
18. And at the Sky,[6104] How it is raised high?—	وَإِلَى ٱلسَّمَآءِ كَيْفَ رُفِعَتْ ١٨
19. And at the Mountains,[6105] How they are fixed firm?—	وَإِلَى ٱلْجِبَالِ كَيْفَ نُصِبَتْ ١٩

6101. The most important point is their inward state of joy and satisfaction, mentioned in verses 8-9. Now are mentioned the outer things of bliss, the chief of which is the Garden. The Garden is in contrast to the Fire. Its chief beauty will be that they will hear there nothing unbecoming, or foolish, or vain. It will be a Garden *on high,* in all senses—fit for the best, highest, and noblest. (R).

6102. Instead of the boiling hot spring (verse 5) there will be a bubbling spring of sparkling water. Instead of the grovelling and grumbling in the place of Wrath, there will be Thrones of Dignity, with all the accompaniments of a brilliant Assembly.

6103. In case men neglect the Hereafter as of no account, they are asked to contemplate four things, which they can see in everyday life, and which are full of meaning, high design, and the goodness of Allah to man. The first mentioned is the domesticated animal, which for Arab countries is *par excellence* the Camel. What a wonderful structure has this Ship of the Desert? He can store water in his stomach for days. He can live on dry and thorny desert shrubs. His limbs are adapted to his life. He can carry men and goods. His flesh can be eaten. Camel's hair can be used in weaving. And withal, he is so gentle! Who can sing his praises enough?

6104. The second thing they should consider is the noble blue vault high above them—with the sun and moon, the stars and planets, and other heavenly bodies. This scene is full of beauty and magnificence, design and order, plainness and mystery. And yet we receive our light and warmth from the sun, and what would our physical lives be without these influences that come from such enormous distances?

6105. From everyday utility and affection in the Camel, to the utility in grandeur in the heavens above us, we had two instances touching our individual as well as our social lives. In the third instance, in the Mountains we come to the utility to mankind generally in the services the Mountains perform in storing water, in moderating climate, and in various other ways which it is the business of Physical Geography to investigate and describe.

20. And at the Earth,[6106] How it is spread out?	وَإِلَى ٱلْأَرْضِ كَيْفَ سُطِحَتْ ﴿٢٠﴾
21. Therefore do thou give Admonition, for thou art One to admonish.	فَذَكِّرْ إِنَّمَآ أَنتَ مُذَكِّرٌ ﴿٢١﴾
22. Thou art not one To manage (men's) affairs.[6107]	لَّسْتَ عَلَيْهِم بِمُصَيْطِرٍ ﴿٢٢﴾
23. But if any turns away And rejects Allah—	إِلَّا مَن تَوَلَّىٰ وَكَفَرَ ﴿٢٣﴾
24. Allah will punish him With a mighty Punishment.	فَيُعَذِّبُهُ ٱللَّهُ ٱلْعَذَابَ ٱلْأَكْبَرَ ﴿٢٤﴾
25. For to Us will be Their Return;	إِنَّ إِلَيْنَآ إِيَابَهُمْ ﴿٢٥﴾
26. Then it will be for Us To call them to account.	ثُمَّ إِنَّ عَلَيْنَا حِسَابَهُم ﴿٢٦﴾

6106. The fourth and last instance given is that of the Earth as a whole, the habitation of mankind in our present phase of life. The Earth is a globe, and yet how marvellously it seems to be spread out before us in plains, valleys, hills, deserts, seas, etc.! Can man, seeing these things, fail to see a Plan and Purpose in his life, or fail to turn to the great Creator before Whom he will have to give an account after this life is done?

6107. The Prophet of Allah is sent to teach and direct people on the way. He is not sent to force their will, or to punish them, except insofar as he may receive authority to do so. Punishment belongs to Allah alone. And Punishment is certain in the Hereafter, when true values will be restored.

INTRODUCTION AND SUMMARY TO SŪRAH 89—*AL FAJR*

This is one of the earliest of the Sūrahs to be revealed—probably within the first ten in chronological order.

Its mystic meaning is suggested by contrasts—contrasts in nature and in man's long history. Thus does it enforce the lesson of Faith in the Hereafter to "those who understand". Man's history and legendary lore show that greatness does not last and the proudest are brought low. For enforcing moral and spiritual truths, the strictest history is no better than legend. Indeed all artistic history is legend, for it is written from a special point of view.

Man is easily cowed by contrasts in his own fortunes, and yet he does not learn from them the lesson of forbearance and kindness to others, and the final elevation of goodness in the Hereafter. When all the things on which his mind and heart are set on this earth shall be crushed to nothingness, he will see the real glory and power, love and beauty, of Allah, for these are the light of the Garden of Paradise.

C. 269.—Man is apt to forget the contrasts
(89:1-30.) In nature and life, and all that they mean
In his spiritual growth. Perchance his mind
Is so absorbed in what he sees,
That he doubts the vast Realities
He does not see. The Present makes
Him blind to the Past and to the Future.
Fooled by glory, he fears not a fall;
And baulked in disaster, he gives up Hope
And sometimes Faith. Let him study
Nature and History, and restore his Faith:
Realising the Sure Event, the Hereafter,
Let him find his fullest fulfilment
In the service and the good pleasure of Allah!

Sūrah 89.

Al Fajr (The Dawn)

الجزء الثلاثون سورة الفجر

In the name of Allah, Most Gracious, Most Merciful.

بِسْمِ اللَّهِ الرَّحْمَٰنِ الرَّحِيمِ

1. By the Break of Day;[6108] وَالْفَجْرِ ①

2. By the Nights twice five;[6109] وَلَيَالٍ عَشْرٍ ②

3. By the Even
And Odd (contrasted);[6110] وَالشَّفْعِ وَالْوَتْرِ ③

4. And by the Night[6111]
When it passeth away— وَاللَّيْلِ إِذَا يَسْرِ ④

5. Is there (not) in these[6112] هَلْ فِي ذَٰلِكَ ⑤

6108. Four striking contrasts are mentioned, to show Allah's Power and Justice, and appeal to "those who understand". The first is the glory and mystery of the Break of Day. It just succeeds the deepest dark of the Night, when the first rays of light break through. Few people except those actually in personal touch with nature can feel its compelling power. In respect both of beauty and terror, of hope and inspiration, of suddenness and continuing increase of light and joy, this "holy time" of night may well stand as the type of spiritual awakening from darkness to Faith, from Death to Resurrection.

6109. By the Ten Nights are usually understood the first ten nights of *D͟hu al Hijjah*, the sacred season of Pilgrimage. From the most ancient times Makkah was the centre of Arab pilgrimage. The story of Abraham is intimately connected with it; see 2:125-127 and notes, also n. 217 to 2:197. In times of Paganism various superstitions were introduced, which Islam swept away. Islam also purified the rites and ceremonies, giving them new meaning. The ten days specially devoted to the Ḥajj introduce a striking contrast in the life of Makkah and of the pilgrims. Makkah, from being a quiet secluded city, is then thronged with thousands of pilgrims from all parts of the world. They discard their ordinary dress—representing every kind of costume—to the simple and ordinary *Iḥrām* (n.217); they refrain from every kind of fighting and quarrel; they abstain from every kind of luxury and self-indulgence; they hold all life sacred, however humble, except in the way of symbolical and carefully regulated sacrifice; and they spend their nights in prayer and meditation.

6110. The contrast between even and odd forms the subject of learned argument among those who deal with the mystic properties of numbers. In any case, even and odd follow each other in regular succession: each is independent, and yet neither is self-sufficient. In ultimate analysis every even number is a pair of odd ones. And all things go in pairs: see 36:36, and n. 3981. In the animal world pairs are but two individuals, and yet each is a complement of the other. Both abstract and concrete things are often understood in contrast with their opposites. Why should we not, in spiritual matters, understand this life better with reference to the Hereafter, and why should we disbelieve in the Hereafter simply because we cannot conceive of anything different from our present life?

6111. That is, the last part of the night, just before full daylight. Note the gradations in spiritual awakening, and their symbols: first, the turn of the night, when just the first rays of daylight break through; secondly, the social and institutional rites of religion, like those during the ten nights of Pilgrimage; thirdly, when the usual contrast between the Here and Hereafter vanishes, and we can see heaven even here; and lastly, when this world vanishes, the full light of Day arrives, and we see Reality face to face.

6112. All these mystic Symbols draw our attention, like solemn adjurations in speech, to the profoundest mystery of our inner life, *viz.*, how from utter depths of darkness—ignorance or even degradation—Allah's wonderful Light or Revelation can lead us by contrast into the most beautiful sunshine of a glorious spiritual Day. But the contrast suggests also the opposite process as a corollary—how resistance to Allah's light would destroy us utterly, converting our greatness or glory to perdition, as happened with the peoples of Arab antiquity, the 'Ād and the T͟hamūd, and the type of the powerful but arrogant and godless monarch, the Pharaoh of Egypt. Like a man with a bounded horizon, the average man does not understand these long range mysteries of life, and we have need to pray that we may be of "those who understand".

An adjuration (or evidence)
For those who understand?

قَسَمٌ لِّذِى حِجْرٍ

6. Seest thou not
How thy Lord dealt
With the 'Ād (people)—[6113]

أَلَمْ تَرَ كَيْفَ فَعَلَ رَبُّكَ بِعَادٍ ٦

7. Of the (city of) Iram,[6114]
With lofty pillars,

إِرَمَ ذَاتِ ٱلْعِمَادِ ٧

8. The like of which
Were not produced
In (all) the land?[6115]

ٱلَّتِى لَمْ يُخْلَقْ مِثْلُهَا فِى ٱلْبِلَٰدِ ٨

9. And with the Thamūd[6116]
(People), who cut out
(Huge) rocks in the valley?—

وَثَمُودَ ٱلَّذِينَ جَابُوا۟ ٱلصَّخْرَ بِٱلْوَادِ ٩

10. And with Pharaoh,
Lord of Stakes?[6117]

وَفِرْعَوْنَ ذِى ٱلْأَوْتَادِ ١٠

11. (All) these transgressed
Beyond bounds in the lands.

ٱلَّذِينَ طَغَوْا۟ فِى ٱلْبِلَٰدِ ١١

12. And heaped therein
Mischief (on mischief).

فَأَكْثَرُوا۟ فِيهَا ٱلْفَسَادَ ١٢

13. Therefore did thy Lord
Pour on them a scourge
Of diverse chastisements:

فَصَبَّ عَلَيْهِمْ رَبُّكَ سَوْطَ عَذَابٍ ١٣

6113. For the 'Ād see n. 1040 to 7:65. They seem to have possessed an ancient civilisation, which succumbed when they persistently broke Allah's law.

6114. Iram would seem to have been an ancient 'Ād capital, in southern Arabia. It boasted of lofty architecture ("lofty pillars"). Some Commentators understand Iram to be the name of an eponymous hero of the 'Ād, in which case the following line, "with lofty pillars", should be construed "of lofty stature". The 'Ād were a tall race.

6115. This tract of southern Arabia was once very prosperous (Arabia Felix) and contains ruins and inscriptions. It has always been an object of great interest to the Arabs. In the time of Mu'āwiyah some precious stones were found among the ruins in this locality. Quite recently, a bronze lion's head and a bronze piece of gutter with a Sabaean inscription, found in Najrān, have been described in the *British Museum Quarterly*, vol. XI, No. 4, Sept. 1937.

6116. For the Thamūd see n. 1043 to 6:73. Their civilisation shows traces of Egyptian, Syrian, and (later) Greek and Roman influences. They built fine temples, tombs, and buildings cut out of the solid rock. The cult of the goddess Lāt flourished among them.

6117. For "Lord of Stakes", see 38:12, n. 4160. For Pharaoh's arrogance and his fall, see 20:43, 78-79. The three examples given, the 'Ād, the Thamūd, and Pharaoh, show that neither nations nor individuals, however mighty, prosperous, or firmly established they may be, can live if they transgress the Law of Allah. The Law of Allah, which is also the law of the higher nature which He has bestowed on us, made them in the first place great and glorious: when they fell from it and "heaped mischief on mischief", they were swept away.

14. For thy Lord is
(As a Guardian)
On a watchtower.[6118]

﴿١٤﴾ إِنَّ رَبَّكَ لَبِالْمِرْصَادِ

15. Now, as for man,[6119]
When his Lord trieth him,
Giving him honour and gifts,
Then saith he, (puffed up),
"My Lord hath honoured me"

﴿١٥﴾ فَأَمَّا الْإِنسَانُ إِذَا مَا ابْتَلَاهُ رَبُّهُ
فَأَكْرَمَهُ وَنَعَّمَهُ فَيَقُولُ رَبِّي أَكْرَمَنِ

16. But when he trieth him,
Restricting his subsistence[6120]
For him, then saith he
(In despair), "My Lord
Hath humiliated me!"

﴿١٦﴾ وَأَمَّا إِذَا مَا ابْتَلَاهُ فَقَدَرَ
عَلَيْهِ رِزْقَهُ فَيَقُولُ رَبِّي أَهَانَنِ

17. Nay, nay! But *ye*[6121]
Honour not the orphans!

﴿١٧﴾ كَلَّا بَل لَّا تُكْرِمُونَ الْيَتِيمَ

18. Nor do ye encourage
One another[6122]
To feed the poor!—

﴿١٨﴾ وَلَا تَحَاضُّونَ عَلَىٰ طَعَامِ الْمِسْكِينِ

19. And ye devour Inheritance—[6123]
All with greed,

﴿١٩﴾ وَتَأْكُلُونَ التُّرَاثَ أَكْلًا لَّمًّا

6118. Even though Allah's punishment is delayed, it is not to be supposed that He does not see all things. Allah's providence is ever vigilant: His punishment of evildoers is a form of justice to the weak and the righteous whom they oppress. It is part of the signification of His title as *Rabb* (Cherisher). (R).

6119. Contrast with Allah's justice and watchful care, man's selfishness and pettiness. Allah tries us both by prosperity and adversity: in the one we should show humility and kindness; and in the other patience and faith. On the contrary, we get puffed up in prosperity and depressed in adversity, putting false values on this world's goods.

6120. *Subsistence,* in both the literal and the figurative sense. Allah provides for all, but people complain if the provision is measured and restricted to their needs, circumstances, and antecedents, and does not come up to their desires or expectations, or is different from that given to people in quite different circumstances.

6121. Even at our own valuation, if we are favoured with superfluities, do we think of the fatherless children, or the struggling poor? On the contrary, too many men are but ready to embezzle the helpless orphan's inheritance, and to waste their own substance in worthless riot instead of supplying the people's real needs.

6122. Kindness and generosity set up standards which even worldly men feel bound to follow out of social considerations even if they are not moved by higher motives. But the wicked find plausible excuses for their own hardheartedness, and by their evil example choke up the springs of charity and kindness in others.

6123. Inheritance is abused in two ways. (1) Guardians and trustees for the inheritance of minors or women or persons unable to look after their own interests should fulfil their trusts with even more care than they devote to their own interests. Instead of that they selfishly "devour" the property. (2) Persons who inherit property in their own rights should remember that in that case, too, it is a sacred trust. They must use it for the purposes, objects, and duties which they also inherit. It gives them no licence to live in idleness or waste their days in riotous show.

20. And ye love wealth
With inordinate love!

وَتُحِبُّونَ ٱلْمَالَ حُبًّا جَمًّا ﴿٢٠﴾

21. Nay! When the earth
Is pounded to powder,[6124]

كَلَّآ إِذَا دُكَّتِ ٱلْأَرْضُ دَكًّا دَكًّا ﴿٢١﴾

22. And thy Lord cometh,
And His angels,
Rank upon rank,

وَجَآءَ رَبُّكَ وَٱلْمَلَكُ صَفًّا صَفًّا ﴿٢٢﴾

23. And Hell, that Day,[6125]
Is brought (face to face)—
On that Day will man
Remember, but how will
That remembrance profit him?

وَجِاْىٓءَ يَوْمَئِذٍۭ بِجَهَنَّمَ ۚ
يَوْمَئِذٍ يَتَذَكَّرُ ٱلْإِنسَٰنُ وَأَنَّىٰ لَهُ ٱلذِّكْرَىٰ ﴿٢٣﴾

24. He will say: "Ah!
Would that I had
Sent forth (Good Deeds)
For (this) my (Future) Life!"

يَقُولُ يَٰلَيْتَنِى
قَدَّمْتُ لِحَيَاتِى ﴿٢٤﴾

25. For, that Day,
His Chastisement will be
Such as none (else)
Can inflict,[6126]

فَيَوْمَئِذٍ لَّا يُعَذِّبُ
عَذَابَهُۥٓ أَحَدٌ ﴿٢٥﴾

26. And His bonds
Will be such as
None (other) can bind.

وَلَا يُوثِقُ وَثَاقَهُۥٓ أَحَدٌ ﴿٢٦﴾

27. (To the righteous soul
Will be said:)
"O (thou) soul,[6127]

يَٰٓأَيَّتُهَا ٱلنَّفْسُ ﴿٢٧﴾

6124. Our attention is now called to the Day of Reckoning. Whether we failed to respect the rights of the helpless here or actually suppressed those rights in our mad love for the good things of this life, we shall have to answer in the realm of Reality. This solid earth, which we imagine to be so real, will crumble to powder like dust before the real Presence, manifested in glory.

6125. The Retribution will at last come, and we shall realise it in our inmost being, all the illusions of this fleeting world having been swept away. Then we shall remember, and wish, too late, that we had repented. Why not repent now? Why not bring forth the fruits of repentance now, as a preparation for the Hereafter?

6126. "Chastisement" in this verse and the "binding in bonds" in the next verse are two distinct phases of the Penalty. "Chastisement" involves pain and agony, such as cannot be imagined anywhere else, or from any other source, for it touches our inmost soul and cannot be compared with anything our bodies may suffer or others may inflict. "Bonds" imply confinement, want of freedom, the closing of a door which was once open but which we deliberately passed by. We see that others accepted in faith and entered that door. This shutting out of what might have been is worse than any other bonds or confinement we can imagine, and may be worse than actual chastisement.

6127. The righteous enter into their inheritance and receive their welcome with a title that suggests freedom from all pain, sorrow, doubt, struggle, disappointment, passion, and even further desire: at rest, in peace; in a state of complete satisfaction.

In Muslim theology, this stage of the soul is the final stage of bliss. The unregenerate human soul, that seeks its satisfaction in the lower earthly desires, is the *Ammārah* (12:53). The self-reproaching soul that feels conscious of sin and resists it is the *Lawwāmah* (75:2, and n. 5810).

In (complete) rest
And satisfaction!

ٱلْمُطْمَئِنَّةُ

28. "Come back thou
To thy Lord—[6128]
Well pleased (thyself),
And well-pleasing
Unto Him!

ٱرْجِعِىٓ إِلَىٰ رَبِّكِ رَاضِيَةً مَّرْضِيَّةً ﴿٢٨﴾

29. "Enter thou, then,
Among my Devotees!

فَٱدْخُلِى فِى عِبَٰدِى ﴿٢٩﴾

30. "Yea, enter thou
My Heaven!"[6129]

وَٱدْخُلِى جَنَّتِى ﴿٣٠﴾

6128. Note that Evil finds itself isolated, and cries out in lonely agony (verse 24), while Good receives a warm welcome from the Lord of Goodness Himself—also that it is the soul which enters heaven, and not the gross body which perishes.

6129. The climax of the whole is: "Enter My Heaven!" Men may have imagined all kinds of heaven before, and many types and symbols are used in the sacred Word itself. But nothing can express the reality itself better than "My Heaven"—Allah's own Heaven! May we reach it through Allah's grace! (R).

INTRODUCTION AND SUMMARY TO SŪRAH 90—*AL BALAD*

This is an early Makkan revelation, and refers to the mystic relation (by divine sanction) of the Holy Prophet with the city of Makkah. He was born in that City, which had already been sacred for ages before. He was nurtured in that City and had (to use a modern phrase) the freedom of that City, belonging, as he did, to the noble family which held the government of its sacred precincts in its hands. But he was an orphan, and orphans in his day had a poor time. But his mind was turned to things divine. He protested against the prevailing idolatry and sin, and his parent City persecuted him and cast him out. He made another City, *Yathrib,* his own: it became the *Madīnah al Nabī,* the City of the Prophet, and it has ever since been called Madīnah. We can speak of Madīnah as the Prophet's child. But the Prophet ever cherished in his heart the love of his parent City of Makkah, and in the fulness of time was received in triumph there. He purified it from all idols and abominations, reestablished the worship of the One True God, overthrew the purse-proud selfish autocracy, restored the sway of the righteous (people of the Right Hand), the liberty of the slave, and the rights of the poor and downtrodden. What a wonderful career centering round a City? It becomes a symbol of the world's spiritual history.

C. 270.—The Prophet's own City persecuted him.
(90:1-20.) Honoured by his nativity, it sought to slay him:
Yet he loved it and purged it of all that was wrong.
What toil and struggle did it not involve?
Man is made for toil and struggle:
Let him not boast of ease and wealth.
He will be called to account for all his doings.
Let him use his God-given faculties, and tread
The steep path that leads to Heaven's Heights:
The steps thereto are Love, unselfish Love,
Given freely to Allah's creatures—all those
In need—and Faith in Allah, and Patience
Joined with self-restraint and kindness.
Thus only can we reach the ranks
Of the blest Companions of the Right Hand!

Sūrah 90.

Al Balad (The City)

الجزء الثلاثون سُورَةُ البَلَدِ

In the name of Allah, Most Gracious, Most Merciful.

بِسۡمِ ٱللَّهِ ٱلرَّحۡمَٰنِ ٱلرَّحِيمِ

1. I do call to witness[6130]
This City—

لَآ أُقۡسِمُ بِهَٰذَا ٱلۡبَلَدِ ۝١

2. And thou art a freeman[6131]
Of this City—

وَأَنتَ حِلُّۢ بِهَٰذَا ٱلۡبَلَدِ ۝٢

3. And (the mystic ties
Of) Parent and Child)—[6132]

وَوَالِدٖ وَمَا وَلَدَ ۝٣

4. Verily We have created
Man into toil and struggle.[6133]

لَقَدۡ خَلَقۡنَا ٱلۡإِنسَٰنَ فِي كَبَدٍ ۝٤

5. Thinketh he, that none
Hath power over him?[6134]

أَيَحۡسَبُ أَن لَّن يَقۡدِرَ عَلَيۡهِ أَحَدٞ ۝٥

6. He may say (boastfully):
Wealth have I squandered

يَقُولُ أَهۡلَكۡتُ مَالٗا ۝٦

6130. The appeal to the mystic ties between the Holy Prophet and his parent city of Makkah has been explained in the Introduction to this Sūrah. It is a symbol of man's own history. Man is born for toil and struggle, and this is the substantive proposition in verse 4 below, which this appeal leads up to.

6131. *Ḥillun:* an inhabitant, a man with lawful rights, a man freed from such obligations as would attach to a stranger to the city, a freeman in a wider sense than the technical sense to which the word is restricted in modern usage. The Prophet should have been honoured in his native city. He was actually being persecuted. He should have been loved, as a parent loves a child. Actually his life was being sought, and those who believed in him were under a ban. But time was to show that he was to come triumphant to his native city after having made Madīnah sacred by his life and work.

6132. A parent loves a child ordinarily: the father is proud and the mother, in spite of her birth pains, experiences supreme joy when the child is born. But in abnormal circumstances there may be misunderstandings, even hatred between parent and child. So Makkah cast out her most glorious son, but it was only for a time. Makkah was sound at heart; only her power had been usurped by an ignorant autocracy which passed away, and Makkah was to receive back her glory at the hands of the son whom she had rejected but whom she welcomed back later. And Makkah retains for all time her sacred character as the centre of Islam.

6133. *Cf.* "Man is born unto troubles as the sparks fly upward" (Job, v. 7); "For all his days are sorrows, and his travail grief" (Ecclesiastes, ii. 23). Man's life is full of sorrow and vexation; but our text has a different shade of meaning: man is born to strive and struggle; and if he suffers from hardships, he must exercise patience, for Allah will make his way smooth for him (65:7; 94:5-6). On the other hand no man should boast of worldly goods or worldly prosperity (see verses 5-7 below).

6134. See the end of last note. If a man has wealth, influence, or power, he should not behave as if it is to last forever, or as if he has no responsibility for his acts and can do what he likes. All his gifts and advantages are given to him for trial. Allah, Who bestowed them on him, can take them away, and will do so if man fails in his trial.

In abundance!"[6135] لُّبَدًا

7. Thinketh he that none
Beholdeth him?[6136] ٧ أَيَحْسَبُ أَن لَّمْ يَرَهُۥٓ أَحَدٌ

8. Have We not made
For him a pair of eyes?— ٨ أَلَمْ نَجْعَل لَّهُۥ عَيْنَيْنِ

9. And a tongue,[6137]
And a pair of lips?— ٩ وَلِسَانًا وَشَفَتَيْنِ

10. And shown him
The two highways?[6138] ١٠ وَهَدَيْنَٰهُ ٱلنَّجْدَيْنِ

11. But he hath made no haste
On the path that is steep.[6139] ١١ فَلَا ٱقْتَحَمَ ٱلْعَقَبَةَ

12. And what will explain
To thee the path that is steep?— ١٢ وَمَآ أَدْرَىٰكَ مَا ٱلْعَقَبَةُ

13. (It is:) freeing the bondman;[6140] ١٣ فَكُّ رَقَبَةٍ

6135. The man who feels no responsibility and thinks that he can do what he likes in life forgets his responsibility to Allah. He boasts of his wealth and scatters it about, thinking that he can thus purchase the support of the world. For a time he may. But a rude awakening must come soon, for he bases his hopes on unsubstantial things. Or if he spends his substance on self-indulgence, he is weakening himself and putting himself into snares that must destroy him.

6136. Allah watches him, and sees all his acts and motives, and all the secret springs of his follies. But lest he should think the higher spiritual forces too remote for him, let him look within himself and use the faculties which Allah has given him. See the next verses following.

6137. The eyes give us the faculty of seeing, and may be taken in both the literal and the metaphorical sense. In the same way the tongue gives us the faculty of tasting in both senses. Along with the lips, it also enables us to speak, to ask for information and seek guidance, and to celebrate the praises of Allah.

6138. The two highways of life are: (1) the steep and difficult path of virtue, which is further described in the verses following, and (2) the easy path of vice and the rejection of Allah, referred to in verses 19-20 below. Allah has given us not only the faculties implied in the eyes, the tongue, and the lips, but also given us the judgement by which we can choose our way; and He has sent us Teachers and Guides, with Revelation, to show us the right and difficult way.

6139. In spite of the faculties with which Allah has endowed man and the guidance which He has given him, man has been remiss. By no means has he been eager to follow the steep and difficult path which is for his own spiritual good. *Cf.* Matt. vii. 14: "Strait is the gate, and narrow is the way, which leadeth unto life, and few there be that find it".

6140. The difficult path of virtue is defined as the path of charity or unselfish love, and three specific instances are given for our understanding: *viz.* (1) freeing the bondman, (2) feeding the orphan, and (3) feeding the indigent down in the dust. As regards the bondman, we are to understand not only a reference to legal slavery, but many other kinds of slavery which flourish especially in advanced societies. There is political slavery, industrial slavery, and social slavery. There is the slavery of conventions, of ignorance, and of superstition. There is slavery to wealth or passions or power. The good man tries to liberate men and women from all kinds of slavery, often at great danger to himself. But he begins by first liberating himself. (R).

14. Or the giving of food
In a day of privation[6141]

١٤ أَوْ إِطْعَٰمٌ فِى يَوْمٍ ذِى مَسْغَبَةٍ

15. To the orphan
With claims of relationship,[6142]

١٥ يَتِيمًا ذَا مَقْرَبَةٍ

16. Or to the indigent
(Down) in the dust.[6143]

١٦ أَوْ مِسْكِينًا ذَا مَتْرَبَةٍ

17. Then will he be[6144]
Of those who believe,
And enjoin patience, (constancy,
And self-restraint), and enjoin
Deeds of kindness and
compassion.

١٧ ثُمَّ كَانَ مِنَ ٱلَّذِينَ ءَامَنُوا۟
وَتَوَاصَوْا۟ بِٱلصَّبْرِ
وَتَوَاصَوْا۟ بِٱلْمَرْحَمَةِ

18. Such are the Companions
Of the Right Hand.[6145]

١٨ أُو۟لَٰٓئِكَ أَصْحَٰبُ ٱلْمَيْمَنَةِ

19. But those who reject
Our Signs, they are
The (unhappy) Companions
Of the Left Hand.[6146]

١٩ وَٱلَّذِينَ كَفَرُوا۟ بِـَٔايَٰتِنَا
هُمْ أَصْحَٰبُ ٱلْمَشْـَٔمَةِ

20. On them will be Fire
Vaulted over (all round).

٢٠ عَلَيْهِمْ نَارٌ مُّؤْصَدَةٌۢ

6141. Feed those who need it, both literally and figuratively; but do so especially when there is privation or famine, literal or figurative, *i.e.*, when or where the sources of sustenance, physical, moral, or spiritual, are cut off.

6142. All orphans should be fed and helped. But ordinary orphans will come under the indigent in verse 16 below. The orphans related to us have a special claim on us. They should be near and dear to us, and if charity begins at home, they have the first claim on us.

6143. Persons down in the dust can only be helped from motives of pure charity, because nothing can be expected of them—neither praise nor advertisement nor any other advantage to the helper. Such help is help indeed. But there may be various degrees, and the help will be suited to the needs.

6144. Such practical charity and love will be the acid test of Faith and the teaching of all virtues. The virtues are summed up under the names of Patience (the Arabic word includes constancy and self-restraint) and compassionate kindness. Not only will they be the test by which the sincerity of their Faith will be judged: they will be the fruit which their Faith will constantly produce.

6145. *Cf.* 56:27-40, also n. 5223. They will be those who achieve salvation.

6146. *Cf.* 56:41-56, also n. 5223. They will be the unfortunate ones enveloped in the Fire of lasting Penalty, heaped over them and all round them.

INTRODUCTION AND SUMMARY TO SŪRAH 91—*AL SHAMS*

This is one of the early Makkan revelations. Beginning with a fine nature passage, and leading up to man's need of realising his spiritual responsibility, it ends with a warning of the terrible consequences for those who fear not the Hereafter.

C. 271.—All nature around us and her pageants,
(91:1-15.) And the soul of man within, proclaim
The goodness of Allah. Allah gave the soul
The power of choice and the sense of Right
And Wrong. Let man keep it pure and attain
Salvation—soil it with sin and reach
Perdition. Inordinate wrongdoing ruined
The Thamūd. They defied Allah's sacred Law
And His Prophet, and went to Destruction for their crime.

Sūrah 91.

Al Shams (The Sun) الجزء الثلاثون سُورَةُ الشَّمْسِ

In the name of Allah, Most Gracious, Most Merciful. بِسْمِ اللَّهِ الرَّحْمَٰنِ الرَّحِيمِ

1. By the Sun[6147]
And its (glorious) splendour; وَالشَّمْسِ وَضُحَاهَا ١

2. By the Moon[6148]
As it follows (the Sun); وَالْقَمَرِ إِذَا تَلَاهَا ٢

3. By the Day as it[6149]
Shows up (the Sun's) glory; وَالنَّهَارِ إِذَا جَلَّاهَا ٣

4. By the Night as it
Conceals it; وَاللَّيْلِ إِذَا يَغْشَاهَا ٤

5. By the Firmament[6150]
And its (wonderful) structure;[6151] وَالسَّمَاءِ وَمَا بَنَاهَا ٥

6. By the Earth
And its (wide) expanse; وَالْأَرْضِ وَمَا طَحَاهَا ٦

6147. Six types are taken in three pairs, from Allah's mighty works in nature, as tokens or evidence of Allah's providence and the contrasts in His sublime creation, which yet conduce to cosmic harmony (verses 1-6). Then (verses 7-8) the soul of man, with internal order and proportion in its capacities and faculties, as made by Allah, is appealed to as having been endowed with the power of discriminating between right and wrong. Then the conclusion is stated in verses 9-10, that man's success or failure, prosperity or bankruptcy, would depend upon his keeping that soul pure or his corrupting it.

6148. The first pair is the glorious sun, the source of our light and physical life, and the moon which follows or acts as second to the sun for illuminating our world. The moon, when she is in the sky with the sun, is pale and inconspicuous; in the sun's absence she shines with reflected light and may metaphorically be called the sun's vicegerent. So with Revelation and the great Prophets who brought it; and the minor Teachers who derive their light reflected, or perhaps doubly reflected, from the original source.

6149. The next contrasted pair consists, not of luminaries, but conditions, or periods of time, Day and Night. The Day reveals the sun's glory and the Night conceals it from our sight. So there may be contrasts in our subjective reception of divine light, but it is there, working all the time, and must reappear in its own good time.

6150. The next contrasted pair is the wonderful firmament on high, and the earth below our feet, stretching away to our wide horizons. The sky gives us rain, and the earth gives us food. Yet both work together: for the rain is moisture sucked up from the earth, and the food cannot grow without the heat and warmth of the sun. There are many other contrasts under this head; yet they all point to unity.

6151. The *mā maṣdariyah* in Arabic, in this and the subsequent clauses, is best translated in English by nouns. Thus what would literally be "and the (wonderful) making or construction of it" or "the fact of its (wonderful) construction" is, idiomatically, "its (wonderful) structure." "The (wide) spreading out" of the earth is rendered "its (wide) expanse," and so on.

7. By the Soul, And the proportion and order Given to it;[6152]	وَنَفْسٍ وَمَا سَوَّىٰهَا ﴿٧﴾
8. And its enlightenment As to its wrong And its right—	فَأَلْهَمَهَا فُجُورَهَا وَتَقْوَىٰهَا ﴿٨﴾
9. Truly he succeeds That purifies it,	قَدْ أَفْلَحَ مَن زَكَّىٰهَا ﴿٩﴾
10. And he fails That corrupts it![6153]	وَقَدْ خَابَ مَن دَسَّىٰهَا ﴿١٠﴾
11. The Thamūd (people) Rejected (their prophet) Through their inordinate Wrongdoing.[6154]	كَذَّبَتْ ثَمُودُ بِطَغْوَىٰهَآ ﴿١١﴾
12. Behold, the most wicked Man among them was Deputed (for impiety).[6155]	إِذِ ٱنۢبَعَثَ أَشْقَىٰهَا ﴿١٢﴾
13. But the Messenger of Allah[6156] Said to them: "It is A She-camel of Allah! And (bar her not From) having her drink!"	فَقَالَ لَهُمْ رَسُولُ ٱللَّهِ نَاقَةَ ٱللَّهِ وَسُقْيَٰهَا ﴿١٣﴾
14. Then they rejected him (As a false prophet),	فَكَذَّبُوهُ ﴿١٤﴾

6152. Allah makes the soul, and gives it order, proportion, and relative perfection, in order to adapt it for the particular circumstances in which it has to live its life. *Cf.* 32:9. See also n. 120 to 2:117. He breathes into it an understanding of what is sin, impiety, wrongdoing and what is piety and right conduct, in the special circumstances in which it may be placed. This is the most precious gift of all to man, the faculty of distinguishing between right and wrong. After the six external evidences mentioned in verses 1-6 above, this internal evidence of Allah's goodness is mentioned as the greatest of all. By these various tokens man should learn that his success, his prosperity, his salvation depends on himself—on his keeping his soul pure as Allah made it; and his failure, his decline, his perdition depends on his soiling his soul by choosing evil.

6153. This is the core of the Sūrah, and it is illustrated by a reference to the story of the Thamūd in the following verses.

6154. The allusion to the story of the Thamūd will be understood by a reference to 7:73-79; see specially n. 1044. Their prophet was Ṣāliḥ but he had to deal with an arrogant people, who oppressed the poor and denied them their rights of watering and pasture for their cattle.

6155. The prophet Ṣāliḥ made a certain she-camel a Sign or Symbol, a test case, "This she-camel of Allah is Sign unto you; so leave her to graze in Allah's earth and let her come to no harm, or ye shall be seized with a grievous punishment" (7:73). but they plotted to kill her and sent the most wicked man among them to dare and do that deed of impiety. It was probably when she came to drink at the stream that she was hamstrung and killed. See 26:155, and 54:27.

6156. That is, Ṣāliḥ: see last note.

فعقروها فدمدم
عليهم ربهم بذنبهم
فسوىها

And they hamstrung her.[6157]
So their Lord, on account
Of their crime, obliterated
Their traces and made them
Equal (in destruction,
High and low)!

ولا يخاف عقبىها ﴿١٥﴾

15. And for Him[6158]
Is no fear
Of its consequences.

6157. The man who was deputed to do the impious deed of hamstringing the she-camel had, of course, the sympathy and cooperation of the whole people. Only he was more daring than the rest.

6158. This verse has been variously construed. I follow the general opinion in referring the pronoun "Him" to "their Lord" in the last verse and the pronoun "its" to the Punishment that was meted out to all, high and low, equally. In that case the meaning would be: God decreed the total destruction of the Thamūd; in the case of creatures any such destruction might cause a loss to them, and they might fear the consequences of such loss or destruction, but Allah has created and can create at will, and there can be no question of any such apprehension in His case. An alternative view is that "him" refers to the prophet Ṣāliḥ, mentioned in verse 13. Then the interpretation would be: Ṣāliḥ had no fear of the consequences for himself; he had warned the wicked according to his commission; he was saved by Allah's mercy as a just and righteous man, and he left them with regrets (7:79). Yet another alternative refers "him" to the wicked man (mentioned in verse 12) who hamstrung the she-camel: he feared not the consequences of his deed.

INTRODUCTION AND SUMMARY TO SŪRAH 92—*AL LAYL*

This was one of the first Sūrahs to be revealed—within the first ten; and may be placed in date close to S. 89 and S. 93. Note that in all these three Sūrahs the mystery and the contrast as between Night and Day are appealed to for the consolation of man in his spiritual yearning. Here we are told to strive our utmost towards Allah, and He will give us every help and satisfaction.

C. 272.—When we consider Allah's wonderful Creation,
(92:1-21.) We see many myteries—many opposites—
Many differences; the succession of nights
And days, the creation of male and female.
Can we wonder at the differences
In the nature and objectives of man?
He is endowed with Will, and he must strive
For the Right through all his diverse paths.
For the righteous, the way is made the smoother
For bliss; for the arrogant crooked will,
The way is the smoother for Misery.
But Allah's guidance is always nigh,
If man will choose it. And what
Is the goal for those who choose aright?—
The sight of the Face of Allah Most High:
For that indeed is happiness supreme.

Sūrah 92.

Al Layl (The Night)

الجزء الثلاثون سورة الليل

In the name of Allah, Most Gracious, Most Merciful.

بِسۡمِ ٱللَّهِ ٱلرَّحۡمَٰنِ ٱلرَّحِيمِ

1. By the Night as it
Conceals (the light);[6159]

(١) وَٱلَّيۡلِ إِذَا يَغۡشَىٰ

2. By the Day as it
Appears in glory;

(٢) وَٱلنَّهَارِ إِذَا تَجَلَّىٰ

3. By (the mystery of)[6160]
The creation of male
And female—[6161]

(٣) وَمَا خَلَقَ ٱلذَّكَرَ وَٱلۡأُنثَىٰٓ

4. Verily, (the ends) ye
Strive for are diverse.[6162]

(٤) إِنَّ سَعۡيَكُمۡ لَشَتَّىٰ

5. So he who gives
(In charity) and fears (Allah),

(٥) فَأَمَّا مَنۡ أَعۡطَىٰ وَٱتَّقَىٰ

6. And (in all sincerity)
Testifies to the Best—[6163]

(٦) وَصَدَّقَ بِٱلۡحُسۡنَىٰ

6159. The evidence of three things is invoked. *viz.*, Night, Day, and the mystery of Sex, and the conclusion is stated in verse 4, that men's aims are diverse. But similarly there are contrasts in nature. What contrast can be greater than between Night and Day? When the Night spreads her veil, the sun's light is hidden, but not lost. The sun is in its place all the time, and will come forth in all its glory again in its own good time. *Cf.* 91:3, 4, and n. 6149. Man pursuing diverse aims may find, owing to his own position, Allah's light obscured from him for a time, but he must strive hard to put himself in a position to reach it in all its glory.

6160. *Mā maṣdarīyah* as in 91:5-7; see there n. 6151.

6161. The mystery of the sexes runs through all life. There is attraction between opposites; each performs its own functions, having special characters, primary and secondary, within limited spheres, and yet both have common characteristics in many other spheres. Each is indispensable to the other. Love in its noblest sense is the type of heavenly love and the highest good; in its debasement it leads to the lowest sins and the worst crimes. Here, then, striving is necessary for the highest good.

6162. There are wide contrasts in the nature and aims of men. These may be broadly divided into two classes, good and evil. As night replaces day on account of certain relative positions, but does not annihilate it, so evil may for a time obscure good but cannot blot it out. Again, night in certain circumstances *(e.g.* for rest) is a blessing; do certain things, which seek the highest truth from the light of Allah. Considering these contrasts, do not be surprised or depressed. Men's immediate aims may be different. The duty of all is to seek the one true Light.

6163. The good are distinguished here by three signs: (1) large-hearted sacrifices for Allah and men: (2) fear of Allah, which shows itself in righteous conduct, for *Taqwā* (see n. 26 to 2:2) includes just action as well as a mental state: and (3) truth and sincerity in recognising and supporting all that is morally beautiful, for *Ḥusn* is the good as well as the beautiful.

7. We will indeed
Make smooth for him
The path to Bliss.[6164]

فَسَنُيَسِّرُهُۥ لِلْيُسْرَىٰ ⑦

8. But he who is
A greedy miser
And thinks himself
Self-sufficient,

وَأَمَّا مَنۢ بَخِلَ وَٱسْتَغْنَىٰ ⑧

9. And gives the lie
To the Best—[6165]

وَكَذَّبَ بِٱلْحُسْنَىٰ ⑨

10. We will indeed
Make smooth for him
The Path to Misery;

فَسَنُيَسِّرُهُۥ لِلْعُسْرَىٰ ⑩

11. Nor will his wealth
Profit him when he
Falls headlong (into the Pit).[6166]

وَمَا يُغْنِى عَنْهُ مَالُهُۥٓ إِذَا تَرَدَّىٰٓ ⑪

12. Verily We take[6167]
Upon Ourselves to guide,

إِنَّ عَلَيْنَا لَلْهُدَىٰ ⑫

13. And verily unto Us
(Belong) the End
And the Beginning.[6168]

وَإِنَّ لَنَا لَلْءَاخِرَةَ وَٱلْأُولَىٰ ⑬

14. Therefore do I warn you
Of a Fire blazing fiercely;

فَأَنذَرْتُكُمْ نَارًا تَلَظَّىٰ ⑭

6164. So far from there being any hardship in a good life, the righteous will enjoy their life more and more, and Allah will make their path smoother and smoother until they reach eventual Bliss.

6165. The evil are distinguished here by three signs: (1) selfish greed and denial of other people's rights; (2) arrogance and self-sufficiency (96:6-7); and (3) knowingly dishonouring Truth out of spite, or seeing ugliness where there is beauty. Such men's downward progress gathers momentum as they go, and their end can be nothing but Misery. Where will be their boasted wealth and possessions, or their self-confidence?

6166. Wealth amassed in this world will be of no use at the Day of Final Judgement, nor will any material advantages of this life bring profit by themselves in the spiritual world. What will count will be a life of truth and righteousness, and of goodness to all the creatures of Allah.

6167. Allah in His infinite mercy has provided full guidance to His creatures. All through His creation there are sign posts indicating the right way. To man He has given the five senses of perception, with mental and spiritual faculties for co-ordinating his physical perceptions and leading him higher and higher in thought and feeling. He has besides sent inspired men for further teaching and guidance.

6168. In the End man will return to Allah, and even from the beginning of man's life Allah's mercies and loving care surround him. In the probationary period of man's life, he has a measure of free will, and he is expected to use it in such a way as to bring his whole being into harmony with the universal Will and Law. For he will have to answer for the right use of his talents and opportunities. If man's will has any meaning, he has the choice of accepting Allah's guidance or rejecting it, and in the latter case he must take the consequences. Hence the warning of the future "Fire" in the next verse.

15. None shall reach it[6169]
But those most unfortunate ones

لَا يَصْلَىٰهَآ إِلَّا ٱلْأَشْقَى ﴿١٥﴾

16. Who give the lie to Truth
And turn their backs.

ٱلَّذِى كَذَّبَ وَتَوَلَّىٰ ﴿١٦﴾

17. But those most devoted
To Allah shall be[6170]
Removed far from it—

وَسَيُجَنَّبُهَا ٱلْأَتْقَى ﴿١٧﴾

18. Those who spend their wealth[6171]
For increase in self-purification,[6172]

ٱلَّذِى يُؤْتِى مَالَهُۥ يَتَزَكَّىٰ ﴿١٨﴾

19. And have in their minds
No favour from anyone
For which a reward
Is expected in return,[6173]

وَمَا لِأَحَدٍ عِندَهُۥ مِن نِّعْمَةٍ تُجْزَىٰٓ ﴿١٩﴾

20. But only the desire
To seek for the Countenance
Of their Lord Most High;[6174]

إِلَّا ٱبْتِغَآءَ وَجْهِ رَبِّهِ ٱلْأَعْلَىٰ ﴿٢٠﴾

21. And soon will they
Attain (complete) satisfaction.

وَلَسَوْفَ يَرْضَىٰ ﴿٢١﴾

6169. The Fire of Punishment will not reach any except those who have deliberately sinned against their conscience and rejected Allah's Truth. The term used for them is *"Ashqā"* (superlative degree). *Cf.* 87:11. The corresponding idea in Christian theology is expressed in the following sentence. "All manner of sin and blasphemy shall be forgiven unto men: but the blasphemy against the Holy Ghost shall not be forgiven unto men" (Matt. xii. 31). (R).

6170. "Those most devoted to Allah": the *Atqā*, the God-fearing men who live lives of purity, and seek only for the "Face of their Lord Most High". See the verses following.

6171. The spending may be for charity, or for good works, such as advancing the cause of knowledge or science, or supporting ideals, etc. *"Wealth"* must be understood not only for money or material goods, but also for any advantage or opportunity which a man happens to enjoy, and which he can place at the service of others.

6172. The Arabic root word *zakā* implies both increase and purification, and both meanings may be understood to be implied here. Wealth (understood both literally and metaphorically) is not for selfish enjoyment or idle show. It is held on trust. It may be a trial in itself, from which a man who emerges successfully is a man all the purer in his life; and even if he was a good man before, his proper use of his wealth increases his position and dignity in the moral and spiritual world.

6173. The good man does not give in charity or do his good deeds with the motive that he is returning someone else's favour and compensating and rewarding someone for some service done to him or expecting some reward in return for his own good deed: the sole motive in his mind is that he desires the Countenance or Good Pleasure of Allah Most High. This "Countenance" or "Face" (Arabic, *Wajh)* implies good pleasure or approval; but it implies something more. It also means the Cause—either the "final cause" or the "efficient cause" of Aristotelian philosophy. For the *Atqā* would refer everything, backwards in origin and forwards in destiny, to Allah. Allah is the source of their goodness, as well as its goal or purpose.

6174. The definition of Righteousness, Charity, or Self-sacrifice, becomes thus highly spiritualised. The *Atqā* are so completely identified with Allah's Will that everything else is blotted out to them. What would seem to be sacrifice from other points of view, becomes their own highest pleasure and satisfaction. Every virtuous man will have his own bliss, for there are degrees in virtue and bliss. This supreme bliss is the portion—not the prize—of supreme virtue. (R).

INTRODUCTION AND SUMMARY TO SŪRAH 93—*AL ḌUḤĀ*

This Sūrah is close in date to Sūrahs 89 and 92, and the imagery drawn from the contrast of Night and Day is common to all three. In this Sūrah the vicissitudes of human life are referred to, and a message of hope and consolation is given to man's soul from Allah's past mercies, and he is bidden to pursue the path of goodness and proclaim the bounties of Allah. This is the general meaning. In particular, the Sūrah seems to have been revealed in a dark period in the outer life of the Holy Prophet, when a man of less resolute will might have been discouraged. But the Prophet is told to hold the present of less account than the glorious Hereafter which awaited him like the glorious morning after a night of stillness and gloom. The Hereafter was, not only in the Future Life, but his later life on this earth, full of victory and satisfaction.

C. 273.—What an example we have in the Prophet's life!
(93:1-11.) When moments of inspiration were still,
His soul yet felt the power of that stillness,
Like one who prays by night and waits
For the dawn, knowing how the light grows brighter
Every hour till noon, and well content
That night and morn and the hours succeeding
Are but steps to the plenary splendour of noon.
He was content and consoled in the thought that Allah
Had bestowed His loving care on him,
In the past, and so the future was sure.
He followed the Light Divine—to help
The helpless, to attend with patience to the call
Of those in need, and to rehearse and proclaim
And share the boundless Bounties of Allah!

Sūrah 93.

Al Ḍuḥā (The Glorious Morning Light)

الجزء الثلاثون سُورَةُ الضُّحَىٰ

In the name of Allah, Most Gracious,
Most Merciful.

بِسْمِ اللَّهِ الرَّحْمَٰنِ الرَّحِيمِ

1. By the Glorious
Morning Light,[6175]

وَالضُّحَىٰ ﴿١﴾

2. And by the Night[6176]
When it is still—

وَاللَّيْلِ إِذَا سَجَىٰ ﴿٢﴾

3. Thy Guardian-Lord
Hath not forsaken thee,[6177]
Nor is He displeased.[6178]

مَا وَدَّعَكَ رَبُّكَ وَمَا قَلَىٰ ﴿٣﴾

4. And verily the hereafter
Will be better for thee
Than the present.[6179]

وَلَلْآخِرَةُ خَيْرٌ لَّكَ مِنَ الْأُولَىٰ ﴿٤﴾

5. And soon will thy
Guardian-Lord give thee

وَلَسَوْفَ يُعْطِيكَ رَبُّكَ ﴿٥﴾

6175. The full morning light of the sun, when its splendour shines forth in contrast with the night which has passed. *Cf.* 91:1. The growing hours of morning light, from sunrise to noon, are the true type of the growth of spiritual life and work, while the stillness of the night is, to those who know, only a preparation for it. We are not to imagine that the stillness or quiescence of the night is wasted, or means stagnation in our spiritual life. The stillness may seem lonely, but we are not alone, nor forsaken by Allah. Nor is such preparation, without immediate visible results, a sign of Allah's displeasure.

6176. *Cf.* 92:1-2. There Night is mentioned first, and Day second, to enforce the lesson of contrasts: the veil of the night naturally comes first before the splendour of daylight is revealed. Here the argument is different: the growing hours of morning light are the main thing and are mentioned first; while the hours of preparation and quiescence, which are subordinate, come second.

6177. As usual, there is the particular assurance to the Holy Prophet, and the general assurance to mankind: see the Introduction to this Sūrah. The early years of the Prophet's ministry might well have seemed blank. After inspiration there were days and periods of waiting. A sense of loneliness might well have weighed on his mind. His own tribe of the Quraysh jeered at him, taunted and threatened him, and slandered and persecuted him as well as those who believe in him. But his faith was never shaken, not even to the extent of that cry of agony of Jesus: "My God! why hast Thou forsaken me?": (Mark, xvi. 34). Much less did it enter the Prophet's mind to think that Allah was angry with him, as the taunts of his enemies suggested.

6178. See last note. The more general meaning is similar. To the man who prepares for spiritual work and spiritual growth the chief thing is typified by the growing hours of the morning. He should not be discouraged, nor overcome with a sense of loneliness in his early struggles or difficulties. The end will crown his work. Allah's care is always around him. If unsympathetic or hostile critics laugh at him or taunt him with being "mad" or "old-fashioned" or "ploughing his lonely furrow", his steady faith will uphold him. He will never believe that his earnest and sincere devotion to Allah, whatever be its results in this world, can be anything but pleasing to Allah.

6179. To the truly devout man, each succeeding moment is better than the one preceding it. In this sense the "hereafter" refers not only to the Future Life after death, but also to "the soul of goodness in things" in this very life. For even though some outward trappings of this shadow world may be wanting, his soul is filled with more and more satisfaction as he goes on.

(That wherewith) thou
Shalt be well-pleased.[6180]

فَتَرْضَىٰ

6. Did He not find thee[6181]
An orphan and give thee
Shelter (and care)?[6182]

أَلَمْ يَجِدْكَ يَتِيمًا فَآوَىٰ ﴿٦﴾

7. And He found thee
Wandering, and He gave
Thee guidance.[6183]

وَوَجَدَكَ ضَالًّا فَهَدَىٰ ﴿٧﴾

8. And He found thee
In need, and made
Thee independent.[6184]

وَوَجَدَكَ عَائِلًا فَأَغْنَىٰ ﴿٨﴾

9. Therefore treat not[6185]
The orphan with harshness,

فَأَمَّا الْيَتِيمَ فَلَا تَقْهَرْ ﴿٩﴾

6180. Allah's good pleasure is sure when we serve Him. But we are assured that even our feelings of doubt and suffering will vanish, and we shall have a sense of complete satisfaction, contentment, and active pleasure when our will is identified with the Will of Allah.

6181. Judge the future from the past. Allah has been good to you in your past experience: trust His goodness in the future also. Again, there is a particular and a general meaning. Three facts are taken from the Holy Prophet's outer life by way of illustration. Metaphorically they also apply to us. And futher, the outer facts are themselves types for the spiritual life. See notes below.

6182. (1) There is the case of the orphan, literally and figuratively. Our Holy Prophet was himself an orphan. His father 'Abd Allah died young before the child was born, leaving no property. The Prophet's mother Āminah was in ailing health, and he was chiefly brought up by his nurse Ḥalīmah. His mother herself died when he was only six years old. His aged grandfather 'Abd al Muṭṭalib treated him as his own son, but died two years later. Thereafter his uncle Abū Ṭālib treated him as his own son. He was thus an orphan in more senses than one, and yet the love he received from each one of these persons was greater than ordinary parental love. Each one of us is an orphan in some sense or another, and yet someone's love and shelter come to us by the grace of Allah. In the spiritual world there is no father or mother: our very first sustenance and shelter must come from the grace of Allah.

6183. (2) The Holy Prophet was born in the midst of the idolatry and polytheism of Makkah, in a family which was the custodian of this false worship. He wandered in quest of Unity and found it by the guidance of Allah. There is no implication whatever of sin or error on his part. But we may err and find ourselves wandering in mazes of error, in thought, motive, or understanding: we must pray for Allah's grace ever to give us guidance.

The Arabic root *ḍalla* has various shades of meaning. In 1:7, I have translated it by the verb "stray". In 53:2 the Prophet is defended from the charge of being "astray" or straying in mind. In 12:8 and 12:95 Jacob's sons use the word for their aged father, to suggest that he was senile and wandering in mind. In 32:10 it is used of the dead, and I have translated it "hidden and lost" (in the earth).

6184. (3) The Holy Prophet inherited no wealth and was poor. The true, pure, and sincere love of K͟hadījah not only raised him above want, but made him independent of worldly needs in his later life, enabling him to devote his whole time to the service of Allah. So do we all find ourselves in some want or another, which, if we work wholeheartedly and sincerely is supplied to us by the grace of Allah. When we have found the Way, it is a laborious task to climb up in our poverty of spiritual equipment: Allah will give us spiritual riches in love and knowledge.

6185. Verses 9-11 carry on, to a step further, the triple argument of verses 6-8, as explained in the preceding notes. The Prophet treated all orphans with tender affection and respect, setting an example to his contemporaries, who frequently took advantage of the helpless position of orphans, and in any case looked upon them as subordinate creatures to be repressed and kept in their place. Such an attitude is common in all ages. Helpless creatures ought, on the contrary, to be treated as sacred trusts, whether they are orphans, or dependants, or creatures of any kind unable to assert themselves, either through age, sex, social rank, artificial conditions, or any cause whatever.

10. Nor repulse the petitioner
(Unheard);[6186]

وَأَمَّا ٱلسَّآئِلَ فَلَا تَنْهَرْ ⑩

11. But the Bounty
Of thy Lord—
Rehearse and proclaim![6187]

وَأَمَّا بِنِعْمَةِ رَبِّكَ فَحَدِّثْ ⑪

6186. Then there are the people who come with petitions—who have to ask for something. They may be genuine beggars asking for financial help, or ignorant people asking for knowledge, or timid people asking for some lead or encouragement. The common attitude is to scorn them or repulse them. The scorn may be shown even when alms or assistance is given to them. Such an attitude is wrong. Charity is of no moral value without sympathy and love. Nor is it charity to give to idle sturdy professional beggars, for show or to get rid of them. They are mere parasites on society. Every petition should be examined and judged on its merits.

6187. Besides the petitioners, who ask for help, there is the case of those who do no ask but are nevertheless poor—poor but contented in worldly goods, or poor in knowledge or resources and not even knowing that they are poor. If you are bountifully endowed by Allah, your duty is to make that Bounty spread far and wide. Proclaim it and share it, as the Holy Prophet always did. Spiritually we all belong to one of these three classes in one sense or another—orphans, petitioners, and victims of poverty. We all receive Allah's grace and guidance in some degree or other. We all owe it as a duty to our fellow-men to be kind and helpful to those less endowed in any respect than ourselves.

INTRODUCTION AND SUMMARY TO SŪRAH 94— *AL SHARḤ* or *AL INSHIRĀḤ*

This short Sūrah gives a message of hope and encouragement in a time of darkness and difficulty. It was revealed to the Holy Prophet soon after the last Sūrah *(Al Ḍuḥā),* whose argument it supplements.

C. 274.—The Prophet's mind and heart had indeed
(94:1-8.) Been expanded and purified; the burden
Which pressed on his soul had been removed;
And his name exalted in this world and the next.
For the righteous man there is no trouble
But is linked with ease and joy: he must strive
At every stage, and look to Allah
Alone as the goal of all his hopes.

Sūrah 94.

الجزء الثلاثون سورة الشرح

Al Sharḥ or *Al Inshirāḥ* (The Expansion of the Breast)

In the name of Allah, Most Gracious, Most Merciful.

بِسْمِ اللَّهِ الرَّحْمَٰنِ الرَّحِيمِ

1. Have We not
Expanded thee thy breast?[6188]

أَلَمْ نَشْرَحْ لَكَ صَدْرَكَ ﴿١﴾

2. And removed from thee
Thy burden[6189]

وَوَضَعْنَا عَنكَ وِزْرَكَ ﴿٢﴾

3. The which did gall
Thy back?—

الَّذِي أَنقَضَ ظَهْرَكَ ﴿٣﴾

4. And raised high the esteem
(In which) thou (art held)?[6190]

وَرَفَعْنَا لَكَ ذِكْرَكَ ﴿٤﴾

5. So, verily,
With every difficulty,
There is relief:[6191]

فَإِنَّ مَعَ الْعُسْرِ يُسْرًا ﴿٥﴾

6. Verily, with every difficulty
There is relief.

إِنَّ مَعَ الْعُسْرِ يُسْرًا ﴿٦﴾

7. Therefore, when thou art
Free (form thine immediate task),

فَإِذَا فَرَغْتَ ﴿٧﴾

6188. *Cf.* the prayer of Moses in 20:25. The breast is symbolically the seat of knowledge and the highest feelings of love and affection, the treasure house in which are stored the jewels of that quality of human character which approaches nearest to the divine. The Holy Prophet's human nature had been purified, expanded, and elevated, so that he became a Mercy to all Creation. Such a nature could afford to ignore the lower motives of ordinary humanity which caused shameful attacks to be made on him. Its strength and courage could also bear the burden of the galling work which it had to do in denouncing sin, subduing it, and protecting Allah's creatures from its oppression.

6189. See last note. It is indeed a grievous and galling burden for a man to fight single-handed against sin. But Allah sends His grace and aid, and that burden is removed, or converted into joy and triumph in the service of the One True God.

6190. The Prophet's virtues, the magnanimity of his character, and his love for mankind were fully recognised even in his lifetime, and his name stands highest among the heroic leaders of mankind. The phrase used is more comprehensive in meaning than that used for various prophets in 37:119 etc.: "We left this blessing for them among generations to come in later times".

6191. This verse is repeated for extra emphasis. Whatever difficulties or troubles are encountered by men, Allah always provides a solution, a way out, a relief, a way to lead to ease and happiness, if we only follow His Path and show our Faith by patience and welldoing. The solution or relief does not merely come *after* the Difficulty: it is provided *with* it. I understand the definite article in *al 'usr* in a generic sense, and translate: "every difficulty", In 92:7, I have translated *Yusr* as Bliss, and in 92:10 *'Usr* as Misery.

Still labour hard,[6192] فَانصَبْ

8. And to thy Lord
Turn (all) thy attention.[6193] وَإِلَىٰ رَبِّكَ فَارْغَب ﴿٨﴾

6192. *When thou art free:* or when thou art relieved. The words understood may be: from thy immediate task, that of preaching to men, denouncing sin, and encouraging righteousness; or, from the difficulties that confronted thee. When that happens, that does not finish the labours of the man of Allah. It is only one step to them. He has constantly and insistently to go on. When there is rest from the task of instructing the world, the contact with the spiritual kingdom continues, and indeed it becomes more intimate and concentrated.

6193. The kingdom of Allah is everything. Other things are incidental, and really do not matter. Worldly greatness or success may be a means to an end, but it may also be a hindrance to true spiritual greatness. Allah is the goal of the righteous man's whole attention and desire.

INTRODUCTION AND SUMMARY TO SŪRAH 95—*AL TĪN*

This is also a very early Sūrah. It appeals to the most sacred symbols to show that Allah created man in the best of moulds, but that man is capable of the utmost degradation unless he has Faith and leads a good life. In subject matter this Sūrah closely resembles S. 103.

C. 275.—Nature and history and the Light of Revelation,
(95:1-8.) Through the ages, show that man,
Created by Allah in the best of moulds,
Can yet fall to the lowest depths, unless
He lives a life of faith and righteousness.
Then will he reach his goal: if not,
He must stand his Judgement—none can doubt—
Before the wisest and justest of Judges.

Sūrah 95.

Al Tīn (The Fig)

In the name of Allah, Most Gracious, Most Merciful.

1. By the Fig[6194]
And the Olive,[6195]

2. And the Mount
Of Sinai,[6196]

3. And this City[6197]
Of security—[6198]

بِسْمِ اللَّهِ الرَّحْمَٰنِ الرَّحِيمِ

وَالتِّينِ وَالزَّيْتُونِ ﴿١﴾

وَطُورِ سِينِينَ ﴿٢﴾

وَهَٰذَا الْبَلَدِ الْأَمِينِ ﴿٣﴾

6194. The substantive proposition is in verse 4-8, and it is clinched by an appeal to four sacred symbols. *viz.*, the Fig, the Olive, Mount Sinai, and the sacred City of Makkah. About the precise interpretation of the first two symbols, and especially of the symbol of the Fig, there is much difference of opinion. If we take the Fig literally to refer to the fruit or the tree, it can stand as a symbol of man's destiny in many ways. Under cultivation it can be one of the finest, most delicious, and most wholesome fruits in existence: in its wild state, it is nothing but tiny seeds, and is insipid, and often full of worms and maggots. So man at his best has a noble destiny: at his worst, he is "the lowest of the low". Christ is said to have cursed a fig tree for having only leaves, and not producing fruit (Matt. xxi. 18-29), enforcing the same lesson. There is also a parable of the fig tree in Matt. xxiv. 32-35. See also the parable of the good and evil figs in Jeremiah, xxiv. 1-10. But see n. 6198 below.

6195. For the sacred symbolism of the Olive, see n. 2880 to 23:20, and notes 3000-3002 to 24:35, where the parable of Allah's Light includes a reference to the Olive. But it is possible that the Olive here refers to the Mount of Olives, just outside the walls of the City of Jerusalem (see n. 5038 to 52:2), for this is the scene in the Gospel story (Matt. xxiv. 3-4) of Christ's description of the Judgement to come.

6196. This was the Mountain on which the Law was given to Moses. See 19:52, and n. 2504. The Law was given, and the glory of Allah was made visible. But did Israel faithfully obey the Law thereafter?

6197. "This City of security" is undoubtedly Makkah. Even in Pagan times its sacred character was respected, and no fighting was allowed in its territory. But the same City, with all its sacred associations, persecuted the greatest of the Prophets and gave itself up for a time to idolatry and sin, thus presenting the contrast of the best and the worst.

6198. Having discussed the four symbols in detail, let us consider them together. It is clear that they refer to Allah's Light or Revelation, which offers man the highest destiny if he will follow the Way. Makkah stands for Islam, Sinai for Israel, and the Mount of Olives for Christ's original and pure Message. It has been suggested that the Fig stands for the *Ficus Indica,* the Bo-tree, under which Gautama Buddha obtained Nirvana. I hesitate to adopt the suggestion, but if accepted it would cover pristine Buddhism and the ancient Vedic religions from which it was an offshoot. In this way all the great religions of the world would be indicated. But even if we refer the Fig and the Olive to the symbolism in their fruit, and not to any particular religion, the contrast of Best and Worst in man's destiny remains, and that is the main thing.

This raises a doctrinal question of considerable importance: how does Islam view the ancient vedic religions and Buddhism, or for that matter, any other religion? As Muslims we are not in a position to affirm whether Budha was a prophet or not. Although the Qur'ān states that Allah sent Prophets to every people (90:78), it does not mention the names of all of them. In fact it mentions by name relatively few of the Prophets of the semitic tradition, or only such as with whom its first audience, the Arabs were generally familiar. As to its present form, we find the doctrines of Buddhism clearly at variance with monotheism and cardinal Principles of the True Religion as explained in the Qur'ān. This may have been the result of distortion or loss by the followers of its original teachings.

As a general rule, we cannot describe anyone as a Prophet or Messenger of Allah unless explicitly mentioned in the Qur'ān, or Ḥadīth. The Message as brought by Prophet Muḥammad preserves in itself all that was essential in the earlier revelations or scriptures: it abrogates all the previous messages sent through earlier Prophets (3:85). (R).

4. We have indeed created man In the best of moulds,[6199]	٤ لَقَدْ خَلَقْنَا الْإِنسَٰنَ فِىٓ أَحْسَنِ تَقْوِيمٍ
5. Then do We abase him (To be) the lowest Of the low—[6200]	٥ ثُمَّ رَدَدْنَٰهُ أَسْفَلَ سَٰفِلِينَ
6. Except such as believe And do righteous deeds: For they shall have A reward unfailing.	٦ إِلَّا الَّذِينَ ءَامَنُوا۟ وَعَمِلُوا۟ الصَّٰلِحَٰتِ فَلَهُمْ أَجْرٌ غَيْرُ مَمْنُونٍ
7. Then what can, After this, contradict thee,[6201] As to the Judgement (To come)?	٧ فَمَا يُكَذِّبُكَ بَعْدُ بِالدِّينِ
8. Is not Allah The wisest of Judges?[6202]	٨ أَلَيْسَ اللَّهُ بِأَحْكَمِ الْحَٰكِمِينَ

6199. *Taqwīm:* mould, symmetry, form, nature, constitution. There is no fault in Allah's creation. To man Allah gave the purest and best nature, and man's duty is to preserve the pattern on which Allah has made him: 30:30. But by making him His vicegerent, Allah exalted him *in posse* even higher than the angels, for the angels had to make obeisance to him (2:30-34, and n. 48). But man's position as vicegerent also gives him will and discretion, and if he uses them wrongly he falls even lower than the beasts. See next note.

6200. This verse should be read with the next. If man rebels against Allah, and follows after evil, he will be abased to the lowest possible position. For Judgement is sure. Those who use their faculties aright and follow Allah's Law will reach the high and noble destiny intended for them. That reward will not be temporary, but unfailing.

6201. *Thee:* may refer to the Holy Prophet, or to man collectively. *After this: i.e.*, when it is clearly shown to you that Allah created man true and pure, that He guides him, and that those who rebel and break His law will be punished and brought down in the Hereafter, who can doubt this, or contradict the Prophet when he gives warning?

6202. Allah is wise and just. Therefore the righteous have nothing to fear, but the evil ones cannot escape punishment.

INTRODUCTION AND SUMMARY TO SŪRAH 96—*AL 'ALAQ* or *IQRA'*

Verses 1-5 of this Sūrah were the first direct Revelation to the Holy Prophet. The circumstances, material and psychical, in which they came, are described in C. 28-30, which should be referred to.

After that there was an interval or break *(Fatrah)*, extending over some months or perhaps over a year. S. 68 is usually considered to have been the next revelation in point of time. But the remainder of this Sūrah (96:6-19) came soon after the *Fatrah*, and that portion is joined on to the first five verses containing the command to preach, because it explains the chief obstacle to the delivery of the message to man, *viz.:* man's own obstinacy, vanity, and insolence.

C. 276.—Noble is the mission of the Prophet, selected
(96:1-19.) To proclaim the Message of Allah, the Lord
And Cherisher of all His Creation, Whose measureless
Bounties include the instruction of man
In new and ever new knowledge. But alas
For man! he fancies himself self-sufficient,
Turns away from the Path, and misleads others.
But nothing is hidden from Allah. He will bring
All untruth and sin and rebellion to Judgement,
And subdue all evil. The righteous bow
In adoration to Allah, and draw closer to Him.

Sūrah 96.

الجزء الثلاثون سورة العلق

Al 'Alaq (The Clinging Clot) or
Iqra' (Read!)

In the name of Allah, Most Gracious,
Most Merciful.

بِسْمِ ٱللَّهِ ٱلرَّحْمَٰنِ ٱلرَّحِيمِ

1. Proclaim! (or Read!)[6203]
In the name[6204]
Of thy Lord and Cherisher,
Who created—

ٱقْرَأْ بِٱسْمِ رَبِّكَ ٱلَّذِى خَلَقَ ١

2. Created man, out of
A (mere) clot
Of congealed blood:[6205]

خَلَقَ ٱلْإِنسَٰنَ مِنْ عَلَقٍ ٢

3. Proclaim! And thy Lord
Is Most Bountiful—

ٱقْرَأْ وَرَبُّكَ ٱلْأَكْرَمُ ٣

4. He Who taught
(The use of) the Pen—[6206]

ٱلَّذِى عَلَّمَ بِٱلْقَلَمِ ٤

6203. *Iqra'* may mean "read", or "recite or rehearse", or "proclaim aloud", the object understood being Allah's Message. For an account of the circumstances in which this first revelation—the divine commission to preach and proclaim Allah's Message came to the Holy Prophet, in the cave of Ḥira', see C. 27-31. In worldly letters he was unversed, but with spiritual knowledge his mind and soul were filled, and now had come the time when he must stand forth to the world and declare his mission.

6204. The declaration or proclamation was to be in the name of Allah the Creator. It was not for any personal benefit to the Prophet: to him there was to come bitter persecution, sorrow, and suffering. It was the call of Allah for the benefit of erring humanity. Allah is mentioned by his title of "thy Lord and Cherisher", to establish a direct nexus between the source of the Message and the one addressed. The Message was not merely an abstract proposition of philosophy, but the direct concrete message of a personal Allah to the creatures whom He loves and cherishes. *Thy* addressed to the Prophet is appropriate in two ways: (1) he was in direct contact with the divine Messenger (Gabriel) and Him Who sent the Messenger; (2) he represented the whole of humanity, in a fuller sense than that in which Christ Jesus is the "Son of Man".

6205. *Cf.* 23:14. The lowly origin of the animal in man is contrasted with the high destiny offered to him in his intellectual, moral, and spiritual nature by his "most bountiful" Creator. No knowledge is withheld from man. On the contrary, through the faculties freely given to him, he acquires it in such measure as outstrips his immediate understanding, and leads him ever to strive for newer and newer meaning.

6206. The symbol of a permanent revelation is the mystic Pen and the mystic Record. See n. 5593 to 68:1.

The Arabic words for "teach" and "knowledge" are from the same root. It is impossible to produce in a Translation the complete orchestral harmony of the words for "read", "teach", "pen" (which implies reading, writing, books, study, research), "knowledge" (including science, self knowledge, spiritual understanding), and "proclaim", an alternative meaning of the word for "to read". This proclaiming or reading implies not only the duty of blazoning forth Allah's message, as going with the prophetic office, but also the duty of promulgation and wide dissemination of the Truth by all who read and understand it. The comprehensive meaning of *qara'* refers not only to a particular person and occasion but also gives a universal direction. And this kind of comprehensive meaning, as we have seen, runs throughout the Qur'ān—for those who will understand.

5. Taught man that
Which he knew not.[6207]

عَلَّمَ ٱلْإِنسَٰنَ مَا لَمْ يَعْلَمْ ﴿٥﴾

6. Nay, but man doth
Transgress all bounds,[6208]

كَلَّآ إِنَّ ٱلْإِنسَٰنَ لَيَطْغَىٰٓ ﴿٦﴾

7. In that he looketh
Upon himself as self-sufficient.

أَن رَّءَاهُ ٱسْتَغْنَىٰٓ ﴿٧﴾

8. Verily, to thy Lord
Is the return (of all).[6209]

إِنَّ إِلَىٰ رَبِّكَ ٱلرُّجْعَىٰٓ ﴿٨﴾

9. Seest thou one
Who forbids—[6210]

أَرَءَيْتَ ٱلَّذِى يَنْهَىٰ ﴿٩﴾

10. A votary when he
(Turns) to pray?

عَبْدًا إِذَا صَلَّىٰٓ ﴿١٠﴾

11. Seest thou if[6211]
He is on (the road
Of) Guidance?—

أَرَءَيْتَ إِن كَانَ عَلَى ٱلْهُدَىٰٓ ﴿١١﴾

12. Or enjoins Righteousness?

أَوْ أَمَرَ بِٱلتَّقْوَىٰٓ ﴿١٢﴾

13. Seest thou if he[6212]
Denies (Truth) and turns away?

أَرَءَيْتَ إِن كَذَّبَ وَتَوَلَّىٰٓ ﴿١٣﴾

6207. Allah teaches us new knowledge at every given moment. Individuals learn more and more day by day; nations and humanity at large learn fresh knowledge at every stage. This is even more noticeable and important in the spiritual world.

6208. All our knowledge and capacities come as gifts from Allah. But man, in his inordinate vanity and insolence, mistakes Allah's gifts for his own achievements. The gifts may be strength or beauty, wealth, position, or power, or the more subtle gifts of knowledge or talents in individuals—or Science, or Art, or Government, or Organisation for mankind in general.

6209. Man is not self-sufficient, either as an individual, or in his collective capacity. If he arrogates Allah's gifts to himself, he is reminded—backwards, of his lowly physical origin (from a drop of animal matter), and forwards, of his responsibility and final return to Allah.

6210. The words, may be applied generally to perverse humanity, which seeks not only to rebel against Allah's Law, but also to prevent others from following it. There may however be a reference here to Abū Jahl, an inveterate enemy of Islam, who used, in its early days, to insult and persecute the Holy Prophet and those who followed his teaching. He used, in particular, to use shameful methods to prevent the Prophet from going to the Ka'bah for devotions, and forbid any who came under his influence, from offering prayers or performing devotions. He was arrogant and purse-proud and met his end in the battle of Badr.

6211. Man's insolence leads to two results: (1) self-destruction through self-misleading; (2) a false example or false guidance to others. The righteous man must therefore test human example or human guidance by the question, "Is there Allah's guidance behind it?" And visible light would be thrown on it by the question, "Does it lead to righteousness?" A flouting of Allah and Allah's truth answers the first question in the negative, and conduct which turns back from the eternal principles of Right answers the second.

6212. The usual trick of the ungodly is to refuse to face Truth. If they are placed in a corner, they deny what is obvious to reasonable men, and turn their backs.

14. Knoweth he not That Allah doth see?	أَلَمْ يَعْلَم بِأَنَّ ٱللَّهَ يَرَىٰ ﴿١٤﴾
15. Let him beware! If he Desist not, We will Drag him by the forelock—[6213]	كَلَّا لَئِن لَّمْ يَنتَهِ لَنَسْفَعًۢا بِٱلنَّاصِيَةِ ﴿١٥﴾
16. A lying, sinful forelock!	نَاصِيَةٍ كَٰذِبَةٍ خَاطِئَةٍ ﴿١٦﴾
17. Then, let him call (For help) to his council[6214] (Of comrades):	فَلْيَدْعُ نَادِيَهُۥ ﴿١٧﴾
18. We will call On the angels of punishment (To deal with him)![6215]	سَنَدْعُ ٱلزَّبَانِيَةَ ﴿١٨﴾
19. Nay, heed him not: But bow down in adoration, And bring thyself The closer (to Allah)![6216]	كَلَّا لَا تُطِعْهُ وَٱسْجُدْ وَٱقْتَرِب ﴿١٩﴾

6213. *Cf.* 11:56, and n. 1551. The forelock is on the forehead, and is thus symbolical of the summit and crown of the man's power or dignity. To be dragged by it is to suffer the lowest dregs of humiliation. *Nasfa'an* is a syncopated form of the emphatic first person plural.

6214. The Pagan Quraysh, who formed an oppressive junta or council to manage the Ka'bah were in sympathy with Abū Jahl, though they did not go to the unbridled lengths to which Abū Jahl went. But they could not, all combined, resist the onward march of the divine mission, though they did all they could to check it.

6215. All the combined forces of evil, though they may have worldly appearances in their favour, and though they may seem to be successful for a time, cannot stand against Allah. He has but to command His forces of punishment to exert themselves, and they will subdue evil, protect Allah's votaries and justify the faith for which the votaries suffer.

6216. The righteous man has no fear. He can disregard all the forces of evil that are brought against him. But he must learn humility: that is his defence. He will bow down in adoration to Allah. He must have the will to bring *himself* closer to Allah. For Allah is always close to him,—closer to him than his life blood in the jugular vein. (50:16). Man's humility and adoration remove him from being an insolent rebel on the one hand and, on the other, prepare his will to realise his nearness to Allah.

INTRODUCTION AND SUMMARY TO SŪRAH 97—*AL QADR*

The chronology of this Sūrah has no significance. It is probably Makkan, though some hold that it was revealed in Madīnah.

The subject matter is the mystic Night of Power (or Honour), in which Revelation comes down to a benighted world—it may be to the wonderful Cosmos of an individual—and transforms the conflict of wrongdoing into Peace and Harmony—through the agency of the angelic host, representing the spiritual powers of the Mercy of Allah.

C. 277.—Blessed indeed is the Night of Power!—
(97:1-5.) When the Mercy of Allah's Revelation breaks through
The darkness of the human soul!
All the Powers, of the world divine,
Speed on their mystic Message of Mercy,
By Allah's command, and bless every nook
And corner of the heart! All jars
Are stilled in the reign supreme of Peace,
Until this mortal night gives place
To the glorious day of an immortal world!

Sūrah 97.

الجزء الثلاثون سورة القدر

Al Qadr (The Night of Power or Honour)

In the name of Allah, Most Gracious,
Most Merciful.

بِسْمِ ٱللَّهِ ٱلرَّحْمَٰنِ ٱلرَّحِيمِ

1. We have indeed revealed
This (Message)
In the Night of Power:[6217]

إِنَّآ أَنزَلْنَٰهُ فِى لَيْلَةِ ٱلْقَدْرِ ﴿١﴾

2. And what will explain
To thee what the Night
Of Power is?

وَمَآ أَدْرَىٰكَ مَا لَيْلَةُ ٱلْقَدْرِ ﴿٢﴾

3. The Night of Power
Is better than
A thousand Months.[6218]

لَيْلَةُ ٱلْقَدْرِ خَيْرٌ مِّنْ أَلْفِ شَهْرٍ ﴿٣﴾

4. Therein come down
The angels and the Spirit[6219]
By Allah's permission,
On every errand:

تَنَزَّلُ ٱلْمَلَٰٓئِكَةُ وَٱلرُّوحُ فِيهَا
بِإِذْنِ رَبِّهِم مِّن كُلِّ أَمْرٍ ﴿٤﴾

5. Peace!...This
Until the rise of Morn![6220]

سَلَٰمٌ هِىَ حَتَّىٰ مَطْلَعِ ٱلْفَجْرِ ﴿٥﴾

6217. *Cf.* 44:3 and n. 4690. The 23rd, 25th or 27th night of *Ramaḍān,* as well as other nights, have been suggested as the Night of Power. See, however, the Introduction to this Sūrah. It is best to take this in the mystic sense, which also accords with verse 3 below, which says that the Night of Power is better than a thousand Months. It transcends Time: for it is Allah's Power dispelling the Darkness of Ignorance, by His Revelation, in every kind of affair. (R).

6218. "A thousand" must be taken in an indefinite sense, as denoting a very long period of time. *Cf.* notes 3632 and 3634 to 32:4-5, and n. 5678 to 70:4. This does not refer to our ideas of time, but to "timeless Time". One moment of enlightenment under Allah's Light is better than thousands of months or years of animal life, and such a moment converts the night of darkness into a period of spiritual glory.

6219. *The Spirit:* usually understood to be the angel Gabriel, the Spirit of Inspiration. (R).

6220. When the Night of spiritual darkness is dissipated by the glory of Allah, a wonderful Peace and a sense of Security arise in the soul. And this lasts on until this life closes, and the glorious Day of the new spiritual world dawns, when everything will be on a different plane, and the chequered nights and days of this world will be even less than a dream.

INTRODUCTION AND SUMMARY TO SŪRAH 98—*AL BAYYINAH*

This Sūrah was probably an early Madīnah Sūrah, or possibly a late Makkan Sūrah.

In subject matter it carries forward the argument of the last Sūrah. The mystic night of revelation is indeed blessed: but those who reject Truth are impervious to Allah's Message, however clear may be the evidence in support of it.

C. 278.—But those who reject the light of Truth
(98:1-8.) Are obstinate. Why should they persist
In evil ways when the Clear Evidence
Has come before them? The straight Religion
Is simple: to adore with a pure heart
The God of Truth, to draw nigh to Him
In Prayer sincere, and to serve
Our fellow-creatures in charity and love.
To do aught else is to fall from Grace.
But Faith and Good Life lead straight to the Goal—
The beauteous Gardens of Bliss Eternal,
And the mutual good pleasure of the Soul in her Lord.

Sūrah 98.

Al Bayyinah (The Clear Evidence)

الجزء الثلاثون سورة البينة

In the name of Allah, Most Gracious,
Most Merciful.

بسم الله الرحمن الرحيم

1. Those who reject (Truth),
Among the People of the Book[6221]
And among the Polytheists,[6222]
Were not going to depart
(From their ways) until
There should come to them
Clear Evidence—[6223]

١ لم يكن الذين كفروا
من أهل الكتب والمشركين
منفكين حتى تأتيهم البينة

2. A messenger from Allah,
Rehearsing scriptures[6224]
Kept pure and Holy:[6225]

٢ رسول من الله يتلوا صحفا مطهرة

3. Wherein are laws (or decrees)
Right and straight.[6226]

٣ فيها كتب قيمة

4. Nor did the People
Of the Book
Make schisms,[6227]
Until after there came
To them Clear Evidence.

٤ وما تفرق الذين أوتوا الكتب
إلا من بعد ما جاءتهم البينة

6221. The People of the Book immediately referred to are the Jews and the Christians, who had received scriptures in the same line of prophecy in which came our Holy Prophet. Their scriptures should have prepared them for the advent of the greatest and last of the Prophets. For the Jewish scriptures promised to the Jews, cousins or brethren to the Arabs, a prophet like Moses: "The Lord thy God will raise up unto thee a Prophet from the midst of thee, of thy brethren, like unto me; unto him ye shall hearken" (Deut. xviii. 15). And Christ promised a Comforter (John, xiv. 16; xv. 26; and xvi. 7; see my n. 5438 to 61:6) almost by name. The People of the Book fell from the true, straight, and standard religion, into devious ways, and would not come to the true Path until (they said) they were convinced by the arrival of the promised Prophet. But when the promised Prophet came in the person of Muḥammad, they rejected him, because they really did not seek for Truth but only followed their own fancies and desires.

6222. The Polytheists, the Pagans, had not previously believed in any scriptures. But yet, when clear evidence came to them, they should have believed. Yet they rejected the Holy Prophet because they were not really searching for Truth, but were only following their own fancies and desires.

6223. The Clear Evidence was the Holy Prophet himself, his life, his personality, and his teaching. .

6224. *Cf.* 2:151.

6225. *Cf.* 80:13-16.

6226. *Qayyimah:* straight, as opposed to crooked; standard as opposed to irregular; definite and permanent, as opposed to casual or temporary. *Cf.* 9:36; 12:40; etc.

6227. The responsibility of the People of the Book is greater than that of Pagans, because the People of the Book had been prepared for the standard and straight Religion by the revelations which they had already received. Yet, when the clear evidence came in Islam, they resisted it. And what is this standard and straight Religion, free of all ambiguity, and free of all casual rights and ceremonies? They are summed up in three eternal principles, as explained in the next verse and the next note.

5. And they have been commanded
No more than this:[6228]
To worship Allah,
Offering Him sincere devotion,
Being True (in faith);[6229]
To establish regular Prayer;
And to practise regular Charity;
And that is the Religion
Right and Straight.[6230]

٥ وَمَآ أُمِرُوٓا۟ إِلَّا
لِيَعْبُدُوا۟ ٱللَّهَ مُخْلِصِينَ لَهُ ٱلدِّينَ حُنَفَآءَ
وَيُقِيمُوا۟ ٱلصَّلَوٰةَ وَيُؤْتُوا۟ ٱلزَّكَوٰةَ ۚ
وَذَٰلِكَ دِينُ ٱلْقَيِّمَةِ

6. Those who reject (Truth),
Among the People of the Book
And among the Polytheists,
Will be in Hellfire,
To dwell therein (for aye).
They are the worst
Of creatures.[6231]

٦ إِنَّ ٱلَّذِينَ كَفَرُوا۟ مِنْ أَهْلِ ٱلْكِتَٰبِ
وَٱلْمُشْرِكِينَ فِى نَارِ جَهَنَّمَ خَٰلِدِينَ فِيهَآ ۚ
أُو۟لَٰٓئِكَ هُمْ شَرُّ ٱلْبَرِيَّةِ

7. Those who have faith
And do righteous deeds—
They are the best
Of creatures.[6232]

٧ إِنَّ ٱلَّذِينَ ءَامَنُوا۟ وَعَمِلُوا۟ ٱلصَّٰلِحَٰتِ
أُو۟لَٰٓئِكَ هُمْ خَيْرُ ٱلْبَرِيَّةِ

8. Their reward is with Allah:
Gardens of Eternity,
Beneath which rivers flow;
They will dwell therein
Forever; Allah well pleased
With them, and they with Him:[6233]
All this for such as
Fear their Lord and Cherisher.[6234]

٨ جَزَآؤُهُمْ عِندَ رَبِّهِمْ جَنَّٰتُ عَدْنٍ
تَجْرِى مِن تَحْتِهَا ٱلْأَنْهَٰرُ خَٰلِدِينَ فِيهَآ أَبَدًا ۖ
رَّضِىَ ٱللَّهُ عَنْهُمْ وَرَضُوا۟ عَنْهُ ۚ
ذَٰلِكَ لِمَنْ خَشِىَ رَبَّهُۥ

6228. The three eternal principles of Religion are: (1) sincere devotion to Allah; (2) Prayer and Praise as drawing man nearer to Allah and to the spiritual world; and (3) the service of Allah's creatures by deeds of practical charity.

6229. *Ḥanīf:* see n. 134 to 2:135.

6230. See n. 6226 above.

6231. To be given the faculty of discrimination between right and wrong, and then to reject truth and right, is the worst folly which a creature endowed with will can commit. It must necessarily bring its own punishment, whether the creature calls himself one of the children of Abraham or one of the redeemed of Christ, or whether he goes by the mere light of nature and reason as a Pagan. Honour in the sight of Allah is not due to race or professions of faith, but to sincere and righteous conduct (49:13).

6232. Contrast this with the preceding verse. Human beings who live a life of faith and good deed justify the purpose of their probation here. They attain the fulfillment of their highest hopes. (R).

6233. The Good Pleasure of Allah is the final Bliss of Salvation. The good pleasure is mutual; the truly saved is he whose will has become completely identified with Allah's Universal Will. (R).

6234. The fear of Allah is the fear to offend against His Holy Law, the fear to do anything which is against His Holy Will. Such fear is akin to love; for with it dawns the consciousness of Allah's loving care for all His creatures.

INTRODUCTION AND SUMMARY TO SŪRAH 99—*AL ZALZALAH*

This Sūrah is close in date to the last: it is generally referred to the early Madīnah period, though it may possibly be of the late Makkan period.

It refers to the tremendous convulsion and uprooting which will take place when the present order of the world is dissolved and the new spiritual world of Justice and Truth takes its place. The symbol used is that of an earthquake which will shake our present material and phenomenal world to its very foundations. The mystic words in which the earthquake is described are remarkable for both power and graphic aptness. With that shaking all hidden mysteries will be brought to light.

C. 279.—The Hour of Judgement must needs be heralded
(99:1-8.) By a mighty Convulsion: the Earth will give up
Her secrets and tell her tale of all
Man's doings: men will march in companies
And clearly see the inwardness
Of all their Deeds: not an atom of Good
Or Evil done, but will be shown
In the final Account of men convinced.

Sūrah 99.

Al Zalzalah (The Earthquake)

In the name of Allah, Most Gracious, Most Merciful.

بِسْمِ ٱللَّهِ ٱلرَّحْمَٰنِ ٱلرَّحِيمِ

1. When the Earth is
Shaken to its (utmost)
convulsion,[6235]

إِذَا زُلْزِلَتِ ٱلْأَرْضُ زِلْزَالَهَا ﴿١﴾

2. And the Earth throws up
Its burdens (from within),[6236]

وَأَخْرَجَتِ ٱلْأَرْضُ أَثْقَالَهَا ﴿٢﴾

3. And man cries (distressed);
'What is the matter with it?'—[6237]

وَقَالَ ٱلْإِنسَٰنُ مَا لَهَا ﴿٣﴾

4. On that Day will it
Declare its tidings:

يَوْمَئِذٍ تُحَدِّثُ أَخْبَارَهَا ﴿٤﴾

5. For that thy Lord will
Have given it inspiration.[6238]

بِأَنَّ رَبَّكَ أَوْحَىٰ لَهَا ﴿٥﴾

6. On that Day will men
Proceed in companies sorted
out,[6239]
To be shown the Deeds
That they (had done).

يَوْمَئِذٍ يَصْدُرُ ٱلنَّاسُ أَشْتَاتًا لِّيُرَوْا۟ أَعْمَٰلَهُمْ ﴿٦﴾

6235. To the ordinary human observer a violent earthquake is a terrifying phenomenon, in its suddenness, in its mysterious origin, and in its power to destroy and uproot the strongest buildings and to bring up strange materials from the bowels of the earth. The Overwhelming Event (S. 88) which ushers in the Judgement will be a bigger and more far-reaching convulsion than any earthquakes that we know. And yet the incidents of earthquakes may give us some idea of that supreme world-shaking Event.

6236. An earthquake, if accompanied by a volcanic eruption, throws up enormous boulders and lava from beneath the crust of the earth. They are thrown up as if they were a burden to the Earth personified. They may be all kinds of minerals, or treasures buried for secrecy. So in the great and final Convulsion, the dead who had been buried and forgotten will rise; matters and motives which had been secretly hidden and metaphorically buried will be brought to the light of day, and justice will be done in the full glare of absolute Truth.

6237. The puzzled agony suffered by the victims of violent earthquakes is as nothing compared to the experience of the new and wonderful world which will then open out to the gaze of man.

6238. The present order may be personified as the earth. It will pass away, but the Deeds done therein, even the most secret, will be brought to the full light of day. And this will be because Allah will give the Command, the inspiration or Word, by which alone all events do proceed. The "inspiration" is the Command or direction conveyed by instruction breathed into the Earth personified: it is directed to tell the whole story of what it knows. *Cf.* 16:68, n. 2097.

6239. In this world good and evil are mixed together. But then they will be sorted out, and each grade of good and evil will be sorted out. So they will proceed in companies to receive judgement. And they will be shown the exact import of everything that they had thought, said, or done, in this life of probation, however they may have concealed or misinterpreted it in this life. Everything will be considered in taking the account, and the account will convince the persons concerned themselves.

7. Then shall anyone who Has done an atom's weight[6240] Of good, see it!	فَمَن يَعْمَلْ مِثْقَالَ ذَرَّةٍ خَيْرًا يَرَهُۥ ﴿٧﴾
8. And anyone who Has done an atom's weight Of evil, shall see it.	وَمَن يَعْمَلْ مِثْقَالَ ذَرَّةٍ شَرًّا يَرَهُۥ ﴿٨﴾

6240. *Dharrah:* the weight of an ant, the smallest living weight an ordinary man can think of. Figuratively the subtlest form of good and evil will then be brought to account, and it will be done openly and convincingly: he "shall see it".

INTRODUCTION AND SUMMARY TO SŪRAH 100—*AL 'ĀDIYĀT*

This is one of the earlier Makkan Sūrahs. In the depth of its mystery and the rhythm and sublimity of its language and symbolism, it may be compared with S. 79. Its subject matter is the irresistible nature of spiritual power and knowledge, contrasted with unregenerate man's ingratitude, pettiness, helplessness, and ignorance.

C. 280.—There are those that fight, with eager charge,
(100:1-11.) The hosts of evil, and storm its citadel.
But unregenerate Man shows less
Than gratitude for Allah's most gracious
Bounties: his life bears witness to his treason
And his greed. Allah's knowledge is all-embracing:
All things hidden will be laid bare at Judgement.

Sūrah 100.

الجزء الثلاثون سورة العاديات

Al 'Ādiyāt (Those That Run)

In the name of Allah, Most Gracious,
Most Merciful.

بِسۡمِ ٱللَّهِ ٱلرَّحۡمَٰنِ ٱلرَّحِيمِ

1. By the (Steeds)[6241]
That run, with panting (breath),

وَٱلۡعَٰدِيَٰتِ ضَبۡحٗا ١

2. And strike sparks of fire,[6242]

فَٱلۡمُورِيَٰتِ قَدۡحٗا ٢

3. And push home the charge
In the morning,[6243]

فَٱلۡمُغِيرَٰتِ صُبۡحٗا ٣

4. And raise the dust
In clouds the while,[6244]

فَأَثَرۡنَ بِهِۦ نَقۡعٗا ٤

5. And penetrate forthwith
Into the midst (of the foe)
En masse—[6245]

فَوَسَطۡنَ بِهِۦ جَمۡعًا ٥

6. Truly Man is,
To his Lord,[6246]
Ungrateful;

إِنَّ ٱلۡإِنسَٰنَ لِرَبِّهِۦ لَكَنُودٞ ٦

6241. The substantive proposition is in verses 6-8 below, and the metaphors and symbols enforcing the lesson are in verses 1-5 here. These symbols have at least three layers of mystic meaning: (1) Look at the chargers (mares or swift camels) panting for war on behalf of their masters. Off they go, striking fire with their hoofs by night at the behest of their riders; they push home the charge in the morning, chivalrously giving the enemy the benefit of daylight; and regardless of flashing steel or the weapons of their enemies they boldly penetrate into the midst of their foe, risking their lives for the Cause. Does unregenerate man show that fidelity to his Lord Allah? On the contrary he is ungrateful to Allah; he shows that by his deeds; he is violently in love with wealth and gain and things that perish. (2) By the figure of metonymy the brave fidelity of the war horse may stand for that of the brave and true men who rally to the standard of Allah and carry it to victory, contrasted with the poltroonery and pettiness of unregenerate man. (3) The whole conflict, fighting, and victory, may be applied to spiritual warfare against those who are caught and overwhelmed by the camp of Evil.

6242. With their hoofs. If we suppose the march to be in the dead of night, the sparks of fire would be still more conspicuous.

6243. We may suppose a surprise attack, but yet a chivalrous attack by daylight. The foe is punished through his own lethargy and unpreparedness, apart from the strength, fire, and spirit of the forces of righteousness.

6244. The clouds of dust typify the ignorance and confusion in the minds of those who oppose Truth.

6245. The forces of evil mass themselves for strength, but their massing itself may become a means of their speedy undoing.

6246. Man, *i.e.*, unregenerate man, in contrast to those who receive guidance and wage unceasing war with Evil, is ungrateful to his Lord and Cherisher, Him Who created him and sustains him, and sends His blessings and favours at all times. The ingratitude may be shown by thoughts, words, and deeds—by forgetting or denying Allah and His goodness, by misusing His gifts, or by injustice to His creatures. He is in this respect worse than the war horse that risks his life in the service of his master.

7. And to that (fact)
He bears witness
(By his deeds);[6247]

وَإِنَّهُۥ عَلَىٰ ذَٰلِكَ لَشَهِيدٌ ۝٧

8. And violent is he
In his love of wealth.[6248]

وَإِنَّهُۥ لِحُبِّ ٱلْخَيْرِ لَشَدِيدٌ ۝٨

9. Does he not know—
When that which is
In the graves is
Scattered abroad[6249]

أَفَلَا يَعْلَمُ إِذَا بُعْثِرَ مَا فِى ٱلْقُبُورِ ۝٩

10. And that which is
(Locked up) in (human) breasts
Is made manifest—

وَحُصِّلَ مَا فِى ٱلصُّدُورِ ۝١٠

11. That their Lord had been
Well-acquainted with them,
(Even to) that Day?[6250]

إِنَّ رَبَّهُم بِهِمْ يَوْمَئِذٍ لَّخَبِيرٌۢ ۝١١

6247. Man himself, by his conduct, proves the charge of treason against himself.

6248. What an evil choice he makes in committing treason against his own Benefactor by going after the petty baubles of this world's wealth of fleeting gains?

6249. Dead bodies, secret plots, evil thoughts and imaginings, long since buried, will yet stand forth before the Judgement Seat of Allah. Instead of being closely hidden or blotted out—as they will have been from the consciousness of mankind—they will stand out as from the consciousness of Allah, which is all-embracing and never suffers from sleep or fatigue.

6250. Allah's knowledge is full and vigilant at all times. But on that day it will reveal to men secrets which they had long forgotten; for the Book of their Deeds will be made manifest at Judgement.

INTRODUCTION AND SUMMARY TO SŪRAH 101—*AL QĀRI'AH*

This Makkan Sūrah describes the Judgement Day as the Day of Clamour, when men will be distracted and the landmarks of this world will be lost, but every deed will be weighed in a just balance, and find its real value and setting.

C. 281.—How will the senses of man stand the Noise
(101:1-11.) And Clamour of the great Day of Account,
Whereon this life's old landmarks will vanish,
And men will be helpless like scattered moths?
Nay, but a Balance of Justice will weigh
And appraise all Deeds: and those whose good
Will show substance and weight will achieve a Life
Of good pleasure and satisfaction, while those
Whose good will be light will find themselves,
Alas, in a blazing Pit of Punishment.

Sūrah 101.

Al Qāri'ah (The Great Calamity)

*In the name of Allah, Most Gracious,
Most Merciful.*

بِسْمِ ٱللَّهِ ٱلرَّحْمَٰنِ ٱلرَّحِيمِ

1. The (Day) of
Noise and Clamour:[6251]

ٱلْقَارِعَةُ ﴿١﴾

2. What is the (Day)
Of Noise and Clamour?

مَا ٱلْقَارِعَةُ ﴿٢﴾

3. And what will explain
To thee what the (Day)
Of Noise and Clamour is?

وَمَآ أَدْرَىٰكَ مَا ٱلْقَارِعَةُ ﴿٣﴾

4. (It is) a Day whereon
Men will be like moths
Scattered about,[6252]

يَوْمَ يَكُونُ ٱلنَّاسُ كَٱلْفَرَاشِ ٱلْمَبْثُوثِ ﴿٤﴾

5. And the mountains
Will be like carded wool.[6253]

وَتَكُونُ ٱلْجِبَالُ كَٱلْعِهْنِ ٱلْمَنفُوشِ ﴿٥﴾

6. Then, he whose
Balance (of good deeds)[6254]
Will be (found) heavy,

فَأَمَّا مَن ثَقُلَتْ مَوَٰزِينُهُۥ ﴿٦﴾

6251. The Day of Noise and Clamour is the Day of Judgement, when the whole of the present order of things will be overthrown with a tremendous convulsion. *Cf.* n. 6235 to 99:1, and n. 6096 to 88. All our present landmarks will be lost. It will be a stunning experience to begin with, but it will inaugurate a new world of true and permanent values, in which every human deed will have its true and just consequences, as if weighed in the balance. See verses 6-11 below.

6252. Moths are frail light things. To see them scattered about in a violent storm gives some idea of the confusion, distress, and helplessness in which men will be at first overwhelmed on the Day of Account. Old memories will be like a book almost blotted out. New hopes will be vague in a new world just rising on the horizon. But it will be a perfectly just world, and no good action will be lost and no evil one but will have its compensating value estimated.

6253. *Cf.* n. 5682 to 70:9. The mountains are solid things, which seem as if nothing could move them. But in that tremendous cataclysm they will be scattered about like flakes of teased or carded wool. This is a metaphor to show that what we consider very substantial in this life will be as an airy nothing in the spiritual world.

6254. The Good Deeds will be weighed and appraised. This appraisement will be of the nicest and justest kind: for it will take into account motives, temptations, provocations, surrounding conditions, antecedents, subsequent amends, and all possible connected circumstances. Against them, presumably, will be deeds of the opposite kind, appraised in the same way. If the good predominates, the judgement will be in the man's favour, and he will be ushered into a life of good pleasure and satisfaction. This will of course be on another plane. (R).

7. Will be in a Life
Of good pleasure and
satisfaction.[6255]

فَهُوَ فِي عِيشَةٍ رَّاضِيَةٍ ﴿٧﴾

8. But he whose
Balance (of good deeds)
Will be (found) light—

وَأَمَّا مَنْ خَفَّتْ مَوَٰزِينُهُۥ ﴿٨﴾

9. Will have his home
In a (bottomless) Pit.[6256]

فَأُمُّهُۥ هَاوِيَةٌ ﴿٩﴾

10. And what will explain
To Thee what this is?

وَمَآ أَدْرَىٰكَ مَا هِيَهْ ﴿١٠﴾

11. (It is) a Fire
Blazing fiercely!

نَارٌ حَامِيَةٌۢ ﴿١١﴾

6255. *Cf.* 98:8, and n. 6233, but perhaps the Bliss is not of the same grade for all men. In every case it is bliss, but bliss suited to the particular nature of the individual concerned.

6256. Just as grades of bliss are indicated for the righteous, so apparently we are to understand grades of punishment suited to the sins of the individual sinners concerned.

INTRODUCTION AND SUMMARY TO SŪRAH 102—*AL TAKĀTHUR*

This probably early Makkan Sūrah gives a warning against acquisitiveness, *i.e.*, the passion for piling up quantities or numbers, whether in the good things of this world, or in manpower or in other forms of megalomania, which leave no time or opportunity for pursuing the higher things of life.

C. 282.—Be not engrossed in things ephemeral,
(102:1-8.) To the neglect of higher things in life.
Life is but short, and Death will soon claim you.
Oh that men would only learn,
Before it is too late, the serious
Issues of the higher life! They must
Taste the consequences of their neglect.
For every good enjoyed they must
In the Hereafter give a strict account.

Sūrah 102.

Al Takāthur (The Piling Up)

الجزء الثلاثون سورة التكاثر

In the name of Allah, Most Gracious,
Most Merciful.

بِسْمِ اللَّهِ الرَّحْمَٰنِ الرَّحِيمِ

1. The mutual rivalry
For piling up (the good things
Of this world) diverts you[6257]
(From the more serious things),

أَلْهَىٰكُمُ ٱلتَّكَاثُرُ ١

2. Until ye visit the graves.[6258]

حَتَّىٰ زُرْتُمُ ٱلْمَقَابِرَ ٢

3. But nay, ye soon shall
Know (the reality).

كَلَّا سَوْفَ تَعْلَمُونَ ٣

4. Again, ye soon shall know!

ثُمَّ كَلَّا سَوْفَ تَعْلَمُونَ ٤

5. Nay, were ye to know
With certainty of mind,[6259]
(Ye would beware!)

كَلَّا لَوْ تَعْلَمُونَ عِلْمَ ٱلْيَقِينِ ٥

6. Ye shall certainly see
Hellfire![6260]

لَتَرَوُنَّ ٱلْجَحِيمَ ٦

7. Again, ye shall see it
With certainty of sight!

ثُمَّ لَتَرَوُنَّهَا عَيْنَ ٱلْيَقِينِ ٧

6257. Acquisitiveness, that is, the passion for seeking an increase in wealth, position, the number of adherents or followers or supporters, mass production and mass organisation, may affect an individual as such, or it may affect whole societies or nations. Other people's example or rivalry in such things may aggravate the situation. Up to a certain point it may be good and necessary. But when it becomes inordinate and monopolises attention, it leaves no time for higher things in life, and a clear warning is here sounded from a spiritual point of view. Man may be engrossed in these things till death approaches, and he looks back on a wasted life, as far as the higher things are concerned.

6258. That is, until the time comes when you must lie down in the graves and leave the pomp and circumstance of an empty life. The true Reality will then appear before you. Why not try to strive for a little understanding of that Reality in this very life?

6259. Three kinds of *yaqīn* (certainty of knowledge) are described in n. 5673 to 69:51. The first is certainty of mind or inference mentioned here: we hear from someone, or we infer from something we know: this refers to our own state of mind. If we instruct our minds in this way, we should value the deeper things of life better, and not waste all our time in ephemeral things. But if we do not use our reasoning faculties now, we shall yet see with our own eyes, the Penalty for our sins. It will be certainty of sight. We shall see Hell. See next verse. But the absolute certainty of assured Truth is that described in 69:51. That is not liable to any human error or psychological defect.

6260. See 19:71-72, and n. 2518.

8. Then, shall ye be
Questioned that Day
About the joy[6261]
(Ye indulged in!)

ثُمَّ لَتُسْـَٔلُنَّ يَوْمَئِذٍ عَنِ ٱلنَّعِيمِ ٨

6261. We shall be questioned, *i.e.*, we shall be held responsible for every kind of joy we indulge in—whether it was false pride or delight in things of no value, or things evil, or the enjoyment of things legitimate—the last, to see whether we kept this within reasonable bounds.

INTRODUCTION AND SUMMARY TO SŪRAH 103—*AL 'AṢR*

This early Makkan Sūrah refers to the testimony of Time through the Ages. All history shows that Evil came to an evil end. But Time is always in favour of those who have Faith, live clean and pure lives, and know how to wait, in patience and constancy. *Cf.* the theme of S. 95.

C. 283.—Waste not, nor misuse, your life. Time
(103:1-3.) Through the Ages bears witness that nothing remains
But Faith and Good Deeds, and the teaching of Truth
And the teaching of Patience and Constancy.
But for these, Man against Time is in loss!

Al 'Aṣr (Time Through the Ages)

In the name of Allah, Most Gracious,
Most Merciful.

بِسْمِ اللَّهِ الرَّحْمَٰنِ الرَّحِيمِ

1. By (the Token of)
Time (through the Ages),[6262]

وَالْعَصْرِ ١

2. Verily Man
Is in loss,[6263]

إِنَّ الْإِنسَانَ لَفِي خُسْرٍ ٢

3. Except such as have Faith,
And do righteous deeds,[6264]
And (join together)[6265]
In the mutual teaching
Of Truth, and of
Patience and Constancy.

إِلَّا الَّذِينَ آمَنُوا وَعَمِلُوا الصَّالِحَاتِ ٣
وَتَوَاصَوْا بِالْحَقِّ
وَتَوَاصَوْا بِالصَّبْرِ

6262. *Al 'Aṣr* may mean: (1) Time through the Ages, or long periods, in which case it comes near to the abstract idea of Time, *Dahr,* which was sometimes deified by the Pagan Arabs (see Introduction to S. 76.); (2) or the late afternoon, from which the *'Aṣr* canonical prayer takes its name (see n. 271 to 2:238). A mystic use of both these ideas is understood here. An appeal is made to Time as one of the creations of Allah, of which everyone knows something but of which no one can fully explain the exact significance. Time searches out and destroys everything material. No one in secular literature has expressed the tyranny of "never-resting Time" better than Shakespeare in his Sonnets. For example, see Sonnets 5 ("never-resting Time"), 12 ("Nothing 'gainst Time's scythe can make defense"), and 64 ("When I have seen by Time's fell hand defaced, the rich proud cost of outworn buried age"). If we merely run a race against Time, we shall lose. It is the spiritual part of us that conquers Time. See verse 3 below. For the "afternoon" idea see next note.

6263. If life be considered under the metaphor of a business bargain, man, by merely attending to his material gains, will lose. When he makes up his day's account in the afternoon, it will show a loss. It will only show profit if he has Faith, leads a good life, and contributes to social welfare by directing and encouraging other people on the Path of Truth and Constancy.

6264. Faith is his armour, which wards off the wounds of the material world; and his righteous life is his positive contribution to spiritual ascent.

6265. If he lived only for himself, he would not fulfil his whole duty. Whatever good he has, especially in moral and spiritual life, he must spread among his brethren, so that they may see the Truth and stand by it in patient hope and unshaken constancy amidst all the storm and stress of outer life. For he and they will then have attained Peace within.

APPENDIX XI

Oaths and Adjurations in the Qur'ān

1. An oath is an invocation of the name of Allah or of some person or object held sacred by the person using the invocation, to witness the truth of a solemn affirmation and to emphasise that affirmation.

2. An adjuration is a solemn appeal to a person or persons to do some act or to believe some important statement by the evidence of something great or sublime or remarkable or out of the ordinary.

3. On these subjects as thus defined, let us review the teaching of the Holy Qur'ān.

4. Among the Pagan Arabs the use of oaths became so common that it almost ceased to have any solemn meaning. On the other hand, when they wanted to suppress the rights of women or do some unjust acts, they would resort to an oath to do so, and then plead that they were bound by their oath when pressure was brought to bear on them to desist from their injustice. Thus, they doubly dishonour oaths: they took the name of Allah lightly, and on the other hand, they made an oath an excuse for not doing what was right and just. It is much to be feared that our own contemporaries are not free from such forms of disrespect to Allah.

5. Such practices are condemned in the strongest terms in the Qur'ān. "Make not Allah's name an excuse in your oaths against doing good, or acting rightly, or making peace between persons" (2:224). Perjury is condemned as deception which hurts both the deceiver and the deceived. "Take not your oaths to practise deception between yourselves, with the result that someone's foot may slip after it was firmly planted, and ye may have to taste the evil consequences of having hindered men from the Path of Allah, and a mighty Wrath descend on you" (16:94). See also 3:77. You must not only fulfil your oaths, but you must fulfil all covenants, express or implied, and all your obligations of every kind, without reference to an oath: 5:1, n. 682.

6. Considering the harm caused by thoughtless oaths, in which there was no intention to deceive or to do wrong, it is provided that they may be expiated for. "Allah will not call you to account for what is futile in your oaths, but He will call you to account for your deliberate oaths: for expiation feed ten indigent persons. . .or clothe them, or give a slave his freedom. If that is beyond your means, fast for three days. That is the expiation for the oaths ye have sworn. But keep to your oaths" (5:92). See also 2:225 and 66:2.

7. Some examples may be cited of the false oaths which were used for deception. The Hypocrites, "in whose hearts is a disease", "swore their strongest oaths by Allah" that they would be with the Muslims, but treachery was in their hearts (5:55-56). See also 24:53. On the other hand, the oath of Joseph's wicked brethren, "By Allah!", in speaking to their father, (12:85), seems to be a mere expletive, used lightly, and therefore worthy of condemnation.

8. In passages like the following, the oath seems to be emphatic and solemn as in a court of law:

12:66 — By Joseph's brethren, at Jacob's request.
12:73 — By Joseph's brethren, to the Egyptains.
21:57 — By Abraham, to the Polytheists.
26:97 — By the denizens of Hell, when they realise their wrong.
37:56 — By the righteous one in heaven, when he realises the great danger he escaped in life.
38:82 — By the Power of Evil, who solemnly swears by the power of Allah.
46:34 — By the denizens of Hell, when they realise the Truth.

9. In the following passages addressed by Allah to men, an appeal is made to man's realisation of Allah's own greatness, goodness, and glory, or Allah's special relationship to man as Creator, Cherisher, and Protector, to teach him the lesson of truth and right conduct. In English phrase it might be rendered: "As I am thy Lord God, believe in Me and follow My Word."

4:65 — "By thy Lord" (they can have no real faith until...).
15:92 — "By thy Lord" (We will call them to account).
16:56 — "By Allah" (ye shall be called to account).
16:63 — "By Allah" (We sent messengers).
19:68 — "By thy Lord" (We shall gather them together).
34: 3 — "By my Lord (said by the Prophet to assure men of the coming of the Hour of Judgement).
64:7 — ,, ,, ,, ,, ,,
51:23 — "By the Lord of heaven and earth" (this is the very Truth). See also 70:40 (paragraph 12 below).

10. Another way in which an appeal is made to men is by the evidence of the life of the Holy Prophet, whose truth and purity were known to them, or by the Holy Qur'ān, whose wonderful power over men's hearts was a miracle which they witnessed before their eyes:

15:72 — "By thy life" (to enforce the lesson of the unspeakable crime of Lot's people).
36:2 — "By thy Qur'ān, Full of wisdom" (to show the Prophet's inspiration).
38:1 — "By thy Qur'ān, Full of admonition" (to show the error of the Unbelievers).
43:2 — "By the Book that Makes things clear" (to show that Revelation is reasonable and conformable to truth).
44:2 — ,, ,, ,, ,, ,,
50:1 — "By the Glorious Qur'ān" (to quell the wonder of the ignorant).

11. Now we come to the great mystic passages in the Makkan Sūrahs, in which men are adjured to turn to the wonders of the spiritual world by striking phrases full of sublimity, full of mystery, full of symbolism, and using the wonders of the heavens and the earth by way of illustration. They are the despair of the translator, because the words used are widely comprehensive, with little that is precise in them. There are layers upon layers of meaning, and only the profoundest spiritual experience can probe their depths. An attempt has been made in the notes to analyse and explain some of their meanings. All that we can do here is to bring them together into juxtaposition, to help the earnest student. They may be divided into three categories: (1) those introduced by the words *"Lā uqsimu"* (I do swear or I do call to witness), (2) those introduced by the particle *wa*, which is the general form of adjuration, and (3) those, mainly concerned with the Judgement to come, which are introduced by the adverb *"idha" (when)*.

12. *Lā Uqsimu* (with the first person singular) implies that special attention is drawn to something by a personal and beneficent God, and an appeal is made to His creatures:

56:75 — "The setting of the stars." Other glories may set, but not the glory of Revelation.
69:38 — "What ye see and what ye see not." Revelation is good for both outer and inner life.
70:40 — "The Lord of all points in the East and the West." Allah's Kingdom extends everywhere.
75:1-2 — "The Resurrection Day and the self-reproaching spirit." Evil should be eschewed.
81:15-18 — "Planets, Night, and Dawn." Nature may vary, but Allah's Light is ever the same.
84:16-18 — "The ruddy glow of sunset, the Night, the Moon." Man must travel from stage to stage.
90:1-3 — "This City (of Makkah) and mystic ties." Man is created for toil and struggle, but Allah has given him guidance.

13. The great mystic Symbols or Signs, introduced by the particle *wa*, by which man is adjured to turn to the higher life, are rich in suggestive imagery, which loses part of its charm by any attempt at precise definition:

37:1 — "By those who range themselves in ranks".
51:1-4 — "By the (Winds) that scatter broadcast" etc.
51:7 — "By the heaven with its numerous Paths" etc.
52:1-6 — "By the Mount (of Revelation)" etc.
53:1 — "By the Star when it goes down."
68:1 — "By the Pen and by the Record which men write".
74:32-34 — "By the Moon, the Night, the Dawn".
77:1-5 — "By the (Winds) sent forth (to man's profit)" etc.
79:1-5 — "By the (angles) who tear out" etc.
85:1-3 — "By the Sky (displaying) the Zodiacal Signs" etc.
86:1 — "By the Sky and the Night-Visitant (therein)".
86:11-12 — "By the Firmament which returns (in its round), and by the Earth" etc.
89:1-5 — "By the Break of Day", etc.
91:1-8 — "By the Sun and its (glorious) splendour, By the Soul. . ." etc.
92:1-3 — "By the Night as it conceals (the light); By the Day as it appears in glory" etc.
93:1-2 — "By the Glorious morning Light" etc.
95:1-3 — "By the Fig and the Olive" etc.
100:1-5 — "By the (Steeds) that run with panting breath" etc.
103:1 — "By (the Token of) Time (through the Ages)".

14. The great mystic Symbols introduced by the adverb "when" *(idha)* do not *in form* belong to the category of Adjurations, but their mystic meaning and imagery bring them within this category. They refer to the end of the present order of things, and the inauguration of the new world of perfect spiritual values, but they need not necessarily be understood in a definite sequence of time such as we know it, for the spiritual world overlaps the material:

77:8-11 — "When the Stars become dim" etc.
81:1-13 — "When the Sun is folded up" etc.
82:1-4 — "When the Sky is cleft asunder" etc.
84:1-5 — "When the Sky is rent asunder" etc.
99:1-3 — "When the Earth is shaken" etc.

15. Every Symbol is connected with the argument of the passage concerned, by way of metaphor or illustration. See n. 5798 to 74:32. The appropriate meaning suggested is explained in the notes to each passage as it occurs.

INTRODUCTION AND SUMMARY TO SŪRAH 104—*AL HUMAZAH*

This Makkan Sūrah condemns all sorts of scandal, backbiting, and selfish hoarding of wealth, as destroying the hearts and affections of men.

C. 284.—Woe to the man or woman who deals
(104:1-9.) In scandal, in word or act, or by insults
Or suggestions. Woe to the backbiter, e'en
If his tale is true, for the taint is in his motive.
Woe to the miser who blocks up the channels
Of use and service and dams up his wealth,
As if he could remain in possession
For all time! The Fire of Wrath will envelop them
And wither up their hearts and minds, and consume
That largeness of life which is the portion of mankind.

Sūrah 104.

Al Humazah (The Scandalmonger)

In the name of Allah, Most Gracious, Most Merciful.

بِسْمِ ٱللَّهِ ٱلرَّحْمَٰنِ ٱلرَّحِيمِ

1. Woe to every
(Kind of) scandalmonger
And backbiter,[6266]

وَيْلٌ لِّكُلِّ هُمَزَةٍ لُّمَزَةٍ ﴿١﴾

2. Who pileth up wealth
And layeth it by,

ٱلَّذِى جَمَعَ مَالًا وَعَدَّدَهُۥ ﴿٢﴾

3. Thinking that his wealth
Would make him last
Forever!

يَحْسَبُ أَنَّ مَالَهُۥٓ أَخْلَدَهُۥ ﴿٣﴾

4. By no means! He will
Be sure to be thrown into
That which Breaks to Pieces.[6267]

كَلَّا ۖ لَيُنۢبَذَنَّ فِى ٱلْحُطَمَةِ ﴿٤﴾

5. And what will explain
To thee That which Breaks
To Pieces?

وَمَآ أَدْرَىٰكَ مَا ٱلْحُطَمَةُ ﴿٥﴾

6. (It is) the Fire
Of (the Wrath of) Allah
Kindled (to a blaze),

نَارُ ٱللَّهِ ٱلْمُوقَدَةُ ﴿٦﴾

7. The which doth mount
(Right) to the Hearts:[6268]

ٱلَّتِى تَطَّلِعُ عَلَى ٱلْأَفْـِٔدَةِ ﴿٧﴾

8. It shall be made
Into a vault over them,

إِنَّهَا عَلَيْهِم مُّؤْصَدَةٌ ﴿٨﴾

9. In columns outstretched.[6269]

فِى عَمَدٍ مُّمَدَّدَةٍ ﴿٩﴾

6266. Three vices are here condemned in the strongest terms: (1) scandalmongering, talking or suggesting evil of men or women by word or innuendo, or behaviour, or mimicry, or sarcasm, or insult; (2) detracting from their character behind their backs, even if the things suggested are true, where the motive is evil; (3) piling up wealth, not for use and service to those who need it, but in miserly hoards, as if such hoards can prolong the miser's life or give him immortality: miserliness is itself a kind of scandal.

6267. *Hutamah:* that which smashes or breaks to pieces: an apt description of the three antisocial vices condemned. For scandalmongering and backbiting make any sort of cohesion or mutual confidence impossible; and the miser's hoards block up the channels of economic service and charity, and the circulation of good-will among men.

6268. This Fire of Punishment mounts right up to the hearts and minds of such men, and shuts them out of the love of their fellows. "Heart" in Arabic means not only the seat of affection, pity, charity, etc., but also of understanding and intelligent appreciation of things.

6269. Those guilty of these vices will be choked and suffocated, for this Vault of Fire will cover them all over, and its scorching columns will extend over a far wider area than they imagine.

INTRODUCTION AND SUMMARY TO SŪRAH 105—*AL FĪL*

This early Makkan Sūrah refers to an event that happened in the year of the birth of our Holy Prophet, say about 570 A.C. Yemen was then under the rule of the Abyssinians (Christians), who had driven out the Jewish Ḥimyarite rulers. Abrahah Ashram was the Abyssinian governor or viceroy. Intoxicated with power and fired by religious fanaticism, he led a big expedition against Makkah, intending to destroy the Ka'bah. He had an elephant or elephants in his train. But his sacrilegious intentions were defeated by a miracle. No defence was offered by the custodians of the Ka'bah as the army was too strong for them. But a shower of stones, thrown by flocks of birds, destroyed the invading army almost to a man. The stones produced sores and pustules on the skin, which spread like a pestilence. (R).

C. 285.—Let not man be intoxicated with power
(105:1-5.) Or material resources: they cannot defeat
The purpose of Allah. So Abrahah Ashram
Found to his cost. His sacrilegious attack
On the holy Fane of Allah brought about
His own undoing: what seemed but frail
Destroyed his mighty hosts in a day!

Sūrah 105.

الجزء الثلاثون سُورَةُ الفِيلِ

Al Fil (The Elephant)

In the name of Allah, Most Gracious,
Most Merciful.

بِسْمِ اللَّهِ الرَّحْمَٰنِ الرَّحِيمِ

1. Seest[6270] thou not
How thy Lord dealt
With the Companions
Of the Elephant?[6271]

أَلَمْ تَرَ كَيْفَ فَعَلَ رَبُّكَ بِأَصْحَٰبِ ٱلْفِيلِ ١

2. Did He not make
Their treacherous plan
Go astray?

أَلَمْ يَجْعَلْ كَيْدَهُمْ فِى تَضْلِيلٍ ٢

3. And He sent against them
Flights of Birds,[6272]

وَأَرْسَلَ عَلَيْهِمْ طَيْرًا أَبَابِيلَ ٣

4. Striking them with stones[6273]
Of baked clay.

تَرْمِيهِم بِحِجَارَةٍ مِّن سِجِّيلٍ ٤

5. Then did He make them
Like an empty field[6274]
Of stalks and straw,
(Of which the corn)
Has been eaten up.[6275]

فَجَعَلَهُمْ كَعَصْفٍ مَّأْكُولٍۭ ٥

6270. *Seest thou not?—i.e.* with thy mental vision. The incident happened in the very year of the Holy Prophet's birth, barely two months before it.

6271. These were the troops of Abrahah the Abyssinian, who invaded Makkah with a large army, in which were some elephants. See Introduction to this Sūrah.

6272. The miracle consisted in the birds coming in large flights and flinging stones at the army which caused a great pestilence to arise and destroy the whole of Abrahah's army.

6273. *Sijjīl:* see n. 1579 to 11:82. The word also occurs at 15:74. Stones of baked clay, or hard as baked clay, are part of the miracle in the story.

6274. A field, from which all the corn has been eaten up and only straw with stalks or stubble is left, is a field dead and useless. And such was the army of Abrahah—dead and useless. Another possible rendering would be: "like eaten straw and stubble found in the dung of animals". The meaning would be the same, but much more emphatic.

6275. The lesson to be drawn is twofold. For the Pagan Quraysh of Makkah it was: Allah will protect His own; if you persecute the Holy Prophet, he is greater than the mere building of the Ka'bah: will not Allah protect him? For men in all ages it is: 'a man intoxicated with power can prepare armies and material resources against Allah's Holy Plan; but such a man's plan will be his own undoing; he cannot prevail against Allah'.

INTRODUCTION AND SUMMARY TO SŪRAH 106—*QURAYSH*

This Makkan Sūrah may well be considered as a pendant to the last. If the Quraysh were fond of Makkah and proud of it, if they profited, by its central position and it guaranteed security, from their caravans of trade and commerce, let them be grateful, adore the One True God, and accept His Message.

C. 286.—Who gave the Quraysh their talents for the arts
(106:1-4.) Of peace, for trade and commerce, and for journeys
South and north at proper seasons,
And made their home inviolable in Makkah?
Surely they, if any, should adore their Lord
And listen to His Message of Unity and Truth.

Sūrah 106.

Qurays͟h (The Tribe of Qurays͟h) الجزء الثلاثون سورة قريش

In the name of Allah, Most Gracious, Most Merciful.

بِسۡمِ ٱللَّهِ ٱلرَّحۡمَٰنِ ٱلرَّحِيمِ

1. For the covenants
(Of security and safeguard
Enjoyed) by the Qurays͟h,[6276]

لِإِيلَٰفِ قُرَيۡشٍ ١

2. Their covenants (covering) journeys
By winter and summer—[6277]

إِۦلَٰفِهِمۡ رِحۡلَةَ ٱلشِّتَآءِ وَٱلصَّيۡفِ ٢

3. Let them adore the Lord
Of this House,[6278]

فَلۡيَعۡبُدُواْ رَبَّ هَٰذَا ٱلۡبَيۡتِ ٣

4. Who provides them
With food against hunger,[6279]
And with security
Against fear (of danger).[6280]

ٱلَّذِيٓ أَطۡعَمَهُم مِّن جُوعٖ وَءَامَنَهُم مِّنۡ خَوۡفِۭ ٤

6276. The Qurays͟h were the noblest tribe of Arabia, the tribe to which belonged the Holy Prophet himself. They had the custody of the Ka'bah, the central shrine of Arabia, and their possession of Makkah gave them a triple advantage: (1) they had a commanding influence over other tribes; (2) their central position facilitated trade and intercourse, which gave them both honour and profit; and (3) the Makkah territory being, by Arabian custom, inviolable from the ravages of war and private feuds, they had a secure position, free from fear of danger. This honour and advantage they owed to their position as servants of the sacred shrine of the Ka'bah. They owed it to Allah. Was it not therefore right and fitting that they should adore the One True God, and listen to His Message of Unity and Purity, brought by His Prophet?

In those days of general insecurity, their prestige as custodians of Makkah enabled them to obtain Covenants of security and safeguard from the rulers of neighbouring countries on all sides—Syria, Persia, Yemen, and Abyssinia—protecting their trade journeys in all seasons.

6277. See last note, especially section (2). On account of their trade journeys to the warmth of Yemen in the winter and the cooler regions of Syria and the north in the summer, The Qurays͟h became practised travellers and merchants, acquired much knowledge of the world and many arts, and perfected their language as a polished medium of literary expression.

6278. The Ka'bah.

6279. Their trade caravans enriched them, and drew people from distant parts to visit Makkah and bring their merchandise and gifts thither.

6280. Their territory being inviolable, they did not suffer from the dangers of constant warfare nor from private feuds of vengeance or breaches of the peace in their secure homes.

INTRODUCTION AND SUMMARY TO SŪRAH 107—*AL MĀ'ŪN*

This Sūrah—at least the first half of it—belongs to the early Makkan period. The subject matter is the meaning of true worship, which requires Faith, the practical and helpful love of those in need, and sincerity rather than show in devotion and charity.

C. 287.—What remains if you deny all Faith
(107:1-7.) And personal Responsibility? Why then
Help the helpless or teach others
Deeds of Charity? Vain were worship
Without heart and soul. What think ye of men
Who make great show, but fail to meet
The simple needs of daily life?

Sūrah 107.

Al Mā'ūn (The Neighbourly Assistance) سورة الماعون

*In the name of Allah, Most Gracious,
Most Merciful.*

بِسْمِ ٱللَّهِ ٱلرَّحْمَٰنِ ٱلرَّحِيمِ

1. Seest thou one
Who denies the Judgement[6281]
(To come)?

أَرَءَيْتَ ٱلَّذِى يُكَذِّبُ بِٱلدِّينِ ١

2. Then such is the (man)
Who repulses the orphan
(With harshness),

فَذَٰلِكَ ٱلَّذِى يَدُعُّ ٱلْيَتِيمَ ٢

3. And encourages not[6282]
The feeding of the indigent.

وَلَا يَحُضُّ عَلَىٰ طَعَامِ ٱلْمِسْكِينِ ٣

4. So woe to the worshippers

فَوَيْلٌ لِّلْمُصَلِّينَ ٤

5. Who are neglectful
Of their Prayers,[6283]

ٱلَّذِينَ هُمْ عَن صَلَاتِهِمْ سَاهُونَ ٥

6. Those who (want but)
To be seen (of men),[6284]

ٱلَّذِينَ هُمْ يُرَآءُونَ ٦

7. But refuse (to supply)
(Even) neighbourly needs.[6285]

وَيَمْنَعُونَ ٱلْمَاعُونَ ٧

6281. *Dīn* may mean either (1) the Judgement to come, the responsibility in the moral and spiritual world, for all actions done by men, or (2) Faith, Religion, the principles of right and wrong in spiritual matters, which often conflict with selfish desires or predilections. It is men who deny Faith or future responsibility, that treat the helpless with contempt and lead arrogant selfish lives.

6282. The Charity or Love which feeds the indigent at the expense of Self is a noble form of virtue, which is beyond the reach of men who are so callous as even to discourage or forbid or look down upon the virtue of charity or kindness in others.

6283. True worship does not consist in the mere form of prayer, without the heart and mind being earnestly applied to seek the realisation of the presence of Allah, and to understand and do His Holy Will.

6284. *Cf.* 4:142: "When they stand up to prayer, they stand without earnestness, to be seen of men, but little do they hold Allah in remembrance."

6285. Hypocrites make a great show of hollow acts of goodness, devotion, and charity. But they fail signally if you test them by little acts of neighbourly help or charity, the thousand little courtesies and kindnesses of daily life, the supply of needs which cost little but mean much.

INTRODUCTION AND SUMMARY TO SŪRAH 108—*AL KAWTHAR*

This very brief early Makkan Sūrah sums up in the single mystic word *Kawthar* (Abundance) the doctrine of spiritual Riches through devotion and sacrifice. The converse also follows: indulgence in hatred means the cutting off of all hopes of this life and the Hereafter.

C. 288.—To the man of God, rich in divine
(108:1-3.) Blessings, is granted a Fountain unfailing,
That will quench the spiritual thirst of millions.
Turn, then, in devotion and sacrifice to Allah,
Nor heed the venom of Hatred, which destroys
Its own hopes, alas, of the present and the future!

Sūrah 108

Al Kawthar (The Abundance)

الجزء الثلاثون سُورَةُ الكَوثَرِ

In the name of Allah, Most Gracious, Most Merciful.

بِسْمِ اللَّهِ الرَّحْمَٰنِ الرَّحِيمِ

1. To thee have We
Granted the Fount
(of Abundance).[6286]

إِنَّآ أَعْطَيْنَٰكَ ٱلْكَوْثَرَ ١

2. Therefore to thy Lord
Turn in Prayer
And Sacrifice.[6287]

فَصَلِّ لِرَبِّكَ وَٱنْحَرْ ٢

3. For he who hateth thee—[6288]
He will be cut off
(From Future Hope).

إِنَّ شَانِئَكَ هُوَ ٱلْأَبْتَرُ ٣

6286. *Kawthar* literally means "good in abundance". It is the abundant bounty which Allah bestowed on Prophet Muḥammad (peace be on him). This includes a river (or fountain) in heaven of this name which Allah has promised the Prophet (peace be on him). [Eds.].

6287. He who grants these belssings is Allah, and to Allah alone must we turn in adoration and thanksgiving, and in sacrifice. *Naḥr* = sacrifice: in a restricted ritual sense, the sacrifice of camels: see n. 2813 to 22:36. But the ritual is a mere Symbol. Behind it is a deep spiritual meaning; the meat slaughtered feeds the poor, and the slaughter is a symbol of the self-sacrifice in our hearts. "It is not their meat nor their blood, that reaches Allah; it is your piety that reaches Him" (22:37).

6288. Hatred and spite are not constructive contributions to the work of this world, but its opposites. Abū Jahl and his Pagan confederates vented their personal spite and venom against the Holy Prophet by taunting him with the loss of his two infant sons by Khadījah, but where were these venomous detractors a few years afterwards, when the divine Light shone more brilliantly than ever? It was these that were cut off from all future hope, in this world and the next.

INTRODUCTION AND SUMMARY TO SŪRAH 109—*AL KĀFIRŪN*

This is another early Makkan Sūrah. It defines the right attitude to those who reject Faith; in matters of Truth we can make no compromise, but there is no need to persecute or abuse anyone for his faith or belief.

C. 289.—The man of Faith holds fast to his faith,
(109:1-6) Because he knows it is true. The man
Of the world, rejecting Faith, clings hard
To worldly interests. Let him mind
His worldly interests, but let him not
Force his interests on men sincere
And true, by favour, force or fraud.

Sūrah 109.

Al Kāfirūn (Those Who Reject Faith)

سورة الكافرون

In the name of Allah, Most Gracious,
Most Merciful.

بِسْمِ ٱللَّهِ ٱلرَّحْمَٰنِ ٱلرَّحِيمِ

1. Say: O ye
That reject Faith![6289]

قُلْ يَٰٓأَيُّهَا ٱلْكَٰفِرُونَ ﴿١﴾

2. I worship not that
Which ye worship,

لَآ أَعْبُدُ مَا تَعْبُدُونَ ﴿٢﴾

3. Nor will ye worship
That which I worship.[6290]

وَلَآ أَنتُمْ عَٰبِدُونَ مَآ أَعْبُدُ ﴿٣﴾

4. And I will not worship
That which ye have been
Wont to worship,

وَلَآ أَنَا۠ عَابِدٌ مَّا عَبَدتُّمْ ﴿٤﴾

5. Nor will ye worship
That which I worship.

وَلَآ أَنتُمْ عَٰبِدُونَ مَآ أَعْبُدُ ﴿٥﴾

6. To you be your Way,
And to me mine.[6291]

لَكُمْ دِينُكُمْ وَلِىَ دِينِ ﴿٦﴾

6289. Faith is a matter of personal conviction, and does not depend on worldly motives. Worship should depend on pure and sincere Faith, but often does not: for motives of worldly gain, ancestral custom, social conventions or imitative instincts, or a lethargic instinct to shrink from enquiring into the real significance of solemn acts and the motives behind them, reduce a great deal of the world's worship to sin, selfishness, or futility. Symbolic idols may themselves be merely instruments for safeguarding the privileges of a selfish priestly class, or the ambitions, greed, or lust of private individuals. Hence the insistence of Islam and its Teacher on the pure worship of the One True God. The Prophet firmly resisted all appeals to worldly motives, and stood firm to his Message of eternal Unity.

6290. Verses 2-3 describe the conditions as they were at the time when this Sūrah was revealed, and may be freely paraphrased: 'I am a worshipper of the One True God, the Lord of all, of you as well as of myself; but you on account of your vested interests have not the will to give up your false worship, of idols and self'. Verses 4-5 describe the psychological reasons; 'I, being a prophet of Allah do not and cannot possibly desire to follow your false ancestral ways; and you, as custodians of the false worship, have not the will to give up your ways of worship, which are wrong'. The "will" in the translation represents less the future tense than the will, the desire, the psychological possibility; it tries to reproduce the Arabic noun-agent.

6291. 'I, having been given the Truth, cannot come to your false ways; you, having your vested interests, will not give them up. For your ways the responsibility is yours: I have shown you the Truth. For my ways the responsibility is mine; you have no right to ask me to abandon the Truth. Your persecutions will be in vain; the Truth must prevail in the end'. This was the attitude of Faith then: but it is true for all time. Hold fast to Truth, "in scorn of consequence".

INTRODUCTION AND SUMMARY TO SŪRAH 110—*AL NAṢR*

This beautiful Sūrah was the last of the Sūrahs to be revealed *as a whole,* though the portion of the verse 5:4, "This day have I perfected your religion for you" etc., contains probably the last *words* of the Qur'ān to be revealed.

The date of this Sūrah was only a few months before the passing away of the Holy Prophet from this world, *Rabī' I,* A.H. 11. The place was either the precincts of Makkah at his Farewell Pilgrimage, *Dhu al Ḥijjah,* A.H. 10, or Madīnah after his return from the Farewell Pilgrimage.

Victory is the crown of service, not an occasion for exultation. All victory comes from the help of Allah.

C. 290.—For that which is right the help of Allah.
(110:1-3) Is ever nigh, and victory!
When the spirit of men is stirred, they come
To the flag of faith in troops and battalions.
They are to be welcomed: but Praise and Glory
Belong to Allah: to Him we humbly
Turn and pray for Grace: for He
Is Oft-Returning in Grace and Mercy.

Sūrah 110.

الجزء الثلاثون سورة النصر

Al Naṣr (The Help)

In the name of Allah, Most Gracious, Most Merciful.

بِسۡمِ ٱللَّهِ ٱلرَّحۡمَٰنِ ٱلرَّحِيمِ

1. When comes the Help
Of Allah, and Victory,

إِذَا جَآءَ نَصۡرُ ٱللَّهِ وَٱلۡفَتۡحُ ١

2. And thou dost see
The People enter Allah's Religion
In crowds,[6292]

وَرَأَيۡتَ ٱلنَّاسَ يَدۡخُلُونَ فِي دِينِ ٱللَّهِ أَفۡوَاجٗا ٢

3. Celebrate the Praises
Of thy Lord, and pray
For His Forgiveness:[6293]
For He is Oft-Returning
(In Grace and Mercy).

فَسَبِّحۡ بِحَمۡدِ رَبِّكَ وَٱسۡتَغۡفِرۡهُۚ إِنَّهُۥ كَانَ تَوَّابَۢا ٣

6292. The Prophet migrated from Makkah to Madīnah, a hunted and persecuted man. In Madīnah all the forces of truth and righteousness rallied round him, and the efforts by the Makkans and their confederates to destroy him and his community recoiled on their own heads. Gradually all the outlying parts of Arabia ranged themselves round his standard and the bloodless conquest of Makkah was the crown and prize of his patience and constant endeavour. After that, whole tribes and tracts of country gave their adhesion to him collectively, and before his earthly ministry was finished, the soil was prepared for the conquest of the wide world of Islam. What was the lesson to be learnt from this little epitome of the world's history? Not man's self-glory, but humility; not power but service; not an appeal to man's selfishness or self-sufficiency, but a realisation of Allah's Grace and Mercy, and the abundant outpouring of Allah's Praises in word and conduct.

6293. Every man should humble himself before Allah, confess his human frailties, and seek Allah's grace—attributing any success that he gets in his work, not to his own merits, but to the goodness and mercy of Allah. But the Prophet of Allah had also another duty and privilege—to pray for grace and forgiveness for his people in case any of them had exulted in their victory or done anything that they should not have done.

INTRODUCTION AND SUMMARY TO SŪRAH 111—*AL MASAD* or *AL LAHAB*

This very early Makkan Sūrah, though it referred in the first instance to a particular incident in a cruel and relentless persecution, carries the general lesson that cruelty ultimately ruins itself. The man who rages against holy things is burnt up in his own rage. His hands, which are the instruments of his action, perish, and he perishes himself. No boasted wealth or position will save him. The women, who are made for nobler emotions, may, if they go wrong, feed unholy rage with fiercer fuel—to their own loss. For they may twist the torturing rope round their own neck. It is a common experience that people perish by the very means by which they seek to destroy others.

C. 291.—The Chosen One of Allah, in his earnest
(111:1-5.) Desire to proclaim the Message, gathered
His kin together to hear and judge
With open minds between error and truth.
Behold, the fiery "Father of Flame"
Blazed up with foul abuse and curses,
And said to the holy one: "Perish thou!"
With his hands he took stones and cast them
At the holy one's head. Purse-proud he headed
Relentless persecution. His wife
Laid snares, tied thorns with twisted ropes
Of prickly palm-leaf fibre, and strewed them
In the holy one's path on darkest nights,
For cruel sport! But lo! the curses,
Insults, spite, harmed not the Innocent,
But hit the wrongdoers themselves
And branded them with eternal infamy!

Sūrah 111.

Al Masad (The Plaited Rope) or *Al Lahab* (The Flame)

الجزء الثلاثون سورة المسد

In the name of Allah, Most Gracious, Most Merciful.

بِسْمِ ٱللَّهِ ٱلرَّحْمَٰنِ ٱلرَّحِيمِ

1. Perish the hands
Of the Father of Flame![6294]
Perish he!

تَبَّتْ يَدَآ أَبِى لَهَبٍ وَتَبَّ ﴿١﴾

2. No profit to him
From all his wealth,
And all his gains!

مَآ أَغْنَىٰ عَنْهُ مَالُهُۥ وَمَا كَسَبَ ﴿٢﴾

3. Burnt soon will he be
In a Fire
Of blazing Flame!

سَيَصْلَىٰ نَارًا ذَاتَ لَهَبٍ ﴿٣﴾

4. His wife shall carry
The (crackling) wood—
As fuel!—[6295]

وَٱمْرَأَتُهُۥ حَمَّالَةَ ٱلْحَطَبِ ﴿٤﴾

5. A twisted rope
Of palm leaf fibre
Round her (own) neck!

فِى جِيدِهَا حَبْلٌ مِّن مَّسَدٍۭ ﴿٥﴾

6294. *Abū Lahab:* "Father of Flame", was the nickname of an uncle of the Holy Prophet, from his fiery hot temper and his ruddy complexion. He was one of the most inveterate enemies of early Islam. When the Holy Prophet called together the Quraysh and his own kith and kin to come and listen to his preaching and his warning against the sins of his people, the "Father of Flame" flared up and cursed the Holy Prophet, saying "Perdition to thee!" According to the English saying, "the causeless curse will not come". His words were futile, but his power and strength were equally futile. The star of Islam rose higher and higher every day, and its persecutors dwindled in strength and power. Many of the leaders of persecution perished at Badr, and Abū Lahab himself perished a week after Badr, consumed with grief and his own fiery passions. Verse 3 was prophetic of his end in this very life, though it also refers to the Hereafter.

6295. Abū Lahab's wife was a woman of equally passionate spite and cruelty against the sacred person of the Holy Prophet. She used to tie bundles of thorns with ropes of twisted palm leaf fibre and carry them and strew them about on dark nights in the paths which the Prophet was expected to take, in order to cause him bodily injury. "To carry firewood" may also be symbolical for carrying tales between people to embroil them. This was also one of her vices. But she was laying up for herself another kind of Fire and another kind of Rope, the Fire of Punishment, and the Rope of Slavery to Evil. Thus does Evil prepare its own fate. This is the general lesson of sustained craft and cruel wrongdoing recoiling on the wrongdoer's head. See also Introduction to this Sūrah.

INTRODUCTION AND SUMMARY TO SŪRAH 112—*AL IKHLĀṢ*

This early Makkan Sūrah sums up in a few terse words the Unity of the Godhead—often professed, but frequently mixed up in the popular mind with debasing superstitions.

C. 292.—Keep Faith all pure and undefiled.
(112:1-4.) There *is* Allah, the One and Only;
Eternal, Free of all needs; on Whom
Depend, to Whom go back, all things;
He hath no son nor father nor partner.
There is no person like unto Him.

Sūrah 112.

Al Ikhlāṣ (The Purity of Faith)

الجزء الثلاثون سورة الإخلاص

In the name of Allah, Most Gracious,
Most Merciful.

بِسْمِ ٱللَّهِ ٱلرَّحْمَٰنِ ٱلرَّحِيمِ

1. Say: He is Allah,[6296]
The One and Only;[6297]

قُلْ هُوَ ٱللَّهُ أَحَدٌ ١

2. Allah, the Eternal, Absolute;[6298]

ٱللَّهُ ٱلصَّمَدُ ٢

3. He begetteth not,
Nor is He begotten;[6299]

لَمْ يَلِدْ وَلَمْ يُولَدْ ٣

4. And there is none
Like unto Him.[6300]

وَلَمْ يَكُن لَّهُۥ كُفُوًا أَحَدٌۢ ٤

6296. The nature of Allah is here indicated to us in a few words, such as we can understand. The qualities of Allah are described in numerous places elsewhere, *e.g.*, in 59:22-24, 62:1, and 2:255. Here we are specially taught to avoid the pitfalls into which men and nations have fallen at various times in trying to understand Allah. The first thing we have to note is that His nature is so sublime, so far beyond our limited conceptions, that the best way in which we can realise Him is to feel that He is a Personality, "He", and not a mere abstract conception of philosophy. He is near us; He cares for us; we owe our existence to Him. Secondly, He is the One and Only God, the Only One to Whom worship is due; all other things or beings that we can think of are His creatures and in no way comparable to Him. Thirdly, He is Eternal, without beginning or end, Absolute, not limited by time or place or circumstance, the Reality before which all other things or places are mere shadows or reflections. Fourthly, we must not think of Him as having a son or a father, for that would be to import animal qualities into our conception of Him. Fifthly, He is not like any other person or thing that we know or can imagine: His qualities and nature are unique.

6297. This is to negate the idea of Polytheism, a system in which people believe in gods many and lords many. Such a system is opposed to our truest and profoundest conceptions of life. For Unity in Design, Unity in the fundamental facts of existence, proclaim the Unity of the Maker.

6298. *Ṣamad* is difficult to translate by one word. I have used two, "Eternal" and "Absolute". The latter implies: (1) that absolute existence can only be predicted of Him; all other existence is temporal or conditional; (2) that He is dependent on no person or things, but all persons or things are dependent on Him, thus negativing the idea of gods and goddesses who ate and drank, wrangled and plotted, depended on the gifts of worshippers, etc.

6299. This is to negative the Christian idea of the godhead, "the Father", "the only-begotten Son" etc.

6300. This sums up the whole argument and warns us specially against Anthropomorphism, the tendency to conceive of Allah after our own pattern, an insidious tendency that creeps in at all times and among all peoples.

INTRODUCTION AND SUMMARY TO SŪRAH 113—*AL FALAQ*

This early Makkan Sūrah provides the antidote to superstition and fear by teaching us to seek refuge in Allah from every kind of ill arising from outer nature and from dark and evil plottings and envy on the part of others.

C. 293.—It is Allah Who brings forth light from darkness,
(113:1-5.) Life and activity from death, spiritual
Enlightenment from ignorance and superstition
Banish fear, and trust His Providence.
No danger, then, from the outer world,
No secret plottings from perverted wills,
No disturbance of your happiness or good,
Can affect the fortress of your inmost soul.

Sūrah 113.

Al Falaq (The Daybreak)

الجزء الثلاثون سورة الفلق

In the name of Allah, Most Gracious,
Most Merciful.

بِسْمِ اللَّهِ الرَّحْمَٰنِ الرَّحِيمِ

1. Say: I seek refuge[6301]
With the Lord of the Dawn,[6302]

قُلْ أَعُوذُ بِرَبِّ ٱلْفَلَقِ ١

2. From the mischief
Of created things;[6303]

مِن شَرِّ مَا خَلَقَ ٢

3. From the mischief
Of Darkness as it overspreads;[6304]

وَمِن شَرِّ غَاسِقٍ إِذَا وَقَبَ ٣

4. From the mischief
Of those who practise
Secret Arts;[6305]

وَمِن شَرِّ ٱلنَّفَّٰثَٰتِ فِى ٱلْعُقَدِ ٤

5. And from the mischief
Of the envious one
As he practises envy.[6306]

وَمِن شَرِّ حَاسِدٍ إِذَا حَسَدَ ٥

6301. In Allah's created world, there are all kinds of forces and counterforces, especially those put in motion by beings who have been endowed with some sort of will. The forces of good may be compared to light, and those of evil to darkness. Allah can cleave the depths of darkness and produce light (6:96), and therefore we should cast off fear and take refuge in divine guidance and goodness.

6302. *Falaq* is the Dawn or Daybreak, the cleaving of darkness and the manifestation of light. This may be understood in various senses: (1) literally, when the darkness of the night is at its worst, rays of light pierce through and produce the dawn; (2) when the darkness of ignorance is at its worst, the light of Allah pierces through the soul and gives it enlightenment: 24:35; (3) non-existence is darkness, and life and activity may be typified by light. The author and source of all true light is Allah, and if we seek Him, we are free from ignorance, superstition, fear, and every kind of evil.

6303. See n. 6301 above. Our trust in Allah is the refuge from every kind of fear and superstition, every kind of danger and evil. Three special kinds of mischief are specified in the next three verses, against which our best guard is our trust in Allah, the Light of the heavens and the earth. They are: (1) physical dangers, typified by darkness, (2) psychical dangers within us, typified by Secret Arts, and (3) psychical dangers from without us, resulting from a perverted will, which seeks to destroy any good that we enjoy.

6304. The darkness of the night, physical darkness, is a good type of physical dangers and difficulties. Many people are afraid of physical darkness, and all are afraid of physical injuries, accidents, and calamities. We should not fear, but having taken reasonable precautions, trust in Allah.

6305. *Those who practise Secret Arts:* literally, 'those (feminine) who blow on knots', this having been a favourite form of witchcraft practised by perverted women. Such secret arts cause psychological terror. They may be what is called magic, or secret plottings, or the display of false and seductive charms (3:14), or the spreading of false and secret rumours or slanders to frighten men or deter them from right action. There is fraud in such things, but men are swayed by it. They should cast off fear and do their duty.

6306. Malignant envy, translated into action, seeks to destroy the happiness or the material or spiritual good enjoyed by other people. The best guard against it is trust in Allah with purity of heart.

INTRODUCTION AND SUMMARY TO SŪRAH 114—*AL NĀS*

This early Makkan Sūrah is a pendant to the last Sūrah, and concludes the Holy Qur'ān, with an appeal to us to trust in Allah, rather than man, as our sure shield and protection. It warns us specially against the secret whispers of evil within our own hearts.

C. 294.—Insidious Evil lies in wait
(114:1-6.) For man, and loves to whisper and withdraw,
Thus testing his will. But man can make
Allah his sure shield; for Allah doth care
For him and cherishes him: Allah is
The heavenly King who gives him laws:
And Allah is the Goal to which he will
Return and be judged. Let man but place
Himself in Allah's hands, and never can Evil
Touch him in his essential and inner life.

Sūrah 114.

Al Nās (Mankind)

In the name of Allah, Most Gracious, Most Merciful.

بِسْمِ اللَّهِ الرَّحْمَٰنِ الرَّحِيمِ

1. Say: I seek refuge[6307]
With the Lord
And Cherisher of Mankind,[6308]

قُلْ أَعُوذُ بِرَبِّ النَّاسِ ﴿١﴾

2. The King (or Ruler)
Of Mankind,

مَلِكِ النَّاسِ ﴿٢﴾

3. The God (or Judge)
Of Mankind—

إِلَٰهِ النَّاسِ ﴿٣﴾

4. From the mischief
Of the Whisperer[6309]
(Of Evil), who withdraws
(After his whisper)—

مِن شَرِّ الْوَسْوَاسِ الْخَنَّاسِ ﴿٤﴾

5. (The same) who whispers
Into the hearts of Mankind—

الَّذِي يُوَسْوِسُ فِي صُدُورِ النَّاسِ ﴿٥﴾

6. Among Jinns
And among Men.[6310]

مِنَ الْجِنَّةِ وَالنَّاسِ ﴿٦﴾

6307. The previous Sūrah pointed to the necessity of seeking Allah's protection against external factors which might affect an individual. Here the need of protection from internal factors, mankind being viewed as a whole, is pointed out. For this reason the threefold relation in which man stands to Allah is mentioned, as explained in the next note.

6308. Man's relation to Allah may be viewed in three aspects: (1) Allah is his Lord, Maker, and Cherisher; Allah sustains him and cares for him; He provides him with all the means for his growth and development, and for his protection against evil; (2) Allah is his king or ruler; more than any earthly king, Allah has authority to guide man's conduct, and lead him to ways which will make for his welfare; and He has given him laws; and (3) Allah is He to Whom mankind must return, to give an account of all their deeds in this life (2:156); Allah will be the Judge; He is the goal of the Hereafter, and the only Being entitled to man's worship at any time. From all these aspects man could and should seek Allah's protection against evil.

6309. Evil insinuates itself in all sorts of insidious ways from within so as to sap man's will, which was given to man by Allah. This power of evil may be Satan or his host of evil ones, or evil men or the evil inclinations within man's own will: for there are "evil ones among men and Jinns, inspiring each other with flowery discourses by way of deception" (6:112). They secretly whisper evil and then withdraw, to make their net the more subtle and alluring.

6310. This last clause amplifies the description of the sources from which the whisper of evil may emanate: they may be men whom you may see or invisible spirits of evil working within. See last note. So long as we put ourselves in Allah's protection, and trust in Allah, evil cannot really touch us in our essential and inner life.

CONCLUSION

C. 295.—Thus spake, inspired, our Holy Prophet,
Muhammad, on whom we invoke Allah's blessings
For ever and ever—we who are heirs
To his teaching, his exemplary life,
And the golden thread which he inwove
Into the web of human history.
In pious retreats he prayed; much thought
He gave to Life's most obstinate tangles;
'Gainst odds he strove with might and main;
Wisely he led; gently he counselled;
And firmly he subdued Evil.

C. 296.—Mantle-clad,[6311] he solved the most baffling
Mysteries. His soul would scale
The heights of Heaven, yet showered its love
On the weak and lowly of this earth.
Like a cloud that catches the glory of the Sun,
He threw his protecting shade on all.
The widow's cry, and the orphan's, found
An answer in his heart, as did
The cry of Penury and Need.
He searched out those who felt no need,
Being by pride or ignorance blinded,
And he fulfilled their real wants.
His last great charge summed up the rule
Of spiritual life in linking Faith
With one universal Brotherhood.
Ah! ne'er shall we see such life again!

C. 297.—But his clarion voice still speaks his message.
His love and wisdom still pour forth
Without stint the inexhaustible Treasures
Of Allah, for whosoe'er will bring
A purified heart to receive them.
And ne'er did the world, improverished
By its own wayword lusts and greed,
Need those treasures more than now!

C. 298.—There's still with us much sorrow and sin,
Injustice, oppression, wrong, and hate.
Still does Arrogance deaden Conscience,
Rob struggling souls of e'en the crumbs
Of Pity, and make, of loathsome flesh
And crumbling dust, fair-seeming Idols
For worship. Still does Ignorance blow
A mighty Horn and try to shame
True Wisdom. Still do man drive Slaves—
Protesting smoothly the end of Slavery!

6311. An epithet applied to the Prophet in the Qur'an. See 74:1, n. 5778. I have in my mind a reminiscence of an Urdu *Na't*, or Song in praise of the Holy Prophet. (R).

Still does Greed devour the substance
Of helpless ones within her power.
Nay, more—the fine Individual Voice
Is smothered in the raucous din
Of Groups and Crowds that madly shout
What they call Slogans New—
Old Falsehoods long discredited.

C.299.— What can we do to make Allah's Light
Shine forth through the Darkness around us?
We must first let it shine in our own true Selves
With that Light in the niche of our inmost hearts
We can walk with steps both firm and sure:
We can humbly visit the comfortless
And guide their steps. Not we but the Light
Will guide! But oh! the joy of being found
Worthy to bear the Torch, and to say
To our brethren: "I too was in Darkness
Comfortless, and behold, I have found
Comfort and Joy in the Grace Divine!"

C. 300.—Thus should we pay the dues of Brotherhood—
By walking humbly, side by side,
In the Ways of the Lord,
With mutual aid and comfort,
And heartfelt prayer,
Backed by action,
That Allah's good Purpose
May be accomplished
In us all together!

L'ENVOI

Cowper wrote: "Oars alone can ne'er prevail to reach the distant coast; the breath of heaven must swell the sail, Or all the toil is lost." I praise and glorify the name of Allah that He has enabled His humble servant to complete in manuscript the work of Interpretation at which he has systematically and unceasingly laboured for the last three years. My manuscript was completed in Lahore on the fourth of April 1937, my sixty-fifth birthday according to the solar calendar. My inner history during these three years has been one of joyful and concentrated exploration, undisturbed by the storms that vexed my outer life. I had not imagined that so much human jealousy, misunderstanding, and painful misrepresentation should pursue one who seeks no worldly gain and pretends to no dogmatic authority. But I have been much consoled by numerous appreciative letters from distant readers. I thank them and wish them to feel that they and I are fellow riders *(Arabice, Zamil)* on a steed of research in a field that is unlimited in scope and sublime compared to all ordinary knowledge. Such relationship is closer in spirit than ties of blood, or country, or any other joint enterprise whatsoever.

The printer and publisher hope now to bring out the whole completed volumes within two months. I have appended a short Index, which yet is fuller than is to be found in most Quranic Translations. A complete analytical Index, covering the text, notes, and commentary, such as I contemplated in my Preface, will take time to prepare, and will, if there is a demand, be issued as a separate volume at some future time.

And so I take leave of thee, Gentle Reader, and pray for thy spiritual advancement, as I wish thee to pray for mine.

'Abdullah Yūsuf 'Alī

19th *Jumādā al Ūlā* 1345 A.H./
14 November 1937 A.C.

عبدالله يوسف علي

ولد عام ١٨٧٢م (١٢٨٩هـ) في مدينة بومباي في بيت من بيوت «البهرة» وكان والده رجلاً متديناً من تجار بومباي فاعتنى بتعليم ولده القرآن الكريم قبل كل شيء، ولما حفظ عبدالله القرآن أقام والده مأدبة كبيرة بمناسبة إكمال ولده حفظ القرآن وذلك ليطبع في ذهن طفله أهمية القرآن وعظمته، وتدرج عبدالله في مراحل تعليمه العصري إلى المراحل العليا وهو لا يفارق تلاوة القرآن، وتلقى مبادىء اللغة العربية في صغره بجانب الثقافة العصرية التي امتاز بها وفاق أترابه وفاز في المسابقة العلمية التي كانت تجري لاختيار الحكام الاداريين والتي يطلق عليها الخدمات المدنية الهندية، وكانت هذه المسابقة تعد من أهم المسابقات العلمية التي يتطلع إليها الأغنياء لأبنائهم من الشباب ولا ينجح فيها إلا ذوو الحظوظ بينهم. وتمكن عبدالله يوسف علي من التشبع بالأدب الانجليزي وبزّ كثيراً من مواطنيه في الكتابة باللغة الانجليزية ، ونشرت له كبرى المجلات العلمية مقالاته مبدية إعجابها بأسلوبه الأدبي المطبوع، وسافر عبدالله يوسف علي إلى عواصم اوروبا وأقام بمدينة لندن مدة طويلة واطلع على ترجمات الكتب المقدسة بجانب شغفه غير المنقطع بالقرآن الكريم وما يتصل به، وعكف على دراسة القرآن والتفاسير القديمة والحديثة ردحاً من الزمن استوعب فيه كثيراً مما كتب عن القرآن في اللغات الأوروبية والشرقية ثم عاد إلى الهند واستقر بمكانه بمدينة لاهور حيث عين فيها عميداً للكلية الإسلامية وبدأ بترجمة معاني القرآن الكريم. وتوفي في مدينة لاهور عام ١٩٤٨م (١٣٦٧هـ)، رحمه الله وتقبل منه وجزاه خير الجزاء.

فهرس بأسماء السور وبيان المكي والمدني منها

كلمة الناشر

نحمد الله سبحانه وتعالى على ما يسّر لنا من إصدار هذه الطبعة الجديدة المنقحة من (ترجمة معاني القرآن الكريم) التي سبق وأن قام بإعدادها العلامة عبدالله يوسف علي رحمه الله.

ويمثل هذا العمل خلاصة التجارب لشركة أمانة للنشر في خدمة كتاب الله العزيز خلال العقدين الأخيرين. وذلك بإصدار تراجم معاني القرآن بعدة لغات.

وقد شُرع في العمل على هذه الطبعة منذ أكثر من ثماني سنوات، حين بدأت تصلنا ملاحظات القراء والعلماء والمراكز والجمعيات الإسلامية تبدي تصويباً أو اعتراضاً أو استفساراً على ما أورده المترجم. ثم كوّنت شركة أمانة لجنة تتضمن نخبة من العلماء المسلمين لاختيار أفضل التراجم المتداولة لمعاني القرآن الكريم باللغة الانجليزية. وقد وقع اختيار تلك اللجنة على العمل الجليل الذي قام به العلامة عبدالله يوسف علي. فدرست الآراء والملاحظات التي تجمعت حول هذا العمل على اختلاف مصادرها. ثم تلتها عدة لجان لمراجعة الردود والآراء وفحص المتن وتحقيق الهوامش عامة. ولقد قام بآخر مراجعة لأعمال تلك اللجان الأستاذ الدكتور اسماعيل راجي الفاروقي (رحمه الله) الذي كان يومها رئيساً للمعهد العالمي للفكر الإسلامي (IIIT) بالولايات المتحدة الأمريكية.

وحرصاً على إتقان هذا العمل المبارك قمنا بالتعاون مع المعهد العالمي للفكر الإسلامي بتأسيس هيئة تحرير لتنفيذ التوصيات ومراجعة التعديلات وإعداد النسخة النهائية وإخراج العمل بشكله الحالي (والمشار اليه بتفصيل في المقدمة الانجليزية الخاصة بهذه الطبعة المنقحة).

نسأل الله تعالى أن يجزي خير الجزاء المعهد العالمي للفكر الإسلامي وكل من أسهم في إخراج هذه الطبعة المنقحة بالرأي أو الجهد أو المال، ونسأله سبحانه أن يثيب العلامة عبدالله يوسف علي ويسكنه فسيح جناته، آمين.

وآخر دعوانا أن الحمد لله رب العالمين

واشنطن
جمادي الآخرة ١٤٠٩هـ
كانون الثاني/ يناير ١٩٨٩م

فخري البرزنجي
رئيس شركة أمانة

توضيح

يسعد شركة أمانة أن تتوجه بالشكر لكل الذين أبدوا ملاحظاتهم حول استعمال التعبير الانجليزي «طبعة جديدة منقحة» لطبعتها التي أصدرتها سنة ١٤٠٩هـ/١٩٨٩م «لترجمة معاني القرآن لكريم» للعلامة عبدالله يوسف علي.

وتفاديًا لأي التباس قد يحدث لدى قراء الترجمة من غير المسلمين اختارت الشركة أن تلغي تلك العبارة من هذه الطبعة الجديدة.

واشنطن
شعبان ١٤١١هـ
شباط / فبراير ١٩٩١م

الناشر

الناشر
شركة أمـانة

٤٤١١ شارع ٤١ ، برنت وود
ميريلاند ٢٠٧٢٢ ، الولايات المتحدة الأمريكية
هاتف ٧٧٧٧ـ ٧٧٩ (٣٠١)
فاكس ٠٥٧٠ـ ٧٧٩ (٣٠١)

رقم الإصدار الدولي: ٦ ـ ٠٨ ـ ٩١٥٩٥٧ ـ ٠
رقم التسجيل في مكتبة الكونجرس : ٣٤٩٧٤ ـ ٨٨

طبع النص القرآني بالرسم العثماني
على مصحف المدينة المنورة

تَرْجَمَةُ

مَعَانِي ٱلْقُرْآنِ ٱلْكَرِيمِ

بِالْإِنْجِلِيزِيَّةِ

عَبْدُ ٱللّٰه يُوسُفُ عَلِي

طَبْعَة جَدِيدَة مُنَقَّحَة

برينت وود ، ميريلاند ، الولايات المتحدة الأمريكية